Compiled by
**H.-C. SASSE,**

M.A. (Adel.), M.Litt. (Cantab.)

*Lecturer in German in the*
*University of Newcastle upon Tyne*

**Dr. J. HORNE**

*Lecturer in German in the*
*University of Birmingham*

**& Dr. Charlotte DIXON**

# Cassell's
*New Compact*
*German - English*
*English - German*
# Dictionary

CASSELL · *London*

## Cassell & Company Ltd.

an imprint of Cassell and Collier
Macmillan Publishers Ltd.
35 Red Lion Square, London, WCIR 4SG
and at Sydney, Johannesburg, Auckland,
Toronto
an affiliate of Macmillan Inc., New York.

© Cassell & Company Ltd., 1966
CASSELL'S COMPACT
GERMAN-ENGLISH ENGLISH-GERMAN DICTIONARY
First published 1925
Fifth Edition (revised and enlarged) 1936
Twentieth Edition 1964

CASSELL'S NEW COMPACT
GERMAN-ENGLISH ENGLISH-GERMAN DICTIONARY
First published 1966
Second Edition 1966
Second Edition, Second Impression, 1968
Second Edition, Third Impression, 1969
Second Edition, Fourth Impression, 1970
Second Edition, Fifth Impression, 1971
Second Edition, Sixth Impression, 1972
Second Edition, Seventh Impression, 1974

I.S.B.N. 0 304 91817 2

Printed in Norway by Grøndahl & Søn.

# Contents

# Preface

Among the difficulties that arise in the compilation of a Compact Dictionary that of the selection of words is undoubtedly the most formidable one. The decision as to what to include and, much more difficult, what to exclude, must to a considerable extent depend on the type of student of a foreign language who is most likely to use it. Primarily a dictionary of this kind is intended for the student in the earlier stages of learning German, whether at school or university. As the study of German, even at an early stage, is likely to include the reading of literary texts from the eighteenth century onwards, it was felt that some attention at least must be paid to the inclusion of words no longer in common use today but frequently found in the prescribed texts, whether poetry, drama or prose. That in this respect severe limitations are imposed by the very concept of a 'Compact' Dictionary is of course obvious, but an attempt has been made to include at least some of the most common literary and poetical terms. However, the main emphasis throughout must of course be on straightforward contemporary German. In addition to the needs of the student, those of the traveller and the tourist, of the reader of contemporary literature and of newspapers and magazines, have been kept in mind. It is hoped that the student of science and technology too will find the dictionary useful, though in his case additional reference must of course be made to one of the growing number of specialized works dealing with the technical vocabulary of his particular discipline.

The aim of a Compact Dictionary must be to achieve some kind of viable compromise between conciseness on the one hand and completeness on the other. To make the dictionary as helpful as possible—given only a limited amount of space—certain economies were called for. Omissions were inevitable. What is similarly inevitable is that, except in the most obvious cases, no two experts are likely

to agree as to what may safely be omitted unless (as was attempted here) one makes frequency of usage and general usefulness the main criteria.

It should be remembered, lastly, that this is a concise dictionary which cannot remotely hope to do justice to all the finer meanings and nuances of two highly developed and complex languages. But it is hoped that the student and reader of German, especially in the earlier stages of learning the language, will find here all the help he needs.

For more detailed reference the user will find Cassell's New German Dictionary (ed. Dr. H. T. Betteridge) of considerable help, while the Duden works of reference on German are regarded as the authoritative last word on matters of controversy. In the final analysis there will always be areas of doubt and dispute. That is the prerogative of a living and developing language.

Finally, thanks are due on behalf of the publishers to Prof. W. E. Collinson, late of the University of Liverpool, who acted in a consultative capacity.

H.-C. Sasse

# Advice to the User

As a guide to the nature of words which have inevitably been omitted from a dictionary of this size, it may be helpful to state that, when a German *Fremdwort* is identical with the corresponding English term and possesses no grammatical peculiarities, it appears only in the English–German section. For example, it was felt that the word *Atom* (and *a fortiori* derivative compounds such as *Atomphysik*) was unlikely to perplex any English reader and it has therefore been omitted from the German–English, but included in the English–German, section. For the same reason, a somewhat similar plan has been followed with regard to the names of countries. These have mostly been given in German–English only, whereas the corresponding nouns and adjectives of nationality or race are given in English–German only.

## *Arrangement of Entries*

Strict alphabetical order seemed to be most helpful in a dictionary intended primarily for readers in the earlier stages of acquiring a knowledge of German. Within the entries themselves literal meanings and frequency of usage determine the sequence of definitions. Admittedly the second criterion is to a considerable extent a matter of personal linguistic judgment, indeed of *Sprachgefühl*, but it is hoped that in most cases the reader will thereby more readily discover the meaning of any particular word. It can generally be assumed that definitions separated by commas have much the same meaning, whereas differences in meaning or usage are marked by semicolons. Where it was thought desirable and feasible to include idiomatic phrases, relative frequency of usage appeared a more helpful criterion than strict alphabetic sequence.

Words which are spelt alike but are etymologically distinct

# Zur Benutzung des Wörterbuches

Ein Hinweis auf die Art der Wörter, auf die in einem Taschenwörterbuch unweigerlich verzichtet werden muss, wird dem Leser die Anwendung dieses Nachschlagwerkes gewiss erleichtern: Ein deutsches Fremdwort, das mit dem entsprechenden englischen Ausdruck identisch ist und keine grammatikalischen Besonderheiten aufweist, erscheint als Stichwort nicht in beiden Sprachen, sondern wird nur im englisch-deutschen Teil aufgeführt. Man darf wohl annehmen, dass ein Wort wie z.B. *Atom* (und *a fortiori* abgeleitete Zusammensetzungen wie *Atomphysik*) einen englischen Leser kaum verwirren wird, weshalb es denn auch im deutsch–englischen Teil weggelassen, indessen im englisch-deutschen Teil berücksichtigt wurde. Aus dem gleichen Grunde wurde bei den Namen von Ländern ein ähnliches Prinzip beachtet. Diese wurden in der Regel nur im deutsch-englischen Teil aufgeführt, während die entsprechenden Substantive und Adjektive der Nationalität oder Rasse nur im englisch–deutschen Teil erscheinen.

### Anordnung der Stichwörter

Die strikte alphabetische Reihenfolge schien vorteilhaft für ein Nachschlagwerk, das in erster Linie für Lernende gedacht ist, die die deutsche Sprache noch nicht völlig beherrschen. Bei den gegebenen Übersetzungen eines Stichwortes bestimmen die wörtliche Übertragung sowie die Häufigkeit des Gebrauches die Folge der Definitionen. Gewiss ist das zweite Kriterium weitgehend eine Angelegenheit der persönlichen linguistischen Beurteilung, in der Tat des Sprachgefühls. Doch ist zu hoffen, dass der Leser in den meisten Fällen gerade dadurch der Bedeutung eines Begriffes näher kommt. Allgemein gilt, dass durch ein Komma getrennte Wörter eine annähernd gleiche Bedeutung haben, während Unterschiede in Bedeutung oder Anwendung

# Advice to the User

have been given separate, numbered entries for the sake of clarity.

A word should be added on the subject of compounds. Most students of German come to realize before long that the notoriously long German nouns, far from complicating the understanding of the language, are merely a matter of syntactical and grammatical convenience, a device for structural conciseness within a given sentence construction. In a 'Compact' Dictionary only such compounds can be given which have a meaning which can be arrived at only with difficulty or not at all. Where a compound is not given, the constituent parts of the word should be looked up. The meaning should then become self-evident.

*Grammar*

*Parts of Speech.* These are indicated by abbreviations in italics (*adj.*, *v.a.* etc.), the meaning of which will be found in the List of Abbreviations. It has not been felt necessary to indicate the nature of English proper names.

*Genders.* In the German-English section nouns are denoted by their gender (*m.*, *f.* or *n.*). In the English-German section gender is shown by the definite article preceding the noun; in a series of nouns the gender is sometimes omitted when it is the same as that of the preceding noun or nouns.

*Declension.* The Genitive singular and Nominative plural of German nouns are given in parentheses after the gender. The plurals of English nouns are not given, except for certain very irregular forms. The cases governed by prepositions have been included.

*Verbs.* In both German and English the indication *irr.* refers the user to the tables of Irregular Verbs. Where a compound irregular verb is not given, its forms are identical with those of the simple irregular verb in the table. "To" is omitted from English infinitives throughout. German inseparable verbs are described as such only when there is any possibility of doubt, *e.g.* in the case of prepositional prefixes. Where prefixes are axiomatically always part of an

durch ein Semikolon markiert sind. Wo es als notwendig und durchführbar erachtet wurde, idiomatische Redewendungen zu zitieren, schien die relative Häufigkeit der Anwendung ein nützlicheres Kriterium als die strenge alphabetische Folge. Orthographisch gleiche Wörter, die sich durch ihre etymologische Herkunft unterscheiden, wurden um der Klarheit willen als einzelne Stichwörter aufgeführt und mit Ziffern versehen. Noch ein Wort zum Thema der Wortzusammensetzungen: Die meisten Deutschlernenden werden bald erkennen, dass die berüchtigt langen deutschen Substantive das Verständnis der Sprache keineswegs erschweren. Sie sind lediglich eine Sache syntaktischer und grammatikalischer Vereinfachung, ein Hilfsmittel zu struktureller Kürze und Prägnanz innerhalb einer gegebenen Satzbildung. In einem Taschenwörterbuch können allein solche Wortverbindungen berücksichtigt werden, die nur mit Mühe oder überhaupt nicht abzuleiten sind. Ist eine Wortverbindung nicht angeführt, so sollten die einzelnen Bestandteile nachgesehen werden. Auf diese Weise wird sich der Sinn der Zusammensetzung von selbst ergeben.

## Grammatik

*Wortarten.* Sie sind in abgekürzter Form durch Kursivschrift gekennzeichnet (*adj.*, *v.a.* etc.). Eine Erläuterung der Abkürzungen findet sich im Verzeichnis der Abkürzungen. Es wurde nicht für nötig befunden, die Zugehörigkeit von Eigennamen anzuzeigen.

*Geschlecht.* Im deutsch–englischen Teil sind die Substantive mit ihrem Geschlecht (*m.*, *f.* oder *n.*) gekennzeichnet. Im englisch–deutschen Teil ist das Geschlecht durch den bestimmten Artikel vor dem Substantiv angegeben. In einer Reihe aufeinanderfolgender Definitionen wurde der Artikel dort weggelassen, wo er mit dem vorhergehenden übereinstimmt.

*Deklination.* Die Endungen des Genitiv Singular und des Nominativ Plural deutscher Substantive sind in Klammern nach der Bezeichnung des Geschlechtes eingefügt. Der

inseparable verb (*be-*, *ent-*, *zer-* etc.) no such information is given, as it is assumed that the student will be familiar with the function of these prefixes long before he comes to use a dictionary.

*Phonetics.* Phonetic transcriptions, using the symbols of the International Phonetic Association, are given throughout for all entries in both sections of the dictionary as a help to correct pronunciation. The mark ′ precedes the syllable which carries the stress. The glottal stop is not indicated.

*Numbers.* Only the most common numerals appear in the body of the dictionary. However, fuller coverage is given in the separate Numerical Tables.

# Zur Benutzung des Wörterbuches

Plural englischer Substantive wurde nicht berücksichtigt ausser bei einigen stark unregelmässigen Formen. Fälle, die von Präpositionen regiert werden, wurden aufgenommen.

*Verben.* Im Deutschen wie im Englischen weist die Anmerkung *irr.* den Leser auf die Tabellen unregelmässiger Verben hin. Ist ein zusammengesetztes Verb nicht angeführt, so sind seine Formen mit denen des einfachen Verbs in der Tabelle identisch. "To" vor englischen Infinitivformen wurde durchgehend weggelassen. Deutsche untrennbare Verben werden nur dort als solche gekennzeichnet, wo Zweifel möglich sind, also bei Verben mit präpositionalen Vorsilben. Wo Vorsilben grundsätzlich Teile eines untrennbaren Verbes (*be-, ent-, zer-* etc.) bilden, ist kein solcher Hinweis angebracht, da angenommen werden darf, dass der Lernende die Funktion dieser Vorsilben kennt, lange bevor er dazu kommt, ein Wörterbuch zu konsultieren.

*Phonetik.* Jedes einzelne Stichwort ist auch in seiner phonetischen Transkription wiedergegeben. Dabei wurden die phonetischen Symbole der *International Phonetic Association* benutzt. Der Akzent ' steht jeweils unmittelbar vor der betonten Silbe. Der Knacklaut ist indessen nicht markiert.

*Zahlwörter.* Nur die gebräuchlichsten Zahlen erscheinen im Hauptteil des Wörterbuches. Eine ausführliche Zusammenstellung findet sich in den besonderen Zahlentabellen.

# Key to Pronunciation

## Vowels

| Phonetic Symbol | German Example | Phonetic Symbol | English Example |
|---|---|---|---|
| a | lassen ['lasən] | i: | seat [si:t] |
| a: | haben ['ha:bən], Haar [ha:r] | i | finish ['finiʃ], physic ['fizik] |
| ɛ | häßlich ['hɛslɪç], Geld [gɛlt] | e | neck [nek] |
| ɛ: | Märchen ['mɛ:rçən], Zähne ['tsɛ:nə] | æ | man [mæn], malefactor ['mælifæktə] |
| e | Medizin [medi'tsi:n] | ɑ: | father ['fɑ:ðə], task [tɑ:sk] |
| e: | leben ['le:bən], See [ze:], lehnen ['le:nən] | ɔ | block [blɔk], waddle [wɔdl] |
| ə | rufen ['ru:fən] | ɔ: | shawl [ʃɔ:l], tortoise ['tɔ:təs] |
| ɪ | Fisch [fɪʃ], Mystik ['mɪstɪk] | o | domain [do'mein] |
| i | Militär [mili'tɛ:r] | u | good [gud], July [dʒu'lai] |
| i: | Berlin [bɛr'li:n], Liebe ['li:bə], ihm [i:m] | u: | moon [mu:n], tooth [tu:θ] |
| ɔ | Kopf [kɔpf] | ʌ | cut [kʌt], somewhere ['sʌmweə] |
| o | mobil [mo'bi:l] | ə: | search [sə:tʃ], surgeon ['sə:dʒən] |
| o: | Rose ['ro:zə], Boot [bo:t], ohne ['o:nə] | ə | cathedral [kə'θi:drəl], never ['nevə] |
| œ | Mörder ['mœrdər] | | |
| ø | möblieren [mø'bli:rən] | | |
| ø: | Löwe ['lø:və], Röhre ['rø:rə] | | |
| u | Hund [hunt] | | |
| u: | gut [gu:t], Uhr [u:r] | | |
| y | fünf [fynf], Symbol [zym'bo:l] | | |
| y: | Lübeck ['ly:bɛk], Mühe ['my:ə] | | |

## Diphthongs

| Phonetic Symbol | German Example | Phonetic Symbol | English Example |
|---|---|---|---|
| aɪ | Eis [aɪs], Waise ['vaɪzə] | ei | great [greit] |
| au | Haus [haus] | ou | show [ʃou] |
| ɔy | Beute ['bɔytə], Gebäude [gə'bɔydə] | ai | high [hai] |
| | | au | crowd [kraud] |
| | | ɔi | boy [bɔi] |
| | | iə | steer [stiə] |
| | | ɛə | hair [hɛə] |
| | | uə | moor [muə] |

## Consonants

| Phonetic Symbol | German Example | Phonetic Symbol | English Example |
|---|---|---|---|
| ç | Blech [blɛç], ich [ɪç] | p | paper ['peipə] |
| f | Vater ['fa:tər] | b | ball [bɔ:l] |
| j | ja [ja:] | t | tea [ti:], train [trein] |
| ŋ | bringen ['brɪŋən] | d | deed [di:d] |
| s | beißen ['baɪsən], wißen ['vɪsən], los [lo:s] | k | cake [keik], quest [kwest] |
| ʃ | schon [ʃo:n] | g | game [geim] |
| ts | Cäcilie [tsɛ'tsi:ljə], Zimmer ['tsɪmər] | m | mammoth ['mæməθ] |
| v | weiß [vaɪs] | n | nose [nouz], nanny ['næni] |
| x | Bach [bax], kochen ['kɔxən], ruchbar ['ru:xba:r] | ŋ | bring [briŋ], finger ['fiŋgə] |
| z | lesen ['le:zən] | f | fair [fɛə], far [fɑ:] |
| b | Biene ['bi:nə] | v | vine [vain] |
| d | Dach [dax] | θ | thin [θin], bath [bɑ:θ] |
| g | geben ['ge:bən] | ð | thine [ðain], bathe [beið] |
| h | hier [hi:r] | | |
| k | Koch [kɔx], quartieren [kwar'ti:rən] | s | since [sins] |
| l | Lied [li:t] | z | busy ['bizi] |
| m | Mirakel [mi'ra:kəl] | l | land [lænd], hill [hil] |
| n | Nase ['na:zə] | ʃ | shield [ʃi:ld], sugar ['ʃugə] |
| p | Probe ['pro:bə] | ʒ | vision ['viʒən] |
| r | rot [ro:t] | r | rat [ræt], train [trein] |
| t | Tisch [tɪʃ] | h | here [hiə], horse [hɔ:s] |
| | | x | coronach ['kɔrənæx], loch [lɔx] |

## Semi-Consonants

| | |
|---|---|
| j | yellow ['jelou], yes [jes] |
| w | wall [wɔ:l] |

# List of Abbreviations

| | | | |
|---|---|---|---|
| *abbr.* | abbreviation (of), abbreviated | *m.* | masculine |
| *Acc.* | Accusative | *Maths.* | Mathematics |
| *adj.* | adjective | *Meas.* | Measurement |
| *adv.* | adverb | *Mech.* | Mechanics |
| *Agr.* | agriculture | *Med.* | Medicine |
| *Am.* | American(ism) | *Met.* | Meteorology |
| *Anat.* | Anatomy | *Metall.* | Metallurgy |
| *Archæol.* | Archæology | *Mil.* | Military |
| *Archit.* | Architecture | *Min.* | Mining |
| *Arith.* | Arithmetic | *Motor.* | Motoring |
| *art.* | article | *Mount.* | Mountaineering |
| *Astrol.* | Astrology | *Mus.* | Music |
| *Astron.* | Astronomy | *Myth.* | Mythology |
| *Austr.* | Austrian | *n.* | neuter |
| *aux.* | auxiliary | *Naut.* | Nautical |
| *Aviat.* | Aviation | *Nav.* | Navigation |
| *Bibl.* | Biblical | *o.('s)* | one('s) |
| *Bot.* | Botany | *o.s.* | oneself |
| *Br.* | British | *obs.* | obsolete |
| *Build.* | Building | *Orn.* | Ornithology |
| *Carp.* | Carpentry | *p.* | person |
| *Chem.* | Chemistry | *Parl.* | Parliament |
| *coll.* | colloquial | *part.* | particle |
| *collec.* | collective | *pej.* | pejorative |
| *Comm.* | Commerce | *pers.* | person(al) |
| *comp.* | comparative | *Phil.* | Philosophy |
| *conj.* | conjunction | *Phonet.* | Phonetics |
| *Cul.* | Culinary | *Phot.* | Photography |
| *Dat.* | Dative | *Phys.* | Physics |
| *def.* | definite | *Physiol.* | Physiology |
| *defect.* | defective | *pl.* | plural |
| *dem.* | demonstrative | *Poet.* | Poetical |
| *dial.* | dialect | *Pol.* | Political |
| *Eccl.* | Ecclesiastical | *poss.* | possessive |
| *Econ.* | Economics | *p.p.* | past participle |
| *Elec.* | Electricity | *prec.* | preceded |
| *emph.* | emphatic | *pred.* | predicative |
| *Engin.* | Engineering | *prep.* | preposition |
| *Ent.* | Entomology | *pron.* | pronoun |
| *excl.* | exclamation | *Psych.* | Psychology |
| *f.* | feminine | *r.* | reflexive |
| *fig.* | figurative | *Rad.* | Radio |
| *Fin.* | Finance | *Railw.* | Railways |
| *Footb.* | Football | *reg.* | regular |
| *Genit.* | Genitive | *Rel.* | Religion |
| *Geog.* | Geography | *rel.* | relative |
| *Geol.* | Geology | *s.* | substantive |
| *Geom.* | Geometry | *Sch.* | School |
| *Gram.* | Grammar | *Scot.* | Scottish |
| *Gymn.* | Gymnastics | *sing.* | singular |
| *Her.* | Heraldry | *sl.* | slang |
| *Hist.* | History | *s.th.* | something |
| *Hunt.* | Hunting | *Tail.* | Tailoring |
| *imper.* | imperative | *Tech.* | Technical |
| *impers.* | impersonal | *Teleph.* | Telephone |
| *Ind.* | Industry | *temp.* | temporal |
| *indecl.* | indeclinable | *Text.* | Textiles |
| *indef.* | indefinite | *Theat.* | Theatre |
| *infin.* | infinitive | *Theol.* | Theology |
| *insep.* | inseparable | *Transp.* | Transport |
| *int.* | interjection | *Typ.* | Typography |
| *interr.* | interrogative | *Univ.* | University |
| *intim.* | intimate | *us.* | usually |
| *iron.* | ironical | *v.a.* | active *or* transitive verb |
| *irr.* | irregular | *v.n.* | neuter *or* intransitive verb |
| *Ling.* | Linguistics | *v.r.* | reflexive verb |
| *Lit.* | Literary | *Vet.* | Veterinary Science |
| *Log.* | Logic | *vulg.* | vulgar |
| | | *Zool.* | Zoology |

# Cassell's German-English Dictionary

# A

**A, a** [a:], *n. das A* (des —s, die —s) the letter A; (*Mus.*) the note A; *A Dur*, A major; *A Moll*, A minor.

**Aal** [a:l], *m.* (—s, *pl.* —e) eel.

**Aas** [a:s], *n.* (—es, *pl.* Äser *or* —e) carcass, carrion.

**ab** [ap], *adv.* off; down; away; (*Theat.*) exit *or* exeunt, — *und zu*, now and again, occasionally; *auf und* —, up and down, to and fro. — *prep.* from; — *Hamburg*, from Hamburg.

**abändern** ['apɛndərn], *v.a.* alter.

**Abart** ['apa:rt], *f.* (—, *pl.* —en) variety, species.

**Abbau** ['apbau], *m.* (—s, *no pl.*) demolition, dismantling; reduction (of staff).

**abberufen** ['apbəru:fən], *v.a. irr.* recall.

**abbestellen** ['apbəʃtɛlən], *v.a.* countermand, annul, cancel (an order).

**Abbild** ['apbɪlt], *n.* (—es, *pl.* —er) copy, image.

**Abbildung** ['apbɪlduŋ], *f.* (—, *pl.* —en) illustration.

**Abbitte** ['apbɪtə], *f.* (—, *pl.* —n) apology; — *tun*, apologise.

**abblenden** ['apblɛndən], *v.a.* dim (lights).

**Abbruch** ['apbrux], *m.* (—s, *pl.* ⁻e) breaking off; demolition; *einer Sache* — *tun*, damage s.th.

**abdanken** ['apdaŋkən], *v.n.* resign, abdicate, retire (from office).

**abdecken** ['apdɛkən], *v.a.* uncover, unroof; clear (the table).

**Abdruck** ['apdruk], *m.* (—s, *pl.* —e) impression, copy, reprint, cast.

**Abend** ['a:bənt], *m.* (—s, *pl.* —e) evening, eve.

**Abendbrot** ['a:bəntbro:t], *n.* (—s, *no pl.*) evening meal, (*Am.*) supper.

**Abendland** ['a:bəntlant], *n.* (—es, *no pl.*) occident, west.

**Abendmahl** ['a:bəntma:l], *n.* (—s, *no pl.*) supper; *das heilige* —, Holy Communion, the Lord's Supper.

**abends** ['a:bənts], *adv.* in the evening, of an evening.

**Abenteuer** ['a:bəntɔyər], *n.* (—s, *pl.* —) adventure.

**aber** ['a:bər], *conj.* but, however; (*emphatic*) — *ja!* yes, indeed! of course! —*prefix.* again, once more.

**Aberglaube** ['a:bərglaubə], *m.* (—ns, *no pl.*) superstition.

**abermals** ['a:bərma:ls], *adv.* again, once more.

**Abessinien** [abɛ'si:njən], *n.* Abyssinia.

**abfahren** ['apfa:rən], *v.n. irr.* (*aux.* sein) set out, depart, drive off.

**Abfall** ['apfal], *m.* (—s, *pl.* ⁻e) scrap, remnant; secession; slope; (*pl.*) waste, refuse.

**abfallen** ['apfalən], *v.n. irr.* (*aux.* sein) fall off; desert; slope.

**abfällig** ['apfɛlɪç], *adj.* derogatory.

**abfangen** ['apfaŋən], *v.a. irr.* intercept, catch.

**abfärben** ['apfɛrbən], *v.n.* (*colours*)run; stain; lose colour.

**abfassen** ['apfasən], *v.a.* compose, draft.

**abfertigen** ['apfɛrtɪgən], *v.a.* despatch; deal with, serve (a customer *or* client).

**abfeuern** ['apfɔyərn], *v.a.* fire (off), launch (rocket, missile).

**abfinden** ['apfɪndən], *v.a.irr.* indemnify, compound with (o.'s creditors). — *v.r. sich* — *mit*, put up with, come to terms with.

**Abflug** ['apflu:k], *m.* (—s, *pl.* ⁻e) take-off, departure (by air).

**Abfluß** ['apflus], *m.* (—sses, *pl.* ⁻sse) flowing off; drain.

**Abfuhr** ['apfu:r], *f.* (—, *pl.* —en) removal, collection (of refuse); (*coll.*) rebuff.

**abführen** ['apfy:rən], *v.a.* arrest, lead away. —*v.n.* (*Med.*) act as a purgative.

**Abführmittel** ['apfy:rmɪtəl], *n.* (—s, *pl.* —) purgative, laxative.

**Abgabe** ['apga:bə], *f.* (—, *pl.* —n) delivery, tax, duty, levy.

**abgabepflichtig** ['apga:bəpflɪçtɪç], *adj.* taxable, subject to duty.

**Abgang** ['apgaŋ], *m.* (—(e)s, *pl.* ⁻e) wastage, loss; departure; *Schul*—, school-leaving.

**abgängig** ['apgɛŋɪç], *adj.* lost, missing; (*of goods*) saleable.

**abgeben** ['apge:bən], *v.a. irr.* deliver, cede; give (an opinion). — *v.r. sich mit etwas*, — concern o.s. with s.th.

**abgedroschen** ['apgədrɔʃən], *adj.* (*phrases etc.*) trite, hackneyed.

**abgefeimt** ['apgəfaɪmt], *adj.* cunning, crafty.

**abgegriffen** ['apgəgrɪfən], *adj.* well thumbed, worn.

**abgehen** ['apge:ən], *v.n. irr.* (*aux.* sein) leave, retire; branch off; (*Theat.*) make an exit.

**abgelebt** ['apgəle:pt], *adj.* (*of humans*) decrepit, worn out.

**abgelegen** ['apgəle:gən], *adj.* remote, distant.

**abgemacht** ['apgəmaxt], *adj., int.* agreed! done!

**abgeneigt** ['apgənaɪkt], *adj.* disinclined, averse.

**Abgeordnete** ['apgəɔrdnətə], *m., f.* (—n, *pl.* —n) political representative, deputy, Member of Parliament.

**Abgesandte** ['apgəzantə], *m., f.* (—n, *pl.* —n) delegate, ambassador.

1

**abgeschieden** ['apgəʃiːdən], *adj.* secluded, remote; deceased.

**abgeschmackt** ['apgəʃmakt], *adj.* insipid.

**abgesehen** ['apgəzeːən], *adv.* — *von*, apart from, except for.

**abgespannt** ['apgəʃpant], *adj.* worn out, run down, exhausted.

**abgestorben** ['apgəʃtɔrbən], *adj.* dead, numb.

**abgetan** ['apgətaːn], *adj.* finished, over, done with; *damit ist die Sache* —, that finishes the matter.

**abgetragen** ['apgətraːgən], *adj.* (*clothes*) shabby, threadbare.

**abgewöhnen** ['apgəvøːnən], *v.a. einem etwas* —, free (rid) s.o. from (of) a habit, wean from.

**abgrasen** ['apgraːzən], *v.a.* (*animals*) graze.

**Abgrund** ['apgrunt], *m.* (—es, *pl.* ⁚e) abyss, precipice.

**Abguss** ['apgus], *m.* (—es, *pl.* ⁚e) cast, plaster-cast, mould.

**abhalten** ['aphaltən], *v.a. irr.* restrain, hold back; hold (meeting etc.).

**abhandeln** ['aphandəln], *v.a. einem etwas* —, bargain for s.th.

**abhanden** [ap'handən], *adv.* mislaid; — *kommen*, get lost.

**Abhandlung** ['aphandluŋ], *f.* (—, *pl.* —en) treatise, dissertation; (*pl.*) proceedings.

**Abhang** ['aphaŋ], *m.* (—es, *pl.* ⁚e) slope; declivity.

**abhängen** ['aphɛŋən], *v.a. irr.* take off, unhook; *von etwas* oder *jemandem* —, depend on s.th. *or* s.o.

**abhärten** ['aphɛrtən], *v.a.* inure against rigours, toughen.

**abheben** ['apheːbən], *v.a. irr.* draw (money from bank).

**abhold** ['aphɔlt], *adj.* averse to (*Dat.*).

**abholen** ['aphoːlən], *v.a. etwas* —, fetch, collect s.th.; *einen* —, meet s.o. (at the station etc.).

**Abitur** [abi'tuːr], *n.* (—s, *no pl.*) matriculation examination.

**Abiturient** [abitu'rjɛnt], *m.* (—en, *pl.* —en) matriculation candidate.

**Abkehr** ['apkeːr], *f.* (—, *no pl.*) turning away, renunciation.

**abklären** ['apkleːrən], *v.a.* (*Chem.*) filter, clear.

**Abkommen** ['apkɔmən], *n.* (—s, *pl.* —) treaty, agreement, contract.

**Abkömmling** ['apkœmliŋ], *m.* (—s, *pl.* —e) descendant.

**abkühlen** ['apkyːlən], *v.a.* cool, chill.

**Abkunft** ['apkunft], *f.* (—, *no pl.*) descent, origin.

**abkürzen** ['apkyrtsən], *v.a.* shorten, abridge, curtail.

**abladen** ['aplaːdən], *v.a. irr.* unload, dump.

**Ablaß** ['aplas], *m.* (—sses, *pl.* ⁚sse) (*Eccl.*) indulgence.

**ablassen** ['aplasən], *v.n. irr. von etwas* —, desist from, refrain from s.th.— *v.a. einem etwas billig* —, reduce the price of s.th. for s.o.

**Ablauf** ['aplauf], *m.* (—es, *no pl.*) (*water*) drainage; (*ticket*) expiration; lapse (of time); (*bill*) maturity.

**ablaufen** ['aplaufən], *v.n. irr.* (*aux.* sein) (*water*) run off; (*ticket*) expire; *gut* —, turn out well.

**Ableben** ['apleːbən], *n.* (—s, *no pl.*) decease, death.

**ablegen** ['apleːgən], *v.a.* (*clothes*) take off; (*documents*) file; *Rechenschaft* —, account for; *eine Prüfung* —, take an examination.

**Ableger** ['apleːgər], *m.* (—s, *pl.* —) (*Hort.*) cutting.

**Ablegung** ['apleːguŋ], *f.* (—, *no pl.*) making (of a vow); taking (of an oath).

**ablehnen** ['apleːnən], *v.a.* refuse, decline.

**ableiten** ['aplaitən], *v.a.* divert, draw off; (*water*) drain; (*words*) derive from.

**ablenken** ['aplɛŋkən], *v.a.* (*aux.* haben) *einen von etwas* —, divert s.o.'s attention from s.th., distract.

**ablesen** ['apleːzən], *v.a. irr.* (*meter*) read off; (*field*) glean.

**abliefern** ['apliːfərn], *v.a.* deliver.

**ablösen** ['apløːzən], *v.a. einen* —, take the place of s.o., (*Mil.*) relieve; detach (a stamp from a letter etc.).

**abmachen** ['apmaxən], *v.a.* undo, detach; settle, arrange.

**abmagern** ['apmaːgərn], *v.n.* (*aux.* sein) get thinner, waste away.

**Abmarsch** ['apmarʃ], *m.* (—es, *no pl.*) (*Mil.*) marching off.

**abmelden** ['apmɛldən], *v.r. sich* —, give notice of departure.

**abmessen** ['apmɛsən], *v.a. irr.* measure (off), gauge.

**abmühen** ['apmyːən], *v.r. sich* —, exert o.s., strive.

**Abnahme** ['apnaːmə], *f.* (—, *pl.* —n) decline, loss of weight; (*moon*) waning; (*goods*) taking delivery.

**abnehmen** ['apneːmən], *v.n. irr.* lose weight; (*moon*) wane. — *v.a.* (*hat*) take off; *einem etwas* —, relieve s.o. (of trouble or work).

**Abneigung** ['apnaiguŋ], *f.* (—, *pl.* —en) antipathy, dislike.

**abnutzen** ['apnutsən], *v.a.* wear out by use.

**Abonnement** [abɔnə'maŋ], *n.* (—s, *pl.* —s) (*newspaper*) subscription; (*railway*) season-ticket.

**Abonnent** [abɔ'nɛnt], *m.* (—en, *pl.* —en) subscriber.

**abonnieren** [abɔ'niːrən], *v.a.* subscribe to (a paper).

**Abordnung** ['apɔrdnuŋ,] *f.* (—, *pl.* —en) delegation, deputation.

**Abort** [a'bɔrt], *m.* (—s, *pl.* —e) lavatory, toilet.

**Abortus** [a'bɔrtus], *m.* (—us, *no pl.*) (*Med.*) abortion.

**abplagen** ['applaːgən], *v.r. sich* —, slave, toil.

**abprallen** ['appralən], *v.n.* (*aux.* sein) *von etwas* —, bounce off, rebound.

**abquälen** ['apkvɛ:lən], v.r. sich —, toil, make o.s. weary (mit, with).

**abraten** ['apra:tən], v.n. irr. einem von etwas —, dissuade s.o. from, advise or warn s.o. against.

**abräumen** ['aprɔymən], v.a. remove; den Tisch —, clear the table.

**abrechnen** ['aprɛçnən], v.a. reckon up. — v.n. mit einem —, settle accounts with s.o., (coll.) get even with s.o.

**Abrede** ['apre:də], f. (—, pl. —n) agreement, arrangement; in — stellen, deny.

**abreißen** ['apraɪsən], v.a. irr. tear off.

**abrichten** ['aprɪçtən], v.a. (dogs) train, (horses) break in.

**abriegeln** ['apri:gəln], v.a. bolt, bar.

**Abriß** ['aprɪs], m. (—sses, pl. —sse) sketch; summary, synopsis.

**abrollen** ['aprɔlən], v.a. uncoil. — v.n. (aux. sein) roll off.

**abrücken** ['aprykən], v.a. move away. —v.n. (aux. sein) (Mil.) march off.

**Abruf** ['apru:f], m. (—es, no pl.) recall (from a post).

**abrunden** ['aprundən], v.a. round off.

**abrupfen** ['aprupfən], v.a. (feathers) pluck; (flowers) pluck off.

**abrüsten** ['aprystən], v.n. disarm.

**Abrüstung** ['aprystuŋ], f. (—, no pl.) disarmament.

**abrutschen** ['aprutʃən], v.n. (aux. sein) slide, slither down.

**Absage** ['apza:gə], f. (—, pl. —n) cancellation, refusal.

**absagen** ['apza:gən], v.n. refuse, beg to be excused, decline (an invitation).

**Absatz** ['apzats], m. (—es, pl. ·e) (shoe) heel; (letter) paragraph; (Comm.) guter —, ready sale.

**abschaffen** ['apʃafən], v.a. abolish, do away with.

**abschälen** ['apʃɛ:lən], v.a. peel. — v.r. sich —, peel off.

**abschätzen** ['apʃɛtsən], v.a. estimate, appraise; (taxes) assess.

**Abschaum** ['apʃaum], m. (—es, no pl.) scum.

**Abscheu** ['apʃɔy], m. (—s, no pl.) abhorrence, detestation, loathing.

**abscheulich** ['apʃɔylɪç], adj. abominable, repulsive.

**abschieben** ['apʃi:bən], v.a. irr. shove off, push off; schieb ab! scram!

**Abschied** ['apʃi:t], m. (—s, pl. —e) leave, departure, farewell; discharge; resignation.

**abschießen** ['apʃi:sən], v.a. irr. shoot off; discharge; (gun) fire; den Vogel —, win the prize.

**abschinden** ['apʃɪndən], v.r. irr. sich —, exhaust o.s. with hard work.

**abschirren** ['apʃɪrən], v.a. unharness.

**abschlagen** ['apʃla:gən], v.a. irr. (attack) beat off; (branches) lop off; einem etwas —, deny s.o. s.th.; eine Bitte —, refuse a request.

**abschlägig** ['apʃlɛgɪç], adj. negative.

**Abschlagszahlung** ['apʃlakstsa:luŋ], f. (—, pl. —en) payment by instalments.

**abschleifen** ['apʃlaɪfən], v.a. irr. grind off.

**abschleppen** ['apʃlɛpən], v.a. (car) tow (away). — v.r. sich —, wear o.s. out by carrying heavy loads.

**abschließen** ['apʃli:sən], v.a. irr. lock up; (work) conclude; (accounts) balance; einen Vertrag —, conclude an agreement.

**Abschluß** ['apʃlus], m. (—sses, pl. ·sse) settlement, winding-up.

**abschneiden** ['apʃnaɪdən], v.a. irr. cut off. — v.n. gut —, come off well.

**Abschnitt** ['apʃnɪt], m. (—es, pl. —e) section; (book) paragraph.

**abschnüren** ['apʃny:rən], v.a. lace up, tie up.

**abschrecken** ['apʃrɛkən], v.a. deter, frighten.

**abschreiben** ['apʃraɪbən], v.a. irr. copy, transcribe; crib; eine Schuld —, write off a debt.

**Abschrift** ['apʃrɪft], f. (—, pl. —en) copy, transcript, duplicate; beglaubigte —, certified copy.

**Abschuß** ['apʃus], m. (—sses, pl. ·sse) act of firing (a gun), shooting down (aircraft).

**abschüssig** ['apʃysɪç], adj. steep.

**abschütteln** ['apʃytəln], v.a. shake off, cast off.

**abschwächen** ['apʃvɛçən], v.a. weaken, diminish.

**abschweifen** ['apʃvaɪfən], v.n. (aux. sein) digress (from), deviate.

**abschwenken** ['apʃvɛŋkən], v.n. (aux. sein) wheel off (or aside).

**abschwören** ['apʃvø:rən], v.a. irr. abjure, renounce by oath.

**absehbar** ['apze:ba:r], adj. imaginable, conceivable, foreseeable.

**absehen** ['apze:ən], v.a., v.n. irr. einem etwas —, copy s.th. from s.o.; auf etwas —, aim at s.th.; von etwas —, waive s.th.; refrain from s.th.

**abseits** ['apzaɪts], adv., prep. (Genit.) aside; — von, away from.

**Absender** ['apzɛndər], m. (—s, pl.—) sender; (Comm.) consigner.

**absetzen** ['apzɛtsən], v.a. set down; dismiss, deprive of office; depose; (Comm.) sell, dispose of.

**Absicht** ['apzɪçt], f. (—, pl. —en) intention, purpose, aim.

**absondern** ['apzɔndərn], v.a. separate, set apart; (Med.) secrete. — v.r. sich —, seclude o.s. from.

**abspannen** ['apʃpanən], v.a. unharness.

**absparen** ['apʃpa:rən], v.n. sich etwas vom Munde —, stint o.s. for s.th.

**abspenstig** ['apʃpenstɪç], adj.—machen, alienate s.o.'s affections, entice s.o. away; — werden, desert.

**absperren** ['apʃpɛrən], v.a. (door) lock, shut up; (street) close, barricade; (gas, water) turn off.

**absprechen** ['apʃprɛçən], v.a. irr. einem das Recht —, deprive s.o. of the right to do s.th.

3

# abspülen

**abspülen** [ˈapʃpyːlən], *v.a.* wash up, rinse.

**abstammen** [ˈapʃtamən], *v.n. (aux. sein)* descend from, originate from.

**Abstand** [ˈapʃtant], *m.* (—es, pl. ⸚e) distance; *von etwas — nehmen,* refrain from doing s.th.

**abstatten** [ˈapʃtatən], *v.a. einen Besuch —,* pay a visit; *einen Bericht —,* report on; *Dank —,* return thanks.

**abstechen** [ˈapʃtɛçən], *v.a. irr. Tiere —,* slaughter animals. — *v.n. von etwas —,* contrast with s.th.

**Abstecher** [ˈapʃtɛçər], *m.* (—s, pl. —) short trip, excursion; detour.

**abstecken** [ˈapʃtɛkən], *v.a.* mark off, peg out.

**absteigen** [ˈapʃtaɪgən], *v.n. irr. (aux. sein)* descend, alight, dismount.

**abstellen** [ˈapʃtɛlən], *v.a.* put s.th. down; *(gas, water)* turn off.

**absterben** [ˈapʃtɛrbən], *v.n. irr. (aux. sein)* wither; die.

**Abstieg** [ˈapʃtiːk], *m.* (—es, no pl.) descent.

**Abstimmung** [ˈapʃtɪmuŋ], *f.* (—, pl. —en) *(Parl.)* division; referendum, voting.

**abstoßen** [ˈapʃtoːsən], *v.a. irr.* push off, kick off. —*v.n. (Naut.)* set sail.

**abstoßend** [ˈapʃtoːsənt], *adj.* repulsive, repugnant.

**abstreifen** [ˈapʃtraɪfən], *v.a. irr.* strip off, pull off; cast, shed.

**abstufen** [ˈapʃtuːfən], *v.a.* grade.

**abstumpfen** [ˈapʃtumpfən], *v.a.* blunt, dull, take the edge off.

**abstürzen** [ˈapʃtyrtsən], *v.n. (aux. sein) (person)* fall; fall down; *(Aviat.)* crash.

**Abt** [apt], *m.* (—es, pl. ⸚e) abbot.

**Abtei** [ˈaptaɪ], *f.* (—, pl. —en) abbey.

**Abteil** [ˈaptaɪl], *n.* (—s, pl. —e) compartment.

**abteilen** [ˈaptaɪlən], *v.a.* divide, partition.

**Abteilung** [apˈtaɪluŋ], *f.* (—, pl. —en) section, department.

**Äbtissin** [ɛpˈtɪsɪn], *f.* (—, pl. —nen) abbess.

**abtöten** [ˈaptøːtən], *v.a.* mortify, deaden.

**abtragen** [ˈaptraːgən], *v.a. irr.* carry away; *(building)* demolish; *(dress, shoes)* wear out; *eine Schuld —,* pay a debt.

**abtreiben** [ˈaptraɪbən], *v.a. irr. (cattle)* drive off; procure an abortion. —*v.n. (aux. sein) (ship)* drift off.

**Abtreibung** [ˈaptraɪbuŋ], *f.* (—, pl. —en) abortion.

**abtrennen** [ˈaptrɛnən], *v.a. (s.th. sewn)* unpick; separate.

**Abtretung** [ˈaptreːtuŋ], *f.* (—, pl. —en) cession; conveyance.

**Abtritt** [ˈaptrɪt], *m.* (—es, pl. —e) W.C.; *(Theat.)* exit *or* exeunt.

**abtrocknen** [ˈaptrɔknən], *v.a.* dry.

**abtrünnig** [ˈaptrynɪç], *adj.* disloyal, faithless.

**aburteilen** [ˈapurtaɪlən], *v.a.* pass judgment on.

**abwägen** [ˈapvɛːgən], *v.a. gegeneinander —,* weigh against each other.

**abwälzen** [ˈapvɛltsən], *v.a. etwas von sich —,* clear o.s. from s.th.

**abwandeln** [ˈapvandəln], *v.n.* change; *(verbs)* conjugate; *(nouns)* decline.

**abwärts** [ˈapvɛrts], *prep., adv.* downward.

**abwaschen** [ˈapvaʃən], *v.a. irr.* wash up.

**abwechseln** [ˈapvɛksəln], *v.a.* vary, alternate.

**Abweg** [ˈapveːk], *m.* (—es, pl. —e) wrong way; *auf —e geraten,* go astray.

**abwehren** [ˈapveːrən], *v.a.* ward off, parry.

**abweichen** [ˈapvaɪçən], *v.n. irr. (aux. sein) — von,* deviate from.

**abweisen** [ˈapvaɪzən], *v.a. irr.* refuse admittance to, rebuff.

**abwenden** [ˈapvɛndən], *v.a. irr.* avert, prevent. — *v.r. sich —,* turn away from.

**abwesend** [ˈapveːzənt], *adj.* absent.

**Abwesenheit** [ˈapveːzənhaɪt], *f.* (—, pl. —en) absence.

**abwickeln** [ˈapvɪkəln], *v.a.* uncoil; *(business)* wind up.

**abwischen** [ˈapvɪʃən], *v.a.* wipe clean; *sich die Stirn —,* mop o.'s brow.

**abzahlen** [ˈaptsaːlən], *v.a.* pay off; pay by instalments.

**abzehren** [ˈaptseːrən], *v.n. (aux. sein)* waste away.

**Abzeichen** [ˈaptsaɪçən], *n.* (—s, pl. —) badge, insignia.

**abzeichnen** [ˈapsaɪçnən], *v.a.* sketch, draw from a model. — *v.r. sich —,* become clear.

**abziehen** [ˈaptsiːən], *v.a. irr.* deduct, subtract; *(knife)* sharpen; strip (a bed). — *v.n. (aux. sein)* depart; *(Mil.)* march off.

**Abzug** [ˈaptsuːk], *m.* (—es, pl. ⸚e) retreat, departure; photographic copy; — *der Kosten,* deduction of charges; *(steam, air)* outlet.

**abzweigen** [ˈaptsvaɪgən], *v.n. (aux. sein)* fork off, branch off.

**Achsel** [ˈaksəl], *f.* (—, pl. —n) shoulder; *die —n zucken,* shrug o.'s shoulders.

**Acht** [axt], *f.* (—, no pl.) attention, care, caution, heed; *achtgeben,* pay attention; *sich in — acht nehmen,* be careful; ban, excommunication, outlawry; *in — und Bann tun,* outlaw, proscribe.

**acht** [axt], *num. adj.* eight; *in — Tagen,* in a week; *vor — Tagen,* a week ago.

**achtbar** [ˈaxtbaːr], *adj.* respectable.

**achten** [ˈaxtən], *v.a.* hold in esteem, value; — *auf,* pay attention to, keep an eye on.

**ächten** [ˈɛxtən], *v.a.* ban, outlaw, proscribe.

**achtlos** [ˈaxtloːs], *adj.* inattentive, negligent.

**achtsam** [ˈaxtzaːm], *adj.* attentive, careful.

**Achtung** [ˈaxtuŋ], *f.* (—, no pl.) esteem, regard; *(Mil.)* attention!

**Ächtung** [ˈɛxtuŋ], *f.* (—, no pl.) ban, proscription.

**achtzehn** [ˈaxtseːn], *num. adj.* eighteen.

4

# Alpdrücken

achtzig ['axtsɪç], *num. adj.* eighty.
ächzen ['ɛçtsən], *v.n.* groan.
Acker ['akər], *m.* (—s, *pl.* ∸) field, arable land; *den — bestellen,* till the soil.
ackern ['akərn], *v.n.* till (the land).
addieren [a'di:rən], *v.a.* add, add up.
Adel ['a:dəl], *m.* (—s, *no pl.*) nobility, aristocracy.
ad(e)lig ['a:dlɪç], *adj.* of noble birth, aristocratic.
Ader ['a:dər], *f.* (—, *pl.* —n) vein; *zu — lassen,* bleed s.o.
Adler ['a:dlər], *m.* (—s, *pl.* —) eagle.
Adresse [a'drɛsə], *f.* (—, *pl.* —n) address.
adrett [a'drɛt], *adj.* neat, adroit, smart.
Affe ['afə], *m.* (—n, *pl.* —n) ape, monkey; (*fig.*) fool.
affektiert [afɛk'ti:rt], *adj.* affected, giving o.s. airs.
äffen ['ɛfən], *v.a.* ape, mimic.
Afghanistan [af'ganistan], *n.* Afghanistan.
Afrika ['a:frika], *n.* Africa.
After ['aftər], *m.* (—s, *pl.* —) anus.
Agentur [agɛn'tu:r], *f.* (—, *pl.* —en) agency.
Agraffe [a'grafə], *f.* (—, *pl.* —n) brooch, clasp.
Agrarier [a'gra:rjər], *m.* (—s, *pl.* —) landed proprietor.
Ägypten [ɛ'gyptən], *n.* Egypt.
Ahle ['a:lə], *f.* (—, *pl.* —n) awl, bodkin.
Ahn [a:n], *m.* (—en, *pl.* —en) ancestor, forefather.
ahnden ['a:ndən], *v.a.* avenge, punish.
Ahne ['a:nə] *see* Ahn.
ähneln ['ɛ:nəln], *v.a.* resemble, look like.
ahnen ['a:nən], *v.a.,* *v.n.* have a presentiment, foresee, have a hunch.
ähnlich ['ɛ:nlɪç], *adj.* resembling, like, similar.
Ahnung ['a:nuŋ], *f.* (—, *pl.* —en) foreboding, presentiment, idea, (*Am.*) hunch.
Ahorn ['a:hɔrn], *m.* (—s, *pl.* —e) (*Bot.*) maple.
Ähre ['ɛ:rə], *f.* (—, *pl.* —n) ear of corn.
Akademiker [aka'de:mɪkər], *m.* (—s, *pl.* —) university graduate.
akademisch [aka'de:mɪʃ], *adj.* academic; — *gebildet,* with a university education.
Akazie [a'ka:tsjə], *f.* (—, *pl.* —n) (*Bot.*) acacia.
akklimatisieren [aklimati'zi:rən], *v.r.* *sich* —, become acclimatised.
Akkord [a'kɔrt], *m.* (—es, *pl.* —e) (*Mus.*) chord; *in* — *arbeiten,* work on piece-rates.
Akt [akt], *m.* (—es, *pl.* —e) deed, action; (*Theat.*) act; (*Art*) (depiction of) the nude.
Akte ['aktə], *f.* (—, *pl.* —n) document, deed; (*pl.*) records, files; *zu den* —*n legen,* pigeonhole, shelve.
Aktenstück ['aktənʃtyk], *n.* (—es, *pl.* —e) official document, file.
Aktie ['aktsjə], *f.* (—, *pl.* —n) (*Comm.*) share, (*Am.*) stock.

Aktiengesellschaft ['aktsjəngəzɛlʃaft], *f.* (—, *pl.* —en) joint stock company.
Aktionär [aktsjo'nɛ:r], *m.* (—s, *pl.* —e) shareholder, (*Am.*) stockholder.
Aktiv ['akti:f], *n.* (—s, *pl.* —e) (*Gram.*) active voice.
Aktiva [ak'ti:va], *n. pl.* (*Comm.*) assets.
aktuell [aktu'ɛl], *adj.* topical.
akzentuieren [aktsɛntu'i:rən], *v.a.* accentuate, stress, emphasize.
Albanien [al'ba:njən], *n.* Albania.
albern ['albərn], *adj.* silly, foolish.
Aliment [ali'mɛnt], *n.* (—es, *pl.* —e) (*usually pl.*—e) alimony, maintenance.
Alkali [al'ka:li], *n.* (—s, *pl.* —en) alkali.
Alkohol ['alkoho:l], *m.* (—s, *no pl.*) alcohol.
Alkoholiker [alko'ho:lɪkər], *m.* (—s, *pl.* —) drunkard, alcoholic.
All [al], *n.* (—s, *no pl.*) the universe, (outer) space.
all [al], *adj.* all, entire, whole; every, each, any.
alle ['alə], *adj.* all, everybody; — *beide,* both of them.
Allee [a'le:], *f.* (—, *pl.* —n) tree-lined walk, avenue.
allein [a'laɪn], *adj.* alone, sole. — *adv.* solely, only, merely. —*conj.* (*obs.*) only, but, however.
alleinig [a'laɪnɪç], *adj.* sole, only, exclusive.
allenfalls [alən'fals], *adv.* possibly, perhaps, if need be.
allenthalben [alənt'halbən], *adv.* everywhere, in all places.
allerdings [alər'dɪŋs], *adv.* of course, indeed, nevertheless.
allerhand [alər'hant], *adj.* of all sorts *or* kinds, various; *das ist ja* —! I say!
Allerheiligen [alər'haɪlɪgən], *pl.* All Saints' Day.
allerlei [alər'laɪ], *adj.* miscellaneous, various.
allerliebst [alər'li:pst], *adj.* (*Am.*) cute; charming.
allerseits ['alərzaɪts], *adv.* generally, on all sides, universally.
alles ['aləs], *adj.* everything, all.
allgemein [algə'maɪn], *adj.* universal, common, general.
alliieren [ali'i:rən], *v.a.,* *v.n.* ally (o.s.).
allmächtig [al'mɛçtɪç], *adj.* omnipotent.
allmählich [al'mɛ:lɪç], *adj.* by degrees, gradual.
allseitig ['alzaɪtɪç], *adj.* universal, (*Am.*) all-round.
Alltag ['alta:k], *m.* (—s, *pl.*—e) working day, week-day.
allwissend [al'vɪsənt], *adj.* omniscient.
allzu ['altzu:], *adv.* too, much too.
Alm [alm], *f.* (—, *pl.* —en) Alpine meadow.
Almosen ['almo:zən], *n.* (—s, *pl.* —) alms, charity.
Alp [alp], *f.* (—, *pl.* —en) (*mostly pl.*) mountain(s), Alps.
Alpdrücken ['alpdrykən], *n.* (—s, *no pl.*) nightmare.

5

# als

**als** [als], *conj.* than; *(after comparatives)* than; as, like; but; *er hat nichts — Schulden,* he has nothing but debts; *(temp.)* when, as.
**alsbald** [als'balt], *adv.* forthwith.
**also** ['alzo:], *adv.* thus, so, in this manner. — *conj.* consequently, therefore.
**Alt** [alt], *m.* (—s, *pl.* —e) *(Mus.)* alto.
**alt** [alt], *adj.* old, ancient; aged; antique.
**Altan** [al'ta:n], *m.* (—s, *pl.* —e) balcony, gallery.
**Altar** [al'ta:r], *m.* (—s, *pl.* ⁇e) altar.
**altbacken** ['altbakən], *adj.* stale.
**Alter** ['altər], *n.* (—s, *no pl.*) age, old age; epoch.
**altern** ['altərn], *v.n.* *(aux.* sein) grow old.
**Altertum** ['altərtu:m], *n.* (—s, *pl.* ⁇er) antiquity.
**Altistin** [al'tıstın], *f.* (—, *pl.* —nen) *(Mus.)* contralto.
**altklug** ['altklu:k], *adj.* precocious.
**ältlich** ['eltlıç], *adj.* elderly.
**Altweibersommer** [alt'vaıbərzəmər], *m.* (—s, *pl.* —) Indian summer.
**Amboß** ['ambɔs], *m.* (—sses, *pl.* —sse) anvil.
**Ameise** ['a:maızə], *f.* (—, *pl.* —n) *(Ent.)* ant.
**Amerika** [a'me:rika], *n.* America.
**Amme** ['amə], *f.* (—, *pl.* —n) wet nurse.
**Ammoniak** [amon'jak], *n.* (—s, *no pl.*) ammonia.
**Ampel** ['ampəl], *f.* (—, *pl.* —n) (hanging) light, lamp, lantern; traffic light.
**Ampfer** ['ampfər], *m.* (—s, *pl.* —) *(Bot.)* sorrel, dock.
**Amsel** ['amzəl], *f.* (—, *pl.* —n) *(Orn.)* blackbird.
**Amt** [amt], *n.* (—es, *pl.* ⁇er) office, post, employment; administration, domain, jurisdiction; place of public business.
**amtlich** ['amtlıç], *adj.* official.
**Amtmann** ['amtman], *m.* (—s, *pl.* ⁇er) bailiff.
**Amtsblatt** ['amtsblat], *n.* (—es, *pl.* ⁇er) official gazette.
**Amtsgericht** ['amtsgərıçt], *n.* (—s, *pl.* —e) county court; *(Am.)* district court.
**amüsieren** [amy'zi:rən], *v.a.* amuse.— *v.r. sich* —, enjoy o.s.
**an** [an], *prep.* *(Dat. or Acc.)*, at, to, on.
**analog** [ana'lo:k], *adj.* analogous.
**Ananas** ['ananas], *f.* (—, *pl.* —) pineapple.
**Anatom** [ana'to:m], *m.* (—en, *pl.* —en) anatomist.
**anbahnen** ['anba:nən], *v.a.* initiate, open up, pave the way for.
**anbändeln** ['anbendəln], *v.n.* — *mit,* flirt with, make up to.
**Anbau** ['anbau], *m.* (—s, *pl.* —ten) *(grain)* cultivation; annex(e), wing (of building).
**anbauen** ['anbauən], *v.a.* cultivate; add to a building.
**anbei** [an'baı], *adv.* enclosed (in letter).
**anbeißen** ['anbaısən], *v.a. irr.* bite at,

take a bite of. — *v.n.* *(fish)* bite; *(coll.)* take the bait.
**anbelangen** ['anbəlaŋən], *v.a.* concern.
**anberaumen** ['anbəraumən], *v.a.* fix (a date).
**anbeten** ['anbe:tən], *v.a.* worship, adore, idolise.
**anbiedern** ['anbi:dərn], *v.r. ʒich mit einem* —, chum up with s.o.
**anbieten** ['anbi:tən], *v.a. irr.* offer.
**anbinden** ['anbındən], *v.a. irr.* tie on, bind to; *kurz angebunden sein,* be curt.
**Anblick** ['anblık], *m.* (—s, *no pl.*) view, sight, aspect, spectacle.
**anbrechen** ['anbreçən], *v.a. irr.* begin; break; start on. — *v.n.* dawn.
**anbrennen** ['anbrenən], *v.a. irr.* light, set fire to, burn. — *v.n.* *(aux.* sein) catch fire; burn.
**anbringen** ['anbrıŋən], *v.a. irr.* fit to, place.
**Anbruch** ['anbrux], *m.* (—s, *no pl.*) beginning; — *der Nacht,* night-fall.
**anbrüllen** ['anbrylən], *v.a.* roar at.
**Andacht** ['andaxt], *f.* (—, *pl.* —en) *(Eccl.)* devotion(s).
**andächtig** ['andɛxtıç], *adj.* devout.
**andauern** ['andauərn], *v.n.* last, continue.
**Andenken** ['andeŋkən], *n.* (—s, *pl.* —) memory; keepsake; souvenir.
**anderer** ['andərər], *adj.* other, different; *ein* —, another.
**andermal** ['andərma:l], *adv. ein* —, another time.
**ändern** ['ɛndərn], *v.a.* alter, change.
**andernfalls** ['andərnfals], *adv.* otherwise, or else.
**anders** ['andərs], *adv.* differently, in another manner, otherwise.
**anderthalb** ['andərthalp], *adj.* one and a half.
**anderweitig** ['andərvaıtıç], *adj.* elsewhere.
**andeuten** ['andɔytən], *v.a.* hint at, intimate, indicate.
**Andrang** ['andraŋ], *m.* (—es, *no pl.*) throng, crowd.
**aneignen** ['anaıgnən], *v.r. sich etwas* —, appropriate s.th.; *(an opinion)* adopt.
**anekeln** ['ane:kəln], *v.a.* disgust.
**Anerbieten** ['anɛrbi:tən], *n.* (—s, *pl.* —) offer.
**anerkennen** ['anɛrkenən], *v.a. irr.* acknowledge, appreciate, recognize, accept.
**anfachen** ['anfaxən], *v.a.* kindle (a flame).
**Anfahrt** ['anfa:rt], *f.* (—, *pl.* —en) drive; *(down a mine)* descent; *(Am.)* drive-way.
**Anfall** ['anfal], *m.* (—s, *pl.* ⁇e) attack, assault; *(Med.)* seizure, fit; *(mood)* fit, burst.
**anfallen** ['anfalən], *v.a. irr. einen* —, attack s.o.
**Anfang** ['anfaŋ], *m.* (—s, *pl.* ⁇e) beginning, start, commencement.

**anfangen** ['anfaŋən], *v.a. irr.* begin, start. — *v.n.* begin, originate.

**Anfänger** ['anfɛŋər], *m.* (—s, *pl.* —) beginner, novice.

**anfänglich** ['anfɛŋlɪç], *adv.* in the beginning, at first, initially.

**anfassen** ['anfasən], *v.a.* take hold of; touch; seize.

**anfechtbar** ['anfɛçtba:r], *adj.* disputable, refutable, debatable.

**anfechten** ['anfɛçtən], *v.a.* (*a will, a verdict*) contest; (*jurors*) challenge.

**anfeinden** ['anfaɪndən], *v.a.* show enmity to.

**anfertigen** ['anfɛrtɪgən], *v.a.* make, manufacture, prepare; (*a list*) draw up.

**anflehen** ['anfle:ən], *v.a.* implore, beseech.

**Anflug** ['anflu:k], *m.* (—s, *pl.* ˙˙e) (*Aviat.*) approach; (*beard*) down; touch.

**anfordern** ['anfɔrdərn], *v.a.* demand, claim.

**Anfrage** ['anfra:gə], *f.* (—, *pl.* —n) enquiry.

**anfügen** ['anfy:gən], *v.a.* join to, annex.

**anführen** ['anfy:rən], *v.a.* lead; adduce, quote (examples), cite; *einen* —, dupe s.o., take s.o. in.

**Anführungszeichen** ['anfy:ruŋstsaɪçən], *n.* (—s, *pl.* —) inverted commas, quotation marks.

**anfüllen** ['anfylən], *v.a. wieder* —, replenish.

**Angabe** ['anga:bə], *f.* (—, *pl.* —n) declaration, statement; data; instruction; bragging.

**angeben** ['ange:bən], *v.a. irr.* declare, state; *den Ton* —, lead the fashion; *den Wert* —, declare the value of.— *v.n. groß* —, brag, show off.

**Angeber** ['ange:bər], *m.* (—s, *pl.* —) informer; braggart.

**Angebinde** ['angəbɪndə], *n.* (—s, *pl.* —) (*obs.*) present, gift.

**angeblich** ['ange:plɪç], *adj.* ostensible, alleged, so-called.

**angeboren** ['angəbo:rən], *adj.* innate, inborn.

**Angebot** ['angəbo:t], *n.* (—es, *pl.* —e) offer, tender, bid; (*Comm.*) — *und Nachfrage*, supply and demand.

**angebracht** ['angəbraxt], *adj.* apt, appropriate, opportune.

**angedeihen** ['angədaɪən], *v.n. einem etwas* — *lassen*, bestow s.th. on s.o.

**angegossen** ['angəgɔsən], *adj. das sitzt wie* —, it fits like a glove.

**angehen** ['ange:ən], *v.a. irr. einen um etwas* —, apply to s.o. for s.th.; *das geht Dich nichts an*, that is none of your business.

**angehören** ['angəhø:rən], *v.n.* belong to.

**Angehörige** ['angəhø:rɪgə], *m., f.* (—n, *pl.* —n) near relative; next of kin.

**Angeklagte** ['angəkla:ktə], *m., f.* (—n, *pl.* —n) the accused, defendant, prisoner at the bar.

**Angel** ['aŋəl], *f.* (—, *pl.* —n) fishing-rod;

(*door*) hinge, pivot; *zwischen Tür und* —, in passing.

**angelegen** ['angəle:gən], *adj. sich etwas* — *sein lassen*, interest o.s. in s.th., concern o.s. in s.th.; *ich werde es mir* — *sein lassen*, I shall make it my business.

**Angelegenheit** ['angəle:gənhaɪt], *f.* (—, *pl.* —en) concern, matter, affair.

**angeln** ['aŋəln], *v.a.* fish, angle.

**angemessen** ['angəmɛsən], *adj.* proper, suitable, appropriate.

**angenehm** ['angəne:m], *adj.* acceptable, agreeable, pleasing, pleasant.

**angenommen** ['angənɔmən], *conj.* — *daß*, given that, supposing that, say.

**Anger** ['aŋər], *m.* (—s, *pl.* —) grassplot; green, common.

**angesehen** ['angəze:ən], *adj.* respected, esteemed, distinguished.

**Angesicht** ['angəzɪçt], *n.* (—s, *pl.* —er) face, countenance.

**angestammt** ['angəʃtamt], *adj.* ancestral, hereditary.

**Angestellte** ['angəʃtɛltə], *m., f.* (—n, *pl.* —n) employee; (*pl.*) staff.

**Angler** ['aŋlər], *m.* (—s, *pl.* —) angler, fisherman.

**angliedern** ['angli:dərn], *v.a.* annex, attach.

**Anglist** [an'glɪst], *m.* (—en, *pl.* —en) (*Univ.*) professor *or* student of English.

**angreifen** ['angraɪfən], *v.a. irr.* handle, touch; (*capital*) break into; attack, assail; *es greift mich an*, it taxes my strength.

**angrenzen** ['angrɛntsən], *v.n.* border upon, adjoin.

**Angriff** ['angrɪf], *m.* (—s, *pl.* —e) offensive, attack, assault.

**Angst** [aŋst], *f.* (—, *pl.* ˙˙e) anxiety; fear; anguish.

**ängstigen** ['ɛŋstɪgən], *v.a.* alarm, frighten. — *v.r. sich* —, feel uneasy, be afraid.

**angucken** ['angukən], *v.a.* look at.

**anhaben** ['anha:bən], *v.a. irr.* have on, be dressed in, wear; *einem etwas* —, hold s.th. against s.o.

**anhaften** ['anhaftən], *v.n.* stick to, adhere to.

**Anhalt** ['anhalt], *m.* (—es, *no pl.*) support, basis.

**anhalten** ['anhaltən], *v.a. irr. einen* —, stop s.o. — *v.n.* stop, pull up, halt; *um ein Mädchen* —, ask for a girl's hand in marriage. — *v.r. sich an etwas halten*, cling to, hang on to s.th.

**Anhaltspunkt** ['anhaltspuŋkt], *m.* (—es, *pl.* —e) clue, (*Am.*) lead.

**Anhang** ['anhaŋ], *m.* (—s, *pl.* ˙˙e) appendix, supplement.

**anhängen** ['anhɛŋən], *v.a. irr.* hang on, fasten to, attach.

**Anhänger** ['anhɛŋər], *m.* (—s, *pl.* —) follower, adherent; (*Footb.*) supporter; pendant (on a necklace); label; (*Transp.*) trailer.

**anhänglich** ['anhɛŋlɪç], *adj.* attached, affectionate.

**Anhängsel** ['anhɛŋsəl], *n.* (—s, *pl.* —) appendage.

**anhauchen** ['anhauxən], *v.a.* breathe upon.

**anhäufen** ['anhɔyfən], *v.a.* heap up, pile up, amass. —*v.r. sich* —, accumulate.

**anheben** ['anhe:bən], *v.a. irr.* lift. — *v.n. (obs.)* begin.

**anheim** [an'haɪm], *adv.* — *stellen,* leave to s.o.'s discretion.

**anheimeln** ['anhaɪməln], *v.a.* remind one of home.

**anheischig** ['anhaɪʃɪç], *adj. sich* — *machen,* undertake, pledge o.s.

**Anhieb** ['anhi:p], *m.* (—s, *pl.* —e) *(fencing)* first stroke; *auf* —, at the first attempt.

**Anhöhe** ['anhø:ə], *f.* (—, *pl.* —n) hill, rising ground.

**anhören** ['anhø:rən], *v.a.* listen to; tell by s.o.'s voice *or* accent.

**animieren** [ani'mi:rən], *v.a.* instigate, egg on.

**ankämpfen** ['ankɛmpfən], *v.n. gegen etwas* —, struggle against s.th.

**ankaufen** ['ankaufən], *v.a.* purchase, buy. — *v.r. sich irgendwo* —, buy land somewhere.

**Anker** ['aŋkər], *m.* (—s, *pl.* —) *(Naut.)* anchor; *den* — *auswerfen,* cast anchor.

**ankern** ['aŋkərn], *v.a., v.n.* anchor, cast anchor.

**Anklage** ['ankla:gə], *f.* (—, *pl.* —n) accusation; *gegen einen* — *erheben,* bring a charge against s.o.

**Ankläger** ['anklɛ:gər], *m.* (—s, *pl.* —) accuser, prosecutor; plaintiff.

**Anklang** ['anklaŋ], *m.* (—s, *pl.* ⁓e) reminiscence; — *finden,* please, meet with approval.

**ankleben** ['ankle:bən], *v.a.* stick to, glue to, paste on.

**ankleiden** ['anklaɪdən], *v.a.* dress. — *v.r. sich* —, dress o.s., get dressed.

**anklingeln** ['anklɪŋəln], *v.a. (coll.) einen* —, ring s.o. up (on the telephone).

**anklopfen** ['anklɔpfən], *v.n.* knock.

**anknüpfen** ['anknypfən], *v.a.* tie; join on to; *ein Gespräch* —, start a conversation; *wieder* —, resume.

**ankommen** ['ankɔmən], *v.n. irr. (aux. sein)* arrive; *es kommt darauf an,* it depends upon.

**ankreiden** ['ankraɪdən], *v.a.* chalk up.

**ankündigen** ['ankyndɪgən], *v.a.* announce, advertise, give notice of, proclaim.

**Ankunft** ['ankunft], *f.* (—, *no pl.*) arrival.

**ankurbeln** ['ankurbəln], *v.a. (Motor.)* crank up.

**Anlage** ['anla:gə], *f.* (—, *pl.* —n) *(capital)* investment; enclosure *(with a letter)*; *(industrial)* plant; *(building)* lay-out; *öffentliche* —, pleasure grounds; talent.

**anlangen** ['anlaŋən], *v.n. (aux. sein)* arrive; concern; *was das anlangt,* as far as this is concerned.

**Anlaß** ['anlas], *m.* (—sses, *pl.* ⁓sse) cause, occasion, motive.

**anlassen** ['anlasən], *v.a. irr.* keep on; *(Motor.)* start. — *v.r. sich gut* —, promise well.

**Anlasser** ['anlasər], *m.* (—s, *pl.* —) *(Motor.)* starter.

**anläßlich** ['anlɛslɪç], *prep. (Genit.)* à propos of, on the occasion of.

**Anlauf** ['anlauf], *m.* (—s, *pl.* ⁓e) start, run, *(Aviat.)* take-off run.

**anlaufen** ['anlaufən], *v.n. irr.* tarnish; call at (port).

**anlegen** ['anle:gən], *v.a. Geld* —, invest money; *Kleider* —, don clothes; *einen Garten* —, lay out a garden; *Hand* —, give a helping hand; *auf einen* —, take aim at s.o.; *(Naut.)* land, dock.

**Anlegestelle** ['anle:gəʃtɛlə], *f.* (—, *pl.* —n) landing place.

**anlehnen** ['anle:nən], *v.r. sich an etwas* —, lean against s. th.

**Anleihe** ['anlaɪə], *f.* (—, *pl.* —n) loan; *öffentliche* —, government loan; *eine* — *machen,* raise a loan.

**anleiten** ['anlaɪtən], *v.a.* train, instruct.

**anlernen** ['anlɛrnən], *v.a. einen* —, train, apprentice s.o. (in a craft).

**Anliegen** ['anli:gən], *n.* (—s, *pl.* —) request, petition, concern.

**anmachen** ['anmaxən], *v.a.* fix, fasten; light (a fire).

**anmaßen** ['anma:sən], *v.a. sich etwas* —, arrogate s.th.

**anmaßend** ['anma:sənt], *adj.* arrogant.

**anmelden** ['anmɛldən], *v.a.* announce, *(claim)* give notice of. — *v.r. sich* —, notify o.'s arrival, make an appointment; *sich* — *lassen,* send in o.'s name.

**Anmeldungsformular** [an'mɛlduŋs-fɔrmula:r], *n.* (—s, *pl.* —e) registration form.

**Anmerkung** ['anmɛrkuŋ], *f.* (—, *pl.* —en) remark, annotation, footnote.

**anmessen** ['anmɛsən], *v.a. irr.* measure (s.o. for a garment).

**Anmut** ['anmu:t], *f.* (—, *no pl.*) grace, charm.

**annähen** ['annɛ:ən], *v.a.* sew on (to).

**annähern** ['annɛ:ərn], *v.r. sich* —, approach, draw near; *(Maths.)* approximate.

**Annäherung** ['annɛ:əruŋ], *f.* (—, *pl.* —en) approach; *(Maths.)* approximation.

**Annahme** ['anna:mə], *f.* (—, *pl.* —n) acceptance; assumption, hypothesis.

**annehmbar** ['anne:mba:r], *adj.* acceptable; *ganz* —, passable.

**annehmen** ['anne:mən], *v.a. irr.* take, accept, take delivery of; suppose, assume, presume; *an Kindes Statt* —, adopt.

**Annehmlichkeit** ['anne:mlɪçkaɪt], *f.* (—, *pl.* —en) amenity, comfort.

**Annonce** [an'nɔ̃:sə], *f.* (—, *pl.* —n) (classified) advertisement (in newspaper).

**anordnen** ['anɔrdnən], *v.a.* arrange, regulate; order, direct.

# anspringen

**anorganisch** [ʼanɔrgaːnɪʃ], *adj.* inorganic.

**anpacken** [ʼanpakən], *v.a.* get hold of, seize, grasp.

**anpassen** [ʼanpasən], *v.a.* fit, suit. — *v.r. sich —,* adapt o.s.

**anpflanzen** [ʼanpflantsən], *v.a.* plant, grow.

**Anprall** [ʼanpral], *m.* (—s, *no pl.*) impact, bounce, shock.

**anpumpen** [ʼanpumpən], *v.a.* (*coll.*) *einen —,* borrow money from s.o.

**anrechnen** [ʼanrɛçnən], *v.a. einem etwas —,* charge s.o. with s.th.; *einem etwas hoch —,* think highly of a person for s.th.

**Anrecht** [ʼanrɛçt], *n.* (—es, *no pl.*) — *auf,* title to, claim to.

**Anrede** [ʼanreːdə], *f.* (—, *pl.* —n) (form of) address, title.

**anreden** [ʼanreːdən], *v.a.* address (s.o.); suggest (s.th.).

**anregen** [ʼanreːgən], *v.a.* stimulate (s.o.); suggest (s.th.).

**Anregung** [ʼanreːguŋ], *f.* (—, *pl.* —en) suggestion, hint.

**Anreiz** [ʼanraɪts], *m.* (—es, *no pl.*) incentive; impulse.

**Anrichte** [ʼanrɪçtə], *f.* (—, *pl.* —n) dresser, sideboard.

**anrichten** [ʼanrɪçtən], *v.a.* (*meal*) prepare, serve (up); *Unheil —,* make mischief.

**anrüchig** [ʼanryːçɪç], *adj.* disreputable.

**anrücken** [ʼanrykən], *v.a.* bring near to. — *v.n.* (*aux.* sein) approach.

**Anruf** [ʼanruːf], *m.* (—s, *pl.* —e) (*by sentry*) challenge; telephone call.

**anrufen** [ʼanruːfən], *v.a. irr.* call to, challenge; implore; ring up; *Gott —,* invoke God.

**anrühren** [ʼanryːrən], *v.a.* handle, touch; (*Cul.*) mix.

**Ansage** [ʼanzaːgə], *f.* (—, *pl.* —n) announcement.

**ansagen** [ʼanzaːgən], *v.a.* announce, notify.

**Ansager** [ʼanzaːgər], *m.* (—s, *pl.* —) announcer; compere.

**ansammeln** [ʼanzaməln], *v.a.* accumulate, gather. — *v.r. sich —,* gather, foregather, congregate, collect.

**ansässig** [ʼanzɛsɪç], *adj.* domiciled, resident; *sich — machen,* settle.

**Ansatz** [ʼanzats], *m.* (—es, *pl.* —e) start; (*Maths.*) construction; disposition (to), tendency (to).

**anschaffen** [ʼanʃafən], *v.a.* buy, purchase, get.

**anschauen** [ʼanʃauən], *v.a.* look at, view.

**anschaulich** [ʼanʃaulɪç], *adj.* clear; *einem etwas — machen,* give s.o. a clear idea of s.th.

**Anschauung** [ʼanʃauuŋ], *f.* (—, *pl.* —en) view, perception; *nach meiner —,* in my opinion.

**Anschein** [ʼanʃaɪn], *m.* (—s, *no pl.*) appearance, semblance.

**anscheinend** [ʼanʃaɪnənt], *adj.* apparent, ostensible, seeming.

**anschicken** [ʼanʃɪkən], *v.r. sich — zu,* prepare for, get ready for.

**anschirren** [ʼanʃɪrən], *v.a.* (*horses*) harness.

**Anschlag** [ʼanʃlaːk], *m.* (—s, *pl.* ⸚e) poster, placard; — *auf das Leben,* attempt at assassination.

**Anschlagbrett** [ʼanʃlaːkbrɛt], *n.* (—es, *pl.* —er) notice-board.

**anschlagen** [ʼanʃlaːgən], *v.a. irr.* (*keys of piano or typewriter*) strike, touch; (*knitting*) cast on; *zu hoch —,* overestimate.

**anschließen** [ʼanʃliːsən], *v.a. irr.* fasten with a lock. — *v.r. sich —,* join in; (*club*) join.

**Anschluß** [ʼanʃlus], *m.* (—sses, *pl.* ⸚sse) (*Railw., telephone*) [connection; (*Pol.*) annexation.

**Anschlußpunkt** [ʼanʃluspuŋkt], *m.* (—es, *pl.* —e) junction; (*Elec.*) inlet point, power point.

**anschmiegen** [ʼanʃmiːgən], *v.r. sich —,* nestle closely to.

**anschmieren** [ʼanʃmiːrən], *v.a. einen —,* (*coll.*) deceive, cheat s.o.

**anschnallen** [ʼanʃnalən], *v.a.* buckle on.

**anschnauzen** [ʼanʃnautsən], *v.a.* snarl at, snap at.

**anschneiden** [ʼanʃnaɪdən], *v.a. irr.* cut into; *ein Thema —,* broach a subject.

**Anschrift** [ʼanʃrɪft], *f.* (—, *pl.* —en) address.

**anschwellen** [ʼanʃvɛlən], *v.n.* (*aux.* sein) swell.

**Ansehen** [ʼanzeːən], *n.* (—s, *no pl.*) respect; reputation; authority.

**ansehen** [ʼanzeːən], *v.a. irr.* look at or upon, consider, regard.

**ansehnlich** [ʼanzeːnlɪç], *adj.* considerable, appreciable.

**anseilen** [ʼanzaɪlən], *v.a.* (*Mount.*) rope together.

**ansetzen** [ʼanzɛtsən], *v.a.* join to; (*Maths.*) start, write out (an equation).

**Ansicht** [ʼanzɪçt], *f.* (—, *pl.* —en) opinion; view; (*Comm.*) approval.

**ansichtig** [ʼanzɪçtɪç], *adj.* — *werden,* get a glimpse of.

**Ansichts(post)karte** [ʼanzɪçts(pɔst)kartə], *f.* (—, *pl.* —n) picture postcard.

**ansiedeln** [ʼanziːdəln], *v.r. sich —,* settle (down), colonize.

**Ansinnen** [ʼanzɪnən], *n.* (—s, *pl.* —) demand, suggestion.

**anspannen** [ʼanʃpanən], *v.a.* tighten yoke, stretch; harness.

**anspielen** [ʼanʃpiːlən], *v.n.* (*Game, Sport*) lead off; *auf etwas —,* allude to s.th.

**Ansporn** [ʼanʃpɔrn], *m.* (—s, *no pl.*) spur, incentive.

**Ansprache** [ʼanʃpraːxə], *f.* (—, *pl.* —n) address, speech, talk.

**ansprechen** [ʼanʃprɛçən], *v.a. irr.* address, accost; please.

**anspringen** [ʼanʃprɪŋən], *v.a. irr.* leap at. — *v.n.* (*Motor.*) start.

9

**Anspruch** ['anʃprux], *m.* (—s, *pl.* ⁻e) (*Law*) claim, title.

**anspruchsvoll** ['anʃpruxsfɔl], *adj.* demanding, hard to please.

**anstacheln** ['anʃtaxəln], *v.a.* goad, prod.

**Anstalt** ['anʃtalt], *f.* (—, *pl.* —en) institution, establishment; —*en treffen*, make arrangements (for).

**Anstand** ['anʃtant], *m.* (—es, *no pl.*) propriety; politeness, good manners, good grace; decency; (*Hunt.*) stand, butts.

**anständig** ['anʃtɛndɪç], *adj.* decent, proper, respectable.

**Anstandsbesuch** ['anʃtantsbəzu:x], *m.* (—es, *pl.* —e) formal visit.

**anstandshalber** ['anʃtantshalbər], *adv.* for decency's sake.

**anstandslos** ['anʃtantslo:s], *adv.* unhesitatingly.

**anstarren** ['anʃtarən], *v.a.* stare at.

**anstatt** [an'ʃtat], *prep.* (*Genit.*), *conj.* instead of, in lieu of, in the place of.

**anstecken** ['anʃtɛkən], *v.a.* pin on; set fire to; infect.

**Ansteckung** ['anʃtɛkuŋ], *f.* (—, *pl.* —en) infection, contagion.

**anstehen** ['anʃte:ən], *v.n. irr.* stand in a queue; — *lassen*, put off, delay.

**ansteigen** ['anʃtaɪgən], *v.n. irr.* (*aux.* sein) rise, increase.

**anstellen** ['anʃtɛlən], *v.a. einen —*, appoint s.o. to a post; employ; *Betrachtungen —*, speculate. — *v.r. sich —*, form a queue, line up.

**anstellig** ['anʃtɛlɪç], *adj.* able, skilful, adroit.

**Anstellung** ['anʃtɛluŋ], *f.* (—, *pl.* —en) appointment, employment.

**anstiften** ['anʃtɪftən], *v.a.* instigate.

**anstimmen** ['anʃtɪmən], *v.a.* intone.

**Anstoß** ['anʃto:s], *m.* (—es, *pl.* ⁻e) (*Footb.*) kick-off; — *erregen*, give offence; *den* — *geben zu*, initiate, give an impetus to; *Stein des* —*es*, stumbling block; — *nehmen*, take offence.

**anstoßen** ['anʃto:sən], *v.a. irr.* knock against, push against; give offence; clink (glasses); border on; *mit der Zunge —*, lisp.

**anstößig** ['anʃtø:sɪç], *adj.* shocking, offensive.

**anstreichen** ['anʃtraɪçən], *v.a. irr.* paint; *Fehler —*, mark wrong.

**Anstreicher** ['anʃtraɪçər], *m.* (—s, *pl.* —) house-painter.

**anstrengen** ['anʃtrɛŋən], *v.a.* strain, exert; *eine Klage gegen einen —*, bring an action against s.o. — *v.r. sich —*, exert o.s.

**Anstrengung** ['anʃtrɛŋuŋ], *f.* (—, *pl.* —en) exertion, effort.

**Anstrich** ['anʃtrɪç], *m.* (—s, *pl.* —e) coat of paint.

**Ansturm** ['anʃturm], *m.* (—s, *no pl.*) attack, assault, charge.

**Ansuchen** ['anzu:xən], *n.* (—s, *pl.* —) application, request, petition.

**ansuchen** ['anzu:xən], *v.n. bei einem um etwas —*, apply to s.o. for s.th.

**Anteil** ['antaɪl], *m.* (—s, *pl.* —e) share, portion; sympathy.

**Anteilnahme** ['antaɪlna:mə], *f.* (—, *no pl.*) sympathy.

**Antenne** [an'tɛnə], *f.* (—, *pl.* —n) aerial; antenna.

**antik** [an'ti:k], *adj.* antique, ancient, classical.

**Antike** [an'ti:kə], *f.* (—, *pl.* —en) (classical) antiquity; ancient work of art (statue etc.).

**Antiquar** [anti'kva:r], *m.* (—s, *pl.* —e) second-hand dealer; antiquary.

**Antiquariat** [antikva'rja:t], *n.* (—s, *pl.* —e) second-hand bookshop.

**antiquarisch** [anti'kva:rɪʃ], *adj.* antiquarian, second-hand.

**Antlitz** ['antlɪts], *n.* (—es, *pl.* —e) countenance, (*Poet.*) face.

**Antrag** ['antra:k], *m.* (—s, *pl.* ⁻e) proposition, proposal, application; *einen — stellen*, bring in a motion; make application.

**antragen** ['antra:gən], *v.a. irr.* propose, make a proposal, offer to.

**Antragsformular** ['antra:ksfɔrmula:r], *n.* (—s, *pl.* —e) (*Insurance*) proposal form; application form.

**Antragsteller** ['antra:kʃtɛlər], *m.* (—s, *pl.* —) applicant, mover of a resolution.

**antreten** ['antre:tən], *v.a. irr. ein Amt —*, enter upon an office; *eine Reise —*, set out on a journey. — *v.n.* (*aux.* sein) (*Mil.*) fall in.

**Antrieb** ['antri:p], *m.* (—s, *pl.* —e) impulse, motive; incentive; *aus eigenem —*, voluntarily.

**Antritt** ['antrɪt], *m.* (—s, *no pl.*) start, commencement.

**Antrittsvorlesung** ['antrɪtsforle:zuŋ], *f.* (*Univ.*) inaugural lecture.

**antun** ['antu:n], *v.a. irr. einem etwas —*, do s.th. to s.o.

**Antwort** ['antvɔrt], *f.* (—, *pl.* —en) answer, reply; *abschlägige —*, refusal, rebuff.

**antworten** ['antvɔrtən], *v.a.* answer, reply to.

**anvertrauen** ['anfɛrtrauən], *v.a. einem etwas —*, entrust s.o. with s.th.; confide in s.o.

**anverwandt** ['anfɛrvant] *see* **verwandt**.

**Anwalt** ['anvalt], *m.* (—s, *pl.* ⁻e) lawyer, barrister, solicitor, attorney, advocate.

**anwandeln** ['anvandəln], *v.a.* befall.

**Anwandlung** ['anvandluŋ], *f.* (—, *pl.* —en) fit, turn.

**Anwartschaft** ['anvartʃaft], *f.* (—, *pl.* —en) (*Law*) reversion; candidacy.

**anweisen** ['anvaɪzən], *v.a. irr.* instruct, direct; *angewiesen sein auf*, depend upon.

**Anweisung** ['anvaɪzuŋ], *f.* (—, *pl.* —en) instruction, advice, method; (*Comm.*) voucher, credit voucher, cheque.

**anwenden** ['anvɛndən], *v.a. irr.* use, make use of, apply.

# armselig

**anwerben** ['anvɛrbən], *v.a. irr.* (*Mil.*) recruit; *sich — lassen,* enlist.
**anwesend** ['anve:zənt], *adj.* at hand, present.
**Anwesenheit** ['anve:zənhaɪt], *f.* (—, *no pl.*) presence, attendance.
**anwidern** ['anvi:dərn], *v.a.* disgust.
**Anzahl** ['antsa:l], *f.* (—, *no pl.*) number, quantity.
**anzahlen** ['antsa:lən], *v.a.* pay a deposit.
**Anzahlung** ['antsa:luŋ], *f.* (—, *pl.* —en) deposit.
**Anzeichen** ['antsaɪçən], *n.* (—s, *pl.* —) indication, omen.
**Anzeige** ['antsaɪgə], *f.* (—, *pl.* —n) notice, (classified) advertisement; denunciation; — *erstatten,* to lay information.
**anzeigen** ['antsaɪgən], *v.a.* point out, indicate; announce; notify; advertise; denounce.
**Anzeiger** ['antsaɪgər], *m.* (—s, *pl.* —) indicator; (*newspaper*) advertiser.
**anzetteln** ['antsɛtəln], *v.a.* plot, contrive.
**anziehen** ['antsi:ən], *v.a. irr.* pull, draw tight, give a tug; attract; stretch; dress; (*screws*) tighten. —, *v.r. sich —,* dress, put on o.'s clothes.
**anziehend** ['antsi:ənt], *adj.* attractive.
**Anziehung** ['antsi:uŋ], *f.* (—, *no pl.*) attraction.
**Anzug** ['antsu:k], *m.* (—s, *pl.* ⁀e) (man's) suit; approach.
**anzüglich** ['antsy:klɪç], *adj.* allusive; suggestive; — *werden,* become offensive.
**anzünden** ['antsyndən], *v.a.* kindle, ignite.
**apart** [a'part], *adj.* charming, delightful; (*Am.*) cute.
**Apfel** ['apfəl], *m.* (—s, *pl.* ⁀) apple.
**Apfelmost** ['apfəlmɔst], *m.* (—s, *no pl.*) cider.
**Apfelsine** [apfəl'zi:nə], *f.* (—, *pl.* —n) orange.
**Apostel** [a'pɔstəl], *m.* (—s, *pl.* —) apostle.
**Apotheke** [apo'te:kə], *f.* (—, *pl.* —n) dispensary, pharmacy, chemist's shop; (*Am.*) drugstore.
**Apparat** [apa'ra:t], *m.* (—(e)s, *pl.* —e) apparatus; radio *or* television set; telephone.
**appellieren** [apɛ'li:rən], *v.n.* — *an,* appeal to.
**appetitlich** [ape'ti:tlɪç], *adj.* appetising, dainty.
**Aprikose** [apri'ko:zə], *f.* (—, *pl.* —en) apricot.
**Aquarell** [akva'rɛl], *n.* (—s, *pl.* —e) water-colour (painting).
**Ära** ['ɛ:ra], *f.* (—, *no pl.*) era.
**Arabien** [a'ra:bjən], *n.* Arabia.
**Arbeit** ['arbaɪt], *f.* (—, *pl.* —en) work, labour; job; employment; workmanship; *an die — gehen,* set to work.
**arbeiten** ['arbaɪtən], *v.a., v.n.* work, labour, toil.
**Arbeiter** ['arbaɪtər], *m.* (—s, *pl.* —) worker, workman, labourer, hand.

**Arbeiterschaft** ['arbaɪtərʃaft], *f.* (—, *no pl.*) working men; workers.
**arbeitsam** ['arbaɪtza:m], *adj.* industrious, diligent.
**Arbeitsamt** ['arbaɪtsamt], *n.* (—s, *pl.* ⁀er) labour exchange.
**arbeitsfähig** ['arbaɪtsfe:ɪç], *adj.* capable of working, able-bodied.
**arbeitslos** ['arbaɪtslo:s], *adj.* unemployed, out of work.
**Arbeitslosigkeit** ['arbaɪtslo:zɪçkaɪt], *f.* (—, *no pl.*) unemployment.
**Arbeitsnachweis** ['arbaɪtsnaxvaɪs], *m.* (—es, *no pl.*) labour exchange; (*Am.*) labour registry-office.
**Arbeitssperre** ['arbaɪtsʃpɛrə], *f.* (—, *pl.* —n) (*Ind.*) lock-out.
**Archäologe** [arçɛo'lo:gə], *m.* (—n, *pl.* —n) archaeologist.
**Arche** ['arçə], *f.* (—, *pl.* —n) ark.
**Archipel** [arçi'pe:l], *m.* (—s, *pl.* —e) archipelago.
**architektonisch** [arçitɛk'to:nɪʃ], *adj.* architectural.
**Archivar** [arçi'va:r], *m.* (—s, *pl.* —e) keeper of archives.
**arg** [ark], *adj.* bad, wicked, mischievous.
**Argentinien** [argən'ti:njən], *n.* Argentina.
**Ärger** ['ɛrgər], *m.* (—s, *no pl.*) anger, annoyance.
**ärgerlich** ['ɛrgərlɪç], *adj.* annoying, aggravating, vexing; angry.
**ärgern** ['ɛrgərn], *v.a.* annoy, vex, make angry. — *v.r. sich —,* get annoyed.
**Ärgernis** ['ɛrgərnɪs], *n.* (—ses, *pl.* —se) scandal, nuisance.
**arglistig** ['arklɪstɪç], *adj.* crafty, sly.
**arglos** ['arklo:s], *adj.* unsuspecting, guileless, naive.
**Argwohn** ['arkvo:n], *m.* (—s, *no pl.*) mistrust, suspicion.
**argwöhnisch** ['arkvø:nɪʃ], *adj.* suspicious, distrustful.
**Arie** ['a:rjə], *f.* (—, *pl.* —n) (*Mus.*) aria.
**Arm** [arm], *m.* (—s, *pl.* —e) arm.
**arm** [arm], *adj.* poor, indigent, needy.
**Armaturenbrett** [arma'tu:rənbrɛt], *n.* (—s, *no pl.*) dashboard.
**Armband** ['armbant], *n.* (—s, *pl.* ⁀er) bracelet.
**Armbanduhr** ['armbantu:r], *f.* (—, *pl.* —en) wrist-watch.
**Armbrust** ['armbrust], *f.* (—, *pl.* —e) cross-bow.
**Ärmel** ['ɛrməl], *m.* (—s, *pl.* —) sleeve.
**Ärmelkanal** ['ɛrməlkana:l], *m.* (—s, *no pl.*) English Channel.
**Armenien** [ar'me:njən], *n.* Armenia.
**Armenhaus** ['armənhaus], *n.* (—es, *pl.* ⁀er) poor-house, almshouse.
**Armenpfleger** ['armənpfle:gər], *m.* (—s, *pl.* —) almoner.
**Armesündermiene** [arma'zyndərmi:nə], *f.* (—, *pl.* —n) hangdog look.
**ärmlich** ['ɛrmlɪç], *adj.* poor, shabby, scanty.
**armselig** ['armze:lɪç], *adj.* poor, miserable, wretched; paltry.

# Armut

**Armut** ['armu:t], *f.* (—, *no pl.*) poverty; *in* — *geraten*, be reduced to penury.

**Arsch** [arʃ], *m.* (—es, ⸚e) (*vulg.*) arse, backside.

**Arsen(ik)** [ar'ze:n(ɪk)], *n.* (—s, *no pl.*) arsenic.

**Art** [a:rt], *f.* (—, *pl.* —en) kind, species; race; sort; method, way, manner.

**artig** ['a:rtɪç], *adj.* well-behaved, polite.

**Artigkeit** ['a:rtɪçkaɪt], *f.* (—, *pl.* —en) politeness, courtesy.

**Artikel** [ar'ti:kəl], *m.* (—s, *pl.* —) article; commodity.

**Artist** [ar'tɪst], *m.* (—en, *pl.* —en) artiste (circus, variety).

**Arznei** [arts'naɪ], *f.* (—, *pl.* —en) medicine.

**Arzneimittel** [arts'naɪmɪtəl], *n.* (—s, *pl.*—) medicine, drug.

**Arzt** [artst], *m.* (—es, *pl.* ⸚e) doctor, physician; *praktischer* —, general practitioner.

**ärztlich** ['ɛrtstlɪç], *adj.* medical.

**As** (1) [as], *n.* (—, *pl.* —) (*Mus.*) A flat; — *Dur*, A flat major, — *Moll*, A flat minor.

**As** (2) [as], *n.* (—sses, *pl.* —sse) (*Sport*, *cards*) ace.

**Asbest** [as'bɛst], *m.* (—s, *no pl.*) asbestos.

**Asche** ['aʃə], *f.* (—, *no pl.*) ashes.

**Aschenbecher** ['aʃənbɛçər], *m.* (—s, *pl.* —) ash-tray.

**Aschenbrödel** ['aʃənbrø:dəl]*or***Aschenputtel** ['aʃənpʊtəl], *n.* Cinderella.

**Aschkraut** ['aʃkraut], *n.* (—s, *pl.* ⸚er) (*Bot.*) cineraria.

**Askese** [as'ke:zə], *f.* (—, *no pl.*) asceticism.

**Asket** [as'ke:t], *m.* (—en, *pl.* —en) ascetic.

**Assessor** [a'sɛsɔr], *m.* (—s, *pl.* —en) assistant; assistant judge.

**Ast** [ast], *m.* (—es, *pl.* ⸚e) branch, bough.

**Astronaut** [astro'naut], *m.* (—en, *pl.* —en) astronaut.

**Astronom** [astro'no:m], *m.* (—en, *pl.* —en) astronomer.

**Asyl** [a'zy:l], *n.* (—s, *pl.* —e) asylum, sanctuary.

**Atem** ['a:təm], *m.* (—s, *no pl.*) breath, breathing, respiration.

**Atemzug** ['a:təmtsu:k], *m.* (—s, *pl.* ⸚e) breath.

**Äthiopien** [eti'o:pjən], *n.* Ethiopia.

**Atlas** (1) ['atlas], *m.* (—sses, *pl.* —sse *and* **Atlanten**) atlas, book of maps.

**Atlas** (2) ['atlas], *m.* (—sses, *pl.* —asse) satin.

**atmen** ['a:tmən], *v.n.* breathe.

**atomar** [ato'ma:r], *adj.* atomic.

**Attentat** [atɛn'ta:t], *n.* (—s, *pl.* —e) attempt on s.o.'s life.

**Attest** [a'tɛst], *n.* (—s, *pl.* —e) (*Med.*) certificate.

**ätzen** ['ɛtsən], *v.a.* corrode; (*Art*) etch; (*Med.*) cauterise.

**auch** [aux], *conj.*, *adv.* also, too. likewise, as well.

**Au(e)** ['au(ə)], *f.* (—, *pl.* —en) green meadow, pasture.

**auf** [auf], *prep.* on, upon; — *der Straße*, in the road; — *eigene Gefahr*, at your own risk; — *Befehl*, by order; — *einige Tage*, for a few days; — *dem Lande*, in the country; — *keinen Fall*, on no account.

**aufatmen** ['aufa:tmən], *v.n.* breathe a sigh of relief.

**Aufbau** ['aufbau], *m.* (—s, *no pl.*) building; (*Lit.*) composition, structure.

**aufbauen** ['aufbauən], *v.a.* erect, build, construct.

**aufbäumen** ['aufbɔymən], *v.r. sich* —, (*horses*) rear.

**aufbewahren** ['aufbəva:rən], *v.a.* keep, store; (*luggage*) take charge of.

**Aufbewahrung** ['aufbəva:ruŋ], *f.* (—, *pl.* —en) storage, safe keeping.

**aufbieten** ['aufbi:tən], *v.a. irr.* call up for service; exert (*energies*).

**aufbinden** ['aufbɪndən], *v.a. irr.* untie; *einem einen Bären* —, to hoax s.o.

**aufblähen** ['aufblɛ:ən], *v.a.* puff up, swell, inflate.

**aufblühen** ['aufbly:ən], *v.n.* (*aux.* sein) flourish, unfold.

**aufbrausen** ['aufbrauzən], *v.n.* (*aux.* sein) fly into a rage.

**Aufbruch** ['aufbrux], *m.* (—s, *no pl.*) departure.

**aufbürden** ['aufbyrdən], *v.a. einem eine Last* —, burden s.o. with a thing.

**aufdecken** ['aufdɛkən], *v.a.* uncover, unveil.

**aufdonnern** ['aufdɔnərn], *v.r. sich* — dress up showily.

**aufdrängen** ['aufdrɛŋən], *v.a. einem etwas* —, press s.th. upon s.o.— *v.r. sich* —, force o.'s company on.

**aufdrehen** ['aufdre:ən], *v.a.* (*tap*) turn on.

**aufdringlich** ['aufdrɪŋlɪç], *adj.* importunate, officious, obtrusive.

**Aufdruck** ['aufdruk], *m.* (—s, *pl.* —e) imprint.

**aufdrücken** ['aufdrykən], *v.a.* press open; press on s.th.

**Aufenthalt** ['aufɛnthalt], *m.* (—s, *pl.* —e) stay, sojourn; delay; stop.

**auferlegen** ['aufɛrle:gən], *v.a.* impose; enjoin.

**auferstehen** ['aufɛrʃte:ən], *v.n. irr.* (*aux.* sein) (*Rel.*) rise from the dead.

**auffahren** ['auffa:rən], *v.n. irr.* (*aux.* sein) start (from o.'s sleep); mount; flare up (in anger).

**Auffahrt** ['auffa:rt], *f.* (—, *pl.* —en) ascent; approach to a house, drive.

**auffallen** ['auffalən], *v.n. irr.* (*aux.* sein) strike the ground; *einem* —, strike s.o., astonish.

**auffangen** ['auffaŋən], *v.a. irr.* (*ball*) catch; (*blow*) parry, ward off; (*letter*) intercept.

**auffassen** ['auffasən], *v.a.* take in, comprehend.

**Auffassung** ['auffasuŋ], *f.* (—, *pl.* —en) conception, interpretation; view.

**aufflackern** ['aufflakərn],*v.n.* (*aux.* sein) flare up, flicker.

**auffordern** ['auffɔrdərn], *v.a.* summon, request, ask, invite.

**aufforsten** ['auffɔrstən], *v.a.* afforest.

**auffressen** ['auffresən], *v.a. irr.* devour; (*of animals*) eat up.

**auffrischen** ['auffrɪʃən], *v.a.* renew, redecorate; (*fig.*) brush up.

**aufführen** ['auffy:rən], *v.a.* (*Theat.*) perform; *einzeln* —, specify, particularise. — *v.r. sich* —, behave, conduct o.s.

**Aufführung** ['auffy:ruŋ], *f.* (—, *pl.* —en) (*Theat.*) performance.

**Aufgabe** ['aufga:bə], *f.* (—, *pl.* —n) giving up, abandonment; (*letters, telegrams*) posting, despatch; (*work*) task; (*Sch.*) exercise; (*Maths.*) problem.

**aufgabeln** ['aufga:bəln], *v.a.* (*sl.*) pick up.

**Aufgang** ['aufgaŋ], *m.* (—s, *pl.* ¨e) ascent, stairs.

**aufgeben** ['aufge:bən], *v.a. irr.* give up, abandon, relinquish; (*Am.*) quit; (*luggage*) register.

**aufgeblasen** ['aufgəbla:zən], *adj.* conceited, stuck up.

**Aufgebot** ['aufgəbo:t], *n.* (—s, *pl.* —e) (*marriage*) banns; (*Mil.*) levy; *mit — aller Kräfte*, with the utmost exertion.

**aufgebracht** ['aufgəbraxt], *adj.* angry, annoyed.

**aufgedunsen** ['aufgədunzən], *adj.* bloated, sodden.

**aufgehen** ['aufge:ən], *v.n. irr.* (*aux.* sein) (*knot*) come undone; (*sun*) rise; (*dough*) swell, rise; (*Maths.*) leave no remainder, cancel out.

**aufgehoben** ['aufgəho:bən], *adj. gut — sein*, be in good hands.

**aufgelegt** ['aufgəle:kt], *adj.* disposed, inclined.

**aufgeräumt** ['aufgərɔymt], *adj.* merry, cheerful, in high spirits.

**aufgeweckt** ['aufgəvekt], *adj.* bright, clever, intelligent.

**aufgießen** ['aufgi:sən], *v.a. irr. Kaffee* —, make coffee.

**aufgreifen** ['aufgraɪfən], *v.a. irr.* seize.

**Aufguß** ['aufgus], *m.* (—sses, *pl.* ¨sse) infusion.

**aufhalsen** ['aufhalzən], *v.a. einem etwas* —, (*coll.*) saddle s.o. with s.th.

**aufhalten** ['aufhaltən], *v.a. irr.* (*door*) hold open; *einen* —, delay s.o. — *v.r. sich an einem Ort* —, stay at a place; *sich über etwas* —, find fault with s.th.

**aufhängen** ['aufhɛŋən], *v.a. irr.* hang (up).

**aufhäufen** ['aufhɔyfən], *v.a.* pile up. — *v.r. sich* —, accumulate.

**Aufheben** ['aufhe:bən], *n.* (—s, *no pl.*) lifting up; ado; *viel —s machen*, make a great fuss.

**aufheben** ['aufhe:bən], *v.a. irr.* lift (up), pick up; keep, preserve; (*laws*) repeal, abolish; (*agreements*) rescind, annul.

**Aufhebung** ['aufhe:buŋ], *f.* (—, *pl.* —en) abolition, abrogation, annulment, repeal.

**aufheitern** ['aufhaɪtərn], *v.a.* cheer up; amuse. — *v.r. sich* —, (*weather*) brighten, clear up.

**aufhelfen** ['aufhɛlfən], *v.n. irr. einem* —, help s.o. up.

**aufhellen** ['aufhɛlən], *v.r. sich* —, (*weather*) clear up; (*face*) brighten up.

**aufhetzen** ['aufhɛtsən],*v.a.* rouse (s.o.); *einen — gegen*, incite s.o. against.

**aufhorchen** ['aufhɔrçən], *v.n.* prick up o.'s ears.

**aufhören** ['aufhø:rən], *v.n.* cease, stop; (*Am.*) quit; *ohne aufzuhören*, incessantly; *da hört sich doch alles auf!* that is the limit!

**aufklären** ['aufkle:rən], *v.a.* enlighten; clear up; *einen* —, enlighten s.o. —*v.r. sich* —, (*weather*) brighten.

**Aufklärung** ['aufkle:ruŋ], *f.* (—, *no pl.*) (age of) Enlightenment.

**aufknacken** ['aufknakən], *v.a.* crack (open).

**aufknöpfen** ['aufknœpfən], *v.a.* unbutton; *aufgeknöpft sein*, be in a talkative mood.

**aufkommen** ['aufkɔmən], *v.n. irr.* (*aux.* sein) come into use, prevail; *für etwas* —, pay for s.th.; *einen nicht — lassen*, give s.o. no chance.

**aufkrempeln** ['aufkrempəln], *v.a.* (*coll.*) roll up (o.'s sleeves).

**aufkündigen** ['aufkyndɪgən], *v.a.* (*money*) recall; *einem die Freundschaft* —, break with s.o.

**Auflage** ['aufla:gə], *f.* (—, *pl.* —n) (*tax*) impost, duty, levy; (*book*) edition, impression; circulation.

**auflassen** ['auflasən], *v.a. irr.* leave open; (*Law*) cede.

**auflauern** ['auflauərn], *v.n. einem* —, lie in wait for s.o., waylay s.o.

**Auflauf** ['auflauf], *m.* (—s, *pl.* ¨e) tumult, noisy street gathering; soufflé.

**auflaufen** ['auflaufən], *v.n. irr.* (*aux.* sein) swell, increase; (*ship*) run aground.

**aufleben** ['aufle:bən], *v.n.* (*aux.* sein) *wieder* —, revive.

**auflegen** ['aufle:gən], *v.a. irr.* lay upon, put on; (*book*) publish; (*tax, punishment*) impose, inflict.

**auflehnen** ['aufle:nən], *v.r. sich gegen einen* (or *etwas*) —, rebel against, mutiny, oppose.

**auflesen** ['aufle:zən], *v.a. irr.* pick up, gather.

**aufleuchten** ['auflɔyçtən], *v.n.* light up; (*eyes*) shine.

**auflockern** ['auflɔkərn], *v.a.* loosen.

**auflodern** ['auflo:dərn], *v.n.* (*aux.* sein) flare up, blaze up.

# auflösen

**auflösen** ['auflø:zən], *v.a.* dissolve, loosen; (*puzzle*) solve, guess; (*meeting*) break up; (*business*) wind up; (*partnership*) dissolve; (*army*) disband. — *v.r. sich —*, melt, dissolve, be broken up.

**aufmachen** ['aufmaxən], *v.a.* (*door, packet*) open; (*knot*) undo; *gut —*, pack nicely. — *v.r. sich —*, get going, set out for.

**Aufmachung** ['aufmaxuŋ], *f.* (—, *pl.* —en) outward appearance, make-up, get-up.

**Aufmarsch** ['aufmarʃ], *m.* (—es, *pl.* ⁒e) (*Mil.*) parade.

**aufmerksam** ['aufmɛrkza:m], *adj.* attentive, observant; civil, kind; *einen — machen auf*, draw s.o.'s attention to.

**aufmuntern** ['aufmuntərn], *v.a.* encourage, cheer up.

**Aufnahme** ['aufna:mə], *f.* (—, *pl.* —n) reception; (*Phot.*) snap, photograph; (*Geog.*) mapping out, survey; (*Mus.*) recording.

**aufnehmen** ['aufne:mən], *v.a. irr.* take up; receive, give shelter to; (*Phot.*) photograph, film; (*Mus.*) record; (*money*) raise, borrow; (*minutes*) draw up; *den Faden wieder —*, take up the thread; *die Arbeit wieder —*, return to work, resume work; *die Fährte —*, (*Hunt.*) recover the scent; *es mit einem —*, be a match for s.o.; (*Comm.*) *Inventar —*, take stock, draw up an inventory.

**aufnötigen** ['aufnø:tɪgən], *v.a. einem etwas —*, force s.th. upon s.o.

**aufpassen** ['aufpasən], *v.n.* attend to, pay attention to, take notice of, take care of.

**aufpeitschen** ['aufpaɪtʃən], *v.a.* whip up.

**aufpflanzen** ['aufpflantsən], *v.a.* mount, erect. — *v.r. sich vor einem —*, plant o.s. in front of s.o.; *mit aufgepflanztem Bajonett*, with bayonets fixed.

**Aufputz** ['aufputs], *m.* (—es, *no pl.*) finery, trimmings.

**aufraffen** ['aufrafən], *v.a.* snatch up, rake up. — *v.r. sich wieder —*, pull o.s. together.

**aufräumen** ['aufrɔymən], *v.a.* put in order, clear away; (*room*) tidy up; *mit etwas —*, make a clean sweep of s.th.; *aufgeräumt sein*, be in a jolly mood.

**aufrechnen** ['aufrɛçnən], *v.a.* reckon up; set off against.

**aufrecht** ['aufrɛçt], *adj.* upright, erect; *etwas — erhalten*, maintain s.th.; (*opinion*) stick to, adhere to, uphold.

**Aufrechterhaltung** ['aufrɛçtərhaltuŋ], *f.* (—, *no pl.*) maintenance, preservation.

**aufregen** ['aufre:gən], *v.a.* excite, enrage.

**aufreiben** ['aufraɪbən], *v.a. irr.* rub sore; (*Mil.*) destroy, wipe out. — *v.r. sich —*, exhaust o.s. with worry (*or* work).

**aufreizen** ['aufraɪtsən], *v.a.* incite, provoke.

**aufrichten** ['aufrɪçtən], *v.a.* raise, erect, set upright; (*fig.*) comfort, console. — *v.r. sich —*, rise, sit up.

**aufrichtig** ['aufrɪçtɪç], *adj.* sincere, frank.

**aufriegeln** ['aufri:gəln], *v.a.* unbolt.

**Aufriß** ['aufrɪs], *m.* (—sses, *pl.* —sse) sketch, draft; (*Archit.*) elevation, section.

**aufrücken** ['aufrykən], *v.n.* (*aux.* sein) rise, be promoted (in rank), advance.

**Aufruf** ['aufru:f], *m.* (—s, *pl.* —e) summons, proclamation, appeal; (*Law*) citation.

**aufrufen** ['aufru:fən], *v.a. irr.* summons; (*Sch.*) call upon.

**Aufruhr** ['aufru:r], *m.* (—s, *pl.* —e) uproar, riot, tumult, rebellion, mutiny.

**aufrühren** ['aufry:rən], *v.a.* stir up, agitate, rouse to rebellion.

**Aufrüstung** ['aufrystuŋ], *f.* (—, *no pl.*) (*Mil.*) (re-)armament.

**aufrütteln** ['aufrytəln], *v.a.* rouse, shake s.o. out of his lethargy.

**aufsagen** ['aufza:gən], *v.a.* recite.

**aufsässig** ['aufzesɪç], *adj.* refractory, rebellious.

**Aufsatz** ['aufzats], *m.* (—es, *pl.* ⁒e) top, head-piece, table centre-piece; (*Sch.*) composition, essay; (*newspaper*) article.

**aufscheuchen** ['aufʃɔyçən], *v.a.* flush (game), startle.

**aufschichten** ['aufʃɪçtən], *v.a.* stack, pile up in layers.

**aufschieben** ['aufʃi:bən], *v.a. irr.* push open; delay, postpone, adjourn; (*Parl.*) prorogue.

**Aufschlag** ['aufʃla:k], *m.* (—s, *pl.* ⁒e) impact, striking; (*sleeve*) cuff; turn-up; (*uniform*) facings; (*Comm.*) increase in price; (*Tennis*) service.

**aufschlagen** ['aufʃla:gən], *v.n. irr.* (*aux.* sein) hit, strike (open); (*Tennis*) serve. — *v.a. die Augen —*, open o.'s eyes; *ein Lager —*, pitch camp; *ein Buch —*, open a book.

**aufschlitzen** ['aufʃlɪtsən], *v.a.* rip open, slit open.

**Aufschluß** ['aufʃlus], *m.* (—sses, *pl.* ⁒sse) disclosure, information.

**aufschneiden** ['aufʃnaɪdən], *v.a. irr.* cut open. — *v.n.* brag, boast.

**Aufschneider** ['aufʃnaɪdər], *m.* (-s, *pl.* —) swaggerer, braggart.

**Aufschnitt** ['aufʃnɪt], *m.* (—s, *no pl.*) slice of cold meat *or* sausage.

**aufschnüren** ['aufʃny:rən], *v.a.* unlace, untie.

**Aufschrei** ['aufʃraɪ], *m.* (—s, *pl.* —e) outcry, screech, scream, shout, shriek.

**Aufschrift** ['aufʃrɪft], *f.* (—, *pl.* —en) inscription, address; heading.

**Aufschub** ['aufʃu:p], *m.* (—s, *pl.* ⁒e) delay, adjournment, postponement.

**aufschütten** ['aufʃytən], *v.a.* (*liquid*) pour upon; (*dam*) raise.

# aufzeichnen

**aufschwingen** ['aufʃvɪŋən], *v.r. irr. sich* —, soar, rise; *ich kann mich dazu nicht* —, I cannot rise to that.

**Aufschwung** ['aufʃvʊŋ], *m.* (—s, *no pl.*) flight, rising; (*Comm.*) improvement, boom.

**Aufsehen** ['aufze:ən], *n.* (—s, *no pl.*) sensation, stir.

**Aufseher** ['aufze:ər], *m.* (—s, *pl.* —) overseer, inspector.

**aufsein** ['aufzaɪn], *v.n. irr.* (*aux.* sein) be out of bed, be up and about.

**aufsetzen** ['aufzɛtsən], *v.a.* (*hat*) put on; (*letter, essay*) draft.

**Aufsicht** ['aufzɪçt], *f.* (—, *no pl.*) inspection, supervision, control.

**Aufsichtsrat** ['aufzɪçtsra:t], *m.* (—s, *pl.* ∸e) (*Comm.*) board of directors.

**aufsitzen** ['aufzɪtsən], *v.n. irr.* sit up, wait up at night; (*horse*) mount.

**aufspannen** ['aufʃpanən], *v.a.* (*umbrella*) put up; (*tent*) pitch.

**aufspeichern** ['aufʃpaɪçərn], *v.a.* store (up), warehouse.

**aufsperren** ['aufʃpɛrən], *v.a.* open wide, unlock.

**aufspielen** ['aufʃpi:lən], *v.n. zum Tanz* —, play music for dancing. — *v.r. sich groß* —, give o.s. airs.

**aufspießen** ['aufʃpi:sən], *v.a.* pierce on a spit; (*joint*) skewer.

**aufspringen** ['aufʃprɪŋən], *v.n. irr.* (*aux.* sein) leap up, jump up; (*door*) fly open; (*hands in winter*) chap.

**aufspüren** ['aufʃpy:rən], *v.a.* track, trace.

**aufstacheln** ['aufʃtaxəln], *v.a.* goad, incite.

**Aufstand** ['aufʃtant], *m.* (—s, *pl.* ∸e) insurrection, revolt, sedition.

**aufstapeln** ['aufʃta:pəln], *v.a.* pile up, stack, store.

**aufstechen** ['aufʃtɛçən], *v.a. irr.* (*Med.*) lance.

**aufstehen** ['aufʃte:ən], *v.n. irr.* (*aux.* sein) (*door*) stand open; stand up; get up (from bed); rise (from a chair).

**aufstellen** ['aufʃtɛlən], *v.a.* set up, arrange; erect; (*Pol.*) put forward (candidate).

**Aufstellung** ['aufʃtɛluŋ], *f.* (—, *pl.* —en) arrangement; statement; inventory; (*Pol.*) nomination.

**aufstemmen** ['aufʃtɛmən], *v.a.* prise open.

**Aufstieg** ['aufʃti:k], *m.* (—s, *pl.* —e) ascent, rise.

**aufstöbern** ['aufʃtø:bərn], *v.a.* stir (up); start; (*fig.*) discover, ferret out.

**aufstoßen** ['aufʃto:sən], *v.a. irr.* push open; bump against. — *v.n.* belch.

**aufstreben** ['aufʃtre:bən], *v.n.* soar; (*fig.*) aspire.

**aufstreichen** ['aufʃtraɪçən], *v.a. irr.* (*paint*) lay on; (*butter*) spread.

**aufstülpen** ['aufʃtylpən], *v.a.* turn up; (*hat*) clap on o.'s head.

**auftakeln** ['aufta:kəln], *v.a.* (*Naut.*) rig.

**Auftakt** ['auftakt], *m.* (—s, *pl.* —e) (*Mus.*) arsis; (*fig.*) opening, prelude.

**auftauchen** ['auftauxən], *v.n.* (*aux.* sein) appear, emerge, surface.

**auftauen** ['auftauən], *v.n.* (*aux.* sein) thaw; (*fig.*) lose o.'s reserve.

**auftischen** ['auftɪʃən], *v.a.* dish up.

**Auftrag** ['auftra:k], *m.* (—s, *pl.* ∸e) assignment, commission, errand; *im* — *von*, on behalf of.

**auftragen** ['auftra:gən], *v.a. irr.* (*food*) serve up; (*paint*) apply; *einem etwas* —, charge s.o. with a job; *stark* —, lay it on thick.

**auftreiben** ['auftraɪbən], *v.a. irr.* raise (*money*); procure, obtain. — *v.n.* (*aux.* sein) (*ship*) run aground.

**auftrennen** ['auftrɛnən], *v.a.* unstitch; (*hem*) unpick.

**Auftreten** ['auftre:tən], *n.* (—s, *no pl.*) (*Theat.*) appearance; behaviour.

**auftreten** ['auftre:tən], *v.n. irr.* (*aux.* sein) tread upon, step upon; (*Theat.*) appear, come on; *energisch* —, take strong measures, put o.'s foot down.

**Auftritt** ['auftrɪt], *m.* (—s, *pl.* —e) (*Theat.*) scene; altercation, row.

**auftun** ['auftu:n], *v.a. irr.* open; *den Mund* —, speak. — *v.r. sich* —, (*abyss*) yawn.

**auftürmen** ['auftyrmən], *v.a.* pile up, heap up. — *v.r. sich* —, tower.

**aufwachen** ['aufvaxən], *v.n.* (*aux.* sein) awake, wake up.

**aufwallen** ['aufvalən], *v.n.* (*aux.* sein) boil up, bubble up, rage.

**Aufwand** ['aufvant], *m.* (—s, *no pl.*) expense, expenditure; sumptuousness.

**aufwarten** ['aufvartən], *v.n.* wait upon, attend on.

**aufwärts** ['aufvɛrts], *adv.* upward(s), aloft.

**Aufwartung** ['aufvartuŋ], *f.* (—, *pl.* —en) attendance; *seine* — *machen*, pay a (formal) visit.

**aufwaschen** ['aufvaʃən], *v.a. irr.* wash the dishes.

**aufweisen** ['aufvaɪzən], *v.a. irr.* show, produce.

**aufwenden** ['aufvɛndən], *v.a. irr.* spend upon, expend upon.

**aufwickeln** ['aufvɪkəln], *v.a.* wind up; unwind.

**aufwiegeln** ['aufvi:gəln], *v.a.* stir up, incite to rebellion.

**aufwiegen** ['aufvi:gən], *v.a. irr.* outweigh, counter-balance, make up for.

**aufwischen** ['aufvɪʃən], *v.a.* wipe away, mop up.

**aufwühlen** ['aufvy:lən], *v.a.* dig, root up, (*fig.*) stir.

**aufzählen** ['auftsɛ:lən], *v.a.* count up, enumerate, list.

**aufzäumen** ['auftsɔymən], *v.a.* bridle (horses).

**aufzehren** ['auftse:rən], *v.a.* eat up, consume.

**aufzeichnen** ['auftsaɪçnən], *v.a.* write down, take a note of, record.

# aufziehen

**aufziehen** ['auftsi:ən], *v.a. irr.* draw up, pull up; pull open; (*pennant*) hoist; (*clock*) wind up; (*child*) bring up, rear; *einen* —, tease s.o.; *gelindere Saiten* —, be more lenient.

**Aufzucht** ['auftsuxt], *f.* (—, *no pl.*) breeding, rearing.

**Aufzug** ['auftsu:k], *m.* (—s, *pl.* ⸚e) lift; (*Am.*) elevator; (*Theat.*) act; dress, array, attire.

**aufzwingen** ['auftsvɪŋən], *v.a. irr. einem etwas* —, force s.th. on s.o.

**Augapfel** ['aukapfəl], *m.* (—s, *pl.* ⸚) eye-ball; (*fig.*) apple of o.'s eye.

**Auge** ['augə], *n.* (—s, *pl.* —n) eye; *aus den* —n, *aus dem Sinn*, out of sight, out of mind; *mit einem blauen* — *davonkommen*, escape by the skin of o.'s teeth, get off cheaply; *es wird mir schwarz vor den* —n, I feel faint.

**Augenblick** ['augənblɪk], *m.* (—s, *pl.* —e) moment, instant; *jeden* —, at any moment.

**augenblicklich** [augən'blɪklɪç], *adj.* momentary, instantaneous.— *adv.* at present, for the moment, immediately.

**Augenbraue** ['augənbrauə], *f.* (—, *pl.* —n) eye-brow.

**augenfällig** ['augənfɛlɪç], *adj.* visible, evident, conspicuous.

**Augenglas** ['augənglas], *n.* (—es, *pl.* ⸚er) eye-glass.

**Augenhöhle** ['augənhø:lə], *f.* (—, *pl.* —n) eye-socket.

**Augenlicht** ['augənlɪçt], *n.* (—s, *no pl.*) eye-sight.

**Augenlid** ['augənli:t], *n.* (—s, *pl.* —er) eye-lid.

**Augenmaß** ['augənma:s], *n.* (—es, *no pl.*) *gutes* —, good measuring ability with the eye, a sure eye.

**Augenmerk** ['augənmɛrk], *n.* (—s, *no pl.*) attention; *sein* — *auf etwas richten*, focus o.'s attention on s.th.

**Augenschein** ['augənʃain], *m.* (—s, *no pl.*) appearance; *in* — *nehmen*, view.

**augenscheinlich** ['augənʃainlɪç], *adj.* apparent, evident.

**Augenweide** ['augənvaidə], *f.* (—, *pl.* —n) delight to the eye, s.th. lovely to look at.

**Augenwimper** ['augənvɪmpər], *f.* (—, *pl.* —n) eye-lash.

**Augenzeuge** ['augəntsɔygə], *m.* (—n, *pl.* —n) eye-witness.

**August** [au'gust], *m.* (—s, *no pl.*) (*month*) August.

**Augustiner** [augus'ti:nər], *m.* (—s, *pl.* —) (*Eccl.*) Augustinian.

**auktionieren** [auktsjo'ni:rən], *v.a.* auction(eer), sell by auction.

**Aula** ['aula], *f.* (—, *pl.* —len) (*Sch., Univ.*) great hall; auditorium maximum.

**Aurikel** [au'ri:kəl], *f.* (—, *pl.* —n) (*Bot.*) auricula.

**aus** [aus], *prep.* (*Dat.*) from, out of, of, off. — *adv.* out, over, finished, done with, spent; *es ist alles* —, it is over and done with; *ich weiß veder ein noch* —, I am at my wits' end.

**ausarten** ['ausartən], *v.n.* (*aux.* sein) degenerate; (*fig.*) deteriorate.

**Ausbau** ['ausbau], *m.* (—s, *no pl.*) enlargement, extension.

**ausbauen** ['ausbauən], *v.a.* enlarge (a house); improve on.

**ausbedingen** ['ausbədɪŋən], *v.a. sich etwas* —, stipulate.

**ausbessern** ['ausbɛsərn], *v.a.* (*garment*) mend, repair.

**Ausbeute** ['ausbɔytə], *f.* (—, *no pl.*) gain, profit, produce.

**Ausbeutung** ['ausbɔytuŋ], *f.* (—, *no pl.*) exploitation, sweating; (*Min.*) working.

**ausbezahlen** ['ausbətsa:lən], *v.a.* pay in full.

**ausbilden** ['ausbɪldən], *v.a.* develop, train; (*Mil.*) drill.

**Ausbildung** ['ausbɪlduŋ], *f.* (—, *pl.* —en) training, education.

**ausbleiben** ['ausblaibən], *v.n. irr.* (*aux.* sein) fail to appear, be absent.

**Ausblick** ['ausblɪk], *m.* (—s, *pl.* —e) view (from window); (*fig.*) prospect, outlook.

**ausborgen** ['ausbɔrgən], *v.a.* (*sich*) *etwas* —, borrow s.th. from.

**ausbreiten** ['ausbraitən], *v.a.* spread (things); stretch out (o.'s arms). — *v.r. sich* —, spread, extend.

**Ausbreitung** ['ausbraituŋ], *f.* (—, *no pl.*) spreading, extension, distribution, expansion.

**ausbringen** ['ausbrɪŋən], *v.a. irr. einen Toast auf einen* —, drink s.o.'s health.

**Ausbruch** ['ausbrux], *m.* (—s, *pl.* ⸚e) breaking out, outbreak, eruption, burst (of laughter).

**ausbrüten** ['ausbry:tən], *v.a.* hatch; (*fig.*) plot.

**Ausbund** ['ausbunt], *m.* (—s, *pl.* ⸚e) paragon, embodiment.

**Ausdauer** ['ausdauər], *f.* (—, *no pl.*) perseverance, persistence, stamina.

**ausdehnen** ['ausde:nən], *v.a.* extend, stretch, distend; (*fig.*) prolong, protract. — *v.r. sich* —, expand, extend, stretch.

**Ausdehnung** ['ausde:nuŋ], *f.* (—, *pl.* —en) extension, expansion; dilation; (*Phys.*) dimension.

**ausdenken** ['ausdɛŋkən], *v.a. irr.* think out. — *v.r. sich etwas* —, devise s.th., invent s.th.; *das ist gar nicht auszudenken*, that is unimaginable, inconceivable.

**Ausdeutung** ['ausdɔytuŋ], *f.* (—, *pl.* —en) interpretation, explanation.

**ausdörren** ['ausdœrən], *v.a.* parch, dry (up).

**ausdrehen** ['ausdre:ən], *v.a.* (*gas, light, water*) turn off, switch off.

**Ausdruck** ['ausdruk], *m.* (—s, *pl.* ⸚e) expression, phrase.

**ausdrücken** ['ausdrykən], *v.a.* squeeze out, press out; (*fig.*) express.

**ausdrücklich** ['ausdryklɪç], *adj.* express, explicit.

**Ausdrucksweise** ['ausdruksvaɪzə], *f.* (—, *pl.* —n) enunciation, manner of speech, (mode of) expression, style.
**ausdünsten** ['ausdynstən], *v.a.* exhale, perspire.
**auseinander** [ausaɪn'andər], *adv.* asunder, apart.
**Auseinandersetzung** [ausaɪn'andər-zetsuŋ], *f.* (—, *pl.* —en) altercation; discussion, explanation.
**auserkoren** ['auserko:rən], *adj.* elect, chosen, selected.
**auserlesen** ['auserle:zən], *adj.* choice, picked, excellent, first class.
**auserwählen** ['auservɛ:lən], *v.a.* choose, select.
**Ausfahrt** ['ausfa:rt], *f.* (—, *pl.* —en) drive; gateway; exit.
**Ausfall** ['ausfal], *m.* (—s, *pl.* ̈e) falling out; (*radioactivity*) fall-out; sortie, sally; deficiency, loss, cancellation; result, outcome.
**ausfallen** ['ausfalən], *v.n. irr.* (*aux.* sein) drop out, fall out; be cancelled, be omitted, fail to take place; turn out (well etc.).
**ausfallend** ['ausfalənt], *adj.* offensive, abusive; — *werden*, become insulting.
**ausfertigen** ['ausfertɪgən], *v.a.* despatch, draw up, make out, issue.
**ausfindig** ['ausfɪndɪç], *adj.* — *machen*, find out, locate, discover.
**ausflicken** ['ausflɪkən], *v.a.* mend, patch.
**Ausflucht** ['ausfluxt], *f.* (—, *pl.* ̈e) evasion, excuse, subterfuge.
**Ausflug** ['ausflu:k], *m.* (—s, *pl.* ̈e) trip, excursion, outing.
**Ausfluß** ['ausflus], *m.* (—sses, *pl.* ̈sse) (*Engin.*) outflow, outlet; (*Med.*) discharge, suppuration.
**ausfragen** ['ausfra:gən], *v.a. einen —*, question, quiz s.o.
**Ausfuhr** ['ausfu:r], *f.* (—, *pl.* —en) export.
**ausführbar** ['ausfy:rba:r], *adj.* practicable, feasible; exportable.
**ausführen** ['ausfy:rən], *v.a.* take out; lead out; export; carry out, perform, fulfil; point out.
**ausführlich** [aus'fy:rlɪç], *adj.* detailed, full.
**Ausführung** ['ausfy:ruŋ], *f.* (—, *pl.* —en) execution, carrying out; finish; workmanship.
**ausfüllen** ['ausfylən], *v.a.* (*forms*) fill up, fill in, complete.
**ausfüttern** ['ausfytərn], *v.a.* line (a dress).
**Ausgabe** ['ausga:bə], *f.* (—, *pl.* —en) issue, distribution; (*goods*) dispatch, issuing counter; delivery; (*book*) edition; (*pl.*) expenses, expenditure.
**Ausgang** ['ausgaŋ], *m.* (—s, *pl.* ̈e) going out; exit; result, upshot; end, conclusion; time off (from duty).
**Ausgangspunkt** ['ausgaŋspuŋkt], *m.* (—s, *pl.* —e) starting-point; point of departure.

**ausgären** ['ausge:rən], *v.n. irr.* (*aux.* sein) ferment; *ausgegoren sein*, have fermented.
**ausgeben** ['ausge:bən], *v.a. irr.* (*work*) give out, distribute; (*money*) expend, spend; (*tickets*) issue. —*v.r. sich — für*, pass o.s. off as.
**ausgebreitet** ['ausgəbraɪtət], *adj.* extensive, widespread.
**Ausgeburt** ['ausgəburt], *f.* (—, *pl.* —en) monstrosity; — *des Hirns*, figment of the imagination.
**ausgefahren** ['ausgəfa:rən], *adj.* (*street*) rutted, well-worn.
**ausgehen** ['ausge:ən], *v.n. irr.* (*aux.* sein) go out; (*hair*) to fall out; (*colour*) come off, fade; (*breath, patience, money*) become exhausted; result, end in.
**ausgelassen** ['ausgəlasən], *adj.* boisterous, exuberant, frolicsome, merry, jolly, unbridled.
**ausgemacht** ['ausgəmaxt], *adj.* arranged, settled, decided; *eine —e Sache*, a matter of course, a foregone conclusion; *ein —er Schurke*, a downright scoundrel.
**ausgeschlossen** ['ausgəʃlɔsən], *p.p. das ist —*, that is impossible, out of the question.
**ausgewachsen** ['ausgəvaksən], *adj.* full-grown, fully grown.
**ausgezeichnet** ['ausgətsaɪçnət], *adj.* excellent, first rate, distinguished.
**ausgiebig** ['ausgi:bɪç], *adj.* abundant, plentiful; (*soil*) fertile, rich.
**ausgießen** ['ausgi:sən], *v.a. irr.* pour out.
**Ausgleich** ['ausglaɪç], *m.* (—s, *no pl.*) settlement, compromise, compensation, equalisation.
**ausgleichen** ['ausglaɪçən], *v.a. irr.* make even, balance, equalise, compensate; (*sport*) equalise, draw.
**ausgraben** ['ausgra:bən], *v.a. irr.* dig out, dig up, excavate, exhume.
**Ausguck** ['ausguk], *m.* (—s, *pl.* —e) look-out; (*Naut.*) crow's nest.
**Ausguß** ['ausgus], *m.* (—sses, *pl.* ̈sse) sink, gutter.
**aushalten** ['aushaltən], *v.a. irr.* sustain, endure, bear, stand.
**aushändigen** ['aushɛndɪgən], *v.a.* deliver up, hand over.
**Aushang** ['aushaŋ], *m.* (—s, *pl.* ̈e) sign, sign-board, placard.
**ausharren** ['ausharən], *v.n.* persevere, hold out, wait patiently.
**aushecken** ['aushɛkən], *v.a.* hatch (a plot).
**aushelfen** ['aushɛlfən], *v.n. irr.* help out.
**Aushilfe** ['aushɪlfə], *f.* (—, *pl.* —n) help, aid, assistance.
**aushilfsweise** ['aushɪlfsvaɪzə], *adv.* temporarily, as a stop-gap.
**aushöhlen** ['aushø:lən], *v.a.* hollow out, excavate.
**ausholen** ['ausho:lən], *v.a.* pump, sound s.o. — *v.n.* strike out; *weit —*, go far back (in a narration).

**auskehren** ['auskeːrən], *v.a.* sweep out.

**auskennen** ['auskɛnən], *v.r. irr.* sich in etwas —, know all about s.th.

**auskleiden** ['ausklaɪdən], *v.a.* undress.

**ausklingen** ['ausklɪŋən], *v.n. irr. (aux. sein) (sound)* die away.

**ausklügeln** ['ausklyːgəln], *v.a.* puzzle out, contrive.

**auskneifen** ['ausknaɪfən], *v.n. irr. (aux. sein) (coll.)* bolt, run away.

**Auskommen** ['auskɔmən], *n.* (—s, *no pl.*) sufficiency, subsistence, livelihood; mit dem ist kein —, there is no getting on with him.

**auskommen** ['auskɔmən], *v.n. irr. (aux. sein)* mit etwas —, have enough or sufficient of s.th., manage; mit einem gut —, be on good terms with s.o., get on well with s.o.

**auskömmlich** ['auskœmlɪç], *adj.* sufficient.

**auskosten** ['auskɔstən], *v.a.* taste or enjoy to the full.

**auskramen** ['auskraːmən], *v.a.* rummage out; (fig.) reminisce; talk freely.

**auskundschaften** ['auskuntʃaftən], *v.a.* spy out, reconnoitre, explore.

**Auskunft** ['auskunft], *f.* (—, *pl.* ⁝e) information; (Tel.) enquiries; (Mil.) intelligence, enquiry.

**auslachen** ['auslaxən], *v.a.* laugh at, deride.

**ausladen** ['auslaːdən], *v.a. irr.* unload, discharge; cancel (invitation).

**Auslage** ['auslaːgə], *f.* (—, *pl.* —n) outlay, expenses, advance; shop-window display.

**Ausland** ['auslant], *n.* (—s, *no pl.*) foreign country; ins — fahren, go abroad.

**Ausländer** ['auslɛndər], *m.* (—s, *pl.* —) foreigner, alien.

**auslassen** ['auslasən], *v.a. irr.* let off (steam); let out (a dress); melt (butter); leave off, omit. — *v.r.* sich über etwas —, speak o.'s mind about s.th.

**Auslassung** ['auslasuŋ], *f.* (—, *pl.* —en) utterance; omission.

**auslaufen** ['auslaufən], *v.n. irr. (aux. sein)* run out, leak out; (ship) put to sea; (result) turn out.

**Ausläufer** ['auslɔyfər], *m.* (—s, *pl.* —) errand boy; (mountain) spur.

**Auslaut** ['auslaut], *m.* (—s, *pl.* —e) (Phonet.) final sound.

**auslegen** ['ausleːgən], *v.a.* lay out, spread out, display; interpret; (money) advance.

**ausleihen** ['auslaɪən], *v.a. irr.* lend, hire out. — *v.r.* sich etwas —, borrow s.th.

**auslernen** ['auslɛrnən], *v.n.* end o.'s apprenticeship.

**ausliefern** ['ausliːfərn], *v.a.* hand over, deliver; surrender, give up, extradite.

**auslöschen** ['auslœʃən], *v.a.* extinguish, put out (fire).

**auslosen** ['auslɔːzən], *v.a.* raffle, draw lots for.

**auslösen** ['ausløːzən], *v.a.* redeem, ransom, recover; (fig.) produce; arouse.

**Auslosung** ['auslɔːzuŋ], *f.* (—, *pl.* —en) raffle, draw.

**Auslösung** ['ausløːzuŋ], *f.* (—, *pl.* —en) ransom.

**auslüften** ['auslyftən], *v.a.* air, ventilate.

**ausmachen** ['ausmaxən], *v.a.* decide, settle; amount to; etwas mit einem —, arrange s.th. with s.o.; es macht nichts aus, it does not matter; wieviel macht das aus? how much is this? würde es Ihnen etwas —? would you mind?

**Ausmaß** ['ausmaːs], *n.* (—es, *pl.* —e) dimension, amount, extent, scale.

**ausmeißeln** ['ausmaɪsəln], *v.a.* chisel out, carve out.

**ausmerzen** ['ausmertsən], *v.a.* expunge, eradicate.

**ausmisten** ['ausmɪstən], *v.a.* clean, clear up (mess).

**ausmustern** ['ausmustərn], *v.a.* eliminate, reject; (Mil.) discharge.

**Ausnahme** ['ausnaːmə], *f.* (—, *pl.* —n) exception.

**ausnehmen** ['ausneːmən], *v.a. irr.* except, exclude; (poultry) draw; (fish) clean.

**ausnutzen** ['ausnutsən], *v.a.* make the most of s.th.; take advantage of s.th.

**ausnützen** ['ausnytsən], *v.a.* exploit.

**auspacken** ['auspakən], *v.a.* unpack. — *v.n.* talk freely; (coll.) open up.

**auspfeifen** ['auspfaɪfən], *v.a. irr.* (Theat.) hiss at, cat-call.

**auspolstern** ['auspɔlstərn], *v.a.* stuff.

**ausprägen** ['auspreːgən], *v.a.* stamp, impress, coin.

**ausprobieren** ['ausprobiːrən], *v.a.* try out.

**Auspuff** ['auspuf], *m.* (—s, *no pl.*) (Motor.) exhaust.

**auspusten** ['auspuːstən], *v.a.* blow out.

**ausputzen** ['ausputsən], *v.a.* clean out; adorn.

**ausquartieren** ['auskvartiːrən], *v.a.* (Mil.) billet out.

**ausquetschen** ['auskvetʃən], *v.a.* squeeze out.

**ausradieren** ['ausradiːrən], *v.a.* erase.

**ausrangieren** ['ausranʒiːrən], *v.a.* cast off, sort out.

**ausräuchern** ['ausrɔyçərn], *v.a.* fumigate.

**ausraufen** ['ausraufən], *v.a.* (obs.) tear or pull out (hair).

**ausräumen** ['ausrɔymən], *v.a.* clear out, clear away.

**ausrechnen** ['ausrɛçnən], *v.a.* reckon, compute, calculate; ausgerechnet du, (emph.) you of all people.

**ausrecken** ['ausrɛkən], *v.a.* sich den Hals —, crane o.'s neck.

**Ausrede** ['ausreːdə], *f.* (—, *pl.* —n) evasion, excuse, subterfuge.

**ausreden** ['ausreːdən], *v.a.* einem etwas —, dissuade s.o. from s.th. — *v.n.* finish speaking; einen — lassen, allow s.o. to finish speaking.

**ausreichen** ['ausraɪçən], v.n. suffice.
**ausreißen** ['ausraɪsən], v.a. irr. pluck, pull out. — v.n. (aux. sein) run away, bolt.
**ausrenken** ['ausrɛŋkən], v.a. dislocate, sprain.
**ausrichten** ['ausrɪçtən], v.a. adjust, make straight; deliver (a message); accomplish; (Mil.) dress.
**ausrotten** ['ausrɔtən], v.a. root up; exterminate, extirpate.
**ausrücken** ['ausrykən], v.n. (aux. sein) (Mil.) march out; (coll.) decamp.
**Ausruf** ['ausru:f], m. (—s, pl. —e) exclamation, interjection, outcry; (public) proclamation.
**Ausruf(ungs)zeichen** ['ausru:f(uŋs)-tsaɪçən], n. (—s, pl. —) exclamation mark.
**ausruhen** ['ausru:ən], v.r. sich —, rest, take a rest.
**ausrüsten** ['ausrystən], v.a. furnish, fit out, equip.
**ausrutschen** ['ausrutʃən], v.n. (aux. sein) slip.
**Aussage** ['ausza:gə], f. (—, pl. —n) declaration, statement, evidence; (Law) deposition, affidavit; (Gram.) predicate.
**aussagen** ['ausza:gən], v.a. say, state, utter, declare; (Law) depose, give evidence.
**Aussatz** ['auszats], m. (—es, no pl.) leprosy.
**Aussätzige** ['auszɛtsɪgə], m. (—n, pl. —n) leper.
**aussaugen** ['auszaugən], v.a. suck dry.
**ausschalten** ['ausʃaltən], v.a. switch off.
**Ausschank** ['ausʃaŋk], m. (—s, no pl.) retail (of alcohol); pub, bar.
**Ausschau** ['ausʃau], f. (—, no pl.) watch; — halten, look out for.
**ausscheiden** ['ausʃaɪdən], v.a. irr. separate; (Med.) secrete. — v.n. (aux. sein) withdraw from, retire, secede.
**Ausscheidung** ['ausʃaɪduŋ], f. (—, pl. —en) retirement, withdrawal; (Med.) secretion.
**Ausschlag** ['ausʃla:k], m. (—s, pl. :e) turn (of the scales); deflection (of the magnetic needle); (Med.) rash, eczema; den — geben, clinch the matter; give the casting vote.
**ausschlagen** ['ausʃla:gən], v.a. irr. knock out; refuse, decline (an invitation); das schlägt dem Faß den Boden aus, that is the last straw. — v.n. (aux. sein) (Hort.) bud, shoot; gut —, turn out well.
**auschlaggebend** ['ausʃla:kge:bənt], adj. decisive; (vote) casting.
**ausschließen** ['ausʃli:sən], v.a. irr. lock out; exclude.
**ausschließlich** ['ausʃli:slɪç], adj. exclusive, sole.
**ausschlüpfen** ['ausʃlypfən], v.n. (aux. sein) hatch out.
**Ausschluß** ['ausʃlus], m. (—sses, pl. :sse) exclusion; unter — der Öffentlichkeit, in camera.

**ausschmücken** ['ausʃmykən], v.a. adorn, decorate, embellish.
**Ausschnitt** ['ausʃnɪt], m. (—s, pl. —e) cutting out; (newspaper) cutting; (dress) neck (line).
**ausschreiben** ['ausʃraɪbən], v.a. irr. write down in full; make out a bill; advertise (post) as vacant.
**ausschreiten** ['ausʃraɪtən], v.n. irr. (aux. sein) step out, stride along.
**Ausschreitungen** ['ausʃraɪtuŋən], f. pl. rioting; excesses.
**Ausschuß** ['ausʃus], m. (—sses, pl. :sse) dross, refuse, rejects, low quality goods; committee, commission, board.
**ausschweifend** ['ausʃvaɪfənt], adj. extravagant; licentious, dissolute.
**aussehen** ['ausze:ən], v.n. irr. look; look like, appear.
**außen** ['ausən], adv. outside, abroad, outward, without.
**Außenhandel** ['ausənhandəl], m. (—s, no pl.) export trade.
**Außenministerium** ['ausənmɪnɪste:r-jum], n. (—s, pl. —terien) Ministry of Foreign Affairs; (U.K.) Foreign Office, (U.S.) State Department.
**Außenstände** ['ausənʃtɛndə], m. pl. outstanding claims, liabilities.
**außer** ['ausər], prep. (Dat.) in addition to, besides, apart from; out of, at the outside of, beside, without; — Dienst, retired. — conj. except, save, but.
**außerdem** ['ausərde:m], adv. besides, moreover, furthermore.
**Äußere** ['ɔysərə], n. (—n, no pl.) exterior.
**außerehelich** ['ausəre:əlɪç], adj. illegitimate.
**außergewöhnlich** ['ausərgəvø:nlɪç], adj. unusual, exceptional.
**außerhalb** ['ausərhalp], prep. outside.
**äußerlich** ['ɔysərlɪç], adj. external.
**Äußerlichkeit** ['ɔysərlɪçkaɪt], f. (—, pl. —en) formality.
**äußern** ['ɔysərn], v.a. utter, express. — v.r. sich zu etwas —, give o.'s opinion on some question; express o.s. on some subject.
**außerordentlich** [ausər'ɔrdəntlɪç], adj. extraordinary, unusual; (Univ.) —er Professor, senior lecturer or reader; (Am.) associate professor.
**äußerst** ['ɔysərst], adj. outermost, most remote; extreme, utmost.
**außerstande** ['ausərʃtandə], adj. unable.
**Äußerung** ['ɔysəruŋ], f. (—, pl. —en) utterance, remark, observation.
**aussetzen** ['auszetsən], v.a. set out, put out; offer (a reward); suspend; etwas an einer Sache —, find fault with s.th.; sich einer Gefahr —, expose o.s. to danger, run a risk. — v.n. pause, discontinue; (Motor.) stop, misfire.
**Aussicht** ['auszɪçt], f. (—, pl. —en) view, panorama; prospect, chance; etwas in — stellen, hold out the prospect of s.th.; in — nehmen, intend.

# aussinnen

**aussinnen** [ˈauszɪnən],*v. a. irr.* imagine, invent, devise.

**aussöhnen** [ˈauszøːnən], *v.r. sich mit einem —*, become reconciled with s.o.

**aussondern** [ˈauszɔndərn], *v.a.* single out.

**ausspannen** [ˈausʃpanən], *v.a. (animals)* unharness. *— v.n. (coll.)* relax.

**ausspeien** [ˈausʃpaɪən], *v.a.* spit out, vomit.

**aussperren** [ˈausʃpɛrən], *v.a.* shut out; *(industrial)* lock out.

**ausspielen** [ˈausʃpiːlən], *v.n.* finish playing; *(Sport, Game)* lead (off).

**Aussprache** [ˈausʃpraːxə], *f. (—, no pl.)* pronunciation; discussion; confidential talk.

**aussprechen** [ˈausʃprɛçən], *v.a. irr.* have o.'s say; utter; pronounce. *— v.r. sich —*, speak o.'s mind.

**Ausspruch** [ˈausʃprux], *m. (—s, pl. ̈e)* utterance, dictum.

**ausspüren** [ˈausʃpyːrən], *v.a. (Hunt.)* track down.

**ausstaffieren** [ˈausʃtafiːrən],*v.a.*furnish, equip.

**Ausstand** [ˈausʃtant], *m. (—s, pl. ̈e)* *(industry)* strike; *(pl.)* outstanding debts, arrears.

**ausständig** [ˈausʃtɛndɪç], *adj.* outstanding; on strike.

**ausstatten** [ˈausʃtatən], *v.a.* endow with, provide with, equip.

**Ausstattung** [ˈausʃtatuŋ], *f. (—, pl. —en)* outfit; (bridal) trousseau; *(coll.)* get-up.

**ausstechen** [ˈausʃtɛçən], *v.a. irr.* pierce; *einen —*, *(fig.)* excel s.o.

**ausstehen** [ˈausʃteːən], *v.n. irr.* stand out; *(money)* be overdue. *— v.a.* endure, suffer, bear, undergo; *ich kann ihn nicht —*, I cannot stand him.

**aussteigen** [ˈausʃtaɪgən], *v.n. irr. (aux. sein)* get out, alight; disembark.

**ausstellen** [ˈausʃtɛlən], *v.a.* exhibit; display; make out (bill etc.).

**Aussteller** [ˈausʃtɛlər], *m. (—s, pl. —)* drawer (of a cheque); exhibitor.

**Ausstellung** [ˈausʃtɛluŋ], *f. (—, pl. —en)* exhibition; *(Am.)* exposition.

**Aussteuer** [ˈausʃtɔyər], *f. (—, pl. —n)* trousseau.

**ausstopfen** [ˈausʃtɔpfən], *v.a.* stuff.

**ausstoßen** [ˈausʃtoːsən], *v.a. irr.* push out, expel; utter.

**Ausstrahlung** [ˈausʃtraːluŋ], *f. (—, pl. —en)* radiation.

**ausstrecken** [ˈausʃtrɛkən], *v.a.* stretch out, reach out, extend.

**ausstreichen** [ˈausʃtraɪçən], *v.a. irr.* strike out, erase, delete; smoothe.

**ausstreuen** [ˈausʃtrɔyən], *v.a.* scatter, spread, sprinkle; *Gerüchte —*, circulate rumours.

**ausstudieren** [ˈausʃtudiːrən], *v.n.* finish o.'s studies; graduate.

**aussuchen** [ˈauszuːxən], *v.a.* select.

**Austausch** [ˈaustauʃ], *m. (—es, pl. —e)* barter, exchange; *(thoughts, letters)* interchange.

**austauschen** [ˈaustauʃən], *v.a.* barter, exchange; *(thoughts, letters)* interchange.

**austeilen** [ˈaustaɪlən], *v.a.* distribute, allocate.

**Auster** [ˈaustər], *f. (—, pl. —n)* oyster.

**Austerbank** [ˈaustərbaŋk], *f. (—, pl. ̈e)* oyster-bed.

**austilgen** [ˈaustɪlgən], *v.a.* exterminate, eradicate, extirpate.

**Australien** [auˈstraːljən], *n.* Australia.

**austreiben** [ˈaustraɪbən], *v.a. irr.* drive out, expel; exorcise.

**austreten** [ˈaustreːtən], *v.a. irr.* tread out; stretch (shoes) by walking; *ausgetretene Stufen*, worn steps. *— v.n. (aux. sein)* retire (from business); withdraw (from a club); *(coll.)* go to the lavatory.

**Austritt** [ˈaustrɪt], *m. (—s, pl. —e)* withdrawal, retirement.

**ausüben** [ˈausyːbən], *v.a.* exercise, practise; exert, commit.

**Ausverkauf** [ˈausfɛrkauf], *m. (—s, pl. ̈e)* selling-off, clearance sale.

**Auswahl** [ˈausvaːl], *f. (—, pl. —en)* choice, selection.

**Auswanderer** [ˈausvandərər], *m. (—s, pl. —)* emigrant.

**auswärtig** [ˈausvɛrtɪç], *adj.* foreign, away.

**auswärts** [ˈausvɛrts], *adv.* outward(s), away from home.

**auswechseln** [ˈausvɛksəln], *v.a.* exchange; fit (spare parts).

**Ausweg** [ˈausveːk], *m. (—s, pl. —e)* expedient; way out; *ich weiß keinen —*, I am at my wits' end.

**ausweichen** [ˈausvaɪçən], *v.n. irr. (aux. sein)* give way; evade, parry.

**Ausweis** [ˈausvaɪs], *m. (—es, pl. —e)* proof of identity, identity card.

**ausweisen** [ˈausvaɪzən], *v.a. irr.* turn out, banish, exile, deport. *— v.r. (aux. haben) sich —*, show proof of o.'s identity.

**auswendig** [ˈausvɛndɪç], *adj.* by heart.

**auswirken** [ˈausvɪrkən], *v.r. sich gut —*, work out well, have a good effect.

**Auswuchs** [ˈausvuːks], *m. (—es, pl. ̈e)* sprouting, outgrowth, *(fig.)* excrescence.

**Auswurf** [ˈausvurf], *m. (—s, pl. ̈e)* excretion; expectoration; *— der Menschheit*, scum of the earth.

**auszählen** [ˈaustsɛːlən], *v.n.* count, number. *— v.a.* count out.

**Auszahlung** [ˈaustsaːluŋ], *f. (—, pl. —en)* payment.

**auszanken** [ˈaustsaŋkən], *v.a.* scold, chide.

**auszehren** [ˈaustseːrən], *v.n. (aux. sein)* waste away, be consumed.

**auszeichnen** [ˈaustsaɪçnən], *v.a.* mark out, honour, decorate. *— v.r. sich —*, distinguish o.s.

**Auszeichnung** [ˈaustsaɪçnuŋ], *f. (—, pl. —en)* distinction, medal.

**ausziehen** ['austsi:ən], *v.a. irr.* undress, take off (clothes); (*Chem.*) extract; stretch. — *v.n.* (*aux.* sein) move out. — *v.r.* sich —, undress.

**auszischen** ['austsɪʃən], *v.a.* (*Theat.*) hiss, cat-call.

**Auszug** ['austsu:k], *m.* (—s, *pl.* ⁀e) removal (from home); marching off; exodus; extract (from a book), abstract (from a deed).

**Auto** ['auto], *n.* (—s, *pl.* —s) motor-car, (*Am.*) automobile.

**Autogramm** [auto'gram], *n.* (—s, *pl.* —e) autograph.

**Automat** [auto'ma:t], *m.* (—en, *pl.* —en) slot machine.

**Autor** ['autor], *m.* (—s, *pl.* —en) author, writer.

**Autorität** [autori'tɛ:t], *f.* (—, *pl.* —en) authority.

**avisieren** [avɪ'zi:rən], *v.a.* notify, advise.

**Axt** [akst], *f.* (—, *pl.* ⁀e) axe.

**Azur** [a'tsu:r], *m.* (—s, *no pl.*) azure.


# B

**B** [be:], *n.* (—s, *pl.*—s) the letter B; (*Mus.*) B flat; — *Dur*, B flat major; — *Moll*, B flat minor.

**Bach** [bax], *m.* (—es, *pl.* ⁀e) brook, rivulet.

**Bachstelze** ['baxʃtɛltsə], *f.* (—, *pl.* —n) wagtail.

**Backe** ['bakə], *f.* (—, *pl.* —n) cheek.

**backen** ['bakən], *v.a.* bake.

**Backenstreich** ['bakənʃtraɪç], *m.* (—s, *pl.* —e) box on the ear.

**Bäcker** ['bɛkər], *m.* (—s, *pl.* —) baker.

**Backfisch** ['bakfɪʃ], *m.* (—es, *pl.* —e) (*fig.*) teenage girl.

**Backhuhn** ['bakhu:n], *n.* (—s, *pl.* ⁀er) fried chicken.

**Backobst** ['bakopst], *n.* (—es, *no pl.*) dried fruit.

**Backpfeife** ['bakpfaɪfə], *f.* (—, *pl.* —n) box on the ear.

**Backpflaume** ['bakpflaumə], *f.* (—, *pl.* —n) prune.

**Backstein** ['bakʃtaɪn], *m.* (—s, *pl.* —e) brick.

**Backwerk** ['bakvɛrk], *n.* (—s, *no pl.*) pastry.

**Bad** [ba:t], *n.* (—es, *pl.* ⁀er) bath; spa, watering-place.

**Badeanstalt** ['ba:dəanʃtalt], *f.* (—, *pl.* —en) public baths.

**baden** ['ba:dən], *v.n.* bathe, have a bath.

**Badewanne** ['ba:dəvanə], *f.* (—, *pl.* —n) bath-tub.

**Bagage** [ba'ga:ʒə], *f.* (—, *no pl.*) luggage; (*Am.*) baggage; (*sl.*) mob, rabble.

**Bagger** ['bagər], *m.* (—s, *pl.* —) dredger, dredging-machine.

**baggern** ['bagərn], *v.a.* dredge.

**Bahn** [ba:n], *f.* (—, *pl.* —en) road, path, course; (*Astr.*) orbit; railway(-line); — *brechen*, open a path.

**bahnbrechend** ['ba:nbrɛçənt], *adj.* pioneering, epoch-making.

**bahnen** ['ba:nən], *v.a.* make passable; pave (the way).

**Bahngleis** ['ba:nglaɪs], *n.* (—es, *pl.* —e) railway-line, railway-track; (*Am.*) railroad-line, railroad-track.

**Bahnhof** ['ba:nho:f], *m.* (—s, *pl.* ⁀e) railway-station, (*Am.*) depot.

**Bahnsteig** ['ba:nʃtaɪk], *m.* (—s, *pl.* —e) platform.

**Bahnwärter** ['ba:nvɛrtər], *m.* (—s, *pl.* —) signal-man.

**Bahre** ['ba:rə], *f.* (—, *pl.* —n) litter, stretcher; bier.

**Bahrtuch** ['ba:rtu:x], *n.* (—s, *pl.* ⁀er) pall, shroud.

**Bai** [baɪ], *f.* (—, *pl.* —en) bay, cove.

**Baisse** ['bɛsə], *f.* (—, *pl.* —n) (*Comm.*) fall in share prices.

**Bakkalaureat** [bakalaure'a:t], *n.* (—s, *pl.* —e) bachelor's degree.

**Bakterie** [bak'te:rjə], *f.* (—, *pl.* —n) bacterium.

**bald** [balt], *adv.* soon, shortly, directly, presently.

**baldig** ['baldɪç], *adj.* quick, speedy; *auf —es Wiedersehen*, see you again soon.

**Baldrian** ['baldria:n], *m.* (—s, *no pl.*) valerian.

**Balearen, die** [bale'a:rən, di:], *pl.* Balearic Islands.

**Balg** (1) [balk], *m.* (—s, *pl.* ⁀e) skin, slough, husk; bellows (of organ *or* forge).

**Balg** (2) [balk], *n.* (—s, *pl.* ⁀er) brat; naughty child.

**balgen** ['balgən], *v.r.* sich —, (*children*) fight, romp.

**Balgerei** ['balgəraɪ], *f.* (—, *pl.* —en) scuffle, scrimmage.

**Balken** ['balkən], *m.* (—s, *pl.* —) beam, joist, rafter.

**Balkenwerk** ['balkənvɛrk], *n.* (—s, *no pl.*) building-frame, timbers, wood-work.

**Balkon** [bal'k5], *m.* (—s, *pl.* —s, —e) balcony.

**Ball** [bal], *m.* (—s, *pl.* ⁀e) ball; globe; sphere; dance.

**ballen** ['balən], *v.a.* form into a ball; clench (o.'s fist).

**Ballen** ['balən], *m.* (—s, *pl.* —) bale, bundle, package; ball (of the hand *or* foot).

**ballförmig** ['balfœrmɪç], *adj.* spherical.

**Ballistik** [ba'lɪstɪk], *f.* (—, *no pl.*) ballistics.

**Ballon** [ba'l5], *m.* (—s, *pl.* —s, —e) balloon.

**Balsam** ['balza:m], *m.* (—s, *pl.* —e) balm, balsam.

**Baltikum** ['baltɪkum], *n.* (—s, *no pl.*) the Baltic countries.

**Bambusrohr** ['bambusro:r], *n.* (—s, *pl.* —e) bamboo (cane).
**Banane** [ba'na:nə], *f.* (—, *pl.* —n) banana.
**Banause** [ba'nauzə], *m.* (—n, *pl.* —n) narrow-minded person, philistine.
**Band** (1) [bant], *n.* (—s, *pl.* ⸚er) ribbon, riband, tape; string; (*Bot.*) band; hoop (*for a cask*); (*Anat.*) ligament, tendon.
**Band** (2) [bant], *n.* (—s, *pl.* —e) (*fig.*) bond, fetter, chain, (*pl.*) bonds, ties (*of friendship*).
**Band** (3) [bant], *m.* (—es, *pl.* ⸚e) volume.
**Bändchen** ['bɛntçən], *n.* (—s, *pl.* —) small ribbon, small piece of string; (*book*) small volume.
**Bande** ['bandə], *f.* (—, *pl.* —n) horde, gang, set.
**bändigen** ['bɛndɪgən], *v.a.* tame, subdue.
**Bandmaß** ['bantma:s], *n.* (—es, *pl.* —e) tape-measure.
**Bandwurm** ['bantvurm], *m.* (—s, *pl.* ⸚er) (*Zool.*) tape-worm.
**bange** ['baŋə], *adj.* afraid, worried, alarmed.
**Bangigkeit** ['baŋɪçkaɪt], *f.* (—, *no pl.*) uneasiness, anxiety.
**Bank** (1) [baŋk], *f.* (—, *pl.* ⸚e) bench, seat (in a park); *auf die lange — schieben*, delay, shelve; *durch die —*, without exception.
**Bank** (2) [baŋk], *f.* (—, *pl.* —en) bank; *die — sprengen*, break the bank.
**Bänkelsänger** ['bɛŋkəlzɛŋər], *m.* (—s, *pl.* —) ballad singer.
**bank(e)rott** [baŋk'rɔt], *adj.* bankrupt.
**Bankett** [baŋ'kɛt], *n.* (—s, *pl.* —e) banquet.
**Bankkonto** ['baŋkkɔnto], *n.* (—s, *pl.* —ten) bank-account.
**Bann** [ban], *m.* (—s, *no pl.*) ban, exile; (*Eccl.*) excommunication; *in den — tun*, outlaw, (*Eccl.*) excommunicate; (*fig.*) charm, spell.
**bannen** ['banən], *v.a.* banish, exile, cast out.
**Banner** ['banər], *n.* (—s, *pl.* —) banner, standard.
**Bannmeile** ['banmaɪlə], *f.* (—, *pl.* —n) boundary.
**bar** [ba:r], *adv.* in cash, ready money.
**Bar** [ba:r], *f.* (—, *pl.* —s) bar (for selling drinks etc.).
**Bär** [bɛ:r], *m.* (—en, *pl.* —en) (*Zool.*) bear; *einem einen —en aufbinden*, to lead s.o. up the garden-path.
**Barauslagen** ['barausla:gən], *f. pl.* cash expenses.
**Barbar** [bar'ba:r], *m.* (—en, *pl.* —en) barbarian, vandal.
**barbarisch** [bar'ba:rɪʃ], *adj.* barbarous.
**Barbestand** ['ba:rbəʃtant], *m.* (—s, *pl.* ⸚e) cash reserve, cash balance.
**bärbeißig** ['bɛ:rbaɪsɪç], *adj.* surly, morose.
**Barchent** ['barçənt], *m.* (—s, *no pl.*) fustian.

**Barde** ['bardə], *m.* (—n, *pl.* —n) bard, minstrel.
**Bärenfell** ['bɛ:rənfɛl], *n.* (—s, *pl.* —e) bear-skin.
**Bärenmütze** ['bɛ:rənmytsə], *f.* (—, *pl.* —n) (*Mil.*) busby.
**Bärenzwinger** ['bɛ:rəntsvɪŋər], *m.* (—s, *pl.* —) bear-garden.
**Barett** [ba'rɛt], *n.* (—s, *pl.* —e) cap, beret; (*Eccl.*) biretta.
**barfuß** ['barfus], *adj.* barefoot(ed).
**Bargeld** ['barɡɛlt], *n.* (—(e)s, *no pl.*) cash.
**barhäuptig** ['barhɔyptɪç], *adj.* bare-headed.
**Barkasse** [bar'kasə], *f.* (—, *pl.* —n) launch.
**Barke** ['barkə], *f.* (—, *pl.* —n) barge, lighter.
**barmherzig** [barm'hɛrtsɪç], *adj.* merciful, charitable, compassionate.
**Barock** [ba'rɔk], *n.* (—s, *no pl.*) Baroque.
**Baronin** [ba'ro:nɪn], *f.* (—, *pl.* —nen) baroness.
**Barren** ['barən], *m.* (—s, *pl.* —) parallel bars.
**Barsch** [barʃ], *m.* (—es, *pl.* —e) (*Zool.*) perch.
**barsch** [barʃ], *adj.* rough, harsh, sharp, abrupt, unfriendly.
**Barschaft** ['ba:rʃaft], *f.* (—, *pl.* —en) ready money.
**Bart** [ba:rt], *m.* (—s, *pl.* ⸚e) beard; (*key*) ward.
**Bartflechte** ['ba:rtflɛçtə], *f.* (—, *pl.* —n) barber's itch.
**bärtig** ['bɛ:rtɪç], *adj.* bearded.
**Basalt** [ba'zalt], *m.* (—s, *pl.* —e) (*Min.*) basalt.
**Base** ['ba:zə], *f.* (—, *pl.* —n) female cousin; (*Chem.*) base.
**Basis** ['ba:zɪs], *f.* (—, *pl.* **Basen**) base, foundation.
**Baskenmütze** ['baskənmytsə], *f.* (—, *pl.* —n) tam-o'-shanter, beret.
**Baß** [bas], *m.* (—sses, *pl.* ⸚sse) (*Mus.*) bass.
**Baßschlüssel** ['basʃlysəl], *m.* (—s, *pl.* —) (*Mus.*) bass-clef.
**Bassin** [ba'sɛ̃], *n.* (—s, *pl.* —s) basin, reservoir.
**Bast** [bast], *m.* (—es, *pl.* —e) inner bark, fibre (*of trees etc.*); bast.
**basta** ['basta], *int.* and that's that!
**Bastei** [bas'taɪ], *f.* (—, *pl.* —en) bastion.
**basteln** ['bastəln], *v.a.* work on a hobby, tinker.
**Batist** [ba'tɪst], *m.* (—s, *pl.* —e) cambric.
**Bau** [bau], *m.* (—es, *pl.* —ten) building, structure, edifice; act of building; *im — begriffen*, in course of construction.
**Bauart** ['bauart], *f.* (—, *pl.* —en) (architectural) style, structure.
**Bauch** [baux], *m.* (—es, *pl.* ⸚e) belly, stomach.
**Bauchfell** ['bauxfɛl], *n.* (—s, *pl.* —e) peritoneum.

**bauchig** ['bauçɪç], adj. bulgy.
**Bauchredner** ['bauxre:dnər], m. (—s, pl. —) ventriloquist.
**bauen** ['bauən], v.a. build, construct, erect. — v.n. auf etwas —, (fig.) rely on s.th., count on s.th.
**Bauer** (1) ['bauər], m. (—n, pl. —n) farmer, peasant; (chess) pawn.
**Bauer** (2) ['bauər], n. (—s, pl. —) (bird) cage.
**Bäuerin** ['bɔyərɪn], f. (—, pl. —nen) farmer's wife.
**Bauernfänger** ['bauərnfɛŋər], m. (—s, pl. —) sharper, rook, confidence-trickster.
**Bauernstand** ['bauərnʃtant], m. (—s, pl. ⸚e) peasantry.
**baufällig** ['baufɛlɪç], adj. dilapidated, ramshackle.
**Baugerüst** ['baugəryst], n. (—s, pl. —e) scaffolding.
**Baugewerbe** ['baugəvɛrbə], n. (—s, no pl.) building trade.
**Baukunst** ['baukunst], f. (—, no pl.) architecture.
**Baum** [baum], m. (—(e)s, pl. ⸚e) tree.
**Baumeister** ['baumaɪstər], m. (—s, pl. —) architect, master-builder.
**baumeln** ['bauməln], v.n. dangle.
**Baumkuchen** ['baumku:xən], m. (—s, pl. —) pyramid-cake.
**Baumschule** ['baumʃu:lə], f. (—, pl. —n) plantation of trees, orchard, tree nursery.
**Baumstamm** ['baumʃtam], m. (—s, pl. ⸚e) stem, trunk.
**Baumwolle** ['baumvɔlə], f. (—, pl. —n) cotton.
**Bauriß** ['baurɪs], m. (—sses, pl. —sse) plan, architect's drawing.
**Bausch** [bauʃ], m. (—es, pl. ⸚e) pad, bolster; in — und Bogen, in the lump; all at once.
**bauschig** ['bauʃɪç], adj. baggy.
**Bauwerk** ['bauvɛrk] see **Gebäude**.
**Bayern** ['baɪərn], n. Bavaria.
**Bazar** [ba'za:r], m. (—s, pl. —e) bazaar, fair, emporium.
**beabsichtigen** [bə'apzɪçtɪgən], v.a. aim at, intend, have in view.
**beachten** [bə'axtən], v.a. observe, pay attention to.
**Beamte** [bə'amtə], m. (—n, pl. —n) official, officer, civil servant.
**Beamtin** [bə'amtɪn], f. (—, pl. —nen) female official, female civil servant.
**beängstigen** [bə'ɛŋstɪgən], v.a. alarm, make afraid.
**beanspruchen** [bə'anʃpruxən], v.a. demand, claim, lay claim to.
**beanstanden** [bə'anʃtandən], v.a. object to, raise objections to, query.
**beantragen** [bə'antra:gən], v.a. move, apply, lodge an application.
**beantworten** [bə'antvɔrtən], v.a. answer, reply to.
**bearbeiten** [bə'arbaɪtən], v.a. work (on); (book, play) adapt, arrange, revise; (Agr.) cultivate; (fig.) einen —, try to influence s.o., try to convince s.o.

**Bearbeitung** [bə'arbaɪtuŋ], f. (—, pl. —en) working, manipulation, operation; (Agr.) culture, cultivation; (book, play) adaptation, revision, arrangement.
**beargwöhnen** [bə'arkvø:nən], v.a. suspect, view with suspicion.
**beaufsichtigen** [bə'aufzɪçtɪgən], v.a. control, supervise, superintend.
**beauftragen** [bə'auftra:gən], v.a. commission, charge, authorize.
**bebauen** [bə'bauən], v.a. build upon; (Agr.) cultivate.
**beben** ['be:bən], v.n. shake, quake, tremble; vor Kälte —, shiver with cold.
**Becher** ['bɛçər], m. (—s, pl. —) beaker, cup, goblet, mug; (dice) box.
**Becken** ['bɛkən], n. (—s, pl. —) basin, bowl; (Anat.) pelvis; (Mus.) cymbal.
**Bedacht** [bə'daxt], m. (—s, no pl.) consideration; mit —, deliberately; ohne —, thoughtlessly.
**bedächtig** [bə'dɛçtɪç], adj. circumspect, deliberate, cautious, slow.
**bedanken** [bə'daŋkən], v.r. sich für etwas —, thank s.o. for s.th., decline with thanks (also iron.).
**Bedarf** [bə'darf], m. (—s, no pl.) need, requirement, demand.
**bedauerlich** [bə'dauərlɪç], adj. regrettable, deplorable.
**bedauern** [bə'dauərn], v.a. pity, commiserate, regret; ich bedaure, daß, I am sorry that . . .
**bedecken** [bə'dɛkən], v.a. cover (up); sich mit Ruhm —, cover o.s. with glory.
**bedeckt** [bə'dɛkt], adj. (sky) overcast.
**bedenken** [bə'dɛŋkən], v.a. irr. consider, bear in mind. — v.r. sich —, deliberate, hesitate; sich anders —, change o.'s mind.
**bedenklich** [bə'dɛŋklɪç], adj. (persons) doubtful, dubious; (things) risky, delicate, precarious; (illness) serious, grave.
**Bedenkzeit** [bə'dɛŋktsaɪt], f. (—, pl. —en) time to consider, respite.
**bedeuten** [bə'dɔytən], v.a. signify, mean, imply; direct, order.
**bedeutend** [bə'dɔytənt], adj. important, eminent, considerable, outstanding.
**bedeutsam** [bə'dɔytza:m], adj. significant.
**Bedeutung** [bə'dɔytuŋ], f. (—, pl. —en) significance, meaning; consequence, importance; nichts von —, nothing to speak of.
**bedienen** [bə'di:nən], v.a. serve, attend to, wait on; (machine) operate; (Cards) follow suit. —v.r. sich —, help o.s., make use of.
**Bediente** [bə'di:ntə], m. (—n, pl. —n) servant, attendant, footman, lackey.
**Bedienung** [bə'di:nuŋ], f. (—, pl. —en) service, attendance.
**bedingen** [bə'dɪŋən], v.a. stipulate, postulate, condition, cause.

**bedingt** [bə'dɪŋkt], *adj.* conditional.
**Bedingung** [bə'dɪŋuŋ], *f.* (—, *pl.* —en) stipulation, condition, term; *unter keiner* —, on no account.
**bedingungsweise** [bə'dɪŋuŋsvaɪzə], *adv.* on condition, conditionally.
**bedrängen** [bə'drɛŋən], *v.a.* oppress; press hard, afflict.
**Bedrängnis** [bə'drɛŋnɪs], *f.* (—, *pl.* —se) oppression, distress.
**bedrohen** [bə'dro:ən], *v.a.* threaten, menace.
**bedrohlich** [bə'dro:lɪç], *adj.* threatening, menacing, ominous.
**bedrücken** [bə'drykən], *v.a.* oppress, harass, depress.
**Beduine** [bedu'i:nə], *m.* (—n, *pl.* —n) Bedouin.
**bedünken** [bə'dyŋkən], *v.a.* appear, seem; *es bedünkt mich,* methinks.
**bedürfen** [bə'dyrfən], *v.n. irr.* want, need, be in need of.
**Bedürfnis** [bə'dyrfnɪs], *n.* (—ses, *pl.* —se) want, need, requirement, necessity; *es ist mir ein* —, I cannot but; *einem dringenden* — *abhelfen,* meet an urgent want *or* need; *ein* — *haben,* (*coll.*) need to relieve o.s.
**Bedürfnisanstalt** [bə'dyrfnɪsanʃtalt], *f.* (—, *pl.* —en) public lavatory, public convenience.
**bedürftig** [bə'dyrftɪç], *adj.* needy, indigent, poor.
**beeidigen** [bə'aɪdɪgən], *v.a.* confirm by oath, swear in.
**beeifern** [bə'aɪfərn], *v.r. sich* —, exert o.s., strive, be zealous.
**beeilen** [bə'aɪlən], *v.r. sich* —, hurry, hasten, make haste.
**beeindrucken** [bə'aɪndrukən], *v.a.* impress.
**beeinflussen** [bə'aɪnflusən], *v.a.* influence.
**beeinträchtigen** [bə'aɪntrɛçtɪgən], *v.a.* injure, lessen, diminish, detract from, curtail.
**beenden** [bə'ɛndən], *v.a.* end, finish, terminate, conclude.
**beendigen** [bə'ɛndɪgən], *v.a.* end, finish, terminate, conclude.
**beengen** [bə'ɛŋən], *v.a.* cramp, narrow.
**beerben** [bə'ɛrbən], *v.a. einen* —, inherit from s.o.
**beerdigen** [bə'ɛːrdɪgən], *v.a.* bury, inter.
**Beere** ['be:rə], *f.* (—, *pl.* —n) berry.
**Beet** [be:t], *n.* (—es, *pl.* —e) (flower) bed.
**befähigen** [bə'fɛ:ɪgən], *v.a.* fit, enable, qualify.
**Befähigung** [bə'fɛ:ɪguŋ], *f.* (—, *pl.* —en) qualification, capacity, aptitude.
**befahren** [bə'fa:rən], *v.a. irr.* pass over, travel over; (*Naut.*) navigate.
**befallen** [bə'falən], *v.a. irr.* befall, fall on; *von Traurigkeit* — *sein,* be overcome by sadness.
**befangen** [bə'faŋən], *adj.* biased, prejudiced; bashful, embarrassed.

**befassen** [bə'fasən], *v.a.* touch, handle. — *v.r. sich mit etwas* —, occupy o.s. with s.th.
**befehden** [bə'fe:dən], *v.a.* make war upon, show enmity towards.
**Befehl** [bə'fe:l], *m.* (—s, *pl.* —e) order, command; (*Mil.*) *zu* —, very good, sir; (*Mil.*) *den* — *führen über,* command.
**befehlen** [bə'fe:lən], *v.a. irr.* order, command.
**befehligen** [bə'fe:lɪgən], *v.a.* (*Mil.*) command, lead.
**Befehlshaber** [bə'fe:lsha:bər], *m.* (—s, *pl.* —) commander, commanding officer, chief.
**befehlswidrig** [bə'fe:lsvi:drɪç], *adj.* contrary to orders.
**befestigen** [bə'fɛstɪgən], *v.a.* fasten, fix, attach, affix; (*Mil.*) fortify; strengthen.
**befeuchten** [bə'fɔʏçtən], *v.a.* wet, moisten, dampen.
**Befinden** [bə'fɪndən], *n.* (—s, *no pl.*) state of health.
**befinden** [bə'fɪndən], *v.a. irr.* think, deem, find. — *v.r. sich an einem Ort* —, be in some place; *sich wohl* —, feel well.
**befindlich** [bə'fɪntlɪç], *adj.* existing; — *sein,* be contained in.
**beflecken** [bə'flɛkən], *v.a.* stain, spot, blot; defile, pollute.
**befleißigen** [bə'flaɪsɪgən], *v.r. sich* —, devote o.s. to, take pains to.
**beflissen** [bə'flɪsən], *adj.* eager to serve, assiduous.
**beflügeln** [bə'fly:gəln], *v.a.* give wings; (*fig.*) accelerate, animate.
**befolgen** [bə'fɔlgən], *v.a.* follow, obey; *einen Befehl* —, comply with an order.
**befördern** [bə'fœrdərn], *v.a.* despatch, forward, send, post, mail, transmit; promote, advance.
**Beförderung** [bə'fœrdəruŋ], *f.* (—, *pl.* —en) forwarding, transmission; (*office*) promotion, advancement.
**Beförderungsmittel** [bə'fœrdəruŋsmɪtəl], *n.* (—s, *pl.* —) conveyance, means of transport.
**befragen** [bə'fra:gən], *v.a.* question, interrogate, examine.
**befreien** [bə'fraɪən], *v.a.* free, liberate.
**befremden** [bə'frɛmdən], *v.a.* appear strange, astonish, surprise.
**befreunden** [bə'frɔʏndən], *v.a.* befriend. — *v.r. sich mit einem* —, make friends with s.o.
**befriedigen** [bə'fri:dɪgən], *v.a.* content, satisfy; appease, calm.
**befruchten** [bə'fruxtən], *v.a.* fertilise, impregnate.
**Befugnis** [bə'fu:knɪs], *f.* (—, *pl.* —se) authority, right, warrant.
**Befund** [bə'funt], *m.* (—s, *pl.* —e) (*Med.*) diagnosis, findings.
**befürchten** [bə'fyrçtən], *v.a.* fear, be afraid of.
**befürworten** [bə'fy:rvɔrtən], *v.a.* support, second.

# belehren

**Beistrich** ['baɪʃtrɪç], *m.* (—(e)s, *pl.* —e) comma.

**beitragen** ['baɪtra:gən], *v.a. irr.* contribute; be conducive to.

**beitreten** ['baɪtre:tən], *v.n. irr. (aux.* sein) join (a club); enter into partnership with (a firm).

**Beitritt** ['baɪtrɪt], *m.* (—s, *no pl.*) accession, joining.

**Beiwagen** ['baɪva:gən], *m.* (—s, *pl.* —) trailer, sidecar (on motor cycle).

**beiwohnen** ['baɪvo:nən], *v.n.* be present at, attend.

**Beiwort** ['baɪvɔrt], *n.* (—s, *pl.* ꞏer) adjective, epithet.

**Beize** ['baɪtsə], *f.* (—, *pl.* —n) caustic fluid; (*wood*) stain.

**beizeiten** [baɪ'tsaɪtən], *adv.* betimes, early, in good time.

**beizen** ['baɪtsən], *v.a.* cauterise; (*wood*) stain.

**bejahen** [bə'ja:ən], *v.a.* answer in the affirmative.

**bejahrt** [bə'ja:rt], *adj.* aged, elderly, old.

**bejammern** [bə'jamərn], *v.a.* bemoan, bewail.

**bekannt** [bə'kant], *adj.* known, well-known; — *mit,* acquainted with.

**Bekannte** [bə'kantə], *m.* (—n, *pl.* —n) acquaintance.

**bekanntlich** [bə'kantlɪç], *adv.* as is well known.

**Bekanntmachung** [bə'kan...tuŋ], *f.* (—, *pl.* —en) publication, announcement.

**Bekanntschaft** [bə'kantʃaft], *f.* (—, *pl.* —en) — *mit einem machen,* strike up an acquaintance with s.o.

**bekehren** [bə'ke:rən], *v.a.* convert. — *v.r. sich* —, be converted *or* become a convert (to); reform.

**bekennen** [bə'kɛnən], *v.a. irr.* confess, profess; admit, own up to.

**Bekenner** [bə'kɛnər], *m.* (—s, *pl.* —) Confessor (as title).

**Bekenntnis** [bə'kɛntnɪs], *n.* (—ses, *pl.* —se) confession (of faith), avowal, creed.

**beklagen** [bə'kla:gən], *v.a.* lament, bewail, deplore. — *v.r. sich* — *über,* complain of.

**Beklagte** [bə'kla:ktə], *m.* (—n, *pl.* —n) (*Law*) defendant.

**bekleiden** [bə'klaɪdən], *v.a.* clothe, dress, cover; (*office*) hold.

**Bekleidung** [bə'klaɪduŋ], *f.* (—, *no pl.*) clothing, clothes; (*office*) administration, holding, exercise.

**beklemmen** [bə'klɛmən], *v.a. irr.* oppress.

**Beklemmung** [bə'klɛmuŋ], *f.* (—, *pl.* —en) oppression, anguish.

**beklommen** [bə'klɔmən], *adj.* anxious, uneasy.

**bekommen** [bə'kɔmən], *v.a. irr.* obtain, get, receive.

**bekömmlich** [bə'kœmlɪç], *adj.* beneficial; digestible, wholesome.

**beköstigen** [bə'kœstɪgən], *v.a.* board; feed.

**bekräftigen** [bə'krɛftɪgən], *v.a.* aver, corroborate, confirm.

**bekränzen** [bə'krɛntsən], *v.a.* wreathe, crown (with a garland).

**bekreuzigen** [bə'krɔytsɪgən], *v.r. sich* —, make the sign of the cross, cross o.s.

**bekriegen** [bə'kri:gən], *v.a.* make war on.

**bekritteln** [bə'krɪtəln], *v.a.* criticise, carp at, find fault with.

**bekritzeln** [bə'krɪtsəln], *v.a.* scrawl on, doodle on.

**bekümmern** [bə'kymərn], *v.a.* grieve, distress, trouble. — *v.r.* trouble o.s. about, grieve over.

**bekunden** [bə'kundən], *v.a.* manifest, show; declare.

**beladen** [bə'la:dən], *v.a. irr.* load.

**Belag** [bə'la:k], *m.* (—s, *pl.* ꞏe) covering, layer; spread (on sandwiches); fur (on the tongue).

**belagern** [bə'la:gərn], *v.a.* besiege.

**Belang** [bə'laŋ], *m.* (—s, *pl.* —e) importance; *von* —, of great moment *or* consequence; (*pl.*) concerns, interests.

**belangen** [bə'laŋən], *v.a.* (*Law*) sue, prosecute.

**belanglos** [bə'laŋlo:s], *adj.* of small account; irrelevant, unimportant.

**belassen** [bə'lasən], *v.a. irr. es dabei* —, leave things as they are.

**belasten** [bə'lastən], *v.a.* load, burden; (*Comm.*) debit, charge; (*Law*) incriminate.

**belästigen** [bə'lɛstɪgən], *v.a.* bother, pester, molest.

**Belastung** [bə'lastuŋ], *f.* (—, *pl.* —en) load, burden; (*Comm.*) debiting; (*house*) mortgage; *erbliche* —, hereditary disposition.

**Belastungszeuge** [bə'lastuŋstsɔygə], *m.* (—n, *pl.* —n) witness for the prosecution.

**belaubt** [bə'laupt], *adj.* covered with leaves, leafy.

**belaufen** [bə'laufən], *v.r. irr. sich* — *auf,* amount to, come to.

**belauschen** [bə'lauʃən], *v.a.* eavesdrop, overhear.

**beleben** [bə'le:bən], *v.a.* animate, enliven.

**Belebtheit** [bə'le:pthaɪt], *f.* (—, *no pl.*) animation, liveliness.

**Beleg** [bə'le:k], *m.* (—s, *pl.* —e) document, proof, receipt, voucher.

**belegen** [bə'le:gən], *v.a.* cover, overlay; reserve, book (*seat*); support by documents, authenticate, prove.

**Belegschaft** [bə'le:kʃaft], *f.* (—, *pl.* —en) workers, personnel, staff; (*Min.*) gang, shift.

**belegt** [bə'le:kt], *adj.* (*tongue*) furred; —*es Brot,* sandwich.

**belehnen** [bə'le:nən], *v.a.* enfeoff, invest (with a fief).

**belehren** [bə'le:rən], *v.a.* instruct, advise, inform.

# Belehrung

**Belehrung** [bə'le:ruŋ], *f.* (—, *pl.* —en) information, instruction, advice.

**beleibt** [bə'laɪpt], *adj.* stout, corpulent, obese.

**beleidigen** [bə'laɪdɪgən], *v.a.* insult, offend, give offence to.

**belesen** [bə'le:zən], *adj.* well-read.

**beleuchten** [bə'lɔyçtən], *v.a.* illumine, illuminate; (*fig.*) throw light on, elucidate.

**Beleuchtungskörper** [bə'lɔyçtuŋskœr-pər], *m.* (—s, *pl.* —) lighting fixture, lamp.

**Belgien** ['bɛlgjən], *n.* Belgium.

**belichten** [bə'lɪçtən], *v.a.* (*Phot.*) expose.

**belieben** [bə'li:bən], *v.a.*, *v.n.* please, like, choose.

**beliebig** [bə'li:bɪç], *adj.* optional; any, whatever.

**beliebt** [bə'li:pt], *adj.* popular, well-liked.

**Beliebtheit** [bə'li:pthaɪt], *f.* (—, *no pl.*) popularity.

**bellen** ['bɛlən], *v.n.* bark.

**beloben** [bə'lo:bən], *v.a.* praise, approve.

**belohnen** [bə'lo:nən], *v.a.* reward, recompense.

**belügen** [bə'ly:gən], *v.a. irr. einen* —, tell lies to s.o., deceive s.o. by lying.

**belustigen** [bə'lustɪgən], *v.a.* amuse, divert, entertain.

**bemächtigen** [bə'mɛçtɪgən], *v.r. sich einer Sache* —, take possession of s.th.

**bemäkeln** [bə'mɛːkəln], *v.a.* find fault with.

**bemalen** [bə'ma:lən], *v.a.* paint (over).

**bemängeln** [bə'mɛŋəln], *v.a.* find fault with.

**bemannen** [bə'manən], *v.a.* man.

**bemänteln** [bə'mɛntəln], *v.a.* cloak, hide.

**bemeistern** [bə'maɪstərn], *v.a.* master.

**bemerkbar** [bə'mɛrkba:r], *adj.* perceptible, noticeable.

**bemerken** [bə'mɛrkən], *v.a.* observe, perceive, notice.

**Bemerkung** [bə'mɛrkuŋ], *f.* (—, *pl.* —en) remark, observation, note.

**bemessen** [bə'mɛsən], *v.a. irr.* measure; curtail.

**bemitleiden** [bə'mɪtlaɪdən], *v.a.* pity, be sorry for.

**bemittelt** [bə'mɪtəlt], *adj.* well-off, well-to-do.

**bemoost** [bə'mo:st], *adj.* mossy.

**bemühen** [bə'my:ən], *v.a.* trouble, give trouble (to). — *v.r. sich* —, take pains, strive, endeavour, try to.

**bemüht** [bə'my:t], *adj.* studious; — *sein*, endeavour, try to.

**bemuttern** [bə'mutərn], *v.a.* mother.

**benachbart** [bə'naxba:rt], *adj.* neighbouring, adjacent.

**benachrichtigen** [bə'naxrɪçtɪgən], *v.a.* inform, give notice of, notify.

**benachteiligen** [bə'naxtaɪlɪgən], *v.a.* prejudice, discriminate against, handicap.

**benagen** [bə'na:gən], *v.a.* gnaw at.

**benebeln** [bə'ne:bəln], *v.a.* befog, cloud; (*fig.*) dim, intoxicate.

**benedeien** [bene'daɪən], *v.a.* bless, glorify.

**Benediktiner** [benedɪk'ti:nər], *m.* (—s, *pl.* —) (monk) Benedictine; Benedictine liqueur.

**Benefiz** [bene'fi:ts], *n.* (—es, *pl.* —e) benefit; benefit performance.

**Benehmen** [bə'ne:mən], *n.* (—s, *no pl.*) conduct, behaviour.

**benehmen** [bə'ne:mən], *v.r. irr. sich* —, behave, conduct o.s.

**beneiden** [bə'naɪdən], *v.a. einen* — *um*, envy s.o. (s.th.).

**benennen** [bə'nɛnən], *v.a.* name.

**benetzen** [bə'nɛtsən], *v.a.* moisten.

**Bengel** ['bɛŋəl], *m.* (—s, *pl.* —) naughty boy, scamp; rascal, lout.

**benommen** [bə'nɔmən], *adj.* dazed, giddy.

**benötigen** [bə'nøːtɪgən], *v.a.* be in need of, require.

**benutzen** [bə'nutsən], *v.a.* make use of, utilise.

**Benzin** [bɛnt'si:n], *n.* (—s, *no pl.*) benzine; (*Motor.*) petrol; (*Am.*) gas, gasoline.

**beobachten** [bə'o:baxtən], *v.a.* watch, observe.

**bequem** [bə'kve:m], *adj.* comfortable, easy; convenient; indolent, lazy.

**bequemen** [bə'kve:mən], *v.r. sich* —, condescend (to), comply (with).

**Bequemlichkeit** [bə'kve:mlɪçkaɪt], *f.* (—, *pl.* —en) convenience, ease; indolence.

**beraten** [bə'ra:tən], *v.a. irr.* advise, assist with advice, counsel. — *v.r. sich* — *mit*, confer with, consult with.

**beratschlagen** [bə'ra:tʃla:gən], *v.n.* deliberate with.

**Beratung** [bə'ra:tuŋ], *f.* (—, *pl.* —en) council, deliberation, consultation.

**berauben** [bə'raubən], *v.a.* rob, deprive (s.o.) of (s.th.).

**berauschen** [bə'rauʃən], *v.a.* intoxicate.

**berechnen** [bə'rɛçnən], *v.a.* compute, charge, calculate, estimate.

**berechtigen** [bə'rɛçtɪgən], *v.a. einen zu etwas* —, entitle s.o. to s.th.; authorise s.o. to have *or* do s.th.

**beredsam** [bə're:tza:m], *adj.* eloquent.

**beredt** [bə're:t], *adj.* eloquent.

**Bereich** [bə'raɪç], *m. & n.* (—s, *pl.* —e) extent, realm, sphere, scope.

**bereichern** [bə'raɪçərn], *v.a.* enrich, enlarge.

**bereisen** [bə'raɪzən], *v.a.* travel over *or* through, tour (a country).

**bereit** [bə'raɪt], *adj.* ready, prepared.

**bereiten** [bə'raɪtən], *v.a.* prepare, get ready.

**bereits** [bə'raɪts], *adv.* already.

**Bereitschaft** [bə'raɪtʃaft], *f.* (—, *no pl.*) readiness, preparedness.

**bereitwillig** [bə'raɪtvɪlɪç], *adj.* willing, ready, obliging.

**bereuen** [bə'rɔyən], *v.a.* repent, be sorry for, regret.

**Berg** [bɛrk], *m.* (**—es**, *pl.* **—e**) mountain, hill.

**bergab** [bɛrk'ap], *adj.* downhill.

**Bergamt** ['bɛrkamt], *n.* (**—s**, *pl.* **ʺer**) mining-office, mine authority.

**bergan** [bɛrk'an], *adj.* uphill.

**Bergarbeiter** ['bɛrkarbaItər], *m.* (**—s**, *pl.* **—**) miner, collier.

**bergauf** [bɛrk'auf], *adj.* uphill.

**Bergbau** ['bɛrkbau], *m.* (**—s**, *no pl.*) mining, mining industry.

**bergen** ['bɛrgən], *v.a. irr.* shelter, protect, save; (*flotsam*) save, recover, salvage.

**bergig** ['bɛrgIç], *adj.* mountainous, hilly.

**Bergkristall** ['bɛrkkrIstal], *m.* (**—s**, *pl.* **—e**) rock-crystal.

**Bergleute** ['bɛrklɔytə], *pl.* miners, colliers.

**Bergmann** ['bɛrkman], *m.* (**—s**, *pl.* **Bergleute**) miner, collier.

**Bergpredigt** ['bɛrkpre:dIçt], *f.* (**—**, *no pl.*) Sermon on the Mount.

**Bergschlucht** ['bɛrkʃluxt], *f.* (**—**, *pl.* **—en**) ravine, gorge.

**Bergsteiger** ['bɛrkʃtaIgər], *m.* (**—s**, *pl.* **—**) mountaineer.

**Bergstock** ['bɛrkʃtɔk], *m.* (**—s**, *pl.* **ʺe**) alpenstock.

**Bergsturz** ['bɛrkʃturts], *m.* (**—es**, *pl.* **ʺe**) landslip, landslide.

**Bergung** ['bɛrguŋ], *f.* (**—**, *pl.* **—en**) sheltering; salvaging; rescue operation.

**Bergwerk** ['bɛrkvɛrk], *n.* (**—s**, *pl.* **—e**) mine, pit.

**Bericht** [bə'rIçt], *m.* (**—s**, *pl.* **—e**) report, account, statement; —*erstatten*, report, give an account of.

**Berichterstatter** [bə'rIçtɛrʃtatər], *m.* (**—s**, *pl.* **—**) reporter.

**berichtigen** [bə'rIçtIgən], *v.a.* set right, correct, rectify, amend.

**berieseln** [bə'ri:zəln], *v.a.* irrigate.

**beritten** [bə'rItən], *adj.* mounted on horseback.

**Berlin** [bɛr'li:n], *n.* Berlin; —*er Blau*, Prussian blue.

**Bern** [bɛrn], *n.* Berne.

**Bernhardiner** [bɛrnhar'di:nər], *m.* (**—s**, *pl.* **—**) Cistercian monk; Newfoundland dog, St. Bernard dog.

**Bernstein** ['bɛrnʃtaIn], *m.* (**—s**, *no pl.*) amber.

**bersten** ['bɛrstən], *v.n. irr.* (*aux.* sein) burst.

**berüchtigt** [bə'ryçtIçt], *adj.* notorious, infamous.

**berücken** [bə'rykən], *v.a.* enchant, fascinate.

**berücksichtigen** [bə'rykzIçtIgən], *v.a.* have regard to, take into consideration, allow for.

**Beruf** [bə'ru:f], *m.* (**—s**, *pl.* **—e**) profession, occupation, calling, trade.

**berufen** [bə'ru:fən], *v.a. irr.* (*meeting*) call, convene; appoint (to an office). — *v.r. sich — auf*, appeal to, refer to. — *adj.* competent, qualified.

**berufsmäßig** [bə'ru:fsmɛ:sIç], *adj.* professional.

**Berufung** [bə'ru:fuŋ], *f.* (**—**, *pl.* **—en**) call, vocation, appointment; (*Law*) appeal.

**beruhen** [bə'ru:ən], *v.n. auf etwas —*, be based on, be founded on.

**beruhigen** [bə'ru:Igən], *v.a.* calm, pacify; comfort, console, set at rest.

**Beruhigung** [bə'ru:Iguŋ], *f.* (**—**, *pl.* **—en**) reassurance, quieting, calming.

**berühmt** [bə'ry:mt], *adj.* famous, celebrated, illustrious, renowned.

**berühren** [bə'ry:rən], *v.a.* touch, handle; (*subject*) mention, touch upon; *peinlich berührt*, unpleasantly affected.

**berußt** [bə'ru:st], *adj.* sooty.

**Beryll** [be'ryl], *m.* (**—s**, *pl.* **—e**) beryl.

**besagen** [bə'za:gən], *v.a.* mean, signify.

**besagt** [bə'za:kt], *adj.* aforesaid, abovementioned.

**besaiten** [bə'zaItən], *v.a.* fit with strings.

**Besan** [bə'za:n], *m.* (**—s**, *pl.* **—e**) (*Naut.*) miz(z)en.

**besänftigen** [bə'zɛnftIgən], *v.a.* calm, appease, pacify.

**Besatz** [bə'zats], *m.* (**—es**, *pl.* **ʺe**) trimming, border.

**Besatzung** [bə'zatsuŋ], *f.* (**—**, *pl.* **—en**) crew; (*Mil.*) garrison, occupation.

**besaufen** [bə'zaufən], *v.r. irr.* (*vulg.*) *sich —*, get drunk.

**beschädigen** [bə'ʃɛ:dIgən], *v.a.* damage.

**beschaffen** [bə'ʃafən], *v.a.* procure, get. — *adj.* conditioned, constituted.

**Beschaffenheit** [bə'ʃafənhaIt], *f.* (**—**, *no pl.*) nature, kind, quality, condition.

**beschäftigen** [bə'ʃɛftIgən], *v.a.* occupy, employ.

**beschämen** [bə'ʃɛ:mən], *v.a.* make ashamed, shame.

**beschatten** [bə'ʃatən], *v.a.* shade, shadow; follow (s.o.).

**Beschau** [bə'ʃau], *f.* (**—**, *no pl.*) examination; inspection.

**beschauen** [bə'ʃauən], *v.a.* view, look at.

**beschaulich** [bə'ʃaulIç], *adj.* tranquil, contemplative.

**Beschaulichkeit** [bə'ʃaulIçkaIt], *f.* (**—**, *pl.* **—en**) tranquillity, contemplation.

**Bescheid** [bə'ʃaIt], *m.* (**—s**, *pl.* **—e**) answer, information; (*Law*) decision; — *wissen*, know o.'s way about; know what's what.

**bescheiden** [bə'ʃaIdən], *v.a. irr.* inform (s.o.); *einen zu sich —*, send for s.o. — *adj.* modest, unassuming.

**Bescheidenheit** [bə'ʃaIdənhaIt], *f.* (**—**, *no pl.*) modesty.

**bescheinen** [bə'ʃaInən], *v.a. irr.* shine upon.

**bescheinigen** [bə'ʃaInIgən], *v.a. einem etwas —*, attest, certify.

**beschenken** [bə'ʃɛŋkən], *v.a.* give a present to.

# bescheren

**bescheren** [bə'ʃeːrən], *v.a.* give (a present to), bestow (s.th. on s.o.).
**Bescherung** [bə'ʃeːruŋ], *f.* (—, *pl.* —en) giving (of present); *das ist eine schöne —*, (*fig.*) this is a nice mess!
**beschicken** [bə'ʃɪkən], *v.a. eine Ausstellung —*, contribute to an exhibition.
**beschießen** [bə'ʃiːsən], *v.a. irr.* shoot at, fire upon, bombard.
**beschiffen** [bə'ʃɪfən], *v.a.* navigate, sail.
**beschimpfen** [bə'ʃɪmpfən], *v.a.* insult, abuse, revile.
**beschirmen** [bə'ʃɪrmən], *v.a.* protect, shelter, defend.
**Beschlag** [bə'ʃlaːk], *m.* (—s, *pl.* ⸚e) mounting; metal fitting; (*on stick*) ferrule; *etwas mit — belegen*, or *in — nehmen*, sequestrate, confiscate, seize.
**beschlagen** [bə'ʃlaːgən], *v.a. irr.* shoe (a horse). — *v.n.* (*window*) mist over.
**Beschlagnahme** [bə'ʃlaːknaːmə], *f.* (—, *pl.* —n) confiscation, seizure.
**beschleunigen** [bə'ʃlɔynɪgən], *v.a.* hasten, speed up, accelerate.
**beschließen** [bə'ʃliːsən], *v.a. irr.* shut, lock up; close, conclude, finish; decide, resolve upon.
**Beschluß** [bə'ʃlus], *m.* (—sses, *pl.* ⸚sse) determination, resolution, decree.
**beschmieren** [bə'ʃmiːrən], *v.a.* soil, smear.
**beschmutzen** [bə'ʃmutsən], *v.a.* soil, dirty, foul.
**beschneiden** [bə'ʃnaɪdən], *v.a. irr.* cut, clip; (*Hort.*) lop, prune; (*animals*) crop; circumcise.
**Beschneidung** [bə'ʃnaɪduŋ], *f.* (—, *pl.* —en) lopping, pruning; circumcision.
**beschönigen** [bə'ʃøːnɪgən], *v.a.* palliate, excuse.
**beschränken** [bə'ʃrɛnkən], *v.a.* limit, restrict.
**beschränkt** [bə'ʃrɛŋkt], *adj.* limited; *etwas —*, a little stupid; *Gesellschaft mit —er Haftung*, limited (liability) company.
**Beschränkung** [bə'ʃrɛŋkuŋ], *f.* (—, *pl.* —en) limitation, restriction.
**beschreiben** [bə'ʃraɪbən], *v.a. irr.* describe; write upon.
**beschreiten** [bə'ʃraɪtən], *v.a. irr.* tread on.
**beschuldigen** [bə'ʃuldɪgən], *v.a.* charge (s.o.), accuse.
**beschützen** [bə'ʃytsən], *v.a.* protect, shelter, guard.
**Beschützer** [bə'ʃytsər], *m.* (—s, *pl.* —) protector, defender.
**Beschwerde** [bə'ʃveːrdə], *f.* (—, *pl.* —n) trouble, hardship, difficulty; complaint, grievance.
**beschweren** [bə'ʃveːrən], *v.a.* make heavier, weight. — *v.r. sich über etwas —*, complain of s.th.
**beschwerlich** [bə'ʃveːrlɪç], *adj.* burdensome, hard, troublesome.

**beschwichtigen** [bə'ʃvɪçtɪgən], *v.a.* soothe, appease, still.
**beschwindeln** [bə'ʃvɪndəln], *v.a.* cheat, swindle (s.o.).
**beschwingt** [bə'ʃvɪŋkt], *adj.* winged, light-footed.
**beschwipst** [bə'ʃvɪpst], *adj.* (*coll.*) tipsy.
**beschwören** [bə'ʃvøːrən], *v.a. irr.* testify on oath; *einen —*, implore s.o.; conjure (up) (ghosts etc.); exorcize.
**beseelen** [bə'zeːlən], *v.a.* animate.
**besehen** [bə'zeːən], *v.a. irr.* look at, inspect.
**beseitigen** [bə'zaɪtɪgən], *v.a.* remove.
**beseligt** [bə'zeːlɪçt], *adj.* enraptured, beatified.
**Besen** ['beːzən], *m.* (—s, *pl.* —) broom, besom.
**Besenstiel** ['beːzənʃtiːl], *m.* (—s, *pl.* —e) broom-stick.
**besessen** [bə'zɛsən], *adj.* possessed, obsessed, mad.
**besetzen** [bə'zɛtsən], *v.a.* (*dress*) trim, lace; (*Mil.*) occupy, garrison; (*office*) fill; (*Theat.*) cast; (*seat*) occupy, take; *besetzt*, engaged.
**Besetzung** [bə'zɛtsuŋ], *f.* (—, *pl.* —en) lacing, trimming; appointment (to post); (*Theat.*) cast.
**besichtigen** [bə'zɪçtɪgən], *v.a.* view, go over, inspect, examine.
**besiedeln** [bə'ziːdəln], *v.a.* colonise.
**besiegeln** [bə'ziːgəln], *v.a.* seal, set o.'s seal to.
**besiegen** [bə'ziːgən], *v.a.* vanquish, conquer, overcome.
**besinnen** [bə'zɪnən], *v.r. irr.* reflect; *sich auf etwas —*, recollect, remember, think of.
**besinnungslos** [bə'zɪnuŋsloːs], *adj.* insensible, unconscious.
**Besitz** [bə'zɪts], *m.* (—es, *no pl.*) possession, property.
**besitzanzeigend** [bə'zɪtsantsaɪgənt], *adj.* (*Gram.*) possessive.
**besitzen** [bə'zɪtsən], *v.a. irr.* possess, own, have.
**Besitzergreifung** [bə'zɪtsɛrgraɪfuŋ], *f.* (—, *no pl.*) occupation, taking possession (of).
**besoffen** [bə'zɔfən], *adj.* (*vulg.*) drunk.
**besohlen** [bə'zoːlən], *v.a.* sole (shoes).
**besolden** [bə'zɔldən], *v.a.* give a salary to, pay.
**besonder** [bə'zɔndər], *adj.* special, particular.
**Besonderheit** [bə'zɔndərhaɪt], *f.* (—, *pl.* —en) particularity, peculiarity, strangeness.
**besonders** [bə'zɔndərs], *adv.* especially.
**besonnen** [bə'zɔnən], *adj.* prudent, cautious, collected, circumspect.
**besorgen** [bə'zɔrgən], *v.a.* take care of, provide, procure.
**Besorgnis** [bə'zɔrknɪs], *f.* (—, *pl.* —se) care, concern, anxiety, fear.
**besorgt** [bə'zɔrkt], *adj.* apprehensive, anxious, worried.

30

**Besorgung** [bə'zɔrguŋ], *f.* (—, *pl.* —en) care, management; purchase, commission; —*en machen*, go shopping.

**bespannen** [bə'ʃpanən], *v.a.* string (a musical instrument); put horses (to a carriage).

**bespötteln** [bə'ʃpœtəln], *v.a.* ridicule.

**besprechen** [bə'ʃpreçən], *v.a. irr.* discuss, talk over; (book) review. — *v.r. sich — mit*, confer with.

**bespritzen** [bə'ʃprɪtsən], *v.a.* sprinkle, splash.

**besser** ['bɛsər], *adj.* better; *um so —*, so much the better; *je mehr desto —*, the more the better; *— sein als*, be better than; be preferable to; *— werden*, (*weather*) clear up; (*health*) improve.

**bessern** ['bɛsərn], *v.a.* better, improve. — *v.r. sich —*, reform, improve, mend o.'s ways.

**Besserung** ['bɛsəruŋ], *f.* (—*pl.* —en) improvement, amendment, reform; (*Med.*) recovery; *gute —*, get well soon.

**Besserungsanstalt** ['bɛsəruŋsanʃtalt], *f.* (—, *pl.* —en) reformatory.

**best** ['bɛst], *adj.* best.

**bestallen** [bə'ʃtalən], *v.a.* appoint.

**Bestand** [bə'ʃtant], *m.* (—s, *pl.* ˙'e) continuance, duration; stock; balance of cash; *— haben*, endure.

**Bestandaufnahme** [bə'ʃtantaufna:mə], *f.* (—, *pl.* —n) (*Comm.*) stock-taking.

**beständig** [bə'ʃtɛndɪç], *adj.* continual, perpetual; (*persons*) steady, steadfast, constant.

**Bestandteil** [bə'ʃtanttaɪl], *m.* (—s, *pl.* —e) constituent part, component, ingredient, essential part.

**bestärken** [bə'ʃtɛrkən], *v.a.* confirm, strengthen.

**bestätigen** [bə'ʃtɛːtɪgən], *v.a.* confirm, ratify, bear out, sanction; *den Empfang eines Briefes —*, acknowledge receipt of a letter.

**bestatten** [bə'ʃtatən], *v.a.* bury, inter.

**bestäuben** [bə'ʃtɔybən], *v.a.* cover with dust, spray; (*Bot.*) pollinate.

**bestechen** [bə'ʃtɛçən], *v.a. irr.* bribe, corrupt; (*fig.*) captivate.

**bestechlich** [bə'ʃtɛçlɪç], *adj.* corruptible.

**Bestechung** [bə'ʃtɛçuŋ], *f.* (—, *pl.* —en) corruption, bribery.

**Besteck** [bə'ʃtɛk], *n.* (—s, *pl.* —e) set of knife, fork and spoon; set *or* case (of instruments).

**Bestehen** [bə'ʃteːən], *n.* (—s, *no pl.*) existence.

**bestehen** [bə'ʃteːən], *v.a. irr.* undergo, endure, pass (an examination). — *v.n.* exist; *aus etwas —*, consist of s.th.; be composed of s.th.; *auf* (*Dat.*) —, insist upon s.th.

**besteigen** [bə'ʃtaɪgən], *v.a. irr.* ascend, mount, climb.

**bestellen** [bə'ʃtɛlən], *v.a.* order, book; appoint; put in order; (*letter, message*) deliver; (*field*) till.

**Bestellung** [bə'ʃtɛluŋ], *f.* (—, *pl.* —en) order, commission, delivery (of letter); tilling (of field); appointment; *auf —*, to order.

**bestens** ['bɛstəns], *adv.* in the best manner.

**besteuern** [bə'ʃtɔyərn], *v.a.* tax.

**bestialisch** [bɛstɪ'aːlɪʃ], *adj.* beastly, bestial.

**Bestie** ['bɛstjə], *f.* (—, *pl.* —n) beast, brute.

**bestimmen** [bə'ʃtɪmən], *v.a.* fix, settle; decide (s.th.); determine, define.

**bestimmt** [bə'ʃtɪmt], *adj.* decided, fixed, appointed; *ganz —*, positively, most decidedly.

**Bestimmtheit** [bə'ʃtɪmthaɪt], *f.* (—, *no pl.*) certainty.

**Bestimmung** [bə'ʃtɪmuŋ], *f.* (—, *pl.* —en) settlement, decision, determination; provision; destiny.

**bestrafen** [bə'ʃtraːfən], *v.a.* punish, chastise.

**bestrahlen** [bə'ʃtraːlən], *v.a.* irradiate; (*Med.*) treat by radiotherapy.

**bestreben** [bə'ʃtreːbən], *v.r. sich —*, exert o.s., strive (for), endeavour.

**Bestrebung** [bə'ʃtreːbuŋ], *f.* (—, *pl.* —en) effort, endeavour, exertion.

**bestreichen** [bə'ʃtraɪçən], *v.a. irr.* spread.

**bestreiten** [bə'ʃtraɪtən], *v.a. irr.* contest, deny, dispute; defray (costs).

**bestreuen** [bə'ʃtrɔyən], *v.a.* sprinkle, strew, powder.

**bestricken** [bə'ʃtrɪkən], *v.a.* ensnare, entangle.

**bestürmen** [bə'ʃtyrmən], *v.a.* storm, assail; (*fig.*) importune.

**bestürzen** [bə'ʃtyrtsən], *v.a.* dismay, confound, perplex.

**Besuch** [bə'zuːx], *m.* (—s, *pl.* —e) visit; (*person*) visitor.

**besuchen** [bə'zuːxən], *v.a.* visit, call on; attend; frequent.

**besudeln** [bə'zuːdəln], *v.a.* soil, foul.

**betagt** [bə'taːkt], *adj.* aged, elderly.

**betätigen** [bə'tɛːtɪgən], *v.a.* practise, operate. — *v.r. sich —*, take an active part, work, participate (in).

**betäuben** [bə'tɔybən], *v.a.* deafen; stun, benumb, anaesthetize.

**Betäubung** [bə'tɔybuŋ], *f.* (—, *pl.* —en) stupor, stupefaction; *örtliche —*, local anaesthetic.

**beteiligen** [bə'taɪlɪgən], *v.a. einen an etwas —*, give s.o. a share of s.th. — *v.r. sich an etwas —*, participate in s.th.; (*Comm.*) have shares in s.th.

**Beteiligte** [bə'taɪlɪçtə], *m.* (—n, *pl.* —n) person concerned.

**Beteiligung** [bə'taɪlɪguŋ], *f.* (—, *pl.* —en) participation, interest.

**beten** ['beːtən], *v.n.* pray, say o.'s prayers.

**beteuern** [bə'tɔyərn], *v.a.* aver, affirm solemnly.

**betiteln** [bə'tiːtəln], *v.a.* entitle, name.

**Beton** [be'tɔ̃], *m.* (—s, *no pl.*) concrete.

31

# betonen

**betonen** [bə'to:nən], *v.a.* accentuate, stress, emphasise.

**Betonung** [bə'to:nuŋ], *f.* (—, *pl.* —en) accentuation, emphasis, stress.

**betören** [bə'tø:rən], *v.a.* delude, infatuate.

**Betracht** [bə'traxt], *m.* (—s, *no pl.*) consideration, respect, regard.

**betrachten** [bə'traxtən], *v.a.* consider, look at, view; *etwas aufmerksam —,* contemplate s.th.

**beträchtlich** [bə'trɛçtlɪç], *adj.* considerable.

**Betrachtung** [bə'traxtuŋ], *f.* (—, *pl.* —en) contemplation, consideration.

**Betrag** [bə'tra:k], *m.* (—s, *pl.* ⁺e) amount, sum total.

**betragen** [bə'tra:gən], *v.a. irr.* amount to, come to. — *v.r. sich —,* behave, conduct o.s.

**Betragen** [bə'tra:gən], *n.* (—s, *no pl.*) behaviour, conduct, demeanour.

**betrauen** [bə'trauən], *v.a. einen mit etwas —,* entrust s.o. with s.th.

**betrauern** [bə'trauərn], *v.a.* mourn for, bemoan.

**Betreff** [bə'trɛf], *m.* (—s, *no pl.*) reference; *in —,* with regard to.

**betreffen** [bə'trɛfən], *v.a. irr.* concern, affect, relate to.

**Betreiben** [bə'traɪbən], *n.* (—s, *no pl.*) *auf — von,* at the instigation of.

**betreiben** [bə'traɪbən], *v.a. irr.* (*business*) carry on; (*factory*) run; (*trade*) follow, practise.

**Betreten** [bə'tre:tən], *n.* (—s, *no pl.*) entry, entering.

**betreten** [bə'tre:tən], *v.a. irr.* step upon, set foot on, enter. — *adj.* disconcerted, embarrassed.

**betreuen** [bə'trɔyən], *v.a.* care for, attend to.

**Betrieb** [bə'tri:p], *m.* (—s, *pl.* —e) management, business, factory, plant; *den — einstellen,* close down; *in — sein,* be in operation; *in — setzen,* start working.

**betriebsam** [bə'tri:pza:m], *adj.* active, busy, industrious, diligent.

**Betriebsamkeit** [bə'tri:pza:mkaɪt], *f.* (—, *pl.* —en) activity, industry, bustle.

**betriebsfertig** [bə'tri:psfɛrtɪç], *adj.* ready for service; operational.

**Betriebsmaterial** [bə'tri:psmaterja:l], *n.* (—s, *pl.* —ien) (*Railw.*) rolling-stock; (*factory*) working-stock.

**Betriebspersonal** [bə'tri:psperzona:l], *n.* (—s, *no pl.*) workmen, employees, staff.

**betrinken** [bə'trɪŋkən], *v.r. irr. sich —,* get drunk.

**betroffen** [bə'trɔfən], *adj.* perplexed, confounded.

**betrüben** [bə'try:bən], *v.a.* afflict, grieve.

**Betrübnis** [bə'try:pnɪs], *f.* (—ses, *pl.* —se) affliction, grief, distress, sorrow.

**betrübt** [bə'try:pt], *adj.* sad, grieved.

**Betrug** [bə'tru:k], *m.* (—s, *pl.* ⁺ereien) fraud, deceit, deception, imposture; *einen — begehen,* commit a fraud.

**betrügen** [bə'try:gən], *v.a. irr.* cheat, deceive.

**Betrüger** [bə'try:gər], *m.* (—s, —) swindler, cheat, deceiver, impostor.

**betrunken** [bə'truŋkən], *adj.* drunk, drunken, tipsy.

**Bett** [bɛt], *n.* (—(e)s, *pl.* —en) bed; (*river*) bed, channel.

**Bettdecke** ['bɛtdɛkə], *f.* (—, *pl.* —n) counterpane; (*Am.*) bedspread; *wollene —,* blanket; *gesteppte —,* quilt.

**Bettel** ['bɛtəl], *m.* (—s, *no pl.*) trash, trifle.

**bettelarm** ['bɛtəlarm], *adj.* destitute.

**Bettelei** [bɛtə'laɪ], *f.* (—, *pl.* —en) begging, beggary, penury.

**betteln** ['bɛtəln], *v.a.* beg, ask alms.

**betten** ['bɛtən], *v.a.* bed, lay to rest. — *v.r.* (*fig.*) *sich —,* make o.'s bed.

**bettlägerig** ['bɛtlɛgərɪç], *adj.* bed-ridden.

**Bettlaken** ['bɛtla:kən], *n.* (—s, *pl.* —) sheet.

**Bettler** ['bɛtlər], *m.* (—s, *pl.* —) beggar.

**Bettstelle** ['bɛtʃtɛlə], *f.* (—, *pl.* —n) bedstead.

**Bettvorleger** ['bɛtfo:rle:gər], *m.* (—s, *pl.* —) bedside-carpet *or* rug.

**Bettwäsche** ['bɛtvɛʃə], *f.* (—, *no pl.*) bed linen, bed clothes.

**Bettzeug** ['bɛttsɔyk], *n.* (—s, *no pl.*) bedding.

**beugen** ['bɔygən], *v.a.* bend, bow. — *v.r. sich —,* bend down, stoop.

**Beugung** ['bɔyguŋ], *f.* (—, *pl.* —en) (*Gram.*) inflection.

**Beule** ['bɔylə], *f.* (—, *pl.* —n) bruise, bump, swelling, boil.

**beunruhigen** [bə'unru:ɪgən], *v.a.* alarm, trouble, disquiet.

**beurkunden** [bə'u:rkundən], *v.a.* authenticate, verify.

**beurlauben** [bə'u:rlaubən], *v.a.* grant leave of absence. — *v.r. sich —,* take leave.

**beurteilen** [bə'urtaɪlən], *v.a.* judge, criticise.

**Beute** ['bɔytə], *f.* (—, *no pl.*) booty, loot; (*animals*) prey; (*Hunt.*) bag.

**Beutel** ['bɔytəl], *m.* (—s, *pl.* —) bag; (*money*) purse; (*Zool.*) pouch.

**Beuteltier** ['bɔytəlti:r], *n.* (—s, *pl.* —e) marsupial.

**bevölkern** [bə'fœlkərn], *v.a.* people, populate.

**Bevölkerung** [bə'fœlkəruŋ], *f.* (—, *pl.* —en) population.

**bevollmächtigen** [bə'fɔlmɛçtɪgən], *v.a.* empower, authorise.

**bevor** [bə'fo:r], *conj.* before, ere, beforehand.

**bevormunden** [bə'fo:rmundən], *v.a. insep.* act as guardian to; (*fig.*) browbeat.

**bevorrechtigt** [bə'fo:rrɛçtɪçt], *adj.* privileged.

**bevorstehen** [bə'fo:rʃte:ən], v.n. irr. impend, lie ahead, be imminent; *einem* —, be in store for s.o.

**bevorzugen** [bə'fo:rtsu:gən], v.a. insep. prefer, favour.

**bewachen** [bə'vaxən], v.a. watch over, guard.

**bewachsen** [bə'vaksən], adj. overgrown.

**bewaffnen** [bə'vafnən], v.a. arm, supply with arms.

**Bewahranstalt** [bə'va:ranʃtalt], f. (—, pl. —en) kindergarten, nursery.

**bewahren** [bə'va:rən], v.a. preserve, keep, take care of.

**bewähren** [bə'vɛ:rən], v.r. sich —, prove o.s.

**bewahrheiten** [bə'va:rhaɪtən], v.r. sich —, come true.

**bewährt** [bə'vɛ:rt], adj. proved.

**Bewährung** [bə'vɛ:ruŋ], f. (—, no pl.) proof, verification.

**Bewährungsfrist** [bə'vɛ:ruŋsfrɪst], f. (—, no pl.) probation.

**bewaldet** [bə'valdət], adj. wooded, woody.

**bewältigen** [bə'vɛltɪgən], v.a. overcome; manage, master; cope or deal with.

**bewandert** [bə'vandərt], adj. versed, skilled, experienced, conversant.

**bewandt** [bə'vant], adj. such; *damit ist es so* —, it is like this.

**Bewandtnis** [bə'vantnɪs], f. (—, pl. —se) circumstance, condition, state; *es hat damit folgende* —, the circumstances are as follows.

**bewässern** [bə'vɛsərn], v.a. water, irrigate.

**bewegen** [bə've:gən], v.a., v.r. move, stir; take exercise. — v.a. irr. persuade, induce.

**Beweggrund** [bə've:kgrunt], m. (—es, pl. —e) motive, reason, motivation.

**beweglich** [bə've:klɪç], adj. movable; agile, brisk, sprightly.

**Bewegung** [bə've:guŋ], f. (—, pl. —en) motion, movement; (mind) emotion, agitation.

**beweinen** [bə'vaɪnən], v.a. lament, bemoan, deplore.

**Beweis** [bə'vaɪs], m. (—es, pl. —e) proof, evidence; (Maths.) demonstration.

**beweisen** [bə'vaɪzən], v.a. irr. prove, show, demonstrate.

**Beweiskraft** [bə'vaɪskraft], f. (—, no pl.) probative force.

**Beweismittel** [bə'vaɪsmɪtəl], n. (—s, pl. —) evidence, proof.

**Bewenden** [bə'vɛndən], n. (—s, no pl.) *es hat damit sein* —, there the matter rests.

**bewenden** [bə'vɛndən], v.n. irr. *es dabei* — *lassen*, leave it at that.

**bewerben** [bə'vɛrbən], v.r. irr. sich um *etwas* —, apply for s.th.

**Bewerber** [bə'vɛrbər], m. (—s, pl. —) applicant, candidate; (marriage) suitor.

**Bewerbung** [bə'vɛrbuŋ], f. (—, pl. —en) application, candidature; (marriage) courtship.

**bewerkstelligen** [bə'vɛrkʃtɛlɪgən], v.a. perform, bring about.

**bewerten** [bə'vɛrtən], v.a. estimate, value.

**bewilligen** [bə'vɪlɪgən], v.a. grant, allow, permit.

**bewillkommnen** [bə'vɪlkɔmnən], v.a. welcome.

**bewirken** [bə'vɪrkən], v.a. effect, bring about.

**bewirten** [bə'vɪrtən], v.a. entertain, act as host (to).

**bewirtschaften** [bə'vɪrtʃaftən], v.a. manage.

**bewohnen** [bə'vo:nən], v.a. inhabit, occupy.

**Bewohner** [bə'vo:nər], m. (—s, pl. —) inhabitant, tenant, resident.

**bewölken** [bə'vœlkən], v.r. sich —, become overcast, become cloudy.

**bewundern** [bə'vundərn], v.a. admire.

**bewundernswert** [bə'vundərnsvert], adj. admirable.

**bewußt** [bə'vust], adj. conscious, aware; *es war mir nicht* —, I was not aware of.

**bewußtlos** [bə'vustlo:s], adj. unconscious; — *werden*, faint, lose consciousness.

**Bewußtsein** [bə'vustsaɪn], n. (—s, no pl.) consciousness; *einem etwas zum* — *bringen*, bring s.th. home to s.o.

**bezahlbar** [bə'tsa:lba:r], adj. payable.

**bezahlen** [bə'tsa:lən], v.a. pay; (bill) settle.

**bezähmen** [bə'tsɛ:mən], v.a. tame, restrain. — v.r. sich —, restrain o.s., control o.s.

**bezaubern** [bə'tsaubərn], v.a. bewitch, enchant, fascinate.

**bezeichnen** [bə'tsaɪçnən], v.a. mark, denote, indicate, designate.

**bezeichnend** [bə'tsaɪçnənt], adj. indicative, characteristic, significant.

**bezeigen** [bə'tsaɪgən], v.a. manifest, show.

**bezeugen** [bə'tsɔygən], v.a. attest, bear witness, testify.

**bezichtigen** [bə'tsɪçtɪgən], v.a. accuse (s.o.) of (s.th.).

**beziehbar** [bə'tsi:ba:r], adj. (goods) obtainable; (house) ready for occupation.

**beziehen** [bə'tsi:ən], v.a. irr. cover; (house etc.) move into; (instrument) string; make up (a bed); *die Wache* —, mount guard. — v.r. sich —, (sky) cloud over; *sich auf etwas* —, refer to s.th.

**Bezieher** [bə'tsi:ər], m. (—s, pl. —) customer; (newspaper) subscriber.

**Beziehung** [bə'tsi:uŋ], f. (—, pl. —en) relation, connection; reference, bearing; *in dieser* —, in this respect; (Comm.) unter — *auf*, with reference to.

**beziehungsweise** [bə'tsi:uŋsvaɪzə], adv. respectively, as the case may be, or.

**beziffern** [bə'tsıfərn], *v.a.* number.
**Bezirk** [bə'tsɪrk], *m.* (—s, *pl.* —e) district; (*Am.*) precinct; (*Parl.*) constituency; (*Law*) circuit.
**Bezirksgericht** [bə'tsɪrksgəriçt], *n.* (—s, *pl.* —e) county court.
**Bezug** [bə'tsu:k], *m.* (—s, *pl.* ˙:e) (*pillow*) case, cover; (*goods*) order, purchase; (*fig.*) relation; — **haben auf,** refer to; *mit* — *auf,* referring to; (*pl.*) emoluments, income.
**bezüglich** [bə'tsy:klıç], *adj.* with regard to, regarding.
**Bezugnahme** [bə'tsu:kna:mə], *f.* (—, *pl.* —n) reference; *unter* — *auf,* with reference to.
**Bezugsbedingung** [bə'tsu:ksbədɪŋuŋ], *f.* (—, *pl.* —en) (*usually pl.*) (*Comm.*) conditions *or* terms of delivery.
**Bezugsquelle** [bə'tsu:kskvɛlə], *f.* (—, *pl.* —n) source of supply.
**bezwecken** [bə'tsvɛkən], *v.a.* aim at, intend.
**bezweifeln** [bə'tsvaɪfəln], *v.a.* doubt, question.
**bezwingen** [bə'tsvıŋən], *v.a.irr.* subdue, conquer. — *v.r. sich* —, restrain o.s.
**Bibel** [bi:bəl], *f.* (—, *pl.* —n) Bible.
**Bibelauslegung** ['bi:bəlausle:guŋ], *f.* (—, *pl.* —en) (Biblical) exegesis.
**Biber** ['bi:bər], *m.* (—s, *pl.* —) (*Zool.*) beaver.
**Bibliothek** [biblio'te:k], *f.* (—, *pl.* —en) library.
**Bibliothekar** [bibliote'ka:r], *m.* (—s, *pl.* —e) librarian.
**biblisch** ['bi:blıʃ], *adj.* biblical, scriptural.
**Bickbeere** ['bıkbe:rə], *f.* (—, *pl.* —n) bilberry.
**bieder** ['bi:dər], *adj.* upright, honest, decent.
**Biederkeit** ['bi:dərkaɪt], *f.* (—, *no pl.*) uprightness, probity.
**Biedermann** ['bi:dərman], *m.* (—s, *pl.* ˙:er) honourable man; (*iron.*) Philistine.
**biegen** ['bi:gən], *v.a. irr.* bend, bow. — *v.n.* (*aux.* sein) *um die Ecke* —, turn the corner. — *v.r. sich* —, curve; — *oder brechen,* by hook or by crook.
**biegsam** ['bi:kza:m], *adj.* flexible, supple, pliant.
**Biegung** ['bi:guŋ], *f.* (—, *pl.* —en) curve, bend; (*Gram.*) inflexion.
**Biene** ['bi:nə], *f.* (—, *pl.* —n) bee.
**Bienenhaus** ['bi:nənhaus], *n.* (—es, *pl.* ˙:er) apiary.
**Bienenkorb** ['bi:nənkɔrp], *m.* (—s, *pl.* ˙:e) beehive.
**Bienenzüchter** ['bi:nəntsyçtər], *m.* (—s, *pl.* —) apiarist, bee-keeper.
**Bier** ['bi:r], *n.* (—(e)s, *pl.* —e) beer.
**Bierkanne** ['bi:rkanə], *f.* (—, *pl.* —n) tankard.
**Biest** [bi:st], *n.* (—es, *pl.* —er) brute, beast.
**bieten** ['bi:tən], *v.a.irr.* offer; (*auction*) bid.

**Bieter** ['bi:tər], *m.* (—s, *pl.* —) (*auction*) bidder.
**Bigotterie** [bıgɔtə'ri:], *f.* (—, *no pl.*) bigotry.
**Bijouterie** [bıʒutə'ri:], *f.* (—, *pl.* —n) trinkets, dress-jewellery.
**Bilanz** [bı'lants], *f.* (—, *pl.* —en) (*Comm.*) balance; (financial) statement.
**Bild** [bılt], *n.* (—es, *pl.* —er) picture, painting, portrait, image; idea; (*coins*) effigy; (*Cards*) court card; (*books*) illustration; (*speech*) figure of speech, metaphor.
**bilden** ['bıldən], *v.a.* form, shape; (*mind*) cultivate. — *v.r. sich* —, improve o.'s mind, educate o.s.
**bildend** ['bıldənt], *adj.* instructive, civilising; *die* —*en Künste,* the fine arts.
**bilderreich** ['bıldəraıç], *adj.* —*e Sprache,* flowery language, figurative style.
**Bilderschrift** ['bıldərʃrıft], *f.* (—, *pl.* —en) hieroglyphics.
**Bilderstürmer** ['bıldərʃtyrmər], *m.* (—s, *pl.* —) iconoclast.
**Bildhauer** ['bılthauər], *m.* (—s, *pl.* —) sculptor.
**bildhübsch** ['bılthypʃ], *adj.* as pretty as a picture.
**bildlich** ['bıltlıç], *adj.* figurative.
**Bildnis** ['bıltnıs], *n.* (—ses, *pl.* —se) portrait, figure, image, effigy.
**bildsam** ['bıltza:m], *adj.* plastic, ductile.
**bildschön** ['bıltʃø:n], *adj.* very beautiful.
**Bildseite** ['bıltzaıtə], *f.* (—, *pl.* —n) (*coin*) face, obverse.
**Bildung** ['bılduŋ], *f.* (—, *pl.* (*rare*) —en) formation; (*mind*) education, culture; knowledge, learning, accomplishments, attainments.
**Billard** ['bıljart], *n.* (—s, *pl.* —s) billiards.
**Billett** [bıl'jɛt], *n.* (—s, *pl.* —s) ticket.
**billig** ['bılıç], *adj.* cheap, inexpensive; equitable, just, fair, reasonable.
**billigen** ['bılıgən], *v.a.* sanction, approve of, consent to.
**Billigkeit** ['bılıçkaıt], *f.* (—, *no pl.*) cheapness; fairness, equitableness, reasonableness.
**Billigung** ['bılıguŋ], *f.* (—, *no pl.*) approbation, approval, sanction.
**Bilsenkraut** ['bılzənkraut], *n.* (—s, *pl.* ˙:er) henbane.
**bimmeln** ['bıməln], *v.n.* (*coll.*) tinkle.
**Bimsstein** ['bımsʃtaın], *m.* (—s, *pl.* —e) pumice stone.
**Binde** ['bındə], *f.* (—, *pl.* —n) band, bandage; tie; ligature; sanitary towel.
**Bindeglied** ['bındəgli:t], *n.* (—s, *pl.* —er) connecting link.
**Bindehaut** ['bındəhaut], *f.* (—, *pl.* ˙:e) (*Anat.*) conjunctiva.
**Bindehautentzündung** ['bındəhautɛntsynduŋ], *f.* (—, *pl.* —en) conjunctivitis.

**binden** ['bɪndən], *v.a. irr.* bind, tie, fasten.

**Bindestrich** ['bɪndəʃtrɪç], *m.* (—(e)s, *pl.* —e) hyphen.

**Bindewort** ['bɪndəvɔrt], *n.* (—s, *pl.* ⁈er) conjunction.

**Bindfaden** ['bɪntfaːdən], *m.* (—s, *pl.* ⁈) string, twine.

**Bindung** ['bɪnduŋ], *f.* (—, *pl.* —en) binding, bond; obligation; (*Mus.*) ligature.

**binnen** ['bɪnən], *prep.* (*Genit. & Dat.*), *adv.* within.

**Binnenhafen** ['bɪnənhaːfən], *m.* (—s, *pl.* ⁈) inland harbour.

**Binnenhandel** ['bɪnənhandəl], *m.* (—s, *no pl.*) inland trade.

**Binse** ['bɪnzə], *f.* (—, *pl.* —n) (*Bot.*) rush, reed.

**Biographie** [biogra'fiː], *f.* (—, *pl.* —n) biography.

**Birke** ['bɪrkə], *f.* (—, *pl.* —n) (*Bot.*) birch, birch-tree.

**Birma** ['bɪrmaː], *n.* Burma.

**Birnbaum** ['bɪrnbaum], *m.* (—s, *pl.* ⁈e) pear-tree.

**Birne** ['bɪrnə], *f.* (—, *pl.* —n) pear; (*Elec.*) bulb.

**birnförmig** ['bɪrnfœrmɪç], *adj.* pear-shaped.

**bis** [bɪs], *prep.* (*time*) till, until; by; (*place*) to, up to; — *auf,* with the exception of. — *conj.* till, until.

**Bisam** ['biːzam], *m.* (—s, *pl.* —e) musk.

**Bischof** ['bɪʃɔf], *m.* (—s, *pl.* ⁈e) bishop.

**bischöflich** ['bɪʃœflɪç], *adj.* episcopal.

**Bischofsstab** ['bɪʃɔfsʃtaːp], *m.* (—s, *pl.* ⁈e) crosier.

**bisher** ['bɪsheːr], *adv.* hitherto, till now.

**bisherig** [bɪs'heːrɪç], *adj.* up to this time, hitherto existing.

**Biskayischer Meerbusen** [bɪs'kaːɪʃər 'meːrbuːzən]. Bay of Biscay.

**Biß** [bɪs], *m.* (—sses, *pl.* —sse) bite, sting.

**Bißchen** ['bɪsçən], *n.* (—s, *pl.* —) morsel; little bit.

**Bissen** ['bɪsən], *m.* (—s, *pl.* —) bite, morsel.

**bissig** ['bɪsɪç], *adj.* biting, cutting; sharp, vicious; sarcastic.

**Bistum** ['bɪstum], *n.* (—s, *pl.* ⁈er) bishopric, diocese; see.

**bisweilen** [bɪs'vaɪlən], *adv.* sometimes, now and then, occasionally.

**Bitte** ['bɪtə], *f.* (—, *pl.* —n) request, entreaty.

**bitte** ['bɪtə], *int.* please.

**bitten** ['bɪtən], *v.a. irr.* ask; request.

**bitter** ['bɪtər], *adj.* bitter.

**Bitterkeit** ['bɪtərkaɪt], *f.* (—, *no pl.*) bitterness.

**bitterlich** ['bɪtərlɪç], *adv.* (*fig.*) bitterly.

**Bittersalz** ['bɪtərzalts], *n.* (—es, *no pl.*) Epsom salts.

**Bittgang** ['bɪtgaŋ], *m.* (—(e)s, *pl.* ⁈e) (*Eccl.*) procession.

**Bittsteller** ['bɪtʃtɛlər], *m.* (—s, *pl.* —) petitioner, suppli(c)ant.

**Biwak** ['biːvak], *m.* (—s, *pl.* —s) bivouac.

**blähen** ['blɛːən], *v.a.* inflate, puff up, swell.

**Blähung** ['blɛːuŋ], *f.* (—, *pl.* —en) (*Med.*) flatulence.

**blaken** ['blaːkən], *v.n.* smoulder; smoke.

**Blamage** [bla'maːʒə], *f.* (—, *pl.* —n) shame, disgrace.

**blamieren** [bla'miːrən], *v.a., v.r.* make (o.s.) ridiculous, make a fool of o.s.

**blank** [blaŋk], *adj.* shining, bright, smooth, polished.

**Bläschen** ['blɛːsçən], *n.* (—s, *pl.* —) little bubble, blister; (*Med.*) vesicle.

**Blase** ['blaːzə], *f.* (—, *pl.* —n) (*soap*) bubble; (*skin*) blister; (*Anat.*) bladder.

**Blasebalg** ['blaːzəbalk], *m.* (—s, *pl.* ⁈e) pair of bellows.

**blasen** ['blaːzən], *v.a. irr.* blow; (*Mus.*) sound.

**Bläser** ['blɛːzər], *m.* (—s, *pl.* —) (*glass*) blower; (*Mus.*) wind player.

**blasiert** [bla'ziːrt], *adj.* blasé, haughty.

**Blasrohr** ['blaːsroːr], *n.* (—s, *pl.* —e) blow-pipe, pea-shooter.

**blaß** [blas], *adj.* pale, wan, pallid.

**Blässe** ['blɛsə], *f.* (—, *no pl.*) paleness, pallor.

**Blatt** [blat], *n.* (—s, *pl.* ⁈er) leaf; (*paper*) sheet; blade.

**Blatter** ['blatər], *f.* (—, *pl.* —n) pustule; (*pl.*) smallpox.

**blättern** ['blɛtərn], *v.a.* turn the leaves (of a book).

**Blätterteig** ['blɛtərtaɪk], *m.* (—s, *no pl.*) puff pastry.

**Blattgold** ['blatgɔlt], *n.* (—es, *no pl.*) gold-leaf.

**Blattlaus** ['blatlaus], *f.* (—, *pl.* ⁈e) (*Ent.*) plant-louse.

**Blattpflanze** ['blatpflantsə], *f.* (—, *pl.* —n) leaf-plant.

**blau** [blau], *adj.* blue; —*en Montag machen,* stay away from work; *sein* —*es Wunder erleben,* be amazed.

**blauäugig** ['blauɔygɪç], *adj.* blue-eyed.

**Blaubeere** ['blaubeːrə], *f.* (—, *pl.* —n) bilberry, blueberry.

**blaublütig** ['blaublyːtɪç], *adj.* aristocratic.

**bläuen** ['blauən], *v.a.* dye blue, rinse in blue.

**bläulich** ['blɔylɪç], *adj.* pale blue, bluish.

**Blausäure** ['blauzɔyrə], *f.* (—, *no pl.*) prussic acid.

**Blaustrumpf** ['blauʃtrumpf], *m.* (—s, *pl.* ⁈e) blue-stocking.

**Blech** [blɛç], *n.* (—s, *pl.* —e) tinplate, sheet metal.

**blechen** ['blɛçən], *v.n.* (*coll.*) fork out money.

**blechern** ['blɛçərn], *adj.* made of tin, tinny.

**Blechinstrument** ['blɛçɪnstrumɛnt], *n.* (—s, *pl.* —e) (*Mus.*) brass instrument.

# Blei

Blei [blaɪ], *n.* (—s, *no pl.*) lead.
bleiben ['blaɪbən], *v.n. irr.* (*aux.* sein) remain, stay.
bleich [blaɪç], *adj.* pale, wan, pallid.
Bleiche ['blaɪçə], *f.* (—, *pl.* —n) pallor; (*laundry*) bleaching-place.
bleichen ['blaɪçən], *v.a. irr.* bleach, whiten.
Bleichsucht ['blaɪçzuxt], *f.* (—, *no pl.*) chlorosis, anaemia.
bleiern ['blaɪərn], *adj.* leaden.
Bleiglanz ['blaɪglants], *m.* (—es, *no pl.*) (*Min.*) lead sulphide.
Bleisoldat ['blaɪzɔldaːt], *m.* (—en, *pl.* —en) tin soldier.
Bleistift ['blaɪʃtɪft], *m.* (—s, *pl.* —e) pencil.
Blende ['blɛndə], *f.* (—, *no pl.*) blind; (*Min.*) blende; (*Phot.*) shutter.
blenden ['blɛndən], *v.a.* dazzle, blind.
Blendlaterne ['blɛntlatɛrnə], *f.* (—, *pl.* —n) dark-lantern.
Blendung ['blɛnduŋ], *f.* (—, *pl.* —en) blinding, dazzling.
Blendwerk ['blɛntvɛrk], *n.* (—s, *no pl.*) (optical) illusion, false show.
Blick [blɪk], *m.* (—s, *pl.* —e) glance, look, glimpse.
blicken ['blɪkən], *v.n.* look, glance.
blind [blɪnt], *adj.* blind, sightless; *—er Passagier,* stowaway.
Blinddarm ['blɪntdarm], *m.* (—s, *pl.* —e) appendix.
Blinddarmentzündung ['blɪntdarmɛntsynduŋ], *f.* (—, *pl.* —en) appendicitis.
Blindekuh [blɪndə'kuː], *f.* (—, *no pl.*) blind man's buff.
Blindgänger ['blɪntgɛŋər], *m.* (—s, *pl.* —) misfire, dud, blind.
Blindheit ['blɪnthaɪt], *f.* (—, *no pl.*) blindness.
blindlings ['blɪntlɪŋs], *adv.* blindly; at random.
Blindschleiche ['blɪntʃlaɪçə], *f.* (—, *pl.* —n) (*Zool.*) blind-worm.
blinken ['blɪŋkən], *v.n.* blink, flash, glitter, gleam.
blinzeln ['blɪntsəln], *v.n.* blink.
Blitz [blɪts], *m.* (—es, *pl.* —e) lightning, flash.
Blitzableiter ['blɪtsaplaɪtər], *m.* (—s, *pl.* —) lightning-conductor.
blitzblank ['blɪtsblaŋk], *adj.* as bright as a new pin; shining.
blitzen ['blɪtsən], *v.n.* flash; *es blitzt,* it is lightning; glitter, shine.
Blitzesschnelle ['blɪtsəsʃnɛlə], *f.* (—, *no pl.*) lightning-speed.
Blitzlicht ['blɪtslɪçt], *n.* (—s, *no pl.*) flashlight.
Blitzschlag ['blɪtsʃlaːk], *m.* (—s, *pl.* —e) flash of lightning.
Blitzstrahl ['blɪtsʃtraːl], *m.* (—s, *pl.* —en) flash of lightning.
Block [blɔk], *m.* (—s, *pl.* —e) block, log; pad.
Blockhaus ['blɔkhaus], *n.* (—es, *pl.* —er) log-cabin.

blockieren [blɔ'kiːrən], *v.a.* block (up); (*Mil.*) blockade.
blöde ['bløːdə], *adj.* stupid, dull, thick-headed, dim.
Blödsinn ['bløːtsɪn], *m.* (—s, *no pl.*) nonsense, idiocy.
blöken ['bløːkən], *v.n.* bleat; (*cows*) low.
blond [blɔnt], *adj.* blond, fair, fair-headed.
bloß [bloːs], *adj.* naked, uncovered; bare, mere.
Blöße ['bløːsə], *f.* (—, *pl.* —n) nakedness, bareness; (*fig.*) weak point.
bloßlegen ['bloːsleːgən], *v.a.* uncover, lay bare; (*fig.*) reveal, expose.
bloßstellen ['bloːsʃtɛlən], *v.a.* compromise, show up. — *v.r. sich —,* compromise o.s.
blühen ['blyːən], *v.n.* bloom, blossom, flower, flourish.
Blümchen ['blyːmçən], *n.* (—s, *pl.* —) small flower.
Blume ['bluːmə], *f.* (—, *pl.* —n) flower, bloom; (*wine*) bouquet; (*beer*) froth.
Blumenblatt ['bluːmənblat], *n.* (—s, *pl.* ̈er) petal.
Blumenerde ['bluːməneːrdə], *f.* (—, *no pl.*) garden mould.
Blumenkelch ['bluːmənkɛlç], *m.* (—es, *pl.* —e) calyx.
Blumenkohl ['bluːmənkoːl], *m.* (—s, *pl.* —e) cauliflower.
Blumenstaub ['bluːmənʃtaup], *m.* (—s, *no pl.*) pollen.
Blumenstrauß ['bluːmənʃtraus], *m.* (—es, *pl.* ̈e) bunch of flowers, posy, nosegay.
Blumenzucht ['bluːməntsuxt], *f.* (—, *no pl.*) floriculture.
Bluse ['bluːzə], *f.* (—, *pl.* —n) blouse.
Blut [bluːt], *n.* (—es, *no pl.*) blood.
blutarm ['bluːtarm], *adj.* anaemic; (*fig.*) very poor.
Blutbad ['bluːtbaːt], *n.* (—es, *pl.* ̈er) massacre.
blutdürstig ['bluːtdyrstɪç], *adj.* bloodthirsty.
Blüte ['blyːtə], *f.* (—, *pl.* —n) blossom, flower, bloom.
Blutegel ['bluːteːgəl], *m.* (—s, *pl.* —) leech.
bluten ['bluːtən], *v.n.* bleed.
Bluterguß ['bluːtergus], *m.* (—es, *pl.* ̈e) effusion of blood.
Blutgefäß ['bluːtgəfɛːs], *n.* (—es, *pl.* —e) blood-vessel.
blutig ['bluːtɪç], *adj.* bloody; cruel.
blutjung ['bluːtjuŋ], *adj.* very young.
Blutkörperchen ['bluːtkœrpərçən], *n.* (—s, *pl.* —) blood-corpuscle.
Blutlassen ['bluːtlasən], *n.* (—s, *no pl.*) (*Med.*) bloodletting.
Blutrache ['bluːtraxə], *f.* (—, *no pl.*) vendetta.
Blutsauger ['bluːtzaugər], *m.* (—s, *pl.* —) vampire.
Blutschande ['bluːtʃandə], *f.* (—, *no pl.*) incest.

# Bösewicht

**blutstillend** ['blu:ʃtɪlənt], *adj.* styptic, blood-stanching.

**Blutsturz** ['blu:tʃturts], *m.* (—es, *no pl.*) haemorrhage; *einen* — *haben*, burst a blood-vessel.

**Blutsverwandte** ['blu:tsfɛrvantə], *m. or f.* (—n, *pl.* —n) blood-relation.

**Blutvergießen** ['blu:tfɛrgi:sən], *n.* (—s, *no pl.*) bloodshed.

**Blutvergiftung** ['blu:tfɛrgɪftuŋ], *f.* (—, *pl.* —en) blood poisoning.

**Blutwurst** ['blu:tvurst], *f.* (—, *pl.* ˙ːe) black-pudding.

**Blutzeuge** ['blu:ttsɔygə], *m.* (—n, *pl.* —n) martyr.

**Bö** [bøː], *f.* (—, *pl.* —en) (*Naut.*) squall, gust of wind.

**Bock** [bɔk], *m.* (—s, *pl.* ˙ːe) buck; he-goat; (*Gymn.*) horse; (*horse-drawn carriage*) box seat.

**bockbeinig** ['bɔkbaɪnɪç], *adj.* bow-legged; pigheaded, obstinate.

**Bockbier** ['bɔkbiːr], *n.* (—s, *no pl.*) bock beer.

**bocken** ['bɔkən], *v.n.* kick, be refractory; sulk.

**Bockfell** ['bɔkfɛl], *n.* (—s, *pl.* —e) buckskin.

**bockig** ['bɔkɪç], *adj.* pigheaded, obstinate.

**Bocksbeutel** ['bɔksbɔytəl], *m.* (—s, *pl.* —) leather bag; Franconian wine (bottle).

**Bockshorn** ['bɔkshɔrn], *n.* (—s, *pl.* ˙ːer) buck horn; *einen ins* — *jagen*, intimidate s.o.

**Boden** ['boːdən], *m.* (—s, *pl.* ˙ː) ground, bottom, soil, floor; garret, loft.

**Bodenfenster** ['boːdənfɛnstər], *n.* (—s, *pl.* —) attic window.

**Bodenkammer** ['boːdənkamər], *f.* (—, *pl.* —n) garret, attic.

**bodenlos** ['boːdənloːs], *adj.* bottomless; (*fig.*) unimaginable, enormous.

**Bodensatz** ['boːdənzats], *m.* (—es, *pl.* ˙ːe) sediment, dregs, deposit.

**Bodensee** ['boːdənzeː], *m.* Lake Constance.

**Bogen** ['boːgən], *m.* (—s, *pl.* —, ˙ː) arch, vault, curve; (*Maths.*) arc; (*violin*) bow; (*paper*) sheet; (*Mus.*) ligature.

**bogenförmig** ['boːgənfœrmɪç], *adj.* arch-shaped, arched.

**Bogenführung** ['boːgənfyːruŋ], *f.* (—, *no pl.*) (*Mus.*) bowing (technique).

**Bogengang** ['boːgəngaŋ], *m.* (—es, *pl.* ˙ːe) arcade.

**Bogenlampe** ['boːgənlampə], *f.* (—, *pl.* —n) arc-lamp.

**Bogenschütze** ['boːgənʃytsə], *m.* (—n, *pl.* —n) archer.

**bogig** ['boːgɪç], *adj.* bent, curved, arched.

**Bohle** ['boːlə], *f.* (—, *pl.* —n) board, plank.

**Böhmen** ['bøːmən], *n.* Bohemia.

**Bohne** ['boːnə], *f.* (—, *pl.* —n) bean; *grüne* —*n*, French (*Am.* string) beans; *dicke* —*n*, broad beans; *blaue* —*n*, (*fig.*) bullets.

**Bohnenstange** ['boːnənʃtaŋə], *f.* (— *pl.* —n) bean-pole.

**Bohnerbürste** ['boːnərbyrstə], *f.* (—, *pl.* —n) polishing-brush.

**bohnern** ['boːnərn], *v.a.* polish, wax.

**bohren** ['boːrən], *v.a.* bore, pierce, drill.

**Bohrer** ['boːrər], *m.* (—s, *pl.* —) gimlet; drill.

**Bohrturm** ['boːrturm], *m.* (—s, *pl.* ˙ːe) derrick.

**Boje** ['boːjə], *f.* (—, *pl.* —n) (*Naut.*) buoy.

**Bolivien** [boˈliːvjən], *n.* Bolivia.

**Böller** ['bœlər], *m.* (—s, *pl.* —) (*Mil.*) small mortar.

**Bollwerk** ['bɔlvɛrk], *n.* (—s, *pl.* —e) bulwark.

**Bolzen** ['bɔltsən], *m.* (—s, *pl.* —) bolt, arrow, pin; (*smoothing iron*) heater.

**Bombe** ['bɔmbə], *f.* (—, *pl.* —n) bomb, bomb-shell.

**Bombenerfolg** ['bɔmbənɛrfɔlk], *m.* (—(e)s, *pl.* —e) (*Theat.*) smash hit.

**Bonbon** [bɔ̃ˈbɔ̃], *m.* (—s, *pl.* —s) sweet(s), bonbon; (*Am.*) candy.

**Bonbonniere** [bɔ̃bɔˈnjeːrə], *f.* (—, *pl.* —n) box of sweets.

**Bonze** ['bɔntsə], *m.* (—n, *pl.* —n) (*coll.*) bigwig, (*Am.*) big shot.

**Boot** [boːt], *n.* (—es, *pl.* —e) boat.

**Bootsanker** ['boːtsaŋkər], *m.* (—s, *pl.* —) grapnel.

**Bootsleine** ['boːtslaɪnə], *f.* (—, *pl.* —n) tow-rope.

**Bor** [boːr], *n.* (—s, *no pl.*) (*Chem.*) boron.

**Bord** [bɔrt], *m.* (—s, *pl.* —e) rim; (*Naut.*) board.

**Bordell** [bɔrˈdɛl], *n.* (—s, *pl.* —e) brothel.

**borgen** ['bɔrgən], *v.a., v.n.* borrow (*von*, from); lend (*Dat.*, to).

**Borke** ['bɔrkə], *f.* (—, *pl.* —n) bark, rind.

**Born** [bɔrn], *m.* (—es, *pl.* —e) (*Poet.*) bourn, spring, well, source.

**borniert** [bɔrˈniːrt], *adj.* narrow-minded.

**Borsäure** ['boːrzɔyrə], *f.* (—, *no pl.*) boric acid.

**Börse** ['bœrzə], *f.* (—, *pl.* —n) purse; (*Comm.*) stock-exchange, bourse.

**Börsenbericht** ['bœrzənbərɪçt], *m.* (—s, *pl.* —e) stock-market report.

**Borste** ['bɔrstə], *f.* (—, *pl.* —n) bristle.

**borstig** ['bɔrstɪç], *adj.* bristly; (*fig.*) irritable.

**Borte** ['bɔrtə], *f.* (—, *pl.* —n) border, trimming.

**bösartig** ['bøːsartɪç], *adj.* malevolent, malicious, vicious; (*disease*) malignant.

**Böschung** ['bøːʃuŋ], *f.* (—, *pl.* —en) slope, scarp.

**böse** ['bøːzə], *adj.* bad, wicked; evil; angry, cross (with, *Dat.*); — *auf* (*Acc.*), angry with s.o., (*Am.*) mad at s.o.

**Bösewicht** ['bøːzəvɪçt], *m.* (—s, *pl.* —er) villain, ruffian; wretch.

# boshaft

**boshaft** ['bo:shaft], *adj.* spiteful, malicious.

**Bosheit** ['bo:shaɪt], *f.* (—, *pl.* —en) malice.

**böswillig** ['bø:svɪlɪç], *adj.* malevolent.

**Botanik** [bo'ta:nɪk], *f.* (—, *no pl.*) botany.

**Botaniker** [bo'ta:nɪkər], *m.* (—s, *pl.* —) botanist.

**Botanisiertrommel** [botanɪ'zi:rtrɔməl], *f.* (—, *pl.* —n) specimen-box.

**Bote** ['bo:tə], *m.* (—n, *pl.* —n) messenger.

**Botengang** ['bo:təngaŋ], *m.* (—s, *pl.* ⁇e) errand.

**botmäßig** ['bo:tmɛ:sɪç], *adj.* subject, subordinate.

**Botschaft** ['bo:tʃaft], *f.* (—, *pl.* —en) message; (*Pol.*) embassy; *gute* —, glad tidings.

**Botschafter** ['bo:tʃaftər], *m.* (—s, *pl.* —) ambassador.

**Böttcher** ['bœtçər], *m.* (—s, *pl.* —) cooper.

**Bottich** ['bɔtɪç], *m.* (—s, *pl.* —e) vat, tub.

**Bouillon** [bul'jõ], *f.* (—, *no pl.*) broth, meat soup.

**Bowle** ['bo:lə], *f.* (—, *no pl.*) bowl; spiced wine.

**boxen** ['bɔksən], *v.n.* box.

**brach** [bra:x], *adj.* fallow, unploughed, untilled.

**Brand** [brant], *m.* (—es, *pl.* ⁇e) burning, fire, combustion, conflagration; (*Med.*) gangrene.

**Brandblase** ['brantbla:zə], *f.* (—, *pl.* —n) blister.

**branden** ['brandən], *v.n.* surge, break (waves).

**brandig** ['brandɪç], *adj.* blighted; (*Med.*) gangrenous.

**Brandmal** ['brantma:l], *n.* (—s, *pl.* —e) burn mark; brand (cattle); (*fig.*) stigma.

**brandmarken** ['brantmarkən], *v.a.* brand; (*fig.*) stigmatise.

**Brandmauer** ['brantmauər], *f.* (—, *pl.* —n) fire-proof wall.

**brandschatzen** ['brantʃatsən], *v.a.* levy contributions (from); pillage, plunder.

**Brandsohle** ['brantzo:lə], *f.* (—, *pl.* —n) inner sole, welt (of shoe).

**Brandstifter** ['brantʃtɪftər], *m.* (—s, *pl.* —) incendiary, fire-raiser.

**Brandstiftung** ['brantʃtɪftuŋ], *f.* (—, *pl.* —en) arson.

**Brandung** ['branduŋ], *f.* (—, *pl.* —en) breakers, surf, surge (of sea).

**Branntwein** ['brantvaɪn], *m.* (—s, *pl.* —e) brandy.

**Brasilien** [bra'zi:ljən], *n.* Brazil.

**Braten** ['bra:tən], *m.* (—s, *pl.* —) roast (meat), joint.

**braten** ['bra:tən], *v.a. reg. & irr.* roast, broil, bake, fry, grill. — *v.n.* (*coll.*) bask (in sun), roast.

**Brathering** ['bra:the:rɪŋ], *m.* (—s, *pl.* —e) grilled herring.

**Brathuhn** ['bra:thu:n], *n.* (—s, *pl.* ⁇er) roast chicken.

**Bratkartoffeln** ['bra:tkartɔfəln], *f. pl.* roast *or* fried potatoes.

**Bratpfanne** ['bra:tpfanə], *f.* (—, *pl.* —n) frying pan.

**Bratsche** ['bra:tʃə], *f.* (—, *pl.* —n) (*Mus.*) viola.

**Bratspieß** ['bra:tʃpi:s], *m.* (—es, *pl.* —e) spit (roasting).

**Bratwurst** ['bra:tvurst], *f.* (—, *pl.* ⁇e) sausage for frying; fried sausage.

**Brau** [brau], **Bräu** [brɔy], *n. & m.* (—s, *no pl.*) brew.

**Brauch** [braux], *m.* (—es, *pl.* ⁇e) usage, custom, habit.

**brauchbar** ['brauxba:r], *adj.* useful, serviceable.

**brauchen** ['brauxən], *v.a.* make use of, employ; need, require, want; (*time*) take.

**Braue** ['brauə], *f.* (—, *pl.* —n) brow, eye-brow.

**brauen** ['brauən], *v.a.* brew.

**Brauer** ['brauər], *m.* (—s, *pl.* —) brewer.

**Brauerei** ['brauəraɪ], *f.* (—, *pl.* —en) brewery.

**Brauhaus** ['brauhaus], *n.* (—es, *pl.* ⁇er) brewery.

**braun** [braun], *adj.* brown.

**bräunen** ['brɔynən], *v.a.* make brown, tan.

**Braunkohl** ['braunko:l], *m.* (—s, *no pl.*) (*Bot.*) broccoli.

**Braunschweig** ['braunʃvaɪk], *n.* Brunswick.

**Braus** [braus], *m.* (—es, *no pl.*) bustle, tumult; *in Saus und — leben*, lead a riotous life.

**Brause** ['brauzə], *f.* (—, *pl.* —n) shower (bath); effervescence, (*coll.*) fizzy drink.

**Brausekopf** ['brauzəkɔpf], *m.* (—es, *pl.* ⁇e) hothead.

**Brauselimonade** ['brauzəlɪmona:də], *f.* (—, *pl.* —n) effervescent *or* fizzy lemonade.

**brausen** ['brauzən], *v.n.* roar, bluster, rush; effervesce.

**Brausepulver** ['brauzəpulvər], *n.* (—s, *pl.* —) effervescent powder.

**Braut** [braut], *f.* (—, *pl.* ⁇e) bride, betrothed, fiancée.

**Brautführer** ['brautfy:rər], *m.* (—s, *pl.* —) best man.

**Bräutigam** ['brɔytɪgam], *m.* (—s, *pl.* —e) bridegroom, betrothed, fiancé.

**Brautjungfer** ['brautjuŋfər], *f.* (—, *pl.* —n) bridesmaid.

**bräutlich** ['brɔytlɪç], *adj.* bridal.

**Brautpaar** ['brautpa:r], *n.* (—es, *pl.* —e) engaged couple.

**Brautschau** ['brautʃau], *f.* (—, *no pl.*) (*obs.*) search for a wife.

**brav** [bra:f], *adj.* honest, upright, worthy, honourable; well-behaved, good.

**bravo!** ['bra:vo], *int.* well done!

Bravourstück [bra'vu:rʃtyk], n. (—s, pl. —e) feat of valour.

Brechbohnen ['breçboːnən], f. pl. kidney-beans.

Brecheisen ['breçaɪzən], n. (—s, pl. —) jemmy.

brechen ['breçən], v.a. irr. break; (flowers) pluck, pick; vomit. — v.n. (aux. sein) break.

Brechmittel ['breçmɪtəl], n. (—s, pl. —) emetic.

Brechruhr ['breçruːr], f. (—, no pl.) cholera.

Brechstange ['breçʃtaŋə], f. (—, pl. —n) crow-bar.

Brechung ['breçuŋ], f. (—, pl. —en) breaking; (Phys.) refraction.

Brei [braɪ], m. (—s, pl. —e) pap, pulp, porridge.

breiartig ['braɪaːrtɪç], adj. pulpy.

breiig ['braɪɪç], adj. pappy.

breit [braɪt], adj. broad, wide.

breitbeinig ['braɪtbaɪnɪç], adj. straddle-legged.

Breite ['braɪtə], f. (—, pl. —n) breadth, width; (Geog.) latitude.

Breitengrad ['braɪtəngraːt], m. (—es, pl. —e) (Geog.) degree of latitude.

Breitenkreis ['braɪtənkraɪs], m. (—es, pl. —e) (Geog.) parallel.

breitschultrig ['braɪtʃultrɪç], adj. broad-shouldered.

Bremse ['bremzə], f. (—, pl. —n) (Ent.) gad-fly; (Motor.) brake; (horse) barnacle.

bremsen ['bremzən], v.a. brake, pull up.

brennbar ['brenbaːr], adj. combustible.

Brenneisen ['brenaɪzən], n. (—s, pl. —) branding iron.

brennen ['brenən], v.a. irr. burn; (Med.) cauterise; (alcohol) distil; (hair) curl; (coffee) roast; (coal) char; (bricks) bake. — v.n. burn; (fig.) sting; (eyes) smart.

Brenner ['brenər], m. (—s, pl. —) (person) distiller; (Tech.) burner.

Brennerei [brenə'raɪ], f. (—, pl. —en) distillery.

Brennessel ['brennesəl], f. (—, pl. —n) stinging nettle.

Brennholz ['brenholts], n. (—es, no pl.) firewood.

Brennmaterial ['brenmaterjaːl], n. (—s, pl. —ien) fuel.

Brennofen ['brenoːfən], m. (—s, pl. ⁓n) kiln.

Brennpunkt ['brenpuŋkt], m. (—s, pl. —e) focus.

Brennschere ['brenʃeːrə], f. (—, pl. —n) curling-irons.

Brennstoff ['brenʃtɔf], m. (—(e)s, pl. —e) fuel.

brenzlich ['brentslɪç], adj. smelling (or tasting) of burning; (fig.) ticklish.

Bresche ['breʃə], f. (—, pl. —n) breach, gap.

Brett [bret], n. (—s, pl. —er) board, plank, shelf.

Brettspiel ['bretʃpiːl], n. (—s, pl. —e) table-game.

Brevier [bre'viːr], n. (—s, pl. (rare) —e) breviary.

Brezel ['breːtsəl], f. (—, pl. —n) cracknel, pretzel.

Brief [briːf], m. (—es, pl. —e) letter; epistle.

Briefanschrift ['briːfanʃrɪft], f. (—, pl. —en) address.

Briefbeschwerer ['briːfbəʃveːrər], m. (—s, pl. —) letter-weight, paper-weight.

Briefbogen ['briːfboːgən], m. (—s, pl. —) sheet of notepaper.

Briefkasten ['briːfkastən], m. (—s, pl. ⁓) (house) letter-box; (street) pillar-box, (Am.) post-box.

brieflich ['briːflɪç], adv. by letter, in writing.

Briefmarke ['briːfmarkə], f. (—, pl. —n) postage stamp.

Briefpapier ['briːfpapiːr], n. (—s, no pl.) notepaper.

Briefporto ['briːfpɔrto], n. (—s, pl. —ti) postage.

Brieftasche ['briːftaʃə], f. (—, pl. —n) portfolio, wallet; (Am.) pocket-book.

Brieftaube ['briːftaubə], f. (—, pl. —n) carrier pigeon.

Briefträger ['briːftreːgər], m. (—s, pl. —) postman.

Briefumschlag ['briːfumʃlaːk], m. (—s, pl. ⁓e) envelope.

Briefwechsel ['briːfvɛksəl], m. (—s, no pl.) correspondence.

Brillant [brɪl'jant], m. (—en, pl. —en) brilliant, diamond. — adj. brilliant.

Brille ['brɪlə], f. (— pl. —n) spectacles, glasses.

Brillenschlange ['brɪlənʃlaŋə], f. (—, pl. —n) (Zool.) hooded cobra.

bringen ['brɪŋən], v.a. irr. bring, fetch, carry to, take to, conduct to.

Brise ['briːzə], f. (—, pl. —n) breeze, light wind.

Britannien [brɪ'tanjən], n. Britain.

bröckeln ['brœkəln], v.a., v.n. crumble.

Brocken ['brɔkən], m. (—s, pl. —) bit, piece, fragment, scrap; (bread) crumb.

bröcklig ['brœklɪç], adj. crumbling.

brodeln ['broːdəln], v.n. bubble, simmer.

Brodem ['broːdəm], m. (—s, no pl.) (Poet.) steam, vapour, exhalation.

Brokat [bro'kaːt], m. (—s, pl. —e) brocade.

Brom [broːm], n. (—s, no pl.) (Chem.) bromine.

Brombeere ['brɔmbeːrə], f. (—, pl. —n) blackberry, bramble.

Bronze ['brõːsə], f. (—, pl. —n) bronze.

Brosamen ['broːzaːmən], pl. crumbs.

Brosche ['brɔʃə], f. (—, pl. —n) brooch.

Broschüre [brɔ'ʃyːrə], f. (—, pl. —n) pamphlet, brochure, folder.

Brösel ['brøːzəl], m. (—s, pl. —) crumb.

Brot [broːt], n. (—es, pl. —e) bread, loaf; (fig.) livelihood.

Brötchen ['brøːtçən], n. (—s, pl. —) roll, bread-roll.

**Broterwerb** ['bro:tərvɛrp], *m.* (—s, *no pl.*) livelihood.

**Brotgeber** ['bro:tge:bər], *m.* (—s, *pl.* —) employer, master.

**Brotherr** ['bro:tɛr], *m.* (—n, *pl.* —en) employer, master.

**Brotkorb** ['bro:tkɔrp], *m.* (—s, *pl.* ˝e) bread-basket.

**brotlos** ['bro:tlo:s], *adj.* unemployed; *(fig.)* unprofitable.

**Brotneid** ['bro:tnaIt], *m.* (—s, *no pl.*) professional jealousy.

**Bruch** [brux], *m.* (—s, *pl.* ˝e) breakage; rupture; *(Med.)* fracture, rupture, hernia; *(Maths.)* fraction.

**Bruchband** ['bruxbant], *f.* (—es, *pl.* ˝er) abdominal belt, truss.

**brüchig** ['bryçIç], *adj.* brittle, full of flaws.

**Bruchlandung** ['bruxlanduŋ], *f.* (—, —en) *(Aviat.)* crash-landing.

**Bruchrechnung** ['bruxrɛçnuŋ], *f.* (—, *pl.* —en) *(Arith.)* fractions.

**Bruchstück** ['bruxʃtyk], *n.* (—s, *pl.* —e) fragment, scrap.

**Bruchteil** ['bruxtaIl], *m.* (—s, *pl.* —e) fraction.

**Brücke** ['brykə], *f.* (—, *pl.* —n) bridge.

**Brückenpfeiler** ['brykənpfaIlər], *m.* (—s, *pl.* —) pier.

**Bruder** ['bru:dər], *m.* (—s, *pl.* ˝) brother; *(Eccl.)* friar.

**brüderlich** ['bry:dərlIç], *adj.* fraternal, brotherly.

**Bruderschaft** ['bru:dərʃaft], *f.* (—, *pl.* —en) fraternity, brotherhood.

**Brügge** ['brygə], *n.* Bruges.

**Brühe** ['bry:ə], *f.* (—, *pl.* —n) broth, meat-soup.

**brühen** ['bry:ən], *v.a.* scald.

**Brühkartoffeln** ['bry:kartɔfəln], *f. pl.* potatoes cooked in broth.

**brüllen** ['brylən], *v.n.* roar howl, yell; *(cows)* low, bellow.

**Brummbaß** ['brumbas], *m.* (—sses, *pl.* ˝sse) *(Mus.)* double-bass.

**Brummeisen** ['brumaIzən], *n.* (—s, *pl.* —) Jew's harp.

**brummen** ['brumən], *v.n.* growl, grumble, hum.

**Brummer** ['brumər], *n.* (—s, *pl.* —) *(Ent.)* blue-bottle.

**Brunnen** ['brunən], *m.* (—s, *pl.* —) well, fountain, spring.

**Brunnenkur** ['brunənku:r], *f.* (—, *pl.* —en) taking of mineral waters.

**Brunst** [brunst], *f.* (—, *pl.* ˝e) *(Zool.)* rut, heat.

**Brust** [brust], *f.* (—, *pl.* ˝e) breast; chest; bosom.

**Brustbein** ['brustbaIn], *n.* (—s, *pl.* —e) breastbone, sternum.

**Brustbild** ['brustbIlt], *n.* (—s, *pl.* —er) half-length portrait.

**brüsten** ['brystən], *v.r. sich* —, boast, brag, plume o.s.

**Brustfell** ['brustfɛl], *n.* (—s, *pl.* —e) pleura.

**Brustfellentzündung** ['brustfɛlɛntsynduŋ], *f.* (—, *no pl.*) pleurisy.

**Brusthöhle** ['brusthø:lə], *f.* (—, *pl.* —n) thoracic cavity.

**Brustkasten** ['brustkastən], *m.* (—s, *pl.* ˝n) chest.

**Brusttee** ['brustte:], *m.* (—s, *no pl.*) pectoral (herbal) tea.

**Brüstung** ['brystuŋ], *f.* (—, *pl.* —en) parapet.

**Brustwarze** ['brustvartsə], *f.* (—, *pl.* —n) nipple.

**Brustwehr** ['brustve:r], *f.* (—, *pl.* —en) breastwork, parapet.

**Brut** [bru:t], *f.* (—, *no pl.*) brood; *(fish)* fry.

**brutal** [bru'ta:l], *adj.* brutal.

**brüten** ['bry:tən], *v.a.* brood, hatch.

**Brutofen** ['bru:to:fən], *m.* (—s, *pl.* ˝) incubator.

**brutto** ['bruto], *adv.* *(Comm.)* gross.

**Bube** ['bu:bə], *m.* (—n, *pl.* —n) boy, lad; *(cards)* knave, *(Am.)* jack; rogue, rascal.

**Bubenstreich** ['bu:bənʃtraIç], *m.* (—s, *pl.* —e) boyish prank; knavish trick.

**Bubikopf** ['bu:bIkɔpf], *m.* (—(e)s, *pl.* ˝e) bobbed hair.

**Buch** [bu:x], *n.* (—s, *pl.* ˝er) book; quire (of paper).

**Buchdruckerei** ['bu:xdrukəraI], *f.* (—, —en) printing works, printing office.

**Buche** ['bu:xə], *f.* (—, *pl.* —n) beech (tree).

**buchen** ['bu:xən], *v.a.* book, enter, reserve; *(fig.)* score.

**Bücherei** [by:çə'raI], *f.* (—, *pl.* —en) library.

**Buchesche** ['bu:xɛʃə], *f.* (—, *pl.* —n) hornbeam.

**Buchfink** ['bu:xfIŋk], *m.* (—en, *pl.* —en) *(Orn.)* chaffinch.

**Buchhalter** ['bu:xhaltər], *m.* (—s, *pl.* —) book-keeper.

**Buchhändler** ['bu:xhɛndlər], *m.* (—s, *pl.* —) bookseller.

**Buchmarder** ['bu:xmardər], *m.* (—s, *pl.* —) *(Zool.)* pine-marten.

**Buchsbaum** ['buksbaum], *m.* (—s, *pl.* ˝e) *(Bot.)* box-tree.

**Büchse** ['byksə], *f.* (—, *pl.* —n) box, case; tin, can; rifle, gun.

**Büchsenfleisch** ['byksənflaIʃ], *n.* (—es, *no pl.*) tinned meat.

**Büchsenlauf** ['byksənlauf], *m.* (—s, *pl.* ˝e) gun-barrel.

**Büchsenöffner** ['byksənœfnər], *m.* (—s, *pl.*—) tin-opener.

**Buchstabe** ['bu:xʃta:bə], *m.* (—n, *pl.* —n) letter, character; *großer* —, capital (letter).

**Buchstabenrätsel** ['bu:xʃta:bənrɛtsəl], *n.* (—s, *pl.* —) anagram.

**buchstabieren** [bu:xʃta'bi:rən], *v.a.* spell (out).

**buchstäblich** ['bu:xʃtɛplIç], *adj.* literal.

**Bucht** [buxt], *f.* (—, *pl.* —en) inlet, bay, creek, bight.

**Buchung** ['bu:xuŋ], *f.* (—, *pl.* —en) *(Comm.)* entry (in a book); booking (of tickets).

**Buchwissen** ['bu:xvɪsən], *n.* (—s, *no pl.*) book-learning.
**Buckel** ['bukəl], *m.* (—s, *pl.* —) hump, humpback; boss, stud; (*coll.*) back.
**bücken** ['bykən], *v.r. sich* —, stoop, bow.
**bucklig** ['buklɪç], *adj.* humpbacked.
**Bückling** ['byklɪŋ], *m.* (—s, *pl.* —e) smoked herring; kipper.
**buddeln** ['budəln], *v.n.* (*coll.*) dig.
**Bude** ['bu:də], *f.* (—, *pl.* —n) booth, stall; (*coll.*) room; (*student's*) digs.
**Büfett** [by'fɛt], *n.* (—s, *pl.* —s) sideboard; buffet.
**Büffel** ['byfəl], *m.* (—s, *pl.* —) buffalo.
**büffeln** ['byfəln], *v.n.* (*coll.*) cram (for an examination), swot.
**Bug** [bu:k], *m.* (—s, *pl.* ̈e, —e) (*Naut.*) bow, (*Aviat.*) nose.
**Buganker** ['bu:kaŋkər], *m.* (—s, *pl.* —) bow-anchor.
**Bügel** ['by:gəl], *m.* (—s, *pl.* —) coathanger; (*trigger*) guard; (*horse*) stirrup.
**bügeln** ['by:gəln], *v.a.* iron, smoothe, press.
**bugsieren** [buk'si:rən], *v.a.* tow.
**Bugspriet** ['bu:kʃpri:t], *n.* (—s, *pl.* —e) bowsprit.
**Buhle** ['bu:lə], *m.* or *f.* (—n, *pl.* —n) (*Poet.*) paramour, lover.
**buhlen** ['bu:lən], *v.n.* (*Poet.*) woo, make love (to).
**buhlerisch** ['bu:lərɪʃ], *adj.* (*Poet.*) amorous, wanton, lewd.
**Bühne** ['by:nə], *f.* (—, *pl.* —n) (*Theat.*) stage; scaffold, platform.
**Bühnenbild** ['by:nənbɪlt], *n.* (—es, *pl.* —er) scenery.
**Bukett** [bu'kɛt], *n.* (—s, *pl.* —s) bunch of flowers, bouquet; bouquet (*wine*).
**Bulgarien** [bul'ga:rjən], *n.* Bulgaria.
**Bulldogge** ['buldɔgə], *f.* (—, *pl.* —n) bulldog.
**Bulle** (1) ['bulə], *m.* (—n, *pl.* —n) bull, bullock.
**Bulle** (2) ['bulə], *f.* (—, *pl.* —n) (*Eccl.*) (Papal) Bull.
**bumm** [bum], *int.* boom! bang!
**Bummel** ['buməl], *m.* (—s, *pl.* —) stroll.
**Bummelei** [bumə'lai], *f.* (—, *pl.* —en) idleness, negligence, casualness, carelessness.
**bummeln** ['buməln], *v.n.* lounge, waste o.'s time, dawdle; stroll.
**Bummelzug** ['buməltsu:k], *m.* (—s, *pl.* ̈e) slow train.
**bums** [bums], *int.* bang! crash!
**Bund** (1) [bunt], *m.* (—es, *pl.* ̈e) bond, tie, league, alliance, federation, confederacy; (*Eccl.*) covenant.
**Bund** (2) [bunt], *n.* (—es, *pl.* —e) bundle, bunch (of keys).
**Bündel** ['byndəl], *n.* (—s, *pl.* —) bundle, package.
**Bundesgenosse** ['bundəsgənɔsə], *m.* (—n, *pl.* —n) confederate, ally.
**Bundesstaat** ['bundəsʃta:t], *m.* (—es, *pl.* —en) federal state; federation.

**Bundestag** ['bundəsta:k], *m.* (—es, *pl.* —e) federal parliament.
**Bundeswehr** ['bundəsve:r], *f.* (—, *no pl.*) federal defence; armed forces.
**bündig** ['byndɪç], *adj.* binding; *kurz und* —, concise, terse, to the point.
**Bündnis** ['byntnɪs], *n.* (—ses, *pl.* —se) alliance.
**Bundschuh** ['buntʃu:], *m.* (—s, *pl.* —e) clog, sandal.
**bunt** [bunt], *adj.* many-coloured, chequered, variegated, motley; *das ist mir zu* —, this is going too far.
**buntscheckig** ['buntʃɛkɪç], *adj.* dappled, spotted.
**Buntspecht** ['buntʃpɛçt], *m.* (—s, *pl.* —e) (*Orn.*) (spotted) woodpecker.
**Bürde** ['byrdə], *f.* (—, *pl.* —n) load, burden.
**Bure** ['bu:rə], *m.* (—n, *pl.* —n) Boer.
**Burg** [burk], *f.* (—, *pl.* —en) castle, fortress, citadel, stronghold.
**Bürge** ['byrgə], *m.* (—n, *pl.* —n) surety, bail, guarantee; *einen —n stellen*, offer bail.
**bürgen** ['byrgən], *v.n.* give security, vouch (for), go bail (for).
**Bürger** ['byrgər], *m.* (—s, *pl.* —) citizen, townsman, bourgeois, commoner.
**bürgerlich** ['byrgərlɪç], *adj.* civic; middle-class, bourgeois; — *e Küche*, plain cooking.
**Bürgermeister** ['byrgərmaistər], *m.* (—s, *pl.* —) burgomaster, mayor.
**Burggraf** ['burkgra:f], *m.* (—en, *pl.* —en) burgrave.
**Bürgschaft** ['byrkʃaft], *f.* (—, *pl.* —en) bail, surety, guarantee; — *leisten*, provide security.
**Burgund** [bur'gunt], *n.* Burgundy.
**Burgvogt** ['burkfo:kt], *m.* (—s, *pl.* —e) (*obs.*) castellan, bailiff.
**Burgwarte** ['burkvartə], *f.* (—, *pl.* —n) watch-tower.
**Büro** [by'ro:], *n.* (—s, *pl.* —s) office, bureau, (professional) chambers.
**Bursche** ['burʃə], *m.* (—n, *pl.* —n) lad, boy, fellow; student; (*Mil.*) batman.
**Burschenschaft** ['burʃənʃaft], *f.* (—, *pl.* —en) students' association.
**Bürste** ['byrstə], *f.* (—, *pl.* —n) brush.
**Burundi** [bu'rundi], *n.* Burundi.
**Busch** [buʃ], *m.* (—es, *pl.* ̈e) bush, shrub, copse, thicket.
**Büschel** ['byʃəl], *n.* (—s, *pl.* —) bunch; (*hair*) tuft.
**buschig** ['buʃɪç], *adj.* bushy, tufted.
**Buschklepper** ['buʃklɛpər], *m.* (—s, *pl.* —) bushranger.
**Busen** ['bu:zən], *m.* (—s, *pl.* —) bosom, breast; (*Geog.*) bay, gulf.
**Bussard** ['busart], *m.* (—s, *pl.* —e) (*Orn.*) buzzard.
**Buße** ['bu:sə], *f.* (—, *pl.* —n) penance; repentance; penalty.
**büßen** ['by:sən], *v.a., v.n.* repent, atone, expiate, make amends.
**bußfertig** ['bu:sfɛrtɪç], *adj.* penitent, repentant.

Büste ['bystə], *f.* (—, *pl.* —n) bust.
Büstenhalter ['bystənhaltər], *m.* (—s, *pl.* —) brassière.
Bütte ['bytə], *f.* (—, *pl.* —n) tub.
Büttel ['bytəl], *m.* (—s, *pl.* —) beadle; bailiff.
Büttenpapier ['bytənpapi:r], *n.* (—s, *no pl.*) hand-made paper.
Butter ['butər], *f.* (—, *no pl.*) butter.
Butterblume ['butərblu:mə], *f.* (—, *pl.* —n) buttercup.
Butterbrot ['butərbro:t], *n.* (—s, *pl.* —e) bread and butter.
buttern ['butərn], *v.a.*, *v.n.* smear with butter; churn.
Butterteig ['butərtaik], *m.* (—es, *pl.* —e) puff-pastry.
Butzenscheibe ['butsənʃaibə], *f.* (—, *pl.* —n) bull's-eyed pane.
Byzanz [by'tsants], *n.* Byzantium, Constantinople.

# C

C [tse:], *n.* (—s, *pl.* —s) the letter C; (*Mus.*) C *dur*, C major; C *Moll*, C minor; C-*Schlüssel*, C clef.
Cäsar ['tse:zar], *m.* Cæsar.
Ceylon ['tseilɔn], *n.* Ceylon.
Chaiselongue [ʃɛːzə'lɔ̃:g], *f.* (—, *pl.* —s) couch, settee, sofa.
Champagner [ʃam'panjər], *m.* (—s, *pl.* —) champagne.
Champignon [ʃampɪn'jɔ̃], *m.* (—s, *pl.* —s) mushroom.
chaotisch [ka'o:tɪʃ], *adj.* chaotic.
Charakter [ka'raktər], *m.* (—s, *pl.* —e) character; mental make-up, disposition.
Charakteristik [karaktər'ɪstɪk], *f.* (—, *pl.* —en) characterisation.
charakteristisch [karaktər'ɪstɪʃ], *adj.* characteristic; typical.
Charge ['ʃarʒə], *f.* (—, *pl.* —n) office, appointment; (*pl.*) (*Mil.*) non-commissioned officers.
Chaussee [ʃɔ'se:], *f.* (—, *pl.* —n) main road, highway.
Chef [ʃef], *m.* (—s, *pl.* —s) chief, head, employer; (*coll.*) boss.
Chefredakteur ['ʃefredaktø:r], *m.* (—s, *pl.* —e) editor-in-chief.
Chemie [çe'mi:], *f.* (—, *no pl.*) chemistry.
Chemikalien [çemɪ'ka:ljən], *f. pl.* chemicals.
Chemiker ['çe:mɪkər], *m.* (—s, *pl.* —) (analytical) chemist.
chemisch ['çe:mɪʃ], *adj.* chemical; — *gereinigt*, dry-cleaned.
Chiffre ['ʃɪfər], *f.* (—, *pl.* —n) cipher.
chiffrieren [ʃɪ'fri:rən], *v.a.* encipher.
Chile ['tʃi:lə, 'çi:lə], *n.* Chile.

China ['çi:na], *n.* China.
Chinarinde [çi:na'rɪndə], *f.* (—, *no pl.*) Peruvian bark.
Chinin [çi'ni:n], *n.* (—s, *no pl.*) quinine.
Chirurg [çi'rurk], *m.* (—en, *pl.* —en) surgeon.
Chirurgie [çirur'gi:], *f.* (—, *no pl.*) surgery.
Chlor [klo:r], *n.* (—s, *no pl.*) chlorine.
Chlorkalk ['klo:rkalk], *m.* (—s, *no pl.*) chloride of lime.
Chlornatrium [klo:r'na:trjum], *n.* (—s, *no pl.*) sodium chloride.
Choleriker [ko'le:rɪkər], *m.* (—s, *pl.* —) irascible person.
Chor [ko:r], *m.* (—s, *pl.* -:e) chorus; choir; (*Archit.*) choir, chancel.
Choral [ko'ra:l], *m.* (—s, *pl.* -:e) hymn, chorale.
Choramt ['ko:ramt], *n.* (—s, *pl.* -:er) cathedral service.
Chorgesang ['ko:rgəsaŋ], *m.* (—s, *pl.* -:e) chorus, choral singing.
Chorhemd ['ko:rhemt], *n.* (—s, *pl.* —en) surplice.
Chorherr ['ko:rhɛr], *m.* (—n, *pl.* —en) canon, prebendary.
Christ [krɪst], *m.* (—en, *pl.* —en) Christian.
Christbaum ['krɪstbaum], *m.* (—s, *pl.* -:e) Christmas tree.
Christentum ['krɪstəntu:m], *n.* (—s, *no pl.*) Christendom, Christianity.
Christkind ['krɪstkɪnt], *n.* (—s, *no pl.*) Infant Christ, Christ child.
christlich ['krɪstlɪç], *adj.* Christian.
Christmette ['krɪstmetə], *f.* (—, *pl.* —n) Christmas matins; midnight mass.
Christus ['krɪstus], *m.* (—i) Christ; *vor* —, B.C.; *nach* —, A.D.
Chrom [kro:m], *n.* (—s, *no pl.*) chrome.
chromatisch [kro'ma:tɪʃ], *adj.* chromatic.
chromsauer ['kro:mzauər], *adj.* — chromate of; —*es Salz*, chromate.
Chronik ['kro:nɪk], *f.* (—, *pl.* —en) chronicle.
chronisch ['kro:nɪʃ], *adj.* chronic.
Chronist [kro'nɪst], *m.* (—en, *pl.* —en) chronicler.
Chrysantheme [kryzan'te:mə], *f.* (—, *pl.* —n) chrysanthemum.
Cis [tsɪs], (*Mus.*) C sharp.
Clique ['klɪkə], *f.* (—, *pl.* —n) clique, set.
Coeur [kø:r], *n.* (*Cards*) hearts.
coulant [ku'lant], *adj.* polite, friendly; (*Comm.*) fair, obliging.
Couleur [ku'lø:r], *f.* (—, *pl.* —en) colour; students' corporation.
Coupé [ku'pe:], *m.* (—s, *pl.* —s) (*train*) compartment.
Couplet [ku'ple:], *n.* (—s, *pl.* —s) comic song.
Coupon [ku'pɔ̃], *m.* (—s, *pl.* —s) coupon, check, dividend voucher.
Cour [ku:r], *f.* (—, *no pl.*) *einem Mädchen die* — *machen*, court a girl.

**Courtage** [kur'ta:ʒə], *f.* (—, *pl.* —n) brokerage.

**Cousin** [ku'zɛ̃], *m.* (—s, *pl.* —s) cousin.

**Cousine** [ku'zi:nə], *f.* (—, *pl.* —n) (female) cousin.

**Cutaway** ['katave:], *m.* (—s, *pl.* —s) morning coat.

**Czar** [tsa:r], *m.* (—en, *pl.* —en) Tsar, Czar.

# D

**D** [de:], *n.* (—s, *pl.* —s) the letter D; (*Mus.*) *D dur*, D major; *D moll*, D minor; *D-Zug*, express train.

**da** [da:], *adv.* (*local*) there; here; (*temporal*) then, at that moment; (*Mil.*) *wer —?* who goes there? (*Poet. obs.*) where. — *conj.* (*temporal*) when, as; (*causal*) as, because, since.

**dabei** [da'baɪ], *adv.* nearby; besides, moreover; as well; —*sein*, be present, be about to (*infin.*); — *bleiben*, persist in.

**Dach** [dax], *n.* (—es, *pl.* ̈er) roof.

**Dachboden** ['daxbo:dən], *m.* (—s, *pl.* ̈) loft.

**Dachdecker** ['daxdɛkər], *m.* (—s, *pl.* —) slater, tiler.

**Dachgiebel** ['daxgi:bəl], *m.* (—s, *pl.* —) gable.

**Dachluke** ['daxlu:kə], *f.* (—, *pl.* —n) dormer window.

**Dachpappe** ['daxpapə], *f.* (—, *pl.* —n) roofing felt.

**Dachrinne** ['daxrɪnə], *f.* (—, *pl.* —n) gutter.

**Dachs** [daks], *m.* (—es, *pl.* —e) badger.

**Dachstube** ['daxʃtu:bə], *f.* (—, *pl.* —n) garret, attic (room).

**Dachtraufe** ['daxtraufə], *f.* (—, *pl.* —n) eaves.

**dadurch** [da'durç], *adv.* (*local*) through it; in that way; (*causal*) thereby.

**dafür** [da'fy:r], *adv.* for it; instead of it, in return for it; *ich kann nichts —*, it is not my fault, I can't help it.

**Dafürhalten** [da'fy:rhaltən], *n.* (—s, *no pl.*) opinion.

**dagegen** [da'ge:gən], *adv.* against it, compared to it. — *conj.* on the other hand.

**daheim** [da'haɪm], *adv.* at home.

**daher** [da'he:r], *adv.* thence, from that. — *conj.* therefore, for that reason.

**dahin** [da'hɪn], *adv.* thither, to that place; there; *bis —*, (*local*) thither; (*temporal*) till then; over, past, lost, gone.

**dahinbringen** [da'hɪnbrɪŋən], *v.a. irr.* *jemanden —*, induce s.o. to; *es —*, succeed in, manage to.

**dahinsiechen** [da'hɪnzi:çən], *v.n.* (*aux.* sein) pine away, be failing (in health).

**dahinter** [da'hɪntər], *adv.* behind that.

**Dahlie** ['da:ljə], *f.* (—, *pl.* —n) (*Bot.*) dahlia.

**Dahome** ['daome:], *n.* Dahomey.

**damalig** ['da:malɪç], *adj.* then; of that time; past.

**damals** ['da:mals], *adv.* then, at that time.

**Damast** [da'mast], *m.* (—s, *no pl.*) damask.

**Damaszener** [damas'tse:nər], *m.* (—s, *pl.* —) Damascene. — *adj.* — *Stahl*, Damascus steel, dagger.

**Dame** ['da:mə], *f.* (—, *pl.* —n) lady; (*cards, chess*) queen; draughts (*game*).

**damit** [da'mɪt], *adv.* therewith, with that, with it; *genug — basta!* and that's all there is to it. — *conj.* in order that, so that; — *nicht*, lest.

**dämlich** ['dɛ:mlɪç], *adj.* (*coll.*) foolish, silly.

**Damm** [dam], *m.* (—es, *pl.* ̈e) dam, dyke, mole; (*street*) roadway, causeway; (*rail*) embankment.

**dämmen** ['dɛmən], *v.a.* dam; (*fig.*) stop, restrain.

**dämmerig** ['dɛmərɪç], *adj.* dusky.

**dämmern** ['dɛmərn], *v.n.* grow dusky; dawn.

**dämonisch** [dɛ'mo:nɪʃ], *adj.* demoniac-(al), demonlike.

**Dampf** [dampf], *m.* (—es, *pl.* ̈e) vapour, steam, mist, fume; smoke.

**dampfen** ['dampfən], *v.n.* smoke, fume, steam.

**dämpfen** ['dɛmpfən], *v.a.* damp, smother, steam; subdue, deaden, muffle, soften down.

**Dampfer** ['dampfər], *m.* (—s, *pl.* —) steamer.

**Dämpfer** ['dɛmpfər], *m.* (—s, *pl.* —) damper; (*Mus.*) mute.

**Dampfkessel** ['dampfkɛsəl], *m.* (—s, *pl.* —) boiler.

**Dämpfung** ['dɛmpfuŋ], *f.* (—, *pl.* —en) damping, smothering, suppression; (*Aviat.*) stabilization.

**danach** [da'na:x], *adv.* after that, thereafter; accordingly, according to that.

**daneben** [da'ne:bən], *adv.* near it, by it, close by; *es geht —*, it goes amiss. — *conj.* besides.

**Dänemark** ['dɛ:nəmark], *n.* Denmark.

**Dank** [daŋk], *m.* (—es, *no pl.*) thanks, gratitude; reward; *Gott sei —*, thank heaven!

**dank** [daŋk], *prep.* (*Dat.*) owing to, thanks to.

**dankbar** ['daŋkba:r], *adj.* grateful, thankful.

**danken** ['daŋkən], *v.n.* (*Dat.*) thank. — *v.a.* owe.

**Dankgebet** ['daŋkgəbe:t], *n.* (—s, *pl.* —e) (prayer of) thanksgiving.

**dann** [dan], *adv.* then, at that time, in that case; — *und wann*, now and then, occasionally.

**Danzig** ['dantsɪç], *n.* Dantzig.

43

# daran

**daran, dran** [da'ran, dran], *adv.* on it, at it, near that; thereon, thereby; *was liegt —?* what does it matter?

**darauf, drauf** [da'rauf, drauf], *adv.* (*local*) upon it, on it; (*temporal*) thereupon, thereon, thereafter.

**daraufhin** [darauf'hɪn], *adv.* thereupon; on the strength of that.

**daraus, draus** [da'raus, draus], *adv.* therefrom, hence, from that; *ich mache mir nichts —,* I do not care for it.

**darben** ['darbən], *v.n.* suffer want, go short; famish.

**darbieten** ['da:rbi:tən], *v.a. irr.* offer, tender, present.

**Darbietung** ['da:rbi:tuŋ], *f.* (—, *pl.* —en) offering, presentation, performance.

**darbringen** ['da:rbrɪŋən], *v.a. irr.* bring, present, offer.

**darein, drein** [da'raɪn, draɪn], *adv.* into it, therein.

**darin, drin** [da'rɪn, drɪn], *adv.* therein, in it, within.

**darinnen, drinnen** [da'rɪnən, 'drɪnən], *adv.* inside, in there.

**darlegen** ['da:rle:gən], *v.a.* demonstrate, explain; expound.

**Darlehen** ['da:rle:ən], *n.* (—s, *pl.* —) loan.

**Darm** [darm], *m.* (—s, *pl.* ⸚e) gut; (*pl.*) intestines, bowels.

**Darmsaite** ['darmzaɪtə], *f.* (—, *pl.* —n) catgut, gut-string.

**darob** [da'rɔp], *adv.* (*obs.*) on that account, on account of it.

**darreichen** ['da:raɪçən], *v.a.* offer, tender, present; (*Eccl.*) administer (sacraments).

**darstellen** ['da:rʃtɛlən], *v.a.* represent, delineate; (*Theat.*) perform.

**Darstellung** ['da:rʃtɛluŋ], *f.* (—, *pl.* —en) representation, exhibition, presentation; (*Theat.*) performance.

**dartun** ['da:rtu:n], *v.a. irr.* prove, demonstrate.

**darüber, drüber** [dar'y:bər, 'dry:bər], *adv.* over that, over it; concerning that.

**darum, drum** [da'rum, drum], *adv.* around it, around that, thereabout; therefore, for that reason.

**darunter, drunter** [da'runtər, 'druntər], *adv.* under that; thereunder; among; — *und drüber,* topsy-turvy.

**das** [das], *def. art. n.* the. — *dem. pron., dem. adj.* that, this. —*rel. pron.* which.

**Dasein** ['da:zaɪn], *n.* (—s, *no pl.*) presence, being, existence.

**daselbst** [da:'zɛlpst], *adv.* there, in that very place.

**daß** [das], *conj.* that; *es sei denn —,* unless; — *nicht,* lest.

**dastehen** ['da:ʃte:ən], *v.n. irr.* stand (there).

**datieren** [da'ti:rən], *v.a.* date, put a date to.

**Dativ** ['da:ti:f], *m.* (—s, *pl.* —e) dative.

**dato** ['da:to], *adv. bis —,* till now, hitherto.

**Dattel** ['datəl], *f.* (—, *pl.* —n) (*Bot.*) date.

**Datum** ['da:tum], *n.* (—s, *pl.* **Daten**) date (*calendar*).

**Dauer** ['dauər], *f.* (—, *no pl.*) duration, length of time; continuance; permanence.

**dauerhaft** ['dauərhaft], *adj.* durable, lasting; (*colours*) fast.

**Dauerkarte** ['dauərkartə], *f.* (—, *pl.* —n) season ticket; (*Am.*) commutation ticket.

**dauern** ['dauərn], *v.n.* continue, last, endure.— *v.a.* move to pity; *er dauert mich,* I am sorry for him.

**Dauerpflanze** ['dauərpflantsə], *f.* (—, *pl.* —n) perennial plant.

**Dauerwelle** ['dauərvɛlə], *f.* (—, *pl.* —n) permanent wave, (*coll.*) perm.

**Daumen** ['daumən], *m.* (—s, *pl.* —) thumb; *einem den — halten,* wish s.o. well, keep o.'s fingers crossed for s.o.

**Daune** ['daunə], *f.* (—, *pl.* —n) down.

**davon** [da'fɔn], *adv.* thereof, therefrom, from that; off, away.

**davonkommen** [da'fɔnkɔmən], *v.n. irr.* (*aux.* sein) get off; *mit einem blauen Auge —,* get off lightly.

**davor** [da'fo:r], *adv.* before that, before it.

**dawider** [da'vi:dər], *adv.* against it.

**dazu** [da'tsu:], *adv.* thereto, to that, to it; in addition to that; for that purpose; *noch —,* besides.

**dazumal** [da'tsuma:l], *adv.* then, at that time.

**dazwischen** [da'tsvɪʃən], *adv.* between, among; — *kommen,* intervene, interfere; — *treten,* intervene.

**debattieren** [deba'ti:rən], *v.a., v.n.* debate.

**Debet** ['de:bɛt], *n.* (—s, *pl.* —s) debit.

**Debüt** [de'by:], *n.* (—s, *pl.* —s) first appearance, début.

**Dechant** [de'çant], *m.* (—en, *pl.* —en) (*Eccl.*) dean.

**dechiffrieren** [deʃɪf'ri:rən], *v.a.* decode, decipher.

**Deck** [dɛk], *n.* (—s, *pl.* —e) (*Naut.*) deck.

**Deckbett** ['dɛkbɛt], *n.* (—s, *pl.* —en) coverlet.

**Deckblatt** ['dɛkblat], *n.* (—s, *pl.* ⸚er) (*Bot.*) bractea; (*cigar*) wrapper.

**Decke** ['dɛkə], *f.* (—, *pl.* —n) cover; blanket, rug; (*bed*) coverlet; (*room*) ceiling.

**Deckel** ['dɛkəl], *m.* (—s, *pl.* —) lid, top; (*book*) cover; (*coll.*) hat.

**decken** ['dɛkən], *v.a.* cover; (*Comm.*) secure, reimburse. — *v.r. sich —,* (*Maths.*) coincide; (*fig.*) square, tally.

**Deckfarbe** ['dɛkfarbə], *f.* (—, *pl.* —n) body colour.

**Deckmantel** ['dɛkmantəl], *m.* (—s, *pl.* ⸚) cloak, disguise.

**Deckung** ['dɛkuŋ], *f.* (—, *pl.* —en) covering, protection; (*Comm.*) reimbursement; security; (*Mil.*) cover.

**dedizieren** [dedɪ'tsi:rən], *v.a.* dedicate.

**deduzieren** [dedu'tsi:rən], *v.a.* deduce.

**defekt** [de'fɛkt], *adj.* defective, incomplete, imperfect.

**defilieren** [defɪ'li:rən], *v.n.* (*Mil.*) pass in review, march past.

**definieren** [defɪ'ni:rən], *v.a.* define.

**Degen** ['de:gən], *m.* (—s, *pl.* —) sword; (*fig.*) brave warrior.

**degradieren** [degra'di:rən], *v.a.* degrade, demote.

**dehnbar** ['de:nba:r], *adj.* extensible, ductile.

**dehnen** ['de:nən], *v.a.* extend, expand, stretch. — *v.r. sich* —, stretch o.s.

**Deich** [daɪç], *m.* (—es, *pl.* —e) dike, dam, embankment.

**Deichsel** ['daɪksəl], *f.* (—, *pl.* —n) thill, shaft, pole.

**deichseln** ['daɪksəln], *v.a.* (*fig.*) engineer; (*coll.*) manage; wangle.

**dein** [daɪn], *poss. adj.* your; (*Poet.*) thy. — *poss. pron.* yours; (*Poet.*) thine.

**deinesgleichen** [daɪnəs'glaɪçən], *adj.*, *pron.* the like of you, such as you.

**deinethalben** ['daɪnəthalbən], *adv.* on your account, for your sake, on your behalf.

**deinetwegen** ['daɪnətve:gən], *adv.* because of you, on your account, for your sake, on your behalf.

**deinetwillen** ['daɪnətvɪlən], *adv. um* —, on your account, for your sake, on your behalf.

**deinige** ['daɪnɪgə], *poss. adj.* your; (*Poet.*) thy. — *poss. pron.* yours; (*Poet.*) thine.

**Dekan** [de'ka:n], *m.* (—s, *pl.* —e) (*Eccl., Univ.*) dean.

**Dekanat** [deka'na:t], *n.* (—s, *pl.* —e) (*Eccl., Univ.*) deanery, office of dean.

**deklamieren** [dekla'mi:rən], *v.a., v.n.* recite, declaim.

**deklarieren** [dekla'ri:rən], *v.a.* declare (for customs duty).

**Deklination** [deklina'tsjo:n], *f.* (—, *pl.* —en) (*Gram.*) declension; (*Phys.*) declination.

**deklinieren** [deklɪ'ni:rən], *v.a.* (*Gram.*) decline.

**dekolletiert** [dekɔle'ti:rt], *adj.* décolleté, low-necked.

**Dekret** [de'kre:t], *n.* (—s, *pl.* —e) decree, edict, official regulation.

**dekretieren** [dekre'ti:rən], *v.a.* decree, ordain.

**delegieren** [dele'gi:rən], *v.a.* delegate.

**Delegierte** [dele'gi:rtə], *m.* (—n, *pl.* —n) delegate.

**delikat** [delɪ'ka:t], *adj.* subtle, dainty; tasty; (*coll.*) tricky, difficult.

**Delikatesse** [delɪka'tɛsə], *f.* (—, *pl.* —n) delicacy, dainty; (*pl.*) (*Am.*) delicatessen.

**Delikt** [de'lɪkt], *n.* (—s, *pl.* —e) (*Law*) crime; misdemeanour.

**Delle** ['dɛlə], *f.* (—, *pl.* —n) dent.

**Delphin** [dɛl'fi:n], *m.* (—s, *pl.* —e) dolphin.

**deltaförmig** ['dɛltafœrmɪç], *adj.* deltoid.

**dem** [de:m], *def. art. Dat.* to the. — *dem. adj.* to this, to that: — *dem. pron.* to this, to that; *wie* — *auch sei*, however that may be. — *rel. pron.* to whom, to which.

**demarkieren** [demar'ki:rən], *v.a.* mark, demarcate.

**Dementi** [de'mɛnti], *n.* (—s, *pl.* —s) (*official*) denial.

**dementieren** [demɛn'ti:rən], *v.a.* (*Pol.*) deny, contradict.

**demgemäß** ['de:mgəme:s], *adv.* accordingly.

**demnach** ['de:mnax], *conj.* therefore, consequently, in accordance with that.

**demnächst** ['de:mnɛ:çst], *adv.* shortly, soon, in the near future.

**demokratisch** [demo'kra:tɪʃ], *adj.* democratic.

**demolieren** [demo'li:rən], *v.a.* demolish.

**demonstrieren** [demɔn'stri:rən], *v.a., v.n.* demonstrate.

**Demut** ['de:mu:t], *f.* (—, *no pl.*) humility, meekness.

**demütig** ['de:mytɪç], *adj.* humble, meek, submissive.

**demütigen** ['de:mytɪgən], *v.a.* humble, humiliate, subdue.

**Denkart** ['dɛŋka:rt], *f.* (—, *pl.* —en) way of thinking.

**denken** ['dɛŋkən], *v.a., v.n. irr.* think, reflect (upon); imagine; (*coll.*) guess.

**Denker** ['dɛŋkər], *m.* (—s, *pl.* —) thinker, philosopher.

**Denkmal** ['dɛŋkma:l], *n.* (—s, *pl.* ⸚er) monument.

**Denkmünze** ['dɛŋkmyntsə], *f.* (—, *pl.* —n) (commemorative) medal.

**Denkschrift** ['dɛŋkʃrɪft], *f.* (—, *pl.* —en) memorandum, memoir.

**Denkspruch** ['dɛŋkʃprux], *m.* (—s, *pl.* ⸚e) aphorism, maxim, motto.

**Denkungsart** ['dɛŋkuŋsart], *f.* (*pl.* —en) *see* Denkart.

**Denkweise** ['dɛŋkvaɪzə], *f.* (—, *pl.* —n) *see* Denkart.

**denkwürdig** ['dɛŋkvyrdɪç], *adj.* memorable.

**Denkzettel** ['dɛŋktsetəl], *m.* (—s, *pl.* —) (*fig.*) reminder, punishment, lesson; *einem einen* — *geben*, give s.o. s.th. to think about *or* a sharp reminder.

**denn** [dɛn], *conj.* for. — *adv.* then; (*after comparatives*) than; *es sei* — *dass*, unless.

**dennoch** ['dɛnɔx], *conj.* yet, nevertheless, notwithstanding.

**Denunziant** [denun'tsjant], *m.* (—en, *pl.* —en) informer.

**denunzieren** [denun'tsi:rən], *v.a.* inform against, denounce.

**Depesche** [de'pɛʃə], *f.* (—, *pl.* —n) dispatch; telegram, wire.

**deponieren** [depo'ni:rən], *v.a.* deposit; (*Law*) depose.

**Depositenbank** [depo'zi:tənbaŋk], *f.* (—, *pl.* —en) deposit-bank.

# deprimieren

**deprimieren** [deprɪ'mi:rən], *v.a.* depress.

**Deputierte** [depu'ti:rtə], *m.* (—n, *pl.* —n) deputy.

**der** [de:r], *def. art. m.* the. — *dem. adj.*, *dem. pron.* this, that. — *rel. pron.* who, which, that.

**derart** ['de:ra:rt], *adv.* so, in such a manner.

**derartig** ['de:ra:rtɪç], *adj.* such.

**derb** [dɛrp], *adj.* firm, solid, coarse, blunt, uncouth; strong, robust.

**dereinst** [de:r'aɪnst], *adv.* one day (in future).

**derenthalben** ['de:rənthalbən], *adv.* for her (their) sake, on her (their) account, on whose account.

**derentwegen** ['de:rəntve:gən], *adv. see* **derenthalben.**

**derentwillen** ['de:rəntvɪlən], *adv. see* **derenthalben.**

**dergestalt** ['de:rgəʃtalt], *adv.* in such a manner; so.

**dergleichen** [de:r'glaɪçən], *adv.* such, such as, suchlike.

**derjenige** [de:r'je:nɪgə], *dem. adj.*, *dem. pron.* that, this; — *welcher*, he who.

**derlei** ['de:rlaɪ], *adj.* of that sort.

**dermaßen** ['de:rma:sən], *adv.* to such an extent, to such a degree.

**derselbe** [de:r'zɛlbə], *pron.* the same.

**derweilen** [de:r'vaɪlən], *adv.* meanwhile.

**Derwisch** ['dɛrvɪʃ], *m.* (—(e)s, *pl.* —e) dervish.

**derzeit** ['de:rtsaɪt], *adv.* at present.

**Des** [dɛs], *n.* (—, *pl.* —) (*Mus.*) D flat; — *Dur*, D flat major; — *Moll*, D flat minor.

**des** [dɛs], *def. art. m. & n. Genit. sing.* of the.

**desgleichen** [dɛs'glaɪçən], *adj.* such, suchlike. — *adv.* likewise, ditto.

**deshalb** ['dɛshalp], *adv., conj.* therefore.

**desinfizieren** [dɛsɪnfɪt'si:rən], *v.a.* disinfect.

**dessen** ['dɛsən], *dem. pron. m & n. Genit. sing.* of it, of that. — *rel. pron. m. & n. Genit. sing.* whose, of whom, of which, whereof.

**dessenungeachtet** [dɛsənunge'axtət], *conj.* notwithstanding that, for all that, despite all that.

**Destillateur** [dɛstɪla'tø:r], *m.* (—s, *pl.* —e) distiller.

**destillieren** [dɛstɪ'li:rən], *v.a.* distil.

**desto** ['dɛsto], *adv.* the; — *besser*, so much the better; *je* . . . —, the . . . the.

**deswegen** ['dɛsve:gən], *adv., conj.* therefore.

**Detaillist** [deta'jɪst], *m.* (—en, *pl.* —en) retailer.

**deucht** [dɔyçt] *see* **dünken**; (*obs.*) *mich deucht*, methinks.

**deuten** ['dɔytən], *v.a.* point to, show; explain, interpret.

**deutlich** ['dɔytlɪç], *adj.* clear, distinct; evident, plain.

**deutsch** [dɔytʃ], *adj.* German.

**Deutschland** ['dɔytʃlant], *n.* Germany.

**Deutschmeister** ['dɔytʃmaɪstər], *m.* (—s, *pl.* —) Grand Master of the Teutonic Order.

**Deutschtum** ['dɔytʃtu:m], *n.* (—s, *no pl.*) German nationality, German customs, German manners.

**Deutung** ['dɔytuŋ], *f.* (—, *pl.* —en) explanation, interpretation.

**Devise** [de'vi:zə], *f.* (—, *pl.* —n) device, motto; (*pl.*) foreign currency.

**devot** [de'vo:t], *adj.* submissive, respectful, humble.

**Dezember** [de'tsɛmbər], *m.* December.

**dezent** [de'tsɛnt], *adj.* modest, decent; unobtrusive.

**Dezernent** [detsɛr'nɛnt], *m.* (—en, *pl.* —en) head of section in ministry or city administration.

**dezimieren** [detsɪ'mi:rən], *v.a.* decimate, reduce.

**Diagramm** [dia'gram], *n.* (—s, *pl.* —e) diagram, graph.

**Diakon** [dia'ko:n], *m.* (—s, *pl.* —e) (*Eccl.*) deacon.

**Diakonisse, Diakonissin** [diako'nɪsə, diako'nɪsɪn], *f.* (—, *pl.* —nen) deaconess.

**Dialektik** [dia'lɛktɪk], *f.* (—, *no pl.*) dialectics.

**Diamant** [dia'mant], *m.* (—en, *pl.* —en) diamond.

**diametral** [diame'tra:l], *adj.* diametrical.

**Diapositiv** [diapozi'ti:f], *n.* (—s, *pl.* —e) (*lantern, Phot.*) slide.

**Diät** [di'ɛ:t], *f.* (—, *pl.* —en) diet; (*pl.*) daily allowance.

**dich** [dɪç], *pers. pron.* you. — *refl. pron.* yourself.

**dicht** [dɪçt], *adj.* tight; impervious (to water); dense, compact, solid, firm; — *bei*, hard by, close to.

**Dichte** ['dɪçtə], *f.* (—, *no pl.*) density.

**dichten** ['dɪçtən], *v.a., v.n.* write poetry, compose (*verses etc.*); (*Tech.*) tighten; (*Naut.*) caulk.

**Dichter** ['dɪçtər], *m.* (—s, *pl.* —) poet.

**dichterisch** ['dɪçtərɪʃ], *adj.* poetic(al).

**Dichtigkeit** ['dɪçtɪçkaɪt], *f.* (—, *no pl.*) closeness, compactness, thickness, density.

**Dichtkunst** ['dɪçtkunst], *f.* (—, *no pl.*) (art of) poetry.

**Dichtung** ['dɪçtuŋ], *f.* (—, *pl.* —en) poetry, poem; fiction; (*Tech.*) caulking; washer, gasket.

**dick** [dɪk], *adj.* thick; fat; (*books*) bulky; voluminous, stout, obese, corpulent.

**Dicke** ['dɪkə], *f.* (—, *no pl.*) thickness, stoutness.

**dickfellig** ['dɪkfɛlɪç], *adj.* thick-skinned.

**Dickicht** ['dɪkɪçt], *n.* (—s, *pl.* —e) thicket.

**die** [di:], *def. art. f. & pl.* the. — *dem. adj.*, *dem. pron. f. & pl.* this, these. — *rel. pron. f. & pl.* who, that which.

**Dieb** [di:p], *m.* (—s, *pl.* —e) thief.

**Diebstahl** ['di:pʃta:l], *m.* (—s, *pl.* ⁀e) theft.

**Diele** ['di:lə], *f.* (—, *pl.* —n) floor; (entrance) hall.

**dielen** ['di:lən], *v.a.* board, floor.

**dienen** ['di:nən], *v.n. einem* —, serve (s.o.); help (s.o.).

**Diener** ['di:nər], *m.* (—s, *pl.* —) servant, attendant; (*coll.*) bow.

**dienlich** ['di:nlɪç], *adj.* serviceable, useful; *für* — *halten*, think fit.

**Dienst** [di:nst], *m.* (—es, *pl.* —e) service, employment, duty; — *haben*, be on duty.

**Dienstag** ['di:nsta:k], *m.* (—s, *pl.* —e) Tuesday.

**Dienstalter** ['di:nstaltər], *n.* (—s, *pl.* —) seniority.

**dienstbar** ['di:nstba:r], *adj.* subject, subservient.

**Dienstbarkeit** ['di:nstba:rkaɪt], *f.* (—, *no pl.*) bondage, servitude.

**dienstbeflissen** ['di:nstbəflɪsən], *adj.* assiduous.

**Dienstbote** ['di:nstbo:tə], *m.* (—n, *pl.* —n) domestic servant.

**dienstfertig** ['di:nstfɛrtɪç], *adj.* obliging, ready to serve.

**Dienstleistung** ['di:nstlaɪstuŋ], *f.* (—, *pl.* —en) service.

**dienstlich** ['di:nstlɪç], *adj.* official.

**Dienstmädchen** ['di:nstmɛ:tçən], *n.* (—s, pl. —) maidservant.

**Dienstmann** ['di:nstman], *m.* (—s, *pl.* ˙er) commissionaire, porter.

**Dienstpflicht** ['di:nstpflɪçt], *f.* (—, *no pl.*) official duty, liability to serve; (*Mil.*) (compulsory) military service.

**Dienststunden** ['di:nstʃtundən], *f. pl.* office hours.

**diensttauglich** ['di:nsttauklɪç], *adj.* (*Mil.*) fit for service.

**Dienstverhältnis** ['di:nstfɛrhɛltnɪs], *n.* (—ses, *pl.* —se) (*pl.*) terms of service.

**dies** [di:s], *abbr. dieses.*

**diesbezüglich** ['di:sbətsy:klɪç], *adj.* concerning this, relating to this matter.

**diese** ['di:zə], *dem. adj., dem. pron. f. & pl.* this, these.

**dieser** ['di:zər], *dem. adj., dem. pron. m.* this.

**dieses** ['di:zəs], *dem. adj., dem. pron. n.* this.

**diesjährig** ['di:sjɛ:rɪç], *adj.* of this year, this year's.

**diesmal** ['di:sma:l], *adv.* this time, for this once.

**Dietrich** (1) ['di:trɪç], *m.* Derek.

**Dietrich** (2) ['di:trɪç], *m.* (—s, *pl.* —e) pick lock, master-key, skeleton key.

**Differentialrechnung** [dɪfərɛnts'ja:l-rɛçnuŋ], *f.* (—, *pl.* —en) differential calculus.

**Differenz** [dɪfə'rɛnts], *f.* (—, *pl.* —en) difference; quarrel.

**Diktat** [dɪk'ta:t], *n.* (—s, *pl.* —e) dictation.

**diktatorisch** [dɪkta'to:rɪʃ], *adj.* dictatorial.

**Diktatur** [dɪkta'tu:r], *f.* (—, *pl.* —en) dictatorship.

**diktieren** [dɪk'ti:rən], *v.a.* dictate.

**Ding** [dɪŋ], *n.* (—s, *pl.* —e) thing, object, matter.

**dingen** ['dɪŋən], *v.a.* hire, engage (a manual worker).

**dingfest** ['dɪŋfɛst], *adj.* — *machen*, arrest.

**dinglich** ['dɪŋlɪç], *adj.* real.

**dinieren** [di'ni:rən], *v.n.* dine.

**Diözese** [diø'tse:zə], *f.* (—, *pl.* —n) diocese.

**Diphtherie** [dɪftə'ri:], *f.* (—, *no pl.*) diphtheria.

**Diplom** [di'plo:m], *n.* (—s, *pl.* —e) diploma.

**Diplomatie** [dɪploma'ti:], *f.* (—, *no pl.*) diplomacy.

**dir** [di:r], *pers. pron. Dat.* to you.

**direkt** [di'rɛkt], *adj.* direct; —*er Wagen*, (*railway*) through carriage; — *danach*, immediately afterwards.

**Direktion** [dirɛkt'sjo:n], *f.* (—, *pl.* —en) direction, management.

**Direktor** [di'rɛktor], *m.* (—s, *pl.* —en) (managing) director, manager; headmaster, principal.

**Direktorium** [dirɛk'to:rjum], *n.* (—s, *pl.* —rien) directorate, board of directors.

**Direktrice** [dirɛk'tri:sə], *f.* (—, *pl.* —n) manageress.

**Dirigent** [diri'gɛnt], *m.* (—en, *pl.* —en) (*Mus.*) conductor; (*Austr. Admin.*) head of section in Ministry.

**dirigieren** [diri'gi:rən], *v.a.* direct, manage; (*Mus.*) conduct.

**Dirndl** ['dɪrndl], *n.* (—s, *pl.* —) (*dial.*) young girl, country wench; (*fig.*) peasant dress, dirndl.

**Dirne** ['dɪrnə], *f.* (—, *pl.* —n) (*Poet.*) girl; prostitute.

**Dis** [dɪs], *n.* (—, *no pl.*) (*Mus.*) D sharp.

**disharmonisch** [dɪshar'mo:nɪʃ], *adj.* discordant.

**Diskant** [dɪs'kant], *m.* (—s, *pl.* —e) (*Mus.*) treble, soprano.

**Diskont** [dɪs'kɔnt], *m.* (—(e)s, *pl.* —e) discount, rebate.

**diskret** [dɪs'kre:t], *adj.* discreet.

**Diskurs** [dɪs'kurs], *m.* (—es, *pl.* —e) discourse.

**diskutieren** [dɪsku'ti:rən], *v.a.* discuss, debate.

**Dispens** [dɪs'pɛns], *m.* (—es, *pl.* —e) dispensation.

**dispensieren** [dɪspɛn'zi:rən], *v.a.* dispense (from), exempt (from).

**disponieren** [dɪspo'ni:rən], *v.n.* — *über*, dispose of; make plans about.

**Dissident** [dɪsi'dɛnt], *m.* (—en, *pl.* —en) dissenter, nonconformist.

**distanzieren** [dɪstan'tsi:rən], *v.r. sich* — *von*, keep o.'s distance from; dissociate o.s. from.

**Distel** ['dɪstəl], *f.* (—, *pl.* —n) thistle.

**Distelfink** ['dɪstəlfɪŋk], *m.* (—s, *pl.* —e) (*Orn.*) gold-finch.

**disziplinarisch** [dɪstsipli'na:rɪʃ], *adj.* diciplinary.

**dito** ['di:to], *adv.* ditto.

# dividieren

**dividieren** [dɪvɪ'diːrən], *v.a.* divide.
**Diwan** ['diːvan], *m.* (—s, *pl.* —e) divan, sofa, couch.
**doch** [dɔx], *adv., conj.* however, though, although, nevertheless, yet, but; after all, (*emphatic*) yes.
**Docht** [dɔxt], *m.* (—es, *pl.* —e) wick.
**Dock** [dɔk], *n.* (—s, *pl.* —s, —e) dock.
**Dogge** ['dɔgə], *f.* (—, *pl.* —n) bulldog, mastiff; Great Dane.
**Dogmatiker** [dɔg'maːtɪkər], *m.* (—s, *pl.* —) dogmatist.
**dogmatisch** [dɔg'maːtɪʃ], *adj.* dogmatic, doctrinal.
**Dohle** ['doːlə], *f.* (—, *pl.* —n) (*Orn.*) jackdaw.
**Doktor** ['dɔktɔr], *m.* (—s, *pl.* —en) doctor; physician, surgeon.
**Dolch** [dɔlç], *m.* (—es, *pl.* —e) dagger, dirk.
**Dolde** ['dɔldə], *f.* (—, *pl.* —n) (*Bot.*) umbel.
**Dolmetscher** ['dɔlmɛtʃər], *m.* (—s, *pl.* —) interpreter.
**dolmetschen** ['dɔlmɛtʃən], *v.a.* interpret.
**Dolomiten** [dolo'miːtən], *pl.* Dolomites.
**Dom** [doːm], *m.* (—s, *pl.* —e) cathedral; dome, cupola.
**Domherr** ['doːmhɛr], *m.* (—n, *pl.* —en) canon, prebendary.
**dominieren** [domi'niːrən], *v.a.* dominate, domineer.
**Dominikaner** [domini'kaːnər], *m.* (—s, *pl.* —) Dominican friar.
**dominikanische Republik** [domini-'kaːnɪʃə repu'bliːk], *f.* Dominican Republic.
**Domizil** [domi'tsiːl], *n.* (—s, *pl.* —e) domicile, residence, address.
**Domkapitel** ['doːmkapiːtəl], *n.* (—s, *pl.* —) dean and chapter.
**Dompfaff** ['doːmpfaf], *m.* (—s, *pl.* —en) (*Orn.*) bullfinch.
**Dompropst** ['doːmproːpst], *m.* (—es, *pl.* ˙e) provost.
**Donau** ['doːnau], *f.* (—, *no pl.*) Danube.
**Donner** ['dɔnər], *m.* (—s, *no pl.*) thunder.
**donnern** ['dɔnərn], *v.n.* thunder; (*fig.*) storm, rage.
**Donnerschlag** ['dɔnərʃlaːk], *m.* (—s, *pl.* ˙e) thunderclap.
**Donnerstag** ['dɔnərstaːk], *m.* (—s, *pl.* —e) Thursday; *Grün* —, Maundy Thursday.
**Donnerwetter** ['dɔnərvɛtər], *n.* (—s, *pl.* —) thunderstorm; *zum* — (*nochmal*)*!* hang it all, confound it!
**doppeldeutig** ['dɔpəldɔytɪç], *adj.* ambiguous.
**Doppelgänger** ['dɔpəlgɛŋər], *m.* (—s, *pl.* —) double.
**Doppellaut** ['dɔpəllaut], *m.* (—s, *pl.* —e) diphthong.
**doppeln** ['dɔpəln] *see* **verdoppeln.**
**doppelsinnig** ['dɔpəlzɪnɪç] *see* **doppeldeutig.**
**doppelt** ['dɔpəlt], *adj.* double, twofold.

**Doppelzwirn** ['dɔpəltsvɪrn], *m.* (—s, *no pl.*) double-thread.
**Dorf** [dɔrf], *n.* (—es, *pl.* ˙er) village.
**dörflich** ['dœrflɪç], *adj.* rural, rustic.
**dorisch** ['doːrɪʃ], *adj.* Doric.
**Dorn** [dɔrn], *m.* (—s, *pl.* —en) thorn, prickle; (*Bot.*) spine; (*buckle*) tongue.
**dornig** ['dɔrnɪç], *adj.* thorny.
**Dornröschen** ['dɔrnrøːsçən], *n.* (—s, *pl.* —) Sleeping Beauty.
**Dorothea** [doro'teːa], *f.* Dorothea, Dorothy.
**dorren** ['dɔrən] *see* **verdorren.**
**dörren** ['dœrən], *v.a.* dry, make dry, parch.
**Dörrobst** ['dœrroːbst], *n.* (—es, *no pl.*) dried fruit.
**Dorsch** [dɔrʃ], *m.* (—es, *pl.* —e) cod, codfish.
**dort** [dɔrt], (*Austr.*) **dorten** ['dɔrtən], *adv.* there, yonder; *von* — *aus*, from that point, from there.
**dorther** ['dɔrtheːr], *adv.* from there, therefrom, thence.
**dorthin** ['dɔrthɪn], *adv.* to that place, thereto, thither.
**dortig** ['dɔrtɪç], *adj.* of that place, local.
**Dose** ['doːzə], *f.* (—, *pl.* —n) box, tin, can.
**dösen** ['døːzən], *v.n.* doze, daydream.
**Dosis** ['doːzɪs], *f.* (—, *pl.* **Dosen**) dose.
**Dotter** ['dɔtər], *n.* (—s, *pl.* —) yolk (of egg).
**Dozent** [do'tsɛnt], *m.* (—en, *pl.* —en) university lecturer; (*Am.*) Assistant Professor.
**dozieren** [do'tsiːrən], *v.n.* lecture.
**Drache** ['draxə], *m.* (—n, *pl.* —n) dragon; kite; (*fig.*) termagant, shrew.
**Dragoner** [dra'goːnər], *m.* (—s, *pl.* —) dragoon.
**Draht** [draːt], *m.* (—es, *pl.* ˙e) wire.
**drahten** ['draːtən], *v.a.* wire, telegraph.
**Drahtgewebe** ['draːtgəveːbə], *n.* (—s, *pl.* —) wire-gauze.
**Drahtgitter** ['draːtgɪtər], *m.* (—s, *pl.* —) wire grating.
**drahtlos** ['draːtloːs], *adj.* wireless.
**Drahtseilbahn** ['draːtsailbaːn], *f.* (—, *pl.* —en) cable (funicular) railway.
**Drahtzange** ['draːttsaŋə], *f.* (—, *pl.* —n) pliers.
**drall** [dral], *adj.* buxom, plump.
**Drama** ['draːma], *n.* (—s, *pl.* —men) drama.
**Dramatiker** [dra'maːtɪkər], *m.* (—s, *pl.* —) dramatist.
**dramatisch** [dra'maːtɪʃ], *adj.* dramatic.
**dran** [dran] *see* **daran.**
**Drang** [draŋ], *m.* (—s, *no pl.*) urge; rush; throng; pressure; impulse.
**drängeln** ['drɛŋəln], *v.a.* jostle.
**drängen** ['drɛŋən], *v.a.* press, urge; *die Zeit drängt*, time presses; *es drängt mich*, I feel called upon.
**Drangsal** ['draŋzaːl], *f. or n.* (—s, *pl.* —e *or* —en) distress, misery.
**drapieren** [dra'piːrən], *v.a.* drape.

48

# Druckerei

**drastisch** ['drastɪʃ], *adj.* drastic.
**drauf** [drauf] *see* **darauf.**
**Draufgänger** ['draufgɛŋər], *m.* (—s, *pl.* —) daredevil.
**draußen** ['drausən], *adv.* outside, without, out of doors.
**drechseln** ['drɛksəln], *v.a.* turn (on a lathe); *Phrasen* —, turn phrases.
**Drechsler** ['drɛkslər], *m.* (—s, *pl.* —) turner.
**Dreck** [drɛk], *m.* (—s, *no pl.*) dirt, mire, dust, filth, dung.
**dreckig** ['drɛkɪç], *adj.* dirty, filthy, muddy.
**drehbar** ['dre:ba:r], *adj.* revolving, swivelling.
**Drehbuch** ['dre:bu:x], *n.* (—s, *pl.* ˙er) (*film*) script.
**drehen** ['dre:ən], *v.a.* turn; (*film*) shoot. — *v.n.* turn round, veer.
**Drehorgel** ['dre:ɔrgəl], *f.* (—, *pl.* —n) barrel-organ.
**Drehrad** ['dre:ra:t], *n.* (—s, *pl.* ˙er) fly-wheel.
**Drehung** ['dre:uŋ], *f.* (—, *pl.* —en) rotation, turn, revolution.
**drei** [draɪ], *num. adj.* three.
**dreiblätterig** ['draɪblɛtərɪç], *adj.* trifoliate.
**Dreieck** ['draɪɛk], *n.* (—s, *pl.* —e) triangle.
**dreieckig** ['draɪɛkɪç], *adj.* triangular, three-cornered.
**dreieinig** [draɪ'aɪnɪç], *adj.* (*Theol.*) triune.
**dreifach** ['draɪfax], *adj.* threefold, triple.
**Dreifaltigkeit** [draɪ'faltɪçkaɪt], *f.* (—, *no pl.*) (*Theol.*) Trinity.
**Dreifuß** ['draɪfu:s], *m.* (—es, *pl.* ˙e) tripod.
**dreijährlich** ['draɪjɛrlɪç], *adj.* triennial.
**Dreikönigsfest** [draɪ'kø:nɪksfɛst], *n.* (—es, *no pl.*) Epiphany.
**dreimonatlich** ['draɪmo:natlɪç], *adj.* quarterly.
**Dreirad** ['draɪra:t], *n.* (—s, *pl.* ˙er) tricycle.
**dreiseitig** ['draɪzaɪtɪç], *adj.* trilateral.
**dreißig** ['draɪsɪç], *num. adj.* thirty.
**dreist** [draɪst], *adj.* bold, audacious; impudent.
**dreistellig** ['draɪʃtɛlɪç], *adj.* —e Zahl, number of three figures.
**dreistimmig** ['draɪʃtɪmɪç], *adj.* for three voices.
**Dreistufenrakete** ['draɪʃtu:fənra'ke:tə], *f.* (—, *pl.* —n) three-stage rocket.
**dreistündig** ['draɪʃtyndɪç], *adj.* lasting three hours.
**dreitägig** ['draɪtɛ:gɪç], *adj.* lasting three days.
**dreiteilig** ['draɪtaɪlɪç], *adj.* tripartite; three-piece.
**dreizehn** ['draɪtse:n], *num. adj.* thirteen.
**Drell** [drɛl], *m.* (—s, *no pl.*) *see* **Drillich.**
**Dresche** ['drɛʃə], *f.* (—, *no pl.*) thrashing, beating.
**dreschen** ['drɛʃən], *v.a. irr.* (*corn*) thresh; (*person*) thrash.

**Dreschflegel** ['drɛʃfle:gəl], *m.* (—s, *pl.* —) flail.
**dressieren** [drɛ'si:rən], *v.a.* (*animal*) train; break in.
**Dressur** [drɛ'su:r], *f.* (—, *pl.* —en) training, breaking-in.
**Drillbohrer** ['drɪlbo:rər], *m.* (—s, *pl.* —) drill.
**drillen** ['drɪlən], *v.a.* (*a hole*) bore; (*soldiers*) drill.
**Drillich** ['drɪlɪç], *m.* (—s, *pl.* —e) drill, canvas.
**Drilling** ['drɪlɪŋ], *m.* (—s, *pl.* —e) three-barrelled gun; (*pl.*) triplets.
**drin** [drɪn] *see* **darin.**
**dringen** ['drɪŋən], *v.n. irr.* penetrate, force o.'s way through; *auf etwas* —, insist on s.th.
**dringlich** ['drɪŋlɪç], *adj.* urgent, pressing.
**drinnen** ['drɪnən], *adv.* inside, within.
**drittens** ['drɪtəns], *adv.* thirdly.
**droben** ['dro:bən], *adv.* up there, above, aloft, overhead.
**Droge** ['dro:gə], *f.* (—, *pl.* —n) drug.
**Drogerie** [dro:gə'ri:], *f.* (—, *pl.* —n) druggist's shop, chemist's; (*Am.*) drugstore.
**drohen** ['dro:ən], *v.a., v.n.* threaten, menace.
**Drohne** ['dro:nə], *f.* (—, *pl.* —n) drone.
**dröhnen** ['drø:nən], *v.n.* boom, roar.
**Drohung** ['dro:uŋ], *f.* (—, *pl.* —en) threat, menace.
**drollig** ['drɔlɪç], *adj.* droll, odd, quaint.
**Dromedar** [drɔmə'da:r], *n.* (—s, *pl.* —e) dromedary.
**Droschke** ['drɔʃkə], *f.* (—, *pl.* —n) cab, hansom, taxi.
**Drossel** ['drɔsəl], *f.* (—, *pl.* —n) thrush.
**Drosselader** ['drɔsəla:dər], *f.* (—, *pl.* —n) jugular vein.
**Drosselbein** ['drɔsəlbaɪn], *n.* (—s, *pl.* —e) collar-bone.
**drosseln** ['drɔsəln], *v.a.* throttle. *See also* **erdrosseln.**
**drüben** ['dry:bən], *adv.* over there, on the other side.
**drüber** ['dry:bər] *see* **darüber.**
**Druck** [druk], *m.* (—s, *pl.* ˙e, —e) pressure, squeeze; (*Phys.*) compression; (*Typ.*) impression, print; (*fig.*) hardship.
**Druckbogen** ['drukbo:gən], *m.* (—s, *pl.* —) proof-sheet, proof.
**Druckbuchstabe** ['drukbu:xʃta:bə], *m.* (—n, *pl.* —n) letter, type.
**Drückeberger** ['drykəbɛrgər], *m.* (—s, *pl.* —) slacker, shirker.
**drucken** ['drukən], *v.a.* print.
**drücken** ['drykən], *v.a.* press, squeeze; trouble, oppress. — *v.r. sich* —, sneak away, shirk.
**Drucker** ['drukər], *m.* (—s, *pl.* —) printer.
**Drücker** ['drykər], *m.* (—s, *pl.* —) (*door*) handle, latch; (*gun*) trigger.
**Druckerei** ['drukəraɪ], *f.* (—, *pl.* —en) printing shop.

# Druckerschwärze

**Druckerschwärze** ['drukərʃvɛrtsə], *f.* (—, *no pl.*) printing-ink.

**Druckfehler** ['drukfeːlər], *m.* (—s, *pl.* —) misprint, printer's error.

**druckfertig** ['drukfɛrtɪç], *adj.* ready for press.

**Drucksache** ['drukzaxə], *f.* (—, *pl.* —n) (*Postal*) printed matter.

**drum** [drum] *see* **darum.**

**drunten** ['druntən], *adv.* down there, below.

**drunter** ['druntər] *see* **darunter.**

**Drüse** ['dryːzə], *f.* (—, *pl.* —n) gland.

**Dschungel** ['dʒuŋəl], *m.* or *n.* (—s, *pl.* —) jungle.

**du** [duː], *pers. pron.* thou, you.

**ducken** ['dukən], *v.a.* bring down, humble. — *v.r. sich* —, duck, stoop, crouch.

**dudeln** ['duːdəln], *v.n.* play the bagpipes; tootle.

**Dudelsack** ['duːdəlzak], *m.* (—s, *pl.* ̈e) bagpipe(s).

**Duft** [duft], *m.* (—s, *pl.* ̈e) scent, odour, fragrance, aroma, perfume.

**duften** ['duftən], *v.n.* be fragrant.

**duftig** ['duftɪç], *adj.* fragrant, odoriferous, perfumed.

**dulden** ['duldən], *v.a.* suffer, endure, bear, tolerate.

**duldsam** ['dultzaːm], *adj.* tolerant, indulgent, patient.

**dumm** [dum], *adj.* stupid, foolish, dull.

**Dummheit** ['dumhaɪt], *f.* (—, *pl.* —en) stupidity, folly.

**dumpf** [dumpf], *adj.* musty; (*air*) close; (*sound*) hollow; (*fig.*) gloomy.

**dumpfig** ['dumpfɪç], *adj.* damp, musty, stuffy.

**Düne** ['dyːnə], *f.* (—, *pl.* —n) dune, sand-hill.

**Düngemittel** ['dyŋəmɪtəl], *n.* (—s, *pl.* —) fertilizer.

**düngen** ['dyŋən], *v.a.* manure, fertilize.

**Dünger** ['dyŋər], *m.* (—s, *no pl.*) compost, artificial manure.

**dunkel** ['duŋkəl], *adj.* dark; (*fig.*) obscure, mysterious.

**Dünkel** ['dyŋkəl], *m.* (—s, *no pl.*) conceit, arrogance.

**dünkelhaft** ['dyŋkəlhaft], *adj.* conceited, arrogant.

**Dunkelheit** ['duŋkəlhaɪt], *f.* (—, *no pl.*) darkness, obscurity.

**dunkeln** ['duŋkəln], *v.n.* grow dark.

**dünken** ['dyŋkən], *v.n.* (*rare*) seem, appear. — *v.r. sich* —, fancy o.s., imagine o.s.

**dünn** [dyn], *adj.* thin, slim, weak.

**Dunst** [dunst], *m.* (—es, *pl.* ̈e) vapour, fume; exhalation; haze; *einem blauen* — *vormachen,* humbug a p.

**dünsten** ['dynstən], *v.a.* stew.

**dunstig** ['dunstɪç], *adj.* misty, hazy.

**Dunstkreis** ['dunstkraɪs], *m.* (—es, *pl.* —e) atmosphere.

**Dunstobst** ['dunstoːpst], *n.* (—es, *no pl.*) stewed fruit.

**duodez** [duo'deːts], *adj.* (*Typ.*) duodecimo (12mo).

**Duodezfürst** [duo'deːtsfyrst], *m.* (—en, *pl.* —en) petty prince, princeling.

**Dur** [duːr], *n.* (*Mus.*) major; sharp.

**durch** [durç], *prep.* (*Acc.*) (*local*) through, across; (*temporal*) during, throughout; (*manner*) by means of, by. — *adv.* thoroughly, through.

**durchaus** [durç'aus], *adv.* throughout, quite, by all means, absolutely.

**Durchblick** ['durçblɪk], *m.* (—s, *pl.* —e) vista, view.

**durchbohren** [durç'boːrən], *v.a. insep.* perforate, pierce.

**durchbrennen** ['durçbrɛnən], *v.n. irr.* (*aux.* sein) abscond, bolt.

**durchbringen** ['durçbrɪŋən], *v.a. irr.* bring through, get through; squander (money); pull (a sick person) through. — *v.r. sich redlich* —, make an honest living.

**Durchbruch** ['durçbrux], *m.* (—s, *pl.* ̈e) breach, break-through.

**durchdrängen** ['durçdrɛŋən], *v.r. sich* —, force o.'s way through.

**durchdringen** ['durçdrɪŋən], *v.n. irr. sep.* (*aux.* sein) get through. — [durç'drɪŋən], *v.a. irr. insep.* penetrate, pierce, permeate, pervade.

**durchdrücken** ['durçdrykən], *v.a.* press through; (*fig.*) carry through.

**durcheilen** [durç'aɪlən], *v.a. insep.* hurry through.

**Durcheinander** [durçaɪn'andər], *n.* (—s, *no pl.*) confusion, muddle.

**durcheinander** [durçaɪn'andər], *adv.* in confusion, pell-mell.

**Durchfall** ['durçfal], *m.* (—s, *no pl.*) diarrhoea; (*exams etc.*) failure.

**durchfallen** ['durçfalən], *v.n. irr.* (*aux.* sein) fall through, come to nought; (*exams etc.*) fail.

**durchflechten** [durç'flɛçtən], *v.a. irr.* interweave, intertwine.

**durchfliegen** [durç'fliːgən], *v.a. irr.* fly through; read superficially, skim through.

**durchforschen** [durç'fɔrʃən], *v.a. insep.* explore, scrutinise, examine thoroughly.

**Durchfuhr** ['durçfuːr], *f.* (—, *pl.* —en) passage, transit.

**durchführbar** ['durçfyːrbaːr], *adj.* practicable, feasible.

**durchführen** ['durçfyːrən], *v.a.* escort through; (*fig.*) execute, bring about, carry through.

**Durchgang** ['durçgaŋ], *m.* (—s, *pl.* ̈e) passage, thoroughfare; (*Comm.*) transit.

**Durchgänger** ['durçgɛŋər], *m.* (—s, *pl.* —) runaway horse, bolter; (*fig.*) hothead.

**durchgängig** ['durçgɛŋɪç], *adj.* general, universal.

**durchgehen** ['durçgeːən], *v.n. irr.* (*aux.* sein) go through; (*fig.*) abscond; (*horse*) bolt; (*proposal*) be carried. — *v.a. irr.* (*aux.* sein) peruse, review, go over.

**durchgreifen** ['durçgraɪfən], *v.n. irr.* act decisively, take strong action.

**durchhauen** ['durçhauən], *v.a. irr.* cut through; *einen* —, flog s.o.

**durchkommen** ['durçkɔmən], *v.n. irr.* (*aux.* sein) get through; (*exams etc.*) pass.

**durchkreuzen** [durç'krɔytsən], *v.a. insep.* cross out; (*fig.*) thwart.

**durchlassen** ['durçlasən], *v.a. irr.* let pass.

**Durchlaucht** ['durçlauxt], *f.* (— *pl.* —en) Highness.

**durchleuchten** [durç'lɔyçtən], *v.a. insep.* (*Med.*) X-ray.

**durchlöchern** [durç'lœçərn], *v.a. insep.* perforate, riddle.

**durchmachen** ['durçmaxən], *v.a.* go through, suffer.

**Durchmesser** ['durçmɛsər], *m.* (—s, *pl.* —) diameter.

**durchnässen** [durç'nɛsən], *v.a. insep.* wet to the skin, soak.

**durchnehmen** ['durçne:mən], *v.a. irr.* go over *or* cover (a subject).

**durchpausen** ['durçpauzən], *v.a.* trace, copy.

**durchqueren** [durç'kve:rən], *v.a. insep.* cross, traverse.

**Durchsage** ['durçza:gə], *f.* (—, *pl.* —n) (radio) announcement.

**durchschauen** [durç'ʃauən], *v.a. insep. einen* —, see through s.o.

**durchscheinend** ['durçʃaɪnənt], *adj.* transparent, translucent.

**Durchschlag** ['durçʃla:k], *m.* (—s, *pl.* ⸚e) strainer, sieve, colander, filter; carbon copy.

**durchschlagen** ['durçʃla:gən], *v.a. irr. insep.* strain, filter. — *v.r. irr. sich* —, fight o.'s way through.

**durchschlagend** ['durçʃla:gənt], *adj.* thorough, complete, effective.

**Durchschnitt** ['durçʃnɪt], *m.* (—s, *pl.* —e) average; (*Med. etc.*) cross section.

**durchschnittlich** ['durçʃnɪtlɪç], *adj.* average; ordinary.

**durchschossen** [durç'ʃɔsən], *adj.* inter-leaved; interwoven.

**durchseihen** ['durçzaɪən], *v.a. see* **durchsieben**.

**durchsetzen** [durç'zɛtsən], *v.a. insep.* intersperse; ['durçzɛtsən], *v.a. sep.* have o.'s way (with s.o.). — *v.r. sep. sich* —, make o.'s way successfully, succeed.

**Durchsicht** ['durçzɪçt], *f.* (—, *no pl.*) revision, inspection, perusal.

**durchsichtig** ['durçzɪçtɪç], *adj.* trans-parent.

**durchsickern** ['durçzɪkərn], *v.n.* (*aux.* sein) trickle through, ooze through.

**durchsieben** ['durçzi:bən], *v.a.* strain, filter, sift.

**durchsprechen** ['durçʃprɛçən], *v.a. irr.* talk over, discuss.

**durchstöbern** [durç'ʃtø:bərn], *v.a. insep.* rummage through.

**durchstreichen** ['durçʃtraɪçən], *v.a. irr.* cross out, delete.

**durchstreifen** [durç'ʃtraɪfən], *v.a. insep.* roam (through).

**durchströmen** [durç'ʃtrø:mən], *v.a. insep.* flow through, permeate.

**durchsuchen** [durç'zu:xən], *v.a. insep.* search thoroughly, examine closely.

**durchtrieben** [durç'tri:bən], *adj.* artful, sly, cunning, crafty.

**durchweben** [durç've:bən], *v.a.* inter-weave.

**durchweg(s)** ['durçvek(s)], *adv.* with-out exception, every time, throughout.

**durchwühlen** [durç'vy:lən], *v.a. insep.* search; ransack.

**durchziehen** [durç'tsi:ən], *v.a. irr. insep.* wander through, traverse; ['durçtsi:ən], *v.a. irr. sep.* interlace (with threads); draw through.

**durchzucken** [durç'tsukən], *v.a. insep.* flash through, convulse.

**Durchzug** ['durçtsu:k], *m.* (—s, *no pl.*) passage, march through; (*air*) draught.

**dürfen** ['dyrfən], *v.n. irr.* be permitted; be allowed; dare; be likely.

**dürftig** ['dyrftɪç], *adj.* paltry, insuffi-cient, poor.

**dürr** [dyr], *adj.* dry, arid, withered; (*wood*) dead; (*persons*) thin, gaunt.

**Dürre** ['dyrə], *f.* (—, *pl.* —n) aridity, dryness; drought; (*persons*) thinness.

**Durst** [durst], *m.* (—es, *no pl.*) thirst.

**dürsten** ['dyrstən], *v.n.* thirst.

**durstig** ['durstɪç], *adj.* thirsty.

**Dusche** ['du:ʃə], *f.* (—, *pl.* —n) shower (bath).

**Düse** ['dy:zə], *f.* (—, *pl.* —n) jet.

**duselig** ['du:zəlɪç], *adj.* drowsy; silly.

**düster** ['dy:stər], *adj.* dark, gloomy; sad, mournful; sombre.

**Dutzend** ['dutsənt], *n.* (—s, *pl.* —e) dozen.

**Duzbruder** ['du:tsbru:dər], *m.* (—s, *pl.* ⸚) crony, chum; close friend.

**duzen** ['du:tsen], *v.a.* be on close terms with.

**dynamisch** [dy'na:mɪʃ], *adj.* dyna-mic(al).

# E

**E** [e:], *n.* (—s, *pl.* —s) the letter E; (*Mus.*) E Dur, E major; E Moll, E minor.

**Ebbe** ['ɛbə], *f.* (—, *pl.* —n) ebb, low tide; — *und Flut*, the tides.

**ebben** ['ɛbən], *v.n.* ebb.

**eben** ['e:bən], *adj.* even, level, plane; (*fig.*) plain. — *adv.* precisely, exactly.

**Ebenbild** ['e:bənbɪlt], *n.* (—es, *pl.* —er) likeness, image.

**ebenbürtig** ['e:bənbyrtɪç], *adj.* of equal birth *or* rank; equal.

# ebenda

**ebenda** ['e:bənda:], *adv.* in the same place.

**ebendeswegen** ['e:bəndɛsve:gən], *adv.* for that very reason.

**Ebene** ['e:bənə], *f.* (—, *pl.* —n) plain; level ground; (*Maths.*) plane; *schiefe* —, inclined plane.

**ebenfalls** ['e:bənfals], *adv.* likewise, also, too, as well.

**Ebenholz** ['e:bənhɔlts], *n.* (—es, *no pl.*) ebony.

**Ebenmaß** ['e:bənma:s], *n.* (—es, *pl.* —e) symmetry.

**ebenmäßig** ['e:bənmɛ:sɪç], *adj.* symmetrical.

**ebenso** ['e:bənzo:], *adv.* in the same way; — *wie*, just as . . .

**Eber** ['e:bər], *m.* (—s, *pl.* —) (*Zool.*) boar.

**Eberesche** ['e:bərɛʃə], *f.* (—, *pl.* —n) (*Bot.*) mountain ash, rowan.

**ebnen** ['e:bnən], *v.a.* even out, level; smoothe.

**echt** [ɛçt], *adj.* genuine, real, true, authentic, pure.

**Ecke** ['ɛkə], *f.* (—, *pl.* —en) corner, nook.

**eckig** ['ɛkɪç], *adj.* angular.

**Eckzahn** ['ɛktsa:n], *m.* (—s, *pl.* ⸚e) eye tooth; canine tooth.

**Eckziegel** ['ɛktsi:gəl], *m.* (—s, *pl.* —) (*Build.*) header.

**edel** ['e:dəl], *adj.* noble; well-born, aristocratic; (*metal*) precious.

**Edelmann** ['e:dəlman], *m.* (—s, *pl.* **Edelleute**) nobleman, aristocrat.

**Edelmut** ['e:dəlmu:t], *m.* (—s, *no pl.*) generosity, magnanimity.

**Edelstein** ['e:dəlʃtain], *m.* (—s, *pl.* —e) precious stone, jewel.

**Edeltanne** ['e:dəltanə], *f.* (—, *pl.* —n) (*Bot.*) silver fir.

**Edelweiß** ['e:dəlvais], *n.* (—sses, *no pl.*) (*Bot.*) edelweiss; lion's foot.

**Eduard** ['e:duart], *m.* Edward.

**Efeu** ['e:fɔy], *m.* (—s, *no pl.*) (*Bot.*) ivy.

**Effekten** [e'fɛktən], *m. pl.* goods and chattels; effects; stocks, securities.

**Effektenbörse** [e'fɛktənbœrzə], *f.* (—, *pl.* —n) Stock Exchange.

**Effekthascherei** [e'fɛkthaʃərai], *f.* (—, *pl.* —en) sensationalism, clap-trap.

**effektuieren** [efɛktu'i:rən], *v.a.* (*Comm.*) execute, effectuate.

**egal** [e'ga:l], *adj.* equal; all the same.

**Egge** ['ɛgə], *f.* (—, *pl.* —n) harrow.

**Egoismus** [ego'ɪsmus], *m.* (—, *no pl.*) selfishness, egoism.

**egoistisch** [ego'ɪstiʃ], *adj.* selfish, egoistic(al).

**Ehe** ['e:ə], *f.* (—, *pl.* —n) marriage.

**ehe** ['e:ə], *conj.* before; *adv.* formerly; *je* —*r*, *desto besser*, the sooner, the better.

**Ehebrecher** ['e:əbrɛçər], *m.* (—s, *pl.* —) adulterer.

**Ehebruch** ['e:əbrux], *m.* (—s, *pl.* ⸚e) adultery.

**Ehefrau** ['e:əfrau], *f.* (—, *pl.* —en) wife, spouse, consort.

**Ehegatte** ['e:əgatə], *m.* (—n, *pl.* —n) husband, spouse.

**ehelich** ['e:əlɪç], *adj.* matrimonial; (*children*) legitimate.

**Ehelosigkeit** ['e:olo:zɪçkait], *f.* (—, *no pl.*) celibacy.

**ehemalig** ['e:əma:lɪç], *adj.* former, late.

**ehemals** ['e:əma:ls], *adv.* formerly, once, of old.

**Ehemann** ['e:əman], *m.* (—s, *pl.* ⸚er) husband.

**ehern** ['e:ərn], *adj.* brazen; of brass, of bronze.

**Ehestand** ['e:əʃtant], *m.* (—s, *no pl.*) matrimony.

**ehestens** ['e:əstəns], *adv.* as soon as possible.

**Ehre** ['e:rə], *f.* (—, *pl.* —n) honour, reputation, respect, distinction, glory.

**ehren** ['e:rən], *v.a.* honour, respect, esteem; *sehr geehrter Herr*, dear Sir.

**Ehrenbezeigung** ['e:rənbətsaiguŋ], *f.* (—, *pl.* —en) mark of respect; (*Mil.*) salute.

**Ehrenbürger** ['e:rənbyrgər], *m.* (—s, *pl.* —) honorary citizen *or* freeman.

**Ehrendame** ['e:rəndaːmə], *f.* (—, *pl.* —n) maid of honour.

**Ehrenerklärung** ['e:rənɛrklɛ:ruŋ], *f.* (—, *pl.* —en) reparation, apology.

**Ehrengericht** ['e:rəngərɪçt], *n.* (—s, *pl.* —e) court of honour.

**ehrenhaft** ['e:rənhaft], *adj.* honourable, worthy.

**Ehrenpreis** ['e:rənprais], *m.* (—es, *pl.* —e) prize; (*no pl.*) (*Bot.*) speedwell.

**Ehrenrettung** ['e:rənretuŋ], *f.* (—, *pl.* —en) vindication.

**ehrenrührig** ['e:rənry:rɪç], *adj.* defamatory, calumnious.

**ehrenvoll** ['e:rənfɔl], *adj.* honourable.

**ehrenwert** ['e:rənvert], *adj.* honourable, respectable.

**ehrerbietig** ['e:rərbi:tɪç], *adj.* reverential, respectful.

**Ehrfurcht** ['e:rfurçt], *f.* (—, *no pl.*) reverence, awe.

**Ehrgefühl** ['e:rgəfy:l], *n.* (—s, *no pl.*) sense of honour.

**Ehrgeiz** ['e:rgaits], *m.* (—es, *no pl.*) ambition.

**ehrlich** ['e:rlɪç], *adj.* honest; — *währt am längsten*, honesty is the best policy.

**ehrlos** ['e:rlo:s], *adj.* dishonourable, infamous.

**ehrsam** ['e:rza:m], *adj.* respectable, honourable.

**Ehrwürden** ['e:rvyrdən], *m. & f.* (*form of address*) *Euer* —, Reverend Sir, Your Reverence.

**ehrwürdig** ['e:rvyrdɪç], *adj.* venerable, reverend.

**Ei** [ai], *n.* (—s, *pl.* —er) egg, ovum.

**ei** [ai], *int.* ay, indeed.

**Eibe** ['aibə], *f.* (—, *pl.* —n) (*Bot.*) yew.

**Eichamt** ['aiçamt], *n.* (—s, *pl.* ⸚er) office of weights and measures; (*Am.*) bureau of standards.

**Eichapfel** ['aɪçapfəl], *m.* (—s, *pl.* ∵) oak apple.

**Eiche** ['aɪçə], *f.* (—, *pl.* —n) (*Bot.*) oak.

**Eichel** ['aɪçəl], *f.* (—, *pl.* —n) acorn; (*Anat.*) glans; (*Cards*) clubs.

**eichen** (1) ['aɪçən], *v.a.* gauge, calibrate.

**eichen** (2) ['aɪçən], *adj.* made of oak.

**Eichhörnchen** ['aɪçhœrnçən] or **Eich-kätzchen** ['aɪçkɛtsçən], *n.* (—s, *pl.* —) squirrel.

**Eid** [aɪt], *m.* (—es, *pl.* —e) oath; *falscher* —, perjury.

**Eidam** ['aɪdam], *m.* (—s, *pl.* —e) (*obs.*) son-in-law.

**eidbrüchig** ['aɪtbryçɪç], *adj.* guilty of perjury.

**Eidechse** ['aɪdɛksə], *f.* (—, *pl.* —n) lizard.

**Eidesleistung** ['aɪdəslaɪstuŋ], *f.* (—, *pl.* —en) affidavit.

**Eidgenosse** ['aɪtgənosə], *m.* (—n, ∵*pl.* —n) confederate.

**Eidgenossenschaft** ['aɪtgenosənʃaft], *f.* (—, *pl.* —en) confederacy.

**eidlich** ['aɪtlɪç], *adj.* by oath, sworn.

**Eidotter** ['aɪdɔtər], *m. & n.* (—s, *pl.* —) yolk of an egg.

**Eierbecher** ['aɪərbɛçər], *m.* (—s, *pl.* —) egg cup.

**Eierkuchen** ['aɪərku:xən], *m.* (—s, *pl.* —) omelet(te), pancake.

**Eierschale** ['aɪərʃa:lə], *f.* (—, *pl.* —n) egg shell.

**Eierspeise** ['aɪərʃpaɪzə], *f.* (—, *pl.* —n) dish prepared with eggs.

**Eierstock** ['aɪərʃtɔk], *m.* (—s, *pl.* ∵e) ovary.

**Eifer** ['aɪfər], *m.* (—s, *no pl.*) zeal, eagerness, ardour, haste, passion, vehemence.

**Eiferer** ['aɪfərər], *m.* (—s, *pl.* —) zealot.

**eifern** ['aɪfərn], *v.n.* be zealous; *gegen einen* —, inveigh against s.o.

**eiförmig** ['aɪfœrmɪç], *adj.* oval, egg-shaped.

**eifrig** ['aɪfrɪç], *adj.* zealous, ardent, eager.

**Eigelb** ['aɪgɛlp], *n.* (—s, *pl.* —) yolk of (an) egg.

**eigen** ['aɪgən], *adj.* own; particular, peculiar.

**Eigenart** ['aɪgəna:rt], *f.* (—, *pl.* —en) peculiarity; idiosyncrasy.

**eigenhändig** ['aɪgənhɛndɪç], *adj.* with o.'s own hand.

**Eigenheit** ['aɪgənhaɪt], *f.* (—, *pl.* —en) peculiarity; idiosyncrasy.

**eigenmächtig** ['aɪgənmɛçtɪç], *adj.* arbitrary, autocratic, high-handed.

**Eigenname** ['aɪgənna:mə], *m.* (—ns, *pl.* —n) proper name.

**Eigennutz** ['aɪgənnuts], *m.* (—es, *no pl.*) self-interest, selfishness.

**eigennützig** ['aɪgənnytsɪç], *adj.* selfish, self-interested, self-seeking.

**eigens** ['aɪgəns], *adv.* particularly, specially.

**Eigenschaft** ['aɪgənʃaft], *f.* (—, *pl.* —en) quality, peculiarity; property.

**Eigenschaftswort** ['aɪgənʃaftsvɔrt], *n.* (—s, *pl.* ∵er) (*Gram.*) adjective.

**Eigensinn** ['aɪgənzɪn], *m.* (—s, *no pl.*) obstinacy.

**eigentlich** ['aɪgəntlɪç], *adj.* true, real; exact, literal.

**Eigentum** ['aɪgəntu:m], *n.* (—s, *pl.* ∵er) property, possession, estate.

**Eigentümer** ['aɪgənty:mər], *m.* (—s, *pl.* —) owner, proprietor.

**eigenwillig** ['aɪgənvɪlɪç], *adj.* self-willed.

**eignen** ['aɪgnən], *v.r. sich* — *für* (*zu*), suit, fit, be suitable *or* fit for (to).

**Eilbote** ['aɪlbo:tə], *m.* (—n, *pl.* —n) special messenger.

**Eile** ['aɪlə], *f.* (—, *no pl.*) haste, hurry.

**eilen** ['aɪlən], *v.n.* (*aux.* sein), *v.r.* (*sich* —), hasten, hurry; be urgent.

**eilends** ['aɪlənts], *adv.* hastily.

**eilfertig** ['aɪlfɛrtɪç], *adj.* hasty.

**Eilgut** ['aɪlgu:t], *n.* (—s, *pl.* ∵er) express goods.

**eilig** ['aɪlɪç], *adj.* hasty, speedy; pressing, urgent.

**Eilzug** ['aɪltsu:k], *m.* (—s, *pl.* ∵e) fast train.

**Eimer** ['aɪmər], *m.* (—s, *pl.* —) pail, bucket.

**ein(e)** ['aɪn(ə)], *indef. art,* a, an; *was für* —; what kind of a(n). — *num. adj.* one; — *jeder*, each one.

**einander** [aɪn'andər], *adv.* each other, one another.

**einarbeiten** ['aɪnarbaɪtən], *v.a.* train, familiarize s.o. with. —*v.r.* (*aux.* haben) *sich* —, familiarize o.s.

**einäschern** ['aɪnɛʃərn], *v.a.* reduce to ashes, incinerate; cremate.

**einatmen** ['aɪna:tmən], *v.a.* breathe in, inhale.

**einätzen** ['aɪnɛtsən], *v.a.* etch in.

**einäugig** ['aɪnɔygɪç], *adj.* one-eyed.

**Einbahnstraße** ['aɪnba:nʃtra:sə], *f.* (—, *pl.* —n) one-way street.

**Einband** ['aɪnbant], *m.* (—s, *pl.* ∵e) binding, cover of book.

**einbändig** ['aɪnbɛndɪç], *adj.* in one volume.

**einbauen** ['aɪnbauən], *v.a.* build in.

**einbegreifen** ['aɪnbəgraɪfən], *v.a. irr.* include, comprise.

**einberufen** ['aɪnbəru:fən], *v.a. irr.* convene, convoke; (*Mil.*) call up.

**einbeziehen** ['aɪnbətsi:ən], *v.a. irr.* include.

**einbiegen** ['aɪnbi:gən], *v.n. irr.* turn into (road).

**einbilden** ['aɪnbɪldən], *v.r. sich* —, imagine, fancy.

**Einbildung** ['aɪnbɪlduŋ], *f.* (—, *pl.* —en) imagination, fancy, delusion; conceit.

**einbinden** ['aɪnbɪndən], *v.a. irr.* (*book*) bind.

**Einblick** ['aɪnblɪk], *m.* (—s, *no pl.*) insight.

**Einbrecher** ['aɪnbrɛçər], *m.* (—s, *pl.* —) burglar; intruder.

**Einbrenne** ['aɪnbrɛnə], *f.* (—, *pl.* **—n**) thickening of soup.
**einbringen** ['aɪnbrɪŋən], *v.a. irr.* bring in, yield, fetch (a price); *wieder* —, retrieve.
**einbrocken** ['aɪnbrɔkən], *v.a.* crumble; *einem etwas* —, (*fig.*) get s.o. into trouble.
**Einbruch** ['aɪnbrux], *m.* (**—s,** *pl.* **¨e**) breaking-in; burglary, house-breaking.
**Einbuchtung** ['aɪnbuxtuŋ], *f.* (—, *pl.* **—en**) bight, bay.
**einbürgern** ['aɪnbyrgərn], *v.a.* naturalise.
**Einbuße** ['aɪnbu:sə], *f.* (—, *pl.* **—n**) loss.
**einbüßen** ['aɪnby:sən], *v.a.* suffer a loss from, lose, forfeit.
**eindämmen** ['aɪndɛmən], *v.a.* dam in (*or* up).
**Eindecker** ['aɪndɛkər], *m.* (**—s,** *pl.* —) (*Aviat.*) monoplane.
**eindeutig** ['aɪndɔytɪç], *adj.* unequivocal, unambiguous.
**eindrängen** ['aɪndrɛŋən], *v.r. sich* —, intrude (into), force o.'s way in(to), interfere.
**eindrillen** ['aɪndrɪlən], *v.a. einem etwas* —, drum s.th. into s.o.
**eindringen** ['aindrɪŋən], *v.n. irr.* (*aux.* sein) enter, intrude; invade; penetrate.
**eindringlich** ['aɪndrɪŋlɪç], *adj.* forceful, urgent; impressive.
**Eindruck** ['aɪndruk], *m.* (**—s,** *pl.* **¨e**) impression.
**eindrücken** ['aɪndrykən], *v.a.* press in, squeeze in.
**eindrucksfähig** ['aɪndruksfɛ:ɪç], *adj.* impressionable.
**einengen** ['aɪnɛŋən], *v.a.* compress, limit, confine, cramp.
**Einer** ['aɪnər], *m.* (**—s,** *pl.* —) (*Maths.*) digit, unit.
**einerlei** ['aɪnərlaɪ], *adj.* the same, all the same.
**einerseits** ['aɪnərzaɪts], *adv.* on the one hand.
**einfach** ['aɪnfax], *adj.* single; simple, plain, uncomplicated; modest, homely.
**einfädeln** ['aɪnfɛ:dəln], *v.a.* thread.
**einfahren** ['aɪnfa:rən], *v.n. irr.* (*aux.* sein) drive in, enter. — *v.a.* run in (new car).
**Einfahrt** ['aɪnfa:rt], *f.* (—, *pl.* **—en**) entrance, gateway, drive; (*Min.*) descent.
**Einfall** ['aɪnfal], *m.* (**—s,** *pl.* **¨e**) falling-in, downfall, fall; (*Mil.*) invasion; (*fig.*) idea, inspiration.
**einfallen** ['aɪnfalən], *v.n. irr.* (*aux.* sein) fall in, fall into; (*Mil.*) invade; (*fig.*) occur to s.o.
**Einfalt** ['aɪnfalt], *f.* (—, *no pl.*) simplicity; silliness.
**Einfaltspinsel** ['aɪnfaltspɪnzəl], *m.* (**—s,** *pl.* —) simpleton, dunce.
**einfangen** ['aɪnfaŋən], *v.a. irr.* catch, get hold of.
**einfarbig** ['aɪnfarbɪç], *adj.* of one colour; monochrome.
**einfassen** ['aɪnfasən], *v.a.* border, trim; (*diamonds*) set.
**Einfassung** ['aɪnfasuŋ], *f.* (—, *pl.* **—en**) bordering, trimming, edging, framing.
**einfetten** ['aɪnfɛtən], *v.a.* grease, lubricate.
**einfinden** ['aɪnfɪndən], *v.r. irr. sich* —, appear, be present.
**einflechten** ['aɪnflɛctən], *v.a. irr.* plait; (*fig.*) insert.
**einfließen** ['aɪnfli:sən], *v.n. irr.* (*aux.* sein) flow in; — *lassen*, (*fig.*) mention casually, slip in (a word).
**einflößen** ['aɪnflø:sən], *v.a.* infuse; (*fig.*) instil, inspire with.
**Einfluß** ['aɪnflus], *m.* (**—sses,** *pl.* **¨sse**) influx; (*fig.*) influence.
**einflußreich** ['aɪnflusraɪç], *adj.* influential.
**einflüstern** ['aɪnflystərn], *v.n.* suggest, insinuate.
**einförmig** ['aɪnfœrmɪç], *adj.* uniform; monotonous.
**einfriedigen** ['aɪnfri:dɪgən], *v.a.* fence in, enclose.
**einfügen** ['aɪnfy:gən], *v.a.* insert, include, fit in. — *v.r. sich* —, adapt o.s., become a part of.
**Einfühlungsvermögen** ['aɪnfyluŋsfɛrmø:gən], *n.* (**—s,** *no pl.*) (*Phil.*) empathy, sympathetic understanding.
**Einfuhr** ['aɪnfu:r], *f.* (—, *pl.* **—en**) importation, import.
**einführen** ['aɪnfy:rən], *v.a.* introduce; (*goods*) import.
**Einführung** ['aɪnfy:ruŋ], *f.* (—, *pl.* **—en**) introduction; (*goods*) importation.
**einfüllen** ['aɪnfylən], *v.a.* fill in, pour into, bottle.
**Eingabe** ['aɪnga:bə], *f.* (—, *pl.* **—n**) petitition; application.
**Eingang** ['aɪngaŋ], *m.* (**—s,** *pl.* **¨e**) entry, entrance; arrival.
**eingangs** ['aɪngaŋs], *adv.* in *or* at the beginning.
**eingeben** ['aɪnge:bən], *v.a. irr.* inspire (with); (*petition*) present, deliver; (*claim*) file; (*complaint*) bring; (*medicine*) administer.
**eingeboren** ['aɪngəbo:rən], *adj.* native; (*Theol.*) only-begotten.
**Eingeborene** ['aɪngəbo:rənə], *m.* (**—n,** *pl.* **—n**) native.
**Eingebrachte** ['aɪngəbraxtə], *n.* (**—n,** *no pl.*) dowry.
**Eingebung** ['aɪnge:buŋ], *f.* (—, *pl.* **—en**) inspiration.
**eingedenk** ['aɪngədɛŋk], *prep.* (*Genit.*) mindful of, remembering.
**eingefleischt** ['aɪngəflaɪʃt], *adj.* inveterate, confirmed.
**eingehen** ['aɪnge:ən], *v.n. irr.* (*aux.* sein) (*Comm.*) arrive; *auf etwas* —, enter into s.th., agree to s.th.; *auf etwas näher* —, enter into the details of s.th.; (*animals, plants*) die; (*cloth*) shrink.

# Einlauf

**eingehend** ['aɪngeːənt], *adj.* thorough, exhaustive.

**Eingemachte** ['aɪngəmaxtə], *n.* (—n, *no pl.*) preserve.

**eingenommen** ['aɪngənɔmən], *adj.* enthusiastic for, infatuated with; — *von sich*, conceited.

**Eingeschlossenheit** ['aɪngəʃlɔsənhaɪt], *f.* (—, *no pl.*) isolation, seclusion.

**eingeschrieben** ['aɪngəʃriːbən], *adj.* registered (letter).

**eingesessen** ['aɪngəzesən], *adj.* old-established; resident.

**Eingeständnis** ['aɪngəʃtentnɪs], *n.* (—ses, *pl.* —se) confession.

**eingestehen** ['aɪngəʃteːən], *v.a. irr.* confess to, avow.

**Eingeweide** ['aɪngəvaɪdə], *n. pl.* bowels, intestines.

**eingewöhnen** ['aɪngəvøːnən], *v.r. sich* —, accustom o.s. to, get used to.

**eingießen** ['aɪngiːsən], *v.a. irr.* pour in; pour out.

**eingleisig** ['aɪnglaɪzɪç], *adj.* single-track.

**eingliedern** ['aɪngliːdərn], *v.r. sich* —, adapt o.s., fit in.

**eingreifen** ['aɪngraɪfən], *v.n. irr.* intervene in; interfere with, encroach on.

**Eingriff** ['aɪngrɪf], *m.* (—s, *pl.* —e) intervention, encroachment, infringement; (*Med.*) operation.

**Einguß** ['aɪngus], *m.* (—sses, *pl.* ¨sse) infusion; enema.

**einhaken** ['aɪnhaːkən], *v.a.* hook in. — *v.r. sich* —, (*fig.*) take a p.'s arm.

**Einhalt** ['aɪnhalt], *m.* (—s, *no pl.*) stop, check, prohibition, cessation; — *gebieten*, check, suppress.

**einhalten** ['aɪnhaltən], *v.a. irr.* observe, adhere to.

**einhändigen** ['aɪnhendɪgən], *v.a.* hand in, deliver.

**einhauen** ['aɪnhauən], *v.a. irr.* hew in, break open.

**Einhebung** ['aɪnheːbuŋ], *f.* (—, *pl.* —en) (*taxes*) collection.

**einheften** ['aɪnheftən], *v.a.* sew in, stitch in; (*papers*) file.

**einhegen** ['aɪnheːgən], *v.a.* fence in, hedge in.

**einheimisch** ['aɪnhaɪmɪʃ], *adj.* native; (*Bot.*) indigenous.

**einheimsen** ['aɪnhaɪmzən], *v.a.* reap.

**Einheit** ['aɪnhaɪt], *f.* (—, *pl.* —en) unit; unity.

**einheitlich** ['aɪnhaɪtlɪç], *adj.* uniform, consistent.

**einheizen** ['aɪnhaɪtsən], *v.a., v.n.* heat the stove, light the fire.

**einhellig** ['aɪnhelɪç], *adj.* unanimous, harmonious.

**einher** [aɪn'heːr], *adv.* forth, along, on.

**einholen** ['aɪnhoːlən], *v.a.* obtain; catch up with. — *v.n.* go shopping.

**Einhorn** ['aɪnhɔrn], *n.* (—s, *pl.* ¨er) unicorn.

**einhüllen** ['aɪnhylən], *v.a.* wrap up, cover, envelop.

**einig** ['aɪnɪç], *adj.* at one. — *adv.* in agreement.

**einige** ['aɪnɪgə], *adj.* some, several.

**einigemal** ['aɪnɪgəmaːl], *adv.* several times.

**einigen** ['aɪnɪgən], *v.a.* unite. — *v.r. sich* — *mit*, come to an agreement with.

**einigermaßen** [aɪnɪgər'maːsən], *adv.* to a certain extent.

**Einigkeit** ['aɪnɪçkaɪt], *f.* (—, *no pl.*) union; unity, unanimity, harmony.

**Einigung** ['aɪnɪguŋ], *f.* (—, *pl.* —en) agreement; union.

**einimpfen** ['aɪnɪmpfən], *v.a.* inoculate, vaccinate.

**einjährig** ['aɪnjeːrɪg], *adj.* one-year-old; annual.

**einkassieren** ['aɪnkasiːrən], *v.a.* cash (*cheque*), collect (*money*).

**Einkauf** ['aɪnkauf], *m.* (—s, *pl.* ¨e) purchase, buy.

**einkaufen** ['aɪnkaufən], *v.a.* purchase, buy. — *v.n.* go shopping.

**Einkäufer** ['aɪnkɔyfər], *m.* (—s, *pl.* —) (*Comm.*) purchaser, buyer.

**Einkehr** ['aɪnkeːr], *f.* (—, *pl.* —en) stopping (at an inn); (*fig.*) meditation.

**einkehren** ['aɪnkeːrən], *v.n.* (*aux.* sein) stop *or* put up (at an inn).

**einkerkern** ['aɪnkerkərn], *v.a.* imprison.

**einklagen** ['aɪnklaːgən], *v.a.* (*Law*) sue for (money).

**einklammern** ['aɪnklamərn], *v.a.* bracket, enclose in brackets.

**Einklang** ['aɪnklaŋ], *m.* (—s, *no pl.*) accord, unison, harmony.

**einkleben** ['aɪnkleːbən], *v.a.* paste in.

**einkleiden** ['aɪnklaɪdən], *v.a.* clothe; (*fig.*) invest; *sich* — *lassen*, (*Eccl.*) take the veil.

**einklemmen** ['aɪnklemən], *v.a.* squeeze in, jam in.

**einkochen** ['aɪnkɔxən], *v.a.* preserve. — *v.n.* (*aux.* sein) boil down.

**Einkommen** ['aɪnkɔmən], *n.* (—s, *no pl.*) income, revenue.

**einkommen** ['aɪnkɔmən], *v.n. irr.* (*aux.* sein) *bei einem wegen etwas* —, apply to s.o. for s.th.

**einkreisen** ['aɪnkraɪzən], *v.a.* encircle, isolate.

**Einkünfte** ['aɪnkynftə], *f. pl.* income, revenue; emoluments.

**einladen** ['aɪnlaːdən], *v.a. irr.* load in; invite.

**Einlage** ['aɪnlaːgə], *f.* (—, *pl.* —n) (*letter*) enclosure; (*Theat.*) addition to programme; (*game*) stake; (*Comm.*) investment.

**einlagern** ['aɪnlaːgərn], *v.a.* (*goods*) store, warehouse; (*Mil.*) billet, quarter.

**Einlaß** ['aɪnlas], *m.* (—sses, *pl.* ¨sse) admission, admittance; (*water*) inlet.

**einlassen** ['aɪnlasən], *v.a. irr.* admit, allow in; let in. — *v.r. sich auf etwas* —, engage in s.th., enter into s.th.

**Einlauf** ['aɪnlauf], *m.* (—s, *no pl.*) entering; (*Med.*) enema.

**55**

# einlaufen

**einlaufen** ['aɪnlaufən], *v.n. irr. (aux. sein) (Naut.)* enter harbour, put into port; *(material)* shrink.

**einleben** ['aɪnle:bən], *v.r. sich* —, grow accustomed to, settle down, acclimatise o.s.

**einlegen** ['aɪnle:gən], *v.a.* put in, lay in; enclose; *(money)* deposit; *(food)* pickle, preserve; *Fürbitte* —, intercede; *eingelegte Arbeit,* inlaid work.

**einleiten** ['aɪnlaɪtən], *v.a.* begin, introduce; institute.

**Einleitung** ['aɪnlaɪtuŋ], *f.* (—, *pl.* —en) introduction; *(book)* preface; *(Mus.)* prelude; *(Law)* institution.

**einlenken** ['aɪnleŋkən], *v.n.* turn in; give in, come round.

**einleuchten** ['aɪnlɔʏçtən], *v.n.* become clear.

**einlösen** ['aɪnlø:zən], *v.a.* redeem; *(bill)* honour; *(cheque)* cash.

**einmachen** ['aɪnmaxən], *v.a.* preserve.

**einmal** ['aɪnma:l], *adv.* once; *es war* —, once upon a time; *auf* —, suddenly; *noch* —, once more; *nicht* —, not even.

**Einmaleins** ['aɪnma:laɪns], *n.* (—es, *no pl.)* multiplication table.

**einmalig** ['aɪnma:lɪç], *adv.* unique, unrepeatable.

**Einmaster** ['aɪnmastər], *m.* (—s, *pl.* —) *(Naut.)* brigantine, cutter.

**einmauern** ['aɪnmauərn], *v.a.* wall in, immure.

**einmengen** ['aɪnmɛŋən], *v.r. sich* —, meddle with, interfere.

**einmieten** ['aɪnmi:tən], *v.r. sich* —, take lodgings.

**einmischen** ['aɪnmɪʃən], *v.r. sich* —, meddle (with), interfere.

**einmütig** ['aɪnmy:tɪç], *adj.* unanimous, in harmony, united.

**Einnahme** ['aɪnna:mə], *f.* (—, *pl.* —n) income, revenue; receipts; *(Mil.)* occupation, capture.

**einnehmen** ['aɪnne:mən], *v.a. irr.* take in; *(money)* receive; *(medicine)* take; *(taxes)* collect; *(place)* take up, occupy; *(Mil.)* occupy, conquer; *(fig.)* captivate, fascinate.

**einnehmend** ['aɪnne:mənt], *adj.* fetching, engaging, charming.

**einnicken** ['aɪnnɪkən], *v.n. (aux. sein)* nod or doze off.

**einnisten** ['aɪnnɪstən], *v.r. sich* —, nestle down; *( fig.)* settle in a place.

**Einöde** ['aɪnø:də], *f.* (—, *pl.* —n) desert, solitude.

**einordnen** ['aɪnɔrdnən], *v.a.* place in order, file, classify.

**einpauken** ['aɪnpaukən], *v.a.* cram.

**einpferchen** ['aɪnpferçən], *v.a.* pen in, coop up.

**einpökeln** ['aɪnpø:kəln], *v.a.* salt, pickle.

**einprägen** ['aɪnprɛ:gən], *v.a.* imprint, impress.

**einquartieren** ['aɪnkvarti:rən], *v.a. (Mil.)* quarter, billet.

**einrahmen** ['aɪnra:mən], *v.a.* frame.

**einräumen** ['aɪnrɔʏmən], *v.a.* stow (things) away; *einem etwas* —, concede s.th. to s.o.

**Einrede** ['aɪnre:də], *f.* (—, *pl.* —n) objection.

**einreden** ['aɪnre:dən], *v.a. einem etwas* —, persuade s.o. to. — *v.r. sich etwas* —, get s.th. into o.'s head.

**einreichen** ['aɪnraɪçən], *v.a.* hand in, deliver; tender.

**einreihen** ['aɪnraɪən], *v.a.* place in line, arrange.

**einreihig** ['aɪnraɪɪç], *adj.* consisting of a single row; *(Tail.)* single-breasted (suit).

**einreißen** ['aɪnraɪsən], *v.a. irr.* make a tear in; *(houses)* pull down. — *v.n. (fig.)* gain ground.

**einrenken** ['aɪnrɛŋkən], *v.a. (Med.)* set; *(fig.)* settle.

**einrichten** ['aɪnrɪçtən], *v.a.* put in order, arrange; equip, set up; furnish.

**Einrichtung** ['aɪnrɪçtuŋ], *f.* (—, *pl.* —en) arrangement, management; furnishing; *(pl.)* facilities; equipment, amenities.

**einrücken** ['aɪnrykən], *v.n. (aux. sein)* march in. — *v.a.* insert (in the newspaper).

**Eins** [aɪns], *f.* (—, *pl.* —en, —er) one; *(Sch.)* top marks.

**eins** [aɪns], *num.* one; *es ist mir alles* —, it is all the same to me.

**einsalzen** ['aɪnzaltsən], *v.a.* salt, pickle, cure.

**einsam** ['aɪnza:m], *adj.* lonely, solitary, secluded.

**Einsamkeit** ['aɪnza:mkaɪt], *f.* (—, *no pl.)* loneliness, solitude, seclusion.

**Einsatz** ['aɪnzats], *m.* (—es, *pl.* ⁖e) *(game)* stake, pool; *(dress)* lace inset; *(Mus.)* entry (of a voice), starting intonation; *(Mil.)* sortie, mission.

**einsaugen** ['aɪnzaugən], *v.a.* suck in; *( fig.)* imbibe.

**einsäumen** ['aɪnzɔʏmən], *v.a.* hem (in).

**einschalten** ['aɪnʃaltən], *v.a.* insert, interpolate; switch on; put in gear.

**einschärfen** ['aɪnʃerfən], *v.a.* impress s.th. on s.o.

**einschätzen** ['aɪnʃetsən], *v.a.* assess.

**einschenken** ['aɪnʃeŋkən], *v.a.* pour in *or* out, fill.

**einschieben** ['aɪnʃi:bən], *v.a.* push in; interpolate, insert.

**Einschiebsel** ['aɪnʃi:psəl], *n.* (—s, *pl.* —) interpolation; interpolated part.

**einschiffen** ['aɪnʃifən], *v.a.* embark; *(goods)* ship. — *v.r. sich* —, go aboard, embark.

**einschlafen** ['aɪnʃla:fən], *v.n. irr. (aux. sein)* fall asleep, go to sleep.

**einschläfern** ['aɪnʃle:fərn], *v.a.* lull to sleep.

**Einschlag** ['aɪnʃla:k], *m.* (—s, *pl.* ⁖e) cover, envelope; *(weaving)* woof, weft; explosion; strike; *( fig.)* streak (of character); touch.

**einschlagen** [ˈaɪnʃlɑːgən], *v.a. irr.* knock in; (*nail*) drive in; (*parcel*) wrap up; (*road*) take. — *v.n.* (*lightning*) strike; be a success.

**einschlägig** [ˈaɪnʃlɛːgɪç], *adj.* bearing on (the subject), pertinent.

**einschleppen** [ˈaɪnʃlɛpən], *v.a.* (*disease*) bring in, introduce.

**einschließen** [ˈaɪnʃliːsən], *v.a. irr.* lock in *or* up; (*enemy*) surround; (*fig.*) include.

**einschlummern** [ˈaɪnʃlumərn], *v.n.* (*aux.* sein) doze off, fall asleep.

**Einschluß** [ˈaɪnʃlus], *m.* (—sses, *pl.* ⸚sse) inclusion; *mit* — *von*, inclusive of.

**einschmeicheln** [ˈaɪnʃmaɪçəln], *v.r. sich bei einem* —, ingratiate o.s. with s.o.

**einschmelzen** [ˈaɪnʃmɛltsən], *v.a. irr.* melt down.

**einschmieren** [ˈaɪnʃmiːrən], *v.a.* smear, grease, oil; (*sore*) put ointment on.

**einschneidend** [ˈaɪnʃnaɪdənt], *adj.* important, sweeping, incisive, trenchant.

**einschneidig** [ˈaɪnʃnaɪdɪç], *adj.* single-edged.

**Einschnitt** [ˈaɪnʃnɪt], *m.* (—s, *pl.* —e) incision, cut, notch; (*verse*) caesura.

**einschnüren** [ˈaɪnʃnyːrən], *v.a.* lace up; (*parcel*) tie up.

**einschränken** [ˈaɪnʃrɛŋkən], *v.a.* confine, limit, restrict. — *v.r. sich* —, curtail o.'s expenses, economize.

**einschrauben** [ˈaɪnʃraubən], *v.a.* screw in.

**einschreiben** [ˈaɪnʃraɪbən], *v.a. irr.* write in *or* down, inscribe; (*letter*) register. — *v.r. sich* —, enter o.'s name; enrol.

**Einschreibesendung** [ˈaɪnʃraɪbəzendun], *f.* (—, *pl.* —en) registered letter, registered parcel.

**einschreiten** [ˈaɪnʃraɪtən], *v.n. irr.* (*aux.* sein) step in, intervene.

**einschrumpfen** [ˈaɪnʃrumpfən], *v.n.* (*aux.* sein) shrink, shrivel.

**einschüchtern** [ˈaɪnʃyçtərn], *v.a.* intimidate, overawe.

**Einschuß** [ˈaɪnʃus], *m.* (—sses, *pl.* ⸚sse) share, advance of capital; (*weaving*) woof, weft.

**einsegnen** [ˈaɪnzeːgnən], *v.a.* consecrate, bless; (*Eccl.*) confirm.

**Einsehen** [ˈaɪnzeːən], *n.* (—s, *no pl.*) realisation; *ein* — *haben*, be reasonable.

**einsehen** [ˈaɪnzeːən], *v.a. irr.* look into, glance over; (*fig.*) comprehend, realise.

**einseifen** [ˈaɪnzaɪfən], *v.a.* soap, lather; (*fig.*) take s.o. in.

**einseitig** [ˈaɪnzaɪtɪç], *adj.* one-sided; (*fig.*) one-track (mind).

**Einsenkung** [ˈaɪnzɛŋkun], *f.* (—, *pl.* —en) depression (of the ground).

**einsetzen** [ˈaɪnzɛtsən], *v.a.* put in, set in; institute, establish; (*money*) stake; (*Hort.*) plant; (*office*) install s.o. — *v.n.* begin.

**Einsetzung** [ˈaɪnzɛtsun], *f.* (—, *pl.* —en) (*office*) investiture, installation; institution.

**Einsicht** [ˈaɪnzɪçt], *f.* (—, *no pl.*) inspection, examination; insight, understanding.

**einsichtig** [ˈaɪnzɪçtɪç], *adj.* intelligent, sensible, judicious.

**Einsichtnahme** [ˈaɪnzɪçtnaːmə], *f. zur* —, (*Comm.*) on approval, for inspection.

**Einsiedler** [ˈaɪnziːdlər], *m.* (—s, *pl.* —) hermit, recluse.

**einsilbig** [ˈaɪnzɪlbɪç], *adj.* monosyllabic; (*fig.*) taciturn, laconic.

**einspannen** [ˈaɪnʃpanən], *v.a.* stretch in a frame; harness; (*coll.*) put to work.

**Einspänner** [ˈaɪnʃpɛnər], *m.* (—s, *pl.* —) one-horse vehicle; one-horse cab, fiacre.

**einsperren** [ˈaɪnʃpɛrən], *v.a.* lock in, shut up, imprison.

**einspinnen** [ˈaɪnʃpɪnən], *v.r. irr. sich* —, spin a cocoon.

**einsprengen** [ˈaɪnʃprɛŋən], *v.a.* sprinkle.

**einspringen** [ˈaɪnʃprɪŋən], *v.n. irr.* (*aux.* sein) *auf einen* —, leap at; (*lock*) catch, snap; *für einen* —, deputize for s.o.

**Einspruch** [ˈaɪnʃprux], *m.* (—s, *pl.* ⸚e) objection, protest; — *erheben*, protest; (*Law*) appeal (against).

**einspurig** [ˈaɪnʃpuːrɪç], *adj.* (*Railw.*) single-track line.

**einst** [aɪnst], *adv.* (*past*) once, once upon a time; (*future*) some day.

**Einstand** [ˈaɪnʃtant], *m.* (—s, *no pl.*) (*Tennis*) deuce.

**einstecken** [ˈaɪnʃtɛkən], *v.a.* put in; pocket; post (a letter).

**einstehen** [ˈaɪnʃteːən], *v.n. irr. zu etwas* —, answer for s.th.; *für einen* —, stand security for s.o.

**einsteigen** [ˈaɪnʃtaɪgən], *v.n. irr.* (*aux.* sein) get in, climb on; board.

**einstellen** [ˈaɪnʃtɛlən], *v.a.* put in; (*persons*) engage, hire; adjust; (*work*) stop, strike; (*payments*) stop; (*hostilities*) suspend, cease fire. — *v.r. sich* —, turn up, appear.

**einstellig** [ˈaɪnʃtɛlɪç], *adj.* (*Maths.*) of one digit.

**Einstellung** [ˈaɪnʃtɛlun], *f.* (—, *pl.* —en) putting in; (*persons*) engagement, hiring; adjustment; (*work*) stoppage, strike; (*payments*) suspension; (*hostilities*) suspension, cessation; (*fig.*) opinion, attitude.

**einstig** [ˈaɪnstɪç], *adj.* (*past*) former, late, erstwhile; (*future*) future, to be, to come.

**einstimmen** [ˈaɪnʃtɪmən], *v.n.* join in, chime in.

**einstimmig** [ˈaɪnʃtɪmɪç], *adj.* (*Mus.*) (for) one voice, unison; (*fig.*) unanimous.

**einstmals** [ˈaɪnstmaːls], *adv.* once, formerly.

# einstöckig

**einstöckig** ['aɪnʃtœkɪç], *adj.* one-storied.

**einstreichen** ['aɪnʃtraɪçən], *v.a. irr.* (*money*) take in, pocket.

**einstreuen** ['aɪnʃtrɔyən], *v.a.* strew; (*fig.*) intersperse.

**einstudieren** ['aɪnʃtudiːrən], *v.a.* study; (*Theat., Mus.*) rehearse.

**einstürmen** ['aɪnʃtyrmən], *v.n.* (*aux.* sein) *auf einen* —, rush at, fall upon.

**Einsturz** ['aɪnʃturts], *m.* (—es, *pl.* ∸e) fall, crash; subsidence, collapse.

**einstürzen** ['aɪnʃtyrtsən], *v.n.* (*aux.* sein) fall in, fall into ruin, fall to pieces, collapse.

**einstweilen** ['aɪnstvaɪlən], *adv.* in the meantime, meanwhile, for the time being, provisionally.

**einstweilig** ['aɪnstvaɪlɪç], *adj.* temporary, provisional.

**eintägig** ['aɪntɛːgɪç], *adj.* one-day, ephemeral.

**Eintagsfliege** ['aɪntaːksfliːgə], *f.* (—, *pl.* —n) dayfly.

**eintauschen** ['aɪntauʃən], *v.a.* — *gegen*, exchange for, barter for.

**einteilen** ['aɪntaɪlən], *v.a.* divide; distribute; classify.

**eintönig** ['aɪntøːnɪç], *adj.* monotonous.

**Eintracht** ['aɪntraxt], *f.* (—, *no pl.*) concord, harmony.

**einträchtig** ['aɪntrɛçtɪç], *adj.* united, harmonious.

**Eintrag** ['aɪntraːk], *m.* (—s, *pl.* ∸e) entry (in a book); prejudice, damage, detriment.

**eintragen** ['aɪntraːgən], *v.a. irr.* enter (in a book), register; bring in, yield.

**einträglich** ['aɪntrɛklɪç], *adj.* profitable, lucrative.

**Eintragung** ['aɪntraːguŋ], *f.* (—, *pl.* —en) entry (in a book); enrolment.

**einträufeln** ['aɪntrɔyfəln], *v.a.* instil.

**eintreffen** ['aɪntrɛfən], *v.n. irr.* (*aux.* sein) arrive; happen, come true.

**eintreiben** ['aɪntraɪbən], *v.a. irr.* drive home (*cattle*); collect (debts etc.).

**eintreten** ['aɪntreːtən], *v.n. irr.* (*aux.* sein) step in, enter; happen, take place; *in einen Verein* —, join a club; *für einen* —, speak up for s.o.

**eintrichtern** ['aɪntrɪçtərn], *v.a. einem etwas* —, cram s.th. into s.o.

**Eintritt** ['aɪntrɪt], *m.* (—s, *no pl.*) entry, entrance; beginning; *kein* —, no admission.

**eintrocknen** ['aɪntrɔknən], *v.n.* (*aux.* sein) shrivel, dry up.

**einüben** ['aɪnyːbən], *v.a.* practise, exercise.

**einverleiben** ['aɪnfɛrlaɪbən], *v.a.* incorporate in, embody in.

**Einvernahme** ['aɪnfɛrnaːmə], *f.* (—, *pl.* —n) (*Austr.*) *see* **Vernehmung**.

**Einvernehmen** ['aɪnfɛrneːmən], *n.* (—s, *no pl.*) understanding; *im besten* —, on the best of terms.

**einvernehmen** ['aɪnfɛrneːmən], *v.a.* (*aux.* haben) (*Austr.*) *see* **vernehmen**.

**einverstanden** ['aɪnfɛrʃtandən], (*excl.*) agreed! — *adj.* — *sein*, agree.

**Einverständnis** ['aɪnfɛrʃtɛntnɪs], *n.* (—ses, *no pl.*) consent, agreement, accord.

**Einwand** ['aɪnvant], *m.* (—s, *pl.* ∸e) objection, exception; — *erheben*, raise objections.

**einwandern** ['aɪnvandərn], *v.n.* (*aux.* sein) immigrate.

**einwandfrei** ['aɪnvantfraɪ], *adj.* irreproachable, unobjectionable.

**einwärts** ['aɪnvɛrts], *adv.* inward(s).

**einwechseln** ['aɪnvɛksəln], *v.a.* change, exchange.

**einweichen** ['aɪnvaɪçən], *v.a.* steep in water, soak.

**einweihen** ['aɪnvaɪən], *v.a.* dedicate; (*Eccl.*) consecrate; open (formally), inaugurate; initiate (into).

**Einweihung** ['aɪnvaɪuŋ], *f.* (—, *pl.* —en) (*Eccl.*) consecration; inauguration, formal opening; initiation.

**einwenden** ['aɪnvɛndən], *v.a. irr.* object to, raise objections, urge against.

**einwerfen** ['aɪnvɛrfən], *v.a. irr.* throw in; smash in; interject.

**einwickeln** ['aɪnvɪkəln], *v.a.* wrap up, envelop.

**einwilligen** ['aɪnvɪlɪgən], *v.n.* consent, assent, agree, accede.

**einwirken** ['aɪnvɪrkən], *v.n. auf einen* —, influence s.o.

**Einwohner** ['aɪnvoːnər], *m.* (—s, *pl.* —) inhabitant.

**Einwohnerschaft** ['aɪnvoːnərʃaft], *f.* (—, *no pl.*) population, inhabitants.

**Einwurf** ['aɪnvurf], *m.* (—s, *pl.* ∸e) (*letter box*) opening, slit; slot; objection.

**einwurzeln** ['aɪnvurtsəln], *v.r. sich* —, take root; *eingewurzelt*, deep-rooted.

**Einzahl** ['aɪntsaːl], *f.* (—, *no pl.*) singular.

**einzahlen** ['aɪntsaːlən], *v.a.* pay in, deposit.

**einzäunen** ['aɪntsɔynən], *v.a.* fence in.

**einzeichnen** ['aɪntsaɪçnən], *v.a.* draw in, sketch in. — *v.r. sich* —, enter o.'s name, sign.

**Einzelhaft** ['aɪntsəlhaft], *f.* (—, *no pl.*) solitary confinement.

**Einzelheit** ['aɪntsəlhaɪt], *f.* (—, *pl.* —en) detail, particular.

**einzeln** ['aɪntsəln], *adj.* single; isolated, detached, apart.

**einziehen** ['aɪntsiːən], *v.a. irr.* draw in, retract; (*Law*) confiscate, impound; (*debts*) collect, call in; (*bill of sight*) discount, cash; (*money*) withdraw (from circulation); (*sails*) furl; (*Mil.*) call up.

**einzig** ['aɪntsɪç], *adj.* sole, single; unique, only.

**Einzug** ['aɪntsuːk], *m.* (—s, *pl.* ∸e) entry, entrance; move (into new house).

**einzwängen** ['aɪntsvɛŋən], *v.a.* force in, squeeze in.

**Eis** [aɪs], *n.* (—es, *no pl.*) ice; ice-cream.

**E-is** ['eːɪs], *n.* (—, *pl.* —) (*Mus.*) E sharp.

**Eisbahn** ['aɪsba:n], *f.* (—, *pl.* —en) ice-rink, skating-rink.

**Eisbär** ['aɪsbɛ:r], *m.* (—en, *pl.* —en) polar bear, white bear.

**Eisbein** ['aɪsbaɪn], *n.* (—s, *pl.* —e) pig's trotters.

**Eisberg** ['aɪsbɛrk], *m.* (—s, *pl.* —e) iceberg.

**Eisblumen** ['aɪsblu:mən], *f. pl.* frost patterns (*on glass*).

**Eisen** ['aɪzən], *n.* (—s, *pl.* —) iron; *altes* —, scrap iron.

**Eisenbahn** ['aɪzənba:n], *f.* (—, *pl.* —en) railway.

**Eisenfleck** ['aɪzənflɛk], *m.* (—s, *pl.* —e) iron mould.

**Eisengießerei** ['aɪzəngi:səraɪ], *f.* (—, *pl.* —en) iron foundry, iron forge.

**Eisenguß** ['aɪzəngus], *m.* (—sses, *pl.* ⁛sse) cast-iron.

**Eisenhändler** ['aɪzənhɛndlər], *m.* (—s, *pl.* —) ironmonger.

**Eisenhütte** ['aɪzənhytə], *f.* (—, *pl.* —n) *see* **Eisengießerei.**

**Eisenschlacke** ['aɪzənʃlakə], *f.* (—, *no pl.*) iron dross, iron slag.

**eisern** ['aɪzərn], *adj.* made of iron; (*coll. & fig.*) strong; strict.

**Eisgang** ['aɪsgaŋ], *m.* (—s, *pl.* ⁛e) drift of ice.

**eisgrau** ['aɪsgrau], *adj.* hoary.

**eiskalt** ['aɪskalt], *adj.* icy cold.

**Eislauf** ['aɪslauf], *m.* (—s, *no pl.*) ice-skating.

**Eismeer** ['aɪsme:r], *n.* (—s, *pl.* —e) polar sea; *nördliches* —, Arctic Ocean; *südliches* —, Antarctic Ocean.

**Eispickel** ['aɪspɪkəl], *m.* (—s, *pl.* —) ice axe.

**Eisvogel** ['aɪsfo:gəl], *m.* (—s, *pl.* ⁛) (*Orn.*) kingfisher.

**Eiszapfen** ['aɪstsapfən], *m.* (—s, *pl.* —) icicle.

**eitel** ['aɪtəl], *adj.* vain, frivolous, conceited; (*obs.*) pure.

**Eiter** ['aɪtər], *m.* (—s, *no pl.*) (*Med.*) pus, matter.

**Eitergeschwür** ['aɪtərgəʃvy:r], *n.* (—s, *pl.* —e) abscess.

**eitern** ['aɪtərn], *v.n.* suppurate.

**Eiterung** ['aɪtəruŋ], *f.* (—, *pl.* —en) suppuration.

**eitrig** ['aɪtrɪç], *adj.* purulent.

**Eiweiß** ['aɪvaɪs], *n.* (—es, *no pl.*) white of egg; albumen.

**Ekel** ['e:kəl], *m.* (—s, *no pl.*) nausea, disgust, distaste, aversion.

**ekelhaft** ['e:kəlhaft], *adj.* loathsome, disgusting, nauseous.

**ekeln** ['e:kəln], *v.r. sich — vor*, be disgusted (by), feel sick, loathe.

**Ekuador** [ekua'dɔr], *n.* Ecuador.

**Elan** [e'lã], *m.* (—s, *no pl.*) verve, vigour.

**elastisch** [e'lastɪʃ], *adj.* elastic, flexible, buoyant.

**Elastizität** [elastɪtsɪ'tɛ:t], *f.* (—, *no pl.*) elasticity; (*mind*) buoyancy.

**Elch** [ɛlç], *m.* (—s, *pl.* —e) (*Zool.*) elk.

**Elegie** [ele'gi:], *f.* (—, *pl.* —n) elegy.

**elektrisieren** [elɛktrɪ'zi:rən], *v.a.* electrify.

**Elektrizität** [elɛktritsɪ'tɛ:t], *f.* (—, *no pl.*) electricity.

**Elend** ['e:lɛnt], *n.* (—s, *no pl.*) misery, distress, wretchedness.

**elend** ['e:lɛnt], *adj.* miserable, wretched, pitiful; weak; *sich — fühlen*, feel poorly.

**elendiglich** ['e:lɛndɪklɪç], *adv.* miserably, wretchedly.

**Elentier** ['e:lɛnti:r], *n.* (—s, *pl.* —e) (*Zool.*) elk.

**elf** [ɛlf], *num. adj.* eleven.

**Elfe** ['ɛlfə], *f.* (—, *pl.* —n) fairy.

**Elfenbein** ['ɛlfənbaɪn], *n.* (—s, *no pl.*) ivory.

**Elisabeth** [e'li:zabɛt], *f.* Elizabeth.

**Ellbogen** ['ɛlbo:gən], *m.* (—s, *pl.* —) elbow.

**Elle** ['ɛlə], *f.* (—, *pl.* —n) yard, ell.

**Elritze** ['ɛlrɪtsə], *f.* (—, *pl.* —n) minnow.

**Elsaß** ['ɛlzas], *n.* Alsace.

**Elster** ['ɛlstər], *f.* (—, *pl.* —n) magpie.

**Eltern** ['ɛltərn], *pl.* parents.

**Emaille** [e'ma:j], *n.* (—s, *no pl.*) enamel.

**emailliert** [ema(l)'ji:rt], *adj.* covered with vitreous enamel, enamelled.

**Empfang** [ɛm'pfaŋ], *m.* (—s, *pl.* ⁛e) receipt; reception.

**empfangen** [ɛm'pfaŋən], *v.a. irr.* receive, accept, take.

**Empfänger** [ɛm'pfɛŋər], *m.* (—s, *pl.* —) recipient, receiver.

**empfänglich** [ɛm'pfɛŋlɪç], *adj.* susceptible, impressionable.

**Empfängnis** [ɛm'pfɛŋnɪs], *f.* (—, *no pl.*) conception.

**empfehlen** [ɛm'pfe:lən], *v.a. irr.* commend, recommend; give compliments to. — *v.r. sich —*, take leave.

**empfinden** [ɛm'pfɪndən], *v.a. irr.* feel, perceive.

**empfindlich** [ɛm'pfɪntlɪç], *adj.* sensitive, susceptible; touchy, thin-skinned.

**empfindsam** [ɛm'pfɪntsa:m], *adj.* sentimental.

**Empfindung** [ɛm'pfɪnduŋ], *f.* (—, *pl.* —en) sensation, feeling, sentiment.

**empor** [ɛm'po:r], *adv.* upward(s), up.

**Empore** [ɛm'po:rə], *f.* (—, *pl.* —n) gallery (*in church*).

**empören** [ɛm'pø:rən], *v.a.* excite, enrage, shock. — *v.r. sich —*, revolt, rebel.

**Emporkömmling** [ɛm'po:rkœmlɪŋ], *m.* (—s, *pl.* —e) upstart.

**empört** [ɛm'pø:rt], *adj.* furious, shocked, disgusted.

**Empörung** [ɛm'pø:ruŋ], *f.* (—, *pl.* —en) rebellion, revolt, mutiny, insurrection; indignation, disgust.

**emsig** ['ɛmzɪç], *adj.* assiduous, industrious, busy.

**Emsigkeit** ['ɛmzɪçkaɪt], *f.* (—, *no pl.*) assiduity, diligence.

**Ende** ['ɛndə], *n.* (—s, *pl.* —n) end, conclusion.

# enden

**enden** ['ɛndən], *v.n.* end, finish, conclude. — *v.a.* terminate, put an end to.
**endgültig** ['ɛntgyltɪç], *adj.* definitive, final.
**Endivie** [ɛn'diːvjə], *f.* (—, *pl.* —n) (*Bot.*) endive.
**endlich** ['ɛntlɪç], *adj.* finite, final, ultimate. — *adv.* at last, at length, finally.
**endlos** ['ɛntloːs], *adj.* endless, never-ending, boundless.
**Endung** ['ɛnduŋ], *f.* (—, *pl.* —en) (*Gram.*) ending, termination.
**Endziel** ['ɛntsiːl], *n.* (—s, *pl.* —e) final aim.
**Energie** [enɛr'giː], *f.* (—, *pl.* —n) energy.
**energisch** [e'nɛrgɪʃ], *adj.* energetic.
**eng** [ɛŋ], *adj.* narrow, tight; tight-fitting.
**engagieren** [ãga'ʒiːrən], *v.a.* engage, hire.
**Enge** ['ɛŋə], *f.* (—, *pl.* —n) narrowness, lack of space; *einen in die — treiben* drive s.o. into a corner.
**Engel** ['ɛŋəl], *m.* (—s, *pl.* —) angel.
**engelhaft** ['ɛŋəlhaft], *adj.* angelic.
**Engelschar** ['ɛŋəlʃaːr], *f.* (—, *pl.* —en) angelic host.
**Engelwurzel** ['ɛŋəlvurtsəl], *f.* (—, *pl.* —n) angelica.
**engherzig** ['ɛŋhɛrtsɪç], *adj.* narrow-minded.
**England** ['ɛŋlant], *n.* England.
**englisch** (1) ['ɛŋlɪʃ], *adj.* (*obs.*) angelic.
**englisch** (2) ['ɛŋlɪʃ], *adj.* English; —*e Krankheit*, rickets.
**Engpaß** ['ɛŋpas], *m.* (—sses, *pl.* ˙e) defile, narrow pass; (*fig.*) bottleneck.
**engros** [ã'groː], *adj.* wholesale.
**engstirnig** ['ɛŋʃtɪrnɪç], *adj.* narrow-minded.
**Enkel** ['ɛŋkəl], *m.* (—s, *pl.* —) grandchild, grandson.
**enorm** [e'nɔrm], *adj.* enormous; (*coll.*) terrific.
**entarten** [ɛnt'artən], *v.n.* (*aux.* sein) degenerate.
**entäußern** [ɛnt'ɔysərn], *v.r. sich einer Sache —*, part with s.th.
**entbehren** [ɛnt'beːrən], *v.a.* lack, be in want of; spare.
**entbehrlich** [ɛnt'beːrlɪç], *adj.* dispensable, unnecessary, superfluous.
**Entbehrung** [ɛnt'beːruŋ], *f.* (—, *pl.* —en) privation, want.
**entbieten** [ɛnt'biːtən], *v.a. irr. Grüße —*, send o.'s respects.
**entbinden** [ɛnt'bɪndən], *v.a. irr. einen von etwas —*, release *or* dispense s.o. from s.th.; (*Med.*) deliver (a woman of a child).
**Entbindung** [ɛnt'bɪnduŋ], *f.* (—, *pl.* —en) (*Med.*) delivery, child-birth.
**entblättern** [ɛnt'blɛtərn], *v.a.* strip of leaves.
**entblößen** [ɛnt'bløːsən], *v.a., v.r.* (*sich*) —, uncover (o.s.), bare (o.s.).
**entdecken** [ɛnt'dɛkən], *v.a.* discover, detect.

**Ente** ['ɛntə], *f.* (—, *pl.* —n) duck; *junge —*, duckling; (*fig.*) hoax, fictitious newspaper report.
**entehren** [ɛnt'eːrən], *v.a.* dishonour, disgrace; deflower, ravish.
**enterben** [ɛnt'ɛrbən], *v.a.* disinherit.
**Enterich** ['ɛntərɪç], *m.* (—s, *pl.* —e) drake.
**entfachen** [ɛnt'faxən], *v.a.* set ablaze, kindle.
**entfahren** [ɛnt'faːrən], *v.n. irr.* (*aux.* sein) slip off, escape.
**entfallen** [ɛnt'falən], *v.n. irr.* (*aux.* sein) escape o.'s memory; be left off.
**entfalten** [ɛnt'faltən], *v.a.* unfold; display. — *v.r. sich —*, develop, open up, expand.
**entfärben** [ɛnt'fɛrbən], *v.r. sich —*, lose colour, grow pale.
**entfernen** [ɛnt'fɛrnən], *v.a.* remove. — *v.r. sich —*, withdraw.
**Entfernung** [ɛnt'fɛrnuŋ], *f.* (—, *pl.* —en) removal; distance.
**entfesseln** [ɛnt'fɛsəln], *v.a.* unfetter; let loose.
**Entfettungskur** [ɛnt'fɛtuŋskuːr], *f.* (—, —en) slimming-cure.
**entflammen** [ɛnt'flamən], *v.a.* inflame.
**entfliegen** [ɛnt'fliːgən], *v.n. irr.* (*aux.* sein) fly away.
**entfliehen** [ɛnt'fliːən], *v.n. irr.* (*aux.* sein) run away, escape, flee.
**entfremden** [ɛnt'frɛmdən], *v.a.* estrange, alienate.
**entführen** [ɛnt'fyːrən], *v.a.* abduct, carry off; kidnap; elope with.
**entgegen** [ɛnt'geːgən], *prep.* (*Dat.*), *adv.* against, contrary to; towards.
**Entgegenkommen** [ɛnt'geːgənkɔmən], *n.* (—s, *no pl.*) obliging behaviour, courtesy.
**entgegenkommen** [ɛnt'geːgənkɔmən], *v.n. irr.* (*aux.* sein) come towards s.o., come to meet s.o.; do a favour, oblige.
**entgegennehmen** [ɛnt'geːgənneːmən], *v.a. irr.* receive, accept.
**entgegensehen** [ɛnt'geːgənzeːən], *v.n. irr.* await, look forward to.
**entgegnen** [ɛnt'geːgnən], *v.a.* reply, retort.
**Entgegnung** [ɛnt'geːgnuŋ], *f.* (—, *pl.* —en) reply, retort, rejoinder.
**entgehen** [ɛnt'geːən], *v.n. irr.* (*aux.* sein) (*Dat.*) escape; — *lassen*, let slip.
**Entgelt** [ɛnt'gɛlt], *n.* (—s, *no pl.*) remuneration, recompense.
**entgelten** [ɛnt'gɛltən], *v.a. irr. einen etwas — lassen*, make s.o. pay for s.th. *or* suffer.
**entgleisen** [ɛnt'glaɪzən], *v.n.* (*aux.* sein) run off the rails, be derailed.
**enthaaren** [ɛnt'haːrən], *v.a.* depilate.
**enthalten** [ɛnt'haltən], *v.a. irr.* hold, contain. — *v.r. sich —*, abstain from, refrain from.
**enthaltsam** [ɛnt'haltzaːm], *adj.* abstinent, abstemious, temperate.
**Enthaltung** [ɛnt'haltuŋ], *f.* (—, *no pl.*) abstention.

**enthaupten** [ɛnt'hauptən], *v.a.* behead, decapitate.

**entheben** [ɛnt'he:bən], *v.a. irr. einen einer Sache* —, exempt *or* dispense from, suspend from, relieve of.

**entheiligen** [ɛnt'haɪlɪgən], *v.a.* profane, desecrate.

**enthüllen** [ɛnt'hylən], *v.a.* unveil; (*fig.*) reveal.

**entkleiden** [ɛnt'klaɪdən], *v.a.* unclothe, undress, strip.

**entkommen** [ɛnt'kɔmən], *v.n. irr.* (*aux.* sein) escape, get off.

**entkräften** [ɛnt'krɛftən], *v.a.* enfeeble, debilitate, weaken; (*fig.*) refute (an argument).

**entladen** [ɛnt'la:dən], *v.a. irr.* unload, discharge. — *v.r. sich* —, burst; (*gun*) go off.

**Entladung** [ɛnt'la:duŋ], *f.* (—, *pl.* —en) unloading, discharge, explosion.

**entlang** [ɛnt'laŋ], *prep.* along.

**entlarven** [ɛnt'larfən], *v.a.* unmask; expose.

**Entlarvung** [ɛnt'larfuŋ], *f.* (—, *pl.* —en) unmasking, exposure.

**entlassen** [ɛnt'lasən], *v.a. irr.* dismiss; (*Am.*) fire; discharge; pension off.

**Entlastung** [ɛnt'lastuŋ], *f.* (—, *no pl.*) exoneration; credit (to s.o.'s bank account).

**entlaufen** [ɛnt'laufən], *v.n. irr.* (*aux.* sein) run away.

**entlausen** [ɛnt'lauzən], *v.a.* delouse.

**entledigen** [ɛnt'le:dɪgən], *v.r. sich einer Sache* —, rid o.s. of *or* get rid of a thing; *sich einer Aufgabe* —, perform a task, discharge a commission.

**entleeren** [ɛnt'le:rən], *v.a.* empty.

**entlegen** [ɛnt'le:gən], *adj.* remote, distant, far off.

**entlehnen** [ɛnt'le:nən], *v.a.* borrow from.

**entleihen** [ɛnt'laɪən], *v.a. irr.* borrow.

**entlocken** [ɛnt'lɔkən], *v.a.* elicit from.

**entmannen** [ɛnt'manən], *v.a.* castrate, emasculate.

**entmündigen** [ɛnt'myndɪgən], *v.a.* place under care of a guardian *or* (*Law*) trustees.

**Entmündigung** [ɛnt'myndɪguŋ], *f.* (—, *no pl.*) placing under legal control.

**entmutigen** [ɛnt'mu:tɪgən], *v.a.* discourage, dishearten.

**Entnahme** [ɛnt'na:mə], *f.* (—, *pl.* —n) (*money*) withdrawal.

**entnehmen** [ɛnt'ne:mən], *v.a. irr.* (*money*) withdraw; understand, gather *or* infer from.

**entnerven** [ɛnt'nɛrfən], *v.a.* enervate.

**entpuppen** [ɛnt'pupən], *v.r. sich* —, burst from the cocoon; (*fig.*) turn out to be.

**enträtseln** [ɛnt'rɛ:tsəln], *v.a.* decipher, make out.

**entreißen** [ɛnt'raɪsən], *v.a. irr.* snatch away from; *einer Gefahr* —, save *or* rescue from danger.

**entrichten** [ɛnt'rɪçtən], *v.a.* pay (off).

**entrinnen** [ɛnt'rɪnən], *v.n. irr.* (*aux.* sein) escape from.

**entrückt** [ɛnt rykt], *adj.* enraptured.

**entrüsten** [ɛnt'rystən], *v.a.* make angry, exasperate. — *v.r. sich* —, become angry, fly into a passion.

**entsagen** [ɛnt'za:gən], *v.n.* renounce; waive; abdicate.

**Entsatz** [ɛnt'zats], *m.* (—es, *no pl.*) (*Mil.*) relief.

**entschädigen** [ɛnt'ʃɛ:dɪgən], *v.a.* indemnify, compensate.

**entscheiden** [ɛnt'ʃaɪdən], *v.a. irr.* decide. — *v.r. sich* — *für*, come to a decision for, decide in favour of.

**Entscheidung** [ɛnt'ʃaɪduŋ], *f.* (—, *pl.* —en) decision; verdict.

**entschieden** [ɛnt'ʃi:dən], *adj.* decided, determined, resolute, peremptory.

**Entschiedenheit** [ɛnt'ʃi:dənhaɪt], *f.* (—, *no pl.*) resolution, firmness, determination.

**entschlafen** [ɛnt'ʃla:fən], *v.n. irr.* (*aux.* sein) fall asleep; (*fig.*) die, depart this life.

**entschleiern** [ɛnt'ʃlaɪərn], *v.a.* unveil.

**entschließen** [ɛnt'ʃli:sən], *v.r. irr. sich* —, decide (upon), resolve, make up o.'s mind.

**Entschlossenheit** [ɛnt'ʃlɔsənhaɪt], *f.* (—, *no pl.*) resoluteness, determination.

**entschlummern** [ɛnt'ʃlumərn], *v.n.* (*aux.* sein) fall asleep.

**entschlüpfen** [ɛnt'ʃlypfən], *v.n.* (*aux.* sein) slip away; escape.

**Entschluß** [ɛnt'ʃlʊ·], *m.* (—sses, *pl.* ⸚sse) resolution; *einen* — *fassen*, resolve (to).

**entschuldigen** [ɛnt'ʃuldɪgən], *v.a.* excuse. — *v.r. sich* —, apologise.

**entschwinden** [ɛnt'ʃvɪndən], *v.n. irr.* (*aux.* sein) disappear, vanish.

**entseelt** [ɛnt'ze:lt], *adj.* inanimate, lifeless.

**entsenden** [ɛnt'zɛndən], *v.a. irr.* send off, despatch.

**Entsetzen** [ɛnt'zɛtsən], *n.* (—s, *no pl.*) horror, terror.

**entsetzen** [ɛnt'zɛtsən], *v.a.* (*Mil.*) relieve; frighten, shock, fill with horror. — *v.r. sich* — *über*, be horrified at.

**entsetzlich** [ɛnt'zɛtslɪç], *adj.* horrible, terrible, dreadful, awful.

**entsiegeln** [ɛnt'zi:gəln], *v.a.* unseal.

**entsinnen** [ɛnt'zɪnən], *v.r. sich einer Sache* —, recollect, remember, call s.th. to mind.

**entspannen** [ɛnt'ʃpanən], *v.a.,v.r.* (*sich*) —, relax.

**entspinnen** [ɛnt'ʃpɪnən], *v.r. irr. sich* —, arise, begin.

**entsprechen** [ɛnt'ʃprɛçən], *v.n. irr.* respond to, correspond to, meet, suit.

**entsprechend** [ɛnt'ʃprɛçənt], *adj.* corresponding, suitable.

**entsprießen** [ɛnt'ʃpri:sən], *v.n. irr.* (*aux.* sein) spring up, sprout.

**entspringen** [ɛnt'ʃprɪŋən], *v.n. irr.* (*aux.* sein) escape, originate from; (*river*) have its source at, rise.

**entstammen** [ɛnt'ʃtamən], *v.n.* (*aux.* sein) spring from, originate from.

**entstehen** [ɛnt'ʃte:ən], *v.n. irr.* (*aux.* sein) arise, originate, begin, result, spring from.

**Entstehung** [ɛnt'ʃte:uŋ], *f.* (—, *no pl.*) origin, rise.

**entstellen** [ɛnt'ʃtɛlən], *v.a.* disfigure, deform, distort; (*fig.*) garble.

**entsühnen** [ɛnt'zy:nən], *v.a.* free from sin, purify, purge.

**enttäuschen** [ɛnt'tɔyʃən], *v.a.* disappoint.

**entthronen** [ɛnt'tro:nən], *v.a.* dethrone.

**entvölkern** [ɛnt'fœlkərn], *v.a.* depopulate.

**entwachsen** [ɛnt'vaksən], *v.n. irr.* (*aux.* sein) grow out of, outgrow.

**entwaffnen** [ɛnt'vafnən], *v.a.* disarm.

**entwässern** [ɛnt'vɛsərn], *v.a.* drain.

**entweder** [ɛnt've:dər], *conj.* either; — ......*oder*, either ...... or.

**entweichen** [ɛnt'vaiçən], *v.n. irr.* escape, run away.

**entweihen** [ɛnt'vaiən], *v.a.* profane, desecrate.

**entwenden** [ɛnt'vɛndən], *v.a.* take away, steal, embezzle.

**entwerfen** [ɛnt'vɛrfən], *v.a. irr.* design, sketch, plan, draw up.

**entwerten** [ɛnt'vɛrtən], *v.a.* reduce in value, depreciate; (*stamps*) cancel.

**entwickeln** [ɛnt'vikəln], *v.a.* unfold, develop; (*ideas*) explain, explicate. — *v.r. sich* —, develop (into), evolve.

**Entwicklung** [ɛnt'vikluŋ], *f.* (—, *pl.* —en) unfolding, development, evolution.

**entwinden** [ɛnt'vindən], *v.a. irr.* wrench from, wrest from.

**entwirren** [ɛnt'virən], *v.a.* unravel, disentangle.

**entwischen** [ɛnt'viʃən], *v.n.* (*aux.* sein) slip away, escape.

**entwöhnen** [ɛnt'vø:nən], *v.a.* disaccustom; break off a habit; (*baby*) wean.

**entwürdigen** [ɛnt'vyrdigən], *v.a.* disgrace, degrade.

**Entwurf** [ɛnt'vurf], *m.* (—s, *pl.* ˙̈e) sketch, design, draft, plan, project.

**entwurzeln** [ɛnt'vurtsəln], *v.a.* uproot.

**entziehen** [ɛnt'tsi:ən], *v.a. irr.* withdraw, take away, deprive of.

**entziffern** [ɛnt'tsifərn], *v.a.* decipher.

**entzücken** [ɛnt'tsykən], *v.a.* enchant, delight, charm.

**entzündbar** [ɛnt'tsyntba:r], *adj.* inflammable.

**entzünden** [ɛnt'tsyndən], *v.a.* set on fire, light the fire; (*fig.*) inflame. — *v.r. sich* —, catch fire, ignite; (*Med.*) become inflamed.

**Entzündung** [ɛnt'tsynduŋ], *f.* (—, *pl.* —en) kindling, setting on fire; (*Med.*) inflammation.

**entzwei** [ɛnt'tsvai], *adv.* in two, broken.

**entzweien** [ɛnt'tsvaiən], *v.a.* disunite.

**Enzian** ['ɛntsjan], *m.* (—s, *pl.* —e) (*Bot.*) gentian.

**Enzyklopädie** [ɛntsyklopɛ'di:], *f.* (—, *pl.* —n) encyclopædia.

**Epidemie** [ɛpide'mi:], *f.* (—, *pl.* —en) epidemic.

**epidemisch** [ɛpi'de:miʃ], *adj.* epidemic(al).

**Epik** ['e:pik], *f.* (—, *no pl.*) epic poetry.

**episch** ['e:piʃ], *adj.* epic.

**Epos** ['e:pɔs], *n.* (—, *pl.* **Epen**) epic poem.

**Equipage** [ɛkvi'pa:ʒə], *f.* (—, *pl.* —n) carriage.

**er** [e:r], *pers. pron.* he.

**Erachten** [ɛr'axtən], *n.* (—s, *no pl.*) opinion, judgment; *meines* —*s*, in my opinion.

**erachten** [ɛr'axtən], *v.a.* think, consider.

**erarbeiten** [ɛr'arbaitən], *v.a.* gain *or* achieve by working.

**erb** ['ɛrb], *adj.* (*in compounds*) hereditary.

**erbarmen** [ɛr'barmən], *v.r. sich* —, have mercy (on), take pity (on).

**erbärmlich** [ɛr'bɛrmliç], *adj.* miserable, pitiful; contemptible.

**erbauen** [ɛr'bauən], *v.a.* build, erect; (*fig.*) edify.

**erbaulich** [ɛr'bauliç], *adj.* edifying.

**Erbauung** [ɛr'bauuŋ], *f.* (—, *no pl.*) building, erection; (*fig.*) edification.

**Erbbesitz** ['ɛrpbəzits], *m.* (—es, *pl.* —e) hereditary possession.

**Erbe** ['ɛrbə], *m.* (—n, *pl.* —n) heir. *n.* (—s, *no pl.*) inheritance; heritage.

**erbeben** [ɛr'be:bən], *v.n.* (*aux.* sein) shake, tremble, quake.

**erbeigen** ['ɛrpaigən], *adj.* inherited.

**erben** ['ɛrbən], *v.a.* inherit.

**erbeten** [ɛr'be:tən], *v.a. sich etwas* —, ask for s.th. by prayer; request.

**erbetteln** [ɛr'betəln], *v.a.* obtain by begging.

**erbeuten** [ɛr'bɔytən], *v.a.* take as booty.

**Erbfeind** ['ɛrpfaint], *m.* (—s, *pl.* —e) sworn enemy.

**Erbfolge** ['ɛrpfɔlgə], *f.* (—, *no pl.*) succession.

**erbieten** [ɛr'bi:tən], *v.r. irr. sich* —, offer to do s.th.; volunteer; *Ehre* —, do homage.

**Erbin** ['ɛrbin], *f.* (—, *pl.* —nen) heiress.

**erbitten** [ɛr'bitən], *v.a. irr.* beg, request, ask for, gain by asking.

**erbittern** [ɛr'bitərn], *v.a.* embitter, anger, exasperate.

**erblassen** [ɛr'blasən], *v.n.* (*aux.* sein) turn pale.

**Erblasser** ['ɛrplasər], *m.* (—s, *pl.* —) testator.

**erbleichen** [ɛr'blaiçən], *v.n. irr.* (*aux.* sein) turn pale, lose colour.

**erblich** ['ɛrpliç], *adj.* hereditary, congenital.

**erblicken** [ɛr'blikən], *v.a.* perceive, behold, catch sight of.

**erblinden** [ɛr'blindən], *v.n.* (*aux.* sein) turn blind.

**erblos** ['ɛrplo:s], *adj.* disinherited; without an heir.

**erblühen** [ɛrˈblyːən], v.n. (aux. sein) blossom (out).

**Erbmasse** [ˈɛrpmasə], f. (—, no pl.) estate.

**erbosen** [ɛrˈboːzən], v.a. make angry. — v.r. sich —, become angry.

**erbötig** [ɛrˈbøːtiç], adj. — sein, be willing, be ready.

**Erbpacht** [ˈɛrppaxt], f. (—, pl. —en) hereditary tenure.

**erbrechen** [ɛrˈbrɛçən], v.a. irr. break open, open by force. — v.r. sich —, vomit.

**Erbrecht** [ˈɛrprɛçt], n. (—s, no pl.) law (or right) of succession.

**Erbschaft** [ˈɛrpʃaft], f. (—, pl. —en) inheritance, heritage, legacy.

**Erbse** [ˈɛrpsə], f. (—, pl. —n) pea.

**Erbstück** [ˈɛrpʃtyk], n. (—s, pl. —e) heirloom.

**Erbsünde** [ˈɛrpzyndə], f. (—, no pl.) original sin.

**Erbteil** [ˈɛrptaɪl], n. (—s, pl. —e) portion of inheritance.

**Erdapfel** [ˈeːrtapfəl], m. (—s, pl. ⁣ ⁣ ⁣˝) (Austr.) potato.

**Erdbahn** [ˈeːrtbaːn], f. (—, no pl.) orbit of the earth.

**Erdball** [ˈeːrtbal], m. (—s, no pl.) terrestrial globe.

**Erdbeben** [ˈeːrtbeːbən], n. (—s, pl. —) earthquake.

**Erdbeere** [ˈeːrtbeːrə], f. (—, pl. —n) strawberry.

**Erde** [ˈeːrdə], f. (—, pl. —n) earth, soil ground.

**erden** [ˈeːrdən], v.a. (Rad.) earth.

**erdenken** [ɛrˈdɛŋkən], v.a.irr. think out, invent. — v.r. sich etwas —, invent s.th., devise s.th.

**erdenklich** [ɛrˈdɛŋkliç], adj. imaginable, conceivable.

**Erdenleben** [ˈeːrdənleːbən], n. (—s, no pl.) life on this earth.

**Erdfall** [ˈeːrtfal], m. (—s, pl. ⁣˝e) landslip.

**Erdfläche** [ˈeːrtflɛçə], f. (—, no pl.) surface of the earth.

**Erdgeschoß** [ˈeːrtgəʃɔs], n. (—sses, pl. —sse) ground floor.

**Erdhügel** [ˈeːrthyːgəl], m. (—s, pl. —) mound of the earth.

**erdichten** [ɛrˈdɪçtən], v.a. think out, invent, feign.

**Erdkunde** [ˈeːrtkundə], f. (—, no pl.) geography.

**Erdleitung** [ˈeːrtlaɪtuŋ], f. (—, pl. —en) earth circuit, earth connexion.

**Erdmaus** [ˈeːrtmaus], f. (—, pl. ⁣˝e) field mouse.

**Erdmolch** [ˈeːrtmɔlç], m. (—s, pl. —e) salamander.

**Erdnuß** [ˈeːrtnus], f. (—, pl. ⁣˝sse) groundnut, peanut.

**Erdöl** [ˈeːrtøːl], n. (—s, no pl.) petroleum, mineral oil.

**erdolchen** [ɛrˈdɔlçən], v.a. stab (with a dagger).

**Erdpech** [ˈeːrtpɛç], n. (—s, no pl.) bitumen.

**erdreisten** [ɛrˈdraɪstən], v.r. sich —, dare, have the audacity.

**erdrosseln** [ɛrˈdrɔsəln], v.a. strangle, throttle.

**erdrücken** [ɛrˈdrykən], v.a. crush to death.

**Erdrutsch** [ˈeːrtrutʃ], m. (—es, no pl.) landslip, landslide.

**Erdschicht** [ˈeːrtʃɪçt], f. (—, pl. —en) (Geol.) layer, stratum.

**Erdschnecke** [ˈeːrtʃnɛkə], f. (—, pl. —n) slug, snail.

**Erdscholle** [ˈeːrtʃɔlə], f. (—, pl. —n) clod (of earth).

**Erdsturz** [ˈeːrtʃturts], m. (—es, no pl.) landslide.

**erdulden** [ɛrˈduldən], v.a. suffer, endure.

**Erdumseg(e)lung** [ˈeːrtumzeːg(ə)luŋ], f. (—, pl. —en) circumnavigation of the earth.

**ereifern** [ɛrˈaɪfərn], v.r. sich —, become heated, get excited.

**ereignen** [ɛrˈaɪgnən], v.r. sich —, happen, come to pass.

**Ereignis** [ɛrˈaɪknɪs], n. (—ses, pl. —se) event, occurrence, happening.

**ereilen** [ɛrˈaɪlən], v.a. overtake, befall.

**Eremit** [ereˈmiːt], m. (—en, pl. —en) hermit, recluse.

**erfahren** [ɛrˈfaːrən], v.a. irr. learn, hear; experience. — adj. experienced, practised; conversant with, versed in.

**Erfahrenheit** [ɛrˈfaːrənhaɪt], f. (—, no pl.) experience, skill.

**Erfahrung** [ɛrˈfaːruŋ], f. (—, pl. —en) experience, knowledge, expertness, skill; in — bringen, ascertain, come to know.

**erfahrungsgemäß** [ɛrˈfaːruŋsgəmɛːs], adj. based on or according to experience.

**erfahrungsmäßig** [ɛrˈfaːruŋsmɛːsɪç], adj. based on experience; empirical.

**erfassen** [ɛrˈfasən], v.a. get hold of, seize, comprehend, grasp.

**erfinden** [ɛrˈfɪndən], v.a. irr. invent, contrive.

**erfinderisch** [ɛrˈfɪndərɪʃ], adj. inventive, ingenious.

**Erfindung** [ɛrˈfɪnduŋ], f. (—, pl. —en) invention; contrivance.

**Erfolg** [ɛrˈfɔlk], m. (—s, pl. —e) success; result; effect; — haben, succeed, be successful; keinen — haben, fail.

**erfolgen** [ɛrˈfɔlgən], v.n. (aux. sein) ensue, follow, result.

**erfolgreich** [ɛrˈfɔlkraɪç], adj. successful.

**erforderlich** [ɛrˈfɔrdərliç], adj. necessary, required.

**erfordern** [ɛrˈfɔrdərn], v.a. demand, require.

**Erfordernis** [ɛrˈfɔrdərnɪs], n. (—ses, pl. —se) necessity, requirement, requisite.

**erforschen** [ɛrˈfɔrʃən], v.a. explore, investigate, conduct research into.

**erfragen** [ɛrˈfraːgən], v.a. find out by asking, ascertain.

**erfreuen** [ɛrˈfrɔyən], v.a. gladden, cheer, delight. — v.r. sich — an, enjoy, take pleasure in.

**erfreulich** [ɛr'frɔylɪç], *adj.* pleasing, gratifying.

**erfrieren** [ɛr'fri:rən], *v.n. irr.* (*aux.* sein) freeze to death, die of exposure; become numb.

**erfrischen** [ɛr'frɪʃən], *v.a.* refresh.

**erfüllen** [ɛr'fylən], *v.a.* fulfil, keep (promise); comply with; perform; *seinen Zweck —*, serve its purpose. — *v.r. sich —*, come true, be fulfilled.

**Erfüllung** [ɛr'fylʊŋ], *f.* (—, *no pl.*) fulfilment; granting; performance; *in — gehen*, come true, be realised.

**ergänzen** [ɛr'gɛntsən], *v.a.* complete, complement.

**Ergänzung** [ɛr'gɛntsʊŋ], *f.* (—, *pl.* —en) completion; complement, supplement.

**ergattern** [ɛr'gatərn], *v.a.* pick up.

**ergeben** [ɛr'ge:bən], *v.a. irr.* give, yield, prove, show. — *v.r. sich —*, surrender (to), acquiesce (in); happen, result, follow. — *adj.* devoted, submissive, humble, obedient.

**Ergebenheit** [ɛr'ge:bənhaɪt], *f.* (—, *no pl.*) devotion, obedience, humility, fidelity.

**ergebenst** [ɛr'ge:bənst], *adj. Ihr —er* (*letter ending*), yours very truly, your obedient servant. — *adv.* respectfully.

**Ergebnis** [ɛr'ge:pnɪs], *n.* (—ses, *pl.* —se) outcome, result; (*Agr.*) yield.

**Ergebung** [ɛr'ge:bʊŋ], *f.* (—, *no pl.*) submission, resignation; surrender.

**Ergehen** [ɛr'ge:ən], *n.* (—s, *no pl.*) health, condition, well-being.

**ergehen** [ɛr'ge:ən], *v.n. irr.* (*aux.* sein) be promulgated *or* issued; — *lassen*, issue, publish; *etwas über sich — lassen*, submit to *or* suffer s.th. patiently. — *v.r. sich —*, (*obs.*) take a stroll.

**ergiebig** [ɛr'gi:bɪç], *adj.* rich, productive, fertile, profitable.

**ergießen** [ɛr'gi:sən], *v.r. irr. sich —*, discharge, flow into.

**erglänzen** [ɛr'glɛntsən], *v.n.* (*aux.* sein) shine forth, sparkle.

**erglühen** [ɛr'gly:ən], *v.n.* (*aux.* sein) glow; blush.

**ergötzen** [ɛr'gœtsən], *v.a.* (*obs.*) amuse, delight. — *v.r. sich — an*, delight in.

**ergrauen** [ɛr'grauən], *v.n.* (*aux.* sein) become grey; grow old.

**ergreifen** [ɛr'graɪfən], *v.a. irr.* seize, grasp, get hold of; move, touch, affect; *Maßnahmen —*, take measures.

**Ergreifung** [ɛr'graɪfʊŋ], *f.* (—, *no pl.*) seizure; (*measure*) adoption.

**ergriffen** [ɛr'grɪfən], *adj.* moved, touched, impressed.

**Ergriffenheit** [ɛr'grɪfənhaɪt], *f.* (—, *no pl.*) emotion.

**ergrimmen** [ɛr'grɪmən], *v.n.* (*aux.* sein) grow angry, be enraged.

**ergründen** [ɛr'gryndən], *v.a.* get to the bottom of, investigate, fathom.

**Erguß** [ɛr'gus], *m.* (—sses, *pl.* ⸚sse) outpouring; (*fig.*) effusion.

**erhaben** [ɛr'ha:bən], *adj.* sublime, exalted; majestic, elevated.

**Erhabenheit** [ɛr'ha:bənhaɪt], *f.* (—, *no pl.*) majesty, sublimity.

**erhalten** [ɛr'haltən], *v.a. irr.* receive, obtain, get, preserve; maintain, keep up. — *v.r. sich — von*, subsist on.

**erhältlich** [ɛr'hɛltlɪç], *adj.* obtainable.

**Erhaltung** [ɛr'haltʊŋ], *f.* (—, *no pl.*) preservation, conservation; (*family*) maintenance.

**erhärten** [ɛr'hɛrtən], *v.a.* make hard; (*fig.*) prove, confirm.

**erhaschen** [ɛr'haʃən], *v.a.* catch, snatch.

**erheben** [ɛr'he:bən], *v.a. irr.* lift up, raise; (*fig.*) elevate, exalt; *Klage —*, bring an action; *Geld —*, raise money; *Steuern —*, levy taxes. — *v.r. sich —*, rise, stand up.

**erheblich** [ɛr'he:plɪç], *adj.* considerable, weighty, appreciable.

**Erhebung** [ɛr'he:bʊŋ], *f.* (—, *pl.* —en) elevation; (*taxes*) levying; revolt, rebellion, rising.

**erheischen** [ɛr'haɪʃən], *v.a.* (*rare*) require, demand.

**erheitern** [ɛr'haɪtərn], *v.a.* cheer, exhilarate.

**erhellen** [ɛr'hɛlən], *v.a.* light up, illuminate; (*fig.*) enlighten. — *v.n.* become evident.

**erhitzen** [ɛr'hɪtsən], *v.a.* heat; (*fig.*) inflame, excite. — *v.r. sich —*, grow hot; grow angry.

**erhöhen** [ɛr'hø:ən], *v.a.* heighten, raise, intensify, increase; (*value*) enhance.

**erholen** [ɛr'ho:lən], *v.r. sich —*, recover, get better; relax (after work); take a rest.

**erholungsbedürftig** [ɛr'ho:lʊŋsbədyrftɪç], *adj.* in need of a rest.

**erhören** [ɛr'hø:rən], *v.a.* hear, vouchsafe, grant.

**Erich** ['e:rɪç], *m.* Eric.

**erinnerlich** [ɛr'ɪnərlɪç], *adj.* remembered; *soweit mir — ist*, as far as I can remember.

**erinnern** [ɛr'ɪnərn], *v.a.* remind. — *v.r. sich —*, remember, recollect, recall, call to mind.

**Erinnerung** [ɛr'ɪnərʊŋ], *f.* (—, *pl.* —en) remembrance; recollection; reminiscences.

**erjagen** [ɛr'ja:gən], *v.a.* hunt (down), chase.

**erkalten** [ɛr'kaltən], *v.n.* (*aux.* sein) grow cold.

**erkälten** [ɛr'kɛltən], *v.r. sich —*, catch cold.

**Erkältung** [ɛr'kɛltʊŋ], *f.* (—, *pl.* —en) cold, chill.

**erkämpfen** [ɛr'kɛmpfən], *v.a.* obtain by fighting; obtain by great exertion.

**erkaufen** [ɛr'kaufən], *v.a.* purchase; bribe, corrupt.

**erkennen** [ɛr'kɛnən], *v.a. irr.* recognise; perceive, distinguish, discern; (*Comm.*) credit; *zu — geben*, give to understand; *sich zu — geben*, make o.s. known. — *v.n.* (*Law*) judge; — *auf*, (*Law*) announce verdict, pass sentence.

**erkenntlich** [ɛr'kɛntlɪç], *adj.* grateful; (*fig.*) *sich — zeigen,* show o.s. grateful.
**Erkenntlichkeit** [ɛr'kɛntlɪçkaɪt], *f.* (—, *no pl.*) gratitude.
**Erkenntnis** [ɛr'kɛntnɪs], *f.* (—, *pl.* —se) perception, knowledge, comprehension, understanding; realisation, (*Phil.*) cognition.
**Erkennung** [ɛr'kɛnuŋ], *f.* (—, *no pl.*) recognition.
**Erker** ['ɛrkər], *m.* (—s, *pl.* —) alcove bay, turret.
**Erkerfenster** ['ɛrkərfɛnstər], *n.* (—s, *pl.* —) bay-window.
**erklären** [ɛr'klɛːrən], *v.a.* explain, expound, account for; make a statement on, declare, state.
**erklärlich** [ɛr'klɛːrlɪç], *adj.* explicable.
**Erklärung** [ɛr'klɛː ruŋ], *f.* (—, *pl.* —en) explanation; declaration, statement; (*income tax*) return.
**erklecklich** [ɛr'klɛklɪç],*adj.*considerable.
**erklettern** [ɛr'klɛtərn], *v.a.* climb.
**erklimmen** [ɛr'klɪmən], *v.a. irr.* climb.
**erklingen** [ɛr'klɪŋən], *v.n. irr.* (*aux.* sein) sound, resound.
**erkoren** [ɛr'koːrən], *adj.* select, chosen.
**erkranken** [ɛr'kraŋkən], *v.n.* (*aux.* sein) fall ill.
**erkühnen** [ɛr'kyːnən], *v.r. sich —,* dare, make bold, venture.
**erkunden** [ɛr'kundən], *v.a.* explore, find out; (*Mil.*) reconnoitre.
**erkundigen** [ɛr'kundɪgən], *v.r. sich —,* enquire (about), make enquiries.
**erlaben** [ɛr'laːbən], *v.r. sich —,* (*obs.*) refresh o.s.
**erlahmen** [ɛr'laːmən],*v.n.*(aux.sein)become lame; lose o.'s drive; grow tired.
**erlangen** [ɛr'laŋən], *v.a.* reach, gain, obtain; acquire; attain.
**Erlaß** [ɛr'las], *m.* (—sses, *pl.* ˙-sse) remission, exemption, release, dispensation; (*Comm.*) deduction; (*Law, Pol.*) proclamation, edict, decree, writ; (*Eccl.*) indulgence; remission.
**erlassen** [ɛr'lasən], *v.a. irr.* remit, release, let off; (*Law, Pol.*) enact, promulgate.
**erläßlich** [ɛr'lɛslɪç], *adj.* remissible, dispensable, venial.
**erlauben** [ɛr'laubən], *v.a.* permit, allow; *sich etwas —,* take the liberty of, make bold to; have the impertinence to.
**Erlaubnis** [ɛr'laupnɪs], *f.* (—, *no pl.*) permission, leave, permit; *die — haben,* be permitted; *um — bitten,* beg leave; *mit Ihrer —,* by your leave.
**erlaucht** [ɛr'lauxt], *adj.* illustrious, noble.
**erlauschen** [ɛr'lauʃən], *v.a.* overhear.
**erläutern** [ɛr'lɔytərn], *v.a.* explain, illustrate, elucidate.
**Erle** ['ɛrlə], *f.* (—, *pl.* —n) (*Bot.*) alder.
**erleben** [ɛr'leːbən], *v.a.* live to see; go through, experience.
**Erlebnis** [ɛr'leːpnɪs], *n.* (—ses, *pl.* —se) experience, adventure, occurrence.

**erledigen** [ɛr'leːdɪgən], *v.a.* settle, finish off, clear up; dispatch; execute (commission etc.).
**erledigt** [ɛr'leːdɪçt], *adj.* (*coll.*) worn-out; exhausted.
**erlegen** [ɛr'leːgən], *v.a.* slay; pay down.
**erleichtern** [ɛr'laɪçtərn], *v.a.* lighten, ease, facilitate.
**erleiden** [ɛr'laɪdən], *v.a. irr.* suffer, endure, bear, undergo.
**erlernen** [ɛr'lɛrnən], *v.a.* learn, acquire.
**erlesen** [ɛr'leːzən], *v.a. irr.* select, choose. — *adj.* select, choice.
**erleuchten** [ɛr'lɔyçtən], *v.a.* illumine, illuminate, floodlight; (*fig.*) enlighten, inspire.
**erliegen** [ɛr'liːgən], *v.n. irr.* (*aux.* sein) succumb.
**Erlkönig** ['ɛrlkøːnɪç], *m.* (—s, *pl.* —e) fairy-king, elf-king.
**erlogen** [ɛr'loːgən], *adj.* false, untrue; trumped-up.
**Erlös** [ɛr'løːs], *m.* (—es, *no pl.*) proceeds.
**erlöschen** [ɛr'lœʃən], *v.n. irr.* (*aux.* sein) be extinguished, die out; (*fire*) go out; (*contract*) expire.
**erlösen** [ɛr'løːzən], *v.a.* redeem; release, save, deliver.
**ermächtigen** [ɛr'mɛçtɪgən], *v.a.* empower; authorize.
**ermahnen** [ɛr'maːnən], *v.a.* admonish, exhort, remind.
**ermäßigen** [ɛr'mɛːsɪgən], *v.a.* reduce.
**ermatten** [ɛr'matən], *v.a.* weaken, weary, tire. — *v.n.* (*aux.* sein) grow weak, become tired.
**Ermessen** [ɛr'mɛsən], *n.* (—s, *no pl.*) judgment, opinion.
**ermitteln** [ɛr'mɪtəln], *v.a.* ascertain, find out.
**ermöglichen** [ɛr'møːklɪçən], *v.a.* make possible.
**ermorden** [ɛr'mɔrdən], *v.a.* murder.
**ermüden** [ɛr'myːdən], *v.a.* tire, fatigue. — *v.n.* (*aux.* sein) get tired, grow weary.
**ermuntern** [ɛr'muntərn], *v.a.* encourage, cheer up.
**ermutigen** [ɛr'muːtɪgən],*v.a.*encourage.
**ernähren** [ɛr'nɛːrən], *v.a.* nourish, feed.
**ernennen** [ɛr'nɛnən], *v.a. irr.* nominate, appoint.
**erneuern** [ɛr'nɔyərn], *v.a.* renew repair, renovate.
**erniedrigen** [ɛr'niːdrɪgən], *v.a.* humble, humiliate, degrade. — *v.r. sich —,* humble o.s., abase o.s.
**Ernst** (1) [ɛrnst], *m.* Ernest.
**Ernst** (2) [ɛrnst], *m.* (—es, *no pl.*) earnestness, seriousness.
**ernst** [ɛrnst], *adj.* earnest, serious.
**Ernte** ['ɛrntə], *f.* (—, *pl.* —n) harvest crop.
**ernüchtern** [ɛr'nyçtərn], *v.a.* sober; (*fig.*) disenchant, disillusion.
**erobern** [ɛr'oːbərn], *v.a.* (*Mil.*) conquer; take, win.
**eröffnen** [ɛr'œfnən], *v.a.* open, inaugurate; inform, reveal.
**erörtern** [ɛr'œrtərn], *v.a.* discuss, debate, argue.

# erpicht

**erpicht** [ɛr'pɪçt], *adj.* eager for, bent on.

**erpressen** [ɛr'prɛsən], *v.a.* extort, blackmail.

**erquicken** [ɛr'kvɪkən], *v.a.* refresh.

**erraten** [ɛr'ra:tən], *v.a. irr.* guess.

**erregen** [ɛr're:gən], *v.a.* cause; stir up, excite, agitate; provoke.

**erreichen** [ɛr'raɪçən], *v.a.* reach, arrive at; (*fig.*) attain, reach.

**erretten** [ɛr'rɛtən], *v.a.* save, rescue.

**errichten** [ɛr'rɪçtən], *v.a.* erect, raise, build.

**erringen** [ɛr'rɪŋən], *v.a. irr.* obtain (by exertion), achieve.

**erröten** [ɛr'rø:tən], *v.n.* (*aux.* sein) blush, redden.

**Errungenschaft** [ɛr'ruŋənʃaft], *f.* (—, *pl.* —en) achievement, acquisition.

**Ersatz** [ɛr'zats], *m.* (—es, *no pl.*) substitute; compensation, amends; (*Mil. etc.*) replacement.

**erschallen** [ɛr'ʃalən], *v.n.* (*aux.* sein) resound, sound.

**erschaudern** [ɛr'ʃaudərn], *v.n.* (*aux.* sein) be seized with horror.

**erscheinen** [ɛr'ʃaɪnən], *v.n. irr.* (*aux.* sein) appear, make o.'s appearance; seem; be published.

**erschießen** [ɛr'ʃi:sən], *v.a. irr.* shoot dead.

**erschlaffen** [ɛr'ʃlafən], *v.n.* (*aux.* sein) flag, slacken.

**erschlagen** [ɛr'ʃla:gən], *v.a. irr.* slay, kill.

**erschließen** [ɛr'ʃli:sən], *v.a. irr.* open up.

**erschöpfen** [ɛr'ʃœpfən], *v.a.* exhaust.

**erschrecken** [ɛr'ʃrɛkən], *v.a. irr.* startle, shock, terrify. — *v.n.* (*aux.* sein) be startled, be frightened, be terrified.

**erschüttern** [ɛr'ʃytərn], *v.a.* shake; (*fig.*) move, affect strongly.

**erschweren** [ɛr'ʃve:rən], *v.a.* (*fig.*) aggravate, make more difficult.

**erschwingen** [ɛr'ʃvɪŋən], *v.a. irr.* afford, be able to pay.

**erschwinglich** [ɛr'ʃvɪŋlɪç], *adj.* attainable, within o.'s means.

**ersehen** [ɛr'ze:ən], *v.a. irr.* — *aus*, gather (from).

**ersehnen** [ɛr'ze:nən], *v.a.* long for, yearn for.

**ersetzen** [ɛr'zɛtsən], *v.a.* replace, take the place of; restore, make good; repair; (*money*) refund.

**ersichtlich** [ɛr'zɪçtlɪç], *adj.* evident.

**ersinnen** [ɛr'zɪnən], *v.a. irr.* think out, imagine, devise, contrive.

**ersparen** [ɛr'ʃpa:rən], *v.a.* save.

**ersprießlich** [ɛr'ʃpri:slɪç], *adj.* useful, profitable, beneficial.

**erst** [e:rst], *num. adj.* first. — *adv.* first, at first, only, but; — *jetzt*, only now; *nun — recht*, now more than ever.

**erstatten** [ɛr'ʃtatən], *v.a.* reimburse, compensate, repay; *Bericht* —, report.

**Erstattung** [ɛr'ʃtatuŋ], *f.* (—, *pl.* —en) reimbursement, restitution.

**Erstaufführung** ['e:rstauffy:ruŋ], *f.* (—, *pl.* —en) (*Theat.*) first night; première.

**Erstaunen** [ɛr'ʃtaunən], *n.* (—s, *no pl.*) amazement, astonishment, surprise.

**erstechen** [ɛr'ʃtɛçən], *v.a. irr.* stab.

**erstehen** [ɛr'ʃte:ən], *v.n. irr.* (*aux.* sein) rise, arise. — *v.a.* buy, purchase.

**ersteigen** [ɛr'ʃtaɪgən], *v.a. irr.* climb, mount, ascend.

**ersticken** [ɛr'ʃtɪkən], *v.a. irr.* choke, stifle, suffocate. — *v.n.* (*aux.* sein) choke, suffocate.

**erstmalig** ['e:rstma:lɪç], *adj.* first. — *adv.* for the first time.

**erstreben** [ɛr'ʃtre:bən], *v.a.* strive after.

**erstrecken** [ɛr'ʃtrɛkən], *v.r. sich* —, extend, reach to.

**ersuchen** [ɛr'zu:xən], *v.a.* request, ask.

**ertappen** [ɛr'tapən], *v.a.* catch, detect.

**erteilen** [ɛr'taɪlən], *v.a.* bestow, impart; *einen Auftrag* —, issue an order; *Unterricht* —, instruct; *die Erlaubnis* —, give permission.

**ertönen** [ɛr'tø:nən], *v.n.* (*aux.* sein) sound, resound.

**Ertrag** [ɛr'tra:k], *m.* (—s, *pl.* ¨e) produce; returns, yield; output; (*sale*) proceeds.

**ertragen** [ɛr'tra:gən], *v.a. irr.* bear, suffer, endure.

**ertränken** [ɛr'trɛnkən], *v.a.* drown.

**ertrinken** [ɛr'trɪŋkən], *v.n. irr.* (*aux.* sein) drown, be drowned.

**erübrigen** [ɛr'y:brɪgən], *v.a.* save, spare.

**erwachen** [ɛr'vaxən], *v.n.* (*aux.* sein) awake, wake up.

**erwachsen** [ɛr'vaksən], *adj.* grown-up, adult. — *v.n. irr.* grow up; ensue, follow, arise.

**erwägen** [ɛr've:gən], *v.a. irr.* weigh, ponder, consider.

**erwähnen** [ɛr've:nən], *v.a.* mention.

**erwärmen** [ɛr'vɛrmən], *v.a.* warm (up), make warm.

**erwarten** [ɛr'vartən], *v.a.* expect, await.

**Erwartung** [ɛr'vartuŋ], *f.* (—, *pl.* —en) expectation.

**erwecken** [ɛr'vɛkən], *v.a.* wake up, awaken, raise; rouse.

**erwehren** [ɛr've:rən], *v.r. sich* — (*Genit.*), defend o.s.; *ich kann mich des Lachens nicht* —; I cannot help laughing.

**erweichen** [ɛr'vaɪçən], *v.a.* soften.

**erweisen** [ɛr'vaɪzən], *v.a. irr.* prove, show; demonstrate.

**erweitern** [ɛr'vaɪtərn], *v.a.* widen, enlarge, expand.

**erwerben** [ɛr'vɛrbən], *v.a. irr.* acquire.

**erwidern** [ɛr'vi:dərn], *v.a.* reply, answer; return.

**erwirken** [ɛr'vɪrkən], *v.a.* effect, secure.

**erwischen** [ɛr'vɪʃən], *v.a. see* **ertappen**.

**erwünschen** [ɛr'vynʃən], *v.a.* desire, wish for.

**erwürgen** [ɛr'vyrgən], *v.a.* strangle, throttle.

**Erz** [erts], (—es, *pl.* —e) ore; brass, bronze.

**erzählen** [ɛr'tsɛ:lən], *v.a.* narrate, relate, tell.

**Erzbischof** ['ɛrtsbɪʃɔf], *m.* (—s, *pl.* ⁝e) archbishop.

**erzeugen** [ɛr'tsɔygən], *v.a.* engender; beget; produce; (*Elec.*) generate.

**Erzherzog** ['ɛrtshɛrtso:k], *m.* (—s, *pl.* ⁝e) archduke.

**erziehen** [ɛr'tsi:ən], *v.a. irr.* educate, train, bring up, rear.

**Erziehungsanstalt** [ɛr'tsi:uŋsanʃtalt], *f.* (—, *pl.* —en) approved school, reformatory.

**erzielen** [ɛr'tsi:lən], *v.a.* obtain; fetch, realize (a price); *Gewinn* —, make a profit.

**erzittern** [ɛr'tsɪtərn], *v.n.* (*aux.* sein) tremble, shake.

**Erzofen** ['ɛrtso:fən], *m.* (—s, *pl.* ⁝n) furnace.

**erzürnen** [ɛr'tsyrnən], *v.a.* make angry. — *v.r. sich* —, grow angry.

**Erzvater** ['ɛrtsfa:tər], *m.* (—s, *pl.* ⁝) patriarch.

**erzwingen** [ɛr'tsvɪŋən], *v.a. irr.* enforce, force, compel.

**es** [ɛs], *pron.* it; — *gibt*, there is; — *sind*, there are; — *lebe*, long live!

**Es** [ɛs], *n.* (—, *pl.* —) (*Mus.*) E flat.

**Esche** ['ɛʃə], *f.* (—, *pl.* —n) (*Bot.*) ash, ashtree.

**Esel** ['e:zəl], *m.* (—s, *pl.* —) ass, donkey.

**Eselsohr** ['e:zəlso:r], *n.* (—s, *pl.* —en) (*fig.*) dog's ear.

**Eskadron** [ɛska'dro:n], *f.* (—, *pl.* —en) squadron.

**Espe** ['ɛspə], *f.* (—, *pl.* —n) (*Bot.*) asp, aspen.

**eßbar** ['ɛsba:r], *adj.* edible.

**Esse** ['ɛsə], *f.* (—, *pl.* —n) chimney, forge.

**Essen** ['ɛsən], *n.* (—s, *no pl.*) meal; eating.

**essen** ['ɛsən], *v.a. irr.* eat, have a meal.

**Essenz** [ɛ'sɛnts], *f.* (—, *pl.* —en) essence.

**Essig** ['ɛsɪç], *m.* (—s, *no pl.*) vinegar.

**Eßlöffel** ['ɛslœfəl], *m.* (—s, *pl.* —) table-spoon.

**Estland** ['ɛstlant], *n.* Estonia.

**Estrade** [ɛ'stra:də], *f.* (—, *pl.* —n) platform.

**Estrich** ['ɛstrɪç], *m.* (—s, *no pl.*) floor, flooring, plaster-floor.

**etablieren** [eta'bli:rən], *v.a.* establish, set up (business).

**Etagenwohnung** [e'ta:ʒənvo:nuŋ], *f.* (—, *pl.* —en) flat; (*Am.*) apartment.

**Etappe** [e'tapə], *f.* (—, *pl.* —n) stage; (*Mil.*) lines of communication.

**Etat** [e'ta:], *m.* (—s, *pl.* —s) (*Parl.*) estimates, budget; (*Comm.*) statement, balance sheet.

**ethisch** [e'tɪʃ], *adj.* ethical.

**Etikett** [eti'kɛt], *n.* (—s, *pl.* —s) label, ticket, tag.

**Etikette** [eti'kɛtə], *f.* (—, *no pl.*) etiquette; ceremonial.

**etikettieren** [etikɛ'ti:rən], *v.a.* label.

**etliche** ['ɛtlɪçə], *pl. adj. & pron.* some, several, sundry.

**Etui** [e'tvi:], *n.* (—s, *pl.* —s) small case, small box.

**etwa** ['ɛtva], *adv.* nearly, about; perhaps, perchance, in some way.

**etwaig** ['ɛtvaɪç], *adj.* possible, any, eventual.

**etwas** ['ɛtvas], *indef. pron.* some, something. — *adj.* some, any. — *adv.* a little, somewhat.

**Etzel** ['ɛtsəl], *m.* Attila.

**euch** [ɔyç], *pers. pron. pl. Dat. & Acc.* you, yourselves.

**euer** ['ɔyər], *poss. adj.* your. — *poss. pron.* yours.

**Eule** ['ɔylə], *f.* (—, *pl.* —n) owl.

**eurige** ['ɔyrɪgə], *poss. pron. der, die, das* —, yours.

**Europa** [ɔy'ro:pa], *n.* Europe.

**Euter** ['ɔytər], *n.* (—s, *pl.* —) udder.

**evangelisch** [evan'ge:lɪʃ], *adj.* Evangelical, Protestant.

**Evangelium** [evan'ge:ljum], *n.* (—s, *pl.* —lien) gospel.

**eventuell** [evɛntu'ɛl], *adj.* possible.

**ewig** ['e:vɪç], *adj.* eternal; perpetual.

**Ewigkeit** ['e:vɪçkaɪt], *f.* (—, *pl.* —en) eternity.

**explodieren** [ɛksplo'di:rən], *v.n.* explode; detonate.

**exponieren** [ɛkspo'ni:rən], *v.a.* set forth, explain at length.

**Extemporale** [ɛkstɛmpo'ra:lə], *n.* (—s, *pl.* —lien) unprepared exercise.

**extrahieren** [ɛkstra'hi:rən], *v.a.* extract.

**Extremitäten** [ɛkstremi'tɛ:tən], *f. pl.* extremities.

# F

**F** [ɛf], *n.* (—s, *pl.* —s) the letter F; (*Mus.*) F *Dur*, F major; F *Moll*, F minor.

**Fabel** ['fa:bəl], *f.* (—, *pl.* —n) fable; (*fig.*) tale, fiction; (*drama*) plot, story.

**fabelhaft** ['fa:bəlhaft], *adj.* fabulous; phenomenal, gorgeous.

**fabeln** ['fa:bəln], *v.n.* tell fables; talk nonsense.

**Fabrik** [fa'bri:k], *f.* (—, *pl.* —en) factory; plant, works.

**Fabrikant** [fabri'kant], *m.* (—en, *pl.* —en) manufacturer.

**fabrizieren** [fabri'tsi:rən], *v.a.* manufacture, make.

**fabulieren** [fabu'li:rən], *v.n.* tell fables; (*fig.*) tell tall stories.

**Fach** [fax], *n.* (—s, *pl.* ⁝er) compartment; pigeon-hole, drawer; (*fig.*) subject of study, department, branch.

**Fachausdruck** ['faxausdruk], *m.* (—s, *pl.* ⁝e) technical term.

**Fächer** ['fɛçər], *m.* (—s, *pl.* —) fan.
**Fächertaube** ['fɛçərtaubə], *f.* (—, *pl.* —n) fantail.
**Fachmann** ['faxman], *m.* (—s, *pl.* ̈er *or* **Fachleute**) expert, specialist.
**Fachschule** ['faxʃuːlə], *f.* (—, *pl.* —n) technical school.
**fachsimpeln** ['faxzɪmpəln], *v.n.* talk shop.
**Fachwerk** ['faxvɛrk], *n.* (—s, *no pl.*) timbered framework.
**Fackel** ['fakəl], *f.* (—, *pl.* —n) torch.
**fade** ['faːdə], *adj.* tasteless; boring, insipid.
**Faden** ['faːdən], *m.* (—s, *pl.* ̈) thread; (*measure*) fathom.
**fadenscheinig** ['faːdənʃaɪnɪç], *adj.* threadbare.
**Fagott** [fa'gɔt], *n.* (—s, *pl.* —e) (*Mus.*) bassoon.
**fähig** ['fɛːɪç], *adj.* able, capable; talented, gifted, competent.
**fahl** [faːl], *adj.* pale, sallow.
**Fähnchen** ['fɛːnçən], *n.* (—s, *pl.* —) small banner; pennon; (*Mil.*) (*obs.*) small troop.
**fahnden** ['faːndən], *v.a.* search for (officially).
**Fahne** ['faːnə], *f.* (—, *pl.* —n) flag, banner, standard, colours; (*weather*) vane; (*Typ.*) galley proof.
**Fahnenflucht** ['faːnənfluxt], *f.* (—, *no pl.*) (*Mil.*) desertion.
**Fähnrich** ['fɛːnrɪç], *m.* (—s, *pl.* —e) ensign.
**Fahrbahn** ['faːrbaːn], *f.* (—, *pl.* —en) traffic lane, roadway.
**fahrbar** ['faːrbaːr], *adj.* passable, navigable, negotiable.
**Fähre** ['fɛːrə], *f.* (—, *pl.* —n) ferry, ferry-boat.
**fahren** ['faːrən], *v.a. irr.* drive. — *v.n.* (*aux.* sein) (*vehicle*) ride (in), be driven; (*vessel*) sail; go, travel.
**Fahrer** ['faːrər], *m.* (—s, *pl.* —) driver, chauffeur.
**Fahrgast** ['faːrgast], *m.* (—s, *pl.* ̈e) passenger.
**fahrig** ['faːrɪç], *adj.* absent-minded, giddy, thoughtless.
**Fahrkarte** ['faːrkartə], *f.* (—, *pl.* —n) ticket.
**fahrlässig** ['faːrlɛsɪç], *adj.* negligent, careless.
**Fährmann** ['fɛːrman], *m.* (—s, *pl.* ̈er) ferry-man.
**Fahrplan** ['faːrplaːn], *m.* (—s, *pl.* ̈e) timetable, railway-guide.
**fahrplanmäßig** ['faːrplanmɛːsɪç], *adj.* according to the timetable, scheduled.
**Fahrpreis** ['faːrpraɪs], *m.* (—es, *pl.* —e) cost of ticket, fare.
**Fahrrad** ['faːrraːt], *n.* (—s, *pl.* ̈er) cycle, bicycle.
**Fahrschein** ['faːrʃaɪn], *m.* (—s, *pl.* —e) ticket.
**Fahrstraße** ['faːrʃtraːsə], *f.* (—, *pl.* —n) roadway.
**Fahrstuhl** ['faːrʃtuːl], *m.* (—s, *pl.* ̈e) lift; (*Am.*) elevator.

**Fahrt** [faːrt], *f.* (—, *pl.* —en) drive, ride, journey; (*sea*) voyage, cruise.
**Fährte** ['fɛːrtə], *f.* (—, *pl.* —n) track, trace, trail.
**Fahrzeug** ['faːrtsɔyk], *n.* (—s, *pl.* —e) vehicle, conveyance; vessel, craft.
**faktisch** ['faktɪʃ], *adj.* real, actual.
**Faktor** ['faktɔr], *m.* (—s, *pl.* —en) foreman, overseer, factor; (*Maths.*) factor, component part.
**Faktura** [fak'tuːra], *f.* (—, *pl.* —ren) (*Comm.*) invoice.
**fakturieren** [faktu'riːrən], *v.a.* (*Comm.*) invoice.
**Fakultät** [fakul'tɛːt], *f.* (—, *pl.* —en) (*Univ.*) faculty.
**fakultativ** [fakulta'tiːf], *adj.* optional.
**Falbel** ['falbəl], *f.* (—, *pl.* —n) flounce, furbelow.
**Falke** ['falkə], *m.* (—n, *pl.* —n) (*Orn.*) falcon, hawk.
**Fall** [fal], *m.* (—s, *pl.* ̈e) fall, falling; case; (*Geog.*) decline, incline, gradient; (*fig.*) fall, decline, downfall, failure.
**Fallbaum** ['falbaum], *m.* (—s, *pl.* ̈e) tollbar, turnpike.
**Fallbeil** ['falbaɪl], *n.* (—s, *pl.* —e) guillotine.
**Fallbrücke** ['falbrykə], *f.* (—, *pl.* —n) draw-bridge.
**Falle** ['falə], *f.* (—, *pl.* —n) trap, snare.
**fallen** ['falən], *v.n. irr.* (*aux.* sein) fall, drop; (*Mil.*) be killed.
**fällen** ['fɛlən], *v.a.* fell, cut down, hew down; *ein Urteil* —, (*Law*) pronounce judgment.
**Fallensteller** ['falənʃtɛlər], *m.* (—s, *pl.* —) trapper.
**fallieren** [fa'liːrən], *v.n.* become bankrupt.
**fällig** ['fɛlɪç], *adj.* due, payable.
**Fälligkeit** ['fɛlɪçkaɪt], *f.* (—, *pl.* —en) (*Comm.*) maturity.
**Fallobst** ['faloːpst], *n.* (—es, *no pl.*) windfall (of fruit).
**falls** [fals], *conj.* in case, if.
**Fallschirm** ['falʃɪrm], *m.* (—s, *pl.* —e) parachute.
**Fallstrick** ['falʃtrɪk], *m.* (—s, *pl.* —e) snare, trap.
**Fallsucht** ['falzuxt], *f.* (—, *no pl.*) (*Med.*) epilepsy.
**Falltür** ['faltyːr], *f.* (—, *pl.* —en) trap-door.
**Fällung** ['fɛluŋ], *f.* (—, *pl.* —en) cutting down.
**falsch** [falʃ], *adj.* false, incorrect, wrong; disloyal; counterfeit.
**fälschen** ['fɛlʃən], *v.a.* falsify, forge, tamper with.
**Falschheit** ['falʃhaɪt], *f.* (—, *pl.* —en) falsehood, deceit, disloyalty.
**fälschlich** ['fɛlʃlɪç], *adv.* wrongly, falsely.
**Fälschung** ['fɛlʃuŋ], *f.* (—, *pl.* —en) falsification; forgery.
**Falte** ['faltə], *f.* (—, *pl.* —n) fold, pleat; (*face*) wrinkle.
**falten** ['faltən], *v.a.* fold, plait, pleat; wrinkle.

# Fehdehandschuh

**Falter** ['faltər], *m.* (—s, *pl.* —) (*Ent.*) butterfly.

**-fältig** [fɛltɪç], *suffix* (*following numbers*). **-fold** (*e.g.* vierfältig, fourfold).

**Falz** [falts], *m.* (—es, *pl.* —e) groove, notch; joint.

**Falzbein** ['faltsbaɪn], *n.* (—s, *pl.* —e) paper-folder, paper-knife.

**Falzmaschine** ['faltsmaʃiːnə], *f.* (—, *pl.* —n) folding-machine.

**familiär** [famil'jɛːr], *adj.* familiar, intimate.

**Familie** [fa'miːljə], *f.* (—, *pl.* —n) family.

**famos** [fa'moːs], *adj.* (*coll.*) excellent, splendid.

**fanatisch** [fa'naːtiʃ], *adj.* fanatic(al), bigoted.

**Fanatismus** [fana'tɪsmus], *m.* (—, *no pl.*) fanaticism.

**Fang** [faŋ], *m.* (—es, *pl.* ⏑e) catch, capture; (*bird*) talon, claw.

**fangen** ['faŋən], *v.a. irr.* catch, seize.

**Fangzahn** ['faŋtsaːn], *m.* (—s, *pl.* ⏑e) fang, tusk.

**Fant** [fant], *m.* (—s, *pl.* —e) fop, cockscomb.

**Farbe** ['farbə], *f.* (—, *pl.* —n) colour, hue, paint, dye.

**färben** ['fɛrbən], *v.a.* dye, stain.

**Farbenbrett** ['farbənbret], *n.* (—s, *pl.* —er) palette.

**Farb(en)druck** ['farpdruk, farbəndruk], *m.* (—s, *pl.* —e) colour-printing.

**Farbenspiel** ['farbənʃpiːl], *n.* (—s, *no pl.*) iridescence.

**Färber** ['fɛrbər], *m.* (—s, *pl.* —) dyer.

**farbig** ['farbɪç], *adj.* coloured.

**Farbstift** ['farpʃtift], *m.* (—s, *pl.* —e) crayon.

**Farbstoff** ['farpʃtɔf], *m.* (—es, *pl.* —e) dye.

**Farbton** ['farptoːn], *m.* (—s, *pl.* ⏑e) hue, tone, tinge, shade.

**Farn** [farn], *m.* (—s, *pl.* —e) (*Bot.*) fern.

**Färse** ['fɛrzə], *f.* (—, *pl.* —n) (*Zool.*) heifer.

**Fasan** [fa'zaːn], *m.* (—s, *pl.* —e) (*Orn.*) pheasant.

**Fasching** ['faʃɪŋ], *m.* (—s, *no pl.*) (Shrovetide) carnival.

**Faschismus** [fa'ʃɪsmus], *m.* (—s, *no pl.*) fascism.

**Faselei** [fazə'laɪ], *f.* (—, *pl.* —en) silly talk, drivel.

**faseln** ['faːzəln], *v.n.* drivel.

**Faser** ['faːzər], *f.* (—, *pl.* —n) thread; string; fibre, filament.

**fasern** ['faːzərn], *v.n.* fray.

**Faß** [fas], *n.* (—sses, *pl.* ⏑sser) barrel, vat, tun, tub, cask, keg; *Bier vom* —, draught beer; *Wein vom* —, wine from the wood.

**Fassade** [fa'saːdə], *f.* (—, *pl.* —n) façade.

**faßbar** ['fasbaːr], *adj.* tangible.

**Faßbinder** ['fasbɪndər], *m.* (—s, *pl.* —) cooper.

**fassen** ['fasən], *v.a.* seize, take hold of, grasp; (*jewels*) set; contain, hold. — *v.r.* (*aux.* haben) *sich* —, compose o.s.; *sich kurz* —, be brief.

**faßlich** ['faslɪç], *adj.* comprehensible, understandable.

**Fasson** [fa'sɔ̃], *f.* (—, *pl.* —s) fashion; (*fig.*) cut, style.

**Fassung** ['fasuŋ], *f.* (—, *pl.* —en) (*jewels*) setting; (*speech*) wording, version; (*fig.*) composure.

**fassungslos** ['fasuŋsloːs], *adj.* bewildered, disconcerted; distraught, speechless.

**fast** [fast], *adv.* almost, nearly.

**fasten** ['fastən], *v.n.* fast.

**Fastenzeit** ['fastəntsaɪt], *f.* (—, *pl.* —en) time of fasting; Lent.

**Fastnacht** ['fastnaxt], *f.* (—, *no pl.*) Shrove Tuesday; Shrovetide.

**fauchen** ['fauxən], *v.n.* spit, hiss.

**faul** [faul], *adj.* (*food*) rotten, putrid, decayed; (*persons*) lazy, idle.

**Fäule** ['fɔylə], *f.* (—, *no pl.*) rot.

**faulen** ['faulən], *v.n.* (*aux.* sein) rot.

**faulenzen** ['faulentsən], *v.n.* laze, idle.

**Faulenzer** ['faulentsər], *m.* (—s, *pl.* —) idler, sluggard, lazybones.

**Faulenzerei** ['faulentsəraɪ], *f.* (—, *pl.* —en) idleness, laziness.

**Faulheit** ['faulhaɪt], *f.* (—, *no pl.*) idleness, laziness, sluggishness.

**faulig** ['faulɪç], *adj.* putrid, rotten.

**Fäulnis** ['fɔylnɪs], *f.* (—, *no pl.*) rottenness, putridity.

**Faust** [faust], *f.* (—, *pl.* ⏑e) fist.

**Fäustchen** ['fɔystçən], *n.* (—s, *pl.* —) small fist; *sich ins* — *lachen*, laugh in o.'s sleeve.

**Faustkampf** ['faustkampf], *m.* (—es, *pl.* ⏑e) boxing (match).

**Faxen** ['faksən], *f. pl.* foolery; — *machen*, play the buffoon.

**Fazit** ['faːtsɪt], *n.* (—s, *no pl.*) sum, amount.

**Februar** ['feːbruaːr], *m.* (—s, *no pl.*) February.

**fechten** ['fɛçtən], *v.n. irr.* fight; fence; (*fig.*) beg.

**Feder** ['feːdər], *f.* (—, *pl.* —n) (*bird*) feather; (*hat*) plume; (*writing*) pen; (*antique*) quill; (*Tech.*) spring.

**Federball** ['feːdərbal], *m.* (—s, *pl.* ⏑e) shuttle-cock.

**federig** ['feːdərɪç], *adj.* feathery; (*Tech.*) springy, resilient.

**Federlesen(s)** ['feːdərleːzən(s)], *n.* (—s, *no pl.*) *nicht viel* — *machen*, make short work of.

**Fee** [feː], *f.* (—, *pl.* —n) fairy.

**feenhaft** ['feːənhaft], *adj.* fairy-like, magical.

**Fegefeuer** ['feːgəfɔyər], *n.* (—s, *no pl.*) purgatory.

**fegen** ['feːgən], *v.a.* clean, sweep. — *v.n.* (*aux.* sein) tear along.

**Fehde** ['feːdə], *f.* (—, *pl.* —n) feud, quarrel.

**Fehdehandschuh** ['feːdəhantʃuː], *m.* (—s, *pl.* —e) gauntlet.

# fehlbar

**fehlbar** ['fe:lba:r], *adj.* fallible.
**Fehlbetrag** ['fe:lbətra:k], *m.* (—s, *pl.* ⁓e) deficit.
**fehlen** ['fe:lən], *v.a.* miss. — *v.n.* err, do wrong; be absent; be wanting; *er fehlt mir*, I miss him.
**Fehler** ['fe:lər], *m.* (—s, *pl.* —) fault, defect; mistake, error.
**Fehlgeburt** ['fe:lgəburt], *f.* (—, *pl.* —en) miscarriage.
**Fehlschlag** ['fe:lʃla:k], *m.* (—s, *pl.* ⁓e) failure, disappointment.
**feien** ['faɪən], *v.a.* einen — gegen, charm s.o. against; *gefeit*, proof.
**Feier** ['faɪər], *f.* (—, *pl.* —n) celebration, festival, holiday, festive day.
**Feierabend** ['faɪəra:bənt], *m.* (—s, *pl.* —e) time for leaving off work; — *machen*, knock off (work).
**feierlich** ['faɪərlɪç], *adj.* festive, solemn, stately.
**feiern** ['faɪərn], *v.a.* celebrate; honour, praise. — *v.n.* rest from work.
**Feiertag** ['faɪərta:k], *m.* (—s, *pl.* —e) holiday, festive day.
**feig** [faɪk], *adj.* cowardly.
**Feige** ['faɪgə], *f.* (—, *pl.* —n) (*Bot.*) fig.
**Feigheit** ['faɪkhaɪt], *f.* (—, *pl.* —en) cowardice, cowardliness.
**Feigling** ['faɪklɪŋ], *m.* (—s, *pl.* —e) coward.
**Feigwurz** ['faɪkvurts], *m.* (—es, *no pl.*) (*Bot.*) fennel.
**feil** [faɪl], *adj.* (*obs.*) for sale; venal.
**feilbieten** ['faɪlbi:tən], *v.a.* offer for sale.
**Feile** ['faɪlə], *f.* (—, *pl.* —n) file.
**feilen** ['faɪlən], *v.a.* file.
**feilhalten** ['faɪlhaltən], *v.a.* have for sale, be ready to sell.
**feilschen** ['faɪlʃən], *v.n.* bargain, haggle.
**Feilspäne** ['faɪlʃpɛ:nə], *m. pl.* filings.
**fein** [faɪn], *adj.* fine; neat, pretty, nice; delicate; (*clothes*) elegant; (*behaviour*) refined, polished.
**Feinbäckerei** ['faɪnbɛkəraɪ], *f.* (—, *pl.* —en) confectioner's shop.
**Feind** [faɪnt], *m.* (—es, *pl.* —e) enemy, foe, adversary.
**Feindschaft** ['faɪntʃaft], *f.* (—, *pl.* —en) enmity, hostility.
**feindselig** ['faɪntze:lɪç], *adj.* hostile, malignant.
**feinfühlend** ['faɪnfy:lənt], *adj.* delicate, sensitive.
**Feinheit** ['faɪnhaɪt], *f.* (—, *pl.* —en) fineness, elegance, politeness, delicacy.
**Feinschmecker** ['faɪnʃmɛkər], *m.* (—s, *pl.* —), gourmet.
**Feinsliebchen** [faɪns'li:pçən], *n.* (—s, *pl.* —) (*Poet. obs.*) sweetheart.
**feist** [faɪst], *adj.* fat, obese.
**Feld** [fɛlt], *n.* (—es, *pl.* —er) field, plain; (*chess*) square; (*fig.*) sphere, province.
**Feldbett** ['fɛltbɛt], *n.* (—s, *pl.* —en) camp-bed.
**Feldherr** ['fɛlthɛr], *m.* (—n, *pl.* —en) commander, general.

**Feldmesser** ['fɛltmɛsər], *m.* (—s, *pl.* —) land-surveyor.
**Feldscher** ['fɛltʃe:r], *m.* (—s, *pl.* —e) army-surgeon.
**Feldstecher** ['fɛltʃtɛçər], *m.* (—s, *pl.* —) field-glass(es).
**Feldwebel** ['fɛltve:bəl], *m.* (—s, *pl.* —) sergeant-major.
**Feldzug** ['fɛlttsu:k], *m.* (—es, *pl.* ⁓e) campaign, expedition.
**Felge** ['fɛlgə], *f.* (—, *pl.* —n) (*wheel*) felloe, felly, rim.
**Fell** [fɛl], *n.* (—s, *pl.* —e) hide, skin, pelt.
**Felsabhang** ['fɛlsaphaŋ], *m.* (—s, *pl.* ⁓e) rocky slope.
**Felsen** ['fɛlzən], *m.* (—s, *pl.* —) rock, cliff.
**Felsengebirge** ['fɛlzəngəbɪrgə], *n.* Rocky Mountains.
**Felsenriff** ['fɛlzənrɪf], *n.* (—s, *pl.* —e) reef.
**felsig** ['fɛlzɪç], *adj.* rocky.
**Feme** ['fe:mə], *f.* (—, *pl.* —n) secret tribunal.
**Fenchel** ['fɛnçəl], *m.* (—s, *no pl.*) (*Bot.*) fennel.
**Fenster** ['fɛnstər], *n.* (—s, *pl.* —) window.
**Fensterbrett** ['fɛnstərbrɛt], *n.* (—s, *pl.* —er) window-sill.
**Fensterflügel** ['fɛnstərfly:gəl], *m.* (—s, *pl.* —) (window) casement.
**Fensterladen** ['fɛnstərla:dən], *m.* (—s, *pl.* ⁓) shutter.
**Fensterscheibe** ['fɛnstərʃaɪbə], *f.* (—, *pl.* —n) pane.
**Ferien** ['fe:rjən], *pl.* holidays.
**Ferkel** ['fɛrkəl], *n.* (—s, *pl.* —) young pig, piglet.
**Fermate** [fɛr'ma:tə], *f.* (—, *pl.* —n) (*Mus.*) pause, fermata.
**fern** [fɛrn], *adj.* far, distant, remote.
**Fernbleiben** ['fɛrnblaɪbən], *n.* (—s, *no pl.*) absence.
**Ferne** ['fɛrnə], *f.* (—, *pl.* —n) distance, remoteness.
**ferner** ['fɛrnər], *adv.* further, furthermore, moreover.
**fernerhin** ['fɛrnərhɪn], *adv.* henceforth.
**Ferngespräch** ['fɛrngəʃprɛx], *n.* (—s, *pl.* —e) long-distance telephone call, trunk call.
**Fernglas** ['fɛrngla:s], *n.* (—es, *pl.* ⁓er) binoculars.
**fernhalten** ['fɛrnhaltən], *v.a. irr.* keep away.
**fernher** ['fɛrnhe:r], *adv.* von —, from afar.
**fernliegen** ['fɛrnli:gən], *v.n. irr.* be far from.
**Fernrohr** ['fɛrnro:r], *n.* (—s, *pl.* —e) telescope.
**Fernschreiber** ['fɛrnʃraɪbər], *m.* (—s, *pl.* —) teleprinter.
**Fernsehen** ['fɛrnze:ən], *n.* (—s, *no pl.*) television.
**fernsehen** ['fɛrnze:ən], *v.n. irr.* watch television.

**feurig**

**Fernsehgerät** ['fɛrnzeːgərɛːt], *n.* (—s, —e) television set.
**Fernsprechamt** ['fɛrnʃprɛçamt], *n.* (—s, *pl.* ⁻er) telephone exchange.
**Fernsprecher** ['fɛrnʃprɛçər], *m.* (—s, *pl.* —) telephone.
**Fernstehende** ['fɛrnʃteːəndə], *m.* (—n, *pl.* —n) outsider.
**Fernverkehr** ['fɛrnfɛrkeːr], *m.* (—s, *no pl.*) long-distance traffic.
**Ferse** ['fɛrzə], *f.* (—, *pl.* —n) heel.
**Fersengeld** ['fɛrzəngɛlt], *n.* (—s, *no pl.*) — *geben,* take to o.'s heels.
**fertig** ['fɛrtɪç], *adj.* ready, finished; (*coll.*) worn-out, ruined, done for.
**Fertigkeit** ['fɛrtɪçkaɪt], *f.* (—, *pl.* —en) dexterity, skill.
**Fes** [fɛs], *n.* (—, *pl.* —) (*Mus.*) F flat.
**fesch** [fɛʃ], *adj.* smart, stylish; (*dial.*) good-looking.
**Fessel** ['fɛsəl], *f.* (—, *pl.* —n) fetter, shackle.
**Fesselballon** ['fɛsəlbalɔ̃], *m.* (—s, *pl.* —s) captive balloon.
**Fesselbein** ['fɛsəlbaɪn], *n.* (—s, *pl.* —e) pastern-joint.
**fesseln** ['fɛsəln], *v.a.* fetter, shackle, chain; (*fig.*) captivate.
**Fest** [fɛst], *n.* (—es, *pl.* —e) feast, festival.
**fest** [fɛst], *adj.* fast, firm; solid, hard; sound; fixed; constant, steadfast.
**Feste** ['fɛstə], *f.* (—, *pl.* —n) fortress, stronghold.
**festigen** ['fɛstɪgən], *v.a.* make firm; strengthen.
**Festland** ['fɛstlant], *n.* (—es, *pl.* ⁻er) continent.
**festlich** ['fɛstlɪç], *adj.* festive, solemn.
**festmachen** ['fɛstmaxən], *v.a.* fasten.
**Festnahme** ['fɛstnaːmə], *f.* (—, *no pl.*) apprehension, arrest.
**festnehmen** ['fɛstneːmən], *v.a. irr.* seize, arrest.
**Festrede** ['fɛstreːdə], *f.* (—, *pl.* —n) formal address.
**festschnallen** ['fɛstʃnalən], *v.a.* buckle on, fasten.
**Festschrift** ['fɛstʃrɪft], *f.* (—, *pl.* —en) commemorative volume (in honour of a person or an occasion).
**festsetzen** ['fɛstzɛtsən], *v.a.* fix, decree.
**Festspiel** ['fɛstʃpiːl], *n.* (—s, *pl.* —e) festival (play).
**feststehen** ['fɛstʃteːən], *v.n. irr.* stand firm; *es steht fest,* it is certain.
**feststellen** ['fɛstʃtɛlən], *v.a.* ascertain; state; find; determine; diagnose; establish.
**Festtag** ['fɛsttaːk], *m.* (—s, *pl.* —e) feast-day, holiday.
**Festung** ['fɛstuŋ], *f.* (—, *pl.* —en) fortress, stronghold, citadel.
**festziehen** ['fɛsttsiːən], *v.a. irr.* tighten.
**Festzug** ['fɛsttsuːk], *m.* (—s, *pl.* ⁻e) procession.
**Fett** [fɛt], *n.* (—s, *pl.* —e) fat, grease, lard.
**fett** [fɛt], *adj.* fat, greasy.
**fettartig** ['fɛtartɪç], *adj.* fatty.

**fetten** ['fɛtən], *v.a.* oil, grease.
**Fettfleck** ['fɛtflɛk], *m.* (—s, *pl.* —e) spot of grease.
**fettgedruckt** ['fɛtgədrukt], *adj.* in heavy type.
**fetthaltig** ['fɛthaltɪç], *adj.* greasy; adipose.
**fettig** ['fɛtɪç], *adj.* greasy.
**fettleibig** ['fɛtlaɪbɪç], *adj.* corpulent, obese.
**Fetzen** ['fɛtsən], *m.* (—s, *pl.* —) piece, rag, tatter, shred.
**feucht** [fɔʏçt], *adj.* moist; (*weather*) muggy, wet; (*room*) damp.
**Feuchtigkeit** ['fɔʏçtɪçkaɪt], *f.* (—, *no pl.*) moisture, humidity, dampness, wetness.
**feudal** [fɔʏ'daːl], *adj.* feudal; (*coll.*) distinguished, magnificent.
**Feuer** ['fɔʏər], *n.* (—s, *pl.* —) fire; (*jewels*) brilliancy; (*fig.*) ardour, passion.
**feuerbeständig** ['fɔʏərbəʃtɛndɪç], *adj.* fire-proof.
**Feuerbestattung** ['fɔʏərbəʃtatuŋ], *f.* (—, *pl.* —en) cremation.
**Feuereifer** ['fɔʏəraɪfər], *m.* (—s, *no pl.*) ardour.
**feuerfest** ['fɔʏərfɛst], *adj.* fire-proof, incombustible.
**feuergefährlich** ['fɔʏərgəfɛːrlɪç], *adj.* inflammable.
**Feuerlilie** ['fɔʏərliːljə], *f.* (—, *pl.* —n) tiger lily.
**Feuermal** ['fɔʏərmaːl], *n.* (—s, *pl.* —e) burn, burn-mark.
**Feuermauer** ['fɔʏərmauər], *f.* (—, *pl.* —n) fire-proof wall, party-wall.
**Feuermelder** ['fɔʏərmɛldər], *m.* (—s, *pl.* —) fire-alarm.
**feuern** ['fɔʏərn], *v.a.* (*Mil.*) fire, discharge; (*coll.*) fire, sack.
**Feuerprobe** ['fɔʏərproːbə], *f.* (—, *pl.* —n) ordeal by fire.
**Feuerrad** ['fɔʏəraːt], *n.* (—s, *pl.* ⁻er) Catherine wheel.
**Feuerrohr** ['fɔʏərroːr], *n.* (—s, *pl.* —e) gun, matchlock.
**Feuersbrunst** ['fɔʏərsbrunst], *f.* (—, *pl.* ⁻e) (*rare*) fire, conflagration.
**Feuerspritze** ['fɔʏərʃprɪtsə], *f.* (—, *pl.* —n) fire-engine.
**Feuerstein** ['fɔʏərʃtaɪn], *m.* (—s, *no pl.*) flint.
**Feuertaufe** ['fɔʏərtaufə], *f.* (—, *pl.* —n) baptism of fire.
**Feuerwarte** ['fɔʏərvartə], *f.* (—, *pl.* —en) beacon; lighthouse.
**Feuerwehr** ['fɔʏərveːr], *f.* (—, *no pl.*) fire-brigade.
**Feuerwerk** ['fɔʏərvɛrk], *n.* (—, *no pl.*) fireworks.
**Feuerwerkskunst** ['fɔʏərvɛrkskunst], *f.* (—, *no pl.*) pyrotechnics.
**Feuerzange** ['fɔʏərtsaŋə], *f.* (—, *pl.* —n) fire-tongs.
**Feuerzeug** ['fɔʏərtsɔʏk], *n.* (—s, *pl.* —e) match-box; cigarette-lighter.
**feurig** ['fɔʏrɪç], *adj.* fiery, burning; (*fig.*) ardent, impassioned, fervent; (*wine*) heady.

71

# Fiaker

**Fiaker** [fi'akər], *m.* (—s, *pl.* —) (*Austr.*) cab, hansom; (*Am.*) coach.

**Fiasko** [fi'asko:], *n.* (—s, *pl.* —s) failure.

**Fibel** ['fi:bəl], *f.* (—, *pl.* —n) primer, spelling-book.

**Fiber** ['fi:bər], *f.* (—, *pl.* —n) fibre.

**Fichte** ['fiçtə], *f.* (—, *pl.* —n) (*Bot.*) pine, pine-tree.

**fidel** [fi'de:l], *adj.* merry, jolly.

**Fidibus** ['fi:dibus], *m.* (—ses, *pl.* —se) spill, fidibus.

**Fidschi** ['fɪdʒi:], Fiji.

**Fieber** ['fi:bər], *n.* (—s, *no pl.*) fever.

**fieberhaft** ['fi:bərhaft], *adj.* feverish, vehement.

**fieberig** ['fi:bərɪç], *adj.* feverish, racked by fever.

**Fieberkälte** ['fi:bərkɛltə], *f.* (—, *no pl.*) chill, shivering (fit).

**fiebern** ['fi:bərn], *v.n.* have a fever; (*fig.*) rave.

**fiebrig** ['fi:brɪç], *see* fieberig.

**Fiedel** ['fi:dəl], *f.* (—, *pl.* —n) (*Mus.*) fiddle, violin.

**Figur** [fi'gu:r], *f.* (—, *pl.* —en) figure, statue, sculpture; chessman.

**figürlich** [fi'gy:rlɪç], *adj.* figurative.

**Filet** [fi'le:], *n.* (—s, *pl.* —s) netting, net-work; (*meat*) fillet.

**Filiale** [fil'ja:lə], *f.* (—, *pl.* —n) branch, branch-establishment, branch-office.

**Filigran** [fili'gra:n], *n.* (—s, *no pl.*) filigree.

**Film** [film], *m.* (—s, *pl.* —e) film; (*motion*) picture.

**Filter** ['fɪltər], *m.* (—s, *pl.* —) filter.

**filtrieren** [fil'tri:rən], *v.a.* filter.

**Filz** [fɪlts], *m.* (—es, *pl.* —e) felt; (*fig.*) niggard, miser, skinflint.

**Filzlaus** ['fɪltslaus], *f.* (—, *pl.* ̈e) crab-louse.

**Finanzamt** [fi'nantsamt], *n.* (—s, *pl.* ̈er) income-tax office; revenue-office.

**Finanzen** [fi'nantsən], *f. pl.* finances, revenue.

**Findelkind** ['fɪndəlkɪnt], *n.* (—s, *pl.* —er) foundling.

**finden** ['fɪndən], *v.a. irr.* find. — *v.r. sich* —, *das wird sich* —, we shall see.

**Finder** ['fɪndər], *m.* (—s, *pl.* —) finder.

**findig** ['fɪndɪç], *adj.* resourceful, ingenious.

**Findling** ['fɪntlɪŋ], *m.* (—s, *pl.* —e) foundling.

**Finger** ['fɪŋər], *m.* (—s, *pl.* —) finger.

**Fingerabdruck** ['fɪŋərapdruk], *m.* (—s, *pl.* ̈e) finger-print.

**fingerfertig** ['fɪŋərfertɪç], *adj.* nimble-fingered.

**Fingerhut** ['fɪŋərhu:t], *m.* (—s, *pl.* ̈e) thimble; (*Bot.*) foxglove.

**fingern** ['fɪŋərn], *v.a.* touch with the fingers, finger.

**Fingersatz** ['fɪŋərzats], *m.* (—es, *pl.* ̈e) (*Mus.*) fingering.

**Fingerspitze** ['fɪŋərʃpɪtsə], *f.* (—, *pl.* —n) finger-tip.

**Fingerzeig** ['fɪŋərtsaɪk], *m.* (—s, *pl.* —e) hint.

**fingieren** [fɪŋ'gi:rən], *v.a.* sham.

**fingiert** [fɪŋ'gi:rt], *adj.* fictitious.

**Fink** [fɪŋk], *m.* (—en, *pl.* —en) (*Orn.*) finch.

**Finne** (1) ['fɪnə], *m.* (—n, *pl.* —n) Finn.

**Finne** (2) ['fɪnə], *f.* (—, *pl.* —n) pimple; (*fish*) fin.

**finnig** ['fɪnɪç], *adj.* pimpled; (*fish*) finny.

**Finnland** ['fɪnlant], *n.* Finland.

**finster** ['fɪnstər], *adj.* dark, obscure; (*fig.*) gloomy, sinister.

**Finsternis** ['fɪnstərnɪs], *f.* (—, *no pl.*) darkness, gloom.

**Finte** ['fɪntə], *f.* (—, *pl.* —n) feint; (*fig.*) pretence, trick.

**Firlefanz** ['fɪrləfants], *m.* (—es, *no pl.*) foolery.

**Firma** ['fɪrma], *f.* (—, *pl.* —men) (*business*) firm, company.

**Firmung** ['fɪrmuŋ], *f.* (—, *pl.* —en) (*Eccl.*) confirmation.

**Firnis** ['fɪrnɪs], *m.* (—ses, *pl.* —se) varnish.

**firnissen** ['fɪrnɪsən], *v.a.* varnish.

**First** [fɪrst], *m.* (—es, *pl.* —e) (*house*) roof-ridge; (*mountain*) top.

**Fis** [fɪs], *n.* (—, *pl.* —) (*Mus.*) F sharp.

**Fisch** [fɪʃ], *m.* (—es, *pl.* —e) fish.

**Fischadler** ['fɪʃa:dlər], *m.* (—s, *pl.* —) osprey, sea-eagle.

**Fischbein** ['fɪʃbaɪn], *n.* (—s, *no pl.*) whalebone.

**fischen** ['fɪʃən], *v.a., v.n.* fish, angle.

**Fischer** ['fɪʃər], *m.* (—s, *pl.* —) fisherman, fisher.

**Fischerei** [fɪʃə'raɪ], *f.* (—, *no pl.*) fishing; fishery.

**Fischergerät** ['fɪʃərgərɛ:t], *n.* (—s, *pl.* —e) fishing-tackle.

**Fischgräte** ['fɪʃgrɛ:tə], *f.* (—, *pl.* —n) fish-bone.

**Fischkelle** ['fɪʃkɛlə], *f.* (—, *pl.* —n) fish-slice.

**Fischlaich** ['fɪʃlaɪç], *m.* (—s, *no pl.*) spawn.

**Fischmilch** ['fɪʃmɪlç], *f.* (—, *no pl.*) soft roe, milt.

**Fischotter** ['fɪʃɔtər], *m.* (—, *pl.* —n) common otter.

**Fischreiher** ['fɪʃraɪər], *m.* (—s, *pl.* —) (*Orn.*) heron.

**Fischreuse** ['fɪʃrɔyzə], *f.* (—, *pl.* —n) bow-net; weir.

**Fischrogen** ['fɪʃro:gən], *m.* (—s, *no pl.*) roe.

**Fischschuppe** ['fɪʃʃupə], *f.* (—, *pl.* —n) scale.

**Fischtran** ['fɪʃtra:n], *m.* (—s, *no pl.*) train-oil.

**Fischzucht** ['fɪʃtsuxt], *f.* (—, *no pl.*) fish-breeding, pisciculture.

**Fiskus** ['fɪskus], *m.* (—, *pl.* —ken) Treasury, Exchequer.

**Fisole** [fi'zo:lə], *f.* (—, *pl.* —n) (*Austr.*) French bean.

72

**Fistelstimme** ['fɪstəlʃtɪmə], f. (—, no pl.) (*Mus.*) falsetto.

**Fittich** ['fɪtɪç], m. (—es, pl. —e) (*Poet.*) wing, pinion.

**fix** [fɪks], adj. quick, sharp; — und fertig, quite ready.

**Fixum** ['fɪksum], n. (—s, pl. —xa) fixed amount; regular salary.

**flach** [flax], adj. flat, plain, smooth, level; (*water*) shallow.

**Fläche** ['flɛçə], f. (—, pl. —n) plain; (*Maths.*) plane; (*crystal*) face.

**Flächeninhalt** ['flɛçənɪnhalt], m. (—s, no pl.) area.

**Flächenmaß** ['flɛçənma:s], n. (—es, pl. —e) square-measure.

**Flächenraum** ['flɛçənraum], m. (—es, no pl.) surface area.

**Flachheit** ['flaxhaɪt], f. (—, no pl.) flatness; (*fig.*) shallowness.

**Flachs** [flaks], m. (—es, no pl.) flax.

**flackern** ['flakərn], v.n. flare, flicker.

**Fladen** ['fla:dən], m. (—s, pl. —) flat cake; cow-dung.

**Flagge** ['flagə], f. (—, pl. —n) flag.

**Flame** ['fla:mə], m. (—n, pl. —n) Fleming.

**flämisch** ['flɛmɪʃ], adj. Flemish.

**Flamme** ['flamə], f. (—, pl. —n) flame; blaze.

**flammen** ['flamən], v.n. flame, blaze, sparkle.

**Flammeri** ['flaməri:], m. (—s, pl. —s) blancmange.

**Flandern** ['flandərn], n. Flanders.

**Flanell** [fla'nɛl], m. (—s, pl. —e) flannel.

**Flaneur** [fla'nøːr], m. (—s, pl. —e) lounger, stroller.

**flanieren** [fla'ni:rən], v.n. lounge, stroll.

**Flanke** ['flaŋkə], f. (—, pl. —n) flank; in die — fallen, (*Mil.*) attack in the flank.

**Flasche** ['flaʃə], f. (—, pl. —en) bottle, flask.

**Flaschenzug** ['flaʃəntsu:k], m. (—es, pl. —e) pulley.

**flatterhaft** ['flatərhaft], adj. fickle, inconstant, flighty.

**flattern** ['flatərn], v.n. flutter.

**flau** [flau], adj. insipid, stale; (*fig.*) dull.

**Flaum** [flaum], m. (—s, no pl.) down.

**Flausch** [flauʃ], m. (—es, no pl.) pilot-cloth.

**Flaute** ['flautə], f. (—, pl. —n) (*Nav.*) calm; (*fig.*) (*Comm.*) depression.

**Flechte** ['flɛçtə], f. (—, pl. —n) twist, plait, braid; (*Med.*) eruption, ring-worm; (*Bot.*) lichen.

**flechten** ['flɛçtən], v.a. irr. plait; wreathe.

**Flechtwerk** ['flɛçtvɛrk], n. (—s, no pl.) wicker-work, basketry.

**Fleck** [flɛk], m. (—s, pl. —e) spot; place, piece (of ground); (*fig.*) stain, blemish.

**Flecken** ['flɛkən], m. (—s, pl. —) market town, small town.

**fleckenlos** ['flɛkənlo:s], adj. spotless.

**fleckig** ['flɛkɪç], adj. spotted, speckled

**Fledermaus** ['fle:dərmaus], f. (—, pl. ⁺e) (*Zool.*) bat.

**Flederwisch** ['fle:dərvɪʃ], m. (—es, pl. —e) feather-duster.

**Flegel** ['fle:gəl], m. (—s, pl. —) flail; (*fig.*) boor.

**flegelhaft** ['fle:gəlhaft], adj. boorish, churlish, rude.

**Flegeljahre** ['fle:gəlja:rə], n. pl. years of indiscretion; teens, adolescence.

**flehen** ['fle:ən], v.a., v.n. implore, supplicate, entreat.

**Fleisch** [flaɪʃ], n. (—es, no pl.) (raw) flesh; (*for cooking*) meat; (*fruit*) pulp.

**Fleischbrühe** ['flaɪʃbry:ə], f. (—, pl. —n) broth, beef-tea.

**Fleischer** ['flaɪʃər], m. (—s, pl. —) butcher.

**fleischfressend** ['flaɪʃfresənt], adj. carnivorous.

**Fleischhacker** ['flaɪʃhakər], **Fleischhauer** ['flaɪʃhauər], m. (—s, pl. —) butcher.

**fleischlich** ['flaɪʃlɪç], adj. fleshly, carnal.

**fleischlos** ['flaɪʃlo:s], adj. vegetarian.

**Fleischpastete** ['flaɪʃpaste:tə], f. (—, pl. —n) meat-pie.

**Fleiß** [flaɪs], m. (—es, no pl.) diligence, assiduity, industry.

**fleißig** ['flaɪsɪç], adj. diligent, assiduous, industrious, hard-working.

**fletschen** ['flɛtʃən], v.a. die Zähne —, show o.'s teeth.

**Flicken** ['flɪkən], m. (—s, pl. —) patch.

**flicken** ['flɪkən], v.a. patch, repair, mend; (*shoes*) cobble; (*stockings*) darn.

**Flieder** ['fli:dər], m. (—s, pl. —) (*Bot.*) elder, lilac.

**Fliege** ['fli:gə], f. (—, pl. —n) (*Ent.*) fly; (*beard*) imperial.

**fliegen** ['fli:gən], v.n. irr. (aux. sein) fly; (*coll.*) get the sack, be fired. — v.a. fly, pilot (an aircraft).

**Flieger** ['fli:gər], m. (—s, pl. —) airman, aviator; pilot.

**fliehen** ['fli:ən], v.n. irr. (aux. sein) flee, run away; zu einem —, take refuge with s.o. — v.a. irr. avoid, shun (s.o.).

**Fliehkraft** ['fli:kraft], f. (—, no pl.) centrifugal force.

**Fliese** ['fli:zə], f. (—, pl. —n) floor-tile, flagstone.

**Fließband** ['fli:sbant], n. (—(e)s, pl. ⁺er) (*Ind.*) assembly line.

**fließen** ['fli:sən], v.n. irr. (aux. sein) flow.

**Fließpapier** ['fli:spapi:r], n. (—s, no pl.) blotting-paper.

**Flimmer** ['flɪmər], m. (—s, no pl.) glittering, sparkling, glimmer.

**flimmern** ['flɪmərn], v.n. glisten, glitter.

**flink** [flɪŋk], adj. brisk, agile, quick, sharp, nimble.

73

**Flinte** ['flɪntə], f. (—, pl. —n) gun, musket, rifle.

**Flitter** ['flɪtər], m. (—s, no pl.) tinsel, spangle, frippery.

**Flitterwochen** ['flɪtərvɔxən], f. pl. honeymoon.

**flitzen** ['flɪtsən], v.n. (aux. sein) vorbei —, flit or rush past, dash along.

**Flocke** ['flɔkə], f. (—, pl. —n) (snow) flake; (wool) flock.

**Floh** [flo:], m. (—s, pl. ꞊e) (Ent.) flea.

**Flor** [flo:r], m. (—s, pl. —e) bloom; gauze, crape; in —, blossoming, blooming.

**Florenz** [flo'rents], n. Florence.

**Florett** [flo'rɛt], n. (—s, pl. —e) (fencing) foil.

**florieren** [flo'ri:rən], v.n. flourish.

**Florstrumpf** ['flo:rʃtrumpf], m. (—s, pl. ꞊e) lisle stocking.

**Floskel** ['flɔskəl], f. (—, pl. —n) rhetorical ornament; oratorical flourish; phrase.

**Floß** [flo:s], n. (—es, pl. ꞊e) raft.

**Flosse** ['flɔsə], f. (—, pl. —n) fin.

**flößen** ['flø:sən], v.a. float.

**Flößer** ['flø:sər], m. (—s, pl. —) raftsman.

**Flöte** ['flø:tə], f. (—, pl. —n) (Mus.) flute.

**Flötenzug** ['flø:təntsu:k], m. (—es, pl. ꞊e) (organ) flute-stop.

**flott** [flɔt], adj. (Naut.) afloat, floating; (fig.) gay, jolly, lively, smart; — leben, lead a fast life.

**Flotte** ['flɔtə], f. (—, pl. —n) fleet, navy.

**Flottille** [flɔ'tɪljə], f. (—, pl. —n) flotilla, squadron.

**Flöz** [flø:ts], n. (—es, pl. —e) layer, stratum; (coal) seam.

**Fluch** [flu:x], m. (—es, pl. ꞊e) curse, spell; (verbal) curse, oath, swear-word.

**fluchen** ['flu:xən], v.n. curse, swear.

**Flucht** [fluxt], f. (—, pl. —en) flight, fleeing; suite (of rooms).

**flüchten** ['flyçtən], v.n. (aux. sein), v.r. flee, run away, escape.

**flüchtig** ['flyçtɪç], adj. fugitive; (Chem.) volatile; (fig.) superficial; evanescent; hasty; slight.

**Flüchtling** ['flyçtlɪŋ], m. (—s, pl. —e) fugitive, refugee.

**Flug** [flu:k], m. (—s, pl. ꞊e) (Aviat.) flight.

**Flugblatt** ['flu:kblat], n. (—s, pl. ꞊er) broadsheet, leaflet.

**Flügel** ['fly:gəl], m. (—s, pl. —) wing; (Mus.) grand piano; (door) leaf.

**Flügelschlag** ['fly:gəlʃla:k], m. (—s, pl. ꞊e) wing-stroke.

**Flügeltür** ['fly:gəlty:r], f. (—, pl. —en) folding-door.

**flügge** ['flygə], adj. fledged.

**Flughafen** ['flu:kha:fən], m. (—s, pl. ꞊) airport, aerodrome.

**Flugpost** ['flu:kpɔst], f. (—, no pl.) air mail.

**flugs** [fluks], adv. quickly, instantly; (Lit., obs.) anon.

**Flugsand** ['flu:kzant], m. (—s, no pl.) quicksand, drifting sand.

**Flugzeug** ['flu:ktsɔyk], n. (—s, pl. —e) aeroplane; (Am.) airplane.

**Flugzeugführer** ['flu:ktsɔykfy:rər], m. (—s, pl. —) (Aviat.) pilot.

**Fluidum** ['flu:idum], n. (—s, pl. —da) fluid; (fig.) atmosphere.

**Flunder** ['flundər], f. (—, pl. —n) (fish) flounder.

**Flunkerer** ['fluŋkərər], m. (—s, pl. —) (coll.) fibber, story-teller.

**Flur** (1) [flu:r], f. (—, pl. —en) field, plain; auf weiter —, in the open.

**Flur** (2) [flu:r], m. (—s, pl. —e) (house) hall, vestibule; corridor.

**Flurschaden** ['flu:rʃa:dən], m. (—s, pl. ꞊) damage to crops.

**Fluß** [flus], m. (—sses, pl. ꞊sse) river, stream; flow, flowing; flux.

**Flußbett** ['flusbɛt], n. (—s, pl. —en) channel, riverbed.

**flüssig** ['flysɪç], adj. fluid, liquid; —e Gelder, ready cash; liquid assets.

**flüstern** ['flystərn], v.a. whisper.

**Flut** [flu:t], f. (—, pl. —en) flood; high-tide, high water; torrent; deluge.

**fluten** ['flu:tən], v.n. flow.

**Fockmast** ['fɔkmast], m. (—s, pl. —en) foremast.

**Focksegel** ['fɔkze:gəl], n. (—s, pl. —) foresail.

**Föderalismus** [fø:dəra'lɪsmus], m. (—, no pl.) federalism.

**Fohlen** ['fo:lən], n. (—s, pl. —) foal.

**fohlen** ['fo:lən], v.n. foal.

**Föhn** [fø:n], m. (—s, pl. —e) (warm) Alpine wind.

**Föhre** ['fø:rə], f. (—, pl. —n) (Bot.) fir, fir-tree.

**Folge** ['fɔlgə], f. (—, pl. —n) succession; series, sequence; continuation; consequence.

**folgen** ['fɔlgən], v.n. (aux. sein) follow; succeed; result from, be the consequence of; obey.

**folgendermaßen** ['fɔlgəndərma:sən], adv. as follows.

**folgenschwer** ['fɔlgənʃve:r], adj. momentous, portentous.

**folgerichtig** ['fɔlgərɪçtɪç], adj. consistent, logical.

**folgern** ['fɔlgərn], v.a. draw a conclusion, infer, conclude, deduce.

**Folgerung** ['fɔlgəruŋ], f. (—, pl. —en) induction, deduction, inference.

**folglich** ['fɔlklɪç], conj. consequently, therefore.

**folgsam** ['fɔlkza:m], adj. obedient.

**Foliant** [fo:'ljant], m. (—en, pl. —en) folio-volume, tome.

**Folie** ['fo:ljə], f. (—, pl. —n) foil.

**Folter** ['fɔltər], f. (—, pl. —n) rack, torture.

**Folterbank** ['fɔltərbaŋk], f. (—, pl. ꞊e) rack.

**Fond** [fɔ̃:], m. (—s, pl. —s) back seat.

**Fontäne** [fɔ̃'tɛ:nə], *f.* (—, *pl.* —n) fountain.

**foppen** ['fɔpən], *v.a.* chaff, banter, tease.

**Fopperei** [fɔpə'raɪ], *f.* (—, *pl.* —en) chaff, banter, teasing.

**forcieren** [fɔr'si:rən], *v.a.* strain, overdo.

**Förderer** ['fœrdərər], *m.* (—s, *pl.* —) promoter, backer.

**Förderkarren** ['fœrdərkarən], *m.* (—s, *pl.* —) (*Min.*) truck, trolley.

**förderlich** ['fœrdərliç], *adj.* useful, conducive (to).

**Fördermaschine** ['fœrdərmaʃi:nə], *f.* (—, *pl.* —n) hauling-machine.

**fordern** ['fɔrdərn], *v.a.* demand, claim, ask for; (*duel*) challenge.

**fördern** ['fœrdərn], *v.a.* further, advance, promote, back; hasten; (*Min.*) haul.

**Förderschacht** ['fœrdərʃaxt], *m.* (—s, *pl.* ̈e) (*Min.*) winding shaft.

**Forderung** ['fɔrdərun], *f.* (—, *pl.* —en) demand, claim; (*duel*) challenge.

**Förderung** ['fœrdərun], *f.* (—, *no pl.*) furtherance, promotion, advancement; (*Min.*) hauling.

**Forelle** [fo'rɛlə], *f.* (—, *pl.* —n) trout.

**Forke** ['fɔrkə], *f.* (—, *pl.* —n) pitchfork, garden-fork.

**Form** [fɔrm], *f.* (—, *pl.* —en) form, shape, figure; manner; condition; (*casting*) mould; (*grammar*) form, voice.

**Formalien** [fɔr'ma:ljən], *pl.* formalities.

**Formalität** [fɔrmali'tɛ:t], *f.* (—, *pl.* —en) formality, form.

**Format** [fɔr'ma:t], *n.* (—s, *pl.* —e) (*book, paper*) size; format; (*fig.*) stature.

**Formel** ['fɔrməl], *f.* (—, *pl.* —n) formula.

**formell** [fɔr'mɛl], *adj.* formal.

**Formfehler** ['fɔrmfe:lər], *m.* (—s, *pl.* —) faux pas, breach of etiquette.

**formieren** [fɔr'mi:rən], *v.a.* form. — *v.r. sich* —, fall into line.

**förmlich** ['fœrmliç], *adj.* formal; downright.

**formlos** ['fɔrmlo:s], *adj.* shapeless; (*fig.*) unconventional, informal, unceremonious.

**Formular** [fɔrmu'la:r], *n.* (—s, *pl.* —e) (printed) form, schedule.

**formulieren** [fɔrmu'li:rən], *v.a.* formulate, word.

**formvollendet** ['fɔrmfɔlɛndət], *adj.* well-rounded, well-finished.

**forsch** [fɔrʃ], *adj.* dashing.

**forschen** ['fɔrʃən], *v.n.* search, enquire (after), do research.

**Forschung** ['fɔrʃun], *f.* (—, *pl.* —en) research, investigation; search, exploration.

**Forst** [fɔrst], *m.* (—es, *pl.* —e) forest.

**Förster** ['fœrstər], *m.* (—s, *pl.* —) forester, forest-keeper; (*Am.*) ranger.

**Forstfrevel** ['fɔrstfre:fəl], *m.* (—s, *no pl.*) infringement of forest-laws.

**Forstrevier** ['fɔrstrevi:r], *n.* (—s, *pl.* —e) section of forest.

**Forstwesen** ['fɔrstve:zən], *n.* (—s, *no pl.*) forestry.

**Forstwirtschaft** ['fɔrstvɪrtʃaft], *f.* (—, *no pl.*) forestry.

**fort** [fɔrt], *adv.* away; lost, gone, forth, forward.

**Fort** [fo:rt], *n.* (—s, *pl.* —s) fort.

**fortan** [fɔrt'an], *adv.* henceforth.

**fortbilden** ['fɔrtbɪldən], *v.r. sich* —, improve o.s., receive further education.

**fortbleiben** ['fɔrtblaɪbən], *v.n. irr.* (*aux.* sein) stay away.

**Fortdauer** ['fɔrtdauər], *f.* (—, *no pl.*) continuance, duration.

**fortfahren** ['fɔrtfa:rən], *v.n. irr.* (*aux.* sein) drive off; (*Naut.*) set sail; (*fig.*) continue, go on.

**Fortgang** ['fɔrtgaŋ], *m.* (—s, *no pl.*) going away, departure; (*fig.*) continuation, progress.

**Fortkommen** ['fɔrtkɔmən], *n.* (—s, *no pl.*) advancement, progress; (*fig.*) livelihood.

**fortkommen** ['fɔrtkɔmən], *v.n. irr.* (*aux.* sein) get on, prosper, succeed.

**fortlassen** ['fɔrtlasən], *v.a. irr.* allow to go; leave out, omit; *nicht* —, detain.

**fortlaufen** ['fɔrtlaufən], *v.n. irr.* (*aux.* sein) run away.

**fortpflanzen** ['fɔrtpflantsən], *v.r. sich* —, propagate, multiply; (*sickness*) spread.

**forträumen** ['fɔrtrɔymən], *v.a.* clear away, remove.

**fortschaffen** ['fɔrtʃafən], *v.a.* carry away, get rid of.

**fortscheren** ['fɔrtʃe:rən], *v.r. sich* — (*coll.*) beat it, go away.

**fortscheuchen** ['fɔrtʃɔyçən], *v.a.* scare away.

**fortschreiten** ['fɔrtʃraɪtən], *v.n. irr.* (*aux.* sein) progress, advance.

**Fortschritt** ['fɔrtʃrɪt], *m.* (—s, *pl.* —e) progress, advancement, proficiency.

**fortsetzen** ['fɔrtzetsən], *v.a.* continue, carry on.

**fortwährend** ['fɔrtvɛ:rənt], *adj.* continual, perpetual, unceasing.

**Fracht** [fraxt], *f.* (—, *pl.* —en) freight, cargo, load.

**Frack** [frak], *m.* (—s, *pl.* —s, ̈e) dress-suit, evening dress.

**Frage** ['fra:gə], *f.* (—, *pl.* —n) question, query.

**Fragebogen** ['fra:gəbo:gən], *m.* (—s, *pl.* —) questionnaire.

**fragen** ['fra:gən], *v.a.* ask, enquire, question.

**Fragesteller** ['fra:gəʃtɛlər], *m.* (—s, *pl* —) interrogator, questioner.

**fraglich** ['fra:kliç], *adj.* questionable, problematic(al).

**fragwürdig** ['fra:kvyrdiç], *adj.* doubtful, questionable.

**Fraktion** [frak'tsjo:n], *f.* (—, *pl.* —en) (*Pol.*) party group.

**Frakturschrift** [frak'tu:rʃrɪft], *f.* (—, *no pl.*) (*lettering*) Gothic type, Old English type, Black Letter type.

**Frank** [fraŋk], *m.* (—en, *pl.* —en) (*coin*) franc.

**Franke** ['fraŋkə], *m.* (—n, *pl.* —n) Frank, Franconian.

**frankieren** [fraŋ'ki:rən], *v.a.* (*post*) prepay, frank.

**franko** ['fraŋko], *adj.* post-paid; *gratis und* —, gratuitously.

**Frankreich** ['frankraɪx], *n.* France.

**Franse** ['franzə], *f.* (—, *pl.* —n) fringe.

**Franzose** [fran'tso:zə], *m.* (—n, *pl.* —n) Frenchman.

**französisch** [fran'tsø:zɪʃ], *adj.* French.

**frappant** [fra'pant], *adj.* striking.

**frappieren** [fra'pi:rən], *v.a.* strike, astonish.

**Fraß** [fra:s], *m.* (—es, *no pl.*) (*animals*) feed, fodder; (*sl.*) grub.

**Fratz** [frats], *m.* (—es, *pl.* —en) brat, little monkey.

**Fratze** ['fratsə], *f.* (—, *pl.* —en) grimace, caricature.

**Frau** [frau], *f.* (—, *pl.* —en) woman, wife, lady; (*title*) Mrs.; *gnädige* —, Madam.

**Frauenkirche** ['frauənkɪrçə], *f.* (—, *no pl.*) Church of Our Lady.

**Frauenzimmer** ['frauəntsɪmər], *n.* (—s, *pl.* —) (*pej.*) woman, female.

**Fräulein** ['frɔylaɪn], *n.* (—s, *pl.* —) young lady; (*title*) Miss.

**frech** [frɛç], *adj.* insolent, impudent, cheeky, pert, saucy.

**Frechheit** ['frɛçhaɪt], *f.* (—, *pl.* —en) insolence, impudence.

**Fregatte** [fre'gatə], *f.* (—, *pl.* —n) frigate.

**frei** [fraɪ], *adj.* free, exempt, unhampered, independent, disengaged; vacant; candid, frank.

**Freibeuter** ['fraɪbɔytər], *m.* (—s, *pl.* —) freebooter, pirate.

**Freibrief** ['fraɪbri:f], *m.* (—s, *pl.* —e) patent, licence; permit.

**freien** ['fraɪən], *v.a.* woo, court.

**Freier** ['fraɪər], *m.* (—s, *pl.* —) (*obs.*) suitor.

**Freigabe** ['fraɪga:bə], *f.* (—, *no pl.*) release.

**freigeben** ['fraɪge:bən], *v.a. irr.* release.

**freigebig** ['fraɪge:bɪç], *adj.* liberal, generous.

**Freigebigkeit** ['fraɪge:bɪçkaɪt], *f.* (—, *no pl.*) liberality, munificence, generosity.

**Freigut** ['fraɪgu:t], *n.* (—s, *pl.* ⸚er) freehold.

**Freiheit** ['fraɪhaɪt], *f.* (—, *pl.* —en) freedom, liberty, immunity, privilege.

**Freiherr** ['fraɪhɛr], *m.* (—n, *pl.* —en) baron.

**Freikorps** ['fraɪko:r], *n.* (—, *no pl.*) volunteer-corps.

**Freilauf** ['fraɪlauf], *m.* (—s, *no pl.*) (*bicycle*) free-wheel.

**freilich** ['fraɪlɪç], *adv.* to be sure, it is true, indeed, of course.

**Freilicht-** ['fraɪlɪçt], *adj.* (*in compounds*) open-air.

**Freimarke** ['fraɪmarkə], *f.* (—, *pl.* —n) postage stamp.

**freimütig** ['fraɪmy:tɪç], *adj.* frank, open, candid.

**Freisprechung** ['fraɪʃprɛçuŋ], *f.* (—, *no pl.*) acquittal; absolution.

**Freistätte** ['fraɪʃtɛtə], *f.* (—, *pl.* —n) refuge, asylum.

**Freistoß** ['fraɪʃto:s], *m.* (—es, *pl.* ⸚e) (*Footb.*) free kick.

**Freitag** ['fraɪta:k], *m.* (—s, *pl.* —e) Friday.

**Freitreppe** ['fraɪtrɛpə], *f.* (—, *pl.* —n) outside staircase.

**Freiübung** ['fraɪy:buŋ], *f.* (—, *pl.* —en) (*mostly pl.*) physical exercises, gymnastics.

**freiwillig** ['fraɪvɪlɪç], *adj.* voluntary, of o.'s own accord; spontaneous.

**Freiwillige** ['fraɪvɪlɪgə], *m.* (—n, *pl.* —n) (*Mil.*) volunteer.

**fremd** [frɛmt], *adj.* strange, foreign, outlandish; odd.

**fremdartig** ['frɛmtartɪç], *adj.* strange, odd.

**Fremde** (1) ['frɛmdə], *f.* (—, *no pl.*) foreign country; *in die — gehen*, go abroad.

**Fremde** (2) ['frɛmdə], *m.* (—n, *pl.* —n) stranger, foreigner.

**Fremdheit** ['frɛmthaɪt], *f.* (—, *no pl.*) strangeness.

**Freßbeutel** ['frɛsbɔytəl], *m.* (—s, *pl.* —) nose-bag.

**Fresse** ['frɛsə], *f.* (—, *pl.* —n) (*vulg.*) mouth, snout.

**fressen** ['frɛsən], *v.a. irr.* (*animals*) eat; (*also fig.*) devour.

**Fresserei** [frɛsəraɪ], *f.* (—, *no pl.*) gluttony.

**Frettchen** ['frɛtçən], *n.* (—s, *pl.* —) (*Zool.*) ferret.

**Freude** ['frɔydə], *f.* (—, *pl.* —n) joy, joyfulness, gladness, enjoyment, delight, pleasure.

**Freudenfest** ['frɔydənfɛst], *n.* (—s, *pl.* —e) feast, jubilee.

**Freudenhaus** ['frɔydənhaus], *n.* (—es, *pl.* ⸚er) brothel.

**Freudenmädchen** ['frɔydənmɛːtçən], *n.* (—s, *pl.* —) prostitute.

**freudig** ['frɔydɪç], *adj.* joyful, cheerful, glad.

**freudlos** ['frɔytlo:s], *adj.* joyless.

**freuen** ['frɔyən], *v.r. sich* —, rejoice (at), be glad (of); *sich auf etwas* —, look forward to s.th.

**Freund** [frɔynt], *m.* (—es, *pl.* —e) friend.

**freundlich** ['frɔyntlɪç], *adj.* friendly, kind, affable, pleasing, cheerful, pleasant, genial.

**Freundschaft** ['frɔyntʃaft], *f.* (—, *pl.* —en) friendship.

**Frevel** ['fre:fəl], *m.* (—s, *pl.* —) crime, misdeed, offence.

# Fühler

**freveln** ['fre:fəln], *v.n.* do wrong, trespass, commit an outrage.
**Friede(n)** ['fri:də(n)], *m.* (—ns, *no pl.*) peace.
**friedfertig** ['fri:tfertıç], *adj.* peaceable.
**Friedhof** ['fri:tho:f], *m.* (—s, *pl.* ⸚e) churchyard, cemetery.
**friedlich** ['fri:tlıç], *adj.* peaceful.
**friedliebend** ['fri:tli:bənt], *adj.* peace-able, peace-loving.
**Friedrich** ['fri:drıç], *m.* Frederic(k).
**friedselig** ['fri:tze:lıç], *adj.* peaceable.
**frieren** ['fri:rən], *v.n. irr.* feel cold, freeze.
**Fries** [fri:s], *m.* (—es, *pl.* —e) frieze.
**Friese** ['fri:zə], *m.* (—n, *pl.* —n) Frisian.
**frisch** [frıʃ], *adj.* fresh; new; (*weather*) crisp; (*fig.*) lively, brisk, gay.
**Frische** ['frıʃə], *f.* (—, *no pl.*) freshness, liveliness, gaiety.
**Friseur** [fri'zø:r], *m.* (—s, *pl.* —e) hairdresser, barber.
**Friseuse** [fri'zø:zə], *f.* (—, *pl.* —n) female hairdresser.
**frisieren** [fri'zi:rən], *v.a.* dress (s.o.'s) hair.
**Frist** [frıst], *f.* (—, *pl.* —en) time, term, period; (fixed) term; delay, respite.
**fristen** ['frıstən], *v.a. das Leben* —, gain a bare living.
**Frisur** [fri'zu:r], *f.* (—, *pl.* —en) coiffure, hair-style.
**frivol** [fri'vo:l], *adj.* frivolous.
**Frivolität** [frivo:li'tɛ:t], *f.* (—, *pl.* —en) frivolity.
**froh** [fro:], *adj.* glad, joyful, joyous.
**frohgelaunt** ['fro:gəlaunt], *adj.* good-humoured, cheerful.
**fröhlich** ['frø:lıç], *adj.* gay, merry.
**frohlocken** [fro:'lɔkən], *v.n.* (*rare*) exult.
**Frohsinn** ['fro:zın], *m.* (—s, *no pl.*) good humour, gaiety.
**fromm** [frɔm], *adj.* pious, religious, devout.
**frommen** ['frɔmən], *v.n.* (*obs.*) be of advantage (to s.o.).
**Frömmigkeit** ['frœmıçkaıt], *f.* (—, *no pl.*) piety, devoutness.
**Fron** [fro:n], *f.* (—, *no pl.*) (feudal) service; statute labour.
**frönen** ['frø:nən], *v.n.* (*fig.*) be a slave to; indulge in (*Dat.*).
**Fronleichnam** [fro:n'laıxna:m], *m.* (*Eccl.*) (feast of) Corpus Christi.
**Front** [frɔnt], *f.* (—, *pl.* —en) front, forepart; (*building*) elevation; (*Mil.*) front line.
**Frosch** [frɔʃ], *m.* (—es, *pl.* ⸚e) (*Zool.*) frog.
**Frost** [frɔst], *m.* (—es, *pl.* ⸚e) frost; coldness, chill.
**Frostbeule** ['frɔstbɔylə], *f.* (—, *pl.* —n) chilblain.
**frösteln** ['frœstəln], *v.n.* feel a chill, shiver.
**frostig** ['frɔstıç], *adj.* frosty; cold, chilly.
**frottieren** [frɔ'ti:rən], *v.a.* rub (down).

**Frottiertuch** [frɔ'ti:rtu:x], *n.* (—s, *pl.* ⸚er) Turkish towel, bath towel.
**Frucht** [fruxt], *f.* (—, *pl.* ⸚e) fruit; (*fig.*) result, effect; (*Med.*) fœtus.
**fruchtbar** ['fruxtba:r], *adj.* fruitful, productive, fertile.
**fruchten** ['fruxtən], *v.n.* produce fruit; (*fig.*) be effectual.
**Fruchtknoten** ['fruxtkno:tən], *m.* (—s, *pl.* —) seed-vessel.
**früh(e)** [fry:(ə)], *adj.* early.
**Frühe** ['fry:ə], *f.* (—, *no pl.*) early morning, dawn.
**früher** ['fry:ər], *adv.* earlier (on), formerly.
**frühestens** ['fry:əstəns], *adv.* at the earliest (possible moment).
**Frühjahr** ['fry:ja:r], *n.*, **Frühling** ['fry:lıŋ], *m.* (—s, *pl.* —e) spring.
**frühreif** ['fry:raıf], *adj.* precocious.
**Frühschoppen** ['fry:ʃɔpən], *m.* (—s, *pl.* —) morning pint (beer *or* wine).
**Frühstück** ['fry:ʃtyk], *n.* (—s, *pl.* —e) breakfast; *zweites* —, lunch.
**Fuchs** [fuks], *m.* (—es, *pl.* ⸚e) fox; chestnut (horse); (*fig.*) cunning chap; (*student*) freshman.
**Fuchsbau** ['fuksbau], *m.* (—s, *pl.* —e) fox-hole.
**Fuchseisen** ['fuksaızən], *n.* (—s, *pl.* —) fox-trap.
**fuchsen** ['fuksən], *v.r. sich* — *über*, be annoyed about.
**Fuchsie** ['fuksjə], *f.* (—, *pl.* —n) (*Bot.*) fuchsia.
**fuchsig** ['fuksıç], *adj.* (*coll.*) very angry.
**Füchsin** ['fyksın], *f.* (—, *pl.* —innen) vixen.
**fuchsrot** ['fuksro:t], *adj.* fox-coloured, sorrel.
**Fuchsschwanz** ['fuksʃvants], *m.* (—es, *pl.* ⸚e) fox-brush; pad saw.
**Fuchtel** ['fuxtəl], *f.* (—, *pl.* —n) sword blade; rod, whip.
**Fuder** ['fu:dər], *n.* (—s, *pl.* —) load, cart-load; wine measure (c. 270 gallons).
**Fug** ['fu:k], *m.* (—s, *no pl.*) (*rare*) right, justice; *mit* — *und Recht*, with every right.
**Fuge** (1) ['fu:gə], *f.* (—, *pl.* —n) joint, groove.
**Fuge** (2) ['fu:gə], *f.* (—, *pl.* —n) (*Mus.*) fugue.
**fügen** ['fy:gən], *v.a.* fit together, join, dovetail. — *v.r. sich* —, submit (to), accommodate o.s. (to).
**fügsam** ['fy:kza:m], *adj.* pliant, submissive, yielding.
**Fügung** ['fy:guŋ], *f.* (—, *pl.* —en) coincidence; dispensation (of Providence); Providence.
**fühlbar** ['fy:lba:r], *adj.* perceptible; tangible; *sich* — *machen*, make o.s. felt.
**fühlen** ['fy:lən], *v.a.* feel, touch, sense, be aware of.
**Fühler** ['fy:lər], *m.* (—s, *pl.* —) tentacle, feeler.

# Fühlhorn

**Fühlhorn** ['fy:lhɔrn], *n.* (—**s**, *pl.* ⁀**er**) feeler, antenna, tentacle.

**Fühlung** ['fy:luŋ], *f.* (—, *no pl.*) — *haben mit*, be in touch with.

**Fuhre** ['fu:rə], *f.* (—, *pl.* —**n**) conveyance, vehicle, cart-load.

**führen** ['fy:rən], *v.a.* lead, guide, conduct, command; (*pen*) wield; (*law-suit*) carry on; (*conversation*) have, keep up; (*name, title*) bear; (*goods*) stock, deal in; *Krieg* —, wage war; *etwas im Schilde* —, have a plan; *das Wort* —, be spokesman; *einen hinters Licht* —, cheat s.o.

**Führer** ['fy:rər], *m.* (—**s**, *pl.* —) leader, guide; head, manager; conductor; driver, pilot.

**Führerschaft** ['fy:rərʃaft], *f.* (—, *no pl.*) leadership.

**Führerschein** ['fy:rərʃain], *m.* (—**s**, *pl.* —**e**) driving-licence.

**Führersitz** ['fy:rərzɪts], *m.* (—**es**, *pl.* —**e**) driver's seat; pilot's cockpit.

**Fuhrlohn** ['fu:rlo:n], *m.* (—**s**, *no pl.*) cartage, carriage.

**Fuhrmann** ['fu:rman], *m.* (—**s**, *pl.* ⁀**er**) carter, carrier.

**Führung** ['fy:ruŋ], *f.* (—, *no pl.*) guidance; leadership; conducted tour; management, direction; behaviour, conduct.

**Führungszeugnis** ['fy:ruŋstsɔyknɪs], *n.* (—**sses**, *pl.* —**sse**) certificate of good conduct.

**Fuhrwerk** ['fu:rvɛrk], *n.* (—**s**, *pl.* —**e**) carriage, vehicle, waggon.

**Fuhrwesen** ['fu:rve:zən], *n.* (—**s**, *no pl.*) transport services, transportation.

**Fülle** ['fylə], *f.* (—, *no pl.*) fullness; abundance, plenty.

**Füllen** ['fylən], *n.* (—**s**, *pl.* —) foal.

**füllen** ['fylən], *v.a.* fill, fill up; stuff.

**Füllfederhalter** ['fylfe:dərhaltər], *m.* (—**s**, *pl.* —) fountain-pen.

**Füllung** ['fyluŋ], *f.* (—, *pl.* —**en**) filling; stuffing; (*door*) panel.

**fummeln** ['fuməln], *v.n.* fumble.

**Fund** [funt], *m.* (—**es**, *pl.* —**e**) find; discovery.

**Fundbüro** ['funtbyro], *n.* (—**s**, *pl.* —**s**) lost property office.

**Fundgrube** ['funtgru:bə], *f.* (—, *pl.* —**n**) gold-mine, source, treasure-house.

**fundieren** [fun'di:rən], *v.a.* found; establish.

**fünf** [fynf], *num. adj.* five.

**Fünfeck** ['fynfɛk], *n.* (—**s**, *pl.* —**e**) pentagon.

**Fünffüßler** ['fynffy:slər], *m.* (—**s**, *pl.* —) (*Poet.*) pentameter.

**fünfjährig** ['fynfjɛ:rɪç], *num. adj.* five-year-old.

**fünfjährlich** ['fynfjɛ:rlɪç], *num. adj.* quinquennial, five-yearly.

**fünfzehn** ['fynftse:n], *num. adj.* fifteen.

**fünfzig** ['fynftsɪç], *num. adj.* fifty.

**fungieren** [fun'gi:rən], *v.n.* — *als*, act as, officiate as.

**Funk** [funk], *m.* (—**s**, *no pl.*) radio; wireless; telegraphy.

**Funke** ['funkə], *m.* (—**n**, *pl.* —**n**) spark, sparkle.

**funkeln** ['funkəln], *v.n.* sparkle, glitter; (*stars*) twinkle.

**funkelnagelneu** ['funkəlna:gəlnɔy], *adj.* (*coll.*) brand-new.

**funken** ['funkən], *v.a.* flash (messages); telegraph, broadcast.

**Funker** ['funkər], *m.* (—**s**, *pl.* —) wireless operator.

**Funksender** ['funkzɛndər], *m.* (—**s**, *pl.* —) radio-transmitter.

**Funkspruch** ['funkʃprux], *m.* (—**s**, *pl.* ⁀**e**) wireless-message.

**Funktelegramm** ['funktelegram], *n.* (—**s**, *pl.* —**e**) radio telegram.

**für** [fy:r], *prep.* (*Acc.*) for, instead of; *ein* — *allemal*, once and for all; *an und* — *sich*, in itself.

**Fürbitte** ['fy:rbɪtə], *f.* (—, *pl.* —**n**) intercession.

**Furche** ['furçə], *f.* (—, *pl.* —**n**) furrow; (*face*) wrinkle.

**furchen** ['furçən], *v.a.* furrow; (*face*) wrinkle.

**Furcht** [furçt], *f.* (—, *no pl.*) fear, worry, anxiety; dread, fright, terror, apprehension.

**furchtbar** ['furçtba:r], *adj.* dreadful, terrible, frightful.

**fürchten** ['fyrçtən], *v.a.* fear, be afraid of. — *v.r. sich* — *vor*, be afraid of.

**fürchterlich** ['fyrçtərlɪç], *adj.* terrible, horrible, awful.

**furchtsam** ['furçtza:m], *adj.* timid, fearful, apprehensive.

**Furie** ['fu:rjə], *f.* (—, *pl.* —**n**) fury, virago.

**fürlieb** [fyr'li:p], *adv. mit etwas* — *nehmen*, put up with, be content with s.th.

**Furnier** [fur'ni:r], *n.* (—**s**, *pl.* —**e**) veneer, inlay.

**Furore** [fu'ro:rə], *n.* (—**s**, *no pl.*) — *machen*, cause a sensation, create an uproar.

**Fürsorge** ['fy:rzɔrgə], *f.* (—, *no pl.*) solicitude; provision; welfare.

**fürsorglich** ['fy:rzɔrglɪç], *adj.* thoughtful, with loving care.

**Fürsprache** ['fy:rʃpra:xə], *f.* (—, *no pl.*) advocacy, intercession.

**Fürst** [fyrst], *m.* (—**en**, *pl.* —**en**) prince, sovereign.

**Furt** [furt], *f.* (—, *pl.* —**en**) ford.

**Furunkel** [fu'ruŋkəl], *m.* (—**s**, *pl.* —) furuncle, boil.

**Fürwort** ['fy:rvɔrt], *n.* (—**s**, *pl.* ⁀**er**) pronoun.

**Fusel** ['fu:zəl], *m.* (—**s**, *no pl.*) bad liquor, (*Am. sl.*) hooch.

**Fuß** [fu:s], *m.* (—**es**, *pl.* ⁀**e**) (*human*) foot; (*object*) base.

**Fußangel** ['fu:saŋəl], *f.* (—, *pl.* —**n**) man-trap.

**Fußball** ['fu:sbal], *m.* (—**s**, *pl.* ⁀**e**) football.

**Fußboden** ['fu:sbo:dən], *m.* (—s, *pl.* ⸚) floor.

**fußen** ['fu:sən], *v.n.* — *auf,* be based upon.

**fußfrei** ['fu:sfraɪ], *adj.* ankle-length.

**Fußgänger** ['fu:sgɛŋər], *m.* (—s, *pl.* —) pedestrian.

**Fußgestell** ['fu:sgəʃtɛl], *n.* (—s, *pl.* —e) pedestal.

**Fußpflege** ['fu:spfle:gə], *f.* (—, *no pl.*) chiropody.

**Fußpunkt** ['fu:spuŋkt], *m.* (—s, *no pl.*) nadir.

**Fußtritt** ['fu:strɪt], *m.* (—s, *pl.* —e) kick.

**futsch** [futʃ], *excl.* (*coll.*) gone, lost.

**Futter** ['futər], *n.* (—s, *no pl.*) (*dress*) lining; (*animals*) fodder, feed.

**Futteral** [futə'ra:l], *n.* (—s, *pl.* —e) case; sheath.

**Futterkräuter** ['futərkrɔytər], *n. pl.* herbage.

**futtern** ['futərn], *v.n.* (*coll.*) feed, stuff o.s.

**füttern** ['fytərn], *v.a.* feed; (*garment*) line.

# G

**G** [ge:], *n.* (—s, *pl.* —s) the letter G; (*Mus.*) *G Dur*, G major; (*Mus.*) *G Moll*, G minor; (*Mus.*) — -*Saite*, G string.

**Gabe** ['ga:bə], *f.* (—, *pl.* —n) gift, present; donation; *barmherzige* —, alms; (*fig.*) gift, talent.

**Gabel** ['ga:bəl], *f.* (—, *pl.* —n) fork; (*deer*) antler; (*cart*) shafts.

**gabelig** ['ga:bəlɪç], *adj.* forked.

**Gabelung** ['ga:bəluŋ], *f.* (—, *pl.* —en) bifurcation, branching (of road).

**Gabelzinke** ['ga:bəltsɪŋkə], *f.* (—, *pl.* —n) prong, tine.

**Gabun** [ga'bu:n], *n.* Gaboon.

**gackern** ['gakərn], *v.n.* cackle; (*fig.*) chatter.

**gaffen** ['gafən], *v.n.* gape (at), stare.

**Gage** ['ga:ʒə], *f.* (—, *pl.* —n) salary, pay, fee.

**gähnen** ['gɛ:nən], *v.n.* yawn, gape.

**Galan** [ga'la:n], *m.* (—s, *pl.* —e) lover, gallant.

**galant** [ga'lant], *adj.* polite, courteous; —*es Abenteuer*, love affair.

**Galanterie** [galantə'ri:], *f.* (—,*pl.*—n) courtesy.

**Galanteriewaren** [galantə'ri:va:rən], *f. pl.* fancy goods.

**Galeere** [ga'le:rə], *f.* (—, *pl.* —n) galley.

**Galerie** [galə'ri:], *f.* (—, *pl.* —n) gallery.

**Galgen** ['galgən], *m.* (—s, *pl.* —) gallows, gibbet; scaffold.

**Galgenfrist** ['galgənfrɪst], *f.* (—, *no pl.*) short delay, respite.

**Galgenhumor** ['galgənhumo:r],*m.* (—s, *no pl.*) wry *or* grim humour.

**Galgenvogel** ['galgənfo:gəl], *m.* (—s, *pl.* ⸚) gallows-bird.

**Galizien** [ga'li:tsjən], *n.* Galicia.

**Gallapfel** ['galapfəl], *m.* (—s, *pl.* ⸚) gall-nut.

**Galle** ['galə], *f.* (—, *pl.* —n) gall, bile.

**Gallenblase** ['galənbla:zə], *f.* (—, *pl.* —n) gall-bladder.

**Gallert** ['galərt], *n.* (—s, *no pl.*) jelly.

**Gallien** ['galjən], *n.* Gaul.

**gallig** ['galɪç], *adj.* bilious.

**galvanisieren** [galvanɪ'zi:rən], *v.a.* galvanize.

**Gamaschen** [ga'maʃən], *f. pl.* spats, gaiters.

**Gang** [gaŋ], *m.* (—es, *pl.* ⸚e) walk, gait; (*horse*) pace; (*house*) passage, corridor; (*meal*) course, dish; (*action*) progress, course; (*sport*) round, bout; (*machine*) motion; stroke; (*Motor.*) gear.

**gang** [gaŋ], *adj.* — *und gäbe,* customary, usual, common.

**Gangart** ['gaŋa:rt], *f.* (—, *pl.* —en) gait; (*horse*) pace.

**gangbar** ['gaŋba:r], *adj.* marketable, saleable; (*road*) passable; practicable.

**Gans** [gans], *f.* (—, *pl.* ⸚e) (*Orn.*) goose.

**Gänseblümchen** ['gɛnzəbly:mçən], *n.* (—s, *pl.*—) daisy.

**Gänsefüßchen** ['gɛnzəfy:sçən], *n. pl.* (*coll.*) inverted commas, quotation marks.

**Gänsehaut** ['gɛnzəhaut], *f.* (—, *no pl.*) goose-flesh, goose-pimples.

**Gänserich** ['gɛnzərɪç], *m.* (—s, *pl.* —e) (*Orn.*) gander.

**ganz** ['gants], *adj.* whole, entire, all; complete, total.

**gänzlich** ['gɛntslɪç], *adj.* whole, total, entire, full, complete.

**gar** [ga:r], *adj.* sufficiently cooked, done. — *adv.* very, quite.

**garantieren** [garan'ti:rən], *v.a.* guarantee, warrant.

**Garaus** ['ga:raus], *m.* (—, *no pl.*) *einem den — machen,* finish s.o., kill s.o.

**Garbe** ['garbə], *f.* (—, *pl.* —n) sheaf.

**Garde** ['gardə], *f.* (—, *pl.* —n) guard, guards.

**Garderobe** [gardə'ro:bə], *f.* (—, *pl.* —n) wardrobe; cloak-room; (*Theat.*) dressing-room.

**Gardine** [gar'di:nə], *f.* (—, *pl.* —n) curtain.

**Gardist** [gar'dɪst], *m.* (—en, *pl.* —en) guardsman.

**gären** ['gɛ:rən], *v.n.* ferment; effervesce.

**Garn** [garn], *n.* (—s, *pl.* —e) yarn, thread.

**Garnele** [gar'ne:lə], *f.* (—, *pl.* —n) (*Zool.*) shrimp; *große* —, prawn.

**garnieren** [gar'ni:rən], *v.a.* trim, garnish.

**Garnison** [garni'zo:n], *f.* (—, *pl.* —en) garrison.

# Garnitur

**Garnitur** [garni'tu:r], *f.* (—, *pl.* —en) trimming; set.

**Garnröllchen** ['garnrœlçən], *n.* (—s, *pl.* —) reel of thread.

**garstig** ['garstiç], *adj.* nasty, loathsome, ugly.

**Garten** ['gartən], *m.* (—s, *pl.* ⁻) garden.

**Gartenlaube** ['gartənlaubə], *f.* (—, *pl.* —n) bower, arbour.

**Gärtner** ['gertnər], *m.* (—s, *pl.* —) gardener.

**Gärtnerei** [gertnə'rai], *f.* (—, *pl.* —en) horticulture; market-garden; (plant) nursery.

**Gärung** ['gɛːruŋ], *f.* (—, *pl.* —en) fermentation, effervescence.

**Gas** [ga:s], *n.* (—es, —e) gas; — geben, (*Motor.*) accelerate.

**gasartig** ['ga:sartiç], *adj.* gaseous.

**Gäßchen** ['gɛsçən], *n.* (—s, *pl.* —) narrow alley; lane.

**Gasse** ['gasə], *f.* (—, *pl.* —n) alleyway, lane; (*rare*) street.

**Gassenbube** ['gasənbu:bə] *see* **Gassenjunge.**

**Gassenhauer** ['gasənhauər], *m.* (—s, *pl.* —), street-song, vulgar ballad; pop song.

**Gassenjunge** ['gasənjuŋə], *m.* (—n, *pl.* —n) street-urchin.

**Gast** [gast], *m.* (—s, *pl.* ⁻e) guest, visitor.

**gastfrei** ['gastfrai], *adj.* hospitable.

**Gastfreund** ['gastfrɔynt], *m.* (—s, *pl.* —e) guest; host.

**Gastfreundschaft** ['gastfrɔyntʃaft], *f.* (—, *no pl.*) hospitality.

**Gastgeber** ['gastge:bər], *m.* (—s, *pl.* —) host.

**Gasthaus** ['gasthaus], *n.* (—es, *pl.* ⁻er), **Gasthof** ['gastho:f], *m.* (—es, *pl.* ⁻e) inn, hotel, public house.

**gastieren** [gas'ti:rən], *v.n.* (*Theat.*) appear as a guest artist; star.

**gastlich** ['gastliç], *adj.* hospitable.

**Gastmahl** ['gastma:l], *n.* (—s, *pl.* —e) banquet, feast.

**Gastrecht** ['gastreçt], *n.* (—s, *no pl.*) right of hospitality.

**Gastspiel** ['gastʃpi:l], *n.* (—s, *pl.* —e) (*Theat.*) performance by visiting company.

**Gaststätte** ['gaststɛtə], *f.* (—, *pl.* —n) restaurant.

**Gaststube** ['gastʃtu:bə], *f.* (—, *pl.* —n) hotel lounge; saloon.

**Gastwirt** ['gastvirt], *m.* (—s, *pl.* —e) landlord.

**Gastwirtin** ['gastvirtin], *f.* (—, *pl.* —nen) landlady.

**Gastzimmer** ['gasttsimər], *n.* (—s, *pl.* —) *see* **Gaststube;** spare bedroom.

**Gatte** ['gatə], *m.* (—n, *pl.* —n) husband, spouse, consort.

**Gatter** ['gatər], *n.* (—s, *pl.* —) grate, lattice, grating.

**Gattin** ['gatin], *f.* (—, *pl.* —nen) wife, spouse, consort.

**Gattung** ['gatuŋ], *f.* (—, *pl.* —en) kind, species, sort, class; breed, genus; (*Lit.*) genre.

**Gau** [gau], *m.* (—s, *pl.* —e) district, province.

**gaukeln** ['gaukəln], *v.n.* juggle. — *v.a.* dazzle.

**Gaul** [gaul], *m.* (—s, *pl.* ⁻e) (old) horse, nag; einem geschenkten — sieht man nicht ins Maul, never look a gift horse in the mouth.

**Gaumen** ['gaumən], *m.* (—s, *pl.* —) palate.

**Gauner** ['gaunər], *m.* (—s, *pl.* —) rogue, sharper, swindler, cheat.

**gaunern** ['gaunərn], *v.n.* cheat, trick, swindle.

**Gaunersprache** ['gaunərʃpra:xə], *f.* (—, *no pl.*) thieves' slang.

**Gaze** ['ga:zə], *f.* (—, *pl.* —n) gauze.

**Gazelle** [ga'tsɛlə], *f.* (—, *pl.* —n) (*Zool.*) gazelle, antelope.

**Geächtete** [gə'ɛçtətə], *m.* (—n, *pl.* —n) outlaw.

**Geächze** [gə'ɛçtsə], *n.* (—s, *no pl.*) moaning, groaning.

**Geäder** [gə'ɛ:dər], *n.* (—s, *no pl.*) veins, arteries; veining.

**geädert** [gə'ɛ:dərt], *adj.* veined, streaked; grained.

**-geartet** [gə'a:rtət], *adj.* (*suffix in compounds*) -natured.

**Gebäck** [gə'bɛk], *n.* (—s, *no pl.*) pastry, rolls, cakes.

**Gebälk** [gə'bɛlk], *n.* (—s, *no pl.*) timberwork, timber-frame.

**Gebärde** [gə'bɛ:rdə], *f.* (—, *pl.* —n) gesture.

**gebärden** [gə'bɛ:rdən], *v.r. sich —,* behave.

**Gebaren** [gə'ba:rən], *n.* (—s, *no pl.*) demeanour.

**gebären** [gə'bɛ:rən], *v.a. irr.* bear, bring forth, give birth to, to be delivered of.

**Gebärmutter** [gə'bɛ:rmutər], *f.* (—, *no pl.*) womb, uterus.

**Gebäude** [gə'bɔydə], *n.* (—s, *pl.* —) building, edifice.

**Gebein** [gə'bain], *n.* (—s, *pl.* —e) bones, skeleton; (*fig.*) remains.

**Gebell** [gə'bɛl], *n.* (—s, *no pl.*) barking.

**geben** ['ge:bən], *v.a. irr.* give, present; confer, bestow; yield; (*cards*) deal. — *v.r. sich —,* show o.s., behave; abate; das gibt sich, that won't last long; es gibt ..., there is ...; was gibt's? what's the matter? 

**Geber** ['ge:bər], *m.* (—s, *pl.* —) giver, donor.

**Gebet** [gə'be:t], *n.* (—s, *pl.* —e) prayer; sein — verrichten, say o.'s prayers; ins — nehmen, question s.o. thoroughly.

**Gebiet** [gə'bi:t], *n.* (—s, *pl.* —e) district, territory; (*Am.*) precinct; jurisdiction; (*fig.*) province, field, sphere, domain.

**gebieten** [gə'bi:tən], *v.a. irr.* command, order.

**Gebieter** [gə'bi:tər], *m.* (—s, *pl.* —) lord, master, ruler.

**Gebilde** [gə'bɪldə], *n.* (—s, *pl.* —) form, thing; formation, structure; figment.

**gebildet** [gə'bɪldət], *adj.* educated, cultured, refined.

**Gebirge** [gə'bɪrgə], *n.* (—s, *pl.* —) mountains.

**Gebirgskamm** [gə'bɪrkskam], *m.* (—s, *pl.* ⁻e) mountain-ridge.

**Gebiß** [gə'bɪs], *n.* (—sses, *pl.* —sse) set of (false) teeth, denture; (*horse*) bit.

**Gebläse** [gə'blɛ:zə], *n.* (—s, *pl.* —) bellows; blower.

**Gebläsemaschine** [gə'blɛ:zəmaʃi:nə], *f.* (—, *pl.* —n) blower.

**Gebläseofen** [gə'blɛ:zəo:fən], *m.* (—s, *pl.* ⁻) blast-furnace.

**geblümt** [gə'bly:mt], *adj.* flowered.

**Geblüt** [gə'bly:t], *n.* (—s, *no pl.*) blood; race, line, lineage, stock.

**geboren** [gə'bo:rən], *adj.* born.

**geborgen** [gə'bɔrgən], *adj.* saved, hidden, sheltered, rescued.

**Gebot** [gə'bo:t], *n.* (—s, *pl.* —e) order, decree, command; (*Bibl.*) Commandment.

**geboten** [gə'bo:tən], *adj.* necessary, advisable.

**Gebräu** [gə'brɔy], *n.* (—s, *no pl.*) brew, concoction, mixture.

**Gebrauch** [gə'braux], *m.* (—s, *pl.* ⁻e) use; employment; custom, usage, habit, practice; (*rare*) rite.

**gebrauchen** [gə'brauxən], *v.a.* use, make use of, employ.

**gebräuchlich** [gə'brɔyçlɪç], *adj.* usual, customary, common.

**Gebrauchsanweisung** [gə'brauxsanvaɪzuŋ], *f.* (—, *pl.* —en) directions for use.

**gebraucht** [gə'brauxt], *adj.* used, second-hand.

**Gebrechen** [gə'brɛçən], *n.* (—s, *pl.* —) infirmity.

**gebrechen** [gə'brɛçən], *v.n. irr. es gebricht mir an*, I am in want of, I lack.

**gebrechlich** [gə'brɛçlɪç], *adj.* infirm, frail, weak.

**gebrochen** [gə'brɔxən], *adj.* broken; —*es Deutsch*, broken German.

**Gebrüder** [gə'bry:dər], *m. pl.* (*Comm.*) brothers.

**Gebrüll** [gə'bryl], *n.* (—s, *no pl.*) roaring; (*cows*) lowing.

**Gebühr** [gə'by:r], *f.* (—, *pl.* —en) charge, due; fee; tax, duty.

**gebühren** [gə'by:rən], *v.n.* be due to s.o. — *v.r. sich* —, *wie es sich gebührt*, as it ought to be, as is right and proper.

**gebunden** [gə'bundən], *adj.* ( *fig.*) bound, committed; (*Poet.*) metrical.

**Geburt** [gə'burt], *f.* (—, *pl.* —en) birth.

**gebürtig** [gə'byrtɪç], *adj.* a native of.

**Geburtsfehler** [gə'burtsfe:lər], *m.* (—s, *pl.* —) congenital defect.

**Geburtshelfer** [gə'burtshɛlfər], *m.* (—s, *pl.* —) obstetrician.

**Geburtshelferin** [gə'burtshɛlfərɪn], *f.* (—, *pl.* —nen) midwife.

**Geburtsort** [gə'burtsɔrt], *m.* (—s, *pl.* —e) birthplace.

**Geburtsschein** [gə'burtsʃaɪn], *m.* (—(e)s, *pl.* —e) birth certificate.

**Geburtswehen** [gə'burtsve:ən], *f. pl.* birthpangs; labour pains.

**Gebüsch** [gə'byʃ], *n.* (—es, *no pl.*) bushes, thicket; underwood.

**Geck** [gɛk], *m.* (—en, *pl.* —en) fop, dandy; (*carnival*) fool.

**geckenhaft** ['gɛkənhaft], *adj.* foppish, dandyish.

**Gedächtnis** [gə'dɛçtnɪs], *n.* (—ses, *pl.* —se) memory; remembrance, recollection; *im — behalten*, keep in mind.

**Gedanke** [gə'daŋkə], *m.* (—ns, *pl.* —n) thought, idea.

**Gedankenfolge** [gə'daŋkənfɔlgə], *f.* (—, *no pl.*), **Gedankengang** [gə'daŋkəŋgaŋ], *m.* (—s, *pl.* ⁻e) sequence of thought, train of thought.

**Gedankenstrich** [gə'daŋkənʃtrɪç], *m.* (—s, *pl.* —e) dash; hyphen.

**Gedärm** [gə'dɛrm], *n.* (—s, *pl.* —e) bowels, intestines, entrails.

**Gedeck** [gə'dɛk], *n.* (—s, *pl.* —e) cover; menu; place laid at a table.

**gedeihen** [gə'daɪən], *v.n. irr.* (*aux.* sein) thrive, prosper; progress.

**gedeihlich** [gə'daɪlɪç], *adj.* thriving, salutary.

**gedenken** [gə'dɛŋkən], *v.n. irr.* (*Genit.*) think of, remember; — *etwas zu tun*, intend to do s.th.

**Gedenken** [gə'dɛŋkən], *n.* (—s, *no pl.*) remembrance.

**Gedenkfeier** [gə'dɛŋkfaɪər], *f.* (—, *pl.* —n) commemoration.

**Gedicht** [gə'dɪçt], *n.* (—s, *pl.* —e) poem.

**gediegen** [gə'di:gən], *adj.* solid, sound, genuine, true, honourable, sterling.

**Gedränge** [gə'drɛŋə], *n.* (—s, *no pl.*) crowd, throng; crush.

**Gedrängtheit** [gə'drɛŋkthaɪt], *f.* (—, *no pl.*) conciseness.

**gedrungen** [gə'druŋən], *adj.* thick-set, stocky; compact; concise (style).

**Geduld** [gə'dult], *f.* (—, *no pl.*) patience, forbearance.

**gedulden** [gə'duldən], *v.r. sich* —, be patient.

**geduldig** [gə'duldɪç], *adj.* patient, forbearing, indulgent.

**Geduld(s)spiel** [gə'dult(s)ʃpi:l], *n.* (—s, *pl.* —e) puzzle; (*Cards*) patience.

**gedunsen** [gə'dunzən], *adj.* bloated.

**geeignet** [gə'aɪgnət], *adj.* suitable, fit, appropriate, apt.

**Gefahr** [gə'fa:r], *f.* (—, *pl.* —en) danger, peril, hazard, risk; — *laufen*, run the risk.

**gefahrden** [gə'fɛ:rdən], *v.a.* endanger,

**gefahrlich** [gə'fɛ:rlɪç], *adj.* dangerous, perilous.

**Gefahrt** [gə'fɛ:rt], *n.* (—s, *pl.* —e) (*obs.*) vehicle, conveyance.

**Gefahrte** [gə'fɛ:rtə], *m.* (—n, *pl.* —n) comrade, companion, fellow.

# Gefälle

**Gefälle** [gə'fɛlə], *n.* (—s, *pl.* —) fall, descent, incline, gradient.

**Gefallen** [gə'falən], *m.* (—s, *no pl.*) pleasure, liking; favour, kindness.

**gefallen** (1) [gə'falən], *v.n. irr.* please; *es gefällt mir,* I like it; *wie gefällt Ihnen . . .?* how do you like . . .?

**gefallen** (2) [gə'falən], *adj.* (*Mil.*) fallen, killed in action.

**gefällig** [gə'fɛlɪç], *adj.* pleasing, accommodating, obliging, anxious to please; *was ist — ?* what can I do for you?

**Gefälligkeit** [gə'fɛlɪçkaɪt], *f.* (—, *pl.* —en) courtesy; favour, service, good turn.

**gefälligst** [gə'fɛlɪçst], *adv.* if you please.

**Gefallsucht** [gə'falzuxt], *f.* (—, *no pl.*) coquetry.

**gefallsüchtig** [gə'falzyçtɪç], *adj.* coquettish.

**gefangen** [gə'faŋən], *adj.* in prison, imprisoned, captive.

**Gefangene** [gə'faŋənə], *m., f.* (—n, *pl.* —n) prisoner, captive.

**Gefangennahme** [gə'faŋənna:mə], *f.* (—, *no pl.*) arrest, capture.

**Gefangenschaft** [gə'faŋənʃaft], *f.* (—, *no pl.*) captivity, imprisonment, detention; *in — geraten,* be taken prisoner.

**Gefängnis** [gə'fɛŋnɪs], *n.* (—ses, *pl.* —se) prison, gaol.

**Gefäß** [gə'fɛːs], *n.* (—es, *pl.* —e) vessel.

**gefaßt** [gə'fast], *adj.* collected, composed, ready; calm; *sich auf etwas — machen,* prepare o.s. for s.th.

**Gefecht** [gə'fɛçt], *n.* (—s, *pl.* —e) fight, battle, combat; action, engagement.

**gefeit** [gə'faɪt], *adj.* proof against.

**Gefieder** [gə'fiːdər], *n.* (—s, *no pl.*) plumage, feathers.

**Gefilde** [gə'fɪldə], *n.* (—s, *pl.* —) (*Poet.*) fields, plain.

**Geflecht** [gə'flɛçt], *n.* (—s, *no pl.*) wicker-work, texture.

**geflissentlich** [gə'flɪsəntlɪç], *adj.* intentional, wilful, with a purpose.

**Geflügel** [gə'flyːgəl], *n.* (—s, *no pl.*) fowls, poultry.

**geflügelt** [gə'flyːgəlt], *adj.* winged; *—e Worte,* household words, familiar quotation.

**Geflüster** [gə'flystər], *n.* (—s, *no pl.*) whispering, whisper.

**Gefolge** [gə'fɔlgə], *n.* (—s, *no pl.*) retinue, following.

**gefräßig** [gə'frɛːsɪç], *adj.* voracious, gluttonous.

**Gefreite** [gə'fraɪtə], *m.* (—n, *pl.* —n) (*Mil.*) lance-corporal.

**gefrieren** [gə'friːrən], *v.n. irr.* (*aux.* sein) freeze; congeal.

**Gefrierpunkt** [gə'friːrpuŋkt], *m.* (—s, *no pl.*) freezing point, zero.

**Gefrorene** [gə'froːrənə], *n.* (—n, *no pl.*) ice-cream.

**Gefüge** [gə'fyːgə], *n.* (—s, *no pl.*) joints, structure, construction; frame.

**gefügig** [gə'fyːgɪç], *adj.* pliant; docile; *einen — machen,* make s.o. amenable, persuade s.o.

**Gefühl** [gə'fyːl], *n.* (—s, *pl.* —e) feeling, sense, sensation.

**gegen** ['geːgən], *prep.* (*Acc.*) against; towards; about, near; in comparison with; in the direction of; opposed to; in exchange for; — *Quittung,* against receipt. — *adv., prefix.* counter, opposing, contrary.

**Gegend** ['geːgənt], *f.* (—, *pl.* —en) region, country, part.

**Gegengewicht** ['geːgəngəvɪçt], *n.* (—s, *pl.* —e) counterweight, counterpoise.

**Gegengift** ['geːgəngɪft], *n.* (—s, *pl.* —e) antidote.

**Gegenleistung** ['geːgənlaɪstuŋ], *f.* (—, *pl.* —en) return; service in return; *Leistung und —,* give and take.

**Gegenrede** ['geːgənreːdə], *f.* (—, *pl.* —n) contradiction; objection.

**Gegensatz** ['geːgənzats], *m.* (—es, *pl.* ⸚e) contrast, opposition, antithesis.

**gegensätzlich** ['geːgənzetslɪç], *adj.* contrary, adverse.

**Gegenseite** ['geːgənzaɪtə], *f.* (—, *pl.* —n) opposite side; (*coin*) reverse.

**gegenseitig** ['geːgənzaɪtɪç], *adj.* reciprocal, mutual.

**Gegenstand** ['geːgənʃtant], *m.* (—s, *pl.* ⸚e) object; subject, matter.

**gegenstandslos** ['geːgənʃtantsloːs], *adj.* superfluous, irrelevant.

**Gegenstück** ['geːgənʃtyk], *n.* (—s, *pl.* —e) counterpart.

**Gegenteil** ['geːgəntaɪl], *n.* (—s, *no pl.*) contrary; *im —,* on the contrary.

**gegenüber** [geːgən'yːbər], *prep.* (*Dat.*) opposite to, facing. — *adv.* opposite.

**Gegenüberstellung** [geːgən'yːbərʃtɛluŋ], *f.* (—, *pl.* —en) confrontation.

**Gegenwart** ['geːgənvart], *f.* (—, *no pl.*) presence; (*Gram.*) present tense.

**Gegenwehr** ['geːgənveːr], *f.* (—, *no pl.*) defence, resistance.

**Gegenwirkung** ['geːgənvɪrkuŋ], *f.* (—, *pl.* —en) reaction, counter-effect.

**gegenzeichnen** ['geːgəntsaɪçnən], *v.a.* countersign.

**Gegner** ['geːgnər], *m.* (—s, *pl.* —) opponent, adversary, antagonist.

**gegnerisch** ['geːgnərɪʃ], *adj.* adverse, antagonistic.

**Gegnerschaft** ['geːgnərʃaft], *f.* (—, *no pl.*) antagonism; opposition.

**Gehalt** (1) [gə'halt], *m.* (—s, *no pl.*) contents; (*fig.*) value, standard.

**Gehalt** (2) [gə'halt], *n.* (—s, *pl.* ⸚er) salary, stipend; pay.

**Gehaltszulage** [gə'haltstsuːlaːgə], *f.* (—, *pl.* —n) rise (in salary); increment; (*Am.*) raise.

**gehaltvoll** [gə'haltfɔl], *adj.* substantial.

**Gehänge** [gə'hɛŋə], *n.* (—s, *pl.* —) slope; festoon, garland.

**geharnischt** [gə'harnɪʃt], *adj.* armoured, steel-clad; (*fig.*) severe.

**gehässig** [gə'hɛsɪç], *adj.* malicious, spiteful.

**Gehäuse** [gə'hɔyzə], *n.* (—s, *pl.* —) casing, case; (*snail*) shell.

**Gehege** [gə'he:gə], *n.* (—s, *pl.* —) enclosure; *einem ins — kommen*, trespass on s.o.'s preserves.

**geheim** [gə'haim], *adj.* secret, clandestine.

**Geheimnis** [gə'haimnis], *n.* (—ses, *pl.* —se) secret, mystery.

**geheimnisvoll** [gə'haimnisfɔl], *adj.* mysterious.

**Geheimrat** [gə'haimra:t], *m.* (—s, *pl.* ⁻e) Privy Councillor.

**Geheimschrift** [gə'haimʃrift], *f.* (—, *pl.* —en) cryptography.

**Geheimsprache** [gə'haimʃpra:xə], *f.* (—, *pl.* —en) cipher.

**Geheiß** [gə'hais], *n.* (—es, *no pl.*) command, order, bidding.

**gehen** ['ge:ən], *v.n. irr.* (*aux.* sein) go, walk; (*Mach.*) work, function; (*goods*) sell; (*dough*) rise; *er lässt sich —*, he lets himself go; *er lässt es sich gut —*, he enjoys himself; *einem an die Hand —*, lend s.o. a hand, assist s.o.; *in Erfüllung —*, come true; *in sich —*, reflect; *wie geht es dir?* how are you? *es geht mir gut*, I am well.

**geheuer** [gə'hɔyər], *adj.* (*only in neg.*) *nicht ganz —*, creepy, eerie, uncanny; (*coll.*) fishy.

**Gehilfe** [gə'hilfə], *m.* (—n, *pl.* —n) assistant, helper.

**Gehirn** [gə'hirn], *n.* (—s, *pl.* —e) brain, brains.

**Gehirnhautentzündung** [gə'hirnhautɛntsyndun], *f.* (—, *pl.* —en) meningitis, cerebral inflammation.

**Gehirnschlag** [gə'hirnʃla:k], *m.* (—s, *pl.* ⁻e) apoplexy.

**Gehöft** [gə'hœft], *n.* (—es, *pl.* —e) farmstead.

**Gehör** [gə'hø:r], (—s, *no pl.*) hearing; *gutes —*, musical ear.

**gehorchen** [gə'hɔrçən], *v.n.* obey; *nicht —*, disobey.

**gehören** [gə'hø:rən], *v.n.* belong. — *v.r. sich —*, be the proper thing to do.

**gehörig** [gə'hø:riç], *adj. dazu —*, belonging to, referring to; due, fit, proper, thorough; (*fig.*) sound.

**Gehörn** [gə'hœrn], *n.* (—s, *pl.* —e) horns, antlers.

**gehörnt** [gə'hœrnt], *adj.* horned; (*fig.*) duped (*husband*).

**Gehorsam** [gə'ho:rza:m], *m.* (—s, *no pl.*) obedience; *— leisten*, show obedience; *den — verweigern*, refuse to obey.

**gehorsam** [gə'ho:rza:m], *adj.* obedient, dutiful, submissive.

**Gehrock** [ge:rɔk], *m.* (—s, *pl.* ⁻e) frock-coat.

**Geier** ['gaiər], *m.* (—s, *pl.* —) (*Orn.*) vulture.

**Geifer** ['gaifər], *m.* (—s, *no pl.*) saliva, drivel; (*animals*) foam; (*fig.*) venom, rancour.

**geifern** ['gaifərn], *v.n.* slaver; drivel; (*fig.*) foam at the mouth; give vent to o.'s anger.

**Geige** ['gaigə], *f.* (—, *pl.* —n) violin, fiddle.

**Geigenharz** ['gaigənha:rts], *n.* (—es, *no pl.*) colophony; rosin.

**Geigensteg** ['gaigənʃte:k], *m.* (—s, *pl.* —e) bridge of a violin.

**Geiger** ['gaigər], *m.* (—s, *pl.* —) violin-player, violinist.

**geil** [gail], *adj.* rank; lecherous, lascivious.

**Geisel** ['gaizəl], *f.* (—, *pl.* —n) hostage.

**Geiß** [gais], *f.* (—, *pl.* —en) goat, she-goat.

**Geißblatt** ['gaisblat], *n.* (—s, *no pl.*) (*Bot.*) honeysuckle.

**Geißbock** ['gaisbɔk], *m.* (—s, *pl.* ⁻e) billy-goat.

**Geißel** ['gaisəl], *f.* (—, *pl.* —n) scourge.

**geißeln** ['gaisəln], *v.a.* scourge, whip, flagellate.

**Geist** [gaist], *m.* (—es, *pl.* —er) spirit, mind; brains, intellect; wit; apparition, ghost.

**Geisterbeschwörung** ['gaistərbəʃvø:run], *f.* (—, *pl.* —en) evocation (of spirits); necromancy; exorcism.

**geisterhaft** ['gaistərhaft], *adj.* ghostly, spectral, weird.

**Geisterwelt** ['gaistərvɛlt], *f.* (—, *no pl.*) world of spirits.

**geistesabwesend** ['gaistəsapve:zənt], *adj.* absent-minded.

**Geistesfreiheit** ['gaistəsfraihait], *f.* (—, *no pl.*) freedom of thought.

**Geistesgegenwart** ['gaistəsgə:gənvart], *f.* (—, *no pl.*) presence of mind.

**Geisteskraft** ['gaistəskraft], *f.* (—, *pl.* ⁻e) faculty of the mind.

**Geistesstörung** ['gaistəsʃtø:run], *f.* (—, *pl.* —en) mental aberration.

**Geistesverfassung** ['gaistəsfɛrfasun], *f.* (—, *no pl.*) state of mind.

**geistesverwandt** ['gaistəsfɛrvant], *adj.* congenial.

**Geistesverwirrung** ['gaistəsfɛrvirun], *f.* (—, *no pl.*) bewilderment.

**Geisteswissenschaften** ['gaistəsvisənʃaftən], *f.pl.* (*Univ.*) Arts, Humanities.

**Geisteszerrüttung** ['gaistəstsɛrytun], *f.* (—, *no pl.*) mental derangement, insanity.

**geistig** ['gaistiç], *adj.* intellectual, mental; spiritual; *—e Getränke*, alcoholic liquors.

**geistlich** ['gaistliç], *adj.* spiritual; religious; ecclesiastical, clerical; *—er Orden*, religious order; *—er Stand*, holy orders, the Clergy.

**Geistliche** ['gaistliçə], *m.* (—n, *pl.* —n) priest, clergyman, cleric; minister of religion.

**Geistlichkeit** ['gaistliçkait], *f.* (—, *no pl.*) clergy.

**geistlos** ['gaistlo:s], *adj.* dull, stupid.

**geistreich** ['gaistraiç], *adj.* clever, witty.

**Geiz** [gaits], *m.* (—es, *no pl.*) avarice, covetousness.

**geizen** ['gaitsən], *v.n.* be miserly.

**Geizhals** ['gaItshals], *m.* (—es, *pl.* ∴e) miser, niggard.

**Geizkragen** ['gaItskra:gən], *m.* (—s, *pl.* —) *see* Geizhals.

**Gekreisch** [gə'kraIʃ], *n.* (—es, *no pl.*) screaming, shrieks.

**Gekritzel** [gə'krItsəl], *n.* (—s, *no pl.*) scrawling, scribbling.

**Gekröse** [gə'krø:zə], *n.* (—s, *no pl.*) tripe; (*Anat.*) mesentery.

**gekünstelt** [gə'kynstəlt], *adj.* artificial, affected.

**Gelächter** [gə'lɛçtər], *n.* (—s, *no pl.*) laughter.

**Gelage** [gə'la:gə], *n.* (—s, *pl.* —) (*obs.*) feast, banquet.

**Gelände** [gə'lɛndə], *n.* (—s, *pl.* —) terrain, region; landscape.

**Geländer** [gə'lɛndər], *n.* (—s, *pl.* —) railing, balustrade, banister.

**gelangen** [gə'laŋən], *v.n.* (*aux.* sein) arrive, come (to).

**Gelaß** [gə'las], *n.* (—sses, *pl.* —sse) (*obs.*) room, chamber.

**gelassen** [gə'lasən], *adj.* calm, composed, collected.

**geläufig** [gə'lɔyfIç], *adj.* fluent.

**gelaunt** [gə'launt], *adj.* disposed.

**Geläute** [gə'lɔytə], *n.* (—s, *no pl.*) ringing, chiming; bells.

**geläutert** [gə'lɔytərt], *adj.* purified, cleansed.

**gelb** [gɛlp], *adj.* yellow, amber.

**Gelbschnabel** ['gɛlpʃna:bəl], *m.* (—s, *pl.* ∴) (*Orn.*) fledg(e)ling; greenhorn.

**Gelbsucht** ['gɛlpzuxt], *f.* (—, *no pl.*) jaundice.

**Geld** [gɛlt], *n.* (—es, *pl.* —er) money, currency, coin; *bares* —, ready money, hard cash; *kleines* —, small change.

**Geldanweisung** ['gɛltanvaIzuŋ], *f.* (—, *pl.* —en) money-order.

**Geldbuße** ['gɛltbu:sə], *f.*(—,*pl.*—n) fine.

**Geldkurs** ['gɛltkurs], *m.* (—es, *pl.* —e) rate of exchange.

**Geldmittel** ['gɛltmItəl], *n. pl.* pecuniary resources, financial resources.

**Geldschrank** ['gɛltʃraŋk], *m.* (—s, *pl.* ∴e) safe.

**Geldstrafe** ['gɛltʃtra:fə], *f.* (—, *pl.* —n) fine.

**Geldverlegenheit** ['gɛltfɛrle:gənhaIt], *f.* (—, *pl.* —en) pecuniary embarrassment, financial difficulty.

**Geldwährung** ['gɛltvɛ:ruŋ], *f.* (—, *pl.* —en) currency.

**Geldwechsel** ['gɛltvɛksəl], *m.* (—s, *no pl.*) exchange.

**Gelee** [ʒə'le:], *n.* (—s, *pl.* —s) jelly.

**gelegen** [gə'le:gən], *adj.* situated, situate; *das kommt mir gerade* —, that suits me; *mir ist daran* —, *dass,* I am anxious that.

**Gelegenheit** [gə'le:gənhaIt], *f.* (—, *pl.* —en) occasion, chance, opportunity; facility; *bei* —, one of these days.

**Gelegenheitskauf** [gə'le:gənhaItskauf], *m.* (—s, *pl.* ∴e) bargain.

**gelegentlich** [gə'le:gəntlIç], *adj.* occasional.

**gelehrig** [gə'le:rIç], *adj.* docile, tractable.

**Gelehrsamkeit** [gə'le:rza:mkaIt], *f.* (—, *no pl.*) learning, erudition.

**gelehrt** [gə'le:rt], *adj.* learned, erudite.

**Gelehrte** [gə'le:rtə], *m.* (—n, *pl.* —n) scholar, man of learning, savant.

**Geleise** [gə'laIzə], *n.* (—s, *pl.* —) *see* Gleis.

**Geleit** [gə'laIt], *n.* (—s, *no pl.*) escort, accompaniment; (*Naut.*) convoy; *sicheres* —, safe conduct.

**geleiten** [gə'laItən], *v.a.* accompany, conduct, escort.

**Gelenk** [gə'lɛŋk], *n.* (—s, *pl.* —e) (*human*) joint; (*chain*) link.

**Gelenkentzündung** [gə'lɛŋkɛnttsynduŋ], *f.* (—, *pl.* —en) (*Med.*) arthritis.

**gelenkig** [gə'lɛŋkIç], *adj.* flexible, pliant, nimble, supple.

**Gelenkrheumatismus** [gə'lɛŋkrɔymatIsmus], *m.* (—, *no pl.*) (*Med.*) rheumatoid arthritis, rheumatic gout.

**Gelichter** [gə'lIçtər], *n.* (—s, *no pl.*) riff-raff.

**Geliebte** [gə'li:ptə], *m.* (—n, *pl.* —n) lover, sweetheart, beloved. — *f.* (—n, *pl.*—n) mistress, beloved.

**gelinde** [gə'lIndə], *adj.* soft, smooth, gentle, mild; — *gesagt,* to say the least.

**Gelingen** [gə'lIŋən], *n.* (—s, *no pl.*) success.

**gelingen** [gə'lIŋən], *v.n. irr.* (*aux.* sein) succeed; *es gelingt mir,* I succeed.

**gellen** ['gɛlən], *v.n.* yell; shrill.

**geloben** [gə'lo:bən], *v.a.* (*aux.* haben) promise solemnly, vow; *das Gelobte Land,* the Promised Land.

**Gelöbnis** [gə'lø:pnIs], *n.* (—ses, *pl.* —se) vow, promise.

**gelt** [gɛlt], *inter.* (*coll.*) isn't it? don't you think so?

**gelten** ['gɛltən], *v.a. irr.* be worth, cost. — *v.n.* count (as), be valid.

**Geltung** ['gɛltuŋ], *f.* (—, *no pl.*) value, importance.

**Gelübde** [gə'lypdə], *n.* (—s, *pl.* —) vow, solemn promise *or* undertaking.

**gelungen** [gə'luŋən], *adj.* (*coll.*) funny, capital.

**Gelüst** [gə'lyst], *n.* (—s, *pl.* —e) appetite, desire.

**gelüsten** [gə'lystən], *v.a.* — *nach,* long for, covet.

**Gemach** [gə'ma:x], *n.* (—es, *pl.* ∴er) (*Poet.*) chamber, room; apartment.

**gemach** [gə'ma:x], *adv.* slowly, softly, by degrees.

**gemächlich** [gə'mɛçlIç], *adj.* slow, soft, easy, unhurried, leisurely.

**Gemahl** [gə'ma:l], *m.* (—s, *pl.* —e) spouse, husband, consort.

**Gemahlin** [gə'ma:lIn], *f.* (—, *pl.* —nen) spouse, wife, consort.

**Gemälde** [gə'mɛ:ldə], *n.* (—s, *pl.* —) picture, painting, portrait.

**gemäß** [gə'mɛ:s], *prep.* (*Dat.*) in accordance with, according to.

**gemäßigt** [gə'mɛːsɪçt], *adj.* temperate, moderate; *—es Klima*, temperate climate.

**Gemäuer** [gə'mɔyər], *n.* (—s, *no pl.*) ancient walls, ruins.

**gemein** [gə'maɪn], *adj.* common, mean, low, vulgar, base.

**Gemeinde** [gə'maɪndə], *f.* (—, *pl.* —n) community, parish, municipality; (*Eccl.*) congregation.

**Gemeindevorstand** [gə'maɪndefor-ʃtant], *m.* (—es, *no pl.*) town *or* borough council.

**gemeingefährlich** [gə'maɪngəfɛːrlɪç], *adj.* dangerous to the public.

**Gemeinheit** [gə'maɪnhaɪt], *f.* (—, *pl.* —en) meanness; baseness; dirty trick.

**gemeinhin** [gə'maɪnhɪn], *adv.* commonly.

**Gemeinplatz** [gə'maɪnplats], *m.* (—es, *pl.* ̈e) commonplace, truism.

**gemeinsam** [gə'maɪnzaːm], *adj.* common, joint; *der — Markt*, (*Pol.*) Common Market; *—e Sache machen*, make common cause. — *adv.* together.

**Gemeinschaft** [gə'maɪnʃaft], *f.* (—, *pl.* —en) community; association; *in — mit*, jointly; *in — haben*, hold in common.

**gemeinschaftlich** [gə'maɪnʃaftlɪç], *adj.* common. — *adv.* in common, together.

**Gemeinsinn** [gə'maɪnzɪn], *m.* (—s, *no pl.*) public spirit.

**Gemeinwesen** [gə'maɪnveːzən], *n.* (—s, *no pl.*) community.

**Gemeinwohl** [gə'maɪnvoːl], *n.* (—s, *no pl.*) common weal; common good.

**Gemenge** [gə'mɛŋə], *n.* (—s, *no pl.*) mixture; (*fig.*) scuffle.

**Gemengsel** [gə'mɛŋsəl], *n.* (—s, *no pl.*) medley, hotchpotch.

**gemessen** [gə'mɛsən], *adj.* deliberate.

**Gemessenheit** [gə'mɛsənhaɪt], *f.* (—, *no pl.*) precision, deliberation.

**Gemetzel** [gə'mɛtsəl], *n.* (—s, *no pl.*) slaughter, massacre.

**Gemisch** [gə'mɪʃ], *n.* (—es, *pl.* —e) mixture, motley.

**Gemme** ['gɛmə], *f.* (—, *pl.* —n) gem, cameo.

**Gemse** ['gɛmzə], *f.* (—, *pl.* —n) chamois.

**Gemüse** [gə'myːzə], *n.* (—s, *pl.* —) vegetables, greens.

**Gemüsehändler** [gə'myːzəhɛndlər], *m.* (—s, *pl.* —) greengrocer.

**gemustert** [gə'mustərt], *adj.* patterned, figured; (*Comm.*) *—e Sendung*, delivery as per sample.

**Gemüt** [gə'myːt], *n.* (—s, *pl.* —er) mind, soul, heart; disposition, nature, spirit, temper; feeling.

**gemütlich** [gə'myːtlɪç], *adj.* cosy, snug, comfortable; genial, friendly, pleasant.

**Gemütlichkeit** [gə'myːtlɪçkaɪt], *f.* (—, *no pl.*) cosiness, snugness; *da hört die — auf*, that is more than I will stand for.

**gemütlos** [gə'myːtloːs], *adj.* unfeeling.

**Gemütsart** [gə'myːtsaːrt], *f.* (—, *no pl.*) disposition; character.

**Gemütsbewegung** [gə'myːtsbəveːguŋ], *f.* (—, *pl.* —en) emotion.

**gemütskrank** [gə'myːtskraŋk], *adj.* sick in mind; melancholy.

**Gemütsleben** [gə'myːtsleːbən], *n.* (—s, *no pl.*) emotional life.

**Gemütsmensch** [gə'myːtsmɛnʃ], *m.* (—en, *pl.* —en) man of feeling *or* sentiment; (*pej.*) sentimentalist.

**gemütvoll** [gə'myːtfɔl], *adj.* full of feeling, sympathetic.

**gen** [gɛn], *prep. contraction* of **gegen**, (*Poet.*) towards, to (*Acc.*).

**Genannte** [gə'nantə], *m.* (—n, *pl.* —n) named person, aforesaid.

**genäschig** [gə'nɛʃɪç], *adj.* fond of sweets, sweet-toothed.

**genau** [gə'nau], *adj.* precise, exact, accurate; strict, parsimonious.

**Genauigkeit** [gə'nauɪçkaɪt], *f.* (—, *no pl.*) accuracy, exactitude, precision.

**Gendarm** [ʒã'darm], *m.* (—en, *pl.* —en) policeman, constable.

**genehm** [gə'neːm], *adj.* agreeable, acceptable, convenient.

**genehmigen** [gə'neːmɪgən], *v.a.* approve of, agree to, permit; (*contract*) ratify.

**geneigt** [gə'naɪkt], *adj.* inclined (to), disposed (to), prone (to); *einem — sein*, be well disposed towards s.o.; (*Lit.*) *der —e Leser*, gentle reader.

**Geneigtheit** [gə'naɪktheit], *f.* (—, *no pl.*) inclination, proneness, propensity; favour, kindness.

**General** [genə'raːl], *m.* (—s, *pl.* —e, ̈e) general.

**Generalfeldmarschall** [genə'raːlfɛlt-marʃal], *m.* (—s, *pl.* ̈e) field marshal.

**Generalkommando** [genə'raːlkɔman-do], *n.* (—s, *pl.* —s) general's headquarters; (corps) headquarters.

**Generalkonsul** [genə'raːlkɔnzul], *m.* (—s, *pl.* —e) consul-general.

**Generalnenner** [genə'raːlnɛnər], *m.* (—s, *pl.* —) (*Maths.*) common denominator.

**Generalprobe** [genə'raːlproːbə], *f.* (—, *pl.* —n) dress-rehearsal.

**Generalvollmacht** [genə'raːlfɔlmaxt], *f.* (—, *pl.* —en) (*Law*) general power of attorney.

**generell** [genə'rɛl], *adj.* general, common.

**generös** [genə'røːs], *adj.* generous, magnanimous.

**genesen** [gə'neːzən], *v.n. irr.* (*aux.* sein) recover, be restored to health; convalesce.

**Genf** [gɛnf], *n.* Geneva.

**genial** [gen'jaːl], *adj.* ingenious; extremely gifted.

**Genick** [gə'nɪk], *n.* (—s, *pl.* —e) nape, neck.

**Genickstarre** [gə'nɪkʃtarə], *f.* (—, *no pl.*) (*Med.*) (cerebrospinal) meningitis.

**Genie** [ʒe'niː], *n.* (—s, *pl.* —s) genius.

**genieren** [ʒe'ni:rən], *v.a.* trouble, embarrass, disturb. — *v.r. sich* —, feel embarrassed; *sich nicht* —, make o.s. at home.
**genießbar** [gə'ni:sba:r], *adj.* eatable, edible, palatable; drinkable; (*fig.*) pleasant, agreeable.
**genießen** [gə'ni:sən], *v.a. irr.* enjoy; have the use of; (*food*) eat, partake of; *Ansehen* —, enjoy respect.
**Geniestreich** [ʒe'ni:ʃtraɪç], *m.* (**—s,** *pl.* **—e**) stroke of genius.
**Genitiv** ['ge:nɪti:f], *m.* (**—s,** *pl.* **—e**) (*Gram.*) genitive.
**Genosse** [gə'nɔsə], *m.* (**—n,** *pl.* **—n**) comrade, mate, colleague; (*crime*) accomplice.
**Genossenschaft** [gə'nɔsənʃaft], *f.* (**—,** *pl.* **—en**) association, company, confederacy, co-operative, union.
**Genre** ['ʒãrə], *n.* (**—s,** *pl.* **—s**) genre; style, kind.
**Gent** [gɛnt], *n.* Ghent.
**Genua** ['ge:nua], *n.* Genoa.
**genug** [gə'nu:k], *indecl. adj.* enough, sufficient; —*!* that will do!
**Genüge** [gə'ny:gə], *f.* (**—,** *no pl.*) *zur* —, sufficiently; *einem — leisten*, give satisfaction to s.o.
**genügen** [gə'ny:gən], *v.n.* be enough, suffice; *sich etwas — lassen*, be content with s.th.
**genügsam** [gə'ny:kza:m], *adj.* easily satisfied; temperate, sober.
**Genügsamkeit** [gə'ny:kza:mkaɪt], *f.* (**—,** *no pl.*) contentedness, moderation; temperateness, sobriety.
**Genugtuung** [gə'nu:ktuuŋ], *f.* (**—,** *no pl.*) satisfaction; reparation; atonement.
**Genuß** [gə'nus], *m.* (**—sses,** *pl.* **¨sse**) enjoyment; use; (*food*) consumption.
**Genußmittel** [gə'nusmɪtəl], *n.* (**—s,** *pl.* **—**) (*mostly pl.*) luxuries; (*Am.*) delicatessen.
**genußreich** [gə'nusraɪç], *adj.* enjoyable, delightful.
**Genußsucht** [gə'nussuxt], *f.* (**—,** *no pl.*) thirst for pleasure.
**Geograph** [geo'gra:f], *m.* (**—en,** *pl.* **—en**) geographer.
**Geographie** [geogra'fi:], *f.* (**—,** *no pl.*) geography.
**Geologe** [geo'lo:gə], *m.* (**—n,** *pl.* **—n**) geologist.
**Geologie** [geolo'gi:], *f.* (**—,** *no pl.*) geology.
**Geometer** [geo'me:tər], *m.* (**—s,** *pl.* **—**) geometrician; land-surveyor.
**Geometrie** [geome'tri:], *f.* (**—,** *no pl.*) geometry.
**Georg** [ge'ɔrk], *m.* George.
**Georgine** [geɔr'gi:nə], *f.* (**—,** *pl.* **—n**) (*Bot.*) dahlia.
**Gepäck** [gə'pɛk], *n.* (**—s,** *no pl.*) luggage; (*Am.*) baggage.
**Gepäckaufbewahrung** [gə'pɛkaufbəva:ruŋ], *f.* (**—,** *pl.* **—en**) left luggage office.
**Gepäckträger** [gə'pɛktrɛ:gər], *m.* (**—s,** *pl.* **—**) porter.
**Gepflogenheit** [gə'pflo:gənhaɪt], *f.* (**—,** *pl.* **—en**) habit, custom, wont.
**Geplänkel** [gə'plɛnkəl], *n.* (**—s,** *pl.* **—**) (*rare*) skirmish.
**Geplärr** [gə'plɛr], *n.* (**—s,** *no pl.*) bawling.
**Geplauder** [gə'plaudər], *n.* (**—s,** *no pl.*) chatting; small talk.
**Gepräge** [gə'prɛ:gə], *n.* (**—s,** *no pl.*) impression, stamp.
**Gepränge** [gə'prɛŋə], *n.* (**—s,** *no pl.*) pomp, ceremony, splendour.
**Ger** [ge:r], *m.* (**—s,** *pl.* **—e**) (*rare*) spear, javelin.
**Gerade** [gə'ra:də], *f.* (**—n,** *pl.* **—n**) (*Maths.*) straight line.
**gerade** [gə'ra:də], *adj.* straight, direct, erect, even; (*fig.*) upright, honest. — *adv.* quite, just; *jetzt* —, now more than ever; *fünf — sein lassen*, stretch a point; — *heraus*, in plain terms.
**geradeaus** [gə'ra:dəaus], *adv.* straight on.
**gerädert** [gə'rɛ:dərt], *adj.* (*fig.*) fatigued, exhausted, worn out.
**geradeswegs** [gə'ra:dəsve:ks], *adv.* straightaway, immediately.
**geradezu** [gə'ra:dətsu:], *adv.* frankly, downright; *das ist — scheußlich*, this is downright nasty.
**Geradheit** [gə'ra:thaɪt], *f.* (**—,** *no pl.*) straightness; (*fig.*) straightforwardness.
**geradlinig** [gə'ra:tlɪnɪç], *adj.* rectilinear.
**geradsinnig** [gə'ra:tzɪnɪç], *adj.* honest, upright.
**gerändert** [gə'rɛndərt], *adj.* with a milled edge.
**Geranie** [gə'ra:njə], *f.* (**—,** *pl.* **—n**) (*Bot.*) geranium.
**Gerät** [gə'rɛ:t], *n.* (**—s,** *pl.* **—e**) tool, implement, device; appliance; (radio, television) set; apparatus.
**geraten** [gə'ra:tən], *v.n. irr.* (*aux.* sein) turn out; *gut* —, turn out well; — *auf*, come upon.
**Geräteturnen** [gə'rɛ:təturnən], *n.* (**—s,** *no pl.*) gymnastics with apparatus.
**Geratewohl** [gə'ra:təvo:l], *n.* (**—s,** *no pl.*) *aufs* —, at random.
**geraum** [gə'raum], *adj.* *—e Zeit*, a long time.
**geräumig** [gə'rɔymɪç], *adj.* spacious, large, wide, roomy.
**Geräusch** [gə'rɔyʃ], *n.* (**—es,** *pl.* **—e**) noise; sound.
**gerben** ['gɛrbən], *v.a.* tan, taw; *einem die Haut* —, give s.o. a hiding.
**Gerber** ['gɛrbər], *m.* (**—s,** *pl.* **—**) tanner.
**Gerbsäure** ['gɛrpsɔyrə], *f.* (**—,** *no pl.*) tannin.
**gerecht** [gə'rɛçt], *adj.* just, fair; (*Bibl.*) righteous; *einem — werden*, do justice to s.o.
**Gerechtigkeit** [gə'rɛçtɪçkaɪt], *f.* (**—,** *no pl.*) justice, fairness; (*Bibl.*) righteousness.

**Gerede** [gə'reːdə], *n.* (—s, *no pl.*) talk, rumour, gossip.
**gereichen** [gə'raɪçən], *v.n.* turn out to be; *einem zur Ehre* —, redound to s.o.'s honour.
**gereizt** [gə'raɪtst], *adj.* irritated, annoyed.
**gereuen** [gə'rɔyən] *see* reuen.
**Gerhard** ['geːrhart], *m.* Gerard, Gerald.
**Gericht** [gə'rɪçt], *n.* (—s, *pl.* —e) court of justice, tribunal; (*food*) course, dish; *das Jüngste* —, Last Judgment.
**gerichtlich** [gə'rɪçtlɪç], *adj.* judicial, legal; *einen* — *belangen*, sue s.o.
**Gerichtsbarkeit** [gə'rɪçtsbarkaɪt], *f.* (—, *no pl.*) jurisdiction.
**Gerichtsdiener** [gə'rɪçtsdiːnər], *m.* (—s, *pl.* —) (*law court*) usher.
**Gerichtshof** [gə'rɪçtshoːf], *m.* (—es, *pl.* ⸚e) court of justice.
**Gerichtskanzlei** [gə'rɪçtskantslaɪ], *f.* (—, *pl.* —en) record office.
**Gerichtskosten** [gə'rɪçtskɔstən], *f. pl.* (*Law*) costs.
**Gerichtsordnung** [gə'rɪçtsɔrdnuŋ], *f.* (—, *pl* —en) legal procedure.
**Gerichtstermin** [gə'rɪçtstɛrmiːn], *m.* (—s, *pl.* —e) day fixed for a hearing.
**Gerichtsverhandlung** [gə'rɪçtsfɛrhandluŋ], *f.* (—, *pl.* —en) hearing; trial.
**Gerichtsvollzieher** [gə'rɪçtsfɔltsiːər], *m.* (—s, *pl.* —) bailiff.
**gerieben** [gə'riːbən], *adj.* ground; crafty, cunning.
**gering** [gə'rɪŋ], *adj.* small, little, mean, petty, unimportant, of little value, trifling; low, base.
**geringfügig** [gə'rɪŋfyːgɪç], *adj.* small, petty, insignificant.
**geringschätzig** [gə'rɪŋʃɛtsɪç], *adj.* contemptuous, disdainful, supercilious; derogatory.
**gerinnen** [gə'rɪnən], *v.n. irr.* (*aux.* sein) coagulate, clot; curdle.
**Gerinnsel** [gə'rɪnzəl], *n.* (—s, *pl.* —) embolism (of the blood); clot.
**Gerippe** [gə'rɪpə], *n.* (—s, *pl.* —) skeleton; frame; (*Aviat.*) air-frame.
**gerippt** [gə'rɪpt], *adj.* ribbed, fluted.
**gerissen** [gə'rɪsən], *adj.* (*coll.*) sharp, cunning.
**Germane** [gɛr'maːnə], *m.* (—n, *pl.* —n) Teuton.
**Germanist** ['gɛrmanɪst], *m.* (—en, *pl.* —en) (*Univ.*) student of *or* expert in German language and/or literature.
**gern** [gɛrn], *adv.* gladly, willingly, readily, with pleasure; — *haben*, like.
**Geröll** [gə'rœl], *n.* (—s, *no pl.*) boulders, rubble.
**Gerste** ['gɛrstə], *f.* (—, *no pl.*) (*Bot.*) barley.
**Gerstenschleim** ['gɛrstənʃlaɪm], *m.* (—s, *no pl.*) barley water.
**Gerte** ['gɛrtə], *f.* (—, *pl.* —n) whip, switch, rod.
**Geruch** [gə'ruːx], *m.* (—s, *pl.* ⸚e) smell, odour, scent; *guter* —, fragrance, aroma.

**geruchlos** [gə'ruːxloːs], *adj.* scentless, odourless, without smell.
**Geruchsinn** [gə'ruːxzɪn], *m.* (—es, *no pl.*) sense of smell.
**Gerücht** [gə'rʏçt], *n.* (—s, *pl.* —e) rumour, report.
**Gerümpel** [gə'rʏmpəl], *n.* (—s, *no pl.*) lumber, trash.
**Gerundium** [gə'rundjum], *n.* (—s, *pl.* —dien) (*Gram.*) gerund.
**Gerüst** [gə'rʏst], *n.* (—es, *pl.* —e) scaffolding.
**Ges** [gɛs], *n.* (—, *pl.* —) (*Mus.*) G flat.
**gesamt** [gə'zamt], *adj.* entire, all, complete.
**Gesamtheit** [gə'zamthaɪt], *f.* (—, *no pl.*) totality.
**Gesandte** [gə'zantə], *m.* (—n, *pl.* —n) messenger; ambassador, envoy; *päpstlicher* —, papal nuncio.
**Gesandtschaft** [gə'zantʃaft], *f.* (—, *pl.* —en) embassy, legation.
**Gesang** [gə'zaŋ], *m.* (—s, *pl.* ⸚e) song, air; hymn; (*Lit.*) canto.
**Gesangbuch** [gə'zaŋbuːx], *n.* (—s, *pl.* ⸚er) hymnal, hymn-book.
**Gesäß** [gə'zɛːs], *n.* (—es, *pl.* —e) seat, buttocks.
**Geschäft** [gə'ʃɛft], *n.* (—s, *pl.* —e) business; trade, commerce; affairs; occupation; shop, (*Am.*) store.
**geschäftig** [gə'ʃɛftɪç], *adj.* active, bustling, busy.
**geschäftlich** [gə'ʃɛftlɪç], *adj.* concerning business. — *adv.* on business.
**Geschäftsführer** [gə'ʃɛftsfyːrər], *m.* (—s, *pl.* —) manager.
**Geschäftshaus** [gə'ʃɛftshaus], *n.* (—es, *pl.* ⸚er) firm; business premises.
**geschäftskundig** [gə'ʃɛftskundɪç], *adj.* experienced in business.
**Geschäftslokal** [gə'ʃɛftsloka:l], *n.* (—s, *pl.* —e) business premises, shop.
**Geschäftsordnung** [gə'ʃɛftsɔrdnuŋ], *f.* (—, *pl.* —en) standing orders; agenda.
**Geschäftsträger** [gə'ʃɛftstrɛːgər], *m.* (—s, *pl.* —) (*Comm.*) agent; (*Pol.*) chargé d'affaires.
**Geschäftsverkehr** [gə'ʃɛftsfɛrkeːr], *m.* (—s, *no pl.*) business dealings.
**Geschehen** [gə'ʃeːən], *n.* (—s, *no pl.*) happening.
**geschehen** [gə'ʃeːən], *v.n. irr.* (*aux.* sein) happen, occur; take place; be done; *das geschieht dir recht*, it serves you right.
**gescheit** [gə'ʃaɪt], *adj.* clever, intelligent.
**Geschenk** [gə'ʃɛŋk], *n.* (—s, *pl.* —e) gift, present, donation.
**Geschichte** [gə'ʃɪçtə], *f.* (—, *pl.* —n) tale; story; history.
**Geschichtenbuch** [gə'ʃɪçtənbuːx], *n.* (—es, *pl.* ⸚er) story-book.
**geschichtlich** [gə'ʃɪçtlɪç], *adj.* historical.
**Geschichtsschreiber** [gə'ʃɪçtsʃraɪbər], *m.* (—s, *pl.* —) historian.
**Geschick** [gə'ʃɪk], *n.* (—es, *no pl.*) fate, destiny; dexterity, skill, knack, aptitude.

87

**Geschicklichkeit** [gə'ʃɪklɪçkaɪt], *f.* (—, *pl.* —en) dexterity, adroitness, skill.
**geschickt** [gə'ʃɪkt], *adj.* skilled, skilful, clever, able.
**Geschirr** [gə'ʃɪr], *n.* (—s, *no pl.*) crockery, plates and dishes; (*horses*) harness.
**Geschlecht** [gə'ʃlɛçt], *n.* (—s, *pl.* —er) sex; kind, race, species, extraction, family; (*Gram.*) gender.
**geschlechtlich** [gə'ʃlɛçtlɪç], *adj.* sexual; generic.
**Geschlechtsart** [gə'ʃlɛçtsa:rt], *f.* (—, *pl.* —en) generic character.
**Geschlechtskrankheit** [gə'ʃlɛçtskraŋkhaɪt], *f.* (—, *pl.* —en) venereal disease.
**Geschlechtskunde** [gə'ʃlɛçtskundə], *f.* (—, *no pl.*) genealogy.
**Geschlechtsreife** [gə'ʃlɛçtsraɪfə], *f.* (—, *no pl.*) puberty.
**Geschlechtsteile** [gə'ʃlɛçtstaɪlə], *m. pl.* genitals.
**Geschlechtstrieb** [gə'ʃlɛçtstri:p], *m.* (—s, *no pl.*) sexual instinct.
**Geschlechtswort** [gə'ʃlɛçtsvɔrt], *n.* (—s, *pl.* ⁝er) (*Gram.*) article.
**geschliffen** [gə'ʃlɪfən], *adj.* polished; (*glass*) cut.
**Geschmack** [gə'ʃmak], *m.* (—s, *pl.* ⁝er) taste, flavour.
**geschmacklos** [gə'ʃmaklo:s], *adj.* tasteless, insipid; in bad taste.
**Geschmacksrichtung** [gə'ʃmaksrɪçtuŋ], *f.* (—, *pl.* —en) prevailing taste; vogue; tendency.
**Geschmeide** [gə'ʃmaɪdə], *n.* (—s, *pl.* —) jewels, jewellery; trinkets.
**geschmeidig** [gə'ʃmaɪdɪç], *adj.* flexible, pliant, supple; (*Tech.*) malleable.
**Geschmeiß** [gə'ʃmaɪs], *n.* (—es, *no pl.*) dung; vermin; (*fig.*) rabble.
**Geschnatter** [gə'ʃnatər], *n.* (—s, *no pl.*) cackling.
**geschniegelt** [gə'ʃni:gəlt], *adj.* spruce, dressed up.
**Geschöpf** [gə'ʃœpf], *n.* (—es, *pl.* —e) creature.
**Geschoß** [gə'ʃɔs], *n.* (—sses, *pl.* —sse) shot, shell, projectile, missile; (*house*) storey.
**geschraubt** [gə'ʃraupt], *adj.* (*style*) stilted, affected.
**Geschrei** [gə'ʃraɪ], *n.* (—s, *no pl.*) shrieking, shouting, screaming; (*fig.*) stir, great noise.
**Geschreibsel** [gə'ʃraɪpsəl], *n.* (—s, *no pl.*) scrawl, scribbling.
**Geschütz** [gə'ʃyts], *n.* (—es, *pl.* —e) artillery, guns; *schweres — auffahren,* bring o.'s. guns into play.
**Geschützweite** [gə'ʃytsvaɪtə], *f.* (—, *no pl.*) calibre.
**Geschwader** [gə'ʃva:dər], *n.* (—s, *pl.*—) squadron.
**Geschwätz** [gə'ʃvɛts], *n.* (—es, *no pl.*) chatter, gossip, prattle, tittle-tattle.
**geschweige** [gə'ʃvaɪgə], *adv.* let alone, to say nothing of.
**geschwind** [gə'ʃvɪnt], *adj.* quick, nimble, fast, swift, fleet.

**Geschwindigkeitsmesser** [gə'ʃvɪndɪçkaɪtsmɛsər], *m.* (—s, *pl.* —) (*Motor.*) speedometer.
**Geschwister** [gə'ʃvɪstər], *pl.* brothers and sisters.
**geschwollen** [gə'ʃvɔlən], *adj.* stilted, turgid, pompous.
**Geschworene** [gə'ʃvo:rənə], *m.* (—n, *pl.* —n), juror, juryman; (*pl.*) jury.
**Geschwulst** [gə'ʃvulst], *f.* (—, *pl.* ⁝e) swelling, tumour.
**Geschwür** [gə'ʃvy:r], *n.* (—s, *pl.* —e) sore, ulcer, abscess.
**Geselle** [gə'zɛlə], *m.* (—n, *pl.* —n) journeyman; companion, comrade, mate.
**gesellen** [gə'zɛlən], *v.a., v.r.* join, associate with, keep company with.
**gesellig** [gə'zɛlɪç], *adj.* sociable, companionable; gregarious.
**Gesellschaft** [gə'zɛlʃaft], *f.* (—, *pl.* —en) society; community; (formal) party; company, club; *geschlossene —,* private party; *einem — leisten,* keep s.o. company; (*Comm.*) *— mit beschränkter Haftung,* (abbr.) *GmbH,* limited company, (*abbr.*) Ltd.
**gesellschaftlich** [gə'zɛlʃaftlɪç], *adj.* social.
**Gesellschaftsanzug** [gə'zɛlʃaftsantsu:k], *m.* (—s, *pl.* ⁝e) evening dress.
**Gesellschaftsspiel** [gə'zɛlʃaftsʃpi:l], *n.* (—s, *pl.* —e) round game, party game.
**Gesellschaftsvertrag** [gə'zɛlʃaftsfɛrtra:k], *m.* (—es, *pl.* ⁝e) (*Law*) partnership agreement; deed of partnership.
**Gesellschaftszimmer** [gə'zɛlʃaftstsɪmər], *n.* (—s, *pl.* —) drawing-room, reception room.
**Gesetz** [gə'zɛts], *n.* (—es, *pl.* —e) law, statute, regulation.
**Gesetzbuch** [gə'zɛtsbu:x], *n.* (—es, *pl.* ⁝er) code of laws; statute book.
**Gesetzentwurf** [gə'zɛtsentvurf], *m.* (—es, *pl.* ⁝er) (*Parl.*) draft bill.
**gesetzgebend** [gə'zɛtsgə:bənt], *adj.* legislative.
**gesetzlich** [gə'zɛtslɪç], *adj.* lawful, legal.
**Gesetzlichkeit** [gə'zɛtslɪçkaɪt], *f.* (—, *no pl.*) lawfulness, legality.
**gesetzlos** [gə'zɛtslo:s], *adj.* lawless, anarchical.
**gesetzmäßig** [gə'zɛtsmɛ:sɪç], *adj.* conforming to law, lawful, legitimate.
**gesetzt** [gə'zɛtst], *adj.* steady, sedate, staid; *von —em Alter,* of mature age; *— daß,* supposing that.
**Gesetztheit** [gə'zɛtsthaɪt], *f.* (—, *no pl.*) sedateness, steadiness.
**gesetzwidrig** [gə'zɛtsvi:drɪç], *adj.* illegal, unlawful.
**Gesicht** (1) [gə'zɪçt], *n.* (—s, *pl.* —er) face, physiognomy, look.
**Gesicht** (2) [gə'zɪçt], *n.* (—s, *pl.* —e) sight; vision, apparition.
**Gesichtsausdruck** [gə'zɪçtsausdruk], *m.* (—s, *no pl.*) face, mien; expression.

# Getöse

**Gesichtsfeld** [gə'zɪçtsfɛlt], *n.* (**—es,** *pl.* **—er**) field of vision.
**Gesichtskreis** [gə'zɪçtskraɪs], *m.* (**—es,** *pl.* **—e**) horizon.
**Gesichtspunkt** [gə'zɪçtspuŋkt], *m.* (**—es,** *pl.* **—e**) point of view.
**Gesichtszug** [gə'zɪçtstsu:k], *m.* (**—s,** *pl.* **-e**) feature.
**Gesims** [gə'zɪms], *n.* (**—es,** *pl.* **—e**) cornice, moulding, ledge.
**Gesinde** [gə'zɪndə], *n.* (**—s,** *no pl.*) (domestic) servants.
**Gesindel** [gə'zɪndəl], *n.* (**—s,** *no pl.*) mob, rabble.
**gesinnt** [gə'zɪnt], *adj.* disposed.
**Gesinnung** [gə'zɪnuŋ], *f.* (**—,** *pl.* **—en**) disposition, sentiment; conviction.
**gesinnungslos** [gə'zɪnuŋslo:s], *adj.* unprincipled.
**gesinnungstreu** [gə'zɪnuŋstrɔy], *adj.* loyal, staunch.
**Gesinnungswechsel** [gə'zɪnuŋsvɛksəl], *m.* (**—s,** *no pl.*) change of opinion, volte-face.
**gesittet** [gə'zɪtət], *adj.* civilised, well-mannered.
**Gesittung** [gə'zɪtuŋ], *f.* (**—,** *no pl.*) (*rare*) civilisation, good manners.
**gesonnen** [gə'zɔnən] *see* gesinnt.
**Gespann** [gə'ʃpan], *n.* (**—s,** *pl.* **—e**) team, yoke (oxen etc.).
**gespannt** [gə'ʃpant], *adj.* stretched; intense, thrilled; tense; filled with suspense.
**Gespanntheit** [gə'ʃpanthaɪt], *f.* (**—,** *no pl.*) tension, strain, suspense.
**Gespenst** [gə'ʃpɛnst], *n.* (**—es,** *pl.* **—er**) ghost, spectre, apparition.
**gespenstisch** [gə'ʃpɛnstɪʃ], *adj.* ghostly, spectral.
**Gespiele** [gə'ʃpi:lə], *m.* (**—n,** *pl.* **—n**) playmate.
**Gespielin** [gə'ʃpi:lɪn], *f.* (**—,** *pl.* **—innen**) (girl) playmate.
**Gespinst** [gə'ʃpɪnst], *n.* (**—es,** *pl.* **—e**) web.
**Gespött** [gə'ʃpœt], *n.* (**—s,** *no pl.*) mocking, mockery, jeering, derision; (*fig.*) laughing stock.
**Gespräch** [gə'ʃprɛ:ç], *n.* (**—s,** *pl.* **—e**) conversation, discourse, talk; (*phone*) call; *ein — anknüpfen*, start a conversation.
**gesprächig** [gə'ʃprɛ:çɪç], *adj.* talkative, communicative.
**gespreizt** [gə'ʃpraɪtst], *adj.* wide apart; (*fig.*) affected, pompous.
**gesprenkelt** [gə'ʃprɛŋkəlt], *adj.* speckled.
**gesprungen** [gə'ʃpruŋən], *adj.* cracked (glass etc.).
**Gestade** [gə'ʃta:də], *n.* (**—s,** *pl.* **—**) shore, coast, bank.
**Gestalt** [gə'ʃtalt], *f.* (**—.** *pl.* **—en**) form, figure, shape; configuration; stature; fashion; manner, way.
**gestalten** [gə'ʃtaltən], *v.a.* form, shape, fashion, make. — *v.r. sich*, turn out.
**Gestaltung** [gə'ʃtaltuŋ], *f.* (**—,** *pl.* **—en**) formation; arrangement; planning.

**geständig** [gə'ʃtɛndɪç], *adj.* confessing; *— sein*, confess.
**Geständnis** [gə'ʃtɛntnɪs], *n.* (**—ses,** *pl.* **—se**) confession, admission.
**Gestank** [gə'ʃtaŋk], *m.* (**—s,** *no pl.*) stink, stench.
**gestatten** [gə'ʃtatən], *v.a.* permit, allow, grant; *wir — uns*, we beg leave to; *— Sie !* pardon me, excuse me.
**Geste** ['gɛstə], *f.* (**—,** *pl.* **—n**) gesture, gesticulation.
**gestehen** [gə'ʃte:ən], *v.a.* confess, admit, own; *offen gestanden*, quite frankly.
**Gestein** [gə'ʃtaɪn], *n.* (**—s,** *pl.* **—e**) (*Poet.*) rock; (*Geol.*) rocks, minerals.
**Gestell** [gə'ʃtɛl], *n.* (**—s,** *pl.* **—e**) rack, frame; (*table*) trestle; (*books*) stand.
**Gestellung** [gə'ʃtɛluŋ], *f.* (**—,** *no pl.*) (*Mil.*) reporting for service.
**gestern** ['gɛstərn], *adv.* yesterday; *— abend*, last night.
**gestiefelt** [gə'ʃti:fəlt], *adj.* booted; *der —e Kater*, Puss in Boots.
**gestielt** [gə'ʃti:lt], *adj.* (*axe*) helved; (*Bot.*) stalked, stemmed.
**gestikulieren** [gɛstiku'li:rən], *v.n.* gesticulate.
**Gestirn** [gə'ʃtɪrn], *n.* (**—s,** *pl.* **—e**) star, constellation.
**gestirnt** [gə'ʃtɪrnt], *adj.* starred, starry.
**Gestöber** [gə'ʃtø:bər], *n.* (**—s,** *pl.* **—**) (*snow, dust*) drift, storm, blizzard.
**Gesträuch** [gə'ʃtrɔyç], *n.* (**—es,** *no pl.*) bushes, shrubs; thicket.
**gestreift** [gə'ʃtraɪft], *adj.* striped.
**gestreng** [gə'ʃtrɛŋ], *adj.* (*obs.*) strict, severe.
**gestrig** ['gɛstrɪç], *adj.* of yesterday.
**Gestrüpp** [gə'ʃtryp], *n.* (**—s,** *no pl.*) bushes, underwood, shrubs, shrubbery.
**Gestüt** [gə'ʃty:t], *n.* (**—s,** *pl.* **—e**) stud (-farm).
**Gestüthengst** [gə'ʃty:thɛŋst], *m.* (**—es,** *pl.* **—e**) stallion.
**Gesuch** [gə'zu:x], *n.* (**—s,** *pl.* **—e**) petition, request, application.
**gesucht** [gə'zu:xt], *adj.* in demand; (*style*) far-fetched; affected; studied.
**gesund** [gə'zunt], *adj.* healthy, wholesome; *der —e Menschenverstand*, common sense.
**Gesundbrunnen** [gə'zuntbrunən], *m.* (**—s,** *pl.* **—**) mineral waters; spa.
**gesunden** [gə'zundən], *v.n.* (*aux.* sein) recover o.'s health.
**Gesundheit** [gə'zunthaɪt], *f.* (**—,** *no pl.*) health.
**Gesundheitslehre** [gə'zunthaɪtsle:rə], *f.* (**—,** *no pl.*) hygiene.
**Getäfel** [gə'tɛ:fəl], *n.* (**—s,** *no pl.*) wainscot, wainscoting, panelling.
**Getändel** [gə'tɛndəl], *n.* (**—s,** *no pl.*) (*rare*) flirting, dallying.
**Getier** [gə'ti:r], *n.* (**—s,** *no pl.*) (*collective term*) animals.
**Getöse** [gə'tø:zə], *n.* (**—s,** *no pl.*) loud noise, din.

89

# Getränk

**Getränk** [gə'trɛŋk], *n.* (**—s**, *pl.* **—e**) drink, beverage.

**getrauen** [gə'trauən], *v.r. sich* —, dare, venture.

**Getreide** [gə'traɪdə], *n.* (**—s**, *pl.* **—**) corn, grain.

**getreu** [gə'trɔy], *adj.* faithful, true, loyal.

**getreulich** [gə'trɔylɪç], *adv.* faithfully, truly, loyally.

**Getriebe** [gə'tri:bə], *n.* (**—s**, *pl.* **—**) machinery; (*Motor.*) gear; drive; *das — der Welt*, the bustle of life.

**getrieben** [gə'tri:bən], *adj.* (*Tech.*) chased (work.)

**Getrödel** [gə'trø:dəl], *n.* (**—s**, *no pl.*) dawdling.

**getrost** [gə'tro:st], *adj.* confident, cheerful; — *sein*, be of good cheer.

**Getto** ['gɛto], *n.* (**—s**, *pl.* **—s**) ghetto.

**Getue** [gə'tu:ə], *n.* (**—s**, *no pl.*) pretence, fuss.

**Getümmel** [gə'tyməl], *n.* (**—s**, *no pl.*) bustle, turmoil.

**geübt** [gə'y:pt], *adj.* skilled, versed.

**Geübtheit** [gə'y:pthaɪt], *f.* (**—**, *no pl.*) skill, experience, dexterity.

**Gevatter** [gə'fatər], *m.* (**—s**, *pl.* **—**) (*obs.*) godfather.

**gevierteilt** [gə'fi:rtaɪlt], *adj.* quartered.

**Gewächs** [gə'vɛks], *n.* (**—es**, *pl.* **—e**) plant, growth; (*Med.*) excrescence.

**gewachsen** [gə'vaksən], *adj. einem (einer Sache)* — *sein*, be equal to s.o. (s.th.).

**Gewächshaus** [gə'vɛkshaus], *n.* (**—es**, *pl.* **⁻er**) green-house, hot-house, conservatory.

**gewagt** [gə'va:kt], *adj.* risky, hazardous; daring.

**gewählt** [gə've:lt], *adj.* choice, select.

**gewahr** [gə'va:r], *adj. einer Sache — werden*, become aware of s.th., perceive s.th.

**Gewähr** [gə've:r], *f.* (**—**, *no pl.*) surety; guarantee; warranty; — *leisten*, guarantee.

**gewahren** [gə'va:rən], *v.a.* perceive, see, become aware of.

**gewähren** [gə'vɛ:rən], *v.a.* allow, grant; *einen — lassen*, let s.o. do as he pleases, let be.

**Gewährleistung** [gə'vɛ:rlaɪstuŋ], *f.* (**—**, *pl.* **—en**) grant of security (*or* bail); guarantee.

**Gewahrsam** [gə'va:rza:m], *m.* (**—s**, *no pl.*) safe-keeping, custody.

**Gewährsmann** [gə'vɛ:rsman], *m.* (**—es**, *pl.* **⁻er**) authority; informant.

**Gewährung** [gə'vɛ:ruŋ], *f.* (**—**, *no pl.*) granting of request).

**Gewalt** [gə'valt], *f.* (**—**, *pl.* **—en**) power, force, might; authority; violence; *höhere* —, (*Law*) act of God, force majeure; *sich in der — haben*, have control over o.s.

**Gewalthaber** [gə'valtha:bər], *m.* (**—s**, *pl.* **—**) tyrant; despot, autocrat; person in authority.

**gewaltig** [gə'valtɪç], *adj.* powerful, mighty, enormous, stupendous.

**gewaltsam** [gə'valtza:m], *adj.* forcible, violent.

**Gewaltstreich** [gə'valtʃtraɪç], *m.* (**—s**, *pl.* **—e**) bold stroke; coup d'état.

**Gewalttat** [gə'valtta:t], *f.* (**—**, *pl.* **—en**) violent action, violence, outrage.

**gewalttätig** [gə'valttɛ:tɪç], *adj.* violent, fierce, outrageous.

**Gewand** [gə'vant], *n.* (**—es**, *pl.* **⁻er**) (*Lit.*) garment, dress; (*Eccl.*) vestment.

**gewandt** [gə'vant], *adj.* nimble, deft, clever; (*mind*) versatile.

**gewärtig** [gə'vɛrtɪç], *adj. einer Sache — sein*, expect s.th. to happen.

**Gewäsch** [gə'vɛʃ], *n.* (**—es**, *no pl.*) stuff and nonsense; rubbish.

**Gewässer** [gə'vɛsər], *n.* (**—s**, *pl.* **—**) waters.

**Gewebe** [gə've:bə], *n.* (**—s**, *pl.* **—**) (*Physiol.*, *Text.*) tissue; web, weft, texture.

**geweckt** [gə'vɛkt], *adj.* smart, wideawake.

**Gewehr** [gə've:r], *n.* (**—s**, *pl.* **—e**) gun, fire-arm, rifle.

**Gewehrlauf** [gə've:rlauf], *m.* (**—s**, *pl.* **⁻e**) barrel.

**Geweih** [gə'vaɪ], *n.* (**—s**, *pl.* **—e**) horns, antlers.

**geweiht** [gə'vaɪt], *adj.* consecrated; holy.

**gewellt** [gə'vɛlt], *adj.* corrugated, wavy.

**Gewerbe** [gə'vɛrbə], *n.* (**—s**, *pl.* **—**) trade, profession, business; calling; industry.

**Gewerbekunde** [gə'vɛrbəkundə], *f.* (**—**, *no pl.*) technology.

**Gewerbeschein** [gə'vɛrbəʃaɪn], *m.* (**—s**, *pl.* **—e**) trade-licence.

**gewerblich** [gə'vɛrplɪç], *adj.* industrial.

**gewerbsmäßig** [gə'vɛrpsmɛ:sɪç], *adj.* professional.

**Gewerkschaft** [gə'vɛrkʃaft], *f.* (**—**, *pl.* **—en**) trade union.

**Gewicht** [gə'vɪçt], *n.* (**—s**, *pl.* **—e**) weight; *schwer ins — fallen*, carry great weight, weigh heavily.

**gewichtig** [gə'vɪçtɪç], *adj.* weighty, ponderous; (*fig.*) momentous, important, strong.

**gewiegt** [gə'vi:kt], *adj.* experienced, clever.

**gewillt** [gə'vɪlt], *adj.* willing.

**Gewimmel** [gə'vɪməl], *n.* (**—s**, *no pl.*) milling crowd, swarm, throng.

**Gewinde** [gə'vɪndə], *n.* (**—s**, *pl.* **—**) (*screw*) thread; (*flowers*) garland.

**Gewinn** [gə'vɪn], *m.* (**—s**, *pl.* **—e**) gain, profit; (*lottery*) prize; (*gambling*) winnings.

**gewinnen** [gə'vɪnən], *v.a. irr.* win, gain, obtain, get, earn.

**gewinnend** [gə'vɪnənt], *adj.* prepossessing; engaging.

**Gewinnung** [gə'vɪnuŋ], *f.* (**—**, *no pl.*) (*Ind.*, *Chem.*) extraction; output, production.

**Gewinsel** [gə'vɪnzəl], *n.* (**—s**, *no pl.*) whimpering.

**Gewinst** [gə'vɪnst], *m.* (—es, *pl.* —e) (*obs.*) gain, profit.

**Gewirr** [gə'vɪr], *n.* (—s, *no pl.*) entanglement, confusion.

**gewiß** [gə'vɪs], *adj.* (*Genit.*) certain, sure. — *adv.* indeed.

**Gewissen** [gə'vɪsən], *n.* (—s, *no pl.*) conscience.

**gewissenhaft** [gə'vɪsənhaft], *adj.* conscientious, scrupulous.

**gewissenlos** [gə'vɪsənloːs], *adj.* unscrupulous.

**Gewissensbiß** [gə'vɪsənsbɪs],*m.*(—sses, *pl.* —sse) (*mostly pl.*) pangs of conscience.

**gewissermaßen** [gə'vɪsərmaːsən], *adv.* to a certain extent, so to speak.

**Gewißheit** [gə'vɪshaɪt], *f.* (—, *no pl.*) certainty.

**gewißlich** [gə'vɪslɪç], *adv.* surely.

**Gewitter** [gə'vɪtər], *n.* (—s, *pl.* —) thunderstorm.

**gewittern** [gə'vɪtərn], *v.n.* thunder.

**gewitzigt, gewitzt** [gə'vɪtsɪçt, gə'vɪtst], *adj.* knowing, clever; shrewd.

**gewogen** [gə'voːɡən], *adj.* kindly disposed, favourable; *einem* — *sein*, be favourably inclined towards s.o.

**Gewogenheit** [gə'voːɡənhaɪt], *f.* (—, *no pl.*) kindness, favour.

**gewöhnen** [gə'vøːnən], *v.a.* accustom to. — *v.r. sich* — *an*, get used to, accustom o.s. to.

**Gewohnheit** [gə'voːnhaɪt], *f.* (—, *pl.* —en) (*general*) custom, usage; (*personal*) habit.

**gewohnheitsmäßig** [gə'voːnhaɪtsmɛːsɪç], *adj.* habitual. — *adv.* by force of habit.

**Gewohnheitsrecht** [gə'voːnhaɪtsreçt], *n.* (—s, *no pl.*) common law.

**gewöhnlich** [gə'vøːnlɪç], *adj.* customary, usual; (*fig.*) common, mean, vulgar.

**gewohnt** [gə'voːnt], *adj.* accustomed to, used to.

**Gewöhnung** [gə'vøːnuŋ], *f.* (—, *no pl.*) habit, use, habituation.

**Gewölbe** [gə'vœlbə], *n.* (—s, *pl.* —) vault, arch.

**Gewölk** [gə'vœlk], *n.* (—s, *no pl.*) clouds, cloud formation.

**Gewühl** [gə'vyːl], *n.* (—s, *no pl.*) crowd, throng, bustle.

**gewunden** [gə'vundən], *adj.* tortuous.

**Gewürm** [gə'vyrm], *n.* (—s, *no pl.*) reptiles, worms; vermin.

**Gewürz** [gə'vyrts], *n.* (—es, *pl.* —e) spice.

**Gewürznelke** [gə'vyrtsnɛlkə], *f.* (—, *pl.* —n) clove.

**Gezänk** [gə'tsɛŋk], *n.* (—s, *no pl.*) quarrelling, bickering.

**Gezeiten** [gə'tsaɪtən], *f. pl.* tides.

**Gezeter** [gə'tseːtər], *n.* (—s, *no pl.*) screaming, yelling; (*fig.*) outcry.

**geziemen** [gə'tsiːmən], *v.r. sich für einen* —, befit or become s.o.

**geziert** [gə'tsiːrt], *adj.* affected.

**Gezischel** [gə'tsɪʃəl], *n.* (—s, *no pl.*) whispering.

**Gezücht** [gə'tsyçt], *n.* (—ⳋs, *no pl.*) brood, breed.

**Gezweig** [gə'tsvaɪk], *n.* (—s, *no pl.*) branches, boughs.

**Gezwitscher** [gə'tsvɪtʃər], *n.* (—s, *no pl.*) chirping.

**Gezwungenheit** [gə'tsvuŋənhaɪt], *f.* (—, *no pl.*) constraint.

**Gicht** [ɡɪçt], *f.* (—, *no pl.*) (*Med.*) gout.

**gichtbrüchig** [ˈɡɪçtbryçɪç], *adj.* (*obs.*) paralytic; gouty.

**gichtig** [ˈɡɪçtɪç], *adj.* gouty.

**Giebel** [ˈɡiːbəl], *m.* (—s, *pl.* —) gable.

**Giebelfenster** [ˈɡiːbəlfɛnstər], *n.* (—s, *pl.*—) gable-window, dormer-window.

**gieb(e)lig** [ˈɡiːb(ə)lɪç], *adj.* gabled.

**Gier** [ɡiːr], *f.* (—, *no pl.*) greediness, eagerness.

**gieren** [ˈɡiːrən], *v.n.* (*rare*) — *nach*, thirst for, yearn for.

**gierig** [ˈɡiːrɪç], *adj.* eager, greedy.

**Gießbach** [ˈɡiːsbax], *m.* (—s, *pl.* ⸚e) mountain-torrent.

**gießen** [ˈɡiːsən], *v.a. irr.* (*liquids*) pour, shed; (*metal*) cast, found.

**Gießer** [ˈɡiːsər], *m.* (—s, *pl.*—) founder.

**Gießerei** [ɡiːsəˈraɪ], *f.* (—, *pl.* —en) foundry.

**Gießform** [ˈɡiːsfɔrm], *f.* (—, *pl.* —en) casting-mould.

**Gießkanne** [ˈɡiːskanə], *f.* (—, *pl.* —n) watering-can.

**Gift** [ɡɪft], *n.* (—es, *pl.* —e) poison, venom; (*fig.*) virulence; (*coll.*) *darauf kannst du* — *nehmen*, you can bet your life on it.

**Giftbaum** [ˈɡɪftbaum], *m.* (—s, *pl.* ⸚e) upas-tree.

**Giftdrüse** [ˈɡɪftdryːzə], *f.* (—, *pl.* —n) poison-gland.

**giftig** [ˈɡɪftɪç], *adj.* poisonous; (*fig.*) venomous; (*Med.*) toxic.

**Giftlehre** [ˈɡɪftleːrə], *f.* (—, *no pl.*) toxicology.

**Giftpilz** [ˈɡɪftpɪlts], *m.* (—es, *pl.* —e) poisonous toadstool.

**Giftschlange** [ˈɡɪftʃlaŋə], *f.* (—, *pl.* —n) poisonous snake.

**Giftstoff** [ˈɡɪftʃtɔf], *m.* (—es, *pl.* —e) poison, virus.

**Gigant** [ɡɪˈɡant], *m.* (—en, *pl.* —en) giant.

**Gigerl** [ˈɡiːɡərl], *m.* (—s, *pl.* —) (*Austr. dial.*) fop, coxcomb.

**Gilde** [ˈɡɪldə], *f.* (—, *pl.* —n) guild, corporation.

**Gimpel** [ˈɡɪmpəl], *m.* (—s, *pl.* —) (*Orn.*) bullfinch, chaffinch; (*fig.*) simpleton.

**Ginster** [ˈɡɪnstər], *m.* (—s, *no pl.*) (*Bot.*) gorse, furze, broom.

**Gipfel** [ˈɡɪpfəl], *m.* (—s, *pl.* —) summit, peak; (*fig.*) acme, culmination, height.

**gipfeln** [ˈɡɪpfəln], *v.n.* culminate.

**Gips** [ɡɪps], *m.* (—es, *no pl.*) gypsum, stucco, plaster of Paris.

**Gipsabdruck** [ˈɡɪpsapdruk], *m.* (—s, *pl.* ⸚e) plaster-cast.

# Gipsbild

**Gipsbild** ['gɪpsbɪlt], *n.* (**—s**, *pl.* **—er**) plaster-figure.

**Gipsverband** ['gɪpsfɛrbant], *m.* (**—es**, *pl.* ˙‐e) (*Med.*) plaster of Paris dressing.

**girieren** [ʒi'ri:rən], *v.a.* (*Comm.*) endorse (a bill).

**Girlande** [gɪr'landə], *f.* (**—**, *pl.* **—n**) garland.

**Girobank** ['ʒi:robaŋk], *f.* (**—**, *pl.* **—en**) transfer *or* clearing bank.

**Gis** [gɪs], *n.* (**—**, *pl.* **—**) (*Mus.*) G sharp; **— Moll,** G sharp minor.

**gischen** ['gɪʃən], *v.n.* foam, froth.

**Gischt** [gɪʃt], *f.* (**—**, *pl.* **—e**) foam, froth; spray.

**Gitarre** [gi'tarə], *f.* (**—**, *pl.* **—n**) guitar.

**Gitter** ['gɪtər], *n.* (**—s**, *pl.* **—**) trellis, grate, fence; railing; lattice; (*colour-printing*) screen.

**Gitterwerk** ['gɪtərverk], *n.* (**—s**, *no pl.*) trellis-work.

**Glacéhandschuh** [gla'se:hantʃu:], *m.* (**—s**, *pl.* **—e**) kid-glove.

**Glanz** [glants], *m.* (**—es**, *no pl.*) brightness, lustre, gloss; polish, sheen; (*fig.*) splendour.

**glänzen** ['glɛntsən], *v.n.* shine, glitter, glisten; (*fig.*) sparkle.

**glänzend** ['glɛntsənt], *adj.* glossy; (*fig.*) splendid, magnificent.

**Glanzfirnis** ['glantsfɪrnɪs], *m.* (**—ses**, *pl.* **—se**) glazing varnish.

**Glanzleder** ['glantsle:dər], *n.* (**—s**, *no pl.*) patent leather.

**Glanzleinwand** ['glantslaɪnvant], *f.* (**—**, *no pl.*) glazed linen.

**glanzlos** ['glantslo:s], *adj.* lustreless, dull.

**glanzvoll** ['glantsfɔl], *adj.* splendid, brilliant.

**Glanzzeit** ['glantstsaɪt], *f.* (**—**, *pl.* **—en**) golden age.

**Glas** [gla:s], *n.* (**—es**, *pl.* ˙‐er) glass, tumbler.

**glasartig** ['gla:sa:rtɪç], *adj.* vitreous, glassy.

**Glaser** ['gla:zər], *m.* (**—s**, *pl.* **—**) glazier.

**Glaserkitt** ['gla:zərkɪt], *m.* (**—s**, *no pl.*) putty.

**gläsern** ['glɛ:zərn], *adj.* vitreous, glassy, made of glass.

**Glashütte** ['gla:shytə], *f.* (**—**, *pl.* **—n**) glass-works.

**glasieren** [gla'zi:rən], *v.a.* glaze; (*cake etc.*) ice.

**glasiert** [gla'zi:rt], *adj.* glazed; (*Cul.*) frosted, iced; (*Art.*) varnished.

**Glasröhre** ['gla:srø:rə], *f.* (**—**, *pl.* **—n**) glass-tube.

**Glasscheibe** ['gla:sʃaɪbə], *f.* (**—**, *pl.* **—n**) glass-pane, sheet of glass.

**Glassplitter** ['gla:sʃplɪtər], *m.* (**—s**, *pl.* **—**) splinter of glass.

**Glasur** [gla'zu:r], *f.* (**—**, *pl.* **—en**) (*potter's*) glaze, glazing; enamel, varnish; (*cake*) icing.

**glatt** [glat], *adj.* smooth, sleek; even, plain, glossy; glib; downright. **—** *adv.* entirely; **— rasiert,** close-shaven.

**Glätte** ['glɛtə], *f.* (**—**, *no pl.*) smoothness, evenness, slipperiness; polish.

**Glatteis** ['glataɪs], *n.* (**—es**, *no pl.*) slippery ice; sheet ice; (*Am.*) glaze; **einen aufs — führen,** lead s.o. up the garden path.

**glätten** ['glɛtən], *v.a.* smooth; (*dial.*) iron.

**Glatze** ['glatsə], *f.* (**—**, *pl.* **—n**) bald head.

**glatzköpfig** ['glatskœpfɪç], *adj.* bald, bald-pated.

**Glaube(n)** ['glaubə(n)], *m.* (**—ns**, *no pl.*) faith, belief; creed, religion.

**glauben** ['glaubən], *v.a.* believe; think, suppose. **—** *v.n.* **an etwas** (*Acc.*) **—,** believe in s.th.

**Glaubensbekenntnis** ['glaubənsbəkɛntnɪs], *n.* (**—ses**, *pl.* **—se**) confession of faith; creed.

**Glaubensgericht** ['glaubənsgərɪçt], *n.* (**—es**, *no pl.*) inquisition.

**Glaubersalz** ['glaubərzalts], *n.* (**—es**, *no pl.*) phosphate of soda, Glauber's salts.

**glaubhaft** ['glauphaft], *adj.* credible, authentic.

**gläubig** ['glɔybɪç], *adj.* believing, faithful; (*Eccl.*) **die Gläubigen,** the faithful.

**Gläubiger** ['glɔybɪgər], *m.* (**—s**, *pl.* **—**) creditor.

**glaublich** ['glauplɪç], *adj.* credible, believable.

**glaubwürdig** ['glaupvyrdɪç], *adj.* authentic, worthy of belief; plausible.

**gleich** [glaɪç], *adj.* same, like, equal, even; **auf —e Weise,** likewise; **es ist mir ganz —,** it is all the same to me. **—** *adv.* alike, at once; almost; just as; **ich komme —,** I shall be there in a moment; **— und — gesellt sich gern,** birds of a feather flock together.

**gleichaltrig** ['glaɪçaltrɪç], *adj.* of the same age.

**gleichartig** ['glaɪçartɪç], *adj.* of the same kind, homogeneous.

**gleichberechtigt** ['glaɪçbərɛçtɪçt], *adj.* entitled to equal rights.

**Gleiche** ['glaɪçə], *n.* (**—n**, *pl.* **—n**) the like; the same; **etwas ins — bringen,** straighten s.th. out.

**gleichen** ['glaɪçən], *v.n. irr.* be like, resemble, be equal to.

**gleichermaßen** ['glaɪçərma:sən], *adv.* in a like manner, likewise.

**gleichfalls** ['glaɪçfals], *adv.* likewise, equally, as well; **danke —,** thanks, the same to you.

**gleichförmig** ['glaɪçfœrmɪç], *adj.* uniform; monotonous.

**gleichgesinnt** ['glaɪçgəzɪnt], *adj.* congenial, of the same mind.

**Gleichgewicht** ['glaɪçgəvɪçt], *n.* (**—s**, *no pl.*) balance, equilibrium.

**gleichgültig** ['glaɪçgyltɪç], *adj.* indifferent; **es ist mir —,** it's all the same to me.

**Gleichheit** ['glaɪçhaɪt], *f.* (**—**, *pl.* **—en**) equality, likeness.

**Gleichklang** ['glaɪçklaŋ], *m.* (—s, *pl.* ˙˙e) consonance.
**gleichmachen** ['glaɪçmaxən], *v.a.* level, equate; *dem Erdboden* —, raze to the ground.
**Gleichmaß** ['glaɪçma:s], *n.* (—es, *no pl.*) proportion, symmetry.
**gleichmäßig** ['glaɪçmε:sɪç], *adj.* proportionate, symmetrical.
**Gleichmut** ['glaɪçmu:t], *m.* (—s, *no pl.*) equanimity, calm.
**gleichmütig** ['glaɪçmy:tɪç], *adj.* even-tempered, calm.
**gleichnamig** ['glaɪçna:mɪç], *adj.* homonymous.
**Gleichnis** ['glaɪçnɪs], *n.* (—ses, *pl.* —se) simile; (*Bibl.*) parable.
**gleichsam** ['glaɪçza:m], *adv.* as it were, as if.
**gleichschenklig** ['glaɪçʃeŋklɪç], *adj.* (*Maths.*) isosceles.
**gleichseitig** ['glaɪçzaɪtɪç], *adj.* (*Maths.*) equilateral.
**Gleichsetzung** ['glaɪçzetsuŋ], *f.* (—, *no pl.*), **Gleichstellung** ['glaɪçʃteluŋ], *f.* (—, *pl.* —en) equalisation.
**Gleichstrom** ['glaɪçʃtro:m], *m.* (—s, *no pl.*) (*Elec.*) direct current.
**gleichtun** ['glaɪçtu:n], *v.a.* irr. es einem —, emulate s.o.
**Gleichung** ['glaɪçuŋ], *f.* (—, *pl.* —en) (*Maths.*) equation.
**gleichwohl** ['glaɪçvo:l], *adv.*, *conj.* nevertheless, however, yet.
**gleichzeitig** ['glaɪçtsaɪtɪç], *adj.* simultaneous, contemporary.
**Gleis** [glaɪs], *n.* (—es, *pl.* —e) (*Railw.*) track; rails; (*Am.*) track.
**gleiten** ['glaɪtən], *v.n.* irr. (aux. sein) glide, slide, slip.
**Gleitflug** ['glaɪtflu:k], *m.* (—es, *pl.* ˙˙e) (*Aviat.*) gliding.
**Gletscher** ['gletʃər], *m.* (—s, *pl.* —) glacier.
**Gletscherspalte** ['gletʃərʃpaltə], *f.* (—, *pl.* —n) crevasse.
**Glied** [gli:t], *n.* (—es, *pl.* —er) limb, joint; member; link; rank, file.
**Gliederlähmung** ['gli:dərle:muŋ], *f.* (—, *no pl.*) paralysis.
**gliedern** ['gli:dərn], *v.a.* articulate, arrange, form.
**Gliederreißen** ['gli:dərraɪsən], *n.* (—s, *no pl.*) pain in the limbs, rheumatism, arthritis etc.
**Gliederung** ['gli:dəruŋ], *f.* (—, *pl.* —en) articulation, disposition, structure, arrangement, organisation.
**Gliedmaßen** ['gli:tma:sən], *f. pl.* limbs.
**glimmen** ['glɪmən], *v.n.* irr. glimmer, glow, burn faintly; —*de Asche*, embers.
**Glimmer** ['glɪmər], *m.* (—s, *no pl.*) (*Min.*) mica.
**glimpflich** ['glɪmpflɪç], *adj.* gentle.
**glitschen** ['glɪtʃən], *v.n.* (aux. sein) (*coll.*) slide.
**glitschig** ['glɪtʃɪç], *adj.* (*coll.*) slippery.
**glitzern** ['glɪtsərn], *v.n.* glisten, glitter.

**Globus** ['glo:bus], *m.* (—ses, *pl.* —se) globe.
**Glöckchen** ['glœkçən], *n.* (—s, *pl.* —) small bell; hand-bell.
**Glocke** ['glɔkə], *f.* (—, *pl.* —n) bell; *etwas an die große* — *hängen*, make a great fuss about s.th.
**Glockenblume** ['glɔkənblu:mə], *f.* (—, *pl.* —n) (*Bot.*) bluebell.
**Glockengießer** ['glɔkəngi:sər], *m.* (—s, *pl.* —) bell-founder.
**glockenklar** ['glɔkənkla:r], *adj.* as clear as a bell.
**Glockenläuter** ['glɔkənlɔytər], *m.* (—s, *pl.* —) bell-ringer.
**Glockenspiel** ['glɔkənʃpi:l], *n.* (—s, *pl.* —e) chime; (*Mus.*) glockenspiel, carillon.
**Glockenstuhl** ['glɔkənʃtu:l], *m.* (—s, *pl.* ˙˙e) belfry.
**Glockenzug** ['glɔkəntsu:k], *m.* (—s, *pl.* ˙˙e) bell-rope; (*Mus.*) bell-stop.
**Glöckner** ['glœknər], *m.* (—s, *pl.* —) bellringer, sexton.
**glorreich** ['glo:raɪç], *adj.* glorious.
**Glosse** ['glɔsə], *f.* (—, *pl.* —n) gloss, comment, annotation; —*n machen über*, comment upon; find fault with; scoff at.
**glotzen** ['glɔtsən], *v.n.* stare wide-eyed; gape.
**Glück** [glyk], *n.* (—s, *no pl.*) luck, good luck, fortune, happiness; — *haben*, be in luck; *auf gut* —, at random; *zum* —, fortunately, luckily; *viel* —, good luck.
**Glucke** ['glukə], *f.* (—, *pl.* —n) (sitting) hen.
**glücken** ['glykən], *v.n.* succeed; *es ist mir geglückt*, I have succeeded in.
**glücklich** ['glyklɪç], *adj.* fortunate, lucky, happy.
**glückselig** [glyk'ze:lɪç], *adj.* blissful, happy.
**glucksen** ['gluksən], *v.n.* gurgle.
**Glücksfall** ['glyksfal], *m.* (—es, *pl.* ˙˙e) lucky chance, windfall, stroke of good fortune.
**Glückspilz** ['glykspɪlts], *m.* (—es, *pl.* —e) (*coll.*) lucky dog.
**glückverheißend** ['glykfεrhaɪsənt], *adj.* auspicious, propitious.
**Glückwunsch** ['glykvunʃ], *m.* (—es, *pl.* ˙˙e) congratulation; felicitation.
**glühen** ['gly:ən], *v.a.* make red-hot; (*wine*) mull. — *v.n.* glow, be red-hot.
**glühend** ['gly:ənt], *adj.* glowing, burning; red-hot; (*coal*) live; (*fig.*) ardent, fervent.
**Glühstrumpf** ['gly:ʃtrumpf], *m.* (—s, *pl.* ˙˙e) incandescent mantle.
**Glühwein** ['gly:vaɪn], *m.* (—s, *no pl.*) mulled wine.
**Glut** [glu:t], *f.* (—, *no pl.*) glowing fire; heat; (*fig.*) ardour.
**glutrot** ['glu:tro:t], *adj.* fiery red.
**Glyzerin** [glytsəri:n], *n.* (—s, *no pl.*) glycerine.

# Gnade

**Gnade** ['gna:də], *f.* (—, *pl.* —n) grace; favour; pardon, clemency, mercy; kindness; *Euer* —n, Your Grace.

**Gnadenakt** ['gna:dənakt], *m.* (—s, *pl.* —e) act of grace.

**Gnadenbrot** ['gna:dənbro:t], *n.* (—s, *no pl.*) *das* — *essen*, live on charity.

**Gnadenfrist** ['gna:dənfrist], *f.* (—, *pl.* —en) respite.

**Gnadenort** ['gna:dənɔrt], *m.* (—(e)s, *pl.* —e) place of pilgrimage.

**Gnadenstoß** ['gna:dənʃto:s], *m.* (—es, *pl.* -̈e) finishing stroke, coup de grâce, death-blow.

**gnadenvoll** ['gna:dənfɔl], *adj.* merciful, gracious.

**Gnadenweg** ['gna:dənve:k], *m.* (—es, *no pl.*) act of grace; *auf dem* —, by reprieve (as an act of grace).

**gnädig** ['gnɛ:dɪç], *adj.* gracious, merciful, kind; —*e Frau*, Madam; —*er Herr*, Sir.

**Gnostiker** ['gnɔstɪkər], *m.* (—s, *pl.* —) gnostic.

**Gnu** [gnu:], *n.* (—s, *pl.* —s) (*Zool.*) gnu.

**Gold** [gɔlt], *n.* (—(e)s, *no pl.*) gold.

**Goldammer** ['gɔltamər], *f.* (—, *pl.* —n) (*Orn.*) yellow-hammer.

**Goldamsel** ['gɔltamzəl], *f.* (—, *pl.* —n) (*Orn.*) yellow-thrush.

**Goldarbeiter** ['gɔltarbaɪtər], *m.* (—s, *pl.* —) goldsmith.

**Goldbarren** ['gɔltbarən], *m.* (—s, *pl.* —) ingot of gold.

**Goldbergwerk** ['gɔltbɛrkvɛrk], *n.* (—s, *pl.* —e) gold-mine.

**Goldfisch** ['gɔltfɪʃ], *m.* (—es, *pl.* —e) goldfish.

**Goldgewicht** ['gɔltgəvɪçt], *n.* (—s, *no pl.*) gold-weight, troy-weight.

**Goldgrube** ['gɔltgru:bə], *f.* (—, *pl.* —n) gold-mine.

**goldig** ['gɔldɪç], *adj.* golden; (*fig.*) sweet, cute, charming.

**Goldklumpen** ['gɔltklumpən], *m.* (—s, *pl.* —) nugget (of gold).

**Goldlack** ['gɔltlak], *m.* (—s, *no pl.*) gold-coloured varnish; (*Bot.*) wall-flower.

**Goldmacher** ['gɔltmaxər], *m.* (—s, *pl.* —) alchemist.

**Goldregen** ['gɔltre:gən], *m.* (—s, *pl.* —) (*Bot.*) laburnum.

**Goldscheider** ['gɔltʃaɪdər], *m.* (—s, *pl.* —) gold-refiner.

**Goldschmied** ['gɔltʃmi:t], *m.* (—s, *pl.* —e) goldsmith.

**Goldschnitt** ['gɔltʃnɪt], *m.* (—s, *no pl.*) gilt edge.

**Golf** (1) [gɔlf], *m.* (—s, *pl.* —e) gulf.

**Golf** (2) [gɔlf], *n.* (—s, *no pl.*) golf.

**Gondel** ['gɔndəl], *f.* (—, *pl.* —n) gondola.

**gondeln** ['gɔndəln], *v.n.* (*aux.* sein) ride in a gondola; (*coll.*) travel, get about.

**gönnen** ['gœnən], *v.a. einem etwas* —, not grudge s.o. s.th.; *wir* — *es ihm*, we are happy for him.

**Gönner** ['gœnər], *m.* (—s, *pl.* —) patron, protector.

**gönnerhaft** ['gœnərhaft], *adj.* patronising.

**Gönnerschaft** ['gœnərʃaft], *f.* (—, *no pl.*) patronage.

**gordisch** ['gɔrdɪʃ], *adj.* Gordian; *der* —*e Knoten*, the Gordian knot.

**Göre** ['gø:rə], *f.* (—, *pl.* —n) (*coll.*) brat; (*Am.*) kid.

**Gosse** ['gɔsə], *f.* (—, *pl.* —n) gutter.

**Gote** ['go:tə], *m.* (—n, *pl.* —n) Goth.

**Gotik** ['go:tɪk], *f.* (—, *no pl.*) Gothic style (architecture etc.).

**gotisch** ['go:tɪʃ], *adj.* Gothic.

**Gott** [gɔt], *m.* (—es, *pl.* -̈er) God, god; — *befohlen*, goodbye; *grüß* —*!* (*Austr.*) good day; — *sei Dank*, thank God, thank heaven.

**gottbegnadet** ['gɔtbəgna:dət], *adj.* favoured by God, inspired.

**Götterbild** ['gœtərbɪlt], *n.* (—es, *pl.* —er) image of a god.

**gottergeben** ['gɔtɛrge:bən], *adj.* submissive to God's will, devout.

**Götterlehre** ['gœtərle:rə], *f.* (—, *pl.* —n) mythology.

**Götterspeise** ['gœtərʃpaɪzə], *f.* (—, *pl.* —n) ambrosia.

**Götterspruch** ['gœtərʃprux], *m.* (—s, *no pl.*) oracle.

**Göttertrank** ['gœtərtraŋk], *m.* (—s, *pl.* -̈e) nectar.

**Gottesacker** ['gɔtəsakər], *m.* (—s, *pl.* —) God's acre, churchyard.

**Gottesdienst** ['gɔtəsdi:nst], *m.* (—es, *pl.* —e) divine service, public worship.

**gottesfürchtig** ['gɔtəsfyrçtɪç], *adj.* God-fearing, pious.

**Gottesgelehrsamkeit** ['gɔtəsgəle:rza:mkaɪt], *f.* (—, *no pl.*) (*rare*) theology, divinity.

**Gottesgericht** ['gɔtəsgərɪçt], *n.* (—s, *pl.* —e) ordeal.

**Gotteshaus** ['gɔtəshaus], *n.* (—es, *pl.* -̈er) house of God; (*rare*) church.

**Gotteslästerer** ['gɔtəslɛstərər], *m.* (—s, *pl.* —) blasphemer.

**Gottesleugner** ['gɔtəslɔygnər], *m.* (—s, *pl.* —) atheist.

**Gottfried** ['gɔtfri:t], *m.* Godfrey, Geoffrey.

**gottgefällig** ['gɔtgəfɛlɪç], *adj.* pleasing to God.

**Gottheit** ['gɔthaɪt], *f.* (—, *pl.* —en) deity, divinity.

**Göttin** ['gœtɪn], *f.* (—, *pl.* —nen) goddess.

**göttlich** ['gœtlɪç], *adj.* divine, godlike; (*fig.*) heavenly.

**gottlob!** [gɔt'lo:p], *excl.* thank God!

**gottlos** ['gɔtlo:s], *adj.* godless, ungodly, impious; (*fig.*) wicked.

**gottvergessen** ['gɔtfɛrgɛsən], *adj.* reprobate, impious.

**gottverlassen** ['gɔtfɛrlasən], *adj.* God-forsaken.

**Götze** ['gœtsə], *m.* (—n, *pl.* —n) idol, false deity.

**Götzenbild** ['gœtsənbɪlt], *n.* (—es, *pl.* —er) idol.

**Götzendienst** ['gœtsəndi:nst], *m.* (—es, *no pl.*) idolatry.

**Gouvernante** [guvɛr'nantə], *f.* (—, *pl.* —n) governess.

**Gouverneur** [guvɛr'nø:r], *m.* (—s, *pl.* —e) governor.

**Grab** [gra:p], *n.* (—s, *pl.* ̈er) grave, tomb; sepulchre.

**Graben** ['gra:bən], *m.* (—s, *pl.* ̈) ditch, trench.

**graben** ['gra:bən], *v.a. irr.* dig.

**Grabgeläute** ['gra:pgələytə], *n.* (—s, *no pl.*) death-knell.

**Grabhügel** ['gra:phy:gəl], *m.* (—s, *pl.* —) tumulus, mound.

**Grablegung** ['gra:ple:guŋ], *f.* (—, *no pl.*) (*rare*) burial, interment.

**Grabmal** ['gra:pma:l], *n.* (—s, *pl.* —e, ̈er) tomb, sepulchre, monument.

**Grabschrift** ['gra:pʃrɪft], *f.* (—, *pl.* —n) epitaph.

**Grabstichel** ['gra:pʃtɪçəl], *m.* (—s, *pl.* —) graving-tool.

**Grad** [gra:t], *m.* (—s, *pl.* —e) degree; rank; grade; extent; point; *in gewissem* —e, to a certain degree; *im höchsten* —e, in the highest degree, extremely.

**Gradeinteilung** ['gra:taɪntaɪluŋ], *f.* (—, *pl* —en) gradation, graduation.

**Gradmesser** ['gra:tmɛsər], *m.* (—s, *pl.* —) graduator; (*fig.*) index.

**gradweise** ['gra:tvaɪzə], *adv.* gradually, by degrees.

**Graf** [gra:f], *m.* (—en, *pl.* —en) count, earl.

**Gräfin** ['grɛfɪn], *f.* (—, *pl.* —en) countess.

**gräflich** ['grɛflɪç], *adj.* belonging to a count *or* earl.

**Grafschaft** ['gra:fʃaft], *f.* (—, *pl.* —en) county, shire.

**Gral** [gra:l], *m.* (—s, *no pl.*) Holy Grail.

**Gram** [gra:m], *m.* (—s, *no pl.*) grief, sorrow.

**grämen** ['grɛ:mən], *v.a.* grieve. — *v.r. sich* —, grieve, fret, worry.

**gramgebeugt** ['gra:mgəbɔykt], *adj.* prostrate with grief.

**grämlich** ['grɛ:mlɪç], *adj.* sullen, morose, ill-humoured.

**Gramm** [gram], *n.* (—s, *pl.* —e) gramme (15.438 grains); (*Am.*) gram.

**Grammatik** [gra'matɪk], *f.* (—, *pl.* —en) grammar.

**grammatikalisch, grammatisch** [gramatɪ'ka:lɪʃ, gra'matɪʃ], *adj.* grammatical.

**Gran** [gra:n], *n.* (—s, *pl.* —e) (*weight*) grain.

**Granat** [gra'na:t], *m.* (—s, *pl.* —e) garnet.

**Granatapfel** [gra'na:tapfəl], *m.* (—s, *pl.* ̈e) (*Bot.*) pomegranate.

**Granate** [gra'na:tə], *f.* (—, *pl.* —n) shell, grenade.

**Grande** ['grandə], *m.* (—n, *pl.* —n) grandee.

**Grandezza** [gran'dɛtsa], *f.* (—, *no pl.*) grandeur; sententiousness; pomposity.

**grandios** [grandɪ'o:s], *adj.* grand.

**Granit** [gra'ni:t], *m.* (—s, *pl.* —e) granite.

**Granne** ['granə], *f.* (—, *pl.* —n) (*corn*) awn, beard.

**graphisch** ['gra:fɪʃ], *adj.* graphic.

**Graphit** [gra'fi:t], *m.* (—s, *no pl.*) blacklead.

**Gras** [gra:s], *n.* (—es, *pl.* ̈er) grass; (*coll.*)ins — beißen, bite the dust.

**grasartig** ['gra:sa:rtɪç], *adj.* gramineous.

**grasen** ['gra:zən], *v.n.* graze.

**Grasfleck** ['gra:sflɛk], *m.* (—s, *pl.* —e) grass-stain.

**Grashalm** ['gra:shalm], *m.* (—s, *pl.* —e) grass-blade.

**Grashüpfer** ['gra:shypfər], *m.* (—s, *pl.* —) (*Ent.*) grass-hopper.

**grasig** ['gra:zɪç], *adj.* grassy.

**Grasmäher** ['gra:smɛ:ər], *m.* (—s, *pl.* —) lawn-mower.

**Grasmücke** ['gra:smykə], *f.* (—, *pl.* —n) (*Orn.*) hedge-sparrow.

**grassieren** [gra'si:rən], *v.n.* (*epidemics etc.*) spread, rage.

**gräßlich** ['grɛslɪç], *adj.* hideous, horrible, ghastly.

**Grasweide** ['gra:svaɪdə], *f.* (—, *pl.* —n) pasture.

**Grat** [gra:t], *m.* (—s, *pl.* —e) edge, ridge.

**Gräte** ['grɛ:tə], *f.* (—, *pl.* —n) fish-bone.

**Grätenstich** ['grɛ:tənʃtɪç], *m.* (—s, *pl.* —e) (*embroidery*) herring-bone stitch.

**grätig** ['grɛ:tɪç], *adj.* full of fishbones; (*fig.*) grumpy.

**gratis** ['gra:tɪs], *adj.* gratis; — *und franko*, for nothing.

**Gratulation** [gratula'tsjo:n], *f.* (—, *pl.* —en) congratulation.

**gratulieren** [gratu'li:rən], *v.n. einem zu etwas* —, congratulate s.o. on s.th.

**grau** [grau], *adj.* grey; (*Am.*) gray; *vor* —*en Zeiten*, in times of yore.

**Grauen** ['grauən], *n.* (—s, *no pl.*) horror, aversion.

**grauen** ['grauən], *v.n.* (*morning*) dawn; *es graut mir vor*, I shudder at.

**grauenhaft** ['grauənhaft], *adj.* horrible, awful, ghastly.

**graulen** ['graulən], *v.r. sich* —, shudder, be afraid (of ghosts etc.).

**graulich** ['graulɪç], *adj. mir ist ganz* —, I shudder.

**Graupe** ['graupə], *f.* (—, *pl.* —n) groats, peeled barley.

**graupeln** ['graupəln], *v.n. imp.* (*coll.*) drizzle, sleet.

**Graus** [graus], *m.* (—es, *no pl.*) horror, dread.

**grausam** ['grauza:m], *adj.* cruel.

**Grauschimmel** ['grauʃɪməl], *m.* (—s, *pl.* —) grey (horse).

**grausen** ['grauzən], *v.n. es graust mir vor*, I shudder at.

**grausig** ['grauzɪç], *adj.* dreadful, gruesome, horrible.

**Graveur** [gra'vø:r], *m.* (—s, *pl.* —e) engraver.

**gravieren** [gra'vi:rən], *v.a.* engrave.

**Gravität** [gravi'tɛ:t], *f.* (—, *no pl.*) gravity.

**gravitätisch** [gravi'tɛ:tɪʃ], *adj.* grave, solemn.

**Grazie** ['gra:tsjə], *f.* (—, *pl.* —n) grace, charm; (*goddess*) Grace.

**graziös** [gra'tsjø:s], *adj.* graceful.

**Greif** [graɪf], *m.* (—(e)s, *pl.* —e) griffin.

**greifbar** ['graɪfba:r], *adj.* to hand; (*fig.*) tangible, palpable.

**greifen** ['graɪfən], *v.a. irr.* grasp, seize, touch, handle; *etwas aus der Luft* —, invent s.th.; *um sich* —, gain ground.

**greinen** ['graɪnən], *v.n.* (*dial. & coll.*) cry, blubber.

**Greis** [graɪs], *m.* (—es, *pl.* —e) old man.

**greisenhaft** ['graɪzənhaft], *adj.* senile.

**grell** [grɛl], *adj.* (*colour*) glaring; (*light*) dazzling; (*tone*) shrill, sharp.

**Grenadier** [grena'di:r], *m.* (—s, *pl.* —e) grenadier.

**Grenadiermütze** [grena'di:rmytsə], *f.* (—, *pl.* —n) busby, bearskin.

**Grenze** ['grɛntsə], *f.* (—, *pl.* —n) boundary; frontier; borders; (*fig.*) limit.

**grenzen** ['grɛntsən], *v.n.* — *an*, border on; (*fig.*) verge on.

**Grenzlinie** ['grɛntsli:njə], *f.* (—, *pl.* —n) boundary-line, line of demarcation.

**Greuel** ['grɔyəl], *m.* (—s, *pl.* —) horror, abomination; *das ist mir ein* —, I abominate it.

**Greueltat** [grɔyəlta:t], *f.* (—, *pl.* —en) atrocity.

**greulich** ['grɔylɪç], *adj.* horrible, dreadful, shocking, heinous.

**Griebe** ['gri:bə], *f.* (—, *pl.* —n) (*mostly pl.*) greaves.

**Griebs** ['gri:ps], *m.* (—es, *pl.* —e) (*dial.*) (*apple*) core.

**Grieche** ['gri:çə], *m.* (—n, *pl.* —n) Greek.

**Griechenland** ['gri:çənlant], *n.* Greece.

**Griesgram** ['gri:sgra:m], *m.* (—s, *pl.* —e) grumbler.

**griesgrämig** ['gri:sgrɛ:mɪç], *adj.* morose, grumbling.

**Grieß** ['gri:s], *m.* (—es, *no pl.*) groats, semolina.

**Grießbrei** ['gri:sbraɪ], *m.* (—s, *pl.* —e) gruel.

**Griff** [grɪf], *m.* (—s, *pl.* —e) grip, hold, handle.

**griffbereit** ['grɪfbəraɪt], *adj.* handy.

**Grille** ['grɪlə], *f.* (—, *pl.* —n) (*Ent.*) cricket; (*fig.*) whim; —*n haben*, be capricious; —*n fangen*, be crotchety, be depressed.

**grillenhaft** ['grɪlənhaft], *adj.* whimsical; capricious.

**Grimasse** [gri'masə], *f.* (—, *pl.* —n) grimace.

**Grimm** [grɪm], *m.* (—s, *no pl.*) fury, rage, wrath.

**Grimmen** ['grɪmən], *n.* (—s, *no pl.*) gripes; (*Med.*) colic.

**grimmig** ['grɪmɪç], *adj.* fierce, furious; grim.

**Grind** [grɪnt], *m.* (—s, *pl.* —e) scab, scurf.

**grinsen** ['grɪnzən], *v.n.* grin.

**Grippe** ['grɪpə], *f.* (—, *pl.* —n) influenza, grippe.

**Grips** [grɪps], *m.* (—es, *no pl.*) (*coll.*) sense, brains; *einen beim* — *nehmen*, take s.o. by the scruff of his neck.

**grob** [grɔp], *adj.* coarse; rough; gross; rude, crude, uncouth, impolite; (*jewels*) rough, unpolished.

**Grobheit** ['grɔphaɪt], *f.* (—, *pl.* —en) rudeness; abusive language.

**Grobian** ['gro:bja:n], *m.* (—s, *pl.* —e) boor, rude fellow.

**Grobschmied** ['grɔpʃmi:t], *m.* (—s, *pl.* —e) blacksmith.

**Grog** [grɔk], *m.* (—s, *pl.* —s) grog, toddy.

**grölen** ['grø:lən], *v.n.* (*coll.*) scream, squall, bawl.

**Groll** [grɔl], *m.* (—s, *no pl.*) resentment, anger, rancour; *einen* — *gegen einen haben*, bear s.o. a grudge.

**grollen** ['grɔlən], *v.n.* (*thunder*) rumble; *einem* —, bear s.o. ill-will; (*Poet.*) be angry (with).

**Grönland** ['grø:nlant], *n.* Greenland.

**Gros** (1) [grɔs], *n.* (—ses, *pl.* —se) gross; twelve dozen.

**Gros** (2) [gro:], *n.* (—, *no pl.*) bulk, majority; *en* —, wholesale.

**Groschen** ['grɔʃən], *m.* (—s, *pl.* —) small coin, penny; one 100th of an Austrian shilling; ten-pfennig piece; *einen schönen* — *verdienen*, make good money.

**groß** [gro:s], *adj.* great, big, large; tall; vast; eminent, famous; intense; —*e Augen machen*, stare; *Grosser Ozean*, Pacific (Ocean).

**großartig** ['gro:sa:rtɪç], *adj.* grand, sublime, magnificent, splendid.

**Großbetrieb** ['gro:sbətri:p], *m.* (—s, *pl.* —e) large business; large (industrial) concern.

**Großbritannien** [gro:sbri'tanjən], *n.* Great Britain.

**Größe** ['grø:sə], *f.* (—, *pl.* —n) size, largeness, greatness; height; quantity; power; celebrity, star; importance.

**Großeltern** ['gro:sɛltərn], *pl.* grandparents.

**Großenkel** ['gro:sɛŋkəl], *m.* (—s, *pl.* —) great-grandson.

**Größenverhältnis** ['grø:sənfɛrhɛltnɪs], *n.* (—ses, *pl.* —se) proportion, ratio.

**Größenwahn** ['grø:sənva:n], *m.* (—s, *no pl.*) megalomania; delusion of grandeur.

**Großfürst** ['gro:sfyrst], *m.* (—en, *pl.* —en) grand-duke.

**Großfürstin** ['gro:sfyrstɪn], *f.* (—, *pl.* —nen) grand-duchess.

**Großgrundbesitz** ['gro:sgruntbəzɪts], *m.* (—es, *pl.* —e) large landed property, estates.

**Großhandel** ['gro:shandəl], *m.* (—s, *no pl.*) wholesale business.

**großherzig** ['gro:shɛrtsɪç], *adj.* magnanimous.

**Grossist** [gro'sɪst], *m.* (—en, *pl.* —en) wholesale merchant.

**großjährig** ['gro:sjɛːrɪç], *adj.* of age; — *werden*, come of age.

**großmächtig** ['gro:smɛçtɪç], *adj.* (*fig.*) high and mighty.

**großmäulig** ['gro:smɔylɪç], *adj.* bragging, swaggering.

**Großmut** ['gro:smu:t], *f.* (—, *no pl.*) magnanimity, generosity.

**Großmutter** ['gro:smutər], *f.* (—, *pl.* ∵) grandmother.

**Großsiegelbewahrer** [gro:s'zi:gəlbəva:rər], *m.* (—s, *pl.* —) Lord Chancellor; Keeper of the Great Seal.

**Großstadt** ['gro:sʃtat], *f.* (—, *pl.* ∵e) large town, city, metropolis.

**Großtat** ['gro:sta:t], *f.* (—, *pl.* —en) achievement, exploit, feat.

**Großtuer** ['gro:stu:ər], *m.* (—s, *pl.* —) boaster, braggart.

**großtun** ['gro:stu:n], *v.r. irr. sich — mit*, brag of; show off, parade.

**Großvater** ['gro:sfa:tər], *m.* (—s, *pl.* ∵) grandfather.

**großziehen** ['gro:stsi:ən], *v.a. irr.* bring up, rear.

**großzügig** ['gro:stsy:gɪç], *adj.* boldly conceived; grand, generous.

**Grotte** ['grɔtə], *f.* (—, *pl.* —n) grotto.

**Grübchen** ['gry:pçən], *n.* (—s, *pl.* —) dimple.

**Grube** ['gru:bə], *f.* (—, *pl.* —n) hole, pit; (*Min.*) mine; *in die — fahren*, (*Bibl.*) go down to the grave.

**Grübelei** ['gry:bəlaɪ], *f.* (—, *pl.* —en) brooding, musing.

**grübeln** ['gry:bəln], *v.n.* brood (over s.th.)

**Grubenarbeiter** ['gru:bənarbaɪtər], *m.* (—s, *pl.* —) miner.

**Grubengas** ['gru:bəngaːs], *n.* (—es, *pl.* —e) fire-damp.

**Grubenlampe** ['gru:bənlampə], *f.* (—, *pl.* —n) miner's lamp.

**Gruft** [gruft], *f.* (—, *pl.* ∵e) tomb, sepulchre; vault, mausoleum.

**grün** [gry:n], *adj.* green; *grüne Bohnen*, French beans, runner beans; (*fig.*) unripe, immature, inexperienced; *am —en Tisch*, at the conference table; (*fig.*) in theory; *auf einen —en Zweig kommen*, thrive, get on in the world; *einem nicht — sein*, dislike s.o.

**Grund** [grunt], *m.* (—s, *pl.* ∵e) ground, soil; earth; land; bottom; foundation, basis; valley; reason, cause, argument; motive.

**Grundbedeutung** ['gruntbədɔytuŋ], *f.* (—, *pl.* —en) primary meaning, basic meaning.

**Grundbesitz** ['gruntbəzɪts], *m.* (—es, *no pl.*) landed property.

**Grundbuch** ['gruntbu:x], *n.* (—s, *pl.* ∵er) land register.

**grundehrlich** ['grunte:rlɪç], *adj.* thoroughly honest.

**Grundeigentum** ['gruntaɪgəntu:m], *n.* (—s, *pl.* ∵er) landed property.

**Grundeis** ['gruntaɪs], *n.* (—es, *no pl.*) ground-ice.

**gründen** ['gryndən], *v.a.* found, establish, float (a company). — *v.r. sich auf*, be based on.

**grundfalsch** ['gruntfalʃ], *adj.* radically false.

**Grundfarbe** ['gruntfarbə], *f.* (—, *pl.* —n) primary colour.

**Grundfläche** ['gruntflɛçə], *f.* (—, *pl.* —n) basis, base.

**Grundherr** ['grunthɛr], *m.* (—n, *pl.* —en) lord of the manor, freeholder.

**grundieren** [grun'di:rən], *v.a.* prime, size, paint the undercoat.

**Grundkapital** ['gruntkapita:l], *n.* (—s, *no pl.*) original stock.

**Grundlage** ['gruntla:gə], *f.* (—, *pl.* —n) foundation, basis.

**Grundlegung** ['gruntle:guŋ], *f.* (— *no pl.*) laying the foundation.

**gründlich** ['gryntlɪç], *adj.* thorough, solid.

**grundlos** ['gruntlo:s], *adj.* bottomless; groundless, unfounded, without foundation.

**Grundmauer** ['gruntmauər], *f.* (—, *pl.* —n) foundation wall.

**Gründonnerstag** [gry:n'dɔnərsta:k], *m.* (—s, *pl.* —e) Maundy Thursday.

**Grundpfeiler** ['gruntpfaɪlər], *m.* (—s, *pl.* —) (main) pillar.

**Grundriß** ['gruntrɪs], *m.* (—sses, *pl.* —sse) design, groundplan; compendium, elements; blueprint.

**Grundsatz** ['gruntzats], *m.* (—es, *pl.* ∵e) principle, maxim; axiom.

**grundschlecht** ['gruntʃlɛçt], *adj.* thoroughly bad.

**Grundschuld** ['gruntʃult], *f.* (—, *pl.* —en) mortgage (on land).

**Grundstein** ['gruntʃtaɪn], *m.* (—s, *pl.* —e) foundation-stone.

**Grundsteuer** ['gruntʃtɔyər], *f.* (—, *pl.* —n) land-tax.

**Grundstoff** ['gruntʃtɔf], *m.* (—es, *pl.* —e) raw material.

**Grundstück** ['gruntʃtyk], *n.* (—s, *pl.* —e) real estate; plot of land; lot.

**Grundtugend** ['grunttu:gənt], *f.* (— *pl.* —en) cardinal virtue.

**Gründung** ['grynduŋ], *f.* (—, *pl.* —en) foundation, establishment.

**grundverschieden** ['gruntferʃi:dən], *adj.* radically different.

**Grundwasser** ['gruntvasər], *n.* (—s, *no pl.*) underground water.

**Grundzahl** ['grunttsa:l], *f.* (—, *pl.* —en) cardinal number.

**Grundzug** ['grunttsu:k], *m.* (—s, *pl.* ∵e) characteristic; distinctive feature.

# Grüne

**Grüne** ['gry:nə], *n.* (—**n**, *no pl.*) greenness, verdure; *ins — gehen,* take a walk in the open country.

**grünen** ['gry:nən], *v.n.* become green; (*fig.*) flourish.

**Grünfutter** ['gry:nfutər], *n.* (—**s**, *no pl.*) green food.

**Grünkohl** ['gry:nko:l], *m.* (—**s**, *no pl.*) green kale.

**Grünkramhändler** ['gry:nkra:mhɛndlər], *m.* (—**s**, *pl.* —) greengrocer.

**Grünschnabel** ['gry:nʃna:bəl], *m.* (—**s**, *pl.* ⸚) greenhorn.

**Grünspan** ['gry:nʃpa:n], *m.* (—**s**, *no pl.*) verdigris.

**Grünspecht** ['gry:nʃpɛçt], *m.* (—**s**, *pl.* —**e**) (*Orn.*) green woodpecker.

**grunzen** ['gruntsən], *v.n.* grunt.

**Grünzeug** ['gry:ntsɔyk], *n.* (—**s**, *no pl.*) greens, herbs.

**Gruppe** ['grupə], *f.* (—, *pl.* —**n**) group.

**gruppieren** [gru'pi:rən], *v.a.* group.

**gruselig** ['gru:zəlɪç], *adj.* creepy, uncanny.

**gruseln** ['gru:zəln], *v.a. es gruselt mir* I shudder, it gives me the creeps.

**Gruß** [gru:s], *m.* (—**es**, *pl.* ⸚**e**) salutation, greeting; (*pl.*) regards; *mit herzlichem —,* with kind regards; *einen — ausrichten,* convey s.o.'s regards.

**grüßen** ['gry:sən], *v.a.* greet; *einen — lassen,* send o.'s regards to s.o.; — *Sie ihn von mir,* remember me to him.

**Grütze** ['grytsə], *f.* (—, *pl.* —**n**) peeled grain, groats; (*fig.*) (*coll.*) gumption, brains.

**Guatemala** [guatə'ma:la], *n.* Guatemala.

**gucken** ['gukən], *v.n.* look, peep.

**Guinea** [gɪ'ne:a], *n.* Guinea.

**Gulasch** ['gulaʃ], *n.* (—**s**, *no pl.*) goulash.

**Gulden** ['guldən], *m.* (—**s**, *pl.* —) florin, guilder.

**gülden** ['gyldən], *adj.* (*Poet.*) golden.

**gültig** ['gyltɪç], *adj.* valid; (*money*) current, legal (tender).

**Gummi** ['gumi:], *m.* (—**s**, *no pl.*) gum, rubber.

**Gummiarabikum** [gumia'ra:bɪkum], *n.* gum arabic.

**gummiartig** ['gumia:rtɪç], *adj.* gummy; like rubber.

**Gummiball** ['gumibal], *m.* (—**s**, *pl.* ⸚**e**) rubber-ball.

**Gummiband** ['gumibant], *n.* (—**s**, *pl.* ⸚**er**) rubber-band, elastic.

**Gummielastikum** [gumie'lastikum], *n.* indiarubber.

**gummieren** [gu'mi:rən], *v.a.* gum.

**Gummireifen** ['gumiraɪfən], *m.* (—**s**, *pl.* —) tyre; (*Am.*) tire.

**Gummischuhe** ['gumiʃu:ə], *m. pl.* galoshes; (*Am.*) rubbers.

**Gunst** [gunst], *f.* (—, *no pl.*) favour; *zu seinen —en,* in his favour.

**Gunstbezeigung** ['gunstbətsaɪguŋ], *f.* (—, *pl.* —**en**) favour, kindness, goodwill.

**günstig** ['gynstɪç], *adj.* favourable, propitious.

**Günstling** ['gynstlɪŋ], *m.* (—**s**, *pl.* —**e**) favourite.

**Gurgel** ['gurgəl], *f.* (—, *pl.* —**n**) gullet, throat.

**gurgeln** ['gurgəln], *v.n.* gargle; gurgle.

**Gurke** ['gurkə], *f.* (—, *pl.* —**n**) (*Bot.*) cucumber; (*pickled*) gherkin.

**Gurt** [gurt], *m.* (—**es**, *pl.* —**e**) belt; strap; harness.

**Gürtel** ['gyrtəl], *m.* (—**s**, *pl.* —) girdle, belt; (*Geog.*) zone.

**Guß** [gus], *m.* (—**sses**, *pl.* ⸚**sse**) gush, downpour; founding; cast; (*Cul.*) icing.

**Gut** [gu:t], *n.* (—(**e**)**s**, *pl.* ⸚**er**) good thing, blessing; property, possession; country seat; estate; (*pl.*) goods.

**gut** [gu:t], *adj.* good; beneficial; kind; virtuous. — *adv.* well; *es — haben,* be well off; —*er Dinge sein,* be of good cheer; *kurz und —,* in short.

**Gutachten** ['gu:taxtən], *n.* (—**s**, *pl.* —) expert opinion, expert evidence.

**gutartig** ['gu:ta:rtɪç], *adj.* good-natured; benign.

**Güte** ['gy:tə], *f.* (—, *no pl.*) goodness, kindness, quality.

**Güterabfertigung** ['gy:tərapfɛrtɪguŋ], *f.* (—, *pl.* —**en**) (*Railw.*) goods-depot, goods-office.

**Güterabtretung** ['gy:təraptre:tuŋ], *f.* (—, *pl.* —**en**) cession of goods; (*Law*) surrender of an estate.

**gutgelaunt** ['gu:tgəlaunt], *adj.* in good spirits, good-humoured.

**gutgemeint** ['gu:tgəmaɪnt], *adj.* well-meant, well-intentioned.

**gutgesinnt** ['gu:tgəzɪnt], *adj.* well-intentioned.

**Guthaben** ['gu:tha:bən], *n.* (—**s**, *pl.* —) credit-balance, assets.

**gutheißen** ['gu:thaɪsən], *v.a. irr.* approve.

**gütig** ['gy:tɪç], *adj.* kind, benevolent.

**gütlich** ['gy:tlɪç], *adj.* amicable, friendly; —*er Vergleich,* amicable settlement; *sich — tun,* indulge o.s.

**gutmachen** ['gu:tmaxən], *v.a. etwas wieder —,* make amends for s.th., compensate.

**gutmütig** ['gu:tmy:tɪç], *adj.* good-natured, good-tempered.

**Gutsbesitzer** ['gu:tsbəzɪtsər], *m.* (—**s**, *pl.* —) landowner; proprietor of an estate.

**gutschreiben** ['gu:tʃraɪbən], *v.a. irr. einem etwas —,* enter a sum to s.o.'s credit.

**Gutsverwalter** ['gu:tsfɛrvaltər], *m.* (—**s**, *pl.* —) land-steward, agent, bailiff.

**gutwillig** ['gu:tvɪlɪç], *adj.* willing, of o.'s own free will.

**Gymnasialbildung** [gymnaz'ja:lbɪlduŋ], *f.* (—, *no pl.*) classical *or* grammar school education.

**Gymnasiast** [gymnaz'jast], *m.* (—**en**, *pl.* —**en**) grammar-school pupil.

# haften

**Gymnasium** [gym'na:zjum], *n.* (—s, *pl.* —sien) grammar-school.
**Gymnastik** [gym'nastɪk], *f.* (—, *no pl.*) gymnastics.
**gymnastisch** [gym'nastɪʃ], *adj.* gymnastic(al); —*e Übungen*, physical exercises.

# H

**H** [ha:], *n.* (—s, *pl.* —s) the letter H; (*Mus.*) *H Dur*, B major; *H Moll*, B minor.
**ha!** [ha:], *excl.* ha!
**Haag, Den** [ha:k, de:n], *m.* The Hague.
**Haar** [ha:r], *n.* (—s, *pl.* —e) hair; wool; nap; *aufs* —, exactly, to a hair; *um ein* —, very nearly, within a hair's breadth.
**haaren** ['ha:rən], *v.r. sich* —, shed o.'s hair.
**haargenau** ['ha:rgənau], *adj.* (very) exactly; to a nicety.
**haarig** ['ha:rɪç], *adj.* hairy.
**Haarlocke** ['ha:rlɔkə], *f.* (—, *pl.* —n) curl, ringlet.
**Haarnadel** ['ha:rna:dəl], *f.* (—, *pl.* —n) hairpin.
**Haaröl** ['ha:rø:l], *n.* (—s, *no pl.*) hair-oil.
**Haarpinsel** ['ha:rpɪnzəl], *m.* (—s, *pl.* —) camel-hair brush.
**Haarröhrchen** ['ha:rrø:rçən], *n.* (—s, *pl.* —) capillary tube.
**Haarschleife** ['ha:rʃlaɪfə], *f.* (—, *pl.* —en) bow in the hair.
**Haarschnitt** ['ha:rʃnɪt], *m.* (—s, *pl.* —e) hair-cut.
**Haarschuppen** ['ha:rʃupən], *f. pl.* dandruff.
**Haarspalterei** ['ha:rʃpaltəraɪ], *f.* (—, *pl.* —en) hair-splitting.
**haarsträubend** ['ha:rʃtrɔybənt], *adj.* hair-raising, monstrous.
**Haarwäsche** ['ha:rvɛʃə], *f.* (—, *no pl.*) shampooing.
**Haarwickel** ['ha:rvɪkəl], *m.* (—s, *pl.* —) curler.
**Haarzange** ['ha:rtsaŋə], *f.* (—, *pl.* —n) tweezers.
**Habe** ['ha:be], *f.* (—, *no pl.*) property, belongings, effects; *Hab und Gut*, all o.'s belongings, goods and chattels.
**Haben** ['ha:bən], *n.* (—s, *no pl.*) credit; *Soll und* —, debit and credit.
**haben** ['ha:bən], *v.a. irr.* have, possess; *da hast du's*, there you are; *es ist nicht zu* —, it is not available.
**Habenichts** ['ha:bənɪçts], *m.* (—es, *no pl.*) have-not.
**Habgier** ['ha:pgi:r], *f.* (—, *no pl.*) greediness, avarice, covetousness.

**habhaft** ['ha:phaft], *adj. einer Sache* — *werden*, get possession of a thing.
**Habicht** ['ha:bɪçt], *m.* (—s, *pl.* —e) (*Orn.*) hawk.
**Habichtsinseln** ['ha:bɪçtsɪnzəln], *f. pl.* the Azores.
**Habichtsnase** ['ha:bɪçtsna:zə], *f.* (—, *pl.* —n) hooked nose, aquiline nose.
**Habilitation** [habilita'tsjo:n], *f.* (—, *pl.* —en) admission *or* inauguration as a university lecturer.
**habilitieren** [habili'ti:rən], *v.r. sich* —, qualify as a university lecturer.
**Habseligkeiten** ['ha:pzelɪçkaɪtən], *f. pl.* property, effects, chattels.
**Habsucht** ['ha:pzuxt], *f.* (—, *no pl.*) avarice, greediness.
**Hackbeil** ['hakbaɪl], *n.* (—s, *pl.* —e) cleaver, chopping-knife.
**Hackbrett** ['hakbret], *n.* (—s, *pl.* —er) chopping-board.
**Hacke** ['hakə], *f.* (—, *pl.* —n) hoe, mattock; heel.
**Hacken** ['hakən], *m.* (—s, *pl.* —) heel; *sich auf die* — *machen*, be off, take to o.'s heels.
**hacken** ['hakən], *v.a.* hack, chop, hoe; mince; (*birds*) peck.
**Hacker** ['hakər], *m.* (—s, *pl.* —) chopper.
**Häckerling** ['hɛkərlɪŋ], *m.* (—s, *no pl.*) chopped straw.
**Hackfleisch** ['hakflaɪʃ], *n.* (—es, *no pl.*) mincemeat.
**Häcksel** ['hɛksəl], *n.* (—s, *no pl.*) chopped straw.
**Hader** ['ha:dər], *m.* (—s, *no pl.*) quarrel, dispute.
**hadern** ['ha:dərn], *v.n.* quarrel, have a dispute.
**Hafen** ['ha:fən], *m.* (—s, *pl.* ⸚) harbour, port; refuge, haven.
**Hafendamm** ['ha:fəndam], *m.* (—s, *pl.* ⸚e) jetty, mole, pier.
**Hafensperre** ['ha:fənʃpɛrə], *f.* (—, *pl.* —n) embargo, blockade.
**Hafenzoll** ['ha:fəntsɔl], *m.* (—s, *no pl.*) anchorage, harbour due.
**Hafer** ['ha:fər], *m.* (—s, *no pl.*) oats; *es sticht ihn der* —, he is getting cheeky, insolent.
**Haferbrei** ['ha:fərbraɪ], *m.* (—s, *no pl.*) porridge.
**Hafergrütze** ['ha:fərgrytsə], *f.* (—, *no pl.*) ground-oats, oatmeal.
**Haferschleim** ['ha:fərʃlaɪm], *m.* (—s, *no pl.*) oat-gruel, porridge.
**Haff** [haf], *n.* (—s, *pl.* —e) bay, lagoon.
**Haft** [haft], *f.* (—, *no pl.*) custody, imprisonment, arrest.
**haftbar** ['haftba:r], *adj.* answerable; (*Law*) liable.
**Haftbefehl** ['haftbəfe:l], *m.* (—s, *pl.* —e) warrant for arrest.
**haften** ['haftən], *v.n.* stick, cling, adhere; *für einen* —, go bail for s.o.; *für etwas* —, answer for, be liable for s.th.

# Häftling

**Häftling** ['hɛftlɪŋ], *m.* (—s, *pl.* —e) prisoner.

**Haftpflicht** ['haftpflɪçt], *f.* (—, *no pl.*) liability.

**Haftung** ['haftuŋ], *f.* (—, *no pl.*) liability, security; (*Comm.*) *Gesellschaft mit beschränkter* —, limited liability company, (*abbr.*) Ltd.

**Hag** [ha:k], *m.* (—es, *pl.* —e) hedge, enclosure.

**Hagebuche** ['ha:gəbu:xə], *f.* (—, *pl.* —n) hornbeam.

**Hagebutte** ['ha:gəbutə], *f.* (—, *pl.* —n) (*Bot.*) hip, haw.

**Hagedorn** ['ha:gədɔrn], *m.* (—s, *no pl.*) (*Bot.*) hawthorn.

**Hagel** ['ha:gəl], *m.* (—s, *no pl.*) hail.

**hageln** ['ha:gəln], *v.n.* hail.

**Hagelschauer** ['ha:gəlʃauər], *m.* (—s, *pl.* —) hailstorm.

**hager** ['ha:gər], *adj.* thin, lean, lank, gaunt.

**Häher** ['hɛ:ər], *m.* (—s, *pl.* —) (*Orn.*) jay.

**Hahn** [ha:n], *m.* (—s, *pl.* ̈e) (*Orn.*) cockerel, cock; (*water, gas*) cock, tap, faucet; — *im Korbe sein,* rule the roost; *da kräht kein* — *danach,* nobody cares two hoots about it.

**Hahnenbalken** ['ha:nənbalkən], *m.* (—s, *pl.* —) cock-loft; hen-roost.

**Hahnenfuß** ['ha:nənfu:s], *m.* (—es, *no pl.*) (*Bot.*) crow-foot.

**Hahnensporn** ['ha:nənʃpɔrn], *m.* (—s, *no pl.*) cockspur.

**Hahnentritt** ['ha:nəntrɪt], *m.* (—s, *no pl.*) cock's tread.

**Hahnrei** ['ha:nraɪ], *m.* (—s, *pl.* —e) cuckold; *einen zum* — *machen,* cuckold s.o.

**Hai** [haɪ], *m.* (—s, *pl.* —e) (*Zool.*) shark.

**Haifisch** ['haɪfɪʃ], *m.* (—es, *pl.* —e) (*Zool.*) shark.

**Hain** [haɪn], *m.* (—s, *pl.* —e) (*Poet.*) grove, thicket.

**Haiti** [ha'ɪti], *n.* Haiti.

**Häkchen** ['hɛ:kçən], *n.* (—s, *pl.* —) small hook, crotchet; apostrophe.

**häkeln** ['hɛ:kəln], *v.a. v.n.* crochet; (*fig.*) tease; (*Am.*) needle.

**Haken** ['ha:kən], *m.* (—s, *pl.* —) hook, clasp; (*fig.*) hitch, snag.

**Hakenkreuz** ['ha:kənkrɔyts], *n.* (—es, *pl.* —e) swastika.

**halb** [halp], *adj.* half; *halb neun,* half past eight.

**halbieren** [hal'bi:rən], *v.a.* halve, divide into halves; (*Maths.*) bisect.

**Halbinsel** ['halpɪnzəl], *f.* (—, *pl.* —n) peninsula.

**Halbmesser** ['halpmɛsər], *m.* (—s, *pl.* —) radius.

**halbpart** ['halppart], *adj.* — *mit einem machen,* go halves with s.o.

**halbstündig** ['halpʃtyndɪç], *adj.* lasting half an hour.

**halbstündlich** ['halpʃtyntlɪç], *adj.* half-hourly, every half-hour.

**halbwegs** ['halpve:ks], *adv.* (*coll.*) reasonably, tolerably.

**Halbwelt** ['halpvɛlt], *f.* (—, *no pl.*) demi-monde.

**halbwüchsig** ['halpvy:ksɪç], *adj.* teenage.

**Halde** ['haldə], *f.* (—, *pl.* —n) declivity, hill; (*Min.*) waste-heap, slag-heap.

**Hälfte** ['hɛlftə], *f.* (—, *pl.* —n) half; (*obs.*) moiety.

**Halfter** ['halftər], *f.* (—, *pl.* —n) halter.

**Hall** [hal], *m.* (—s, *no pl.*) sound, echo.

**Halle** ['halə], *f.* (—, *pl.* —n) hall, vestibule; portico; porch.

**hallen** ['halən], *v.n.* sound, resound; clang.

**Halm** [halm], *m.* —es, *pl.* —e) stalk; (*grass*) blade.

**Hals** [hals], *m.* (—es, *pl.* ̈e) neck, throat; — *über Kopf,* head over heels, hastily, hurriedly.

**Halsader** ['halsa:dər], *f.* (—, *pl.* —n) jugular vein.

**Halsbinde** ['halsbɪndə], *f.* (—, *pl.* —n) scarf, tie.

**Halsentzündung** ['halsɛntsynduŋ], *f.* (—, *pl.* —en) inflammation of the throat.

**Halskrause** ['halskrauzə], *f.* (—, *pl.* —n) frill, ruff.

**halsstarrig** ['halsʃtarɪç], *adj.* stubborn, obstinate.

**Halsweh** ['halsve:], *n.* (—s, *no pl.*) sore throat.

**Halt** [halt], *m.* (—es, *no pl.*) halt; stop; hold; (*also fig.*) support.

**haltbar** ['haltba:r], *adj.* durable, strong; tenable, valid.

**halten** ['haltən], *v.a. irr.* hold; keep; detain; deliver (speech, lecture); observe, celebrate. — *v.n.* stop; stand firm; insist; *halt!* stop! stop it! — *v.r. sich* —, hold out, keep, behave.

**haltlos** ['haltlo:s], *adj.* unprincipled; floundering, unsteady.

**Haltung** ['haltuŋ], *f.* (—, *pl.* —en) carriage, posture, attitude; (*fig.*) behaviour, demeanour; attitude.

**Halunke** [ha'luŋkə], *m.* (—n, *pl.* —n) scoundrel, rascal, scamp.

**hämisch** ['hɛ:mɪʃ], *adj.* malicious, spiteful.

**Hammel** ['haməl], *m.* (—s, *pl.* —) (*meat*) mutton.

**Hammelkeule** ['haməlkɔylə], *f.* (—, *pl.* —n) leg of mutton.

**Hammer** ['hamər], *m.* (—s, *pl.* ̈) hammer; *unter den* — *kommen,* be sold by auction.

**Hämorrhoiden** [hɛmo'ri:dən], *f. pl.* (*Med.*) piles, haemorrhoids.

**Hand** [hant], *f.* (—, *pl.* ̈e) hand.

**Handarbeit** ['hantarbaɪt], *f.* (—, *pl.* —en) manual labour; needlework.

**Handel** ['handəl], *m.* (—s, *no pl.*) trade, commerce; — *treiben,* carry on trade, do business.

**Händel** ['hɛndəl], *m. pl.* quarrel, difference, dispute.

**handeln** ['handəln], *v.n.* act; — *in*, deal in; *es handelt sich um* ... it is a question of ... ; *es handelt von* ..., it deals with ....

**handelseinig** ['handəlsaınıç], *adj.* — *werden*, come to terms.

**Handelsgenossenschaft** ['handəls-gənɔsənʃaft], *f.* (—, *pl.* —en) trading company.

**Handelsgeschäft** ['handəlsgəʃɛft], *n.* (—es, *pl.* —e) commercial transaction.

**Handelsgesellschaft** ['handəlsgəzɛl-ʃaft], *f.* (—, *pl.* —en) trading company; joint-stock company.

**Handelskammer** ['handəlskamər], *f.* (—, *pl.* —n) chamber of commerce.

**Handelsmarke** ['handəlsmarkə], *f.* (—, *pl.* —n) trade-mark.

**Handelsreisende** ['handəlsraızəndə], *m.* (—n, *pl.* —n) commercial traveller.

**händelsüchtig** ['hɛndəlzyçtıç], *adj.* quarrelsome; litigious.

**Handelsvertrag** ['handəlsfɛrtra:k], *m.* (—es, *pl.* ˙e) commercial treaty; contract.

**Handelszweig** ['handəlstsvaık], *m.* (—es, *pl.* —e) branch of trade.

**Handfeger** ['hantfe:gər], *m.* (—s, *pl.* —) hand-broom, handbrush.

**Handfertigkeit** ['hantfɛrtıçkaıt], *f.* (—, *no pl.*) dexterity, manual skill; handicrafts.

**Handfessel** ['hantfɛsəl], *f.* (—, *pl.* —n) handcuff.

**handfest** ['hantfɛst], *adj.* robust, strong.

**Handgeld** ['hantgɛlt], *n.* (—es, *no pl.*) earnest; (*money*) advance.

**Handgelenk** ['hantgəlɛŋk], *n.* (—s, *pl.* —e) wrist.

**handgemein** ['hantgəmaın], *adj.* — *werden*, come to blows.

**Handgemenge** ['hantgəmɛŋə], *n.* (—s, *no pl.*) fray, scuffle.

**handgreiflich** ['hantgraıflıç], *adj.* palpable; evident, plain.

**Handgriff** ['hantgrıf], *m.* (—es, *pl.* —e) handle; (*fig.*) knack.

**Handhabe** ['hantha:bə], *f.* (—, *pl.* —n) (*fig.*) hold, handle.

**handhaben** ['hantha:bən], *v.a.* handle, manage; operate.

**Handlanger** ['hantlaŋər], *m.* (—s, *pl.* —) helper, carrier.

**Händler** ['hɛndlər], *m.* (—s, *pl.* —) dealer, merchant.

**handlich** ['hantlıç], *adj.* handy, manageable.

**Handlung** ['handluŋ], *f.* (—, *pl.* —en) shop; (*Am.*) store; commercial house, mercantile business; action, act, deed; (*Lit.*) plot.

**Handrücken** ['hantrykən], *m.* (—s, *pl.* —) back of the hand.

**Handschelle** ['hantʃɛlə], *f.* (—, *pl.* —n) manacle, handcuff.

**Handschlag** ['hantʃla:k], *m.* (—s, *pl.* ˙e) handshake.

**Handschuh** ['hantʃu:], *m.* (—s, *pl.* —e) glove; (*of iron*) gauntlet.

**Handstreich** ['hantʃtraıç], *m.* (—es, *pl.* —e) (*Mil.*) surprise attack, coup de main.

**Handtuch** ['hanttu:x], *n.* (—es, *pl.* ˙er) towel.

**Handumdrehen** ['hantumdre:ən], *n.* (—s, *no pl.*) im —, in no time, in a jiffy.

**Handwerk** ['hantvɛrk], *n.* (—s, *pl.* —e) handicraft, trade, craft.

**Handwörterbuch** ['hantvœrtərbu:x], *n.* (—es, *pl.* ˙er) compact dictionary.

**Handwurzel** ['hantvurtsəl], *f.* (—, *pl.* —n) wrist.

**Hanf** [hanf], *m.* (—es, *no pl.*) hemp.

**Hänfling** ['hɛnflıŋ], *m.* (—s, *pl.* —e) (*Orn.*) linnet.

**Hang** [haŋ], *m.* (—es, *pl.* ˙e) slope, declivity; (*fig.*) (*no pl.*) inclination, propensity.

**Hängematte** ['hɛŋəmatə], *f.* (—, *pl.* —n) hammock.

**hängen** ['hɛŋən], *v.a. irr.* hang, suspend. — *v.r. sich* —, hang o.s. — *v.n.* hang, be suspended; be hanged (*execution*).

**Hannover** [ha'no:fər], *n.* Hanover.

**Hänselei** ['hɛnzəlaı], *f.* (—, *pl.* —en) chaffing, leg-pulling, teasing.

**hänseln** ['hɛnzəln], *v.a.* tease, chaff.

**Hantel** ['hantəl], *f.* (—, *pl.* —n) dumbbell.

**hantieren** [han'ti:rən], *v.n.* busy o.s., work, occupy o.s. (with).

**hapern** ['ha:pərn], *v.n.* lack, be deficient; *da hapert es*, that's the snag.

**Häppchen** ['hɛpçən], *n.* (—s, *pl.* —) morsel.

**Happen** ['hapən], *m.* (—s, *pl.* —) mouthful.

**happig** ['hapıç], *adj.* greedy; excessive.

**Härchen** ['hɛ:rçən], *n.* (—s, *pl.* —) short hair.

**Harfe** ['harfə], *f.* (—, *pl.* —n) (*Mus.*) harp.

**Harke** ['harkə], *f.* (—, *pl.* —n) rake.

**Harm** [harm], *m.* (—es, *no pl.*) grief, sorrow; injury, wrong.

**härmen** ['hɛrmən], *v.r. sich* — *um*, grieve over.

**harmlos** ['harmlo:s], *adj.* harmless, innocuous.

**Harmonielehre** [harmo'ni:le:rə], *f.* (—, *pl.* —n) (*Mus.*) harmonics; harmony.

**harmonieren** [harmo'ni:rən], *v.n. mit einem* —, be in concord with s.o., agree with s.o.

**Harmonika** [har'mo:nıka], *f.* (—, *pl.* —ken) (*Mus.*) accordion, concertina; mouth-organ.

**Harn** [harn], *m.* (—s, *no pl.*) urine.

**Harnisch** ['harnıʃ], *m.* (—es, *pl.* —e) harness, armour; *in* — *bringen*, enrage.

**Harpune** [har'pu:nə], *f.* (—, *pl.* —n) harpoon.

**harren** ['harən], *v.n.* wait for, hope for.

**harsch** [harʃ], *adj.* harsh; rough; unfriendly.

**hart** [hart], *adj.* hard, severe, cruel, austere.

**Härte** ['hɛrtə], *f.* (—, *pl.* —n) hardness, severity.

**härten** ['hɛrtən], *v.a.* harden.

**hartleibig** ['hartlaɪbɪç], *adj.* constipated.

**hartnäckig** ['hartnɛkɪç], *adj.* stubborn, obstinate; undaunted.

**Harz** (1) [harts], *m.* (*Geog.*) (—es, *no pl.*) the Hartz mountains.

**Harz** (2) [harts], *n.* (—es, *pl.* —e) resin, rosin.

**harzig** ['hartsɪç], *adj.* resinous.

**Hasardspiel** [ha'zartʃpiːl], *n.* (—es, *pl.* —e) game of chance, gamble.

**Haschee** [ha'ʃeː], *n.* (—s, *pl.* —s) puree, hash, mash.

**haschen** ['haʃən], *v.a.* catch, snatch, seize. — *v.n.* — nach, strain after, snatch at.

**Häschen** ['hɛːsçən], *n.* (—s, *pl.* —) (*Zool.*) small hare, leveret.

**Häscher** ['hɛʃər], *m.* (—s, *pl.* —) bailiff.

**Hase** ['haːzə], *m.* (—n, *pl.* —n) (*Zool.*) hare.

**Haselrute** ['haːzəlruːtə], *f.* (—, *pl.* —n) hazel-switch.

**Hasenfuß** ['haːzənfuːs], *m.* (—es, *no pl.*) coward.

**Hasenklein** ['haːzənklaɪn], *n.* (—s, *no pl.*) jugged hare.

**Hasenscharte** ['haːzənʃartə], *f.* (—, *pl.* —n) hare-lip.

**Haspe** ['haspə], *f.* (—, *pl.* —n) hasp, hinge.

**Haspel** ['haspəl], *f.* (—, *pl.* —n) reel.

**haspeln** ['haspəln], *v.a.* wind on a reel; (*fig.*) rattle off.

**Haß** [has], *m.* (—sses, *no pl.*) hatred, hate, detestation.

**hassen** ['hasən], *v.a.* hate, detest.

**haßerfüllt** ['hasərfylt], *adj.* full of spite, full of hatred.

**häßlich** ['hɛslɪç], *adj.* ugly, repulsive; (*fig.*) unpleasant, unkind; unseemly.

**Hast** [hast], *f.* (—, *no pl.*) haste, hurry, hastiness, rashness.

**hastig** ['hastɪç], *adj.* hasty, hurried.

**hätscheln** ['hɛtʃəln], *v.a.* pamper, caress, fondle.

**Hatz** [hats], *f.* (—, *pl.* —en) baiting; hunt; revelry.

**Haube** ['haubə], *f.* (—, *pl.* —n) bonnet, cap; (*Motor.*) bonnet, (*Am.*) hood.

**Haubenlerche** ['haubənlɛrçə], *f.* (—, *pl.* —n) (*Orn.*) crested lark.

**Haubitze** [hau'bɪtsə], *f.* (—, *pl.* —n) howitzer.

**Hauch** [haux], *m.* (—es, *no pl.*) breath, whiff; (*fig.*) touch, tinge.

**hauchdünn** ['hauxˈdyn], *adj.* extremely thin.

**hauchen** ['hauxən], *v.n.* breathe.

**Hauchlaut** ['hauxlaut], *m.* (—es, *pl.* —e) (*Phonet.*) aspirate.

**Haudegen** ['haudeːgən], *m.* (—s, *pl.* —) broad-sword; *ein alter* —, an old bully.

**Haue** ['hauə], *f.* (—, *no pl.*) (*coll.*) thrashing.

**hauen** ['hauən], *v.a.* hew; cut; strike; hit; give a hiding to. — *v.n. über die Schnur* —, kick over the traces.

**Hauer** ['hauər], *m.* (—s, *pl.* —) hewer, cutter; (*animal*) fang, tusk.

**Häuer** ['hɔyər], *m.* (—s, *pl.* —) miner.

**Haufen** ['haufən], *m.* (—s, *pl.* —) heap, pile.

**häufen** ['hɔyfən], *v.a.* heap, pile. — *v.r. sich* —, accumulate, multiply, increase.

**häufig** ['hɔyfɪç], *adj.* frequent, abundant. — *adv.* frequently, often.

**Häufung** ['hɔyfuŋ], *f.* (—, *pl.* —en) accumulation.

**Haupt** [haupt], *n.* (—es, *pl.* ˸er) head; leader; chief, principal; (*compounds*) main—; *aufs* — *schlagen*, inflict a total defeat on; *ein bemoostes* —, an old student.

**Hauptaltar** ['hauptaltaːr], *m.* (—s, *pl.* —e) (*Eccl.*) high altar.

**Hauptbuch** ['hauptbuːx], *n.* (—es, *pl.* ˸er) ledger.

**Häuptling** ['hɔyptlɪŋ], *m.* (—s, *pl.* —e) chieftain.

**Hauptmann** ['hauptman], *m.* (—s, *pl.* ˸er, **Hauptleute**) (*Mil.*) captain.

**Hauptnenner** ['hauptnenər], *m.* (—s, *pl.* —) (*Maths.*) common denominator.

**Hauptquartier** ['hauptkvartiːr], *n.* (—es, *pl.* —e) headquarters.

**Hauptsache** ['hauptzaxə], *f.* (—, *pl.* —n) main thing, substance, main point; *in der* —, in the main.

**hauptsächlich** ['hauptzɛçlɪç], *adj.* chief, main, principal, essential.

**Hauptsatz** ['hauptzats], *m.* (—es, *pl.* ˸e) (*Gram.*) principal sentence.

**Hauptschriftleiter** ['hauptʃrɪftlaɪtər], *m.* (—s, *pl.* —) editor-in-chief.

**Hauptschule** ['hauptʃuːlə], *f.* (—, *pl.* —n) intermediate school.

**Hauptstadt** ['hauptʃtat], *f.* (—, *pl.* ˸e) capital, metropolis.

**Hauptton** ['hauptoːn], *m.* (—s, *pl.* ˸e) (*Mus.*) key-note; (*Phonet.*) primary accent.

**Haupttreffer** ['haupttrefər], *m.* (—s, *pl.* —) first prize; jackpot.

**Hauptverkehrsstunden** ['hauptfɛrkeːrsʃtundən], *f. pl.* (*traffic etc.*) rush-hour.

**Hauptwache** ['hauptvaxə], *f.* (—, *pl.* —n) central guardroom.

**Hauptwort** ['hauptvɔrt], *n.* (—es, *pl.* ˸er) noun, substantive.

**Hauptzahl** ['hauptsaːl], *f.* (—, *pl.* —en) cardinal number.

**Haus** [haus], *n.* (—es, *pl.* ˸er) house; home; household; firm; *zu* —*e*, at home; *nach* —*e*, in the main.

**Hausarbeit** ['hausarbaɪt], *f.* (—, *pl.* —en) housework, domestic work; homework.

**Hausarrest** ['hausarɛst], *m.* (—es, *no pl.*) house arrest.

**Hausarzt** ['hausartst], *m.* (—es, *pl.* ˙e) family doctor.

**hausbacken** ['hausbakən], *adj.* homemade; homely; humdrum.

**Häuschen** ['hɔysçən], *n.* (—s, *pl.* —) small house, cottage; *ganz aus dem — sein,* be beside o.s.

**Hausen** ['hauzən], *m.* (—s, *pl.* —) sturgeon.

**hausen** ['hauzən], *v.n.* reside, be domiciled; *übel —,* play havoc among.

**Hausflur** ['hausflu:r], *m.* (—s, *pl.* —e) entrance hall (of a house), vestibule.

**Hausfrau** ['hausfrau], *f.* (—, *pl.* —en) housewife, mistress of the house.

**Hausfriedensbruch** ['hausfri:dənsbrux], *m.* (—es, *pl.* ˙e) (*Law*) intrusion, trespass.

**Hausgenosse** ['hausgənɔsə], *m.* (—n, *pl.* —n) fellow-lodger.

**Haushalt** ['haushalt], *m.* (—es, *no pl.*) household.

**Haushaltung** ['haushaltuŋ], *f.* (—, *no pl.*) housekeeping.

**Hausherr** ['hausher], *m.* (—n, *pl.* —en) master of the house, householder.

**Haushofmeister** ['haushofmaistər], *m.* (—s, *pl.* —) steward; butler.

**hausieren** [hau'zi:rən], *v.n.* peddle, hawk.

**Hauslehrer** ['hausle:rər], *m.* (—s, *pl.* —) private tutor.

**Häusler** ['hɔyslər], *m.* (—s, *pl.* —) cottager.

**häuslich** ['hɔyslɪç], *adj.* domestic, domesticated.

**Hausmädchen** ['hausmɛdçən], *n.* (—s, *pl.* —) housemaid.

**Hausmannskost** ['hausmanskɔst], *f.* (—, *no pl.*) plain fare.

**Hausmeister** ['hausmaistər], *m.* (—s, *pl.* —) house-porter, caretaker.

**Hausmittel** ['hausmɪtəl], *n.* (—s, *pl.* —) household remedy.

**Hausrat** ['hausra:t], *m.* (—s, *no pl.*) household furnishings, household effects.

**Hausschlüssel** ['hausʃlysəl], *m.* (—s, *pl.* —) latch-key.

**Hausschuh** ['hausʃu:], *m.* (—s, *pl.* —e) slipper.

**Hausstand** ['hausʃtant], *m.* (—es, *pl.* ˙e) household.

**Haustier** ['hausti:r], *n.* (—es, *pl.* —e) domestic animal.

**Hausvater** ['hausfa:tər], *m.* (—s, *pl.* ˙ ) paterfamilias.

**Hausverwalter** ['hausfɛrvaltər], *m.* (—s, *pl.* —) steward, caretaker; (*Am.*) janitor.

**Hauswesen** ['hausve:zən], *n.* (—s, *no pl.*) household management *or* affairs.

**Hauswirt** ['hausvɪrt], *m.* (—es, *pl.* —e) landlord.

**Hauswirtin** ['hausvɪrtɪn], *f.* (—, *pl.* —nen) landlady.

**Hauswirtschaft** ['hausvɪrtʃaft], *f.* (—, *no pl.*) housekeeping, domestic economy.

**Haut** [haut], *f.* (—, *pl.* ˙e) (*human*) skin; (*animal*) hide; (*fruit*) peel; (*on liquid*) skin; membrane; film; *aus der — fahren,* flare up.

**Hautausschlag** ['hautausʃla:k], *m.* (—s, *pl.* ˙e) rash, eczema.

**Häutchen** ['hɔytçən], *n.* (—s, *pl.* —) cuticle, pellicle, membrane.

**häuten** ['hɔytən], *v.a.* skin, flay, strip off the skin. — *v.r. sich —,* cast off (skin) *or* slough.

**Hebamme** ['he:pamə], *f.* (—, *pl.* —n) midwife.

**Hebel** ['he:bəl], *m.* (—s, *pl.* —) lever.

**heben** ['he:bən], *v.a. irr.* raise, lift, hoist, heave; elevate; improve; *aus der Taufe —,* be godfather (godmother) to (s.o.).

**Heber** ['he:bər], *m.* (—s, *pl.* —) siphon.

**Hebräer** [he'brɛ:ər], *m.* (—s, *pl.* —) Hebrew.

**Hechel** ['hɛçəl], *f.* (—, *pl.* —n) hackle, flax-comb.

**hecheln** ['hɛçəln], *v.a.* dress flax; hackle; (*fig.*) taunt, heckle.

**Hecht** [hɛçt], *m.* (—es, *pl.* —e) (*Zool.*) pike; (*swimming*) dive.

**Hechtsprung** ['hɛçtʃpruŋ], *m.* header.

**Heck** [hɛk], *n.* (—s, *pl.* —e) (*Naut.*) stern; (*Motor.*) rear; (*Aviat.*) tail.

**Heckbord** ['hɛkbɔrt], *m.* (—s, *pl.* —e) (*Naut.*) taffrail.

**Hecke** ['hɛkə], *f.* (—, *pl.* —n) hedge.

**hecken** ['hɛkən], *v.n.* breed, bring forth.

**Heckpfennig** ['hɛkpfɛnɪç], *m.* (—s, *pl.* —e) lucky sixpence.

**heda!** ['he:da:], *excl.* hey, you!

**Heer** [he:r], *n.* (—es, *pl.* —e) army; multitude; *stehendes —,* regular army.

**Heeresmacht** ['he:rəsmaxt], *f.* (—, *pl.* ˙e) armed forces, troops.

**Heerschar** ['he:rʃa:r], *f.* (—, *pl.* —en) host; corps, legion; (*Bibl.*) *der Herr der —en,* the Lord of Hosts.

**Heerschau** ['he:rʃau], *f.* (—, *pl.* —en) review, muster, parade.

**Heerstraße** ['he:rʃtra:sə], *f.* (—, *pl.* —en) military road; highway; (*Am.*) highroad.

**Heerwesen** ['he:rve:zən], *n.* (—s, *no pl.*) military affairs.

**Hefe** ['he:fə], *f.* (—, *no pl.*) yeast; dregs, sediment.

**Hefeteig** ['he:fətaɪk], *m.* (—s, *pl.* —e) leavened dough.

**Heft** [hɛft], *n.* (—es, *pl.* —e) exercise-book, copy-book; haft, handle, hilt.

**heften** ['hɛftən], *v.a.* fasten; baste, stitch, fix, pin.

**heftig** ['hɛftɪç], *adj.* vehement, violent.

**Heftnadel** ['hɛftna:dəl], *f.* (—, *pl.* —n) stitching-needle.

**hegen** ['he:gən], *v.a.* enclose, protect, preserve; (*fig.*) cherish; entertain; hold; *— und pflegen,* nurse carefully.

**Hehl** [he:l], *n.* (—es, *no pl.*) concealment, secret.

**hehlen** ['he:lən], *v.n.* receive stolen goods.

**Hehler** ['hɔːlər], *m.* (—s, *pl.* —) receiver of stolen goods, (*sl.*) fence.

**hehr** [he:r], *adj.* (*Lit.*) exalted, august, sublime.

**Heide** (1) ['haɪdə], *m.* (—n, *pl.* —n) heathen, pagan.

**Heide** (2) ['haɪdə], *f.* (—, *pl.* —n) heath.

**Heidekraut** ['haɪdəkraut], *n.* (—es, *no pl.*) heath, heather.

**Heidelbeere** ['haɪdəlbeːrə], *f.* (—, *pl.* —n) (*Bot.*) bilberry; (*Am.*) blueberry.

**Heidenangst** ['haɪdənaŋst], *f.* (—, *no pl.*) mortal fear.

**Heidenlärm** ['haɪdənlɛrm], *m.* (—es, *no pl.*) hullaballoo.

**Heidenröschen** ['haɪdənrøːsçən], *n.* (—s, *pl.* —) (*Bot.*) sweet-briar.

**Heidentum** ['haɪdəntuːm], *n.* (—s, *no pl.*) paganism.

**heidnisch** ['haɪdnɪʃ], *adj.* pagan, heathen.

**Heidschnuke** ['haɪtʃnuːkə], *f.* (—, *pl.* —n) moorland sheep.

**heikel** ['haɪkəl], *adj.* delicate, sensitive, critical.

**Heil** [haɪl], *n.* (—(e)s, *no pl.*) safety, welfare; (*Theol.*) salvation; *sein — versuchen*, have a try, try o.'s luck. — *int.* hail! — *der Königin*, God save the Queen.

**heil** [haɪl], *adj.* unhurt, intact.

**Heiland** ['haɪlant], *m.* (—s, *no pl.*) Saviour, Redeemer.

**Heilanstalt** ['haɪlanʃtalt], *f.* (—, *pl.* —en) sanatorium, convalescent home; (*Am.*) sanitarium.

**heilbar** ['haɪlbaːr], *adj.* curable.

**heilbringend**['haɪlbrɪŋənt],*adj.*salutary.

**heilen** ['haɪlən], *v.a.* cure, heal. — *v.n.* (*aux.* sein) heal.

**heilig** ['haɪlɪç], *adj.* holy, sacred; *der Heilige Abend*, Christmas Eve; — *sprechen*, canonise; (*before name*) *der*, *die* —*e*, Saint.

**Heiligenschein** ['haɪlɪɡənʃaɪn], *m.* (—s, *pl.* —e) halo; (*clouds*) nimbus.

**Heiligkeit** ['haɪlɪçkaɪt], *f.* (—, *no pl.*) holiness, sanctity, sacredness.

**Heiligtum** ['haɪlɪçtuːm], *n.* (—s, *pl.* ̈er) sanctuary, shrine; holy relic.

**Heiligung** ['haɪlɪɡuŋ], *f.* (—, *pl.* —en) sanctification, consecration.

**heilkräftig** ['haɪlkrɛftɪç], *adj.* curative, salubrious.

**Heilkunde** ['haɪlkundə], *f.* (—, *no pl.*) therapeutics.

**heillos** ['haɪloːs], *adj.* wicked, mischievous; (*fig.*) awful.

**Heilmittel** ['haɪlmɪtəl], *n.* (—s, *pl.* —) remedy.

**heilsam** ['haɪlzaːm], *adj.* salubrious, salutary.

**Heilsamkeit** ['haɪlzaːmkaɪt], *f.* (—, *no pl.*) salubrity, salubriousness.

**Heilsarmee** ['haɪlsarmeː], *f.* (—, *no pl.*) Salvation Army.

**Heilslehre** ['haɪlsleːrə], *f.* (—, *pl.* —n) doctrine of salvation.

**Heiltrank** ['haɪltraŋk], *m.* (—es, *no pl.*) (medicinal) potion.

**Heim** [haɪm], *n.* (—es, *pl.* —e) home.

**heim** [haɪm], *adv. prefix* (*to verbs*) home.

**Heimat** ['haɪmat], *f.* (—, *no pl.*) native place, home, homeland.

**Heimatschein** ['haɪmatʃaɪn], *m.* (—es, *pl.* —e) certificate of origin *or* domicile.

**Heimchen** ['haɪmçən], *n.* (—s, *pl.* —) (*Ent.*) cricket.

**heimführen** ['haɪmfyːrən], *v.a.* bring home (a bride); (*fig.*) marry.

**Heimgang** ['haɪmgaŋ], *m.* (—es, *no pl.*) going home; (*fig.*) decease, death.

**heimisch** ['haɪmɪʃ], *adj.* native, indigenous; *sich — fühlen*, feel at home.

**heimkehren** ['haɪmkeːrən], *v.n.* return (home).

**heimleuchten** ['haɪmlɔyçtən], *v.n. einem —*, tell s.o. the plain truth, give s.o. a piece of o.'s mind.

**heimlich** ['haɪmlɪç], *adj.* secret, clandestine, furtive.

**heimsuchen** ['haɪmzuːxən], *v.a.* visit; afflict, punish.

**Heimtücke** ['haɪmtykə], *f.* (—, *no pl.*) malice.

**heimwärts** ['haɪmvɛrts], *adv.* homeward.

**Heimweh** ['haɪmveː], *n.* (—s, *no pl.*) homesickness; nostalgia.

**heimzahlen** ['haɪmtsaːlən], *v.a.* pay back, retaliate.

**Hein** [haɪn], *m.* (*coll.*) *Freund —*, Death.

**Heinzelmännchen** ['haɪntsəlmɛnçən], *n.* (—s, *pl.* —) goblin, brownie, imp.

**Heirat** ['haɪraːt], *f.* (—, *pl.* —en) marriage, wedding.

**heiraten** ['haɪraːtən], *v.a.* marry, wed.

**Heiratsgut** ['haɪraːtsguːt], *n.* (—es, *pl.* ̈er) dowry.

**heischen** ['haɪʃən], *v.a.* (*Poet.*) ask, demand.

**heiser** ['haɪzər], *adj.* hoarse.

**heiß** [haɪs], *adj.* hot; (*fig.*) ardent; (*climate*) torrid.

**heißen** ['haɪsən], *v.a. irr.* bid, command. — *v.n.* be called; be said; signify, mean; *es heißt*, it is said; *das heißt (d.h.)*, that is to say; *wie — Sie?* what is your name?

**heißgeliebt** ['haɪsɡəliːpt], *adj.* dearly beloved.

**heiter** ['haɪtər], *adj.* clear; serene; cheerful.

**Heiterkeit** ['haɪtərkaɪt], *f.* (—, *no pl.*) serenity; cheerfulness.

**heizen** ['haɪtsən], *v.a., v.n.* heat.

**Heizkissen** ['haɪtskɪsən], *n.* (—s, *pl.* —) electric pad *or* blanket.

**Heizkörper** ['haɪtskœrpər], *m.* (—s, *pl.* —) radiator; heater.

**Heizung** ['haɪtsuŋ], *f.* (—, *pl.* —en) heating.

**hektisch** ['hɛktɪʃ], *adj.* hectic.

**hektographieren** [hɛktogra'fi:rən], *v.a.* stencil, duplicate.

**Hektoliter** ['hɛktoli:tər], *m.* (—s, *pl.* —) hectolitre (22 gallons).

**Held** [hɛlt], *m.* (—en, *pl.* —en) hero.

**Heldengedicht** ['hɛldəngədɪçt], *n.* (—es, *pl.* —e) heroic poem, epic.

**heldenhaft** ['hɛldənhaft], *adj.* heroic. — *adv.* heroically.

**Heldenmut** ['hɛldənmu:t], *m.* (—es, *no pl.*) heroism.

**helfen** ['hɛlfən], *v.n. irr.* (*Dat.*) help, aid, assist.

**Helfershelfer** ['hɛlfərshɛlfər], *m.* (—s, *pl.* —) accomplice, accessory.

**Helgoland** ['hɛlgolant], *n.* Heligoland.

**hell** [hɛl], *adj.* clear, bright, light; (*coll.*) clever, wide awake.

**Helldunkel** ['hɛlduŋkəl], *n.* (—s, *no pl.*) twilight; (*Art*) chiaroscuro.

**Helle** ['hɛlə], *f.* (—, *no pl.*) clearness, brightness; daylight.

**Heller** ['hɛlər], *m.* (—s, *pl.* —) small coin, farthing.

**hellhörig** ['hɛlhø:rɪç], *adj.* keen of hearing.

**Helligkeit** ['hɛlɪçkaɪt], *f.* (—, *no pl.*) clearness; daylight.

**Hellseher** ['hɛlze:ər], *m.* (—s, *pl.* —) clairvoyant.

**hellsichtig** ['hɛlzɪxtɪç], *adj.* clairvoyant; clear-sighted.

**Helm** [hɛlm], *m.* (—es, *pl.* —e) helmet.

**Helmbusch** ['hɛlmbuʃ], *m.* (—es, *pl.* ⏜e) crest (of helmet).

**Helmgitter** ['hɛlmgɪtər], *n.* (—s, *pl.* —) eye-slit (in helmet).

**Helsingfors** ['hɛlzɪŋfors], *n.* Helsinki.

**Helsingör** [hɛlzɪŋ'ø:r], *n.* Elsinore.

**Hemd** [hɛmt], *n.* (—es, *pl.* —en) shirt; vest.

**Hemdenstoff** ['hɛmdənʃtɔf], *m.* (—es, *pl.* —e) shirting.

**hemmen** ['hɛmən], *v.a.* stop, hamper, hinder, restrain; (*fig.*) inhibit.

**Hemmschuh** ['hɛmʃu:], *m.* (—s, *pl.* —e) brake; (*fig.*) drag, obstruction.

**Hemmung** ['hɛmuŋ], *f.* (—, *pl.* —en) stoppage, hindrance, restraint; (*watch*) escapement; (*fig.*) inhibition, reluctance.

**Hengst** [hɛŋkst], *m.* (—es, *pl.* —e) stallion.

**Henkel** ['hɛŋkəl], *m.* (—s, *pl.* —) handle.

**henken** ['hɛŋkən], *v.a* hang (s.o.).

**Henker** ['hɛŋkər], *m.* (—s, *pl.* —) hangman, executioner.

**Henne** ['hɛnə], *f.* (—, *pl.* —n) (*Zool.*) hen; *junge* —, pullet.

**her** [he:r], *adv.* hither, here, to me; (*temp.*) since, ago; *von alters* —, from olden times; *von je* —, from time immemorial; *wo kommst du* —? where do you come from? *wie lange ist es* —? how long ago was it?

**herab** [hɛ'rap], *adv.* downwards, down to; *die Treppe* —, downstairs.

**herablassen** [hɛ'raplasən], *v.r. irr. sich — etwas zu tun*, condescend to do s.th.

**herabsehen** [hɛ'rapze:ən], *v.n. irr.* look down; (*fig.*) look down upon s.o.

**herabsetzen** [hɛ'rapzɛtsən], *v.a.* put down; degrade; (*value*) depreciate; (*price*) reduce, lower; (*fig.*) disparage.

**herabwürdigen** [hɛ'rapvyrdɪgən], *v.a.* degrade, abase.

**herabziehen** [hɛ'raptsi:ən], *v.a. irr.* pull down.

**Heraldik** [he'raldɪk], *f.* (—, *no pl.*) heraldry.

**heran** [hɛ'ran], *adv.* up to, on, near.

**heranbilden** [hɛ'ranbɪldən], *v.a.* train. — *v.r. sich* —, train, qualify.

**herangehen** [hɛ'range:ən], *v.n. irr.* (*aux. sein*) approach, sidle up (to); *an etwas* —, set to work on s.th.

**heranmachen** [hɛ'ranmaxən], *v.r. sich an etwas* —, set to work on s.th., set about s.th.

**herannahen** [hɛ'ranna:ən], *v.n.* (*aux. sein*) approach, draw near.

**heranrücken** [hɛ'ranrykən], *v.a.* move near. — *v.n.* (*aux. sein*) advance, draw near.

**heranschleichen** [hɛ'ranʃlaɪçən], *v.r. irr. sich — an*, sneak up to.

**heranwachsen** [hɛ'ranvaksən], *v.n. irr.* (*aux. sein*) grow up.

**heranwagen** [hɛ'ranva:gən], *v.r. sich* —, venture near.

**heranziehen** [hɛ'rantsi:ən], *v.a. irr.* draw near; *als Beispiel* —, cite as an example; (*fig.*) enlist (s.o.'s aid). — *v.n.* (*aux. sein*) draw near, approach.

**herauf** [hɛ'rauf], *adv.* up, upwards.

**heraufbeschwören** [hɛ'raufbeʃvø:rən], *v.a.* conjure up.

**heraus** [hɛ'raus], *adv.* out, out of.

**herausfordern** [hɛ'rausfordərn], *v.a.* challenge.

**Herausgabe** [hɛ'rausga:bə], *f.* (—, *pl.* —n) delivery; (*book*) publication; editing.

**herausgeben** [hɛ'rausge:bən], *v.a. irr.* give out, deliver; (*money*) give change; (*book*) publish, edit.

**Herausgeber** [hɛ'rausge:bər], *m.* (—s, *pl.* —) publisher; editor.

**heraushaben** [hɛ'rausha:bən], *v.a. irr. etwas* —, have the knack of s.th.

**herausputzen** [hɛ'rausputsən], *v.r. sich* —, dress up.

**herausrücken** [hɛ'rausrykən], *v.n. mit Geld* —, fork out money; *mit der Sprache* —, speak out, come out with.

**herausschlagen** [hɛ'rausʃla:gən], *v.a. irr. die Kosten* —, recover expenses; *viel* —, make the most of; profit by.

**herausstellen** [hɛ'rausʃtɛlən], *v.a.* put out, expose. — *v.r. sich — als*, turn out to be.

**herausstreichen** [hɛ'rausʃtraɪçən], *v.a. irr.* extol, praise.

**heraussuchen** [hɛ'raussu:xən], *v.a.* pick out.

# herauswollen

**herauswollen** [hɛˈrausvɔlən], *v.n. nicht mit der Sprache —,* hesitate to speak out.

**herb** [hɛrp], *adj.* sour, sharp, tart, acrid; (*fig.*) austere, harsh, bitter; (*wine*) dry.

**herbei** [hɛrˈbaɪ], *adv.* hither, near.

**herbeischaffen** [hɛrˈbaɪʃafən], *v.a.* procure.

**herbeiströmen** [hɛrˈbaɪʃtrøːmən], *v.n.* (*aux.* sein) crowd, flock.

**Herberge** [ˈhɛrbɛrgə], *f.* (—, *pl.* —n) shelter, lodging, inn.

**Herbst** [hɛrpst], *m.* (—es, *pl.* —e) autumn; (*Am.*) fall.

**Herbstrose** [ˈhɛrpstroːzə], *f.* (—, *pl.* —n) (*Bot.*) hollyhock.

**Herbstzeitlose** [ˈhɛrpsttsaɪtloːzə], *f.* (—, *pl.* —n) (*Bot.*) meadow-saffron.

**Herd** [heːrt], *m.* (—es, *pl.* —e) hearth, fireplace; cooking-stove; (*fig.*) focus.

**Herde** [ˈheːrdə], *f.* (—, *pl.* —n) flock, herd; (*fig.*) troop.

**herein** [hɛˈraɪn], *adv.* in, inside. — *int.* —! come in!

**hereinbrechen** [hɛˈraɪnbrɛçən], *v.n. irr.* (*aux.* sein) *über einen —,* befall s.o., overtake s.o.; (*night*) close in.

**hereinfallen** [hɛˈraɪnfalən], *v.n. irr.* (*aux.* sein) (*fig.*) be taken in, fall for s.th.

**herfallen** [ˈheːrfalən], *v.n. irr.* (*aux.* sein) *über einen —,* go for s.o., set upon s.o.

**Hergang** [ˈheːrgaŋ], *m.* (—es, *no pl.*) proceedings, course of events; circumstances; story, plot.

**hergeben** [ˈheːrgeːbən], *v.a. irr.* give up, surrender.

**hergebracht** [ˈheːrgəbraxt], *adj.* traditional, time-honoured.

**hergehen** [ˈheːrgeːən], *v.n. irr.* (*aux.* sein) proceed; *es geht lustig her,* they are having a gay time.

**hergelaufen** [ˈheːrgəlaufən], *adj. ein —er Kerl,* an adventurer, an upstart.

**herhalten** [ˈheːrhaltən], *v.n. irr.* suffer, serve (as a butt).

**Hering** [ˈheːrɪŋ], *m.* (—s, *pl.* —e) (*Zool.*) herring; *geräucherter —,* smoked herring, bloater; *gesalzener —,* pickled herring.

**herkommen** [ˈheːrkɔmən], *v.n. irr.* (*aux.* sein) come here; be derived from, descend from.

**herkömmlich** [ˈheːrkœmlɪç], *adj.* traditional, customary, usual.

**Herkunft** [ˈheːrkunft], *f.* (—, *no pl.*) descent, extraction; origin.

**herleiern** [ˈheːrlaɪərn], *v.a.* recite monotonously; reel off.

**herleiten** [ˈheːrlaɪtən], *v.a.* derive from.

**Hermelin** [hɛrməˈliːn], *m.* (—s, *no pl.*) ermine (*fur*).

**hermetisch** [hɛrˈmeːtɪʃ], *adj.* hermetical.

**hernach** [hɛrˈnaːx], *adv.* after, afterwards; hereafter.

**hernehmen** [ˈheːrneːmən], *v.a. irr.* take, get (from); take (s.o.) to task.

**hernieder** [hɛrˈniːdər], *adv.* down.

**Herr** [hɛr], *m.* (—n, *pl.* —en) master; lord; nobleman; gentleman; (*Theol.*) Lord; principal, governor; *mein —,* Sir; *meine Herren,* gentlemen; *— Schmidt,* Mr. Smith; *einer Sache — werden,* master s.th.

**Herrenhaus** [ˈhɛrənhaus], *n.* (—es, *pl.* ˸er) mansion, manor house; (*Parl.*) House of Lords.

**Herrenhof** [ˈhɛrənhoːf], *m.* (—es, *pl.* ˸e) manor, country-seat.

**Herrenstand** [ˈhɛrənʃtant], *m.* (—es, *no pl.*) nobility, gentry.

**Herrenzimmer** [ˈhɛrəntsɪmər], *n.* (—s, *pl.* —) study.

**Herrgott** [ˈhɛrgɔt], the Lord God.

**herrichten** [ˈheːrrɪçtən], *v.a.* prepare, fix up.

**Herrin** [ˈhɛrɪn], *f.* (—, *pl.* —innen) mistress, lady.

**herrisch** [ˈhɛrɪʃ], *adj.* imperious, lordly.

**herrlich** [ˈhɛrlɪç], *adj.* magnificent, splendid, glorious, excellent.

**Herrnhuter** [ˈhɛrnhuːtər], *m.* (—s, *pl.* —) Moravian; (*pl.*) Moravian brethren.

**Herrschaft** [ˈhɛrʃaft], *f.* (—, *pl.* —en) mastery, rule, dominion; master, mistress; *meine —en!* ladies and gentlemen!

**herrschaftlich** [ˈhɛrʃaftlɪç], *adj.* belonging to a lord; (*fig.*) elegant, fashionable, distinguished.

**herrschen** [ˈhɛrʃən], *v.n.* rule, govern, reign.

**Herrscher** [ˈhɛrʃər], *m.* (—s, *pl.* —) ruler.

**herrühren** [ˈheːrryːrən], *v.n.* come from, originate in.

**hersagen** [ˈheːrzaːgən], *v.a.* recite, reel off.

**herschaffen** [ˈheːrʃafən], *v.a.* procure.

**herstammen** [ˈheːrʃtamən], *v.n.* come from, stem from, originate from; be derived from.

**herstellen** [ˈheːrʃtɛlən], *v.a.* place here; manufacture; *wieder —,* restore; (*sick person*) restore to health.

**Herstellung** [ˈheːrʃtɛluŋ], *f.* (—, *no pl.*) manufacture, production.

**herstürzen** [ˈheːrʃtyrtsən], *v.n.* (*aux.* sein) *über einen —,* rush at s.o.

**herüber** [hɛˈryːbər], *adv.* over, across; *— und hinüber,* there and back.

**herum** [hɛˈrum], *adv.* round, about; around.

**herumbalgen** [hɛˈrumbalgən], *v.r. sich —,* scrap; scuffle.

**herumbekommen** [hɛˈrumbəkɔmən], *v.a. irr.* (*coll.*) talk s.o. over, win s.o. over.

**herumbummeln** [hɛˈrumbuməln], *v.n.* loaf about.

**herumstreichen** [hɛˈrumʃtraɪçən], *v.n. irr.* (*aux.* sein) gad about.

**herumtreiben** [hɛˈrumtraɪbən], *v.r. irr. sich —,* loaf about, gad about.

**herumzanken** [hɛˈrumtsaŋkən], *v.r. sich —,* squabble, quarrel; live like cat and dog.

**herumziehen** [hɛ'rʊmtsi:ən], *v.a. irr.* drag about. — *v.n.* (*aux.* sein) wander about, move from place to place.

**herunter** [hɛ'rʊntər], *adj.* down, downward; *ich bin ganz* —, I feel poorly.

**heruntergekommen** [hɛ'rʊntərgəkɔmən], *adj.* decayed, broken down; in straitened circumstances; depraved.

**herunterhandeln** [hɛ'rʊntərhandəln], *v.a. einem etwas* —, beat s.o. down (in price).

**herunterwürgen** [hɛ'rʊntərvyrgən], *v.a.* swallow s.th. with dislike.

**hervor** [hɛr'fo:r], *adv.* forth, forward, out.

**hervorheben** [hɛr'fo:rhe:bən], *v.a. irr.* emphasize, stress.

**hervorragen** [hɛr'fo:rra:gən], *v.n.* stand out, project; (*fig.*) be distinguished, excel.

**hervorragend** [hɛr'fo:rra:gənt], *adj.* prominent; (*fig.*) outstanding, excellent.

**hervorrufen** [hɛr'fo:rru:fən], *v.a. irr.* call forth; (*fig.*) evoke, bring about, create, cause.

**hervorstechen** [hɛr'fo:rʃtɛçən], *v.n. irr.* be predominant, stand out.

**hervortun** [hɛr'fo:rtu:n], *v.r. irr. sich* —, distinguish o.s.

**Herz** [hɛrts], *n.* (—ens, *pl.* —en) heart; courage; mind; spirit; feeling; core; (*Cards*) hearts; (*coll.*) darling; *einem etwas ans* — *legen*, impress s.th. upon s.o.; *von* —en *gern*, with all my heart; *sich etwas zu* —en *nehmen*, take s.th. to heart.

**herzählen** [hɛ:rtsɛ:lən], *v.a.* enumerate.

**Herzanfall** [hɛrtsanfal], *m.* (—s, *pl.* ̈e) (*Med.*) heart attack.

**Herzbube** [hɛrtsbu:bə], *m.* (—n, *pl.* —n) (*Cards*) knave *or* jack of hearts.

**Herzdame** [hɛrtsda:mə], *f.* (—, *pl.* —n) (*Cards*) queen of hearts.

**Herzeleid** [hɛrtsəlaɪt], *n.* (—es, *no pl.*) heartbreak, sorrow, anguish, grief.

**herzen** [hɛrtsən], *v.a.* hug.

**Herzenseinfalt** [hɛrtsənsaɪnfalt], *f.* (—, *no pl.*) simple-mindedness.

**Herzensgrund** [hɛrtsənsgrunt], *m.* (—es, *no pl.*) *aus* —, with all my heart.

**Herzenslust** [hɛrtsənslust], *f.* (—, *no pl.*) heart's delight; *nach* —, to o.'s heart's content.

**Herzfehler** [hɛrtsfe:lər], *m.* (—s, *pl.* —) (*Med.*) cardiac defect; organic heart disease.

**Herzfell** [hɛrtsfɛl], *n.* (—s, *pl.* —e) pericardium.

**herzförmig** [hɛrtsfœrmɪç], *adj.* heart-shaped.

**herzhaft** [hɛrtshaft], *adj.* stout-hearted; courageous, bold; resolute; hearty.

**herzig** [hɛrtsɪç], *adj.* lovely, charming, sweet; (*Am.*) cute.

**Herzkammer** [hɛrtskamər], *f.* (—, *pl.* —n) ventricle (of the heart).

**Herzklappe** [hɛrtsklapə], *f.* (—, *pl.* —n) valve of the heart.

**Herzklopfen** [hɛrtsklɔpfən], *n.* (—s, *no pl.*) palpitations.

**herzlich** [hɛrtslɪç], *adj.* hearty, cordial, affectionate; — *gern*, with pleasure; —e *Grüße*, kind regards.

**Herzog** [hɛrtso:k], *m.* (—s, *pl.* ̈e) duke.

**Herzogtum** [hɛrtso:ktu:m], *n.* (—s, *pl.* ̈er) duchy, dukedom.

**Herzschlag** [hɛrtsʃla:k], *m.* (—es, *pl.* ̈e) heartbeat; (*Med.*) heart attack, cardiac failure.

**Hetäre** [he'tɛ:rə], *f.* (—, *pl.* —n) courtesan.

**Hetzblatt** [hɛtsblat], *n.* (—s, *pl.* ̈er) gutter press.

**Hetze** [hɛtsə], *f.* (—, *pl.* —n) chase, hunt, hurry, rush; agitation.

**hetzen** [hɛtsən], *v.a.* bait, fluster, chase, hunt, incite. — *v.n. herum* —, rush around.

**Hetzer** [hɛtsər], *m.* (—s, *pl.* —) instigator, rabble-rouser.

**Heu** [hɔy], *n.* (—s, *'no pl.*) hay.

**Heuboden** [hɔybo:dən], *m.* (—s, *pl.* ̈) hayloft.

**Heuchelei** [hɔyçə'laɪ], *f.* (—, *pl.* —en) hypocrisy.

**heucheln** [hɔyçəln], *v.n.* play the hypocrite, dissemble. — *v.a.* simulate, affect, feign.

**Heuchler** [hɔyçlər], *m.* (—s, *pl.* —) hypocrite.

**Heuer** [hɔyər], *f.* (—, *pl.* —n) (*Naut.*) engagement; hire, wages.

**heuer** [hɔyər], *adv.* (*dial.*) this year, this season.

**heuern** [hɔyərn], *v.a.* (*Naut.*) engage, hire.

**Heugabel** [hɔyga:bəl], *f.* (—, *pl.* —n) pitchfork.

**heulen** [hɔylən], *v.n.* howl; roar; cry, yell, scream.

**Heupferd** [hɔypfɛrt], *n.* (—es, *pl.* —e) (*Ent.*) grasshopper.

**heurig** [hɔyrɪç], *adj.* of this year, this year's (*wine etc.*).

**Heuschnupfen** [hɔyʃnupfən], *m.* (—s, *no pl.*) hay-fever.

**Heuschober** [hɔyʃo:bər], *m.* (—s, *pl.* —) hayrick.

**Heuschrecke** [hɔyʃrɛkə], *f.* (—, *pl.* —n) (*Ent.*) locust.

**heute** [hɔytə], *adv.* today, this day; — *in acht Tagen*, today week, a week today; — *abend*, tonight.

**heutig** [hɔytɪç], *adj.* today's, this day's; modern.

**heutzutage** [hɔytsuta:gə], *adv.* nowadays.

**Hexe** [hɛksə], *f.* (—, *pl.* —n) witch, sorceress, hag.

**hexen** [hɛksən], *v.n.* use witchcraft; practise sorcery.

**Hexenschuß** [hɛksənʃus], *m.* (—sses, *no pl.*) (*Med.*) lumbago.

# Hexerei

**Hexerei** [hɛksə'raɪ], *f.* (—, *pl.* **—en**) witchcraft, sorcery, juggling.

**hie** [hi:], *adv.* (*dial.*) here.

**Hieb** [hi:p], *m.* (**—es**, *pl.* **—e**) cut, stroke; hit, blow; (*pl.*) a thrashing.

**hienieden** [hi:'ni:dən], *adv.* here below, down here.

**hier** [hi:r], *adv.* here, in this place.

**Hiersein** ['hi:rzaɪn], *n.* (**—s**, *no pl.*) presence, attendance.

**hiesig** ['hi:zɪç], *adj.* of this place, of this country, local.

**Hifthorn** ['hɪfthɔrn], *n.* (**—s**, *pl.* ¨**er**) hunting-horn.

**Hilfe** ['hɪlfə], *f.* (—, *pl.* **—n**) help, aid, assistance, succour, relief.

**hilflos** ['hɪlflo:s], *adj.* helpless.

**hilfreich** ['hɪlfraɪç], *adj.* helpful.

**Hilfsmittel** ['hɪlfsmɪtəl], *n.* (**—s**, *pl.* —) expedient, remedy.

**Hilfsschule** ['hɪlfsʃu:lə], *f.* (—, *pl.* **—n**) school for backward children.

**Hilfszeitwort** ['hɪlfstsaɪtvɔrt], *n.* (**—s**, *pl.* ¨**er**) (*Gram.*) auxiliary verb.

**Himbeere** ['hɪmbe:rə], *f.* (—, *pl.* **—n**) raspberry.

**Himmel** ['hɪməl], *m.* (**—s**, *pl.* —) heaven, heavens; sky; firmament.

**himmelan** [hɪməl'an], *adv.* heavenward.

**himmelangst** ['hɪməlaŋkst], *adv. ihm war —*, he was panic-stricken.

**Himmelbett** ['hɪməlbet], *n.* (**—s**, *pl.* **—en**) fourposter.

**himmelblau** ['hɪməlblau], *adj.* sky-blue.

**Himmelfahrt** ['hɪməlfa:rt], *f.* (—, *no pl.*) Ascension.

**Himmelschlüssel** ['hɪməlʃlysəl], *m.* (**—s**, *pl.* —) (*Bot.*) primrose.

**himmelschreiend** ['hɪməlʃraɪənt], *adj.* atrocious, revolting.

**Himmelsgewölbe** ['hɪməlsgəvœlbə], *n.* (**—s**, *pl.* —) firmament.

**Himmelsstrich** ['hɪməlsʃtrɪç], *m.* (**—s**, *pl.* **—e**) climate, zone.

**Himmelszeichen** ['hɪməlstsaɪçən], *n.* (**—s**, *pl.* —) sign of the zodiac.

**himmelweit** ['hɪməlvaɪt], *adj.* enormous; *— entfernt*, poles apart.

**himmlisch** ['hɪmlɪʃ], *adj.* celestial, heavenly.

**hin** [hɪn], *adv.* there, towards that place; finished, gone; ruined; *— und her*, to and fro.

**hinab** [hɪn'ap], *adv.* down.

**hinan** [hɪn'an], *adv.* up.

**hinarbeiten** ['hɪnarbaɪtən], *v.n. auf etwas —*, work towards s.th.

**hinauf** [hɪn'auf], *adv.* up, up to.

**hinaus** [hɪn'aus], *adv.* out, out of; *es kommt auf dasselbe —*, it comes to the same thing.

**hinauswollen** [hɪn'ausvɔlən], *v.n.* wish to go out; (*fig.*) *hoch —*, aim high.

**hinausziehen** [hɪn'austsi:ən], *v.a. irr.* draw out; drag on; (*fig.*) protract.

**Hinblick** ['hɪnblɪk], *m.* (**—es**, *no pl.*) *im — auf*, in consideration of, with regard to.

**hinbringen** ['hɪnbrɪŋən], *v.a. irr.* bring to; escort; *Zeit —*, while away time.

**hinderlich** ['hɪndərlɪç], *adj.* obstructive, cumbersome.

**hindern** ['hɪndərn], *v.a.* hinder, obstruct, hamper, impede.

**hindeuten** ['hɪndɔytən], *v.n. auf etwas —*, point to s.th., hint at s.th.

**Hindin** ['hɪndɪn], *f.* (—, *pl.* **—innen**) (*Poet.*) hind.

**hindurch** [hɪn'durç], *adv.* through; throughout; *die ganze Zeit —*, all the time.

**hinein** [hɪn'aɪn], *adv.* in, into; *in den Tag — leben*, live for the present, lead a life of carefree enjoyment.

**hineinfinden** [hɪn'aɪnfɪndən], *v.r. irr. sich in etwas —*, reconcile *or* adapt o.s. to s.th.

**hinfällig** ['hɪnfɛlɪç], *adj.* frail, feeble, weak; shaky, void, invalid.

**Hingabe** ['hɪnga:bə], *f.* (—, *no pl.*) surrender; (*fig.*) devotion.

**hingeben** ['hɪnge:bən], *v.a. irr.* give up, surrender. *— v.r. sich einer Sache —*, devote o.s. to a task.

**hingegen** [hɪn'ge:gən], *adv.* on the other hand.

**hinhalten** ['hɪnhaltən], *v.a. irr.* (*thing*) hold out; (*person*) keep in suspense, put off.

**hinken** ['hɪŋkən], *v.n.* limp.

**hinlänglich** ['hɪnlɛŋlɪç], *adj.* sufficient.

**hinlegen** ['hɪnle:gən], *v.a.* lay down, put away. *— v.r. sich —*, lie down, go to bed.

**hinnehmen** ['hɪnne:mən], *v.a. irr.* take, submit to, accept.

**hinreichen** ['hɪnraɪçən], *v.a.* pass to. *— v.n.* suffice, be sufficient.

**Hinreise** ['hɪnraɪzə], *f.* (—, *pl.* **—n**) outward journey.

**hinreißen** ['hɪnraɪsən], *v.r. irr. sich — lassen*, allow o.s. to be carried away.

**hinreißend** ['hɪnraɪsənt], *adj.* charming, ravishing, enchanting.

**hinrichten** ['hɪnrɪçtən], *v.a.* execute, put to death.

**hinscheiden** ['hɪnʃaɪdən], *v.n. irr.* die, pass away.

**hinschlängeln** ['hɪnʃlɛŋəln], *v.r. sich —*, meander, wind along.

**Hinsicht** ['hɪnzɪçt], *f.* (—, *no pl.*) view, consideration, regard.

**hinsichtlich** ['hɪnzɪçtlɪç], *prep.* (*Genit.*) with regard to.

**hinstellen** ['hɪnʃtelən], *v.a.* put down; make out to be.

**hinten** ['hɪntən], *adv.* behind; *von —*, from behind.

**hinter** ['hɪntər], *prep.* (*Dat.*) behind, after.

**Hinterachse** ['hɪntəraksə], *f.* (—, *pl.* **—n**) (*Motor.*) rear-axle.

**Hinterbein** ['hɪntərbaɪn], *n.* (**—s**, *pl.* **—e**) hind-leg; (*fig.*) *sich auf die —e stellen*, get up on o.'s hind-legs.

**Hinterbliebene** [hɪntər'bliːbənə], *m.* (—n, *pl.* —n) survivor; mourner; (*pl.*) the bereaved.

**hinterbringen** [hɪntər'brɪŋən], *v.a. irr.* give information about, (*coll.*) tell on.

**Hinterdeck** ['hɪntərdɛk], *n.* (—s, *no pl.*) (*Naut.*) quarter deck.

**hinterdrein** ['hɪntərdraɪn], *adv.* afterwards, after; behind.

**hintereinander** [hɪntəraɪn'andər], *adv.* in succession, one after another.

**Hintergedanke** ['hɪntərgədaŋkə], *m.* (—n, *pl.* —n) mental reservation, ulterior motive.

**hintergehen** [hɪntər'geːən], *v.a. irr.* deceive, circumvent.

**Hintergrund** ['hɪntərgrunt], *m.* (—es, *pl.* ˙e) background; (*Theat.*) backcloth, back-drop.

**Hinterhalt** ['hɪntərhalt], *m.* (—s, *pl.* —e) ambush; (*fig.*) reserve.

**hinterhältig** ['hɪntərhɛltɪç], *adj.* furtive, secretive; insidious.

**hinterher** [hɪntər'heːr], *adv.* behind; in the rear; afterwards.

**Hinterindien** ['hɪntərɪndjən], *n.* Indo-China.

**Hinterkopf** ['hɪntərkɔpf], *m.* (—es, *pl.* ˙e) occiput, back of the head.

**Hinterlader** ['hɪntərlaːdər], *m.* (—s, *pl.* —) breech-loader.

**hinterlassen** [hɪntər'lasən], *v.a. irr.* leave (a legacy), bequeath; leave (word).

**Hinterlassenschaft** [hɪntər'lasənʃaft], *f.* (—, *pl.* —en) inheritance, bequest.

**Hinterlegung** [hɪntər'leːguŋ], *f.* (—, *pl.* —en) deposition.

**Hinterlist** ['hɪntərlɪst], *f.* (—, *no pl.*) fraud, deceit; cunning.

**hinterrücks** [hɪntər'ryks], *adv.* from behind; (*fig.*) treacherously, behind s.o.'s back.

**Hintertreffen** ['hɪntərtrɛfən], *n.* (—s, *no pl.*) *ins — geraten*, be left out in the cold, fall behind.

**hintertreiben** [hɪntər'traɪbən], *v.a. irr.* prevent, frustrate.

**Hintertreppe** ['hɪntərtrɛpə], *f.* (—, *pl.* —n) back-stairs.

**Hintertreppenroman** ['hɪntərtrɛpənromaːn], *m.* (—s, *pl.* —e) (*Lit.*) cheap thriller.

**hinterziehen** ['hɪntərtsiːən], *v.a. irr. insep.* defraud.

**hinträumen** ['hɪntrɔymən], *v.n. vor sich —*, daydream.

**hinüber** [hɪn'yːbər], *adv.* over, across.

**hinunter** [hɪn'untər], *adv.* down; *den Berg —*, downhill.

**hinweg** [hɪn'vɛk], *adv.* away, off.

**hinwegsetzen** [hɪn'vɛkzɛtsən], *v.r. sich über etwas —*, make light of s.th.

**Hinweis** ['hɪnvaɪs], *m.* (—es, *pl.* —e) hint, indication, reference; *unter — auf*, with reference to.

**hinweisen** ['hɪnvaɪzən], *v.a. irr. auf etwas —*, refer to, point to s.th.

**hinwerfen** ['hɪnvɛrfən], *v.a. irr.* throw down; *hingeworfene Bemerkung*, casual remark.

**hinziehen** ['hɪntsiːən], *v.a. irr.* draw along; attract. — *v.r. sich —*, march along. — *v.r. sich —*, drag on.

**hinzielen** ['hɪntsiːlən], *v.n. auf etwas —*, aim at s.th., have s.th. in mind.

**hinzu** [hɪn'tsuː], *adv.* to, near; besides, in addition.

**hinzufügen** [hɪn'tsuːfyːgən], *v.a.* add.

**hinzukommen** [hɪn'tsuːkɔmən], *v.n. irr.* (*aux.* sein) be added.

**hinzuziehen** [hɪn'tsuːtsiːən], *v.a. irr.* include, add; call in (expert).

**Hiobsbotschaft** ['hiːɔpsboːtʃaft], *f.* (—, *no pl.*) bad news.

**Hirn** [hɪrn], *n.* (—es, *pl.* —e) brain, brains. *See also* **Gehirn**.

**Hirngespinst** ['hɪrngəʃpɪnst], *n.* (—es, *pl.* —e) fancy, chimera, illusion, figment of the imagination.

**hirnverbrannt** ['hɪrnfɛrbrant], *adj.* crazy, insane, mad; (*coll.*) crackbrained.

**Hirsch** [hɪrʃ], *m.* (—es, *pl.* —e) (*Zool.*) stag, hart.

**Hirschbock** ['hɪrʃbɔk], *m.* (—s, *pl.* ˙e) (*Zool.*) stag.

**Hirschfänger** ['hɪrʃfɛŋər], *m.* (—s, *pl.* —) hunting-knife.

**Hirschgeweih** ['hɪrʃgəvaɪ], *n.* (—s, *pl.* —e) horns, antlers.

**Hirschhorn** ['hɪrʃhorn], *m.* (—s, *no pl.*) (*Chem.*) hartshorn.

**Hirschkäfer** ['hɪrʃkɛːfər], *m.* (—s, *pl.* —) (*Ent.*) stag beetle.

**Hirschkeule** ['hɪrʃkɔylə], *f.* (—, *pl.* —n) haunch of venison.

**Hirschkuh** ['hɪrʃkuː], *f.* (—, *pl.* ˙e) (*Zool.*) hind, doe.

**Hirse** ['hɪrzə], *f.* (—, *no pl.*) (*Bot.*) millet.

**Hirt** [hɪrt], *m.* (—en, *pl.* —en) shepherd, herdsman.

**Hirtenbrief** ['hɪrtənbriːf], *m.* (—s, *pl.* —e) (*Eccl.*) pastoral letter.

**His** [hɪs], *n.* (—, *pl.* —) (*Mus.*) B sharp.

**hissen** ['hɪsən], *v.a.* hoist (the flag).

**Historiker** [hɪ'stoːrɪkər], *m.* (—s, *pl.* —) historian.

**historisch** [hɪ'stoːrɪʃ], *adj.* historical.

**Hitzblase** ['hɪtsblaːzə], *f.* (—, *pl.* —n) blister, heat-rash.

**Hitze** ['hɪtsə], *f.* (—, *no pl.*) heat, hot weather.

**hitzig** ['hɪtsɪç], *adj.* hot-headed, hasty, passionate.

**Hitzschlag** ['hɪtsʃlaːk], *m.* (—es, *pl.* ˙e) sunstroke, heat-stroke.

**Hobel** ['hoːbəl], *m.* (—s, *pl.* —) (*tool*) plane.

**Hoch** [hoːx], *n.* (—s, *no pl.*) toast (*drink*); (*Met.*) high.

**hoch, hoh** [hoːx, hoː], *adj.* high; (*fig.*) eminent, sublime.

**Hochachtung** ['hoːxaxtuŋ], *f.* (—, *no pl.*) esteem, regard, respect.

**hochachtungsvoll** ['hoːxaxtuŋsfɔl], *adj., adv.* (*letters*) yours faithfully.

# Hochamt

**Hochamt** ['ho:xamt], *n.* (—es, *pl.* ⁻er) (*Eccl.*) High Mass.

**Hochbau** ['ho:xbau], *m.* (—s, *pl.* —ten) superstructure.

**hochbetagt** ['ho:xbəta:kt], *adj.* advanced in years.

**Hochburg** ['ho:xburk], *f.* (—, *pl.* —en) (*fig.*) stronghold, citadel.

**Hochebene** ['ho:xe:bənə], *f.* (—, *pl.* —n) table-land, plateau.

**hochfahrend** ['ho:xfa:rənt], *adj.* haughty, high-flown; (*coll.*) stuck-up.

**Hochgefühl** ['ho:xɡəfy:l], *n.* (—s, *no pl.*) exaltation.

**Hochgenuß** ['ho:xɡənus], *m.* (—sses, *pl.* ⁻sse) exquisite enjoyment; treat.

**Hochgericht** ['ho:xɡəriçt], *n.* (—s, *pl.* —e) place of execution, scaffold.

**hochherzig** ['ho:xhɛrtsɪç], *adj.* magnanimous.

**Hochmeister** ['ho:xmaɪstər], *m.* (—s, *pl.* —) Grand Master.

**Hochmut** ['ho:xmu:t], *m.* (—s, *no pl.*) haughtiness, pride.

**hochnäsig** ['ho:xnɛ:zɪç], *adj.* supercilious, stuck-up.

**hochnotpeinlich** ['ho:xno:tpaɪnlɪç], *adj.* (*obs.*) penal, criminal; —es Verhör, criminal investigation.

**Hochofen** ['ho:xo:fən], *m.* (—s, *pl.* ⁻) blast-furnace.

**Hochschule** ['ho:xʃu:lə], *f.* (—, *pl.* —n) academy; university.

**Hochschüler** ['ho:xʃy:lər], *m.* (—s, *pl.* —) student, undergraduate.

**höchst** [hø:çst], *adj.* highest, most. — *adv.* most, extremely.

**Hochstapler** ['ho:xʃta:plər], *m.* (—s, *pl.* —) confidence trickster, swindler.

**höchstens** ['hœ:çstəns], *adv.* at most, at best.

**hochtrabend** ['ho:xtra:bənt], *adj.* (*horse*) high-stepping; (*fig.*) high-sounding, bombastic.

**hochverdient** ['ho:xfɛrdi:nt], *adj.* highly meritorious.

**Hochverrat** ['ho:xfɛra:t], *m.* (—s, *no pl.*) high treason.

**Hochwild** ['ho:xvɪlt], *n.* (—es, *no pl.*) deer; big game.

**hochwohlgeboren** ['ho:xvo:lɡəbo:rən], *adj.* (*obs.*) noble; Euer Hochwohlgeboren, Right Honourable Sir.

**hochwürden** ['ho:xvyrdən], *adj.* Euer Hochwürden, Reverend Sir.

**Hochzeit** ['hoxtsaɪt], *f.* (—, *pl.* —en) wedding; nuptials.

**hochzeitlich** ['hoxtsaɪtlɪç], *adj.* nuptial, bridal.

**Hochzeitsreise** ['hoxtsaɪtsraɪzə], *f.* (—, *pl.* —n) honeymoon.

**Hocke** ['hokə], *f.* (—, *pl.* —n) squatting posture; shock, stook.

**hocken** ['hokən], *v.n.* crouch, squat; zu Hause —, be a stay-at-home.

**Hocker** ['hokər], *m.* (—s, *pl.* —) stool.

**Höcker** ['hœkər], *m.* (—s, *pl.* —) hump.

**höckerig** ['hœkərɪç], *adj.* hump-backed, hunch-backed.

**Hode** ['ho:də], *f.* (—, *pl.* —n) testicle.

**Hof** [ho:f], *m.* (—es, *pl.* ⁻e) yard, courtyard; farm(stead); (*royal*) court; (*moon*) halo; einem den — machen, court s.o.

**Hofarzt** ['ho:fartst], *m.* (—es, *pl.* ⁻e) court physician.

**hoffähig** ['ho:ffɛ:ɪç], *adj.* presentable at court.

**Hoffart** ['hofart], *f.* (—, *no pl.*) pride, arrogance.

**hoffärtig** ['hofɛrtɪç], *adj.* proud, arrogant.

**hoffen** ['hofən], *v.n.* hope; fest auf etwas —, trust.

**hoffentlich** ['hofəntlɪç], *adv.* as I hope, I trust that.

**Hoffnung** ['hofnuŋ], *f.* (—, *pl.* —en) hope, expectation, anticipation, expectancy; guter — sein, be full of hope; be expecting a baby; sich — machen auf, cherish hopes of.

**hoffnungslos** ['hofnuŋslo:s], *adj.* hopeless, past hope.

**hofieren** [ho'fi:rən], *v.a.* court.

**höfisch** ['hø:fɪʃ], *adj.* courtlike, courtly.

**höflich** ['hø:flɪç], *adj.* courteous, civil, polite.

**Hoflieferant** ['ho:fli:fərant], *m.* (—en, *pl.* —en) purveyor to His or Her Majesty.

**Höfling** ['hø:flɪŋ], *m.* (—s, *pl.* —e) courtier.

**Hofmarschall** ['ho:fmarʃal], *m.* (—s, *pl.* —e) Lord Chamberlain.

**Hofmeister** ['ho:fmaɪstər], *m.* (—s, *pl.* —) (*obs.*) steward; tutor.

**Hofnarr** ['ho:fnar], *m.* (—en, *pl.* —en) court jester, court fool.

**Hofrat** ['ho:fra:t], *m.* (—s, *pl.* ⁻e) Privy Councillor.

**Hofschranze** ['ho:fʃrantsə], *m.* (—n, *pl.* —n) courtier; flunkey.

**Hofsitte** ['ho:fzɪtə], *f.* (—, *pl.* —n) court etiquette.

**Höhe** ['hø:ə], *f.* (—, *pl.* —n) height, altitude; bis zur — von, up to the level of; in die —, upwards; in die — fahren, give a start, get excited.

**Hoheit** ['ho:haɪt], *f.* (—, *pl.* —en) grandeur; sovereignty; (*title*) Highness.

**Hohelied** [ho:ə'li:t], *n.* (—s, *no pl.*) Song of Solomon.

**Höhenmesser** ['hø:ənmɛsər], *m.* (—s, *pl.* —) (*Aviat.*) altimeter.

**Höhensonne** ['hø:ənzonə], *f.* (—, *pl.* —n) Alpine sun; (*Med.*) ultra-violet lamp.

**Höhenzug** ['hø:əntsu:k], *m.* (—s, *pl.* ⁻e) mountain range.

**Höhepunkt** ['hø:əpuŋkt], *m.* (—s, *pl.* —e) climax, culmination, acme; peak.

**höher** ['hø:ər], *comp. adj.* higher.

**hohl** [ho:l], *adj.* hollow; (*tooth*) decayed, hollow.

**Höhle** ['hø:lə], *f.* (—, *pl.* —n) cave, cavern, den.

**hohlgeschliffen** [ˈhoːlgəʃlɪfən], *adj.* concave, hollow-ground.
**Hohlheit** [ˈhoːlhaɪt], *f.* (—, *no pl.*) hollowness.
**Hohlleiste** [ˈhoːllaɪstə], *f.* (—, *pl.* —n) groove, channel.
**Hohlmaß** [ˈhoːlmaːs], *n.* (—es, *pl.* —e) dry measure.
**Hohlmeißel** [ˈhoːlmaɪsəl], *m.* (—s, *pl.* —) gouge.
**Hohlsaum** [ˈhoːlzaum], *m.* (—s, *pl.* ⁀e) hemstitch.
**Hohlspiegel** [ˈhoːlʃpiːgəl], *m.* (—s, *pl.* —) concave mirror.
**Höhlung** [ˈhøːluŋ], *f.* (—, *pl.* —en) hollow, cavity.
**Hohlziegel** [ˈhoːltsiːgəl], *m.* (—s, *pl.* —) hollow brick.
**Hohn** [hoːn], *m.* (—s, *no pl.*) scorn, derision, mockery; sneer.
**höhnen** [ˈhøːnən], *v.a.* deride, sneer at; *see* **verhöhnen**.
**Höker** [ˈhøːkər], *m.* (—s, *pl.* —) hawker, huckster.
**hold** [hɔlt], *adj.* kind, friendly; gracious; graceful; sweet.
**Holder** [ˈhɔldər] *see* **Holunder**.
**holdselig** [ˈhɔltzeːlɪç], *adj.* sweet, charming, gracious.
**holen** [ˈhoːlən], *v.a.* fetch, collect, get.
**Holland** [ˈhɔlant], *n.* Holland.
**Hölle** [ˈhœlə], *f.* (—, *no pl.*) hell.
**Holm** [hɔlm], *m.* (—es, *pl.* —e) islet, holm; (*Gymn.*) bar.
**holperig** [ˈhɔlpərɪç], *adj.* rough, bumpy.
**holpern** [ˈhɔlpərn], *v.n.* jolt, stumble; (*fig.*) falter.
**Holunder** [hoˈlundər], *m.* (—s, *pl.* —) (*Bot.*) elder; *spanischer* —, lilac.
**Holz** [hɔlts], *n.* (—es, *pl.* ⁀er) wood, timber; (*Am.*) lumber; (*no pl.*) forest; bush.
**Holzapfel** [ˈhɔltsapfəl], *m.* (—s, *pl.* ⁀) (*Bot.*) crab-apple.
**holzartig** [ˈhɔltsartɪç], *adj.* woody, ligneous.
**holzen** [ˈhɔltsən], *v.a.* cut *or* gather wood.
**hölzern** [ˈhœltsərn], *adj.* wooden; (*fig.*) stiff.
**Holzhändler** [ˈhɔltshɛndlər], *m.* (—s, *pl.* —) timber-merchant; (*Am.*) lumber-merchant.
**Holzhauer** [ˈhɔltshauər], *m.* (—s, *pl.* —) wood-cutter.
**holzig** [ˈhɔltsɪç], *adj.* woody, wooded; (*asparagus*) woody, hard; (*beans*) stringy.
**Holzkohle** [ˈhɔltskoːlə], *f.* (—, *no pl.*) charcoal.
**Holzscheit** [ˈhɔltsʃaɪt], *n.* (—s, *pl.* —e) log of wood.
**Holzschlag** [ˈhɔltsʃlaːk], *m.* (—es, *pl.* ⁀e) clearing; felling area.
**Holzschnitt** [ˈhɔltsʃnɪt], *m.* (—es, *pl.* —e) wood-cut.
**Holzschuh** [ˈhɔltsʃuː], *m.* (—s, *pl.* —e) clog.

**Holzweg** [ˈhɔltsveːk], *m.* (—s, *pl.* —e) timbertrack; (*fig.*) *auf dem* — *sein*, be on the wrong tack.
**Holzwolle** [ˈhɔltsvɔlə], *f.* (—, *no pl.*) wood shavings.
**homogen** [homoˈgeːn], *adj.* homogeneous.
**homolog** [homoˈloːg], *adj.* homologous.
**honett** [hɔˈnɛt], *adj.* (*obs.*) respectable, genteel.
**Honig** [ˈhoːnɪç], *m.* (—s, *no pl.*) honey.
**Honigkuchen** [ˈhoːnɪçkuːxən], *m.* (—s, *pl.* —) ginger-bread.
**Honigwabe** [ˈhoːnɪçvaːbə], *f.* (—, *pl.* —n) honeycomb.
**Honorar** [honoˈraːr], *n.* (—s, *pl.* —e) remuneration; (*professional*) fee; honorarium.
**Honoratioren** [honoraˈtsjoːrən], *m. pl.* people of rank; dignitaries.
**honorieren** [honoˈriːrən], *v.a.* pay a fee to, remunerate.
**Hopfen** [ˈhɔpfən], *m.* (—s, *no pl.*) (*Bot.*) hop, hops; *an dem ist* — *und Malz verloren*, he is beyond help.
**Hopfenstange** [ˈhɔpfənʃtaŋə], *f.* (—, *pl.* —n) hop-pole; (*fig.*) tall thin person.
**hopsen** [ˈhɔpsən], *v.n.* (*aux.* sein) (*coll.*) hop, jump.
**hörbar** [ˈhøːrbaːr], *adj.* audible.
**horchen** [ˈhɔrçən], *v.n.* listen, eavesdrop.
**Horde** [ˈhɔrdə], *f.* (—, *pl.* —n) horde.
**hören** [ˈhøːrən], *v.a., v.n.* hear.
**Hörer** [ˈhøːrər], *m.* (—s, *pl.* —) listener; (*Univ.*) student; (*telephone*) receiver.
**Hörerin** [ˈhøːrərɪn], *f.* (—, *pl.* —innen) female listener; (*Univ.*) woman student.
**Hörerschaft** [ˈhøːrərʃaft], *f.* (—, *no pl.*) audience.
**Hörgerät** [ˈhøːrgərɛːt], *n.* (—es, *pl.* —e) hearing-aid.
**hörig** [ˈhøːrɪç], *adj.* in bondage, a slave to.
**Horizont** [horiˈtsɔnt], *m.* (—es, *pl.* —e) horizon.
**Horizontale** [horitsɔnˈtaːlə], *f.* (—, *pl.* —n) horizontal line.
**Horn** [hɔrn], *n.* (—s, *pl.* ⁀er) horn; (*Mus.*) French horn.
**Hörnchen** [ˈhœrnçən], *n.* (—s, *pl.* —) French roll, croissant.
**hörnern** [ˈhœrnərn], *adj.* horny, made of horn.
**Hornhaut** [ˈhɔrnhaut], *f.* (—, *pl.* ⁀te) horny skin; (*eye*) cornea.
**Hornhautverpflanzung** [ˈhɔrnhautfɛrpflantsuŋ], *f.* (—, *no pl.*) corneal graft.
**hornig** [ˈhɔrnɪç], *adj.* hard, horny.
**Hornisse** [hɔrˈnɪsə], *f.* (—, *pl.* —n) (*Ent.*) hornet.
**horrend** [hɔˈrɛnt], *adj.* exorbitant; stupendous.
**Hörrohr** [ˈhøːrroːr], *n.* (—s, *pl.* —e) ear-trumpet.
**Hörsaal** [ˈhøːrzaːl], *m.* (—s, *pl.* —säle) auditorium, lecture-room.

# Hörspiel

**Hörspiel** ['hø:rʃpi:l], *n.* (—s, *pl.* —e) radio play.

**Horst** [hɔrst], *m.* (—es, *pl.* —e) eyrie.

**Hort** [hɔrt], *m.* (—es, *pl.* —e) (*Poet.*) treasure; stronghold.

**Hortensie** [hɔr'tɛnzjə], *f.* (—, *pl.* —n) (*Bot.*) hydrangea.

**Hose** ['ho:zə], *f.* (—, *pl.* —n) trousers, pants, breeches; (*women*) slacks.

**Hosenband** ['ho:zənbant], *n.* (—es, *pl.* ̈er) garter.

**Hosenträger** ['ho:zəntregər], *m. pl.* braces, (*Am.*) suspenders.

**Hospitant** [hɔspɪ'tant], *m.* (—en, *pl.* —en) (*Univ.*) temporary student, non-registered student.

**hospitieren** [hɔspɪ'ti:rən], *v.n.* attend lectures as a visitor.

**Hostie** ['hɔstjə], *f.* (—, *pl.* —n) (*Eccl.*) the Host.

**hüben** ['hy:bən], *adv.* on this side; — *und drüben*, on either side.

**hübsch** [hypʃ], *adj.* pretty, attractive; handsome; good-looking.

**Hubschrauber** ['hu:pʃraubər], *m.* (—s, *pl.* —) (*Aviat.*) helicopter.

**huckepack** ['hukəpak], *adv.* — *tragen*, carry pick-a-back.

**Huf** [hu:f], *m.* (—es, *pl.* —e) hoof.

**Hufe** ['hu:fə], *f.* (—, *pl.* —n) hide (of land).

**Hufeisen** ['hu:faɪzən], *n.* (—s, *pl.* —) horseshoe.

**Huflattich** ['hu:flatɪç], *m.* (—s, *pl.* —e) (*Bot.*) colt's foot.

**Hufschlag** ['hu:fʃla:k], *m.* (—s, *pl.* ̈e) (*of a horse*) hoof-beat.

**Hüfte** ['hyftə], *f.* (—, *pl.* —n) (*Anat.*) hip; (*animals*) haunch.

**Hügel** ['hy:gəl], *m.* (—s, *pl.* —) hill, hillock.

**hügelig** ['hy:gəlɪç], *adj.* hilly.

**Huhn** [hu:n], *n.* (—s, *pl.* ̈er) fowl; hen.

**Hühnchen** ['hy:nçən], *n.* (—s, *pl.* —) pullet, chicken.

**Hühnerauge** ['hy:nəraugə], *n.* (—s, *pl.* —n) corn (*on the foot*).

**Huld** [hult], *f.* (—, *no pl.*) grace, favour.

**huldigen** ['huldɪgən], *v.n.* pay homage.

**huldvoll** ['hultfɔl], *adj.* gracious.

**Hülle** ['hylə], *f.* (—, *pl.* —n) cover, covering; veil; *in — und Fülle*, in abundance, in profusion.

**hüllen** ['hylən], *v.a.* cover, veil, wrap.

**Hülse** ['hylzə], *f.* (—, *pl.* —n) hull, husk, shell; cartridge-case.

**Hülsenfrucht** ['hylzənfruxt], *f.* (—, *pl.* ̈e) (*Bot.*) leguminous plant.

**human** [hu'ma:n], *adj.* humane.

**humanistisch** [huma'nɪstɪʃ], *adj.* classical; humanistic.

**Hummel** ['huməl], *f.* (—, *pl.* —n) (*Ent.*) bumble-bee.

**Hummer** ['humər], *m.* (—s, *pl.* —) (*Zool.*) lobster.

**Humor** [hu'mo:r], *m.* (—s, *no pl.*) humour.

**humoristisch** [humo'rɪstɪʃ], *adj.* humorous, witty.

**humpeln** ['humpəln], *v.n.* hobble, limp.

**Humpen** ['humpən], *m.* (—s, *pl.* —) deep drinking-cup, bowl, tankard.

**Humus** ['hu:mus], *m.* (—, *no pl.*) garden-mould, humus.

**Hund** [hunt], *m.* (—es, *pl.* —e) dog; (*hunting*) hound; (*fig.*) rascal, scoundrel.

**Hundehaus** ['hundəhaus], *n.* (—es, *pl.* ̈er) dog-kennel.

**hundert** ['hundərt], *num. adj.* a hundred, one hundred.

**Hündin** ['hyndɪn], *f.* (—, *pl.* —innen) bitch.

**Hundstage** ['huntsta:gə], *m. pl.* dog days (July to August).

**Hundszahn** ['huntstsa:n], *m.* (—es, *pl.* ̈e) (*Bot.*) dandelion.

**Hüne** ['hy:nə], *m.* (—n, *pl.* —n) giant, colossus; (*fig.*) tall man.

**Hünengrab** ['hy:nəngra:p], *n.* (—es, *pl.* ̈er) tumulus, burial mound, barrow, cairn.

**Hunger** ['huŋər], *m.* (—s, *no pl.*) hunger; starvation.

**hungern** ['huŋərn], *v.n.* hunger, be hungry.

**Hungertuch** ['huŋərtu:x], *n.* (—es, *no pl.*) *am — nagen*, go without food; live in poverty.

**hungrig** ['huŋrɪç], *adj.* hungry; (*fig.*) desirous (of).

**Hupe** ['hu:pə], *f.* (—, *pl.* —n) motor-horn, hooter (of a car).

**hüpfen** ['hypfən], *v.n.* (*aux.* sein) hop, skip.

**Hürde** ['hyrdə], *f.* (—, *pl.* —n) hurdle.

**Hure** ['hu:rə], *f.* (—, *pl.* —n) whore, prostitute, harlot; (*coll.*) tart.

**hurtig** ['hurtɪç], *adj.* nimble, agile; quick, speedy, swift.

**Husar** [hu'za:r], *m.* (—en, *pl.* —en) hussar.

**husch!** [huʃ], *excl.* quick!

**huschen** ['huʃən], *v.n.* (*aux.* sein) scurry, whip away.

**hüsteln** ['hystəln], *v.n.* cough slightly; clear o.'s throat.

**husten** ['hu:stən], *v.n.* cough.

**Hut** (1) [hu:t], *m.* (—es, *pl.* ̈e) hat; *steifer —*, bowler.

**Hut** (2) [hu:t], *f.* (—, *no pl.*) guard, keeping, care.

**hüten** ['hy:tən], *v.a.* guard, tend, care for; *Kinder —*, baby-sit; *das Bett —*, be confined to o.'s bed, be ill in bed. — *v.r. sich — vor*, be on o.'s guard against, beware of.

**Hüter** ['hy:tər], *m.* (—s, *pl.* —) guardian, keeper; (*cattle*) herdsman.

**Hutkrempe** ['hu:tkrɛmpə], *f.* (—, *pl.* —n) hat-brim.

**Hütte** ['hytə], *f.* (—, *pl.* —n) hut, cottage; (*Tech.*) furnace, forge, foundry.

**Hüttenarbeiter** ['hytənarbaɪtər], *m.* (—s, *pl.* —) smelter, foundry-worker.

**Hyäne** [hy'ɛ:nə], *f.* (—, *pl.* —n) (*Zool.*) hyena.

**Hyazinthe** [hyat'sɪntə], f. (—, pl. —n) (Bot.) hyacinth.

**Hyperbel** [hy'pɛrbəl], f. (—, pl. —n) hyperbola.

**hypnotisch** [hyp'no:tɪʃ], adj. hypnotic.

**hypnotisieren** [hypnoti'zi:rən], v.a. hypnotise.

**Hypochonder** [hypo'xɔndər], m. (—s, pl. —) hypochondriac.

**Hypothek** [hypo'te:k], f. (—, pl. —en) mortgage.

**Hysterie** [hyste'ri:], f. (—, no pl.) hysterics, hysteria.

**hysterisch** [hys'te:rɪʃ], adj. hysterical.

# I

**I** [i:], n. (—, no pl.) the letter I. — excl. **i wo!** (dial.) certainly not! of course not!

**ich** [ɪç], pers. pron. I, myself.

**ideal** [ide'a:l], adj. ideal.

**idealisieren** [ideali'zi:rən], v.a. idealise.

**Idealismus** [idea'lɪsmus], m. (—, no pl.) idealism.

**Idee** [i'de:], f. (—, pl. —n) idea, notion, conception.

**identifizieren** [ɪdɛntifi'tsi:rən], v.a. identify.

**identisch** [i'dɛntɪʃ], adj. identical.

**Identität** [ɪdɛnti'tɛ:t], f. (—, no pl.) identity.

**idiomatisch** [idio'ma:tɪʃ], adj. idiomatic.

**Idyll** [i'dyl], n. (—s, pl. —e) idyll.

**Idylle** [i'dylə], f. (—, pl. —n) idyll.

**idyllisch** [i'dylɪʃ], adj. idyllic.

**Igel** [i:gəl], m. (—s, pl. —) (Zool.) hedgehog.

**ignorieren** [ɪgno'ri:rən], v.a. ignore, take no notice of.

**ihm** [i:m], pers. pron. Dat. to him, it.

**ihn** [i:n], pers. pron. Acc. him, it.

**Ihnen** [i':nən], pers. pron. Dat. you, to you.

**ihnen** [i':nən], pers. pron. pl. Dat. them, to them.

**Ihr** [i:r], poss. adj. your; of your. — poss. pron. yours.

**ihr** [i:r], pers. pron. to her; (pl.) (intim.) you. — poss. adj. her, their. — poss. pron. hers, theirs.

**Ihrer** [i':rər], pers. pron. of you. — poss. adj. of your.

**ihrer** [i':rər], pers. pron. of her, of it; (pl.) of them. — poss. adj of her; to her; (pl.) of them.

**ihresgleichen** [i':rəsglaɪçən], adv. of her, its or their kind.

**ihrethalben** [i':rəthalbən], adv. for her sake, for their sake, on her account, on their account.

**ihretwegen** [i':rətve:gən] see **ihrethalben.**

**ihretwillen** [i':rətvɪlən] see **ihrethalben.**

**Ihrige** [i:rɪgə], poss. pron. yours.

**ihrige** [i':rɪgə], poss. pron. hers, its, theirs.

**illegitim** [ɪlegi'ti:m], adj. illegitimate.

**illuminieren** [ɪlumi'ni:rən], v.a. illuminate, floodlight.

**illustrieren** [ɪlu'stri:rən], v.a. illustrate.

**Iltis** ['ɪltɪs], m. (—ses, pl. —se) (Zool.) polecat, fitchet.

**im** [ɪm], contraction of **in dem**, in the.

**Imbiß** ['ɪmbɪs], m. (—sses, pl. —sse) snack, refreshment, light meal.

**Imker** ['ɪmkər], m. (—s, pl. —) beekeeper.

**immatrikulieren** [ɪmmatriku'li:rən], v.a. (Univ.) matriculate, enrol.

**Imme** ['ɪmə], f. (—, pl. —n) (dial., Poet.) bee.

**immer** ['ɪmər], adv. always, ever; — mehr, more and more; — noch, still; — wieder, time and again; — größer, larger and larger; auf —, for ever.

**immerdar** ['ɪmərda:r], adv. for ever.

**immerhin** ['ɪmərhɪn], adv. nevertheless, still, after all.

**immerzu** ['ɪmərtsu:], adv. always, constantly.

**Immobilien** [ɪmo'bi:ljən], pl. real estate.

**Immortelle** [ɪmɔr'tɛlə], f. (—, pl. —n) (Bot.) everlasting flower.

**immun** [ɪ'mu:n], adj. immune.

**impfen** ['ɪmpfən], v.a. vaccinate, inoculate; (Hort.) graft.

**imponieren** [ɪmpo'ni:rən], v.n. impress.

**Import** [ɪm'pɔrt], m. (—s, pl. —e) import, importation.

**imposant** [ɪmpo'zant], adj. imposing, impressive.

**imstande** [ɪm'ʃtandə], adv. capable, able; — sein, be able.

**in** [ɪn], prep. (Dat., Acc.) in, into; at; within.

**Inangriffnahme** [ɪn'angrɪfna:mə], f. (—, no pl.) start, beginning, inception.

**Inbegriff** ['ɪnbəgrɪf], m. (—es, no pl.) essence, epitome.

**inbegriffen** ['ɪnbəgrɪfən], adv. inclusive.

**Inbrunst** ['ɪnbrunst], f. (—, no pl.) ardour, fervour.

**indem** [ɪn'de:m], adv. meanwhile. — conj. while, whilst; as, because, in that.

**indessen** [ɪn'dɛsən], adv. meanwhile, in the meantime. — conj. however, nevertheless, yet.

**Indien** ['ɪndjən], n. India.

**Individualität** [ɪndividuali'tɛ:t], f. (—, pl. —en) individuality, personality.

**individuell** [ɪndividu'ɛl], adj. individual.

**Individuum** [ɪndi'vi:duum], n. (—s, pl. —duen) individual.

**Indizienbeweis** [ɪn'di:tsjənbəvaɪs], *m.* (—es, *pl.* —e) (*Law*) circumstantial evidence *or* proof.

**indossieren** [ɪndɔ'si:rən], *v.a.* endorse.

**Industrie** [ɪndus'tri:], *f.* (—, *pl.* —n) industry; manufacture.

**industriell** [ɪndustri'ɛl], *adj.* industrial.

**Industrielle** [ɪndustri'ɛlə], *m.* (—n, *pl.* —n) manufacturer, industrialist.

**ineinander** [ɪnaɪ'nandər], *adv.* into each other, into one another.

**infam** [ɪn'fa:m], *adj.* infamous.

**Infantin** [ɪn'fantɪn], *f.* (—, *pl.* —en) Infanta.

**infizieren** [ɪnfi'tsi:rən], *v.a.* infect.

**infolge** [ɪn'fɔlgə], *prep.* (*Genit.*) in consequence of, owing to.

**informieren** [ɪnfɔr'mi:rən], *v.a.* inform, advise.

**Ingenieur** [ɪnʒen'jø:r], *m.* (—s, *pl.* —e) engineer.

**Ingrimm** ['ɪngrɪm], *m.* (—s, *no pl.*) anger, rage, wrath.

**Ingwer** ['ɪŋvər], *m.* (—s, *no pl.*) ginger.

**Inhaber** ['ɪnha:bər], *m.* (—s, *pl.* —) possessor, owner; proprietor; occupant.

**inhaftieren** [ɪnhaf'ti:rən], *v.a.* imprison; arrest.

**inhalieren** [ɪnha'li:rən], *v.a.* inhale.

**Inhalt** ['ɪnhalt], *m.* (—(e)s, *no pl.*) content; contents; tenor.

**Inhaltsverzeichnis** ['ɪnhaltsfɛrtsaɪçnɪs], *n.* (—ses, *pl.* —se) (table of) contents; index.

**inhibieren** [ɪnhi'bi:rən], *v.a.* inhibit, prevent.

**Inkasso** [ɪn'kaso], *n.* (—s, *pl.* —s) encashment.

**inklinieren** [ɪnkli'ni:rən], *v.n.* be inclined to.

**inklusive** [ɪnklu'zi:və], *adv.* inclusive of, including.

**inkonsequent** ['ɪnkɔnzəkvɛnt], *adj.* inconsistent.

**Inkrafttreten** [ɪn'krafttre:tən], *n.* (—s, *no pl.*) enactment; coming into force.

**Inland** ['ɪnlant], *n.* (—s, *no pl.*) inland, interior.

**Inländer** ['ɪnlɛndər], *m.* (—s, *pl.* —) native.

**Inlett** ['ɪnlɛt], *n.* (—s, *pl.* —e) bed-tick, ticking.

**inliegend** ['ɪnli:gənt], *adj.* enclosed.

**inmitten** [ɪn'mɪtən], *prep.* (*Genit.*) in the midst of.

**innehaben** ['ɪnəha:bən], *v.a. irr.* possess; occupy; hold.

**innehalten** ['ɪnəhaltən], *v.a. irr.* (*conditions*) keep to, observe; (*time*) come promptly at. — *v.n.* stop, pause.

**innen** ['ɪnən], *adv.* within; nach —, inwards; von —, from within.

**Innenminister** ['ɪnənmɪnɪstər], *m.* (—s, *pl.* —) Minister for Internal Affairs; Home Secretary; (*Am.*) Secretary of the Interior.

**inner** ['ɪnər], *adj.* inner, interior, internal; intrinsic.

**innerhalb** ['ɪnərhalp], *prep.* (*Genit.*) within.

**innerlich** ['ɪnərlɪç], *adj.* internal; inside o.s.; inward.

**innerste** ['ɪnərstə], *adj.* inmost, innermost.

**innewerden** ['ɪnəve:rdən], *v.a. irr.* (*aux.* sein) perceive, become aware of.

**innewohnen** ['ɪnəvo:nən], *v.n.* be inherent in.

**innig** ['ɪnɪç], *adj.* heartfelt, cordial.

**Innung** ['ɪnuŋ], *f.* (—, *pl.* —en) guild, corporation.

**Insasse** ['ɪnzasə], *m.* (—n, *pl.* —n) inmate; occupant.

**insbesondere** [ɪnsbə'zɔndərə], *adv.* especially, particularly, in particular.

**Inschrift** ['ɪnʃrɪft], *f.* (—, *pl.* —en) inscription.

**Insel** ['ɪnzəl], *f.* (—, *pl.* —n) island.

**Inserat** [ɪnzə'ra:t], *n.* (—es, *pl.* —e) classified advertisement; (*coll.*) (small) ad.

**inserieren** [ɪnzə'ri:rən], *v.a.* advertise; insert.

**insgeheim** [ɪnsgə'haɪm], *adv.* privately, secretly.

**insgesamt** [ɪnsgə'zamt], *adv.* altogether, in a body.

**insofern** [ɪnzo'fɛrn], *conj.* — als, in so far as, inasmuch as, so far as.

**inspirieren** [ɪnspi'ri:rən], *v.a.* inspire.

**installieren** [ɪnsta'li:rən], *v.a.* install, fit.

**instandhalten** [ɪn'ʃtanthaltən], *v.a. irr.* maintain, preserve, keep in repair.

**inständig** ['ɪnʃtɛndɪç], *adj.* urgent; fervent.

**instandsetzen** [ɪn'ʃtantzɛtsən], *v.a.* restore, repair; *einen — etwas zu tun*, enable s.o. to do s.th.

**Instanz** [ɪn'stants], *f.* (—, *pl.* —en) (*Law*) instance; *letzte —*, highest court of appeal, last resort.

**Institut** [ɪnsti'tu:t], *n.* (—es, *pl.* —e) institute, institution, establishment; (*Univ.*) department.

**instruieren** [ɪnstru'i:rən], *v.a.* instruct.

**Insulaner** [ɪnzu'la:nər], *m* (—s, *pl.* —) islander.

**inszenieren** [ɪnstse'ni:rən], *v.a.* put on the stage, produce.

**Inszenierung** [ɪnstse'ni:ruŋ], *f.* (—, *pl.* —en) (*Theat.*) production, staging.

**intellektuell** [ɪntɛlektu'ɛl], *adj.* intellectual.

**Intendant** [ɪntɛn'dant], *m.* (—en, *pl.* —en) (*Theat.*) director.

**interessant** [ɪntərɛ'sant], *adj.* interesting.

**Interesse** [ɪntə'rɛsə], *n.* (—s, *pl.* —n) interest.

**Interessent** [ɪntərɛ'sɛnt], *m.* (—en, *pl.* —en) interested party.

**interessieren** [ɪntərɛ'si:rən], *v.a.* interest. — *v.r. sich* —, be interested (in).

**intern** [ɪn'tɛrn], *adj.* internal.

**Internat** [ɪntɛr'na:t], *n.* (—es, *pl.* —e) boarding-school.

**Interne** [ɪn'tɛrnə], *m.* (—n, *pl.* —n) resident (pupil *or* doctor), boarder.

**Internist** [ɪntɛr'nɪst], *m.* (—en, *pl.* —en) specialist in internal diseases.

**interpunktieren** [ɪntərpunk'ti:rən], *v.a.* punctuate.

**Interpunktion** [ɪntərpunkts'jo:n], *f.* (—, *pl.* —en) punctuation.

**intim** [ɪn'ti:m], *adj.* intimate; *mit einem — sein*, be on close terms with s.o.

**intonieren** [ɪnto'ni:rən], *v.n.* intone.

**Intrigant** [ɪntri'gant], *m.* (—en, *pl.* —en) intriguer, schemer.

**intrigieren** [ɪntri'gi:rən], *v.n.* intrigue, scheme.

**Inventar** [ɪnvɛn'ta:r], *n.* (—s, *pl.* —e) inventory; *ein — aufnehmen*, draw up an inventory.

**Inventur** [ɪnvɛn'tu:r], *f.* (—, *pl.* —en) stock-taking.

**inwärts** ['ɪnvɛrts], *adv.* inwards.

**inwendig** ['ɪnvɛndɪç], *adj.* inward, internal, inner.

**inwiefern** [ɪnvi:'fɛrn], *adv.* to what extent.

**inwieweit** [ɪnvi:'vaɪt], *adv.* how far.

**Inzucht** ['ɪntsuxt], *f.* (—, *no pl.*) inbreeding.

**inzwischen** [ɪn'tsvɪʃən], *adv.* meanwhile, in the meantime.

**Irak** [i'ra:k], *m., n.* Iraq.

**Iran** [i'ra:n], *n.* Iran.

**irden** ['ɪrdən], *adj.* earthen.

**irdisch** ['ɪrdɪʃ], *adj.* earthly, worldly; terrestrial, temporal.

**irgend** ['ɪrgənt], *adv.* any, some; *wenn es — geht*, if it can possibly be done.

**irgendein** [ɪrgənt'aɪn], *pron.* any, some.

**Irland** ['ɪrlant], *n.* Ireland.

**ironisch** [i'ro:nɪʃ], *adj.* ironic, ironical.

**Irre** (1) ['ɪrə], *f.* (—, *no pl.*) *in die — gehen*, go astray.

**Irre** (2) ['ɪrə], *m.* (—n, *pl.* —n) madman, lunatic.

**irre** ['ɪrə], *adj.* astray; wrong, confused; crazy, demented.

**irren** ['ɪrən], *v.n.* err, go astray, be wrong. — *v.r. sich* —, be mistaken.

**Irrenarzt** ['ɪrənartst], *m.* (—es, *pl.* ⸚e) psychiatrist.

**Irrenhaus** ['ɪrənhaus], *n.* (—es, *pl.* ⸚er) lunatic asylum, mental hospital.

**Irrfahrt** ['ɪrfa:rt], *f.* (—, *pl.* —en) wandering.

**Irrglaube** ['ɪrglaubə], *m.* (—ns, *no pl.*) heresy.

**irrig** ['ɪrɪç], *adj.* erroneous.

**irritieren** [ɪri'ti:rən], *v.a.* irritate.

**Irrlicht** ['ɪrlɪçt], *n.* (—s, *pl.* —er) will-o'-the-wisp.

**Irrsinn** ['ɪrzɪn], *m.* (—s, *no pl.*) madness, insanity, lunacy.

**irrsinnig** ['ɪrzɪnɪç], *adj.* insane, deranged.

**Irrtum** ['ɪrtu:m], *m.* (—s, *pl.* ⸚er) error, mistake, fault, oversight.

**Irrweg** ['ɪrve:k], *m.* (—s, *pl.* —e) wrong track.

**Irrwisch** ['ɪrvɪʃ], *m.* (—es, *pl.* —e) will-o'-the-wisp.

**Ischias** ['ɪsçias], *f., m.* (*Med.*) sciatica.

**Isegrim** ['i:zəgrɪm], *m.* (—s, *pl.* —e) (*fable*) the wolf; a bear (with a sore head) (*also fig.*).

**Island** ['i:slant], *n.* Iceland.

**isolieren** [izo'li:rən], *v.a.* (*Electr.*) insulate; (*fig.*) isolate.

**Isolierung** [izo'li:ruŋ], *f.* (—, *pl.* —en) (*Electr.*) insulation; (*fig.*) isolation.

**Italien** [i'ta:ljən], *n.* Italy.

# J

**J** [jɔt], *n.* (—, *no pl.*) the letter J.

**ja** [ja:], *adv., part.* yes; indeed, certainly; even; — *doch*, to be sure; — *freilich*, certainly.

**Jacht** [jaxt], *f.* (—, *pl.* —en) yacht.

**Jacke** ['jakə], *f.* (—, *pl.* —n) jacket, tunic.

**Jackett** [ja'kɛt], *n.* (—s, *pl.* —s) jacket, short coat.

**Jagd** [ja:kt], *f.* (—, *pl.* —en) hunt, hunting; shooting; chase.

**Jagdhund** ['ja:kthunt], *m.* (—es, *pl.* —e) retriever, setter; hound.

**Jagdrevier** ['ja:ktrevi:r], *n.* (—s, *pl.* —e) hunting-ground.

**jagen** ['ja:gən], *v.a.* hunt; chase; (*fig.*) tear along.

**Jäger** ['jɛ:gər], *m.* (—s, *pl.* —) hunter, huntsman; game-keeper.

**Jägerei** [jɛ:gə'raɪ], *f.* (—, *no pl.*) huntsmanship.

**jäh** [jɛ:], *adj.* abrupt; steep, precipitous; (*fig.*) hasty, rash, sudden.

**jählings** ['jɛ:lɪŋs], *adv.* abruptly, suddenly, hastily.

**Jahr** [ja:r], *n.* (—es, *pl.* —e) year.

**jähren** ['jɛ:rən], *v.r. sich* —, (*anniversary*) come round.

**Jahresfeier** ['ja:rəsfaɪər], *f.* (—, *pl.* —n) anniversary.

**Jahresrente** ['ja:rəsrɛntə], *f.* (—, *pl.* —n) annuity.

**Jahreszeit** ['ja:rəstsaɪt], *f.* (—, *pl.* —en) season.

**Jahrgang** ['ja:rgaŋ], *m.* (—s, *pl.* ⸚e) age group; class; year of publication; vintage.

**Jahrhundert** [ja:r'hundərt], *n.* (—s, *pl.* —e) century.

**jährig** ['jɛ:rɪç], *adj.* year-old.

**jährlich** ['jɛ:rlɪç], *adj.* yearly, annual. — *adv.* every year.

**Jahrmarkt** ['ja:rmarkt], *m.* (—s, *pl.* ⸚e) annual fair.

**Jahrtausend** [ja:r'tauzənt], *n.* (—s, *pl.* —e) millennium.

**Jahrzehnt** [ja:r'tse:nt], *n.* (—s, *pl.* —e) decade.

**Jähzorn** ['jɛ:tsɔrn], *m.* (—s, *no pl.*) irascibility.

**Jalousie** [ʒalu'ziː], *f.* (—, *pl.* —n) Venetian blind.

**Jamaika** [ja'maika], *n.* Jamaica.

**Jambus** ['jambus], *m.* (—, *pl.* —ben) (*Poet.*) iambic foot.

**Jammer** ['jamər], *m.* (—s, *no pl.*) lamentation; misery; (*fig.*) pity.

**jämmerlich** ['jɛmərlɪç], *adj.* lamentable, miserable, wretched, piteous.

**Jammerschade** ['jamərʃaːdə], *adv.* a thousand pities.

**Jänner** ['jɛnər] (*Austr.*) *see* **Januar**.

**Januar** ['januaːr], *m.* (—s, *pl.* —e) January.

**Japan** ['jaːpan], *n.* Japan.

**Jaspis** ['jaspɪs], *m.* (—ses, *pl.* —se) jasper.

**jäten** ['jɛːtən], *v.a.* weed.

**Jauche** ['jauxə], *f.* (—, *pl.* —n) liquid manure.

**jauchzen** ['jauxtsən], *v.n.* exult, shout with joy.

**Jauchzer** ['jauxtsər], *m.* (—s, *pl.* —) shout of joy.

**jawohl** [ja'voːl], *int.* yes, indeed! certainly, of course.

**je** [jeː], *adv.* ever; at any time; at a time; each; *von — her*, always; *— nachdem*, it depends; *— zwei*, in twos; *— eher — besser*, the sooner the better.

**jedenfalls** ['jeːdənfals], *adv.* at all events, in any case, at any rate, anyway.

**jeder, -e, -es** ['jeːdər], *adj.* every, each; *— beliebige*, any. *— pron.* each, each one; everybody.

**jederlei** ['jeːdərlai], *adj.* of every kind.

**jedoch** [je'dɔx], *adv.*, however, nevertheless, yet, notwithstanding.

**jeglicher, -e, -es** ['jeːklɪçər], *adj.* every, each. *— pron.* every man, each.

**jemals** ['jeːmals], *adv.* ever, at any time.

**jemand** ['jeːmant], *pron.* somebody, someone; anybody, anyone.

**Jemen** ['jeːmən], *n.* Yemen.

**jener, -e, -es** ['jeːnər], *dem. adj.* that, (*Poet.*) yonder. *— dem. pron.* that one, the former.

**Jenseits** ['jɛnzaits], *n.* (—, *no pl.*) the next world, the hereafter, the life to come.

**jenseits** ['jɛnzaits], *prep.* (*Genit.*) on the other side, beyond.

**jetzig** ['jɛtsɪç], *adj.* present, now existing, current, extant.

**jetzt** [jɛtst], *adv.* now, at this time, at present.

**jeweilig** ['jeːvailɪç], *adj.* momentary; actual, for the time being.

**Joch** [jɔx], *n.* (—es, *pl.* —e) yoke.

**Jochbein** ['jɔxbain], *n.* (—s, *pl.* —e) cheek-bone.

**Jockei** ['jɔkai], *m.* (—s, *pl.* —s) jockey.

**Jod** [joːt], *n.* (—s, *no pl.*) iodine.

**jodeln** ['joːdəln], *v.n.* yodel.

**Jodler** ['joːdlər], *m.* (—s, *pl.* —) (*person*) yodeler; (*sound*) yodelling.

**Johannisbeere** [jo'hanisbeːrə], *f.* (—, *pl.* —n) (*Bot.*) red-currant.

**Johannisfest** [jo'hanisfɛst], *n.* (—s, *pl.* —e) Midsummer Day, St. John the Baptist's Day (June 24th).

**Johanniskäfer** [jo'haniskɛːfər], *m.* (—s, *pl.* —) (*Ent.*) glow-worm.

**Johannisnacht** [jo'hanisnaxt], *f.* (—, *pl.* ⁓e) Midsummer Eve.

**johlen** [joːlən], *v.n.* bawl.

**Joppe** ['jɔpə], *f.* (—, *pl.* —n) shooting-jacket.

**Jota** ['joːta], *n.* (—s, *pl.* —s) iota, jot.

**Journalismus** [ʒurna'lɪsmus], *m. see* **Journalistik**.

**Journalistik** [ʒurna'lɪstɪk], *f.* (—, *no pl.*) journalism.

**jubeln** ['juːbəln], *v.n.* rejoice, exult.

**Jubilar** [ju:bi'laːr], *m.* (—s, *pl.* —e) person celebrating a jubilee.

**Jubiläum** [ju:bi'lɛːum], *n.* (—s, *pl.* —läen) jubilee.

**jubilieren** [ju:bi'liːrən], *v.n.* exult, shout with glee.

**juchhe** [jux'heː], *excl.* hurrah!

**Juchten** ['juxtən], *m.* (—, *no pl.*) Russian leather.

**jucken** ['jukən], *v.a.* scratch. *— v.n.* itch.

**Jude** ['juːdə], *m.* (—n, *pl.* —n) Jew, Israelite.

**Judentum** ['juːdəntuːm], *n.* (—s, *no pl.*) Judaism.

**Judenviertel** ['juːdənfiːrtəl], *n.* (—s, *pl.* —) Jewish quarter, ghetto.

**Jüdin** ['jyːdɪn], *f.* (—, *pl.* —innen) Jewess.

**jüdisch** ['jyːdɪʃ], *adj.* Jewish.

**Jugend** ['juːgənt], *f.* (—, *no pl.*) youth.

**jugendlich** ['juːgəntlɪç], *adj.* youthful, juvenile.

**Jugoslawien** [ju:go'slaːvjən], *n.* Jugoslavia.

**Julfest** ['juːlfɛst], *n.* (—es, *pl.* —e) Yule.

**Juli** ['juːli], *m.* (—, *pl.* —s) July.

**jung** [juŋ], *adj.* young.

**Junge** (1) ['juŋə], *m.* (—n, *pl.* —n) boy, lad.

**Junge** (2) ['juŋə], *n.* (—n, *pl.* —n) young animal.

**jungenhaft** ['juŋənhaft], *adj.* boyish.

**Jünger** ['jyŋər], *m.* (—s, *pl.* —) disciple, devotee, follower.

**Jungfer** ['juŋfər], *f.* (—, *pl.* —n) (*obs.*) virgin, maid, maiden; lady's maid.

**jüngferlich** ['jyŋfərlɪç], *adj.* maidenly, coy, prim.

**Jungfrau** ['juŋfrau], *f.* (—, *pl.* —en) virgin.

**Junggeselle** ['juŋgəzɛlə], *m.* (—n, *pl.* —n) bachelor; *eingefleischter —*, confirmed bachelor.

**Jüngling** ['jyŋlɪŋ], *m.* (—s, *pl.* —e) young man.

**jüngst** [jyŋst], *adv.* lately, recently.

**Juni** ['juːni], *m.* (—s, *pl.* —s) June.

**Junker** ['juŋkər], *m.* (—s, *pl.* —) country squire; titled landowner.

**Jura** ['juːra], *n. pl.* jurisprudence, law; (*Univ.*) *— studieren*, read law.

**Jurisprudenz** [ju:rɪspru'dɛnts], *f.* (—, *no pl.*) jurisprudence.

**Jurist** [ju:'rɪst], *m.* (—en, *pl.* —en) lawyer, jurist.

**juristisch** [ju:'rɪstɪʃ], *adj.* juridical; legal.
**just** [just], *adv.* just now.
**Justiz** [jus'ti:ts], *f.* (—, *no pl.*) administration of the law *or* of justice.
**Justizrat** [jus'ti:tsra:t], *m.* (—s, *pl.* ⸚e) (*Law*) Counsellor; King's (Queen's) Counsel.
**Jute** ['ju:tə], *f.* (—, *no pl.*) jute.
**Juwel** [ju've:l], *n.* (—s, *pl.* —en) jewel; (*pl.*) jewellery; (*Am.*) jewelry.
**Juwelier** [juvə'li:r], *m.* (—s, *pl.* —e) jeweller, goldsmith.


# K

**K** [ka:], *n.* (—, *no pl.*) the letter K.
**Kabel** ['ka:bəl], *n.* (—s, *pl.* —) cable.
**Kabeljau** [kabəl'jau], *m.* (—s, *pl.* —e) (*Zool.*) cod, codfish.
**kabeln** ['ka:bəln], *v.n.* cable, send a cablegram.
**Kabine** [ka'bi:nə], *f.* (—, *pl.* —n) cabin, cubicle.
**Kabinett** [kabi'nɛt], *n.* (—s, *pl.* —e) closet; cabinet.
**Kabinettsrat** [kabi'nɛtsra:t], *m.* (—s, *pl.* ⸚e) cabinet *or* ministerial committee; political adviser.
**Kabüse** [ka'by:zə], *f.* (—, *pl.* —n) ship's galley.
**Kachel** ['kaxəl], *f.* (—, *pl.* —n) glazed tile.
**Kadaver** [ka'da:vər], *m.* (—s, *pl.* —) carrion, carcass; corpse.
**Kadenz** [ka'dɛnts], *f.* (—, *pl.* —en) (*Mus.*) cadenza.
**Kadett** [ka'dɛt], *m.* (—en, *pl.* —en) cadet.
**Käfer** ['kɛ:fər], *m.* (—s, *pl.* —) (*Ent.*) beetle, (*Am.*) bug.
**Kaffee** ['kafe], *m.* (—s, *no pl.*) coffee.
**Käfig** ['kɛ:fɪç], *m.* (—s, *pl.* —e) cage.
**kahl** [ka:l], *adj.* bald; (*trees*) leafless; (*landscape*) barren; — *geschoren*, close-cropped.
**Kahn** ['ka:n], *m.* (—s, *pl.* ⸚e) boat; punt.
**Kai** [kaɪ], *m.* (—s, *pl.* —s) quay, wharf, landing-place.
**Kaimeister** ['kaɪmaɪstər], *m.* (—s, *pl.* —) wharfinger.
**Kaiser** ['kaɪzər], *m.* (—s, *pl.* —) emperor; *um des* —s *Bart streiten*, quarrel about nothing.
**kaiserlich** ['kaɪzərlɪç], *adj.* imperial.
**Kaiserschnitt** ['kaɪzərʃnɪt], *m.* (—es, *pl.* —e) (*Med.*) Caesarean operation.
**Kajüte** [ka'jy:tə], *f.* (—, *pl.* —n) cabin.
**Kakadu** ['kakadu:], *m.* (—s, *pl.* —s) (*Orn.*) cockatoo.
**Kakao** [ka'ka:o], *m.* (—s, *no pl.*) cocoa.
**Kalauer** ['ka:lauər], *m.* (—s, *no pl.*) pun; stale joke.

**Kalb** [kalp], *n.* (—es, *pl.* ⸚er) calf; (*roe*) fawn; (*fig.*) colt, calf.
**Kalbfleisch** ['kalpflaɪʃ], *n.* (—es, *no pl.*) veal.
**Kälberei** [kɛlbə'raɪ], *f.* (—, *pl.* —en) friskiness.
**kälbern** ['kɛlbərn], *v.n.* frisk, frolic.
**Kalbsbraten** ['kalpsbra:tən], *m.* (—s, *pl.* —) roast veal.
**Kalbshaxe** ['kalpshaksə], *f.* (—, *pl.* —n) knuckle of veal.
**Kalbskeule** ['kalpskɔylə], *f.* (—, *pl.* —n) leg of veal.
**Kalbsmilch** ['kalpsmɪlç], *f.* (—, *no pl.*) sweetbread.
**Kaldaunen** [kal'daunən], *f. pl.* (*dial.*) tripe.
**Kalesche** [ka'lɛʃə], *f.* (—, *pl.* —n) chaise, light carriage.
**Kali** ['ka:li], *n.* (—s, *no pl.*) potash.
**Kaliber** [ka'li:bər], *n.* (—s, *pl.* —) calibre; (*fig.*) sort, quality.
**kalibrieren** [kali'bri:rən], *v.a.* (*Tech.*) calibrate, graduate, gauge.
**Kalifornien** [kali'fɔrnjən], *n.* California.
**Kalium** ['ka:ljum], *n.* (—s, *no pl.*) (*Chem.*) potassium.
**Kalk** [kalk], *m.* (—s, *pl.* —e) lime; *gebrannter* —, quicklime; *mit* — *bewerfen*, rough-cast.
**kalkartig** ['kalka:rtɪç], *adj.* calcareous.
**Kalkbewurf** ['kalkbəvurf], *m.* (—es, *pl.* ⸚e) coat of plaster.
**kalken** ['kalkən], *v.a.* whitewash; (*Agr.*) lime.
**kalkig** ['kalkɪç], *adj.* limy, calcareous.
**kalkulieren** [kalku'li:rən], *v.n.* calculate, reckon.
**kalt** [kalt], *adj.* cold, frigid; *mir ist* —, I am cold.
**kaltblütig** ['kaltbly:tɪç], *adj.* cold-blooded, cool.
**Kälte** ['kɛltə], *f.* (—, *no pl.*) cold, coldness.
**Kaltschale** ['kaltʃa:lə], *f.* (—, *pl.* —n) cold beer (*or* wine) soup.
**Kambodscha** [kam'bɔtʃa], *f.* Cambodia.
**Kamee** [ka'me:], *f.* (—, *pl.* —n) cameo.
**Kamel** [ka'me:l], *n.* (—s, *pl.* —e) (*Zool.*) camel.
**Kamelziege** [ka'me:ltsi:gə], *f.* (—, *pl.* —n) (*Zool.*) Angora-goat, llama.
**Kamerad** [kamə'ra:t], *m.* (—en, *pl.* —en) comrade, companion, mate.
**Kameradschaft** [kamə'ra:tʃaft], *f.* (—, *pl.* —en) comradeship, fellowship.
**Kamerun** [kamə'ru:n], *n.* the Cameroons.
**Kamille** [ka'mɪlə], *f.* (—, *pl.* —n) camomile.
**Kamin** [ka'mi:n], *m.* (—s, *pl.* —e) chimney; funnel; fireplace, fireside.
**Kaminaufsatz** [ka'mi:naufzats], *m.* (—es, *pl.* ⸚e) mantel-piece, over-mantel.
**Kaminfeger** [ka'mi:nfe:gər], *m.* (—s, *pl.* —) chimney-sweep.

117

**Kaminsims** [ka'mi:nzɪms], *m.* or *n.* (—es, *pl.* —e) mantel-piece.

**Kamm** [kam], *m.* (—es, *pl.* ⁓e) comb; (*cock*) crest; (*mountains*) ridge.

**kämmen** ['kɛmən], *v.a.* comb; (*wool*) card.

**Kammer** ['kamər], *f.* (—, *pl.* —n) chamber, small room; (*Am.*) closet; (*authority*) board; (*Parl. etc.*) chamber.

**Kammerdiener** ['kamərdi:nər], *m.* (—s, *pl.* —) valet.

**Kämmerer** ['kɛmərər], *m.* (—s, *pl.* —) Chamberlain, Treasurer.

**Kammergericht** ['kamərgərɪçt], *n.* (—s, *pl.* —e) Supreme Court of Justice.

**Kammergut** ['kamərgu:t], *n.* (—s, *pl.* ⁓er) domain, demesne; crown land.

**Kammerherr** ['kamərhɛr], *m.* (—n, *pl.* —en) chamberlain.

**Kammersänger** ['kamərzɛŋər], *m.* (—s, *pl.* —) court singer; title given to prominent singers.

**Kammgarn** ['kamgarn], *n.* (—s, no *pl.*) worsted.

**Kammwolle** ['kamvɔlə], *f.* (—, no *pl.*) carded wool.

**Kampagne** [kam'panjə], *f.* (—, *pl.* —n) (*Mil.*) campaign.

**Kämpe** ['kɛmpe], *m.* (—n, *pl.* —n) (*Poet.*) champion, warrior; *alter* —, old campaigner.

**Kampf** [kampf], *m.* (—es, *pl.* ⁓e) combat, fight, struggle; (*fig.*) conflict.

**kämpfen** ['kɛmpfən], *v.n.* fight, combat, struggle.

**Kampfer** ['kampfər], *m.* (—s, no *pl.*) camphor.

**Kämpfer** ['kɛmpfər], *m.* (—s, *pl.* —) fighter, combatant.

**kampfunfähig** ['kampfunfɛ:ɪç], *adj.* (*Mil.*) disabled; — *machen*, disable, put out of action.

**kampieren** [kam'pi:rən], *v.n.* be encamped, camp.

**Kanada** ['kanada], *n.* Canada.

**Kanal** [ka'na:l], *m.* (—s, *pl.* ⁓e) (*natural*) channel; (*artificial*) canal; sewer; *der Ärmelkanal*, the English Channel.

**kanalisieren** [kanali'zi:rən], *v.a.* canalise; (*streets*) drain by means of sewers.

**Kanapee** ['kanape:], *n.* (—s, *pl.* —s) sofa, divan.

**Kanarienvogel** [ka'na:rjənfo:gəl], *m.* (—s, *pl.* ⁓) (*Orn.*) canary.

**Kanarische Inseln** [ka'na:rɪʃə 'ɪnzəln], *f.pl.* Canary Islands.

**Kandare** [kan'da:rə], *f.* (—, *pl.* —n) bridle, bit.

**Kandelaber** [kandə'la:bər], *m.* (—s, *pl.* —) candelabrum, chandelier.

**kandidieren** [kandi'di:rən], *v.n.* be a candidate (for), apply (for) (*post*); (*Parl.*) stand (for), (*Am.*) run (for election).

**kandieren** [kan'di:rən], *v.a.* candy.

**Kandiszucker** ['kandɪstsukər], *m.* (—, no *pl.*) sugar-candy.

**Kanevas** ['kanəvas], *m.* (—ses, *pl.* —se) canvas.

**Känguruh** ['kɛŋguru:], *n.* (—s, *pl.* —s) (*Zool.*) kangaroo.

**Kaninchen** [ka'ni:nçən], *n.* (—s, *pl.* —) (*Zool.*) rabbit.

**Kaninchenbau** [ka'ni:nçənbau], *m.* (—s, *pl.* —e) rabbit-warren, burrow.

**Kanne** ['kanə], *f.* (—, *pl.* —n) can, tankard, mug; jug; pot; quart.

**Kannegießer** ['kanəgi:sər], *m.* (—s, *pl.* —) pot-house politician.

**kannelieren** [kanə'li:rən], *v.a.* flute, channel.

**Kannibale** [kani'ba:lə], *m.* (—n, *pl.* —n) cannibal.

**Kanoe** [ka'nu:], *n.* see Kanu.

**Kanone** [ka'no:nə], *f.* (—, *pl.* —n) cannon, gun; *unter aller* —, beneath contempt; beneath criticism.

**Kanonier** [kano'ni:r], *m.* (—s, *pl.* —e) gunner.

**Kanonikus** [ka'no:nikus], *m.* (—, *pl.* —ker) canon, prebendary.

**kanonisieren** [kanoni'zi:rən], *v.a.* canonise.

**Kante** ['kantə], *f.* (—, *pl.* —n) edge, rim, brim, brink, ledge; (*cloth*) list, selvedge.

**Kanten** ['kantən], *m.* (—s, *pl.* —) (*bread*) crust.

**kanten** ['kantən], *v.a.* edge, tilt.

**Kanthaken** ['kantha:kən], *m.* (—s, *pl.* —) cant-hook; grapple; grappling hook.

**kantig** ['kantɪç], *adj.* angular.

**Kantine** [kan'ti:nə], *f.* (—, *pl.* —n), canteen, mess.

**Kanton** [kan'to:n], *m.* (—s, *pl.* —e) (*Swiss*) canton; district, region.

**Kantonist** [kanto'nɪst], *m.* (—en, *pl.* —en) *unsicherer* —, shifty fellow.

**Kantor** ['kantor], *m.* (—s, *pl.* —en) precentor; organist; cantor.

**Kanu** [ka'nu:], *n.* (—s, *pl.* —s) canoe.

**Kanzel** ['kantsəl], *f.* (—, *pl.* —n) pulpit; (*Aviat.*) cockpit.

**Kanzlei** [kants'lai], *f.* (—, *pl.* —en) office, secretariat; chancellery; chancery-office; lawyer's office.

**Kanzleipapier** [kants'laipapi:r], *n.* (—s, no *pl.*) foolscap (paper).

**Kanzleistil** [kants'laiʃti:l], *m.* (—s, no *pl.*) legal jargon.

**Kanzler** ['kantslər], *m.* (—s, *pl.* —) Chancellor.

**Kanzlist** [kants'lɪst], *m.* (—en, *pl.* —en) chancery clerk; copying clerk.

**Kap** [kap], *n.* (—s, *pl.* —s) (*Geog.*) cape, promontory.

**Kapaun** [ka'paun], *m.* (—s, *pl.* —e) capon.

**Kapazität** [kapatsi'tɛ:t], *f.* (—, *pl.* —en) capacity; (*fig.*) (*person*) authority.

**Kapelle** [ka'pɛlə], *f.* (—, *pl.* —n) chapel; (*Mus.*) band.

**Kapellmeister** [ka'pɛlmaistər], *m.* (—s, *pl.* —) (*Mus.*) band leader, conductor.

**Kaper** ['ka:pər], *f.* (—, *pl.* —n) (*Bot.*) caper.

**kapern** ['ka:pərn], *v.a.* capture, catch.
**kapieren** [ka'pi:rən], *v.a.* (*coll.*) understand, grasp.
**Kapital** [kapi'ta:l], *n.* (—s, *pl.* —ien) (*money*) capital, stock.
**Kapitäl, Kapitell** [kapɪ'tɛ:l, kapɪ'tɛl], *n.* (—s, *pl.* —e) (*Archit.*) capital.
**Kapitalanlage** [kapi'ta:lanla:gə], *f.* (—, *pl.* —n) investment.
**kapitalisieren** [kapitali'zi:rən], *v.a.* capitalise.
**kapitalkräftig** [kapi'ta:lkrɛftɪç], *adj.* wealthy, moneyed, affluent; (*business, firm*) sound.
**Kapitalverbrechen** [kapi'ta:lfɛrbrɛçən], *n.* (—s, *pl.* —) capital offence.
**Kapitän** [kapi'tɛ:n], *m.* (—s, *pl.* —e) captain (of a ship), master.
**Kapitel** [ka'pɪtəl], *n.* (—s, *pl.* —) chapter.
**Kapitulation** [kapitulats'jo:n], *f.* (—, *pl.* —en) surrender.
**kapitulieren** [kapitu'li:rən], *v.n.* surrender; capitulate.
**Kaplan** [kap'la:n], *m.* (—s, *pl.* ̈e) chaplain; assistant priest.
**Kapotte** [ka'pɔtə], *f.* (—, *pl.* —n) hood.
**Kappe** ['kapə], *f.* (—, *pl.* —n) cap, bonnet; (*shoe*) toe-cap.
**Käppi** ['kɛpi], *n.* (—s, *pl.* —s) military cap.
**Kapriole** [kapri'o:lə], *f.* (—, *pl.* —n) caper.
**kaprizieren** [kapri'tsi:rən], *v.r. sich auf etwas —*, set o.'s heart on s.th., be obstinate about s.th.
**kapriziös** [kapri'tsjø:s], *adj.* whimsical, capricious.
**Kapsel** ['kapzəl], *f.* (—, *pl.* —n) capsule.
**kaputt** [ka'put], *adj.* broken, ruined, done for; *— machen*, break, ruin.
**Kapuze** [ka'pu:tsə], *f.* (—, *pl.* —n) hood; monk's cowl.
**Kapuziner** [kapu'tsi:nər], *m.* (—s, *pl.* —) Capuchin (friar); (*coffee*) cappuccino.
**Kapuzinerkresse** [kapu'tsi:nərkrɛsə], *f.* (—, *no pl.*) (*Bot.*) nasturtium.
**Karabiner** [kara'bi:nər], *m.* (—s, *pl.* —) (*rifle*) carbine.
**Karaffe** [ka'rafə], *f.* (—, *pl.* —n) carafe; decanter.
**Karambolage** [karambo'la:ʒə], *f.* (—, *pl.* —n) collision; (*billiards*) cannon.
**Karawane** [kara'va:nə], *f.* (—, *pl.* —n) convoy; caravan.
**Karbol** [kar'bo:l], *n.* (—s, *no pl.*) carbolic acid.
**Karbunkel** [kar'buŋkəl], *m.* (—s, *pl.* —) (*Med.*) carbuncle.
**Karfreitag** [kar'fraita:k], *m.* Good Friday.
**Karfunkel** [kar'fuŋkəl], *m.* (—s, *pl.* —) (*Min.*) carbuncle.
**karg** [kark], *adj.* scant; meagre; parsimonious.
**kargen** ['kargən], *v.n.* be stingy, be niggardly.
**kärglich** ['kɛrklɪç], *adj.* sparing, scanty poor, paltry.

**karieren** [ka'ri:rən], *v.a.* chequer.
**kariert** [ka'ri:rt], *adj.* checked, chequered.
**Karikatur** [karika'tu:r], *f.* (—, *pl.* —en) caricature, cartoon.
**karikieren** [kari'ki:rən], *v.a.* caricature, distort.
**Karl** [karl], *m.* Charles; *— der Grosse,* Charlemagne.
**Karmeliter** [karme'li:tər], *m.* (—s, *pl.* —) Carmelite (friar).
**karminrot** [kar'mi:nro:t], *adj.* carmine.
**karmoisin** [karmoa'zi:n], *adj.* crimson.
**Karneol** [karne'o:l], *m.* (—s, *pl.* —e) (*Min.*) cornelian, carnelian.
**Karneval** ['karnəval], *m.* (—s, *pl.* —s) carnival; Shrovetide festivities.
**Karnickel** [kar'nɪkəl], *n.* (—s, *pl.* —) rabbit; *er war das —,* he was the scapegoat.
**Kärnten** ['kɛrntən], *n.* Carinthia.
**Karo** ['ka:ro], *n.* (—s, *pl.* —s) check, square; (*cards*) diamonds.
**Karosse** [ka'rɔsə], *f.* (—, *pl.* —n) state-coach.
**Karosserie** [karɔsə'ri:], *f.* (—, *pl.* —n) (*Motor.*) body(-work).
**Karotte** [ka'rɔtə], *f.* (—, *pl.* —n) (*Bot.*) carrot.
**Karpfen** ['karpfən], *m.* (—s, *pl.* —) (*fish*) carp.
**Karre** ['karə], *f.* (—, *pl.* —n) cart, wheelbarrow.
**Karren** ['karən], *m.* (—s, *pl.* —) cart, wheelbarrow, dray.
**Karrete** [ka're:tə], *f.* (—, *pl.* —n) (*Austr.*) rattletrap, rickety coach.
**Karriere** [ka'rjɛ:rə], *f.* (—, *pl.* —n) career; *— machen,* get on well.
**Kärrner** ['kɛrnər], *m.* (—s, *pl.* —) (*obs.*) carter.
**Karst** [karst], *m.* (—s, *pl.* —e) mattock.
**Karthago** [kar'ta:go], *n.* Carthage.
**Kartätsche** [kar'tɛ:tʃə], *f.* (—, *pl.* —n) grape-shot, shrapnel.
**Kartäuser** [kar'tɔyzər], *m.* (—s, *pl.* —) Carthusian (monk).
**Karte** ['kartə], *f.* (—, *pl.* —n) card; ticket; map; chart; (*pl.*) pack ((*Am.*) deck) of cards.
**Kartei** [kar'tai], *f.* (—, *pl.* —en) card index.
**Kartell** [kar'tɛl], *n.* (—s, *pl.* —e) cartel; ring; syndicate.
**Kartoffel** [kar'tɔfəl], *f.* (—, *pl.* —n) (*Bot.*) potato.
**Kartoffelpuffer** [kar'tɔfəlpufər], *m.* (—s, *pl.* —) potato-pancake.
**Karton** [kar'tɔŋ], *m.* (—s, *pl.* —s) carton, cardboard-box; (*material*) cardboard, paste-board; cartoon.
**Kartusche** [kar'tuʃə], *f.* (—, *pl.* —n) cartridge.
**Karussell** [karu'sɛl], *m.* (—s, *pl.* —e) merry-go-round; roundabout.
**Karwoche** ['ka:rvɔxə], *f.* Holy Week.
**Karzer** ['kartsər], *m.* (—s, *pl.* —) lock-up, prison.
**Kaschmir** ['kaʃmi:r], *m.* (—s, *no pl.*) cashmere.

# Käse

Käse ['kɛːzə], m. (—s, pl. —) cheese.

käseartig ['kɛːzəaːrtɪç], adj. like cheese; caseous.

Kaserne [ka'zɛrnə], f. (—, pl. —n) barracks.

kasernieren [kazɛr'niːrən], v.a. put into barracks.

Käsestoff ['kɛːzəʃtɔf], m. (—s, pl. —e) casein.

käseweiß ['kɛːzəvaɪs], adj. deathly pale.

käsig ['kɛːzɪç], adj. cheese-like, cheesy, caseous; (fig.) sallow.

Kasperle ['kaspɛrlə], n. (—s, pl. —) Punch.

Kasperl(e)theater ['kaspɛrl(ə)teaːtər], n. (—s, pl. —) Punch-and-Judy show.

Kaspisches Meer ['kaspɪʃəsmeːr], n. Caspian Sea.

Kasse ['kasə], f. (—, pl. —n) money-box, till; cash-desk; box-office; cash, ready money.

Kassenanweisung ['kasənanvaɪzuŋ], f. (—, pl. —en) treasury-bill; cash voucher.

Kassenbuch ['kasənbuːx], n. (—es, pl. ⏑er) cash-book.

Kassenschrank ['kasənʃraŋk], m. (—s, pl. ⏑e) strong-box, safe.

Kasserolle [kasə'rɔlə], f. (—, pl. —n) stew-pot, casserole.

Kassette [ka'sɛtə], f. (—, pl. —n) deed-box; casket; (Phot.) plate-holder.

kassieren [ka'siːrən], v.a. cash, collect (money); cashier, annul, discharge.

Kassierer [ka'siːrər], m. (—s, pl. —) cashier; teller.

Kastagnette [kastan'jɛtə], f. (—, pl. —n) castanet.

Kastanie [ka'staːnjə], f. (—, pl. —n) (Bot.) chestnut, (coll.) conker; chestnut-tree.

Kästchen ['kɛstçən], n. (—s, pl. —) casket, little box.

Kaste ['kastə], f. (—, pl. —n) caste.

kasteien [ka'staɪən], v.r. sich —, castigate or mortify o.s.

Kastell [ka'stɛl], n. (—s, pl. —e) citadel, small fort; castle.

Kastellan [kaste'laːn], m. (—s, pl. —e) castellan; caretaker.

Kasten ['kastən], m. (—s, pl. ⏑) box, chest, case, crate.

Kastengeist ['kastəngaɪst], m. (—es, no pl.) exclusiveness; class consciousness.

Kastilien [ka'stiːljən], n. Castile.

Kastrat [ka'straːt], m. (—en, pl. —en) eunuch.

kastrieren [ka'striːrən], v.a. castrate.

Katafalk [kata'falk], m. (—s, pl. —e) catafalque.

katalogisieren [katalogi'ziːrən], v.a. catalogue.

Katarakt [kata'rakt], m. (—es, pl. —e) cataract; waterfall.

Katasteramt [ka'tastəramt], n. (—es, pl. ⏑er) land-registry office.

katechisieren [kateçi'ziːrən], v.a. catechise, instruct.

kategorisch [kate'goːrɪʃ], adj. categorical, definite.

Kater ['kaːtər], m. (—s, pl. —) tom-cat; (fig.) hangover; der gestiefelte —, Puss-in-Boots.

Katheder [ka'teːdər], n. (—s, pl. —) desk; rostrum; lecturing-desk; (fig.) professorial chair.

Kathedrale [kate'draːlə], f. (—, pl. —n) cathedral.

Katholik [kato'liːk], m. (—en, pl. —en) (Roman) Catholic.

katholisch [ka'toːlɪʃ], adj. (Roman) Catholic.

Kattun [ka'tuːn], m. (—s, pl. —e) calico, cotton.

Kätzchen ['kɛtsçən], n. (—s, pl. —) kitten; (Bot.) catkin.

Katze ['katsə], f. (—, pl. —n) cat; die — im Sack kaufen, buy a pig in a poke; für die —, no good at all, useless.

katzenartig ['katsənaːrtɪç], adj. cat-like, feline.

Katzenauge ['katsənaugə], n. (—s, pl. —n) cat's-eye.

Katzenbuckel ['katsənbukəl], m. (—s, pl. —) arched back of a cat.

Katzenjammer ['katsənjamər], m. (—s, pl. —) hangover.

Katzenmusik ['katsənmuziːk], f. (—, no pl.) caterwauling; cacophony, discordant music.

Katzensprung ['katsənʃpruŋ], m. (—es, no pl.) (fig.) stone's throw.

Kauderwelsch ['kaudərvɛlʃ], n. (—es, no pl.) gibberish, double-Dutch.

kauen ['kauən], v.a., v.n. chew.

kauern ['kauərn], v.n. cower, squat, crouch.

Kauf [kauf], m. (—es, pl. ⏑e) purchase, buy; bargain.

Kaufbummel ['kaufbuməl], m. (—s, no pl.) shopping-spree.

kaufen ['kaufən], v.a. (things) buy, purchase; (persons) bribe.

Käufer ['kɔyfər], m. (—s, pl. —) buyer, purchaser.

Kaufhaus ['kaufhaus], n. (—es, pl. ⏑er) department-store, emporium.

Kaufladen ['kaufˌlaːdən], m. (—s, pl. ⏑) shop.

käuflich ['kɔyflɪç], adj. (things) purchasable, marketable; (persons) open to bribery, venal.

Kaufmann ['kaufman], m. (—s, pl. Kaufleute) merchant; shopkeeper; (Am.) store-keeper.

kaufmännisch ['kaufmɛnɪʃ], adj. commercial, mercantile.

Kaugummi ['kaugumi], m. (—s, no pl.) chewing-gum.

Kaukasus ['kaukazus], m. Caucasus (Mountains).

Kaulquappe ['kaulkvapə], f. (—, pl. —n) (Zool.) tadpole.

kaum [kaum], adv. scarcely, hardly; no sooner.

Kaurimuschel ['kaurimuʃəl], f. (— pl. —n) (Zool.) cowrie-shell.

# Kettenstich

**Kautabak** ['kautabak], *m.* (—s, *no pl.*) chewing-tobacco.

**Kaution** [kau'tsjo:n], *f.* (—, *pl.* —en) security, bail, surety; *eine — stellen,* go, give *or* stand bail.

**Kautschuk** ['kautʃuk], *m.* (—s, *no pl.*) caoutchouc, India-rubber.

**Kauz** [kauts], *m.* (—es, *pl.* ⁺e) (*Orn.*) screech-owl; (*fig.*) *komischer —,* queer customer.

**Käuzchen** ['kɔytsçən], *n.* (—s, *pl.* —) little owl; (*fig.*) imp.

**Kavalier** [kava'li:r], *m.* (—s, *pl.* —e) gentleman; lady's man.

**keck** [kɛk], *adj.* bold, daring; pert, saucy.

**Kegel** ['ke:gəl], *m.* (—s, *pl.* —) ninepin, skittle; (*Geom.*) cone; *mit Kind und —,* bag and baggage.

**Kegelbahn** ['ke:gəlba:n], *f.* (—, *pl.* —en) skittle-alley, bowling-alley.

**kegelförmig** ['ke:gəlfœrmiç], *adj.* conical.

**kegeln** ['ke:gəln], *v.n.* bowl, play at ninepins.

**Kehle** ['ke:lə], *f.* (—, *pl.* —n) throat, windpipe.

**Kehlkopf** ['ke:lkɔpf], *m.* (—es, *pl.* ⁺e) larynx.

**Kehllaut** ['ke:llaut], *m.* (—es, *pl.* —e) (*Phonet.*) guttural sound.

**Kehlung** ['ke:luŋ], *f.* (—, *pl.* —en) channel, flute, groove.

**Kehraus** ['ke:raus], *m.* (—, *no pl.*) last dance; (*fig.*) break-up, end.

**kehren** ['ke:rən], *v.a.* sweep; turn; *den Rücken —,* turn o.'s back. — *v.r. sich — an,* pay attention to, regard.

**Kehricht** ['ke:riçt], *m.* (—s, *no pl.*) sweepings; rubbish.

**Kehrreim** ['ke:rraim], *m.* (—s, *pl.* —e) refrain.

**Kehrseite** ['ke:rzaitə], *f.* (—, *pl.* —n) reverse.

**kehrtmachen** ['ke:rtmaxən], *v.n.* turn around; (*Mil.*) face about; turn back.

**keifen** ['kaifən], *v.n.* scold, nag.

**Keil** [kail], *m.* (—s, *pl.* —e) wedge.

**Keile** ['kailə], *f.* (—, *no pl.*) blows; (*coll.*) hiding; — *kriegen,* get a thrashing.

**keilen** ['kailən], *v.a.* wedge; (*coll.*) thrash.

**Keilerei** [kailə'rai], *f.* (—, *pl.* —en) brawl, fight.

**keilförmig** ['kailfœrmiç], *adj.* wedge-shaped.

**Keilschrift** ['kailʃrift], *f.* (—, *pl.* —en) cuneiform writing.

**Keim** [kaim], *m.* (—es, *pl.* —e) germ, seed.

**keimen** ['kaimən], *v.n.* germinate.

**keimfrei** ['kaimfrai], *adj.* sterile, germ-free.

**keiner, -e, -es** ['kainər], *adj.* no, not a, not any. — *pron.* no one, none.

**keinerlei** ['kainərlai], *adj.* no, of no sort, no ... whatever.

**keineswegs** ['kainəsve:ks], *adv.* by no means, on no account.

**Keks** [ke:ks], *m.* (—es, *pl.* —e) biscuit.

**Kelch** [kɛlç], *m.* (—es, *pl.* —e) cup; (*Eccl.*) chalice; (*Bot.*) calyx.

**Kelchblatt** ['kɛlçblat], *n.* (—es, *pl.* ⁺er) sepal.

**kelchförmig** ['kɛlçfœrmiç], *adj.* cup-shaped.

**Kelle** ['kɛlə], *f.* (—, *pl.* —n) ladle; (*mason*) trowel.

**Keller** ['kɛlər], *m.* (—s, *pl.* —) cellar, basement.

**Kellergewölbe** ['kɛlərgəvœlbə], *n.* (—s, *pl.* —) vault.

**Kellner** ['kɛlnər], *m.* (—s, *pl.* —) waiter.

**keltern** ['kɛltərn], *v.a.* press (*grapes*).

**Kenia** ['ke:nja], *n.* Kenya.

**kennbar** ['kɛnba:r], *adj.* recognisable, conspicuous.

**kennen** ['kɛnən], *v.a. irr.* know, be acquainted with.

**Kenner** ['kɛnər], *m.* (—s, *pl.* —) connoisseur, expert.

**Kennkarte** ['kɛnkartə], *f.* (—, *pl.* —n) identity card.

**kenntlich** ['kɛntliç], *adj.* distinguishable.

**Kenntnis** ['kɛntnis], *f.* (—, *pl.* —se) knowledge; (*language*) command.

**Kennzeichen** ['kɛntsaiçən], *n.* (—s, *pl.* —) characteristic, distinguishing mark; sign; symptom; criterion.

**Kenterhaken** ['kɛntərha:kən], *m.* (—s, *pl.* —) grappling-iron.

**kentern** ['kɛntərn], *v.n.* (*aux.* sein) capsize.

**keramisch** [ke'ra:miʃ], *adj.* ceramic.

**Kerbe** ['kɛrbə], *f.* (—, *pl.* —n) notch, indentation.

**kerben** ['kɛrbən], *v.a.* notch.

**Kerbholz** ['kɛrphɔlts], *n.* (—es, *no pl.*) tally; *auf dem —,* on o.'s conscience, charged against o.

**Kerbtier** ['kɛrpti:r], *n.* (—es, *pl.* —e) insect.

**Kerker** ['kɛrkər], *m.* (—s, *pl.* —) prison, jail, gaol; dungeon.

**Kerl** [kɛrl], *m.* (—s, *pl.* —e) fellow, chap; (*Am.*) guy.

**Kern** [kɛrn], *m.* (—es, *pl.* —e) (*nut*) kernel; (*fruit*) stone; (*fig.*) heart, crux; pith; (*Phys.*) nucleus.

**kerngesund** ['kɛrngəzunt], *adj.* hale and hearty, fit as a fiddle.

**kernig** ['kɛrniç], *adj.* solid, pithy.

**Kernphysik** ['kɛrnfyzi:k], *f.* (—, *no pl.*) nuclear physics.

**Kernpunkt** ['kɛrnpuŋkt], *m.* (—es, *pl.* —e) gist, essential point.

**Kernwaffe** ['kɛrnvafə], *f.* (—, *pl.* —n) nuclear weapon.

**Kerze** ['kɛrtsə], *f.* (—, *pl.* —n) candle.

**Kessel** ['kɛsəl], *m.* (—s, *pl.* —) kettle, cauldron; (*steam*) boiler.

**Kesselschmied** ['kɛsəlʃmi:t], *m.* (—s, *pl.* —e) boiler-maker.

**Kesselstein** ['kɛsəlʃtain], *m.* (—s, *no pl.*) fur, deposit, scale (on boiler).

**Kette** ['kɛtə], *f.* (—, *pl.* —n) chain.

**ketten** ['kɛtən], *v.a.* chain, fetter.

**Kettenstich** ['kɛtənʃtiç], *m.* (—es, *pl.* —e) chain-stitch; (*Naut.*) chain-knot.

# Ketzer

Ketzer ['kɛtsər], m. (—s, pl. —) heretic.
Ketzerei [kɛtsə'raɪ], f. (—, pl. —en) heresy.
ketzerisch ['kɛtsərɪʃ], adj. heretical.
keuchen ['kɔʏçən], v.n. pant, puff, gasp.
Keuchhusten ['kɔʏçhu:stən], m. (—s, no pl.) whooping-cough.
Keule ['kɔʏlə], f. (—, pl. —n) club; (meat) leg.
keusch [kɔʏʃ], adj. chaste, pure.
kichern ['kɪçərn], v.n. titter, giggle.
Kiebitz ['ki:bɪts], m. (—es, pl. —e) (Orn.) lapwing, peewit; (fig.) on-looker; (Am.) rubber-neck (at chess or cards).
Kiefer (1) ['ki:fər], m. (—s, pl. —) jaw, jaw-bone.
Kiefer (2) ['ki:fər], f. (—, pl. —n) (Bot.) pine.
Kiel [ki:l], m. (—es, pl. —e) keel; (pen) quill.
Kielwasser ['ki:lvasər], n. (—s, no pl.) wake.
Kieme ['ki:mə], f. (—, pl. —n) (fish) gill.
Kien [ki:n], m. (—s, no pl.) pine-resin, resinous pinewood.
Kienspan ['ki:nʃpa:n], m. (—s, pl. —e) pine-splinter.
Kiepe ['ki:pə], f. (—, pl. —n) (dial.) creel, wicker basket.
Kies [ki:s], m. (—es, no pl.) gravel.
Kiesel ['ki:zəl], m. (—s, pl. —) pebble; flint.
Kieselsäure ['ki:zəlzɔʏrə], f. (—, no pl.) silicic acid.
Kieselstein ['ki:zəlʃtaɪn], m. (—s, pl. —e) pebble.
Kilogramm ['ki:logram], n. (—s, pl. —e) kilogramme (1000 grammes).
Kilometer ['ki:lome:tər], m. (—s, pl. —) kilometre; (Am.) kilometer (1000 metres).
Kimme ['kɪmə], f. (—, pl. —n) notch.
Kind [kɪnt], n. (—es, pl. —er) child; (law) infant; — und Kegel, bag and baggage.
Kind(e)l ['kɪnt(ə)l], n. (—s, pl. —) (dial.) small child, baby; Münchner —, Munich beer.
Kinderei [kɪndə'raɪ], f. (—, pl. —en) childishness; childish prank.
Kinderfräulein ['kɪndərfrɔʏlaɪn], n. (—s, pl. —) nurse, (coll.) nannie.
Kindergarten ['kɪndərgartən], m. (—s, pl. ˙) kindergarten, infant-school.
Kinderhort ['kɪndərhɔrt], m. (—s, pl. —e) crèche.
kinderleicht ['kɪndərlaɪçt], adj. ex-tremely easy, child's play.
Kindermärchen ['kɪndərmɛ:rçən], n. (—s, pl. —) fairy-tale.
Kinderstube ['kɪndərʃtu:bə], f. (—, pl. —n) nursery; eine gute —, a good upbringing.
Kinderwagen ['kɪndərva:gən], m. (—s, pl. —) perambulator, pram.
Kindesbeine ['kɪndəsbaɪnə], n. pl. von —n an, from infancy.

Kindeskind ['kɪndəskɪnt], n. (—es, pl. —er) (obs.) grandchild.
Kindheit ['kɪnthaɪt], f. (—, no pl.) childhood, infancy.
kindisch ['kɪndɪʃ], adj. childish.
kindlich ['kɪntlɪç], adj. childlike; naïve.
Kinn [kɪn], n. (—s, pl. —e) chin.
Kinnbacken ['kɪnbakən], m. (—s, pl. —) (Anat.) jaw-bone.
Kinnbackenkrampf ['kɪnbakən-krampf], m. (—s, pl. ˙e) (Med.) lock-jaw.
Kinnlade ['kɪnla:də], f. (—, pl. —n) (Anat.) jaw-bone.
Kino ['ki:no], n. (—s, pl. —s) cinema; (coll.) pictures; (Am.) motion picture theatre; motion pictures, (coll.) movies.
Kipfel ['kɪpfəl], n. (—s, pl. —) (dial.) roll, croissant.
kippen ['kɪpən], v.a. tilt, tip over.
Kirche ['kɪrçə], f. (—, pl. —n) church.
Kirchenbann ['kɪrçənban], m. (—s, no. pl.) excommunication.
Kirchenbuch ['kɪrçənbu:x], n. (—es, pl. ˙er) parish-register.
Kirchengut ['kɪrçəngu:t], n. (—es, pl. ˙er) church-property.
Kirchenlicht ['kɪrçənlɪçt], n. (—es, pl. —er) (fig.) shining light, bright spark.
Kirchenrecht ['kɪrçənrɛçt], n. (—es, no pl.) canon law.
Kirchenschiff ['kɪrçənʃɪf], n. (—es, pl. —e) nave.
Kirchenstuhl ['kɪrçənʃtu:l], n. (—es, pl. ˙e) pew.
Kirchenversammlung ['kɪrçənfer-zamluŋ], f. (—, pl. —en) synod; convocation.
Kirchenvorsteher ['kɪrçənforʃte:ər], m. (—s, pl. —) churchwarden.
kirchlich ['kɪrçlɪç], adj. ecclesiastic(al), religious.
Kirchspiel ['kɪrçʃpi:l], n. (—es, pl. —e) parish.
Kirchsprengel ['kɪrçʃprɛŋəl], m. (—s, pl. —) diocese.
Kirchturm ['kɪrçturm], m. (—es, pl. ˙e) steeple.
Kirchweih ['kɪrçvaɪ], f. (—, pl. —en) (dial.) church fair, parish fair.
Kirmes ['kɪrməs], f. (—, pl. —sen) see Kirchweih.
kirre ['kɪrə], adj. tame; (fig.) amenable.
kirren ['kɪrən], v.a. tame, allure. — v.n. coo.
Kirsch(branntwein) [kɪrʃ(brantvaɪn)], m. (—s, no pl.) cherry-brandy.
Kirsche ['kɪrʃə], f. (—, pl. —n) (Bot.) cherry; mit ihr ist nicht gut —n essen, she is hard to get on with or not pleasant to deal with.
Kirschsaft ['kɪrʃzaft], m. (—es, no pl.) cherry-juice.
Kirschwasser ['kɪrʃvasər], n. (—s, no pl.) cherry-brandy.
Kissen ['kɪsən], n. (—s, pl. —s) cushion, pillow.

# kleiden

**Kiste** ['kɪstə], *f.* (—, *pl.* —n) box, case, chest; crate; coffer.

**Kitsch** [kɪtʃ], *m.* (—es, *no pl.*) trash; rubbish.

**Kitt** [kɪt], *m.* (—s, *pl.* —e) cement; (*Glazing*) putty.

**Kittel** ['kɪtəl], *m.* (—s, *pl.* —) smock; overall, tunic; frock.

**kitten** ['kɪtən], *v.a.* cement, glue.

**Kitzchen** ['kɪtsçən], *n.* (—s, *pl.* —) kid; fawn; kitten.

**Kitzel** ['kɪtsəl], *m.* (—s, *no pl.*) tickling, titillation; itch; (*fig.*) desire, appetite.

**kitzeln** ['kɪtsəln], *v.a.* tickle, titillate.

**kitzlich** ['kɪtslɪç], *adj.* ticklish; (*fig.*) delicate.

**Kladderadatsch** ['kladəradatʃ], *m.* (—es, *no pl.*) bang; mess, muddle.

**klaffen** ['klafən], *v.n.* gape, yawn.

**kläffen** ['klɛfən], *v.n.* bark, yelp.

**Klafter** ['klaftər], *f.* (—, *pl.* —n) fathom; (*wood*) cord.

**klagbar** ['kla:kba:r], *adj.* (*Law*) actionable.

**Klage** ['kla:gə], *f.* (—, *pl.* —n) complaint; (*Law*) suit, action.

**Klagelied** ['kla:gəli:t], *n.* (—es, *pl.* —er) dirge, lamentation.

**klagen** ['kla:gən], *v.n.* complain, lament; (*Law*) sue.

**Kläger** ['klɛ:gər], *m.* (—s, *pl.* —) complainant; (*Law*) plaintiff.

**Klageschrift** ['kla:gəʃrɪft], *f.* (—, *pl.* —en) bill of indictment; written complaint.

**kläglich** ['klɛ:klɪç], *adj.* woeful, pitiful, deplorable.

**klaglos** ['kla:klo:s], *adj.* uncomplaining.

**Klamm** [klam], *f.* (—, *pl.* —en) gorge, ravine.

**klamm** [klam], *adj.* tight, narrow; numb; clammy.

**Klammer** ['klamər], *f.* (—, *pl.* —n) clamp, clasp, hook; peg; clip; bracket, parenthesis.

**klammern** ['klamərn], *v.a.* fasten, peg. — *v.r. sich — an*, cling to.

**Klang** [klaŋ], *m.* (—es, *pl.* ˙-e) sound, tone; *ohne Sang und —*, unheralded and unsung.

**klanglos** ['klaŋlo:s], *adj.* soundless.

**klangnachahmend** ['klaŋnaxa:mənt], *adj.* onomatopoeic.

**klangvoll** ['klaŋfɔl], *adj.* sonorous.

**Klappe** ['klapə], *f.* (—, *pl.* —en) flap; (*Tech.*) valve; (*vulg.*) *halt die —!* shut up!

**klappen** ['klapən], *v.n.* flap; (*fig.*) tally, square; *es hat geklappt*, it worked.

**Klapper** ['klapər], *f.* (—, *pl.* —n) rattle.

**klappern** ['klapərn], *v.n.* rattle; (*teeth*) chatter.

**Klapperschlange** ['klapərʃlaŋə], *f.* (—, *pl.* —n) (*Zool.*) rattle-snake.

**Klapphut** ['klaphu:t], *m.* (—es, *pl.* ˙-e) opera-hat; chapeau-claque.

**Klapps** [klaps], *m.* (—es, *pl.* ˙-e) slap, smack; (*fig.*) touch of madness, kink.

**Klappstuhl** ['klapʃtu:l], *m.* (—s, *pl.* ˙-e) camp-stool, folding-chair.

**Klapptisch** ['klaptɪʃ], *m.* (—es, *pl.* —e) folding-table.

**klar** [kla:r], *adj.* clear; bright; (*fig.*) evident; plain, distinct.

**Kläranlage** ['klɛ:ranla:gə], *f.* (—, *pl.* —n) sewage-farm; filter plant.

**klären** ['klɛ:rən], *v.a.* clear.

**Klarheit** ['kla:rhaɪt], *f.* (—, *no pl.*) clearness, plainness.

**Klarinette** [klari'nɛtə], *f.* (—, *pl.* —n) (*Mus.*) clarinet.

**Klärmittel** ['klɛ:rmɪtəl], *n.* (—s, *pl.* —) clarifier.

**Klärung** ['klɛ:ruŋ], *f.* (—, *pl.* —en) clarification; (*fig.*) elucidation.

**Klasse** ['klasə], *f.* (—, *pl.* —n) class, order; (*Sch.*) form.

**klassifizieren** [klasifi'tsi:rən], *v.a.* classify.

**Klassiker** ['klasıkər], *m.* (—s, *pl.* —) classic.

**klassisch** ['klasɪʃ], *adj.* classic(al), standard.

**Klatsch** [klatʃ], *m.* (—es, *no pl.*) gossip, scandal.

**klatschen** ['klatʃən], *v.n.* clap; gossip; (*rain*) patter; *Beifall —*, applaud.

**Klatscherei** [klatʃə'raɪ], *f.* (—, *pl.* —en) gossip, scandalmongering.

**klauben** ['klaubən], *v.a.* pick.

**Klaue** ['klauə], *f.* (—, *pl.* —n) claw, talon; paw.

**klauen** ['klauən], *v.a.* steal, (*coll.*) pinch.

**Klauenseuche** ['klauənzɔyçə], *f.* (—, *pl.* —n) *Maul und —*, foot and mouth disease.

**Klause** ['klauzə], *f.* (—, *pl.* —n) cell, hermitage; (*coll.*) den.

**Klausel** ['klauzəl], *f.* (—, *pl.* —n) clause, paragraph.

**Klausner** ['klausnər], *m.* (—s, *pl.* —) hermit, recluse, anchorite.

**Klausur** [klau'zu:r], *f.* (—, *pl.* —en) seclusion; written examination.

**Klaviatur** [klavja'tu:r], *f.* (—, *pl.* —en) keyboard.

**Klavier** [kla'vi:r], *n.* (—s, *pl.* —e) piano, pianoforte.

**Klavierstück** [kla'vi:rʃtyk], *n.* (—s, *pl.* —e) piece of piano music.

**Klebemittel** ['kle:bəmɪtəl], *n.* (—s, *pl.* —) adhesive, glue.

**kleben** ['kle:bən], *v.a.* paste, stick, glue. — *v.n.* stick, adhere.

**klebrig** ['kle:brɪç], *adj.* sticky; clammy.

**Klebstoff** ['kle:pʃtɔf], *m.* (—es, *no pl.*) gum; glue.

**Klecks** [klɛks], *m.* (—es, *pl.* —e) blot; blotch.

**Kleckser** ['klɛksər], *m.* (—s, *pl.* —) scrawler; (*painter*) dauber.

**Klee** [kle:], *m.* (—s, *no pl.*) (*Bot.*) clover, trefoil.

**Kleid** [klaɪt], *n.* (—es, *pl.* —er) frock, garment, dress; gown; (*Poet.*) garb; (*pl.*) clothes; *—er machen Leute*, clothes make the man.

**Kleidchen** ['klaɪtçən], *n.* (—s, *pl.* —) child's dress.

**kleiden** ['klaɪdən], *v.a.* dress, clothe.

123

**Kleiderbügel** ['klaɪdərby:gəl], *m.* (—s, *pl.* —) coat-hanger.

**Kleiderpuppe** ['klaɪdərpupə], *f.* (—, *pl.* —n) tailor's dummy.

**Kleiderschrank** ['klaɪdərʃraŋk], *m.* (—s, *pl.* ⸚e) wardrobe.

**kleidsam** ['klaɪtza:m], *adj.* becoming; well-fitting, a good fit.

**Kleidung** ['klaɪduŋ], *f.* (—, *no pl.*) clothing, clothes, dress.

**Kleie** ['klaɪə], *f.* (—, *no pl.*) bran.

**klein** [klaɪn], *adj.* little, small; minute; petty; *ein — wenig,* a little bit.

**Kleinasien** [klaɪn'a:zjən], *n.* Asia Minor.

**Kleinbahn** ['klaɪnba:n], *f.* (—, *pl.* —en) narrow-gauge railway.

**kleinbürgerlich** ['klaɪnbyrgərlɪç], *adj.* (petit) bourgeois.

**Kleingeld** ['klaɪngɛlt], *n.* (—(e)s, *no pl.*) small change.

**kleingläubig** ['klaɪnglɔybɪç], *adj.* faint-hearted.

**Kleinhandel** ['klaɪnhandəl], *m.* (—s, *no pl.*) retail-trade.

**Kleinigkeit** ['klaɪnɪçkaɪt], *f.* (—, *pl.* —en) trifle, small matter.

**Kleinkram** ['klaɪnkra:m], *m.* (—s, *no pl.*) trifles.

**kleinlaut** ['klaɪnlaut], *adj.* subdued, dejected, low-spirited.

**kleinlich** ['klaɪnlɪç], *adj.* petty; mean; narrow-minded; pedantic.

**Kleinmut** ['klaɪnmu:t], *m.* (—es, *no pl.*) faint-heartedness; dejection.

**Kleinod** ['klaɪno:t], *n.* (—s, *pl.* —ien) jewel; trinket.

**Kleinstadt** ['klaɪnʃtat], *f.* (—, *pl.* ⸚e) small town.

**Kleister** ['klaɪstər], *m.* (—s, *no pl.*) paste.

**Klemme** ['klɛmə], *f.* (—, *pl.* —n) (*Tech.*) vice; clamp; (*fig.*) difficulty, straits; (*coll.*) fix, jam.

**klemmen** ['klɛmən], *v.a.* pinch, squeeze, jam.

**Klemmer** ['klɛmər], *m.* (—s, *pl.*—) (*eye*) glasses, pince-nez.

**Klempner** ['klɛmpnər], *m.* (—s, *pl.*—) tin-smith; plumber.

**Klerus** ['kle:rus], *m.* (—, *no pl.*) clergy.

**Klette** ['klɛtə], *f.* (—, *pl.* —n) burdock, bur(r); (*fig.*) hanger-on.

**klettern** ['klɛtərn], *v.n.* (*aux.* sein) climb, clamber.

**Klima** ['kli:ma], *n.* (—s, *pl.* —s) climate.

**Klimaanlage** ['kli:maanla:gə], *f.* (—, *pl.* —n) air conditioning plant.

**Klimbim** ['klɪm'bɪm], *m.* (—s, *no pl.*) goings-on; festivity; fuss; *der ganze —,* the whole caboodle.

**klimpern** ['klɪmpərn], *v.n.* (*piano*) strum; (*money*) jingle.

**Klinge** ['klɪŋə], *f.* (—, *pl.* —n) blade.

**Klingel** ['klɪŋəl], *f.* (—, *pl.* —n) (*door, telephone*) bell.

**Klingelbeutel** ['klɪŋəlbɔytəl], *m.* (—s, *pl.*—) collecting-bag.

**klingeln** ['klɪŋəln], *v.n.* ring, tinkle.

**Klingelzug** ['klɪŋəltsu:k], *m.* (—es, *pl.* ⸚e) bell-rope, bell-pull.

**klingen** ['klɪŋən], *v.n. irr.* sound; (*metals*) clang; (*ears*) tingle; —*de Münze,* hard cash, ready money.

**Klinke** ['klɪŋkə], *f.* (—, *pl.* —en) (*door*) handle, latch.

**klipp** [klɪp], *adv.* — *und klar,* as clear as daylight.

**Klippe** ['klɪpə], *f.* (—, *pl.* —n) cliff, crag, rock.

**klirren** ['klɪrən], *v.n.* clatter, rattle.

**Klischee** [kli'ʃe:], *n.* (—s, *pl.* —s) (*Typ.*) plate, printing-block; (*fig.*) cliché, hackneyed expression, tag.

**Klistier** [klɪ'sti:r], *n.* (—s, *pl.* —e) (*Med.*) enema.

**Kloake** [klo'a:kə], *f.* (—, *pl.* —n) sewer, drain.

**Kloben** ['klo:bən], *m.* (—s, *pl.* —) log, block (of wood); pulley.

**klopfen** ['klɔpfən], *v.a., v.n.* knock, beat.

**Klöppel** ['klœpəl], *m.* (—s, *pl.* —) mallet; (*bell*) tongue, clapper; (*drum*) stick; (*lace*) bobbin.

**klöppeln** ['klœpəln], *v.a* make (bone) lace.

**Klöppelspitze** ['klœpəlʃpɪtsə], *f.* (—, *no pl.*) bone-lace.

**Klops** [klɔps], *m.* (—es, *pl.* —e) meat-dumpling.

**Klosett** [klo'zɛt], *n.* (—s, *pl.* —e) lavatory, water-closet, toilet.

**Kloß** [klo:s], *m.* (—es, *pl.* ⸚e) dumpling.

**Kloster** ['klo:stər], *n.* (—s, *pl.* ⸚) cloister; monastery; convent.

**Klostergang** ['klo:stərgaŋ], *m.* (—es, *pl.* ⸚e) cloisters.

**Klotz** [klɔts], *m.* (—es, *pl.* ⸚e) block, trunk, stump; (*fig.*) *ein grober —,* a great lout.

**klotzig** ['klɔtsɪç], *adj.* cloddy; lumpish; (*sl.*) enormous.

**Klub** [klup], *m.* (—s, *pl.* —s) club.

**Kluft** [kluft], *f.* (—, *pl.* ⸚e) gap; gulf, chasm; (*fig.*) cleavage.

**klug** [klu:k], *adj.* clever, wise, prudent, judicious, sagacious; *ich kann daraus nicht — werden,* I cannot make head nor tail of it.

**klügeln** ['kly:gəln], *v.n.* ponder; quibble.

**Klugheit** ['klu:khaɪt], *f.* (—, *no pl.*) cleverness, wisdom, prudence, judiciousness.

**Klumpfuß** ['klumpfu:s], *m.* (—es, *pl.* ⸚e) club-foot.

**Klumpen** ['klumpən], *m.* (—s, *pl.* —) lump, mass, clod; (*blood*) clot; (*metal*) ingot; (*gold*) nugget.

**Klüngel** ['klyŋəl], *m.* (—s, *pl.* —) clique, set.

**knabbern** ['knabərn], *v.n.* nibble.

**Knabe** ['kna:bə], *m.* (—n, *pl.* —n) boy.

**Knäblein** ['knɛ:blaɪn], *n.* (—s, *pl.* —) (*Poet.*) baby boy, small boy.

**knack** [knak], *int.* crack! snap!

**Knäckebrot** ['knɛkəbro:t], *n.* (—es, *no pl.*) crispbread.

**knacken** ['knakən], *v.a.* crack.

**Knackmandel** ['knakmandəl], *f.* (—, *pl.* —n) shell-almond.

**Knackwurst** ['knakvurst], *f.* (—, *pl.* ⸚e) saveloy.

**Knacks** [knaks], *m.* (—es, *pl.* —e) crack.

**knacksen** ['knaksən], *v.n.* (*coll.*) crack.

**Knall** [knal], *m.* (—es, *pl.* —e) report, bang, detonation; — *und Fall*, quite suddenly, then and there.

**Knallbüchse** ['knalbyksə], *f.* (—, *pl.* —n) pop-gun.

**Knalleffekt** ['knalɛfɛkt], *m.* (—s, *pl.* —e) coup de théâtre; sensation.

**knallen** ['knalən], *v.n.* pop, explode, crack.

**Knallgas** ['knalga:s], *n.* (—es, *no pl.*) oxyhydrogen gas.

**knallrot** ['knalro:t], *adj.* scarlet; glaring red.

**knapp** [knap], *adj.* tight; scarce, insufficient; (*style*) concise; (*majority*) narrow, bare.

**Knappe** ['knapə], *m.* (—n, *pl.* —n) esquire, shield-bearer; miner.

**Knappheit** ['knaphaɪt], *f.* (—, *no pl.*) scarcity, shortage.

**Knappschaft** ['knapʃaft], *f.* (—, *pl.* —en) miners' association.

**Knarre** ['knarə], *f.* (—, *pl.* —n) rattle.

**knarren** ['knarən], *v.n.* rattle, creak.

**Knaster** ['knastər], *m.* (—s, *pl.* —) tobacco.

**knattern** ['knatərn], *v.n.* crackle.

**Knäuel** ['knɔyəl], *m., n.* (—s, *pl.* —) skein, clew, ball.

**Knauf** [knauf], *m.* (—es, *pl.* ⸚e) (*stick*) knob, head; (*Archit.*) capital.

**Knauser** ['knauzər], *m.* (—s, *pl.* —) niggard, skinflint.

**knausern** ['knauzərn], *v.n.* be stingy, scrimp.

**Knebel** ['kne:bəl], *m.* (—s, *pl.* —) cudgel; gag.

**knebeln** ['kne:bəln], *v.a.* tie, bind; gag; (*fig.*) muzzle.

**Knecht** [knɛçt], *m.* (—es, *pl.* —e) servant, farm hand, menial; vassal, slave.

**Knechtschaft** ['knɛçtʃaft], *f.* (—, *no pl.*) servitude, slavery.

**kneifen** ['knaɪfən], *v.a. irr.* pinch. — *v.n.* (*fig. coll.*) back out (of), shirk.

**Kneifer** ['knaɪfər], *m.* (—s, *pl.* —) pince-nez.

**Kneifzange** ['knaɪftsaŋə], *f.* (—, *pl.* —n) pincers.

**Kneipe** ['knaɪpə], *f.* (—, *pl.* —n) pub; saloon.

**kneten** ['kne:tən], *v.a.* knead; massage.

**knick(e)beinig** ['knɪk(ə)baɪnɪç], *adj.* knock-kneed.

**knicken** ['knɪkən], *v.a.* crack, break.

**Knicks** [knɪks], *m.* (—es, *pl.* —e) curtsy.

**knicksen** ['knɪksən], *v.n.* curtsy.

**Knie** [kni:], *n.* (—s, *pl.* —) knee; *etwas übers — brechen*, make short work of.

**Kniekehle** ['kni:ke:lə], *f.* (—, *pl.* —n) hollow of the knee.

**knien** ['kni:ən], *v.n.* kneel.

**Kniescheibe** ['kni:ʃaɪbə], *f.* (—, *pl.* —n) knee-cap.

**Kniff** [knɪf], *m.* (—es, *pl.* —e) fold; (*fig.*) trick, knack, dodge.

**knipsen** ['knɪpsən], *v.a.* (*tickets*) clip, punch; (*Phot.*) take a snap of.

**Knirps** [knɪrps], *m.* (—es, *pl.* —e) pigmy; (*fig.*) urchin.

**knirschen** ['knɪrʃən], *v.n.* crunch, grate, gnash (teeth).

**knistern** ['knɪstərn], *v.n.* crackle.

**knittern** ['knɪtərn], *v.a.* rumple, wrinkle, crinkle, crease.

**Knobel** ['kno:bəl], *m. pl.* dice.

**Knoblauch** ['kno:blaux], *m.* (—s, *no pl.*) (*Bot.*) garlic.

**Knöchel** ['knœçəl], *m.* (—s, *pl.* —) knuckle, joint; ankle.

**Knochen** ['knɔxən], *m.* (—s, *pl.* —) bone.

**Knochengerüst** ['knɔxəngəryst], *n.* (—es, *pl.* —e) skeleton.

**knöchern** ['knœçərn], *adj.* made of bone.

**knochig** ['knɔxɪç], *adj.* bony.

**Knödel** ['knø:dəl], *m.* (—s, *pl.* —) dumpling.

**Knollen** ['knɔlən], *m.* (—s, *pl.* —) lump, clod; (*Bot.*) tuber, bulb.

**knollig** ['knɔlɪç], *adj.* knobby, bulbous.

**Knopf** [knɔpf], *m.* (—es, *pl.* ⸚e) button; stud; (*stick*) head, knob.

**knöpfen** ['knœpfən], *v.a.* button.

**Knorpel** ['knɔrpəl], *m.* (—s, *pl.* —) gristle, cartilage.

**knorplig** ['knɔrplɪç], *adj.* gristly.

**knorrig** ['knɔrɪç], *adj.* knotty, gnarled.

**Knospe** ['knɔspə], *f.* (—, *pl.* —n) bud.

**Knote** ['kno:tə], *m.* (—n, *pl.* —n) (*fig.*) bounder; lout.

**Knoten** ['kno:tən], *m.* (—s, *pl.* —) knot; (*fig.*) difficulty; (*Theat.*) plot.

**Knotenpunkt** ['kno:tənpuŋkt], *m.* (—es, *pl.* —e) (*Railw.*) junction.

**Knotenstock** ['kno:tənʃtɔk], *m.* (—es, *pl.* ⸚e) knotty stick.

**knotig** ['kno:tɪç], *adj.* knotty, nodular.

**knüllen** ['knylən], *v.a.* crumple.

**knüpfen** ['knypfən], *v.a.* tie; knot; form (a friendship etc.).

**Knüppel** ['knypəl], *m.* (—s, *pl.* —) cudgel.

**knurren** ['knurən], *v.n.* grunt, snarl; (*fig.*) growl, grumble.

**knurrig** ['knurɪç], *adj.* surly, grumpy.

**knusprig** ['knusprɪç], *adj.* crisp, crunchy.

**Knute** ['knu:tə], *f.* (—, *pl.* —n) knout.

**knutschen** ['knu:tʃən], *v.r. sich* —, (*coll.*) cuddle; (*Am.*) neck.

**Knüttel** [knytəl], *m.* (—s, *pl.* —) cudgel, bludgeon.

**Knüttelvers** ['knytəlfɛrs], *m.* (—es, *pl.* —e) doggerel, rhyme.

**Kobalt** ['ko:balt], *m.* (—s, *no pl.*) cobalt.

**Kobaltblau** ['ko:baltblau], *n.* (—s, *no pl.*) smalt.

# Koben

**Koben** ['ko:bən], *m.* (—s, *pl.* —) pig-sty.

**Kober** ['ko:bər], *m.* (—s, *pl.* —) (*dial.*) basket, hamper.

**Kobold** ['ko:bɔlt], *m.* (—(e)s, *pl.* —e) goblin, hobgoblin.

**Koch** [kɔx], *m.* (—es, *pl.* ⁓e) cook, chef.

**kochen** ['kɔxən], *v.a.* cook, boil. — *v.n.* boil; (*fig.*) seethe.

**Kocher** ['kɔxər], *m.* (—s, *pl.* —) boiler.

**Köcher** ['kœçər], *m.* (—s, *pl.* —) quiver.

**Köchin** ['kœçin], *f.* (—, *pl.* —nen) (female) cook.

**Kochsalz** ['kɔxzalts], *n.* (—es, *no pl.*) common salt.

**Köder** ['kø:dər], *m.* (—s, *pl.* —) bait, lure; (*fig.*) decoy.

**ködern** ['kø:dərn], *v.a.* bait; (*fig.*) decoy.

**Kodex** ['ko:dɛks], *m.* (—es, *pl.* —e) codex; old MS.; (*Law*) code.

**kodifizieren** [kodifi'tsi:rən], *v.a.* codify.

**Koffein** [kɔfɛ'i:n], *n.* (—s, *no pl.*) caffeine.

**Koffer** ['kɔfər], *m.* (—s, *pl.* —) box, trunk, suitcase, portmanteau.

**Kofferradio** ['kɔfərra:djo], *n.* (—s, *pl.* —s) portable radio.

**Kofferraum** ['kɔfərraum], *m.* (—s, *no pl.*) (*Motor.*) boot, (*Am.*) trunk.

**Kohl** [ko:l], *m.* (—s, *pl.* ⁓e) (*Bot.*) cabbage; (*no pl.*) (*fig.*) nonsense, rot.

**Kohle** ['ko:lə], *f.* (—, *pl.* —n) coal.

**Kohlenflöz** ['ko:lənflø:ts], *n.* (—es, *pl.* —e) coal-seam.

**Kohlenoxyd** ['ko:lənɔksy:t], *n.* (—s, *no pl.*) carbon monoxide.

**Kohlensäure** ['ko:lənzɔyrə], *f.* (—, *no pl.*) carbonic acid.

**Kohlenstift** ['ko:lənʃtift], *m.* (—es, *pl.* —e) charcoal-crayon.

**Köhler** ['kø:lər], *m.* (—s, *pl.* —) charcoal-burner.

**Koje** ['ko:jə], *f.* (—, *pl.* —n) (*Naut.*) berth, bunk.

**Kokarde** [kɔ'kardə], *f.* (—, *pl.* —n) cockade.

**kokett** [ko'kɛt], *adj.* coquettish.

**Kokette** [ko'kɛtə], *f.* (—, *pl.* —n) coquette, flirt.

**kokettieren** [kokɛ'ti:rən], *v.n.* flirt.

**Kokon** [ko'kɔ̃], *m.* (—s, *pl.* —s) cocoon.

**Kokosnuß** ['ko:kɔsnus], *f.* (—, *pl.* ⁓sse) (*Bot.*) coconut.

**Koks** [ko:ks], *m.* (—es, *pl.* —e) coke.

**Kolben** ['kɔlbən], *m.* (—s, *pl.* —) club: (*rifle*) butt-end; (*engine*) piston; (*Chem.*) retort.

**Kolbenstange** ['kɔlbənʃtaŋə], *f.* (—, *pl.* —n) piston-rod.

**Kolibri** ['ko:libri:], *m.* (—s, *pl.* —s) (*Orn.*) humming-bird.

**Kolkrabe** ['kɔlkra:bə], *m.* (—n, *pl.* —n) (*Orn.*) raven.

**Kolleg** [kɔ'le:k], *n.* (—s, *pl.* —ien) course of lectures; lecture.

**Kollege** [kɔ'le:gə], *m.* (—n, *pl.* —n) colleague.

**Kollekte** [kɔ'lɛktə], *f.* (—, *pl.* —n) collection; (*Eccl.*) collect.

**Koller** ['kɔlər], *m.* (—s, *no pl.*) frenzy, rage.

**kollidieren** [kɔli'di:rən], *v.n.* collide.

**Köln** [kœln], *n.* Cologne.

**kölnisch** ['kœlniʃ], *adj.* of Cologne; —*Wasser*, eau de Cologne.

**kolonisieren** [koloni'zi:rən], *v.a.* colonise.

**Kolonnade** [kolo'na:də], *f.* (— *pl.* —n) colonnade.

**Koloratur** [kolora'tu:r], *f.* (—, *pl.* —n) coloratura.

**kolorieren** [kolo'ri:rən], *v.a.* colour.

**Koloß** [ko'lɔs], *m.* (—sses, *pl.* —sse) colossus.

**Kolportage** [kɔlpɔr'ta:ʒə], *f.* (—, *pl.* —n) colportage, door-to-door sale of books; sensationalism.

**Kolportageroman** [kɔlpɔr'ta:ʒəroma:n], *m.* (—s, *pl.* —e) penny dreadful, shocker.

**kolportieren** [kɔlpɔr'ti:rən], *v.a.* hawk; spread, disseminate.

**Kombinationsgabe** [kɔmbina'tsjo:nsga:bə], *f.* (—, *pl.* —n) power of deduction.

**kombinieren** [kɔmbi'ni:rən], *v.a.* combine; deduce.

**Kombüse** [kɔm'by:zə], *f.* (— *pl.* —n) galley, caboose.

**Komik** ['ko:mik], *f.* (—, *no pl.*) comicality; humour; funny side.

**Komiker** ['ko:mikər], *m.* (—s, *pl.* —) comedian.

**komisch** ['ko:miʃ], *adj.* comical, funny; peculiar, strange, odd.

**Kommandantur** [kɔmandan'tu:r], *f.* (—, *pl.* —en) commander's office; garrison headquarters

**kommandieren** [kɔman'di:rən], *v.a.* command.

**Kommanditgesellschaft** [kɔman'di:tgəzɛlʃaft], *f.* (—, *pl.* —en) limited partnership.

**Kommando** [kɔ'mando], *n.* (—s, *pl.* —s) command.

**kommen** ['kɔmən], *v.n. irr.* (*aux.* sein) come, arrive; come about; *um etwas* —, lose s.th.; *zu etwas* —, come by s.th.; *zu sich* —, come to, regain consciousness.

**Kommentar** [kɔmɛn'ta:r], *m.* (—s, *pl.* —e) comment, commentary.

**Kommers** [kɔ'mɛrs], *m.* (—es, *pl.* —e) students' festivity; drinking party.

**Kommersbuch** [kɔ'mɛrsbu:x], *n.* (—es, *pl.* ⁓er) students' song-book.

**kommerziell** [kɔmɛrts'jɛl], *adj.* commercial.

**Kommerzienrat** [kɔ'mɛrtsjənra:t], *m.* (—s, *pl.* ⁓e) Councillor to the Chamber of Commerce.

**Kommilitone** [kɔmili'to:nə], *m.* (—n, *pl.* —n) fellow-student.

**Kommis** [kɔ'mi:], *m.* (—, *pl.* —) clerk.

**Kommiß** [kɔ'mis], *m.* (—sses, *pl.* —) military fatigue-dress; (*fig.*) military service.

**Kommissar** [kɔmɪ'saːr], m. (—s, pl. —e) commissioner.

**Kommissariat** [kɔmɪsar'jaːt], n. (—s, pl. —e) commissioner's office.

**Kommißbrot** [kɔ'mɪsbroːt], n. (—es, no pl.) (coarse) army bread.

**Kommission** [kɔmɪs'joːn], f. (—, pl. —en) commission, mission, committee.

**kommod** [kɔ'moːd], adj. (coll.) snug, comfortable.

**Kommode** [kɔ'moːdə], f. (—, pl. —n) chest of drawers.

**Kommune** [kɔ'muːnə], f. (—, pl. —n) (coll.) Communist Party; Reds.

**Kommunismus** [kɔmu'nɪsmus], m. (—, no pl.) Communism.

**kommunistisch** [kɔmu'nɪstɪʃ], adj. Communist.

**Komödiant** [kɔmød'jant], m. (—en, pl. —en) comedian, player; humbug.

**Komödie** [kɔ'møːdjə], f. (—, pl. —n) comedy, play; make-believe; — spielen, a (fig.) sham, pretend, play-act.

**Kompagnon** ['kɔmpanjɔ̃], m. (—s, pl. —s) partner, associate.

**Kompanie** [kɔmpa'niː], f. (—, pl. —n) (Mil.) company; (Comm.) partnership, company.

**Kompaß** ['kɔmpas], m. (—sses, pl. —sse) compass.

**Kompaßrose** ['kɔmpasroːzə], f. (—, pl. —n) compass-card.

**kompensieren** [kɔmpɛn'ziːrən], v.a. compensate.

**komplementär** [kɔmpləmɛn'tɛːr], adj. complementary.

**komplett** [kɔm'plɛt], adj. complete.

**komplimentieren** [kɔmplimɛn'tiːrən], v.a. compliment, flatter.

**Komplize** [kɔm'pliːtsə], f. (—n, pl. —n) accomplice.

**kompliziert** [kɔmpli'tsiːrt], adj. complicated.

**Komplott** [kɔm'plɔt], n. (—s, pl. —e) plot, conspiracy.

**Komponente** [kɔmpo'nɛntə], f. (—, pl. —n) component part; constituent.

**komponieren** [kɔmpo'niːrən], v.a. compose, set to music.

**Komponist** [kɔmpo'nɪst], m. (—en, pl. —en) composer.

**Kompositum** [kɔm'poːzɪtum], n. (—s, pl. —ta) (Gram.) compound word.

**Kompott** [kɔm'pɔt], n. (—s, pl. —e) stewed fruit, compote; sweet, dessert.

**Kompresse** [kɔm'prɛsə], f. (—, pl. —n) compress.

**komprimieren** [kɔmpri'miːrən], v.a. compress.

**Kompromiß** [kɔmpro'mɪs], m. (—sses, pl. —sse) compromise, settlement.

**kompromittieren** [kɔmprɔmɪ'tiːrən], v.a. compromise. — v.r. sich —, compromise o.s.

**kondensieren** [kɔndɛn'ziːrən], v.a. condense.

**Konditor** [kɔn'diːtɔr], m. (—s, pl. —en) confectioner, pastry-cook.

**Konditorei** [kɔnditɔ'raɪ], f. (—, pl. —en) confectioner's shop, pastry-shop; café.

**kondolieren** [kɔndo'liːrən], v.n. condole with s.o.

**Kondukteur** [kɔnduk'tøːr], m. (—s, pl. —e) (Swiss & Austr. dial.) guard (on train), conductor (on tram or bus).

**Konfekt** [kɔn'fɛkt], n. (—s, pl. —e) chocolates; candy.

**Konfektion** [kɔnfɛk'tsjoːn], f. (—, no pl.) ready-made clothes; outfitting.

**Konfektionär** [kɔnfɛktsjo'nɛːr], m. (—s, pl. —e) outfitter.

**Konferenz** [kɔnfe'rɛnts], f. (—, pl. —en) conference.

**konfessionell** [kɔnfɛsjo'nɛl], adj. denominational, confessional.

**Konfirmand** [kɔnfɪr'mant], m. (—en, pl. —en) confirmation candidate.

**konfirmieren** [kɔnfɪr'miːrən], v.a. (Eccl.) confirm.

**konfiszieren** [kɔnfɪs'tsiːrən], v.a. confiscate.

**Konfitüren** [kɔnfi'tyːrən], f. pl. confectionery, candied fruit, preserves.

**konform** [kɔn'fɔrm], adj. in conformity (with).

**konfus** [kɔn'fuːs], adj. confused, puzzled, disconcerted.

**Kongo** ['kɔŋgo], m. Congo.

**Kongruenz** [kɔŋgru'ɛnts], f. (—, no pl.) congruity.

**König** ['køːnɪç], m. (—s, pl. —e) king.

**Königin** ['køːnɪgɪn], f. (—, pl. —nen) queen.

**königlich** ['køːnɪçlɪç], adj. royal, regal, kingly, king-like.

**Königreich** ['køːnɪçraɪç], n. (—(e)s, pl. —e) kingdom.

**Königsadler** ['køːnɪçsaːdlər], m. (—s, pl. —) golden eagle.

**Königsschlange** ['køːnɪçsʃlaŋə], f. (—, pl. —n) (Zool.) boa constrictor.

**Königstiger** ['køːnɪçstiːgər], m. (—s, pl. —) (Zool.) Bengal tiger.

**Königtum** ['køːnɪçtuːm], n. (—s, pl.) kingship.

**Konjunktur** [kɔnjuŋk'tuːr], f. (—, pl. —en) state of the market, (coll.) boom.

**Konkordat** [kɔnkɔr'daːt], n. (—s, pl. —e) concordat.

**konkret** [kɔn'kreːt], adj. concrete.

**Konkurrent** [kɔnku'rɛnt], m. (—en, pl. —en) competitor, (business) rival.

**Konkurrenz** [kɔnku'rɛnts], f. (—, no pl.) competition.

**konkurrieren** [kɔnku'riːrən], v.n. compete.

**Konkurs** [kɔn'kurs], m. (—es, pl. —e) bankruptcy.

**Konkursmasse** [kɔn'kursmasə], f. (—, pl. —n) bankrupt's estate, bankrupt's stock.

**Können** ['kœnən], n. (—s, no pl.) ability; knowledge.

**können** ['kœnən], v.a., v.n. irr. be able to, be capable of; understand; ich kann, I can; er kann Englisch, he speaks English.

# konsequent

**konsequent** [kɔnzeˈkvɛnt], *adj.* consistent.

**Konsequenz** [kɔnzeˈkvɛnts], *f.* (—, *pl.* —en) (*characteristic*) consistency; (*result*) consequence.

**Konservatorium** [kɔnzɛrvaˈtoːrjum], *n.* (—s, *pl.* —rien) (*Mus.*) conservatoire, conservatorium.

**Konserve** [kɔnˈzɛrvə], *f.* (—, *pl.* —n) preserve; tinned *or* (*Am.*) canned food.

**konservieren** [kɔnzɛrˈviːrən], *v.a.* preserve.

**Konsistorium** [kɔnzɪsˈtoːrjum], *n.* (—s, *pl.* —rien) (*Eccl.*) consistory.

**Konsole** [kɔnˈzoːlə], *f.* (—, *pl.* —n) bracket.

**konsolidieren** [kɔnzoliˈdiːrən], *v.a.* consolidate.

**Konsonant** [kɔnzoˈnant], *m.* (—en, *pl.* —en) (*Phonet.*) consonant.

**Konsorte** [kɔnˈzɔrtə], *m.* (—n, *pl.* —n) associate, accomplice.

**Konsortium** [kɔnˈzɔrtsjum], *n.* (—s, *pl.* —tien) syndicate.

**konstatieren** [kɔnstaˈtiːrən], *v.a.* state, note, assert.

**konsternieren** [kɔnstɛrˈniːrən], *v.a.* dismay, disconcert.

**konstituieren** [kɔnstituˈiːrən], *v.a.* constitute.

**konstitutionell** [kɔnstitutsjoˈnɛl], *adj.* constitutional.

**konstruieren** [kɔnstruˈiːrən], *v.a.* construct; (*Gram.*) construe.

**konsularisch** [kɔnzuˈlaːrɪʃ], *adj.* consular.

**Konsulat** [kɔnzuˈlaːt], *n.* (—s, *pl.* —e) consulate.

**Konsulent** [kɔnzuˈlɛnt], *m.* (—en, *pl.* —en) (*Law*) counsel; consultant.

**konsultieren** [kɔnzulˈtiːrən], *v.a.* consult.

**Konsum** [kɔnˈzuːm], *m.* (—s, *no pl.*) (*Econ.*) consumption.

**konsumieren** [kɔnzuˈmiːrən], *v.a.* consume.

**Konsumverein** [kɔnˈzuːmfɛraɪn], *m.* (—s, *pl.* —e) cooperative society.

**Konterbande** [kɔntɛrˈbandə], *f.* (—, *no pl.*) contraband.

**Konterfei** [kɔntɛrˈfaɪ], *n.* (—s, *pl.* —e) (*obs.*) portrait, likeness.

**Kontertanz** [ˈkɔntɛrtants], *m.* (—es, *pl.* ⁀e) square dance, quadrille.

**kontinuierlich** [kɔntinuˈiːrlɪç], *adj.* continuous.

**Kontinuität** [kɔntinuiˈtɛːt], *f.* (—, *no pl.*) continuity.

**Konto** [ˈkɔnto], *n.* (—s, *pl.* —ten) (*bank*) account; à —, on account.

**Kontokorrent** [kɔntokoˈrɛnt], *n.* (—s, *pl.* —e) current account.

**Kontor** [kɔnˈtoːr], *n.* (—s, *pl.* —e) (*obs.*) office.

**Kontorist** [kɔntoˈrɪst], *m.* (—en, *pl.* —en) clerk.

**Kontrabaß** [ˈkɔntrabas], *m.* (—sses, *pl.* ⁀sse) double-bass.

**Kontrapunkt** [ˈkɔntrapuŋkt], *m.* (—es, *pl.* —e) (*Mus.*) counterpoint.

**kontrastieren** [kɔntrasˈtiːrən], *v.a., v.n.* contrast.

**kontrollieren** [kɔntrɔˈliːrən], *v.a.* check, verify.

**Kontroverse** [kɔntroˈvɛrzə], *f.* (—, *pl.* —n) controversy.

**Kontur** [kɔnˈtuːr], *f.* (—, *pl.* —en) outline, (*pl.*) contours.

**Konvent** [kɔnˈvɛnt], *m.* (—s, *pl.* —e) convention, assembly, congress.

**konventionell** [kɔnvɛntsjoˈnɛl], *adj.* conventional, formal.

**Konversationslexikon** [kɔnvɛrzaˈtsjoːnslɛksɪkɔn], *n.* (—s, *pl.* —s) encyclopaedia.

**konvertieren** [kɔnvɛrˈtiːrən], *v.a., v.n.* convert.

**Konvertit** [kɔnvɛrˈtɪt], *m.* (—en, *pl.* —en) convert.

**Konvolut** [kɔnvoˈluːt], *n.* (—s, *pl.* —e) bundle; scroll.

**konvulsivisch** [kɔnvulˈziːvɪʃ], *adj.* convulsive.

**konzentrieren** [kɔntsɛnˈtriːrən], *v.a., v.r.* concentrate; *auf etwas* —, centre upon.

**konzentrisch** [kɔnˈtsɛntrɪʃ], *adj.* concentric.

**Konzept** [kɔnˈtsɛpt], *n.* (—es, *pl.* —e) rough draft, sketch; *aus dem* — *bringen*, unsettle, disconcert.

**Konzeptpapier** [kɔnˈtsɛptpapiːr], *n.* (—s, *no pl.*) scribbling paper.

**Konzern** [kɔnˈtsɛrn], *m.* (—s, *pl.* —e) (*Comm.*) combine.

**Konzert** [kɔnˈtsɛrt], *n.* (—es, *pl.* —e) concert, (*musical*) recital; concerto.

**Konzertflügel** [kɔnˈtsɛrtflyːgəl], *m.* (—s, *pl.* —) grand piano.

**konzertieren** [kɔntsɛrˈtiːrən], *v.n.* give recitals; play in a concert.

**Konzertmeister** [kɔnˈtsɛrtmaɪstər], *m.* (—s, *pl.* —) leader (*of orchestra*).

**Konzession** [kɔntseˈsjoːn], *f.* (—, *pl.* —en) concession, licence.

**konzessionieren** [kɔntsesjoˈniːrən], *v.a.* license.

**Konzil** [kɔnˈtsiːl], *n.* (—s, *pl.* —ien) (*Eccl.*) council.

**konzipieren** [kɔntsiˈpiːrən], *v.a.* draft, plan.

**Koordinierung** [koːɔrdiˈniːruŋ], *f.* (—, *pl.* —en) co-ordination.

**Kopf** [kɔpf], *m.* (—es, *pl.* ⁀e) head; top; heading; (*fig.*) mind, brains, judgment; *aus dem* —, by heart.

**köpfen** [ˈkœpfən], *v.a.* behead, decapitate; (*Bot.*) lop.

**Kopfhaut** [ˈkɔpfhaut], *f.* (—, *no pl.*) scalp.

**Kopfhörer** [ˈkɔpfhøːrər], *m.* (—s, *pl.* —) headphone, receiver.

**Kopfkissen** [ˈkɔpfkɪsən], *n.* (—s, *pl.* —) pillow.

**Kopfsalat** [ˈkɔpfzalaːt], *m.* (—s, *pl.* —e) (*garden*) lettuce.

**kopfscheu** [ˈkɔpfʃɔy], *adj.* afraid, alarmed, timid; — *machen*, scare; — *werden*, take fright, jib.

**Kopfschmerz** ['kɔpfʃmɛrts], *m.* (—es, *pl.* —en) (*mostly pl.*) headache.

**Kopfsprung** ['kɔpfʃpruŋ], *m.* (—s, *pl.* ⁝e) (*diving*) header.

**kopfüber** [kɔpf'yːbər], *adv.* head over heels; headlong.

**Kopfweh** ['kɔpfveː], *n.* (—s, *no pl.*) headache.

**Kopfzerbrechen** ['kɔpftsɛrbrɛçən], *n.* (—s, *no pl.*) racking o.'s brains.

**Kopie** [ko'piː] *f.* (—, *pl.* —n) copy, duplicate.

**kopieren** [ko'piːrən], *v.a.* copy, ape, mimic, take off.

**Koppe** ['kɔpə], *f. see* Kuppe.

**Koppel** ['kɔpəl], *f.* (—, *pl.* —n) (*dogs*) couple, leash; (*ground*) enclosure, paddock.

**koppeln** ['kɔpəln], *v.a.* couple, leash.

**kopulieren** [kopu'liːrən], *v.a.* (*obs.*) marry; pair; (*Hort.*) graft.

**Koralle** [ko'ralə], *f.* (—, *pl.* —n) coral.

**Korallenriff** [ko'ralənrɪf], *n.* (—es, *pl.* —e) coral-reef.

**Korb** [kɔrp], *m.* (—s, *pl.* ⁝e) basket, hamper; *einen — geben,* turn s.o. down, refuse an offer of marriage.

**Korbweide** ['kɔrpvaɪdə], *f.* (—, *pl.* —n) (*Bot.*) osier.

**Kord** [kɔrt], *m.* (—s, *no pl.*) corduroy.

**Kordel** ['kɔrdəl], *f.* (—, *pl.* —n) cord, twine, thread.

**Korea** [ko'reːa], *n.* Korea.

**Korinthe** [ko'rɪntə], *f.* (—, *pl.* —n) (*Bot.*) currant.

**Korken** ['kɔrkən], *m.* (—s, *pl.* —) cork, stopper.

**Korkenzieher** ['kɔrkəntsiːər], *m.* (—s, *pl.* —) cork-screw.

**Korn** [kɔrn], *n.* (—s, *pl.* —e, ⁝er) (*Bot.*) corn, grain, cereal, rye; (*gun*) sight, *aufs — nehmen,* take aim at.

**Kornblume** ['kɔrnbluːmə], *f.* (—, *pl.* —n) (*Bot.*) corn-flower.

**Kornbranntwein** ['kɔrnbrantvaɪn], *m.* (—s, *no pl.*) corn-brandy, whisky.

**Kornett** [kɔr'nɛt], *m.* (—s, *pl.* —e) (*Mil., Mus.*) cornet.

**körnig** ['kœrnɪç], *adj.* granular, granulous; grained.

**Kornrade** ['kɔrnraːdə], *f.* (—, *pl.* —n) (*Bot.*) corn-cockle.

**Kornspeicher** ['kɔrnʃpaɪçər], *m.* (—s, *pl.* —) granary, corn-loft.

**Körper** ['kœrpər], *m.* (—s, *pl.* —) body; (*Phys.*) solid.

**Körperbau** ['kœrpərbau], *m.* (—s, *no pl.*) build, frame.

**Körpergeruch** ['kœrpərgəruːx], *m.* (—s, *no pl.*) body odour.

**körperlich** ['kœrpərlɪç], *adj.* bodily, physical; *—e Züchtigung,* corporal punishment.

**Körpermaß** ['kœrpərmaːs], *n.* (—es, *pl.* —e) cubic measure.

**Körperschaft** ['kœrpərʃaft], *f.* (—, *pl.* —en) corporation.

**Korps** [koːr], *n.* (—, *pl.* —) (*Mil.*) corps; students' corporation.

**Korrektheit** [kɔ'rɛkthaɪt], *f.* (—, *no pl.*) correctness.

**Korrektionsanstalt** [kɔrɛk'tsjoːnsanʃtalt], *f.* (—, *pl.* —en) penitentiary, Borstal institution.

**Korrektor** [kɔ'rɛktɔr], *m.* (—s, *pl.* —en) proof-reader.

**Korrektur** [kɔrɛk'tuːr], *f.* (—, *pl.* —en) correction; proof-correction; revision.

**Korrekturbogen** [kɔrɛk'tuːrboːgən], *m.* (—s, *pl.* —) (*Typ.*) proof-sheet, galley.

**Korrespondenzkarte** [kɔrɛspɔn'dɛntskartə], *f.* (—, *pl.* —n) post-card.

**korrigieren** [kɔri'giːrən], *v.a.* correct, revise; read (proofs).

**Korsett** [kɔr'zɛt], *n.* (—s, *pl.* —s) corset, bodice, stays.

**Koryphäe** [kɔri'fɛːə], *m.* (—n, *pl.* —n) celebrity, authority, master mind.

**Koseform** ['koːzəfɔrm], *f.* (—, *pl.* —en) term of endearment, pet-name, diminutive.

**kosen** ['koːzən], *v.a., v.n.* caress, fondle; make love (to).

**Kosinus** ['koːzinus], *m.* (—, *pl.* —) (*Maths.*) cosine.

**Kosmetik** [kɔs'meːtɪk], *f.* (—, *no pl.*) cosmetics.

**kosmetisch** [kɔs'meːtɪʃ], *adj.* cosmetic.

**kosmisch** ['kɔzmɪʃ], *adj.* cosmic.

**Kosmopolit** [kɔsmopo'liːt], *m.* (—en, *pl.* —en) cosmopolitan.

**kosmopolitisch** [kɔsmopo'liːtɪʃ], *adj.* cosmopolitan.

**Kost** [kɔst], *f.* (—, *no pl.*) food, fare; board.

**Kostarika** [kɔsta'rika], *n.* Costa Rica.

**kostbar** ['kɔstbaːr], *adj.* valuable, precious, costly.

**Kostbarkeit** ['kɔstbaːrkaɪt], *f.* (—, *pl.* —en) costliness, preciousness; (*pl.*) (*goods*) valuables.

**Kosten** ['kɔstən], *pl.* cost(s), expenses, charges; (*Law*) costs.

**kosten** ['kɔstən], *v.a.* taste; (*money*) cost; take, require; *was kostet das?* how much is this?

**Kosten(vor)anschlag** ['kɔstən(for)anʃlaːk], *m.* (—s, *pl.* ⁝e) estimate.

**Kostenaufwand** ['kɔstənaufvant], *m.* (—s, *pl.* ⁝e) expenditure.

**Kostenersatz** ['kɔstənɛrzats], *m.* (—es, *no pl.*) refund of expenses, compensation.

**kostenfrei** ['kɔstənfraɪ], *adj.* free (of charge), gratis.

**kostenlos** ['kɔstənloːs], *see* kostenfrei.

**Kostgänger** ['kɔstgɛŋər], *m.* (—s, *pl.* —) boarder.

**Kostgeld** ['kɔstgɛlt], *n.* (—es, *no pl.*) maintenance *or* board allowance.

**köstlich** ['kœstlɪç], *adj.* excellent, precious; delicious; *ein —er Witz,* a capital joke.

**kostspielig** ['kɔstʃpiːlɪç], *adj.* expensive, costly.

**Kostüm** [kɔs'tyːm], *n.* (—s, *pl.* —e) costume; fancy dress.

**Kostümfest** [kɔs'tyːmfɛst], *n.* (—s, *pl.* —e) fancy-dress ball.

**kostümieren** [kɔsty'miːrən], *v.a.* dress up.

**Kot** [koːt], *m.* (—es, *no pl.*) mud, dirt; filth, mire; excrement.

**Kotelett** [kɔt'let], *n.* (—s, *pl.* —s) cutlet.

**Köter** [ˈkøːtər], *m.* (—s, *pl.* —) cur, mongrel.

**Koterie** [koːtəˈriː], *f.* (—, *pl.* —n) clique, set, coterie.

**Kotflügel** [ˈkoːtflyːgəl], *m.* (—s, *pl.* —) (*Motor.*) mudguard.

**kotig** [ˈkoːtɪç], *adj.* dirty, miry.

**kotzen** [ˈkɔtsən], *v.n.* (*vulg.*) vomit.

**Koweit** [ˈkɔvaɪt], *n.* Kuwait.

**Krabbe** [ˈkrabə], *f.* (—, *pl.* —n) (*Zool.*) crab; shrimp; (*fig.*) brat, imp.

**krabbeln** [ˈkrabəln], *v.n.* crawl.

**Krach** [krax], *m.* (—es, *pl.* —e) crack, crash; din, noise; (*Comm.*) slump; quarrel, row.

**krachen** [ˈkraxən], *v.n.* crack, crash.

**krächzen** [ˈkrɛçtsən], *v.n.* croak.

**Kraft** [kraft], *f.* (—, *pl.* ¨e) strength, vigour; force; power, energy; intensity; *in — treten,* come into force.

**kraft** [kraft], *prep.* (*Genit.*) by virtue of, by authority of, on the strength of.

**Kraftausdruck** [ˈkraftausdruk], *m.* (—s, *pl.* ¨e) forcible expression; expletive.

**Kraftbrühe** [ˈkraftbryːə], *f.* (—, *pl.* —n) meat-soup, beef-tea.

**Kraftfahrer** [ˈkraftfaːrər], *m.* (—s, *pl.* —) motorist.

**kräftig** [ˈkrɛftɪç], *adj.* strong, powerful, vigorous, energetic; (*food*) nourishing.

**Kraftlehre** [ˈkraftleːrə], *f.* (—, *no pl.*) dynamics.

**kraftlos** [ˈkraftloːs], *adj.* weak, feeble.

**Kraftwagen** [ˈkraftvaːgən], *m.* (—s, *pl.* —) motor car, automobile, car, lorry, truck.

**Kragen** [ˈkraːgən], *m.* (—s, *pl.* —) collar; *es geht mir an den —,* it will cost me dearly.

**Krähe** [ˈkrɛːə], *f.* (—, *pl.* —n) (*Orn.*) crow.

**krähen** [ˈkrɛːən], *v.n.* crow.

**Krähenfüße** [ˈkrɛːənfyːsə], *m. pl.* crow's feet (wrinkles).

**Krakau** [ˈkraːkau], *n.* Cracow.

**krakeelen** [kraˈkeːlən], *v.n.* (*coll.*) kick up a row.

**Kralle** [ˈkralə], *f.* (—, *pl.* —n) claw, talon.

**Kram** [kraːm], *m.* (—s, *no pl.*) small wares (trade); stuff, rubbish, litter; *es paßt mir nicht in den —,* it does not suit my purpose.

**kramen** [ˈkraːmən], *v.n.* rummage.

**Krämer** [ˈkrɛːmər], *m.* (—s, *pl.* —) retailer, general dealer, shopkeeper.

**Kramladen** [ˈkraːmlaːdən], *m.* (—s, *pl.* ¨) small retail-shop, general shop *or* store.

**Krampe** [ˈkrampə], *f.* (—, *pl.* —n) staple.

**Krampf** [krampf], *m.* (—es, *pl.* ¨) cramp, spasm, convulsion.

**Krampfader** [ˈkrampfaːdər], *f.* (—, *pl.* —n) varicose vein.

**krampfartig** [ˈkrampfaːrtɪç], *adj.* spasmodic.

**krampfhaft** [ˈkrampfhaft], *adj.* convulsive.

**Kran** [kraːn], *m.* (—s, *pl.* ¨e) (*Engin.*) crane.

**Kranich** [ˈkraːnɪç], *m.* (—s, *pl.* —e) (*Orn.*) crane.

**krank** [kraŋk], *adj.* sick, ill.

**kränkeln** [ˈkrɛŋkəln], *v.n.* be ailing, be in poor health.

**kranken** [ˈkraŋkən], *v.n. an etwas —,* suffer from s.th., be afflicted with s.th.

**kränken** [ˈkrɛŋkən], *v.a.* vex, grieve; offend, insult.

**Krankenbahre** [ˈkraŋkənbaːrə], *f.* (—, *pl.* —n) stretcher.

**Krankenhaus** [ˈkraŋkənhaus], *n.* (—es, *pl.* ¨er) hospital.

**Krankenkasse** [ˈkraŋkənkasə], *f.* (—, *pl.* —n) sick-fund; health insurance.

**Krankenkost** [ˈkraŋkənkɔst], *f.* (—, *no pl.*) invalid diet.

**Krankenschwester** [ˈkraŋkənʃvestər], *f.* (—, *pl.* —n) nurse.

**Krankenstuhl** [ˈkraŋkənʃtuːl], *m.* (—s, *pl.* ¨e) invalid chair.

**Krankenversicherung** [ˈkraŋkənfɛrzɪçəruŋ], *f.* (—, *pl* —en) health insurance.

**Krankenwärter** [ˈkraŋkənvertər], *m.* (—s, *pl.* —) attendant, male nurse.

**krankhaft** [ˈkraŋkhaft], *adj.* morbid.

**Krankheit** [ˈkraŋkhaɪt], *f.* (—, *pl.* —en) illness, sickness, disease, malady; complaint; *englische —,* rickets.

**Krankheitserscheinung** [ˈkraŋkhaɪtsɛrʃaɪnuŋ], *f.* (—, *pl.* —en) symptom.

**kränklich** [ˈkrɛŋklɪç], *adj.* sickly, infirm, in poor health.

**Kränkung** [ˈkrɛŋkuŋ], *f.* (—, *pl.* —en) grievance, annoyance; offence, insult.

**Kranz** [krants], *m.* (—es, *pl.* ¨e) wreath, garland.

**Kränzchen** [ˈkrɛntsçən], *n.* (—s, *pl.* —) little garland; (*fig.*) (ladies') weekly tea party; circle, club.

**kränzen** [ˈkrɛntsən], *v.a.* garland, wreathe.

**Krapfen** [ˈkrapfən], *m.* (—s, *pl.* —) doughnut.

**kraß** [kras], *adj.* crass, crude.

**Krater** [ˈkraːtər], *m.* (—s, *pl.* —) crater.

**Kratzbürste** [ˈkratsbyrstə], *f.* (—, *pl.* —n) scraper; (*fig.*) cross-patch, irritable person.

**Krätze** [ˈkrɛtsə], *f.* (—, *no pl.*) (*Med.*) scabies, itch, mange.

**kratzen** [ˈkratsən], *v.a., v.n.* scratch, scrape, itch.

**krauen** [ˈkrauən], *v.a.* scratch softly.

**kraus** [kraus], *adj.* frizzy, curly; crisp, fuzzy; creased; (*fig.*) abstruse; *die Stirn — ziehen,* frown, knit o.'s brow.

**Krause** [ˈkrauzə], *f.* (—, *pl.* —n) ruff.

**kräuseln** [ˈkrɔyzəln], *v.a., v.r.* crisp, curl; ripple.

**Krauskohl** [ˈkrauskoːl], *m.* (—s, *no pl.*) Savoy cabbage.

**Kraut** [kraut], *n.* (—es, *pl.* ̈er) herb; plant; (*dial.*) cabbage; *wie — und Rüben,* higgledy-piggledy.

**krautartig** [ˈkrautaːrtiç], *adj.* herbaceous.

**Kräuterkäse** [ˈkrɔytərkɛːzə], *m.* (—s, *pl.* —) green cheese.

**Kräutertee** [ˈkrɔytərteː], *m.* (—s, *no pl.*) herb-tea, infusion of herbs.

**Krawall** [kraˈval], *m.* (—s, *pl.* —e) (*coll.*) row, uproar; shindy.

**Krawatte** [kraˈvatə], *f.* (—, *pl.* —n) cravat, tie.

**kraxeln** [ˈkraksəln], *v.n.* (*coll.*) climb, clamber.

**Krebs** [kreːps], *m.* (—es, *pl.* —e) (*Zool.*) crayfish, crab; (*Med.*) cancer, carcinoma; (*Geog.*) Tropic of Cancer.

**krebsartig** [ˈkreːpsaːrtiç], *adj.* cancerous.

**Krebsbutter** [ˈkreːpsbutər], *f.* (—, *no pl.*) crab-cheese.

**Krebsgang** [ˈkreːpsgaŋ], *m.* (—es, *no pl.*) crab's walk, sidling; *den — gehen,* retrograde, decline.

**Krebsschaden** [ˈkreːpsʃaːdən], *m.* (—s, *pl.* ̈) cancerous sore *or* affection; (*fig.*) canker, inveterate evil.

**Kredenz** [kreˈdɛnts], *f.* (—, *pl.* —en) buffet, serving table, sideboard.

**kredenzen** [kreˈdɛntsən], *v.a.* taste (*wine*); (*obs.*) present, offer.

**kreditieren** [krediˈtiːrən], *v.a. einem etwas —,* credit s.o. with s.th.

**Kreide** [ˈkraɪdə], *f.* (—, *pl.* —n) chalk; (*Art*) crayon.

**kreieren** [kreˈiːrən], *v.a.* create.

**Kreis** [kraɪs], *m.* (—es, *pl.* —e) circle; (*Astron.*) orbit; district; range; sphere.

**Kreisabschnitt** [ˈkraɪsapʃnɪt], *m.* (—s, *pl.* —e) segment.

**Kreisausschnitt** [ˈkraɪsausʃnɪt], *m.* (—s, *pl.* —e) sector.

**Kreisbogen** [ˈkraɪsboːgən], *m.* (—s, *pl.* ̈) arc.

**kreischen** [ˈkraɪʃən], *v.n.* scream, shriek.

**Kreisel** [ˈkraɪzəl], *m.* (—s, *pl.* —) (*toy*) (spinning) top; gyroscope.

**kreisen** [ˈkraɪzən], *v.n.* circle, revolve; circulate.

**Kreislauf** [ˈkraɪslauf], *m.* (—es, *pl.* ̈e) circular course; (*Astron.*) orbit; (*blood*) circulation.

**kreißen** [ˈkraɪsən], *v.n.* (*Med.*) be in labour.

**Kreisstadt** [ˈkraɪsʃtat], *f.* (—, *pl.* ̈e) county town.

**Kreisumfang** [ˈkraɪsumfaŋ], *m.* (—s, *pl.* ̈e) circumference.

**Kreml** [kreml], *m.* (—s, *no pl.*) the Kremlin.

**Krempe** [ˈkrɛmpə], *f.* (—, *pl.* —n) (*hat*) brim.

**Krempel** [ˈkrɛmpəl], *m.* (—s, *no pl.*) (*coll.*) refuse, rubbish; stuff.

**Kren** [kreːn], *m.* (—s, *no pl.*) (*Austr.*) horse-radish.

**krepieren** [kreˈpiːrən], *v.n.* (*aux. sein*) (*animals*) die; (*humans*) (*coll.*) perish miserably; explode.

**Krepp** [krɛp], *m.* (—s, *no pl.*) crape, crêpe.

**Kresse** [ˈkrɛsə], *f.* (—, *pl.* —n) cress.

**Kreta** [ˈkreːta], *n.* Crete.

**Kreuz** [krɔyts], *n.* (—es, *pl.* —e) cross, crucifix; (*Anat.*) small of the back; (*fig.*) calamity; affliction; *kreuz und quer,* in all directions.

**Kreuzband** [ˈkrɔytsbant], *n.* (—es, *pl.* ̈er) wrapper (for printed matter).

**kreuzbrav** [ˈkrɔytsbraːf], *adj.* as good as gold.

**kreuzen** [ˈkrɔytsən], *v.a.* cross. — *v.r. sich —,* make the sign of the cross.

**Kreuzfahrer** [ˈkrɔytsfaːrər], *m.* (—s, *pl.* —) crusader.

**kreuzfidel** [ˈkrɔytsfideːl], *adj.* jolly, merry, as merry as a cricket.

**Kreuzgang** [ˈkrɔytsgaŋ], *m.* (—es, *pl.* ̈e) cloisters.

**kreuzigen** [ˈkrɔytsɪgən], *v.a.* crucify.

**Kreuzritter** [ˈkrɔɪtsrɪtər], *m.* (—s, *pl.* —) Knight of the Cross; crusader.

**Kreuzschmerzen** [ˈkrɔytsʃmɛrtsən], *m. pl.* lumbago.

**Kreuzstich** [ˈkrɔytsʃtɪç], *m.* (—es, *no pl.*) (*Embroidery*) cross-stitch.

**Kreuzung** [ˈkrɔytsuŋ], *f.* (—, *pl.* —en) (*road*) crossing; (*animals*) cross-breeding.

**Kreuzverhör** [ˈkrɔytsfɛrhøːr], *n.* (—s, *pl.* —e) cross-examination.

**Kreuzweg** [ˈkrɔytsveːk], *m.* (—s, *pl.* —e) crossroads; (*Eccl.*) Stations of the Cross.

**Kreuzworträtsel** [ˈkrɔytsvɔrtrɛːtsəl], *n.* (—s, *pl.* —) crossword-puzzle.

**Kreuzzug** [ˈkrɔytstsuːk], *m.* (—es, *pl.* ̈e) crusade.

**kriechen** [ˈkriːçən], *v.n. irr.* (*aux. sein*) creep, crawl; (*fig.*) cringe, fawn.

**kriecherisch** [ˈkriːçəriʃ], *adj.* fawning, cringing.

**Kriechtier** [ˈkriːçtiːr], *n.* (—s, *pl.* —e) reptile.

**Krieg** [kriːk], *m.* (—es, *pl.* —e) war.

**kriegen** [ˈkriːgən], *v.a.* get, obtain.

**Krieger** [ˈkriːgər], *m.* (—s, *pl.* —) warrior.

**kriegerisch** [ˈkriːgəriʃ], *adj.* warlike, martial.

**kriegführend** [ˈkriːkfyːrənt], *adj.* belligerent.

**Kriegsfuß** [ˈkriːksfuːs], *m.* (—es, *no pl.*) *auf —,* at logger-heads.

**Kriegsgewinner** [ˈkriːksgəvɪnlər], *m.* (—s, *pl.* —) war-profiteer.

**Kriegslist** [ˈkriːkslɪst], *f.* (—, *pl.* —en) stratagem.

**Kriegsschauplatz** [ˈkriːksʃauplats], *m.* (—es, *pl.* ̈e) theatre of war.

**Kriegsschiff** [ˈkriːksʃɪf], *n.* (—es, *pl.* —e) man-of-war, warship.

**Kriegswesen** [ˈkriːksveːzən], *n.* (—s, *no pl.*) military affairs.

**Kriegszug** [ˈkriːkstsuːk], *m.* (—es, *pl.* ̈e) campaign.

**Krim** [krɪm], *f.* the Crimea.

**Kriminalbeamte** [krɪmiˈnaːlbeamtə], *m.* (—n, *pl.* —n) crime investigator.

**Kriminalprozeß** [krɪmɪˈnaːlprotsɛs], *m.* (—**sses**, *pl.* —**sse**) criminal procedure *or* trial.

**Krimskrams** [ˈkrɪmskrams], *m.* (—, *no pl.*) whatnots, knick-knacks, medley.

**Krippe** [ˈkrɪpə], *f.* (—, *pl.* —**n**) crib, manger; crèche.

**Krise** [ˈkriːzə], *f.* (—, *pl.* —**n**) crisis.

**Kristall** [krɪˈstal], *m.* (—**s**, *pl.* —**e**) crystal; cut glass.

**kristallartig** [krɪˈstalaːrtɪç], *adj.* crystalline.

**kristallisieren** [krɪstaliˈziːrən], *v.a.*, *v.n.* (*aux.* sein), crystallise.

**Kristallkunde** [krɪˈstalkundə], *f.* (—, *no pl.*) crystallography.

**Kriterium** [kriˈteːrjum], *n.* (—**s**, *pl.* —**rien**) criterion, test.

**Kritik** [kriˈtiːk], *f.* (—, *pl.* —**en**) criticism, review; *unter aller* —, extremely bad.

**Kritiker** [ˈkriːtɪkər], *m.* (—**s**, *pl.* —) critic.

**kritisch** [ˈkriːtɪʃ], *adj.* critical; precarious, crucial.

**kritisieren** [kritiˈziːrən], *v.a.* criticise; review; censure.

**kritteln** [ˈkrɪtəln], *v.n.* cavil (at), find fault.

**Krittler** [ˈkrɪtlər], *m.* (—**s**, *pl.* —) caviller, fault-finder.

**Kritzelei** [krɪtsəˈlaɪ], *f.* (—, *pl.* —**en**) scrawling, scribbling.

**kritzeln** [ˈkrɪtsəln], *v.a.* scrawl, scribble.

**Kroatien** [kroˈaːtsjən], *n.* Croatia.

**Krokodil** [krokoˈdiːl], *n.* (—**s**, *pl.* —**e**) (*Zool.*) crocodile.

**Kronbewerber** [ˈkroːnbevɛrbər], *m.* (—**s**, *pl.* —) aspirant to the crown, pretender.

**Krone** [ˈkroːnə], *f.* (—, *pl.* —**n**) crown; (*Papal*) tiara; (*fig.*) head, top, flower.

**krönen** [ˈkrøːnən], *v.a.* crown.

**Kronerbe** [ˈkroːnɛrbə], *m.* (—**n**, *pl.* —**n**) heir apparent.

**Kronleuchter** [ˈkroːnlɔʏçtər], *m.* (—**s**, *pl.* —) chandelier.

**Kronsbeere** [ˈkroːnsbeːrə], *f.* (—, *pl.* —**n**) (*Bot.*) cranberry.

**Krönung** [ˈkrøːnuŋ], *f.* (—, *pl.* —**en**) coronation.

**Kropf** [krɔpf], *m.* (—**es**, *pl.* —**e**) (*human*) goitre, wen; (*birds*) crop, craw.

**kropfartig** [ˈkrɔpfaːrtɪç], *adj.* goitrous.

**kröpfen** [ˈkrœpfən], *v.a.* (*birds*) cram.

**Kropftaube** [ˈkrɔpftaubə], *f.* (—, *pl.* —**n**) (*Orn.*) pouter-pigeon.

**Kröte** [ˈkrøːtə], *f.* (—, *pl.* —**n**) toad.

**Krücke** [ˈkrykə], *f.* (—, *pl.* —**n**) crutch; (*fig.*) rake.

**Krückstock** [ˈkrykʃtɔk], *m.* (—**s**, *pl.* —**e**) crutch.

**Krug** [kruːk], *m.* (—**es**, *pl.* —**e**) jug, pitcher, mug; (*fig.*) pub, inn.

**Krüger** [ˈkryːgər], *m.* (—**s**, *pl.* —) pub-keeper, tapster.

**Krume** [ˈkruːmə], *f.* (—, *pl.* —**n**) crumb.

**krüm(e)lig** [ˈkryːm(ə)lɪç], *adj.* crumbly, crumby.

**krümeln** [ˈkryːmeln], *v.n.* crumble.

**krumm** [krum], *adj.* crooked, curved; *etwas* — *nehmen*, take s.th. amiss.

**krummbeinig** [ˈkrumbaɪnɪç], *adj.* bandy-legged.

**krümmen** [ˈkrymən], *v.a.* crook, bend, curve. — *v.r. sich* —, (*fig.*) writhe, cringe.

**Krummholz** [ˈkrumhɔlts], *n.* (—**es**, *no pl.*) (*Bot.*) dwarf-pine.

**Krummschnabel** [ˈkrumʃnaːbəl], *m.* (—**s**, *pl.* ⏑) (*Orn.*) curlew, crook-bill.

**Krümmung** [ˈkrymuŋ], *f.* (—, *pl.* —**en**) curve; turning, winding.

**Krüppel** [ˈkrypəl], *m.* (—**s**, *pl.* —**e**) cripple.

**krüppelhaft** [ˈkrypəlhaft], *adj.* crippled, lame.

**krüpp(e)lig** [ˈkryp(ə)lɪç], *adj.* crippled, lame.

**Kruste** [ˈkrustə], *f.* (—, *pl.* —**n**) crust.

**Kübel** [ˈkyːbəl], *m.* (—**s**, *pl.* —) tub, bucket.

**Kubikfuß** [kuˈbiːkfuːs], *m.* (—**es**, *pl.* —) cubic foot.

**Kubikinhalt** [kuˈbiːkɪnhalt], *m.* (—**s**, *no pl.*) cubic content.

**Kubismus** [kuˈbɪsmus], *m.* (—, *no pl.*) cubism.

**Küche** [ˈkyçə], *f.* (—, *pl.* —**n**) (*room*) kitchen; (*food*) cooking, cookery, cuisine.

**Kuchen** [ˈkuːxən], *m.* (—**s**, *pl.* —) cake.

**Küchengeschirr** [ˈkyçəngəʃɪr], *n.* (—**s**, *no pl.*) kitchen utensils.

**Küchenherd** [ˈkyçənheːrt], *m.* (—**es**, *pl.* —**e**) kitchen-range.

**Küchenlatein** [ˈkyçənlataɪn], *n.* (—**s**, *no pl.*) dog-Latin.

**Küchenmeister** [ˈkyçənmaɪstər], *m.* (—**s**, *pl.* —) chef, head cook.

**Küchenschrank** [ˈkyçənʃraŋk], *m.* (—**s**, *pl.* ⏑**e**) dresser.

**Kuchenteig** [ˈkuːxəntaɪk], *m.* (—**s**, *pl.* —**e**) dough (for cake).

**Küchenzettel** [ˈkyçəntsetəl], *m.* (—**s**, *pl.* —) bill of fare.

**Küchlein** [ˈkyːçlaɪn], *n.* (—**s**, *pl.* —) young chicken, pullet.

**Kücken** [ˈkykən], *n.* (—**s**, *pl.* —) young chicken, pullet.

**Kuckuck** [ˈkukuk], *m.* (—**s**, *pl.* —**e**) (*Orn.*) cuckoo; *scher Dich zum* —! go to blazes!

**Kufe** [ˈkuːfə], *f.* (—, *pl.* —**n**) tub, vat; (*sleigh*) runner; (*cradle*) rocker.

**Küfer** [ˈkyːfər], *m.* (—**s**, *pl.* —) cooper.

**Kugel** [ˈkuːgəl], *f.* (—, *pl.* —**n**) ball, bullet, sphere; globe.

**kugelfest** [ˈkuːgəlfɛst], *adj.* bulletproof.

**kugelförmig** [ˈkuːgəlfœrmɪç], *adj.* spherical, globular.

**Kugelgelenk** [ˈkuːgəlgələŋk], *n.* (—**s**, *pl.* —**e**) ball and socket joint.

**Kugellager** [ˈkuːgəllaːgər], *n.* (—**s**, *pl.* —) ball-bearing.

**Kugelmaß** [ˈkuːgəlmaːs], *n.* (—**es**, *pl.* —**e**) ball-calibre.

**kugeln** [ˈkuːgəln], *v.a.* roll; bowl.

**Kugelregen** ['ku:gəlre:gən], *m.* (—s, *no pl.*) hail of bullets.
**kugelrund** ['ku:gəlrunt], *adj.* round as a ball, well-fed.
**Kugelschreiber** ['ku:gəlʃraɪbər], *m.* (—s, *pl.* —) ball-point pen.
**Kuh** [ku:] *f.* (—, *pl.* ˙-e) cow; *junge* —, heifer.
**Kuhblattern** ['ku:blatərn], *f. pl.* cow-pox.
**Kuhblume** ['ku:blu:mə], *f.* (—, *pl.* —n) (*Bot.*) marigold.
**Kuhfladen** ['ku:fla:dən], *m.* (—s, *pl.* —) cow-dung.
**Kuhhaut** ['ku:haut], *f.* (—, *pl.* ˙-e) cow-hide; *das geht auf keine* —, that defies description.
**kühl** [ky:l], *adj.* cool, fresh; (*behaviour*) reserved.
**Kühle** ['ky:lə], *f.* (—, *no pl.*) coolness, freshness; (*behaviour*) reserve.
**kühlen** ['ky:lən], *v.a.* cool, freshen.
**Kühlraum** ['ky:lraum], *m.* (—es, *pl.* ˙-e) refrigerating-chamber.
**Kühlschrank** ['ky:lʃraŋk], *m.* (—s, *pl.* ˙-e) refrigerator, (*coll.*) fridge.
**Kühltruhe** ['ky:ltru:ə], *f.* (—, *pl.* —n) deep freeze.
**Kühlung** ['ky:luŋ], *f.* (—, *pl.* —en) refrigeration.
**Kuhmist** ['ku:mɪst], *m.* (—s, *no pl.*) cow-dung.
**kühn** [ky:n], *adj.* bold, daring, audacious.
**Kühnheit** ['ky:nhaɪt], *f.* (—, *no pl.*) boldness, daring, audacity.
**Kujon** [ku'jo:n], *m.* (—s, *pl.* —e) bully, scoundrel.
**kujonieren** [kujo'ni:rən], *v.a.* bully, exploit.
**Kukuruz** ['kukuruts], *m.* (—es, *no pl.*) (*Austr.*) maize.
**kulant** [ku'lant], *adj.* obliging; (*terms*) easy.
**Kulanz** [ku'lants], *f.* (—, *no pl.*) accommodating manner.
**Kuli** ['ku:li:], *m.* (—s, *pl.* —s) coolie.
**kulinarisch** [kuli'na:rɪʃ], *adj.* culinary.
**Kulisse** [ku'lɪsə], *f.* (—, *pl.* —n) (*Theat.*) back-drop, side-scene, wings.
**Kulissenfieber** [ku'lɪsənfi:bər], *n.* (—s, *no pl.*) stage-fright.
**kulminieren** [kulmi'ni:rən], *v.n.* culminate.
**kultivieren** [kulti'vi:rən], *v.a.* cultivate.
**Kultur** [kul'tu:r], *f.* (—, *pl.* —en) (*Agr.*) cultivation; (*fig.*) culture, civilization.
**Kultus** ['kultus], *m.* (—, *pl.* Kulte) cult, worship.
**Kultusministerium** ['kultusmɪnɪste:rjum], *n.* (—s, *pl.* —rien) Ministry of Education.
**Kümmel** ['kyməl], *m.* (—s, *no pl.*) caraway-seed; (*drink*) kümmel.
**Kummer** ['kumər], *m.* (—s, *no pl.*) grief, sorrow, trouble.
**kümmerlich** ['kymərlɪç], *adj.* miserable, pitiful.
**kummerlos** ['kumərlo:s], *adj.* untroubled.

**kümmern** ['kymərn], *v.r. sich* — *um*, mind, look after, be worried about, care for.
**Kümmernis** ['kymərnɪs], *f.* (—, *pl.* —se) grief, sorrow.
**kummervoll** ['kumərfɔl], *adj.* sorrowful, painful, grievous.
**Kumpan** [kum'pa:n], *m.* (—s, *pl.* —e) companion; mate; *lustiger* —, jolly fellow, good companion.
**kund** [kunt], *adj.* known, public; *etwas* — *tun*, make s.th. public; — *und zu wissen sei hiermit*, (*obs.*) we hereby give notice.
**kundbar** ['kuntba:r], *adj.* known; *etwas* — *machen*, announce s.th., make s.th. known.
**kündbar** ['kyntba:r], *adj.* (*loan, capital etc.*) redeemable; capable of being called in, terminable.
**Kunde** (1) ['kundə], *m.* (—n, *pl.* —n) customer; *ein schlauer* —, an artful dodger.
**Kunde** (2) ['kundə], *f.* (—, *pl.* —n) news; information, notification; (*compounds*) science.
**Kundgebung** ['kuntge:buŋ], *f.* (—, *pl.* —en) publication; rally; demonstration.
**kundig** ['kundɪç], *adj.* versed in, conversant with.
**Kundige** ['kundɪgə], *m.* (—n, *pl.* —n) expert, initiate.
**kündigen** ['kyndɪgən], *v.n.* give notice (*Dat.*).
**Kundmachung** ['kuntmaxuŋ], *f.* (—, *pl.* —en) publication.
**Kundschaft** ['kuntʃaft], *f.* (—, *no pl.*) clientele, customers; information, reconnaissance.
**kundschaften** ['kuntʃaftən], *v.n.* reconnoitre, scout.
**künftig** ['kynftɪç], *adj.* future, prospective, to come.
**Kunst** [kunst], *f.* (—, *pl.* ˙-e) art; skill.
**Kunstbutter** ['kunstbutər], *f.* (—, *no pl.*) margarine.
**Künstelei** [kynstə'laɪ], *f.* (—, *pl.* —en) affectation, mannerism.
**kunstfertig** ['kunstfertɪç], *adj.* skilled, skilful.
**Kunstfreund** ['kunstfrɔynt], *m.* (—es, *pl.* —e) art-lover.
**kunstgerecht** ['kunstgəreçt], *adj.* workmanlike.
**Kunstgewerbe** ['kunstgəverbə], *n.* (—s, *no pl.*) arts and crafts.
**Kunstgriff** ['kunstgrɪf], *m.* (—es, *pl.* —e) trick, dodge, artifice, knack.
**Kunsthändler** ['kunsthendlər], *m.* (—s, *pl.* —) art-dealer.
**Kunstkenner** ['kunstkenər], *m.* (—s, *pl.* —) connoisseur.
**Künstler** ['kynstlər], *m.* (—s, *pl.* —) artist, performer.
**künstlerisch** ['kynstlərɪʃ], *adj.* artistic, elaborate, ingenious.
**künstlich** ['kynstlɪç], *adj.* artificial.
**kunstlos** ['kunstlo:s], *adj.* artless, unaffected.

**kunstreich** ['kunstraɪç], *adj.* ingenious.
**Kunstseide** ['kunstzaɪdə], *f.* (—, *no pl.*) artificial silk.
**Kunststickerei** ['kunstʃtɪkəraɪ], *f.* (—, *no pl.*) art needlework.
**Kunststoff** ['kunstʃtɔf], *m.* (—es, *pl.* —e) plastics.
**Kunststopfen** ['kunstʃtɔpfən], *n.* (—s, *no pl.*) invisible mending.
**Kunststück** ['kunstʃtyk], *n.* (—es, *pl.* —e) trick, feat.
**Kunstverständige** ['kunstfɛrʃtɛndɪgə], *m.* (—n, *pl.* —n) art expert.
**Küpe** ['ky:pə], *f.* (—, *pl.* —n) large tub; (dyeing) copper.
**Kupfer** ['kupfər], *n.* (—s, *no pl.*) copper.
**Kupferblech** ['kupfərblɛç], *n.* (—es, *no pl.*) copper-sheet.
**Kupferdraht** ['kupfərdra:t], *m.* (—es, *pl.* ̈e) copper-wire.
**kupferhaltig** ['kupfərhaltɪç], *adj.* containing copper.
**Kupferrost** ['kupfərrɔst], *m.* (—es, *no pl.*) verdigris.
**Kupferstecher** ['kupfərʃtɛçər], *m.* (—s, *pl.* —) (copperplate) engraver.
**kupieren** [ku'pi:rən], *v.a.* (rare) (ticket) punch; (Austr.) (horse) dock.
**Kuppe** ['kupə], *f.* (—, *pl.* —n) (hill) top, summit.
**Kuppel** ['kupəl], *f.* (—, *pl.* —n) cupola, dome.
**kuppeln** ['kupəln], *v.n.* procure, pimp; make a match.
**Kuppler** ['kuplər], *m.* (—s, *pl.* —) procurer, pimp; matchmaker.
**Kupplung** ['kupluŋ], *f.* (—, *pl.* —en) (Railw.) coupling, joint; (Motor.) clutch.
**Kur** [ku:r], *f.* (—, *pl.* —en) cure; *eine — machen,* undergo medical treatment.
**Kuranstalt** ['ku:ranʃtalt], *f.* (—, *pl.* —en) sanatorium; (Am.) sanitarium.
**Küraß** ['ky:ras], *m.* (—sses, *pl.* —sse) cuirass.
**Kuratel** [kura'tɛl], *f.* (—, *pl.* —en) guardianship, trusteeship.
**Kuratorium** [kura'to:rjum], *n.* (—s, *pl.* —rien) board of guardians *or* trustees; council, governing body.
**Kurbel** ['kurbəl], *f.* (—, *pl.* —n) crank, winch.
**Kurbelstange** ['kurbəlʃtaŋə], *f.* (—, *pl.* —n) connecting rod.
**Kurbelwelle** ['kurbəlvɛlə], *f.* (—, *pl.* —n) crankshaft.
**Kürbis** ['kyrbɪs], *m.* (—ses, *pl.* —se) (Bot.) pumpkin, gourd.
**küren** ['ky:rən], *v.a. irr.* (Poet.) choose, elect.
**Kurfürst** ['ku:rfyrst], *m.* (—en, *pl.* —en) Elector (of the Holy Roman Empire).
**Kurhaus** ['ku:rhaus], *n.* (—es, *pl.* ̈er) spa; hotel; pump room.
**Kurie** ['ku:rjə], *f.* (—, *pl.* —n) (Eccl.) Curia; Papal Court.

**Kurier** [ku'ri:r], *m.* (—s, *pl.* —e) courier.
**kurieren** [ku'ri:rən], *v.a.* cure.
**kurios** [kur'jo:s], *adj.* curious, queer, strange.
**Kuriosität** [kurjozi'tɛ:t], *f.* (—, *pl.* —en) curio, curiosity.
**Kurort** ['ku:rɔrt], *m.* (—es, *pl.* —e) spa, watering-place, health-resort.
**Kurrentschrift** [ku'rɛntʃrɪft], *f.* (—, *no pl.*) running hand, cursive writing.
**Kurs** [kurs], *m.* (—es, *pl.* —e) rate of exchange; quotation; circulation; course.
**Kursaal** ['ku:rza:l], *m.* (—s, *pl.* —säle) hall, (spa) pump-room, casino.
**Kursbericht** ['kursbərɪçt], *m.* (—es, *pl.* —e) market report.
**Kursbuch** ['kursbu:x], *n.* (—es, *pl.* ̈er) railway-guide, time-table.
**Kürschner** ['kyrʃnər], *m.* (—s, *pl.* —) furrier, skinner.
**kursieren** [kur'zi:rən], *v.n.* be current, circulate.
**Kursivschrift** [kur'zi:fʃrɪft], *f.* (—, *no pl.*) italics.
**Kursstand** ['kursʃtant], *m.* (—es, *no pl.*) rate of exchange.
**Kursus** ['kurzus], *m.* (—, *pl.* **Kurse**) course (of lectures).
**Kurszettel** ['kursʃtɛtəl], *m.* (—s, *pl.* —) quotation-list.
**Kurve** ['kurvə], *f.* (—, *pl.* —n) curve.
**kurz** [kurts], *adj.* short, brief, concise; curt, abrupt.
**kurzangebunden** [kurts'angəbundən], *adj.* terse, abrupt, curt.
**kurzatmig** ['kurtsa:tmɪç], *adj.* short-winded, short of breath.
**Kürze** ['kyrtsə], *f.* (—, *no pl.*) shortness, brevity.
**kürzen** ['kyrtsən], *v.a.* shorten, abbreviate, condense; (Maths.) reduce.
**kürzlich** ['kyrtslɪç], *adv.* lately, recently, the other day.
**Kurzschluß** ['kurtsʃlus], *m.* (—sses, *pl.* ̈sse) short circuit.
**Kurzschrift** ['kurtsʃrɪft], *f.* (—, *no pl.*) shorthand.
**kurzsichtig** ['kurtszɪçtɪç], *adj.* short-sighted.
**kurzum** [kurts'um], *adv.* in short.
**Kürzung** ['kyrtsuŋ], *f.* (—, *pl.* —en) abbreviation, abridgement.
**Kurzwaren** ['kurtsva:rən], *f. pl.* haberdashery.
**kurzweg** ['kurts've:k], *adv.* simply, off-hand, briefly.
**Kurzweil** ['kurtsvaɪl], *f.* (—, *no pl.*) pastime.
**kurzweilig** ['kurtsvaɪlɪç], *adj.* amusing, diverting, entertaining.
**kusch!** [kuʃ], *excl.* (to dogs) lie down!
**kuschen** ['kuʃən], *v.n., v.r.* crouch, lie down.
**Kuß** [kus], *m.* (—sses, *pl.* ̈sse) kiss.
**küssen** ['kysən], *v.a., v.n., v.r.* kiss.
**Küste** ['kystə], *f.* (—, *pl.* —n) coast, shore.

**Küstenstadt** ['kystənʃtat], *f.* (—, *pl.* ⸚e) seaside town.
**Küster** ['kystər], *m.* (—s, *pl.* —) sacristan, sexton, verger.
**Kustos** ['kustɔs], *m.* (—, *pl.* —oden) custodian; director of museum.
**Kutschbock** ['kutʃbɔk], *m.* (—s, *pl.* ⸚e) box(-seat).
**Kutsche** ['kutʃə], *f.* (—, *pl.* —n) coach, carriage.
**kutschieren** [kut'ʃi:rən], *v.n.* drive a coach.
**Kutte** ['kutə], *f.* (—, *pl.* —n) cowl.
**Kutter** ['kutər], *m.* (—s, *pl.* —) (*Naut.*) cutter.
**Kuvert** [ku've:r], *n.* (—s, *pl.* —s) envelope; (*dinner*) place laid.
**kuvertieren** [kuver'ti:rən], *v.a.* envelop, wrap.
**Kux** [kuks], *m.* (—es, *pl.* —e) share in a mining concern.
**Kybernetik** [ky:ber'ne:tɪk], *f.* (—, *no pl.*) cybernetics.

# L

**L** [ɛl], *n.* (—, *pl.* —) the letter L.
**Lab** [la:p], *n.* (—es, *pl.* —e) rennet.
**labbern** ['labərn], *v.a.*, *v.n.* dribble, slobber; blab.
**Labe** ['la:bə], *f.* (—, *no pl.*) (*Poet.*) refreshment; comfort.
**laben** ['la:bən], *v.a.* refresh, restore, revive.
**labil** [la'bi:l], *adj.* unstable.
**Laborant** [labo'rant], *m.* (—en, *pl.* —en) laboratory assistant.
**Laboratorium** [labora'to:rjum], *n.* (—s, *pl.* —rien) laboratory.
**laborieren** [labo'ri:rən], *v.n.* experiment; suffer (from).
**Labsal** ['la:pza:l], *n.* (—s, *pl.* —e) restorative, refreshment.
**Labung** ['la:buŋ], *f.* (—, *pl.* —en) refreshment, comfort.
**Lache** ['laxə], *f.* (—, *pl.* —n) pool, puddle.
**Lächeln** ['lɛçəln], *n.* (—s, *no pl.*) smile; *albernes* —, smirk; *höhnisches* —, sneer.
**lächeln** ['lɛçəln], *v.n.* smile.
**Lachen** ['laxən], *n.* (—s, *no pl.*) laugh, laughter.
**lachen** ['laxən], *v.n.* laugh.
**lächerlich** ['lɛçərlɪç], *adj.* laughable, ridiculous; preposterous; ludicrous; *sich* — *machen*, make a fool of o.s.; *etwas* — *machen*, ridicule s.th.
**Lachgas** ['laxga:s], *n.* (—es, *no pl.*) nitrous oxide, laughing-gas.
**lachhaft** ['laxhaft], *adj.* laughable, ridiculous.

**Lachkrampf** ['laxkrampf], *m.* (—es, *pl.* ⸚e) hysterical laughter, a fit of laughter.
**Lachs** [laks], *m.* (—es, *pl.* —e) salmon.
**Lachsalve** ['laxzalvə], *f.* (—, *pl.* —n) peal of laughter.
**Lack** [lak], *m.* (—s, *pl.* —e) lac, lacquer, varnish.
**lackieren** [la'ki:rən], *v.a.* lacquer, varnish.
**Lackmus** ['lakmus], *n.* (—, *no pl.*) litmus.
**Lackschuh** ['lakʃu:], *m.* (—s, *pl.* —e) patent-leather shoe.
**Lackwaren** ['lakva:rən], *f. pl.* japanned goods.
**Lade** ['la:də], *f.* (—, *pl.* —n) box, chest, case, drawer.
**Ladebaum** ['la:dəbaum], *m.* derrick.
**Ladefähigkeit** ['la:dəfɛ:ɪçkaɪt], *f.* (—, *pl.* —en), carrying capacity, loading capacity; tonnage.
**Ladegeld** ['la:dəgɛlt], *n.* (—es, *pl.* —er) loading charges.
**Laden** ['la:dən], *m.* (—s, *pl.* ⸚) (*window*) shutter; shop, store.
**laden** ['la:dən], *v.a. irr.* load; (*Elec.*) charge; (*Law*) summon, (*fig.*) incur.
**Ladenhüter** ['la:dənhy:tər], *m.* (—s, *pl.* —) unsaleable article.
**Ladenpreis** ['la:dənpraɪs], *m.* (—es, *pl.* —e) retail-price.
**Ladentisch** ['la:dəntɪʃ], *m.* (—es, *pl.* —e) counter.
**Ladeschein** ['la:dəʃaɪn], *m.* (—s, *pl.* —e) bill of lading.
**Ladestock** ['la:dəʃtɔk], *m.* (—es, *pl.* ⸚e) ramrod.
**Ladung** ['la:duŋ], *f.* (—, *pl.* —en) loading, lading, freight; shipment, cargo; (*gun*) charge; (*Law*) summons.
**Laffe** ['lafə], *m.* (—n, *pl.* —n) fop.
**Lage** ['la:gə], *f.* (—, *pl.* —n) site, position, situation; state, condition; stratum, layer.
**Lager** ['la:gər], *n.* (—s, *pl.* —) couch, bed, divan; (*Geol.*) seam, vein; (*Tech.*) bearing; (*Comm.*) warehouse, store; camp.
**Lageraufnahme** ['la:gəraufna:mə], *f.* (—, *pl.* —n) stock-taking, inventory.
**Lager(bier)** ['la:gər(bi:r)], *n.* (—s, *pl.* —e) lager.
**Lagergeld** ['la:gərgɛlt], *n.* (—es, *pl.* —er) storage charge.
**Lagerist** [la:gə'rɪst], *m.* (—en, *pl.* —en) warehouse-clerk.
**lagern** ['la:gərn], *v.a.* store, warehouse.
**Lagerstätte** ['la:gərʃtɛtə], *f.* (—, *pl.* —n) couch, resting-place; camp site.
**Lagerung** ['la:gəruŋ], *f.* (—, *pl.* —en) encampment; storage; stratification.
**Lagune** [la'gu:nə], *f.* (—, *pl.* —n) lagoon.
**lahm** [la:m], *adj.* lame, paralysed, crippled.
**lahmen** ['la:mən], *v.n.* be lame, limp.
**lähmen** ['lɛ:mən], *v.a.* paralyse.
**lahmlegen** ['la:mle:gən], *v.a.* paralyse.

# Lähmung

**Lähmung** ['lɛ:muŋ], *f.* (—, *pl.* —en) paralysis.
**Laib** [laɪp], *m.* (—es, *pl.* —e) (*bread*) loaf.
**Laich** [laɪç], *m.* (—es, *pl.* —e) spawn.
**laichen** ['laɪçən], *v.n.* spawn.
**Laie** ['laɪə], *m.* (—n, *pl.* —n) layman, (*pl.*) laity.
**Lakai** [la'kaɪ], *m.* (—en, *pl.* —en) lackey, flunkey, footman.
**Lake** ['la:kə], *f.* (—, *pl.* —n) brine, pickle.
**Laken** ['la:kən], *n.* (—s, *pl.* —) (*bed*) sheet.
**lakonisch** [la'ko:nɪʃ], *adj.* laconic.
**Lakritze** [ la'krɪtsə], *f.* (—, *pl.* —n) liquorice.
**lallen** ['lalən], *v.a., v.n.* stammer; babble.
**Lama** (1) ['la:ma:], *n.* (—s, *pl.* —s) (*animal*) llama.
**Lama** (2) ['la:ma:], *m.* (—s, *pl.* —s) (*priest*) lama.
**lamentieren** [lamɛn'ti:rən], *v.n.* lament, wail.
**Lamm** [lam], *n.* (—es, *pl.* ̈er) (*Zool.*) lamb.
**Lämmchen** ['lɛmçən], *n.* (—s, *pl.* —) (*Zool.*) lamb.
**Lämmergeier** ['lɛmərgaɪər], *m.* (—s, *pl.* —) (*Orn.*) great bearded vulture.
**Lampe** ['lampə], *f.* (—, *pl.* —n) lamp.
**Lampenfieber** ['lampənfi:bər], *n.* (—s, *no pl.*) stage-fright.
**Lampenputzer** ['lampənputsər], *m.* (—s, *pl.* —) lamplighter.
**Lampenschirm** ['lampənʃɪrm], *m.* (—s, *pl.* —e) lampshade.
**Lampion** [lam'pjɔ̃], *m. & n.* (—s, *pl.* —s) Chinese lantern.
**lancieren** [lãˈsi:rən], *v.a.* thrust; launch.
**Land** [lant], *n.* (—es, *pl.* —e (*Poet.*) and ̈er) land, country; state; ground, soil; *das Gelobte* —, the Promised Land; *an* — *gehen*, go ashore; *aufs* — *gehen*, go into the country.
**Landadel** ['lanta:dəl], *m.* (—s, *no pl.*) landed gentry.
**Landarbeiter** ['lantarbaɪtər], *m.* (—s, *pl.* —) farm-worker.
**Landauer** ['landauər], *m.* (—s, *pl.* —) landau.
**Landebahn** ['landəba:n], *f.* (—, *pl.* —en) (*Aviat.*) runway.
**landen** ['landən], *v.n.* (*aux. sein*) land, disembark; (*aircraft*) land, touch down.
**Landenge** ['lantɛŋə], *f.* (—, *pl.* —n) isthmus.
**Ländereien** ['lɛndəraɪən], *f. pl.* landed property, estate.
**Landeserzeugnis** ['landəsɛrtsɔyknɪs], *n.* (—sses, *pl.* —sse) home produce.
**Landesfürst** ['landəsfyrst], *m.* (—en, *pl.* —en) sovereign.
**Landesherr** ['landəshɛr], *m.* (—n, *pl.* —en) (reigning) prince; sovereign.
**Landeshoheit** ['landəshohaɪt], *f.* (—, *no pl.*) sovereignty.

**Landeskirche** ['landəskɪrçə], *f.* (—, *pl.* —n) established church; national church.
**Landesschuld** ['landəsʃult], *f.* (—, *no pl.*) national debt.
**Landessprache** ['landəsʃpra:xə], *f.* (—, *pl.* —n) vernacular.
**Landestracht** ['landəstraxt], *f.* (—, *pl.* —en) national costume.
**landesüblich** ['landəsy:plɪç], *adj.* conventional, usual, customary.
**Landesverweisung** ['landəsfɛrvaɪzuŋ], *f.* (—, *pl.* —en) exile, banishment.
**landflüchtig** ['lantflyçtɪç], *adj.* fugitive.
**Landfrieden** ['lantfri:dən], *m.* (—s, *no pl.*) King's (*or* Queen's) peace; (*medieval*) public peace.
**Landgericht** ['lantgərɪçt], *n.* (—es, *pl.* —e) district court; county court.
**Landgraf** ['lantgra:f], *m.* (—en, *pl.* —en) landgrave, count.
**Landhaus** ['lanthaus], *n.* (—es, *pl.* ̈er) country house.
**Landjunker** ['lantjuŋkər], *m.* (—s, *pl.* —) country squire.
**Landkarte** ['lantkartə], *f.* (—, *pl.* —n) map.
**landläufig** ['lantlɔyfɪç], *adj.* customary, conventional.
**ländlich** ['lɛntlɪç], *adj.* rural, rustic.
**Landmann** ['lantman], *m.* (—es, *pl.* **Landleute**) rustic, peasant.
**Landmesser** ['lantmɛsər], *m.* (—s, *pl.* —) surveyor.
**Landpartie** ['lantparti:], *f.* (—, *pl.* —n) country excursion, picnic.
**Landplage** ['lantpla:gə], *f.* (—, *pl.* —n) scourge, calamity; *eine richtige* —, a public nuisance.
**Landrat** ['lantra:t], *m.* (—s, *pl.* ̈e) district president *or* magistrate.
**Landratte** ['lantratə], *f.* (—, *pl.* —n) landlubber.
**Landrecht** ['lantrɛçt], *n.* (—es, *no pl.*) common law.
**Landregen** ['lantre:gən], *m.* (—s, *no pl.*) steady downpour; persistent rain.
**Landschaft** ['lantʃaft], *f.* (—, *pl.* —en) landscape.
**landschaftlich** ['lantʃaftlɪç], *adj.* scenic.
**Landsknecht** ['lantsknɛçt], *m.* (—es, *pl.* —e) mercenary; hired soldier.
**Landsmann** ['lantsman], *m.* (—es, *pl.* **Landsleute**) fellow-countryman, compatriot.
**Landspitze** ['lantʃpɪtsə], *f.* (—, *pl.* —n) cape, headland, promontory.
**Landstraße** ['lantʃtra:sə], *f.* (—, *pl.* —n) open road, main road, highway.
**Landstreicher** ['lantʃtraɪçər], *m.* (—s, *pl.* —) vagabond, tramp, (*Am.*) hobo.
**Landstrich** ['lantʃtrɪç], *m.* (—es, *pl.* —e) tract of land.
**Landsturm** ['lantʃturm], *m.* (—s, *no pl.*) (*Milit.*) militia; Home Guard.
**Landtag** ['lantta:k], *m.* (—s, *pl.* —e) (*Parl.*) diet.
**Landung** ['landuŋ], *f.* (—, *pl.* —en) landing.
**Landvermesser** *see* **Landmesser**.

**Landvogt** ['lantfo:kt], *m.* (—es, *pl.* ⁀e) (provincial) governor.
**Landweg** ['lantve:k], *m.* (—s, *pl.* —e) overland route.
**Landwehr** ['lantve:r], *f.* (—, *pl.* —en) militia.
**Landwirt** ['lantvɪrt], *m.* (—s, *pl.* —e) farmer, husbandman.
**Landwirtschaft** ['lantvɪrtʃaft], *f.* (—, *no pl.*) agriculture.
**Landzunge** ['lanttsuŋə], *f.* (—, *pl.* —n) spit of land.
**lang** [laŋ], *adj.* long, tall. — *adv.*, *prep.* (*prec. by Acc.*) for, during, long.
**langatmig** ['laŋa:tmɪç], *adj.* long-winded.
**lange** ['laŋə], *adv.* a long time; *wie —?* how long? *so — wie*, as long as.
**Länge** ['lɛŋə], *f.* (—, *pl.* —n) length; (*Geog.*) longitude.
**langen** ['laŋən], *v.a.* reach, hand, give s.o. s.th. — *v.n.* suffice, be enough.
**Längengrad** ['lɛŋəŋgra:t], *m.* (—s, *pl.* —e) degree of longitude.
**Längenkreis** ['lɛŋəŋkraɪs], *m.* (—es, *pl.* —e) meridian.
**Längenmaß** ['lɛŋənma:s], *n.* (—es, *pl.* —e) linear measure.
**Langeweile** ['laŋəvaɪlə], *f.* (—, *no pl.*) boredom, ennui.
**Langfinger** ['laŋfɪŋər], *m.* (—s, *pl.* —) pickpocket.
**langjährig** ['laŋjɛ:rɪç], *adj.* of long standing.
**Langlebigkeit** ['laŋle:bɪçkaɪt], *f.* (—, *no pl.*) longevity.
**länglich** ['lɛŋlɪç], *adj.* oblong.
**Langmut** ['laŋmu:t], *f.* (—, *no pl.*) forbearance, patience.
**längs** [lɛŋs], *prep.* (*Genit.*, *Dat.*) along.
**langsam** ['laŋza:m], *adj.* slow; deliberate.
**längst** [lɛŋst], *adv.* long ago, long since.
**längstens** ['lɛŋstəns], *adv.* at the longest; at the latest.
**Languste** [laŋ'gustə], *f.* (—, *pl.* —n) (*Zool.*) spiny lobster.
**langweilen** ['laŋvaɪlən],*v.a.(insep.)* bore, tire. — *v.r. sich —*, feel bored, be bored.
**langwierig** ['laŋvi:rɪç], *adj.* lengthy, protracted, wearisome.
**Lanze** ['lantsə], *f.* (—, *pl.* —n) lance, spear; *eine — brechen*, take up the cudgels, stand up for (s.th. *or* s.o.).
**Lanzenstechen** ['lantsənʃtɛçən], *n.* (—s, *no pl.*) tournament.
**Lanzette** [lan'tsetə], *f.* (—, *pl.* —n) lancet.
**Lanzknecht** ['lantsknɛçt], *m.* (—es, *pl.* —e) see **Landsknecht**.
**Laos** ['la:ɔs], *n.* Laos.
**Lappalie** [la'pa:ljə], *f.* (—, *pl.* —n) trifle.
**Lappen** ['lapən], *m.* (—s, *pl.* —) rag, duster, patch; (*ear*) lobe.
**Läpperschulden** ['lɛpərʃuldən], *f. pl.* petty debts.
**läppisch** ['lɛpɪʃ], *adj.* silly, foolish, trifling.
**Lappland** ['lapland], *n.* Lapland.

**Lärche** ['lɛrçə], *f.* (—, *pl.* —n) (*Bot.*) larch.
**Lärm** [lɛrm], *m.* (—s, *no pl.*) noise, din.
**lärmen** ['lɛrmən], *v.n.* make a noise, brawl.
**Larve** ['larfə], *f.* (—, *pl.* —n) mask; (*Ent.*) grub, larva.
**lasch** [laʃ], *adj.* limp; insipid.
**Lasche** ['laʃə], *f.* (—, *pl.* —n) flap; (*shoe*) gusset, strip.
**lassen** ['lasən], *v.a.*, *v.n. irr.* let, allow, suffer, permit; leave; make, cause; order, command; desist.
**läßlich** ['lɛslɪç], *adj.* (*Eccl.*) venial (*sin*).
**lässig** ['lɛsɪç], *adj.* indolent, sluggish, inactive.
**Lässigkeit** ['lɛsɪçkaɪt], *f.* (—, *no pl.*) lassitude, inaction, indolence; negligence.
**Last** [last], *f.* (—, *pl.* —en) load, burden, weight, charge.
**lasten** ['lastən], *v.n.* be heavy; weigh (on).
**lastenfrei** ['lastənfraɪ], *adj.* unencumbered.
**Laster** ['lastər], *n.* (—s, *pl.* —) vice.
**Lästerer** ['lɛstərər], *m.* (—s, *pl.* —) slanderer, calumniator; blasphemer.
**lasterhaft** ['lastərhaft], *adj.* vicious, wicked; corrupt.
**Lasterhöhle** ['lastərhø:lə], *f.* (—, *pl.* —n) den of vice.
**lästerlich** ['lɛstərlɪç], *adj.* blasphemous.
**lästern** ['lɛstərn], *v.a.* slander, defame; blaspheme.
**lästig** ['lɛstɪç], *adj.* tiresome, troublesome.
**Lasttier** ['lasttí:r], *n.* (—es, *pl.* —e) beast of burden.
**Lastwagen** ['lastva:gən], *m.* (—s, *pl.* —) lorry, (*Am.*) truck.
**Lasur** [la'zu:r], *m.* (—s, *pl.* —e) lapis-lazuli; ultramarine.
**Latein** [la'taɪn], *n.* (—s, *no pl.*) Latin.
**lateinisch** [la'taɪnɪʃ], *adj.* Latin.
**Laterne** [la'tɛrnə], *f.* (—, *pl.* —n) lantern; (*street*) lamp.
**latschen** ['la:tʃən], *v.n.* shuffle along.
**Latte** ['latə], *f.* (—, *pl.* —n) lath, batten; *eine lange —*, lanky person.
**Lattich** ['latɪç], *m.* (—s, *pl.* —e) lettuce.
**Latz** [lats], *m.* (—es, *pl.* ⁀e) flap, bib; pinafore.
**lau** [lau], *adj.* tepid, lukewarm, insipid; (*fig.*) half-hearted.
**Laub** [laup], *n.* (—es, *no pl.*) foliage, leaves.
**Laube** ['laubə], *f.* (—, *pl.* —n) arbour, summer-house.
**Laubengang** ['laubəŋgaŋ], *m.* (—es, *pl.* ⁀e) arcade, covered walk.
**Laubfrosch** ['laupfrɔʃ], *m.* (—es, *pl.* ⁀e) (*Zool.*) tree-frog.
**Laubsäge** ['laupzɛ:gə], *f.* (—, *pl.* —n) fret-saw.
**Lauch** [laux], *m.* (—es, *no pl.*) (*Bot.*) leek.
**Lauer** ['lauər], *f.* (—, *no pl.*) ambush, hiding-place; *auf der — sein*, lie in wait.

**lauern** ['lauərn], v.n. lurk, lie in wait (for), watch (for).

**Lauf** [lauf], m. (—es, pl. ⸚e) course, run; running; operation; (river) current; (gun) barrel; (fig.) rein.

**Laufbahn** ['laufba:n], f. (—, pl. —en) career, running; die medizinische — einschlagen, enter upon a medical career.

**Laufband** ['laufbant], n. (—s, pl. ⸚er) (baby) rein, leading-string; (Tech.) conveyor-belt.

**Laufbrücke** ['laufbrykə], f. (—, pl. —n) gangway.

**Laufbursche** ['laufburʃə], m. (—n, pl. —n) errand-boy.

**laufen** ['laufən], v.n. irr. (aux. sein) run; walk; (wheel) turn; flow, trickle down.

**laufend** ['laufənt], adj. current.

**Läufer** ['lɔyfər], m. (—s, pl. —) runner; (carpet) rug; (Chess) bishop; (Footb.) half-back.

**Lauffeuer** ['lauffɔyər], n. (—s, no pl.) wildfire.

**Laufgraben** ['laufgra:bən], m. (—s,, pl. ⸚) trench.

**läufig** ['lɔyfɪç], adj. (animals) ruttish.

**Laufpaß** ['laufpas], m. (—sses, no pl.) den — geben, give (s.o.) the sack.

**Laufschritt** ['laufʃrɪt], m. (—es, pl. —e) march; im —, at the double.

**Laufzeit** ['lauftsait], f. (—, pl. —en) running-time; currency; (animals) rutting time.

**Lauge** ['laugə], f. (—, pl. —en) (Chem.) lye, alkali.

**Lauheit** ['lauhait], f. (—, no pl.) tepidity, lukewarmness; (fig.) half-heartedness.

**Laune** ['launə], f. (—, pl. —n) humour, temper, mood, whim.

**launenhaft** ['launənhaft], adj. moody.

**launig** ['launɪç], adj. humorous.

**launisch** ['launɪʃ], adj. moody, fitful, bad-tempered.

**Laus** [laus], f. (—, pl. ⸚e) (Zool.) louse.

**Lausbub** ['lausbu:p], m. (—en, pl. —en) young scamp, rascal.

**lauschen** ['lauʃən], v.n. listen, eavesdrop.

**Lausejunge** ['lauzəjuŋə], m. (—n, pl. —n) rascal, lout.

**lausig** ['lauzɪç], adj. (vulg.) sordid, lousy.

**laut** [laut], adj. loud, noisy, audible, clamorous. — prep. (Genit.) as per, according to, in virtue of.

**Laut** [laut], m. (—es, pl. —e) sound.

**lautbar** ['lautba:r], adj. — machen, make known.

**Laute** ['lautə], f. (—, pl. —n) (Mus.) lute.

**lauten** ['lautən], v.n. purport, run, read.

**läuten** ['lɔytən], v.a., v.n. ring; toll; es läutet, the bell is ringing.

**lauter** ['lautər], adj. clear, pure; (fig.) single-minded; genuine; nothing but. — adv. merely.

**Lauterkeit** ['lautərkait], f. (—, no pl.) clearness, purity; (fig.) single-mindedness, integrity.

**läutern** ['lɔytərn], v.a. clear, purify; refine.

**Läuterung** ['lɔytəruŋ], f. (—, pl. —en) clearing, purification; refinement.

**lautieren** [lau'ti:rən], v.a. read phonetically.

**Lautlehre** ['lautle:rə], f. (—, no pl.) phonetics.

**lautlich** ['lautlɪç], adj. phonetic.

**lautlos** ['lautlo:s], adj. mute, silent; noiseless.

**Lautmalerei** ['lautma:lərai], f. (—, no pl.) onomatopoeia.

**Lautsprecher** ['lautʃpreçər], m. (—s, pl. —) loudspeaker.

**Lautverschiebung** ['lautferʃi:buŋ], f. (—, pl. —en) sound shift.

**lauwarm** ['lauvarm], adj. lukewarm, tepid; (fig.) half-hearted.

**Lava** ['la:va], f. (—, no pl.) lava.

**Lavendel** [la'vendəl], m. (—s, no pl.) (Bot.) lavender.

**lavieren** [la'vi:rən], v.n. tack; (fig.) wangle.

**Lawine** [la'vi:nə], f. (—, pl. —n) avalanche.

**lax** [laks], adj. lax, loose.

**Laxheit** ['lakshait], f. (—, pl. —en) laxity.

**Laxiermittel** [lak'si:rmɪtəl], n. (—s, pl. —) laxative, aperient.

**Lazarett** [latsa'ret], n. (—s, pl. —e) infirmary, military hospital.

**Lebemann** ['le:bəman], m. (—es, pl. ⸚er) man about town.

**Leben** ['le:bən], n. (—s, pl. —) life; (fig.) existence; activity; animation, bustle, stir.

**leben** ['le:bən], v.n. live, be alive.

**lebend** ['le:bənt], adj. alive, living; (language) modern.

**lebendig** [le'vbendɪç], adj. living, alive, quick.

**Lebensanschauung** ['le:bənsanʃauuŋ], f. (—, pl. —en) conception of life, philosophy of life.

**Lebensart** ['le:bənsa:rt], f. (—, no pl.) way of living; (fig.) behaviour; gute —, good manners.

**lebensfähig** ['le:bənsfɛ:ɪç], adj. capable of living, viable.

**lebensgefährlich** ['le:bənsgəfɛ:rlɪç], adj. perilous, extremely dangerous.

**Lebensgeister** ['le:bənsgaistər], m. pl. spirits.

**lebensgroß** ['le:bənsgro:s], adj. life-size.

**lebenslänglich** ['le:bənslɛŋlɪç], adj. lifelong, for life; —e Rente, life annuity.

**Lebenslauf** ['le:bənslauf], m. (—es, pl. ⸚e) curriculum vitae.

**Lebensmittel** ['le:bənsmɪtəl], n. pl. food, provisions, victuals.

**lebensmüde** ['le:bənsmy:də], adj. weary of life.

**Lebensunterhalt** ['le:bənsuntərhalt], m. (—s, no pl.) livelihood.

**Lebenswandel** ['le:bənsvandəl], m. (—s, no pl.) conduct, mode of life.

**Lebensweise** ['le:bənsvaɪzə], *f.* (—, *no pl.*) habits, way of life.

**Leber** ['le:bər], *f.* (—, *pl.* —n) liver; *frisch von der — weg*, frankly, without mincing matters.

**Leberblümchen** ['le:bərbly:mçən], *n.* (—s, *pl.* —) (*Bot.*) liverwort.

**Leberfleck** ['le:bərflɛk], *m.* (—s, *pl.* —e) mole.

**Lebertran** ['le:bərtra:n], *m.* (—s, *no pl.*) cod-liver oil.

**Leberwurst** ['le:bərvurst], *f.* (—, *pl.* ⸚e) liver sausage.

**Lebewesen** ['le:bəve:zən], *n.* (—s, *pl.* —) living creature.

**Lebewohl** ['le:bəvo:l], *n.*, *excl.* farewell, good-bye; — *sagen*, bid farewell.

**lebhaft** ['le:phaft], *adj.* lively, vivacious, brisk, animated.

**Lebkuchen** ['le:pku:xən], *m.* (—s, *pl.* —) gingerbread.

**Lebzeiten** ['le:ptsaɪtən], *f. pl. zu — von* (*Genit.*), in the lifetime of.

**lechzen** ['lɛçtsən], *v.n.* be parched with thirst; *nach etwas —*, (*fig.*) long for s.th., thirst for s.th.

**Leck** [lɛk], *n.* (—s, *pl.* —e) leak; *ein — bekommen*, spring a leak.

**leck** [lɛk], *adj.* leaky.

**lecken** ['lɛkən], *v.a.* lick, lap.

**lecker** ['lɛkər], *adj.* delicate, delicious, dainty.

**Leckerbissen** ['lɛkərbɪsən], *m.* (—s, *pl.* —) delicacy; dainty, tit-bit.

**Leckerei** [lɛkə'raɪ], *f.* (—, *pl.* —en) delicacy.

**Leder** ['le:dər], *n.* (—s, *no pl.*) leather.

**ledern** ['le:dərn], *adj.* (of) leather, leathery; (*fig.*) dull, boring.

**ledig** ['le:dɪç], *adj.* unmarried, single; (*fig.*) rid of, free from.

**lediglich** ['le:dɪklɪç], *adv.* merely, only, solely.

**leer** [le:r], *adj.* empty, void; blank; (*fig.*) hollow, futile, empty, vain, inane.

**Leere** ['le:rə], *f.* (—, *no pl.*) emptiness, void, vacuum.

**leeren** ['le:rən], *v.a.* empty, evacuate.

**Leerlauf** ['le:rlauf], *m.* (—s, *no pl.*) (*Motor.*) idling; (*gear*) neutral.

**legalisieren** [legali'zi:rən], *v.a.* legalise, authenticate.

**Legat** (1) [le'ga:t], *m.* (—en, *pl.* —en) legate.

**Legat** (2) [le'ga:t], *n.* (—s, *pl.* —e) legacy, bequest.

**Legationsrat** [lega'tsjo:nsra:t], *m.* (—s, *pl.* ⸚e) counsellor in a legation.

**legen** ['le:gən], *v.a.* lay, put, place. — *v.r. sich —*, lie down; cease, subside.

**Legende** [le'gɛndə], *f.* (—, *pl.* —n) legend.

**Legierung** [lə'gi:ruŋ], *f.* (—, *pl.* —en) alloy.

**Legion** [le'gjo:n], *f.* (—, *pl.* —en) legion.

**Legionär** [le:gjo'nɛ:r], *m.* (—s, *pl.* —e) legionary.

**legitim** [legi'ti:m], *adj.* legitimate.

**Legitimation** [legitima'tsjo:n], *f.* (—, *pl.* —en) proof of identity.

**legitimieren** [legiti'mi:rən], *v.a.* legitimise. — *v.r. sich —*, prove o.'s identity.

**Lehen** ['le:ən], *n.* (—s, *pl.* —) fief; *zu — geben*, invest with, enfeoff; *zu — tragen*, hold in fee.

**Lehensdienst** *see* Lehnsdienst.

**Lehenseid** *see* Lehnseid.

**Lehensmann** *see* Lehnsmann.

**Lehm** [le:m], *m.* (—s, *no pl.*) loam, clay, mud.

**lehmig** ['le:mɪç], *adj.* clayey, loamy.

**Lehne** ['le:nə], *f.* (—, *pl.* —n) support, prop; (*chair*) back, arm-rest.

**lehnen** ['le:nən], *v.a., v.n.* lean. — *v.r. sich — an*, lean against.

**Lehnsdienst** ['le:nsdi:nst], *m.* (—es, *pl.* —e) feudal service.

**Lehnseid** ['le:nsaɪt], *m.* (—es, *pl.* —e) oath of allegiance.

**Lehnsmann** ['le:nsman], *m.* (—es, *pl.* ⸚er) feudal tenant, vassal.

**Lehnstuhl** ['le:nʃtu:l], *m.* (—s, *pl.* ⸚e) armchair, easy chair.

**Lehramt** ['le:ramt], *n.* (—es, *pl.* ⸚er) professorship; teaching post *or* profession.

**Lehrbrief** ['le:rbri:f], *m.* (—es, *pl.* —e) apprentice's indentures; certificate of apprenticeship.

**Lehrbuch** ['le:rbu:x], *n.* (—es, *pl.* ⸚er) textbook, manual.

**Lehre** ['le:rə], *f.* (—, *pl.* —n) teaching, advice, rule, doctrine, dogma, moral; (*craft*) apprenticeship.

**lehren** ['le:rən], *v.a.* teach, inform, instruct; profess.

**Lehrer** ['le:rər], *m.* (—s, *pl.* —) teacher, instructor, schoolmaster.

**Lehrgang** ['le:rgaŋ], *m.* (—es, *pl.* ⸚e) course (of instruction).

**Lehrgegenstand** ['le:rge:gənʃtant], *m.* (—es, *pl.* ⸚e) subject of instruction; branch of study.

**Lehrgeld** ['le:rgɛlt], *n.* (—es, *pl.* —er) premium for apprenticeship; — *zahlen*, (*fig.*) pay for o.'s experience.

**Lehrkörper** ['le:rkœrpər], *m.* (—s, *no pl.*) teaching staff; (*Univ.*) faculty.

**Lehrling** ['le:rlɪŋ], *m.* (—s, *pl.* —e) apprentice.

**Lehrmädchen** ['le:rmɛːtçən], *n.* (—s, *pl.* —) girl apprentice.

**Lehrmeister** ['le:rmaɪstər], *m.* (—s, *pl.* —) teacher, instructor, master.

**Lehrmittel** ['le:rmɪtəl], *n.* (—s, *pl.* —) teaching appliance *or* aid.

**lehrreich** ['le:rraɪç], *adj.* instructive.

**Lehrsatz** ['le:rzats], *m.* (—es, *pl.* ⸚e) tenet, dogma, rule; (*Maths.*) theorem.

**Lehrstuhl** ['le:rʃtu:l], *m.* (—s, *pl.* ⸚e) (*Univ.*) chair; professorship.

**Lehrzeit** ['le:rtsaɪt], *f.* (—, *pl.* —en) apprenticeship.

**Leib** [laɪp], *m.* (—es, *pl.* —er) body; abdomen; womb.

**Leibarzt** ['laɪpa:rtst], *m.* (—es, *pl.* ⸚e) court surgeon.

**Leibbinde** ['laɪpbɪndə], *f.* (—, *pl.* —n) abdominal belt.

**Leibchen** ['laɪpçən], *n.* (—s, *pl.* —) bodice, corset; vest.

**leibeigen** [laɪp'aɪgən], *adj.* in bondage, in thraldom, in serfdom.

**Leibeserbe** ['laɪbəserbə], *m.* (—n, *pl.* —n) heir, descendant, offspring; (*pl.*) issue.

**Leibesfrucht** ['laɪbəsfruxt], *f.* (—, *pl.* ̈e) embryo, foetus.

**Leibeskraft** ['laɪbəskraft], *f.* (—, *pl.* ̈e) bodily strength; *aus* —en, with might and main.

**Leibesübung** ['laɪbəsy:buŋ], *f.* (—, *pl.* —en) physical exercise; (*pl.*) gymnastic exercises.

**Leibgericht** ['laɪpgərɪçt], *n.* (—s, *pl.* —e) favourite dish.

**leibhaftig** [laɪp'haftɪç], *adj.* real, incarnate, in person.

**leiblich** ['laɪplɪç], *adj.* bodily, corporeal.

**Leibrente** ['laɪprɛntə], *f.* (—, *pl.* —n) life-annuity.

**Leibschmerzen** ['laɪpʃmɛrtsən], *m. pl.* stomach-ache.

**Leibspeise** ['laɪpʃpaɪzə], *f.* (—, *pl.* —n) favourite dish.

**Leibwache** ['laɪpvaxə], *f.* (—, *no pl.*) body-guard.

**Leibwäsche** ['laɪpvɛʃə], *f.* (—, *no pl.*) underwear.

**Leiche** ['laɪçə], *f.* (—, *pl.* —n) (dead) body, corpse; (*dial.*) funeral.

**Leichenbegängnis** ['laɪçənbəgɛŋnɪs], *n.* (—ses, *pl.* —se) funeral, burial, interment.

**Leichenbeschauer** ['laɪçənbəʃauər], *m.* (—s, *pl.* —) coroner.

**Leichenbestatter** ['laɪçənbəʃtater], *m.* (—s, *pl.* —) undertaker; (*Am.*) mortician.

**leichenhaft** ['laɪçenhaft], *adj.* corpse-like, cadaverous.

**Leichenschau** ['laɪçənʃau], *f.* (—, *no pl.*) post mortem (examination), (coroner's) inquest.

**Leichentuch** ['laɪçəntu:x], *n.* (—es, *pl.* ̈er) shroud, pall.

**Leichenverbrennung** ['laɪçənferbrennuŋ], *f.* (—, *pl.* —en) cremation.

**Leichenwagen** ['laɪçənva:gən], *m.* (—s, *pl.* —) hearse.

**Leichenzug** ['laɪçəntsu:k], *m.* (—es, *pl.* ̈e) funeral procession.

**Leichnam** ['laɪçna:m], *m.* (—s, *pl.* —e) (dead) body, corpse.

**leicht** [laɪçt], *adj.* light; slight; weak; easy.

**leichtfertig** ['laɪçtfertɪç], *adj.* frivolous, irresponsible.

**leichtgläubig** ['laɪçtglɔybɪç], *adj.* credulous, gullible.

**leichthin** ['laɪçthɪn], *adv.* lightly.

**Leichtigkeit** ['laɪçtɪçkaɪt], *f.* (—, *no pl.*) ease, facility.

**Leichtsinn** ['laɪçtzɪn], *m.* (—s, *no pl.*) thoughtlessness, carelessness; frivolity.

**Leid** [laɪt], *n.* (—es, *no pl.*) sorrow, grief; harm, hurt; *einem etwas zu* —e *tun,* harm s.o.

**leid** [laɪt], *adj. es tut mir* —, I am sorry; *du tust mir* —, I am sorry for you.

**Leiden** ['laɪdən], *n.* (—s, *pl.* —) suffering, misfortune; (*illness*) affliction, complaint; *das* — *Christi,* the Passion.

**leiden** ['laɪdən], *v.a., v.n. irr.* suffer, bear, endure, undergo.

**Leidenschaft** ['laɪdənʃaft], *f.* (—, *pl.* —en) passion.

**leider** ['laɪdər], *adv.* unfortunately.

**leidig** ['laɪdɪç], *adj.* tiresome, unpleasant.

**leidlich** ['laɪtlɪç], *adj.* tolerable, moderate.

**leidtragend** ['laɪttra:gənt], *adj.* in mourning.

**Leidtragende** ['laɪttra:gəndə], *m. or f.* (—n, *pl.* —n) mourner.

**Leidwesen** ['laɪtve:zən], *n.* (—s, *no pl.*) *zu meinem* —, to my regret.

**Leier** ['laɪər], *f.* (—, *pl.* —n) lyre.

**Leierkasten** ['laɪərkastən], *m.* (—s, *pl.* ̈) barrel organ.

**leiern** ['laɪərn], *v.n.* drone, drawl on.

**leihen** ['laɪən], *v.a. irr. einem etwas* —, lend s.o. s.th.; *von einem etwas* —, borrow s.th. from s.o.

**Leim** [laɪm], *m.* (—s, *no pl.*) glue; *einem auf den* — *gehen,* be taken in by s.o., fall for s.th.

**Leimfarbe** ['laɪmfarbə], *f.* (—, *pl.* —en) water-colour, distemper.

**Lein** [laɪn], *m.* (—s, *pl.* —e) linseed, flax.

**Leine** ['laɪnə], *f.* (—, *pl.* —n) line, cord.

**Leinen** ['laɪnən], *n.* (—s, *no pl.*) linen.

**Leinöl** ['laɪnø:l], *n.* (—s, *no pl.*) linseed oil.

**Leintuch** ['laɪntu:x], *n.* (—es, *pl.* ̈er) linen sheet, sheeting.

**Leinwand** ['laɪnvant], *f.* (—, *no pl.*) linen, sheeting; (*Art*) canvas; (*film*) screen.

**leise** ['laɪzə], *adj.* low, soft, gentle, faint, slight; delicate.

**Leiste** ['laɪstə], *f.* (—, *pl.* —n) ledge, border; groin.

**Leisten** ['laɪstən], *m.* (—s, *pl.* —) (*shoe*) last, form.

**leisten** ['laɪstən], *v.a.* do, perform; accomplish; *ich kann es mir nicht* —, I cannot afford it.

**Leistenbruch** ['laɪstənbrux], *m.* (—es, *pl.* ̈e) hernia, rupture.

**Leistung** ['laɪstuŋ], *f.* (—, *pl.* —en) performance, accomplishment, achievement.

**leistungsfähig** ['laɪstuŋksfe:ɪç], *adj.* efficient.

**leiten** ['laɪtən], *v.a.* lead, guide, manage; preside over.

**Leiter** (1) ['laɪtər], *m.* (—s, *pl.* —) leader, manager; conductor; head.

**Leiter** (2) ['laɪtər], *f.* (—, *pl.* —) ladder.

**Leiterwagen** ['laɪtərva:gən], *m.* (—s, *pl.* —) rack-wagon; (*Austr.*) small hand-cart.

# Liebhaberin

**Leitfaden** ['laɪtfaːdən], *m.* (—s, *pl.* ∵) (*book*) manual, textbook, guide.

**Leitstern** ['laɪtʃtɛrn], *m.* (—s, *pl.* —e) pole-star; (*fig.*) lodestar, guiding star.

**Leitung** ['laɪtuŋ], *f.* (—, *pl.* —en) management, direction; (*Elec.*) lead, connection; line; (water- *or* gas-) main(s); pipeline; *eine lange — haben*, be slow in the uptake.

**Leitungsvermögen** ['laɪtuŋsfɛrmøːgən], *n.* (—s, *no pl.*) conductivity.

**Leitwerk** ['laɪtvɛrk], *n.* (—s, *no pl.*) (*Aviat.*) tail unit.

**Lektion** [lɛktsˈjoːn], *f.* (—, *pl.* —en) lesson; *einem eine — geben*, lecture s.o.

**Lektor** ['lɛktɔr], *m.* (—s, *pl.* —en) publisher's reader; teacher, lector.

**Lektüre** [lɛkˈtyːrə], *f.* (—, *pl.* —n) reading matter, books.

**Lende** ['lɛndə], *f.* (—, *pl.* —n) (*Anat.*) loin.

**lendenlahm** ['lɛndənlaːm], *adj.* weak-kneed, lame.

**lenkbar** ['lɛŋkbaːr], *adj.* dirigible, manageable, tractable, governable.

**lenken** ['lɛŋkən], *v.a.* drive, steer; (*fig.*) direct, rule, manage.

**Lenkstange** ['lɛŋkʃtaŋə], *f.* (—, *pl.* —n) connecting-rod; (*bicycle*) handle-bar.

**Lenz** [lɛnts], *m.* (—es, *pl.* —e) (*Poet.*) spring.

**Lepra** ['leːpra], *f.* (—, *no pl.*) leprosy.

**Lerche** ['lɛrçə], *f.* (—, *pl.* —n) (*Orn.*) lark, skylark.

**lernbegierig** ['lɛrnbəgiːrɪç], *adj.* studious, eager to learn.

**lernen** ['lɛrnən], *v.a.* learn; study; *einen kennen —*, make s.o.'s acquaintance; *auswendig —*, learn by heart.

**Lesart** ['leːsaːrt], *f.* (—, *pl.* —en) reading, version.

**lesbar** ['leːsbaːr], *adj.* legible; readable.

**Lese** ['leːzə], *f.* (—, *pl.* —n) gathering (of fruit); vintage.

**lesen** ['leːzən], *v.a. irr.* gather; glean; read; *die Messe —*, celebrate *or* say mass; *über etwas —*, (*Univ.*) lecture on s.th.

**lesenswert** ['leːzənsvɛrt], *adj.* worth reading.

**Leser** ['leːzər], *m.* (—s, *pl.* —) gatherer, gleaner; reader.

**leserlich** ['leːzərlɪç], *adj.* legible.

**Lettland** ['lɛtlant], *n.* Latvia.

**letzen** ['lɛtsən], *v.a.* (*Poet.*) comfort, cheer, refresh.

**letzt** [lɛtst], *adj.* last, extreme, ultimate, final.

**letztens** ['lɛtstəns], *adv.* lastly, in the end.

**letztere** ['lɛtstərə], *adj.* latter.

**letzthin** ['lɛtsthɪn], *adv.* (*rare*) lately, the other day, recently.

**Leu** [lɔy], *m.* (—en, *pl.* —en) (*Poet.*) lion.

**Leuchte** ['lɔyçtə], *f.* (—, *pl.* —n) light, lamp, lantern; (*fig.*) luminary, star.

**leuchten** ['lɔyçtən], *v.n.* light, shine.

**leuchtend** ['lɔyçtənt], *adj.* shining, bright; luminous.

**Leuchter** ['lɔyçtər], *m.* (—s, *pl.* —) candlestick, candelabrum.

**Leuchtrakete** ['lɔyçtrakeːtə], *f.* (—, *pl.* —n) Roman candle; flare.

**Leuchtturm** ['lɔyçtturm], *m.* (—s, *pl.* ∵e) lighthouse.

**leugnen** ['lɔygnən], *v.a.* deny, disclaim; *nicht zu —*, undeniable.

**Leumund** ['lɔymunt], *m.* (—es, *no pl.*) renown, reputation.

**Leute** ['lɔytə], *pl.* persons, people, men; servants, domestic staff.

**Leutnant** ['lɔytnant], *m.* (—s, *pl.* —s) lieutenant.

**leutselig** ['lɔytzeːlɪç], *adj.* affable, friendly; condescending.

**Levkoje** [lɛfˈkoːjə], *f.* (—, *pl.* —n) (*Bot.*) stock.

**Lexikon** ['lɛksɪkɔn], *n.* (—s, *pl.* —s, —ka) dictionary, lexicon, encyclopaedia.

**Libanon** ['liːbanɔn], *m.* Lebanon.

**Libelle** [liˈbɛlə], *f.* (—, *pl.* —n) (*Ent.*) dragonfly.

**Liberia** [liˈbeːrja], *n.* Liberia.

**Libyen** ['liːbɨ̯ən], *n.* Libya.

**Licht** [lɪçt], *n.* (—es, *pl.* —er) light, candle; luminary.

**licht** [lɪçt], *adj.* light, clear, open.

**Lichtbild** ['lɪçtbɪlt], *n.* (—es, *pl.* —er) photograph.

**Lichtbrechung** ['lɪçtbrɛçuŋ], *f.* (—, *pl.* —en) refraction of light.

**lichten** ['lɪçtən], *v.a.* clear, thin; *den Anker —*, weigh anchor.

**lichterloh** ['lɪçtərloː], *adj.* blazing, ablaze.

**Lichthof** ['lɪçthoːf], *m.* (—s, *pl.* ∵e) well of a court, quadrangle.

**Lichtmeß** ['lɪçtmɛs], *f.* (—, *no pl.*) (*Eccl.*) Candlemas.

**Lichtschirm** ['lɪçtʃɪrm], *m.* (—s, *pl.* —e) screen, lamp-shade.

**Lichtspieltheater** ['lɪçtʃpiːlteatər], *n.* (—s, *pl.* —) cinema.

**Lichtung** ['lɪçtuŋ], *f.* (—, *pl.* —en) glade, clearing.

**Lid** [liːt], *n.* (—s, *pl.* —er) eye-lid.

**lieb** [liːp], *adj.* dear; beloved; good; *das ist mir —*, I am glad of it; *der —e Gott*, God; *unsere —e Frau*, Our Lady; *bei einem — Kind sein*, be a favourite with s.o., curry favour with s.o.

**liebäugeln** ['liːpɔygəln], *v.n. insep.* ogle.

**Liebchen** ['liːpçən], *n.* (—s, *pl.* —) sweetheart, love, darling.

**Liebe** ['liːbə], *f.* (—, *no pl.*) love.

**Liebelei** [liːbəˈlaɪ], *f.* (—, *pl.* —en) flirtation.

**lieben** ['liːbən], *v.a.* love, like, be fond of.

**liebenswürdig** ['liːbənsvyrdɪç], *adj.* amiable, kind, charming.

**lieber** ['liːbər], *adv.* rather, better, sooner; *etwas — tun*, prefer to do s.th.

**Liebhaber** ['liːphaːbər], *m.* (—s, *pl.* —) lover; (*fig.*) amateur, dilettante; (*Theat.*) leading man.

**Liebhaberin** ['liːphaːbərɪn], *f.* leading lady.

141

# liebkosen

**liebkosen** ['li:pko:zən], *v.a. insep.* fondle, caress.
**lieblich** ['li:plɪç], *adj.* lovely, charming, sweet.
**Liebling** ['li:plɪŋ], *m.* (—s, *pl.* —e) darling, favourite.
**lieblos** ['li:plo:s], *adj.* hard-hearted; unkind.
**Liebreiz** ['li:praɪts], *m.* (—es, *no pl.*) charm, attractiveness.
**liebreizend** ['li:praɪtsənt], *adj.* charming.
**Liebschaft** ['li:pʃaft], *f.* (—, *pl.* —en) love affair.
**Lied** [li:t], *n.* (—es, *pl.* —er) song, air, tune; *geistliches* —, hymn.
**liederlich** ['li:dərlɪç], *adj.* careless, slovenly; dissolute, debauched; —*es Leben,* profligacy.
**Lieferant** [li:fə'rant], *m.* (—en, *pl.* —en) supplier, purveyor, contractor; *Eingang für —en,* tradesmen's entrance.
**liefern** ['li:fərn], *v.a.* deliver, furnish, supply.
**Lieferschein** ['li:fərʃaɪn], *m.* (—s, *pl.* —e) delivery note.
**liegen** ['li:gən], *v.n. irr.* lie; be situated; *es liegt mir daran,* it is of importance to me, I have it at heart; *es liegt mir nichts daran,* it is of no consequence to me.
**Liegenschaft** ['li:gənʃaft], *f.* (—, *pl.* —en) landed property, real estate.
**Liga** ['li:ga:], *f.* (—, *pl.* —gen) league.
**Liguster** [li'gustər], *m.* (—s, *no pl.*) privet.
**liieren** [li'i:rən], *v.r.* (*aux.* haben) *sich* — *mit,* unite with, combine with.
**Likör** [li'kø:r], *m.* (—s, *pl.* —e) liqueur.
**lila** ['li:la:] *adj.* (*colour*) lilac.
**Lilie** ['li:ljə], *f.* (—, *pl.* —n) (*Bot.*) lily.
**Limonade** [limo'na:də], *f.* (—, *pl.* —n) lemonade.
**lind** [lɪnt], *adj.* soft, gentle, mild.
**Linde** ['lɪndə], *f.* (—, *pl.* —n) (*Bot.*) lime-tree, linden.
**lindern** ['lɪndərn], *v.a.* soften, assuage, mitigate, soothe, allay.
**Lindwurm** ['lɪntvurm], *m.* (—s, *pl.* ̈er) (*Poet.*) dragon.
**Lineal** [line'a:l], *n.* (—s, *pl.* —e) ruler, rule.
**Linie** ['li:njə], *f.* (—, *pl.* —n) line; lineage, descent; *in erster* —, in the first place.
**Linienschiff** ['li:njənʃɪf], *n.* (—es, *pl.* —e) (*Naut.*) liner.
**lin(i)ieren** [lin'(j)i:rən], *v.a.* rule.
**linkisch** ['lɪŋkɪʃ], *adj.* awkward, clumsy.
**links** [lɪŋks], *adv.* to the left, on the left-hand side; —*um!* left about turn!
**Linnen** ['lɪnən], *n.* (—s, *no pl.*) (*Poet.*) linen.
**Linse** ['lɪnzə], *f.* (—, *pl.* —n) (*vegetable*) lentil; (*optical*) lens.
**linsenförmig** ['lɪnzənfœrmɪç], *adj.* lens-shaped.
**Linsengericht** ['lɪnzəngərɪçt], *n.* (—s, *pl.* —e) (*Bibl.*) mess of pottage.

**Lippe** ['lɪpə], *f.* (—, *pl.* —n) lip; (*coll.*) *eine* — *riskieren,* be cheeky.
**Lippenlaut** ['lɪpənlaut], *m.* (—s, *pl.* —e) (*Phonet.*) labial.
**Lippenstift** ['lɪpənʃtɪft], *m.* (—s, *pl.* —e) lipstick.
**liquidieren** [lɪkvi'di:rən], *v.a.* liquidate, wind up, settle; charge.
**lispeln** ['lɪspəln], *v.n.* lisp.
**Lissabon** [lɪsa'bɔn], *n.* Lisbon.
**List** [lɪst], *f.* (—, *pl.* —en) cunning, craft; trick, stratagem, ruse.
**Liste** ['lɪstə], *f.* (—, *pl.* —n) list, roll, catalogue.
**listig** ['lɪstɪç], *adj.* cunning, crafty, sly.
**Listigkeit** ['lɪstɪçkaɪt], *f.* (—, *no pl.*) slyness, craftiness.
**Litanei** [lita'naɪ], *f.* (—, *pl.* —en) litany.
**Litauen** ['lɪtauən], *n.* Lithuania.
**Liter** ['li:tər], *m. & n.* (—s, *pl.* —) litre.
**literarisch** [litə'ra:rɪʃ], *adj.* literary.
**Literatur** [litəra'tu:r], *f.* (—, *pl.* —en) literature, letters.
**Litfaßsäule** ['lɪtfaszɔylə], *f.* (—, *pl.* —n) advertisement pillar.
**Liturgie** [litur'gi:], *f.* (—, *pl.* —n) liturgy.
**Litze** ['lɪtsə], *f.* (—, *pl.* —n) lace, braid, cord; (*Elec.*) flex.
**Livland** ['li:flant], *n.* Livonia.
**Livree** [li'vre:], *f.* (—, *pl.* —n) livery.
**Lizenz** [li'tsɛnts], *f.* (—, *pl.* —en) licence.
**Lob** [lo:p], *n.* (—es, *no pl.*) praise, commendation.
**loben** ['lo:bən], *v.a.* praise, commend.
**lobesam** ['lo:bəza:m], *adj.* (*Poet.*) worthy, honourable.
**Lobgesang** ['lo:pgəzaŋ], *m.* (—s, *pl.* ̈e) hymn of praise.
**Lobhudelei** [lo:phu:də'laɪ], *f.* (—, *pl.* —en) adulation, flattery, toadying.
**löblich** ['lø:plɪç], *adj.* laudable, commendable, meritorious.
**lobpreisen** ['lo:ppraɪzən], *v.a. insep.* eulogise, extol.
**Lobrede** ['lo:prɛːdə], *f.* (—, *pl.* —n) panegyric, eulogy.
**Loch** [lɔx], *n.* (—es, *pl.* ̈er) hole.
**Lochbohrer** ['lɔxbo:rər], *m.* (—s, *pl.* —) auger.
**lochen** ['lɔxən], *v.a.* perforate, punch.
**Locher** ['lɔxər], *m.* (—s, *pl.* —) perforator, punch.
**löcherig** ['lœçərɪç], *adj.* full of holes.
**Lochmeißel** ['lɔxmaɪsəl], *m.* (—s, *pl.* —) mortice-chisel.
**Locke** ['lɔkə], *f.* (—, *pl.* —n) curl, lock, ringlet, tress.
**locken** ['lɔkən], *v.a.* allure, decoy, entice.
**locker** ['lɔkər], *adj.* loose; slack; spongy; dissolute; *nicht* — *lassen,* stick to o.'s guns.
**lockern** ['lɔkərn], *v.a.* loosen.
**lockig** ['lɔkɪç], *adj.* curled, curly.
**Lockmittel** ['lɔkmɪtəl], *n.* (—s, *pl.* —) inducement, lure, bait.
**Lockspeise** ['lɔkʃpaɪzə], *f.* (—, *pl.* —n) lure, bait.

# Lotrechtstarter

**Lockung** ['lɔkuŋ], f. (—, pl. —en) allurement, enticement.

**Lockvogel** ['lɔkfoːgəl], m. (—s, pl. ˙) decoy-bird.

**Loden** ['loːdən], m. (—s, pl. —) coarse cloth, frieze.

**lodern** ['loːdərn], v.n. blaze, flame.

**Löffel** ['lœfəl], m. (—s, pl. —) spoon; (animal) ear; einen über den — barbieren, take s.o. in.

**Logarithmus** [loga'rɪtmus], m. (—, pl. —men) logarithm.

**Logbuch** ['lɔkbuːx], n. (—es, pl. ˙er) logbook.

**Loge** ['loːʒə], f. (—, pl. —n) (Theat.) box; (Freemasonry) lodge.

**Logenschließer** ['loːʒənʃliːsər], m. (—s, pl. —) (Theat.) attendant.

**logieren** [lo'ʒiːrən], v.n. board (with).

**Logis** [lo'ʒiː], n. (—, pl. —) lodgings.

**logisch** ['loːgɪʃ], adj. logical.

**Lohe** ['loːhə], f. (—, pl. —n) tanning bark; flame.

**Lohgerber** ['loːgɛrbər], m. (—s, pl. —) tanner.

**Lohn** [loːn], m. (—s, pl. ˙e) wages, pay; reward; recompense.

**lohnen** ['loːnən], v.a. reward, recompense, remunerate; pay wages to; es lohnt sich nicht, it is not worth while.

**Lohnstopp** ['loːnʃtɔp], m. (—s, pl. —s) pay pause, wage freeze.

**Löhnung** ['løːnuŋ], f. (—, pl. —en) pay, payment.

**Lokal** [lo'kaːl], n. (—s, pl —e) locality, premises; inn, pub, café.

**lokalisieren** [lokali'ziːrən], v.a. localise.

**Lokalität** [lokali'tɛːt], f. (—, pl. —en) see Lokal.

**Lokomotive** [lokomo'tiːvə], f. (—, pl. —n) (Railw.) locomotive, engine.

**Lokomotivführer** [lokomo'tiːffyːrər], m. (—s, pl. —) (Railw.) engine-driver.

**Lombard** [lɔm'bart], m. (—s, pl. —e) deposit-bank, loan bank.

**Lombardei** [lɔmbar'daɪ], f. Lombardy.

**Lorbeer** ['lɔrbeːr], m. (—s, pl. —en) laurel.

**Lorbeerbaum** ['lɔrbeːrbaum], m. (—s, pl. ˙e) laurel-tree, bay-tree.

**Lorbeerspiritus** ['lɔrbeːrʃpiːritus], m. (—, no pl.) bay rum.

**Lorgnon** [lɔrn'jõ], n. (—s, pl. —s) monocle, eye-glass.

**Los** [loːs], n. (—es, pl. —e) share, ticket; lot, fate; das große —, first prize.

**los** [loːs], adj. loose, untied; free from, released from, rid of; (Am.) quit of; was ist los? what is going on? what's the matter? etwas — werden, get rid of s.th.; schieß los! fire away!

**lösbar** ['løːsbaːr], adj. (question, riddle) soluble.

**losbinden** ['loːsbɪndən], v.a. irr. untie, unbind, loosen.

**losbrechen** ['loːsbrɛçən], v.a. irr. break off. — v.n. (aux. sein) break loose.

**Löschblatt** ['lœʃblat], n. (—es, pl. ˙er) blotting-paper.

**Löscheimer** ['lœʃaɪmər], m. (—s, pl. —) fire-bucket.

**löschen** ['lœʃən], v.a. put out; extinguish; (debt) cancel; (writing) efface, blot; (freight) (Naut.) unload; (thirst) quench.

**Löschpapier** ['lœʃpapiːr], n. (—s, no pl.) blotting-paper.

**Löschung** ['lœʃuŋ], f. (—, pl. —en) (freight) (Naut.) discharging, landing, unloading.

**losdrücken** ['loːsdrykən], v.n. discharge, fire.

**lose** ['loːzə], adj. loose, slack; (fig.) dissolute; —s Maul, malicious tongue.

**Lösegeld** ['løːzəgɛlt], n. (—es, pl. —er) ransom.

**losen** ['loːzən], v.n. draw lots.

**lösen** ['løːzən], v.a. loosen, untie; absolve, free, deliver; dissolve; solve; (relations) break off; (tickets) take, buy.

**losgehen** ['loːsgeːən], v.n. irr. (aux. sein) begin; (gun) go off; auf einen —, go for s.o.; jetzt kann's —, now for it.

**loskaufen** ['loːskaufən], v.a. redeem, ransom.

**loskommen** ['loːskɔmən], v.n. irr. (aux. sein) come loose; von etwas —, get rid of s.th.

**löslich** ['løːslɪç], adj. (Chem.) soluble.

**loslösen** ['loːsløːzən], v.a. detach.

**losmachen** ['loːsmaxən], v.a. free from. — v.r. sich — von, disengage o.s. from.

**losreißen** ['loːsraɪsən], v.a. irr. pull away, separate. — v.n. (aux. sein), break loose. — v.r. sich — von, tear o.s. away from.

**lossagen** ['loːszaːgən], v.r. sich — von, renounce s.th., dissociate o.s. from s.th.

**losschlagen** ['loːsʃlaːgən], v.a. knock loose; let fly; (fig.) sell, dispose of.

**lossprechen** ['loːsʃprɛçən], v.a. irr. (Eccl.) absolve; (Law) acquit.

**lossteuern** ['loːsʃtɔyərn], v.n. — auf, make for.

**Losung** ['loːzuŋ], f. (—, pl. —en) watchword, motto, password, slogan.

**Lösung** ['løːzuŋ], f. (—, pl. —en) loosening; solution.

**losziehen** ['loːstsiːən], v.n. irr. (Mil.) set out; gegen einen —, inveigh against s.o.; (fig., coll.) run s.o. down.

**Lot** [loːt], n. (—es, pl. —e) lead, plummet; (weight) half an ounce; (Maths.) perpendicular (line).

**Löteisen** ['løːtaɪzən], n. (—s, pl. —) soldering iron.

**loten** ['loːtən], v.a., v.n. (Naut.) take soundings, plumb.

**löten** ['løːtən], v.a. solder.

**Lothringen** ['loːtrɪŋən], n. Lorraine.

**Lötkolben** ['løːtkɔlbən], m. (—s, pl. —) soldering iron.

**Lotleine** ['loːtlaɪnə], f. (—, pl. —n) sounding-line.

**Lotrechtstarter** ['loːtrɛçtʃtartər], m. (—s, pl. —) (Aviat.) vertical take-off plane (V.T.O.L.).

# Lötrohr

**Lötrohr** ['løːtroːr], *n.* (—s, *pl.* —e) soldering-pipe.

**Lotse** ['loːtsə], *m.* (—n, *pl.* —n) (*Naut.*) pilot.

**Lotterbett** ['lɔtərbɛt], *n.* (—es, *pl.* —en) bed of idleness; (*obs.*) couch.

**Lotterie** [lɔtə'riː], *f.* (—, *pl.* —n) lottery, sweep-stake.

**Lotterleben** ['lɔtərleːbən], *n.* (—s, *no pl.*) dissolute life.

**Löwe** ['løːvə], *m.* (—n, *pl.* —n) (*Zool.*) lion.

**Löwenbändiger** ['løːvənbɛndɪgər], *m.* (—s, *pl.*—) lion tamer.

**Löwengrube** ['løːvəngruːbə], *f.* (—, *pl.* —n) lion's den.

**Löwenmaul** ['løːvənmaul], *n.* (—s, *no pl.*) (*Bot.*) snapdragon.

**Löwenzahn** ['løːvəntsaːn], *m.* (—s, *no pl.*) (*Bot.*) dandelion.

**Löwin** ['løːvɪn], *f.* (—, *pl.* —nen) (*Zool.*) lioness.

**Luchs** [luks], *m.* (—es, *pl.* —e) lynx.

**Lücke** ['lykə], *f.* (—, *pl.* —n) gap, breach; (*fig.*) omission, defect, blank.

**Lückenbüßer** ['lykənbyːsər], *m.* (—s, *pl.* —) stop-gap, stand-in.

**lückenhaft** ['lykənhaft], *adj.* fragmentary, incomplete, imperfect.

**Luder** ['luːdər], *n.* (—s, *pl.* —) (*rare*) carrion; (*vulg.*) beast, trollop; *dummes* —, silly ass, fathead.

**Luderleben** ['luːdərleːbən], *n.* (—s, *no pl.*) dissolute life.

**ludern** ['luːdərn], *v.n.* lead a dissolute life.

**Luft** [luft], *f.* (—, *pl.* ːe) air.

**Luftbrücke** ['luftbrykə], *f.* (—, *no pl.*) air-lift.

**Lüftchen** ['lyftçən], *n.* (—s, *pl.* —) gentle breeze.

**luftdicht** ['luftdɪçt], *adj.* airtight.

**Luftdruck** ['luftdruk], *m.* (—s, *no pl.*) air pressure, atmospheric pressure; blast.

**Luftdruckmesser** ['luftdrukmɛsər], *m.* (—s, *pl.* —) barometer, pressure-gauge.

**lüften** ['lyftən], *v.a.* air, ventilate.

**luftförmig** ['luftfœrmɪç], *adj.* gaseous.

**luftig** ['luftɪç], *adj.* airy, windy.

**Luftklappe** ['luftklapə], *f.* (—, *pl.* —n) air-valve.

**Luftkurort** ['luftkuːrɔrt], *m.* (—s, *pl.* —e) health resort.

**Luftlinie** ['luftliːnjə], *f.* (—, *pl.* —n) beeline; *in der* —, as the crow flies; (*Aviat.*) airline.

**Luftloch** ['luftlɔx], *m.* (—s, *pl.* ːer) air-pocket.

**Luftraum** ['luftraum], *m.* (—s, *no pl.*) atmosphere; air space.

**Lufröhre** ['luftrøːrə], *f.* (—, *pl.* —n) windpipe.

**Luftschiff** ['luftʃif], *n.* (—es, *pl.* —e) air-ship.

**Luftschiffahrt** ['luftʃifaːrt], *f.* (—, *no pl.*) aeronautics.

**Luftspiegelung** ['luftʃpiːgəluŋ], *f.* (—, *pl.* —en) mirage.

**Luftsprung** ['luftʃpruŋ], *m.* (—s, *pl.* ːe) caper, gambol; ːe *machen*, caper, gambol.

**Lüftung** ['lyftuŋ], *f.* (—, *no pl.*) airing, ventilation.

**Lug** [luːk], *m.* (—s, *no pl.*) (*obs.*) lie; — *und Trug*, a pack of lies.

**Lüge** ['lyːgə], *f.* (—, *pl.* —n) lie, falsehood, fib; *einen* — *strafen*, give s.o. the lie.

**lügen** ['lyːgən], *v.n. irr.* lie, tell a lie.

**lügenhaft** ['lyːgənhaft], *adj.* lying, false, untrue.

**Lügner** ['lyːgnər], *m.* (—s, *pl.* —) liar.

**Luke** ['luːkə], *f.* (—, *pl.* —n) dormerwindow; (*ship*) hatch.

**Lümmel** ['lyməl], *m.* (—s, *pl.* —) lout; hooligan.

**Lump** ['lump], *m.* (—s, —en, *pl.* —e, —en) scoundrel, blackguard.

**Lumpen** ['lumpən], *m.* (—s, *pl.* —) rag, tatter.

**Lumpengesindel** ['lumpəngəzɪndəl], *n.* (—s, *no pl.*) rabble, riffraff.

**Lumpenpack** ['lumpənpak], *n.* (—s, *no pl.*) rabble, riffraff.

**Lumpensammler** ['lumpənzamlər], *m.* (—s, *pl.* —) rag-and-bone-man.

**Lumperei** [lumpə'rai], *f.* (—, *pl.* —en) shabby trick; meanness; trifle.

**lumpig** ['lumpɪç], *adj.* ragged; (*fig.*) shabby, mean.

**Lunge** ['luŋə], *f.* (—, *pl.* —n) (*human*) lung; (*animals*) lights.

**Lungenentzündung** ['luŋənɛntsynduŋ], *f.* (—, *pl.* —en) pneumonia.

**Lungenkrankheit** ['luŋənkraŋkhait], *f.* (—, *pl.* —en) pulmonary disease.

**Lungenkraut** ['luŋənkraut], *n.* (—s, *pl.* ːer) lungwort.

**Lungenschwindsucht** ['luŋənʃvɪntzuxt], *f.* (—, *no pl.*) pulmonary consumption, tuberculosis.

**lungern** ['luŋərn], *v.n.* idle, loiter.

**Lunte** ['luntə], *f.* (—, *pl.* —n) fuse, slow-match; — *riechen*, smell a rat.

**Lupe** ['luːpə], *f.* (—, *pl.* —n) magnifying glass, lens; *etwas durch die* — *besehen*, examine s.th. closely, scrutinise s.th.; *unter die* — *nehmen*, examine closely.

**lüpfen** ['lypfən], *v.a.* lift.

**Lupine** [lu'piːnə], *f.* (—, *pl.* —n) (*Bot.*) lupin.

**Lust** [lust], *f.* (—, *pl.* ːe) enjoyment, pleasure, delight; desire, wish, inclination, liking; — *bekommen zu*, feel inclined to; — *haben auf*, have a mind to, feel like; *nicht übel* — *haben*, have half a mind to.

**Lustbarkeit** ['lustbaːrkait], *f.* (—, *pl.* —en) amusement, diversion, entertainment, pleasure.

**Lustdirne** ['lustdɪrnə], *f.* (—, *pl.* —n) prostitute.

**lüstern** ['lystərn], *adj.* lustful, lascivious.

**lustig** ['lustɪç], *adj.* gay, merry, cheerful, amusing, funny; — *sein*, make merry; *sich über einen* — *machen*, poke fun at s.o.

# Mahlzahn

**Lüstling** ['lʏstlɪŋ], *m.* (—s, *pl.* —e) libertine, lecher.

**Lustmord** ['lustmɔrt], *m.* (—es, *pl.* —e) sex murder.

**Lustreise** ['lustraɪzə], *f.* (—, *pl.* —n) pleasure trip.

**Lustschloß** ['lustʃlɔs], *n.* (—sses, *pl.* ∺sser) country house, country seat.

**Lustspiel** ['lustʃpiːl], *n.* (—s, *pl.* —e) comedy.

**lustwandeln** ['lustvandəln], *v.n. insep.* (*aux.* sein) stroll, promenade.

**Lutherisch** ['lutərɪʃ], *adj.* Lutheran.

**lutschen** ['lutʃən], *v.a.* suck.

**Lüttich** ['lʏtɪç], *n.* Liège.

**Luxus** ['luksus], *m.* (—, *no pl.*) luxury.

**Luzern** [lu'tsɛrn], *n.* Lucerne.

**Luzerne** [lut'sɛrnə], *f.* (—, *pl.* —n) (*Bot.*) lucerne.

**Lymphe** ['lʏmfə], *f.* (—, *pl.* —n) lymph.

**lynchen** ['lʏnçən], *v.a.* lynch.

**Lyrik** ['lyːrɪk], *f.* (—, *no pl.*) lyric poetry.

**lyrisch** ['lyːrɪʃ], *adj.* lyric(al).

**Lyzeum** [ly'tseːum], *n.* (—s, *pl.* Lyzeen) lyceum, grammar school *or* high school for girls.

# M

**M** [ɛm], *n.* (—s, *pl.* —s) the letter M.

**Maas** [maːs], *f.* River Meuse.

**Maat** [maːt], *m.* (—s, *pl.* —s, —en) (*Naut.*) mate.

**Mache** ['maxə], *f.* (—, *no pl.*) put-up job, humbug, sham, eyewash.

**machen** ['maxən], *v.a.* make, do, produce, manufacture; cause; amount to; *mach schon,* be quick; *das macht nichts,* it does not matter; *mach's kurz,* cut it short; *etwas — lassen,* have s.th. made; *sich auf den Weg —,* set off; *sich viel (wenig) aus etwas —,* care much (little) for s.th.; *mach, daß du fortkommst,* get out, scram.

**Macherlohn** ['maxərloːn], *m.* (—es, *pl.* ∺e) charge for making s.th.

**Macht** [maxt], *f.* (—, *pl.* ∺e) might, power; force, strength; authority; *mit aller —,* with might and main.

**Machtbefugnis** ['maxtbəfuːknɪs], *f.* (—, *pl.* —se) competence.

**Machtgebot** ['maxtgəboːt], *n.* (—s, *pl.* —e) authoritative order.

**Machthaber** ['maxthaːbər], *m.* (—s, *pl.* —) potentate, ruler.

**mächtig** ['mɛçtɪç], *adj.* mighty, powerful; *einer Sache — sein,* to have mastered s.th.

**machtlos** ['maxtloːs], *adj.* powerless.

**Machtspruch** ['maxtʃprux], *m.* (—s, *pl.* ∺e) authoritative dictum; command; decree.

**Machtvollkommenheit** ['maxtfɔlkɔmənhaɪt], *f.* (—, *pl.* —en) absolute power; sovereignty; *aus eigner —,* of o.'s own authority.

**Machtwort** ['maxtvɔrt], *n.* (—es, *pl.* —e) word of command, fiat; *ein — sprechen,* bring o.'s authority to bear, speak with authority.

**Machwerk** ['maxvɛrk], *n.* (—s, *pl.* —e) shoddy product; bad job; concoction; (*story*) pot-boiler.

**Madagaskar** [mada'gaskar], *n.* Madagascar.

**Mädchen** ['mɛːtçən], *n.* (—s, *pl.* —) girl; (*servant*) maid; *— für alles,* maid-of-all-work.

**mädchenhaft** ['mɛːtçənhaft], *adj.* girlish, maidenly.

**Mädchenhandel** ['mɛːtçənhandəl], *m.* (—s, *no pl.*) white slave trade.

**Made** ['maːdə], *f.* (—, *pl.* —n) maggot, mite.

**Mädel** ['mɛːdəl], *n.* (—s, *pl.* —) (*coll.*) *see* **Mädchen.**

**madig** ['maːdɪç], *adj.* maggoty.

**Magazin** [maga'tsiːn], *n.* (—s, *pl.* —e) warehouse, storehouse; journal.

**Magd** [maːkt], *f.* (—, *pl.* ∺e) maid, maidservant; (*Poet.*) maiden.

**Magen** ['maːgən], *m.* (—s, *pl.* —) (*human*) stomach; (*animals*) maw.

**Magengrube** ['maːgəngruːbə], *f.* (—, *pl.* —n) pit of the stomach.

**Magensaft** ['maːgənzaft], *m.* (—es, *pl.* ∺e) gastric juice.

**mager** ['maːgər], *adj.* lean, thin, slender, slim; (*fig.*) meagre.

**Magerkeit** ['maːgərkaɪt], *f.* (—, *no pl.*) leanness, thinness, slenderness.

**Magie** [ma'giː], *f.* (—, *no pl.*) magic.

**Magier** ['maːgjər], *m.* (—s, *pl.* —) magician.

**Magister** [ma'gɪstər], *m.* (—s, *pl.* —) schoolmaster; (*Univ.*) Master; *— der freien Künste,* Master of Arts.

**Magistrat** [magɪs'traːt], *m.* (—s, *pl.* —e) municipal board, local authority.

**magnetisch** [mag'neːtɪʃ], *adj.* magnetic.

**magnetisieren** [magneti'ziːrən], *v.a.* magnetise.

**Magnetismus** [magne'tɪsmus], *m.* (—, *pl.* —men) magnetism; (*person*) mesmerism; *Lehre vom —,* magnetics.

**Magnifizenz** [magnifi'tsɛnts], *f.* (—, *pl.* —en) magnificence; *seine —,* (*Univ.*) title of Vice-Chancellor.

**Mahagoni** [maha'goːni], *n.* (—s, *no pl.*) mahogany.

**Mahd** [maːt], *f.* (—, *pl.* —en) mowing.

**mähen** ['mɛːən], *v.a.* mow.

**Mäher** ['mɛːər], *m.* (—s, *pl.* —) mower.

**Mahl** [maːl], *n.* (—s, *pl.* —e, ∺er) meal, repast.

**mahlen** ['maːlən], *v.a.* grind.

**Mahlstrom** ['maːlʃtroːm], *m.* (—s, *no pl.*) maelstrom, whirlpool, eddy.

**Mahlzahn** ['maːltsaːn], *m.* (—s, *pl.* ∺e) molar, grinder.

**Mahlzeit** [ˈmaːltsaɪt], f. (—, pl. —en) meal, repast.

**Mähmaschine** [ˈmɛːmaʃiːnə], f. (—, pl. —n) reaping-machine; lawn-mower.

**Mähne** [ˈmɛːnə], f. (—, pl. —n) mane.

**mahnen** [ˈmaːnən], v.a. remind, admonish, warn; (debtor) demand payment, dun.

**Mähre** [ˈmɛːrə], f. (—, pl. —n) mare.

**Mähren** [ˈmɛːrən], n. Moravia.

**Mai** [maɪ], m. (—s, pl. —e) May.

**Maid** [maɪt], f. (—, no pl.) (Poet.) maiden.

**Maiglöckchen** [ˈmaɪɡlœkçən], n. (—s, pl. —) (Bot.) lily of the valley.

**Maikäfer** [ˈmaɪkɛːfər], m. (—s, pl. —) (Ent.) cockchafer.

**Mailand** [ˈmaɪlant], n. Milan.

**Mais** [maɪs], m. (—es, no pl.) (Bot.) maize, Indian corn.

**Majestät** [majɛsˈtɛːt], f. (—, pl. —en) majesty.

**majestätisch** [majɛsˈtɛːtiʃ], adj. majestic.

**Major** [maˈjoːr], m. (—s, pl. —e) (Mil.) major.

**Majoran** [majoˈraːn], m. (—s, no pl.) (Bot.) marjoram.

**Majorat** [majoˈraːt], n. (—s, pl. —e) primogeniture; entail.

**majorenn** [majoˈrɛn], adj. (obs.) of age, over twenty-one.

**Majorität** [majoriˈtɛːt], f. (—, pl. —en) majority.

**Makel** [ˈmaːkəl], m. (—s, pl. —) spot, blot; (fig.) blemish, flaw, defect.

**Mäkelei** [mɛːkəˈlaɪ], f. (—, pl. —en) fault-finding, carping; fastidiousness.

**makellos** [ˈmaːkəlloːs], adj. spotless, immaculate.

**mäkeln** [ˈmɛːkəln], v.n. find fault (with), cavil (at).

**Makkabäer** [makaˈbɛːər], m. Maccabee.

**Makler** [ˈmaːklər], m. (—s, pl. —) broker.

**Mäkler** [ˈmɛːklər], m. (—s, pl. —) fault-finder, caviller.

**Maklergebühr** [ˈmaːklərɡəbyːr], f. (—, pl. —en) brokerage.

**Makrele** [maˈkreːlə], f. (—, pl. —n) (Zool.) mackerel.

**Makrone** [maˈkroːnə], f. (—, pl. —n) macaroon.

**Makulatur** [makulaˈtuːr], f. (—, no pl.) waste paper.

**Mal** [maːl], n. (—s, pl. —e) mark, sign, token; monument; mole, birthmark; stain; time; dieses —, this time, this once; manches —, sometimes; mehrere —e, several times; mit einem —, all of a sudden.

**mal** [maːl], adv. & part. once; noch—, once more; (coll.) hör —, I say.

**Malaya** [maˈlaɪa], n. Malaya.

**malen** [ˈmaːlən], v.a. paint.

**Maler** [ˈmaːlər], m. (—s, pl. —) painter.

**Malerei** [maːləˈraɪ], f. (—, pl. —en) painting; picture.

**malerisch** [ˈmaːlərɪʃ], adj. picturesque.

**Malerleinwand** [ˈmaːlərlaɪnvant], f. (—, no pl.) canvas.

**Malheur** [maˈløːr], n. (—s, pl. —e) misfortune, mishap.

**Mali** [maːli] n. Mali.

**maliziös** [maliˈtsjøːs], adj. malicious.

**Malkasten** [ˈmaːlkastən], m. (—s, pl. ⸚) paint-box.

**Malstein** [ˈmaːlʃtaɪn], m. (—s, pl. —e) monument; boundary stone.

**Malstock** [ˈmaːlʃtɔk], m. (—s, pl. ⸚e) maulstick, mahlstick.

**Malteserorden** [malˈteːzərɔrdən], m. (—s, no pl.) Order of the Knights of Malta.

**malträtieren** [maltrɛˈtiːrən], v.a. ill-treat.

**Malve** [ˈmalvə], f. (—, pl. —n) (Bot.) mallow.

**Malz** [malts], n. (—es, no pl.) malt; an ihm ist Hopfen und — verloren, he is hopeless.

**Malzbonbon** [ˈmaltsbɔbɔ̃], m. (—s, pl. —s) cough-lozenge, malt drop.

**Mälzer** [ˈmɛltsər], m. (—s, pl. —) maltster.

**Mama** [maˈmaː], f. (—, pl. —s) (fam.) mummy, mum, (Am.) mammy.

**Mammon** [ˈmamɔn], m. (—s, no pl.) mammon; schnöder —, filthy lucre.

**Mammut** [ˈmamut], n. (—s, pl. —e) mammoth.

**Mamsell** [mamˈzɛl], f. (—, pl. —en) housekeeper.

**man** [man], indef. pron. one, they, people, men; — sagt, they say.

**manch** [manç], pron. (—er, —e, —es) many a, some, several.

**mancherlei** [mançərˈlaɪ], adj. several; of several kinds.

**Manchester** [manˈçɛstər], m. (—s, no pl.) corduroy.

**manchmal** [ˈmançmaːl], adv. sometimes.

**Mandant** [manˈdant], m. (—en, pl. —en) client.

**Mandantin** [manˈdantin], f. (—, pl. —innen) female client.

**Mandarine** [mandaˈriːnə], f. (—, pl. —n) mandarin (orange), tangerine.

**Mandat** [manˈdaːt], n. (—s, pl. —e) mandate.

**Mandel** [ˈmandəl], f. (—, pl. —n) almond; (Anat.) tonsil; (quantity) fifteen; eine — Eier, fifteen eggs.

**Mandoline** [mandoˈliːnə], f. (—, pl. —n) mandolin.

**Mangan** [manˈɡaːn], n. (—s, no pl.) (Chem.) manganese.

**Mangel** (1) [ˈmaŋəl], f. (—, pl. —n) mangle, wringer.

**Mangel** (2) [ˈmaŋəl], m. (—s, pl. ⸚) deficiency, defect; blemish; lack, shortage, want; aus — an, for want of; — haben an, be short of, lack (s.th.).

**mangelhaft** [ˈmaŋəlhaft], adj. defective, imperfect.

**mangeln** (1) [ˈmaŋəln], v.a. (laundry) mangle.

**mangeln** (2) ['maŋəln], v.n. be in want of, be short of; *es mangelt uns an ...*, we lack ....

**mangels** ['maŋəls], *prep.* (*Genit.*) for lack of, for want of.

**Mangold** ['maŋgɔlt], m. (—s, *no pl.*) (*Bot.*) beet, mangel-wurzel.

**Manie** [ma'ni:], f. (—, *pl.* —n) mania, craze.

**Manier** [ma'ni:r], f. (—, *pl.* —en) manner, habit; *gute —en haben*, have good manners.

**maniert** [mani'ri:rt], *adj.* affected; (*Art*) mannered.

**manierlich** [ma'ni:rlɪç], *adj.* well behaved, civil, polite.

**manipulieren** [manipu'li:rən], v.a. manipulate.

**Manko** ['maŋko:], n. (—s, *pl.* —s) deficit, deficiency.

**Mann** [man], m. (—(e)s, *pl.* ˝er, (*Poet.*) —en) man; husband; *etwas an den — bringen*, get s.th. off o.'s hands, dispose of s.th.; *seinen — stehen*, hold o.'s own; *bis auf den letzten —*, to a man.

**Mannbarkeit** ['manbaːrkaɪt], f. (—, *no pl.*) puberty; marriageable age.

**Männchen** ['mɛnçən], n. (—s, *pl.* —) little man, manikin; (*Zool.*) male; *mein —*, (*coll.*) my hubby; *— machen*, (*dogs*) sit on the hindlegs, beg.

**mannhaft** ['manhaft], *adj.* manly, stout, valiant.

**mannigfaltig** ['manɪçfaltɪç], *adj.* manifold, multifarious.

**männlich** ['mɛnlɪç], *adj.* male; (*fig.*) manly; (*Gram.*) masculine.

**Mannsbild** ['mansbɪlt], n. (—es, *pl.* —er) (*coll.*) man, male person.

**Mannschaft** ['manʃaft], f. (—, *pl.* —en) men; crew, team.

**mannstoll** ['manstɔl], *adj.* man-mad.

**Mannszucht** ['manstsuxt], f. (—, *no pl.*) discipline.

**Manöver** [ma'nøːvər], n. (—s, *pl.* —) manoeuvre.

**manövrieren** [manø'vriːrən], v.a. manoeuvre.

**Mansarde** [man'zardə], f. (—, *pl.* —n) garret, attic.

**manschen** ['manʃən], v.a., v.n. dabble; splash (about).

**Manschette** [man'ʃɛtə], f. (—, *pl.* —n) cuff.

**Mantel** ['mantəl], m. (—s, *pl.* ˝) cloak, overcoat, coat, mantle, wrap; *den — nach dem Winde hängen*, be a time-server.

**Manufaktur** [manufak'tuːr], f. (—, *pl.* —en) manufacture.

**Mappe** ['mapə], f. (—, *pl.* —n) portfolio, case, file.

**Mär** [mɛːr], f. (—, *pl.* —en) (*Poet.*) tale, tidings, legend.

**Märchen** ['mɛːrçən], n. (—s, *pl.* —) fairy-tale, fable; fib.

**märchenhaft** ['mɛːrçənhaft], *adj.* fabulous, legendary; (*coll.*) marvellous.

**Marder** ['mardər], m. (—s, *pl.* —) (*Zool.*) marten.

**Maria** [ma'riːa], f. Mary; *die Jungfrau —*, the Virgin Mary.

**Marienbild** [ma'riːənbɪlt], n. (—es, *pl.* —er) image of the Virgin Mary.

**Marienblume** [ma'riːənbluːmə], f. (—, *no pl.*) (*Bot.*) daisy.

**Marienglas** [ma'riːənglas], n. (—es, *no pl.*) mica.

**Marienkäfer** [ma'riːənkɛːfər], m. (—s, *pl.* —) (*Ent.*) lady-bird.

**Marine** [ma'riːnə], f. (—, *pl.* —n) navy.

**marinieren** [mari'niːrən], v.a. pickle.

**Marionette** [mario'nɛtə], f. (—, *pl.* —n) puppet, marionette.

**Mark** (1) [mark], n. (—s, *no pl.*) (*bone*) marrow; (*fruit*) pith, pulp.

**Mark** (2) [mark], f. (—, *pl.* —en) boundary, frontier province.

**Mark** (3) [mark], f. (—, *pl.* —) (*coin*) mark.

**markant** [mar'kant], *adj.* striking, prominent; (*remark*) pithy.

**Marke** ['markə], f. (—, *pl.* —n) (*trade*) mark, brand; (*postage*) stamp; (*game*) counter.

**markieren** [mar'kiːrən], v.a. mark.

**markig** ['markɪç], *adj.* marrowlike; (*fig.*) pithy, strong.

**Markise** [mar'kiːzə], f. (—, *pl.* —n) (sun)blind, awning.

**Markt** [markt], m. (—es, *pl.* ˝e) market, market-square, fair.

**Marktflecken** ['marktflɛkən], m. (—s, *pl.* —) borough; (small) market town.

**Marktschreier** ['marktʃraɪər], m. (—s, *pl.* —) cheap-jack, quack, charlatan.

**Markus** ['markus], m. Mark.

**Marmel** ['marməl], f. (—, *pl.* —n) (*obs.*) marble.

**Marmelade** [marmə'laːdə], f. (—, *pl.* —n) marmalade, jam.

**Marmor** ['marmɔr], m. (—s, *no pl.*) marble.

**Marokko** [ma'rɔko], n. Morocco.

**Marone** [ma'roːnə], f. (—, *pl.* —n) sweet chestnut.

**Maroquin** [maro'kɛ̃], n. (—s, *no pl.*) Morocco leather.

**Marotte** [ma'rɔtə], f. (—, *pl.* —n) whim; fad.

**Marquise** [mar'kiːzə], f. (—, *pl.* —n) marchioness.

**Marsch** (1) [marʃ], m. (—es, *pl.* ˝e) march; *sich in — setzen*, set out; march off.

**Marsch** (2) [marʃ], f. (—, *pl.* —en) fen, marsh.

**marsch!** [marʃ], *int.* march! be off! get out!

**Marschboden** ['marʃboːdən], m. (—s, *no pl.*) marshy soil, marshland.

**marschieren** [mar'ʃiːrən], v.n. (*aux.* sein) march.

**Marstall** ['marʃtal], m. (—s, *pl.* ˝e) royal stud.

**Marter** ['martər], f. —, *pl.* —n) torture, torment.

# martern

**martern** ['martǝrn], *v.a.* torture, torment.

**Märtyrer** ['mɛrtyrǝr], *m.* (—s, *pl.* —) martyr.

**Martyrium** [mar'ty:rjum], *n.* (—s, *pl.* —rien) martyrdom.

**März** [mɛrts], *m.* (—es, *pl.* —e) (*month*) March.

**Masche** ['maʃǝ], *f.* (—, *pl.* —n) mesh; (*knitting*) stitch; (*dial.*) bow tie; (*coll.*) racket.

**Maschine** [ma'ʃi:nǝ], *f.* (—, *pl.* —n) machine; engine; *mit der — geschrieben*, typewritten.

**Maschinengarn** [ma'ʃi:nǝngarn], *n.* (—s, *no pl.*) twist.

**Maschinerie** [maʃinǝ'ri:], *f.* (—, *pl.* —en) machinery.

**Maser** ['ma:zǝr], *f.* (—, *pl.* —n) (*wood*) vein, streak.

**Masern** ['ma:zǝrn], *f. pl.* measles.

**Maske** ['maskǝ], *f.* (—, *pl.* —n) mask, visor.

**Maskerade** [maskǝ'ra:dǝ], *f.* (—, *pl.* —n) masquerade.

**maskieren** [mas'ki:rǝn], *v.a.* mask. — *v.r. sich* —, put on a mask.

**Maß** (1) [ma:s], *n.* (—es, *pl.* —e) measure, size; moderation, propriety; degree, extent; proportion; *— halten*, be moderate; *einem — nehmen*, measure s.o. (for); *in starkem —*, to a high degree; *mit —*, in moderation; *nach —*, to measure; *ohne — und Ziel*, immoderately, with no holds barred; *über alle —en*, exceedingly.

**Maß** (2) [ma:s], *m. & f.* (—, *pl.* —e) (*drink*) quart.

**massakrieren** [masa'kri:rǝn], *v.a.* massacre, slaughter.

**Maßarbeit** ['ma:sarbaɪt], *f.* (—, *pl.* —en) (*work*) made to measure; bespoke tailoring.

**Masse** ['masǝ], *f.* (—, *pl.* —n) mass, bulk; multitude; *eine —*, a lot.

**Maßeinheit** ['ma:saɪnhaɪt], *f.* (—, *pl.* —n) measuring-unit.

**massenhaft** ['masǝnhaft], *adj.* abundant.

**Maßgabe** ['ma:sga:bǝ], *f.* (—, *pl.* —n) *nach —*, according to, in proportion to.

**maßgebend** ['ma:sge:bǝnt], *adj.* standard; (*fig.*) authoritative.

**massieren** [ma'si:rǝn], *v.a.* massage.

**mäßig** ['mɛ:sɪç], *adj.* moderate, temperate, frugal.

**Mäßigkeit** ['mɛ:sɪçkaɪt], *f.* (—, *no pl.*) moderation, temperance, frugality.

**Mäßigung** ['mɛ:sɪguŋ], *f.* (—, *no pl.*) moderation.

**Massiv** [ma'si:f], *n.* (—s, *pl.* —e) (*mountains*) massif, range.

**Maßliebchen** ['ma:sli:pçǝn], *n.* (—s, *pl.* —) (*Bot.*) daisy.

**maßlos** ['ma:slo:s], *adj.* immoderate; (*fig.*) extravagant.

**Maßnahme** ['ma:sna:mǝ], *f.* (—, *pl.* —n) measure; *—n ergreifen*, take steps.

**Maßregel** ['ma:sre:gǝl], *f.* (—, *pl.* —n) measure.

**maßregeln** ['ma:sre:gǝln], *v.a.* reprove, reprimand.

**Maßstab** ['ma:sʃta:p], *m.* (—es, *pl.* ∵e) standard; (*maps*) scale; *in kleinem (großem) —*, on a small (large) scale.

**maßvoll** ['ma:sfɔl], *adj.* moderate.

**Mast** (1) [mast], *m.* (—es, *pl.* —e) mast; pylon.

**Mast** (2) [mast], *f.* (—, *no pl.*) fattening.

**Mastbaum** ['mastbaum], *m.* (—s, *pl.* ∵e) mast.

**Mastdarm** ['mastdarm], *m.* (—s, *pl.* ∵e) rectum.

**mästen** ['mɛstǝn], *v.a.* feed, fatten.

**Mastkorb** ['mastkɔrp], *m.* (—s, *pl.* ∵e) masthead.

**Mästung** ['mɛstuŋ], *f.* (—, *no pl.*) fattening, cramming.

**Materialwaren** [mate'rjalva:rǝn], *f. pl.* groceries; household goods.

**materiell** [mate'rjɛl], *adj.* material, real; materialistic.

**Mathematik** [matema'ti:k], *f.* (—, *no pl.*) mathematics.

**mathematisch** [mate'ma:tɪʃ], *adj.* mathematical.

**Matratze** [ma'tratsǝ], *f.* (—, *pl.* —n) mattress.

**Matrikel** [ma'tri:kǝl], *f.* (—, *pl.* —n) register, roll.

**Matrize** [ma'tri:tsǝ], *f.* (—, *pl.* —n) matrix, die, stencil.

**Matrose** [ma'tro:zǝ], *m.* (—n, *pl.* —n) sailor, seaman.

**Matsch** [matʃ], *m.* (—es, *no pl.*) slush; mud.

**matt** [mat], *adj.* tired, exhausted, spent; languid; weak, feeble; (*light*) dim; (*gold*) dull; (*silver*) tarnished; (*Chess*) (check-)mate; *— setzen*, (*Chess*) to (check-)mate.

**Matte** ['matǝ], *f.* (—, *pl.* —n) mat, matting.

**Matthäus** [ma'tɛ:us], *m.* Matthew.

**Mattheit** ['mathaɪt], *f.* (—, *no pl.*) tiredness, exhaustion, languor, feebleness; (*light*) dimness; (*gold*) dullness.

**mattherzig** ['mathɛrtsɪç], *adj.* poorspirited, faint-hearted.

**Matura** [ma'tu:ra], *f.* (—, *pl.* —en) (*Austr.*) school-leaving *or* matriculation examination.

**Mätzchen** ['mɛtsçǝn], *n.* (—s, *pl.* —) nonsense; trick; *mach keine —*, don't be silly.

**Mauer** ['mauǝr], *f.* (—, *pl.* —n) wall.

**Mauerkelle** ['mauǝrkɛlǝ], *f.* (—, *pl.* —n) trowel.

**mauern** ['mauǝrn], *v.a.* build. — *v.n.* lay bricks, construct a wall.

**Mauerwerk** ['mauǝrvɛrk], *n.* (—s, *no pl.*) brick-work.

**Maul** [maul], *n.* (—es, *pl.* ∵er) (*animals*) mouth, muzzle; (*vulg.*) mouth; *das — halten*, shut up, hold o.'s tongue; *ein loses — haben*, have a loose tongue; *nicht aufs — gefallen sein*, have a quick tongue; (*vulg.*) *halt's —*, shut up.

148

**Maulaffe** ['maulafə], *m.* (—n, *pl.* —n) booby; —*n feilhalten*, stand gaping.

**Maulbeere** ['maulbe:rə], *f.* (—, *pl.* —n) (*Bot.*) mulberry.

**maulen** ['maulən], *v.n.* pout, sulk.

**Maulesel** ['maulɛ:zəl], *m.* (—s, *pl.* —) (*Zool.*) mule.

**maulfaul** ['maulfaul], *adj.* tongue-tied; taciturn.

**Maulheld** ['maulhɛlt], *m.* (—en *pl.* —en) braggart.

**Maulkorb** ['maulkɔrp], *m.* (—s, *pl.* ¨e) muzzle.

**Maulschelle** ['maulʃɛlə], *f.* (—, *pl.* —n) box on the ear.

**Maultier** ['maulti:r], *n.* (—s, *pl.* —e) (*Zool.*) mule.

**Maulwerk** ['maulvɛrk], *n.* (—s, *no pl.*) *ein großes — haben*, (*coll.*) have the gift of the gab.

**Maulwurf** ['maulvurf], *m.* (—s, *pl.* ¨e) (*Zool.*) mole.

**Maurer** ['maurər], *m.* (—s, *pl.* —) mason, bricklayer.

**Maus** [maus], *f.* (—, *pl.* ¨e) mouse.

**Mausefalle** ['mauzəfalə], *f.* (—, *pl.* —n) mouse-trap.

**mausen** ['mauzən], *v.n.* catch mice. — *v.a.* (*fig.*) pilfer, pinch.

**Mauser** ['mauzər], *f.* (—, *no pl.*) moulting.

**mausern** ['mauzərn], *v.r. sich* —, moult.

**mausetot** ['mauzəto:t], *adj.* dead as a door-nail.

**mausig** ['mauzɪç], *adj. sich — machen*, put on airs.

**Maxime** [mak'si:mə], *f.* (—, *pl.* —n) maxim, motto, device.

**Mazedonien** [matsə'do:njən], *n.* Macedonia.

**Mäzen** [mɛ:'tse:n], *m.* (—s, *pl.* —e) patron of the arts, Maecenas.

**Mechanik** [me'ça:nɪk], *f.* (—, *no pl.*) mechanics.

**Mechaniker** [me'ça:nɪkər], *m.* (—s, *pl.* —) mechanic.

**mechanisch** [me'ça:nɪʃ], *adj.* mechanical.

**meckern** ['mɛkərn], *v.n.* bleat; (*fig.*) grumble, complain.

**Medaille** [me'daljə], *f.* (—, *pl.* —n) medal.

**Medaillon** [medal'jõ], *n.* (—s, *pl.* —s) locket.

**meditieren** [medi'ti:rən], *v.n.* meditate.

**Medizin** [medi'tsi:n], *f.* (—, *pl.* —en) medicine, physic.

**Mediziner** [medi'tsi:nər], *m.* (—s, *pl.* —) physician, medical practitioner, student of medicine.

**medizinisch** [medi'tsi:nɪʃ], *adj.* medical, medicinal.

**Meer** [me:r], *n.* (—es, *pl.* —e) sea, ocean; *offnes* —, high seas; *am* —, at the seaside; *auf dem* —, at sea; *übers* —, overseas.

**Meerbusen** ['me:rbu:zən], *m.* (—s, *pl.* —) bay, gulf, bight.

**Meerenge** ['me:rɛŋə], *f.* (—, *pl.* —n) straits.

**Meeresspiegel** ['me:rəsʃpi:gəl], *m.* (—s, *no pl.*) sea-level.

**Meerkatze** ['me:rkatsə], *f.* (—, *pl.* —n) long-tailed monkey.

**Meerrettich** ['me:rrɛtɪç], *m.* (—s, *pl.* —e) (*Bot.*) horse-radish.

**Meerschaum** ['me:rʃaum], *m.* (—s, *no pl.*) sea-foam; (*pipe*) meerschaum.

**Meerschwein** ['me:rʃvain], *n.* (—s, *pl.* —e) (*Zool.*) porpoise.

**Meerschweinchen** ['me:rʃvainçən], *n.* (—s, *pl.* —) (*Zool.*) guinea-pig.

**Mehl** [me:l], *n.* (—es, *no pl.*) flour; meal; dust, powder.

**Mehlkleister** ['me:lklaistər], *m.* (—s, *no pl.*) flour paste.

**Mehlspeise** ['me:lʃpaizə], *f.* (—, *pl.* —n) (*dial.*) pudding, sweet.

**mehr** [me:r], *indecl. adj., adv.* more; *umso* —, all the more; *immer* —, more and more; — *als genug*, enough and to spare.

**Mehrbetrag** ['me:rbətra:k], *m.* (—s, *pl.* ¨e) surplus.

**mehrdeutig** ['me:rdɔytɪç], *adj.* ambiguous.

**mehren** ['me:rən], *v.r. sich* —, multiply, increase in numbers.

**mehrere** ['me:rərə], *pl. adj.* several.

**mehrfach** ['me:rfax], *adj.* repeated.

**Mehrheit** ['me:rhait], *f.* (—, *pl.* —en) majority.

**mehrmals** ['me:rma:ls], *adv.* several times.

**Mehrzahl** ['me:rtsa:l], *f.* (—, *no pl.*) (*Gram.*) plural; majority; bulk.

**meiden** ['maidən], *v.a. irr.* shun, avoid.

**Meierei** [maiə'rai], *f.* (—, *pl.* —en) (*dairy*) farm.

**Meile** ['mailə], *f.* (—, *pl.* —n) mile; league.

**Meiler** ['mailər], *m.* (—s, *pl.* —) charcoal-kiln, charcoal-pile.

**mein(e)** ['main(ə)], *poss. adj.* my.—*poss. pron.* mine.

**Meineid** ['mainait], *m.* (—s, *pl.* —e) perjury; *einen — schwören*, perjure o.s.

**meineidig** ['mainaidɪç], *adj.* perjured, forsworn.

**meinen** ['mainən], *v.a.* mean, intend, think.

**meinerseits** ['mainərzaits], *adv.* I, for my part.

**meinethalben** ['mainəthalbən], *adv.* on my account, speaking for myself, for my sake; I don't care, I don't mind.

**meinetwegen** ['mainətve:gən], *adv. see* **meinethalben**.

**meinetwillen** ['mainətvilən], *adv. um* —, for my sake, on my behalf.

**meinige** ['mainigə], *poss. pron.* mine.

**Meinung** ['mainuŋ], *f.* (—, *pl.* —en) opinion; meaning; notion; *öffentliche* —, public opinion; *der — sein*, be of the opinion, hold the opinion; *einem die — sagen*, give s.o. a piece of o.'s mind; *meiner — nach*, in my opinion.

**Meinungsverschiedenheit** ['maɪnuŋs-fɛrʃi:dənhaɪt], *f.* (—, *pl.* —en) difference of opinion, disagreement.

**Meise** ['maɪzə], *f.* (—, *pl.* —n) (*Orn.*) titmouse.

**Meißel** ['maɪsəl], *m.* (—s, *pl.* —) chisel.

**meißeln** ['maɪsəln], *v.a.* chisel, sculpt.

**meist** [maɪst], *adj.* most. — *adv.* usually, generally.

**meistens** ['maɪstəns], *adv.* mostly.

**Meister** ['maɪstər], *m.* (—s, *pl.* —) (*craft*) master; (*sport*) champion; *seinen — finden*, meet o.'s match.

**meisterhaft** ['maɪstərhaft], *adj.* master-ly.

**meisterlich** ['maɪstərlɪç], *adj.* masterly.

**meistern** ['maɪstərn], *v.a.* master.

**Meisterschaft** ['maɪstərʃaft], *f.* (—, *pl.* —en) mastery; (*sport*) champion-ship.

**Mekka** ['mɛka], *n.* Mecca.

**Meldeamt** ['mɛldəamt], *n.* (—s, *pl.* ̈er) registration office.

**melden** ['mɛldən], *v.a.* announce, inform, notify; (*Mil.*) report. — *v.r. sich —*, answer the phone; *sich — lassen*, send in o.'s name, have o.s. announced; *sich zu etwas —*, apply for s.th.

**Meldezettel** ['mɛldətsetəl], *m.* (—s, *pl.* —) registration form.

**meliert** [me'li:rt], *adj.* mixed; (*hair*) iron grey, streaked with grey.

**melken** ['mɛlkən], *v.a. irr.* milk.

**Melodie** [melo'di:], *f.* (—, *pl.* —n) melody, tune.

**Melone** [me'lo:nə], *f.* (—, *pl.* —n) (*Bot.*) melon; (*coll.*) bowler hat.

**Meltau** ['me:ltau], *m.* (—s, *no pl.*) mildew.

**Membrane** [mɛm'bra:nə], *f.* (—, *pl.* —n) membrane, diaphragm.

**Memme** ['mɛmə], *f.* (—, *pl.* —n) coward, poltroon.

**memorieren** [memo'ri:rən], *v.a.* memorise, learn by heart.

**Menage** [me'na:ʒə], *f.* (—, *pl.* —n) household.

**Menge** ['mɛŋə], *f.* (—, *pl.* —n) quantity, amount; multitude, crowd; *eine —*, a lot.

**mengen** ['mɛŋən], *v.a.* mix. — *v.r. sich — in*, interfere in.

**Mensch** (1) [mɛnʃ], *m.* (—en, *pl.* —en) human being; man; person; *kein —*, nobody.

**Mensch** (2) [mɛnʃ], *n.* (—s, *pl.* —er) (*vulg.*) wench.

**Menschenfeind** ['mɛnʃənfaɪnt], *m.* (—es, *pl.* —e) misanthropist.

**Menschenfreund** ['mɛnʃənfrɔynt], *m.* (—es, *pl.* —e) philanthropist.

**Menschengedenken** ['mɛnʃəngədeŋkən], *n.* (—s, *no pl.*) *seit —*, from time immemorial.

**Menschenhandel** ['mɛnʃənhandəl], *m.* (—s, *no pl.*) slave-trade.

**Menschenkenner** ['mɛnʃənkɛnər], *m.* (—s, *pl.* —) judge of character.

**Menschenmenge** ['mɛnʃənmɛŋə], *f.* (—, *no pl.*) crowd.

**Menschenraub** ['mɛnʃənraup], *m.* (—s, *no pl.*) kidnapping.

**Menschenverstand** ['mɛnʃənfɛrʃtant], *m.* (—es, *no pl.*) human under-standing; *gesunder —*, common-sense.

**Menschheit** ['mɛnʃhaɪt], *f.* (—, *no pl.*) mankind, human race.

**menschlich** ['mɛnʃlɪç], *adj.* human.

**Menschwerdung** ['mɛnʃverduŋ], *f.* (—, *no pl.*) incarnation.

**Mensur** [mɛn'zu:r], *f.* (—, *pl.* —en) students' duel.

**Mergel** ['mɛrgəl], *m.* (—s, *no pl.*) marl.

**merkbar** ['mɛrkba:r], *adj.* perceptible, noticeable.

**merken** ['mɛrkən], *v.a.* note, perceive, observe, notice; *sich etwas —*, bear in mind; *sich nichts — lassen*, show no sign.

**merklich** ['mɛrklɪç], *adj.* perceptible, appreciable.

**Merkmal** ['mɛrkma:l], *n.* (—s, *pl.* —e) mark, characteristic, feature.

**merkwürdig** ['mɛrkvyrdɪç], *adj.* re-markable, curious, strange.

**Merle** ['mɛrlə], *f.* (—, *pl.* —n) (*dial.*) blackbird.

**Mesner** ['mɛsnər], *m.* (—s, *pl.* —) sexton, sacristan.

**meßbar** ['mɛsba:r], *adj.* measurable.

**Meßbuch** ['mɛsbu:x], *n.* (—es, *pl.* ̈er) missal.

**Messe** ['mɛsə], *f.* (—, *pl.* —n) (*Eccl.*) Mass; *stille —*, Low Mass; (*Comm.*) fair; (*Mil.*) mess.

**messen** ['mɛsən], *v.a. irr.* measure, gauge. — *v.r. sich mit einem —*, pit oneself against s.o.

**Messer** (1) ['mɛsər], *m.* (—s, *pl.* —) gauge, meter.

**Messer** (2) ['mɛsər], *n.* (—s, *pl.* —) knife.

**Messerheld** ['mɛsərhɛlt], *m.* (—en, *pl.* —en) cut-throat, hooligan, rowdy.

**Messias** [mɛ'si:as], *m.* Messiah.

**Meßgewand** ['mɛsgəvant], *n.* (—es, *pl.* ̈er) chasuble, vestment.

**Meßkunst** ['mɛskunst], *f.* (—, *no pl.*) surveying.

**Messing** ['mɛsɪŋ], *n.* (—s, *no pl.*) brass; *aus —*, brazen.

**Metall** [me'tal], *n.* (—s, *pl.* —e) metal; *unedle —e*, base metals.

**Metallkunde** [me'talkundə], *f.* (—, *no pl.*) metallurgy.

**meteorologisch** [meteoro'lo:gɪʃ], *adj.* meteorological.

**Meter** ['me:tər], *n. & m.* (—s, *pl.* —) (*linear measure*) metre; (*Am.*) meter; (*Poet.*) metre.

**methodisch** [me'to:dɪʃ], *adj.* meth-odical.

**Metrik** ['me:trɪk], *f.* (—, *no pl.*) prosody, versification.

**Mette** ['mɛtə], *f.* (—, *pl.* —n) (*Eccl.*) matins.

**Metze** ['mɛtsə], *f.* (—, *pl.* —n) (*obs.*) prostitute.

**Metzelei** [mɛtsə'laɪ], *f.* (—, *pl.* —en) slaughter, massacre.

**metzeln** ['mɛtsəln], *v.a.* massacre, butcher.

**Metzger** ['mɛtsgər], *m.* (—s, *pl.* —) butcher.

**Meuchelmörder** ['mɔyçəlmœrdər], *m.* (—s, *pl.* —) assassin.

**meucheln** ['mɔyçəln], *v.a.* assassinate.

**meuchlings** ['mɔyçlɪŋs], *adv.* treacherously, insidiously.

**Meute** ['mɔytə], *f.* (—, *pl.* —n) pack of hounds; (*fig.*) gang.

**Meuterei** [mɔytə'raɪ], *f.* (—, *pl.* —en) mutiny, sedition.

**meutern** ['mɔytərn], *v.n.* mutiny.

**Mezzanin** ['mɛtsanɪn], *m.* (—s, *pl.* —e) half-storey, mezzanine.

**miauen** [mi'auən], *v.n.* mew.

**mich** [mɪç], *pers. pron.* me, myself.

**Michaeli(s)** [mɪça'e:li(s)], *n.* Michaelmas.

**Michel** ['mɪçəl], *m.* Michael; *deutscher* —, plain honest German.

**Mieder** ['mi:dər], *n.* (—s, *pl.* —) bodice.

**Miene** ['mi:nə], *f.* (—, *pl.* —n) mien, air; (facial) expression.

**Miete** ['mi:tə], *f.* (—, *pl.* —n) rent; hire; (*corn*) rick, stack.

**mieten** ['mi:tən], *v.a.* rent, hire.

**Mieter** ['mi:tər], *m.* (—s, *pl.* —) tenant, lodger.

**Mietskaserne** ['mi:tskazɛrnə], *f.* (—, *pl.* —en) tenement house.

**Mietszins** ['mi:tstsɪns], *m.* (—es, *pl.* —e) rent.

**Milbe** ['mɪlbə], *f.* (—, *pl.* —n) mite.

**Milch** [mɪlç], *f.* (—, *no pl.*) milk; (*fish*) soft roe; *abgerahmte* —, skim(med) milk; *geronnene* —, curdled milk.

**Milchbart** ['mɪlçba:rt], *m.* (—s, *pl.* ⁻e) milksop.

**Milchbruder** ['mɪlçbru:dər], *m.* (—s, *pl.* ⁻) foster-brother.

**milchen** ['mɪlçən], *v.n.* yield milk.

**Milcher** ['mɪlçər], *m.* (—s, *pl.* —) (*fish*) milter.

**Milchgesicht** ['mɪlçgəzɪçt], *n.* (—s, *pl.* —er) baby face; smooth complexion.

**Milchglas** ['mɪlçglas], *n.* (—es, *no pl.*) opalescent glass, frosted glass.

**Milchstraße** ['mɪlçʃtra:sə], *f.* (—, *no pl.*) Milky Way.

**Milde** ['mɪldə], *f.* (—, *no pl.*) mildness, softness; (*fig.*) gentleness, (*rare*) charity, generosity.

**mildern** ['mɪldərn], *v.a.* soften, alleviate, mitigate, soothe, allay; —*de Umstände*, extenuating circumstances.

**Milderung** ['mɪldərʊŋ], *f.* (—, *pl.* —en) mitigation, moderation; soothing.

**mildtätig** ['mɪltte:tɪç], *adj.* charitable, benevolent, munificent.

**Militär** [mili'tɛ:r], *n.* (—s, *no pl.*) military, army; *beim* — *sein*, serve in the army.

**Miliz** [mi'li:ts], *f.* (—, *no pl.*) militia.

**Milliarde** [mɪl'jardə], *f.* (—, *pl.* —n) a thousand millions; (*Am.*) billion.

**Million** [mɪl'jo:n], *f.* (—, *pl.* —en) million.

**Millionär** [mɪljo'nɛ:r], *m.* (—s, *pl.* —e) millionaire.

**Milz** [mɪlts], *f.* (—, *pl.* —en) spleen.

**Mime** ['mi:mə], *m.* (—n, *pl.* —n) mime, actor.

**Mimik** ['mi:mɪk], *f.* (—, *no pl.*) mime, miming.

**Mimiker** ['mi:mɪkər], *m.* (—s, *pl.* —) mimic.

**Mimose** [mi'mo:zə], *f.* (—, *pl.* —n) (*Bot.*) mimosa.

**minder** ['mɪndər], *adj.* lesser, smaller, minor, inferior.

**Minderheit** ['mɪndərhaɪt], *f.* (—, *pl.* —en) minority.

**minderjährig** ['mɪndərjɛ:rɪç], *adj.* (*Law*) under age.

**mindern** ['mɪndərn], *v.a.* diminish, lessen.

**minderwertig** ['mɪndərvɛrtɪç], *adj.* inferior, of poor quality.

**Minderwertigkeitskomplex** ['mɪndərvɛrtɪçkaɪtskɔmplɛks], *m.* (—es, *pl.* —e) inferiority complex.

**mindest** ['mɪndəst], *adj.* least, smallest, minimum, lowest; *nicht im* —*en*, not in the least, not at all.

**mindestens** ['mɪndəstəns], *adv.* at least.

**Mine** ['mi:nə], *f.* (—, *pl.* —n) mine; (*ball point pen*) refill; (*pencil*) lead.

**minimal** [mini'ma:l], *adj.* infinitesimal, minimum.

**Ministerialrat** [minister'ja:lra:t], *m.* (—s, *pl.* ⁻e) senior civil servant.

**ministeriell** [minister'jɛl], *adj.* ministerial.

**Ministerium** [mini'ste:rjum], *n.* (—s, *pl.* —rien) ministry.

**Ministerpräsident** [mi'nɪstərprɛ:zident], *m.* (—en, *pl.* —en) prime minister; premier.

**Ministerrat** [mi'nɪstərra:t], *m.* (—s, *pl.* ⁻e) cabinet, council of ministers.

**Ministrant** [mini'strant], *m.* (—en, *pl.* —en) acolyte; sacristan.

**Minne** ['mɪnə], *f.* (—, *no pl.*) (*obs.*, *Poet.*) love.

**Minnesänger** [mɪnə'zɛŋər], *m.* (—s, *pl.* —) minnesinger; troubadour, minstrel.

**Minus** ['mi:nus], *n.* (—, *no pl.*) deficit.

**Minze** ['mɪntsə], *f.* (—, *pl.* —n) (*Bot.*) mint.

**mir** [mi:r], *pers. pron.* to me.

**Mirakel** [mi'ra:kəl], *n.* (—s, *pl.* —) miracle, marvel, wonder.

**mischen** ['mɪʃən], *v.a.* mix; (*Cards*) shuffle; (*coffee, tea*) blend.

**Mischling** ['mɪʃlɪŋ], *m.* (—s, *pl.* —e) mongrel, hybrid.

**Mischrasse** ['mɪʃrasə], *f.* (—, *pl.* —n) cross-breed.

**Mischung** ['mɪʃuŋ], *f.* (—, *pl.* —en) mixture, blend.

**Misere** [mi'ze:rə], *f.* (—, *no pl.*) unhappiness, misery.

**Mispel** ['mɪspəl], *f.* (—, *pl.* —n) (*Bot.*) medlar (tree).

**mißachten** [mɪs'axtən], *v.a.* disregard, despise.

**mißarten** [mɪs'a:rtən], *v.n.* (*aux.* sein) degenerate.

**Mißbehagen** ['mɪsbəha:gən], *n.* (—s, *no pl.*) displeasure, uneasiness.

**mißbilligen** [mɪs'bɪlɪgən], *v.a.* object (to), disapprove (of).

**Mißbrauch** ['mɪsbraux], *m.* (—s, *pl.* ⁀e) abuse, misuse.

**missen** ['mɪsən], *v.a.* lack, be without, feel the lack of.

**Missetat** ['mɪsəta:t], *f.* (—, *pl.* —en) misdeed, felony.

**mißfallen** [mɪs'falən], *v.n. irr.* displease.

**mißförmig** ['mɪsfœrmɪç], *adj.* deformed, misshapen.

**Mißgeburt** ['mɪsgəburt], *f.* (—, *pl.* —en) abortion; monster.

**mißgelaunt** ['mɪsgəlaunt], *adj.* ill-humoured.

**Mißgeschick** ['mɪsgəʃɪk], *n.* (—s, *no pl.*) mishap, misfortune.

**mißgestimmt** ['mɪsgəʃtɪmt], *adj.* grumpy, out of sorts.

**mißglücken** [mɪs'glykən], *v.n.* (*aux.* sein) fail, be unsuccessful.

**Mißgriff** ['mɪsgrɪf], *m.* (—s, *pl.* —e) blunder, mistake.

**Mißgunst** ['mɪsgunst], *f.* (—, *no pl.*) jealousy, envy.

**mißhandeln** [mɪs'handəln], *v.a.* ill-treat.

**Missionar** [mɪsjo'na:r], *m.* (—s, *pl.* —e) missionary.

**mißlich** ['mɪslɪç], *adj.* awkward; difficult, unpleasant.

**mißliebig** ['mɪsli:bɪç], *adj.* unpopular, odious.

**mißlingen** [mɪs'lɪŋən], *v.n. irr.* (*aux.* sein) miscarry, go wrong, misfire, prove a failure, turn out badly.

**mißraten** [mɪs'ra:tən], *v.n. irr.* (*aux.* sein) miscarry, turn out badly.

**Mißstand** ['mɪsʃtant], *m.* (—es, *pl.* ⁀e) grievance, abuse.

**Mißton** ['mɪsto:n], *m.* (—s, *pl.* ⁀e) dissonance.

**mißtrauen** [mɪs'trauən], *v.n.* distrust, mistrust.

**Mißverhältnis** ['mɪsfɛrhɛltnɪs], *n.* (—ses, *no pl.*) disproportion.

**Mißverständnis** ['mɪsfɛrʃtɛntnɪs], *n.* (—ses, *pl.* —se) misunderstanding.

**Mist** [mɪst], *m.* (—es, *no pl.*) dung, manure, muck; (*fig.*) rubbish.

**Mistel** ['mɪstəl], *f.* (—, *pl.* —n) (*Bot.*) mistletoe.

**Mistfink** ['mɪstfɪŋk], *m.* (—s, *pl.* —e) (*fig.*) dirty child; mudlark.

**mit** [mɪt], *prep.* (*Dat.*) with. — *adv.* also, along with.

**mitarbeiten** ['mɪtarbaɪtən], *v.n.* collaborate, cooperate; (*lit. work*) contribute.

**mitbringen** ['mɪtbrɪŋən], *v.a. irr.* bring along.

**Mitbürger** ['mɪtbyrgər], *m.* (—s, *pl.* —) fellow-citizen.

**mitempfinden** ['mɪtɛmpfɪndən], *v.a. irr.* sympathise with.

**Mitesser** ['mɪtɛsər], *m.* (—s, *pl.* —) (*Med.*) blackhead.

**mitfahren** ['mɪtfa:rən], *v.n. irr.* (*aux.* sein) ride with s.o.; *einen — lassen*, give s.o. a lift.

**mitfühlen** ['mɪtfy:lən], *v.n.* sympathise.

**mitgehen** ['mɪtge:ən], *v.n. irr.* (*aux.* sein) go along (with), accompany (s.o.); *etwas — heißen* or *lassen*, pilfer, pocket, pinch.

**Mitgift** ['mɪtgɪft], *f.* (—, *no pl.*) dowry.

**Mitglied** ['mɪtgli:t], *n.* (—s, *pl.* —er) member, fellow, associate.

**mithin** [mɪt'hɪn], *adv.*, *conj.* consequently, therefore.

**Mitläufer** ['mɪtlɔyfər], *m.* (—s, *pl.* —) (*Polit.*) fellow-traveller.

**Mitlaut** ['mɪtlaut], *m.* (—s, *pl.* —e) (*Phonet.*) consonant.

**Mitleid** ['mɪtlaɪt], *n.* (—s, *no pl.*) compassion, sympathy, pity; *mit einem — haben*, take pity on s.o.

**Mitleidenschaft** ['mɪtlaɪdənʃaft], *f.* (—, *no pl.*) *einen in — ziehen*, involve s.o., implicate s.o.

**mitmachen** ['mɪtmaxən], *v.a.*, *v.n.* join in, participate (in), do as others do; go through, suffer.

**Mitmensch** ['mɪtmɛnʃ], *m.* (—en, *pl.* —en) fellow-man; fellow-creature.

**mitnehmen** ['mɪtne:mən], *v.a. irr.* take along, take with o.; strain, take it out of o., weaken.

**mitnichten** [mɪt'nɪçtən], *adv.* by no means.

**mitreden** ['mɪtre:dən], *v.n.* join in a conversation; contribute.

**mitsamt** [mɪt'zamt], *prep.* (*Dat.*) together with.

**Mitschuld** ['mɪtʃult], *f.* (—, *no pl.*) complicity.

**Mitschüler** ['mɪtʃy:lər], *m.* (—s, *pl.* —) schoolfellow, fellow-pupil, fellow-student, classmate.

**Mittag** ['mɪta:k], *m.* (—s, *pl.* —e) midday, noon, noontide; *zu — essen*, have dinner *or* lunch.

**Mittagessen** ['mɪta:kɛsən], *n.* (—s, *pl.* —) lunch, luncheon.

**Mittagsseite** ['mɪta:kszaɪtə], *f.* (—, *no pl.*) south side.

**Mittäter** ['mɪttɛtər], *m.* (—s, *pl.* —) accomplice.

**Mitte** ['mɪtə], *f.* (—, *no pl.*) middle, midst.

**mitteilen** ['mɪttaɪlən], *v.a.* (*Dat.*) communicate, inform, impart.

**mitteilsam** ['mɪttaɪlzaːm], adj. communicative.
**Mitteilung** ['mɪttaɪluŋ], f. (—, pl. —en) communication.
**Mittel** ['mɪtəl], n. (—s, pl.) means, expedient, way, resource; remedy; (pl.) money, funds; als — zum Zweck, as a means to an end; sich ins — legen, mediate, intercede.
**Mittelalter** ['mɪtəlaltər], n. (—s, no pl.) Middle Ages.
**mittelbar** ['mɪtəlbaːr], adj. indirect.
**Mittelding** ['mɪtəldɪŋ], n. (—s, pl. —e) medium; something in between.
**Mittelgebirge** ['mɪtəlgəbɪrgə], n. (—s, pl. —) hills; (subalpine) mountains.
**mittelländisch** ['mɪtəllɛndɪʃ], adj. Mediterranean.
**mittellos** ['mɪtəlloːs], adj. penniless, impecunious.
**Mittelmaß** ['mɪtəlmaːs], n. (—es, pl. —e) average.
**mittelmäßig** ['mɪtəlmɛːsɪç], adj. mediocre.
**Mittelmeer** ['mɪtəlmeːr], n. (—s, no pl.) Mediterranean.
**Mittelpunkt** ['mɪtəlpuŋkt], m. (—s, pl. —e) centre; focus.
**mittels** ['mɪtəls], prep. (Genit.) by means of.
**Mittelschule** ['mɪtəlʃuːlə], f. (—, pl. —n) secondary (intermediate) school; (Austr.) grammar school; (Am.) high school.
**Mittelstand** ['mɪtəlʃtant], m. (—es, no pl.) middle class.
**mittelste** ['mɪtəlstə], adj. middlemost, central.
**Mittelstürmer** ['mɪtəlʃtyrmər], m. (—s, pl. —) (Footb.) centre-forward.
**Mittelwort** ['mɪtəlvɔrt], n. (—es, pl. ⁓er) (Gram.) participle.
**mitten** ['mɪtən], adv. in the midst; — am Tage, in broad daylight.
**Mitternacht** ['mɪtərnaxt], f. (—, no pl.) midnight.
**Mittler** ['mɪtlər], m. (—s, pl. —) mediator.
**mittlere** ['mɪtlərə], adj. middle; average; mean.
**Mittwoch** ['mɪtvɔx], m. (—s, pl. —e) Wednesday.
**mitunter** [mɪt'untər], adv. now and then, occasionally, sometimes.
**mitunterzeichnen** ['mɪtuntərtsaɪçnən], v.a., v.n. countersign; add o.'s signature (to).
**Miturheber** ['mɪtuːrheːbər], m. (—s, pl. —) co-author.
**Mitwelt** ['mɪtvɛlt], f. (—, no pl.) the present generation, contemporaries, our own times; the world outside.
**mitwirken** ['mɪtvɪrkən], v.n. cooperate.
**Mnemotechnik** [mnemo'tɛçnɪk], f. (—, no pl.) mnemonics.
**Möbel** ['møːbəl], n. (—s, pl. —) piece of furniture; (pl.) furniture.
**mobil** [mo'biːl], adj. mobile, active, quick; — machen, mobilise, put in motion.

**Mobiliar** [mobil'jaːr], n. (—s, pl. Mobilien) furniture, movables.
**mobilisieren** [mobili'ziːrən], v.a. mobilise.
**möblieren** [mø'bliːrən], v.a. furnish; neu —, refurnish.
**Mode** ['moːdə], f. (—, pl. —n) mode, fashion; custom, use; in der —, in fashion, in vogue.
**Modell** [mo'dɛl], n. (—s, pl. —e) model; — stehen, model; (fig.) be the prototype.
**modellieren** [modɛ'liːrən], v.a. (dresses) model; (Art) mould.
**Moder** ['moːdər], m. (—s, no pl.) mould.
**moderig** ['moːdrɪç] see modrig.
**modern** (1) ['moːdərn], v.n. moulder, rot.
**modern** (2) [mo'dɛrn], adj. modern, fashionable, up-to-date.
**modernisieren** [modɛrni'ziːrən], v.a. modernise.
**modifizieren** [modifi'tsiːrən], v.a. modify.
**modisch** ['moːdɪʃ], adj. stylish, fashionable.
**Modistin** [mo'dɪstɪn], f. (—, pl. —nen) milliner.
**modrig** ['moːdrɪç], adj. mouldy.
**modulieren** [modu'liːrən], v.a. modulate.
**Modus** ['moːdus], m. (—, pl. Modi) (Gram.) mood; mode, manner.
**mogeln** ['moːgəln], v.n. cheat.
**mögen** ['møːgən], v.n. irr. like, desire, want, be allowed, have a mind to; (modal auxiliary) may, might; ich möchte gern, I should like to.
**möglich** ['møːklɪç], adj. possible, practicable; feasible; sein —stes tun, do o.'s utmost; nicht —! you don't say (so)!
**Möglichkeit** ['møːklɪçkaɪt], f. (—, pl. —en) possibility, feasibility, practicability; (pl.) potentialities; contingencies, prospects (of career).
**Mohn** [moːn], m. (—es, no pl.) poppy(seed).
**Mohr** [moːr], m. (—en, pl. —en) Moor; negro.
**Möhre** ['møːrə], f. (—, pl. —n) carrot.
**Mohrenkopf** ['moːrənkɔpf], m. (—es, pl. ⁓e) chocolate éclair.
**Mohrrübe** ['moːrryːbə], f. (—, pl. —n) carrot.
**mokieren** [mo'kiːrən], v.r. sich — über, sneer at, mock at, be amused by.
**Mokka** ['mɔka], m. (—s, no pl.) Mocha coffee.
**Molch** [mɔlç], m. (—es, pl. —e) (Zool.) salamander.
**Moldau** ['mɔldau], f. Moldavia.
**Mole** ['moːlə], f. (—, pl. —n) breakwater, jetty, pier.
**Molekül** [mole'kyːl], n. (—s, pl. —e) molecule.
**Molke** ['mɔlkə], f. (—, pl. —n) whey.
**Molkerei** [mɔlke'raɪ], f. (—, pl. —en) dairy.
**moll** [mɔl], adj. (Mus.) minor.

# Molluske

**Molluske** [mɔ'luskə], f. (—, pl. —n) (Zool.) mollusc.

**Moment** (1) [mo'mɛnt], m. (—s, pl. —e) moment, instant.

**Moment** (2) [mo'mɛnt], n. motive, factor; (Phys.) momentum.

**Momentaufnahme** [mo'mɛntaufna:-mə], f. (—, pl. —n) snapshot.

**momentan** [momɛn'ta:n], adv. at the moment, for the present, just now.

**Monarch** [mo'narç], m. (—en, pl. —en) monarch.

**Monarchie** [monar'çi:], f. (—, pl. —n) monarchy.

**Monat** [mo'na:t], m. (—s, pl. —e) month.

**monatlich** ['mo:natlɪç], adj. monthly.

**Monatsfluß** ['mo:natsflus], m. (—sses, pl. ⁀sse) menses.

**Monatsschrift** ['mo:natsʃrɪft], f. (—, pl. —en) monthly (journal).

**Mönch** [mœnç], m. (—es, pl. —e) monk, friar.

**Mönchskappe** ['mœnçskapə], f. (—, pl. —n) cowl, monk's hood.

**Mönchskutte** ['mœnçskutə], f. (—, pl. —n) cowl.

**Mond** [mo:nt], m. (—es, pl. —e) moon; zunehmender —, waxing moon; abnehmender —, waning moon.

**Mondfinsternis** ['mo:ntfɪnstɛrnɪs], f. (—, pl. —se) eclipse of the moon.

**mondsüchtig** ['mo:ntzyçtɪç], adj. given to sleep-walking; (fig.) moon-struck.

**Mondwandlung** ['mo:ntvandluŋ], f. (—, pl. —en) phase of the moon.

**Moneten** [mo'ne:tən], pl. (sl.) money, cash, funds.

**Mongolei** [mɔŋgo'laɪ], f. Mongolia.

**monieren** [mo'ni:rən], v.a. remind (a debtor); censure.

**monogam** [mono'ga:m], adj. monogamous.

**Monopol** [mono'po:l], n. (—s, pl. —e) monopoly.

**monoton** [mono'to:n], adj. monotonous.

**Monstrum** ['mɔnstrum], n. (—s, pl. Monstra) monster, monstrosity.

**Monsun** [mɔn'zu:n], m. (—s, pl. —e) monsoon.

**Montag** ['mo:nta:k], m. (—s, pl. —e) Monday; blauer —, Bank Holiday Monday.

**Montage** [mɔn'ta:ʒə], f. (—, pl. —n) fitting (up), setting up, installation, assembling.

**Montanindustrie** [mɔn'ta:nɪndustri:], f. (—, no pl.) mining industry.

**Montanunion** [mɔn'ta:nunjo:n], f. (—, no pl.) (Pol.) European Coal and Steel Community.

**Monteur** [mɔn'tø:r], m. (—s, pl. —e) fitter.

**montieren** [mɔn'ti:rən], v.a. fit (up), set up, mount, install.

**Montur** [mɔn'tu:r], f. (—, pl. —en) uniform, livery.

**Moor** [mo:r], n. (—es, pl. —e) swamp, fen, bog.

**Moos** [mo:s], n. (—es, pl. —e) moss; (sl.) cash.

**Moped** ['mo:pɛt], n. (—s, pl. —s) moped, motorised pedal cycle.

**Mops** [mɔps], m. (—es, pl. ⁀e) pug (dog).

**mopsen** ['mɔpsən], v.r. sich —, feel bored.

**Moral** [mo'ra:l], f. (—, no pl.) moral, morals.

**moralisch** [mo'ra:lɪʃ], adj. moral.

**Morast** [mo'rast], m. (—es, pl. ⁀e) morass, bog, fen, mire.

**Moratorium** [mora'to:rjum], n. (—s, pl. —rien) (payments etc.) respite.

**Morchel** ['mɔrçəl], f. (—, pl. —n) (Bot.) morel (edible fungus).

**Mord** [mɔrt], m. (—es, pl. —e) murder.

**morden** ['mɔrdən], v.a., v.n. murder.

**Mörder** ['mœrdər], m. (—s, pl. —) murderer.

**Mordsgeschichte** ['mɔrtsgəʃɪçtə], f. (—, pl. —n) (coll.) cock-and-bull story.

**Mordskerl** ['mɔrtskɛrl], m. (—s, pl. —e) devil of a fellow; (Am.) great guy.

**Mordtat** ['mɔrtta:t], f. (—, pl. —en) murder.

**Morelle** [mo'rɛlə], f. (—, pl. —n) (Bot.) morello cherry.

**Morgen** ['mɔrgən], m. (—s, pl. —) morning, daybreak; (Poet.) east; measure of land; eines —s, one morning.

**morgen** ['mɔrgən], adv. tomorrow; — früh, tomorrow morning; heute —, this morning.

**Morgenblatt** ['mɔrgənblat], n. (—s, pl. ⁀er) morning paper.

**morgendlich** ['mɔrgəntlɪç], adj. of or in the morning; matutinal.

**Morgenland** ['mɔrgənlant], n. (—es, pl. —er) orient, east.

**Morgenrot** ['mɔrgənro:t], n. (—s, no pl.) dawn, sunrise.

**morgens** ['mɔrgəns], adv. in the morning.

**morgig** ['mɔrgɪç], adj. tomorrow's.

**Morphium** ['mɔrfjum], n. (—s, no pl.) morphia, morphine.

**morsch** [mɔrʃ], adj. brittle, rotten, decayed.

**Mörser** ['mœrzər], m. (—s, pl. —) mortar.

**Mörserkeule** ['mœrzərkɔylə], f. (—, pl. —n) pestle.

**Mörtel** ['mœrtəl], m. (—s, no pl.) mortar, plaster.

**Mörtelkelle** ['mœrtəlkɛlə], f. (—, pl. —n) trowel.

**Mosaik** [moza'i:k], n. (—s, pl. —e) mosaic (work); inlaid work.

**mosaisch** [mo'za:ɪʃ], adj. Mosaic.

**Moschee** [mo'ʃe:], f. (—, pl. —n) mosque.

**Moschus** ['mɔʃus], m. (—, no pl.) musk.

**Mosel** ['mo:zəl], f. Moselle.

**Moskau** ['mɔskau], n. Moscow.

# mürrisch

**Moskito** [mɔs'ki:to], *m.* (—s, *pl.* —s) (*Ent.*) mosquito.
**Most** [mɔst], *m.* (—es, *no pl.*) new wine, cider.
**Mostrich** ['mɔstrɪç], *m.* (—s, *no pl.*) mustard.
**Motiv** [mo'ti:f], *n.* (—es, *pl.* —e) motive; (*Mus., Lit.*) motif, theme.
**motivieren** [moti'vi:rən], *v.a.* motivate.
**Motorrad** ['mo:tɔrra:t], *n.* (—es, *pl.* ⸚er) motor-cycle.
**Motte** ['mɔtə], *f.* (—, *pl.* —n) (*Ent.*) moth.
**moussieren** [mu'si:rən], *v.n.* effervesce, sparkle.
**Möwe** ['mø:və], *f.* (—, *pl.* —n) (*Orn.*) seagull.
**Mucke** ['mukə], *f.* (—, *pl.* —n) whim, caprice; obstinacy.
**Mücke** ['mykə], *f.* (—, *pl.* —n) (*Ent.*) gnat, fly, mosquito.
**Muckerei** [mukə'rai], *f.* (—, *pl.* —en) cant.
**mucksen** ['muksən], *v.n.* stir, move, budge.
**müde** ['my:də], *adj.* tired, weary; — *machen,* tire.
**Muff** [muf], *m.* (—es, *pl.* —e) muff.
**muffig** ['mufɪç], *adj.* musty, fusty, stuffy.
**Mühe** ['my:ə], *f.* (—, *pl.* —n) trouble, pains; effort, labour, toil; *sich — geben,* take pains.
**mühelos** ['my:əlo:s], *adj.* effortless, easy.
**mühen** ['my:ən], *v.r. sich* —, exert o.s., take pains.
**Mühewaltung** ['my:əvaltuŋ], *f.* (—, *pl.* —en) exertion, effort.
**Mühle** ['my:lə], *f.* (—, *pl.* —n) (*flour*) mill; (*coffee*) grinder; game.
**Muhme** ['mu:mə], *f.* (—, *pl.* —n) (*obs.*) aunt.
**Mühsal** ['my:za:l], *f.* (—, *pl.* —e) hardship, misery, toil.
**mühsam** ['my:za:m], *adj.* troublesome, laborious.
**mühselig** ['my:ze:lɪç], *adj.* painful, laborious; miserable.
**Mulatte** [mu'latə], *m.* (—n, *pl.* —n) mulatto.
**Mulde** ['muldə], *f.* (—, *pl.* —n) trough.
**muldenförmig** ['muldənfœrmɪç], *adj.* trough-shaped.
**Mull** [mul], *m.* (—s, *no pl.*) Indian muslin.
**Müll** [myl], *m.* (—s, *no pl.*) dust, rubbish; (*Am.*) garbage.
**Müller** ['mylər], *m.* (—s, *pl.* —) miller.
**mulmig** ['mulmɪç], *adj.* dusty, mouldy, decayed.
**multiplizieren** [multipli'tsi:rən], *v.a.* multiply.
**Mumie** ['mu:mjə], *f.* (—, *pl.* —n) (*Archæol.*) mummy.
**Mummenschanz** ['mumənʃants], *m.* (—es, *no pl.*) mummery, masquerade.
**München** ['mynçən], *n.* Munich.

**Mund** [munt], *m.* (—es, *pl.* —e, ⸚er) mouth; *den — halten,* keep quiet; *einen großen — haben,* talk big; *sich den — verbrennen,* put o.'s foot in it.
**Mundart** ['munta:rt], *f.* (—, *pl.* —en) (local) dialect.
**Mündel** ['myndəl], *m., f. & n.* (—s, *pl.* —) ward, minor, child under guardianship.
**mündelsicher** ['myndəlzɪçər], *adj.* gilt-edged.
**munden** ['mundən], *v.n. es mundet mir,* I like the taste, I relish it.
**münden** ['myndən], *v.n.* discharge (into), flow (into).
**mundfaul** ['muntfaul], *adj.* tonguetied; taciturn.
**mundgerecht** ['muntgərɛçt], *adj.* palatable; (*fig.*) suitable.
**Mundharmonika** ['muntharmo:nɪka], *f.* (—, *pl.* —kas, —ken) mouth organ.
**mündig** ['myndɪç], *adj.* of age; — *werden,* come of age.
**mündlich** ['myntlɪç], *adj.* verbal, oral, by word of mouth; (*examination*) viva voce.
**Mundschenk** ['muntʃɛŋk], *m.* (—s, *pl.* —e) cupbearer.
**mundtot** ['muntto:t], *adj.* — *machen,* silence, gag.
**Mündung** ['mynduŋ], *f.* (—, *pl.* —en) (*river*) estuary, mouth; (*gun*) muzzle.
**Mundvorrat** ['muntforra:t], *m.* (—s, *pl.* ⸚e) provisions, victuals.
**Mundwerk** ['muntverk], *n.* (—s, *no pl.*) mouth; (*fig.*) gift of the gab.
**Munition** [muni'tsjo:n], *f.* (—, *no pl.*) ammunition.
**munkeln** ['muŋkəln], *v.n.* whisper; *man munkelt,* it is rumoured.
**Münster** ['mynstər], *n.* (—s, *pl.* —) minster, cathedral.
**munter** ['muntər], *adj.* awake; lively, active, sprightly, vivacious, cheerful, gay.
**Münze** ['myntsə], *f.* (—, *pl.* —n) coin.
**Münzeinheit** ['myntsaɪnhaɪt], *f.* (—, *no pl.*) monetary unit.
**Münzfälscher** ['myntsfɛlʃər], *m.* (—s, *pl.* —) (counterfeit) coiner.
**Münzkunde** ['myntskundə], *f.* (—, *no pl.*) numismatics.
**Münzprobe** ['myntspro:bə], *f.* (—, *pl.* —n) assay of a coin.
**mürbe** ['myrbə], *adj.* mellow; (*meat*) tender; (*cake*) crisp; brittle; *einen — machen,* soften s.o. up, force s.o. to yield.
**Murmel** ['murməl], *f.* (—, *pl.* —n) (*toy*) marble.
**murmeln** ['murməln], *v.n.* murmur, mutter.
**Murmeltier** ['murməlti:r], *n.* (—s, *pl.* —e) (*Zool.*) marmot; *wie ein — schlafen,* sleep like a log.
**murren** ['murən], *v.n.* grumble, growl.
**mürrisch** ['myrɪʃ], *adj.* morose, surly, sulky, peevish, sullen.

155

**Mus** [mu:s], *n.* (—es, *no pl.*) purée, (apple) sauce; pulp.
**Muschel** ['muʃəl], *f.* (—, *pl.* —n) mussel, shell; (*telephone*) ear-piece.
**Muse** ['mu:zə], *f.* (—, *pl.* —n) muse.
**Muselman** ['mu:zəlman], *m.* (—en, *pl.* —en) Muslim, Moslem.
**Musik** [mu'zi:k], *f.* (—, *no pl.*) music.
**musikalisch** [muzi'ka:lɪʃ], *adj.* musical.
**Musikant** [muzi'kant], *m.* (—en, *pl.* —en) musician; performer.
**Musiker** ['mu:zɪkər], *m.* (—s, *pl.* —) musician.
**musizieren** [muzi'tsi:rən], *v.n.* play music.
**Muskateller** [muska'tɛlər], *m.* (—s, *no pl.*) muscatel (wine).
**Muskatnuß** [mus'ka:tnus], *f.* (—, *pl.* ⁚sse) nutmeg.
**Muskel** ['muskəl], *m.* (—s, *pl.* —n) muscle.
**muskelig** ['musklɪç] *see* **musklig**.
**Muskete** [mus'ke:tə], *f.* (—, *pl.* —n) musket.
**Musketier** [muske'ti:r], *m.* (—s, *pl.* —e) musketeer.
**musklig** ['musklɪç], *adj.* muscular.
**muskulös** [musku'lø:s], *adj.* muscular.
**Muße** ['mu:sə], *f.* (—, *no pl.*) leisure; *mit* —, leisurely, at leisure.
**Musselin** [musə'li:n], *m.* (—s, *pl.* —e) muslin.
**müssen** ['mysən], *v.n. irr.* have to, be forced, be compelled, be obliged; *ich muß*, I must, I have to.
**müßig** ['my:sɪç], *adj.* idle, lazy, unemployed.
**Müßiggang** ['my:sɪçgaŋ], *m.* (—s, *no pl.*) idleness, laziness, sloth.
**Muster** ['mustər], *n.* (—s, *pl.* —) sample; pattern; (proto-)type; (*fig.*) example.
**Musterbild** ['mustərbɪlt], *n.* (—s, *pl.* —er) paragon.
**mustergültig** ['mustərgyltɪç], *adj.* exemplary; standard; excellent.
**musterhaft** ['mustərhaft], *adj.* exemplary.
**mustern** ['mustərn], *v.a.* examine, muster, scan; (*troops*) review, inspect.
**Musterung** ['mustəruŋ], *f.* (—, *pl.* —en) review; examination, inspection.
**Mut** ['mu:t], *m.* (—es, *no pl.*) courage, spirit; — *fassen*, take heart, muster up courage.
**Mutation** [muta'tsjo:n], *f.* (—, *pl.* —en) change.
**mutieren** [mu'ti:rən], *v.n.* change; (*voice*) break.
**mutig** ['mu:tɪç], *adj.* courageous, brave.
**mutlos** ['mu:tlo:s], *adj.* discouraged, dejected, despondent.
**mutmaßen** ['mu:tma:sən], *v.a. insep.* surmise, suppose, conjecture.
**Mutter** ['mutər], *f.* (—, *pl.* ⁚) mother; (*screw*) nut.
**Mutterkorn** ['mutərkɔrn], *n.* (—s, *no pl.*) ergot.

**Mutterkuchen** ['mutərku:xən], *m.* (—s, *pl.* —) placenta, after-birth.
**Mutterleib** ['mutərlaip], *m.* (—s, *no pl.*) womb, uterus.
**Muttermal** ['mutərma:l], *n.* (—s, *pl.* —e) birth-mark.
**Mutterschaft** ['mutərʃaft], *f.* (—, *no pl.*) motherhood, maternity.
**mutterseelenallein** ['mutərze:lənalain], *adj.* quite alone; (*coll.*) all on o.'s own.
**Muttersöhnchen** ['mutərz:ønçən], *n.* (—s, *pl.* —) mother's darling, spoilt child.
**Mutterwitz** ['mutərvɪts], *m.* (—es, *no pl.*) mother-wit, native wit, common sense.
**Mutwille** ['mu:tvɪlə], *m.* (—ns, *no pl.*) mischievousness, wantonness.
**Mütze** ['mytsə], *f.* (—, *pl.* —n) cap; bonnet; beret.
**Myrrhe** ['mɪrə], *f.* (—, *pl.* —n) myrrh.
**Myrte** ['mɪrtə], *f.* (—, *pl.* —n) (*Bot.*) myrtle.
**Mysterium** [mɪs'te:rjum], *n.* (—s, *pl.* —rien) mystery.
**Mystik** ['mɪstɪk], *f.* (—, *no pl.*) mysticism.
**Mythologie** [mytolo'gi:], *f.* (—, *pl.* —n) mythology.
**Mythus** ['mytus], *m.* (—, *pl.* **Mythen**) myth.

# N

**N** [ɛn], *n.* (—s, *pl.* —s) the letter N.
**na** [na], *int.* well, now; —*nu!* well, I never! — *und?* so what?
**Nabe** ['na:bə], *f.* (—, *pl.* —n) hub.
**Nabel** ['na:bəl], *m.* (—s, *pl.* —) navel.
**Nabelschnur** ['na:bəlʃnu:r], *f.* (—, *pl.* ⁚e) umbilical cord.
**nach** [na:x], *prep.* (*Dat.*) after, behind, following; to, towards; according to, in conformity or accordance with; in imitation of. — *adv., prefix.* after, behind; afterwards, later; — *und* —, little by little, by degrees, gradually.
**nachäffen** ['na:xɛfən], *v.a.* ape, mimic, imitate; (*coll.*) take off.
**nachahmen** ['na:xa:mən], *v.a.* imitate, copy; counterfeit.
**nacharbeiten** ['na:xarbaitən], *v.n.* work after hours or overtime. — *v.a.* copy (*Dat.*).
**nacharten** ['na:xa:rtən], *v.n.* (*aux.* sein) resemble, (*coll.*) take after.
**Nachbar** ['na:xba:r], *m.* (—s, —n, *pl.* —n) neighbour.
**Nachbarschaft** ['naxba:rʃaft], *f.* (—, *no pl.*) neighbourhood, vicinity; (*people*) neighbours.
**nachbestellen** ['na:xbəʃtɛlən], *v.a.* order more, re-order.

**nachbilden** ['na:xbɪldən], *v.a.* copy, reproduce.

**nachdem** [na:x'de:m], *adv.* afterwards, after that. — *conj.* after, when; *je* —, according to circumstances, that depends.

**nachdenken** ['na:xdɛŋkən], *v.n. irr.* think (over), meditate, muse, ponder.

**nachdenklich** ['na:xdɛŋklɪç], *adj.* reflective, pensive, wistful; — *stimmen*, set thinking.

**Nachdruck** ['na:xdruk], *m.* (—s, *pl.* —e) reprint; stress, emphasis.

**nachdrucken** ['na:xdrukən], *v.a.* reprint.

**nachdrücklich** ['na:xdryklɪç], *adj.* emphatic; — *betonen*, emphasise.

**nacheifern** ['na:xaɪfərn], *v.n. einem* —, emulate s.o.

**nacheinander** ['na:xaɪnandər], *adv.* one after another.

**nachempfinden** ['na:xɛmpfɪndən], *v.a. irr.* sympathize with, feel for.

**Nachen** ['naxən], *m.* (—s, *pl.* —) (*Poet.*) boat, skiff.

**Nachfolge** ['na:xfɔlgə], *f.* (—, *pl.* —n) succession.

**nachfolgend** ['na:xfɔlgənt], *adj.* following, subsequent.

**Nachfolger** ['na:xfɔlgər], *m.* (—s, *pl.* —) successor.

**nachforschen** ['na:xfɔrʃən], *v.a.* search after; enquire into, investigate.

**Nachfrage** ['na:xfra:gə], *f.* (—, *no pl.*) enquiry; (*Comm.*) demand; *Angebot und* —, supply and demand.

**nachfühlen** ['na:xfy:lən], *v.a. einem etwas* —, enter into s.o.'s feelings, sympathize with s.o.

**nachfüllen** ['na:xfylən], *v.a.* replenish, fill up.

**nachgeben** ['na:xge:bən], *v.n. irr.* relax, slacken, yield; give in, relent, give way.

**nachgehen** ['na:xge:ən], *v.n. irr.* (*aux.* sein) *einem* —, follow s.o., go after s.o.; (*clock*) be slow; follow up, investigate.

**nachgerade** ['na:xgəra:də], *adv.* by this time, by now; gradually.

**nachgiebig** ['na:xgi:bɪç], *adj.* yielding, compliant.

**nachgrübeln** ['na:xgry:bəln], *v.n.* speculate.

**Nachhall** ['na:xhal], *m.* (—s, *no pl.*) echo, resonance.

**nachhaltig** ['na:xhaltɪç], *adj.* lasting, enduring.

**nachhängen** ['na:xhɛŋən], *v.n. irr. seinen Gedanken* —, muse.

**nachher** ['na:xhe:r], *adv.* afterwards, later on.

**nachherig** ['na:xhe:rɪç], *adj.* subsequent, later.

**Nachhilfestunde** ['na:xhɪlfəʃtundə], *f.* (—, *pl.* —n) private coaching.

**nachholen** ['na:xho:lən], *v.a.* make good; make up for.

**Nachhut** ['na:xhu:t], *f.* (—, *no pl.*) (*Mil.*) rearguard.

**nachjagen** ['na:xja:gən], *v.n.* (*aux.* sein) pursue.

**Nachklang** ['na:xklaŋ], *m.* (—s, *pl.* ⁘e) echo; (*fig.*) after-effect, reminiscence.

**Nachkomme** ['na:xkɔmə], *m.* (—n, *pl.* —n) descendant, offspring.

**nachkommen** ['na:xkɔmən], *v.n. irr.* (*aux.* sein) come after, follow; *seiner Pflicht* —, do o.'s duty; comply with; *einem Versprechen* —, keep a promise; *seinen Verpflichtungen nicht* — *können*, be unable to meet o.'s commitments.

**Nachkommenschaft** ['na:xkɔmənʃaft], *f.* (—, *no pl.*) descendants, offspring, issue, progeny.

**Nachlaß** ['na:xlas], *m.* (—sses, *pl.* ⁘sse) inheritance, estate, bequest; remission, discount, allowance.

**nachlassen** ['na:xlasən], *v.a. irr.* leave behind, bequeath; (*trade*) give a discount of. — *v.n.* abate, subside, slacken.

**nachlässig** ['na:xlɛsɪç], *adj.* negligent, remiss, careless.

**nachlaufen** ['na:xlaufən], *v.n. irr.* (*aux.* sein) *einem* —, run after s.o.

**Nachlese** ['na:xle:zə], *f.* (—, *pl.* —n) gleaning.

**nachliefern** ['na:xli:fərn], *v.a.* supply subsequently, complete delivery of.

**nachmachen** ['na:xmaxən], *v.a.* copy, imitate; counterfeit, forge.

**nachmals** ['na:xma:ls], *adv.* afterwards, subsequently.

**Nachmittag** ['na:xmɪta:k], *m.* (—s, *pl.* —e) afternoon.

**Nachnahme** ['na:xna:mə], *f.* (—, *no pl.*) *per* —, cash *or* (*Am.*) collect (payment) on delivery (*abbr.* C.O.D.).

**nachplappern** ['na:xplapərn], *v.a.* repeat mechanically.

**Nachrede** ['na:xre:də], *f.* (—, *pl.* —n) epilogue; *üble* —, slander.

**Nachricht** ['na:xrɪçt], *f.* (—, *pl.* —en) news, information; (*Mil.*) intelligence; — *geben*, send word.

**nachrücken** ['na:xrykən], *v.n.* (*aux.* sein) move up.

**Nachruf** ['na:xru:f], *m.* (—s, *pl.* —e) obituary.

**nachrühmen** ['na:xry:mən], *v.a. einem etwas* —, speak well of s.o.

**Nachsatz** ['na:xzats], *m.* (—es, *pl.* ⁘e) concluding clause; postscript.

**nachschauen** ['na:xʃauən], *v.n. jemandem* —, gaze after s.o.

**nachschlagen** ['na:xʃla:gən], *v.a. irr.* look up, consult (a book).

**Nachschlagewerk** ['na:xʃla:gəveɪk], *n.* (—s, *pl.* —e) work of reference, reference book.

**Nachschlüssel** ['na:xʃlysəl], *m.* (—s, *pl.* —) master-key, skeleton-key.

**Nachschrift** ['na:xʃrɪft], *f.* (—, *pl.* —en) postscript (*abbr.* P.S.).

**Nachschub** ['na:xʃu:p], *m.* (—s, *pl.* ⁘e) (fresh) supply; (*Mil.*) reinforcements.

**Nachsehen** ['na:xze:ən], *n.* (—s, *no pl.*) *das* — *haben*, be left out in the cold.

# nachsehen

**nachsehen** ['na:xze:ən], *v.a., v.n. irr.* look for, look s.th. up, refer to s.th.; *einem etwas* —, be indulgent with s.o.

**Nachsicht** ['na:xzıçt], *f.* (—, *no pl.*) forbearance, indulgence.

**Nachsilbe** ['na:xzılbə], *f.* (—, *pl.* —n) suffix.

**nachsinnen** ['na:xzınən], *v.n.* muse, reflect.

**nachsitzen** ['na:xzitsən], *v.n.* be kept in after school.

**Nachsommer** ['na:xzɔmər], *m.* (—s, *pl.* —) Indian summer.

**Nachspeise** ['na:xʃpaızə], *f.* (—, *pl.* —n) dessert.

**nachspüren** ['na:xʃpy:rən], *v.n. einem* —, trace, track.

**nächst** [nɛ:çst], *prep.* (*Dat.*) next to, nearest to. — *adj.* next.

**Nächste** ['nɛ:çstə], *m.* (—n, *pl.* —n) fellow-man, neighbour.

**nachstehen** ['na:xʃte:ən], *v.n. irr. einem* —, be inferior to s.o.; *keinem* —, be second to none.

**nachstehend** ['na:xʃte:ənt], *adv.* below, hereinafter. — *adj.* following.

**nachstellen** ['na:xʃtɛlən], *v.n. einem* —, lie in wait for s.o.

**Nachstellung** ['na:xʃtɛluŋ], *f.* (—, *pl.* —en) persecution, ambush; (*Gram.*) postposition.

**nächstens** ['nɛ:çstəns], *adv.* soon, shortly.

**nachstöbern** ['na:xʃtø:bərn], *v.n.* rummage.

**nachströmen** ['na:xʃtrø:mən], *v.n.* (*aux.* sein) crowd after.

**Nacht** [naxt], *f.* (—, *pl.* ⁀e) night; *die ganze* — *hindurch*, all night; *bei* —, at night; *gute* — *wünschen*, bid good-night; *über* —, overnight; *in der* —, during the night; *bei* — *und Nebel*, in the dead of night.

**Nachteil** ['na:xtaıl], *m.* (—s, *pl.* —e) disadvantage, damage.

**Nachtessen** ['naxtɛsən], *n.* (—s, *pl.* —) supper; evening meal.

**Nachtfalter** ['naxtfaltər], *m.* (—s, *pl.* —) (*Ent.*) moth.

**Nachtgeschirr** ['naxtgəʃɪr], *n.* (—s, *pl.* —e) chamber-pot.

**Nachtgleiche** ['naxtglaıçə], *f.* (—, *pl.* —n) equinox.

**Nachthemd** ['naxthɛmt], *n.* (—es, *pl.* —en) night-dress, night-gown.

**Nachtigall** ['naxtıgal], *f.* (—, *pl.* —en) (*Orn.*) nightingale.

**nächtigen** ['nɛçtıgən], *v.n.* spend the night.

**Nachtisch** ['naxtıʃ], *m.* (—es, *pl.* —e) dessert.

**Nachtlager** ['naxtla:gər], *n.* (—s, *pl.* —) lodgings for the night; (*Mil.*) bivouac.

**Nachtmahl** ['naxtma:l], *n.* (—s, *pl.* —e) (*Austr.*) supper.

**nachtönen** ['na:xtø:nən], *v.n.* resound.

**Nachtrag** ['na:xtra:k], *m.* (—s, *pl.* ⁀e) supplement, postscript, addition; (*pl.*) addenda.

**nachtragen** ['na:xtra:gən], *v.a. irr.* carry after; add; (*fig.*) *einem etwas* —, bear s.o. a grudge.

**nachträglich** ['na:xtrɛ:klıç], *adj.* subsequent; supplementary; additional; further; later.

**Nachtrupp** ['na:xtrup], *m.* (—s, *no pl.*) rearguard.

**Nachtschwärmer** ['naxtʃvɛrmər], *m.* (—s, *pl.* —) night-reveller.

**Nachttisch** ['naxttıʃ], *m.* (—es, *pl.* —e) bedside-table.

**nachtun** ['na:xtu:n], *v.a. irr. einem etwas* —, imitate s.o., emulate s.o.

**Nachtwächter** ['naxtvɛçtər], *m.* (—s, *pl.* —) night-watchman.

**Nachtwandler** ['naxtvandlər], *m.* (—s, *pl.* —) sleep-walker, somnambulist.

**Nachwahl** ['na:xva:l], *f.* (—, *pl.* —en) by(e)-election.

**Nachwehen** ['na:xve:ən], *f. pl.* aftermath; unpleasant consequences.

**Nachweis** ['na:xvaıs], *m.* (—es, *pl.* —e) proof; (*Lit.*) reference; agency.

**nachweisen** ['na:xvaızən], *v.a. irr.* prove, establish; (*Lit.*) refer.

**Nachwelt** ['na:xvɛlt], *f.* (—, *no pl.*) posterity.

**Nachwort** ['na:xvɔrt], *n.* (—es, *pl.* —e) epilogue.

**Nachwuchs** ['na:xvu:ks], *m.* (—es, *no pl.*) coming generation; recruits.

**Nachzahlung** ['na:xtsa:luŋ], *f.* (—, *pl.* —en) additional payment, supplementary payment.

**Nachzählung** ['na:xtsɛ:luŋ], *f.* (—, *pl.* —en) recount.

**nachziehen** ['na:xtsi:ən], *v.a. irr.* drag, tow; tighten; trace, pencil. — *v.n.* follow.

**Nachzügler** ['na:xtsy:glər], *m.* (—s, *pl.* —) straggler.

**Nacken** ['nakən], *m.* (—s, *pl.* —) nape, scruff of the neck.

**nackend** ['nakənt], *adj.* naked.

**nackt** [nakt], *adj.* nude, naked; (*bird*) callow; (*fig.*) bare; *sich* — *ausziehen*, strip.

**Nadel** ['na:dəl], *f.* (—, *pl.* —n) needle, pin; *wie auf* —*n sitzen*, be on tenter-hooks.

**Nadelöhr** ['na:dəlø:r], *n.* (—s, *pl.* —e) eye of a needle.

**Nagel** ['na:gəl], *m.* (—s, *pl.* ⁀) nail; (*wooden*) peg; (*ornament*) stud; *etwas an den* — *hängen*, lay s.th. aside, give s.th. up.

**nagelneu** ['na:gəlnɔy], *adj.* brand new.

**nagen** ['na:gən], *v.a., v.n.* gnaw; (*fig.*) rankle.

**Näharbeit** ['nɛ:arbaıt], *f.* (—, *pl.* —en) sewing, needlework.

**nahe** ['na:ə], *adj., adv.* near, close, nigh; — *bei*, close to; — *daran sein*, be on the point of; *es geht mir* —, it grieves me, it touches me; *einem zu* — *treten*, hurt s.o.'s feelings; *es liegt* —, it is obvious, it suggests itself.

**Nähe** ['nɛ:ə], *f.* (—, *no pl.*) nearness, proximity; *in der* —, at hand, close by.

**nahen** ['na:ən], *v.n.* (*aux.* sein) draw near, approach.

**nähen** ['nɛːən], *v.a.* sew, stitch.

**Nähere** ['nɛːərə], *n.* (—n, *no pl.*) details, particulars.

**Näherin** ['nɛːərɪn], *f.* (—, *pl.* — innen) seamstress, needlewoman.

**nähern** ['nɛːərn], *v.r. sich* —, draw near, approach.

**nahestehen** ['na:əʃteːən], *v.n.* be closely connected *or* friendly (with s.o.).

**Nährboden** ['nɛːrboːdən], *m.* (—s, *pl.* ") rich soil; (*Med., Biol.*) culture-medium.

**nähren** ['nɛːrən], *v.a.* nourish, feed. — *v.r. sich* — *von*, feed on; (*fig.*) gain a livelihood.

**nahrhaft** ['na:rhaft], *adj.* nourishing, nutritive, nutritious.

**Nährstand** ['nɛːrʃtant], *m.* (—es, *no pl.*) peasants, producers.

**Nahrung** ['na:ruŋ], *f.* (—, *no pl.*) nourishment.

**Nahrungsmittel** ['na:ruŋsmɪtəl], *n.* (—s, *pl.* —) food, provisions, victuals.

**Naht** [na:t], *f.* (—, *pl.* "e) seam.

**Nähzeug** ['nɛːtsɔyk], *n.* (—s, *no pl.*) sewing kit, work box.

**naiv** [na'iːf], *adj.* naïve, artless, guileless.

**Naivität** [naivi'tɛːt], *f.* (—, *no pl.*) artlessness, guilelessness, naïveté.

**Name** ['na:mə], *m.* (—ns, *pl.* —n) name; *guter* —, good name, renown, reputation; *dem* — *nach*, by name; *etwas beim rechten* —n *nennen*, call a spade a spade.

**namens** ['na:məns], *adv.* called; by the name of.

**Namensvetter** ['na:mənsfɛtər], *m.* (—s, *pl.* —n) namesake.

**namentlich** ['na:məntlɪç], *adj.* by name; particularly.

**Namenverzeichnis** ['na:mɛnfɛrtsaɪçnɪs], *n.* (—ses, *pl.* —se) list of names; (*scientific*) nomenclature.

**namhaft** ['na:mhaft], *adj.* distinguished, renowned; considerable; — *machen*, name.

**nämlich** ['nɛːmlɪç], *adv.* namely, to wit.

**Napf** [napf], *m.* (—es, *pl.* "e) bowl, basin.

**Napfkuchen** ['napfku:xən], *m.* (—s, *pl.* —) pound-cake, large cake.

**Narbe** ['narbə], *f.* (—, *pl.* —n) scar; (*leather*) grain.

**Narkose** [nar'ko:zə], *f.* (—, *pl.* —n) anaesthesia; narcosis.

**Narr** [nar], *m.* (—en, *pl.* —en) fool; jester, buffoon; *einen zum* —en *haben*, make a fool of s.o.; *an einem einen* —en *gefressen haben*, dote on, be infatuated with s.o.

**Narrheit** ['narhaɪt], *f.* (—, *pl.* —en) foolishness, folly.

**närrisch** ['nɛrɪʃ], *adj.* foolish, comical; odd; merry; eccentric, mad; — *werden*, go mad.

**Narzisse** [nar'tsɪsə], *f.* (—, *pl.* —n) (*Bot.*) narcissus; *gelbe* —, daffodil.

**naschen** ['naʃən], *v.a., v.n.* pilfer titbits; nibble at, eat sweets.

**Näscherei** [nɛʃər'aɪ], *f.* (—, *pl.* —en) sweets, dainties, sweetmeats.

**naschhaft** ['naʃhaft], *adj.* sweet-toothed.

**Naschkatze** ['naʃkatsə], *f.* (—, *pl.* —n) sweet tooth.

**Nase** ['na:zə], *f.* (—, *pl.* —n) nose; (*animal*) snout; scent; *stumpfe* —, snub nose; *gebogene* —, Roman nose; *immer der* — *nach*, follow your nose; *die* — *hoch tragen*, be stuck-up; *eine feine* (*gute*) — *haben*, be good at; not miss much; *die* — *rümpfen*, turn up o.'s nose; *seine* — *in alles stecken*, poke o.'s nose into everything; *einem etwas unter die* — *reiben*, bring s.th. home to s.o.

**näseln** ['nɛːzəln], *v.n.* speak with a twang.

**Nasenbein** ['na:zənbaɪn], *n.* (—s, *pl.* —e) nasal bone.

**Nasenbluten** ['na:zənbluːtən], *n.* (—s, *no pl.*) nose-bleed.

**Nasenflügel** ['na:zənflyːgəl], *m.* (—s, *pl.* —) side of the nose; nostril.

**naseweis** ['na:zəvaɪs], *adj.* pert, saucy.

**Nashorn** ['na:shɔrn], *n.* (—s, *pl.* "er) (*Zool.*) rhinoceros.

**Naß** [nas], *n.* (—sses, *no pl.*) (*Poet.*) fluid.

**naß** [nas], *adj.* wet, moist, damp.

**Nässe** ['nɛsə], *f.* (—, *no pl.*) wetness, dampness, moisture, humidity.

**nationalisieren** [natsjonali'ziːrən], *v.a.* nationalise.

**Nationalität** [natsjonali'tɛːt], *f.* (—, *pl.* —en) nationality.

**Natrium** ['na:trjum], *n.* (—s, *no pl.*) sodium.

**Natron** ['natrɔn], *n.* (—s, *no pl.*) sodium carbonate; *doppelkohlensaures* —, sodium bicarbonate; bicarbonate of soda.

**Natter** ['natər], *f.* (—, *pl.* —n) (*Zool.*) adder, viper.

**Natur** [na'tuːr], *f.* (—, *pl.* —en) nature; (*body*) constitution; (*mind*) disposition; *von* —, by nature, constitutionally; *nach der* — *zeichnen*, draw from nature.

**naturalisieren** [naturali'ziːrən], *v.a.* naturalise.

**Naturalleistung** [natu'ra:llaɪstuŋ], *f.* (—, *pl.* —en) payment in kind.

**Naturell** [natu'rɛl], *n.* (—s, *pl.* —e) natural disposition, temper.

**Naturforscher** [na'tuːrfɔrʃər], *m.* (—s, *pl.* —) naturalist.

**naturgemäß** [na'tuːrgəmɛːs], *adj.* natural.

**Naturgeschichte** [na'tuːrgəʃɪçtə], *f.* (—, *no pl.*) natural history.

**naturgetreu** [na'tuːrgətrɔy], *adj.* true to nature, lifelike.

**Naturkunde** [na'tuːrkundə], *f.* (—, *no pl.*) natural history.

**Naturlehre** [na'tuːrleːrə], *f.* (—, *no pl.*) natural philosophy; physics.

# natürlich

**natürlich** [na'ty:rlıç], *adj.* natural; innate, inherent; unaffected, artless. — *adv.* of course, naturally.

**Naturspiel** [na'tu:rʃpi:l], *n.* (—s, *pl.* —e) freak of nature.

**Naturtrieb** [na'tu:rtri:p], *m.* (—s, *no pl.*) natural impulse, instinct.

**naturwidrig** [na'tu:rvi:drıç], *adj.* contrary to nature, unnatural.

**Naturwissenschaft** [na'tu:rvısənʃaft], *f.* (—, *pl.* —en) (natural) science.

**naturwüchsig** [na'tu:rvy:ksıç], *adj.* original; unsophisticated.

**Nautik** ['nautık], *f.* (—, *no pl.*) nautical science.

**nautisch** ['nautıʃ], *adj.* nautical.

**Nazi** ['na:tsi], *abbr.* National Socialist.

**Neapel** [ne'a:pəl], *n.* Naples.

**Nebel** ['ne:bəl], *m.* (—s, *pl.* —) fog; *leichter* —, haze, mist; *dichter* —, (*London*) pea-souper; (*with soot*) smog.

**Nebelschicht** ['ne:bəlʃıçt], *f.* (—, *pl.* —n) fog-bank.

**neben** ['ne:bən], *prep.* (*Dat., Acc.*) near, by, beside, besides, close to, next to; (*in compounds*) secondary, subsidiary, side-. — *adv.* beside, besides.

**nebenan** [ne:bən'an], *adv.* next door, nearby.

**nebenbei** [ne:bən'baı], *adv.* besides, by the way, incidentally.

**Nebenbuhler** [ne:bənbu:lər], *m.* (—s, *pl.* —) rival.

**nebeneinander** [ne:bənaın'andər], *adv.* side by side, abreast.

**Nebenfluß** ['ne:bənflus], *m.* (—sses, *pl.* ˙sse) tributary, affluent.

**nebenher** [ne:bən'he:r], *adv.* by the side of, along with.

**Nebenmensch** ['ne:bənmɛnʃ], *m.* (—en, *pl.* —en) fellow creature.

**Nebensatz** ['ne:bənzats], *m.* (—es, *pl.* ˙e) (*Gram.*) subordinate clause.

**Nebenzimmer** ['ne:bəntsımər], *n.* (—s, *pl.* —) adjoining room.

**neblig** ['ne:blıç], *adj.* foggy, misty, hazy.

**nebst** [ne:pst], *prep.* (*Dat.*) together with, including.

**necken** ['nɛkən], *v.a.* tease, chaff, banter.

**neckisch** ['nɛkıʃ], *adj.*, droll, playful, arch.

**Neffe** ['nɛfə], *m.* (—n, *pl.* —n) nephew.

**Neger** ['ne:gər], *m.* (—s, *pl.* —) Negro.

**negerartig** ['ne:gəra:rtıç], *adj.* Negroid.

**negieren** [ne'gi:rən], *v.a.* deny, negate, negative.

**nehmen** ['ne:mən], *v.a. irr.* take, seize; receive, accept; *einem etwas* —, take s.th. from s.o.; *das lasse ich mir nicht* —, I insist on that, I am not to be done out of that; *ein Ende* —, come to an end; *etwas in die Hand* —, take s.th. in hand; *Schaden* —, suffer damage; *einen beim Wort* —, take s.o. at his word; *sich in acht* —, take care.

**Nehrung** ['ne:run], *f.* (—, *pl.* —en) narrow tongue of land, spit.

**Neid** [naıt], *m.* (—es, *no pl.*) envy, grudge.

**Neidhammel** ['naıthaməl], *m.* (—s, *pl.* —) dog in the manger.

**neidisch** ['naıdıʃ], *adj.* envious, grudging, jealous.

**Neige** ['naıgə], *f.* (—, *pl.* —n) remnant, sediment; *zur* — *gehen*, be on the decline, run short, dwindle.

**neigen** ['naıgən], *v.a., v.n.* incline, bow, bend; *zu etwas* —, be inclined to, be prone to. — *v.r. sich* —, bow.

**Neigung** ['naıgun], *f.* (—, *pl.* —en) inclination, proneness; affection; (*ground*) dip, slope, gradient; (*ship*) list.

**Neigungsfläche** ['naıgunsflɛçə], *f.* (—, *pl.* —n) inclined plane.

**nein** [naın], *adv.* no.

**Nekrolog** [nekro'lo:k], *m.* (—(e)s, *pl.* —e) obituary.

**Nelke** ['nɛlkə], *f.* (—, *pl.* —n) (*Bot.*) pink, carnation; (*condiment*) clove.

**nennen** ['nɛnən], *v.a. irr.* name, call by name, term, style.

**Nenner** ['nɛnər], *m.* (—s, *pl.* —) denominator.

**Nennung** ['nɛnun], *f.* (—, *pl.* —en) naming, mentioning.

**Nennwert** ['nɛnve:rt], *m.* (—s, *pl.* —e) nominal value.

**Nepal** ['ne:pal], *n.* Nepal.

**Nerv** [nɛrf], *m.* (—s, *pl.* —en) nerve, sinew; *einem auf die* —*en gehen*, get on s.o.'s nerves.

**Nervenlehre** ['nɛrfənle:rə], *f.* (—, *no pl.*) neurology.

**nervig** ['nɛrvıç], *adj.* strong; (*fig.*) pithy.

**nervös** [nɛr'vø:s], *adj.* nervous, irritable, fidgety.

**Nerz** [nɛrts], *m.* (—es, *pl.* —e) mink.

**Nessel** ['nɛsəl], *f.* (—, *pl.* —n) nettle.

**Nesseltuch** ['nɛsəltu:x], *n.* (—es, *no pl.*) muslin.

**Nest** [nɛst], *n.* (—es, *pl.* —er) nest; (*eagle*) eyrie; *kleines* —, small town.

**Nesthäkchen** ['nɛsthe:kçən], *n.* (—s, *pl.* —) youngest child.

**nett** [nɛt], *adj.* nice, kind, friendly; neat, trim.

**netto** ['nɛto], *adv.* (*Comm.*) net, clear.

**Netz** [nɛts], *n.* (—es, *pl.* —e) net; (*Electr.*) grid; *Eisenbahn* —, railway network *or* system.

**netzen** ['nɛtsən], *v.a.* (*obs., Poet.*) wet, moisten.

**Netzhaut** ['nɛtshaut], *f.* (—, *pl.* ˙e) retina.

**neu** [nɔy], *adj.* new, fresh; modern; recent; *aufs* —*e, von* —*em*, anew, afresh; —*e,* —*ere Sprachen*, modern languages.

**Neuenburg** ['nɔyənburk], *n.* Neuchâtel.

**neuerdings** ['nɔyərdıŋs], *adv.* newly, lately.

**Neuerer** ['nɔyərər], *m.* (—s, *pl.* —) innovator.

160

**neuerlich** ['nɔyərlɪç], *adj.* late, repeated.
**Neufundland** [nɔy'funtlant], *n.* Newfoundland.
**Neugier(de)** ['nɔygi:r(də)], *f.* (—, *no pl.*) inquisitiveness, curiosity.
**neugierig** ['nɔygi:rɪç], *adj.* curious, inquisitive.
**Neuheit** ['nɔyhaɪt], *f.* (—, *pl.* —en) novelty.
**Neuigkeit** ['nɔyɪçkaɪt], *f.* (—, *pl.* —en) piece of news.
**neulich** ['nɔylɪç], *adv.* lately, recently.
**Neuling** ['nɔylɪŋ], *m.* (—s, *pl.* —e) novice, beginner, tyro, newcomer; (*Am.*) greenhorn.
**neumodisch** ['nɔymo:dɪʃ], *adj.* newfangled, in vogue.
**Neumond** ['nɔymo:nt], *m.* (—s, *pl.* —e) new moon.
**neun** [nɔyn], *num. adj.* nine.
**Neunauge** ['nɔynaugə], *n.* (—s, *pl.* —n) river lamprey.
**neunzehn** ['nɔyntse:n], *num. adj.* nineteen.
**neunzig** ['nɔyntsɪç], *num. adj.* ninety.
**Neuregelung** ['nɔyre:gəluŋ], *f.* (—, *pl.* —en) rearrangement.
**Neuseeland** [nɔy'ze:lant], *n.* New Zealand.
**neutralisieren** [nɔytrali'zi:rən], *v.a.* neutralise.
**Neutralität** [nɔytrali'tɛ:t], *f.* (—, *no pl.*) neutrality.
**Neutrum** ['nɔytrum], *n.* (—s, *pl.* —ren) (*Gram.*) neuter.
**Neuzeit** ['nɔytsaɪt], *f.* (—, *no pl.*) modern times.
**nicht** [nɪçt], *adv.* not; *auch* —, nor; — *doch*, don't; — *einmal*, not even; *durchaus* —, not at all, by no means; — *mehr*, no more, no longer; not any more; *noch* —, not yet; — *wahr?* isn't it? aren't you? (*in compounds*) non–, dis–, a– (*negativing*).
**Nichte** ['nɪçtə], *f.* (—, *pl.* —n) niece.
**nichten** ['nɪçtən], *adv.* (*obs.*) *mit*—, by no means, not at all.
**nichtig** ['nɪçtɪç], *adj.* null, void, invalid.
**Nichtigkeit** ['nɪçtɪçkaɪt], *f.* (—, *no pl.*) invalidity, nullity.
**nichts** [nɪçts], *pron.* nothing, nought; — *als*, nothing but.
**nichtsdestoweniger** [nɪçtsdesto've:nɪgər], *adv.* nevertheless.
**Nichtsnutz** ['nɪçtsnuts], *m.* (—es, *pl.* —e) good for nothing.
**Nickel** ['nɪkəl], *n.* (—s, *no pl.*) (*metal*) nickel.
**nicken** ['nɪkən], *v.n.* nod.
**nie** [ni:], *adv.* never, at no time.
**nieder** ['ni:dər], *adj.* low, lower, nether; mean, inferior. — *adv.* down.
**niedergeschlagen** ['ni:dərgəʃla:gən], *adj.* dejected, low-spirited, depressed.
**niederkommen** ['ni:dərkɔmən], *v.n. irr.* (*aux.* sein) (*rare*) be confined.
**Niederkunft** ['ni:dərkunft], *f.* (—, *no pl.*) confinement, childbirth.

**Niederlage** ['ni:dərla:gə], *f.* (—, *pl.* —n) (*enemy*) defeat, overthrow; (*goods*) depot, warehouse; agency.
**Niederlande** ['ni:dərlandə], *n. pl.* the Netherlands.
**niederlassen** ['ni:dərlasən], *v.a. irr.* let down. — *v.r. sich* —, sit down, take a seat; settle; establish o.s. in business.
**Niederlassung** ['ni:dərlasuŋ], *f.* (—, *pl.* —en) establishment; settlement, colony; branch, branch establishment.
**niederlegen** ['ni:dərle:gən], *v.a.* lay down, put down; (*office*) resign, abdicate. — *v.r. sich* —, lie down.
**Niederschlag** ['ni:dərʃla:k], *m.* (—s, *pl.* ˙e) precipitation, sediment, deposit; rain.
**niederschlagen** ['ni:dərʃla:gən], *v.a. irr.* strike down; (*fig.*) depress, discourage; (*Law*) quash, cancel; (*eyes*) cast down; (*Chem.*) precipitate; (*Boxing*) knock out.
**Niedertracht** ['ni:dərtraxt], *f.* (—, *no pl.*) baseness, meanness, villainy, beastliness.
**Niederung** ['ni:dəruŋ], *f.* (—, *pl.* —en) low ground, marsh.
**niedlich** ['ni:tlɪç], *adj.* pretty, dainty; (*Am.*) cute.
**niedrig** ['ni:drɪç], *adj.* low; (*fig.*) base, vile.
**niemals** ['ni:ma:ls], *adv.* never, at no time.
**niemand** ['ni:mant], *pron.* nobody, no one.
**Niere** ['ni:rə], *f.* (—, *pl.* —n) kidney.
**Nierenbraten** ['ni:rənbra:tən], *m.* (—s, *no pl.*) roast loin.
**Nierenfett** ['ni:rənfet], *n.* (—s, *no pl.*) suet.
**nieseln** ['ni:zəln], *v.n. imp.* drizzle.
**niesen** ['ni:zən], *v.n.* sneeze.
**Nießbrauch** ['ni:sbraux], *m.* (—s, *no pl.*) usufruct, benefit.
**Niete** ['ni:tə], *f.* (—, *pl.* —n) blank; (*Engin.*) rivet; failure.
**Niger** ['ni:gər], *n.* Niger.
**Nigeria** [ni'ge:rja], *n.* Nigeria.
**Nikaragua** [nika'ra:gua], *n.* Nicaragua.
**Nikolaus** ['nikolaus], *m.* Nicholas; *Sankt* —, Santa Claus.
**Nil** [ni:l], *m.* (—s, *no pl.*) Nile.
**Nilpferd** ['ni:lpfe:rt], *n.* (—s, *pl.* —e) (*Zool.*) hippopotamus.
**nimmer (mehr)** ['nɪmər (me:r)], *adv.* never, never again.
**nippen** ['nɪpən], *v.a., v.n.* sip, (take a) nip (of).
**Nippsachen** ['nɪpzaxən], *f. pl.* knickknacks.
**nirgends** ['nɪrgənts], *adv.* nowhere.
**Nische** ['ni:ʃə], *f.* (—, *pl.* —n) niche.
**Nisse** ['nɪsə], *f.* (—, *pl.* —n) nit.
**nisten** ['nɪstən], *v.n.* nest.
**Niveau** [ni'vo:], *n.* (—s, *pl.* —s) level, standard.
**nivellieren** [nive'li:rən], *v.a.* level.
**Nixe** ['nɪksə], *f.* (—, *pl.* —n) waternymph, mermaid, water-sprite.

# Nizza

**Nizza** ['nɪtsa], *n.* Nice.

**nobel** ['no:bəl], *adj.* noble, smart; (*Am.*) swell; munificent, openhanded, magnanimous.

**noch** [nɔx], *adv.* still, yet; — *einmal*, —*mals*, once more; *weder* ... — ..., neither ... nor ...; — *nicht*, not yet; — *nie*, never yet, never before.

**nochmalig** ['nɔxma:lɪç], *adj.* repeated.

**Nomade** [no'ma:də], *m.* (—n, *pl.* —n) nomad.

**nominell** [nomi'nɛl], *adj.* nominal.

**nominieren** [nomi'ni:rən], *v.a.* nominate.

**Nonne** ['nɔnə], *f.* (—, *pl.* —n) nun.

**Noppe** ['nɔpə], *f.* (—, *pl.* —n) nap.

**Norden** ['nɔrdən], *m.* (—s, *no pl.*) north.

**nördlich** ['nœrtlɪç], *adj.* northern, northerly.

**Nordsee** ['nɔrtze:], *f.* North Sea.

**nörgeln** ['nœrgəln], *v.n.* find fault, cavil, carp, nag.

**Norm** ['nɔrm], *f.* (—, *pl.* —en) standard, rule, norm.

**normal** [nɔr'ma:l], *adj.* normal, standard.

**Norwegen** ['nɔrve:gən], *n.* Norway.

**Not** [no:t], *f.* (—, *pl.* ˙e) need, necessity; misery, want, trouble, distress; (*in compounds*) emergency.

**not** [no:t], *pred. adj.* — *tun*, be necessary.

**Nota** ['no:ta], *f.* (—, *pl.* —s) bill, statement.

**Notar** [no'ta:r], *m.* (—s, *pl.* —e) notary.

**Notdurft** ['no:tdurft], *f.* (—, *pl.* ˙e) want, necessaries, necessity; *seine* — *verrichten*, ease o.s.

**notdürftig** ['no:tdyrftɪç], *adj.* scanty, makeshift.

**Note** ['no:tə], *f.* (—, *pl.* —n) note; (*Mus.*) sobriety; (*School*) mark(s); *nach* —*n*, (*fig.*) with a vengeance.

**Notenbank** ['no:tənbaŋk], *f.* (—, *pl.* —en) bank of issue.

**Notenblatt** ['no:tənblat], *n.* (—s, *pl.* ˙er) sheet of music.

**notgedrungen** ['no:tgədruŋən], *adj.* compulsory, forced; perforce.

**Nothelfer** ['no:thɛlfər], *m.* (—s, *pl.* —) helper in time of need.

**notieren** [no'ti:rən], *v.a.* note, book; (*Comm.*) quote.

**notifizieren** [notifi'tsi:rən], *v.a.* notify.

**nötig** ['nø:tɪç], *adj.* necessary; — *haben*, want, need.

**nötigen** ['nø:tɪgən], *v.a.* compel, press, force, urge; necessitate; *sich* — *lassen*, stand upon ceremony.

**Notiz** [no'ti:ts], *f.* (—, *pl.* —en) note, notice; — *nehmen von*, take notice of; (*pl.*) notes, jottings.

**notleidend** ['no:tlaɪdənt], *adj.* financially distressed, indigent, needy.

**notorisch** [no'to:rɪʃ], *adj.* notorious.

**Notstand** ['no:tʃtant], *m.* (—s, *no pl.*) state of distress; emergency.

**Notverband** ['no:tfɛrbant], *m.* (—es, *pl.* ˙e) first-aid dressing.

**Notwehr** ['no:tve:r], *f.* (—, *no pl.*) self-defence.

**notwendig** ['no:tvɛndɪç], *adj.* necessary, essential, needful.

**Notzucht** ['no:ttsuxt], *f.* (—, *no pl.*) rape, violation.

**Novelle** [no'vɛlə], *f.* (—, *pl.* —n) (*Lit.*) novella, short story, short novel.

**Novize** [no'vi:tsə], *m.* (—n, *pl.* —n) or *f.* (—, *pl.* —n) novice.

**Nu** [nu:], *m. & n.* (—, *no pl.*) moment; *im* —, in no time, in an instant.

**Nubien** ['nu:bjən], *n.* Nubia.

**nüchtern** ['nyçtərn], *adj.* fasting; sober; jejune; (*fig.*) dry, matter-of-fact, realistic.

**Nüchternheit** ['nyçtərnhaɪt], *f.* (—, *no pl.*) sobriety; (*fig.*) dryness.

**Nudel** ['nu:dəl], *f.* (—, *pl.* —n) noodles, macaroni, vermicelli; *eine komische* —, a funny person.

**Null** [nul], *f.* (—, *pl.* —en) nought, zero; (*fig.*) nonentity.

**null** [nul], *adj.* null; nil; — *und nichtig*, null and void; *etwas für* —'*und nichtig erklären*, annul.

**numerieren** [nume'ri:rən], *v.a.* number.

**Nummer** ['numər], *f.* (—, *pl.* —n) number, size, issue.

**nun** [nu:n], *adv., conj.* now, at present; since; —! now! well! *von* — *an*, henceforth; — *und nimmermehr*, nevermore; *was* —? what next?

**nunmehr** ['nu:nme:r], *adv.* now, by this time.

**Nunzius** ['nuntsjus], *m.* (—, *pl.* —zien) (Papal) nuncio.

**nur** [nu:r], *adv.* only, solely, merely, but; *wenn* —, if only, provided that; — *das nicht*, anything but that; — *zu*, go to it!

**Nürnberg** ['nyrnbɛrk], *n.* Nuremberg.

**Nuß** [nus], *f.* (—, *pl.* ˙sse) nut.

**Nußhäher** ['nushɛ:ər], *m.* (—s, *pl.* —) (*Orn.*) jay.

**Nüster** ['nystər], *f.* (—, *pl.* —n) (*horse*) nostril.

**Nutzanwendung** ['nutsanvɛnduŋ], *f.* (—, *pl.* —en) practical application.

**nutzbar** ['nutsba:r], *adj.* useful, usable, productive.

**nütze** ['nytsə], *adj.* useful, of use.

**Nutzen** ['nutsən], *m.* (—s, *pl.* —) use, utility; profit, gain, advantage, benefit; — *bringen*, yield profit; — *ziehen aus*, derive profit from.

**nützen** ['nytsən], *v.a.* make use of, use. — *v.n.* be of use, serve, be effective, work.

**nützlich** ['nytslɪç], *adj.* useful.

**nutzlos** ['nutslo:s], *adj.* useless.

**Nutznießer** ['nutsni:sər], *m.* (—s, *pl.* —) beneficiary, usufructuary.

**Nymphe** ['nymfə], *f.* (—, *pl.* —en) nymph.

162

# O

O [o:], n. (—s, pl. —s) the letter O.
o! [o:], excl. oh!
Oase [o'a:zə], f. (—, pl. —n) oasis.
ob [ɔp], conj. whether; if; als —, as if;
und —! rather! yes, indeed! — prep.
(Genit., Dat.) on account of; upon, on.
Obacht ['o:baxt], f. (—, no pl.) heed,
care; — geben, pay attention, look out.
Obdach ['ɔpdax], n. (—es, no pl.)
shelter, lodging.
Obduktion [ɔpduk'tsjo:n], f. (—, pl.
—en) post-mortem examination.
oben [o:bən], adv. above, aloft, on top;
(house) upstairs; (water) on the
surface; von — bis unten, from top to
bottom; von — herab, from above;
(fig.) haughtily, superciliously.
obendrein [o:bən'draɪn], adv. besides,
into the bargain.
obengenannt ['o:bəngənant], adj.
above-mentioned.
Ober ['o:bər], m. (—s, pl. —) head
waiter; Herr —!, waiter!; (in compounds) upper, chief.
ober ['o:bər], adj. upper, higher; chief;
superior.
Oberfläche ['o:bərflɛçə], f. (—, pl.
—n) surface.
oberflächlich ['o:bərflɛçlɪç], adj.
superficial, casual.
oberhalb ['o:bərhalp], adv., prep.
(Genit.) above.
Oberin ['o:bərɪn], f. (—, pl. —innen)
(Eccl.) Mother Superior; hospital
matron.
Oberschule ['o:bərʃu:lə], f. (—, pl.
—n) high school, secondary school.
Oberst ['o:bərst], m. (—en, pl. —en)
colonel.
Oberstaatsanwalt ['o:bərʃta:tsanvalt],
m. (—s, pl. ꞏe) Attorney-General.
oberste ['o:bərstə], adj. uppermost,
highest, supreme.
Oberstimme ['o:bərʃtɪmə], f. (—, pl.
—n) (Mus.) treble, soprano.
Oberstübchen ['o:bərʃty:pçən], n. (—s,
pl. —) (fig.) nicht richtig im — sein,
have bats in the belfry.
Obervolta ['o:bərvɔlta], n. Upper Volta.
obgleich [ɔp'glaɪç], conj. though,
although.
Obhut ['ɔphu:t], f. (—, no pl.) keeping,
care, protection.
obig ['o:bɪç], adj. foregoing, above-
mentioned, aforementioned, aforesaid.
objektiv [ɔpjɛk'ti:f], adj. objective,
impartial, unprejudiced.
Oblate [o'bla:tə], f. (—, pl. —n)
wafer; (Eccl.) Host.

obliegen ['ɔpli:gən], v.n. irr. be incumbent upon s.o.; be o.'s duty;
apply o.s. to.
Obmann ['ɔpman], m. (—es, pl. ꞏer)
chairman; (jury) foreman.
Obrigkeit ['o:brɪçkaɪt], f. (—, pl. —en)
authorities.
obschon [ɔp'ʃo:n] see under obwohl.
Observatorium [ɔpzɛrva'to:rjum], n.
(—s, pl. —rien) observatory.
obsiegen ['ɔpzi:gən], v.n. (rare) be
victorious.
Obst [o:pst], n. (—es, no pl.) fruit.
obszön [ɔps'tsø:n], adj. obscene.
obwalten ['ɔpvaltən], v.n. (rare) exist,
prevail, obtain; unter den —den
Umständen, in the circumstances, as
matters stand.
obwohl [ɔp'vo:l] (also obschon
[ɔp'ʃo:n], obzwar [ɔp'tsva:r]), conj.
though, although.
Ochse ['ɔksə], m. (—n, pl. —n) (Zool.)
ox; bullock; (fig.) blockhead.
ochsen ['ɔksən], v.n. (sl.) swot,
cram.
Ochsenauge ['ɔksənaugə], n. (—s, pl.
—n) ox-eye, bull's eye; (Archit.)
oval dormer window; porthole light.
Ochsenziemer ['ɔksəntsi:mər], m. (—s,
pl. —) (obs.) horse-whip.
Ocker ['ɔkər], m. (—s, no pl.) ochre.
Öde ['ø:də], f. (—, pl. —n) wilderness.
öde ['ø:də], adj. desolate, bleak,
dreary.
Odem ['o:dəm], m. (—s, no pl.) (Poet.)
breath.
oder ['o:dər], conj. or; — aber, or else;
— auch, or rather.
Ofen ['o:fən], m. (—s, pl. ꞏ) stove;
oven, furnace.
Ofenpest [o:fən'pɛst], n. Budapest.
offen ['ɔfən], adj. open; (fig.) candid,
sincere, frank; — gestanden, frankly
speaking.
offenbar [ɔfən'ba:r], adj. obvious,
manifest, evident.
offenbaren [ɔfən'ba:rən], v.a. insep.
make known, reveal, disclose. — v.r.
sich einem —, open o.'s heart to s.o.;
unbosom o.s.
Offenheit ['ɔfənhaɪt], f. (—, no pl.)
frankness, candour.
offenkundig ['ɔfənkundɪç], adj. obvious, manifest.
offensichtlich ['ɔfənzɪçtlɪç], adj. obvious; apparent.
öffentlich ['œfəntlɪç], adj. public.
offerieren [ɔfə'ri:rən], v.a. offer.
Offerte [ɔ'fɛrtə], f. (—, pl. —n) offer,
tender.
offiziell [ɔfi'tsjɛl], adj. official.
Offizier [ɔfi'tsi:r], m. (—s, pl. —e)
officer, lieutenant.
Offizierspatent [ɔfi'tsi:rspatɛnt], n.
(—s, pl. —e) (Mil.) commission.
offiziös [ɔfi'tsjø:s], adj. semi-official.
öffnen ['œfnən], v.a. open.
oft [ɔft], oftmals ['ɔftma:ls], adv.
often, frequently.
öfters ['œftərs], adv. often, frequently.

**Oheim** ['o:haɪm], *m.* (**—s**, *pl* **—e**) (*Poet.*) uncle.

**ohne** ['o:nə], *prep.* (*Acc.*) without, but for, except.

**ohnehin** ['o:nəhɪn], *adv.* as it is.

**Ohnmacht** ['o:nmaxt], *f.* (**—**, *pl.* **—en**) fainting-fit, swoon; impotence; *in — fallen*, faint.

**Ohr** [o:r], *n.* (**—es**, *pl.* **—en**) ear; *bis über beide —en*, head over heels; *die —en spitzen*, prick up o.'s ears.

**Ohrenbläser** ['o:rənblɛ:zər], *m.* (**—s**, *pl.* **—**) tale-bearer.

**Ohrensausen** ['o:rənzauzən], *n.* (**—s**, *no pl.*) humming in the ears.

**Ohrenschmaus** ['o:rənʃmaus], *m.* (**—es**, *no pl.*) musical treat.

**Ohrfeige** ['o:rfaɪgə], *f.* (**—**, *pl.* **—n**) box on the ear.

**Ohrläppchen** ['o:rlɛpçən], *n.* (**—s**, *pl.* **—**) lobe of the ear.

**Ohrmuschel** ['o:rmuʃəl], *f.* (**—**, *pl.* **—n**) auricle.

**oktav** [ɔk'ta:f], *adj.* octavo.

**Oktober** [ɔk'to:bər], *m.* (**—s**, *pl.* **—**) October.

**oktroyieren** [ɔktroa'ji:rən], *v.a.* dictate, force s.th. upon s.o.

**okulieren** [oku'li:rən], *v.a.* (*trees*) graft.

**Öl** [ø:l], *n.* (**—s**, *pl.* **—e**) oil; (*rare*) olive-oil.

**Ölanstrich** ['ø:lanʃtrɪç], *m.* (**—s**, *pl.* **—e**) coat of oil-paint.

**ölen** ['ø:lən], *v.a.* oil, lubricate; (*rare*) anoint.

**Ölgemälde** ['ø:lgəmɛ:ldə], *n.* (**—s**, *pl.* **—**) oil painting.

**Ölung** ['ø:luŋ], *f.* (**—**, *pl.* **—en**) oiling; anointing; (*Eccl.*) *die letzte —*, Extreme Unction.

**Olymp** [o'lymp], *m.* Mount Olympus.

**olympisch** [o'lympɪʃ], *adj.* Olympian.

**Omelett** [ɔmə'lɛt], *n.* (**—s**, *pl.* **—s**) omelette.

**Onkel** ['ɔŋkəl], *m.* (**—s**, *pl.* **—**) uncle.

**Oper** ['o:pər], *f.* (**—**, *pl.* **—n**) opera.

**operieren** [opə'ri:rən], *v.a., v.n.* operate (on); *sich — lassen*, be operated on; undergo an operation.

**Opfer** ['ɔpfər], *n.* (**—s**, pl. **—**) sacrifice; victim.

**opfern** ['ɔpfərn], *v.a., v.n.* offer (up), sacrifice, immolate.

**opponieren** [ɔpo'ni:rən], *v.n.* oppose.

**Optiker** ['ɔptɪkər], *m.* (**—s**, *pl.* **—**) optician.

**oratorisch** [ora'to:rɪʃ], *adj.* oratorical.

**Orchester** [ɔr'kɛstər], *n.* (**—s**, *pl.* **—**) orchestra, band.

**orchestrieren** [ɔrkɛs'tri:rən], *v.a.* orchestrate, score for orchestra.

**Orchidee** [ɔrçi'de:], *f.* (**—**, *pl.* **—n**) (*Bot.*) orchid.

**Orden** ['ɔrdən], *m.* (**—s**, *pl.* **—**) medal; (*Eccl.*) (religious) order.

**ordentlich** ['ɔrdəntlɪç], *adj.* orderly, tidy, methodical, neat; regular; respectable, steady; sound; *—er Professor*, (full) professor.

**Order** ['ɔrdər], *f.* (**—**, *pl.* **—s**) (*Comm.*) order.

**ordinär** [ɔrdi'nɛ:r], *adj.* common, vulgar.

**Ordinarius** [ɔrdi'na:rjus], *m.* (**—**, *pl.* **—ien**) (*Univ.*) professor; (*Eccl.*) ordinary.

**ordnen** ['ɔrdnən], *v.a.* put in order, tidy, arrange, dispose.

**Ordnung** ['ɔrdnuŋ], *f.* (**—**, *pl.* **—en**) order, arrangement, disposition, routine; tidiness; class, rank; *in —*, all right, in good trim; *nicht in —*, out of order, wrong.

**ordnungsgemäß** ['ɔrdnuŋsgəmɛ:s], *adv.* duly.

**ordnungsmäßig** ['ɔrdnuŋsmɛsɪç], *adj.* regular.

**ordnungswidrig** ['ɔrdnuŋsvi:drɪç], *adj.* irregular.

**Ordnungszahl** ['ɔrdnuŋstsa:l], *f.* (**—**, *pl.* **—en**) ordinal number.

**Ordonnanz** [ɔrdɔ'nants], *f.* (**—**, *pl.* **—en**) ordinance; (*Mil.*) orderly.

**Organ** [ɔr'ga:n], *n.* (**—s**, *pl.* **—e**) organ.

**organisieren** [ɔrgani'zi:rən], *v.a.* organise.

**Orgel** ['ɔrgəl], *f.* (**—**, *pl.* **—n**) (*Mus.*) organ.

**Orgelzug** ['ɔ:rgəltsu:k], *m.* (**—s**, *pl.* **—̈e**) organ-stop.

**Orgie** ['ɔrgjə], *f.* (**—**, *pl.* **—n**) orgy.

**orientalisch** [ɔrjɛn'ta:lɪʃ], *adj.* oriental, eastern.

**orientieren** [ɔrjɛn'ti:rən], *v.a.* inform, orientate; set s.o. right. — *v.r. sich — über*, orientate o.s., find out about; get o.'s bearings.

**Orkan** [ɔr'ka:n], *m.* (**—s**, *pl.* **—e**) hurricane, gale, typhoon.

**Ornat** [ɔr'na:t], *m.* (**—es**, *pl.* **—e**) official robes; vestments.

**Ort** [ɔrt], *m.* (**—es**, *pl.* **—e**, **—̈er**) place, spot; region; (*in compounds*) local.

**örtlich** ['œrtlɪç], *adj.* local.

**Ortschaft** ['ɔrtʃaft], *f.* (**—**, *pl.* **—en**) place, township, village.

**Öse** ['ø:zə], *f.* (**—**, *pl.* **—n**) loop; *Haken und —n*, hooks and eyes.

**Ostasien** ['ɔsta:zjən], *n.* Eastern Asia, the Far East.

**Ost(en)** ['ɔst(ən)], *m.* (**—s**, *no pl.*) east.

**ostentativ** [ɔstɛnta'ti:f], *adj.* ostentatious.

**Osterei** ['o:stəraɪ], *n.* (**—s**, *pl.* **—er**) Easter egg.

**Ostern** ['o:stərn], *f. pl.* (*used as n. sing.*) Easter.

**Österreich** ['ø:stərraɪç], *n.* Austria.

**Ostindien** ['ɔstɪndjən], *n.* the East Indies.

**östlich** ['œstlɪç], *adj.* eastern, easterly.

**Oxyd** [ɔk'sy:t], *n.* (**—es**, *pl.* **—e**) oxide.

**oxydieren** [ɔksy'di:rən], *v.a., v.n.* oxidise.

**Ozean** ['o:tsea:n], *m.* (**—s**, *pl.* **—e**) ocean, sea; *Grosser —*, Pacific (Ocean).

**Ozon** [o'tso:n], *n.* (**—s**, *no pl.*) ozone.

# P

**P** [pe:], *n.* (—s, *pl.* —s) the letter P.
**Paar** [pa:r], *n.* (—es, *pl.* —e) pair, couple.
**paar** [pa:r], *adj.* ein —, a few, some.
**Pacht** [paxt], *f.* (—, *pl.* —en) lease; *in — nehmen*, take on lease.
**Pachthof** ['paxtho:f], *m.* (—s, *pl.* ⁝e) leasehold estate, farm.
**Pack** (1) [pak], *m.* (—s, *pl.* ⁝e) pack, bale, packet; *mit Sack und —*, (with) bag and baggage.
**Pack** (2) [pak], *n.* (—s, *no pl.*) rabble, mob.
**Päckchen** ['pɛkçən], *n.* (—s, *pl.* —) pack, packet; (small) parcel.
**packen** ['pakən], *v.a.* pack; seize; (*fig.*) —*d*, thrilling; *pack dich!* be off! scram!
**pädagogisch** [pe:da'go:gɪʃ], *adj.* educational, pedagogic(al).
**paddeln** ['padəln], *v.n.* paddle.
**paff** [paf], *excl.* bang! *ich bin ganz —*, I am astounded.
**paffen** ['pafən], *v.n.* puff; draw (at a pipe).
**Page** ['pa:ʒə], *m.* (—n, *pl.* —n) page-boy.
**Paket** [pa'ke:t], *n.* (—s, *pl.* —e) packet, package, parcel.
**paktieren** [pak'ti:rən], *v.n.* come to terms.
**Palast** [pa'last], *m.* (—es, *pl.* ⁝e) palace.
**Palästina** [palɛ'sti:na], *n.* Palestine.
**Paletot** ['paləto:], *m.* (—s, *pl.* —s) overcoat.
**Palisanderholz** [pali'zandərhɔlts], *n.* (—es, *no pl.*) rosewood.
**Palme** ['palmə], *f.* (—, *pl.* —n) (*Bot.*) palm-tree.
**Palmkätzchen** ['palmkɛtsçən], *n.* (—s, *pl.* —) (*Bot.*) catkin.
**Palmwoche** ['palmvɔxə], *f.* Holy Week.
**Pampelmuse** ['pampəlmu:zə], *f.* (—, *pl.* —n) (*Bot.*) grapefruit.
**Panama** ['pa:nama], *n.* Panama.
**Panier** [pa'ni:r], *n.* (—s, *pl.* —e) standard, banner.
**panieren** [pa'ni:rən], *v.a.* dress (*meat etc.*), roll in bread-crumbs.
**Panne** ['panə], *f.* (—, *pl.* —n) puncture; (*Motor.*) break-down; mishap.
**panschen** ['panʃən], *v.n.* splash about in water. — *v.a.* adulterate.
**Pantoffel** [pan'tɔfəl], *m.* (—s, *pl.* —n) slipper; *unter dem — stehen*, be henpecked.
**Pantoffelheld** [pan'tɔfəlhɛlt], *m.* (—en, *pl.* —en) henpecked husband.

**Panzer** ['pantsər], *m.* (—s, *pl.* —) armour, breast-plate, coat of mail; (*Mil.*) tank.
**Papagei** [papa'gaɪ], *m.* (—s, *pl.* —en) (*Orn.*) parrot.
**Papier** [pa'pi:r], *n.* (—s, *pl.* —e) paper; (*Comm.*) stocks; (*pl.*) papers, documents; *ein Bogen —*, a sheet of paper.
**Papierkrieg** [pa'pi:rkri:k], *m.* (—s, *no pl.*) (*coll.*) red tape.
**Papierwaren** [pa'pi:rva:rən], *f. pl.* stationery.
**Pappdeckel** ['papdɛkəl], *m.* (—s, *pl.* —) pasteboard.
**Pappe** ['papə], *f.* (—, *no pl.*) paste, cardboard, pasteboard.
**Pappel** ['papəl], *f.* (—, *pl.* —n) poplar.
**pappen** ['papən], *v.a.* stick; glue, paste.
**Pappenstiel** ['papənʃti:l], *m.* (—s, *pl.* —e) trifle.
**papperlapapp** ['papərlapap], *excl.* fiddlesticks! nonsense!
**Papst** [pa:pst], *m.* (—es, *pl.* ⁝e) Pope.
**päpstlich** ['pɛ:pstlɪç], *adj.* papal; *—er als der Papst*, fanatically loyal, outheroding Herod; over-zealous.
**Parabel** [pa'ra:bəl], *f.* (—, *pl.* —n) parable; (*Maths.*) parabola.
**paradieren** [para'di:rən], *v.n.* parade, make a show.
**Paradies** [para'di:s], *n.* (—es, *pl.* —e) paradise.
**paradox** [para'dɔks], *adj.* paradoxical.
**Paragraph** [para'gra:f], *m.* (—en, *pl.* —en) paragraph, article, clause, section.
**Paraguay** ['paragvaɪ, para'gua:ɪ], *n.* Paraguay.
**Paralyse** [para'ly:zə], *f.* (—, *pl.* —n) paralysis.
**parat** [pa'ra:t], *adj.* prepared, ready.
**Pardon** [par'dõ], *m.* (—s, *no pl.*) pardon, forgiveness.
**Parfüm** [par'fy:m], *n.* (—s, *pl.* —e) perfume, scent.
**pari** ['pa:ri:], *adv.* at par.
**parieren** [pa'ri:rən], *v.a.* parry, keep off. — *v.n.* obey; *aufs Wort —*, obey implicitly or to the letter.
**Parität** [pari'tɛ:t], *f.* (—, *no pl.*) parity; (religious) equality.
**Parkanlagen** [park'anla:gən], *f. pl.* parks; public gardens.
**parken** ['parkən], *v.a.* park.
**Parkett** [par'kɛt], *n.* (—s, *pl.* —e) parquet flooring; (*Theat.*) stalls.
**Parkuhr** [park'u:r], *f.* (—, *pl.* —en) parking-meter.
**Parlament** [parla'mɛnt], *n.* (—s, *pl.* —e) parliament.
**Parlamentär** [parlamen'tɛ:r], *m.* (—s, *pl.* —e) officer negotiating a truce.
**Parlamentarier** [parlamen'ta:rjər], *m.* (—s, *pl.* —) parliamentarian, member of a parliament.
**Parole** [pa'ro:lə], *f.* (—, *pl.* —n) watchword, cue, motto, slogan, password.

# Partei

**Partei** [par'taɪ], *f.* (—, *pl.* —en) party, faction; — *nehmen für,* side with.

**Parteigänger** [par'taɪɡɛŋər], *m.* (—s, *pl.* —) partisan.

**Parteigenosse** [par'taɪɡənɔsə], *m.* (—n, *pl.* —n) party member (especially National Socialist); comrade.

**parteiisch** [par'taɪɪʃ], *adj.* partial, biased, prejudiced.

**Parteinahme** [par'taɪnaːmə], *f.* (—, *no pl.*) partisanship.

**Parteitag** [par'taɪtaːk], *m.* (—s, *pl.* —e) party conference; congress.

**Parterre** [par'tɛrə], *n.* (—s, *pl.* —s) ground floor; (*Theat.*) pit; stalls.

**Partie** [par'tiː], *f.* (—, *pl.* —n) (*Comm.*) parcel; (*marriage*) match; (*chess etc.*) game; (*bridge*) rubber; outing, excursion, trip.

**Partitur** [parti'tuːr], *f.* (—, *pl.* —en) (*Mus.*) score.

**Partizip** [parti'tsiːp], *n.* (—s, *pl.* —e, —ien) (*Gram.*) participle.

**Parzelle** [par'tsɛlə], *f.* (—, *pl.* —n) allotment, lot, parcel.

**paschen** [ˈpaʃən], *v.a.* smuggle.

**Paß** [pas], *m.* (—sses, *pl.* ⸚sse) (*mountain*) pass; (*travelling*) passport; (*horse*) amble.

**Passagier** [pasaˈʒiːr], *m.* (—s, *pl.* —e) passenger; *blinder* —, stowaway.

**Passant** [paˈsant], *m.* (—en, *pl.* —en) passer-by.

**Passatwind** [paˈsaːtvɪnt], *m.* (—s, *pl.* —e) trade-wind.

**passen** [ˈpasən], *v.n.* fit, suit, be suitable, be convenient; (*Cards*) pass.

**passieren** [paˈsiːrən], *v.a.* sieve; (*road*) pass, cross, negotiate. — *v.n.* (*aux.* sein) pass; happen, take place, come about.

**Passif, Passivum** [paˈsiːf *or* ˈpasiːf, paˈsiːvum], *n.* (—s, *pl.* —e, —, *pl.* —va) (*Gram.*) passive voice; (*Comm.*) (*pl.*) debts, liabilities.

**Passus** [ˈpasus], *m.* (—, *pl.* —) passage (in book).

**Pasta, Paste** [ˈpasta, ˈpastə], *f.* (—, *pl.* —ten) paste.

**Pastell** [paˈstɛl], *m.* (—s, *pl.* —e) pastel, crayon; — *malen,* draw in pastel.

**Pastete** [paˈsteːtə], *f.* (—, *pl.* —n) pie, pastry.

**Pastille** [paˈstɪlə], *f.* (—, *pl.* —n) lozenge, pastille.

**Pastor** [ˈpastɔr], *m.* (—s, *pl.* —en) minister, pastor; parson; vicar, rector.

**Pate** [ˈpaːtə], *m.* (—n, *pl.* —n) godparent; — *stehen,* be godfather to.

**patent** [paˈtɛnt], *adj.* fine, grand, (*sl.*) smashing.

**Patent** [paˈtɛnt], *n.* (—(e)s, *pl.* —e) patent; charter, licence.

**patentieren** [patɛnˈtiːrən], *v.a.* patent, license.

**pathetisch** [paˈteːtɪʃ], *adj.* elevated, solemn, moving.

**Patin** [ˈpaːtɪn], *f.* (—, *pl.* —innen) godmother.

**patriotisch** [patriˈoːtɪʃ], *adj.* patriotic.

**Patrone** [paˈtroːnə], *f.* (—, *pl.* —n) cartridge; stencil, pattern.

**Patrouille** [paˈtruljə], *f.* (—, *pl.* —n) (*Mil.*) patrol.

**Patsche** [ˈpatʃə], *f.* (—, *pl.* —n) (*dial.*) hand; (*fig.*) mess, pickle; *in eine — geraten,* get into a jam.

**patschen** [ˈpatʃən], *v.n.* (*aux.* sein) splash.

**Patt** [pat], *n.* (—s, *pl.* —s) (*Chess*) stalemate.

**patzig** [ˈpatsɪç], *adj.* rude; cheeky, saucy.

**Pauke** [ˈpaukə], *f.* (—, *pl.* —n) kettledrum; *mit —n und Trompeten,* with drums beating and colours flying.

**pauken** [ˈpaukən], *v.n.* beat the kettledrum; (*coll.*) swot, plod, grind; fight a duel.

**pausbackig** [ˈpausbakɪç], *adj.* chubby-faced, bonny.

**Pauschale** [pauˈʃaːlə], *f.* (—, *pl.* —n) lump sum.

**Pause** [ˈpauzə], *f.* (—, *pl.* —n) pause, stop; (*Theat.*) interval; (*Sch.*) playtime, break; (*Tech.*) tracing.

**pausen** [ˈpauzən], *v.a.* trace.

**pausieren** [pauˈziːrən], *v.n.* pause.

**Pavian** [ˈpaːvjaːn], *m.* (—s, *pl.* —e) (*Zool.*) baboon.

**Pech** [pɛç], *n.* (—es, *no pl.*) pitch; (*shoemaker's*) wax; (*fig.*) bad luck, rotten luck.

**pechschwarz** [ˈpɛçʃvarts], *adj.* black as pitch.

**Pechvogel** [ˈpɛçfoːɡəl], *m.* (—s, *pl.* ⸚) unlucky fellow.

**Pedell** [peˈdɛl], *m.* (—s, *pl.* —e) beadle; porter, caretaker; (*Univ. sl.*) bulldog.

**Pegel** [ˈpeːɡəl], *m.* (—s, *pl.* —) water-gauge.

**peilen** [ˈpaɪlən], *v.a., v.n.* sound, measure, take bearings (of).

**Pein** [paɪn], *f.* (—, *no pl.*) pain, torment.

**peinigen** [ˈpaɪnɪɡən], *v.a.* torment; harass, distress.

**peinlich** [ˈpaɪnlɪç], *adj.* painful, disagreeable; embarrassing; delicate; strict, punctilious; (*Law*) capital, penal.

**Peitsche** [ˈpaɪtʃə], *f.* (—, *pl.* —n) whip.

**pekuniär** [pekunˈjɛːr], *adj.* financial.

**Pelerine** [peləˈriːnə], *f.* (—, *pl.* —n) cape.

**Pelle** [ˈpɛlə], *f.* (—, *pl.* —n) peel, husk.

**Pellkartoffeln** [ˈpɛlkartɔfəln], *f. pl.* potatoes in their jackets.

**Pelz** [pɛlts], *m.* (—es, *pl.* —e) pelt, fur; fur coat.

**pelzig** [ˈpɛltsɪç], *adj.* furry.

**Pendel** [ˈpɛndəl], *n.* (—s, *pl.* —) pendulum.

**pendeln** [ˈpɛndəln], *v.n.* swing, oscillate.

**pennen** [ˈpɛnən], *v.n.* (*sl.*) sleep.

**Pension** [på'sjo:n], *f.* (—, *pl.* —en) pension; boarding-house; board and lodging.
**Pensionat** [påsjo'na:t], *n.* (—s, *pl.* —e) boarding-school.
**pensionieren** [påsjo'ni:rən], *v.a.* pension off; *sich — lassen*, retire.
**Pensum** ['penzum], *n.* (—s, *pl.* —sen) task; curriculum, syllabus.
**per** [pɛr], *prep. — Adresse*, care of.
**Perfekt** [per'fɛkt], *n.* (—s, *pl.* —e) (*Gram.*) perfect (tense).
**perforieren** [perfo'ri:rən], *v.a.* perforate, punch.
**Pergament** [pɛrga'mɛnt], *n.* (—s, *pl.* —e) parchment, vellum.
**Perle** ['perlə], *f.* (—, *pl.* —n) pearl; (*glass*) bead; (*fig.*) gem, treasure.
**perlen** ['perlən], *v.n.* sparkle.
**Perlgraupe** ['perlgraupə], *f.* (—, no *pl.*) (*Bot.*) pearl-barley.
**Perlhuhn** ['perlhu:n], *n.* (—s, *pl.* ¨er) (*Zool.*) guinea-fowl.
**Perlmutter** ['perlmutər], *f.* (—, no *pl.*) mother-of-pearl.
**Perpendikel** [pɛrpən'dɪkəl], *m. & n.* (—s, *pl.* —) pendulum.
**Perser** ['perzər], *m.* (—s, *pl.* —) Persian; *echter —*, genuine Persian carpet.
**Persien** ['perzjən], *n.* Persia.
**Personal** [perzo'na:l], *n.* (—s, no *pl.*) personnel, staff.
**Personalien** [perzo'na:ljən], *n. pl.* particulars (of a person).
**Personenverkehr** [per'zo:nənfɛrke:r], *m.* (—s, no *pl.*) passenger-traffic.
**Personenzug** [per'zo:nəntsu:k], *m.* (—s, *pl.* ¨e) (slow) passenger train.
**personifizieren** [pɛrzonifi'tsi:rən], *v.a.* personify, embody, impersonate.
**Persönlichkeit** [per'zø:nlıçkaıt], *f.* (—, *pl.* —en) personality, person.
**perspektivisch** [pɛrspɛk'ti:vıʃ], *adj.* perspective.
**Peru** [pe'ru:], *n.* Peru.
**Perücke** [pɛ'rykə], *f.* (—, *pl.* —n) wig.
**Pest** [pɛst], *f.* (—, no *pl.*) plague, pestilence.
**pestartig** ['pɛsta:rtıç], *adj.* pestilential.
**Petersilie** [pe:tər'zi:ljə], *f.* (—, no *pl.*) (*Bot.*) parsley.
**petitionieren** [petitsjo'ni:rən], *v.a.* petition.
**Petschaft** ['petʃaft], *n.* (—s, *pl.* —e) seal, signet.
**Petz** [pets], *m.* (—es, *pl.* —e) *Meister —*, Bruin (the bear).
**petzen** ['petsən], *v.n.* tell tales (about), sneak.
**Pfad** [pfa:t], *m.* (—es, *pl.* —e) path.
**Pfadfinder** ['pfa:tfɪndər], *m.* (—s, *pl.* —) Boy Scout.
**Pfaffe** ['pfafə], *m.* (—n, *pl.* —n) (*pej.*) cleric, priest.
**Pfahl** [pfa:l], *m.* (—s, *pl.* ¨e) post, stake.
**Pfahlbauten** ['pfa:lbautən], *m. pl.* lake dwellings.

**pfählen** ['pfɛ:lən], *v.a.* fasten with stakes; impale.
**Pfand** [pfant], *n.* (—s, *pl.* ¨er) pawn, pledge; security; (*game*) forfeit; *ein — einlösen*, redeem a pledge.
**pfänden** ['pfɛndən], *v.a.* take in pledge; seize.
**Pfänderspiel** ['pfɛndərʃpi:l], *n.* (—s, *pl.* —e) game of forfeits.
**Pfandgeber** ['pfantge:bər], *m.* (—s, *pl.* —) pawner.
**Pfandleiher** ['pfantlaıər], *m.* (—s, *pl.* —) pawnbroker.
**Pfandrecht** ['pfantreçt], *n.* (—s, no *pl.*) lien.
**Pfändung** ['pfɛnduŋ], *f.* (—, *pl.* —en) seizure, attachment, distraint.
**Pfanne** ['pfanə], *f.* (—, *pl.* —n) pan, frying-pan.
**Pfannkuchen** ['pfanku:xən], *m.* (—s, *pl.* —) pancake; *Berliner —*, doughnut.
**Pfarre** ['pfarə], *f.* (—, *pl.* —n) living, parish; (*house*) vicarage, parsonage, manse.
**Pfarrer** ['pfarər], *m.* (—s, *pl.* —) parson; vicar, (parish) priest.
**Pfau** [pfau], *m.* (—en, *pl.* —en) (*Orn.*) peacock.
**Pfauenauge** ['pfauənaugə], *n.* (—s, *pl.* —n) (*Ent.*) peacock butterfly.
**Pfeffer** ['pfɛfər], *m.* (—s, no *pl.*) pepper; *spanischer —*, red pepper, cayenne.
**Pfefferkuchen** ['pfɛfərku:xən], *m.* (—s, *pl.* —) gingerbread, spiced cake.
**Pfefferminz** ['pfɛfərmɪnts], *n.* (—, no *pl.*) peppermint.
**Pfeife** ['pfaıfə], *f.* (—, *pl.* —n) whistle, fife; pipe.
**pfeifen** ['pfaıfən], *v.a., v.n. irr.* whistle, play the fife; (*Theat.*) boo, hiss; (*bullets*) whiz(z).
**Pfeifenrohr** ['pfaıfənro:r], *n.* (—s, *pl.* —e) pipe-stem.
**Pfeil** [pfaıl], *m.* (—es, *pl.* —e) arrow, dart, bolt.
**Pfeiler** ['pfaılər], *m.* (—s, *pl.* —) pillar.
**Pfeilwurz** ['pfaılvurts], *f.* (—, no *pl.*) (*Bot.*) arrow root.
**Pfennig** ['pfenıç], *m.* (—s, *pl.* —e) one hundredth of a mark; (*loosely*) penny.
**Pferch** [pfɛrç], *m.* (—es, *pl.* —e) fold, pen.
**Pferd** [pfe:rt], *n.* (—es, *pl.* —e) horse; *zu —*, on horseback; *vom — steigen*, dismount.
**Pferdeknecht** ['pfe:rdəknɛçt], *m.* (—es, *pl.* —e) groom.
**Pferdestärke** ['pfe:rdəʃtɛrkə], *f.* (—, no *pl.*) horse-power (*abbr.* PS).
**Pfiff** [pfɪf], *m.* (—es, *pl.* —e) whistle.
**Pfifferling** ['pfɪfərlıŋ], *m.* (—s, *pl.* —e) (*Bot.*) mushroom; chanterelle; *einen — wert*, worthless.
**pfiffig** ['pfɪfıç], *adj.* cunning, sly, crafty.
**Pfiffikus** ['pfɪfɪkus], *m.* (—, *pl.* —se) (*coll.*) sly dog.

167

**Pfingsten** ['pfɪŋkstən], *n.* Whitsun (-tide), Pentecost.
**Pfingstrose** ['pfɪŋkstro:zə], *f.* (—, *pl.* (*Bot.*) (*Bot.*)) peony.
**Pfirsich** ['pfɪrzɪç], *m.* (—s, *pl.* —e) (*Bot.*) peach.
**Pflanze** ['pflantsə], *f.* (—, *pl.* —n) plant.
**pflanzen** ['pflantsən], *v.a.* plant.
**Pflanzer** ['pflantsər], *m.* (—s, *pl.* —) planter.
**pflanzlich** ['pflantslɪç], *adj.* vegetable, botanical.
**Pflänzling** ['pflɛntslɪŋ], *m.* (—s, *pl.* —e) seedling, young plant.
**Pflanzung** ['pflantsuŋ], *f.* (—, *pl.* —en) plantation.
**Pflaster** ['pflastər], *n.* (—s, *pl.* —) (*Med.*) plaster; (*street*) pavement; *ein teures* —, an expensive place to live in.
**Pflaume** ['pflaumə], *f.* (—, *pl.* —n) plum; *getrocknete* —, prune.
**Pflege** ['pfle:gə], *f.* (—, *no pl.*) care, attention, nursing, fostering.
**Pflegeeltern** ['pfle:gəɛltərn], *pl.* foster-parents.
**pflegen** ['pfle:gən], *v.a.* nurse, look after, take care of; *Umgang* — *mit*, associate with. — *v.n.* be used to, be in the habit of.
**Pflegling** ['pfle:klɪŋ], *m.* (—s, *pl.* —e) foster-child, ward.
**Pflicht** [pflɪçt], *f.* (—, *pl.* —en) duty, obligation.
**Pflichtgefühl** ['pflɪçtgəfy:l], *n.* (—s, *no pl.*) sense of duty.
**pflichtgemäß** ['pflɪçtgəmɛ:s], *adj.* dutiful.
**pflichtschuldig** ['pflɪçtʃuldɪç], *adj.* in duty bound.
**Pflock** [pflɔk], *m.* (—s, *pl.* ⸚e) plug, peg.
**pflücken** ['pflykən], *v.a.* pluck, pick, gather.
**Pflug** [pflu:k], *m.* (—es, *pl.* ⸚e) plough.
**Pflugschar** ['pflu:kʃa:r], *f.* (—, *pl.* —en) ploughshare.
**Pforte** ['pfɔrtə], *f.* (—, *pl.* —n) gate, door, porch.
**Pförtner** ['pfœrtnər], *m.* (—s, *pl.* —) door-keeper, porter.
**Pfosten** ['pfɔstən], *m.* (—s, *pl.* —) post, stake; (*door*) jamb.
**Pfote** ['pfo:tə], *f.* (—, *pl.* —n) paw.
**Pfriem** [pfri:m], *m.* (—es, *pl.* —e) awl.
**Pfropf(en)** ['pfrɔpf(ən)], *m.* (—s, *pl.* —en) cork, stopper; (*gun*) wad.
**pfropfen** ['pfrɔpfən], *v.a.* graft; cork.
**Pfründe** ['pfryndə], *f.* (—, *pl.* —n) living, benefice.
**Pfuhl** [pfu:l], *m.* (—es, *pl.* —e) pool, puddle.
**Pfühl** [pfy:l], *m.* (—es, *pl.* —e) (*Poet.*) bolster, pillow, cushion.
**pfui!** [pfui], *excl.* shame! ugh! — *Teufel!* shame! a damned shame!
**Pfund** [pfunt], *n.* (—es, *pl.* —e) pound.
**pfuschen** ['pfuʃən], *v.n.* botch; *einem ins Handwerk* —, poach on s.o. else's preserve.

**Pfütze** ['pfytsə], *f.* (—, *pl.* —n) puddle.
**Phänomen** [fɛno'me:n], *n.* (—s, *pl.* —e) phenomenon.
**Phantasie** [fanta'zi:], *f.* (—, *pl.* —n) fancy, imagination; (*Mus.*) fantasia.
**phantasieren** [fanta'zi:rən], *v.n.* indulge in fancies; (*sick person*) rave, wander, be delirious; (*Mus.*) improvise.
**Phantast** [fan'tast], *m.* (—en, *pl.* —en) dreamer, visionary.
**Pharisäer** [fari'zɛ:ər], *m.* (—s, *pl.* —) Pharisee.
**Phase** ['fa:zə], *f.* (—, *pl.* —n) phase, stage (of process or development).
**Philippinen** [fili'pi:nən], *f. pl.* Philippines.
**Philister** [fi'lɪstər], *m.* (—s, *pl.* —) Philistine.
**philisterhaft** [fi'lɪstərhaft], *adj.* philistine, narrow-minded, conventional.
**Philologie** [filolo'gi:], *f.* (—, *no pl.*) philology; study of languages.
**Philosoph** [filo'zo:f], *m.* (—en, *pl.* —en) philosopher.
**Philosophie** [filozo'fi:], *f.* (—, *pl.* —n) philosophy.
**Phiole** [fi'o:lə], *f.* (—, *pl.* —n) phial, vial.
**Phlegma** ['flɛgma], *n.* (—s, *no pl.*) phlegm.
**Phonetik** [fo'ne:tɪk], *f.* (—, *no pl.*) phonetics.
**photogen** [foto'ge:n], *adj.* photogenic.
**Photograph** [foto'gra:f], *m.* (—en, *pl.* —en) photographer.
**Photographie** [fotogra'fi:], *f.* (—, *pl.* —n) photograph, photo; (*Art*) photography.
**photographieren** [fotogra'fi:rən], *v.a.* photograph.
**Physik** [fy'zi:k], *f.* (—, *no pl.*) physics.
**physikalisch** [fyzi'ka:lɪʃ], *adj.* physical (of physics).
**Physiker** ['fy:zɪkər], *m.* (—s, *pl.* —) physicist.
**Physiologe** [fyzjo'lo:gə], *m.* (—en, *pl.* —en) physiologist.
**physiologisch** [fyzjo'lo:gɪʃ], *adj.* physiological.
**physisch** ['fy:zɪʃ], *adj.* physical.
**Picke** ['pɪkə], *f.* (—, *pl.* —n) pickaxe, axe.
**Pickel** ['pɪkəl], *m.* (—s, *pl.* —) pimple.
**Piedestal** ['pje:dɛsta:l], *n.* (—s, *pl.* —e) pedestal.
**piepen** ['pi:pən], *v.n.* squeak, chirp.
**piepsen** ['pi:psən], *v.n.* squeak, chirp.
**Pietät** [pie'tɛ:t], *f.* (—, *no pl.*) piety, reverence.
**Pik** [pi:k], *n.* (—s, *pl.* —s) (*cards*) spades.
**pikant** [pi'kant], *adj.* piquant, spicy; (*fig.*) risqué.
**Pikee** [pi'ke:], *m.* (—s, *pl.* —s) piqué.
**pikiert** [pi'ki:rt], *adj.* irritated, annoyed, piqued.
**Pikkolo** ['pɪkolo], *m.* (—s, *pl.* —s) apprentice waiter, boy (waiter); (*Mus.*) piccolo, flute.

**Pilger** ['pɪlgər], *m.* (—s, *pl.* —) pilgrim.
**Pille** ['pɪlə], *f.* (—, *pl.* —n) pill.
**Pilz** [pɪlts], *m.* (—es, *pl.* —e) fungus, mushroom.
**Piment** [pi'mɛnt], *n.* (—s, *pl.* —e) pimento, Jamaican pepper, all-spice.
**pimplig** ['pɪmplɪç], *adj.* effeminate.
**Pinguin** [pɪŋgu'iːn], *m.* (—s, *pl.* —e) (*Orn.*) penguin.
**Pinie** ['piːnjə], *f.* (—, *pl.* —n) (*Bot.*) stone-pine.
**Pinne** ['pɪnə], *f.* (—, *pl.* —n) drawing-pin; peg.
**Pinscher** ['pɪnʃər], *m.* (—s, *pl.* —) terrier.
**Pinsel** ['pɪnzəl], *m.* (—s, *pl.* —) (*Painting*) brush, pencil; (*fig.*) simpleton.
**Pinzette** [pɪn'tsɛtə], *f.* (—, *pl.* —n) pincers, tweezers.
**Pirsch** [pɪrʃ], *f.* (—, *no pl.*) (deer-)stalking.
**Piste** ['pɪstə], *f.* (—, *pl.* —n) track; (*Aviat.*) runway.
**pittoresk** [pɪto'rɛsk], *adj.* picturesque.
**placken** ['plakən], *v.r. sich* —, toil, drudge.
**plädieren** [plɛ'diːrən], *v.n.* plead.
**Plädoyer** [plɛ:doa'je:], *n.* (—s, *pl.* —s) speech for the prosecution *or* the defence (in a court of law), plea, pleading.
**Plage** ['plaːgə], *f.* (—, *pl.* —n) torment, trouble; calamity; plague.
**plagen** ['plaːgən], *v.a.* plague, trouble, torment, vex. — *v.r. sich* —, toil.
**Plagiat** [plag'jaːt], *n.* (—es, *pl.* —e) plagiarism.
**Plaid** [ple:t], *n.* (—s, *pl.* —s) travelling-rug.
**Plakat** [pla'kaːt], *n.* (—(e)s, *pl.* —e) poster, placard, bill.
**Plan** [plaːn], *n.* (—es, *pl.* ːe) plan, scheme, plot; map, ground-plan.
**Plane** ['plaːnə], *f.* (—, *pl.* —n) awning, cover.
**planieren** [pla'niːrən], *v.a.* level, plane down; bulldoze, flatten.
**Planke** ['plaŋkə], *f.* (—, *pl.* —n) plank, board.
**Plänkelei** [plɛnkə'laɪ], *f.* (—, *pl.* —en) skirmish.
**planmäßig** ['plaːnmɛːsɪç], *adj.* according to plan.
**planschen** ['planʃən], *v.n.* splash; paddle.
**Plantage** [plan'taːʒə], *f.* (—, *pl.* —n) plantation.
**planvoll** ['plaːnfɔl], *adj.* systematic, well-planned.
**Planwagen** ['plaːnvaːgən], *m.* (—s, *pl.* —) tilt-cart.
**plappern** ['plapərn], *v.n.* prattle, chatter.
**plärren** |['plɛrən], *v.n.* blubber, bawl.
**Plastik** ['plastɪk], *f.* (—, *pl.* —en) plastic art; plastic (material).
**Platane** [pla'taːnə], *f.* (—, *pl.* —n) plane-tree.

**Platin** ['plaːtiːn], *n.* (—s, *no pl.*) platinum.
**platonisch** [pla'toːnɪʃ], *adj.* platonic.
**plätschern** ['plɛtʃərn], *v.n.* splash about.
**platt** [plat], *adj.* flat, level, even; insipid; downright; —*e Redensart*, commonplace, platitude; (*coll.*) *ich bin ganz* —, I am astonished *or* dumbfounded.
**Plättbrett** ['plɛtbrɛt], *n.* (—es, *pl.* —er) ironing board.
**plattdeutsch** ['platdɔytʃ], *adj.* Low German.
**Platte** ['platə], *f.* (—, *pl.* —n) plate; dish; board; slab; sheet; ledge; (*fig.*) bald head; (*Mus.*) (gramophone) record.
**plätten** ['plɛtən], *v.a.* iron (clothes).
**Plattfisch** ['platfɪʃ], *m.* (—es, *pl.* —e) (*Zool.*) plaice.
**Plattfuß** ['platfuːs], *n.* (—es, *pl.* ːe) flat foot.
**Plattheit** ['plathaɪt], *f.* (—, *pl.* —en) flatness; (*fig.*) platitude.
**Platz** [plats], *m.* (—es, *pl.* ːe) place, town, spot, site; space, room; (*town*) square; seat; — *nehmen*, take a seat, be seated.
**Platzanweiserin** ['platsanvaɪzərɪn], *f.* (—, *pl.* —nen) usherette.
**Plätzchen** ['plɛtsçən], *n.* (—s, *pl.* —) small place; drop; biscuit.
**platzen** ['platsən], *v.n.* (*aux.* sein) burst, explode.
**Platzregen** ['platsreːgən], *m.* (—s, *no pl.*) downpour, heavy shower.
**Plauderei** [plaudə'raɪ], *f.* (—, *pl.* —en) chat.
**Plaudertasche** ['plaudərtaʃə], *f.* (—, *pl.* —n) chatterbox.
**Pleite** ['plaɪtə], *f.* (—, *pl.* —n) (*coll.*) bankruptcy; — *machen*, go bankrupt.
**Plenum** ['pleːnum], *n.* (—s, *no pl.*) plenary session.
**Pleuelstange** ['plɔyəlʃtaŋə], *f.* (—, *pl.* —n) connecting-rod.
**Plinsen** ['plɪnzən], *f. pl.* (*Austr.*) fritters.
**Plissee** [plɪ'se:], *n.* (—s, *pl.* —s) pleating.
**Plombe** ['plɔmbə], *f.* (—, *pl.* —n) lead, seal; (*teeth*) filling.
**plombieren** [plɔm'biːrən], *v.a.* seal with lead; (*teeth*) fill.
**plötzlich** ['plœtslɪç], *adj.* sudden.
**plump** [plump], *adj.* clumsy, ungainly, awkward; crude, coarse.
**plumps** [plumps], *excl.* bump! oops!
**Plunder** ['plundər], *m.* (—s, *no pl.*) lumber, trash.
**plündern** ['plyndərn], *v.a.* plunder, pillage.
**Plüsch** [ply:ʃ], *m.* (—es, *no pl.*) plush.
**pneumatisch** [pnɔy'maːtɪʃ], *adj.* pneumatic.
**Pöbel** ['pø:bəl], *m.* (—s, *no pl.*) mob, rabble.
**pochen** ['pɔxən], *v.a., v.n.* knock, beat, throb.

# Pocke

**Pocke** ['pɔkə], *f.* (—, *pl.* —n) pock-mark; (*pl.*) smallpox.
**pockennarbig** ['pɔkənnarbɪç], *adj.* pockmarked.
**Podagra** ['po:dagra:], *n.* (—s, *no pl.*) (*Med.*) gout.
**Pointe** [po'ɛ̃tə], *f.* (—, *pl.* —n) (*of a story*) point.
**Pokal** [po'ka:l], *m.* (—s, *pl.* —e) goblet, cup; trophy.
**Pökelfleisch** ['pø:kəlflaɪʃ], *n.* (—es, *no pl.*) salted meat.
**Pol** [po:l], *m.* (—s, *pl.* —e) pole.
**polemisch** [po'le:mɪʃ], *adj.* polemic(al), controversial.
**Polen** ['po:lən], *n.* Poland.
**Police** [po'li:sə], *f.* (—, *pl.* —n) insurance policy.
**polieren** [po'li:rən], *v.a.* polish, furbish, burnish.
**Poliklinik** ['po:likli:nɪk], *f.* (—, *pl.* —en) (*Med.*) out-patients' department.
**Politik** [poli'ti:k], *f.* (—, *no pl.*) politics; policy.
**politisieren** [politi'zi:rən], *v.n.* talk politics.
**Politur** [poli'tu:r], *f.* (—, *no pl.*) polish, gloss.
**Polizei** [poli'tsaɪ], *f.* (—, *no pl.*) police.
**polizeilich** [poli'tsaɪlɪç], *adj.* of the police.
**Polizeistunde** [poli'tsaɪʃtundə], *f.* (—, *no pl.*) closing time.
**Polizeiwache** [poli'tsaɪvaxə], *f.* (—, *pl.* —n) police station.
**Polizist** [poli'tsɪst], *m.* (—en, *pl.* —en) policeman, constable.
**Polizze** [po'lɪtsə], *f.* (—, *pl.* —n) (*Austr. dial.*) insurance policy.
**polnisch** ['pɔlnɪʃ], *adj.* Polish.
**Polster** ['pɔlstər], *n.* (—s, *pl.* —) cushion, bolster.
**Polterabend** ['pɔltəra:bənt], *m.* (—s, *pl.* —e) wedding-eve party.
**Poltergeist** ['pɔltərgaɪst], *m.* (—es, *pl.* —er) poltergeist, hobgoblin.
**poltern** ['pɔltərn], *v.n.* rumble; make a noise; bluster.
**Polyp** [po'ly:p], *m.* (—en, *pl.* —en) (*Zool.*) polyp; (*Med.*) polypus.
**Pomeranze** [pomə'rantsə], *f.* (—, *pl.* —n) (*Bot.*) orange.
**Pommern** ['pɔmərn], *n.* Pomerania.
**Pope** ['po:pə], *m.* (—n, *pl.* —n) Greek Orthodox priest.
**Popo** [po'po:], *m.* (—s, *pl.* —s) (*coll.*) backside, bottom.
**populär** [popu'lɛ:r], *adj.* popular.
**porös** [po'rø:s], *adj.* porous.
**Porree** ['pɔre:], *m.* (—s, *no pl.*) leek.
**Portefeuille** [pɔr'tjœːj], *n.* (—s, *pl.* —s) portfolio.
**Portier** [pɔr'tje:], *m.* (—s, *pl.* —s) doorkeeper, caretaker; porter.
**Porto** ['pɔrto:], *n.* (—s, *pl.* **Porti**) postage.
**Porzellan** [pɔrtsɛ'la:n], *n.* (—s, *pl.* —e) china, porcelain; *Meißner* —, Dresden china.

**Posamenten** [poza'mɛntən], *n. pl.* trimmings.
**Posaune** [po'zaunə], *f.* (—, *pl.* —n) (*Mus.*) trombone.
**Positur** [pozi'tu:r], *f.* (—, *pl.* —en) posture; *sich in* — *setzen*, strike an attitude.
**Posse** ['pɔsə], *f.* (—, *pl.* —n) (*Theat.*) farce, skit.
**Possen** ['pɔsən], *m.* (—s, *pl.* —) trick; *einem einen* — *spielen*, play a trick on s.o.
**possierlich** [po'si:rlɪç], *adj.* droll, funny, comic(al).
**Post** [pɔst], *f.* (—, *pl.* —en) post, mail; (*building*) post-office.
**Postament** [pɔsta'mɛnt], *n.* (—s, *pl.* —e) plinth, pedestal.
**Postanweisung** ['pɔstanvaɪzuŋ], *f.* (—, *pl.* —en) postal order, money order.
**Posten** ['pɔstən], *m.* (—s, *pl.* —) post, station; place; (*goods*) parcel, lot, job lot; (*Comm.*) item; (*Mil.*) outpost; — *stehen*, stand sentry; *nicht auf dem* — *sein*, be unwell.
**Postfach** ['pɔstfax], *n.* (—es, *pl.* —er) post-office box.
**postieren** [pɔs'ti:rən], *v.a.* post, place, station.
**postlagernd** ['pɔstla:gərnt], *adj.* poste restante, to be called for.
**Postschalter** ['pɔstʃaltər], *m.* (—s, *pl.* —) post-office counter.
**postulieren** [pɔstu'li:rən], *v.a.* postulate.
**postwendend** ['pɔstvɛndənt], *adj.* by return of post.
**Postwertzeichen** ['pɔstvɛːrtsaɪçən], *n.* (—s, *pl.* —) stamp.
**Potenz** [po'tɛnts], *f.* (—, *pl.* —en) (*Maths.*) power; *zur dritten* —, cubed, to the power of three.
**potenzieren** [potɛn'tsi:rən], *v.a.* (*Math.*) raise; intensify.
**Pottasche** ['pɔtaʃə], *f.* (—, *no pl.*) potash.
**potzblitz** ['pɔtsblɪts], *excl.* good Heavens! good gracious!
**potztausend** ['pɔtstauzənt], *excl.* great Scott! good Heavens!
**Pracht** [praxt], *f.* (—, *no pl.*) splendour, magnificence; (*in compounds*) de luxe.
**prächtig** ['prɛ:çtɪç], *adj.* splendid, magnificent, sumptuous.
**prachtvoll** ['praxtfɔl], *adj.* gorgeous, magnificent.
**Prädikat** [prɛdi'ka:t], *n.* (—s, *pl.* —e) mark; (*Gram.*) predicate.
**Prag** [pra:k], *n.* Prague.
**prägen** ['prɛ:gən], *v.a.* coin, mint, stamp.
**prägnant** [prɛg'nant], *adj.* meaningful, precise.
**prahlen** ['pra:lən], *v.n.* boast, brag, talk big, show off.
**Praktikant** [prakti'kant], *m.* (—en, *pl.* —en) probationer; apprentice.
**Praktiken** ['praktɪkən], *f. pl.* machinations.

**praktisch** ['praktɪʃ], *adj.* practical;
—*er Arzt*, general practitioner.
**praktizieren** [prakti'tsi:rən], *v.a.* practise.
**Prall** [pral], *m.* (—es, *pl.* —e) impact.
**prall** [pral], *adj.* tense, tight; (*cheeks*) chubby.
**prallen** ['pralən], *v.n.* (*aux.* sein) *auf etwas* —, bounce against s.th.
**Prämie** ['prɛ:mjə], *f.* (—, *pl.* —n) prize; (*insurance*) premium; (*dividend*) bonus.
**prangen** ['praŋən], *v.n.* shine, glitter, make a show.
**Pranger** ['praŋər], *m.* (—s, *pl.* —) pillory; *etwas an den* — *stellen*, expose s.th., pillory.
**präparieren** [prɛpa'ri:rən], *v.a.*, *v.r.* prepare.
**Präsens** ['prɛ:zɛns], *n.* (—, *pl.* —ntia) (*Gram.*) present tense.
**präsentieren** [prɛzɛn'ti:rən], *v.a.* present; *präsentiert das Gewehr!* present arms!
**prasseln** ['prasəln], *v.n.* (*fire*) crackle; rattle.
**prassen** ['prasən], *v.n.* revel, gorge (o.s.), guzzle, feast.
**Prätendent** [prɛtɛn'dɛnt], *m.* (—en, *pl.* —en) pretender, claimant.
**Präteritum** [prɛ'tɛ:ritum], *n.* (—s, *pl.* —ta) (*Gram.*) preterite, past tense.
**Praxis** ['praksɪs], *f.* (—, *no pl.*) practice.
**präzis** [prɛ'tsi:s], *adj.* precise, exact.
**präzisieren** [prɛtsi'zi:rən], *v.a.* define exactly.
**predigen** ['prɛ:dɪgən], *v.a.*, *v.n.* preach.
**Predigt** ['prɛ:dɪçt], *f.* (—, *pl.* —en) sermon; (*fig.*) homily, lecture.
**Preis** [praɪs], *m.* (—es, *pl.* —e) price, rate, value; (*reward*) prize; praise; *um jeden* —, at any price, at all costs; *um keinen* —, not for all the world; *feste* —*e*, fixed prices; no rebate, no discount.
**Preisausschreiben** ['praɪsausʃraɪbən], *n.* (—s, *pl.* —) prize competition.
**Preiselbeere** ['praɪzəlbe:rə], *f.* (—, *pl.* —n) (*Bot.*) bilberry, cranberry.
**preisen** ['praɪzən], *v.a.* irr. praise, laud; glorify.
**preisgeben** ['praɪsge:bən], *v.a.* irr. give up, abandon, part with; *dem Spott preisgegeben sein*, become a laughing-stock.
**Preisunterbietung** ['praɪsuntərbi:tuŋ], *f.* (—, *pl.* —en) under-cutting.
**Prellbock** ['prɛlbɔk], *m.* (—s, *pl.* ⁻e) buffer (-block).
**prellen** ['prɛlən], *v.a.* cheat, defraud.
**Prellstein** ['prɛlʃtaɪn], *m.* (—s, *pl.* —e) kerbstone.
**pressant** [prɛ'sant], *adj.* (*Austr.*) urgent.
**Presse** ['prɛsə], *f.* (—, *pl.* —n) press; newspapers; (*coll.*) coaching establishment, crammer.
**pressieren** [prɛ'si:rən], *v.n.* be urgent.
**Preßkohle** ['prɛsko:lə], *f.* (—, *no pl.*) briquette(s).

**Preßkolben** ['prɛskɔlbən], *m.* (—s, *pl.* —) piston.
**Preßluft** ['prɛsluft], *f.* (—, *no pl.*) compressed air.
**Preußen** ['prɔysən], *n.* Prussia.
**prickeln** ['prɪkəln], *v.n.* prick, prickle, sting, tickle.
**Prieme** ['pri:mə], *f.* (—, *pl.* —n) chew, quid.
**Priester** ['pri:stər], *m.* (—s, *pl.* —) priest; *zum* — *weihen*, ordain to the priesthood.
**Prima** ['pri:ma:], *f.* (—, *pl.* **Primen**) highest form at a grammar school (sixth form).
**prima** ['pri:ma:], *adj.* excellent, splendid, first-rate.
**Primaner** [pri'ma:nər], *m.* (—s, *pl.* —) pupil in the highest form at a grammar school, sixth form boy.
**Primel** ['pri:məl], *f.* (—, *pl.* —n) (*Bot.*) primrose, primula.
**Primus** ['pri:mus], *m.* (—, *no pl.*) (*School*) head boy, captain of the school.
**Prinzip** [prɪn'tsi:p], *n.* (—s, *pl.* —ien) principle.
**Priorität** [priori'tɛ:t], *f.* (—, *no pl.*) priority, precedence.
**Prise** ['pri:zə], *f.* (—, *pl.* —n) pinch of snuff.
**Prisma** ['prɪsma:], *n.* (—s, *pl.* —men) prism.
**Pritsche** ['prɪtʃə], *f.* (—, *pl.* —n) plank-bed.
**Privatdozent** [pri'va:tdotsɛnt], *m.* (—en, *pl.* —en) (*Univ.*) (unsalaried) lecturer.
**privatisieren** [privati'zi:rən], *v.n.* have private means.
**Probe** ['pro:bə], *f.* (—, *pl.* —n) experiment, trial, probation, test; (*Theat.*, *Mus.*) rehearsal; sample, pattern; *auf* —, on trial; *auf die* — *stellen*, put to the test *or* on probation.
**Probeabzug** ['pro:bəaptsu:k], *m.* (—s, *pl.* ⁻e) (*Printing*) proof.
**proben** ['pro:bən], *v.a.* rehearse.
**probieren** [pro'bi:rən], *v.a.* try, attempt; taste.
**Probst** [pro:pst], *m.* (—es, *pl.* ⁻e) provost.
**Produzent** [produ'tsɛnt], *m.* (—en, *pl.* —en) producer (of goods), manufacturer.
**produzieren** [produ'tsi:rən], *v.a.* produce (goods). — *v.r. sich* —, perform, show off.
**profanieren** [profa'ni:rən], *v.a.* desecrate, profane.
**Professur** [profɛ'su:r], *f.* (—, *pl.* —en) (*Univ.*) professorship, Chair.
**profitieren** [profi'ti:rən], *v.a.*, *v.n.* profit (by), take advantage (of).
**projizieren** [proji'tsi:rən], *v.a.* project.
**Prokura** [pro'ku:ra:], *f.* (—, *no pl.*) (*Law*) power of attorney.
**Prokurist** [proku'rɪst], *m.* (—en, *pl.* —en) confidential clerk; company secretary.

171

# prolongieren

**prolongieren** [prolɔŋˈgiːrən], v.a. prolong, extend.
**promenieren** [proməˈniːrən], v.n. take a stroll.
**Promotion** [promoˈtsjoːn], f. (—, pl. —en) graduation, degree ceremony.
**promovieren** [promoˈviːrən], v.n. graduate, take a degree.
**promulgieren** [promulˈgiːrən], v.a. promulgate.
**Pronomen** [proˈnoːmən], n. (—s, pl. —mina) (Gram.) pronoun.
**prophezeien** [profeˈtsaɪən], v.a. prophesy, predict, forecast.
**prophylaktisch** [profyˈlaktɪʃ], adj. preventive, prophylactic.
**Propst** [proːpst], m. (—es, pl. ⸚e) provost.
**Prosa** [ˈproːzaː], f. (—, no pl.) prose.
**prosit** [ˈproːzɪt], excl. cheers! here's to you! your health!
**Prospekt** [proˈspɛkt], m. (—es, pl. —e) prospect; (booklet) prospectus.
**Prostituierte** [prostituˈiːrtə], f. (—n, pl. —n) prostitute; (coll.) tart.
**protegieren** [proteˈʒiːrən], v.a. favour, patronize.
**Protektion** [protɛkˈtsjoːn], f. (—, no pl.) patronage, favouritism.
**protestieren** [protɛsˈtiːrən], v.n. make a protest, protest (against s.th.).
**Protokoll** [protoˈkɔl], n. (—s, pl. —e) minutes, record; protocol; regulations.
**Protokollführer** [protoˈkɔlfyːrər], m. (—s, pl. —) recorder, clerk of the minutes.
**Protz** [prɔts], m. (—en, pl. —en) snob, upstart; show-off.
**Proviant** [proˈvjant], m. (—s, no pl.) provisions, stores.
**provinziell** [provɪnˈtsjɛl], adj. provincial.
**Provinzler** [proˈvɪntslər], m. (—s, pl. —) provincial.
**Provision** [proviˈzjoːn], f. (—, pl. —en) (Comm.) commission, brokerage.
**Provisor** [proˈviːzɔr], m. (—s, pl. —en) dispenser.
**provisorisch** [proviˈzoːrɪʃ], adj. provisional, temporary.
**provozieren** [provoˈtsiːrən], v.a. provoke.
**Prozedur** [protseˈduːr], f. (—, pl. —en) proceedings, procedure.
**Prozent** [proˈtsɛnt], m. & n. (—s, pl. —e) per cent.
**Prozentsatz** [proˈtsɛntzats], m. (—es, pl. ⸚e) percentage, rate of interest.
**Prozeß** [proˈtsɛs], m. (—es, pl. —e) process; lawsuit, litigation; trial; mit etwas kurzem — machen, deal summarily with.
**Prozeßwesen** [proˈtsɛsveːzən], n. (—s, no pl.) legal procedure.
**prüde** [ˈpryːdə], adj. prudish, prim.
**prüfen** [ˈpryːfən], v.a. test, examine.
**Prüfung** [ˈpryːfuŋ], f. (—, pl. —en) trial, test; examination; (fig.) temptation, affliction.

**Prügel** [ˈpryːgəl], m. (—s, pl.—) cudgel; (pl.) thrashing; eine Tracht —, a good hiding.
**prügeln** [ˈpryːgəln], v.a. beat, give a hiding to.
**Prunk** [pruŋk], m. (—(e)s, no pl.) splendour, ostentation, pomp.
**prusten** [ˈpruːstən], v.n. snort.
**Psalm** [psalm], m. (—es, pl. —e) psalm.
**Psalter** [ˈpsaltər], m. (—s, pl. —) (book) psalter; (instrument) psaltery.
**Psychiater** [psyçiˈaːtər], m. (—s, pl.—) psychiatrist.
**Psychologe** [psyçoˈloːgə], m. (—n, pl. —n) psychologist.
**Pubertät** [pubɛrˈtɛːt], f. (—, no pl.) puberty.
**Publikum** [ˈpuːblɪkum], n. (—s, no pl.) public; (Theat.) audience.
**publizieren** [publiˈtsiːrən], v.a. publish; promulgate.
**Pudel** [ˈpuːdəl], m. (—s, pl. —) poodle; des —s Kern, the gist of the matter.
**Puder** [ˈpuːdər], m. (—s, no pl.) powder, face-powder.
**pudern** [ˈpuːdərn], v.a. powder.
**Puff** [puf], m. (—s, pl. ⸚e) cuff, thump.
**puffen** [ˈpufən], v.a. cuff, thump.
**Puffer** [ˈpufər], m. (—s, pl. —) buffer.
**Puffspiel** [ˈpufʃpiːl], n. (—s, pl. —e) backgammon.
**pullen** [ˈpulən], v.n. rein in (a horse); (coll.) piddle.
**Pulsader** [ˈpulsaːdər], f. (—, pl. —n) artery; aorta.
**pulsieren** [pulˈziːrən], v.n. pulsate; pulse, throb.
**Pulsschlag** [ˈpulsʃlaːk], m. (—s, pl. ⸚e) pulse-beat; pulsation.
**Pult** [pult], n. (—es, pl. —e) desk, writing-table; lectern.
**Pulver** [ˈpulvər], n. (—s, pl. —) powder.
**Pump** [pump], m. (—s, no pl.) (sl.) credit; auf —, on tick.
**pumpen** [ˈpumpən], v.a., v.n. pump; (fig.) (sl.) sich etwas —, borrow s.th., touch s.o. for s.th.; lend.
**Pumpenschwengel** [ˈpumpənʃvɛŋəl], m. (—s, pl. —) pump-handle.
**Pumpernickel** [ˈpumpərnɪkəl], m. (—s, pl. —) black bread, Westphalian rye-bread.
**Pumphosen** [ˈpumphoːzən], f. pl. plus-fours.
**Punkt** [puŋkt], m. (—es, pl. —e) point, dot, spot; (Gram.) full stop.
**punktieren** [puŋkˈtiːrən], v.a. dot; punctuate.
**pünktlich** [ˈpyŋktlɪç], adj. punctual.
**punktum** [ˈpuŋktum], excl. und damit —, that's the end of it; that's it.
**Puppe** [ˈpupə], f. (—, pl. —n) doll; (Ent.) pupa, chrysalis.
**pur** [puːr], adj. pure, sheer; (drink) neat.

**Puritaner** [puri'taːnər], *m.* (—s, *pl.* —) puritan.

**Purpur** ['purpur], *m.* (—s, *no pl.*) purple.

**Purzelbaum** ['purtsəlbaum], *m.* (—s, *pl.* ⸚e) somersault.

**purzeln** ['purtsəln], *v.n.* tumble.

**Pustel** ['pustəl], *f.* (—, *pl.* —n) pustule.

**pusten** ['puːstən], *v.n.* puff, blow.

**Pute** ['puːtə], *f.* (—, *pl.* —n) (*Orn.*) turkey-hen; *dumme* —, silly goose.

**Puter** ['puːtər], *m.* (—s, *pl.* —) turkey-cock.

**puterrot** ['puːtərroːt], *adj.* as red as a turkey-cock.

**Putsch** [putʃ], *m.* (—es, *pl.* —e) coup de main, insurrection, riot.

**Putz** [puts], *m.* (—es, *no pl.*) finery; cleaning; rough-cast.

**putzen** ['putsən], *v.a.* polish, shine; clean. — *v.r. sich* —, dress up.

**Putzfrau** ['putsfrau], *f.* (—, *pl.* —en) charwoman.

**Putzmacherin** ['putsmaxərɪn], *f.* (—, *pl.* —nen) milliner.

**Pyramide** [pyra'miːdə], *f.* (—, *pl.* —n) pyramid.

**Pyrenäen** [pyrə'nɛːən], *pl.* Pyrenees; —*halbinsel*, Iberian Peninsula.


# Q

**Q** [kuː], *n.* (—s, *pl.* —s) the letter Q.

**quabbeln** ['kvabəln], *v.n.* shake, wobble.

**Quacksalber** ['kvakzalbər], *m.* (—s, *pl.* —) quack, mountebank.

**Quacksalberei** [kvakzalbə'rai], *f.* (—, *pl.* —en) quackery.

**Quaderstein** ['kvaːdərʃtain], *m.* (—s, *pl.* —e) ashlar, hewn stone.

**Quadrat** [kva'draːt], *n.* (—es, *pl.* —e) square; *zum* (or *ins*) — *erheben*, square (a number).

**Quadratur** [kvadra'tuːr], *f.* (—, *pl.* —en) quadrature; *die* — *des Kreises finden*, square the circle.

**quadrieren** [kva'driːrən], *v.a.* square.

**quaken** ['kvaːkən], *v.n.* (*frog*) croak; (*duck*) quack.

**quäken** ['kvɛːkən], *v.n.* squeak.

**Quäker** ['kvɛːkər], *m.* (—s, *pl.* —) Quaker.

**Qual** [kvaːl], *f.* (—, *pl.* —en) anguish, agony, torment.

**quälen** ['kvɛːlən], *v.a.* torment, torture, vex. — *v.r. sich* —, toil.

**qualifizieren** [kvalifi'tsiːrən], *v.a.* qualify.

**Qualität** [kvali'tɛːt], *f.* (—, *pl.* —en) quality.

**Qualle** ['kvalə], *f.* (—, *pl.* —n) (*Zool.*) jelly-fish.

**Qualm** [kvalm], *m.* (—es, *no pl.*) dense smoke.

**Quantität** [kvanti'tɛːt], *f.* (—, *pl.* —en) quantity.

**Quantum** ['kvantum], *n.* (—s, *pl.* —ten) portion, quantity.

**Quappe** ['kvapə], *f.* (—, *pl.* —n) (*Zool.*) tadpole.

**Quarantäne** [kvaran'tɛːnə], *f.* (—, *no pl.*) quarantine.

**Quark** [kvark], *m.* (—s, *no pl.*) curds; cream-cheese; (*fig.*) trash, rubbish, nonsense, bilge.

**Quarta** ['kvarta:], *f.* (—, *no pl.*) fourth form.

**Quartal** [kvar'taːl], *n.* (—s, *pl.* —e) quarter of a year; term.

**Quartier** [kvar'tiːr], *n.* (—s, *pl.* —e) quarters, lodging; (*Mil.*) billet.

**Quarz** [kvarts], *m.* (—es, *no pl.*) quartz.

**Quaste** ['kvastə], *f.* (—, *pl.* —n) tassel.

**Quatember** [kva'tɛmbər], *m.* (—s, *pl.* —) quarter day; (*Eccl.*) Ember Day.

**Quatsch** [kvatʃ], *m.* (—es, *no pl.*) nonsense, drivel.

**Quecke** ['kvɛkə], *f.* (—, *pl.* —n) couch-grass, quick-grass.

**Quecksilber** ['kvɛkzɪlbər], *n.* (—s, *no pl.*) quicksilver, mercury.

**Quelle** ['kvɛlə], *f.* (—, *pl.* —n) well, spring, fountain; (*fig.*) source; *aus sicherer* —, on good authority.

**Quentchen** ['kvɛntçən], *n.* (—s, *pl.* —) small amount, dram.

**quer** [kveːr], *adj.* cross, transverse, oblique, diagonal. — *adv.* across; *kreuz und* —, in all directions.

**Querbalken** ['kveːrbalkən], *m.* (—s, *pl.* —) cross-beam.

**querdurch** ['kveːrdurç], *adv.* across.

**querfeldein** ['kveːrfɛltain], *adv.* cross-country.

**Querkopf** ['kveːrkopf], *m.* (—es, *pl.* ⸚e) crank.

**Quersattel** ['kveːrzatəl], *m.* (—s, *pl.* ⸚) side-saddle.

**Querschiff** ['kveːrʃif], *n.* (—es, *pl.* —e) (*church*) transept.

**Querschnitt** ['kveːrʃnɪt], *m.* (—s, *pl.* —e) cross-section; (*fig.*) average.

**Querulant** [kveru'lant], *m.* (—en, *pl.* —en) grumbler.

**quetschen** ['kvɛtʃən], *v.a.* squeeze, crush, mash; bruise.

**Queue** [køː], *n.* (—s, *pl.* —s) (*Billiards*) cue.

**quieken** ['kviːkən], *v.n.* squeak.

**Quinta** ['kvɪnta:], *f.* (—, *no pl.*) fifth form.

**Quinte** ['kvɪntə], *f.* (—, *pl.* —n) (*Mus.*) fifth.

**Quirl** [kvɪrl], *m.* (—s, *pl.* —e) whisk; (*Bot.*) whorl.

**quitt** [kvɪt], *adj.* — *sein*, be quits.

**Quitte** ['kvɪtə], *f.* (—, *pl.* —n) (*Bot.*) quince.

**quittegelb** [ˈkvɪtəɡɛlp], *adj.* bright yellow.
**quittieren** [kvɪˈtiːrən], *v.a.* receipt; give a receipt; *den Dienst* —, leave the service.
**Quittung** [ˈkvɪtuŋ], *f.* (—, *pl.* —en) receipt.
**Quodlibet** [ˈkvɔdliːbɛt], *n.* (—s, *pl.* —s) medley.
**Quote** [ˈkvoːtə], *f.* (—, *pl.* —n) quota, share.
**quotieren** [kvoˈtiːrən], *v.a.* (*stock exchange*) quote (prices).

# R

**R** [ɛr], *n.* (—s, *pl.* —s) the letter R.
**Rabatt** [raˈbat], *m.* (—s, *pl.* —e) rebate, discount.
**Rabatte** [raˈbatə], *f.* (—, *pl.* —n) flower-border.
**Rabbiner** [raˈbiːnər], *m.* (—s, *pl.* —) rabbi.
**Rabe** [ˈraːbə], *m.* (—n, *pl.* —n) (*Orn.*) raven; *ein weißer* —, a rare bird.
**Rabenaas** [ˈraːbənaːs], *n.* (—es, *pl.* —e) carrion.
**rabiat** [raˈbjaːt], *adj.* furious, rabid.
**Rache** [ˈraxə], *f.* (—, *no pl.*) revenge, vengeance.
**Rachen** [ˈraxən], *m.* (—s, *pl.* —) jaws, throat.
**rächen** [ˈrɛːçən], *v.a.* avenge. — *v.r.* *sich* —, avenge o.s., take vengeance.
**Rachenbräune** [ˈraxənbrɔynə], *f.* (—, *no pl.*) croup, quinsy.
**Rachitis** [raˈxiːtɪs], *f.* (—, *no pl.*) (*Med.*) rickets.
**rachsüchtig** [ˈraxzyçtɪç], *adj.* vindictive, vengeful.
**rackern** [ˈrakərn], *v.r. sich* —, (*coll.*) toil, work hard.
**Rad** [raːt], *n.* (—es, *pl.* —er) wheel; bicycle; *ein* — *schlagen*, turn a cart-wheel; (*peacock*) spread the tail.
**Radau** [raˈdau], *m.* (—s, *no pl.*) noise, din, shindy.
**Rade** [ˈraːdə], *f.* (—, *pl.* —n) corn-cockle.
**radebrechen** [ˈraːdəbrɛçən], *v.a. insep.* murder a language.
**radeln** [ˈraːdəln], *v.n.* (*aux.* sein) (*coll.*) cycle.
**Rädelsführer** [ˈrɛːdəlsfyːrər], *m.* (—s, *pl.* —) ringleader.
**rädern** [ˈrɛːdərn], *v.a.* break on the wheel; *gerädert sein*, (*fig.*) ache in all o.'s bones, be exhausted.
**Radfahrer** [ˈraːtfaːrər], *m.* (—s, *pl.* —) cyclist.
**radieren** [raˈdiːrən], *v.n.* erase; etch.
**Radierung** [raˈdiːruŋ], *f.* (—, *pl.* —en) etching.

**Radieschen** [raˈdiːsçən], *n.* (—s, *pl.* —) (*Bot.*) radish.
**Radio** [ˈraːdjo], *n.* (—s, *pl.* —s) wireless, radio.
**raffen** [ˈrafən], *v.a.* snatch up, gather up.
**Raffinade** [rafiˈnaːdə], *f.* (—, *no pl.*) refined sugar.
**Raffinement** [rafinəˈmãː], *n.* (—s, *no pl.*) elaborateness.
**raffinieren** [rafiˈniːrən], *v.a.* refine.
**raffiniert** [rafiˈniːrt], *adj.* refined; elaborate, crafty, wily, cunning.
**ragen** [ˈraːɡən], *v.n.* tower, soar.
**Rahm** [raːm], *m.* (—es, *no pl.*) cream; *den* — *abschöpfen*, skim; (*fig.*) skim the cream off.
**Rahmen** [ˈraːmən], *m.* (—s, *pl.* —) frame; milieu, limit, scope, compass; *im* — *von*, within the framework of.
**rahmig** [ˈraːmɪç], *adj.* creamy.
**raisonnieren** [rɛzɔˈniːrən], *v.n.* reason, argue; (*fig.*) grumble, answer back.
**Rakete** [raˈkeːtə], *f.* (—, *pl.* —n) rocket, sky-rocket.
**Rakett** [raˈkɛt], *n.* (—s, *pl.* —s) (*tennis*) racket.
**rammen** [ˈramən], *v.a.* ram.
**Rampe** [ˈrampə], *f.* (—, *pl.* —n) ramp, slope; platform; (*Theat.*) apron.
**ramponiert** [rampoˈniːrt], *adj.* battered, damaged.
**Ramsch** [ramʃ], *m.* (—es, *pl.* —e) odds and ends; (*Comm.*) job lot.
**Rand** [rant], *m.* (—es, *pl.* —er) edge, border, verge, rim; (*book*) margin; (*hat*) brim; *am* — *des Grabes*, with one foot in the grave; *außer* — *und Band geraten*, get completely out of hand.
**randalieren** [randaˈliːrən], *v.n.* kick up a row.
**Randbemerkung** [ˈrantbəmɛrkuŋ], *f.* (—, *pl.* —en) marginal note, gloss.
**rändern** [ˈrɛndərn], *v.a.* border, edge, mill.
**Ränftchen** [ˈrɛnftçən], *n.* (—s, *pl.* —) crust (of bread).
**Rang** [raŋ], *m.* (—es, *pl.* —e) rank, grade, rate; order, class; standing (in society); (*Theat.*) circle, tier, gallery.
**Range** [ˈraŋə], *m.* (—n, *pl.* —n) scamp, rascal. — *f.* (—, *pl.* —n) tomboy, hoyden.
**rangieren** [rãˈʒiːrən], *v.a.* (*Railw.*) shunt. — *v.n.* rank.
**Ranke** [ˈraŋkə], *f.* (—, *pl.* —n) tendril, shoot.
**Ränke** [ˈrɛŋkə], *m. pl.* intrigues, tricks.
**ranken** [ˈraŋkən], *v.r.* (*aux.* haben) *sich* —, (*plant*) climb (with tendrils).
**Ränkeschmied** [ˈrɛŋkəʃmiːt], *m.* (—es, *pl.* —e) plotter, intriguer.
**Ranzen** [ˈrantsən], *m.* (—s, *pl.* —) satchel, knapsack, rucksack.
**ranzig** [ˈrantsɪç], *adj.* rancid, rank.
**Rappe** [ˈrapə], *m.* (—n, *pl.* —n) black horse.

**Rappel** ['rapəl], m. (—s, no pl.) (coll.) slight madness; rage, fit.

**Rappen** ['rapən], m. (—s, pl. —) small Swiss coin; centime.

**rapportieren** [rapor'ti:rən], v.a. report.

**Raps** [raps], m. (—es, no pl.) rapeseed.

**rar** [ra:r], adj. rare, scarce; exquisite.

**rasch** [raʃ], adj. quick, swift.

**rascheln** ['raʃəln], v.n. rustle.

**Rasen** ['ra:zən], m. (—s, pl. —) lawn, turf, sod.

**rasen** ['ra:zən], v.n. rave, rage, be delirious; rush, speed; in —der Eile, in a tearing hurry.

**Raserei** [ra:zə'rai], f. (—, pl. —en) madness; (fig.) fury.

**Rasierapparat** [ra'zi:rapara:t], m. (—s, pl. —e) (safety-)razor; shaver.

**rasieren** [ra'zi:rən], v.a. shave; sich — lassen, be shaved, get a shave.

**Rasierzeug** [ra'zi:rtsɔyk], n. (—s, no pl.) shaving-tackle.

**Raspel** ['raspəl], f. (—, pl. —n) rasp.

**Rasse** ['rasə], f. (—, pl. —n) race; breed; reine —, thoroughbred; gekreuzte —, cross-breed.

**Rassel** ['rasəl], f. (—, pl. —n) rattle.

**rasseln** ['rasəln], v.n. rattle, clank.

**Rassendiskriminierung** ['rasəndiskrimini:ruŋ], f. (—, no pl.) racial discrimination.

**Rast** [rast], f. (—, no pl.) rest, repose.

**rasten** ['rastən], v.n. rest, take a rest; halt.

**Raster** ['rastər], m. (—s, pl. —) (Phot.) screen.

**rastlos** ['rastlo:s], adj. restless.

**Rat** (1) [ra:t], m. (—es, pl. —schläge) advice, counsel; deliberation; mit — und Tat, with advice and assistance; einem einen — geben, give s.o. advice, counsel s.o.; einen um — fragen, consult s.o.; — schaffen, find ways and means.

**Rat** (2) [ra:t], m. (—es, pl. —e) council, councillor.

**Rate** ['ra:tə], f. (—, pl. —n) instalment, rate.

**raten** ['ra:tən], v.a., v.n., irr. advise; guess, conjecture.

**Ratgeber** ['ra:tge:bər], m. (—s, pl. —) adviser, counsellor.

**Rathaus** ['ra:thaus], n. (—es, pl. —er) town-hall.

**Ratifizierung** [ratifi'tsi:ruŋ], f. (—, pl. —en) ratification.

**Ration** [ra'tsjo:n], f. (—, pl. —en) ration, share, portion.

**rationell** [ratsjo'nel], adj. rational.

**ratlos** ['ra:tlo:s], adj. helpless, perplexed.

**ratsam** ['ra:tza:m], adj. advisable.

**Ratschlag** ['ra:tʃla:k], m. (—s, pl. —e) advice, counsel.

**Ratschluß** ['ra:tʃlus], m. (—sses, pl. —sse) decision, decree.

**Ratsdiener** ['ra:tsdi:nər], m. (—s, pl. —) beadle, tipstaff, summoner.

**Rätsel** ['rɛ:tsəl], n. (—s, pl. —) riddle, puzzle, mystery, enigma, conundrum.

**Ratsherr** ['ra:tsher], m. (—n, pl. —en) alderman, (town-)councillor, senator.

**Ratte** ['ratə], f. (—, pl. —n) (Zool.) rat.

**Raub** [raup], m. (—es, no pl.) robbery; booty, prey.

**rauben** ['raubən], v.a. rob, plunder; es raubt mir den Atem, it takes my breath away.

**Räuber** ['rɔybər], m. (—s, pl. —) robber, thief; highwayman; — und Gendarm, cops and robbers.

**Raubgier** ['raupgi:r], f. (—, no pl.) rapacity.

**Rauch** [raux], m. (—s, no pl.) smoke, vapour.

**Rauchen** ['rauxən], n. (—s, no pl.) smoking; — verboten, no smoking.

**rauchen** ['rauxən], v.a., v.n. smoke.

**räuchern** ['rɔyçərn], v.a. (meat, fish) smoke-dry, cure; (disinfect) fumigate. — v.n. (Eccl.) burn incense.

**Rauchfang** ['rauxfaŋ], m. (—s, pl. —e) chimney-flue.

**Räude** ['rɔydə], f. (—, no pl.) mange.

**Raufbold** ['raufbolt], m. (—s, pl. —e) brawler, bully.

**raufen** ['raufən], v.a. (hair) tear out, pluck. — v.n. fight, brawl. — v.r. sich — mit, scuffle with, fight, have a scrap with.

**rauh** [rau], adj. rough; (fig.) harsh, rude; hoarse; (weather) raw, inclement.

**Rauheit** ['rauhait], f. (—, no pl.) roughness; hoarseness; (fig.) harshness, rudeness; (weather) inclemency; (landscape) ruggedness.

**rauhen** ['rauən], v.a. (cloth) nap.

**Raum** [raum], m. (—es, pl. —e) space, room; outer space; (fig.) scope; dem Gedanken — geben, entertain an idea.

**räumen** ['rɔymən], v.a. clear, empty; quit, leave; das Feld —, abandon the field, clear out.

**Rauminhalt** ['raumInhalt], m. (—s, no pl.) volume.

**räumlich** ['rɔymlɪç], adj. spatial; (in compounds) space-.

**Räumlichkeiten** ['rɔymlɪçkaitən], f. pl. premises.

**Raumschiff** ['raumʃif], n. (—es, pl. —e) spaceship, spacecraft.

**Räumung** ['rɔymuŋ], f. (—, pl. —en) evacuation.

**raunen** ['raunən], v.a., v.n. whisper.

**Raupe** ['raupə], f. (—, pl. —n) (Ent.) caterpillar.

**Rausch** [rauʃ], m. (—es, pl. —e) intoxication; delirium, frenzy; einen — haben, be drunk, intoxicated; seinen — ausschlafen, sleep it off.

**rauschen** ['rauʃən], v.n. rustle, rush, roar.

**Rauschgift** ['rauʃgift], n. (—s, pl. —e) drug; narcotic.

**Rauschgold** ['rauʃgolt], n. (—es, no pl.) tinsel.

**räuspern** ['rɔyspərn], v.r. sich —, clear o.'s throat.

**Raute** ['rautə], f. (—, pl. —n) (Maths.) rhombus; lozenge; (Bot.) rue.

# Razzia

**Razzia** ['ratsja], *f.* (—, *pl.* —zzien) (police-)raid, swoop.

**reagieren** [rea'gi:rən], *v.n.* react (on).

**realisieren** [reali'zi:rən], *v.a.* convert into money, realise.

**Realschule** [re'a:lʃu:lə], *f.* (—, *pl.* —n) technical grammar school; secondary modern school.

**Rebe** ['re:bə], *f.* (—, *pl.* —n) vine.

**Rebell** [re'bɛl], *m.* (—en, *pl.* —en) rebel, mutineer, insurgent.

**Rebensaft** ['re:bənzaft], *m.* (—s, *pl.* ⁻e) grape-juice, wine.

**Rebhuhn** ['re:phu:n], *n.* (—s, *pl.* ⁻er) (*Orn.*) partridge.

**Reblaus** ['re:plaus], *f.* (—, *pl.* ⁻e) (*Ent.*) phylloxera.

**Rechen** ['reçən], *m.* (—s, *pl.* —) (*garden*) rake; (*clothes*) rack.

**Rechenaufgabe** ['reçənaufga:bə], *f.* (—, *pl.* —n) sum; mathematical *or* arithmetical problem.

**Rechenmaschine** ['reçənmaʃi:nə], *f.* (—, *pl.* —n) calculating machine, adding-machine.

**Rechenschaft** ['reçənʃaft], *f.* (—, *no pl.*) account; — *ablegen,* account for; *zur* — *ziehen,* call to account.

**Rechenschieber** ['reçənʃi:bər], *m.* (—s, *pl.* —) slide-rule.

**Rechentabelle** ['reçəntabɛlə], *f.* (—, *pl.* —n) ready reckoner.

**rechnen** ['reçnən], *v.a., v.n.* reckon, calculate, do sums, compute; *auf etwas* —, count on s.th.; *auf einen* —, rely on s.o.

**Rechnung** ['reçnuŋ], *f.* (—, *pl.* —en) reckoning, account, computation; (*document*) invoice, bill, statement, account; *einer Sache* — *tragen,* make allowances for s.th.; *take s.th. into account; einem einen Strich durch die* — *machen,* put a spoke in s.o.'s wheel; *eine* — *begleichen,* settle an account.

**Rechnungsabschluß** ['reçnuŋsapʃlus], *m.* (—sses, *pl.* ⁻sse) balancing of accounts, balance-sheet.

**Rechnungsprüfer** ['reçnuŋspry:fər], *m.* (—s, *pl.* —) auditor.

**Rechnungsrat** ['reçnuŋsra:t], *m.* (—s, *pl.* ⁻e) member of the board of accountants, (senior government) auditor.

**Recht** [reçt], *n.* (—es, *pl.* —e) right, justice; claim on, title to; law, jurisprudence; *von* —s *wegen,* by right; — *sprechen,* administer justice; *die* —e *studieren,* study law.

**recht** [reçt], *adj.* right; just; real, true; suitable; proper; *zur* —en *Zeit,* in time; *es geht nicht mit* —en *Dingen zu,* there is s.th. queer about it; *was den einen* —, *ist dem andern billig,* what is sauce for the goose is sauce for the gander; *einem* — *geben,* agree with s.o.; — *haben,* be (in the) right.

**Rechteck** ['reçtɛk], *n.* (—s, *pl.* —e) rectangle.

**rechten** ['reçtən], *v.n. mit einem* —, dispute, remonstrate with s.o.

**rechtfertigen** ['reçtfɛrtɪgən], *v.a. insep.* justify. — *v.r. sich* —, exculpate o.s.

**rechtgläubig** ['reçtglɔybɪç], *adj.* orthodox.

**rechthaberisch** ['reçtha:bərɪʃ], *adj.* stubborn, obstinate.

**rechtlich** ['reçtlɪç], *adj.* legal, lawful, legitimate; (*Law*) judicial, juridical.

**rechtmäßig** ['reçtmɛ:sɪç], *adj.* lawful, legitimate, legal.

**rechts** [reçts], *adv.* to the right, on the right.

**Rechtsabtretung** ['reçtsaptre:tuŋ], *f.* (—, *pl.* —en) cession, assignment.

**Rechtsanwalt** ['reçtsanvalt], *m.* (—s, *pl.* ⁻e) lawyer, solicitor, attorney.

**Rechtsbeistand** ['reçtsbaɪʃtant], *m.* (—s, *pl.* ⁻e) (legal) counsel.

**rechtschaffen** ['reçtʃafən], *adj.* upright, honest, righteous.

**Rechtschreibung** ['reçtʃraibuŋ], *f.* (—, *no pl.*) orthography, spelling.

**Rechtshandel** ['reçtshandəl], *m.* (—s, *pl.* ⁻) action, case, lawsuit.

**rechtskräftig** ['reçtskrɛftɪç], *adj.* legal, valid.

**Rechtslehre** ['reçtsle:rə], *f.* (—, *pl.* —n) jurisprudence.

**Rechtsspruch** ['reçtsʃprux], *m.* (—(e)s, *pl.* ⁻e) verdict.

**Rechtsverhandlung** ['reçtsfɛrhandluŋ], *f.* (—, *pl.* —en) legal proceedings.

**Rechtsweg** ['reçtsve:k], *m.* (—(e)s, *pl.* —e) course of law.

**rechtswidrig** ['reçtsvi:drɪç], *adj.* against the law, illegal.

**Rechtszuständigkeit** ['reçtstsu:ʃtɛndɪçkaɪt], *f.* (—, *pl.* —en) (legal) competence.

**rechtwinklig** ['reçtvɪŋklɪç], *adj.* rectangular.

**rechtzeitig** ['reçttsaitɪç], *adj.* opportune. — *adv.* in time, at the right time.

**Reck** [rɛk], *n.* (—s, *pl.* —e) horizontal bar.

**Recke** ['rɛkə], *m.* (—n, *pl.* —n) (*Poet.*) hero.

**recken** ['rɛkən], *v.a.* stretch, extend.

**Redakteur** [redak'tø:r], *m.* (—s, *pl.* —e) editor (newspaper, magazine).

**Redaktion** [redak'tsjo:n], *f.* (—, *pl.* —en) editorship, editorial staff; (*room*) editorial office.

**Rede** ['re:də], *f.* (—, *pl.* —n) speech, oration; address; *es geht die* —, people say; *es ist nicht der* — *wert,* it is not worth mentioning; *eine* — *halten,* deliver a speech; *zur* — *stellen,* call to account.

**reden** ['re:dən], *v.a.* speak, talk, discourse; *einem nach dem Munde* —, humour s.o.; *in den Wind* —, speak in vain, preach to the winds; *mit sich* — *lassen,* be amenable to reason.

**Redensart** ['re:dənsa:rt], *f.* (—, *pl.* —en) phrase, idiom; cliché; *einen mit leeren —en abspeisen,* put s.o. off with fine words.

**Redewendung** ['re:dəvenduŋ], *f.* (—, *pl.* —en) turn of phrase.

**redigieren** [redi'gi:rən], *v.a.* edit.

**redlich** ['re:tlɪç], *adj.* honest, upright.

**Redner** ['re:dnər], *m.* (—s, *pl.* —) speaker, orator.

**Reede** ['re:də], *f.* (—, *pl.* —n) (*Naut.*) roadstead.

**Reederei** [re:də'raɪ], *f.* (—, *pl.* —en) shipping-business.

**reell** [re'ɛl], *adj.* honest, fair, sound, bona fide.

**Reep** [re:p], *n.* (—s, *pl.* —e) (*Naut.*) rope.

**Referat** [refe'ra:t], *n.* (—s, *pl.* —e) report; paper (to a learned society), lecture.

**Referendar** [referɛn'da:r], *m.* (—s, *pl.* —e) junior barrister *or* teacher.

**Referent** [refe'rɛnt], *m.* (—en, *pl.* —en) reporter, reviewer; lecturer; expert (adviser).

**Referenz** [refe'rɛnts], *f.* (—, *pl.* —en) reference (to s.o. *or* s.th.).

**referieren** [refe'ri:rən], *v.a., v.n.* report (on), give a paper (on).

**reflektieren** [reflɛk'ti:rən], *v.a.* reflect. — *v.n. auf etwas —,* be a prospective buyer of s.th., have o.'s eye on s.th.

**Reformator** [refor'ma:tor], *m.* (—s, *pl.* —en) reformer.

**reformieren** [refor'mi:rən], *v.a.* reform.

**Regal** [re'ga:l], *n.* (—s, *pl.* —e) shelf.

**rege** ['re:gə], *adj.* brisk, lively, animated.

**Regel** ['re:gəl], *f.* (—, *pl.* —n) rule precept, principle; *in der —,* as a rule, generally.

**regelmäßig** ['re:gəlmɛ:sɪç], *adj.* regular.

**regeln** ['re:gəln], *v.a.* regulate, arrange, order.

**Regelung** ['re:gəluŋ], *f.* (—, *pl.* —en) regulation.

**regelwidrig** ['re:gəlvi:drɪç], *adj.* contrary to rule, irregular, foul.

**Regen** ['re:gən], *m.* (—s, *no pl.*) rain.

**regen** ['re:gən], *v.r. sich —,* move, stir.

**Regenbogen** ['re:gənbo:gən], *m.* (—s, *pl.* —) rainbow.

**Regenbogenhaut** ['re:gənbo:gənhaut], *f.* (—, *pl.* ⸚e) (*eye*) iris.

**Regenguß** ['re:gəngus], *m.* (—sses, *pl.* ⸚sse) downpour, violent shower.

**Regenmantel** ['re:gənmantəl], *m.* (—s, *pl.* ⸚) waterproof, raincoat, mac.

**Regenpfeifer** ['re:gənpfaɪfər], *m.* (—s, *pl.* —) (*Orn.*) plover.

**Regenrinne** ['re:gənrɪnə], *f.* (—, *pl.* —n) eaves.

**Regenschirm** ['re:gənʃɪrm], *m.* (—s, *pl.* —e) umbrella.

**Regentschaft** [re'gɛntʃaft], *f.* (—, *pl.* —en) regency.

**Regie** [re'ʒi:], *f.* (—, *pl.* —n) stage management, production, direction.

**regieren** [re'gi:rən], *v.a.* rule, reign over, govern. — *v.n.* reign; (*fig.*) prevail, predominate.

**Regierung** [re'gi:ruŋ], *f.* (—, *pl.* —en) government; reign.

**Regierungsrat** [re'gi:ruŋsra:t], *m.* (—s, *pl.* ⸚e) government adviser.

**Regiment** (1) [regi'mɛnt], *n.* (—s, *pl.* —e) rule, government.

**Regiment** (2) [regi'mɛnt], *n.* (—s, *pl.* —er) (*Mil.*) regiment.

**Regisseur** [reʒi'sø:r], *m.* (—s, *pl.* —e) stage-manager, producer, director.

**Registrator** [regɪs'tra:tor], *m.* (—s, *pl.* —en) registrar, recorder; registering machine.

**Registratur** [regɪstra'tu:r], *f.* (—, *pl.* —en) record office, registry; filing-cabinet.

**registrieren** [regɪs'tri:rən], *v.a.* register, record, file.

**reglos** ['re:klo:s], *adj.* motionless.

**regnen** ['re:gnən], *v.n.* rain; *es regnet in Strömen,* it is raining cats and dogs.

**Regreß** [re'grɛs], *m.* (—sses, *pl.* —sse) recourse, remedy.

**regsam** ['re:kza:m], *adj.* quick, alert, lively.

**regulieren** [regu'li:rən], *v.a.* regulate.

**Regung** ['re:guŋ], *f.* (—, *pl.* —en) movement; impulse.

**Reh** [re:], *n.* (—(e)s, *pl.* —e) doe, roe.

**rehabilitieren** [rehabili'ti:rən], *v.a.* rehabilitate.

**Rehbock** ['re:bɔk], *m.* (—s, *pl.* ⸚e) (*Zool.*) roe-buck.

**Rehkeule** ['re:kɔylə], *f.* (—, *pl.* —n) haunch of venison.

**reiben** ['raɪbən], *v.a. irr.* rub, grate, grind; *einem etwas unter die Nase —,* throw s.th. in s.o.'s teeth, bring s.th. home to s.o.

**Reibung** ['raɪbuŋ], *f.* (—, *pl.* —en) friction.

**Reich** [raɪç], *n.* (—(e)s, *pl.* —e) kingdom, realm, empire, state.

**reich** [raɪç], *adj.* rich, wealthy, opulent.

**reichen** ['raɪçən], *v.a.* reach, pass, hand; *einem die Hand —,* shake hands with s.o. — *v.n.* reach, extend; be sufficient.

**reichhaltig** ['raɪçhaltɪç], *adj.* abundant, copious.

**reichlich** ['raɪçlɪç], *adj.* ample, plentiful.

**Reichskammergericht** [raɪçs'kamərgərɪçt], *n.* (—s, *no pl.*) Imperial High Court of Justice (*Holy Roman Empire*).

**Reichskanzlei** ['raɪçskantslaɪ], *f.* (—, *pl.* —en) (Imperial) Chancery.

**Reichskanzler** ['raɪçskantslər], *m.* (—s, *pl.* —) (Imperial) Chancellor.

**Reichsstände** ['raɪçsʃtɛndə], *m. pl.* Estates (of the Holy Roman Empire).

**Reichstag** ['raɪçsta:k], *m.* (—s, *pl.* —e) Imperial Parliament, Reichstag, Diet.

**Reichtum** ['raɪçtu:m], *m.* (—s, *pl.* ⁻er) riches, wealth, opulence.

**Reif** (1) [raɪf], *m.* (—s, *no pl.*) hoarfrost.

**Reif** (2) [raɪf], *m.* (—s, *pl.* —e) ring.

**reif** [raɪf], *adj.* ripe, mature.

**Reifen** ['raɪfən], *m.* (—s, *pl.* —) hoop; tyre; — *schlagen*, trundle a hoop.

**reifen** ['raɪfən], *v.n.* (*aux.* sein) ripen, mature, grow ripe.

**Reifeprüfung** ['raɪfəpry:fuŋ], *f.* (—, *pl.* —en) matriculation examination.

**reiflich** ['raɪflɪç], *adj.* *sich etwas* — *überlegen*, give careful consideration to s.th.

**Reigen** ['raɪgən], *m.* (—s, *pl.* —) round-dance, roundelay.

**Reihe** ['raɪə], *f.* (—, *pl.* —n) series; file; row; progression, sequence; (*Theat.*) tier; *in* — *und Glied*, in closed ranks; *nach der* —, in turns; *ich bin an der* —, it is my turn.

**Reihenfolge** ['raɪənfɔlgə], *f.* (—, *no pl.*) succession.

**Reiher** ['raɪər], *m.* (—s, *pl.* —) (*Orn.*) heron.

**Reim** [raɪm], *m.* (—(e)s, *pl.* —e) rhyme.

**rein** [raɪn], *adj.* clean, pure, clear, neat; —*e Wahrheit*, plain truth; *ins* —*e bringen*, settle, clear up; *ins* —*e schreiben*, make a fair copy of; *einem* —*en Wein einschenken*, have a straight talk with s.o.

**Reineke** ['raɪnəkə], *m.* (—, *no pl.*) — *Fuchs*, Reynard the Fox.

**Reinertrag** ['raɪnɛrtra:k], *m.* (—(e)s, *pl.* ⁻e) net proceeds.

**Reinfall** ['raɪnfal], *m.* (—s, *pl.* ⁻e) sell, wild-goose chase; disappointment.

**reinfallen** ['raɪnfalən], *v.n. irr.* (*aux.* sein) be unsuccessful.

**Reingewinn** ['raɪngəvɪn], *m.* (—s, *pl.* —e) net proceeds.

**Reinheit** ['raɪnhaɪt], *f.* (—, *no pl.*) purity.

**reinigen** ['raɪnɪgən], *v.a.* clean, cleanse; dry-clean; purge.

**Reinigung** ['raɪnɪguŋ], *f.* (—, *pl.* —en) cleaning; (*fig.*) purification, cleansing; *chemische* —, dry-cleaning.

**reinlich** ['raɪnlɪç], *adj.* clean, neat.

**Reis** (1) [raɪs], *m.* (—es, *no pl.*) rice.

**Reis** (2) [raɪs], *n.* (—es, *pl.* —er) twig, sprig; scion; cutting.

**Reisbesen** ['raɪsbe:zən], *m.* (—s, *pl.* —) birch-broom, besom.

**Reise** ['raɪzə], *f.* (—, *pl.* —n) tour, trip, journey, travels; voyage; *gute* —! bon voyage!

**reisefertig** ['raɪzəfɛrtɪç], *adj.* ready to start.

**Reisegeld** ['raɪzəgɛlt], *n.* (—es, *pl.* —er) travel allowance.

**reisen** ['raɪzən], *v.n.* (*aux.* sein) travel, tour, journey, take a trip.

**Reisende** ['raɪzəndə], *m.* (—n, *pl.* —n) traveller; commercial traveller.

**Reisig** ['raɪzɪç], *n.* (—s, *no pl.*) brushwood.

**Reisige** ['raɪzɪgə], *m.* (—n, *pl.* —n) (*obs.*) trooper, horseman.

**Reißaus** [raɪs'aus], *n.* (—, *no pl.*) — *nehmen*, take to o.'s heels.

**Reißbrett** ['raɪsbrɛt], *n.* (—es, *pl.* —er) drawing-board.

**reißen** ['raɪsən], *v.a. irr.* tear; rend; pull; snatch; *etwas an sich* —, seize s.th., usurp.

**reißend** ['raɪsənt], *adj.* rapid; ravening; carnivorous; (*Comm.*) brisk, rapid (sales).

**Reißnagel** ['raɪsna:gəl], *m. see* **Reißzwecke.**

**Reißschiene** ['raɪsʃi:nə], *f.* (—, *pl.* —n) T-square.

**Reißverschluß** ['raɪsfɛrʃlus], *m.* (—sses, *pl.* ⁻sse) zip-fastener.

**Reißzwecke** ['raɪstsvɛkə], *f.* (—, *pl.* —n) drawing-pin.

**reiten** ['raɪtən], *v.a. irr.* ride (a horse). — *v.n.* (*aux.* sein) ride, go on horseback.

**Reiterei** [raɪtə'raɪ], *f.* (—, *pl.* —en) cavalry.

**Reitknecht** ['raɪtknɛçt], *m.* (—es, *pl.* —e) groom.

**Reiz** [raɪts], *m.* (—es, *pl.* —e) charm, attraction, fascination, allure; stimulus; irritation; (*Phys.*) impulse.

**reizbar** ['raɪtsba:r], *adj.* susceptible; irritable.

**reizen** ['raɪtsən], *v.a.* irritate; stimulate, charm, entice.

**reizend** ['raɪtsənt], *adj.* charming.

**Reizmittel** ['raɪtsmɪtəl], *n.* (—s, *pl.* —) stimulant; irritant.

**rekeln** ['re:kəln], *v.r.* (*dial.*) *sich* —, loll about.

**Reklame** [re'kla:mə], *f.* (—, *pl.* —n) propaganda, advertisement, advertising, publicity.

**reklamieren** [rekla'mi:rən], *v.a.* claim, reclaim. — *v.n.* complain.

**rekognoszieren** [rekɔgnɔs'tsi:rən], *v.a.* reconnoitre.

**rekommandieren** [rekɔman'di:rən], *v.a.* (*Austr.*) register (a letter).

**Rekonvaleszent** [rekɔnvalɛs'tsɛnt], *m.* (—en, *pl.* —en) convalescent.

**Rekrut** [re'kru:t], *m.* (—en, *pl.* —en) recruit.

**rekrutieren** [rekru'ti:rən], *v.a.* recruit. — *v.r. sich* — *aus*, be recruited from.

**rektifizieren** [rɛktifi'tsi:rən], *v.a.* rectify.

**Rektor** ['rɛktɔr], *m.* (—s, *pl.* —en) (school) headmaster; (*Univ.*) chancellor.

**Rektorat** [rɛkto'ra:t], *n.* (—es, *pl.* —e) rectorship, chancellorship.

**relativ** [rela'ti:f], *adj.* relative, comparative.

**relegieren** [rele'gi:rən], *v.a.* expel; (*Univ.*) send down, rusticate.

**Relief** [rɛl'jef], *n.* (—s, *pl.* —s) (*Art*) relief.

**religiös** [reli'gjø:s], *adj.* religious.

**Reliquie** [re'li:kvjə], *f.* (—, *pl.* —n) (*Rel.*) relic.

**Remise** [re′mi:zə], *f.* (—, *pl.* —n) coach-house.

**Remittent** [remɪ′tɛnt], *m.* (—en, *pl.* —en) remitter.

**Renegat** [rene′ga:t], *m.* (—en, *pl.* —en) renegade.

**Renette** [rɛ′nɛtə], *f.* (—, *pl.* —n) rennet(-apple).

**renken** [′rɛŋkən], *v.a.* wrench, bend, twist.

**Rennbahn** [′rɛnba:n], *f.* (—, *pl.* —en) race-course; (cinder-)track; (*Motor.*) racing-circuit.

**rennen** [′rɛnən], *v.n. irr.* (*aux.* sein) run, race, rush.

**Renommé** [reno′me:], *n.* (—s, *no pl.*) renown, repute, reputation.

**renommieren** [reno′mi:rən], *v.n.* brag, boast.

**renovieren** [reno′vi:rən], *v.a.* renovate, restore, redecorate, renew.

**rentabel** [rɛn′ta:bəl], *adj.* profitable, lucrative.

**Rente** [′rɛntə], *f.* (—, *pl.* —n) pension, annuity.

**Rentier** [rɛn′tje:], *m.* (—s, *pl.* —s) rentier, person of independent means.

**rentieren** [rɛn′ti:rən], *v.r. sich* —, be profitable, be worthwhile, pay.

**Rentner** [′rɛntnər], *m.* (—s, *pl.* —) pensioner.

**Reparatur** [repara′tu:r], *f.* (—, *pl.* —en) repair.

**reparieren** [repa′ri:rən], *v.a.* repair.

**Repräsentant** [reprezɛn′tant], *m.* (—en, *pl.* —en) representative.

**Repräsentantenkammer** [reprezɛn′tantənkamər], *f.* (—, *pl.* —n) (*Am.*) House of Representatives.

**Repressalien** [reprɛ′sa:ljən], *f. pl.* reprisals, retaliation.

**reproduzieren** [reprodu′tsi:rən], *v.a.* reproduce.

**Republikaner** [republi′ka:nər], *m.* (—s, *pl.* —) republican.

**requirieren** [rekvi′ri:rən], *v.a.* requisition.

**Reseda** [re′ze:da], *f.* (—, *pl.* —s) (*Bot.*) mignonette.

**Reservat** [rezɛr′va:t], *n.* (—es, *pl.* —e) reservation, reserve.

**Residenz** [rezi′dɛnts], *f.* (—, *pl.* —en) residence, seat of the Court.

**residieren** [rezi′di:rən], *v.n.* reside.

**Residuum** [re′zi:duum], *n.* (—s, *pl.* —duen) residue, dregs.

**resignieren** [rezɪg′ni:rən], *v.n., v.r.* resign; be resigned (to s.th.); give up.

**Respekt** [re′spɛkt], *m.* (—es, *no pl.*) respect, regard; *mit* — *zu sagen*, with all due respect.

**respektieren** [rɛspɛk′ti:rən], *v.a.* respect, honour.

**Ressort** [re′so:r], *n.* (—s, *pl.* —s) department, domain.

**Rest** [rɛst], *m.* (—es, *pl.* —e) rest, residue, remainder; remnant; (*money*) balance.

**restaurieren** [rɛsto′ri:rən], *v.a.* restore, renovate.

**Resultat** [rezul′ta:t], *n.* (—es, *pl.* —e) result, outcome.

**Resümee** [rezy′me:], *n.* (—s, *pl.* —s) résumé, précis, digest, summary, synopsis, abstract.

**retten** [′rɛtən], *v.a.* save, preserve; rescue, deliver; *die Ehre* —, vindicate o.'s honour.

**Rettich** [′rɛtɪç], *m.* (—s, *pl.* —e) radish.

**Rettung** [′rɛtuŋ], *f.* (—, *pl.* —en) saving, rescue, deliverance.

**retuschieren** [retu′ʃi:rən], *v.a.* retouch.

**Reue** [′rɔyə], *f.* (—, *no pl.*) repentance, remorse, contrition.

**reuen** [′rɔyən], *v.a., v.n.* repent, regret; *es reut mich,* I am sorry.

**Reugeld** [′rɔygɛlt], *n.* (—es, *pl.* —er) forfeit-money, penalty.

**reüssieren** [rey′si:rən], *v.n.* succeed.

**Revanche** [re′vã:ʃə], *f.* (—, *pl.* —n) revenge; (*fig.*) return.

**revanchieren** [revã′ʃi:rən], *v.r. sich* —, repay a service, have *or* take o.'s revenge.

**Reverenz** [reve′rɛnts], *f.* (—, *pl.* —en) bow, curtsy.

**revidieren** [revi′di:rən], *v.a.* revise, check.

**Revier** [re′vi:r], *n.* (—s, *pl.* —e) district, precinct, quarter; preserve.

**Revisor** [re′vi:zɔr], *m.* (—s, *pl.* —en) accountant, auditor.

**revoltieren** [revɔl′ti:rən], *v.n.* rise, revolt.

**revolutionieren** [revolutsjo′ni:rən], *v.a.* revolutionise.

**Revolverblatt** [re′vɔlvərblat], *n.* (—s, *pl.* —er) gutter press.

**Revue** [re′vy:], *f.* (—, *pl.* —n) revue; review; — *passieren lassen*, pass in review.

**Rezensent** [retsɛn′zɛnt], *m.* (—en, *pl.* —en) reviewer, critic.

**rezensieren** [retsɛn′zi:rən], *v.a.* review.

**Rezept** [re′tsɛpt], *n.* (—es, *pl.* —e) (*Med.*) prescription; (*Cul.*) recipe.

**rezitieren** [retsi′ti:rən], *v.a.* recite.

**Rhabarber** [ra′barbər], *m.* (—s, *no pl.*) (*Bot.*) rhubarb.

**Rhein** [raɪn], *m.* (—s, *no pl.*) (*River*) Rhine.

**Rhodesien** [ro′de:zjən], *n.* Rhodesia.

**Rhodus** [′ro:dus], *n.* Rhodes.

**Rhythmus** [′rytmus], *m.* (—, *pl.* —men) rhythm.

**Richtbeil** [′rɪçtbaɪl], *n.* (—s, *pl.* —e) executioner's axe.

**richten** [′rɪçtən], *v.a., v.n.* direct, point at; prepare; *die Augen* — *auf*, fix o.'s eyes upon; *einen zugrunde* —, ruin s.o.; judge, try, pass sentence on, condemn. —*v.r. sich nach* (*Dat.*) —, be guided by.

**Richter** [′rɪçtər], *m.* (—s, *pl.* —) judge; justice.

**richtig** [′rɪçtɪç], *adj.* right, correct, exact, true; *nicht ganz* — *sein*, be not quite right in the head.

# Richtlot

**Richtlot** ['rɪçtlo:t], *n.* (—s, *pl.* —e) plumb-line.

**Richtschnur** ['rɪçtʃnu:r], *f.* (—, *pl.* —en) plumb-line; (*fig.*) rule, precept.

**Richtung** ['rɪçtuŋ], *f.* (—, *pl.* —en) direction.

**riechen** ['ri:çən], *v.a., v.n. irr.* smell, scent, reek; *Lunte* —, smell a rat.

**Riege** ['ri:gə], *f.* (—, *pl.* —n) row, section.

**Riegel** ['ri:gəl], *m.* (—s, *pl.* —) bar, bolt; *ein* — *Schokolade*, a bar of chocolate.

**Riemen** ['ri:mən], *m.* (—s, *pl.* —) strap, thong; oar.

**Ries** [ri:s], *n.* (—es, *pl.* —e) (*paper*) ream.

**Riese** ['ri:zə], *m.* (—n, *pl.* —n) giant.

**rieseln** ['ri:zəln], *v.n.* murmur, babble, ripple, trickle; drizzle.

**Riesenschlange** ['ri:zənʃlaŋə], *f.* (—, *pl.* —n) anaconda.

**Riff** [rɪf], *n.* (—es, *pl.* —e) reef.

**rigoros** [rigo'ro:s], *adj.* strict, rigorous.

**Rille** ['rɪlə], *f.* (—, *pl.* —n) groove, small furrow; (*Archit.*) flute, chamfer.

**Rind** [rɪnt], *n.* (—es, *pl.* —er) ox, cow; (*pl.*) cattle, horned cattle, head of cattle.

**Rinde** ['rɪndə], *f.* (—, *pl.* —n) rind, bark, peel; (*bread*) crust.

**Rinderbraten** ['rɪndərbra:tən], *m.* (—s, *pl.* —) roast beef.

**Rindfleisch** ['rɪntflaɪʃ], *n.* (—es, *no pl.*) beef.

**Rindvieh** ['rɪntfi:], *n.* (—s, *no pl.*) cattle; (*fig.*) blockhead, ass.

**Ring** [rɪŋ], *m.* (—(e)s, *pl.* —e) ring; (*chain*) link; (*under the eye*) dark circle; (*Comm.*) syndicate, trust.

**Ringelblume** ['rɪŋəlblu:mə], *f.* (—, *pl.* —n) (*Bot.*) marigold.

**ringeln** ['rɪŋəln], *v.r. sich* —, curl.

**ringen** ['rɪŋən], *v.a. irr.* wring. — *v.n.* wrestle.

**Ringer** ['rɪŋər], *m.* (—s, *pl.* —) wrestler.

**Ringmauer** ['rɪŋmauər], *f.* (—, *pl.* —n) city *or* town wall.

**rings** [rɪŋs], *adv.* around.

**ringsum(her)** [rɪŋ'sum(he:r)], *adv.* round about.

**Rinne** ['rɪnə], *f.* (—, *pl.* —n) furrow, gutter; groove.

**rinnen** ['rɪnən], *v.n. irr.* (*aux,* sein) run, leak, drip.

**Rinnsal** ['rɪnza:l], *n.* (—s, *pl.* —e) channel, water-course.

**Rinnstein** ['rɪnʃtaɪn], *m.* (—s, *pl.* —e) gutter.

**Rippe** ['rɪpə], *f.* (—, *pl.* —n) rib.

**Rippenfellentzündung** ['rɪpənfɛlɛnt-tsynduŋ], *f.* (—, *pl.* —en) pleurisy.

**Rippenspeer** ['rɪpənʃpe:r], *m.* (—s, *pl.* —e) (*Casseler* —), spare-rib, ribs of pork.

**Rippenstoß** ['rɪpənʃto:s], *m.* (—es, *pl.* -̈e) dig in the ribs, nudge.

**Rips** [rɪps], *m.* (—es, *no pl.*) rep.

**Risiko** ['ri:ziko], *n.* (—s, *pl.* —ken) risk.

**riskant** [rɪs'kant], *adj.* risky.

**riskieren** [rɪs'ki:rən], *v.a.* risk.

**Riß** [rɪs], *m.* (—sses, *pl.* —sse) rent, tear; sketch, design, plan.

**rissig** ['rɪsɪç], *adj.* cracked, torn.

**Ritt** [rɪt], *m.* (—(e)s, *pl.* —e) ride.

**Ritter** ['rɪtər], *m.* (—s, *pl.* —) knight; *einen zum* — *schlagen*, dub s.o. a knight.

**ritterlich** ['rɪtərlɪç], *adj.* knightly; (*fig.*) chivalrous, valiant, gallant.

**Ritterschlag** ['rɪtərʃla:k], *m.* (—(e)s, *pl.* -̈e) accolade.

**Rittersporn** ['rɪtərʃpɔrn], *m.* (—s, *pl.* —e) (*Bot.*) larkspur.

**rittlings** ['rɪtlɪŋs], *adv.* astride.

**Rittmeister** ['rɪtmaɪstər], *m.* (—s, *pl.* —) captain (of cavalry).

**Ritus** ['ri:tus], *m.* (—, *pl.* **Riten**) rite.

**Ritz** [rɪts], *m.* (—es, *pl.* —e) chink, fissure, cleft, crevice; (*glacier*) crevasse.

**ritzen** ['rɪtsən], *v.a.* scratch.

**Rivale** [ri'va:lə], *m.* (—n, *pl.* —n) rival.

**Rivalität** [rivali'tɛ:t], *f.* (—, *pl.* —en) rivalry.

**Rizinusöl** ['ri:tsinusø:l], *n.* (—s, *no pl.*) castor oil.

**Robbe** ['rɔbə], *f.* (—, *pl.* —n) (*Zool.*) seal.

**Robe** ['ro:bə], *f.* (—, *pl.* —n) dress, robe; gown.

**röcheln** ['rœçəln], *v.n.* rattle in o.'s throat.

**rochieren** [rɔ'xi:rən], *v.n.* (*Chess*) castle.

**Rock** [rɔk], *m.* (—(e)s, *pl.* -̈e) (*woman*) skirt; (*man*) coat.

**rodeln** ['ro:dəln], *v.n.* (*aux.* haben & sein) toboggan.

**roden** ['ro:dən], *v.a.* clear, weed, thin out (plants).

**Rogen** ['ro:gən], *m.* (—s, *no pl.*) (*fish*) roe, spawn.

**Roggen** ['rɔgən], *m.* (—s, *no pl.*) rye.

**roh** [ro:], *adj.* raw; rough, rude, coarse, crude; *ein* —*er Mensch*, a brute; (*in compounds*) rough-; preliminary, unrefined.

**Rohbilanz** ['ro:bilants], *f.* (—, *pl.* —en) trial balance.

**Roheisen** ['ro:aɪzən], *n.* (—s, *no pl.*) pig-iron.

**Roheit** ['ro:haɪt], *f.* (—, *pl.* —en) coarseness, rudeness, crudity.

**Rohr** [ro:r], *n.* (—es, *pl.* —e, -̈en) tube, pipe; reed, cane; (*gun*) barrel.

**Rohrdommel** ['ro:rdɔməl], *f.* (—, *pl.* —n) (*Orn.*) bittern.

**Röhre** ['rø:rə], *f.* (—, *pl.* —n) tube, pipe; (*Radio*) valve.

**Röhricht** ['rø:rɪçt], *n.* (—s, *pl.* —e) reeds.

**Rohrpfeife** ['ro:rpfaɪfə], *f.* (—, *pl.* —n) reed-pipe.

**Rohrpost** ['ro:rpɔst], *f.* (—, *no pl.*) pneumatic post.

**Rohrzucker** ['ro:rtsukər], *m.* (—s, *no pl.*) cane-sugar.

# Rückhalt

**Rolladen** ['rɔladən], *m.* (—s, *pl.* ˝) sliding shutter, roller blind.

**Rollbahn** ['rɔlba:n], *f.* (—, *pl.* —en) (*Aviat.*) runway, tarmac.

**Rolle** ['rɔlə], *f.* (—, *pl.* —n) reel, roll; pulley; (*Theat.*) part; rôle; (*laundry*) mangle.

**rollen** ['rɔlən], *v.a.* roll, reel; (*laundry*) mangle. — *v.n.* (*aux.* sein) roll (along); (*thunder*) roar, roll.

**Roller** ['rɔlər], *m.* (—s, *pl.* —) scooter.

**Rollmops** ['rɔlmɔps], *m.* (—es, *pl.* ˝e) soused herring.

**Rollschuh** ['rɔlʃu:], *m.* (—s, *pl.* —e) roller-skate.

**Rollstuhl** ['rɔlʃtu:l], *m.* (—s, *pl.* ˝e) wheel-chair, bath-chair.

**Rolltreppe** ['rɔltrɛpə], *f.* (—, *pl.* —n) escalator, moving staircase.

**Rom** [ro:m], *n.* Rome.

**Roman** [ro'ma:n], *m.* (—s, *pl.* —e) novel.

**romanisch** [ro'ma:nɪʃ], *adj.* Romanesque.

**Romanliteratur** [ro'ma:nlitəratu:r], *f.* (—, *pl.*) fiction.

**Romanschriftsteller** [ro'ma:nʃrɪftʃtelər], *m.* (—s, *pl.* —) novelist.

**Römer** ['rø:mər], *m.* (—s, *pl.* —) Roman; (*glass*) rummer.

**Rondell** [rɔn'dɛl], *n.* (—s, *pl.* —e) circular flower-bed.

**Röntgenstrahlen** ['rœntgənʃtra:lən], *m. pl.* X-rays.

**rosa** ['ro:za:], *adj.* pink, rose-coloured.

**Rose** ['ro:zə], *f.* (—, *pl.* —n) rose.

**Rosenkranz** ['ro:zənkrants], *m.* (—es, *pl.* ˝e) garland of roses; (*Eccl.*) rosary.

**Rosenkreuzer** ['ro:zənkrɔytsər], *m.* (—s, *pl.* —) Rosicrucian.

**Rosine** [ro'zi:nə], *f.* (—, *pl.* —n) sultana, raisin.

**Rosmarin** ['rɔsmari:n], *m.* (—s, *no pl.*) (*Bot.*) rosemary.

**Roß** [rɔs], *n.* (—sses, *pl.* —sse) horse, steed.

**Roßbremse** ['rɔsbrɛmzə], *f.* (—, *pl.* —n) (*Ent.*) horsefly, gadfly.

**Rössel** ['rœsəl], *n.* (—s, *pl.* —) (*Chess*) knight.

**Roßhaarmatratze** ['rɔsha:rmatratsə], *f.* (—, *pl.* —n) hair-mattress.

**Roßkastanie** ['rɔskasta:njə], *f.* (—, *pl.* —n) (*Bot.*) horse-chestnut.

**Rost** (1) [rɔst], *m.* (—es, *no pl.*) rust.

**Rost** (2) [rɔst], *m.* (—s, *pl.* —e) grate; gridiron.

**Rostbraten** ['rɔstbra:tən], *m.* (—s, *pl.* —) roast meat.

**rosten** ['rɔstən], *v.n.* go rusty; rust; *alte Liebe rostet nicht*, love that's old rusts not away.

**rösten** ['rø:stən], *v.a.* toast, roast, grill.

**rot** [ro:t], *adj.* red; — *werden*, redden, blush.

**Rotauge** ['ro:taugə], *n.* (—s, *pl.* —n) (*Zool.*) roach.

**Röte** ['rø:tə], *f.* (—, *no pl.*) redness, red colour.

**Röteln** ['rø:təln], *m. pl.* (*Med.*) German measles, rubella.

**Rotfink** ['ro:tfɪŋk], *m.* (—en, *pl.* —en) (*Orn.*) bullfinch.

**Rotfuchs** ['ro:tfuks], *m.* (—es, *pl.* ˝e) (*Zool.*) sorrel horse.

**rotieren** [ro'ti:rən], *v.n.* rotate.

**Rotkäppchen** ['ro:tkɛpçən], *n.* Little Red Riding Hood.

**Rotkehlchen** ['ro:tke:lçən], *n.* (—s, *pl.* —) robin.

**Rotlauf** ['ro:tlauf], *m.* (—s, *no pl.*) (*Med.*) erysipelas.

**Rotschimmel** ['ro:tʃɪməl], *m.* (—s, *pl.* —) roan-horse.

**Rotspon** ['ro:tʃpo:n], *m.* (—s, *no pl.*) (*dial.*) claret.

**Rotte** ['rɔtə], *f.* (—, *pl.* —n) band, gang, rabble; (*Mil.*) file, squad.

**Rotwild** ['ro:tvɪlt], *n.* (—s, *no pl.*) red deer.

**Rotz** [rɔts], *m.* (—es, *no pl.*) (*vulg.*) mucus; snot.

**Rouleau** [ru'lo:], *n.* (—s, *pl.* —s) sun-blind, roller-blind.

**routiniert** [ruti'ni:rt], *adj.* smart; experienced.

**Rübe** ['ry:bə], *f.* (—, *pl.* —n) (*Bot.*) turnip; *rote* —, beetroot; *gelbe* —, carrot.

**Rubel** ['ru:bəl], *m.* (—s, *pl.* —) rouble.

**Rübenzucker** ['ry:bəntsukər], *m.* (—s, *no pl.*) beet-sugar.

**Rubin** [ru'bi:n], *m.* (—s, *pl.* —e) ruby.

**Rubrik** [ru'bri:k], *f.* (—, *pl.* —en) rubric; title, heading, category, column.

**Rübsamen** ['ry:pza:mən], *m.* (—s, *no pl.*) rape-seed.

**ruchbar** ['ru:xba:r], *adj.* manifest, known, notorious.

**ruchlos** ['ru:xlo:s], *adj.* wicked, profligate, vicious.

**Ruck** [ruk], *m.* (—(e)s, *pl.* —e) pull, jolt, jerk.

**Rückblick** ['rykblɪk], *m.* (—s, *pl.* —e) retrospect, retrospective view.

**Rücken** ['rykən], *m.* (—s, *pl.* —) back; (*mountains*) ridge; *einem den* — *kehren*, turn o.'s back upon s.o.

**rücken** ['rykən], *v.a.* move, push. — *v.n.* move along.

**Rückenmark** ['rykənmark], *n.* (—s, *no pl.*) spinal marrow.

**Rückenwirbel** ['rykənvɪrbəl], *m.* (—s, *pl.* —) dorsal vertebra.

**rückerstatten** ['rykərʃtatən], *v.a.* refund.

**Rückfahrkarte** ['rykfa:rkartə], *f.* (—, *pl.* —n) return ticket.

**Rückfall** ['rykfal], *m.* (—s, *pl.* ˝e) relapse.

**rückgängig** ['rykgɛŋɪç], *adj.* — *machen*, cancel, annul, reverse (a decision).

**Rückgrat** ['rykgra:t], *n.* (—s, *pl.* —e) backbone, spine.

**Rückhalt** ['rykhalt], *m.* (—s, *no pl.*) reserve; support, backing.

181

**Rückkehr** ['rykkeːr], *f.* (—, *no pl.*) return.

**Rücklicht** ['ryklɪçt], *n.* (—s, *pl.* —er) (*Motor. etc.*) tail-light.

**rücklings** ['ryklɪŋks], *adv.* from behind.

**Rucksack** ['rukzak], *m.* (—s, *pl.* ⸚e) rucksack; knapsack.

**Rückschritt** ['rykʃrɪt], *m.* (—es, *pl.* —e) step backward, retrograde step, regression.

**Rücksicht** ['rykzɪçt], *f.* (—, *pl.* —en) consideration, regard.

**Rücksprache** ['rykʃpraːxə], *f.* (—, *pl.* —n) conference, consultation; — *nehmen mit*, consult, confer with.

**rückständig** ['rykʃtɛndɪç], *adj.* outstanding; old-fashioned; backward.

**Rücktritt** ['ryktrɪt], *m.* (—s, *no pl.*) resignation.

**ruckweise** ['rukvaɪzə], *adv.* by fits and starts; jerkily.

**Rückwirkung** ['rykvɪrkuŋ], *f.* (—, *pl.* —en) reaction, retroaction.

**Rüde** ['ryːdə], *m.* (—n, *pl.* —n) male (dog, fox etc.).

**Rudel** ['ruːdəl], *n.* (—s, *pl.* —) flock, herd, pack.

**Ruder** ['ruːdər], *n.* (—s, *pl.* —) oar, rudder, paddle; *am — sein*, be at the helm; (*Pol.*) be in power.

**rudern** ['ruːdərn], *v.a.*, *v.n.* row.

**Ruf** [ruːf], *m.* (—(e)s, *pl.* —e) call; shout; reputation, renown; *einen guten (schlechten) — haben*, have a good (bad) reputation, be well (ill) spoken of.

**rufen** ['ruːfən], *v.a.*, *v.n. irr.* call, shout; *einen — lassen*, send for s.o.

**Rüffel** ['ryfəl], *m.* (—s, *pl.* —) (*coll.*) reprimand; (*sl.*) rocket.

**Rüge** ['ryːgə], *f.* (—, *pl.* —n) censure, blame, reprimand.

**Ruhe** ['ruːə], *f.* (—, *no pl.*) rest, repose; quiet, tranquillity; *sich zur — setzen*, retire (from business etc.).

**Ruhegehalt** ['ruːəgəhalt], *n.* (—es, *pl.* ⸚er) retirement pension, superannuation.

**ruhen** ['ruːən], *v.n.* rest, repose, take a rest.

**Ruhestand** ['ruːəʃtant], *m.* (—es, *no pl.*) retirement.

**ruhig** ['ruːɪç], *adj.* quiet, tranquil, peaceful, calm; *sich — verhalten*, keep quiet.

**Ruhm** [ruːm], *m.* (—(e)s, *no pl.*) glory, fame, renown; *einem zum — gereichen*, be *or* redound to s.o.'s credit.

**rühmen** ['ryːmən], *v.a.* praise, extol, glorify. — *v.r. sich —*, boast.

**Ruhr** (1) [ruːr], *f.* (River) Ruhr.

**Ruhr** (2) [ruːr], *f.* (—, *no pl.*) dysentery.

**Rührei** ['ryːraɪ], *n.* (—s, *pl.* —er) scrambled egg.

**rühren** ['ryːrən], *v.a.* stir, move, touch. — *v.r. sich —*, move, stir; get a move on.

**rührig** ['ryːrɪç], *adj.* active, alert.

**rührselig** ['ryːrzeːlɪç], *adj.* oversentimental; lachrymose.

**Rührung** ['ryːruŋ], *f.* (—, *no pl.*) emotion.

**Ruin** [ru'iːn], *m.* (—s, *no pl.*) (*fig.*) ruin; decay; bankruptcy.

**Ruine** [ru'iːnə], *f.* (—, *pl.* —n) ruin(s).

**rülpsen** ['rylpsən], *v.n.* belch.

**Rum** [rum], *m.* (—s, *no pl.*) rum.

**Rumänien** [ru'mɛːnjən], *n.* Rumania.

**Rummel** ['ruməl], *m.* (—s, *no pl.*) tumult, row, hubbub.

**Rumor** [ru'moːr], *m.* (—s, *no pl.*) noise; rumour.

**rumoren** [ru'moːrən], *v.n.* make a noise.

**Rumpelkammer** ['rumpəlkamər], *f.* (—, *pl.* —n) lumber-room, junk-room.

**rumpeln** ['rumpəln], *v.n.* rumble.

**Rumpf** [rumpf], *m.* (—(e)s, *pl.* ⸚e) (*Anat.*) trunk; (*ship*) hull; (*Aviat.*) fuselage.

**rümpfen** ['rympfən], *v.a. die Nase —*, turn up o.'s nose.

**rund** [runt], *adj.* round, rotund; — *heraus*, flatly; *etwas — abschlagen*, refuse s.th. flatly; — *herum*, round about.

**Runde** ['rundə], *f.* (—, *pl.* —n) round; (*Sport*) round, bout; *die — machen*, (*watchman*) patrol.

**Rundfunk** ['runtfuŋk], *m.* (—s, *no pl.*) broadcasting, wireless; radio.

**Rundgang** ['runtgaŋ], *m.* (—s, *pl.* ⸚e) round, tour (of inspection).

**rundlich** ['runtlɪç], *adj.* plump.

**Rundschau** ['runtʃau], *f.* (—, *no pl.*) panorama; review, survey.

**Rundschreiben** ['runtʃraɪbən], *n.* (—s, *pl.* —) circular letter.

**rundweg** ['runtveːk], *adv.* flatly, plainly.

**Rune** ['ruːnə], *f.* (—, *pl.* —n) rune; runic writing.

**Runkelrübe** ['ruŋkəlryːbə], *f.* (—, *pl.* —n) beetroot.

**Runzel** ['runtsəl], *f.* (—, *pl.* —n) wrinkle, pucker.

**Rüpel** ['ryːpəl], *m.* (—s, *pl.* —) bounder, lout.

**rupfen** ['rupfən], *v.a.* pluck; *einen —*, (*fig.*) fleece s.o.

**Rupie** ['ruːpjə], *f.* (—, *pl.* —n) rupee.

**ruppig** ['rupɪç], *adj.* unfriendly, rude; scruffy.

**Ruprecht** ['ruːprɛçt], *m. Knecht —*, Santa Claus.

**Rüsche** ['ryːʃə], *f.* (—, *pl.* —n) ruche.

**Ruß** [ruːs], *m.* (—es, *no pl.*) soot.

**Rüssel** ['rysəl], *m.* (—s, *pl.* —) snout; (*elephant*) trunk.

**Rußland** ['ruslant], *n.* Russia.

**rüsten** ['rystən], *v.a.* prepare, fit (out); equip; (*Mil.*) arm, mobilise.

**Rüster** ['rystər], *f.* (—, *pl.* —n) elm.

**rüstig** ['rystɪç], *adj.* vigorous, robust.

**Rüstung** ['rystuŋ], *f.* (—, *pl.* —en) armour; preparation; (*Mil.*) armament.

**Rüstzeug** ['rysttsɔyk], *n.* (—s, *no pl.*) equipment.
**Rute** ['ru:tə], *f.* (—, *pl.* —n) rod, twig; (*fox*) brush.
**Rutengänger** ['ru:təngɛŋər], *m.* (—s, *pl.* —) water-diviner.
**rutschen** ['rutʃən], *v.n.* (*aux.* sein) slip, slide, skid, slither.
**rütteln** ['rytəln], *v.a., v.n.* shake, jolt.

# S

**S** [ɛs], *n.* (—s, *pl.* —s) the letter S.
**Saal** [za:l], *m.* (—(e)s, *pl.* Säle) hall, large room.
**Saat** [za:t], *f.* (—, *pl.* —en) seed; sowing; standing corn.
**Sabbat** ['zabat], *m.* (—s, *pl.* —e) sabbath.
**sabbern** ['zabərn], *v.n.* (*sl.*) slaver, drivel.
**Säbel** ['zɛ:bəl], *m.* (—s, *pl.* —) sabre; *krummer* —, falchion, scimitar.
**säbeln** ['zɛ:bəln], *v.a.* sabre, hack at.
**sachdienlich** ['zaxdi:nlıç], *adj.* relevant, pertinent.
**Sache** ['zaxə], *f.* (—, *pl.* —n) thing, matter, affair; (*Law*) action, case; *die — ist (die) daß*, the fact is that; *das gehört nicht zur —*, that is beside the point; *bei der — sein*, pay attention to the matter in hand; *das ist meine —*, that is my business; *die — der Unterdrückten verteidigen*, take up the cause of the oppressed.
**Sachlage** ['zaxla:gə], *f.* (—, *no pl.*) state of affairs.
**sachlich** ['zaxlıç], *adj.* pertinent; objective.
**sächlich** ['zɛçlıç], *adj.* (*Gram.*) neuter.
**Sachse** ['zaksə], *m.* (—n, *pl.* —n) Saxon.
**Sachsen** ['zaksən], *n.* Saxony.
**sachte** ['zaxtə], *adj.* soft, slow, quiet, careful, gentle.
**Sachverhalt** ['zaxfɛrhalt], *m.* (—s, *no pl.*) facts (of a case), state of things, circumstances.
**sachverständig** ['zaxfɛrʃtɛndıç], *adj.* expert, competent, experienced.
**Sachwalter** ['zaxvaltər], *m.* (—s, *pl.* —) manager, counsel, attorney.
**Sack** [zak], *m.* (—(e)s, *pl.* ⁀e) sack, bag; *mit — und Pack*, (with) bag and baggage.
**Säckel** ['zɛkəl], *m.* (—s, *pl.* —) purse.
**Sackgasse** ['zakgasə], *f.* (—, *pl.* —n) cul-de-sac, blind alley; *einen in eine — treiben*, corner s.o.
**Sackpfeife** ['zakpfaıfə], *f.* (—, *pl.* —n) bagpipe.
**Sacktuch** ['zaktu:x], *n.* (—es, *pl.* ⁀er) sacking; (*dial.*) pocket-handkerchief.

**säen** ['zɛ:ən], *v.a.* sow.
**Saffian** ['zafja:n], *m.* (—s, *no pl.*) morocco-leather.
**Saft** [zaft], *m.* (—(e)s, *pl.* ⁀e) juice; (*tree*) sap; (*meat*) gravy; *ohne — und Kraft*, insipid; *im eigenen — schmoren*, stew in o.'s own juice.
**Sage** ['za:gə], *f.* (—, *pl.* —n) legend, fable, myth; *es geht die —*, it is rumoured.
**Säge** ['zɛ:gə], *f.* (—, *pl.* —n) saw.
**sagen** ['za:gən], *v.a.* say, tell; *einem etwas — lassen*, send word to s.o.; *es hat nichts zu —*, it does not matter; *was Du nicht sagst!* you don't say (so)!
**sägen** ['zɛ:gən], *v.a., v.n.* saw; (*fig.*) snore.
**sagenhaft** ['za:gənhaft], *adj.* legendary, mythical; (*fig.*) fabulous.
**Sahne** ['za:nə], *f.* (—, *no pl.*) cream.
**Saite** ['zaıtə], *f.* (—, *pl.* —n) string; *strengere —n aufziehen*, (*fig.*) take a stricter line.
**Sakko** ['zako], *m.* (—s, *pl.* —s) lounge jacket.
**Sakristei** [zakrı'staı], *f.* (—, *pl.* —en) vestry.
**Salat** [za'la:t], *m.* (—(e)s, *pl.* —e) salad; (*plant*) lettuce; (*sl.*) mess.
**salbadern** ['zalba:dərn], *v.n.* prate, talk nonsense.
**Salbe** ['zalbə], *f.* (—, *pl.* —n) ointment, salve.
**Salbei** ['zalbaı], *m.* (—s, *no pl.*) (*Bot.*) sage.
**salben** ['zalbən], *v.a.* anoint.
**salbungsvoll** ['zalbuŋsfɔl], *adj.* unctuous.
**Saldo** ['zaldo], *m.* (—s, *pl.* —s) balance.
**Saline** [za'li:nə], *f.* (—, *pl.* —n) salt-mine, salt-works.
**Salkante** ['za:lkantə], *f.* (—, *pl.* —n) selvedge, border.
**Salm** [zalm], *m.* (—s, *pl.* —e) (*Zool.*) salmon.
**Salmiakgeist** ['zalmjakgaıst], *m.* (—s, *no pl.*) ammonia.
**Salon** [za'lɔ̃], *m.* (—s, *pl.* —s) salon; saloon; drawing-room.
**salonfähig** [za'lɔ̃fɛ:ıç], *adj.* presentable, socially acceptable.
**salopp** [za'lɔp], *adj.* careless, slovenly, shabby, sloppy.
**Salpeter** [zal'pe:tər], *m.* (—s, *no pl.*) nitre, saltpetre.
**salutieren** [zalu'ti:rən], *v.a., v.n.* salute.
**Salve** ['zalvə], *f.* (—, *pl.* —n) volley, discharge, salute.
**Salz** [zalts], *n.* (—es, *pl.* —e) salt.
**Salzfaß** ['zaltsfas], *n.* (—sses, *pl.* ⁀sser) salt-cellar.
**Salzlake** ['zaltsla:kə], *f.* (—, *pl.* —n) brine.
**Salzsäure** ['zaltssɔyrə], *f.* (—, *no pl.*) hydrochloric acid.
**Sämann** ['zɛ:man], *m.* (—s, *pl.* ⁀ner) sower.
**Sambia** ['zambia], *n.* Zambia.

**Same(n)** ['za:mə(n)], *m.* (**—ns**, *pl.* **—n**) seed; sperm; spawn.

**Samenstaub** ['za:mənʃtaup], *m.* (**—s**, *no pl.*) pollen.

**Sämereien** [zɛ:mə'raɪən], *f. pl.* seeds, grain.

**sämisch** ['zɛ:mɪʃ], *adj.* chamois.

**Sammelband** ['zaməlbant], *m.* (**—es**, *pl.* ˝e) miscellany, anthology.

**sammeln** ['zaməln], *v.a.* collect, gather. — *v.r. sich* —, meet; collect o.'s thoughts, compose o.s.

**Sammler** ['zamlər], *m.* (**—s**, *pl.* —) collector; accumulator.

**Samstag** ['zamsta:k], *m.* (**—s**, *pl.* —e) Saturday.

**Samt** [zamt], *m.* (**—(e)s**, *pl.* —e) velvet.

**samt** [zamt], *adv.* together, all together; — *und sonders*, jointly and severally.— *prep.* (*Dat.*) together with.

**sämtlich** ['zɛmtlɪç], *adj.* each and every.

**Sand** [zant], *m.* (**—es**, *no pl.*) sand; *feiner* —, grit; *grober* —, gravel.

**Sandtorte** ['zanttɔrtə], *f.* (**—**, *pl.* **—n**) sponge-cake, madeira-cake.

**Sanduhr** ['zantu:r], *f.* (**—**, *pl.* **—en**) hourglass.

**sanft** [zanft], *adj.* soft, gentle.

**Sänfte** ['zɛnftə], *f.* (**—**, *pl.* **—n**) sedan-chair.

**Sang** [zaŋ], *m.* (**—es**, *pl.* **Gesänge**) song; *ohne* — *und Klang*, (*fig.*) unostentatiously, without fuss, without ceremony.

**sanieren** [za'ni:rən], *v.a.* cure; (*company*) reconstruct, put on a sound financial basis.

**sanitär** [zani'tɛ:r], *adj.* sanitary.

**Sanitäter** [zani'tɛ:tər], *m.* (**—s**, *pl.*—) medical orderly; ambulance man.

**Sankt** [zaŋkt], *indecl. adj.* Saint; (*abbr.*) St.

**sanktionieren** [zaŋktsjo'ni:rən], *v.a.* sanction.

**Sansibar** ['zanziba:r], *n.* Zanzibar.

**Sardelle** [zar'dɛlə], *f.* (**—**, *pl.* **—n**) (*Zool.*) anchovy.

**Sardinien** [zar'di:njən], *n.* Sardinia.

**Sarg** [zark], *m.* (**—es**, *pl.* ˝e) coffin.

**sarkastisch** [zar'kastɪʃ], *adj.* sarcastic.

**Satellit** [zatə'li:t], *m.* (**—en**, *pl.* **—en**) satellite.

**Satiriker** [za'ti:rɪkər], *m.* (**—s**, *pl.* —) satirist.

**satt** [zat], *adj.* sated, satiated, satisfied; (*colours*) deep, rich; *sich* — *essen*, eat o.'s fill; *einer Sache* — *sein*, be sick of s.th., have had enough of s.th.

**Sattel** ['zatəl], *m.* (**—s**, *pl.* ˝) saddle; *einen aus dem* — *heben*, (*fig.*) oust s.o.; *fest im* — *sitzen*, (*fig.*) be master of a situation; *in allen* ˝n *gerecht*, versatile.

**satteln** ['zatəln], *v.a.* saddle.

**Sattheit** ['zathaɪt], *f.* (**—**, *no pl.*) satiety.

**sättigen** ['zetɪgən], *v.a.* satisfy, sate, satiate; (*Chem.*) saturate.

**sattsam** ['zatza:m], *adv.* enough, sufficiently.

**saturieren** [zatu'ri:rən], *v.a.* (*Chem.*) saturate.

**Satz** [zats], *m.* (**—es**, *pl.* ˝e) sentence; proposition; thesis; (*Mus.*) movement; (*Typ.*) composition; (*dregs*) sediment; (*gambling*) stake; *mit einem* —, with one leap (*or* jump *or* bound).

**Satzbildung** ['zatsbɪlduŋ], *f.* (**—**, *pl.* **—en**) (*Gram.*) construction; (*Chem.*) sedimentation.

**Satzlehre** ['zatsle:rə], *f.* (**—**, *no pl.*) syntax.

**Satzung** ['zatsuŋ], *f.* (**—**, *pl.* **—en**) statute.

**Satzzeichen** ['zatstsaɪçən], *n.* (**—s**, *pl.* —) punctuation-mark.

**Sau** [zau], *f.* (**—**, *pl.* ˝e) sow; (*vulg.*) dirty person, slut.

**sauber** ['zaubər], *adj.* clean, neat, tidy.

**säubern** ['zɔybərn], *v.a.* clean, cleanse; (*fig.*) purge.

**Saubohne** ['zaubo:nə], *f.* (**—**, *pl.* **—n**) broad bean.

**Saudiarabien** ['zaudiara:bjən], *n.* Saudi Arabia.

**sauer** ['zauər], *adj.* sour, acid; (*fig.*) troublesome; morose.

**Sauerbrunnen** ['zauərbrunən], *m.* (**—s**, *pl.* —) mineral water.

**Sauerei** [zauə'raɪ], *f.* (**—**, *pl.* **—en**) (*sl.*) filthiness; mess.

**Sauerkraut** ['zauərkraut], *n.* (**—s**, *no pl.*) pickled cabbage.

**säuerlich** ['zɔyərlɪç], *adj.* acidulous.

**Sauerstoff** ['zauərʃtɔf], *m.* (**—(e)s**, *no pl.*) oxygen.

**Sauerteig** ['zauərtaɪk], *m.* (**—(e)s**, *pl.* —e) leaven.

**sauertöpfisch** ['zauərtœpfɪʃ], *adj.* morose, peevish.

**saufen** ['zaufən], *v.a., v.n. irr.* (*animals*) drink; (*humans*) drink to excess.

**Säufer** ['zɔyfər], *m.* (**—s**, *pl.* —) drunkard, drinker, alcoholic.

**saugen** ['zaugən], *v.a., v.n.* suck.

**säugen** ['zɔygən], *v.a.* suckle.

**Säugetier** ['zɔygəti:r], *n.* (**—s**, *pl.* —e) mammal.

**Saugheber** ['zaukhe:bər], *m.* (**—s**, *pl.* —) suction-pump; siphon.

**Säugling** ['zɔyklɪŋ], *m.* (**—s**, *pl.* —e) suckling, baby.

**Saugwarze** ['zaukvartsə], *f.* (**—**, *pl.* **—n**) nipple.

**Säule** ['zɔylə], *f.* (**—**, *pl.* **—n**) pillar, column.

**Säulenbündel** ['zɔylənbyndəl], *n.* (**—s**, *pl.* —) (*Archit.*) clustered column.

**Säulenfuß** ['zɔylənfu:s], *m.* (**—es**, *pl.* ˝e) (*Archit.*) base, plinth.

**Säulengang** ['zɔyləngaŋ], *m.* (**—s**, *pl.* ˝e) colonnade.

**Saum** [zaum], *m.* (**—(e)s**, *pl.* ˝e) seam, hem, border, edge; selvedge.

**saumäßig** ['zaumɛ:sɪç], *adj.* (*sl.*) beastly, filthy, piggish; enormous.

**säumen** (1) ['zɔymən], *v.a.* hem.

**säumen** (2) ['zɔymən], *v.n.* delay, tarry.

**säumig** ['zɔymɪç], *adj.* tardy, slow, dilatory.

**Saumpferd** ['zaumpfe:rt], *n.* (—s, *pl.* —e) pack-horse.
**saumselig** ['zaumze:lɪç], *adj.* tardy, dilatory.
**Säure** ['zɔyrə], *f.* (—, *pl.* —n) acid; (*Med.*) acidity.
**Saurier** ['zaurjər], *m.* (—s, *pl.* —) saurian.
**Saus** [zaus], *m.* (—es, *no pl.*) rush; revel, riot; *in — und Braus leben,* live a wild life, live riotously.
**säuseln** ['zɔyzəln], *v.n.* rustle, murmur.
**sausen** ['zauzən], *v.n.* bluster, blow, howl, whistle; (*coll.*) rush, dash.
**Saustall** ['zauʃtal], *m.* (—s, *pl.* ⁻e) pigsty.
**Schabe** ['ʃa:bə], *f.* (—, *pl.* —n) (*Ent.*) cockroach.
**schaben** ['ʃa:bən], *v.a.* scrape, shave, rub.
**Schabernack** ['ʃa:bərnak], *m.* (—s, *pl.* —e) practical joke, trick.
**schäbig** ['ʃɛ:bɪç], *adj.* shabby.
**Schablone** [ʃa'blo:nə], *f.* (—, *pl.* —n) model, mould, pattern, stencil; (*fig.*) routine.
**Schach** [ʃax], *n.* (—(e)s, *no pl.*) chess; — *bieten,* check; — *spielen,* play chess; *in — halten,* keep in check.
**Schacher** ['ʃaxər], *m.* (—s, *no pl.*) haggling, bargaining, barter.
**Schächer** ['ʃɛçər], *m.* (—s, *pl.* —) wretch, felon, robber.
**Schacht** [ʃaxt], *m.* (—(e)s, *pl.* ⁻e) shaft.
**Schachtel** ['ʃaxtəl], *f.* (—, *pl.* —n) box, (cardboard) box, (small) case.
**Schachtelhalm** ['ʃaxtəlhalm], *m.* (—s, *pl.* —e) (*grass*) horse-tail.
**Schächter** ['ʃɛçtər], *m.* (—s, *pl.* —) (kosher) butcher.
**schade** ['ʃa:də], *int.* a pity, a shame, unfortunate; *wie —,* what a pity; *sehr —,* a great pity.
**Schädel** ['ʃɛ:dəl], *m.* (—s, *pl.* —) skull.
**Schaden** ['ʃa:dən], *m.* (—s, *pl.* ⁻) damage, injury, detriment; *zu — kommen,* come to grief.
**schaden** ['ʃa:dən], *v.n.* do harm, do damage, do injury; *es schadet nichts,* it does not matter.
**Schadenersatz** ['ʃa:dənɛrzats], *m.* (—es, *no pl.*) indemnity, compensation, indemnification; (*money*) damages.
**Schadenfreude** ['ʃa:dənfrɔydə], *f.* (—, *no pl.*) malicious pleasure.
**Schadensforderung** ['ʃa:dənsfordəruŋ], *f.* (—, *pl.* —en) claim (for damages).
**schadhaft** ['ʃa:thaft], *adj.* defective, faulty.
**schädlich** ['ʃɛ:tlɪç], *adj.* injurious, noxious, pernicious, noisome.
**schadlos** ['ʃa:tlo:s], *adj.* indemnified; *einen — halten,* indemnify s.o., compensate s.o.; *sich an einem — halten,* recoup o.s. from s.o.
**Schadlosigkeit** ['ʃa:tlo:zɪçkaɪt], *f.* (—, *no pl.*) harmlessness.
**Schaf** [ʃa:f], *n.* (—(e)s, *pl.* —e) sheep.

**Schafblattern** ['ʃa:fblatərn], *f. pl.* (*Med.*) chicken-pox.
**Schafdarm** ['ʃa:fdarm], *m.* (—s, *pl.* ⁻e) sheep-gut.
**Schäfer** ['ʃɛ:fər], *m.* (—s, *pl.* —) shepherd.
**Schäferstündchen** ['ʃɛ:fərʃtyntçən], *n.* (—s, *pl.* —) tryst; rendezvous.
**schaffen** ['ʃafən], *v.a., v.n. irr.* make, produce, create. — *v.a. reg.* provide; manage; *aus dem Wege —,* remove. — *v.n. reg.* work; *einem zu — machen,* give s.o. trouble.
**Schaffner** ['ʃafnər], *m.* (—s, *pl.* —) (*Railw. etc.*) guard, conductor.
**Schafgarbe** ['ʃa:fgarbə], *f.* (—, *pl.* —n) (*Bot.*) common yarrow.
**Schafhürde** ['ʃa:fhyrdə], *f.* (—, *pl.* —n) sheep-fold.
**Schafott** [ʃa'fɔt], *n.* (—(e)s, *pl.* —e) scaffold.
**Schafschur** ['ʃa:fʃu:r], *f.* (—, *pl.* —en) sheep-shearing.
**Schaft** [ʃaft], *m.* (—(e)s, *pl.* ⁻e) shaft; (*gun*) stock.
**Schafwolle** ['ʃa:fvɔlə], *f.* (—, *no pl.*) sheep's wool, fleece.
**Schakal** [ʃa'ka:l], *m.* (—s, *pl.* —e) (*Zool.*) jackal.
**Schäkerei** [ʃɛ:kə'raɪ], *f.* (—, *pl.* —en) playfulness, teasing, dalliance, flirtation.
**Schal** [ʃa:l], *m.* (—s, *pl.* —e) scarf, shawl.
**schal** [ʃa:l], *adj.* stale, flat, insipid.
**Schale** ['ʃa:lə], *f.* (—, *pl.* —n) (*nut, egg*) shell; (*fruit*) peel, rind; dish, bowl; (*Austr.*) cup; (*fig.*) outside.
**schälen** ['ʃɛ:lən], *v.a.* shell; peel.
**Schalk** [ʃalk], *m.* (—(e)s, *pl.* —e) knave, rogue; wag, joker.
**Schall** [ʃal], *m.* (—(e)s, *no pl.*) sound.
**Schallbecken** ['ʃalbɛkən], *n.* (—s, *pl.* —) cymbal.
**Schallehre** ['ʃalle:rə], *f.* (—, *no pl.*) acoustics.
**schallen** ['ʃalən], *v.n.* sound, reverberate.
**Schalmei** [ʃal'maɪ], *f.* (—, *pl.* —en) (*Poet., Mus.*) shawm.
**Schallplatte** ['ʃalplatə], *f.* (—, *pl.* —n) (gramophone) record.
**schalten** ['ʃaltən], *v.n.* rule; switch; (*Motor.*) change gear; — *und walten,* manage.
**Schalter** ['ʃaltər], *m.* (—s, *pl.* —) (*Elec.*) switch; booking-office; counter.
**Schalthebel** ['ʃalthe:bəl], *m.* (—s, *pl.* —) (*Motor.*) gear lever.
**Schaltier** ['ʃa:lti:r], *n.* (—s, *pl.* —e) (*Zool.*) crustacean.
**Schaltjahr** ['ʃaltja:r], *n.* (—s, *pl.* —e) leap year.
**Schalttafel** ['ʃaltta:fəl], *f.* (—, *pl.* —n) switch-board.
**Scham** [ʃa:m], *f.* (—, *no pl.*) shame, modesty; private parts.
**schämen** ['ʃɛ:mən], *v.r. sich —,* be ashamed (of).
**schamlos** ['ʃa:mlo:s], *adj.* shameless.
**schamrot** ['ʃa:mro:t], *adj.* blushing; — *werden,* blush.

# schandbar

**schandbar** [ˈʃantbaːr], *adj.* ignominious, infamous.
**Schande** [ˈʃandə], *f.* (—, *no pl.*) shame, disgrace; dishonour, ignominy.
**schänden** [ˈʃɛndən], *v.a.* dishonour, disgrace; violate, ravish.
**Schandfleck** [ˈʃantflɛk], *m.* (—s, *pl.* —e) stain, blemish.
**schändlich** [ˈʃɛntlɪç], *adj.* shameful, disgraceful, infamous.
**Schändung** [ˈʃɛnduŋ], *f.* (—, *pl.* —en) violation.
**Schank** [ʃaŋk], *m.* (—s, *no pl.*) sale of liquor.
**Schanzarbeiter** [ˈʃantsarbaɪtər], *m.* (—s, *pl.* —) sapper.
**Schanze** [ˈʃantsə], *f.* (—, *pl.* —n) redoubt, bulwark; *in die — schlagen*, risk, venture.
**Schar** [ʃaːr], *f.* (—, *pl.* —en) troop, band; host.
**Scharade** [ʃaˈraːdə], *f.* (—, *pl.* —n) charade.
**scharen** [ˈʃaːrən], *v.r. sich — um*, assemble, congregate, gather round.
**Schären** [ˈʃɛːrən], *f. pl.* reefs, skerries.
**scharf** [ʃarf], *adj.* sharp, keen, acute, acrid, pungent; piercing; (*fig.*) severe, rigorous.
**Schärfe** [ˈʃɛrfə], *f.* (—, *no pl.*) sharpness, keenness, acuteness; pungency, acridness; severity, rigour.
**schärfen** [ˈʃɛrfən], *v.a.* sharpen, whet; (*fig.*) strengthen, intensify.
**Scharfrichter** [ˈʃarfrɪçtər], *m.* (—s, *pl.* —) executioner.
**scharfsichtig** [ˈʃarfzɪçtɪç], *adj.* sharp-eyed, (*fig.*) penetrating, astute.
**scharfsinnig** [ˈʃarfzɪnɪç], *adj.* clear-sighted, sagacious, ingenious.
**Scharlach** [ˈʃarlax], *m.* (—s, *no pl.*) scarlet; (*Med.*) scarlet-fever.
**Scharlatan** [ˈʃarlataːn], *m.* (—s, *pl.* —e) charlatan, humbug.
**scharmant** [ʃarˈmant], *adj.* charming.
**Scharmützel** [ʃarˈmytsəl], *n.* (—s, *pl.* —) skirmish.
**Scharnier** [ʃarˈniːr], *n.* (—s, *pl.* —e) hinge, joint.
**Schärpe** [ˈʃɛrpə], *f.* (—, *pl.* —n) sash.
**Scharpie** [ʃarˈpiː], *f.* (—, *no pl.*) lint.
**scharren** [ˈʃarən], *v.a., v.n.* scrape, rake.
**Scharte** [ˈʃartə], *f.* (—, *pl.* —n) notch, crack; *eine — auswetzen*, repair a mistake, make up for s.th.
**Scharteke** [ʃarˈteːkə], *f.* (—, *pl.* —n) worthless book, trash; *eine alte —*, an old fuddy-duddy, frump.
**scharwenzeln** [ʃarˈvɛntsəln], *v.n.* dance attendance, be obsequious.
**Schatten** [ˈʃatən], *m.* (—s, *pl.* —) shade, shadow.
**Schattenbild** [ˈʃatənbɪlt], *n.* (—s, *pl.* —er) silhouette.
**Schattenriß** [ˈʃatənrɪs], *m.* (—sses, *pl.* —sse) silhouette.
**schattieren** [ʃaˈtiːrən], *v.a.* shade (drawing).
**schattig** [ˈʃatɪç], *adj.* shady.

**Schatulle** [ʃaˈtulə], *f.* (—, *pl.* —n) cashbox; privy purse.
**Schatz** [ʃats], *m.* (—es, *pl.* ˸e) treasure; (*fig.*) sweetheart, darling.
**Schatzamt** [ˈʃatsamt], *n.* (—s, *pl.* ˸er) Treasury, Exchequer.
**schätzbar** [ˈʃɛtsbaːr], *adj.* estimable.
**Schätzchen** [ˈʃɛtsçən], *n.* (—s, *pl.* —) (*coll.*) sweetheart.
**schätzen** [ˈʃɛtsən], *v.a.* value, estimate; esteem; reckon at.
**Schatzkammer** [ˈʃatskamər], *f.* (—, *pl.* —n) treasury.
**Schatzmeister** [ˈʃatsmaɪstər], *m.* (—s, *pl.* —) treasurer.
**Schätzung** [ˈʃɛtsuŋ], *f.* (—, *pl.* —en) valuation, estimate; (*fig.*) esteem.
**Schau** [ʃau], *f.* (—, *pl.* —en) show, view, spectacle; *zur — stellen*, display; parade.
**Schauder** [ˈʃaudər], *m.* (—s, *pl.* —) shudder, shiver; horror.
**schaudern** [ˈʃaudərn], *v.n.* shudder, shiver.
**schauen** [ˈʃauən], *v.a.* see, view. — *v.n.* look, gaze (*auf*, at), *schau mal*, look here.
**Schauer** [ˈʃauər], *m.* (—s, *pl.* —) shiver, paroxysm; (*fig.*) thrill, awe; (*rain*) shower.
**schauern** [ˈʃauərn], *v.n.* shudder, shiver; (*rain*) shower.
**Schauerroman** [ˈʃauərromaːn], *m.* (—s, *pl.* —e) (*novel*) penny dreadful, thriller.
**Schaufel** [ˈʃaufəl], *f.* (—, *pl.* —n) shovel.
**Schaufenster** [ˈʃaufɛnstər], *n.* (—s, *pl.* —) shop-window.
**Schaukel** [ˈʃaukəl], *f.* (—, *pl.* —n) swing.
**schaulustig** [ˈʃaulustɪç], *adj.* curious.
**Schaum** [ʃaum], *m.* (—es, *pl.* ˸e) foam, froth; bubbles; scum; *— schlagen*, whip cream.
**schäumen** [ˈʃɔymən], *v.n.* foam, froth, sparkle.
**Schauplatz** [ˈʃauplats], *m.* (—es, *pl.* ˸e) scene, stage.
**schaurig** [ˈʃaurɪç], *adj.* grisly, horrid, horrible.
**Schauspiel** [ˈʃauʃpiːl], *n.* (—s, *pl.* —e) spectacle; drama, play.
**Schauspieler** [ˈʃauʃpiːlər], *m.* (—s, *pl.* —) actor, player.
**Schaustellung** [ˈʃauʃteluŋ], *f.* (—, *pl.* —en) exhibition.
**Scheck** [ʃɛk], *m.* (—s, *pl.* —s) cheque.
**scheckig** [ˈʃɛkɪç], *adj.* piebald, spotted, dappled.
**scheel** [ʃeːl], *adj.* squint-eyed; envious; *einen — ansehen*, look askance at s.o.
**Scheffel** [ˈʃɛfəl], *m.* (—s, *pl.* —) bushel.
**scheffeln** [ˈʃɛfəln], *v.a.* rake in; accumulate.
**Scheibe** [ˈʃaɪbə], *f.* (—, *pl.* —n) disc; (*window*) pane; (*shooting*) target; (*bread*) slice.
**Scheibenhonig** [ˈʃaɪbənhoːnɪç], *m.* (—s, *no pl.*) honey in the comb.

**Scheibenschießen** ['ʃaɪbənʃiːsən], n. (—s, no pl.) target-practice.

**Scheich** [ʃaɪç], m. (—s, pl. —e) sheikh.

**Scheide** ['ʃaɪdə], f. (—, pl. —n) sheath, scabbard; (Anat.) vagina.

**Scheidemünze** ['ʃaɪdəmyntsə], f. (—, pl. —n) small coin, change.

**scheiden** ['ʃaɪdən], v.a. irr. divide; separate, divorce; sich — lassen, obtain a divorce. — v.n. (aux. sein) part, depart; aus dem Amte —, resign office.

**Scheidewand** ['ʃaɪdəvant], f. (—, pl. ̈e) partition-wall.

**Scheideweg** ['ʃaɪdəveːk], m. (—s, pl. —e) cross-roads; am — stehen, be at the parting of the ways.

**Scheidung** ['ʃaɪduŋ], f. (—, pl. —en) divorce.

**Schein** [ʃaɪn], m. (—(e)s, no pl.) shine, sheen, lustre, splendour; semblance, pretence; den — wahren, keep up appearances; der — trügt, appearances are deceptive; (in compounds) mock, would-be, apparent; (pl. —e) (piece of) paper, chit, note; (fig.) attestation, certificate.

**scheinbar** ['ʃaɪnbaːr], adj. apparent; ostensible, seeming. — adv. seemingly.

**scheinen** ['ʃaɪnən], v.n. irr. shine, sparkle; seem, appear.

**scheinheilig** ['ʃaɪnhaɪlɪç], adj. hypocritical.

**Scheinheiligkeit** ['ʃaɪnhaɪlɪçkaɪt], f. (—, no pl.) hypocrisy.

**scheintot** ['ʃaɪntoːt], adj. in a cataleptic trance; seemingly dead.

**Scheinwerfer** ['ʃaɪnvɛrfər], m. (—s, pl. —) headlight; searchlight; floodlight.

**Scheit** [ʃaɪt], n. (—(e)s, pl. —e) piece of wood, billet.

**Scheitel** ['ʃaɪtəl], m. (—s, pl. —) (hair) parting; top, vertex.

**Scheiterhaufen** ['ʃaɪtərhaufən], m. (—s, pl. —) stake; funeral pyre.

**scheitern** ['ʃaɪtərn], v.n. (aux. sein) (ship) founder, be wrecked; (fig.) miscarry, fail.

**Schelle** ['ʃɛlə], f. (—, pl. —n) bell.

**Schellen** ['ʃɛlən], f. pl. (Cards) diamonds.

**schellen** ['ʃɛlən], v.n. ring the bell.

**Schellfisch** ['ʃɛlfɪʃ], m. (—es, pl. —e) (Zool.) haddock.

**Schelm** [ʃɛlm], m. (—(e)s, pl. —e) rogue, knave, villain.

**schelten** ['ʃɛltən], v.a. irr. scold, chide, rebuke, reprimand.

**Schema** ['ʃeːma], n. (—s, pl. —s) schedule, model, plan, scheme.

**Schemel** ['ʃeːməl], m. (—s, pl. —) foot-stool.

**Schenk** [ʃɛŋk], m. (—en, pl. —en) cupbearer; publican.

**Schenke** ['ʃɛŋkə], f. (—, pl. —n) alehouse, tavern, pub.

**Schenkel** ['ʃɛŋkəl], m. (—s, pl. —) thigh; (Geom.) side of triangle.

**schenken** ['ʃɛŋkən], v.a. present s.o. with, donate, give.

**Schenkstube** ['ʃɛŋkʃtuːbə], f. (—, pl. —n) tap-room.

**Scherbe** ['ʃɛrbə], f. (—, pl. —n) potsherd; fragment of glass etc.

**Schere** ['ʃeːrə], f. (—, pl. —n) scissors; (garden) shears; (crab) claw.

**scheren** ['ʃeːrən], v.a. shave; clip, shear; bother, concern. — v.r. sich —, clear off; scher dich zum Teufel! go to blazes!

**Schererereien** [ʃeːrəˈraɪən], f. pl. vexation, bother, trouble.

**Scherflein** ['ʃɛrflaɪn], n. (—s, pl. —) mite; sein — beitragen, contribute o.'s share.

**Scherge** ['ʃɛrgə], m. (—n, pl. —n) (obs.) beadle.

**Scherz** [ʃɛrts], m. (—es, pl. —e) jest, joke; — beiseite, joking apart.

**scheu** [ʃɔy], adj. shy, bashful, timid; skittish.

**scheuchen** ['ʃɔyçən], v.a. scare away.

**scheuen** ['ʃɔyən], v.a. shun, avoid, fight shy of, fear. — v.n. take fright.

**Scheuer** ['ʃɔyər], f. (—, pl. —n) barn.

**scheuern** ['ʃɔyərn], v.a. scour, scrub.

**Scheuklappe** ['ʃɔyklapə], f. (—, pl. —n) blinker.

**Scheune** ['ʃɔynə], f. (—, pl. —n) barn.

**Scheusal** ['ʃɔyzaːl], n. (—s, pl. —e) monster.

**scheußlich** ['ʃɔyslɪç], adj. frightful, dreadful, abominable, hideous.

**Schicht** [ʃɪçt], f. (—, pl. —en) layer, stratum, seam; (society) class; (work) shift.

**schick** [ʃɪk], adj. stylish, chic.

**schicken** ['ʃɪkən], v.a. send, despatch, convey. — v.r. sich —, be proper; sich in etwas —, put up with s.th., resign o.s. to s.th.

**schicklich** ['ʃɪklɪç], adj. proper, becoming, suitable, seemly.

**Schicksal** ['ʃɪkzaːl], n. (—s, pl. —e) fate, destiny, lot.

**Schickung** ['ʃɪkuŋ], f. (—, pl. —en) Divine Will, Providence.

**schieben** ['ʃiːbən], v.a. irr. shove, push; die Schuld auf einen —, put the blame on s.o.

**Schieber** ['ʃiːbər], m. (—s, pl. —) bolt, slide; (fig.) profiteer, spiv.

**Schiedsgericht** ['ʃiːtsgəriçt], n. (—es, pl. —e) arbitration tribunal.

**Schiedsrichter** ['ʃiːtsrɪçtər], m. (—s, pl. —) referee, umpire, arbiter.

**schief** [ʃiːf], adj. slanting, oblique, bent, crooked; wry; —e Ebene, inclined plane; — gehen, go wrong.

**Schiefe** ['ʃiːfə], f. (—, no pl.) obliquity.

**Schiefer** ['ʃiːfər], m. (—s, no pl.) slate.

**schiefrig** ['ʃiːfrɪç], adj. slaty.

**schielen** ['ʃiːlən], v.n. squint, be cross-eyed.

**Schienbein** ['ʃiːnbaɪn], n. (—s, pl. —e) shin-bone, shin.

# Schiene

**Schiene** ['ʃiːnə], *f.* (—, *pl.* —n) rail; (*Med.*) splint.
**schier** [ʃiːr], *adj.* (*rare*) sheer, pure. — *adv.* almost, very nearly.
**Schierling** ['ʃiːrlɪŋ], *m.* (—s, *pl.* —e) (*Bot.*) hemlock.
**schießen** ['ʃiːsən], *v.a., v.n.* irr. shoot, fire, discharge; (*fig.*) rush; *etwas — lassen,* let go of s.th.; *die Zügel — lassen,* loosen o.'s hold on the reins; *ein Kabel — lassen,* pay out a cable; *das ist zum —,* that's very funny.
**Schiff** [ʃɪf], *n.* (—(e)s, *pl.* —e) ship, vessel, boat; (*church*) nave.
**schiffbar** ['ʃɪfbaːr], *adj.* navigable.
**Schiffbruch** ['ʃɪfbrux], *m.* (—s, *pl* ˙e) shipwreck.
**Schiffbrücke** ['ʃɪfbrykə], *f.* (—, *pl.* —n) pontoon-bridge.
**schiffen** ['ʃɪfən], *v.n.* sail; navigate.
**Schiffsboden** ['ʃɪfsboːdən], *m.* (—s, *pl.* ˙) (ship's) hold.
**Schiffsmaat** ['ʃɪfsmaːt], *m.* (—s, *pl.* —e) shipmate.
**Schiffsrumpf** ['ʃɪfsrumpf], *m.* (—es, *pl.* ˙e) hull.
**Schiffsschnabel** ['ʃɪfsʃnaːbəl], *m.* (—s, *pl.* ˙) prow, bows.
**Schiffsvorderteil** ['ʃɪfsfɔrdərtaɪl], *n.* (—s, *pl.* —e) forecastle, prow.
**Schiffszwieback** ['ʃɪfstsviːbak], *m.* (—s, *no pl.*) ship's biscuit.
**Schikane** [ʃiˈkaːnə], *f.* (—, *pl.* —n) chicanery.
**Schild** (1) [ʃɪlt], *m.* (—(e)s, *pl.* —e) shield, buckler, escutcheon; *etwas im — führen,* have designs on s.th., plan s.th.
**Schild** (2) [ʃɪlt], *n.* (—s, *pl.* —er) signboard, plate.
**Schilderhaus** ['ʃɪldərhaus], *n.* (—es, *pl.* ˙er) sentry-box.
**Schildermaler** ['ʃɪldərmaːlər], *m.* (—s, *pl.* —) sign-painter.
**schildern** ['ʃɪldərn], *v.a.* describe, depict.
**Schildknappe** ['ʃɪltknapə], *m.* (—n, *pl.* —n) shield-bearer, squire.
**Schildkrot** ['ʃɪltkroːt], *n.* (—s, *no pl.*) tortoise-shell.
**Schildkröte** ['ʃɪltkrøːtə], *f.* (—, *pl.* —n) (*Zool.*) turtle, tortoise.
**Schildpatt** ['ʃɪltpat], *n.* (—s, *no pl.*) tortoise-shell.
**Schildwache** ['ʃɪltvaxə], *f.* (—, *pl.* —n) sentinel, sentry; — *stehen,* be on sentry duty, stand guard.
**Schilf(rohr)** ['ʃɪlf(roːr)], *n.* (—(e)s, *no pl.*) (*Bot.*) reed, rush, sedge.
**schillern** ['ʃɪlərn], *v.n.* opalesce, glitter, change colour, be iridescent.
**Schilling** ['ʃɪlɪŋ], *m.* (—s, *pl.* —e) Austrian coin; shilling.
**Schimmel** (1) ['ʃɪməl], *m.* (—s, *pl.* —) white horse.
**Schimmel** (2) ['ʃɪməl], *m.* (—s, *no pl.*) mould, mustiness.
**schimmeln** ['ʃɪməln], *v.n.* (*aux.* sein) go mouldy, moulder.

**Schimmer** ['ʃɪmər], *m.* (—s, *pl.* —) glitter, gleam; *ich habe keinen —,* I haven't a clue.
**schimmlig** ['ʃɪmlɪç], *adj.* mouldy, musty, mildewed.
**Schimpanse** [ʃɪmˈpanzə], *m.* (—n, *pl.* —n) (*Zool.*) chimpanzee.
**Schimpf** [ʃɪmpf], *m.* (—es, *no pl.*) abuse, affront, insult; *mit — und Schande,* in disgrace.
**schimpfen** ['ʃɪmpfən], *v.n.* curse, swear; — *auf,* (*fig.*) run (s.o.) down. — *v.a.* insult (s.o.), call (s.o.) names; scold.
**Schindel** ['ʃɪndəl], *f.* (—, *pl.* —n) shingle.
**schinden** ['ʃɪndən], *v.a.* irr. flay; (*fig.*) grind, oppress, sweat. — *v.r. sich —,* slave, drudge.
**Schindluder** ['ʃɪntluːdər], *n.* (—s, *pl.* —) worn-out animal; *mit einem — treiben,* exploit s.o.
**Schinken** ['ʃɪŋkən], *m.* (—s, *pl.* —) ham.
**Schinkenspeck** ['ʃɪŋkənʃpɛk], *m.* (—s, *no pl.*) bacon.
**Schippe** ['ʃɪpə], *f.* (—, *pl.* —n) shovel, spade.
**Schirm** [ʃɪrm], *m.* (—(e)s, *pl.* —e) screen; umbrella; parasol, sunshade; lampshade; (*fig.*) shield, shelter, cover.
**schirmen** ['ʃɪrmən], *v.a.* protect (from), shelter.
**Schirmherr** ['ʃɪrmhɛr], *m.* (—n, *pl.* —en) protector, patron.
**Schlacht** [ʃlaxt], *f.* (—, *pl.* —en) battle; fight; *eine — liefern,* give battle; *die — gewinnen,* carry the day, win the battle.
**Schlachtbank** ['ʃlaxtbaŋk], *f.* (—, *pl.* ˙e) shambles; *zur — führen,* lead to the slaughter.
**schlachten** ['ʃlaxtən], *v.a.* kill, butcher, slaughter.
**Schlachtenbummler** ['ʃlaxtənbumlər], *m.* (—s, *pl.* —) camp follower.
**Schlachtfeld** ['ʃlaxtfɛlt], *n.* (—s, *pl.* —er) battlefield.
**Schlachtruf** ['ʃlaxtruːf], *m.* (—s, *pl.* —e) battle-cry.
**Schlacke** ['ʃlakə], *f.* (—, *pl.* —n) slag, clinker, dross.
**Schlackwurst** ['ʃlakvurst], *f.* (—, *pl.* ˙e) (*North German*) sausage.
**Schlaf** [ʃlaːf], *m.* (—(e)s, *no pl.*) sleep; slumber, rest; *in tiefem —,* fast asleep; *in den — wiegen,* rock to sleep.
**Schläfchen** ['ʃlɛːfçən], *n.* (—s, *pl.* —) nap; *ein — machen,* have forty winks.
**Schläfe** ['ʃlɛːfə], *f.* (—, *pl.* —n) temple.
**schlafen** ['ʃlaːfən], *v.n.* irr. sleep; *schlaf wohl,* sleep well; — *gehen,* go to bed.
**schlaff** [ʃlaf], *adj.* slack, loose, lax, flabby; weak; remiss.
**schlaflos** ['ʃlaːfloːs], *adj.* sleepless.
**Schlafmittel** ['ʃlaːfmɪtəl], *n.* (—s, *pl.* —) soporific, sleeping tablet, sleeping draught.
**schläfrig** ['ʃlɛːfrɪç], *adj.* drowsy, sleepy.

**Schlafrock** ['ʃla:frɔk], *m.* (—s, *pl.* ⸚e) dressing-gown; *Apfel im* —, apple fritters.

**schlafwandeln** ['ʃla:fvandəln], *v.n.* (*aux.* sein) walk in o.'s sleep, sleep-walk.

**Schlag** [ʃla:k], *m.* (—(e)s, *pl.* ⸚e) blow, stroke; beat; (*Elec.*) shock; *ein Mann von gutem* —, a good type of man; *vom — gerührt*, struck by apoplexy; — *fünf*, at five o'clock sharp.

**Schlagader** ['ʃla:ka:dər], *f.* (—, *pl.* —n) artery.

**Schlaganfall** ['ʃla:kanfal], *m.* (—s, *pl.* ⸚e) stroke, apoplexy.

**Schlagballspiel** ['ʃla:kbalʃpi:l], *n.* (—s, *pl.* —e) rounders.

**Schlagbaum** ['ʃla:kbaum], *m.* (—s, *pl.* ⸚e) turnpike.

**schlagen** ['ʃla:gən], *v.a. irr.* beat, strike, hit; (*tree*) fell; (*money*) coin; *Alarm* —, sound the alarm; *ans Kreuz* —, crucify; *ein Kreuz* —, make the sign of the cross. — *v.n.* (*clock*) strike; (*heart*) beat; (*birds*) warble; *aus der Art* —, degenerate. — *v.r. sich* —, fight; *sich auf Säbel* —, fight with sabres; *sich an die Brust* —, beat o.'s breast.

**Schlager** ['ʃla:gər], *m.* (—s, *pl.* —) hit, pop song; (*fig.*) success.

**Schläger** ['ʃle:gər], *m.* (—s, *pl.* —) rapier; bat; (*tennis-*)racket; (*golf-*)club.

**Schlägerei** [ʃle:gə'raɪ], *f.* (—, *pl.* —en) fray, scuffle.

**schlagfertig** ['ʃla:kfertɪç], *adj.* quick-witted.

**Schlagkraft** ['ʃla:kkraft], *f.* (—, *no pl.*) striking power.

**Schlaglicht** ['ʃla:klɪçt], *n.* (—s, *pl.* —er) strong direct light.

**Schlagsahne** ['ʃla:kza:nə], *f.* (—, *no pl.*) double cream, raw cream; whipped cream.

**Schlagschatten** ['ʃla:kʃatən], *m.* (—s, *pl.* —) deep shadow.

**Schlagseite** ['ʃla:kzaɪtə], *f.* (—, *no pl.*) — *bekommen*, (*Naut.*) list.

**Schlagwort** ['ʃla:kvɔrt], *n.* (—s, *pl.* ⸚er) catchword, slogan; trite saying.

**Schlagzeile** ['ʃla:ktsaɪlə], *f.* (—, *pl.* —n) headline.

**Schlamm** [ʃlam], *m.* (—(e)s, *no pl.*) mud, mire.

**Schlampe** ['ʃlampə], *f.* (—, *pl.* —n) slut.

**Schlange** ['ʃlaŋə], *f.* (—, *pl.* —n) snake, serpent; (*fig.*) queue.

**schlängeln** ['ʃleŋəln], *v.r. sich* —, wind, meander.

**schlangenartig** ['ʃlaŋəna:rtɪç], *adj.* snaky, serpentine.

**schlank** [ʃlaŋk], *adj.* slim, slender.

**schlapp** [ʃlap], *adj.* limp, tired, weak, slack; — *machen*, break down, collapse.

**Schlappe** ['ʃlapə], *f.* (—, *pl.* —n) reverse, defeat; *eine* — *erleiden*, suffer a set-back.

**Schlappschwanz** ['ʃlapʃvants], *m.* (—es, *pl.* ⸚e) weakling; milksop.

**Schlaraffenland** [ʃla'rafənlant], *n.* (—(e)s, *pl.* ⸚er) land of milk and honey.

**schlau** [ʃlau], *adj.* cunning, crafty, sly, shrewd.

**Schlauch** [ʃlaux], *m.* (—(e)s, *pl.* ⸚e) hose; tube.

**Schlaukopf** ['ʃlaukɔpf], *m.* (—(e)s, *pl.* ⸚e) slyboots; (*Am.*) wiseacre.

**schlecht** [ʃlɛçt], *adj.* bad, evil, wicked; poor; *mir ist* —, I feel ill; —*e Zeiten*, hard times; —*es Geld*, base money.

**schlechterdings** ['ʃlɛçtərdɪŋs], *adv.* simply, positively, absolutely.

**schlechthin** ['ʃlɛçthɪn], *adv.* simply, plainly.

**Schlechtigkeit** ['ʃlɛçtɪçkaɪt], *f.* (—, *pl.* —en) wickedness, baseness.

**Schlegel** ['ʃle:gəl], *m.* (—s, *pl.* —) mallet; drumstick; (*bell*) clapper.

**Schlehdorn** ['ʃle:dɔrn], *m.* (—s, *pl.* —e) blackthorn, sloe-tree.

**schleichen** ['ʃlaɪçən], *v.n. irr.* (*aux.* sein) sneak, prowl, slink; —*de Krankheit*, lingering illness.

**Schleichhandel** ['ʃlaɪçhandəl], *m.* (—s, *no pl.*) smuggling, black marketeering.

**Schleie** ['ʃlaɪə], *f.* (—, *pl.* —n) tench.

**Schleier** ['ʃlaɪər], *m.* (—s, *pl.* —) veil.

**Schleife** ['ʃlaɪfə], *f.* (—, *pl.* —n) bow, loop, noose.

**schleifen** ['ʃlaɪfən], *v.a. irr.* drag along, trail; grind, polish, sharpen, whet, hone; cut.

**Schleim** [ʃlaɪm], *m.* (—(e)s, *no pl.*) slime, mucus, phlegm.

**Schleimhaut** ['ʃlaɪmhaut], *f.* (—, *pl.* ⸚e) mucous membrane.

**Schleimsuppe** ['ʃlaɪmzupə], *f.* (—, *pl.* —n) gruel.

**schleißen** ['ʃlaɪsən], *v.a. irr.* split, slit; (*feathers*) strip.

**schlemmen** ['ʃlemən], *v.n.* carouse, gormandise.

**schlendern** ['ʃlendərn], *v.n.* (*aux.* sein) saunter along, stroll.

**Schlendrian** ['ʃlendria:n], *m.* (—s, *no pl.*) old jog-trot, routine.

**schlenkern** ['ʃleŋkərn], *v.a.* dangle, swing.

**Schleppdampfer** ['ʃlepdampfər], *m.* (—s, *pl.* —) steam-tug, tug-boat, tow-boat.

**Schleppe** ['ʃlepə], *f.* (—, *pl.* —n) train (of a dress).

**schleppen** ['ʃlepən], *v.a.* carry (s.th. heavy), drag, tow.

**Schleppenträger** ['ʃlepəntre:gər], *m.* (—s, *pl.* —) train-bearer.

**Schleppnetz** ['ʃlepnets], *n.* (—es, *pl.* —e) dragnet.

**Schlesien** ['ʃle:zjən], *n.* Silesia.

**Schleuder** ['ʃlɔydər], *f.* (—, *pl.* —n) sling; catapult.

**schleudern** ['ʃlɔydərn], *v.a.* sling, throw, fling away. — *v.n.* (*Motor.*) skid; (*Comm.*) sell cheaply, under-sell.

189

# schleunigst

**schleunigst** [ˈʃlɔynɪçst], *adv.* very quickly, with the utmost expedition, promptly.

**Schleuse** [ˈʃlɔyzə], *f.* (—, *pl.* —n) sluice, flood-gate, lock.

**Schlich** [ʃlɪç], *m.* (—es, *pl.* —e) trick, dodge; *einem hinter seine —e kommen*, be up to s.o.'s tricks.

**schlicht** [ʃlɪçt], *adj.* plain, simple, homely; *—er Abschied*, curt dismissal.

**schlichten** [ˈʃlɪçtən], *v.a.* level; (*argument*) settle; adjust, compose.

**Schlichtheit** [ˈʃlɪçthaıt], *f.* (—, *no pl.*) plainness, simplicity, homeliness.

**schließen** [ˈʃliːsən], *v.a. irr.* shut, close; contract; *etwas — aus*, conclude s.th. from; (*meeting*) close; *Frieden —*, make peace; *einen in die Arme —*, embrace s.o.; *etwas in sich —*, imply, entail.

**Schließer** [ˈʃliːsər], *m.* (—s, *pl.* —) doorkeeper; (*prison*) jailer, turnkey.

**schließlich** [ˈʃliːslɪç], *adv.* lastly, finally, in conclusion.

**Schliff** [ʃlɪf], *m.* (—(e)s, *no pl.*) polish, refinement.

**schlimm** [ʃlɪm], *adj.* bad, evil, ill; sad; serious, sore; disagreeable; naughty; *um so —er*, so much the worse, worse luck.

**Schlinge** [ˈʃlɪŋə], *f.* (—, *pl.* —n) loop, knot; noose, snare.

**Schlingel** [ˈʃlɪŋəl], *m.* (—s, *pl.* —) little rascal.

**schlingen** [ˈʃlɪŋən], *v.a. irr.* sling, wind; swallow, devour.

**Schlips** [ʃlɪps], *m.* (—es, *pl.* —e) (neck-)tie, cravat.

**Schlitten** [ˈʃlɪtən], *m.* (—s, *pl.* —) sledge, sled, sleigh.

**Schlittschuh** [ˈʃlɪtʃuː], *m.* (—s, *pl.* —e) skate; *— laufen*, skate.

**Schlitz** [ʃlɪts], *m.* (—es, *pl.* —e) slit.

**schlohweiß** [ˈʃloːvaıs], *adj.* white as sloe-blossom, snow-white.

**Schloß** [ʃlɔs], *n.* (—sses, *pl.* ⁔sser) (*door*) lock, padlock; (*gun*) lock; palace, castle; *unter — und Riegel*, under lock and key.

**Schloße** [ˈʃloːsə], *f.* (—, *pl.* —n) hailstone.

**Schlosser** [ˈʃlɔsər], *m.* (—s, *pl.* —) locksmith.

**Schlot** [ʃloːt], *m.* (—(e)s, *pl.* —e) chimney, funnel.

**schlottern** [ˈʃlɔtərn], *v.n.* wobble, dodder; tremble.

**Schlucht** [ʃluxt], *f.* (—, *pl.* —en) deep valley, defile, cleft, glen, ravine, gorge.

**schluchzen** [ˈʃluxtsən], *v.n.* sob.

**schlucken** [ˈʃlukən], *v.a.* gulp down, swallow. — *v.n.* hiccup.

**Schlucker** [ˈʃlukər], *m.* (—s, *pl.* —) *armer —*, poor wretch.

**Schlummer** [ˈʃlumər], *m.* (—s, *no pl.*) slumber.

**Schlumpe** [ˈʃlumpə], *f.* (—, *pl.* —n) slut, slattern.

**Schlund** [ʃlunt], *m.* (—(e)s, *pl.* ⁔e) throat, gorge, gullet; gulf, abyss.

**schlüpfen** [ˈʃlypfən], *v.n.* (*aux.* sein) slip, slide, glide.

**Schlüpfer** [ˈʃlypfər], *m. pl.* knickers.

**schlüpfrig** [ˈʃlypfrɪç], *adj.* slippery; (*fig.*) obscene, indecent.

**schlürfen** [ˈʃlyrfən], *v.a.* drink noisily, lap up. — *v.n.* (*aux.* sein) (*dial.*) shuffle along.

**Schluß** [ʃlus], *m.* (—sses, *pl.* ⁔sse) end, termination; conclusion.

**Schlüssel** [ˈʃlysəl], *m.* (—s, *pl.* —) key; (*Mus.*) clef.

**Schlüsselbein** [ˈʃlysəlbaın], *n.* (—s, *pl.* —e) collar-bone.

**Schlüsselblume** [ˈʃlysəlbluːmə], *f.* (—, *pl.* —n) (*Bot.*) cowslip, primrose.

**Schlußfolgerung** [ˈʃlusfɔlgərʊŋ], *f.* (—, *pl.* —en) conclusion, inference, deduction.

**schlüssig** [ˈʃlysɪç], *adj.* resolved, determined; sure; (*Law*) well-grounded; *sich — werden über*, resolve on.

**Schmach** [ʃmaːx], *f.* (—, *no pl.*) disgrace, ignominy.

**schmachten** [ˈʃmaxtən], *v.n.* languish, pine.

**schmächtig** [ˈʃmɛçtɪç], *adj.* slender, slim, spare.

**schmackhaft** [ˈʃmakhaft], *adj.* tasty, savoury.

**schmähen** [ˈʃmɛːən], *v.a.* revile, abuse, calumniate.

**Schmähschrift** [ˈʃmɛːʃrɪft], *f.* (—, *pl.* —en) lampoon.

**schmal** [ʃmaːl], *adj.* narrow.

**schmälen** [ˈʃmɛːlən], *v.a.* chide, scold.

**schmälern** [ˈʃmɛːlərn], *v.a.* lessen, diminish, curtail; detract from, belittle.

**Schmalz** [ʃmalts], *n.* (—es, *no pl.*) grease, lard, fat.

**schmarotzen** [ʃmaˈrɔtsən], *v.n.* sponge on others.

**Schmarren** [ˈʃmarən], *m.* (—s, *pl.* —) trash; (*dial.*) omelette.

**Schmatz** [ʃmats], *m.* (—es, *pl.* ⁔e) (*dial.*) smacking kiss.

**schmauchen** [ˈʃmauxən], *v.a., v.n.* smoke.

**Schmaus** [ʃmaus], *m.* (—es, *pl.* —e) feast, banquet.

**schmecken** [ˈʃmɛkən], *v.a.* taste. — *v.n.* taste; *es schmeckt mir*, I like it.

**Schmeichelei** [ʃmaıçəˈlaı], *f.* (—, *pl.* —en) flattery, adulation.

**schmeicheln** [ˈʃmaıçəln], *v.n.* flatter; fondle, pet.

**schmeißen** [ˈʃmaısən], *v.a. irr.* throw, hurl, fling; (*sl.*) *ich werde die Sache schon —*, I shall pull it off.

**Schmeißfliege** [ˈʃmaısfliːgə], *f.* (—, *pl.* —n) (*Ent.*) bluebottle.

**Schmelz** [ʃmɛlts], *m.* (—es, *no pl.*) enamel; melting; (*voice*) mellowness.

**schmelzbar** [ˈʃmɛltsbaːr], *adj.* fusible.

**schmelzen** [ˈʃmɛltsən], *v.a. irr.* smelt, melt. — *v.n.* (*aux.* sein) (*ice*) melt; (*fig.*) decrease, diminish.

# schnellen

**Schmelztiegel** ['ʃmɛltsti:gəl], *m.* (—s, *pl.* —) crucible; melting pot.

**Schmelztopf** ['ʃmɛltstɔpf], *m. see* Schmelztiegel.

**Schmerbauch** ['ʃme:rbaux], *m.* (—(e)s, *pl.* ⁴e) (*coll.*) paunch, belly.

**Schmerz** [ʃmɛrts], *m.* (—es, *pl.* —en) ache, pain; grief, sorrow; *einem —en verursachen*, give *or* cause s.o. pain.

**schmerzlich** ['ʃmɛrtslɪç], *adj.* painful, distressing.

**Schmetterling** ['ʃmɛtərlɪŋ], *m.* (—s, *pl.* —e) (*Ent.*) butterfly, moth.

**schmettern** ['ʃmɛtərn], *v.n.* resound; (*trumpets*) blare; (*bird*) warble.

**Schmied** [ʃmi:t], *m.* (—s, *pl.* —e) (black)smith.

**Schmiede** ['ʃmi:də], *f.* (—, *pl.* —n) forge, smithy.

**schmiegen** ['ʃmi:gən], *v.r. sich —*, bend, yield; *sich an einen —*, cling to s.o., nestle against s.o.

**Schmiere** ['ʃmi:rə], *f.* (—, *pl.* —n) grease, salve; (*Theat.*) troop of strolling players.

**schmieren** ['ʃmi:rən], *v.a.* smear, grease, spread; (*fig.*) bribe; (*bread*) butter. — *v.n.* scrawl, scribble.

**Schmierfink** ['ʃmi:rfɪŋk], *m.* (—en, *pl.* —en) dirty person; muckraker.

**Schmiermittel** ['ʃmi:rmɪtəl], *n.* (—s, *pl.* —) lubricant.

**Schmierseife** ['ʃmi:rzaɪfə], *f.* (—, *no pl.*) soft soap.

**Schminke** ['ʃmɪŋkə], *f.* (—, *pl.* —n) greasepaint; rouge; make-up, cosmetics.

**Schmirgel** ['ʃmɪrgəl], *m.* (—s, *no pl.*) emery.

**Schmiß** [ʃmɪs], *m.* (—sses, *pl.* —sse) cut in the face, (duelling) scar; (*fig.*) smartness, verve.

**Schmöker** ['ʃmøːkər], *m.* (—s, *pl.* —) trashy book.

**schmollen** ['ʃmɔlən], *v.n.* sulk, pout.

**Schmorbraten** ['ʃmo:rbra:tən], *m.* (—s, *pl.* —) stewed meat.

**Schmuck** [ʃmuk], *m.* (—(e)s, *pl.* —stücke) ornament, jewels, jewellery; (*Am.*) jewelry.

**schmuck** [ʃmuk], *adj.* neat, spruce, dapper, smart.

**schmücken** ['ʃmykən], *v.a.* adorn, embellish.

**Schmucksachen** ['ʃmukzaxən], *f. pl.* jewels, finery, jewellery, articles of adornment; (*Am.*) jewelry.

**schmuggeln** ['ʃmugəln], *v.a.* smuggle.

**schmunzeln** ['ʃmuntsəln], *v.n.* smirk, grin.

**Schmutz** [ʃmuts], *m.* (—es, *no pl.*) dirt, filth.

**schmutzen** ['ʃmutsən], *v.n.* get soiled, get dirty.

**Schmutzkonkurrenz** ['ʃmutskɔnkurɛnts], *f.* (—, *no pl.*) unfair competition.

**Schnabel** ['ʃna:bəl], *m.* (—s, *pl.* ⁴) bill, beak; (*ship*) prow; *halt den —*, keep your mouth shut; *er spricht, wie ihm*

*der — gewachsen ist*, he calls a spade a spade.

**Schnabeltier** ['ʃna:bəlti:r], *n.* (—s, *pl.* —e) duck-bill, duck-billed platypus.

**Schnaderhüpfel** ['ʃna:dərhypfəl], *n.* (—s, *pl.* —) (*dial.*) Alpine folk-song.

**Schnalle** ['ʃnalə], *f.* (—, *pl.* —n) buckle.

**schnalzen** ['ʃnaltsən], *v.n.* click; snap.

**schnappen** ['ʃnapən], *v.n.* snap; snatch at s.th.; *nach Luft —*, gasp for breath.

**Schnaps** [ʃnaps], *m.* (—es, *pl.* ⁴e) spirits, brandy, gin.

**schnarchen** ['ʃnarçən], *v.n.* snore.

**Schnarre** ['ʃnarə], *f.* (—, *pl.* —n) rattle.

**schnattern** ['ʃnatərn], *v.n.* cackle; gabble; chatter.

**schnauben** ['ʃnaubən], *v.n.* puff and blow; snort; *vor Zorn —*, fret and fume.

**schnaufen** ['ʃnaufən], *v.n.* breathe heavily, pant.

**Schnauze** ['ʃnautsə], *f.* (—, *pl.* —n) (*animals*) snout; (*vulg.*) mouth, trap; nozzle.

**schnauzen** ['ʃnautsən], *v.n.* snarl, shout (at).

**Schnecke** ['ʃnɛkə], *f.* (—, *pl.* —n), (*Zool.*) snail, slug.

**Schnee** [ʃne:], *m.* (—s, *no pl.*) snow.

**Schneegestöber** ['ʃne:gəʃtøːbər], *n.* (—s, *pl.* —) snow-storm.

**Schneeglöckchen** ['ʃne:glœkçən], *n.* (—s, *pl.* —) (*Bot.*) snowdrop.

**Schneeschläger** ['ʃne:ʃle:gər], *m.* (—s, *pl.* —) whisk.

**Schneetreiben** ['ʃne:traɪbən], *n.* (—s, *no pl.*) snow-storm, blizzard.

**Schneewittchen** [ʃne:'vɪtçən], *n.* (—s, *no pl.*) Snow White.

**Schneid** [ʃnaɪt], *m.* (—s, *no pl.*) go, push, dash, courage.

**Schneide** ['ʃnaɪdə], *f.* (—, *pl.* —n) edge.

**Schneidebohne** ['ʃnaɪdəbo:nə], *f.* (—, *pl.* —n) French bean, string-bean.

**Schneidemühle** ['ʃnaɪdəmy:lə], *f.* (—, *pl.* —n) saw mill.

**schneiden** ['ʃnaɪdən], *v.a. irr.* cut, trim, carve; (*fig.*) ignore, cut; *Gesichter —*, make faces. — *v.r. sich —*, cut o.s.; (*Maths.*) intersect; *sich die Haare — lassen*, have o.'s hair cut.

**Schneider** ['ʃnaɪdər], *m.* (—s, *pl.* —) tailor.

**Schneiderei** [ʃnaɪdə'raɪ], *f.* (—, *no pl.*) tailoring; dressmaking.

**Schneidezahn** ['ʃnaɪdətsa:n], *m.* (—s, *pl.* ⁴e) incisor.

**schneidig** ['ʃnaɪdɪç], *adj.* dashing.

**schneien** ['ʃnaɪən], *v.n.* snow.

**Schneise** ['ʃnaɪzə], *f.* (—, *pl.* —n) (*forest*) glade, cutting.

**schnell** [ʃnɛl], *adj.* quick, swift, speedy, fast, rapid; *mach —*, hurry up.

**Schnelle** ['ʃnɛlə], *f.* (—, *pl.* —n) (*river*) rapids.

**schnellen** ['ʃnɛlən], *v.n.* spring, jump.

# Schnelligkeit

**Schnelligkeit** [ˈʃnɛlɪçkaɪt], *f.* (—, *no pl.*) quickness, speed, swiftness, rapidity; (*Tech.*) velocity.
**Schnepfe** [ˈʃnɛpfə], *f.* (—, *pl.* —n) (*Orn.*) snipe, woodcock.
**schneuzen** [ˈʃnɔytsən], *v.r.* sich (die *Nase*) —, blow o.'s nose.
**schniegeln** [ˈʃniːgəln], *v.r.* sich —, (*coll.*) dress up, deck out; *geschniegelt und gebügelt*, spick and span.
**Schnippchen** [ˈʃnɪpçən], *n.* (—s, *pl.* —) einem ein — schlagen, play a trick on s.o.
**schnippisch** [ˈʃnɪpɪʃ], *adj.* pert, perky.
**Schnitt** [ʃnɪt], *m.* (—(e)s, *pl.* —e) cut, incision; section; (*beer*) small glass; (*dress*) cut-out pattern; (*book*) edge.
**Schnittbohne** [ˈʃnɪtboːnə], *f.* (—, *pl.* —n) (*Bot.*) French bean.
**Schnitte** [ˈʃnɪtə], *f.* (—, *pl.* —n) slice (of bread).
**Schnitter** [ˈʃnɪtər], *m.* (—s, *pl.* —) reaper.
**Schnittlauch** [ˈʃnɪtlaux], *m.* (—s, *no pl.*) (*Bot.*) chives.
**Schnittmuster** [ˈʃnɪtmʊstər], *n.* (—s, *pl.* —) cut-out pattern.
**Schnittwaren** [ˈʃnɪtvaːrən], *f. pl.* dry goods, drapery.
**Schnitzel** [ˈʃnɪtsəl], *n.* (—s, *pl.* —) (*Cul.*) cutlet; *Wiener* —, veal cutlet; snip; (*pl.*) shavings.
**schnitzen** [ˈʃnɪtsən], *v.a.* carve (in wood).
**schnodd(e)rig** [ˈʃnɔd(ə)rɪç], *adj.* (*coll.*) cheeky, insolent.
**schnöde** [ˈʃnøːdə], *adj.* base, heinous, mean, vile; —*r Mammon*, filthy lucre; —*r Undank*, rank ingratitude.
**Schnörkel** [ˈʃnœrkəl], *m.* (—s, *pl.* —) (*writing*) flourish.
**schnorren** [ˈʃnɔrən], *v.n.* (*rare*) cadge, beg.
**schnüffeln** [ˈʃnyfəln], *v.n.* sniff; (*fig.*) pry, snoop.
**Schnuller** [ˈʃnʊlər], *m.* (—s, *pl.* —) baby's dummy; (*Am.*) comforter.
**Schnupfen** [ˈʃnʊpfən], *m.* (—s, *pl.* —) cold (in the head); *den* — *haben*, have a (running) cold; *den* — *bekommen*, catch cold.
**schnupfen** [ˈʃnʊpfən], *v.a., v.n.* take snuff.
**Schnupftuch** [ˈʃnʊpftuːx], *n.* (—(e)s, *pl.* —er) (*dial.*) (pocket-) handkerchief.
**schnuppe** [ˈʃnʊpə], *adj.* (*sl.*) *mir ist alles* —, it is all the same to me, I don't care.
**schnuppern** [ˈʃnʊpərn], *v.n.* smell, snuffle.
**Schnur** [ʃnuːr], *f.* (—, *pl.* —en, —e) twine, cord, string; (*Elec.*) lead, flex.
**Schnürchen** [ˈʃnyːrçən], *n.* (—s, *pl.* —) *wie am* —, like clockwork.
**schnüren** [ˈʃnyːrən], *v.a.* lace, tie up; *sein Ränzel* —, pack o.'s bag.
**Schnurrbart** [ˈʃnurbaːrt], *m.* (—s,

*pl.* —e) moustache; *sich einen* — *wachsen lassen*, grow a moustache.
**Schnurre** [ˈʃnurə], *f.* (—, *pl.* —n) funny story, yarn.
**schnurren** [ˈʃnurən], *v.n.* purr.
**Schnürsenkel** [ˈʃnyːrzɛŋkəl], *m.* (—s, *pl.* —) (*shoe*) lace.
**schnurstracks** [ˈʃnuːrʃtraks], *adv.* directly, immediately, on the spot.
**Schober** [ˈʃoːbər], *m.* (—s, *pl.* —) stack, rick.
**Schock** (1) [ʃɔk], *n.* (—(e)s, *pl.* —e) sixty, three score.
**Schock** (2) [ʃɔk], *m.* (—(e)s, *pl.* —s) shock; blow; stroke.
**Schöffe** [ˈʃœfə], *m.* (—n, *pl.* —n) (*Law*) juror; member of jury.
**Schokolade** [ʃokoˈlaːdə], *f.* (—, *pl.* —n) chocolate; *eine Tafel* —, a bar of chocolate.
**Scholle** [ˈʃɔlə], *f.* (—, *pl.* —n) plaice; (*ice*) floe; clod; soil.
**schon** [ʃoːn], *adv.* already; indeed; yet; *na wenn* —, so what; — *gut*, that'll do; — *gestern*, as early as yesterday.
**schön** [ʃøːn], *adj.* beautiful, fair, handsome, lovely; —*e Literatur*, belles-lettres, good books.
**schonen** [ˈʃoːnən], *v.a.* spare, save; treat considerately.
**Schoner** [ˈʃoːnər], *m.* (—s, *pl.* —) antimacassar; (*Naut.*) schooner.
**Schönheit** [ˈʃøːnhaɪt], *f.* (—, *no pl.*) beauty.
**Schonung** [ˈʃoːnʊŋ], *f.* (—, *pl.* —en) forbearance, considerate treatment; (*forest*) plantation of young trees.
**Schonzeit** [ˈʃoːntsaɪt], *f.* (—, *pl.* —en) close season.
**Schopf** [ʃɔpf], *m.* (—es, *pl.* —e) tuft, head of hair; (*bird*) crest; *das Glück beim* —*e fassen*, take time by the forelock, make hay while the sun shines.
**Schöpfbrunnen** [ˈʃœpfbrunən], *m.* (—s, *pl.* —) (draw-)well.
**schöpfen** [ˈʃœpfən], *v.a.* (*water*) draw; derive; *Verdacht* —, become suspicious; *frische Luft* —, get a breath of fresh air; *Mut* —, take heart.
**Schöpfer** [ˈʃœpfər], *m.* (—s, *pl.* —) creator.
**Schöpfkelle** [ˈʃœpfkɛlə], *f.* (—, *pl.* —n) scoop.
**Schopflerche** [ˈʃɔpflɛrçə], *f.* (—, *pl.* —n) (*Orn.*) crested lark.
**Schöpfung** [ˈʃœpfʊŋ], *f.* (—, *pl.* —en) creation.
**Schoppen** [ˈʃɔpən], *m.* (—s, *pl.* —) (*approx.*) half a pint.
**Schöps** [ʃœps], *m.* (—es, *pl.* —e) (*Zool.*) wether; (*fig.*) simpleton.
**Schorf** [ʃɔrf], *m.* (—(e)s, *pl.* —e) scab, scurf.
**Schornstein** [ˈʃɔrnʃtaɪn], *m.* (—s, *pl.* —e) chimney; (*ship*) funnel.
**Schoß** [ʃoːs], *m.* (—es, *pl.* —e) lap; (*Poet.*) womb; skirt, tail; *die Hände in den* — *legen*, be idle, fold o.'s arms, twiddle o.'s thumbs.

# schuldig

**Schößling** [ˈʃœslɪŋ], *m.* (—s, *pl.* —e) shoot, sprig.
**Schote** [ˈʃoːtə], *f.* (—, *pl.* —n) pod, husk, shell; (*pl.*) green peas.
**Schotter** [ˈʃɔtər], *m.* (—s, *no pl.*) road-metal, broken stones, gravel.
**Schottland** [ˈʃɔtlant], *n.* Scotland.
**schraffieren** [ʃraˈfiːrən], *v.a.* (*Art*) hatch.
**schräg** [ˈʃrɛːk], *adj.* oblique, sloping, slanting, diagonal.
**Schramme** [ˈʃramə], *f.* (—, *pl.* —n) scratch, scar.
**Schrank** [ʃraŋk], *m.* (—(e)s, *pl.* ˸e) cupboard, wardrobe.
**Schranken** [ˈʃraŋkən], *f. pl.* barriers, (level crossing) gates, limits, bounds; *in — halten*, limit, keep within bounds.
**schränken** [ˈʃrɛŋkən], *v.a.* cross; fold.
**Schranze** [ˈʃrantsə], *m.* (—n, *pl.* —n) sycophant, toady.
**Schraube** [ˈʃraubə], *f.* (—, *pl.* —n) screw; bolt; propeller.
**Schraubengewinde** [ˈʃraubəngəvɪndə], *n.* (—s, *pl.* —) thread of a screw.
**Schraubenmutter** [ˈʃraubənmutər], *f.* (—, *pl.* —n) female screw, nut.
**Schraubenzieher** [ˈʃraubəntsiːər], *m.* (—s, *pl.* —) screw-driver.
**Schraubstock** [ˈʃraupʃtɔk], *m.* (—s, *pl.* ˸e) (*tool*) vice.
**Schreck(en)** [ˈʃrɛk(ən)], *m.* (—s, *pl.* —) fright, terror, alarm, horror; shock.
**Schrecknis** [ˈʃrɛknɪs], *n.* (—ses, *pl.* —se) terror, horror.
**Schrei** [ʃrai], *m.* (—s, *pl.* —e) cry; scream.
**Schreiben** [ˈʃraibən], *n.* (—s, *pl.* —) letter, missive.
**schreiben** [ˈʃraibən], *v.a. irr.* write; *ins Reine —*, make a fair copy.
**Schreibfehler** [ˈʃraipfeːlər], *m.* (—s, *pl.* —) slip of the pen.
**Schreibkrampf** [ˈʃraipkrampf], *m.* (—(e)s, *pl.* ˸e) writer's cramp.
**Schreibmaschine** [ˈʃraipmaʃiːnə], *f.* (—, *pl.* —n) typewriter.
**Schreibwaren** [ˈʃraipvaːrən], *f. pl.* stationery.
**Schreibweise** [ˈʃraipvaizə], *f.* (—, *pl.* —n) style; spelling.
**schreien** [ˈʃraiən], *v.a., v.n. irr.* cry, shout, scream, yell.
**Schreihals** [ˈʃraihals], *m.* (—es, *pl.* ˸e) cry-baby, noisy child.
**Schrein** [ʃrain], *m.* (—(e)s, *pl.* —e) box, chest; shrine.
**schreiten** [ˈʃraitən], *v.n. irr.* (*aux.* sein) stride, step, pace.
**Schrift** [ʃrɪft], *f.* (—, *pl.* —en) writing; handwriting, calligraphy; publication; type; *Heilige —*, Holy Writ, Holy Scripture.
**Schriftführer** [ˈʃrɪftfyːrər], *m.* (—s, *pl.* —) secretary.
**Schriftgießerei** [ˈʃrɪftgiːsərai], *f.* (—, *pl.* —en) type-foundry.
**Schriftleiter** [ˈʃrɪftlaitər], *m.* (—s, *pl.* —) editor.

**schriftlich** [ˈʃrɪftlɪç], *adj.* written. — *adv.* in writing, by letter.
**Schriftsetzer** [ˈʃrɪftzɛtsər], *m.* (—s, *pl.* —) compositor.
**Schriftsteller** [ˈʃrɪftʃtelər], *m.* (—s, *pl.* —) writer, author.
**Schriftstück** [ˈʃrɪftʃtyk], *n.* (—s, *pl.* —e) document, deed.
**Schriftwechsel** [ˈʃrɪftvɛksəl], *m.* (—s, *no pl.*) exchange of notes, correspondence.
**Schriftzeichen** [ˈʃrɪftsaiçən], *n.* (—s, *pl.* —) character, letter (of alphabet).
**schrill** [ʃrɪl], *adj.* shrill.
**Schritt** [ʃrɪt], *m.* (—(e)s, *pl.* —e) step, pace, move; *lange —e machen*, stride; *— halten*, keep pace; *— fahren*, drive slowly, drive at walking pace; *aus dem —*, out of step; *in einer Sache —e tun*, make a move *or* take steps about s.th.
**schrittweise** [ˈʃrɪtvaizə], *adv.* step by step, gradually.
**schroff** [ʃrɔf], *adj.* steep, precipitous; (*fig.*) gruff, blunt, rough, harsh.
**schröpfen** [ˈʃrœpfən], *v.a.* (*Med.*) cup; (*fig.*) fleece.
**Schrot** [ʃroːt], *m. & n.* (—(e)s, *pl.* —e) grape-shot, small shot; *ein Mann vom alten —*, a man of the utmost probity.
**Schrotbrot** [ˈʃroːtbroːt], *n.* (—es, *no pl.*) wholemeal bread.
**Schrott** [ʃrɔt], *m.* (—(e)s, *pl.* —e), old iron, scrap metal.
**Schrulle** [ˈʃrulə], *f.* (—, *pl.* —n) fad, whim.
**schrumpfen** [ˈʃrumpfən], *v.n.* (*aux.* sein) shrink, shrivel.
**Schub** [ʃup], *m.* (—s, *pl.* ˸e) shove, push; batch.
**Schubkarren** [ˈʃupkarən], *m.* (—s, *pl.* —) wheelbarrow.
**Schublade** [ˈʃuplaːdə], *f.* (—, *pl.* —n) drawer.
**schüchtern** [ˈʃyçtərn], *adj.* shy, bashful, timid.
**Schuft** [ʃuft], *m.* (—(e)s, *pl.* —e) blackguard, scoundrel.
**schuften** [ˈʃuftən], *v.n.* work hard, toil.
**Schufterei** [ʃuftəˈrai], *f.* (—, *no pl.*) drudgery.
**schuftig** [ˈʃuftɪç], *adj.* rascally, mean.
**Schuh** [ʃuː], *m.* (—s, *pl.* —e) shoe; *einem etwas in die —e schieben*, lay the blame at s.o.'s door.
**Schuhwerk** [ˈʃuːvɛrk], *n.* (—s, *no pl.*) footwear.
**Schuhwichse** [ˈʃuːvɪksə], *f.* (—, *no pl.*) shoe-polish.
**Schuld** [ʃult], *f.* (—, *pl.* —en) guilt, offence, sin; fault; blame; cause; (*money*) debt; *in —en geraten*, run into debt.
**schuld** [ʃult], *adj. ich bin —*, it is my fault, I am to blame.
**schulden** [ˈʃuldən], *v.a.* owe, be indebted to.
**schuldig** [ˈʃuldɪç], *adj.* guilty, culpable; *sich — bekennen*, plead guilty; *einen — sprechen*, pronounce s.o. guilty;

193

# Schuldigkeit

*ihm ist Anerkennung* —, appreciation is due to him.

**Schuldigkeit** ['ʃuldɪçkaɪt], *f.* (—, *no pl.*) obligation, duty.

**schuldlos** ['ʃultlo:s], *adj.* innocent, guiltless.

**Schuldner** ['ʃuldnər], *m.* (—s, *pl.* —) debtor.

**Schule** ['ʃu:lə], *f.* (—, *pl.* —n) school; *in die* — *gehen*, go to school, attend school; *die* — *schwänzen*, play truant; *hohe* —, (*Riding*) advanced horsemanship.

**schulen** ['ʃu:lən], *v.a.* train, instruct.

**Schüler** ['ʃy:lər], *m.* (—s, *pl.* —) schoolboy, pupil, student, scholar.

**Schulklasse** ['ʃu:lklasə], *f.* (—, *pl.* —n) class, form.

**Schulleiter** ['ʃu:llaɪtər], *m.* (—s, *pl.* —) headmaster.

**Schulrat** ['ʃu:lra:t], *m.* (—s, *pl.* ˙e) school-inspector.

**Schulter** ['ʃultər], *f.* (—, *pl.* —n) shoulder.

**Schulterblatt** ['ʃultərblat], *n.* (—s, *pl.* ˙er) shoulder-blade.

**Schultheiß** ['ʃulthaɪs], *m.* (—en, *pl.* —en) village magistrate, mayor.

**Schulunterricht** ['ʃu:luntərrɪçt], *m.* (—s, *no pl.*) school teaching, lessons.

**schummeln** ['ʃuməln], *v.n.* (*coll.*) cheat.

**Schund** [ʃunt], *m.* (—(e)s, *no pl.*) trash.

**Schuppe** ['ʃupə], *f.* (—, *pl.* —n) scale; (*pl.*) dandruff.

**Schuppen** ['ʃupən], *m.* (—s, *pl.* —) shed.

**Schuppentier** ['ʃupənti:r], *n.* (—s, *pl.* —e) (*Zool.*) armadillo.

**Schur** [ʃu:r], *f.* (—, *pl.* —en) shearing.

**schüren** ['ʃy:rən], *v.a.* (*fire*) poke, rake; (*fig.*) stir up, fan, incite.

**schürfen** ['ʃyrfən], *v.a.* scratch. — *v.n.* (*Min.*) prospect.

**schurigeln** ['ʃu:rɪgəln], *v.a.* bully, pester.

**Schurke** ['ʃurkə], *m.* (—n, *pl.* —n) scoundrel, villain, blackguard.

**Schurz** [ʃurts], *m.* (—es, *pl.* —e) apron, overall.

**Schürze** ['ʃyrtsə], *f.* (—, *pl.* —n) apron, pinafore.

**schürzen** ['ʃyrtsən], *v.a.* tuck up, pin up.

**Schürzenjäger** ['ʃyrtsənje:gər], *m.* (—s, *pl.* —) ladies' man.

**Schurzfell** ['ʃurtsfel], *n.* (—s, *pl.* —e) leather apron.

**Schuß** [ʃus], *m.* (—sses, *pl.* ˙sse) shot, report; dash; *weit vom* —, out of harm's way; wide of the mark.

**Schüssel** ['ʃysəl], *f.* (—, *pl.* —n) dish.

**Schußwaffe** ['ʃusvafə], *f.* (—, *pl.* —n) fire-arm.

**Schuster** ['ʃu:stər], *m.* (—s, *pl.* —) shoemaker, cobbler; *auf* —s *Rappen*, on Shanks's pony.

**schustern** ['ʃu:stərn], *v.n.* cobble, make *or* mend shoes.

**Schutt** [ʃut], *m.* (—(e)s, *no pl.*) rubbish, refuse; — *abladen*,

dump refuse.

**Schütte** ['ʃytə], *f.* (—, *pl.* —n) (*dial.* bundle, truss.

**schütteln** ['ʃytəln], *v.a.* shake, jolt.

**schütten** ['ʃytən], *v.a.* shoot, pour; pour out.

**schütter** ['ʃytər], *adj.* (*dial.*) (*hair*) thin; scarce.

**Schutz** [ʃuts], *m.* (—es, *no pl.*) protection, shelter, cover; *einen in* — *nehmen gegen*, defend s.o. against.

**Schutzbefohlene** ['ʃutsbəfo:lənə], *m.* (—n, *pl.* —n) charge, person in o.'s care, ward.

**Schutzbündnis** ['ʃutsbyntnɪs], *n.* (—ses, *pl.* —se) defensive alliance.

**Schütze** ['ʃytsə], *m.* (—n, *pl.* —n) rifleman, sharpshooter, marksman; (*Astrol.*) Sagittarius.

**schützen** ['ʃytsən], *v.a.* protect, shelter, defend. — *v.r. sich* — *vor*, guard o.s. against.

**Schützengraben** ['ʃytsəngra:bən], *m.* (—s, *pl.* ˙) trench.

**Schutzgebiet** ['ʃutsgəbi:t], *n.* (—s, *pl.* —e) protectorate.

**Schutzgitter** ['ʃutsgɪtər], *n.* (—s, *pl.* —) grid, guard.

**Schutzheilige** ['ʃutshaɪlɪgə], *m.* (—n, *pl.* —n) patron saint.

**Schützling** ['ʃytslɪŋ], *m.* (—s, *pl.* —e) protégé, charge.

**Schutzmann** ['ʃutsman], *m.* (—s, *pl.* ˙er, **Schutzleute**) policeman, constable.

**Schutzmarke** ['ʃutsmarkə], *f.* (—, *pl.* —n) trade-mark.

**Schutzzoll** ['ʃutstsol], *m.* (—s, *pl.* ˙e) protective duty, tariff.

**Schwaben** ['ʃva:bən], *n.* Swabia.

**Schwabenstreich** ['ʃva:bənʃtraɪç], *m.* (—s, *pl.* —e) tomfoolery.

**schwach** [ʃvax], *adj.* weak, frail, feeble; (*noise*) faint; (*pulse*) low; —*e Seite*, foible; —*e Stunde*, unguarded moment.

**Schwäche** ['ʃvɛçə], *f.* (—, *pl.* —n) weakness, faintness; infirmity.

**schwächen** ['ʃvɛçən], *v.a.* weaken, debilitate.

**Schwächling** ['ʃvɛçlɪŋ], *m.* (—s, *pl.* —e) weakling.

**Schwachsinn** ['ʃvaxzɪn], *m.* (—s, *no pl.*) feeble-mindedness.

**Schwächung** ['ʃvɛçuŋ], *f.* (—, *pl.* —en) weakening, lessening.

**Schwadron** [ʃva'dro:n], *f.* (—, *pl.* —en) squadron.

**Schwadroneur** [ʃvadro'nø:r], *m.* (—s, *pl.* —e) swaggerer.

**schwadronieren** [ʃvadro'ni:rən], *v.n.* talk big, swagger.

**schwafeln** ['ʃva:fəln], *v.n.* (*sl.*) talk nonsense, waffle.

**Schwager** ['ʃva:gər], *m.* (—s, *pl.* ˙) brother-in-law.

**Schwägerin** ['ʃvɛ:gərɪn], *f.* (—, *pl.* —nen) sister-in-law.

**Schwalbe** ['ʃvalbə], *f.* (—, *pl.* —n) (*Orn.*) swallow.

# Schwellung

**Schwalbenschwanz** ['ʃvalbənʃvants], *m.* (—es, *pl.* ⸚e) (*butterfly*) swallow's tail; (*joinery*) dovetail.

**Schwall** [ʃval], *m.* (—(e)s, *no pl.*) flood; (*fig.*) deluge, torrent.

**Schwamm** [ʃvam], *m.* (—(e)s, *pl.* ⸚e) sponge; fungus, mushroom; dry rot.

**schwammig** ['ʃvamɪç], *adj.* spongy, fungous.

**Schwan** [ʃvaːn], *m.* (—(e)s, *pl.* ⸚e) swan; *junger* —, cygnet.

**schwanen** ['ʃvaːnən], *v.n. imp. es schwant mir,* I have a foreboding.

**Schwang** [ʃvaŋ], *m. im —e sein,* be in fashion, be the rage.

**schwanger** ['ʃvaŋər], *adj.* pregnant.

**schwängern** ['ʃvɛŋərn], *v.a.* make pregnant, get with child; (*fig.*) impregnate.

**Schwangerschaft** ['ʃvaŋərʃaft], *f.* (—, *pl.* —en) pregnancy.

**Schwank** [ʃvaŋk], *m.* (—(e)s, *pl.* ⸚e) funny story, joke; (*Theat.*) farce.

**schwank** [ʃvaŋk], *adj.* flexible, supple; *ein —es Rohr,* a reed shaken by the wind.

**schwanken** ['ʃvaŋkən], *v.n.* totter, stagger; (*fig.*) waver, vacillate; (*prices*) fluctuate.

**Schwanz** [ʃvants], *m.* (—es, *pl.* ⸚e) tail.

**schwänzeln** ['ʃvɛntsəln], *v.n.* (*animal*) wag the tail; (*fig.*) fawn, cringe.

**schwänzen** ['ʃvɛntsən], *v.a. die Schule* —, play truant.

**Schwären** ['ʃvɛːrən], *m.* (—s, *pl.* —) ulcer, abscess.

**schwären** ['ʃvɛːrən], *v.n.* fester, suppurate.

**Schwarm** [ʃvarm], *m.* (—(e)s, *pl.* ⸚e) (*insects*) swarm; (*humans*) crowd; (*birds*) flight.

**Schwärmerei** [ʃvɛrmə'raɪ], *f.* (—, *pl.* —en) enthusiasm, passion, craze.

**Schwarte** ['ʃvartə], *f.* (—, *pl.* —n) rind; crust; *alte —,* (*fig.*) old volume; tome.

**schwarz** [ʃvarts], *adj.* black.

**Schwarzamsel** ['ʃvartsamzəl], *f.* (—, *pl.* —n) (*Orn.*) blackbird.

**Schwarzdorn** ['ʃvartsdɔrn], *m.* (—s, *no pl.*) (*Bot.*) blackthorn, sloe.

**Schwärze** ['ʃvɛrtsə], *f.* (—, *no pl.*) blackness; printer's ink.

**schwärzen** ['ʃvɛrtsən], *v.a.* blacken.

**Schwarzkünstler** ['ʃvartskynstlər], *m.* (—s, *pl.* —) magician, necromancer.

**Schwarzwald** ['ʃvartsvalt], *m.* Black Forest.

**Schwarzwild** ['ʃvartsvɪlt], *n.* (—(e)s, *no pl.*) wild boar.

**schwatzen** ['ʃvatsən], *v.n.* chat, chatter, prattle.

**Schwätzer** ['ʃvɛtsər], *m.* (—s, *pl.* —) chatterbox.

**Schwatzhaftigkeit** ['ʃvatshaftɪçkaɪt], *f.* (—, *no pl.*) loquacity, talkativeness.

**Schwebe** ['ʃveːbə], *f.* (—, *pl.* —n) suspense; suspension.

**Schwebebaum** ['ʃveːbəbaum], *m.* (—s, *pl.* ⸚e) horizontal bar.

**schweben** ['ʃveːbən], *v.n.* be suspended, hover; (*fig.*) be pending; *in Gefahr* —, be in danger; *es schwebt mir auf der Zunge,* it is on the tip of my tongue.

**Schwede** ['ʃveːdə], *m.* (—n, *pl.* —n) Swede; *alter —,* (*fig.*) old boy.

**Schweden** ['ʃveːdən], *n.* Sweden.

**Schwedenhölzer** ['ʃveːdənhœltsər], *n. pl.* (*rare*) matches.

**Schwefel** ['ʃveːfəl], *m.* (—s, *no pl.*) sulphur, brimstone.

**Schwefelhölzchen** ['ʃveːfəlhœltsçən], *n.* (—s, *pl.* —) (*obs.*) match.

**schwefeln** ['ʃveːfəln], *v.a.* impregnate with sulphur, fumigate.

**Schwefelsäure** ['ʃveːfəlzɔyrə], *f.* (—, *no pl.*) sulphuric acid.

**Schweif** [ʃvaɪf], *m.* (—(e)s, *pl.* —e) tail.

**schweifen** ['ʃvaɪfən], *v.n.* (*aux.* sein) ramble, stray, wander.

**schweifwedeln** ['ʃvaɪfveːdəln], *v.n.* fawn.

**Schweigegeld** ['ʃvaɪgəgelt], *n.* (—(e)s, *pl.* —er) (*coll.*) hush-money.

**Schweigen** ['ʃvaɪgən], *n.* (—s, *no pl.*) silence.

**schweigen** ['ʃvaɪgən], *v.n. irr.* be silent; be quiet; *ganz zu — von,* to say nothing of.

**schweigsam** ['ʃvaɪkzaːm], *adj.* taciturn.

**Schwein** [ʃvaɪn], *n.* (—(e)s, *pl.* —e) pig, hog; swine; *wildes —,* boar; (*fig.*) luck, fluke; — *haben,* be lucky.

**Schweinekoben** ['ʃvaɪnəkoːbən], *m.* (—s, *pl.* —) pigsty.

**Schweinerei** [ʃvaɪnə'raɪ], *f.* (—, *pl.* —en) filth; (*fig.*) smut, filthiness, obscenity; mess.

**Schweineschmalz** ['ʃvaɪnəʃmalts], *n.* (—es, *no pl.*) lard.

**Schweinigel** ['ʃvaɪnɪgəl], *m.* (—s, *pl.* —) (*Zool.*) hedgehog, porcupine; (*fig.*) dirty pig, filthy wretch.

**Schweinskeule** ['ʃvaɪnskɔylə], *f.* (—, *pl.* —n) leg of pork.

**Schweiß** [ʃvaɪs], *m.* (—es, *no pl.*) sweat, perspiration.

**schweißen** ['ʃvaɪsən], *v.a.* weld, solder.

**Schweiz** [ʃvaɪts], *f.* Switzerland.

**Schweizer** ['ʃvaɪtsər], *m.* (—s, *pl.* —) Swiss; (*fig.*) dairyman.

**Schweizerei** [ʃvaɪtsə'raɪ], *f.* (—, *pl.* —en) dairy.

**schwelen** ['ʃveːlən], *v.n.* burn slowly, smoulder.

**schwelgen** ['ʃvelgən], *v.n.* carouse, revel.

**Schwelgerei** [ʃvelgə'raɪ], *f.* (—, *pl.* —en) revelry.

**schwelgerisch** ['ʃvelgərɪʃ], *adj.* luxurious, voluptuous.

**Schwelle** ['ʃvelə], *f.* (—, *pl.* —n) threshold; (*Railw.*) sleeper.

**schwellen** ['ʃvelən], *v.n. irr.* (*aux.* sein) swell; (*water*) rise.

**Schwellung** ['ʃveluŋ], *f.* (—, *pl.* —en) swelling.

195

**schwemmen** [ˈʃvɛmən], *v.a.* wash, soak, carry off.
**Schwengel** [ˈʃvɛŋəl], *m.* (—s, *pl.* —) (*bell*) clapper; (*pump*) handle.
**schwenken** [ˈʃvɛŋkən], *v.a.* swing; shake, brandish; (*glasses*) rinse.
**Schwenkung** [ˈʃvɛŋkuŋ], *f.* (—, *pl.* —en) change; (*Mil.*) wheeling.
**schwer** [ʃveːr], *adj.* heavy; difficult, hard; ponderous; severe; — *von Begriff*, obtuse, slow in the uptake; —*e Speise*, indigestible food; *einem das Herz — machen*, grieve s.o.
**schwerblütig** [ˈʃveːrblyːtɪç], *adj.* phlegmatic.
**Schwere** [ˈʃveːrə], *f.* (—, *no pl.*) weight, heaviness; gravity.
**Schwerenöter** [ˈʃveːrənøːtər], *m.* (—s, *pl.* —) gay dog, ladies' man.
**schwerfällig** [ˈʃveːrfɛlɪç], *adj.* ungainly, cumbrous, unwieldy; (*fig.*) thick-headed, dense.
**Schwergewicht** [ˈʃveːrgəvɪçt], *n.* (—s, *no pl.*) (*Sport*) heavyweight; (*fig.*) emphasis.
**schwerhörig** [ˈʃveːrhøːrɪç], *adj.* hard of hearing, deaf.
**Schwerkraft** [ˈʃveːrkraft], *f.* (—, *no pl.*) gravity.
**schwerlich** [ˈʃveːrlɪç], *adv.* hardly, scarcely.
**schwermütig** [ˈʃveːrmyːtɪç], *adj.* melancholy.
**Schwerpunkt** [ˈʃveːrpuŋkt], *m.* (—s, *pl.* —e) centre of gravity.
**Schwert** [ʃveːrt], *n.* (—(e)s, *pl.* —er) sword.
**Schwertgriff** [ˈʃveːrtgrɪf], *m.* (—s, *pl.* —e) hilt.
**Schwertlilie** [ˈʃveːrtliːljə], *f.* (—, *pl.* —n) (*Bot.*) iris; fleur-de-lys.
**Schwertstreich** [ˈʃveːrtʃtraɪç], *m.* (—(e)s, *pl.* —e) sword-blow, sword-stroke.
**schwerwiegend** [ˈʃveːrviːgənt], *adj.* weighty.
**Schwester** [ˈʃvɛstər], *f.* (—, *pl.* —n) sister; *barmherzige* —, sister of mercy.
**Schwesternschaft** [ˈʃvɛstərnʃaft], *f.* (—, *pl.* —en) sisterhood; (*Am.*) sorority.
**Schwibbogen** [ˈʃvɪpboːgən], *m.* (—s, *pl.* —en) (*Archit.*) flying buttress.
**Schwiegersohn** [ˈʃviːgərzoːn], *m.* (—s, *pl.* ⁓e) son-in-law.
**Schwiegertochter** [ˈʃviːgərtɔxtər], *f.* (—, *pl.* ⁓) daughter-in-law.
**Schwiele** [ˈʃviːlə], *f.* (—, *pl.* —n) hard skin, callus, weal.
**schwielig** [ˈʃviːlɪç], *adj.* callous, horny.
**schwierig** [ˈʃviːrɪç], *adj.* difficult, hard.
**Schwierigkeit** [ˈʃviːrɪçkaɪt], *f.* (—, *pl.* —en) difficulty; *auf* —*en stoßen*, meet with difficulties.
**schwimmen** [ˈʃvɪmən], *v.n. irr.* (*aux.* sein) swim, float.
**Schwimmer** [ˈʃvɪmər], *m.* (—s, *pl.* —) swimmer.

**Schwimmgürtel** [ˈʃvɪmgyrtəl], *m.* (—s, *pl.* —) life-belt.
**Schwindel** [ˈʃvɪndəl], *m.* (—s, *pl.* —) giddiness, dizziness, vertigo; swindle, fraud.
**Schwindelanfall** [ˈʃvɪndəlanfal], *m.* (—s, *pl.* ⁓e) attack of giddiness, vertigo.
**Schwindelei** [ʃvɪndəˈlaɪ], *f.* (—, *pl.* —en) swindle, fraud, deceit.
**schwindelhaft** [ˈʃvɪndəlhaft], *adj.* fraudulent.
**schwinden** [ˈʃvɪndən], *v.n. irr.* (*aux.* sein) dwindle; disappear, vanish.
**Schwindler** [ˈʃvɪndlər], *m.* (—s, *pl.* —) swindler, humbug, cheat.
**schwindlig** [ˈʃvɪndlɪç], *adj.* dizzy, giddy.
**Schwindsucht** [ˈʃvɪntzuxt], *f.* (—, *no pl.*) (*Med.*) tuberculosis, consumption.
**schwindsüchtig** [ˈʃvɪntzyçtɪç], *adj.* (*Med.*) tubercular.
**Schwinge** [ˈʃvɪŋə], *f.* (—, *pl.* —n) wing.
**schwingen** [ˈʃvɪŋən], *v.a. irr.* brandish. — *v.n.* swing, vibrate. — *v.r. sich* —, vault; *sich auf den Thron* —, usurp *or* take possession of the throne.
**Schwingung** [ˈʃvɪŋuŋ], *f.* (—, *pl.* —en) vibration, oscillation.
**Schwips** [ʃvɪps], *m.* (—es, *pl.* —e) (*coll.*) tipsiness; *einen — haben*, be tipsy.
**schwirren** [ˈʃvɪrən], *v.n.* whir, buzz.
**Schwitzbad** [ˈʃvɪtsbaːt], *n.* (—es, *pl.* ⁓er) Turkish bath, steam-bath.
**schwitzen** [ˈʃvɪtsən], *v.n.* sweat, perspire.
**schwören** [ˈʃvøːrən], *v.a., v.n. irr.* swear, take an oath; *darauf kannst du* —, you can be quite sure of that, you bet; *falsch* —, forswear o.s., perjure o.s.
**schwül** [ʃvyːl], *adj.* sultry, close.
**Schwüle** [ˈʃvyːlə], *f.* (—, *no pl.*) sultriness.
**Schwulst** [ʃvulst], *m.* (—es, *no pl.*) bombast.
**schwülstig** [ˈʃvylstɪç], *adj.* bombastic, turgid.
**Schwülstigkeit** [ˈʃvylstɪçkaɪt], *f.* (—, *pl.* —en) bombastic style, turgidity.
**Schwund** [ʃvunt], *m.* (—(e)s, *no pl.*) dwindling, decline; shrinkage.
**Schwung** [ʃvuŋ], *m.* (—(e)s, *pl.* ⁓e) swing, leap, bound; (*fig.*) verve, élan; (*Poet.*) flight, soaring.
**schwunghaft** [ˈʃvuŋhaft], *adj.* flourishing, soaring.
**Schwungkraft** [ˈʃvuŋkraft], *f.* (—, *no pl.*) centrifugal force; (*mental*) resilience.
**Schwungrad** [ˈʃvuŋraːt], *n.* (—s, *pl.* ⁓er) fly-wheel.
**schwungvoll** [ˈʃvuŋfɔl], *adj.* spirited.
**Schwur** [ʃvuːr], *m.* (—(e)s, *pl.* ⁓e) oath.
**Schwurgericht** [ˈʃvuːrgərɪçt], *n.* (—s, *pl.* —e) (*Law*) assizes.
**sechs** [zɛks], *num. adj.* six.
**Sechseck** [ˈzɛksɛk], *n.* (—s, *pl.* —e) hexagon.
**sechseckig** [ˈzɛksɛkɪç], *adj.* hexagonal.

**Sechser** ['zɛksər], *m.* (—s, *pl.* —) coin of small value.

**sechsspännig** ['zɛksʃpɛnɪç], *adj.* drawn by six horses.

**sechzehn** ['zɛçtse:n], *num. adj.* sixteen.

**sechzig** ['zɛçtsɪç], *num. adj.* sixty.

**Sediment** [zedi'mɛnt], *n.* (—s, *pl.* —e) sediment.

**See** (1) [ze:], *m.* (—s, *pl.* —n) lake, pool.

**See** (2) [ze:], *f.* (—, *no pl.*) sea, ocean; *hohe* —, high seas; *zur* — *gehen*, go to sea, become a sailor.

**Seeadler** ['ze:adlər], *m.* (—s, *pl.* —) (*Orn.*) osprey.

**Seebad** ['ze:ba:t], *n.* (—s, *pl.* ⸚er) seaside resort; bathe in the sea.

**Seebär** ['ze:bɛ:r], *m.* (—en, *pl.* —en) (*fig.*) old salt.

**Seefahrer** ['ze:fa:rər], *m.* (—s, *pl.* —) mariner, navigator.

**Seefahrt** ['ze:fa:rt], *f.* (—, *pl.* —en) seafaring; voyage, cruise.

**seefest** ['ze:fɛst], *adj.* (*ship*) seaworthy; (*person*) a good sailor.

**Seefischerei** ['ze:fɪʃərai], *f.* (—, *no pl.*) deep-sea fishing.

**Seeflotte** ['ze:flɔtə], *f.* (—, *pl.* —n) navy, fleet.

**Seegang** ['ze:gaŋ], *m.* (—s, *no pl.*) swell.

**Seegras** ['ze:gra:s], *n.* (—es, *no pl.*) seaweed.

**Seehandel** ['ze:handəl], *m.* (—s, *no pl.*) maritime trade.

**Seehund** ['ze:hunt], *m.* (—s, *pl.* —e) (*Zool.*) seal.

**Seeigel** ['ze:i:gəl], *m.* (—s, *pl.* —) (*Zool.*) sea-urchin.

**Seejungfrau** ['ze:juŋfrau], *f.* (—, *pl.* —en) mermaid.

**Seekadett** ['ze:kadɛt], *m.* (—en, *pl.* —en) midshipman; (*naval*) cadet.

**Seekarte** ['ze:kartə], *f.* (—, *pl.* —n) chart.

**seekrank** ['ze:kraŋk], *adj.* seasick.

**Seekrieg** ['ze:kri:k], *m.* (—s, *pl.* —e) naval war.

**Seeküste** ['ze:kystə], *f.* (—, *pl.* —n) sea-coast, shore, beach.

**Seele** ['ze:lə], *f.* (—, *pl.* —n) soul; *mit ganzer* —, with all my heart.

**Seelenamt** ['ze:lənamt], *n.* (—s, *pl.* ⸚er) (*Eccl.*) office for the dead, requiem.

**Seelenangst** ['ze:lənaŋkst], *f.* (—, *pl.* ⸚e) anguish, agony.

**Seelenheil** ['ze:lənhail], *n.* (—s, *no pl.*) (*Theol.*) salvation.

**Seelenhirt** ['ze:lənhɪrt], *m.* (—en, *pl.* —en) pastor.

**seelenlos** ['ze:lənlo:s], *adj.* inanimate.

**Seelenmesse** ['ze:lənmɛsə], *f.* (—, *pl.* —n) requiem; Mass for the dead.

**Seelenruhe** ['ze:lənru:ə], *f.* (—, *no pl.*) tranquillity of mind.

**seelenruhig** ['ze:lənru:ɪç], *adj.* cool, calm, collected, unperturbed.

**Seelenstärke** ['ze:lənʃtɛrkə], *f.* (—, *no pl.*) fortitude; composure.

**seelenvergnügt** ['ze:lənfɛrgny:kt], *adj.* blissfully happy.

**Seelenverwandtschaft** ['ze:lənfɛrvant-ʃaft], *f.* (—, *pl.* —en) mental affinity, (mutual) understanding.

**seelenvoll** ['ze:lənfɔl], *adj.* wistful, soulful.

**Seelenwanderung** ['ze:lənvandəruŋ], *f.* (—, *no pl.*) transmigration of souls, metempsychosis.

**Seeleute** ['ze:lɔytə] *see under* **Seemann.**

**seelisch** ['ze:lɪʃ], *adj.* mental, psychological, psychic(al).

**Seelsorge** ['ze:lsɔrgə], *f.* (—, *no pl.*) (*Eccl.*) cure of souls; pastoral duties *or* work.

**Seemann** ['ze:man], *m.* (—s, *pl.* ⸚er, **Seeleute**) seaman, sailor, mariner.

**Seemeile** ['ze:mailə], *f.* (—, *pl.* —n) knot, nautical mile.

**Seemöwe** ['ze:mø:və], *f.* (—, *pl.* —n) (*Orn.*) seagull.

**Seemuschel** ['ze:muʃəl], *f.* (—, *pl.* —n) sea-shell.

**Seepflanze** ['ze:pflantsə], *f.* (—, *pl.* —n) marine plant.

**Seerabe** ['ze:ra:bə], *m.* (—n, *pl.* —n) (*Orn.*) cormorant.

**Seeräuber** ['ze:rɔybər], *m.* (—s, *pl.* —) pirate.

**Seerose** ['ze:ro:zə], *f.* (—, *pl.* —n) (*Bot.*) water-lily.

**Seesalz** ['ze:zalts], *n.* (—es, *no pl.*) bay salt, sea salt.

**Seeschlacht** ['ze:ʃlaxt], *f.* (—, *pl.* —en) naval engagement, naval battle.

**Seestern** ['ze:ʃtɛrn], *m.* (—s, *pl.* —e) (*Zool.*) starfish.

**Seestille** ['ze:ʃtɪlə], *f.* (—, *no pl.*) calm (at sea).

**Seetang** ['ze:taŋ], *m.* (—s, *no pl.*) (*Bot.*) seaweed.

**seetüchtig** ['ze:tyçtɪç], *adj.* seaworthy.

**Seeuhr** ['ze:u:r], *f.* (—, *pl.* —en) marine chronometer.

**Seeuntüchtigkeit** ['ze:untyçtɪçkait], *f.* (—, *no pl.*) unseaworthiness.

**Seewasser** ['ze:vasər], *n.* (—s, *no pl.*) sea-water, brine.

**Seewesen** ['ze:ve:zən], *n.* (—s, *no pl.*) naval affairs.

**Seezunge** ['ze:tsuŋə], *f.* (—, *pl.* —n) sole (*fish*).

**Segel** ['ze:gəl], *n.* (—s, *pl.* —) sail; *großes* —, mainsail; *unter* — *gehen*, set sail, put to sea; *die* — *streichen*, strike sail.

**segelfertig** ['ze:gəlfɛrtɪç], *adj.* ready to sail; *sich* — *machen*, get under sail.

**Segelflugzeug** ['ze:gəlflu:ktsɔyk], *n.* (—s, *pl.* —e) glider(-plane).

**Segelschiff** ['ze:gəlʃɪf], *n.* (—s, *pl.* —e) sailing-vessel.

**Segelstange** ['ze:gəlʃtaŋə], *f.* (—, *pl.* —n) sail-yard.

**Segen** ['ze:gən], *m.* (—s, *no pl.*) blessing, benediction; (*fig.*) abundance; — *sprechen*, give the blessing, say grace.

**segensreich** ['ze:gənsraɪç], *adj.* blessed, full of blessings; prosperous.

**Segenswunsch** ['ze:gənsvunʃ], *m.* (—es, *pl.* ⁓e) good wish.

**segnen** ['ze:gnən], *v.a.* bless.

**sehen** ['ze:ən], *v.a. irr.* see, behold, perceive; *etwas gern* —, like s.th., approve of s.th. — *v.n.* look, see; *sich lassen*, parade, show o.s., *wir werden* —, that remains to be seen, we shall see.

**sehenswert** ['ze:ənsveːrt], *adj.* worth seeing.

**Sehenswürdigkeit** ['ze:ənsvyrdɪçkaɪt], *f.* (—, *pl.* —en) curiosity, object of interest, tourist attraction; (*pl.*) sights.

**Seher** ['ze:ər], *m.* (—s, *pl.* —) seer, prophet.

**Sehne** ['ze:nə], *f.* (—, *pl.* —n) sinew, tendon; string.

**sehnig** ['ze:nɪç], *adj.* sinewy, muscular; (*meat*) tough.

**sehnlich** ['ze:nlɪç], *adj.* earnest, passionate, eager.

**Sehnsucht** ['ze:nzuxt], *f.* (—, *no pl.*) longing, yearning, desire.

**sehr** [ze:r], *adv.* very, much, greatly, very much; *zu* —, too much; — *gut*, very good; — *wohl*, very well.

**Sehweite** ['ze:vaɪtə], *f.* (—, *no pl.*) range of vision.

**seicht** [zaɪçt], *adj.* shallow, superficial.

**Seide** ['zaɪdə], *f.* (—, *pl.* —n) silk.

**Seidel** ['zaɪdəl], *n.* (—s, *pl.* —) (*dial.*) mug, tankard; pint.

**seiden** ['zaɪdən], *adj.* silk, silken, silky.

**Seidenpapier** ['zaɪdənpapiːr], *n.* (—s, *no pl.*) tissue-paper.

**Seidenraupe** ['zaɪdənraupə], *f.* (—, *pl.* —n) (*Ent.*) silkworm.

**Seidenstoff** ['zaɪdənʃtɔf], *m.* (—es, *pl.* —e) spun silk.

**Seife** ['zaɪfə], *f.* (—, *pl.* —n) soap; *ein Stück* —, a cake of soap.

**seifen** ['zaɪfən], *v.a.* soap.

**Seifenschaum** ['zaɪfənʃaum], *m.* (—s, *no pl.*) lather.

**Seifenwasser** ['zaɪfənvasər], *n.* (—s, *no pl.*) soap-suds.

**seifig** ['zaɪfɪç], *adj.* soapy, saponaceous.

**seihen** ['zaɪən], *v.a.* strain, filter.

**Seil** [zaɪl], *n.* (—(e)s, *pl.* —e) rope; *straffes* —, taut rope, tight rope; *schlaffes* —, slack rope.

**Seilbahn** ['zaɪlbaːn], *f.* (—, *pl.* —en) funicular railway; cable car.

**Seilbrücke** ['zaɪlbrykə], *f.* (—, *pl.* —n) rope bridge.

**Seiltänzer** ['zaɪltɛntsər], *m.* (—s, *pl.* —) tight-rope walker.

**Seilziehen** ['zaɪltsiːən], *n.* (—s, *no pl.*) tug of war.

**Seim** [zaɪm], *m.* (—(e)s, *pl.* —e) strained honey.

**Sein** [zaɪn], *n.* (—s, *no pl.*) being, existence.

**sein** (1) [zaɪn], *v.n. irr.* (*aux.* sein) be, exist.

**sein** (2) [zaɪn], *poss. adj.* his, her, its; one's. — *pers. pron.* his.

**seinerseits** ['zaɪnərzaɪts], *adv.* for his part.

**seinerzeit** ['zaɪnərtsaɪt], *adv.* at that time, at the time, formerly.

**seinesgleichen** ['zaɪnəsglaɪçən], *indecl. adj. & pron.* of his sort, such as he.

**seinethalben** ['zaɪnəthalbən], *adv.* on his account, for his sake, on his behalf.

**seinetwegen** ['zaɪnətveːgən], *adv.* on his account, for his sake, on his behalf.

**Seinige** ['zaɪnɪgə], *n.* (—n, *pl.* —n) his, his property; (*pl.*) his family, his people; *das* — *tun*, do o.'s share.

**seit** [zaɪt], *prep.* (*Dat.*) since, for; — *gestern*, since yesterday, from yesterday onwards; — *einiger Zeit*, for some time past. — *conj. see* **seitdem**.

**seitdem** [zaɪt'deːm], *adv.* since then, since that time. — *conj.* since.

**Seite** ['zaɪtə], *f.* (—, *pl.* —n) side, flank; (*book*) page; *etwas auf die* — *bringen*, put s.th. aside; *ich bin auf seiner* —, I side with him, I am on his side; *er hat seine guten* —*n*, he has his good points.

**Seitenansicht** ['zaɪtənanzɪçt], *f.* (—, *pl.* —en) profile.

**Seitengleis** ['zaɪtənglaɪs], *n.* (—es, *pl.* —e) (railway) siding.

**Seitenhieb** ['zaɪtənhiːp], *m.* (—s, *pl.* —e) innuendo, sly hit, dig.

**seitens** ['zaɪtəns], *prep.* (*Genit.*) on the part of.

**Seitensprung** ['zaɪtənʃpruŋ], *m.* (—s, *pl.* ⁓e) side-leap, caper; (*fig.*) (amorous) escapade.

**Seitenstraße** ['zaɪtənʃtraːsə], *f.* (—, *pl.* —n) side-street.

**Seitenstück** ['zaɪtənʃtyk], *n.* (—s, *pl.* —e) companion-piece.

**Seitenzahl** ['zaɪtəntsaːl], *f.* (—, *pl.* —en) page-number; number of pages.

**seither** ['zaɪtheːr], *adv.* since that time, since then.

**seitlich** ['zaɪtlɪç], *adj.* lateral.

**Sekretär** [zekre'teːr], *m.* (—s, *pl.* —e) secretary.

**Sekretariat** [zekreta'rjaːt], *n.* (—s, *pl.* —e) secretariat, secretary's office.

**Sekt** [zɛkt], *m.* (—s, *pl.* —e) champagne.

**Sekte** ['zɛktə], *f.* (—, *pl.* —n) sect.

**Sektierer** [zɛk'tiːrər], *m.* (—s, *pl.* —) sectarian.

**Sektion** [zɛk'tsjoːn] *f.* (—, *pl.* —en) section; (*Med.*) dissection.

**Sekundaner** [zekun'daːnər], *m.* (—s, *pl.* —) pupil in the second (highest) form.

**Sekundant** [zekun'dant], *m.* (—en, *pl.* —en) (*Duelling*) second.

**sekundär** [zekun'deːr], *adj.* secondary.

**Sekunde** [ze'kundə], *f.* (—, *pl.* —n) (*time*) second.

**Sekundenzeiger** [ze'kundəntsaɪgər], *m.* (—s, *pl.* —) (*clock*) second-hand.

**sekundieren** [zekun'diːrən], *v.n. einem* —, second s.o.

**selber** ['zɛlbər], *indecl. adj. & pron.* self.

**selb(ig)** ['zɛlb(ɪg)], *adj.* the same.

**selbst** [zɛlpst], *indecl. adj. & pron.* self; — *ist der Mann*, depend on yourself; *von* —, of its own accord, spontaneously. — *adv.* even; — *wenn*, even if, even though; — *dann nicht*, not even then.

**selbständig** ['zɛlpʃtɛndiç], *adj.* independent.

**Selbstbestimmung** ['zɛlpstbəʃtɪmuŋ], *f.* (—, *no pl.*) self-determination, autonomy.

**selbstbewußt** ['zɛlpstbəvust], *adj.* self-assertive, self-confident, conceited.

**selbstherrlich** ['zɛlpstherlɪç], *adj.* autocratic, tyrannical.

**Selbstlaut** ['zɛlpstlaut], *m.* (—s, *pl.* —e) vowel.

**selbstlos** ['zɛlpstloːs], *adj.* unselfish, selfless, altruistic.

**Selbstlosigkeit** [zɛlpst'loːzɪçkaɪt], *f.* (—, *no pl.*) unselfishness, altruism.

**Selbstmord** ['zɛlpstmɔrt], *m.* (—s, *pl.* —e) suicide.

**selbstredend** ['zɛlpstre:dənt], *adj.* self-evident, obvious.

**Selbstsucht** ['zɛlpstzuxt], *f.* (—, *no pl.*) selfishness, ego(t)ism.

**selbstsüchtig** ['zɛlpstzyçtɪç], *adj.* selfish, ego(t)istic(al).

**selbstverständlich** ['zɛlpstferʃtentlɪç], *adj.* self-evident. — *adv.* of course, obviously.

**Selbstzweck** ['zɛlpsttsvɛk], *m.* (—s, *no pl.*) end in itself.

**selig** ['ze:lɪç], *adj.* blessed, blissful; (*fig.*) delighted; deceased, late; — *sprechen*, beatify.

**Seligkeit** ['ze:lɪçkaɪt], *f.* (—, *pl.* —en) bliss, blissfulness; (*Eccl.*) salvation, beatitude.

**Seligsprechung** ['ze:lɪçʃpreçuŋ], *f.* (—, *pl.* —en) beatification.

**Sellerie** ['zɛləri:], *m.* (—s, *pl.* —s) (*Bot.*) celery.

**selten** ['zɛltən], *adj.* rare, scarce; (*fig.*) remarkable. — *adv.* seldom, rarely, infrequently.

**Seltenheit** ['zɛltənhaɪt], *f.* (—, *pl.* —en) rarity, curiosity, scarcity; (*fig.*) remarkableness.

**Selterswasser** ['zɛltərvasər], *n.* (—s, *no pl.*) soda-water.

**seltsam** ['zɛltza:m], *adj.* strange, unusual, odd, curious.

**Semester** [ze'mestər], *n.* (—s, *pl.* —) university term, semester.

**Semit** [ze'mi:t], *m.* (—en, *pl.* —en) Semite, Jew.

**semmelblond** ['zɛməlblɔnt], *adj.* flaxen-haired.

**Semmelkloß** ['zɛməlkloːs], *m.* (—es, *pl.* ⏜e) bread dumpling.

**Senator** [ze'na:tɔr], *m.* (—s, *pl.* —en) senator.

**senden** ['zɛndən], *v.a. irr.* send, despatch; (*money*) remit. — *v.a. reg.* (*Rad.*) broadcast.

**Sender** ['zɛndər], *m.* (—s, *pl.* —) sender; (*Rad.*) (broadcasting) station, transmitter.

**Sendling** ['zɛntlɪŋ], *m.* (—s, *pl.* —e) (*Poet.*) emissary.

**Sendschreiben** ['zɛntʃraɪbən], *n.* (—s, *pl.* —) epistle, missive.

**Sendung** ['zɛnduŋ], *f.* (—, *pl.* —en) (*Comm.*) shipment, consignment; (*fig.*) mission; (*Rad.*) broadcast, transmission.

**Senegal** ['ze:nəgal], *n.* Senegal.

**Senf** [zɛnf], *m.* (—s, *no pl.*) mustard.

**sengen** ['zɛŋən], *v.a.* singe, scorch; — *und brennen*, lay waste.

**Senkblei** ['zɛŋkblaɪ], *n.* (—s, *pl.* —e) plummet.

**Senkel** ['zɛŋkəl], *m.* (—s, *pl.* —) shoe-lace.

**senken** ['zɛŋkən], *v.a.* lower, sink. — *v.r. sich* —, sink, go down; dip, slope, subside.

**senkrecht** ['zɛŋkreçt], *adj.* perpendicular.

**Senkung** ['zɛŋkuŋ], *f.* (—, *pl.* —en) depression, dip, subsidence.

**Senn(e)** ['zɛn(ə)], *m.* (—n, *pl.* —(e)n) Alpine herdsman.

**Sennerin** ['zɛnərɪn], *f.* (—, *pl.* —nen) Alpine dairy-woman.

**Senneschoten** ['zɛnəʃo:tən], *f. pl.* senna pods.

**Sennhütte** ['zɛnhytə], *f.* (—, *pl.* —n) Alpine dairy; chalet.

**sensationell** [zɛnzatsjo'nɛl], *adj.* sensational.

**Sense** ['zɛnzə], *f.* (—, *pl.* —n) scythe.

**sensibel** [zɛn'zi:bəl], *adj.* sensitive.

**Sentenz** [zɛn'tɛnts], *f.* (—, *pl.* —en) aphorism.

**sentimental** [zɛntimɛn'ta:l], *adj.* sentimental.

**separat** [zepa'ra:t], *adj.* separate, special.

**September** [zɛp'tɛmbər], *m.* (—s, *pl.* —) September.

**Serbien** ['zɛrbjən], *n.* Serbia.

**Serie** ['ze:rjə], *f.* (—, *pl.* —n) series.

**Service** [zɛr'vi:s], *n.* (—s, *pl.* —) dinner-set, dinner-service.

**servieren** [zɛr'vi:rən], *v.a., v.n.* serve, wait at table.

**Serviertisch** [zɛr'vi:rtɪʃ], *m.* (—es, *pl.* —e) sideboard.

**Sessel** ['zɛsəl], *m.* (—s, *pl.* —) arm-chair, easy-chair; (*Austr. dial.*) chair.

**seßhaft** ['zɛshaft], *adj.* settled, domiciled.

**setzen** ['zɛtsən], *v.a.* set, put, place; (*monument*) erect; (*bet*) stake; (*Typ.*) compose. — *v.r. sich* —, sit down; (*coffee*) settle; *sich bei einem in Gunst* —, ingratiate o.s. with s.o.

**Setzer** ['zɛtsər], *m.* (—s, *pl.* —) compositor.

**Setzling** ['zɛtslɪŋ], *m.* (—s, *pl.* —e) young tree, young plant.

**Seuche** ['zɔyçə], *f.* (—, *pl.* —n) pestilence; epidemic.

**seufzen** ['zɔyftsən], *v.n.* sigh.

**Seufzer** ['zɔyftsər], *m.* (—s, *pl.* —) sigh.

**Sexta** ['zɛksta:], *f.* (—, *pl.* —s) (*Sch.*) sixth form, lowest form.

199

**Sextant** [zɛks'tant], *m.* (—en, *pl.* —en) sextant.

**sexuell** [zɛksu'ɛl], *adj.* sexual.

**sezieren** [ze'tsi:rən], *v.a.* dissect.

**Seziersaal** [ze'tsi:rza:l], *m.* (—s, *pl.* —säle) dissecting-room.

**Sibirien** [zi'bi:rjən], *n.* Siberia.

**sich** [zɪç], *pron.* oneself, himself, herself, itself, themselves; each other.

**Sichel** ['zɪçəl], *f.* (—, *pl.* —n) sickle.

**sicher** ['zɪçər], *adj.* certain, sure, secure, safe; confident, positive; *seiner Sache — sein,* be sure of o.'s ground; — *stellen,* secure.

**Sicherheit** ['zɪçərhaɪt], *f.* (—, *pl.* —en) certainty; security, safety; confidence, positiveness; *in — bringen,* secure.

**sichern** ['zɪçərn], *v.a.* secure, make secure; assure, ensure.

**Sicherung** ['zɪçəruŋ], *f.* (—, *pl.* —en) securing; (*Elec.*) fuse; (*gun*) safety-catch.

**Sicht** [zɪçt], *f.* (—, *no pl.*) sight.

**sichtbar** ['zɪçtba:r], *adj.* visible; conspicuous.

**sichten** ['zɪçtən], *v.a.* sift, sort out; sight.

**sichtlich** ['zɪçtlɪç], *adv.* visibly.

**Sichtwechsel** ['zɪçtvɛksəl], *m.* (—s, *pl.* —) (*Banking*) sight-bill, bill payable on sight.

**Sichtweite** ['zɪçtvaɪtə], *f.* (—, *no pl.*) range of vision.

**sickern** ['zɪkərn], *v.n.* (*aux.* sein) leak, ooze, seep.

**Sie** [zi:], *pron.* (*formal*) you.

**sie** [zi:], *pers. pron.* she, her; they, them.

**Sieb** [zi:p], *n.* (—(e)s, *pl.* —e) sieve; riddle; colander.

**sieben** (1) ['zi:bən], *v.a.* (*Cul.*) sift, strain.

**sieben** (2) ['zi:bən], *num. adj.* seven; *meine — Sachen,* my belongings.

**Siebeneck** ['zi:bənɛk], *n.* (—s, *pl.* —e) heptagon.

**Siebengestirn** ['zi:bəngəʃtɪrn], *n.* (—s, *no pl.*) Pleiades.

**siebenmal** ['zi:bənma:l], *adv.* seven times.

**Siebenmeilenstiefel** [zi:bən'maɪlənʃti:fəl], *m. pl.* seven-league boots.

**Siebenschläfer** ['zi:bənʃle:fər], *m.* (—s, *pl.* —) lazy-bones.

**siebzehn** ['zi:ptse:n], *num. adj.* seventeen.

**siebzig** ['zi:ptsɪç], *num. adj.* seventy.

**siech** [zi:ç], *adj.* (*rare*) sick, infirm.

**siechen** ['zi:çən], *v.n.* be in bad health.

**sieden** ['zi:dən], *v.a., v.n.* boil, seethe.

**siedeln** ['zi:dəln], *v.n.* settle.

**Siedlung** ['zi:dluŋ], *f.* (—, *pl.* —en) settlement; housing estate.

**Sieg** [zi:k], *m.* (—(e)s, *pl.* —e) victory; *den — davontragen,* win the day.

**Siegel** ['zi:gəl], *n.* (—s, *pl.* —) seal; *Brief und —,* sign and seal.

**Siegelbewahrer** ['zi:gəlbəva:rər], *m.* (—s, *pl.* —) Lord Privy Seal; keeper of the seal.

**Siegellack** ['zi:gəllak], *n.* (—s, *no pl.*) sealing wax.

**siegeln** ['zi:gəln], *v.a.* seal.

**siegen** ['zi:gən], *v.n.* conquer, win, be victorious, triumph (over).

**Sieger** ['zi:gər], *m.* (—s, *pl.* —) victor, conqueror.

**Siegesbogen** ['zi:gəsbo:gən], *m.* (—s, *pl.* ⸚) triumphal arch.

**Siegeszeichen** ['zi:gəstsaɪçən], *n.* (—s, *pl.* —) sign of victory, trophy.

**sieghaft** ['zi:khaft], *adj.* victorious, triumphant.

**siegreich** ['zi:kraɪç], *adj.* victorious, triumphant.

**siehe!** ['zi:ə], *excl.* see! look! lo and behold!

**Sierra Leone** ['siɛra le'o:nə], *f.* Sierra Leone.

**Signal** [zɪg'na:l], *n.* (—s, *pl.* —e) signal.

**Signalement** [zɪgnalə'mã], *n.* (—s, *pl.* —s) personal description.

**Signalglocke** [zɪg'na:lglɔkə], *f.* (—, *pl.* —n) warning-bell.

**signalisieren** [zɪgnali'zi:rən], *v.a.* signal.

**Signatarmacht** [zɪgna'ta:rmaxt], *f.* (—, *pl.* ⸚e) signatory power.

**signieren** [zɪg'ni:rən], *v.a.* sign.

**Silbe** ['zɪlbə], *f.* (—, *pl.* —n) syllable.

**Silbenmaß** ['zɪlbənma:s], *n.* (—es, *pl.* —e) (*Poet.*) metre.

**Silbenrätsel** ['zɪlbənrɛ:tsəl], *n.* (—s, *pl.* —) charade.

**Silber** ['zɪlbər], *n.* (—s, *no pl.*) silver; plate.

**Silberbuche** ['zɪlbərbu:xə], *f.* (—, *pl.* —n) white beech(-tree).

**Silberfuchs** ['zɪlbərfuks], *m.* (—es, *pl.* ⸚e) (*Zool.*) silver fox.

**silbern** ['zɪlbərn], *adj.* made of silver, silvery.

**Silberpappel** ['zɪlbərpapəl], *f.* (—, *pl.* —n) (*Bot.*) white poplar(-tree).

**Silberschimmel** ['zɪlbərʃɪməl],*m.* (—s, *pl.* —) grey-white horse.

**Silberzeug** ['zɪlbərtsɔyk], *n.* (—s, *no pl.*) (silver) plate.

**Silvester** [zɪl'vɛstər], *m.* (—s, *pl.* —) New Year's Eve.

**Similistein** ['zi:miliʃtaɪn], *m.* (—s, *pl.* —e) imitation *or* paste jewellery.

**Sims** [zɪms], *m.* (—es, *pl.* —e) cornice, moulding, shelf, ledge.

**Simulant** [zimu'lant], *m.* (—en, *pl.* —en) malingerer.

**simulieren** [zimu'li:rən], *v.a.* simulate.

**simultan** [zimul'ta:n], *adj.* simultaneous.

**Singapur** [zɪŋga'pu:r], *n.* Singapore.

**Singdrossel** ['zɪŋdrɔsəl], *f.* (—, *pl.* —n) (*Orn.*) common thrush.

**singen** ['zɪŋən], *v.a., v.n. irr.* sing.

**Singspiel** ['zɪŋʃpi:l], *n.* (—s, *pl.* —e) musical comedy, light opera, opera buffa.

**Singular** ['zɪŋgula:r], *m.* (—s, *pl.* —e) singular.

**sinken** ['zɪŋkən], *v.n. irr. (aux.* sein) sink; *(price)* decline, drop, fall; *den Mut — lassen,* lose heart.

**Sinn** [zɪn], *m.* (—(e)s, *pl.* —e) sense; intellect, mind; consciousness, memory; taste, meaning, purport; wish; *etwas im — haben,* have s.th. in mind, intend s.th.; *leichter —,* lightheartedness; *andern —es werden,* change o's mind; *das hat keinen —,* there is no sense in that; *von —en sein,* be out of o.'s senses; *seine fünf —e beisammen haben,* be in o.'s right mind; *sich etwas aus dem — schlagen,* dismiss s.th. from o.'s mind; *es kommt mir in den —,* it occurs to me.

**Sinnbild** ['zɪnbɪlt], *n.* (—s, *pl.* —er) symbol, emblem.

**sinnen** ['zɪnən], *v.n. irr.* meditate, reflect.

**Sinnesänderung** ['zɪnəsɛndərʊŋ], *f.* (—, *pl.* —en) change of mind.

**Sinnesart** ['zɪnəsaːrt], *f.* (—, *no pl.*) disposition, character.

**Sinnesorgan** ['zɪnəsɔrgaːn], *n.* (—s, *pl.* —e) sense-organ.

**Sinnestäuschung** ['zɪnəstɔyʃʊŋ], *f.* (—, *pl.* —en) illusion, hallucination.

**sinnfällig** ['zɪnfɛlɪç], *adj.* obvious, striking.

**Sinngedicht** ['zɪngədɪçt], *n.* (—es, *pl.* —e) epigram.

**sinnig** ['zɪnɪç], *adj.* thoughtful, meaningful; judicious, fitting.

**sinnlich** ['zɪnlɪç], *adj.* sensual, sensuous.

**Sinnlichkeit** ['zɪnlɪçkaɪt], *f.* (—, *no pl.*) sensuality, sensuousness.

**sinnlos** ['zɪnloːs], *adj.* senseless, meaningless, pointless.

**sinnreich** ['zɪnraɪç], *adj.* ingenious.

**Sinnspruch** ['zɪnʃprʊx], *m.* (—es, *pl.* —e) sentence, maxim, device, motto.

**sinnverwandt** ['zɪnfɛrvant], *adj.* synonymous.

**sinnvoll** ['zɪnfɔl], *adj.* meaningful, significant.

**sinnwidrig** ['zɪnviːdrɪç], *adj.* nonsensical, absurd.

**Sintflut** ['zɪntfluːt], *f.* (—, *no pl.*) *(Bibl.)* the Flood.

**Sinus** ['ziːnus], *m.* (—, *pl.* —se) *(Maths.)* sine.

**Sippe** ['zɪpə], *f.* (—, *pl.* —n) kin, tribe, family, clan.

**Sippschaft** ['zɪpʃaft], *f.* (—, *pl.* —en) kindred; *die ganze —,* the whole caboodle.

**Sirene** [zi're:nə], *f.* (—, *pl.* —n) siren.

**Sirup** ['ziːrup], *m.* (—s, *no pl.*) syrup, treacle.

**Sitte** ['zɪtə], *f.* (—, *pl.* —n) custom, mode, fashion; *(pl.)* manners, morals; *—n und Gebräuche,* manners and customs.

**Sittengesetz** ['zɪtəngəzɛts], *n.* (—es, *pl.* —e) moral law.

**Sittenlehre** ['zɪtənleːrə], *f.* (—, *no pl.*) moral philosophy, ethics.

**sittenlos** ['zɪtənloːs], *adj.* immoral, profligate, licentious.

**Sittenprediger** ['zɪtənpreːdɪgər], *m.* (—s, *pl.* —) moraliser.

**Sittich** ['zɪtɪç], *m.* (—s, *pl.* —e) *(Orn.)* budgerigar; parakeet.

**sittig** ['zɪtɪç], *adj.* well-behaved.

**sittlich** ['zɪtlɪç], *adj.* moral.

**Sittlichkeit** ['zɪtlɪçkaɪt], *f.* (—, *no pl.*) morality, morals.

**sittsam** ['zɪtzaːm], *adj.* modest, demure.

**situiert** [zitu'iːrt], *adj. gut (schlecht) —,* well (badly) off.

**Sitz** [zɪts], *m.* (—es, *pl.* —e) seat, chair; residence, location, place; *(Eccl.)* see.

**Sitzarbeit** ['zɪtsarbaɪt], *f.* (—, *pl.* —en) sedentary work.

**Sitzbad** ['zɪtsbaːt], *n.* (—(e)s, *pl.* ⁼er) hip bath.

**sitzen** ['zɪtsən], *v.n. irr.* sit, be seated; *(fig.)* be in prison; *(dress)* fit; *— lassen,* throw over, jilt; *— bleiben,* remain seated; *(school)* stay in the same class, not be moved up; be a wallflower; remain unmarried.

**Sitzfleisch** ['zɪtsflaɪʃ], *n.* (—es, *no pl.*) *(coll.) kein — haben,* be restless, lack application.

**Sitzplatz** ['zɪtsplats], *m.* (—es, *pl.* ⁼e) seat.

**Sitzung** ['zɪtsʊŋ], *f.* (—, *pl.* —en) meeting, sitting, session.

**Sitzungsprotokoll** ['zɪtsʊŋsprotokɔl], *n.* (—s, *pl.* —e) minutes of a meeting.

**Sitzungssaal** ['zɪtsʊŋszaːl], *m.* (—s, *pl.* —säle) board-room, conference room.

**Sizilien** [zi'tsiːljən], *n.* Sicily.

**Skala** ['skaːla], *f.* (—, *pl.* —len) scale; *(Mus.)* gamut.

**Skandal** [skan'daːl], *m.* (—s, *pl.* —e) scandal; row, riot; *— machen,* kick up a row.

**skandalös** [skanda'løːs], *adj.* scandalous.

**skandieren** [skan'diːrən], *v.a. (Poet.)* scan.

**Skandinavien** [skandɪ'naːvjən], *n.* Scandinavia.

**Skelett** [ske'lɛt], *n.* (—s, *pl.* —e) skeleton.

**Skepsis** ['skɛpsɪs], *f.* (—, *no pl.*) scepticism, doubt.

**skeptisch** ['skɛptɪʃ], *adj.* sceptical, doubtful.

**Skizze** ['skɪtsə], *f.* (—, *pl.* —n) sketch.

**skizzieren** [skɪ'tsiːrən], *v.a.* sketch.

**Sklave** ['sklaːvə], *m.* (—n, *pl.* —n) slave; *zum — machen,* enslave.

**Sklavendienst** ['sklaːvəndiːnst], *m.* (—es, *no pl.*) slavery.

**Sklaverei** [sklaːvə'raɪ], *f.* (—, *no pl.*) slavery, thraldom.

**Skonto** ['skɔnto], *m. & n.* (—s, *pl.* —s) discount.

**Skrupel** ['skruːpəl], *m.* (—s, *pl.* —) scruple; *sich — machen,* have scruples.

**skrupulös** [skrupu'løːs], *adj.* scrupulous, meticulous.

**Skulptur** [skulp'tuːr], *f.* (—, *pl.* —en) sculpture.

**skurril** [sku'riːl], *adj.* ludicrous.

**Slawe** ['slaːvə], *m.* (—n, *pl.* —n) Slav.

**slawisch** ['slaːvɪʃ], *adj.* Slav, Slavonic.

**Slowake** [slo'vaːkə], *m.* (—n, *pl.* —n) Slovakian.

**Slowene** [slo've:nə], *m.* (—n, *pl.* —n) Slovenian.

**Smaragd** [sma'rakt], *m.* (—(e)s, *pl.* —e) emerald.

**smaragden** [sma'raktən], *adj.* emerald.

**Smoking** ['smoːkɪŋ], *m.* (—s, *pl.* —s) dinner-jacket.

**so** [zoː], *adv.* so, thus, in this way, like this; —? really? — *ist es*, that is how it is; — *daß*, so that; — ... *wie*, as ... as; *na — was!* well, I never! — *conj.* then, therefore.

**sobald** [zo'balt], *conj.* as soon as, directly.

**Socke** ['zɔkə], *f.* (—, *pl.* —n) sock.

**Sockel** ['zɔkəl], *m.* (—s, *pl.* —) pedestal, plinth, stand, base.

**Soda** ['zoːda], *n.* (—s, *no pl.*) (carbonate of) soda.

**sodann** [zo'dan], *adv. conj.* then.

**Sodbrennen** ['zoːtbrɛnən], *n.* (—s, *no pl.*) heartburn.

**soeben** [zo'eːbən], *adv.* just now.

**sofern** [zo'fɛrn], *conj.* if, in case, so far as.

**sofort** [zo'fɔrt], *adv.* at once, immediately.

**Sog** [zoːk], *m.* (—(e)s, *pl.* —e) undertow, suction.

**sogar** [zo'gaːr], *adv.* even.

**sogenannt** [zogə'nant], *adj.* so-called, would-be.

**sogleich** [zo'glaɪç], *adv.* at once, immediately.

**Sohle** ['zoːlə], *f.* (—, *pl.* —n) sole; (*mine*) floor.

**Sohn** [zoːn], *m.* (—(e)s, *pl.* ⁺e) son; *der verlorene* —, the prodigal son.

**solange** [zo'laŋə], *conj.* as long as.

**Solbad** ['zoːlbaːt], *n.* (—s, *pl.* ⁺er) saline bath.

**solch** [zɔlç], *adj., dem. pron.* such.

**solcherlei** ['zɔlçərlaɪ], *adj.* of such a kind, suchlike.

**Sold** [zɔlt], *m.* (—(e)s, *no pl.*) army pay.

**Soldat** [zɔl'daːt], *m.* (—en, *pl.* —en) soldier.

**Soldateska** [zɔlda'tɛska], *f.* (—, *pl.* —s) soldiery.

**Söldner** ['zœldnər], *m.* (—s, *pl.* —) mercenary, hireling.

**Sole** ['zoːlə], *f.* (—, *pl.* —n) salt-water, brine.

**Solei** ['zoːlaɪ], *n.* (—s, *pl.* —er) pickled egg.

**solidarisch** [zoli'daːrɪʃ], *adj.* joint, jointly responsible; unanimous.

**Solidarität** [zolidari'tɛːt], *f.* (—, *no pl.*) solidarity.

**Solist** [zo'lɪst], *m.* (—en, *pl.* —en) soloist.

**Soll** [zɔl], *n.* (—s, *no pl.*) debit; — *und Haben*, debit and credit.

**sollen** ['zɔlən], *v.n. irr.* be obliged, be compelled; have to; be supposed to; (*aux.*) shall, should etc.; *ich soll*, I must, I am to; *er soll krank sein*, he is said to be ill; *ich sollte eigentlich*, I really ought to.

**Söller** ['zœlər], *m.* (—s, *pl.* —) loft, garret, balcony.

**Somali** [zo'maːli], *n.* Somalia.

**somit** [zo'mɪt], *adv.* consequently, therefore, accordingly.

**Sommer** ['zɔmər], *m.* (—s, *pl.* —) summer.

**Sommerfäden** ['zɔmərfɛːdən], *m. pl.* gossamer.

**Sommerfrische** ['zɔmərfrɪʃə], *f.* (—, *pl.* —n) holiday resort.

**Sommergetreide** ['zɔmərgətraɪdə], *n.* (—s, *no pl.*) spring corn.

**Sommersonnenwende** ['zɔmərzɔnən-vendə], *f.* (—, *pl.* —n) summer solstice.

**Sommersprosse** ['zɔmərʃprɔsə], *f.* (—, *pl.* —n) freckle.

**sonach** [zo'naːx], *adv.* therefore, consequently.

**Sonate** [zo'naːtə], *f.* (—, *pl.* —n) sonata.

**Sonde** ['zɔndə], *f.* (—, *pl.* —n) sounding-lead, plummet; probe.

**sonder** ['zɔndər], (*obs.*) *prep.* (*Acc.*) without.

**Sonderausgabe** ['zɔndərausgaːbə], *f.* (—, *pl.* —n) separate edition; special edition.

**Sonderausschuß** ['zɔndərausʃus], *m.* (—sses, *pl.* ⁺sse) select committee.

**sonderbar** ['zɔndərbaːr], *adj.* strange, odd, queer, singular, peculiar.

**sonderlich** ['zɔndərlɪç], *adj.* special, especial, particular. — *adv. nicht* —, not much.

**Sonderling** ['zɔndərlɪŋ], *m.* (—s, *pl.* —e) freak, odd character, crank.

**sondern** ['zɔndərn], *v.a.* separate, distinguish, differentiate. — *conj.* but; *nicht nur*, ... — *auch*, not only ... but also.

**Sonderrecht** ['zɔndərrɛçt], *n.* (—s, *pl.* —e) special privilege.

**sonders** ['zɔndərs], *adv. samt und* —, all and each, all and sundry.

**Sonderstellung** ['zɔndərʃtɛluŋ], *f.* (—, *no pl.*) exceptional position.

**Sonderung** ['zɔndəruŋ], *f.* (—, *pl.* —en) separation.

**Sonderzug** ['zɔndərtsuːk], *m.* (—s, *pl.* ⁺e) special train.

**sondieren** [zɔn'diːrən], *v.a.* (*wound*) probe; (*ocean*) plumb; (*fig.*) sound.

**Sonett** [zo'nɛt], *n.* (—(e)s, *pl.* —e) sonnet.

**Sonnabend** ['zɔnaːbənt], *m.* (—s, *pl.* —e) Saturday.

**Sonne** ['zɔnə], *f.* (—, *pl.* —n) sun.

**sonnen** ['zɔnən], *v.r. sich* —, sun o.s., bask in the sun, sunbathe.

**Sonnenaufgang** ['zɔnənaufgaŋ], *m.* (—s, *pl.* ⁺e) sunrise.

**Sonnenbrand** ['zɔnənbrant], *m.* (—s, *pl.* ⁺e) sunburn.

**Sonnendeck** ['zɔnəndɛk], *n.* (—s, *pl.* —e) awning.

**Sonnenfinsternis** ['zɔnənfɪnstərnɪs], *f.* (—, *pl.* —se) eclipse of the sun.

**sonnenklar** ['zɔnənkla:r], *adj.* very clear, as clear as daylight.

**Sonnenschirm** ['zɔnənʃɪrm], *m.* (—s, *pl.* —e) parasol, sunshade.

**Sonnenstich** ['zɔnənʃtiç], *n.* (—(e)s, *no pl.*) sunstroke.

**Sonnenuhr** ['zɔnənu:r], *f.* (—, *pl.* —en) sundial.

**Sonnenuntergang** ['zɔnənuntərgaŋ], *m.* (—s, *pl.* ⸚e) sunset.

**Sonnenwende** ['zɔnənvɛndə], *f.* (—, *no pl.*) solstice.

**Sonntag** ['zɔnta:k], *m.* (—s, *pl.* —e) Sunday.

**sonntags** ['zɔnta:ks], *adv.* on Sundays, of a Sunday.

**Sonntagsjäger** ['zɔnta:ksjɛ:gər], *m.* (—s, *pl.* —) amateur sportsman.

**sonor** [zo'no:r], *adj.* sonorous.

**sonst** [zɔnst], *adv.* else, otherwise, besides, at other times; — *noch etwas?* anything else?

**sonstig** ['zɔnstiç], *adj.* other, existing besides.

**sonstwo** ['zɔnstvo], *adv.* elsewhere, somewhere else.

**Sopran** [zo'pra:n], *m.* (—s, *pl.* —e) soprano.

**Sorbett** ['zɔrbɛt], *n.* (—s, *pl.* —e) sherbet.

**Sorge** ['zɔrgə], *f.* (—, *pl.* —n) care; grief, worry; sorrow; anxiety; concern; (*pl.*) troubles, worries; — *tragen dass...*, see to it that...; — *tragen zu,* take care of; — *um,* concern for.

**sorgen** ['zɔrgən], *v.n.* — *für,* care for, provide for, look after. — *v.r. sich* — *um,* worry about.

**sorgenvoll** ['zɔrgənfɔl], *adj.* uneasy, troubled, anxious.

**Sorgfalt** ['zɔrkfalt], *f.* (—, *no pl.*) care, attention.

**sorgfältig** ['zɔrkfɛltiç], *adj.* careful, painstaking; elaborate.

**sorglos** ['zɔrklo:s], *adj.* careless, irresponsible, unconcerned, indifferent; carefree.

**sorgsam** ['zɔrkza:m], *adj.* careful, heedful.

**Sorte** ['zɔrtə], *f.* (—, *pl.* —n) sort, kind, species, brand.

**sortieren** [zɔr'ti:rən], *v.a.* sort (out).

**Sortiment** [zɔrti'mɛnt], *n.* (—s, *pl.* —e) assortment; bookshop.

**Sortimentsbuchhändler** [zɔrti'mentsbu:xhɛndlər], *m.* (—s, *pl.* —) retail bookseller.

**Soße** ['zo:sə], *f.* (—, *pl.* —n) sauce, gravy.

**Souffleur** [suf'lø:r], *m.* (—s, *pl.* —e) prompter.

**Soutane** [su'ta:nə], *f.* (—, *pl.* —n) cassock, soutane.

**Souterrain** [sutɛ'rɛ̃], *n.* (—s, *pl.* —s) basement.

**souverän** [su:və're:n], *adj.* sovereign; (*fig.*) supremely good.

**Souveränität** [su:vərɛ:ni'tɛ:t], *f.* (—, *no pl.*) sovereignty.

**soviel** [zo'fi:l], *adv.* so much; — *wie,* as much as. — *conj.* so far as; — *ich weiß,* as far as I know.

**sowie** [zo'vi:], *conj.* as, as well as, as soon as.

**Sowjet** [sɔv'jɛt], *m.* (—s, *pl.* —s) Soviet.

**sowohl** [zo'vo:l], *conj.* — *wie,* as well as.

**sozial** [zo'tsja:l], *adj.* social.

**sozialisieren** [zotsjali'zi:rən], *v.a.* nationalise.

**Sozialwissenschaft** [zo'tsja:lvɪsənʃaft], *f.* (—, *pl.* —en) sociology; social science.

**Sozietät** [zotsje'tɛ:t], *f.* (—, *pl.* —en) partnership.

**Sozius** ['zotsjus], *m.* (—, *pl.* —se, Socii) partner; pillion-rider; —*sitz,* (*motor cycle*) pillion (seat).

**sozusagen** ['zo:tsuza:gən], *adv.* as it were, so to speak.

**Spagat** [ʃpa'ga:t], *m.* (—(e)s, *no pl.*) (*dial.*) string, twine; (*Dancing*) the splits.

**spähen** ['ʃpɛ:ən], *v.n.* look out, watch; (*Mil.*) scout; spy.

**Späher** ['ʃpɛ:ər], *m.* (—s, *pl.* —) scout; spy.

**Spalier** [ʃpa'li:r], *n.* (—s, *pl.* —e) trellis; — *bilden,* form a lane (*of people*).

**Spalierobst** [ʃpa'li:ro:pst], *n.* (—(e)s, *no pl.*) wall-fruit.

**Spalt** [ʃpalt], *m.* (—(e)s, *pl.* —e) crack, rift, cleft, rent; (*glacier*) crevasse.

**Spalte** ['ʃpaltə], *f.* (—, *pl.* —n) (*newspaper*) column.

**spalten** ['ʃpaltən], *v.a.* split, cleave, slit. — *v.r. sich* —, divide, break up, split up; (*in two*) bifurcate.

**Spaltholz** ['ʃpalthɔlts], *n.* (—es, *no pl.*) fire-wood.

**Spaltpilz** ['ʃpaltpɪlts], *m.* (—es, *pl.* —e) fission-fungus.

**Spaltung** ['ʃpaltuŋ], *f.* (—, *pl.* —en) cleavage; (*atomic*) fission; (*fig.*) dissension, rupture; (*Eccl.*) schism.

**Span** [ʃpa:n], *m.* (—(e)s, *pl.* ⸚e) chip, chippings, shavings.

**Spange** ['ʃpaŋə], *f.* (—, *pl.* —n) clasp, buckle.

**Spanien** ['ʃpa:njən], *n.* Spain.

**spanisch** ['ʃpa:nɪʃ], *adj.* Spanish; —*e Wand,* folding screen; *es kommt mir* — *vor,* it is Greek to me.

**Spann** [ʃpan], *m.* (—(e)s, *pl.* —e) instep.

**Spanne** ['ʃpanə], *f.* (—, *pl.* —n) span; *eine* — *Zeit,* a short space of time.

**spannen** ['ʃpanən], *v.a.* stretch, strain, span.

**spannend** ['ʃpanənt], *adj.* thrilling, tense.

**Spannkraft** ['ʃpankraft], *f.* (—, *no pl.*) elasticity.

**Spannung** ['ʃpanuŋ], *f.* (—, *pl.* —en) tension, suspense, strain; (*fig.*) eager expectation, curiosity, suspense, close attention; (*Elec.*) voltage.

**Sparbüchse** [ˈʃpaːrbyksə], f. (—, pl. —n) money-box.

**sparen** [ˈʃpaːrən], v.a., v.n. save, economise, put by, lay by.

**Spargel** [ˈʃpargəl], m. (—s, pl. —) asparagus.

**Spargelder** [ˈʃpaːrgɛldər], n. pl. savings.

**Sparkasse** [ˈʃpaːrkasə], f. (—, pl. —n) savings bank.

**spärlich** [ˈʃpɛːrlɪç], adj. scant, scanty, sparse.

**Sparpfennig** [ˈʃpaːrpfɛnɪç], m. (—s, pl. —e) nest-egg.

**Sparren** [ˈʃparən], m. (—s, pl. —) spar, rafter; er hat einen —, he has a screw loose.

**sparsam** [ˈʃpaːrzaːm], adj. economical, thrifty, frugal.

**Spaß** [ʃpaːs], m. (—es, pl. ⸚e) jest, fun, joke; aus —, im —, zum —, in fun; — verstehen, take a joke; es macht mir —, it amuses me, it is fun for me.

**spaßen** [ˈʃpaːsən], v.n. jest, joke.

**spaßhaft** [ˈʃpaːshaft], adj. funny, facetious, jocular.

**Spaßverderber** [ˈʃpaːsfɛrdɛrbər], m. (—s, pl. —) spoil-sport.

**Spaßvogel** [ˈʃpaːsfoːgəl], m. (—s, pl. ⸚) wag.

**Spat** [ʃpaːt], m. (—(e)s, pl. —e) (Min.) spar.

**spät** [ʃpɛːt], adj. late; wie — ist es? what is the time? zu — kommen, be late.

**Spätabend** [ˈʃpɛːtaːbənt], m. (—s, pl. —e) latter part of the evening, late evening.

**Spatel** [ˈʃpaːtəl], m. (—s, pl. —) spatula.

**Spaten** [ˈʃpaːtən], m. (—s, pl. —) spade.

**Spatenstich** [ˈʃpaːtənʃtɪç], m. (—(e)s, pl. —e) den ersten — tun, turn the first sod.

**später** [ˈʃpɛːtər], adv. later (on), afterwards.

**spätestens** [ˈʃpɛːtəstəns], adv. at the latest.

**Spätling** [ˈʃpɛːtlɪŋ], m. (—s, pl. —e) late arrival; late fruit.

**Spätsommer** [ˈʃpɛːtzɔmər], m. (—s, pl. —) Indian summer.

**Spatz** [ʃpats], m. (—en pl. —en) (Orn.) sparrow.

**spazieren** [ʃpaˈtsiːrən], v.n. (aux. sein) walk leisurely, stroll; — gehen, go for a walk, take a stroll; — führen, take for a walk.

**Spazierfahrt** [ʃpaˈtsiːrfaːrt], f. (—, pl. —en) (pleasure-)drive.

**Spazierstock** [ʃpaˈtsiːrʃtɔk], m. (—s, pl. ⸚e) walking-stick.

**Spazierweg** [ʃpaˈtsiːrveːk], m. (—s, pl. —e) walk, promenade.

**Specht** [ʃpɛçt], m. (—(e)s, pl. —e) (Orn.) woodpecker.

**Speck** [ʃpɛk], m. (—(e)s, no pl.) bacon; eine Scheibe —, a rasher of bacon.

**speckig** [ˈʃpɛkɪç], adj. fat.

**Speckschwarte** [ˈʃpɛkʃvartə], f. (—, pl. —n) bacon-rind.

**Speckseite** [ˈʃpɛkzaɪtə], f. (—, pl. —n) flitch of bacon.

**spedieren** [ʃpeˈdiːrən], v.a. forward; despatch.

**Spediteur** [ʃpediˈtøːr], m. (—s, pl. —e) forwarding agent, furniture-remover, carrier.

**Spedition** [ʃpediˈtsjoːn], f. (—, pl. —en) conveyance; forwarding agency.

**Speer** [ʃpeːr], m. (—(e)s, pl. —e) spear, lance.

**Speiche** [ˈʃpaɪçə], f. (—, pl. —n) spoke.

**Speichel** [ˈʃpaɪçəl], m. (—s, no pl.) spittle, saliva.

**Speicher** [ˈʃpaɪçər], m. (—s, pl. —) granary; warehouse, storehouse; loft.

**speien** [ˈʃpaɪən], v.a., v.n. irr. spit; vomit, be sick.

**Speise** [ˈʃpaɪzə], f. (—, pl. —n) food, nourishment, dish.

**Speisekammer** [ˈʃpaɪzəkamər], f. (—, pl. —n) larder, pantry.

**Speisekarte** [ˈʃpaɪzəkartə], f. (—, pl. —n) bill of fare, menu.

**speisen** [ˈʃpaɪzən], v.a. feed, give to eat. — v.n. eat, dine, sup, lunch.

**Speiseröhre** [ˈʃpaɪzərøːrə], f. (—, pl. —n) gullet.

**Speisewagen** [ˈʃpaɪzəvaːgən], m. (—s, pl. —) (Railw.) dining-car.

**Spektakel** [ʃpɛkˈtaːkəl], m. (—s, no pl.) uproar, hubbub; shindy, rumpus; noise, row.

**Spektrum** [ˈʃpɛktrum], n. (—s, pl. Spektren) spectrum.

**Spekulant** [ʃpekuˈlant], m. (—en, pl. —en) speculator.

**spekulieren** [ʃpekuˈliːrən], v.n. speculate; theorise.

**Spende** [ˈʃpɛndə], f. (—, pl. —n) gift, donation; bounty.

**spenden** [ˈʃpɛndən], v.a. bestow, donate, contribute.

**Spender** [ˈʃpɛndər], m. (—s, pl. —) donor, giver, benefactor.

**spendieren** [ʃpɛnˈdiːrən], v.a. (give a) treat, pay for, stand.

**Sperber** [ˈʃpɛrbər], m. (—s, pl. —) (Orn.) sparrow-hawk.

**Sperling** [ˈʃpɛrlɪŋ], m. (—s, pl. —e) (Orn.) sparrow.

**sperrangelweit** [ˈʃpɛraŋəlvaɪt], adv. wide open.

**Sperre** [ˈʃpɛrə], f. (—, pl. —n) shutting, closing, blockade, blocking; closure; ban; (Railw.) barrier.

**sperren** [ˈʃpɛrən], v.a. spread out; (Typ.) space; shut, close, block; cut off; ins Gefängnis —, put in prison. — v.r. sich — gegen, offer resistance to.

**Sperrhaken** [ˈʃpɛrhaːkən], m. (—s, pl. —) catch, ratchet.

**Sperrsitz** [ˈʃpɛrzɪts], m. (—es, pl. —e) (Theat.) stall.

**Sperrung** [ˈʃpɛruŋ], f. (—, pl. —en) barring, obstruction, block, blockade; (Comm.) embargo.

**Sperrzeit** [ˈʃpɛrtsaɪt], f. (—, pl. —en) closing-time.

**Spesen** [ˈʃpeːzən], f. pl. charges, expenses.

**spesenfrei** ['∫peːzənfraɪ], *adj.* free of charge; expenses paid.

**Spezereien** [∫peːtsəˈraɪən], *f. pl.* spices.

**spezialisieren** [∫petsjaliˈziːrən], *v.a.* specify. — *v.r. sich* —, specialise.

**Spezialist** [∫petsjaˈlɪst], *m.* (—en, *pl.* —en) specialist, expert.

**Spezialität** [∫petsjaliˈtɛːt], *f.* (—, *pl.* —en) speciality, (*Am.*) specialty.

**speziell** [∫peˈtsjɛl], *adj.* special, particular.

**Spezies** ['∫peːtsjɛs], *f.* (—, *pl.* —) species; (*Maths.*) rule.

**Spezifikation** [∫petsifikaˈtsjoːn], *f.* (—, *pl.* —en) specification.

**spezifisch** [∫peˈtsiːfɪ∫], *adj.* specific.

**spezifizieren** [∫petsifiˈtsiːrən], *v.a.* specify.

**Spezifizierung** [∫petsifiˈtsiːruŋ], *f.* (— *pl.* —en) specification.

**Spezimen** ['∫peːtsimən], *n.* (—s, *pl.* —mina) specimen.

**Sphäre** ['sfɛːrə], *f.* (—, *pl.* —n) sphere.

**sphärisch** ['sfɛːrɪ∫], *adj.* spherical.

**Spickaal** ['∫pɪkaːl], *m.* (—s, *pl.* —e) smoked eel.

**spicken** ['∫pɪkən], *v.a.* lard; *den Beutel* —, fill o.'s purse.

**Spiegel** ['∫piːgəl], *m.* (—s, *pl.* —) mirror, looking-glass.

**spiegelblank** ['∫piːgəlblaŋk], *adj.* sparkling, shiny, polished.

**Spiegelei** ['∫piːgəlaɪ], *n.* (—s, *pl.* —er) fried egg.

**Spiegelfechterei** ['∫piːgəlfɛçtəraɪ], *f.* (—, *pl.* —en) shadow-boxing, make-believe.

**Spiegelfenster** ['∫piːgəlfɛnstər], *n.* (—s, *pl.* —) plate-glass window.

**spiegeln** ['∫piːgəln], *v.n.* glitter, shine. — *v.a.* reflect. — *v.r. sich* —, be reflected.

**Spiegelscheibe** ['∫piːgəl∫aɪbə], *f.* (—, *pl.* —n) plate-glass pane.

**Spiegelung** ['∫piːgəluŋ], *f.* (—, *pl.* —en) reflection; mirage.

**Spiel** [∫piːl], *n.* (—(e)s, *pl.* —e) play; game; sport; (*Theat.*) acting, performance; (*Mus.*) playing; *ehrliches (unehrliches)* —, fair (foul) play; *leichtes* —, walk-over; *auf dem* — *stehen*, be at stake; *aufs* — *setzen*, stake, risk; *die Hand im* — *haben*, have a finger in the pie; *gewonnenes* — *haben*, gain o.'s point; *ein gewagtes* — *treiben*, play a bold game; *sein* — *mit einem treiben*, trifle with s.o.

**Spielart** ['∫piːlaːrt], *f.* (—, *pl.* —en) manner of playing; variety.

**Spielbank** ['∫piːlbaŋk], *f.* (—, *pl.* —en) casino; gambling-table.

**Spieldose** ['∫piːldoːzə], *f.* (—, *pl.* —n) musical box.

**spielen** ['∫piːlən], *v.a., v.n.* play; gamble; (*Mus.*) play; (*Theat.*) act; *eine Rolle* —, play a part; *mit dem Gedanken* —, toy with the idea.

**spielend** ['∫piːlənt], *adv.* easily.

**Spieler** ['∫piːlər], *m.* (—s, *pl.* —) player; gambler; gamester.

**Spielerei** [∫piːləˈraɪ], *f.* (—, *pl.* —en) child's play; trivialities.

**Spielhölle** ['∫piːlhœlə], *f.* (—, *pl.* —n) gambling-den.

**Spielmann** ['∫piːlman], *m.* (—s, *pl.* **Spielleute**) musician, fiddler; (*Middle Ages*) minstrel.

**Spielmarke** ['∫piːlmarkə], *f.* (—, *pl.* —n) counter, chip.

**Spielplan** ['∫piːlplaːn], *m.* (—s, *pl.* ⸚e) (*Theat.*) repertory.

**Spielplatz** ['∫piːlplats], *m.* (—es, *pl.* ⸚e) playground.

**Spielraum** ['∫piːlraum], *m.* (—s, *no pl.*) elbow-room; (*fig.*) scope; margin; clearance.

**Spielsache** ['∫piːlzaxə], *f.* (—, *pl.* —n) toy, plaything.

**Spielschule** ['∫piːl∫uːlə], *f.* (—, *pl.* —n) infant-school, kindergarten.

**Spieltisch** ['∫piːltɪ∫], *m.* (—es, *pl.* —e) card-table.

**Spieluhr** ['∫piːluːr], *f.* (—, *pl.* —en) musical clock.

**Spielverderber** ['∫piːlfɛrderbər], *m.* (—s, *pl.* —) spoilsport.

**Spielwaren** ['∫piːlvaːrən], *f. pl.* toys.

**Spielzeit** ['∫piːltsaɪt], *f.* (—, *pl.* —en) playtime; (*Theat.*) season.

**Spielzeug** ['∫piːltsɔyk], *n.* (—s, *pl.* —e) plaything, toy.

**Spieß** [∫piːs], *m.* (—es, *pl.* —e) spear, pike; (*Cul.*) spit.

**Spießbürger** ['∫piːsbyrgər], *m.* (—s, *pl.* —) Philistine.

**spießen** ['∫piːsən], *v.a.* spear, pierce.

**Spießer** ['∫piːsər], *m.* (—s, *pl.* —) Philistine.

**Spießgeselle** ['∫piːsgəzɛlə], *m.* (—n, *pl.* —n) accomplice, companion *or* partner in crime.

**spießig** ['∫piːsɪç], *adj.* (*coll.*) Philistine, uncultured, narrow-minded.

**Spießruten** ['∫piːsruːtən], *f. pl.* — *laufen*, run the gauntlet.

**Spinat** [∫piˈnaːt], *m.* (—s, *no pl.*) spinach.

**Spind** [∫pɪnt], *n.* (—(e)s, *pl.* —e) cupboard.

**Spindel** ['∫pɪndəl], *f.* (—, *pl.* —n) spindle; distaff; (*staircase*) newel.

**spindeldürr** ['∫pɪndəldyr], *adj.* as thin as a lath.

**Spindelholz** ['∫pɪndəlhɔlts], *n.* (—es, *no pl.*) spindle-tree wood.

**Spinett** [∫piˈnɛt], *n.* (—s, *pl.* —e) spinet.

**Spinne** ['∫pɪnə], *f.* (—, *pl.* —n) spider.

**spinnefeind** ['∫pɪnəfaɪnt], *adj. einander* — *sein*, hate each other like poison.

**spinnen** ['∫pɪnən], *v.a. irr.* spin. — *v.n.* (*coll.*) be off o.'s head, be crazy.

**Spinnerei** [∫pɪnəˈraɪ], *f.* (—, *pl.* —en) spinning-mill.

**Spinngewebe** ['∫pɪŋgəveːbə], *n.* (—s, *pl.* —) cobweb.

**Spinnrocken** ['∫pɪnrɔkən], *m.* (—s, *pl.* —) distaff.

**spintisieren** [∫pɪntiˈziːrən], *v.n.* muse, meditate.

# Spion

**Spion** [ʃpiˈoːn], *m.* (—s, *pl.* —e) spy.
**spionieren** [ʃpioˈniːrən], *v.n.* spy, pry.
**Spirale** [ʃpiˈraːlə], *f.* (—, *pl.* —n) spiral.
**Spirituosen** [ʃpirituˈoːzən], *pl.* spirits, liquors.
**Spiritus** [ˈʃpiːritus], *m.* (—, *pl.* —se) alcohol, spirits of wine; *denaturierter* —, methylated spirits.
**Spiritusbrennerei** [ˈʃpiːritusbrenəraɪ], *f.* (—, *pl.* —en) distillery.
**Spiritusgehalt** [ˈʃpiːritusgəhalt], *m.* (—s, *pl.* —e) (*alcoholic*) strength, proof.
**Spital** [ʃpiˈtaːl], *n.* (—s, *pl.* ⁻er) infirmary; hospital.
**Spitz** [ʃpɪts], *m.* (—es, *pl.* —e) Pomeranian dog; *einen — haben,* (*coll.*) be slightly tipsy.
**spitz** [ʃpɪts], *adj.* pointed; (*fig.*) snappy, biting.
**Spitzbart** [ˈʃpɪtsbaːrt], *m.* (—s, *pl.* ⁻e) imperial (beard), pointed beard.
**Spitzbogen** [ˈʃpɪtsboːgən], *m.* (—s, *pl.* —) pointed arch, Gothic arch.
**Spitzbogenfenster** [ˈʃpɪtsboːgənfenstər], *n.* (—s, *pl.* —) lancet window.
**Spitzbube** [ˈʃpɪtsbuːbə], *m.* (—n, *pl.* —n) rogue; rascal; scamp.
**Spitzbubenstreich** [ˈʃpɪtsbuːbənʃtraɪç], *m.* (—(e)s, *pl.* —e) act of roguery, knavery.
**spitzbübisch** [ˈʃpɪtsbyːbɪʃ], *adj.* roguish.
**Spitze** [ˈʃpɪtsə], *f.* (—, *pl.* —n) point; tip; top, peak; extremity; (*pipe*) mouthpiece; (*cigarette*) holder; (*pen*) nib; lace; *etwas auf die — treiben,* carry s.th. to extremes; *an der — stehen,* be at the head of.
**Spitzel** [ˈʃpɪtsəl], *m.* (—s, *pl.* —) police-agent; informer.
**spitzen** [ˈʃpɪtsən], *v.a.* sharpen; *die Ohren —,* prick up o.'s ears; *sich auf etwas —,* await s.th. eagerly, be all agog for s.th.
**Spitzenbelastung** [ˈʃpɪtsənbəlastuŋ], *f.* (—, *pl.* —en) peak load.
**Spitzenleistung** [ˈʃpɪtsənlaɪstuŋ], *f.* (—, *pl.* —en) maximum output; peak performance.
**Spitzentuch** [ˈʃpɪtsəntuːx], *n.* (—(e)s, *pl.* ⁻er) lace scarf.
**spitzfindig** [ˈʃpɪtsfɪndɪç], *adj.* subtle, crafty; hair-splitting.
**Spitzhacke** [ˈʃpɪtshakə], *f.* (—, *pl.* —n) pickaxe.
**spitzig** [ˈʃpɪtsɪç], *adj.* pointed, sharp; (*fig.*) biting, pungent.
**Spitzmaus** [ˈʃpɪtsmaus], *f.* (—, *pl.* ⁻e) (*Zool.*) shrew.
**Spitzname** [ˈʃpɪtsnaːmə], *m.* (—ns, *pl.* —n) nickname.
**spitzwinklig** [ˈʃpɪtsvɪŋklɪç], *adj.* acute-angled.
**spleißen** [ˈʃplaɪsən], *v.a. irr.* split, cleave.
**Splitter** [ˈʃplɪtər], *m.* (—s, *pl.* —) splinter, chip.
**splittern** [ˈʃplɪtərn], *v.n.* (*aux.* sein) splinter.

**splitternackt** [ˈʃplɪtərnakt], *adj.* stark naked.
**spontan** [ʃpɔnˈtaːn], *adj.* spontaneous.
**sporadisch** [ʃpoˈraːdɪʃ], *adj.* sporadic.
**Spore** [ˈʃpoːrə], *f.* (—, *pl.* —n) spore.
**Sporn** [ʃpɔrn], *m.* (—s, *pl.* **Sporen**) spur.
**spornstreichs** [ˈʃpɔrnʃtraɪçs], *adv.* post-haste, at once.
**Sportler** [ˈʃpɔrtlər], *m.* (—s, *pl.* —) athlete, sportsman.
**sportlich** [ˈʃpɔrtlɪç], *adj.* athletic; sporting.
**sportsmäßig** [ˈʃpɔrtsmɛːsɪç], *adj.* sportsmanlike.
**Spott** [ʃpɔt], *m.* (—(e)s, *no pl.*) mockery; scorn; *Gegenstand des —s,* laughing-stock; *— treiben mit,* mock, deride; *zum Schaden den — hinzufügen,* add insult to injury.
**spottbillig** [ˈʃpɔtbɪlɪç], *adj.* ridiculously cheap, dirt-cheap.
**Spöttelei** [ʃpœtəˈlaɪ], *f.* (—, *pl.* —en) sarcasm.
**spötteln** [ˈʃpœtəln], *v.n.* mock, jeer.
**spotten** [ˈʃpɔtən], *v.a., v.n.* deride, scoff (at); *es spottet jeder Beschreibung,* it defies description.
**Spötter** [ˈʃpœtər], *m.* (—s, *pl.* —) mocker, scoffer.
**Spötterei** [ʃpœtəˈraɪ], *f.* (—, *pl.* —en) mockery, derision.
**Spottgedicht** [ˈʃpɔtgədɪçt], *n.* (—(e)s, *pl.* —e) satirical poem.
**spöttisch** [ˈʃpœtɪʃ], *adj.* mocking, satirical, ironical, scoffing.
**spottlustig** [ˈʃpɔtlustɪç], *adj.* flippant, satirical.
**Spottschrift** [ˈʃpɔtʃrɪft], *f.* (—, *pl.* —en) satire, lampoon.
**Sprache** [ˈʃpraːxə], *f.* (—, *pl.* —n) speech, language; tongue; expression; diction; discussion; *etwas zur — bringen,* bring a subject up; *zur — kommen,* come up for discussion; *heraus mit der —!* speak out!
**Sprachfehler** [ˈʃpraːxfeːlər], *m.* (—s, *pl.* —) impediment in o.'s speech.
**sprachfertig** [ˈʃpraːxfertɪç], *adj.* having a ready tongue; a good linguist, fluent.
**Sprachgebrauch** [ˈʃpraːxgəbraux], *m.* (—(e)s, *pl.* ⁻e) (linguistic) usage.
**Sprachkenner** [ˈʃpraːxkenər], *m.* (—s, *pl.* —) linguist.
**sprachkundig** [ˈʃpraːxkundɪç], *adj.* proficient in languages.
**Sprachlehre** [ˈʃpraːxleːrə], *f.* (—, *no pl.*) grammar.
**sprachlich** [ˈʃpraːxlɪç], *adj.* linguistic.
**sprachlos** [ˈʃpraːxloːs], *adj.* speechless, tongue-tied; *— dastehen,* be dumb-founded.
**Sprachrohr** [ˈʃpraːxroːr], *n.* (—s, *pl.* —e) megaphone, speaking-tube; (*fig.*) mouthpiece.
**Sprachschatz** [ˈʃpraːxʃats], *m.* (—es, *no pl.*) vocabulary.
**Sprachvergleichung** [ˈʃpraːxfɛrglaɪçuŋ], *f.* (—, *no pl.*) comparative philology.

**Sprachwerkzeug** [ˈʃpraːxvərktsɔyk], *n.*
(—s, *pl.* —e) organ of speech.
**Sprachwissenschaft** [ˈʃpraːxvisənʃaft],
*f.* (—, *pl.* —en) linguistics, philology.
**sprechen** [ˈʃprɛçən], *v.a.,v.n. irr.* speak,
declare, say; talk; *für einen* —, put in
a good word for s.o., speak up for s.o.;
*er ist nicht zu* —, he is not available;
*auf einen gut zu* — *sein*, feel well
disposed towards s.o.; *schuldig* —,
pronounce guilty; *das Urteil* —, pass
sentence.
**sprechend** [ˈʃprɛçənt], *adj.* expressive;
— *ähnlich*, strikingly alike.
**Sprecher** [ˈʃprɛçər], *m.* (—s, *pl.* —)
speaker, orator, spokesman; (*Rad.*) announcer.
**Sprechstunde** [ˈʃprɛçʃtundə], *f.* (—,
*pl.* —n) consulting hours, surgery
hours; office hours.
**Sprechzimmer** [ˈʃprɛçtsimər], *n.* (—s,
*pl.*—) consulting-room.
**spreizen** [ˈʃpraitsən], *v.a.* spread open;
*die Beine* —, plant o.'s legs wide apart,
straddle. — *v.r. sich* —, give o.s. airs.
**Sprengbombe** [ˈʃprɛŋbɔmbə], *f.* (—,
*pl.* —n) (high explosive) bomb.
**Sprengel** [ˈʃprɛŋəl], *m.* (—s, *pl.* —)
diocese.
**sprengen** [ˈʃprɛŋən], *v.a.* sprinkle;
water; burst, explode; burst open,
blow up; *eine Versammlung* —, break
up a meeting. — *v.n.* (*aux.* sein) ride
at full speed, gallop.
**Sprengpulver** [ˈʃprɛŋpulvər], *n.* (—s,
*no pl.*) blasting-powder.
**Sprengstoff** [ˈʃprɛŋʃtɔf], *m.* (—es, *pl.*
—e) explosive.
**Sprengwagen** [ˈʃprɛŋvaːgən], *m.* (—s,
*pl.* —) sprinkler; water-cart.
**sprenkeln** [ˈʃprɛŋkəln], *v.a.* speckle.
**Spreu** [ʃprɔy], *f.* (—, *no pl.*) chaff.
**Sprichwort** [ˈʃpriçvɔrt], *n.* (—s, *pl.*
ˈer) proverb, adage, saying.
**sprießen** [ˈʃpriːsən], *v.n. irr.* sprout,
shoot, germinate.
**Springbrunnen** [ˈʃpriŋbrunən], *m.*
(—s, *pl.* —) fountain.
**springen** [ˈʃpriŋən], *v.n. irr.* (*aux.* sein)
spring, leap, jump; (*glass*) burst;
*etwas* — *lassen*, (*coll.*) treat s.o. to
s.th.
**Springer** [ˈʃpriŋər], *m.* (—s, *pl.* —)
jumper, acrobat; (*Chess*) knight.
**Springflut** [ˈʃpriŋfluːt], *f.* (—, *pl.* —en)
spring-tide.
**Springtau** [ˈʃpriŋtau], *n.* (—s, *pl.* —e)
skipping-rope; (*Naut.*) slip-rope.
**Sprit** [ʃprit], *m.* (—s, *pl.* —e) spirit
alcohol; (*sl.*) fuel, petrol.
**Spritze** [ˈʃpritsə], *f.* (—, *pl.* —n) squirt,
syringe; fire-engine; (*coll.*) injection.
**spritzen** [ˈʃpritsən], *v.a.* squirt, spout,
spray, sprinkle; (*coll.*) inject. — *v.n.*
gush forth.
**Spritzkuchen** [ˈʃpritskuːxən], *m.* (—s,
*pl.* —) fritter.
**Spritztour** [ˈʃpritstuːr], *f.* (—, *pl.* —en)
(*coll.*) pleasure trip, outing; (*coll.*)
spin.

**spröde** [ˈʃprøːdə], *adj.* (*material*) brittle;
(*person*) stubborn; coy, prim, prudish.
**Sprödigkeit** [ˈʃprøːdiçkait], *f.* (—, *no
pl.*) (*material*) brittleness; (*person*)
stubbornness; coyness, primness, prudery.
**Sproß** [ʃprɔs], *m.* (—sses, *pl.* —sse)
sprout, shoot, germ; (*fig.*) scion,
offspring.
**Sprosse** [ˈʃprɔsə], *f.* (—, *pl.* —n)
(*ladder*) step, rung.
**Sprößling** [ˈʃprœsliŋ], *m.* (—s, *pl.* —e)
scion, offspring.
**Sprotte** [ˈʃprɔtə], *f.* (—, *pl.* —n) sprat.
**Spruch** [ʃprux], *m.* (—(e)s, *pl.* ˈe)
saying, aphorism; proverb; (*obs.*)
saw; (*judge*) sentence, verdict.
**spruchreif** [ˈʃpruxraif], *adj.* ripe for
judgment; ready for a decision.
**Sprudel** [ˈʃpruːdəl], *m.* (—s, *pl.* —)
bubbling spring; (*coll.*) soda water.
**sprudeln** [ˈʃpruːdəln], *v.n.* bubble, gush.
**sprühen** [ˈʃpryːən], *v.a.* sprinkle, scatter, spray. — *v.n.* sparkle, emit
sparks; (*rain*) drizzle.
**sprühend** [ˈʃpryːənt], *adj.* (*fig.*) sparkling, scintillating, brilliant.
**Sprühregen** [ˈʃpryːreːgən], *m.* (—s,
*no pl.*) drizzling rain, drizzle.
**Sprung** [ʃpruŋ], *m.* (—(e)s, *pl.* ˈe) leap,
bound, jump; chink, crack; *nur auf
einen* — *zu Besuch kommen*, pay a
flying visit; *auf dem* — *sein zu*, be on
the point of; *sich auf den* — *machen*,
cut and run, (*coll.*) fly; *große* ˈe
*machen*, (*coll.*) live it up, cut a dash.
**Sprungfeder** [ˈʃpruŋfeːdər], *f.* (—,
*pl.* —n) spring.
**Sprungkraft** [ˈʃpruŋkraft], *f.* (—, *no
pl.*) springiness, elasticity, buoyancy.
**Spucke** [ˈʃpukə], *f.* (—, *no pl.*) spittle,
saliva.
**spucken** [ˈʃpukən], *v.a.,v.n.* spit.
**Spuk** [ʃpuːk], *m.* (—s, *pl.* —e) haunting;
ghost, spectre, apparition; (*coll.*) spook.
**spuken** [ˈʃpuːkən], *v.n.* haunt; be
haunted.
**spukhaft** [ˈʃpuːkhaft], *adj.* uncanny,
phantom-like, ghost-like, spooky.
**Spule** [ˈʃpuːlə], *f.* (—, *pl.* —n) spool;
(*Elec.*) coil.
**Spüleimer** [ˈʃpyːlaimər], *m.* (—s,
*pl.* —) slop-pail.
**spülen** [ˈʃpyːlən], *v.a.* rinse, wash.
**Spülicht** [ˈʃpyːliçt], *n.* (—s, *no pl.*)
dish-water.
**Spund** [ʃpunt], *m.* (—(e)s, *pl.* ˈe) bung.
**Spundloch** [ˈʃpuntlɔx], *n.* (—s, *pl.*
ˈer) bung-hole.
**Spur** [ʃpuːr], *f.* (—, *pl.* —en) footprint,
track, trail; spoor; (*fig.*) trace,
vestige; *frische* —, hot scent; *einer
Sache auf die* — *kommen*, be on the
track of s.th.; *keine* — *von*, not a
trace of, not an inkling of.
**spüren** [ˈʃpyːrən], *v.a.* trace, track
(down); feel, sense, notice.
**Spürhund** [ˈʃpyːrhunt], *m.* (—s, *pl.* —e)
tracker dog, setter, beagle; (*fig.*) spy,
sleuth.

# spurlos

**spurlos** [ˈʃpuːrloːs], *adj.* trackless, without a trace; *es ging — an ihm vorüber,* it left no mark on him; *—verschwinden,* vanish into thin air.

**Spürsinn** [ˈʃpyːrzɪn], *m.* (—s, *no pl.*) scent; flair; sagacity, shrewdness.

**Spurweite** [ˈʃpuːrvaɪtə], *f.* (—, *pl.* —n) gauge, width of track.

**sputen** [ˈʃpuːtən], *v.r. sich* —, make haste, hurry.

**Staat** [ʃtaːt], *m.* (—(e)s, *pl.* —en) state; government; pomp, show, parade; *— machen,* make a show of.

**Staatenbund** [ˈʃtaːtənbunt], *m.* (—(e)s, *pl.* ⁻e) confederacy, federation.

**staatlich** [ˈʃtaːtlɪç], *adj.* belonging to the state, public, national.

**Staatsangehörige** [ˈʃtaːtsangəhøːrɪgə], *m.* (—n, *pl.* —n) citizen (of a country), subject, national.

**Staatsangehörigkeit** [ˈʃtaːtsangəhøːrɪçkaɪt], *f.* (—, *pl.* —en) nationality.

**Staatsanwalt** [ˈʃtaːtsanvalt], *m.* (—s, *pl.* ⁻e) public prosecutor, Attorney-General.

**Staatsbeamte** [ˈʃtaːtsbəamtə], *m.* (—n, *pl.* —n) civil servant, employee of the state.

**Staatsbürger** [ˈʃtaːtsbyrgər], *m.* (—s, *pl.* —) citizen, national.

**Staatsdienst** [ˈʃtaːtsdiːnst], *m.* (—(e)s, *pl.* —e) civil service, government service.

**Staatseinkünfte** [ˈʃtaːtsaɪnkynftə], *f. pl.* public revenue.

**Staatsgesetz** [ˈʃtaːtsgəzɛts], *n.* (—es, *pl.* —e) statute law.

**Staatsgewalt** [ˈʃtaːtsgəvalt], *f.* (—, *no pl.*) executive power.

**Staatshaushalt** [ˈʃtaːtshaushalt], *m.* (—s, *no pl.*) state finances, budget.

**Staatshaushaltsanschlag** [ˈʃtaːtshaushaltsanʃlaːk], *m.* (—s, *pl.* ⁻e) budget estimates.

**Staatskanzler** [ˈʃtaːtskantslər], *m.* (—s, *pl.* —) Chancellor.

**Staatskasse** [ˈʃtaːtskasə], *f.* (—, *no pl.*) public exchequer, treasury.

**Staatskörper** [ˈʃtaːtskœrpər], *m.* (—s, *pl.* —) body politic.

**Staatskosten** [ˈʃtaːtskɔstən], *f. pl. auf* —, at (the) public expense.

**Staatskunst** [ˈʃtaːtskunst], *f.* (—, *no pl.*) statesmanship; statecraft.

**Staatsminister** [ˈʃtaːtsminɪstər], *m.* (—s, *pl.* —) cabinet minister; minister of state.

**Staatsrat** [ˈʃtaːtsraːt], *m.* (—(e)s, *pl.* ⁻e) council of state; (*pl.* ⁻e) councillor of state.

**Staatsrecht** [ˈʃtaːtsrɛçt], *n.* (—(e)s, *no pl.*) constitutional law.

**Staatssiegel** [ˈʃtaːtsziːgəl], *n.* (—s, *pl.* —) Great Seal, official seal.

**Staatsstreich** [ˈʃtaːtsʃtraɪç], *m.* (—(e)s, *pl.* —e) coup d'état.

**Staatswirtschaft** [ˈʃtaːtsvɪrtʃaft], *f.* (—, *no pl.*) political economy.

**Staatszimmer** [ˈʃtaːtstsɪmər], *n.* (—s, *pl.* —) state apartment.

**Stab** [ʃtaːp], *m.* (—(e)s, *pl.* ⁻e) staff; stick, rod, pole; crosier; mace; (*Mil.*) field-officers, staff; *den — über einen brechen,* condemn s.o. (to death).

**stabil** [ʃtaˈbiːl], *adj.* steady, stable, firm.

**stabilisieren** [ʃtabiliˈziːrən], *v.a.* stabilise.

**Stabreim** [ˈʃtaːbraɪm], *m.* (—s, *no pl.*) alliteration.

**Stabsarzt** [ˈʃtaːpsartst], *m.* (—es, *pl.* ⁻e) (*Mil.*) medical officer.

**Stabsquartier** [ˈʃtaːpskvartiːr], *n.* (—s, *pl.* —e) (*Mil.*) headquarters.

**Stachel** [ˈʃtaxəl], *m.* (—s, *pl.* —n) (*animal*) sting; (*plant*) prickle, thorn; (*fig.*) keen edge, sting; stimulus; *wider den — löcken,* kick against the pricks.

**Stachelbeere** [ˈʃtaxəlbeːrə], *f.* (—, *pl.* —n) (*Bot.*) gooseberry.

**Stachelschwein** [ˈʃtaxəlʃvaɪn], *n.* (—s, *pl.* —e) (*Zool.*) hedgehog, porcupine.

**stachlig** [ˈʃtaxlɪç], *adj.* prickly, thorny; (*fig.*) disagreeable.

**Stadion** [ˈʃtaːdjon], *n.* (—s, *pl.* —dien) sports-arena, stadium.

**Stadium** [ˈʃtaːdjum], *n.* (—s, *pl.* —dien) stage (of development), phase.

**Stadt** [ʃtat], *f.* (—, *pl.* ⁻e) town; city.

**Stadtbahn** [ˈʃtatbaːn], *f.* (—, *pl.* —en) metropolitan railway.

**Städtchen** [ˈʃtɛtçən], *n.* (—s, *pl.* —) small town, township.

**Städter** [ˈʃtɛtər], *m.* (—s, *pl.* —) townsman.

**Stadtgemeinde** [ˈʃtatgəmaɪndə], *f.* (—, *pl.* —n) municipality.

**städtisch** [ˈʃtɛtɪʃ], *adj.* municipal.

**Stadtmauer** [ˈʃtatmauər], *f.* (—, *pl.* —n) town wall, city wall.

**Stadtrat** [ˈʃtatraːt], *m.* (—s, *no pl.*) town council; (*pl.* ⁻e) town councillor; alderman.

**Stadtteil** [ˈʃtattaɪl], *m.* (—s, *pl.* —e) ward, district, part of a town.

**Stadttor** [ˈʃtattoːr], *n.* (—s, *pl.* —e) city-gate.

**Stadtverordnete** [ˈʃtatfɛrɔrdnətə], *m.* (—n, *pl.* —n) town councillor.

**Stafette** [ʃtaˈfɛtə], *f.* (—, *pl.* —n) courier; relay.

**Staffel** [ˈʃtafəl], *f.* (—, *pl.* —n) step, rundle, rung, round; relay; (*fig.*) degree; (*Aviat.*) squadron.

**Staffelei** [ʃtafəˈlaɪ], *f.* (—, *pl.* —en) easel.

**staffeln** [ˈʃtafəln], *v.a.* grade; differentiate; stagger.

**Staffelung** [ˈʃtafəluŋ], *f.* (—, *pl.* —en) gradation.

**stagnieren** [ʃtagˈniːrən], *v.n.* stagnate.

**Stahl** [ʃtaːl], *m.* (—(e)s, *pl.* ⁻e) steel.

**stählen** [ˈʃtɛːlən], *v.a.* steel, harden, temper; brace.

**stählern** [ˈʃtɛːlərn], *adj.* made of steel, steely.

**Stahlquelle** [ˈʃtaːlkvelə], *f.* (—, *pl.* —n) chalybeate spring; mineral spring.

**Stahlstich** [ˈʃtaːlʃtɪç], *m.* (—(e)s, *pl.* —e) steel-engraving.

**Stählung** ['ʃtɛːluŋ], f. (—, no pl.) steeling; (fig.) bracing.

**Stahlwaren** ['ʃtaːlvaːrən], f. pl. hardware, cutlery.

**Stall** [ʃtal], m. (—(e)s, pl. ⸚e) stable; (pig) sty; (dog) kennel.

**Stallbursche** ['ʃtalburʃə], m. (—n, pl. —n) stable-boy, groom.

**Stallungen** ['ʃtaluŋən], f. pl. stabling, stables.

**Stambul** ['stambul], n. Istanbul.

**Stamm** [ʃtam], m. (—(e)s, pl. ⸚e) (tree) trunk; (people) tribe, family, race; (words) stem; root.

**Stammaktie** ['ʃtamaktsjə], f. (—, pl. —n) (Comm.) original share.

**Stammbaum** ['ʃtambaum], m. (—s, pl. ⸚e) pedigree; family tree.

**Stammbuch** ['ʃtambuːx], n. (—(e)s, pl. ⸚er) album.

**stammeln** ['ʃtaməln], v.a., v.n. stammer, stutter; falter.

**stammen** ['ʃtamən], v.n. (aux. sein) be descended from, spring from, originate from, stem from; be derived from.

**Stammesgenosse** ['ʃtaməsgənɔsə], m. (—n, pl. —n) kinsman, clansman.

**Stammgast** ['ʃtamgast], m. (—es, pl. ⸚e) regular customer.

**Stammgut** ['ʃtamguːt], n. (—s, pl. ⸚er) family estate.

**Stammhalter** ['ʃtamhaltər], m. (—s, pl. —) son and heir; eldest son.

**Stammhaus** ['ʃtamhaus], n. (—es, pl. ⸚er) ancestral mansion; (royalty) dynasty; (Comm.) business headquarters, head office.

**stämmig** ['ʃtɛmɪç], adj. sturdy, strong.

**Stammler** ['ʃtamlər], m. (—s, pl. —) stammerer, stutterer.

**Stammsilbe** ['ʃtamzɪlbə], f. (—, pl. —n) (Ling.) radical syllable.

**Stammtafel** ['ʃtamtaːfəl], f. (—, pl. —n) genealogical table.

**Stammvater** ['ʃtamfaːtər], m. (—s, pl. ⸚) ancestor, progenitor.

**stammverwandt** ['ʃtamfɛrvant], adj. cognate, kindred.

**stampfen** ['ʃtampfən], v.a. stamp, pound, ram down. — v.n. stamp, trample.

**Stand** [ʃtant], m. (—(e)s, pl. ⸚e) stand; (market) stall; situation, state (of affairs), condition; reading, position; rank, station (in life); (pl.) the classes, the estates.

**Standarte** [ʃtan'dartə], f. (—, pl. —n) standard, banner.

**Standbild** ['ʃtantbɪlt], n. (—(e)s, pl. —er) statue.

**Ständchen** ['ʃtɛntçən], n. (—s, pl. —) serenade; einem ein — bringen, serenade s.o.

**Ständehaus** ['ʃtɛndəhaus], n. (—es, pl. ⸚er) state assembly-hall.

**Ständer** ['ʃtɛndər], m. (—s, pl. —) stand, pedestal; post; (upright) desk.

**Standesamt** ['ʃtandəsamt], n. (—s, pl. ⸚er) registry office.

**Standesbeamte** ['ʃtandəsbəamtə], m. (—n, pl. —n) registrar (of births, marriages and deaths).

**Standesbewußtsein** ['ʃtandəsbəvust-zaɪn], n. (—s, no pl.) class-feeling, class-consciousness.

**Standesperson** ['ʃtandəspɛrzoːn], f. (—, pl. —en) person of rank.

**Standgericht** ['ʃtantgərɪçt], n. (—es, pl. —e) court-martial; summary court of justice.

**standhaft** ['ʃtanthaft], adj. constant, firm, steadfast.

**standhalten** ['ʃtanthaltən], v.n. irr. bear up, stand o.'s ground, withstand, resist.

**ständig** ['ʃtɛndɪç], adj. permanent.

**ständisch** ['ʃtɛndɪʃ], adj. relating to the estates (of the realm).

**Standort** ['ʃtantɔrt], m. (—s, pl. —e) location; station.

**Standpauke** ['ʃtantpaukə], f. (—, pl. —n) (coll.) harangue; severe reprimand.

**Standpunkt** ['ʃtantpuŋkt], m. (—(e)s, pl. —e) standpoint; point of view; den — vertreten, take the line; einem den — klar machen, give s.o. a piece of o.'s mind.

**Standrecht** ['ʃtantrɛçt], n. (—(e)s, no pl.) martial law.

**Standuhr** ['ʃtantuːr], f. (—, pl. —en) grandfather-clock.

**Stange** ['ʃtaŋə], f. (—, pl. —n) stick, pole; bei der — bleiben, stick to the point, persevere.

**Stank** [ʃtaŋk], m. (—s, no pl.) (dial.) stench; discord, trouble.

**Stänker** ['ʃtɛŋkər], m. (—s, pl. —) (coll.) mischief-maker, quarrelsome person.

**stänkern** ['ʃtɛŋkərn], v.n. pick quarrels; ferret about, make trouble.

**Stanniol** [ʃta'njoːl], n. (—s, no pl.) tinfoil.

**stanzen** ['ʃtantsən], v.a. punch, stamp.

**Stapel** ['ʃtaːpəl], m. (—s, pl. —) pile, heap; (Naut.) slipway; ein Schiff vom — lassen, launch a ship.

**Stapellauf** ['ʃtaːpəllauf], m. (—s, pl. ⸚e) (Naut.) launch, launching.

**stapeln** ['ʃtaːpəln], v.a. pile up.

**Stapelnahrung** ['ʃtaːpəlnaːruŋ], f. (—, no pl.) staple diet.

**Stapelplatz** ['ʃtaːpəlplats], m. (—es, pl. ⸚e) mart, emporium.

**Stapelware** ['ʃtaːpəlvaːrə], f. (—, pl. —n) staple goods.

**Stapfen** ['ʃtapfən], m. or f. pl. footsteps.

**Star** (1) [ʃtaːr], m. (—(e)s, pl. —e) (Med.) cataract; einem den — stechen, operate for cataract; (fig.) open s.o's eyes.

**Star** (2) [ʃtaːr], m. (—(e)s, pl. —en) (Orn.) starling.

**stark** [ʃtark], adj. strong, stout; robust; vigorous; heavy; considerable; —er Esser, hearty eater. — adv. very much.

# Stärke

**Stärke** [ˈʃtɛrkə], *f.* (—, *no pl.*) strength, vigour, robustness; strong point; starch.

**Stärkekleister** [ˈʃtɛrkəklaɪstər], *m.* (—s, *no pl.*) starch-paste.

**Stärkemehl** [ˈʃtɛrkəmeːl], *n.* (—s, *no pl.*) starch-flour.

**stärken** [ˈʃtɛrkən], *v.a.* strengthen; corroborate; starch. — *v.r. sich* —, take some refreshment.

**stärkend** [ˈʃtɛrkənt], *adj.* strengthening, restorative; —*es Mittel*, tonic.

**starkleibig** [ˈʃtarklaɪbɪç], *adj.* corpulent, stout, obese.

**Stärkung** [ˈʃtɛrkuŋ], *f.* (—, *pl.* —en) strengthening, invigoration; refreshment.

**starr** [ʃtar], *adj.* stiff, rigid; fixed; inflexible; stubborn; *einen — ansehen*, stare at s.o.

**starren** [ˈʃtarən], *v.n.* stare.

**Starrheit** [ˈʃtarhaɪt], *f.* (—, *no pl.*) stiffness, rigidity; fixedness; inflexibility; stubbornness.

**starrköpfig** [ˈʃtarkœpfɪç], *adj.* headstrong, stubborn, obstinate, pigheaded.

**Starrkrampf** [ˈʃtarkrampf], *m.* (—(e)s, *no pl.*) (*Med.*) tetanus.

**Starrsinn** [ˈʃtarzɪn], *m.* (—s, *no pl.*) stubbornness, obstinacy.

**Station** [ʃtaˈtsjoːn], *f.* (—, *pl.* —en) (*Railw.*) station; (*main*) terminus; stop, stopping-place; (*hospital*) ward; *freie* —, board and lodging found.

**stationär** [ʃtatsjoˈnɛːr], *adj.* stationary.

**stationieren** [ʃtatsjoˈniːrən], *v.a.* station.

**Stationsvorsteher** [ʃtatˈsjoːnsfɔrʃteːər], *m.* (—s, *pl.* —) station-master.

**statisch** [ˈʃtatɪʃ], *adj.* static.

**Statist** [ʃtaˈtɪst], *m.* (—en, *pl.* —en) (*Theat.*) extra, walking-on part; (*pl.*) supers.

**Statistik** [ʃtaˈtɪstɪk], *f.* (—, *pl.* —en) statistics.

**Statistiker** [ʃtaˈtɪstɪkər], *m.* (—s, *pl.* —) statistician.

**Stativ** [ʃtaˈtiːf], *n.* (—s, *pl.* —e) stand, tripod.

**Statt** [ʃtat], *f.* (—, *no pl.*) place, stead; *an seiner* —, in his place.

**statt** [ʃtat], *prep.* (*Genit.*) instead of, in lieu of.

**Stätte** [ˈʃtɛtə], *f.* (—, *pl.* —n) place, abode.

**stattfinden** [ˈʃtatfɪndən], *v.n.* irr. take place.

**stattgeben** [ˈʃtatgeːbən], *v.n.* irr. *einer Bitte* —, grant a request.

**statthaft** [ˈʃtathaft], *adj.* admissible, allowable, lawful.

**Statthalter** [ˈʃtathaltər], *m.* (—s, *pl.* —) governor.

**stattlich** [ˈʃtatlɪç], *adj.* stately, handsome, distinguished, comely; portly; considerable; *eine* —*e Summe*, a tidy sum.

**statuieren** [ʃtatuˈiːrən], *v.a.* decree; *ein Exempel* —, make an example of.

**Statut** [ʃtaˈtuːt], *n.* (—s, *pl.* —en) statute, regulation.

**Staub** [ʃtaup], *m.* (—(e)s, *no pl.*) dust, powder; *sich aus dem — machen*, take French leave; abscond.

**Stäubchen** [ˈʃtɔypçən], *n.* (—s, *pl.* —) mote, particle of dust.

**stauben** [ˈʃtaubən], *v.n. es staubt*, it is dusty.

**Staubgefäß** [ˈʃtaupɡəfɛːs], *n.* (—es, *pl.* —e) stamen.

**staubig** [ˈʃtaubɪç], *adj.* dusty.

**Staubkamm** [ˈʃtaupkam], *m.* (—s, *pl.* ⸚e) fine-tooth comb.

**Staublappen** [ˈʃtauplapən], *m.* (—s, *pl.* —) duster.

**Staubmantel** [ˈʃtaupmantəl], *m.* (—s, *pl.* ⸚) overall, smock; dust(er)coat, (*Am.*) duster.

**Staubsauger** [ˈʃtaupzauɡər], *m.* (—s, *pl.* —) vacuum cleaner.

**Staubtuch** [ˈʃtauptuːx], *n.* (—es, *pl.* ⸚er) duster.

**Staubwedel** [ˈʃtaupveːdəl], *m.* (—s, *pl.* —) feather duster.

**Staubwolke** [ˈʃtaupvɔlkə], *f.* (—, *pl.* —n) cloud of dust.

**Staubzucker** [ˈʃtauptsukər], *m.* (—s, *no pl.*) castor-sugar, icing-sugar.

**Staudamm** [ˈʃtaudam], *m.* (—s, *pl.* ⸚e) dam, dyke.

**Staude** [ˈʃtaudə], *f.* (—, *pl.* —n) shrub, bush.

**stauen** [ˈʃtauən], *v.a.* stow; (*water*) dam. — *v.r. sich* —, be congested.

**staunen** [ˈʃtaunən], *v.n.* be astonished, be surprised, wonder (at).

**Staupe** [ˈʃtaupə], *f.* (—, *pl.* —n) (*animals*) distemper.

**stäupen** [ˈʃtɔypən], *v.a.* (*obs.*) scourge, flog.

**Stauung** [ˈʃtauuŋ], *f.* (—, *pl.* —en) stowage; (*water*) damming-up, swell, rising; (*blood*) congestion; (*traffic*) jam, build-up.

**stechen** [ˈʃtɛçən], *v.a.* irr. prick, sting; stab; (*cards*) trump.

**stechend** [ˈʃtɛçənt], *adj.* pungent, biting.

**Stechmücke** [ˈʃtɛçmykə], *f.* (—, *pl.* —n) (*Ent.*) gnat, mosquito.

**Stechpalme** [ˈʃtɛçpalmə], *f.* (—, *pl.* —n) (*Bot.*) holly.

**Steckbrief** [ˈʃtɛkbriːf], *m.* (—s, *pl.* —e) warrant (for arrest).

**stecken** [ˈʃtɛkən], *v.a.* stick into, put, place, fix; (*plants*) set, plant; *in Brand* —, set on fire, set fire to. — *v.n. irgendwo* —, be about somewhere; — *bleiben*, get stuck, break down; *er steckt dahinter*, he is at the bottom of it. — *v.r. sich hinter einen* —, shelter behind s.o.

**Stecken** [ˈʃtɛkən], *m.* (—s, *pl.* —) stick, staff.

**Stecker** [ˈʃtɛkər], *m.* (—s, *pl.* —) (*Elec.*) plug.

**Steckkontakt** [ˈʃtɛkkɔntakt], *m.* (—(e)s, *pl.* —e) (*Elec.*) plug, point.

**Stecknadel** [ˈʃtɛknaːdəl], *f.* (—, *pl.* —n) pin.

**Steg** [ʃteːk], *m.* (—(e)s, *pl.* —e) plank, foot-bridge; jetty; (*violin*) bridge.

# Stelzbein

**Stegreif** ['ʃteːkraɪf], m. (—s, pl. —e) (obs.) stirrup; *aus dem — sprechen*, extemporise, improvise.

**stehen** ['ʃteːən], v.n. irr. stand; be; stand still; *einem gut —*, fit or suit s.o. well; *mit einem gut —*, be on good terms with s.o.; *gut —*, be in a fair way, look promising; *was steht zu Diensten?* what can I do for you? *— bleiben*, stand still, stop, pull up.

**stehlen** ['ʃteːlən], v.a. irr. steal.

**Steiermark** ['ʃtaɪərmark], f. Styria.

**steif** [ʃtaɪf], adj. stiff; (grog) strong; awkward; ceremonious, punctilious, formal. *— adv. etwas — und fest behaupten*, swear by all that's holy.

**steifen** ['ʃtaɪfən], v.a. stiffen, starch.

**Steifheit** ['ʃtaɪfhaɪt], f. (—, no pl.) stiffness; (fig.) formality.

**Steifleinen** ['ʃtaɪflaɪnən], n. (—s, no pl.) buckram.

**Steig** [ʃtaɪk], m. (—(e)s, pl. —e) path, (mountain) track.

**Steigbügel** ['ʃtaɪkbyːgəl], m. (—s, pl. —) stirrup.

**Steigen** ['ʃtaɪgən], n. (—s, no pl.) rising, increase; (price) advance, rise; *im —*, on the increase.

**steigen** ['ʃtaɪgən], v.n. irr. (aux. sein) climb, mount, ascend; (barometer) rise; (population) increase; (horse) rear; (price) advance, rise.

**Steiger** ['ʃtaɪgər], m. (—s, pl. —) climber, mountaineer; mining-surveyor, overseer.

**steigern** ['ʃtaɪgərn], v.a. (price) raise; (fig.) enhance, increase. *— v.r. sich —*, increase.

**Steigerung** ['ʃtaɪgərʊŋ], f. (—, pl. —en) raising; (fig.) enhancement; increase; (Gram.) comparison.

**Steigung** ['ʃtaɪgʊŋ], f. (—, pl. —en) gradient.

**steil** [ʃtaɪl], adj. steep.

**Stein** [ʃtaɪn], m. (—(e)s, pl. —e) stone, rock; flint; jewel, gem; monument; (Chess) piece, chessman; (Draughts) man; (fruit) stone, kernel; *— des Anstoßes*, stumbling block; *mir fällt ein — vom Herzen*, it is a load off my mind; *bei einem einen — im Brett haben*, be in s.o.'s good books; *einem —e in den Weg legen*, put obstacles in s.o.'s way; *der — des Weisen*, the philosopher's stone.

**Steinadler** ['ʃtaɪnaːdlər], m. (—s, pl. —) (Orn.) golden eagle.

**steinalt** ['ʃtaɪnalt], adj. very old.

**Steinbock** ['ʃtaɪnbɔk], m. (—s, pl. ̈e) ibex; (Astrol.) Capricorn.

**Steinbruch** ['ʃtaɪnbrux], m. (—s, pl. ̈e) stone-pit, quarry.

**Steinbutt** ['ʃtaɪnbut], m. (—s, pl. —e) (Zool.) turbot.

**Steindruck** ['ʃtaɪndruk], m. (—s, no pl.) lithography.

**steinern** ['ʃtaɪnərn], adj. stony; built of stone.

**Steingut** ['ʃtaɪnguːt], n. (—s, no pl.) earthenware, stoneware, pottery.

**Steinhagel** ['ʃtaɪnhaːgəl], m. (—s, no pl.) shower of stones.

**Steinhaue** ['ʃtaɪnhauə], f. (—, pl. —n) pickaxe.

**Steinhügel** ['ʃtaɪnhyːgəl], m. (—s, pl. —) cairn.

**steinig** ['ʃtaɪnɪç], adj. stony, rocky.

**steinigen** ['ʃtaɪnɪgən], v.a. stone.

**Steinkalk** ['ʃtaɪnkalk], m. (—s, no pl.) quicklime.

**Steinkohle** ['ʃtaɪnkoːlə], f. (—, no pl.) pit-coal.

**Steinkrug** ['ʃtaɪnkruːk], m. (—s, pl. ̈e) stone jar.

**Steinmarder** ['ʃtaɪnmardər], m. (—s, pl. —) (Zool.) stone-marten.

**Steinmetz** ['ʃtaɪnmets], m. (—es, pl. —e) stone-cutter, stone-mason.

**Steinobst** ['ʃtaɪnoːpst], n. (—es, no pl.) stone-fruit.

**Steinplatte** ['ʃtaɪnplatə], f. (—, pl. —n) slab, flagstone.

**steinreich** ['ʃtaɪnraɪç], adj. as rich as Croesus.

**Steinsalz** ['ʃtaɪnzalts], n. (—es, no pl.) rock-salt, mineral-salt.

**Steinwurf** ['ʃtaɪnvurf], m. (—s, pl. ̈e) *einen — entfernt*, within a stone's throw.

**Steiß** [ʃtaɪs], m. (—es, pl. —e) rump; (coll.) buttocks, posterior.

**Stellage** [ʃteˈlaːʒə], f. (—, pl. —n) stand, frame.

**Stelldichein** ['ʃteldɪçaɪn], n. (—s, no pl.) assignation, rendezvous, tryst; (coll.) date.

**Stelle** ['ʃtelə], f. (—, pl. —n) place, spot; job, position; situation; (book) passage; figure, digit; department; *offene —*, vacancy; *auf der —*, at once, immediately; *an deiner —*, if I were you; *nicht von der — kommen*, remain stationary; *zur — sein*, be at hand.

**stellen** ['ʃtelən], v.a. put, place, set; *richtig —*, regulate, correct, amend; (clock) set right; *seinen Mann —*, play o.'s part, pull o.'s weight. *— v.r. sich —*, come forward; pretend; *sich krank —*, feign illness, malinger, pretend to be ill.

**Stellenbewerber** ['ʃtelənbəverbər], m. (—s, pl. —) applicant (for a job).

**Stellengesuch** ['ʃteləngəzuːx], n. (—s, pl. —e) application (for a job).

**Stellenvermittlung** ['ʃtelənfermɪtlʊŋ], f. (—, pl. —en) employment office, employment exchange.

**stellenweise** ['ʃtelənvaɪzə], adv. in parts, here and there.

**Stellmacher** ['ʃtelmaxər], m. (—s, pl. —) wheelwright.

**Stellung** ['ʃtelʊŋ], f. (—, pl. —en) position, posture; attitude; situation; job; (Mil.) trenches; *— nehmen zu*, express o.'s views on.

**Stellvertreter** ['ʃtelfertreːtər], m. (—s, pl. —) representative, deputy; substitute, supply, proxy, relief; (doctor) locum.

**Stelzbein** ['ʃteltsbaɪn], n. (—s, pl. —e) wooden leg.

211

# Stemmeisen

**Stemmeisen** ['ʃtɛmaɪzən], *n.* (**—s**, *pl.* **—**) crowbar.

**stemmen** ['ʃtɛmən], *v.a.* (*water*) stem, dam; (*weight*) lift. — *v.r.* sich — *gegen*, resist fiercely.

**Stempel** ['ʃtɛmpəl], *m.* (**—s**, *pl.* **—**) stamp, rubber-stamp, die; pounder; (*Bot.*) pistil.

**Stempelgebühr** ['ʃtɛmpəlɡəbyːr], *f.* (**—**, *pl.* **—en**) stamp-duty.

**stempeln** ['ʃtɛmpəln], *v.a.* stamp, hallmark; brand; cancel (*postage stamp*). — *v.n.* (*coll.*) — *gehen*, be on the dole.

**Stengel** ['ʃtɛŋəl], *m.* (**—s**, *pl.* **—**) stalk.

**Stenografie** [ʃtenoɡraˈfiː], *f.* (**—**, *no pl.*) stenography, shorthand.

**stenografisch** [ʃtenoˈɡrafɪʃ], *adj.* in shorthand.

**Stenogramm** [ʃtenoˈɡram], *n.* (**—s**, *pl.* **—e**) shorthand-note.

**Stenotypistin** [ʃtenotyˈpɪstɪn], *f.* (**—**, *pl.* **—nen**) shorthand-typist.

**Stephan** ['ʃtefan], *m.* Stephen.

**Steppdecke** ['ʃtɛpdɛkə], *f.* (**—**, *pl.* **—n**) quilt.

**Steppe** ['ʃtɛpə], *f.* (**—**, *pl.* **—n**) steppe.

**steppen** ['ʃtɛpən], *v.a.* stitch, quilt.

**Sterbeglocke** ['ʃtɛrbəɡlɔkə], *f.* (**—**, *pl.* **—n**) passing bell, death bell.

**Sterbehemd** ['ʃtɛrbəhɛmt], *n.* (**—(e)s**, *pl.* **—en**) shroud, winding-sheet.

**sterben** ['ʃtɛrbən], *v.n. irr.* (*aux.* sein) die.

**Sterbenswörtchen** ['ʃtɛrbənsvœrtçən], *n.* (**—s**, *pl.* **—**) *nicht ein* —, not a syllable.

**Sterbesakramente** ['ʃtɛrbəzakramɛntə], *n. pl.* (*Eccl.*) last sacraments, last rites.

**sterblich** ['ʃtɛrplɪç], *adj.* mortal; — *verliebt*, desperately in love.

**Sterblichkeit** ['ʃtɛrplɪçkaɪt], *f.* (**—**, *no pl.*) mortality.

**stereotyp** [stereoˈtyːp], *adj.* stereotyped.

**sterilisieren** [ster;iliˈziːrən], *v.a.* sterilise.

**Sterilität** [steriliˈtɛːt], *f.* (**—**, *no pl.*) sterility.

**Stern** [ʃtɛrn], *m.* (**—(e)s**, *pl.* **—e**) star; (*Typ.*) asterisk.

**Sternbild** ['ʃtɛrnbɪlt], *n.* (**—s**, *pl.* **—er**) constellation.

**Sterndeuter** ['ʃtɛrndɔytər], *m.* (**—s**, *pl.* **—**) astrologer.

**Sterndeutung** ['ʃtɛrndɔytuŋ], *f.* (**—**, *no pl.*) astrology.

**Sternenschimmer** ['ʃtɛrnənʃɪmər], *m.* (**—s**, *no pl.*) starlight.

**sternförmig** ['ʃtɛrnfœrmɪç], *adj.* star-like, star-shaped.

**Sterngucker** ['ʃtɛrnɡukər], *m.* (**—s**, *pl.* **—**) stargazer.

**sternhagelvoll** ['ʃtɛrnhaːɡəlfɔl], *adj.* (*coll.*) as drunk as a lord.

**Sternkunde** ['ʃtɛrnkundə], *f.* (**—**, *no pl.*) astronomy.

**Sternkundige** ['ʃtɛrnkundɪɡə], *m.* (**—n**, *pl.* **—n**) astronomer.

**Sternschnuppe** ['ʃtɛrnʃnupə], *f.* (**—**, *pl.* **—n**) falling star, shooting star, meteorite.

**Sternwarte** ['ʃtɛrnvartə], *f.* (**—**, *pl.* **—n**) observatory.

**stetig** ['ʃteːtɪç], *adj.* continual, continuous, constant.

**stets** [ʃteːts], *adv.* always, ever, continually.

**Steuer** (1) ['ʃtɔyər], *n.* (**—s**, *pl.* **—**) rudder, helm, steering wheel.

**Steuer** (2) ['ʃtɔyər], *f.* (**—**, *pl.* **—n**) tax; (*local*) rate; (*import*) customs duty.

**Steueramt** ['ʃtɔyəramt], *n.* (**—s**, *pl.* **—er**) inland revenue office, tax office.

**Steuerbeamte** ['ʃtɔyərbəamtə], *m.* (**—n**, *pl.* **—n**) revenue officer, tax collector.

**Steuerbord** ['ʃtɔyərbort], *n.* (**—s**, *no pl.*) starboard.

**Steuereinnehmer** ['ʃtɔyəraɪnneːmər], *m.* (**—s**, *pl.* **—**) tax collector.

**steuerfrei** ['ʃtɔyərfraɪ], *adj.* duty-free, exempt from taxes.

**Steuerhinterziehung** ['ʃtɔyərhɪntərtsiːuŋ], *f.* (**—**, *pl.* **—en**) tax evasion.

**steuerlos** ['ʃtɔyərloːs], *adj.* rudderless, adrift.

**Steuermann** ['ʃtɔyərman], *m.* (**—s**, *pl.* **—er**) mate; helmsman.

**steuern** ['ʃtɔyərn], *v.a.* steer; *einem Unheil* —, avoid *or* steer clear of an evil.

**steuerpflichtig** ['ʃtɔyərpflɪçtɪç], *adj.* taxable, liable to tax, dutiable.

**Steuerrad** ['ʃtɔyərraːt], *n.* (**—s**, *pl.* **—er**) steering-wheel.

**Steuerung** ['ʃtɔyəruŋ], *f.* (**—**, *no pl.*) steering, controls.

**Steuerveranlagung** ['ʃtɔyərfɛranlaːɡuŋ], *f.* (**—**, *pl.* **—en**) tax-assessment.

**stibitzen** [ʃtiˈbɪtsən], *v.a.* (*coll.*) pilfer, filch.

**Stich** [ʃtɪç], *m.* (**—(e)s**, *pl.* **—e**) sting; prick; stitch; stab; (*Cards*) trick; (*Art*) engraving; *einen im — lassen*, leave s.o. in the lurch.

**Stichel** ['ʃtɪçəl], *m.* (**—s**, *pl.* **—**) (*Art*) graver.

**Stichelei** [ʃtɪçəˈlaɪ], *f.* (**—**, *pl.* **—en**) taunt, sneer, gibe.

**sticheln** ['ʃtɪçəln], *v.a.* taunt, nag.

**stichhaltig** ['ʃtɪçhaltɪç], *adj.* valid, sound.

**Stichhaltigkeit** ['ʃtɪçhaltɪçkaɪt], *f.* (**—**, *no pl.*) validity, cogency.

**Stichprobe** ['ʃtɪçproːbə], *f.* (**—**, *pl.* **—n**) sample taken at random, sampling.

**Stichwahl** ['ʃtɪçvaːl], *f.* (**—**, *pl.* **—en**) second ballot.

**Stichwort** ['ʃtɪçvɔrt], *n.* (**—s**, *pl.* **—e**) key-word; (*Theat.*) cue.

**sticken** ['ʃtɪkən], *v.a., v.n.* embroider.

**Stickerei** [ʃtɪkəˈraɪ], *f.* (**—**, *pl.* **—en**) embroidery.

**Stickgarn** ['ʃtɪkɡarn], *n.* (**—s**, *pl.* **—e**) embroidery cotton *or* silk.

**Stickhusten** ['ʃtɪkhuːstən], *m.* (**—s**, *no pl.*) choking cough.

**stickig** ['ʃtɪkɪç], *adj.* stuffy.
**Stickmuster** ['ʃtɪkmustər], *n.* (—s, *pl.* —) embroidery-pattern.
**Stickstoff** ['ʃtɪkʃtɔf], *m.* (—(e)s, *no pl.*) nitrogen.
**stieben** ['ʃtiːbən], *v.n.* (*aux.* sein) scatter, spray; *auseinander —*, disperse.
**Stiefbruder** ['ʃtiːfbruːdər], *m.* (—s, *pl.* ⸚) step-brother.
**Stiefel** ['ʃtiːfəl], *m.* (—s, *pl.* —) boot.
**Stiefelknecht** ['ʃtiːfəlknɛçt], *m.* (—(e)s, *pl.* —e) boot-jack.
**Stiefelputzer** ['ʃtiːfəlputsər], *m.* (—s, *pl.* —) shoe-black; (*Am.*) shoe-shine; (*hotel*) boots.
**Stiefeltern** ['ʃtiːfɛltern], *pl.* step-parents.
**Stiefmütterchen** ['ʃtiːfmytərçən], *n.* (—s, *pl.* —) (*Bot.*) pansy.
**stiefmütterlich** ['ʃtiːfmytərlɪç], *adj.* like a stepmother; niggardly.
**Stiefsohn** ['ʃtiːfzoːn], *m.* (—s, *pl.* ⸚e) stepson.
**Stiege** ['ʃtiːɡə], *f.* (—, *pl.* —n) staircase.
**Stieglitz** ['ʃtiːɡlɪts], *m.* (—es, *pl.* —e) goldfinch.
**Stiel** [ʃtiːl], *m.* (—(e)s, *pl.* —e) handle; (*plant*) stalk.
**Stier** [ʃtiːr], *m.* (—(e)s, *pl.* —e) bull; *junger —*, bullock; (*Astrol.*) Taurus.
**stieren** ['ʃtiːrən], *v.n.* stare (at), goggle.
**Stift** (1) [ʃtɪft], *m.* (—(e)s, *pl.* —e) tack, pin, peg; pencil; (*coll.*) apprentice; young chap.
**Stift** (2) [ʃtɪft], *n.* (—(e)s, *pl.* —e) charitable *or* religious foundation.
**stiften** ['ʃtɪftən], *v.a.* establish, give, donate; found, set on foot, originate; *Frieden —*, bring about peace.
**Stifter** ['ʃtɪftər], *m.* (—s, *pl.* —) founder, originator, donor.
**Stiftung** ['ʃtɪftuŋ], *f.* (—, *pl.* —en) establishment, foundation; institution; charitable foundation; endowment, donation.
**Stil** [ʃtiːl], *m.* (—(e)s, *pl.* —e) style; (*fig.*) manner.
**stilisieren** [ʃtiːliˈziːrən], *v.a.* word, draft.
**Stilistik** [ʃtiːˈlɪstɪk], *f.* (—, *no pl.*) art of composition.
**stilistisch** [ʃtiːˈlɪstɪʃ], *adj.* stylistic.
**still** [ʃtɪl], *adj.* quiet, still, silent; calm; *—er Teilhaber*, sleeping partner; *im —en*, secretly, on the sly.
**Stille** ['ʃtɪlə], *f.* (—, *no pl.*) silence, quietness, tranquillity; calm, calmness; *in der —*, silently; *in der — der Nacht*, at dead of night.
**stillen** ['ʃtɪlən], *v.a.* allay; (*blood*) staunch; (*baby*) suckle, feed, nurse; (*thirst*) quench; (*hunger*) appease.
**stillos** ['ʃtiːlloːs], *adj.* incongruous; in bad taste.
**Stillung** ['ʃtɪluŋ], *f.* (—, *no pl.*) allaying; (*blood*) staunching; (*baby*) suckling, feeding, nursing; (*thirst*) quenching; (*hunger*) appeasing.

**stilvoll** ['ʃtiːlfɔl], *adj.* harmonious; stylish; in good taste.
**Stimmband** ['ʃtɪmbant], *n.* (—s, *pl.* ⸚er) vocal chord.
**stimmberechtigt** ['ʃtɪmbərɛçtɪçt], *adj.* entitled to vote, enfranchised.
**Stimmbruch** ['ʃtɪmbrux], *m.* (—s, *no pl.*) breaking of the voice.
**Stimme** ['ʃtɪmə], *f.* (—, *pl.* —n) voice; (*election*) vote, suffrage; *die — abgeben*, vote.
**stimmen** ['ʃtɪmən], *v.a.* (*piano*) tune; *einen günstig —*, dispose s.o. favourably towards s.th. — *v.n.* agree, tally (with), square (with), accord (with); vote.
**Stimmeneinheit** ['ʃtɪmənaɪnhaɪt], *f.* (—, *no pl.*) unanimity.
**Stimmengleichheit** ['ʃtɪmənɡlaɪçhaɪt], *f.* (—, *no pl.*) equality of votes, tie.
**Stimmer** ['ʃtɪmər], *m.* (—s, *pl.* —) (*piano*) tuner.
**Stimmführer** ['ʃtɪmfyːrər], *m.* (—s, *pl.* —) leader, spokesman.
**Stimmgabel** ['ʃtɪmɡaːbəl], *f.* (—, *pl.* —n) tuning fork.
**stimmhaft** ['ʃtɪmhaft], *adj.* (*Phonet.*) voiced.
**Stimmlage** ['ʃtɪmlaːɡə], *f.* (—, *pl.* —n) (*Mus.*) register.
**stimmlos** ['ʃtɪmloːs], *adj.* voiceless; (*Phonet.*) unvoiced.
**Stimmrecht** ['ʃtɪmrɛçt], *n.* (—s, *no pl.*) suffrage, right to vote; *allgemeines —*, universal suffrage.
**Stimmung** ['ʃtɪmuŋ], *f.* (—, *no pl.*) tuning; (*fig.*) disposition, humour, mood; atmosphere; *in guter —*, in high spirits, *in gedrückter —*, in low spirits.
**stimmungsvoll** ['ʃtɪmuŋsfɔl], *adj.* impressive, full of atmosphere.
**Stimmwechsel** ['ʃtɪmvɛksəl], *m.* (—s, *no pl.*) breaking of the voice.
**Stimmzettel** ['ʃtɪmtsɛtəl], *m.* (—s, *pl.* —) ballot-paper.
**stinken** ['ʃtɪŋkən], *v.n. irr.* stink, reek, smell.
**Stinktier** ['ʃtɪŋktiːr], *n.* (—s, *pl.* —e) (*Zool.*) skunk.
**Stipendium** [ʃtiˈpɛndjum], *n.* (—s, *pl.* —dien) scholarship.
**Stirn** [ʃtɪrn], *f.* (—, *pl.* —en) forehead, brow; *die — runzeln*, frown, knit o.'s brow; *die — haben zu*, have the cheek to; *einem die — bieten*, face s.o., defy s.o.
**Stirnhöhle** ['ʃtɪrnhøːlə], *f.* (—, *pl.* —en) frontal cavity.
**Stirnseite** ['ʃtɪrnzaɪtə], *f.* (—, *pl.* —n) front.
**stöbern** ['ʃtøːbərn], *v.n.* rummage about; (*snow*) drift.
**stochern** ['ʃtɔxərn], *v.a., v.n.* (*food*) pick (at); (*teeth*) pick.
**Stock** (1) [ʃtɔk], *m.* (—(e)s, *pl.* ⸚e) stick, cane, walking-stick; *über — und Stein*, over hedges and ditches.
**Stock** (2) [ʃtɔk], *m.* (—es, *pl.* —werke) storey, floor.

213

# stocken

**stocken** ['ʃtɔkən], v.n. stop; (blood) run cold; (linen) go mildewed; hesitate, falter; (conversation) flag.

**stockfinster** ['ʃtɔkfɪnstər], adj. pitch dark.

**Stockfisch** ['ʃtɔkfɪʃ], m. (—es, pl. —e) dried cod; dried fish.

**stöckisch** ['ʃtœkɪʃ], adj. obstinate, stubborn.

**Stockrose** ['ʃtɔkro:zə], f. (—, pl. —n) (Bot.) hollyhock.

**Stockschnupfen** ['ʃtɔkʃnupfən], m. (—s, no pl.) heavy or chronic cold.

**stocksteif** ['ʃtɔkʃtaɪf], adj. stiff as a poker.

**stockstill** ['ʃtɔkʃtɪl], adj. quite still, stock-still.

**stocktaub** ['ʃtɔktaup], adj. deaf as a post.

**Stockung** ['ʃtɔkuŋ], f. (—, pl. —en) stagnation; hesitation; block, blockage; stopping, standstill.

**Stockwerk** ['ʃtɔkverk], n. (—s, pl. —e) storey, floor.

**Stoff** [ʃtɔf], m. (—(e)s, pl. —e) fabric, material; substance; subject matter.

**Stoffwechsel** ['ʃtɔfveksəl], m. (—s, no pl.) metabolism.

**stöhnen** ['ʃtø:nən], v.n. groan, moan.

**Stoiker** ['sto:ikər], m. (—s, pl. —) stoic.

**Stola** ['sto:la:], f. (—, pl. —len) (Eccl.) stole.

**Stollen** ['ʃtɔlən], m. (—s, pl. —) fruit-cake; (Min.) gallery, adit.

**stolpern** ['ʃtɔlpərn], v.n. (aux. sein) stumble, trip.

**Stolz** [ʃtɔlts], m. (—es, no pl.) haughtiness, pride.

**stolz** [ʃtɔlts], adj. haughty, proud; stuck-up, conceited; (fig.) majestic.

**stolzieren** [ʃtɔl'tsi:rən], v.n. (aux. sein) strut; prance.

**stopfen** ['ʃtɔpfən], v.a. stuff; fill; darn, mend; einem den Mund —, cut s.o. short.

**Stopfgarn** ['ʃtɔpfgarn], n. (—s, pl. —e) darning-thread.

**Stoppel** ['ʃtɔpəl], f. (—, pl. —n) stubble.

**stoppeln** ['ʃtɔpəln], v.a. glean; etwas zusammen —, compile s.th. badly.

**Stöpsel** ['ʃtœpsəl], m. (—s, pl. —) stopper, cork; kleiner —, little mite.

**stöpseln** ['ʃtœpsəln], v.a. cork.

**Stör** [ʃtø:r], m. (—(e)s, pl. —e) (Zool.) sturgeon.

**Storch** [ʃtɔrç], m. (—(e)s, pl. ˙-e) (Orn.) stork.

**Storchschnabel** ['ʃtɔrçʃna:bəl], m. (—s, pl. ˙-) stork's bill; (Tech.) pantograph.

**stören** ['ʃtø:rən], v.a. disturb, trouble; (Rad.) jam. — v.n. intrude, be in the way.

**Störenfried** ['ʃtø:rənfri:d], m. (—s, pl. —e) intruder, mischief-maker, nuisance.

**Störer** ['ʃtø:rər], m. (—s, pl. —) disturber.

**stornieren** [ʃtɔr'ni:rən], v.a. cancel, annul.

**störrisch** ['ʃtœrɪʃ], adj. stubborn obstinate.

**Störung** ['ʃtø:ruŋ], f. (—, pl. —en) disturbance, intrusion; (Rad.) jamming.

**Stoß** [ʃto:s], m. (—es, pl. ˙-e) push, thrust; impact; blow, stroke, jolt; (papers) heap, pile; (documents) bundle.

**Stoßdegen** ['ʃto:sde:gən], m. (—s, pl. —) rapier.

**Stößel** ['ʃtø:səl], m. (—s, pl. —) pestle; (Motor.) tappet.

**stoßen** ['ʃto:sən], v.a. irr. thrust, push; pound; vor den Kopf —, offend. — v.n. bump, jolt; — an, border upon; auf etwas —, come across s.th., stumble on s.th.; ins Horn —, blow a horn. — v.r. sich —, hurt o.s.; sich an etwas —, take offence at s.th., take exception to s.th.

**Stoßseufzer** ['ʃto:szɔyftsər], m. (—s, pl. —) deep sigh.

**Stoßwaffe** ['ʃto:svafə], f. (—, pl. —n) thrusting or stabbing weapon.

**stoßweise** ['ʃto:svaɪzə], adv. by fits and starts.

**Stotterer** ['ʃtɔtərər], m. (—s, pl. —) stutterer, stammerer.

**stottern** ['ʃtɔtərn], v.n. stutter, stammer.

**stracks** [ʃtraks], adv. straight away, directly.

**Strafanstalt** ['ʃtra:fanʃtalt], f. (—, pl. —en) penitentiary, prison.

**Strafarbeit** ['ʃtra:farbaɪt], f. (—, pl. —en) (Sch.) imposition.

**strafbar** ['ʃtra:fba:r], adj. punishable, criminal, culpable.

**Strafbarkeit** ['ʃtra:fba:rkaɪt], f. (—, no pl.) culpability.

**Strafe** ['ʃtra:fə], f. (—, pl. —n) punishment; (money) fine, penalty; bei — von, on pain of.

**strafen** ['ʃtra:fən], v.a. punish, rebuke; (money) fine.

**Straferlaß** ['ʃtra:fərlas], m. (—sses, pl. —sse) remission of penalty, amnesty.

**straff** [ʃtraf], adj. tight, tense, taut.

**Strafgericht** ['ʃtra:fgərɪçt], n. (—es, no pl.) punishment; judgment; (Law) Criminal Court.

**Strafgesetzbuch** ['ʃtra:fgəzɛtsbu:x], n. (—(e)s, pl. ˙-er) penal code.

**sträflich** ['ʃtrɛ:flɪç], adj. punishable; culpable; reprehensible, blameworthy.

**Sträfling** ['ʃtrɛ:flɪŋ], m. (—s, pl. —e) convict.

**Strafporto** ['ʃtra:fpɔrto], n. (—s, pl. —ti) excess postage.

**Strafpredigt** ['ʃtra:fpre:dɪçt], f. (—, pl. —en) severe admonition, stern reprimand.

**Strafprozess** ['ʃtra:fprɔtsɛs], m. (—es, pl. —e) criminal proceedings.

**Strafrecht** ['ʃtra:frɛçt], n. (—(e)s, no pl.) criminal law.

**Strafverfahren** ['ʃtra:fferfa:rən], n. (—s, pl. —) criminal procedure.

**Strahl** [ʃtraːl], *m.* (—(e)s, *pl.* —en) beam, ray; (*water etc.*) jet, spout; (*lightning*) flash; —en werfen, emit rays.

**Strahlantrieb** [ˈʃtraːlantriːp], *m.* (—s, *no pl.*) (*Aviat.*) jet propulsion.

**strahlen** [ˈʃtraːlən], *v.n.* radiate, shine, beam, emit rays; (*fig.*) beam (with joy).

**strählen** [ˈʃtrɛːlən], *v.a.* (*rare*) comb.

**Strahlenbrechung** [ˈʃtraːlənbrɛçuŋ], *f.* (—, *pl.* —en) refraction.

**strahlenförmig** [ˈʃtraːlənfœrmɪç], *adj.* radiate.

**Strahlenkrone** [ˈʃtraːlənkroːnə], *f.* (—, *pl.* —n) aureole, halo.

**Strahlung** [ˈʃtraːluŋ], *f.* (—, *pl.* —en) radiation; (*fig.*) radiance.

**Strähne** [ˈʃtrɛːnə], *f.* (—, *pl.* —n) skein, hank; eine — Pech, a spell of bad luck.

**Stramin** [ʃtraˈmiːn], *m.* (—s, *pl.* —e) embroidery canvas.

**stramm** [ʃtram], *adj.* tight; rigid; sturdy, strapping.

**strampeln** [ˈʃtrampəln], *v.n.* struggle; (*baby*) kick.

**Strand** [ʃtrant], *m.* (—(e)s, *pl.* —e) shore, beach, strand.

**stranden** [ˈʃtrandən], *v.n.* be stranded, founder.

**Strandkorb** [ˈʃtrantkɔrp], *m.* (—s, *pl.* ⁀e) beach-chair.

**Strandwache** [ˈʃtrantvaxə], *f.* (—, *no pl.*) coast-guard.

**Strang** [ʃtraŋ], *m.* (—(e)s, *pl.* ⁀e) rope, cord; über die ⁀e schlagen, kick over the traces; zum — verurteilen, condemn to be hanged.

**strangulieren** [ʃtraŋguˈliːrən], *v.a.* strangle.

**Strapaze** [ʃtraˈpaːtsə], *f.* (—, *pl.* —n) over-exertion, fatigue, hardship.

**strapazieren** [ʃtrapaˈtsiːrən], *v.a.* over-exert, fatigue.

**strapaziös** [ʃtrapaˈtsjøːs], *adj.* fatiguing, exacting.

**Straße** [ˈʃtraːsə], *f.* (—, *pl.* —n) (*city*) street; (*country*) road, highway; (*sea*) strait; auf der —, in the street; über die — gehen, cross the street.

**Straßenbahn** [ˈʃtraːsənbaːn], *f.* (—, *pl.* —en) tram; tramcar, (*Am.*) streetcar.

**Straßendamm** [ˈʃtraːsəndam], *m.* (—s, *pl.* ⁀e) roadway.

**Straßendirne** [ˈʃtraːsəndɪrnə], *f.* (—, *pl.* —n) prostitute, street-walker.

**Straßenfeger** [ˈʃtraːsɔnfeːgər], *m.* (—s, *pl.* —) roadman, road-sweeper, scavenger, crossing-sweeper.

**Straßenpflaster** [ˈʃtraːsənpflastər], *n.* (—s, *no pl.*) pavement.

**Straßenraub** [ˈʃtraːsənraup], *m.* (—s, *no pl.*) highway-robbery.

**Stratege** [ʃtraˈteːgə], *m.* (—n, *pl.* —n) strategist.

**sträuben** [ˈʃtrɔybən], *v.r.* sich —, bristle; (*fig.*) struggle (against), oppose.

**Strauch** [ʃtraux], *m.* (—(e)s, *pl.* ⁀er) bush, shrub.

**straucheln** [ˈʃtrauxəln], *v.n.* (*aux.* sein) stumble.

**Strauchritter** [ˈʃtrauxrɪtər], *m.* (—s, *pl.* —) footpad, vagabond, highwayman.

**Strauß** (1) [ʃtraus], *m.* (—es, *pl.* ⁀e) (*Poet.*) fight, tussle; (*flowers*) bunch, bouquet, nosegay.

**Strauß** (2) [ʃtraus], *m.* (—es, *pl.* —e) (*Orn.*) ostrich.

**Sträußchen** [ˈʃtrɔysçən], *n.* (—s, *pl.* —) small bunch of flowers, nosegay.

**Straußfeder** [ˈʃtrausfeːdər], *f.* (—, *pl.* —n) ostrich-feather.

**Strazze** [ˈʃtratsə], *f.* (—, *pl.* —n) scrapbook.

**Strebe** [ˈʃtreːbə], *f.* (—, *pl.* —n) buttress, prop, stay.

**Strebebogen** [ˈʃtreːbəboːgən], *m.* (—s, *pl.* —) (*Archit.*) arch, buttress; flying buttress.

**Streben** [ˈʃtreːbən], *n.* (—s, *no pl.*) ambition, aspiration; effort, endeavour, striving.

**streben** [ˈʃtreːbən], *v.n.* strive, aspire, endeavour.

**Streber** [ˈʃtreːbər], *m.* (—s, *pl.* —) pushing person, (social) climber. (*Am. coll.*) go-getter.

**strebsam** [ˈʃtreːpzaːm], *adj.* ambitious, assiduous, industrious.

**streckbar** [ˈʃtrɛkbaːr], *adj.* ductile, extensible.

**Streckbett** [ˈʃtrɛkbɛt], *n.* (—s, *pl.* —en) orthopaedic bed.

**Strecke** [ˈʃtrɛkə], *f.* (—, *pl.* —n) stretch, reach, extent; distance; tract; line; zur — bringen, (*Hunt.*) bag, run to earth.

**strecken** [ˈʃtrɛkən], *v.a.* stretch, extend; (*metal*) hammer out, roll; make (s.th.) last; die Waffen —, lay down arms.

**Streich** [ʃtraiç], *m.* (—(e)s, *pl.* —e) stroke, blow; (*fig.*) prank; trick; dummer —, piece of folly, lark.

**streicheln** [ˈʃtraiçəln], *v.a.* stroke, caress.

**streichen** [ˈʃtraiçən], *v.a.* irr. stroke, touch; spread; paint; cancel; strike; (*sail*) lower. — *v.n.* move past, fly past; wander.

**Streichholz** [ˈʃtraiçhɔlts], *n.* (—es, *pl.* ⁀er) match.

**Streichinstrument** [ˈʃtraiçɪnstrumɛnt], *n.* (—s, *pl.* —e) stringed instrument.

**Streif** [ʃtraif], *m.* (—(e)s, *pl.* —e) stripe, strip, streak.

**Streifband** [ˈʃtraifbant], *n.* (—s, *pl.* ⁀er) wrapper.

**Streifblick** [ˈʃtraifblɪk], *m.* (—s, *pl.* —e) glance.

**Streife** [ˈʃtraifə], *f.* (—, *pl.* —n) raid; patrol (*police etc.*).

**Streifen** [ˈʃtraifən], *m.* (—s, *pl.* —) stripe, streak; (*Mil.*) bar.

**streifen** ['ʃtraɪfən], *v.a.* graze, touch in passing; take off (*remove*). — *v.n.* (*aux.* sein) ramble, roam, rove.

**streifig** ['ʃtraɪfɪç], *adj.* striped, streaky.

**Streik** [ʃtraɪk], *m.* (—(e)s, *pl.* —s) strike; *in den — treten*, go on strike.

**Streikbrecher** ['ʃtraɪkbreçər], *m.* (—s, *pl.* —) blackleg.

**streiken** ['ʃtraɪkən], *v.n.* (*workers*) strike, be on strike.

**Streit** [ʃtraɪt], *m.* (—(e)s, *pl.* —e) dispute, quarrel, conflict; (*words*) argument; *einen — anfangen*, pick a quarrel.

**Streitaxt** ['ʃtraɪtakst], *f.* (—, *pl.* ¨e) battle-axe.

**streitbar** ['ʃtraɪtbaːr], *adj.* warlike, martial.

**streiten** ['ʃtraɪtən], *v.n. irr.* quarrel, fight; *—de Kirche*, Church Militant.

**Streitfrage** ['ʃtraɪtfraːgə], *f.* (—, *pl.* —n) moot point, point at issue; controversy.

**Streithammel** ['ʃtraɪthaməl], *m.* (—s, *pl.* —) squabbler.

**Streithandel** ['ʃtraɪthandəl], *m.* (—s, *pl.* ¨) law-suit.

**streitig** ['ʃtraɪtɪç], *adj.* disputable, doubtful, at issue; *einem etwas — machen*, contest s.o.'s right to s.th.

**Streitkräfte** ['ʃtraɪtkreftə], *f. pl.* (*Mil.*) forces.

**streitlustig** ['ʃtraɪtlustɪç], *adj.* argumentative.

**Streitschrift** ['ʃtraɪtʃrɪft], *f.* (—, *pl.* —en) pamphlet, polemical treatise.

**Streitsucht** ['ʃtraɪtzuxt], *f.* (—, *no pl.*) quarrelsomeness; (*Law*) litigiousness.

**streitsüchtig** ['ʃtraɪtzyçtɪç], *adj.* quarrelsome, litigious.

**streng** [ʃtrɛŋ], *adj.* severe, strict, rigorous; *—e Kälte*, biting cold; *im —sten Winter*, in the depth of winter. — *adv.* —*genommen*, strictly speaking.

**Strenge** ['ʃtrɛŋə], *f.* (—, *no pl.*) severity, rigour.

**strenggläubig** ['ʃtrɛŋglɔybɪç], *adj.* strictly orthodox.

**Streu** [ʃtrɔy], *f.* (—, *pl.* —en) litter, bed of straw.

**Streubüchse** ['ʃtrɔybyksə], *f.* (—, *pl.* —n) castor.

**streuen** ['ʃtrɔyən], *v.a.* strew, scatter, sprinkle.

**streunen** ['ʃtrɔynən], *v.n.* roam (about).

**Streuung** ['ʃtrɔyuŋ], *f.* (—, *pl.* —en) strewing; (*shot*) dispersion.

**Streuzucker** ['ʃtrɔytsukər], *m.* (—s, *no pl.*) castor-sugar.

**Strich** [ʃtrɪç], *m.* (—(e)s, *pl.* —e) stroke, line, dash; (*land*) tract; (*Art*) touch; region; *gegen den —*, against the grain; *einem einen — durch die Rechnung machen*, put a spoke in s.o.'s wheel, frustrate s.o.

**Strichpunkt** ['ʃtrɪçpuŋkt], *m.* (—s, *pl.* —e) semicolon.

**Strichregen** ['ʃtrɪçreːgən], *m.* (—s, *pl.* —) passing shower.

**Strick** [ʃtrɪk], *m.* (—(e)s, *pl.* —e) cord, line, rope; *du —*, (*fig.*) you scamp! *einem einen — drehen*, give s.o. enough rope to hang himself, lay a trap for s.o.

**stricken** ['ʃtrɪkən], *v.a., v.n.* knit.

**Strickerei** [ʃtrɪkə'raɪ], *f.* (—, *pl.* —en) knitting; knitting business, workshop.

**Strickleiter** ['ʃtrɪklaɪtər], *f.* (—, *pl.* —n) rope-ladder.

**Strickzeug** ['ʃtrɪktsɔyk], *n.* (—s, *pl.* —e) knitting.

**Striegel** ['ʃtriːgəl], *m.* (—s, *pl.* —) curry-comb.

**striegeln** ['ʃtriːgəln], *v.a.* curry.

**Strieme** ['ʃtriːmə], *f.* (—, *pl.* —n) weal, stripe.

**Strippe** ['ʃtrɪpə], *f.* (—, *pl.* —n) strap, band, string; cord.

**strittig** ['ʃtrɪtɪç], *adj.* contentious, debatable.

**Stroh** [ʃtroː], *n.* (—s, *no pl.*) straw; (*roof*) thatch; *mit — decken*, thatch; *leeres — dreschen*, beat the air.

**Strohfeuer** ['ʃtroːfɔyər], *n.* (—s, *no pl.*) (*fig.*) flash in the pan; short-lived enthusiasm.

**Strohhalm** ['ʃtroːhalm], *m.* (—s, *pl.* —e) straw.

**Strohhut** ['ʃtroːhuːt], *m.* (—s, *pl.* ¨e) straw-hat.

**Strohkopf** ['ʃtroːkɔpf], *m.* (—(e)s, *pl.* ¨e) (*coll.*) stupid person.

**Strohmann** ['ʃtroːman], *m.* (—s, *pl.* ¨er) (*coll.*) man of straw; (*Cards*) dummy.

**Strohmatte** ['ʃtroːmatə], *f.* (—, *pl.* —n) straw-mat.

**Strohwitwe** ['ʃtroːvɪtvə], *f.* (—, *pl.* —n) grass-widow.

**Strolch** [ʃtrɔlç], *m.* (—(e)s, *pl.* —e) vagabond; (*fig.*) scamp.

**Strom** [ʃtroːm], *m.* (—(e)s, *pl.* ¨e) river, torrent; (*also fig.*) flood; stream; (*also Elec.*) current; (*coll.*) electricity; *gegen den — schwimmen*, swim against the current, be an individualist.

**stromab** ['ʃtroːmap], *adv.* downstream.

**stromauf** ['ʃtroːmauf], *adv.* upstream.

**strömen** ['ʃtrøːmən], *v.n.* (*aux.* sein) flow, stream; (*rain*) pour; (*people*) flock.

**Stromer** ['ʃtroːmər], *m.* (—s, *pl.* —) vagabond, tramp, vagrant.

**Stromkreis** ['ʃtroːmkraɪs], *m.* (—es, *pl.* —e) (*Elec.*) circuit.

**Stromschnelle** ['ʃtroːmʃnɛlə], *f.* (—, *pl.* —n) rapids.

**Strömung** ['ʃtrøːmuŋ], *f.* (—, *pl.* —en) current; (*fig.*) tendency.

**Strophe** ['ʃtroːfə], *f.* (—, *pl.* —n) verse, stanza.

**strotzen** ['ʃtrɔtsən], *v.n.* be puffed up; overflow, burst, teem.

**strotzend** ['ʃtrɔtsənt], *adj. vor Gesundheit —*, bursting with health.

**Strudel** ['ʃtruːdəl], *m.* (—s, *pl.* —) whirl, whirlpool, vortex, eddy; pastry.

**Struktur** [ʃtruk'tuːr], *f.* (—, *pl.* —en) structure.

# Sturmglocke

**Strumpf** [ʃtrumpf], *m.* (—(e)s, *pl.* ⸚e) stocking; (*short*) sock.
**Strumpfband** [ʃtrumpfbant], *n.* (—(e)s, *pl.* ⸚er) garter.
**Strumpfwaren** [ʃtrumpfvaːrən], *f. pl.* hosiery.
**Strumpfwirker** [ʃtrumpfvɪrkər], *m.* (—s, *pl.* —) stocking-weaver.
**Strunk** [ʃtruŋk], *m.* (—(e)s, *pl.* ⸚e) (*tree*) stump, trunk; (*plant*) stalk.
**struppig** [ʃtrupɪç], *adj.* rough, unkempt, frowsy.
**Stube** [ʃtuːbə], *f.* (—, *pl.* —n) room, chamber; *gute* —, sitting-room.
**Stubenarrest** [ʃtuːbənarɛst], *m.* (—s, *pl.* —e) confinement to quarters.
**Stubenhocker** [ʃtuːbənhɔkər], *m.* (—s, *pl.* —) stay-at-home.
**Stubenmädchen** [ʃtuːbənmɛːtçən], *n.* (—s, *pl.* —) housemaid.
**Stuck** [ʃtuk], *m.* (—(e)s, *no pl.*) stucco, plaster.
**Stück** [ʃtyk], *n.* (—(e)s, *pl.* —e) piece; part; lump; (*Theat.*) play; *aus freien —en*, of o.'s own accord; *große —e auf einen halten*, think highly of s.o.
**Stückarbeit** [ʃtykarbaɪt], *f.* (—, *pl.* —en) piece-work.
**Stückchen** [ʃtykçən], *n.* (—s, *pl.* —) small piece, morsel, bit.
**stückeln** [ʃtykəln], *v.a.* cut in(to) pieces; patch, mend.
**stückweise** [ʃtykvaɪzə], *adv.* piecemeal.
**Stückwerk** [ʃtykvɛrk], *n.* (—s, *no pl.*) (*fig.*) patchy *or* imperfect work, a bungled job.
**Stückzucker** [ʃtyktsukər], *m.* (—s, *no pl.*) lump sugar.
**Student** [ʃtuˈdɛnt], *m.* (—en, *pl.* —en) (*Univ.*) student, undergraduate.
**studentenhaft** [ʃtuˈdɛntənhaft], *adj.* student-like.
**Studentenverbindung** [ʃtuˈdɛntənfɛrbɪnduŋ], *f.* (—, *pl.* —en) students' association *or* union.
**Studie** [ʃtuːdjə], *f.* (—, *pl.* —n) study, (*Art*) sketch; (*Lit.*) essay; (*pl.*) studies.
**Studienplan** [ʃtuːdiːənplaːn], *m.* (—s, *pl.* ⸚e) curriculum.
**Studienrat** [ʃtuːdiːənraːt], *m.* (—s, *pl.* ⸚e) grammar school teacher, assistant master.
**studieren** [ʃtuˈdiːrən], *v.a., v.n.* study, read (a subject); be at (the) university.
**studiert** [ʃtuˈdiːrt], *adj.* educated; (*fig.*) affected, deliberate, studied.
**Studierte** [ʃtuˈdiːrtə], *m.* (*coll.*) egghead.
**Studium** [ʃtuːdjum], *n.* (—s, *pl.* —dien) study, pursuit; university education.
**Stufe** [ʃtuːfə], *f.* (—, *pl.* —n) step; (*fig.*) degree; *auf gleicher — mit*, on a level with.
**stufenweise** [ʃtuːfənvaɪzə], *adv.* gradually, by degrees.
**Stuhl** [ʃtuːl], *m.* (—s, *pl.* ⸚e) chair, seat; *der Heilige —*, the Holy See.
**Stuhlgang** [ʃtuːlɡaŋ], *m.* (—s, *no pl.*) (*Med.*) stool, evacuation (of the bowels), movement, motion.

**Stukkatur** [ʃtukaˈtuːr], *f.* (—, *no pl.*) stucco-work.
**Stulle** [ʃtulə], *f.* (—, *pl.* —n) (*dial.*) slice of bread and butter.
**Stulpe** [ʃtulpə], *f.* (—, *pl.* —n) cuff.
**stülpen** [ʃtylpən], *v.a.* turn up, invert.
**Stulpnase** [ʃtulpnaːzə], *f.* (—, *pl.* —n) turned-up nose, pug-nose.
**Stulpstiefel** [ʃtulpʃtiːfəl], *m.* (—s, *pl.* —) top-boot.
**stumm** [ʃtum], *adj.* mute, dumb, silent.
**Stumme** [ʃtumə], *m. & f.* (—n, *pl.* —n) dumb person, mute.
**Stummel** [ʃtuməl], *m.* (—s, *pl.* —) stump; (*cigarette*) end, butt.
**Stummheit** [ʃtumhaɪt], *f.* (—, *no pl.*) dumbness.
**Stümper** [ʃtympər], *m.* (—s, *pl.* —) bungler, botcher.
**stümperhaft** [ʃtympərhaft], *adj.* bungling, botchy.
**stümpern** [ʃtympərn], *v.a., v.n.* bungle, botch.
**Stumpf** [ʃtumpf], *m.* (—(e)s, *pl.* ⸚e) stump, trunk; *mit — und Stiel ausrotten*, destroy root and branch.
**stumpf** [ʃtumpf], *adj.* blunt; (*angle*) obtuse; (*fig.*) dull; — *machen*, blunt, dull.
**Stumpfsinn** [ʃtumpfzɪn], *m.* (—s, *no pl.*) stupidity, dullness.
**stumpfwinklig** [ʃtumpfvɪŋklɪç], *adj.* obtuse-angled.
**Stunde** [ʃtundə], *f.* (—, *pl.* —n) hour; lesson.
**stunden** [ʃtundən], *v.a.* give a respite, allow time (to pay up).
**Stundenglas** [ʃtundənɡlas], *n.* (—es, *pl.* ⸚er) hour-glass.
**Stundenplan** [ʃtundənplaːn], *m.* (—s, *pl.* ⸚e) (*Sch.*) time-table.
**Stundenzeiger** [ʃtundəntsaɪɡər], *m.* (—s, *pl.* —) hour-hand.
**Stündlein** [ʃtyntlaɪn], *n.* (—s, *pl.* —) *sein — hat geschlagen*, his last hour has come.
**Stundung** [ʃtunduŋ], *f.* (—, *pl.* —en) respite, grace.
**stupend** [ʃtuˈpɛnt], *adj.* stupendous.
**stur** [ʃtuːr], *adj.* obdurate, unwavering, stolid, dour, stubborn.
**Sturm** [ʃturm], *m.* (—(e)s, *pl.* ⸚e) storm, gale, tempest, hurricane; (*Mil.*) attack, assault; — *und Drang*, (*Lit.*) Storm and Stress; — *im Wasserglas*, storm in a teacup; — *laufen gegen*, storm against.
**Sturmband** [ʃturmbant], *n.* (—s, *pl.* ⸚er) chinstrap.
**Sturmbock** [ʃturmbɔk], *m.* (—s, *pl.* ⸚e) battering-ram.
**stürmen** [ʃtyrmən], *v.a.* storm, take by assault. — *v.n.* be violent, be stormy; (*Mil.*) advance.
**Stürmer** [ʃtyrmər], *m.* (—s, *pl.* —) assailant; (*football*) centre-forward.
**Sturmglocke** [ʃturmɡlɔkə], *f.* (—, *pl.* —n) tocsin, alarm-bell.

# Sturmhaube

**Sturmhaube** [ˈʃturmhaubə], f. (—, pl. —en) (Mil.) morion, helmet.

**stürmisch** [ˈʃtyrmɪʃ], adj. stormy, tempestuous; (fig.) boisterous, turbulent, tumultuous, impetuous; —er Beifall, frantic applause; —e Überfahrt, rough crossing.

**Sturmschritt** [ˈʃturmʃrɪt], m. (—s, no pl.) double march.

**Sturmvogel** [ˈʃturmfoːgəl], m. (—s, pl. ") (Orn.) stormy petrel.

**Sturz** [ʃturts], m. (—es, pl. "e) fall, tumble; crash; collapse; (Comm.) failure, smash; (government) overthrow.

**Sturzacker** [ˈʃturtsakər], m. (—s, pl. ") freshly ploughed field.

**Sturzbach** [ˈʃturtsbax], m. (—(e)s, pl. "e) torrent.

**Stürze** [ˈʃtyrtsə], f. (—, pl. —n) pot-lid, cover.

**stürzen** [ˈʃtyrtsən], v.a. hurl, overthrow; ruin. — v.n. (aux. sein) (person) have a fall; (object) tumble down; (business) fail; crash; plunge; (water) rush. — v.r. throw oneself; sich — auf, rush at, plunge into.

**Sturzhelm** [ˈʃturtshelm], m. (—s, pl. —e) crash-helmet.

**Sturzsee** [ˈʃturtszeː], f. (—, no pl.) heavy sea.

**Sturzwelle** [ˈʃturtsvelə], f. (—, pl. —n) breaker, roller.

**Stute** [ˈʃtuːtə], f. (—, pl. —n) mare.

**Stutzbart** [ˈʃtutsbaːrt], m. (—s, pl. "e) short beard.

**Stütze** [ˈʃtytsə], f. (—, pl. —n) prop, support, stay.

**Stutzen** [ˈʃtutsən], m. (—s, pl. —) short rifle, carbine.

**stutzen** [ˈʃtutsən], v.a. (hair) clip, trim; (horse) dock, crop; (tree) prune, lop. — v.n. be taken aback, hesitate.

**stützen** [ˈʃtytsən], v.a. prop, support; base or found (on). — v.r. sich — auf, lean upon; (fig.) rely upon.

**Stutzer** [ˈʃtutsər], m. (—s, pl. —) dandy, fop, beau.

**stutzerhaft** [ˈʃtutsərhaft], adj. dandified.

**stutzig** [ˈʃtutsɪç], adj. startled, puzzled; — werden, be nonplussed, be taken aback or puzzled.

**Stützmauer** [ˈʃtytsmauər], f. (—, pl. —n) buttress, retaining wall.

**Stützpunkt** [ˈʃtytspuŋkt], m. (—s, pl. —e) point of support; foothold; (Mil.) base; (Tech.) fulcrum.

**Subjekt** [zupˈjɛkt], n. (—s, pl. —e) subject; (fig.) creature.

**subjektiv** [zupjɛkˈtiːf], adj. subjective, personal, prejudiced.

**sublimieren** [zubliˈmiːrən], v.a. sublimate.

**Substantiv** [zupstanˈtiːf], n. (—(e)s, pl. —e) (Gram.) substantive, noun.

**subtil** [zupˈtiːl], adj. subtle.

**subtrahieren** [zuptraˈhiːrən], v.a. subtract.

**Subvention** [zupvɛnˈtsjoːn], f. (—, pl. —en) subsidy, grant-in-aid.

**Suche** [ˈzuːxə], f. (—, no pl.) search, quest; auf der — nach, in quest of.

**suchen** [ˈzuːxən], v.a., v.n. seek, look for; attempt, endeavour.

**Sucht** [zuxt], f. (—, pl. "e) mania, addiction, passion.

**süchtig** [ˈzyçtɪç], adj. addicted (to).

**Sud** [zuːd], m. (—(e)s, pl. —e) boiling, brewing; suds.

**Sudan** [ˈzuːdan], m. the Sudan.

**sudeln** [ˈzuːdəln], v.a., v.n. smear, daub, make a mess (of).

**Süden** [ˈzyːdən], m. (—s, no pl.) south.

**Südfrüchte** [ˈzyːtfryçtə], f. pl. Mediterranean or tropical fruit.

**südlich** [ˈzyːtlɪç], adj. southern, southerly; in —er Richtung, southward.

**Südosten** [zyːtˈɔstən], m. (—s, no pl.) south-east.

**Suff** [zuf], m. (—(e)s, no pl.) (sl.) boozing, tippling.

**suggerieren** [zugeˈriːrən], v.a. suggest.

**Sühne** [ˈzyːnə], f. (—, no pl.) expiation, atonement.

**sühnen** [ˈzyːnən], v.a. expiate, atone for.

**Sühneopfer** [ˈzyːnɔpfər], n. (—s, pl. —) expiatory sacrifice; atonement.

**Suite** [ˈsviːtə], f. (—, pl. —n) retinue, train.

**sukzessiv** [zuktseˈsiːf], adj. gradual, successive.

**Sülze** [ˈzyltsə], f. (—, pl. —n) brawn, aspic, jelly.

**Summa** [zuˈmaː], f. (—, pl. Summen) — summarum, sum total.

**summarisch** [zuˈmaːrɪʃ], adj. summary.

**Summe** [ˈzumə], f. (—, pl. —n) sum, amount.

**summen** [ˈzumən], v.a. hum. — v.n. buzz, hum.

**summieren** [zuˈmiːrən], v.a. sum up, add up. — v.r. sich —, mount up.

**Sumpf** [zumpf], m. (—(e)s, pl. "e) bog, morass, marsh, moor, swamp.

**sumpfig** [ˈzumpfɪç], adj. boggy, marshy.

**Sund** [zunt], m. (—(e)s, pl. —e) straits, sound.

**Sünde** [ˈzyndə], f. (—, pl. —n) sin.

**Sündenbock** [ˈzyndənbɔk], m. (—s, pl. "e) scapegoat.

**Sündenfall** [ˈzyndənfal], m. (—s, no pl.) (Theol.) fall of man.

**Sündengeld** [ˈzyndəngelt], n. (—(e)s, no pl.) ill-gotten gains; (coll.) vast sum of money.

**sündenlos** [ˈzyndənloːs], adj. sinless, impeccable.

**Sündenpfuhl** [ˈzyndənpfuːl], m. (—s, pl. —e) sink of iniquity.

**Sünder** [ˈzyndər], m. (—s, pl. —) sinner; armer —, poor devil; du alter —, you old scoundrel.

**sündhaft** [ˈzynthaft], adj. sinful, iniquitous.

**sündig** [ˈzyndɪç], adj. sinful.

**sündigen** [ˈzyndɪgən], v.n. sin, err.

**Sündigkeit** [ˈzyndɪçkaɪt], f. (—, no pl.) sinfulness.

**Superlativ** [ˈzuːpərlatiːf], m. (—s, pl. —e) superlative (degree).

**Suppe** [´zupə], *f.* (—, *pl.* —n) soup; *eingebrannte* —, thick soup; *einem die* — *versalzen*, spoil s.o.'s little game.
**Suppenfleisch** [´zupənflaɪʃ], *n.* (—es, *no pl.*) stock-meat.
**Suppenkelle** [´zupənkɛlə], *f.* (—, *pl.* —n) soup ladle.
**Suppenterrine** [´zupənteri:nə], *f.* (—, *pl.* —n) tureen.
**Surrogat** [zuro´ga:t], *n.* (—s, *pl.* —e) substitute.
**süß** [zy:s], *adj.* sweet.
**Süße** [´zy:sə], *f.* (—, *no pl.*) sweetness.
**süßen** [´zy:sən], *v.a.* sweeten.
**Süßholz** [´zy:shɔlts], *n.* (—es, *no pl.*) liquorice; — *raspeln*, talk sweet nothings, pay compliments.
**Süßigkeit** [´zy:sɪçkaɪt], *f.* (—, *pl.* —en) sweetness; (*pl.*) sweets.
**süßlich** [´zy:slɪç], *adj.* sweetish; (*fig.*) fulsome, mawkish, cloying.
**Süßspeise** [´zy:sʃpaɪzə], *f.* (—, *pl.* —n) dessert.
**Süßwasser** [´zy:svasər], *n.* (—s, *no pl.*) fresh water.
**Symbolik** [zym´bo:lɪk], *f.* (—, *no pl.*) symbolism.
**symbolisch** [zym´bo:lɪʃ], *adj.* symbolic(al).
**symbolisieren** [zymbɔli´zi:rən], *v.a.* symbolize.
**symmetrisch** [zy´me:trɪʃ], *adj.* symmetrical.
**Sympathie** [zympa´ti:], *f.* (—, *pl.* —n) fondness, congeniality, sympathy.
**sympathisch** [zym´pa:tɪʃ], *adj.* congenial, likeable.
**Synagoge** [zyna´go:gə], *f.* (—, *pl.* —n) synagogue.
**synchronisieren** [zynkroni´zi:rən], *v.a.* synchronise.
**Syndikus** [´zyndikus], *m.* (—, *pl.* Syndizi) syndic.
**Synode** [zy´no:də], *f.* (—, *pl.* —n) synod.
**synthetisch** [zyn´te:tɪʃ], *adj.* synthetic.
**Syrien** [zy:rjən], *n.* Syria.
**systematisch** [zyste´ma:tɪʃ], *adj.* systematic(al).
**Szenarium** [stse´na:rjum], *n.* (—s, *pl.* —rien) scenario, stage, scene.
**Szene** [´stse:nə], *f.* (—, *pl.* —n) scene; *in* — *setzen*, stage, produce; (*coll.*) get up; *sich in* — *setzen*, show off.
**Szenerie** [stsenə´ri:], *f.* (—, *pl.* —n) scenery.
**szenisch** [´stse:nɪʃ], *adj.* scenic.
**Szepter** [´stsɛptər], *n.* (—s, *pl.* —) sceptre, mace.

# T

**T** [te:], *n.* (—, *pl.* —) the letter T.
**Tabak** [´tabak], *m.* (—s, *pl.* —e) tobacco.

**Tabaksbeutel** [´tabaksbɔytəl], *m.* (—s, *pl.* —) tobacco-pouch.
**Tabatiere** [taba´tjɛ:rə], *f.* (—, *pl.* —n) snuff-box.
**tabellarisch** [tabɛ´la:rɪʃ], *adj.* in tables, tabular.
**Tabelle** [ta´bɛlə], *f.* (—, *pl.* —n) table, index, schedule.
**Tablett** [ta´blɛt], *n.* (—s, *pl.* —s) tray.
**Tablette** [ta´blɛtə], *f.* (—, *pl.* —n) tablet, pill.
**Tabulatur** [tabula´tu:r], *f.* (—, *pl.* —en) tablature, tabling, index.
**Tadel** [´ta:dəl], *m.* (—s, *pl.* —) blame, censure, reproach; (*Sch.*) bad mark; *ohne* —, blameless.
**tadellos** [´ta:dəllo:s], *adj.* blameless, faultless, impeccable.
**tadeln** [´ta:dəln], *v.a.* blame, censure, find fault with; reprimand.
**tadelnswert** [´ta:dəlnsve:rt], *adj.* blameworthy, culpable.
**Tafel** [´ta:fəl], *f.* (—, *pl.* —n) board; (*Sch.*) blackboard; slate; (*fig.*) (*obs.*) dinner, banquet; festive fare; (*chocolate*) slab, bar.
**Täfelchen** [´tɛ:fəlçən], *n.* (—s, *pl.* —) tablet.
**tafelförmig** [´ta:fəlfœrmɪç], *adj.* tabular.
**tafeln** [´ta:fəln], *v.n.* dine, feast.
**täfeln** [´tɛ:fəln], *v.a.* wainscot, panel.
**Täfelung** [´tɛ:fəluŋ], *f.* (—, *pl.* —en) wainscoting, panelling.
**Taft, Taffet** [taft, ´tafət], *m.* (—(e)s, *pl.* —e) taffeta.
**Tag** [ta:k], *m.* (—(e)s, *pl.* —e) day; (*fig.*) light; *der jüngste* —, Doomsday; *bei* —*e*, in the daytime, by daylight; *sich etwas bei* —*e besehen*, examine s.th. in the light of day; — *für* —, day by day; *von* — *zu* —, from day to day; *dieser* —*e*, one of these days, shortly; *etwas an den* — *bringen*, bring s.th. to light; *in den* — *hinein leben*, live improvidently; — *und Nachtgleiche*, equinox.
**Tagbau** [´ta:kbau], *m.* (—s, *no pl.*) opencast mining.
**Tageblatt** [´ta:gəblat], *n.* (—s, *pl.* ̈er) daily paper.
**Tagebuch** [´ta:gəbu:x], *n.* (—(e)s, *pl.* ̈er) diary, journal.
**Tagedieb** [´ta:gədi:p], *m.* (—(e)s, *pl.* —e) idler, wastrel.
**Tagelöhner** [´ta:gəlø:nər], *m.* (—s, *pl.* —) day-labourer.
**tagen** [´ta:gən], *v.n.* dawn; (*gathering*) meet; (*Law*) sit.
**Tagesanbruch** [´ta:gəsanbrux], *m.* (—s, *pl.* ̈e) daybreak, dawn.
**Tagesbericht** [´ta:gəsbərɪçt], *m.* (—(e)s, *pl.* —e) daily report.
**Tagesgespräch** [´ta:gəsgəʃprɛ:ç], *n.* (—(e)s, *pl.* —e) topic of the day.
**Tagesordnung** [´ta:gəsɔrdnuŋ], *f.* (—, *pl.* —en) agenda.
**Tagewerk** [´ta:gəverk], *n.* (—s, *no pl.*) day's work, daily round.
**täglich** [´tɛ:klɪç], *adj.* daily.

**tagsüber** ['ta:ksy:bər], *adv.* in the daytime, during the day.

**Taille** ['taljə], *f.* (—, *pl.* —n) waist.

**takeln** ['ta:kəln], *v.a.* tackle, rig.

**Takelwerk** ['ta:kəlvɛrk], *n.* (—s, *no pl.*) rigging.

**Takt** (1) [takt], *m.* (—es, *pl.* —e) (*Mus.*) time, measure, bar; — *schlagen*, beat time.

**Takt** (2) [takt], *m.* (—es, *no pl.*) tact, discretion.

**taktfest** ['taktfest], *adj.* (*Mus.*) good at keeping time; (*fig.*) firm.

**taktieren** [tak'ti:rən], *v.n.* (*Mus.*) beat time.

**Taktik** ['taktɪk], *f.* (—, *pl.* —en) tactics.

**Taktiker** ['taktɪkər], *m.* (—s, *pl.* —) tactician.

**taktisch** ['taktɪʃ], *adj.* tactical.

**taktlos** ['taktlo:s], *adj.* tactless.

**Taktmesser** ['taktmɛsər], *m.* (—s, *pl.* —) metronome.

**Taktstock** ['taktʃtɔk], *m.* (—s, *pl.* ⁀e) baton.

**Tal** [ta:l], *n.* (—(e)s, *pl.* ⁀er) valley, dale, glen.

**talab** [ta:l'ap], *adv.* downhill.

**Talar** [ta'la:r], *m.* (—s, *pl.* —e) gown.

**Talent** [ta'lɛnt], *n.* (—(e)s, *pl.* —e) talent, accomplishment, gift.

**talentiert** [talən'ti:rt], *adj.* talented, gifted, accomplished.

**talentvoll** [ta'lɛntfɔl], *adj.* talented, gifted, accomplished.

**Taler** ['ta:lər], *m.* (—s, *pl.* —) old German coin; thaler.

**Talfahrt** ['ta:lfa:rt], *f.* (—, *pl.* —en) descent.

**Talg** [talk], *m.* (—(e)s, *no pl.*) tallow.

**Talk** [talk], *m.* (—(e)s, *no pl.*) talc.

**Talkerde** ['talkeːrdə], *f.* (—, *no pl.*) magnesia.

**Talkessel** ['ta:lkɛsəl], *m.* (—s, *pl.* —) (*Geog.*) hollow, narrow valley.

**Talmulde** ['ta:lmuldə], *f.* (—, *pl.* —n) narrow valley, trough.

**Talschlucht** ['ta:lʃluxt], *f.* (—, *pl.* —en) glen.

**Talsohle** ['ta:lzo:lə], *f.* (—, *pl.* —n) floor of a valley.

**Talsperre** ['ta:lʃpɛrə], *f.* (—, *pl.* —n) dam (across valley); barrage.

**Tambour** ['tambu:r], *m.* (—s, *pl.* —e) drummer.

**Tamtam** ['tamtam], *n.* (—s, *no pl.*) tom-tom; (*fig.*) palaver.

**Tand** [tant], *m.* (—(e)s, *no pl.*) knick-knack, trifle; rubbish.

**Tändelei** [tɛndə'laɪ], *f.* (—, *pl.* —en) trifling, toying; (*fig.*) flirting.

**Tändelmarkt** ['tɛndəlmarkt], *m.* (—s, *pl.* ⁀e) rag-fair.

**tändeln** ['tɛndəln], *v.n.* trifle, dally, toy; (*fig.*) flirt.

**Tang** [taŋ], *m.* (—s, *pl.* —e) (*Bot.*) seaweed.

**Tanganjika** [taŋga'nji:ka], *n.* Tanganyika.

**Tangente** [taŋ'gɛntə], *f.* (—, *pl.* —n) tangent.

**Tanger** ['taŋər], *n.* Tangier.

**Tank** [taŋk], *m.* (—(e)s, *pl.* —e) tank.

**tanken** ['taŋkən], *v.n.* refuel; fill up (with petrol).

**Tankstelle** ['taŋkʃtelə], *f.* (—, *pl.* —n) filling-station.

**Tanne** ['tanə], *f.* (—, *pl.* —n) (*Bot.*) fir.

**Tannenbaum** ['tanənbaum], *m.* (—s, *pl.* ⁀e) (*Bot.*) fir-tree.

**Tannenholz** ['tanənhɔlts], *n.* (—es, *no pl.*) (*timber*) deal.

**Tannenzapfen** ['tanəntsapfən], *m.* (—s, *pl.* —) (*Bot.*) fir-cone.

**Tansania** [tanza'ni:a], *n.* Tanzania.

**Tante** ['tantə], *f.* (—, *pl.* —n) aunt.

**Tantieme** [tã'tje:mə], *f.* (—, *pl.* —n) royalty, share (in profits), percentage.

**Tanz** [tants], *m.* (—es, *pl.* ⁀e) dance.

**Tanzboden** ['tantsbo:dən], *m.* (—s, *pl.* ⁀) ballroom, dance-hall.

**tänzeln** ['tɛntsəln], *v.n.* skip about, frisk; (*horses*) amble.

**tanzen** ['tantsən], *v.a., v.n.* dance.

**tanzlustig** ['tantslustɪç], *adj.* fond of dancing.

**Tapet** [ta'pe:t], *n.* (—s, *no pl.*) *aufs — bringen*, broach, bring up for discussion.

**Tapete** [ta'pe:tə], *f.* (—, *pl.* —n) wallpaper.

**tapezieren** [tapə'tsi:rən], *v.a.* paper.

**Tapezierer** [tapə'tsi:rər], *m.* (—s, *pl.* —) paperhanger; upholsterer.

**tapfer** ['tapfər], *adj.* brave, valiant, gallant, courageous.

**Tapferkeit** ['tapfərkaɪt], *f.* (—, *no pl.*) valour, bravery, gallantry.

**Tapisserie** [tapɪsə'ri:], *f.* (—, *no pl.*) needlework; tapestry.

**tappen** ['tapən], *v.n.* grope about.

**täppisch** ['tɛpɪʃ], *adj.* clumsy, awkward, unwieldy.

**tarnen** ['tarnən], *v.a.* camouflage.

**Tasche** ['taʃə], *f.* (—, *pl.* —n) pocket; bag, pouch; *in die — stecken*, pocket; *in die — greifen*, pay, fork out, put o.'s hand in o.'s pocket.

**Taschendieb** ['taʃəndi:p], *m.* (—(e)s, *pl.* —e) pickpocket; *vor —en wird gewarnt*, beware of pickpockets.

**Taschenformat** ['taʃənfɔrma:t], *n.* (—s, *no pl.*) pocket-size.

**Taschenspieler** ['taʃənʃpi:lər], *m.* (—s, *pl.* —) juggler, conjurer.

**Taschentuch** ['taʃəntu:x], *n.* (—s, *pl.* ⁀er) (pocket-)handkerchief.

**Taschenuhr** ['taʃənu:r], *f.* (—, *pl.* —en) pocket-watch.

**Tasse** ['tasə], *f.* (—, *pl.* —n) cup.

**Tastatur** [tasta'tu:r], *f.* (—, *pl.* —en) keyboard.

**Taste** ['tastə], *f.* (—, *pl.* —n) (*Mus.*) key.

**tasten** ['tastən], *v.n.* grope about, feel o.'s way.

**Tastsinn** ['tastzɪn], *m.* (—s, *no pl.*) sense of touch.

**Tat** [taːt], *f.* (—, *pl.* —en) deed, act, action; feat, exploit; *in der* —, in fact, indeed; *auf frischer* —, in the very act; *einem mit Rat und* — *beistehen*, give s.o. advice and guidance, help by word and deed.

**Tatbestand** [ˈtaːtbəʃtant], *m.* (—es, *pl.* ˸e) (*Law*) facts of the case.

**Tatendrang** [ˈtaːtəndraŋ], *m.* (—(e)s, *no pl.*) urge for action; impetuosity.

**tatenlos** [ˈtaːtənloːs], *adj.* inactive.

**Täter** [ˈtɛːtər], *m.* (—s, *pl.* —) perpetrator, doer; culprit.

**tätig** [ˈtɛːtɪç], *adj.* active, busy.

**Tätigkeit** [ˈtɛːtɪçkaɪt], *f.* (—, *pl.* —en) activity.

**Tätigkeitswort** [ˈtɛːtɪçkaɪtsvɔrt], *n.* (—(e)s, *pl.* ˸er) (*Gram.*) verb.

**Tatkraft** [ˈtaːtkraft], *f.* (—, *no pl.*) energy.

**tätlich** [ˈtɛːtlɪç], *adj.* — *werden*, become violent.

**tätowieren** [tɛːtoˈviːrən], *v.a.* tattoo.

**Tatsache** [ˈtaːtzaxə], *f.* (—, *pl.* —en) fact, matter of fact.

**tatsächlich** [ˈtaːtzɛçlɪç], *adj.* actual. — *excl.* really!

**tätscheln** [ˈtɛːtʃəln], *v.a.* fondle.

**Tatterich** [ˈtatərɪç], *m.* (—s, *no pl.*) (*coll.*) trembling, shakiness.

**Tatze** [ˈtatsə], *f.* (—, *pl.* —n) paw.

**Tau** (1) [tau], *m.* (—s, *no pl.*) thaw; dew.

**Tau** (2) [tau], *n.* (—s, *pl.* —e) rope, cable.

**taub** [taup], *adj.* deaf; (*nut*) hollow, empty; — *machen*, deafen; — *sein gegen*, turn a deaf ear to.

**Täubchen** [ˈtɔypçən], *n.* (—s, *pl.* —) little dove; (*fig.*) sweetheart.

**Taube** [ˈtaubə], *f.* (—, *pl.* —n) (*Orn.*) pigeon, dove.

**Taubenschlag** [ˈtaubənʃlaːk], *m.* (—s, *pl.* ˸e) dovecote.

**Taubenschwanz** [ˈtaubənʃvants], *m.* (—es, *pl.* ˸e) (*Ent.*) hawkmoth.

**Tauber** [ˈtaubər], *m.* (—s, *pl.* —) (*Orn.*) cock-pigeon.

**Taubheit** [ˈtauphaɪt], *f.* (—, *no pl.*) deafness.

**Taubnessel** [ˈtaupnɛsəl], *f.* (—, *pl.* —n) (*Bot.*) deadnettle.

**taubstumm** [ˈtaupʃtum], *adj.* deaf and dumb, deaf-mute.

**tauchen** [ˈtauçən], *v.n.* (*aux.* haben & sein) dive, plunge. — *v.a.* immerse, dip.

**Tauchsieder** [ˈtauçziːdər], *m.* (—s, *pl.* —) (*Elec.*) immersion heater.

**tauen** [ˈtauən], *v.a.*, *v.n.* thaw, melt.

**Taufbecken** [ˈtaufbɛkən], *n.* (—s, *pl.* —) (baptismal) font.

**Taufe** [ˈtaufə], *f.* (—, *pl.* —n) baptism, christening; *aus der* — *heben*, stand godparent.

**taufen** [ˈtaufən], *v.a.* baptise, christen.

**Taufkleid** [ˈtaufklaɪt], *n.* (—s, *pl.* —er) christening robe.

**Täufling** [ˈtɔyflɪŋ], *m.* (—s, *pl.* —e) infant presented for baptism; neophyte.

**Taufname** [ˈtaufnaːmə], *n.* (—ns, *pl.* —n) Christian name.

**Taufpate** [ˈtaufpaːtə], *m.* (—n, *pl.* —n) godfather, godmother.

**Taufstein** [ˈtaufʃtaɪn], *n.* (—s, *pl.* —e) (baptismal) font.

**taugen** [ˈtaugən], *v.n.* be good for, be fit for; *nichts* —, be good for nothing.

**Taugenichts** [ˈtaugənɪçts], *m.* (—, *pl.* —e) ne'er-do-well, scapegrace, good-for-nothing.

**tauglich** [ˈtauklɪç], *adj.* able; useful, fit, suitable.

**Taumel** [ˈtauməl], *m.* (—s, *no pl.*) giddiness, dizziness, staggering; (*fig.*) whirl; ecstasy, frenzy, delirium, intoxication.

**taumeln** [ˈtauməln], *v.n.* (*aux.* sein) reel, stagger.

**Tausch** [tauʃ], *m.* (—es, *no pl.*) exchange, barter.

**tauschen** [ˈtauʃən], *v.a.* exchange for, barter against, swop; *die Rollen* —, change places.

**täuschen** [ˈtɔyʃən], *v.a.* deceive, delude. — *v.r. sich* —, be mistaken.

**Tauschhandel** [ˈtauʃhandəl], *m.* (—s, *no pl.*) barter.

**Tauschmittel** [ˈtauʃmɪtəl], *n.* (—s, *pl.* —) medium of exchange.

**Täuschung** [ˈtɔyʃuŋ], *f.* (—, *pl.* —en) deceit, deception; illusion.

**Täuschungsversuch** [ˈtɔyʃuŋsferzuːç], *m.* (—es, *pl.* —e) attempt at deception; (*Mil.*) diversion.

**tausend** [ˈtauzənt], *num. adj.* a thousand.

**tausendjährig** [ˈtauzəntjɛːrɪç], *adj.* millennial, of a thousand years; *das* —*e Reich*, the millennium.

**Tausendsasa** [ˈtauzəntzasa], *m.* (—s, *pl.* —) devil of a fellow.

**Tautropfen** [ˈtautrɔpfən], *m.* (—s, *pl.* —) dew-drop.

**Tauwetter** [ˈtauvɛtər], *n.* (—s, *no pl.*) thaw.

**Taxameter** [taksaˈmeːtər], *m.* (—s, *pl.* —) taximeter.

**Taxe** [ˈtaksə], *f.* (—, *pl.* —n) set rate, tariff; (taxi)cab; *nach der* — *verkauft werden*, be sold ad valorem.

**taxieren** [takˈsiːrən], *v.a.* appraise, value.

**Taxus** [ˈtaksus], *m.* (—, *pl.* —) (*Bot.*) yew(-tree).

**Technik** [ˈtɛçnɪk], *f.* (—, *pl.* —en) technology, engineering; technique; skill, execution.

**Techniker** [ˈtɛçnɪkər], *m.* (—s, *pl.* —) technician, technical engineer.

**Technikum** [ˈtɛçnɪkum], *n.* (—s, *pl.* —s) technical school, college.

**technisch** [ˈtɛçnɪʃ], *adj.* technical; —*er Ausdruck*, technical term; —*e Störung*, technical hitch *or* breakdown.

**technologisch** [tɛçnoˈloːgɪʃ], *adj.* technological.

221

# Techtelmechtel

**Techtelmechtel** ['tɛçtəlmɛçtəl], *n.* (—s, *pl.* —) (*coll.*) love affair, flirtation.

**Tee** [te:], *m.* (—s, *no pl.*) tea.

**Teedose** ['te:do:zə], *f.* (—, *pl.* —n) tea-caddy.

**Teekanne** ['te:kanə], *f.* (—, *pl.* —n) tea-pot.

**Teelöffel** ['te:lœfəl], *m.* (—s, *pl.* —) tea-spoon.

**Teemaschine** ['te:maʃinə], *f.* (—, *pl.* —n) tea-urn.

**Teer** [te:r], *m.* (—(e)s, *no pl.*) tar.

**Teerleinwand** ['te:rlaɪnvant], *f.* (—, *no pl.*) tarpaulin.

**Teerose** ['te:ro:zə], *f.* (—, *pl.* —n) (*Bot.*) tea rose.

**Teerpappe** ['te:rpapə], *f.* (—, *no pl.*) roofing-felt.

**teeren** ['te:rən], *v.a.* tar.

**Teesieb** ['te:zi:p], *n.* (—(e)s, *pl.* —e) tea-strainer.

**Teich** [taɪç], *m.* (—es, *pl.* —e) pond.

**Teig** [taɪk], *m.* (—(e)s, *pl.* —e) dough, paste.

**teigig** ['taɪgɪç], *adj.* doughy.

**Teigrolle** ['taɪkrɔlə], *f.* (—, *pl.* —n) rolling-pins.

**Teil** [taɪl], *m. & n.* (—(e)s, *pl.* —e) part; portion; piece, component; share; *edler* —, vital part; *zum* —, partly; *zu gleichen* —*en*, share and share alike.

**teilbar** ['taɪlba:r], *adj.* divisible.

**Teilchen** ['taɪlçən], *n.* (—s, *pl.* —) particle.

**teilen** ['taɪlən], *v.a.* divide; share; partition off. — *v.r. sich* —, share in; (*road*) fork.

**Teiler** ['taɪlər], *m.* (—s, *pl.* —) divider; (*Maths.*) divisor.

**teilhaben** ['taɪlha:bən], *v.n. irr.* (have a) share in, participate in.

**Teilhaber** ['taɪlha:bər], *m.* (—s, *pl.* —) partner.

**teilhaftig** ['taɪlhaftɪç], *adj.* sharing, participating; *einer Sache* — *werden*, partake of s.th., come in for s.th.

**Teilnahme** ['taɪlna:mə], *f.* (—, *no pl.*) participation; (*fig.*) sympathy, interest.

**teilnahmslos** ['taɪlna:mslo:s], *adj.* unconcerned, indifferent.

**Teilnahmslosigkeit** ['taɪlna:mslo:zɪçkaɪt], *f.* (—, *no pl.*) unconcern; listlessness, indifference.

**teilnahmsvoll** ['taɪlna:msfɔl], *adj.* solicitous.

**teilnehmen** ['taɪlne:mən], *v.n. irr.* take part (in), participate, partake; (*fig.*) sympathise.

**Teilnehmer** ['taɪlne:mər], *m.* (—s, *pl.* —) member, participant; (*telephone*) subscriber.

**teils** [taɪls], *adv.* partly.

**Teilstrecke** ['taɪlʃtrɛkə], *f.* (—, *pl.* —n) section (of a railway).

**Teilung** ['taɪluŋ], *f.* (—, *pl.* —en) division, partition; distribution.

**Teilungszahl** ['taɪluŋstsa:l], *f.* (—, *pl.* —en) (*Maths.*) dividend; quotient.

**teilweise** ['taɪlvaɪzə], *adv.* partly, in part.

**Teilzahlung** ['taɪltsa:luŋ], *f.* (—, *pl.* —en) part-payment, instalment.

**Teint** [tɛ̃], *m.* (—s, *no pl.*) complexion.

**telephonieren** [telefo'ni:rən], *v.a., v.n.* telephone.

**Telegraphie** [telegra'fi:], *f.* (—, *no pl.*) telegraphy.

**telegraphisch** [tele'gra:fɪʃ], *adj.* telegraphic, by telegram.

**Telegramm** [tele'gram], *n.* (—s, *pl.* —e) telegram, wire, cable.

**Telegrammadresse** [tele'gramadrɛsə], *f.* (—, *pl.* —n) telegraphic address.

**Telegrammformular** [tele'gramformula:r], *n.* (—s, *pl.* —e) telegram-form.

**Teleskop** [teles'ko:p], *n.* (—s, *pl.* —e) telescope.

**Teller** ['tɛlər], *m.* (—s, *pl.* —) plate.

**Tempel** ['tɛmpəl], *m.* (—s, *pl.* —) temple.

**Temperament** [tɛmpəra'mɛnt], *n.* (—s, *pl.* —e) temperament, disposition; (*fig.*) spirits.

**temperamentvoll** [tɛmpəra'mɛntfɔl], *adj.* full of spirits, vivacious; lively.

**Temperatur** [tɛmpəra'tu:r], *f.* (—, *pl.* —en) temperature.

**Temperenzler** [tɛmpə'rɛntslər], *m.* (—s, *pl.* —) total abstainer, tee-totaller.

**temperieren** [tɛmpə'ri:rən], *v.a.* temper.

**Tempo** ['tɛmpo:], *n.* (—s, *pl.* —s, Tempi) time, measure, speed.

**temporisieren** [tɛmpori'zi:rən], *v.n.* temporise.

**Tendenz** [tɛn'dɛnts], *f.* (—, *pl.* —en) tendency.

**tendenziös** [tɛndɛn'tsjø:s], *adj.* biased, coloured, tendentious.

**Tender** ['tɛndər], *m.* (—s, *pl.* —) (*Railw.*) tender.

**Tenne** ['tɛnə], *f.* (—, *pl.* —n) threshing floor.

**Tenor** [te'no:r], *m.* (—s, *pl.* ⁻e) (*Mus.*) tenor.

**Teppich** ['tɛpɪç], *m.* (—s, *pl.* —e) carpet.

**Termin** [tɛr'mi:n], *m.* (—s, *pl.* —e) time, date, appointed day; *einen* — *ansetzen*, fix a day (for a hearing, examination etc.).

**Termingeschäft** [tɛr'mi:ngəʃɛft], *n.* (—s, *pl.* —e) (business) in futures.

**Terminologie** [tɛrminolo'gi:], *f.* (—, *pl.* —n) terminology.

**Terpentin** [tɛrpɛn'ti:n], *n.* (—s, *no pl.*) turpentine.

**Terrain** [tɛ'rɛ̃], *n.* (—s, *pl.* —s) ground, terrain.

**Terrasse** [tɛ'rasə], *f.* (—, *pl.* —n) terrace.

**Terrine** [tɛ'ri:nə], *f.* (—, *pl.* —n) tureen.

**territorial** [tɛrɪto'rja:l], *adj.* territorial.

**Territorium** [tɛrɪ'to:rjum], *n.* (—s, *pl.* —torien) territory.

**tertiär** [tɛr'tsjɛ:r], *adj.* tertiary.
**Terzett** [tɛr'tsɛt], *n.* (—s, *pl.* —e) trio.
**Testament** [tɛsta'mɛnt], *n.* (—s, *pl.* —e) testament, will; (*Bibl.*) Testament; *ohne* —, intestate.
**testamentarisch** [tɛstamɛn'ta:rɪʃ], *adj.* testamentary.
**Testamentseröffnung** [tɛsta'mɛntser-œfnuŋ], *f.* (—, *pl.* —en) reading of the will.
**Testamentsvollstrecker** [tɛsta'mɛnts-fɔlʃtrɛkər], *m.* (—s, *pl.* —) executor.
**teuer** ['tɔyər], *adj.* dear; costly, expensive; *einem — zu stehen kommen*, cost s.o. dear.
**Teuerung** ['tɔyəruŋ], *f.* (—, *pl.* —en) scarcity, dearth.
**Teufel** ['tɔyfəl], *m.* (—s, *pl.* —) devil, fiend; *armer —*, poor devil; *scher dich zum —*, go to blazes; *den — an die Wand malen*, talk of the devil.
**Teufelei** [tɔyfə'laɪ], *f.* (—, *pl.* —en) devilry, devilish trick.
**teuflisch** ['tɔyflɪʃ], *adj.* devilish, diabolical.
**Thailand** ['taɪlant], *n.* Thailand.
**Theater** [te'a:tər], *n.* (—s, *pl.* —) theatre, stage.
**Theaterkarte** [te'a:tərkartə], *f.* (—, *pl.* —n) theatre-ticket.
**Theaterkasse** [te'a:tərkasə], *f.* (—, *pl.* —n) box-office.
**Theaterstück** [te'a:tərʃtyk], *n.* (—(e)s, *pl.* —e) play, drama.
**Theatervorstellung** [te'a:tərfo:rʃtɛluŋ], *f.* (—, *pl.* —en) theatre performance.
**Theaterzettel** [te'a:tərtsɛtəl], *m.* (—s, *pl.* —) play-bill.
**theatralisch** [tea'tra:lɪʃ], *adj.* theatrical; dramatic; histrionic.
**Thema** ['te:ma:], *n.* (—s, *pl.* —men, Themata) theme, subject, topic.
**Themse** ['tɛmzə], *f.* Thames.
**Theologe** [teo'lo:gə], *m.* (—n, *pl.* —n) theologian.
**Theologie** [teolo'gi:], *f.* (—, *no pl.*) theology, divinity.
**theoretisch** [teo're:tɪʃ], *adj.* theoretical.
**theoretisieren** [teoreti'zi:rən], *v.n.* theorise.
**Theorie** [teo'ri:], *f.* (—, *pl.* —n) theory.
**Therapie** [tera'pi:], *f.* (—, *no pl.*) therapy.
**Therme** ['tɛrmə], *f.* (—, *pl.* —n) hot spring.
**Thermometer** [tɛrmo'me:tər], *n.* (—s, *pl.* —) thermometer.
**Thermosflasche** ['tɛrmɔsflaʃə], *f.* (—, *pl.* —n) thermos-flask.
**These** ['te:zə], *f.* (—, *pl.* —n) thesis.
**Thron** [tro:n], *m.* (—(e)s, *pl.* —e) throne; *auf den — setzen*, place on the throne, enthrone; *vom — stoßen*, dethrone, depose.
**Thronbesteigung** ['tro:nbəʃtaɪguŋ], *f.* (—, *pl.* —en) accession (to the throne).
**Thronbewerber** ['tro:nbəvɛrbər], *m.* (—s, *pl.* —) claimant to the throne, pretender.
**thronen** ['tro:nən], *v.n.* sit enthroned.

**Thronerbe** ['tro:nɛrbə], *m.* (—n, *pl.* —n) heir apparent, crown prince.
**Thronfolge** ['tro:nfɔlgə], *f.* (—, *no pl.*) line *or* order of succession.
**Thronfolger** ['tro:nfɔlgər], *m.* (—s, *pl.* —) heir to the throne, heir apparent.
**Thronhimmel** ['tro:nhɪməl], *m.* (—s, *pl.* —) canopy.
**Thronrede** ['tro:nre:də], *f.* (—, *pl.* —n) speech from the throne.
**Thunfisch** ['tu:nfɪʃ], *m.* (—es, *pl.* —e) (*Zool.*) tunny, (*Am.*) tuna.
**Thüringen** ['ty:rɪŋən], *n.* Thuringia.
**Thymian** ['ty:mja:n], *m.* (—s, *no pl.*) (*Bot.*) thyme.
**ticken** ['tɪkən], *v.n.* tick.
**tief** [ti:f], *adj.* deep, profound, low; far; extreme; (*voice*) bass; (*fig.*) profound; *in —ster Nacht*, in the dead of night; *aus —stem Herzen*, from the bottom of o.'s heart. — *adv.* — *atmen*, take a deep breath; — *in Schulden*, head over ears in debt; — *verletzt*, cut to the quick.
**Tiefbau** ['ti:fbau], *m.* (—s, *no pl.*) underground workings.
**tiefbedrückt** ['ti:fbədrykt], *adj.* deeply distressed; very depressed.
**tiefbewegt** ['ti:fbəve:kt], *adj.* deeply moved.
**Tiefe** ['ti:fə], *f.* (—, *pl.* —en) depth; (*fig.*) profundity.
**tiefgebeugt** ['ti:fgəbɔykt], *adj.* bowed down.
**tiefgreifend** ['ti:fgraɪfənt], *adj.* radical, sweeping.
**tiefschürfend** ['ti:fʃyrfənt], *adj.* profound; thoroughgoing.
**Tiefsee** ['ti:fze:], *f.* (—, *no pl.*) [deep sea.
**Tiefsinn** ['ti:fzɪn], *m.* (—s, *no pl.*) pensiveness, melancholy.
**tiefsinnig** ['ti:fzɪnɪç], *adj.* pensive, melancholy, melancholic(al).
**Tiegel** ['ti:gəl], *m.* (—s, *pl.* —) crucible; saucepan.
**Tier** [ti:r], *n.* (—(e)s, *pl.* —e) animal, beast; *ein großes —*, (*coll.*) a V.I.P., a bigwig; (*Am.*) a swell, a big shot.
**Tierart** ['ti:ra:rt], *f.* (—, *pl.* —en) (*Zool.*) species.
**Tierarzt** ['ti:ra:rtst], *m.* (—es, *pl.* ⸚e) veterinary surgeon.
**Tierbändiger** ['ti:rbɛndɪgər], *m.* (—s, *pl.* —) animal-tamer.
**Tiergarten** ['ti:rgartən], *m.* (—s, *pl.* ⸚) zoological gardens, zoo.
**tierisch** ['ti:rɪʃ], *adj.* animal, brute, brutal, bestial.
**Tierkreis** ['ti:rkraɪs], *m.* (—es, *no pl.*) zodiac.
**Tierkunde** ['ti:rkundə], *f.* (—, *no pl.*) zoology.
**Tierquälerei** ['ti:rkvɛ:ləraɪ], *f.* (—, *pl.* —en) cruelty to animals.
**Tierreich** ['ti:rraɪç], *n.* (—(e)s, *no pl.*) animal kingdom.
**Tierschutzverein** ['ti:rʃutsfəraɪn], *m.* (—s, *pl.* —e) society for the prevention of cruelty to animals.

223

**Tierwärter** ['ti:rvɛrtər], *m.* (—s, *pl.* —) keeper (at a zoo).

**Tiger** ['ti:gər], *m.* (—s, *pl.* —) (*Zool.*) tiger.

**Tigerin** ['ti:gərɪn], *f.* (—, *pl.* —nen) (*Zool.*) tigress.

**tilgbar** ['tɪlkba:r], *adj.* extinguishable; (*debt*) redeemable.

**tilgen** ['tɪlgən], *v.a.* strike out, efface, annul; (*debt*) discharge; (*sin*) expiate, atone for.

**Tilgung** ['tɪlguŋ], *f.* (—, *pl.* —en) striking out, obliteration; annulment, payment; redemption.

**Tilgungsfonds** ['tɪlguŋsfɔ̃], *m.* (—, *pl.* —) sinking fund.

**Tingeltangel** ['tɪŋəltaŋəl], *m. & n.* (—s, *pl.* —) (*coll.*) music-hall.

**Tinktur** [tɪŋk'tu:r], *f.* (—, *pl.* —en) tincture.

**Tinte** ['tɪntə], *f.* (—, *pl.* —n) ink; *in der — sein,* be in a jam, be in the soup.

**Tintenfaß** ['tɪntənfas], *n.* (—sses, *pl.* ⁻sser) ink-pot, ink-stand.

**Tintenfisch** ['tɪntənfɪʃ], *m.* (—es, *pl.* —e) (*Zool.*) cuttle-fish.

**Tintenfleck** ['tɪntənflɛk], *m.* (—s, *pl.* —e) blot, ink-spot.

**Tintenklecks** ['tɪntənklɛks], *m.* (—es, *pl.* —e) blot.

**Tintenstift** ['tɪntənʃtɪft], *m.* (—s, *pl.* —e) indelible pencil.

**Tintenwischer** ['tɪntənvɪʃər], *m.* (—s, *pl.* —) pen-wiper.

**tippen** ['tɪpən], *v.a.* tap; (*coll.*) type.

**Tirol** [ti'ro:l], *n.* Tyrol.

**Tisch** [tɪʃ], *m.* (—es, *pl.* —e) table, board; *den — decken,* lay the table; *zu — gehen,* sit down to dinner.

**Tischdecke** ['tɪʃdɛkə], *f.* (—, *pl.* —n) tablecloth.

**Tischgebet** ['tɪʃgəbe:t], *n.* (—s, *pl.* —e) grace.

**Tischler** ['tɪʃlər], *m.* (—s, *pl.* —) joiner, cabinet-maker, carpenter.

**Tischlerei** [tɪʃlə'rai], *f.* (—, *no pl.*) joinery, cabinet-making, carpentry.

**Tischrede** ['tɪʃre:də], *f.* (—, *pl.* —n) after-dinner speech.

**Tischrücken** ['tɪʃrykən], *n.* (—s, *no pl.*) table-turning.

**Tischtennis** ['tɪʃtɛnɪs], *n.* (—, *no pl.*) table-tennis, ping-pong.

**Tischtuch** ['tɪʃtu:x], *n.* (—(e)s, *pl.* ⁻er) tablecloth.

**Tischzeit** ['tɪʃtsait], *f.* (—, *pl.* —en) mealtime.

**Titane** [ti'ta:nə], *m.* (—n, *pl.* —n) Titan.

**titanenhaft** [ti'ta:nənhaft], *adj.* titanic.

**Titel** ['ti:təl], *m.* (—s, *pl.* —) title; claim; heading, headline.

**Titelbild** ['ti:təlbɪlt], *n.* (—(e)s, *pl.* —er) frontispiece.

**Titelblatt** ['ti:təlblat], *n.* (—(e)s, *pl.* ⁻er) title page.

**Titelrolle** ['ti:təlrɔlə], *f.* (—, *pl.* —n) title role.

**titulieren** [titu'li:rən], *v.a.* style, address.

**toben** ['to:bən], *v.n.* rave; rage, roar; be furious; be wild.

**tobsüchtig** ['to:pzyçtɪç], *adj.* raving, mad.

**Tochter** ['tɔxtər], *f.* (—, *pl.* ⁻) daughter.

**töchterlich** ['tœçtərlɪç], *adj.* filial, daughterly.

**Tod** [to:t], *m.* (—es, *pl.* —esfälle *or* (*rare*) —e) death, decease, demise; *dem — geweiht,* doomed; *Kampf auf — und Leben,* fight to the death; *zum — verurteilen,* condemn to death.

**Todesangst** ['to:dəsaŋst], *f.* (—, *pl.* ⁻e) agony, mortal terror.

**Todesanzeige** ['to:dəsantsaigə], *f.* (—, *pl.* —n) announcement of death; obituary notice.

**Todesfall** ['to:dəsfal], *m.* (—(e)s, *pl.* ⁻e) death, decease; fatality.

**Todesgefahr** ['to:dəsgəfa:r], *f.* (—, *pl.* —en) mortal danger.

**Todeskampf** ['to:dəskampf], *m.* (—(e)s, *pl.* ⁻e) death agony.

**todesmutig** ['to:dəsmu:tɪç], *adj.* death-defying.

**Todesstoß** ['to:dəsʃto:s], *m.* (—es, *pl.* ⁻e) death-blow.

**Todesstrafe** ['to:dəsʃtra:fə], *f.* (—, *no pl.*) capital punishment.

**Todfeind** ['to:tfaint], *m.* (—es, *pl.* —e) mortal enemy.

**todkrank** ['to:tkraŋk], *adj.* sick unto death, dangerously *or* mortally ill.

**tödlich** ['tœ:tlɪç], *adj.* mortal, deadly, fatal.

**todmüde** ['to:tmy:də], *adj.* tired to death.

**Todsünde** ['to:tzyndə], *f.* (—, *pl.* —n) mortal sin.

**Togo** ['to:go], *n.* Togo.

**Toilette** [toa'lɛtə], *f.* (—, *pl.* —n) lavatory, toilet; (*fig.*) dress.

**tolerant** [tole'rant], *adj.* tolerant.

**Toleranz** [tole'rants], *f.* (—, *no pl.*) toleration; tolerance.

**tolerieren** [tole'ri:rən], *v.a.* tolerate.

**toll** [tɔl], *adj.* mad, frantic; wild; *—er Streich,* mad prank; *zum — werden,* enough to drive o. mad.

**Tolle** ['tɔlə], *f.* (—, *pl.* —n) (*dial.*) forelock, tuft of hair, top-knot.

**Tollhaus** ['tɔlhaus], *n.* (—es, *pl.* ⁻er) madhouse, lunatic asylum.

**Tollheit** ['tɔlhait], *f.* (—, *pl.* —en) foolhardiness, mad prank.

**Tollkirsche** ['tɔlkɪrʃə], *f.* (—, *pl.* —n) belladonna, deadly nightshade.

**Tollwut** ['tɔlvu:t], *f.* (—, *no pl.*) frenzy; rabies.

**Tolpatsch** ['tɔlpatʃ], *m.* (—es, *pl.* —e) clumsy person.

**Tölpel** ['tœlpəl], *m.* (—s, *pl.* —) blockhead, lout, hobbledehoy.

**Tölpelei** [tœlpə'lai], *f.* (—, *pl.* —en) clumsiness, awkwardness.

**tölpelhaft** ['tœlpəlhaft], *adj.* clumsy, doltish, loutish.

**Tomate** [to'ma:tə], *f.* (—, *pl.* —n) tomato.

**Ton** (1) [to:n], *m.* (—(e)s, *pl.* ⸚e) sound, tone, accent, note; shade; manners; *guter (schlechter)* —, good (bad) form, etiquette; *den — angeben,* set the fashion.

**Ton** (2) [to:n], *m.* (—s, *no pl.*) clay, potter's earth.

**Tonabnehmer** ['to:napne:mər], *m.* (—s, *pl.* —) *(gramophone)* pick-up.

**tonangebend** ['to:nange:bənt], *adj.* leading in fashion, setting the pace; leading, fashionable.

**Tonart** ['to:na:rt], *f.* (—, *pl.* —en) *(Mus.)* key.

**Tonbandgerät** ['to:nbantgɛrɛ:t], *n.* (—s, *pl.* —e) tape-recorder.

**tönen** ['tø:nən], *v.n.* sound.

**Tonerde** ['to:ne:rdə], *f.* (—, *no pl.*) clay.

**tönern** ['tø:nərn], *adj.* earthen.

**Tonfall** ['to:nfal], *m.* (—s, *no pl.*) cadence, intonation (of voice).

**Tonfolge** ['to:nfɔlgə], *f.* (—, *pl.* —n) *(Mus.)* succession of notes.

**Tonführung** ['to:nfy:ruŋ], *f.* (—, *no pl.*) modulation.

**Tonkunst** ['to:nkunst], *f.* (—, *no pl.*) music.

**Tonkünstler** ['to:nkynstlər], *m.* (—s, *pl.* —) musician.

**Tonleiter** ['to:nlaɪtər], *f.* (—, *pl.* —n) scale, gamut.

**Tonne** ['tɔnə], *f.* (—, *pl.* —n) tun, cask, barrel; ton.

**Tonnengewölbe** ['tɔnəngəvœlbə], *n.* (—s, *pl.* —n) cylindrical vault.

**Tonpfeife** ['to:npfaɪfə], *f.* (—, *pl.* —n) clay-pipe.

**Tonsatz** ['to:nzats], *m.* (—es, *pl.* ⸚e) *(Mus.)* composition.

**Tonsur** [tɔn'zu:r], *f.* (—, *pl.* —en) tonsure.

**Tonwelle** ['to:nvɛlə], *f.* (—, *pl.* —n) sound-wave.

**Topas** [to'pa:s], *m.* (—es, *pl.* —e) topaz.

**Topf** [tɔpf], *m.* (—(e)s, *pl.* ⸚e) pot; *alles in einen — werfen,* lump everything together.

**Topfblume** ['tɔpfblu:mə], *f.* (—, *pl.* —n) pot-plant.

**Topfdeckel** ['tɔpfdekəl], *m.* (—s, *pl.* —) lid of a pot.

**Töpfer** ['tœpfər], *m.* (—s, *pl.* —) potter.

**Töpferarbeit** ['tœpfərarbaɪt], *f.* (—, *pl.* —en) pottery.

**Töpferscheibe** ['tœpfərʃaɪbə], *f.* (—, *pl.* —n) potter's wheel.

**Töpferware** ['tœpfərva:rə], *f.* (—, *pl.* —n) pottery, earthenware.

**Topfgucker** ['tɔpfgukər], *m.* (—s, *pl.* —) busybody; inquisitive person.

**Topographie** [topogra'fi:], *f.* (—, *no pl.*) topography.

**Tor** (1) [to:r], *m.* (—en, *pl.* —en) *(obs.)* fool, simpleton.

**Tor** (2) [to:r], *n.* (—(e)s, *pl.* —e) gate; *(Footb.)* goal.

**Torangel** ['to:raŋəl], *f.* (—, *pl.* —n) hinge.

**Tor(es)schluß** ['to:r(əs)ʃlus], *m.* (—es, *no pl.*) shutting of the gate; *noch gerade vor* —, at the eleventh hour.

**Torf** [tɔrf], *m.* (—(e)s, *no pl.*) peat, turf.

**Torfgrube** ['tɔrfgru:bə], *f.* (—, *pl.* —n) turf-pit.

**Torfmoor** ['tɔrfmo:r], *n.* (—s, *pl.* —e) peat-bog.

**Torfstecher** ['tɔrfʃteçər], *m.* (—s, *pl.* —) peat-cutter.

**Torheit** ['to:rhaɪt], *f.* (—, *pl.* —en) foolishness, folly.

**Torhüter** ['to:rhy:tər], *m.* (—s, *pl.* —) gate-keeper.

**töricht** ['tø:rɪçt], *adj.* foolish, silly.

**Törin** ['tø:rɪn], *f.* (—, *pl.* —nen) *(rare)* foolish woman.

**torkeln** ['tɔrkəln], *v.n.* *(coll.)* stagger, reel.

**Tornister** [tɔr'nɪstər], *m.* (—s, *pl.* —) knapsack, satchel.

**Torpedo** [tɔr'pe:do], *m.* (—s, *pl.* —s) torpedo.

**Torso** ['tɔrzo], *m.* (—s, *pl.* —s) trunk, torso.

**Tort** [tɔrt], *m.* (—s, *no pl.*) injury, wrong; *einem einen — antun,* wrong s.o., play a trick on s.o.

**Torte** ['tɔrtə], *f.* (—, *pl.* —n) cake, pastry, tart.

**Tortur** [tɔr'tu:r], *f.* (—, *pl.* —en) torture.

**Torwächter** ['to:rvɛçtər], *m.* (—s, *pl.* —) gate-keeper; porter.

**tosen** ['to:zən], *v.n.* roar.

**tot** [to:t], *adj.* dead, deceased.

**total** [to'ta:l], *adj.* total, complete.

**Totalisator** [totali'za:tɔr], *m.* (—s, *pl.* —en) totalisator; (coll.) tote.

**Totalleistung** [to'ta:llaɪstuŋ], *f.* (—, *pl.* —en) full effect; total output.

**Tote** ['to:tə], *m.,f.* (—n, *pl.* —n) dead person, the deceased.

**töten** ['tø:tən], *v.a.* kill, put to death.

**Totenacker** ['to:tənakər], *m.* (—s, *pl.* ⸚) churchyard, cemetery.

**Totenamt** ['to:tənamt], *n.* (—s, *no pl.*) office for the dead, requiem, Mass for the dead.

**Totenbahre** ['to:tənba:rə], *f.* (—, *pl.* —n) bier.

**Totengräber** ['to:təngrɛ:bər], *m.* (—s, *pl.* —) grave-digger.

**Totenhemd** ['to:tənhɛmt], *n.* (—(e)s, *pl.* —en) shroud, winding-sheet.

**Totenklage** ['to:tənkla:gə], *f.* (—, *no pl.*) lament.

**Totenschein** ['to:tənʃaɪn], *m.* (—(e)s, *pl.* —e) death-certificate.

**Totenstille** ['to:tənʃtɪlə], *f.* (—, *no pl.*) dead calm.

**Totenwache** ['to:tənvaxə], *f.* (—, *no pl.*) wake.

**totgeboren** ['to:tgəbo:rən], *adj.* stillborn, born dead.

**Totschlag** ['to:tʃla:k], *m.* (—s, *no pl.*) manslaughter.

**totschlagen** ['to:tʃla:gən], *v.a.* *irr.* kill, strike dead.

# Totschläger

**Totschläger** ['to:tʃlɛ:gər], *m.* (—s, *pl.* —) loaded cane, life-preserver.

**totschweigen** ['to:tʃvaɪgən], *v.a. irr.* hush up.

**Tötung** ['tø:tuŋ], *f.* (—, *pl.* —en) killing.

**Tour** [tu:r], *f.* (—, *pl.* —en) tour, excursion; *in einer* —, ceaselessly; *auf —en bringen,(coll.) (Motor.)* rev up.

**Tournee** [tur'ne:], *f.* (—, *pl.* —n) *(Theat.)* tour.

**Trab** [tra:p], *m.* (—(e)s, *no pl.)* trot.

**Trabant** [tra'bant], *m.* (—en, *pl.* —en) satellite.

**traben** ['tra:bən], *v.n. (aux.* sein) trot.

**Trabrennen** ['tra:prɛnən], *n.* (—s, *pl.* —) trotting-race.

**Tracht** [traxt], *f.* (—, *pl.* —en) dress, costume; national costume; native dress; *eine — Prügel,* a good hiding.

**trachten** ['traxtən], *v.n.* strive, aspire, endeavour; *einem nach dem Leben —,* seek to kill s.o.

**trächtig** ['trɛçtɪç], *adj. (animal)* pregnant, with young.

**Trafik** [tra'fɪk], *m.* (—s, *pl.* —s) *(Austr.)* tobacco-kiosk.

**Tragbahre** ['tra:kba:rə], *f.* (—, *pl.* —n) stretcher.

**Tragbalken** ['tra:kbalkən], *m.* (—s *pl.,* —) girder.

**tragbar** ['tra:kba:r], *adj.* portable; tolerable.

**träge** ['trɛ:gə], *adj.* lazy, indolent, inert, sluggish.

**tragen** ['tra:gən], *v.a. irr.* bear, carry; *(dress)* wear; *( fig.)* bear, endure; *Bedenken —,* hesitate, have doubts; *Zinsen —,* yield interest; *einen auf Händen —,* care lovingly for s.o.

**Träger** ['trɛ:gər], *m.* (—s, *pl.* —) porter, carrier; girder.

**Trägheit** ['trɛ:khaɪt], *f.* (—, *no pl.)* indolence, laziness, inertia.

**tragisch** ['tra:gɪʃ], *adj.* tragic(al).

**Tragkraft** ['tra:kkraft], *f.* (—, *no pl.)* carrying *or* load capacity; lifting power.

**Tragödie** [tra'gø:djə], *f.* (—, *pl.* —n) tragedy.

**Tragsessel** ['tra:kzɛsəl], *m.* (—s, *pl.* —) sedan-chair.

**Tragweite** ['tra:kvaɪtə], *f.* (—, *no pl.)* significance, importance, range.

**trainieren** [trɛ'ni:rən], *v.a.* train.

**Traktat** [trak'ta:t], *n.* (—s, *pl.* —e) treatise, tract.

**Traktätchen** [trak'tɛ:tçən], *n.* (—s, *pl.* —) (short) tract.

**traktieren** [trak'ti:rən], *v.a.* treat; treat badly.

**trällern** ['trɛlərn], *v.n.* trill, hum.

**Trambahn** ['tramba:n], *f.* (—, *pl.* —en) tram; *(Am.)* streetcar.

**Trampel** ['trampəl], *n.* (—s, *pl.* —) clumsy person, bumpkin; *(Am.)* hick.

**trampeln** ['trampəln], *v.n.* trample.

**Trampeltier** ['trampəlti:r], *n.* (—s, *pl.* —e) camel; *( fig.)* clumsy person.

**Tran** [tra:n], *m.* (—(e)s, *no pl.)* whale-oil.

**tranchieren** [trã'ʃi:rən], *v.a.* carve.

**Tranchiermesser** [trã'ʃi:rmɛsər], *n.* (—s, *pl.* —) carving-knife.

**Träne** ['trɛ:nə], *f.* (—, *pl.* —n) tear, teardrop; *zu —n gerührt,* moved to tears.

**tränen** ['trɛ:nən], *v.n. (eyes)* water.

**Tränendrüse** ['trɛ:nəndry:zə], *f.* (—, *pl.* —n) lachrymal gland.

**tränenleer** ['trɛ:nənle:r], *adj.* tearless.

**Tränenstrom** ['trɛ:nənʃtro:m], *m.* (—s, *pl.* ̈e) flood of tears.

**tränenvoll** ['trɛ:nənfɔl], *adj.* tearful.

**tranig** ['tra:nɪç], *adj.* dull, slow.

**Trank** [traŋk], *m.* (—(e)s, *pl.* ̈e) drink, beverage, potion.

**Tränke** ['trɛŋkə], *f.* (—, *pl.* —n) *(horse)* watering-place.

**tränken** ['trɛŋkən], *v.a.* give to drink, water; impregnate, saturate.

**transitiv** ['tranziti:f], *adj.* transitive.

**Transitlager** ['tranzɪtla:gər], *n.* (—s, *pl.* —) bonded warehouse; transit camp.

**transitorisch** [tranzi'to:rɪʃ], *adj.* transitory.

**transpirieren** [transpi'ri:rən], *v.n.* perspire.

**transponieren** [transpo'ni:rən], *v.a.* transpose.

**Transportkosten** [trans'pɔrtkɔstən], *f. pl.* shipping charges.

**Transportmittel** [trans'pɔrtmɪtəl], *n.* (—s, *pl.* —) means of carriage, conveyance, transport.

**Trapez** [tra'pe:ts], *n.* (—es, *pl.* —e) trapeze; *(Maths.)* trapezoid.

**Tratsch** [tra:tʃ], *m.* (—es, *no pl.) (coll.)* gossip, tittle-tattle.

**tratschen** ['tra:tʃən], *v.n. (coll.)* gossip.

**Tratte** ['tratə], *f.* (—, *pl.* —n) *(Comm.)* draft, bill of exchange.

**Traube** ['traubə], *f.* (—, *pl.* —n) *(Bot.)* grape, bunch of grapes.

**Traubensaft** ['traubənzaft], *m.* (—s, *pl.* ̈e) grape-juice; *(Poet.)* wine.

**traubig** ['traubɪç], *adj.* clustered, grape-like.

**trauen** ['trauən], *v.a.* marry; join in marriage; *sich — lassen,* get married. — *v.n. einem —,* trust s.o., confide in s.o. — *v.r. sich —,* dare, venture.

**Trauer** ['trauər], *f.* (—, *no pl.)* mourning; sorrow, grief.

**Trauermarsch** ['trauərmarʃ], *m.* (—es, *pl.* ̈e) funeral march.

**trauern** ['trauərn], *v.n.* mourn, be in mourning.

**Trauerspiel** ['trauərʃpi:l], *n.* (—s, *pl.* —e) tragedy.

**Trauerweide** ['trauərvaɪdə], *f.* (—, *pl.* —n) *(Bot.)* weeping willow.

**Traufe** ['traufə], *f.* (—, *pl.* —n) eaves; *vom Regen in die —,* out of the frying pan into the fire.

**träufeln** ['trɔyfəln], *v.a.* drip, drop.

**Traufröhre** ['traufrø:rə], *f.* (—, *pl.* —n) gutter-pipe.

**traulich** ['traulɪç], *adj.* familiar, homely, cosy.

**Traum** [traum], *m.* (—(e)s, *pl.* ⁓e) dream; *das fällt mir nicht im —e ein*, I should not dream of it.

**Traumbild** ['traumbɪlt], *n.* (—s, *pl.* —er) vision.

**Traumdeutung** ['traumdɔytuŋ], *f.* (—, *no pl.*) interpretation of dreams.

**träumen** ['trɔymən], *v.n.* dream; *sich etwas nicht — lassen*, have no inkling of, not dream of s.th.; not believe s.th.

**Träumer** ['trɔymər], *m.* (—s, *pl.* —) dreamer; (*fig.*) visionary.

**Träumerei** [trɔymə'raɪ], *f.* (—, *pl.* —en) dreaming, reverie.

**traumhaft** ['traumhaft], *adj.* dream-like.

**traurig** ['traurɪç], *adj.* sad, mournful, sorrowful.

**Traurigkeit** ['traurɪçkaɪt], *f.* (—, *no pl.*) sadness, melancholy.

**Trauring** ['trauriŋ], *m.* (—s, *pl.* —e) wedding-ring.

**Trauschein** ['trauʃaɪn], *m.* (—s, *pl.* —e) marriage certificate.

**traut** [traut], *adj.* dear, beloved; cosy; *—es Heim Glück allein*, east, west, home's best; there's no place like home.

**Trauung** ['trauuŋ], *f.* (—, *pl.* —en) marriage ceremony.

**Trauzeuge** ['trautsɔygə], *m.* (—n, *pl.* —n) witness to a marriage.

**trecken** ['trɛkən], *v.a.* (*dial.*) draw, drag, tug.

**Trecker** ['trɛkər], *m.* (—s, *pl.* —) tractor.

**Treff** [trɛf], *n.* (—s, *no pl.*) (*Cards*) clubs.

**Treffen** ['trɛfən], *n.* (—s, *no pl.*) action, battle, fight; meeting, gathering; *etwas ins — führen*, put s.th. forward, urge s.th.

**treffen** ['trɛfən], *v.a. irr.* hit, meet; *nicht —*, miss; *wie vom Donner getroffen*, thunderstruck; *ins Schwarze —*, hit the mark, score a bull's eye. — *v.r. sich —*, happen.

**treffend** ['trɛfənt], *adj.* appropriate, pertinent.

**Treffer** ['trɛfər], *m.* (—s, *pl.* —) (*lottery*) win, prize; (*Mil.*) hit.

**trefflich** ['trɛflɪç], *adj.* excellent.

**Treffpunkt** ['trɛfpuŋkt], *m.* (—s, *pl.* —e) meeting-place.

**Treffsicherheit** ['trɛfzɪçərhaɪt], *f.* (—, *no pl.*) accurate aim.

**Treibeis** ['traɪpaɪs], *n.* (—es, *no pl.*) floating-ice, ice floe.

**treiben** ['traɪbən], *v.a. irr.* drive, urge; incite; (*trade*) carry on, ply; *Studien —*, study; *was treibst du?* what are you doing? *etwas zu weit —*, carry s.th. too far; *einen in die Enge —*, drive s.o. into a corner. — *v.n.* be adrift, drift.

**Treiben** ['traɪbən], *n.* (—s, *no pl.*) driving; doings; bustle.

**Treiber** ['traɪbər], *m.* (—s, *pl.* —) (*Hunt.*) driver; beater.

**Treibhaus** ['traɪphaus], *n.* (—es, *pl.* ⁓er) hothouse, greenhouse.

**Treibkraft** ['traɪpkraft], *f.* (—, *no pl.*) impulse, driving power.

**Treibriemen** ['traɪpri:mən], *m.* (—s, *pl.* —) driving-belt.

**Treibsand** ['traɪpzant], *m.* (—s, *no pl.*) quicksand, shifting sand.

**Treibstange** ['traɪpʃtaŋə], *f.* (—, *pl.* —en) main rod, connecting-rod.

**Treibstoff** ['traɪpʃtɔf], *m.* (—(e)s, *pl.* —e) fuel.

**treideln** ['traɪdəln], *v.a.* (*Naut.*) tow.

**Treidelsteig** ['traɪdəlʃtaɪk], *m.* (—s, *pl.* —e) towpath.

**trennbar** ['trɛnba:r], *adj.* separable.

**trennen** ['trɛnən], *v.a.* separate, sever. — *v.r. sich —*, part.

**Trennung** ['trɛnuŋ], *f.* (—, *pl.* —en) separation, segregation; parting; division.

**Trennungsstrich** ['trɛnuŋsʃtrɪç], *m.* (—es, *pl.* —e) hyphen, dash.

**treppab** [trɛp'ap], *adv.* downstairs.

**treppauf** [trɛp'auf], *adv.* upstairs.

**Treppe** ['trɛpə], *f.* (—, *pl.* —n) stairs, staircase, flight of stairs.

**Treppenabsatz** ['trɛpənapzats], *m.* (—es, *pl.* ⁓e) (*staircase*) landing.

**Treppengeländer** ['trɛpəngələndər], *n.* (—s, *pl.* —) balustrade, banisters.

**Treppenhaus** ['trɛpənhaus], *n.* (—es, *pl.* ⁓er) stair-well, staircase.

**Treppenläufer** ['trɛpənlɔyfər], *m.* (—s, *pl.* —) stair-carpet.

**Treppenstufe** ['trɛpənʃtu:fə], *f.* (—, *pl.* —n) step, stair.

**Treppenwitz** ['trɛpənvɪts], *m.* (—es, *no pl.*) afterthought, esprit de l'escalier.

**Tresor** [tre'zo:r], *m.* (—s, *pl.* —e) safe, strongroom.

**Tresse** ['trɛsə], *f.* (—, *pl.* —n) braid, lace, galloon.

**treten** ['tre:tən], *v.a., v.n. irr.* tread, step, trample upon; go; *— Sie näher*, step this way; *in Verbindung — mit*, make contact with; *in den Ehestand —*, get married; *einem zu nahe —*, offend s.o., tread on s.o.'s toes.

**treu** [trɔy], *adj.* faithful, loyal, true; conscientious.

**Treubruch** ['trɔybrux], *m.* (—(e)s, *pl.* ⁓e) breach of faith, disloyalty.

**Treue** ['trɔyə], *f.* (—, *no pl.*) faithfulness, loyalty, fidelity; *meiner Treu!* upon my soul! *auf Treu und Glauben*, on trust.

**Treueid** ['trɔyaɪt], *m.* (—s, *pl.* —e) oath of allegiance.

**Treuhänder** ['trɔyhɛndər], *m.* (—s, *pl.* —) trustee.

**treuherzig** ['trɔyhɛrtsɪç], *adj.* guileless, trusting.

**treulich** ['trɔylɪç], *adv.* faithfully.

**treulos** ['trɔylo:s], *adj.* faithless, perfidious; unfaithful.

**Treulosigkeit** ['trɔylo:zɪçkaɪt], *f.* (—, *no pl.*) faithlessness, perfidy, disloyalty.

**Tribüne** [tri'by:nə], *f.* (—, *pl.* —n) tribune, platform; (*racing*) grandstand.

**Tribut** [tri'bu:t], *m.* (—s, *pl.* —e) tribute.

**tributpflichtig** [tri'bu:tpflɪçtɪç], *adj.* tributary.

**Trichter** ['trɪçtər], *m.* (—s, *pl.* —) funnel.

**trichterförmig** ['trɪçtərfœrmɪç], *adj.* funnel-shaped.

**Trieb** [tri:p], *m.* (—(e)s, *pl.* —e) (*plant*) shoot, growth; instinct, bent, propensity, inclination; (*Psych.*) drive.

**Triebfeder** ['tri:pfe:dər], *f.* (—, *pl.* —n) mainspring; (*fig.*) motive, guiding principle.

**Triebkraft** ['tri:pkraft], *f.* (—, *pl.* ⸚e) motive power.

**Triebwagen** ['tri:pva:gən], *m.* (—s, *pl.* —) rail-car.

**Triebwerk** ['tri:pvɛrk], *n.* (—s, *pl.* —e) power unit, drive.

**triefen** ['tri:fən], *v.n. irr. & reg.* trickle, drip; be wet through, be soaking wet.

**Trient** [tri'ɛnt], *n.* Trent.

**Trier** [tri:r], *n.* Trèves.

**Triest** [tri'ɛst], *n.* Trieste.

**Trift** [trɪft], *f.* (—, *pl.* —en) pasture, pasturage, common, meadow.

**triftig** ['trɪftɪç], *adj.* weighty, valid, conclusive, cogent.

**Trikot** [tri'ko:], *m. & n.* (—s, *pl.* —s) stockinet; (*circus, ballet*) tights.

**Triller** ['trɪlər], *m.* (—s, *pl.* —) (*Mus.*) trill, shake.

**trillern** ['trɪlərn], *v.n.* trill, quaver, shake; warble.

**Trinität** [trini'tɛ:t], *f.* (—, *no pl.*) Trinity.

**trinkbar** ['trɪŋkba:r], *adj.* drinkable.

**Trinkbecher** ['trɪŋkbeçər], *m.* (—s, *pl.* —) drinking-cup.

**trinken** ['trɪŋkən], *v.a., v.n. irr.* drink.

**Trinker** ['trɪŋkar], *m.* (—s, *pl.* —) drinker, drunkard.

**Trinkgelage** ['trɪŋkgəla:gə], *n.* (—s, *pl.* —) drinking-bout.

**Trinkgeld** ['trɪŋkgɛlt], *n.* (—s, *pl.* —er) tip, gratuity.

**Trinkhalle** ['trɪŋkhalə], *f.* (—, *pl.* —n) (*spa*) pump-room.

**Trinkspruch** ['trɪŋkʃprux], *m.* (—(e)s, *pl.* ⸚e) toast.

**Trinkstube** ['trɪŋkʃtu:bə], *f.* (—, *pl.* —n) tap-room.

**Tripolis** ['tri:polɪs], *n.* Tripoli.

**trippeln** ['trɪpəln], *v.n.* trip (daintily), patter.

**Tripper** ['trɪpər], *m.* (—s, *no pl.*) (*Med.*) gonorrhoea.

**Tritt** [trɪt], *m.* (—(e)s, *pl.* —e) step, pace; kick.

**Trittbrett** ['trɪtbrɛt], *n.* (—s, *pl.* —er) foot-board; carriage-step; (*organ*) pedal.

**Triumph** [tri'umf], *m.* (—(e)s, *pl.* —e) triumph.

**Triumphzug** [tri'umftsu:k], *m.* (—(e)s, *pl.* ⸚e) triumphal procession.

**Trivialität** [trivjali'tɛ:t], *f.* (—, *pl.* —en) triviality, platitude.

**trocken** ['trɔkən], *adj.* dry, arid; (*fig.*) dull, dry as dust; (*wine*) dry.

**Trockenboden** ['trɔkənbo:dən], *m.* (—s, *pl.* ⸚) loft.

**Trockenfäule** ['trɔkənfɔylə], *f.,* **Trockenfäulnis** ['trɔkənfɔylnɪs], *f.* (—, *no pl.*) dry rot.

**Trockenfutter** ['trɔkənfutər], *n.* (—s, *no pl.*) fodder.

**Trockenfütterung** ['trɔkənfytərʊŋ], *f.* (—, *pl.* —en) dry feeding.

**Trockenhaube** ['trɔkənhaubə], *f.* (—, *pl.* —n) hair drier.

**Trockenheit** ['trɔkənhaɪt], *f.* (—, *no pl.*) dryness; drought.

**Trockenschleuder** ['trɔkənʃlɔydər], *f.* (—, *pl.* —n) spin-drier.

**trocknen** ['trɔknən], *v.a., v.n.* dry, air.

**Troddel** ['trɔdəl], *f.* (—, *pl.* —n) tassel.

**Trödel** ['trø:dəl], *m.* (—s, *no pl.*) junk, lumber, rubbish.

**Trödelladen** ['trø:dəlla:dən], *m.* (—s, *pl.* ⸚) junk-shop.

**Trödelmarkt** ['trø:dəlmarkt], *m.* (—s, *no pl.*) kettle market, jumble sale.

**trödeln** ['trø:dəln], *v.n.* dawdle, loiter.

**Trödler** ['trø:dlər], *m.* (—s, *pl.* —) second-hand dealer; (*coll.*) dawdler, loiterer.

**Trog** [tro:k], *m.* (—(e)s, *pl.* ⸚e) trough.

**Troja** ['tro:ja], *n.* Troy.

**trollen** ['trɔlən], *v.r. sich* —, decamp, toddle off, make o.s. scarce.

**Trommel** ['trɔməl], *f.* (—, *pl.* —n) drum; cylinder, barrel; tin box; *die* — *rühren,* beat the big drum.

**Trommelfell** ['trɔməlfɛl], *n.* (—s, *pl.* —e) drum-skin; ear-drum.

**trommeln** ['trɔməln], *v.n.* drum, beat the drum.

**Trommelschlegel** ['trɔməlʃle:gəl], *m.* (—s, *pl.* —) drumstick.

**Trommelwirbel** ['trɔməlvɪrbəl], *m.* (—s, *pl.* —) roll of drums.

**Trommler** ['trɔmlər], *m.* (—s, *pl.* —) drummer.

**Trompete** [trɔm'pe:tə], *f.* (—, *pl.* —n) trumpet; *die* — *blasen,* blow the trumpet.

**trompeten** [trɔm'pe:tən], *v.n.* trumpet, sound the trumpet.

**Trompetengeschmetter** [trɔm'pe:təngəʃmɛtər], *n.* (—s, *no pl.*) flourish of trumpets.

**Tropen** ['tro:pən], *f. pl.* the tropics.

**Tropenfieber** ['tro:pənfi:bər], *n.* (—s, *no pl.*) tropical fever.

**tröpfeln** ['trœpfəln], *v.a., v.n.* trickle, sprinkle.

**Tropfen** ['trɔpfən], *m.* (—s, *pl.* —) drop; *steter* — *höhlt den Stein,* constant dripping wears away a stone.

**tropfen** ['trɔpfən], *v.n.* drop, drip.

**Trophäe** [tro'fɛə], f. (—, pl. —n) trophy.

**tropisch** ['tro:pɪʃ], adj. tropical, tropic.

**Troß** [trɔs], m. (—sses, pl. -sse) (*Mil.*) baggage-train; (*fig.*) hangers-on, camp-followers.

**Troßpferd** ['trɔspfe:rt], n. (—s, pl. —e) pack-horse.

**Trost** [tro:st], m. (—es, no pl.) consolation, comfort; *geringer* —, cold comfort; *du bist wohl nicht bei* —? have you taken leave of your senses?

**trösten** ['trø:stən], v.a. comfort, console; *tröste dich*, cheer up.

**Tröster** ['trø:stər], m. (—s, pl. —) comforter, consoler; (*Theol.*) Holy Ghost, Comforter.

**tröstlich** ['trø:stlɪç], adj. consoling, comforting.

**trostlos** ['tro:stlo:s], adj. disconsolate, inconsolable; desolate, bleak.

**Trostlosigkeit** ['tro:stlo:zɪçkaɪt], f. (—, no pl.) disconsolateness; (*fig.*) wretchedness; dreariness.

**Trott** [trɔt], m. (—s, no pl.) trot.

**Trottel** ['trɔtəl], m. (—s, pl. —) (*coll.*) idiot.

**Trottoir** [trɔto'a:r], n. (—s, pl. —e) pavement, footpath; (*Am.*) sidewalk.

**trotz** [trɔts], prep. (*Genit., Dat.*) in spite of, despite; — *alledem*, all the same.

**Trotz** [trɔts], m. (—es, no pl.) defiance, obstinacy, refractoriness; *einem* — *bieten*, defy s.o.; *einem etwas zum* — *machen*, do s.th. in defiance of s.o.

**trotzdem** [trɔts'de:m], conj. notwithstanding that, albeit, although. — adv. nevertheless.

**trotzen** ['trɔtsən], v.n. defy; sulk, be obstinate; *Gefahren* —, brave dangers.

**trotzig** ['trɔtsɪç], adj. defiant; sulky, refractory; headstrong, stubborn, obstinate.

**Trotzkopf** ['trɔtskɔpf], m. (—(e)s, pl. —e) obstinate child; pig-headed person.

**trübe** ['try:bə], adj. dim, gloomy; (*weather*) dull, cloudy, overcast; (*water*) troubled; (*glass*) misted; —s *Lächeln*, wan smile.

**Trubel** ['tru:bəl], m. (—s, no pl.) tumult, turmoil, disturbance.

**trüben** ['try:bən], v.a. darken, sadden, trouble; (*glass*) mist; (*metal*) tarnish; (*fig.*) obscure.

**Trübsal** ['try:pza:l], f. (—, pl. —e), n. (—s, pl. —e) misery, trouble, distress; — *blasen*, mope.

**trübselig** ['try:pze:lɪç], adj. woeful, lamentable; woebegone, forlorn.

**Trübsinn** ['try:pzɪn], m. (—s, no pl.) sadness, dejection.

**trübsinnig** ['try:pzɪnɪç], adj. sad, dejected.

**Trüffel** ['tryfəl], f. (—, pl. —n) truffle.

**Trug** [tru:k], m. (—(e)s, no pl.) deceit, fraud; *Lug und* —, a pack of lies.

**Trugbild** ['tru:kbɪlt], n. (—es, pl. —er) phantom.

**trügen** ['try:gən], v.a. irr. deceive.

**trügerisch** ['try:gərɪs], adj. deceptive, illusory, fallacious.

**Truggewebe** ['tru:kgəve:bə], n. (—s, pl. —) tissue of lies.

**Trugschluß** ['tru:kʃlus], m. (—sses, pl. ⸚sse) fallacy, false deduction.

**Truhe** ['tru:ə], f. (—, pl. —n) chest, trunk, coffer.

**Trumm** [trum], m. (—s, pl. ⸚er) lump, broken piece.

**Trümmer** ['trymər], m. pl. fragments, debris, ruins; *in* — *gehen*, go to wrack and ruin; *in* — *schlagen*, wreck.

**Trümmerhaufen** ['trymərhaufən], m. (—s, pl. —) heap of ruins, heap of rubble.

**Trumpf** [trumpf], m. (—(e)s, pl. ⸚e) trump, trump-card.

**trumpfen** ['trumpfən], v.a. trump.

**Trumpffarbe** ['trumpffarbə], f. (—, pl. —n) trump-suit.

**Trunk** [truŋk], m. (—(e)s, pl. ⸚e) draught, potion, drinking; *sich dem* — *ergeben*, take to drink.

**trunken** ['truŋkən], adj. drunk, intoxicated; (*fig.*) elated.

**Trunkenbold** ['truŋkənbɔlt], m. (—s, pl. —e) drunkard.

**Trunkenheit** ['truŋkənhaɪt], f. (—, no pl.) drunkenness, intoxication.

**Trunksucht** ['truŋkzuxt], f. (—, no pl.) dipsomania, alcoholism.

**trunksüchtig** ['truŋkzyçtɪç], adj. dipsomaniac, addicted to drinking.

**Trupp** [trup], m. (—s, pl. —s) troop, band.

**Truppe** ['trupə], f. (—, pl. —n) (*Mil.*) company, troops, forces; (*actors*) troupe.

**Truppengattung** ['trupəngatuŋ], f. (—, pl. —en) branch of the armed forces.

**Truthahn** ['tru:tha:n], m. (—s, pl. ⸚e) (*Orn.*) turkey cock.

**Truthenne** ['tru:thɛnə], f. (—, pl. —n) (*Orn.*) turkey hen.

**Trtuhühner** ['tru:thy:nər], n. pl. (*Orn.*) turkey-fowl.

**Trutz** [truts], m. (—es, no pl.) (*Poet.*) defiance; *zum Schutz und* —, offensively and defensively.

**Tschad** [tʃat], n. Chad.

**Tschechoslowakei** [tʃɛçɔslova'kaɪ], f. Czechoslovakia.

**Tuch** (1) [tu:x], n. (—(e)s, pl. ⸚er) shawl, wrap.

**Tuch** (2) [tu:x], n. (—s, pl. —e) cloth, fabric.

**Tuchhändler** ['tu:xhɛndlər], m. (—s, pl. —) draper, clothier.

**tüchtig** ['tyçtɪç], adj. able, competent, efficient. — adv. largely, much, heartily.

**Tüchtigkeit** ['tyçtɪçkaɪt], f. (—, no pl.) ability, competence, efficiency.

**Tücke** ['tykə], f. (—, pl. —n) malice, spite.

# tückisch

**tückisch** ['tykɪʃ], *adj.* malicious, insidious.

**Tugend** ['tu:gənt], *f.* (—, *pl.* **—en**) virtue.

**Tugendbold** ['tu:gəntbɔlt], *m.* (**—s**, *pl.* **—e**) paragon.

**tugendhaft** ['tu:gənthaft], *adj.* virtuous.

**Tugendlehre** ['tu:gəntleːrə], *f.* (—, *no pl.*) ethics, morals.

**Tüll** [tyl], *m.* (**—s**, *pl.* **—e**) tulle.

**Tulpe** ['tulpə], *f.* (—, *pl.* **—n**) (*Bot.*) tulip.

**Tulpenzwiebel** ['tulpəntsviːbəl], *f.* (—, *pl.* **—n**) tulip-bulb.

**tummeln** ['tuməln], *v.r. sich* —, romp about; make haste.

**Tummelplatz** ['tuməlplats], *m.* (**—es**, *pl.* ˙̈**e**) playground, fairground.

**Tümpel** ['tympəl], *m.* (**—s**, *pl.* —) pond, pool, puddle.

**Tun** [tuːn], *n.* (**—s**, *no pl.*) doing; *sein — und Lassen*, his conduct.

**tun** [tuːn], *v.a. irr.* do, make; put; *tut nichts*, it does not matter; *viel zu — haben*, have a lot to do, be busy; *not —*, be necessary; *Buße —*, repent.

**Tünche** ['tynçə], *f.* (—, *pl.* **—n**) whitewash.

**tünchen** ['tynçən], *v.a.* whitewash.

**Tunichtgut** ['tuːnɪçtguːt], *m.* (**—s**, *no pl.*) ne'er-do-well, scamp.

**Tunke** ['tuŋkə], *f.* (—, *pl.* **—n**) sauce, gravy.

**tunken** ['tuŋkən], *v.a.* dip, steep; (*Am.*) dunk.

**tunlich** ['tuːnlɪç], *adj.* feasible, practicable, expedient.

**tunlichst** ['tuːnlɪçst], *adv.* if possible, possibly.

**Tunnel** ['tunəl], *m.* (**—s**, *pl.* —) tunnel.

**Tunnelbau** ['tunəlbau], *m.* (**—s**, *no pl.*) tunnelling.

**tüpfeln** ['typfəln], *v.a.* dot, spot.

**Tupfen** ['tupfən], *m.* (**—s**, *pl.* —) dot, polka-dot.

**Tür** [tyːr], *f.* (—, *pl.* **—en**) door; *einem die — weisen*, show s.o. the door; *vor der — stehen*, be imminent; *kehr vor deiner eigenen —*, mind your own business; *put your own house in order; offene —en einrennen*, flog a willing horse; *zwischen — und Angel stecken*, be undecided.

**Türangel** ['tyːraŋəl], *f.* (—, *pl.* **—n**) door-hinge.

**Türhüter** ['tyːrhyːtər], *m.* (**—s**, *pl.* —) doorkeeper.

**Türkei** [tyrˈkai], *f.* Turkey.

**Türkensäbel** ['tyrkənzɛːbəl], *m.* (**—s**, *pl.* —) scimitar.

**Türkis** [tyrˈkiːs], *m.* (**—es**, *pl.* **—e**) turquoise.

**Türklinke** ['tyːrklɪŋkə], *f.* (—, *pl.* **—n**) door-handle.

**Turm** [turm], *m.* (**—(e)s**, *pl.* ˙̈**e**) tower; spire, steeple; belfry; (*Chess*) castle.

**Turmalin** [turmaˈliːn], *m.* (**—s**, *pl.* **—e**) tourmaline.

**Türmchen** ['tyrmçən], *n.* (**—s**, *pl.* —) turret.

**türmen** ['tyrmən], *v.a.* pile up. — *v.n.* (*coll.*) bolt, run away. — *v.r. sich* —, rise high, be piled high.

**Turmspitze** ['turmʃpɪtsə], *f.* (—, *pl.* **—n**) spire.

**turnen** ['turnən], *v.n.* do exercises *or* gymnastics.

**Turnen** ['turnən], *n.* (**—s**, *no pl.*) gymnastics, physical training.

**Turner** ['turnər], *m.* (**—s**, *pl.* —) gymnast.

**Turngerät** ['turngəreːt], *n.* (**—es**, *pl.* **—e**) gymnastic apparatus.

**Turnhalle** ['turnhalə], *f.* (—, *pl.* **—n**) gymnasium.

**Turnier** [turˈniːr], *n.* (**—s**, *pl.* **—e**) tournament.

**Turnübung** ['turnyːbuŋ], *f.* (—, *pl.* **—en**) gymnastic exercise.

**Turnverein** ['turnfərain], *m.* (**—s**, *pl.* **—e**) athletics club, gymnastic club.

**Türpfosten** ['tyːrpfostən], *m.* (**—s**, *pl.* —) door-post.

**Türriegel** ['tyːrriːgəl], *m.* (**—s**, *pl.* —) bolt.

**Türschild** ['tyːrʃɪlt], *n.* (**—(e)s**, *pl.* **—e**) (door)plate.

**Türschloß** ['tyːrʃlɔs], *n.* (**—sses**, *pl.* ˙̈**sser**) lock.

**Türschlüssel** ['tyːrʃlysəl], *m.* (**—s**, *pl.* —) door-key, latch-key.

**Türschwelle** ['tyːrʃvɛlə], *f.* (—, *pl.* **—n**) threshold.

**Tusch** [tuʃ], *m.* (**—es**, *pl.* **—e**) (*Mus.*) flourish.

**Tusche** ['tuʃə], *f.* (—, *pl.* **—n**) water-colour; Indian ink.

**tuscheln** ['tuʃəln], *v.n.* whisper.

**tuschen** ['tuʃən], *v.a.* draw in Indian ink.

**Tuschkasten** ['tuʃkastən], *m.* (**—s**, *pl.* ˙̈) paint-box.

**Tüte** ['tyːtə], *f.* (—, *pl.* **—n**) paper bag.

**Tutel** [tuˈteːl], *f.* (—, *no pl.*) guardianship.

**tuten** ['tuːtən], *v.n.* hoot, honk, blow a horn.

**Tütendreher** ['tyːtəndreːər], *m.* (**—s**, *pl.* —) (*sl.*) small shopkeeper.

**Typ** [typ], *m.* (**—s**, *pl.* **—en**) type.

**Type** ['typə], *f.* (—, *pl.* **—n**) (*Typ.*) type; (*fig.*) queer fish.

**Typhus** ['tyːfus], *m.* (—, *no pl.*) (*Med.*) typhoid (fever).

**typisch** ['tyːpɪʃ], *adj.* typical.

**Typus** ['tyːpus], *m.* (—, *pl.* **Typen**) type.

**Tyrann** [tyˈran], *m.* (**—en**, *pl.* **—en**) tyrant.

**Tyrannei** [tyraˈnai], *f.* (—, *pl.* **—en**) tyranny, despotism.

**tyrannisch** [tyˈranɪʃ], *adj.* tyrannical, despotic.

**tyrannisieren** [tyraniˈziːrən], *v.a.* tyrannise over, oppress, bully.

# U

**U** [u:], *n.* (—s, *pl.* —s) the letter U.
**U-Bahn** ['u:baːn], *f.* (—, *no pl.*) underground (railway); tube, (*Am.*) subway.
**Übel** ['y:bəl], *n.* (—s, *pl.* —) evil, trouble; misfortune; disease.
**übel** ['y:bəl], *adj.* evil, ill, bad; *mir ist* —, I feel sick; *nicht* —, not too bad; — *daran sein*, be in a bad way, be in a mess.
**übelgesinnt** ['y:bəlgəzɪnt], *adj.* evilminded; ill-disposed; *einem* — *sein*, bear s.o. a grudge.
**Übelkeit** ['y:bəlkaɪt], *f.* (—, *pl.* —en) nausea, sickness.
**übellaunig** ['y:bəllaunɪç], *adj.* illhumoured, bad-tempered.
**übelnehmen** ['y:bəlneːmən], *v.a. irr.* take amiss, resent, be offended at.
**übelnehmerisch** ['y:bəlneːmərɪʃ], *adj.* touchy, easily offended.
**Übelstand** ['y:bəlʃtant], *m.* (—(e)s, *pl.* ᵉe) inconvenience, drawback; (*pl.*) abuses.
**Übeltat** ['y:bəltaːt], *f.* (—, *pl.* —en) misdeed.
**Übeltäter** ['y:bəltɛːtər], *m.* (—s, *pl.* —) evildoer, malefactor.
**übelwollend** ['y:bəlvɔlənt], *adj.* malevolent.
**üben** ['y:bən], *v.a.* practise, exercise; *Rache* —, wreak vengeance.
**über** ['y:bər], *prep.* (*Dat., Acc.*) over, above; across; about; more than, exceeding; via, by way of; concerning, on. — *adv.* over, above; — *und* —, all over; — *kurz oder lang*, sooner or later; *heute* —*s Jahr*, a year from today.
**überall** ['y:bəral], *adv.* everywhere, anywhere.
**überanstrengen** [y:bər'anʃtrɛŋən], *v.a. insep.* overtax s.o.'s strength, strain. — *v.r. sich* —, overtax o.'s strength, overexert o.s.
**Überanstrengung** [y:bər'anʃtrɛŋuŋ], *f.* (—, *pl.* —en) over-exertion, strain.
**überantworten** [y:bər'antvɔrtən], *v.a. insep.* deliver up, surrender.
**überarbeiten** [y:bər'arbaɪtən], *v.a. insep.* revise, do again. — *v.r. sich* —, overwork o.s.
**überarbeitet** [y:bər'arbaɪtət], *adj.* overwrought, overworked.
**überaus** ['y:bəraus], *adv.* exceedingly, extremely.
**überbauen** [y:bər'bauən], *v.a. insep.* build over.
**überbieten** [y:bər'biːtən], *v.a. irr. insep.* outbid (s.o.); (*fig.*) surpass.

**Überbleibsel** ['y:bərblaɪpsəl], *n.* (—s, *pl.* —) remainder, remnant, residue, rest.
**Überblick** ['y:bərblɪk], *m.* (—(e)s, *pl.* —e) survey, general view.
**überblicken** [y:bər'blɪkən], *v.a. insep.* survey, look over.
**überbringen** [y:bər'brɪŋən], *v.a. irr. insep.* bear, deliver, hand in.
**Überbringung** [y:bər'brɪŋuŋ], *f.* (—, *no pl.*) delivery.
**überbrücken** [y:bər'brykən], *v.a. insep.* bridge, span.
**überdachen** [y:bər'daxən], *v.a. insep.* roof (over).
**überdauern** [y:bər'dauərn], *v.a. insep.* outlast; tide over.
**überdenken** [y:bər'dɛŋkən], *v.a. irr. insep.* think over, consider.
**überdies** [y:bər'diːs], *adv.* besides, moreover.
**überdrucken** [y:bər'drukən], *v.a. insep.* overprint.
**Überdruß** ['y:bərdrus], *m.* (—sses, *no pl.*) weariness; disgust; *zum* —, ad nauseam.
**überdrüssig** ['y:bərdrysɪç], *adj.* weary of.
**Übereifer** ['y:bəraɪfər], *m.* (—s, *no pl.*) excessive zeal.
**übereifrig** ['y:bəraɪfrɪç], *adj.* excessively zealous, officious.
**übereilen** [y:bər'aɪlən], *v.r. insep. sich* —, hurry too much, overshoot the mark.
**übereilt** [y:bər'aɪlt], *adj.* overhasty, rash.
**übereinkommen** [y:bər'aɪnkɔmən], *v.n. irr.* (*aux.* sein) agree.
**Übereinkunft** [y:bər'aɪnkunft], *f.* (—, *pl.* ᵉe) agreement, convention.
**übereinstimmen** [y:bər'aɪnʃtɪmən], *v.n.* agree, concur, harmonize, be of one mind, be of the same opinion; (*things*) tally, square.
**Übereinstimmung** [y:bər'aɪnʃtɪmuŋ], *f.* (—, *no pl.*) accord, agreement, conformity, harmony.
**überfahren** (1) [y:bər'faːrən], *v.a. irr. insep.* traverse, pass over; run over (s.o.).
**überfahren** (2) ['y:bərfaːrən], *v.a. irr.* ferry across. — *v.n.* (*aux.* sein) cross.
**Überfahrt** ['y:bərfaːrt], *f.* (—, *pl.* —en) passage, crossing.
**Überfall** ['y:bərfal], *m.* (—s, *pl.* ᵉe) sudden attack, raid.
**überfallen** (1) ['y:bərfalən], *v.n. irr.* (*aux.* sein) (*p.p.* übergefallen) fall over.
**überfallen** (2) [y:bər'falən], *v.a. irr., insep.* (*p.p.* überfallen) attack suddenly, raid.
**überfällig** ['y:bərfɛlɪç], *adj.* overdue.
**überfliegen** [y:bər'fliːgən], *v.a. irr. insep.* fly over; (*fig.*) glance over, skim.
**überfließen** ['y:bərfliːsən], *v.n. irr.* (*aux.* sein) overflow.

231

**überflügeln** [y:bər′fly:gəln], *v.a. insep.* surpass, outstrip.

**Überfluß** [′y:bərflus], *m.* (—**sses**, *no pl.*) abundance, plenty, profusion; surplus; — *haben an*, abound in, have too much of.

**überflüssig** [′y:bərflysɪç], *adj.* superfluous, unnecessary.

**überfluten** [y:bər′flu:tən], *v.a. insep.* overflow, flood.

**überführen** (1) [′y:bərfy:rən], *v.a.* convey, conduct (across).

**überführen** (2) [y:bər′fy:rən], *v.a. insep.* convict; transport a coffin.

**Überführung** [y:bər′fy:ruŋ], *f.* (—, *pl.* —**en**) conviction (for a crime); transport (of a coffin).

**Überfüllung** [y:bər′fyluŋ], *f.* (—, *no pl.*) overcrowding.

**Übergabe** [′y:bərga:bə], *f.* (—, *no pl.*) surrender, yielding up; delivery, handing over.

**Übergang** [′y:bərgaŋ], *m.* (—**s**, *pl.* ̈**e**) passage; (*Railw.*) crossing; (*fig.*) change-over, transition.

**übergeben** [y:bər′ge:bən], *v.a. irr. insep.* deliver up, hand over. — *v.r. sich* —, vomit.

**übergehen** (1) [′y:bərge:ən], *v.n. irr.* (*aux.* sein) (*p.p.* übergegangen) go over, change over, turn (into); *zum Feinde* —, go over to the enemy; *in andre Hände* —, change hands.

**übergehen** (2) [y:bər′ge:ən], *v.a. irr. insep.* (*p.p.* übergangen) pass over, pass by.

**Übergehung** [y:bər′ge:uŋ], *f.* (—, *no pl.*) omission; passing over.

**übergeordnet** [′y:bərgəɔrdnət], *adj.* superior.

**Übergewicht** [′y:bərgəvɪçt], *n.* (—(e)**s**, *no pl.*) overweight; (*fig.*) preponderance, superiority.

**übergießen** [y:bər′gi:sən], *v.a. irr. insep.* pour over, douse with.

**überglücklich** [′y:bərglyklɪç], *adj.* overjoyed.

**übergreifen** [′y:bərgraɪfən], *v.n. irr.* overlap; encroach (upon); spread.

**Übergriff** [′y:bərgrɪf], *m.* (—(e)**s**, *pl.* —**e**) encroachment.

**übergroß** [′y:bərgro:s], *adj.* excessively large, overlarge.

**überhaben** [′y:bərha:bən], *v.a. irr.* have enough of, be sick of.

**überhandnehmen** [y:bər′hantne:mən], *v.n. irr.* gain the upper hand; run riot.

**überhangen** [′y:bərhaŋən], *v.n. irr.* hang over.

**überhängen** [y:bər′hɛŋən], *v.a. irr.* cover, hang upon.

**überhäufen** [y:bər′hɔyfən], *v.a. insep.* overwhelm.

**überhaupt** [y:bər′haupt], *adv.* in general, altogether; at all; after all.

**überheben** [y:bər′he:bən], *v.r. irr. insep. sich* —, strain o.s. by lifting; (*fig.*) be overbearing.

**überheblich** [y:bər′he:plɪç], *adj.* overbearing, arrogant.

**überheizen** [y:bər′haɪtsən], *v.a. insep.* overheat.

**überhitzt** [y:bər′hɪtst], *adj.* overheated; impassioned.

**überholen** [y:bər′ho:lən], *v.a. insep.* overtake, out-distance; (*fig.*) overhaul.

**überhören** [y:bər′hø:rən], *v.a. insep.* hear s.o.'s lessons; ignore; miss (s.th.).

**überirdisch** [′y:bərɪrdɪʃ], *adj.* celestial, superterrestrial.

**Überkleid** [′y:bərklaɪt], *n.* (—(e)**s**, *pl.* —**er**) outer garment; overall.

**überklug** [′y:bərklu:k], *adj.* too clever by half, conceited.

**überkochen** [′y:bərkɔxən], *v.n.* (*aux.* sein) boil over.

**überkommen** [y:bər′kɔmən], *adj.* — *sein von*, be seized with.

**überladen** [y:bər′la:dən], *v.a. irr. insep.* overload. — *adj.* overdone, too elaborate; bombastic.

**überlassen** [y:bər′lasən], *v.a. irr. insep.* leave, relinquish, give up, yield.

**überlasten** [y:bər′lastən], *v.a. insep.* overburden.

**überlaufen** (1) [′y:bərlaufən], *v.a. irr.* run over; (*to the enemy*) desert.

**überlaufen** (2) [y:bər′laufən], *v.a. insep.* (*p.p.* überlaufen) overrun.

**Überläufer** [′y:bərlɔyfər], *m.* (—**s**, *pl.* —) deserter, runaway.

**überleben** [y:bər′le:bən], *v.a. insep.* survive, outlive; (*fig.*) live (s.th.) down; *sich überlebt haben*, be out of date, be dated.

**Überlebende** [y:bər′le:bəndə], *m.* (—**n**, *pl.* —**n**) survivor.

**überlegen** (1) [′y:bərle:gən], *v.a.* lay over, cover.

**überlegen** (2) [y:bər′le:gən], *v.a. insep.* (*p.p.* überlegt) think over, consider, turn over in o.'s mind. — *adj.* superior; — *sein*, outdo, be superior to.

**Überlegenheit** [y:bər′le:gənhaɪt], *f.* (—, *no pl.*) superiority.

**Überlegung** [y:bər′le:guŋ], *f.* (—, *pl.* —**en**) consideration, deliberation; *bei näherer* —, on second thoughts, on thinking it over.

**überliefern** [y:bər′li:fərn], *v.a. insep.* hand down (to posterity), hand on, pass on.

**Überlieferung** [y:bər′li:fəruŋ], *f.* (—, *pl.* —**en**) tradition.

**überlisten** [y:bər′lɪstən], *v.a. insep.* outwit.

**Übermacht** [′y:bərmaxt], *f.* (—, *no pl.*) superiority, superior force.

**übermalen** [y:bər′ma:lən], *v.a. insep.* paint over.

**übermangansauer** [y:bərman′ga:nzauər], *adj.* permanganate of; —*es Kali*, permanganate of potash.

**übermannen** [y:bər′manən], *v.a. insep.* overpower.

**Übermaß** [′y:bərma:s], *n.* (—**es**, *no pl.*) excess; *im* —, to excess.

überspannt

**übermäßig** ['y:bərmɛ:sɪç], *adj.* excessive, immoderate.

**Übermensch** ['y:bərmɛnʃ], *m.* (**—en,** *pl.* **—en**) superman.

**übermenschlich** ['y:bərmɛnʃlɪç], *adj.* superhuman.

**übermitteln** [y:bər'mɪtəln], *v.a. insep.* convey.

**übermorgen** ['y:bərmɔrgən], *adv.* the day after tomorrow.

**Übermut** ['y:bərmu:t], *m.* (**—s,** *no pl.*) wantonness; high spirits.

**übermütig** ['y:bərmy:tɪç], *adj.* wanton; full of high spirits.

**übernachten** [y:bər'naxtən], *v.n. insep.* pass *or* spend the night.

**übernächtig** [y:bər'nɛçtɪç], *adj.* haggard, tired by a sleepless night.

**Übernahme** ['y:bərna:mə], *f.* (**—,** *no pl.*) taking possession, taking charge.

**übernatürlich** ['y:bərnaty:rlɪç], *adj.* supernatural.

**übernehmen** [y:bər'ne:mən], *v.a. irr. insep.* take possession of, take upon o.s., take over. — *v.r. sich* —, overtax o.'s strength.

**überordnen** ['y:bərɔrdnən], *v.a.* place above.

**überprüfen** [y:bər'pry:fən], *v.a. insep.* examine, overhaul.

**überquellen** ['y:bərkvɛlən], *v.n. irr. insep.* (*aux.* sein) bubble over.

**überqueren** [y:bər'kve:rən], *v.a. insep.* cross.

**überragen** [y:bər'ra:gən], *v.a. insep.* tower above, overtop; (*fig.*) surpass, outstrip.

**überraschen** [y:bər'raʃən], *v.a. insep.* surprise, take by surprise.

**Überraschung** [y:bər'raʃuŋ], *f.* (**—,** *pl.* **—en**) surprise.

**überreden** [y:bər're:dən], *v.a. insep.* persuade, talk (s.o.) into (s.th.).

**Überredung** [y:bər're:duŋ], *f.* (**—,** *no pl.*) persuasion.

**überreichen** [y:bər'raɪçən], *v.a. insep.* hand over, present formally.

**überreichlich** ['y:bərraɪçlɪç], *adj.* superabundant.

**Überreichung** [y:bər'raɪçuŋ], *f.* (**—,** *no pl.*) formal presentation.

**überreizen** [y:bər'raɪtsən], *v.a. insep.* over-excite, over-stimulate.

**überrennen** [y:bər'rɛnən], *v.a. irr. insep.* take by storm, overrun.

**Überrest** ['y:bərrɛst], *m.* (**—es,** *pl.* **—e**) remainder, remnant, residue.

**überrumpeln** [y:bər'rumpəln], *v.a. insep.* catch unawares, surprise.

**übersättigen** [y:bər'zɛtɪgən], *v.a. insep.* saturate; surfeit, cloy.

**Übersättigung** [y:bər'zɛtɪguŋ], *f.* (**—,** *no pl.*) saturation; surfeit.

**Überschallgeschwindigkeit** ['y:bərʃalgəʃvɪndɪçkaɪt], *f.* (**—,** *no pl.*) supersonic speed.

**überschatten** [y:bər'ʃatən], *v.a. insep.* overshadow.

**überschätzen** [y:bər'ʃɛtsən], *v.a. insep.* overrate, over-estimate.

**überschauen** [y:bər'ʃauən], *v.a. insep.* survey.

**überschäumen** ['y:bərʃɔymən], *v.n.* (*aux.* sein) bubble over.

**überschäumend** ['y:bərʃɔymənt], *adj.* ebullient, exuberant.

**Überschlag** ['y:bərʃla:k], *m.* (**—s,** *pl.* **—e**) somersault; estimate.

**überschlagen** [y:bər'ʃla:gən], *v.a. irr. insep.* (*pages*) miss, skip; estimate, compute. — *v.r. sich* —, turn a somersault, overturn. — *adj.* tepid, lukewarm.

**überschnappen** ['y:bərʃnapən], *v.n.* (*aux.* sein) snap; (*fig., coll.*) go out of o.'s mind.

**überschreiben** [y:bər'ʃraɪbən], *v.a. irr. insep.* superscribe, entitle.

**überschreiten** [y:bər'ʃraɪtən], *v.a. irr. insep.* cross; go beyond, exceed.

**Überschrift** ['y:bərʃrɪft], *f.* (**—,** *pl.* **—en**) heading, headline.

**Überschuß** ['y:bərʃus], *m.* (**—sses,** *pl.* **—sse**) surplus.

**überschüssig** ['y:bərʃysɪç], *adj.* surplus, remaining.

**überschütten** [y:bər'ʃytən], *v.a. insep.* shower with, overwhelm with.

**Überschwang** ['y:bərʃvaŋ], *m.* (**—s,** *no pl.*) exaltation, rapture.

**überschwemmen** [y:bər'ʃvɛmən], *v.a. insep.* flood, inundate.

**Überschwemmung** [y:bər'ʃvɛmuŋ], *f.* (**—,** *pl.* **—en**) inundation, flood, deluge.

**überschwenglich** [y:bər'ʃvɛŋlɪç], *adj.* exuberant, exalted.

**Übersee** ['y:bərze:], *f.* (**—,** *no pl.*) overseas.

**übersehen** [y:bər'ze:ən], *v.a. irr. insep.* survey, look over; overlook, disregard.

**übersenden** [y:bər'zɛndən], *v.a. irr. insep.* send, forward, transmit; (*money*) remit.

**Übersendung** [y:bər'zɛnduŋ], *f.* (**—,** *pl.* **—en**) sending, forwarding, transmission; remittance.

**übersetzen** (1) ['y:bərzɛtsən], *v.a.* (*p.p.* übergesetzt) ferry across, cross (a river).

**übersetzen** (2) [y:bər'zɛtsən], *v.a. insep.* (*p.p.* übersetzt) translate.

**Übersetzer** [y:bər'zɛtsər], *m.* (**—s,** *pl.* **—**) translator.

**Übersetzung** [y:bər'zɛtsuŋ], *f.* (**—,** *pl.* **—en**) translation.

**Übersicht** ['y:bərzɪçt], *f.* (**—,** *pl.* **—en**) survey, summary; epitome.

**übersichtlich** ['y:bərzɪçtlɪç], *adj.* clearly arranged, readable at a glance, lucid.

**übersiedeln** [y:bər'zi:dəln], *v.n.* (*aux.* sein) remove, move, settle in a different place.

**Übersiedlung** [y:bər'zi:dluŋ], *f.* (**—,** *pl.* **—en**) removal.

**überspannen** [y:bər'ʃpanən], *v.a. insep.* overstretch.

**überspannt** [y:bər'ʃpant], *adj.* eccentric, extravagant.

# Überspanntheit

**Überspanntheit** [y:bər'ʃpanthaɪt], *f.*
(—, *pl.* —en) eccentricity.

**überspringen** [y:bər'ʃprɪŋən], *v.a. irr.*
*insep.* jump over; (*fig.*) skip.

**übersprudeln** [y:bər'ʃpru:dəln], *v.n.*
(*aux.* sein) bubble over.

**überstechen** [y:bər'ʃtɛçən], *v.a. irr.*
(*cards*) trump higher.

**überstehen** [y:bər'ʃte:ən], *v.a. irr.*
*insep.* overcome, endure, get over,
weather.

**übersteigen** [y:bər'ʃtaɪgən], *v.a. irr.*
*insep.* exceed, surpass.

**überstrahlen** [y:bər'ʃtra:lən], *v.a. insep.*
outshine, surpass in splendour.

**überstreichen** [y:bər'ʃtraɪçən], *v.a. irr.*
*insep.* paint over.

**überströmen** [y:bər'ʃtrø:mən], *v.a.*
*insep.* flood, overflow.

**Überstunde** [y:bər'ʃtundə], *f.* (—, *pl.*
—n) extra working time, overtime.

**überstürzen** [y:bər'ʃtyrtsən], *v.r. insep.*
*sich* —, act in haste.

**übertäuben** [y:bər'tɔybən], *v.a. insep.*
deafen.

**überteuern** [y:bər'tɔyərn], *v.a. insep.*
overcharge.

**übertölpeln** [y:bər'tœlpəln], *v.a. insep.*
cheat.

**übertönen** [y:bər'tø:nən], *v.a. insep.*
(*sound*) drown.

**übertragen** [y:bər'tra:gən], *v.a. irr.*
*insep.* transfer, hand over; convey;
broadcast; translate; (*Comm.*) carry
over; *einem ein Amt* —, confer an
office on s.o.

**Übertragung** [y:bər'tra:guŋ], *f.* (—, *pl.*
—en) cession; transference; handing
over; (*Comm.*) carrying over; (*Rad.*)
transmission; (*Med.*) transfusion.

**übertreffen** [y:bər'trɛfən], *v.a. irr.*
*insep.* surpass, excel, outdo.

**übertreiben** [y:bər'traɪbən], *v.a. irr.*
*insep.* exaggerate.

**Übertreibung** [y:bər'traɪbuŋ], *f.* (—,
*pl.* —en) exaggeration.

**übertreten** (1) [y:bər'tre:tən], *v.n. irr.*
(*aux.* sein) go over to; (*river*) overflow; (*religion*) change to, join (*church,
party*).

**übertreten** (2) [y:bər'tre:tən], *v.a. irr.*
*insep.* transgress, trespass against,
infringe, violate.

**Übertretung** [y:bər'tre:tuŋ], *f.* (—, *pl.*
—en) transgression, trespass, violation, infringement.

**übertrieben** [y:bər'tri:bən], *adj.* excessive, immoderate, exaggerated.

**Übertritt** [y:bər'trɪt], *m.* (—s, *no pl.*)
defection, going over; (*Rel.*) change,
conversion.

**übertünchen** [y:bər'tynçən], *v.a. insep.*
whitewash, rough-cast; (*fig.*) gloss
over.

**Übervölkerung** [y:bər'fœlkəruŋ], *f.*
(—, *no pl.*) overpopulation.

**übervoll** [y:bər'fɔl], *adj.* overful, brimful, chock-full.

**übervorteilen** [y:bər'fo:rtaɪlən], *v.a.*
*insep.* cheat, defraud.

**überwachen** [y:bər'vaxən], *v.a. insep.*
watch over, superintend, supervise.

**Überwachung** [y:bər'vaxuŋ], *f.* (—,
*no pl.*) superintendence, supervision.

**überwachsen** [y:bər'vaksən], *v.a. irr.*
*insep.* overgrow.

**überwältigen** [y:bər'vɛltɪgən], *v.a.*
*insep.* overcome, overpower, subdue.

**überwältigend** [y:bər'vɛltɪgənt], *adj.*
overwhelming.

**Überwältigung** [y:bər'vɛltɪguŋ], *f.*
(—, *no pl.*) overpowering.

**überweisen** [y:bər'vaɪzən], *v.a. irr.*
*insep.* assign; (*money*) remit.

**Überweisung** [y:bər'vaɪzuŋ], *f.* (—, *pl.*
—en) assignment; (*money*) remittance.

**überwerfen** (1) ['y:bərvɛrfən], *v.a. irr.*
throw over; (*clothes*) slip on.

**überwerfen** (2) [y:bər'vɛrfən], *v.r. irr.*
*insep. sich — mit*, fall out with s.o.

**überwiegen** [y:bər'vi:gən], *v.n. irr.*
*insep.* prevail.

**überwiegend** [y:bər'vi:gənt], *adj.* paramount, overwhelming, predominant.

**überwinden** [y:bər'vɪndən], *v.a. irr.*
*insep.* overcome, conquer. — *v.r.*
*sich* —, prevail upon o.s., bring o.s.
(to).

**Überwindung** [y:bər'vɪnduŋ], *f.* (—,
*no pl.*) conquest; reluctance.

**überwintern** [y:bər'vɪntərn], *v.n. insep.*
winter, hibernate.

**Überwinterung** [y:bər'vɪntəruŋ], *f.*
(—, *no pl.*) hibernation.

**überwölkt** [y:bər'vœlkt], *adj.* overcast.

**Überwurf** ['y:bərvurf], *m.* (—s, *pl.* ⸚e)
wrap, shawl, cloak.

**Überzahl** ['y:bərtsa:l], *f.* (—, *no pl.*) *in
der* —, in the majority.

**überzählig** ['y:bərtsɛ:lɪç], *adj.* super-
numerary, surplus.

**überzeichnen** [y:bər'tsaɪçnən], *v.a.*
*insep.* (*Comm.*) over-subscribe.

**überzeugen** [y:bər'tsɔygən], *v.a. insep.*
convince. — *v.r. sich* —, satisfy o.s.

**Überzeugung** [y:bər'tsɔyguŋ], *f.* (—,
*no pl.*) conviction, certainty.

**überziehen** (1) ['y:bərtsi:ən], *v.a. irr.*
put on (a garment).

**überziehen** (2) [y:bər'tsi:ən], *v.a. irr.*
*insep.* cover; (*bed*) put fresh linen on;
(*Bank*) overdraw.

**Überzieher** ['y:bərtsi:ər], *m.* (—s, *pl.*
—) overcoat.

**Überzug** ['y:bərtsu:k], *m.* (—s, *pl.* ⸚e)
case, cover; bed-tick; coating.

**üblich** ['y:plɪç], *adj.* usual, customary;
*nicht mehr* —, out of use, obsolete.

**übrig** ['y:brɪç], *adj.* remaining, left
over; *die* —*en*, the others; — *bleiben*,
be left, remain; — *haben*, have left;
— *sein*, be left; *im* —*en*, for the rest;
*ein* —*es tun*, stretch a point; *für
einen etwas* — *haben*, like s.o.

**übrigens** ['y:brɪgəns], *adv.* besides,
moreover; by the way.

**Übung** ['y:buŋ], *f.* (—, *pl.* —en)
exercise, practice.

234

**Ufer** ['uːfər], *n.* (—s, *pl.* —) (*river*) bank; (*sea*) shore, beach.

**Uganda** [u'ganda], *n.* Uganda.

**Uhr** [uːr], *f.* (—, *pl.* —en) clock; watch; *elf* —, eleven o'clock; *wieviel* — *ist es?* what is the time?

**Uhrmacher** ['uːrmaxər], *m.* (—s, *pl.* —) watchmaker, clockmaker.

**Uhrwerk** ['uːrvɛrk], *n.* (—s, *pl.* —e) clockwork.

**Uhrzeiger** ['uːrtsaɪgər], *m.* (—s, *pl.* —) hand (of clock *or* watch).

**Uhu** ['uːhuː], *m.* (—s, *pl.* —s) (*Orn.*) eagle-owl.

**ulkig** ['ulkiç], *adj.* funny.

**Ulme** ['ulmə], *f.* (—, *pl.* —en) (*Bot.*) elm, elm-tree.

**Ultrakurzwelle** ['ultrakurtsvɛlə], *f.* (—, *pl.* —n) ultra-short wave.

**ultrarot** ['ultraroːt], *adj.* infra-red.

**Ultrastrahlung** ['ultraʃtraːluŋ], *f.* (—, *pl.* —en) cosmic radiation.

**ultraviolett** ['ultraviolet], *adj.* ultra-violet.

**um** [um], *prep.* (*Acc.*) about, around; approximately, near; for, because of; by; — *Geld bitten*, ask for money; — 5 *Uhr*, at five o'clock. — *conj.* to, in order to. — *adv.* up, past, upside down; round about; around.

**umarbeiten** ['umarbaɪtən], *v.a.* do again, remodel, revise; recast.

**umarmen** [um'armən], *v.a. insep.* embrace.

**Umarmung** [um'armuŋ], *f.* (—, *pl.* —en) embrace.

**umbauen** (1) ['umbauən], *v.a.* rebuild.

**umbauen** (2) [um'bauən], *v.a. insep.* surround with buildings.

**umbiegen** ['umbiːgən], *v.a. irr.* bend.

**umbilden** ['umbɪldən], *v.a.* transform, reform, recast, remould.

**umbinden** ['umbɪndən], *v.a. irr. sich etwas* —, tie s.th. around o.s.

**umblicken** ['umblɪkən], *v.r. sich* —, look round.

**umbringen** ['umbrɪŋən], *v.a. irr.* kill, slay, murder.

**umdrehen** ['umdreːən], *v.a.* turn over, turn round, revolve. — *v.r. sich* —, turn round.

**Umdrehung** [um'dreːuŋ], *f.* (—, *pl.* —en) revolution, rotation.

**umfahren** (1) [um'faːrən], *v.a. irr. insep.* drive round, circumnavigate.

**umfahren** (2) ['umfaːrən], *v.a. irr.* run down.

**umfallen** ['umfalən], *v.n. irr.* (*aux.* sein) fall down, fall over.

**Umfang** ['umfaŋ], *m.* (—s, *pl.* ⸚e) circumference; (*fig.*) extent.

**umfangen** [um'faŋən], *v.a. irr. insep.* encircle, embrace.

**umfangreich** ['umfaŋraɪç], *adj.* extensive, voluminous.

**umfassen** [um'fasən], *v.a. insep.* comprise, contain.

**umfassend** [um'fasənt], *adj.* comprehensive.

**umfließen** [um'fliːsən], *v.a. irr. insep.* surround by water.

**umformen** ['umfɔrmən], *v.a.* transform, remodel.

**Umformung** ['umfɔrmuŋ], *f.* (—, *pl.* —en) transformation, remodelling.

**Umfrage** ['umfraːgə], *f.* (—, *pl.* —n) enquiry, poll, quiz.

**Umfriedung** [um'friːduŋ], *f.* (—, *pl.* —en) enclosure.

**Umgang** ['umgaŋ], *m.* (—s, *pl.* ⸚e) circuit, procession; (*fig.*) acquaintance, association; relations, connection; — *haben mit*, associate with.

**umgänglich** ['umgɛŋliç], *adj.* sociable, companionable.

**Umgangsformen** ['umgaŋsfɔrmən], *f. pl.* manners.

**Umgangssprache** ['umgaŋsʃpraːxə], *f.* (— *pl.* —en) colloquial speech.

**umgeben** [um'geːbən], *v.a. irr. insep.* surround.

**Umgebung** [um'geːbuŋ], *f.* (—, *pl.* —en) environment, surroundings.

**umgehen** (1) ['umgeːən], *v.n. irr.* (*aux.* sein) associate with s.o.; handle s.th.; — *in*, haunt.

**umgehen** (2) [um'geːən], *v.a. irr. insep.* go round; (*flank*) turn; (*fig.*) evade, shirk.

**umgehend** ['umgeːənt], *adv.* immediately; (*letter*) by return of post.

**Umgehung** [um'geːuŋ], *f.* (—, *pl.* —en) shirking, evasion; detour; (*Mil.*) flank movement, turning.

**umgekehrt** ['umgəkeːrt], *adj.* reverse. — *adv.* conversely.

**umgestalten** ['umgəʃtaltən], *v.a.* transform, recast.

**Umgestaltung** ['umgəʃtaltuŋ], *f.* (—, *pl.* —en) transformation; recasting.

**umgraben** ['umgraːbən], *v.a. irr.* dig up.

**umgrenzen** [um'grɛntsən], *v.a. insep.* limit, set bounds to.

**Umgrenzung** [um'grɛntsuŋ], *f.* (—, *pl.* —en) boundary; limitation.

**umgucken** ['umgukən], *v.r. sich* —, look about o.

**umhalsen** [um'halzən], *v.a. insep.* hug, embrace.

**Umhang** ['umhaŋ], *m.* (—s, *pl.* ⸚e) shawl, cloak.

**umher** [um'heːr], *adv.* around, round, about.

**umherblicken** [um'heːrblɪkən], *v.n.* look round.

**umherflattern** [um'heːrflatərn], *v.n.* (*aux.* sein) flutter about.

**umherlaufen** [um'heːrlaufən], *v.n. irr.* (*aux.* sein) run about; roam about, ramble, wander.

**umherziehend** [um'heːrtsiːənt], *adj.* itinerant.

**umhüllen** [um'hylən], *v.a. insep.* envelop, wrap up.

**Umkehr** ['umkeːr], *f.* (—, *no pl.*) return; change; (*fig.*) conversion.

**umkehren** ['umke:rən], *v.a.* turn (back), upset, overturn. — *v.n.* (*aux.* sein) turn back, return.

**Umkehrung** ['umke:ruŋ], *f.* (—, *pl.* —en) inversion.

**umkippen** ['umkɪpən], *v.a.* upset, overturn. — *v.n.* (*aux.* sein) capsize, tilt over.

**umklammern** [um'klamərn], *v.a. insep.* clasp; clutch; (*fig.*) cling to.

**umkleiden** (1) ['umklaɪdən], *v.r. sich* —, change o.'s clothes.

**umkleiden** (2) [um'klaɪdən], *v.a. insep.* cover.

**umkommen** ['umkɔmən], *v.n. irr.* (*aux.* sein) perish, die.

**Umkreis** ['umkraɪs], *m.* (—es, *pl.* —e) circumference, compass.

**Umlauf** ['umlauf], *m.* (—s, *no pl.*) circulation; *in — bringen,* put into circulation.

**Umlaut** ['umlaut], *m.* (—s, *pl.* —e) (*Phonet.*) modification of vowels.

**umlegen** ['umle:gən], *v.a.* lay down, move, shift, put about; (*sl.*) kill.

**umleiten** ['umlaɪtən], *v.a.* (*traffic*) divert.

**umlernen** ['umlɛrnən], *v.a., v.n.* relearn; retrain (for new job).

**umliegend** ['umli:gənt], *adj.* surrounding.

**ummodeln** ['ummo:dəln], *v.a.* remodel, recast, change, fashion differently.

**Umnachtung** [um'naxtuŋ], *f.* (—, *no pl.*) mental derangement.

**umpacken** ['umpakən], *v.a.* repack.

**umpflanzen** ['umpflantsən], *v.a.* transplant.

**Umpflanzung** ['umpflantsuŋ], *f.* (—, *pl.* —en) transplantation.

**umrahmen** [um'ra:mən], *v.a. insep.* frame, surround.

**umrändern** [um'rɛndərn], *v.a. insep.* border, edge.

**umrechnen** ['umrɛçnən], *v.a.* (*figures*) reduce, convert.

**umreißen** (1) ['umraɪsən], *v.a. irr.* pull down, break up.

**umreißen** (2) [um'raɪsən], *v.a. irr. insep.* sketch, outline.

**umrennen** ['umrɛnən], *v.a. irr.* run down, knock over.

**umringen** [um'rɪŋən], *v.a. insep.* encircle, surround.

**Umriß** ['umrɪs], *m.* (—sses, *pl.* —sse) outline, contour.

**umrühren** ['umry:rən], *v.a.* (*Cul.*) stir.

**umsatteln** ['umzatəln], *v.n.* (*fig.*) change o.'s profession.

**Umsatz** ['umzats], *m.* (—es, *pl.* —e) turnover.

**umschalten** ['umʃaltən], *v.a.* (*Elec.*) switch (over); reverse (current).

**Umschau** ['umʃau], *f.* (—, *no pl.*) review, survey; — *halten,* look round, muster, review.

**umschauen** ['umʃauən], *v.r. sich —,* look round.

**umschichtig** ['umʃɪçtɪç], *adv.* turn and turn about, in turns.

**umschiffen** (1) ['umʃɪfən], *v.a.* transship, transfer (cargo, passengers).

**umschiffen** (2) [um'ʃɪfən], *v.a. insep.* sail round, circumnavigate.

**Umschlag** ['umʃla:k], *m.* (—(e)s, *pl.* ̈e) (*weather*) break, sudden change; (*letter*) envelope; (*Med.*) poultice, compress.

**umschlagen** ['umʃla:gən], *v.n. irr.* (*aux.* sein) (*weather*) change suddenly; capsize; turn sour.

**umschließen** [um'ʃli:sən], *v.a. irr. insep.* enclose, surround; comprise.

**umschlingen** [um'ʃlɪŋən], *v.a. irr. insep.* embrace.

**umschnallen** ['umʃnalən], *v.a.* buckle on.

**umschreiben** (1) ['umʃraɪbən], *v.a. irr.* rewrite, write differently.

**umschreiben** (2) [um'ʃraɪbən], *v.a. irr. insep.* circumscribe, paraphrase.

**Umschreibung** [um'ʃraɪbuŋ], *f.* (—, *pl.* —en) paraphrase.

**Umschweife** [um'ʃvaɪfə], *m.pl.* fuss, talk; circumlocution; *ohne —,* point-blank.

**Umschwung** ['umʃvuŋ], *m.* (—s, *no pl.*) sudden change, revolution.

**umsegeln** [um'ze:gəln], *v.a. insep.* sail round.

**umsehen** ['umze:ən], *v.r. irr. sich —,* look round; look out (for), cast about (for).

**Umsicht** ['umzɪçt], *f.* (—, *no pl.*) circumspection.

**umsichtig** ['umzɪçtɪç], *adj.* cautious, circumspect.

**umsinken** ['umzɪŋkən], *v.n. irr.* (*aux.* sein) sink down.

**umsonst** [um'zɔnst], *adv.* without payment, gratis, for nothing; in vain, vainly, to no purpose.

**umspannen** (1) ['umʃpanən], *v.a.* change horses.

**umspannen** (2) [um'ʃpanən], *v.a. insep.* encompass, span.

**umspringen** ['umʃprɪŋən], *v.n. irr.* (*aux.* sein) (*wind*) change suddenly; *mit einem —,* (*fig.*) deal with s.o.

**Umstand** ['umʃtant], *m.* (—s, *pl.* ̈e) circumstance; fact; factor; (*pl.*) fuss; *in anderen ̈en sein,* be expecting a baby; *unter keinen ̈en,* on no account.

**umständlich** ['umʃtɛntlɪç], *adj.* circumstantial; ceremonious; complicated, fussy.

**Umstandswort** ['umʃtantsvɔrt], *n.* (—es, *pl.* ̈er) (*Gram.*) adverb.

**umstehend** ['umʃte:ənt], *adv.* on the next page.

**Umstehenden** ['umʃte:əndən], *pl.* bystanders.

**umsteigen** ['umʃtaɪgən], *v.n. irr.* (*aux.* sein) change (trains etc.).

**umstellen** (1) ['umʃtɛlən], *v.a.* place differently, transpose, change over.

**umstellen** (2) [um'ʃtɛlən], *v.a. insep.* surround, beset.

**Umstellung** ['umʃtɛluŋ], *f.* (—, *pl.* —en) transposition; (*Gram.*) inversion; change of position in team.

**umstimmen** ['umʃtɪmən], *v.a.* turn s.o. from his opinion, bring s.o. round to (s.th.).

**umstoßen** ['umʃtoːsən], *v.a. irr.* knock down, upset, overthrow; (*judgment*) reverse.

**umstricken** [um'ʃtrɪkən], *v.a. insep.* ensnare.

**umstritten** [um'ʃtrɪtən], *adj.* controversial, disputed.

**umstülpen** ['umʃtylpən], *v.a.* turn up, turn upside down.

**Umsturz** ['umʃturts], *m.* (—es, *no pl.*) downfall; subversion; revolution.

**umstürzen** ['umʃtyrtsən], *v.a.* upset, overturn; overthrow.

**umtaufen** ['umtaufən], *v.a.* rename, rechristen.

**Umtausch** ['umtauʃ], *m.* (—s, *no pl.*) exchange.

**umtauschen** ['umtauʃən], *v.a.* exchange, change.

**Umtriebe** ['umtriːbə], *m. pl.* plots, goings-on, intrigues.

**umtun** ['umtuːn], *v.r. irr. sich — nach*, look for, cast about for.

**Umwälzung** ['umvɛltsuŋ], *f.* (—, *pl.* —en) turning-about; (*fig.*) revolution.

**umwandeln** ['umvandəln], *v.a.* change, transform; (*Gram.*) inflect.

**umwechseln** ['umvɛksəln], *v.a.* exchange.

**Umweg** ['umveːk], *m.* (—s, *pl.* —e) roundabout way, detour.

**Umwelt** ['umvɛlt], *f.* (—, *no pl.*) environment, milieu.

**umwenden** ['umvɛndən], *v.a. irr.* turn round; turn over. — *v.r. sich* —, turn round.

**umwerben** [um'vɛrbən], *v.a. irr. insep.* court.

**umwerfen** ['umvɛrfən], *v.a. irr.* overturn, knock over, upset.

**umwickeln** [um'vɪkəln], *v.a. insep.* wrap round, wind round.

**umwölken** [um'vœlkən], *v.r. insep. sich* —, (*sky*) darken, become overcast.

**umzäunen** [um'tsɔynən], *v.a. insep.* hedge in, fence in, enclose.

**umziehen** (1) ['umtsiːən], *v.a. irr.* change (clothes). — *v.n.* (*aux.* sein) move house. — *v.r. sich* —, change o.'s clothes.

**umziehen** (2) [um'tsiːən], *v.r. irr. insep. sich* —, get overcast, cloud over.

**umzingeln** [um'tsɪŋəln], *v.a. insep.* surround.

**Umzug** ['umtsuːk], *m.* (—s, *pl.* ⁻e) procession; removal; move.

**unabänderlich** [unap'ɛndərlɪç], *adj.* unalterable, irrevocable.

**Unabänderlichkeit** ['unapɛndərlɪçkaɪt], *f.* (—, *no pl.*) unchangeableness, irrevocability.

**unabhängig** ['unaphɛŋɪç], *adj.* independent, autonomous; unrelated.

**Unabhängigkeit** ['unaphɛŋɪçkaɪt], *f.* (—, *no pl.*) independence, self-sufficiency.

**unabkömmlich** ['unapkœmlɪç], *adj.* indispensable.

**unablässig** ['unaplɛsɪç], *adj.* unceasing, continual, unremitting.

**unabsehbar** ['unapzeːbaːr], *adj.* immeasurable, immense; unfathomable.

**unabsichtlich** ['unapzɪçtlɪç], *adj.* unintentional, accidental.

**unabwendbar** [unap'vɛntbaːr], *adj.* irremediable; unavoidable.

**unachtsam** ['unaxtzaːm], *adj.* unattentive, inadvertent, negligent, careless.

**Unachtsamkeit** ['unaxtzaːmkaɪt], *f.* (—, *pl.* —en) inadvertence, inattention, negligence, carelessness.

**unähnlich** ['unɛːnlɪç], *adj.* unlike, dissimilar.

**unanfechtbar** ['unanfɛçtbaːr], *adj.* indisputable, incontestable.

**unangebracht** ['unangəbraxt], *adj.* out of place, inapposite.

**unangefochten** ['unangəfɔxtən], *adj.* undisputed, uncontested.

**unangemeldet** ['unangəmɛldət], *adj.* unannounced, unheralded.

**unangemessen** ['unangəmɛsən], *adj.* unsuitable, inappropriate, inadequate.

**unangenehm** ['unangəneːm], *adj.* disagreeable, unpleasant; *einen* — *berühren*, jar, grate on s.o.

**unangetastet** ['unangətastət], *adj.* untouched.

**unangreifbar** ['unangraɪfbaːr], *adj.* unassailable, secure.

**unannehmbar** ['unanneːmbaːr], *adj.* unacceptable.

**Unannehmlichkeit** ['unanneːmlɪçkaɪt], *f.* (—, *pl.* —en) unpleasantness, annoyance.

**unansehnlich** ['unanzeːnlɪç], *adj.* insignificant; unattractive.

**unanständig** ['unanʃtɛndɪç], *adj.* improper, indecent.

**Unanständigkeit** ['unanʃtɛndɪçkaɪt], *f.* (—, *pl.* —en) indecency, immodesty, impropriety.

**unantastbar** ['unantastbaːr], *adj.* unimpeachable.

**unappetitlich** ['unapetiːtlɪç], *adj.* distasteful, unsavoury, unappetising.

**Unart** ['unaːrt], *f.* (—, *pl.* —en) bad habit, naughtiness.

**unartig** ['unaːrtɪç], *adj.* ill-behaved, naughty.

**unästhetisch** ['unɛsteːtɪʃ], *adj.* offensive, coarse; inartistic.

**unauffällig** ['unauffɛlɪç], *adj.* unobtrusive.

**unaufgefordert** ['unaufgəfɔrdərt], *adj.* unbidden.

**unaufgeklärt** ['unaufgəkleːrt], *adj.* unexplained, unsolved.

**unaufgeschnitten** ['unaufgəʃnɪtən], *adj.* uncut.

**unaufhaltsam** ['unaufhaltzaːm], *adj.* incessant, irresistible.

# unaufhörlich

**unaufhörlich** ['unaufhø:rlɪç], *adj.* incessant, continual.
**unauflöslich** ['unauflø:slɪç], *adj.* indissoluble.
**unaufmerksam** ['unaufmɛrkza:m], *adj.* inattentive.
**unaufrichtig** ['unaufrɪçtɪç], *adj.* insincere.
**unaufschiebbar** ['unaufʃi:pba:r], *adj.* urgent, pressing, brooking no delay.
**unausbleiblich** ['unausblaɪplɪç], *adj.* inevitable, unfailing.
**unausführbar** ['unausfy:rba:r], *adj.* impracticable.
**unausgebildet** ['unausgəbɪldət], *adj.* untrained, unskilled.
**unausgefüllt** ['unausgəfylt], *adj.* not filled up; (*form*) blank.
**unausgegoren** ['unausgəgo:rən], *adj.* crude; (*wine*) unfermented.
**unausgesetzt** ['unausgəzɛtst], *adj.* continual, continuous.
**unausgesprochen** ['unausgəʃprɔxən], *adj.* unsaid; (*fig.*) implied.
**unauslöschlich** ['unausløʃlɪç], *adj.* indelible, inextinguishable.
**unaussprechlich** ['unausʃpreçlɪç], *adj.* inexpressible, unspeakable.
**unausstehlich** ['unausʃte:lɪç], *adj.* insufferable.
**unausweichlich** ['unausvaɪçlɪç], *adj.* inevitable.
**unbändig** ['unbɛndɪç], *adj.* intractable, unmanageable; (*fig.*) extreme.
**unbarmherzig** ['unbarmhɛrtsɪç], *adj.* merciless.
**unbeabsichtigt** ['unbəapzɪçtɪçt], *adj.* unintentional.
**unbeanstandet** ['unbəanʃtandət], *adj.* unexceptionable; unopposed; with impunity.
**unbeantwortbar** ['unbəantvɔrtba:r], *adj.* unanswerable.
**unbeaufsichtigt** ['unbəaufzɪçtɪçt], *adj.* unattended to, not looked after; without supervision.
**unbebaut** ['unbəbaut], *adj.* (*Agr.*) uncultivated; undeveloped (by building).
**unbedacht** ['unbədaxt], *adj.* thoughtless.
**unbedenklich** ['unbədɛŋklɪç], *adj.* harmless, innocuous. — *adv.* without hesitation.
**unbedeutend** ['unbədɔytənt], *adj.* insignificant.
**unbedingt** ['unbədɪŋkt], *adj.* unconditional, unlimited, absolute. — *adv.* quite definitely; without fail.
**unbeeinflußt** ['unbəaɪnflust], *adj.* uninfluenced.
**unbefahrbar** ['unbəfa:rba:r], *adj.* impassable, impracticable.
**unbefangen** ['unbəfaŋən], *adj.* unbiased, unprejudiced; easy, unselfconscious, unembarrassed, uninhibited; natural.
**Unbefangenheit** ['unbəfaŋənhaɪt], *f.*

(—, *no pl.*) impartiality; ease of manner, unselfconsciousness, openness, naturalness.
**unbefestigt** ['unbəfɛstɪçt], *adj.* unfortified.
**unbefleckt** ['unbəflɛkt], *adj.* immaculate; —*e Empfängnis*, Immaculate Conception.
**unbefriedigend** ['unbəfri:dɪgənt], *adj.* unsatisfactory.
**unbefriedigt** ['unbəfri:dɪçt], *adj.* not satisfied, unsatisfied.
**unbefugt** ['unbəfu:kt], *adj.* unauthorised.
**unbegreiflich** ['unbəgraɪflɪç], *adj.* incomprehensible, inconceivable.
**unbegrenzt** ['unbəgrɛntst], *adj.* unlimited, unbounded.
**unbegründet** ['unbəgryndət], *adj.* unfounded, groundless.
**Unbehagen** ['unbəha:gən], *n.* (—s, *no pl.*) uneasiness, discomfort.
**unbehaglich** ['unbəha:klɪç], *adj.* uncomfortable; *sich — fühlen*, feel ill at ease.
**unbehelligt** ['unbəhɛlɪçt], *adj.* unmolested.
**unbeholfen** ['unbəhɔlfən], *adj.* awkward, clumsy.
**unbeirrt** ['unbəɪrt], *adj.* unswerving, uninfluenced, unperturbed.
**unbekannt** ['unbəkant], *adj.* unknown, unacquainted; *ich bin hier —*, I am a stranger here.
**unbekümmert** ['unbəkymərt], *adj.* unconcerned, careless, indifferent.
**unbelehrt** ['unbəle:rt], *adj.* uninstructed.
**unbeliebt** ['unbəli:pt], *adj.* unpopular.
**unbemannt** ['unbəmant], *adj.* without crew, unmanned.
**unbemerkbar** ['unbəmɛrkba:r], *adj.* unnoticeable, imperceptible.
**unbemerkt** ['unbəmɛrkt], *adj.* unnoticed.
**unbemittelt** ['unbəmɪtəlt], *adj.* impecunious, poor.
**unbenommen** ['unbənɔmən], *adj.* *es bleibt dir —*, you are free to.
**unbenutzt** ['unbənutst], *adj.* unused.
**unbequem** ['unbəkve:m], *adj.* uncomfortable, inconvenient, troublesome.
**Unbequemlichkeit** ['unbəkve:mlɪçkaɪt], *f.* (—, *pl.* —en) inconvenience.
**unberechenbar** ['unbəreçənba:r], *adj.* incalculable; (*fig.*) erratic.
**unberechtigt** ['unbəreçtɪçt], *adj.* unwarranted, unjustified.
**unberücksichtigt** ['unbərykzɪçtɪçt], *adj.* disregarded; — *lassen*, ignore.
**unberufen** ['unbəru:fən], *adj.* unauthorized. — *excl.* touch wood!
**unbeschadet** ['unbəʃa:dət], *prep.* (*Genit.*) without prejudice to.
**unbeschädigt** ['unbəʃe:dɪçt], *adj.* undamaged.
**unbeschäftigt** ['unbəʃɛftɪçt], *adj.* unemployed, disengaged.

238

**unbescheiden** ['unbəʃaɪdən], adj. presumptuous, greedy, immodest; unblushing; exorbitant; arrogant.

**Unbescheidenheit** ['unbəʃaɪdənhaɪt], f. (—, no pl.) presumptuousness, greed.

**unbescholten** ['unbəʃɔltən], adj. irreproachable, of unblemished character.

**Unbescholtenheit** ['unbəʃɔltənhaɪt], f. (—, no pl.) blamelessness, good character, unsullied reputation.

**unbeschränkt** ['unbəʃrɛŋkt], adj. unlimited, unbounded; —e Monarchie, absolute monarchy.

**unbeschreiblich** ['unbəʃraɪplɪç], adj. indescribable.

**unbeschrieben** ['unbəʃriːbən], adj. unwritten; ein —es Papier, a blank sheet of paper.

**unbeschwert** ['unbəʃveːrt], adj. unburdened; easy.

**unbeseelt** ['unbəzeːlt], adj. inanimate.

**unbesiegbar** [unbə'ziːkbaːr], adj. invincible.

**unbesoldet** ['unbəzɔldət], adj. unpaid, unsalaried.

**unbesonnen** ['unbəzɔnən], adj. thoughtless, rash.

**Unbesonnenheit** ['unbəzɔnənhaɪt], f. (—, pl. —en) thoughtlessness.

**unbesorgt** ['unbəzɔrkt], adj. unconcerned; sei —, never fear.

**unbeständig** ['unbəʃtɛndɪç], adj. fickle, inconstant; (weather) unsettled.

**unbestechlich** ['unbəʃtɛçlɪç], adj. incorruptible.

**unbestellbar** ['unbəʃtɛlbaːr], adj. not deliverable; (letters etc.) address(ee) unknown.

**unbestellt** ['unbəʃtɛlt], adj. not ordered; (Agr.) uncultivated, untilled.

**unbestimmt** ['unbəʃtɪmt], adj. uncertain, not settled; indefinite; irresolute; vague.

**unbestraft** ['unbəʃtraːft], adj. unpunished; without previous conviction.

**unbestreitbar** ['unbəʃtraɪtbaːr], adj. indisputable, incontestable.

**unbestritten** ['unbəʃtrɪtən], adj. uncontested, undoubted, undisputed.

**unbeteiligt** ['unbətaɪlɪçt], adj. unconcerned, indifferent.

**unbeträchtlich** ['unbətrɛçtlɪç], adj. inconsiderable, trivial.

**unbetreten** ['unbətreːtən], adj. untrodden, untouched.

**unbeugsam** ['unbɔykzaːm], adj. inflexible, unyielding.

**unbewacht** ['unbəvaxt], adj. unguarded.

**unbewaffnet** ['unbəvafnət], adj. unarmed; mit —em Auge, with the naked eye.

**unbewandert** ['unbəvandərt], adj. unversed in, unfamiliar with.

**unbezahlt** ['unbətsaːlt], adj. unpaid.

**unbezähmbar** ['unbətsɛːmbaːr], adj. uncontrollable; indomitable.

**unbezwinglich** ['unbətsvɪŋlɪç], adj. invincible, unconquerable.

**Unbildung** ['unbɪlduŋ], f. (—, no pl.) lack of education or knowledge or culture.

**Unbill** ['unbɪl], f. (—, pl. **Unbilden**) injustice, wrong, injury; (weather) inclemency.

**unbillig** ['unbɪlɪç], adj. unreasonable, unfair.

**Unbilligkeit** ['unbɪlɪçkaɪt], f. (—, no pl.) unreasonableness, injustice, unfairness.

**unbotmäßig** ['unboːtmɛːsɪç], adj. unruly, insubordinate.

**unbußfertig** ['unbuːsfertɪç], adj. impenitent, unrepentant.

**und** [unt], conj. and; — nicht, nor; — so weiter (abbr. usw.), etc., and so on, and so forth; — wenn, even if.

**Undank** ['undaŋk], m. (—s, no pl.) ingratitude.

**undankbar** ['undaŋkbaːr], adj. ungrateful; eine —e Aufgabe, a thankless task.

**Undankbarkeit** ['undaŋkbaːrkaɪt], f. (—, no pl.) ingratitude.

**undenkbar** ['undɛŋkbaːr], adj. unthinkable, unimaginable, inconceivable.

**undenklich** ['undɛŋklɪç], adj. seit —en Zeiten, from time immemorial.

**undeutlich** ['undɔytlɪç], adj. indistinct; inarticulate; (fig.) unintelligible.

**Unding** ['undɪŋ], n. (—s, no pl.) absurdity.

**unduldsam** ['undultzaːm], adj. intolerant.

**undurchdringlich** ['undurçdrɪŋlɪç], adj. impenetrable.

**undurchführbar** ['undurçfyːrbaːr], adj. impracticable, unworkable.

**undurchsichtig** ['undurçzɪçtɪç], adj. opaque, not transparent.

**uneben** ['uneːbən], adj. uneven, rugged; (coll.) nicht —, not bad.

**unecht** ['unɛçt], adj. false, not genuine, spurious, counterfeit.

**unedel** ['uneːdəl], adj. (metal) base.

**unehelich** ['uneːəlɪç], adj. illegitimate.

**Unehre** ['uneːrə], f. (—, no pl.) dishonour, disgrace, discredit.

**unehrlich** ['uneːrlɪç], adj. dishonest.

**Unehrlichkeit** ['uneːrlɪçkaɪt], f. (—, pl. —en) dishonesty.

**uneigennützig** ['unaɪgənnytsɪç], adj. unselfish, disinterested, public-spirited.

**uneingedenk** ['unaɪngədɛŋk], adj. (Genit.) unmindful, forgetful.

**uneingeschränkt** ['unaɪngəʃrɛŋkt], adj. unrestrained, unlimited.

**uneinig** ['unaɪnɪç], **uneins** ['unaɪns], adj. disunited, divided; — werden, fall out; — sein, disagree.

**Uneinigkeit** ['unaɪnɪçkaɪt], f. (—, pl. —en) disharmony, discord.

**uneinnehmbar** ['unaɪnneːmbaːr], adj. unconquerable, impregnable.

**uneins** see under **uneinig.**

**unempfänglich** ['unɛmpfɛŋlıç], adj. insusceptible; unreceptive.

**unempfindlich** ['unɛmpfɪntlıç], adj. insensitive, indifferent; unfeeling.

**unendlich** [un'ɛntlıç], adj. endless, infinite.

**unentbehrlich** ['unɛntbeːrlıç], adj. indispensable, (absolutely) essential.

**unentgeltlich** [unɛnt'gɛltlıç], adj. free (of charge).

**unentschieden** ['unɛntʃiːdən], adj. undecided, undetermined; irresolute; (game) drawn, tied.

**unentschlossen** ['unɛntʃlɔsən], adj. irresolute.

**Unentschlossenheit** ['unɛntʃlɔsənhaɪt], f. (—, no pl.) irresolution, indecision.

**unentschuldbar** ['unɛntʃultbaːr], adj. inexcusable.

**unentstellt** ['unɛntʃtɛlt], adj. undistorted.

**unentwegt** ['unɛntveːkt], adj. steadfast, unflinching, unswerving.

**unentwickelt** ['unɛntvɪkəlt], adj. undeveloped; —e Länder, underdeveloped countries.

**unentwirrbar** ['unɛntvɪrbaːr], adj. inextricable.

**unentzifferbar** ['unɛnttsɪfərbaːr], adj. indecipherable.

**unentzündbar** ['unɛnttsyntbaːr], adj. non-inflammable.

**unerachtet** ['unɛraxtət], prep. (Genit.) (obs.) notwithstanding.

**unerbeten** ['unɛrbeːtən], adj. unsolicited.

**unerbittlich** ['unɛrbɪtlıç], adj. inexorable.

**unerfahren** ['unɛrfaːrən], adj. inexperienced.

**unerforschlich** ['unɛrfɔrʃlıç], adj. inscrutable.

**unerfreulich** ['unɛrfrɔylıç], adj. unpleasant, displeasing, disagreeable.

**unerfüllbar** ['unɛrfylbaːr], adj. unrealisable.

**unerfüllt** ['unɛrfylt], adj. unfulfilled.

**unergründlich** ['unɛrgryntlıç], adj. unfathomable, impenetrable.

**unerheblich** ['unɛrheːplıç], adj. trifling, unimportant.

**unerhört** ['unɛrhøːrt], adj. unprecedented, unheard of, shocking, outrageous; not granted; turned down.

**unerkannt** ['unɛrkant], adj. unrecognised.

**unerkennbar** ['unɛrkɛnbaːr], adj. unrecognisable.

**unerklärlich** ['unɛrklɛːrlıç], adj. inexplicable.

**unerläßlich** ['unɛrlɛslıç], adj. indispensable.

**unerlaubt** ['unɛrlaupt], adj. unlawful, illicit.

**unermeßlich** ['unɛrmɛslıç], adj. immense, vast.

**unermüdlich** ['unɛrmyːtlıç], adj. untiring, indefatigable.

**unerquicklich** ['unɛrkvɪklıç], adj. unedifying, disagreeable.

**unerreichbar** ['unɛrraɪçbaːr], adj. unattainable, inaccessible.

**unerreicht** ['unɛrraɪçt], adj. unequalled.

**unersättlich** ['unɛrzɛtlıç], adj. insatiable, greedy.

**unerschöpflich** ['unɛrʃœpflıç], adj. inexhaustible.

**unerschöpft** ['unɛrʃœpft], adj. unexhausted.

**unerschrocken** ['unɛrʃrɔkən], adj. intrepid, undaunted.

**unerschütterlich** ['unɛrʃytərlıç], adj. imperturbable.

**unerschüttert** ['unɛrʃytərt], adj. unshaken, unperturbed.

**unerschwinglich** ['unɛrʃvɪŋlıç], adj. prohibitive, exorbitant, unattainable.

**unersetzlich** ['unɛrzɛtslıç], adj. irreplaceable.

**unersprießlich** ['unɛrʃpriːslıç], adj. unprofitable.

**unerträglich** ['unɛrtrɛːklıç], adj. intolerable, insufferable.

**unerwartet** ['unɛrvartət], adj. unexpected.

**unerwidert** ['unɛrviːdərt], adj. (love) unrequited; (letter) unanswered.

**unerwünscht** ['unɛrvynʃt], adj. undesirable, unwelcome.

**unerzogen** ['unɛrtsoːgən], adj. uneducated; ill-bred, unmannerly.

**unfähig** ['unfɛːıç], adj. incapable, unable, unfit.

**Unfähigkeit** ['unfɛːıçkaɪt], f. (—, no pl.) incapability, inability, unfitness.

**Unfall** ['unfal], m. (—s, pl. ⸚e) accident.

**unfaßbar** ['unfasbaːr], adj. incomprehensible, inconceivable.

**unfehlbar** ['unfeːlbaːr], adj. inevitable; infallible.

**Unfehlbarkeit** ['unfeːlbaːrkaɪt], f. (—, no pl.) infallibility.

**unfein** ['unfaɪn], adj. indelicate, coarse, impolite.

**unfern** ['unfɛrn], prep. (Genit., Dat.) not far from.

**unfertig** ['unfɛrtıç], adj. unfinished, unready.

**unflätig** ['unflɛːtıç], adj. obscene, nasty, filthy.

**unfolgsam** ['unfɔlkzaːm], adj. disobedient, recalcitrant.

**unförmig** ['unfœrmıç], adj. deformed, ill-shaped, misshapen.

**unförmlich** ['unfœrmlıç], adj. shapeless; free and easy, unceremonious.

**unfrankiert** ['unfraŋkiːrt], adj. (letter) not prepaid, unstamped, unfranked.

**unfrei** ['unfraɪ], adj. not free; subjugated; constrained.

**unfreiwillig** ['unfraɪvɪlıç], adj. involuntary.

**unfreundlich** ['unfrɔyntlɪç], *adj.* unfriendly, unkind; (*weather*) inclement.

**Unfreundlichkeit** ['unfrɔyntlɪçkaɪt], *f.* (—, *pl.* —en) unfriendliness, unkindness; (*weather*) inclemency.

**Unfrieden** ['unfri:dən], *m.* (—s, *no pl.*) discord, dissension.

**unfruchtbar** ['unfruxtba:r], *adj.* barren, sterile; (*fig.*) fruitless.

**Unfug** ['unfu:k], *m.* (—s, *no pl.*) disturbance, misconduct; mischief; *grober* —, public nuisance.

**unfühlbar** ['unfy:lba:r], *adj.* imperceptible.

**ungangbar** ['unganba:r], *adj.* impassable.

**Ungarn** ['ungarn], *n.* Hungary.

**ungastlich** ['ungastlɪç], *adj.* inhospitable.

**ungeachtet** ['ungəaxtət], *prep.* (*Genit.*) notwithstanding.

**ungeahndet** ['ungəa:ndət], *adj.* unpunished, with impunity.

**ungeahnt** ['ungəa:nt], *adj.* unexpected, unsuspected, undreamt of.

**ungebändigt** ['ungəbɛndɪçt], *adj.* untamed.

**ungebärdig** ['ungəbɛ:rdɪç], *adj.* unmannerly, refractory.

**ungebeten** ['ungəbe:tən], *adj.* uninvited, unbidden.

**ungebleicht** ['ungəblaɪçt], *adj.* unbleached.

**ungebraucht** ['ungəbrauxt], *adj.* unused.

**Ungebühr** ['ungəby:r], *f.* (—, *no pl.*) unseemliness, impropriety, excess.

**ungebührlich** ['ungəby:rlɪç], *adj.* unseemly.

**ungebunden** ['ungəbundən], *adj.* unbound, in sheets; unrestrained, loose; unlinked; —*e Rede*, prose.

**Ungeduld** ['ungədult], *f.* (—, *no pl.*) impatience.

**ungeduldig** ['ungəduldɪç], *adj.* impatient.

**ungeeignet** ['ungəaɪgnət], *adj.* unfit, unsuitable.

**ungefähr** ['ungəfɛ:r], *adj.* approximate, rough. — *adv.* approximately, roughly, about, round.

**ungefährlich** ['ungəfɛ:rlɪç], *adj.* not dangerous, harmless, safe.

**ungefällig** ['ungəfɛlɪç], *adj.* ungracious, disobliging.

**ungefärbt** ['ungəfɛrpt], *adj.* uncoloured; (*fig.*) unvarnished.

**ungefüge** ['ungəfy:gə], *adj.* clumsy.

**ungehalten** ['ungəhaltən], *adj.* indignant, angry.

**ungeheißen** ['ungəhaɪsən], *adj.* unbidden. — *adv.* of o.'s own accord.

**ungehemmt** ['ungəhɛmt], *adj.* unchecked, uninhibited.

**ungeheuchelt** ['ungəhɔyçəlt], *adj.* unfeigned.

**Ungeheuer** ['ungəhɔyər], *n.* (—s, *pl.* —) monster, monstrosity.

**ungeheuer** ['ungəhɔyər], *adj.* huge, immense; atrocious, frightful.

**ungehobelt** ['ungəho:bəlt], *adj.* unplaned; (*fig.*) boorish, uncultured, unpolished.

**ungehörig** ['ungəhø:rɪç], *adj.* unseemly, improper.

**Ungehorsam** ['ungəho:rza:m], *m.* (—s, *no pl.*) disobedience.

**ungehorsam** ['ungəho:rza:m], *adj.* disobedient; — *sein*, disobey.

**Ungehorsamkeit** ['ungəho:rza:mkaɪt], *f.* (—, *pl.* —en) disobedience, insubordination.

**ungekämmt** ['ungəkɛmt], *adj.* unkempt.

**ungekünstelt** ['ungəkynstəlt], *adj.* artless, unstudied.

**ungeladen** ['ungəla:dən], *adj.* (*gun*) unloaded, not charged; uninvited.

**ungeläutert** ['ungəlɔytərt], *adj.* unrefined; unpurified.

**ungelegen** ['ungəle:gən], *adj.* inconvenient, inopportune.

**Ungelegenheit** ['ungəle:gənhaɪt], *f.* (—, *pl.* —en) inconvenience, trouble.

**ungelehrig** ['ungəle:rɪç], *adj.* intractable, unintelligent.

**ungelenk** ['ungəlɛŋk], *adj.* clumsy, awkward; ungainly.

**ungelöscht** ['ungəlœʃt], *adj.* unquenched; (*lime*) unslaked; (*mortgage*) unredeemed.

**Ungemach** ['ungəma:x], *n.* (—(e)s, *no pl.*) adversity, toil, privation.

**ungemein** ['ungəmaɪn], *adj.* uncommon, extraordinary. — *adv.* very much, exceedingly.

**ungemütlich** ['ungəmy:tlɪç], *adj.* uncomfortable, cheerless, unpleasant.

**ungeniert** ['unʒeni:rt], *adj.* free and easy, unceremonious, unabashed.

**ungenießbar** ['ungə'ni:sba:r], *adj.* unpalatable, uneatable, inedible.

**ungenügend** ['ungəny:gənt], *adj.* insufficient, unsatisfactory.

**ungenügsam** ['ungəny:kza:m], *adj.* insatiable, greedy.

**ungeordnet** ['ungəɔrdnət], *adj.* illassorted, confused.

**ungepflegt** ['ungəpfle:kt], *adj.* uncared for, neglected.

**ungerade** ['ungəra:də], *adj.* uneven; — *Zahl*, odd number.

**ungeraten** ['ungəra:tən], *adj.* abortive, unsuccessful, spoiled; undutiful; illbred.

**ungerecht** ['ungəreçt], *adj.* unjust, unfair.

**ungerechtfertigt** ['ungəreçtfɛrtɪçt], *adj.* unwarranted, unjustified.

**Ungerechtigkeit** ['ungəreçtɪçkaɪt], *f.* (—, *pl.* —en) injustice.

**ungeregelt** ['ungəre:gəlt], *adj.* not regulated, irregular.

**ungereimt** ['ungəraɪmt], *adj.* rhymeless; —*es Zeug*, nonsense, absurdity.

**ungern** ['ungern], *adv.* unwillingly, reluctantly.

**ungerufen** ['ungəru:fən], *adj.* unbidden.

**ungerührt** ['ungəry:rt], *adj.* unmoved.

**ungesäumt** ['ungəzɔymt], *adj.* unseamed, unhemmed; (*fig.*) immediate. — *adv.* immediately, without delay.

**ungeschehen** ['ungəʃe:ən], *adj.* undone; — *machen*, undo.

**Ungeschick** ['ungəʃɪk], *n.* (—s, *no pl.*) awkwardness, clumsiness.

**Ungeschicklichkeit** ['ungəʃɪklɪçkaɪt], *f.* (—, *pl.* —en) awkwardness, clumsiness.

**ungeschickt** ['ungəʃɪkt], *adj.* awkward, clumsy, unskilful.

**ungeschlacht** ['ungəʃlaxt], *adj.* uncouth, unwieldy; coarse, rude.

**ungeschliffen** ['ungəʃlɪfən], *adj.* unpolished; (*fig.*) coarse.

**Ungeschliffenheit** ['ungəʃlɪfənhaɪt], *f.* (—, *no pl.*) coarseness, uncouthness.

**ungeschmälert** ['ungəʃmɛ:lərt], *adj.* undiminished, unimpaired.

**ungeschminkt** ['ungəʃmɪŋkt], *adj.* without cosmetics *or* make-up, not made up; (*truth*) plain, unvarnished.

**ungeschoren** ['ungəʃo:rən], *adj.* unshorn; *laß mich —*, leave me alone.

**ungeschult** ['ungəʃu:lt], *adj.* untrained.

**ungeschwächt** ['ungəʃvɛçt], *adj.* unimpaired.

**ungesellig** ['ungəzɛlɪç], *adj.* unsociable.

**ungesetzlich** ['ungəzɛtslɪç], *adj.* illegal, unlawful, illicit.

**ungesetzmäßig** ['ungəzɛtsmɛ:sɪç], *adj.* illegitimate, lawless; exceptional; not regular.

**ungesiegelt** ['ungəzi:gəlt], *adj.* unsealed.

**Ungestalt** ['ungəʃtalt], *f.* (—, *no pl.*) deformity.

**ungestalt** ['ungəʃtalt], *adj.* misshapen, deformed.

**ungestempelt** ['ungəʃtɛmpəlt], *adj.* unstamped, uncancelled, not postmarked.

**ungestillt** ['ungəʃtɪlt], *adj.* unquenched, unslaked; not fed, unsatisfied.

**ungestört** ['ungəʃtø:rt], *adj.* undisturbed.

**ungestraft** ['ungəʃtra:ft], *adj.* unpunished. — *adv.* with impunity.

**ungestüm** ['ungəʃty:m], *adj.* impetuous.

**Ungestüm** ['ungəʃty:m], *m. & n.* (—s, *no pl.*) impetuosity.

**ungesund** ['ungəzunt], *adj.* unwholesome, unhealthy, sickly; (*fig.*) unnatural, morbid.

**ungetan** ['ungəta:n], *adj.* not done, left undone.

**ungetreu** ['ungətrɔy], *adj.* disloyal, faithless.

**ungetrübt** ['ungətry:pt], *adj.* untroubled.

**ungewandt** ['ungəvant], *adj.* unskilful.

**ungewaschen** ['ungəvaʃən], *adj.* unwashed; (*sl.*) *—es Mundwerk*, malicious tongue.

**ungeweiht** ['ungəvaɪt], *adj.* unconsecrated.

**ungewiß** ['ungəvɪs], *adj.* uncertain, doubtful.

**Ungewißheit** ['ungəvɪshaɪt], *f.* (—, *no pl.*) uncertainty, suspense.

**Ungewitter** ['ungəvɪtər], *n.* (—s, *pl.* —) storm, thunderstorm.

**ungewöhnlich** ['ungəvø:nlɪç], *adj.* unusual, uncommon.

**Ungewohntheit** ['ungəvo:nthaɪt], *f.* (—, *no pl.*) strangeness; want of practice.

**ungezähmt** ['ungətsɛ:mt], *adj.* untamed; (*fig.*) uncurbed.

**Ungeziefer** ['ungətsi:fər], *n.* (—s, *pl.* —) vermin.

**ungeziert** ['ungətsi:rt], *adj.* unaffected, natural.

**ungezogen** ['ungətso:gən], *adj.* illmannered, naughty.

**ungezügelt** ['ungətsy:gəlt], *adj.* unbridled; (*fig.*) unruly.

**ungezwungen** ['ungətsvuŋən], *adj.* unforced; (*fig.*) unaffected.

**Ungezwungenheit** ['ungətsvuŋənhaɪt], *f.* (—, *no pl.*) naturalness, ease.

**Unglaube** ['unglaubə], *m.* (—ns, *no pl.*) disbelief.

**unglaubhaft** ['unglauphaft], *adj.* unauthenticated, incredible.

**ungläubig** ['unglɔybɪç], *adj.* incredulous, disbelieving.

**Ungläubige** ['unglɔybɪgə], *m.* (—n, *pl.* —n) unbeliever.

**unglaublich** ['unglauplɪç], *adj.* incredible, unbelievable.

**unglaubwürdig** ['unglaupvyrdɪç], *adj.* unauthenticated, incredible.

**ungleichartig** ['unglaɪça:rtɪç], *adj.* dissimilar, heterogeneous.

**ungleichförmig** ['unglaɪçfœrmɪç], *adj.* not uniform; dissimilar.

**Ungleichheit** ['unglaɪçhaɪt], *f.* (—, *pl.* —en) inequality; unlikeness, dissimilarity; unevenness.

**ungleichmäßig** ['unglaɪçmɛ:sɪç], *adj.* unequal, irregular; changeable, fitful.

**Unglimpf** ['unglɪmpf], *m.* (—(e)s, *no pl.*) harshness; insult.

**Unglück** ['unglyk], *n.* (—s, *pl.* —sfälle) misfortune, adversity, ill-luck; accident, disaster; distress, sorrow, affliction.

**unglückbringend** ['unglykbrɪŋənt], *adj.* disastrous, unpropitious.

**unglücklich** ['unglyklɪç], *adj.* unfortunate, unhappy, unlucky; *—e Liebe*, unrequited love.

**unglücklicherweise** ['unglyklɪçərvaɪzə], *adv.* unfortunately, unluckily.

**Unglücksbotschaft** ['unglyksbo:tʃaft], *f.* (—, *pl.* —en) bad news.

**unglückselig** ['unglykze:lɪç], *adj.* luckless, wretched, unfortunate, calamitous.

**Unglücksfall** ['unglyksfal], *m.* (—(e)s, *pl.* ⁻e) accident.

**Unglücksgefährte** [ˈʊnglyksgəfɛːrtə], m. (**—n,** pl. **—n**) companion in misfortune.

**Ungnade** [ˈʊngnaːdə], f. (**—,** no pl.) disgrace.

**ungültig** [ˈʊngyltɪç], adj. invalid, void; **— machen,** invalidate, annul.

**Ungunst** [ˈʊngunst], f. (**—,** no pl.) disfavour; unpropitiousness; (weather) inclemency.

**ungünstig** [ˈʊngynstɪç], adj. unfavourable, adverse.

**ungut** [ˈʊnguːt], adv. etwas für **—** nehmen, take s.th. amiss.

**unhaltbar** [ˈʊnhaltbaːr], adj. untenable.

**Unheil** [ˈʊnhaɪl], n. (**—s,** no pl.) mischief, harm; disaster.

**unheilbar** [ˈʊnhaɪlbaːr], adj. incurable.

**unheilbringend** [ˈʊnhaɪlbrɪŋənt], adj. ominous, unlucky; disastrous.

**Unheilstifter** [ˈʊnhaɪlʃtɪftər], m. (**—s,** pl. **—)** mischief-maker.

**unheilvoll** [ˈʊnhaɪlfɔl], adj. calamitous, disastrous.

**unheimlich** [ˈʊnhaɪmlɪç], adj. weird, eerie, uncanny.

**unhöflich** [ˈʊnhøːflɪç], adj. impolite, uncivil, discourteous.

**Unhold** [ˈʊnhɔlt], m. (**—s,** pl. **—e)** fiend, monster.

**Unhörbarkeit** [ˈʊnhøːrbaːrkaɪt], f. (**—,** no pl.) inaudibility.

**Uniformität** [ʊnifɔrmiˈtɛːt], f. (**—,** no pl.) uniformity.

**Unikum** [ˈuːnikum], n. (**—s,** pl. **—s)** unique thing or person; eccentric.

**Universalmittel** [ʊnivɛrˈzaːlmɪtəl], n. (**—s,** pl. **—)** panacea, universal remedy.

**Universität** [ʊnivɛrziˈtɛːt], f. (**—,** pl. **—en)** university.

**Universitätsdozent** [ʊnivɛrziˈtɛːtsdoːtsent], m. (**—en,** pl. **—en)** university lecturer.

**Universum** [ʊniˈvɛrzum], n. (**—s,** no pl.) universe.

**unkaufmännisch** [ˈʊnkaufmɛnɪʃ], adj. unbusinesslike.

**Unke** [ˈʊŋkə], f. (**—,** pl. **—n)** (Zool.) toad; (fig.) grumbler, pessimist.

**unken** [ˈʊŋkən], v.n. grumble, grouse.

**unkenntlich** [ˈʊnkɛntlɪç], adj. indiscernible, unrecognisable.

**Unkenntlichkeit** [ˈʊnkɛntlɪçkaɪt], f. (**—,** no pl.) bis zur **—,** past recognition.

**Unkenntnis** [ˈʊnkɛntnɪs], f. (**—,** no pl.) ignorance.

**unklug** [ˈʊnkluːk], adj. imprudent.

**Unkosten** [ˈʊnkɔstən], f. pl. expenses, costs, charges; overheads.

**Unkraut** [ˈʊnkraut], n. (**—s,** no pl.) weed(s).

**unkündbar** [ˈʊnkyntbaːr], adj. irredeemable; irrevocable, permanent.

**unkundig** [ˈʊnkundɪç], adj. ignorant (of), unacquainted (with).

**unlängst** [ˈʊnlɛŋst], adv. recently, lately, not long ago.

**unlauter** [ˈʊnlautər], adj. sordid, squalid; unfair.

**unleidlich** [ˈʊnlaɪtlɪç], adj. intolerable.

**unleserlich** [ˈʊnleːzərlɪç], adj. illegible.

**unleugbar** [ˈʊnlɔykbaːr], adj. undeniable, indisputable.

**unlieb** [ˈʊnliːp], adj. disagreeable.

**unliebenswürdig** [ˈʊnliːbənsvyrdɪç], adj. sullen, surly.

**unlösbar** [ˈʊnløːsbaːr], adj. insoluble.

**unlöslich** [ˈʊnløːslɪç], adj. (substance) indissoluble, insoluble.

**Unlust** [ˈʊnlust], f. (**—,** no pl.) aversion, disinclination; slackness.

**unlustig** [ˈʊnlustɪç], adj. averse, disinclined.

**unmanierlich** [ˈʊnmaniːrlɪç], adj. ill-mannered.

**unmännlich** [ˈʊnmɛnlɪç], adj. unmanly, effeminate.

**Unmaß** [ˈʊnmaːs], n. (**—es,** no pl.) excess.

**Unmasse** [ˈʊnmasə], f. (**—,** pl. **—n)** vast quantity.

**unmaßgeblich** [ˈʊnmaːsgeːplɪç], adj. unauthoritative, open to correction; (fig.) humble.

**unmäßig** [ˈʊnmɛːsɪç], adj. intemperate, excessive.

**Unmenge** [ˈʊnmɛŋə], f. (**—,** pl. **—n)** vast quantity.

**Unmensch** [ˈʊnmɛnʃ], m. (**—en,** pl. **—en)** brute.

**unmenschlich** [ˈʊnmɛnʃlɪç], adj. inhuman, brutal; (coll.) vast.

**unmerklich** [ˈʊnmɛrklɪç], adj. imperceptible.

**unmeßbar** [ˈʊnmɛsbaːɪ], adj. immeasurable.

**unmittelbar** [ˈʊnmɪtəlbaːr], adj. immediate, direct.

**unmöglich** [ˈʊnmøːklɪç], adj. impossible.

**unmündig** [ˈʊnmyndɪç], adj. under age, minor.

**Unmündige** [ˈʊnmyndɪgə], m. (**—n,** pl. **—n)** (Law) minor.

**Unmündigkeit** [ˈʊnmyndɪçkaɪt], f. (**—,** no pl.) minority.

**Unmut** [ˈʊnmuːt], m. (**—s,** no pl.) ill-humour; displeasure, indignation, petulance.

**unmutig** [ˈʊnmuːtɪç], adj. ill-humoured, petulant, indignant.

**unnachahmlich** [ˈʊnnaxaːmlɪç], adj. inimitable.

**unnachgiebig** [ˈʊnnaxgiːbɪç], adj. relentless, unyielding.

**unnachsichtig** [ˈʊnnaxzɪçtɪç], adj. unrelenting, relentless.

**unnahbar** [ˈʊnnaːbaːr], adj. unapproachable, stand-offish.

**unnennbar** [ˈʊnnɛnbaːr], adj. unutterable.

**unnütz** [ˈʊnnyts], adj. useless.

**unordentlich** [ˈʊnɔrdəntlɪç], adj. untidy, slovenly.

**Unordnung** [ˈʊnɔrdnuŋ], f. (**—,** no pl.) disorder, untidiness, muddle, confusion.

**unparteiisch** [ˈunpartaɪʃ], *adj.* impartial, unbiased, objective.

**unpassend** [ˈunpasənt], *adj.* unsuitable, inappropriate; improper.

**unpassierbar** [ˈunpasiːrbaːr], *adj.* impassable.

**unpäßlich** [ˈunpɛslɪç], *adj.* indisposed, unwell, out of sorts.

**Unpäßlichkeit** [ˈunpɛslɪçkaɪt], *f.* (—, *pl.* —en) indisposition.

**unproportioniert** [ˈunproportsjoniːrt], *adj.* disproportionate; unshapely.

**unqualifizierbar** [ˈunkvalifitsiːrbaːr], *adj.* unspeakable, nameless.

**Unrat** [ˈunraːt], *m.* (—(e)s, *no pl.*) dirt, rubbish.

**unratsam** [ˈunraˈtzaːm], *adj.* inadvisable.

**Unrecht** [ˈunrɛçt], *n.* (—(e)s, *no pl.*) wrong, injustice; — *haben*, be in the wrong.

**unrecht** [ˈunrɛçt], *adj.* wrong, unjust.

**unrechtmäßig** [ˈunrɛçtmɛːsɪç], *adj.* unlawful, illegal.

**unredlich** [ˈunreːtlɪç], *adj.* dishonest.

**unregelmäßig** [ˈunreːgəlmɛːsɪç], *adj.* irregular.

**unreif** [ˈunraɪf], *adj.* unripe, immature; (*fig.*) crude, raw.

**Unreife** [ˈunraɪfə], *f.* (—, *no pl.*) immaturity.

**unrein** [ˈunraɪn], *adj.* unclean; (*fig.*) impure.

**Unreinheit** [ˈunraɪnhaɪt], *f.* (—, *pl.* —en) impurity.

**Unreinlichkeit** [ˈunraɪnlɪçkaɪt], *f.* (—, *no pl.*) uncleanliness.

**unrentabel** [ˈunrɛntaˈbəl], *adj.* unprofitable.

**unrettbar** [ˈunrɛtbaːr], *adj.* irretrievable, hopelessly lost.

**unrichtig** [ˈunrɪçtɪç], *adj.* incorrect, erroneous, wrong.

**Unrichtigkeit** [ˈunrɪçtɪçkaɪt], *f.* (—, *no pl.*) error, falsity, incorrectness.

**Unruhe** [ˈunruːə], *f.* (—, *pl.* —en) unrest, restlessness; disquiet, uneasiness; riot, disturbance; (*clock*) balance.

**Unruhestifter** [ˈunruːəʃtɪftər], *m.* (—s, *pl.* —) disturber (of the peace); troublemaker.

**unruhig** [ˈunruːɪç], *adj.* restless; troublesome, turbulent, uneasy (about), fidgety.

**unrühmlich** [ˈunryːmlɪç], *adj.* inglorious.

**uns** [uns], *pers. pron.* us, ourselves; to us.

**unsachlich** [ˈunzaxlɪç], *adj.* subjective; irrelevant.

**unsagbar** [ˈunzaˈkbaːr], *adj.* unutterable, unspeakable.

**unsanft** [ˈunzanft], *adj.* harsh, violent.

**unsauber** [ˈunzaubər], *adj.* unclean, dirty; (*fig.*) squalid.

**unschädlich** [ˈunʃeːtlɪç], *adj.* harmless, innocuous.

**unschätzbar** [ˈunʃɛtsbaːr], *adj.* invaluable.

**unscheinbar** [ˈunʃaɪnbaːr], *adj.* plain, homely, insignificant.

**unschicklich** [ˈunʃɪklɪç], *adj.* unbecoming, indecent, improper, unseemly.

**unschlüssig** [ˈunʃlysɪç], *adj.* irresolute, undecided.

**Unschuld** [ˈunʃult], *f.* (—, *no pl.*) innocence; *verfolgte* —, injured innocence.

**unschuldig** [ˈunʃuldɪç], *adj.* innocent, guiltless; chaste; —*es Vergnügen*, harmless pleasure.

**unschwer** [ˈunʃveːr], *adv.* easily.

**Unsegen** [ˈunzeːgən], *m.* (—s, *no pl.*) misfortune; curse.

**unselbständig** [ˈunzɛlpʃtɛndɪç], *adj.* dependent.

**unselig** [ˈunzeːlɪç], *adj.* unfortunate, luckless, fatal.

**unser** [ˈunzər], *poss. adj.* our. — *pers. pron.* of us.

**unsereiner** [ˈunzəraɪnər], *pron.* s.o. in our position; one of us, people in our position.

**unserthalben, unsertwegen** [ˈunzərthalbən, unzərtveːgən], *adv.* for our sake, on our account.

**unsertwillen** [ˈunzərtvɪlən], *adv. um —*, for our sake, on our account.

**unsicher** [ˈunzɪçər], *adj.* unsafe; uncertain, doubtful; (*route*) precarious; (*hand*) unsteady; (*legs*) shaky.

**unsichtbar** [ˈunzɪçtbaːr], *adj.* invisible.

**Unsinn** [ˈunzɪn], *m.* (—s, *no pl.*) nonsense.

**unsinnig** [ˈunzɪnɪç], *adj.* nonsensical; mad, insane.

**Unsitte** [ˈunzɪtə], *f.* (—, *pl.* —n) abuse, nuisance; bad habit.

**unsittlich** [ˈunzɪtlɪç], *adj.* immoral.

**unstät, unstet** [ˈunʃteːt, ˈunʃteːt], *adj.* unsteady, inconstant; restless.

**unstatthaft** [ˈunʃtathaft], *adj.* illicit.

**unsterblich** [ˈunʃtɛrplɪç], *adj.* immortal.

**Unsterblichkeit** [ˈunʃtɛrplɪçkaɪt], *f.* (—, *no pl.*) immortality.

**unstillbar** [ˈunʃtɪlbaːr], *adj.* unappeasable, unquenchable.

**unstreitig** [ˈunʃtraɪtɪç], *adj.* indisputable, unquestionable.

**Unsumme** [ˈunzuməə], *f.* (—, *pl.* —n) vast amount (of money).

**unsympathisch** [ˈunzympaˈtɪʃ], *adj.* uncongenial, disagreeable; *er ist mir* —; I dislike him.

**untadelhaft, untadelig** [ˈuntaːdəlhaft, ˈuntaːdəlɪç], *adj.* blameless, irreproachable, unimpeachable.

**Untat** [ˈuntaːt], *f.* (—, *pl.* —en) misdeed, crime.

**untätig** [ˈunteːtɪç], *adj.* inactive, idle, supine.

**untauglich** [ˈuntauklɪç], *adj.* unfit, useless; incompetent; (*Mil.*) disabled.

**unteilbar** [ˈunˈtaɪlbaːr], *adj.* indivisible.

**unten** ['untən], *adv.* below, beneath; (*house*) downstairs.
**unter** ['untər], *prep.* (*Dat.*, *Acc.*) under, beneath, below, among, between.
**Unterbau** ['untərbau], *m.* (—**s**, *pl.* —**ten**) substructure, foundation.
**Unterbewußtsein** ['untərbəvustzaɪn], *n.* (—**s**, *no pl.*) subconscious mind, subconsciousness.
**unterbieten** [untər'bi:tən], *v.a. irr. insep.* underbid, undersell.
**Unterbilanz** ['untərbilants], *f.* (—, *pl.* —**en**) deficit.
**unterbinden** [untər'bɪndən], *v.a. irr. insep.* tie up, bind up; (*fig.*) prevent, check.
**unterbleiben** [untər'blaɪbən], *v.n. irr. insep.* (*aux.* sein) remain undone, be left undone, cease.
**unterbrechen** [untər'brɛçən], *v.a. irr. insep.* interrupt; (*journey*) break; (*speech*) cut short.
**Unterbrechung** [untər'brɛçuŋ], *f.* (—, *pl.* —**en**) interruption.
**unterbreiten** (1) ['untərbraɪtən], *v.a.* spread under.
**unterbreiten** (2) [untər'braɪtən], *v.a. insep.* submit, lay before.
**unterbringen** ['untərbrɪŋən], *v.a. irr.* provide (*a place*) for; (*goods*) dispose of; (*money*) invest; (*people*) accommodate, put up.
**Unterbringung** ['untərbrɪŋuŋ], *f.* (—, *no pl.*) provision for; (*goods*) disposal of; (*money*) investment; (*people*) accommodation.
**unterdessen** [untər'dɛsən], *adv.*, *conj.* in the meantime, meanwhile.
**unterdrücken** [untər'drykən], *v.a. insep.* suppress, curb, check; oppress.
**Unterdrückung** [untər'drykuŋ], *f.* (—, *no pl.*) oppression, suppression.
**untereinander** [untəraɪn'andər], *adv.* with each other, mutually, among themselves.
**unterfangen** [untər'faŋən], *v.r. irr. insep.* *sich* —, dare, venture, presume.
**Untergang** ['untərgaŋ], *m.* (—**s**, *pl.* ⸚**e**) (*sun*) setting; (*ship*) sinking; (*fig.*) decline.
**untergeben** [untər'ge:bən], *adj.* subject, subordinate.
**Untergebene** [untər'ge:bənə], *m.* (—**n**, *pl.* —**n**) subordinate.
**untergehen** ['untərge:ən], *v.n. irr.* (*aux.* sein) (*sun*) go down, set; (*ship*) sink; (*fig.*) perish; decline.
**Untergeschoß** ['untərgəʃɔs], *n.* (—**sses**, *pl.* —**sse**) ground floor.
**Untergestell** ['untərgəʃtɛl], *n.* (—**s**, *pl.* —**e**) undercarriage, chassis.
**untergraben** [untər'gra:bən], *v.a. irr. insep.* undermine.
**unterhalb** ['untərhalp], *prep.* (*Genit.*) below, under.
**Unterhalt** ['untərhalt], *m.* (—**s**, *no pl.*) maintenance, support, livelihood.
**unterhalten** (1) ['untərhaltən], *v.a. irr.* hold under.
**unterhalten** (2) [untər'haltən], *v.a. irr. insep.* maintain, keep, support; entertain. — *v.r. sich* —, converse, make conversation; *sich gut* —, enjoy o.s.
**unterhaltend** [untər'haltənt], *adj.* entertaining, amusing, lively.
**Unterhaltskosten** ['untərhaltskɔstən], *f. pl.* maintenance; (*house*) cost of repairs.
**Unterhaltung** [untər'haltuŋ], *f.* (—, *pl.* —**en**) maintenance; conversation; amusement, entertainment.
**Unterhaltungslektüre** [untər'haltuŋslɛkty:rə], *f.* (—, *no pl.*) light reading, fiction.
**unterhandeln** [untər'handəln], *v.n. insep.* negotiate.
**Unterhändler** ['untərhɛndlər], *m.* (—**s**, *pl.* —) negotiator, mediator.
**Unterhandlung** [untər'handluŋ], *f.* (—, *pl.* —**en**) negotiation.
**Unterhaus** ['untərhaus], *n.* (—**es**, *pl.* ⸚**er**) ground floor; (*Parl.*) lower house; House of Commons.
**Unterhemd** ['untərhɛmt], *n.* (—(**e**)**s**, *pl.* —**en**) vest.
**unterhöhlen** [untər'hø:lən], *v.a. insep.* undermine.
**Unterholz** ['untərhɔlts], *n.* (—**es**, *no pl.*) undergrowth, underwood.
**Unterhosen** ['untərho:zən], *f. pl.* (*women*) briefs; (*men*) underpants.
**unterirdisch** ['untərɪrdɪʃ], *adj.* subterranean, underground.
**unterjochen** [untər'jɔxən], *v.a. insep.* subjugate, subdue.
**Unterkiefer** ['untərki:fər], *m.* (—**s**, *pl.* —) lower jaw.
**Unterkleid** ['untərklaɪt], *n.* (—**s**, *pl.* —**er**) under-garment.
**unterkommen** ['untərkɔmən], *v.n. irr.* (*aux.* sein) find accommodation *or* shelter; (*fig.*) find employment.
**Unterkommen** ['untərkɔmən], *n.* (—**s**, *no pl.*) shelter, accommodation; (*fig.*) employment, place.
**Unterkörper** ['untərkœrpər], *m.* (—**s**, *pl.* —) lower part of the body.
**unterkriegen** ['untərkri:gən], *v.a.* get the better of; *lass dich nicht* —, stand firm.
**Unterkunft** ['untərkunft], *f.* (—, *pl.* ⸚**e**) shelter, accommodation; employment.
**Unterlage** ['untərla:gə], *f.* (—, *pl.* —**n**) foundation, base; blotting pad; (*pl.*) documents, files.
**unterlassen** [untər'lasən], *v.a. irr. insep.* omit (to do), fail (to do), neglect; forbear.
**Unterlassung** [untər'lasuŋ], *f.* (—, *pl.* —**en**) omission, neglect.
**Unterlassungssünde** [untər'lasuŋszyndə], *f.* (—, *pl.* —**n**) sin of omission.
**Unterlauf** ['untərlauf], *m.* (—(**e**)**s**, *pl.* ⸚**e**) (*river*) lower course.

# Unterlaufen

unterlaufen [untər'laufən], *v.n. irr. insep. (aux.* sein) run under; *(mistake)* creep in. — *adj.* suffused, blood-shot.

unterlegen (1) ['untərle:gən], *v.a.* lay under; *einen anderen Sinn —,* put a different construction upon.

unterlegen (2) [untər'le:gən], *adj.* inferior.

Unterleib ['untərlaip], *m.* (—s, *no pl.*) abdomen.

unterliegen [untər'li:gən], *v.n. irr. insep. (aux.* sein) succumb, be overcome; be subject (to).

Untermieter ['untərmi:tər], *m.* (—s, *pl.* —) subtenant.

unterminieren [untərmi'ni:rən], *v.a. insep.* undermine.

unternehmen [untər'ne:mən], *v.a. irr. insep.* undertake, take upon o.s., attempt.

Unternehmen [untər'ne:mən], *n.* (—s, *pl.* —) enterprise, undertaking.

unternehmend [untər'ne:mənt], *adj.* bold, enterprising.

Unternehmer [untər'ne:mər], *m.* (—s, *pl.* —) contractor, entrepreneur.

Unteroffizier ['untərɔfitsi:r], *m.* (—s, *pl.* —e) *(army)* non-commissioned officer; *(navy)* petty officer.

unterordnen ['untərɔrdnən], *v.a.* subordinate. — *v.r. sich —,* submit (to).

Unterordnung ['untərɔrdnuŋ], *f.* (—, *no pl.*) subordination, submission; (Biol.) sub-order.

Unterpacht ['untərpaxt], *f.* (—, *no pl.*) sublease.

Unterpfand ['untərpfant], *n.* (—(e)s, *no pl.*) *(obs.)* pawn, pledge.

Unterredung [untər're:duŋ], *f.* (—, *pl.* —en) conference, interview, talk.

Unterricht ['untərrɪçt], *m.* (—(e)s, *no pl.*) instruction, tuition, teaching.

unterrichten [untər'rɪçtən], *v.a. insep.* instruct, teach.

Unterrichtsanstalt ['untərrɪçtsanʃtalt], *f.* (—, *pl.* —en) educational establishment *or* institution.

Unterrichtsgegenstand ['untərrɪçtsge:gənʃtant], *m.* (—s, *pl.* ¨e) subject of instruction.

Unterrock ['untərrɔk], *m.* (—s, *pl.* ¨e) petticoat, slip; underskirt.

untersagen [untər'za:gən], *v.a. insep.* forbid; *Rauchen untersagt,* smoking prohibited.

Untersatz ['untərzats], *m.* (—es, *pl.* ¨e) basis, holder, stand, trestle; saucer.

unterschätzen [untər'ʃɛtsən], *v.a. insep.* underrate, underestimate.

unterscheiden [untər'ʃaidən], *v.a. irr. insep.* distinguish, discriminate, discern, differentiate. — *v.r. sich —,* differ; *ich kann sie nicht —,* I cannot tell them apart.

Unterscheidung [untər'ʃaiduŋ], *f.* (—, *pl.* —en) distinction, differentiation.

Unterscheidungsmerkmal [untər-'ʃaiduŋsmɛrkma:l], *n.* (—s, *pl.* —e) distinctive mark, characteristic.

Unterscheidungsvermögen [untər-'ʃaiduŋsfɛrmø:gən], *n.* (—s, *no pl.*) power of discrimination.

Unterscheidungszeichen [untər'ʃaiduŋstsaiçən], *n.* (—s, *pl.* —) criterion.

Unterschenkel [untər'ʃɛŋkəl], *m.* (—s, *pl.* —) shank, lower part of the thigh.

Unterschicht [untər'ʃɪçt], *f.* (—, *pl.* —en) substratum, subsoil.

unterschieben (1) ['untərʃi:bən], *v.a. irr.* substitute; interpolate; forge; foist upon.

unterschieben (2) [untər'ʃi:bən], *v.a. irr. insep. (fig.)* attribute falsely, pass s.o. off as.

Unterschiebung [untər'ʃi:buŋ], *f.* (—, *pl.* —en) substitution; forgery.

Unterschied ['untərʃi:t], *m.* (—(e)s, *pl.* —e) difference.

unterschiedlich ['untərʃi:tlɪç], *adj.* different, diverse.

unterschiedslos ['untərʃi:tslo:s], *adv.* indiscriminately.

unterschlagen [untər'ʃla:gən], *v.a. irr. insep.* embezzle, intercept.

Unterschlagung [untər'ʃla:guŋ], *f.* (—, *pl.* —en) embezzlement.

Unterschlupf ['untərʃlupf], *m.* (—es, *pl.* ¨e) shelter, refuge.

unterschlüpfen ['untərʃlypfən], *v.n. (aux.* sein) find shelter, slip away; *(fig.)* hide.

unterschreiben [untər'ʃraibən], *v.a. irr. insep.* sign, subscribe to.

Unterschrift [untər'ʃrɪft], *f.* (—, *pl.* —en) signature.

Unterseeboot [untərze:bo:t], *n.* (—s, *pl.* —e) submarine.

untersetzt [untər'zɛtst], *adj.* thickset, dumpy.

untersinken ['untərzɪŋkən], *v.n. irr. (aux.* sein) go down.

unterst ['untərst], *adj.* lowest, undermost, bottom.

Unterstaatssekretär [untər'ʃta:tszekrete:r], *m.* (—s, *pl.* —e) under-secretary of state.

unterstehen (1) ['untərʃte:ən], *v.n. irr. (aux.* sein) find shelter (under).

unterstehen (2) [untər'ʃte:ən], *v.n. irr. insep.* be subordinate. — *v.r. sich —,* dare, venture.

unterstellen (1) ['untərʃtɛlən], *v.a.* place under. — *v.r. sich —,* take shelter (under).

unterstellen (2) [untər'ʃtɛlən], *v.a. insep.* put under the authority of; impute (s.th. to s.o.).

Unterstellung [untər'ʃtɛluŋ], *f.* (—, *pl.* —en) imputation, insinuation.

unterstreichen [untər'ʃtraiçən], *v.a. irr. insep.* underline.

Unterstreichung [untər'ʃtraiçuŋ], *f.* (—, *pl.* —en) underlining.

Unterströmung [untər'ʃtrø:muŋ], *f.* (—, *pl.* —en) undercurrent.

unterstützen [untər'ʃtytsən], *v.a. insep.* support, assist, aid; *(fig.)* countenance.

**Unterstützung** [untər'ʃtytsuŋ], f. (—, pl. —en) support, aid, assistance, relief.
**Unterstützungsanstalt**[untər'ʃtytsuŋs-anʃtalt], f. (—, pl. —en) charitable institution.
**unterstützungsbedürftig** [untər'ʃtyt-suŋsbədyrftɪç], adj. indigent.
**untersuchen** [untər'zu:xən], v.a. insep. investigate, examine, look over.
**Untersuchung** [untər'zu:xuŋ], f. (—, pl. —en) investigation, inquiry; (medical) examination.
**Untersuchungshaft** [untər'zu:xuŋs-haft], f. (—, no pl.) imprisonment pending investigation.
**Untersuchungsrichter** [untər'zu:-xuŋsrɪçtər], m. (—s, pl. —) examining magistrate.
**Untertan** ['untərta:n], m. (—s, pl. —en) subject, vassal.
**untertan** ['untərta:n], adj. subject.
**untertänig** ['untərte:nɪç], adj. humble, obsequious, submissive, servile.
**Untertasse** ['untərtasə], f. (—, pl. —n) saucer.
**untertauchen** ['untərtauxən], v.a. dip, duck, submerge. — v.n. (aux. sein) dive.
**unterwegs** [untər've:ks], adv. on the way.
**unterweisen** [untər'vaizən], v.a. irr. insep. teach, instruct.
**Unterweisung** [untər'vaizuŋ], f. (—, pl. —en) instruction, teaching.
**Unterwelt** ['untərvelt], f. (—, no pl.) Hades, the underworld.
**unterwerfen** [untər'verfən], v.a. irr. insep. subject, subdue. — v.r. sich —, submit (to), resign o.s. (to).
**Unterwerfung** [untər'verfuŋ], f. (—, no pl.) subjection, submission.
**unterwühlen** [untər'vy:lən], v.a. insep. root up; (fig.) undermine.
**unterwürfig** [untər'vyrfɪç], adj. submissive, subject; obsequious.
**Unterwürfigkeit** [untər'vyrfɪçkait], f. (—, no pl.) submissiveness; obsequiousness.
**unterzeichnen** [untər'tsaiçnən], v.a. insep. sign.
**Unterzeichner** [untər'tsaiçnər], m. (—s, pl. —) signatory; (insurance) underwriter.
**Unterzeichnete** [untər'tsaiçnətə], m. (—n, pl. —n) undersigned.
**Unterzeichnung** [untər'tsaiçnuŋ], f. (—, pl. —en) signature.
**unterziehen** [untər'tsi:ən], v.r. irr. insep. sich —, submit to, undertake; (operation) undergo.
**Untiefe** ['unti:fə], f. (—, pl. —n) shallow water, flat, shoal, sands.
**Untier** ['unti:r], n. (—s, pl. —e) monster.
**untilgbar** ['untɪlkba:r], adj. indelible; (debt) irredeemable.
**untrennbar** ['untrenba:r], adj. inseparable.
**untreu** ['untrɔy], adj. faithless, unfaithful, disloyal, perfidious.

**Untreue** ['untrɔyə], f. (—, no pl.) faithlessness, unfaithfulness, disloyalty, perfidy.
**untröstlich** ['untrø:stlɪç], adj. inconsolable, disconsolate.
**untrüglich** ['untry:klɪç], adj. unmistakable, infallible.
**untüchtig** ['untyçtɪç], adj. inefficient; incompetent.
**unüberlegt** ['uny:bərle:kt], adj. inconsiderate, thoughtless; rash.
**unübersehbar** ['uny:bərze:ba:r], adj. immense, vast.
**unübersteiglich** ['uny:bərʃtaiklɪç], adj. insurmountable.
**unübertrefflich** ['uny:bərtreflɪç], adj. unsurpassable, unequalled, unrivalled.
**unübertroffen** ['uny:bərtrɔfən], adj. unsurpassed.
**unüberwindlich** ['uny:bərvɪntlɪç], adj. invincible, unconquerable.
**unumgänglich** ['unumgeŋlɪç], adj. indispensable, unavoidable, inevitable.
**unumschränkt** ['unumʃreŋkt], adj. unlimited, absolute.
**unumstößlich** ['unumʃtø:slɪç], adj. irrefutable.
**unumwunden** ['unumvundən], adj. frank, plain.
**ununterbrochen** ['ununtərbrɔxən], adj. uninterrupted, unremitting.
**unveränderlich** ['unferendərlɪç], adj. unchangeable, unalterable.
**unverändert** ['unferendərt], adj. unchanged, unaltered.
**unverantwortlich** ['unferantvortlɪç], adj. irresponsible, inexcusable, unjustifiable.
**unveräußerlich** ['unferɔysərlɪç], adj. not for sale; inalienable.
**unverbesserlich** ['unferbesərlɪç], adj. incorrigible.
**unverbindlich** ['unferbɪntlɪç], adj. not binding, without prejudice, without obligation.
**unverblümt** ['unferblymt], adj. blunt, point-blank.
**unverbrennlich** ['unferbrenlɪç], adj. incombustible.
**unverbrüchlich** ['unferbryçlɪç], adj. inviolable.
**unverbürgt** ['unferbyrkt], adj. unwarranted, unofficial; unconfirmed.
**unverdaulich** ['unferdaulɪç], adj. indigestible.
**unverdaut** ['unferdaut], adj. undigested.
**unverdient** ['unferdi:nt], adj. unmerited, undeserved.
**unverdientermaßen** ['unferdi:ntərma:sən], adv. undeservedly.
**unverdorben** ['unferdɔrbən], adj. unspoiled, uncorrupted, innocent.
**unverdrossen** ['unferdrɔsən], adj. indefatigable.
**unvereidigt** ['unferaidɪçt], adj. unsworn.
**unvereinbar** ['unferainba:r], adj. incompatible, inconsistent.

# Unvereinbarkeit

**Unvereinbarkeit** ['unfɛraɪnba:rkaɪt], *f.* (—, *no pl.*) incompatibility, inconsistency.

**unverfälscht** ['unfɛrfɛlʃt], *adj.* unadulterated, genuine, pure.

**unverfänglich** ['unfɛrfɛŋlɪç], *adj.* harmless.

**unverfroren** ['unfɛrfro:rən], *adj.* cheeky, impudent.

**unvergeßlich** ['unfɛrgɛslɪç], *adj.* memorable, not to be forgotten, unforgettable.

**unvergleichlich** ['unfɛrglaɪçlɪç], *adj.* incomparable.

**unverhältnismäßig** ['unfɛrhɛltnɪsmɛ:sɪç], *adj.* disproportionate.

**unverheiratet** ['unfɛrhaɪra:tət], *adj.* unmarried.

**unverhofft** ['unfɛrhɔft], *adj.* unexpected.

**unverhohlen** ['unfɛrho:lən], *adj.* unconcealed, undisguised, candid.

**unverkennbar** ['unfɛrkɛnba:r], *adj.* unmistakable.

**unverlangt** ['unfɛrlaŋkt], *adj.* unsolicited, not ordered.

**unverletzlich** ['unfɛrlɛtslɪç], *adj.* invulnerable; (*fig.*) inviolable.

**unverletzt** ['unfɛrlɛtst], *adj.* (*persons*) unhurt; (*things*) undamaged, intact.

**unvermeidlich** ['unfɛrmaɪtlɪç], *adj.* inevitable, unavoidable.

**unvermindert** ['unfɛrmɪndərt], *adj.* undiminished.

**unvermittelt** ['unfɛrmɪtəlt], *adj.* sudden, abrupt.

**Unvermögen** ['unfɛrmø:gən], *n.* (—s, *no pl.*) inability, incapacity.

**unvermögend** ['unfɛrmø:gənt], *adj.* incapable; impecunious.

**unvermutet** ['unfɛrmu:tət], *adj.* unexpected, unforeseen.

**unverrichtet** ['unfɛrrɪçtət], *adj.* —er *Sache*, empty-handed; unsuccessfully.

**unverschämt** ['unfɛrʃɛ:mt], *adj.* impudent, brazen.

**unverschuldet** ['unfɛrʃuldət], *adj.* not in debt, unencumbered; (*fig.*) undeserved.

**unversehens** ['unfɛrze:əns], *adv.* unexpectedly, unawares.

**unversehrt** ['unfɛrze:rt], *adv.* (*persons*) unhurt, safe; (*things*) undamaged.

**unversiegbar** ['unfɛrzi:kba:r], *adj.* inexhaustible.

**unversiegt** ['unfɛrzi:kt], *adj.* unexhausted.

**unversöhnlich** ['unfɛrzø:nlɪç], *adj.* implacable, irreconcilable.

**unversöhnt** ['unfɛrzø:nt], *adj.* unreconciled.

**unversorgt** ['unfɛrzɔrkt], *adj.* unprovided for.

**Unverstand** ['unfɛrʃtant], *m.* (—(e)s, *no pl.*) want of judgment, indiscretion.

**unverständig** ['unfɛrʃtɛndɪç], *adj.* foolish, unwise, imprudent.

**unverständlich** ['unfɛrʃtɛntlɪç], *adj.* unintelligible, incomprehensible.

**unversteuert** ['unfɛrʃtɔyərt], *adj.* with duty *or* tax unpaid.

**unversucht** ['unfɛrzu:xt], *adj.* untried; *nichts — lassen*, leave no stone unturned.

**unverträglich** ['unfɛrtrɛ:klɪç], *adj.* quarrelsome.

**unverwandt** ['unfɛrvant], *adj.* unrelated; fixed, constant; immovable.

**unverwundbar** ['unfɛrvuntba:r], *adj.* invulnerable.

**unverwüstlich** ['unfɛrvy:stlɪç], *adj.* indestructible.

**unverzagt** ['unfɛrtsa:kt], *adj.* undaunted, intrepid.

**unverzeihlich** ['unfɛrtsaɪlɪç], *adj.* unpardonable.

**unverzinslich** ['unfɛrtsɪnslɪç], *adj.* (*money*) gaining no interest.

**unverzollt** ['unfɛrtsɔlt], *adj.* duty unpaid.

**unverzüglich** ['unfɛrtsy:klɪç], *adj.* immediate.

**unvollendet** ['unfɔlɛndət], *adj.* unfinished.

**unvollständig** ['unfɔlʃtɛndɪç], *adj.* incomplete.

**unvorbereitet** ['unfo:rbəraɪtət], *adj.* unprepared.

**unvordenklich** ['unfo:rdɛŋklɪç], *adj.* *seit —en Zeiten*, from time immemorial.

**unvorhergesehen** ['unfo:rhe:rgəze:ən], *adj.* unforeseen, unlooked for.

**unvorsichtig** ['unfo:rzɪçtɪç], *adj.* imprudent, incautious, careless.

**unvorteilhaft** ['unfo:rtaɪlhaft], *adj.* unprofitable, disadvantageous; *— aussehen*, not look o.'s best.

**unwägbar** ['unvɛ:kba:r], *adj.* imponderable.

**unwahr** ['unva:r], *adj.* untrue, false.

**Unwahrhaftigkeit** ['unva:rhaftɪçkaɪt], *f.* (—, *no pl.*) want of truthfulness, unreliability, dishonesty.

**Unwahrheit** ['unva:rhaɪt], *f.* (—, *pl.* —en) lie, untruth, falsehood.

**unwegsam** ['unve:kza:m], *adj.* impassable, impracticable.

**unweigerlich** ['unvaɪgərlɪç], *adj.* unhesitating, unquestioning. *— adv.* without fail.

**unweit** ['unvaɪt], *prep.* (*Genit.*) not far from, near.

**Unwesen** ['unve:zən], *n.* (—s, *no pl.*) nuisance; *sein — treiben*, be up to o.'s tricks.

**Unwetter** ['unvɛtər], *n.* (—s, *pl.* —) bad weather, thunderstorm.

**unwichtig** ['unvɪçtɪç], *adj.* unimportant; insignificant, of no consequence.

**unwiderleglich** ['unvi:dərle:klɪç], *adj.* irrefutable.

**unwiderruflich** ['unvi:dərru:flɪç], *adj.* irrevocable.

**unwidersprechlich** ['unvi:dərʃprɛçlɪç], *adj.* incontestable.

**unwidersprochen** ['unvi:dərʃprɔxən], *adj.* uncontradicted.

unwiderstehlich [ˈunviːdərʃteˈliç], adj. irresistible.
unwiederbringlich [ˈunviːdərbrɪŋliç], adj. irrecoverable, irretrievable.
Unwille [ˈunvɪlə], m. (—ns, no pl.) displeasure, indignation.
unwillkürlich [ˈunvɪlkyːrliç], adj. involuntary; instinctive.
unwirsch [ˈunvɪrʃ], adj. petulant, testy; curt, uncivil.
unwirtlich [ˈunvɪrtliç], adj. inhospitable.
unwirtschaftlich [ˈunvɪrtʃaftliç], adj. not economic, uneconomic.
unwissend [ˈunvɪsənt], adj. illiterate, ignorant.
Unwissenheit [ˈunvɪsənhaɪt], f. (—, no pl.) ignorance.
unwissenschaftlich [ˈunvɪsənʃaftliç], adj. unscholarly; unscientific.
unwissentlich [ˈunvɪsəntliç], adv. unknowingly, unconsciously.
unwohl [ˈunvoːl], adj. unwell, indisposed.
Unwohlsein [ˈunvoːlzaɪn], n. (—s, no pl.) indisposition.
unwürdig [ˈunvyrdiç], adj. unworthy, undeserving.
Unzahl [ˈuntsaːl], f. (—, no pl.) vast number.
unzählbar [unˈtseːlbaːr], adj. innumerable, numberless.
unzählig [unˈtseːliç], adj. innumerable; —e Male, over and over again.
unzart [ˈuntsaːrt], adj. indelicate, rude, rough; unceremonious.
Unzeit [ˈuntsaɪt], f. (—, no pl.) zur —, out of season, inopportune.
unzeitgemäß [ˈuntsaɪtgəmeːs], adj. out of date, behind the times; unfashionable.
unzeitig [ˈuntsaɪtiç], adj. unseasonable; untimely, inopportune.
unziemlich [ˈuntsiːmliç], adj. unseemly, unbecoming.
Unzier [ˈuntsiːr], f. (—, no pl.) disfigurement; flaw.
Unzucht [ˈuntsuxt], f. (—, no pl.) unchastity; lewdness; fornication.
unzüchtig [ˈuntsyçtiç], adj. unchaste, lascivious, lewd.
unzufrieden [ˈuntsufriːdən], adj. discontented, dissatisfied.
unzugänglich [ˈuntsugeŋliç], adj. inaccessible.
unzulänglich [ˈuntsuleŋliç], adj. inadequate, insufficient.
Unzulänglichkeit [ˈuntsuleŋliçkaɪt], f. (—, no pl.) inadequacy.
unzulässig [ˈuntsulesiç], adj. inadmissible.
unzurechnungsfähig [ˈuntsureçnuŋsfeːiç], adj. not accountable (for o.'s actions), non compos mentis, insane.
Unzurechnungsfähigkeit [ˈuntsureçnuŋsfeːiçkaɪt], f. (—, no pl.) irresponsibility; feeblemindedness.
unzusammenhängend [ˈuntsuzamənheŋənt], adj. incoherent.
unzuständig [ˈuntsuʃtendiç], adj. incompetent, not competent (Law etc.).

unzuträglich [ˈuntsutreːkliç], adj. unwholesome.
unzutreffend [ˈuntsutrefənt], adj. inapposite; unfounded; inapplicable.
unzuverlässig [ˈuntsufɛrlesiç], adj. unreliable.
unzweckmäßig [ˈuntsvɛkmeːsiç], adj. inexpedient.
unzweideutig [ˈuntsvaɪdɔytiç], adj. unequivocal, explicit, unambiguous.
üppig [ˈypiç], adj. abundant; opulent, luxurious, luxuriant, voluptuous.
uralt [ˈuːralt], adj. very old, old as the hills; ancient.
uranfänglich [ˈuːranfeŋliç], adj. primordial, primeval.
Uraufführung [ˈuːrauffyːruŋ], f. (—, pl. —en) (Theat.) first night, première.
urbar [ˈuːrbaːr], adj. arable, under cultivation; — machen, cultivate.
Urbarmachung [ˈuːrbaːrmaxuŋ], f. (—, no pl.) cultivation.
Urbild [ˈuːrbɪlt], n. (—(e)s, pl. —er) prototype; (fig.) ideal.
ureigen [ˈuːraɪgən], adj. quite original; idiosyncratic.
Ureltern [ˈuːrɛltərn], pl. ancestors.
Urenkel [ˈuːrɛŋkəl], m. (—s, pl. —) great-grandson, great-grandchild.
Urenkelin [ˈuːrɛŋkəlɪn], f. (—, pl. —nen) great-granddaughter.
Urfehde [ˈuːrfeːdə], f. (—, no pl.) oath to keep the peace.
Urform [ˈuːrfɔrm], f. (—, pl. —en) primitive form; original form; archetype.
Urgroßmutter [ˈuːrgroːsmutər], f. (—, pl. ⸚) great-grandmother.
Urgroßvater [ˈuːrgroːsfaːtər], m. (—s, pl. ⸚) great-grandfather.
Urheber [ˈuːrheːbər], m. (—s, pl. —) author, originator.
Urheberrecht [ˈuːrheːbərreçt], n. (—s, pl. —e) copyright.
Urheberschaft [ˈuːrheːbərʃaft], f. (—, no pl.) authorship.
Urin [uˈriːn], m. (—s, no pl.) urine.
Urkunde [ˈuːrkundə], f. (—, pl. —n) document, deed, charter; zur — dessen, (obs.) in witness whereof.
Urkundenbeweis [ˈuːrkundənbəvaɪs], m. (—es, pl. —e) documentary evidence.
urkundlich [ˈuːrkuntliç], adj. documentary.
Urlaub [ˈuːrlaup], m. (—s, pl. —e) leave of absence; vacation; (Mil.) furlough.
urplötzlich [ˈuːrplœtsliç], adj. sudden. — adv. all at once, suddenly.
Urquell [ˈuːrkvɛl], m. (—s, pl. —en) fountain-head, original source.
Ursache [ˈuːrzaxə], f. (—, pl. —n) cause; keine —, don't mention it.
Urschrift [ˈuːrʃrɪft], f. (—, pl. —en) original text.
Ursprache [ˈuːrʃpraːxə], f. (—, pl. —n) original language.
Ursprung [ˈuːrʃpruŋ], m. (—s, pl. ⸚e) origin; extraction.

**ursprünglich** [ˈuːrʃpryŋlɪç], *adj.* original.

**Urteil** [ˈurtaɪl], *n.* (**—s,** *pl.* **—e**) opinion; (*Law*) judgment, verdict, sentence; *ein — fällen,* pass judgment on; *nach meinem —,* in my opinion.

**urteilen** [ˈurtaɪlən], *v.n.* judge.

**Urteilsspruch** [ˈurtaɪlsʃprux], *m.* (**—s,** *pl.* **⸚e**) judgment, sentence.

**Uruguay** [uruˈgwaːɪ], *n.* Uruguay.

**Urureltern** [ˈuːruːrɛltərn], *pl.* ancestors.

**Urvater** [ˈuːrfaːtər], *m.* (**—s,** *pl.* **⸚**) forefather.

**Urvolk** [ˈuːrfɔlk], *n.* (**—(e)s,** *pl.* **⸚er**) primitive people, aborigines.

**Urwald** [ˈuːrvalt], *m.* (**—(e)s,** *pl.* **⸚er**) primæval forest, virgin forest.

**Urwelt** [ˈuːrvɛlt], *f.* (**—,** *no pl.*) primæval world.

**Urzeit** [ˈuːrtsaɪt], *f.* (**—,** *pl.* **—en**) prehistoric times.

# V

**V** [fau], *n.* (**—s,** *pl.* **—s**) the letter V.

**vag** [va:k], *adj.* vague.

**Vagabund** [vagaˈbunt], *m.* (**—en,** *pl.* **—en**) vagabond, tramp; (*Am.*) hobo.

**Vakuumbremse** [ˈva:kuumbrɛmzə], *f.* (**—,** *pl.* **—n**) air-brake, vacuum-brake.

**Vase** [ˈva:zə], *f.* (**—,** *pl.* **—n**) vase.

**Vater** [ˈfa:tər], *m.* (**—s,** *pl.* **⸚**) father.

**Vaterland** [ˈfa:tərlant], *n.* (**—(e)s,** *pl.* **⸚er**) mother-country, native country; **—sliebe,** patriotism.

**vaterländisch** [ˈfa:tərlɛndɪʃ], *adj.* patriotic.

**vaterlandslos** [ˈfa:tərlantslo:s], *adj.* having no mother country; unpatriotic.

**väterlich** [ˈfɛ:tərlɪç], *adj.* fatherly, paternal. — *adv.* like a father.

**vaterlos** [ˈfa:tərlo:s], *adj.* fatherless.

**Vatermord** [ˈfa:tərmɔrt], *m.* (**—(e)s,** *pl.* **—e**) parricide; patricide.

**Vatermörder** [ˈfa:tərmœrdər], *m.* (**—s,** *pl.* **—**) parricide; (*fig.*) high *or* stand-up collar.

**Vaterschaft** [ˈfa:tərʃaft], *f.* (**—,** *no pl.*) paternity.

**Vatersname** [ˈfa:tərsna:mə], *m.* (**—ns,** *pl.* **—n**) surname, family name.

**Vaterstadt** [ˈfa:tərʃtat], *f.* (**—,** *pl.* **⸚e**) native town.

**Vaterstelle** [ˈfa:tərʃtɛlə], *f.* (**—,** *pl.* **—n**) — *vertreten,* act as a father, be a father (to).

**Vaterunser** [fa:tərˈunzər], *n.* (**—s,** *pl.* **—n**) Lord's Prayer.

**Vatikan** [vatiˈka:n], *m.* (**—s,** *no pl.*) Vatican.

**vegetieren** [vegeˈti:rən], *v.n.* vegetate.

**Veilchen** [ˈfaɪlçən], *n.* (**—s,** *pl.* **—**) (*Bot.*) violet.

**Vene** [ˈve:nə], *f.* (**—,** *pl.* **—n**) vein.

**Venezuela** [vɛnətsuˈe:la], *n.* Venezuela.

**Ventil** [vɛnˈti:l], *n.* (**—s,** *pl.* **—e**) valve.

**ventilieren** [vɛntiˈli:rən], *v.a.* ventilate, air; (*fig.*) discuss, ventilate.

**verabfolgen** [fɛrˈapfɔlgən], *v.a.* deliver, hand over, remit; serve.

**Verabfolgung** [fɛrˈapfɔlguŋ], *f.* (**—,** *no pl.*) delivery.

**verabreden** [fɛrˈapre:dən], *v.a.* agree (upon); stipulate; *etwas mit einem —,* agree on s.th. with s.o. — *v.r. sich mit einem —,* make an appointment with s.o.; (*coll.*) have a date.

**Verabredung** [fɛrˈapre:duŋ], *f.* (**—,** *pl.* **—en**) agreement, arrangement, appointment; (*coll.*) date.

**verabreichen** [fɛrˈapraɪçən], *v.a.* deliver, dispense.

**verabsäumen** [fɛrˈapzɔymən], *v.a.* neglect, omit.

**verabscheuen** [fɛrˈapʃɔyən], *v.a.* detest, loathe, abhor.

**Verabscheuung** [fɛrˈapʃɔyuŋ], *f.* (**—,** *no pl.*) abhorrence, detestation, loathing.

**verabscheuungswürdig** [fɛrˈapʃɔyuŋsvyrdɪç], *adj.* abominable, detestable.

**verabschieden** [fɛrˈapʃi:dən], *v.a.* dismiss, discharge. — *v.r. sich —,* take leave, say good-bye; (*Pol.*) pass (of an Act).

**Verabschiedung** [fɛrˈapʃi:duŋ], *f.* (**—,** *no pl.*) dismissal; discharge; (*Pol.*) passing (of an Act).

**verachten** [fɛrˈaxtən], *v.a.* despise, scorn.

**verächtlich** [fɛrˈɛçtlɪç], *adj.* despicable, contemptible; contemptuous, scornful.

**Verachtung** [fɛrˈaxtuŋ], *f.* (**—,** *no pl.*) contempt, disdain, scorn.

**verallgemeinern** [fɛralgəˈmaɪnərn], *v.a., v.n.* generalise.

**veralten** [fɛrˈaltən], *v.n.* (*aux.* sein) become obsolete, date.

**veraltet** [fɛrˈaltət], *adj.* obsolete.

**Veranda** [veˈranda], *f.* (**—,** *pl.* **—den**) verandah, porch.

**veränderlich** [fɛrˈɛndərlɪç], *adj.* changeable, variable; (*fig.*) inconstant, fickle.

**verändern** [fɛrˈɛndərn], *v.a.* change, alter. — *v.r. sich —,* change, vary; change o.'s job.

**verankern** [fɛrˈaŋkərn], *v.a.* anchor.

**veranlagt** [fɛrˈanla:kt], *adj.* inclined; gifted; having a propensity (to); *gut —,* talented; (*tax*) assessed.

**Veranlagung** [fɛrˈanla:guŋ], *f.* (**—,** *pl.* **—en**) bent; talent: predisposition; (*tax*) assessment.

**veranlassen** [fɛrˈanlasən], *v.a.* bring about, cause, motivate; *einen —,* induce s.o., cause s.o.; *etwas —,* bring s.th. about, cause s.th.

# verbrämen

**Veranlassung** [fɛr'anlasuŋ], *f.* (—, *no pl.*) cause, motive; occasion; inducement; *auf seine* —, at his suggestion; *ohne irgend eine* —, without the slightest provocation.

**veranschaulichen** [fɛr'anʃaulɪçən], *v.a.* illustrate, make clear.

**veranschlagen** [fɛr'anʃla:gən], *v.a.* estimate, assess.

**Veranschlagung** [fɛr'anʃla:guŋ], *f.* (—, *pl.* —en) estimate.

**veranstalten** [fɛr'anʃtaltən], *v.a.* organise, arrange.

**Veranstalter** [fɛr'anʃtaltər], *m.* (—s, *pl.* —) organiser.

**Veranstaltung** [fɛr'anʃtaltuŋ], *f.* (—, *pl.* —en) arrangement; entertainment; show; event; (sporting) fixture.

**verantworten** [fɛr'antvɔrtən], *v.a.* account for. — *v.r. sich* —, answer (for), justify o.s.

**verantwortlich** [fɛr'antvɔrtlɪç], *adj.* responsible, answerable, accountable.

**Verantwortlichkeit** [fɛr'antvɔrtlɪçkaɪt], *f.* (—, *no pl.*) responsibility.

**Verantwortung** [fɛr'antvɔrtuŋ], *f.* (—, *no pl.*) responsibility, justification, excuse; defence; *auf deine* —, at your own risk; *einen zur — ziehen*, call s.o. to account.

**verantwortungsvoll** [fɛr'antvɔrtuŋsfɔl], *adj.* responsible.

**verarbeiten** [fɛr'arbaɪtən], *v.a.* manufacture, process; (*fig.*) digest.

**Verarbeitung** [fɛr'arbaɪtuŋ], *f.* (—, *no pl.*) manufacture; process; finish; (*fig.*) digestion.

**verargen** [fɛr'argən], *v.a. einem etwas* —, blame *or* reproach s.o. for s.th.

**verärgern** [fɛr'ɛrgərn], *v.a.* annoy, make angry.

**Verarmung** [fɛr'armuŋ], *f.* (—, *no pl.*) impoverishment.

**verausgaben** [fɛr'ausga:bən], *v.r. sich* —, overspend, run short of money; spend o.s., wear o.s. out.

**veräußern** [fɛr'ɔysərn], *v.a.* dispose of, sell.

**Veräußerung** [fɛr'ɔysəruŋ], *f.* (—, *no pl.*) sale; alienation.

**Verband** [fɛr'bant], *m.* (—s, *pl.* ːe) bandage, dressing; association, union; unit.

**verbannen** [fɛr'banən], *v.a.* banish, exile, outlaw.

**Verbannte** [fɛr'bantə], *m.* (—n, *pl.* —n) exile, outlaw.

**Verbannung** [fɛr'banuŋ], *f.* (—, *pl.* —en) banishment, exile.

**verbauen** [fɛr'bauən], *v.n.* obstruct; build up; use up *or* spend in building.

**verbeißen** [fɛr'baɪsən], *v.a. irr. sich etwas* —, suppress s.th.; *sich das Lachen* —, stifle a laugh. — *v.r. sich in etwas* —, stick doggedly to s.th.

**verbergen** [fɛr'bɛrgən], *v.a. irr.* conceal, hide.

**verbessern** [fɛr'bɛsərn], *v.a.* improve, correct, mend.

**Verbesserung** [fɛr'bɛsəruŋ], *f.* (—, *pl.* —en) improvement; correction.

**verbeugen** [fɛr'bɔygən], *v.r. sich* —, bow.

**Verbeugung** [fɛr'bɔyguŋ], *f.* (—, *pl.* —en) bow, obeisance.

**verbiegen** [fɛr'bi:gən], *v.a. irr.* twist, distort, bend the wrong way.

**verbieten** [fɛr'bi:tən], *v.a. irr.* forbid, prohibit.

**verbilligen** [fɛr'bɪlɪgən], *v.a.* cheapen, reduce the price of.

**verbinden** [fɛr'bɪndən], *v.a. irr.* tie up, bind up, connect; (*Med.*) dress, bandage; unite, join; *die Augen* —, blindfold. — *v.r. sich* —, unite, join; (*Chem.*) combine.

**verbindlich** [fɛr'bɪntlɪç], *adj.* binding; obligatory; obliging; *—en Dank*, my best thanks.

**Verbindlichkeit** [fɛr'bɪntlɪçkaɪt], *f.* (—, *pl.* —en) liability, obligation; compliment.

**Verbindung** [fɛr'bɪnduŋ], *f.* (—, *pl.* —en) connexion, connection, junction; association; alliance; (*Railw.*) connection; (*Chem.*) compound.

**Verbindungsglied** [fɛr'bɪnduŋsgli:t], *n.* (—(e)s, *pl.* —er) connecting link.

**Verbindungslinie** [fɛr'bɪnduŋsli:njə], *f.* (—, *pl.* —n) line of communication.

**verbissen** [fɛr'bɪsən], *adj.* obstinate, grim; soured. — *adv.* doggedly.

**verbitten** [fɛr'bɪtən], *v.a. irr. sich etwas* —, forbid s.th. determinedly; insist on s.th. not being done, object to.

**verbittern** [fɛr'bɪtərn], *v.a.* embitter.

**Verbitterung** [fɛr'bɪtəruŋ], *f.* (—, *no pl.*) exasperation.

**verblassen** [fɛr'blasən], *v.n.* (*aux. sein*) turn pale.

**Verbleib** [fɛr'blaɪp], *m.* (—(e)s, *no pl.*) whereabouts.

**verbleiben** [fɛr'blaɪbən], *v.n. irr.* (*aux. sein*) remain.

**verblenden** [fɛr'blɛndən], *v.a.* dazzle, delude, blind.

**Verblendung** [fɛr'blɛnduŋ], *f.* (—, *no pl.*) infatuation; delusion.

**verblüffen** [fɛr'blyfən], *v.n.* amaze, stagger, dumbfound.

**Verblüffung** [fɛr'blyfuŋ], *f.* (—, *no pl.*) bewilderment.

**verblühen** [fɛr'bly:ən], *v.n.* (*aux. sein*) wither, fade.

**verblümt** [fɛr'bly:mt], *adj.* veiled.

**verbluten** [fɛr'blu:tən], *v.n.* (*aux. sein*) bleed to death.

**verborgen** (1) [fɛr'bɔrgən], *v.a.* lend out.

**verborgen** (2) [fɛr'bɔrgən], *adj.* concealed, hidden; *im —en*, secretly.

**Verborgenheit** [fɛr'bɔrgənhaɪt], *f.* (—, *no pl.*) concealment, seclusion.

**Verbot** [fɛr'bo:t], *n.* (—(e)s, *pl.* —e) prohibition.

**verboten** [fɛr'bo:tən], *adj.* forbidden, prohibited.

**verbrämen** [fɛr'brɛ:mən], *v.a.* (*garment*) edge, border.

251

# verbrauchen

**verbrauchen** [fɛr'brauxən], *v.a.* consume, use up; spend.

**Verbraucher** [fɛr'brauxər], *m.* (—s, *pl.* —) consumer.

**Verbrechen** [fɛr'brɛçən], *n.* (—s, *pl.* —) crime.

**verbrechen** [fɛr'brɛçən], *v.a. irr.* commit, perpetrate.

**Verbrecher** [fɛr'brɛçər], *m.* (—s, *pl.* —) criminal.

**Verbrecheralbum** [fɛr'brɛçəralbum], *n.* (—s, *no pl.*) rogues' gallery.

**verbreiten** [fɛr'braɪtən], *v.a.* spread, diffuse.

**verbreitern** [fɛr'braɪtərn], *v.a.* widen.

**Verbreitung** [fɛr'braɪtuŋ], *f.* (—, *no pl.*) spread(ing), propaganda, extension.

**verbrennbar** [fɛr'brɛnbaːr], *adj.* combustible.

**verbrennen** [fɛr'brɛnən], *v.a. irr.* burn; cremate; *von der Sonne verbrannt*, sunburnt. — *v.n.* (*aux.* sein) get burnt. — *v.r. sich* —, scald o.s., burn o.s.

**Verbrennung** [fɛr'brɛnuŋ], *f.* (—, *pl.* —en) burning, combustion; cremation.

**verbrieft** [fɛr'briːft], *adj.* vested; documented.

**verbringen** [fɛr'brɪŋən], *v.a. irr.* (*time*) spend, pass.

**verbrüdern** [fɛr'bryːdərn], *v.r. sich* —, fraternise.

**verbrühen** [fɛr'bryːən], *v.a.* scald.

**verbummeln** [fɛr'buməln], *v.a. die Zeit* —, fritter the time away.

**verbunden** [fɛr'bundən], *adj. einem* — *sein*, be obliged to s.o.

**verbünden** [fɛr'byndən], *v.r. sich* — *mit*, ally o.s. with.

**Verbündete** [fɛr'byndətə], *m.* (—n, *pl.* —n) ally, confederate.

**verbürgen** [fɛr'byrgən], *v.a.* warrant, guarantee. — *v.r. sich für etwas* —, vouch for s.th.; guarantee s.th.

**Verdacht** [fɛr'daxt], *m.* (—(e)s, *no pl.*) suspicion.

**verdächtig** [fɛr'dɛçtɪç], *adj.* suspicious, doubtful, questionable.

**verdächtigen** [fɛr'dɛçtɪgən], *v.a.* throw suspicion on, suspect.

**verdammen** [fɛr'damən], *v.a.* condemn, damn.

**verdammenswert** [fɛr'damənsveːrt], *adj.* damnable.

**Verdammung** [fɛr'damuŋ], *f.* (—, *no pl.*) condemnation.

**verdampfen** [fɛr'dampfən], *v.n.* (*aux.* sein) evaporate.

**verdanken** [fɛr'daŋkən], *v.a. einem etwas* —, be indebted to s.o. for s.th.; owe s.th. to s.o.

**verdauen** [fɛr'dauən], *v.a.* digest.

**verdaulich** [fɛr'dauliç], *adj.* digestible.

**Verdauung** [fɛr'dauuŋ], *f.* (—, *no pl.*) digestion.

**Verdauungsstörung** [fɛr'dauuŋsʃtøːruŋ], *f.* (—, *pl.* —en) indigestion.

**Verdeck** [fɛr'dɛk], *n.* (—s, *pl.* —e) awning; (*Naut.*) deck.

**verdecken** [fɛr'dɛkən], *v.a.* cover, hide.

**verdenken** [fɛr'dɛŋkən], *v.a. irr. einem etwas* —, blame s.o. for s.th.

**Verderb** [fɛr'dɛrp], *m.* (—s, *no pl.*) ruin, decay.

**verderben** [fɛr'dɛrbən], *v.a. irr.* spoil, corrupt, pervert. — *v.n.* (*aux.* sein) decay, go bad.

**Verderben** [fɛr'dɛrbən], *n.* (—s, *no pl.*) corruption, ruin.

**Verderber** [fɛr'dɛrbər], *m.* (—s, *pl.* —) corrupter, perverter.

**verderblich** [fɛr'dɛrplɪç], *adj.* ruinous, pernicious, destructive; (*goods*) perishable.

**Verderbnis** [fɛr'dɛrpnɪs], *f.* (—, *no pl.*) corruption, depravity; perversion; perdition.

**Verderbtheit** [fɛr'dɛrptthaɪt], *f.* (—, *no pl.*) corruption, perversion, depravity.

**verdeutlichen** [fɛr'dɔytlɪçən], *v.a.* illustrate, clarify.

**verdichten** [fɛr'dɪçtən], *v.a., v.r.* thicken, condense, liquefy.

**Verdichtung** [fɛr'dɪçtuŋ], *f.* (—, *no pl.*) condensation; solidification.

**verdicken** [fɛr'dɪkən], *v.a.* thicken; solidify.

**verdienen** [fɛr'diːnən], *v.a.* earn; deserve.

**Verdienst** (1) [fɛr'diːnst], *m.* (—es, *pl.* —e) profit, gain, earnings.

**Verdienst** (2) [fɛr'diːnst], *n.* (—es, *pl.* —e) merit, deserts.

**verdienstvoll** [fɛr'diːnstfɔl], *adj.* meritorious, deserving; distinguished.

**verdient** [fɛr'diːnt], *adj. sich* — *machen um*, deserve well of, serve well (a cause etc.).

**verdientermaßen** [fɛr'diːntərmasən], *adv.* deservedly.

**verdingen** [fɛr'dɪŋən], *v.r. irr. sich* —, enter service (with), take a situation (with).

**verdolmetschen** [fɛr'dɔlmɛtʃən], *v.a.* interpret, translate.

**verdoppeln** [fɛr'dɔpəln], *v.a.* double.

**verdorben** [fɛr'dɔrbən], *adj.* spoilt; corrupted, depraved, debauched.

**verdrängen** [fɛr'drɛŋən], *v.a.* crowd out; (*Phys.*) displace; (*fig.*) supplant, supersede; (*Psych.*) inhibit, repress.

**Verdrängung** [fɛr'drɛŋuŋ], *f.* (—, *no pl.*) supplanting; (*Phys.*) displacement; (*Psych.*) inhibition, repression.

**verdrehen** [fɛr'dreːən], *v.a.* twist (the wrong way); (*fig.*) misrepresent, distort.

**verdreht** [fɛr'dreːt], *adj.* cracked, cranky, crazy, queer.

**Verdrehtheit** [fɛr'dreːthaɪt], *f.* (—, *no pl.*) crankiness.

**Verdrehung** [fɛr'dreːuŋ], *f.* (—, *pl.* —en) distortion; (*fig.*) misrepresentation.

**verdrießen** [fɛr'driːsən], *v.a. irr.* vex, annoy.

**verdrießlich** [fɛr'driːslɪç], *adj.* (*thing*) vexatious, tiresome; (*person*) morose, peevish.

# Verfälschung

**verdrossen** [fɛr'drɔsən], *adj.* annoyed; fretful, sulky.

**Verdrossenheit** [fɛr'drɔsənhaɪt], *f.* (—, *no pl.*) annoyance; fretfulness, sulkiness.

**verdrücken** [fɛr'drykən], *v.a.* (*sl.*) eat o.'s fill of. — *v.r.* (*coll.*) *sich* —, slink away; sneak away.

**Verdruß** [fɛr'drus], *m.* (—sses, *no pl.*) vexation, annoyance; — *bereiten*, give trouble, cause annoyance.

**verduften** [fɛr'duftən], *v.n.* (*aux.* sein) evaporate; (*fig.*) (*coll.*) take French leave, clear out.

**verdummen** [fɛr'dumən], *v.n.* (*aux.* sein) become stupid.

**verdunkeln** [fɛr'duŋkəln], *v.a.* black-out, obscure; (*fig.*) eclipse.

**Verdunk(e)lung** [fɛr'duŋk(ə)luŋ], *f.* (—, *no pl.*) darkening, eclipse; black-out.

**Verdunk(e)lungsgefahr** [vɛr'duŋk(ə)-luŋsɡəfaːr], *f.* (—, *no pl.*) (*Law*) danger of prejudicing the course *or* administration of justice.

**verdünnen** [fɛr'dynən], *v.a.* thin out, dilute.

**Verdünnung** [fɛr'dynuŋ], *f.* (—, *no pl.*) attenuation; dilution.

**verdunsten** [fɛr'dunstən], *v.n.* (*aux.* sein) evaporate.

**verdursten** [fɛr'durstən], *v.n.* (*aux.* sein) die of thirst, perish with thirst.

**verdüstern** [fɛr'dyːstərn], *v.a.* darken, make gloomy.

**verdutzen** [fɛr'dutsən], *v.a.* disconcert, bewilder, nonplus.

**Veredlung** [fɛr'eːdluŋ], *f.* (—, *no pl.*) improvement, refinement.

**verehelichen** [fɛr'eːəlɪçən], *v.r.* (*obs.*) *sich* —, get married.

**verehren** [fɛr'eːrən], *v.a.* respect, revere, esteem; worship, adore.

**Verehrer** [fɛr'eːrər], *m.* (—s, *pl.* —) admirer; lover.

**verehrlich** [fɛr'eːrlɪç], *adj.* venerable.

**verehrt** [fɛr'eːrt], *adj.* honoured; *sehr —er Herr*, dear Sir.

**Verehrung** [fɛr'eːruŋ], *f.* (—, *no pl.*) reverence, veneration; worship, adoration.

**verehrungswürdig** [fɛr'eːruŋsvyrdɪç], *adj.* venerable.

**vereidigt** [fɛr'aɪdɪçt], *adj.* sworn in, bound by oath, under oath; —*er Bücherrevisor*, chartered accountant.

**Vereidigung** [fɛr'aɪdɪɡuŋ], *f.* (—, *no pl.*) swearing in; oathtaking.

**Verein** [fɛr'aɪn], *m.* (—s, *pl.* —e) union, association, society; club.

**vereinbar** [fɛr'aɪnbaːr], *adj.* compatible.

**vereinbaren** [fɛr'aɪnbaːrən], *v.a.* agree upon, arrange.

**Vereinbarung** [fɛr'aɪnbaːruŋ], *f.* (—, *pl.* —en) arrangement, agreement.

**vereinen** [fɛr'aɪnən], *v.a.* unite.

**vereinfachen** [fɛr'aɪnfaxən], *v.a.* simplify.

**vereinigen** [fɛr'aɪnɪɡən], *v.a.* unite. — *v.r. sich* — *mit*, associate o.s. with, join with.

**Vereinigung** [fɛr'aɪnɪɡuŋ], *f.* (—, *pl.* —en) union; association.

**vereinnahmen** [fɛr'aɪnaːmən], *v.a.* receive, take (*money*).

**vereinsamen** [fɛr'aɪnzaːmən], *v.n.* (*aux.* sein) become isolated, become lonely.

**vereint** [fɛr'aɪnt], *adj.* united, joined. — *adv.* in concert, (all) together.

**vereinzelt** [fɛr'aɪntsəlt], *adj.* sporadic, isolated. — *adv.* here and there, now and then.

**Vereinzelung** [fɛr'aɪntsəluŋ], *f.* (—, *pl.* —en) isolation; individualization.

**vereisen** [fɛr'aɪzən], *v.n.* become frozen, freeze; congeal.

**Vereisung** [fɛr'aɪzuŋ], *f.* (—, *pl.* —en) freezing, icing (up).

**vereiteln** [fɛr'aɪtəln], *v.a.* frustrate, thwart.

**Vereitelung** [fɛr'aɪtəluŋ], *f.* (—, *pl.* —en) frustration, thwarting.

**vereitern** [fɛr'aɪtərn], *v.n.* suppurate.

**Vereiterung** [fɛr'aɪtəruŋ], *f.* (—, *pl.* —en) suppuration.

**verenden** [fɛr'ɛndən], *v.n.* (*aux.* sein) (*animal*) die.

**verengen** [fɛr'ɛŋən], *v.a.* narrow, straighten, constrict.

**Verengung** [fɛr'ɛŋuŋ], *f.* (—, *pl.* —en) narrowing, straightening, contraction.

**vererben** [fɛr'ɛrbən], *v.a.* leave (by will), bequeath. — *v.r. sich* — *auf*, devolve upon, be hereditary.

**vererblich** [fɛr'ɛrplɪç], *adj.* (in)heritable, hereditary.

**Vererbung** [fɛr'ɛrbuŋ], *f.* (—, *no pl.*) heredity.

**verewigen** [fɛr'eːvɪɡən], *v.a.* immortalise.

**Verewigte** [fɛr'eːvɪçtə], *m.* (—n, *pl.* —n) (*Poet.*) deceased.

**Verfahren** [fɛr'faːrən], *n.* (—s, *pl.* —) process; (*Law*) procedure; proceedings; *das — einstellen*, quash proceedings.

**verfahren** [fɛr'faːrən], *v.n. irr.* (*aux.* sein) proceed, act, operate. — *v.a.* spend (*money etc.*) on travelling. — *v.r. sich* —, (*Motor.*) lose o.'s way.

**Verfall** [fɛr'fal], *m.* (—s, *no pl.*) decay, decline; downfall, ruin; (*Comm.*) expiration, maturity; *in — geraten*, fall into ruin, decay.

**verfallen** [fɛr'falən], *v.n. irr.* (*aux.* sein) decay; go to ruin; lapse; (*Comm.*) fall due, expire; (*pledge*) become forfeit; *einem —*, become the property of, accrue to, devolve upon s.o.; (*fig.*) become the slave of s.o.; (*health*) decline, fail; *auf etwas —*, hit upon an idea. — *adj.* decayed, ruined.

**Verfalltag** [fɛr'faltaːk], *m.* (—s, *pl.* —e) day of payment; maturity.

**verfälschen** [fɛr'fɛlʃən], *v.a.* falsify; adulterate.

**Verfälschung** [fɛr'fɛlʃuŋ], *f.* (—, *pl.* —en) falsification; adulteration.

253

# verfangen

**verfangen** [fɛr'faŋən], *v.r. irr. sich* —, get entangled; *sich in ein Lügennetz* —, entangle o.s. in a tissue of lies.

**verfänglich** [fɛr'fɛŋlɪç], *adj.* risky; insidious.

**verfärben** [fɛr'fɛrbən], *v.r. sich* —, change colour.

**verfassen** [fɛr'fasən], *v.a.* compose, write, be the author of.

**Verfasser** [fɛr'fasər], *m.* (—s, *pl.* —) author, writer.

**Verfassung** [fɛr'fasuŋ], *f.* (—, *pl.* —en) composition; (*state*) constitution; state, condition, disposition.

**verfassungsgemäß** [fɛr'fasuŋsgəmɛːs], *adj.* constitutional.

**verfassungswidrig** [fɛr'fasuŋsviːdrɪç], *adj.* unconstitutional.

**verfaulen** [fɛr'faulən], *v.n.* (*aux.* sein) rot, putrefy.

**verfechten** [fɛr'fɛçtən], *v.a. irr.* defend, advocate; maintain.

**verfehlen** [fɛr'feːlən], *v.a.* fail, miss; fail to meet; fail to do; *den Weg* —, lose o.'s way.

**verfehlt** [fɛr'feːlt], *adj.* unsuccessful, false, abortive; *eine* —*e Sache*, a failure.

**Verfehlung** [fɛr'feːluŋ], *f.* (—, *pl.* —en) lapse.

**verfeinern** [fɛr'fainərn], *v.a.* refine, improve.

**Verfeinerung** [fɛr'fainəruŋ], *f.* (—, *pl.* —en) refinement, polish.

**verfertigen** [fɛr'fɛrtɪgən], *v.a.* make, manufacture.

**verfilmen** [fɛr'fɪlmən], *v.a.* make a film of, film.

**verfinstern** [fɛr'fɪnstərn], *v.r. sich* —, get dark; be eclipsed.

**verflechten** [fɛr'flɛçtən], *v.a. irr.* interweave, interlace. — *v.r. sich* —, (*fig.*) become entangled, become involved.

**verfließen** [fɛr'fliːsən], *v.n. irr.* (*aux.* sein) flow away; (*time*) elapse, pass.

**verflossen** [fɛr'flɔsən], *adj.* past, bygone.

**verfluchen** [fɛr'fluːxən], *v.a.* curse, execrate.

**verflucht** [fɛr'fluːxt], *excl.* damn!

**verflüchtigen** [fɛr'flyçtɪgən], *v.r. sich* —, become volatile; evaporate; (*coll.*) make off, make o.s. scarce.

**Verfluchung** [fɛr'fluːxuŋ], *f.* (—, *pl.* —en) malediction, curse.

**Verfolg** [fɛr'fɔlk], *m.* (—(e)s, *no pl.*) progress, course.

**verfolgen** [fɛr'fɔlgən], *v.a.* pursue; persecute; prosecute.

**Verfolger** [fɛr'fɔlgər], *m.* (—s, *pl.* —) pursuer; persecutor.

**Verfolgung** [fɛr'fɔlguŋ], *f.* (—, *pl.* —en) pursuit; persecution; prosecution.

**Verfolgungswahn** [fɛr'fɔlguŋsvaːn], *m.* (—s, *no pl.*) persecution mania.

**verfrüht** [fɛr'fryːt], *adj.* premature.

**verfügbar** [fɛr'fyːkbaːr], *adj.* available.

**verfügen** [fɛr'fyːgən], *v.a.* decree, order. — *v.n.* — *über etwas*, have control of s.th, have s.th. at o.'s disposal.

**Verfügung** [fɛr'fyːguŋ], *f.* (—, *pl.* —en) decree, ordinance; disposition, disposal; *einem zur* — *stehen*, be at s.o.'s service *or* disposal.

**verführen** [fɛr'fyːrən], *v.a.* seduce.

**verführerisch** [fɛr'fyːrərɪʃ], *adj.* seductive, alluring; (*coll.*) fetching.

**Verführung** [fɛr'fyːruŋ], *f.* (—, *no pl.*) seduction.

**vergällen** [fɛr'gɛlən], *v.a.* spoil, mar.

**vergallopieren** [fɛrgalo'piːrən], *v.r.* (*coll.*) *sich* —, blunder, overshoot the mark.

**vergangen** [fɛr'gaŋən], *adj.* past, gone, last.

**Vergangenheit** [fɛr'gaŋənhait], *f.* (—, *no pl.*) past, time past; (*Gram.*) past tense.

**vergänglich** [fɛr'gɛŋlɪç], *adj.* transient, transitory.

**Vergaser** [fɛr'gaːzər], *m.* (—s, *pl.* —) (*Motor.*) carburettor.

**vergeben** [fɛr'geːbən], *v.a. irr.* give away; forgive, pardon; confer, bestow.

**vergebens** [fɛr'geːbəns], *adv.* in vain, vainly.

**vergeblich** [fɛr'geːplɪç], *adj.* vain, futile, fruitless. — *adv.* in vain.

**Vergebung** [fɛr'geːbuŋ], *f.* (—, *no pl.*) forgiveness, pardon; (*office*) bestowal.

**vergegenwärtigen** [fɛrgeːgən'vɛrtɪgən], *v.a.* bring to mind, imagine.

**Vergehen** [fɛr'geːən], *n.* (—s, *pl.* —) offence lapse.

**vergehen** [fɛr'geːən], *v.n. irr.* (*aux.* sein) go away, pass (away); elapse; perish; (*time*) pass. — *v.r. sich* —, go wrong; offend; violate (*Law,* person).

**vergelten** [fɛr'gɛltən], *v.a. irr.* repay, reward, recompense.

**Vergeltung** [fɛr'gɛltuŋ], *f.* (—, *no pl.*) requital, retribution; reward, recompense.

**vergessen** [fɛr'gɛsən], *v.a. irr.* forget; *bei einem* —, leave behind.

**Vergessenheit** [fɛr'gɛsənhait], *f.* (— *no pl.*) oblivion.

**vergeßlich** [fɛr'gɛslɪç], *adj.* forgetful.

**vergeuden** [fɛr'gɔydən], *v.a.* waste, squander.

**vergewaltigen** [fɛrgə'valtɪgən], *v.a.* assault criminally, rape, violate; (*fig.*) coerce, force.

**Vergewaltigung** [fɛrgə'valtɪguŋ], *f.* (—, *no pl.*) criminal assault; rape; (*fig.*) coercion.

**vergewissern** [fɛrgə'vɪsərn], *v.r. sich* —, ascertain, make sure.

**vergießen** [fɛr'giːsən], *v.a. irr.* spill; shed.

**vergiften** [fɛr'gɪftən], *v.a.* poison.

**Vergiftung** [fɛr'gɪftuŋ], *f.* (—, *pl.* —en) poisoning.

**vergilbt** [fɛr'gɪlpt], *adj.* yellow with age.

**Vergißmeinnicht** [fɛr'gɪsmainnɪçt], *n.* (—s, *pl.* —e) (*Bot.*) forget-me-not.

**Vergleich** [fɛr'glaɪç], *m.* (—(e)s, *pl.* —e) comparison; agreement; (*Law*) compromise.

**vergleichbar** [fɛr'glaɪçbaːr], *adj.* comparable.

**vergleichen** [fɛr'glaɪçən], *v.a. irr.* compare.

**vergleichsweise** [fɛr'glaɪçsvaɪzə], *adv.* by way of comparison; comparatively; (*Law*) by way of agreement.

**Vergnügen** [fɛr'gnyːgən], *n.* (—s, *no pl.*) pleasure, enjoyment, fun.

**vergnügen** [fɛr'gnyːgən], *v.a.* amuse, delight.

**Vergnügung** [fɛr'gnyːguŋ], *f.* (—, *pl.* —en) entertainment, amusement.

**vergönnen** [fɛr'gœnən], *v.a.* grant, allow; not (be)grudge.

**vergöttern** [fɛr'gœtərn], *v.a.* idolise, worship.

**vergraben** [fɛr'graːbən], *v.a. irr.* hide in the ground, bury.

**vergrämt** [fɛr'grɛːmt], *adj.* careworn.

**vergreifen** [fɛr'graɪfən], *v.r. irr. sich — an*, lay violent hands on, violate.

**vergriffen** [fɛr'grɪfən], *adj.* out of stock, out of print.

**vergrößern** [fɛr'grøːsərn], *v.a.* enlarge, expand; increase; magnify; (*fig.*) exaggerate.

**Vergrößerung** [fɛr'grøːsəruŋ], *f.* (—, *pl.* —en) magnification, enlargement, increase.

**Vergrößerungsglas** [fɛr'grøːsəruŋsglas], *n.* (—es, *pl.* ⸚er) magnifying glass.

**Vergünstigung** [fɛr'gynstɪguŋ], *f.* (—, *pl.* —en) privilege, favour, special facility, concession.

**vergüten** [fɛr'gyːtən], *v.a. einem etwas —*, compensate s.o. for s.th.; reimburse s.o. for s.th.

**Vergütung** [fɛr'gyːtuŋ], *f.* (—, *pl.* —en) indemnification, compensation, reimbursement.

**verhaften** [fɛr'haftən], *v.a.* arrest.

**Verhaftung** [fɛr'haftuŋ], *f.* (—, *pl.* —en) arrest.

**verhallen** [fɛr'halən], *v.n.* (*aux.* sein) (*sound*) fade, die away.

**verhalten** [fɛr'haltən], *v.r. irr. sich —*, act, behave.

**Verhalten** [fɛr'haltən], *n.* (—s, *no pl.*) behaviour, conduct, demeanour.

**Verhältnis** [fɛr'hɛltnɪs], *n.* (—ses, *pl.* —se) (*Maths.*) proportion, ratio; relation; footing; love-affair, liaison; (*coll.*) mistress.

**verhältnismäßig** [fɛr'hɛltnɪsmɛːsɪç], *adj.* proportionate, comparative.

**Verhältniswort** [fɛr'hɛltnɪsvɔrt], *n.* (—es, *pl.* ⸚er) preposition.

**Verhältniszahl** [fɛr'hɛltnɪstsaːl], *f.* (—, *pl.* —en) proportional number.

**Verhaltungsmaßregel** [fɛr'haltuŋsmaːsreːgəl], *f.* (—, *pl.* —n) rule of conduct; instruction.

**verhandeln** [fɛr'handəln], *v.a.* discuss, transact. — *v.n.* negotiate.

**Verhandlung** [fɛr'handluŋ], *f.* (—, *pl.* —en) discussion, negotiation, transaction; (*Law*) proceedings.

**verhängen** [fɛr'hɛŋən], *v.a.* cover with; decree; inflict (a penalty) on s.o.

**Verhängnis** [fɛr'hɛŋnɪs], *n.* (—ses, *pl.* —se) fate, destiny; misfortune.

**Verhängnisglaube** [fɛr'hɛŋnɪsglaubə], *m.* (—ns, *no pl.*) fatalism.

**verhängnisvoll** [fɛr'hɛŋnɪsfɔl], *adj.* fateful, portentous; fatal.

**verhärmt** [fɛr'hɛrmt], *adj.* careworn.

**verharren** [fɛr'harən], *v.n.* remain; persist.

**Verhärtung** [fɛr'hɛrtuŋ], *f.* (—, *pl.* —en) hardening, hardened state; (*skin*) callosity; (*fig.*) obduracy.

**verhaßt** [fɛr'hast], *adj.* hated, odious.

**verhätscheln** [fɛr'hɛtʃəln], *v.a.* pamper, coddle.

**verhauen** [fɛr'hauən], *v.a.* beat, thrash.

**Verheerung** [fɛr'heːruŋ], *f.* (—, *pl.* —en) devastation.

**verhehlen** [fɛr'heːlən], *v.a.* conceal, hide.

**verheilen** [fɛr'haɪlən], *v.n.* (*aux.* sein) heal.

**verheimlichen** [fɛr'haɪmlɪçən], *v.a.* keep secret, hush up.

**verheiraten** [fɛr'haɪraːtən], *v.a.* give in marriage, marry off. — *v.r. sich —*, marry, get married.

**verheißen** [fɛr'haɪsən], *v.a. irr.* promise.

**Verheißung** [fɛr'haɪsuŋ], *f.* (—, *pl.* —en) promise.

**verhelfen** [fɛr'hɛlfən], *v.n. irr. einem zu etwas —*, help s.o. to s.th.

**Verherrlichung** [fɛr'hɛrlɪçuŋ], *f.* (—, *no pl.*) glorification.

**Verhetzung** [fɛr'hɛtsuŋ], *f.* (—, *pl.* —en) incitement, instigation.

**verhexen** [fɛr'hɛksən], *v.a.* bewitch.

**verhindern** [fɛr'hɪndərn], *v.a.* hinder, prevent.

**Verhinderung** [fɛr'hɪndəruŋ], *f.* (—, *pl.* —en) prevention, obstacle.

**verhöhnen** [fɛr'høːnən], *v.a.* deride, scoff at, jeer at.

**Verhöhnung** [fɛr'høːnuŋ], *f.* (—, *pl.* —en) derision.

**Verhör** [fɛr'høːr], *n.* (—s, *pl.* —e) hearing; (judicial) examination; *ins — nehmen*, question, interrogate, cross-examine.

**verhören** [fɛr'høːrən], *v.a.* examine judicially, interrogate. — *v.r. sich —*, misunderstand.

**verhüllen** [fɛr'hylən], *v.a.* cover, wrap up, veil.

**verhungern** [fɛr'huŋərn], *v.n.* (*aux.* sein) starve.

**verhungert** [fɛr'huŋərt], *adj.* famished.

**verhunzen** [fɛr'huntsən], *v.a.* spoil, bungle.

**verhüten** [fɛr'hyːtən], *v.a.* prevent, avert.

**Verhütung** [fɛr'hyːtuŋ], *f.* (—, *no pl.*) prevention, warding off.

**verirren** [fɛr'ɪrən], *v.r. sich —*, go astray, lose o.'s way.

**verirrt** [fɛr'ɪrt], *adj.* stray, straying, lost.
**verjagen** [fɛr'ja:gən], *v.a.* drive away, chase away.
**verjährt** [fɛr'jɛ:rt], *adj.* statute-barred; prescriptive; obsolete; old.
**verjubeln** [fɛr'ju:bəln], *v.a.* play ducks and drakes with; squander.
**verjüngen** [fɛr'jyŋən], *v.a.* make younger; (*Archit.*) taper. — *v.r. sich* —, grow younger.
**Verjüngung** [fɛr'jyŋuŋ], *f.* (—, *pl.* —en) rejuvenation.
**verkannt** [fɛr'kant], *adj.* misunderstood.
**verkappt** [fɛr'kapt], *adj.* disguised, secret, in disguise.
**Verkauf** [fɛr'kauf], *m.* (—(e)s, *pl.* ⁻e) sale.
**verkaufen** [fɛr'kaufən], *v.a.* sell.
**Verkäufer** [fɛr'kɔyfər], *m.* (—s, *pl.* —) seller; shop assistant, salesman.
**verkäuflich** [fɛr'kɔyflɪç], *adj.* for sale, saleable; mercenary.
**Verkaufspreis** [fɛr'kaufsprais], *m.* (—es, *pl.* —e) selling-price.
**Verkehr** [fɛr'ke:r], *m.* (—s, *no pl.*) traffic; commerce; intercourse; communication; — *mit*, association with; service (*trains, buses etc.*), transport.
**verkehren** [fɛr'ke:rən], *v.a.* turn upside down; transform; pervert. — *v.n.* frequent (a place), visit, associate (with); run, operate.
**Verkehrsstockung** [fɛr'ke:rsʃtɔkuŋ], *f.* (—, *pl.* —en) traffic jam.
**Verkehrsstraße** [fɛr'ke:rsʃtra:sə], *f.* (—, *pl.* —n) thoroughfare.
**verkehrt** [fɛr'ke:rt], *adj.* upside down; (*fig.*) wrong.
**Verkehrtheit** [fɛr'ke:rthait], *f.* (—, *pl.* —en) absurdity, piece of folly.
**Verkehrung** [fɛr'ke:ruŋ], *f.* (—, *pl.* —en) turning; inversion; perversion; misrepresentation; (*Gram.*) inversion.
**verkennen** [fɛr'kɛnən], *v.a. irr.* mistake, fail to recognize; misjudge (s.o.'s intentions).
**verklagen** [fɛr'kla:gən], *v.a.* sue; accuse.
**verklären** [fɛr'klɛ:rən], *v.a.* transfigure, illumine.
**verklärt** [fɛr'klɛ:rt], *adj.* transfigured; radiant.
**verkleben** [fɛr'kle:bən], *v.a.* paste over.
**verkleiden** [fɛr'klaidən], *v.a., v.r.* disguise (o.s.).
**Verkleidung** [fɛr'klaiduŋ], *f.* (— *pl.* —en) disguise.
**verkleinern** [fɛr'klainərn], *v.a.* make smaller, diminish, reduce; belittle, disparage.
**Verkleinerung** [fɛr'klainəruŋ], *f.* (—, *pl.* —en) diminution, reduction; belittling, detraction.
**Verkleinerungswort** [fɛr'klainəruŋs-vɔrt], *n.* (—s, *pl.* ⁻er) (*Gram.*) diminutive.
**verkneifen** [fɛr'knaifən], *v.r. irr.* (*coll.*) *sich etwas* —, deny o.s. s.th.

**verkniffen** [fɛr'knifən], *adj.* pinched; shrewd; hard-bitten.
**verknöchern** [fɛr'knœçərn], *v.n.* (*aux.* sein) ossify; (*fig.*) become fossilised *or* inflexible.
**Verknöcherung** [fɛr'knœçəruŋ], *f.* (—, *pl.* —en) ossification; (*fig.*) fossilisation.
**verknüpfen** [fɛr'knypfən], *v.a.* tie, connect, link.
**verkochen** [fɛr'kɔxən], *v.n.* (*aux.* sein) boil away.
**verkommen** [fɛr'kɔmən], *v.n. irr.* (*aux.* sein) go from bad to worse, go to seed, decay, become depraved. — *adj.* demoralised, down and out, depraved.
**Verkommenheit** [fɛr'kɔmənhait], *f.* (—, *no pl.*) demoralisation; depravity.
**verkörpern** [fɛr'kœrpərn], *v.a.* embody.
**verkrachen** [fɛr'kraxən], *v.r. sich* —, quarrel, (*coll.*) have a row.
**verkriechen** [fɛr'kri:çən], *v.r. irr. sich* —, creep *or* crawl away; slink away, lie low.
**verkümmern** [fɛr'kymərn], *v.n.* (*aux.* sein) wear away, waste away; pine away.
**verkünden** [fɛr'kyndən], *v.a.* proclaim, announce, publish, prophesy.
**Verkündigung** [fɛr'kyndɪguŋ], *f.* (—, *pl.* —en) announcement, proclamation; prediction.
**Verkündung** [fɛr'kynduŋ], *f.* (—, *pl.* —en) publication, proclamation.
**Verkürzung** [fɛr'kyrtsuŋ], *f.* (—, *pl.* —en) shortening, curtailment.
**verlachen** [fɛr'laxən], *v.a.* laugh at, deride.
**verladen** [fɛr'la:dən], *v.a. irr.* load, ship, freight.
**Verladung** [fɛr'la:duŋ], *f.* (—, *pl.* —en) loading, shipping.
**Verlag** [fɛr'la:k], *m.* (—(e)s, *pl.* —e) publication; publishing house, (firm of) publishers.
**Verlagsrecht** [fɛr'la:ksrɛçt], *n.* (—s, *pl.* —e) copyright.
**Verlangen** [fɛr'laŋən], *n.* (—s, *no pl.*) demand, request; longing, desire.
**verlangen** [fɛr'laŋən], *v.a.* ask, demand, request.
**verlängern** [fɛr'lɛŋərn], *v.a.* lengthen, prolong, extend.
**Verlängerung** [fɛr'lɛŋəruŋ], *f.* (—, *pl.* —en) lengthening; (*period*) prolongation, extension.
**verlangsamen** [fɛr'laŋza:mən], *v.a.* slow down, slacken, decelerate.
**Verlaß** [fɛr'las], *m.* (—sses, *no pl.*) *es ist kein — auf dich*, you cannot be relied on.
**verlassen** [fɛr'lasən], *v.a. irr.* leave, abandon. — *v.r. sich* — *auf*, rely on, depend upon. — *adj.* forlorn, forsaken, deserted, desolate, lonely.
**Verlassenheit** [fɛr'lasənhait], *f.* (—, *no pl.*) desolation, loneliness, solitude.
**verläßlich** [fɛr'lɛslɪç], *adj.* reliable, trustworthy.

**Verlauf** [fɛr'lauf], *m.* (—(e)s, *no pl.*) lapse, expiration; course.

**verlaufen** [fɛr'laufən], *v.n. irr.* (*aux.* sein) (*time*) pass; (*period*) expire, elapse; develop(e), turn out. — *v.r. sich* —, lose o.'s way; (*colour*) run.

**verlauten** [fɛr'lautən], *v.n.* transpire.

**verleben** [fɛr'le:bən], *v.a.* pass, spend.

**verlebt** [fɛr'le:pt], *adj.* worn out; spent; (*Am.*) played out.

**verlegen** [fɛr'le:gən], *v.a.* (*domicile*) move, remove; (*things*) mislay; (*books*) publish; obstruct; adjourn; change to another date or place. — *v.r. sich auf etwas* —, devote o.s. to s.th. — *adj.* embarrassed, ill at ease.

**Verlegenheit** [fɛr'le:gənhaɪt], *f.* (—, *pl.* —en) embarrassment, perplexity; predicament, difficulty.

**Verleger** [fɛr'le:gər], *m.* (—s, *pl.* —) publisher.

**verleiden** [fɛr'laɪdən], *v.a. einem etwas* —, spoil s.th. for s.o.

**verleihen** [fɛr'laɪən], *v.a. irr.* lend; (*honour, title*) confer, bestow, award.

**Verleiher** [fɛr'laɪər], *m.* (—s, *pl.* —) lender.

**Verleihung** [fɛr'laɪuŋ], *f.* (—, *pl.* —en) lending, loan; (*medal, prize*) investiture; grant, conferring.

**verleiten** [fɛr'laɪtən], *v.a.* mislead, entice, induce; seduce.

**Verleitung** [fɛr'laɪtuŋ], *f.* (—, *no pl.*) misleading, enticement, inducement; seduction.

**verlernen** [fɛr'lɛrnən], *v.a.* unlearn; forget.

**verlesen** [fɛr'le:zən], *v.a. irr.* read aloud, read out, recite. — *v.r. sich* —, misread.

**verletzen** [fɛr'lɛtsən], *v.a.* injure, hurt, wound, violate.

**verletzend** [fɛr'lɛtsənt], *adj.* offensive, insulting; cutting.

**verletzlich** [fɛr'lɛtslɪç], *adj.* vulnerable.

**Verletzlichkeit** [fɛr'lɛtslɪçkaɪt], *f.* (—, *no pl.*) vulnerability.

**Verletzung** [fɛr'lɛtsuŋ], *f.* (—, *pl.* —en) hurt, wound; (*Law*) violation.

**verleugnen** [fɛr'lɔygnən], *v.a.* deny, renounce, disown.

**Verleugnung** [fɛr'lɔygnuŋ], *f.* (—, *pl.* —en) denial, abnegation.

**verleumden** [fɛr'lɔymdən], *v.a.* slander, calumniate, traduce.

**Verleumdung** [fɛr'lɔymduŋ], *f.* (—, *pl.* —en) slander, libel, calumny.

**verlieben** [fɛr'li:bən], *v.r. sich* — *in*, fall in love with.

**Verliebte** [fɛr'li:ptə], *m. or f.* (—n, *pl.* —n) person in love, lover.

**Verliebtheit** [fɛr'li:pthaɪt], *f.* (—, *no pl.*) infatuation, amorousness.

**verlieren** [fɛr'li:rən], *v.a. irr.* lose.

**Verlierer** [fɛr'li:rər], *m.* (—s, *pl.* —) loser.

**Verlies** [fɛr'li:s], *n.* (—(s)es, *pl.* —(s)e) dungeon.

**verloben** [fɛr'lo:bən], *v.r. sich* — *mit*, become engaged to.

**Verlöbnis** [fɛr'lø:pnɪs], *n.* (—ses, *pl.* —se) (*rare*) engagement.

**Verlobte** [fɛr'lo:ptə], *m.* (—n, *pl.* —n) and *f.* (—n, *pl.* —n) fiancé(e), betrothed.

**Verlobung** [fɛr'lo:buŋ], *f.* (—, *pl.* —en) engagement, betrothal.

**verlocken** [fɛr'lɔkən], *v.a.* tempt, entice.

**verlogen** [fɛr'lo:gən], *adj.* lying, mendacious.

**Verlogenheit** [fɛr'lo:gənhaɪt], *f.* (—, *no pl.*) mendacity.

**verlohnen** [fɛr'lo:nən], *v. impers.* be worth while.

**verlöschen** [fɛr'lœʃən], *v.a.* extinguish.

**verlosen** [fɛr'lo:zən], *v.a.* raffle; draw *or* cast lots for.

**Verlosung** [fɛr'lo:zuŋ], *f.* (—, *pl.* —en) raffle, lottery.

**verlöten** [fɛr'lø:tən], *v.a.* solder.

**verlottern** [fɛr'lɔtərn], *v.n.* (*aux.* sein) go to the dogs.

**Verlust** [fɛr'lust], *m.* (—es, *pl.* —e) loss; (*death*) bereavement; (*Mil.*) casualty.

**verlustig** [fɛr'lustɪç], *adj.* — *gehen*, lose s.th., forfeit s.th.

**vermachen** [fɛr'maxən], *v.a. einem etwas* —, bequeath s.th. to s.o.

**Vermächtnis** [fɛr'mɛçtnɪs], *n.* (—ses, *pl.* —sse) will; legacy, bequest; (*fig.*) *heiliges* —, sacred trust.

**vermahlen** [fɛr'ma:lən], *v.a.* grind (down).

**Vermählung** [fɛr'mɛ:luŋ], *f.* (—, *pl.* —en) marriage, wedding.

**Vermahnung** [fɛr'ma:nuŋ], *f.* (—, *pl.* —en) admonition, exhortation.

**vermauern** [fɛr'mauərn], *v.a.* wall up.

**vermehren** [fɛr'me:rən], *v.a.* augment, multiply, increase. — *v.r. sich* —, multiply.

**Vermehrung** [fɛr'me:ruŋ], *f.* (—, *pl.* —en) increase, multiplication.

**vermeiden** [fɛr'maɪdən], *v.a. irr.* avoid, shun, shirk.

**vermeidlich** [fɛr'maɪtlɪç], *adj.* avoidable.

**Vermeidung** [fɛr'maɪduŋ], *f.* (—, *no pl.*) avoidance.

**vermeintlich** [fɛr'maɪntlɪç], *adj.* supposed, alleged, pretended; (*heir*) presumptive.

**vermelden** [fɛr'mɛldən], *v.a.* announce, notify.

**vermengen** [fɛr'mɛŋən], *v.a.* mingle, mix.

**Vermerk** [fɛr'mɛrk], *m.* (—s, *pl.* —e) entry, notice, note.

**vermerken** [fɛr'mɛrkən], *v.a.* observe, jot down.

**vermessen** [fɛr'mɛsən], *v.a. irr.* measure; (*land*) survey. — *adj.* bold, daring, audacious; arrogant.

**Vermessenheit** [fɛr'mɛsənhaɪt], *f.* (—, *no pl.*) boldness, audacity; arrogance.

**Vermesser** [fɛr'mɛsər], *m.* (—s, *pl.* —) (*land*) surveyor.

# Vermessung

**Vermessung** [fɛr'mɛsuŋ], *f.* (—, *pl.* —en) (*land*) survey; measuring.

**vermieten** [fɛr'mi:tən], *v.a.* let, lease, hire out.

**Vermieter** [fɛr'mi:tər], *m.* (—s, *pl.* —) landlord; hirer.

**vermindern** [fɛr'mɪndərn], *v.a.* diminish, lessen.

**Verminderung** [fɛr'mɪndəruŋ], *f.* (—, *pl.* —en) diminution, reduction, decrease, lessening.

**vermischen** [fɛr'mɪʃən], *v.a.* mix, mingle, blend.

**vermissen** [fɛr'mɪsən], *v.a.* miss; *vermißt sein*, be missing; *vermißt werden*, be missed.

**vermitteln** [fɛr'mɪtəln], *v.n.* mediate. — *v.a.* adjust; negotiate, secure.

**Vermittler** [fɛr'mɪtlər], *m.* (—s, *pl.* —) mediator; agent, middleman.

**Vermittlung** [fɛr'mɪtluŋ], *f.* (—, *pl.* —en) mediation, intervention.

**vermöbeln** [fɛr'mø:bəln], *v.a.* (*sl.*) *einen* —, thrash s.o.

**vermodern** [fɛr'mo:dərn], *v.n.* (*aux.* sein) moulder, rot.

**vermöge** [fɛr'mø:gə], *prep.* (*Genit.*) by virtue of, by dint of, on the strength of.

**Vermögen** [fɛr'mø:gən], *n.* (—s, *pl.* —) faculty, power; means, assets; fortune, wealth, riches; *er hat* —, he is a man of property; *nach bestem* —, to the best of o.'s ability.

**vermögen** [fɛr'mø:gən], *v.a. irr.* be able to, have the power to, be capable of.

**vermögend** [fɛr'mø:gənt], *adj.* wealthy.

**Vermögensbestand** [fɛr'mø:gənsbə-ʃtant], *m.* (—s, *pl.* ⁻e) assets.

**Vermögenssteuer** [fɛr'mø:gənsʃtɔyər], *f.* (—, *pl.* —n) property tax.

**vermorscht** [fɛr'mɔrʃt], *adj.* mouldering, rotten.

**vermuten** [fɛr'mu:tən], *v.a.* suppose, conjecture, surmise, presume; guess.

**vermutlich** [fɛr'mu:tlɪç], *adj.* likely, probable.

**Vermutung** [fɛr'mu:tuŋ], *f.* (—, *pl.* —en) guess, supposition, conjecture.

**vernachlässigen** [fɛr'naxlɛsɪgən], *v.a.* neglect.

**Vernachlässigung** [fɛr'naxlɛsɪguŋ], *f.* (—, *pl.* —en) neglect, negligence.

**vernarren** [fɛr'narən], *v.r. sich* — (*in, Acc.*), become infatuated (with).

**vernarrt** [fɛr'nart], *adj.* madly in love.

**vernaschen** [fɛr'naʃən], *v.a.* squander (money) on sweets.

**vernehmbar** [fɛr'ne:mba:r], *adj.* audible; *sich* — *machen*, make o.s. heard.

**Vernehmen** [fɛr'ne:mən], *n.* (—s, *no pl.*) *dem* — *nach*, from what o. hears.

**vernehmen** [fɛr'ne:mən], *v.a. irr.* hear, learn; (*Law*) examine, interrogate.

**vernehmlich** [fɛr'ne:mlɪç], *adj.* audible, distinct, clear.

**Vernehmlichkeit** [fɛr'ne:mlɪçkaɪt], *f.* (—, *no pl.*) audibility.

**Vernehmung** [fɛr'ne:muŋ], *f.* (—, *pl.* —en) (*Law*) interrogation, examination.

**verneigen** [fɛr'naɪgən], *v.r. sich* —, curts(e)y, bow.

**Verneigung** [fɛr'naɪguŋ], *f.* (—, *pl.* —en) curts(e)y, bow.

**verneinen** [fɛr'naɪnən], *v.a.* deny, answer in the negative.

**Verneinung** [fɛr'naɪnuŋ], *f.* (—, *pl.* —en) negation, denial; (*Gram.*) negation, negative.

**vernichten** [fɛr'nɪçtən], *v.a.* annihilate, destroy utterly, exterminate.

**Vernichtung** [fɛr'nɪçtuŋ], *f.* (—, *no pl.*) annihilation, extinction, destruction.

**vernieten** [fɛr'ni:tən], *v.a.* rivet.

**Vernunft** [fɛr'nunft], *f.* (—, *no pl.*) reason, sense, intelligence; judgment; *gesunde* —, common sense; — *annehmen*, listen to reason; *einen zur* — *bringen*, bring s.o. to his senses.

**vernünftig** [fɛr'nynftɪç], *adj.* sensible, reasonable, rational.

**veröden** [fɛr'ø:dən], *v.n.* (*aux.* sein) become desolate, become devastated.

**Verödung** [fɛr'ø:duŋ], *f.* (—, *no pl.*) devastation, desolation.

**veröffentlichen** [fɛr'œfəntlɪçən], *v.a.* publish.

**Veröffentlichung** [fɛr'œfəntlɪçuŋ], *f.* (—, *pl.* —en) publication.

**verordnen** [fɛr'ɔrdnən], *v.a.* order, command, ordain; (*Med.*) prescribe.

**Verordnung** [fɛr'ɔrdnuŋ], *f.* (—, *pl.* —en) order; (*Law*) decree, edict, statute; (*Med.*) prescription.

**verpassen** [fɛr'pasən], *v.a.* lose by delay, let slip; (*train etc.*) miss.

**verpfänden** [fɛr'pfɛndən], *v.a.* pawn, pledge.

**Verpfänder** [fɛr'pfɛndər], *m.* (—s, *pl.* —) mortgager.

**Verpfändung** [fɛr'pfɛnduŋ], *f.* (—, *pl.* —en) pawning, pledging.

**verpflanzen** [fɛr'pflantsən], *v.a.* transplant.

**Verpflanzung** [fɛr'pflantsuŋ], *f.* (—, *pl.* —en) transplantation.

**verpflegen** [fɛr'pfle:gən], *v.a.* board, provide food for, feed; nurse.

**Verpflegung** [fɛr'pfle:guŋ], *f.* (—, *no pl.*) board, catering; food.

**Verpflegungskosten** [fɛr'pfle:guŋskos-tən], *f. pl.* (cost of) board and lodging.

**verpflichten** [fɛr'pflɪçtən], *v.a.* bind, oblige, engage.

**verpflichtend** [fɛr'pflɪçtənt], *adj.* obligatory.

**Verpflichtung** [fɛr'pflɪçtuŋ], *f.* (—, *pl.* —en) obligation, duty; liability, engagement.

**verplaudern** [fɛr'plaudərn], *v.a.* spend (time) chatting.

**verplempern** [fɛr'plɛmpərn], *v.a.* (*coll.*) spend foolishly, fritter away.

**verpönt** [fɛr'pø:nt], *adj.* frowned upon; taboo.

**verprassen** [fɛr'prasən], *v.a.* squander (money) in riotous living.

**verpuffen** [fɛr'pufən], *v.n.* (*aux.* sein) (*coll.*) fizzle out.

**verpulvern** [fɛr'pulvərn], *v.a.* fritter away.

**Verputz** [fɛr'puts], *m.* (—es, *no pl.*) plaster.

**verquicken** [fɛr'kvɪkən], *v.a.* amalgamate; mix up.

**Verrat** [fɛr'ra:t], *m.* (—(e)s, *no pl.*) treachery, treason.

**verraten** [fɛr'ra:tən], *v.a. irr.* betray; disclose; *das verrät die Hand des Künstlers*, this proclaims the hand of the artist.

**Verräter** [fɛr'rɛ:tər], *m.* (—s, *pl.* —) traitor.

**verräterisch** [fɛr'rɛ:tərɪʃ], *adj.* treacherous, treasonable, perfidious; (*fig.*) tell-tale.

**verrauchen** [fɛr'rauxən], *v.n.* (*aux.* sein) evaporate; (*fig.*) blow over; cool down.

**verräuchern** [fɛr'rɔyçərn], *v.a.* smoke, fill with smoke.

**verräumen** [fɛr'rɔymən], *v.a.* misplace, mislay.

**verrauschen** [fɛr'rauʃən], *v.n.* (*aux.* sein) (*sound*) die away; pass away.

**verrechnen** [fɛr'rɛçnən], *v.a.* reckon up. — *v.r. sich* —, miscalculate.

**Verrechnung** [fɛr'rɛçnuŋ], *f.* (—, *pl.* — en) reckoning-up.

**Verrechnungsscheck** [fɛr'rɛçnuŋs-ʃɛk], *m.* (—s, *pl.* —e, —s) crossed cheque.

**verregnen** [fɛr're:gnən], *v.a.* spoil by rain.

**verreiben** [fɛr'raibən], *v.a. irr.* rub away; rub hard.

**verreisen** [fɛr'raizən], *v.n.* (*aux.* sein) go on a journey.

**verrenken** [fɛr'rɛŋkən], *v.a.* sprain, dislocate.

**Verrenkung** [fɛr'rɛŋkuŋ], *f.* (—, *pl.* —en) sprain, dislocation.

**verrichten** [fɛr'rɪçtən], *v.a.* do, perform, acquit o.s. of; execute; (*prayer*) say.

**verriegeln** [fɛr'ri:gəln], *v.a.* bolt.

**verringern** [fɛr'rɪŋərn], *v.a.* reduce, diminish.

**Verringerung** [fɛr'rɪŋəruŋ], *f.* (—, *no pl.*) diminution, reduction.

**verrinnen** [fɛr'rɪnən], *v.n. irr.* (*aux.* sein) run off; (*fig.*) pass, elapse.

**verrosten** [fɛr'rɔstən], *v.n.* (*aux.* sein) rust.

**verrottet** [fɛr'rɔtət], *adj.* rotten.

**verrucht** [fɛr'ru:xt], *adj.* villainous, atrocious, heinous, infamous.

**Verruchtheit** [fɛr'ru:xthait], *f.* (—, *no pl.*) villainy.

**verrücken**[fɛr'rykən], *v.a.*shift,displace.

**verrückt** [fɛr'rykt], *adj.* crazy, mad.

**Verrückte** [fɛr'ryktə], *m.* (—n, *pl.* —n) madman. — *f.* (—n, *pl.* —n) madwoman.

**Verrücktheit** [fɛr'rykthait], *f.* (—, *pl.* —en) craziness; mad act.

**Verruf** [fɛr'ru:f], *m.* (—s, *no pl.*) discredit, ill repute.

**verrufen** [fɛr'ru:fən], *adj.* notorious, of ill repute.

**Vers** [fɛrs], *m.* (—es, *pl.* —e) verse.

**versagen** [fɛr'za:gən], *v.a. einem etwas* —, deny s.o. s.th., refuse s.o. s.th. — *v.n.* fail, break down; (*voice*) falter; *sich etwas* —, abstain from s.th., deny o.s. s.th.

**Versager** [fɛr'za:gər], *m.* (—s, *pl.* —) misfire; failure, unsuccessful person, flop.

**versammeln** [fɛr'zaməln], *v.a.* gather around, convene. — *v.r. sich* —, assemble, meet.

**Versammlung** [fɛr'zamluŋ], *f.* (—, *pl.* —en) assembly, meeting, gathering, convention.

**Versand** [fɛr'zant], *m.* (—s, *no pl.*) dispatch, forwarding, shipping, shipment.

**versanden** [fɛr'zandən], *v.n.* (*aux.* sein) silt up.

**Versandgeschäft** [fɛr'zantgəʃɛft], *n.* (—s, *pl.* —e) export business; mail order business.

**Versatzamt** [fɛr'zatsamt], *n.* (—s, *pl.* ⁀er) pawn-shop.

**versauen** [fɛr'zauən], *v.a.* (*sl.*) make a mess of.

**versauern** [fɛr'zauərn], *v.n.* (*aux.* sein) turn sour; (*fig.*) become morose.

**versaufen** [fɛr'zaufən], *v.a. irr.* (*sl.*) squander (money) on drink, drink away.

**versäumen** [fɛr'zɔymən], *v.a.* miss, omit, lose by delay; leave undone; neglect.

**Versäumnis** [fɛr'zɔymnɪs], *n.* (—ses, *pl.* —se) neglect, omission; (*time*) loss.

**Versbau** ['fɛrsbau], *m.* (—s, *no pl.*) versification; verse structure.

**verschachern** [fɛr'ʃaxərn], *v.a.* barter away.

**verschaffen** [fɛr'ʃafən], *v.a.* provide, procure, obtain, get.

**verschämt** [fɛr'ʃɛ:mt], *adj.* shamefaced, bashful.

**verschanzen** [fɛr'ʃantsən], *v.a.* fortify.

**Verschanzung** [fɛr'ʃantsuŋ], *f.* (—, *pl.* —en) fortification, entrenchment.

**verschärfen** [fɛr'ʃɛrfən], *v.a.* heighten, intensify, sharpen.

**verscharren** [fɛr'ʃarən], *v.a.* cover with earth; bury hurriedly.

**verscheiden** [fɛr'ʃaidən], *v.n. irr.* (*aux.* sein) die, pass away.

**verschenken** [fɛr'ʃɛŋkən], *v.a.* make a present of, give away.

**verscherzen** [fɛr'ʃɛrtsən], *v.a. sich etwas* —, forfeit s.th.

**verscheuchen** [fɛr'ʃɔyçən], *v.a.* scare away, frighten away; *Sorgen* —, banish care.

**verschicken** [fɛr'ʃɪkən], *v.a.* send on, send out, forward, transmit; evacuate.

**Verschickung** [fɛr'ʃɪkuŋ], *f.* (—, *no pl.*) forwarding, transmission; evacuation; banishment, exile.

# verschieben

**verschieben** [fɛr'ʃiːbən], v.a. irr. shift, move; delay, put off, defer, postpone.

**Verschiebung** [fɛr'ʃiːbuŋ], f. (—, pl. —en) removal; postponement; (fig.) black marketeering.

**verschieden** [fɛr'ʃiːdən], adj. different, diverse; deceased, departed; (pl.) some, several, sundry.

**verschiedenartig** [fɛr'ʃiːdənaːrtɪç], adj. varied, various, heterogeneous.

**verschiedenerlei** [fɛr'ʃiːdənərlaɪ], indecl. adj. diverse, of various kinds.

**Verschiedenheit** [fɛr'ʃiːdənhaɪt], f. (—, pl. —en) difference; diversity, variety.

**verschiedentlich** [fɛr'ʃiːdəntlɪç], adv. variously, severally; repeatedly.

**verschiffen** [fɛr'ʃɪfən], v.a. export, ship.

**verschimmeln** [fɛr'ʃɪməln], v.n. (aux. sein) go mouldy.

**verschlafen** [fɛr'ʃlaːfən], v.a. irr. sleep through, sleep away. — v.r. sich —, oversleep. — adj. sleepy, drowsy.

**Verschlag** [fɛr'ʃlaːk], m. (—s, pl. ⁀e) partition, box, cubicle.

**verschlagen** [fɛr'ʃlaːgən], v.a. irr. es verschlägt mir den Atem, it takes my breath away. — adj. cunning, crafty, sly.

**verschlechtern** [fɛr'ʃlɛçtərn], v.a. worsen, make worse. — v.r. sich —, deteriorate.

**Verschlechterung** [fɛr'ʃlɛçtəruŋ], f. (—, no pl.) deterioration.

**verschleiern** [fɛr'ʃlaɪərn], v.a. veil.

**Verschleierung** [fɛr'ʃlaɪəruŋ], f. (—, pl. —en) veiling, concealment; camouflage.

**verschleißen** [fɛr'ʃlaɪsən], v.a. irr. wear out, waste.

**verschlemmen** [fɛr'ʃlɛmən], v.a. squander on eating and drinking.

**verschleppen** [fɛr'ʃlɛpən], v.a. carry off, deport; kidnap; protract, spread; put off, procrastinate.

**verschleudern** [fɛr'ʃlɔydərn], v.a. waste; sell at cut prices.

**verschließen** [fɛr'ʃliːsən], v.a. irr. lock, lock up.

**verschlimmern** [fɛr'ʃlɪmərn], v.a. make worse. — v.r. sich —, get worse, worsen, deteriorate.

**Verschlimmerung** [fɛr'ʃlɪməruŋ], f. (—, no pl.) worsening, deterioration.

**verschlingen** [fɛr'ʃlɪŋən], v.a. irr. swallow up, devour.

**verschlossen** [fɛr'ʃlɔsən], adj. reserved, uncommunicative, withdrawn.

**Verschlossenheit** [fɛr'ʃlɔsənhaɪt], f. (—, no pl.) reserve.

**verschlucken** [fɛr'ʃlukən], v.a. swallow, gulp down; (fig.) suppress. — v.r. sich —, swallow the wrong way.

**verschlungen** [fɛr'ʃluŋən], adj. intricate, complicated.

**Verschluß** [fɛr'ʃlus], m. (—sses, pl. ⁀sse) lock; clasp; fastening; unter — haben, keep under lock and key.

**Verschlußlaut** [fɛr'ʃluslaut], m. (—s, pl. —e) (Phon.) explosive, plosive, stop.

**verschmachten** [fɛr'ʃmaxtən], v.n. (aux. sein) languish, pine; be parched.

**Verschmähung** [fɛr'ʃmɛːuŋ], f. (—, no pl.) disdain, scorn, rejection.

**Verschmelzung** [fɛr'ʃmɛltsuŋ], f. (—, no pl.) coalescence, fusion, blending.

**verschmerzen** [fɛr'ʃmɛrtsən], v.a. get over; bear stoically, make the best of.

**verschmitzt** [fɛr'ʃmɪtst], adj. cunning, crafty, mischievous.

**verschmutzen** [fɛr'ʃmutsən], v.n. (aux. sein) get dirty.

**verschnappen** [fɛr'ʃnapən], v.r. sich —, blurt out a secret, give o.s. away, let the cat out of the bag.

**verschneiden** [fɛr'ʃnaɪdən], v.a. irr. (wings) clip; (trees) prune; (animals) castrate; (wine) blend.

**verschneien** [fɛr'ʃnaɪən], v.n. (aux. sein) be snowed up, be covered with snow, be snowbound.

**Verschnitt** [fɛr'ʃnɪt], m. (—s, no pl.) blended wine, blend.

**Verschnittene** [fɛr'ʃnɪtənə], m. (—n, pl. —n) eunuch.

**verschnörkelt** [fɛr'ʃnœrkəlt], adj. adorned with flourishes.

**verschnupft** [fɛr'ʃnupft], adj. — sein, have a cold in the head; (fig.) be vexed.

**verschnüren** [fɛr'ʃnyːrən], v.a. (shoes) lace up; (parcel) tie up.

**verschonen** [fɛr'ʃoːnən], v.a. spare, exempt from.

**verschönern** [fɛr'ʃøːnərn], v.a. embellish, beautify.

**Verschönerung** [fɛr'ʃøːnəruŋ], f. (—, pl. —en) embellishment, adornment.

**Verschonung** [fɛr'ʃoːnuŋ], f. (—, no pl.) exemption; forbearance.

**verschossen** [fɛr'ʃɔsən], adj. faded, discoloured; (fig.) madly in love.

**verschreiben** [fɛr'ʃraɪbən], v.a. irr. prescribe. — v.r. sich —, make a mistake in writing.

**verschrien** [fɛr'ʃriːən], adj. notorious.

**verschroben** [fɛr'ʃroːbən], adj. cranky, eccentric.

**Verschrobenheit** [fɛr'ʃroːbənhaɪt], f. (—, pl. —en) crankiness, eccentricity.

**verschrumpfen** [fɛr'ʃrumpfən], v.n. (aux. sein) shrivel up.

**verschüchtern** [fɛr'ʃʏçtərn], v.a. intimidate.

**verschulden** [fɛr'ʃuldən], v.a. bring on, be the cause of; be guilty of.

**verschuldet** [fɛr'ʃuldət], adj. in debt.

**Verschuldung** [fɛr'ʃulduŋ], f. (—, no pl.) indebtedness.

**verschütten** [fɛr'ʃʏtən], v.a. spill; bury alive.

**verschwägern** [fɛr'ʃvɛːgərn], v.r. sich —, become related by marriage.

**Verschwägerung** [fɛr'ʃvɛːgəruŋ], f. (—, no pl.) relationship by marriage.

**verschwatzen** [fɛr'ʃvatsən], v.a. gossip (the time) away, spend o.'s time gossiping.

**verschweigen** [fɛr'ʃvaɪgən], v.a. irr. keep secret, keep (news) from, hush up.

**verschwenden** [fɛrˈʃvɛndən], *v.a.* squander, waste.

**verschwenderisch** [fɛrˈʃvɛndərɪʃ], *adj.* prodigal, profuse, lavish; wasteful.

**Verschwendung** [fɛrˈʃvɛnduŋ], *f.* (—, *no pl.*) waste, extravagance.

**Verschwendungssucht** [fɛrˈʃvɛnduŋs-zuxt], *f.* (—, *no pl.*) prodigality; extravagance.

**verschwiegen** [fɛrˈʃviːgən], *adj.* discreet, close, secretive.

**Verschwiegenheit** [fɛrˈʃviːgənhaɪt], *f.* (—, *no pl.*) discretion, secrecy.

**verschwimmen** [fɛrˈʃvɪmən], *v.n.* irr. (*aux.* sein) become blurred.

**verschwinden** [fɛrˈʃvɪndən], *v.n.* irr. (*aux.* sein) disappear, vanish.

**verschwommen** [fɛrˈʃvɔmən], *adj.* vague, blurred.

**verschwören** [fɛrˈʃvøːrən], *v.r.* irr. sich —, plot, conspire.

**Verschwörer** [fɛrˈʃvøːrer], *m.* (—s, *pl.* —) conspirator.

**Verschwörung** [fɛrˈʃvøːruŋ], *f.* (—, *pl.* —en) conspiracy.

**Versehen** [fɛrˈzeːən], *n.* (—s, *pl.* —) error, mistake, oversight.

**versehen** [fɛrˈzeːən], *v.a.* irr. provide; perform; fill (an office); einen — mit, furnish s.o. with. — *v.r.* sich —, make a mistake.

**versehren** [fɛrˈzeːrən], *v.a.* wound; disable.

**versenden** [fɛrˈzɛndən], *v.a.* irr. forward, consign, send off.

**Versender** [fɛrˈzɛndər], *m.* (—s, *pl.*—) consigner, exporter.

**Versendung** [fɛrˈzɛnduŋ], *f.* (—, *no pl.*) transmission, shipping.

**Versendungskosten** [fɛrˈzɛnduŋskɔs-tən], *f. pl.* forwarding charges.

**versengen** [fɛrˈzɛŋən], *v.a.* singe, scorch.

**versenken** [fɛrˈzɛŋkən], *v.a.* sink; (*ship*) scuttle.

**Versenkung** [fɛrˈzɛŋkuŋ], *f.* (—, *no pl.*) sinking; hollow; (*ship*) scuttling; (*Theat.*) trap-door.

**versessen** [fɛrˈzɛsən], *adj.* — sein auf, be bent upon, be mad on.

**versetzen** [fɛrˈzɛtsən], *v.a.* transplant, remove; give; pawn, pledge; transfer; (*pupil*) promote to a higher form. — *v.r.* sich in die Lage eines anderen —, put o.s. in s.o. else's position.

**versichern** [fɛrˈzɪçərn], *v.a.* assert, declare, aver, assure (s.o. of s.th) insure (s.th.).

**Versicherung** [fɛrˈzɪçəruŋ], *f.* (—, *pl.* —en) assurance, assertion; insurance.

**Versicherungsgesellschaft** [fɛrˈzɪçə-ruŋsgəzɛlʃaft], *f.* (—, *pl.* —en) insurance company.

**Versicherungsprämie** [fɛrˈzɪçəruŋs-prɛːmjə], *f.* (—, *pl.* —n) insurance premium.

**versiegbar** [fɛrˈziːkbaːr], *adj.* exhaustible.

**versiegeln** [fɛrˈziːgəln], *v.a.* seal (up).

**versiegen** [fɛrˈziːgən], *v.n.* (*aux.* sein) dry up, be exhausted.

**versilbern** [fɛrˈzɪlbərn], *v.a.* plate with silver; (*fig.*) convert into money.

**versinken** [fɛrˈzɪŋkən], *v.n.* irr. sink; (*ship*) founder; sink; versunken sein, be absorbed (in s.th.).

**Versmaß** [ˈfɛrsmaːs], *n.* (—es, *pl.* —e) metre.

**versoffen** [fɛrˈzɔfən], *adj.* (*vulg.*) drunken.

**versohlen** [fɛrˈzoːlən], *v.a.* (*coll.*) thrash (s.o.).

**versöhnen** [fɛrˈzøːnən], *v.r.* sich mit einem —, become reconciled with s.o.

**versöhnlich** [fɛrˈzøːnlɪç], *adj.* propitiatory, conciliatory.

**Versöhnung** [fɛrˈzøːnuŋ], *f.* (—, *no pl.*) reconciliation.

**versorgen** [fɛrˈzɔrgən], *v.a.* provide with; take care of; support, maintain.

**Versorger** [fɛrˈzɔrgər], *m.* (—s, *pl.* —) provider.

**Versorgung** [fɛrˈzɔrguŋ], *f.* (—, *no pl.*) provision, maintenance.

**verspäten** [fɛrˈʃpɛːtən], *v.r.* sich —, be late, be behind time; (*train*) be overdue.

**Verspätung** [fɛrˈʃpɛːtuŋ], *f.* (—, *no pl.*) delay; lateness.

**verspeisen** [fɛrˈʃpaɪzən], *v.a.* eat up.

**versperren** [fɛrˈʃpɛrən], *v.a.* block up, barricade, close.

**verspielen** [fɛrˈʃpiːlən], *v.a.* lose (at play); gamble away. — *v.r.* sich —, play wrong.

**verspielt** [fɛrˈʃpiːlt], *adj.* playful.

**verspotten** [fɛrˈʃpɔtən], *v.a.* deride, scoff at.

**versprechen** [fɛrˈʃprɛçən], *v.a.* irr. promise. — *v.r.* sich —, make a slip of the tongue.

**Versprechen** [fɛrˈʃprɛçən], *n.* (—s, *pl.* —) promise.

**versprengen** [fɛrˈʃprɛŋən], *v.a.* disperse.

**verspüren** [fɛrˈʃpyːrən], *v.a.* feel, perceive.

**verstaatlichen** [fɛrˈʃtaːtlɪçən], *v.a.* nationalise.

**Verstand** [fɛrˈʃtant], *m.* (—(e)s, *no pl.*) intellect, intelligence, sense; understanding, reason, mind.

**verstandesmäßig** [fɛrˈʃtandəsmɛːsɪç], *adj.* rational, reasonable.

**Verstandesschärfe** [fɛrˈʃtandəsʃɛrfə], *f.* (—, *no pl.*) penetration, acumen.

**verständig** [fɛrˈʃtɛndɪç], *adj.* judicious, sensible, reasonable.

**verständigen** [fɛrˈʃtɛndɪgən], *v.a.* inform, notify. — *v.r.* sich mit einem —, come to an agreement with s.o.

**Verständigung** [fɛrˈʃtɛndɪguŋ], *f.* (—, *pl.* —en) understanding, agreement; information; arrangement.

**verständlich** [fɛrˈʃtɛntlɪç], *adj.* intelligible, clear, understandable.

**Verständnis** [fɛrˈʃtɛntnɪs], (—ses, *no pl.*) comprehension, understanding, perception, insight.

**verständnisinnig** [fɛrˈʃtɛntnɪsɪnɪç], *adj.* sympathetic; having profound insight.

**verstärken** [fɛrˈʃtɛrkən], *v.a.* strengthen, reinforce, intensify.

**Verstärker** [fɛrˈʃtɛrkər], *m.* (—s, *pl.* —) amplifier; magnifier.

**Verstärkung** [fɛrˈʃtɛrkuŋ], *f.* (—, *pl.* —en) strengthening, intensification, amplification; (*Mil.*) reinforcements.

**verstauben** [fɛrˈʃtaubən], *v.n.* (*aux.* sein) get dusty.

**verstauchen** [fɛrˈʃtauxən], *v.a.* wrench, sprain, dislocate.

**verstauen** [fɛrˈʃtauən], *v.a.* stow away.

**Versteck** [fɛrˈʃtɛk], *n.* (—s, *pl.* —e) hiding-place; place of concealment; —(en) *spielen*, play hide-and-seek.

**verstecken** [fɛrˈʃtɛkən], *v.a.* hide, conceal.

**versteckt** [fɛrˈʃtɛkt], *adj.* indirect, veiled.

**verstehen** [fɛrˈʃteːən], *v.a. irr.* understand, comprehend.

**versteigen** [fɛrˈʃtaɪgən], *v.r. irr. sich* —, climb too high; (*fig.*) go too far.

**versteigern** [fɛrˈʃtaɪgərn], *v.a.* sell by auction.

**Versteigerung** [fɛrˈʃtaɪgəruŋ], *f.* (—, *pl.* —en) auction, public sale.

**versteinern** [fɛrˈʃtaɪnərn], *v.n.* (*aux.* sein) turn into stone, petrify.

**verstellbar** [fɛrˈʃtɛlbaːr], *adj.* adjustable.

**verstellen** [fɛrˈʃtɛlən], *v.a.* adjust; (*voice*) disguise. — *v.r. sich* —, sham, pretend.

**versterben** [fɛrˈʃtɛrbən], *v.n. irr.* (*aux.* sein) (*Poet.*) die.

**versteuern** [fɛrˈʃtɔyərn], *v.a.* pay tax on.

**verstiegen** [fɛrˈʃtiːgən], *adj.* eccentric, extravagant.

**verstimmen** [fɛrˈʃtɪmən], *v.a.* (*Mus.*) put out of tune; (*fig.*) put out of humour, annoy.

**Verstimmtheit** [fɛrˈʃtɪmthaɪt], *f.* (—, *no pl.*) ill-humour, ill-temper, pique.

**Verstimmung** [fɛrˈʃtɪmuŋ], *f.* (—, *pl.* —en) bad temper, ill-feeling.

**verstockt** [fɛrˈʃtɔkt], *adj.* stubborn, obdurate.

**Verstocktheit** [fɛrˈʃtɔkthaɪt], *f.* (—, *no pl.*) stubbornness, obduracy.

**verstohlen** [fɛrˈʃtoːlən], *adj.* surreptitious, clandestine, furtive.

**verstopfen** [fɛrˈʃtɔpfən], *v.a.* stop up; block (up); *verstopft sein*, be constipated.

**Verstopfung** [fɛrˈʃtɔpfuŋ], *f.* (—, *pl.* —en) obstruction; constipation.

**verstorben** [fɛrˈʃtɔrbən], *adj.* deceased, late.

**verstört** [fɛrˈʃtøːrt], *adj.* troubled, worried; distracted.

**Verstörtheit** [fɛrˈʃtøːrthaɪt], *f.* (—, *no pl.*) consternation, agitation; distraction; haggardness.

**Verstoß** [fɛrˈʃtoːs], *m.* (—es, *pl.* ⁝e) blunder, mistake; offence.

**verstoßen** [fɛrˈʃtoːsən], *v.a. irr.* cast off, disown, repudiate. — *v.n.* —

*gegen*, offend against, act in a manner contrary to.

**verstreichen** [fɛrˈʃtraɪçən], *v.n. irr.* (*aux.* sein) (*time*) elapse, pass away.

**verstricken** [fɛrˈʃtrɪkən], *v.a.* entangle, ensnare.

**Verstrickung** [fɛrˈʃtrɪkuŋ], *f.* (—, *pl.* —en) entanglement.

**verstümmeln** [fɛrˈʃtyməln], *v.a.* mutilate, mangle.

**verstummen** [fɛrˈʃtumən], *v.n.* (*aux.* sein) grow silent; become speechless.

**Verstümmlung** [fɛrˈʃtymluŋ], *f.* (—, *pl.* —en) mutilation.

**Versuch** [fɛrˈzuːx], *m.* (—s, *pl.* —e) attempt, trial, endeavour; (*science*) experiment; (*Lit.*) essay.

**versuchen** [fɛrˈzuːxən], *v.a.* try, attempt, endeavour; (*food*) taste; *einen* —, tempt s.o.

**Versucher** [fɛrˈzuːxər], *m.* (—s, *pl.* —) tempter.

**Versuchskaninchen** [fɛrˈzuːxskaniːnçən], *n.* (—s, *pl.* —) (*fig.*) guinea-pig.

**Versuchung** [fɛrˈzuːxuŋ], *f.* (—, *pl.* —en) temptation.

**versündigen** [fɛrˈzyndɪgən], *v.r. sich* —, sin (against).

**Versunkenheit** [fɛrˈzuŋkənhaɪt], *f.* (—, *no pl.*) absorption, preoccupation.

**vertagen** [fɛrˈtaːgən], *v.a.* adjourn, prorogue.

**Vertagung** [fɛrˈtaːguŋ], *f.* (—, *pl.* —en) adjournment, prorogation.

**vertauschen** [fɛrˈtauʃən], *v.a.* exchange, barter, mistake, confuse.

**verteidigen** [fɛrˈtaɪdɪgən], *v.a.* defend, uphold, vindicate; (*fig.*) maintain.

**Verteidiger** [fɛrˈtaɪdɪgər], *m.* (—s, *pl.* —) defender; (*Law*) counsel for the defence.

**Verteidigung** [fɛrˈtaɪdɪguŋ], *f.* (—, *no pl.*) defence; justification.

**Verteidigungskrieg** [fɛrˈtaɪdɪguŋskriːk], *m.* (—(e)s, *pl.* —e) defensive war.

**verteilen** [fɛrˈtaɪlən], *v.a.* distribute, allot, allocate.

**Verteilung** [fɛrˈtaɪluŋ], *f.* (—, *pl.* —en) distribution, apportionment.

**verteuern** [fɛrˈtɔyərn], *v.a.* make dearer, raise the price of.

**verteufelt** [fɛrˈtɔyfəlt], *adj.* devilish. — *adv.* (*coll.*) awfully, infernally.

**vertiefen** [fɛrˈtiːfən], *v.a.* deepen.

**vertieft** [fɛrˈtiːft], *adj.* absorbed, deep in thought.

**Vertiefung** [fɛrˈtiːfuŋ], *f.* (—, *pl.* —en) cavity, recess, hollow; (*knowledge*) deepening; (*fig.*) absorption.

**vertilgen** [fɛrˈtɪlgən], *v.a.* wipe out, exterminate; (*food*) (*coll.*) polish off.

**Vertilgung** [fɛrˈtɪlguŋ], *f.* (—, *no pl.*) extermination, extirpation.

**Vertrag** [fɛrˈtraːk], *m.* (—(e)s, *pl.* ⁝e) contract, agreement; (*Pol.*) treaty, pact, convention.

**vertragen** [fɛrˈtraːgən], *v.a. irr.* suffer, endure; (*food*) digest. — *v.r. sich* — *mit*, get on well with.

# Verwandlung

**vertraglich** [fɛr'traːklɪç], *adj.* as per contract, according to agreement.
**verträglich** [fɛr'trɛːklɪç], *adj.* accommodating, peaceable.
**vertragsmäßig** [fɛr'traːksmɛːsɪç], *adj.* according to contract.
**vertragswidrig** [fɛr'traːksviːdrɪç], *adj.* contrary to contract.
**vertrauen** [fɛr'trauən], *v.n.* rely (upon), trust (in).
**Vertrauen** [fɛr'trauən], *n.* (—s, *no pl.*) confidence, trust, reliance.
**vertrauenerweckend** [fɛr'trauənɛrvɛkənt], *adj.* inspiring confidence.
**Vertrauensbruch** [fɛr'trauənsbrux], *m.* (—es, *pl.* ̈e) breach of faith.
**Vertrauensmann** [fɛr'trauənsman], *m.* (—s, *pl.* ̈er) confidant; delegate; person entrusted with s.th.; (*Ind.*) shop steward.
**vertrauensselig** [fɛr'trauənszeːlɪç], *adj.* confiding, trusting.
**Vertrauensvotum** [fɛr'trauənsvoːtum], *n.* (—s, *pl.* —ten) vote of confidence.
**vertrauenswürdig** [fɛr'trauənsvyrdɪç], *adj.* trustworthy.
**vertraulich** [fɛr'traulɪç], *adj.* confidential; familiar.
**Vertraulichkeit** [fɛr'traulɪçkaɪt], *f.* (—, *pl.* —en) familiarity.
**verträumt** [fɛr'trɔymt], *adj.* dreamy.
**vertraut** [fɛr'traut], *adj.* intimate, familiar; conversant.
**Vertraute** [fɛr'trautə], *m.* (—n, *pl.* —n) close friend, confidant.
**Vertrautheit** [fɛr'trauthaɪt], *f.* (—, *no pl.*) familiarity.
**vertreiben** [fɛr'traɪbən], *v.a. irr.* drive away, expel; eject; (*person*) banish; (*time*) pass, kill; (*goods*) sell.
**Vertreibung** [fɛr'traɪbuŋ], *f.* (—, *no pl.*) expulsion; banishment.
**vertreten** [fɛr'treːtən], *v.a. irr.* represent (s.o.), deputise for (s.o.).
**Vertreter** [fɛr'treːtər], *m.* (—s, *pl.* —) representative, deputy; (*Comm.*) agent.
**Vertretung** [fɛr'treːtuŋ], *f.* (—, *pl.* —en) representation, agency.
**Vertrieb** [fɛr'triːp], *m.* (—s, *pl.* —e) sale; distribution.
**vertrinken** [fɛr'trɪŋkən], *v.a. irr.* spend *or* waste money on drink.
**vertrocknen** [fɛr'trɔknən], *v.n.* (*aux.* sein) dry up, wither.
**vertrödeln** [fɛr'trøːdəln], *v.a.* fritter (o.'s time) away.
**vertrösten** [fɛr'trøːstən], *v.a.* console; put off; put (s.o.) off with fine words; fob (s.o.) off with vain hopes.
**Vertröstung** [fɛr'trøːstuŋ], *f.* (—, *pl.* —en) comfort; empty promises.
**vertun** [fɛr'tuːn], *v.a. irr.* squander, waste.
**vertuschen** [fɛr'tuʃən], *v.a.* hush up.
**verübeln** [fɛr'yːbəln], *v.a.* take amiss.
**verüben** [fɛr'yːbən], *v.a.* commit, perpetrate.
**verunehren** [fɛr'uneːrən], *v.a.* dishonour, disgrace.

**verunglimpfen** [fɛr'unglɪmpfən], *v.a.* bring into disrepute; defame, calumniate.
**Verunglimpfung** [fɛr'unglɪmpfuŋ], *f.* (—, *pl.* —en) defamation, detraction, calumny.
**verunglücken** [fɛr'unglykən], *v.n.* (*aux.* sein) (*person*) meet with an accident; be killed; (*thing*) misfire, fail.
**verunreinigen** [fɛr'unraɪnɪgən], *v.a.* contaminate.
**Verunreinigung** [fɛr'unraɪnɪguŋ], *f.* (—, *pl.* —en) contamination.
**verunstalten** [fɛr'unʃtaltən], *v.a.* disfigure, deface.
**Verunstaltung** [fɛr'unʃtaltuŋ], *f.* (—, *pl.* —en) disfigurement.
**Veruntreuung** [fɛr'untrɔyuŋ], *f.* (—, *pl.* —en) embezzlement, misappropriation.
**verunzieren** [fɛr'untsiːrən], *v.a.* disfigure, spoil.
**verursachen** [fɛr'uːrzaxən], *v.a.* cause, occasion.
**verurteilen** [fɛr'urtaɪlən], *v.a.* condemn; (*Law*) sentence.
**Verurteilung** [fɛr'urtaɪluŋ], *f.* (—, *no pl.*) condemnation; (*Law*) sentence.
**vervielfältigen** [fɛr'fiːlfɛltɪgən], *v.a.* multiply; duplicate, make copies of.
**Vervielfältigung** [fɛr'fiːlfɛltɪguŋ], *f.* (—, *pl.* —en) multiplication; duplication, copying.
**vervollkommnen** [fɛr'fɔlkɔmnən], *v.a.* improve, perfect.
**Vervollkommnung** [fɛr'fɔlkɔmnuŋ], *f.* (—, *no pl.*) improvement, perfection.
**vervollständigen** [fɛr'fɔlʃtɛndɪgən], *v.a.* complete.
**Vervollständigung** [fɛr'fɔlʃtɛndɪguŋ], *f.* (—, *no pl.*) completion.
**verwachsen** [fɛr'vaksən], *v.n. irr.* (*aux.* sein) grow together; be overgrown. — *adj.* deformed.
**verwahren** [fɛr'vaːrən], *v.a.* take care of, preserve, secure. — *v.r. sich —* gegen, protest against.
**verwahrlosen** [fɛr'vaːrloːzən], *v.a.* neglect. — *v.n.* (*aux.* sein) be in need of care and protection, be neglected.
**Verwahrlosung** [fɛr'vaːrloːzuŋ], *f.* (—, *no pl.*) neglect.
**Verwahrung** [fɛr'vaːruŋ], *f.* (—, *no pl.*) keeping; charge; *in — geben*, deposit, give into s.o.'s charge; *— einlegen gegen*, enter a protest against.
**verwalten** [fɛr'valtən], *v.a.* manage, administer.
**Verwalter** [fɛr'valtər], *m.* (—s, *pl.* —) administrator, manager; steward, bailiff.
**Verwaltung** [fɛr'valtuŋ], *f.* (—, *pl.* —en) administration, management; Civil Service.
**Verwaltungsbezirk** [fɛr'valtuŋsbətsɪrk], *m.* (—s, *pl.* —e) administrative district.
**Verwandlung** [fɛr'vandluŋ], *f.* (—, *pl.* —en) alteration, transformation.

263

**Verwandlungskünstler** [fɛr'vandluŋs-kynstlər], *m.* (—s, *pl.* —) quick-change artist.

**verwandt** [fɛr'vant], *adj.* related; cognate; congenial.

**Verwandte** [fɛr'vantə], *m.* (—n, *pl.* —n) relative, relation; kinsman; *der nächste* —, next of kin.

**Verwandtschaft** [fɛr'vantʃaft], *f.* (—, *pl.* —en) relationship; relations, family; congeniality, sympathy.

**verwarnen** [fɛr'varnən], *v.a.* admonish, forewarn.

**Verwarnung** [fɛr'varnuŋ], *f.* (—, *pl.* —en) admonition.

**Verwässerung** [fɛr'vɛsərun], *f.* (—, *pl.* —en) dilution.

**verwechseln** [fɛr'vɛksəln], *v.a.* confuse; mistake for.

**Verwechslung** [fɛr'vɛkslun], *f.* (—, *pl.* —en) confusion, mistake.

**verwegen** [fɛr've:gən], *adj.* bold, audacious.

**Verwegenheit** [fɛr've:gənhaɪt], *f.* (—, *pl.* —en) boldness, audacity.

**verweichlichen** [fɛr'vaɪçlɪçən], *v.a.* coddle. — *v.n.* (*aux.* sein) become effeminate.

**verweigern** [fɛr'vaɪgərn], *v.a.* refuse, deny; reject.

**Verweigerung** [fɛr'vaɪgərun], *f.* (—, *pl.* —en) refusal, denial; rejection.

**verweilen** [fɛr'vaɪlən], *v.n.* remain; tarry; stay (with), dwell (on).

**verweint** [fɛr'vaɪnt], *adj.* (*eyes*) red with weeping.

**Verweis** [fɛr'vaɪs], *m.* (—es, *pl.* —e) reproof, reprimand, rebuke.

**verweisen** [fɛr'vaɪzən], *v.a. irr.* reprimand; banish, exile; — *auf etwas*, refer to s.th., hint at s.th.

**Verweisung** [fɛr'vaɪzuŋ], *f.* (—, *pl.* —en) banishment, exile; reference.

**verweltlichen** [fɛr'vɛltlɪçən], *v.a.* secularise, profane.

**verwenden** [fɛr'vɛndən], *v.a.* use, make use of; apply to, employ in, utilize.

**Verwendung** [fɛr'vɛnduŋ], *f.* (—, *pl.* —en) application, use, expenditure, employment.

**verwerfen** [fɛr'vɛrfən], *v.a. irr.* reject, disapprove of.

**verwerflich** [fɛr'vɛrflɪç], *adj.* objectionable.

**Verwertung** [fɛr've:rtuŋ], *f.* (—, *no pl.*) utilisation.

**verwesen** [fɛr've:zən], *v.a.* administer. — *v.n.* (*aux.* sein) rot, decompose, putrefy.

**Verweser** [fɛr've:zər], *m.* (—s, *pl.* —) administrator.

**Verwesung** [fɛr've:zuŋ], *f.* (—, *no pl.*) (*office*) administration; putrefaction, rotting.

**verwickeln** [fɛr'vɪkəln], *v.a.* entangle, involve.

**verwickelt** [fɛr'vɪkəlt], *adj.* intricate, complicated, involved.

**Verwicklung** [fɛr'vɪkluŋ], *f.* (—, *pl.*

—en) entanglement, involvement, complication.

**verwildern** [fɛr'vɪldərn], *v.n.* (*aux.* sein) run wild.

**verwildert** [fɛr'vɪldərt], *adj.* wild, uncultivated, overgrown; (*fig.*) intractable.

**Verwilderung** [fɛr'vɪldəruŋ], *f.* (—, *no pl.*) running wild, growing wild.

**verwirken** [fɛr'vɪrkən], *v.a.* forfeit.

**verwirklichen** [fɛr'vɪrklɪçən], *v.a.* realise. — *v.r.* sich —, materialise, come true.

**Verwirklichung** [fɛr'vɪrklɪçuŋ], *f.* (—, *no pl.*) realisation, materialisation.

**Verwirkung** [fɛr'vɪrkuŋ], *f.* (—, *no pl.*) forfeiture.

**verwirren** [fɛr'vɪrən], *v.a.* disarrange, throw into disorder, entangle; puzzle, bewilder, confuse, disconcert.

**Verwirrung** [fɛr'vɪruŋ], *f.* (—, *pl.* —en) bewilderment, confusion.

**verwischen** [fɛr'vɪʃən], *v.a.* blot out, smudge, obliterate.

**verwittern** [fɛr'vɪtərn], *v.n.* (*aux.* sein) be weather-beaten.

**verwöhnen** [fɛr'vø:nən], *v.a.* spoil, pamper, coddle.

**verworfen** [fɛr'vɔrfən], *adj.* profligate; rejected, reprobate.

**verworren** [fɛr'vɔrən], *adj.* confused, perplexed; intricate; (*speech*) rambling.

**verwundbar** [fɛr'vuntba:r], *adj.* vulnerable.

**verwunden** [fɛr'vundən], *v.a.* wound, hurt, injure.

**verwundern** [fɛr'vundərn], *v.r.* sich —, be surprised, wonder, be amazed.

**Verwunderung** [fɛr'vundəruŋ], *f.* (—, *no pl.*) surprise, astonishment, amazement.

**Verwundung** [fɛr'vunduŋ], *f.* (—, *pl.* —en) wounding, wound, injury.

**verwunschen** [fɛr'vunʃən], *adj.* enchanted, spellbound, bewitched.

**verwünschen** [fɛr'vynʃən], *v.a.* curse; cast a spell on, bewitch.

**verwünscht** [fɛr'vynʃt], *excl.* confound it!

**Verwünschung** [fɛr'vynʃuŋ], *f.* (—, *pl.* —en) curse, malediction.

**verwüsten** [fɛr'vy:stən], *v.a.* devastate, ravage, lay waste.

**Verwüstung** [fɛr'vy:stuŋ], *f.* (—, *pl.* —en) devastation.

**verzagen** [fɛr'tsa:gən], *v.n.* (*aux.* sein) lose heart, lose courage.

**verzagt** [fɛr'tsa:kt], *adj.* fainthearted, discouraged.

**Verzagtheit** [fɛr'tsa:kthaɪt], *f.* (—, *no pl.*) faintheartedness.

**verzählen** [fɛr'tsɛ:lən], *v.r.* sich —, miscount.

**verzapfen** [fɛr'tsapfən], *v.a.* sell (liquor) on draught; (*fig.*) tell (a story), talk (nonsense).

**verzärteln** [fɛr'tsɛ:rtəln], *v.a.* pamper, coddle; spoil.

**verzaubern** [fɛr'tsaubərn], *v.a.* bewitch, charm, put a spell on.

# Vision

**verzehren** [fɛr'tseːrən], *v.a.* consume, eat. — *v.r.* sich — in, pine away with, be consumed with.

**Verzehrung** [fɛr'tseːruŋ], *f.* (—, *no pl.*) (*obs.*) consumption, tuberculosis.

**verzeichnen** [fɛr'tsaɪçnən], *v.a.* draw badly; note down, register, record.

**Verzeichnis** [fɛr'tsaɪçnɪs], *n.* (—ses, *pl.* —se) catalogue, list, register.

**verzeihen** [fɛr'tsaɪən], *v.a. irr.* forgive, pardon.

**verzeihlich** [fɛr'tsaɪlɪç], *adj.* pardonable, forgivable, excusable, venial.

**Verzeihung** [fɛr'tsaɪuŋ], *f.* (—, *no pl.*) pardon, forgiveness; *ich bitte um* —, I beg your pardon.

**verzerren** [fɛr'tsɛrən], *v.a.* distort.

**Verzerrung** [fɛr'tsɛruŋ], *f.* (—, *pl.* —en) distortion; (*face*) grimace.

**verzetteln** [fɛr'tsɛtəln], *v.a.* disperse, scatter.

**Verzicht** [fɛr'tsɪçt], *m.* (—(e)s, *no pl.*) renunciation, resignation.

**verzichten** [fɛr'tsɪçtən], *v.n.* forgo, renounce.

**verziehen** [fɛr'tsiːən], *v.a. irr.* distort; spoil (*child*). — *v.n.* (*aux.* sein) go away, move away.

**Verzierung** [fɛr'tsiːruŋ], *f.* (—, *pl.* —en) decoration, ornament.

**verzögern** [fɛr'tsøːgərn], *v.a.* delay, defer, retard, protract, procrastinate. — *v.r.* sich —, be delayed.

**Verzögerung** [fɛr'tsøːgəruŋ], *f.* (—, *pl.* —en) delay, retardation, procrastination; time-lag.

**verzollen** [fɛr'tsɔlən], *v.a.* pay duty on.

**Verzücktheit** [fɛr'tsʏkthaɪt], *f.* (—, *no pl.*) ecstasy, rapture.

**Verzug** [fɛr'tsuːk], *m.* (—s, *no pl.*) delay.

**verzweifeln** [fɛr'tsvaɪfəln], *v.n.* despair, be desperate.

**Verzweiflung** [fɛr'tsvaɪfluŋ], *f.* (—, *no pl.*) despair.

**verzwickt** [fɛr'tsvɪkt], *adj.* complicated, intricate, tricky.

**Vesuv** [ve'zuːf], *m.* Mount Vesuvius.

**Vetter** ['vɛtər], *m.* (—s, *pl.* —n) cousin.

**Vetternwirtschaft** ['vɛtərnvɪrtʃaft], *f.* (—, *no pl.*) nepotism.

**Vexierbild** [vɛ'ksiːrbɪlt], *n.* (—s, *pl.* —er) picture-puzzle.

**Vexierspiegel** [vɛ'ksiːrʃpiːgəl], *m.* (—s, *pl.*—) distorting mirror.

**vibrieren** [vi'briːrən], *v.n.* vibrate.

**Vieh** [fiː], *n.* (—s, *no pl.*) cattle, livestock.

**Viehfutter** ['fiːfutər], *n.* (—s, *no pl.*) forage, fodder, feeding-stuff.

**viehisch** ['fiːɪʃ], *adj.* beastly, brutal.

**Viehwagen** ['fiːvaːgən], *m.* (—s, *pl.* —) cattle-truck.

**Viehweide** ['fiːvaɪdə], *f.* (—, *pl.* —n) pasture, pasturage.

**Viehzüchter** ['fiːtsʏçtər], *m.* (—s, *pl.* —) cattle-breeder.

**viel** [fiːl], *adj.* much, a great deal, a lot; (*pl.*) many.

**vielartig** ['fiːlartɪç], *adj.* multifarious.

**vieldeutig** ['fiːldɔytɪç], *adj.* ambiguous, equivocal.

**Vieleck** ['fiːlɛk], *n.* (—s, *pl.* —e) polygon.

**vielerlei** ['fiːlərlaɪ], *adj.* of many kinds, various.

**vielfältig** ['fiːlfɛltɪç], *adj.* manifold.

**vielfarbig** ['fiːlfarbɪç], *adj.* multicoloured, variegated.

**Vielfraß** ['fiːlfraːs], *m.* (—es, *pl.* —e) glutton.

**vielgeliebt** ['fiːlgəliːpt],*adj.* much loved, well-beloved, dearly loved.

**vielgereist** ['fiːlgəraɪst], *adj.* much travelled.

**vielleicht** [fi'laɪçt],*adv.* perhaps, maybe.

**vielmals** ['fiːlmaːls], *adv.* many times, frequently, much.

**Vielmännerei** [fiːlmɛnə'raɪ], *f.* (—, *no pl.*) polyandry.

**vielmehr** [fiːl'meːr], *adv.* rather, much more. — *conj.* rather, on the other hand.

**vielsagend** ['fiːlzaːgənt], *adj.* expressive, full of meaning.

**vielseitig** ['fiːlzaɪtɪç], *adj.* multilateral; (*fig.*) versatile.

**Vielseitigkeit** ['fiːlzaɪtɪçkaɪt], *f.* (—, *no pl.*) versatility.

**vielverheißend** ['fiːlfɛrhaɪsənt], *adj.* promising, auspicious.

**Vielweiberei** [fiːlvaɪbə'raɪ], *f.* (—, *no pl.*) polygamy.

**vier** [fiːr], *num. adj.* four.

**Viereck** ['fiːrɛk], *n.* (—s, *pl.* —e) square, quadrangle.

**viereckig** ['fiːrɛkɪç], *adj.* square.

**vierfüßig** ['fiːrfyːsɪç], *adj.* four-footed.

**vierhändig** ['fiːrhɛndɪç], *adj.* four-handed; — *spielen*, (*piano*) play duets.

**vierschrötig** ['fiːrʃrøːtɪç], *adj.* robust, thick-set, stocky.

**vierseitig** ['fiːrzaɪtɪç], *adj.* quadrilateral.

**vierstimmig** ['fiːrʃtɪmɪç], *adj.* (*Mus.*) four-part; for four voices.

**vierteilen** ['fiːrtaɪlən], *v.a.* quarter, divide into four parts.

**Viertel** ['fɪrtəl], *n.* (—s, *pl.* —) quarter, fourth part.

**Viertelstunde** [fɪrtəl'ʃtundə], *f.* (—, *pl.* —n) quarter of an hour.

**viertens** ['fiːrtəns], *num. adv.* fourthly, in the fourth place.

**Vierwaldstättersee** [fiːr'valtʃtɛtərzeː], *m.* Lake Lucerne.

**vierzehn** ['fɪrtseːn], *num. adj.* fourteen; — *Tage*, a fortnight.

**vierzig** ['fɪrtsɪç], *num. adj.* forty.

**Vietnam** [vjɛt'naːm], *n.* Vietnam.

**Violinschlüssel** [vio'liːnʃlysəl], *m.* (—s, *pl.* —) (*Mus.*) treble clef.

**Virtuosität** [vɪrtuozi'tɛːt], *f.* (—, *no pl.*) mastery, virtuosity.

**Visage** [vi'zaːʒə], *f.* (—, *pl.* —n) (*coll.*) face.

**Visier** [vi'ziːr], *n.* (—, *pl.* —e) visor; (*gun*) sight.

**Vision** [vi'zjoːn], *f.* (—, *pl.* —en) vision.

# Visionär

**Visionär** [vizjo'nɛːr], *m.* (**—s**, *pl.* **—e**) visionary.

**Visitenkarte** [vi'ziːtənkartə], *f.* (**—**, *pl.* **—n**) card, visiting card.

**Visum** ['viːzum], *n.* (**—s**, *pl.* **Visa**) visa.

**Vizekönig** ['viːtsəkøːnɪç], *m.* (**—s**, *pl.* **—e**) viceroy.

**Vlies** [fliːs], *n.* (**—es**, *pl.* **—e**) fleece.

**Vogel** ['foːgəl], *m.* (**—s**, *pl.* **¨**) bird; (*coll.*) fellow; *einen — haben*, be off o.'s head.

**Vogelbauer** ['foːgəlbauər], *n.* (**—s**, *pl.* **—**) bird-cage.

**Vogelfänger** ['foːgəlfɛŋər], *m.* (**—s**, *pl.* **—**) fowler, bird-catcher.

**vogelfrei** ['foːgəlfraɪ], *adj.* outlawed, proscribed.

**Vogelfutter** ['foːgəlfutər], *n.* (**—s**, *no pl.*) bird-seed.

**Vogelhändler** ['foːgəlhɛndlər], *m.* (**—s**, *pl.* **—**) bird-dealer.

**Vogelhaus** ['foːgəlhaus], *n.* (**—es**, *pl.* **¨er**) aviary.

**Vogelkenner** ['foːgəlkɛnər], *m.* (**—s**, *pl.* **—**) ornithologist.

**Vogelkunde** ['foːgəlkundə], *f.* (**—**, *no pl.*) ornithology.

**Vogelperspektive** ['foːgəlpɛrspɛktiːvə], *f.* (**—**, *no pl.*) bird's-eye view.

**Vogelschau** ['foːgəlʃau], *f.* (**—**, *no pl.*) bird's-eye view.

**Vogelsteller** ['foːgəlʃtɛlər], *m.* (**—s**, *pl.* **—**) fowler, bird-catcher.

**Vogesen** [vo'geːzən], *pl.* Vosges Mountains.

**Vogler** ['foːglər], *m.* (**—s**, *pl.* **—**) fowler.

**Vogt** [foːkt], *m.* (**—(e)s**, *pl.* **¨e**) prefect, bailiff, steward, provost.

**Vogtei** [foːk'taɪ], *f.* (**—**, *pl.* **—en**) prefecture, bailiwick.

**Vokabel** [vo'kaːbəl], *f.* (**—**, *pl.* **—n**) word, vocable.

**Vokabelbuch** [vo'kaːbəlbuːx], *n.* (**—(e)s**, *pl.* **¨er**) vocabulary (book).

**Vokal** [vo'kaːl], *m.* (**—s**, *pl.* **—e**) vowel.

**Vokativ** [voka'tiːf], *m.* (**—s**, *pl.* **—e**) (*Gram.*) vocative.

**Volk** [fɔlk], *n.* (**—(e)s**, *pl.* **¨er**) people, nation; *das gemeine —*, mob, the common people.

**Völkerkunde** ['fœlkərkundə], *f.* (**—**, *no pl.*) ethnology.

**Völkerrecht** ['fœlkərrɛçt], *n.* (**—s**, *no pl.*) international law.

**Völkerschaft** ['fœlkərʃaft], *f.* (**—**, *pl.* **—en**) tribe, people.

**Völkerwanderung** ['fœlkərvandəruŋ], *f.* (**—**, *pl.* **—en**) mass migration.

**Volksabstimmung** ['fɔlksapʃtɪmuŋ], *f.* (**—**, *pl.* **—en**) referendum.

**Volksausgabe** ['fɔlksausgaːbə], *f.* (**—**, *pl.* **—n**) popular edition.

**Volksbeschluß** ['fɔlksbəʃlus], *m.* (**—sses**, *pl.* **¨sse**) plebiscite.

**Volksbibliothek** ['fɔlksbiblioteːk], *f.* (**—**, *pl.* **—en**) public library.

**Volkscharakter** ['fɔlkskaraktər], *m.* (**—s**, *no pl.*) national character.

**Volksentscheid** ['fɔlksɛntʃaɪt], *m.* (**—s**, *pl.* **—e**) plebiscite.

**Volksführer** ['fɔlksfyːrər], *m.* (**—s**, *pl.* **—**) demagogue.

**Volksheer** ['fɔlksheːr], *n.* (**—s**, *pl.* **—e**) national army.

**Volksherrschaft** ['fɔlkshɛrʃaft], *f.* (**—**, *no pl.*) democracy.

**Volkshochschule** ['fɔlkshoxʃuːlə], *f.* (**—**, *no pl.*) adult education (classes).

**Volksjustiz** ['fɔlksjustiːts], *f.* (**—**, *no pl.*) lynch-law.

**Volkskunde** ['fɔlkskundə], *f.* (**—**, *no pl.*) folklore.

**Volkslied** ['fɔlksliːt], *n.* (**—s**, *pl.* **—er**) folk-song.

**Volksschicht** ['fɔlksʃɪçt], *f.* (**—**, *pl.* **—en**) class.

**Volksschule** ['fɔlksʃuːlə], *f.* (**—**, *pl.* **—n**) primary school; elementary school.

**Volkssitte** ['fɔlkszɪtə], *f.* (**—**, *pl.* **—n**) national custom.

**Volkssprache** ['fɔlksʃpraːxə], *f.* (**—**, *pl.* **—n**) vernacular.

**Volksstamm** ['fɔlksʃtam], *m.* (**—s**, *pl.* **¨e**) tribe.

**Volkstracht** ['fɔlkstraxt], *f.* (**—**, *pl.* **—en**) national costume.

**volkstümlich** ['fɔlkstyːmlɪç], *adj.* national, popular.

**Volksvertretung** ['fɔlksfɛrtreːtuŋ], *f.* (**—**, *no pl.*) representation of the people, parliamentary representation.

**Volkswirt** ['fɔlksvɪrt], *m.* (**—s**, *pl.* **—e**) political economist.

**Volkswirtschaft** ['fɔlksvɪrtʃaft], *f.* (**—**, *no pl.*) political economy.

**Volkszählung** ['fɔlkstseːluŋ], *f.* (**—**, *pl.* **—en**) census.

**voll** [fɔl], *adj.* full, filled; whole, complete, entire.

**vollauf** ['fɔlauf], *adv.* abundantly.

**Vollbart** ['fɔlbaːrt], *m.* (**—s**, *pl.* **¨e**) beard.

**vollberechtigt** ['fɔlbərɛçtɪçt], *adj.* fully entitled.

**Vollbild** ['fɔlbɪlt], *n.* (**—s**, *pl.* **—er**) full-length portrait, full-page illustration.

**Vollblut** ['fɔlbluːt], *n.* (**—s**, *pl.* **¨er**) thoroughbred.

**vollblütig** ['fɔlblyːtɪç], *adj.* full-blooded, thoroughbred.

**vollbringen** [fɔl'brɪŋən], *v.a. irr.* accomplish, achieve, complete.

**Vollbringung** [fɔl'brɪŋuŋ], *f.* (**—**, *no pl.*) achievement.

**Volldampf** ['fɔldampf], *m.* (**—es**, *no pl.*) full steam.

**vollenden** [fɔl'ɛndən], *v.a.* finish, complete.

**vollendet** [fɔl'ɛndət], *adj.* finished; accomplished.

**vollends** ['fɔlɛnts], *adv.* quite, altogether, wholly, entirely, moreover.

**Vollendung** [fɔl'ɛnduŋ], *f.* (**—**, *no pl.*) completion; perfection.

**Völlerei** [fœlə'raɪ], *f.* (**—**, *pl.* **—en**) gluttony.

# Vorbereitung

**vollführen** [fɔl'fy:rən], *v.a.* execute, carry out.
**Vollgefühl** ['fɔlgəfy:l], *n.* (—s, *no pl.*) consciousness, full awareness.
**Vollgenuß** ['fɔlgənus], *m.* (—sses, *no pl.*) full enjoyment.
**vollgültig** ['fɔlgyltıç], *adj.* fully valid; unexceptionable.
**Vollheit** ['fɔlhaɪt], *f.* (—, *no pl.*) fullness, plenitude.
**völlig** ['fœlıç], *adj.* entire, whole, complete.
**vollinhaltlich** ['fɔlınhaltlıç], *adv.* to its full extent.
**volljährig** ['fɔljɛ:rɪç], *adj.* of age.
**Volljährigkeit** ['fɔljɛ:rɪçkaɪt], *f.* (—, *no pl.*) adult years, majority.
**vollkommen** ['fɔlkɔmən], *adj.* perfect. — *adv.* entirely.
**Vollkommenheit** [fɔl'kɔmənhaɪt], *f.* (—, *no pl.*) perfection.
**Vollmacht** ['fɔlmaxt], *f.* (—, *pl.* —en) authority; fullness of power; power of attorney.
**vollsaftig** ['fɔlzaftıç], *adj.* juicy, succulent.
**vollständig** ['fɔlʃtɛndıç], *adj.* complete, full. — *adv.* entirely.
**vollstrecken** [fɔl'ʃtrɛkən], *v.a.* execute, carry out.
**Vollstrecker** [fɔl'ʃtrɛkər], *m.* (—s, *pl.* —) executor.
**volltönig** ['fɔltø:nıç], *adj.* sonorous.
**vollwertig** ['fɔlvɛrtıç], *adj.* standard, sterling.
**vollzählig** ['fɔltsɛ:lıç], *adj.* complete.
**vollziehen** [fɔl'tsi:ən], *v.a. irr.* execute, carry out, ratify.
**vollziehend** [fɔl'tsi:ənt], *adj.* executive.
**Vollziehungsgewalt** [fɔl'tsi:uŋsgəvalt], *f.* (—, *no pl.*) executive power.
**Vollzug** [fɔl'tsu:k], *m.* (—s, *no pl.*) execution; fulfilment.
**Volontär** [vɔlɔ'tɛ:r], *m.* (—s, *pl.* —e) volunteer.
**von** [fɔn] (*von dem* becomes **vom**), *prep.* (*Dat.*) by, from; of; on; concerning, about; — *Shakespeare,* by Shakespeare; — *Beruf,* by profession; *er kommt — London,* he comes from London; — *fern,* from afar; — *jetzt an,* from now on; — *einem sprechen,* speak of s.o.; *dein Brief vom 15.,* your letter of the 15th.
**vonnöten** [fɔn'nø:tən], *adv.* — *sein,* be necessary.
**vonstatten** [fɔn'ʃtatən], *adv.* — *gehen,* progress; go off.
**vor** [fo:r], *prep.* (*Dat., Acc.*) (*place*) before, ahead of, in front of; (*time*) before, prior to, earlier than; from; of; with; above; in presence of, because of; more than; — *dem Hause,* in front of the house; — *Sonnenaufgang,* before sunrise; —*zwei Tagen,* two days ago; *sich — einem verstecken,* hide from s.o.; *sich hüten —,* beware of; *starr — Kälte,* stiff with cold; — *allem,* above all. — *adv.* before; *nach wie —,* now as before.

**Vorabend** ['fo:ra:bənt], *m.* (—s, *pl.* —e) eve.
**Vorahnung** ['fo:ra:nuŋ], *f.* (—, *pl.* —en) presentiment, foreboding.
**voran** [fo'ran], *adv.* before, in front, forward, on.
**vorangehen** [fo'range:ən], *v.n. irr.* (*aux.* sein) take the lead, go ahead.
**Voranzeige** ['fo:rantsaɪgə], *f.* (—, *pl.* —n) advance notice; (*film*) trailer.
**Vorarbeiter** ['fo:rarbaɪtər], *m.* (—s, *pl.* —) foreman.
**voraus** [fo'raus], *adv.* before, in front, foremost; in advance; *im* or *zum* —, beforehand; (*thanks*) in anticipation.
**vorauseilen** [fo'rausaɪlən], *v.n.* (*aux.* sein) run ahead.
**vorausgehen** [fo'rausge:ən], *v.n. irr.* (*aux.* sein) walk ahead; *einem* —, go before; precede s.o.
**voraushaben** [fo'rausha:bən], *v.n. irr. etwas vor einem —,* have the advantage over s.o.
**Voraussage** [fo'rausza:gə], *f.* (—, *pl.* —n) prediction, prophecy; (*weather*) forecast.
**voraussagen** [fo'rausza:gən], *v.a.* predict, foretell; (*weather*) forecast.
**voraussehen** [fo'rausze:ən], *v.a. irr.* foresee.
**voraussetzen** [fo'rauszɛtsən], *v.a.* presuppose, take for granted.
**Voraussetzung** [fo'rauszɛtsuŋ], *f.* (—, *pl.* —en) supposition, presupposition; *unter der —,* on the understanding.
**Voraussicht** [fo'rauszɪçt], *f.* (—, *no pl.*) foresight, forethought; *aller — nach,* in all probability.
**voraussichtlich** [fo'rauszɪçtlıç], *adj.* prospective, presumptive, probable, expected. — *adv.* probably, presumably.
**Vorbau** ['fo:rbau], *m.* (—s, *pl.* —ten) frontage.
**Vorbedacht** ['fo:rbədaxt], *m.* (—s, *no pl.*) premeditation; *mit —,* on purpose, deliberately.
**vorbedacht** ['fo:rbədaxt], *adj.* premeditated.
**Vorbedeutung** ['fo:rbədɔytuŋ], *f.* (—, *pl.* —en) omen.
**Vorbehalt** ['fo:rbəhalt], *m.* (—s, *pl.* —e) reservation, proviso.
**vorbehalten** ['fo:rbəhaltən], *v.a. irr.* reserve; make reservation that.
**vorbehaltlich** ['fo:rbəhaltlıç], *prep.* (*Genit.*) with the proviso that.
**vorbei** [fo:r'baɪ], *adv.* by; along; past, over, finished, gone.
**vorbeigehen** [fo:r'baɪge:ən], *v.n. irr.* (*aux.* sein) pass by; go past; march past.
**vorbeilassen** [fo:r'baɪlasən], *v.a. irr.* let pass.
**Vorbemerkung** ['fo:rbəmɛrkuŋ], *f.* (—, *pl.* —en) preface, prefatory note.
**vorbereiten** ['fo:rbəraɪtən], *v.a.* prepare.
**Vorbereitung** ['fo:rbəraɪtuŋ], *f.* (—, *pl.* —en) preparation.

# Vorbesitzer

**Vorbesitzer** ['fo:rbəzɪtsər], *m.* (—s, *pl.* —) previous owner.
**Vorbesprechung** ['fo:rbəʃprɛçuŋ], *f.* (—, *pl.* —en) preliminary discussion.
**vorbestimmen** ['fo:rbəʃtɪmən], *v.a.* predestine, predetermine.
**Vorbestimmung** ['fo:rbəʃtɪmuŋ], *f.* (—, *no pl.*) predestination.
**vorbestraft** ['fo:rbəʃtra:ft], *adj.* previously convicted.
**vorbeten** ['fo:rbe:tən], *v.n.* lead in prayer.
**vorbeugen** ['fo:rbɔygən], *v.n.* prevent, preclude, obviate. — *v.r. sich* —, bend forward.
**Vorbeugung** ['fo:rbɔyguŋ], *f.* (—, *no pl.*) prevention; prophylaxis.
**Vorbeugungsmaßnahme** ['fo:rbɔyguŋsma:sna:mə], *f.* (—, *pl.* —n) preventive measure.
**Vorbild** ['fo:rbɪlt], *n.* (—s, *pl.* —er) model, example, pattern, ideal.
**vorbildlich** ['fo:rbɪltlɪç], *adj.* exemplary; typical; — *sein*, be a model.
**Vorbildung** ['fo:rbɪlduŋ], *f.* (—, *no pl.*) preparatory training.
**Vorbote** ['fo:rbo:tə], *m.* (—n, *pl.* —n) herald, precursor, forerunner.
**vorbringen** ['fo:rbrɪŋən], *v.a. irr.* produce, proffer; advance, utter, allege, assert, claim.
**vordatieren** ['fo:rdati:rən], *v.a.* antedate.
**vordem** [for'de:m], *adv.* (obs.) formerly, once.
**Vorderachse** ['fordəraksə], *f.* (—, *pl.* —n) front axle.
**Vorderansicht** ['fordəranzɪçt], *f.* (—, *pl.* —en) front view.
**Vorderarm** ['fordərarm], *m.* (—s, *pl.* —e) forearm.
**Vordergrund** ['fordərgrunt], *m.* (—s, *pl.* —e) foreground.
**vorderhand** ['fordərhant], *adv.* for the present.
**Vorderseite** ['fordərzaɪtə], *f.* (—, *pl.* —n) front.
**vorderst** ['fordərst], *adj.* foremost, first.
**Vordertür** ['fordərty:r], *f.* (—, *pl.* —en) front door.
**Vordertreffen** ['fordərtrɛfən], *n.* (—s, *no pl.*) *ins — kommen*, be in the vanguard, come to the fore.
**vordrängen** ['fo:rdrɛŋən], *v.r. sich* —, press forward, jump the queue.
**vordringen** ['fo:rdrɪŋən], *v.n. irr.* (aux. sein) advance, push forward.
**vordringlich** ['fo:rdrɪŋlɪç], *adj.* urgent; forward, importunate.
**Vordruck** ['fo:rdruk], *m.* (—s, *pl.* —e) (printed) form.
**voreilen** ['fo:raɪlən], *v.n.* (aux. sein) rush forward.
**voreilig** ['fo:raɪlɪç], *adj.* over-hasty, rash.
**Voreiligkeit** ['fo:raɪlɪçkaɪt], *f.* (—, *no pl.*) hastiness, rashness.
**voreingenommen** ['fo:raɪŋənɔmən], *adj.* biased, prejudiced.
**Voreingenommenheit** ['fo:raɪŋənɔmənhaɪt], *f.* (—, *no pl.*) bias, prejudice.
**Voreltern** ['fo:rɛltərn], *pl.* forefathers, ancestors.
**vorenthalten** ['fo:rɛnthaltən], *v.a. irr. sep. & insep.* withhold.
**Vorentscheidung** ['fo:rɛntʃaɪduŋ], *f.* (—, *pl.* —en) preliminary decision.
**vorerst** [fo:r'e:rst], *adv.* first of all, firstly; for the time being.
**vorerwähnt** ['fo:rɛrvɛ:nt], *adj.* aforementioned.
**Vorfahr** ['fo:rfa:r], *m.* (—en, *pl.* —en) ancestor.
**vorfahren** ['fo:rfa:rən], *v.n. irr.* (aux. sein) drive up (to a house *etc.*).
**Vorfall** ['fo:rfal], *m.* (—s, *pl.* —e) occurrence, incident.
**vorfinden** ['fo:rfɪndən], *v.a. irr.* find, find present, meet with.
**Vorfrage** ['fo:rfra:gə], *f.* (—, *pl.* —n) preliminary question.
**vorführen** ['fo:rfy:rən], *v.a.* bring forward, produce.
**Vorführung** ['fo:rfy:ruŋ], *f.* (—, *pl.* —en) production, presentation; performance.
**Vorgang** ['fo:rgaŋ], *m.* (—s, *pl.* —e) occurrence, event, happening; proceeding, precedent; procedure.
**Vorgänger** ['fo:rgɛŋər], *m.* (—s, *pl.* —) predecessor.
**Vorgarten** ['fo:rgartən], *m.* (—s, *pl.* —) front garden.
**vorgeben** ['fo:rge:bən], *v.a. irr.* pretend; allow (in advance).
**Vorgebirge** ['fo:rgəbɪrgə], *n.* (—s, *no pl.*) cape, promontory.
**vorgeblich** ['fo:rge:plɪç], *adj.* pretended; ostensible.
**vorgefaßt** ['fo:rgəfast], *adj.* preconceived.
**Vorgefühl** ['fo:rgəfy:l], *n.* (—s, *pl.* —e) presentiment.
**vorgehen** ['fo:rge:ən], *v.n. irr.* (aux. sein) advance, walk ahead; proceed; (*clock*) be fast, gain; (*fig.*) take precedence; occur, happen; *was geht hier vor?* what's going on here?
**Vorgehen** ['fo:rge:ən], *n.* (—s, *no pl.*) (course of) action, (manner of) procedure.
**vorgenannt** ['fo:rgənant], *adj.* aforenamed.
**Vorgericht** ['fo:rgərɪçt], *n.* (—s, *pl.* —e) hors d'œuvre, entrée.
**Vorgeschichte** ['fo:rgəʃɪçtə], *f.* (—, *no pl.*) prehistory; early history; antecedents.
**vorgeschichtlich** ['fo:rgəʃɪçtlɪç], *adj.* prehistoric.
**Vorgeschmack** ['fo:rgəʃmak], *m.* (—s, *no pl.*) foretaste.
**Vorgesetzte** ['fo:rgəzɛtstə], *m.* (—n, *pl.* —n) superior, senior; boss.
**vorgestern** ['fo:rgɛstərn], *adv.* the day before yesterday.
**vorgreifen** ['fo:rgraɪfən], *v.n. irr.* anticipate, forestall.

**Vorhaben** ['fo:rha:bən], *m.* (—s, *no pl.*) intention, purpose, design.
**vorhaben** ['fo:rha:bən], *v.a. irr.* intend; be busy with; *etwas mit einem —*, have designs on s.o.; have plans for s.o.
**Vorhalle** ['fo:rhalə], *f.* (—, *pl.* —n) vestibule, hall, porch.
**vorhalten** ['fo:rhaltən], *v.a. irr.* hold s.th. before s.o.; (*fig.*) remonstrate (with s.o. about s.th.); reproach. — *v.n.* last.
**Vorhaltungen** ['fo:rhaltuŋən], *f. pl.* remonstrances, expostulations.
**vorhanden** [for'handən], *adj.* at hand, present, in stock, on hand.
**Vorhandensein** [for'handənzaɪn], *n.* (—s, *no pl.*) existence; availability.
**Vorhang** ['fo:rhaŋ], *m.* (—s, *pl.* ⁓e) curtain.
**Vorhängeschloß** ['fo:rhɛŋəʃlɔs], *n.* (—sses, *pl.* ⁓sser) padlock.
**vorher** ['fo:rhe:r], *adv.* before, beforehand, in advance.
**vorhergehen** [fo:r'he:rge:ən], *v.n. irr.* (*aux.* sein) go before, precede.
**vorhergehend** [fo:r'he:rge:ənt], *adj.* foregoing, aforesaid, preceding.
**vorherig** [fo:r'he:rɪç], *adj.* preceding, previous, former.
**vorherrschen** ['fo:rhɛrʃən], *v.n.* prevail, predominate.
**vorhersagen** [fo:r'he:rza:gən], *v.a.* predict, foretell.
**vorhersehen** [fo:r'he:rze:ən], *v.a. irr.* foresee.
**vorheucheln** ['fo:rhɔyçəln], *v.a. einem etwas —*, pretend s.th. to s.o.
**vorhin** [fo:r'hɪn], *adv.* just before, a short while ago.
**Vorhof** ['fo:rho:f], *m.* (—s, *pl.* ⁓e) forecourt.
**Vorhölle** ['fo:rhœlə], *f.* (—, *no pl.*) limbo.
**Vorhut** ['fo:rhu:t], *f.* (—, *no pl.*) vanguard.
**vorig** ['fo:rɪç], *adj.* former, preceding.
**Vorjahr** ['fo:rja:r], *n.* (—s, *pl.* —e) preceding year.
**vorjammern** ['fo:rjamərn], *v.n. einem etwas —*, moan to s.o. about s.th.
**Vorkämpfer** ['fo:rkɛmpfər], *m.* (—s, *pl.* —) champion; pioneer.
**vorkauen** ['fo:rkauən], *v.a.* (*fig.*) predigest; spoon-feed.
**Vorkaufsrecht** ['fo:rkaufsrɛçt], *n.* (—s, *no pl.*) right of first refusal, right of pre-emption.
**Vorkehrung** ['fo:rke:ruŋ], *f.* (—, *pl.* —en) preparation; precaution; (*pl.*) arrangements.
**Vorkenntnisse** ['fo:rkɛntnɪsə], *f. pl.* rudiments, elements, grounding; previous knowledge.
**vorkommen** ['fo:rkɔmən], *v.n. irr.* (*aux.* sein) occur, happen; be found.
**Vorkommnis** ['fo:rkɔmnɪs], *n.* (—ses, *pl.* —se) occurrence, event, happening.
**Vorkriegs-** ['fo:rkri:ks], *prefix.* pre-war.

**Vorladung** ['fo:rla:duŋ], *f.* (—, *pl.* —en) summons, writ, subpœna.
**Vorlage** ['fo:rla:gə], *f.* (—, *pl.* —n) pattern, master-copy.
**vorlagern** ['fo:rla:gərn], *v.n.* (*aux.* sein) extend (in front of).
**Vorland** ['fo:rlant], *n.* (—s, *pl.* ⁓er) cape, foreland, foreshore.
**vorlassen** ['fo:rlasən], *v.a. irr.* give precedence to; admit, show in.
**Vorläufer** ['fo:rlɔyfər], *m.* (—s, *pl.* —) forerunner, precursor.
**vorläufig** ['fo:rlɔyfɪç], *adj.* provisional, preliminary, temporary. — *adv.* for the time being.
**vorlaut** ['fo:rlaut], *adj.* pert, forward.
**Vorleben** ['fo:rle:bən], *n.* (—s, *no pl.*) antecedents, past life.
**vorlegen** ['fo:rle:gən], *v.a.* put before s.o.; submit, propose; (*food*) serve.
**Vorleger** ['fo:rle:gər], *m.* (—s, *pl.* —) rug, mat.
**Vorlegeschloß** ['fo:rle:gəʃlɔs], *n.* (—sses, *pl.* ⁓sser) padlock.
**vorlesen** ['fo:rle:zən], *v.a. irr.* read aloud, read out.
**Vorlesung** ['fo:rle:zuŋ], *f.* (—, *pl.* —en) lecture.
**vorletzte** ['fo:rlɛtstə], *adj.* last but one, penultimate.
**Vorliebe** ['fo:rli:bə], *f.* (—, *no pl.*) predilection, partiality.
**vorliebnehmen** [for'li:pne:mən], *v.n. — mit etwas*, be content with s.th., take pot luck.
**vorliegen** ['fo:rli:gən], *v.n. irr.* (*aux.* sein) be under consideration.
**vorlügen** ['fo:rly:gən], *v.a. irr. einem etwas —*, tell lies to s.o.
**vormachen** ['fo:rmaxən], *v.a. einem etwas —*, show s.o. how a thing is done; (*fig.*) play tricks on s.o., deceive s.o.
**vormalig** ['fo:rma:lɪç], *adj.* former, erstwhile, late.
**vormals** ['fo:rma:ls], *adv.* formerly.
**Vormarsch** ['fo:rmarʃ], *m.* (—es, *pl.* ⁓e) (*Mil.*) advance.
**vormerken** ['fo:rmɛrkən], *v.a.* make a note of, take down; book.
**Vormittag** ['fo:rmɪta:k], *m.* (—s, *pl.* —e) morning, forenoon.
**vormittags** ['fo:rmɪta:ks], *adv.* in the morning; before noon.
**Vormund** ['fo:rmunt], *m.* (—s, *pl.* ⁓er) guardian.
**Vormundschaft** ['fo:rmuntʃaft], *f.* (—, *pl.* —en) guardianship.
**Vormundschaftsgericht** ['fo:rmuntʃaftsgərɪçt], *n.* (—s, *pl.* —e) Court of Chancery.
**vorn** [fɔrn], *adv.* before, in front of; in front; (*Naut.*) fore.
**Vorname** ['fo:rna:mə], *m.* (—ns, *pl.* —n) first name, Christian name.
**vornehm** ['fo:rne:m], *adj.* of noble birth, refined; distinguished, elegant.
**vornehmen** ['fo:rne:mən], *v.a. irr.* take in hand; *sich etwas —*, undertake s.th.; plan *or* intend to do s.th.

**Vornehmheit** ['foːrneːmhaɪt], *f.* (—, *no pl.*) refinement, distinction.
**vornehmlich** ['foːrneːmlɪç], *adv.* chiefly, principally, especially.
**vornherein** ['fɔrnheraɪn], *adv. von* —, from the first; from the beginning.
**Vorort** ['foːrɔrt], *m.* (—s, *pl.* —e) suburb.
**Vorortsbahn** ['foːrɔrtsbaːn], *f.* (—, *pl.* —en) suburban (railway) line.
**Vorplatz** ['foːrplats], *m.* (—es, *pl.* ˙e) forecourt.
**Vorposten** ['foːrpɔstən], *m.* (—s, *pl.* —) (*Mil.*) outpost, pickets.
**Vorpostengefecht** ['foːrpɔstəngəfeçt], *n.* (—s, *pl.* —e) outpost skirmish.
**Vorprüfung** ['foːrpryːfuŋ], *f.* (—, *pl.* —en) preliminary examination.
**Vorrang** ['foːrraŋ], *m.* (—s, *no pl.*) precedence, first place, priority.
**Vorrat** ['foːrraːt], *m.* (—s, *pl.* ˙e) store, stock, provision.
**Vorratskammer** ['foːrraːtskamər], *f.* (—, *pl.* —n) store-room; larder.
**Vorrecht** ['foːrreçt], *n.* (—s, *pl.* —e) privilege, prerogative.
**Vorrede** ['foːrreːdə], *f.* (—, *pl.* —n) preface; introduction.
**Vorredner** ['foːrreːdnər], *m.* (—s, *pl.* —) previous speaker.
**vorrichten** ['foːrrɪçtən], *v.a.* prepare, fix up, get ready.
**Vorrichtung** ['foːrrɪçtuŋ], *f.* (—, *pl.* —en) appliance, device, contrivance.
**vorrücken** ['foːrrykən], *v.a.* move forward, advance; (*clock*) put on. — *v.n.* (*aux.* sein) (*Mil.*) advance.
**Vorsaal** ['foːrzaːl], *m.* (—s, *pl.* —säle) hall, entrance hall.
**Vorsatz** ['foːrzats], *m.* (—es, *pl.* ˙e) purpose, design, intention.
**vorsätzlich** ['foːrzetslɪç], *adj.* intentional, deliberate.
**Vorschein** ['foːrʃaɪn], *m.* *zum* — *kommen*, turn up; appear.
**vorschießen** ['foːrʃiːsən], *v.a.* irr. (*money*) advance, lend.
**Vorschlag** ['foːrʃlaːk], *m.* (—s, *pl.* ˙e) proposal, offer, proposition.
**vorschlagen** ['foːrʃlaːgən], *v.a.* irr. put forward, propose, suggest; recommend.
**vorschnell** ['foːrʃnel], *adj.* hasty, rash, precipitate.
**vorschreiben** ['foːrʃraɪbən], *v.a.* irr. write out (for s.o.); (*fig.*) prescribe, order.
**Vorschrift** ['foːrʃrɪft], *f.* (—, *pl.* —en) prescription, direction, order, command, regulation.
**vorschriftsmäßig** ['foːrʃrɪftsmeːsɪç], *adj.* according to regulations.
**vorschriftswidrig** ['foːrʃrɪftsviːdrɪç], *adj.* contrary to regulations.
**Vorschub** ['foːrʃuːp], *m.* (—s, *no pl.*) aid, assistance; — *leisten*, countenance, encourage, abet.
**Vorschule** ['foːrʃuːlə], *f.* (—, *pl.* —n) preparatory school.
**Vorschuß** ['foːrʃus], *m.* (—sses, *pl.* ˙sse) advance (of cash).

**vorschützen** ['foːrʃytsən], *v.a.* use as a pretext, pretend, plead.
**vorschweben** ['foːrʃveːbən], *v.n.* be present in o.'s mind.
**vorsehen** ['foːrzeːən], *v.r.* irr. sich —, take heed, be careful, look out, beware.
**Vorsehung** ['foːrzeːuŋ], *f.* (—, *no pl.*) Providence.
**vorsetzen** ['foːrzetsən], *v.a.* set before; serve; (*word*) prefix.
**Vorsicht** ['foːrzɪçt], *f.* (—, *no pl.*) care, precaution, caution, circumspection.
**vorsichtig** ['foːrzɪçtɪç], *adj.* cautious, careful, circumspect.
**vorsichtshalber** ['foːrzɪçtshalbər], *adv.* as a precautionary measure.
**Vorsichtsmaßnahme** ['foːrzɪçtsmaːsnaːmə], *f.* (—, *pl.* —n) precautionary measure, precaution.
**Vorsilbe** ['foːrzɪlbə], *f.* (—, *pl.* —n) prefix.
**vorsintflutlich** ['foːrzɪntfluːtlɪç], *adj.* antediluvian; (*fig.*) out-of-date.
**Vorsitzende** ['foːrzɪtsəndə], *m.* (—n, *pl.* —n) chairman, president.
**Vorsorge** ['foːrzɔrgə], *f.* (—, *no pl.*) care, precaution.
**vorsorglich** ['foːrzɔrklɪç], *adj.* provident, careful.
**vorspiegeln** ['foːrʃpiːgəln], *v.a. einem etwas* —, deceive s.o.; pretend.
**Vorspiegelung** ['foːrʃpiːgəluŋ], *f.* (—, *pl.* —en) pretence; — *falscher Tatsachen*, false pretences.
**Vorspiel** ['foːrʃpiːl], *n.* (—s, *pl.* —e) prelude; overture.
**vorsprechen** ['foːrʃpreçən], *v.n.* irr. *bei einem* —, call on s.o. — *v.a. einem etwas* —, say s.th. for s.o.; repeat.
**vorspringen** ['foːrʃprɪŋən], *v.n.* irr. (*aux.* sein) leap forward; jut out, project.
**Vorsprung** ['foːrʃpruŋ], *m.* (—s, *pl.* ˙e) projection, prominence; (*fig.*) advantage (over), start, lead.
**Vorstadt** ['foːrʃtat], *f.* (—, *pl.* ˙e) suburb.
**vorstädtisch** ['foːrʃtetɪʃ], *adj.* suburban.
**Vorstand** ['foːrʃtant], *m.* (—s, *pl.* ˙e) board of directors; director, principal.
**Vorstandssitzung** ['foːrʃtantszɪtsuŋ], *f.* (—, *pl.* —en) board meeting.
**vorstehen** ['foːrʃteːən], *v.n.* irr. project, protrude; (*office*) administer, govern, direct, manage.
**vorstehend** ['foːrʃteːənt], *adj.* projecting, protruding; above-mentioned, foregoing.
**Vorsteher** ['foːrʃteːər], *m.* (—s, *pl.* —) director, manager; supervisor.
**Vorsteherdrüse** ['foːrʃteːərdryːzə], *f.* (—, *pl.* —n) prostate gland.
**vorstellbar** ['foːrʃtelbaːr], *adj.* imaginable.
**vorstellen** ['foːrʃtelən], *v.a.* (*thing*) put forward; (*person*) present, introduce; (*Theat.*) impersonate; represent; (*clock*) put on; *sich etwas* —, visualise s.th., imagine s.th.

# vulkanisch

**vorstellig** ['foːrʃtɛlɪç], *adj.* — *werden*, petition; lodge a complaint.
**Vorstellung** ['foːrʃtɛluŋ], *f.* (—, *pl.* —en) (*person*) presentation, introduction; (*Theat.*) performance; idea, notion, image; representation.
**Vorstellungsvermögen** ['foːrʃtɛluŋsfɛrˌmøːgən], *n.* (—s, *no pl.*) imagination, imaginative faculty.
**Vorstoß** ['foːrʃtoːs], *m.* (—es, *pl.* ˙ˑe) (*Mil.*) sudden advance, thrust.
**vorstoßen** ['foːrʃtoːsən], *v.a. irr.* push forward. — *v.n.* (*aux.* sein) (*Mil.*) advance suddenly.
**Vorstrafe** ['foːrʃtraːfə], *f.* (—, *pl.* —n) previous conviction.
**vorstrecken** ['foːrʃtrɛkən], *v.a.* stretch forward, protrude; (*money*) advance.
**Vorstufe** ['foːrʃtuːfə], *f.* (—, *pl.* —n) first step.
**Vortänzerin** ['foːrtɛntsərɪn], *f.* (—, *pl.* —nen) prima ballerina.
**Vorteil** ['fɔrtaɪl], *m.* (—s, *pl.* —e) advantage, profit.
**vorteilhaft** ['fɔrtaɪlhaft], *adj.* advantageous, profitable, lucrative.
**Vortrag** ['foːrtraːk], *m.* (—s, *pl.* ˙ˑe) recitation, delivery, rendering; statement, report; talk, speech, lecture.
**vortragen** ['foːrtraːgən], *v.a. irr.* make a report; (*poem*) recite, declaim; make a request; (*Comm.*) carry forward; lecture on.
**Vortragskunst** ['foːrtraːkskunst], *f.* (—, *no pl.*) elocution; (art of) public speaking.
**vortrefflich** [fɔrˈtrɛflɪç], *adj.* excellent, splendid.
**Vortrefflichkeit** [fɔrˈtrɛflɪçkaɪt], *f.* (—, *no pl.*) excellence.
**vortreten** ['foːrtreːtən], *v.n. irr.* (*aux.* sein) step forward.
**Vortritt** ['foːrtrɪt], *m.* (—s, *no pl.*) precedence.
**vorüber** [fɔrˈyːbər], *adv.* past, gone, over, finished, done with.
**vorübergehen** [fɔrˈyːbərgeːən], *v.n. irr.* (*aux.* sein) pass by, pass, go past.
**vorübergehend** [fɔrˈyːbərgeːənt], *adj.* passing, temporary, transitory.
**Vorübung** ['foːryːbuŋ], *f.* (—, *pl.* —en) preliminary exercise.
**Voruntersuchung** ['foːruntərzuːxuŋ], *f.* (—, *pl.* —en) preliminary inquiry; trial in magistrate's court.
**Vorurteil** ['foːrurtaɪl], *n.* (—s, *pl.* —e) bias, prejudice.
**vorurteilslos** ['foːrurtaɪlsloːs], *adj.* impartial, unprejudiced, unbiased.
**Vorvater** ['foːrfaːtər], *m.* (—s, *pl.* ˙ˑ) progenitor, ancestor.
**Vorverkauf** ['foːrfɛrkauf], *m.* (—s, *pl.* ˙ˑe) booking in advance, advance booking.
**vorwagen** ['foːrvaːgən], *v.r. sich* —, dare to go (*or* come) forward.
**vorwaltend** ['foːrvaltənt], *adj.* prevailing, predominating.

**Vorwand** ['foːrvant], *m.* (—s, *pl.* ˙ˑe) pretence, pretext; *unter dem* —, under pretence of.
**vorwärts** ['fɔrvɛrts], *adv.* forward.
**vorwärtskommen** ['fɔrvɛrtskɔmən], *v.n. irr.* (*aux.* sein) make headway, get on.
**vorweg** [fɔrˈvɛk], *adv.* before.
**vorwegnehmen** [fɔrˈvɛkneːmən], *v.a. irr.* anticipate.
**vorweisen** ['foːrvaɪzən], *v.a. irr.* show, produce, exhibit.
**Vorwelt** ['foːrvɛlt], *f.* (—, *no pl.*) primitive world; former ages.
**vorweltlich** ['foːrvɛltlɪç], *adj.* primæval, prehistoric.
**vorwerfen** ['foːrvɛrfən], *v.a. irr. einem etwas* —, blame s.o. for s.th.; charge s.o. with s.th., tax s.o. with s.th.
**vorwiegen** ['foːrviːgən], *v.n. irr.* prevail.
**vorwiegend** ['foːrviːgənt], *adv.* mostly, for the most part.
**Vorwissen** ['foːrvɪsən], *n.* (—s, *no pl.*) foreknowledge, prescience.
**Vorwitz** ['foːrvɪts], *m.* (—es, *no pl.*) pertness.
**vorwitzig** ['foːrvɪtsɪç], *adj.* forward, pert, meddlesome.
**Vorwort** (1) ['foːrvɔrt], *n.* (—s, *pl.* —e) preface.
**Vorwort** (2) ['foːrvɔrt], *n.* (—s, *pl.* ˙ˑer) (*Gram.*) preposition.
**Vorwurf** ['foːrvurf], *m.* (—s, *pl.* ˙ˑe) reproach; theme, subject.
**vorwurfsfrei** ['foːrvurfsfraɪ], *adj.* free from blame, irreproachable.
**vorwurfsvoll** ['foːrvurfsfɔl], *adj.* reproachful.
**Vorzeichen** ['foːrtsaɪxən], *n.* (—s, *pl.* —) omen, token; (*Maths.*) sign.
**vorzeigen** ['foːrtsaɪgən], *v.a.* show, produce, exhibit, display.
**Vorzeit** ['foːrtsaɪt], *f.* (—, *no pl.*) antiquity, olden times.
**vorzeiten** [fɔrˈtsaɪtən], *adv.* (*Poet.*) in olden times, formerly.
**vorzeitig** ['foːrtsaɪtɪç], *adj.* premature.
**vorziehen** ['foːrtsiːən], *v.a. irr.* prefer.
**Vorzimmer** ['foːrtsɪmər], *n.* (—s, *pl.* —) anteroom, antechamber.
**Vorzug** ['foːrtsuːk], *m.* (—s, *pl.* ˙ˑe) preference, advantage; excellence, superiority.
**vorzüglich** [fɔrˈtsyːklɪç], *adj.* superior, excellent, exquisite.
**Vorzüglichkeit** [fɔrˈtsyːklɪçkaɪt], *f.* (—, *no pl.*) excellence, superiority.
**Vorzugsaktie** ['foːrtsuːksaktsjə], *f.* (—, *pl.* —n) preference share.
**vorzugsweise** ['foːrtsuːksvaɪzə], *adv.* for choice, preferably.
**vulgär** [vulˈgɛːr], *adj.* vulgar.
**Vulkan** [vulˈkaːn], *m.* (—s, *pl.* —e) volcano.
**vulkanisch** [vulˈkaːnɪʃ], *adj.* volcanic.

# W

**W** [ve:] *n.* (—s, *pl.* —s) the letter W.

**Waage** ['va:gə], *f.* (—, *pl.* —n) balance, pair of scales.

**waag(e)recht** ['va:g(ə)rɛçt], *adj.* horizontal.

**Waagschale** ['va:kʃa:lə], *f.* (—, *pl.* —n) pan of a balance.

**Wabe** ['va:bə], *f.* (—, *pl.* —n) honeycomb.

**Waberlohe** ['va:bərlo:ə], *f.* (—, *no pl.*) (*Poet.*) flickering flames, magic fire.

**wach** [vax], *adj.* awake; alert; *völlig* —, wide awake.

**Wachdienst** ['vaxdi:nst], *m.* (—es, *no pl.*) guard, sentry duty.

**Wache** ['vaxə], *f.* (—, *pl.* —n) guard, watch; (*person*) sentry, sentinel.

**wachen** ['vaxən], *v.n.* be awake; guard; — *über*, watch, keep an eye on.

**Wacholder** [va'xɔldər], *m.* (—s, *pl.* —) (*Bot.*) juniper.

**wachrufen** [vax'ru:fən], *v.a. irr.* (*fig.*) call to mind.

**Wachs** [vaks], *n.* (—es, *no pl.*) wax.

**wachsam** ['vaxza:m], *adj.* watchful, vigilant.

**Wachsamkeit** ['vaxza:mkaɪt], *f.* (—, *no pl.*) watchfulness, vigilance.

**Wachsbild** ['vaksbɪlt], *n.* (—s, *pl.* —er) waxen image.

**wachsen** ['vaksən], *v.n. irr.* (*aux.* sein) grow, increase.

**wächsern** ['vɛksərn], *adj.* waxen, made of wax.

**Wachsfigur** ['vaksfigu:r], *f.* (—, *pl.* —en) wax figure.

**Wachsfigurenkabinett** ['vaksfigu:rənkabinɛt], *n.* (—s, *pl.* —e) waxworks.

**Wachsleinwand** ['vakslaɪnvant], *f.* (—, *no pl.*) oil-cloth.

**Wachstuch** ['vakstu:x], *n.* (—(e)s, *no pl.*) oil-cloth; American cloth.

**Wachstum** ['vakstu:m], *n.* (—s, *no pl.*) growth, increase.

**Wacht** [vaxt], *f.* (—, *pl.* —en) watch, guard.

**Wachtdienst** ['vaxtdi:nst] *see* **Wachdienst**.

**Wachtel** ['vaxtəl], *f.* (—, *pl.* —n) (*Orn.*) quail.

**Wachtelhund** ['vaxtəlhunt], *m.* (—(e)s, *pl.* —e) (*Zool.*) spaniel.

**Wächter** ['vɛçtər], *m.* (—s, *pl.* —) watchman, warder, guard.

**wachthabend** ['vaxtha:bənt], *adj.* on duty.

**Wachtmeister** ['vaxtmaɪstər], *m.* (—s, *pl.* —) sergeant.

**Wachtparade** ['vaxtpara:də], *f.* (—, *pl.* —n) mounting of the guard.

**Wachtposten** ['vaxtpɔstən], *m.* (—s, *pl.* —) guard, picket.

**Wachtraum** ['vaxtraum], *m.* (—s, *pl.* ⸚e) day-dream, waking dream.

**Wachtturm** ['vaxtturm], *m.* (—s, *pl.* ⸚e) watch-tower.

**wackeln** ['vakəln], *v.n.* totter, shake, wobble.

**wacker** ['vakər], *adj.* gallant, brave, valiant; upright.

**wacklig** ['vaklɪç], *adj.* tottering, shaky; (*furniture*) rickety; (*tooth*) loose.

**Wade** ['va:də], *f.* (—, *pl.* —n) calf (of the leg).

**Wadenbein** ['va:dənbaɪn], *n.* (—s, *pl.* —e) shin-bone.

**Waffe** ['vafə], *f.* (—, *pl.* —n) weapon, arm; *die —n strecken*, surrender.

**Waffel** ['vafəl], *f.* (—, *pl.* —n) wafer; waffle.

**Waffeleisen** ['vafəlaɪzən], *n.* (—s, *pl.* —) waffle-iron.

**Waffenbruder** ['vafənbru:dər], *m.* (—s, *pl.* ⸚) brother-in-arms, comrade.

**waffenfähig** ['vafənfɛ:ɪç], *adj.* able to bear arms.

**Waffengewalt** ['vafəngəvalt], *f.* (—, *no pl.*) *mit* —, by force of arms.

**Waffenglück** ['vafənglyk], *n.* (—s, *no pl.*) fortunes of war.

**Waffenrock** ['vafənrɔk], *m.* (—s, *pl.* ⸚e) tunic.

**Waffenruf** ['vafənru:f], *m.* (—s, *no pl.*) call to arms.

**Waffenschmied** [vafənʃmi:t], *m.* (—s, *pl.* —e) armourer.

**Waffenstillstand** ['vafənʃtɪlʃtant], *m.* (—s, *no pl.*) armistice, truce.

**waffnen** ['vafnən], *v.a.* arm.

**Wage** *see* **Waage**.

**Wagebalken** ['va:gəbalkən], *m.* (—s, *pl.* —) scale-beam.

**Wagen** ['va:gən], *m.* (—s, *pl.* —) vehicle, conveyance, carriage, coach, car, cab, wagon, cart, truck, van, dray.

**wagen** ['va:gən], *v.a., v.n.* dare, venture, risk.

**wägen** ['vɛ:gən], *v.a., irr.* weigh, balance; (*words*) consider.

**Wagenverkehr** ['va:gənfɛrke:r], *m.* (—s, *no pl.*) vehicular traffic.

**wagerecht** *see* **waagerecht**.

**Waggon** [va'gɔ̃], *m.* (—s, *pl.* —s) railway carriage; goods van.

**waghalsig** ['va:khalzɪç], *adj.* foolhardy, rash, daring.

**Wagnis** ['va:knɪs], *n.* (—ses, *pl.* —se) venture, risky undertaking; risk.

**Wagschale** *see* **Waagschale**.

**Wahl** [va:l], *f.* (—, *pl.* —en) choice; election; selection; alternative.

**Wahlakt** ['va:lakt], *m.* (—s, *pl.* —e) poll, election.

**Wahlaufruf** ['va:laufru:f], *m.* (—s, *pl.* —e) manifesto, election address.

**wählbar** ['vɛ:lba:r], *adj.* eligible.

**Wählbarkeit** ['vɛ:lba:rkaɪt], *f.* (—, *no pl.*) eligibility.

**wahlberechtigt** ['va:lbəreçtıçt], *adj.* entitled to vote.

**wählen** ['vɛːlən], *v.a.* choose; (*Parl.*) elect; (*Telephone*) dial.

**Wähler** ['vɛːlər], *m.* (—s, *pl.* —) elector; constituent.

**wählerisch** ['vɛːlərıʃ], *adj.* fastidious, particular.

**Wählerschaft** ['vɛːlərʃaft], *f.* (—, *pl.* —en) constituency.

**wahlfähig** ['va:lfɛːıç], *adj.* eligible.

**Wahlliste** ['va:llıstə], *f.* (—, *pl.* —n) electoral list, register (of electors).

**wahllos** ['va:llo:s], *adj.* indiscriminate.

**Wahlrecht** ['va:lrɛçt], *n.* (—s, *no pl.*) franchise.

**Wahlspruch** ['va:lʃprux], *m.* (—s, *pl.* ⁝e) device, motto.

**wahlunfähig** ['va:lunfɛːıç], *adj.* ineligible.

**Wahlurne** ['va:lurnə], *f.* (—, *pl.* —n) ballot-box.

**Wahlverwandtschaft** ['va:lfɛrvantʃaft], *f.* (—, *no pl.*) elective affinity, congeniality.

**Wahlzettel** ['va:ltsɛtəl], *m.* (—s, *pl.* —) ballot-paper.

**Wahn** [va:n], *m.* (—(e)s, *no pl.*) delusion.

**Wahnbild** ['va:nbılt], *n.* (—s, *pl.* —er) hallucination, delusion; phantasm.

**wähnen** ['vɛːnən], *v.a.* fancy, believe.

**Wahnsinn** ['va:nzın], *m.* (—s, *no pl.*) madness, lunacy.

**wahnsinnig** ['va:nzınıç], *adj.* insane, mad, lunatic; (*coll.*) terrific.

**Wahnsinnige** ['va:nzınıgə], *m.* (—n, *pl.* —n) madman, lunatic.

**Wahnwitz** ['va:nvıts], *m.* (—es, *no pl.*) madness.

**wahnwitzig** ['va:nvıtsıç], *adj.* mad.

**wahr** [va:r], *adj.* true, real, genuine.

**wahren** ['va:rən], *v.a.* guard, watch over.

**währen** ['vɛːrən], *v.n.* last.

**während** ['vɛːrənt], *prep.* (*Genit.*) during. — *conj.* while, whilst; whereas.

**wahrhaft** ['va:rhaft], *adj.* truthful, veracious.

**wahrhaftig** [va:r'haftıç], *adv.* truly, really, in truth.

**Wahrhaftigkeit** [va:r'haftıçkaıt], *f.* (—, *no pl.*) truthfulness, veracity.

**Wahrheit** ['va:rhaıt], *f.* (—, *pl.* —en) truth; reality; *die — sagen*, tell the truth.

**Wahrheitsliebe** ['va:rhaıtsli:bə], *f.* (—, *no pl.*) love of truth, truthfulness.

**wahrlich** ['va:rlıç], *adv.* truly, in truth.

**wahrnehmbar** ['va:rne:mba:r], *adj.* perceptible.

**wahrnehmen** ['va:rne:mən], *v.a. irr.* perceive, observe.

**Wahrnehmung** ['va:rne:mun], *f.* (—, *pl.* —en) perception, observation.

**wahrsagen** ['va:rza:gən], *v.n.* prophesy; tell fortunes.

**Wahrsager** ['va:rza:gər], *m.* (—s, *pl.* —) fortune-teller, soothsayer.

**wahrscheinlich** [va:r'ʃaınlıç], *adj.* likely, probable; *es wird — regnen*, it will probably rain.

**Wahrscheinlichkeit** [va:r'ʃaınlıçkaıt], *f.* (—, *pl.* —en) likelihood, probability.

**Wahrung** ['va:run], *f.* (—, *no pl.*) protection, preservation, maintenance.

**Währung** ['vɛːrun], *f.* (—, *pl.* —en) currency, standard.

**Wahrzeichen** ['va:rtsaıçən], *n.* (—s, *pl.* —) landmark; (*fig.*) sign, token.

**Waibling(er)** ['vaıblın(ər)], *m.* Ghibelline.

**Waidmann** ['vaıtman], *m.* (—s, *pl.* ⁝er) huntsman, hunter.

**waidmännisch** ['vaıtmɛnıʃ], *adj.* sportsmanlike.

**Waise** ['vaızə], *f.* (—, *pl.* —n) orphan.

**Waisenhaus** ['vaızənhaus], *n.* (—es, *pl.* ⁝er) orphanage.

**Waisenmutter** ['vaızənmutər], *f.* (—, *pl.* ⁝) foster-mother.

**Waisenvater** ['vaızənfa:tər], *m.* (—s, *pl.* ⁝) foster-father.

**Wald** [valt], *m.* (—es, *pl.* ⁝er) wood, forest; woodland.

**Waldbrand** ['valtbrant], *m.* (—s, *pl.* ⁝e) forest-fire.

**Waldlichtung** ['valtlıçtun], *f.* (—, *pl.* —en) forest glade, clearing.

**Waldmeister** ['valtmaıstər], *m.* (—s, *no pl.*) (*Bot.*) woodruff.

**Waldung** ['valdun], *f.* (—, *pl.* —en) woods, woodland.

**Waldwiese** ['valtvi:zə], *f.* (—, *pl.* —en) forest-glade.

**Walfisch** ['va:lfıʃ], *m.* (—es, *pl.* —e) whale.

**Walfischfang** ['va:lfıʃfan], *m.* (—s, *no pl.*) whaling.

**Walfischfänger** ['va:lfıʃfɛnər], *m.* (—s, *pl.* —) whaler, whale fisher.

**Walfischtran** ['va:lfıʃtra:n], *m.* (—s, *no pl.*) train-oil.

**Walküre** [val'ky:rə], *f.* (—, *pl.* —n) Valkyrie.

**Wall** [val], *m.* (—(e)s, *pl.* ⁝e) rampart, dam, vallum; mound.

**Wallach** ['valax], *m.* (—s, *pl.* —e) castrated horse, gelding.

**wallen** ['valən], *v.n.* bubble, boil up; wave, undulate.

**Wallfahrer** ['valfa:rər], *m.* (—s, *pl.* —) pilgrim.

**Wallfahrt** ['valfa:rt], *f.* (—, *pl.* —en) pilgrimage.

**wallfahrten** ['valfa:rtən], *v.n.* (*aux. sein*) go on a pilgrimage.

**Walnuß** ['valnus], *f.* (—, *pl.* ⁝sse) (*Bot.*) walnut.

**Walpurgisnacht** [val'purgısnaxt], *f.* witches' sabbath.

**Walroß** ['valros], *n.* (—sses, *pl.* —sse) sea-horse, walrus.

**Walstatt** ['valʃtat], *f.* (—, *pl.* ⁝en) (*Poet.*) battlefield.

**walten** ['valtən], *v.n.* rule; *seines Amtes —*, do o.'s duty, carry out o.'s duties.

**Walze** ['valtsə], *f.* (—, *pl.* —n) roller, cylinder.

# walzen

**walzen** ['valtsən], *v.a.* roll. — *v.n.* waltz.

**wälzen** ['vɛltsən], *v.a.* roll, turn about.

**walzenförmig** ['valtsənfœrmɪç], *adj.* cylindrical.

**Walzer** ['valtsər], *m.* (—s, *pl.* —) waltz.

**Wälzer** ['vɛltsər], *m.* (—s, *pl.* —) tome; thick volume.

**Walzwerk** ['valtsvɛrk], *n.* (—s, *pl.* —e) rolling-mill.

**Wams** [vams], *n.* (—es, *pl.* ·e) (*obs.*) doublet, jerkin.

**Wand** [vant], *f.* (—, *pl.* ·e) wall; side.

**Wandbekleidung** ['vantbəklaɪduŋ], *f.* (—, *pl.* —en) wainscot, panelling.

**Wandel** ['vandəl], *m.* (—s, *no pl.*) mutation, change; behaviour, conduct; *Handel und* —, trade and traffic.

**wandelbar** ['vandəlbaːr], *adj.* changeable, inconstant.

**Wandelgang** ['vandəlgaŋ], *m.* (—s, *pl.* ·e) lobby; lounge, foyer; (*in the open*) covered way, covered walk.

**wandeln** ['vandəln], *v.a.* (*aux.* haben) change. — *v.n.* (*aux.* sein) walk, wander. — *v.r. sich* —, change.

**Wanderbursche** ['vandərburʃə], *m.* (—n, *pl.* —n) travelling journeyman.

**Wanderer** ['vandərər], *m.* (—s, *pl.* —) wanderer, traveller; hiker.

**Wanderleben** ['vandərleːbən], *n.* (—s, *no pl.*) nomadic life.

**Wanderlehrer** ['vandərleːrər], *m.* (—s, *pl.* —) itinerant teacher.

**Wanderlust** ['vandərlust], *f.* (—, *no pl.*) urge to travel; call of the open.

**wandern** ['vandərn], *v.n.* (*aux.* sein) wander, travel; migrate.

**Wanderschaft** ['vandərʃaft], *f.* (—, *no pl.*) wanderings.

**Wandersmann** ['vandərsman], *m.* (—s, *pl.* ·er) wayfarer.

**Wandertruppe** ['vandərtrupə], *f.* (—, *pl.* —n) (*Theat.*) strolling players.

**Wanderung** ['vandəruŋ], *f.* (—, *pl.* —en) walking tour; hike.

**Wandervolk** ['vandərfɔlk], *n.* (— (e)s, *pl.* ·er) nomadic tribe.

**Wandgemälde** ['vantgəmeːldə], *n.* (—s, *pl.* —) mural painting, mural.

**Wandlung** ['vandluŋ], *f.* (—, *pl.* —en) transformation; (*Theol.*) transubstantiation.

**Wandspiegel** ['vantʃpiːgəl], *m.* (—s, *pl.* —) pier-glass.

**Wandtafel** ['vanttaːfəl], *f.* (—, *pl.* —n) blackboard.

**Wange** ['vaŋə], *f.* (—, *pl.* —n) cheek.

**Wankelmut** ['vaŋkəlmuːt], *m.* (—s, *no pl.*) fickleness, inconstancy.

**wankelmütig** ['vaŋkəlmyːtɪç], *adj.* inconstant, fickle.

**wanken** ['vaŋkən], *v.n.* totter, stagger; (*fig.*) waver, be irresolute.

**wann** [van], *adv.* when; *dann und* —, now and then, sometimes.

**Wanne** ['vanə], *f.* (—, *pl.* —n) tub, bath.

**wannen** ['vanən], *adv.* (*obs.*) *von* —, whence.

**Wannenbad** ['vanənbaːt], *n.* (—s, *pl.* ·er) bath.

**Wanst** [vanst], *m.* (—es, *pl.* ·e) belly, paunch.

**Wanze** ['vantsə], *f.* (—, *pl.* —n) (*Ent.*) bug.

**Wappen** ['vapən], *n.* (—s, *pl.* —) crest, coat-of-arms.

**Wappenbild** ['vapənbɪlt], *n.* (—s, *pl.* —er) heraldic figure.

**Wappenkunde** ['vapənkundə], *f.* (—, *no pl.*) heraldry.

**Wappenschild** ['vapənʃɪlt], *m.* (—s, *pl.* —e) escutcheon.

**Wappenspruch** ['vapənʃprux], *m.* (—(e)s, *pl.* ·e) motto, device.

**wappnen** ['vapnən], *v.a.* arm.

**Ware** ['vaːrə], *f.* (—, *pl.* —n) article, commodity; (*pl.*) merchandise, goods, wares.

**Warenausfuhr** ['vaːrənausfuːr], *f.* (—, *no pl.*) exportation, export.

**Warenbörse** ['vaːrənbœrzə], *f.* (—, *pl.* —n) commodity exchange.

**Wareneinfuhr** ['vaːrənaɪnfuːr], *f.* (—, *no pl.*) importation, import.

**Warenhaus** ['vaːrənhaus], *n.* (—es, *pl.* ·er) department store, emporium; (*Am.*) store.

**Warenlager** ['vaːrənlaːgər], *n.* (—s, *pl.* —) magazine; stock; warehouse.

**Warensendung** ['vaːrənzɛnduŋ], *f.* (—, *pl.* —en) consignment of goods.

**Warentausch** ['vaːrəntauʃ], *m.* (—es, *no pl.*) barter.

**warm** [varm], *adj.* warm, hot.

**warmblütig** ['varmblyːtɪç], *adj.* warm-blooded.

**Wärme** ['vɛrmə], *f.* (—, *no pl.*) warmth; heat.

**Wärmeeinheit** ['vɛrməaɪnhaɪt], *f.* (—, *pl.* —en) thermal unit; calorie.

**Wärmegrad** ['vɛrməgraːt], *m.* (—s, *pl.* —e) degree of heat; temperature.

**Wärmeleiter** ['vɛrmələɪtər], *m.* (—s, *pl.* —) conductor of heat.

**Wärmemesser** ['vɛrməmɛsər], *m.* (—s, *pl.* —s) thermometer.

**wärmen** ['vɛrmən], *v.a.* warm, heat.

**Wärmflasche** ['vɛrmflaʃə], *f.* (—, *pl.* —n) hot-water bottle.

**warnen** ['varnən], *v.a.* warn; caution.

**Warnung** ['varnuŋ], *f.* (—, *pl.* —en) warning, caution, admonition; notice.

**Warschau** ['varʃau], *n.* Warsaw.

**Warte** ['vartə], *f.* (—, *pl.* —n) watch-tower, belfry, look-out.

**Wartegeld** ['vartəgɛlt], *n.* (—s, *pl.* —er) half pay; (*ship*) demurrage charges.

**warten** ['vartən], *v.n.* wait; — *auf* (*Acc.*), wait for, await. — *v.a.* tend, nurse.

**Wärter** ['vɛrtər], *m.* (—s, *pl.* —) keeper, attendant; warder; male nurse.

**Wartesaal** ['vartəzaːl], *m.* (—s, *pl.* —säle) (*Railw.*) waiting-room.

**Wartung** ['vartuŋ], *f.* (—, *no pl.*) nursing, attendance; servicing; maintenance.

**warum** [va'rum], *adv., conj.* why, for what reason.

**Warze** ['vartsə], *f.* (—, *pl.* —n) wart.

**was** [vas], *interr. pron.* what? — *rel. pron.* what, that which.

**Waschanstalt** ['vaʃanʃtalt], *f.* (—, *pl.* —en) laundry.

**waschbar** ['vaʃbaːr], *adj.* washable.

**Waschbär** ['vaʃbɛːr], *m.* (—en, *pl.* —en) (*Zool.*) raccoon.

**Waschbecken** ['vaʃbɛkən], *n.* (—s, *pl.* —) wash-basin.

**Wäsche** ['vɛʃə], *f.* (—, *no pl.*) washing, wash, laundry; linen.

**waschecht** ['vaʃɛçt], *adj.* washable; (*fig.*) genuine.

**waschen** ['vaʃən], *v.a. irr.* wash.

**Wäscherin** ['vɛʃərɪn], *f.* (—, *pl.* —nen) washerwoman, laundress.

**Waschhaus** ['vaʃhaus], *n.* (—es, *pl.* ̈er) wash-house, laundry; (*reg. trade name*) launderette.

**Waschkorb** ['vaʃkɔrp], *m.* (—s, *pl.* ̈e) clothes-basket.

**Waschküche** ['vaʃkyçə], *f.* (—, *pl.* —en) wash-house.

**Waschlappen** ['vaʃlapən], *m.* (—s, *pl.* —) face-flannel, face-cloth, face-washer; (*fig.*) milksop.

**Waschleder** ['vaʃleːdər], *n.* (—s, *no pl.*) chamois leather, wash-leather.

**Waschmaschine** ['vaʃmaʃiːnə], *f.* (—, *pl.* —n) washing-machine.

**Waschtisch** ['vaʃtɪʃ], *m.* (—es, *pl.* —e) wash-stand.

**Waschwanne** ['vaʃvanə], *f.* (—, *pl.* —n) wash-tub.

**Wasser** ['vasər], *n.* (—s, *pl.* —) water; *stille — sind tief*, still waters run deep.

**wasserarm** ['vasərarm], *adj.* waterless, dry, arid.

**Wasserbehälter** ['vasərbəhɛltər], *m.* (—s, *pl.* —) reservoir, cistern, tank.

**Wasserblase** ['vasərblaːzə], *f.* (—, *pl.* —en) bubble.

**Wässerchen** ['vɛsərçən], *n.* (—s, *pl.* —) brook, streamlet; *er sieht aus, als ob er kein — trüben könnte*, he looks as if butter would not melt in his mouth.

**Wasserdampf** ['vasərdampf], *m.* (—(e)s, *no pl.*) steam.

**wasserdicht** ['vasərdɪçt], *adj.* water-proof.

**Wasserdruck** ['vasərdruk], *m.* (—s, *no pl.*) hydrostatic pressure, hydraulic pressure.

**Wassereimer** ['vasəraimər], *m.* (—s, *pl.* —) pail, water-bucket.

**Wasserfall** ['vasərfal], *m.* (—s, *pl.* ̈e) waterfall, cataract, cascade.

**Wasserfarbe** ['vasərfarbə], *f.* (—, *pl.* —n) water-colour.

**Wasserheilanstalt** ['vasərhailanʃtalt], *f.* (—, *pl.* —en) spa.

**wässerig** ['vɛsərɪç], *adj.* watery; (*fig.*) insipid, flat, diluted.

**Wasserkanne** ['vasərkanə], *f.* (—, *pl.* —n) pitcher, ewer.

**Wasserkessel** ['vasərkɛsəl], *m.* (—s, *pl.* —) boiler; kettle.

**Wasserkopf** ['vasərkɔpf], *m.* (—(e)s, *pl.* ̈e) (*Med.*) hydrocephalus.

**Wasserkur** ['vasərkuːr], *f.* (—, *pl.* —en) hydropathic treatment.

**Wasserleitung** ['vasərlaituŋ], *f.* (—, *pl.* —en) aqueduct; water main.

**Wasserlinsen** ['vasərlɪnzən], *f. pl.* (*Bot.*) duck-weed.

**Wassermann** ['vasərman], *m.* (—s, *no pl.*) (*Astrol.*) Aquarius.

**wässern** ['vɛsərn], *v.a.* water, irrigate, soak.

**Wassernixe** ['vasərnɪksə], *f.* (—, *pl.* —n) water nymph.

**Wassernot** ['vasərnoːt], *f.* (—, *no pl.*) drought, scarcity of water.

**Wasserrabe** ['vasərraːbə], *m.* (—n, *pl.* —n) (*Orn.*) cormorant.

**Wasserrinne** ['vasərrɪnə], *f.* (—, *pl.* —n) gutter.

**Wasserröhre** ['vasərrøːrə], *f.* (—, *pl.* —n) water-pipe.

**Wasserscheide** ['vasərʃaidə], *f.* (—, *pl.* —n) watershed.

**Wasserscheu** ['vasərʃɔy], *f.* (—, *no pl.*) hydrophobia.

**Wasserspiegel** ['vasərʃpiːgəl], *m.* (—s, *pl.* —) water-level.

**Wasserspritze** ['vasərʃprɪtsə], *f.* (—, *pl.* —n) squirt; sprinkler.

**Wasserstand** ['vasərʃtant], *m.* (—s, *no pl.*) water-level.

**Wasserstiefel** ['vasərʃtiːfəl], *m.* (—s, *pl.* —n) wader, gumboot.

**Wasserstoff** ['vasərʃtɔf], *m.* (—(e)s, *no pl.*) hydrogen.

**Wassersucht** ['vasərzuxt], *f.* (—, *no pl.*) dropsy.

**Wassersuppe** ['vasərzupə], *f.* (—, *pl.* —n) water-gruel.

**Wässerung** ['vɛsəruŋ], *f.* (—, *pl.* —en) watering, irrigation.

**Wasserverdrängung** ['vasərfɛrdrɛŋuŋ], *f.* (—, *no pl.*) displacement (of water).

**Wasserwaage** ['vasərvaːgə], *f.* (—, *pl.* —n) water-balance, water-level; hydrometer.

**Wasserweg** ['vasərveːk], *m.* (—s, *pl.* —e) waterway; *auf dem —*, by water, by sea.

**Wasserzeichen** ['vasərtsaiçən], *n.* (—s, *pl.* —) watermark.

**waten** ['vaːtən], *v.n.* (*aux.* sein) wade.

**watscheln** ['vaːtʃəln], *v.n.* (*aux.* sein) waddle.

**Watt** (1) [vat], *n.* (—s, *pl.* —e) sand-bank; (*pl.*) shallows.

**Watt** (2) [vat], *n.* (—s, *pl.* —) (*Elec.*) watt.

**Watte** ['vatə], *f.* (—, *no pl.*) wadding, cotton-wool.

**wattieren** [va'tiːrən], *v.a.* pad.

**Webe** ['veːbə], *f.* (—, *pl.* —n) web, weft.

**weben** ['veːbən], *v.a.* weave.

**Weber** ['veːbər], *m.* (—s, *pl.* —) weaver.

**Weberei** [veːbə'rai], *f.* (—, *pl.* —en) weaving-mill.

# Weberschiffchen

**Weberschiffchen** [ˈveːbərʃɪfçən], *n.*
(—s, *pl.* —) shuttle.

**Wechsel** [ˈvɛksəl], *m.* (—s, *pl.* —)
change; turn, variation; vicissitude;
(*Comm.*) bill of exchange.

**Wechselbalg** [ˈvɛksəlbalk], *m.* (—s,
*pl.* ˙e) changeling.

**Wechselbank** [ˈvɛksəlbaŋk], *f.* (—,
*pl.* ˙e) discount-bank.

**Wechselbeziehung** [ˈvɛksəlbətsiːuŋ], *f.*
(—, *pl.* —en) reciprocal relation, cor-
relation.

**Wechselfälle** [ˈvɛksəlfɛlə], *m. pl.* vicis-
situdes.

**Wechselfieber** [ˈvɛksəlfiːbər], *n.* (—s,
*pl.* —) intermittent fever.

**Wechselfolge** [ˈvɛksəlfɔlgə], *f.* (—, *no
pl.*) rotation, alternation.

**Wechselgeld** [ˈvɛksəlgɛlt], *n.* (—(e)s,
*no pl.*) change.

**wechseln** [ˈvɛksəln], *v.a.* change, exchange. — *v.n.* change, alternate,
change places.

**wechselseitig** [ˈvɛksəlzaɪtɪç], *adj.* reciprocal, mutual.

**Wechselstrom** [ˈvɛksəlʃtroːm], *m.* (—s,
*no pl.*) alternating current.

**Wechselstube** [ˈvɛksəlʃtuːbə], *f.* (—,
*pl.* —n) exchange office.

**wechselvoll** [ˈvɛksəlfɔl], *adj.* eventful,
chequered; changeable.

**wechselweise** [ˈvɛksəlvaɪzə], *adv.* reci-
procally, mutually; by turns, alter-
nately.

**Wechselwinkel** [ˈvɛksəlvɪŋkəl], *m.* (—s,
*pl.* —) alternate angle.

**Wechselwirkung** [ˈvɛksəlvɪrkuŋ], *f.*
(—, *pl.* —en) reciprocal effect.

**Wechselwirtschaft** [ˈvɛksəlvɪrtʃaft], *f.*
(—, *no pl.*) rotation of crops.

**Wecken** [ˈvɛkən], *m.* (—s, *pl.* —) (*dial.*)
bread-roll.

**wecken** [ˈvɛkən], *v.a.* wake, rouse,
awaken.

**Wecker** [ˈvɛkər], *m.* (—s, *pl.* —) alarm-
clock.

**Weckuhr** [ˈvɛkuːr], *f.* (—, *pl.* —en)
alarm-clock.

**Wedel** [ˈveːdəl], *m.* (—s, *pl.* —) feather-
duster, fan; tail.

**wedeln** [ˈveːdəln], *v.n. mit dem Schwanz*
—, wag its tail.

**weder** [ˈveːdər], *conj.* neither; — ...
*noch,* neither ... nor.

**Weg** [veːk], *m.* (—(e)s, *pl.* —e) way,
path, route, road; walk, errand; *am*
—, by the wayside.

**weg** [vɛk], *adv.* away, gone, off, lost.

**wegbegeben** [ˈvɛkbəgeːbən], *v.r. irr.
sich* —, go away, leave.

**wegbekommen** [ˈvɛkbəkɔmən], *v.a.
irr. etwas* —, get the hang of s.th.;
get s.th. off *or* away.

**Wegbereiter** [ˈveːkbəraɪtər], *m.* (—s,
*pl.* —) forerunner, pathfinder, pioneer.

**wegblasen** [ˈvɛkblaːzən], *v.a. irr.* blow
away; *wie weggeblasen,* without leaving a trace.

**wegbleiben** [ˈvɛkblaɪbən], *v.n. irr.*
(*aux.* sein) stay away.

**wegblicken** [ˈvɛkblɪkən], *v.n.* look the
other way.

**wegbringen** [ˈvɛkbrɪŋən], *v.a. irr.
einen* —, get s.o. away.

**wegdrängen** [ˈvɛkdrɛŋən], *v.a.* push
away.

**Wegebau** [ˈveːgəbau], *m.* (—s, *no pl.*)
road-making.

**wegeilen** [ˈvɛkaɪlən], *v.n.* (*aux.* sein)
hasten away, hurry off.

**wegelagern** [ˈveːgəlaːgərn], *v.a.* waylay.

**wegen** [ˈveːgən], *prep.* (*Genit., Dat.*)
because of, on account of, owing to,
by reason of.

**Wegfall** [ˈvɛkfal], *m.* (—s, *no pl.*)
omission.

**wegfallen** [ˈvɛkfalən], *v.n. irr.* (*aux.*
sein) fall off; be omitted; cease.

**Weggang** [ˈvɛkgaŋ], *m.* (—s, *no pl.*)
departure, going away.

**weggießen** [ˈvɛkgiːsən], *v.a. irr.* pour
away.

**weghaben** [ˈvɛkhaːbən], *v.a. irr. etwas*
—, understand how to do s.th, have
the knack of doing s.th.

**wegkommen** [ˈvɛkkɔmən], *v.n. irr.*
(*aux.* sein) get away; be lost.

**wegkönnen** [ˈvɛkkœnən], *v.n. irr. nicht*
—, not be able to get away.

**Weglassung** [ˈvɛklasuŋ], *f.* (—, *pl.*
—en) omission.

**wegmachen** [ˈvɛkmaxən], *v.r. sich* —,
decamp, make off.

**wegmüssen** [ˈvɛkmysən], *v.n. irr.* be
obliged to go; have to go.

**Wegnahme** [ˈvɛknaːmə], *f.* (—, *no
pl.*) taking, seizure, capture.

**Wegreise** [ˈvɛkraɪzə], *f.* (—, *no pl.*)
departure.

**Wegscheide** [ˈveːkʃaɪdə], *f.* (—, *pl.*
—n) crossroads, crossways.

**wegscheren** [ˈvɛkʃeːrən], *v.a.* clip;
shave off. — *v.r. sich* —, be off.

**wegschnappen** [ˈvɛkʃnapən], *v.a.*
snatch away.

**wegsehnen** [ˈvɛkzeːnən], *v.r. sich* —,
wish o.s. far away; long to get
away.

**wegsein** [ˈvɛkzaɪn], *v.n. irr.* (*aux.* sein)
(*person*) be gone, be away; have gone
off; (*things*) be lost; *ganz* —, (*coll.*)
be beside o.s. *or* amazed.

**wegsetzen** [ˈvɛkzɛtsən], *v.a.* put
away.

**wegspülen** [ˈvɛkʃpyːlən], *v.a.* wash
away.

**Wegstunde** [ˈvɛkʃtundə], *f.* (—, *pl.*
—n) an hour's walk.

**Wegweiser** [ˈveːkvaɪzər], *m.* (—s,
*pl.* —) signpost, road-sign.

**wegwenden** [ˈvɛkvɛndən], *v.r. irr. sich*
—, turn away.

**wegwerfen** [ˈvɛkvɛrfən], *v.a. irr.* throw
away.

**wegwerfend** [ˈvɛkvɛrfənt], *adj.* dis-
paraging, disdainful.

**Wegzehrung** [ˈveːktseːruŋ], *f.* (—, *no
pl.*) food for the journey; (*Eccl.*)
viaticum.

**wegziehen** ['vɛktsiːən], *v.a. irr.* draw away, pull away. — *v.n.* (*aux.* sein) march away; (*fig.*) move, remove.

**Wegzug** ['vɛktsuːk], *m.* (—s, *no pl.*) removal; moving away.

**Weh** [veː], *n.* (—s, *no pl.*) pain; grief, pang; misfortune.

**weh** [veː], *adj.* painful, sore; *mir ist — uns Herz,* I am sick at heart; my heart aches. — *adv.* — *tun,* ache; pain, hurt, offend, distress, grieve. — *int.* — *mir !* woe is me!

**Wehen** ['veːən], *n. pl.* birth-pangs, labour-pains.

**wehen** ['veːən], *v.n.* (*wind*) blow.

**Wehgeschrei** ['veːgəʃraɪ], *n.* (—s, *no pl.*) wailings.

**Wehklage** ['veːklaːgə], *f.* (—, *pl.* —n) lamentation.

**wehklagen** ['veːklaːgən], *v.n. insep.* lament, wail.

**wehleidig** ['veːlaɪdɪç], *adj.* tearful; easily hurt; self-pitying.

**wehmütig** ['veːmyːtɪç], *adj.* sad, melancholy, wistful.

**Wehr** (1) [veːr], *n.* (—s, *pl.* —e) weir.

**Wehr** (2) [veːr], *f.* (—, *pl.* —en) defence, bulwark.

**wehren** ['veːrən], *v.r. sich —,* defend o.s., offer resistance.

**wehrhaft** ['veːrhaft], *adj.* capable of bearing arms, able-bodied.

**wehrlos** ['veːrloːs], *adj.* defenceless, unarmed; (*fig.*) weak, unprotected.

**Wehrpflicht** ['veːrpflɪçt], *f.* (—, *no pl.*) compulsory military service, conscription.

**Wehrstand** ['veːrʃtant], *m.* (—s, *no pl.*) the military.

**Weib** [vaɪp], *n.* (—(e)s, *pl.* —er) woman; (*Poet.*) wife.

**Weibchen** ['vaɪpçən], *n.* (—s, *pl.* —) (*animal*) female.

**Weiberfeind** ['vaɪbərfaɪnt], *m.* (—s, *pl.* —e) woman-hater, misogynist.

**Weiberherrschaft** ['vaɪbərhɛrʃaft], *f.* (—, *no pl.*) petticoat rule.

**weibisch** ['vaɪbɪʃ], *adj.* womanish, effeminate.

**weiblich** ['vaɪplɪç], *adj.* female, feminine; womanly.

**Weiblichkeit** ['vaɪplɪçkaɪt], *f.* (—, *no pl.*) womanliness, femininity.

**Weibsbild** ['vaɪpsbɪlt], *n.* (—s, *pl.* —er) (*sl.*) female; wench.

**weich** [vaɪç], *adj.* weak; soft; tender, gentle; effeminate; sensitive; — *machen,* soften; — *werden,* relent.

**Weichbild** ['vaɪçbɪlt], *n.* (—s, *no pl.*) precincts; city boundaries.

**Weiche** ['vaɪçə], *f.* (—, *pl.* —n) (*Railw.*) switch, points.

**weichen** (1) ['vaɪçən], *v.a.* steep, soak, soften.

**weichen** (2) ['vaɪçən], *v.n. irr.* (*aux.* sein) yield, make way, give ground.

**Weichensteller** ['vaɪçənʃtɛlər], *m.* (—s, *pl.* —) (*Railw.*) pointsman, signalman.

**Weichheit** ['vaɪçhaɪt], *f.* (—, *no pl.*) softness; (*fig.*) weakness, tenderness.

**weichherzig** ['vaɪçhɛrtsɪç], *adj.* softhearted, tender-hearted.

**weichlich** ['vaɪçlɪç], *adj.* soft; (*fig.*) weak, effeminate.

**Weichling** ['vaɪçlɪŋ], *m.* (—s, *pl.* —e) weakling.

**Weichsel** ['vaɪksəl], *f.* Vistula.

**Weichselkirsche** ['vaɪksəlkɪrʃə], *f.* (—, *pl.* —n) sour cherry; morello.

**Weide** ['vaɪdə], *f.* (—, *pl.* —n) pasture, pasturage; (*Bot.*) willow.

**Weideland** ['vaɪdəlant], *n.* (—s, *pl.* ⁻er) pasture-ground.

**weiden** ['vaɪdən], *v.a., v.n.* pasture, feed.

**Weidenbaum** ['vaɪdənbaum], *m.* (—s, *pl.* ⁻e) willow-tree.

**Weiderich** ['vaɪdərɪç], *m.* (—s, *pl.* —e) willow-herb, loose-strife, rose bay.

**Weidgenosse** ['vaɪtgənɔsə], *m.* (—en, *pl.* —en) fellow huntsman.

**weidlich** ['vaɪtlɪç], *adv.* (*rare*) greatly, thoroughly.

**Weidmann** ['vaɪtman], *m.* (—s, *pl.* ⁻er) sportsman, huntsman.

**Weidmannsheil!** ['vaɪtmanshaɪl], *excl.* tally-ho!

**weigern** ['vaɪgərn], *v.r. sich —,* refuse, decline.

**Weigerung** ['vaɪgərʊŋ], *f.* (—, *pl.* —en) refusal, denial.

**Weih** [vaɪ], *m.* (—en, *pl.* —en) (*Orn.*) kite.

**Weihbischof** ['vaɪbɪʃɔf], *m.* (—s, *pl.* ⁻e) suffragan bishop.

**Weihe** ['vaɪə], *f.* (—, *pl.* —en) consecration; (*priest*) ordination; initiation; (*fig.*) solemnity.

**weihen** ['vaɪən], *v.a.* bless, consecrate; ordain. — *v.r. sich —,* devote o.s. (to).

**Weiher** ['vaɪər], *m.* (—s, *pl.* —) pond, fishpond.

**weihevoll** ['vaɪəfɔl], *adj.* solemn.

**Weihnachten** ['vaɪnaxtən], *n. or f.* Christmas.

**Weihnachtsabend** ['vaɪnaxtsaːbənt], *m.* (—s, *pl.* —e) Christmas Eve.

**Weihnachtsfeiertag** ['vaɪnaxtsfaɪərtaːk], *m.* (—s, *pl.* —e) Christmas Day; *zweiter —,* Boxing Day.

**Weihnachtsgeschenk** ['vaɪnaxtsgəʃɛŋk], *n.* (—s, *pl.* —e) Christmas box, Christmas present.

**Weihnachtslied** ['vaɪnaxtsliːt], *n.* (—(e)s, *pl.* —er) Christmas carol.

**Weihnachtsmann** ['vaɪnaxtsman], *m.* (—(e)s, *pl.* ⁻er) Santa Claus, Father Christmas.

**Weihrauch** ['vaɪraux], *m.* (—s, *no pl.*) incense.

**Weihwasser** ['vaɪvasər], *n.* (—s, *no pl.*) holy water.

**weil** [vaɪl], *conj.* because, as, since.

**weiland** ['vaɪlant], *adv.* (*obs.*) formerly, once.

**Weile** ['vaɪlə], *f.* (—, *no pl.*) while, short time; leisure.

**weilen** ['vaɪlən], *v.n.* tarry, stay, abide.

**Wein** [vaɪn], *m.* (—(e)s, *pl.* —e) wine; (*plant*) vine; *einem reinen — einschenken,* tell s.o. the truth.

# Weinbau

**Weinbau** ['vaɪnbau], *m.* (—s, *no pl.*) vine growing, viticulture.

**Weinbeere** ['vaɪnbeːrə], *f.* (—, *pl.* —n) grape.

**Weinberg** ['vaɪnbɛrk], *m.* (—s, *pl.* —e) vineyard.

**Weinbrand** ['vaɪnbrant], *m.* (—s, *no pl.*) brandy.

**weinen** ['vaɪnən], *v.n.* weep, cry.

**Weinernte** ['vaɪnɛrntə], *f.* (—, *pl.* —n) vintage.

**Weinessig** ['vaɪnɛsɪç], *m.* (—s, *no pl.*) (wine) vinegar.

**Weinfaß** ['vaɪnfas], *n.* (—sses, *pl.* ⸚sser) wine-cask.

**Weingeist** ['vaɪngaɪst], *m.* (—es, *no pl.*) spirits of wine, alcohol.

**Weinhändler** ['vaɪnhɛndlər], *m.* (—s, *pl.* —) wine merchant.

**Weinkarte** ['vaɪnkartə], *f.* (—, *pl.* —n) wine-list.

**Weinkeller** ['vaɪnkɛlər], *m.* (—s, *pl.* —) wine-cellar; wine-tavern.

**Weinkellerei** ['vaɪnkɛləraɪ], *f.* (—, *pl.* —en) wine-store.

**Weinkelter** ['vaɪnkɛltər], *f.* (—, *pl.* —n) wine-press.

**Weinkneipe** ['vaɪnknaɪpə], *f.* (—, *pl.* —n) wine-tavern.

**Weinkoster** ['vaɪnkɔstər], *m.* (—s, *pl.* —) wine-taster.

**Weinlaub** ['vaɪnlaup], *n.* (—s, *no pl.*) vine-leaves.

**Weinlese** ['vaɪnleːzə], *f.* (—, *pl.* —n) vintage, grape harvest.

**Weinranke** ['vaɪnraŋkə], *f.* (—, *pl.* —n) vine-branch, tendril.

**Weinschenke** ['vaɪnʃɛŋkə], *f.* (—, *pl.* —n) wine-house, tavern.

**weinselig** ['vaɪnzeːlɪç], *adj.* tipsy.

**Weinstein** ['vaɪnʃtaɪn], *m.* (—s, *no pl.*) tartar.

**Weinsteinsäure** ['vaɪnʃtaɪnzɔyrə], *f.* (—, *no pl.*) tartaric acid.

**Weinstock** ['vaɪnʃtɔk], *m.* (—s, *pl.* ⸚e) vine.

**Weintraube** ['vaɪntraubə], *f.* (—, *pl.* —n) grape, bunch of grapes.

**weinumrankt** ['vaɪnumraŋkt], *adj.* vine-clad.

**weise** ['vaɪzə], *adj.* wise, prudent.

**Weise** (1) ['vaɪzə], *m.* (—n, *pl.* —n) wise man, sage.

**Weise** (2) ['vaɪzə], *f.* (—, *pl.* —n) manner, fashion; method, way; tune, melody.

**weisen** ['vaɪzən], *v.a. irr.* point to, point out, show.

**Weiser** ['vaɪzər], *m.* (—s, *pl.* —) signpost; indicator; (*clock*) hand.

**Weisheit** ['vaɪshaɪt], *f.* (—, *pl.* —en) wisdom, prudence.

**Weisheitszahn** ['vaɪshaɪtstsaːn], *m.* (—s, *pl.* ⸚e) wisdom tooth.

**weislich** ['vaɪslɪç], *adv.* wisely, prudently, advisedly.

**weismachen** ['vaɪsmaxən], *v.a. einem etwas* —, (*coll.*) spin a yarn to s.o.; *laß dir nichts* —, don't be taken in.

**weiß** [vaɪs], *adj.* white, clean, blank.

**weissagen** ['vaɪszaːgən], *v.a. insep.* prophesy, foretell.

**Weissager** ['vaɪszaːgər], *m.* (—s, *pl.* —) prophet, soothsayer.

**Weissagung** ['vaɪszaːguŋ], *f.* (—, *pl.* —en) prophecy.

**Weißbuche** ['vaɪsbuːxə], *f.* (—, *pl.* —n) (*Bot.*) hornbeam.

**Weiße** ['vaɪsə], *f.* (—, *no pl.*) whiteness; (*fig.*) (*dial.*) pale ale.

**weißglühend** ['vaɪsglyːənt], *adj.* at white heat, incandescent, white hot.

**Weißnäherin** ['vaɪsnɛːərɪn], *f.* (—, *pl.* —nen) seamstress.

**Weißwaren** ['vaɪsvaːrən], *f. pl.* linen.

**Weisung** ['vaɪzuŋ], *f.* (—, *pl.* —en) order, direction, instruction; directive.

**weit** [vaɪt], *adj.* distant, far, far off; wide, broad, vast, extensive; (*clothing*) loose, too big.

**weitab** [vaɪt'ap], *adv.* far away.

**weitaus** [vaɪt'aus], *adv.* by far.

**weitblickend** ['vaɪtblɪkənt], *adj.* far-sighted.

**Weite** ['vaɪtə], *f.* (—, *pl.* —n) width, breadth; distance.

**weiten** ['vaɪtən], *v.a.* widen, expand.

**weiter** ['vaɪtər], *adj.* further, farther, wider.

**weiterbefördern** ['vaɪtərbəfœrdərn], *v.a.* send, forward, send on.

**weiterbilden** ['vaɪtərbɪldən], *v.a.* improve, develop(e), extend.

**Weitere** ['vaɪtərə], *n.* (—n, *no pl.*) rest, remainder.

**weiterführen** ['vaɪtərfyːrən], *v.a.* continue, carry on.

**weitergeben** ['vaɪtərgeːbən], *v.a. irr.* pass on.

**weitergehen** ['vaɪtərgeːən], *v.n. irr.* (*aux.* sein) walk on.

**weiterhin** ['vaɪtərhɪn], *adv.* furthermore; in time to come; in future.

**weiterkommen** ['vaɪtərkɔmən], *v.n. irr.* (*aux.* sein) get on.

**Weiterung** ['vaɪtəruŋ], *f.* (—, *pl.* —en) widening, enlargement.

**weitgehend** ['vaɪtgeːənt], *adj.* far-reaching, sweeping.

**weitläufig** ['vaɪtlɔyfɪç], *adj.* ample, large; detailed, elaborate; distant, widespread; diffuse, long-winded.

**weitschweifig** ['vaɪtʃvaɪfɪç], *adj.* prolix, diffuse, rambling.

**weitsichtig** ['vaɪtzɪçtɪç], *adj.* long-sighted.

**weittragend** ['vaɪttraːgənt], *adj.* portentous, far-reaching.

**weitverbreitet** ['vaɪtfɛrbraɪtət], *adj.* widespread.

**Weizen** ['vaɪtsən], *m.* (—s, *no pl.*) wheat.

**Weizengrieß** ['vaɪtsəngriːs], *m.* (—es, *no pl.*) semolina; grits.

**welch** [vɛlç], *pron.* what (a).

**welcher, -e, -es** ['vɛlçər], *interr. pron.* which? what? — *rel. pron.* who, which, that; (*indef.*) (*coll.*) some.

# werktätig

**welcherlei** ['vɛlçərlaɪ], *indecl. adj.* of what kind.

**Welfe** ['vɛlfə], *m.* (—n, *pl.* —n) Guelph.

**welk** [vɛlk], *adj.* faded, withered; — *werden*, fade, wither.

**welken** ['vɛlkən], *v.n.* (*aux.* sein) wither, fade, decay.

**Wellblech** ['vɛlblɛç], *n.* (—s, *no pl.*) corrugated iron.

**Welle** ['vɛlə], *f.* (—, *pl.* —n) wave, billow.

**wellen** ['vɛlən], *v.a.* wave.

**Wellenbewegung** ['vɛlənbəveːɡuŋ], *f.* (—, *pl.* —en) undulation.

**Wellenlinie** ['vɛlənliːnjə], *f.* (—, *pl.* —n) wavy line.

**wellig** ['vɛlɪç], *adj.* wavy, undulating.

**welsch** [vɛlʃ], *adj.* foreign; Italian; French.

**Welschkohl** ['vɛlʃkoːl], *m.* (—s, *no pl.*) (*Bot.*) savoy cabbage.

**Welschkorn** ['vɛlʃkɔrn], *n.* (—s, *no pl.*) (*Bot.*) Indian corn.

**Welt** [vɛlt], *f.* (—, *pl.* —en) world, earth; universe; society.

**Weltall** ['vɛltal], *n.* (—s, *no pl.*) universe, cosmos; (outer) space.

**Weltanschauung** ['vɛltanʃauuŋ], *f.* (—, *pl.* —en) view of life, philosophy of life, ideology.

**Weltbeschreibung** ['vɛltbəʃraɪbuŋ], *f.* (—, *no pl.*) cosmography.

**Weltbürger** ['vɛltbyrɡər], *m.* (—s, *pl.* —) cosmopolitan.

**welterschütternd** ['vɛltərʃytərnt], *adj.* world-shaking.

**weltfremd** ['vɛltfrɛmt], *adj.* unworldy, unsophisticated.

**Weltgeschichte** ['vɛltɡəʃɪçtə], *f.* (—, *no pl.*) world history.

**Weltherrschaft** ['vɛltherʃaft], *f.* (—, *no pl.*) world dominion.

**Weltkenntnis** ['vɛltkɛntnɪs], *f.* (—, *no pl.*) worldly wisdom.

**weltklug** ['vɛltkluːk], *adj.* astute, worldly-wise.

**Weltkrieg** ['vɛltkriːk], *m.* (—es, *pl.* —e) world war.

**weltlich** ['vɛltlɪç], *adj.* worldly; (*Eccl.*) temporal, secular.

**Weltmacht** ['vɛltmaxt], *f.* (—, *pl.* ⁻e) world power, great power.

**Weltmeer** ['vɛltmeːr], *n.* (—s, *pl.* —e) ocean.

**Weltmeisterschaft** ['vɛltmaɪstərʃaft], *f.* (—, *pl.* —en) world championship.

**Weltordnung** ['vɛltɔrdnuŋ], *f.* (— *pl.* —en) cosmic order.

**Weltraum** ['vɛltraum], *m.* (—s, *no pl.*) space.

**Weltraumflug** ['vɛltraumfluːk], *m.* (—(e)s, *pl.* ⁻e) space flight.

**Weltraumforschung** ['vɛltraumfor-ʃuŋ], *f.* (—, *no pl.*) space exploration.

**Weltraumgeschoß** ['vɛltraumɡəʃoːs], *n.* (—sses, *pl.* —sse) space rocket.

**Weltruf** ['vɛltruːf], *m.* (—s, *no pl.*) world-wide renown.

**Weltschmerz** ['vɛltʃmɛrts], *m.* (—es, *no pl.*) world-weariness, Wertherism; melancholy.

**Weltsprache** ['vɛltʃpraːxə], *f.* (—, *pl.* —en) universal language; world language.

**Weltstadt** ['vɛltʃtat], *f.* (—, *pl.* ⁻e) metropolis.

**Weltumseglung** ['vɛltumzeːɡluŋ], *f.* (—, *pl.* —en) circumnavigation (of the globe).

**Weltuntergang** ['vɛltuntərɡaŋ], *m.* (—s, *no pl.*) end of the world.

**Weltwirtschaft** ['vɛltvɪrtʃaft], *f.* (—, *no pl.*) world trade.

**wem** [veːm], *pers. pron.* (*Dat. of* wer) to whom. — *interr. pron.* to whom?

**wen** [veːn], *pers. pron.* (*Acc. of* wer) whom. — *interr. pron.* whom?

**Wende** ['vɛndə], *f.* (—, *pl.* —n) turn, turning(-point).

**Wendekreis** ['vɛndəkraɪs], *m.* (—es, *pl.* —e) tropic.

**Wendeltreppe** ['vɛndəltrepə], *f.* (—, *pl.* —n) spiral staircase.

**wenden** ['vɛndən], *v.a.* reg. & irr. turn.

**Wendepunkt** ['vɛndəpuŋkt], *m.* (—es, *pl.* —e) turning point; crisis.

**Wendung** ['vɛnduŋ], *f.* (—, *pl.* —en) turn, turning; crisis; (*speech*) phrase.

**wenig** ['veːnɪç], *adj.* little, few; *ein* —, a little.

**weniger** ['veːnɪɡər], *adj.* less, fewer.

**wenigstens** ['veːnɪçstəns], *adv.* at least.

**wenn** [vɛn], *conj.* if; when; whenever; in case; — *nicht*, unless.

**wenngleich** [vɛn'ɡlaɪç], *conj.* though, although.

**wer** [veːr], *rel. pron.* who, he who; — *auch*, whoever. — *interr. pron.* who? which? — *da?* who goes there?

**Werbekraft** ['vɛrbəkraft], *f.* (—, *no pl.*) (*Advertising*) attraction; appeal; publicity value.

**werben** ['vɛrbən], *v.n.* irr. advertise, canvass; court, woo. — *v.a.* (*soldiers*) recruit.

**Werbung** ['vɛrbuŋ], *f.* (—, *pl.* —en) advertising, publicity, propaganda; recruiting; courtship.

**Werdegang** ['veːrdəɡaŋ], *m.* (—s, *no pl.*) evolution, development.

**werden** ['veːrdən], *v.n.* irr. (*aux.* sein) become, get; grow; turn; *Arzt* —, become a doctor; *alt* —, grow old; *bleich* — turn pale.

**werdend** ['veːrdənt], *adj.* becoming; nascent, incipient, budding.

**werfen** ['vɛrfən], *v.a.* irr. throw, cast.

**Werft** (1) [vɛrft], *m.* (—(e)s, *pl.* —e) warp.

**Werft** (2) [vɛrft], *f.* (—, *pl.* —en) dockyard, shipyard, wharf.

**Werk** [vɛrk], *n.* (—(e)s, *pl.* —e) work, action, deed; undertaking; (*Ind.*) works, plant, mill, factory.

**Werkführer** ['vɛrkfyːrər], *m.* (—s, *pl.* —) foreman.

**Werkleute** ['vɛrklɔytə], *pl.* workmen.

**Werkmeister** ['vɛrkmaɪstər], *m.* (—s, *pl.* —) overseer, foreman.

**werktätig** ['vɛrktɛːtɪç], *adj.* active, practical; hard-working.

279

# Werkzeug

**Werkzeug** ['vɛrktsɔyk], *n.* (—s, *pl.* —e) implement, tool, jig, instrument.

**Wermut** ['veːrmuːt], *m.* (—s, *no pl.*) absinthe, vermouth.

**Wert** [veːrt], *m.* (—e)s, *pl.* —e) value, worth, price; use; merit; importance.

**wert** [veːrt], *adj.* valuable; worth; dear, esteemed.

**Wertangabe** ['veːrtangaːbə], *f.* (—, *pl.* —n) valuation; declared value.

**Wertbestimmung** ['veːrtbəʃtɪmuŋ], *f.* (—, *no pl.*) appraisal, assessment, valuation.

**Wertbrief** ['veːrtbriːf], *m.* (—s, *pl.* —e) registered letter.

**werten** ['veːrtən], *v.a.* value.

**Wertgegenstand** ['veːrtgeːgənʃtant], *m.* (—s, *pl.* ⁈e) article of value.

**Wertmesser** ['veːrtmɛsər], *m.* (—s, *pl.* —) standard.

**Wertpapiere** ['veːrtpapiːrə], *n. pl.* securities.

**Wertsachen** ['veːrtzaxən], *f. pl.* valuables.

**wertschätzen** ['veːrtʃɛtsən], *v.a.* esteem (highly).

**wertvoll** ['veːrtfɔl], *adj.* of great value, valuable.

**Wertzeichen** ['veːrttsaɪçən], *n.* (—s, *pl.* —) stamp; coupon.

**wes** [vɛs], *pers. pron.* (*obs.*) whose.

**Wesen** ['veːzən], *n.* (—s, *pl.* —) being, creature; reality; essence, nature, substance; character, demeanour; (*in compounds*) organisation, affairs.

**wesenlos** ['veːzənloːs], *adj.* disembodied, unsubstantial, shadowy; trivial.

**wesensgleich** ['veːzənsglaɪç], *adj.* identical, substantially the same.

**wesentlich** ['veːzəntlɪç], *adj.* essential, material.

**weshalb** [vɛs'halp], *conj., adv.* wherefore, why; therefore.

**Wespe** ['vɛspə], *f.* (—, *pl.* —n) (*Ent.*) wasp.

**Wespennest** ['vɛspənnɛst], *n.* (—s, *pl.* —er) wasps' nest; *in ein — stechen*, stir up a hornets' nest.

**wessen** ['vɛsən], *pers. pron.* (*Genit. of* wer) whose. — *interr. pron.* whose?

**Weste** ['vɛstə], *f.* (—, *pl.* —n) waistcoat.

**Westen** ['vɛstən], *m.* (—s, *no pl.*) west; *nach* —, westward.

**Westfalen** [vɛst'faːlən], *n.* Westphalia.

**Westindien** [vɛst'ɪndjən], *n.* the West Indies.

**weswegen** [vɛs'veːgən] *see* **weshalb**.

**Wettbewerb** ['vɛtbəvɛrp], *m.* (—s, *pl.* —e) competition, rivalry; *unlauterer* —, unfair competition.

**Wettbewerber** ['vɛtbəvɛrbər], *m.* (—s, *pl.* —) rival, competitor.

**Wette** ['vɛtə], *f.* (—, *pl.* —n) bet, wager; *um die — laufen*, race one another.

**Wetteifer** ['vɛtaɪfər], *m.* (—s, *no pl.*) rivalry.

**wetteifern** ['vɛtaɪfərn], *v.n. insep.* vie (with), compete.

**wetten** ['vɛtən], *v.a., v.n.* bet, lay a wager, wager.

**Wetter** ['vɛtər], *n.* (—s, *pl.* —) weather; bad weather, storm; *schlagende* —, (*Min.*) fire-damp.

**Wetterbeobachtung** ['vɛtərbəobax-tuŋ], *f.* (—, *pl.* —en) meteorological observation.

**Wetterbericht** ['vɛtərbərɪçt], *m.* (—s, *pl.* —e) weather report *or* forecast.

**Wetterfahne** ['vɛtərfaːnə], *f.* (—, *pl.* —en) weather-cock, vane; (*fig.*) turncoat.

**wetterfest** ['vɛtərfɛst], *adj.* weatherproof.

**Wetterglas** ['vɛtərglaːs], *n.* (—es, *pl.* ⁈er) barometer.

**Wetterhahn** ['vɛtərhaːn], *m.* (—s, *pl.* ⁈e) weather-cock.

**Wetterkunde** ['vɛtərkundə], *f.* (—, *no pl.*) meteorology.

**Wetterleuchten** ['vɛtərlɔyçtən], *n.* (—s, *no pl.*) summer lightning; sheet lightning.

**wettern** ['vɛtərn], *v.n.* be stormy; (*fig.*) curse, swear, thunder (against), storm.

**Wettervorhersage** ['vɛtərfoːrheːrzaː-gə], *f.* (—, *pl.* —n) weather forecast.

**wetterwendisch** ['vɛtərvendɪʃ], *adj.* changeable; irritable, peevish.

**Wettkampf** ['vɛtkampf], *m.* (—(e)s, *pl.* ⁈e) contest, tournament.

**Wettlauf** ['vɛtlauf], *m.* (—s, *pl.* ⁈e) race.

**wettmachen** ['vɛtmaxən], *v.a.* make up for.

**Wettrennen** ['vɛtrɛnən], *n.* (—s, *pl.* —) race.

**Wettstreit** ['vɛtʃtraɪt], *m.* (—s, *pl.* —e) contest, contention.

**wetzen** ['vɛtsən], *v.a.* whet, hone, sharpen.

**Wichse** ['vɪksə], *f.* (—, *pl.* —n) blacking, shoe-polish; (*fig.*) thrashing.

**wichsen** ['vɪksən], *v.a.* black, shine; (*fig.*) thrash.

**Wicht** [vɪçt], *m.* (—(e)s, *pl.* —e) creature; (*coll.*) chap.

**Wichtelmännchen** ['vɪçtəlmɛnçən], *n.* (—s, *pl.* —) pixie, goblin.

**wichtig** ['vɪçtɪç], *adj.* important; weighty; significant; *sich — machen*, put on airs.

**Wichtigkeit** ['vɪçtɪçkaɪt], *f.* (—, *no pl.*) importance; significance.

**Wicke** ['vɪkə], *f.* (—, *pl.* —n) (*Bot.*) vetch.

**Wickel** ['vɪkəl], *m.* (—s, *pl.* —) roller; (*hair*) curler; (*Med.*) compress.

**Wickelkind** ['vɪkəlkɪnt], *n.* (—s, *pl.* —er) babe in arms.

**wickeln** ['vɪkəln], *v.a.* roll, coil; wind; wrap (up); (*babies*) swaddle; (*hair*) curl.

**Widder** ['vɪdər], *m.* (—s, *pl.* —) ram; (*Astrol.*) Aries.

**wider** ['viːdər], *prep.* (*Acc.*) against, in opposition to, contrary to.

**widerfahren** [vi:dər'fa:rən], *v.n. irr.
insep. (aux.* sein) happen to s.o.,
befall s.o.; *einem Gerechtigkeit —
lassen,* give s.o. his due.
**Widerhaken** ['vi:dərha:kən], *m.* (—s,
*pl.* —) barb.
**Widerhall** ['vi:dərhal], *m.* (—s, *pl.* —e)
echo, resonance; ( *fig.*) response.
**widerlegen** [vi:dər'le:gən], *v.a. insep.*
refute, disprove, prove (s.o.) wrong.
**Widerlegung** [vi:dər'le:guŋ], *f.* (—,
*pl.* —en) refutation, rebuttal.
**widerlich** ['vi:dərlɪç], *adj.* disgusting,
nauseating, repulsive.
**widernatürlich** ['vi:dərnaty:rlɪç], *adj.*
unnatural; perverse.
**widerraten** [vi:dər'ra:tən], *v.a. irr.
insep.* advise against; dissuade from.
**widerrechtlich** ['vi:dərreçtlɪç], *adj.*
illegal, unlawful.
**Widerrede** ['vi:dərre:də], *f.* (—, *pl.*
—n) contradiction.
**Widerruf** ['vi:dərru:f], *m.* (—s, *pl.* —e)
revocation, recantation.
**widerrufen** [vi:dər'ru:fən], *v.a. irr.
insep.* recant, retract, revoke.
**Widersacher** ['vi:dərzaxər], *m.* (—s,
*pl.* —) adversary, antagonist.
**Widerschein** ['vi:dərʃaɪn], *m.* (—s,
*no pl.*) reflection.
**widersetzen** [vi:dər'zetsən], *v.r. insep.
sich* —, resist, (*Dat.*) oppose.
**widersetzlich** [vi:dər'zetslɪç], *adj.* refractory, insubordinate.
**Widersinn** [vi:dərzɪn], *m.* (—s, *no pl.*)
nonsense, absurdity; paradox.
**widersinnig** ['vi:dərzɪnɪç], *adj.* nonsensical, absurd; paradoxical.
**widerspenstig** ['vi:dərʃpenstɪç], *adj.*
refractory, rebellious, obstinate, stubborn.
**widerspiegeln** [vi:dər'ʃpi:gəln], *v.a.*
reflect, mirror.
**widersprechen** [vi:dər'ʃpreçən], *v.n.
irr. insep.* (*Dat.*) contradict, gainsay.
**Widerspruch** ['vi:dərʃprux], *m.* (—(es),
*pl.* ⸚e) contradiction.
**widerspruchsvoll** ['vi:dərʃpruxsfɔl],
*adj.* contradictory.
**Widerstand** ['vi:dərʃtant], *m.* (—s, *pl.*
⸚e) resistance, opposition.
**widerstandsfähig** ['vi:dərʃtantsfɛ:ɪç],
*adj.* resistant, hardy.
**widerstehen** [vi:dər'ʃte:ən], *v.n. irr.
insep.* (*Dat.*) resist, withstand; be
distasteful (to).
**Widerstreben** [vi:dər'ʃtre:bən], *n.* (—s,
*no pl.*) reluctance.
**widerstreben** [vi:dər'ʃtre:bən], *v.n.
insep.* (*Dat.*) strive against; oppose; be
distasteful to a p.
**Widerstreit** ['vi:dərʃtraɪt], *m.* (—s, *no
pl.*) contradiction, opposition; conflict.
**widerwärtig** ['vi:dərvertɪç], *adj.* unpleasant, disagreeable, repugnant,
repulsive; hateful, odious.
**Widerwille** ['vi:dərvɪlə], *m.* (—ns, *no
pl.*) aversion (to).

**widmen** ['vɪdmən], *v.a.* dedicate.
**Widmung** ['vɪdmuŋ], *f.* (—, *pl.* —en)
dedication.
**widrig** ['vi:drɪç], *adj.* contrary, adverse,
inimical, unfavourable.
**widrigenfalls** ['vi:drɪgənfals], *adv.* failing this, otherwise, else.
**wie** [vi:], *adv.* how. — *conj.* as, just as,
like; — *geht's?* how are you?
**wieder** ['vi:dər], *adv.* again, anew,
afresh; back, in return.
**Wiederabdruck** ['vi:dərapdruk], *m.*
(—s, *pl.* —e) reprint.
**Wiederaufbau** [vi:dər'aufbau], *m.* (—s,
*no pl.*) rebuilding.
**Wiederaufnahme** [vi:dər'aufna:mə], *f.*
(—, *no pl.*) resumption.
**Wiederbelebungsversuch** ['vi:dərbə-
le:buŋsfɛrzu:x], *m.* (—es, *pl.* —e) attempt at resuscitation.
**Wiederbezahlung** ['vi:dərbətsa:luŋ], *f.*
(—, *pl.* —en) reimbursement.
**wiederbringen** ['vi:dərbrɪŋən], *v.a.
irr.* bring back, restore.
**Wiedereinrichtung** ['vi:dəraɪnrɪçtuŋ],
*f.* (—, *no pl.*) reorganisation, re-estab-
lishment.
**Wiedereinsetzung** ['vi:dəraɪnzetsuŋ],
*f.* (—, *pl.* —en) restoration, reinstate-
ment, rehabilitation.
**wiedererkennen** ['vi:dərerkenən], *v.a.
irr.* recognise.
**Wiedererstattung** ['vi:dərerʃtatuŋ], *f.*
(—, *no pl.*) restitution.
**Wiedergabe** ['vi:dərga:bə], *f.* (—, *no pl.*)
restitution, return; ( *fig.*) rendering,
reproduction.
**wiedergeben** ['vi:dərge:bən], *v.a. irr.*
return, give back; ( *fig.*) render.
**Wiedergeburt** ['vi:dərgəbu:rt], *f.* (—,
*no pl.*) rebirth, regeneration, rena-
scence.
**Wiedergutmachung** [vi:dər'gu:t-
maxuŋ], *f.* (—, *no pl.*) reparation.
**Wiederherstellung** [vi:dər'he:rʃteluŋ],
*f.* (—, *no pl.*) restoration; recovery.
**Wiederherstellungsmittel** [vi:dər-
'he:rʃteluŋsmɪtəl], *n.* (—s, *pl.* —)
restorative, tonic.
**wiederholen** [vi:dər'ho:lən], *v.a. insep.*
repeat, reiterate.
**Wiederholung** [vi:dər'ho:luŋ], *f.* (—,
*pl.* —en) repetition.
**Wiederkäuer** ['vi:dərkɔyər], *m.* (—s,
*pl.* —) ruminant.
**Wiederkehr** ['vi:dərke:r], *f.* (—, *no pl.*)
return; recurrence.
**wiederkehren** ['vi:dərke:rən], *v.n. (aux.*
sein) return.
**wiederklingen** ['vi:dərklɪŋən], *v.n. irr.*
reverberate.
**wiederkommen** ['vi:dərkɔmən], *v.n.
irr. (aux.* sein) return, come back.
**Wiedersehen** ['vi:dərze:ən], *n.* (—s,
*no pl.*) reunion, meeting after separation; *auf* —, good-bye! so long! see
you again!
**wiedersehen** ['vi:dərze:ən], *v.a. irr.* see
again, meet again.

281

**wiederum** ['vi:dərum], *adv.* again, anew, afresh.

**Wiedervereinigung** ['vi:dərfɛraɪnɪgun̩], *f.* (—, *pl.* —en) reunion, reunification.

**Wiedervergeltung** ['vi:dərfɛrgɛltun̩], *f.* (—, *no pl.*) requital, retaliation, reprisal.

**Wiederverkauf** ['vi:dərfɛrkauf], *m.* (—s, *no pl.*) resale.

**Wiederverkäufer** ['vi:dərfɛrkɔyfər], *m.* (—s, *pl.* —) retailer.

**Wiederversöhnung** ['vi:dərfɛrzø:nun̩], *f.* (—, *no pl.*) reconciliation.

**Wiederwahl** ['vi:dərva:l], *f.* (—, *no pl.*) re-election.

**Wiege** ['vi:gə], *f.* (—, *pl.* —n) cradle.

**wiegen** ['vi:gən], *v.a.* rock (the cradle). — *v.r. sich* — *in*, delude o.s. with. — *v.a., v.n. irr.* weigh.

**Wiegenfest** ['vi:gənfɛst], *n.* (—es, *pl.* —e) (*Poet., Lit.*) birthday.

**Wiegenlied** ['vi:gənli:t], *n.* (—s, *pl.* —er) cradle-song, lullaby.

**wiehern** ['vi:ərn], *v.n.* neigh.

**Wien** [vi:n], *n.* Vienna.

**Wiese** ['vi:zə], *f.* (—, *pl.* —n) meadow.

**Wiesel** ['vi:zəl], *n.* (—s, *pl.* —) (*Zool.*) weasel.

**wieso** [vi'zo:] *adv.* why? how do you mean? in what way?

**wieviel** [vi'fi:l], *adv.* how much, how many; *den* —*ten haben wir heute?* what is the date today?

**wiewohl** [vi'vo:l], *conj.* although, though.

**Wild** [vɪlt], *n.* (—(e)s, *no pl.*) game; venison.

**wild** [vɪlt], *adj.* wild, savage, fierce; furious.

**Wildbach** ['vɪltbax], *m.* (—s, *pl.* ¨e) (mountain) torrent.

**Wilddieb** ['vɪltdi:p], *m.* (—(e)s, *pl.* —e) poacher.

**Wilde** ['vɪldə], *m.* (—n, *pl.* —n) savage.

**wildern** ['vɪldərn], *v.n.* poach.

**Wildfang** ['vɪltfaŋ], *m.* (—s, *pl.* ¨e) scamp, tomboy.

**wildfremd** ['vɪltfrɛmt], *adj.* completely strange.

**Wildhüter** ['vɪlthy:tər], *m.* (—s, *pl.* —) gamekeeper.

**Wildleder** ['vɪltle:dər], *n.* (—s, *no pl.*) suède, doeskin, buckskin.

**Wildnis** ['vɪltnɪs], *f.* (—, *pl.* —se) wilderness, desert.

**Wildpark** ['vɪltpark], *m.* (—s, *pl.* —s) game-reserve.

**Wildpret** ['vɪltprɛt], *n.* (—s, *no pl.*) game; venison.

**Wildschwein** ['vɪltʃvaɪn], *n.* (—s, *pl.* —e) wild boar.

**Wille** ['vɪlə], *m.* (—ns, *no pl.*) will, wish, design, purpose.

**willenlos** ['vɪlənlo:s], *adj.* weak-minded.

**willens** ['vɪləns], *adv.* — *sein*, be willing, have a mind to.

**Willenserklärung** ['vɪlənsɛrkle:run̩], *f.* (—, *pl.* —en) (*Law*) declaratory act.

**Willensfreiheit** ['vɪlənsfraɪhaɪt], *f.* (—, *no pl.*) free will.

**Willenskraft** ['vɪlənskraft], *f.* (—, *no pl.*) strength of will, will-power.

**willentlich** ['vɪləntlɪç], *adv.* purposely, on purpose, intentionally, wilfully.

**willfahren** [vɪl'fa:rən], *v.n. insep.* (*Dat.*) comply with, gratify.

**willfährig** ['vɪlfɛ:rɪç], *adj.* compliant, complaisant.

**willig** ['vɪlɪç], *adj.* willing, ready, docile.

**willkommen** [vɪl'kɔmən], *adj.* welcome; — *heißen*, welcome.

**Willkür** ['vɪlky:r], *f.* (—, *no pl.*) free will; discretion; caprice, arbitrariness.

**willkürlich** ['vɪlky:rlɪç], *adj.* arbitrary.

**wimmeln** ['vɪməln], *v.n.* swarm, teem (with).

**wimmern** ['vɪmərn], *v.n.* whimper.

**Wimpel** ['vɪmpəl], *m.* (—s, *pl.* —) pennon, pennant, streamer.

**Wimper** ['vɪmpər], *f.* (—, *pl.* —n) eyelash; *ohne mit der* — *zu zucken*, without turning a hair, without batting an eyelid.

**Wind** [vɪnt], *m.* (—(e)s, *pl.* —e) wind, breeze; *von etwas* — *bekommen*, get wind of.

**Windbeutel** ['vɪntbɔytəl], *m.* (—s, *pl.* —) cream puff; (*fig.*) windbag.

**Windbüchse** ['vɪntbyksə], *f.* (—, *pl.* —n) air-gun.

**Winde** ['vɪndə], *f.* (—, *pl.* —n) (*Tech.*) windlass; (*Bot.*) bindweed.

**Windel** ['vɪndəl], *f.* (—, *pl.* —n) (baby's) napkin; (*Am.*) diaper.

**windelweich** ['vɪndəlvaɪç], *adj.* very soft, limp; *einen* — *schlagen*, beat s.o. to a jelly.

**winden** ['vɪndən], *v.a. irr.* wind, reel; wring; (*flowers*) make a wreath of. — *v.r. sich* —, writhe.

**Windeseile** ['vɪndəsaɪlə], *f.* (—, *no pl.*) lightning speed.

**Windfahne** ['vɪntfa:nə], *f.* (—, *pl.* —n) weather-cock, vane.

**windfrei** ['vɪntfraɪ], *adj.* sheltered.

**Windhund** ['vɪnthunt], *m.* (—s, *pl.* —e) greyhound; (*fig.*) windbag.

**windig** ['vɪndɪç], *adj.* windy.

**Windklappe** ['vɪntklapə], *f.* (—, *pl.* —n) air-valve.

**Windlicht** ['vɪntlɪçt], *n.* (—s, *pl.* —er) torch; storm lantern.

**Windmühle** ['vɪntmy:lə], *f.* (—, *pl.* —n) windmill.

**Windpocken** ['vɪntpɔkən], *f. pl.* (*Med.*) chicken-pox.

**Windrichtung** ['vɪntrɪçtun̩], *f.* (—, *pl.* —en) direction of the wind.

**Windrose** ['vɪntro:zə], *f.* (—, *pl.* —n) compass card; windrose.

**Windsbraut** ['vɪntsbraut], *f.* (—, *no pl.*) gust of wind, squall; gale.

**windschief** ['vɪntʃi:f], *adj.* warped, bent.

**Windschutzscheibe** ['vɪntʃutsʃaɪbə], *f.* (—, *pl.* —n) (*Motor.*) windscreen.

**Windseite** ['vɪntzaɪtə], *f.* (—, *pl.* —n) windward side.

# Witterungsverhältnisse

**Windspiel** ['vɪntʃpi:l], *n.* (—s, *pl.* —e) greyhound.

**windstill** ['vɪntʃtɪl], *adj.* calm.

**Windung** ['vɪnduŋ], *f.* (—, *pl.* —en) winding; convolution; twist, loop; coil; meandering.

**Wink** [vɪŋk], *m.* (—(e)s, *pl.* —e) sign, nod; (*fig.*) hint, suggestion.

**Winkel** ['vɪŋkəl], *m.* (—s, *pl.* —) corner; (*Maths.*) angle.

**Winkeladvokat** ['vɪŋkəlatvoka:t], *m.* (—en, *pl.* —en) quack lawyer.

**Winkelmaß** ['vɪŋkəlma:s], *n.* (—es, *pl.* —e) set-square.

**Winkelmesser** ['vɪŋkəlmesər], *m.* (—s, *pl.* —) protractor.

**Winkelzug** ['vɪŋkəltsu:k], *m.* (—s, *pl.* ⁓e) evasion, trick, shift.

**winken** ['vɪŋkən], *v.n.* signal, nod, beckon, wave.

**winklig** ['vɪŋklɪç], *adj.* angular.

**winseln** ['vɪnzəln], *v.n.* whimper, whine, wail.

**Winter** ['vɪntər], *m.* (—s, *pl.* —) winter.

**Wintergarten** ['vɪntərgartən], *m.* (—s, *pl.* ⁓) conservatory.

**Wintergewächs** ['vɪntərgəveks], *n.* (—es, *pl.* —e) perennial plant.

**Wintergrün** ['vɪntərgry:n], *n.* (—s, no *pl.*) evergreen; wintergreen.

**wintern** ['vɪntərn], *v.n.* become wintry.

**Winterschlaf** ['vɪntərʃla:f], *m.* (—s, no *pl.*) hibernation; den — halten, hibernate.

**Winzer** ['vɪntsər], *m.* (—s, *pl.* —) vine-grower.

**winzig** ['vɪntsɪç], *adj.* tiny, diminutive.

**Wipfel** ['vɪpfəl], *m.* (—s, *pl.* —) top (of a tree), tree-top.

**Wippe** ['vɪpə], *f.* (—, *pl.* —n) seesaw.

**wippen** ['vɪpən], *v.n.* balance, see-saw.

**wir** [vi:r], *pers. pron.* we.

**Wirbel** ['vɪrbəl], *m.* (—s, *pl.* —) (*water*) whirlpool, eddy; whirlwind; (*drum*) roll; (*head*) crown; (*back*) vertebra.

**wirbeln** ['vɪrbəln], *v.a., v.n.* whirl.

**Wirbelsäule** ['vɪrbəlzɔylə], *f.* (—, *pl.* —n) spine, vertebral column.

**Wirbelwind** ['vɪrbəlvɪnt], *m.* (—s, *pl.* —e) whirlwind.

**Wirken** ['vɪrkən], *n.* (—s, no *pl.*) activity.

**wirken** ['vɪrkən], *v.a.* effect, work; bring to pass; (*materials*) weave; (*dough*) knead. — *v.n.* work.

**Wirker** ['vɪrkər], *m.* (—s, *pl.* —) weaver.

**wirklich** ['vɪrklɪç], *adj.* real, actual; true, genuine.

**Wirklichkeit** ['vɪrklɪçkaɪt], *f.* (—, no *pl.*) reality.

**wirksam** ['vɪrkza:m], *adj.* effective, efficacious.

**Wirksamkeit** ['vɪrkza:mkaɪt], *f.* (—, no *pl.*) efficacy, efficiency.

**Wirkung** ['vɪrkuŋ], *f.* (—, *pl.* —en) working, operation; reaction; efficacy; effect, result, consequence; force, in-

fluence; eine — ausüben auf, have an effect on; influence s.o. or s.th.

**Wirkungskreis** ['vɪrkuŋskraɪs], *m.* —es, *pl.* —e) sphere of activity.

**wirkungslos** ['vɪrkuŋslo:s], *adj.* ineffectual.

**wirkungsvoll** ['vɪrkuŋsfɔl], *adj.* effective, efficacious; (*fig.*) impressive.

**wirr** [vɪr], *adj.* tangled, confused; — durcheinander, higgledy-piggledy; mir ist ganz — im Kopf, my head is going round.

**Wirren** ['vɪrən], *f. pl.* troubles, disorders, disturbances.

**wirrköpfig** ['vɪrkœpfɪç], *adj.* muddle-headed.

**Wirrsal** ['vɪrza:l], *n.* (—s, *pl.* —e) confusion, disorder.

**Wirrwarr** ['vɪrvar], *m.* (—s, no *pl.*) jumble, hurly-burly, hubbub.

**Wirt** [vɪrt], *m.* (—(e)s, *pl.* —e) host; innkeeper; landlord.

**Wirtin** ['vɪrtɪn], *f.* (—, *pl.* —innen) hostess, landlady, innkeeper's wife.

**wirtlich** ['vɪrtlɪç], *adj.* hospitable.

**Wirtschaft** ['vɪrtʃaft], *f.* (—, *pl.* —en) housekeeping; administration; economy; household; housekeeping; inn, ale-house; (*coll.*) mess.

**wirtschaften** ['vɪrtʃaftən], *v.n.* keep house, housekeep; administer, run; (*coll.*) rummage.

**Wirtschafterin** ['vɪrtʃaftərɪn], *f.* (—, *pl.* —innen) housekeeper.

**wirtschaftlich** ['vɪrtʃaftlɪç], *adj.* economical, thrifty.

**Wirtschaftlichkeit** ['vɪrtʃaftlɪçkaɪt], *f.* (—, no *pl.*) economy; profitability.

**Wirtschaftsgeld** ['vɪrtʃaftsgelt], *n.* (—s, *pl.* —er) housekeeping-money.

**Wirtshaus** ['vɪrtshaus], *n.* (—es, *pl.* ⁓er) inn.

**Wisch** [vɪʃ], *m.* (—es, *pl.* —e) scrap of paper, rag.

**wischen** ['vɪʃən], *v.a.* wipe.

**wispern** ['vɪspərn], *v.a., v.n.* whisper.

**Wißbegier(de)** ['vɪsbəgi:r(də)], *f.* (—, no *pl.*) craving for knowledge; curiosity.

**Wissen** ['vɪsən], *n.* (—s, no *pl.*) knowledge, learning, erudition.

**wissen** ['vɪsən], *v.a. irr.* know, be aware of (a fact); be able to.

**Wissenschaft** ['vɪsənʃaft], *f.* (—, *pl.* —en) learning, scholarship; science.

**wissenschaftlich** ['vɪsənʃaftlɪç], *adj.* learned, scholarly; scientific.

**wissenswert** ['vɪsənsve:rt], *adj.* worth knowing.

**Wissenszweig** ['vɪsənstsvaɪk], *m.* (—s, *pl.* —e) branch of knowledge.

**wissentlich** ['vɪsəntlɪç], *adj.* deliberate, wilful. — *adv.* knowingly.

**wittern** ['vɪtərn], *v.a.* scent, smell; (*fig.*) suspect.

**Witterung** ['vɪtəruŋ], *f.* (—, no *pl.*) weather; trail; scent.

**Witterungsverhältnisse** ['vɪtəruŋsfer-heltnɪsə], *n. pl.* atmospheric conditions.

283

**Witterungswechsel** ['vɪtəruŋsvɛksəl], *m.* (—s, *no pl.*) change in the weather.

**Witwe** ['vɪtvə], *f.* (—, *pl.* —n) widow.

**Witwer** ['vɪtvər], *m.* (—s, *pl.* —) widower.

**Witz** [vɪts], *m.* (—es, *pl.* —e) wit, brains; joke, jest, witticism; funny story.

**Witzblatt** ['vɪtsblat], *n.* (—s, *pl.* ˙-er) satirical *or* humorous journal.

**Witzbold** ['vɪtsbɔlt], *m.* (—es, *pl.* —e) wag; wit.

**witzeln** ['vɪtsəln], *v.n.* poke fun (at).

**witzig** ['vɪtsɪç], *adj.* witty; funny, comical; bright.

**wo** [voː], *interr. adv.* where? — *conj.* when.

**wobei** [voːˈbaɪ], *adv.* by which, at which, in connection with which; whereby; in doing so.

**Woche** ['vɔxə], *f.* (—, *pl.* —n) week.

**Wochenbericht** ['vɔxənbərɪçt], *m.* (—s, *pl.* —e) weekly report.

**Wochenbett** ['vɔxənbet], *n.* (—s, *no pl.*) confinement.

**Wochenblatt** ['vɔxənblat], *n.* (—s, *pl.* ˙-er) weekly (paper).

**Wochenlohn** ['vɔxənloːn], *m.* (—s, *pl.* ˙-e) weekly wage(s).

**Wochenschau** ['vɔxənʃau], *f.* (—, *no pl.*) newsreel.

**Wochentag** ['vɔxəntaːk], *m.* (—s, *pl.* —e) week-day.

**wöchentlich** ['vœçəntlɪç], *adj.* weekly, every week.

**wodurch** [voːˈdurç], *adv.* whereby, by which, through which; (*interr.*) by what?

**wofern** [voːˈfɛrn], *conj.* if, provided that.

**wofür** [voːˈfyːr], *adv.* for what, for which, wherefore.

**Woge** ['voːgə], *f.* (—, *pl.* —n) wave, billow.

**wogegen** [voːˈgeːgən], *adv.* against what, against which, in return for which.

**wogen** ['voːgən], *v.n.* heave, sway; (*fig.*) fluctuate.

**woher** [voːˈheːr], *adv.* whence, from what place, how.

**wohin** [voːˈhɪn], *adv.* whither, where.

**wohingegen** [voːhɪnˈgeːgən], *conj.* (*obs.*) whereas.

**Wohl** [voːl], *n.* (—(e)s, *no pl.*) welfare, health; *auf dein* —, your health! cheers!

**wohl** [voːl], *adv.* well, fit; indeed, doubtless, certainly; *ja* —, to be sure.

**wohlan!** [voːlˈan], *excl.* well! now then!

**wohlauf!** [voːlˈauf], *excl.* cheer up! — *sein*, be in good health.

**wohlbedacht** ['voːlbədaxt], *adj.* well considered.

**Wohlbefinden** ['voːlbəfɪndən], *n.* (—s, *no pl.*) good health.

**Wohlbehagen** ['voːlbəhaːgən], *n.* (—s, *no pl.*) comfort, ease, wellbeing.

**wohlbehalten** ['voːlbəhaltən], *adj.* safe.

**wohlbekannt** ['voːlbəkant], *adj.* well known.

**wohlbeleibt** ['voːlbəlaɪpt], *adj.* corpulent, stout.

**wohlbestallt** ['voːlbəʃtalt], *adj.* duly installed.

**Wohlergehen** ['voːlɛrgeːən], *n.* (—s, *no pl.*) welfare, wellbeing.

**wohlerhalten** ['voːlɛrhaltən], *adj.* well preserved.

**wohlerzogen** ['voːlɛrtsoːgən], *adj.* well bred, well brought up.

**Wohlfahrt** ['voːlfaːrt], *f.* (—, *no pl.*) welfare, prosperity.

**wohlfeil** ['voːlfaɪl], *adj.* cheap, inexpensive.

**Wohlgefallen** ['voːlgəfalən], *n.* (—s, *no pl.*) pleasure, delight, approval.

**wohlgefällig** ['voːlgəfɛlɪç], *adj.* pleasant, agreeable.

**Wohlgefühl** ['voːlgəfyːl], *n.* (—s, *no pl.*) comfort, ease.

**wohlgelitten** ['voːlgəlɪtən], *adj.* popular.

**wohlgemeint** ['voːlgəmaɪnt], *adj.* well meant.

**wohlgemerkt** ['voːlgəmɛrkt], *adv.* mind you! mark my words!

**wohlgemut** ['voːlgəmuːt], *adj.* cheerful, merry.

**wohlgeneigt** ['voːlgənaɪkt], *adj.* well disposed (towards).

**wohlgepflegt** ['voːlgəpfleːkt], *adj.* well kept.

**wohlgeraten** ['voːlgəraːtən], *adj.* successful; well turned out; good, well behaved.

**Wohlgeruch** ['voːlgəruːx], *m.* (—es, *pl.* ˙-e) sweet scent, perfume, fragrance.

**Wohlgeschmack** ['voːlgəʃmak], *m.* (—s, *no pl.*) pleasant flavour, agreeable taste.

**wohlgesinnt** ['voːlgəzɪnt], *adj.* well disposed.

**wohlgestaltet** ['voːlgəʃtaltət], *adj.* well shaped.

**wohlgezielt** ['voːlgətsiːlt], *adj.* well aimed.

**wohlhabend** ['voːlhaːbənt], *adj.* well-to-do, wealthy, well off.

**wohlig** ['voːlɪç], *adj.* comfortable, cosy.

**Wohlklang** ['voːlklaŋ], *m.* (—s, *pl.* ˙-e) harmony, euphony.

**wohlklingend** ['voːlklɪŋənt], *adj.* harmonious, euphonious, sweet-sounding.

**Wohlleben** ['voːlleːbən], *n.* (—s, *no pl.*) luxurious living.

**wohllöblich** ['voːlløːplɪç], *adj.* worshipful.

**wohlmeinend** ['voːlmaɪnənt], *adj.* well-meaning.

**wohlschmeckend** ['voːlʃmɛkənt], *adj.* savoury, tasty, delicious.

**Wohlsein** ['voːlzaɪn], *n.* (—s, *no pl.*) good health, wellbeing.

**Wohlstand** ['voːlʃtant], *m.* (—s, *no pl.*) prosperity.

**Wohltat** ['voːltaːt], *f.* (—, *pl.* —en) benefit; kindness; (*pl.*) benefaction, charity; (*fig.*) treat.

**Wohltäter** ['vo:ltɛ:tər], *m.* (—s, *pl.* —) benefactor.

**Wohltätigkeit** ['vo:ltɛ:tɪçkaɪt], *f.* (—, *no pl.*) charity.

**wohltuend** ['vo:ltu:ənt], *adj.* soothing.

**wohltun** ['vo:ltu:n], *v.n. irr.* do good; be comforting.

**wohlweislich** ['vo:lvaɪslɪç], *adj.* wisely.

**Wohlwollen** ['vo:lvɔlən], *n.* (—s, *no pl.*) benevolence; favour, patronage.

**wohnen** ['vo:nən], *v.n.* reside, dwell, live.

**wohnhaft** ['vo:nhaft], *adj.* domiciled, resident; — *sein*, reside, be domiciled.

**Wohnhaus** ['vo:nhaus], *n.* (—es, *pl.* ‥er) dwelling-house.

**wohnlich** ['vo:nlɪç], *adj.* comfortable; cosy.

**Wohnort** ['vo:nɔrt], *m.* (—s, *pl.* —e) place of residence.

**Wohnsitz** ['vo:nzɪts], *m.* (—es, *pl.* —e) domicile, abode, residence.

**Wohnstätte** ['vo:nʃtɛtə], *f.* (—, *pl.* —n) abode, home.

**Wohnung** ['vo:nuŋ], *f.* (—, *pl.* —en) residence, dwelling; house, flat, lodging; apartment.

**Wohnungsmangel** ['vo:nuŋsmaŋəl], *m.* (—s, *no pl.*) housing shortage.

**Wohnwagen** ['vo:nva:gən], *m.* (—s, *pl.* —) caravan.

**Wohnzimmer** ['vo:ntsɪmər], *n.* (—s, *pl.* —) sitting-room, living-room.

**wölben** ['vœlbən], *v.r. sich* —, vault, arch.

**Wölbung** ['vœlbuŋ], *f.* (—, *pl.* —en) vault, vaulting.

**Wolf** [vɔlf], *m.* (—(e)s, *pl.* ‥e) wolf.

**Wolke** ['vɔlkə], *f.* (—, *pl.* —n) cloud.

**Wolkenbruch** ['vɔlkənbrux], *m.* (—s, *pl.* ‥e) cloudburst, violent downpour.

**Wolkenkratzer** ['vɔlkənkratsər], *m.* (—s, *pl.* —) sky-scraper.

**Wolkenkuckucksheim** [vɔlkən'kukuks-haɪm], *n.* (—s, *no pl.*) Utopia, cloud cuckoo land.

**Wolldecke** ['vɔldɛkə], *f.* (—, *pl.* —n) blanket.

**Wolle** ['vɔlə], *f.* (—, *pl.* —n) wool.

**wollen** (1) ['vɔlən], *v.a., v.n. irr.* wish, want to, be willing, intend; *was* — *Sie*, what do you want?

**wollen** (2) ['vɔlən], *adj.* woollen, made of wool.

**Wollgarn** ['vɔlgarn], *n.* (—s, *pl.* —e) woollen yarn.

**Wollhandel** ['vɔlhandəl], *m.* (—s, *no pl.*) wool-trade.

**wollig** ['vɔlɪç], *adj.* woolly.

**Wollsamt** ['vɔlzamt], *m.* (—s, *no pl.*) plush, velveteen.

**Wollust** ['vɔlust], *f.* (—, *pl.* ‥e) voluptuousness; lust.

**wollüstig** ['vɔlystɪç], *adj.* voluptuous.

**Wollwaren** ['vɔlva:rən], *f. pl.* woollen goods.

**Wollzupfen** ['vɔltsupfən], *n.* (—s, *no pl.*) wool-picking.

**womit** [vo:'mɪt], *adv.* wherewith, with which; (*interr.*) with what?

**womöglich** [vo:'mø:klɪç], *adv.* if possible, perhaps.

**wonach** [vo:'na:x], *adv.* whereafter, after which; according to which.

**Wonne** ['vɔnə], *f.* (—, *pl.* —n) delight, bliss, rapture.

**wonnetrunken** ['vɔnətruŋkən], *adj.* enraptured.

**wonnig** ['vɔnɪç], *adj.* delightful.

**woran** [vo:'ran], *adv.* whereat, whereby; (*interr.*) by what? at what?

**worauf** [vo:'rauf], *adv.* upon which, at which; whereupon; (*interr.*) on what?

**woraufhin** [vo:rauf'hɪn], *conj.* whereupon.

**woraus** [vo:'raus], *adv.* (*rel. & interr.*) whence, from which; by or out of which.

**worein** [vo:'raɪn], *adv.* (*rel. & interr.*) into which; into what.

**worin** [vo:'rɪn], *adv.* (*rel.*) wherein; (*interr.*) in what?

**Wort** [vɔrt], *n.* (—(e)s, *pl.* ‥er, —e) word, term; expression, saying.

**wortarm** ['vɔrtarm], *adj.* poor in words, deficient in vocabulary.

**Wortarmut** ['vɔrtarmu:t], *f.* (—, *no pl.*) paucity of words, poverty of language.

**Wortbildung** ['vɔrtbɪlduŋ], *f.* (—, *pl.* —en) word-formation.

**wortbrüchig** ['vɔrtbryçɪç], *adj.* faithless, disloyal.

**Wörterbuch** ['vœrtərbu:x], *n.* (—(e)s, *pl.* ‥er) dictionary.

**Worterklärung** ['vɔrtɛrklɛ:ruŋ], *f.* (—, *pl.* —en) definition.

**Wortforschung** ['vɔrtfɔrʃuŋ], *f.* (—, *no pl.*) etymology.

**Wortfügung** ['vɔrtfy:guŋ], *f.* (—, *no pl.*) syntax.

**Wortführer** ['vɔrtfy:rər], *m.* (—s, *pl.* —) spokesman.

**Wortgefecht** ['vɔrtgəfɛçt], *n.* (—es, *pl.* —e) verbal battle.

**wortgetreu** ['vɔrtgətrɔy], *adj.* literal, verbatim.

**wortkarg** ['vɔrtkark], *adj.* laconic, sparing of words, taciturn.

**Wortlaut** ['vɔrtlaut], *m.* (—s, *pl.* —e) wording, text.

**wörtlich** ['vœrtlɪç], *adj.* verbal; literal; word for word.

**wortlos** ['vɔrtlo:s], *adj.* speechless. — *adv.* without uttering a word.

**wortreich** ['vɔrtraɪç], *adj.* (*language*) rich in words; (*fig.*) verbose, wordy.

**Wortreichtum** ['vɔrtraɪçtum], *m.* (—s, *no pl.*) (*language*) wealth of words; (*fig.*) verbosity, wordiness.

**Wortschwall** ['vɔrtʃval], *m.* (—s, *no pl.*) bombast; torrent of words.

**Wortspiel** ['vɔrtʃpi:l], *n.* (—s, *pl.* —e) pun.

**Wortversetzung** ['vɔrtfɛrzɛtsuŋ], *f.* (—, *pl.* —en) inversion (of words).

**Wortwechsel** ['vɔrtvɛksəl], *m.* (—s, *pl.* —) dispute, altercation.

**worüber** [vo:'ry:bər], *adv.* (*rel.*) about which, whereof; (*interr.*) about what?

**worunter** [vo'runtər], *adv.* (*rel.*) whereunder; (*interr.*) under what?

**woselbst** [vo:'zɛlpst], *adv.* where.

**wovon** [vo:'fɔn], *adv.* (*rel.*) whereof; (*interr.*) of what?

**wovor** [vo:'fo:r], *adv.* (*rel.*) before which; (*interr.*) before what?

**wozu** [vo:'tsu:], *adv.* (*rel.*) whereto; (*interr.*) why? for what purpose? to what end?

**Wrack** [vrak], *n.* (**—s**, *pl.* **—s**) wreck.

**wringen** ['vrɪŋən], *v.a.* wring.

**Wringmaschine** ['vrɪŋmaʃi:nə], *f.* (**—**, *pl.* **—n**) wringer, mangle.

**Wucher** ['vu:xər], *m.* (**—s**, *no pl.*) usury.

**wucherisch** ['vu:xərɪʃ], *adj.* usurious, extortionate.

**wuchern** ['vu:xərn], *v.n.* practise usury; (*plants*) luxuriate, grow profusely.

**Wucherungen** ['vu:xəruŋən], *f. pl.* (*Med.*) excrescence, growth.

**Wuchs** [vu:ks], *m.* (**—es**, *no pl.*) growth; shape, build.

**Wucht** [vuxt], *f.* (**—**, *no pl.*) power, force; weight; impetus.

**wuchten** ['vuxtən], *v.n.* (*Poet.*) press heavily. — *v.a.* prise up.

**wuchtig** ['vuxtɪç], *adj.* weighty, forceful.

**Wühlarbeit** ['vy:larbaɪt], *f.* (**—**, *pl.* **—en**) subversive activity.

**wühlen** ['vy:lən], *v.a., v.n.* dig, burrow; (*fig.*) agitate.

**Wühler** ['vy:lər], *m.* (**—s**, *pl.* **—**) agitator, demagogue.

**Wühlmaus** ['vy:lmaus], *f.* (**—**, *pl.* **:e**) (*Zool.*) vole.

**Wulst** [vulst], *m.* (**—es**, *pl.* **:e**) roll, pad; swelling.

**wülstig** ['vylstɪç], *adj.* padded, stuffed; swollen.

**wund** [vunt], *adj.* sore, wounded.

**Wundarzt** ['vuntartst], *m.* (**—es**, *pl.* **:e**) (*obs.*) surgeon.

**Wundbalsam** ['vuntbalzam], *m.* (**—s**, *pl.* **—e**) balm.

**Wunde** ['vundə], *f.* (**—**, *pl.* **—n**) wound, hurt.

**Wunder** ['vundər], *n.* (**—s**, *pl.* **—**) marvel, wonder, miracle.

**wunderbar** ['vundərba:r], *adj.* wonderful, marvellous.

**Wunderding** ['vundərdɪŋ], *n.* (**—s**, *pl.* **—e**) marvel.

**Wunderdoktor** ['vundərdɔktər], *m.* (**—s**, *pl.* **—en**) quack doctor.

**Wunderglaube** ['vundərglaubə], *m.* (**—ns**, *no pl.*) belief in miracles.

**wunderhübsch** [vundər'hypʃ], *adj.* exceedingly pretty.

**Wunderkind** ['vundərkɪnt], *n.* (**—s**, *pl.* **—er**) infant prodigy.

**Wunderlampe** ['vundərlampə], *f.* (**—**, *pl.* **—n**) magic lantern.

**wunderlich** ['vundərlɪç], *adj.* strange, odd, queer.

**wundern** ['vundərn], *v.r. sich — über*, be surprised at, be astonished at.

**wundersam** ['vundərza:m], *adj.* wonderful, strange.

**wunderschön** ['vundərʃø:n], *adj.* lovely,

gorgeous; exquisite.

**Wundertat** ['vundərta:t], *f.* (**—**, *pl.* **—en**) miraculous deed.

**wundertätig** ['vundərtε:tɪç], *adj.* miraculous.

**Wundertier** ['vundərti:r], *n.* (**—s**, *pl.* **—e**) monster; (*fig.*) prodigy.

**Wunderwerk** ['vundərverk], *n.* (**—s**, *pl.* **—e**) miracle.

**Wundmal** ['vuntma:l], *n.* (**—s**, *pl.* **—e**) scar.

**Wunsch** [vunʃ], *m.* (**—es**, *pl.* **:e**) wish, desire, aspiration.

**Wünschelrute** ['vynʃəlru:tə], *f.* (**—**, *pl.* **—n**) divining-rod.

**wünschen** ['vynʃən], *v.a.* wish, desire, long for.

**wünschenswert** ['vynʃənsve:rt], *adj.* desirable.

**Wunschform** ['vunʃfɔrm], *f.* (**—**, *no pl.*) (*Gram.*) optative form.

**wuppdich!** ['vupdɪç], *excl.* here goes!

**Würde** ['vyrdə], *f.* (**—**, *pl.* **—n**) dignity, honour.

**Würdenträger** ['vyrdəntrε:gər], *m.* (**—s**, *pl.* **—**) dignitary.

**würdevoll** ['vyrdəfɔl], *adj.* dignified.

**würdig** ['vyrdɪç], *adj.* worthy (of), deserving, meritorious.

**würdigen** ['vyrdɪgən], *v.a.* honour; *ich weiss es zu —*, I appreciate it.

**Würdigung** ['vyrdɪguŋ], *f.* (**—**, *pl.* **—en**) appreciation.

**Wurf** [vurf], *m.* (**—(e)s**, *pl.* **:e**) cast, throw.

**Würfel** ['vyrfəl], *m.* (**—s**, *pl.* **—**) die; (*Geom.*) cube; — *spielen*, play at dice.

**würfelförmig** ['vyrfəlfœrmɪç], *adj.* cubic, cubiform.

**würfeln** ['vyrfəln], *v.n.* play at dice.

**Wurfgeschoß** ['vurfgəʃo:s], *n.* (**—sses**, *pl.* **—sse**) missile, projectile.

**Wurfmaschine** ['vurfmaʃi:nə], *f.* (**—**, *pl.* **—n**) catapult.

**Wurfscheibe** ['vurfʃaɪbə], *f.* (**—**, *pl.* **—n**) discus, quoit.

**Wurfspieß** ['vurfʃpi:s], *m.* (**—es**, *pl.* **—e**) javelin.

**würgen** ['vyrgən], *v.a.* strangle, throttle. — *v.n.* choke.

**Würgengel** ['vyrgɛŋəl], *m.* (**—s**, *no pl.*) avenging angel.

**Würger** ['vyrgər], *m.* (**—s**, *pl.* **—**) strangler, murderer; (*Poet.*) slayer; (*Orn.*) shrike, butcher-bird.

**Wurm** [vurm], *m.* (**—(e)s**, *pl.* **:er**) worm; (*apple*) maggot.

**wurmen** ['vurmən], *v.a.* vex.

**wurmstichig** ['vurmʃtɪçɪç], *adj.* worm-eaten.

**Wurst** [vurst], *f.* (**—**, *pl.* **:e**) sausage.

**wurstig** ['vurstɪç], *adj.* (*sl.*) quite indifferent.

**Wurstigkeit** ['vurstɪçkaɪt], *f.* (**—**, *no pl.*) callousness, indifference.

**Würze** ['vyrtsə], *f.* (**—**, *pl.* **—n**) seasoning, spice, condiment.

**Wurzel** ['vurtsəl], *f.* (**—**, *pl.* **—n**) root.

**wurzeln** ['vurtsəln], *v.n.* be rooted.

**würzen** ['vyrtsən], *v.a.* season, spice.

**würzig** ['vyrtsɪç], *adj.* spicy, fragrant.

**Wust** [vust], *m.* (**—es,** *no pl.*) chaos, trash.

**wüst** [vy:st], *adj.* waste, desert; desolate; dissolute.

**Wüste** ['vy:stə], *f.* (**—,** *pl.* **—n**) desert, wilderness.

**Wüstling** ['vy:stliŋ], *m.* (**—s,** *pl.* **—e**) profligate, libertine.

**Wut** [vu:t], *f.* (**—,** *no pl.*) rage, fury, passion.

**wüten** ['vy:tən], *v.n.* rage, storm, fume.

**wutentbrannt** ['vu:təntbrant], *adj.* enraged, infuriated.

**Wüterich** ['vy:tərIç], *m.* (**—s,** *pl.* **—e**) tyrant; ruthless fellow.

**Wutgeschrei** ['vu:tgəʃraɪ], *n.* (**—s,** *no pl.*) yell of rage.

**wutschnaubend** ['vu:tʃnaubənt], *adj.* foaming with rage.

# X

**X** [Iks], *n.* (**—s,** *pl.* **—s**) the letter X.

**X-Beine** ['Iksbaɪnə], *n. pl.* knock-knees.

**x-beliebig** ['Iksbəli:bIç], *adj.* any, whatever (one likes).

**Xenie** ['kse:njə], *f.* (**—,** *pl.* **—n**) epigram.

**Xereswein** ['kse:rəsvaɪn], *m.* (**—s,** *pl.* **—e**) sherry.

**x-mal** ['Iksma:l], *adv.* (*coll.*) so many times, umpteen times.

**X-Strahlen** ['Iksʃtra:lən], *m. pl.* X-rays.

**Xylographie** [ksylogra'fi:], *f.* (**—,** *no pl.*) wood-engraving.

**Xylophon** [ksylo'fo:n], *n.* (**—s,** *pl.* **—e**) (*Mus.*) xylophone.

# Y

**Y** ['ypsilɔn], *n.* (**—s,** *pl.* **—s**) the letter Y

**Yak** [jak], *m.* (**—s,** *pl.* **—s**) (*Zool.*) yak.

**Yamswurzel** ['jamsvurtsəl], *f.* (**—,** *pl.* **—n**) yam.

**Ysop** [y'zo:p], *m.* (**—s,** *no pl.*) hyssop.

# Z

**Z** [tsɛt], *n.* (**—s,** *pl.* **—s**) the letter Z.

**Zabel** ['tsa:bəl], *m.* (**—s,** *pl.* **—**) (*obs.*) chess-board.

**Zacke** ['tsakə], *f.* (**—,** *pl.* **—n**) tooth, spike; (*fork*) prong.

**zackig** ['tsakIç], *adj.* pronged, toothed, indented; (*rock*) jagged; (*sl.*) smart.

**zagen** ['tsa:gən], *v.n.* quail, blench, be disheartened, be fainthearted.

**zaghaft** ['tsa:xaft], *adj.* faint-hearted.

**Zaghaftigkeit** ['tsa:xaftIçkaɪt], *f.* (**—,** *no pl.*) faintheartedness, timidity.

**zäh** [tsɛ:], *adj.* tough.

**Zähigkeit** ['tsɛ:Içkaɪt], *f.* (**—,** *no pl.*) toughness.

**Zahl** [tsa:l], *f.* (**—,** *pl.* **—en**) number, figure.

**zahlbar** ['tsa:lba:r], *adj.* payable, due.

**zählbar** ['tsɛ:lba:r], *adj.* calculable.

**zahlen** ['tsa:lən], *v.a.* pay; *Ober!* **—,** waiter! the bill, please.

**zählen** ['tsɛ:lən], *v.a.,* *v.n.* count, number.

**Zahlenfolge** ['tsa:lənfɔlgə], *f.* (**—,** *no pl.*) numerical order.

**Zahlenlehre** ['tsa:lənle:rə], *f.* (**—,** *no pl.*) arithmetic.

**Zahlenreihe** ['tsa:lənraɪə], *f.* (**—,** *pl.* **—n**) numerical progression.

**Zahlensinn** ['tsa:lənzIn], *m.* (**—s,** *no pl.*) head for figures.

**Zahler** ['tsa:lər], *m.* (**—s,** *pl.* **—**) payer.

**Zähler** ['tsɛ:lər], *m.* (**—s,** *pl.* **—**) counter, teller; meter; (*Maths.*) numerator.

**Zahlkellner** ['tsa:lkɛlnər], *m.* (**—s,** *pl.* **—**) head waiter.

**Zahlmeister** ['tsa:lmaɪstər], *m.* (**—s,** *pl.* **—**) paymaster, treasurer, bursar.

**zahlreich** ['tsa:lraɪç], *adj.* numerous.

**Zahltag** ['tsa:lta:k], *m.* (**—s,** *pl.* **—e**) pay-day.

**Zahlung** ['tsa:luŋ], *f.* (**—,** *pl.* **—en**) payment; *— leisten,* make payment; *die —en einstellen,* stop payment.

**Zählung** ['tsɛ:luŋ], *f.* (**—,** *pl.* **—en**) counting, computation; census.

**Zahlungseinstellung** ['tsa:luŋsaɪnʃtɛluŋ], *f.* (**—,** *pl.* **—en**) suspension of payment.

**zahlungsfähig** ['tsa:luŋsfɛ:Iç], *adj.* solvent.

**Zahlungsmittel** ['tsa:luŋsmItəl], *n.* (**—s,** *pl.* **—**) means of payment; *gesetzliches —,* legal tender.

**Zahlungstermin** ['tsa:luŋstermi:n], *m.* (**—s,** *pl.* **—e**) time of payment.

**zahlungsunfähig** ['tsa:luŋsunfɛ:Iç], *adj.* insolvent.

**Zahlwort** ['tsa:lvɔrt], *n.* (**—s,** *pl.* **⸚er**) (*Gram.*) numeral.

**zahm** [tsa:m], *adj.* tame; domestic(ated); *— machen,* tame.

**zähmen** ['tsɛ:mən], *v.a.* tame, domesticate.

**Zähmer** ['tsɛ:mər], *m.* (**—s,** *pl.* **—**) tamer.

**Zahmheit** ['tsa:mhaɪt], *f.* (**—,** *no pl.*) tameness.

**Zähmung** ['tsɛ:muŋ], *f.* (**—,** *no pl.*) taming, domestication.

**Zahn** [tsa:n], *m.* (**—(e)s,** *pl.* **⸚e**) tooth; (*wheel*) cog.

# Zahnarzt

**Zahnarzt** ['tsa:nartst], *m.* (**—es**, *pl.* ‥**e**) dentist, dental surgeon.

**Zahnbürste** ['tsa:nbyrstə], *f.* (**—**, *pl.* **—n**) tooth-brush.

**Zähneklappern** ['tsɛ:nəklapərn], *n.* (**—s**, *no pl.*) chattering of teeth.

**Zähneknirschen** ['tsɛ:nəknɪrʃən], *n.* (**—s**, *no pl.*) gnashing of teeth.

**zahnen** ['tsa:nən], *v.n.* teethe, cut o.'s teeth.

**zähnen** ['tsɛ:nən], *v.a.* indent, notch.

**Zahnfleisch** ['tsa:nflaɪʃ], *n.* (**—es**, *no pl.*) gums.

**Zahnfüllung** ['tsa:nfylun], *f.* (**—**, *pl.* **—en**) filling, stopping (of tooth).

**Zahnheilkunde** ['tsa:nhaɪlkundə], *f.* (**—**, *no pl.*) dentistry, dental surgery.

**Zahnlücke** ['tsa:nlykə], *f.* (**—**, *pl.* **—n**) gap in the teeth.

**Zahnpaste** ['tsa:npastə], *f.* (**—**, *no pl.*) tooth-paste.

**Zahnpulver** ['tsa:npulvər], *n.* (**—s**, *no pl.*) tooth-powder.

**Zahnrad** ['tsa:nra:t], *n.* (**—s**, *pl.* ‥**er**) cog-wheel.

**Zahnradbahn** ['tsa:nra:tba:n], *f.* (**—**, *pl.* **—en**) rack-railway.

**Zahnschmerzen** ['tsa:nʃmɛrtsən], *m. pl.* toothache.

**Zahnstocher** ['tsa:nʃtɔxər], *m.* (**—s**, *pl.* **—**) tooth-pick.

**Zähre** ['tsɛ:rə], *f.* (**—**, *pl.* **—n**) (*Poet.*) tear.

**Zander** ['tsandər], *m.* (**—s**, *pl.* **—**) (*fish*) pike.

**Zange** ['tsaŋə], *f.* (**—**, *pl.* **—n**) tongs; pincers; tweezers; nippers; (*Med.*) forceps.

**Zank** [tsaŋk], *m.* (**—es**, *pl.* ‥**ereien**) quarrel, altercation, tiff.

**Zankapfel** ['tsaŋkapfəl], *m.* (**—s**, *pl.* ‥) bone of contention.

**zanken** ['tsaŋkən], *v.r. sich* **—**, quarrel, dispute.

**zänkisch** ['tsɛnkɪʃ], *adj.* quarrelsome.

**Zanksucht** ['tsaŋkzuxt], *f.* (**—**, *no pl.*) quarrelsomeness.

**zanksüchtig** ['tsaŋkzyçtɪç], *adj.* quarrelsome, cantankerous.

**Zapfen** ['tsapfən], *m.* (**—s**, *pl.* **—**) pin, peg; (*cask*) bung, spigot; (*fir*) cone.

**zapfen** ['tsapfən], *v.a.* tap, draw.

**Zapfenstreich** ['tsapfənʃtraɪç], *m.* (**—s**, *no pl.*) (*Mil.*) tattoo, retreat.

**zapp(e)lig** ['tsap(ə)lɪç], *adj.* fidgety.

**zappeln** ['tsapəln], *v.n.* kick, struggle, wriggle.

**Zar** [tsa:r], *m.* (**—en**, *pl.* **—en**) Czar, Tsar.

**zart** [tsart], *adj.* tender, sensitive, delicate, gentle; **—** *besaitet*, (*iron.*) sensitive, highly strung.

**Zartgefühl** ['tsartgəfy:l], *n.* (**—s**, *no pl.*) delicacy, sensitivity.

**Zartheit** ['tsarthaɪt], *f.* (**—**, *no pl.*) tenderness, gentleness.

**zärtlich** ['tsɛ:rtlɪç], *adj.* loving, amorous, tender.

**Zärtlichkeit** ['tsɛ:rtlɪçkaɪt], *f.* (**—**, *pl.* **—en**) tenderness; caresses.

**Zartsinn** ['tsartzɪn], *m.* (**—s**, *no pl.*) delicacy.

**Zauber** ['tsaubər], *m.* (**—s**, *no pl.*) charm, spell, enchantment; magic; fascination.

**Zauberei** [tsaubə'raɪ], *f.* (**—**, *pl.* **—en**) magic, witchcraft, sorcery.

**Zauberer** ['tsaubərər], *m.* (**—s**, *pl.* **—**) magician, sorcerer, wizard.

**zauberisch** ['tsaubərɪʃ], *adj.* magical; (*fig.*) enchanting.

**Zauberkraft** ['tsaubərkraft], *f.* (**—**, *no pl.*) magic power, witchcraft.

**Zaubermittel** ['tsaubərmɪtəl], *n.* (**—s**, *pl.* **—**) charm.

**zaubern** ['tsaubərn], *v.n.* practise magic; conjure.

**Zauberspruch** ['tsaubərʃprux], *m.* (**—s**, *pl.* ‥**e**) spell, charm.

**Zauberstab** ['tsaubərʃta:p], *m.* (**—s**, *pl.* ‥**e**) magic wand.

**Zauderer** ['tsaudərər], *m.* (**—s**, *pl.* **—**) loiterer, temporizer, procrastinator.

**zaudern** ['tsaudərn], *v.n.* delay; hesitate, procrastinate.

**Zaum** [tsaum], *m.* (**—(e)s**, *pl.* ‥**e**) bridle; *im* **—** *halten*, check, restrain.

**zäumen** ['tsɔymən], *v.a.* bridle.

**Zaun** [tsaun], *m.* (**—(e)s**, *pl.* ‥**e**) hedge, fence; *einen Streit vom* **—** *brechen*, pick a quarrel.

**Zaungast** ['tsaungast], *m.* (**—s**, *pl.* ‥**e**) onlooker, outsider; intruder.

**Zaunkönig** ['tsaunkø:nɪç], *m.* (**—s**, *pl.* **—e**) (*Orn.*) wren.

**Zaunpfahl** ['tsaunpfa:l], *m.* (**—s**, *pl.* ‥**e**) pale, hedge-pole; *mit dem* **—** *winken*, give s.o. a broad hint.

**Zaunrebe** ['tsaunre:bə], *f.* (**—**, *pl.* **—n**) (*Bot.*) Virginia creeper.

**zausen** ['tsauzən], *v.a.* tousle; (*hair*) disarrange, ruffle.

**Zechbruder** ['tsɛçbru:dər], *m.* (**—s**, *pl.* ‥) tippler, toper.

**Zeche** ['tsɛçə], *f.* (**—**, *pl.* **—n**) bill (in a restaurant); mine; *die* **—** *bezahlen*, foot the bill, pay the piper.

**Zeder** ['tse:dər], *f.* (**—**, *pl.* **—n**) (*Bot.*) cedar.

**zedieren** [tsɛ'di:rən], *v.a.* cede.

**Zehe** ['tse:ə], *f.* (**—**, *pl.* **—n**) toe.

**Zehenspitze** ['tse:ənʃpɪtsə], *f.* (**—**, *pl.* **—n**) tip of the toe, tiptoe.

**zehn** [tse:n], *num. adj.* ten.

**Zehneck** ['tse:nɛk], *n.* (**—s**, *pl.* **—e**) decagon.

**Zehnte** ['tse:ntə], *m.* (**—n**, *pl.* **—n**) tithe.

**zehren** ['tse:rən], *v.n. von etwas* **—**, live on s.th., prey upon s.th.

**Zehrfieber** ['tse:rfi:bər], *n.* (**—s**, *no pl.*) hectic fever.

**Zehrgeld** ['tse:rgɛlt], *n.* (**—s**, *pl.* **—er**) subsistence, allowance.

**Zehrvorrat** ['tse:rfo:rra:t], *m.* (**—s**, *pl.* ‥**e**) provisions.

**Zehrung** ['tse:run], *f.* (**—**, *pl.* **—en**) consumption; victuals; (*Eccl.*) *letzte* **—**, viaticum.

**Zeichen** ['tsaɪçən], *n.* (**—s**, *pl.* **—**) sign, token, symptom, omen; indication; badge; signal.

**Zeichenbrett** ['tsaɪçənbrɛt], n. (—s, pl. —er) drawing-board.

**Zeichendeuter** ['tsaɪçəndɔytər], m. (—s, pl. —) astrologer.

**Zeichendeuterei** [tsaɪçəndɔytə'raɪ], f. (—, no pl.) astrology.

**Zeichenerklärung** ['tsaɪçənɛrklɛːruŋ], f. (— pl.—en) legend, key.

**Zeichensprache** ['tsaɪçənʃpraːxə], f. (—, no pl.) sign-language.

**Zeichentinte** ['tsaɪçəntɪntə], f. (—, no pl.) marking ink.

**zeichnen** ['tsaɪçnən], v.a. draw; mark; (money) subscribe; (letter) sign.

**Zeichner** ['tsaɪçnər], m. (—s, pl. —) draughtsman, designer.

**Zeichnung** ['tsaɪçnuŋ], f. (—, pl. —en) drawing.

**Zeigefinger** ['tsaɪgəfɪŋər], m. (—s, pl. —) forefinger, index finger.

**zeigen** ['tsaɪgən], v.a. show, point to, prove.

**Zeiger** ['tsaɪgər], m. (—s, pl. —) indicator; hand (of watch, clock).

**zeihen** ['tsaɪən], v.a. irr. einen einer Sache —, tax s.o. with s.th.

**Zeile** ['tsaɪlə], f. (—, pl. —n) line; furrow; (pl.) letter.

**Zeisig** ['tsaɪzɪç], m. (—s, pl. —e) (Orn.) siskin.

**Zeit** [tsaɪt], f. (—, pl. —en) time; zur —, at present; auf —, on credit.

**Zeitabschnitt** ['tsaɪtapʃnɪt], m. (—s, pl. —e) period; epoch.

**Zeitalter** ['tsaɪtaltər], n. (—s, pl. —) age, era.

**Zeitdauer** ['tsaɪtdauər], f. (—, no pl.) space of time.

**Zeitfrage** ['tsaɪtfraːgə], f. (—, pl. —n) topical question; question of time.

**Zeitgeist** ['tsaɪtgaɪst], m. (—s, no pl.) spirit of the age.

**zeitgemäß** ['tsaɪtgəmɛːs], adj. timely, seasonable, opportune, modern.

**Zeitgenosse** ['tsaɪtgənɔsə], m. (—n, pl. —n) contemporary.

**zeitig** ['tsaɪtɪç], adj. early, timely.

**zeitigen** ['tsaɪtɪgən], v.a. engender, generate. — v.n. mature, ripen.

**Zeitkarte** ['tsaɪtkartə], f. (—, pl. —n) season ticket.

**Zeitlauf** ['tsaɪtlauf], m. (—s, pl. ⁝e) course of time, conjuncture.

**zeitlebens** ['tsaɪtleːbəns], adv. for life, (for) all his (or her) life.

**zeitlich** ['tsaɪtlɪç], adj. temporal, earthly; secular; temporary, transient.

**zeitlos** ['tsaɪtloːs], adj. lasting, permanent.

**Zeitmangel** ['tsaɪtmaŋəl], m. (—s, no pl.) lack of time.

**Zeitmesser** ['tsaɪtmɛsər], m. (—s, pl. —) chronometer, timepiece; metronome.

**Zeitpunkt** ['tsaɪtpuŋkt], m. (—s, pl. —e) moment, date; point of time.

**zeitraubend** ['tsaɪtraubənt], adj. time-consuming.

**Zeitraum** ['tsaɪtraum], m. (—s, pl. ⁝e) space of time, period.

**Zeitschrift** ['tsaɪtʃrɪft], f. (—, pl. —en) periodical, journal, magazine.

**Zeitung** ['tsaɪtuŋ], f. (—, pl. —en) newspaper.

**Zeitungsente** ['tsaɪtuŋsɛntə], f. (—, pl. —n) canard, newspaper hoax.

**Zeitungskiosk** ['tsaɪtuŋskiɔsk], m. (—s, pl. —e) newspaper-stall.

**Zeitungsnachricht** ['tsaɪtuŋsnaːxrɪçt], f. (—, pl. —en) newspaper report.

**Zeitungswesen** ['tsaɪtuŋsveːzən], n. (—s, no pl.) journalism.

**Zeitverlust** ['tsaɪtfɛrlust], m. (—s, no pl.) loss of time; ohne —, without delay.

**Zeitvertreib** ['tsaɪtfɛrtraɪp], m. (—s, no pl.) pastime, amusement; zum —, to pass the time.

**zeitweilig** ['tsaɪtvaɪlɪç], adj. temporary.

**zeitweise** ['tsaɪtvaɪzə], adv. from time to time.

**Zeitwort** ['tsaɪtvɔrt], n. (—s, pl. ⁝er) (Gram.) verb.

**Zelle** ['tsɛlə], f. (—, pl. —n) cell.

**Zelt** [tsɛlt], n. (—(e)s, pl. —e) tent.

**Zeltdecke** ['tsɛltdɛkə], f. (—, pl. —n) awning, marquee.

**Zement** [tse'mɛnt], m. (—s, no pl.) cement.

**Zenit** [tse'niːt], m. (—s, no pl.) zenith.

**zensieren** [tsɛn'ziːrən], v.a. review, censure; (Sch.) mark.

**Zensor** ['tsɛnzɔr], m. (—s, pl. —en) censor.

**Zensur** [tsɛn'zuːr], f. (—, pl. —en) censure; (Sch.) report, mark; censorship.

**Zentimeter** ['tsɛntimeːtər], m. (—s, pl. —) centimetre.

**Zentner** ['tsɛntnər], m. (—s, pl. —) hundredweight.

**zentral** [tsɛn'traːl], adj. central.

**Zentrale** [tsɛn'traːlə], f. (—, pl. —n) control room; head office.

**zentralisieren** [tsɛntrali'ziːrən], v.a. centralise.

**Zentrum** ['tsɛntrum], n. (—s, pl. —tren) centre; (Am.) center.

**Zephir** ['tseːfiːr], m. (—s, pl. —e) zephyr.

**Zepter** ['tsɛptər], m. & n. (—s, pl. —) sceptre, mace.

**zerbrechen** [tsɛr'brɛçən], v.a., v.n. irr. (aux. sein) break to pieces; shatter; sich den Kopf —, rack o.'s brains.

**zerbrechlich** [tsɛr'brɛçlɪç], adj. brittle, fragile.

**zerbröckeln** [tsɛr'brœkəln], v.a., v.n. (aux. sein) crumble.

**zerdrücken** [tsɛr'drykən], v.a. crush, bruise.

**Zeremonie** [tseremo'niː], f. (—, pl. —n) ceremony.

**zeremoniell** [tseremo'njɛl], adj. ceremonial, formal.

**Zerfahrenheit** [tsɛr'faːrənhaɪt], f. (—, no pl.) absent-mindedness.

**Zerfall** [tsɛr'fal], m. (—s, no pl.) disintegration; decay.

**zerfallen** [tsɛr'falən], v.n. irr. (aux. sein) fall to pieces. — adj. in ruins.

T—M    289

# zerfleischen

**zerfleischen** [tsɛrˈflaɪʃən], v.a. lacerate, tear to pieces.

**zerfließen** [tsɛrˈfliːsən], v.n. irr. (aux. sein) dissolve, melt.

**zerfressen** [tsɛrˈfrɛsən], v.a. irr. gnaw, corrode.

**zergehen** [tsɛrˈgeːən], v.n. irr. (aux. sein) dissolve, melt.

**zergliedern** [tsɛrˈgliːdərn], v.a. dissect; (fig.) analyse.

**zerhauen** [tsɛrˈhauən], v.a. hew in pieces, chop up.

**zerkauen** [tsɛrˈkauən], v.a. chew.

**zerkleinern** [tsɛrˈklaɪnərn], v.a. cut into small pieces; (firewood) chop.

**zerklüftet** [tsɛrˈklʏftət], adj. rugged.

**zerknirscht** [tsɛrˈknɪrʃt], adj. contrite.

**Zerknirschung** [tsɛrˈknɪrʃuŋ], f. (—, no pl.) contrition.

**zerknittern** [tsɛrˈknɪtərn], v.a. crumple.

**zerknüllen** [tsɛrˈknʏlən], v.a. rumple.

**zerlassen** [tsɛrˈlasən], v.a. irr. melt, liquefy.

**zerlegen** [tsɛrˈleːgən], v.a. resolve; take to pieces; cut up, carve; (fig.) analyse.

**zerlumpt** [tsɛrˈlumpt], adj. ragged, tattered.

**zermahlen** [tsɛrˈmaːlən], v.a. grind to powder.

**zermalmen** [tsɛrˈmalmən], v.a. crush.

**zermartern** [tsɛrˈmartərn], v.a. torment; sich das Hirn —, rack o.'s brains.

**zernagen** [tsɛrˈnaːgən], v.a. gnaw (away).

**zerquetschen** [tsɛrˈkvɛtʃən], v.a. squash, crush.

**zerraufen** [tsɛrˈraufən], v.a. dishevel.

**Zerrbild** [ˈtsɛrbɪlt], n. (—s, pl. —er) caricature.

**zerreiben** [tsɛrˈraɪbən], v.a. irr. grind to powder, pulverise.

**zerreißen** [tsɛrˈraɪsən], v.a. irr. tear, rend, tear up; break; rupture. — v.n. (aux. sein) be torn; (clothes) wear out.

**zerren** [ˈtsɛrən], v.a. pull, tug, drag; strain.

**zerrinnen** [tsɛrˈrɪnən], v.n. irr. (aux. sein) dissolve, melt; (fig.) vanish.

**zerrütten** [tsɛrˈrʏtən], v.a. unsettle, disorder, unhinge; ruin, destroy.

**zerschellen** [tsɛrˈʃɛlən], v.n. (aux. sein) be dashed to pieces, be wrecked.

**zerschlagen** [tsɛrˈʃlaːgən], v.a. irr. break, smash to pieces, batter.

**zerschmettern** [tsɛrˈʃmɛtərn], v.a. dash to pieces, break, crush; shatter, overwhelm.

**zersetzen** [tsɛrˈzɛtsən], v.a., v.r. break up; disintegrate.

**zerspalten** [tsɛrˈʃpaltən], v.a. cleave, split, slit.

**zersprengen** [tsɛrˈʃprɛŋən], v.a. explode, burst; (crowd) disperse; (Mil.) rout.

**zerspringen** [tsɛrˈʃprɪŋən], v.n. irr. (aux. sein) crack; fly to pieces, split.

**zerstampfen** [tsɛrˈʃtampfən], v.a. crush, pound.

**zerstäuben** [tsɛrˈʃtɔybən], v.a. spray, atomize.

**zerstörbar** [tsɛrˈʃtøːrbaːr], adj. destructible.

**zerstören** [tsɛrˈʃtøːrən], v.a. destroy, devastate.

**Zerstörer** [tsɛrˈʃtøːrər], m. (—s, pl. —) destroyer.

**Zerstörung** [tsɛrˈʃtøːruŋ], f. (—, pl. —en) destruction.

**Zerstörungswut** [tsɛrˈʃtøːruŋsvuːt], f. (—, no pl.) vandalism.

**zerstoßen** [tsɛrˈʃtoːsən], v.a. irr. bruise, pound.

**zerstreuen** [tsɛrˈʃtrɔyən], v.a. scatter, disperse; divert.

**zerstreut** [tsɛrˈʃtrɔyt], adj. absent-minded.

**Zerstreuung** [tsɛrˈʃtrɔyuŋ], f. (—, pl. —en) dispersion; amusement, diversion, distraction.

**zerstückeln** [tsɛrˈʃtʏkəln], v.a. dismember.

**Zerstückelung** [tsɛrˈʃtʏkəluŋ], f. (—, no pl.) dismemberment.

**zerteilen** [tsɛrˈtaɪlən], v.a. divide, separate; disperse, dissipate. — v.r. sich —, dissolve.

**Zertifikat** [tsɛrtifiˈkaːt], n. (—s, pl. —e) certificate, attestation.

**zertrennen** [tsɛrˈtrɛnən], v.a. rip up, unstitch.

**zertrümmern** [tsɛrˈtrʏmərn], v.a. destroy, break up, demolish.

**Zerwürfnis** [tsɛrˈvyrfnɪs], n. (—ses, pl. —se) discord, dissension.

**zerzausen** [tsɛrˈtsauzən], v.a. dishevel, tousle.

**zerzupfen** [tsɛrˈtsupfən], v.a. pick to pieces, pluck.

**Zession** [tsɛsˈjoːn], f. (—, pl. —en) cession, assignment, transfer.

**Zetergeschrei** [ˈtseːtərgəʃraɪ], n. (—s, no pl.) outcry, hullabaloo.

**zetern** [ˈtseːtərn], v.n. yell; (coll.) kick up a row.

**Zettel** [ˈtsɛtəl], m. (—s, pl. —) slip of paper; label, chit.

**Zettelkasten** [ˈtsɛtəlkastən], m. (—s, pl. ⁜) card-index, filing cabinet.

**Zeug** [tsɔyk], n. (—(e)s, no pl.) stuff, material; implements, kit, utensils; (coll.) things.

**Zeuge** [ˈtsɔygə], m. (—n, pl. —n) witness; zum —n aufrufen, call to witness.

**zeugen** [ˈtsɔygən], v.a. beget, generate, engender. — v.n. give evidence.

**Zeugenaussage** [ˈtsɔygənausaːgə], f. (—, pl. —n) evidence, deposition.

**Zeugenbeweis** [ˈtsɔygənbəvaɪs], m. (—es, pl. —e) evidence, proof.

**Zeugeneid** [ˈtsɔygənaɪt], m. (—s, pl. —e) oath of a witness.

**Zeughaus** [ˈtsɔykhaus], n. (—es, pl. ⁜er) (obs.) arsenal.

**Zeugin** [ˈtsɔygɪn], f. (—, pl. —innen) female witness.

**Zeugnis** ['tsɔyknıs], n. (—ses, pl. —se) (*Law.*) deposition; testimonial, certificate, reference; character; school report; — *ablegen*, give evidence, bear witness; *einem ein gutes — ausstellen*, give s.o. a good reference.

**Zeugung** ['tsɔygun], f. (—, pl. —en) procreation, generation.

**Zeugungskraft** ['tsɔygunskraft], f. (—, no pl.) generative power.

**Zeugungstrieb** ['tsɔygunstri:p], m. (—s, no pl.) procreative instinct.

**Zichorie** [tsɪ'çɔ:rjə], f. (—, pl. —n) chicory.

**Zicke** ['tsɪkə], f. (—, pl. —n) dial. for **Ziege.**

**Ziege** ['tsi:gə], f. (—, pl. —n) goat.

**Ziegel** ['tsi:gəl], m. (—s, pl. —) (*roof*) tile; (*wall*) brick.

**Ziegelbrenner** ['tsi:gəlbrenər], m. (—s, pl. —) tile-maker, tiler; brickmaker.

**Ziegelbrennerei** [tsi:gəlbrenə'rai], f. (—, pl. —en) brickyard.

**Ziegeldach** ['tsi:gəldax], n. (—s, pl. ⁙er) tiled roof.

**Ziegeldecker** ['tsi:gəldɛkər], m. (—s, pl. —) tiler.

**Ziegelei** [tsi:gə'lai], f. (—, pl. —en) brickyard, brickworks.

**Ziegelerde** ['tsi:gəle:rdə], f. (—, no pl.) brick-clay.

**Ziegenbart** ['tsi:gənba:rt], m. (—s, pl. ⁙e) goat's beard; (*human*) goatee.

**Ziegenleder** ['tsi:gənle:dər], n. (—s, no pl.) kid (leather).

**Ziegenpeter** ['tsi:gənpe:tər], m. (—s, no pl.) (*Med.*) mumps.

**ziehen** ['tsi:ən], v.a. irr. draw, pull, drag; pull out; cultivate; breed; (*game*) move. — v.n. draw, be an attraction; (aux. sein) go, move. — v.r. sich —, extend.

**Ziehkind** ['tsi:kɪnt], n. (—s, pl. —er) foster-child.

**Ziehmutter** ['tsi:mutər], f. (—, pl. ⁙) foster-mother.

**Ziehung** ['tsi:un], f. (—, pl. —en) draw (in a lottery).

**Ziehvater** ['tsi:fa:tər], m. (—s, pl. ⁙) foster-father.

**Ziel** [tsi:l], n. (—s, pl. —e) goal, aim, purpose, intention, end; butt, target; (*Mil.*) objective; (*sports*) winning-post.

**zielbewußt** ['tsi:lbəvust], adj. purposeful; systematic.

**zielen** ['tsi:lən], v.n. aim (at), take aim (at).

**Ziellosigkeit** ['tsi:llo:zıçkait], f. (—, no pl.) aimlessness.

**Zielscheibe** ['tsi:lʃaibə], f. (—, pl. —en) target, butt.

**ziemen** ['tsi:mən], v.r. sich —, become s.o., behove s.o., be proper for, befit.

**Ziemer** ['tsi:mər], n. & m. (—s, pl. —) whip.

**ziemlich** ['tsi:mlıç], adj. moderate, tolerable, middling, fairly considerable, fair. — adv. rather, fairly.

**Zier** [tsi:r], f. (—, pl. —den) ornament.

**Zieraffe** ['tsi:rafə], m. (—n, pl. —n) fop, affected person.

**Zierat** ['tsi:ra:t], m. (—s, no pl.) ornament, finery.

**Zierde** ['tsi:rdə], f. (—, pl. —n) decoration, embellishment; (*fig.*) credit, pride.

**Ziererei** [tsi:rə'rai], f. (—, pl. —en) affectation.

**Ziergarten** ['tsi:rgartən], m. (—s, pl. ⁙) flower-garden, ornamental garden.

**zierlich** ['tsi:rlıç], adj. dainty, graceful, pretty.

**Zierpflanze** ['tsi:rpflantsə], f. (—, pl. —n) ornamental plant.

**Zierpuppe** ['tsi:rpupə], f. (—, pl. —n) overdressed woman.

**Ziffer** ['tsɪfər], f. (—, pl. —n) figure, numeral.

**Zifferblatt** ['tsɪfərblat], n. (—s, pl. ⁙er) dial, face.

**ziffernmäßig** ['tsɪfərnme:sıç], adj. statistical.

**Ziffernschrift** ['tsɪfərnʃrift], f. (—, pl. —en) code.

**Zigarette** [tsiga'retə], f. (—, pl. —n) cigarette.

**Zigarettenetui** [tsiga'retənetvi:], n. (—s, pl. —s) cigarette-case.

**Zigarettenspitze** [tsiga'retənʃpitsə], f. (—, pl. —n) cigarette-holder.

**Zigarettenstummel** [tsiga'retənʃtuməl], m. (—s, pl. —) cigarette-end.

**Zigarre** [tsi'garə], f. (—, pl. —n) cigar.

**Zigarrenkiste** [tsi'garənkıstə], f. (—, pl. —n) cigar-box.

**Zigarrenstummel** [tsi'garənʃtuməl], m. (—s, pl. —) cigar-end.

**Zigeuner** [tsi'gɔynər], m. (—s, pl. —) gipsy.

**Zikade** [tsi'ka:də], f. (—, pl. —n) (*Ent.*) grasshopper.

**Zimmer** ['tsɪmər], n. (—s, pl. —) room.

**Zimmermädchen** ['tsɪmərme:tçən], n. (—s, pl. —) chambermaid.

**Zimmermann** ['tsɪmərman], m. (—s, pl. **Zimmerleute**) carpenter, joiner.

**zimmern** ['tsɪmərn], v.a. carpenter, construct, build.

**Zimmernachweis** ['tsɪmərna:xvais], m. (—es, pl. —e) accommodation bureau.

**Zimmerreihe** ['tsɪmərraiə], f. (—, pl. —n) suite of rooms.

**Zimmervermieter** ['tsɪmərfermi:tər], m. (—s, pl. —) landlord.

**zimperlich** ['tsɪmpərlıç], adj. simpering; prim; finicky, hypersensitive.

**Zimt** [tsɪmt], m. (—(e)s, no pl.) cinnamon.

**Zink** [tsɪnk], n. (—s, no pl.) zinc.

**Zinke** ['tsɪnkə], f. (—, pl. —n) prong, tine.

**Zinn** [tsɪn], n. (—s, no pl.) tin; pewter.

**Zinnblech** ['tsɪnblɛç], n. (—s, no pl.) tin-plate.

**Zinne** ['tsɪnə], f. (—, pl. —n) battlement, pinnacle.

**zinnern** ['tsɪnern], *adj.* made of pewter, of tin.

**Zinnober** [tsɪn'o:bər], *m.* (—s, *no pl.*) cinnabar; (*coll.*) fuss.

**Zinnsäure** ['tsɪnzɔyrə], *f.* (—, *no pl.*) stannic acid.

**Zins** [tsɪns], *m.* (—es, *pl.* —en) duty, tax; rent; (*pl.*) interest.

**zinsbar** ['tsɪnsba:r], *adj.* tributary; — *anlegen,* invest at interest; — *machen,* force to pay a tribute.

**Zinsen** ['tsɪnzən], *m. pl.* interest.

**zinsentragend** ['tsɪnzəntra:gənt], *adj.* interest-bearing.

**Zinseszins** ['tsɪnzəstsɪns], *m.* (—, *no pl.*) compound interest.

**Zinsfuß** ['tsɪnsfu:s], *m.* (—es, *pl.* —e) rate of interest.

**zinspflichtig** ['tsɪnspflɪçtɪç], *adj.* subject to tax.

**Zinsrechnung** ['tsɪnsrɛçnuŋ], *f.* (—, *pl.* —en) interest account, calculation of interest.

**Zinsschein** ['tsɪnsʃaɪn], *m.* (—s, *pl.* —e) coupon, dividend warrant.

**Zipfel** ['tsɪpfəl], *m.* (—s, *pl.* —) tassel, edge, point, tip.

**Zipperlein** ['tsɪpərlaɪn], *n.* (—s, *no pl.*) (*coll.*) gout.

**zirka** ['tsɪrka], *adv.* circa, about, approximately.

**Zirkel** ['tsɪrkəl], *m.* (—s, *pl.* —) circle; (*Maths.*) pair of compasses; gathering.

**zirkulieren** [tsɪrku'li:rən], *v.n.* circulate; — *lassen,* put in circulation.

**Zirkus** ['tsɪrkus], *m.* (—, *pl.* —se) circus.

**zirpen** ['tsɪrpən], *v.n.* chirp.

**zischeln** ['tsɪʃəln], *v.n.* whisper.

**zischen** ['tsɪʃən], *v.n.* hiss; sizzle.

**Zischlaut** ['tsɪʃlaut], *m.* (—s, *pl.* —e) (*Phon.*) sibilant.

**Zisterne** [tsɪs'tɛrnə], *f.* (—, *pl.* —n) cistern.

**Zisterzienser** [tsɪstɛr'tsjɛnzər], *m.* (—s, *pl.* —) Cistercian (monk).

**Zitadelle** [tsɪta'dɛlə], *f.* (—, *pl.* —n) citadel.

**Zitat** [tsi'ta:t], *n.* (—(e)s, *pl.* —e) quotation, reference; *falsches* —, misquotation.

**Zither** ['tsɪtər], *f.* (—, *pl.* —n) zither.

**zitieren** [tsi'ti:rən], *v.a.* cite, quote; *falsch* —, misquote.

**Zitronat** [tsitro'na:t], *n.* (—s, *no pl.*) candied lemon peel.

**Zitrone** [tsi'tro:nə], *f.* (—, *pl.* —n) lemon.

**Zitronenlimonade** [tsi'tro:nənlimo-na:də], *f.* (—, *pl.* —n) lemonade, lemon drink.

**Zitronensaft** [tsi'tro:nənzaft], *m.* (—s, *pl.* —e) lemon-juice.

**Zitronensäure** [tsi'tro:nənzɔyrə], *f.* (—, *no pl.*) citric acid.

**Zitronenschale** [tsi'tro:nənʃa:lə], *f.* (—, *pl.* —n) lemon-peel.

**zitterig** ['tsɪtərɪç], *adj.* shaky, shivery.

**zittern** ['tsɪtərn], *v.n.* tremble, shiver, quake.

**Zitterpappel** ['tsɪtərpapəl], *f.* (—, *pl.* —n) (*Bot.*) aspen-tree.

**Zivil** [tsi'vi:l], *n.* (—s, *no pl.*) civilians, *in* —, in plain clothes; (*coll.*) in civvies or mufti.

**Zivilbeamte** [tsi'vi:lbəamtə], *m.* (—n, *pl.* —n) civil servant.

**Zivildienst** [tsi'vi:ldi:nst], *m.* (—es, *no pl.*) civil service.

**Zivilehe** [tsi'vi:le:ə], *f.* (—, *pl.* —n) civil marriage.

**Zivilgesetzbuch** [tsi'vi:lgəzɛtsbu:x], *n.* (—s, *pl.* ∵er) code of civil law.

**Zivilingenieur** [tsi'vi:lɪnʒenjø:r], *m.* (—s, *pl.* —e) civil engineer.

**Zivilisation** [tsiviliza'tsjo:n], *f.* (—, *pl.* —en) civilisation.

**zivilisatorisch** [tsiviliza'to:rɪʃ], *adj.* civilising.

**zivilisieren** [tsivili'zi:rən], *v.a.* civilise.

**Zivilist** [tsivi'lɪst], *m.* (—en, *pl.* —en) civilian.

**Zivilkleidung** [tsi'vi:lklaɪduŋ], *f.* (—, *no pl.*) civilian dress, plain clothes.

**Zobel** ['tso:bəl], *m.* (—s, *pl.* —) sable.

**Zobelpelz** ['tso:bəlpɛlts], *m.* (—es, *pl.* —e) sable fur; sable-coat.

**Zofe** ['tso:fə], *f.* (—, *pl.* —n) lady's maid.

**zögern** ['tsø:gərn], *v.n.* hesitate, tarry, delay.

**Zögerung** ['tsø:gəruŋ], *f.* (—, *pl.* —en) hesitation, delay.

**Zögling** ['tsø:klɪŋ], *m.* (—s, *pl.* —e) (*obs.*) pupil; charge, ward.

**Zölibat** [tsø:li'ba:t], *m. & n.* (—s, *no pl.*) celibacy.

**Zoll** (1) [tsɔl], *m.* (—s, *no pl.*) inch.

**Zoll** (2) [tsɔl], *m.* (—s, *pl.* ∵e) customs duty; (*bridge*) toll.

**Zollabfertigung** ['tsɔlapfɛrtɪguŋ], *f.* (—, *no pl.*) customs clearance.

**Zollamt** ['tsɔlamt], *n.* (—s, *pl.* ∵er) custom house.

**Zollaufschlag** ['tsɔlaufʃla:k], *m.* (—s, *pl.* ∵e) additional duty.

**Zollbeamte** ['tsɔlbəamtə], *m.* (—n, *pl.* —n) customs officer.

**zollbreit** ['tsɔlbraɪt], *adj.* one inch wide.

**zollen** ['tsɔlən], *v.a. Ehrfurcht* —, pay o.'s respects; *Beifall* —, applaud; *Dank* —, show gratitude.

**zollfrei** ['tsɔlfraɪ], *adj.* duty-free, exempt from duty.

**Zöllner** ['tsœlnər], *m.* (—s, *pl.* —) tax-gatherer.

**zollpflichtig** ['tsɔlpflɪçtɪç], *adj.* liable to duty, dutiable.

**Zollsatz** ['tsɔlzats], *m.* (—es, *pl.* ∵e) customs tariff.

**Zollverein** ['tsɔlfəraɪn], *m.* (—s, *no pl.*) customs union.

**Zollverschluß** ['tsɔlfɛrʃlus], *m.* (—sses, *pl.* ∵sse) bond.

**Zone** ['tso:nə], *f.* (—, *pl.* —n) zone.

**Zoologe** [tso:o'lo:gə], *m.* (—n, *pl.* —n) zoologist.

**Zoologie** [tso:olo'gi:], *f.* (—, *no pl.*) zoology.

# Zuflucht

**zoologisch** [tsoːoˈloːgiʃ], *adj.* zoological; *—er Garten,* zoological gardens, zoo.

**Zopf** [tsɔpf], *m.* (—(e)s, *pl.* ⸚e) plait, pigtail; (*coll.*) (old-fashioned) pedantry.

**Zorn** [tsɔrn], *m.* (—(e)s, *no pl.*) wrath, anger, indignation; *seinen — auslassen,* vent o.'s anger; *in — geraten,* get angry.

**zornglühend** [ˈtsɔrnglyːənt], *adj.* boiling with rage.

**zornig** [ˈtsɔrnɪç], *adj.* angry, wrathful, irate; *— werden,* get angry.

**Zote** [ˈtsoːtə], *f.* (—, *pl.* —n) smutty story, ribaldry, bawdiness.

**zotig** [ˈtsoːtɪç], *adj.* loose, ribald, smutty.

**zottig** [ˈtsɔtɪç], *adj.* shaggy.

**zu** [tsuː], *prep.* (*Dat.*) to, towards; in addition to; at, in, on; for; *— Anfang,* in the beginning; *— Fuß,* on foot; *— Hause,* at home; *— Wasser,* at sea, by sea; *— deinem Nutzen,* for your benefit. *— adv. & prefix,* to, towards; closed; too; *— sehr,* too; *— viel,* too much.

**Zubehör** [ˈtsuːbəhøːr], *n.* (—s, *no pl.*) accessory, appurtenance.

**zubekommen** [ˈtsuːbəkɔmən], *v.a. irr.* get in addition.

**Zuber** [ˈtsuːbər], *m.* (—s, *pl.* —) tub.

**zubereiten** [ˈtsuːbəraɪtən], *v.a.* prepare.

**Zubereitung** [ˈtsuːbəraɪtuŋ], *f.* (—, *no pl.*) preparation.

**zubilligen** [ˈtsuːbɪlɪgən], *v.a.* allow, grant.

**zubleiben** [ˈtsuːblaɪbən], *v.n. irr.* (*aux. sein*) remain shut.

**zubringen** [ˈtsuːbrɪŋən], *v.a. irr. die Zeit —,* spend the time.

**Zubringerdienst** [ˈtsuːbrɪŋərdiːnst], *m.* (—es, *pl.* —e) shuttle-service, tender-service.

**Zubuße** [ˈtsuːbuːsə], *f.* (—, *pl.* —n) (additional) contribution.

**Zucht** [tsuxt], *f.* (—, *no pl.*) race, breed; discipline; breeding, rearing; education, discipline; (good) manners; *in — halten,* keep in hand.

**züchten** [ˈtsyçtən], *v.a.* cultivate; rear, breed; grow.

**Züchter** [ˈtsyçtər], *m.* (—s, *pl.* —) (*plants*) nurseryman; (*animals*) breeder.

**Zuchthaus** [ˈtsuxthaus], *n.* (—es, *pl.* ⸚er) penitentiary, convict prison.

**Zuchthäusler** [ˈtsuxthɔyslər], *m.* (—s, *pl.* —) convict.

**Zuchthengst** [ˈtsuxthɛŋst], *m.* (—es, *pl.* —e) stallion.

**züchtig** [ˈtsyçtɪç], *adj.* modest, chaste.

**züchtigen** [ˈtsyçtɪgən], *v.a.* chastise, lash.

**Züchtigkeit** [ˈtsyçtɪçkaɪt], *f.* (—, *no pl.*) modesty, chastity.

**Züchtigung** [ˈtsyçtɪguŋ], *f.* (—, *pl.* —en) chastisement; *körperliche —,* corporal punishment.

**Zuchtlosigkeit** [ˈtsuxtloːzɪçkaɪt], *f.* (—, *no pl.*) want of discipline.

**Zuchtmeister** [ˈtsuxtmaɪstər], *m.* (—s, *pl.* —) disciplinarian, taskmaster.

**Zuchtochse** [ˈtsuxtɔksə], *m.* (—n, *pl.* —n) bull.

**Zuchtstute** [ˈtsuxtʃtuːtə], *f.* (—, *pl.* —n) brood-mare.

**Züchtung** [ˈtsyçtuŋ], *f.* (—, *pl.* —en) (*plants*) cultivation; (*animals*) rearing, breeding.

**Zuchtvieh** [ˈtsuxtfiː], *n.* (—s, *no pl.*) breeding stock.

**Zuchtwahl** [ˈtsuxtvaːl], *f.* (—, *no pl.*) (*breeding*) selection.

**zucken** [ˈtsukən], *v.n.* quiver, twitch; wince; start, jerk.

**Zucken** [ˈtsukən], *n.* (—s, *no pl.*) palpitation, convulsion, twitch, tic.

**Zucker** [ˈtsukər], *m.* (—s, *no pl.*) sugar.

**Zuckerbäcker** [ˈtsukərbɛkər], *m.* (—s, *pl.* —) confectioner.

**Zuckerguß** [ˈtsukərgus], *m.* (—es, *no pl.*) (sugar-)icing.

**Zuckerkandis** [ˈtsukərkandɪs], *m.* (—, *no pl.*) sugar-candy.

**zuckerkrank** [ˈtsukərkraŋk], *adj.* (*Med.*) diabetic.

**Zuckerkrankheit** [ˈtsukərkraŋkhaɪt], *f.* (—, *no pl.*) (*Med.*) diabetes.

**zuckern** [ˈtsukərn], *v.a.* sugar.

**Zuckerpflanzung** [ˈtsukərpflantsuŋ], *f.* (—, *pl.* —en) sugar-plantation.

**Zuckerraffinerie** [ˈtsukərrafinəriː], *f.* (—, *pl.* —n) sugar-refinery.

**Zuckerrohr** [ˈtsukərroːr], *n.* (—s, *no pl.*) sugar-cane.

**Zuckerrübe** [ˈtsukərryːbə], *f.* (—, *pl.* —n) sugar-beet.

**Zuckerwerk** [ˈtsukərvɛrk], *n.* (—s, *no pl.*) confectionery.

**Zuckerzange** [ˈtsukərtsaŋə], *f.* (—, *pl.* —n) sugar-tongs.

**Zuckung** [ˈtsukuŋ], *f.* (—, *pl.* —en) convulsion, spasm.

**zudecken** [ˈtsuːdɛkən], *v.a.* cover up.

**zudem** [tsuˈdeːm], *adv.* besides, moreover.

**Zudrang** [ˈtsuːdraŋ], *m.* (—s, *no pl.*) crowd(ing); rush (on), run (on).

**zudrehen** [ˈtsuːdreːən], *v.a.* turn off.

**zudringlich** [ˈtsuːdrɪŋlɪç], *adj.* importunate; intruding.

**zudrücken** [ˈtsuːdrykən], *v.a.* close (by pressing), shut.

**zueignen** [ˈtsuːaɪgnən], *v.a.* dedicate.

**zuerkennen** [ˈtsuːɛrkɛnən], *v.a. irr.* award, adjudicate.

**zuerst** [tsuˈeːrst], *adv.* at first, first, in the first instance.

**Zufahrt** [ˈtsuːfaːrt], *f.* (—, *no pl.*) approach, drive.

**Zufall** [ˈtsuːfal], *m.* (—s, *pl.* ⸚e) chance, coincidence; *durch —,* by chance.

**zufallen** [ˈtsuːfalən], *v.n. irr.* (*aux. sein*) close, fall shut; *einem —,* devolve upon s.o., fall to s.o.'s lot.

**zufällig** [ˈtsuːfɛlɪç], *adj.* accidental, casual, fortuitous. *— adv.* by chance.

**Zuflucht** [ˈtsuːfluxt], *f.* (—, *no pl.*) refuge, shelter, haven, recourse.

293

# Zufluchtsort

**Zufluchtsort** ['tsu:fluxtsɔrt], *m.* (—(e)s, *pl.* —e) asylum, shelter, place of refuge.

**Zufluß** ['tsu:flus], *m.* (—sses, *pl.* ‟sse) supply; influx.

**zuflüstern** ['tsu:flystərn], *v.a.* einem etwas —, whisper s.th. to s.o.

**zufolge** [tsu'fɔlgə], *prep.* (Genit., Dat.) in consequence of, owing to, due to, on account of.

**zufrieden** [tsu'fri:dən], *adj.* content, contented, satisfied; — lassen, leave alone.

**zufriedenstellen** [tsu'fri:dənʃtɛlən], *v.a.* satisfy.

**zufügen** ['tsu:fy:gən], *v.a.* add (to); inflict.

**Zufuhr** ['tsu:fu:r], *f.* (—, *pl.* —en) (goods) supplies.

**Zug** [tsu:k], *m.* (—(e)s, *pl.* ‟e) drawing, pull, tug; draught; march, procession; (Railw.) train; (face) feature; (chess) move; (character) trait; (pen) stroke; (birds) flight; migration; (mountains) range.

**Zugabe** ['tsu:ga:bə], *f.* (—, *pl.* —n) addition, make-weight, extra; (concert) encore; als —, into the bargain.

**Zugang** ['tsu:gaŋ], *m.* (—s, *pl.* ‟e) approach, entry, entrance, admittance, access.

**zugänglich** ['tsu:gɛŋlɪç], *adj.* accessible, available; (person) affable.

**Zugbrücke** ['tsu:kbrykə], *f.* (—, *pl.* —n) drawbridge.

**zugeben** ['tsu:ge:bən], *v.a. irr.* give in addition; concede, admit.

**zugegen** [tsu'ge:gən], *adv.* present.

**zugehen** ['tsu:ge:ən], *v.n. irr.* (aux. sein) (door) shut (of itself), close; happen; auf einen —, walk towards s.o.; so geht es im Leben zu, such is life; das geht nicht mit rechten Dingen zu, there is something uncanny about it.

**zugehörig** ['tsu:gəhø:rɪç], *adj.* belonging, appertaining.

**zugeknöpft** ['tsu:gəknœpft], *adj.* reserved, taciturn.

**Zügel** ['tsy:gəl], *m.* (—s, *pl.* —) rein, bridle.

**zügeln** ['tsy:gəln], *v.a.* bridle, curb, check.

**zugesellen** ['tsu:gəzɛlən], *v.r. sich —*, associate with, join.

**Zugeständnis** ['tsu:gəʃtɛntnɪs], *n.* (—sses, *pl.* —sse) admission; concession.

**zugestehen** ['tsu:gəʃte:ən], *v.a. irr.* admit; concede; einem etwas —, allow s.o. s.th.

**zugetan** ['tsu:gəta:n], *adj.* attached, devoted.

**Zugführer** ['tsu:kfy:rər], *m.* (—s, *pl.* —) (Railw.) guard; (Mil.) platoon commander.

**zugießen** ['tsu:gi:sən], *v.a. irr.* fill up, pour on.

**zugig** ['tsu:gɪç], *adj.* windy, draughty.

**Zugkraft** ['tsu:kkraft], *f.* (—, *no pl.*) tractive power, magnetic attraction;

(fig.) pull, attraction; publicity value.

**zugleich** [tsu'glaɪç], *adv.* at the same time; — mit, together with.

**Zugluft** ['tsu:kluft], *f.* (—, *no pl.*) draught (of air).

**zugreifen** ['tsu:graɪfən], *v.n. irr.* grab; lend a hand; (at table) help o.s.

**Zugrolle** ['tsu:krɔlə], *f.* (—, *pl.* —n) pulley.

**zugrunde** [tsu'grundə], *adv.* — gehen, perish, go to ruin, go to the dogs; — legen, base upon.

**Zugstück** ['tsu:kʃtyk], *n.* (—s, *pl.* —e) (Theat.) popular show; (coll.) success, hit.

**zugucken** ['tsu:gukən], *v.n.* look on, watch.

**zugunsten** [tsu'gunstən], *prep.* (Genit.) for the benefit of.

**zugute** [tsu'gu:tə], *adv.* — halten, make allowances.

**Zugvogel** ['tsu:kfo:gəl], *m.* (—s, *pl.* ‟) bird of passage.

**zuhalten** ['tsu:haltən], *v.a. irr.* keep closed.

**Zuhälter** ['tsu:hɛltər], *m.* (—s, *pl.* —) souteneur; pimp.

**Zuhilfenahme** [tsu'hɪlfəna:mə], *f.* (—, *no pl.*) unter —, with the help of, by means of.

**zuhören** ['tsu:hø:rən], *v.n.* listen to, attend to.

**Zuhörerschaft** ['tsu:hø:rərʃaft], *f.* (—, *pl.* —en) audience.

**zujubeln** ['tsu:ju:bəln], *v.n.* einem —, acclaim s.o., cheer s.o.

**zukehren** ['tsu:ke:rən], *v.a.* einem den Rücken —, turn o.'s back on s.o.

**zuknöpfen** ['tsu:knœpfən], *v.a.* button (up).

**zukommen** ['tsu:kɔmən], *v.n. irr.* (aux. sein) auf einen —, advance towards s.o.; einem —, be due to s.o.; become s.o.; reach s.o.

**Zukost** ['tsu:kɔst], *f.* (—, *no pl.*) (food) trimmings, extras.

**Zukunft** ['tsu:kunft], *f.* (—, *no pl.*) future; prospects.

**zukünftig** ['tsu:kynftɪç], *adj.* future, prospective.

**Zukunftsmusik** ['tsu:kunftsmuzi:k], *f.* (—, *no pl.*) daydreams, pipedreams.

**zulächeln** ['tsu:lɛçəln], *v.a.* einem —, smile at s.o.

**Zulage** ['tsu:la:gə], *f.* (—, *pl.* —n) addition; increase of salary, rise; (Am.) raise.

**zulangen** ['tsu:laŋən], *v.n.* be sufficient; (at table) help o.s.

**zulänglich** ['tsu:lɛŋlɪç], *adj.* sufficient, adequate.

**zulassen** ['tsu:lasən], *v.a. irr.* leave unopened; allow; admit; permit.

**zulässig** ['tsu:lɛsɪç], *adj.* admissible; das ist nicht —, that is not allowed.

**Zulassung** ['tsu:lasuŋ], *f.* (—, *pl.* —en) admission.

**Zulauf** ['tsu:lauf], *m.* (—s, *no pl.*) run (of customers); crowd, throng.

**zulaufen** ['tsu:laufən], *v.n. irr.* (*aux.* sein) *auf einen —,* run towards s.o.; *spitz —,* taper, come to a point.

**zulegen** ['tsu:le:gən], *v.a.* add; increase; *sich etwas —,* make o.s. a present of s.th.; get s.th.

**zuletzt** [tsu'lɛtst], *adv.* last, at last, lastly, finally, eventually, in the end.

**zuliebe** [tsu'li:bə], *adv. einem etwas — tun,* oblige s.o.; do s.th. for s.o.'s sake.

**zum = zu dem.**

**zumachen** ['tsu:maxən], *v.a.* shut, close.

**zumal** [tsu'ma:l], *adv.* especially, particularly. — *conj.* especially since.

**zumeist** [tsu'maIst], *adv.* mostly, for the most part.

**zumute** [tsu'mu:tə], *adv. mir ist nicht gut —,* I don't feel well.

**zumuten** ['tsu:mu:tən], *v.a. einem etwas —,* expect *or* demand s.th. of s.o.

**Zumutung** ['tsu:mu:tuŋ], *f.* (—, *pl.* —en) unreasonable demand.

**zunächst** [tsu'nɛ:çst], *adv.* first, above all.

**Zunahme** ['tsu:na:mə], *f.* (—, *pl.* —n) increase.

**Zuname** ['tsu:na:mə], *m.* (—ns, *pl.* —n) surname, family name.

**zünden** ['tsyndən], *v.n.* catch fire, ignite.

**Zunder** ['tsundər], *m.* (—s, *no pl.*) tinder.

**Zünder** ['tsyndər], *m.* (—s, *pl.* —) lighter, detonator, fuse.

**Zündholz** ['tsynthɔlts], *n.* (—es, *pl.* ‥er) match.

**Zündkerze** ['tsyntkɛrtsə], *f.* (—,*pl.*—n) (*Motor.*) sparking-plug.

**Zündstoff** ['tsyntʃtɔf], *m.* (—s, *pl.* —e) fuel.

**Zündung** ['tsynduŋ], *f.* (—, *pl.* —en) ignition; detonation.

**zunehmen** ['tsu:ne:mən], *v.n. irr.* increase, put on weight; (*moon*) wax.

**zuneigen** ['tsu:naIgən], *v.r. sich —,* incline towards.

**Zuneigung** ['tsu:naIguŋ], *f.* (—, *pl.* —en) affection, inclination.

**Zunft** [tsunft], *f.* (—, *pl.* ‥e) company, guild, corporation; (*fig.*) brotherhood.

**Zunftgenosse** ['tsunftgənɔsə], *m.* (—n, *pl.* —n) member of a guild.

**zünftig** ['tsynftıç], *adj.* professional; proper.

**zunftmäßig** ['tsunftmɛ:sıç], *adj.* professional; competent.

**Zunge** ['tsuŋə], *f.* (—, *pl.* —n) tongue; (*buckle*) catch; (*fig.*) language; (*fish*) sole.

**züngeln** ['tsyŋəln], *v.n.* (*flame*) shoot out, lick.

**Zungenband** ['tsuŋənbant], *n.* (—s, *pl.* ‥er) ligament of the tongue.

**zungenfertig** ['tsuŋənfɛrtıç], *adj.* voluble, glib.

**Zungenlaut** ['tsuŋənlaut], *m.* (—s, *pl.* —e) (*Phon.*) lingual sound.

**Zungenspitze** ['tsuŋənʃpItsə], *f.* (—, *pl.* —n) tip of the tongue.

**zunichte** [tsu'nIçtə], *adv. — machen,* ruin, undo, destroy; *— werden,* come to nothing.

**zupfen** ['tsupfən], *v.a.* pick, pluck.

**zurechnungsfähig** ['tsu:rɛçnuŋsfɛ:Iç], *adj.* accountable, of sane mind, compos mentis.

**zurecht** [tsu'rɛçt], *adv.* aright, right(ly), in order.

**zurechtfinden** [tsu'rɛçtfIndən], *v.r. irr. sich —,* find o.'s way about.

**zurechtkommen** [tsu'rɛçtkɔmən], *v.n. irr.* (*aux.* sein) arrive in (good) time; *mit einem gut —,* get on well with s.o.

**zurechtlegen** [tsu'rɛçtle:gən], *v.a.* put in order, get ready.

**zurechtmachen** [tsu'rɛçtmaxən], *v.a.* get s.th. ready, prepare s.th. — *v.r. sich—,* prepare o.s.; (*women*) make up (*coll.*) put on o.'s face.

**zurechtweisen** [tsu'rɛçtvaIzən], *v.a. irr.* reprove (s.o.), set (s.o.) right; direct.

**Zurechtweisung** [tsu'rɛçtvaIzuŋ], *f.* (—, *pl.* —en) reprimand.

**Zureden** ['tsu:re:dən], *n.* (—s, *no pl.*) encouragement; entreaties.

**zureden** ['tsu:re:dən], *v.n.* encourage (s.o.), persuade (s.o.).

**zureichen** ['tsu:raIçən], *v.a.* reach, hand. — *v.n.* be sufficient, be enough, suffice.

**zurichten** ['tsu:rIçtən], *v.a. etwas (einen) übel —,* maltreat s.th. (s.o.).

**zürnen** ['tsyrnən], *v.n.* be angry (with).

**zurück** [tsu'ryk], *adv.* back; behind; backwards; — *excl.* stand back!

**zurückbegeben** [tsu'rykbəge:bən], *v.r. irr. sich —,* go back, return.

**zurückbehalten** [tsu'rykbəhaltən], *v.a. irr.* retain, keep back.

**zurückbekommen** [tsu'rykbəkɔmən], *v.a. irr.* get back, recover (s.th.).

**zurückberufen** [tsu'rykbəru:fən], *v.a. irr.* recall.

**zurückfordern** [tsu'rykfɔrdərn], *v.a.* demand back, demand the return of.

**zurückführen** [tsu'rykfy:rən], *v.a.* lead back; *auf etwas —,* attribute to; trace back to.

**zurückgeblieben** [tsu'rykgəbli:bən], *adj.* retarded, mentally deficient, backward.

**zurückgezogen** [tsu'rykgətso:gən], *adj.* secluded, retired.

**zurückhalten** [tsu'rykhaltən], *v.a. irr.* keep back, retain.

**zurückhaltend** [tsu'rykhaltənt], *adj.* reserved.

**zurückkehren** [tsu'rykke:rən], *v.n.* (*aux.* sein) return.

**zurückkommen** [tsu'rykkɔmən], *v.n. irr.* (*aux.* sein) come back.

**zurücklassen** [tsu'ryklasən], *v.a. irr.* leave behind, abandon.

# zurücklegen

**zurücklegen** [tsu'rykleːgən], *v.a.* lay aside, put by; *eine Strecke* —, cover a distance. — *v.r. sich* —, lean back; *zurückgelegter Gewinn,* undistributed profits.

**zurückmüssen** [tsu'rykmysən], *v.n. irr.* be obliged to return.

**zurücknehmen** [tsu'rykneːmən], *v.a. irr.* take back.

**zurückschrecken** [tsu'rykʃrɛkən], *v.a.* frighten away. — *v.n. irr. (aux.* sein) recoil (from).

**zurücksehnen** [tsu'rykzeːnən], *v.r. sich* —, long to return, wish o.s. back.

**zurücksetzen** [tsu'rykzetsən], *v.a.* put back; slight; discriminate against; neglect.

**Zurücksetzung** [tsu'rykzetsuŋ], *f.* (—, *pl.* —en) slight, rebuff.

**zurückstrahlen** [tsu'rykʃtraːlən], *v.a.* reflect.

**zurücktreten** [tsu'ryktreːtən], *v.n. irr. (aux.* sein) stand back, withdraw; resign.

**zurückverlangen** [tsu'rykfɛrlaŋən], *v.a.* demand back, request the return of.

**zurückversetzen** [tsu'rykfɛrzetsən], *v.a. (Sch.)* put in a lower form. — *v.r. sich* —, turn o.'s thoughts back (to), hark back.

**zurückweichen** [tsu'rykvaɪçən], *v.n.irr. (aux.* sein) withdraw, retreat.

**zurückweisen** [tsu'rykvaɪzən], *v.a. irr.* refuse, reject, repulse.

**zurückwollen** [tsu'rykvɔlən], *v.n.* wish to return.

**zurückziehen** [tsu'ryktsiːən], *v.a. irr.* draw back; *(fig.)* withdraw, retract, countermand. — *v.r. sich* —, retire, withdraw.

**Zuruf** [ˈtsuːruːf], *m.* (—s, *pl.* —e) call, acclaim, acclamation.

**Zusage** [ˈtsuːzaːgə], *f.* (—, *pl.* —n) promise; acceptance.

**zusagen** [ˈtsuːzaːgən], *v.a.* promise; *es sagt mir zu,* I like it. — *v.n.* accept.

**zusagend** [ˈtsuːzaːgənt], *adj.* affirmative; agreeable.

**zusammen** [tsu'zamən], *adv.* together, jointly.

**zusammenbeißen** [tsu'zamənbaɪsən], *v.a. irr. die Zähne* —, set o.'s teeth.

**zusammenbetteln** [tsu'zamənbetəln], *v.a. sich etwas* —, collect (by begging).

**zusammenbrechen** [tsu'zamənbre-çən], *v.n. irr. (aux.* sein) break down, collapse.

**Zusammenbruch** [tsu'zamənbrux], *m.* (—s, *pl.* ⁝e) breakdown, collapse, débâcle.

**zusammendrängen** [tsu'zaməndreŋ-ən], *v.a.* press together; *(fig.)* abridge, condense.

**zusammendrücken** [tsu'zaməndry-kən], *v.a.* compress.

**zusammenfahren** [tsu'zamənfaːrən], *v.n. irr. (aux.* sein) collide; give a start.

**zusammenfallen** [tsu'zamənfalən], *v.n. irr. (aux.* sein) collapse.

**zusammenfassen** [tsu'zamənfasən], *v.a.* sum up, summarize.

**Zusammenfassung** [tsu'zamənfasuŋ], *f.* (—, *no pl.*) summing-up, summary.

**zusammenfinden** [tsu'zamənfɪndən], *v.r. irr. sich* —, discover a mutual affinity, come together.

**Zusammenfluß** [tsu'zamənflus], *m.* (—sses, *pl.* ⁝sse) confluence.

**zusammengeben** [tsu'zaməngeːbən], *v.a. irr.* join in marriage.

**Zusammengehörigkeit** [tsu'zaməngə-høːrɪçkaɪt], *f.* (—, *no pl.*) solidarity; *(Am.)* togetherness.

**zusammengesetzt** [tsu'zaməngəzɛtst], *adj.* composed (of), consisting (of); complicated; *(Maths.)* composite.

**zusammengewürfelt** [tsu'zaməngə-vyrfəlt], *adj.* motley, mixed.

**Zusammenhalt** [tsu'zamənhalt], *m.* (—s, *no pl.*) holding together; unity.

**Zusammenhang** [tsu'zamənhaŋ], *m.* (—s, *pl.* ⁝e) coherence; connection, context.

**zusammenhängen** [tsu'zamənhɛŋən], *v.n. irr.* hang together, cohere; *(fig.)* be connected (with).

**Zusammenklang** [tsu'zamənklaŋ], *m.* (—s, *pl.* ⁝e) unison, harmony.

**Zusammenkunft** [tsu'zamənkunft], *f.* (—, *pl.* ⁝e) meeting, convention, conference; reunion.

**zusammenlaufen** [tsu'zamənlaufən], *v.n. irr. (aux.* sein) crowd together, converge; flock together; *(milk)* curdle; *(material)* shrink.

**zusammenlegen** [tsu'zamənleːgən], *v.a.* put together; *(money)* collect; *(letter)* fold up.

**zusammennehmen** [tsu'zamənneː-mən], *v.a. irr.* gather up. — *v.r. sich* —, get a firm grip on o.s., pull o.s. together.

**zusammenpassen** [tsu'zamənpasən], *v.n.* fit together, match; agree; be compatible.

**zusammenpferchen** [tsu'zamənpfɛr-çən], *v.a.* pen up, crowd together in a small space.

**zusammenpressen** [tsu'zamənpresən], *v.a.* squeeze together.

**zusammenraffen** [tsu'zamənrafən], *v.a.* gather up hurriedly, collect. — *v.r. sich* —, pluck up courage; pull o.s. together.

**zusammenrechnen** [tsu'zamənreç-nən], *v.a.* add up.

**zusammenreimen** [tsu'zamənraɪmən], *v.a. sich etwas* —, figure s.th. out.

**zusammenrücken** [tsu'zamənrykən], *v.a.* move together, draw closer. — *v.n.* move closer together, move up.

**zusammenschießen** [tsu'zamənʃiːsən], *v.a. irr.* shoot to pieces, shoot down; *Geld* —, club together, raise a subscription.

**zusammenschlagen** [tsu'zamənʃlaː-gən], *v.a. irr.* beat up; strike together; clap, fold.

296

**zusammenschließen** [tsu'zamənʃliː-sən], v.r. irr. sich —, join, unite, ally o.s. (with).

**zusammenschweißen** [tsu'zamənʃvai-sən], v.a. weld together.

**Zusammensein** [tsu'zamənzain], n. (—s, no pl.) meeting, social gathering.

**Zusammensetzung** [tsu'zamənzetsuŋ], f. (—, no pl.) construction; composition.

**Zusammenspiel** [tsu'zamənʃpiːl], n. (—s, no pl.) (Theat., Mus.) ensemble.

**zusammenstellen** [tsu'zamənʃtɛlən], v.a. compose, concoct; put together, compile.

**Zusammenstellung** [tsu'zamənʃtɛluŋ], f. (—, pl. —en) combination, compilation; juxtaposition.

**zusammenstoppeln** [tsu'zamənʃtɔp-əln], v.a. string together, patch up.

**Zusammenstoß** [tsu'zamənʃtoːs], m. (—es, pl. ⸚e) clash, conflict; collision.

**zusammenstoßen** [tsu'zamənʃtoːsən], v.n. irr. (aux. sein) clash; crash, come into collision, collide.

**zusammentragen** [tsu'zaməntraːgən], v.a. irr. collect, compile.

**zusammentreffen** [tsu'zaməntrɛfən], v.n. irr. meet; coincide.

**zusammentreten** [tsu'zaməntreːtən], v.n. irr. (aux. sein) meet.

**zusammentun** [tsu'zaməntuːn], v.r. irr. sich — mit, associate with, join.

**zusammenwirken** [tsu'zamənvirkən], v.n. cooperate, collaborate.

**zusammenwürfeln** [tsu'zamənvyr-fəln], v.a. jumble up.

**zusammenzählen** [tsu'zaməntsɛːlən], v.a. add up.

**zusammenziehen** [tsu'zaməntsiːən], v.n. irr. (aux. sein) move in together. — v.a. draw together, contract. — v.r. sich —, shrink; (storm) gather; Zahlen —, add up.

**Zusammenziehung** [tsu'zaməntsiːuŋ], f. (—, no pl.) contraction.

**Zusatz** [tsu'zats], m. (—es, pl. ⸚e) addition, supplement, admixture; (will) codicil.

**zuschanzen** [tsu'ʃantsən], v.a. einem etwas —, obtain s.th. for s.o.

**zuschauen** [tsu'ʃauən], v.n. look on, watch.

**Zuschauer** [tsu'ʃauər], m. (—s, pl. —) onlooker, spectator.

**Zuschauerraum** [tsu'ʃauərraum], m. (—s, pl. ⸚e) (Theat.) auditorium.

**zuschaufeln** [tsu'ʃaufəln], v.a. shovel in, fill up.

**zuschieben** [tsu'ʃiːbən], v.a. irr. push towards; shut; einem etwas —, shove (blame) on to s.o.

**zuschießen** [tsu'ʃiːsən], v.a. irr. Geld —, put money into (an undertaking).

**Zuschlag** [tsu'ʃlaːk], m. (—s, pl. ⸚e) addition; (Railw.) excess fare.

**zuschlagen** [tsu'ʃlaːgən], v.a. irr. add; (door) bang; (auction) knock down to (s.o.). — v.n. strike hard.

**zuschlag(s)pflichtig** [tsu'ʃlaːk(s)pflɪç-tɪç], adj. liable to a supplementary charge.

**zuschmeißen** [tsu'ʃmaisən], v.a. irr. (door) slam to, bang.

**zuschneiden** [tsu'ʃnaidən], v.a. irr. (pattern) cut out; cut up.

**Zuschneider** [tsu'ʃnaidər], m. (—s, pl.—) (Tail.) cutter.

**Zuschnitt** [tsu'ʃnit], m. (—s, no pl.) (clothing) cut.

**zuschreiben** [tsu'ʃraibən], v.a. irr. einem etwas —, impute s.th. to s.o.; attribute or ascribe s.th. to s.o

**Zuschrift** [tsu'ʃrift], f. (—, pl. —en) communication, letter.

**Zuschuß** [tsu'ʃus], m. (—sses, pl. ⸚sse) additional money, supplementary allowance, subsidy.

**zuschütten** [tsu'ʃytən], v.a. fill up.

**Zusehen** [tsu'zeːən], n. (—s, no pl.) das — haben, be left out in the cold.

**zusehen** [tsu'zeːən], v.n. irr. look on, watch; be a spectator; see to it.

**zusehends** [tsu'zeːənts], adv. visibly.

**zusetzen** [tsu'zɛtsən], v.a. add to, admix; lose. — v.n. einem —, pester s.o.; attack s.o.

**zusichern** [tsu'zɪçərn], v.a. promise, assure.

**Zusicherung** [tsu'zɪçəruŋ], f. (—, pl. —en) promise, assurance.

**Zuspeise** [tsu'ʃpaizə], f. (—, no pl.) (dial.) (food) trimmings; vegetables.

**zusperren** [tsu'ʃpɛrən], v.a. shut, close, lock up.

**zuspitzen** [tsu'ʃpitsən], v.a. sharpen to a point. — v.r. sich —, come to a climax.

**zusprechen** [tsu'ʃprɛçən], v.n. irr. dem Wein —, drink heavily. — v.a. Mut —, comfort.

**Zuspruch** [tsu'ʃprux], m. (—s, pl. ⸚e) exhortation; consolation.

**Zustand** [tsu'ʃtant], m. (—s, pl. ⸚e) condition, state of affairs, situation.

**zustande** [tsu'ʃtandə], adv. — kommen, come off, be accomplished; — bringen, accomplish.

**zuständig** [tsu'ʃtɛndɪç], adj. competent; appropriate.

**Zuständigkeit** [tsu'ʃtɛndɪçkait], f. (—, no pl.) competence.

**zustecken** [tsu'ʃtɛkən], v.a. pin up; einem etwas —, slip s.th. into s.o.'s hand.

**zustehen** [tsu'ʃteːən], v.n. irr. be due to, belong to; be s.o.'s business to.

**zustellen** [tsu'ʃtɛlən], v.a. deliver, hand over; (Law) serve (a writ).

**Zustellung** [tsu'ʃtɛluŋ], f. (—, pl. —en) delivery; (Law) service.

**zusteuern** [tsu'ʃtɔyərn], v.a. contribute. — v.n. (aux. sein) steer for; (fig.) aim at.

**zustimmen** [tsu'ʃtɪmən], v.n. agree to.

**Zustimmung** [tsu'ʃtɪmuŋ], f. (—, pl. —en) assent, consent, agreement.

# zustopfen

**zustopfen** ['tsu:ʃtɔpfən], *v.a.* fill up, stop up, plug; darn, mend.

**zustoßen** ['tsu:ʃto:sən], *v.a. irr.* push to, shut.

**zustürzen** ['tsu:ʃtyrtsən], *v.n.* (*aux.* sein) *auf einen* —, rush at *or* towards s.o.

**Zutaten** ['tsu:ta:tən], *f. pl.* ingredients, garnishings.

**zuteil** [tsu'taɪl], *adv.* — *werden*, fall to s.o.'s share.

**zutragen** ['tsu:tra:gən], *v.a. irr.* report, tell. — *v.r. sich* —, happen.

**Zuträger** ['tsu:trɛ:gər], *m.* (—s, *pl.* —) informer, tale-bearer.

**zuträglich** ['tsu:trɛ:klɪç], *adj.* advantageous, wholesome.

**Zutrauen** ['tsu:trauən], *n.* (—s, *no pl.*) confidence.

**zutrauen** ['tsu:trauən], *v.a. einem etwas* —, credit s.o. with s.th.

**zutraulich** ['tsu:traulɪç], *adj.* trusting; familiar, intimate; tame.

**zutreffen** ['tsu:trɛfən], *v.n. irr.* prove correct, take place.

**zutreffend** ['tsu:trɛfənt], *adj.* apposite, pertinent.

**Zutritt** ['tsu:trɪt], *m.* (—s, *no pl.*) entry; access, admittance; — *verboten*, no admittance.

**zutunlich** ['tsu:tu:nlɪç], *adj.* confiding; obliging.

**zuverlässig** ['tsu:fɛrlɛsɪç], *adj.* reliable; authentic.

**Zuversicht** ['tsu:fɛrzɪçt], *f.* (—, *no pl.*) trust, confidence.

**zuversichtlich** ['tsu:fɛrzɪçtlɪç], *adj.* confident.

**zuvor** [tsu'fo:r], *adv.* before, first, formerly.

**zuvorkommend** [tsu'fo:rkɔmənt], *adj.* obliging, polite.

**Zuwachs** ['tsu:vaks], *m.* (—es, *no pl.*) increase, accretion, growth.

**zuwachsen** ['tsu:vaksən], *v.n. irr.* (*aux.* sein) become overgrown.

**zuwandern** ['tsu:vandərn], *v.n.* (*aux.* sein) immigrate.

**zuwegebringen** [tsu've:gəbrɪŋən], *v.a. irr.* bring about, effect.

**zuweilen** [tsu'vaɪlən], *adv.* sometimes, at times.

**zuweisen** ['tsu:vaɪzən], *v.a. irr.* assign, apportion.

**zuwenden** ['tsu:vɛndən], *v.a.* turn towards; give.

**zuwerfen** ['tsu:vɛrfən], *v.a. irr.* throw towards, cast; (*door*) slam.

**zuwider** [tsu'vi:dər], *prep.* (*Dat.*) against, contrary to. — *adv.* repugnant.

**Zuwiderhandlung** [tsu'vi:dərhandluŋ], *f.* (—, *pl.* —en) contravention.

**zuwiderlaufen** [tsu'vi:dərlaufən], *v.n. irr.* (*aux.* sein) be contrary to, fly in the face of.

**zuzählen** ['tsu:tsɛ:lən], *v.a.* add to.

**zuziehen** ['tsu:tsi:ən], *v.a. irr.* draw together; tighten; consult; (*curtain*) draw. — *v.r. sich eine Krankheit* —, catch a disease.

**Zuzug** ['tsu:tsu:k], *m.* (—s, *no pl.*) immigration; population increase.

**zuzüglich** ['tsu:tsy:klɪç], *prep.* (*Genit.*) in addition to, including, plus.

**Zwang** [tsvaŋ], *m.* (—s, *no pl.*) coercion, force; compulsion; (*fig.*) constraint; *sich* — *auferlegen*, restrain o.s.; *tu deinen Gefühlen keinen* — *an*, let yourself go.

**zwanglos** ['tsvaŋlo:s], *adj.* informal, free and easy.

**Zwangsarbeit** ['tsvaŋsarbaɪt], *f.* (—, *pl.* —en) forced labour.

**Zwangsjacke** ['tsvaŋsjakə], *f.* (—, *pl.* —en) strait-jacket.

**Zwangsmaßnahme** ['tsvaŋsma:sna:mə], *f.* (—, *pl.* —en) compulsory measure, compulsion.

**Zwangsversteigerung** ['tsvaŋsfɛrʃtaɪgəruŋ], *f.* (—, *pl.* —en) enforced sale.

**Zwangsvollstreckung** ['tsvaŋsfɔlʃtrekuŋ], *f.* (—, *pl.* —en) distraint.

**zwangsweise** ['tsvaŋsvaɪzə], *adv.* by force, compulsorily.

**Zwangswirtschaft** ['tsvaŋsvɪrtʃaft], *f.* (—, *no pl.*) price control, controlled economy.

**zwanzig** ['tsvantsɪç], *num. adj.* twenty.

**zwar** [tsva:r], *adv.* to be sure, indeed, it is true, true; (*Am.*) sure.

**Zweck** [tsvɛk], *m.* (—(e)s, *pl.* —e) end, object, purpose.

**zweckdienlich** ['tsvɛkdi:nlɪç], *adj.* useful, expedient.

**Zwecke** ['tsvɛkə], *f.* (—, *pl.* —n) tack, drawing-pin.

**zweckentsprechend** ['tsvɛkɛntʃprɛçənt], *adj.* suitable, appropriate.

**zweckmäßig** ['tsvɛkmɛ:sɪç], *adj.* expedient, suitable, proper.

**zwecks** [tsvɛks], *prep.* (*Genit.*) for the purpose of.

**zwei** [tsvaɪ], *num. adj.* two.

**zweibändig** ['tsvaɪbɛndɪç], *adj.* in two volumes.

**zweideutig** ['tsvaɪdɔytɪç], *adj.* ambiguous, equivocal; (*fig.*) suggestive.

**Zweideutigkeit** ['tsvaɪdɔytɪçkaɪt], *f.* (—, *pl.* —en) ambiguity.

**Zweifel** ['tsvaɪfəl], *m.* (—s, *pl.* —) doubt, scruple; *ohne* —, no doubt.

**zweifelhaft** ['tsvaɪfəlhaft], *adj.* doubtful, dubious.

**zweifellos** ['tsvaɪfəllo:s], *adv.* doubtless.

**zweifeln** ['tsvaɪfəln], *v.n.* doubt, question; *ich zweifle nicht daran*, I have no doubt about it.

**Zweifelsfall** ['tsvaɪfəlsfal], *m.* (—s, *pl.* ⸚e) doubtful matter; *im* —, in case of doubt.

**Zweifler** ['tsvaɪflər], *m.* (—s, *pl.* —) doubter, sceptic.

**Zweig** [tsvaɪk], *m.* (—(e)s, *pl.* —e) twig, bough, branch.

**zweigen** ['tsvaɪgən], *v.r. sich* —, bifurcate, fork, branch.

**Zweigniederlassung** ['tsvaɪkni:dərlasuŋ], *f.* (—, *pl.* —en) branch establishment.

# zwitschern

**zweihändig** ['tsvaɪhɛndɪç], *adj.* two-handed; (*keyboard music*) solo.
**Zweihufer** ['tsvaɪhuːfər], *m.* (—s, *pl.* —) cloven-footed animal.
**zweijährig** ['tsvaɪjɛːrɪç], *adj.* two-year-old; of two years' duration.
**zweijährlich** ['tsvaɪjɛːrlɪç], *adj.* biennial. — *adv.* every two years.
**Zweikampf** ['tsvaɪkampf], *m.* (— (e)s, *pl.* ⁓e) duel.
**zweimal** ['tsvaɪmal], *adv.* twice; — *soviel,* twice as much.
**zweimotorig** ['tsvaɪmotoːrɪç], *adj.* twin-(or two-) engined.
**Zweirad** ['tsvaɪraːt], *n.* (—s, *pl.* ⁓er) bicycle.
**zweireihig** ['tsvaɪraɪɪç], *adj.* (*suit*) double-breasted.
**zweischneidig** ['tsvaɪʃnaɪdɪç], *adj.* two-edged.
**zweiseitig** ['tsvaɪzaɪtɪç], *adj.* two-sided, bilateral.
**zweisprachig** ['tsvaɪʃpraːxɪç], *adj.* bilingual, in two languages.
**zweitälteste** ['tsvaɪtɛltəstə], *adj.* second (eldest).
**zweitbeste** ['tsvaɪtbɛstə], *adj.* second best.
**zweite** ['tsvaɪtə], *num. adj.* second; *aus —r Hand,* secondhand; *zu zweit,* in twos, two of (us, them).
**Zweiteilung** ['tsvaɪtaɪluŋ], *f.* (—, *pl.* —en) bisection.
**zweitens** ['tsvaɪtəns], *adv.* secondly, in the second place.
**zweitletzte** ['tsvaɪtletstə], *adj.* last but one, penultimate.
**zweitnächste** ['tsvaɪtnɛçstə], *adj.* next but one.
**Zwerchfell** ['tsvɛrçfel], *n.* (—s, *pl.* —e) diaphragm, midriff.
**zwerchfellerschütternd** ['tsvɛrçfelərʃytərnt], *adj.* side-splitting.
**Zwerg** [tsvɛrk], *m.* (—s, *pl.* —e) dwarf, pigmy.
**zwerghaft** ['tsvɛrkhaft], *adj.* dwarfish.
**Zwetsche** ['tsvetʃə], *f.* (—, *pl.* —n) (*Bot.*) damson.
**Zwickel** ['tsvɪkəl], *m.* (—s, *pl.* —) gusset; *komischer —,* (*coll.*) queer fish.
**zwicken** ['tsvɪkən], *v.a.* pinch, nip.
**Zwicker** ['tsvɪkər], *m.* (—s, *pl.* —) pince-nez.
**Zwickmühle** ['tsvɪkmyːlə], *f.* (—, *pl.* —n) *in der — sein,* be on the horns of a dilemma, be in a jam.
**Zwickzange** ['tsvɪktsaŋə], *f.* (—, *pl.* —n) pincers.
**Zwieback** ['tsviːbak], *m.* (—s, *pl.* —e) rusk.
**Zwiebel** ['tsviːbəl], *f.* (—, *pl.* —n) onion; bulb.
**zwiebelartig** ['tsviːbəlaːrtɪç], *adj.* bulbous.
**zwiebeln** ['tsviːbəln], *v.a. einen —,* bully, torment s.o.
**Zwielicht** ['tsviːlɪçt], *n.* (—s, *no pl.*) twilight.
**Zwiespalt** ['tsviːʃpalt], *m.* (—s, *pl.* —e) difference, dissension; schism.

**Zwiesprache** ['tsviːʃpraːxə], *f.* (—, *pl.* —n) dialogue; discussion.
**Zwietracht** ['tsviːtraxt], *f.* (—, *no pl.*) discord, disharmony.
**zwieträchtig** ['tsviːtrɛçtɪç], *adj.* discordant, at variance.
**Zwillich** ['tsvɪlɪç], *m.* (—s, *pl.* —e) ticking.
**Zwilling** ['tsvɪlɪŋ], *m.* (—s, *pl.* —e) twin; (*pl.*) (*Astrol.*) Gemini.
**Zwingburg** ['tsvɪŋburk], *f.* (—, *pl.* —en) stronghold.
**Zwinge** ['tsvɪŋə], *f.* (—, *pl.* —n) ferrule.
**zwingen** ['tsvɪŋən], *v.a. irr.* force, compel; master, overcome, get the better of. — *v.r. sich —,* force o.s. (to), make a great effort (to).
**zwingend** ['tsvɪŋənt], *adj.* cogent, imperative, convincing.
**Zwinger** ['tsvɪŋər], *m.* (—s, *pl.* —) keep, donjon, fort; bear-pit.
**Zwingherrschaft** ['tsvɪŋhɛrʃaft], *f.* (—, *pl.* —en) despotism, tyranny.
**zwinkern** ['tsvɪŋkərn], *v.n.* wink; (*stars*) twinkle.
**Zwirn** [tsvɪrn], *m.* (—(e)s, *pl.* —e) thread, sewing cotton.
**Zwirnrolle** ['tsvɪrnrɔlə], *f.* (—, *pl.* —n) ball of thread, reel of cotton.
**zwischen** ['tsvɪʃən], *prep.* (*Dat., Acc.*) between; among, amongst.
**Zwischenakt** ['tsvɪʃənakt], *m.* (—s, *pl.* —e) (*Theat.*) interval.
**Zwischenbemerkung** ['tsvɪʃənbəmɛrkuŋ], *f.* (—, *pl.* —en) interruption, digression.
**Zwischendeck** ['tsvɪʃəndɛk], *n.* (—s, *pl.* —e) (*ship*) steerage, between decks.
**zwischendurch** ['tsvɪʃəndurç], *adv.* in between, at intervals.
**Zwischenfall** ['tsvɪʃənfal], *m.* (—s, *pl.* ⁓e) incident; episode.
**Zwischengericht** ['tsvɪʃəngərɪçt], *n.* (—s, *pl.* —e) (*food*) entrée, entremets.
**Zwischenglied** ['tsvɪʃəngliːt], *n.* (—s, *pl.* —er) link.
**Zwischenhändler** ['tsvɪʃənhɛndlər], *m.* (—s, *pl.* —) middleman.
**Zwischenpause** ['tsvɪʃənpauzə], *f.* (—, *pl.* —n) interval; pause.
**Zwischenraum** ['tsvɪʃənraum], *m.* (—s, *pl.* ⁓e) intermediate space, gap.
**Zwischenrede** ['tsvɪʃənreːdə], *f.* (—, *pl.* —n) interruption.
**Zwischenruf** ['tsvɪʃənruːf], *m.* (—s, *pl.* —e) interruption, interjection.
**Zwischensatz** ['tsvɪʃənzats], *m.* (—es, *pl.* ⁓e) parenthesis; interpolation.
**Zwischenspiel** ['tsvɪʃənʃpiːl], *n.* (—s, *pl.* —e) interlude, intermezzo.
**Zwischenzeit** ['tsvɪʃəntsaɪt], *f.* (—, *no pl.*) interval, interim, meantime; *in der —,* meanwhile.
**Zwist** [tsvɪst], *m.* (—es, *pl.* —e) discord, quarrel, dispute.
**Zwistigkeiten** ['tsvɪstɪçkaɪtən], *f. pl.* hostilities.
**zwitschern** ['tsvɪtʃərn], *v.n.* chirp, twitter.

# Zwitter

**Zwitter** ['tsvɪtər], *m.* (—s, *pl.* —) hybrid, cross-breed, mongrel; hermaphrodite.

**zwitterhaft** ['tsvɪtərhaft], *adj.* hybrid; bisexual.

**zwölf** [tsvœlf], *num. adj.* twelve.

**Zwölffingerdarm** ['tsvœlffɪŋərdarm], *m.* (—s, *pl.* ∸e) duodenum.

**Zyankali** [tsy:an'ka:li], *n.* (—s, *no pl.*) potassium cyanide.

**Zyklon** [tsy'klo:n], *m.* (—s, *pl.* —e) cyclone.

**Zyklus** ['tsyklus], *m.* (—, *pl.* Zyklen) cycle; course, series.

**zylinderförmig** [tsy'lɪndərfœrmɪç], *adj.* cylindric(al).

**Zylinderhut** [tsy'lɪndərhu:t], *m.* (—s, *pl.* ∸e) top-hat, silk-hat.

**zylindrisch** [tsy'lɪndrɪʃ], *adj.* cylindric(al).

**Zyniker** ['tsy:nɪkər], *m.* (—s, *pl.* —) cynic.

**zynisch** ['tsy:nɪʃ], *adj.* cynical.

**Zynismus** [tsy'nɪsmus], *m.* (—, *no pl.*) cynicism.

**Zypern** ['tsy:pərn], *n.* Cyprus.

**Zypresse** [tsy'prɛsə], *f.* (—, *pl.* —n) (*Bot.*) cypress.

# Cassell's English-German Dictionary

# A

**A** [ei]. das A (*also Mus.*).

**a** [ə, ei] (**an** [ən, æn] *before vowel or silent* h), *indef. art.* ein, eine, ein; *two at a time*, zwei auf einmal; *many a*, mancher; *two shillings a pound*, zwei Schilling das Pfund.

**abacus** ['æbəkəs], *s.* das Rechenbrett.

**abandon** [ə'bændən], *v.a.* (*give up*) aufgeben; (*forsake*) verlassen; (*surrender*) preisgeben.

**abandonment** [ə'bændənmənt], *s.* das Verlassen (*active*); das Verlassensein (*passive*); die Wildheit, das Sichgehenlassen.

**abasement** [ə'beismənt], *s.* die Demütigung, Erniedrigung.

**abash** [ə'bæʃ], *v.a.* beschämen.

**abate** [ə'beit], *v.n.* nachlassen.

**abbess** ['æbes], *s.* die Äbtissin.

**abbey** ['æbi], *s.* die Abtei.

**abbot** ['æbət], *s.* der Abt.

**abbreviate** [ə'bri:vieit], *v.a.* abkürzen.

**abbreviation** [əbri:vi'eiʃən], *s.* die Abkürzung.

**abdicate** ['æbdikeit], *v.a., v.n.* entsagen (*Dat.*), abdanken.

**abdomen** [æb'doumən, 'æbdəmən], *s.* (*Anat.*) der Unterleib, Bauch.

**abdominal** [æb'dɔminəl], *adj.* (*Anat.*) Bauch-, Unterleibs-.

**abduct** [æb'dʌkt], *v.a.* entführen.

**abed** [ə'bed], *adv.* zu Bett, im Bett.

**aberration** [æbə'reiʃən], *s.* die Abirrung; die Verirrung; (*Phys.*) die Strahlenbrechung.

**abet** [ə'bet], *v.a.* helfen (*Dat.*), unterstützen.

**abeyance** [ə'beiəns], *s.* die Unentschiedenheit, (der Zustand der) Ungewißheit; *in* —, unentschieden.

**abhor** [əb'hɔː], *v.a.* verabscheuen.

**abhorrence** [əb'hɔrəns], *s.* die Abscheu (*of*, vor, *Dat.*).

**abhorrent** [əb'hɔrənt], *adj.* widerlich, ekelhaft.

**abide** [ə'baid], *v.n. irr.* bleiben, verweilen; (*last*) dauern. — *v.a.* aushalten.

**ability** [ə'biliti], *s.* die Fähigkeit, Tüchtigkeit; (*pl.*) die Geisteskräfte, *f. pl.*

**abject** ['æbdʒekt], *adj.* elend; (*submissive*) unterwürfig, verächtlich.

**ablaze** [ə'bleiz], *adj., adv.* in Flammen.

**able** [eibl], *adj.* fähig; (*clever*) geschickt; (*efficient*) tüchtig.

**ablution** [ə'blu:ʃən], *s.* die Abwaschung, Waschung.

**abnormal** [æb'nɔːməl], *adj.* abnorm, ungewöhnlich.

**abnormality** [æbnɔː'mæliti], *s.* die Ungewöhnlichkeit.

**aboard** [ə'bɔːd], *adv.* an Bord.

**abode** [ə'boud], *s.* der Wohnsitz, Wohnort.

**abolish** [ə'bɔliʃ], *v.a.* aufheben, abschaffen.

**abolition** [æbo'liʃən], *s.* die Abschaffung, Aufhebung.

**abominable** [ə'bɔminəbl], *adj.* abscheulich, scheußlich.

**abominate** [ə'bɔmineit], *v.a.* verabscheuen.

**abomination** [əbɔmi'neiʃən], *s.* der Abscheu, Greuel.

**aboriginal** [æbə'ridʒinəl], *adj.* eingeboren, einheimisch. — *s.* der Eingeborene.

**aborigines** [æbə'ridʒini:z], *s. pl.* die Eingeborenen, Ureinwohner.

**abortion** [ə'bɔːʃən], *s.* die Fehlgeburt; die Abtreibung.

**abortive** [ə'bɔːtiv], *adj.* mißlungen.

**abound** [ə'baund], *v.n.* wimmeln von (*Dat.*).

**about** [ə'baut], *prep.* um; (*toward*) gegen; *about 3 o'clock*, gegen drei; (*concerning*) über, betreffend. — *adv.* umher, herum; (*round*) rund herum; (*nearly*) etwa, ungefähr; (*everywhere*) überall; *to be* — *to*, im Begriffe sein *or* stehen zu …

**above** [ə'bʌv], *prep.* über; — *all things*, vor allen Dingen; *this is* — *me*, das ist mir zu hoch; — *board*, offen, ehrlich. — *adv.* oben, darüber, *over and* —, obendrein; —*mentioned*, obenerwähnt.

**abrade** [ə'breid], *v.a.* abschaben, abschürfen.

**abrasion** [ə'breiʒən], *s.* die Abschürfung; Abnutzung.

**abreast** [ə'brest], *adj., adv.* nebeneinander, Seite an Seite; *keep* —, (sich) auf dem Laufenden halten; Schritt halten (mit).

**abridge** [ə'bridʒ], *v.a.* (ab)kürzen.

**abridgement** [ə'bridʒmənt], *s.* die (Ab)kürzung; (*book etc.*) der Auszug.

**abroad** [ə'brɔːd], *adv.* im Ausland, auswärts; *to go* —, ins Ausland reisen.

**abrogate** ['æbrogeit], *v.a.* abschaffen.

**abrogation** [æbro'geiʃən], *s.* (*Pol.*) die Abschaffung.

**abrupt** [ə'brʌpt], *adj.* plötzlich; (*curt*) schroff; kurz; jäh.

**abruptness** [ə'brʌptnis], *s.* (*speech*) die Schroffheit; (*suddenness*) die Plötzlichkeit; (*drop*) die Steilheit.

**abscess** ['æbses], *s.* das Geschwür, die Schwellung, der Abszeß.

# abscond

**abscond** [əb'skɔnd], *v.n.* sich davon-machen.

**absence** ['æbsəns], *s.* die Abwesenheit; *leave of* —, der Urlaub.

**absent** (1) ['æbsənt], *adj.* abwesend; — *minded*, zerstreut.

**absent** (2) [æb'sent], *v.r.* — *oneself*, fehlen, fernbleiben; (*go away*) sich entfernen.

**absentee** [æbsən'ti:], *s.* der Abwesende.

**absolute** ['æbsəlu:t], *adj.* absolut, un-umschränkt.

**absolve** [əb'zɔlv], *v.a.* freisprechen (*from*, von), lossprechen, entbinden.

**absorb** [əb'sɔ:b], *v.a.* absorbieren, aufsaugen; (*attention*) in Anspruch nehmen.

**absorbed** [əb'sɔ:bd], *adj.* versunken.

**absorbent** [əb'sɔ:bənt], *adj.* absorbie-rend.

**absorption** [əb'sɔ:pʃən], *s.* (*Chem.*) die Absorption; (*attention*) das Versun-kensein.

**abstain** [əb'stein], *v.n.* sich enthalten; — *from voting*, sich der Stimme enthalten.

**abstainer** [əb'steinə], *s.* der Abstinenz-ler, Antialkoholiker.

**abstemious** [əb'sti:miəs], *adj.* enthalt-sam.

**abstention** [əb'stenʃən], *s.* die Enthaltung.

**abstinence** ['æbstinəns], *s.* die Ent-haltsamkeit, das Fasten (*food*).

**abstract** [æb'strækt], *v.a.* abstrahieren, abziehen; (*summarize*) kürzen, aus-ziehen.—['æbstrækt], *adj.* abstrakt; (*Maths.*) rein. — *s.* der Auszug, Abriß (*of article, book, etc.*).

**abstracted** [æb'stræktid], *adj.* zerstreut, geistesabwesend.

**abstraction** [æb'strækʃən], *s.* die Ab-straktion; der abstrakte Begriff.

**abstruse** [æb'stru:s], *adj.* schwerver-ständlich, tiefsinnig.

**absurd** [əb'sə:d], *adj.* absurd, töricht; (*unreasonable*) unvernünftig, gegen alle Vernunft; (*laughable*) lächerlich.

**absurdity** [əb'sə:diti], *s.* die Torheit, Unvernünftigkeit.

**abundance** [ə'bʌndəns], *s.* die Fülle, der Überfluß.

**abundant** [ə'bʌndənt], *adj.* reichlich.

**abuse** [ə'bju:z], *v.a.* mißbrauchen; (*insult*) beschimpfen; (*violate*) schän-den.—[ə'bju:s], *s.* der Mißbrauch; (*language*) die Beschimpfung; (*vio-lation*) die Schändung.

**abusive** [ə'bju:siv], *adj.* (*language*) grob; schimpfend, schmähend.

**abut** [ə'bʌt], *v.n.* anstoßen, angrenzen.

**abysmal** [ə'bizməl], *adj.* bodenlos.

**abyss** [ə'bis], *s.* der Abgrund, Schlund.

**Abyssinian** [æbi'sinjən], *adj.* abes-sinisch. — *s.* der Abessinier.

**acacia** [ə'keiʃə], *s.* (*Bot.*) die Akazie.

**academic** [ækə'demik], *adj.* akademisch. — *s.* der Akademiker.

**academy** [ə'kædəmi], *s.* die Akademie.

**acajon** ['ækəʒu:], *s.* (*Bot.*) der Nieren-baum.

**accede** [æk'si:d], *v.n.* beistimmen; ein-willigen; — *to the throne*, den Thron besteigen.

**accelerate** [æk'seləreit], *v.a.* beschleu-nigen. — *v.n.* schneller fahren.

**acceleration** [ækselə'reiʃən], *s.* die Beschleunigung.

**accelerator** [æk'seləreitə], *s.* (*Motor.*) der Gashebel, das Gaspedal.

**accent** (1), **accentuate** [æk'sent, æk-'sentjueit], *v.a.* akzentuieren, betonen.

**accent** (2), ['æksənt], *s.* (*Phon.*) der Ton, Wortton, die Betonung; der Akzent (*dialect*), die Aussprache.

**accentuation** [æksentju'eiʃən], *s.* die Aussprache, Akzentuierung, Beto-nung.

**accept** [æk'sept], *v.a.* annehmen.

**acceptable** [æk'septəbl], *adj.* angenehm, annehmbar, annehmlich.

**acceptance** [æk'septəns], *s.* die An-nahme; (*Comm.*) das Akzept.

**access** ['ækses], *s.* der Zugang, Zutritt.

**accessible** [æk'sesibl], *adj.* erreichbar, zugänglich.

**accession** [æk'seʃən], *s.* der Zuwachs; — *to the throne*, die Thronbesteigung.

**accessory** [æk'sesəri], *adj.* zugehörig; hinzukommend; (*subsidiary*) nebensächlich. — *s.* (*Law*) der Mitschuldige; (*pl.*) das Zubehör.

**accidence** ['æksidəns], *s.* (*Gram.*) die Flexionslehre.

**accident** ['æksidənt], *s.* (*chance*) der Zufall; (*mishap*) der Unfall, Unglücks-fall.

**accidental** [æksi'dentəl], *adj.* zufällig; (*inessential*) unwesentlich; durch Un-fall.

**acclaim** [ə'kleim], *v.a.* akklamieren, mit Beifall aufnehmen. — *v.n.* zujubeln. — *s.* der Beifall.

**acclamation** [æklə'meiʃən], *s.* der Beifall, Zuruf.

**acclimatize** [ə'klaimətaiz], *v.a.*, *v.r.* akklimatisieren; sich anpassen, einge-wöhnen.

**accommodate** [ə'kɔmədeit], *v.a.* (*adapt*) anpassen; (*lodge*) unter-bringen, beherbergen, aufnehmen; einem aushelfen; (*with money*) jeman-dem Geld leihen. — *v.r.* — *oneself to*, sich an etwas anpassen, sich in etwas fügen.

**accommodating** [ə'kɔmədeitiŋ], *adj.* gefällig, entgegenkommend.

**accommodation** [əkɔmə'deiʃən], *s.* (*adaptation*) die Anpassung; (*dispute*) die Beilegung; (*room*) die Unterkunft.

**accompaniment** [ə'kʌmpənimənt], *s.* die Begleitung.

**accompany** [ə'kʌmpəni], *v.a.* begleiten.

**accomplice** [ə'kʌmplis *or* ə'kɔmplis], *s.* der Komplize, Mitschuldige, Mit-täter.

**accomplish** [ə'kʌmpliʃ *or* ə'kɔmpliʃ], *v.a.* vollenden, zustandebringen, voll-bringen; (*objective*) erreichen.

**accomplished** [ə'kʌmpliʃd *or* ə'kɔm-pliʃd], *adj.* vollendet.

# actual

**accomplishment** [ə'kʌmpliʃmənt *or* ə'kɔmpliʃmənt], *s.* (*of project*) die Ausführung; (*of task*) die Vollendung; (*of prophecy*) die Erfüllung; (*pl.*) die Talente, *n. pl.*, Gaben, Kenntnisse, *f. pl.*

**accord** [[ə'kɔːd], *s.* (*agreement*) die Übereinstimmung; (*unison*) die Eintracht. — *v.n.* übereinstimmen (*with,* mit). — *v.a.* bewilligen.

**accordance** [ə'kɔːdəns], *s.* die Übereinstimmung.

**according** [ə'kɔːdiŋ], *prep.* — *to,* gemäß, nach, laut.

**accordingly** [ə'kɔːdiŋli], *adv.* demgemäß, demnach, folglich.

**accordion** [ə'kɔːdiən], *s.* (*Mus.*) die Ziehharmonika, das Akkordeon.

**accost** [ə'kɔst], *v.a.* ansprechen, anreden.

**account** [ə'kaunt], *s.* die Rechnung; (*report*) der Bericht; (*narrative*) die Erzählung; (*importance*) die Bedeutung; (*Fin.*) das Konto, Guthaben; *cash* —, die Kassenrechnung; *on no* —, auf keinen Fall; *on his* —, seinetwegen, um seinetwillen; *on* — *of,* wegen (*Genit.*); *on that* —, darum; *of no* —, unbedeutend. — *v.n.* — *for,* Rechenschaft ablegen über (*Acc.*); (*explain*) erklären.

**accountable** [ə'kauntəbl], *adj.* verrechenbar (*item*); verantwortlich (*person*).

**accountant** [ə'kauntənt], *s.* der Bücherrevisor, Rechnungsführer; *junior* —, der Buchhalter.

**accredit** [ə'kredit], *v.a.* akkreditieren, beglaubigen; (*authorize*) ermächtigen, bevollmächtigen.

**accretion** [ə'kriːʃən], *s.* der Zuwachs.

**accrue** [ə'kruː], *v.n.* (*Comm.*) zuwachsen, erwachsen, zufallen.

**accumulate** [ə'kjuːmjuleit], *v.a., v.n.* anhäufen; sich anhäufen, zunehmen, sich ansammeln.

**accumulation** [əkjuːmju'leiʃən], *s.* die Ansammlung, Anhäufung.

**accuracy** ['ækjurəsi], *s.* die Genauigkeit.

**accurate** ['ækjurit], *adj.* genau, richtig.

**accursed** [ə'kɔːsid], *adj.* verflucht, verwünscht.

**accusation** [ækju'zeiʃən], *s.* die Anklage.

**accusative** [ə'kjuːzətiv], *s.* (*Gram.*) der Akkusativ.

**accuse** [ə'kjuːz], *v.a.* anklagen, beschuldigen (*of, Genit.*).

**accustom** [ə'kʌstəm], *v.a.* gewöhnen (*to,* an, *Acc.*).

**ace** [eis], *s.* (*Cards*) das As, die Eins.

**acerbity** [ə'sɔːbiti], *s.* die Rauheit, Herbheit; (*manner*) die Grobheit.

**acetate** ['æsiteit], *s.* das Azetat; essigsaures Salz.

**acetic** [ə'siːtik, ə'setik], *adj.* essigsauer.

**acetylene** [ə'setiliːn], *s.* das Azetylen.

**ache** [eik], *s.* der Schmerz. — *v.n.* schmerzen, weh(e)tun.

**achieve** [ə'tʃiːv], *v.a.* erreichen, erlangen; (*accomplish*) vollenden; (*perform*) ausführen; (*gain*) erlangen, erwerben.

**achievement** [ə'tʃiːvmənt], *s.* (*accomplishment*) die Leistung, der Erfolg; die Errungenschaft; (*gain*) die Erwerbung.

**achromatic** [ækro'mætik], *adj.* achromatisch, farblos.

**acid** ['æsid], *adj.* sauer, scharf. — *s.* (*Chem.*) die Säure.

**acidulated** [ə'sidjuleitid], *adj.* (*Chem.*) angesäuert.

**acknowledge** [æk'nɔlidʒ], *v.a.* anerkennen; (*admit*) zugeben; (*confess*) bekennen; (*letter*) den Empfang bestätigen.

**acknowledgement** [æk'nɔlidʒmənt], *s.* die Anerkennung, (*receipt*) Bestätigung, Quittung; (*pl.*) die Dankesbezeigung; die Erkenntlichkeit.

**acme** ['ækmi], *s.* der Gipfel, Höhepunkt.

**acorn** ['eikɔːn], *s.* (*Bot.*) die Eichel.

**acoustics** [ə'kuːstiks], *s. pl.* die Akustik; (*subject, study*) die Schallehre.

**acquaint** [ə'kweint], *v.a.* bekanntmachen; (*inform*) mitteilen (*Dat.*), informieren; unterrichten.

**acquaintance** [ə'kweintəns], *s.* die Bekanntschaft; der Bekannte, die Bekannte (*person*); die Kenntnis (*with,* von).

**acquiesce** [ækwi'es], *v.n.* einwilligen, sich fügen.

**acquiescence** [ækwi'esəns], *s.* die Einwilligung (*in,* in, *Acc.*), Zustimmung (*in,* zu, *Dat.*).

**acquiescent** [ækwi'esənt], *adj.* fügsam.

**acquire** [ə'kwaiə], *v.a.* erlangen, erwerben; (*language*) erlernen.

**acquisition** [ækwi'ziʃən], *s.* die Erlangung, Erwerbung.

**acquit** [ə'kwit], *v.a.* freisprechen.

**acre** ['eikə], *s.* der Acker (*appr.* 0.4 Hektar).

**acrid** ['ækrid], *adj.* scharf, beißend.

**acrimonious** [ækri'mouniəs], *adj.* scharf, bitter.

**across** [ə'krɔs, ə'krɔːs], *adv.* kreuzweise, (quer) hinüber. — *prep.* quer durch, über; *come* —, (zufällig) treffen; *come* — *a problem,* auf ein Problem stoßen.

**act** [ækt], *s.* (*deed*) die Tat; (*Theat.*) der Akt; (*Parl. etc.*) die Akte. — *v.a.* (*Theat.*) spielen. — *v.n.* handeln (*do something*); sich benehmen *or* tun, als ob (*act as if, pretend*); (*Theat.*) spielen; (*Chem.*) wirken (*react*).

**action** ['ækʃən], *s.* die Handlung (*play, deed*); Wirkung (*effect*); (*Law*) der Prozeß; der Gang.

**active** ['æktiv], *adj.* (*person, Gram.*) aktiv; tätig; rührig (*industrious*); wirksam (*effective*).

**activity** [æk'tiviti], *s.* die Tätigkeit; (*Chem.*) Wirksamkeit.

**actor** ['æktə], *s.* der Schauspieler.

**actress** ['æktrəs], die Schauspielerin.

**actual** ['æktjuəl], *adj.* tatsächlich, wirklich.

# actuality

**actuality** [æktju'æliti], *s.* die Wirklichkeit.
**actuary** ['æktjuəri], *s.* der Aktuar, Versicherungsbeamte.
**actuate** ['æktjueit], *v.a.* betreiben, in Bewegung setzen.
**acuity** [ə'kju:iti], *s.* der Scharfsinn (*mind*), die Schärfe (*vision etc.*).
**acute** [ə'kju:t], *adj.* scharf, scharfsinnig (*mind*); spitz (*angle*); fein (*sense*); — *accent*, der Akut.
**adage** ['ædidʒ], *s.* das Sprichwort.
**adamant** ['ædəmənt], *adj.* sehr hart, unerbittlich (*inexorable*).
**adapt** [ə'dæpt], *v.a.* anpassen, angleichen; bearbeiten.
**adaptable** [ə'dæptəbl], *adj.* anpassungsfähig.
**adaptation** [ædæp'teiʃən], *s.* die Anpassung, die Bearbeitung (*of book*).
**adaptive** [ə'dæptiv], *adj.* anpassungsfähig.
**add** [æd], *v.a.* hinzufügen, (*Maths.*) addieren.
**adder** ['ædə], *s.* (*Zool.*) die Natter.
**addict** ['ædikt], *s.* der Süchtige.
**addiction** [ə'dikʃən], *s.* die Sucht.
**addicted** [ə'diktid], *adj.* verfallen.
**addition** [ə'diʃən], *s.* die Hinzufügung, Zugabe, (*Maths.*) Addition.
**additional** [ə'diʃənəl], *adj.* zusätzlich, nachträglich.
**address** [ə'dres], *s.* die Anschrift, Adresse (*letter*); die Ansprache (*speech*). — *v.a.* (*letter*) adressieren, richten an (*Acc.*).
**addressee** [ædre'si:], *s.* der Adressat, der Empfänger.
**adduce** [ə'dju:s], *v.a.* anführen (*proof, Beweis*).
**adenoid** ['ædinɔid], *s.* (*usually pl.*) (*Med.*) die Wucherung.
**adept** ['ædept], *adj.* geschickt, erfahren.
**adequacy** ['ædikwəsi], *s.* die Angemessenheit, das Gewachsensein, die Zulänglichkeit.
**adequate** ['ædikwət], *adj.* gewachsen (*Dat.*); angemessen, hinreichend (*sufficient*).
**adhere** [əd'hiə], *v.n.* haften, anhängen; — *to one's opinion*, bei seiner Meinung bleiben.
**adherence** [əd'hiərəns], *s.* das Festhalten (an, *Dat.*).
**adhesion** [əd'hi:ʒən], *s.* (*Phys.*) die Adhäsion; das Anhaften.
**adhesive** [əd'hi:ziv], *adj.* haftend, klebrig; — *plaster*, das Heftpflaster.
**adipose** ['ædipous], *adj.* fett, feist.
**adjacent** [ə'dʒeisənt], *adj.* naheliegend, benachbart, angrenzend.
**adjective** ['ædʒəktiv], *s.* (*Gram.*) das Adjektiv; Eigenschaftswort.
**adjoin** [ə'dʒɔin], *v.a.* anstoßen, angrenzen.
**adjourn** [ə'dʒə:n], *v.a.* vertagen, aufschieben.
**adjudicate** [ə'dʒu:dikeit], *v.a.* beurteilen, richten.
**adjunct** ['ædʒʌŋkt], *s.* der Zusatz.

**adjust** [ə'dʒʌst], *v.a.* ordnen; (*adapt*) anpassen; regulieren, einstellen.
**adjustable** [ə'dʒʌstəbl], *adj.* verstellbar, einstellbar.
**adjustment** [ə'dʒʌstmənt], *s.* die Einstellung, Anpassung; (*Law*) Schlichtung; Berichtigung.
**administer** [əd'ministə], *v.a.* verwalten (*an enterprise*); verabreichen (*medicine*); abnehmen (*an oath*, einen Eid).
**administration** [ədminis'treiʃən], *s.* die Verwaltung, Regierung; die Darreichung (*sacraments*).
**administrative** [əd'ministrətiv], *adj.* Verwaltungs-; verwaltend.
**admirable** ['ædmirəbl], *adj.* bewundernswert.
**admiral** ['ædmirəl], *s.* der Admiral.
**Admiralty** ['ædmirəlti], *s.* die Admiralität.
**admiration** [ædmi'reiʃən], *s.* die Bewunderung.
**admire** [əd'maiə], *v.a.* bewundern, verehren.
**admirer** [əd'maiərə], *s.* der Bewunderer, Verehrer.
**admissible** [əd'misibl], *adj.* zulässig.
**admission** [əd'miʃən], *s.* die Zulassung; (*entry*) der Eintritt; Zutritt; (*confession*) das Eingeständnis, Zugeständnis.
**admit** [əd'mit], *v.a.* zulassen; aufnehmen; zugeben (*deed*); gelten lassen (*argument*).
**admittance** [əd'mitəns], *s.* der Zugang, Eintritt, Zutritt.
**admixture** [əd'mikstʃə], *s.* die Beimischung, Beigabe.
**admonish** [əd'mɔniʃ], *v.a.* ermahnen, mahnen, warnen.
**admonition** [ædmə'niʃən], *s.* die Ermahnung, Warnung.
**ado** [ə'du:], *s.* der Lärm, das Tun, das Treiben; *without further* —, ohne weiteres.
**adolescence** [ædo'lesəns], *s.* die Adoleszenz, Jugend, Jugendzeit.
**adolescent** [ædo'lesənt], *s.* der Jugendliche. — *adj.* jugendlich.
**adopt** [ə'dɔpt], *v.a.* (*Law*) annehmen, adoptieren.
**adoption** [ə'dɔpʃən], *s.* (*Law*) die Annahme, Adoption.
**adoptive** [ə'dɔptiv], *adj.* Adoptiv-, angenommen.
**adorable** [ə'dɔ:rəbl], *adj.* anbetungswürdig; (*coll.*) wunderbar, schön.
**adoration** [ædo'reiʃən], *s.* die Anbetung.
**adore** [ə'dɔ:], *v.a.* anbeten; verehren.
**adorn** [ə'dɔ:n], *v.a.* (aus)schmücken, zieren.
**Adriatic (Sea)** [eidri'ætik (si:)]. *das* adriatische Meer.
**adrift** [ə'drift], *adv.* treibend; *cut o.s.* —, sich absondern.
**adroit** [ə'drɔit], *adj.* gewandt, geschickt.
**adroitness** [ə'drɔitnis], *s.* die Gewandtheit, die Geschicklichkeit.

304

**adulation** [ædju'leiʃən], *s.* die Schmeichelei.

**adulator** ['ædjuleitə], *s.* der Schmeichler.

**adulatory** ['ædjuleitəri], *adj.* schmeichlerisch.

**adult** [ə'dʌlt *or* 'ædʌlt], *adj.* erwachsen. — *s.* der Erwachsene.

**adulterate** [ə'dʌltəreit], *v.a.* verfälschen; verwässern.

**adulterer** [ə'dʌltərə], *s.* der Ehebrecher.

**adultery** [ə'dʌltəri], *s.* der Ehebruch.

**adumbrate** [ə'dʌmbreit *or* 'æd-], *v.a.* skizzieren, entwerfen, andeuten.

**advance** [əd'vɑ:ns], *v.a.* fördern (*a cause*); vorschießen (*money*); geltend machen (*claim*). — *v.n.* vorrücken, vorstoßen; (*make progress, gain promotion*) aufsteigen. — *s.* der Fortschritt (*progress*); der Vorschuß (*money*); *in* —, im voraus.

**advancement** [əd'vɑ:nsmənt], *s.* der Fortschritt (*progress*), der Aufstieg, die Beförderung (*promotion*); die Förderung (*of a cause*).

**advantage** [əd'vɑ:ntidʒ], *s.* der Vorteil, Nutzen; (*superiority*) die Überlegenheit.

**Advent** ['ædvent]. (*Eccl.*) der Advent.

**advent** ['ædvənt], *s.* die Ankunft.

**adventitious** [ædven'tiʃəs], *adj.* zufällig.

**adventure** [əd'ventʃə], *s.* das Abenteuer. — *v.n.* auf Abenteuer ausgehen, wagen.

**adventurer** [əd'ventʃərə], *s.* der Abenteurer.

**adventurous** [əd'ventʃərəs], *adj.* abenteuerlich, unternehmungslustig.

**adverb** ['ædvə:b], *s.* (*Gram.*) das Adverb(ium), Umstandswort.

**adverbial** [əd'və:biəl], *adj.* adverbial.

**adversary** ['ædvəsəri], *s.* der Gegner, Widersacher.

**adverse** ['ædvə:s], *adj.* widrig, feindlich, ungünstig.

**adversity** [əd'və:siti], *s.* das Unglück, Mißgeschick; *in* —, im Unglück.

**advert** [əd'və:t], *v.n.* hinweisen.

**advertise** ['ædvətaiz], *v.a.* anzeigen, annoncieren (*in press*), Reklame machen.

**advertisement** [əd'və:tizmənt], *s.* die Anzeige, Annonce; Reklame.

**advertiser** ['ædvətaizə], *s.* der Anzeiger.

**advice** [əd'vais], *s.* der Rat, Ratschlag; die Nachricht (*information*).

**advise** [əd'vaiz], *v.a.* raten (*Dat.*), beraten; benachrichtigen (*inform*); verständigen.

**advisable** [əd'vaizəbl], *adj.* ratsam.

**advisedly** [əd'vaizidli], *adv.* absichtlich, mit Bedacht.

**adviser** [əd'vaizə], *s.* der Berater.

**advisory** [əd'vaizəri], *adj.* beratend, ratgebend, Rats-.

**advocacy** ['ædvəkəsi], *s.* (*Law*) die Verteidigung; die Fürsprache (*championing of*, für, *Acc.*); die Vertretung (*of view*).

**Aegean (Sea)** [i:'dʒi:ən (si:)]. das ägäische Meer.

**aerated** ['εəreitid], *adj.* kohlensauer.

**aerial** ['εəriəl], *s.* (*Rad.*) die Antenne. — *adj.* luftig, Luft-.

**aerie** ['εəri, 'iəri], *s. see* **eyrie**.

**aerodrome** ['εərodroum], *s.* der Flugplatz, Flughafen.

**aeronautical** [εərə'nɔ:tikəl], *adj.* aeronautisch.

**aeronautics** [εərə'nɔ:tiks], *s. pl.* die Aeronautik, Luftfahrt.

**aeroplane**, (*Am.*) **airplane** ['εəroplein, 'εərplein], *s.* das Flugzeug.

**aesthetic(al)** [i:s'θetik(əl)], *adj.* ästhetisch.

**aesthetics** [i:s'θetiks], *s.* die Ästhetik.

**afar** [ə'fɑ:], *adv.* fern, weit entfernt; *from* —, von weitem, (von) weit her.

**affability** [æfə'biliti], *s.* die Leutseligkeit, Freundlichkeit.

**affable** ['æfəbl], *adj.* freundlich, leutselig.

**affair** [ə'fεə], *s.* die Affäre; die Angelegenheit (*matter*); das Anliegen (*concern*).

**affect** [ə'fekt], *v.a.* beeinflußen; rühren; wirken auf; vortäuschen (*pretend*); zur Schau tragen (*exhibit*).

**affectation** [æfek'teiʃən], *s.* die Ziererei, das Affektieren, die Affektiertheit.

**affected** [ə'fektid], *adj.* affektiert, gekünstelt, geziert; befallen, angegriffen (*illness*).

**affection** [ə'fekʃən], *s.* die Zuneigung, Zärtlichkeit.

**affectionate** [ə'fekʃənit], *adj.* zärtlich, liebevoll; (*in letters*) *yours* —*ly*, herzlichst.

**affinity** [ə'finiti], *s.* (*Chem.*) die Affinität; die Verwandtschaft (*relationship*).

**affirm** [ə'fə:m], *v.a.* behaupten, bestätigen, versichern; bekräftigen (*confirm*).

**affirmation** [æfə'meiʃən], *s.* die Behauptung, Bekräftigung.

**affirmative** [ə'fə:mətiv], *adj.* bejahend, positiv; *in the* —, bejahend.

**affix** [ə'fiks], *v.a.* anheften, aufkleben (*stick*); anbringen (*join to*, an, *Acc.*).

**afflict** [ə'flikt], *v.a.* quälen, plagen.

**affliction** [ə'flikʃən], *s.* die Plage, Qual; das Mißgeschick; die Not; das Leiden.

**affluence** ['æfluəns], *s.* der Überfluß (*abundance*); der Reichtum.

**affluent** ['æfluənt], *adj.* reich, wohlhabend. — *s.* der Nebenfluß (*tributary*).

**afford** [ə'fɔ:d], *v.a.* geben, bieten; (*sich*) leisten (*have money for*); gewähren (*give*); hervorbringen (*yield*).

**afforest** [ə'fɔrist], *v.a.* aufforsten.

**affray** [ə'frei], *s.* die Schlägerei.

**African** ['æfrikən], *adj.* afrikanisch. — *s.* der Afrikaner.

**affront** [ə'frʌnt], *s.* die Beleidigung. — *v.a.* beleidigen.

**Afghan** ['æfgæn], *adj.* afghanisch. — *s.* der Afghane.

**afield** [ə'fi:ld], *adj.*, *adv.* im Felde; weit umher; weit weg.

**afire** [ə'faiə], *adv.*, *adv.* in Flammen.

# aflame

aflame [ə'fleim], *adj.*, *adv.* in Flammen.
afloat [ə'flout], *adj.*, *adv.* schwimmend, dahintreibend.
afoot [ə'fut], *adj.*, *adv.* im Gange.
afore [ə'fɔ:], *adv.* vorher.
aforesaid [ə'fɔːsed], *adj.* the —, das Obengesagte, der Vorhergenannte.
afraid [ə'freid], *adj.* ängstlich, furchtsam; *be* —, fürchten (*of s.th.*, etwas, *Acc.*); sich fürchten.
afresh [ə'freʃ], *adv.* von neuem.
aft [ɑːft], *adv.* (*Naut.*) achtern.
after [ɑːftə], *prep.* nach (*time*); nach, hinter (*place*); *the day* — *tomorrow*, übermorgen. — *adj.* hinter, später. — *adv.* hinterher, nachher (*time*); darauf, dahinter (*place*). — *conj.* nachdem.
afternoon [ɑːftə'nuːn], *s.* der Nachmittag.
afterwards [ɑːftəwədz], *adv.* nachher, darauf hin, später.
again [ə'gein], *adv.* wieder, abermals, noch einmal; zurück (*back*); dagegen (*however*); *as much* —, noch einmal soviel; — *and* —, immer wieder.
against [ə'geinst], *prep.* gegen, wider; nahe bei (*near*, *Dat.*); bis an (*up to*, *Acc.*); — *the grain*, wider *or* gegen den Strich.
agate ['ægeit], *s.* der Achat.
agave [ə'geivi], *s.* (*Bot.*) die Agave.
age [eidʒ], *s.* das Alter (*person*); das Zeitalter (*period*); die Reife; *come of* —, volljährig werden; mündig werden; *old* —, das Greisenalter; *for* —*s*, seit einer Ewigkeit. — *v.n.* altern, alt werden.
aged ['eidʒid], *adj.* bejahrt.
agency ['eidʒənsi], *s.* die Agentur (*firm*); die Mitwirkung (*participation*); die Hilfe (*assistance*); die Vermittlung (*mediation*).
agenda [ə'dʒendə], *s.* das Sitzungsprogramm; die Tagesordnung.
agent ['eidʒənt], *s.* der Agent, Vertreter.
agglomerate [ə'glɔməreit], *v.a.* zusammenhäufen. — *v.n.* sich zusammenhäufen, sich ballen.
aggrandisement [ə'grændizmənt], *s.* die Überhebung, Übertreibung, Erweiterung.
aggravate ['ægrəveit], *v.a.* verschlimmern; ärgern.
aggravation [ægrə'veiʃən], *s.* die Verschlimmerung (*of condition*); der Ärger (*annoyance*).
aggregate ['ægrigit], *adj.* gesamt, vereinigt, vereint. — *s.* das Aggregat.
aggregation [ægri'geiʃən], *s.* (*Geol.*, *Chem.*) die Vereinigung, Anhäufung, Ansammlung.
aggression [ə'greʃən], *s.* der Angriff, Überfall.
aggressive [ə'gresiv], *adj.* aggressiv, angreifend.
aggressor [ə'gresə], *s.* der Angreifer.
aggrieve [ə'griːv], *v.a.* kränken.

aghast [ə'gɑːst], *adj.* bestürzt; sprachlos; entsetzt.
agile ['ædʒail], *adj.* behend, flink, beweglich.
agitate ['ædʒiteit], *v.a.* bewegen; beunruhigen; aufrühren; stören.
agitation [ædʒi'teiʃən], *s.* (*Pol.*) die Agitation; die Unruhe (*unrest*); der Aufruhr (*revolt*).
agitator ['ædʒiteitə], *s.* (*Pol.*) der Agitator; der Aufwiegler (*inciter*).
aglow [ə'glou], *adj.* glühend.
agnostic [æg'nɔstik], *s.* der Agnostiker.
ago [ə'gou], *adv.* vor; *long* —, vor langer Zeit; *not long* —, kürzlich; *a month* —, vor einem Monat.
agog [ə'gɔg], *adv.* erregt, gespannt, neugierig (*for*, auf, *Acc.*).
agonize ['ægənaiz], *v.a.* quälen, martern. — *v.n.* Qual erleiden; mit dem Tode ringen *or* kämpfen.
agonising ['ægənaiziŋ], *adj.* schmerzhaft, qualvoll.
agony ['ægəni], *s.* die Pein, Qual; der Todeskampf; — *column*, die Seufzerspalte.
agrarian [ə'grɛəriən], *adj.* landwirtschaftlich; *party*, die Bauernpartei.
agree [ə'griː], *v.n.* übereinstimmen (*be in agreement*); übereinkommen (*come to an agreement*), sich einigen.
agreeable [ə'griːəbl], *adj.* angenehm, gefällig.
agreement [ə'griːmənt], *s.* die Übereinstimmung, das Übereinkommen; der Vertrag, die Verständigung (*understanding*).
agricultural [ægri'kʌltʃərəl], *adj.* landwirtschaftlich.
agriculture ['ægrikʌltʃə], *s.* die Landwirtschaft.
aground [ə'graund], *adj.*, *adv.* (*Naut.*) gestrandet; *to run* —, stranden.
ague ['eigjuː], *s.* (*Med.*) der Schüttelfrost.
ah! [ɑː], *interj.* ach!; aha! (*surprise*).
aha! [ɑ'hɑː], *interj.* ach so!
ahead [ə'hed], *adv.* vorwärts, voran (*movement*), voraus (*position*), go — (*carry on*), fortfahren; go — (*make progress*), vorwärtskommen.
ahoy! [ə'hɔi], *interj.* (*Naut.*) ahoi!
aid [eid], *v.a.* helfen (*Dat.*), unterstützen (*Acc.*), beistehen (*Dat.*). — *s.* die Hilfe, der Beistand.
aide-de-camp ['eiddə'kɑ̃], *s.* der Adjutant (eines Generals).
ail [eil], *v.n.* schmerzen; krank sein.
ailing ['eiliŋ], *adj.* kränklich, leidend.
ailment ['eilmənt], *s.* das Leiden.
aim [eim], *v.a.* (*weapon*, *blow etc.*) richten (*at*, auf). — *v.n.* zielen (auf, *Acc.*); trachten (nach, *strive for*). — *s.*, das Ziel, der Zweck (*purpose*); die Absicht (*intention*).
aimless ['eimlis], *adj.* ziellos, zwecklos.

306

# allow

**air** [ɛə], *s.* die Luft; die Melodie (*tune*); die Miene (*mien*); *air force,* die Luftwaffe; *air pocket,* das Luftloch; *air raid,* der Luftangriff; *in the open —,* im Freien; *on the —,* im Rundfunk; *to give oneself —s,* vornehm tun. — *v.a.* lüften (*room*); trocknen (*washing*); aussprechen (*views*).

**airbase** ['ɛəbeis], *s.* der Fliegerstützpunkt.

**airconditioning** ['ɛəkəndiʃəniŋ], *s.* die Klimaanlage.

**aircraft** ['ɛəkrɑ:ft], *s.* das Luftfahrzeug, Flugzeug.

**airgun** ['ɛəgʌn], *s.* die Windbüchse, das Luftgewehr.

**airiness** ['ɛərinis], *s.* die Luftigkeit, Leichtigkeit.

**airletter** ['ɛələtə], *s.* der Luftpostbrief.

**airliner** ['ɛəlainə], *s.* das Verkehrsflugzeug.

**airmail** ['ɛəmeil], *s.* die Luftpost.

**airman** ['ɛəmən], *s.* der Flieger.

**airplane** *see* **aeroplane.**

**airport** ['ɛəpɔ:t], *s.* der Flughafen.

**airtight** ['ɛətait], *adj.* luftdicht.

**airy** ['ɛəri], *adj.* luftig.

**aisle** [ail], *s.* das Seitenschiff (*church*); der Gang.

**Aix-la-Chapelle** ['eikslaʃæ'pel].Aachen, *n.*

**ajar** [ə'dʒɑ:], *adv.* angelehnt, halb offen.

**akimbo** [ə'kimbou], *adv.* Hände an den Hüften, Arme in die Seiten gestemmt.

**akin** [ə'kin], *adj.* verwandt (*to,* mit, *Dat.*).

**alack** [ə'læk], *interj.* ach! oh, weh! *alas and —,* ach und wehe!

**alacrity** [ə'lækriti], *s.* die Bereitwilligkeit; Munterkeit.

**alarm** [ə'lɑ:m], *s.* der Alarm; Lärm (*noise*); die Warnung; Angst, Bestürzung; — *clock,* der Wecker. — *v.a.* erschrecken.

**alas!** [ə'læs], *interj.* ach, wehe!

**Albanian** [æl'beiniən], *adj.* albanisch. — *s.* der Albanier.

**album** ['ælbəm], *s.* das Album.

**albumen** [æl'bju:mən], *s.* das Eiweiß, (*Chem.*) der Eiweißstoff.

**albuminous** [æl'bju:minəs], *adj.* eiweißhaltig, Eiweiß-.

**alchemist** ['ælkimist], *s.* der Alchimist.

**alchemy** ['ælkəmi], *s.* die Alchimie.

**alcohol** ['ælkəhɔl], *s.* der Alkohol.

**alcoholic** [ælkə'hɔlik], *adj.* alkoholisch. — *s.* der Trinker, Alkoholiker.

**alcove** ['ælkouv], *s.* der Alkoven.

**alder** ['ɔ:ldə], *s.* (*Bot.*) die Erle.

**alderman** ['ɔ:ldəmən], *s.* der Ratsherr, der Stadtrat.

**ale** [eil], *s.* englisches Bier.

**alert** [ə'lə:t], *adj.* wachsam, aufmerksam; *on the —,* auf der Hut.

**algebra** ['ældʒibrə], *s.* die Algebra.

**Algerian** [æl'dʒiəriən], *adj.* algerisch. — *s.* der Algerier.

**Algiers** [æl'dʒiəz]. Algier, *n.*

**alias** ['eiliəs], *adv.* sonst genannt.

**alien** ['eiliən], *adj.* fremd, ausländisch. — *s.* der Fremde, Ausländer.

**alienate** ['eiliəneit], *v.a.* entfremden.

**alienation** [eiliə'neiʃən], *s.* die Entfremdung; — *of mind,* die Geisteserkrankung, Geistesgestörtheit.

**alienist** ['eiliənist], *s.* der Irrenarzt.

**alight** (1) [ə'lait], *v.n.* absteigen (*from horse*); aussteigen (*from carriage etc.*).

**alight** (2) [ə'lait], *adj.* brennend, in Flammen.

**alike** [ə'laik], *adj.* gleich, ähnlich. — *adv. great and small —,* sowohl große wie kleine.

**alimentary** [æli'mentəri], *adj.* Nahrungs-, Verdauungs-; — *canal,* (*Anat.*) der Darmkanal.

**alimentation** [ælimen'teiʃən], *s.* die Beköstigung; (*Law*) der Unterhalt.

**alimony** ['æliməni], *s.* der Unterhaltsbeitrag; (*pl.*) Alimente, *s.n.pl.*

**alive** [ə'laiv], *adj.* lebendig; — *and kicking,* wohlauf, munter; — *to,* empfänglich für.

**alkali** ['ælkəlai], *s.* (*Chem.*) das Laugensalz, Alkali.

**alkaline** ['ælkəlain], *adj.* (*Chem.*) alkalisch, laugensalzig.

**all** [ɔ:l], *adj., pron.* all, ganz (*whole*); sämtliche, alle; *above —,* vor allem; *once and for —,* ein für allemal; *not at —,* keineswegs; *All Saints,* Allerheiligen; *All Souls,* Allerseelen. — *adv.* ganz, gänzlich, völlig; — *the same,* trotzdem; — *the better,* umso besser.

**allay** [ə'lei], *v.a.* lindern, beruhigen, unterdrücken.

**allegation** [æli'geiʃən], *s.* die Behauptung.

**allege** [ə'ledʒ], *v.a.* behaupten, aussagen.

**allegiance** [ə'li:dʒəns], *s.* die Treue, Ergebenheit; Untertanenpflicht.

**allegorical** [æli'gɔrikəl], *adj.* allegorisch, sinnbildlich.

**alleviate** [ə'li:vieit], *v.a.* erleichtern, mildern.

**alleviation** [əli:vi'eiʃən], *s.* die Erleichterung, Milderung.

**alley** ['æli], *s.* die Gasse; Seitenstraße; *bowling —,* die Kegelbahn.

**alliance** [ə'laiəns], *s.* (*Pol.*) die Allianz, das Bündnis (*treaty*); der Bund (*league*).

**allied** [ə'laid, 'ælaid], *adj.* verbündet, vereinigt; alliiert; verwandt.

**alliteration** [əlitə'reiʃən], *s.* die Alliteration, der Stabreim.

**allocate** ['æləkeit], *v.a.* zuweisen, zuteilen.

**allot** [ə'lɔt], *v.a.* zuteilen (*assign*); verteilen (*distribute*).

**allotment** [ə'lɔtmənt], *s.* der Anteil; die Zuteilung; die Landparzelle; die Laubenkolonie, der Schrebergarten (*garden*).

**allow** [ə'lau], *v.a.* gewähren (*grant*); erlauben (*permit*); zulassen (*admit*). — *v.n.* — *for,* Rücksicht nehmen auf (*Acc.*); in Betracht ziehen.

**allowance** [ə′lauəns], *s.* die Rente; das Taschengeld (*money*); die Erlaubnis (*permission*); die Genehmigung (*approval*); die Nachsicht (*indulgence*).

**alloy** [ə′lɔi, ′ælɔi], *s.* die Legierung. — *v.a.* (*Metall.*) legieren.

**allude** [ə′lu:d], *v.a.* anspielen (*to,* auf).

**allure** [ə′ljuə], *v.a.* locken, anlocken.

**allurement** [ə′ljuəmənt], *s.* der Reiz, die Lockung.

**allusion** [ə′lu:ʒən], *s.* die Anspielung.

**alluvial** [ə′lu:viəl], *adj.* angeschwemmt.

**alluvium** [ə′lu:viəm], *s.* das Schwemmgebiet, Schwemmland.

**ally** [′ælai], *s.* der Verbündete, Bundesgenosse, Alliierte. — [ə′lai], *v.a.,* *v.r.* (sich) vereinigen, (sich) verbünden.

**almanac** [′ɔ:lmənæk], *s.* der Almanach.

**almighty** [ɔ:l′maiti], *adj.* allmächtig; *God Almighty!* allmächtiger Gott!

**almond** [′ɑ:mənd], *s.* (*Bot.*) die Mandel.

**almoner** [′ælmənə], *s.* der Wohlfahrtsbeamte, die Fürsorgerin.

**almost** [′ɔ:lmoust], *adv.* fast, beinahe.

**alms** [ɑ:mz], *s.* das Almosen.

**aloe** [′ælou], *s.* (*Bot.*) die Aloe.

**aloft** [ə′lɔft], *adv.* droben, (hoch) oben; empor.

**alone** [ə′loun], *adj., adv.* allein; *all* —, ganz allein; *leave* —, in Ruhe lassen; *let* —, geschweige (denn).

**along** [ə′lɔŋ], *adv.* längs, der Länge nach; entlang, weiter; *come* —*!* komm mit!; *get* — (*with*), auskommen. — *prep.* längs; entlang.

**alongside** [ələŋ′said], *adv.* nebenan. — [ə′lɔŋsaid], *prep.* neben.

**aloof** [ə′lu:f], *adj., adv.* fern, weitab; *keep* —, sich fernhalten.

**aloofness** [ə′lu:fnis], *s.* das Sichfernhalten; das Vornehmtun.

**aloud** [ə′laud], *adj., adv.* laut; hörbar.

**alphabet** [′ælfəbet], *s.* das Alphabet,Abc.

**Alpine** [′ælpain], *adj.* alpinisch, Alpen-.

**Alps, The** [ælps, ðil]. die Alpen, *pl.*

**already** [ɔ:l′redi], *adv.* schon, bereits.

**Alsatian** [æl′seiʃən], *adj.* elsässisch. — *s.* der Elsässer; (*dog*) der Wolfshund, deutscher Schäferhund.

**also** [′ɔ:lsou], *adv.* (*likewise*) auch, ebenfalls; (*moreover*) ferner.

**altar** [′ɔ:ltə], *s.* der Altar.

**alter** [′ɔ:ltə], *v.a.* ändern, verändern. — *v.n.* sich (ver)ändern.

**alterable** [′ɔ:ltərəbl], *adj.* veränderlich.

**alteration** [ɔ:ltə′reiʃən], *s.* die Änderung, Veränderung.

**altercation** [ɔ:ltə′keiʃən], *s.* der Zank, Streit; Wortwechsel.

**alternate** [′ɔ:ltəneit], *v.a., v.n.* abwechseln lassen, abwechseln.

**alternative** [ɔ:l′tə:nətiv], *adj.* abwechselnd, alternativ, zur Wahl gestellt. — *s.* die Alternative, die Wahl.

**although** [ɔ:l′ðou], *conj.* obgleich, obwohl, obschon.

**altimeter** [′æltimi:tə], *s.* der Höhenmesser.

**altitude** [′æltitju:d], *s.* die Höhe.

**alto** [′æltou], *s.* (*Mus.*) die Altstimme, der Alt.

**altogether** [ɔ:ltu′geðə], *adv.* zusammen, zusammengenommen, allesamt; (*wholly*) ganz und gar, durchaus.

**alum** [′æləm], *s.* (*Chem.*) der Alaun.

**aluminium** [ælju′minjəm], (*Am.*) **aluminum** [ə′lu:minəm], *s.* das Aluminium.

**always** [′ɔ:lweiz], *adv.* immer, stets.

**am** [æm] *see* **be.**

**amalgamate** [ə′mælgəmeit], *v.a.* amalgamieren. — *v.n.* sich vereinigen, vermischen.

**amalgamation** [əmælgə′meiʃən], *s.* die Verbindung, Vereinigung.

**amass** [ə′mæs], *v.a.* anhäufen, zusammentragen.

**amateur** [æmə′tə: *or* ′æmətjuə], *s.* der Amateur, Liebhaber.

**amatory** [′æmətəri], *adj.* Liebes-, verliebt, sinnlich.

**amaze** [ə′meiz], *v.a.* erstaunen, in Erstaunen versetzen; verblüffen (*baffle*).

**amazement** [ə′meizmənt], *s.* das Erstaunen, Staunen, die Verwunderung.

**amazing** [ə′meiziŋ], *adj.* erstaunlich, wunderbar.

**Amazon** (1) [′æməzən], *s.* (*Myth.*) die Amazone.

**Amazon** (2) [′æməzən], *s.* (*river*) der Amazonas.

**ambassador** [æm′bæsədə], *s.* der Botschafter.

**ambassadorial** [æmbæsə′dɔ:riəl], *adj.* Botschafts-.

**amber** [′æmbə], *s.* der Bernstein.

**ambidextrous** [æmbi′dekstrəs], *adj.* (mit beiden Händen gleich) geschickt.

**ambiguity** [æmbi′gju:iti], *s.* die Zweideutigkeit, der Doppelsinn.

**ambiguous** [æm′bigjuəs], *adj.* zweideutig; dunkel (*sense*).

**ambit** [′æmbit], *s.* der Umkreis, die Umgebung.

**ambition** [æm′biʃən], *s.* die Ambition, der Ehrgeiz.

**ambitious** [æm′biʃəs], *adj.* ehrgeizig.

**amble** [æmbl], *v.n.* schlendern, (gemächlich) spazieren.

**ambulance** [′æmbjuləns], *s.* der Krankenwagen.

**ambush** [′æmbuʃ], *v.a.* überfallen (*Acc.*), auflauern (*Dat.*). — *s.* die Falle, der Hinterhalt.

**ameliorate** [ə′mi:liəreit], *v.a.* verbessern.

**amenable** [ə′mi:nəbl], *adj.* zugänglich; unterworfen.

**amend** [ə′mend], *v.a.* verbessern, berichtigen; ändern.

**amendment** [ə′mendmənt], *s.* die Verbesserung; der Zusatz, die zusätzliche Änderung (*proviso*).

**amends** [ə′mendz], *s. pl.* der Schadenersatz; *make* —, Schadenersatz leisten; wiedergutmachen.

**amenity** [ə'mi:niti *or* ə'meniti], *s.* die Behaglichkeit, Annehmlichkeit; (*pl.*) die Vorzüge, *m pl.*; die Einrichtungen, *f, pl.*

**American** [ə'merikən], *adj.* amerikanisch; — *cloth*, das Wachstuch. — *s.* der Amerikaner.

**amiability** [eimjə'biliti], *s.* die Liebenswürdigkeit.

**amiable** ['eimjəbl], *adj.* liebenswürdig.

**amicable** ['æmikəbl], *adj.* freundschaftlich.

**amidst** [ə'midst], *prep.* mitten in, mitten unter (*Dat.*), inmitten (*Gen.*).

**amiss** [ə'mis], *adj.*, *adv.* übel; verkehrt; *take* —, übelnehmen.

**amity** ['æmiti], *s.* die Freundschaft.

**ammonia** [ə'mouniə], *s.* das Ammoniak; *liquid* —, der Salmiakgeist.

**ammunition** [æmju'niʃən], *s.* die Munition.

**amnesty** ['æmnisti], *s.* die Amnestie, Begnadigung.

**among(st)** [ə'mʌŋ(st)], *prep.* (mitten) unter, zwischen, bei.

**amorous** ['æmərəs], *adj.* verliebt.

**amorphous** [ə'mɔ:fəs], *adj.* amorph, gestaltlos, formlos.

**amortization** [əmɔ:ti'zeiʃən], *s.* die Amortisierung (*debt*); (*Comm.*) Tilgung, Abtragung.

**amount** [ə'maunt], *s.* der Betrag (*sum of money*); die Menge (*quantity*). — *v.n.* betragen; — *to*, sich belaufen auf (*Acc.*).

**amphibian** [æm'fibiən], *adj.* amphibisch. — *s.* (*Zool.*) die Amphibie.

**amphibious** [æm'fibiəs], [*adj.* amphibienhaft.

**ample** ['æmpl], *adj.* weit, breit (*scope*); voll, reichlich; ausgebreitet; genügend.

**amplification** [æmplifi'keiʃən], *s.* die Ausbreitung; Verbreiterung, Erklärung, Erweiterung; (*Elec.*) die Verstärkung (*sound*).

**amplifier** ['æmplifaiə], *s.* der Verstärker; der Lautsprecher.

**amplify** ['æmplifai], *v.a.* erweitern, ausführen, vergrößern; verstärken (*sound*).

**amputate** ['æmpjuteit], *v.a.* amputieren.

**amputation** [æmpju'teiʃən], *s.* die Amputation.

**amuck** [ə'mʌk], *adv.* amok.

**amulet** ['æmjulit], *s.* das Amulett.

**amuse** [ə'mju:z], *v.a.* unterhalten, amüsieren.

**amusement** [ə'mju:zmənt], *s.* die Unterhaltung, das Vergnügen.

**an** *see under* a.

**Anabaptist** [ænə'bæptist], *s.* der Wiedertäufer.

**anachronism** [ə'nækrənizm], *s.* der Anachronismus.

**anaemia** [ə'ni:miə], *s.* (*Med.*) die Blutarmut.

**anaemic** [ə'ni:mik], *adj.* (*Med.*) blutarm.

**anaesthetic** [ænəs'θetik], *adj.* schmerzbetäubend. — *s.* die Narkose.

**analogous** [ə'næləgəs], *adj.* analog.

**analogy** [ə'nælədʒi], *s.* die Analogie.

**analyse** ['ænəlaiz], *v.a.* analysieren.

**analysis** [ə'nælisis], *s.* die Analyse.

**anarchic(al)** [ə'na:kik(əl)], *adj.* anarchisch.

**anarchy** ['ænəki], *s.* die Anarchie.

**anathema** [ə'næθimə], *s.* (*Eccl.*) der Kirchenbann.

**anatomical** [ænə'tɔmikəl], *adj.* anatomisch.

**anatomist** [ə'nætəmist], *s.* der Anatom.

**anatomize** [ə'nætəmaiz], *v.a.* zergliedern, zerlegen.

**anatomy** [ə'nætəmi], *s.* die Anatomie.

**ancestor** ['ænsəstə], *s.* der Vorfahre, Ahnherr.

**ancestry** ['ænsəstri], *s.* die Ahnenreihe, Herkunft, der Stammbaum (*family tree*).

**anchor** ['æŋkə], *s.* der Anker. — *v.a.* verankern. — *v.n.* ankern.

**anchorage** ['æŋkəridʒ], *s.* die Verankerung; der Ankerplatz.

**anchovy** [æn'tʃouvi *or* 'æntʃəvi], *s.* (*Zool.*) die Sardelle.

**ancient** ['einʃənt], *adj.* alt, uralt, antik; althergebracht (*traditional*). — *s.* (*pl.*) die Alten (Griechen und Römer).

**and** [ænd], *conj.* und.

**Andes, the** ['ændi:z, ði]. die Anden, *pl.*

**anecdote** ['ænekdout], *s.* die Anekdote.

**anemone** [ə'neməni], *s.* (*Bot.*) die Anemone, das Windröschen; (*Zool.*) *sea* —, die Seeanemone.

**anew** [ə'nju:], *adv.* von neuem.

**angel** ['eindʒəl], *s.* der Engel.

**angelic** [æn'dʒelik], *adj.* engelhaft, engelgleich.

**anger** ['æŋgə], *s.* der Zorn, Unwille, Ärger. — *v.a.* erzürnen, verärgern, ärgerlich machen.

**angle** [æŋgl], *s.* (*Geom.*) der Winkel; die Angel (*fishing*). — *v.n.* angeln (*for*, nach).

**Angles** ['æŋglz], *s. pl.* die Angeln, *m. pl.*

**Anglo-Saxon** [æŋglou'sæksən], *adj.* angelsächsisch. — *s.* der Angelsachse.

**anglicism** ['æŋglisizm], *s.* der Anglizismus (*style*).

**anguish** ['æŋgwiʃ], *s.* die Qual, Pein.

**angular** ['æŋgjulə], *adj.* winklig, eckig.

**anhydrous** [æn'haidrəs], *adj.* wasserfrei, (*Chem.*) wasserlos.

**aniline** ['ænilain], *s.* das Anilin. — *adj.* — *dye*, die Anilinfarbe.

**animal** ['æniməl], *s.* das Tier, Lebewesen.

**animate** ['ænimeit], *v.a.* beleben, beseelen; (*fig.*) anregen.

**animated** ['ænimeitid], *adj.* belebt; munter.

**animation** [æni'meiʃən], *s.* die Belebung.

**animosity** [æni'mɔsiti], *s.* die Feindseligkeit, Abneigung, Erbitterung.

**anise** ['ænis], *s.* (*Bot.*) der Anis.

ankle

**ankle** [´æŋkl], *s.* (*Anat.*) der Fußknöchel; — socks, kurze Socken.
**anklet** [´æŋklit], *s.* der Fußring.
**annalist** [´ænəlist], *s.* der Chronist, Geschichtsschreiber.
**annals** [´ænlz], *s. pl.* die Annalen (*f. pl.*); die Chronik (*sing.*).
**anneal** [ə´niːl], *v.a.* ausglühen.
**annex** [ə´neks], *v.a.* annektieren, angliedern, sich aneignen.
**annex(e)** [´æneks], *s.* der Anhang, der Anbau.
**annexation** [ænek´seiʃən], *s.* die Angliederung, Aneignung.
**annihilate** [ə´naiileit], *v.a.* vernichten, zerstören.
**annihilation** [ənaii´leiʃən], *s.* die Vernichtung, Zerstörung.
**anniversary** [æni´vəːsəri], *s.* der Jahrestag, die Jahresfeier.
**annotate** [´ænoteit], *v.a.* anmerken, mit Anmerkungen versehen.
**annotation** [æno´teiʃən], *s.* die Anmerkung, Notiz.
**announce** [ə´nauns], *v.a.* melden, ankündigen; anzeigen; (*Rad.*) ansagen.
**announcement** [ə´naunsmənt], *s.* die Ankündigung, Bekanntmachung; (*Rad.*) die Ansage.
**announcer** [ə´naunsə], *s.* (*Rad.*) der Ansager.
**annoy** [ə´nɔi], *v.a.* ärgern; belästigen.
**annoyance** [ə´nɔiəns], *s.* das Ärgernis; die Belästigung.
**annual** [´ænjuəl], *adj.* jährlich, Jahres-. — *s.* der Jahresband (*serial publication*); das Jahrbuch; (*Bot.*) die einjährige Pflanze.
**annuity** [ə´njuːiti], *s.* die Jahresrente, Lebensrente.
**annul** [ə´nʌl], *v.a.* annullieren, ungültig machen, für ungültig erklären.
**annulment** [ə´nʌlmənt], *s.* die Annullierung, Ungültigkeitserklärung.
**Annunciation** [ənʌnsi´eiʃən], *s.* (*Eccl.*) die Verkündigung.
**anode** [´ænoud], *s.* die Anode.
**anodyne** [´ænodain], *adj.* schmerzstillend.
**anoint** [ə´nɔint], *v.a.* salben.
**anomalous** [ə´nɔmələs], *adj.* abweichend, unregelmäßig, anomal.
**anomaly** [ə´nɔməli], *s.* die Anomalie, Abweichung, Unregelmäßigkeit.
**anon** [ə´nɔn], *adv.* sogleich, sofort.
**anonymous** [ə´nɔniməs], *adj.* (*abbr.* anon.) anonym; namenlos; unbekannt.
**anonymity** [æno´nimiti], *s.* die Anonymität.
**another** [ə´nʌðə], *adj. & pron.* ein anderer; ein zweiter; noch einer; one —, einander.
**answer** [´ɑːnsə], *v.a.* beantworten. — *v.n.* antworten. — *s.* die Antwort, Erwiderung.
**answerable** [´ɑːnsərəbl], *adj.* verantwortlich (*responsible*); beantwortbar (*capable of being answered*).
**ant** [ænt], *s.* (*Ent.*) die Ameise.

**antagonise** [æn´tægənaiz], *v.a.* sich (*Dat.*) jemanden zum Gegner machen.
**antagonism** [æn´tægənizm], *s.* der Widerstreit, Konflikt; der Antagonismus.
**Antarctic** [ænt´ɑːktik], *adj.* Südpol-, antarktisch. — *s.* der südliche Polarkreis.
**antecedence** [ænti´siːdəns], *s.* der Vortritt (*rank*).
**antecedent** [ænti´siːdənt], *s.* (*pl.*) das Vorhergehende, die Vorgeschichte.
**antedate** [´æntideit], *v.a.* vordatieren.
**antediluvian** [æntidi´luːviən], *adj.* vorsintflutlich; (*fig.*) überholt; altmodisch.
**antelope** [´æntiloup], *s.* (*Zool.*) die Antilope.
**antenna** [æn´tenə], *s.* (*Ent.*) der Fühler; (*Rad.*) die Antenne.
**anterior** [æn´tiəriə], *adj.* vorder (*in space*), älter, vorherig, vorhergehend, (*in time*).
**anteroom** [´æntiruːm], *s.* das Vorzimmer.
**anthem** [´ænθəm], *s.* die Hymne, der Hymnus.
**anther** [´ænθə], *s.* (*Bot.*) der Staubbeutel.
**antic** [´æntik], *s.* die Posse; (*pl.*) komisches Benehmen.
**anticipate** [æn´tisipeit], *v.a.* vorwegnehmen; zuvorkommen; ahnen (*guess*); erwarten (*await*); vorgreifen.
**anticipation** [æntisi´peiʃən], *s.* die Vorwegnahme; die Erwartung.
**antidote** [´æntidout], *s.* das Gegengift.
**antipathy** [æn´tipəθi], *s.* die Antipathie, der Widerwille.
**antipodal** [æn´tipədəl], *adj.* antipodisch; entgegengesetzt.
**antiquarian** [ænti´kwɛəriən], *adj.* altertümlich; antiquarisch.
**antiquary** [´æntikwəri], *s.* der Altertumsforscher, Antiquar.
**antiquated** [´æntikweitid], *adj.* überholt, unmodern, veraltet.
**antique** [æn´tiːk], *s.* die Antike; das alte Kunstwerk. — *adj.* alt, antik; altmodisch.
**antiquity** [æn´tikwiti], *s.* die Antike, das Altertum; die Vorzeit (*period of history*).
**antiseptic** [ænti´septik], *adj.* antiseptisch — *s.* das antiseptische Mittel.
**antler** [´æntlə], *s.* die Geweihsprosse; (*pl.*) das Geweih.
**anvil** [´ænvil], *s.* der Amboß.
**anxiety** [æn´zaiəti], *s.* die Angst (*fear*); Besorgnis (*uneasiness*); Unruhe.
**anxious** [´æŋkʃəs], *adj.* ängstlich (*afraid*); besorgt (*worried*); eifrig bemüht (*keen*, um, on, *Acc.*).
**any** [´eni], *adj. & pron.* jeder; irgendein; etwas; (*pl.*) einige; (*neg.*) not —, kein.
**anybody, anyone** [´enibɔdi, ´eniwʌn], *pron.* irgendeiner; jemand; jeder.
**anyhow, anyway** [´enihau, ´eniwei], *adv.* irgendwie, auf irgendeine Weise; auf alle Fälle.
**anyone** *see under* **anybody**.

**anything** ['eniθiŋ], s. irgend etwas; alles.

**anyway** see under **anyhow**.

**anywhere** ['enihwɛə], adv. irgendwo; überall; not —, nirgends.

**apace** [ə'peis], adv. geschwind, hurtig, flink.

**apart** [ə'pɑːt], adv. für sich, abgesondert; einzeln; poles —, weit entfernt; take —, zerlegen; — from, abgesehen von.

**apartment** [ə'pɑːtmənt], s. das Zimmer; (Am.) die Wohnung (flat).

**apathy** ['æpəθi], s. die Apathie, Interesselosigkeit, Gleichgültigkeit.

**apathetic** [æpə'θetik], adj. apathisch, uninteressiert; teilnahmslos.

**ape** [eip], s. (Zool.) der Affe. — v.a. nachäffen, nachahmen.

**aperient** [ə'piəriənt], adj. (Med.) abführend. — s. (Med.) das Abführmittel.

**aperture** ['æpətʃə], s. die Öffnung.

**apex** ['eipeks], s. die Spitze, der Gipfel.

**aphorism** ['æfərizm], s. der Aphorismus.

**apiary** ['eipiəri], s. das Bienenhaus.

**apiece** [ə'piːs], adv. pro Stück, pro Person.

**apologetic** [əpɔlə'dʒetik], adj. entschuldigend, reumütig; verteidigend.

**apologize** [ə'pɔlədʒaiz], v.n. sich entschuldigen (for, wegen; to, bei).

**apology** [ə'pɔlədʒi], s. die Entschuldigung; Abbitte; Rechtfertigung.

**apoplectic** [æpə'plektik], adj. (Med.) apoplektisch.

**apoplexy** ['æpəpleksi], s. (Med.) der Schlagfluß, Schlaganfall (fit).

**apostle** [ə'pɔsl], s. der Apostel.

**apostolic** [æpəs'tɔlik], adj. apostolisch.

**apostrophe** [ə'pɔstrəfi], s. der Apostroph (punctuation); die Anrede (speech).

**apostrophize** [ə'pɔstrəfaiz], v.a. apostrophieren; anreden (speak to).

**apotheosis** [əpɔθi'ousis], s. die Apotheose.

**appal** [ə'pɔːl], v.a. erschrecken.

**appalling** [ə'pɔːliŋ], adj. schrecklich.

**apparatus** [æpə'reitəs], s. das Gerät, die Apparatur; (coll.) der Apparat.

**apparel** [ə'pærəl], s. die Kleidung.

**apparent** [ə'pærənt], adj. scheinbar; offensichtlich; augenscheinlich; heir —, der rechtmäßige Erbe.

**apparition** [æpə'riʃən], s. die Erscheinung; der Geist, das Gespenst (ghost).

**appeal** [ə'piːl], v.n. appellieren (make an appeal); (Law) Berufung einlegen; gefallen (please). — s. (public, Mil.) der Appell; die Bitte (request).

**appear** [ə'piə], v.n. erscheinen; scheinen; auftreten.

**appearance** [ə'piərəns], s. die Erscheinung; das Auftreten (stage, etc.); der Schein (semblance); keep up —s, den Schein wahren; to all —s, allem Anschein nach.

**appease** [ə'piːz], v.a. besänftigen.

**appeasement** [ə'piːzmənt], s. die Besänftigung, (Pol.) die Befriedung.

**appellation** [æpe'leiʃən], s. die Benennung.

**append** [ə'pend], v.a. anhängen, beifügen.

**appendicitis** [əpendi'saitis], s. (Med.) die Blinddarmentzündung.

**appendix** [ə'pendiks], s. der Anhang; (Med.) der Blinddarm.

**appertain** [æpə'tein], v.n. gehören (to, zu).

**appetite** ['æpitait], s. der Appetit.

**appetizing** ['æpitaizin], adj. appetitlich, appetitanregend.

**applaud** [ə'plɔːd], v.a., v.n. applaudieren, Beifall klatschen (Dat.).

**applause** [ə'plɔːz], s. der Applaus, Beifall.

**apple** [æpl], s. der Apfel.

**appliance** [ə'plaiəns], s. das Gerät, die Vorrichtung.

**applicable** ['æplikəbl], adj. anwendbar, passend (to, auf).

**applicant** ['æplikənt], s. der Bewerber (for, um).

**application** [æpli'keiʃən], s. die Bewerbung (for, um); das Gesuch; die Anwendung (to, auf); letter of —, der Bewerbungsbrief; — form, das Bewerbungsformular.

**apply** [ə'plai], v.a. anwenden (to, Acc.); gebrauchen. — v.n. sich bewerben (um, for, Acc.); (Dat.) this does not —, das trifft nicht zu; — within, drinnen nachfragen.

**appoint** [ə'pɔint], v.a. bestimmen; ernennen; ausrüsten.

**appointment** [ə'pɔintmənt], s. die Festsetzung; die Ernennung; die Bestellung, die Stellung (position); make an —, jemanden ernennen (fill a post), sich verabreden (arrange to meet); by —, Hoflieferant (to, Genit.).

**apportion** [ə'pɔːʃən], v.a. zuteilen, zuweisen, zumessen.

**apposite** ['æpəzit], adj. passend, angemessen.

**appositeness** ['æpəzitnis], s. die Angemessenheit.

**appraise** [ə'preiz], v.a. beurteilen.

**appraisal** [ə'preizəl], s. die Beurteilung, Abschätzung.

**appreciable** [ə'priːʃəbl], adj. merklich; nennenswert.

**appreciate** [ə'priːʃieit], v.a. würdigen, schätzen.

**appreciation** [əpriːʃi'eiʃən], s. die Schätzung, Würdigung.

**apprehend** [æpri'hend], v.a. verhaften, ergreifen (arrest); befürchten (fear).

**apprehension** [æpri'henʃən], s. die Verhaftung (arrest); die Befürchtung (fear).

**apprehensive** [æpri'hensiv], adj. besorgt, in Furcht (for, um), furchtsam.

**apprentice** [ə'prentis], s. der Lehrling; Praktikant. — v.a. in die Lehre geben (with, bei, Dat.).

**apprenticeship** [ə'prentiʃip], *s.* die Lehre, Lehrzeit, Praktikantenzeit; *student* —, die Studentenpraxis.

**apprise** [ə'praiz], *v.a.* benachrichtigen, informieren.

**approach** [ə'proutʃ], *v.a.*, *v.n.* sich nähern (*Dat.*). — *s.* die Annäherung, das Herankommen, Näherrücken.

**approachable** [ə'proutʃəbl], *adj.* zugänglich, freundlich.

**approbation** [æpro'beiʃən], *s.* die (offizielle) Billigung, Zustimmung.

**appropriate** [ə'proupriit], *adj.* angemessen, gebührend, geeignet (*suitable*). — [ə'prouprieit], *v.a.* requirieren, sich aneignen.

**appropriation** [əproupri'eiʃən], *s.* die Requisition, Aneignung, Übernahme, Besitznahme.

**approval** [ə'pru:vəl], *s.* die Billigung, der Beifall, die Zustimmung.

**approve** [ə'pru:v], *v.a.* loben, billigen; genehmigen; annehmen (*work*).

**approved** [ə'pru:vd], *adj.* anerkannt.

**approximate** [ə'prɔksimit], *adj.* ungefähr, annähernd. — [ə'prɔksimeit], *v.a.*, *v.n.* sich nähern.

**approximation** [əprɔksi'meiʃən], *s.* die Annäherung.

**approximative** [ə'prɔksimətiv], *adj.* annähernd.

**appurtenance** [ə'pə:tənəns], *s.* das (*or* der) Zubehör.

**appurtenant** [ə'pə:tənənt], *adj.* zugehörig.

**apricot** ['eiprikɔt], *s.* (*Bot.*) die Aprikose.

**April** ['eipril], der April.

**apron** ['eiprən], *s.* die Schürze; der Schurz; — *stage*, die Vorbühne, das Proszenium.

**apropos** [ɑ:prɔ'pou], *adv.* beiläufig; mit Bezug auf, diesbezüglich.

**apse** [æps], *s.* (*Archit.*) die Apsis.

**apt** [æpt], *adj.* geeignet, passend; fähig.

**aptitude** ['æptitju:d], *s.* die Eignung, Fähigkeit.

**aptness** ['æptnis], *s.* die Angemessenheit, Eignung.

**aquatic** [ə'kwɔtik *or* ə'kwætik], *adj.* Wasser-, wasser-; — *display*, Wasserkünste. — *s.* (*pl.*) der Wassersport.

**aqueduct** ['ækwidʌkt], *s.* die Wasserleitung; der Aquädukt.

**aqueous** ['eikwiəs], *adj.* (*Chem.*) wässerig.

**aquiline** ['ækwilain], *adj.* adlerartig, Adler-.

**Arab** ['ærəb], *s.* der Araber.

**Arabian** [ə'reibiən], *adj.* arabisch; — *Nights*, Tausend-und-eine-Nacht.

**Arabic** ['ærəbik], *adj.* arabisch (*language, literature*).

**arable** ['ærəbl], *adj.* pflügbar, bestellbar.

**arbiter** ['ɑ:bitə], *s.* der Schiedsrichter.

**arbitrary** ['ɑ:bitrəri], *adj.* willkürlich.

**arbitrate** ['ɑ:bitreit], *v.n.* vermitteln.

**arbitration** [ɑ:bi'treiʃən], *s.* die Vermittlung; Entscheidung; (*Comm.*) Arbitrage.

**arboriculture** ['ɑ:bɔrikʌltʃə], *s.* die Baumzucht.

**arbour** ['ɑ:bə], *s.* die Laube, Gartenlaube.

**arc** [ɑ:k], *s.* (*Geom.*) der Bogen; — *lamp*, die Bogenlampe; — *welding*, das Lichtschweißen.

**arcade** [ɑ:'keid], *s.* die Arkade.

**Arcadian** [ɑ:'keidiən], *adj.* arkadisch. — *s.* der Arkadier.

**arch** [ɑ:tʃ], *s.* der Bogen, die Wölbung; —*way*, der Bogengang. — *v.a.*, *v.n.* wölben, sich wölben. — *adj.* schelmisch, listig. — *prefix.* oberst; erst, Haupt-; — *-enemy*, der Erzfeind.

**archaeological** [ɑ:kiə'lɔdʒikəl], *adj.* archäologisch.

**archaeologist** [ɑ:ki'ɔlədʒist], *s.* der Archäologe.

**archaeology** [ɑ:ki'ɔlədʒi], *s.* die Archäologie.

**archaic** [ɑ:'keiik], *adj.* altertümlich.

**archaism** ['ɑ:keiizm], *s.* der Archaismus (*style*).

**archbishop** [ɑ:tʃ'biʃəp], *s.* der Erzbischof.

**archduke** [ɑ:tʃ'dju:k], *s.* der Erzherzog.

**archer** ['ɑ:tʃə], *s.* der Bogenschütze.

**archery** ['ɑ:tʃəri], *s.* das Bogenschießen.

**architect** ['ɑ:kitekt], *s.* der Architekt, Baumeister.

**architecture** ['ɑ:kitektʃə], *s.* die Architektur, Baukunst.

**archives** ['ɑ:kaivz], *s. pl.* das Archiv.

**Arctic** ['ɑ:ktik], *adj.* arktisch. — *s.* die Nordpolarländer, *n. pl.*

**ardent** ['ɑ:dənt], *adj.* heiß, glühend, brennend.

**ardour** ['ɑ:də], *s.* die Hitze, die Inbrunst, der Eifer.

**arduous** ['ɑ:djuəs], *adj.* schwierig, mühsam.

**area** ['ɛəriə], *s.* das Areal (*measurement*); das Gebiet, die Zone; die Fläche (*region*).

**arena** [ə'ri:nə], *s.* die Arena, der Kampfplatz.

**Argentine** ['ɑ:dʒəntain], *adj.* argentinisch. — (*Republic*), Argentinien, *n.*

**Argentinian** [ɑ:dʒən'tiniən], *adj.* argentinisch. — *s.* der Argentin(i)er.

**argue** ['ɑ:gju:], *v.n.* disputieren, streiten; folgern, schließen.

**argument** ['ɑ:gjumənt], *s.* das Argument; (*Log.*) der Beweis; der Streit (*dispute*).

**argumentative** [ɑ:gju'mentətiv], *adj.* streitsüchtig.

**arid** ['ærid], *adj.* trocken, dürr.

**aright** [ə'rait], *adv.* richtig, zurecht.

**arise** [ə'raiz], *v.n. irr.* aufstehen; sich erheben; entstehen (*originate*); *arising from the minutes*, es ergibt sich aus dem Protokoll.

**aristocracy** [æris'tɔkrəsi], *s.* die Aristokratie, der Adel.

**aristocratic** [æristo'krætik], *adj.* aristokratisch, adlig.

**arithmetic** [ə'riθmətik], *s.* die Arithmetik.

**arithmetical** [æriθ'metikəl], *adj.* arith-metisch.

**ark** [a:k], *s.* die Arche; — *of the Covenant*, die Bundeslade.

**arm** (1) [a:m], *s.* (*Anat.*) der Arm.

**arm** (2) [a:m], *s.* die Waffe; *up in* —*s*, in Aufruhr. — *v.a., v.n.* bewaffnen, sich bewaffnen, rüsten, sich rüsten.

**armament** ['a:məmənt], *s.* die Rüstung, Bewaffnung.

**armature** ['a:mətiuə], *s.* die Armatur.

**armchair** ['a:mtʃɛə], *s.* der Lehnstuhl; der Sessel.

**Armenian** [a:'mi:niən], *adj.* armenisch. — *s.* der Armenier.

**armistice** ['a:mistis], *s.* der Waffen-stillstand.

**armour** ['a:mə], *s.* die Rüstung, der Harnisch; —*plated*, gepanzert; —*ed car*, der Panzerwagen.

**armourer** ['a:mərə], *s.* der Waffen-schmied.

**armoury** ['a:məri], *s.* die Rüstkammer, Waffenschmiede.

**army** ['a:mi], *s.* die Armee, das Heer.

**aroma** [ə'roumə], *s.* das Aroma, der Duft.

**aromatic** [ærə'mætik], *adj.* aromatisch. —*s.* (*Chem.*) das Aromat.

**around** [ə'raund], *adv.* herum, rund-ringsherum, umher, im Kreise; *stand* —, herumstehen; *be* —, sich in der Nähe halten. — *prep.* um; bei, um ... herum.

**arouse** [ə'rauz], *v.a.* aufwecken, aufrüt-teln.

**arraignment** [ə'reinmənt], *s.* die Anklage.

**arrange** [ə'reindʒ], *v.a.* anordnen, arrangieren, einrichten, vereinbaren.

**arrangement** [ə'reindʒmənt], *s.* die Anordnung; die Einrichtung; die Vereinbarung (*agreement*); (*Law*) die Vergleichung, der Vergleich.

**arrant** ['ærənt], *adj.* durchtrieben.

**array** [ə'rei], *v.a.* schmücken, aufstellen. — *s.* die Ordnung; Aufstellung.

**arrears** [ə'riəz], *s. pl.* der Rückstand, die Schulden.

**arrest** [ə'rest], *v.a.* (*Law*) festnehmen, verhaften; festhalten; aufhalten (*hinder*). — *s.* die Festnahme; die Festhaltung.

**arrival** [ə'raivəl], *s.* die Ankunft.

**arrive** [ə'raiv], *v.n.* ankommen.

**arrogance** ['ærəgəns], *s.* die An-maßung, Überheblichkeit.

**arrogant** ['ærəgənt], *adj.* anmaßend, hochfahrend, überheblich.

**arrow** ['ærou], *s.* der Pfeil.

**arrowroot** ['ærouru:t], *s.* (*Bot.*) die Pfeilwurz.

**arsenal** ['a:sinəl], *s.* das Arsenal, Zeughaus.

**arsenic** ['a:sənik], *s.* das Arsen.

**arson** ['a:sən], *s.* die Brandstiftung.

**art** [a:t], *s.* die Kunst; *fine* —, schöne Kunst; (*Univ.*) —*s faculty*, die philo-sophische Fakultät; —*s* (*subject*), das humanistische Fach, die Geistes-wissenschaften.

**arterial** [a:'tiəriəl], *adj.* Pulsader-, Schlagader-; — *road*, die Hauptver-kehrsader, die Hauptstraße.

**artery** ['a:təri], *s.* die Pulsader, Schlag-ader; der Hauptverkehrsweg.

**artesian** [a:'ti:ʒən], *adj.* artesisch.

**artful** ['a:tful], *adj.* listig, schlau.

**article** ['a:tikl], *s.* (*Gram., Law, Press*) der Artikel; der Posten (*item in list*). — *v.a. be* —*d to a solicitor*, bei einem Advokaten assistieren.

**articulate** [a:'tikjuleit], *v.a.* artikulieren (*pronounce clearly*). — [—lit], *adj.* deutlich (*speech*).

**articulation** [a:tikju'leiʃən], *s.* die Artikulation, deutliche Aussprache.

**artifice** ['a:tifis], *s.* der Kunstgriff, die List.

**artificer** [a:'tifisə], *s.* der Handwerker.

**artificial** [a:ti'fiʃəl], *adj.* künstlich, Kunst-; — *silk*, die Kunstseide.

**artillery** [a:'tiləri], *s.* die Artillerie.

**artisan** [a:ti'zæn], *s.* der Handwerker.

**artist** ['a:tist], *s.* der Künstler, die Künstlerin.

**artistic** [a:'tistik], *adj.* künstlerisch.

**artless** ['a:tlis], *adj.* arglos, natürlich, naiv.

**Aryan** ['ɛəriən], *adj.* arisch. — *s.* der Arier.

**as** [æz], *adv., conj.* so, als, wie, ebenso; als, während, weil; — *big* —, so groß wie; — *well* —, sowohl als auch; *such* —, wie; — *it were*, gleichsam.

**asbestos** [æz'bestɔs], *s.* der Asbest.

**ascend** [ə'send], *v.a., v.n.* ersteigen, be-steigen; emporsteigen.

**ascendancy, -ency** [ə'sendənsi], *s.* der Aufstieg; der Einfluß; das Über-gewicht.

**ascendant, -ent** [ə'sendənt], *s. in the* —, aufsteigend.

**ascent** [ə'sent], *s.* der Aufstieg, die Besteigung.

**ascension** [ə'senʃən], *s.* (*Astron.*) das Aufsteigen; *Ascension Day*, Himmel-fahrt(stag).

**ascertain** [æsə'tein], *v.a.* in Erfah-rung bringen, erkunden, feststellen.

**ascertainable** [æsə'teinəbl], *adj.* er-kundbar, feststellbar.

**ascetic** [ə'setik], *adj.* asketisch.

**asceticism** [ə'setisizm], *s.* die Askese.

**ascribe** [ə'skraib], *v.a.* zuschreiben.

**ascribable** [ə'skraibəbl], *adj.* zuzu-schreiben, zuschreibbar.

**ash** (1) [æʃ], *s.* (*Bot.*) die Esche.

**ash** (2) [æʃ], *s.* die Asche.

**ashamed** [ə'ʃeimd], *adj.* beschämt; *be* —, sich schämen.

**ashcan** ['æʃkæn] (*Am.*) *see* dustbin.

**ashen** ['æʃən], *adj.* aschgrau, asch-farben.

**ashore** [ə'ʃɔ:], *adv.* am Land; am Ufer, ans Ufer *or* Land.

**ashtray** ['æʃtrei], *s.* der Aschenbecher.

**Ash Wednesday** [æʃ'wenzdei], *s.* der Aschermittwoch.

**Asiatic** [eiʃi'ætik], *adj.* asiatisch. — *s.* der Asiat.

# aside

**aside** [əˈsaid], *adv.* seitwärts, zur Seite; abseits.

**ask** [ɑːsk], *v.a., v.n.* fragen (*question*); bitten (*request*); fordern (*demand*); einladen (*invite*).

**asleep** [əˈsliːp], *pred. adj., adv.* schlafend, im Schlaf; eingeschlafen.

**asp** [æsp], *s.* (*Zool.*) die Natter.

**asparagus** [æsˈpærəgəs], *s.* (*Bot.*) der Spargel.

**aspect** [ˈæspekt], *s.* der Anblick, die Ansicht (*view, angle*); der Gesichtspunkt.

**aspen** [ˈæspən], *s.* (*Bot.*) die Espe.

**asperity** [æsˈperiti], *s.* die Härte; Rauheit.

**aspersion** [æsˈpəːʃən], *s.* die Verleumdung; Schmähung.

**asphalt** [ˈæsfælt], *s.* der Asphalt.

**asphyxia** [æsˈfiksjə], *s.* (*Med.*) die Erstickung.

**aspirant** [əˈspaiərənt, ˈæsp-], *s.* der Bewerber, Anwärter.

**aspirate** [ˈæspireit], *v.a.* (*Phon.*) aspirieren. — [—rit] *adj.* aspiriert. — *s.* der Hauchlaut.

**aspiration** [æspiˈreiʃən], *s.* der Atemzug; das Streben (*striving*) ; (*Phon.*) die Aspiration.

**aspire** [əˈspaiə], *v.n.* streben, verlangen.

**ass** [æs], *s.* der Esel.

**assail** [əˈseil], *v.a.* angreifen, anfallen.

**assailable** [əˈseiləbl], *adj.* angreifbar.

**assassin** [əˈsæsin], *s.* der Meuchelmörder.

**assassinate** [əˈsæsineit], *v.a.* meuchlings ermorden.

**assassination** [əsæsiˈneiʃən], *s.* der Meuchelmord, die Ermordung.

**assault** [əˈsɔːlt], *v.a.* angreifen, überfallen. — *s.* der Überfall, Angriff.

**assay** [əˈsei], *s.* die Metallprobe. — *v.a.* (auf Edelmetall hin) prüfen.

**assemble** [əˈsembl], *v.a., v.n.* versammeln, sich versammeln.

**assembly** [əˈsembli], *s.* die Versammlung (*assemblage*); — line, das laufende Band, das Fließband.

**assent** [əˈsent], *v.n.* beistimmen (*Dat.*), billigen (*Acc.*). — *s.* die Zustimmung (zu, *Dat.*), Billigung (*Genit.*).

**assert** [əˈsəːt], *v.a.* behaupten.

**assertion** [əˈsəːʃən], *s.* die Behauptung.

**assess** [əˈses], *v.a.* schätzen, beurteilen.

**assessment** [əˈsesmənt], *s.* die Beurteilung, Schätzung, Wertung.

**assessor** [əˈsesə], *s.* der Beurteiler, Einschätzer, Bewerter, Assessor; der Beisitzer (*second examiner*).

**assets** [ˈæsets], *s. pl.* (*Comm.*) die Aktiva; Vorzüge (*personal*).

**assiduity** [æsiˈdjuːiti], *s.* der Fleiß, die Emsigkeit.

**assiduous** [əˈsidjuəs], *adj.* fleißig, unablässig, emsig.

**assign** [əˈsain], *v.a.* zuteilen, anweisen, zuweisen (*apportion*), festsetzen (*fix*).

**assignable** [əˈsainəbl], *adj.* zuteilbar; bestimmbar.

**assignation** [æsigˈneiʃən], *s.* die Zuweisung; (*Law*) die Übertragung; die Verabredung.

**assignment** [əˈsainmənt], *s.* die Zuweisung, Übertragung; die Aufgabe.

**assimilate** [əˈsimileit], *v.a., v.n.* assimilieren, angleichen; sich assimilieren, sich angleichen, ähnlich werden.

**assist** [əˈsist], *v.a., v.n.* beistehen (*Dat.*), helfen (*Dat.*), unterstützen (*Acc.*).

**assistance** [əˈsistəns], *s.* der Beistand, die Hilfe; die Aushilfe; (*financial*) der Zuschuß.

**assistant** [əˈsistənt], *s.* der Assistent, Helfer.

**assize** [əˈsaiz], *s.* die Gerichtssitzung; (*pl.*) das Schwurgericht.

**associate** [əˈsouʃieit], *v.a.* verbinden (*link*). — *v.n.* verkehren (*company*); sich verbinden; (*Comm.*) sich vereinigen. — [—iit], *s.* (*Comm.*) der Partner.

**association** [əsousiˈeiʃən], *s.* die Vereinigung, der Bund, Verein; die Gesellschaft; der Verkehr.

**assonance** [ˈæsənəns], *s.* (*Phon.*) die Assonanz, der Gleichlaut.

**assort** [əˈsɔːt], *v.a.* ordnen, aussuchen, sortieren; —ed sweets, gemischte Bonbons.

**assortment** [əˈsɔːtmənt], *s.* die Sammlung, Mischung, Auswahl.

**assuage** [əˈsweidʒ], *v.a.* mildern, besänftigen, stillen.

**assume** [əˈsjuːm], *v.a.* annehmen; übernehmen, ergreifen.

**assuming** [əˈsjuːmiŋ], *adj.* anmaßend; — that, angenommen daß . . ., gesetzt den Fall.

**assumption** [əˈsʌmpʃən], *s.* die Annahme (*opinion*); Übernahme (*taking up*); Aneignung (*appropriation*); Assumption of the Blessed Virgin, Mariä Himmelfahrt.

**assurance** [əˈʃuərəns], *s.* die Versicherung; Sicherheit (*manner*).

**assure** [əˈʃuə], *v.a.* versichern, sicher stellen, ermutigen.

**assuredly** [əˈʃuəridli], *adv.* sicherlich, gewiß.

**aster** [ˈæstə], *s.* (*Bot.*) die Aster.

**asterisk** [ˈæstərisk], *s.* (*Typ.*) das Sternchen.

**astern** [əˈstəːn], *adv.* (*Naut.*) achteraus.

**asthma** [ˈæsθmə], *s.* das Asthma.

**asthmatic** [æsθˈmætik], *adj.* asthmatisch.

**astir** [əˈstəː], *adv.* wach, in Bewegung.

**astonish** [əˈstɔniʃ], *v.a.* in Erstaunen versetzen, verblüffen.

**astonishment** [əˈstɔniʃmənt], *s.* das Erstaunen, die Verwunderung; die Bestürzung.

**astound** [əˈstaund], *v.a.* in Erstaunen versetzen, bestürzen.

**astounding** [əˈstaundiŋ], *adj.* erstaunlich, verblüffend.

**astral** [ˈæstrəl], *adj.* Stern(en)-, gestirnt.

auctioneer

**astray** [əˈstrei], *pred. adj., adv.* irre; *go* —, sich verirren; (*fig.*) abschweifen.
**astride**[əˈstraid],*pred.adj.,adv.*rittlings.
**astringent** [əˈstrindʒənt], *adj.* zusammenziehend.
**astrologer** [əˈstrɔlədʒə], *s.* der Sterndeuter, Astrolog(e).
**astrological** [æstrəˈlɔdʒikəl], *adj.* astrologisch.
**astrology** [əˈstrɔlədʒi],*s.* die Astrologie, Sterndeuterei.
**astronaut** [ˈæstrɔnɔ:t], *s.* der Astronaut.
**astronomer** [əˈstrɔnəmə], *s.* der Astronom.
**astronomical**[æstrəˈnɔmikəl],*adj.*astronomisch.
**astronomy** [əˈstrɔnəmi], *s.* die Astronomie, Sternkunde.
**astute** [əˈstju:t], *adj.* listig, schlau.
**astuteness** [əˈstju:tnis], *s.* die Schlauheit, Listigkeit, der Scharfsinn.
**asunder** [əˈsʌndə], *adv.* auseinander, entzwei.
**asylum** [əˈsailəm], *s.* das Asyl, der Zufluchtsort (*refuge*); *lunatic* —, das Irrenhaus.
**at** [æt], *prep.* an; auf; bei, für; in, nach; mit, gegen; um, über; von, aus, zu; — *my expense*, auf meine Kosten; — *all*, überhaupt; — *first*, zuerst; — *last*, zuletzt, endlich; — *peace*, in Frieden; *what are you driving* —? worauf wollen sie hinaus?
**atheism** [ˈeiθiizm], *s.* der Atheismus.
**atheist** [ˈeiθiist], *s.* der Atheist.
**atheistic** [eiθiˈistik], *adj.* atheistisch, gottlos.
**Athenian** [əˈθi:njən], *s.* der Athener. — *adj.* athenisch.
**Athens** [ˈæθənz] Athen, *n.*
**athlete** [ˈæθli:t], *s.* der Athlet.
**athletic** [æθˈletik], *adj.* athletisch.
**athletics** [æθˈletiks], *s. pl.* die Leichtathletik, Athletik.
**Atlantic (Ocean)** [ətˈlæntik (ˈouʃən)]. der Atlantik.
**atlas** [ˈætləs], *s.* der Atlas.
**atmosphere** [ˈætməsfiə], *s.* die Atmosphäre.
**atmospheric(al)** [ætməsˈferik(əl)], *adj.* atmosphärisch. — *s.* (*pl.*) atmosphärische Störungen, *f. pl.*
**atoll**[əˈtɔl],*s.*die Koralleninsel,dasAtoll.
**atom** [ˈætəm], *s.* das Atom.
**atomic** [əˈtɔmik], *adj.* (*Phys.*) Atom-, atomisch, atomar; (*theory*) atomistisch; — *bomb*, die Atombombe; — *pile*, der Atomreaktor; — *armament*, die atomare Aufrüstung.
**atone** [əˈtoun], *v.n.* sühnen, büßen.
**atonement** [əˈtounmənt], *s.* die Buße, Sühne, Versöhnung.
**atonic** [eiˈtɔnik], *adj.* tonlos, unbetont.
**atrocious** [əˈtrouʃəs], *adj.* gräßlich, schrecklich, entsetzlich.
**atrocity** [əˈtrɔsiti], *s.* die Gräßlichkeit, Grausamkeit, Greueltat.
**atrophy** [ˈætrəfi], *s.* (*Med.*) die Abmagerung, Atrophie. — [ˈætrəfai], *v.n.* absterben, auszehren.

**attach** [əˈtætʃ], *v.a.* anheften, beilegen, anhängen; (*fig.*) beimessen (*attribute*).
**attachment** [əˈtætʃmənt], *s.* das Anhaften (*sticking to*, an, *Acc.*); das Anhängsel (*appendage*); die Freundschaft (*to*, für, *Acc.*); die Anhänglichkeit (*loyalty*, an, *Acc.*).
**attack** [əˈtæk], *v.a.* angreifen. — *s.* die Attacke, der Angriff; (*Med.*) der Anfall.
**attain** [əˈtein], *v.a.* erreichen, erlangen.
**attainable** [əˈteinəbl], *adj.* erreichbar.
**attainment** [əˈteinmənt], *s.* die Erlangung, Erreichung; Errungenschaft; (*pl.*) Kenntnisse, *f. pl.*
**attempt** [əˈtempt], *s.* der Versuch. — *v.a.* versuchen.
**attend** [əˈtend], *v.a., v.n.* begleiten, anwesend sein (*be present*, at, bei, *Dat.*); beiwohnen (*be present as guest*); zuhören (*listen to*); bedienen (*customer*); behandeln (*patient*).
**attendance** [əˈtendəns], *s.* die Begleitung (*accompaniment*); die Anwesenheit (*presence*); die Zuhörerschaft (*audience*); *to be in* —, Dienst tun (*at*, bei); anwesend sein (*be present*).
**attendant** [əˈtendənt], *s.* der Diener, Wärter.
**attention** [əˈtenʃən], *s.* die Aufmerksamkeit, Achtung.
**attentive** [əˈtentiv], *adj.* aufmerksam.
**attenuate** [əˈtenjueit], *v.a.* verdünnen (*dilute*). — *v.n.* abmagern.
**attest** [əˈtest], *v.a.* attestieren, bezeugen, bescheinigen.
**attestation** [ætesˈteiʃən], *s.* die Bescheinigung; das Zeugnis.
**Attic** [ˈætik], *adj.* attisch, klassisch.
**attic** [ˈætik], *s.* die Dachkammer, die Dachstube.
**attire** [əˈtaiə], *v.a.* ankleiden, kleiden. — *s.* die Kleidung.
**attitude** [ˈætitju:d], *s.* die Haltung, Stellung (*toward*, zu), Einstellung.
**attorney** [əˈtə:ni], *s.* der Anwalt; *Attorney-General*, der Kronanwalt, (*Am.*) der Staatsanwalt; — *at law*, Rechtsanwalt.
**attract** [əˈtrækt], *v.a.* anziehen.
**attraction** [əˈtrækʃən], *s.* die Anziehung; der Reiz (*appeal*); die Anziehungskraft.
**attractive** [əˈtræktiv], *adj.* anziehend, reizvoll.
**attribute** [əˈtribju:t], *v.a.* zuschreiben, beimessen. — *s.* [ˈætribju:t], (*Gram.*) das Attribut, die Eigenschaft.
**attributive** [əˈtribjutiv], *adj.* (*Gram.*) attributiv; beilegend.
**attrition** [əˈtriʃən], *s.* die Zermürbung, Aufreibung, Reue.
**attune** [əˈtju:n], *v.a.* (*Mus.*) stimmen, anpassen (*adapt to*, an, *Acc.*).
**auburn** [ˈɔ:bə:n], *adj.* rotbraun.
**auction** [ˈɔ:kʃən], *s.* die Auktion, die Versteigerung.
**auctioneer** [ɔ:kʃəˈniə], *s.* der Auktionator, Versteigerer.

315

**audacious** [ɔː'deiʃəs], *adj.* waghalsig, kühn, dreist.

**audacity** [ɔː'dæsiti], *s.* die Kühnheit (*valour*); Frechheit (*impudence*).

**audible** ['ɔːdibl], *adj.* hörbar.

**audibility** [ɔːdi'biliti], *s.* die Hörbarkeit, Vernehmbarkeit.

**audience** ['ɔːdjəns], *s.* die Audienz (*of the Pope*, beim Papst); (*Theat.*) das Publikum; (*listeners*) die Zuhörer.

**audit** ['ɔːdit], *s.* die Rechnungsprüfung, Revision. — *v.a.* revidieren, prüfen.

**auditor** [ɔː'ditə], *s.* der Rechnungsrevisor, Buchprüfer.

**auditory** ['ɔːditəri], *adj.* Gehör-, Hör-.

**auditorium** [ɔːdi'tɔːriəm], *s.* der Hörsaal, Vortragssaal.

**auger** ['ɔːgə], *s.* der (große) Bohrer.

**aught** [ɔːt], *pron.* (*obs.*) irgend etwas (*opp. to* naught).

**augment** [ɔː'gment], *v.a., v.n.* vermehren, vergrößern; zunehmen.

**augmentation** [ɔːgmen'teiʃən], *s.* die Vergrößerung, Erhöhung, Zunahme.

**augur** ['ɔːgə], *v.a.* weissagen, prophezeien.

**August** ['ɔːgəst]. der August.

**august** [ɔː'gʌst], *adj.* erhaben.

**aunt** [ɑːnt], *s.* die Tante.

**aurora** [ɔː'rɔːrə], *s.* die Morgenröte.

**auscultation** [ɔːskəl'teiʃən], *s.*(*Med.*) die Auskultation, Untersuchung.

**auspices** ['ɔːspisiz], *s.* die Auspizien.

**auspicious** [ɔː'spiʃəs], *adj.* unter glücklichem Vorzeichen, verheißungsvoll, günstig.

**austere** [ɔː'stiə], *adj.* streng, ernst, schmucklos.

**austerity** [ɔː'teriti], *s.* die Strenge.

**Australian** [ə'streiljən], *adj.* australisch. — *s.* der Australier.

**Austrian** ['ɔːstriən], *adj.* österreichisch. — *s.* der Österreicher.

**authentic** [ɔː'θentik], *adj.* authentisch, echt.

**authenticity** [ɔːθen'tisiti], *s.* die Authentizität, Echtheit.

**author, authoress** ['ɔːθə, ɔː'θər'es], *s.* der Autor, die Autorin; der Verfasser, die Verfasserin.

**authoritative** [ɔː'θɔritətiv], *adj.* autoritativ, maßgebend.

**authority** [ɔː'θɔriti], *s.* die Autorität, Vollmacht (*power of attorney*); das Ansehen; *the authorities*, die Behörden.

**authorization** [ɔːθɔrai'zeiʃən], *s.* die Bevollmächtigung, Befugnis.

**authorize** ['ɔːθəraiz], *v.a.* autorisieren, bevollmächtigen, berechtigen.

**authorship** ['ɔːθəʃip], *s.* die Autorschaft.

**autobiographical** [ɔːtobaiə'græfikl], *adj.* autobiographisch.

**autobiography** [ɔːtobai'ɔgrəfi], *s.* die Autobiographie.

**autocracy** [ɔː'tɔkrəsi], *s.* die Selbstherrschaft.

**autocrat** ['ɔːtokræt], *s.* der Autokrat, Selbstherrscher.

**autograph** ['ɔːtogræf, -grɑːf], *s.* die eigene Handschrift, Unterschrift; das Autogramm.

**automatic** [ɔːto'mætik], *adj.* automatisch.

**automatize** [ɔː'tɔmətaiz], *v.a.* automatisieren, auf Automation umstellen.

**automation** [ɔːto'meiʃən], *s.* (*Engin.*) die Automation; Automatisierung.

**automaton** [ɔː'tɔmətən], *s.* der Automat.

**automobile** ['ɔːtomobiːl], *s.* der Kraftwagen, das Auto.

**autonomous** [ɔː'tɔnəməs], *adj.* autonom, unabhängig.

**autonomy** [ɔː'tɔnəmi], *s.* die Autonomie, Unabhängigkeit.

**autopsy** ['ɔːtɔpsi], *s.* die Autopsie; Obduktion, Leichenschau.

**autumn** ['ɔːtəm], *s.* der Herbst.

**autumnal** [ɔː'tʌmnəl], *adj.* herbstlich.

**auxiliary** [ɔːg'ziljəri], *adj.* Hilfs-.

**avail** [ə'veil], *v.n.* nützen, helfen, von Vorteil sein. — *v.r.* — *o.s of a th.*, sich einer Sache bedienen. — *s.* der Nutzen; *of no* —, nutzlos.

**available** [ə'veiləbl], *adj.* vorrätig, verfügbar, zur Verfügung (stehend).

**avalanche** ['ævəlɑːnʃ], *s.* die Lawine.

**avarice** ['ævəris], *s.* der Geiz, die Habsucht, Gier.

**avaricious** [ævə'riʃəs], *adj.* geizig, habsüchtig, habgierig.

**avenge** [ə'vendʒ], *v.a.* rächen.

**avenue** ['ævənjuː], *s.* die Allee; der Zugang.

**average** ['ævəridʒ], *adj.* durchschnittlich; *not more than* —, mäßig. — *s.* der Durchschnitt; *on an* —, durchschnittlich, im Durchschnitt. — *v.a.* den Durchschnitt nehmen.

**averse** [ə'vəːs], *adj.* abgeneigt (*to, Dat.*).

**aversion** [ə'vəːʃən], *s.* die Abneigung, der Widerwille.

**avert** [ə'vəːt], *v.a.* abwenden.

**aviary** ['eiviəri], *s.* das Vogelhaus.

**aviation** [eivi'eiʃən], *s.* das Flugwesen.

**aviator** ['eivieitə], *s.* der Flieger.

**avid** ['ævid], *adj.* begierig (*of* or *for*, nach).

**avidity** [æ'viditi], *s.* die Begierde, Gier (*for*, nach).

**avoid** [ə'vɔid], *v.a.* vermeiden.

**avoidable** [ə'vɔidəbl], *adj.* vermeidlich, vermeidbar.

**avoidance** [ə'vɔidəns], *s.* die Vermeidung, das Meiden.

**avow** [ə'vau], *v.a.* eingestehen, anerkennen (*acknowledge*).

**avowal** [ə'vauəl], *s.* das Geständnis; die Erklärung.

**await** [ə'weit], *v.a.* erwarten, warten auf (*Acc.*).

**awake(n)** [ə'weik(ən)], *v.a., v.n. irr.* aufwecken, wecken; aufwachen (*wake up*). — *adj. wide awake*, schlau, auf der Hut.

**award** [ə'wɔ:d], s. die Zuerkennung, Auszeichnung; Belohnung (money); (Law) das Urteil. — v.a. zuerkennen; — damages, Schadenersatz zusprechen; verleihen (grant).

**aware** [ə'wɛə], adj. gewahr, bewußt (Genit.).

**away** [ə'wei], adv. weg; hinweg, fort.

**awe** [ɔ:], s. die Ehrfurcht; Furcht.

**awful** ['ɔ:ful], adj. furchtbar, schrecklich.

**awhile** [ə'wail], adv. eine Weile, eine kurze Zeit.

**awkward** ['ɔ:kwəd], adv. ungeschickt, unbeholfen, ungelenk; unangenehm (difficult); — situation, peinliche Situation, Lage.

**awkwardness** ['ɔkwədnis], s. die Ungeschicklichkeit, Unbeholfenheit.

**awl** [ɔ:l], s. die Ahle, der Pfriem.

**awning** ['ɔ:niŋ], s. die Plane; das Sonnendach.

**awry** [ə'rai], adj. schief, verkehrt.

**axe** [æks], s. die Axt, das Beil.

**axiom** ['æksiəm], s. das Axiom, der Satz, Lehrsatz, Grundsatz.

**axiomatic** [æksiə'mætik], adj. axiomatisch, grundsätzlich; gewiß.

**axis** ['æksis], s. die Achse.

**axle** [æksl], s. die Achse, das Beil.

**ay(e)** (1) [ai], adv. ja, gewiß.

**ay(e)** (2) [ei], adv. ständig, ewig.

**azalea** [ə'zeiliə], s. (Bot.) die Azalie.

**azure** ['æʒə, 'eiʒə], adj. himmelblau, azurblau.


# B

**B** [bi:]. das B; (Mus.) das H.

**baa** [ba:], v.n. blöken.

**babble** [bæbl], v.n. schwatzen, schwätzen. — s. das Geschwätz; das Murmeln (water).

**babe, baby** [beib, 'beibi], s. der Säugling, das Baby, das kleine Kind, das Kindlein.

**baboon** [bə'bu:n], s. (Zool.) der Pavian.

**bachelor** ['bætʃələ], s. der Junggeselle; (Univ.) Bakkalaureus.

**back** [bæk], s. der Rücken, die Rückseite. — adj. Hinter-, Rück-; — door, die Hintertür; — stairs, die Hintertreppe. — adv. rückwärts, zurück. — v.a. unterstützen; (Comm.) indossieren; gegenzeichnen; wetten auf (Acc.) (bet on).

**backbone** ['bækboun], s. (Anat.) das Rückgrat.

**backfire** ['bækfaiə], s. (Motor.) die Frühzündung; (gun) die Fehlzündung. — [bæk'faiə], v.n. (Motor.) frühzünden; (gun) fehlzünden.

**backgammon** [bæk'gæmən], s. das Bordspiel, das Puffspiel.

**background** ['bækgraund], s. der Hintergrund.

**backhand** ['bækhænd], s. (Sport) die Rückhand; a —ed compliment, eine verblümte Grobheit.

**backside** [bæk'said], s. (vulg.) der Hintere.

**backslide** [bæk'slaid], v.n. abfallen, abtrünnig werden.

**backward** ['bækwəd], adj. zurückgeblieben. **backward(s)** adv. rückwärts, zurück.

**backwater** ['bækwɔ:tə], s. das Stauwasser.

**backwoods** ['bækwudz], s. pl. der Hinterwald.

**bacon** ['beikən], s. der Speck.

**bad** [bæd], adj. schlecht, schlimm; böse (immoral); (coll.) unwohl (unwell); not too —, ganz gut; from — to worse, immer schlimmer; — language, unanständige Worte, das Fluchen; — luck, Unglück, Pech; want —ly, nötig brauchen.

**badge** [bædʒ], s. das Abzeichen; Kennzeichen (mark).

**badger** (1) ['bædʒə], s. (Zool.) der Dachs.

**badger** (2) ['bædʒə], v.a. ärgern, stören, belästigen.

**badness** ['bædnis], s. die Schlechtigkeit, Bosheit, das schlechte Wesen, die Bösartigkeit.

**baffle** [bæfl], v.a. täuschen, verblüffen. — s. (obs.) die Täuschung; (Build.) Verkleidung; (Elec.) Verteilerplatte.

**bag** [bæg], s. der Sack, Beutel; die Tasche; shopping —, Einkaufstasche; travelling —, Reisehandtasche. — v.a. einstecken, als Beute behalten (hunt).

**bagatelle** [bægə'tel], s. die Bagatelle, Lappalie, Kleinigkeit; das Kugelspiel (pin-table ball-game).

**baggage** ['bægidʒ], s. das Gepäck.

**bagging** ['bægiŋ], s. die Sackleinwand.

**baggy** ['bægi], adj. ungebügelt; bauschig.

**bagpipe** ['bægpaip], s. der Dudelsack.

**bagpiper** ['bægpaipə], s. der Dudelsackpfeifer.

**bail** [beil], s. der Bürge; die Bürgschaft; stand —, für einen bürgen; allow —, Bürgschaft zulassen. — v.a. Bürgschaft leisten; — out, (durch Kaution) in Freiheit setzen.

**bailiff** ['beilif], s. der Amtmann; Gerichtsvollzieher.

**bait** [beit], s. der Köder. — v.a. ködern, locken (attract).

**baiter** ['beitə], s. der Hetzer, Verfolger.

**baiting** ['beitiŋ], s. die Hetze.

**bake** [beik], v.a., v.n. backen.

**baker** ['beikə], s. der Bäcker; —'s dozen, 13 Stück.

**bakery** ['beikəri], s. die Bäckerei.

**baking** ['beikiŋ], s. das Backen.

# balance

**balance** ['bæləns], s. die Waage (*scales*); die Bilanz (*audit*); das Gleichgewicht (*equilibrium*); (*Comm.*) der Saldo, der Überschuß (*profit*); die Unruhe (*watch*). — *v.a., v.n.* wägen, abwägen (*scales*); ausgleichen (— *up*); einen Saldo ziehen (— *an account*); ins Gleichgewicht bringen (*bring into equilibrium*).

**balcony** ['bælkəni], s. der Balkon, der Söller (*castle*); Altan (*villa*).

**bald** [bɔːld], *adj.* kahl, haarlos; (*fig.*) armselig, schmucklos.

**baldness** ['bɔːldnis], s. die Kahlheit (*hairlessness*); Nacktheit (*bareness*).

**bale** (1) [beil], s. der Ballen.

**bale** (2) [beil], *v.n.* — *out*, abspringen; aussteigen.

**Balearic Islands** [bæli'ærik ailəndz], *s. pl.* die Balearen, Balearischen Inseln. — *adj.* balearisch.

**baleful** ['beilful], *adj.* unheilvoll.

**balk** [bɔːk], *v.a.* aufhalten, hemmen. — *v.n.* scheuen, zurückscheuen (*at*, vor).

**ball** (1) [bɔːl], s. der Ball; die Kugel; — *cock*, der Absperrhahn; —*point pen*, der Kugelschreiber.

**ball** (2) [bɔːl], s. der Ball (*dance*).

**ballad** ['bæləd], s. die Ballade.

**ballast** ['bæləst], s. der Ballast.

**ballet** ['bælei], s. das Ballett.

**balloon** [bə'luːn], s. der Ballon.

**ballot** ['bælət], s. die geheime Wahl, Abstimmung; — *box*, die Wahlurne; —*paper*, der Stimmzettel. —*v. n.* wählen, abstimmen.

**balm** [baːm], s. der Balsam.

**balsam** ['bɔlsəm], s. der Balsam.

**Baltic** ['bɔːltik], *adj.* baltisch. — (*Sea*), die Ostsee; —*Provinces*, das Baltikum, die Ostsee.

**balustrade** ['bæləstreid], s. die Balustrade, das Geländer.

**bamboo** [bæm'buː], s. (*Bot.*) der Bambus.

**bamboozle** [bæm'buːzl], *v.a.* verblüffen; beschwindeln (*cheat*).

**ban** [bæn], *v.a.* bannen, verbannen; verbieten. — s. der Bann, das Verbot.

**banal** [bæ'næl, 'beinəl], *adj.* banal.

**banality** [bæ'næliti], s. die Banalität, Trivialität.

**banana** [bə'naːnə], s. die Banane.

**band** [bænd], s. das Band (*ribbon etc.*); (*Mus.*) die Kapelle; die Bande (*robbers*). — *v.n.* — *together*, sich verbinden; sich zusammentun.

**bandage** ['bændidʒ], s. der Verband, die Bandage.

**bandit** ['bændit], s. der Bandit.

**bandmaster** ['bændmaːstə], s. der Kapellmeister.

**bandstand** ['bændstænd], s. der Musikpavillon.

**bandy** ['bændi], *adj.* —*legged*, krummbeinig. — *v.a.* — *words*, Worte wechseln; streiten.

**bane** [bein], s. das Gift; (*fig.*) Verderben.

**baneful** ['beinful], *adj.* verderblich.

**bang** [bæŋ], s. der Knall (*explosion*), das Krachen (*clap*). — *v.n.* knallen, krachen lassen. — *v.a.* — *a door*, eine Türe zuwerfen.

**banish** ['bæniʃ], *v.a.* verbannen, bannen.

**banisters** ['bænistəz], *s. pl.* das Treppengeländer.

**bank** [bæŋk], s. (*Fin.*) die Bank; das Ufer (*river*); der Damm (*dam*). — *v.a.* einlegen, einzahlen, auf die Bank bringen (*sum of money*); eindämmen (*dam up*). — *v.n.* ein Konto haben (*have an account, with*, bei).

**banker** ['bæŋkə], s. der Bankier.

**bankrupt** ['bæŋkrʌpt], *adj.* bankrott; zahlungsunfähig; (*coll.*) pleite.

**bankruptcy** ['bæŋkrʌptsi], s. der Bankrott.

**banns** [bænz], *s. pl.* das Heiratsaufgebot.

**banquet** ['bæŋkwit], s. das Bankett, Festessen.

**bantam** ['bæntəm], s. das Bantamhuhn, Zwerghuhn; (*Boxing*) —*-weight*, das Bantamgewicht.

**banter** ['bæntə], *v.n.* scherzen, necken. — s. das Scherzen, der Scherz.

**baptism** ['bæptizm], s. die Taufe.

**Baptist** ['bæptist], s. der Täufer; Baptist.

**baptize** [bæp'taiz], *v.a.* taufen.

**bar** [baː], s. die Barre, Stange (*pole*); der Riegel; Balken; Schlagbaum (*barrier*); (*fig.*) das Hindernis; der Schenktisch, die Bar (*in public house*); *prisoner at the*—, Gefangener vor (dem) Gericht; *call to the* —, zur Gerichtsadvokatur (*or* als Anwalt) zulassen; (*Mus.*) der Takt. — *v.a.* verriegeln (*door*); (*fig.*) hindern (*from action*); verbieten (*prohibit*); ausschließen (*exclude*).

**barb** [baːb], s. die Spitze (*of wire*); der Widerhaken (*hook*).

**barbed** [baːbd], *adj.* spitzig; — *remark*, die spitze Bemerkung; — *wire*, der Stacheldraht.

**barbarian** [baː'bɛəriən], s. der Barbar. — *adj.* barbarisch.

**barbarism** ['baːbərizm], s. die Roheit; der Barbarismus.

**barber** ['baːbə], s. der Barbier, Friseur.

**barberry** ['baːbəri], s. (*Bot.*) die Berberitze.

**bard** [baːd], s. der Barde, Sänger.

**bare** [bɛə], *adj.* nackt, bloß; —*headed*, barhäuptig. — *v.a.* entblößen.

**barefaced** ['bɛəfeist], *adj.* schamlos.

**barely** ['bɛəli], *adv.* kaum.

**bargain** ['baːgin], s. der Kauf, Gelegenheitskauf; der Handel (*trading*); das Geschäft; *into the* —, noch dazu, obendrein. — *v.n.* feilschen, handeln (*haggle*) (*for*, um).

**barge** [baːdʒ], s. der Lastkahn, die Barke. — *v.n.* (*coll.*) — *in*, stören.

**bargee** [baː'dʒiː], s. der Flußschiffer, Bootsmann.

**baritone** ['bæritoun], s. (*Mus.*) der Bariton.

**beam**

bark (1) [bɑːk], *s.* die Rinde (*of tree*).
bark (2) [bɑːk], *v.n.* bellen (*dog*); — *up the wrong tree*, auf falscher Fährte sein. — *s.* das Gebell (*dog*).
barley ['bɑːli], *s.* (*Bot.*) die Gerste.
barmaid ['bɑːmeid], *s.* die Kellnerin.
barman ['bɑːmən], *s.* der Kellner.
barn [bɑːn], *s.* die Scheune; — *owl*, die Schleiereule.
barnacle ['bɑːnəkl], *s.* die Entenmuschel; die Klette.
barnstormer ['bɑːnstɔːmə], *s.* der Schmierenkomödiant.
barometer [bə'rɔmitə], *s.* das Barometer.
baron ['bærən], *s.* der Baron, Freiherr.
barony ['bærəni], *s.* die Baronswürde.
baroque [bə'rɔk], *adj.* barock. — *s.* das Barock.
barque [bɑːk], *s.* die Bark.
barracks ['bærəks], *s. pl.* die Kaserne.
barrage ['bærɑːʒ, 'bæridʒ], *s.* das Sperrfeuer (*firing*); das Wehr, der Damm.
barrel ['bærəl], *s.* das Faß (*vat*), die Tonne (*tun*); der Gewehrlauf (*rifle*); die Trommel (*cylinder*); — *organ*, die Drehorgel.
barren ['bærən], *adj.* unfruchtbar, dürr.
barrenness ['bærənnis], *s.* die Unfruchtbarkeit.
barricade [bæri'keid], *s.* die Barrikade. — *v.a.* verrammeln, verschanzen.
barrier ['bæriə], *s.* die Barriere, der Schlagbaum; das Hindernis; (*Railw.*) die Schranke.
barrister ['bæristə], *s.* der Rechtsanwalt, Advokat.
barrow (1) ['bærou], *s.* der Schubkarren, Handkarren; — *boy*, der Höker, Schnellverkäufer.
barrow (2) ['bærou], *s.* (*Archaeol.*) das Hünengrab, Heldengrab.
barter ['bɑːtə], *v.a.* tauschen, austauschen. — *s.* der Tauschhandel.
Bartholomew ['bɑːθɔləmju]. Bartholomäus, *m.*; *Massacre of St. Bartholomew's Eve*, Bartholomäusnacht, Pariser Bluthochzeit.
basalt ['bæsɔːlt, bæ'sɔːlt], *s.* der Basalt.
base [beis], *s.* die Basis, Grundlage; der Sockel; (*Chem.*) die Base. — *adj.* niedrig, gemein; (*Metall.*) unedel. — *v.a.* basieren, beruhen, fundieren (*upon*, auf).
baseless ['beislis], *adj.* grundlos.
basement ['beismənt], *s.* das Kellergeschoß.
baseness ['beisnis], *s.* die Gemeinheit, Niedrigkeit.
bashful ['bæʃful], *adj.* verschämt, schamhaft, schüchtern.
basic ['beisik], *adj.* grundlegend.
basin ['beisən], *s.* das Becken.
basis ['beisis], *s.* die Basis, Grundlage.
bask [bɑːsk], *v.n.* sich sonnen.
basket ['bɑːskit], *s.* der Korb.
bass (1) [beis], *s.* (*Mus.*) der Baß, die Baßstimme.

bass (2) [bæs], *s.* (*Zool.*) der Barsch.
bassoon [bə'suːn], *s.* (*Mus.*) das Fagott.
bastard ['bæstəd], *s.* der Bastard.
baste [beist], *v.a.* mit Fett begießen (*roast meat*); (*coll.*) prügeln.
bastion ['bæstiən], *s.* die Bastion, Festung, das Bollwerk.
bat (1) [bæt], *s.* die Fledermaus.
bat (2) [bæt], *s.* der Schläger. — *v.n.* (den Ball) schlagen; (*cricket*) am Schlagen sein (*be batting*).
batch [bætʃ], *s.* der Stoß (*pile*); die Menge (*people*); (*Mil.*) der Trupp.
bath [bɑːθ], *s.* das Bad; (*Am.*) —*robe*, der Schlafrock, Bademantel; —*tub*, die Badewanne.
bathe [beið], *v.n.* baden; *bathing pool*, das Schwimmbad; *bathing suit*, der Badeanzug.
batman ['bætmən], *s.* der Offiziersbursche.
baton ['bætən], *s.* der Stab.
batsman ['bætsmən], *s.* der Schläger (*cricket*).
batten [bætn], *s.* die Holzlatte. — *v.a.* mästen, füttern. — *v.n.* fett werden.
batter ['bætə], *s.* der Schlagteig. — *v.a.* schlagen, zertrümmern; —*ing ram*, (*Mil.*) der Sturmbock.
battery ['bætəri], *s.* die Batterie.
battle [bætl], *s.* die Schlacht; — *cruiser*, der Schlachtkreuzer; —*ship*, das Schlachtschiff. — *v.n.* kämpfen (*for*, um).
Bavarian [bə'vɛəriən], *adj.* bayrisch. — *s.* der Bayer.
bawl [bɔːl], *v.n.* plärren, schreien.
bay (1) [bei], *adj.* rötlich braun.
bay (2) [bei], *s.* die Bucht, Bai; — *window*, das Erkerfenster.
bay (3) [bei], *s. keep at* —, in Schach halten, *stand at* —, sich zur Wehr setzen.
bay (4) [bei], *s.* (*Bot.*) der Lorbeer.
bay (5) [bei], *v.n.* bellen, heulen; — *for the moon*, das Unmögliche wollen.
bayonet ['beiənet], *s.* das Bajonett.
bazaar [bə'zɑː], *s.* der Basar.
be [biː], *v.n. irr.* sein, existieren; sich befinden; vorhanden sein; — *off*, sich fortmachen (*move*); ungenießbar sein (*meat, food*); nicht mehr da sein (— *off the menu*).
beach [biːtʃ], *s.* der Strand, das Gestade.
beacon ['biːkən], *s.* das Leuchtfeuer; der Leuchtturm; das Lichtsignal.
bead [biːd], *s.* das Tröpfchen (*drop*); die Perle (*pearl*); (*pl.*) die Perlschnur; der Rosenkranz.
beadle ['biːdl], *s.* (*Univ.*) der Pedell; (*Eccl.*) Kirchendiener.
beagle ['biːgl], *s.* der Jagdhund, Spürhund.
beak [biːk], *s.* der Schnabel.
beaker ['biːkə], *s.* der Becher.
beam [biːm], *s.* der Balken (*wood*); der Strahl (*ray*), Glanz. — *v.n.* strahlen.

# bean

**bean** [bi:n], *s.* (*Bot.*) die Bohne; *not a* —, keinen Heller *or* Pfennig.

**bear** (1) [bɛə], *s.* (*Zool.*) der Bär.

**bear** (2) [bɛə], *v.a. irr.* tragen, ertragen; gebären (*a child*); hegen (*sorrow etc.*). — *v.n.* — *upon*, drücken auf (*pressure*), Einfluß haben (*effect*); — *up*, geduldig sein.

**bearable** [ˈbɛərəbl], *adj.* tragbar, erträglich.

**beard** [biəd], *s.* der Bart. — *v.a.* trotzen (*Dat.*).

**bearded** [ˈbiədid], *adj.* bärtig.

**bearer** [ˈbɛərə], *s.* der Träger, Überbringer.

**bearing** [ˈbɛəriŋ], *s.* das Benehmen, die Haltung (*manner*); (*pl.*) (*Geog.*) die Richtung; *lose o.'s* —*s*, sich verlaufen; *ball* —*s*, (*Engin.*) das Kugellager.

**bearpit** [ˈbɛəpit], *s.* der Bärenzwinger.

**beast** [bi:st], *s.* das Tier; die Bestie.

**beastliness** [ˈbi:stlinis], *s.* das tierische Benehmen; die Grausamkeit (*cruelty*); die Gemeinheit.

**beastly** [ˈbi:stli], *adj.* grausam, (*coll.*) schrecklich.

**beat** [bi:t], *s.* der Schlag, das Schlagen; (*Mus.*) der Takt; die Runde, das Revier (*patrol district*). — *v.a. irr.* schlagen; — *time*, den Takt schlagen; — *carpets*, Teppich klopfen. — *v.n.* — *it*, sich davonmachen.

**beater** [ˈbi:tə], *s.* (*Hunt.*) der Treiber.

**beatify** [bi:ˈætifai], *v.a.* seligsprechen.

**beau** [bou], *s.* der Stutzer, Geck.

**beautiful** [ˈbju:tiful], *adj.* schön.

**beautify** [ˈbju:tifai], *v.a.* schön machen, verschönern.

**beauty** [ˈbju:ti], *s.* die Schönheit; — *salon*, der Schönheitssalon; *Sleeping Beauty*, das Dornröschen.

**beaver** [ˈbi:və], *s.* (*Zool.*) der Biber.

**becalm** [biˈka:m], *v.a.* besänftigen.

**because** [biˈkɔz], *conj.* weil, da; — *of*, wegen, um ... willen.

**beck** [bek], *s.* der Wink; *be at s.o.'s* — *and call*, jemandem zu Gebote stehen.

**beckon** [ˈbekən], *v.a., v.n.* winken, heranwinken, zuwinken (*Dat.*).

**become** [biˈkʌm], *v.n. irr.* werden. — *v.a.* anstehen, sich schicken, passen (*Dat.*).

**becoming** [biˈkʌmiŋ], *adj.* passend, kleidsam.

**bed** [bed], *s.* das Bett; Beet (*flowers*); (*Geol.*) das Lager, die Schicht. — *v.a.* betten, einbetten.

**bedaub** [biˈdɔ:b], *v.a.* beflecken, beschmieren.

**bedding** [ˈbediŋ], *s.* das Bettzeug.

**bedevil** [biˈdevəl], *v.a.* behexen, verhexen.

**bedew** [biˈdju:], *v.a.* betauen.

**bedlam** [ˈbedləm], *s.* (*coll.*) das Irrenhaus; *this is* —, die Hölle ist los.

**Bedouin** [ˈbeduin], *s.* der Beduine.

**bedpost** [ˈbedpoust], *s.* der Bettpfosten.

**bedraggle** [biˈdrægl], *v.a.* beschmutzen.

**bedridden** [ˈbedridn], *adj.* bettlägerig, ans Bett gefesselt.

**bedroom** [ˈbedru:m], *s.* das Schlafzimmer.

**bedtime** [ˈbedtaim], *s.* die Schlafenszeit.

**bee** [bi:], *s.* (*Ent.*) die Biene; *have a* — *in o.'s bonnet*, einen Vogel haben.

**beech** [bi:tʃ], *s.* (*Bot.*) die Buche.

**beef** [bi:f], *s.* das Rindfleisch; — *tea*, die Fleischbrühe.

**beehive** [ˈbi:haiv], *s.* der Bienenkorb.

**beeline** [ˈbi:lain], *s.* die Luftlinie, gerade Linie; *make a* — *for s.th.*, schnurstracks auf etwas losgehen.

**beer** [biə], *s.* das Bier; *small* —, Dünnbier, (*fig.*) unbedeutend.

**beet** [bi:t], *s.* (*Bot.*) die Runkelrübe; *sugar* —, die Zuckerrübe.

**beetle** [bi:tl], *s.* (*Ent.*) der Käfer; — *brows*, buschige Augenbrauen.

**beetroot** [ˈbi:tru:t], *s.* (*Bot.*) die rote Rübe.

**befall** [biˈfɔ:l], *v.a. irr.* widerfahren (*Dat.*). — *v.n.* zustoßen (*happen*, *Dat.*).

**befit** [biˈfit], *v.a.* sich geziemen, sich gebühren.

**befog** [biˈfɔg], *v.a.* in Nebel hüllen; umnebeln.

**before** [biˈfɔ:], *adv.* vorn; voraus, voran; (*previously*) vorher, früher; (*already*) bereits, schon. — *prep.* vor. — *conj.* bevor, ehe.

**beforehand** [biˈfɔ:hænd], *adv.* im voraus, vorher.

**befoul** [biˈfaul], *v.a.* beschmutzen.

**befriend** [biˈfrend], *v.a.* befreunden, unterstützen (*support*).

**beg** [beg], *v.a., v.n.* betteln (um, *for*); ersuchen, bitten (*request*).

**beget** [biˈget], *v.a. irr.* zeugen.

**beggar** [ˈbegə], *s.* der Bettler.

**begin** [biˈgin], *v.a., v.n. irr.* beginnen, anfangen.

**beginner** [biˈginə], *s.* der Anfänger.

**beginning** [biˈginiŋ], *s.* der Anfang.

**begone** [biˈgɔn], *interj.* hinweg! fort! mach dich fort!

**begrudge** [biˈgrʌdʒ], *v.a.* nicht gönnen, mißgönnen.

**beguile** [biˈgail], *v.a.* bestricken, betrügen; — *the time*, die Zeit vertreiben.

**behalf** [biˈha:f], *s.* *on* — *of*, um ... (*Genit.*) willen; im Interesse von, im Namen von.

**behave** [biˈheiv], *v.n.* sich benehmen, sich betragen.

**behaviour** [biˈheivjə], *s.* das Benehmen, Gebaren.

**behead** [biˈhed], *v.a.* enthaupten.

**behind** [biˈhaind], *adv.* hinten, zurück; hinterher. — *prep.* hinter.

**behindhand** [biˈhaindhænd], *adj., adv.* im Rückstand (*in arrears*); zurück (*backward*).

**behold** [biˈhould], *v.a. irr.* ansehen; er blicken; *lo and* —! siehe da!

**beholden** [biˈhouldən], *adj.* verpflichtet (*to, Dat.*).

**beholder** [biˈhouldə], *s.* der Zuschauer.

320

**behove** [bi'houv], *v.a.* sich geziemen, ziemen, gebühren.

**being** ['bi:iŋ], *pres. part for the time* —, vorläufig, für jetzt. — *s.* das Sein, die Existenz; das Wesen (*creature*).

**belated** [bi'leitid], *adj.* verspätet.

**belch** [beltʃ], *v.n.* rülpsen, aufstoßen.

**belfry** ['belfri], *s.* der Glockenturm.

**Belgian** ['beldʒən], *adj.* belgisch. — *s.* der Belgier.

**belie** [bi'lai], *v.a.* täuschen, Lügen strafen.

**belief** [bi'li:f], *s.* der Glaube, die Meinung.

**believable** [bi'li:vəbl], *adj.* glaubhaft, glaublich.

**believe** [bi'li:v], *v.a., v.n.* glauben (*an, Acc.*), vertrauen (*Dat.*).

**believer** [bi'li:və], *s.* der Gläubige.

**belittle** [bi'litl], *v.a.* schmälern, verkleinern, verächtlich machen.

**bell** [bel], *s.* die Glocke; Schelle, Klingel; — *-founder,* der Glockengießer; — *-boy,* (*Am.*) — *-hop,* der Hotelpage.

**belligerent** [bi'lidʒərənt], *adj.* kriegführend. — *s.* der Kriegführende.

**bellow** ['belou], *v.n.* brüllen. — *s.* das Gebrüll.

**bellows** ['belouz], *s.* der Blasebalg.

**belly** ['beli], *s.* der Bauch.

**belong** [bi'lɔŋ], *v.n.* gehören (*Dat.*), angehören (*Dat.*).

**belongings** [bi'lɔŋiŋz], *s. pl.* die Habe, das Hab und Gut, der Besitz.

**beloved** [bi'lʌvd, -vid], *adj.* geliebt, lieb.

**below** [bi'lou], *adv.* unten. — *prep.* unterhalb (*Genit.*), unter (*Dat.*).

**Belshazzar** [bel'ʃæzə]. Belsazar, *m.*

**belt** [belt], *s.* der Gürtel, Gurt; der Riemen; (*Tech.*) Treibriemen; *below the* —, unfair. — *v.a.* umgürten; (*coll.*) prügeln.

**bemoan** [bi'moun], *v.a.* beklagen.

**bench** [bentʃ], *s.* die Bank; der Gerichtshof (*court of law*); *Queen's Bench,* der oberste Gerichtshof.

**bend** [bend], *v.a., v.n. irr.* biegen; beugen; sich krümmen. — *s.* die Biegung, Krümmung, Kurve.

**bendable** ['bendəbl], *adj.* biegsam.

**beneath** [bi'ni:θ] *see* **below.**

**Benedictine** [beni'dikti:n], *s.* der Benediktiner.

**benediction** [beni'dikʃən], *s.* der Segensspruch, der Segen; die Segnung.

**benefaction** [beni'fækʃən], *s.* die Wohltat.

**benefactor** ['benifæktə], *s.* der Wohltäter.

**benefactress** ['benifæktris], *s.* die Wohltäterin.

**beneficent** [be'nefisənt], *adj.* wohltätig.

**beneficial** [beni'fiʃəl], *adj.* vorteilhaft, gut (*for,* für), wohltuend.

**benefit** ['benifit], *s.* der Vorteil, Nutzen. — *v.n.* Nutzen ziehen. — *v.a.* nützen.

**benevolence** [be'nevələns], *s.* das Wohlwollen.

**benevolent** [be'nevələnt], *adj.* wohlwollend; — *society,* der Unterstützungsverein, — *fund,* der Unterstützungsfond.

**Bengali** [ben'gɔ:li], *adj.* bengalisch. — *s.* der Bengale.

**benign** [bi'nain], *adj.* gütig, mild.

**bent** [bent], *adj.* gebogen, krumm; — *on something,* versessen auf etwas. — *s.* die Neigung, der Hang; — *for,* Vorliebe für.

**benzene** ['benzi:n], *s.* das Benzol, Kohlenbenzin.

**benzine** ['benzi:n], *s.* das Benzin.

**bequeath** [bi'kwi:θ], *v.a.* vermachen, hinterlassen.

**bequest** [bi'kwest], *s.* das Vermächtnis.

**bereave** [bi'ri:v], *v.a. irr.* berauben (*durch Tod*).

**bereavement** [bi'ri:vmənt], *s.* der Verlust (*durch Tod*).

**beret** ['berei], *s.* die Baskenmütze.

**Bernard** ['bə:nəd]. Bernhard, *m.*; *St.* — *dog,* der Bernhardiner.

**berry** ['beri], *s.* die Beere.

**berth** [bə:θ], *s.* (*Naut.*) der Ankerplatz; die Koje. — *v.a.,* sich anlegen; vor Anker gehen (*boat*).

**beseech** [bi'si:tʃ], *v.a. irr.* bitten, anflehen.

**beset** [bi'set], *v.a. irr.* bedrängen, bedrücken, umringen.

**beside** [bi'said], *prep.* außer, neben, nahe bei; — *the point,* unwesentlich; *quite* — *the mark,* weit vom Schuß.

**besides** [bi'saidz], *adv.* überdies, außerdem.

**besiege** [bi'si:dʒ], *v.a.* belagern.

**besmirch** [bi'smə:tʃ], *v.a.* besudeln.

**besom** ['bi:zəm], *s.* der Besen.

**bespatter** [bi'spætə], *v.a.* bespritzen.

**bespeak** [bi'spi:k], *v.a. irr.* bestellen; (*Tail.*) *bespoke,* nach Maß gemacht *or* gearbeitet.

**best** [best], *adj.* (*superl. of* **good**) best; — *adv.* am besten. — *s. want the* — *of both worlds,* alles haben wollen; *to the* — *of my ability,* nach besten Kräften; *to the* — *of my knowledge,* soviel ich weiß.

**bestial** ['bestjəl], *adj.* bestialisch, tierisch.

**bestow** [bi'stou], *v.a.* verleihen, erteilen.

**bet** [bet], *s.* die Wette. — *v.a., v.n. irr.* wetten.

**betray** [bi'trei], *v.a.* verraten.

**betrayal** [bi'treiəl], *s.* der Verrat.

**betrayer** [bi'treiə], *s.* der Verräter.

**betroth** [bi'trouð], *v.a.* verloben.

**betrothal** [bi'trouðəl], *s.* die Verlobung.

**better** ['betə], *adj.* (*comp. of* **good**) besser. — *adv. you had* — *go,* es wäre besser, Sie gingen; *think* — *of it,* sich eines Besseren besinnen, sich's überlegen. — *s. get the* —, überwinden; *so much the* —, desto *or* umso besser. — *v.a.* verbessern; — *oneself,* seine Lage verbessern.

**betterment** ['betəmənt], *s.* die Verbesserung.

**between** [bi'twi:n], *adv.* dazwischen.
— *prep.* zwischen; unter (*among*).

**bevel** ['bevəl], *s.* der Winkelpasser;
die Schräge. — *v.a.* abkanten.

**beverage** ['bevəridʒ], *s.* das Getränk.

**bevy** ['bevi], *s.* die Schar (*of beauties,
von Schönen*).

**bewail** [bi'weil], *v.a., v.n.* betrauern,
beweinen; trauern um.

**beware** [bi'wɛə], *v.n.* sich hüten (*of,
vor*).

**bewilder** [bi'wildə], *v.a.* verwirren.

**bewitch** [bi'witʃ], *v.a.* bezaubern.

**beyond** [bi'jɔnd], *adv.* jenseits, drüben.
— *prep.* über ... hinaus; jenseits;
außer.

**biannual** [bai'ænjuəl], *adj.* halbjährlich.

**bias** ['baiəs], *s.* die Neigung; das
Vorurteil (*prejudice*). — *v.a.* beeinflussen.

**bias(s)ed** ['baiəsd], *adj.* voreingenommen.

**bib** [bib], *s.* der Schürzenlatz; das
Lätzchen.

**Bible** [baibl], *s.* die Bibel.

**Biblical** ['biblikəl], *adj.* biblisch.

**bibliography** [bibli'ɔgrəfi], *s.* die Bib-
liographie.

**bibliophile** ['bibliɔfail], *s.* der Bücher-
freund.

**biceps** ['baiseps], *s.* der Bizeps, Arm-
muskel.

**bicker** ['bikə], *v.n.* zanken, hadern.

**bickering** ['bikəriŋ], *s.* das Gezänk,
Hadern, der Hader.

**bicycle** ['baisikl], (*coll.*) **bike** [baik], *s.*
das Fahrrad.

**bicyclist** ['baisiklist], *s.* der Radfahrer.

**bid** [bid], *v.a., v.n. irr.* gebieten, befehlen (*Dat.*) (*order*); bieten (*at auction*);
— *farewell*, Lebewohl sagen. — *s.* das
Gebot, Angebot (*at auction*).

**bidding** ['bidiŋ], *s.* der Befehl (*order*);
das Bieten (*at auction*); die Einladung
(*invitation*).

**bide** [baid], *v.n. irr.* verbleiben, verharren (*in, by, bei*).

**biennial** [bai'eniəl], *adj.* zweijährig,
alle zwei Jahre.

**bier** [biə], *s.* die Bahre, Totenbahre.

**big** [big], *adj.* groß, dick (*fat*); *talking
—*, großsprecherisch; *talk —*,
prahlen.

**bigamy** ['bigəmi], *s.* die Bigamie, die
Doppelehe.

**bigness** ['bignis], *s.* die Größe, Dicke.

**bigoted** ['bigɔtid], *adj.* bigott, fanatisch.

**bigotry** ['bigɔtri], *s.* die Bigotterie.

**bigwig** ['bigwig], *s.* (*coll.*) die vornehme Person, der Würdenträger.

**bike** *see* **bicycle.**

**bilberry** ['bilbəri], *s.* (*Bot.*) die Heidelbeere.

**bile** [bail], *s.* die Galle.

**bilge** [bildʒ], *s.* die Bilge, der Schiffsboden; (*coll.*) Unsinn (*nonsense*).

**bilious** ['biljəs], *adj.* gallig.

**bill** (1) [bil], *s.* der Schnabel (*bird*).

**bill** (2) [bil], die Rechnung (*account*);
— *of exchange*, der Wechsel; — *of
entry*, die Zolldeklaration; — *of fare*,
die Speisekarte; (*Parl.*) der Gesetzentwurf; das Plakat (*poster*). — *v.a.*
anzeigen.

**billboard** ['bilbɔ:d], *s.* (*Am.*) das
Anschlagbrett.

**billet** ['bilit], *s.* das Billett (*card*); das
Quartier, die Unterkunft (*army*).

**billfold** ['bilfould], *s.* (*Am.*) die
Brieftasche.

**billhook** ['bilhuk], *s.* die Hippe.

**billiards** ['biljədz], *s.* das Billard-
spiel.

**billow** ['bilou], *s.* die Woge. — *v.n.*
wogen.

**bin** [bin], *s.* der Behälter.

**bind** [baind], *v.a. irr.* binden, verpflichten; (*Law*) — *over*, zu gutem
Benehmen verpflichten.

**binder** ['baində], *s.* der Binder, Buchbinder.

**bindery** ['baindəri], *s.* die Buch-
binderei, Binderwerkstatt.

**binding** ['baindiŋ], *s.* der Einband.

**binnacle** ['binəkl], *s.* das Kompaß-
häuschen.

**binocular** [bi'nɔkjulə], *adj.* für beide
Augen. — *s.* (*pl.*) das Fernglas, der
Feldstecher.

**binomial** [bai'noumiəl], *adj.* bino-
misch. — *s.* (*pl.*) (*Maths.*) das Binom,
der zweigliedrige Ausdruck.

**biochemical** [baio'kemikəl], *adj.* bio-
chemisch.

**biochemistry** [baio'kemistri], *s.* die
Biochemie.

**biographer** [bai'ɔgrəfə], *s.* der Bio-
graph.

**biographical** [baio'græfikəl], *adj.* bio-
graphisch.

**biography** [bai'ɔgrəfi], *s.* die Biographie, die Lebensbeschreibung.

**biological** [baio'lɔdʒikəl], *adj.* biologisch.

**biology** [bai'ɔlədʒi], *s.* die Biologie.

**biometric(al)** [baio'metrik(əl)], *adj.*
biometrisch.

**biometry** [bai'ɔmitri], *s.* die Biometrie.

**biophysical** [baio'fizikəl], *adj.* bio-
physisch.

**biophysics** [baio'fiziks], *s.* die Bio-
physik.

**biped** ['baiped], *s.* der Zweifüßler.

**biplane** ['baiplein], *s.* (*Aviat.*) der
Doppeldecker.

**birch** [bə:tʃ], *s.* (*Bot.*) die Birke; die
Birkenrute, Rute (*cane*). — *v.a.*
(mit der Rute) züchtigen.

**bird** [bə:d], *s.* der Vogel; — *of passage,*
der Wandervogel, Zugvogel; —*cage,*
der Vogelkäfig, das Vogelbauer; —
*fancier,* der Vogelzüchter; —*'s-eye
view,* die Vogelperspektive.

**birth** [bə:θ], *s.* die Geburt; — *certificate,*
der Geburtsschein.

**birthday** ['bə:θdei], *s,* der Geburts-
tag.

**biscuit** ['biskit], *s.* der *or* das Keks;
der Zwieback.

bisect [bai'sekt], v.a. entzweischneiden, halbieren.

bisection [bai'sekʃən], s. die Zweiteilung, Halbierung.

bishop ['biʃəp], s. der Bischof; (Chess) der Läufer.

bishopric ['biʃəprik], s. das Bistum.

bismuth ['bizməθ], s. der or das Wismut.

bison ['baisən], s. (Zool.) der Bison.

bit [bit], s. der Bissen (bite), das Bißchen (little —); das Gebiß (bridle); der Bart (of key).

bitch [bitʃ], s. die Hündin.

bite [bait], v.a. irr. beißen. — s. das Beißen (mastication); der Biß (morsel).

biting ['baitiŋ], adj. (also fig.) beißend, scharf. — adv. — cold, bitterkalt.

bitter ['bitə], adj. bitter.

bittern ['bitə:n], s. (Orn.) die Rohrdommel.

bitterness ['bitənis], s. die Bitterkeit.

bitumen [bi'tju:mən], s. der Bergteer, Asphalt.

bivouac ['bivuæk], s. (Mil.) das Biwak, Lager.

bizarre [bi'za:], adj. bizarr, wunderlich.

blab [blæb], v.a., v.n. schwatzen, ausplaudern (give away).

blabber ['blæbə], s. (coll.) der Schwätzer.

black [blæk], adj. schwarz; — sheep, der Taugenichts; — pudding, die Blutwurst; Black Forest, der Schwarzwald; Black Maria, der Polizeiwagen; (coll.) die grüne Minna; Black Sea, das schwarze Meer.

blackberry ['blækbəri], s. (Bot.) die Brombeere.

blackbird ['blækbə:d], s. (Orn.) die Amsel.

blackguard ['blæga:d], s. der Spitzbube, Schurke.

blackmail ['blækmeil], v.a. erpressen. — s. die Erpressung.

blacksmith ['blæksmiθ], s. der Grobschmied.

bladder ['blædə], s. (Anat.) die Blase.

blade [bleid], s. die Klinge (razor); der Halm (grass); shoulder —, das Schulterblatt.

blamable ['bleiməbl], adj. tadelnswert, tadelhaft.

blame [bleim], s. der Tadel, die Schuld. — v.a. tadeln, beschuldigen, die Schuld zuschreiben (Dat.).

blameless ['bleimlis], adj. tadellos, schuldlos.

blanch [bla:ntʃ], v.n. erbleichen, weiß werden. — v.a. weiß machen.

bland [blænd], adj. mild, sanft.

blandish ['blændiʃ], v.a. schmeicheln (Dat.).

blandishment ['blændiʃmənt], s. (mostly in pl.) die Schmeichelei.

blandness ['blændnis], s. die Milde, Sanftheit.

blank [blæŋk], adj. blank, leer; reimlos (verse); leave a —, einen Raum freilassen; — cartridge, die Platzpatrone.

blanket ['blæŋkit], s. die Decke; (coll.) a wet —, ein langweiliger Kerl, der Spielverderber.

blare [blɛə], v.n. schmettern.

blaspheme [blæs'fi:m], v.a., v.n. lästern, fluchen.

blasphemous ['blæsfiməs], adj. lästerlich.

blasphemy ['blæsfəmi], s. die Gotteslästerung.

blast [bla:st], v.a. sprengen, zerstören. — s. der Windstoß (gust); der Stoß (trumpets); die Explosion (bomb); — furnace, der Hochofen. — excl. (sl.) —! zum Teufel!

blasting ['bla:stiŋ], s. das Sprengen.

blatant ['bleitənt], adj. laut, lärmend; dreist.

blaze [bleiz], s. die Flamme (flame); das Feuer; der Glanz (colour etc.). — v.n. flammen; leuchten (shine). — v.a. ausposaunen, bekannt machen (make known).

blazer ['bleizə], s. die Sportjacke, Klubjacke.

blazon ['bleizən], v.a. verkünden.

bleach [bli:tʃ], v.a. bleichen. — s. das Bleichmittel.

bleak [bli:k], adj. öde, rauh; trübe, freudlos.

bleakness ['bli:knis], s. die Öde (scenery); Traurigkeit, Trübheit.

bleary ['bliəri], adj. trübe; — eyed, triefäugig.

bleat [bli:t], v.n. blöken.

bleed [bli:d], v.n. irr. bluten. — v.a. bluten lassen; erpressen (blackmail).

blemish ['blemiʃ], s. der Makel, der Fehler. — v.a. schänden, entstellen.

blench [blentʃ], v.n. zurückweichen, stutzen.

blend [blend], v.a., v.n. mischen, vermengen; sich mischen. — s. die Mischung, Vermischung.

bless [bles], v.a. segnen; beglücken; loben.

blessed [blest, 'blesid], adj. gesegnet, selig.

blessing ['blesiŋ], s. der Segen.

blight [blait], s. der Meltau. — v.a. verderben.

blind [blaind], adj. blind; — man's buff, Blinde Kuh; — spot, der schwache Punkt. — s. die Blende, das Rouleau; Venetian —, die Jalousie. — v.a. blind machen, täuschen.

blindfold ['blaindfould], adj. mit verbundenen Augen.

blindness ['blaindnis], s. die Blindheit.

blindworm ['blaindwə:m], s. (Zool.) die Blindschleiche.

blink [bliŋk], s. das Blinzeln. — v.n. blinzeln, blinken. — v.a. nicht sehen wollen.

blinkers ['bliŋkəz], s. pl. die Scheuklappen.

bliss [blis], s. die Wonne, Seligkeit.

blissful ['blisful], adj. wonnig, selig.

blister ['blistə], s. die Blase. — v.n. Blasen ziehen, Blasen bekommen.

# blithe

**blithe** [blaið], *adj.* munter, lustig, fröhlich.
**blitheness** ['blaiðnis], *s.* die Munterkeit, Fröhlichkeit.
**blizzard** ['blizəd], *s.* der Schneesturm.
**bloated** ['bloutid], *adj.* aufgeblasen, aufgedunsen.
**bloater** ['bloutə], *s.* (*Zool.*) der Bückling.
**blob** [blɔb], *s.* der Kleks.
**block** [blɔk], *s.* der Block, Klotz (*wood*); Häuserblock (*houses*); — *letters*, große Druckschrift. — *v.a.* blockieren, hemmen (*hinder*); sperren (*road*).
**blockade** [blɔ'keid], *s.* die Blockade.
**blockhead** ['blɔkhed], *s.* der Dummkopf.
**blonde** [blɔnd], *adj.* blond. — *s.* die Blondine.
**blood** [blʌd], *s.* das Blut; — *vessel*, das Blutgefäß.
**bloodcurdling** ['blʌdkə:dliŋ], *adj.* haarsträubend.
**bloodless** ['blʌdlis], *adj.* blutlos, unblutig.
**bloodthirsty** ['blʌdθə:sti], *adj.* blutdürstig.
**bloody** ['blʌdi], *adj.* blutig; (*vulg.*) verflucht.
**bloom** [blu:m], *s.* die Blüte; die Blume. — *v.n.* blühen.
**bloomers** ['blu:məz], *s. pl.* altmodische Unterhosen für Damen.
**blooming** ['blu:miŋ], *adj.* blühend.
**blossom** ['blɔsəm], *s.* die Blüte. — *v.n.* blühen, Blüten treiben.
**blot** [blɔt], *s.* der Klecks; Fleck; (*fig.*) der Schandfleck. — *v.a.* beflecken; löschen (*ink*); — *out*, ausmerzen, austilgen; *blotting paper*, das Löschpapier.
**blotch** [blɔtʃ], *s.* der Hautfleck; die Pustel; der Klecks (*blot*).
**blotter** ['blɔtə], *s.* der Löscher.
**blouse** [blauz], *s.* die Bluse.
**blow** (1) [blou], *s.* der Schlag.
**blow** (2) [blou], *v.a. irr.* blasen; wehen; — *o.'s own trumpet*, prahlen; anfachen (*fire*); — *o.'s nose*, sich schneuzen. — *v.n.* schnaufen, keuchen; — *up*, in die Luft sprengen.
**blower** ['blouə], *s.* das Gebläse; der Bläser.
**blowpipe** ['bloupaip], *s.* das Lötrohr.
**blubber** ['blʌbə], *s.* der Walfischspeck, der Tran. — *v.n.* schluchzen, heulen, flennen.
**bludgeon** ['blʌdʒən], *s.* der Knüppel; die Keule (*club*). — *v.a.* niederschlagen.
**blue** [blu:], *adj.* blau; schwermütig (*sad*); — *blooded*, aus edlem Geblüte.
**bluebell** ['blu:bell], *s.* (*Bot.*) die Glockenblume.
**bluebottle** ['blu:bɔtl], *s.* (*Ent.*) die Schmeißfliege.
**bluestocking** ['blu:stɔkiŋ], *s.* der Blaustrumpf.

**bluff** [blʌf], *adj.* grob, schroff. — *s.* der Bluff, die Täuschung, der Trick. — *v.a.*, *v.n.* vortäuschen (*pretend*), bluffen; verblüffen (*deceive*).
**blunder** ['blʌndə], *s.* der Fehler, Schnitzer. — *v.n.* einen Fehler machen.
**blunderer** ['blʌndərə], *s.* der Tölpel.
**blunderbuss** ['blʌndəbʌs], *s.* die Donnerbüchse.
**blunt** [blʌnt], *adj.* stumpf (*edge*); derb, offen (*speech*). — *v.a.* abstumpfen; verderben (*appetite*).
**bluntness** ['blʌntnis], *s.* die Stumpfheit (*edge*); die Derbheit (*speech*).
**blur** [blə:], *s.* der Fleck. — *v.a.* verwischen.
**blurt** [blə:t], *v.a.* — *out*, herausplatzen.
**blush** [blʌʃ], *v.n.* erröten. — *s.* die Schamröte, das Erröten.
**bluster** ['blʌstə], *s.* das Toben, Brausen. — *v.n.* toben, brausen.
**blustering** ['blʌstəriŋ], *adj.* lärmend, tobend.
**boa** ['bouə], *s.* (*Zool.*) die Boa.
**boar** [bɔ:], *s.* (*Zool.*) der Eber.
**board** [bɔ:d], *s.* das Brett (*wood*); die Tafel (*notice* —); die Verpflegung (*food*); — *and lodging*, die Vollpension; die Behörde, der Ausschuß (*officials*). — *v.a.* — *up*, vernageln, zumachen; — *someone*, verpflegen; — *a steamer*, an Bord gehen; — *ing school*, das Internat, das Pensionat.
**boarder** ['bɔ:də], *s.* der Internatsschüler; der Pensionär.
**boast** [boust], *v.n.* prahlen, sich rühmen. — *s.* der Stolz (*pride*).
**boastful** ['boustful], *adj.* prahlerisch.
**boat** [bout], *s.* das Boot; *rowing-* —, das Ruderboot; der Kahn.
**bob** [bɔb], *s.* der Knicks; (*coll.*) der Schilling. — *v.n.* baumeln; springen; *bobbed hair*, der Bubikopf.
**bobbin** ['bɔbin], *s.* die Spule, der Klöppel.
**bobsleigh** ['bɔbslei], *s.* der Bob(sleigh), Rennschlitten.
**bodice** ['bɔdis], *s.* das Mieder, Leibchen.
**bodied** ['bɔdid], *adj. suffix;* *able-* —, gesund, stark.
**body** ['bɔdi], *s.* der Körper; die Körperschaft (*organisation*).
**bodyguard** ['bɔdiga:d], *s.* die Leibwache.
**Boer** ['bouə], *s.* der Bure.
**bog** [bɔg], *s.* der Sumpf. — *v.a.* (*coll.*) — *down*, einsinken. — *adj.* böhmisch; künstlerhaft.
**Bohemian** [bo'hi:mjən], *s.* der Böhme. — *adj.* böhmisch; künstlerhaft.
**boil** (1) [bɔil], *v.a.*, *v.n.* kochen, sieden. — *s.* das Kochen; *—ing point,* der Siedepunkt.
**boil** (2) [bɔil], *s.* (*Med.*) die Beule, der Furunkel.
**boisterous** ['bɔistərəs], *adj.* ungestüm; laut (*noisy*).
**boisterousness** ['bɔistərəsnis], *s.* die Heftigkeit, Lautheit.

**bold** [bould], *adj.* kühn, dreist; *make* —, sich erkühnen.
**boldness** ['bouldnis], *s.* die Kühnheit, Dreistigkeit.
**Bolivian** [bə'livjən], *adj.* bolivianisch. —*s.* der Bolivianer.
**bolster** ['boulstə], *s.* das Polster, Kissen.
**bolt** [boult], *s.* der Bolzen, Riegel (*on door*); der Pfeil (*arrow*). — *v.a.* verriegeln (*bar*); verschlingen (*devour*). — *v.n.* davonlaufen (*run away*), durchgehen (*abscond*).
**bomb** [bɔm], *s.* die Bombe. — *v.a.* bombardieren.
**bombard** [bɔm'ba:d], *v.a.* bombardieren.
**bombardment** [bɔm'ba:dmənt], *s.* die Beschießung.
**bombastic** [bɔm'bæstik], *adj.* schwülstig, bombastisch (*style*).
**bombproof** ['bɔmpru:f], *adj.* bombensicher.
**bond** [bɔnd], *s.* das Band (*link*); die Schuldverschreibung (*debt*); *in* —, unter Zollverschluß; (*pl.*) die Fesseln (*fetters*). — *v.a.* (*Chem.*) binden; (*Comm.*) zollpflichtig erklären (*declare dutiable*).
**bondage** ['bɔndidʒ], *s.* die Knechtschaft.
**bone** [boun], *s.* der Knochen; die Gräte (*fish*); — *china*, feines Geschirr, das Porzellan; — *of contention*, der Zankapfel; — *dry*, staubtrocken; — *idle*, stinkfaul; — *lace*, die Klöppelspitze. — *v.a.* Knochen oder Gräten entfernen.
**bonfire** ['bɔnfaiə], *s.* das Freudenfeuer.
**bonnet** ['bɔnit], *s.* die Haube, das Häubchen.
**bonny** ['bɔni], *adj.* hübsch, nett.
**bony** ['bouni], *adj.* beinern, knöchern.
**book** [buk], *s.* das Buch. — *v.a.* belegen (*seat*); eine Karte lösen (*ticket*); engagieren (*engage*).
**bookbinder** ['bukbaində], *s.* der Buchbinder.
**bookcase** ['bukkeis], *s.* der Bücherschrank.
**bookie** *see* bookmaker.
**booking-office** ['bukiɲɔfis], *s.* der Fahrkartenschalter; die Kasse (*Theat. etc.*)
**book-keeper** ['bukki:pə], *s.* der Buchhalter.
**book-keeping** ['bukki:piɲ], *s.* die Buchhaltung; *double entry* —, doppelte Buchführung, *single entry* —, einfache Buchführung.
**bookmaker** ['bukmeikə] (*abbr.* **bookie** ['buki]), *s.* (*Racing*) der Buchmacher.
**bookmark(er)** ['bukma:k(ə)], *s.* das Lesezeichen.
**bookseller** ['bukselə], *s.* der Buchhändler.
**bookshop** ['bukʃɔp], *s.* die Buchhandlung.
**bookstall** ['bukstɔ:l], *s.* der Bücherstand.

**bookworm** ['bukwə:m], *s.* der Bücherwurm.
**boom** (1) [bu:m], *s.* der Aufschwung; Boom; (*Comm.*) die Konjunktur; Hausse.
**boom** (2) [bu:m], *v.n.* dröhnen, (dumpf) schallen.
**boon** [bu:n], *s.* die Wohltat.
**boor** [buə], *s.* der Lümmel.
**boorish** ['buəriʃ], *adj.* lümmelhaft.
**boot** [bu:t], *s.* der Stiefel, hohe Schuh. — *v.a.* mit dem Stiefel stoßen, kicken.
**booth** [bu:ð], *s.* die (Markt) Bude; Kabine, Zelle.
**bootlace** ['bu:tleis], *s.* der Schnürsenkel, der Schnürriemen.
**booty** ['bu:ti], *s.* die Beute.
**booze** [bu:z], *v.n.* (*coll.*) saufen.
**boozy** ['bu:zi], *adj.* (*coll.*) angeheitert, leicht betrunken.
**border** ['bɔ:də], *s.* der Rand; die Grenze. — *v.a.*, *v.n.* angrenzen (*on*); einsäumen (*surround*).
**borderer** ['bɔ:dərə], *s.* der Grenzbewohner.
**bore** [bɔ:], *v.a.* bohren; langweilen (*be boring*). — *s.* das Bohrloch (*drill-hole*), die Bohrung (*drilling*); der langweilige Kerl (*person*).
**boredom** ['bɔ:dəm], *s.* die Langeweile.
**borer** ['bɔ:rə], *s.* der Bohrer (*drill*).
**born** [bɔ:n], *adj.* geboren.
**borrow** ['bɔrou], *v.a.* borgen, entlehnen.
**borrowing** ['bɔrouiɲ], *s.* das Borgen, Entlehnen.
**bosom** ['buzəm], *s.* der Busen.
**boss** [bɔs], *s.* der Beschlag, der Buckel; (*coll.*) der Chef.
**botanical** [bə'tænikəl], *adj.* botanisch.
**botanist** ['bɔtənist], *s.* der Botaniker.
**botany** ['bɔtəni], *s.* die Botanik.
**botch** [bɔtʃ], *s.* das Flickwerk. — *v.a.* verderben, verhunzen.
**both** [bouθ], *adj.*, *pron.* beide, beides; — *of them*, beiden. — *conj.* — ... *and*, sowohl ... als auch.
**bother** ['bɔðə], *v.a.* plagen, stören, belästigen; — *it!* zum Henker damit! — *v.n.* sich bemühen. — *s.* die Belästigung, das Ärgernis.
**bottle** [bɔtl], *s.* die Flasche. — *v.a.* in Flaschen abfüllen.
**bottom** ['bɔtəm], *s.* der Boden, Grund (*ground*); die Ursache (*cause*); (*Naut.*) der Schiffsboden.
**bottomless** ['bɔtəmlis], *adj.* grundlos, bodenlos.
**bough** [bau], *s.* der Zweig, Ast.
**boulder** ['bouldə], *s.* der Felsblock.
**bounce** [bauns], *v.a.* aufprallen lassen (*ball*). — *v.n.* aufprallen. — *s.* der Rückprall, Aufprall.
**bound** (1) [baund], *s.* der Sprung; *by leaps and* —*s*, sehr schnell, sprunghaft. — *v.n.* springen, prallen.
**bound** (2) [baund], *v.a.* begrenzen, einschränken. — *adj.* verpflichtet; *he is* — *to* (*inf.*), er wird sicherlich ...

**bound** (3) [baund], *adj.* — *for*, auf dem Wege nach.
**boundary** ['baundəri], *s.* die Grenzlinie, Grenze.
**bounder** ['baundə], *s.* der ungezogene Bursche.
**boundless** ['baundlis], *adj.* grenzenlos, unbegrenzt.
**bounteous** ['bauntiəs], *adj.* freigebig; reichlich (*plenty*).
**bounty** ['baunti], *s.* die Freigebigkeit (*generosity*); (*Comm.*) Prämie.
**bouquet** [bu'kei], *s.* das Bukett, der Blumenstrauß; die Blume (*wine*).
**bourgeois** ['buəʒwɑ:], *s.* der Bürger; Philister. — *adj.* kleinbürgerlich, philisterhaft.
**bow** (1) [bau], *s.* (*Naut.*) der Bug; —*sprit*, das Bugspriet.
**bow** (2) [bau], *s.* die Verbeugung, Verneigung. — *v.n.* sich verneigen, sich verbeugen. — *v.a.* neigen.
**bow** (3) [bou], *s.* (*Mus.*) der Bogen; die Schleife (*ribbon*). — *v.a.* streichen (*violin*).
**bowel** ['bauəl], *s.* der Darm; (*pl.*) die Eingeweide.
**bowl** (1) [boul], *s.* die Schale, der Napf, die Schüssel.
**bowl** (2) [boul], *s.* die Holzkugel; (*pl.*) das Rasenkugelspiel, Bowlingspiel. — *v.n.* (*Cricket*) den Ball werfen.
**bowler** (1) ['boulə], *s.* (*hat*) der steife Hut, die Melone.
**bowler** (2) ['boulə], *s.* (*Sport*) der Ballmann.
**box** (1) [bɔks], *s.* (*Bot.*) der Buchsbaum.
**box** (2) [bɔks], *s.* die Büchse, Dose, Schachtel, der Kasten; (*Theat.*) die Loge; — *office*, die Theaterkasse.
**box** (3) [bɔks], *s.* der Schlag; — *on the ear*, die Ohrfeige. — *v.n.* boxen.
**boxer** ['bɔksə], *s.* der Boxer; Boxkämpfer.
**Boxing Day** ['bɔksiŋ'dei], der zweite Weihnachtstag.
**boy** [bɔi], *s.* der Junge, Knabe; Diener (*servant*).
**boyish** ['bɔiiʃ], *adj.* knabenhaft.
**boyhood** ['bɔihud], *s.* das Knabenalter.
**brace** [breis], *s.* das Band; die Klammer (*clamp*); — *of partridges*, das Paar Rebhühner; die Spange (*denture*). — *v.a.* spannen, straffen. — *v.r.* — *yourself!* stähle dich!
**bracelet** ['breislit], *s.* das Armband.
**braces** ['breisiz], *s. pl.* die Hosenträger.
**bracken** ['brækən], *s.* (*Bot.*) das Farnkraut.
**bracket** ['brækit], *s.* die Klammer; *income* —, die Einkommensgruppe. — *v.a.* (ein-)klammern; (*Maths.*) in Klammern setzen.
**brackish** ['brækiʃ], *adj.* salzig.
**brad** [bræd], *s.* der kopflose Nagel; — *awl*, der Vorstechbohrer.
**brag** [bræg], *v.n.* prahlen.

**braggart** ['brægət], *s.* der Prahlhans.
**Brahmin** ['brɑ:min], *s.* der Brahmane.
**braid** [breid], *s.* die Borte; der Saumbesatz. — *v.a.* (mit Borten) besetzen.
**Braille** [breil], *s.* die Blindenschrift.
**brain** [brein], *s.* das Gehirn, Hirn; *scatter*-—*ed*, zerstreut.
**brainwave** ['breinweiv], *s.* der Geistesblitz.
**brake** [breik], *s.* die Bremse. — *v.a.* bremsen.
**bramble** [bræmbl], *s.* der (*Bot.*) Brombeerstrauch.
**bran** [bræn], *s.* die Kleie.
**branch** [brɑ:ntʃ], *s.* der Ast, Zweig; (*Comm.*) die Zweigstelle, Filiale. — *v.n.* — *out*, sich verzweigen; — *out into*, sich ausbreiten, etwas Neues anfangen; — *off*, abzweigen.
**brand** [brænd], *s.* der (Feuer) Brand; das Brandmal (*on skin*); die Sorte, Marke (*make*); — *new*, funkelnagelneu. — *v.a.* brandmarken, kennzeichnen.
**brandish** ['brændiʃ], *v.a.* schwingen, herumschwenken.
**brandy** ['brændi], *s.* der Branntwein, Kognac, Weinbrand.
**brass** [brɑ:s], *s.* das Messing; — *band*, die Blechmusik, Militärmusikkapelle; — *founder*, Erzgießer; Gelbgießer; (*sl.*) die Frechheit (*impudence*).
**brassiere** ['bræsiəə], *s.* der Büstenhalter.
**brat** [bræt], *s.* (*coll.*) das Kind, der Balg.
**brave** [breiv], *adj.* tapfer, kühn. — *v.a.* trotzen, standhalten (*Dat.*). — *s.* der Held, Krieger; der Indianer (*redskin*).
**bravery** ['breivəri], *s.* die Tapferkeit.
**brawl** [brɔ:l], *s.* der Krawall, die Rauferei. — *v.n.* zanken, lärmen.
**brawn** [brɔ:n], *s.* die Sülze; (*fig.*) die Körperkraft, Stärke.
**brawny** ['brɔ:ni], *adj.* stark, sehnig.
**bray** [brei], *v.n.* iah sagen, Eselslaute von sich geben (*donkey*). — *s.* das Iah des Esels, das Eselsgeschrei.
**brazen** [breizn], *adj.* (*Metall.*) aus Erz; unverschämt (*shameless*).
**brazenfaced** ['breiznfeisd], *adj.* unverschämt.
**brazier** ['breiziə], *s.* der Kupferschmied; die Kohlenpfanne.
**Brazil** [brə'zil]. Brasilien, *n.*; — *nut*, die Paranuß.
**Brazilian** [brə'ziliən], *adj.* brasilianisch. — *s.* der Brasilianer.
**breach** [bri:tʃ], *s.* die Bresche; der Bruch (*break*); die Verletzung; der Vertragsbruch (*of contract*); der Verstoß (*of, gegen, etiquette etc.*).
**bread** [bred], *s.* das Brot; *brown* —, das Schwarzbrot; — *and butter*, das Butterbrot.
**breadth** [bretθ], *s.* die Breite, Weite.

**break** [breik], *s.* der Bruch (*breach*); die Lücke (*gap*); die Chance (*chance*); *a lucky* —, ein glücklicher Zufall, ein Glücksfall; die Pause (*from work*). — *v.a., v.n. irr.* brechen; — *off*, Pause machen; — *in*, unterbrechen (*interrupt*); — *in*, (*horse*) einschulen, zureiten; — *up*, abbrechen (*school, work*); — *away*, sich trennen, absondern; — *down*, zusammenbrechen (*health*); (*Am.*) analysieren; auflösen.

**breakage** ['breikidʒ], *s.* der Bruch, der Schaden (*damage*).

**breakdown** ['breikdoun], *s.* der Zusammenbruch (*health*); die Panne (*car*); (*Am.*) die Analyse (*analysis*).

**breaker** ['breikə], *s.* die Brandungswelle, Brandung.

**breakfast** ['brekfəst], *s.* das Frühstück. — *v.n.* frühstücken.

**breast** [brest], *s.* die Brust.

**breath** [breθ], *s.* der Atem; der Hauch (*exhalation*); *with bated* —, mit verhaltenem Atem.

**breathe** [bri:ð], *v.a., v.n.* atmen.

**breathing** ['bri:ðiŋ], *s.* die Atmung.

**breathless** ['breθlis], *adj.* atemlos.

**breech** [bri:tʃ], *s.* der Boden.

**breeches** ['britʃiz], *s.pl.* Reithosen, *f. pl.*

**breed** [bri:d], *v.a. irr.* zeugen, züchten (*cattle, etc.*). — *v.n.* sich vermehren. — *s.* die Zucht, die Art (*type*); die Rasse (*race*).

**breeder** ['bri:də], *s.* der Züchter.

**breeding** ['bri:diŋ], *s.* die gute Kinderstube (*manners*); die Erziehung; das Züchten (*of plants, cattle etc.*).

**breeze** [bri:z], *s.* die Briese.

**breezy** ['bri:zi], *adj.* windig; lebhaft (*manner*), beschwingt (*tone*).

**brethren** ['breðrən], *s. pl.* (*obs.*) die Brüder.

**Breton** [bretn], *adj.* bretonisch. — *s.* der Bretagner, Bretone.

**brevet** ['brevit], *s.* das Patent.

**breviary** ['bri:viəri], *s.* das Brevier.

**brevity** ['breviti], *s.* die Kürze.

**brew** [bru:], *v.a.* brauen. — *s.* das Gebräu, das Bier (*beer*).

**brewer** ['bru:ə], *s.* der Brauer, Bierbrauer.

**brewery** ['bru:əri], *s.* die Brauerei, das Brauhaus.

**briar, brier** ['braiə], *s.* (*Bot.*) der Dornstrauch, die wilde Rose.

**bribe** [braib], *v.a.* bestechen. — *s.* das Bestechungsgeld.

**bribery** ['braibəri], *s.* die Bestechung.

**brick** [brik], *s.* der Ziegel, Backstein; *drop a* —, eine Taktlosigkeit begehen, einen Schnitzer machen.

**bricklayer** ['brikleiə], *s.* der Maurer.

**bridal** [braidl], *adj.* bräutlich.

**bride** [braid], *s.* die Braut.

**bridegroom** ['braidgru:m], *s.* der Bräutigam.

**bridesmaid** ['braidzmeid], *s.* die Brautjungfer.

**bridge** [bridʒ], *s.* die Brücke. — *v.a.* überbrücken; — *the gap*, die Lücke füllen.

**bridle** [braidl], *s.* der Zaum, Zügel. — *v.a.* aufzäumen. — *v.n.* sich brüsten.

**brief** [bri:f], *adj.* kurz, bündig, knapp. — *s.* der Schriftsatz, der Rechtsauftrag, die Instruktionen, *f. pl.* (*instructions*). — *v.a.* instruieren, beauftragen; informieren (*inform*).

**brigade** [bri'geid], *s.* die Brigade.

**brigand** ['brigənd], *s.* der Brigant, Straßenräuber.

**bright** [brait], *adj.* hell, glänzend (*shiny*); klug, intelligent (*clever*).

**brighten** [braitn], *v.a.* glänzend machen (*polish etc.*); erhellen, aufheitern (*cheer*).

**brightness** ['braitnis], *s.* der Glanz; die Helligkeit; die Klugheit (*cleverness*).

**brill** [bril], *s.* (*Zool.*) der Glattbutt.

**brilliance, brilliancy** ['briljəns, -jənsi], *s.* der Glanz, die Pracht.

**brim** [brim], *s.* der Rand (*glass*); die Krempe (*hat*). — *v.n.* — (*over*) *with*, überfließen von.

**brimful** ['brimful], *adj.* übervoll.

**brimstone** ['brimstoun], *s.* der Schwefel; — *butterfly*, der Zitronenfalter.

**brindled** [brindld], *adj.* scheckig, gefleckt.

**brine** [brain], *s.* die Salzsole, das Salzwasser.

**bring** [briŋ], *v.a. irr.* bringen; — *about*, zustande bringen; — *forth*, hervorbringen; gebären; — *forward*, fördern; anführen; — *on*, herbeiführen; — *up*, erziehen, aufziehen.

**brink** [briŋk], *s.* (*fig.*) der Rand; — *of a precipice*, Rand eines Abgrundes.

**briny** ['braini], *adj.* salzig.

**brisk** [brisk], *adj.* frisch, munter, feurig (*horse*).

**brisket** ['briskit], *s.* die Brust (eines Tieres).

**briskness** ['brisknis], *s.* die Lebhaftigkeit.

**bristle** [brisl], *s.* die Borste. — *v.n.* sich sträuben.

**British** ['britiʃ], *adj.* britisch.

**Britisher, Briton** ['britiʃə, 'britən], *s.* der Brite.

**brittle** [britl], *adj.* zerbrechlich, spröde.

**brittleness** ['britlnis], *s.* die Sprödigkeit, Zerbrechlichkeit.

**broach** [broutʃ], *v.a.* anzapfen, anschneiden; — *a subject*, ein Thema berühren.

**broad** [brɔ:d], *adj.* breit, weit; ordinär, derb (*joke*); — *-minded*, duldsam, weitherzig.

**broadcast** ['brɔ:dka:st], *v.a.* senden, übertragen (*radio*). — *s.* die Sendung, das Programm.

**broadcaster** ['brɔ:dka:stə], *s.* der im Radio Vortragende *or* Künstler (*artist*); Ansager.

**broadcasting** ['brɔ:dka:stiŋ], *s.* das Senden, der Rundfunk; — *station*, der Sender, die Rundfunkstation.

# broadcloth

**broadcloth** ['brɔːdklɔθ], *s.* das feine Tuch.

**broaden** [brɔːdn], *v.a.* erweitern, verbreitern.

**brocade** [bro'keid], *s.* der Brokat.

**brogue** [broug], *s.* der grobe Schuh; der irische Akzent.

**broil** [brɔil], *v.a.* braten, rösten.

**broke** [brouk], *adj.* (*coll.*) pleite.

**broken** ['broukən], *adj.* gebrochen; zerbrochen; unterbrochen (*interrupted*).

**broker** ['broukə], *s.* der Makler.

**bronchial** ['brɔŋkjəl], *adj.* (*Anat.*) bronchial, in *or* von der Luftröhre, Luftröhren-.

**bronchitis** [brɔŋ'kaitis], *s.* (*Med.*) die Luftröhrenentzündung, Bronchitis.

**bronze** [brɔnz], *s.* (*Metall.*) die Bronze, Bronzefarbe.

**brooch** [broutʃ], *s.* die Brosche.

**brood** [bruːd], *s.* die Brut. — *v.n.* brüten; grübeln (*meditate*).

**brook** (1) [bruk], *s.* der Bach.

**brook** (2) [bruk], *v.a.* ertragen, leiden.

**brooklet** ['bruklit], *s.* das Bächlein.

**broom** [bruːm], *s.* der Besen; (*Bot.*) der Ginster.

**broth** [brɔθ], *s.* die Brühe; *meat* —, Fleischbrühe.

**brothel** ['brɔθəl], *s.* das Bordell.

**brother** ['brʌðə], *s.* der Bruder; — *-in-law*, der Schwager.

**brotherhood** ['brʌðəhud], *s.* die Bruderschaft.

**brotherly** ['brʌðəli], *adj.* brüderlich.

**brow** [brau], *s.* die Braue, Augenbraue; der Kamm (*hill*); die Stirn(e) (*forehead*).

**browbeat** ['braubiːt], *v.a.* einschüchtern.

**brown** [braun], *adj.* braun; *in a — study*, in tiefem Nachsinnen.

**browse** [brauz], *v.n.* weiden (*cattle*); stöbern, (durch-)blättern (*in books etc.*).

**Bruin** ['bruːin]. Braun, Meister Petz, der Bär.

**bruise** [bruːz], *v.a.* quetschen, stoßen; (wund) schlagen. — *s.* die Quetschung.

**Brunswick** ['brʌnzwik]. Braunschweig, *n.*

**brunt** [brʌnt], *s.* der Anprall; *bear the* —, der Wucht ausgesetzt sein, den Stoß auffangen.

**brush** [brʌʃ], *s.* die Bürste (*clothes*); der Pinsel (*paint, painting*); — *stroke*, der Pinselstrich. — *v.a., v.n.* bürsten, abbürsten; — *against s.o.*, mit jemandem zusammenstoßen, streifen (*an, Acc.*); — *up one's English*, das Englisch auffrischen; — *off*, abschütteln.

**brushwood** ['brʌʃwud], *s.* das Gestrüpp.

**brusque** [brusk], *adj.* brüsk, barsch.

**Brussels** ['brʌsəlz]. Brüssel, *n.*; — *sprouts*, (*Bot.*) der Rosenkohl.

**brutal** [bruːtl], *adj.* brutal, grausam.

**brutality** [bruː'tæliti], *s.* die Brutalität.

**brute** [bruːt], *s.* der Unmensch.

**bubble** [bʌbl], *s.* die Blase; (*fig.*) der Schwindel (*swindle*). — *v.n.* sprudeln, wallen, schäumen.

**buccaneer** [bʌkə'niə], *s.* der Seeräuber.

**buck** [bʌk], *s.* (*Zool.*) der Bock; (*Am. sl.*) der Dollar. — *v.a.* — *up*, aufmuntern. — *v.n.* — *up*, sich zusammenraffen.

**bucket** ['bʌkit], *s.* der Eimer, Kübel.

**buckle** [bʌkl], *s.* die Schnalle. — *v.a.* zuschnallen; biegen. — *v.n.* sich krümmen.

**buckler** ['bʌklə], *s.* der Schild.

**buckram** ['bʌkrəm], *s.* die Steifleinwand.

**buckskin** ['bʌkskin], *s.* das Wildleder.

**buckwheat** ['bʌkwiːt], *s.* (*Bot.*) der Buchweizen.

**bucolic** [bjuː'kɔlik], *adj.* bukolisch, ländlich, Schäfer-.

**bud** [bʌd], *s.* (*Bot.*) die Knospe. — *v.n.* knospen.

**buddy** ['bʌdi], *s.* (*Am.*) der Freund, Kamerad.

**budge** [bʌdʒ], *v.n.* sich rühren, sich regen.

**budget** ['bʌdʒit], *s.* das Budget; der Haushaltsplan; der Etat; *present the* —, den Staatsetat vorlegen. — *v.n.* voranschlagen (*for*), planen.

**buff** [bʌf], *adj.* ledergelb.

**buffalo** ['bʌfəlou], *s.* (*Zool.*) der Büffel.

**buffer** ['bʌfə], *s.* der Puffer.

**buffet** (1) ['bʌfit], *s.* der Puff, Faustschlag (*blow*). — *v.a.* schlagen, stoßen.

**buffet** (2) ['bufei], *s.* das Buffet, der Anrichtetisch.

**buffoon** [bʌ'fuːn], *s.* der Possenreißer.

**buffoonery** [bʌ'fuːnəri], *s.* die Possen, *f. pl.*; das Possenreißen.

**bug** [bʌg], *s.* (*Ent.*) die Wanze; (*Am.*) der Käfer; (*coll.*) das Insekt.

**buggy** ['bʌgi], *s.* der Einspänner.

**bugle** [bjuːgl], *s.* (*Mus.*) das Signalhorn, die Signaltrompete.

**bugler** ['bjuːglə], *s.* (*Mus.*) der Trompeter.

**build** [bild], *v.a., v.n. irr.* bauen; errichten; — *on*, sich verlassen auf (*rely on*). — *s.* die Statur, Figur (*figure*).

**builder** ['bildə], *s.* der Bauherr, Baumeister (*employer*); Bauarbeiter (*worker*).

**building** ['bildiŋ], *s.* das Gebäude, der Bau; — *site*, der Bauplatz.

**bulb** [bʌlb], *s.* (*Bot.*) der Knollen, die Zwiebel; *Dutch* —, die Tulpe; (*Elec.*) die Birne.

**bulbous** ['bʌlbəs], *adj.* zwiebelartig; dickbäuchig.

**Bulgarian** [bʌl'gɛəriən], *adj.* bulgarisch. — *s.* der Bulgare.

**bulge** [bʌldʒ], *s.* die Ausbauchung; die Ausbuchtung (*in fighting line*). — *v.n.* herausragen, anschwellen.

**bulk** [bʌlk], *s.* die Masse, Menge; *buy in* —, im Großen einkaufen.

# buttery

**bulky** [ˈbʌlki], *adj.* schwer (*heavy*); massig (*stodgy*); unhandlich.
**bull** (1) [bul], *s.* (*Zool.*) der Bulle, Stier; —'s eye, das Schwarze (*target*).
**bull** (2) [bul], *s.* (*Papal*) die Bulle, der Erlass.
**bulldog** [ˈbuldɔg], *s.* der Bullenbeißer.
**bullet** [ˈbulit], *s.* die Kugel, das Geschoß.
**bulletin** [ˈbulitin], *s.* das Bulletin, der Tagesbericht.
**bullfight** [ˈbulfait], *s.* der Stierkampf.
**bullfinch** [ˈbulfintʃ], *s.* (*Orn.*) der Dompfaff.
**bullfrog** [ˈbulfrɔg], *s.* (*Zool.*) der Ochsenfrosch.
**bullion** [ˈbuljən], *s.* der Goldbarren, Silberbarren.
**bullock** [ˈbulək], *s.* (*Zool.*) der Ochse.
**bully** [ˈbuli], *s.* der Raufbold, Angeber, Großtuer (*braggart*); der Tyrann. — *v.a.* tyrannisieren, einschüchtern.
**bulrush** [ˈbulrʌʃ], *s.* (*Bot.*) die Binse.
**bulwark** [ˈbulwək], *s.* das Bollwerk, die Verteidigung.
**bump** [bʌmp], *s.* der Schlag, der Stoß. — *v.a.* stoßen.
**bun** [bʌn], *s.* das Rosinenbrötchen; das süße Brötchen; (*hair*) der Knoten.
**bunch** [bʌntʃ], *s.* der Bund (*keys*); der Strauß (*flowers*); die Traube (*grapes*). — *v.a.* zusammenfassen, zusammenbinden, zusammenraffen.
**bundle** [bʌndl], *s.* das Bündel.
**bung** [bʌŋ], *s.* der Spund (*in barrel*).
**bungle** [bʌŋgl], *v.a.* verpfuschen, verderben.
**bungler** [ˈbʌŋglə], *s.* der Stümper.
**bunion** [ˈbʌnjən], *s.* die Fußschwiele.
**bunk** (1) [bʌŋk], *s.* die (Schlaf-)Koje.
**bunk** (2) [bʌŋk], *s.* (*coll.*) der Unsinn.
**bunker** [ˈbʌŋkə], *s.* der Kohlenraum, Bunker.
**bunting** [ˈbʌntiŋ], *s.* das Flaggentuch.
**buoy** [bɔi], *s.* die Boje.
**buoyant** [ˈbɔiənt], *adj.* schwimmend; lebhaft, heiter.
**buoyancy** [ˈbɔiənsi], *s.* die Schwimmkraft; die Schwungkraft.
**burden** (1) [bəːdn], *s.* die Bürde, Last. — *v.a.* belasten, beladen.
**burden** (2) [bəːdn], *s.* der Refrain; der Hauptinhalt.
**burdensome** [ˈbəːdnsəm], *adj.* beschwerlich.
**bureau** [bjuəˈrou], *s.* der Schreibtisch; das Büro.
**bureaucracy** [bjuəˈrɔkrəsi], *s.* die Bürokratie.
**burgess** [ˈbəːdʒis], *s.* der Bürger.
**burglar** [ˈbəːglə], *s.* der Einbrecher.
**burglary** [ˈbəːgləri], *s.* der Einbruch, der Diebstahl.
**burgomaster** [ˈbəːgomɑːstə], *s.* der Bürgermeister.
**Burgundian** [bəːˈgʌndiən], *adj.* burgundisch. —, *s.* der Burgunder.
**Burgundy** (1) [ˈbəːgəndi], das Burgund.
**Burgundy** (2) [ˈbəːgəndi], *s.* der Burgunder(-wein).

**burial** [ˈberiəl], das Begräbnis; — *ground*, der Kirchhof, Friedhof; — *service*, die Totenfeier, Trauerfeier.
**burlesque** [bəːˈlesk], *s.* die Burleske, Posse.
**burly** [ˈbəːli], *adj.* dick, stark.
**Burmese** [bəːˈmiːz], *adj.* birmesisch. — *s.* der Birmese.
**burn** [bəːn], *v.a., v.n. irr.* brennen, verbrennen. — *s.* das Brandmal.
**burner** [ˈbəːnə], *s.* der Brenner.
**burnish** [ˈbəːniʃ], *v.a.* polieren.
**burred** [bəːd], *adj.* überliegend; (*Metall.*) ausgehämmert; — *over*, (*Metall.*) breitgeschmiedet.
**burrow** [ˈbʌrou], *s.* der Bau, (*rabbits etc.*). —*v.n.* sich eingraben; wühlen.
**burst** [bəːst], *v.a., v.n. irr.* bersten, platzen, explodieren (*explode*); — *out laughing*, laut auflachen; — *into tears*, in Tränen ausbrechen; — *into flames*, aufflammen; sprengen (*blow up*). — *s.* der Ausbruch; die Explosion.
**bury** [ˈberi], *v.a.* begraben; beerdigen.
**bus** [bʌs], *s.* der Autobus, Omnibus.
**busby** [ˈbʌzbi], *s.* (*Mil.*) die Bärenmütze.
**bush** [buʃ], *s.* der Busch.
**bushel** [buʃl], *s.* der Scheffel.
**bushy** [ˈbuʃi], *adj.* buschig.
**business** [ˈbiznis], *s.* das Geschäft; die Beschäftigung, die Tätigkeit (*activity*); Aufgabe, Obliegenheit; der Handel (*trade*); on —, geschäftlich.
**businesslike** [ˈbiznislaik], *adj.* geschäftsmäßig, nüchtern, praktisch.
**businessman** [ˈbiznismæn], *s.* der Geschäftsmann.
**bust** (1) [bʌst], *s.* die Büste.
**bust** (2) [bʌst], *v.a., v.n.* (*coll.*) sprengen; *go* —, bankrott machen.
**bustard** [ˈbʌstəd], *s.* (*Orn.*) die Trappe.
**bustle** [bʌsl], *s.* der Lärm, die Aufregung. — *v.n.* aufgeregt umherlaufen; rührig sein (*be active*).
**busy** [ˈbizi], *adj.* geschäftig (*active*); beschäftigt (*engaged*, mit, *in*); *be* —, zu tun haben.
**but** [bʌt], *conj.* aber, jedoch; sondern. — *adv.* nur, bloß; — *yesterday*, erst gestern. — *prep.* außer; *all* — *two*, alle außer zwei.
**butcher** [ˈbutʃə], *s.* der Metzger, Fleischer; —'s *knife*, das Fleischmesser.
**butchery** [ˈbutʃəri], *s.* die Schlächterei; das Blutbad, das Gemetzel.
**butler** [ˈbʌtlə], *s.* der oberste Diener; Kellermeister.
**butt** [bʌt], *s.* das dicke Ende; der Kolben (*rifle*); der Stoß (*blow*); die Zielscheibe (*target*). — *v.a.* stoßen, spießen.
**butter** [ˈbʌtə], *s.* die Butter. — *v.a.* mit Butter bestreichen; — *up*, schmeicheln (*Dat.*).
**butterfly** [ˈbʌtəflai], *s.* (*Ent.*) der Schmetterling.
**buttery** [ˈbʌtəri], *s.* die Speisekammer.

329

# buttock(s)

**buttock(s)** [ˈbʌtək(s)], *s.* der Hintere, das Gesäß.
**button** [bʌtn], *s.* der Knopf. — *v.a.* — *up*, knöpfen, zumachen.
**buttress** [ˈbʌtris], *s.* der Strebepfeiler.
**buxom** [ˈbʌksəm], *adj.* drall, gesund.
**buy** [bai], *v.a. irr.* kaufen.
**buzz** [bʌz], *s.* das Summen. — *v.n.* summen.
**buzzard** [ˈbʌzəd], *s.* (*Orn.*) der Bussard.
**by** [bai], *prep.* (*beside*) neben, an; (*near*) nahe; (*before*) gegen, um, bei; (*about*) bei; (*from, with*) durch, von, mit; — *the way*, nebenbei bemerkt; — *way of*, mittels. — *adv.* (*nearby*) nahe; nebenan.
**by-election** [ˈbaiilekʃən], *s.* die Nachwahl; Ersatzwahl.
**bygone** [ˈbaigɔn], *adj.* vergangen.
**bylaw, byelaw** [ˈbailɔ:], *s.* die Bestimmung.
**Byzantine** [baiˈzæntain], *adj.* byzantinisch.

# C

**C** [si:]. das C (*also Mus.*).
**cab** [kæb], *s.* (*horse-drawn*) die Droschke, der Wagen; das Taxi; —*stand*, der Droschkenhalteplatz; (*Motor.*) der Taxiplatz, Taxistand.
**cabaret** [ˈkæbərei], *s.* das Kabarett, die Kleinbühne.
**cabbage** [ˈkæbidʒ], *s.* (*Bot.*) der Kohl.
**cabin** [ˈkæbin], *s.* die Kabine (*boat*); die Hütte (*hut*); — *-boy*, der Schiffsjunge.
**cabinet** [ˈkæbinet], *s.* das Kabinett (*government*); der Schrank (*cupboard*); das kleine Zimmer *or* Nebenzimmer (*mainly Austr.*); (*Rad.*) das Gehäuse; — *maker*, der Kunsttischler.
**cable** [keibl], *s.* das Kabel (*of metal*), das Seil (*metal or rope*); das Telegramm. — *v.a.* kabeln, telegraphieren.
**cablegram** [ˈkeiblgræm], *s.* die (Kabel-) Depesche.
**cabman** [ˈkæbmən], *s.* der Taxichauffeur.
**caboose** [kəˈbu:s], *s.* die Schiffsküche.
**cabriolet** [kæbrioˈlei], *s.* das Kabriolett.
**cackle** [kækl], *v.n.* gackern (*hens*); schnattern (*geese*); (*fig.*) schwatzen.
**cacophony** [kəˈkɔfəni], *s.* der Mißklang.
**cad** [kæd], *s.* der gemeine Kerl, Schuft.
**cadaverous** [kəˈdævərəs], *adj.* leichenhaft.
**caddie** [ˈkædi], *s.* der Golfjunge.
**caddy** [ˈkædi], *s.* *tea* —, die Teebüchse, Teedose.
**cadence** [ˈkeidəns], *s.* (*Phonet.*) der Tonfall; (*Mus.*) die Kadenz.
**cadet** [kəˈdet], *s.* (*Mil.*) der Kadett.
**cadge** [kædʒ], *v.a.* erbetteln.

**Caesar** [ˈsi:zə]. Cäsar, *m.*
**Caesarean** [siˈzɛəriən], *adj.* cäsarisch; — *operation* or *section*, (*Med.*) der Kaiserschnitt.
**cafeteria** [kæfəˈtiəriə], *s.* das Selbstbedienungsrestaurant.
**cage** [keidʒ], *s.* (*Zool.*) der Käfig; (*Orn.*) das Vogelbauer. — *v.a.* einfangen, einsperren.
**cagey** [ˈkeidʒi], *adj.* (*coll.*) argwöhnisch, zurückhaltend; schlau.
**cairn** [kɛən], *s.* (*Archaeol.*) der Steinhaufen, der Grabhügel.
**caitiff** [ˈkeitif], *adj.* niederträchtig. — *s.* der Schuft.
**cajole** [kəˈdʒoul], *v.a.* schmeicheln (*Dat.*).
**cake** [keik], *s.* der Kuchen; — *of soap*, das Stück Seife; *have o.'s* — *and eat it*, alles haben. — *v.a., v.n.* zusammenbacken; —*d with dirt*, mit Schmutz beschmiert.
**calamity** [kəˈlæmiti], *s.* das Unheil, Unglück; Elend.
**calcareous** [kælˈkɛəriəs], *adj.* (*Geol.*) kalkartig.
**calculate** [ˈkælkjuleit], *v.a.* berechnen.
**calculation** [kælkjuˈleiʃən], *s.* die Berechnung.
**calendar** [ˈkæləndə], *s.* der Kalender.
**calf** [kɑ:f], *s.* (*Zool.*) das Kalb; (*Anat.*) die Wade; — *love*, die Jugendliebe.
**calibre** [ˈkælibə], *s.* das Kaliber.
**calico** [ˈkælikou], *s.* der Kaliko, Kattun.
**Caliph** [ˈkeilif], *s.* der Kalif.
**calk** (1) [kɔ:k], *v.a.* beschlagen (*horse*).
**calk** (2), **caulk** [kɔ:k], *v.a.* (*Naut.*) abdichten.
**call** [kɔ:l], *v.a., v.n.* rufen, herbeirufen; (*Am.*) antelefonieren, anrufen (*ring up*); (*name*) nennen; — *to account*, zur Rechenschaft ziehen; (*summon*) kommen lassen; — *for*, abholen; *this* —*s for*, das berechtigt zu. — *s.* der Ruf, Anruf; die (*innere*) Berufung, der Beruf.
**callbox** [ˈkɔ:lbɔks] *see* **phone box**.
**calling** [ˈkɔ:liŋ], *s.* der Beruf, das Gewerbe (*occupation*).
**callous** [ˈkæləs], *adj.* schwielig (*hands*); (*fig.*) unempfindlich, hart, gemein.
**callow** [ˈkælou], *adj.* ungefiedert (*bird*); (*fig.*) unerfahren.
**calm** [kɑ:m], *adj.* ruhig, still; gelassen. — *s.* die Ruhe; (*Naut.*) Windstille. — *v.a.* beruhigen. — *v.n.* — *down*, sich beruhigen, sich legen (*storm etc.*).
**caloric** [kæˈlɔrik], *adj.* Wärme-, warm; (*Chem.*) kalorisch.
**calorie, calory** [ˈkæləri], *s.* die Kalorie.
**calumny** [ˈkæləmni], *s.* die Verleumdung.
**calve** [kɑ:v], *v.n.* kalben, Kälber kriegen.
**cambric** [ˈkæmbrik],*s.*der Batist(*textile*).
**camel** [ˈkæməl], *s.* (*Zool.*) das Kamel.
**cameo** [ˈkæmiou], *s.* die Kamee.
**camera** [ˈkæmərə], *s.* (*Phot.*) die Kamera.
**camomile** [ˈkæməmail], *s.* (*Bot.*) die Kamille.

**camp** [kæmp], *s.* das Lager; Zeltlager.
— *v.n.* sich lagern, ein Lager aufschlagen, zelten.
**campaign** [kæm'pein], *s.* der Feldzug.
— *v.n.* einen Feldzug mitmachen;
(*fig.*) Propaganda machen.
**camphor** ['kæmfə], *s.* der Kampfer.
**camping** ['kæmpiŋ], *s.* die Lagerausrüstung (*equipment*); das Lagern
(*activity*), das Zelten.
**can** (1) [kæn], *s.* die Kanne; die Büchse;
*watering* —, die Gießkanne. — *v.a.*
(*Am.*) einmachen, einkochen (*fruit*).
**can** (2) [kæn], *v. aux. irr.* können,
imstande sein, vermögen.
**Canadian** [kə'neidiən], *adj.* kanadisch.
— *s.* der Kanadier.
**canal** [kə'næl], *s.* der Kanal; — *lock*,
die Kanalschleuse.
**canalize** ['kænəlaiz], *v.a.* kanalisieren,
leiten.
**cancel** ['kænsəl], *v.a.* widerrufen, absagen
(*show*); aufheben, ungültig machen.
**cancellation** [kænsə'leiʃən], *s.* die
Aufhebung, Absage, Widerrufung.
**cancer** ['kænsə], *s.* (*Med., Astrol.*) der
Krebs.
**cancerous** ['kænsərəs], *adj.* (*Med.*)
krebsartig.
**candelabra** [kændi'laːbrə], *s.* der
Kandelaber, Leuchter.
**candid** ['kændid], *adj.* offen, aufrichtig.
**candidate** ['kændideit], *s.* der Kandidat, Bewerber.
**candidature** ['kændiditʃə], *s.* die
Kandidatur, die Bewerbung.
**candied** ['kændid], *adj.* gezuckert,
kandiert (*fruit*).
**candle** [kændl], *s.* die Kerze, das Licht.
**Candlemas** ['kændlməs], (*Eccl.*)
Lichtmeß.
**candlestick** ['kændlstik], *s.* der Kerzenleuchter.
**candlewick** ['kændlwik], *s.* der Kerzendocht (*textile*).
**candour** ['kændə], *s.* die Offenheit,
Aufrichtigkeit.
**candy** ['kændi], *s.* (*Am.*) das Zuckerwerk, (*pl.*) Süßigkeiten. — *v.a.*
verzuckern.
**cane** [kein], *s.* (*Bot.*) das Rohr, der
Rohrstock; Spazierstock. — *v.a.* (mit
dem Stock) schlagen.
**canine** ['kænain], *adj.* Hunde-, hündisch; — *tooth*, der Eckzahn.
**canister** ['kænistə], *s.* die Blechbüchse,
der Kanister.
**canker** ['kæŋkə], *s.* (*Bot.*) der Brand;
(*Bot.*) der Pflanzenrost; (*fig.*) eine
zerfressende Krankheit.
**cannibal** ['kænibəl], *s.* der Kannibale,
Menschenfresser.
**cannon** ['kænən], *s.* die Kanone, das
Geschütz.
**canoe** [kə'nuː], *s.* das Kanu.
**canon** ['kænən], *s.* (*Mus., Eccl.*) der
Kanon; die Regel; (*Eccl.*) der Domherr; — *law*, das kanonische Recht.
**canonize** ['kænənaiz], *v.a.* (*Eccl.*)
kanonisieren, heiligsprechen.

**canopy** ['kænəpi], *s.* der Baldachin.
**cant** [kænt], *s.* die Heuchelei.
**can't, cannot** [kaːnt, 'kænɔt] see **can** (2).
**cantankerous** [kæn'tæŋkərəs], *adj.*
zänkisch, mürrisch.
**cantata** [kæn'taːtə], *s.* (*Mus.*) die
Kantate.
**canteen** [kæn'tiːn], *s.* die Kantine (*restaurant*); die Besteckgarnitur (*set of
cutlery*).
**canter** ['kæntə], *s.* der Galopp, der
Kurzgalopp.
**canticle** ['kæntikl], *s.* (*Eccl.*) der
Lobgesang, das Loblied.
**canto** ['kæntou], *s.* (*Lit.*) der Gesang.
**canton** ['kæntɔn], *s.* (*Pol.*) der Kanton,
der Bezirk.
**canvas** ['kænvəs], *s.* das Segeltuch;
(*Art*) die Malerleinwand; die Zeltplane (*tent*).
**canvass** ['kænvəs], *v.a., v.n.* (*Pol.*)
um Stimmen werben.
**canvasser** ['kænvəsə], *s.* (*Pol.*) der
Werber, Stimmensammler.
**cap** [kæp], *s.* die Kappe, Mütze; die
Haube; der Deckel. —*v.a.* übertreffen.
**capability** [keipə'biliti], *s.* die Fähigkeit.
**capable** ['keipəbl], *adj.* fähig (*Genit.*),
imstande (*of*, zu); tüchtig.
**capacious** [kə'peiʃəs], *adj.* geräumig.
**capacity** [kə'pæsiti], *s.* der Inhalt, die
Geräumigkeit; die Fassungskraft
(*intellect*); die Leistungsfähigkeit
(*ability*); der Fassungsraum (*space*).
**cape** (1) [keip], *s.* (*Tail.*) der Kragenmantel.
**cape** (2) [keip], *s.* (*Geog.*) das Kap, das
Vorgebirge.
**caper** ['keipə], *s.* der Sprung, Luftsprung. — *v.n.* in die Luft springen.
**capillary** [kə'piləri], *adj.* haarfein; —
*tubing*, die Haarröhre, die Kapillarröhre.
**capital** ['kæpitl], *s.* (*Comm.*) das
Kapital; die Hauptstadt (*capital city*);
— *punishment*, die Todesstrafe; —
*letter*, der Großbuchstabe. — *adj.*
(*coll.*) ausgezeichnet, vorzüglich.
**capitalize** ['kæpitəlaiz], *v.a.* (*Comm.*)
kapitalisieren; ausmünzen.
**capitation** [kæpi'teiʃən], *s.* die Kopfsteuer.
**capitulate** [kə'pitjuleit], *v.n.* kapitulieren.
**capon** ['keipən], *s.* (*Zool.*) der Kapaun.
**caprice** [kə'priːs], *s.* die Kaprize, Laune.
**capricious** [kə'priʃəs], *adj.* launenhaft,
eigensinnig.
**Capricorn** ['kæprikɔːn], (*Astrol.*) der
Steinbock; *tropic of* —, der Wendekreis des Steinbocks.
**capriole** ['kæprioul], *s.* der Luftsprung.
**capsize** [kæp'saiz], *v.n.* umkippen,
kentern (*boat*).
**capstan** ['kæpstən], *s.* (*Engin.*) die
Ankerwinde; (*Mech.*) die Erdwinde;
(*Naut.*) das Gangspill.
**capsular** ['kæpsjulə], *adj.* kapselförmig.
**capsule** ['kæpsjuːl], *s.* die Kapsel.
**captain** ['kæptin], *s.* (*Naut.*) der
Kapitän; (*Mil.*) der Hauptmann.

331

# captious

**captious** ['kæpʃəs], *adj.* zänkisch, streitsüchtig; verfänglich.

**captivate** ['kæptiveit], *v.a.* einnehmen, gewinnen.

**captive** ['kæptiv], *s.* der Gefangene. — *adj.* gefangen.

**capture** ['kæptʃə], *s.* die Gefangennahme (*men*); Erbeutung (*booty*).

**Capuchin** ['kæputʃin], *s.* (*Eccl.*) der Kapuziner.

**car** [kɑ:], *s.* (*Motor.*) der Wagen; das Auto; (*Am.*) der Eisenbahnwagen.

**carafe** [kæ'ræf], *s.* die Karaffe, Wasserflasche.

**caravan** ['kærəvæn], *s.* die Karawane; der Wohnwagen.

**caraway** ['kærəwei], *s.*(*Bot.*)der Kümmel.

**carbine** ['kɑ:bain], *s.* der Karabiner.

**carbolic** [kɑ:'bolik], *adj.* — **acid**, (*Chem.*) die Karbolsäure.

**carbon** ['kɑ:bən], *s.* (*Chem.*) der Kohlenstoff.

**carbonate** ['kɑ:bəneit], *s.* (*Chem.*) das kohlensaure Salz, Karbonat.

**carbonize** ['kɑ:bənaiz], *v.a.* verkohlen. — *v.n.* (*Chem., Geol.*) zu Kohle werden.

**carbuncle** ['kɑ:bʌŋkl], *s.* (*Min.*) der Karfunkel; (*Med.*) der Karbunkel.

**carburettor** [kɑ:bju'retə], *s.* (*Motor.*) der Vergaser.

**carcase, carcass** ['kɑ:kəs], *s.* der Kadaver.

**card** (1) [kɑ:d], *s.* die Karte, Postkarte; *playing* —, die Spielkarte; *put your* — *on the table*, rück mit der Wahrheit heraus!

**card** (2) [kɑ:d], *v.a.* krempeln (*wool*); kardätschen (*cotton*).

**cardboard** ['kɑ:dbɔ:d], *s.* die Pappe, der Pappendeckel.

**cardiac** ['kɑ:diæk], *adj.* (*Med.*) Herz-.

**cardinal** ['kɑ:dinl], *s.* (*Eccl.*) der Kardinal. — *adj.* Kardinal-, grundlegend.

**cardiogram** [kɑ:'diogræm], *s.* (*Med.*) das Kardiogramm.

**cardsharper** ['kɑ:dʃɑ:pə], *s.* der Falschspieler.

**care** [kɛə], *s.* die Sorge (*anxiety*, um, for); *with* —, mit Sorgfalt, genau; *care of* (*abbr. c/o on letters*), bei; *take* —, sich in acht nehmen. — *v.n.* — *for*, sich interessieren, gern haben.

**careen** [kə'ri:n], *v.a.* (*Naut.*) kielholen, umlegen.

**career** [kə'riə], *s.* die Karriere, Laufbahn.

**careful** ['kɛəful], *adj.* sorgfältig, vorsichtig, umsichtig.

**carefulness** ['kɛəfulnis], *s.* die Vorsicht, Sorgfalt, Umsicht.

**careless** ['kɛəlis], *adj.* unachtsam, nachlässig.

**carelessness** ['kɛəlisnis], *s.* die Nachlässigkeit, Unachtsamkeit.

**caress** [kə'res], *v.a.* liebkosen, herzen. — *s.* die Liebkosung, die Zärtlichkeit.

**caretaker** ['kɛəteikə], *s.* der Hausmeister.

**careworn** ['kɛəwɔ:n], *adj.* abgehärmt, von Sorgen gebeugt.

**cargo** ['kɑ:gou], *s.* die Fracht, die Ladung.

**caricature** [kærikə'tjuə *or* 'kærikətʃə], *s.* die Karikatur. — *v.a.* karikieren, verzerren.

**Carinthian** [kə'rinθjən], *adj.* kärntnerisch.

**carmine** ['kɑ:main], *s.* der Karmin.

**carnage** ['kɑ:nidʒ], *s.* das Blutbad.

**carnal** [kɑ:nl], *adj.* fleischlich, sinnlich.

**carnation** [kɑ:'neiʃən], *s.* (*Bot.*) die Nelke.

**carnival** ['kɑ:nivl], *s.* der Karneval.

**carnivorous** [kɑ:'nivərəs], *adj.* fleischfressend.

**carol** ['kærəl], *s. Christmas* —, das Weihnachtslied.

**carotid** [kə'rɔtid], *s.* (*Anat.*) die Halspulsader.

**carousal** [kə'rauzəl], *s.* das Gelage, das Gezeche.

**carouse** [kə'rauz], *v.n.* zechen, schmausen.

**carp** (1) [kɑ:p], *s.* (*Zool.*) der Karpfen.

**carp** (2) [kɑ:p], *v.n.* bekritteln, tadeln.

**Carpathian Mountains** [kɑ:'peiθjən 'mauntinz], das die Karpathen, *f. pl.*

**carpenter** ['kɑ:pəntə], *s.* der Zimmermann; Tischler.

**carpentry** ['kɑ:pəntri], *s.* die Tischlerei, das Zimmerhandwerk.

**carpet** ['kɑ:pit], *s.* der Teppich; — *bag*, die Reisetasche.

**carriage** ['kæridʒ], *s.* der Wagen, Waggon; das Verhalten, die Haltung (*bearing*); (*Comm.*) — *paid*, einschließlich Zustellung; — *way*, der Straßendamm.

**carrier** ['kæriə], *s.* der Fuhrmann, Fuhrunternehmer.

**carrion** ['kæriən], *s.* das Aas.

**carrot** ['kærət], *s.* (*Bot.*) die Mohrrübe; die Karotte.

**carry** ['kæri], *v.a.* tragen; bringen; führen (*on vehicle*), fahren (*convey*); — *interest*, Zinsen tragen; (*Comm.*) — *forward*, übertragen; — *two* (*in adding up*), zwei weiter; — *on*, weitermachen, fortfahren; — *through*, durchführen, durchhalten. — *v.n.* vernehmbar sein (*of sound*); — *on*, weiterarbeiten, weiterexistieren.

**cart** [kɑ:t], *s.* der Karren, Frachtwagen.

**cartel** [kɑ:'tel], *s.* (*Comm.*) das Kartell.

**Carthage** ['kɑ:θidʒ]. Karthago, *n.*

**carthorse** ['kɑ:θɔ:s], *s.* das Zugpferd.

**cartilage** ['kɑ:tilidʒ], *s.* der Knorpel.

**carton** ['kɑ:tən], *s.* (*cardboard box*) der Karton, die Schachtel.

**cartoon** [kɑ:'tu:n], *s.* die Karikatur; — *film*, der Trickfilm.

**cartridge** ['kɑ:tridʒ], *s.* die Patrone.

**cartwright** ['kɑ:trait], *s.* der Stellmacher, Wagenbauer.

**carve** [kɑ:v], *v.a.* schneiden (*cut*); schnitzen (*wood*), meißeln (*stone*), tranchieren (*meat*).

# caustic

**carver** ['kɑːvə], s. der Schnitzer (wood); das Tranchiermesser (carving knife).

**cascade** [kæs'keid], s. der Wasserfall.

**case** (1) [keis], s. der Kasten, Behälter; das Futteral, Etui (spectacles); das Gehäuse (watch); die Kiste (wooden box); (Typ.) der Schriftkasten.

**case** (2) [keis], s. der Fall (event); (Law) der Rechtsfall, der Umstand (circumstance); in —, falls.

**casement** ['keismənt], s. der Fensterflügel, das Fenster (frame).

**caseous** ['keisjəs], adj. käsig.

**cash** [kæʃ], s. bares Geld; die Barzahlung; — box, die Kasse. — v.a. einlösen (cheque).

**cashier** [kæ'ʃiə], s. der Kassierer. — v.a. (Mil.) entlassen.

**cashmere** ['kæʃmiə], s. die Kaschmirwolle (wool).

**casing** ['keisiŋ], s. die Hülle; das Gehäuse (case); die Haut (sausage skin).

**cask** ['kɑːsk], s. das Faß.

**casket** ['kɑːskit], s. das Kästchen; (Am.) der Sarg.

**Caspian (Sea)** ['kæspiən (siː)], das kaspische Meer.

**cassock** ['kæsək], s. die Soutane.

**cast** [kɑːst], v.a. irr. werfen (throw); (Metall.) gießen; (Theat.) besetzen; (plaster) formen; — off, abwerfen; — anchor, ankern; — o.'s skin, sich häuten; — down, niederschlagen; — a vote, die Stimme abgeben. — s. der Wurf; (Metall.) der Guß; (Theat.) die Besetzung; der Abguß (plaster). — adj. — iron, das Gußeisen; — steel, der Gußstahl.

**castanets** [kæstə'nets], s. pl. (Mus.) die Kastagnetten, f. pl.

**castaway** ['kɑːstəwei], adj. weggeworfen; (Naut.) schiffbrüchig.

**caste** [kɑːst], s. die Kaste.

**caster** ['kɑːstə], s. der Streuer, die Streubüchse; — sugar, Streuzucker.

**casting** ['kɑːstiŋ], s. (Metall.) das Gießen, der Guß.

**castle** [kɑːsl], s. die Burg, das Schloß; (Chess) der Turm.

**castor** (1) ['kɑːstə], s. (Zool.) der Biber.

**castor** (2) ['kɑːstə] see **caster**.

**castor** (3) **oil** ['kɑːstər 'ɔil], s. das Rizinusöl.

**castrate** [kæs'treit], v.a. kastrieren.

**castration** [kæs'treiʃən], s. die Kastration.

**casual** ['kæʒjuəl], adj. zufällig; gelassen (manner); gelegentlich, flüchtig.

**casualty** ['kæʒjuəlti], s. der Unglücksfall; — ward, die Unfallstation; (pl.) die Verluste, m. pl.

**cat** [kæt], s. die Katze; tom —, der Kater; — burglar, der Fassadenkletterer; —'s eye, das Katzenauge, der Rückstrahler; der Reflektor.

**cataclysm** ['kætəklizm], s. die Sintflut, die Überschwemmung.

**catacomb** ['kætəkuːm], s. die Katakombe.

**catalogue** ['kætəlɔg], s. der Katalog,

das Verzeichnis. — v.a. im Katalog verzeichnen, katalogisieren.

**catapult** ['kætəpʌlt], s. die Schleuder (hand); (Mil.) die Wurfmaschine. — v.a. schleudern.

**cataract** ['kætərækt], s. der Wasserfall (water); (Med.) der Star.

**catarrh** [kə'tɑː], s. (Med.) der Katarrh.

**catastrophe** [kə'tæstrəfi], s. die Katastrophe, das Unglück.

**catastrophic** [kætəs'trɔfik], adj. katastrophal, unheilvoll.

**catch** [kætʃ], v.a. irr. fangen, auffangen, fassen; überfallen (— unawares, ambush); — a cold, sich einen Schnupfen zuziehen, sich erkälten; erreichen (train, etc.); — redhanded, bei frischer Tat ertappen. — s. der Fang (fish); die Beute (prey, booty); der Haken (hook, also fig.).

**catchpenny** ['kætʃpeni], s. der Flitterkram, Lockartikel. — adj. marktschreierisch.

**catchphrase, catchword** ['kætʃfreiz, 'kætʃwəːd], s. das (billige) Schlagwort.

**catechism** ['kætikizm], s. der Katechismus.

**categorical** [kæti'gɔrikəl], adj. kategorisch, entschieden.

**category** ['kætigəri], s. die Kategorie, Klasse, Gruppe, Gattung.

**cater** ['keitə], v.n. Lebensmittel einkaufen; verpflegen; (fig.) sorgen (for, für).

**caterer** ['keitərə], s. der Lebensmittellieferant.

**catering** ['keitəriŋ], s. die Verpflegung.

**caterpillar** ['kætəpilə], s. (Ent.) die Raupe; —tractor, der Raupenschlepper.

**caterwaul** ['kætəwɔːl], v.n. miauen.

**cathedral** [kə'θiːdrəl], s. der Dom, die Kathedrale.

**Catholic** ['kæθəlik], adj. katholisch. — s. der Katholik.

**catholic** ['kæθəlik], adj. allumfassend.

**Catholicism** [kə'θɔlisizm], s. der Katholizismus.

**catkin** ['kætkin], s. (Bot.) das Kätzchen; pussy-willow —, das Palmkätzchen.

**cattle** [kætl], s. pl. das Vieh; — plague, die Rinderpest; — show, die Viehausstellung.

**caucus** ['kɔːkəs], s. die Wahlversammlung; der Wahlausschuß.

**caul** [kɔːl], s. das Haarnetz; (Anat.) die Eihaut.

**cauldron** ['kɔːldrən], s. der Kessel.

**cauliflower** ['kɔliflauə], s. (Bot.) der Blumenkohl.

**caulk** [kɔːk], v.a. kalfatern (see under **calk** (2)).

**causal** ['kɔːzəl], adj. ursächlich.

**causality** [kɔː'zæliti], s. der ursächliche Zusammenhang; (Log.) die Kausalität.

**cause** [kɔːz], s. die Ursache. — v.a. verursachen.

**causeway** ['kɔːzwei], s. der Damm.

**caustic** ['kɔːstik], adj. ätzend; beißend.

333

# cauterize

**cauterize** ['kɔ:təraiz], *v.a.* (*Med.*) ätzen, ausbrennen.

**caution** ['kɔ:ʃən], *s.* die Vorsicht (*care*); die Warnung (*warning*). — *v.a.* (*Law*) ermahnen; warnen.

**cautionary** ['kɔ:ʃənəri], *adj.* warnend.

**cautious** ['kɔ:ʃəs], *adj.* vorsichtig, behutsam.

**cautiousness** ['kɔ:ʃəsnis], *s.* die Vorsicht, Behutsamkeit.

**cavalcade** [kævəl'keid], *s.* die Kavalkade; (*Mil.*) der Reiterzug.

**cavalry** ['kævəlri], *s.* die Kavallerie, die Reiterei.

**cave** [keiv], *s.* die Höhle. — *v.a.* aushöhlen. — *v.n.* — *in*, einstürzen, einfallen.

**caveat** ['keiviæt], *s.* (*Law*) die Warnung; der Vorbehalt.

**cavern** ['kævən], *s.* die Höhle.

**cavernous** ['kævənəs], *adj.* (*Geog.*, *Geol.*) voll Höhlen.

**caviare** [kævi'ɑ:], *s.* der Kaviar.

**cavil** ['kævil], *v.n.* nörgeln (*at*, über), tadeln (*Acc.*).

**cavity** ['kæviti], *s.* die Höhlung.

**caw** [kɔ:], *v.n.* (*Orn.*) krächzen.

**cease** [si:s], *v.a.* einstellen; — *v.n.* aufhören.

**ceaseless** ['si:slis], *adj.* unaufhörlich.

**cedar** ['si:də], *s.* (*Bot.*) die Zeder.

**cede** [si:d], *v.a.* überlassen. — *v.n.* nachgeben.

**ceiling** ['si:liŋ], *s.* die Decke (*room*); (*Comm.*) die Preisgrenze.

**celebrate** ['selibreit], *v.a.* feiern; zelebrieren.

**celebrated** ['selibreitid], *adj.* berühmt.

**celebration** [seli'breiʃən], *s.* die Feier.

**celebrity** [si'lebriti], *s.* die Berühmtheit; der „Star".

**celerity** [si'leriti], *s.* die Behendigkeit, Schnelligkeit.

**celery** ['seləri], *s.* (*Bot.*) der Sellerie.

**celestial** [si'lestjəl], *adj.* himmlisch.

**celibacy** ['selibəsi], *s.* die Ehelosigkeit; (*Eccl.*) das Zölibat.

**celibate** ['selibit], *adj.* unverheiratet.

**cell** [sel], *s.* die Zelle.

**cellar** ['selə], *s.* der Keller; *salt* —, das Salzfaß.

**cellarage** ['seləridʒ], *s.* die Kellerei; die Einkellerung (*storage*).

**cellarer** ['selərə], *s.* der Kellermeister.

**cellular** ['seljulə], *adj.* zellartig, Zell-.

**Celt** [kelt, selt], *s.* der Kelte.

**Celtic** ['keltik, 'seltik], *adj.* keltisch.

**cement** [si'ment], *s.* der Zement, Mörtel. — *v.a.* auszementieren, verkitten.

**cemetery** ['semətri], *s.* der Kirchhof, der Friedhof.

**cenotaph** ['senotæf *or* -tɑ:f], *s.* das Ehrengrabmal, Ehrendenkmal.

**censer** ['sensə], *s.* (*Eccl.*) das Weihrauchfaß.

**censor** ['sensə], *s.* der Zensor.

**censorious** [sen'sɔ:riəs], *adj.* kritisch, tadelsüchtig.

**censure** ['senʃə], *s.* der Tadel, Verweis. — *v.a.* tadeln.

**census** ['sensəs], *s.* die Volkszählung.

**cent** [sent], *s.* (*Am.*) der Cent (*coin*); (*Comm.*) *per* —, das Prozent.

**centenarian** [senti'nɛəriən], *adj.* hundertjährig. — *s.* der Hundertjährige.

**centenary** [sen'ti:nəri], *s.* die Hundertjahrfeier.

**centennial** [sen'tenjəl], *adj.* alle hundert Jahre, hundertjährig.

**centipede** ['sentipi:d], *s.* (*Zool.*) der Tausendfüßler.

**central** ['sentrəl], *adj.* zentral.

**centralize** ['sentrəlaiz], *v.a.* zentralisieren.

**centre** ['sentə], *s.* das Zentrum, der Mittelpunkt; die Mitte.

**centric(al)** ['sentrik(əl)], *adj.* (*Engin.*, *Maths.*) zentral.

**centrifugal** [sen'trifjugəl], *adj.* zentrifugal.

**centrifuge** [sen'trifju:dʒ], *s.* die Zentrifuge.

**centripetal** [sen'tripitl], *adj.* zentripetal, zum Mittelpunkt hinstrebend.

**century** ['sentʃuri], *s.* das Jahrhundert.

**cereal** ['siəriəl], *adj.* vom Getreide, Getreide—. — *s.* die Kornmehlspeise.

**cerebral** ['seribrəl], *adj.* Gehirn-.

**ceremonial** [seri'mounjəl], *adj.* feierlich, förmlich (*formal*). — *s.* das Zeremoniell.

**ceremonious** [seri'mounjəs], *adj.* feierlich, zeremoniell.

**ceremony** ['seriməni], *s.* die Zeremonie, die Feier.

**certain** ['sə:tin], *adj.* sicher, gewiß.

**certainty** ['sə:tinti], *s.* die Gewißheit.

**certificate** [sə:'tifikit], *s.* das Zeugnis, die Bescheinigung.

**certification** [sə:tifi'keiʃən], *s.* die Bescheinigung, Bezeugung.

**certify** ['sə:tifai], *v.a.* bescheinigen, bezeugen, beglaubigen.

**certitude** ['sə:titju:d], *s.* die Gewißheit.

**cerulean** [si'ru:ljən], *adj.* himmelblau.

**cesspool** ['sespu:l], *s.* die Senkgrube.

**cessation** [se'seiʃən], *s.* das Aufhören; (*of hostilities*) der Waffenstillstand.

**cession** ['seʃən], *s.* die Abtretung, der Verzicht (*of*, auf).

**chafe** [tʃeif], *v.a.* wärmen, warmreiben; erzürnen (*annoy*); wundreiben (*skin*). — *v.n.* toben, wüten.

**chafer** ['tʃeifə], *s.* (*Ent.*) der Käfer.

**chaff** [tʃɑ:f], *s.* die Spreu; die Neckerei (*teasing*). — *v.a.* necken.

**chaffer** ['tʃæfə], *v.n.* handeln, schachern (*haggle*).

**chaffinch** ['tʃæfintʃ], *s.* (*Orn.*) der Buchfink.

**chagrin** [ʃæ'gri:n], *s.* der Verdruß, der Ärger.

**chain** [tʃein], *s.* die Kette. — *v.a.* anketten.

**chair** [tʃɛə], *s.* der Stuhl; (*Univ.*) Lehrstuhl. — *v.a.* vorsitzen (*Dat.*).

**chairman** ['tʃɛəmən], *s.* der Vorsitzende.

**chalice** ['tʃælis], *s.* (*Eccl.*) der Kelch.

# chassis

**chalk** [tʃɔ:k], *s.* die Kreide. — *v.a.* — up, ankreiden, anschreiben.

**chalky** [ˈtʃɔ:ki], *adj.* (Geol.) kreidig, kreideartig.

**challenge** [ˈtʃælindʒ], *v.a.* herausfordern; in Frage stellen (*question*); anhalten (*of a sentry*). — *s.* die Herausforderung; das Anhalten (*by a sentry*); die Einwendung.

**chalybeate** [kəˈlibiət], *adj.* (Med.) eisenhaltig.

**chamber** [ˈtʃeimbə], *s.* das Zimmer, die Kammer.

**chamberlain** [ˈtʃeimbəlin], *s.* der Kammerherr.

**chambermaid** [ˈtʃeimbəmeid], *s.* das Zimmermädchen, Kammermädchen.

**chameleon** [kəˈmi:ljən], *s.* (Zool.) das Chamäleon.

**chamois** [ˈʃæmwa:], *s.* (Zool.) die Gemse.

**champagne** [ʃæmˈpein], *s.* der Champagner, der Sekt.

**champion** [ˈtʃæmpjən], *s.* der Meister, Verteidiger. — *v.a.* vertreten (*cause*); beschützen (*person*).

**chance** [tʃɑ:ns], *s.* der Zufall; die Gelegenheit (*opportunity*); die Möglichkeit (*possibility*); take a —, es darauf ankommen lassen; by —, zufällig. — *v.a.* zufällig tun, geraten; riskieren (*risk*).

**chancel** [ˈtʃɑ:nsəl], *s.* (Eccl.) der Chor, der Altarplatz.

**chancellor** [ˈtʃɑ:nsələ], *s.* der Kanzler.

**chancery** [ˈtʃɑ:nsəri], *s.* das Kanzleigericht.

**chandelier** [ʃændəˈliə], *s.* der Armleuchter, Kronleuchter.

**chandler** [ˈtʃɑ:ndlə], *s.* der Lichtzieher; Krämer; (corn merchant) der Kornhändler.

**change** [tʃeindʒ], *s.* die Änderung, das Umsteigen (*trains*); small —, das Kleingeld; die Veränderung; Abwechslung. — *v.a.* ändern (*alter*); wechseln (*money*); umsteigen (*trains*); eintauschen, umtauschen (*exchange*); sich umziehen (*clothes*). — *v.n.* sich (ver)ändern, anders werden, umschlagen; (Railw.) — for, umsteigen nach.

**changeable** [ˈtʃeindʒəbl], *adj.* veränderlich.

**changeling** [ˈtʃeindʒliŋ], *s.* der Wechselbalg.

**changeover** [ˈtʃeindʒouvə], *s.* der Wechsel; der Umschalter; die Umstellung.

**channel** [ˈtʃænəl], *s.* der Kanal. — *v.a.* leiten, kanalisieren.

**chant** [tʃɑ:nt], *v.a., v.n.* (Eccl.) singen. — *s.* (Mus.) der Kantus, der liturgische Gesang.

**chaos** [ˈkeiɔs], *s.* das Chaos.

**chaotic** [keiˈɔtik], *adj.* chaotisch.

**chap** (1) [tʃæp], *s.* der Riss (skin etc.). — *v.n.* Risse bekommen.

**chap** (2) [tʃæp], *s.* (usually in pl.) der Kinnbacken.

**chap** (3) [tʃæp], *s.* (coll.) der Kerl, der Bursche.

**chapel** [ˈtʃæpəl], *s.* (Eccl.) die Kapelle.

**chaperon** [ˈʃæpəroun], *s.* die Anstandsdame. — *v.a.* begleiten, bemuttern.

**chaplain** [ˈtʃæplin], *s.* der Kaplan.

**chapter** [ˈtʃæptə], *s.* das Kapitel.

**char** [tʃɑ:], *v.a.* verkohlen. — *v.n.* (coll.) putzen, Hausarbeit verrichten (do housework). — *s.* (coll.) die Haushilfe, die Hausgehilfin, Putzfrau.

**character** [ˈkærəktə], *s.* der Charakter (*personality*); das Zeichen (sign, symbol); (Maths.) die Ziffer; das Zeugnis (testimonial).

**characteristic** [kærəktəˈristik], *adj.* charakteristisch, typisch.

**characterize** [ˈkærəktəraiz], *v.a.* charakterisieren, kennzeichnen.

**charade** [ʃəˈrɑ:d], *s.* die Scharade, das Silbenrätsel.

**charcoal** [ˈtʃɑ:koul], *s.* die Holzkohle; — burner, der Köhler.

**charge** [tʃɑ:dʒ], *v.a.* laden, aufladen; (Law) beschuldigen; (Mil.) angreifen; belasten (with a bill); — up to s.o., jemandem etwas anrechnen; verlangen (price). — *s.* die Ladung, der Auftrag (order); die Aufsicht; to be in —, die Aufsicht haben; (Law) die Beschuldigung, Anklage; das Mündel (of a guardian); (pl.) die Kosten, Spesen.

**chargeable** [ˈtʃɑ:dʒəbl], *adj.* anzurechnend; steuerbar (of objects).

**charger** [ˈtʃɑ:dʒə], *s.* das Schlachtroß.

**chariness** [ˈtʃɛərinis], *s.* die Behutsamkeit.

**chariot** [ˈtʃæriət], *s.* der Kriegswagen.

**charioteer** [tʃæriəˈtiə], *s.* der Wagenlenker.

**charitable** [ˈtʃæritəbl], *adj.* wohltätig, mild, mildtätig.

**charitableness** [ˈtʃæritəblnis], *s.* die Wohltätigkeit, Milde.

**charity** [ˈtʃæriti], *s.* die Güte; Nächstenliebe; Mildtätigkeit (alms); die Barmherzigkeit (charitableness); der wohltätige Zweck (cause); sister of —, barmherzige Schwester.

**charlatan** [ˈʃɑ:lətən], *s.* der Scharlatan, Pfuscher.

**charm** [tʃɑ:m], *s.* der Zauber (magic); der Reiz. — *v.a.* bezaubern.

**chart** [tʃɑ:t], *s.* (Geog.) die Karte. — *v.a.* auf der Karte einzeichnen.

**charter** [ˈtʃɑ:tə], *s.* die Urkunde; (Naut.) die Schiffsmiete. — *v.a.* mieten, chartern, heuern (ship, plane); ein Privileg geben, bevorrechtigen.

**charwoman** [ˈtʃɑ:wumən], *s.* die Putzfrau, Reinemacherin.

**chary** [ˈtʃɛəri], *adj.* behutsam; vorsichtig (cautious); sparsam (thrifty).

**chase** [tʃeis], *v.a.* jagen, verfolgen. — *s.* die Jagd (hunt); das Gehege (game preserve).

**chaser** [ˈtʃeisə], *s.* der Verfolger (pursuer); die Schiffskanone (gun).

**chasm** [kæzm], *s.* die Kluft; der Abgrund.

**chassis** [ˈʃæsi], *s.* (Motor.) das Fahrgestell.

# chaste

chaste [tʃeist], *adj.* keusch, züchtig.
chasten [tʃeisn], *v.a.* züchtigen; reinigen.
chastize [tʃæs'taiz], *v.a.* züchtigen.
chastity [tʃæstiti], *s.* die Keuschheit, Züchtigkeit.
chasuble [tʃæzjubl], *s.* (*Eccl.*) das Meßgewand.
chat [tʃæt], *v.n.* plaudern. — *s.* das Geplauder.
chattel [tʃætl], *s.* (*usually in pl.*) die Habe; *goods and* —*s,* Hab und Gut.
chatter [tʃætə], *v.n.* schwätzen; schnattern. — *s.* das Geschwätz (*talk*).
chatterbox [tʃætəbɔks], *s.* die Plaudertasche.
chatty [tʃæti], *adj.* geschwätzig.
chauffeur [ʃoufə, ʃou'fə:], *s.* (*Motor.*) der Fahrer.
chauffeuse [ʃou'fə:z], *s.* die Fahrerin.
chauvinism [ʃouvinizm], *s.* der Chauvinismus.
cheap [tʃi:p], *adj.* billig.
cheapen [tʃi:pən], *v.a.* herabsetzen, erniedrigen (*value*).
cheapness [tʃi:pnis], *s.* die Billigkeit (*price*).
cheat [tʃi:t], *v.a.,* *v.n.* betrügen. — *s.* der Betrüger.
cheating [tʃi:tiŋ], *s.* das Betrügen; der Betrug.
check [tʃek], *s.* der Einhalt, der Halt; die Kontrolle; das Hindernis (*obstacle*); (*Chess*) Schach; (*Am.*) *see* cheque. — *v.a.* zurückhalten, aufhalten (*stop*); überprüfen. — *v.n.* Schach bieten (*Dat.*).
checker *see under* chequer.
checkmate [tʃekmeit], *s.* das Schachmatt.
cheek [tʃi:k], *s.* die Wange, die Backe; die Unverschämtheit (*impertinence*). — *v.a.* unverschämt sein *or* handeln (*s.o.*), an jemandem.
cheeky [tʃi:ki], *adj.* frech, unverschämt.
cheer [tʃiə], *v.a.* anfeuern, anspornen; zujubeln; — *up,* aufmuntern. — *v.n.* — *up,* Mut fassen. — *s.* der Zuruf; der Beifallsruf (*acclaim*); *three* —*s,* ein dreifaches Hoch (*for,* auf).
cheerful [tʃiəful], *adj.* fröhlich, froh.
cheerless [tʃiəlis], *adj.* unfreundlich, freudlos.
cheese [tʃi:z], *s.* der Käse; — *straw,* die Käsestange.
cheesecloth [tʃi:zklɔθ], *s.* (*Am.*) das Nesseltuch.
cheeseparing [tʃi:zpɛəriŋ], *adj.* knauserig.
cheesy [tʃi:zi], *adj.* käsig; schlecht aussehend.
cheetah [tʃi:tə], *s.* (*Zool.*) der Jagdleopard.
chemical [kemikəl], *adj.* chemisch. — *s.* die Chemikalie, das chemische Element; das chemische Produkt.
chemise [ʃi'mi:z], *s.* das Frauenhemd.
chemist [kemist], *s.* der Chemiker; Drogist; Apotheker (*dispenser*).

chemistry [kemistri], *s.* die Chemie.
cheque, (*Am.*) check [tʃek], *s.* (*Fin.*) der Scheck.
chequer, checker [tʃekə], *s.* das scheckige Muster, Würfelmuster. — *v.a.* würfelig machen, bunt machen.
cherish [tʃeriʃ], *v.a.* hegen, wertschätzen, lieben.
cherry [tʃeri], *s.* (*Bot.*) die Kirsche; — *brandy,* das Kirschwasser.
chess [tʃes], *s.* das Schachspiel; —*man,* die Schachfigur; —*board,* das Schachbrett.
chest [tʃest], *s.* die Truhe (*box*); die Kiste; (*Anat.*) Brust; — *of drawers,* die Kommode.
chestnut [tʃestnʌt], *s.* (*Bot.*) die Kastanie; (*horse*) der Braune. — *adj.* kastanienbraun.
chew [tʃu:], *v.a.* kauen; —*ing gum,* der Kaugummi.
chic [ʃi:k], *adj.* elegant, schick.
chicanery [ʃi'keinəri], *s.* die Schikane, Haarspalterei, Kleinlichkeit.
chicken [tʃikin], *s.* das Huhn, Kücken; — *soup,* die Hühnersuppe.
chickenpox [tʃikinpɔks], *s.* (*Med.*) die Windpocken.
chicory [tʃikəri], *s.* (*Bot.*) die Zichorie.
chide [tʃaid], *v.a. irr.* schelten.
chief [tʃi:f], *s.* der Häuptling (*of tribe*); (*Am. coll.*) der Chef (*boss*). — *adj.* hauptsächlich, Haupt-, oberst.
chieftain [tʃi:ftin], *s.* der Häuptling (*of tribe*); Anführer (*leader*).
chilblain [tʃilblein], *s.* die Frostbeule.
child [tʃaild], *s.* das Kind.
childbirth [tʃaildbə:θ], *s.* die Niederkunft.
childhood [tʃaildhud], *s.* die Kindheit.
childish [tʃaildiʃ], *adj.* kindisch.
childlike [tʃaildlaik], *adj.* kindlich, wie ein Kind.
Chilean [tʃiliən], *adj.* chilenisch. — *s.* der Chilene.
chill [tʃil], *s.* die Kälte, der Frost; die Erkältung. — *v.a.* kalt machen (*freeze*); erstarren lassen (*make rigid*); entmutigen (*discourage*).
chilly [tʃili], *adj.* frostig, eisig, eiskalt.
chime [tʃaim], *s.* das Glockengeläute. — *v.n.* klingen, läuten.
chimera [ki'miərə], *s.* das Hirngespinst, das Trugbild.
chimney [tʃimni], *s.* der Kamin, der Schornstein; —*pot,* —*stack,* der Schornstein; —*sweep,* der Kaminfeger, Schornsteinfeger.
chimpanzee [tʃimpæn'zi:], *s.* (*Zool.*) der Schimpanse.
chin [tʃin], *s.* (*Anat.*) das Kinn.
china [tʃainə], *s.* das Porzellan; — *ware,* das Küchengeschirr.
chine (1) [tʃain], *s.* das Rückgrat.
chine (2) [tʃain], *s.* (*Geog.*) der Kamm.
Chinaman [tʃainəmən], *s.* (*obs.*) der Chinese.
Chinese [tʃai'ni:z], *adj.* chinesisch. — *s.* der Chinese.
chink [tʃink], *s.* die Ritze, der Spalt.

# Circassian

**chip** [tʃip], v.a. schnitzeln (wood); ausbrechen (stone); in kleine Stücke schneiden. — in, (coll.) sich hineinmischen. —s. der Span (wood); der Splitter (glass, stone); (pl.) Pommes frites (pl.) (potatoes).

**chiromancy** ['kaiərəmænsi], s. das Handlesen.

**chiropodist** [ki'rɔpədist], s. der Fußpfleger.

**chirp** [tʃəːp], v.n. zwitschern (birds), zirpen (crickets).

**chirping** ['tʃəːpiŋ], s. das Gezwitscher (birds), das Gezirpe (crickets).

**chisel** [tʃizl], s. der Meißel. — v.a. meißeln.

**chit** [tʃit], s. das Stück Papier; (coll.) junges Ding; —chat, das Geplauder.

**chivalrous** ['ʃivlrəs], adj. ritterlich; tapfer (brave).

**chivalry** ['ʃivlri], s. die Ritterlichkeit (courtesy); Tapferkeit (bravery).

**chive** [tʃaiv], s. (Bot.) der Schnittlauch.

**chlorate** ['klɔːreit], s. (Chem.) das Chlorsalz.

**chlorine** ['klɔːriːn], s. (Chem.) das Chlor, Chlorgas.

**chloroform** ['klɔrəfɔːm], s. das Chloroform. — v.a. chloroformieren.

**chocolate** ['tʃɔkəlit], s. die Schokolade. — adj. schokoladefarben.

**choice** [tʃɔis], s. die Wahl; Auswahl (selection). — adj. auserlesen.

**choir** ['kwaiə], s. der Chor.

**choke** [tʃouk], v.a., v.n. ersticken; verstopfen (block). — s. (Elec.) die Drosselspule; (Motor.) die Starterklappe.

**choler** ['kɔlə], s. die Galle; (fig.) der Zorn (anger).

**cholera** ['kɔlərə], s. (Med.) die Cholera.

**choleric** ['kɔlərik], adj. jähzornig, cholerisch.

**choose** [tʃuːz], v.a. irr. wählen, auswählen (select).

**choosy** ['tʃuːzi], adj. wählerisch.

**chop** [tʃɔp], v.a. abhacken (cut off), hacken (meat). — s. das Kotelett (meat).

**chopper** ['tʃɔpə], s. das Hackbeil (axe); das Hackmesser (knife).

**choppy** ['tʃɔpi], adj. bewegt (sea), stürmisch.

**chopstick** ['tʃɔpstik], s. das Eßstäbchen.

**choral** ['kɔːrəl], adj. Chor-; — society, der Gesangverein.

**chorale** [kɔ'rɑːl], s. (Eccl., Mus.) der Choral.

**chord** [kɔːd], s. die Saite; (Geom.) die Sehne; (Mus.) der Akkord.

**chorister** ['kɔristə], s. der Chorknabe (boy), Chorsänger.

**chorus** ['kɔːrəs], s. der Chor (opera); der Refrain (song).

**Christ** [kraist], Christus, m.

**christen** [krisn], v.a. taufen (baptize); nennen (name).

**Christendom** ['krisndəm], s. die Christenheit.

**christening** ['krisniŋ], s. die Taufe.

**Christian** ['kristjən], s. der Christ (believer in Christ). — adj. christlich; — name, der Vorname.

**Christianity** [kristi'æniti], s. die christliche Religion, das Christentum.

**Christmas** ['krisməs], s. (die) Weihnachten; das Weihnachtsfest; —Eve, der heilige Abend.

**chromatic** [kro'mætik], adj. (Mus.) chromatisch.

**chrome** [kroum], s. das Chrom.

**chronic** ['krɔnik], adj. chronisch.

**chronicle** ['krɔnikl], s. die Chronik. — v.a. (in einer Chronik) verzeichnen.

**chronological** [krɔnə'lɔdʒikəl], adj. chronologisch.

**chronology** [krɔ'nɔlədʒi], s. die Chronologie.

**chronometer** [krɔ'nɔmitə], s. das Chronometer.

**chrysalis** ['krisəlis], s. (Ent.) die Puppe.

**chrysanthemum** [kri'zænθəməm], s. (Bot.) die Chrysantheme.

**chub** [tʃʌb], s. (Zool.) der Döbel.

**chubby** ['tʃʌbi], adj. pausbäckig, plump.

**chuck** [tʃʌk], v.a. (coll.) — out, hinauswerfen. — v.n. glucken (chicken).

**chuckle** [tʃʌkl], v.n. kichern. — s. das Kichern.

**chum** [tʃʌm], s. (coll.) der Freund, Kamerad. — v.n. (coll.) — up, sich befreunden (with, mit).

**chump** [tʃʌmp], s. der Klotz (wood).

**chunk** [tʃʌŋk], s. das große Stück (meat etc.).

**church** [tʃəːtʃ], s. die Kirche.

**churchwarden** [tʃəː'tʃwɔːdn], s. der Kirchenvorsteher.

**churchyard** ['tʃəːtʃjɑːd], s. der Friedhof.

**churl** [tʃəːl], s. der Grobian, der grobe Kerl.

**churlish** ['tʃəːliʃ], adj. grob, unfein.

**churn** [tʃəːn], s. das Butterfaß. — v.a. mischen, schütteln (butter etc.); — up, aufwühlen (stir up).

**chute** [ʃuːt], s. die Gleitbahn.

**cider** ['saidə], s. der Apfelmost.

**cigar** [si'gɑː], s. die Zigarre; — case, das Zigarrenetui.

**cigarette** [sigə'ret], s. die Zigarette; — holder, die Zigarettenspitze; — lighter, das Feuerzeug.

**cinder** ['sində], s. (usually in pl.) die Asche (fire); die Schlacke (furnace).

**Cinderella** [sində'relə], s. das Aschenbrödel, Aschenputtel.

**cinema** ['sinimə], s. das Kino.

**cinematography** [sinimə'tɔgrəfi], s. die Filmkunst.

**Cingalese** see **Singhalese**.

**cinnamon** ['sinəmən], s. der Zimt.

**cipher** ['saifə], s. die Ziffer; die Geheimschrift (code). — v.n. rechnen. — v.a. chiffrieren (code).

**Circassian** [səː'kæsiən], adj. tscherkessisch. — s. der Tscherkesse.

# circle

circle ['sə:kl], s. der Zirkel, Kreis; (social) Gesellschaftskreis; (Theat.) der Rang. — v.a. umringen. — v.n. umkreisen; sich drehen (revolve).

circuit ['sə:kit], s. der Kreislauf; (Elec.) der Stromkreis.

circuitous [sə:'kju:itəs], adj. weitschweifig, weitläufig.

circular ['sə:kjulə], adj. rund, kreisförmig, Rund-; — tour, die Rundreise. — s. das Rundschreiben (letter); der Werbebrief (advertising).

circulate ['sə:kjuleit], v.a. in Umlauf setzen. — v.n. umlaufen, kreisen, zirkulieren.

circulation [sə:kju'leiʃən], s. die Zirkulation, der Kreislauf (blood); die Verbreitung, Auflage (newspaper); der Umlauf (banknotes).

circumcise ['sə:kəmsaiz], v.a. beschneiden.

circumference [sə:'kʌmfərəns], s. der Umfang.

circumscribe ['sə:kəmskraib], v.a. beschränken, einengen (narrow down); umschreiben (paraphrase).

circumspect ['sə:kəmspekt], adj. umsichtig, vorsorglich.

circumspection [sə:kəm'spekʃən], s. die Umsicht, Vorsicht.

circumstance ['sə:kəmstæns, -staːns], s. der Umstand; pomp and —, großer Aufmarsch.

circumstantial [sə:kəm'stænʃəl], adj. umständlich; zu einem Umstand gehörig; eingehend; — evidence, der Indizienbeweis.

circumvent [sə:kəm'vent], v.a. überlisten, hintergehen.

circus ['sə:kəs], s. der Zirkus; der Platz.

cirrhus ['sirəs], s. die Federwolke.

Cistercian [sis'tə:ʃən], s. der Zisterzienser (monk).

cistern ['sistən], s. die Zisterne, der Wasserbehälter.

citadel ['sitədəl], s. die Zitadelle, die Burg.

citation [sai'teiʃən], s. das Zitat; (Law) die Zitierung, Vorladung; (Mil.) die rühmliche Erwähnung.

cite [sait], v.a. zitieren (quote); (Law) vorladen.

citizen ['sitizən], s. der Bürger, Staatsbürger (national); fellow —, der Mitbürger.

citizenship ['sitizənʃip], s. das Bürgerrecht, die Staatsangehörigkeit.

citrate ['sitreit], s. (Chem.) das Zitrat.

citric ['sitrik], adj. (Chem.) Zitronen-.

citron ['sitrən], s. die Zitrone. — adj. zitronenfarben.

city ['siti], s. die Stadt; die Großstadt; die City. — adj. städtisch.

civic ['sivik], adj. Stadt-, städtisch (ceremonial); bürgerlich.

civil ['sivil], adj. zivil; höflich (polite); — engineer, der Zivilingenieur; — service, der Beamtendienst, die Beamtenlaufbahn, der Staatsdienst; — war, der Bürgerkrieg.

civilian [si'viljən], s. der Zivilist.

civility [si'viliti], s. die Höflichkeit.

civilization [sivilai'zeiʃən], s. die Zivilisation.

civilize ['sivilaiz], v.a. zivilisieren, verfeinern (refine).

clack [klæk], v.n. klappern (wood etc.); plaudern, plappern.

clad [klæd], adj. gekleidet.

claim [kleim], v.a. Anspruch erheben (to, auf); fordern (demand); behaupten (assert). — s. der Anspruch; die Forderung (demand); das Recht.

claimant ['kleimənt], s. der Beanspruchende, Ansprucherheber.

clairvoyance [klɛə'vɔiəns], s. das Hellsehen.

clairvoyant [klɛə'vɔiənt], s. der Hellseher.

clam [klæm], s. (Zool.) die Venusmuschel; shut up like a —, verschwiegen sein.

clamber ['klæmbə], v.n. klettern.

clamminess ['klæminis], s. die Feuchtigkeit, Klebrigkeit.

clammy ['klæmi], adj. feucht, klebrig.

clamorous ['klæmərəs], adj. lärmend, laut, ungestüm.

clamour ['klæmə], s. das Geschrei, der Lärm. — v.n. laut schreien (for, nach, Dat.).

clamp [klæmp], s. die Klammer, die Klampe. — v.a. festklammern.

clan [klæn], s. die Sippe, die Familie.

clandestine [klæn'destin], adj. heimlich, verstohlen.

clang [klæŋ], s. der Schall, das Geklirr. — v.n. erschallen. — v.a. erschallen lassen.

clangour ['klæŋə], s. das Getöse, der Lärm.

clank [klæŋk], s. das Geklirre, das Gerassel (metal).

clannish ['klæniʃ], adj. stammesbewußt; engherzig (narrow).

clap [klæp], v.a. schlagen, zusammenschlagen (hands). — v.n. Beifall klatschen (Dat.).

clapperboard ['klæpəbɔ:d], s. (Film) das Klappbrett, die Klapptafel; der Klöppel (beater, in lacemaking).

claptrap ['klæptræp], s. der billige Effekt, das eitle Geschwätz (gossip).

claret ['klærit], s. der Rotwein.

clarification [klærifi'keiʃən], s. die Klarstellung, Aufklärung.

clarify ['klærifai], v.a. klarstellen.

clari(o)net [klæri(ə)'net], s. (Mus.) die Klarinette.

clarion ['klæriən], s. (Mus.) die Zinke, Trompete; — call, der laute Ruf.

clash [klæʃ], v.a. zusammenschlagen. — v.n. aufeinanderprallen, zusammenfallen (dates); widerstreiten (views). — s. (fig.) der Zusammenstoß, der Widerstreit.

clasp [klaːsp], v.a. ergreifen, festhalten. — s. der Haken (hook); die Schnalle, die Spange (buckle, brooch); — knife, das Taschenmesser.

**class** [klɑːs], *s.* die Klasse.
**classic(al)** [ˈklæsik(əl)], *adj.* klassisch.
**classics** [ˈklæsiks], *s. pl.* die Klassiker, *m. pl.*; die klassische Philologie (*subject of study*).
**classification** [klæsifiˈkeiʃən], *s.* die Klassifizierung.
**classify** [ˈklæsifai], *v.a.* klassifizieren.
**clatter** [ˈklætə], *s.* das Getöse, Geklirr. — *v.a., v.n.* klappern, klirren.
**Claus** [klɔːz]. Claus, Nicholas, *m.*; *Santa* —, der heilige Nikolaus, Knecht Ruprecht, Weihnachtsmann.
**clause** [klɔːz], *s.* (*Gram.*) der Nebensatz; die Klausel (*contract*); (*Law*) der Vertragspunkt.
**claw** [klɔː], *s.* die Klaue, die Kralle. — *v.a.* kratzen.
**clay** [klei], *s.* der Ton, Lehm.
**clayey** [kleii], *adj.* lehmig, tonig.
**clean** [kliːn], *adj.* rein, reinlich (*habits*); sauber; — *shaven*, glattrasiert. — *v.a.* reinigen, putzen.
**cleaner** [ˈkliːnə], *s.* die Reinemacherin, die Putzfrau.
**cleanliness** [ˈklenlinis], *s.* die Reinlichkeit, Sauberkeit.
**cleanse** [klenz], *v.a.* reinigen.
**clear** [kliə], *adj.* klar, hell; deutlich (*meaning*); schuldlos (*not guilty*). — *s. in the* —, nicht betroffen, schuldlos. — *v.a.* (*Chem.*) klären; (*Law*) für unschuldig erklären; verzollen (*pass through customs*); springen (über, *Acc.*) — *v.n.* (— *up*), sich aufklären, aufhellen (*weather*).
**clearance** [ˈkliərəns], *s.* die Räumung; — *sale*, der Ausverkauf; die Verzollung (*customs*).
**clearing** [ˈkliəriŋ], *s.* die Lichtung (*in wood*); (*Comm.*) die Verrechnung.
**clearness** [ˈkliənis], *s.* die Deutlichkeit, die Klarheit, Helle.
**cleave** [kliːv], *v.a. irr.* spalten (*wood*). — *v.n.* sich spalten.
**cleaver** [ˈkliːvə], *s.* das Hackmesser.
**cleek** [kliːk], *s.* der Golfschläger.
**clef** [klef], *s.* (*Mus.*) der Schlüssel.
**cleft** [kleft], *s.* der Spalt. — *adj.* — *palate*, die Gaumenspalte.
**clemency** [ˈklemənsi], *s.* die Milde, Gnade (*mercy*).
**clement** [ˈklemənt], *adj.* mild (*climate*); gnädig (*merciful*).
**clench** [klentʃ], *v.a.* zusammenpressen; ballen (*fist*).
**clergy** [ˈkləːdʒi], *s.* (*Eccl.*) die Geistlichkeit.
**clergyman** [ˈkləːdʒimən], *s.* (*Eccl.*) der Geistliche.
**clerical** [ˈklerikl], *adj.* (*Eccl.*) geistlich; beamtlich, Beamten-, Büro- (*office*); — *work*, die Büroarbeit.
**clerk** [klɑːk], *s.* der Schreiber, der Bürogehilfe (*junior*), der Bürobeamte, Büroangestellte (*senior*); *bank* —, der Bankbeamte.
**clever** [ˈklevə], *adj.* klug; intelligent; geschickt (*deft*); gewandt, listig (*cunning*).

**cleverness** [ˈklevənis], *s.* die Klugheit (*intelligence*); die Schlauheit (*cunning*); die Begabung (*talent*); die Geschicklichkeit (*skill*).
**clew** [kluː] *see* **clue.**
**click** [klik], *s.a., v.n.* einschnappen (*lock*); zusammenschlagen (*o.'s heels*, die Hacken); schnalzen (*o.'s tongue*); (*sl.*) zusammenpassen (*of two people*). — *s.* das Einschnappen (*lock*); das Zusammenschlagen (*heels*); das Schnalzen (*tongue*).
**client** [ˈklaiənt], *s.* (*Law*) der Klient; (*Comm.*) der Kunde.
**clientele** [kliːənˈtel], *s.* die Klientel, die Kundschaft.
**cliff** [klif], *s.* die Klippe.
**climate** [ˈklaimit], *s.* das Klima.
**climatic** [klaiˈmætik], *adj.* klimatisch.
**climax** [ˈklaimæks], *s.* der Höhepunkt.
**climb** [klaim], *v.a.* erklettern, erklimmen. — *v.n.* klettern, bergsteigen; (*Aviat.*) steigen. — *s.* der Aufstieg, die Ersteigung.
**climber** [ˈklaimə], *s.* der Bergsteiger (*mountaineer*); (*Bot.*) die Schlingpflanze.
**clinch** [klintʃ], *v.a.* vernieten, befestigen; — *a deal*, einen Handel abschließen. — *s.* der feste Griff; die Umklammerung (*boxing*).
**cling** [kliŋ], *v.n. irr.* sich anklammern, festhalten (*to*, an).
**clinic** [ˈklinik], *s.* die Klinik.
**clinical** [ˈklinikl], *adj.* klinisch.
**clink** [kliŋk], *s.* das Geklirre; (*coll.*) das Gefängnis. — *v.a.* — *glasses*, mit den Gläsern anstoßen.
**clinker** [ˈkliŋkə], *s.* der Backstein; die Schlacke.
**clip** (1) [klip], *v.a.* stutzen, beschneiden; lochen (*ticket*).
**clip** (2) [klip], *v.a.* befestigen. — *s. paper* —, die Büroklammer.
**clippings** [ˈklipiŋz], *s. pl.* die Abschnitte; die Schnitzel (*waste*); Zeitungsausschnitte, *m. pl.*
**cloak** [klouk], *s.* der Mantel, der Deckmantel (*cover*). — *v.a.* verbergen.
**cloakroom** [ˈkloukruːm], *s.* die Garderobe; — *free*, keine Garderobegebühr; (*Railw.*) die Gepäckaufbewahrung.
**clock** [klɔk], *s.* die (große) Uhr, Wanduhr; — *face*, das Zifferblatt. — *v.n.* — *in*, die Zeitkarte (Kontrollkarte) stempeln lassen, eintreffen (*arrive*).
**clockwise** [ˈklɔkwaiz], *adv.* im Uhrzeigersinne.
**clod** [klɔd], *s.* die Erdscholle, der Erdklumpen; (*sl.*) der Lümmel (*lout*).
**clog** [klɔg], *v.a.* belasten, hemmen, verstopfen. — *v.n.* sich verstopfen. — *s.* der Holzschuh.
**cloisters** [ˈklɔistəz], *s. pl.* (*Eccl., Archit.*) der Kreuzgang.

# close

**close** [klouz], *v.a.* schließen, verschließen; beenden (*meeting etc.*). — *v.n.* — *in on*, über einen hereinbrechen, umzingeln. — *s.* das Ende, der Schluß; [klous] der Domplatz. — [klous], *adj.* nahe (*near*); knapp (*narrow*); nahestehend, vertraut ( *friend*); schwül (*weather*); geizig (*miserly*).

**closeness** ['klousnis], *s.* die Nähe (*nearness*); die Schwüle (*weather*); die Vertrautheit ( *familiarity*).

**closet** ['klɔzit], *s.* der Wandschrank (*cupboard*); das kleine Zimmer; das Klosett (*W.C.*). — *v.r.* — *o.s. with,* sich mit jemandem zurückziehen, vertraulich beraten.

**closure** ['klouʒə], *s.* der Schluß; der Abschluß (einer Debatte).

**clot** [klɔt], *s.* das Klümpchen. — *v.n.* sich verdicken, gerinnen; —*ted cream,* dicke Sahne.

**cloth** [klɔθ], *s.* das Tuch; der Stoff; die Leinwand (*bookbinding*); American —, das Wachstuch; — *printing,* der Zeugdruck.

**clothe** [klouð], *v.a.* kleiden. — *v.r.* sich kleiden.

**clothes** [klouðz], *s. pl.* die Kleider, *n. pl.*; die Kleidung; die Wäsche (*washing*); — *basket,* der Wäschekorb; — *press,* der Kleiderschrank.

**clothier** ['klouðiə], *s.* der Tuchmacher (*manufacturer*); der Tuchhändler (*dealer*).

**clothing** ['klouðiŋ], *s.* die Kleidung.

**cloud** [klaud], *s.* die Wolke; *under a —,* in Ungnade; —*burst,* der Wolkenbruch. — *v.a.* bewölken, verdunkeln. — *v.n.* — *over,* sich umwölken.

**cloudiness** ['klaudinis], *s.* die Umwölkung, der Wolkenhimmel.

**cloudy** ['klaudi], *adj.* wolkig, bewölkt, umwölkt.

**clout** [klaut], *s. (obs.)* der Lappen (*rag*); (*coll.*) der Schlag (*hit*). — *v.a.* schlagen (*hit*).

**clove** [klouv], *s.* die Gewürznelke (*spice*).

**clove(n)** [klouv(n)], *adj.* gespalten.

**clover** ['klouvə], *s. (Bot.)* der Klee; *to be in —,* Glück haben, es gut haben.

**clown** [klaun], *s.* der Hanswurst. — *v.n.* den Hanswurst spielen.

**clownish** ['klauniʃ], *adj.* tölpelhaft.

**clownishness** ['klauniʃnis], *s.* die Derbheit, Tölpelhaftigkeit.

**cloy** [klɔi], *v.n.* übersättigen, anwidern, anekeln.

**club** (1) [klʌb], *s.* die Keule (*stick*). — *v.a.* (einen) mit einer Keule schlagen.

**club** (2) [klʌb], *s.* der Klub, der Verein. — *v.n.* — *together,* zusammen beitragen, zusammensteuern (*contribute jointly*).

**club** (3) [klʌb], *s.* (*cards*) das Treff, die Eichel (*German cards*).

**clubfoot** ['klʌbfut], *s.* der Klumpfuß.

**cluck** [klʌk], *v.n.* glucken (*hen*).

**clue** [klu:], *s.* der Anhaltspunkt, Leitfaden, die Richtlinie, die Angabe (*crossword*); *no —,* keine blasse Ahnung.

**clump** [klʌmp], *s.* der Klumpen; die Gruppe.

**clumsiness** ['klʌmzinis], *s.* die Unbeholfenheit, Ungeschicklichkeit.

**clumsy** ['klʌmzi], *adj.* unbeholfen, schwerfällig, ungeschickt.

**Cluniac** ['klu:njæk]. (*Eccl.*) der Kluniazenser.

**cluster** ['klʌstə], *s.* die Traube (*grapes*), der Büschel. — *v.n.* in Büschen wachsen *or* stehen, dicht gruppiert sein.

**clutch** [klʌtʃ], *v.a.* ergreifen, packen (*grip*). — *s.* der Griff; (*Motor.*) die Kupplung.

**coach** [koutʃ], *s.* die Kutsche; der Wagen, der Autobus; der Privatlehrer (*teacher*). — *v.a.* unterrichten, vorbereiten ( *for examinations etc.*).

**coachman** ['koutʃmən], *s.* der Kutscher.

**coagulate** [kou'ægjuleit], *v.a.* gerinnen lassen. — *v.n.* gerinnen.

**coagulation** [kouægju'leiʃən], *s.* das Gerinnen.

**coal** [koul], *s.* die Kohle; — *mine,* das Kohlenbergwerk; die Kohlengrube; — *miner,* der Bergmann.

**coalesce** [kouə'les], *v.n.* zusammenwachsen, sich vereinigen.

**coalescence** [kouə'lesəns], *s.* die Verschmelzung.

**coalition** [kouə'liʃən], *s.* (*Pol.*) die Koalition, das Bündnis.

**coarse** [kɔ:s], *adj.* grob; gemein (*manner*).

**coarseness** ['kɔ:snis], *s.* die Grobheit, Unfeinheit.

**coast** [koust], *s.* die Küste. — *v.n.* (an der Küste) entlangfahren; gleiten, rodeln.

**coat** [kout], *s.* der Mantel, Rock; die Jacke (*jacket*); das Fell (*animal*); — *of arms,* das Wappenschild; — *of mail,* der Panzerhemd; — *of paint,* der Anstrich. — *v.a.* überziehen, bemalen (*paint*).

**coathanger** ['kouthæŋə], *s.* der Kleiderbügel.

**coating** ['koutiŋ], *s.* der Überzug.

**coax** [kouks], *v.a.* beschwatzen; überreden (*persuade*).

**cob** (1) [kɔb], *s.* der Gaul.

**cob** (2) [kɔb], *s.* (*Orn.*) der Schwan.

**cob** (3) [kɔb], *s.* der (Mais)Kolben (*corn on the —*).

**cobble** [kɔbl], *v.a.* flicken (*shoes*).

**cobbled** ['kɔbld], *adj.* mit Kopfsteinen gepflastert.

**cobbler** ['kɔblə], *s.* der Schuhflicker.

**cobble(stone)** ['kɔbl(stoun)], *s.* das Kopfsteinpflaster.

**cobweb** ['kɔbweb], *s.* das Spinngewebe.

**cock** [kɔk], *s.* (*Orn.*) der Hahn; (*Engin.*) der Sperrhahn, Hahn; — *sparrow,* das Sperlingsmännchen; — *-a-doodle-doo!* kikeriki!

**cockade** [kɔ'keid], *s.* die Kokarde.

**cockatoo** [kɔkə'tu:], *s.* (*Orn.*) der Kakadu.

**collier**

cockchafer ['kɔktʃeifə], s. (Ent.) der Maikäfer.
cockerel ['kɔkərəl], s. (Orn.) der junge Hahn.
cockle [kɔkl], s. (Zool.) die Herzmuschel.
cockney ['kɔkni], s. der geborene Londoner.
cockpit ['kɔkpit], s. (Aviat.) der Pilotensitz, die Kanzel, der Führerraum.
cockroach ['kɔkroutʃ], s. (Ent.) die Schabe.
cocksure ['kɔkʃuə], adj. zuversichtlich, allzu sicher.
cockswain [kɔksn] see coxswain.
cocoa ['kɔukou], s. der Kakao.
coconut ['koukonʌt], s. die Kokosnuß.
cocoon [kə'ku:n], s. der Kokon, die Puppe (of silkworm).
cod [kɔd], s. der Kabeljau, Dorsch; — liver oil, der Lebertran; dried —, der Stockfisch.
coddle [kɔdl], v.a. verhätscheln, verweichlichen.
code [koud], s. das Gesetzbuch, der Kodex; die Chiffre (cipher). — v.a. chiffrieren, schlüsseln.
codify ['koudifai], v.a. kodifizieren.
coerce [kou'ə:s], v.a. zwingen.
coercion [kou'ə:ʃən], s. der Zwang.
coercive [kou'ə:siv], adj. zwingend.
coeval [kou'i:vəl], adj. gleichaltrig, gleichzeitig.
coexist [kouig'zist], v.n. zugleich existieren, nebeneinander leben.
coffee ['kɔfi], s. der Kaffee; — grinder, die Kaffeemühle; — grounds, der Kaffeesatz; — pot, die Kaffeekanne; — set, das Kaffeeservice.
coffer ['kɔfə], s. der Kasten, die Truhe.
coffin ['kɔfin], s. der Sarg.
cog [kɔg], s. der Zahn (on wheel); — wheel, das Zahnrad.
cogency ['koudʒənsi], s. die zwingende Kraft, Triftigkeit.
cogent ['koudʒənt], adj. zwingend, triftig.
cogitate ['kɔdʒiteit], v.n. nachdenken.
cogitation [kɔdʒi'teiʃən], s. die Überlegung, das Nachdenken.
cognate ['kɔgneit], adj. verwandt.
cognition [kɔg'niʃən], s. die Kenntnis, das Erkennen.
cognizance ['kɔgnizəns], s. die Erkenntnis; die Kenntnisnahme; (Law) die gerichtliche Kenntnisnahme.
cognizant ['kɔgnizənt], adj. wissend, in vollem Wissen (of, Genit.).
cohabit [kou'hæbit], v.n. zusammenleben.
cohabitation [kouhæbi'teiʃən], s. das Zusammenleben.
coheir [kou'ɛə], s. der Miterbe.
cohere [kou'hiə], v.n. zusammenhängen.
coherence [kou'hiərəns], s. der Zusammenhang.
coherent [kou'hiərənt], adj. zusammenhängend.

cohesion [kou'hi:ʒən], s. (Phys.) die Kohäsion.
coiffure [kwæ'fjuə], s. die Frisur, die Haartracht.
coil [kɔil], s. (Elec.) die Spule; die Windung. — v.a. aufwickeln; umwickeln, (auf)spulen. — v.n. sich winden.
coin [kɔin], s. die Münze, das Geldstück. — v.a. münzen, prägen; — a phrase, eine Redewendung prägen.
coinage ['kɔinidʒ], s. die Prägung.
coincide [kouin'said], v.n. zusammenfallen, zusammentreffen.
coincidence [kou'insidəns], s. das Zusammenfallen, Zusammentreffen; der Zufall (chance).
coincident [kou'insidənt], adj. zusammentreffend.
coke [kouk], s. der Koks. — v.a. (Chem., Engin.) verkoken.
cold [kould], adj. kalt; gefühllos, kühl. — s. die Kälte (temperature); die Erkältung (indisposition).
coldish ['kouldiʃ], adj. kühl.
coldness ['kouldnis], s. die Kälte (temperature); die Kaltherzigkeit (heartlessness).
colic ['kɔlik], s. die Kolik.
collaborate [kə'læbəreit], v.n. zusammenarbeiten.
collaboration [kəlæbə'reiʃən], s. die Zusammenarbeit; die Mitwirkung, Mitarbeit (assistance).
collaborator [kə'læbəreitə], s. der Mitarbeiter.
collapse [kə'læps], s. der Zusammenbruch. — v.n. zusammenbrechen (disintegrate); zerfallen, einstürzen.
collapsible [kə'læpsibl], adj. zerlegbar, zusammenlegbar, zusammenklappbar.
collar ['kɔlə], s. der Kragen; —bone, das Schlüsselbein (Anat.); dog —, das Halsband; (coll.) der Priesterkragen; —stud, der Kragenknopf. — v.a. beim Kragen fassen, ergreifen.
collate [kə'leit], v.a. vergleichen (texts etc.).
collateral [kɔ'lætərəl], adj. Seiten-, von beiden Seiten. — s. (Am.) die Garantie, Bürgschaft.
collation [kə'leiʃən], s. die Vergleichung, der Vergleich (texts etc.); der Imbiß.
colleague ['kɔli:g], s. der Kollege, die Kollegin.
collect [kə'lekt], v.a. sammeln, zusammenbringen. — v.n. sich versammeln. — ['kɔlikt], s. (Eccl.) die Kollekte.
collection [kə'lekʃən], s. die Sammlung.
collective [kə'lektiv], adj. kollektiv, gemeinsam. — s. (Pol.) das Kollektiv.
collector [kə'lektə], s. der Sammler.
college ['kɔlidʒ], s. das Kollegium; das College; die Hochschule, Universität.
collide [kə'laid], v.a. vergleichen (texts).
collie ['kɔli], s. der Schäferhund.
collier ['kɔliə], s. der Kohlenarbeiter; das Kohlenfrachtschiff (boat).

341

# collision

collision [kəˈliʒən], s. der Zusammenstoß, Zusammenprall.
collocate [ˈkɔləkeit], v.a. ordnen.
collodion [kəˈloudjən], s. (Chem.) das
Kollodium.
colloquial [kəˈloukwiəl], adj. umgangssprachlich, Umgangs-.
colloquy [ˈkɔlekwi], s. die Unterredung,
das Gespräch (formal).
collusion [kəˈluːʒən], s. das heimliche
Einverständnis, die unstatthafte Partnerschaft; die Verdunkelung.
collusive [kəˈluːziv], adj. abgekartet.
Cologne [kəˈloun]. Köln, n.; eau de —,
Kölnisch Wasser.
Colombian [kɔˈlɔmbjən], adj. kolum-
bisch. — s. der Kolumbier.
colon (1) [ˈkoulən], s. das Kolon, der
Doppelpunkt.
colon (2) [ˈkoulɔn], s. (Med.) der
Dickdarm.
colonel [kəːnl], s. (Mil.) der Oberst; —
-in-chief, der Generaloberst, der oberste Befehlshaber; lieutenant- —, der
Oberstleutnant.
colonial [kəˈlounjəl], adj. kolonial, aus
den Kolonien.
colonist [ˈkɔlənist], s. der Siedler;
Ansiedler.
colonization [kɔlənaiˈzeiʃən], s. die
Kolonisierung, Besiedelung.
colonize [ˈkɔlənaiz], v.a. besiedeln,
kolonisieren.
colonnade [kɔləˈneid], s. die Kolonnade,
der Säulengang.
colony [ˈkɔləni], s. die Kolonie.
colophony [kɔˈlɔfəni], s. das Kolo-
phonium (resin).
coloration [kʌləˈreiʃən], s. die Färbung,
Tönung.
colossal [kəˈlɔsəl], adj. kolossal, riesig,
riesenhaft.
colour [ˈkʌlə], s. die Farbe; (complexion) die Gesichtsfarbe; (paint)
die Farbe, der Anstrich; (dye) die
Färbung. — v.a. färben; anstreichen
(paint house etc.).
colt [koult], s. das Füllen.
columbine [ˈkɔləmbain], s. (Bot.) die
Akelei.
column [ˈkɔləm], s. die Säule; die
Spalte (press); (also Mil.) die Kolonne.
colza [ˈkɔlzə], s. (Bot.) der Raps.
coma [ˈkoumə], s. (Med.) das Koma,
die Schlafsucht.
comb [koum], s. der Kamm. — v.a.
kämmen; (fig.) genau untersuchen.
combat [ˈkʌmbət, ˈkɔmbət], s. der
Kampf, das Gefecht; in single —, im
Duell, Zweikampf. — v.a. kämpfen,
bekämpfen.
combatant [ˈkʌmbətənt, ˈkɔmb-], s. der
Kämpfer.
comber [ˈkoumə], s. der Wollkämmer.
combination [kɔmbiˈneiʃən], s. die
Kombination, die Verbindung.
combine [kəmˈbain], v.a. kombinieren,
verbinden. — v.n. sich verbinden. —
[ˈkɔmbain], s. (Comm.) der Trust,
Ring.

combustible [kəmˈbʌstibl], adj. verbrennbar; feuergefährlich.
combustion [kəmˈbʌstʃən], s. die
Verbrennung.
come [kʌm], v.n. irr. kommen; — about,
sich ereignen (event); — across,
stoßen auf (Acc.); — by (s.th.),
ergattern, erwerben; — for, abholen;
— forth, forward, hervorkommen,
hervortreten; — from, herkommen
von, — in, hereinkommen; — off, (of
object) loskommen, (succeed) glücken;
— out (appear), herauskommen;
— to o.s., zu sich kommen; — of age,
mündig werden; — to o.'s senses,
zur Besinnung or Vernunft kommen;
that is still to — , das steht uns noch
bevor.
comedian [kəˈmiːdjən], s. der Komödiant, Komiker (stage).
comedy [ˈkɔmədi], s. die Komödie, das
Lustspiel.
comeliness [ˈkʌmlinis], s. die Anmut,
Schönheit.
comely [ˈkʌmli], adj. anmutig, schön.
comestible [kəˈmestibl], s. (usually pl.)
die Eßwaren, f. pl.
comet [ˈkɔmit], s. der Komet.
comfit [ˈkʌmfit], s. das Konfekt, die
Bonbons.
comfort [ˈkʌmfət], s. der Trost (solace);
der Komfort, die Bequemlichkeit. —
v.a. trösten.
comforter [ˈkʌmfətə], s. der Tröster;
(Am.) die Steppdecke.
comfortless [ˈkʌmfətlis], adj. trostlos,
unbehaglich.
comic [ˈkɔmik], adj. komisch; —
writer, humoristischer Schriftsteller.
— s. die Bilderzeitung (children's
paper).
comical [ˈkɔmikl], adj. lächerlich, zum
Lachen, komisch.
comma [ˈkɔmə], s. das Komma, der
Beistrich; inverted —s, die Anführungszeichen.
command [kəˈmɑːnd], v.a., v.n. (Mil.)
kommandieren; über jemanden verfügen (have s.o. at o.'s disposal). — s.
der Befehl.
commandant [kɔmənˈdænt], s. der
Kommandant, Befehlshaber.
commander [kəˈmɑːndə], s. der Befehlshaber.
commandment [kəˈmɑːndmənt], s.
(Rel.) das Gebot.
commemorate [kəˈmeməreit], v.a.
feiern, gedenken (Genit.).
commemoration [kəmeməˈreiʃən], s.
die Feier, die Gedächtnisfeier.
commemorative [kəˈmemərətiv], adj.
Gedächtnis-.
commence [kəˈmens], v.a., v.n. beginnen, anfangen.
commencement [kəˈmensmənt], s. der
Anfang, der Beginn.
commend [kəˈmend], v.a. empfehlen,
loben (praise).
commendable [kəˈmendəbl], adj. emp-
fehlenswert.

342

**commendation** [kɔmen'deiʃən], s. die Empfehlung.

**commensurable, commensurate** [kə'menʃərəbl, kə'menʃərit], adj. kommensurabel, entsprechend; angemessen.

**comment** ['kɔment], v.n. kommentieren (on, zu, Dat.). — s. der Kommentar; die Bemerkung (remark).

**commentary** ['kɔməntəri], s. der Kommentar.

**commentator** ['kɔmənteitə], s. der Kommentator, Berichterstatter.

**commerce** ['kɔmə:s], s. der Handel; college of —, die Handelsschule.

**commercial** [kə'mə:ʃəl], adj. kommerziell, kaufmännisch, Handels-; — traveller, der Handelsreisende, Vertreter; — manager, der geschäftliche Leiter.

**commingle** [kə'miŋgl], v.a. vermischengefühl.

**commiserate** [kə'mizəreit], v.n. bemitleiden; — with s.o., mit einem Mitgefühl haben.

**commissariat** [kɔmi'sɛəriət], s. (Pol.) das Kommissariat.

**commissary** ['kɔmisəri], s. der Kommissar. — adj. kommissarisch.

**commission** [kə'miʃən], s. die Kommission; (Mil.) der Offiziersrang; die Begehung (of crime); (Law) der (offizielle) Kommission; der Auftrag, die Bestellung (order).

**commissionaire** [kəmiʃən'ɛə], s. der Portier.

**commissioned** [kə'miʃənd], adj. bevollmächtigt.

**commissioner** [kə'miʃənə], s. (Pol.) der Kommissar, der Bevollmächtigte.

**commit** [kə'mit], v.a. begehen (do); übergeben (consign); anvertrauen (entrust). — v.r. sich verpflichten.

**committal** [kə'mitl], s. das Übergeben; die Überantwortung.

**committee** [kə'miti], s. das Kommitee, der Ausschuß.

**commodious** [kə'moudiəs], adj. bequem, geräumig.

**commodity** [kə'mɔditi], s. (Comm.) die Ware, der Artikel.

**commodore** ['kɔmədɔ:], s. (Naut.) der Kommodore, der Kommandant eines Geschwaders.

**common** ['kɔmən], adj. gewöhnlich (usual); gemein (vulgar); allgemein (general); in —, gemeinschaftlich; — sense, der gesunde Menschenverstand; the — man, der kleine Mann. — n. pl. House of Commons, das Unterhaus.

**commoner** ['kɔmənə], s. der Bürger; (Parl.) Mitglied des Unterhauses.

**commonness** ['kɔmənnis], s. die Gemeinheit (vulgarity); das häufige Vorkommen (frequency).

**commonplace** ['kɔmənpleis], adj. alltäglich. — s. der Gemeinplatz.

**commonwealth** ['kɔmənwelθ], s. die Staatengemeinschaft, der Staatenbund; das Commonwealth.

**commotion** [kə'mouʃən], s. die Erschütterung; der Aufruhr; der Lärm.

**communal** ['kɔmjunəl], adj. gemeinschaftlich, allgemein; (Pol.) Kommunal-.

**commune** ['kɔmju:n], s. (Pol.) die Kommune. — [kə'mju:n], v.n. sich unterhalten.

**communicable** [kə'mju:nikəbl], adj. mitteilbar; übertragbar.

**communicate** [kə'mju:nikeit], v.a. mitteilen; verkünden (proclaim); benachrichtigen. — v.n. in Verbindung stehen.

**communication** [kəmju:ni'keiʃən], s. die Mitteilung; Verlautbarung; die Verkündigung (proclamation); die Information; (Elec.) die Verbindung; (pl.), die Verbindungslinie; —s engineering, Fernmeldetechnik.

**communion** [kə'mju:njən], s. (Eccl.) die Kommunion; das heilige Abendmahl; die Gemeinschaft (fellowship).

**Communism** ['kɔmjunizm], s. (Pol.) der Kommunismus.

**Communist** ['kɔmjunist], s. der Kommunist. — adj. kommunistisch.

**community** [kə'mju:niti], s. die Gemeinschaft.

**commutable** [kə'mju:təbl], adj. umtauschbar, auswechselbar.

**commutation** [kɔmju'teiʃən], s. der Austausch; (Law) die Herabsetzung (of sentence).

**commutator** ['kɔmjuteitə], s. (Elec.) der Umschalter.

**commute** [kə'mju:t], v.n. hin und her fahren, pendeln, mit Zeitkarte fahren (travel). — v.a. herabsetzen (sentence).

**compact** ['kɔmpækt], adj. kompakt, fest; gedrängt (succinct); kurz, bündig (short).

**companion** [kəm'pænjən], s. der Gefährte, die Gefährtin.

**companionable** [kəm'pænjənəbl], adj. gesellig, freundlich.

**companionship** [kəm'pænjənʃip], s. die Geselligkeit; die Gesellschaft.

**company** ['kʌmpəni], s. die Gesellschaft; (Mil.) die Kompanie; der Freundeskreis (circle of friends); (Comm.) die Handelsgesellschaft; limited (liability) —, Gesellschaft mit beschränkter Haftung; public (private) —, Gesellschaft des öffentlichen (privaten) Rechtes.

**comparative** [kəm'pærətiv], adj. vergleichend, relativ. — s. (Gram.) der Komparativ.

**compare** [kəm'pɛə], v.a. vergleichen. — v.n. sich vergleichen lassen.

**comparison** [kəm'pærisən], s. der Vergleich; das Gleichnis (simile).

**compartment** [kəm'pɑ:tmənt], s. (Railw.) das Abteil; die Abteilung.

**compass** ['kʌmpəs], s. der Umkreis, Umfang (scope); (Naut.) der Kompaß; point of the —, der Kompaßstrich; (Engin.) der Zirkel.

**compassion** [kəm'pæʃən], s. die Barmherzigkeit, das Mitleid, das Erbarmen.
**compassionate** [kəm'pæʃənit], adj. mitleidig; (Mil.) — leave, der Sonderurlaub.
**compatibility** [kəmpæti'biliti], s. die Verträglichkeit, Vereinbarkeit.
**compatible** [kəm'pætibl], adj. verträglich, vereinbar.
**compatriot** [kəm'peitriət], s. der Landsmann.
**compel** [kəm'pel], v.a. zwingen, nötigen.
**compendium** [kəm'pendjəm], s. das Kompendium, die kurze Schrift, die kurze Darstellung.
**compensate** ['kɔmpənseit], v.a. kompensieren, einem Ersatz leisten.
**compensation** [kɔmpən'seiʃən], s. der Ersatz, die Wiedergutmachung.
**compensatory** [kɔmpən'seitəri], adj. ausgleichend, Ersatz-.
**compete** [kəm'pi:t], v.n. wetteifern, konkurrieren.
**competence, competency** ['kɔmpitəns, -nsi], s. die Kompetenz; Zuständigkeit; Befähigung (capability); Tüchtigkeit (ability).
**competent** ['kɔmpitənt], adj. kompetent; zuständig; fähig (capable); tüchtig (able).
**competition** [kɔmpi'tiʃən], s. die Konkurrenz; die Mitbewerbung (for job).
**competitive** [kəm'petitiv], adj. Konkurrenz-, konkurrierend.
**competitor** [kəm'petitə], s. (Comm.) der Konkurrent; der Mitbewerber (fellow applicant), Teilnehmer (sport).
**complacent** [kəm'pleisənt], adj. selbstzufrieden, selbstgefällig.
**complain** [kəm'plein], v.n. sich beklagen (of, über, Acc.).
**complaint** [kəm'pleint], s. die Klage; Beschwerde (grievance); das Leiden (illness).
**complement** ['kɔmplimənt], s. die Ergänzung, Gesamtzahl. — [-'ment], v.a. ergänzen.
**complementary** [kɔmpli'mentəri], adj. Ergänzungs-, ergänzend.
**complete** [kəm'pli:t], adj. komplett; voll (full up); vollkommen (perfect). — v.a. vollenden (end); ergänzen (make whole).
**completeness** [kəm'pli:tnis], s. die Vollendung (condition); Ganzheit (wholeness).
**completion** [kəm'pli:ʃən], s. die Vollendung (fulfilment); die Beendigung (ending); der Abschluß.
**complex** ['kɔmpleks], adj. (Maths.) komplex; kompliziert (complicated). — s. der Komplex (Archit., Psych.).
**complexion** [kəm'plekʃən], s. die Gesichtsfarbe; (fig.) das Aussehen.
**complexity** [kəm'pleksiti], s. die Kompliziertheit; die Schwierigkeit.
**compliance** [kəm'plaiəns], s. die Willfährigkeit, Einwilligung.
**compliant** [kəm'plaiənt], adj. willig, willfährig.

**complicate** ['kɔmplikeit], v.a. komplizieren, erschweren.
**complication** [kɔmpli'keiʃən], s. die Komplikation, die Erschwerung.
**complicity** [kəm'plisiti], s. (Law) die Mitschuld.
**compliment** ['kɔmplimənt], s. das Kompliment. — [-'ment], v.n. Komplimente machen.
**complimentary** [kɔmpli'mentəri], adj. lobend; — ticket, die Freikarte.
**comply** [kəm'plai], v.n. einwilligen (with, in, Acc.); sich halten (an, Acc.).
**compose** [kəm'pouz], v.a., v.n. (Mus.) komponieren; beruhigen (the mind); (Lit.) verfassen; (Typ.) setzen.
**composed** [kəm'pouzd], adj. ruhig, gefaßt.
**composer** [kəm'pouzə], s. (Mus.) der Komponist.
**composite** ['kɔmpəzit], adj. zusammengesetzt.
**composition** [kɔmpə'ziʃən], s. (Mus. etc.) die Komposition; Beschaffenheit Zusammensetzung.
**compositor** [kəm'pɔzitə], s. (Typ.) der Schriftsetzer.
**compost** ['kɔmpɔst], s. (Agr.) der Dünger, Kompost.
**composure** [kəm'pouʒə], s. die Gelassenheit, die Gemütsruhe, die Fassung.
**compound** ['kɔmpaund], s. (Chem.) die Verbindung; die Zusammensetzung. — adj. zusammengesetzt; kompliziert; (Comm.) — interest, die Zinseszinsen. — [kəm'paund], v.a. (Chem.) mischen, zusammensetzen.
**comprehend** [kɔmpri'hend], v.a. verstehen (understand); einschließen (include).
**comprehensible** [kɔmpri'hensibl], adj. verständlich, begreiflich.
**comprehension** [kɔmpri'henʃən], s. das Verstehen, das Erfassen; (Psych.) — tests, die Verständnisprüfung.
**comprehensive** [kɔmpri'hensiv], adj. umfassend.
**compress** [kəm'pres], v.a. komprimieren; zusammendrücken (press together). — ['kɔmpres], s. (Med.) die Kompresse, der Umschlag (poultice).
**compression** [kəm'preʃən], s. der Druck, das Zusammendrücken (pressing together); die Kürzung (abridgment).
**comprise** [kəm'praiz], v.a. umfassen, einschließen.
**compromise** ['kɔmprəmaiz], v.a. kompromittieren. — v.n. einen Kompromiß schließen. — s. der or das Kompromiß.
**compulsion** [kəm'pʌlʃən], s. der Zwang.
**compulsory** [kəm'pʌlsəri], adj. zwingend; Zwangs-; — subject, das obligatorische Fach.
**compunction** [kəm'pʌŋkʃən], s. die Gewissensbisse, m. pl.
**computation** [kɔmpju'teiʃən], s. die Berechnung.

# condition

compute [kəm'pju:t], *v.a., v.n.* berechnen.

computer [kəm'pju:tə], *s.* die automatische Rechenmaschine.

comrade ['kɔmrid], *s.* der Kamerad.

comradeship ['kɔmridʃip], *s.* die Kameradschaft.

con [kɔn], *v.a.* genau betrachten, studieren; (*ship*) steuern.

concave ['kɔnkeiv], *adj.* (*Phys.*) konkav.

conceal [kən'si:l], *v.a.* verbergen, verstecken.

concealment [kən'si:lmənt], *s.* die Verhehlung, die Verheimlichung (*act of concealing*); *place of* —, das Versteck.

concede [kən'si:d], *v.a.* zugestehen, einräumen.

conceit [kən'si:t], *s.* die Einbildung, der Eigendünkel (*presumption*); (*obs.*) die Idee; (*Lit.*) die (gedankliche) Spielerei.

conceited [kən'si:tid], *adj.* eingebildet, eitel.

conceivable [kən'si:vəbl], *adj.* denkbar; begreiflich (*understandable*).

conceive [kən'si:v], *v.a., v.n.* empfangen (*become pregnant*); begreifen (*understand*).

concentrate ['kɔnsəntreit], *v.a.* konzentrieren. — *v.n.* sich konzentrieren (*on*, auf, *Acc.*). — *s.* (*Chem.*) das Konzentrat.

concentrated ['kɔnsəntreitid], *adj.* konzentriert.

concentration [kɔnsən'treiʃən], *s.* die Konzentration.

concentric [kɔn'sentrik], *adj.* (*Geom.*) konzentrisch.

conception [kən'sepʃən], *s.* die Vorstellung, der Begriff (*idea*); die Empfängnis (*of a child*).

concern [kən'sə:n], *v.a.* (*affect*) betreffen, angehen; *be concerned with,* zu tun haben (mit, *Dat.*). — *s.* die Angelegenheit (*affair*); die Sorge (*care, business*); das Geschäft, das Unternehmen; *cause grave* —, tiefe Besorgnis erregen.

concerned [kən'sə:nd], *adj.* (*worried*) besorgt; (*involved*) interessiert (*in*, an, *Dat.*).

concerning [kən'sə:niŋ], *prep.* betreffend (*Acc.*), hinsichtlich (*Genit.*).

concert ['kɔnsət], *s.* (*Mus.*) das Konzert; Einverständnis.

concerted [kən'sə:tid], *adj.* gemeinsam, gemeinschaftlich.

concertina [kɔnsə'ti:nə], *s.* (*Mus.*) die Ziehharmonika.

concerto [kən'tʃə:tou], *s.* (*Mus.*) das Konzert.

concession [kən'seʃən], *s.* die Konzession (*licence*); das Zugeständnis.

conch [kɔŋk], *s.* die (große) Muschel.

conciliate [kən'silieit], *v.a.* versöhnen.

conciliation [kɔnsili'eiʃən], *s.* die Versöhnung.

conciliatory [kən'siliətəri], *adj.* versöhnlich.

concise [kən'sais], *adj.* kurz, knapp.

conciseness [kən'saisnis], *s.* die Kürze, Knappheit.

conclave ['kɔnkleiv], *s.* (*Eccl.*) das Konklave.

conclude [kən'klu:d], *v.a., v.n.* schließen, beenden (*speech etc.*); (*infer*) folgern (*from*, aus, *Dat.*); abschließen (*treaty*).

conclusion [kən'klu:ʒən], *s.* der Abschluß (*treaty*); die Folgerung (*inference*); der Beschluß (*decision*).

conclusive [kən'klu:siv], *adj.* entscheidend, überzeugend.

concoct [kən'kɔkt], *v.a.* zusammenbrauen, aushecken.

concoction [kən'kɔkʃən], *s.* das Gebräu, die Mischung.

concomitant [kən'kɔmitənt], *adj.* begleitend; Begleit-, Neben-. — *s.* der Begleitumstand.

concord ['kɔnkɔ:d], *s.* die Eintracht, die Harmonie.

concordance [kən'kɔ:dəns], *s.* die Übereinstimmung; die Konkordanz (*of Bible etc.*).

concordant [kən'kɔ:dənt], *adj.* in Eintracht (mit), übereinstimmend (mit) (*Dat.*).

concordat [kən'kɔ:dæt], *s.* (*Eccl., Pol.*) das Konkordat.

concourse ['kɔnkɔ:s], *s.* das Gedränge (*crowd*).

concrete ['kɔnkri:t], *s.* (*Build.*) der Beton; (*Log.*) das Konkrete. — *adj.* konkret, wirklich.

concur [kən'kə:], *v.n.* übereinstimmen (*with*, mit, *Dat.*).

concurrence [kən'kʌrəns], *s.* die Übereinstimmung.

concurrent [kən'kʌrənt], *adj.* gleichzeitig (*simultaneous*); mitwirkend (*accompanying*).

concussion [kən'kʌʃən], *s.* (*Med.*) die (Gehirn)Erschütterung.

condemn [kən'dem], *v.a.* verurteilen, verdammen.

condemnable [kən'demnəbl], *adj.* verwerflich, verdammenswert.

condemnation [kɔndem'neiʃən], *s.* die Verurteilung, die Verdammung.

condensate ['kɔndenseit], *s.* (*Chem.*) das Kondensat, das Ergebnis der Kondensation.

condensation [kɔnden'seiʃən], *s.* die Kondensation; Verdichtung.

condensed [kən'densd], *adj.* (*Chem.*) kondensiert; (*Chem., Engin.*) verdichtet; gekürzt (*abridged*).

condenser [kən'densə], *s.* (*Chem., Engin.*) der Kondensator; (*Elec.*) der Verstärker.

condescend [kɔndi'send], *v.n.* sich herablassen.

condescending [kɔndi'sendiŋ], *adj.* herablassend.

condescension [kɔndi'senʃən], *s.* die Herablassung.

condiment ['kɔndimənt], *s.* die Würze.

condition [kən'diʃən], *s.* der Zustand; Umstand; die Bedingung (*proviso*); der Gesundheitszustand (*physical state*).

# conditional

**conditional** [kən'diʃənəl], *adj.* bedingt; unter der Bedingung; konditionell.
**conditioned** [kən'diʃənd], *adj.* vorbereitet (*for action*); geartet.
**condole** [kən'doul], *v.n.* Beileid ausdrücken (*with, Dat.*), kondolieren (*with, Dat.*).
**condolence** [kən'douləns], *s.* das Beileid.
**condone** [kən'doun], *v.a.* verzeihen.
**conducive** [kən'djuːsiv], *adj.* förderlich, dienlich, nützlich (*to, Dat.*).
**conduct** [kən'dʌkt], *v.a.* leiten, führen; (*Phys.*) ein Leiter sein; (*Mus.*) dirigieren. — *v.r.* sich aufführen, sich benehmen. — ['kɔndʌkt], *s.* das Benehmen (*behaviour*); — *of a war*, die Kriegsführung.
**conductive** [kən'dʌktiv], *adj.* (*Elec.*) leitend.
**conductor** [kən'dʌktə], *s.* der Leiter, Führer (*leader*); (*Phys., Elec.*) der Leiter; (*Am.*) der Schaffner (*train*); (*Mus.*) der Dirigent.
**conduit** ['kʌn-, 'kɔndit], *s.* die Leitung, die Röhre.
**cone** [koun], *s.* (*Geom.*) der Kegel; (*Bot.*) der Zapfen.
**coney** ['kouni], *s.* (*Zool.*) das Kaninchen.
**confection** [kən'fekʃən], *s.* das Konfekt.
**confectioner** [kən'fekʃənə], *s.* der Zuckerbäcker, Konditor.
**confectionery** [kən'fekʃənəri], *s.* die Zuckerwaren, *f.pl.* (*sweets*); Konditoreiwaren, *f.pl.* (*cakes*); die Zuckerbäckerei (*sweet shop*); die Konditorei.
**confederacy** [kən'fedərəsi], *s.* der Bund (*of states*); das Bündnis (*treaty*).
**confederate** [kən'fedərit], *s.* der Bundesgenosse, der Verbündete. — *adj.* verbündet; — *state*, der Bundesstaat. — [-reit], *v.n.* sich verbünden (*with, mit, Dat.*).
**confederation** [kənfedə'reiʃən], *s.* das Bündnis (*treaty*); der Bund (*state*).
**confer** [kən'fəː], *v.a.* verleihen (*degree, title*). — *v.n.* beraten (*with, mit, Dat.*), unterhandeln (*negotiate*).
**conference** ['kɔnfərəns], *s.* die Konferenz, die Besprechung, die Beratung, Tagung.
**confess** [kən'fes], *v.a.* bekennen; beichten (*sin*); zugestehen (*acknowledge*).
**confession** [kən'feʃən], *s.* das Bekenntnis; die Beichte (*sin*); das Glaubensbekenntnis (*creed*).
**confessor** [kən'fesə], *s.* der Bekenner; *father* —, der Beichtvater.
**confidant** [kɔnfi'dænt], *s.* der Vertraute.
**confide** [kən'faid], *v.a.* anvertrauen. — *v.n.* vertrauen (*Dat.*).
**confidence** ['kɔnfidəns], *s.* das Vertrauen; die Zuversicht; — *trick*, die Bauernfängerei, der Schwindel.
**confident** ['kɔnfidənt], *adj.* zuversichtlich; dreist (*bold*).
**confidential** [kɔnfi'denʃəl], *adj.* vertraulich, privat.

**confine** [kən'fain], *v.a.* einschränken (*hem in*); einsperren; *be —d to bed*, bettlägerig sein.
**confinement** [kən'fainmənt], *s.* die Einschränkung (*limitation*); das Wochenbett, die Niederkunft (*childbirth*).
**confines** ['kɔnfainz], *s. pl.* die Grenzen, *f. pl.* (*physical*); die Einschränkungen, *f. pl.* (*limitations*).
**confirm** [kən'fəːm], *v.a.* bestätigen, bekräftigen (*corroborate*); (*Eccl.*) firmen, konfirmieren.
**confirmation** [kɔnfə'meiʃən], *s.* die Bestätigung (*corroboration*); (*Eccl.*) die Firmung, Konfirmation.
**confirmed** [kən'fəːmd], *adj.* eingefleischt; unverbesserlich.
**confiscate** ['kɔnfiskeit], *v.a.* konfiszieren, einziehen, beschlagnahmen.
**confiscation** [kɔnfis'keiʃən], *s.* die Konfiszierung, die Einziehung, die Beschlagnahme (*customs etc.*).
**conflagration** [kɔnflə'greiʃən], *s.* der (große) Brand.
**conflict** ['kɔnflikt], *s.* der Konflikt, der Zusammenstoß. — [kən'flikt], *v.n.* in Konflikt geraten; in Widerspruch stehen.
**confluence** [kən'fluəns], *s.* (*Geog.*) der Zusammenfluß.
**confluent** ['kɔnfluənt], *adj.* zusammenfließend. — *s.* der Nebenfluß (*tributary*).
**conform** [kən'fɔːm], *v.n.* sich anpassen.
**conformation** [kɔnfɔː'meiʃən], *s.* die Anpassung.
**conformist** [kən'fɔːmist], *adj.* fügsam. — *s.* das Mitglied der Staatskirche.
**conformity** [kən'fɔːmiti], *s.* die Gleichförmigkeit; *in — with*, gerade so; gemäß (*Dat.*); die Gleichheit (*equality*.)
**confound** [kən'faund], *v.a.* verwirren (*confuse*); vernichten (*overthrow*).
**confounded** [kən'faundid], *adj.* verdammt, verwünscht.
**confront** [kən'frʌnt], *v.a.* (*Law*) — *s.o. with*, gegenüberstellen (*put in front of*); gegenüberstehen (*stand in front of*).
**confrontation** [kɔnfrʌn'teiʃən], *s.* die Gegenüberstellung.
**confuse** [kən'fjuːz], *v.a.* verwirren (*muddle*); bestürzen (*perplex*); verwechseln (*mix up*).
**confusion** [kən'fjuːʒən], *s.* die Verwirrung, das Durcheinander (*muddle*); die Bestürzung (*astonishment*); die Verlegenheit (*dilemma*).
**confutation** [kɔnfjuː'teiʃən], *s.* die Widerlegung.
**confute** [kən'fjuːt], *v.a.* widerlegen.
**congeal** [kən'dʒiːl], *v.n.* gefrieren (*freeze*); gerinnen.
**congenial** [kən'dʒiːniəl], *adj.* geistesverwandt, geistig ebenbürtig, sympathisch.
**congeniality** [kəndʒiːni'æliti], *s.* die Geistesverwandtschaft.
**conger** ['kɔŋgə], *s.* (*Zool.*) der Meeraal.

**congest** [kən'dʒest], v.a. anhäufen, überfüllen.

**congestion** [kən'dʒestʃən], s. die Überfüllung; Stauung; die Übervölkerung (overpopulation); (Med.) der Blutandrang.

**conglomerate** [kən'glɔməreit], v.n. sich zusammenballen. — [-rit], s. das Konglomerat, die Ballung.

**conglomeration** [kənglɔmə'reiʃən], s. die Zusammenhäufung, Zusammenballung.

**Congolese** [kɔŋgo'li:z], adj. kongolesisch. — s. der Kongolese.

**congratulate** [kən'grætjuleit], v.n. gratulieren (on, zu, Dat.).

**congratulation** [kəngrætju'leiʃən], s. (usually pl.) die Glückwünsche, m. pl.

**congratulatory** [kən'grætjuleitəri], adj. Glückwunsch-.

**congregate** [kɔŋgrigeit], v.a. sammeln. — v.n. sich versammeln, sich scharen (round, um, Acc.).

**congregation** [kɔŋgri'geiʃən], s. die Versammlung, die Schar; (Eccl.) die Gemeinde.

**congregational** [kɔŋgri'geiʃənəl], adj. (Eccl.) Gemeinde-; Congregational Church, unabhängige Gemeindekirche.

**congress** [kɔŋgres], s. der Kongreß.

**congruence** [kɔŋgruəns], s. (Geom.) die Kongruenz.

**congruent** [kɔŋgruənt], adj. (Geom.) kongruent.

**congruity** [kɔŋ'gru:iti], s. (Geom.) die Übereinstimmung; die Kongruenz.

**congruous** [kɔŋgruəs], adj. übereinstimmend, angemessen.

**conic(al)** [kɔnik(əl)], adj. konisch, kegelförmig; (Geom.) — section, der Kegelschnitt.

**conifer** [kɔnifə], s. (Bot.) der Nadelbaum.

**conjecture** [kən'dʒektʃə], s. die Mutmaßung, die Annahme. — v.a. mutmaßen, annehmen.

**conjoin** [kən'dʒɔin], v.a. (Law) verbinden.

**conjugal** [kɔndʒugəl], adj. ehelich.

**conjugate** [kɔndʒugeit], v.a. (Gram.) konjugieren.

**conjugation** [kɔndʒu'geiʃən], s. (Gram.) die Konjugation.

**conjunction** [kən'dʒʌŋkʃən], s. (Gram.) das Bindewort.

**conjunctive** [kən'dʒʌŋktiv], adj. verbindend; (Gram.) — mood, der Konjunktiv.

**conjunctivitis** [kəndʒʌŋkti'vaitis], s. (Med.) die Bindehautentzündung.

**conjuncture** [kən'dʒʌŋktʃə], s. der Wendepunkt; die Krise (of events).

**conjure** [kʌndʒə], v.a. beschwören; — up, heraufbeschwören. — v.n. zaubern.

**conjurer** [kʌndʒərə], s. der Zauberer.

**connect** [kə'nekt], v.a. verbinden, in Zusammenhang bringen.

**connection, connexion** [kə'nekʃən],s die Verbindung, der Zusammenhang.

**connivance** [kə'naivəns], s. die Nachsicht, das Gewährenlassen.

**connive** [kə'naiv], v.n. nachsichtig sein (at, bei, Dat.); gewähren lassen.

**connoisseur** [kɔnə'sə:], s. der Kenner.

**connubial** [kə'nju:biəl], adj. ehelich.

**conquer** [kɔŋkə], v.a. besiegen (foe); erobern (place).

**conqueror** [kɔŋkərə], s. der Eroberer, der Sieger.

**conquest** [kɔŋkwest], s. der Sieg, die Eroberung.

**consanguinity** [kɔnsæŋ'gwiniti], s. die Blutsverwandtschaft.

**conscience** [kɔnʃəns], s. das Gewissen; in all — wahrhaftig.

**conscientious** [kɔnʃi'enʃəs], adj. gewissenhaft.

**conscientiousness** [kɔnʃi'enʃəsnis], s. die Gewissenhaftigkeit.

**conscious** [kɔnʃəs], adj. bewußt (Genit.).

**consciousness** [kɔnʃəsnis], s. das Bewußtsein.

**conscript** [kən'skript], v.a. (Mil.) einziehen, einberufen. — [kɔnskript], s. (Mil.) der Rekrut, der Dienstpflichtige.

**conscription** [kən'skripʃən], s. die allgemeine Wehrpflicht.

**consecrate** [kɔnsikreit], v.a. weihen, widmen.

**consecrated** [kɔnsikreitid], adj. geweiht (Dat.).

**consecration** [kɔnsi'kreiʃən], s. die Weihe, Einweihung (of church); die Weihung.

**consecutive** [kən'sekjutiv], adj. aufeinanderfolgend, fortlaufend.

**consecutiveness** [kən'sekjutivnis], s. die Aufeinanderfolge.

**consent** [kən'sent], v.n. zustimmen, beistimmen (to, Dat.). — s. die Zustimmung, die Einwilligung.

**consequence** [kɔnsikwəns], s. die Konsequenz; (Log.) Folgerung; die Folge; die Wichtigkeit (importance).

**consequent** [kɔnsikwənt], adj. folgend, nachfolgend.

**consequential** [kɔnsi'kwenʃəl], adj. wichtigtuend, anmaßend; (Log.) folgerichtig.

**consequently** [kɔnsikwəntli], adv. folglich, infolgedessen.

**conservatism** [kən'sə:vətizm], s. (Pol.) der Konservatismus; die konservative Denkweise.

**conservative** [kən'sə:vətiv], adj. (Pol.) konservativ.

**conservatoire** [kən'sə:vətwa:], s. (Mus.) das Konservatorium, die Musikhochschule.

**conservatory** [kən'sə:vətəri], s. (Bot.) das Gewächshaus.

**conserve** [kən'sə:v], v.a. konservieren, erhalten, einmachen. — s. (fruit) das Eingemachte.

**consider** [kən'sidə], v.a. betrachten, in Betracht ziehen (think over, look at); berücksichtigen (have regard to); nachdenken über (Acc.) (ponder).

# considerable

**considerable** [kən'sidərəbl], *adj.* beträchtlich, ansehnlich.
**considerate** [kən'sidərit], *adj.* rücksichtsvoll (*thoughtful*).
**consideration** [kənsidə'reifən], *s.* die Betrachtung (*contemplation*); die Rücksicht (*regard*) (*for*, auf, *Acc.*); die Entschädigung (*compensation*); die Belohnung (*reward*).
**considering** [kən'sidəriŋ], *prep.* in Anbetracht (*Genit.*).
**consign** [kən'sain], *v.a.* überliefern (*hand over*); übersenden (*remit*).
**consignee** [kənsai'ni:], *s.* (*Comm.*) der Empfänger, der Adressat (*recipient*).
**consigner** [kən'sainə], *s.* der Absender (*of goods*).
**consignment** [kən'sainmənt], *s.* die Sendung (*of goods*).
**consist** [kən'sist], *v.n.* bestehen (*of*, aus, *Dat.*).
**consistency** [kən'sistənsi], *s.* die Festigkeit, Dichtigkeit; (*Chem.*) die Konsistenz.
**consistent** [kən'sistənt], *adj.* konsequent; — *with*, übereinstimmend, gemäß (*Dat.*); (*Chem.*) dicht, fest.
**consistory** [kən'sistəri], *s.* (*Eccl.*) das Konsistorium.
**consolable** [kən'souləbl], *adj.* tröstlich, zu trösten.
**consolation** [kənso'leifən], *s.* der Trost; *draw* —, Trost schöpfen.
**console** (1) [kən'soul], *v.a.* trösten.
**console** (2) ['kɔnsoul], *s.* (*Archit.*) die Konsole.
**consolidate** [kən'sɔlideit], *v.a.* befestigen, konsolidieren. — *v.n.* fest werden.
**consolidation** [kənsɔli'deifən], *s.* die Befestigung; Festigung, Bestärkung (*confirmation*).
**consonance** ['kɔnsənəns], *s.* (*Phonet.*) die Konsonanz; der Einklang, die Harmonie.
**consonant** ['kɔnsənənt], *adj.* in Einklang (*with*, mit, *Dat.*). — *s.* der Konsonant.
**consort** ['kɔnsɔ:t], *s.* der Gemahl, Gatte; die Gemahlin, die Gattin. — [kən'sɔ:t], *v.n.* verkehren (*with*, mit, *Dat.*).
**conspicuous** [kən'spikjuəs], *adj.* auffallend, deutlich sichtbar, hervorragend.
**conspiracy** [kən'spirəsi], *s.* die Verschwörung.
**conspirator** [kən'spirətə], *s.* der Verschwörer.
**conspire** [kən'spaiə], *v.n.* sich verschwören.
**constable** ['kʌnstəbl], *s.* der Polizist, der Schutzmann.
**Constance** ['kɔnstəns], Konstanze, *f.* (*name*); Konstanz, *n.* (*town*); *Lake* —, der Bodensee.
**constancy** ['kɔnstənsi], *s.* die Beständigkeit, Treue.
**constant** ['kɔnstənt], *adj.* (*Chem.*) konstant; treu, beständig.

**constellation** [kɔnstə'leifən], *s.* die Konstellation; das Sternbild.
**consternation** [kɔnstə'neifən], *s.* die Bestürzung.
**constipation** [kɔnsti'peifən], *s.* die Verstopfung.
**constituency** [kən'stitjuənsi], *s.* der Wahlkreis (*electoral district*); die Wählerschaft (*voters*).
**constituent** [kən'stitjuənt], *adj.* wesentlich. — *s.* der Bestandteil (*component*); (*Pol.*) der Wähler.
**constitute** ['kɔnstitju:t], *v.a.* ausmachen (*make up*); bilden (*form*); festsetzen (*establish*); (*Pol.*) errichten (*set up*).
**constitution** [kɔnsti'tju:fən], *s.* die Konstitution (*physique*); die Errichtung (*establishment*); die Beschaffenheit, Natur (*nature*); (*Pol.*) die Verfassung.
**constitutional** [kɔnsti'tju:fənəl], *adj.* körperlich bedingt; (*Pol.*) verfassungsmäßig.
**constrain** [kən'strein], *v.a.* nötigen, zwingen.
**constraint** [kən'streint], *s.* der Zwang.
**constrict** [kən'strikt], *v.a.* zusammenziehen.
**constriction** [kən'strikfən], *s.* die Zusammenziehung, Beengtheit.
**construct** [kən'strʌkt], *v.a.* errichten, bauen, konstruieren.
**construction** [kən'strʌkfən], *s.* die Errichtung, der Bau, die Konstruktion.
**constructive** [kən'strʌktiv], *adj.* (*Engin.*) konstruktiv; behilflich (*positive*).
**constructor** [kən'strʌktə], *s.* der Konstrukteur, der Erbauer (*builder*).
**construe** [kən'stru:], *v.a.* konstruieren, deuten (*interpret*).
**consul** ['kɔnsəl], *s.* der Konsul; — *general*, der Generalkonsul.
**consular** ['kɔnsjulə], *adj.* konsularisch.
**consulate** ['kɔnsjulit], *s.* das Konsulat; — *general*, das Generalkonsulat.
**consult** [kən'sʌlt], *v.a.* konsultieren, zu Rate ziehen; nachschlagen (*a book*). — *v.n.* sich beraten (*with*, mit, *Dat.*); (*Comm.*) als Berater hinzuziehen.
**consultant** [kən'sʌltənt], *s.* (*Med.*) der Facharzt; der Berater.
**consultation** [kɔnsəl'teifən], *s.* die Beratung (*advice*); die Besprechung (*discussion*); (*Med.*, *Engin.*) die Konsultation.
**consume** [kən'sju:m], *v.a.* verzehren (*eat up*); verbrauchen (*use up*).
**consumer** [kən'sju:mə], *s.* der Verbraucher; (*Comm.*) der Konsument.
**consummate** [kən'sʌmit], *adj.* vollendet. — ['kɔnsəmeit], *v.a.* vollenden, vollziehen.
**consummation** [kɔnsə'meifən], *s.* die Vollziehung, Vollendung.
**consumption** [kən'sʌmpfən], *s.* (*Comm.*) der Verbrauch; (*Med.*) die Schwindsucht.
**consumptive** [kən'sʌmptiv], *adj.* (*Med.*) schwindsüchtig.

**contact** ['kɔntækt], *v.a.* berühren (*touch*); in Verbindung treten (mit) (*get into touch* (*with*)). — *s.* (*Elec.*) der Kontakt; die Berührung (*touch*); die Verbindung (*connexion*).

**contagion** [kən'teidʒən], *s.* (*Med.*) die Ansteckung.

**contagious** [kən'teidʒəs],*adj.*ansteckend.

**contain** [kən'tein], *v.a.* enthalten (*hold*); zurückhalten (*restrain*).

**container** [kən'teinə], *s.* der Behälter.

**contaminate** [kən'tæmineit], *v.a.* verunreinigen; vergiften.

**contemplate** ['kɔntəmpleit], *v.a.* betrachten (*consider*). — *v.n.* nachdenken (*ponder*).

**contemplation** [kɔntəm'pleiʃən], *s.* die Betrachtung (*consideration*); das Sinnen (*pondering*).

**contemplative** [kən'templətiv], *adj.* nachdenklich, kontemplativ.

**contemporaneous** [kɔntempə'reiniəs], *adj.* gleichzeitig.

**contemporary** [kən'tempərəri], *adj.* zeitgenössisch. — *s.* der Zeitgenosse.

**contempt** [kən'tempt], *s.* die Verachtung; — *of court*, die Gerichtsbeleidigung.

**contemptible** [kən'temptibl], *adj.* verächtlich, verachtungswert.

**contemptibleness** [kən'temptiblnis], *s.* die Verächtlichkeit.

**contemptuous** [kən'temptjuəs], *adj.* höhnisch, verachtungsvoll.

**contemptuousness** [kən'temptjuəsnis], *s.* der Hohn, der verachtungsvolle Ton, der Hochmut.

**contend** [kən'tend], *v.n.* streiten; bestreiten, behaupten.

**content** [kən'tent], *adj.* zufrieden. — *v.a.* zufriedenstellen. — ['kɔntent], *s.* (*often pl.*) der Inhalt.

**contented** [kən'tentid], *adj.* zufrieden.

**contentedness, contentment** [kən-'tentidnis, kən'tentmənt], *s.* die Zufriedenheit.

**contention** [kən'tenʃən], *s.* der Streit, die Behauptung.

**contentious** [kən'tenʃəs], *adj.* streitsüchtig (*person*); strittig (*question*).

**contest** ['kɔntest], *s.* der Streit, Wettstreit, Wettkampf. — [kən'test], *v.a.* um etwas streiten, bestreiten.

**context** ['kɔntekst], *s.* der Zusammenhang.

**contexture** [kən'tekstʃə], *s.* (*Engin.*) der Bau, die Zusammensetzung; das Gewebe (*textile*).

**contiguity** [kɔnti'gju:iti], *s.* die Berührung; die Nachbarschaft.

**contiguous** [kən'tigjuəs], *adj.* anstossend, anliegend.

**continence** ['kɔntinəns], *s.* die Mäßigung (*moderation*); die Enthaltsamkeit (*abstemiousness*).

**continent** (1) ['kɔntinənt], *adj.* enthaltsam, mässig.

**continent** (2) ['kɔntinənt], *s.* das Festland, der Kontinent.

**contingency** [kən'tindʒənsi], *s.* der Zufall; die Möglichkeit (*possibility*).

**contingent** [kən'tindʒənt], *s.* der Beitrag, das Kontingent (*share*). — *adj.* möglich.

**continual** [kən'tinjuəl], *adj.* fortwährend, beständig.

**continuance** [kən'tinjuəns], *s.* die Fortdauer.

**continuation** [kəntinju'eiʃən], *s.* die Fortsetzung.

**continue** [kən'tinju:], *v.a.* fortsetzen (*go on with*); verlängern (*prolong*). — *v.n.* weitergehen, weiterführen (*of story*).

**continuity** [kɔnti'nju:iti], *s.* der Zusammenhang, die ununterbrochene Folge, Kontinuität (*Film*); — *girl*, die Drehbuchsekretärin.

**continuous** [kən'tinjuəs], *adj.* zusammenhängend, ununterbrochen, andauernd.

**contort** [kən'tɔ:t], *v.a.* verdrehen.

**contortion** [kən'tɔ:ʃən], *s.* die Verdrehung, Verkrümmung, Verzerrung.

**contortionist** [kən'tɔ:ʃənist], *s.* der Schlangenmensch.

**contour** ['kɔntuə], *s.* die Kontur, der Umriß.

**contraband** ['kɔntrəbænd], *adj.* Schmuggel-, geschmuggelt. — *s.* die Bannware, Schmuggelware.

**contract** [kən'trækt], *v.a.* zusammenziehen (*pull together*); verengen (*narrow down*); verkürzen (*shorten*); sich eine Krankheit zuziehen (— *a disease*); Schulden machen (— *debts*). — *v.n.* sich zusammenziehen, kürzer werden; einen Kontrakt abschließen (*come to terms*). — ['kɔntrækt], *s.* der Vertrag (*pact*); (*Comm.*) der Kontrakt.

**contraction** [kən'trækʃən], *s.* die Zusammenziehung; (*Phonet.*) die Kürzung.

**contractor** [kən'træktə], *s.* (*Comm.*) der Kontrahent; der Lieferant (*supplier*); *building* —, der Bauunternehmer.

**contradict** [kɔntrə'dikt], *v.n.* widersprechen (*Dat.*).

**contradiction** [kɔntrə'dikʃən], *s.* der Widerspruch.

**contradictory** [kɔntrə'diktəri], *adj.* in Widerspruch stehend, widersprechend.

**contrarily** ['kɔntrərili], *adv.* im Gegensatz dazu, hingegen, dagegen.

**contrary** ['kɔntrəri], *adj.* entgegengesetzt, *on the* —, im Gegenteil; [kən'trɛəri], widersprechend.

**contrast** [kən'trɑ:st], *v.a.* einander entgegenstellen, gegenüberstellen. — *v.n.* einen Gegensatz darstellen *or* bilden. — ['kɔntrɑ:st], *s.* der Kontrast (*colours*); der Gegensatz.

**contravene** [kɔntrə'vi:n], *v.a.* übertreten, zuwiderhandeln (*Dat.*).

**contribute** [kən'tribju:t], *v.a.* beitragen; beisteuern (*money, energy*).

**contribution** [kɔntri'bju:ʃən], *s.* der Beitrag.

# contributive

**contributive, contributory** [kən'tri-bjutiv, kən'tribjutəri], *adj.* beitragend, Beitrags-.

**contributor** [kən'tribjutə], *s.* der Beitragende, der Spender (*of money*); der Mitarbeiter (*journalist etc.*).

**contrite** ['kɔntrait], *adj.* zerknirscht, reuevoll.

**contrition** [kən'triʃən], *s.* die Zerknirschung, die Reue.

**contrivance** [kən'traivəns], *s.* die Vorrichtung, die Erfindung.

**contrive** [kən'traiv], *v.a.* ausdenken, erfinden; fertigbringen (*accomplish*).

**control** [kən'troul], *v.a.* kontrollieren (*check*); die Leitung haben (*have command of*); die Aufsicht führen (*supervise*). — *s.* die Kontrolle; die Aufsicht; die Leitung; (*pl.*) (*Motor.*) die Steuerung; (*Aviat.*) das Leitwerk.

**controller** [kən'troulə], *s.* der Aufseher (*supervisor*); der Direktor (*of corporation*); der Revisor (*examiner, auditor*).

**controversial** [kɔntro'və:ʃəl], *adj.* umstritten, strittig.

**controversy** ['kɔntrovə:si], *s.* die Kontroverse, die Streitfrage.

**controvert** ['kɔntrovə:t], *v.a.* bestreiten, widersprechen (*Dat.*).

**contumacious** [kɔntju'meiʃəs], *adj.* widerspenstig, halsstarrig.

**contumacy** ['kɔntjuməsi], *s.* die Widerspenstigkeit (*obstreperousness*); der Ungehorsam (*disobedience*).

**contumelious** [kɔntju'mi:liəs], *adj.* frech, unverschämt (*insolent*).

**contuse** [kən'tju:z], *v.a.* quetschen.

**conundrum** [kə'nʌndrəm], *s.* das Scherzrätsel.

**convalescence** [kɔnvə'lesəns], *s.* die Gesundung, die Genesung.

**convalescent** [kɔnvə'lesənt], *adj.* genesend. — *s.* der Genesende, der Rekonvaleszent.

**convene** [kən'vi:n], *v.a.* zusammenrufen, versammeln. — *v.n.* zusammentreten, sich versammeln.

**convenience** [kən'vi:niəns], *s.* die Bequemlichkeit; *at your early* —, umgehend; *public* —, öffentliche Bedürfnisanstalt.

**convenient** [kən'vi:niənt], *adj.* bequem, gelegen; passend (*time*).

**convent** ['kɔnvənt], *s.* das (Nonnen)-Kloster.

**convention** [kən'venʃən], *s.* die Konvention, der Kongress (*meeting*); der Vertrag (*treaty*); die Sitte (*tradition, custom*).

**conventional** [kən'venʃənəl], *adj.* herkömmlich, traditionell.

**conventual** [kən'ventjuəl], *adj.* klösterlich.

**conversation** [kɔnvə'seiʃən], *s.* die Konversation, Unterhaltung; das Gespräch.

**conversational** [kɔnvə'seiʃənəl], *adj.* gesprächig, umgangssprachlich.

**converse** (1) [kən'və:s], *v.n.* sich unterhalten (*with*, mit, *Dat.*).

**converse** (2) ['kɔnvə:s], *adj.* umgekehrt.

**conversely** ['kɔnvə:sli], *adv.* hingegen, dagegen.

**conversion** [kən'və:ʃən], *s.* die Umkehrung (*reversal*); (*Rel.*) die Bekehrung; (*Comm.*) die Umwechslung.

**convert** ['kɔnvə:t], *s.* (*Rel.*) der Bekehrte, die Bekehrte; der Konvertit. — [kən'və:t], *v.a.* (*Rel.*) bekehren; (*Comm.*) umwechseln.

**converter** [kən'və:tə], *s.* (*Rel.*) der Bekehrer; (*Metall., Elec.*) der Umformer.

**convertible** [kən'və:tibl], *adj.* umwandelbar. — *s.* (*Motor.*) der or das Konvertible.

**convex** ['kɔnveks], *adj.* (*Phys.*) konvex.

**convey** [kən'vei], *v.a.* transportieren; führen (*bear, carry*); mitteilen (*impart*).

**conveyance** [kən'veiəns], *s.* die Beförderung (*transport*); das Fuhrwerk (*vehicle*); die Übertragung (*Law*) das Übertragungsdokument.

**conveyancing** [kən'veiənsiŋ], *s.* (*Law*) die legale or rechtliche Übertragung.

**convict** [kən'vikt], *s.* der Sträfling. — [kən'vikt], *v.a.* für schuldig erklären.

**conviction** [kən'vikʃən], *s.* die Überzeugung; (*Law*) die Überführung, die Schuldbesprechung.

**convince** [kən'vins], *v.a.* überzeugen.

**convivial** [kən'viviəl], *adj.* gesellig (*sociable*).

**conviviality** [kənvivi'æliti], *s.* die Geselligkeit.

**convocation** [kɔnvə'keiʃən], *s.* die Zusammenberufung, Festversammlung; (*Eccl.*) die Synode.

**convoke** [kən'vouk], *v.a.* zusammenberufen.

**convolvulus** [kən'vɔlvjuləs], *s.* (*Bot.*) die Winde.

**convoy** ['kɔnvɔi], *s.* das Geleit, die Bedeckung; (*Mil.*) der Begleitzug. — [kən'vɔi], *v.a.* geleiten; (*Mil.*) im Geleitzug mitführen.

**convulse** [kən'vʌls], *v.a.* erschüttern.

**convulsion** [kən'vʌlʃən], *s.* der Krampf, die Zuckung.

**convulsive** [kən'vʌlsiv], *adj.* krampfhaft, zuckend.

**coo** [ku:], *v.n.* girren (*of birds*); *bill and* —, schnäbeln.

**cook** [kuk], *v.a., v.n.* kochen; (*coll.*) *the books*, die Bücher(Bilanz)fälschen or frisieren. — *s.* der Koch, die Köchin; *too many cooks* (*spoil the broth*), zu viele Köche (verderben den Brei).

**cookery** ['kukəri], *s.* die Kochkunst; — *school*, die Kochschule.

**cool** [ku:l], *adj.* kühl (*climate*); kaltblütig (*coldblooded*); unverschämt (*brazen*). — *s.* die Kühle. — *v.a.* abkühlen; (*fig.*) besänftigen. — *v.n.* sich abkühlen.

**cooler** ['ku:lə], *s.* (*Chem.*) das Kühlfaß; (*coll.*) das Gefängnis; (*sl.*) das Kittchen.

**coop** [ku:p], *s.* die Kufe; das Faß; *hen* —, der Hühnerkorb. — *v.a.* — *up*, einsperren.
**cooper** ['ku:pə], *s.* der Böttcher, der Faßbinder.
**cooperate** [kou'ɔpəreit], *v.n.* zusammenarbeiten; mitarbeiten, mitwirken.
**cooperation** [kouɔpə'reiʃən], *s.* die Zusammenarbeit, die Mitarbeit.
**cooperative** [kou'ɔpərətiv], *adj.* willig; mitwirkend. — *s.* die Konsumgenossenschaft, der Konsum.
**coordinate** [kou'ɔ:dineit], *v.a.* koordinieren, beiordnen. — [-nit], *adj.* (*Gram.*) koordiniert.
**coordination** [kouɔ:di'neiʃən], *s.* die Koordinierung.
**coot** [ku:t], *s.* (*Orn.*) das Wasserhuhn.
**copartnership** [kou'pɑ:tnəʃip], *s.* die Teilhaberschaft; die Partnerschaft in der Industrie.
**cope** (1) [koup], *s.* (*Eccl.*) das Pluviale, der Priesterrock; (*Build.*) die Decke.
**cope** (2) [koup], *v.n.* — *with s.th.*, mit etwas fertig werden, es schaffen.
**coping** ['koupiŋ], *s.* (*Build.*) die Kappe; — *-stone* or *copestone*, der Firststein, Schlußstein, Kappstein.
**copious** ['koupiəs], *adj.* reichlich; wortreich (*style*).
**copiousness** ['koupiəsnis], *s.* die Reichhaltigkeit, Fülle.
**copper** ['kɔpə], *s.* (*Metall.*) das Kupfer; (*sl.*) der Polizist; (*coll.*) der Penny, das Pennystück. — *adj.* kupfern.
**copperplate** ['kɔpəpleit], *s.* der Kupferstich (*etching*); (*Typ.*) die Kupferplatte.
**coppery** ['kɔpəri], *adj.* Kupfer-, kupfern, kupferfarben (*colour*).
**coppice, copse** ['kɔpis, kɔps], *s.* das Unterholz, das Dickicht.
**copulate** ['kɔpjuleit], *v.n.* sich paaren, begatten.
**copulation** [kɔpju'leiʃən], *s.* die Paarung; der Beischlaf (*human*).
**copy** ['kɔpi], *v.a.* kopieren, abschreiben (*write*); imitieren, nachahmen (*imitate*). — *s.* die Kopie; *carbon* —, die Durchschrift; Abschrift; die Nachahmung (*imitation*); die Fälschung (*forgery*).
**copybook** ['kɔpibuk], *s.* das Heft.
**copyist** ['kɔpiist], *s.* der Kopist.
**coquet, coquette** (1) [kɔ'ket], *v.n.* kokettieren.
**coquette** (2) [kɔ'ket], *s.* die Kokette.
**coquettish** [kɔ'ketiʃ], *adj.* kokett.
**coral** ['kɔrəl], *s.* die Koralle. — *adj.* Korallen-.
**cord** [kɔ:d], *s.* die Schnur, der Strick (*rope*); (*Am.*) der Bindfaden (*string*); die Klafter (*wood measure*); der Kordstoff (*textile*); *vocal* —, das Stimmband.
**cordage** ['kɔ:didʒ], *s.* (*Naut.*) das Tauwerk.
**cordial** (1) ['kɔ:diəl], *adj.* herzlich.
**cordial** (2) ['kɔ:diəl], *s.* der Fruchtsaft (konzentriert), Magenlikör.
**cordiality** [kɔ:di'æliti], *s.* die Herzlichkeit.

**corduroy** ['kɔ:djurɔi], *s.* der Kordsamt.
**core** [kɔ:], *s.* der Kern; das Innere (*innermost part*).
**cork** [kɔ:k], *s.* der Kork, der Korken. — *v.a.* verkorken.
**corkscrew** ['kɔ:kskru:], *s.* der Korkzieher.
**cormorant** ['kɔ:mərənt], *s.* (*Orn.*) der Kormoran, die Scharbe.
**corn** (1) [kɔ:n], *s.* das Korn, das Getreide (*wheat etc.*); (*Am.*) *sweet* —, der Mais.
**corn** (2) [kɔ:n], *s.* das Hühnerauge (*on foot*).
**corned** [kɔ:nd], *adj.* eingesalzt; — *beef*, das Pökelrindfleisch.
**cornea** ['kɔ:niə], *s.* (*Anat.*) die Hornhaut.
**cornel-tree** ['kɔ:nəltri:], *s.* (*Bot.*) der Kornelkirschbaum.
**cornelian** [kɔ:'ni:liən], *s.* (*Geol.*) der Karneol.
**corner** ['kɔ:nə], *s.* die Ecke; (*Footb.*) der Eckstoß. — *v.a.* in eine Ecke treiben; in die Enge treiben (*force*).
**cornered** ['kɔ:nəd], *adj.* eckig (*angular*); in die Enge getrieben, gefangen (*caught*).
**cornet** ['kɔ:nit], *s.* (*Mus.*) die Zinke, das Flügelhorn; (*Mil.*) der Kornett, der Fähnrich.
**cornflower** ['kɔ:nflauə], *s.* (*Bot.*) die Kornblume.
**cornice** ['kɔ:nis], *s.* (*Archit.*) das Gesims.
**cornucopia** [kɔ:nju'koupjə], *s.* das Füllhorn.
**corollary** [kə'rɔləri], *s.* (*Log.*) der Folgesatz; die Folgeerscheinung (*consequence*).
**corona** [kə'rounə], *s.* (*Astron.*) der Hof, Lichtkranz.
**coronation** [kɔrə'neiʃən], *s.* die Krönung.
**coroner** ['kɔrənə], *s.* der Leichenbeschauer.
**coronet** ['kɔrənet], *s.* die Adelskrone.
**corporal** (1) ['kɔ:pərəl], *s.* (*Mil.*) der Korporal, der Unteroffizier, Obergefreite.
**corporal** (2) ['kɔ:pərəl], *adj.* körperlich; — *punishment*, die Züchtigung.
**corporate** ['kɔ:pərit], *adj.* (*Law, Comm.*) als Körperschaft; gemeinschaftlich, einheitlich (*as a group or unit*).
**corporation** [kɔ:pə'reiʃən], *s.* (*Law, Comm.*) die Körperschaft; die Korporation; die Gemeinde (*municipal*); (*sl.*) der Schmerbauch (*stoutness*).
**corps** [kɔ:], *s.* das Korps.
**corpse** [kɔ:ps], *s.* der Leichnam.
**corpulence** ['kɔ:pjuləns], *s.* die Korpulenz, die Beleibtheit.
**corpulent** ['kɔ:pjulənt], *adj.* korpulent, dick.
**Corpus Christi** ['kɔ:pəs 'kristi], (der) Fronleichnam, das Fronleichnamsfest.
**corpuscle** ['kɔ:pʌsl], *s.* (*Anat.*) das Körperchen.

# correct

**correct** [kɔ'rekt], *v.a.* korrigieren (*remove mistakes*); verbessern; tadeln (*reprove*); berichtigen (*rectify*). — *adj.* korrekt, tadellos, richtig.

**correction** [kɔ'rekʃən], *s.* die Korrektur (*of mistakes*); die Verbesserung (*improvement*); die Richtigstellung (*restoration*); der Verweis (*censure*).

**corrective** [kɔ'rektiv], *adj.* zur Besserung. — *s.* das Korrektiv.

**correctness** [kə'rektnis], *s.* die Korrektheit (*of manner, action etc.*).

**corrector** [kə'rektə], *s.* der Korrektor (*proof reader etc.*).

**correlate** ['kɔrileit], *v.a.* in Beziehung setzen, aufeinander beziehen. — [-lit], *s.* (*Log.*) das Korrelat.

**correlative** [kɔ'relətiv], *adj.* in Wechselbeziehung stehend.

**correspond** [kɔris'pɔnd], *v.n.* korrespondieren (*exchange letters*); entsprechen (*to, Dat.*).

**correspondence** [kɔris'pɔndəns], *s.* die Korrespondenz; der Briefwechsel (*letters*); die Übereinstimmung (*harmony*).

**correspondent** [kɔris'pɔndənt], *s.* der Korrespondent (*letter-writer*); der Journalist, Berichterstatter (*newspaper*).

**corridor** ['kɔridɔ:], *s.* der Korridor; der Gang.

**corrigible** ['kɔridʒibl], *adj.* verbesserlich.

**corroborate** [kə'rɔbəreit], *v.a.* bestätigen (*confirm*); bestärken (*strengthen*).

**corroboration** [kərɔbə'reiʃən], *s.* die Bestätigung, die Bekräftigung.

**corroborative** [kə'rɔbərətiv], *adj.* bekräftigend.

**corrode** [kə'roud], *v.a.* zerfressen, zersetzen, ätzen (*acid*).

**corrosion** [kə'rouʒən], *s.* die Anfressung, Ätzung.

**corrosive** [kə'rouziv], *adj.* ätzend.

**corrugated** ['kɔrugeitid], *adj.* gewellt, Well-; — *iron*, das Wellblech; — *paper*, die Wellpappe.

**corrupt** [kə'rʌpt], *v.a.* verderben (*spoil*); bestechen (*bribe*). — *adj.* korrupt (*morals*); verdorben (*spoilt*).

**corruptible** [kə'rʌptibl], *adj.* verderblich; bestechlich.

**corruption** [kə'rʌpʃən], *s.* die Korruption; die Bestechung (*bribery*).

**corruptness** [kə'rʌptnis], *s.* die Verdorbenheit, der Verfall.

**corsair** ['kɔ:sɛə], *s.* der Korsar, der Seeräuber.

**corset** [kɔ:sit], *s.* das Korsett.

**coruscate** ['kɔrəskeit], *v.n.* schimmern, leuchten.

**corvette** [kɔ:'vet], *s.* (*Naut.*) die Korvette.

**cosine** ['kousain], *s.* (*Maths.*) der Kosinus.

**cosiness** ['kouzinis], *s.* die Bequemlichkeit, die Behaglichkeit (*comfort*).

**cosmetic** [kɔz'metik], *adj.* kosmetisch. — *s.* (*pl.*) das *or* die (*pl.*) Schönheitsmittel.

**cosmic** ['kɔzmik], *adj.* kosmisch.

**cosmopolitan** [kɔzmo'pɔlitən], *adj.* kosmopolitisch, weltbürgerlich. — *s.* der Kosmopolit, der Weltbürger.

**Cossack** ['kɔsæk], *s.* der Kosak.

**cost** [kɔst], *v.a. irr.* kosten. — *v.n. irr.* zu stehen kommen. — *s.* die Kosten, *f. pl.* (*expenses*); at all —s, um jeden Preis.

**costermonger** ['kɔstəmʌŋgə], *s.* der Straßenhändler.

**costly** ['kɔstli], *adj.* kostspielig.

**costume** ['kɔstju:m], *s.* das Kostüm; — *play*, das Zeitstück.

**cosy** ['kouzi], *adj.* behaglich, bequem.

**cot** (1) [kɔt], *s.* das Bettchen, Kinderbett.

**cot** (2) [kɔt], *s.* (*obs.*) die Hütte (*hut*).

**cottage** ['kɔtidʒ], *s.* die Hütte, das Häuschen.

**cottager** ['kɔtidʒə], *s.* der Kleinhäusler.

**cotton** [kɔtn], *s.* die Baumwolle. — *v.n.* — *on to*, (*coll.*) sich anhängen, sich anschließen (*Dat.*); — *on*, folgen können (*understand*).

**couch** [kautʃ], *s.* die Chaiselongue; der Diwan. — *v.a.* (*express*) in Worte fassen.

**cough** [kɔf], *v.n.* husten. — *s.* der Husten; *whooping* —, der Keuchhusten.

**council** ['kaunsil], *s.* der Rat (*body*); die Ratsversammlung.

**councillor** ['kaunsilə], *s.* der Rat, das Ratsmitglied; der Stadtrat.

**counsel** ['kaunsəl], *s.* der Rat (*advice*); der Berater (*adviser*); der Anwalt (*lawyer*). — *v.a.* einen Rat geben, beraten (*Acc.*).

**counsellor** ['kaunsələ], *s.* der Ratgeber; der Ratsherr; (*Am.*) der Anwalt (*lawyer*).

**count** (1) [kaunt], *v.a., v.n.* zählen; — *on s.o.*, sich auf jemanden verlassen. — *s.* die Zählung.

**count** (2) [kaunt], *s.* der Graf.

**countenance** ['kauntənəns], *s.* das Gesicht, die Miene. — *v.a.* begünstigen, unterstützen, zulassen.

**counter** (1) ['kauntə], *s.* der Rechner, der Zähler (*chip*); die Spielmarke; der Zahltisch (*desk*); Ladentisch (*in shop*); Schalter (*in office*).

**counter** (2) ['kauntə], *adv.* entgegen.

**counteract** [kauntə'rækt], *v.a.* entgegenwirken (*Dat.*).

**counteraction** [kauntə'rækʃən], *s.* die Gegenwirkung; der Widerstand (*resistance*).

**counterbalance** ['kauntəbæləns], *s.* das Gegengewicht. — [-'bæləns], *v.a.* ausbalancieren, ausgleichen.

**countercharge** ['kauntətʃa:dʒ], *s.* die Gegenklage.

**counterfeit** ['kauntəfi:t, -fit], *s.* die Fälschung (*forgery*); die Nachahmung (*imitation*). — *adj.* gefälscht, falsch.

**counterfoil** ['kauntəfɔil], *s.* das Kontrollblatt; der Kupon.

**counter–intelligence** ['kauntərintelidʒəns], *s.* die Spionageabwehr.

**countermand** [kauntə'ma:nd], *v.a.* widerrufen.

**counterpane** ['kauntəpein], *s.* die Steppdecke.

**counterpart** ['kauntəpa:t], *s.* das Gegenbild, das Gegenstück.

**counterplot** ['kauntəplɔt], *s.* der Gegenplan. — *v.n.* einen Gegenplan machen.

**counterpoint** ['kauntəpɔint], *s.* (*Mus.*) der Kontrapunkt.

**counterpoise** ['kauntəpɔiz], *s.* das Gegengewicht. — *v.a.* das Gleichgewicht halten.

**countersign** ['kauntəsain], *v.a.* gegenzeichnen, mitunterschreiben. — *s.* das Gegenzeichen.

**countess** ['kauntes], *s.* die Gräfin.

**counting-house** ['kauntiŋhaus], *s.* das Kontor.

**countless** ['kauntlis], *adj.* zahllos.

**country** ['kʌntri], *s.* das Land. — *adj.* Land–, ländlich, Bauern–.

**county** ['kaunti], *s.* die Grafschaft (*British*); der Landbezirk (*U.S.A.*).

**couple** [kʌpl], *s.* das Paar. — *v.a.* paaren, verbinden. — *v.n.* sich paaren (*pair*); sich verbinden.

**couplet** ['kʌplit], *s.* das Verspaar.

**coupling** ['kʌpliŋ], *s.* (*Mech.*) die Kupplung.

**courage** ['kʌridʒ], *s.* der Mut.

**courageous** [kə'reidʒəs], *adj.* mutig, tapfer.

**courier** ['kuriə], *s.* der Eilbote (*messenger*); der Reisebegleiter (*tour leader*).

**course** [kɔ:s], *s.* der Kurs; der Lauf (*time*); der Ablauf (*lapse of a period etc.*); die Bahn (*racing track*); *in due* —, zu gegebener Zeit; *of* —, natürlich.

**courser** ['kɔ:sə], *s.* das schnelle Pferd.

**court** [kɔ:t], *s.* der Hof (*royal etc.*); (*Law*) der Gerichtshof. — *v.a.* (*a lady*) den Hof machen (*Dat.*); — *disaster*, das Unglück herausfordern.

**courteous** ['kə:tiəs], *adj.* höflich.

**courtesan** ['kɔ:tizən *or* kɔ:ti'zæn], *s.* die Kurtisane, die Buhlerin.

**courtesy** ['kə:təsi], *s.* die Höflichkeit; *by* — *of*, mit freundlicher Erlaubnis von.

**courtier** ['kɔ:tiə], *s.* der Höfling.

**courtly** ['kɔ:tli], *adj.* höfisch, Hof–.

**court-martial** [kɔ:t'ma:ʃəl], *s.* das Kriegsgericht.

**courtship** ['kɔ:tʃip], *s.* das Werben, die Werbung, das Freien.

**courtyard** ['kɔ:tja:d], *s.* der Hof, der Hofraum.

**cousin** [kʌzn], *s.* der Vetter (*male*); die Kusine (*female*).

**cove** [kouv], *s.* die (kleine) Bucht.

**covenant** ['kʌvənənt], *s.* (*Bibl.*) der Bund; (*Comm.*) der Vertrag.

**cover** ['kʌvə], *v.a.* decken, bedecken (*table etc.*); schützen (*protect*); — *up*, bemänteln. — *s.* die Decke (*blanket*); der Deckel (*lid*); der Einband (*book*); das Gedeck (*table*); (*Comm.*) die Deckung; — *point*, (*Cricket*) die Deckstellung; *under* —, (*Mil.*) verdeckt, unter Deckung; — *girl*, das Mädchen auf dem Titelblatt (einer Illustrierten.)

**covering** ['kʌvəriŋ], *s.* die Bedeckung, die Bekleidung (*clothing*).

**coverlet, coverlid** ['kʌvəlit, 'kʌvəlid], *s.* die Bettdecke.

**covert** ['kʌvə:t], *s.* der Schlupfwinkel (*hideout*); das Dickicht (*thicket*). — *adj.* verborgen, bedeckt (*covered*); heimlich (*secret*).

**covet** ['kʌvit], *v.a.*, *v.n.* begehren (*Acc.*), gelüsten (nach (*Dat.*)).

**covetous** ['kʌvitəs], *adj.* begierig, habsüchtig.

**covetousness** ['kʌvitəsnis], *s.* die Begierde, die Habsucht.

**covey** ['kʌvi], *s.* der Flug *or* die Kette (Rebhühner, *partridges*).

**cow** (1) [kau], *s.* die Kuh; — — *shed*, der Kuhstall.

**cow** (2) [kau], *v.a.* einschüchtern.

**coward** ['kauəd], *s.* der Feigling.

**cowardice** ['kauədis], *s.* die Feigheit.

**cower** ['kauə], *v.n.* sich kauern.

**cowherd** ['kauhə:d], *s.* der Kuhhirt.

**cowl** [kaul], *s.* die Kappe (*of monk*), die Kapuze (*hood*).

**cowslip** ['kauslip], *s.* (*Bot.*) die Primel, die Schlüsselblume.

**coxswain** ['kɔksn], *s.* (*Naut.*) der Steuermann.

**coy** [kɔi], *adj.* scheu, spröde, zurückhaltend.

**coyness** ['kɔinis], *s.* die Sprödigkeit.

**crab** [kræb], *s.* (*Zool.*) die Krabbe; — *apple*, (*Bot.*) der Holzapfel.

**crabbed** [kræbd], *adj.* mürrisch (*temper*); unleserlich (*handwriting*).

**crack** [kræk], *s.* der Riß (*fissure*); der Krach, Schlag; der Sprung; die komische Bemerkung (*remark*). — *adj.* (*coll.*) erstklassig; — *shot*, der Meisterschütze. — *v.a.* aufbrechen; aufknacken (*nut*, *safe*); — *a joke*, eine witzige Bemerkung machen. — *v.n.* — *under strain*, unter einer Anstrengung zusammenbrechen; bersten (*break*).

**cracked, crackers** [krækd, 'krækəz], *adj.* (*coll.*) verrückt.

**cracker** ['krækə], *s.* der Keks; der Frosch (*firework*).

**crackle** [krækl], *v.n.* knistern, prasseln (*fire*); knallen, platzen (*rocket*).

**cracknel** ['kræknəl], *s.* die Brezel.

**crackpot** ['krækpɔt], *s.* (*coll.*) der verrückte Kerl.

**cradle** [kreidl], *s.* die Wiege. — *v.a.* einwiegen.

**craft** [kra:ft], *s.* die Fertigkeit (*skill*); das Handwerk (*trade*); die List (*cunning*); *arts and* —*s*, die Handwerkskünste.

# craftsman

**craftsman** ['krɑ:ftsmən], *s.* der (ge-lernte) Handwerker.
**crafty** ['krɑ:fti], *adj.* listig, schlau.
**crag** [kræg], *s.* die Klippe.
**cragged, craggy** [krægd, 'krægi], *adj.* felsig, schroff.
**cram** [kræm], *v.a.* vollstopfen (*stuff full*); (*coll.*) pauken (*coach*). — *v.n.* büffeln.
**crammer** ['kræmə], *s.* (*coll.*) der Einpauker, Privatlehrer (*tutor*).
**cramp** [kræmp], *s.* (*Med.*) der Krampf; die Klammer (*tool*). — *v.a.* einengen (*narrow*); verkrampfen.
**cramped** [kræmpd], *adj.* krampfhaft; eingeengt, beengt (*enclosed*).
**cranberry** ['krænbəri], *s.* (*Bot.*) die Preiselbeere.
**crane** [krein], *s.* (*Orn.*) der Kranich; (*Engin.*) der Kran. — *v.a.* — *o.'s neck*, den Hals ausrecken.
**crank** (1) [kræŋk], *s.* (*Motor.*) die Kurbel; — -*handle*, die Andrehwelle; (*Motor., Engin.*) —*shaft*, die Kurbelwelle, die Kurbel.
**crank** (2) [kræŋk], *s.* der Sonderling, der sonderbare Kauz (*eccentric*).
**cranky** ['kræŋki], *adj.* sonderbar.
**cranny** ['kræni], *s.* der Spalt, der Riß; *nook and* —, Eck und Spalt.
**crape** [kreip], *s.* der Krepp, Flor.
**crash** [kræʃ], *s.* der Krach; (*Motor.*) Zusammenstoß; (*Aviat.*) Absturz. — *v.n.* krachen (*noise*); stürzen, abstürzen (*fall*).
**crass** [kræs], *adj.* derb, grob, kraß.
**crate** [kreit], *s.* der Packkorb (*basket*); die Kiste (*wood*).
**crater** ['kreitə], *s.* (*Geol.*) der Krater.
**cravat** [krə'væt], *s.* die breite Halsbinde, das Halstuch (*scarf*); die Krawatte.
**crave** [kreiv], *v.a.* (dringend) verlangen (*for*, nach, *Dat.*).
**craven** [kreivn], *adj.* feig, mutlos. — *s.* der Feigling.
**craving** ['kreiviŋ], *s.* das starke Verlangen.
**craw** [krɔ:], *s.* (*Zool.*) der Vogelkropf.
**crawl** [krɔ:l], *v.n.* kriechen; kraulen (*swim*).
**crawling** ['krɔ:liŋ], *s.* das Kriechen; das Kraulschwimmen.
**crayon** ['kreiən], *s.* der Farbstift, der Pastellstift.
**craze** [kreiz], *s.* die Manie; die verrückte Mode (*fashion*).
**craziness** ['kreizinis], *s.* die Verrücktheit.
**crazy** ['kreizi], *adj.* verrückt.
**creak** [kri:k], *v.n.* knarren.
**cream** [kri:m], *s.* der Rahm, die Sahne; *whipped* —, die Schlagsahne, (*Austr.*) der Schlagobers. — *v.a.* — *off*, (die Sahne) abschöpfen; (*fig.*) das Beste abziehen.
**creamery** ['kri:məri], *s.* die Molkerei.
**creamy** ['kri:mi], *adj.* sahnig.
**crease** [kri:s], *s.* die Falte (*trousers etc.*); — -*resistant*, knitterfrei. — *v.a.* falten (*fold*). — *v.n.* knittern.

**create** [kri'eit], *v.a.* erschaffen, schaffen.
**creation** [kri'eiʃən], *s.* die Schöpfung.
**creative** [kri'eitiv], *adj.* schöpferisch.
**creator** [kri'eitə], *s.* der Schöpfer.
**creature** ['kri:tʃə], *s.* das Geschöpf.
**credence** ['kri:dəns], *s.* der Glaube.
**credentials** [kri'denʃəlz], *s. pl.* das Zeugnis, das Beglaubigungsschreiben; die Legitimation (*proof of identity*).
**credibility** [kredi'biliti], *s.* die Glaubwürdigkeit.
**credible** ['kredibl], *adj.* glaubwürdig, glaublich.
**credit** ['kredit], *s.* (*Comm.*) der Kredit; der gute Ruf (*reputation*); das Guthaben (*assets*). — *v.a.* — *s.o. with s.th.*, jemandem etwas gutschreiben; glauben (*believe*).
**creditable** ['kreditəbl], *adj.* ehrenwert, lobenswert.
**creditor** ['kreditə], *s.* (*Comm.*) der Gläubiger.
**credulity** [kre'dju:liti], *s.* die Leichtgläubigkeit.
**credulous** ['kredjuləs], *adj.* leichtgläubig.
**creed** [kri:d], *s.* das Glaubensbekenntnis.
**creek** [kri:k], *s.* die kleine Bucht; das Flüßchen (*small river*).
**creel** [kri:l], *s.* der Fischkorb.
**creep** [kri:p], *s.* (*Geol.*) der Rutsch; (*pl., coll.*) *the* —*s*, die Gänsehaut, das Gruseln. — *v.n. irr.* kriechen; (*furtively*) sich einschleichen.
**creeper** ['kri:pə], *s.* die Schlingpflanze, das Rankengewächs; (*Sch.*) der Kriecher; *Virginia* —, der wilde Wein.
**creepy** ['kri:pi], *adj.* kriechend; gruselig (*frightening*).
**cremate** [kri'meit], *v.a.* einäschern.
**cremation** [kri'meiʃən], *s.* die Verbrennung, Einäscherung.
**crematorium,** (*Am.*) **crematory** [kremə'tɔ:riəm, 'kremətəri], *s.* das Krematorium.
**Creole** ['kri:oul], *s.* der Kreole.
**crepuscular** [kri'pʌskjulə], *adj.* dämmerig.
**crescent** ['kresənt], *adj.* wachsend, zunehmend. — *s.* der (zunehmende) Mond, die Mondsichel; das Hörnchen.
**cress** [kres], *s.* (*Bot.*) die Kresse; *mustard and* —, die Gartenkresse.
**crest** [krest], *s.* der Kamm (*cock*); der Gipfel (*hill*); der Kamm (*wave*); der Busch (*helmet*); das Wappenschild (*Heraldry*).
**crestfallen** ['krestfɔ:lən], *adj.* entmutigt, mutlos, niedergeschlagen.
**Cretan** ['kri:tən], *adj.* kretisch. — *s.* der Kreter, die Kreterin.
**cretonne** ['kretən], *s.* die Kretonne.
**crevasse** [krə'væs], *s.* die Gletscherspalte.
**crevice** ['krevis], *s.* der Riß.
**crew** (1) [kru:], *s.* (*Naut., Aviat.*) die Besatzung; (*Naut.*) die Schiffsmannschaft; die Mannschaft (*team*); (*Am.*) — *cut*, die Bürstenfrisur.

**crew** (2) [kru:] *see* **crow.**
**crib** [krib], *s.* die Krippe (*Christmas*);
die Wiege (*cradle*); (*Sch.*) die Esels-
brücke. — *v.a.* (*Sch.*) abschreiben
(*copy*).
**crick** [krik], *s.* (*in neck*) der steife Hals.
**cricket** ['krikit], *s.* (*Ent.*) das Heimchen,
die Grille; (*Sport*) das Cricket(spiel).
**crime** [kraim], *s.* das Verbrechen; —
*fiction*, die Detektivromane, *m. pl.*
**criminal** ['kriminəl], *s.* der Verbrecher.
— *adj.* — *case*, der Kriminalfall;
verbrecherisch (*act*); — *investigation*, die Fahndung.
**crimp** [krimp], *v.a.* kräuseln (*hair*).
**crimson** ['krimzən], *adj.* karmesinrot.
**cringe** [krindʒ], *v.n.* kriechen.
**crinkle** ['kriŋkl], *v.a., v.n.* kräuseln. — *s.*
die Falte.
**crinoline** ['krinəlin], *s.* der Reifrock.
**cripple** [kripl], *s.* der Krüppel. — *v.a.*
verkrüppeln; lahmlegen (*immobilize*).
**crisis** ['kraisis], *s.* die Krise, der
Wendepunkt; die Notlage.
**crisp** [krisp], *adj.* kraus (*hair*); knusperig (*bread*); frisch.
**criss-cross** ['kriskrɔs], *adv.* kreuz und
quer.
**criterion** [krai'tiəriən], *s.* das Kennzeichen, das Kriterium.
**critic** ['kritik], *s.* der Kritiker; Rezensent (*reviewer*).
**critical** ['kritikəl], *adj.* kritisch.
**criticism** ['kritisizm], *s.* die Kritik (*of,
an, Dat.*); Rezension, Besprechung
(*review*).
**criticize** ['kritisaiz], *v.a.* kritisieren.
**croak** [krouk], *v.n.* krächzen (*raven*);
quaken (*frog*).
**croaking** ['kroukiŋ], *s.* das Krächzen,
das Gekrächze (*raven*); das Quaken
(*frog*).
**Croat** ['krouæt], *s.* der Kroate.
**Croatian** [krou'eiʃən], *adj.* kroatisch.
**crochet** ['krouʃei], *s.* die Häkelei; —
*hook*, die Häkelnadel. — *v.a., v.n.*
häkeln.
**crock** [krɔk], *s.* der Topf, der irdene
Krug; der alte Topf; (*coll.*) *old* —, der
Invalide, Krüppel.
**crockery** ['krɔkəri], *s.* (*Comm.*) die
Töpferware; das Geschirr (*household*).
**crocodile** ['krɔkədail], *s.* das Krokodil.
**crocus** ['kroukəs], *s.* (*Bot.*) der Krokus,
die Safranblume.
**croft** [krɔft], *s.* das Kleinbauerngut.
**crofter** ['krɔftə], *s.* der Kleinbauer.
**crone** [kroun], *s.* das alte Weib; die
Hexe (*witch*).
**crony** ['krouni], *s.* (*coll.*) *old* —, der alte
Freund.
**crook** [kruk], *s.* der Krummstab (*staff*);
der Schwindler (*cheat*). — *v.a.*
krümmen, biegen.
**crooked** ['krukid], *adj.* krumm; (*fig.*)
schwindlerisch, verbrecherisch.
**crookedness** ['krukidnis], *s.* die Krumm-
heit; die Durchtriebenheit (*slyness*).
**croon** [kru:n], *v.n.* leise singen; (*Am.*)
im modernen Stil singen.

**crooner** ['kru:nə], *s.* der Jazzsänger.
**crop** [krɔp], *s.* der Kropf (*bird*); die
Ernte (*harvest*); der (kurze) Haarschnitt; *riding* —, die Reitpeitsche.
— *v.a.* stutzen (*cut short*). — *v.n.*
— *up*, auftauchen.
**crosier** ['krouziə], *s.* (*Eccl.*) der Bischofsstab.
**cross** [krɔs], *s.* das Kreuz. — *v.a.* (*Zool.,
Bot.*) kreuzen; überqueren (*road,
on foot*); — *s.o.'s path*, einem in die
Quere kommen. — *v.n.* überfahren
(übers Wasser); hinübergehen; —
*over*, übersetzen (*on boat or ferry*).
— *v.r.* sich bekreuzigen. — *adj.*
mürrisch (*grumpy*), verstimmt; *at* —
*purposes*, ohne einander zu verstehen;
*make* —, verstimmen. — *adv.* kreuzweise; — *-eyed*, schielend; — *-grained*,
wider den Strich, schlecht aufgelegt.
**crossbow** ['krɔsbou], *s.* die Armbrust.
**crossbreed** ['krɔsbri:d], *s.* die Mischrasse, der Mischling.
**cross-examine** [krɔsig'zæmin], *v.a.,
v.n.* (*Law*) ins (Kreuz–)Verhör
nehmen.
**crossing** ['krɔsiŋ], *s.* die Straßen-
kreuzung; (*Naut.*) die Überfahrt; der
Straßenübergang; Kreuzweg.
**crossroads** ['krɔsroudz], *s.* der Kreuzweg, die Kreuzung.
**crossword** ['krɔswə:d], *s.* das Kreuzworträtsel.
**crotch** [krɔtʃ], *s.* der Haken.
**crotchet** ['krɔtʃit], *s.* (*Mus.*) die
Viertelnote; die Grille (*mood*).
**crotchety** ['krɔtʃiti], *adj.* grillenhaft,
verschroben.
**crouch** [krautʃ], *v.n.* sich ducken
(*squat*); sich demütigen (*cringe*).
**croup** (1) [kru:p], *s.* (*Med.*) der Krupp.
**croup** (2) [kru:p], *s.* die Kruppe.
**crow** [krou], *s.* (*Orn.*) die Krähe; das
Krähen (*of cock*). — *v.n. irr.* krähen
(*cock*).
**crowbar** ['krouba:], *s.* das Brecheisen.
**crowd** [kraud], *s.* die Menge (*multitude*);
das Gedränge (*throng*). — *v.n.*
— *in*, sich hineindrängen, dazu-
drängen; — *around*, sich herum-
scharen um (*Acc.*).
**crown** [kraun], *s.* die Krone (*diadem
or coin*); der Gipfel (*mountain*);
(*Anat.*) der Scheitel; — *lands*,
Krongüter (*n. pl.*), Landeigentum der
Krone, *n.*; — *prince*, der Kronprinz; —
*of thorns*, die Dornenkrone. — *v.a.*
krönen.
**crucial** ['kru:ʃəl], *adj.* entscheidend,
kritisch.
**crucifix** ['kru:sifiks], *s.* das Kruzifix.
**crucify** ['kru:sifai], *v.a.* kreuzigen.
**crude** [kru:d], *adj.* roh, ungekocht,
unreif; grob (*manners*), ungeschliffen.
**crudity** ['kru:diti], *s.* die Rohheit;
Grobheit (*manners*).
**cruel** ['kru:əl], *adj.* grausam.
**cruelty** ['kru:əlti], *s.* die Grausamkeit.
**cruet** ['kru:it], *s.* das Salz- *oder* Pfeffer-
fäßchen; das Fläschchen.

# cruise

**cruise** [kru:z], *v.n.* (*Naut.*) kreuzen. — *s.* die Seefahrt, die Seereise; *pleasure* —, die Vergnügungsreise (zu Wasser).

**cruiser** ['kru:zə], *s.* (*Naut.*) der Kreuzer; *battle* —, der Panzerkreuzer.

**crumb** [krʌm], *s.* die Krume. — *v.a.* zerbröckeln, zerkrümeln.

**crumble** [krʌmbl], *v.n.* zerfallen, zerbröckeln.

**crumpet** ['krʌmpit], *s.* das Teebrötchen, das Teeküchlein.

**crumple** [krʌmpl], *v.a.* zerknittern (*material*). — *v.n.* — *up*, zusammenbrechen.

**crunch** [krʌntʃ], *v.a.* zerstoßen, zermalmen. — *v.n.* knirschen.

**crusade** [kru:'seid], *s.* der Kreuzzug.

**crusader** [kru:'seidə], *s.* der Kreuzfahrer.

**crush** [krʌʃ], *v.a.* zerdrücken; zerstoßen (*pulverize*); drängen (*crowd*); zertreten (*tread down*); (*fig.*) vernichten. — *s.* das Gedränge (*throng*); (*coll.*) have a — *on*, verknallt sein, in einen verliebt sein.

**crust** [krʌst], *s.* die Kruste, die Rinde (*bread*). — *v.a.* mit einer Kruste bedecken. — *v.n.* verkrusten.

**crustaceous** [krʌs'teiʃəs], *adj.* (*Zool.*) krustenartig, Krustentier-.

**crusty** ['krʌsti], *adj.* krustig, knusperig (*pastry, bread*); mürrisch (*grumpy*).

**crutch** [krʌtʃ], *s.* die Krücke.

**crux** [krʌks], *s.* der entscheidende Punkt, der springende Punkt, die Schwierigkeit.

**cry** [krai], *v.n.* schreien, rufen; weinen (*weep*). — *v.a.* — *down*, niederschreien. — *s.* der Schrei; der Zuruf (*call*).

**crypt** [kript], *s.* (*Eccl.*) die Krypta, die Gruft.

**crystal** ['kristəl], *s.* der Kristall.

**crystallize** ['kristəlaiz], *v.n.* sich kristallisieren, Kristalle bilden.

**cub** [kʌb], *s.* (*Zool.*) das Junge. — *v.n.* Junge haben, Junge werfen.

**Cuban** ['kju:bən], *adj.* kubanisch. — *s.* der Kubaner.

**cube** [kju:b], *s.* der Würfel; (*Maths.*) — *root*, die Kubikwurzel. — *v.a.* zur Dritten (Potenz) erheben; kubieren.

**cubic(al)** ['kju:bik(əl)], *adj.* kubisch, zur dritten Potenz.

**cubit** ['kju:bit], *s.* die Elle.

**cuckoo** ['kuku:], *s.* (*Orn.*) der Kuckuck.

**cucumber** ['kju:kʌmbə], *s.* (*Bot.*) die Gurke; *cool as a —*, ruhig und gelassen.

**cud** [kʌd], *s.* das wiedergekäute Futter; *chew the —*, wiederkäuen (*also fig.*).

**cuddle** [kʌdl], *v.a.* liebkosen, an sich drücken. — *v.n.* sich anschmiegen.

**cudgel** ['kʌdʒəl], *s.* der Knüttel; *take up the — for*, sich für etwas einsetzen.

**cue** (1) [kju:], *s.* (*Theat.*) das Stichwort. — *v.a.* einem (*Theat.*) das Stichwort or (*Mus.*) den Einsatz geben.

**cue** (2) [kju:], *s.* der Billardstock. — *v.a.* (*Billiards*) abschießen.

**cuff** (1) [kʌf], *s.* die Manschette, der Aufschlag (*shirt*); —*links*, die Manschettenknöpfe, *m.pl.*

**cuff** (2) [kʌf], *s.* der Schlag. — *v.a.* schlagen, puffen.

**culinary** ['kju:linəri], *adj.* kulinarisch; Küchen-, Eß-, Speisen-.

**cull** [kʌl], *v.a.* auswählen, auslesen (*from books*).

**culminate** ['kʌlmineit], *v.n.* kulminieren, den Höhepunkt erreichen.

**culpable** ['kʌlpəbl], *adj.* schuldig; strafbar.

**culprit** ['kʌlprit], *s.* der Schuldige, Verbrecher.

**cult** [kʌlt], *s.* der Kult, die Verehrung; der Kultus.

**cultivate** ['kʌltiveit], *v.a.* kultivieren; (*Agr.*) anbauen; pflegen (*acquaintance*); bilden (*mind*).

**cultivation** [kʌlti'veiʃən], *s.* (*Agr.*) der Anbau; die Bildung (*mind*).

**culture** ['kʌltʃə], *s.* die Kultur, die Bildung.

**cumbersome** ['kʌmbəsəm], *adj.* beschwerlich, lästig.

**cunning** ['kʌniŋ], *s.* die List, die Schlauheit. — *adj.* listig, schlau.

**cup** [kʌp], *s.* die Tasse (*tea*—); der Becher (*handleless*); (*Eccl.*) der Kelch; der Pokal (*sports*); — *final*, das Endspiel. — *v.a.* (*Med.*) schröpfen.

**cupboard** ['kʌbəd], *s.* der Schrank.

**cupola** ['kju:pələ], *s.* (*Archit.*, *Metall.*) die Kuppel.

**cur** [kə:], *s.* der Köter; (*fig.*) der Schurke.

**curable** ['kjuərəbl], *adj.* heilbar.

**curate** ['kjuərit], *s.* der Hilfsgeistliche.

**curative** ['kjuərətiv], *adj.* heilsam, heilend.

**curator** [kjuə'reitə], *s.* der Kurator, Verwalter, Direktor.

**curb** [kə:b], *v.a.* zügeln, bändigen. — *s.* der Zaum (*bridle*).

**curd** [kə:d], *s.* der Rahmkäse, der Milchkäse; (*pl.*) der Quark.

**curdle** [kə:dl], *v.a.* gerinnen lassen. — *v.n.* gerinnen; erstarren.

**cure** [kjuə], *s.* die Kur, die Heilung. — *v.a.* kurieren, wieder gesundmachen; einpökeln (*foodstuffs*).

**curfew** ['kə:fju:], *s.* die Abendglocke (*bells*); das Ausgehverbot, die Polizeistunde (*police*).

**curio** ['kjuəriou], *s.* die Kuriosität, das Sammlerstück; die Rarität.

**curiosity** [kjuəri'ɔsiti], *s.* die Neugier; Merkwürdigkeit.

**curious** ['kjuəriəs], *adj.* neugierig (*inquisitive*); seltsam, sonderbar (*strange*).

**curl** [kə:l], *v.a.* kräuseln, (in Locken) wickeln. — *v.n.* sich kräuseln. — *s.* die Haarlocke.

**curler** ['kə:lə], *s.* der Lockenwickler.

**curlew** ['kə:lju:], *s.* (*Orn.*) der Brachvogel.

**curly** ['kə:li], *adj.* lockig.

**currant** ['kʌrənt], *s.* (*Bot.*) die Korinthe, die Johannisbeere.

**currency** ['kʌrənsi], s. die Währung (*money*); der Umlauf (*circulation*).
**current** ['kʌrənt], *adj.* im Umlauf; allgemein gültig, eben gültig; jetzig (*modern*). — *s.* (*Elect.*) der Strom; die Strömung (*river*); der Zug (*air*).
**curry** (1) ['kʌri], *v.a.* gerben (*tan*); — *comb*, der Pferdestriegel; — *favour*, sich einschmeicheln.
**curry** (2) ['kʌri], *s.* das indische Ragout. — *v.a.* würzen.
**curse** [kə:s], *v.a.*, *v.n.* verfluchen; verwünschen. — *s.* der Fluch; die Verwünschung.
**cursive** ['kə:siv], *adj.* kursiv, Kursiv-.
**cursory** ['kə:səri], *adj.* kursorisch, oberflächlich.
**curt** [kə:t], *adj.* kurz angebunden (*speech, manner*).
**curtail** [kə:'teil], *v.a.* stutzen, beschränken (*scope*); verkürzen (*time*).
**curtain** ['kə:tin], *s.* die Gardine; der Vorhang; (*Mil.*) — *fire*, das Sperrfeuer; — *lecture*, die Gardinenpredigt; — *speech*, die Ansprache vor dem Vorhang. — *v.a.* verhüllen (*hide*); mit Vorhängen versehen (*hang curtains*).
**curtness** ['kə:tnis], *s.* die Kürze; die Barschheit.
**curts(e)y** ['kə:tsi], *s.* der Knicks. — *v.n.* knicksen, einen Knicks machen.
**curve** [kə:v], *s.* die Krümmung; (*Geom.*) die Kurve. — *v.a.* krümmen, biegen. — *v.n.* sich biegen.
**curved** [kə:vd], *adj.* krumm, gebogen.
**cushion** ['kuʃən], *s.* das Kissen. — *v.a.* polstern.
**custody** ['kʌstədi], *s.* die Obhut; Bewachung, Haft.
**custom** ['kʌstəm], *s.* die Sitte, die Tradition; der Gebrauch, Brauch (*usage*); die Kundschaft (*trade*); (*pl.*) der Zoll (*duty*).
**customary** ['kʌstəməri], *adj.* gewohnt, althergebracht, gebräuchlich.
**customer** ['kʌstəmə], *s.* der Kunde, die Kundin.
**cut** [kʌt], *v.a.* irr. schneiden; — (*s.o.*), ignorieren; — *o.'s teeth*, zahnen; *this won't* — *any ice*, das wird nicht viel nützen; — *both ways*, das ist ein zweischneidiges Schwert; — *a lecture*, eine Vorlesung schwänzen; — *short*, unterbrechen. — *adj.* — *out for*, wie gerufen zu *or* für; — *to the quick*, aufs tiefste verletzt; — *glass*, das geschliffene Glas; — *price*, verbilligt. — *s.* der Schnitt (*section*); der Hieb (*gash*); (*Art*) der Stich; — *in salary*, eine Gehaltskürzung; die Abkürzung, die Kürzung (*abridgement*).
**cute** [kju:t], *adj.* klug, aufgeweckt; (*Am.*) süß, niedlich.
**cutler** ['kʌtlə], *s.* der Messerschmied.
**cutlery** ['kʌtləri], *s.* das Besteck (*tableware*); (*Comm.*) die Messerschmiedwaren, *f. pl.*
**cutlet** ['kʌtlit], *s.* das Kotelett, das Rippchen.

**cut-throat** ['kʌtθrout], *s.* der Halsabschneider; — *competition*, Konkurrenz auf Leben und Tod.
**cuttle** [kʌtl], *s.* (*Zool.*) der Tintenfisch.
**cyanide** ['saiənaid], *s.* (*Chem.*) zyanidsaures Salz; das Zyanid, die Blausäure.
**cyclamen** ['sikləmən], *s.* (*Bot.*) das Alpenveilchen.
**cycle** [saikl], *s.* (*Geom.*) der Kreis; (*Mus., Zool.*) der Zyklus; (*coll.*) das Fahrrad. — *v.n.* (*coll.*) radfahren; zirkulieren (*round*, um, *Acc.*).
**cyclone** ['saikloun], *s.* der Wirbelwind, der Wirbelsturm.
**cyclopaedia** [saiklo'pi:djə] *see* **encyclopædia**.
**cylinder** ['silində], *s.* der Zylinder; die Walze.
**cymbal** ['simbəl], *s.* (*Mus.*) die Zimbel, das Becken.
**cynic** ['sinik], *s.* der Zyniker.
**cynical** ['sinikəl], *adj.* zynisch.
**cypress** ['saiprəs], *s.* (*Bot.*) die Zypresse.
**Cypriot** ['sipriət], *adj.* zyprisch. — *s.* der Zypriote.
**czar** [zɑ:], *s.* der Zar.
**Czech, Czechoslovak(ian)** [tʃek, tʃeko'slouvæk, tʃekoslo'vækjən], *adj.* tschechisch. —*s.* der Tscheche.

# D

**D** [di:]. das D (*also Mus.*).
**dab** [dæb], *v.a.* leicht berühren. — *s.* der leichte Schlag (*blow*).
**dabble** [dæbl], *v.n.* sich in etwas versuchen, pfuschen (*in*, in, *Dat.*).
**dabbler** ['dæblə], *s.* der Pfuscher, Stümper.
**dace** [deis], *s.* (*Zool.*) der Weißfisch.
**dad, daddy** [dæd, 'dædi], *s.* der Papa; Vati; *daddy longlegs*, die Bachmücke, die langbeinige Mücke.
**dado** ['deidou], *s.* die Täfelung.
**daffodil** ['dæfədil], *s.* (*Bot.*) die Narzisse.
**dagger** ['dægə], *s.* der Dolch; *at* —*s drawn*, spinnefeind; *look* —*s*, mit Blicken durchbohren.
**dahlia** ['deiliə], *s.* (*Bot.*) die Dahlie, die Georgine.
**daily** ['deili], *adj.* täglich; Tages-. — *s.* (*newspaper*) die Tageszeitung; (*woman*) die Putzfrau.
**dainties** ['deintiz], *s. pl.* das Backwerk, das kleine Gebäck, das Teegebäck.
**daintiness** ['deintinis], *s.* die Feinheit; die Kleinheit; die Leckerhaftigkeit.
**dainty** ['deinti], *adj.* fein, klein, zierlich; lecker (*food*).
**dairy** ['dɛəri], *s.* die Molkerei, die Meierei.
**dairyman** ['dɛərimən], *s.* der Milchmann; der Senne (*in Alps*).
**dais** [deis, 'deiis], *s.* das Podium.

# daisy

daisy ['deizi], s. (Bot.) das Gänseblümchen, das Marienblümchen.
dale [deil], s. das Tal.
dalliance ['dæliəns], s. die Tändelei, Liebelei; Verzögerung.
dally ['dæli], v.n. die Zeit vertrödeln.
dam (1) [dæm], s. der Damm. — v.a. eindämmen, abdämmen.
dam (2) [dæm], s. (Zool.) die Tiermutter.
damage ['dæmidʒ], s. der Schaden; der Verlust (loss); (pl.) (Law) der Schadenersatz. — v.a. beschädigen.
damageable ['dæmidʒəbl], adj. leicht zu beschädigen.
damask ['dæməsk], s. der Damast (textile). — adj. damasten, aus Damast.
dame [deim], s. die Dame (title); (Am.) (coll.) die junge Dame, das Fräulein.
damn [dæm], v.a. verdammen.
damnable ['dæmnəbl], adj. verdammenswert, verdammt.
damnation [dæm'neiʃən], s. die Verdammung, Verdammnis.
damn(ed) [dæm(d)], adj. & adv. verwünscht, verdammt.
damp [dæmp], adj. feucht, dumpfig. — s. die Feuchtigkeit; (Build.) course, die Schutzschicht. — v.a. dämpfen, befeuchten; — the spirits, die gute Laune verderben.
damsel ['dæmzəl], s. die Jungfer; das Mädchen.
damson ['dæmzən], s. (Bot.) die Damaszenerpflaume.
dance [da:ns], v.a., v.n. tanzen. — s. der Tanz; lead s.o. a —, einem viel Mühe machen.
dandelion ['dændilaiən], s. (Bot.) der Löwenzahn.
dandle [dændl], v.a. hätscheln; schaukeln.
dandy ['dændi], s. der Geck, der Stutzer.
Dane [dein], s. der Däne.
dane [dein], s. great —, die Dogge.
Danish ['deiniʃ], adj. dänisch.
danger ['deindʒə], s. die Gefahr.
dangerous ['deindʒərəs], adj. gefährlich.
dangle [dæŋgl], v.a. baumeln lassen. — v.n. baumeln, hängen.
dank [dæŋk], adj. feucht, naßkalt.
Danube ['dænju:b], die Donau.
dapper ['dæpə], adj. schmuck; niedlich; elegant.
dappled [dæpld], adj. scheckig, bunt.
Dardanelles, The [da:də'nelz], die Dardanellen, pl.
dare [dɛə], v.n. irr. wagen; I — say, das meine ich wohl, ich gebe zu.
daredevil ['dɛədevl], s. der Wagehals, der Draufgänger.
daring ['dɛəriŋ], s. die Kühnheit.
dark [da:k], adj. dunkel, finster. — s. die Dunkelheit; shot in the —, ein Schuß aufs Geratewohl, ins Blaue.
darken ['da:kən], v.a. verdunkeln, verfinstern. — v.n. dunkel werden.

darkish ['da:kiʃ], adj. nahezu dunkel.
darkness ['da:knis], s. die Dunkelheit, Finsternis.
darkroom ['da:kru:m], s. die Dunkelkammer.
darling ['da:liŋ], s. der Liebling. — adj. lieb, teuer.
darn (1) [da:n], v.a. stopfen.
darn (2) [da:n], v.a. verdammen.
darn(ed) [da:n(d)], (excl.) verdammt.
darning ['da:niŋ], s. das Stopfen; — needle, die Stopfnadel.
dart [da:t], s. der Pfeil; der Spieß (spear); (pl.) das Pfeilwurfspiel. — v.n. losstürmen, sich stürzen.
dash [dæʃ], v.a. zerschmettern, zerstören (hopes). — v.n. stürzen. — s. der Schlag (blow); die Eleganz; (Typ.) der Gedankenstrich; (Motor.)— board, das Schaltbrett, Armaturenbrett.
dashing ['dæʃiŋ], adj. schneidig.
dastard ['dæstəd], s. der Feigling, die Memme.
dastardly ['dæstədli], adj., adv. feige.
data ['deitə], s. pl. (Science) die Angaben, die Daten.
date (1) [deit], s. das Datum; (Am.) die Verabredung; out of —, vertetal (antiquated), altmodisch (out of fashion). — v.a. datieren; (Am.) ausführen. — v.n. das Datum tragen.
date (2) [deit], s. (Bot.) die Dattel.
dative ['deitiv], s. (Gram.) der Dativ.
daub [dɔ:b], v.a. beklecksen; (coll.) bemalen. — s. die Kleckserei; (coll.) die Malerei.
daughter ['dɔ:tə], s. die Tochter;— inlaw, die Schwiegertochter.
daunt [dɔ:nt], v.a. einschüchtern.
dauphin ['dɔ:fin], s. der Dauphin.
daw [dɔ:], s. (Orn.) die Dohle.
dawdle ['dɔ:dl], v.n. trödeln, die Zeit vertrödeln.
dawdler ['dɔ:dlə], s. der Trödler, Tagedieb, die Schlafmütze.
dawn [dɔ:n], s. das Morgengrauen, die Morgendämmerung. — v.n. dämmern, tagen.
day [dei], s. der Tag; the other —, neulich; every —, täglich; one —, eines Tages; by —, bei or am Tage.
daybreak ['deibreik], s. der Tagesanbruch.
daytime ['deitaim], s. in the —, bei Tage.
daze [deiz], v.a. blenden (dazzle); betäuben (stupefy).
dazzle [dæzl], v.a. blenden.
deacon ['di:kən], s. (Eccl.) der Diakon.
deaconess ['di:kənes], s. (Eccl.) die Diakonisse.
dead [ded], adj. tot; stop —, plötzlich anhalten; as — as mutton, mausetot; — from the neck up, (coll.) dumm wie die Nacht. — adv. — beat, erschöpft; (Am.)—sure, ganz sicher. — s. in the — of night, in tiefster Nacht; (pl.) die Toten).

**deaden** [dedn], *v.a.* abschwächen (*weaken*); abtöten (*anæsthetise*).
**deadly** ['dedli], *adj.* tödlich.
**deadness** ['dednis], *s.* die Leblosigkeit; Mattheit (*tiredness*).
**deaf** [def], *adj.* taub; — *and dumb,* taubstumm.
**deafen** [defn], *v.a.* betäuben.
**deafmute** ['defmju:t], *s.* der Taubstumme.
**deal** (1) [di:l], *s.* das Geschäft; die Anzahl; *a fair* or *square* —, eine anständige Behandlung; *a good* —, beträchtlich; *a great* — *of,* sehr viel; *make a* —, ein Geschäft abschliessen; *it's a* —! abgemacht! — *v.a. irr.* austeilen; Karten geben (*cards*); — *a blow,* einen Schlag erteilen. — *v.n. irr.* — *with s.th.,* etwas behandeln.
**deal** (2) [di:l], *s.* (*Bot.*) das Kiefernholz, die Kiefer; — *board,* das Kiefernholzbrett.
**dealer** ['di:lə], *s.* der Händler.
**dean** [di:n], *s.* der Dekan.
**dear** [diə], *adj.* teuer, lieb (*beloved*); teuer, kostspielig (*expensive*); — *me!* ach, Du lieber Himmel! —, —! du liebe Zeit! — *John!* Lieber Hans!
**dearness** ['diənis], *s.* die Teuerung, das Teuersein.
**dearth** [də:θ], *s.* der Mangel (*of, an, Dat.*).
**death** [deθ], *s.* der Tod; der Todesfall; — *penalty,* die Todesstrafe; — *warrant,* das Todesurteil.
**deathbed** ['deθbed], *s.* das Totenbett, Sterbebett.
**deathblow** ['deθblou], *s.* der Todesstoß.
**deathless** ['deθlis], *adj.* unsterblich.
**debar** [di'ba:], *v.a.* ausschließen (*from, von, Dat.*).
**debase** [di'beis], *v.a.* erniedrigen, verschlechtern.
**debatable** [di'beitəbl], *adj.* strittig.
**debate** [di'beit], *s.* die Debatte. — *v.a., v.n.* debattieren.
**debauch** [di'bɔ:tʃ], *v.a., v.n.* verführen; verderben.
**debauchee** [di'bɔ:tʃi:], *s.* der Schwelger, der Wüstling.
**debenture** [di'bentʃə], *s.* der Schuldschein.
**debilitate** [di'biliteit], *v.a.* schwächen.
**debit** ['debit], *s.* die Schuldseite, das Soll (*in account*). — *v.a.* belasten.
**debt** [det], *s.* die Schuld; *run into* — or *incur* —*s,* Schulden machen.
**debtor** ['detə], *s.* der Schuldner.
**decade** ['dekəd, 'dekeid], *s.* das Jahrzehnt; die Dekade.
**decadence** ['dekədəns], *s.* die Dekadenz, der Verfall.
**decalogue** ['dekələg], *s.* (*Bibl.*) die zehn Gebote.
**decamp** [di'kæmp], *v.n.* aufbrechen, ausreißen.
**decant** [di'kænt], *v.a.* abfüllen, abgießen.
**decanter** [di'kæntə], *s.* die Karaffe.

**decapitate** [di'kæpiteit], *v.a.* enthaupten köpfen.
**decapitation** [di:kæpi'teiʃən], *s.* die Enthauptung.
**decay** [di'kei], *v.n.* in Verfall geraten. — *s.* der Verfall, die Verwesung.
**decease** [di'si:s], *s.* das Hinscheiden, der Tod. — *v.n.* sterben, dahinscheiden, verscheiden.
**deceit** [di'si:t], *s.* der Betrug; die List (*cunning*).
**deceive** [di'si:v], *v.a.* betrügen.
**deceiver** [di'si:və], *s.* der Betrüger.
**December** [di'sembə]. der Dezember.
**decency** ['di:sənsi], *s.* der Anstand; die Anständigkeit, Ehrlichkeit; die Schicklichkeit.
**decent** ['di:sənt], *adj.* anständig.
**decentralize** [di:'sentrəlaiz], *v.a.* dezentralisieren.
**deception** [di'sepʃən], *s.* der Betrug.
**deceptive** [di'septiv], *adj.* trügerisch.
**decide** [di'said], *v.a., v.n.* entscheiden; bestimmen (*determine*).
**decimal** ['desiməl], *adj.* dezimal.
**decimate** ['desimeit], *v.a.* dezimieren, herabsetzen (*reduce*).
**decipher** [di'saifə], *v.a.* entziffern (*read*); dechiffrieren (*decode*).
**decision** [di'siʒən], *s.* die Entscheidung, der Beschluß (*resolution*); die Entschlossenheit (*decisiveness*).
**decisive** [di'saisiv], *adj.* entscheidend.
**decisiveness** [di'saisivnis], *s.* die Entschiedenheit.
**deck** [dek], *s.* (*Naut.*) das Deck; — *chair,* der Liegestuhl. — *v.a.* — (*out*), ausschmücken.
**declaim** [di'kleim], *v.a.* deklamieren.
**declamation** [deklə'meiʃən], *s.* die Deklamation.
**declamatory** [di'klæmətəri], *adj.* Deklamations-, deklamatorisch, Vortrags-.
**declaration** [deklə'reiʃən], *s.* die Erklärung; die Deklaration.
**declare** [di'kleə], *v.a.* erklären. — *v.n.* sich erklären.
**declared** [di'kleəd], *adj.* erklärt, offen.
**declension** [di'klenʃən], *s.* (*Gram.*) die Deklination, die Abwandlung.
**declinable** [di'klainəbl], *adj.* (*Gram.*) deklinierbar.
**declination** [dekli'neiʃən], *s.* (*Phys.*) die Abweichung, Deklination.
**decline** [di'klain], *v.n.* abweichen (*deflect*); abnehmen (*decrease*); sich weigern (*refuse*); fallen (*price*). — *v.a.* (*Gram.*) deklinieren; ablehnen (*turn down*). — *s.* die Abnahme (*decrease*); der Verfall (*decadence*); der Abhang (*slope*).
**declivity** [di'kliviti], *s.* der Abhang.
**decode** [di:'koud], *v.a.* entziffern, dechiffrieren.
**decompose** [di:kəm'pouz], *v.n.* verwesen; zerfallen, sich zersetzen. — *v.a.* auflösen.

# decorate

**decorate** [ˈdekəreit], *v.a.* dekorieren (*honour*); ausschmücken (*beautify*); ausmalen (*paint*).

**decoration** [dekəˈreiʃən], *s.* die Dekoration, der Orden (*medal*); die Ausschmückung (*ornamentation*); die Ausmalung (*décor*).

**decorator** [ˈdekəreitə], *s.* der Zimmermaler.

**decorous** [ˈdekərəs *or* diˈkɔːrəs], *adj.* anständig, sittsam.

**decorum** [diˈkɔːrəm], *s.* das Dekorum, das anständige Benehmen.

**decoy** [diˈkɔi], *s.* der Köder (*bait*). — *v.a.* locken, verlocken.

**decrease** [diˈkriːs], *v.a.* vermindern, verringern. — *v.n.* abnehmen. — [ˈdiːkriːs], *s.* die Abnahme, die Verringerung.

**decree** [diˈkriː], *s.* der Beschluß (*resolution*); (*Law*) das Urteil; — *nisi*, das provisorische Scheidungsurteil. — *v.a., v.n.* eine Verordnung erlassen; beschließen (*decide*).

**decrepit** [diˈkrepit], *adj.* abgelebt; gebrechlich (*frail*).

**decry** [diˈkrai], *v.a.* verrufen; in Verruf bringen.

**dedicate** [ˈdedikeit], *v.a.* widmen, weihen, zueignen (*to, Dat.*).

**dedication** [dediˈkeiʃən], *s.* die Widmung, Weihung; die Zueignung.

**dedicatory** [ˈdedikeitəri], *adj.* zueignend.

**deduce** [diˈdjuːs], *v.a.* schließen (*conclude*); ableiten (*derive*).

**deduct** [diˈdʌkt], *v.a.* abziehen (*subtract*); abrechnen (*take off*).

**deduction** [diˈdʌkʃən], *s.* der Abzug (*subtraction*); die Folgerung (*inference*); der Rabatt (*in price*).

**deductive** [diˈdʌktiv], *adj.* (*Log.*) deduktiv.

**deed** [diːd], *s.* die Tat, die Handlung (*action*); (*Law*) die Urkunde, das Dokument.

**deem** [diːm], *v.a.* erachten, halten für.

**deep** [diːp], *adj.* tief; — *freeze*, die Tiefkühlung; (*fig.*) dunkel. — *s.* die Tiefe (des Meeres).

**deepen** [ˈdiːpn], *v.a.* vertiefen. — *v.n.* tiefer werden; sich vertiefen.

**deer** [diə], *s.* (*Zool.*) das Rotwild, der Hirsch; — *stalking*, die Pirsch.

**deface** [diˈfeis], *v.a.* entstellen, verunstalten.

**defalcate** [diˈfælkeit], *v.n.* Gelder unterschlagen.

**defamation** [defəˈmeiʃən], *s.* die Verleumdung.

**defamatory** [diˈfæmətəri], *adj.* verleumderisch.

**defame** [diˈfeim], *v.a.* verleumden.

**default** [diˈfɔːlt], *v.n.* (vor Gericht) ausbleiben. — *s.* der Fehler (*error*); die Unterlassung (*omission*).

**defaulter** [diˈfɔːltə], *s.* der Pflichtvergessene; (*Law*) der Schuldige.

**defeat** [diˈfiːt], *v.a.* schlagen, besiegen. — *s.* die Niederlage.

**defect** [diˈfekt], *s.* der Fehler, Makel. — *v.n.* abfallen (*desert, from,* von, *Dat.*).

**defection** [diˈfekʃən], *s.* der Abfall.

**defective** [diˈfektiv], *adj.* fehlerhaft, mangelhaft.

**defectiveness** [diˈfektivnis], *s.* die Mangelhaftigkeit, die Fehlerhaftigkeit.

**defence** [diˈfens], *s.* die Verteidigung.

**defenceless** [diˈfenslis], *adj.* wehrlos.

**defencelessness** [diˈfenslisnis], *s.* die Wehrlosigkeit.

**defend** [diˈfend], *v.a.* verteidigen.

**defendant** [diˈfendənt], *s.* (*Law*) der Angeklagte.

**defensive** [diˈfensiv], *adj.* verteidigend. — *s.* die Defensive; *be on the* —, sich verteidigen.

**defer** [diˈfəː], *v.a.* aufschieben (*postpone*). — *v.n.* sich unterordnen, sich fügen (*to, Dat.*).

**deference** [ˈdefərəns], *s.* der Respekt, die Achtung (*to,* vor, *Dat.*).

**deferential** [defəˈrenʃəl], *adj.* ehrerbietig, respektvoll.

**defiance** [diˈfaiəns], *s.* der Trotz, die Herausforderung.

**defiant** [diˈfaiənt], *adj.* trotzig, herausfordernd.

**deficiency** [diˈfiʃənsi], *s.* die Unzulänglichkeit, der Mangel (*quantity*); die Fehlerhaftigkeit (*quality*).

**deficient** [diˈfiʃənt], *adj.* unzulänglich (*quantity*); fehlerhaft (*quality*).

**deficit** [ˈdefisit], *s.* das Defizit, der Fehlbetrag.

**defile** (1) [diˈfail], *v.a.* schänden, beflecken.

**defile** (2) [ˈdiːfail], *v.n.* vorbeimarschieren (*march past*) (an, *Dat.*). — *s.* der Engpaß.

**defilement** [diˈfailmənt], *s.* die Schändung.

**define** [diˈfain], *v.a.* definieren, begrenzen; bestimmen (*determine*).

**definite** [ˈdefinit], *adj.* bestimmt (*certain*); klar, deutlich (*clear*); endgültig (*final*).

**definition** [defiˈniʃən], *s.* die Definition, die Klarheit; (*Maths.*) die Bestimmung.

**definitive** [diˈfinitiv], *adj.* definitiv, endgültig (*final*); bestimmt (*certain*).

**deflect** [diˈflekt], *v.a.* ablenken (*divert*). — *v.n.* abweichen (von, *Dat.*).

**defoliation** [diːfouliˈeiʃən], *s.* der Blätterfall.

**deform** [diˈfɔːm], *v.a.* verunstalten, entstellen. — *v.n.* (*Metall.*) sich verformen.

**deformity** [diˈfɔːmiti], *s.* die Entstellung; die Häßlichkeit (*ugliness*).

**defraud** [diˈfrɔːd], *v.a.* betrügen.

**defray** [diˈfrei], *v.a.* bestreiten, bezahlen (*costs*).

**deft** [deft], *adj.* geschickt, gewandt.

**deftness** [ˈdeftnis], *s.* die Gewandtheit, die Geschicktheit.

**defunct** [diˈfʌŋkt], *adj.* verstorben. — *s.* der Verstorbene.

**defy** [di'fai], *v.a.* trotzen (*Dat.*).

**degenerate** [di'dʒenəreit], *v.n.* entarten; herabsinken (*sink low*). —[-rit], *adj.* degeneriert, entartet.

**degradation** [degri'deiʃən], *s.* die Absetzung, Entsetzung, Degradierung.

**degrade** [di'greid], *v.a.* (*Mil.*) degradieren; entwürdigen; vermindern.

**degraded** [di'greidid], *adj.* heruntergekommen.

**degrading** [di'greidiŋ], *adj.* entehrend.

**degree** [di'gri:], *s.* (*Meas., Univ.*) der Grad; (*Univ.*) die akademische Würde; die Stufe (*step, stage*); die Ordnung, die Klasse (*order, class*); *by* —*s,* nach und nach, allmählich.

**deify** ['di:ifai], *v.a.* vergöttern.

**deign** [dein], *v.n.* geruhen, belieben.

**deity** ['di:iti], *s.* die Gottheit.

**dejected** [di'dʒektid], *adj.* niedergeschlagen.

**dejection** [di'dʒekʃən], *s.* die Niedergeschlagenheit.

**delay** [di'lei], *v.a., v.n.* aufschieben (*put off*); verzögern (*retard*). — *s.* der Aufschub; die Verzögerung.

**delectable** [di'lektəbl], *adj.* erfreulich, köstlich.

**delectation** [delek'teiʃən], *s.* die Freude, das Ergötzen (*in, an, Dat.*).

**delegate** ['deligit], *s.* der Delegierte, Abgeordnete; der Vertreter. — ['deligeit], *v.a.* delegieren, entsenden.

**delegation** [deli'geiʃən], *s.* die Delegation, die Abordnung.

**delete** [di'li:t], *v.a.* tilgen, (aus)streichen, auslöschen (*writing*).

**deleterious** [deli'tiəriəs], *adj.* schädlich.

**deletion** [di'li:ʃən], *s.* die Tilgung, die Auslöschung.

**delf** [delf], *s.* das Delfter Porzellan.

**deliberate** [di'libərit], *adj.* absichtlich (*intentional*); vorsichtig (*careful*); bedächtig (*thoughtful*). — [-reit], *v.n.* beratschlagen, Rat halten. — *v.a.* überlegen, bedenken.

**deliberateness** [di'libəritnis], *s.* die Bedächtigkeit (*thoughtfulness*); die Absichtlichkeit (*intention*).

**deliberation** [dilibə'reiʃən], *s.* die Überlegung, die Beratung.

**delicacy** ['delikəsi], *s.* die Feinheit, Zartheit (*manner*); der Leckerbissen (*luxury food*); die Schwächlichkeit (*health*).

**delicate** ['delikit], *adj.* fein (*manner*); schwächlich (*sickly*); kitzlig, heikel (*difficult*).

**delicious** [di'liʃəs], *adj.* köstlich (*food*).

**deliciousness** [di'liʃəsnis], *s.* die Köstlichkeit.

**delight** [di'lait], *s.* das Entzücken, das Vergnügen; *Turkish* —, türkisches Konfekt; *take* — *in,* an etwas Gefallen finden, sich freuen (an, über). — *v.a., v.n.* entzücken, erfreuen (*in, an, Dat.*).

**delightful** [di'laitful], *adj.* entzückend, bezaubernd.

**delimit** [di:'limit], *v.a.* abgrenzen, begrenzen.

**delimitation** [di:limi'teiʃən], *s.* die Begrenzung, Abgrenzung.

**delineate** [di'linieit], *v.a.* umreißen, entwerfen, skizzieren (*draft, sketch*); schildern, beschreiben (*describe*).

**delineation** [dilini'eiʃən], *s.* die Skizze, der Entwurf (*sketch, draft*); die Schilderung (*description*).

**delinquency** [di'liŋkwənsi], *s.* das Verbrechen.

**delinquent** [di'liŋkwənt], *adj.* verbrecherisch. — *s.* der Verbrecher, Missetäter (*criminal*).

**deliquesce** [deli'kwes], *v.n.* (*Chem.*) zergehen, zerschmelzen.

**deliquescence** [deli'kwesəns], *s.* das Zerschmelzen, die Schmelzbarkeit.

**deliquescent** [deli'kwesənt], *adj.* leicht schmelzbar (*melting*); leicht zerfliessend (*butter etc.*).

**delirious** [di'liriəs], *adj.* (*Med.*) phantasierend, wahnsinnig.

**delirium** [di'liriəm], *s.* (*Med.*) das Delirium; der Wahnsinn (*madness*); das Phantasieren (*raving*); — *tremens,* der Säuferwahnsinn.

**deliver** [di'livə], *v.a.* abliefern, überreichen (*hand over*); liefern (*goods*); befreien (*free*); erlösen (*redeem*); zustellen (*letters etc.*); entbinden (*woman of child*).

**deliverance** [di'livərəns], *s.* die Erlösung (*redemption*); die Befreiung (*liberation*); die Übergabe.

**delivery** [di'livəri], *s.* die Befreiung (*liberation*); (*Med.*) die Niederkunft, Entbindung; der Vortrag (*speech*); die Lieferung, die Zustellung (*goods*); — *man,* der Zustellbote; — *van,* der Lieferwagen.

**dell** [del], *s.* das enge Tal.

**delude** [di'lu:d], *v.a.* betrügen, täuschen.

**deluge** ['delju:dʒ], *s.* die Überschwemmung. — *v.a.* überschwemmen.

**delusion** [di'lu:ʒən], *s.* die Täuschung, das Blendwerk.

**delusive, delusory** [di'lu:ziv, di'lu:zəri], *adj.* täuschend, trügerisch.

**delve** [delv], *v.n.* graben.

**demagogic(al)** [deməˈgɔdʒik(əl)], *adj.* demagogisch.

**demagogue** ['deməgɔg], *s.* der Demagoge, der Aufrührer.

**demand** [di'ma:nd], *v.a.* verlangen, fordern. — *s.* die Forderung, das Begehren (*desire*); *on* —, auf Verlangen; *in great* —, viel gefragt; *supply and* —, Angebot und Nachfrage.

**demarcate** ['di:ma:keit], *v.a.* abgrenzen; abstecken (*field*).

**demarcation** [di:ma:'keiʃən], *s.* die Abgrenzung; — *line,* die Grenzlinie.

**demeanour** [di'mi:nə], *s.* das Benehmen.

**demented** [di'mentid], *adj.* wahnsinnig, von Sinnen, toll.

**demerit** [di:'merit], *s.* der Fehler.

# demesne

**demesne** [di'mi:n *or* -'mein], *s.* das Erbgut; die Domäne.

**demi-** ['demi], *prefix.* halb-.

**demigod** ['demigɔd], *s.* der Halbgott.

**demijohn** ['demidʒɔn], *s.* der Glasballon.

**demise** [di'maiz], *s.* der Tod, das Hinscheiden. — *v.a.* (*Law*) vermachen.

**demisemiquaver** ['demisemikweivə], *s.* (*Mus.*) die Zweiunddreißigstelnote.

**demobilize** [di:'moubilaiz], *v.a.* demobilisieren.

**democracy** [di'mɔkrəsi], *s.* die Demokratie.

**democratic** [demo'krætik], *adj.* demokratisch.

**demolish** [di'mɔliʃ], *v.a.* demolieren, zerstören, niederreißen.

**demon** ['di:mən], *s.* der Dämon, der Teufel; *a* — *for work*, ein unersättlicher Arbeiter.

**demoniac** [di'mouniæk], **demoniacal** [di:mə'naiəkl], *adj.* besessen, teuflisch.

**demonstrable** [di'mɔnstrəbl], *adj.* beweisbar, nachweislich (*verifiable*).

**demonstrate** ['demənstreit], *v.a., v.n.* beweisen (*prove*); demonstrieren.

**demonstration** [demən'streiʃən], *s.* der Beweis (*theoretical*); die Demonstration (*practical*); (*Pol.*) Kundgebung.

**demonstrative** [di'mɔnstrətiv], *adj.* (*Gram.*) demonstrativ; überschwenglich (*emotional*).

**demoralize** [di:'mɔrəlaiz], *v.a.* demoralisieren.

**demote** [di:'mout], *v.a.* (*Mil.*, *official*) degradieren.

**demotion** [di:'mouʃən], *s.* (*Mil.*, *official*) die Degradierung.

**demur** [di'mə:], *v.n.* Anstand nehmen; Einwendungen machen (*raise objections*); zögern, zaudern (*hesitate*). — *s.* der Zweifel, der Skrupel.

**demure** [di'mjuə], *adj.* sittsam, zimperlich; spröde (*prim*).

**demureness** [di'mjuənis], *s.* die Sittsamkeit; die Sprödigkeit (*primness*).

**den** [den], *s.* die Höhle, Grube; *lion's* —, die Löwengrube.

**denial** [di'naiəl], *s.* die Verneinung, das Dementi (*negation*); das Ableugnen (*disclaimer*); die Absage (*refusal*).

**denizen** ['denizən], *s.* der Bürger, der Alteingesessene.

**denominate** [di'nɔmineit], *v.a.* nennen, benennen (*name*).

**denomination** [dinɔmi'neiʃən], *s.* die Bezeichnung, der Nennwert (*currency*); (*Rel.*) das Bekenntnis.

**denominational** [dinɔmi'neiʃənəl], *adj.* konfessionell.

**denominator** [di'nɔmineitə], *s.* (*Maths.*) der Nenner.

**denote** [di'nout], *v.a.* bezeichnen, kennzeichnen.

**dénouement** [dei'nu:mɑ̃], *s.* die Entwicklung, die Darlegung, die Lösung.

**denounce** [di'nauns], *v.a.* denunzieren, angeben; (*Law*) anzeigen.

**dense** [dens], *adj.* dicht; (*coll.*) beschränkt (*stupid*).

**density** ['densiti], *s.* die Dichte; — *of population*, die Bevölkerungsdichte.

**dent** (1) [dent], *s.* die Beule.

**dent** (2) [dent], *s.* die Kerbe (*in wood*); der Einschnitt (*cut*).

**dental** [dentl], *adj.* Zahn-; — *studies*, zahnärztliche Studien; — *treatment*, die Zahnbehandlung. — *s.* (*Phonet.*) der Zahnlaut.

**dentist** ['dentist], *s.* der Zahnarzt.

**dentistry** ['dentistri], *s.* die Zahnheilkunde.

**denude** [di'nju:d], *v.a.* entblößen, berauben (*of, Genit.*).

**denunciation** [dinʌnsi'eiʃən], *s.* die Denunzierung, die Anzeige.

**deny** [di'nai], *v.a.* verneinen (*negate*); abschlagen (*refuse*); verleugnen (*refuse to admit*).

**deodorant, deodorizer** [di:'oudərənt, di:'oudəraizə], *s.* der Geruchsentzieher (*apparatus*); der Deodorant.

**deodorize** [di:'oudəraiz], *v.a.* geruchlos machen.

**depart** [di'pɑ:t], *v.n.* abreisen, abfahren (*for*, nach, *Dat.*); scheiden.

**department** [di'pɑ:tmənt], *s.* die Abteilung; — *store*, das Kaufhaus.

**departmental** [di:pɑ:t'mentl], *adj.* Abteilungs-.

**departure** [di'pɑ:tʃə], *s.* die Abreise, die Abfahrt.

**depend** [di'pend], *v.n.* abhängen, abhängig sein (*upon*, von, *Dat.*); sich verlassen (*upon*, auf, *Acc.*); *that* —*s*, das kommt darauf an.

**dependable** [di'pendəbl], *adj.* verläßlich, zuverlässig.

**dependant** [di'pendənt], *s.* das abhängige Familienmitglied (*member of family*); der Angehörige, Abhängige.

**dependence** [di'pendəns], *s.* die Abhängigkeit (*need*); das Vertrauen, der Verlaß (*reliance*).

**dependency** [di'pendənsi], *s.* (*Pol.*) die abhängige Kolonie.

**dependent** [di'pendənt], *adj.* abhängig (*upon*, von, *Dat.*).

**depict** [di'pikt], *v.a.* schildern, beschreiben.

**deplete** [di'pli:t], *v.a.* entleeren (*make empty*); erschöpfen (*exhaust*).

**depletion** [di'pli:ʃən], *s.* die Entleerung.

**deplorable** [di'plɔ:rəbl], *adj.* bedauernswert, bedauerlich.

**deplore** [di'plɔ:], *v.a.* beklagen.

**deploy** [di'plɔi], *v.a.* entfalten. — *v.n.* sich entfalten; (*Mil.*) aufmarschieren.

**deployment** [di'plɔimənt], *s.* (*Mil.*) das Deployieren; die Entfaltung.

**deponent** [di'pounənt], *s.* (*Law*) der vereidigte Zeuge. — *adj.* (*Gram.*) (*verb*) das Deponens.

**depopulate** [di:'pɔpjuleit], *v.a.* entvölkern.

**deport** [di'pɔ:t], *v.a.* deportieren.

**deportation** [di:pɔ:'teiʃən], *s.* die Deportation.

# design

**deportment** [di'pɔ:tmənt], s. die körperliche Haltung (*physical*); das Benehmen (*social*).

**depose** [di'pouz], v.a. absetzen (*remove from office*); (*Law*) zu Papier bringen (*write down*); schriftlich erklären (*declare in writing*).

**deposit** [di'pɔzit], s. (*Comm.*) die Anzahlung; (*Geol., Chem.*) der Niederschlag; (*Geol.*) die Ablagerung; (*Comm.*) — *account*, das Depositenkonto. — v.a. (*Geol., Chem.*) absetzen; (*Comm.*) anzahlen, einzahlen.

**deposition** [di:pə'ziʃən], s. die Niederschrift, die schriftliche Erklärung; die Absetzung (*removal from office*).

**depositor** [di'pɔzitə], s. (*Comm.*) der Einzahler.

**depository** [di'pɔzitəri], s. das Lagerhaus.

**depot** ['depou], s. das Depot, das Lagerhaus (*store*); (*Am.*) der Bahnhof.

**deprave** [di'preiv], v.a. verderben.

**depraved** [di'preivd], adj. (moralisch) verdorben.

**depravity** [di'præviti], s. die Verdorbenheit, die Verworfenheit.

**deprecate** ['deprikeit], v.a. mißbilligen (*disapprove of*; *Acc.*); sich verbitten.

**deprecation** [depri'keiʃən], s. die Abbitte; die Mißbilligung (*disapproval*).

**depreciate** [di'pri:ʃieit], v.a. abwerten, herabwürdigen. — v.n. an Wert verlieren, im Wert sinken.

**depreciation** [dipri:ʃi'eiʃən], s. die Abwertung; der Verlust (*loss*); (*Pol., Comm.*) die Entwertung.

**depredation** [depri'deiʃən], s. das Plündern, der Raub.

**depress** [di'pres], v.a. niederdrücken (*press down*); deprimieren (*morale*).

**depressed** [di'prest], adj. niedergeschlagen.

**depression** [di'preʃən], s. das Niederdrücken (*action*); (*Pol.*) die Depression; die Niedergeschlagenheit (*despondency*); das Tief (*weather*).

**deprivation** [depri'veiʃən], s. der Verlust (*lack*); die Beraubung (*robbery*).

**deprive** [di'praiv], v.a. berauben (*of, Genit.*); wegnehmen (*of, Acc.*).

**depth** [depθ], s. die Tiefe; — *charge*, die Unterwasserbombe; *in the* —*s of night*, in tiefster Nacht; (*Phys.*) — *of focus*, die Tiefenschärfe; *be out of o.'s* —, den Grund unter seinen Füßen verloren haben, ratlos sein (*be helpless*); — *sounder*, das Echolot.

**deputation** [depju'teiʃən], s. die Deputation, die Abordnung.

**depute** [di'pju:t], v.a. abordnen, entsenden.

**deputize** ['depjutaiz], v.n. vertreten (*for, Acc.*).

**deputy** ['depjuti], s. der Abgeordnete, der Deputierte (*delegate*); der Vertreter (*replacement*).

**derail** [di:'reil], v.a. zum Entgleisen bringen. — v.n. entgleisen.

**derailment** [di:'reilmənt], s. die Entgleisung.

**derange** [di'reindʒ], v.a. verwirren, stören.

**derangement** [di'reindʒmənt], s. die Verwirrung; die Geistesstörung (*madness*).

**derelict** ['derilikt], adj. verlassen.

**dereliction** [deri'likʃən], s. das Verlassen; — *of duty*, die Pflichtvergessenheit.

**deride** [di'raid], v.a. verlachen, verhöhnen.

**derision** [di'riʒən], s. die Verhöhnung.

**derisive** [di'raisiv], adj. höhnisch, spöttisch.

**derivable** [di'raivəbl], adj. ableitbar.

**derivation** [deri'veiʃən], s. die Ableitung.

**derivative** [di'rivətiv], adj. abgeleitet. — s. das abgeleitete Wort.

**derive** [di'raiv], v.a., v.n. ableiten, herleiten.

**derogation** [dero'geiʃən], s. die Herabsetzung.

**derrick** ['derik], s. der Ladebaum.

**dervish** ['də:viʃ], s. der Derwisch.

**descant** ['deskænt], s. (*Mus.*) der Diskant oder der Sopran. — [dis'kænt], v.n. sich verbreiten (*on, über, Acc.*).

**descend** [di'send], v.n. hinab- oder herabsteigen (*go down*); abstammen (*stem from*).

**descendant** [di'sendənt], s. der Nachkomme.

**descent** [di'sent], s. der Abstieg (*going down*); der Fall (*decline*); die Abstammung (*forebears*); der Abhang (*slope*); (*Aviat.*) die Landung.

**describable** [dis'kraibəbl], adj. zu beschreiben, beschreibbar.

**describe** [dis'kraib], v.a. beschreiben, schildern.

**description** [dis'kripʃən], s. die Beschreibung; *of any* —, jeder Art.

**descriptive** [dis'kriptiv], adj. schildernd, beschreibend.

**desecrate** ['desikreit], v.a. entweihen, entheiligen.

**desecration** [desi'kreiʃən], s. die Entweihung, die Schändung.

**desert** (1) ['dezət], s. die Wüste.

**desert** (2) [di'zə:t], v.a. verlassen, im Stiche lassen. — v.n. desertieren.

**desert** (3) [di'zə:t], s. (*usually pl.*) das Verdienst.

**desertion** [di'zə:ʃən], s. (*Mil.*) die Fahnenflucht.

**deserve** [di'zə:v], v.a. verdienen.

**deserving** [di'zə:viŋ], adj. verdienstvoll.

**design** [di'zain], v.a. entwerfen (*plan*); vorhaben (*intend*); bestimmen (*determine*). — s. der Entwurf (*sketch*); der Plan (*draft*); die Absicht, das Vorhaben (*intention*); das Muster (*pattern*).

363

# designate

**designate** ['dezigneit], *v.a.* bezeichnen (*mark*); ernennen (*appoint*). — [-nit], *adj.* ernannt; *chairman* —, der künftige Vorsitzende.

**designation** [dezig'neiʃən], *s.* die Bestimmung, Ernennung (*appointment*); die Bezeichnung (*mark*).

**designer** [di'zainə], *s.* der Zeichner, der Graphiker (*artist*); der Ränkeschmied (*schemer*).

**designing** [di'zainiŋ], *adj.* hinterlistig, schlau.

**desirable** [di'zaiərəbl], *adj.* erwünscht, wünschenswert.

**desire** [di'zaiə], *s.* der Wunsch, die Begierde; das Verlangen, die Sehnsucht (*longing*). — *v.a.* verlangen, begehren.

**desirous** [di'zaiərəs], *adj.* begierig (*of, inf.*).

**desist** [di'zist], *v.n.* ablassen, aufhören.

**desk** [desk], *s.* der Schreibtisch; das Pult; — *lamp,* die Tischlampe *or* Bürolampe.

**desolate** ['desəlit], *adj.* verlassen, öde; trostlos (*sad*). — [-leit], *v.a.* verwüsten (*lay waste*).

**desolation** [desə'leiʃən], *s.* die Verwüstung (*of land*); die Trostlosigkeit (*sadness*).

**despair** [dis'pɛə], *v.n.* verzweifeln (*of, an, Dat.*). — *s.* die Verzweiflung.

**despatch, dispatch** [dis'pætʃ], *v.a.* absenden, befördern (*post*); abfertigen (*send*); erledigen (*deal with*); töten (*kill*). — *s.* die Abfertigung (*clearance*); die Eile (*speed*); die Depesche (*message*).

**desperado** [despə'reidou, -'rɑ:dou], *s.* der Wagehals, der Draufgänger.

**desperate** ['despərit], *adj.* verzweifelt.

**desperation** [despə'reiʃən], *s.* die Verzweiflung.

**despicable** ['despikəbl], *adj.* verächtlich.

**despise** [dis'paiz], *v.a.* verachten.

**despite** [dis'pait], *prep.* trotz (*Genit., Dat.*).

**despoil** [dis'pɔil], *v.a.* plündern, ausrauben.

**despondency** [dis'pɔndənsi], *s.* die Verzweiflung, Verzagtheit.

**despondent** [dis'pɔndənt], *adj.* verzagend, verzweifelnd, mutlos.

**despot** ['despɔt], *s.* der Despot, der Tyrann.

**despotic** [des'pɔtik], *adj.* despotisch.

**despotism** ['despətizm], *s.* (*Pol.*) der Despotismus.

**dessert** [di'zə:t], *s.* das Dessert, der Nachtisch.

**destination** [desti'neiʃən], *s.* die Bestimmung, das Ziel; der Bestimmungsort (*address*); das Reiseziel (*journey*).

**destine** ['destin], *v.a.* bestimmen.

**destiny** ['destini], *s.* das Geschick; das Schicksal, das Verhängnis (*fate*).

**destitute** ['destitju:t], *adj.* verlassen (*deserted*); hilflos, mittellos (*poor*); in bitterer Not (*in great distress*).

**destitution** [desti'tju:ʃən], *s.* die Notlage, die bittere Not.

**destroy** [dis'trɔi], *v.a.* zerstören (*buildings*); verwüsten; vernichten (*lives*).

**destroyer** [dis'trɔiə], *s.* der Zerstörer.

**destructible** [dis'trʌktibl], *adj.* zerstörbar.

**destruction** [dis'trʌkʃən], *s.* die Zerstörung (*of buildings*), die Verwüstung; die Vernichtung.

**destructive** [dis'trʌktiv], *adj.* zerstörend, verderblich.

**destructiveness** [dis'trʌktivnis], *s.* die Zerstörungswut, der Zerstörungssinn.

**desultory** ['dezəltəri], *adj.* unmethodisch, sprunghaft; oberflächlich (*superficial*).

**detach** [di'tætʃ], *v.a.* absondern, trennen.

**detachment** [di'tætʃmənt], *s.* die Absonderung (*separation*); (*Mil.*) das Kommando.

**detail** [di'teil], *v.a.* im einzelnen beschreiben (*describe minutely*); (*Mil.*) abkommandieren. — ['di:teil], *s.* die Einzelheit.

**detailed** ['di:teild], *adj.* ausführlich; detailliert, ins Einzelne gehend (*report etc.*); [di'teild], (*Mil.*) abkommandiert.

**detain** [di'tein], *v.a.* aufhalten, zurückhalten; festhalten (*in prison*).

**detect** [di'tekt], *v.a.* entdecken, aufdecken.

**detection** [di'tekʃən], *s.* die Entdeckung, die Aufdeckung.

**detective** [di'tektiv], *s.* der Detektiv.

**detention** [di'tenʃən], *s.* (*Law*) die Haft; die Vorenthaltung (*of articles*).

**deter** [di'tə:], *v.a.* abschrecken.

**detergent** [di'tə:dʒənt], *s.* das Reinigungsmittel.

**deteriorate** [di'tiəriəreit], *v.n.* sich verschlimmern, verschlechtern.

**deterioration** [ditiəriə'reiʃən], *s.* die Verschlimmerung.

**determinable** [di'tə:minəbl], *adj.* bestimmbar.

**determinate** [ditə:minit], *adj.* festgesetzt, bestimmt.

**determination** [di'tə:mi'neiʃən], *s.* die Entschlossenheit (*resoluteness*); die Bestimmung (*identification*); der Entschluß (*resolve*).

**determine** [di'tə:min], *v.a.* bestimmen (*ascertain*); beschließen (*resolve*).

**deterrent** [di'terənt], *s.* das Abschreckungsmittel.

**detest** [di'test], *v.a.* verabscheuen.

**detestable** [di'testəbl], *adj.* abscheulich.

**detestation** [detes'teiʃən], *s.* der Abscheu (*of, vor, Dat.*).

**dethrone** [di'θroun], *v.a.* entthronen, vom Thron verdrängen.

**detonate** ['di:- *or* 'detoneit], *v.n.* detonieren, explodieren. — *v.a.* explodieren, detonieren lassen, zum Detonieren bringen.

dice

**detonation** [deto'neiʃən], s. die Detonation, die Explosion.

**detonator** ['detoneitə], s. der Zünder, die Zündpatrone; (*Railw.*) die Knallpatrone.

**detour** ['deituə or di'tuə], s. der Umweg; (*Civil Engin.*) die Umleitung. — v.n. (*Am.*) einen Umweg machen. — v.a. (*Am.*) umleiten (*re-route*).

**detract** [di'trækt], v.a., v.n. abziehen; schmälern.

**detraction** [di'trækʃən], s. die Schmälerung, die Verleumdung (*slander*).

**detractive** [di'træktiv], adj. verleumderisch.

**detractor** [di'træktə], s. der Verleumder.

**detriment** ['detrimənt], s. der Nachteil, der Schaden.

**detrimental** [detri'mentl], adj. nachteilig; abträglich; schädlich (*harmful*).

**deuce** (1) [dju:s], s. die Zwei (*game*); (*Tennis*) der Einstand.

**deuce** (2) [dju:s], s. (*coll.*) der Teufel.

**devastate** ['devəsteit], v.a. verwüsten, verheeren.

**devastating** ['devəsteitiŋ], adj. schrecklich, verheerend.

**devastation** [devəs'teiʃən], s. die Verheerung, die Verwüstung.

**develop** [di'veləp], v.a. entwickeln. — v.n. sich entwickeln; sich entfalten (*prove, turn out*).

**developer** [di'veləpə], s. (*Phot.*) das Entwicklungsmittel.

**development** [di'veləpmənt], s. die Entwicklung.

**developmental** [divelɔp'mentl], adj. Entwicklungs-.

**deviate** ['di:vieit], v.n. abweichen.

**deviation** [di:vi'eiʃən], s. die Abweichung.

**device** [di'vais], s. die Vorrichtung (*equipment*); der Kunstgriff (*trick*).

**devil** [devl], s. der Teufel; der Lehrling, Laufbursche (*printer's, lawyer's*); *the — take the hindmost!* der Teufel hol was dann kommt! — v.n. in der Lehre sein (*for*, bei, *Dat.*).

**devilish** ['devəliʃ], adj. teuflisch.

**devilment, devilry** ['devəlmənt, 'devəlri], s. die Teufelei, die Teufelslaune.

**devious** ['di:viəs], adj. abweichend; abgelegen; abwegig.

**deviousness** ['di:viəsnis], s. die Abschweifung, Verirrung.

**devise** [di'vaiz], v.a. erfinden (*invent*); ersinnen (*think out*).

**deviser, devisor** [di'vaizə], s. der Erfinder (*inventor*); der Erblasser (*testator*).

**devoid** [di'vɔid], adj. frei (*of*, von, *Dat.*); ohne (*Acc.*).

**devolve** [di'vɔlv], v.a. übertragen (*transfer*); abwälzen (*pass on burden*) (*to*, auf, *Acc.*). — v.n. zufallen (*Dat.*).

**devote** [di'vout], v.a. widmen; aufopfern (*sacrifice*).

**devoted** [di'voutid], adj. ergeben (*affectionate*); geweiht (*consecrated*).

**devotee** [devo'ti:], s. der Anhänger; der Verehrer (*fan*).

**devotion** [di'vouʃən], s. die Hingabe; die Aufopferung (*sacrifice*); die Andacht (*prayer*).

**devotional** [di'vouʃənəl], adj. Andachts-.

**devour** [di'vauə], v.a. verschlingen.

**devout** [di'vaut], adj. andächtig, fromm.

**devoutness** [di'vautnis], s. die Frömmigkeit.

**dew** [dju:], s. der Tau.

**dewy** [dju:i], adj. betaut, taufeucht.

**dexterity** [deks'teriti], s. die Gewandtheit, die Fertigkeit.

**dexterous** ['dekstərəs], adj. gewandt, geschickt.

**diabetes** [daiə'bi:ti:z], s. (*Med.*) die Zuckerkrankheit.

**diabetic** [daiə'betik], s. (*Med.*) der Zuckerkranke. — adj. zuckerkrank.

**diabolic(al)** [daiə'bɔlik(əl)], adj. teuflisch.

**diadem** ['daiədem], s. das Diadem, das Stirnband.

**diæresis** [dai'iərəsis], s. die Diärese.

**diagnose** [daiəg'nouz], v.a. diagnostizieren, als Diagnose finden, befinden.

**diagnosis** [daiəg'nousis], s. die Diagnose, der Befund.

**diagonal** [dai'ægənəl], adj. diagonal, schräg. — s. (*Geom.*) die Diagonale.

**diagram** ['daiəgræm], s. das Diagramm.

**dial** ['daiəl], s. das Zifferblatt; (*Teleph.*) die Wählerscheibe. — v.a., v.n. (*Teleph.*) wählen.

**dialect** ['daiəlekt], s. der Dialekt, die Mundart.

**dialectic** [daiə'lektik], s. (*Phil.*) die Dialektik.

**dialektical** [daiə'lektikəl], adj. dialektisch, logisch.

**dialogue** ['daiəlɔg], s. der Dialog, das Zwiegespräch.

**diameter** [dai'æmitə], s. der Durchmesser.

**diametrical** [daiə'metrikəl], adj. diametral; gerade entgegengesetzt.

**diamond** ['daiəmənd], s. der Diamant; (*Cards*) das Karo.

**diaper** ['daiəpə], s. (*Am.*) die Windel.

**diaphragm** ['daiəfræm], s. (*Anat.*) das Zwerchfell; (*Phys.*) die Membran.

**diarrhœa** [daiə'riə], s. (*Med.*) der Durchfall.

**diary** ['daiəri], s. das Tagebuch, der Kalender.

**diatribe** ['daiətraib], s. der Tadel, der Angriff (*verbal*), die Schmähschrift (*written*).

**dibble** [dibl], s. der Pflanzstock. — v.n. Pflanzen stecken, anpflanzen.

**dice** [dais], s. pl. die Würfel (*sing.* **die**). — v.a. würfeln, werfen.

365

# dicker

**dicker** [′dikə], *v.n.* (*Am.*) feilschen, handeln.

**dicky** [′diki], *s.* das Vorhemd.

**dictate** [dik′teit], *v.a.*, *v.n.* diktieren, vorschreiben.

**dictation** [dik′teiʃən], *s.* (*Sch.*) das Diktat.

**dictator** [dik′teitə], *s.* der Diktator.

**dictatorship** [dik′teitəʃip], *s.* die Diktatur.

**diction** [′dikʃən], *s.* die Ausdrucksweise (*speech*).

**dictionary** [′dikʃənri], *s.* das Wörterbuch.

**didactic** [di′dæktik], *adj.* lehrhaft, Lehr-.

**die** (1) [dai], *v.n.* sterben (*of*, an, *Dat.*); — *away*, verebben.

**die** (2) [dai], *s.* der Würfel (*cube*); die Gießform (*mould*); der Stempel (*punch*); (*Metall.*) das Gesenk (*swage*); — *casting*, der Spritzguß; — *castings*, die Spritzgußteile, Gußteile; — *forging*, das Gesenkschmiedestück.

**die** (3) [dai] *see under* dice.

**dielectric** [daii′lektrik], *adj.* dielektrisch.

**diet** (1) [′daiət], *s.* (*Pol.*) der Landtag, Reichstag.

**diet** (2) [′daiət], *s.* (*Med.*) die Diät. — *v.n.* (*Med.*) eine Diät halten. — *v.a.* (*Med.*) eine Diät vorschreiben.

**dietary, dietetic** [′daiətəri, daiə′tetik], *adj.* diätetisch.

**differ** [′difə], *v.n.* sich unterscheiden (*be different from*, von, *Dat.*); anderer Meinung sein (*be of different opinion*).

**difference** [′difərəns], *s.* (*Maths.*) die Differenz; der Unterschied (*discrepancy*); die Meinungsverschiedenheit (*divergence of opinion*).

**different** [′difərənt], *adj.* verschieden, verschiedenartig.

**differentiate** [difə′renʃieit], *v.n.* (*Maths.*) differenzieren; einen Unterschied machen (*between*, zwischen, *Dat.*).

**difficult** [′difikəlt], *adj.* schwierig, schwer.

**difficulty** [′difikəlti], *s.* die Schwierigkeit.

**diffidence** [′difidəns], *s.* die Schüchternheit.

**diffident** [′difidənt], *adj.* schüchtern.

**diffraction** [di′frækʃən], *s.* die Ablenkung, (*Phys.*, *Optics*) die Brechung.

**diffuse** [di′fju:z], *v.a.* ausgießen (*pour*); verbreiten (*spread*). — [di′fju:s], *adj.* verbreitet, weitschweifig (*style*); zerstreut.

**diffuseness** [di′fju:snis], *s.* die Weitläufigkeit (*style*).

**diffusion** [di′fju:ʒən], *s.* (*Phys.*) die Diffusion, die Zerstreuung, die Verbreitung.

**dig** (1) [dig], *v.a.* *irr.* graben; — *in the ribs*, in die Rippen stoßen. — *v.n.* (*coll.*) wohnen (*live in lodgings*).

**dig** (2) [dig], *v.a.* (*coll.*) verstehen.

**digest** [di′dʒest], *v.a.* (*Anat.*) verdauen. — [′daidʒest], *s.* (*Am.*) die Sammlung von Auszügen; (*pl.*) Pandekten.

**digestibility** [didʒesti′biliti], *s.* die Verdaulichkeit.

**digestible** [di′dʒestibl], *adj.* verdaulich.

**digestion** [di′dʒestʃən], *s.* die Verdauung.

**digestive** [di′dʒestiv], *adj.* Verdauungs-; — *biscuit*, das Kornmehlkeks; — *organs*, die Verdauungsorgane.

**digger** [′digə], *s.* der Gräber; (*coll.*) der Australier.

**digit** [′didʒit], *s.* (*Maths.*) die (einstellige) Zahl; der Zahlenwert.

**digitalis** [didʒi′teilis], *s.* (*Bot.*) der Fingerhut.

**dignified** [′dignifaid], *adj.* würdig, würdevoll.

**dignify** [′dignifai], *v.a.* ehren (*honour*); zieren (*decorate*).

**dignitary** [′dignitəri], *s.* der Würdenträger.

**dignity** [′digniti], *s.* die Würde.

**digress** [dai′gres], *v.n.* abweichen, abschweifen.

**digression** [dai′greʃən], *s.* die Abweichung, die Abschweifung.

**digressive** [dai′gresiv], *adj.* abschweifend (*style*).

**digs** [digz], *s.* *pl.* (*coll.*) das (möblierte) Zimmer, die Wohnung.

**dike** [daik], *s.* der Graben, der Deich. — *v.a.* eindeichen, eindämmen.

**dilapidated** [di′læpideitid], *adj.* baufällig.

**dilapidation** [dilæpi′deiʃən], *s.* die Baufälligkeit, der Verfall.

**dilate** [d(a)i′leit], *v.a.* erweitern, ausdehnen. — *v.n.* sich ausdehnen; sich auslassen (*speak*) (*on*, über, *Acc.*).

**dilation** [d(a)i′leiʃən], *s.* die Erweiterung (*expansion*); die Auslassung (*speaking*).

**dilatoriness** [′dilətərinis], *s.* die Saumseligkeit.

**dilatory** [′dilətəri], *adj.* zögernd, aufschiebend, saumselig.

**dilemma** [d(a)i′lemə], *s.* das Dilemma, die Klemme.

**diligence** [′dilidʒəns], *s.* der Fleiß, die Emsigkeit.

**diligent** [′dilidʒənt], *adj.* fleißig, arbeitsam.

**dilly-dally** [′dili′dæli], *v.n.* tändeln, zaudern, Zeit vertrödeln.

**dilute** [d(a)i′lju:t], *v.a.* (*Chem.*) verdünnen; schwächen (*weaken*).

**dilution** [d(a)i′lju:ʃən], *s.* die Verdünnung.

**diluvial, diluvian** [d(a)i′lju:viəl, -iən], *adj.* Diluvial-, die Diluviums-; sintflutlich.

**dim** [dim], *adj.* trübe, unklar; (*Phys.*) abgeblendet. — *v.a.* abdunkeln, abblenden.

**dimension** [d(a)i′menʃən], *s.* die Dimension, das Maß.

**dimensional** [d(a)i′menʃənəl], *adj.* dimensional.

**diminish** [di'miniʃ], *v.a.* vermindern. — *v.n.* sich vermindern.

**diminution** [dimi'nju:ʃən], *s.* die Verringerung, die Verminderung.

**diminutive** [di'minjutiv], *adj.* verkleinernd, klein. — *s.* (*Gram.*) das Verkleinerungswort.

**dimness** ['dimnis], *s.* die Trübheit; die Düsterkeit (*dark*).

**dimple** [dimpl], *s.* das Grübchen.

**dimpled** [dimpld], *adj.* mit einem Grübchen.

**din** [din], *s.* das Getöse, der Lärm.

**dine** [dain], *v.n.* speisen, essen.

**dinginess** ['dindʒinis], *s.* die Dunkelheit, die Schäbigkeit.

**dingy** ['dindʒi], *adj.* dunkel, schäbig.

**dinner** ['dinə], *s.* das Essen; das Festessen (*formal*); — *jacket*, der Smoking.

**dint** [dint], *s.* der Nachdruck, der Schlag; *by* — *of*, mittels (*Genit.*).

**diocesan** [dai'osisən], *adj.* (*Eccl.*) einer Diözese angehörig, Diözesan-.

**diocese** ['daiəsis], *s.* (*Eccl.*) die Diözese.

**dip** [dip], *v.a.* eintauchen, eintunken; abblenden (*lights*). — *v.n.* (unter)tauchen; sinken; sich flüchtig einlassen (*into*, in). — *s.* die Senke; der Abhang (*slope*).

**diphtheria** [dif'θiəriə], *s.* (*Med.*) die Diphtherie.

**diphthong** ['difθɒŋ], *s.* (*Phonet.*) der Diphthong.

**diploma** [di'plouma], *s.* das Diplom; *teaching* —, das Lehrerdiplom.

**diplomacy** [di'plouməsi], *s.* die Diplomatie.

**diplomatic** [diplo'mætik], *adj.* diplomatisch, taktvoll; urkundlich (*documents*). — *s.* (*pl*) das Studium der Urkunden.

**diplomat(ist)** ['diploumæt, di'ploumətist], *s.* (*Pol.*) der Diplomat.

**dipper** ['dipə], *s.* der Taucher.

**dire** [daiə), *adj.* fürchterlich, schrecklich; — *necessity*, bittere Not.

**direct** [d(a)i'rekt], *adj.* direkt, unmittelbar. — *v.a.* leiten (*be in charge of*); hinweisen, hinlenken; den Weg zeigen (*tell the way to*); anordnen (*arrange for*).

**direction** [d(a)i'rekʃen], *s.* die Leitung (*management*); (*Geog.*) die Richtung, Himmelsrichtung; die Anordnung (*arrangement*, *order*); —*s for use*, die Gebrauchsanweisung.

**director** [d(a)i'rektə], *s.* der Direktor; der Leiter.

**directory** [d(a)i'rektəri], *s.* das Adreßbuch; das Telephonbuch.

**dirge** [də:dʒ], *s.* der Trauergesang.

**dirigible** ['diridʒibl], *adj.* lenkbar, leitbar.

**dirt** [də:t], *s.* der Schmutz, der Kot, Dreck. — *adj.* — *cheap*, spottbillig.

**dirty** ['də:ti], *adj.* schmutzig; gemein (*joke*).

**disability** [disə'biliti], *s.* die Unfähigkeit, das Unvermögen (*inability*); die Schädigung (*impairment of health*).

**disable** [dis'eibl], *v.a.* unfähig *or* untauglich machen.

**disablement** [dis'eiblmənt], *s.* die Versehrung, die Verkrüppelung.

**disabuse** [disə'bju:z], *v.a.* aufklären, eines Besseren belehren.

**disaccustom** [disə'kʌstəm], *v.a.* entwöhnen, abgewöhnen.

**disadvantage** [disəd'va:ntidʒ], *s.* der Nachteil.

**disaffection** [disə'fekʃən], *s.* die Abneigung; der Widerwille.

**disagree** [disə'gri:], *v.n.* nicht übereinstimmen, nicht einer Meinung sein.

**disagreeable** [disə'griəbl], *adj.* unangenehm, verdrießlich; unfreundlich.

**disagreement** [disə'gri:ment], *s.* die Uneinigkeit (*disunity*); die Meinungsverschiedenheit (*difference of opinion*).

**disallow** [disə'lau], *v.a.* nicht gestatten; in Abrede stellen.

**disappear** [disə'piə], *v.n.* verschwinden.

**disappearance** [disə'piərəns], *s.* das Verschwinden.

**disappoint** [disə'pɔint], *v.a.* enttäuschen.

**disappointment** [disə'pɔintmənt], *s.* die Enttäuschung.

**disapprobation** [disæpro'beiʃən], *s.* die Mißbilligung.

**disapproval** [disə'pru:vəl], *s.* die Mißbilligung.

**disapprove** [disə'pru:v], *v.a.* mißbilligen (*of*, *Acc.*).

**disarm** [dis'a:m], *v.a.* entwaffnen. —*v.n.* abrüsten.

**disarmament** [dis'a:məmənt], *s.* die Abrüstung.

**disarray** [disə'rei], *v.a.* in Unordnung bringen. — *s.* die Unordnung (*disorder*); die Verwirrung (*confusion*).

**disaster** [di'za:stə], *s.* das Unglück; das Unheil, die Katastrophe.

**disastrous** [di'za:strəs], *adj.* unheilvoll, schrecklich.

**disavow** [disə'vau], *v.a.* ableugnen.

**disavowal** [disə'vauəl], *s.* das Ableugnen.

**disband** [dis'bænd], *v.a.* entlassen (*dismiss*); auflösen (*dissolve*).

**disbar** [dis'ba:], *v.a.* (*Law*) von der Rechtspraxis ausschließen.

**disbelief** [disbi'li:f], *s.* der Unglaube (*incredulity*); der Zweifel (*doubt*).

**disbelieve** [disbi'li:v], *v.a.* nicht glauben; bezweifeln.

**disburse** [dis'bə:s], *v.a.* auszahlen, ausgeben.

**disbursement** [dis'bə:smənt], *s.* die Auszahlung, die Ausgabe.

**disc** [disk], *s.* (*also Med.*) die Scheibe; die Platte (*record*).

**discard** [dis'ka:d], *v.a.* ablegen, beiseite legen, aufgeben.

**discern** [di'zə:n *or* di'sə:n], *v.a.* unterscheiden; wahrnehmen, bemerken.

**discernment** [di'sə:nmənt], *s.* die Urteilskraft (*powers of judgment*); die Einsicht.

# discharge

**discharge** [dis'tʃɑːdʒ], *v.a.* entlassen (*dismiss*); abfeuern (*pistol*); abladen, ausladen (*cargo*); bezahlen (*debt*); tun, erfüllen (*duty*). — *s.* die Entladung (*gun*); die Entlassung (*dismissal*); die Bezahlung (*debt*); die Erfüllung (*duty*).

**disciple** [di'saipl], *s.* (*Bibl.*) der Jünger; der Schüler.

**disciplinarian** [disipli'nɛəriən], *s.* der Zuchtmeister.

**disciplinary** ['disiplinəri], *adj.* disziplinarisch.

**discipline** ['disiplin], *s.* die Disziplin, die Zucht. — *v.a.* disziplinieren, züchtigen.

**disclaim** [dis'kleim], *v.a.* verleugnen (*deny*); nicht anerkennen (*refuse to acknowledge*); verzichten (*renounce*).

**disclaimer** [dis'kleimə], *s.* der Widerruf.

**disclose** [dis'klouz], *v.a.* eröffnen, enthüllen.

**disclosure** [dis'klouʒə], *s.* die Eröffnung, die Enthüllung.

**discoloration** [diskʌlə'reiʃən], *s.* die Entfärbung, Verfärbung.

**discomfiture** [dis'kʌmfitʃə], *s.* die Verwirrung.

**discomfort** [dis'kʌmfət], *s.* das Unbehagen; die Beschwerde.

**disconcert** [diskən'səːt], *v.a.* außer Fassung bringen (*upset*); vereiteln (*frustrate*).

**disconnect** [diskə'nekt], *v.a.* trennen (*separate*); abstellen.

**disconsolate** [dis'kɔnsəlit], *adj.* trostlos, untröstlich.

**discontent** [diskən'tent], *s.* die Unzufriedenheit, das Mißvergnügen. — *v.a.* mißvergnügt stimmen.

**discontinuance** [diskən'tinjuəns], *s.* die Beendigung (*finish*); das Aufhören (*suspension*); die Unterbrechung (*interruption*).

**discontinue** [diskən'tinjuː], *v.a.* nicht fortsetzen; unterbrechen (*interrupt*); einstellen.

**discord** ['diskɔːd], *s.* die Zwietracht (*disagreement*); (*Mus.*) der Mißklang.

**discordance** [dis'kɔːdəns], *s.* die Uneinigkeit.

**discordant** [dis'kɔːdənt], *adj.* uneinig, widersprechend.

**discount** ['diskaunt], *s.* (*Comm.*) der Abzug, der Rabatt; *allow a* —, einen Rabatt gewähren; *be at a* —, unbeliebt sein, nicht geschätzt sein; *sell at a* —, unter dem Preis verkaufen. — [dis'kaunt], *v.a.* (*Comm.*) diskontieren, einen Rabatt gewähren; nur mit Vorsicht aufnehmen (*accept with doubt*).

**discountable** [dis'kauntəbl], *adj.* diskontierbar, in Abzug zu bringen.

**discountenance** [dis'kauntinəns], *v.a.* mißbilligen.

**discourage** [dis'kʌridʒ], *v.a.* entmutigen; abraten (*from*, von, *Dat.*).

**discouragement** [dis'kʌridʒmənt], *s.* die Entmutigung.

**discourse** [dis'kɔːs], *v.n.* einen Vortrag halten (*on*, über, *Acc.*); sprechen. — ['diskɔːs], *s.* der Vortrag; das Gespräch, die Rede.

**discourteous** [dis'kəːtiəs], *adj.* unhöflich.

**discourtesy** [dis'kəːtəsi], *s.* die Unhöflichkeit.

**discover** [dis'kʌvə], *v.a.* entdecken.

**discovery** [dis'kʌvəri], *s.* die Entdeckung.

**discredit** [dis'kredit], *s.* der üble Ruf; die Schande. — *v.a.* in schlechten Ruf bringen; diskreditieren.

**discreditable** [dis'kreditəbl], *adj.* schimpflich.

**discreet** [dis'kriːt], *adj.* diskret, verschwiegen; vorsichtig (*cautious*).

**discrepancy** [dis'krepənsi], *s.* die Diskrepanz, der Widerspruch; der Unterschied (*difference*).

**discretion** [dis'kreʃən], *s.* die Diskretion; die Klugheit; der Takt (*tact*); die Verschwiegenheit (*silence*); *at your* —, nach Ihrem Belieben; *use your* —, handle nach deinem Ermessen; handeln Sie nach Ihrem Ermessen.

**discretionary** [dis'kreʃənəri], *adj.* willkürlich, uneingeschränkt.

**discriminate** [dis'krimineit], *v.n.* unterscheiden (*distinguish*); absondern (*separate*).

**discriminating** [dis'krimineitiŋ], *adj.* scharfsinnig; einsichtig.

**discriminatory** [dis'krimineitəri], *adj.* einen Unterschied machend; — *legislation*, das Ausnahmegesetz.

**discursive** [dis'kəːsiv], *adj.* diskursiv, ohne Zusammenhang.

**discuss** [dis'kʌs], *v.a.* besprechen, erörtern.

**discussion** [dis'kʌʃən], *s.* die Diskussion, das Gespräch.

**disdain** [dis'dein], *s.* die Verachtung. — *v.a.* verachten, verschmähen; herabsetzen (*belittle*).

**disdainful** [dis'deinful], *adj.* geringschätzig, verächtlich.

**disease** [di'ziːz], *s.* die Krankheit.

**diseased** [di'ziːzd], *adj.* krank.

**disembark** [disim'bɑːk], *v.n.* aussteigen, landen. — *v.a.* aussteigen lassen, ausschiffen.

**disembarkation** [disembɑː'keiʃən], *s.* die Ausschiffung; die Landung.

**disenchant** [disin'tʃɑːnt], *v.a.* ernüchtern.

**disenchantment** [disin'tʃɑːntmənt], *s.* die Ernüchterung.

**disengage** [disin'geidʒ], *v.a.* losmachen, befreien (*release*); freigeben. — *v.n.* (*Mil.*) sich absetzen.

**disengaged** [disin'geidʒd], *adj.* frei (*unoccupied*).

**disentangle** [disin'tæŋgl], *v.a.* entwirren; befreien (*free*).

**disentanglement** [disin'tæŋglmənt], *s.* die Entwirrung; die Befreiung.

dispel

**disfavour** [dis'feivə], *s.* die Ungunst, die Ungnade.
**disfigure** [dis'figə], *v.a.* entstellen, verunstalten.
**disfiguration** [disfigjuə'reiʃən], *s.* die Entstellung, die Verunstaltung.
**disfranchise** [dis'fræntʃaiz], *v.a.* das Wahlrecht entziehen (*Dat.*).
**disgorge** [dis'gɔ:dʒ], *v.a.* ausspeien.
**disgrace** [dis'greis], *v.a.* entehren, Schande bringen. — *s.* die Ungnade, Schande (*shame*); die Entehrung (*putting to shame*).
**disgraceful** [dis'greisful], *adj.* schändlich, entehrend.
**disgruntled** [dis'grʌntld], *adj.* verstimmt, unzufrieden.
**disguise** [dis'gaiz], *v.a.* verkleiden (*dress*); (*fig.*) verstellen. — *s.* die Verkleidung; die Verstellung.
**disgust** [dis'gʌst], *s.* der Ekel, der Widerwille. — *v.a.* anekeln; *be* —*ed*, sehr ärgerlich sein; *be* —*ed with s. th.*, etwas verabscheuen.
**dish** [diʃ], *s.* die Schüssel (*bowl*); das Gericht (*food*). — *v.a.* (*coll.*) abtun (*frustrate*); — *up*, auftragen (*food*).
**dishcloth** [dishklɔθ], *s.* das Wischtuch; der Abwaschlappen.
**dishearten** [dis'hɑ:tn], *v.a.* entmutigen, verzagt machen.
**dishevelled** [di'ʃevəld], *adj.* aufgelöst (*hair*); zerzaust (*hair, clothes*).
**dishonest** [dis'ɔnist], *adj.* unehrlich.
**dishonesty** [dis'ɔnisti], *s.* die Unehrlichkeit.
**dishonour** [dis'ɔnə], *s.* die Schande. — *v.a.* schänden, Schande bringen (über, *Acc.*).
**dishonourable** [dis'ɔnərəbl], *adj.* ehrlos, schimpflich.
**dishwater** [dishwɔ:tə], *s.* das Spülwasser.
**disillusion** [disi'lu:ʒən], *s.* die Enttäuschung, die Ernüchterung. — *v.a.* enttäuschen, ernüchtern.
**disinclination** [disinkli'neiʃən], *s.* die Abneigung.
**disincline** [disin'klain], *v.a.* abgeneigt machen (*Dat.*).
**disinfect** [disin'fekt], *v.a.* desinfizieren.
**disinfectant** [disin'fektənt], *s.* das Desinfektionsmittel.
**disinfection** [disin'fekʃən], *s.* die Desinfektion.
**disingenuous** [disin'dʒenjuəs], *adj.* unaufrichtig, unredlich.
**disinherit** [disin'herit], *v.a.* enterben.
**disinter** [disin'tə:], *v.a.* exhumieren, ausgraben.
**disinterested** [dis'intrəstid], *adj.* uneigennützig.
**disinterestedness** [dis'intrəstidnis], *s.* die Selbstlosigkeit, die Uneigennützigkeit.
**disjoin** [dis'dʒɔin], *v.a.* trennen.
**disjoint** [dis'dʒɔint], *v.a.* zerlegen, zerstückeln.
**disjointedness** [dis'dʒɔintidnis], *s.* die Zerstücktheit, die Zusammenhangslosigkeit (*style of writing etc.*).

**disjunction** [dis'dʒʌŋkʃən], *s.* die Trennung, die Abtrennung.
**disjunctive** [dis'dʒʌŋktiv], *adj.* (*Gram.*) trennend, disjunktiv.
**disk** [disk] *see* **disc.**
**dislike** [dis'laik], *v.a.* nicht leiden mögen, nicht gerne haben. — *s.* die Abneigung (*of*, gegen, *Acc.*).
**dislocate** [dislokeit], *v.a.* verrenken (*bone*); (*fig.*) in Unordnung bringen.
**dislocation** [dislo'keiʃən], *s.* (*Med.*) die Verrenkung; die Verwirrung (*traffic etc.*).
**dislodge** [dis'lɔdʒ], *v.a.* vertreiben (*drive out*); entfernen (*remove*).
**disloyal** [dis'lɔiəl], *adj.* ungetreu; verräterisch.
**disloyalty** [dis'lɔiəlti], *s.* die Untreue (*sentiment*); der Verrat (*act*).
**dismal** ['dizməl], *adj.* trostlos, traurig (*mood*); düster, trüb (*weather*).
**dismantle** [dis'mæntl], *v.a.* niederreißen, zerlegen; abbauen.
**dismay** [dis'mei], *v.a.* erschrecken, entmutigen. — *s.* die Furcht, der Schrecken, die Bangigkeit.
**dismember** [dis'membə], *v.a.* zerstückeln.
**dismemberment** [dis'membəmənt], *s.* die Zerstückelung, die Aufteilung.
**dismiss** [dis'mis], *v.a.* entlassen (*person*); aufgeben (*idea*).
**dismissal** [dis'misəl], *s.* die Entlassung; (*Law*) die Abweisung.
**dismount** [dis'maunt], *v.n.* vom Pferd absteigen. — *v.a.* (die Truppen) absteigen lassen.
**disobedience** [diso'bi:djəns], *s.* der Ungehorsam.
**disobedient** [diso'bi:djənt], *adj.* ungehorsam.
**disobey** [diso'bei], *v.a.*, *v.n.* nicht gehorchen.
**disoblige** [diso'blaidʒ], *v.a.* verletzen, unhöflich behandeln.
**disorder** [dis'ɔ:də], *s.* die Unordnung; der Aufruhr (*riot*). — *v.a.* verwirren, in Unordnung bringen.
**disorderliness** [dis'ɔ:dəlinis], *s.* die Unordentlichkeit.
**disorderly** [dis'ɔ:dəli], *adj.* unordentlich (*unsystematic*); aufrührerisch, liederlich.
**disorganization** [disɔ:gəni'zeiʃən *or* -nai'zeiʃən], *s.* die Zerrüttung, die Auflösung (*dissolution*).
**disorganize** [dis'ɔ:gənaiz], *v.a.* auflösen.
**disown** [dis'oun], *v.a.* verleugnen.
**disparage** [dis'pæridʒ], *v.a.* verunglimpfen (*slight*); herabsetzen (*minimize*).
**disparagement** [dis'pæridʒmənt], *s.* die Herabsetzung.
**disparity** [dis'pæriti], *s.* die Ungleichheit.
**dispatch** [dis'pætʃ] *see* **despatch.**
**dispel** [dis'pel], *v.a.* vertreiben, verscheuchen.

369

# dispensable

**dispensable** [dis'pensəbl], *adj.* erläß-lich, entbehrlich.
**dispensary** [dis'pensəri], *s.* die Apotheke.
**dispensation** [dispen'seiʃən], *s.* die Austeilung; (*Eccl.*) die Dispensation.
**dispense** [dis'pens], *v.a.* ausgeben, austeilen (*distribute*); — *with*, entbehren können, verzichten (auf, *Acc.*).
**dispenser** [dis'pensə], *s.* der Apotheker, der Pharmazeut.
**dispersal** [dis'pə:səl], *s.* das Zerstreuen, die Verteilung.
**disperse** [dis'pə:s], *v.a.* zerstreuen. — *v.n.* sich zerstreuen, sich verteilen.
**dispirit** [dis'pirit], *v.a.* mutlos machen, entmutigen.
**displace** [dis'pleis], *v.a.* verlegen, versetzen; (*Phys.*) verdrängen; —*d person*, der Heimatlose, der Verschleppte, der Flüchtling.
**displacement** [dis'pleismənt], *s.* die Versetzung (*from one place to another*); die Entwurzelung (*uprooting*); (*Phys.*) die Verdrängung; (*Naut.*) das Deplacement.
**display** [dis'plei], *v.a.* entfalten, ausstellen, zur Schau stellen (*show*). — *s.* die Entfaltung (*showing*), die Schaustellung, Ausstellung (*exhibition*).
**displease** [dis'pli:z], *v.a.* mißfallen (*Dat.*).
**displeased** [dis'pli:zd], *adj.* ungehalten (*at*, über, *Acc.*).
**displeasure** [dis'pleʒə], *s.* das Mißvergnügen, das Mißfallen (— *at*, an, *Dat.*).
**disposable** [dis'pouzəbl], *adj.* (*Comm.*) disponibel; zur Verfügung stehend.
**disposal** [dis'pouzl], *s.* die Verfügung (*ordering*); die Übergabe (*handing over*); *at o.'s* —, zur Verfügung; *bomb* —, die Unschädlichmachung der Bomben.
**dispose** [dis'pouz], *v.a.* einrichten (*thing*); geneigt machen (*person*); — *of*, etwas loswerden (*Acc.*). — *v.n.* anordnen (*ordain*).
**disposed** [dis'pouzd], *adj.* geneigt; *be well — towards s.o.*, jemandem zugeneigt sein *or* wohlwollend gegenüberstehen; *well —*, (in) guter Laune.
**disposition** [dispə'ziʃən], *s.* (*Psych.*) die Anlage; die Gemütsart (*temperament*); die Anordnung (*sequence*); der Plan, die Anlage (*of book etc.*); die Verfügung (*arrangement*).
**dispossess** [dispə'zes], *v.a.* enteignen, (des Besitzes) entsetzen (*Genit.*).
**disproof** [dis'pru:f], *s.* die Widerlegung.
**disproportion** [disprə'pɔ:ʃən], *s.* das Mißverhältnis.
**disproportionate** [disprə'pɔ:ʃənit], *adj.* unverhältnismäßig.
**disprove** [dis'pru:v], *v.a.* widerlegen.
**disputable** [dis'pju:təbl], *adj.* bestreitbar.

**disputant** ['dispjutənt], *s.* der Opponent, der Disputant.
**disputation** [dispju'teiʃən], *s.* der gelehrte Streit, die Disputation.
**dispute** [dis'pju:t], *s.* der Disput, die Meinungsverschiedenheit. — *v.a.*, *v.n.* streiten, verschiedener Ansicht sein; disputieren (*debate*); mit Worten streiten (*argue*).
**disqualification** [diskwɔlifi'keiʃən], *s.* die Disqualifizierung.
**disqualify** [dis'kwɔlifai], *v.a.* disqualifizieren, ausschließen.
**disquiet** [dis'kwaiət], *v.a.* beunruhigen, stören. — *s.* die Unruhe, die Störung.
**disquisition** [diskwi'ziʃən], *s.* die (lange) Abhandlung *or* Rede.
**disregard** [disri'ga:d], *v.a.* mißachten, nicht beachten. — *s.* die Außerachtlassung, die Mißachtung.
**disreputable** [dis'repjutəbl], *adj.* verrufen, in üblem Rufe stehend.
**disrepute** [disri'pju:t], *s.* der schlechte Name, der üble Ruf.
**disrespect** [disris'pekt], *s.* die Geringschätzung, der Mangel an Respekt. — *v.a.* mißachten, geringschätzen, respektlos behandeln.
**disrespectful** [disris'pektful], *adj.* respektlos, unhöflich.
**disrobe** [dis'roub], *v.a.* entkleiden. — *v.n.* sich entkleiden.
**disrupt** [dis'rʌpt], *v.a.* abreißen, unterbrechen, stören (*disturb*).
**disruption** [dis'rʌpʃən], *s.* die Störung, die Unterbrechung (*interruption*); der Bruch.
**dissatisfaction** [dissætis'fækʃən], *s.* die Unzufriedenheit.
**dissatisfied** [dis'sætisfaid], *adj.* unzufrieden, unbefriedigt.
**dissatisfy** [dis'sætisfai], *v.a.* unzufrieden lassen.
**dissect** [di'sekt], *v.a.* zergliedern, zerlegen; (*Anat.*) sezieren.
**dissection** [di'sekʃən], *s.* die Zergliederung; (*Anat.*) die Sektion.
**dissemble** [di'sembl], *v.a.*, *v.n.* heucheln; sich verstellen.
**disseminate** [di'semineit], *v.a.* verbreiten.
**dissemination** [disemi'neiʃən], *s.* die Verbreitung.
**dissension** [di'senʃən], *s.* die Uneinigkeit, der Zwist (*conflict*).
**dissent** [di'sent], *v.n.* anderer Meinung sein; abweichen (*from*, von, *Dat.*). — *s.* die Abweichung, die abweichende Meinung.
**dissenter** [di'sentə], *s.* der Dissenter, das Mitglied der Freikirche.
**dissertation** [disə'teiʃən], *s.* die Dissertation, die Abhandlung.
**dissever** [di'sevə], *v.a.* trennen (*separate*); zerteilen (*divide*).
**dissidence** ['disidəns], *s.* die Uneinigkeit.
**dissident** ['disidənt], *adj.* uneinig, anders denkend.

# disunite

**dissimilar** [di'similə], *adj.* unähnlich, ungleichartig.

**dissimilarity** [disimi'læriti], *s.* die Unähnlichkeit, die Ungleichartigkeit.

**dissimulate** [di'simjuleit], *v.a.* verhehlen (*conceal*). — *v.n.* sich verstellen, heucheln.

**dissimulation** [disimju'leiʃən], *s.* die Verstellung, Heuchelei, das Vorgeben (*pretence*).

**dissipate** ['disipeit], *v.a.* zerstreuen (*spread*); verschwenden (*waste*).

**dissipation** [disi'peiʃən], *s.* die Zerstreuung, die Verschwendung; die Ausschweifung.

**dissociate** [di'souʃieit], *v.a.* trennen, lösen. — *v.r.* abrücken (von).

**dissociation** [disouʃi'eiʃən], *s.* die Trennung; die Dissoziation.

**dissolubility** [disɔlju'biliti], *s.* die Auflösbarkeit.

**dissoluble** [di'sɔljubl], *adj.* auflösbar.

**dissolute** ['disɔlju:t], *adj.* ausschweifend, lose, liederlich.

**dissolution** [disə'lju:ʃən], *s.* die Auflösung; der Tod (*death*).

**dissolvable** [di'zɔlvəbl], *adj.* auflösbar, löslich.

**dissolve** [di'zɔlv], *v.a.* auflösen; lösen. — *v.n.* sich auflösen, zergehen (*melt*).

**dissonance** ['disənəns], *s.* die Dissonanz, der Mißklang.

**dissonant** ['disənənt], *adj.* (*Mus.*) dissonant; mißhellig (*discordant*).

**dissuade** [di'sweid], *v.a.* abraten (*from*, von, *Dat.*).

**dissuasion** [di'sweiʒən], *s.* das Abraten.

**dissuasive** [di'sweisiv], *adj.* abratend.

**distaff** ['dista:f], *s.* der Spinnrocken (*spinning*); *on the — side*, auf der weiblichen Linie.

**distance** ['distəns], *s.* die Entfernung; die Ferne (*remoteness*). — *v.a.* hinter sich lassen, sich distanzieren (von, *Dat.*)

**distant** ['distənt], *adj.* entfernt, fern (*space*); kühl (*manner*).

**distaste** [dis'teist], *s.* die Abneigung (vor, *Dat.*); der Widerwille (gegen, *Acc.*).

**distasteful** [dis'teistful], *adj.* widerwärtig, zuwider.

**distastefulness** [dis'teistfulnis], *s.* die Widerwärtigkeit.

**distemper** (1) [dis'tempə], *s.* die Krankheit; die Staupe (*dogs*).

**distemper** (2) [dis'tempə], *s.* die Wasserfarbe (*paint*). — *v.a.* mit Wasserfarbe streichen.

**distend** [dis'tend], *v.a.* (*Med.*) ausdehnen, strecken. — *v.n.* sich ausdehnen.

**distension, distention** [dis'tenʃən], *s.* das Dehnen; (*Med.*) die Ausdehnung, die Streckung.

**distich** ['distik], *s.* (*Poet.*) das Distichon.

**distil** [dis'til], *v.a.* destillieren. — *v.n.* (*Chem.*) destillieren, herauströpfeln.

**distillation** [disti'leiʃən], *s.* die Destillierung, (*Chem.*) der Destilliervorgang.

**distiller** [dis'tilə], *s.* der Branntweinbrenner.

**distillery** [dis'tiləri], *s.* die (Branntwein)brennerei.

**distinct** [dis'tiŋkt], *adj.* deutlich, klar; — *from*, verschieden von (*Dat.*).

**distinction** [dis'tiŋkʃən], *s.* der Unterschied, die Unterscheidung (*differentiation*); die Auszeichnung (*eminence*).

**distinctive** [dis'tiŋktiv], *adj.* unterscheidend (*differentiating*); deutlich (*clear*); leicht zu unterscheiden (*easy to distinguish*).

**distinctiveness** [dis'tiŋktivnis], *s.* die Deutlichkeit (*of voice etc.*); die Eigenart, Eigentümlichkeit (*peculiarity*).

**distinguish** [dis'tiŋgwiʃ], *v.a.* unterscheiden. — *v.r.* — *o.s.*, sich auszeichnen.

**distinguishable** [dis'tiŋgwiʃəbl], *adj.* unterscheidbar.

**distinguished** [dis'tiŋgwiʃd], *adj.* berühmt, vornehm.

**distort** [dis'tɔ:t], *v.a.* verdrehen; verzerren, verrenken.

**distortion** [dis'tɔ:ʃən], *s.* die Verdrehung, Verzerrung; (*fig.*) die Entstellung (*of truth etc.*).

**distract** [dis'trækt], *v.a.* abziehen, ablenken (*divert*); stören (*disturb*).

**distracted** [dis'træktid], *adj.* zerstreut; verrückt (*mentally deranged*).

**distraction** [dis'trækʃən], *s.* die Ablenkung; die Störung (*disturbance*); *to —*, bis zur Raserei.

**distrain** [dis'trein], *v.a.* beschlagnahmen, in Beschlag nehmen.

**distraint** [dis'treint], *s.* die Beschlagnahme.

**distress** [dis'tres], *s.* die Not, die Trübsal. — *v.a.* betrüben (*sadden*); quälen (*torture*).

**distribute** [dis'tribju:t], *v.a.* verteilen, austeilen (*among*, unter, *Acc.*).

**distribution** [distri'bju:ʃən], *s.* die Verteilung; die Austeilung (*giving out*); (*Comm.*) der Vertrieb.

**distributive** [dis'tribjutiv], *adj.* (*Gram.*) distributiv; — *trades*, die Vertriebsgewerbe.

**district** ['distrikt], *s.* (*Geog., Pol.*) der Bezirk; die Gegend (*region*); der Kreis (*administrative*); — *commissioner*, der Kreisbeamte, Kreisvorsteher.

**distrust** [dis'trʌst], *v.a.* mißtrauen (*Dat.*). — *s.* das Mißtrauen (*of*, gegen, *Acc.*).

**distrustful** [dis'trʌstful], *adj.* mißtrauisch (*of*, gegen, *Acc.*).

**disturb** [dis'tə:b], *v.a.* stören (*trouble*); in Unordnung bringen (*disorder*).

**disturbance** [dis'tə:bəns], *s.* die Störung (*interruption etc.*); der Aufruhr (*riot*).

**disunion** [dis'ju:njən], *s.* die Entzweiung, die Zwietracht.

**disunite** [disju'nait], *v.a.* entzweien, Zwietracht säen zwischen. — *v.n.* sich trennen.

371

**disuse** [dis'ju:z], *v.a.* außer Gebrauch setzen. — [-'ju:s], *s.* der Nichtgebrauch (*abeyance*); die Entwöhnung (*cessation of practice*).

**ditch** [ditʃ], *s.* der Graben; *dull as —water*, uninteressant, langweilig. — *v.a.* mit einem Graben umgeben (*dig around*); graben.

**ditto** ['ditou], *adv.* desgleichen, dito.

**ditty** ['diti], *s.* das Liedchen.

**diurnal** [dai'ə:nəl], *adj.* täglich.

**divan** [di'væn], *s.* der Diwan.

**dive** [daiv], *v.n.* tauchen, springen (ins Wasser); (*Aviat.*) sturzfliegen, einen Sturzflug machen. — *s.* der Hechtsprung (ins Wasser); der Wassersprung; der Kopfsprung; (*Aviat.*) der Sturzflug.

**diver** ['daivə], *s.* (*Sport, Orn.*) der Taucher.

**diverge** [dai'və:dʒ], *v.n.* abweichen, auseinandergehen.

**divergence** [dai'və:dʒəns], *s.* die Abweichung, die Divergenz, Meinungsverschiedenheit.

**divergent** [dai'və:dʒənt], *adj.* auseinandergehend, abweichend.

**divers** ['daivəz], *adj. pl.* etliche, verschiedene.

**diverse** [dai'və:s], *adj.* verschieden, mannigfaltig.

**diversify** [dai'və:sifai], *v.a.* verschieden machen.

**diversion** [dai'və:ʃən], *s.* die Zerstreuung; (*Traffic*) die Umleitung.

**diversity** [dai'və:siti], *s.* die Verschiedenheit; die Ungleichheit (*disparity*).

**divert** [dai'və:t], *v.a.* ablenken, zerstreuen.

**divest** [di'vest *or* dai'-], *v.a.* entkleiden, berauben (*of office*, eines Amtes). — *v.r.* — *o.s. of*, auf etwas verzichten (*give up*).

**divide** [di'vaid], *v.a.* (*Maths.*) dividieren; teilen (*share*); aufteilen (*proportion*); sondern, trennen (*separate*). — *v.n.* sich teilen; (*Maths.*) sich dividieren lassen.

**dividend** ['dividənd], *s.* (*Comm.*) die Dividende; (*Maths.*) der Dividend.

**dividers** [di'vaidəz], *s.pl.* der Stechzirkel.

**divination** [divi'neiʃən], *s.* die Wahrsagung (*prophecy*); die Ahnung.

**divine** [di'vain], *v.a.* weissagen (*prophesy*); erraten (*guess*). — *adj.* göttlich; (*coll.*) herrlich. —*s.* (*obs.*) der Geistliche (*clergyman*).

**divinity** [di'viniti], *s.* die Göttlichkeit; die Gottheit (*deity*); die Theologie.

**divisibility** [divizi'biliti], *s.* (*Maths.*) die Teilbarkeit.

**divisible** [di'vizibl], *adj.* teilbar.

**division** [di'viʒən], *s.* (*Maths., Mil.*) die Division; die Teilung (*partition*); die Abteilung (*department*); (*Parl.*) die Abstimmung.

**divisor** [di'vaizə], *s.* (*Maths.*) der Divisor; der Teiler.

**divorce** [di'vɔ:s], *s.* (*Law*) die Scheidung; die Trennung (*separation*). — *v.a.* sich von einem scheiden lassen.

**divulge** [dai'vʌldʒ], *v.a.* ausplaudern; verraten (*betray*); verbreiten (*spread*).

**dizziness** ['dizinis], *s.* der Schwindel.

**dizzy** ['dizi], *adj.* schwindlig.

**do** [du:], *v.a. irr.* tun, machen; — *o.'s duty*, seine Pflicht erfüllen; — *o.'s bit*, das Seinige leisten; — *o.'s homework*, seine Aufgaben machen; — *a favour*, einen Gefallen erweisen; vollbringen (*accomplish*); — *away with*, abschaffen (*Acc.*); einpacken. — *v.n.* *this will —*, das genügt; *this won't —*, so geht's nicht; — *without*, ohne etwas auskommen; *how — you — ?* sehr angenehm (*on introduction to people*).

**docile** ['dousail], *adj.* gelehrig, lenksam, fügsam.

**docility** [do'siliti], *s.* die Gelehrigkeit, die Fügsamkeit.

**dock** (1) [dɔk], *s.* (*Bot.*) das Ampferkraut; — *leaf*, das Ampferblatt.

**dock** (2) [dɔk], *s.* (*Naut.*) das Dock; —*yard*, der Schiffswerft; (*Law*) der Anklagebank. — *v.a.* (*Naut.*) ein Schiff ins Dock bringen.

**dock** (3) [dɔk], *v.a.* stutzen (*clip*); kürzen (*wages*).

**docket** ['dɔkit], *s.* der Zettel (*chit*); der Lieferschein.

**doctor** ['dɔktə], *s.* (*Med.*) der Arzt, der Doktor. — *v.a.* operieren, kastrieren (*a cat etc.*).

**doctorate** ['dɔktərit], *s.* das Doktorat, die Doktorwürde.

**doctrinaire** [dɔktri'nɛə], *s.* der Doktrinär. — *adj.* doktrinär.

**doctrinal** [dɔk'trainəl], *adj.* Lehr-.

**doctrine** ['dɔktrin], *s.* die Lehre, die Doktrin.

**document** ['dɔkjumənt], *s.* das Dokument, die Urkunde.

**documentary** [dɔkju'mentəri], *adj.* Dokumentar- (*film*); dokumentarisch (*evidence*).

**documentation** [dɔkjumen'teiʃən], *s.* die Dokumentation, Heranziehung von Dokumenten.

**dodge** [dɔdʒ], *v.a.* ausweichen (*Dat.*). — *s.* der Kniff.

**dodger** ['dɔdʒə], *s.* der Schwindler.

**doe** [dou], *s.* (*Zool.*) das Reh.

**doeskin** ['douskin], *s.* das Rehleder.

**doff** [dɔf], *v.a.* abnehmen, ablegen (*clothes*).

**dog** [dɔg], *s.* der Hund; —*'s ear*, das Eselsohr (*in book*). — *v.a.* verfolgen, auf Schritt und Tritt folgen (*Dat.*) (*follow closely*).

**dogfish** ['dɔgfiʃ], *s.* (*Zool.*) der Dornhai.

**dogged** ['dɔgid], *adj.* unverdrossen, zäh.

**doggedness** ['dɔgidnis], *s.* die Zähigkeit.

**doggerel** ['dɔgərəl], *s.* der Knüttelvers.

**dogma** ['dɔgmə], *s.* das Dogma, der Glaubenssatz.

**dogmatic** [dɔg'mætik], *adj.* dogmatisch.
**dogmatism** ['dɔgmətizm], *s.* der Dogmatismus.
**dogmatize** ['dɔgmətaiz], *v.n.* dogmatisieren.
**doldrums** ['douldrəmz], *s. pl.* die Schwermut, die Depression; (*Naut.*) die Windstillen, *f.pl.*
**dole** [doul], *s.* das Almosen; die Arbeitslosenunterstützung (*unemployment benefit*); *be on the* —, stempeln gehen, Arbeitslosenunterstützung beziehen. — *v.a.* — *out*, austeilen, verteilen.
**doleful** ['doulful], *adj.* traurig, bekümmert.
**doll** [dɔl], *s.* die Puppe.
**dollar** ['dɔlə], *s.* der Dollar.
**dolman** ['dɔlmən], *s.* der Dolman.
**dolorous** ['dɔlərəs], *adj.* (*Lit.*) schmerzlich, schmerzhaft.
**dolphin** ['dɔlfin], *s.* (*Zool.*) der Delphin.
**dolt** [doult], *s.* der Tölpel.
**doltish** ['doultiʃ], *adj.* tölpelhaft.
**doltishness** ['doultiʃnis], *s.* die Tölpelhaftigkeit.
**domain** [do'mein], *s.* das Gebiet, der Bereich.
**dome** [doum], *s.* (*Archit.*) die Kuppel, die Wölbung; der Dom.
**domed** [doumd], *adj.* gewölbt.
**domestic** [do'mestik], *adj.* Haus-, häuslich; — *animal*, das Haustier.
**domesticate** [do'mestikeit], *v.a.* zähmen (*tame*), zivilisieren.
**domesticity** [domes'tisiti], *s.* die Häuslichkeit.
**domicile** ['dɔmisail], *s.* das Domizil; der Wohnort.
**domiciled** ['dɔmisaild], *adj.* wohnhaft (*at*, in, *Dat.*).
**dominant** ['dɔminənt], *adj.* vorherrschend. — *s.* (*Mus.*) die Dominante.
**dominate** ['dɔmineit], *v.a.* beherrschen. — *v.n.* herrschen.
**domination** [dɔmi'neiʃən], *s.* die Herrschaft.
**domineer** [dɔmi'niə], *v.n.* tyrannisieren.
**domineering** [dɔmi'niəriŋ], *adj.* überheblich, gebieterisch.
**Dominican** [do'minikən], *s.* der Dominikaner (*friar*).
**dominion** [do'minjən], *s.* die Herrschaft (*rule*); das Dominion (*Br. Commonwealth*).
**domino** ['dɔminou], *s.* (*pl.* —noes) der Domino (*mask*); (*pl.*) das Domino (*game*).
**don** (1) [dɔn], *s.* der Universitätsgelehrte, Universitätsdozent (*scholar*); Don (*Spanish nobleman*).
**don** (2) [dɔn], *v.a.* anziehen.
**donate** [do'neit], *v.a.* schenken, stiften.
**donation** [do'neiʃən], *s.* die Schenkung, die Stiftung; die Gabe (*gift*).
**donkey** ['dɔŋki], *s.* (*Zool.*) der Esel; — *engine*, die Hilfsmaschine.
**donor** ['dounə], *s.* der Spender, der Stifter; *blood* —, der Blutspender.

**doom** [du:m], *s.* die Verurteilung (*judgment*); der Untergang; das jüngste Gericht.
**doomed** [du:md], *adj.* verurteilt, verdammt (*to*, zu, *Dat.*).
**Doomsday** ['du:msdei]. der jüngste Tag, der Tag des jüngsten Gerichtes.
**door** [dɔ:], *s.* die Tür(e); *next* —, nebenan; *out of* —*s*, draußen, im Freien; —*bell*, die Türklingel; — *latch*, die Klinke.
**doorman** ['dɔ:mæn], *s.* der Türsteher, der Pförtner.
**dormant** ['dɔ:mənt], *adj.* schlafend; unbenutzt.
**dormer window** ['dɔ:mə 'windou], *s.* das Dachfenster.
**dormitory** ['dɔ:mitri], *s.* der Schlafsaal.
**dormouse** ['dɔ:maus], *s.* (*Zool.*) die Haselmaus.
**dose** [dous], *s.* (*Med.*) die Dosis. — *v.a.* dosieren.
**dot** [dɔt], *s.* der Punkt, das Tüpfel. — *v.a.* punktieren; *sign on the* —*ted line*, unterschreiben; — *the i's and cross the t's*, äußerst genau sein.
**dotage** ['doutidʒ], *s.* die Altersschwäche, das Greisenalter.
**dotard** ['doutəd], *s.* der alte Dummkopf.
**dote** [dout], *v.n.* vernarrt sein (*on*, in, *Acc.*).
**double** [dʌbl], *adj.* (*Maths.*) doppelt; zweideutig (*meaning*); falsch (*false*); — *entry book-keeping*, doppelte Buchführung. — *s.* der Doppelgänger, die Doppelgängerin; *at the* —, im Sturmschritt. — *v.a.* (*Maths.*) verdoppeln; zusammenlegen (*fold in two*). — *v.n.* — *up with pain*, sich vor Schmerzen winden *or* krümmen.
**doublet** ['dʌblit], *s.* der Wams; — *and hose*, Wams und Hosen; der Pasch (*dice*); (*Ling.*) die Dublette, Doppelform.
**doubt** [daut], *s.* der Zweifel. — *v.a.* zweifeln (an, *Dat.*); bezweifeln.
**doubtful** ['dautful], *adj.* zweifelhaft, fraglich (*uncertain*).
**doubtless** ['dautlis], *adj.* zweifellos, ohne Zweifel.
**douche** [du:ʃ], *s.* die Dusche.
**dough** [dou], *s.* der Teig.
**doughnut** ['dounʌt], *s.* der Krapfen, Pfannkuchen.
**doughy** ['doui], *adj.* weich, teigig.
**douse** [daus], *v.a.* begießen, mit Wasser beschütten.
**dove** [dʌv], *s.* (*Orn.*) die Taube.
**dovecote** ['dʌvkɔt], *s.* der Taubenschlag.
**dovetail** ['dʌvteil], *v.a.*, *v.n.* einpassen; fügen; —*ing*, die Einpassung, die Verzinkung.
**dowager** ['dauədʒə], *s.* die Witwe (*of noble family*, von Stande).
**dowdy** ['daudi], *adj.* schlampig, unordentlich, unelegant.
**dower** ['dauə], *s.* die Mitgift, die Ausstattung.

# down

**down** (1) [daun], *s.* der Flaum, die Daune.

**down** (2) [daun], *s.* das Hügelland.

**down** (3) [daun], *adv.* hinunter, herunter; nieder; unter; hinab. — *prep.* herab; hinunter. — *adj.* the — *train,* der Zug aus London. — *v.a.* niederzwingen, hinunterstürzen.

**downcast** ['daunkɑːst], *adj.* niedergeschlagen.

**downfall** ['daunfɔːl], *s.* der Sturz.

**downhill** [daun'hil], *adv.* bergab. — ['daunhil], *adj.* abschüssig.

**downpour** ['daunpɔː], *s.* der Platzregen.

**downright** ['daunrait], *adj.* völlig. — *adv.* geradezu.

**downward** ['daunwəd], *adj.* abschüssig. — *adv.* (also **downwards**) *see* **down**.

**dowry** ['dauri] *see* **dower**.

**doze** [douz], *v.n.* dösen, schlummern.

**dozen** [dʌzn], *s.* das Dutzend.

**drab** [dræb], *adj.* eintönig; langweilig (*boring*).

**draft** [drɑːft], *s.* (*Comm.*) die Tratte; der Entwurf (*sketch*); (*Mil.*) das Detachement. — *v.a.* entwerfen (*sketch*); (*Mil.*) abordnen; (*Am.*) einziehen.

**drag** [dræg], *v.a.* schleppen. — *s.* (*Engin.*) die Schleppbremse, der Dregghaken; der Hemmschuh (*wedge*); —*net*, das Schleppnetz; —*wheel*, das Schlepprad.

**dragoman** ['drægomən], *s.* der Dolmetscher.

**dragon** ['drægən], *s.* der Drache.

**dragonfly** ['drægənflai], *s.* (*Ent.*) die Libelle.

**dragoon** [drə'guːn], *v.a.* unterdrücken. — *s.* (*Mil.*) der Dragoner.

**drain** [drein], *v.a.* entwässern, austrocknen; trockenlegen. — *v.n.* ablaufen, abfließen, auslaufen. — *s.* der Abguß, Abzug, die Gosse (*in street*); (*Engin.*) die Dränage; —*ing board*, das Ablauf- *or* Abwaschbrett; (*Phot.*) —*ing rack*, der Trockenständer; *a — on o.'s income*, eine Belastung des Einkommens.

**drainage** ['dreinidʒ], *s.* die Trockenlegung, die Kanalisierung.

**drainpipe** ['dreinpaip], *s.* das Abflußrohr; — *trousers*, die Röhrenhosen, *f. pl.*

**drake** [dreik], *s.* (*Orn.*) der Enterich.

**dram** [dræm], *s.* der Trunk; Schluck (*spirits*).

**drama** ['drɑːmə], *s.* das Drama, das Schauspiel.

**dramatic** [drə'mætik], *adj.* dramatisch.

**dramatist** ['drɑːm- *or* 'dræmətist], *s.* der Dramatiker.

**dramatize** ['dræmətaiz], *v.a.* dramatisieren.

**drape** [dreip], *v.a.* drapieren, bedecken; einhüllen (*wrap*). — *s.* (*Am.*) der Vorhang.

**draper** ['dreipə], *s.* der Stoffhändler, der Tuchhändler.

**drapery** ['dreipəri], *s.* — *department*, die Stoff- *or* Tuchabteilung; die Tuchhandlung (*shop*).

**drastic** ['drɑːstik *or* 'dræstik], *adj.* drastisch, radikal.

**draught** [drɑːft], *s.* der Zug (*air*); der Tiefgang (— *of ship*); der Schluck (*drink*); der Schlaftrunk (*sleeping* —); — *horse*, das Zugpferd; — *beer*, das Faßbier; —*board*, das Damespielbrett; (*pl.*) das Damespiel.

**draw** [drɔː], *v.a. irr.* ziehen (*pull*); zeichnen (*sketch*); anlocken (*attract*); ausschreiben (*cheque*); —*well*, der Ziehbrunnen. — *s.* das Los, die Verlosung (*lottery*); (*Sport*) das Unentschieden.

**drawback** ['drɔːbæk], *s.* der Nachteil, die Schattenseite.

**drawbridge** ['drɔːbridʒ], *s.* die Zugbrücke.

**drawer** ['drɔːə], *s.* die Schublade; *chest of* —*s*, die Kommode; (*pl.*) die Unterhosen, *f. pl.*

**drawing** ['drɔːiŋ], *s.* (*Art*) die Zeichnung; —*board*, das Reißbrett; — *office*, das Zeichenbüro, der Zeichensaal.

**drawing room** ['drɔːiŋ rum], *s.* das Wohnzimmer, der Salon.

**drawl** [drɔːl], *v.n.* gedehnt sprechen. — *s.* die gedehnte Sprechweise.

**drawn** [drɔːn], *adj.* (*Sport*) unentschieden.

**dray** [drei], *s.* der Rollwagen, der Karren; —*man*, der Kutscher, der Fuhrmann.

**dread** [dred], *s.* der Schrecken. — *adj.* schrecklich. — *v.a.* fürchten. — *v.n.* sich fürchten (vor, *Dat.*).

**dreadful** ['dredful], *adj.* schrecklich, furchtbar.

**dreadnought** ['drednɔːt], *s.* (*Naut.*) das große Schlachtschiff.

**dream** [driːm], *s.* der Traum. — *v.n. irr.* träumen; *I would not — of it*, es würde mir nicht im Traum einfallen, ich denke nicht daran.

**dreamt** [dremt] *see* **dream**.

**dreamy** ['driːmi], *adj.* verträumt, träumerisch.

**dreariness** ['driərinis], *s.* die Öde.

**dreary** ['driəri], *adj.* traurig, öde.

**dredge** [dredʒ], *s.* das Schleppnetz. — *v.a.* (*Engin.*) ausbaggern; (*Naut.*) dreggen.

**dredger** ['dredʒə], *s.* der Bagger, das Baggerschiff; (*Cul.*) die Streubüchse.

**dregs** [dregz], *s. pl.* der Bodensatz (*in cup etc.*); die Hefe (*yeast*).

**drench** [drentʃ], *v.a.* durchnässen, tränken.

**Dresden** ['drezdən]. (*china*) das Meißner Porzellan.

**dress** [dres], *s.* das Kleid; die Kleidung; *evening* —, die Abendkleidung; *full* —, die Gala(kleidung); — *circle*, erster Rang; —*maker*, die Schneiderin; — *rehearsal*, die Generalprobe; — *shirt*, das Frackhemd; — *suit*, der Frackanzug. — *v.a., v.n.* (sich) anziehen.

**dresser** ['dresə], s. der Ankleider (*valet*); der Anrichtetisch (*table*).

**dressing** ['dresiŋ], s. (*Build.*) die Verkleidung; der Verband (*bandage*); der Verputz (*interior decoration*); — *gown*, der Schlafrock, Bademantel; (*Theat.*) — *room*, das Künstlerzimmer; Ankleidezimmer; — *table*, der Toilettentisch.

**dressy** ['dresi], adj. elegant; modesüchtig.

**dribble** [dribl], v.n. tröpfeln (*trickle*); geifern (*slaver*); (*Footb.*) dribbeln.

**driblet** ['driblit], s. die Kleinigkeit, die Lappalie.

**drift** [drift], s. die Richtung (*direction*); die Strömung (*stream*); das Treiben; Gestöber (*snow*). — v.a. treiben. — v.n. dahintreiben.

**drill** (1) [dril], v.a. drillen, bohren (*bore*); (*Mil.*) exerzieren; (*Agr.*) eine Furche ziehen; einstudieren (*coach*). — s. (*Mil.*) das Exerzieren; (*Agr.*) die Furche; der Bohrer (*tool*); — *hall*, die Übungs- or Exerzierhalle.

**drill** (2) [dril], s. der Drillich (*textile*).

**drily** ['draili], adv. trocken.

**drink** [driŋk], v.a., v.n. irr. trinken. — s. das Getränk, der Trank (*potion*); etwas zum Trinken (*a* —); come, have *a* —, trinken wir ein Glas (zusammen); strong —, geistiges Getränk.

**drinkable** ['driŋkəbl], adj. trinkbar; zum Trinken.

**drinker** ['driŋkə], s. der Trinker, Säufer; der Zecher; der Trunkenbold (*drunkard*).

**drip** [drip], v.n. tröpfeln. — s. das Tröpfeln.

**dripping** ['dripiŋ], s. (*Cul.*) das Bratenfett, das Schmalz.

**drive** [draiv], v.a. irr. treiben (*sheep etc.*); fahren (*a car*). — v.n. fahren; dahinfahren (— *along*). — s. die Ausfahrt, Fahrt (*trip*); die Einfahrt (*approach to house*).

**driving** ['draiviŋ], s. das Fahren; — *licence*, der Führerschein; — *school*, die Fahrschule; — *test*, die Fahrprüfung.

**drivel** [drivl], s. der Geifer; der Unsinn (*nonsense*). — v.n. Unsinn reden.

**driver** ['draivə], s. der Fahrer, der Chauffeur; (*Railw.*) Führer; (*Hunt.*) der Treiber.

**drizzle** [drizl], v.n. rieseln; leicht regnen. — s. das Rieseln, der feine Regen, der Sprühregen.

**droll** [droul], adj. drollig, possierlich.

**drollery** ['drouləri], s. die Possierlichkeit; die Schnurre.

**dromedary** ['drʌmədəri or 'drɔm-], s. (*Zool.*) das Dromedar.

**drone** (1) [droun], s. das Gedröhn, das Gesumme (*noise*). — v.n. dröhnen, summen (*hum loudly*).

**drone** (2) [droun], s. (*Ent.*) die Drohne; der Faulpelz (*lazybones*).

**droop** [dru:p], v.a. hängen lassen. — v.n. herabhängen; verwelken (*flowers*); ermatten (*tire*).

**drop** [drɔp], s. der Tropfen (*liquid*); das Fallen (*fall*). — v.a. fallen lassen; — *a brick*, eine taktlose Bemerkung machen; — *a hint*, andeuten, auf etwas hindeuten. — v.n. fallen.

**droppings** ['drɔpiŋz], s. pl. der Mist, Dünger (*of animals*).

**dropsical** ['drɔpsikəl], adj. (*Med.*) wassersüchtig.

**dropsy** ['drɔpsi], s. (*Med.*) die Wassersucht.

**dross** [drɔs], s. (*Metall.*) die Schlacke; der Unrat, das wertlose Zeug.

**drought** [draut], s. die Dürre, die Trockenheit.

**drove** [drouv], s. die Herde, die Trift (*cattle*).

**drover** ['drouvə], s. der Viehtreiber.

**drown** [draun], v.a. ertränken; überschwemmen (*flood*); übertönen (*noise*). — v.n. ertrinken.

**drowse** [drauz], v.n. schlummern, schläfrig sein.

**drowsy** ['drauzi], adj. schläfrig.

**drub** [drʌb], v.a. prügeln.

**drudge** [drʌdʒ], s. das Packtier; der Sklave, der Knecht.

**drudgery** ['drʌdʒəri], s. die Plackerei, die Plagerei (*hard toil*).

**drug** [drʌg], s. die Droge; die Medizin; das Rauschgift. — v.a. betäuben.

**drugget** ['drʌgit], s. der (grobe) Wollstoff.

**drum** [drʌm], s. die Trommel. — v.n. trommeln, austrommeln.

**drunk** [drʌŋk], adj. betrunken.

**drunkard** ['drʌŋkəd], s. der Trunkenbold.

**drunkenness** ['drʌŋkənnis], s. die Trunkenheit.

**dry** [drai], adj. trocken, dürr; ausgetrocknet, durstig (*thirsty*). — v.a. austrocknen, trocken machen, dörren. — v.n. trocken werden, trocknen.

**dryad** ['draiæd], s. die Baumnymphe, Dryade.

**dryness** ['drainis], s. die Trockenheit, die Dürre.

**dual** ['dju:əl], adj. doppelt; Zwei-.

**dub** (1) [dʌb], v.a. zum Ritter schlagen; nennen (*name*).

**dub** (2) [dʌb], v.a. (*Films*) synchronisieren.

**dubious** ['dju:bjəs], adj. zweifelhaft.

**ducal** ['dju:kəl], adj. herzoglich.

**duchess** ['dʌtʃis], s. die Herzogin.

**duchy** ['dʌtʃi], s. das Herzogtum.

**duck** (1) [dʌk], s. (*Orn.*) die Ente.

**duck** (2) [dʌk], v.n. sich ducken, sich bücken; untertauchen (*in water*).— v.a. untertauchen, ins Wasser tauchen.

**duckling** ['dʌkliŋ], s. (*Orn.*) das Entchen.

**duct** [dʌkt], s. (*Anat.*) der Kanal; die Röhre.

**ductile** ['dʌktail], adj. dehnbar; fügsam.

**dud** [dʌd], *s.* (*Mil.*) der Blindgänger; der Fehlschlag.
**dude** [dju:d], *s.* (*Am.*) der Geck.
**dudgeon** [ˈdʌdʒən], *s.* der Groll, der Unwille; *in high* —, sehr aufgebracht.
**due** [dju:], *adj.* gebührend, fällig, schuldig (*to, Dat.*); angemessen, recht; *this is* — *to carelessness*, das ist auf Nachlässigkeit zurückzuführen. — *adv.* direkt, gerade. — *s.* (*pl.*) die Gebühren.
**duel** [ˈdju:əl], *s.* das Duell. — *v.n.* sich duellieren (mit, *Dat.*).
**duet** [dju:ˈet], *s.* (*Mus.*) das Duett.
**duffer** [ˈdʌfə], *s.* der Tölpel; (*obs.*) der Hausierer.
**duffle, duffel** [dʌfl], *s.* der Düffel, das Düffeltuch.
**dug** [dʌg], *s.* die Zitze.
**dug-out** [ˈdʌg-aut], *s.* der Unterstand, der Bunker.
**duke** [dju:k], *s.* der Herzog; *Grand Duke*, der Großherzog.
**dukedom** [ˈdju:kdəm], *s.* das Herzogtum.
**dull** [dʌl], *adj.* fade, langweilig (*boring*); träge, schwerfällig (*slow to grasp*); stumpfsinnig (*obtuse*); schal, abgeschmackt (*tasteless*); schwach (*perception*); dumpf (*thud, noise*); matt (*colour*); trüb, überwölkt (*weather*); flau (*trade*). — *v.a.* abstumpfen!(*senses*).
**dullness** [ˈdʌlnis], *s.* die Stumpfheit (*senses*); die Langweile (*boredom*); die Schwerfälligkeit (*stolidity*); die Schwäche (*vision etc.*); die Stumpfsinnigkeit (*stupidity*).
**dumb** [dʌm], *adj.* stumm; (*sl.*) dumm; —*founded*, verblüfft; — *show*, die Pantomime; —*bell*, (*Gymn.*) die Hantel.
**dumbness** [ˈdʌmnis], *s.* die Stummheit.
**dummy** [ˈdʌmi], *s.* der Strohmann (*cards*); die Kleiderpuppe (*wax figure*); der Blindgänger (*dud shell*); der Schnuller (*baby's*).
**dump** [dʌmp], *v.a.* kippen, abladen; —*ing ground*, der Abladeplatz. — *s.* (*Am. coll.*) das Bumslokal.
**dumpling** [ˈdʌmpliŋ], *s.* der Kloß, (*Austr.*) der Knödel.
**dumps** [dʌmps], *s. pl.* der Unmut, der Mißmut, die Depression.
**dumpy** [ˈdʌmpi], *adj.* untersetzt, kurz und dick.
**dun** (1) [dʌn], *adj.* schwarzbraun.
**dun** (2) [dʌn], *s.* der Gläubiger. — *v.a.* energisch mahnen.
**dunce** [dʌns], *s.* der Dummkopf.
**dune** [dju:n], *s.* die Düne.
**dung** [dʌŋ], *s.* der Dünger. —*v.n.* düngen.
**dungeon** [ˈdʌndʒən], *s.* der Kerker.
**dupe** [dju:p], *s.* der Betrogene. — *v.a.* betrügen.
**duplicate** [ˈdju:plikeit], *v.a.* verdoppeln; doppelt schreiben *or* ausfüllen (*write twice*); vervielfältigen (*stencil*). — [-kit], *s.* das Duplikat.
**duplicity** [dju:ˈplisiti], *s.* die Falschheit, die Doppelzüngigkeit.
**durability** [djuərəˈbiliti], *s.* die Dauerhaftigkeit.

**durable** [ˈdjuərəbl], *adj.* dauerhaft.
**duration** [djuəˈreiʃən], *s.* die Dauer, die Länge (*time*).
**duress** [djuəˈres], *s.* der Zwang; *under* —, zwangsweise.
**during** [ˈdjuəriŋ], *prep.* während.
**dusk** [dʌsk], *s.* die Dämmerung.
**dusky** [ˈdʌski], *adj.* dunkel, trüb; düster.
**dust** [dʌst], *s.* der Staub. — *v.a.* abstauben (*clean*); bestäuben (*pollinate*); bestreuen.
**dustbin** [ˈdʌstbin], *s.* der Mülleimer.
**dusty** [ˈdʌsti], *adj.* staubig; *not so* —, (*coll.*) nicht so übel.
**Dutch** [dʌtʃ], *adj.* holländisch; niederländisch; — *treat*, auf getrennte Kosten; *double* —, Kauderwelsch, Unsinn.
**Dutchman** [ˈdʌtʃmən], *s.* der Holländer, der Niederländer.
**dutiful** [ˈdju:tiful], *adj.* gehorsam, pflichttreu, pflichtbewußt.
**duty** [ˈdju:ti], *s.* die Pflicht; die Abgabe (*tax*); *customs* —, der Zoll; *be on* —, Dienst haben; (*being*) *on* —, diensthabend; *off* —, dienstfrei; — *free*, zollfrei; *in* — *bound*, von Rechts wegen, pflichtgemäß.
**dwarf** [dwɔ:f], *s.* der Zwerg. — *v.a.* am Wachstum hindern (*stunt*); klein erscheinen lassen (*overshadow*).
**dwell** [dwel], *v.n. irr.* wohnen (*be domiciled*); verweilen (*remain*).
**dwelling** [ˈdweliŋ], *s.* die Wohnung; — *place*, der Wohnort.
**dwindle** [dwindl], *v.n.* abnehmen, kleiner werden.
**dye** [dai], *v.a.* färben. — *s.* die Farbe; (*Chem.*) der Farbstoff.
**dyeing** [ˈdaiiŋ], *s.* das Färben; Färbereigewerbe.
**dyer** [ˈdaiə], *s.* der Färber.
**dying** [ˈdaiiŋ], *s.* das Sterben; *the* —, (*pl.*) die Sterbenden, *pl.* — *adj.* sterbend.
**dynamic** [daiˈnæmik], *adj.* dynamisch.
**dynamics** [daiˈnæmiks], *s. pl.* die Dynamik.
**dynamite** [ˈdainəmait], *s.* das Dynamit.
**dynamo** [ˈdainəmou], *s.* der Dynamo, die Dynamomaschine.
**dynasty** [ˈdinəsti], *s.* die Dynastie.
**dysentery** [ˈdisəntri], *s.* (*Med.*) die Ruhr.
**dyspepsia** [disˈpepsiə], *s.* (*Med.*) die Magenverstimmung.
**dyspeptic** [disˈpeptik], *adj.* mit verstimmtem Magen; schlecht aufgelegt (*grumpy*).

# E

**E** [i:]. das E (*also Mus.*); *E flat*, Es; *E sharp*, Eis; *E minor*, E-moll.

# edible

**each** [i:tʃ], *adj., pron.* jeder, jede, jedes; — *other*, einander; — *one*, jeder einzelne.

**eager** ['i:gə], *adj.* eifrig, begierig.

**eagerness** ['i:gənis], *s.* der Eifer, die Begierde.

**eagle** [i:gl], *s.* (*Orn.*) der Adler; (*Am.*) das Zehndollarstück.

**ear** [iə], *s.* das Ohr; —*lap*, das Ohrläppchen; —*phones*, die Kopfhörer; — *piece*, die Hörmuschel; —*drum*, das Trommelfell; — *of corn*, die Ähre.

**earl** [ə:l], *s.* der Graf.

**earldom** ['ə:ldəm], *s.* die (englische) Grafschaft.

**early** ['ə:li], *adj.* früh, frühzeitig.

**earmark** ['iəmɑ:k], *v.a.* kennzeichnen, bezeichnen.

**earn** [ə:n], *v.a.* verdienen; erwerben.

**earnest** [ə:nist], *s.* der Ernst; der ernste Beweis, das Handgeld; (*Comm.*) die Anzahlung; (*fig.*) der Vorgeschmack. — *adj.* ernst, ernsthaft.

**earnings** ['ə:ninz], *s.* das Einkommen.

**earshot** ['iəʃɔt], *s.* die Hörweite.

**earth** [ə:θ], *s.* die Erde; der Erdboden (*soil*); der Fuchsbau (*of fox*); *down to* —, praktisch denkend; *move heaven and* —, alles daransetzen; *where on* —, wo in aller Welt.

**earthen** ['ə:θən], *adj.* irden, aus Erde; —*ware*, das Steingut.

**earthquake** ['ə:θkweik], *s.* das Erdbeben.

**earthly** ['ə:θli], *adj.* irdisch.

**earthworm** ['ə:θwə:m], *s.* (*Zool.*) der Regenwurm.

**earthy** ['ə:θi], *adj.* erdig; irdisch.

**earwig** ['iəwig], *s.* (*Ent.*) der Ohrwurm.

**ease** [i:z], *s.* die Leichtigkeit (*facility*); die Bequemlichkeit (*comfort*); *feel at* —, sich wie zu Hause fühlen; (*Mil.*) *stand at* —! rührt euch! *ill at* —, unbehaglich. — *v.a.* erleichtern, leichter machen; lindern (*pain*). — *v.n.* — *off*, (*Mil.*) sich auflockern.

**easel** [i:zl], *s.* das Gestell; die Staffelei.

**easiness** ['i:zinis], *s.* die Leichtigkeit, die Ungezwungenheit.

**east** [i:st], *adj., adv.* Ost-, ostwärts (*direction*). — *s.* der Osten, der Orient.

**Easter** ['i:stə]. das *or* (*n.* or *f. pl.*) die Ostern.

**eastern** ['i:stən], *adj.* östlich; morgenländisch, orientalisch (*oriental*).

**easy** ['i:zi], *adj.* leicht, frei; — *chair*, der Lehnstuhl, Sessel; *stand* —! rührt Euch! *take it* —, nimm's nicht so ernst; es sich (*Dat.*) bequem machen (*make o.s. comfortable*); (*Comm.*) — *terms*, Zahlungserleichterungen; — *-going*, gemütlich.

**eat** [i:t], *v.a., v.n. irr.* essen, speisen (*dine*); fressen (*of animals*); — *humble pie*, sich demütigen; — *o.'s hat*, einen Besen fressen; — *o.'s words*, seine Worte bereuen.

**eatable** ['i:təbl], *adj.* genießbar, eßbar.

**eaves** [i:vz], *s. pl.* die Dachrinne, die Traufe.

**eavesdrop** ['i:vzdrɔp], *v.n.* belauschen (*on s.o., Acc.*).

**eavesdropper** ['i:vzdrɔpə], *s.* der Lauscher.

**ebb** [eb], *s.* die Ebbe. — *v.n.* nachlassen, abebben, abfließen.

**ebonize** ['ebənaiz], *v.a.* wie Ebenholz *or* schwarz beizen.

**ebony** ['ebəni], *s.* das Ebenholz.

**ebullient** [i'bʌljənt], *adj.* aufwallend.

**eccentric** [ik'sentrik], *adj.* exzentrisch, überspannt, wunderlich.

**eccentricity** [eksen'trisiti], *s.* die Exzentrizität, die Überspanntheit.

**ecclesiastic** [ikli:zi'æstik], *s.* der Geistliche. — *adj.* (*also* -*ical*) geistlich, kirchlich.

**echo** ['ekou], *s.* das Echo, der Widerhall. — *v.a., v.n.* widerhallen (*resound*); wiederholen (*repeat*).

**eclectic** [i'klektik], *adj.* eklektisch. — *s.* der Eklektiker.

**eclecticism** [i'klektisizm], *s.* (*Phil.*) der Eklektizismus.

**eclipse** [i'klips], *s.* die Verfinsterung, Finsternis (*darkness*); die Verdunklung (*darkening*). — *v.a.* verdunkeln.

**ecliptic** [i'kliptik], *s.* die Ekliptik, die Sonnenbahn.

**economic** [i:kə'nɔmik], *adj.* ökonomisch, wirtschaftlich.

**economical** [i:kə'nɔmikl], *adj.* (*frugal*) sparsam, wirtschaftlich.

**economics** [i:kə'nɔmiks], *s.* (*pl.*) die Wirtschaftslehre, die Ökonomie.

**economist** [i'kɔnəmist], *s.* der Ökonom der Wirtschaftsfachmann.

**economize** [i'kɔnəmaiz], *v.n.* sparen (*on*, mit, *Dat.*); sparsam sein mit (*Dat.*).

**economy** [i'kɔnəmi], *s.* die Wirtschaft; *political* —, die Nationalökonomie, Staatswirtschaftslehre.

**ecstasy** ['ekstəsi], *s.* die Ekstase, die Entzückung, die Verzückung.

**ecstatic** [iks'tætik], *adj.* ekstatisch, verzückt; entzückt (*delighted*).

**Ecuadorean** [ekwə'dɔ:riən], *adj.* ekuadorianisch. — *n.* der Ekuadorianer.

**ecumenical** [i:kju'menikəl], *adj.* ökumenisch.

**eddy** ['edi], *s.* der Wirbel, Strudel. — *v.n.* wirbeln.

**edge** [edʒ], *s.* die Schärfe, die Schneide (*blade*); die Kante (*ledge*); der Rand (*brink*); der Saum (*border*); die Ecke (*corner*); der Schnitt (*book*); die Schärfe (*wit, keenness*); *put an* — *on*, schärfen; *be on* —, nervös sein. — *v.a.* besetzen (*decorate*); umgeben; *double-* —*d*, zweischneidig; *two-* —*d*, zweischneidig, zweikantig; —*d with lace*, mit Spitze eingefaßt. — *v.n.* sich bewegen; — *forward*, langsam vorrücken; — *off*, sich abseits halten, sich drücken; — *away from*, abrücken.

**edgy** ['edʒi], *adj.* kantig, eckig; (*fig.*) nervös, reizbar.

**edible** ['edibl], *adj.* eßbar.

377

# edict

edict ['i:dikt], s. die Verordnung.
edification [edifi'keiʃən], s. die Erbauung.
edifice ['edifis], s. der Bau, das Gebäude.
edify ['edifai], v.a. erbauen.
edit ['edit], v.a. herausgeben (book etc.).
edition [i'diʃən], s. die Ausgabe.
editor ['editə], s. der Herausgeber, der Schriftleiter; (newspaper) der Redakteur.
editorial [edi'tɔ:riəl], adj. Redaktions-. — s. der Leitartikel.
editorship ['editəʃip], s. die Redaktion; die Schriftleitung.
educate ['edjukeit], v.a. erziehen, (heran)bilden.
education [edju'keiʃən], s. die Erziehung (upbringing); die Bildung (general culture); das Bildungwesen, das Schulwesen (educational system); primary —, die Grundschulung, das Volksschulwesen; secondary —, das Mittelschulwesen, das höhere Schulwesen; university —, das Hochschulwesen (system), die Universitätsbildung (of individual); local — authority, das Schulamt, die Schulbehörde; Professor of Education, Professor der Pädagogik; further —, adult —, weitere Ausbildung, Erwachsenenbildung.
educational [edju'keiʃənəl], adj. erzieherisch (educative); Bildungs-, Unterrichts- ( for education); — attainment, der Bildungsgrad, die Schulstufe (grade); — facilities, die Lehrmittel, Bildungs- or Schulungsmöglichkeiten, f. pl.
education(al)ist [edju'keiʃən(əl)ist], s. der Erzieher, der Pädagoge; der Erziehungsfachmann (theorist).
eel [i:l], s. (Zool.) der Aal.
eerie ['iəri], adj. gespenstisch, unheimlich.
efface [i'feis], v.a. auslöschen, austilgen.
effacement [i'feismənt], s. die Austilgung; self- —, die Selbstaufopferung.
effect [i'fekt], s. die Wirkung; die Folge, das Ergebnis (consequence); der Eindruck (impression); of no —, ohne jede Wirkung; carry into —, ausführen; take — from, vom . . . in Kraft treten. — v.a. bewirken (bring about).
effective [i'fektiv], adj. wirksam (having an effect); gültig (in force); dienstfähig (usable); wirklich (actual).
effectual [i'fektjuəl], adj. wirksam (effective); kräftig, energisch (strong).
effectuate [i'fektjueit], v.a. bewerkstelligen (get done); bewirken (bring about).
effeminacy [i'feminəsi], s. die Verweichlichung.
effeminate [i'feminit], adj. weichlich, verweichlicht.
effervescence [efə'vesəns], s. das Aufbrausen, Schäumen.
effervescent [efə'vesənt], adj. aufbrausend, aufschäumend.

effete [i'fi:t], adj. abgenutzt, erschöpft.
efficacious [efi'keiʃəs], adj. wirksam. energisch.
efficacy ['efikəsi], s. die Wirksamkeit, die Energie.
efficiency [i'fiʃənsi], s. die Tüchtigkeit (of person); die Wirksamkeit; die Leistung.
efficient [i'fiʃənt], adj. tüchtig; leistungsfähig; wirksam (drug etc.).
effigy ['efidʒi], s. das Bild, das Abbild.
efflorescent [eflɔ:'resənt], adj. aufblühend.
effluent ['efluənt], adj. ausfließend.
effluvium [i'flu:viəm], s. die Ausdünstung.
effort ['efət], s. die Anstrengung, die Bemühung; make an —, sich bemühen, sich anstrengen; make every —, alle Kräfte anspannen.
effrontery [i'frʌntəri], s. die Frechheit (cheek); die Unverschämtheit (impertinence).
effortless ['efətlis], adj. mühelos.
effulgence [i'fʌldʒəns], s. der Glanz, das Strahlen.
effulgent [i'fʌldʒənt], adj. schimmernd, strahlend.
effusion [i'fju:ʒən], s. die Ausgießung; der Erguß (verse etc.); der Überschwang.
effusive [i'fju:ziv], adj. überschwenglich.
egg [eg], s. das Ei; fried —, das Spiegelei; scrambled —, das Rührei; —flip, der Eierpunsch; —shell, die Eierschale. — v.a. — on, anspornen, anreizen.
eglantine ['egləntain], s. (Bot.) die wilde Rose.
egoism ['egouizm], s. der Egoismus.
ego(t)ist ['ego(t)ist], s. der Egoist.
egregious [i'gri:dʒəs], adj. ungeheuer- (lich).
egress ['i:gres], s. der Ausgang, der Ausfluß (water etc.).
Egyptian [i'dʒipʃən], adj. ägyptisch. — s. der Ägypter.
eiderdown ['aidədaun], s. die Daunendecke, Steppdecke.
eiderduck ['aidədʌk], s. (Orn.) die Eidergans.
eight [eit], num. adj. acht.
eighteen [ei'ti:n], num. adj. achtzehn.
eighty ['eiti], num. adj. achtzig.
either ['aiðə], adj., pron. einer von beiden. — conj. entweder (or, oder).
ejaculate [i'dʒækjuleit], v.a., v.n. ausstoßen.
eject [i'dʒekt], v.a. hinauswerfen; ausstoßen.
ejection [i'dʒekʃən], s. die Ausstoßung.
eke [i:k], v.a. — out, verlängern, ergänzen; — out an existence, ein spärliches Auskommen finden.
elaborate [i'læbəreit], v.a. ausarbeiten, im einzelnen ausarbeiten. — [-rit], adj. detailliert, ausgearbeitet; kunstvoll (intricate); umständlich (involved).

**elaboration** [ilæbə'reiʃən], s. die Ausarbeitung (im einzelnen); die Detailarbeit.

**elapse** [i'læps], v.n. verstreichen, verfließen (time).

**elastic** [i'læstik], adj. elastisch. — s. das Gummiband.

**elasticity** [elæs'tisiti], s. (Phys.) die Elastizität.

**elate** [i'leit], v.a. stolz machen; ermutigen.

**elated** [i'leitid], adj. in gehobener Stimmung.

**elation** [i'leiʃən], s. der Stolz; die Begeisterung.

**elbow** ['elbou], s. (Anat.) der Ellenbogen; at o.'s —, bei der Hand; — room, der Spielraum. — v.a. — o.'s way through, sich durchdrängen.

**elder** (1) ['eldə], comp. adj. älter. — s. der Alte, der Älteste; Kirchenälteste.

**elder** (2) ['eldə], s. (Bot.) der Holunder.

**elderly** ['eldəli], adj. älter; alt; ältlich.

**elect** [i'lekt], v.a. erwählen (to, zu, Dat.); auswählen (choose). — adj. erwählt, auserwählt; chairman —, der gewählte Vorsitzende.

**election** [i'lekʃən], s. die Auswahl (selection); (Pol.) die Wahlen, f.pl.; die Wahl (choice); by(e) —, die Bezirkswahl, die Neuwahl; — broadcast, eine Radiowahlrede.

**electioneering** [ilekʃən'iəriŋ], s. das Wahlmanöver, die Wahlpropaganda, der Wahlkampf.

**elective** [i'lektiv], adj. durch Wahl bestimmt; Wahl-.

**elector** [i'lektə], s. (Pol.) der Wähler; das Mitglied eines Wahlausschusses (academic etc.); der Kurfürst (prince).

**electorate** [i'lektərit], s. die Wählerschaft.

**electress** [i'lektrəs], s. die Kurfürstin (princess).

**electric(al)** [i'lektrik(əl)], adj. elektrisch; electrical engineer, der Elektrotechniker; der Student der Elektrotechnik (trainee); electric switch, der elektrische Schalter; — razor, der elektrische Rasierapparat.

**electrician** [elek'triʃən], s. der Elektriker.

**electricity** [ilek- or elek'trisiti], s. die Elektrizität.

**electrocution** [ilektro'kju:ʃən], s. die Hinrichtung or der Unfall (accidental) durch Elektrizität.

**electron** [i'lektrɔn], s. das Elektron.

**electroplate** [i'lektropleit], v.a. galvanisch versilbern.

**electrotype** [i'lektrotaip], s. der galvanische Abdruck, die Galvanographie.

**elegance** ['eligəns], s. die Eleganz.

**elegant** ['eligənt], adj. elegant, fein.

**elegy** ['elidʒi], s. (Lit.) die Elegie.

**element** ['elimənt], s. das Element; der Bestandteil (component).

**elemental** [eli'mentl], adj. elementar.

**elementary** [eli'mentri], adj. einfach (simple); elementar (for beginners).

**elephant** ['elifənt], s. (Zool.) der Elefant.

**elevate** ['eliveit], v.a. erheben, erhöhen.

**elevation** [eli'veiʃən], s. die Erhebung (lifting); (Geom.) die Elevation; die Erhöhung (rise); der Aufriß (Engin. drawing).

**elevator** ['eliveitə], s. (Am.) der Lift, der Aufzug, der Fahrstuhl; (Agr.) der Getreideheber.

**eleven** [i'levn], num. adj. elf.

**elf** [elf], s. der Elf, der Kobold.

**elfin** ['elfin], adj. Elfen-, elfenhaft.

**elicit** [i'lisit], v.a. herauslocken, entlocken.

**eligibility** [elidʒi'biliti], s. die Wählbarkeit.

**eligible** ['elidʒibl], adj. wählbar, passend.

**eliminate** [i'limineit], v.a. ausschalten, ausscheiden, eliminieren.

**elimination** [ilimi'neiʃən], s. die Ausschaltung, die Ausscheidung.

**elision** [i'liʒən], s. (Phonet.) die Auslassung, die Weglassung.

**elixir** [i'liksə], s. das Elixier.

**elk** [elk], s. (Zool.) der Elch.

**ell** [el], s. die Elle.

**ellipse** [i'lips], s. (Geom.) die Ellipse.

**ellipsis** [i'lipsis], s. (Gram.) die Ellipse.

**elliptic(al)** [i'liptik(əl)], adj. (Gram., Geom.) elliptisch.

**elm** [elm], s. (Bot.) die Ulme.

**elocution** [elə'kju:ʃən], s. der Vortrag (delivery); die Vortragskunst.

**elocutionist** [elə'kju:ʃənist], s. der Vortragskünstler.

**elongate** ['i:lɔŋgeit], v.a. verlängern.

**elongation** [i:lɔŋ'geiʃən], s. die Verlängerung.

**elope** [i'loup], v.n. entlaufen, von zu Hause fliehen.

**elopement** [i'loupmənt], s. das Entlaufen, die Flucht von zu Hause.

**eloquence** ['eləkwəns], s. die Beredsamkeit.

**eloquent** ['eləkwənt], adj. beredt, redegewandt.

**else** [els], adv. sonst, außerdem, anders; or —, sonst . . . ; how —? wie denn sonst? nobody —, sonst niemand; anyone —? sonst noch jemand? — conj. sonst.

**elsewhere** [els'wɛə], adv. anderswo; anderswohin.

**Elsinore** ['elsinɔ:], Helsingör, n.

**elucidate** [i'lju:sideit], v.a. erläutern, erklären (to s.o., Dat.).

**elucidation** [ilju:si'deiʃən], s. die Erläuterung, die Erklärung.

**elude** [i'lju:d], v.a. ausweichen, entgehen (Dat.).

**elusive** [i'lju:siv], adj. schwer faßbar, täuschend.

**Elysian** [i'liziən], adj. elysisch.

**emaciate** [i'meiʃieit], v.a. abmagern, dünn werden.

**emaciation** [imeiʃi'eiʃən], s. die Abmagerung.

**emanate** ['emǝneit], *v.n.* ausgehen, herrühren (*derive*); ausstrahlen (*radiate*).

**emancipate** [i'mænsipeit], *v.a.* befreien, emanzipieren.

**emancipation** [imænsi'peiʃǝn], *s.* die Emanzipation.

**embalm** [im'ba:m], *v.a.* einbalsamieren.

**embankment** [im'bæŋkmǝnt], *s.* der Flußdamm, der Eisenbahndamm; die Eindämmung.

**embarcation** *see* **embarkation**.

**embargo** [im'ba:gou], *s.* die Handelssperre.

**embark** [im'ba:k], *v.a.* einschiffen. — *v.n.* sich einschiffen; — *upon s.th.*, an etwas herangehen, unternehmen.

**embarkation** [emba:'keiʃǝn], *s.* die Einschiffung.

**embarrass** [im'bærǝs], *v.a.* verlegen machen, in Verlegenheit bringen.

**embarrassment** [im'bærǝsmǝnt], *s.* die Verlegenheit.

**embassy** ['embǝsi], *s.* (*Pol.*) die Botschaft, die Gesandtschaft.

**embed** [im'bed], *v.a.* einbetten.

**embellish** [im'beliʃ], *v.a.* verschönern, ausschmücken; ausmalen (*story*).

**embers** ['embǝz], *s. pl.* die glühende Asche; die Kohlen, *f. pl.*; *Ember Days*, (*Eccl.*) die Quatembertage, *m. pl.*

**embezzle** [im'bezl], *v.a.* veruntreuen, unterschlagen.

**embitter** [im'bitǝ], *v.a.* verbittern.

**emblazon** [im'bleizn], *v.a.* ausmalen, auf ein Schild setzen.

**emblem** ['emblǝm], *s.* das Emblem, das Abzeichen.

**emblematic(al)** [emblǝ'mætik(ǝl)], *adj.* sinnbildlich, symbolisch.

**embodiment** [im'bɔdimǝnt], *s.* die Verkörperung.

**embody** [im'bɔdi], *v.a.* verkörpern.

**embolden** [im'bouldn], *v.a.* erkühnen, anfeuern, anspornen; *be emboldened*, sich erkühnen.

**emboss** [im'bɔs], *v.a.* in getriebener Arbeit verfertigen, prägen.

**embossed** [im'bɔst], *adj.* getrieben, in erhabener Arbeit; gestanzt.

**embrace** [im'breis], *v.a.* (*fig.*) umarmen, umfassen. — *s.* die Umarmung.

**embrasure** [im'breiʒǝ], *s.* die Schießscharte.

**embrocation** [embro'keiʃǝn], *s.* die Einreibung (*act*); (*Pharm.*) die Einreibsalbe.

**embroider** [im'brɔidǝ], *v.a.* sticken; verzieren, ausschmücken (*adorn*).

**embroidery** [im'brɔidǝri], *s.* die Stickerei; die Verzierung, Ausschmückung (*of story etc.*).

**embroil** [im'brɔil], *v.a.* verwickeln.

**embryo** ['embriou], *s.* der Keim; Embryo.

**embryonic** [embri'ɔnik], *adj.* im Embryostadium, im Werden.

**emend** [i'mend], *v.a.* verbessern (*text*), berichtigen.

**emendation** [i:men'deiʃǝn], *s.* die Textverbesserung.

**emendator** ['i:mendeitǝ], *s.* der Berichtiger.

**emerald** ['emǝrǝld], *s.* der Smaragd.

**emerge** [i'mǝ:dʒ], *v.n.* auftauchen, hervortreten, an den Tag kommen.

**emergence** [i'mǝ:dʒǝns], *s.* das Auftauchen, das Hervortreten.

**emergency** [i'mǝ:dʒǝnsi], *s.* der Notfall; die kritische Lage; *in case of* —, im Notfalle; — *exit*, der Notausgang; — *landing*, die Notlandung; — *measures*, Notmaßnahmen; — *brake*, die Notbremse.

**emery** ['emǝri], *s.* — *paper*, das Schmirgelpapier.

**emetic** [i'metik], *s.* das Brechmittel.

**emigrant** ['emigrǝnt], *s.* der Auswanderer.

**emigrate** ['emigreit], *v.n.* auswandern.

**emigration** [emi'greiʃǝn], *s.* die Auswanderung.

**eminence** ['eminǝns], *s.* die Anhöhe; die Eminenz, der hohe Ruf (*fame*); die eminente Stellung, die Autorität (*authority*); *Your Eminence*, Eure Eminenz.

**eminent** ['eminǝnt], *adj.* eminent, hervorragend.

**emissary** ['emisǝri], *s.* der Abgesandte, der Sendbote.

**emission** [i'miʃǝn], *s.* die Aussendung (*sending out*); die Ausstrahlung (*radiation*).

**emit** [i'mit], *v.a.* aussenden; ausstrahlen; ausströmen.

**emolument** [i'mɔljumǝnt], *s.* das (Neben)einkommen, das Zusatzgehalt, das Honorar (*fee*).

**emotion** [i'mouʃǝn], *s.* die Rührung, die Bewegung, das Gefühl, die Gemütsbewegung.

**emotional** [i'mouʃǝnǝl], *adj.* gefühlvoll.

**emperor** ['empǝrǝ], *s.* der Kaiser.

**emphasis** ['emfǝsis], *s.* der Nachdruck.

**emphasize** ['emfǝsaiz], *v.a.* betonen.

**empire** ['empaiǝ], *s.* das Reich, das Kaiserreich.

**empiric(al)** [emp'irik(ǝl)], *adj.* (*Phil.*) empirisch.

**empiricism** [em'pirisizm], *s.* (*Phil.*) der Empirizismus.

**employ** [im'plɔi], *v.a.* benutzen (*thing*); beschäftigen, anstellen (*person*).

**employee** [im'plɔii:], *s.* der Angestellte.

**employer** [im'plɔiǝ], *s.* der Arbeitgeber.

**employment** [im'plɔimǝnt], *s.* die Beschäftigung, die Arbeit.

**emporium** [em'pɔ:riǝm], *s.* der Handelsplatz; (*Naut.*) der Stapelplatz; das Warenhaus (*stores*).

**empower** [em'pauǝ], *v.a.* bevollmächtigen.

**empress** ['empres], *s.* die Kaiserin.

**emptiness** ['emptinis], *s.* die Leere, die Öde.

**empty** ['empti], *adj.* leer; — *-headed*, geistlos.

**emulate** [′emjuleit], *v.a.* nacheifern (*Dat.*).

**emulation** [emju′leiʃən], *s.* der Wetteifer, das Nacheifern.

**emulous** [′emjuləs], *adj.* nacheifernd, wetteifernd; eifersüchtig (*jealous*).

**emulsion** [i′mʌlʃən], *s.* (*Pharm.*) die Emulsion.

**enable** [i′neibl], *v.a.* befähigen; ermächtigen (*empower*).

**enact** [i′nækt], *v.a.* (*Pol.*) verordnen; verfügen (*order*); darstellen, aufführen (*on stage*).

**enactment** [i′næktmənt], *s.* die Verordnung.

**enamel** [i′næml], *v.a.* emaillieren. — *s.* die Emaille; (*Med.*) der Schmelz.

**enamour** [i′næmə], *v.a.* verliebt machen.

**encamp** [in′kæmp], *v.n.* (sich) lagern, das Lager aufschlagen.

**encampment** [in′kæmpmənt], *s.* das Lager.

**encase** [in′keis], *v.a.* einschließen, in ein Gehäuse schließen.

**encashment** [in′kæʃmənt], *s.* (*Comm.*) das Inkasso, die Einkassierung.

**enchain** [in′tʃein], *v.a.* in Ketten legen, anketten.

**enchant** [in′tʃɑ:nt], *v.a.* bezaubern.

**enchantment** [in′tʃɑ:ntmənt], *s.* die Bezauberung; der Zauber (*spell*).

**encircle** [in′sə:kl], *v.a.* umringen, umkreisen; (*Mil.*) einkreisen.

**encirclement** [in′sə:klmənt], *s.* die Einkreisung.

**enclose** [in′klouz], *v.a.* einschließen; einlegen (*in letter*).

**enclosure** [in′klouʒə], *s.* die Einfriedigung; die Beilage, Einlage (*in letter*).

**encompass** [in′kʌmpəs], *v.a.* umfassen, umspannen (*comprise*).

**encore** [′ɔŋkɔ:, ɔŋ′kɔ:], *int.* noch einmal! — *s.* die Wiederholung, Zugabe.

**encounter** [in′kauntə], *v.a.* treffen; begegnen (*Dat.*). — *s.* das Zusammentreffen.

**encourage** [in′kʌridʒ], *v.a.* ermutigen, anspornen.

**encouragement** [in′kʌridʒmənt], *s.* die Ermutigung; die Förderung (*promotion*).

**encroach** [in′kroutʃ], *v.n.* eingreifen (*interfere*); übergreifen.

**encroachment** [in′kroutʃmənt], *s.* der Eingriff, der Übergriff.

**encrust** [in′krʌst], *v.a.* inkrustieren; verkrusten.

**encumber** [in′kʌmbə], *v.a.* belasten.

**encumbrance** [in′kʌmbrəns], *s.* die Belastung, das Hindernis.

**encyclical** [en′siklikl], *s.* das (päpstliche) Rundschreiben, die Enzyklika.

**encyclopaedia** [insaiklo′pi:djə], *s.* das Lexikon, die Enzyklopädie.

**encyclopaedic** [insaiklo′pi:dik], *adj.* enzyklopädisch.

**end** [end], *s.* das Ende; der Schluß; das Ziel (*aim*); die Absicht (*intention*); *in the —*, am Ende, letzten Endes; *to*

*that —*, zu dem Zweck; *put an — to*, einer Sache ein Ende machen; *make —s meet*, sein Auskommen finden; *burn the candle at both —s*, seine Kräfte verschwenden. — *v.a.* beenden. — *v.n.* enden, Schluß machen.

**ending** [′endiŋ], *s.* das Ende (*of play etc.*); (*Gram.*) die Endung.

**endanger** [in′deindʒə], *v.a.* gefährden, in Gefahr bringen.

**endear** [in′diə], *v.a.* beliebt machen. — *v.r.* — *o.s. to*, sich lieb Kind machen bei.

**endearment** [in′diəmənt], *s.* term of —, ein Kosewort.

**endeavour** [in′devə], *v.n.* sich bemühen, sich bestreben. — *s.* das Streben, die Bestrebung, die Bemühung.

**endemic(al)** [en′demik(əl)], *adj.* einheimisch; endemisch.

**endive** [′endiv], *s.* (*Bot.*) die Endivie.

**endless** [′endlis], *adj.* unendlich, endlos.

**endorse** [in′dɔ:s], *v.a.* bestätigen (*confirm*); beipflichten; (*Fin.*) indossieren (*cheque*).

**endorsement** [in′dɔ:smənt], *s.* die Bestätigung (*confirmation*); (*Fin.*) das Indossament (*cheque*).

**endow** [en′dau], *v.a.* begaben (*talents*); ausstatten (*equip*); stiften.

**endowment** [en′daumənt], *s.* die Begabung (*talents*); die Stiftung; — *policy*, die abgekürzte Lebensversicherung.

**endurable** [in′djuərəbl], *adj.* erträglich.

**endurance** [in′djuərəns], *s.* die Ausdauer (*toughness*); die Dauer, Fortdauer (*time*); das Ertragen (*suffering*); — *test*, die Dauerprüfung; (*fig.*) die Geduldsprobe (*patience*).

**endure** [in′djuə], *v.a.* aushalten, ertragen; leiden (*suffer*).

**endways, endwise** [′endweiz, -waiz], *adv.* mit dem Ende nach vorne; aufrecht (*vertical*).

**enemy** [′enəmi], *s.* der Feind, der Gegner.

**energetic** [enə′dʒetik], *adj.* energisch, tatkräftig.

**energy** [′enədʒi], *s.* die Energie, die Tatkraft; der Nachdruck (*vehemence*).

**enervate** [′enə:veit], *v.a.* entkräften, schwächen.

**enervation** [enə:′veiʃən], *s.* die Entkräftigung, die Schwächung.

**enfeeble** [in′fi:bl], *v.a.* entkräften, schwächen.

**enfold** [in′fould], *v.a.* umschließen, umfassen; einhüllen (*veil*).

**enforce** [in′fɔ:s], *v.a.* erzwingen, durchsetzen.

**enforcement** [in′fɔ:smənt], *s.* die Erzwingung, die Durchsetzung.

**enfranchise** [in′fræntʃaiz], *v.a.* freilassen, befreien (*emancipate*); (*Pol.*) das Stimmrecht geben.

**enfranchisement** [in′fræntʃizmənt], *s.* die Befreiung, die Gewährung des Stimmrechts.

**engage** [in'geidʒ], *v.a.* verpflichten, engagieren (*pledge, bind*); anstellen (*employ*); verwickeln (*in conversation*); become —d, sich verloben. — *v.n.* — *in*, sich einlassen in (*Acc.*), sich befassen mit (*Dat.*).

**engagement** [in'geidʒmənt], *s.* das Verpflichtung (*pledge*); die Verlobung (*betrothal*); die Verabredung (*appointment*); das Gefecht (*with enemy*).

**engaging** [in'geidʒiŋ], *adj.* freundlich, verbindlich (*smile etc.*); einnehmend.

**engender** [in'dʒendə], *v.a.* erzeugen, hervorrufen (*cause*).

**engine** ['endʒin], *s.* die Maschine; der Motor; (*Railw.*) die Lokomotive; *fire* —, die Feuerspritze; — *driver*, (*Railw.*) der Lokomotivführer.

**engineer** [endʒi'niə], *s.* der Ingenieur (*professional*); der Techniker (*technician*); (*Am.*) der Lokomotivführer (*engine driver*).

**engineering** [endʒi'niəriŋ], *s.* das Ingenieurwesen; der Maschinenbau; *chemical* —, die chemische Technik *or* Technologie; *civil* —, das Zivilingenieurwesen; *electrical* —, die Elektrotechnik *or* die Elektrotechnologie; *mechanical* —, der Maschinenbau, die Strukturtechnik; — *laboratory*, das technische Labor; — *workshop*, die technische Werkstatt.

**English** ['iŋgliʃ], *adj.* englisch; britisch. — *s.* die englische Sprache, das Englisch; (*pl.*) the —, die Engländer, *m.pl.*

**Englishman** ['iŋgliʃmən], *s.* der Engländer.

**Englishwoman** ['iŋgliʃwumən], *s.* die Engländerin.

**engrain** [in'grein], *v.a.* tief einprägen.

**engrave** [in'greiv], *v.a.* gravieren, eingravieren (*art*); einprägen (*impress*).

**engraver** [in'greivə], *s.* der Graveur, der Kupferstecher.

**engraving** [in'greiviŋ], *s.* der Kupferstich.

**engross** [in'grous], *v.a.* ganz in Anspruch nehmen, gefangen halten(*mind*).

**engulf** [in'gʌlf], *v.a.* verschlingen.

**enhance** [in'hɑːns], *v.a.* erhöhen (*raise*); steigern (*increase*).

**enhancement** [in'hɑːnsmənt], *s.* die Erhöhung (*pleasure*); die Steigerung (*growth*).

**enigma** [i'nigmə], *s.* das Rätsel.

**enigmatic(al)** [enig'mætik(əl)], *adj.* rätselhaft (*puzzling*); dunkel (*obscure*).

**enjoin** [in'dʒɔin], *v.a.* (an)befehlen (*s.o., Dat.*), einschärfen (*s.o., Dat.*).

**enjoy** [in'dʒɔi], *v.a.* genießen (*Acc.*); sich freuen (über, *Acc.*). — *v.r.* — *o.s.*, sich amüsieren.

**enjoyable** [in'dʒɔiəbl], *adj.* erfreulich, angenehm, genießbar.

**enjoyment** [in'dʒɔimənt], *s.* der Genuß, die Freude (*of*, an, *Dat.*).

**enlarge** [in'lɑːdʒ], *v.a.* vergrößern (*premises etc.*); erweitern (*expand*). —

*v.n.* sich verbreiten (*on* or *upon*, über, *Acc.*).

**enlargement** [in'lɑːdʒmənt], *s.* die Vergrößerung (*also Phot.*).

**enlighten** [in'laitn], *v.a.* erleuchten, aufklären (*explain to*).

**enlightenment** [in'laitnmənt], *s.* (*Eccl.*) die Erleuchtung; (*Phil.*)die Aufklärung.

**enlist** [in'list], *v.a.* anwerben (*Mil.*); gewinnen (*cooperation*). — *v.n.* (*Mil.*) sich anwerben lassen.

**enliven** [in'laivn], *v.a.* beleben, aufmuntern.

**enmity** ['enmiti], *s.* die Feindschaft.

**ennoble** [i'noubl], *v.a.* adeln; veredeln.

**enormity** [i'nɔːmiti], *s.* die Ungeheuerlichkeit.

**enormous** [i'nɔːməs], *adj.* ungeheuer; ungeheuerlich.

**enough** [i'nʌf], *adj., adv.* genug; ausreichend; *sure* —, gewiß!; *well* —, ziemlich gut.

**enquire** *see under* inquire.

**enquiry** *see under* inquiry.

**enrage** [in'reidʒ], *v.a.* wütend machen.

**enraged** [in'reidʒd], *adj.* wütend, entrüstet.

**enrapture** [in'ræptʃə], *v.a.* in Entzückung versetzen, entzücken (*delight*).

**enrich** [in'ritʃ], *v.a.* bereichern; (*Chem.*) verbessern.

**enrol** [in'roul], *v.a.* einschreiben (*inscribe*); (*Mil.*) anwerben. — *v.n.* sich einschreiben; beitreten (*Dat.*).

**enrolment** [in'roulmənt], *s.* die Einschreibung; — *form*, das Einschreibeformular.

**ensconce** [in'skɔns], *v.r.* — *o.s.*, sich niederlassen.

**enshrine** [in'ʃrain], *v.a.* umhüllen, einschließen; in einem Schrein aufbewahren.

**enshroud** [in'ʃraud], *v.a.* einhüllen.

**ensign** ['ensin *or* 'enzən, 'ensain], *s.* (*Naut.*) die Fahne, die Flagge; (*Mil. rank*) der Fähnrich.

**enslave** [in'sleiv], *v.a.* unterjochen, versklaven.

**ensnare** [in'snɛə], *v.a.* umgarnen, verführen (*seduce*).

**ensue** [in'sjuː], *v.n.* folgen.

**ensure** [in'ʃuə], *v.a.* versichern (*assure*); sicherstellen (*make sure*).

**entail** [in'teil], *v.a.* zur Folge haben, mit sich bringen.

**entangle** [in'tæŋgl], *v.a.* verwickeln, verwirren (*confuse*).

**entanglement** [in'tæŋglmənt], *s.* die Verwicklung; die Verwirrung (*confusion*).

**enter** ['entə], *v.a.* betreten; eintreten; — *o.'s name*, seinen Namen einschreiben. — *v.n.* eintreten (*in*, in, *Acc.*); — *into agreement*, einen Vertrag eingehen; — *on*, sich einlassen in (*Acc.*); — *upon a career*, eine Laufbahn antreten.

**enterprise** ['entəpraiz], *s.* das Unternehmen; das Wagnis (*daring*); *private* —, das Privatunternehmen; (*Econ.*)

die freie Wirtschaft; *public* —, das staatliche *or* Staatsunternehmen.

**enterprising** ['entəpraiziŋ], *adj.* unternehmungslustig.

**entertain** [entə'tein], *v.a.* unterhalten (*amuse*); zu Tisch haben (*person*); hegen (*opinion*).

**entertaining** [entə'teiniŋ], *adj.* amüsant, unterhaltend.

**entertainment** [entə'teinmənt], *s.* die Unterhaltung, Vergnügung.

**enthral** [in'θrɔ:l], *v.a.* fesseln, bannen.

**enthrone** [in'θroun], *v.a.* auf den Thron bringen *or* setzen.

**enthusiasm** [in'θju:ziæzm], *s.* die Begeisterung; die Schwärmerei.

**enthusiast** [in'θju:ziæst], *s.* der Enthusiast, der Schwärmer.

**enthusiastic** [inθju:zi'æstik], *adj.* enthusiastisch, begeistert, schwärmerisch.

**entice** [in'tais], *v.a.* locken, anlocken, verlocken (*lure*).

**enticement** [in'taismənt], *s.* die Lockung.

**entire** [in'taiə], *adj.* gesamt, ganz; völlig; vollständig (*complete*).

**entirety** [in'taiəriti], *s.* die Gesamtheit (*totality*); das Ganze (*total*).

**entitle** [in'taitl], *v.a.* berechtigen; betiteln (*title*).

**entitlement** [in'taitlmənt], *s.* die Berechtigung.

**entity** ['entiti], *s.* das Wesen.

**entomb** [in'tu:m], *v.a.* begraben.

**entomologist** [entə'mɔlədʒist], *s.* der Entomologe.

**entomology** [entə'mɔlədʒi], *s.* die Entomologie.

**entrails** ['entreilz], *s.pl.* die Eingeweide, *n.pl.*

**entrain** [in'trein], *v.a.* (*Railw., Mil.*) einsteigen lassen. — *v.n.* (*Railw.*) (in den Zug) einsteigen.

**entrance** (1) ['entrəns], *s.* der Eingang (*door*); — *fee*, der Eintritt; — *hall*, der Hausflur, die Vorhalle; *university* —, Zulassung zur Universität.

**entrance** (2) [in'tra:ns], *v.a.* entzücken, hinreißen.

**entrant** [in'trənt], *s.* (*to school, university etc.*) der (neu) Zugelassene; Teilnehmer.

**entrap** [in'træp], *v.a.* fangen, verstricken.

**entreat** [in'tri:t], *v.a.* anflehen, ersuchen.

**entreaty** [in'tri:ti], *s.* die flehentliche *or* dringende Bitte, (*obs.*) das Ansuchen.

**entrench** [in'trentʃ], *v.a.* verschanzen, festsetzen.

**entrenchment** [in'trentʃmənt], *s.* (*Mil.*) die Verschanzung.

**entrust** [in'trʌst], *v.a.* anvertrauen (*s. th.*); betreuen (*s.o. with, mit, Dat.*).

**entry** ['entri], *s.* das Eintreten, der Eintritt; der Eingang (*house*); (*Comm.*) die Eintragung (*book-keeping*); *double* —, doppelte Buchführung; die Einfuhr (*import*); — *permit*, die

Einreisebewilligung; *no* —, Eintritt verboten!

**entwine** [in'twain], *v.a.* verflechten, herumwickeln.

**enumerate** [i'nju:məreit], *v.a.* aufzählen.

**enumeration** [inju:mə'reiʃən], *s.* die Aufzählung.

**enunciate** [i'nʌnsieit], *v.a.* aussprechen.

**enunciation** [inʌnsi'eiʃən], *s.* (*Phonet.*) die Aussprache; die Kundgebung (*declaration*).

**envelop** [in'veləp], *v.a.* einhüllen, umhüllen.

**envelope** ['enviloup, 'ɔnvəloup], *s.* die Hülle; der Umschlag, Briefumschlag (*letter*).

**enviable** ['enviəbl], *adj.* beneidenswert.

**envious** ['enviəs], *adj.* neidisch (*of s.o., auf, Acc.*).

**environment** [in'vairənmənt], *s.* die Umgebung; (*Geog., Zool.*) die Umwelt.

**environs** [in'vairənz], *s. pl.* die Umgebung, die Umgegend.

**envisage** [in'vizidʒ], *v.a.* sich vorstellen.

**envoy** ['envɔi], *s.* (*Pol.*) der Gesandte, der Bote.

**envy** ['envi], *s.* der Neid. — *v.a.* beneiden.

**epaulette** [epə'let], *s.* (*Mil.*) das Achselstück, die Epaulette.

**ephemeral** [i'femərəl], *adj.* Eintags-, Tages-; eintägig, vergänglich (*transient*).

**epic** ['epik], *adj.* episch. — *s.* das Epos.

**epicure** ['epikjuə], *s.* der Epikureer, der Feinschmecker, der Genießer.

**epidemic** [epi'demik], *s.* die Epidemie.

**epigram** ['epigræm], *s.* das Epigramm.

**epigrammatic** [epigrə'mætik], *adj.* epigrammatisch, kurz; treffend (*apt*).

**epilepsy** ['epilepsi], *s.* (*Med.*) die Epilepsie, die Fallsucht.

**epileptik** [epi'leptik], *s.* (*Med.*) der Epileptiker.

**epilogue** ['epilɔg], *s.* der Epilog.

**Epiphany** [i'pifəni], *s.* (*Eccl.*) das Fest der heiligen drei Könige, Epiphanias.

**episcopal** [i'piskəpəl], *adj.* bischöflich.

**episcopate** [i'piskəpit], *s.* die Bischofswürde, das Episkopat (*collective*).

**episode** ['episoud], *s.* die Episode.

**epistle** [i'pisl], *s.* die Epistel, das Sendschreiben.

**epistolary** [i'pistələri], *adj.* brieflich, Brief-.

**epitaph** ['epita:f], *s.* die Grabschrift.

**epithet** ['epiθet], *s.* das Beiwort, die Benennung.

**epitome** [i'pitəmi], *s.* die Epitome, der Auszug; der Abriß (*summary*).

**epitomize** [i'pitəmaiz], *v.a.* kürzen; einen Auszug machen von (*Dat.*).

**epoch** ['i:pɔk], *s.* die Epoche; — — *making*, bahnbrechend.

**equable** ['ekwəbl], *adj.* gleich, gleichmäßig; gleichmütig (*tranquil*).

**equal** ['i:kwəl], *adj.* gleich, ebenbürtig (*to, Dat.*).

**equality** [i'kwɔliti], *s.* die Gleichheit, Ebenbürtigkeit.
**equalization** [i:kwəlai'zeiʃən], *s.* der Ausgleich; — *of burdens,* der Lastenausgleich.
**equalize** ['i:kwəlaiz], *v.a.* gleichmachen. — *v.n.* (*Footb.*) ausgleichen.
**equanimity** [i:kwə'nimiti], *s.* der Gleichmut.
**equate** [i'kweit], *v.a.* (*Maths.*) gleichsetzen.
**equation** [i'kweiʃən], *s.* die Gleichung.
**equator**[i'kweitə], *s.* (*Geog.*)der Äquator.
**equatorial** [ekwə'tɔ:riəl], *adj.* (*Geog.*) äquatorial.
**equerry** ['ekwəri], *s.* der Stallmeister; diensttuender Kammerherr (*of King*).
**equestrian** [i'kwestriən], *adj.* beritten; Reit-; — *art,* die Reitkunst.
**equidistant** [i:kwi'distənt], *adj.* gleich weit entfernt.
**equilateral** [i:kwi'lætərəl], *adj.* gleichseitig.
**equilibrium** [i:kwi'libriəm], *s.* das Gleichgewicht.
**equine** ['i:kwain], *adj.* Pferd-, pferdeartig.
**equinoctial** [i:kwi'nɔkʃəl], *adj.* äquinoktial.
**equinox** ['i:kwinɔks], *s.* die Tag- und Nachtgleiche.
**equip** [i'kwip], *v.a.* (*Mil.*) ausrüsten; ausstatten (*furnish*).
**equipment** [i'kwipmənt], *s.* die Ausrüstung, die Ausstattung; das Zeug.
**equitable** ['ekwitəbl], *adj.* unparteiisch, gerecht, billig.
**equity** ['ekwiti], *s.* die Billigkeit, die Unparteilichkeit.
**equivalence** [i'kwivələns], *s.* die Gleichwertigkeit, die Gleichheit.
**equivalent** [i'kwivələnt], *adj.* gleichwertig. — *s.* das Äquivalent, der gleiche Wert, der Gegenwert.
**equivocal** [i'kwivəkəl], *adj.* zweideutig, doppelsinnig, zweifelhaft.
**era** ['iərə], *s.* die Ära, die Zeitrechnung.
**eradicate** [i'rædikeit], *v.a.* ausrotten, austilgen, vertilgen.
**eradication** [irædi'keiʃən], *s.* die Ausrottung, die Vertilgung.
**erase** [i'reiz], *v.a.* ausradieren.
**eraser** [i'reizə], *s.* der Radiergummi (*India rubber*).
**erasure** [i'reiʒə], *s.* die Ausradierung; die Auskratzung (*scratching*).
**ere** [ɛə], *prep.* (*obs.*) vor. — *conj.* (*obs.*) ehe, bevor.
**erect** [i'rekt], *adj.* aufrecht, gerade. — *v.a.* aufrichten; errichten (*build*).
**erection** [i'rekʃən], *s.* die Errichtung (*structure*); die Aufrichtung (*putting up*).
**ermine** ['ə:min], *s.* der *or* das Hermelin.
**erode** [i'roud], *v.a.* (*Geog., Geol.*) ausfressen.
**erosion** [i'rouʒən], *s.* die Erosion.
**erotic** [i'rɔtik], *adj.* erotisch.
**err** [ə:], *v.n.* irren.
**errand** ['erənd], *s.* der Auftrag, Gang;

der Botengang; — *boy,* der Laufbursche.
**errant** ['erənt], *adj.* herumstreifend; *knight* —, fahrender Ritter.
**errata** *see under* **erratum.**
**erratic** [i'rætik], *adj.* regellos, unberechenbar, ohne Verlaß.
**erratum** [e'reitəm, e'rɑ:təm], *s.* (*pl.* **errata** [e'reitə, e'rɑ:tə]) der Druckfehler.
**erroneous** [i'rouniəs], *adj.* irrig, irrtümlich.
**error** ['erə], *s.* der Irrtum, der Fehler.
**erudite** ['erudait], *adj.* gelehrt.
**erudition** [eru'diʃən], *s.* die Gelehrsamkeit.
**erupt** [i'rʌpt], *v.n.* ausbrechen.
**eruption** [i'rʌpʃən], *s.* der Ausbruch.
**eruptive** [i'rʌptiv], *adj.* Ausbruchs-, ausbrechend.
**escalator** ['eskəleitə], *s.* die Rolltreppe.
**escapade** [eskə'peid], *s.* der Streich (*prank*).
**escape** [is'keip], *v.a.,* *v.n.* entkommen, entgehen, entfliehen.
**escapism** [is'keipizm], *s.* die Philosophie der Weltflucht.
**escapist** [is'keipist], *s.* der Weltflüchtling.
**escarpment** [is'kɑ:pmənt], *s.* die Böschung.
**eschew** [is'tʃu:], *v.a.* vermeiden.
**escort** [is'kɔ:t], *v.a.* geleiten; decken (*cover*). — ['eskɔ:t], *s.* (*Mil.*) die Garde, die Deckung; Begleitung (*persons*); (*Mil.*) das Geleit (*conduct*).
**escutcheon** [is'kʌtʃən], *s.* das Wappenschild.
**esoteric** [eso'terik], *adj.* (*Phil.*) esoterisch, geheim, dunkel.
**espalier** [es'pæljə], *s.* (*Mil.*) das Spalier.
**especial** [is'peʃəl],*adj.* besonder, außergewöhnlich.
**espionage** ['espiənɑ:ʒ *or* -nidʒ], *s.* die Spionage, das Spionieren.
**espouse** [is'pauz], *v.a.* (ver)-heiraten; (*fig.*) eintreten (für, *Acc.*).
**espy** [is'pai], *v.a.* ausspähen, erspähen.
**essay** [e'sei], *v.a.* versuchen, probieren. — ['esei], *s.* der Versuch; der Aufsatz, Essay (*composition*).
**essayist** ['eseiist], *s.* der Essayist.
**essence** ['esəns], *s.* (*Phil., Chem.*) die Essenz.
**essential** [i'senʃəl], *adj.* wesentlich; wichtig (*important*).
**establish** [is'tæbliʃ], *v.a.* feststellen, (*ascertain*); gründen (*found*); —*ed Church,* die englische Staatskirche.
**establishment** [is'tæbliʃmənt], *s.* die Feststellung (*ascertainment*); die Gründung (*foundation*); das Unternehmen, das Geschäft (*business*); (*Mil.*) die Aufstellung, der Bestand; (*Eccl.*) die Staatskirche.
**estate** [is'teit], *s.* (*Pol.*) der Stand; das Vermögen; das Gut; (*property*) — *duty,* die Vermögenssteuer; — *manager,* der Gutsverwalter; — *agent,* der

Grundstückmakler; *real* —, der Grundbesitz; (*pl.*) Immobilien, *pl.*

**esteem** [is'ti:m], *v.a.* schätzen (*value*); achten (*respect*). — *s.* die Wertschätzung, die Achtung.

**estimable** ['estiməbl], *adj.* schätzenswert.

**estimate** ['estimeit], *v.a.* schätzen (*evaluate*); berechnen (*calculate*). — ['estimit], *s.* die. Schätzung, der Voranschlag.

**estimation** [esti'meiʃən], *s.* die Wertschätzung; die Achtung (*respect*).

**Estonian** [es'touniən], *adj.* estnisch, estländisch. — *s.* der Este, Estländer.

**estrange** [is'treindʒ], *v.a.* entfremden.

**estrangement** [is'treindʒmənt], *s.* die Entfremdung.

**estuary** ['estjuəri], *s.* die Mündung (*river*); der Meeresarm (*bay*).

**etch** [etʃ], *v.a.* (*Metall.*) ätzen; (*Art*) radieren.

**etching** ['etʃiŋ], *s.* (*Art*) die Radierung.

**eternal** [i'tə:nl], *adj.* ewig; immerwährend.

**eternity** [i'tə:niti], *s.* die Ewigkeit.

**ether** ['i:θə], *s.* der Äther.

**ethereal** [i'θiəriəl], *adj.* ätherisch, luftig.

**ethical** ['eθikl], *adj.* ethisch, sittlich.

**ethics** ['eθiks], *s. pl.* die Ethik, die Sittenlehre; *professional* —, das Berufsethos.

**Ethiopian** [i:θi'oupiən], *adj.* äthiopisch. — *s.* der Äthiopier.

**ethnography** [eθ'nɔgrəfi], *s.* die Ethnographie, die Völkerkunde.

**etymology** [eti'mɔlədʒi], *s.* die Etymologie, die Wortableitung.

**eucharist** ['ju:kərist], *s.* (*Eccl.*) die Eucharistie; das heilige Abendmahl.

**eulogize** ['ju:lədʒaiz], *v.a.* loben, preisen.

**euphonium** [ju'founiəm], *s.* (*Mus.*) das Bombardon, Baritonhorn.

**euphony** ['ju:fəni], *s.* der Wohlklang.

**European** [juərə'piən], *adj.* europäisch. — *s.* der Europäer.

**euphemism** ['ju:fimizm], *s.* der Euphemismus.

**euphuism** ['ju:fjuizm], *s.* (*Lit.*) der gezierte Stilart.

**evacuate** [i'vækjueit], *v.a.* evakuieren, räumen.

**evacuation** [ivækju'eiʃən], *s.* die Evakuierung, die Räumung.

**evade** [i'veid], *v.a.* ausweichen (*Dat.*); entgehen (*escape, Dat.*).

**evanescent** [evæ'nesənt], *adj.* verschwindend.

**evangelical** [i:væn'dʒelikəl], *adj.* evangelisch.

**evangelist** [i'vændʒəlist], *s.* der Evangelist.

**evangelize** [i'vændʒəlaiz], *v.a., v.n.* das Evangelium lehren *or* predigen.

**evaporate** [i'væpəreit], *v.a.* verdunsten lassen, verdampfen lassen. — *v.n.* (*Chem.*) verdunsten.

**evaporation** [ivæpə'reiʃən], *s.* die Verdampfung, die Verdunstung.

**evasion** [i'veiʒən], *s.* die Flucht (*escape*) (*from*, von, *Dat.*); die Ausflucht, das Ausweichen.

**evasive** [i'veiziv], *adj.* ausweichend.

**eve, even** (1) [i:v,i:vn], *s.* (*Poet.*) der Vorabend; Abend.

**even** (2) [i:vn], *adj.* eben, glatt (*smooth*); gerade (*number*); quitt (*quits*); gelassen (*temper*); gleich (*equal*). — *v.a.* — *out*, gleichmachen, ebnen.

**even** (3) [i:vn], *adv.* gerade, selbst, sogar (*emphatic*); *not* —, nicht einmal; — *though*, obwohl.

**evening** ['i:vniŋ], *s.* der Abend; — *gown*, das Abendkleid; — *dress*, der Abendanzug; der Smoking (*dinner jacket*); der Frack (*tails*).

**evenness** ['i:vənnis], *s.* die Ebenheit (*of surface*); die Gelassenheit (*of temper*).

**event** [i'vent], *s.* die Begebenheit, der Vorfall (*happening*); das (große) Ereignis (*state occasion*); *at all* —*s*, auf alle Fälle; *in the* —, im Falle, daß.

**eventful** [i'ventful], *adj.* ereignisreich.

**eventual** [i'ventjuəl], *adj.* schließlich, endlich.

**ever** ['evə], *adv.* je; immer, stets; nur, überhaupt; *for* —, für immer; — *so*, so sehr, noch so; — *since*, seitdem.

**evergreen** ['evəgri:n], *adj.* immergrün. — *s.* (*Bot.*) das Immergrün.

**everlasting** [evə'la:stiŋ], *adj.* ewig; dauernd; fortwährend (*continual*).

**every** ['evri], *adj.* jeder, jeder einzelne (*pl.* alle); — *one*, jeder einzelne; — *now and then*, dann und wann; — *other day*, jeden zweiten Tag; — *day*, alle Tage.

**everybody, everyone** ['evribɔdi, 'evriwʌn], *s.* jedermann, ein jeder.

**everyday** ['evridei], *adj.* alltäglich.

**everyone** *see under* everybody.

**everything** ['evriθiŋ], *s.* alles.

**everywhere** ['evriʰwɛə], *adv.* überall.

**evict** [i'vikt], *v.a.* vertreiben (*eject*); (*Law*) (gerichtlich) kündigen (*Dat.*).

**eviction** [i'vikʃən], *s.* die Kündigung, die Vertreibung.

**evidence** ['evidəns], *s.* der Beweis (*proof*); (*Law*) das Zeugnis; *documentary* —, (*Law*) das Beweisstück; (*Law*) *give* —, eine Zeugenaussage machen.

**evident** ['evidənt], *adj.* klar, deutlich (*obvious*); augenscheinlich (*visible*); *self*— —, selbstverständlich.

**evil** ['i:vil], *s.* das Übel, das Böse. — *adj.* übel, böse; — *speaking*, die üble Nachrede.

**evildoer** ['i:vildu:ə], *s.* der Übeltäter.

**evince** [i'vins], *v.a.* zeigen, dartun, an den Tag legen.

**evocation** [i:vo'keiʃən], *s.* die Beschwörung (*magic*); das Hervorrufen.

**evocative** [i'vɔkətiv], *adj.* hervorrufend, voll Erinnerungen (*of, Genit.*).

**evoke** [i'vouk], *v.a.* hervorrufen (*call forth*); beschwören (*conjure up*).

**evolution** [i:və'lju:ʃən, ev–], *s.* die Entwicklung, Evolution.

# evolutionary

**evolutionary** [i:vəˈlju:ʃənri], *adj.* Evolutions-, Entwicklungs-.

**evolve** [iˈvɔlv], *v.a.* entwickeln. — *v.n.* sich entwickeln.

**ewe** [ju:], *s.* (*Zool.*) das Mutterschaf.

**ewer** [ˈjuə], *s.* die Wasserkanne.

**exact** [igˈzækt], *adj.* genau, gewissenhalf, exakt. — *v.a.* fordern; erpressen; eintreiben (*dept.*).

**exacting** [igˈzæktiŋ], *adj.* genau, anspruchsvoll.

**exactitude** [igˈzæktitju:d], *s.* die Genauigkeit.

**exactly** [igˈzæktli], *adv.* (*coll.*) ganz richtig!

**exactness** [igˈzæktnis], *s.* die Genauigkeit.

**exaggerate** [igˈzædʒəreit], *v.a.* übertreiben.

**exaggeration** [igzædʒəˈreiʃən], *s.* die Übertreibung.

**exalt** [igˈzɔ:lt], *v.a.* erhöhen, erheben.

**exaltation** [egzɔ:lˈteiʃən], *s.* die Erhöhung, die Erhebung.

**exalted** [igˈzɔ:ltid], *adj.* erhaben, hoch.

**examination** [igzæmiˈneiʃən], *s.* die Prüfung. (*Med.*) die Untersuchung; (*Law*) das Verhör, das Untersuchungsverhör; die Ausfragung (*scrutiny*); — *board,* die Prüfungskommission.

**examine** [igˈzæmin], *v.a.* prüfen; (*Med.*) untersuchen; (*Law*) verhören; ausfragen.

**examiner** [igˈzæminə], *s.* der Examinator.

**example** [igˈza:mpl], *s.* das Beispiel; *for* —, zum Beispiel; *set an* —, ein Beispiel geben.

**exasperate** [igˈzæspəreit], *v.a.* aufreizen; ärgern, aufbringen.

**exasperation** [igzæspəˈreiʃən], *s.* die Entrüstung, die Erbitterung.

**excavate** [ˈekskəveit], *v.a.* ausgraben.

**excavation** [ekskəˈveiʃən], *s.* die Ausgrabung.

**exceed** [ikˈsi:d], *v.a.* überschreiten (*go beyond*); übertreffen (*surpass*). — *v.n.* zu weit gehen.

**exceeding** [ikˈsi:diŋ], *adj.* (*obs.*) übermäßig, übertrieben.

**exceedingly** [ikˈsi:diŋli], *adv.* außerordentlich; äußerst.

**excel** [ikˈsel], *v.a.* übertreffen. — *v.n.* sich auszeichnen (*in*, in, *Dat.*).

**excellence** [ˈeksələns], *s.* die Vortrefflichkeit.

**excellent** [ˈeksələnt], *adj.* ausgezeichnet, hervorragend.

**except** [ikˈsept], *v.a.* ausnehmen, ausschließen. — *conj.* außer (es sei denn) daß. — *prep.* ausgenommen, mit Ausnahme von (*Dat.*).

**exception** [ikˈsepʃən], *s.* die Ausnahme (*exemption*); der Einwand, Einwurf (*objection*).

**exceptionable** [ikˈsepʃənəbl], *adj.* anfechtbar (*disputable*); anstößig.

**exceptional** [ikˈsepʃənəl], *adj.* außergewöhnlich.

**exceptionally** [ikˈsepʃənəli], *adv.* ausnahmsweise.

**excerpt** [ikˈsə:pt], *v.a.* ausziehen, exzerpieren. — [ˈeksə:pt], *s.* der Auszug, das Exzerpt.

**excess** [ikˈses], *s.* das Übermaß; *carry to* —, übertreiben; — *fare,* der Zuschlag; — *luggage,* das Übergewicht.

**excessive** [ikˈsesiv], *adj.* übermäßig, allzuviel.

**exchange** [iksˈtʃeindʒ], *s.* der Austausch; *stock* —, die Börse; *rate of* —, der Kurs; *bill of* —, der Wechsel; der Tausch (*barter*). — *v.a.* wechseln; tauschen (*barter*) (*against,* für, *Acc.*); austauschen (*messages etc.*).

**exchangeable** [iksˈtʃeindʒəbl], *adj.* (*Comm.*) austauschbar.

**exchequer** [iksˈtʃekə], *s.* die Staatskasse; das Finanzamt (*office*); *Chancellor of the Exchequer,* der Schatzkanzler.

**excise** [ˈeksaiz], *s.* die Akzise; *customs and* —, das Zollamt, der Zoll; — *officer,* der Zollbeamte, Steuerbeamte.

**excise** (2) [ekˈsaiz], *v.a.* (her)ausschneiden.

**excision** [ekˈsiʒən], *s.* das Ausschneiden, die Entfernung.

**excitable** [ikˈsaitəbl], *adj.* erregbar, reizbar.

**excitation** [eksiˈteiʃən], *s.* (*Phys.*, *Chem.*) die Erregung.

**excitement** [ikˈsaitmənt], *s.* die Erregung, Aufregung (*mood*).

**exciting** [ikˈsaitiŋ], *adj.* erregend, aufregend, packend (*thrilling*).

**exclaim** [iksˈkleim], *v.a.* ausrufen.

**exclamation** [ekskləˈmeiʃən], *s.* der Ausruf (*interjection*); das Geschrei (*shouting*).

**exclude** [iksˈklu:d], *v.a.* ausschließen.

**exclusion** [iksˈklu:ʒən], *s.* der Ausschluß.

**exclusive** [iksˈklu:siv], *adj.* ausschließlich (*sole*); exklusiv (*select*).

**exclusiveness** [iksˈklu:sivnis], *s.* der exklusive Charakter, die Exklusivität.

**excommunicate** [ekskəˈmju:nikeit], *v.a.* (*Eccl.*) von der Kirchengemeinde ausschließen, bannen, exkommunizieren.

**excommunication** [ekskəmju:niˈkeiʃən], *s.* (*Eccl.*) die Exkommunikation, der Bann.

**excoriate** [eksˈkɔ:rieit], *v.a.* häuten; abschälen (*peel*).

**excrement** [ˈekskrimənt], *s.* das Exkrement, der Kot.

**excrescence** [iksˈkresəns], *s.* der Auswuchs.

**excretion** [eksˈkri:ʃən], *s.* die Ausscheidung, der Auswurf.

**excruciate** [iksˈkru:ʃieit], *v.a.* martern, peinigen; *excruciatingly funny,* furchtbar komisch.

**exculpate** [ˈekskʌlpeit], *v.a.* rechtfertigen, entschuldigen.

**exculpation** [ekskʌl'peiʃən], s. die Entschuldigung, die Rechtfertigung.

**excursion** [iks'kə:ʃən], s. der Ausflug, die Exkursion (*outing*); die Digression (*irrelevance*); der Abstecher (*deviation*).

**excusable** [iks'kju:zəbl], adj. entschuldbar, verzeihlich.

**excuse** [iks'kju:s], s. die Entschuldigung. — [-'kju:z], v.a. entschuldigen (*Acc.*), verzeihen (*Dat.*).

**execrable** ['eksikrəbl], adj. abscheulich.

**execrate** ['eksikreit], v.a. verfluchen, verwünschen.

**execute** ['eksikju:t], v.a. ausführen (*carry out*); (*Law*) hinrichten (*kill*).

**execution** [eksi'kju:ʃən], s. die Ausführung (*of an order*); (*Law*) die Hinrichtung; die Pfändung (*official forfeit*).

**executioner** [eksi'kju:ʃənə], s. der Henker, der Scharfrichter.

**executive** [ik'sekjutiv], adj. ausübend, vollziehend (*of power etc.*). — s. (*Pol.*) die Exekutive; (*Comm.*) das Direktionsmitglied.

**executor** [ik'sekjutə], s. der Testamentsvollstrecker (*of a will*).

**exemplar** [ig'zemplə], s. das Muster, das Beispiel.

**exemplary** [ig'zempləri], adj. musterhaft, vorbildlich.

**exemplify** [ig'zemplifai], v.a. durch Beispiel(e) erläutern.

**exempt** [ig'zempt], v.a. ausnehmen, befreien, verschonen (*spare*).

**exemption** [ig'zempʃən], s. die Ausnahme.

**exequies** ['eksikwiz], s. pl. das Leichenbegängnis, die Totenfeier.

**exercise** ['eksəsaiz], s. die Übung (*practice*); die körperliche Betätigung (*exertion*). — v.a. üben; — o.'s rights, von seinen Rechten Gebrauch machen; — discretion, Diskretion walten lassen; (*Mil.*) — troops, exerzieren.

**exert** [ig'zə:t], v.a. ausüben; — pressure, Druck ausüben (*upon*, auf, *Acc.*). — v.r. — o.s., sich anstrengen.

**exertion** [ig'zə:ʃən], s. die Anstrengung, die Bemühung.

**exhalation** [eksho'leiʃən], s. die Ausatmung, die Ausdünstung.

**exhale** [eks'heil], v.a. ausatmen; aushauchen; ausdünsten.

**exhaust** [ig'zɔ:st], v.a. erschöpfen. — s. (*Motor.*) der Auspuff.

**exhaustible** [ig'zɔ:stibl], adj. erschöpflich.

**exhaustion** [ig'zɔ:stʃən], s. die Erschöpfung.

**exhibit** [ig'zibit], v.a. ausstellen (*display*); zeigen (*demonstrate*). — ['eksibit], s. das Ausstellungsobjekt; (*Law*) das Beweisstück.

**exhibition** [eksi'biʃən], s. die Ausstellung (*display*); (*Films*) die Vorführung (*showing*); das Stipendium (*scholarship*).

**exhibitioner** [eksi'biʃənə], s. der Stipendiat.

**exhilarate** [ig'ziləreit], v.a. aufheitern.

**exhilaration** [igzilə'reiʃən], s. die Aufheiterung.

**exhort** [ig'zɔ:t], v.a. ermahnen.

**exhortation** [egzɔ:'teiʃən], s. die Ermahnung.

**exigence, exigency** ['eksidʒəns, -si], s. das Bedürfnis, Erfordernis (*necesity*); der dringende Notfall (*emergency*).

**exigent** ['eksidʒənt], adj. dringend.

**exile** ['eksail], s. der Verbannte (*person*); das Exil, die Verbannung (*state*). — v.a. verbannen; des Landes verweisen.

**exist** [ig'zist], v.n. existieren.

**existence** [ig'zistəns], s. das Dasein, die Existenz.

**existent** [ig'zistənt], adj. seiend, wirklich, existierend.

**existentialism** [egzis'tenʃəlizm], s. der Existentialismus.

**exit** ['eksit], s. der Ausgang; (*Theat.*) der Abgang.

**exonerate** [ig'zonəreit], v.a. entlasten.

**exorbitant** [ig'zɔ:bitənt], adj. übertrieben, übermäßig.

**exorcise** ['eksɔ:saiz], v.a. bannen, beschwören.

**exorcism** ['eksɔ:sizm], s. die Geisterbeschwörung.

**exotic** [ig'zɔtik], adj. exotisch.

**expand** [iks'pænd], v.a. erweitern, ausbreiten, ausdehnen. — v.n. sich erweitern (*broaden*); sich ausdehnen (*stretch*).

**expansion** [iks'pænʃən], s. die Ausdehnung, die Ausbreitung.

**expansive** [iks'pænsiv], adj. ausgedehnt; Ausdehnungs- (*forces*); (*fig.*) mitteilsam.

**expatiate** [iks'peiʃieit], v.n. sich verbreiten (*on*, über, *Acc.*).

**expatriate** [eks'peitrieit], v.a. verbannen.

**expect** [iks'pekt], v.a. erwarten (*wait for*); glauben (*believe*); hoffen (*hope for*); — a baby, ein Kind erwarten.

**expectant** [iks'pektənt], adj. schwanger (*with child*); voll Erwartung.

**expectation** [ekspek'teiʃən], s. die Erwartung, die Hoffnung.

**expedience, expediency** [iks'pi:diəns, -si], s. die Zweckmäßigkeit, die Schicklichkeit.

**expedient** [iks'pi:diənt], adj. zweckmäßig, schicklich, ratsam. — s. das Mittel; der Ausweg.

**expedite** ['ekspidait], v.a. beschleunigen.

**expedition** [ekspi'diʃən], s. (*Mil. etc.*) die Expedition; die schnelle Abfertigung.

**expeditious** [ekspi'diʃəs], adj. schleunig, schnell.

**expel** [iks'pel], v.a. vertreiben, austreiben; (*Sch.*) verweisen (*from*, von, aus).

**expend** [iks'pend], v.a. ausgeben.

**expenditure** [iks'penditʃə], s. (*Comm.*) die Ausgabe; der Aufwand (*of energy*).

**expense** [iks'pens], *s.* die Ausgabe; (*pl.*) die Kosten, Auslagen, Spesen, *f. pl.*

**expensive** [iks'pensiv], *adj.* teuer, kostspielig.

**experience** [iks'piəriəns], *s.* die Erfahrung, das Erlebnis. — *v.a.* erfahren.

**experienced** [iks'piəriənsd], *adj.* erfahren.

**experiment** [iks'perimənt], *s.* das Experiment, der Versuch. — *v.n.* experimentieren, Versuche machen.

**experimental** [iksperi'mentl], *adj.* Probe-, probeweise, experimentell.

**expert** ['ekspə:t], *s.* der Fachmann; der Sachverständige.

**expertise** [ekspə'ti:z], *s.* die Expertise, die Fachkenntnis.

**expertness** [iks'pə:tnis], *s.* die Gewandtheit.

**expiable** ['ekspiəbl], *adj.* sühnbar.

**expiation** [ekspi'eiʃən], *s.* die Sühnung, die Sühne.

**expiration** [ekspi'reiʃən], *s.* das Ausatmen; (*fig.*) der Tod; der Ablauf (*time*); die Verfallszeit (*lapse of validity*).

**expire** [iks'paiə], *v.n.* aushauchen (*breathe*); ablaufen (*run out*); sterben (*die*).

**expiry** [iks'paiəri], *s.* die Ablaufsfrist (*of papers*).

**explain** [iks'plein], *v.a.* erklären, erläutern.

**explanation** [eksplə'neiʃən], *s.* die Erklärung, Erläuterung.

**expletive** [iks'pli:tiv], *s.* das Fluchwort, der Kraftausdruck.

**explicable** ['eksplikəbl], *adj.* erklärlich, erklärbar.

**explication** [ekspli'keiʃən], *s.* die Erklärung.

**explicit** [iks'plisit], *adj.* ausdrücklich, deutlich.

**explicitness** [iks'plisitnis], *s.* die Deutlichkeit, die Bestimmtheit.

**explode** [iks'ploud], *v.n.* explodieren; (*Mil.*) platzen (*of a shell*). — *v.a.* explodieren lassen.

**exploit** [iks'plɔit], *v.a.* ausbeuten; ausnützen (*utilize*). — ['eksplɔit], *s.* die Heldentat, die Großtat.

**exploitation** [eksplɔi'teiʃən], *s.* die Ausbeutung, die Ausnützung.

**exploration** [eksplɔ:'reiʃən], *s.* die Erforschung.

**explore** [iks'plɔ:], *v.a.* erforschen, untersuchen (*investigate*).

**explosion** [iks'plouʒən], *s.* die Explosion.

**explosive** [iks'plousiv], *adj.* explosiv. — *s.* der Sprengstoff.

**exponent** [iks'pounənt], *s.* (*Maths.*) der Exponent; der Vertreter (*of a theory*).

**export** [iks'pɔ:t], *v.a.* ausführen, exportieren. — ['ekspɔ:t], *s.* der Export, die Ausfuhr.

**exporter** [eks'pɔ:tə], *s.* der Exporteur, der Ausfuhrhändler, der Exportkaufmann.

**expose** [iks'pouz], *v.a.* entblößen; aussetzen (*to cold etc.*); bloßstellen (*display*); (*Phot.*) belichten; darlegen (*set forth*); ausstellen (*exhibit*).

**exposition** [ekspo'ziʃən], *s.* die Aussetzung; die Auslegung (*interpretation*); die Darlegung (*deposition, declaration*); die Ausstellung (*exhibition*).

**exposure** [iks'pouʒə], *s.* die Aussetzung (*to cold etc.*); die Bloßstellung; (*Phot.*) die Belichtung.

**expostulate** [iks'pɔstjuleit], *v.n.* zur Rede stellen.

**expound** [iks'paund], *v.a.* auslegen, darlegen.

**express** [iks'pres], *v.a.* ausdrücken; zum Ausdruck bringen. — *adj.* ausdrücklich, eilig, Eil-; besonder; — *letter*, der Eilbrief; — *train*, der Schnellzug. — *s.* der Eilzug.

**expression** [iks'preʃən], *s.* der Ausdruck.

**expressive** [iks'presiv], *adj.* ausdrucksvoll.

**expressly** [iks'presli], *adv.* ausdrücklich, besonders.

**expropriate** [eks'prouprieit], *v.a.* enteignen.

**expropriation** [eksproupri'eiʃən], *s.* die Enteignung.

**expulsion** [iks'pʌlʃən], *s.* die Ausstoßung; der Ausschluß; die Vertreibung (*of a large number*).

**expunge** [iks'pʌndʒ], *v.a.* austilgen, auslöschen.

**expurgate** ['ekspə:geit], *v.a.* reinigen.

**exquisite** ['ekskwizit], *adj.* auserlesen, vortrefflich.

**extant** ['ekstənt, ek'stænt], *adj.* noch vorhanden, existierend.

**extempore** [eks'tempəri], *adv.* aus dem Stegreif, extemporiert.

**extemporize** [eks'tempəraiz], *v.a.* extemporieren, improvisieren.

**extend** [iks'tend], *v.a.* ausdehnen (*boundaries etc.*); ausstrecken (*a helping hand*); verlängern (*time*); bieten (*a welcome*); erweitern (*enlarge*). — *v.n.* sich erstrecken, sich ausdehnen; dauern (*time*).

**extensible** [iks'tensibl], *adj.* ausdehnbar.

**extension** [iks'tenʃən], *s.* die Ausdehnung; die Verlängerung (*time*); *university — classes*, Abendkurse, *m.pl.* (der Erwachsenenbildung); (*Telephone*) der Apparat.

**extensive** [iks'tensiv], *adj.* ausgedehnt, umfassend.

**extent** [iks'tent], *s.* die Ausdehnung, die Weite; die Größe (*size*); *to a certain —*, bis zu einem gewissen Grade; *to the — of £x*, bis zu einem Betrage von x Pfund.

**extenuate** [iks'tenjueit], *v.a.* beschönigen; mildern; *extenuating circumstances*, (*Law*) mildernde Umstände, *m. pl.*

**extenuation** [ikstenju'eiʃən], *s.* die Beschönigung, die Abschwächung.

**exterior** [eks'tiəriə], *adj.* äußerlich. — *s.* das Äußere.

**exterminate** [iks'tə:mineit], *v.a.* ausrotten, vertilgen.

**extermination** [ikstə:mi'neiʃən], *s.* die Ausrottung, die Vertilgung.

**external** [eks'tə:nl], *adj.* äußerlich; auswärtig.

**extinct** [iks'tiŋkt], *adj.* ausgestorben.

**extinction** [iks'tiŋkʃən], *s.* das Erlöschen (*dying*); die Vernichtung (*annihilation*); das Aussterben.

**extinguish** [iks'tiŋgwiʃ], *v.a.* auslöschen; vernichten (*annihilate*). — *v.n.* auslöschen, ausgehen (*of fire* or *life*).

**extirpate** ['ekstə:peit], *v.a.* ausrotten.

**extol** [iks'toul], *v.a.* preisen, erheben.

**extort** [iks'tɔ:t], *v.a.* erpressen.

**extortion** [iks'tɔ:ʃən], *s.* die Erpressung.

**extortionate** [iks'tɔ:ʃənit], *adj.* erpresserisch.

**extra** ['ekstrə], *adj.* zusätzlich. — *s.* (*pl.*) die Nebenausgaben, *f. pl.*

**extract** [iks'trækt], *v.a.* (aus)ziehen (*pull out*). — ['ekstrækt], *s.* (*Chem.*) der Extrakt; der Auszug (*book*).

**extraction** [iks'trækʃən], *s.* das Ausziehen (*pulling out*); das Zahnziehen (*tooth*); das Verfertigen eines Auszuges (*book*); die Herkunft (*origin*).

**extradite** ['ekstrədait], *v.a.* (*Pol.*) ausliefern.

**extradition** [ekstrə'diʃən], *s.* (*Pol.*) die Auslieferung.

**extraneous** [eks'treiniəs], *adj.* nicht zur Sache gehörig, unwesentlich.

**extraordinary** [iks'trɔ:dnəri], *adj.* außerordentlich.

**extravagance** [iks'trævəgəns], *s.* die Extravaganz; die Verschwendung (*waste*).

**extravagant** [iks'trævəgənt], *adj.* extravagant; verschwenderisch.

**extravaganza** [ikstrævə'gænzə], *s.* fantastisches Werk, die Burleske, Posse.

**extreme** [iks'tri:m], *adj.* äußerst (*uttermost*); höchst (*highest*); extrem (*stringent*); letzt (*last*); — **unction**, (*Eccl.*) die Letzte Ölung; **in the —**, äußerst.

**extremity** [iks'tremiti], *s.* die äußerste Grenze (*limit*); die Notlage (*straits*, *emergency*); (*pl.*) die Extremitäten, *f. pl.*

**extricate** ['ekstrikeit], *v.a.* herauswinden, herauswickeln (*disentangle*), befreien.

**extrude** [eks'tru:d], *v.a.* ausstoßen; (*Metall.*) ausziehen.

**extrusion** [eks'tru:ʒən], *s.* die Ausstoßung; die Ausziehung (*of steel etc.*).

**exuberant** [ig'zju:bərənt], *adj.* überschwenglich, überschäumend.

**exude** [ig'sju:d], *v.a.* ausschwitzen; von sich geben (*give out*).

**exult** [ig'zʌlt], *v.n.* frohlocken.

**exultant** [ig'zʌltənt], *adj.* triumphierend.

**exultation** [egzʌl'teiʃən], *s.* das Frohlocken, der Jubel.

**eye** [ai], *v.a.* ansehen, betrachten. — *s.* das Auge; — *of a needle*, das Nadelöhr; **an — for an —**, Aug' um Auge; **— witness**, der Augenzeuge.

**eyeball** ['aibɔ:l], *s.* der Augapfel.

**eyebrow** ['aibrau], *s.* die Augenbraue.

**eyeglass** ['aiglɑ:s], *s.* der Zwicker, Klemmer.

**eyelash** ['ailæʃ], *s.* die Augenwimper.

**eyelid** ['ailid], *s.* das Augenlid.

**eyesight** ['aisait], *s.* die Sehkraft, das Augenlicht.

**eyrie** ['ɛəri, 'iəri], *s.* der Adlerhorst.

# F

**F** [ef]. das F (*also Mus.*).

**fable** [feibl], *s.* die Fabel; das Märchen.

**fabric** ['fæbrik], *s.* das Gewebe, der Stoff.

**fabricate** ['fæbrikeit], *v.a.* herstellen; (*fig.*) fabrizieren; erfinden.

**fabrication** [fæbri'keiʃən], *s.* (*fig.*) die Erdichtung, die Erfindung.

**fabulous** ['fæbjuləs], *adj.* fabelhaft; wunderbar.

**façade** [fə'sɑ:d], *s.* die Fassade.

**face** [feis], *v.a.* jemandem ins Gesicht sehen (*s.o.*); gegenüberstehen, gegenüberliegen (*lie opposite, Dat.*); — *west*, nach Westen gehen (*of house, window*). — *v.n.* — *about*, sich umdrehen. — *s.* das Gesicht, (*Poet.*) das Angesicht; — *to* — *with*, gegenüber (*Dat.*); *on the* — *of it*, auf den ersten Blick; *lose* —, sich blamieren; *have the* — *to*, die Frechheit haben etwas zu tun.

**facet** ['fæsit], *s.* die Facette; der Zug (*feature*).

**facetious** [fə'si:ʃəs], *adj.* scherzhaft.

**facetiousness** [fə'si:ʃəsnis], *s.* die Scherzhaftigkeit, die Witzigkeit.

**facile** ['fæsail], *adj.* leicht.

**facilitate** [fə'siliteit], *v.a.* erleichtern, leicht machen.

**facility** [fə'siliti], *s.* die Leichtigkeit (*ease*); die Gewandtheit (*deftness*); die Möglichkeit (*possibility*); (*pl.*) die Einrichtungen, die Möglichkeiten, *f. pl. (amenities).*

**facing** ['feisiŋ], *s.* (*Tail.*) der Besatz, der Aufschlag; (*Build.*) die Verkleidung; (*Mil.*) die Schwenkung, die Wendung.

**facsimile** [fæk'simili], *s.* das Faksimile.

**fact** [fækt], *s.* die Tatsache; *as a matter of* —, tatsächlich, in Wirklichkeit; **—s *and figures*,** der Bericht mit Tatsachen und Zahlen; *in* —, tatsächlich; *in point of* —, in der Tat, in Wirklichkeit.

**faction** ['fækʃən], *s.* (*Pol.*) die Partei, die Faktion.

**factitious** [fæk'tiʃəs], *adj.* nachgemacht, künstlich.

**factor** ['fæktə], *s.* der Faktor; (*Comm.*) der Agent; der Umstand (*fact*).

# factory

**factory** ['fæktəri], *s.* die Fabrik; — *hand*, der Fabrikarbeiter.

**factual** ['fæktjuel], *adj.* Tatsachen-, tatsächlich.

**faculty** ['fækəlti], *s.* (*Univ.*) die Fakultät; die Fähigkeit (*sense*); (*pl.*) die Talente, *n. pl.*, die Begabung; Kräfte, *f. pl.*

**fad** [fæd], *s.* die Grille, die Laune; die Marotte.

**faddy** ['fædi], *adj.* schrullig.

**fade** [feid], *v.n.* verschießen (*colour*); verwelken (*flower*); vergehen.

**fag** [fæg], *v.a.* ermüden. — *v.n.* (*Sch.*) Dienste tun, Diener sein (*for*, für). — *s.* die Plackerei; (*coll.*) die Zigarette; (*Sch.*) der Fuchs, der neue Schüler; — *end*, der Zigarettenstummel; (*Naut.*) das offene Tauende; der letze Rest (*remnant*).

**faggot** ['fægət], *s.* das Reisigbündel.

**fail** [feil], *v.a.* im Stiche lassen (*let down*); (*Sch.*) durchfallen (*an examination*, in einer Prüfung). — *v.n.* — *to do*, etwas nicht tun, fehlgehen, scheitern; versagen.

**failing** ['feiliŋ], *adj.* schwach, versagend. — *s.* der Mangel, Fehler.

**failure** ['feiljə], *s.* der Fehlschlag; das Versagen (*weakness*); das Nichteinhalten (*non-compliance*); das Durchfallen (*in examinations*); der Versager (*person*).

**fain** [fein], *adv.* (*obs.*) gern, gerne.

**faint** [feint], *v.n.* in Ohnmacht fallen, ohnmächtig werden. — *adj.* leise, schwach (*noise etc.*); — *hearted*, kleinmütig.

**fair** (1) [fɛə], *adj.* hübsch, schön (*beautiful*); unparteiisch, fair (*impartial*); anständig, angemessen (*equitable*); blond.

**fair** (2) [fɛə], *s.* der Jahrmarkt (*market*); (*Comm.*) die Messe, die Handelsmesse.

**fairness** ['fɛənis], *s.* die Schönheit (*beauty*); die Unparteilichkeit, Fairneß (*objectivity*); die Sportlichkeit (*sportsmanship*); die Anständigkeit (*equity*).

**fairy** ['fɛəri], *s.* die Fee.

**faith** [feiθ], *s.* der Glaube; die Treue (*loyalty*); das Vertrauen (*trust*).

**faithful** ['feiθful], *adj.* (*Rel.*) gläubig; treu (*loyal*); ergeben (*devoted*).

**faithless** ['feiθlis], *adj.* (*Rel.*) ungläubig; treulos, untreu (*disloyal*).

**fake** [feik], *s.* der Schwindel.

**falcon** ['fɔ:(l)kən], *s.* (*Orn.*) der Falke.

**falconer** ['fɔ:(l)kənə], *s.* der Falkner.

**falconry** ['fɔ:(l)kənri], *s.* die Falknerei.

**fall** [fɔ:l], *v.n. irr.* fallen, abfallen (*leaves*); einbrechen (*night*); sich legen (*wind*); heruntergehen, sinken (*price*); geboren werden (*pigs, lambs*); — *through*, mißlingen, zunichte werden. — *s.* der Fall; (*Am.*) der Herbst (*autumn*); der Abhang (*precipice*); der Verfall (*decay*);der Untergang (*decline*).

**fallacious** [fə'leifəs], *adj.* trügerisch, trüglich, falsch (*assumption etc.*).

**fallacy** ['fæləsi], *s.* die Täuschung, der Irrtum, Trugschluß.

**fallible** ['fælibl], *adj.* fehlbar.

**falling** ['fɔ:liŋ], *s.* das Fallen; — *sickness*, die Fallsucht; — *off*, das Abnehmen (*decrease*); — *out*, der Zwist, der Streit (*disunity*). — *adj.* — *star*, die Sternschnuppe.

**fallow** (1) ['fælou], *adj.* brach.

**fallow** (2) ['fælou], *adj.* fahl.

**false** [fɔ:ls], *adj.* falsch, unrichtig (*untrue*); — *alarm*, der blinde Alarm; — *bottom*, der Doppelboden; — *start*, der Fehlstart; — *step*, der Fehltritt; — *verdict*, das Fehlurteil; — *pretences*, die Vorspiegelung falscher Tatsachen.

**falsehood** ['fɔ:lshud], *s.* die Lüge, die Unwahrheit.

**falseness** ['fɔ:lsnis], *s.* die Falschheit; die Unfrichtigkeit (*insincerity*).

**falsify** ['fɔl'sifai], *v.a.* (ver-)fälschen.

**falsity** ['fɔ:lsiti] *see* falseness.

**falter** ['fɔ:ltə], *v.n.* straucheln (*stumble*); stammeln (*stammer*).

**fame** [feim], *s.* der Ruhm; der Ruf; *ill* —, der üble Ruf.

**familiar** [fə'miljə], *adj.* vertraut, wohlbekannt, intim; gewohnt (*habitual*); *be on* — *terms*, auf vertrautem Fuß stehen.

**familiarity** [fəmili'æriti],*s.*die Vertrautheit, die Vertraulichkeit (*intimacy*).

**familiarize** [fə'miljəraiz], *v.a.* vertraut machen, bekannt machen.

**family** ['fæmili], *s.* die Familie; — *doctor*, der Hausarzt; (*Chem.*) die Gruppe; *be in the* — *way*, in anderen Umständen sein, guter Hoffnung sein, schwanger sein; — *tree*, der Stammbaum.

**famine** ['fæmin], *s.* die Hungersnot; — *relief*, Hilfe für die Hungernden.

**famish** ['fæmiʃ], *v.n.* verhungern, hungern; verschmachten.

**famous** ['feiməs], *adj.* berühmt, wohlbekannt (*for*, wegen).

**fan** [fæn], *s.* der Fächer (*lady's*); der Ventilator; (*sl.*) der leidenschaftliche Anhänger, der Fan; (*coll.*) Fanatiker (*admirer*). — *v.a.* fächeln; anfachen (*flames*); entfachen (*hatred*). — *v.n.* (*Mil.*) — *out*, sich ausbreiten, ausschwärmen.

**fanatic** [fə'nætik], *s.* der Fanatiker.

**fanatical** [fə'nætikəl], *adj.* fanatisch.

**fanaticism** [fə'nætisizm], *s.* der Fanatismus, die Schwärmerei.

**fancier** ['fænsiə] *s. pigeon* —, der Taubenzüchter; *bird* —, der Vogelzüchter.

**fanciful** ['fænsiful], *adj.* schwärmerisch, wunderlich.

**fancy** ['fænsi], *s.* die Vorliebe (*preference*); die Phantasie; die Laune (*whim*); *take a* — *to*, leibgewinnen. — *adj.* — *dress*, der Maskenanzug, das Kostüm; — *goods*, Galanteriewaren; — *cakes*, Torten, *f.pl.*; das Feingebäck. — *v.a.* denken, gern haben; (*coll.*) —*oneself as*, sich einbilden, man sei; *just*—*!* denk doch mal! denk mal an!

**fanfare** ['fænfɛə], s. (Mus.) die Fanfare, der Tusch.

**fang** [fæŋ], s. (Zool.) der Hauzahn, der Giftzahn (of snake); (Engin.) der Zapfen. — v.a. (Engin.) vollpumpen, aufpumpen und in Tätigkeit setzen.

**fanlight** ['fænlait], s. die Lünette, das Lichtfenster.

**fantastic(al)** [fæn'tæstik(əl)], adj. fantastisch.

**fantasy** ['fæntəsi], s. (Poet., Mus.) die Phantasie; das Hirngespinst (chimæra).

**far** [fɑ:], adj. weit; fern, entfernt (distant). — adv. — and wide, weit und breit; by —, bei weitem; go too —, zu weit gehen; he will go —, er wird seinen Weg machen; — sighted, weitsichtig.

**farce** [fɑ:s], s. die Farce, die Posse.

**fare** [fɛə], s. das Fahrgeld; der Fahrpreis (of taxi etc.); der Fahrgast (one travelling in taxi); — stage, die Teilstrecke; das Essen, die Kost (food); bill of —, die Speisekarte. — v.n. ergehen (Dat.), daran sein.

**farewell** [fɛə'wel], interj. lebewohl! — dinner, das Abschiedsessen; — party, die Abschiedsgesellschaft.

**farinaceous** [færi'neiʃəs], adj. mehlig, aus Mehl.

**farm** [fɑ:m], s. der Pachthof, der Bauernhof; die Farm; — hand, der Landarbeiter, der Farmarbeiter; — bailiff, der Gutsverwalter. — v.a. bebauen; — out, verpachten. — v.n. Landwirt sein.

**farmer** ['fɑ:mə], s. der Bauer, Landwirt; der Pächter (tenant).

**farmland** ['fɑ:mlænd], s. das Ackerland.

**farmyard** ['fɑ:mjɑ:d], s. der Bauernhof, Gutshof.

**farrier** ['færiə], s. der Hufschmied.

**farrow** ['færou], s. der Wurf (pigs). — v.n. ferkeln, Junge haben.

**farther** ['fɑ:ðə], comp. adj., adv. ferner, weiter.

**farthest** ['fɑ:ðist], superl. adj., adv. fernst, weitest.

**farthing** ['fɑ:ðiŋ], s. der Farthing, der Heller.

**fascinate** ['fæsineit], v.a. bezaubern, faszinieren.

**fascination** [fæsi'neiʃən], s. die Bezauberung; der Reiz, der Zauberbann (spell).

**fascism** ['fæʃizm], s. (Pol.) der Faschismus.

**fashion** ['fæʃən], s. die Mode; out of —, außer Mode; die Art und Weise (manner). — v.a. gestalten, bilden (shape); fully —ed, vollgeformt or geformt, angepaßt.

**fashionable** ['fæʃnəbl], adj. modisch, modern; elegant.

**fast** (1) [fɑ:st], adj. schnell (runner); fest (firm); my watch is —, meine Uhr geht vor; a — woman, eine leichtlebige Frau; — train, der Schnellzug; — and furious, schnell wie der Wind. — adv. fest.

**fast** (2) [fɑ:st], v.n. (Rel.) fasten; (Rel.) — day, der Fasttag.

**fasten** [fɑ:sn], v.a. festbinden, festmachen (fix). — v.n. sich festhalten (on to, an, Dat.).

**fastidious** [fəs'tidiəs], adj. wählerisch, anspruchsvoll.

**fastidiousness** [fəs'tidiəsnis], s. die anspruchsvolle Art.

**fat** [fæt], adj. fett; dick (person). — s. das Fett; (Cul.) das Speisefett.

**fatal** ['feitəl], adj. tödlich (lethal); verhängnisvoll.

**fatalism** ['feitəlizm], s. der Fatalismus.

**fatality** [fə'tæliti], s. das Verhängnis; der Todesfall; der tödliche Unfall.

**fate** [feit], s. das Schicksal, Geschick; das Verhängnis (doom, destiny).

**fated** ['feitid], adj. dem Verderben (Untergang) geweiht.

**fateful** ['feitful], adj. verhängnisvoll, unselig.

**father** ['fɑ:ðə], s. der Vater; (Eccl.) Pater; — -in-law, der Schwiegervater. — v.a. Vater sein or werden von (Dat.); zeugen (procreate).

**fatherland** ['fɑ:ðəlænd], s. das Vaterland.

**fatherly** ['fɑ:ðəli], adj. väterlich; wie ein Vater.

**fathom** ['fæðəm], s. die Klafter. — v.a. ergründen, erforschen.

**fatigue** [fə'ti:g], s. die Ermüdung, die Erschöpfung; (Mil.) der Arbeitsdienst. — v.a. ermüden, erschöpfen.

**fatling** ['fætliŋ], s. (Agr.) das Mastvieh.

**fatness** ['fætnis], s. die Beleibtheit (person); die Fettheit (animals).

**fatten** [fætn], v.a. — up, mästen (animals); fett werden lassen. — v.n. fett werden, sich mästen (an, Dat.).

**fatty** ['fæti], adj. (Chem.) fett, fettig. — s. (coll.) der Dickwanst.

**fatuity** [fə'tju:iti], s. die Albernheit, die Dummheit.

**fatuous** ['fætjuəs], adj. albern, dumm, nichtssagend.

**faucet** ['fɔ:sit], s. der Zapfen, der Hahn.

**fault** [fɔ:lt], s. der Fehler; die Schuld; find — with, etwas kritisieren; tadeln; it is my —, es ist meine Schuld; at —, im Irrtum.

**faultless** ['fɔ:ltlis], adj. fehlerlos, fehlerfrei.

**faultlessness** ['fɔ:ltlisnis], s. die Fehlerlosigkeit, die fehlerlose Ausführung.

**faulty** ['fɔ:lti], adj. fehlerhaft, mangelhaft.

**faun** [fɔ:n], s. (Myth.) der Faun.

**fauna** ['fɔ:nə], s. die Fauna, die Tierwelt.

**favour** ['feivə], s. die Gunst, das Wohlwollen; (Comm.) in — of, zugunsten; do a —, einen Gefallen tun or erweisen; be in —, sehr begehrt sein, in hoher Gunst stehen. — v.a. bevorzugen, begünstigen, wohlwollend gegenüberstehen (Dat.).

**favourable** ['feivərəbl], adj. günstig, vorteilhaft.

# favourite

**favourite** ['feivərit], s. der Favorit, der Liebling; der Günstling (of kings). — adj. Lieblings-, bevorzugt.

**fawn** (1) [fɔ:n], s. (Zool.) das junge Reh, das Rehkalb; — coloured, rehfarben. — adj. rehfarben, hellbraun.

**fawn** (2) [fɔ:n], v.n. schmeicheln, kriecherisch sein ((up)on, Dat.).

**fawning** ['fɔ:niŋ], adj. kriecherisch, kriechend.

**fear** [fiə], s. die Furcht, die Angst; stand in — of s.o., sich vor jemandem fürchten; for — of, aus Angst vor (Dat.). — v.a. fürchten, befürchten.

**fearful** ['fiəful], adj. furchtsam (full of fear); furchtbar (causing fear).

**fearless** ['fiəlis], adj. furchtlos (of, vor, Dat.).

**fearlessness** ['fiəlisnis], s. die Furchtlosigkeit.

**feasibility** [fi:zi'biliti], s. die Tunlichkeit, die Möglichkeit.

**feasible** ['fi:zibl], adj. tunlich, möglich.

**feast** [fi:st], s. das Fest, der Festtag; der Schmaus (good meal). — v.n. schmausen (upon, von, Dat.). — v.a. festlich bewirten.

**feat** [fi:t], s. die Tat, die Heldentat; das Kunststück.

**feather** ['feðə], s. die Feder; show the white —, Feigheit an den Tag legen; — bed, das Federbett. — v.a. federn; o.'s nest, sich ein Schäfchen ins Trockene bringen.

**feature** ['fi:tʃə], s. der Zug (characteristic); der Gesichtszug (facial). — v.a. charakterisieren; (Film) in der Hauptrolle zeigen.

**February** ['februəri], der Februar.

**feckless** ['feklis], adj. hilflos, unfähig.

**feculence** ['fekjuləns], s. (Chem.) der Bodensatz, der Hefesatz.

**fecund** ['fekənd], adj. fruchtbar.

**fecundate** ['fekəndeit], v.a. fruchtbar machen, befruchten.

**fecundity** [fi'kʌnditi], s. die Fruchtbarkeit.

**federacy** ['fedərəsi], s. der Bund, die Föderation.

**federal** ['fedərəl], adj. Bundes-, föderativ.

**federalism** ['fedərəlizm], s. der Föderalismus.

**federalize** ['fedərəlaiz], v.a. verbünden.

**federation** [fedə'reiʃən], s. die Föderation, die Verbündung; (Pol.) der Bund.

**fee** [fi:], s. die Gebühr (official dues); das Honorar (of doctor etc.); (pl.) (Sch.) das Schulgeld.

**feeble** [fi:bl], adj. schwach, matt; — minded, schwachsinnig.

**feed** [fi:d], v.a. irr. füttern; verköstigen (humans); unterhalten (maintain); zuführen (into machine, Dat.); be fed up with, etwas satt haben; — pipe, die Speiseröhre. — v.n. sich nähren (on, von, Dat.); weiden (graze).

**feeder** ['fi:də], s. der Kinderlatz (bib); (Tech.) der Zubringer.

**feel** [fi:l], v.n. irr. sich fühlen (sense); meinen (think). — v.a. berühren, betasten (touch); empfinden (be aware of).

**feeler** ['fi:lə], s. der Fühler; put out a —, einen Fühler ausstrecken.

**feeling** ['fi:liŋ], s. das Gefühl; with —, bewegt, gerührt (moved); grimmig (in anger).

**feign** [fein], v.a. vortäuschen, heucheln.

**feint** [feint], s. die Verstellung (disguise); die Finte (fencing).

**felicitate** [fi'lisiteit], v.a. Glück wünschen (upon, zu, Dat.), beglückwünschen (Acc.).

**felicitation** [filisi'teiʃən], s. die Beglückwünschung, der Glückwunsch.

**felicitous** [fi'lisitəs], adj. glücklich ausgedrückt, gut gesagt (in speaking).

**felicity** [fi'lisiti], s. die Glückseligkeit; die glückliche Ausdrucksweise (style).

**feline** ['fi:lain], adj. Katzen-, katzenartig.

**fell** (1) [fel], adj. grausam; at one — swoop, mit einem wilden Schwung.

**fell** (2) [fel], v.a. fällen (timber); töten (kill).

**fell** (3) [fel], s. das Gebirge, das Felsengelände.

**fell** (4) [fel], s. das Fell, die Haut (skin).

**fellow** ['felou], s. der Gefährte, Genosse (companion); das Mitglied eines College or einer Universität; (coll.) der Kerl; queer —, seltsamer Kauz; — feeling, das Mitgefühl; — traveller, der Weggenosse; (Pol.) der Mitläufer.

**fellowship** ['felouʃip], s. die Mitgliedschaft (einer Hochschule etc.) (membership); die Freundschaft (friendship); good —, die Geselligkeit.

**felly, felloe** ['feli,'felou], s. die Radfelge.

**felon** ['felən], s. der Verbrecher.

**felonious** [fi'louniəs], adj. verbrecherisch.

**felt** [felt], s. der Filz.

**female** ['fi:meil], adj. weiblich. — s. (Zool.) das Weibchen.

**feminine** ['feminin], adj. weiblich. — s. (Gram.) das weibliche Geschlecht; das Weibliche.

**fen** [fen], s. das Moor, das Marschland.

**fence** [fens], s. der Zaun, das Staket. — v.a. umzäunen, einzäunen (enclose). — v.n. fechten (fight with rapiers).

**fencing** ['fensiŋ], s. die Einzäunung (fence); das Fechten (with rapiers); — master, der Fechtmeister.

**fend** [fend], v.a. — off, abwehren, parieren. — v.n. — for oneself, sich allein behelfen.

**fennel** [fenl], s. (Bot.) der Fenchel.

**ferment** [fə'ment], v.a. zur Gärung bringen. — v.n. gären, fermentieren. — ['fə:ment], s. das Gärmittel (also fig.); (Chem.) das Gärungsprodukt.

**fermentation** [fə:men'teiʃən], s. die Gärung.

**fern** [fə:n], s. (Bot.) das Farnkraut.

**ferocious** [fə'rouʃəs], adj. wild, grimmig.

**ferocity** [fə'rɔsiti], *s.* die Wildheit.
**ferret** ['ferit], *s.* (*Zool.*) das Frett, das Frettchen. — *v.a.* — *out*, ausspüren.
**ferry** ['feri], *s.* die Fähre. — *v.a.* — *across*, hinüberrudern, hinüberfahren, übersetzen.
**fertile** ['fə:tail], *adj.* fruchtbar.
**fertility** [fə:'tiliti], *s.* die Fruchtbarkeit.
**fertilize** ['fə:tilaiz], *v.a.* befruchten.
**fertilizer** ['fə:tilaizə], *s.* das Düngemittel, der Dünger.
**fervent** ['fə:vənt], *adj.* inbrünstig (*prayer*); heiß (*wish*).
**fervid** ['fə:vid], *adj.* glühend, heiß (*with zeal*).
**fervour** ['fə:və], *s.* die Inbrunst (*prayer*); die Sehnsucht (*wish*).
**fester** ['festə], *v.n.* schwären, eitern.
**festival** ['festivəl], *s.* das Fest, die Festspiele, *n. pl.*
**festive** ['festiv], *adj.* festlich, Fest-.
**festivity** [fes'tiviti], *s.* die Festlichkeit.
**festoon** [fes'tu:n], *s.* die Girlande. — *v.a.* behängen, mit Girlanden verzieren, schmücken.
**fetch** [fetʃ], *v.a.* holen, bringen.
**fetching** ['fetʃiŋ], *adj.* einnehmend.
**fetter** ['fetə], *v.a.* fesseln, binden. — *s.* (*pl.*) die Fesseln, *f. pl.*
**feud** [fju:d], *s.* die Fehde.
**feudal** ['fju:dl], *adj.* feudal, Lehns-.
**fever** ['fi:və], *s.* das Fieber.
**few** [fju:], *adj.* einige; wenige; *a* —, ein paar.
**fiancé** [fi'ɔ:nsei], *s.* der Verlobte, Bräutigam.
**fiancée** [fi'ɔ:nsei], *s.* die Verlobte, Braut.
**fib** [fib], *s.* (*coll.*) die Lüge. — *v.n.* (*coll.*) lügen.
**fibre** ['faibə], *s.* die Fiber, Faser.
**fibrous** ['faibrəs], *adj.* faserartig.
**fickle** [fikl], *adj.* unbeständig, wankelmütig.
**fiction** ['fikʃən], *s.* die Erdichtung (*figment*); (*Lit.*) die Romanliteratur.
**fictitious** [fik'tiʃəs], *adj.* erdichtet, in der Phantasie.
**fiddle** [fidl], *s.* (*coll.*) die Geige, Fiedel, Violine. — *v.n.* (*coll.*, *Mus.*) geigen; schwindeln (*cheat*).
**fiddlesticks!** ['fidlstiks], *int.* Unsinn!
**fidelity** [fi'deliti], *s.* die Treue (*loyalty*); Genauigkeit; (*Engin.*) high —, Präzision, High Fidelity.
**fidget** ['fidʒit], *v.n.* unruhig sein.
**fidgety** ['fidʒiti], *adj.* nervös.
**fie!** [fai], *int.* pfui!
**field** [fi:ld], *s.* das Feld; (*fig.*) das Gebiet; — *glass*, der Feldstecher; (*Hunt.*) — *sports*, die Feldübungen, der Jagdsport. — *v.a.*, *v.n.* abfangen, abpassen (*cricket*).
**fiend** [fi:nd], *s.* der Unhold, böse Geist; *fresh air* —, ein Freund der frischen Luft.
**fiendish** ['fi:ndiʃ], *adj.* teuflisch, boshaft.
**fierce** [fiəs], *adj.* wild, wütend (*beast*); — *weather*, — *cold*, die grimmige Kälte, der grimmige Winter.

**fiery** ['faiəri], *adj.* feurig; hitzig.
**fife** [faif], *s.* (*Mus.*) die Querpfeife.
**fifteen** [fif'ti:n], *num. adj.* fünfzehn.
**fifth** [fifθ], *num. adj.* der fünfte.
**fifty** ['fifti], *num. adj.* fünfzig.
**fig** [fig], *s.* (*Bot.*) die Feige.
**fight** [fait], *v.a.*, *v.n. irr.* kämpfen, bekämpfen (*in battle*); raufen (*of boys*). — *s.* der Kampf; die Rauferei.
**figment** ['figmənt], *s.* die Erdichtung.
**figurative** ['figjuərətiv], *adj.* bildlich (*style*).
**figure** ['figə], *s.* die Figur (*body*); die Gestalt, Form (*shape*); (*Maths.*) die Zahl, die Ziffer; *cut a* —, einen Eindruck machen; *a fine* — *of a man!* ein fabelhafter Kerl! — *v.a.* — *out*, ausdenken, ausrechnen. — *v.n.* eine Rolle spielen, rangieren.
**figured** ['figəd], *adj.* figuriert.
**figurehead** ['figəhed], *s.* der scheinbare Leiter, die Representationsfigur.
**filament** ['filəmənt], *s.* der Faden, der Glühfaden (*bulb*).
**filbert** ['filbə:t], *s.* (*Bot.*) die Haselnuß.
**filch** [filtʃ], *v.a.* stehlen, klauen.
**file** [fail], *s.* (*Engin.*) die Feile; (*Mil.*) die Reihe; (*Comm.*) der Aktenstoß, das Aktenbündel, der Ordner; (*pl.*) die Akten, *f. pl.*; *single* —, im Gänsemarsch; *rank and* —, die große Masse; *on the* —, in den Akten. — *v.a.* feilen (*metal*); zu den Akten legen (*papers*); einreichen (*petition*).
**filial** ['filiəl], *adj.* kindlich.
**filibuster** ['filibastə], *s.* der Freibeuter; (*Am.*) (*Pol.*) die Obstruktion.
**filigree** ['filigri:], *s.* die Filigranarbeit.
**filing** ['failiŋ], *s.* (*pl.*) die Feilspäne; das Einheften (*of papers*); — *cabinet*, die Kartei.
**fill** [fil], *v.a.* füllen; ausfüllen (*place, job*); plombieren (*tooth*); — *up*, tanken (*with petrol*). — *s.* das volle Maß; *eat o.'s* —, sich satt essen.
**fillet** ['filit], *s.* das Filet (*meat*); das Band, die Binde (*band*).
**filling** ['filiŋ], *s.* die Plombe (*in tooth*); — *station*, die Tankstelle.
**filly** ['fili], *s.* das Füllen.
**film** [film], *s.* der Film (*cinema*, *Phot.*); die Haut, das Häutchen (*skin*); der Belag (*coating*). — *v.a.* aufnehmen, verfilmen, filmen (*photograph*).
**filter** ['filtə], *v.a.* filtrieren, filtern. — *v.n.* durchfiltern. — *s.* das Filter.
**filth** [filθ], *s.* der Schmutz.
**filthy** ['filθi], *adj.* schmutzig.
**filtration** [fil'treiʃən], *s.* das Filtrieren, das Durchsickern.
**fin** [fin], *s.* (*Zool.*) die Finne, die Flosse.
**final** [fainl], *adj.* letzt, endlich; endgültig. — *s.* (*Sport*) die Endrunde, das Endspiel.
**finale** [fi'nɑ:li], *s.* (*Mus.*) das Finale.
**finality** [fai'næliti], *s.* die Endgültigkeit.
**finance** [fi'næns *or* 'fai-], *s.* die Finanz, das Finanzwesen. — *v.a.* finanzieren.

**financial** [fiˈnænʃəl], *adj.* finanziell, Geld-, Finanz-.

**finch** [fintʃ], *s.* (*Orn.*) der Fink.

**find** [faind], *v.a. irr.* finden; — *fault with,* jemanden kritisieren; *all found,* volle Verpflegung (inbegriffen). — *s.* der Fund.

**finding** [ˈfaindiŋ], *s.* das Finden, der Befund; (*Law*) der Wahrspruch.

**fine** (1) [fain], *adj.* fein (*delicate*); dünn (*thin*); schön (*beautiful*); scharf (*distinct*); großartig(*splendid*).

**fine** (2) [fain], *v.a.* zu einer Geldstrafe verurteilen. — *s.* die Geldstrafe.

**finery** [ˈfainəri], *s.* der Putz; (*Engin.*) der Frischofen.

**finger** [ˈfiŋgə], *s.* der Finger; *have a — in the pie,* die Hand im Spiel haben. — *v.a.* berühren, antasten.

**finish** [ˈfiniʃ], *v.a.* beenden, fertig machen, vollenden; —*ing touch,* die letzte Hand. — *v.n.* aufhören, enden. — *s.* das Ende (*end*); der letzte Schliff; die Appretur, die Fertigung.

**finite** [ˈfainait], *adj.* endlich.

**Finn** [fin], *s.* der Finne.

**Finnish** [ˈfiniʃ], *adj.* finnisch.

**fir** [fəː], *s.* (*Bot.*) die Föhre, die Tanne; — *cone,* der Tannenzapfen.

**fire** [faiə], *s.* das Feuer; — *brigade,* die Feuerwehr; — *damp,* (*Min.*) schlagende Wetter, *n.pl.*; — *engine,* die Feuerspritze; — *extinguisher,* der Löschapparat, Feuerlöscher; — *escape,* der Rettungsleiter. — *v.a.* brennen (*clay*); anzünden, in Gang setzen (*furnace*); anspornen (*enthuse*); (*coll.*) entlassen (*dismiss*). — *v.n.* feuern (*at,* auf, *Acc.*).

**firebrand** [ˈfaiəbrænd], *s.* der Aufwiegler.

**fireman** [ˈfaiəmən], *s.* der Heizer.

**fireplace** [ˈfaiəpleis], *s.* der Kamin.

**fireproof** [ˈfaiəpruːf], *adj.* feuerfest.

**fireside** [ˈfaiəsaid], *s.* der (häusliche) Herd, der Kamin.

**firewood** [ˈfaiəwud], *s.* das Brennholz.

**firework** [ˈfaiəwəːk], *s.* (*usually pl.*) das Feuerwerk.

**firm** [fəːm], *adj.* fest, hart (*solid*); entschlossen (*decided*). — *s.* die Firma.

**firmament** [ˈfəːməmənt], *s.* das Firmament, Himmelsgewölbe; der Sternenhimmel.

**firmness** [ˈfəːmnis], *s.* die Festigkeit, Entschlossenheit.

**first** [fəːst], *num. adj., adv.* erst; zuerst; — *of all,* zuallererst; — *born,* erstgeboren; — *rate,* erstklassig. — *s. from the —,* von Anfang an.

**fiscal** [ˈfiskəl], *adj.* fiskalisch, von der Staatskasse, Finanz-.

**fish** [fiʃ], *s.* der Fisch; *like a — out of water,* nicht in seinem Element; *a queer —,* ein seltsamer Kauz; — *bone,* die Gräte. — *v.n.* fischen; — *for compliments,* nach Lob haschen, nach Komplimenten fischen.

**fisherman** [ˈfiʃəmən], *s.* der Fischer.

**fishery** [ˈfiʃəri], *s.* der Fischfang.

**fishing** [ˈfiʃiŋ], *s.* das Fischen, der Fischfang; — *fly,* die Angelfliege; — *line,* die Angelschnur; — *rod,* die Angelrute; — *tackle,* das Angelgerät.

**fishy** [ˈfiʃi], *adj.* (*coll.*) anrüchig, verdächtig.

**fissile** [ˈfisail], *adj.* (*Phys.*) spaltbar.

**fission** [ˈfiʃ(ə)n], *s.* (*Phys.*) die Spaltung.

**fist** [fist], *s.* die Faust; *hand over —,* im Überfluß; *tight —ed,* geizig.

**fisticuffs** [ˈfistikʌfs], *s.* die Schlägerei, das Raufen.

**fistula** [ˈfistjulə], *s.* (*Anat.*) die Fistel.

**fit** (1) [fit], *v.a.* passen, anpassen (*Dat.*); einfügen (— *into s.th.*); — *in,* hineinpassen; — *on a suit,* einen Anzug anprobieren (*Dat.*); — *for a career,* zu einer Laufbahn vorbereiten; — *out,* ausrüsten. — *v.n.* passen, sich fügen (— *into*); — *in,* passen (*in, zu, Dat.*). — *adj.* geeignet, fähig (*suitable*); — *to drop,* todmüde; gesund, stark (*healthy*); schicklich (*proper*); (*Sport*) in guter Form.

**fit** (2) [fit], *s.* der Anfall; *by —s and starts,* ruckweise.

**fitful** [ˈfitful], *adj.* launenhaft; unbeständig.

**fitness** [ˈfitnis], *s.* die Tauglichkeit (*health*); die Schicklichkeit (*propriety*); die Fähigkeit (*ability*); (*Sport*) die gute Form.

**fitter** [ˈfitə], *s.* der Monteur.

**fitting, fitment** [ˈfitiŋ, ˈfitmənt], *s.* die Armatur; die Montage. — *adj.* passend (*suitable*); geeignet (*appropriate*).

**five** [faiv], *num. adj.* fünf.

**fiver** [ˈfaivə], *s.* (*coll.*) die Fünfpfundnote.

**fix** [fiks], *v.a.* festmachen, befestigen (*make firm*); festsetzen (*a time*); (*Am.*) herrichten, anrichten (*a meal*); — *with a glare or stare,* mit den Augen fixieren, scharf ansehen; — *up* (*coll.*), etwas erledigen (*something*); bedienen (*serve s.o.*). — *s.* (*coll.*) die Klemme, die Schwierigkeit, das Dilemma.

**fixture** [ˈfikstʃə], *s.* (*Sport*) die Veranstaltung; das Inventarstück (*furniture*).

**fizz** [fiz], *v.n.* brausen (*drink*).

**fizzle** [fizl], *v.n.* zischen (*flame*); — *out,* verebben, ausgehen, zunichte werden; (*Am., coll.*) durchfallen (*fail in school*).

**fizzy** [ˈfizi], *adj.* mit Kohlensäure, sprudelnd.

**flabbergast** [ˈflæbəgɑːst], *v.a.* (*coll.*) verblüffen.

**flabby** [ˈflæbi], *adj.* schlaff.

**flaccid** [ˈflæksid], *adj.* schlapp, schlaff.

**flag** (1) [flæg], *s.* (*Mil.*) die Flagge; die Fahne; — *officer,* der Flaggoffizier; —*staff,* die Fahnenstange.

**flag** (2) [flæg], *v.n.* ermatten, erschlaffen.

**flag** (3) [flæg], *s.* (—*stone*) der Fliesstein, die Fliese. — *v.a.* mit Fliesen auslegen, mit Fliessteinen pflastern.

**flagon** ['flægən], s. die Doppelflasche.
**flagrant** ['fleigrənt], adj. entsetzlich (shocking); schamlos (impudent).
**flail** [fleil], s. der Dreschflegel.
**flair** [fleə], s. der Instinkt; (coll.) die Nase (for, für, Acc.).
**flake** [fleik], s. die Flocke. — v.n. — off, abblättern.
**flame** [fleim], s. die Flamme; (coll.) old —, die (alte) Liebe, Geliebte(r), die Flamme. — v.n. flammen, lodern.
**flamingo** [flə'mingou], s. (Orn.) der Flamingo.
**flange** [flændʒ], s. (Engin.) der Flan(t)sch.
**flank** [flæŋk], s. die Flanke, die Seite; die Weiche (of animal). — v.a. flankieren.
**flannel** [flænl], s. der Flanell.
**flap** [flæp], s. die Klappe; das Ohrläppchen (earlobe); der Flügelschlag (— of wings).
**flare** [fleə], v.n. flammen, flackern; — up, aufbrausen (in temper). — s. das Aufflammen, das Aufflackern; die Leuchtkugel.
**flash** [flæʃ], s. der Blitz (of lightning); das Afflammen; (phot.) —light, das Blitzlicht. — v.a. aufflammen lassen, aufblitzen lassen. — v.n. aufflammen, aufblitzen.
**flashy** ['flæʃi], adj. großtuend, angeberisch (bragging); buntfarbig (gaudy).
**flask** [flɑːsk], s. die kleine Flasche, das Fläschchen.
**flat** [flæt], adj. flach, eben; abgestanden, schal (drink); (Mus.) zu tief, vermindert; platt, albern (conversation); —footed, plattfüßig; — tyre, die Panne. — adv. — out, ausgepumpt, erschöpft. — s. die Mietwohnung, Wohnung (lodgings); (Mus.) das B; (pl.) das Flachland; (Theat.) (pl.) die Bühnenbilder, n. pl.
**flatness** ['flætnis], s. die Flachheit, die Plattheit (of conversation etc.).
**flatten** [flætn], v.a. flach machen; glätten (smooth).
**flatter** ['flætə], v.a. schmeicheln (Dat.).
**flattery** ['flætəri], s. die Schmeichelei.
**flaunt** [flɔːnt], v.a. prahlen, prunken (s.th., mit, Dat.).
**flavour** ['fleivə], s. der Geschmack, die Würze; das Aroma; die Blume (bouquet of wine). — v.a. würzen.
**flaw** [flɔː], s. der Riß (chink); der Fehler (fault).
**flawless** ['flɔːlis], adj. fehlerlos.
**flax** [flæks], s. (Bot.) der Flachs.
**flay** [flei], v.a. schinden, die Haut abziehen (Dat.).
**flea** [fliː], s. (Ent.) der Floh.
**fleck** [flek], v.a. sprenkeln.
**fledge** [fledʒ], v.a. befiedern; fully —d, flügge; selbständig.
**fledgling** ['fledʒliŋ], s. der Grünschnabel, der Novize.
**flee** [fliː], v.a., v.n. irr. fliehen, entfliehen (from, von, Dat.); flüchten (vor, Dat.).

**fleece** [fliːs], s. das Vlies. — v.a. scheren (sheep); ausnützen (exploit); berauben.
**fleet** [fliːt], s. die Flotte. — adj. (Poet.) schnellfüßig.
**Fleming** ['flemiŋ], s. der Flame.
**Flemish** ['flemiʃ], adj. flämisch.
**flesh** [fleʃ], s. das (lebende) Fleisch; die Frucht (of fruit).
**flex** [fleks], s. (Elec.) die Kontaktschnur.
**flexible** ['fleksibl], adj. biegsam; (fig.) anpassungsfähig.
**flexion** ['flekʃən], s. (Gram.) die Flexion, die Biegung.
**flick** [flik], s. der leichte Schlag. — v.a. leicht schlagen, berühren.
**flicker** ['flikə], s. das Flackern, das Flimmern. — v.n. flackern, flimmern.
**flight** [flait], s. (Aviat.) der Flug; die Flucht (escape); — of stairs, die Treppe, Treppenflucht.
**flimsy** ['flimzi], adj. hauchdünn (material); schwach (argument).
**flinch** [flintʃ], v.n. zurückweichen, zurückzucken (from, vor, Dat.).
**fling** [fliŋ], v.a. irr. schleudern, werfen, — s. der Wurf; highland —, schottischer Tanz; have a last —, sich zum letzten Mal austoben.
**flint** [flint], s. der Feuerstein.
**flippancy** ['flipənsi], s. die Leichtfertigkeit.
**flippant** ['flipənt], adj. leichtfertig, leichtsinnig, schnippisch.
**flirt** [fləːt], v.n. flirten, liebeln, (with, mit, Dat.).
**flirtation** [fləː'teiʃən], s. die Liebelei.
**flit** [flit], v.n. hin und her flitzen; huschen.
**flitch** [flitʃ], s. die Speckseite.
**flitter** ['flitə], v.n. flattern.
**float** [flout], v.n. obenauf schwimmen, dahingleiten; —ing ice, das Treibeis. — v.a. schwimmen lassen; (Naut.) flott machen; (Comm.) gründen (a company); ausgeben (a loan). — s. das Floß (raft); der ausgeschmückte Wagen (decorated vehicle).
**flock** [flok], s. die Herde (sheep). — v.n. zusammenlaufen, sich scharen.
**floe** [flou], s. die Eisscholle.
**flog** [flog], v.a. peitschen (whip); antreiben; (coll.) verkaufen;— a dead horse, sich umsonst bemühen.
**flood** [flʌd], s. die Flut; das Hochwasser, die Überschwemmung (flooding); (fig.) die Fülle; — gate, die Schleuse. — v.a. überfluten, überschütten (with requests). — v.n. überschwemmen (of river).
**floodlight** ['flʌdlait], s. das Flutlicht, Scheinwerferlicht.
**floor** [flɔː], s. der Boden, der Fußboden; das Stockwerk, der Stock (storey); from the —, aus dem Plenum; — walker, die Aufsicht (in stores). — v.a. zu Boden strecken, überrumpeln (surprise).
**flop** [flɔp], v.n. (coll.) hinsinken, hinplumpsen; versagen (fail). — s. der Versager, Mißerfolg (play, film etc.).

# Florentine

**Florentine** ['flɔrəntain], *adj.* florentinisch. — *s.* der Florentiner.
**florid** ['flɔrid], *adj.* blühend; überladen.
**florin** ['flɔrin], *s.* das Zweischillingstück.
**florist** ['flɔrist], *s.* der Blumenhändler.
**flotsam** ['flɔtsəm], *s.* das Strandgut, Wrackgut.
**flounce** (1) [flauns], *v.n.* hastig bewegen.
**flounce** (2) [flauns], *v.a.* mit Falbeln besetzen (*dress*). — *s.* die Falbel (*on dress*).
**flounder** (1) ['flaundə], *v.n.* umhertappen, unsicher sein.
**flounder** (2) ['flaundə], *s.* (*Zool.*) die Flunder.
**flour** ['flauə], *s.* das Mehl.
**flourish** ['flʌriʃ], *v.n.* blühen; wirken; gedeihen (*thrive*); schnörkeln, verzieren (*in writing*); Fanfaren blasen, schmettern (*trumpets*). — *s.* der Schnörkel; der Trompetenstoß, Tusch (*of trumpets*).
**flout** [flaut], *v.a.* verhöhnen, verspotten. — *s.* der Hohn, der Spott.
**flow** [flou], *v.n. irr.* fließen, strömen. — *s.* der Fluß (*of water, goods etc.*); — *of words,* der Redeschwall.
**flower** ['flauə], *s.* die Blume; die Blüte (*blossom*). — *v.n.* blühen, in Blüte stehen.
**flowery** ['flauəri], *adj.* gewählt, umständlich, geziert (*style*).
**fluctuate** ['flʌktjueit], *v.n.* schwanken.
**fluctuation** [flʌktju'eiʃen], *s.* das Schwanken.
**flue** [flu:], *s.* der Rauchfang (*of chimney*).
**fluency** ['flu:ənsi], *s.* das fließende Sprechen, die Geläufigkeit.
**fluent** ['flu:ənt], *adj.* geläufig, fließend.
**fluid** ['flu:id], *adj.* fließend, flüssig (*liquid*). — *s.* die Flüssigkeit.
**fluke** [flu:k], *s.* der glückliche Zufall (*chance*).
**flunkey** ['flʌŋki], *s.* der Diener, der Bediente.
**flurry** ['flʌri], *s.* die Unruhe; die Aufregung (*excitement*).
**flush** (1) [flʌʃ], *s.* das Erröten (*blushing*); die Aufwallung (*of anger*). — *v.a.* nachspülen (*basin*); erröten machen (*make blush*). — *v.n.* erröten.
**flush** (2) [flʌʃ], *adj.* in gleicher Ebene, eben.
**flush** (3) [flʌʃ], *v.a.* (*Hunt.*) aufscheuchen.
**fluster** ['flʌstə], *v.a.* verwirren (*muddle*); aufregen (*excite*).
**flute** [flu:t], *s.* (*Mus.*) die Flöte; (*Carp.*) die Hohlkehle. — *v.a.* (*Carp., Archit.*) aushöhlen. — *v.n.* (*Mus.*) flöten, Flöte spielen.
**flutter** ['flʌtə], *v.n.* flattern, unruhig sein. — *s.* die Unruhe.
**flux** [flʌks], *s.* das Fließen; *be in* —, in der Schwebe sein.
**fly** [flai], *v.a. irr.* wehen lassen, hissen (*flag*). — *v.n. irr.* (*Aviat.*) fliegen;

fliehen (*escape*); eilen (*hurry*). — *s.* (*Ent.*) die Fliege.
**flyleaf** ['flaili:f], *s.* das Vorsatzblatt.
**flying** ['flaiiŋ], *adj.* fliegend, Flug-; — *squad,* das Überfallkommando.
**flyover** ['flaiouvə], *s.* die Brückenkreuzung, Überführung.
**flywheel** ['flaiwi:l], *s.* das Schwungrad.
**foal** [foul], *s.* (*Zool.*) das Füllen. — *v.n.* fohlen.
**foam** [foum], *s.* der Schaum; — *rubber,* der Schaumgummi. — *v.n.* schäumen.
**fob** [fɔb], *v.a.* — *off,* abfertigen, abspeisen.
**focus** ['foukəs], *s.* der Brennpunkt; der Mittelpunkt (*of interest*). — *v.a.* (*Phot.*) einstellen. — *v.n.* — *upon,* sich konzentrieren auf (*Acc.*).
**fodder** ['fɔdə], *s.* das Futter.
**foe** [fou], *s.* der Feind.
**fog** [fɔg], *s.* der Nebel.
**fogey** ['fougi], *s.* der Kerl, Kauz.
**foible** ['fɔibl], *s.* die Schwäche, die schwache Seite.
**foil** (1) [fɔil], *v.a.* vereiteln.
**foil** (2) [fɔil], *s.* die Folie; der Hintergrund (*background*).
**foil** (3) [fɔil], *s.* das Florett (*fencing*).
**foist** [fɔist], *v.a.* aufschwatzen (*upon, Dat.*).
**fold** (1) [fould], *v.a.* falten (*clothes etc.*); umarmen (*in o.'s arms*). — *v.n.* schließen, sich falten. — *s.* die Falte; (*Geol.*) die Vertiefung.
**fold** (2) [fould], *s.* die Herde (*sheep*); *return to the* —, zu den Seinen zurückkehren.
**folder** ['fouldə], *s.* die Mappe (*papers*); das Falzbein.
**folding** ['fouldiŋ], *adj.* Klapp-; — *chair,* der Klappstuhl; — *door,* die Flügeltür.
**foliage** ['fouljidʒ], *s.* (*Bot.*) das Laub.
**folio** ['fouliou], *s.* das Folio, der Foliant.
**folk** [fouk], *s.* (*also pl.*) die Leute; (*pl.*) (*Am.*) (*mode of address*).
**folklore** ['foukl:ɔ] *s.* die Volkskunde.
**folksong** ['fouksɔŋ], *s.* das Volkslied.
**follow** ['fɔlou], *v.a., v.n.* folgen (*Dat.*); — *suit,* dasselbe tun, Farbe bekennen.
**follower** ['fɔlouə], *s.* der Anhänger (*supporter*); der Nachfolger (*successor*); *camp* —, der Mitläufer.
**folly** ['fɔli], *s.* die Narrheit; die törichte Handlung (*action*).
**foment** [fo'ment], *v.a.* anregen (*stimulate*); pflegen (*cultivate*); warm baden.
**fond** [fɔnd], *adj.* zärtlich, lieb; *be* — *of,* gern haben.
**fondle** [fɔndl], *v.a.* liebkosen.
**fondness** ['fɔndnis], *s.* die Zärtlichkeit, die (Vor-)liebe.
**font** [fɔnt], *s.* der Taufstein (*baptismal*).
**food** [fu:d], *s.* die Nahrung, Speise (*nourishment*) (*n.pl.*); das Futter (*for animals*); *some* —, etwas zum Essen; — *store,* das Lebensmittelgeschäft.
**fool** [fu:l], *s.* der Narr, Tor. — *v.a.* zum Narren halten, übertülpeln.

# formality

**foolish** ['fuːliʃ], *adj.* töricht, albern, närrisch (*person*); unsinnig (*act*).
**foolscap** ['fuːlskæp], *s.* das Kanzleipapier.
**foot** [fut], *s.* der Fuß; *on* —, zu Fuß; — *board*, das Trittbrett; *put o.'s* — *in it*, eine taktlose Bemerkung fallen lassen, ins Fettnäpfchen treten. — *v.a.* — *the bill*, bezahlen.
**footage** ['futidʒ], *s.* die Länge in Fuß.
**football** ['futbɔːl], *s.* der Fußball.
**footbridge** ['futbridʒ], *s.* der Steg.
**footing** ['futiŋ], *s.* die Grundlage, Basis.
**footlight** ['futlait], *s.* (*usually pl.*) die Rampenlichter, *n. pl.*
**footman** ['futmən], *s.* der Bediente.
**footprint** ['futprint], *s.* die Fußstapfe.
**footstool** ['futstuːl], *s.* der Schemel.
**fop** [fɔp], *s.* der Geck.
**for** [fɔː], *prep.* für (*Acc.*); anstatt (*Genit.*) (*instead of*); *in exchange* —, für, um; — *example*, zum Beispiel; — *heaven's sake*, um Himmels willen; — *two days*, zwei Tage lang; auf zwei Tage; seit zwei Tagen; *now you are* — *it!* jetzt hast du's! *as* — *me*, meinetwegen, was mich anbelangt; — *all that*, trotz alledem. — *conj.* denn, weil.
**forage** ['fɔridʒ], *s.* das Futter. — *v.n.* furagieren.
**forasmuch** [fɔrəz'mʌtʃ], *conj.* (*obs.*) — *as*, insofern als.
**foray** ['fɔrei], *s.* der Raubzug.
**forbear** [fɔː'bɛə], *v.a. irr.* vermeiden, unterlassen (*avoid*); sich enthalten (*abstain*). — *v.n.* (geduldig) hinnehmen, ertragen.
**forbid** [fɔ'bid], *v.a. irr.* verbieten; *God* —*!* Gott behüte!
**forbidding** [fɔ'bidiŋ], *adj.* abschreckend.
**force** [fɔːs], *s.* (*Phys.*) die Kraft; die Macht (*might*); die Gewalt (*brute* —); (*pl.*) die Streitkräfte, *f. pl.*; (*Phys.*) die Kräfte. — *v.a.* zwingen, nötigen.
**forceful** ['fɔːsful], *adj.* kräftig, energisch, kraftvoll.
**forceps** ['fɔːseps], *s.* (*Med.*) die Zange; die Pinzette.
**forcible** ['fɔːsibl], *adj.* heftig, stark (*strong*); gewaltsam (*violent*).
**ford** [fɔːd], *s.* die Furt.
**fore-** [fɔː], *pref.* Vorder-, vorder.
**forebear** ['fɔːbɛə], *s.* der Vorfahre.
**forebode** [fɔː'boud], *v.a.* voraussagen, vorbedeuten.
**forecast** [fɔː'kɑːst], *v.a.* vorhersagen, voraussagen. — ['fɔːkɑːst], *s.* die Vorhersage.
**foreclose** [fɔː'klouz], *v.a.* ausschließen.
**forefather** ['fɔːfɑːðə], *s.* der Ahne, der Vorvater.
**forefinger** ['fɔːfiŋgə], *s.* (*Anat.*) der Zeigefinger.
**forego** [fɔː'gou], *v.a. irr.* vorhergehen.
**foreground** ['fɔːgraund], *s.* der Vordergrund.
**forehead** ['fɔrid], *s.* die Stirne.
**foreign** ['fɔrin], *adj.* fremd; ausländisch.

**foreigner** ['fɔrinə], *s.* der Fremde, der Ausländer.
**foreland** ['fɔːlənd], *s.* das Vorgebirge.
**foreman** ['fɔːmən], *s.* der Werkführer, Vorarbeiter.
**foremast** ['fɔːmɑːst], *s.* (*Naut.*) der Fockmast.
**foremost** ['fɔːmoust], *adj.* vorderst, vornehmlichst, führend. — *adv.* zuerst; *first and* —, zuallererst.
**forenoon** ['fɔːnuːn], *s.* der Vormittag.
**forensic** [fɔ'rensik], *adj.* forensisch, gerichtsmedizinisch.
**forerunner** ['fɔːrʌnə], *s.* der Vorläufer.
**foresail** ['fɔːseil, 'fɔːsəl], *s.* (*Naut.*) das Focksegel.
**foresee** [fɔː'siː], *v.a. irr.* vorhersehen.
**foreshadow** [fɔː'ʃædou], *v.a.* vorher andeuten.
**foreshorten** [fɔː'ʃɔːtn], *v.a.* verkürzen.
**foresight** ['fɔːsait], *s.* die Vorsorge, der Vorbedacht.
**forest** ['fɔrist], *s.* der Wald; der Urwald (*jungle*).
**forestall** [fɔː'stɔːl], *v.a.* vorwegnehmen, zuvorkommen (*Dat.*).
**forester** ['fɔristə], *s.* der Förster.
**forestry** ['fɔristri], *s.* die Forstwissenschaft (*science*); das Forstwesen (*management*).
**foretaste** ['fɔːteist], *s.* der Vorgeschmack.
**foretell** [fɔː'tel], *v.a. irr.* voraussagen.
**forethought** ['fɔːθɔːt], *s.* der Vorbedacht.
**forewarn** [fɔː'wɔːn], *v.a.* warnen.
**forfeit** ['fɔːfit], *s.* das Pfand (*pledge*); die Einbuße (*fine*); (*pl.*) das Pfänderspiel. — *v.a.* verlieren, verwirken.
**forfeiture** ['fɔːfitʃə], *s.* die Verwirkung, die Einbuße, der Verlust.
**forge** [fɔːdʒ], *v.a.* schmieden (*iron*); fälschen (*falsify*). — *v.n.* — *ahead*, sich vorwärtsarbeiten. — *s.* die Schmiede (*iron*); der Eisenhammer (*hammer*).
**forget** [fə'get], *v.a., v.n. irr.* vergessen; —*-me-not*, das Vergißmeinnicht.
**forgetful** [fə'getful], *adj.* vergeßlich.
**forgive** [fə'giv], *v.a., v.n. irr.* vergeben, verzeihen.
**forgo** [fɔː'gou], *v.a. irr.* verzichten; aufgeben.
**fork** [fɔːk], *s.* die Gabel; die Abzweigung (*road*). — *v.n.* sich gabeln, sich spalten.
**forlorn** [fɔː'lɔːn], *adj.* verlassen, verloren, elend.
**form** [fɔːm], *s.* die Form, die Gestalt (*shape*); die Formalität (*formality*); das Formular (*document*); *in good* —, (*Sport*) in guter Form; *bad* —, gegen den guten Ton; *a matter of* —, eine Formsache. — *v.a.* formen, gestalten (*shape*); bilden (*an association etc. of*, über, *Acc.*).
**formal** [fɔː'məl], *adj.* formal, äußerlich; formell.
**formality** [fɔː'mæliti], *s.* die Formalität.

# formation

**formation** [fɔː'meiʃən], *s.* (*Mil.*) die Formation; (*Geol.*) die Bildung; die Formung; die Aufstellung (*sports team*).

**former** ['fɔːmə], *adj.* früher, vorig.

**formidable** ['fɔːmidəbl], *adj.* schrecklich, furchtbar.

**formula** ['fɔːmjulə], *s.* die Formel.

**formulate** ['fɔːmjuleit], *v.a.* formulieren.

**forsake** [fɔː'seik], *v.a. irr.* verlassen, im Stich lassen.

**forsooth** [fɔː'suːθ], *adv.* (*Poet.*) wahrlich, wirklich!

**forswear** [fɔː'swɛə], *v.a. irr.* abschwören; — *oneself*, einen Meineid schwören.

**fort** [fɔːt], *s.* das Fort, die Festung.

**forth** [fɔːθ], *adv.* vorwärts; weiter (*further*); *and so* —, und so weiter (*u.s.w.*); *fort* (*away*).

**forthcoming** [fɔːθ'kʌmiŋ], *adj.* bevorstehend.

**forthwith** [fɔːθ'wiθ], *adv.* sogleich.

**fortieth** ['fɔːtiəθ], *num. adj.* vierzigst. — *s.* der Vierzigste.

**fortification** [fɔːtifi'keiʃən], *s.* die Befestigung.

**fortify** ['fɔːtifai], *v.a.* befestigen; bestärken.

**fortitude** ['fɔːtijuːd], *s.* die Tapferkeit.

**fortnight** ['fɔːtnait], *s.* vierzehn Tage, *m. pl.*

**fortress** ['fɔːtris] *see* **fort**.

**fortuitous** [fɔː'tjuːitəs], *adj.* zufällig.

**fortunate** ['fɔːtʃənit], *adj.* glücklich, günstig.

**fortune** [fɔː'tjuːn], *s.* das Glück, das Schicksal; das Vermögen (*wealth*); — *teller*, die Wahrsagerin.

**forty** ['fɔːti], *num. adj.* vierzig.

**forward** ['fɔːwəd], *adj.* vorder (*in front*); voreilig, vorlaut (*rash*); früh (*early*). — *adv.* vorne; — *march!* vorwärts! *carry* —, (*Comm.*) übertragen. — *s.* (*Footb.*) der Stürmer, — *line*, der Angriff. — *v.a.* weiterleiten, expedieren; (*letter*) *please* —, bitte nachsenden.

**forwardness** ['fɔːwədnis], *s.* die Frühreife; die Voreiligkeit, Dreistigkeit.

**fossil** ['fɔsil], *s.* das Fossil.

**foster** ['fɔstə], *v.a.* nähren (*feed*); aufziehen (*bring up*); — *a thought*, einen Gedanken hegen; — *mother*, die Pflegemutter; — *brother*, der Pflegebruder.

**foul** [faul], *adj.* schmutzig; faul (*rotten*). — *v.a.* beschmutzen. — *v.n.* (*Footb.*) einen Verstoß begehen. — *s.* (*Footb.*) der Verstoß.

**found** (1) [faund], *v.a.* gründen, begründen.

**found** (2) [faund], *v.a.* (*Metall.*) gießen (*cast*).

**foundation** [faun'deiʃən], *s.* das Fundament; die Unterlage; die Begründung, die Gründung (*initiation*); die Stiftung (*establishment*); — *stone*, der Grundstein.

**founder** (1) ['faundə], *s.* der Gründer, Stifter.

**founder** (2) ['faundə], *v.n.* scheitern, Schiffbruch erleiden (*on*, an, *Dat.*).

**foundling** ['faundliŋ], *s.* das Findelkind, der Findling.

**foundry** ['faundri], *s.* (*Metall.*) die Gießerei.

**fount** (1) [faunt], *s.* (*Typ.*) der Schriftguss.

**fount** (2) [faunt] (*Poet.*) *see* **fountain**.

**fountain** ['fauntin], *s.* die Quelle, der Brunnen; der Springbrunnen; — *pen*, die Füllfeder; — *head*, der Urquell.

**four** [fɔː], *num. adj.* vier; — *-in-hand*, das Viergespann.

**fowl** [faul], *s.* (*Orn.*) das Huhn, das Geflügel.

**fowler** ['faulə], *s.* der Vogelsteller, Vogelfänger.

**fox** [fɔks], *s.* (*Zool.*) der Fuchs; (*fig.*) der listige Kauz, Schlauberger (*cunning fellow*). — *v.a.* (*coll.*) überlisten, täuschen.

**fraction** ['frækʃən], *s.* (*Maths.*) der Bruch; (*Mech.*) der Bruchteil.

**fractional** ['frækʃənəl], *adj.* (*Maths.*) Bruch–, gebrochen.

**fractionate** ['frækʃəneit], *v.a.* (*Chem.*) fraktionieren (*oil*).

**fractious** ['frækʃəs], *adj.* zänkisch, streitsüchtig.

**fracture** ['fræktʃə], *s.* (*Med.*) der Bruch. — *v.a.* brechen; — *o.'s leg*, sich das Bein brechen.

**fragile** ['frædʒail], *adj.* zerbrechlich; gebrechlich (*feeble*).

**fragment** ['frægmənt], *s.* das Bruchstück, das Fragment.

**fragrance** ['freigrəns], *s.* der Wohlgeruch, Duft.

**fragrant** ['freigrənt], *adj.* wohlriechend, duftend.

**frail** [freil], *adj.* gebrechlich, schwach (*feeble*).

**frailty** ['freilti], *s.* die Schwäche.

**frame** [freim], *s.* der Rahmen (*of picture*); das Gerüst (*scaffold*); die Form (*shape*). — *v.a.* einrahmen (*a picture*); (*Am.*) in die Enge treiben, reinlegen (*get s.o. wrongly blamed*); (*Comm.*) entwerfen (*a letter*).

**framework** ['freimwəːk], *s.* der Rahmen (*outline*); das Fachwerk (*construction*).

**franchise** ['fræntʃaiz], *s.* das Wahlrecht.

**Franciscan** [fræn'siskən], *s.* der Franziskaner (*friar*).

**frank** [fræŋk], *adj.* offen, aufrichtig. — *v.a.* frankieren (*letter*). — *s.* der Frankovermerk.

**frankincense** ['fræŋkinsens], *s.* der Weihrauch.

**frantic** ['fræntik], *adj.* wahnsinnig, außer sich.

**fraternal** [frə'təːnəl], *adj.* brüderlich.

**fraternity** [frə'təːniti], *s.* die Bruderschaft; (*Am.*) der Studentenbund, -klub.

**fraternize** ['frætənaiz], *v.n.* sich verbrüdern, fraternisieren.

**fraud** [frɔːd], *s.* der Betrug.

**fraudulent** ['frɔːdjulənt], *adj.* betrügerisch.

**fraught** [frɔːt], *adj.* voll (*with*, von, *Dat.*).

**fray** (1) [frei], *v.a.* abnutzen; — *the nerves*, auf die Nerven gehen (*Dat.*).

**fray** (2) [frei], *s.* der Kampf, die Schlägerei.

**freak** [friːk], *s.* das Monstrum, die Mißgeburt.

**freakish** ['friːkiʃ], *adj.* seltsam; grotesk.

**freckle** [frekl], *s.* die Sommersprosse.

**freckled** [frekld], *adj.* sommersprossig.

**free** [friː], *adj.* frei; offen (*frank*); — *trade area*, die Freihandelszone; *of my own — will*, aus freien Stücken. — *v.a.* befreien.

**freebooter** ['friːbuːtə], *s.* der Freibeuter.

**freedom** ['friːdəm], *s.* die Freiheit; — *of a city*, das Ehrenbürgerrecht.

**freehold** ['friːhould], *s.* der freie Grundbesitz, der Freigrundbesitz.

**freeholder** ['friːhouldə], *s.* der (freie) Grundbesitzer.

**freeman** ['friːmən], *s.* der Freibürger, Ehrenbürger.

**freemason** ['friːmeisn], *s.* der Freimaurer.

**freewheel** ['friːwiːl], *s.* der Freilauf, das Freilaufrad. — *v.n.* mit Freilauf fahren.

**freeze** [friːz], *v.a. irr.* gefrieren lassen. — *v.n.* frieren, gefrieren; — *up*, zufrieren.

**freight** [freit], *s.* die Fracht. — *v.a.* verfrachten.

**freighter** ['freitə], *s.* (*Naut.*) der Frachtdampfer.

**French** [frentʃ], *adj.* französisch; — *bean*, die Schnittbohne; — *horn*, (*Mus.*) das Horn.

**Frenchman** ['frentʃmən], *s.* der Franzose.

**Frenchwoman** ['frentʃwumən], *s.* die Französin.

**frenzied** ['frenzid], *adj.* wahnsinnig, außer sich.

**frequency** ['friːkwənsi], *s.* (*Phys.*) die Frequenz; die Häufigkeit (*of occurrence*).

**frequent** ['friːkwənt], *adj.* häufig. — [fri'kwent], *v.a.* (häufig) besuchen.

**fresh** [freʃ], *adj.* frisch, neu; ungesalzen (*water*); (*sl.*) frech; — *water*, das Süßwasser.

**fresher, freshman** ['freʃə, 'freʃmən], *s.* der Neuankömmling; (*Univ.*) der Fuchs, Anfänger.

**fret** (1) [fret], *s.* (*Carp.*) das Gitterwerk, Laubsägewerk. — *v.a.* (*Carp.*) durchbrochen verzieren.

**fret** (2) [fret], *s.* der Verdruß, Ärger. — *v.n.* sich Sorgen machen.

**fretful** ['fretful], *adj.* verdrießlich, ärgerlich, mißmutig.

**fretsaw** ['fretsɔː], *s.* (*Carp.*) die Laubsäge.

**friar** ['fraiə], *s.* (*Eccl.*) der Mönch, Bettelmönch.

**friction** ['frikʃən], *s.* die Reibung; (*fig.*) die Unstimmigkeit.

**Friday** ['fraid(e)i]. der Freitag; *Good —*, der Karfreitag.

**friend** [frend], *s.* der (die) Freund(in).

**friendly** ['frendli], *adj.* freundlich.

**friendship** ['frendʃip], *s.* die Freundschaft.

**frigate** ['frigit], *s.* (*Naut.*) die Fregatte.

**fright** [frait], *s.* die Furcht, der Schreck, das Entsetzen.

**frighten** [fraitn], *v.a.* erschrecken (*s.o.*).

**frightful** ['fraitful], *adj.* schrecklich.

**frigid** ['fridʒid], *adj.* kalt, frostig; kühl.

**frill** [fril], *s.* die Krause; die Ausschmückung (*style*).

**frilly** ['frili], *adj.* gekräuselt, geziert.

**fringe** [frindʒ], *s.* die Franse (*fringed edge*); der Rand (*edge, brink*). — *v.a.* mit Fransen besetzen, einsäumen. — *v.n.* — *on*, grenzen an (*Acc.*).

**Frisian** ['friːʒən], *adj.* friesisch.

**frisk** [frisk], *v.a.* (*sl.*) durchsuchen (*search*). — *v.n.* hüpfen (*of animals*). — *s.* der Sprung (*of animals*).

**frisky** ['friski], *adj.* lebhaft, munter.

**fritter** ['fritə], *s.* der Pfannkuchen; *apple —*, Äpfel im Schlafrock. — *v.a.* zerstückeln (*cut up*); vertrödeln (*waste*), vergeuden.

**frivolity** [fri'vɔliti], *s.* der Leichtsinn, die Leichtfertigkeit.

**frivolous** ['frivələs], *adj.* leichtsinnig, leichtfertig.

**fro** [frou], *adv. to and —*, auf und ab, hin und her.

**frock** [frɔk], *s.* der Kittel, das Kleid; (*Eccl.*) die Soutane, Kutte.

**frog** [frɔg], *s.* (*Zool.*) der Frosch.

**frogman** ['frɔgmən], *s.* der Tauchschwimmer, Froschmann.

**frolic** ['frɔlik], *s.* der Scherz; der Spaß. — *v.n.* scherzen, ausgelassen sein.

**from** [frɔm], *prep.* von; von ... her (*hence*); aus ... heraus (*out of*); von ... an (*starting*); vor (*in the face of*).

**front** [frʌnt], *s.* die Stirn; die Vorderseite; (*Mil.*) die Front; *in — of*, vor (*Dat.*); — *door*, die Haustür.

**frontage** ['frʌntidʒ], *s.* die Front, Vorderfront (*of building*).

**frontal** ['frʌntl], *adj.* Stirn-, Vorder-; (*Mil.*) — *attack*, der Frontalangriff. — *s.* (*Eccl.*) die Altardecke.

**frontier** ['frʌntjə], *s.* die Grenze; — *police*, die Grenzpolizei.

**frontispiece** ['frʌntispiːs], *s.* das Titelbild.

**frost** [frɔst], *s.* der Frost, der Reif.

**frostbite** ['frɔstbait], *s.* die Frostbeule.

**frosted** ['frɔstid], *adj.* bereift.

**froth** [frɔθ], *s.* der Schaum. — *v.n.* schäumen.

**frown** [fraun], *v.n.* die Stirn runzeln, finster dreinschauen. — *s.* das Stirnrunzeln.

**frugal** ['fru:gəl], *adj.* frugal, sparsam, einfach.

**fruit** [fru:t], *s.* die Frucht (*singular*); das Obst (*plural or collective*). — *v.n.* (*Bot.*) Früchte tragen.

**frustrate** [frʌs'treit], *v.a.* verhindern; vereiteln (*bring to nought*).

**fry** (1) [frai], *v.a.* braten; *fried potatoes,* Bratkartoffeln, *f. pl.*

**fry** (2) [frai], *s.* der Rogen (*of fish*); (*fig.*) die Brut, Menge.

**frying pan** ['fraiiŋpæn], *s.* die Bratpfanne; *out of the — into the fire,* vom Regen in die Traufe.

**fuchsia** ['fju:ʃə], *s.* (*Bot.*) die Fuchsie.

**fudge** [fʌdʒ], *s.* weiches Zuckerwerk; (*coll.*) Unsinn!

**fuel** ['fjuəl], *s.* der Brennstoff, Treibstoff; das Heizmaterial. — *v.a., v.n.* tanken.

**fugitive** ['fju:dʒitiv], *adj.* flüchtig, auf der Flucht. — *s.* der Flüchtling.

**fugue** [fju:g], *s.* (*Mus.*) die Fuge.

**fulcrum** ['fʌlkrəm], *s.* der Stützpunkt, Hebelpunkt.

**fulfil** [ful'fil], *v.a.* erfüllen; — *a requirement,* einem Gesetz genüge tun.

**full** [ful], *adj.* voll; vollständig (*complete*); — *time,* hauptberuflich.

**fuller** ['fulə], *s.* der Walker.

**fullness** ['fulnis], *s.* die Fülle.

**fulsome** ['fulsəm], *adj.* widerlich, ekelhaft; übermäßig.

**fumble** [fambl], *v.n.* tappen (*for,* nach, *Dat.*).

**fume** [fju:m], *s.* der Rauch, Dunst; der Zorn (*anger*). — *v.n.* zornig sein, wüten (*be angered*).

**fun** [fʌn], *s.* der Spaß, Scherz; *have —,* sich gut unterhalten, sich amüsieren; *make — of,* zum besten haben.

**function** ['fʌŋkʃən], *s.* (*also Maths.*) die Funktion; das Amt (*office*); die Feier(lichkeit) (*formal occasion*). — *v.n.* funktionieren (*be in working order*); fungieren (*officiate*).

**fund** [fʌnd], *s.* der Fonds (*financial*); (*fig.*) die Fülle (*of,* an); *public —s,* die Staatsgelder.

**fundamental** [fʌndə'mentl], *adj.* grundsätzlich, wesentlich. — *s.* (*pl.*) die Grundlagen, *f.pl.*

**funeral** ['fju:nərəl], *s.* die Bestattung, Beerdigung.

**funereal** [fju:'niəriəl], *adj.* wie bei einem Begräbnis, betrübt, traurig.

**fungus** ['fʌŋgəs], *s.* (*Bot.*) der Pilz; der Schwamm (*mushroom*).

**funk** [fʌŋk], *s.* (*sl.*) die Angst, Panik. — *v.a.* fürchten.

**funnel** [fʌnl], *s.* der Trichter.

**funny** ['fʌni], *adj.* spaßhaft, komisch.

**fur** [fə:], *s.* der Pelz, das Fell (*coat of animal*); (*Med.*) der Belag (*on tongue*).

**furbelow** ['fə:bilou], *s.* die Falbel.

**furbish** ['fə:biʃ], *v.a.* aufputzen.

**furious** ['fjuəriəs], *adj.* wild, rasend, wütend.

**furl** [fə:l], *v.a.* (zusammen-)rollen; (*Naut.*) aufrollen.

**furlong** ['fə:lɔŋ], *s.* ein Achtel einer englischen Meile.

**furlough** ['fə:lou], *s.* der Urlaub.

**furnace** ['fə:nis], *s.* der Ofen, Hochofen (*steel*); (*Metall.*) der Schmelzofen.

**furnish** ['fə:niʃ], *v.a.* ausstatten, versehen (*equip*); möblieren (*a room etc.*).

**furnisher** ['fə:niʃə], *s.* der Möbelhändler; der Lieferant.

**furniture** ['fə:nitʃə], *s.* die Möbel, *n. pl.*; die Einrichtung.

**furrier** ['fʌriə], *s.* der Kürschner.

**furrow** ['fʌrou], *s.* die Furche (*field*); die Runzel (*brow*). — *v.a.* runzeln (*brow*); Furchen ziehen (*plough up*).

**further** ['fə:ðə], *comp. adj., adv. see* **farther**. — *v.a.* fördern (*advance*).

**furtherance** ['fə:ðərəns], *s.* die Förderung (*advancement*).

**furthermore** ['fə:ðəmɔ:], *adv.* ferner.

**furthest** ['fə:ðist], *superl. adj., adv. see* **farthest**.

**furtive** ['fə:tiv], *adj.* verstohlen, heimlich.

**fury** ['fjuəri], *s.* die Wut; (*Myth.*) die Furie.

**furze** [fə:z], *s.* (*Bot.*) der Stechginster.

**fuse** [fju:z], *v.a., v.n.* schmelzen (*melt*); vereinigen (*unite*). — *s.* (*Elec.*) die Sicherung; *blow a —,* eine Sicherung durchbrennen; — *box,* der Sicherungskasten; — *wire,* der Schmelzdraht.

**fuselage** ['fju:zilɑ:ʒ *or* -lidʒ], *s.* (*Aviat.*) der (Flugzeug-)rumpf.

**fusible** ['fju:zibl], *adj.* schmelzbar.

**fusilier** [fju:zi'liə], *s.* (*Mil.*) der Füsilier.

**fusion** ['fju:ʒən], *s.* die Verschmelzung; die Vereinigung.

**fuss** [fʌs], *s.* das Getue, die Umständlichkeit; *make a — about,* viel Aufhebens machen.

**fussy** ['fʌsi], *adj.* übertrieben genau; umständlich; geschäftig (*busy*); — *about,* genau in (*Dat.*).

**fusty** ['fʌsti], *adj.* moderig, muffig.

**futile** ['fju:tail], *adj.* nutzlos, vergeblich.

**futility** [fju:'tiliti], *s.* die Nutzlosigkeit.

**future** ['fju:tʃə], *s.* die Zukunft. — *adj.* (zu-)künftig.

**fuzzy** ['fʌzi], *adj.* kraus.

# G

**G** [dʒi:]. das G (*also Mus.*); — *sharp,* das Gis; — *flat,* das Ges; *key of —,* der G Schlüssel, Violinschlüssel.

**gab** [gæb], *s.* das Geschwätz; *the gift of the* —, ein gutes Mundwerk.
**gabble** [gæbl], *v.n.* schwatzen.
**gable** [geibl], *s.* der Giebel.
**gad** [gæd], *v.n.* — *about*, umherstreifen.
**gadfly** [ˈgædflai], *s.* (*Ent.*) die Bremse.
**gag** [gæg], *s.* der Knebel; (*sl.*) der Witz. — *v.a.* knebeln.
**gaiety** [ˈgeiəti], *s.* die Fröhlichkeit.
**gain** [gein], *v.a.* gewinnen, erwerben (*earn*); — *possession*, Besitz ergreifen. — *s.* der Gewinn, Vorteil.
**gainful** [ˈgeinful], *adj.* — *employment*, die einträgliche Beschäftigung.
**gainsay** [ˈgeinsei *or* geinˈsei], *v.a.* widersprechen (*pers.*, *Dat.*).
**gait** [geit], *s.* das Schreiten, der Schritt, Gang.
**gaiter** [ˈgeitə], *s.* die Gamasche.
**galaxy** [ˈgæləksi], *s.* (*Astron.*) die Milchstraße; (*fig.*) die glänzende Versammlung.
**gale** [geil], *s.* der Sturm.
**gall** [gɔ:l], *s.* die Galle. — *v.a.* verbittern, ärgern.
**gallant** [ˈgælənt], *adj.* tapfer (*of soldier*); gallant, höflich (*polite*).
**gallantry** [ˈgæləntri], *s.* die Tapferkeit; die Höflichkeit, Galanterie.
**gallery** [ˈgæləri], *s.* die Gallerie.
**galley** [ˈgæli], *s.* (*Naut.*) die Galeere; (*Typ.*) — *proof*, der Fahnenabzug.
**gallon** [ˈgælən], *s.* die Gallone.
**gallop** [ˈgæləp], *v.n.* galoppieren. — *s.* der Galopp.
**gallows** [ˈgælouz], *s.* der Galgen.
**galosh** [gəˈlɔʃ], *s.* die Galosche.
**galvanic** [gælˈvænik], *adj.* galvanisch.
**galvanize** [ˈgælvənaiz], *v.a.* galvanisieren.
**gamble** [gæmbl], *v.n.* um Geld spielen; — *away*, verspielen. — *s.* das Risiko.
**gambol** [gæmbl], *v.n.* herumspringen.
**game** [geim], *s.* das Spiel (*play*); das Wild, Wildbret (*pheasants etc.*); *fair* —, Freiwild, *n.*, offene Beute, *f.*
**gamecock** [ˈgeimkɔk], *s.* (*Orn.*) der Kampfhahn.
**gamekeeper** [ˈgeimki:pə], *s.* der Wildhüter.
**gammon** [ˈgæmən], *s.* der (geräucherte) Schinken (*bacon*).
**gamut** [ˈgæmət], *s.* die Tonleiter.
**gander** [ˈgændə], *s.* (*Orn.*) der Gänserich.
**gang** [gæŋ], *s.* die Bande; die Mannschaft (*workmen*). — *v.n.* — *up*, eine Bande bilden; — *up on s.o.*, sich gegen jemanden verbünden.
**gangrene** [ˈgæŋgri:n], *s.* (*Med.*) der Brand; die Fäulnis.
**gangway** [ˈgæŋwei], *s.* die Planke, der Laufgang (*on boat*); der Durchgang.
**gaol, jail** [dʒeil], *s.* das Gefängnis. — *v.a.* einsperren.
**gaoler, jailer** [ˈdʒeilə], *s.* der Kerkermeister.
**gap** [gæp], *s.* die Lücke; die Bresche (*breach*).
**gape** [geip], *v.n.* gähnen, (*fig.*) klaffen.

**garage** [ˈgærɑ:ʒ *or* ˈgæridʒ], *s.* die Garage, die Tankstelle.
**garb** [gɑ:b], *s.* die Tracht, Kleidung.
**garbage** [ˈgɑ:bidʒ], *s.* der Abfall; (*Am.*) — *can*, der Mülleimer.
**garble** [gɑ:bl], *v.a.* verstümmeln.
**garden** [gɑ:dn], *s.* der Garten. — *v.n.* im Garten arbeiten.
**gardener** [ˈgɑ:dnə], *s.* der Gärtner.
**gargle** [gɑ:gl], *v.n.* gurgeln, spülen.
**gargoyle** [ˈgɑ:gɔil], *s.* (*Archit.*) der Wasserspeier.
**garish** [ˈgɛəriʃ], *adj.* grell, auffallend.
**garland** [ˈgɑ:lənd], *s.* der Blumenkranz, die Girlande.
**garlic** [ˈgɑ:lik], *s.* (*Bot.*) der Knoblauch.
**garment** [ˈgɑ:mənt], *s.* das Gewand.
**garner** [ˈgɑ:nə], *v.a.* aufspeichern (*store*).
**garnet** [ˈgɑ:nit], *s.* der Granat.
**garnish** [ˈgɑ:niʃ], *v.a.* ausschmücken, verzieren.
**garret** [ˈgærət], *s.* die Dachkammer.
**garrison** [ˈgærisən], *s.* (*Mil.*) die Garnison. — *v.a.* stationieren.
**garrulity** [gæˈru:liti], *s.* die Schwatzhaftigkeit.
**garter** [ˈgɑ:tə], *s.* das Strumpfband, das Hosenband; *Order of the Garter*, der Hosenbandorden.
**gas** [gæs], *s.* das Gas; (*Am.*) *see* **gasoline**.
**Gascon** [ˈgæskən], *s.* der Gaskogner.
**gaseous** [ˈgeisiəs], *adj.* gasförmig, gasartig.
**gash** [gæʃ], *s.* die Schnittwunde.
**gasoline** [ˈgæsoli:n], *s.* (*Am.*) das Benzin.
**gasp** [gɑ:sp], *v.n.* keuchen; nach Luft schnappen. — *s.* das Keuchen, das Luftschnappen.
**gastric** [ˈgæstrik], *adj.* (*Anat.*) gastrisch; — *ulcer*, das Magengeschwür.
**gate** [geit], *s.* das Tor, der Eingang. — *v.a.* einsperren, Hausarrest geben (*Dat.*).
**gateway** [ˈgeitwei], *s.* die Einfahrt.
**gather** [ˈgæðə], *v.a.* sammeln, einsammeln (*collect*); versammeln (*assemble*). — *v.n.* entnehmen, schließen (*infer*); sich versammeln (*come together*); aufziehen (*storm*).
**gathering** [ˈgæðəriŋ], *s.* die Versammlung (*meeting*).
**gauche** [gouʃ], *adj.* linkisch, ungeschickt.
**gaudy** [ˈgɔ:di], *adj.* übertrieben, grell, prunkhaft.
**gauge** [geidʒ], *v.a.* (*Engin.*) ausmessen, kalibrieren; eichen (*officially*). — *s.* der Maßstab (*scale*); (*Railw.*) die Spurweite.
**gauger** [ˈgeidʒə], *s.* der Eichmeister.
**Gaul** [gɔ:l], *s.* der Gallier.
**gaunt** [gɔ:nt], *adj.* mager; hager.
**gauntlet** [ˈgɔ:ntlit], *s.* der (Panzer)handschuh.
**gauze** [gɔ:z], *s.* die Gaze.
**gavotte** [gəˈvɔt], *s.* (*Mus.*) die Gavotte.

**gay** [gei], *adj.* fröhlich, heiter; bunt (*colour*).

**gaze** [geiz], *v.n.* starren.

**gazelle** [gə'zel], *s.* (*Zool.*) die Gazelle.

**gazette** [gə'zet], *s.* die (amtliche) Zeitung; das Amtsblatt.

**gear** [giə], *s.* das Gerät; (*Mech.*) das Triebwerk; (*Naut.*) das Geschirr; *switch—*, das Schaltgerät; (*Motor.*) der Gang; — *ratio*, die Übersetzung; *differential —*, der Achsenantrieb; *steering —*, die Lenkung (*of car*); — *box*, das Schaltgetriebe, die Gangschaltung; *out of —*, in Unordnung; *in top —*, mit Höchstgeschwindigkeit; *change to bottom —*, auf erste Geschwindigkeit (*or*, auf langsam) einschalten. — *v.a. — down*, herabsetzen; (*Engin.*) — *up*, übersetzen; — *to*, anpassen.

**gelatine** ['dʒeləti:n], *s.* die Gallerte, die Geleemasse.

**gem** [dʒem], *s.* die Gemme, der Edelstein.

**gender** ['dʒendə], *s.* (*Gram.*) das Geschlecht.

**gene** [dʒi:n], *s.* (*Biol.*) das Gen.

**geneaology** [dʒi:ni'ælədʒi], *s.* die Genealogie; der Stammbaum (*family tree*).

**general** ['dʒenərəl], *s.* (*Mil.*) der General; *lieutenant- —*, der Generalleutnant. — *adj.* allgemein, General-; — *-purpose*, für alle Zwecke; Allzweck-.

**generalization** [dʒenərəlai'zeifən], *s.* die Verallgemeinerung.

**generalize** ['dʒenərəlaiz], *v.a.* verallgemeinern.

**generate** ['dʒenəreit], *v.a.* erzeugen; (*Elec.*) Strom erzeugen.

**generation** [dʒenə'reifən], *s.* die Generation (*contemporaries*); das Zeugen (*production*); (*Elec.*) die Stromerzeugung.

**generosity** [dʒenə'rɔsiti], *s.* die Großmut (*magnanimity*); die Freigebigkeit (*liberality*).

**generous** ['dʒenərəs], *adj.* großmütig; freigebig (*with gifts*).

**Genevan** [dʒi'ni:vən], *adj.* genferisch. — *s.* der Genfer.

**genial** ['dʒi:niəl], *adj.* freundlich, mild.

**geniality** [dʒi:ni'æliti], *s.* die Freundlichkeit, Leutseligkeit.

**genital** ['dʒenitəl], *adj.* Zeugungs-. — *s.* (*pl.*) die Geschlechtsteile, Genitalien, *pl.*

**genitive** ['dʒenitiv], *s.* (*Gram.*) der Wesfall, Genitiv.

**genius** ['dʒi:niəs], *s.* das Genie; der Genius.

**Genoese** [dʒenou'i:z], *adj.* genuesisch. — *s.* der Genuese.

**Gentile** ['dʒentail], *s.* heidnisch; nicht jüdisch.

**gentility** [dʒen'tiliti], *s.* die Herkunft aus vornehmem Haus, Vornehmheit.

**gentle** [dʒentl], *adj.* sanft, mild; gelind (*breeze*).

**gentlefolk** ['dʒentlfouk], *s.* bessere *or* vornehme Leute, *pl.*

**gentleman** ['dʒentlmən], *s.* der Gentleman, Herr; feiner Herr.

**gentleness** ['dʒentlnis], *s.* die Milde, Sanftheit.

**gentry** ['dʒentri], *s.* der niedere Adel.

**genuine** ['dʒenjuin], *adj.* echt.

**genus** ['dʒi:nəs], *s.* (*Biol.*) die Gattung.

**geographer** [dʒi'ɔgrəfə], *s.* der Geograph.

**geographical** [dʒi:o'græfikəl], *adj.* geographisch.

**geography** [dʒi'ɔgrəfi], *s.* die Geographie, Erdkunde.

**geological** [dʒi:o'lɔdʒikəl], *adj.* geologisch.

**geologist** [dʒi'ɔlədʒist], *s.* der Geologe.

**geology** [dʒi'ɔlədʒi], *s.* die Geologie.

**geometric(al)** [dʒi:o'metrik(əl)], *adj.* geometrisch.

**geometrist** [dʒi'ɔmətrist], *s.* der Geometer.

**geometry** [dʒi'ɔmətri], *s.* die Geometrie.

**geranium** [dʒə'reiniəm], *s.* (*Bot.*) die Geranie, das Geranium.

**germ** [dʒə:m], *s.* der Keim; (*pl.*) die Bakterien, *f. pl.*

**German** ['dʒə:mən], *adj.* deutsch. — *s.* der, die Deutsche.

**germane** [dʒə:'mein], *adj.* zur Sache gehörig, zugehörig.

**Germanic** [dʒə:'mænik], *adj.* germanisch.

**germinate** ['dʒə:mineit], *v.n.* keimen.

**gerund** ['dʒerənd], *s.* (*Gram.*) das Gerundium.

**gerundive** [dʒe'rʌndiv], *s.* (*Gram.*) das Gerundiv(um).

**gesticulate** [dʒes'tikjuleit], *v.n.* Gebärden machen, gestikulieren.

**gesture** ['dʒestfə], *s.* die Geste; der Gebärde.

**get** [get], *v.a. irr.* bekommen, (*coll.*) kriegen; erhalten (*receive*); erwischen (*catch up with*); einholen (*fetch*); — *over* or *across*, klar machen. — *v.n.* gelangen (*arrive*); werden (*become*); — *along*, weiterkommen; — *on* or (*Am.*) *along with s.o.*, mit jemandem auskommen; — *on in the world*, Karriere machen; — *away*, entkommen; — *down to it*, zur Sache kommen; — *in*, hineinkommen; — *off*, aussteigen; *show s.o. where he —s off*, jemandem seine Meinung sagen; (*Sch.*) — *through*, durchkommen (*in examination*); — *up*, aufstehen.

**get-up** ['getʌp], *s.* das Kostüm; die Ausstattung (*attire*).

**Ghanaian** [ga:'neiən], *adj.* ghanaisch. — *s.* der Ghanaer.

**ghastly** ['ga:stli], *adj.* furchtbar, schrecklich.

**gherkin** ['gə:kin], *s.* (*Bot.*) die Essiggurke.

**ghost** [goust], *s.* der Geist, das Gespenst.

**giant** ['dʒaiənt], *s.* der Riese.

**gibberish** ['dʒibərif], *s.* das Kauderwelsch.

**gibbet** ['dʒibit], *s.* der Galgen.

**gibe** [dʒaib], *v.n.* spotten, höhnen (*at*, *über*, *Acc.*). — *s.* der Spott, Hohn; die spöttische Bemerkung (*remark*).

**giblets** ['dʒiblits], *s. pl.* das Gänseklein.

**giddiness** ['gidinis], *s.* das Schwindelgefühl.

**giddy** ['gidi], *adj.* schwindelig.

**gift** [gift], *s.* die Gabe, das Geschenk.

**gifted** ['giftid], *adj.* begabt.

**gig** [gig], *s.* der leichte Wagen; (*Naut.*) der Nachen, das Gig.

**gigantic** [dʒai'gæntik], *adj.* riesig, riesengroß.

**giggle** [gigl], *v.n.* kichern. — *s.* das Kichern, Gekicher.

**gild** [gild], *v.a.* vergolden; verschönern; —*ing the pill*, etwas Unangenehmes (die Pille) versüßen.

**gill** (1) [gil], *s.* (*Biol.*) die Kieme.

**gill** (2) [dʒil], *s.* das Viertel einer Pinte (0.14 *l.*).

**gilt** [gilt], *s.* die Vergoldung; — *edged*, mit Goldschnitt; (*Comm.*) hochwertige *or* mündelsichere Staatspapiere.

**gimlet** ['gimlit], *s.* (*Carp.*) der Handbohrer.

**gin** [dʒin], *s.* der Gin, der Wachholderbranntwein; — *and tonic*, Gin und Tonic.

**ginger** ['dʒindʒə], *s.* der Ingwer; — -*haired*, rothaarig; — *nut*, das Ingweror Pfeffernüßchen, Ingwerkeks; — *beer*, Ingwerbier. — *v.a.* — *up*, aufstacheln, anreizen.

**gingerbread** ['dʒindʒəbred], *s.* der Lebkuchen, Pfefferkuchen.

**gipsy** ['dʒipsi], *s.* der Zigeuner.

**giraffe** [dʒi'rɑːf], *s.* (*Zool.*) die Giraffe.

**gird** [gəːd], *v.a.* reg. & irr. (*Poet.*) gürten.

**girder** ['gəːdə], *s.* der Balken, Träger.

**girdle** [gəːdl], *v.a.* gürten, umgürten; — *the earth*, die Erde umkreisen.

**girl** [gəːl], *s.* das Mädchen.

**girlhood** ['gəːlhud], *s.* die Mädchenzeit, die Mädchenjahre, *n. pl.*

**girlish** ['gəːliʃ], *adj.* mädchenhaft, wie ein Mädchen.

**gist** [dʒist], *s.* das Wesentliche.

**give** [giv], *v.a. irr.* geben; — *out*, bekanntgeben, bekanntmachen; — *up*, aufgeben; — *way to*, Platz machen. — *v.n.* sich dehnen, sich strecken (*of wood, metal etc.*); — *in*, nachgeben (*to*, *Dat.*).

**glacial** ['gleiʃəl], *adj.* eisig, Gletscher-.

**glacier** ['glæsiə], *s.* der Gletscher.

**glad** [glæd], *adj.* froh, erfreut (*at*, *über*, *Acc.*).

**gladden** [glædn], *v.a.* erheitern, erfreuen.

**glade** [gleid], *s.* die Lichtung.

**glamorous** ['glæmərəs], *adj.* bezaubernd, blendend glanzvoll.

**glamour** ['glæmə], *s.* der Zauber; der Glanz.

**glance** [glɑːns], *s.* der Blick; *at a* —, auf den ersten Blick. — *v.n.* flüchtig blicken.

**gland** [glænd], *s.* (*Anat.*) die Drüse.

**glandular** ['glændjulə], *adj.* Drüsen-, drüsig.

**glare** [glɛə], *s.* der blendende Glanz, das Schimmern; der (scharf) durchbohrende Blick (*stare*).

**glaring** ['glɛəriŋ], *adj.* schreiend (*of colour*); auffallend (*obvious*).

**glass** [glɑːs], *s.* das Glas; der Spiegel (*mirror*); das Wetterglas (*barometer*); (*pl.*) die Brille (*spectacles*).

**glassblower** ['glɑːsbləuə], *s.* der Glasbläser.

**glassworks** ['glɑːswəːks], *s.* die Glashütte.

**glassy** ['glɑːsi], *adj.* gläsern.

**glaze** [gleiz], *s.* die Glasur. — *v.a.* glasieren; verglasen.

**glazier** ['gleiziə], *s.* der Glaser.

**gleam** [gliːm], *v.n.* strahlen, glänzen (*with*, vor, *Dat.*). — *s.* der Glanz, das Strahlen.

**glean** [gliːn], *v.a.* auflesen; erfahren (*learn*).

**glebe** [gliːb], *s.* das Pfarrgut.

**glee** (1) [gliː], *s.* die Freude, Heiterkeit.

**glee** (2) [gliː], *s.* (*Mus.*) der Rundgesang; — *club*, die Liedertafel.

**glen** [glen], *s.* das enge Tal.

**glib** [glib], *adj.* glatt, geläufig, zungenfertig.

**glide** [glaid], *v.n.* gleiten. — *s.* das Gleiten.

**glider** ['glaidə], *s.* (*Aviat.*) das Segelflugzeug.

**glimmer** ['glimə], *s.* der Schimmer, Glimmer. — *v.n.* schimmern, glimmen.

**glimpse** [glimps], *s.* der (flüchtige) Blick; *catch a* —, einen Blick erhaschen. — *v.a.* flüchtig blicken (*auf*, *Acc.*).

**glisten** [glisn], *v.n.* glitzern, glänzen.

**glitter** ['glitə], *v.n.* glänzen, schimmern.

**gloaming** ['gləumiŋ], *s.* die Dämmerung.

**globe** [gləub], *s.* der Globus, der Erdball; die Kugel.

**globular** ['glɔbjulə], *adj.* kugelförmig.

**gloom** [gluːm], *s.* das Dunkel; der Trübsinn, die Traurigkeit.

**gloomy** ['gluːmi], *adj.* deprimiert, trübsinnig, düster.

**glorify** ['glɔːrifai], *v.a.* verherrlichen.

**glorious** ['glɔːriəs], *adj.* herrlich; (*Mil.*) glorreich.

**glory** ['glɔːri], *s.* die Herrlichkeit, der Ruhm. — *v.n.* frohlocken (*in*, über, *Acc.*).

**gloss** [glɔs], *s.* der Glanz; (*Lit.*) die Glosse, Anmerkung. — *v.a.* — *over*, beschönigen; (*Lit.*) glossieren, mit Anmerkungen versehen.

**glossary** ['glɔsəri], *s.* das Glossar, die Spezialwörterliste; das Wörterbuch.

**glossy** ['glɔsi], *adj.* glänzend.

**glove** [glʌv], *s.* der Handschuh.

**glow** [gləu], *v.n.* glühen. — *s.* die Glut, das Glühen; Wohlbehagen.

**glower** ['glauə], *v.n.* — *at*, feindselig ansehen, anstarren.

**glue** [glu:], *s.* der Leim. — *v.a.* leimen, zusammenleimen.

**glum** [glʌm], *adj.* mürrisch, finster.

**glut** [glʌt], *s.* die Überfülle. — *v.a.* überladen, überfüllen.

**glutinous** [ˈgluːtinəs], *adj.* zähe, klebrig.

**glutton** [glʌtn], *s.* der Vielfraß.

**gluttony** [ˈglʌtəni], *s.* die Schwelgerei, Gefräßigkeit.

**glycerine** [ˈglisəriːn], *s.* das Glyzerin.

**gnarled** [nɑːld], *adj.* knorrig.

**gnash** [næʃ], *v.a.* knirschen (*teeth*).

**gnat** [næt], *s.* (*Ent.*) die Mücke.

**gnaw** [nɔː], *v.a.*, *v.n.* nagen (an, *Dat.*), zernagen, zerfressen (at, *Acc.*).

**gnome** [noum], *s.* der Erdgeist, der Zwerg, Gnom.

**go** [gou], *v.n. irr.* gehen, fahren, laufen; arbeiten (*engine*); verlaufen (*event*); sich erstrecken (*distance*); — *down in the general esteem*, in der Achtung sinken; — *on*, fortfahren; — *mad*, verrückt werden; — *bald*, die Haare verlieren; — *without*, leer ausgehen, entbehren; *let* —, loslassen; — *for*, auf jemanden losgehen; — *in for*, sich interessieren für (*Acc.*); — *all out for*, energisch unternehmen; *a* —*ing concern*, ein gutgehendes Unternehmen; —*ing on for 20*, fast 20 Jahre. — *s.* der Versuch; (*coll.*) *plenty of* —, recht lebhaft, voller Schwung.

**goad** [goud], *v.a.* anstacheln.

**goal** [goul], *s.* das Ziel; (*Footb.*) das Tor.

**goalkeeper** [ˈgoulkiːpə], *s.* der Torwart.

**goalpost** [ˈgoulpoust], *s.* der Torpfosten.

**goat** [gout], *s.* (*Zool.*) die Geiß, Ziege; *billy* —, der Ziegenbock; *nanny* —, die Geiß.

**gobble** [gɔbl], *v.a.* verschlingen, gierig essen.

**goblet** [ˈgɔblit], *s.* der Becher.

**goblin** [ˈgɔblin], *s.* der Kobold, der Gnom; der Schelm.

**go-cart** [ˈgoukɑːt], *s.* der Kinderwagen, Gängelwagen.

**God** [gɔd], *s.* Gott.

**god** [gɔd], *s.* der Gott.

**godchild** [ˈgɔdtʃaild], *s.* das Patenkind.

**goddess** [ˈgɔdes], *s.* die Göttin.

**godfather** [ˈgɔdfɑːðə], *s.* der Pate.

**godhead** [ˈgɔdhed], *s.* die Gottheit.

**godless** [ˈgɔdlis], *adj.* gottlos, ungläubig.

**godmother** [ˈgɔdmʌðə], *s.* die Patin.

**goggle** [gɔgl], *v.n.* glotzen, starren (*stare*). — *s.* (*pl.*) die Schutzbrille.

**going** [ˈgouiŋ], *s.* das Gehen, das Funktionieren (*of machinery*); *while the* — *is good*, zur rechten Zeit.

**gold** [gould], *s.* das Gold; (*Fin.*) — *standard*, die Goldwährung.

**goldfinch** [ˈgouldfintʃ], *s.* (*Orn.*) der Stieglitz.

**goldsmith** [ˈgouldsmiθ], *s.* der Goldschmied.

**gondola** [ˈgɔndələ], *s.* die Gondel.

**good** [gud], *adj.* gut; artig, brav; *for* —, auf immer; *in* — *time*, rechtzeitig; — *and proper*, (*coll.*) wie es sich gehört, anständig; *as* — *as*, so gut wie; — *looking*, hübsch; — *natured*, gutmütig. — *s. for your own* —, in Ihrem eigenen Interesse; *that's no* —, das taugt nichts; (*pl.*) die Güter, *n.pl.*, Waren, *f.pl.*; *goods station*, der Frachbahnhof; *goods train*, der Güterzug; *goods yard*, der Güterstapelplatz.

**goodbye** [gudˈbai], *interj.*, *s.*—*! leb wohl! auf Wiedersehen!*

**goodness** [ˈgudnis], *s.* die Güte.

**goodwill** [gudˈwil], *s.* das Wohlwollen; (*Comm.*) die Kundschaft.

**goose** [guːs], *s.* (*Orn.*) die Gans.

**gooseberry** [ˈguzbəri], *s.* (*Bot.*) die Stachelbeere.

**gore** [gɔː], *s.* das geronnene Blut. — *v.a.* durchbohren (*pierce, stab*).

**gorge** [gɔːdʒ], *s.* die Felsenschlucht (*ravine*); (*Anat.*) die Kehle. — *v.a.* gierig verschlingen.

**gorgeous** [ˈgɔːdʒəs], *adj.* prachtvoll, prächtig.

**gorse** [gɔːs], *s.* (*Bot.*) der Stechginster.

**gory** [ˈgɔːri], *adj.* blutig.

**goshawk** [ˈgɔshɔːk], *s.* (*Orn.*) der Hühnerhabicht.

**gosling** [ˈgɔzliŋ], *s.* (*Orn.*) das Gänschen.

**gospel** [ˈgɔspəl], *s.* das Evangelium; *the* — *according to*, das ... Evangelium, das Evangelium des ...

**gossamer** [ˈgɔsəmə], *s.* das feine Gewebe, die Sommerfäden.

**gossip** [ˈgɔsip], *v.n.* klatschen; schwatzen, plaudern. — *s.* der Klatsch; der Schwätzer; die Klatschbase.

**Gothic** [ˈgɔθik], *adj.* gotisch.

**gouge** [gaudʒ], *s.* der Hohlmeißel. — *v.a.* aushöhlen, ausstechen.

**gourd** [guəd], *s.* der Kürbis.

**gout** [gaut], *s.* (*Med.*) die Gicht.

**govern** [ˈgʌvən], *v.a.*, *v.n.* (*Pol.*) regieren; beherrschen; (*fig.*) leiten, herrschen.

**governable** [ˈgʌvənəbl], *adj.* lenkbar, lenksam.

**governess** [ˈgʌvənis], *s.* die Erzieherin, die Gouvernante.

**government** [ˈgʌvənmənt], *s.* die Regierung; (*Pol.*) — *benches*, die Regierungssitze; — *loan*, die Staatsanleihe.

**governor** [ˈgʌvənə], *s.* der Gouverneur, Statthalter.

**gown** [gaun], *s.* das Kleid (*lady's*); (*Univ.*) der Talar; (*official robe*) die Amtstracht.

**grab** [græb], *v.a.* packen, ergreifen. — *s.* der Zugriff.

**grace** [greis], *s.* die Gnade; Gunst (*favour*); der Anmut (*gracefulness*); *Your Grace*, Euer Gnaden; das Tischgebet (*prayer at table*); (*Mus.*) — *note*, die Fermate; *ten minutes'* —, zehn Minuten Aufschub. — *v.a.* schmücken, zieren, ehren.

**graceful** [ˈgreisful], *adj.* anmutig, reizend; graziös (*movement*).

**graceless** ['greislis], *adj.* ungraziös.
**gracious**['greiʃəs],*adj.*gnädig,huldreich.
**gradation** [grə'deiʃən], *s.* die Abstufung, die Stufenleiter.
**grade** [greid], *s.* der Grad, Rang (*rank*); (*Am.*) (*Sch.*) die Klasse. — *v.a.* sortieren, ordnen.
**gradient** ['greidiənt], *s.* (*Geog.*) die Steigung; der Steigungswinkel (*angle*).
**gradual** ['grædjuəl], *adj.* allmählich.
**graduate** ['grædjueit], *v.n.* promovieren (*receive degree*); — *as a doctor*, als Doktor promovieren, den Doktor machen.— [-djuit], *s.* der Akademiker, Graduierte.
**graft** (1) [grɑːft], *s.* (*Hort., Med.*) die (Haut)übertragung. — *v.a.* (*Hort., Med.*) übertragen, anheften (*on to*, auf, *Acc.*).
**graft** (2) [grɑːft], *s.* (*Am.*) der unerlaubte Gewinn; das Schmiergeld; der Betrug (*swindle*).
**grain** [grein], *s.* das Korn, Samenkorn; das Getreide; das Gran (=0·065 *gramme*); die Maserung (*in wood*); *against the* —, gegen den Strich.
**grammar** ['græmə], *s.* die Grammatik; — *school*, das Gymnasium.
**grammatical** [grə'mætikəl], *adj.* grammatisch.
**gramme** [græm], *s.* das Gramm.
**gramophone** ['græməfoun], *s.* das Grammophon.
**granary** ['grænəri], *s.* der (Korn)-speicher, die Kornkammer.
**grand** [grænd], *adj.* groß, großartig; wunderbar; *Grand Duke*, der Großherzog. — *s.* (*Am.*) (*sl.*) 1000 Dollar; (*piano*) der Flügel; *baby* —, der Stutzflügel.
**grandchild** ['græntʃaild], *s.* der Enkel, die Enkelin.
**grandee** [græn'diː], *s.* der spanische Grande.
**grandeur** ['grændjə], *s.* die Größe, Pracht.
**grandfather** ['grændfɑːðə], *s.* der Großvater.
**grandiloquent** [græn'dilokwənt], *adj.* großsprecherisch.
**grandmother** ['grændmʌðə], *s.* die Großmutter.
**grange** [greindʒ], *s.* der Meierhof, das Landhaus.
**granite** ['grænit], *s.* der Granit.
**grannie, granny** ['græni], *s.* (*coll.*) die Oma.
**grant** [grɑːnt], *s.* die Gewährung (*of permission etc.*); die Zuwendung (*subsidy*); (*Sch.*) das Stipendium. — *v.a.* geben, gewähren; *take for* —*ed*, als selbstverständlich hinnehmen.
**granular** ['grænjulə], *adj.* körnig.
**granulated** ['grænjuleitid], *adj.* feinkörnig, Kristall- (*sugar*).
**grape** [greip], *s.* (*Bot.*) die Weinbeere; die Traube; — *sugar*, der Traubenzucker; *bunch of* —*s*,Weintrauben,*f.pl.*
**grapefruit** ['greipfruːt], *s.* die Pampelmuse.

**graphic** ['græfik], *adj.* (*Art*) graphisch; deutlich, bildhaft, anschaulich.
**grapnel** ['græpnəl], *s.* (*Naut.*) der Dregganker.
**grapple** [græpl], *v.n.* — *with*, raufen, (miteinander) ringen.
**grasp** [grɑːsp], *v.a.* (mit der Hand) ergreifen, erfassen. — *s.* das Fassungsvermögen, die Auffassung; der Griff (*hand*).
**grasping** ['grɑːspiŋ], *adj.* habgierig, gewinnsüchtig.
**grass** [grɑːs], *s.* (*Bot.*) das Gras; der Rasen (*lawn*); — *widow*, die Strohwitwe.
**grasshopper** ['grɑːshɔpə], *s.* (*Ent.*) die Heuschrecke.
**grate** (1) [greit], *s.* der Feuerrost, der Kamin.
**grate** (2) [greit], *v.a.* reiben (*cheese*); schaben, kratzen. — *v.n.* knirschen; auf die Nerven gehen.
**grateful** ['greitful], *adj.* dankbar.
**grater** ['greitə], *s.* das Reibeisen; die Reibe (*electrical*).
**gratification** [grætifi'keiʃən], *s.* die Genugtuung, Befriedigung.
**gratify** ['grætifai], *v.a.* befriedigen, erfreuen.
**grating** ['greitiŋ], *s.* das Gitter.
**gratis** ['greitis], *adv.* gratis, umsonst, frei, unentgeltlich.
**gratitude** ['grætitjuːd], *s.* die Dankbarkeit.
**gratuitous** [grə'tjuːitəs], *adj.* frei, freiwillig (*voluntary*); unentgeltlich (*free of charge*); grundlos (*baseless*).
**gratuity** [grə'tjuːiti], *s.* das Trinkgeld (*tip*); die Gratifikation.
**grave** (1) [greiv], *adj.* schwer, ernst (*serious*); feierlich (*solemn*).—*s.* (*Mus.*) das Grave.
**grave** (2) [greiv], *s.* das Grab (*tomb*).
**gravel** [grævl], *s.* der Kies.
**graveyard** ['greivjɑːd], *s.* der Friedhof.
**gravitate** ['græviteit], *v.n.* gravitieren, hinstreben.
**gravitation** [grævi'teiʃən], *s.* die Schwerkraft.
**gravitational** [grævi'teiʃənəl], *adj.* (*Phys.*) Schwerkrafts-.
**gravity** ['græviti], *s.* der Ernst (*seriousness*); (*Phys.*) die Schwere, Schwerkraft.
**gravy** ['greivi], *s.* die Sauce, Soße; der Saft des Fleisches, des Bratens; — *boat*, die Sauciere.
**gray, grey** [grei], *adj.* grau.
**graze** (1) [greiz], *v.n.* weiden.
**graze** (2) [greiz], *v.a.* streifen (*pass closely*), abschürfen.
**grazier** ['greiziə], *s.* der Viehzüchter.
**grease** [griːs], *s.* das Fett; das Schmieröl (*machine*). — *v.a.* einfetten (*pans*); schmieren, einschmieren (*machinery*).
**greasy** ['griːsi], *adj.* fett, schmierig, ölig.
**great** [greit], *adj.* groß, bedeutend, wichtig; (*Am.*) wundervoll, wunderbar.

**greatcoat** ['greitcout], *s.* der Wintermantel.

**great-grandfather** [greit'grændfɑːðə], *s.* der Urgroßvater.

**greatly** ['greitli], *adv.* stark, sehr.

**greatness** ['greitnis], *s.* die Größe, Bedeutung.

**greedy** ['griːdi], *adj.* gierig; gefräßig (*eater*).

**Greek** [griːk], *adj.* griechisch. — *s.* der Grieche.

**green** [griːn], *adj.* grün; neu (*new*), frisch (*fresh*).

**greengage** ['griːngeidʒ], *s.* (*Bot.*) die Reineclaude.

**greengrocer** ['griːngrousə], *s.* der Grünwarenhändler, Gemüsehändler.

**greenhorn** ['griːnhɔːn], *s.* der Grünschnabel.

**greenhouse** ['griːnhaus], *s.* das Gewächshaus, Treibhaus.

**Greenlander** ['griːnləndə], *s.* der Grönländer.

**greet** [griːt], *v.a.* grüßen, begrüßen.

**greeting** ['griːtiŋ], *s.* die Begrüßung; (*pl.*) Grüße, *m. pl.*

**gregarious** [gri'gɛəriəs], *adj.* gesellig.

**grenade** [gri'neid], *s.* die Granate.

**grey** *see under* **gray**.

**greyhound** ['greihaund], *s.* (*Zool.*) das Windspiel, der Windhund.

**grid** [grid], *s.* (*Elec.*) das Stromnetz; (*Phys.*) das Gitter.

**gridiron** ['gridaiən], *s.* der Bratrost, das Bratrostgitter.

**grief** [griːf], *s.* der Kummer, die Trauer.

**grievance** ['griːvəns], *s.* die Klage, Beschwerde.

**grieve** [griːv], *v.a.* kränken. — *v.n.* sich grämen, sich kränken (*over*, über, *Acc.*), wegen, *Genit.*).

**grievous** ['griːvəs], *adj.* schmerzlich.

**grill** [gril], *s.* der Rostbraten, Bratrost. — *v.a.* grillieren, rösten (*meat*); verhören (*question closely*).

**grilling** ['griliŋ], *s.* das Verhör.

**grim** [grim], *adj.* grimmig, finster.

**grimace** [gri'meis], *s.* die Grimasse, die Fratze.

**grime** [graim], *s.* der Schmutz, der Ruß.

**grimy** ['graimi], *adj.* schmutzig, rußig.

**grin** [grin], *v.n.* grinsen; (*coll.*) — *and bear it*, mach gute Miene zum bösen Spiel. — *s.* das Grinsen.

**grind** [graind], *v.a. irr.* zerreiben (*rub*); schleifen (*sharpen*); mahlen (*pulverize*); — *o.'s teeth*, mit den Zähnen knirschen. — *s.* (*coll.*) die ungeheuere Anstrengung, die Plackerei.

**grinder** ['graində], *s.* coffee —, die Kaffeemühle; *knife* —, der Schleifer, Wetzer; der Backzahn (*molar*).

**grindstone** ['graindstoun], *s.* der Schleifstein; *keep o.'s nose to the* —, fest bei der Arbeit bleiben.

**grip** [grip], *s.* der Griff; *lose o.'s* —, nicht mehr bewältigen können (wie bisher); (*Tech.*) der Handgriff (*handle*). — *v.a.* ergreifen, festhalten.

**gripe** [graip], *v.n.* (*sl.*) meckern.

**gripes** [graips], *s. pl.* (*Med.*) das Bauchgrimmen, die Kolik.

**gripping** ['gripiŋ], *adj.* fesselnd (*story*).

**grisly** ['grizli], *adj.* scheußlich, gräßlich.

**grist** [grist], *s.* das Mahlgut, Gemahlene; — *to o.'s mill*, Wasser auf seine Mühle.

**gristle** [grisl], *s.* der Knorpel.

**grit** [grit], *s.* das Schrot, der Kies; der Mut (*courage*).

**gritty** ['griti], *adj.* körnig, kiesig, sandig.

**grizzled** [grizld], *adj.* grau, graumeliert.

**groan** [groun], *v.n.* stöhnen.

**groats** [grouts], *s. pl.* die Hafergrütze.

**grocer** ['grousə], *s.* der Kolonialwarenhändler, Feinkosthändler.

**groin** [grɔin], *s.* (*Anat.*) die Leiste; (*Archit.*) die Gewölbekante, Rippe.

**groom** [gruːm], *s.* der Stallknecht (*stables*); (*obs.*) der Junge (*inn*). — *v.a.* schniegeln, bürsten; schön machen.

**groove** [gruːv], *s.* die Rinne; die Rille (*of gramophone record*). — *v.a.* rillen; furchen (*dig a furrow*).

**grope** [group], *v.n.* tappen, tasten (*around*, umher).

**gross** [grous], *adj.* dick (*fat*); plump (*heavy-handed*); grob (*ill-mannered*); — *weight*, das Bruttogewicht; ungeheuer (*error*).

**grotto** ['grotou], *s.* die Grotte.

**ground** [graund], *s.* der Grund, Boden (*also pl.*); die Ursache (*cause*); — *floor*, das Erdgeschoß. — *v.n.* stranden (*of ship*).

**groundwork** ['graundwəːk], *s.* die Grundlagen, *f. pl.*

**group** [gruːp], *s.* die Gruppe. — *v.a.* gruppieren, anordnen.

**grouse** (1) [graus], *v.n.* (*coll.*) meckern, sich beklagen. — *s.* der Grund zur Klage, die Beschwerde.

**grouse** (2) [graus], *s.* (*Orn.*) das Birkhuhn, Moorhuhn.

**grove** [grouv], *s.* der Hain, das Wäldchen.

**grovel** [grɔvl], *v.n.* kriechen, schöntun (*Dat.*).

**grow** [grou], *v.n. irr.* wachsen, sich mehren (*increase*); werden (*become*). — *v.a.* anbauen, anpflanzen.

**growl** [graul], *v.n.* brummen, knurren. — *s.* das Gebrumme, Geknurre.

**grown-up** ['groun'ʌp], *s.* der Erwachsene. — *adj.* erwachsen.

**growth** [grouθ], *s.* das Anwachsen (*increase*); das Wachstum (*growing*).

**grub** [grʌb], *s.* (*Zool.*) die Larve; (*coll.*) das Essen. — *v.n.* — *about*, wühlen.

**grudge** [grʌdʒ], *s.* der Groll; Neid (*jealousy*). — *v.a.* mißgönnen (*envy*). — *v.n.* — *doing s.th.*, etwas ungerne tun.

**gruel** ['gruːəl], *s.* der Haferschleim.

**gruesome** ['gruːsəm], *adj.* schauerlich, schrecklich.

**gruff** [grʌf], *adj.* mürrisch.

**grumble** [grʌmbl], *v.n.* murren, klagen.

**grumbler** ['grʌmblə], s. der Unzufriedene, Nörgler.
**grunt** [grʌnt], v.n. grunzen. — s. das Grunzen.
**guarantee** [gæræn'tiː], v.a. bürgen, garantieren. — s. die Bürgschaft; (Comm.) die Garantie.
**guarantor** [gæræn'tɔː], s. der Bürge; (Comm.) der Garant.
**guard** [gɑːd], s. die Wache (watch or watchman); (Railw.) der Schaffner; die Schutzvorrichtung (protective device); (fire) —, das Kamingitter; (for sword) das Stichblatt. — v.a. bewachen; behüten (protect). — v.n. auf der Hut sein; — against, sich hüten (vor, Dat.); vorbeugen.
**guarded** ['gɑːdid], adj. behutsam, vorsichtig.
**guardian** ['gɑːdjən], s. der Vormund (of child); der Wächter.
**guardianship** ['gɑːdjənʃip], s. (Law) die Vormundschaft.
**Guatemalan** [gwæti'mɑːlən], adj. guatemaltekisch. — s. der Guatemalteke.
**Guelph** [gwelf], s. der Welfe.
**guess** [ges], v.a. raten (a riddle). — v.n. (Am.) glauben, meinen. — s. die Vermutung; have a —, rate mal!
**guest** [gest], s. der Gast; paying —, der Pensionär.
**guffaw** [gʌ'fɔː], s. das (laute) Gelächter.
**guidance** ['gaidəns], s. die Führung, Anleitung.
**guide** [gaid], s. der Führer, Wegweiser, Reiseführer; (Phot.) die Führung. — v.a. führen, anleiten.
**guided** ['gaidid], adj. gelenkt; — missile, das Ferngeschoß, die Rakete.
**guild** [gild], s. die Gilde, Zunft, Innung.
**guildhall** ['gildhɔːl], s. das Rathaus.
**guile** [gail], s. der Betrug, die Arglist.
**guileless** ['gaillis], adj. arglos.
**guilt** [gilt], s. die Schuld.
**guilty** ['gilti], adj. schuldig.
**guinea** ['gini], s. die Guinee (21 shilings); — fowl, das Perlhuhn; — pig, das Meerschweinchen.
**guise** [gaiz], s. die Verkleidung (costume); die Erscheinung (appearance).
**guitar** [gi'tɑː], s. (Mus.) die Gitarre.
**gulf** [gʌlf], s. der Meerbusen, Golf; der Abgrund (abyss).
**gull** [gʌl], s. (Orn.) die Möwe.
**gullet** ['gʌlit], s. (Anat.) der Schlund, die Gurgel.
**gullible** ['gʌlibl], adj. leichtgläubig.
**gully** ['gʌli], s. die Schlucht (abyss).
**gulp** [gʌlp], v.a. schlucken. — s. der Schluck, Zug.
**gum** (1) [gʌm], s. (Bot.) der Gummi. — v.a. gummieren; (coll.) — up, verderben (spoil).
**gum** (2) [gʌm], s. (Anat.) das Zahnfleisch.
**gun** [gʌn], s. das Gewehr (rifle); die Kanone (cannon); — carriage, die Lafette.

**gunpowder** ['gʌnpaudə], s. das Schießpulver.
**gunsmith** ['gʌnsmiθ], s. der Büchsenmacher.
**gurgle** [gəːgl], v.n. glucksen.
**gush** [gʌʃ], v.n. sich ergießen; schwärmen.
**gusset** ['gʌsit], s. (Tail.) der Zwickel.
**gust** [gʌst], s. der Windstoß.
**gut** [gʌt], s. (Anat.) der Darm; (pl.) die Eingeweide, n. pl.; (pl.) (coll.) der Mut. — v.a. ausnehmen; ausleeren.
**gutter** ['gʌtə], s. die Rinne, Gosse.
**guttersnipe** ['gʌtəsnaip], s. der Lausbube.
**guttural** ['gʌtərəl], adj. Kehl-. — s. (Phon.) der Kehllaut.
**guy** [gai], s. die Vogelscheuche, die verkleidete Puppe; (Am.) der Kerl.
**guzzle** [gʌzl], v.n. schlemmen.
**gymnasium** [dʒim'neiziəm], s. die Turnhalle.
**gymnastics** [dʒim'næstiks], s. pl. das Turnen; die Gymnastik.
**gypsum** ['dʒipsəm], s. der Gips; der schwefelsaure Kalk.
**gyrate** [dʒaiə'reit], v.n. sich im Kreise bewegen, sich drehen, kreisen.

# H

**H** [eitʃ]. das H.
**haberdasher** ['hæbədæʃə], s. der Kurzwarenhändler.
**haberdashery** ['hæbədæʃəri], s. die Kurzwarenhandlung.
**habit** ['hæbit], s. die Gewohnheit (custom); force of —, aus Gewohnheit, die Macht der Gewohnheit; die Kleidung (costume); riding —, das Reitkostüm.
**habitable** ['hæbitəbl], adj. bewohnbar.
**habitation** [hæbi'teiʃən], s. die Wohnung.
**habitual** [hə'bitjuəl], adj. gewohnheitsmäßig.
**habituate** [hə'bitjueit], v.a. gewöhnen.
**hack** (1) [hæk], v.a. hacken (wood); treten.
**hack** (2) [hæk], s. der Lohnschreiber; der (alte) Gaul, das Mietpferd (horse).
**hackle** [hækl], v.a. hecheln.
**hackney** ['hækni], s. — carriage, die Mietskutsche; das Taxi.
**haddock** ['hædək], s. (Zool.) der Schellfisch.
**haemorrhage** ['heməridʒ], s. (Med.) die Blutung, der Blutsturz.
**haemorrhoids** ['heməroidz], s.pl. (Med.) die Hämorrhoiden, f. pl.
**hag** [hæg], s. das alte Weib; die Hexe (witch).

**haggard** ['hægəd], *adj.* hager (*lean*); häßlich, abgehärmt.
**haggle** [hægl], *v.n.* feilschen.
**haggler** ['hæglə], *s.* der Feilscher.
**hail** (1) [heil], *s.* der Hagel. — *v.n.* hageln.
**hail** (2) [heil], *v.a.* (mit einem Ruf) begrüßen; rufen. — *interj.* Heil, willkommen! — *s.* der Zuruf, Gruß.
**hair** [hɛə], *s.* das Haar; *split* —*s*, Haarspalterei treiben.
**haircut** ['hɛəkʌt], *s.* der Haarschnitt.
**hairdresser** ['hɛədresə], *s.* der Friseur.
**hale** [heil], *adj.* — *and hearty*, frisch und gesund, rüstig.
**half** [hɑ:f], *adj.* halb. — *adv.* —*baked*, unreif; unterentwickelt (*stupid*); (*coll.*) *not* —, und wie! sehr gern. — *s.* die Hälfte; *too clever by* —, allzu gescheit.
**halfcaste** ['hɑ:fkɑ:st], *s.* der Mischling.
**halfpenny** ['heipni], *s.* der halbe Penny.
**halfwit** ['hɑ:fwit], *s.* der Dummkopf.
**halibut** ['hælibət], *s.* (*Zool.*) der Heilbutt.
**hall** [hɔ:l], *s.* der Saal; die Halle; der Hausflur (*entrance* —); (*Univ.*) — (*of residence*), das Studentenheim; — *porter*, der Portier.
**hallmark** ['hɔ:lmɑ:k], *s.* das Kennzeichen.
**hallow** ['hælou], *v.a.* weihen, heiligen.
**Halloween** [hælou'i:n], der Allerheiligenabend.
**hallucination** [həlu:si'neiʃən], *s.* die Halluzination.
**halo** ['heilou], *s.* der Heiligenschein (*of saint*); der Hof (*round the moon*).
**halt** [hɔ:lt], *v.n.* halten, haltmachen; zögern (*tarry*); —! Halt!—*ing speech*, die Sprechhemmung. — *v.a.* anhalten, zum Halten bringen. — *s.* (*Railw.*) die (kleine) Haltestelle.
**halve** [hɑ:v], *v.a.* halbieren.
**ham** [hæm], *s.* (*Cul.*) der Schinken; (*Anat.*) der Schenkel; — *acting*, das Schmierentheater.
**hammer** ['hæmə], *s.* der Hammer. — *v.a., v.n.* hämmern; — *away at*, an etwas emsig arbeiten; — *out a problem*, ein Problem zur Lösung bringen.
**hammock** ['hæmək], *s.* die Hängematte.
**hamper** (1) ['hæmpə], *s.* der Packkorb.
**hamper** (2) ['hæmpə], *v.a.* behindern.
**hand** [hænd], *s.* die Hand; *a fair* —, eine gute Handschrift; der Uhrzeiger (*on watch, clock*); die Seite (*right, left* —); die Karten, *f. pl.* (*card game*); *play a strong* —, starke Karten halten *or* spielen; *on* —, vorrätig, auf Lager; *get out of* —, unkontrollierbar werden. — *v.a.* — *in*, einhändigen, einreichen; — *out*, austeilen; — *over*, übergeben, einhändigen.
**handbag** ['hændbæg], *s.* die Handtasche.
**handbill** ['hændbil], *s.* der Zettel, Reklamezettel (*advertising*).

**handful** ['hændful], *s.* die Handvoll; *to be quite a* —, genug zu schaffen geben; das Sorgenkind.
**handicap** ['hændikæp], *s.* das Hindernis. — *v.a.* hindern, behindern.
**handicraft** ['hændikrɑ:ft], *s.* das Handwerk; Kunsthandwerk.
**handkerchief** ['hæŋkətʃif], *s.* das Taschentuch.
**handle** [hændl], *s.* der Griff; der Henkel (*pot, vase*). — *v.a.* handhaben (*machine*); behandeln (*person*); anpacken (*problem*).
**handlebar** ['hændlbɑ:], *s.* die Lenkstange (*bicycle*).
**handmaid(en)** ['hændmeid(n)], *s.* (*obs.*) die Magd.
**handrail** ['hændreil], *s.* das Geländer.
**handshake** ['hændʃeik], *s.* der Händedruck.
**handsome** ['hænsəm], *adj.* hübsch, schön, stattlich.
**handy** ['hændi], *adj.* geschickt; — *man*, der Gelegenheitsarbeiter, Mann für alles.
**hang** [hæŋ], *v.a. reg. & irr.* hängen; aufhängen (*suspend*); — *it!* zum Henker; — *paper*, ein Zimmer austapezieren; — *dog expression*, den Kopf hängen lassen, die betrübte Miene. — *v.n.* hängen; (*coll.*) — *on!* warte einen Moment! — *about*, herumstehen; herumlungern (*loiter*).
**hanger-on** [hæŋər'ɔn], *s.* der Anhänger, Mitläufer.
**hangman** ['hæŋmən], *s.* der Henker.
**hanker** ['hæŋkə], *v.n.* sich sehnen.
**Hanoverian** [hæno'viəriən], *adj.* hannöversch. — *s.* der Hannoveraner.
**hansom** ['hænsəm], *s.* die zweirädrige Droschke.
**haphazard** [hæp'hæzəd], *s.* der Zufall, das Geratewohl.
**hapless** ['hæplis], *adj.* unglücklich.
**happen** ['hæpn], *v.n.* sich ereignen, passieren; — *to . . .*, zufällig . . .
**happiness** ['hæpinis], *s.* das Glück; die Glückseligkeit.
**happy** ['hæpi], *adj.* glücklich, glückselig.
**harangue** [hə'ræŋ], *s.* die Ansprache. — *v.a.* einsprechen (auf, *Acc.*); anreden.
**harass** ['hærəs], *v.a.* plagen, quälen.
**harbinger** ['hɑ:bindʒə], *s.* der Vorbote, Bote.
**harbour** ['hɑ:bə], *s.* der Hafen. — *v.a.* beherbergen (*shelter*); hegen (*cherish*).
**hard** [hɑ:d], *adj.* schwer (*difficult*); hart (*tough*); hartherzig (*miserly*); — *up*, in Not, in Geldverlegenheit; — *of hearing*, schwerhörig.
**harden** [hɑ:dn], *v.a.* härten. — *v.n.* hart werden.
**hardiness** ['hɑ:dinis], *s.* die Kraft, Stärke; die Rüstigkeit.
**hardly** ['hɑ:dli], *adv.* kaum.
**hardship** ['hɑ:dʃip], *s.* die Not, Bedrängnis (*need*); die Beschwerde (*complaint*).

**hardware** ['hɑ:dwɛə], s. die Eisenware(n).
**hardy** ['hɑ:di], adj. abgehärtet, stark; (Bot.) — annual, ein widerstandsfähiges Jahresgewächs.
**hare** [hɛə], s. (Zool.) der Hase; — brained, unbedacht, gedankenlos; —lip, die Hasenscharte.
**harebell** ['hɛəbel], s. (Bot.) die Glockenblume.
**haricot** ['hærikou], s. (Bot.) — bean, die welsche Bohne.
**hark** [hɑ:k], v.n. horchen.
**harlequin** ['hɑ:likwin], s. der Harlekin.
**harlot** ['hɑ:lət], s. die Hure.
**harm** [hɑ:m], s. das Leid, Unrecht; do — to, Schaden zufügen (Dat.). — v.a. verletzen (hurt); schaden (damage, Dat.).
**harmful** ['hɑ:mful], adj. schädlich.
**harmless** ['hɑ:mlis], adj. harmlos.
**harmonious** [hɑ:'mouniəs], adj. harmonisch; einmütig (of one mind).
**harmonize** ['hɑ:mənaiz], v.a. in Einklang bringen. — v.n. harmonieren, in Einklang stehen.
**harmony** ['hɑ:məni], s. (Mus.) die Harmonie; (fig.) der Einklang, die Einmütigkeit.
**harness** ['hɑ:nis], s. der Harnisch. — v.a. anschirren, anspannen (horse); (fig.) nutzbar machen.
**harp** [hɑ:p], s. (Mus.) die Harfe. — v.n. (coll.) — upon, herumreiten auf (Dat.).
**harpoon** [hɑ:'pu:n], s. die Harpune. — v.a. harpunieren.
**harrow** ['hærou], s. die Egge, Harke. — v.a. harken, eggen; quälen.
**harry** ['hæri], v.a. verheeren, quälen.
**harsh** [hɑ:ʃ], adj. herb, rauh (rough); streng (severe).
**hart** [hɑ:t], s. (Zool.) der Hirsch.
**harvest** ['hɑ:vist], s. die Ernte; — home, das Erntefest.
**hash** [hæʃ], v.a. zerhacken; vermischen (mix up). — s. das Hackfleisch; make a — of things, verpfuschen, alles verderben.
**hasp** [hæsp or hɑ:sp], s. der Haken, die Spange.
**haste** [heist], s. die Hast, Eile (hurry); die Voreiligkeit (rashness).
**hasten** [heisn], v.n. eilen, sich beeilen.
**hasty** ['heisti], adj. voreilig.
**hat** [hæt], s. der Hut; (coll.) talk through o.'s —, Unsinn reden.
**hatch** (1) [hætʃ], s. die Brut (chickens). — v.a., v.n. (aus-)brüten; aushecken (cunning).
**hatch** (2) [hætʃ], s. das Servierfenster (for serving food); (Naut.) die Luke.
**hatch** (3) [hætʃ], v.a. (Art) schraffieren.
**hatchet** ['hætʃit], s. das Beil, die Axt; bury the —, das Kriegsbeil begraben.
**hate** [heit], v.a., v.n. hassen; — to ..., nicht ... wollen. — s. der Haß, Widerwille, die Abneigung.
**hateful** ['heitful], adj. verhaßt (hated); gehässig (hating).

**hatred** ['heitrid], s. der Haß.
**hatter** ['hætə], s. der Hutmacher.
**haughty** ['hɔ:ti], adj. übermütig (supercilious); hochmütig, stolz (proud); hochnäsig (giving o.s. airs).
**haul** [hɔ:l], v.a. schleppen, ziehen. — s. das Schleppen; (coll.) die Beute.
**haulage** ['hɔ:lidʒ], s. der Schleppdienst, die Spedition.
**haunch** [hɔ:ntʃ], s. (Anat.) die Hüfte; der Schenkel (horse); die Keule (venison).
**haunt** [hɔ:nt], v.a. heimsuchen, spuken (in, Dat.); it is —ed, hier spukt es.
**have** [hæv], v.a. irr. haben, besitzen (possess); erhalten; lassen; — to, müssen; — s.th. made, done, etwas machen lassen.
**haven** [heivn], s. der Zufluchtsort.
**haversack** ['hævəsæk], s. der Brotbeutel.
**havoc** ['hævək], s. die Verwüstung, Verheerung.
**hawk** (1) [hɔ:k], s. (Orn.) der Habicht; der Falke (falcon).
**hawk** (2) [hɔ:k], v.a. hausieren.
**hawker** ['hɔ:kə], s. der Hausierer.
**hawthorn** ['hɔ:θɔ:n], s. (Bot.) der Hagedorn.
**hay** [hei], s. das Heu; — fever, der Heuschnupfen; —loft, der Heuboden; — rick, der Heuschober.
**hazard** ['hæzəd], s. der Zufall (chance); die Gefahr (danger); das Risiko (risk). — v.a. aufs Spiel setzen, riskieren.
**hazardous** ['hæzədəs], adj. gefährlich, gewagt.
**haze** [heiz], s. der Dunst, Nebeldunst.
**hazel** [heizl], s. (Bot.) die Haselstaude; — nut, die Haselnuß.
**hazy** ['heizi], adj. dunstig, nebelig.
**he** [hi:] pers. pron. er; — who, derjenige, welcher, wer.
**head** [hed], s. der Kopf; die Spitze (of arrow); der Leiter (of firm); (Sch.) der Direktor; die Überschrift (heading); die Krisis (climax); (Pol.) der Führer, das (Staats-)Oberhaupt. — v.a. anführen, führen; (Mil.) befehligen; — v.n. (Naut.) — for, Kurs nehmen auf (Acc.).
**headache** ['hedeik], s. (Med.) die Kopfschmerzen, m. pl.
**headlamp** ['hedlæmp], s. der Scheinwerfer.
**headphone** ['hedfoun], s. (usually pl.) der Kopfhörer.
**headstrong** ['hedstrɔŋ], adj. halsstarrig.
**heady** ['hedi], adj. hastig, ungestüm; berauschend (liquor).
**heal** [hi:l], v.a. heilen. — v.n. (zu)heilen, verheilen.
**health** [helθ], s. die Gesundheit; — resort, der Kurort; your (good) —! Gesundheit! auf Ihr Wohl! Prosit! (drinking toast).
**healthy** ['helθi], adj. gesund.
**heap** [hi:p], s. der Haufen, die Menge. — v.a. häufen, aufhäufen.

# hear

**hear** [hiə], *v.a.*, *v.n. irr.* hören; erfahren (*learn*); (*Law*) verhören (*evidence*).

**hearing** ['hiəriŋ], *s.* das Gehör (*auditory perception*); within —, in Hörweite; (*Law*) das Verhör.

**hearsay** ['hiəsei], *s.* das Hörensagen.

**hearse** [həːs], *s.* der Leichenwagen.

**heart** [hɑːt], *s.* das Herz; der Mut (*courage*); das Innerste (*core*); by —, auswendig; *take to* —, beherzigen; *take — from*, Mut fassen (aus, *Dat.*).

**heartburn** ['hɑːtbəːn], *s.* (*Med.*) das Sodbrennen.

**heartfelt** ['hɑːtfelt], *adj.* herzlich.

**hearth** [hɑːθ], *s.* der Herd.

**hearty** ['hɑːti], *adj.* herzlich; aufrichtig (*sincere*); herzhaft.

**heat** [hiːt], *s.* die Hitze, Wärme; die Brunst (*animals*). — *v.a.* heizen (*fuel*); erhitzen (*make hot*).

**heath** [hiːθ], *s.* die Heide.

**heathen** ['hiːðən], *s.* der Heide, Ungläubige.

**heather** ['heðə], *s.* (*Bot.*) das Heidekraut.

**heating** ['hiːtiŋ], *s.* die Heizung.

**heave** [hiːv], *v.a. reg. & irr.* heben, hieben. — *v.n.* sich heben und senken.

**heaven** [hevn], *s.* der Himmel; *good* —*s!* ach, du lieber Himmel!

**heaviness** ['hevinis], *s.* die Schwere.

**heavy** ['hevi], *adj.* schwer; schwerwiegend (*grave*).

**Hebrew** ['hiːbruː], *adj.* hebräisch. — *s.* der Hebräer, der Jude.

**hectic** ['hektik], *adj.* hektisch, aufgeregt.

**hector** ['hektə], *v.a.* tyrannisieren (*bully*). — *v.n.* renommieren, prahlen.

**hedge** [hedʒ], *s.* die Hecke. — *v.a.* einhegen, einzäunen.

**hedgehog** ['hedʒhɔg], *s.* (*Zool.*) der Igel.

**hedgerow** ['hedʒrou], *s.* die Baumhecke.

**heed** [hiːd], *s.* die Hut, Aufmerksamkeit. — *v.a.* beachten.

**heedless** ['hiːdlis], *adj.* unachtsam.

**heel** [hiːl], *s.* die Ferse (*foot*); der Absatz (*shoe*); *take to o.'s* —*s*, die Flucht ergreifen; (*Am. sl.*) der Lump.

**heifer** ['hefə], *s.* (*Zool.*) die junge Kuh.

**height** [hait], *s.* die Höhe, Anhöhe; die Größe (*tallness*); der Hügel (*hill*).

**heighten** [haitn], *v.a.* erhöhen.

**heir** [ɛə], *s.* der Erbe (*to, Genit.*).

**heiress** ['ɛəres], *s.* die Erbin.

**heirloom** ['ɛəluːm], *s.* das Erbstück.

**helicopter** ['helikɔptə], *s.* (*Aviat.*) der Hubschrauber.

**hell** [hel], *s.* die Hölle. — *interj.* zum Teufel!

**hellish** ['heliʃ], *adj.* höllisch.

**helm** [helm], *s.* das Steuer, Steuerruder.

**helmet** ['helmit], *s.* der Helm.

**helmsman** ['helmzmən], *s.* (*Naut.*) der Steuermann.

**help** [help], *v.a.*, *v.n.* helfen (*Dat.*); *I cannot — laughing*, ich muß lachen; *I cannot — it*, ich kann nichts dafür. — *v.r.* — *o.s.*, sich bedienen. — *s.* die Hilfe, Unterstützung.

**helpful** ['helpful], *adj.* behilflich, hilfreich.

**helping** ['helpiŋ], *s.* die Portion.

**helpless** ['helplis], *adj.* hilflos.

**helpmate, helpmeet** ['helpmeit, -miːt], *s.* der Gehilfe, die Gehilfin.

**helter-skelter** ['heltə'skeltə], *adv.* Hals über Kopf.

**hem** [hem], *s.* der Saum. — *v.a.* (*Tail.*) einsäumen, säumen.

**hemisphere** ['hemisfiə], *s.* die Halbkugel, Hemisphäre.

**hemlock** ['hemlɔk], *s.* der Schierling.

**hemp** [hemp], *s.* der Hanf.

**hemstitch** ['hemstitʃ], *s.* der Hohlsaum.

**hen** [hen], *s.* die Henne (*poultry*); das Weibchen (*other birds*).

**hence** [hens], *adv.* von hier; von jetzt an.

**henceforth** ['hens'fɔːθ], *adv.* fortan, von nun an.

**henpecked** ['henpekd], *adj.* unter dem Pantoffel stehend.

**her** [həː], *pers. pron.* sie (*Acc.*), ihr (*Dat.*). — *poss. adj.* ihr.

**herald** ['herəld], *s.* der Herold. — *v.a.* ankündigen.

**heraldry** ['herəldri], *s.* die Wappenkunde.

**herb** [həːb], *s.* (*Bot.*) das Kraut.

**herbaceous** [həː'beiʃəs], *adj.* krautartig.

**herbage** ['həːbidʒ], *s.* das Gras; (*Law*) das Weiderecht.

**herbal** ['həːbəl], *adj.* krautartig, Kräuter-, Kraut-.

**herd** [həːd], *s.* die Herde. — *v.n.* sich zusammenfinden.

**here** [hiə], *adv.* hier.

**hereafter** [hiər'ɑːftə], *adv.* hernach, künftig. — *s.* die Zukunft; das Jenseits.

**hereby** [hiə'bai], *adv.* hiermit.

**hereditary** [hi'reditəri], *adj.* erblich.

**heredity** [hi'rediti], *s.* (*Biol.*) die Erblichkeit, Vererbung.

**heresy** ['herisi], *s.* die Ketzerei.

**heretic** ['heritik], *s.* der Ketzer.

**heretofore** ['hiətufɔː], *adv.* zuvor, vormals.

**heritage** ['heritidʒ], *s.* die Erbschaft.

**hermetic** [həː'metik], *adj.* luftdicht.

**hermit** ['həːmit], *s.* der Eremit, Einsiedler.

**hero** ['hiərou], *s.* der Held.

**heroic** [hi'rouik], *adj.* heldenhaft, heldenmütig.

**heroine** ['heroin], *s.* die Heldin.

**heroism** ['heroizm], *s.* der Heldenmut.

**heron** ['herən], *s.* (*Orn.*) der Reiher.

**herring** ['heriŋ], *s.* (*Zool.*) der Hering; *red* —, die Ablenkungsfinte, das Ablenkungsmanöver; — *bone*, die Gräte; *pickled* —, der eingemachte Hering.

**hers** [həːz], *poss. pron.* ihr, der ihre, der ihrige.

**herself** [həː'self], *pers. pron.* sich; sie selbst.

**hesitate** ['heziteit], *v.n.* zögern, zaudern; unschlüssig sein (*be undecided*).

**hesitation** [hezi'teiʃən], s. das Zögern, Zaudern; das Bedenken (*deliberation*).

**Hessian** ['heʃən], adj. hessisch. — s. der Hesse.

**hessian** ['hesiən], s. die Sackleinwand (*textile*).

**heterodox** ['hetərədɔks], adj. irrgläubig.

**heterogeneous** [hetəro'dʒi:niəs], adj. heterogen, ungleichartig.

**hew** [hju:], v.a. irr. hauen.

**hexagonal** [hek'sægənəl], adj. sechseckig.

**hiatus** [hai'eitəs], s. die Lücke.

**hibernate** ['haibəneit], v.n. überwintern.

**hibernation** [haibə'neiʃən], s. der Winterschlaf.

**hiccup** ['hikʌp], s. (*usually pl.*) (*Med.*) der Schlucken, Schluckauf.

**hickory** ['hikəri], s. (*Bot.*) das Hickoryholz.

**hide** (1) [haid], v.a. irr. verstecken, verbergen. — v.n. irr. sich verbergen; — and seek, das Versteckspiel.

**hide** (2) [haid], s. die Haut (*of animal*), das Fell, (*tanned*) das Leder.

**hideous** ['hidiəs], adj. häßlich, scheußlich, furchtbar.

**hiding** (1) ['haidiŋ], s. das Versteck.

**hiding** (2) ['haidiŋ], s. die Tracht Prügel.

**hierarchy** ['haiəra:ki], s. die Hierarchie.

**higgle** [higl] see haggle.

**higgledy-piggledy** ['higldi'pigldi], adv. wüst durcheinander.

**high** [hai], adj. hoch; erhaben, vornehm; angegangen (*meat*); — school, die höhere Schule; — time, höchste Zeit; (*Am.*) vergnügliche Zeit; High Church, die Hochkirche. — s. (*Meteor.*) das Hoch.

**Highness** ['hainis], s. die Hoheit (*title*).

**highroad, highway** ['hairoud, 'haiwei], s. die Haupt- or Landstraße.

**highwayman** ['haiweimən], s. der Straßenräuber.

**hike** [haik], v.n. wandern, einen Ausflug machen. — s. die Wanderung, der Ausflug.

**hilarious** [hi'lɛəriəs], adj. fröhlich, lustig, ausgelassen.

**hill** [hil], s. der Hügel, Berg.

**hilt** [hilt], s. der Griff.

**him** [him], pers. pron. ihn, ihm.

**himself** [him'self], pers. pron. sich; er selbst.

**hind** [haind], s. (*Zool.*) die Hirschkuh, Hindin.

**hinder** ['hində], v.a. hindern.

**hindmost** ['haindmoust], adj. hinterst; the devil take the —, den letzten hol der Teufel! nach mir die Sintflut!

**hindrance** ['hindrəns], s. das Hindernis; (*Law*) without let or —, ohne Hinderung.

**Hindu** [hin'du:], s. der Hindu.

**hinge** [hindʒ], s. die Angel, der Angelpunkt. — v.n. sich um etwas drehen; von etwas abhängen (on, *Dat.*).

**hint** [hint], v.n. zu verstehen geben, auf etwas hindeuten (at, auf, *Acc.*), andeuten. — s. die Andeutung, der Fingerzeig.

**hip** (1) [hip], s. (*Anat.*) die Hüfte.

**hip** (2) [hip], s. (*Bot.*) die Hagebutte.

**hire** ['haiə], v.a. (ver-)mieten (car etc.); anstellen (man etc.). — s. die Miete; der Lohn (wage); — purchase, der Abzahlungskauf, die Ratenzahlung.

**hireling** ['haiəliŋ], s. der Mietling.

**hirsute** ['hə:sju:t], adj. behaart, haarig.

**his** [hiz], poss. adj. sein, seine. — poss. pron. sein, der seinige, der seine.

**hiss** [his], v.n. zischen (at, auf, *Acc.*). — s. das Zischen.

**historian** [his'tɔ:riən], s. der Historiker, der Geschichtsschreiber.

**historical** [his'tɔrikəl], adj. historisch, geschichtlich.

**history** ['histəri], s. die Geschichte, die Geschichtswissenschaft.

**histrionic** [histri'ɔnik], adj. schauspielerisch.

**hit** [hit], v.a. irr. schlagen, stoßen. — s. der Schlag, der Treffer (on the target); (*Am.*) der Schlager, Erfolg (success); — parade, die Schlagerparade.

**hitch** [hitʃ], v.a. anhaken (hook); anhängen; — a lift, — hike, per Anhalter fahren. — s. der Nachteil, der Haken.

**hither** ['hiðə], adv. hierher.

**hitherto** [hiðə'tu:], adv. bisher.

**hive** [haiv], s. der Bienenkorb; Bienenstock; — of bees, der Schwarm.

**hoar** [hɔ:], adj. eisgrau, weißlich; — frost, der Reif.

**hoard** [hɔ:d], v.a. hamstern. — s. der Vorrat, Schatz.

**hoarding** ['hɔ:diŋ], s. die Umzäunung, die Bretterwand; die Reklamewand.

**hoarse** [hɔ:s], adj. heiser.

**hoarseness** ['hɔ:snis], s. die Heiserkeit.

**hoax** [houks], s. der Betrug, die Irreführung; der Schabernack (in fun). — v.a. betrügen; foppen (in fun).

**hobble** [hɔbl], v.n. humpeln. — v.a. an den Füßen fesseln.

**hobby** ['hɔbi], s. das Steckenpferd, Hobby, die Liebhaberei.

**hobgoblin** [hɔb'gɔblin], s. der Kobold.

**hobnail** ['hɔbneil], s. der Hufnagel.

**hobnailed** ['hɔbneild], adj. — boots, genagelte Stiefel, m. pl.

**hobnob** [hɔb'nɔb], v.n. (coll.) vertraulich sein.

**hock** (1) [hɔk], s. (*Anat.*) das Sprunggelenk.

**hock** (2) [hɔk], s. (wine) der Rheinwein.

**hod** [hɔd], s. (*Build.*) der Trog; der Eimer (coal).

**hodge-podge** see under hotchpotch.

**hoe** [hou], s. die Hacke, Harke. — v.a., v.n. hacken, harken.

**hog** [hɔg], s. das Schwein. — v.a. verschlingen (food); an sich reißen (grasp).

**hogshead** ['hɔgzhed], s. das Oxhoft.

**hoist** [hɔist], v.a. hissen.

411

# hold

**hold** [hould], *v.a.*, *v.n. irr.* halten (*keep*); enthalten (*contain*); behaupten (*assert*); meinen (*think*); gelten (*be valid*); — *forth*, deklamieren; — *good*, sich bewähren; — *out*, hinhalten (*hope*); (*endure*) aushalten;—*up*, aufhalten. — *s.* (*Naut.*) der Schiffsraum; die Macht (*power*).
**holder** ['houldə], *s.* der Inhaber, Besitzer.
**holding** ['houldiŋ], *s.* das Pachtgut (*farm*); der Besitz (*property*); (*Comm.*) der Trust.
**hole** [houl], *s.* das Loch; die Höhle (*cavity*). — *v.a.* aushöhlen; (*Golf*) ins Loch spielen.
**holiday** ['holidei], *s.* der Feiertag; der Urlaub (*vacation*); (*pl.*) die Ferien, *pl.*
**holiness** ['houlinis], *s.* die Heiligkeit.
**hollow** ['holou], *adj.* hohl. — *s.* die Höhlung; die Höhle.
**holly** ['holi], *s.* (*Bot.*) die Stechpalme.
**hollyhock** ['holihok], *s.* (*Bot.*) die Stockrose.
**holocaust** ['holoko:st], *s.* das Brandopfer; die Katastrophe.
**holster** ['houlstə], *s.* die Pistolentasche, die Halfter.
**holy** ['houli], *adj.* heilig; *Holy Week*, die Karwoche.
**homage** ['homidʒ], *s.* die Huldigung; *pay — to*, huldigen (*Dat.*).
**home** [houm], *s.* das Heim, die Wohnung; die Heimat; *at —*, zu Hause; *Home Office*, das Innenministerium; *— Rule*, (*Pol.*) die Selbstverwaltung.
**homer** ['houmə], (*Am.*) *see* **homing pigeon**.
**homesick** ['houmsik], *adj.* an Heimweh leidend.
**homestead** ['houmsted], *s.* der Bauernhof.
**homicide** ['homisaid], *s.* der Mord (*crime*); der Mörder (*killer*).
**homily** ['homili], *s.* die Predigt; Moralpredigt.
**homing pigeon** ['houmiŋ'pidʒən], *s.* die Brieftaube.
**homogeneous** [homə'dʒi:niəs], *adj.* homogen; gleichartig.
**hone** [houn], *s.* der Wetzstein. — *v.a.* (*blade, knife*) abziehen.
**honest** ['onist], *adj.* ehrlich, aufrichtig.
**honesty** ['onisti], *s.* die Ehrlichkeit.
**honey** ['hʌni], *s.* der Honig; (*Am., coll.*) Liebling!
**honeycomb** ['hʌnikoum], *s.* die Honigwabe.
**honeymoon** ['hʌnimu:n], *s.* die Flitterwochen.
**honorarium** [onə'rɛəriəm], *s.* das Honorar.
**honorary** ['onərəri], *adj.* Ehren-, ehrenamtlich.
**honour** ['onə], *s.* die Ehre; *your —*, Euer Ehrwürden, Euer Gnaden (*title*). — *v.a.* ehren, auszeichnen.
**honourable** ['onərəbl], *adj.* ehrenwert, ehrenvoll; Hochwohlgeboren (*title*).

**hood** [hud], *s.* die Kapuze; das akademische Gradabzeichen über dem Talar; (*Hunt.*) die Haube; —*ed falcon*, der Jagdfalke (mit Haube).
**hoodwink** ['hudwiŋk], *v.a.* täuschen.
**hoof** [hu:f *or* huf], *s.* der Huf (*horse*); die Klaue.
**hook** [huk], *s.* der Haken; *by — or by crook*, mit allen Mitteln. — *v.a.* angeln, fangen.
**hooked** [hukd], *adj.* gekrümmt, hakenförmig.
**hooligan** ['hu:ligən], *s.* der Rowdy.
**hoop** [hu:p], *s.* der Reifen. — *v.a.* (ein Faß) binden.
**hooper** ['hu:pə], *s.* der Böttcher.
**hoopoe** ['hu:pou], *s.* (*Orn.*) der Wiedehopf.
**hoot** [hu:t], *v.n.* schreien (*owl*); ertönen (*siren*); hupen (*car*).
**hooter** ['hu:tə], *s.* die Sirene (*siren*); die Hupe (*car*).
**hop** (1) [hop], *v.n.* hüpfen, tanzen; —*ping mad*, ganz verrückt.
**hop** (2) [hop], *s.* (*Bot.*) der Hopfen. —*v.a.* (*beer*) hopfen, Hopfen zusetzen (*Dat.*). — *v.n.* Hopfen ernten.
**hope** [houp], *s.* die Hoffnung. — *v.n.* hoffen (*for*, auf, *Acc.*).
**hopeless** ['houplis], *adj.* hoffnungslos.
**horizon** [hə'raizən], *s.* der Horizont.
**horizontal** [hori'zontl], *adj.* horizontal, waagrecht.
**horn** [ho:n], *s.* das Horn; (*Mus.*) *French —*, das Waldhorn, Horn; (*Motor.*) die Hupe.
**hornet** ['ho:nit], *s.* (*Ent.*) die Hornisse.
**hornpipe** ['ho:npaip], *s.* (*Mus.*) der Matrosentanz; die Hornpfeife.
**horrible** ['horibl], *adj.* schrecklich.
**horrid** ['horid], *adj.* abscheulich.
**horrific** [ho'rifik], *adj.* schrecklich, schreckenerregend.
**horror** ['horə], *s.* der Schrecken, das Entsetzen; (*fig.*) der Greuel.
**horse** [ho:s], *s.* das Pferd, Roß; *on —back*, zu Pferd.
**horseman** ['ho:smən], *s.* der Reiter.
**horsepower** ['ho:spauə], *s.* die Pferdestärke.
**horseradish** ['ho:srædiʃ], *s.* der Meerrettich.
**horseshoe** ['ho:sʃu:], *s.* das Hufeisen.
**horticulture** ['ho:tikʌltʃə], *s.* der Gartenbau.
**hose** [houz], *s.* die Strümpfe, *m. pl.* (*stockings*); der Schlauch (*water pipe*).
**hosiery** ['houʒəri], *s.* die Strumpfwarenindustrie; die Strumpfwaren.
**hospitable** [hos'pitəbl], *adj.* gastlich, gastfreundlich.
**hospital** ['hospitl], *s.* das Krankenhaus.
**hospitality** [hospi'tæliti], *s.* die Gastlichkeit, Gastfreundschaft.
**host** (1) [houst], *s.* der Gastwirt (*landlord*); der Gastgeber.
**host** (2) [houst], *s.* (*Rel.*) *angelic —*, die Engelschar; (*Mil.*) das Heer, die Heerschar.
**host** (3) [houst], *s.* (*Eccl.*) die Hostie.

**hostage** ['hɔstidʒ], s. die Geisel.
**hostess** ['houstis or –tes], s. die Gastgeberin; air —, die Stewardeß.
**hostile** ['hɔstail], adj. feindlich; feindselig (inimical).
**hot** [hɔt], adj. heiß; hitzig (temperament); scharf, gewürzt (of spices); (fig.) heftig, erbittert.
**hotchpotch, hodge-podge** ['hɔtʃpɔtʃ, 'hɔdʒpɔdʒ], s. das Mischmasch.
**hotel** [(h)ou'tel],s.das Hotel,der Gasthof.
**hothouse** ['hɔthaus], s. das Treibhaus.
**hound** [haund], s. (Zool.) der Jagdhund. — v.a. hetzen.
**hour** ['auə], s. die Stunde; — hand, der Stundenzeiger; for —s, stundenlang; keep early (late) —s, früh (spät) zu Bett gehen.
**hourglass** ['auəglɑ:s], s. die Sanduhr.
**hourly** ['auəli], adj., adv. stündlich.
**house** [haus], s. das Haus; (Comm.) die Firma. — [hauz], v.a. beherbergen, unterbringen.
**houseboat** ['hausbout], s. das Wohnboot.
**housebreaking** ['hausbreikiŋ], s. der Einbruch.
**household** ['haushould], s. der Haushalt.
**housekeeper** ['hauski:pə], s. die Haushälterin.
**housewife** ['hauswaif], s. die Hausfrau.
**housing** ['hauziŋ], s. die Unterbringung; — department, das Wohnungsamt.
**hovel** [hɔvl or hʌvl], s. die Hütte.
**hover** ['hɔvə or 'hʌvə], v.n. schweben, schwanken.
**how** [hau], adv. wie; — do you do? (in introduction) sehr angenehm; — are you? wie geht es Ihnen or Dir?
**however** [hau'evə], adv. wie immer, wie auch immer, wie sehr auch. — conj. doch, jedoch, dennoch.
**howl** [haul], v.n. heulen. — s. das Geheul.
**hoyden** [hɔidn], s. das wilde Mädchen.
**hub** [hʌb], s. die Nabe (am Rad); — of the universe, die Mitte der Welt.
**hubbub** ['hʌbʌb], s. der Tumult, Lärm.
**huckaback** ['hʌkəbæk], s. der Zwillich (textile).
**huckle** [hʌkl], s. die Hüfte.
**huddle** [hʌdl], v.n. sich drängen, sich zusammendrücken. — s. das Gedränge.
**hue** [hju:], s. der Farbton, die Tönung.
**huff** [hʌf], s. die schlechte Laune, die Mißstimmung.
**huffy** ['hʌfi], adj. mißmutig, übel gelaunt.
**hug** [hʌg], v.a. umarmen. — s. die Umarmung.
**huge** [hju:dʒ], adj. riesig, groß, ungeheuer.
**Huguenot** ['hju:gənou or –nɔt], s. der Hugenotte. — adj. hugenottisch, Hugenotten-.

**hulk** [hʌlk], s. (Naut.) das Schiffsinnere, der Schiffsrumpf; der schwerfällige Mensch.
**hull** [hʌl], s. die Hülse, Schale; (Naut., Aviat.) der Rumpf. — v.a. (Engin.) hülsen.
**hullo!** [hə'lou], interj. hallo!
**hum** [hʌm], v.n. summen, brummen. — s. das Summen, Brummen, Gemurmel (murmuring).
**human** ['hju:mən], adj. menschlich. — s. der Mensch.
**humane** [hju:'mein], adj. menschenfreundlich.
**humanity** [hju:'mæniti], s. die Menschheit (mankind); die Menschlichkeit (compassion); (pl.) die klassischen Fächer, n. pl., die humanistischen Wissenschaften, f. pl.
**humanize** ['hju:mənaiz], v.a. menschlich oder gesittet machen.
**humble** [hʌmbl], adj. demütig; bescheiden (modest); unterwürfig (servile). — v.a. erniedrigen (humiliate).
**humbug** ['hʌmbʌg], s. die Schwindelei (swindle); der Schwindler (crook); der Unsinn (nonsense).
**humdrum** ['hʌmdrʌm], adj. langweilig, eintönig.
**humid** ['hju:mid], adj. feucht.
**humidity** [hju:'miditi], s. die Feuchtigkeit.
**humiliate** [hju:'milieit], v.a. erniedrigen.
**humility** [hju:'militi], s. die Demut.
**humming-bird** ['hʌmiŋbə:d], s. (Orn.) der Kolibri.
**humming-top** ['hʌmiŋtɔp], s. der Brummkreisel.
**humorous** ['hju:mərəs], adj. humoristisch, spaßhaft, komisch.
**humour** ['hju:mə], s. der Humor, die (gute) Laune. — v.a. in guter Laune erhalten, gut stimmen; willfahren (Dat.).
**hump** [hʌmp], s. der Buckel, der Höcker.
**hunch** [hʌntʃ], s. der Buckel; have a —, das Gefühl haben.
**hunchback** ['hʌntʃbæk], s. der Bucklige.
**hundred** ['hʌndrəd], num. adj. a —, hundert.
**hundredweight** ['hʌndrədweit], s. der (englische) Zentner.
**Hungarian** [hʌŋ'geəriən],adj.ungarisch. — s. der Ungar.
**hunger** ['hʌŋgə], s. der Hunger.
**hungry** ['hʌŋgri], adj. hungrig.
**hunt** [hʌnt], s. die Jagd. — v.a., v.n. jagen.
**hunter** ['hʌntə], s. der Jäger.
**hurdle** [hə:dl], s. die Hürde.
**hurdy-gurdy** ['hə:digə:di], s. der Leierkasten.
**hurl** [hə:l], v.a. schleudern, werfen.
**hurly-burly** ['hə:libə:li], s. der Wirrwarr.
**hurricane** ['hʌrikin], s. der Orkan; — lamp, die Sturmlaterne.
**hurried** ['hʌrid], adj. eilig, hastig.

# hurry

**hurry** ['hʌri], *v.n.* eilen, sich beeilen; — *to do*, eiligst tun. — *v.a.* beschleunigen. — *s.* die Eile, Hast, Beschleunigung.

**hurt** [hə:t], *v.a. irr.* verletzen; wehetun (*Dat.*); (*verbally*) kränken. — *s.* die Verletzung, Kränkung.

**hurtful** ['hə:tful], *adj.* schädlich, kränkend.

**husband** ['hʌzbənd], *s.* der Mann, Ehemann, Gemahl. — *v.a.* verwalten, sparsam verfahren mit (*Dat.*).

**husbandman** ['hʌzbəndmən], *s.* der Landwirt.

**husbandry** ['hʌzbəndri], *s.* die Landwirtschaft.

**hush** [hʌʃ], *v.a.* zum Schweigen bringen. — *s.* die Stille; — *money*, das Schweigegeld.

**husky** (1) ['hʌski], *adj.* heiser (*voice*).

**husky** (2) ['hʌski], *s.* (*Zool.*) der Eskimohund.

**hussy** ['hʌzi], *s.* (*coll.*) das Frauenzimmer.

**hustings** ['hʌstiŋz], *s.* die Wahltribüne.

**hustle** [hʌsl], *v.a.* drängen, stoßen. — *s.* das Gedränge.

**hut** [hʌt], *s.* die Hütte, Baracke.

**hutch** [hʌtʃ], *s.* der Trog, Kasten (*chest*).

**hybrid** ['haibrid], *adj.* Bastard-. — *s.* der Bastard.

**hydraulic** [hai'drɔ:lik], *adj.* hydraulisch.

**hydroelectric** [haidroui'lektrik], *adj.* hydroelektrisch.

**hydrogen** ['haidrədʒən], *s.* der Wasserstoff.

**hyena** [hai'i:nə], *s.* (*Zool.*) die Hyäne.

**hygiene** ['haidʒi:n], *s.* die Hygiene, Gesundheitslehre.

**hymn** [him], *s.* die Hymne, das Kirchenlied.

**hymnal** ['himnəl], *s.* das Gesangbuch.

**hyper-** ['haipə], *prefix.* über-.

**hyperbole** [hai'pə:bəli], *s.* die Übertreibung.

**hyphen** ['haifən], *s.* der Bindestrich.

**hypnosis** [hip'nousis], *s.* die Hypnose.

**hypochondriac** [haipo'kɔndriæk], *adj.* hypochondrisch. — *s.* der Hypochonder.

**hypocrisy** [hi'pɔkrisi], *s.* die Heuchelei.

**hypocrite** ['hipəkrit], *s.* der Heuchler.

**hypothesis** [hai'pɔθisis], *s.* die Hypothese.

**hypothetical** [haipə'θetikəl], *adj.* hypothetisch, angenommen.

**hysteria** [his'tiəriə], *s.* die Hysterie.

# I

**I** [ai]. das I.
**I** [ai], *pers. pron.* ich.

**ice** [ais], *s.* das Eis; — *bound*, eingefroren; (*Naut.*) — *breaker*, der Eisbrecher; (*Am.*) — *box*, der Kühlschrank; — *cream*, das Eis; das Gefrorene. — *v.a.* (*confectionery*) verzuckern; (*cake*) glasieren.

**Icelander** ['aislændə], *s.* der Isländer.

**Icelandic** [ais'lændik], *adj.* isländisch.

**icicle** ['aisikl], *s.* der Eiszapfen.

**icy** ['aisi], *adj.* eisig.

**idea** [ai'diə], *s.* die Idee.

**ideal** [ai'diəl], *adj.* ideal. — *s.* das Ideal.

**idealize** [ai'diəlaiz], *v.a.* idealisieren.

**identical** [ai'dentikəl], *adj.* identisch, gleich.

**identification** [aidentifi'keiʃən], *s.* die Gleichsetzung, Identifizierung.

**identify** [ai'dentifai], *v.a.* identifizieren, gleichsetzen.

**identity** [ai'dentiti], *s.* die Identität, Gleichheit.

**idiocy** ['idiəsi], *s.* der Blödsinn.

**idiom** ['idiəm], *s.* das Idiom, die sprachliche Eigentümlichkeit.

**idiomatic** [idio'mætik], *adj.* idiomatisch.

**idiosyncrasy** [idio'siŋkrəsi], *s.* die Empfindlichkeit; die Abneigung (gegen, *Acc.*); die Idiosynkrasie.

**idiot** ['idiət], *s.* der Idiot.

**idle** [aidl], *adj.* unnütz (*useless*); müßig, faul (*lazy*). — *v.n.* träge sein.

**idleness** ['aidlnis], *s.* der Müßiggang, die Faulheit.

**idol** [aidl], *s.* das Götzenbild; das Idol.

**idolatry** [ai'dɔlətri], *s.* die Götzenverehrung.

**idolize** ['aidolaiz], *v.a.* vergöttern, abgöttisch lieben.

**idyll** ['aidil *or* 'idil], *s.* die Idylle, das Idyll.

**idyllic** [ai'dilik *or* i'dilik], *adj.* idyllisch.

**if** [if], *conj.* wenn, falls (*in case*); ob (*whether*).

**igneous** ['igniəs], *adj.* feurig.

**ignite** [ig'nait], *v.a.* entzünden. — *v.n.* zur Entzündung kommen, sich entzünden.

**ignition** [ig'niʃən], *s.* die Zündung.

**ignoble** [ig'noubl], *adj.* unedel, gemein.

**ignominious** [igno'miniəs], *adj.* schimpflich, schmählich.

**ignominy** ['ignomini], *s.* die Schande, Schmach.

**ignoramus** [ignə'reiməs], *s.* der Unwissende.

**ignorance** ['ignərəns], *s.* die Unwissenheit, Unkenntnis.

**ignorant** ['ignərənt], *adj.* unwissend.

**ignore** [ig'nɔ:], *v.a.* ignorieren, nicht beachten.

**ill** [il], *adj.* böse, schlimm (*bad*); krank (*sick*); — *feeling*, die Verstimmung. — *adv.* — *at ease*, unbequem, verlegen; *can* — *afford*, kann sich kaum leisten …; — *timed*, zu unrechter Zeit.

**illbred** [il'bred], *adj.* unerzogen.

**illegal** [i'li:gəl], *adj.* illegal, ungesetzlich.

**illegibility** [iledʒi'biliti], *s.* die Unleserlichkeit.

# impel

**illegible** [i'ledʒibl], *adj.* unleserlich.
**illegitimacy** [ili'dʒitiməsi], *s.* die Unehelichkeit, Illegitimität.
**illegitimate** [ili'dʒitimit], *adj.* illegitim, unehelich.
**illicit** [i'lisit], *adj.* unerlaubt.
**illiteracy** [i'litərəsi], *s.* die Unkenntnis des Schreibens und Lesens, das Analphabetentum.
**illiterate** [i'litərit], *s.* der Analphabet.
**illness** ['ilnis], *s.* die Krankheit.
**illogical** [i'lɔdʒikəl], *adj.* unlogisch.
**illuminate** [i'lju:mineit], *v.a.* erleuchten; (*fig.*) aufklären.
**illuminating** [i'lju:mineitiŋ], *adj.* aufschlußreich.
**illumination** [ilju:mi'neiʃən], *s.* die Erleuchtung; die Erklärung (*explanation*).
**illusion** [i'lju:ʒən], *s.* die Illusion, Täuschung.
**illusive, illusory** [i'lju:ziv, i'lju:zəri], *adj.* trügerisch, täuschend.
**illustrate** ['iləstreit], *v.a.* erläutern; illustrieren (*with pictures*).
**illustration** [iləs'treiʃən], *s.* die Illustration (*pictorial*); Erläuterung, Erklärung; das Beispiel (*instance*).
**illustrious** [i'lʌstriəs], *adj.* glänzend, berühmt.
**image** ['imidʒ], *s.* das Bild; das Ebenbild; die Erscheinung (*appearance*).
**imagery** ['imidʒəri], *s.* der Gebrauch von Stilbildern (*style*), die Bildersprache.
**imaginable** [i'mædʒinəbl], *adj.* denkbar.
**imaginary** [i'mædʒinəri], *adj.* eingebildet, nicht wirklich, vermeintlich.
**imagination** [imædʒi'neiʃən], *s.* die Einbildung; die Vorstellung; die Phantasie.
**imaginative** [i'mædʒinətiv], *adj.* erfinderisch, voll Phantasie.
**imagine** [i'mædʒin], *v.a.* sich vorstellen, sich denken.
**imbecile** ['imbisail *or* 'imbisi:l], *adj.* schwachsinnig. — *s.* der Idiot.
**imbecility** [imbi'siliti], *s.* der Schwachsinn.
**imbibe** [im'baib], *v.a.* trinken; (*fig.*) in sich aufnehmen.
**imbroglio** [im'brouliou], *s.* die Verwicklung.
**imbue** [im'bju:], *v.a.* erfüllen, sättigen (*fig.*).
**imitate** ['imiteit], *v.a.* nachahmen, imitieren.
**imitation** [imi'teiʃən], *s.* die Nachahmung, Imitation; — *leather*, das Kunstleder.
**immaculate** [i'mækjulit], *adj.* unbefleckt, makellos.
**immaterial** [imə'tiəriəl], *adj.* unwesentlich, unwichtig.
**immature** [imə'tjuə], *adj.* unreif.
**immeasurable** [i'meʒərəbl], *adj.* unermeßlich, unmeßbar.
**immediate** [i'mi:djit], *adj.* unmittelbar, direkt, sofortig.

**immediately** [i'mi:djətli], *adv.* sofort.
**immemorial** [imi'mɔ:riəl], *adj.* undenklich, ewig.
**immense** [i'mens], *adj.* unermeßlich, ungeheuer.
**immerse** [i'mə:s], *v.a.* eintauchen.
**immersion** [i'mə:ʃən], *s.* das Eintauchen, die Versenkung; — *heater*, der Tauchsieder.
**immigrant** ['imigrənt], *s.* der Einwanderer.
**imminent** ['iminənt], *adj.* bevorstehend.
**immobile** [i'moubail], *adj.* unbeweglich.
**immoderate** [i'mɔdərit], *adj.* unmäßig.
**immodest** [i'mɔdist], *adj.* unbescheiden; unsittlich, unanständig (*immoral*).
**immodesty** [i'mɔdisti], *s.* die Unanständigkeit (*indecency*); Unbescheidenheit (*presumption*).
**immolate** ['imoleit], *v.a.* opfern.
**immoral** [i'mɔrəl], *adj.* unsittlich, unmoralisch.
**immortal** [i'mɔ:tl], *adj.* unsterblich.
**immortalize** [i'mɔ:təlaiz], *v.a.* verewigen, unsterblich machen.
**immovable** [i'mu:vəbl], *adj.* unbeweglich (*fig.*).
**immunity** [i'mju:niti], *s.* die Freiheit, Straffreiheit; Immunität.
**immutable** [im'ju:təbl], *adj.* unabänderlich; unveränderlich.
**imp** [imp], *s.* der Knirps, Kobold, kleine Schelm.
**impair** [im'pɛə], *v.a.* beeinträchtigen; vermindern (*reduce*).
**impale** [im'peil], *v.a.* aufspießen; durchbohren.
**impalpable** [im'pælpəbl], *adj.* unfühlbar, unmerklich.
**impart** [im'pɑ:t], *v.a.* erteilen; verleihen (*confer*); mitteilen (*inform*).
**impartial** [im'pɑ:ʃəl], *adj.* unparteiisch.
**impartiality** [impɑ:ʃi'æliti], *s.* die Unparteilichkeit, Objektivität.
**impassable** [im'pɑ:səbl], *adj.* unwegsam, unpassierbar.
**impasse** [im'pæs], *s.* der völlige Stillstand.
**impassioned** [im'pæʃənd], *adj.* leidenschaftlich.
**impassive** [im'pæsiv], *adj.* unempfindlich.
**impatience** [im'peiʃəns], *s.* die Ungeduld.
**impatient** [im'peiʃənt], *adj.* ungeduldig.
**impeach** [im'pi:tʃ], *v.a.* anklagen.
**impeachment** [im'pi:tʃmənt], *s.* die Anklage.
**impecunious** [impi'kju:niəs], *adj.* unbemittelt, mittellos.
**impede** [im'pi:d], *v.a.* behindern, verhindern.
**impediment** [im'pedimənt], *s.* das Hindernis.
**impel** [im'pel], *v.a.* antreiben; zwingen (*force*).

415

# impending

**impending** [im'pendiŋ], *adj.* bevorstehend, drohend.
**impenetrable** [im'penitrəbl], *adj.* undurchdringlich, unerforschlich.
**impenitent** [im'penitənt], *adj.* reuelos, unbußfertig.
**imperative** [im'perətiv], *adj.* zwingend (*cogent*); dringend notwendig. — *s.* (*Gram.*) der Imperativ, die Befehlsform.
**imperceptible** [impə'septibl], *adj.* unmerklich.
**imperfect** [im'pə:fikt], *adj.* unvollständig, unvollkommen; fehlerhaft (*goods etc.*). — *s.* (*Gram.*) das Imperfekt.
**imperial** [im'piəriəl], *adj.* kaiserlich, Kaiser-, Reichs-.
**imperil** [im'peril], *v.a.* gefährden; in Gefahr bringen, einer Gefahr aussetzen.
**imperious** [im'piəriəs], *adj.* gebieterisch.
**imperishable** [im'periʃəbl], *adj.* unverwüstlich, unvergänglich.
**impermeable** [im'pə:miəbl], *adj.* undurchdringlich.
**impersonal** [im'pə:sənəl], *adj.* unpersönlich.
**impersonate** [im'pə:səneit], *v.a.* verkörpern, darstellen; sich ausgeben als.
**impertinence** [im'pə:tinəns], *s.* die Anmaßung, Frechheit, Unverschämtheit.
**impertinent** [im'pə:tinənt], *adj.* anmaßend, frech, unverschämt.
**imperturbable** [impə'tə:bəbl], *adj.* unerschütterlich, ruhig, gelassen.
**impervious** [im'pə:viəs], *adj.* unwegsam, undurchdringlich.
**impetuous** [im'petjuəs], *adj.* ungestüm, heftig.
**impetus** ['impitəs], *s.* die Triebkraft, der Antrieb.
**impinge** [im'pindʒ], *v.n.* verstoßen (*on*, gegen); übergreifen (*on*, in).
**implacable** [im'plækəbl], *adj.* unversöhnlich.
**implement** ['implimənt], *s.* das Gerät. — [impli'ment], *v.a.* (*Law*) erfüllen, in Wirkung setzen, in Kraft treten lassen.
**implementation** [implimen'teiʃən], *s.* das Inkrafttreten, die Erfüllung, Ausführung.
**implicate** ['implikeit], *v.a.* verwickeln.
**implicit** [im'plisit], *adj.* unbedingt; einbegriffen.
**implore** [im'plɔ:], *v.a.* anflehen.
**imply** [im'plai], *v.a.* besagen, meinen; andeuten.
**impolite** [impə'lait], *adj.* unhöflich, grob.
**impolitic** [im'pɔlitik], *adj.* unklug, unpolitisch, undiplomatisch.
**imponderable** [im'pɔndərəbl], *adj.* unwägbar. — *s. pl.* unwägbare, unvorhersehbare Umstände, *m.pl.*
**import** [im'pɔ:t], *v.a.* einführen, importieren; bedeuten, besagen. —

['impɔ:t], *s.* (*Comm.*) die Einfuhr, der Import; die Bedeutung (*importance, meaning*), Wichtigkeit (*significance*); (*Comm.*) — licence, die Einfuhrgenehmigung.
**importance** [im'pɔ:təns], *s.* die Bedeutung, Wichtigkeit.
**important** [im'pɔ:tənt], *adj.* bedeutend, wichtig.
**importation** [impɔ:'teiʃən], *s.* die Einfuhr.
**importune** [impɔ:'tju:n], *v.a.* belästigen, angehen, dringend bitten.
**impose** [im'pouz], *v.a.* aufbürden, auferlegen. — *v.n.* — upon s.o., einen belästigen.
**imposition** [impə'ziʃən], *s.* die Belästigung; (*Sch.*) die Strafarbeit.
**impossible** [im'pɔsibl], *adj.* unmöglich.
**impostor** [im'pɔstə], *s.* der Schwindler, Betrüger.
**impotent** ['impətənt], *adj.* schwach, machtlos; impotent (*sexually*).
**impound** [im'paund], *v.a.* beschlagnahmen, in Beschlag nehmen.
**impoverish** [im'pɔvəriʃ], *v.a.* arm machen.
**impoverished** [im'pɔvəriʃd], *adj.* verarmt, armselig.
**impracticability** [impræktikə'biliti], *s.* die Unmöglichkeit, Unausführbarkeit.
**impracticable** [im'præktikəbl], *adj.* unausführbar.
**imprecate** ['imprikeit], *v.a.* verwünschen.
**impregnable** [im'pregnəbl], *adj.* uneinnehmbar, unbezwinglich.
**impregnate** [im'pregneit], *v.a.* impregnieren; (*Chem.*) sättigen.
**impress** [im'pres], *v.a.* beeindrucken, imponieren (*fig.*); einprägen, einpressen (*print*). — ['impres], *s.* der Eindruck, (*Typ.*) Abdruck.
**impression** [im'preʃən], *s.* (*fig.*) der Eindruck; die Auflage (*books*).
**impressionable** [im'preʃənəbl], *adj.* eindrucksfähig, empfänglich.
**impressive** [im'presiv], *adj.* ergreifend, eindrucksvoll.
**imprint** ['imprint], *s.* der Name des Verlags oder Druckers. — [im'print], *v.a.* drucken.
**imprison** [im'prizn], *v.a.* gefangensetzen, in Haft nehmen.
**imprisonment** [im'priznmənt], *s.* die Haft; (*Law*) der Arrest.
**improbability** [imprɔbə'biliti], *s.* die Unwahrscheinlichkeit.
**improbable** [im'prɔbəbl], *adj.* unwahrscheinlich.
**improbity** [im'proubiti], *s.* die Unredlichkeit.
**impromptu** [im'prɔmptju:], *adj., adv.* aus dem Stegreif, unvorbereitet.
**improper** [im'prɔpə], *adj.* unpassend; unanständig (*indecent*).
**impropriety** [imprə'praiiti], *s.* die Unanständigkeit (*indecency*); die Ungehörigkeit.

**improve** [imˈpruːv], *v.a.* verbessern; (*Hort.*) veredeln. — *v.n.* besser werden, sich bessern; (*Med.*) sich erholen.

**improvement** [imˈpruːvmənt], *s.* die Verbesserung; (*Med.*) die Besserung, der Fortschritt.

**improvident** [imˈprɔvidənt], *adj.* unvorsichtig, nicht auf die Zukunft bedacht.

**improvise** [ˈimprəvaiz], *v.a.* improvisieren.

**imprudent** [imˈpruːdənt], *adj.* unklug, unvorsichtig.

**impudent** [ˈimpjudənt], *adj.* unverschämt.

**impugn** [imˈpjuːn], *v.a.* anfechten, angreifen.

**impulse** [ˈimpʌls], *s.* der Impuls; der Anstoß.

**impulsive** [imˈpʌlsiv], *adj.* impulsiv.

**impunity** [imˈpjuːniti], *s.* die Straffreiheit.

**impure** [imˈpjuə], *adj.* (*also Metall., Chem.*) unrein, unedel; unsauber.

**impute** [imˈpjuːt], *v.a.* beimessen; zurechnen, die Schuld geben für.

**in** [in], *prep.* in; an; zu, auf; bei; nach, unter; über; von; mit; — *the morning,* vormittags; — *case,* falls; — *any case,* auf jeden Fall; — *German,* auf deutsch; — *my opinion,* meiner Meinung nach; — *the street,* auf der Straße; — *time,* rechtzeitig. — *adv.* drinnen, innen; herein, hinein; zu Hause.

**inability** [inəˈbiliti], *s.* die Unfähigkeit.

**inaccessible** [inækˈsesibl], *adj.* unzugänglich.

**inaccurate** [iˈnækjurit], *adj.* ungenau.

**inaction** [iˈnækʃən], *s.* die Untätigkeit.

**inactive** [iˈnæktiv], *adj.* untätig.

**inadequate** [iˈnædikwit], *adj.* unzulänglich.

**inadmissible** [inədˈmisibl], *adj.* unzulässig.

**inadvertent** [inədˈvəːtənt], *adj.* unbeabsichtigt; unachtsam.

**inadvertently** [inədˈvəːtəntli], *adv.* unversehens; versehentlich.

**inalienable** [inˈeiliənəbl], *adj.* unveräußerlich.

**inane** [iˈnein], *adj.* hohl, leer, sinnlos.

**inanimate** [iˈnænimit], *adj.* unbeseelt, leblos.

**inanity** [iˈnæniti], *s.* die Leere, Nichtigkeit.

**inapplicable** [iˈnæplikəbl], *adj.* unanwendbar; unzutreffend.

**inappropriate** [inəˈproupriit], *adj.* unpassend.

**inarticulate** [inɑːˈtikjulit], *adj.* unartikuliert.

**inasmuch** [inəzˈmʌtʃ], *adv.* insofern (als).

**inattentive** [inəˈtentiv], *adj.* unaufmerksam.

**inaudible** [iˈnɔːdibl], *adj.* unhörbar.

**inaugural** [iˈnɔːgjurəl], *adj.* Inaugural-, Eröffnungs-, Antritts-.

**inaugurate** [iˈnɔːgjureit], *v.a.* einweihen, eröffnen.

**inauspicious** [inɔːˈspiʃəs], *adj.* ungünstig.

**inborn** [ˈinbɔːn], *adj.* angeboren.

**inbred** [ˈinbred], *adj.* in Inzucht geboren; angeboren, ererbt.

**inbreeding** [ˈinbriːdiŋ], *s.* die Inzucht.

**incalculable** [inˈkælkjuləbl], *adj.* unberechenbar.

**incandescence** [inkænˈdesəns], *s.* die Weißglut.

**incandescent** [inkænˈdesənt], *adj.* weißglühend.

**incantation** [inkænˈteiʃən], *s.* die Beschwörung.

**incapable** [inˈkeipəbl], *adj.* unfähig (*of doing s.th.,* etwas zu tun).

**incapacitate** [inkəˈpæsiteit], *v.a.* unfähig machen.

**incapacity** [inkəˈpæsiti], *s.* die Unfähigkeit.

**incarcerate** [inˈkɑːsəreit], *v.a.* einkerkern, einsperren.

**incarnate** [inˈkɑːnit], *adj.* eingefleischt; (*Theol.*) verkörpert.

**incarnation** [inkɑːˈneiʃən], *s.* die Verkörperung; (*Theol.*) Menschwerdung.

**incautious** [inˈkɔːʃəs], *adj.* unvorsichtig.

**incendiary** [inˈsendjəri], *adj.* Brand-, brennend. — *s.* der Brandstifter.

**incense** [inˈsens], *v.a.* aufregen, erzürnen (*make angry*); (*Eccl.*) beweihräuchern. — [ˈinsens], *s.* (*Eccl.*) der Weihrauch.

**incentive** [inˈsentiv], *adj.* Ansporn-, Anreiz-. — *s.* der Ansporn, Anreiz; (*Comm.*) — *scheme,* das Inzentivsystem, Akkordsystem.

**incessant** [inˈsesənt], *adj.* unaufhörlich, ununterbrochen.

**incest** [ˈinsest], *s.* die Blutschande.

**incestuous** [inˈsestjuəs], *adj.* blutschänderisch.

**inch** [intʃ], *s.* der Zoll. — *v.n.* — *away,* abrücken.

**incident** [ˈinsidənt], *s.* der Vorfall, Zwischenfall; das Ereignis.

**incidental** [insiˈdentl], *adj.* zufällig. — *s.* (*pl.*) zufällige Ausgaben, *f. pl.*; das Zusätzliche, Nebenausgaben, *f. pl.*

**incipient** [inˈsipiənt], *adj.* beginnend, anfangend.

**incise** [inˈsaiz], *v.a.* einschneiden, (*Med.*) einen Einschnitt machen.

**incision** [inˈsiʒən], *s.* der Einschnitt.

**incisive** [inˈsaisiv], *adj.* einschneidend; energisch (*person*).

**incite** [inˈsait], *v.a.* aufreizen, anspornen.

**incivility** [insiˈviliti], *s.* die Unhöflichkeit.

**inclement** [inˈklemənt], *adj.* unfreundlich (*weather, climate*).

**inclination** [inkliˈneiʃən], *s.* die Neigung (*also fig.*).

**incline** [inˈklain], *v.n.* neigen, sich neigen. — [ˈinklain], *s.* der Neigungswinkel; der Abhang.

**include** [inˈkluːd], *v.a.* einschließen (*contain*); umfassen (*enclose*).

# including

**including** [in'klu:diŋ], *prep.* einschließlich.
**inclusive** [in'klu:siv], *adj.* einschließlich, mitgerechnet.
**incoherent** [inko'hiərənt], *adj.* unzusammenhängend.
**incombustible** [inkəm'bʌstibl], *adj.*
unverbrennbar.
**income** ['inkʌm], *s.* das Einkommen.
**incommensurable, incommensu-
rate** [inkə'menʃərəbl, inkə'menʃərit],
*adj.* unvereinbar, unmeßbar.
**incomparable** [in'kɔmpərəbl], *adj.* unvergleichlich.
**incompatible** [inkəm'pætibl], *adj.* unvereinbar.
**incompetence, incompetency** [in-
'kɔmpitəns, -tənsi], *s.* die Inkompe-
tenz; Unzulänglichkeit.
**incompetent** [in'kɔmpitənt], *adj.* unzuständig, inkompetent; unzulänglich.
**incomplete** [inkəm'pli:t], *adj.* unvollständig.
**incomprehensible** [inkɔmpri'hensibl],
*adj.* unverständlich.
**inconceivable** [inkən'si:vəbl], *adj.* unbegreiflich.
**inconclusive** [inkən'klu:siv], *adj.* unvollständig (*incomplete*); unüberzeu-
gend; ergebnislos.
**incongruity** [inkən'gru:iti], *s.* (*Maths.*)
die Inkongruenz; (*fig.*) die Unan-
gemessenheit.
**incongruous** [in'kɔŋgruəs], *adj.* in-
kongruent; unangemessen.
**inconsequent** [in'kɔnsikwənt], *adj.* fol-
gewidrig.
**inconsequential** [inkɔnsi'kwenʃəl], *adj.*
inkonsequent (*inconsistent*); unzusammenhängend.
**inconsiderate** [inkən'sidərit], *adj.* rücksichtslos, unbedachtsam.
**inconsistent** [inkən'sistənt], *adj.* inkonsequent.
**inconsolable** [inkən'souləbl], *adj.* untröstlich.
**inconstancy** [in'kɔnstənsi], *s.* die Unbeständigkeit; Untreue (*fickleness*).
**incontestable** [inkən'testəbl], *adj.* unanfechtbar, unbestreitbar.
**incontinent** [in'kɔntinənt], *adj.* unent-
haltsam.
**incontrovertible** [inkɔntro'və:tibl], *adj.*
unstreitig, unanfechtbar.
**inconvenience** [inkən'vi:niəns], *s.* die
Unbequemlichkeit, Unannehmlich-
keit.
**inconvenient** [inkən'vi:niənt], *adj.* unangenehm, unpassend.
**inconvertible** [inkən'və:tibl], *adj.* unveränderlich; (*Comm.*) unumsetzbar.
**incorporate** [in'kɔ:pəreit], *v.a.* einverleiben (*Dat.*), eingliedern (*Acc.*).
**incorporated** [in'kɔ:pəreitid], *adj.*
(*Am.*) eingetragene Körperschaft,
eingetragener Verein.
**incorrect** [inkə'rekt], *adj.* unrichtig,
fehlerhaft; unschicklich, unpassend.
**incorrigible** [in'kɔridʒibl], *adj.* unverbesserlich.

**incorruptible** [inkə'rʌptibl], *adj.* unbestechlich.
**increase** [in'kri:s], *v.a.* vermehren,
vergrößern (*size, volume*); steigern
(*heat, intensity*); erhöhen (*price*). —
*v.n.* sich vermehren, sich erhöhen;
wachsen (*grow*). — ['inkri:s], *s.* die
Zunahme; der Zuwachs (*family*); die
Erhöhung.
**incredible** [in'kredibl], *adj.* unglaublich.
**incredulity** [inkre'dju:liti], *s.* die
Ungläubigkeit, der Unglaube.
**incredulous** [in'kredjuləs], *adj.* ungläubig, schwer zu überzeugen.
**increment** ['inkrimənt], *s.* (*Comm.*) die
Zulage, Gehaltserhöhung.
**incriminate** [in'krimineit], *v.a.* beschuldigen, inkriminieren.
**incubate** ['inkjubeit], *v.a.* brüten, ausbrüten. — *v.n.* brüten.
**incubator** ['inkjubeitə], *s.* der Brutap-
parat.
**inculcate** ['inkʌlkeit], *v.a.* einprägen.
**inculpate** ['inkʌlpeit], *v.a.* beschuldigen.
**incumbent** [in'kʌmbənt], *adj.* (*upon,
Dat.*) obliegend, nötig. — *s.* der
Pfründner, Amtsinhaber.
**incur** [in'kə:], *v.a.* auf sich laden, sich
zuziehen.
**incurable** [in'kjuərəbl], *adj.* unheilbar.
**incursion** [in'kə:ʃən], *s.* der Einfall,
Streifzug.
**indebted** [in'detid], *adj.* verpflichtet,
dankbar (*grateful*); verschuldet (*in
debt*).
**indecent** [in'di:sənt], *adj.* unschicklich,
unanständig.
**indecision** [indi'siʒən], *s.* die Unentschlossenheit.
**indecisive** [indi'saisiv], *adj.* unentschlossen.
**indeclinable** [indi'klainəbl], *adj.*
(*Gram.*) undeklinierbar.
**indecorous** [indi'kɔ:rəs *or* in'dekɔrəs],
*adj.* unrühmlich, unanständig.
**indeed** [in'di:d], *adv.* in der Tat,
tatsächlich.
**indefatigable** [indi'fætigəbl], *adj.* unermüdlich.
**indefensible** [indi'fensibl], *adj.* unhaltbar; unverzeihlich (*unforgivable*).
**indefinable** [indi'fainəbl], *adj.* unbestimmbar, undefinierbar.
**indefinite** [in'definit], *adj.* unbestimmt.
**indelible** [in'delibl], *adj.* unauslöschlich.
**indelicate** [in'delikit], *adj.* unfein.
**indemnify** [in'demnifai], *v.a.* entschädigen.
**indemnity** [in'demniti], die Entschädigung.
**indent** [in'dent], *v.a.* auszacken, einschneiden.
**indenture** [in'dentʃə], *s.* der Lehrbrief
(*apprentice*); Vertrag.
**independence** [indi'pendəns], *s.* die
Unabhängigkeit, Freiheit.
**independent** [indi'pendənt], *adj.* unabhängig, frei.

**indescribable** [indi'skraibəbl], *adj.* unbeschreiblich.

**indestructible** [indi'strʌktibl], *adj.* unverwüstlich; unzerstörbar.

**indeterminable** [indi'tə:minəbl], *adj.* unbestimmbar.

**indeterminate** [indi'tə:minit], *adj.* unbestimmt.

**index** ['indeks], *s.* (*pl.* **indexes**) das Inhaltsverzeichnis; (*pl.* **indices**) (*Maths.*) der Exponent; — *finger*, der Zeigefinger; (*pl.*) die Finger, Zeiger, *m. pl.* (*pointers*).

**India** ['indjə], das Indien; — *paper*, das Dünnpapier.

**Indian** ['indjən], *adj.* indisch; — *ink*, die Tusche. — *s.* der Ind(i)er.

**indiarubber** ['indjə'rʌbə], *s.* der Radiergummi.

**indicate** ['indikeit], *v.a.* anzeigen, angeben.

**indication** [indi'keiʃən], *s.* das Anzeichen, Merkmal, der Hinweis.

**indicative** [in'dikətiv], *adj.* bezeichnend (für, *Acc.*). — *s.* (*Gram.*) der Indikativ.

**indict** [in'dait], *v.a.* anklagen.

**indictment** [in'daitmənt], *s.* die Anklage.

**indifference** [in'difrəns], *s.* die Gleichgültigkeit.

**indifferent** [in'difrənt], *adj.* gleichgültig.

**indigence** ['indidʒəns], *s.* die Armut.

**indigenous** [in'didʒinəs], *adj.* eingeboren, einheimisch.

**indigent** ['indidʒənt], *adj.* arm, dürftig.

**indigestible** [indi'dʒestibl], *adj.* unverdaulich.

**indigestion** [indi'dʒestʃən], *s.* die Magenbeschwerden, *f. pl.*; die Magenverstimmung.

**indignant** [in'dignənt], *adj.* empört, unwillig, entrüstet.

**indignation** [indig'neiʃən], *s.* die Entrüstung, der Unwille.

**indignity** [in'digniti], *s.* die Schmach, der Schimpf.

**indirect** [indi'rekt], *adj.* indirekt, mittelbar.

**indiscreet** [indis'kri:t], *adj.* indiskret, unvorsichtig; unbescheiden (*immodest*); taktlos.

**indiscretion** [indis'kreʃən], *s.* die Indiskretion, Taktlosigkeit.

**indiscriminate** [indis'kriminit], *adj.* ohne Unterschied, wahllos, kritiklos.

**indispensable** [indis'pensəbl], *adj.* unerläßlich, unentbehrlich.

**indisposed** [indis'pouzd], *adj.* unwohl (*health*); unwillig (*unwilling*).

**indisposition** [indispə'ziʃən], *s.* das Unwohlsein (*health*); das Abgeneigtsein (*disinclination*).

**indisputable** [indis'pju:təbl], *adj.* unbestreitbar.

**indissoluble** [indi'sɔljubl], *adj.* unauflöslich.

**indistinct** [indis'tiŋkt], *adj.* undeutlich.

**indistinguishable** [indis'tiŋgwiʃəbl], *adj.* nicht zu unterscheiden, ununterscheidbar.

**individual** [indi'vidjuəl], *adj.* individuell, persönlich; einzeln (*single*). — *s.* das Individuum, Einzelwesen.

**individuality** [individju'æliti], *s.* die Individualität.

**indivisible** [indi'vizibl], *adj.* unteilbar.

**Indo-Chinese** [indotʃai'ni:z], *adj.* hinterindisch. — *s.* der Hinterind(i)er.

**indolent** ['indələnt], *adj.* indolent, träge.

**Indonesian** [indo'ni:ʒən], *adj.* indonesisch. — *s.* der Indonesier.

**indoor** ['indɔ:], *adj.* im Haus; drinnen (*inside*).

**indoors** [in'dɔ:z], *adv.* im Hause, zu Hause.

**indubitable** [in'dju:bitəbl], *adj.* zweifellos, unzweifelhaft.

**induce** [in'dju:s], *v.a.* veranlassen, bewegen, verleiten (*incite*).

**inducement** [in'dju:smənt], *s.* der Beweggrund (*cause*); der Anlaß (*reason*); die Verleitung (*incitement*).

**induction** [in'dʌkʃən], *s.* die Einführung; (*Elec.*) die Induktion.

**inductive** [in'dʌktiv], *adj.* (*Log.*, *Elec.*) induktiv.

**indulge** [in'dʌldʒ], *v.a.* nachgeben (*Dat.*); verwöhnen. — *v.n.* — *in*, frönen (*Dat.*).

**indulgence** [in'dʌldʒəns], *s.* die Nachsicht; das Wohlleben; (*Eccl.*) der Ablaß.

**industrial** [in'dʌstriəl], *adj.* industriell, Industrie-.

**industrious** [in'dʌstriəs], *adj.* fleißig, arbeitsam.

**industry** ['indəstri], *s.* die Industrie (*production*); der Fleiß (*industriousness*).

**inebriate** [i'ni:brieit], *v.a.* berauschen. — [-iit], *adj.* berauscht.

**ineffable** [i'nefəbl], *adj.* unaussprechlich.

**ineffective, ineffectual** [ini'fektiv, ini'fektjuəl], *adj.* unwirksam, wirkungslos; unfähig.

**inefficiency** [ini'fiʃənsi], *s.* die Erfolglosigkeit, Untauglichkeit.

**inefficient** [ini'fiʃənt], *adj.* untauglich, untüchtig.

**ineligible** [in'elidʒibl], *adj.* nicht wählbar.

**inept** [i'nept], *adj.* untüchtig, albern, dumm.

**ineptitude** [i'neptitju:d], *s.* die Unfähigkeit; die Dummheit (*stupidity*).

**inequality** [ini'kwoliti], *s.* die Ungleichheit.

**inert** [i'nə:t], *adj.* träg.

**inestimable** [in'estiməbl], *adj.* unschätzbar.

**inevitable** [in'evitəbl], *adj.* unumgänglich, unvermeidlich.

**inexcusable** [iniks'kju:zəbl], *adj.* unverzeihlich, unentschuldbar.

**inexhaustible** [inig'zɔ:stibl], *adj.* unerschöpflich.

**inexpedient** [iniks′pi:djənt], *adj.* unzweckmäßig, unpraktisch, unpassend.

**inexpensive** [iniks′pensiv], *adj.* billig, nicht kostspielig.

**inexperience** [iniks′piəriəns], *s.* die Unerfahrenheit, Naivität.

**inexpert** [iniks′pə:t], *adj.* ungeübt, unerfahren.

**inexpiable** [i′nekspiəbl], *adj.* unsühnbar, nicht wieder gut zu machen.

**inexplicable** [i′neksplikəbl], *adj.* unerklärlich.

**inexpressible** [iniks′presibl], *adj.* unaussprechlich.

**inexpressive** [iniks′presiv], *adj.* ausdruckslos.

**inextinguishable** [iniks′tiŋgwiʃəbl], *adj.* unauslöschlich.

**inextricable** [i′nekstrikəbl], *adj.* unentwirrbar.

**infallible** [in′fælibl], *adj.* unfehlbar.

**infamous** [′infəməs], *adj.* verrufen, abscheulich, berüchtigt.

**infamy** [′infəmi], *s.* die Schande; Ehrlosigkeit (*dishonour*).

**infancy** [′infənsi], *s.* die Kindheit, Unmündigkeit; (*fig.*) der Anfang.

**infant** [′infənt], *s.* das Kind, (*Law*) der Unmündige, das Mündel.

**infantry** [′infəntri], *s.* die Infanterie.

**infatuate** [in′fætjueit], *v.a.* betören.

**infect** [in′fekt], *v.a.* anstecken, infizieren.

**infection** [in′fekʃən], *s.* (*Med.*) die Ansteckung, Infektion.

**infectious** [in′fekʃəs], *adj.* (*Med.*) ansteckend.

**infer** [in′fə:], *v.a.* schließen, herleiten, folgern.

**inference** [′infərəns], *s.* die Folgerung.

**inferior** [in′fiəriə], *comp. adj.* geringer; untergeordnet (*subordinate*); schlechter (*worse*).

**inferiority** [infiəri′oriti], *s.* die Inferiorität, Minderwertigkeit.

**infernal** [in′fə:nəl], *adj.* höllisch.

**infest** [in′fest], *v.a.* heimsuchen, plagen.

**infidel** [′infidəl], *adj.* ungläubig. — *s.* der Heide, Ungläubige.

**infiltrate** [′infiltreit], *v.n.* durchsickern, durchdringen, infiltrieren.

**infinite** [′infinit], *adj.* unendlich.

**infinitive** [in′finitiv], *s.* (*Gram.*) der Infinitiv, die Nennform.

**infirm** [in′fə:m], *adj.* gebrechlich, schwach; siech (*sick*).

**infirmary** [in′fə:məri], *s.* das Krankenhaus.

**infirmity** [in′fə:miti], *s.* die Schwäche, Gebrechlichkeit.

**inflame** [in′fleim], *v.a.* entzünden.

**inflammation** [inflə′meiʃən], *s.* die Entzündung.

**inflate** [in′fleit], *v.a.* aufblasen, aufblähen; (*Comm.*) künstlich erhöhen (*values*).

**inflation** [in′fleiʃən], *s.* die Aufblähung; (*Comm.*) die Inflation.

**inflect** [in′flekt], *v.a.* (*Gram.*) biegen, flektieren, deklinieren, konjugieren.

**inflection** [in′flekʃən], *s.* (*Gram.*) die Biegung; (*Phonet.*) der Tonfall.

**inflexible** [in′fleksibl], *adj.* unbiegsam.

**inflexion** *see* **inflection.**

**inflict** [in′flikt], *v.a.* auferlegen (*impose*); beibringen (*administer*).

**infliction** [in′flikʃən], *s.* die Verhängung, das Beibringen.

**influence** [′influəns], *v.a.* beeinflussen. — *s.* der Einfluß.

**influential** [influ′enʃəl], *adj.* einflußreich.

**influenza** [influ′enzə], *s.* (*Med.*) die Grippe.

**inform** [in′fo:m], *v.a., v.n.* informieren, benachrichtigen; — *against*, jemanden denunzieren.

**informal** [in′fo:məl], *adj.* nicht formell; ungezwungen, zwanglos.

**informant** [in′fo:mənt], *s.* der Angeber.

**information** [infə′meiʃən], *s.* die Information, Nachricht, Auskunft.

**infrequent** [in′fri:kwənt], *adj.* selten.

**infringe** [in′frindʒ], *v.a.* übertreten.

**infuriate** [in′fjuərieit], *v.a.* wütend machen.

**infuse** [in′fju:z], *v.a.* einflößen, aufgießen, begießen.

**infusion** [in′fju:ʒən], *s.* die Eingießung; der Aufguß (*tea*); (*Chem.*) die Infusion.

**ingenious** [in′dʒi:niəs], *adj.* geistreich, genial.

**ingenuity** [indʒi′nju:iti], *s.* der Scharfsinn.

**ingenuous** [in′dʒenjuəs], *adj.* offen, unbefangen, arglos.

**ingot** [′iŋgət], *s.* der Barren.

**ingrained** [in′greind], *adj.* eingefleischt.

**ingratiate** [in′greiʃieit], *v.r.* — *o.s.*, sich beliebt machen, sich einschmeicheln (*with*, bei).

**ingratitude** [in′grætitju:d], *s.* die Undankbarkeit.

**ingredient** [in′gri:diənt], *s.* der Bestandteil; die Zutat.

**inhabit** [in′hæbit], *v.a.* bewohnen.

**inhabitant** [in′hæbitənt], *s.* der Bewohner; Einwohner.

**inhale** [in′heil], *v.a.* einatmen.

**inherent** [in′hiərənt], *adj.* eigen, angeboren (*innate*); in der Sache selbst (*intrinsic*).

**inherit** [in′herit], *v.a.* erben.

**inheritance** [in′heritəns], *s.* die Erbschaft, das Erbgut (*patrimony*); (*fig.*) das Erbe.

**inhibit** [in′hibit], *v.a.* hindern; —*ing factor*, der Hemmfaktor.

**inhibition** [ini′biʃən], *s.* (*Psych.*) die Hemmung.

**inhospitable** [inhɔs′pitəbl], *adj.* ungastlich, ungastfreundlich.

**inhuman** [in′hju:mən], *adj.* unmenschlich.

**inhume** [in′hju:m], *v.a.* beerdigen.

**inimical** [i′nimikəl], *adj.* feindlich (gesinnt), feindselig.

**inimitable** [i'nimitəbl], *adj.* unnachahmlich.

**iniquitous** [i'nikwitəs], *adj.* ungerecht, schlecht, boshaft.

**iniquity** [i'nikwiti], *s.* die Ungerechtigkeit (*injustice*); die Schändlichkeit (*shame*).

**initial** [i'niʃəl], *adj.* anfänglich. — *s.* (*Typ.*) der Anfangsbuchstabe.

**initiate** [i'niʃieit], *v.a.* einweihen, anfangen.

**initiative** [i'niʃiətiv], *s.* die Initiative; der erste Anstoß (*impulse*).

**injection** [in'dʒekʃən], *s.* (*Med.*) die Einspritzung, Injektion.

**injudicious** [indʒu'diʃəs], *adj.* unbedacht, unbesonnen; übereilt (*rash*).

**injunction** [in'dʒʌŋkʃən], *s.* die Vorschrift, (*Law*) die gerichtliche Verfügung.

**injure** ['indʒə], *v.a.* verletzen.

**injurious** [in'dʒuəriəs], *adj.* verletzend; schädlich (*harmful*).

**injury** ['indʒəri], *s.* die Verletzung, Verwundung; der Schaden (*damage*).

**injustice** [in'dʒʌstis], *s.* die Ungerechtigkeit.

**ink** [iŋk], *s.* die Tinte.

**inkling** ['iŋkliŋ], *s.* die Ahnung.

**inkstand** ['iŋkstænd], *s.* das Schreibzeug.

**inlaid** [in'leid], *adj.* eingelegt.

**inland** [in'lænd], *adj.* inländisch, Binnen-; — *revenue office*, das Steueramt, Finanzamt.

**inlet** ['inlit], *s.* (*Geog.*) die kleine Bucht.

**inmate** ['inmeit], *s.* der Insasse, Bewohner.

**inmost** ['inmoust], *adj.* innerst.

**inn** [in], *s.* der Gasthof, das Wirtshaus; *Inns of Court*, die Londoner Rechtskammern, *f. pl.*

**innate** [i'neit], *adj.* angeboren.

**inner** ['inə], *adj.* inner; geheim (*secret*).

**innings** ['iniŋz], *s.* das Daransein (*in Cricket*); die Reihe.

**innocence** ['inəsəns], *s.* die Unschuld.

**innocuous** [i'nɔkjuəs], *adj.* unschädlich.

**innovate** [i'nouveit], *v.a., v.n.* als Neuerung einführen, Neuerungen machen.

**innovation** [ino'veiʃən], *s.* die Neuerung.

**innuendo** [inju'endou], *s.* das Innuendo, die Anspielung.

**innumerable** [i'nju:mərəbl], *adj.* unzählig, unzählbar.

**inoculate** [i'nɔkjuleit], *v.a.* impfen.

**inoffensive** [ino'fensiv], *adj.* harmlos, unschädlich.

**inopportune** [in'ɔpətju:n], *adj.* ungelegen.

**inordinate** [i'nɔ:dinit], *adj.* unmäßig.

**inorganic** [inɔ:'gænik], *adj.* anorganisch.

**inquest** ['inkwest], *s.* die gerichtliche Untersuchung (*Law*); *coroner's* —, die Leichenschau.

**inquire, enquire** [in'kwaiə], *v.n.* sich erkundigen (*after*, nach, *Dat.*), nachfragen.

**inquiry, enquiry** [in'kwaiəri], *s.* die Nachfrage; — *office*, die Auskunftsstelle.

**inquisition** [inkwi'ziʃən], *s.* (*Eccl.*) die Inquisition; die gerichtliche Untersuchung.

**inquisitive** [in'kwizitiv], *adj.* neugierig.

**inquisitiveness** [in'kwizitivnis], *s.* die Neugier(de).

**inroad** ['inroud], *s.* der Eingriff, Überfall.

**insane** [in'sein], *adj.* wahnsinnig.

**insanity** [in'sæniti], *s.* der Wahnsinn.

**insatiable** [in'seiʃəbl], *adj.* unersättlich.

**inscribe** [in'skraib], *v.a.* einschreiben (*enrol*); widmen (*book*).

**inscription** [in'skripʃən], *s.* die Inschrift.

**inscrutable** [in'skru:təbl], *adj.* unergründlich, unerforschlich.

**insect** ['insekt], *s.* das Insekt, Kerbtier.

**insecure** [insi'kjuə], *adj.* unsicher.

**insensate** [in'sensit], *adj.* unsinnig (*senseless*); gefühllos..

**insensible** [in'sensibl], *adj.* unempfindlich; gefühllos.

**insensitive** [in'sensitiv], *adj.* ohne feineres Gefühl, unempfindlich.

**inseparable** [in'sepərəbl], *adj.* unzertrennlich, untrennbar.

**insert** [in'sə:t], *v.a.* einsetzen, einschalten (*add*); inserieren (*in newspaper*).

**insertion** [in'sə:ʃən], *s.* die Einschaltung (*addition*); die Annonce, das Inserat (*press*).

**inside** [in'said], *adj.* inner. — *adv.* im Innern. — *prep.* innerhalb. — *s.* das Innere.

**insidious** [in'sidiəs], *adj.* heimtückisch.

**insight** ['insait], *s.* der Einblick.

**insignia** [in'signiə], *s. pl.* die Insignien.

**insignificance** [insig'nifikəns], *s.* die Geringfügigkeit, Bedeutungslosigkeit.

**insignificant** [insig'nifikənt], *adj.* unbedeutend, geringfügig.

**insincere** [insin'siə], *adj.* unaufrichtig.

**insincerity** [insin'seriti], *s.* die Unaufrichtigkeit.

**insinuate** [in'sinjueit], *v.a.* zu verstehen geben, andeuten, anspielen auf (*Acc.*).

**insinuation** [insinju'eiʃən], *s.* der Wink, die Andeutung, Anspielung.

**insipid** [in'sipid], *adj.* schal, geschmacklos.

**insist** [in'sist], *v.n.* bestehen (*upon*, auf, *Dat.*).

**insistence** [in'sistəns], *s.* das Bestehen, Beharren.

**insolence** ['insələns], *s.* die Frechheit.

**insolent** ['insələnt], *adj.* frech, unverschämt.

**insoluble** [in'sɔljubl], *adj.* unlösbar; (*Chem.*) unlöslich.

**insolvent** [in'sɔlvənt], *adj.* insolvent, zahlungsunfähig, bankrott.

**inspect** [in'spekt], *v.a.* inspizieren; besichtigen.

# inspection

**inspection** [inˈspekʃən], *s.* die Inspektion; Besichtigung.
**inspiration** [inspiˈreiʃən], *s.* die Inspiration, Erleuchtung, Begeisterung.
**inspire** [inˈspaiə], *v.a.* inspirieren, begeistern.
**instability** [instəˈbiliti], *s.* die Unbeständigkeit, Labilität.
**install** [inˈstɔːl], *v.a.* einsetzen (*in office*); einbauen.
**installation** [instəˈleiʃən], *s.* die Einsetzung (*inauguration*); die Installation.
**instalment** [inˈstɔːlmənt], *s.* die Rate; *by* —*s*, auf Abzahlung; die Fortsetzung (*serial*).
**instance** [ˈinstəns], *s.* das Beispiel (*example*); (*Law*) die Instanz; *at my* —, auf meine dringende Bitte; *for* —, zum Beispiel. — *v.a.* als Beispiel anführen.
**instant** [ˈinstənt], *s.* der Augenblick. — *adj.* gegenwärtig; sofortig; laufend (*current month*).
**instantaneous** [instənˈteiniəs], *adj.* augenblicklich, sofortig.
**instead** [inˈsted], *adv.* dafür, stattdessen;—*of*, (an)statt (*Genit.*).
**instep** [ˈinstep], *s.* (*Anat.*) der Rist.
**instigate** [ˈinstigeit], *v.a.* aufhetzen, anreizen, anstiften.
**instil** [inˈstil], *v.a.* einflößen.
**instinct** [ˈinstiŋkt], *s.* der Instinkt, Naturtrieb.
**institute** [ˈinstitjuːt], *s.* das Institut. — *v.a.* einrichten (*install*); stiften (*found*).
**institution** [instiˈtjuːʃən], *s.* die Stiftung (*foundation*); die Anstalt (*establishment*).
**instruct** [inˈstrʌkt], *v.a.* unterrichten, unterweisen.
**instruction** [inˈstrʌkʃən], *s.* der Unterricht (*in schools etc.*); (*pl.*) die Instruktionen, *f. pl.*; die Direktive.
**instructive** [inˈstrʌktiv], *adj.* instruktiv, lehrreich.
**instrument** [ˈinstrumənt], *s.* das Instrument; Werkzeug (*tool*).
**insubordination** [insəbɔːdiˈneiʃən], *s.* der Ungehorsam.
**insufferable** [inˈsʌfərəbl], *adj.* unerträglich.
**insufficient** [insəˈfiʃənt], *adj.* ungenügend, unzulänglich.
**insular** [ˈinsjulə], *adj.* Insel-; insular (*narrow-minded*).
**insulate** [ˈinsjuleit], *v.a.* absondern (*separate*); (*Elec.*) isolieren; *insulating tape*, das Isolierband.
**insult** [inˈsʌlt], *v.a.* beleidigen.
**insuperable** [inˈsjuːpərəbl], *adj.* unüberwindlich.
**insupportable** [insəˈpɔːtəbl], *adj.* unhaltbar (*argument*); unerträglich (*insufferable*).
**insurance** [inˈʃuərəns], *s.* die Versicherung; — *policy*, die Police; — *premium*, die Prämie; — *broker*, der Versicherungsmakler.

**insure** [inˈʃuə], *v.a.* versichern.
**insurgent** [inˈsəːdʒənt], *s.* der Aufständische, Aufrührer.
**insurmountable** [insəˈmauntəbl], *adj.* unüberwindlich.
**insurrection** [insəˈrekʃən], *s.* der Aufstand, Aufruhr; die Empörung.
**intact** [inˈtækt], *adj.* unversehrt, intakt.
**intangible** [inˈtændʒibl], *adj.* unberührbar (*untouchable*); (*Log.*) abstrakt. — *s. pl.* (*Log.*) die Intangibilien, *pl.*
**integer** [ˈintidʒə], *s.* (*Maths.*) das Ganze, die ganze Zahl.
**integral** [ˈintigrəl], *adj.* wesentlich; vollständig. — *s.* (*Maths.*) das Integral.
**integrate** [ˈintigreit], *v.a.* (*Maths.*) integrieren.
**integration** [intiˈgreiʃən], *s.* (*Maths.*) die Integrierung; (*fig.*) die Integration, das völlige Aufgehen.
**integrity** [inˈtegriti], *s.* die Rechtschaffenheit, Redlichkeit (*probity*).
**intellect** [ˈintilekt], *s.* der Geist, Intellekt, Verstand.
**intellectual** [intiˈlektjuəl], *adj.* intellektuell. — *s.* der Intellektuelle.
**intelligence** [inˈtelidʒəns], *s.* die Intelligenz; die Nachricht (*news*).
**intelligent** [inˈtelidʒənt], *adj.* intelligent.
**intelligible** [inˈtelidʒibl], *adj.* verständlich.
**intemperance** [inˈtempərəns], *s.* die Unmäßigkeit.
**intemperate** [inˈtempərit], *adj.* unmäßig.
**intend** [inˈtend], *v.a.* beabsichtigen, vorhaben.
**intendant** [inˈtendənt], *s.* der Intendant, Verwalter.
**intense** [inˈtens], *adj.* intensiv, heftig.
**intent** [inˈtent], *adj.* gespannt, begierig; bedacht (*on*, auf, *Acc.*). — *s.* die Absicht.
**intention** [inˈtenʃən], *s.* die Absicht.
**intentioned** [inˈtenʃənd], *adj.* *well-* —, wohlgesinnt.
**inter** [inˈtəː], *v.a.* beerdigen.
**intercede** [intəˈsiːd], *v.n.* vermitteln (*between*); sich verwenden (*on behalf of*, für, *Acc.*).
**intercept** [intəˈsept], *v.a.* abfangen, auffangen, hemmen.
**intercession** [intəˈseʃən], *s.* die Vermittlung, Fürsprache, Fürbitte.
**interchange** [intətˈʃeindʒ], *s.* der Austausch. — [-ˈtʃeindʒ], *v.a.* austauschen.
**intercourse** [ˈintəkɔːs], *s.* der Verkehr, Umgang.
**interdict** [intəˈdikt], *v.a.* untersagen, verbieten.
**interest** [ˈintrəst], *s.* das Interesse; die Beteiligung; (*Comm.*) die Zinsen, *m. pl.*; *compound* —, die Zinseszinsen, *m. pl.* — *v.a.* interessieren.
**interested** [ˈintrəstid], *adj.* (*in*, an, *Dat.*) interessiert; *be* — *in*, sich interessieren für.

**interesting** ['intrəstiŋ], *adj.* interessant.
**interfere** [intə'fiə], *v.n.* sich einmischen, eingreifen (*in*, in, *Acc.*)
**interference** [intə'fiərəns], *s.* die Einmischung; (*Rad.*) die Störung.
**interim** ['intərim], *adj.* vorläufig, Zwischen-.
**interior** [in'tiəriə], *adj.* innerlich. — *s.* das Innere; das Binnenland; — *decorator*, der Innenraumgestalter, der Innenarchitekt; *Ministry of the Interior*, das Innenministerium.
**interjection** [intə'dʒekʃən], *s.* die Interjektion; der Ausruf.
**interlace** [intə'leis], *v.a.* einflechten.
**interleave** [intə'li:v], *v.a.* durchschießen (*a book*).
**interlinear** [intə'liniə], *adj.* zwischenzeilig.
**interlocutor** [intə'lɔkjutə], *s.* der Gesprächspartner.
**interloper** ['intəloupə], *s.* der Eindringling.
**interlude** ['intəlju:d], *s.* das Zwischenspiel.
**intermarry** [intə'mæri], *v.n.* untereinander heiraten.
**intermediate** [intə'mi:diit],*adj.* Mittel-; (*Sch.*) — *certificate*, das Mittelstufenzeugnis.
**interment** [in'tə:mənt], *s.* die Beerdigung.
**interminable** [in'tə:minəbl], *adj.* endlos, langwierig.
**intermingle** [intə'miŋgl], *v.n.* sich vermischen.
**intermission** [intə'miʃən], *s.* die Pause, Unterbrechung.
**intermit** [intə'mit], *v.a.* unterbrechen.
**intermittent** [intə'mitənt], *adj.* Wechsel-, aussetzend.
**internal** [in'tə:nl], *adj.* intern, innerlich.
**international** [intə'næʃənəl], *adj.* international; — *law*, das Völkerrecht.
**interpolate** [in'tə:poleit], *v.a.* interpolieren, einschalten.
**interpose** [intə'pouz], *v.a.* dazwischenstellen. — *v.n.* vermitteln (*mediate*).
**interpret** [in'tə:prit], *v.a.* verdolmetschen; erklären (*explain*); auslegen, interpretieren.
**interpretation** [intə:pri'teiʃən], *s.* die Auslegung, Interpretation.
**interpreter** [in'tə:pritə], *s.* der Dolmetscher.
**interrogate** [in'terogeit], *v.a.* ausfragen, befragen, vernehmen.
**interrogation** [intero'geiʃən], *s.* die Befragung; (*Law*) das Verhör, die Vernehmung.
**interrogative** [intə'rɔgətiv], *adj.* (*Gram.*) Frage-, Interrogativ-.
**interrupt** [intə'rʌpt], *v.a.* unterbrechen; stören (*disturb*).
**interruption** [intə'rʌpʃən], *s.* die Unterbrechung; Störung (*disturbance*).
**intersect** [intə'sekt], *v.a.* durchschneiden.

**intersperse** [intə'spə:s], *v.a.* untermengen, vermischen, einstreuen.
**intertwine** [intə'twain], *v.a.*, *v.n.* (sich) durchflechten.
**interval** ['intəvəl], *s.* der Zwischenraum; die Pause; (*Mus.*) das Interval.
**intervene** [intə'vi:n], *v.n.* eingreifen; als Vermittler dienen (*act as mediator*).
**intervention** [intə'venʃən], *s.* die Vermittlung, Intervention.
**interview** ['intəvju:], *v.a.* zur Vorsprache einladen (*a candidate*); interviewen. — *s.* die Vorsprache, das Interview.
**intestate** [in'testit], *adj.* ohne Testament.
**intestines** [in'testinz], *s. pl.* (*Anat.*) die Eingeweide, *n. pl.*
**intimacy** ['intiməsi], *s.* die Vertraulichkeit, Intimität.
**intimate** ['intimit], *adj.* intim, vertraut, vertraulich. — [-meit], *v.a.* andeuten, zu verstehen geben.
**intimation** [inti'meiʃən], *s.* der Wink, die Andeutung.
**intimidate** [in'timideit], *v.a.* einschüchtern.
**into** ['intu], *prep.* (*Acc.*) in, in ... hinein (*towards*).
**intolerable** [in'tɔlərəbl], *adj.* unerträglich.
**intolerance** [in'tɔlərəns], *s.* die Unduldsamkeit, Intoleranz.
**intonation** [into'neiʃən], *s.* (*Phonet.*) die Intonation; (*Mus.*) das Anstimmen, der Tonansatz (*of instruments*).
**intoxicate** [in'tɔksikeit], *v.a.* berauschen.
**intractable** [in'træktəbl], *adj.* unbändig, unlenksam.
**intransitive** [in'trænsitiv *or* in'trɑ:ns-], *adj.* (*Gram.*) intransitiv.
**intrepid** [in'trepid], *adj.* unerschrocken, furchtlos.
**intricacy** ['intrikəsi], *s.* die Verwicklung (*tangle*), Schwierigkeit (*difficulty*).
**intricate** ['intrikit], *adj.* verwickelt, schwierig.
**intrigue** [in'tri:g], *s.* die Intrige. — *v.n.* intrigieren.
**intrinsic** [in'trinsik], *adj.* wesentlich; innerlich (*inner*).
**introduce** [intrə'dju:s], *v.a.* einführen, einleiten (*book etc.*); vorstellen (*person*).
**introduction** [intrə'dʌkʃən], *s.* die Einführung, das Bekanntmachen, die Einleitung (*preface*); die Vorstellung (*presentation to s.o.*, *Dat.*).
**introductory** [intrə'dʌktəri], *adj.* einführend.
**introspection** [intrə'spekʃən], *s.* die Selbstbetrachtung, Introspektion.
**introspective** [intrə'spektiv], *adj.* nachdenklich, beschaulich.
**intrude** [in'tru:d], *v.n.* eindringen, sich eindrängen; stören (*be in the way*).
**intrusion** [in'tru:ʒən], *s.* das Eindringen.

423

# intuition

**intuition** [intjuˈiʃən], *s.* die Intuition, Eingebung.
**intuitive** [inˈtjuːitiv], *adj.* intuitiv, gefühlsmäßig.
**inundate** [ˈinʌndeit], *v.a.* überschwemmen.
**inure** [iˈnjuə], *v.a.* gewöhnen; abhärten (*harden*).
**invade** [inˈveid], *v.a.* angreifen, einfallen (in, *Dat.*).
**invalid** [inˈvælid], *adj.* ungültig (*void*); [ˈinvəlid] krank (*sick*). — *s.* der Kranke, Invalide.
**invalidate** [inˈvælideit], *v.a.* ungültig machen, für ungültig erklären.
**invalidity** [invəˈliditi], *s.* die Ungültigkeit.
**invaluable** [inˈvæljuəbl], *adj.* von hohem Wert, wertvoll, unschätzbar.
**invariable** [inˈvɛəriəbl], *adj.* unveränderlich. — *s.* (*Maths.*) die unveränderliche Größe, die Konstante, Unveränderliche.
**invasion** [inˈveiʒən], *s.* die Invasion, der Einfall; Angriff (*of*, auf, *Acc.*).
**invective** [inˈvektiv], *adj.* schmähend. — *s.* die Schmähung.
**inveigh** [inˈvei], *v.n.* schmähen, losziehen (gegen); schimpfen (auf, *Acc.*).
**inveigle** [inˈveigl], *v.a.* verleiten, verführen.
**invent** [inˈvent], *v.a.* erfinden.
**invention** [inˈvenʃən], *s.* die Erfindung.
**inventor** [inˈventə], *s.* der Erfinder.
**inventory** [ˈinvəntri], *s.* der Bestand, das Inventar; die Liste (*list*).
**inverse** [inˈvəːs,ˈinvəːs], *adj.* umgekehrt.
**inversion** [inˈvəːʃən], *s.* die Umkehrung; (*Gram.*, *Maths.*) die Inversion.
**invert** [inˈvəːt], *v.a.* umstellen, umkehren. — [ˈinvəːt], *s.* (*Chem.*) — *sugar*, der Invertzucker.
**invest** [inˈvest], *v.a.* bekleiden; bedecken; (*Comm.*) investieren, anlegen.
**investigate** [inˈvestigeit], *v.a.* untersuchen, erforschen.
**investiture** [inˈvestitʃə], *s.* die Investitur; die Belehnung.
**investment** [inˈvestmənt], *s.* die Investierung, Kapitalanlage.
**inveterate** [inˈvetərit], *adj.* eingewurzelt, eingefleischt.
**invidious** [inˈvidiəs], *adj.* neiderregend, verhaßt.
**invigorate** [inˈvigəreit], *v.a.* stärken, beleben.
**invincible** [inˈvinsibl], *adj.* unbesiegbar, unüberwindlich.
**inviolable** [inˈvaiələbl], *adj.* unverletzlich.
**invisible** [inˈvizibl], *adj.* unsichtbar.
**invitation** [inviˈteiʃən], *s.* die Einladung.
**invite** [inˈvait], *v.a.* einladen.
**invocation** [invoˈkeiʃən], *s.* die Anrufung.
**invoice** [ˈinvɔis], *s.* die Rechnung, Faktura. — *v.a.* fakturieren.
**invoke** [inˈvouk], *v.a.* anrufen.
**involuntary** [inˈvɔləntri], *adj.* unfreiwillig (*unwilling*); unwillkürlich (*reflex*).

**involve** [inˈvɔlv], *v.a.* verwickeln.
**involved** [inˈvɔlvd], *adj.* schwierig, verwickelt, kompliziert.
**invulnerable** [inˈvʌlnərəbl], *adj.* unverwundbar, unverletzlich.
**inward** [ˈinwəd], *adj.* inner(lich). — *adv.* (*also* **inwards**) einwärts, nach innen, ins Innere.
**iodine** [ˈaiədain *or* ˈaiədiːn], *s.* (*Chem.*) das Jod.
**Iraki, Iraqi** [iˈrɑːki], *adj.* irakisch. — *s.* der Iraker.
**Iranian** [iˈreinjən], *adj.* iranisch. — *s.* der Iranier.
**irascible** [iˈræsibl], *adj.* jähzornig, aufbrausend.
**irate** [aiˈreit], *adj.* erzürnt, zornig.
**ire** [aiə], *s.* (*Poet.*) der Zorn.
**iridescent** [iriˈdesənt], *adj.* irisierend, schillernd.
**iris** [ˈaiəris], *s.* (*Anat.*) die Regenbogenhaut; (*Bot.*) die Schwertlilie.
**Irish** [ˈairiʃ], *adj.* irisch, ersisch. — *s.* (*pl.*) *the* —, die Irländer, Iren, *pl.*
**Irishman** [ˈairiʃmən], *s.* der Irländer, Ire.
**irk** [əːk], *v.a.* verdrießen, verärgern.
**irksome** [ˈəːksəm], *adj.* lästig, ärgerlich.
**iron** [ˈaiən], *s.* (*Metall.*) das Eisen; (*pl.*) die eisernen Fesseln. — *adj.* eisern, Eisen-. — *v.a.* bügeln, plätten; — *out*, schlichten, beilegen.
**ironical** [aiˈrɔnikəl], *adj.* ironisch.
**ironmonger** [ˈaiənmʌŋgə], *s.* der Eisenhändler.
**ironmould** [ˈaiənmould], *s.* der Rostfleck.
**irony** [ˈaiərəni], *s.* die Ironie.
**irradiate** [iˈreidieit], *v.a.* bestrahlen.
**irrational** [iˈræʃənəl], *adj.* (*Log.*,*Maths.*) irrational; unvernünftig (*without reason*).
**irreconcilable** [irekənˈsailəbl], *adj.* unversöhnlich; unvereinbar (*incompatible*).
**irregular** [iˈregjulə], *adj.* unregelmäßig, gegen die Regel.
**irrelevant** [iˈreləvənt], *adj.* belanglos.
**irremediable** [iriˈmiːdiəbl], *adj.* unheilbar; nicht wieder gut zu machen.
**irreparable** [iˈrepərəbl], *adj.* unersetzlich.
**irrepressible** [iriˈpresibl], *adj.* nicht zu unterdrücken, unbezähmbar.
**irreproachable** [iriˈproutʃəbl], *adj.* untadelhaft, tadellos.
**irresistible** [iriˈzistibl], *adj.* unwiderstehlich.
**irresolute** [iˈrezoljuːt], *adj.* unschlüssig, unentschlossen.
**irrespective** [irisˈpektiv], *adj.* ohne Rücksicht (*of*, auf, *Acc.*).
**irresponsible** [irisˈpɔnsibl], *adj.* unverantwortlich.
**irretrievable** [iriˈtriːvəbl], *adj.* unersetzlich, unwiederbringlich.
**irreverent** [iˈrevərənt], *adj.* unehrerbietig.
**irrevocable** [iˈrevəkəbl], *adj.* unwiderruflich.

**irrigate** ['irigeit], *v.a.* bewässern.
**irritable** ['iritəbl], *adj.* reizbar.
**irritant** ['iritənt], *s.* das Reizmittel.
**irritate** ['iriteit], *v.a.* reizen (*also Med.*), ärgern.
**irritation** [iri'teiʃən], *s.* die Reizung, das Reizen; die Erzürnung.
**irruption** [i'rʌpʃən], *s.* der Einbruch.
**island** ['ailənd], *s.* die Insel.
**isle** [ail], *s.* (*Poet.*) die Insel.
**isolate** ['aisəleit], *v.a.* (*Med.*) isolieren; absondern; (*Chem.*) darstellen.
**isolation** [aisə'leiʃən], *s.* die Absonderung, Isolierung.
**Israeli** [iz'reili], *adj.* den Staat Israel betreffend. — *s.* der Israeli.
**Israelite** ['izreiəlait], *adj.* israelitisch. — *s.* der Israelit.
**issue** ['isju: *or* 'iʃu:], *s.* der Ausgang, Erfolg (*result*); main —, der Hauptpunkt; die Nachkommenschaft (*children*); die Ausgabe (*edition*); Herausgabe (*publication*). — *v.a.* herausgeben; erlassen (*proclaim*); veröffentlichen (*publish*). — *v.n.* herrühren, stammen (*from*).
**isthmus** ['isθməs], *s.* die Landenge.
**it** [it], *pron.* es; *with* —, damit.
**Italian** [i'tæljən], *adj.* italienisch. — *s.* der Italiener.
**italics** [i'tæliks], *s. pl.* (*Typ.*) der Kursivdruck, die Kursivschrift.
**itch** [itʃ], *s.* das Jucken. — *v.n.* jucken; — *to do s.th.*, (*coll.*) darauf brennen, etwas zu tun.
**item** ['aitəm], *s.* der Posten (*in bill*); der Programmpunkt (*agenda*); die Einzelheit.
**itemize** ['aitəmaiz], *v.a.* (*Comm.*) aufführen; verzeichnen.
**iterate** ['itəreit], *v.a.* wiederholen.
**itinerant** [i'tinərənt], *adj.* wandernd.
**its** [its], *poss. adj.* sein, ihr; dessen, deren.
**itself** [it'self], *pron.* selber, sich; *of* —, von selbst.
**ivory** ['aivəri], *s.* das Elfenbein. — *adj.* aus Elfenbein, elfenbeinern.
**ivy** ['aivi], *s.* (*Bot.*) der Efeu.

# J

**J** [dʒei]. das J.
**jabber** ['dʒæbə], *v.n.* schnattern.
**Jack** [dʒæk]. Hans; *Union* —, die britische Flagge; (*Cards*) der Bube.
**jack** [dʒæk], *s.* (*Motor.*) der Wagenheber. — *v.a.* — *up*, (*Motor.*) hochwinden.
**jackal** ['dʒækɔ:l], *s.* (*Zool.*) der Schakal.
**jackass** ['dʒækæs], *s.* (*Zool.*) der Esel.
**jackdaw** ['dʒækdɔ:], *s.* die Dohle.
**jacket** ['dʒækit], *s.* das Jackett, die Jacke; *dinner* —, der Smoking;

*potatoes in their* —*s*, Kartoffeln in der Schale, *f. pl.*
**jade** [dʒeid], *s.* der Nierenstein.
**jaded** ['dʒeidid], *adj.* abgeplagt, abgehärmt, ermüdet.
**jag** [dʒæg], *s.* die Kerbe. — *v.a.* kerben, zacken.
**jagged** ['dʒægid], *adj.* zackig.
**jail** *see under* gaol.
**jailer** *see under* gaoler.
**jam** (1) [dʒæm], *s.* die Marmelade, Konfitüre.
**jam** (2) [dʒæm], *s. traffic* —, die Verkehrsstauung; (*coll.*) *in a* —, in der Klemme. — *v.a.* zusammenpressen (*press together*); (*Rad.*) stören.
**Jamaican** [dʒə'meikən], *adj.* jamaikanisch. — *s.* der Jamaikaner.
**jamb** [dʒæm], *s.* der Türpfosten.
**jangle** [dʒæŋgl], *v.n.* klirren, rasseln. — *s.* das Geklirr, Gerassel.
**janitor** ['dʒænitə], *s.* der Portier.
**January** ['dʒænjuəri]. der Januar.
**japan** [dʒə'pæn], *s.* lakierte Arbeit. — *v.a.* lackieren.
**Japanese** [dʒæpə'ni:z], *adj.* japanisch. — *s.* der Japaner.
**jar** (1) [dʒɑ:], *s.* der Topf, das Glas (*preserves*).
**jar** (2) [dʒɑ:], *v.n.* offenstehen (*door*); mißtönen, knarren.
**jargon** ['dʒɑ:gən], *s.* der Jargon.
**jasmine** ['dʒæzmin], *s.* (*Bot.*) der Jasmin.
**jasper** ['dʒæspə], *s.* der Jaspis.
**jaundice** ['dʒɔ:ndis], *s.* (*Med.*) die Gelbsucht; (*fig.*) der Neid (*envy*); —*d outlook*, die Verbitterung, Mißstimmung.
**jaunt** [dʒɔ:nt], *s.* der Ausflug, Spaziergang. — *v.n.* herumstreifen, spazieren.
**jaunty** ['dʒɔ:nti], *adj.* leicht, munter, lebhaft.
**jaw** [dʒɔ:], *s.* (*Anat.*) der Kinnbacken; der Rachen (*animals*).
**jay** [dʒei], *s.* (*Orn.*) der Häher.
**jazz** [dʒæz], *s.* die Jazzmusik.
**jealous** ['dʒeləs], *adj.* eifersüchtig.
**jealousy** ['dʒeləsi], *s.* die Eifersucht.
**jeer** ['dʒiə], *v.a.*, *v.n.* spotten, verhöhnen.
**jejune** [dʒi'dʒu:n], *adj.* nüchtern, trocken.
**jelly** ['dʒeli], *s.* das Gelee.
**jellyfish** ['dʒelifiʃ], *s.* (*Zool.*) die Qualle.
**jeopardize** ['dʒepədaiz], *v.a.* gefährden.
**jeopardy** ['dʒepədi], *s.* die Gefahr.
**jerk** [dʒə:k], *v.a.* rucken, stoßen (*push*); plötzlich bewegen (*move suddenly*). — *v.n.* zusammenzucken. — *s.* (*Am. coll.*) der Kerl; der Ruck, Stoß.
**jersey** ['dʒə:zi], *s.* die Wolljacke.
**jessamine** ['dʒesəmin], *s.* (*Bot.*) der Jasmin.
**jest** [dʒest], *s.* der Spaß, Scherz. — *v.n.* scherzen.
**jester** ['dʒestə], *s.* der Spaßmacher, Hofnarr.

# jet

**jet** (1) [dʒet], *s.* der Strahl, Wasserstrahl; (*Aviat.*) die Düse; — *engine*, der Düsenmotor; —*plane*, das Düsenflugzeug. — *v.n.* hervorspringen.
**jet** (2) [dʒet], *s.* der Gagat; — *black*, pechschwarz.
**jetsam** [ˈdʒetsəm], *s.* das Strandgut.
**jetty** [ˈdʒeti], *s.* der Hafendamm, die Landungsbrücke (*landing stage*).
**Jew** [dʒuː], *s.* der Jude.
**jewel** [ˈdʒuəl], *s.* das Juwel, der Edelstein.
**jewel(le)ry** [ˈdʒuəlri], *s.* der Schmuck; die Juwelen, *n. pl.*
**Jewish** [ˈdʒuːiʃ], *adj.* jüdisch.
**Jewry** [ˈdʒuəri], *s.* die Judenschaft, das Judentum.
**jiffy** [ˈdʒifi], *s.* (*coll.*) der Augenblick.
**jig** (1) [dʒig], *s.* die Gigue (*dance*).
**jig** (2) [dʒig], *s.* das Werkzeug (*tool*); —*saw*, die Säge; —*saw puzzle*, das Zusammenlegspiel, -setzspiel.
**jilt** [dʒilt], *v.a.* sitzen lassen.
**jingle** [dʒingl], *v.a.* klimpern, klimpern lassen (*coins etc.*). — *s.* das Geklimper.
**job** [dʒɔb], *s.* die Arbeit, Anstellung; die Stellung; das Geschäft; — *in hand*, die Beschäftigung.
**jobber** [ˈdʒɔbə], *s.* der Makler, Spekulant (*stock exchange*).
**jockey** [ˈdʒɔki], *s.* der Jockei, Reiter.
**jocular** [ˈdʒɔkjulə], *adj.* scherzhaft, lustig.
**jocund** [ˈdʒɔkənd], *adj.* munter, heiter.
**jog** [dʒɔg], *v.a.* stoßen, antreiben. — *v.n.* gemächlich traben, trotten. — *s.* der Trott.
**join** [dʒɔin], *v.a.* verbinden, zusammenfügen; (*club etc.*) beitreten (*Dat.*). — *v.n.* (*rivers*) zusammenfließen (mit, *Dat.*); (*Comm.*) sich vereinigen (mit, *Dat.*).
**joiner** [ˈdʒɔinə], *s.* der Tischler, Schreiner.
**joint** [dʒɔint], *s.* (*Anat.*) das Gelenk; das Stück Fleisch, der Braten (*meat*); (*sl.*) das Lokal, die Spelunke. — *adj.* vereint, gemeinsam; (*Comm.*) — *stock company*, die Aktiengesellschaft; — *heir*, der Miterbe.
**joist** [dʒɔist], *s.* (*Carp.*) der Querbalken.
**joke** [dʒouk], *s.* der Scherz, Witz.
**jollity** [ˈdʒɔliti], *s.* die Heiterkeit.
**jolly** [ˈdʒɔli], *adj.* fröhlich, heiter, lustig.
**jolt** [dʒoult], *v.a.* schütteln, erschüttern (*shake up*). — *s.* der Stoß.
**jostle** [dʒɔsl], *v.a.* stoßen, drängen. — *v.n.* drängeln.
**jot** [dʒɔt], *s.* der Punkt, das Iota. — *v.a.* — (*down*), notieren, niederschreiben.
**journal** [ˈdʒəːnəl], *s.* die Zeitschrift (*periodical*).
**journalism** [ˈdʒəːnəlizm], *s.* das Zeitungswesen, der Journalistenberuf.
**journalist** [ˈdʒəːnəlist], *s.* der Journalist.
**journey** [ˈdʒəːni], *s.* die Reise.
**joust** [dʒuːst], *s.* das Turnier.

**jovial** [ˈdʒouviəl], *adj.* jovial, freundlich; lustig (*gay*).
**joy** [dʒɔi], *s.* die Freude.
**jubilant** [ˈdʒuːbilənt], *adj.* frohlockend.
**jubilation** [dʒuːbiˈleiʃən], *s.* der Jubel.
**jubilee** [ˈdʒuːbiliː], *s.* das Jubiläum.
**Judaism** [dʒuˈdeiizm], *s.* das Judentum.
**judge** [dʒʌdʒ], *s.* der Richter. — *v.a.* richten, beurteilen, entscheiden.
**judgment** [ˈdʒʌdʒmənt], *s.* das Urteil; das Urteilsvermögen (*discretion*), die Urteilskraft.
**judicial** [dʒuːˈdiʃəl], *adj.* richterlich, gerichtlich.
**judicious** [dʒuːˈdiʃəs], *adj.* klug, scharfsinnig.
**jug** [dʒʌg], *s.* der Krug.
**juggle** [dʒʌgl], *v.n.* jonglieren, gaukeln.
**juggler** [ˈdʒʌglə], *s.* der Jongleur.
**Jugoslav** *see* **Yugoslav.**
**jugular** [ˈdʒuːg- *or* ˈdʒʌgjulə], *adj.* Kehl-, Hals-, Gurgel-. — *s.* (*vein*) die Halsader.
**juice** [dʒuːs], *s.* der Saft.
**July** [dʒuˈlai], der Juli.
**jumble** [ˈdʒʌmbl], *v.a.* zusammenmischen, vermischen. — *s.* das gemischte Zeug; — *sale*, der Verkauf, Ausverkauf gebrauchter Dinge, Ramschverkauf.
**jump** [dʒʌmp], *v.n.* springen. — *s.* der Sprung.
**junction** [ˈdʒʌŋkʃən], *s.* (*Railw.*) der Knotenpunkt; die Kreuzung.
**juncture** [ˈdʒʌŋktʃə], *s.* der (kritische) Zeitpunkt.
**June** [dʒuːn], der Juni.
**jungle** [dʒʌŋgl], *s.* der Dschungel.
**junior** [ˈdʒuːnjə], *adj.* jünger; Unter-.
**juniper** [ˈdʒuːnipə], *s.* (*Bot.*) der Wacholder.
**junk** [dʒʌŋk], *s.* (*coll.*) das alte Zeug, alte Möbelstücke, *n. pl.*
**junket** [ˈdʒʌŋkit], *s.* der Schmaus, das Fest; (*Cul.*) dicke Milch mit Sahne. — *v.n.* schmausen, feiern (*celebrate*).
**juridical** [dʒuəˈridikəl], *adj.* rechtlich; gerichtlich (*in Court*).
**jurisdiction** [dʒuərizˈdikʃən], *s.* die Gerichtsbarkeit.
**juror** [ˈdʒuərə], *s.* der, die Geschworene.
**jury** [ˈdʒuəri], *s.* die Jury, das Geschworenengericht.
**just** [dʒʌst], *adj.* gerecht; rechtschaffen (*decent*); gehörig (*proper*). — *adv.* soeben, eben; —*as*, eben als, gerade wie.
**justice** [ˈdʒʌstis], *s.* die Gerechtigkeit; der Richter (*judge*).
**justifiable** [ˈdʒʌstifaiəbl], *adj.* zu rechtfertigen, berechtigt.
**justify** [ˈdʒʌstifai], *v.a.* rechtfertigen.
**jut** [dʒʌt], *v.n.* — (*out*), hervorragen. — *s.* der Vorsprung.
**jute** [dʒuːt], *s.* die Jute.
**juvenile** [ˈdʒuːvənail], *adj.* jugendlich, unreif.
**juxtaposition** [dʒʌkstəpəˈziʃən], *s.* die Nebeneinanderstellung, Gegenüberstellung.

# knowledge

## K

**K** [kei]. das K.
**kale** [keil], *s.* (*Bot.*) der Krauskohl.
**kaleidoscope** [kə'laidəskoup], *s.* das Kaleidoskop.
**kangaroo** [kæŋgə'ru:], *s.* (*Zool.*) das Känguruh.
**keel** [ki:l], *s.* der Kiel; *on an even —,* bei ruhiger See; (*also fig.*) ruhig. *— v.n. — over,* umkippen.
**keen** [ki:n], *adj.* eifrig (*intent*); scharfsinnig (*perspicacious*); scharf (*blade*).
**keenness** ['ki:nnis], *s.* der Eifer; Scharfsinn; die Schärfe (*blade*).
**keep** [ki:p], *v.a. irr.* halten (*hold*); behalten (*retain*); führen (*a shop*); hüten (*gate, dog etc.*). *— v.n. — doing,* in etwas fortfahren, *— going,* weitergehen; *— away,* sich fernhalten; *— in, indoors,* zu Hause bleiben; *— off,* abhalten; sich fernhalten; *— out,* draußen bleiben; *— up,* aufrechterhalten. *— s.* das Burgverlies; der Unterhalt.
**keeper** ['ki:pə], *s.* der Hüter, Wärter; Museumsbeamte.
**keeping** ['ki:piŋ], *s.* die Verwahrung; *in safe —,* in guten Händen, in guter Obhut.
**keepsake** ['ki:pseik], *s.* das Andenken.
**keg** [keg], *s.* das Fäßchen.
**ken** [ken], *s.* die Kenntnis; *in my —,* meines Wissens. *— v.a.* (*Scottish*) kennen.
**kennel** [kenl], *s.* die Hundehütte.
**kerb(stone)** ['kə:b(stoun)], *s.* der Prellstein.
**kerchief** ['kə:tʃif], *s.* das Kopftuch, Halstuch.
**kernel** [kə:nl], *s.* der Kern.
**kettle** [ketl], *s.* der Kessel; *— drum,* die Kesselpauke.
**key** [ki:], *s.* der Schlüssel; (*Mus.*) die Tonart; die Taste (*on piano etc.*); *— man,* eine wichtige Person, Person in einer Schlüsselstellung. *— v.a. — (in),* einfügen, befestigen.
**keyboard** ['ki:bɔ:d], *s.* die Klaviatur; Tastatur (*typewriter*); *— instrument,* das Tasteninstrument.
**keyhole** ['ki:houl], *s.* das Schlüsselloch.
**keystone** ['ki:stoun], *s.* der Schlußstein.
**kick** [kik], *v.a., v.n.* mit dem Fuße stoßen *or* treten; *— against s.th.,* sich wehren. *— s.* der Fußstoß, Tritt; (*Footb.*) *— off,* der Ankick; *free —,* der Freistoß; *penalty —,* der Strafstoß, der Elfmeterstoß.
**kid** (1) [kid], *s.* (*Zool.*) das Geißlein, Zicklein; *with — gloves,* mit Glacéhandschuhen; (*coll.*) das Kind.
**kid** (2) [kid], *v.a.* (*Am. coll.*) zum Narren haben, aufziehen (*tease*).

**kidnap** ['kidnæp], *v.a.* entführen.
**kidney** ['kidni], *s.* (*Anat.*) die Niere; *— bean,* die französische Bohne.
**kill** [kil], *v.a.* töten; schlachten (*animal*).
**kiln** [kiln], *s.* der Darrofen; der Ziegelofen (*tiles, bricks*).
**kilt** [kilt], *s.* der Schottenrock.
**kin** [kin], *s.* die Verwandtschaft; *kith and —,* die Verwandten, *m. pl.*
**kind** [kaind], *s.* die Art, Gattung, Art und Weise. *— adj.* freundlich, gütig, liebenswürdig.
**kindle** [kindl], *v.a.* anzünden, anfachen.
**kindliness, kindness** ['kaindlinis, 'kaindnis], *s.* die Güte, Freundlichkeit.
**kindred** ['kindrid], *adj.* verwandt.
**king** [kiŋ], *s.* der König.
**kingdom** ['kiŋdəm], *s.* das Königreich.
**kink** [kiŋk], *s.* der Knoten; (*coll.*) der Vogel, die Grille (*obsession etc.*).
**kinship** ['kinʃip], *s.* die Sippe, Verwandtschaft.
**kipper** ['kipə], *s.* der geräucherte Hering.
**kiss** [kis], *v.a.* küssen. *— s.* der Kuß.
**kit** [kit], *s.* (*Mil.*) die Ausrüstung.
**kitbag** ['kitbæg], *s.* der Tornister.
**kitchen** ['kitʃən], *s.* die Küche; *— garden,* der Gemüsegarten.
**kite** [kait], *s.* der Drache, Papierdrache; *fly a —,* einen Drachen steigen lassen; (*Orn.*) der Gabelweih, der (rote) Milan; (*sl.*) der Schwindler.
**kith** [kiθ], *s.* now only in *— and kin,* die Verwandten, *m. pl.*
**kitten** [kitn], *s.* das Kätzchen.
**knack** [næk], *s.* der Kniff, Kunstgriff.
**knacker** ['nækə], *s.* der Abdecker (*horse*).
**knapsack** ['næpsæk], *s.* der Rucksack, Tornister.
**knave** [neiv], *s.* der Kerl, Schurke; Bube (*cards*).
**knead** [ni:d], *v.a.* kneten.
**knee** [ni:], *s.* (*Anat.*) das Knie.
**kneel** [ni:l], *v.n. irr.* knien, niederknieen.
**knell** [nel], *s.* die Totenglocke.
**knick-knack** ['niknæk], *s.* die Nippsache.
**knife** [naif], *s.* das Messer. *— v.a.* erstechen.
**knight** [nait], *s.* der Ritter; der Springer (*chess*).
**knit** [nit], *v.a., v.n. reg. & irr.* stricken; *knitting needle,* die Stricknadel.
**knob** [nɔb], *s.* der (Tür)knopf, die Türklinke; der Knorren (*wood*).
**knock** [nɔk], *v.n.* klopfen, schlagen. *— s.* der Schlag, Stoß.
**knoll** [noul], *s.* der kleine Hügel.
**knot** [nɔt], *s.* der Knoten; die Schwierigkeit (*difficulty*).
**know** [nou], *v.a. irr.* kennen (*be acquainted with*); wissen (*possess knowledge (of)*).
**knowing** ['nouiŋ], *adj.* wissend.
**knowledge** ['nɔlidʒ], *s.* die Kenntnis (*acquaintance with*); das Wissen (*by*

427

# knuckle

study, information etc.); die Kenntnisse (of language etc.).
**knuckle** [nakl], s. (Anat.) der Knöchel. — v.n. — under, sich fügen.
**Kremlin** ['kremlin], s. der Kreml.
**kudos** ['kju:dɔs], s. der Ruhm, das Ansehen.

# L

**L** [el]. das L.
**label** [leibl], s. die Etikette, das Schildchen.
**labial** ['leibiəl], adj. (Phonet.) labial, Lippen-. — s. (Phonet.) der Lippenlaut.
**laboratory** [lə'bɔrətəri, (Am.) 'læbərətəri], s. das Laboratorium, (coll.) das Labor.
**laborious** [lə'bɔːriəs], adj. mühsam.
**labour** ['leibə], s. die Arbeit, Mühe; Labour Party, die Arbeiterpartei; (Med.) die Geburtswehen, f. pl. — v.n. sich abmühen, leiden; sich anstrengen.
**labourer** ['leibərə], s. der Arbeiter, Taglöhner.
**lace** [leis], s. die Spitze, Tresse. — v.a. verbrämen (trim with lace); zuschnüren (shoe); stärken (coffee with rum etc.).
**lacerate** ['læsəreit], v.a. zerreißen.
**lack** [læk], v.a. ermangeln (Genit.). — v.n. fehlen (an, Dat.). — s. der Mangel, das Fehlen.
**lackadaisical** [lækə'deizikəl], adj. schlaff, (coll.) schlapp, unbekümmert.
**lackey** ['læki], s. der Lakai, Diener, Bediente.
**laconic** [lə'kɔnik], adj. lakonisch.
**lacquer** ['lækə], s. der Lack. — v.a. lackieren.
**lad** [læd], s. der Bursche, Junge.
**ladder** ['lædə], s. die Leiter.
**lading** ['leidiŋ], s. (Comm.) das Laden; die Fracht; bill of —, der Frachtbrief.
**ladle** [leidl], s. der Schöpflöffel, Suppenlöffel; die Kelle. — v.a. ausschöpfen, austeilen.
**lady** ['leidi], s. die Dame; —-in-waiting, die Hofdame.
**ladybird** ['leidibə:d], s. (Ent.) der Marienkäfer.
**ladyship** ['leidiʃip], s. (Title) gnädige Frau.
**lag** [læg], v.n. zurückbleiben. — v.a. verkleiden, isolieren (tank).
**laggard** ['lægəd], s. der Zauderer. — adj. zögernd, zaudernd.
**lagoon** [lə'gu:n], s. die Lagune.
**lair** [lɛə], s. das Lager (of animal).
**laird** [lɛəd], s. der schottische Gutsherr.

**laity** ['leiiti], s. die Laien, m. pl.
**lake** [leik], s. der See.
**lamb** [læm], s. (Zool.) das Lamm. — v.n. lammen.
**lambent** ['læmbənt], adj. brennend, lodernd, strahlend.
**lame** [leim], adj. lahm. — v.a. lähmen.
**lament** [lə'ment], v.a., v.n. betrauern, beweinen. — s. das Klagelied, die Wehklage.
**lamp** [læmp], s. die Lampe; — -post, der Laternenpfahl.
**lampoon** [læm'pu:n], v.a. schmähen, lächerlich machen. — s. die Schmähschrift.
**lamprey** ['læmpri], s. (Zool.) das Neunauge.
**lance** [lɑ:ns], s. (Mil.) die Lanze. — v.a. durchbohren; (Med.) lancieren.
**lancer** ['lɑ:nsə], s. (Mil.) der Ulan.
**lancet** ['lɑ:nsit], s. (Med.) die Lanzette.
**land** [lænd], s. das Land; das Grundstück (plot); — tax, die Grundsteuer. — v.a. ans Land bringen, fangen (fish). — v.n. landen.
**landlord** ['lændlɔ:d], s. der Eigentümer, der Hausherr; Wirt (pub).
**landmark** ['lændmɑ:k], s. der Grenzstein, das Wahrzeichen.
**landscape** ['lændskeip], s. die Landschaft.
**landslide, landslip** ['lændslaid, 'lændslip], s. der Erdrutsch.
**lane** [lein], s. der Heckenweg, Pfad; die Gasse; (Motor.) die Fahrbahn.
**language** ['læŋgwidʒ], s. die Sprache.
**languid** ['læŋgwid], adj. flau, matt.
**languor** ['læŋgə], s. die Mattigkeit, Flauheit.
**lank** [læŋk], adj. mager, schlank.
**lantern** ['læntən], s. die Laterne.
**Laotian** ['lauʃən], adj. laotisch. — s. der Laote.
**lap** (1) [læp], s. der Schoß.
**lap** (2) [læp], s. das Plätschern (of waves). — v.a. auflecken (lick up). — v.n. plätschern.
**lapel** [lə'pel], s. der Aufschlag (of jacket).
**lapidary** ['læpidəri], adj. lapidarisch; wuchtig.
**lapse** [læps], v.n. gleiten, fallen; verlaufen (time). — s. der Verlauf (time); der Fehler (mistake); das Verfallen (into laziness etc.).
**lapwing** ['læpwiŋ], s. (Orn.) der Kiebitz.
**larceny** ['lɑ:səni], s. der Diebstahl.
**larch** [lɑ:tʃ], s. (Bot.) die Lärche.
**lard** [lɑ:d], s. das Schweinefett, Schweineschmalz.
**larder** ['lɑ:də], s. die Speisekammer.
**large** [lɑ:dʒ], adj. groß; weit; dick, stark.
**largesse** ['lɑ:dʒes], s. die Freigebigkeit (generosity); die Schenkung (donation).
**lark** (1) [lɑ:k], s. (Orn.) die Lerche.
**lark** (2) [lɑ:k], s. (coll.) der Scherz. — v.n. scherzen.
**larkspur** ['lɑ:kspə:], s. (Bot.) der Rittersporn.
**larva** ['lɑ:və], s. (Zool.) die Larve.

# leave

**larynx** ['læriŋks], s. (Anat.) der Kehlkopf.

**lascivious** [lə'siviəs], adj. wollüstig.

**lash** [læʃ], s. die Wimper (eye); die Peitschenschnur (whip); der Peitschenhieb (stroke of whip). — v.a. peitschen.

**lass** [læs], s. (coll.) das Mädchen.

**lassitude** ['læsitju:d], s. die Mattigkeit.

**lasso** [lə'su: or 'læsou], s. das Lasso. — v.a. mit einem Lasso fangen.

**last** (1) [lɑ:st], adj. letzt, vorig, äußerst; at long —, endlich.

**last** (2) [lɑ:st], s. der Leisten (shoemaking).

**last** (3) [lɑ:st], v.n. dauern, anhalten; hinreichen (be sufficient).

**lastly** ['lɑ:stli], adv. zuletzt.

**latch** [lætʃ], v.a. verschließen.

**latchkey** ['lætʃki:], s. der Hausschlüssel.

**late** [leit], adj. spät; verspätet; verstorben, selig (deceased); neulich (recent); the train is —, der Zug hat Verspätung; of late, jüngst.

**latent** ['leitənt], adj. (Med.) latent; verborgen.

**lateral** ['lætərəl], adj. seitlich, Seiten-.

**lath** [lɑ:θ], s. die Latte.

**lathe** [leið], s. die Drehbank.

**lather** ['læðə], s. der Seifenschaum. — v.n., v.a. (sich) einseifen.

**Latin** ['lætin], adj. lateinisch. — s. das Latein, die lateinische Sprache.

**latitude** ['lætitju:d], s. die geographische Breite; die Weite (width); (fig.) der Spielraum (scope).

**latter** ['lætə], adj. letzter; später (later). — s. der Letztere.

**latterly** ['lætəli], adv. neulich, neuerdings.

**lattice** ['lætis], s. das Gitter. — v.a. vergittern.

**Latvian** ['lætviən], adj. lettisch. — s. der Lette.

**laud** [lɔ:d], v.a. loben, preisen.

**laudable** ['lɔ:dəbl], adj. lobenswert.

**laudatory** ['lɔ:dətəri], adj. belobend.

**laugh** [lɑ:f], v.n. lachen; —ing stock, der Gegenstand des Gelächters.

**laughter** ['lɑ:ftə], s. das Lachen, Gelächter.

**launch** [lɔ:ntʃ], s. die Barkasse. — v.a. vom Stapel lassen.

**launching** ['lɔ:ntʃiŋ], s. der Stapellauf.

**laundress** ['lɔ:ndris], s. die Wäscherin.

**laundry** ['lɔ:ndri], s. die Wäsche (clothes); Wäscherei (place).

**laureate** ['lɔ:riit], s. der Hofdichter.

**laurel** ['lɔrəl], s. (Bot.) der Lorbeer.

**lavatory** ['lævətri], s. das W.C., der Abort, Waschraum; die Toilette; public —, die Bedürfnisanstalt.

**lavender** ['lævəndə], s. (Bot.) der Lavendel.

**lavish** ['læviʃ], adj. freigebig, verschwenderisch. — v.a. verschwenden.

**lavishness** ['læviʃnis], s. die Freigebigkeit, Verschwendung.

**law** [lɔ:], s. das Gesetz (statute); das Recht (justice); die Jura, Jurisprudenz (subject of study).

**lawful** ['lɔ:ful], adj. gesetzlich, gesetzmäßig.

**lawless** ['lɔ:lis], adj. gesetzlos; unrechtmäßig (illegal).

**lawn** (1) [lɔ:n], s. der Rasen.

**lawn** (2) [lɔ:n], s. der Batist.

**lawsuit** ['lɔ:su:t], s. der Prozeß.

**lawyer** ['lɔ:jə], s. der Advokat, Rechtsanwalt, Jurist.

**lax** [læks], adj. locker, lax.

**laxative** ['læksətiv], s. das Abführmittel.

**laxity** ['læksiti], s. die Schlaffheit, Lockerheit (of rope etc.).

**lay** (1) [lei], v.a. irr. legen; setzen (put); stellen (place); bannen (ghost); — up, sammeln. — v.n. legen (eggs); wetten (wager); — about one, um sich schlagen.

**lay** (2) [lei], s. (Poet.) das Lied.

**lay** (3) [lei], adj. Laien-.

**layer** ['leiə], s. die Schicht; — cake, die Cremetorte.

**layman** ['leimən], s. der Laie.

**laziness** ['leizinis], s. die Faulheit.

**lazy** ['leizi], adj. faul, träge.

**lea** [li:], s. (Poet.) die Aue.

**lead** (1) [li:d], v.a., v.n. irr. führen, leiten; ausspielen (cards). — s. die Führung; (Elec.) Leitung.

**lead** (2) [led], s. das Blei; Bleilot (plumbline).

**leader** ['li:də], s. der Führer; (Mus.) der Konzertmeister; der Leitartikel (leading article).

**leaf** [li:f], s. (Bot.) das Blatt; (Build.) der Türflügel. — v.a. (coll.) — through, durchblättern.

**leafy** ['li:fi], adj. belaubt.

**league** (1) [li:g], s. drei englische Meilen, f.pl.

**league** (2) [li:g], s. das Bündnis (pact); be in —, verbündet sein; League of Nations, der Völkerbund.

**leak** [li:k], v.n. lecken, ein Loch haben. — s. das Leck; (Naut.) das Leck.

**leaky** ['li:ki], adj. leck.

**lean** (1) [li:n], v.n. irr. (sich) lehnen (an, Acc.), stützen (auf, Acc.).

**lean** (2) [li:n], adj. mager, hager.

**leap** [li:p], v.n. irr. springen. — s. der Sprung; — year, das Schaltjahr.

**learn** [lə:n], v.a. irr. lernen, erfahren.

**learned** ['lə:nid], adj. gelehrt.

**learning** ['lə:niŋ], s. die Gelehrsamkeit.

**lease** [li:s], s. die Pacht, der Mietvertrag (of house). — v.a. (ver)pachten.

**leasehold** ['li:should], s. die Pachtung.

**leash** [li:ʃ], v.a. koppeln, anbinden. — s. die Koppel.

**least** [li:st], adj. wenigst, geringst, mindest, kleinst. — s. at (the) —, wenigstens, mindestens.

**leather** ['leðə], s. das Leder. — adj. Leder-, ledern.

**leave** [li:v], v.a. irr. verlassen (quit); lassen (let); hinterlassen (bequeath). — v.n. Abschied nehmen, abreisen. — s. der Urlaub; der Abschied (farewell); die Erlaubnis (permission).

429

**leaven** [levn], s. der Sauerteig. — v.a. säuern.
**Lebanese** [lebə'ni:z], adj. libanesisch. — s. der Libanese.
**lecture** ['lektʃə], s. die Vorlesung; der Vortrag.
**lecturer** ['lektʃərə], s. (Univ.) der Dozent; der Vortragende (speaker).
**ledge** [ledʒ], s. der Sims (window).
**ledger** ['ledʒə], s. (Comm.) das Hauptbuch.
**lee** [li:], s. die Leeseite (shelter).
**leech** [li:tʃ], s. (Zool.) der Blutegel.
**leek** [li:k], s. (Bot.) der Lauch.
**leer** ['liə], s. das Starren; der Seitenblick. — v.n. schielen (at, auf, nach); starren.
**lees** [li:z], s. pl. der Bodensatz, die Hefe.
**left** [left], adj. link. — adv. inks. — s. die linke Seite.
**leg** [leg], s. (Anat.) das Bein; der Schaft.
**legacy** ['legəsi], s. das Vermächtnis, das Erbe, Erbgut.
**legal** ['li:gəl], adj. gesetzlich.
**legality** [li'gæliti], s. die Gesetzlichkeit.
**legatee** [legə'ti:], s. (Law) der Erbe, die Erbin.
**legation** [li'geiʃən], s. die Gesandtschaft.
**legend** ['ledʒənd], s. die Legende, Sage; die Inschrift (inscription).
**legendary** ['ledʒəndəri], adj. legendär, sagenhaft.
**leggings** ['leginz], s. pl. die Gamaschen.
**legible** ['ledʒibl], adj. leserlich.
**legislation** [ledʒis'leiʃən], s. die Gesetzgebung.
**legislative** ['ledʒislətiv], adj. gesetzgebend.
**legislator** ['ledʒisleitə], s. der Gesetzgeber.
**legitimacy** [li'dʒitiməsi], s. die Gesetzmäßigkeit; (Law) die eheliche Geburt (of birth).
**legitimate** [li'dʒitimit], adj. gesetzmäßig; (Law) ehelich (child). — [-meit], v.a. für gesetzlich erklären.
**legitimize** [li'dʒitimaiz], v.a. legitimieren.
**leguminous** [li'gju:minəs], adj. Hülsen–; hülsentragend.
**leisure** ['leʒə], s. die Freizeit, Muße.
**leisurely** ['leʒəli], adj., adv. gelassen, gemächlich.
**lemon** ['lemən], s. (Bot.) die Zitrone.
**lemonade** [lemən'eid], s. die Limonade.
**lend** [lend], v.a. irr. leihen; —ing library, die Leihbibliothek.
**length** [leŋθ], s. die Länge (extent); die Dauer (duration); at —, ausführlich.
**lengthen** ['leŋθən], v.a., v.n. (sich) verlängern.
**lengthy** ['leŋθi], adj. langwierig, lang.
**lenient** ['li:niənt], adj. nachsichtig, milde.
**lens** [lenz], s. die Linse (optics); das Objektiv.
**Lent** [lent]. die Fastenzeit.
**lentil** ['lentil], s. (Bot.) die Linse.
**leprosy** ['leprəsi], s. der Aussatz, die Leprakrankheit.

**leprous** ['leprəs], adj. aussätzig.
**lesion** ['li:ʒən], s. die Verletzung.
**less** [les], comp. adj., adv. weniger, kleiner.
**lessee** [le'si:], s. der Pächter, Mieter.
**lessen** [lesn], v.a., v.n. (sich) verringern, vermindern.
**lesser** ['lesə], comp. adj. geringer; kleiner.
**lesson** [lesn], s. die Lehrstunde, Lektion; (pl.) der Unterricht; (Rel.) der Bibeltext.
**lessor** ['lesə], s. der Eigentümer, Vermieter.
**lest** [lest], conj. damit nicht; aus Furcht, daß.
**let** [let], v.a. irr. lassen; zulassen; vermieten; (room); — down, blamieren, enttäuschen; (pl.), abschießen. — s. without — or hindrance, ohne Hinderung.
**lethal** ['li:θəl], adj. tödlich.
**letter** ['letə], s. der Brief; der Buchstabe (character); — box, der Briefkasten; (pl.) die Literatur.
**letterpress** ['letəpres], s. die Kopierpresse.
**lettuce** ['letis], s. (Bot.) der Salat.
**level** [levl], adj. eben, gleich. — s. die Ebene; das Niveau. — v.a. ebnen, ausgleichen; (Build.) planieren.
**lever** ['li:və], s. der Hebel.
**levity** ['leviti], s. der Leichtsinn.
**levy** ['levi], v.a. erheben (tax); auferlegen (penalty). — s. die Steuer.
**lewd** [lju:d or lu:d], adj. liederlich, gemein, unzüchtig.
**liability** [laiə'biliti], s. die Verantwortlichkeit; limited —, beschränkte Haftung; die Steuerpflichtigkeit (to tax), Zollpflichtigkeit (to duty).
**liable** ['laiəbl], adj. haftbar, zahlungspflichtig.
**liar** ['laiə], s. der Lügner.
**libel** ['laibl], s. die Verleumdung. — v.a. verleumden, schmähen.
**libellous** ['laibələs], adj. verleumderisch.
**liberal** ['libərəl], adj. (Pol.) liberal; freigebig (generous); — arts, Geisteswissenschaften, f. pl.
**liberate** ['libəreit], v.a. befreien, freisetzen; (Law) in Freiheit setzen.
**Liberian** [lai'bi:riən], adj. liberisch. — s. der Liberier.
**libertine** ['libəti:n], s. der Wüstling.
**liberty** ['libəti], s. die Freiheit; die Erlaubnis (permission).
**librarian** [lai'brɛəriən], s. der Bibliothekar, die Bibliothekarin.
**library** ['laibrəri], s. die Bibliothek.
**Libyan** ['libjən], adj. libysch. — s. der Libyer.
**licence** ['laisəns], s. die Genehmigung, Erlaubnis (permit); driving —, der Führerschein; die Zügellosigkeit (licentiousness).
**license** ['laisəns], v.a. genehmigen, bewilligen; licensing laws, Ausschanksgesetze, n. pl. (for alcohol).

**licentiate** [lai'senʃiit], s. der Lizenziat (*degree*).

**licentious** [lai'senʃəs], *adj.* ausschweifend, liederlich, locker (*in morals*).

**lichen** ['laikən, 'litʃən], s. (*Bot.*) die Flechte.

**lichgate** ['litʃgeit], s. das Friedhofstor.

**lick** [lik], *v.a.* lecken; (*Am.*) prügeln, verhauen.

**lid** [lid], s. das Augenlid; der Deckel.

**lie** [lai], (1) *v.n.* lügen. — s. die Lüge (*untruth*).

**lie** [lai], (2) *v.n. irr.* liegen; — *down*, sich legen, hinlegen; sich fügen (*fig.*).

**lieu** [lju:], s. *in* —, an Stelle, anstatt (*Genit.*).

**lieutenant** [lef'tenənt], s. der Leutnant.

**life** [laif], s. das Leben.

**lifebelt** ['laifbelt], s. der Rettungsgürtel.

**lifeboat** ['laifbout], s. das Rettungsboot.

**lifetime** ['laiftaim], s. die Lebenszeit, Zeit seines Lebens.

**lift** [lift], s. der Aufzug, Fahrstuhl; (*coll.*) *give a* — *to*, mitnehmen (im Auto). — *v.a.* heben; aufheben (*abolish*); (*coll.*) klauen, stehlen.

**ligament** ['ligəmənt], s. das Band; (*Anat.*) die Flechse, die Sehne.

**ligature** ['ligətʃə], s. (*Typ.*) die Ligatur; die Verbindung.

**light** [lait], *adj.* hell, licht; blond (*hair*); leicht (*weight*). — s. das Licht; *give a* —, ein Streichholz geben, Feuer geben. — *v.a. irr.* beleuchten (*room*); anzünden (*fire*). — *v.n. irr.* — (*up*), hell werden, leuchten; (*fig.*) aufleuchten.

**lighten** [laitn], *v.a.* erhellen (*brighten*); erleichtern (*ease*).

**lighter** ['laitə], s. das Feuerzeug (*smoker's*); (*Naut.*) das Lichterschiff.

**lighthouse** ['laithaus], s. der Leuchtturm.

**lightning** ['laitniŋ], s. der Blitz; — *conductor*, der Blitzableiter; — *speed*, die Blitzesschnelle.

**ligneous** ['ligniəs], *adj.* holzig.

**lignite** ['lignait], s. die Braunkohle.

**like** (1) [laik], *v.a.* gern haben; *I* — *to sing*, ich singe gern. — *v.n.* belieben, wollen; *as you* —, wie Sie wollen. — s. *his* —*s and dislikes*, seine Wünsche und Abneigungen.

**like** (2) [laik], *adj.* gleich, ähnlich. — s. *his* —, seinesgleichen. — *prep.* gleich, wie; *just* — *him!* das sieht ihm ähnlich! *feel* —, möchte gern; *what is it* —? wie sieht es aus?

**likelihood** ['laiklihud], s. die Möglichkeit; Wahrscheinlichkeit (*probability*).

**likely** ['laikli], *adj.* möglich; wahrscheinlich (*probable*).

**liken** ['laikən], *v.a.* vergleichen.

**likeness** ['laiknis], s. die Ähnlichkeit.

**likewise** ['laikwaiz], *adv.* ebenso, gleichfalls, auch.

**liking** ['laikiŋ], s. die Vorliebe (*for*, für, *Acc.*); Neigung (*for*, zu, *Dat.*); *to my*

—, nach meinem Geschmack *or* Wunsch.

**lilac** ['lailək], s. (*Bot.*) der Flieder.

**lilt** [lilt], *v.a., v.n.* trällern, summen. — s. die Melodie, Weise.

**lily** ['lili], (*Bot.*) s. die Lilie; — *of the valley*, das Maiglöckchen.

**limb** [lim], s. das Glied.

**limber** ['limbə], *adj.* geschmeidig.

**lime** (1) [laim], s. der Leim, Kalk (*chalk*).

**lime** (2) [laim], s. (*Bot.*) die Linde (*tree*); die Limone (*fruit*); — *juice*, der Limonensaft.

**limestone** ['laimstoun], s. der Kalkstein.

**limit** ['limit], s. die Grenze, das Ende. — *v.a.* begrenzen, beschränken.

**limitation** [limi'teiʃən], s. die Begrenzung.

**limn** [lim], *v.a.* (*Art.*) zeichnen, malen.

**limp** [limp], *v.n.* hinken. — *adj.* müde, schlaff.

**limpid** ['limpid], *adj.* klar, durchsichtig.

**linden** ['lindən], s. (*Bot.*) die Linde.

**line** (1) [lain], s. die Linie, Eisenbahnlinie (*Railw.*); die Zeile; der Strich; (*Mil.*) die Reihe; — *of business*, die Geschäftsbranche; (*Genealogy*) die Abstammung; *take a strong* —, entschlossen auftreten.

**line** (2) [lain], *v.a.* füttern (*a garment*).

**lineage** ['liniidʒ], s. die Abstammung.

**lineament** ['liniəmənt], s. der Gesichtszug.

**linear** ['liniə], *adj.* linear, geradlinig.

**linen** ['linin], s. die Leinwand; *bed* —, die Laken, Bettwäsche. — *adj.* leinen.

**liner** ['lainə], s. (*Naut.*) das Passagierschiff.

**linger** ['liŋgə], *v.n.* zögern; verweilen.

**lingerie** ['lɛ̃ʒəri:], s. die Damenunterwäsche.

**linguist** ['liŋgwist], s. der Sprachkundige, Philologe, Linguist.

**liniment** ['linimənt], s. (*Med.*) die Salbe.

**lining** ['lainiŋ], s. das Futter (*of garment*).

**link** [liŋk], s. das Glied (*in chain*); die Verbindung (*connexion*). — *v.a.* verbinden, verknüpfen.

**linnet** ['linit], s. (*Orn.*) der Hänfling.

**linseed** ['linsi:d], s. der Leinsamen; — *oil*, das Leinöl.

**lint** [lint], s. die Scharpie, das Verbandzeug.

**lion** ['laiən], s. (*Zool.*) der Löwe.

**lioness** ['laiənes], s. (*Zool.*) die Löwin.

**lip** [lip], s. (*Anat., Bot.*) die Lippe (*mouth*); der Rand (*of jug*).

**lipstick** ['lipstik], s. der Lippenstift.

**liquefy** ['likwifai], *v.a., v.n.* flüssig machen *or* werden.

**liqueur** [li'kjuə], s. der Likör.

**liquid** ['likwid], *adj.* flüssig. — s. die Flüssigkeit.

**liquidate** ['likwideit], *v.a.* liquidieren; (*Comm.*) flüssig machen (*assets*); bezahlen (*pay off*).

431

**liquor** ['likə], s. der Alkohol.
**liquorice** ['likəris], s. die Lakritze.
**lisp** [lisp], v.n. lispeln. — s. der Sprachfehler, das Anstoßen, Lispeln.
**list** [list], s. die Liste, das Verzeichnis; (Naut.) die Schlagseite.
**listen** ['lisn], v.n. horchen, zuhören.
**listless** ['listlis], adj. teilnahmslos.
**litany** ['litəni], s. (Eccl.) die Litanei.
**literal** ['litərəl], adj. buchstäblich.
**literary** ['litərəri], adj. literarisch, Literatur-.
**literature** ['litrətʃə], s. die Literatur.
**lithe** [laið], adj. geschmeidig.
**Lithuanian** [liθju'einiən], adj. litauisch. — s. der Litauer.
**litigate** ['litigeit], v.n. einen Prozeß anstrengen, litigieren, prozessieren.
**litigation** [liti'geiʃən], s. die Litigation, der Prozeß.
**litter** ['litə], s. (Zool.) die Jungen, n. pl.; die Brut; die Sänfte (carriage); der Abfall, die Abfälle (waste paper etc.). — v.n. Junge haben, werfen. — v.a. Abfälle wegwerfen, unsauber machen.
**little** [litl], adj. klein (size, value); gering (value); — by —, nach und nach.
**liturgy** ['litədʒi], s. (Eccl.) die Liturgie.
**live** [liv], v.n. leben; wohnen (dwell).
**livelihood** ['laivlihud], s. der Lebensunterhalt.
**liveliness** ['laivlinis], s. die Lebhaftigkeit.
**lively** ['laivli], adj. lebhaft.
**liven** [laivn], v.a. — up, beleben.
**liver** ['livə], s. (Anat.) die Leber.
**livery** ['livəri], s. die Livree (uniform); — company, die Zunftgenossenschaft.
**livid** ['livid], adj. bleich, blaß.
**living** ['liviŋ], s. das Auskommen, der Unterhalt; die Lebensweise; (Eccl.) die Pfründe, Pfarrstelle.
**lizard** ['lizəd], s. (Zool.) die Eidechse.
**lo!** [lou], excl. (obs.) sieh, da! siehe!
**load** [loud], s. die Last, Belastung. — v.a. beladen, belasten. — v.n. laden, aufladen.
**loadstone** see **lodestone.**
**loaf** [louf], s. der Laib (bread); sugar —, der Zuckerhut. — v.n. herumlungern, nichts tun.
**loafer** ['loufə], s. der Faulenzer, Drückeberger.
**loam** [loum], s. der Lehm.
**loan** [loun], s. die Anleihe. — v.a. leihen.
**loath** [louθ], adj. unwillig, abgeneigt.
**loathe** [louð], v.a. verabscheuen, hassen.
**loathing** ['louðiŋ], s. der Abscheu, Ekel.
**loathsome** ['louθsəm], adj. abscheulich, ekelhaft.
**lobby** ['lɔbi], s. die Vorhalle. — v.a. (Pol.) einen beeinflußen.
**lobe** [loub], s. das Läppchen.
**lobster** ['lɔbstə], s. (Zool.) der Hummer.
**local** ['loukəl], adj. lokal, örtlich. — s. (coll.) das Stammgasthaus (pub).

**locality** [lo'kæliti], s. die Lokalität, die Örtlichkeit, der Ort.
**localize** ['loukəlaiz], v.a. lokalisieren, auf einen Ort beschränken.
**locate** [lo'keit], v.a. finden (find); ausfindig machen.
**location** [lo'keiʃən], s. die Plazierung (position); die Lage; der Standort; on —, auf dem Gelände, auf Außenaufnahme (film).
**loch** [lɔx], s. (Scot.) der See.
**lock** [lɔk], s. das Schloß (on door); die Schleuse (on waterway); die Locke (hair). — v.a. schließen, abschließen (door); hemmen (wheel). — v.n. sich schließen; — in, ineinandergreifen (cogs).
**locker** ['lɔkə], s. der Schließschrank, das Schließfach.
**locket** ['lɔkit], s. das Medaillon.
**locksmith** ['lɔksmiθ], s. der Schlosser.
**lock-up** ['lɔkʌp], s. der Arrest, die Haftzelle; (coll.) die Garage.
**locust** ['loukəst], s. (Ent.) die Heuschrecke.
**lodestone** ['loudstoun], s. der Magnetstein, Magnet.
**lodge** [lɔdʒ], v.n. wohnen; logieren (temporary). — v.a. beherbergen (accommodate); einbringen (a complaint, protest). — s. das Haus, das Häuschen; die Loge (Freemasons).
**lodger** ['lɔdʒə], s. der (Unter)mieter.
**lodgings** ['lɔdʒiŋz], s. pl. das möblierte Zimmer, die Wohnung.
**loft** [lɔft], s. der Boden, Dachboden.
**lofty** ['lɔfti], adj. hoch; erhaben; stolz (proud).
**log** [lɔg], s. der Holzklotz, das Scheit; —cabin, —house, das Blockhaus; (Naut.) das Log, das Schiffstagebuch. — v.a. (Naut.) eintragen.
**loggerheads** ['lɔgəhedz], s. pl. at —, in Widerspruch, Widerstreit, im Konflikt.
**logic** ['lɔdʒik], s. die Logik.
**logical** ['lɔdʒikəl], adj. logisch.
**loin** [lɔin], s. (Anat.) die Lende.
**loincloth** ['lɔinklɔθ], s. der Lendenschurz.
**loiter** ['lɔitə], v.n. herumlungern; bummeln.
**loiterer** ['lɔitərə], s. der Lungerer, Faulenzer.
**loitering** ['lɔitəriŋ], s. das Herumlungern, Herumstehen, Faulenzen.
**loll** [lɔl], v.n. herumlungern.
**lollipop** ['lɔlipɔp], s. das Zuckerwerk, die Süßigkeit; (fig.) der Leckerbissen.
**loneliness** ['lounlinis], s. die Einsamkeit.
**lonely,** (Am.) **lonesome** ['lounli, 'lounsəm], adj. einsam.
**long** [lɔŋ], adj. lang. — adv. — ago, vor langer Zeit; before —, in kurzer Zeit. — v.n. sich sehnen (for, nach, Dat.).
**longitude** ['lɔndʒitju:d], s. die Länge; (Geog.) der Längengrad.

**longitudinal** [lɔndʒi'tjuːdinəl], *adj.* in der geographischen Länge, Längen-.

**look** [luk], *v.n.* blicken, sehen, schauen (*at,* auf, *Acc.*); — *to it,* dafür sorgen; — *out for,* Ausschau halten nach (*Dat.*); — *out!* paß auf! — *after s.o.,* sich um jemanden kümmern; — *into,* prüfen, untersuchen; — *forward to,* sich freuen (auf, *Acc.*); — *over,* durchsehen. — *s.* der Blick (*glance*); das Aussehen (*appearance*).

**looking-glass** ['lukiŋglɑːs], *s.* der Spiegel.

**look-out** ['lukaut], *s.* der Ausblick; die Ausschau.

**loom** [luːm], *s.* der Webstuhl. —*v.n.* in der Ferne auftauchen (*emerge*).

**loon** [luːn], *s.* (*Orn.*) der Eisvogel, Eistaucher; (*coll.*) der Narr.

**loony** ['luːni], *adj.* (*coll.*) wahnsinnig, närrisch.

**loop** [luːp], *s.* die Schlinge, das Schlingband; (*Railw.*) — *line,* die Schleife.

**loophole** ['luːphoul], *s.* der Ausweg, die Hintertür.

**loose** [luːs], *adj.* locker, lose; liederlich (*morals*). — *v.a.* lösen.

**loosen** [luːsn], *v.a.* auflockern, locker machen.

**lop** [lɔp], *v.a.* stutzen (*trees*).

**lopsided** [lɔp'saidid], *adj.* einseitig.

**loquacious** [lo'kweiʃəs], *adj.* geschwätzig.

**loquacity** [lo'kwæsiti], *s.* die Schwatzhaftigkeit.

**Lord** [lɔːd], *s.* (*Rel.*) the —, Gott der Herr; der Lord (*nobleman's title*); — *Mayor,* der Oberbürgermeister.

**lord** [lɔːd], *s.* der Herr.

**lordly** ['lɔːdli], *adj.* vornehm, stolz.

**lore** [lɔː], *s.* die Kunde.

**lose** [luːz], *v.a.,v.n. irr.* verlieren; nachgehen (*of timepiece*).

**loser** ['luːzə], *s.* der Verlierende.

**loss** [lɔs], *s.* der Verlust.

**lot** [lɔt], *s.* das Los; der Anteil (*share*); die Menge (*quantity*); die Partie (*auction*); (*Am.*) das Stück Land.

**loth** *see* **loath.**

**lotion** ['louʃən], *s.* das Waschmittel, das Wasser.

**loud** [laud], *adj.* laut; grell (*colour*).

**lounge** [laundʒ], *s.* der Gesellschaftsraum; (*Obs.*) die Chaiselongue; — *suit,* der Straßenanzug. — *v.n.* nichts tun, herumlungern, herumsitzen.

**louse** [laus], *s.* (*Zool.*) die Laus.

**lout** [laut], *s.* der Tölpel.

**lovable** ['lʌvəbl], *adj.* liebenswürdig, liebenswert.

**love** [lʌv], *s.* die Liebe; *for the* — *of God,* um Gottes Willen; *for* —, um nichts; *not for* — *nor money,* weder für Geld noch gute Worte, auf keinen Fall. — *v.a., v.n.* lieben; — *to,* gern tun.

**lover** ['lʌvə], *s.* der Liebhaber, der *or* die Geliebte.

**low** [lou], *adj.* niedrig; nieder, tief; leise; (*Mus.*) tief; (*spirits*) niedergeschlagen. — *v.n.* muhen (*of cattle*).

**lowlands** ['loulændz], *s. pl.* die Niederungen,*f.pl.* ;die Ebene; das Unterland.

**lowliness** ['loulinis], *s.* die Demut, Bescheidenheit.

**lowness** ['lounis], *s.* die Niedrigkeit; Tiefe.

**loyal** ['lɔiəl], *adj.* treu, ergeben, loyal.

**loyalty** ['lɔiəlti], *s.* die Treue, Ergebenheit, Loyalität.

**lozenge** ['lɔzindʒ], *s.* die Pastille; (*Geom.*) die Raute.

**lubricant** ['luːbrikənt], *s.* das Schmiermittel, Schmieröl.

**lubricate** ['luːbrikeit], *v.a.* ölen, schmieren.

**lucid** ['luːsid], *adj.* klar, deutlich.

**lucidity** [luː'siditi], *s.* die Klarheit.

**luck** [lʌk], *s.* das Glück, der Glücksfall.

**luckily** ['lʌkili], *adv.* glücklicherweise.

**lucky** ['lʌki], *adj.* mit Glück gesegnet, glücklich.

**lucrative** ['luːkrətiv], *adj.* einträglich.

**lucre** ['luːkə], *s.* der Gewinn.

**ludicrous** ['luːdikrəs], *adj.* lächerlich, komisch.

**lug** [lʌg], *v.a.* schleifen, zerren; (*burden*) schleppen.

**luggage** ['lʌgidʒ], *s.* das Gepäck.

**lugger** ['lʌgə], *s.* (*Naut.*) der Logger, Lugger.

**lugubrious** [luː'gjuːbriəs], *adj.* traurig.

**lukewarm** ['luːkwɔːm], *adj.* lauwarm.

**lull** [lʌl], *s.* die (Wind)stille. — *v.a.* einlullen, beschwichtigen.

**lullaby** ['lʌləbai], *s.* das Wiegenlied.

**lumbago** [lʌm'beigou], *s.* (*Med.*) der Hexenschuß.

**lumbar** ['lʌmbə], *adj.* (*Anat.*) zu den Lenden gehörig, Lenden-.

**lumber** ['lʌmbə], *s.* der Kram, das alte Zeug; (*timber*) das Bauholz; — *room,* die Rumpelkammer.

**luminous** ['luːminəs], *adj.* leuchtend, Leucht-.

**lump** [lʌmp], *s.* der Klumpen, Haufen; — *sugar,* der Würfelzucker; — *sum,* die Pauschalsumme. — *v.a.* (*together*), zusammenwerfen.

**lumpy** ['lʌmpi], *adj.* klumpig.

**lunacy** ['luːnəsi], *s.* der Wahnsinn.

**lunatic** ['luːnətik], *adj.* wahnsinnig. — *s.* der Wahnsinnige; — *asylum,* das Irrenhaus, die Irrenanstalt.

**lunch** [lʌntʃ], *v.n.* zu Mittag essen. — *s.* (*also* **luncheon** ['lʌntʃən]) das Mittagessen.

**lung** [lʌŋ], *s.* (*Anat.*) die Lunge.

**lunge** [lʌndʒ], *v.n.* stoßen, stürzen. — *s.* der Stoß.

**lurch** [ləːtʃ], *s. leave in the* —, im Stiche lassen. — *v.n.* taumeln.

**lure** [luə], *v.a.* locken, ködern (*bait*). — *s.* der Köder (*bait*), die Lockung.

**lurid** ['ljuərid], *adj.* unheimlich, grell.

**lurk** [ləːk], *v.n.* lauern.

**luscious** ['lʌʃəs], *adj.* saftig, süß.

**lush** [lʌʃ], *adj.* üppig (*vegetation*); übermäßig.

# lust

lust [lʌst], s. die Wollust, Sucht. —
v.n. gelüsten (for, nach, Dat.).
lustre ['lʌstə], s. der Glanz.
lusty ['lʌsti], adj. kräftig, laut.
lute [luːt], s. (Mus.) die Laute.
lutanist ['luːtənist], s. (Mus.) der
Lautenspieler.
Lutheran ['luːθərən], adj. lutherisch.
— s. der Lutheraner.
luxuriate [lʌg'zjuərieit, lʌk'sjuə-], v.n.
schwelgen; (Bot.) üppig wachsen.
luxurious [lʌg'zjuəriəs, lʌk'sjuə-], adj.
üppig; (rich) reich ausgeschmückt,
prächtig, luxuriös.
luxury ['lʌkʃəri], s. der Luxus, Aufwand.
lymph [limf], s. die Lymphe.
lynx [links], s. (Zool.) der Luchs.
lyric ['lirik], s. die Lyrik.
lyrical ['lirikəl], adj. lyrisch.

# M

M [em]. das M.
macaroon [mækə'ruːn], s. die Makrone.
mace [meis], s. das Zepter.
macerate ['mæsəreit], v.a. abzehren.
machination [mæki'neiʃən], s. die
Machenschaft, Ränke, m.pl.
machine [mə'ʃiːn], s. die Maschine.
mackerel ['mækərəl], s. (Zool.) die
Makrele.
mackintosh ['mækintɔʃ], s. der Regenmantel.
mad [mæd], adj. verrückt, wahnsinnig.
madam ['mædəm], s. (addr.) gnädige
Frau.
madden [mædn], v.a. verrückt machen.
madman ['mædmən], s. der Wahnsinnige.
madness ['mædnis], s. der Wahnsinn.
magazine [mægə'ziːn], s. die (illu-
strierte) Zeitschrift; (gun) der Ladestock; der Lagerraum (storeroom).
maggot ['mægət], s. (Ent.) die Made.
magic ['mædʒik], adj. zauberhaft; —
lantern, die Laterna Magica. — s. der
Zauber; die Magie, Zauberei.
magician [mə'dʒiʃən], s. der Zauberer.
magistracy ['mædʒistrəsi], s. die
Obrigkeit (authority).
magistrate ['mædʒistr(e)it], s. der
Richter.
magnanimity [mægnə'nimiti], s. der
Großmut.
magnanimous [mæg'næniməs], adj.
großmütig.
magnate ['mægneit], s. der Magnat,
Großunternehmer.
magnet ['mægnit], s. der Magnet.
magnetic [mæg'netik], adj. magnetisch.
magnetize ['mægnitaiz], v.a. magnetisieren.

magnificence [mæg'nifisəns], s. die
Herrlichkeit.
magnificent [mæg'nifisənt], adj. herrlich, großartig.
magnify ['mægnifai], v.a. vergrößern
(make larger); (Rel.) verherrlichen.
magnitude ['mægnitjuːd], s. die Größe;
order of —, die Größenordnung.
magpie ['mægpai], s. (Orn.) die
Elster.
Magyar ['mægjaː], adj. madjarisch.
— s. der Magyar, Madjar.
mahogany [mə'hɔgəni], s. das Maha-
goni(holz).
maid [meid], s. (Poet.) das Mädchen;
das Stubenmädchen (servant).
maiden [meidn], s. (Poet.) die Jungfrau,
das Mädchen; — aunt, die unverheiratete Tante.
mail (1) [meil], s. die Post. — v.a.
aufgeben, mit der Post senden.
mail (2) [meil], s. (Mil.) der Panzer.
maim [meim], v.a. verstümmeln,
lähmen.
main (1) [mein], adj. hauptsächlich,
Haupt-; (Railw.) — line, die Haupt-
strecke. — s. der Hauptteil; in the —,
hauptsächlich; (Poet.) das Weltmeer;
(pl.) das Hauptrohr, die Hauptleitung.
main (2) [mein], s. with might and —,
mit allen Kräften.
mainstay ['meinstei], s. die Haupt-
grundlage, Hauptstütze.
maintain [mein'tein], v.a. erhalten,
unterhalten (keep); behaupten
(assert).
maintenance ['meintənəns], s. der
Unterhalt, die Unterhaltskosten,pl. die
Erhaltung.
maize [meiz], s. (Bot.) der Mais.
majestic [mə'dʒestik], adj. majestätisch, prunkvoll.
majesty ['mædʒəsti], s. die Majestät.
major ['meidʒə], adj. größer, älter
(elder brother); wichtig (more important). — s. (Mil.) der Major; (Law)
der Mündige. — v.n. (Am.) sich
spezialisieren.
majority [mə'dʒɔriti], s. die Mehrheit
(in numbers); (Law) die Mündigkeit;
(Mil.) der Majorsrang.
make [meik], v.a. irr. machen, schaffen,
herstellen (produce); (coll.) verdienen
(money); he has made it! (coll.) er
hat's geschafft!; — out, ausfüllen
(cheque etc.); entziffern (decipher);
— up, erfinden (invent); schminken
(o.'s face). — v.n. what do you — of
him? was halten Sie von ihm? —
s. die Marke.
make-believe ['meikbəliːv], s. der
Vorwand. — adj. vorgeblich.
maladjustment [mælə'dʒʌstmənt], s.
die Unfähigkeit sich anzupassen; die
falsche Einstellung; das Missverhält-
nis.
maladroit [mælə'drɔit], adj. ungeschickt, ungewandt.
malady ['mælədi], s. das Leiden, die
Krankheit.

**Malagasy** [mælə'gæsi], *adj.* madagassisch. — *s.* der Madagasse.
**Malaysian** [mə'leiziən], *adj.* malaysisch. — *s.* der Malaysier.
**malcontent** ['mælkɔntent], *adj.* mißvergnügt.
**male** [meil], *adj.* männlich; — *screw,* die Schraubenspindel. — *s.* der Mann; (*Zool.*) das Männchen.
**malefactor** ['mælifæktə], *s.* der Übeltäter.
**malice** ['mælis], *s.* die Bosheit.
**malicious** [mə'liʃəs], *adj.* boshaft, böswillig.
**malign** [mə'lain], *v.a.* lästern, verleumden.
**malignant** [mə'lignənt], *adj.* bösartig.
**malignity** [mə'ligniti], *s.* die Bösartigkeit.
**malinger** [mə'liŋgə], *v.n.* sich krank stellen.
**malleable** ['mæliəbl], *adj.* (*Metall.*) leicht zu hämmern; (*fig.*) geschmeidig.
**mallet** ['mælit], *s.* der Schlegel, Holzhammer.
**mallow** ['mælou], *s.* (*Bot.*) die Malve.
**malpractice** [mæl'præktis], *s.* das gesetzwidrige Handeln, der Mißbrauch; die Amtsvergehung.
**malt** [mɔ:lt], *s.* das Malz.
**Maltese** [mɔ:l'ti:z], *adj.* maltesisch. — *s.* der Malteser.
**maltreat** [mæl'tri:t], *v.a.* mißhandeln.
**mammal** ['mæməl], *s.* (*Zool.*) das Säugetier.
**man** [mæn], *s.* der Mann (*adult male*); der Mensch (*human being*); — *of war,* das Kriegsschiff. — *v.a.* bemannen.
**manacle** ['mænəkl], *s.* die Handschelle. — *v.a.* fesseln.
**manage** ['mænidʒ], *v.a.* leiten, handhaben, verwalten; *how did you — it?* wie haben Sie's fertiggebracht?
**management** ['mænidʒmənt], *s.* die Leitung, Führung.
**manager** ['mænədʒə], *s.* der Leiter, Geschäftsführer, Manager.
**mandatary** *see* **mandatory.**
**mandate** ['mændeit], *s.* das Mandat.
**mandatory** ['mændətəri], *adj.* befehlend, bevollmächtigt, beauftragt. — *s.* der Bevollmächtigte, Beauftragte.
**mandrake** ['mændreik], *s.* die Alraun.
**mane** [mein], *s.* die Mähne.
**manganese** ['mæŋgəni:z], *s.* (*Chem.*) das Mangan.
**mange** [meindʒ], *s.* die Räude.
**manger** ['meindʒə], *s.* die Krippe.
**mangle** (1) [mæŋgl], *s.* die Mangel. — *v.a.* rollen; mangeln (*laundry*).
**mangle** (2) [mæŋgl], *v.a.* verstümmeln (*disfigure*).
**mango** ['mæŋgou], *s.* (*Bot.*) die Mangofrucht.
**manhood** ['mænhud], *s.* die Mannbarkeit, das Mannesalter.
**mania** ['meiniə], *s.* der Wahnsinn, die Manie.
**maniac** ['meiniæk], *s.* der Wahnsinnige. — *adj.* wahnsinnig.

**manifest** ['mænifest], *adj.* deutlich, klar, offenbar.
**manifestation** [mænifes'teiʃən], *s.* die Offenbarung.
**manifesto** [mæni'festou], *s.* das Manifest.
**manifold** ['mænifould], *adj.* mannigfach.
**manipulate** [mə'nipjuleit], *v.a.* manipulieren, handhaben.
**mankind** [mæn'kaind], *s.* die Menschheit.
**manly** ['mænli], *adj.* mannhaft, männlich.
**manner** ['mænə], *s.* die Art, Sitte (*custom*); die Manier (*bearing*); das Benehmen (*behaviour*); (*pl.*) gute Sitten.
**mannered** ['mænəd], *adj.* gesittet, geartet; maniriert, gekünstelt (*artificial*).
**manor** ['mænə], *s.* — *house,* das Herrenhaus, Schloß.
**manorial** [mə'nɔ:riəl], *adj.* des Herrenhauses, herrschaftlich.
**manservant** ['mænsə:vənt], *s.* der Bediente, Diener.
**mansion** ['mænʃən], *s.* das (herrschaftliche) Wohnhaus, Herrenhaus.
**manslaughter** ['mænslɔ:tə], *s.* der Totschlag.
**mantelpiece** ['mæntlpi:s], *s.* der Kaminsims.
**mantle** [mæntl], *s.* (*gas*) der Glühstrumpf; (*Tail.*) der Mantel. — *v.a.* verhüllen (*cloak*).
**manual** ['mænjuəl], *s.* das Handbuch; (*Mus.*) das Handregister. — *adj.* Hand-.
**manufacture** [mænju'fæktʃə], *s.* die Herstellung, Erzeugung (*production*); (*Comm.*) das Fabrikat (*product*).
**manufacturer** [mænju'fæktʃərə], *s.* der Fabrikant, Erzeuger.
**manure** [mə'njuə], *s.* der Dünger; der Mist. — *v.a.* düngen.
**manuscript** ['mænjuskript], *s.* die Handschrift, das Manuskript.
**many** ['meni], *adj.* viele; *as — as,* ganze ... (*emphatically*); — *a,* mancher.
**map** [mæp], *s.* die Landkarte. — *v.a.* —(*out*), nach der Karte planen.
**maple** [meipl], *s.* (*Bot.*) der Ahorn.
**mar** [mɑ:], *v.a.* verderben.
**marauder** [mə'rɔ:də], *s.* der Plünderer.
**marble** [mɑ:bl], *s.* der Marmor (*rock*); (*pl.*) die Murmel (*game*). — *adj.* marmorn.
**March** [mɑ:tʃ]. der März.
**march** [mɑ:tʃ], *s.* der Marsch. — *v.n.* marschieren; *steal a — on s.o.,* jemandem zuvorkommen.
**marchioness** [mɑ:ʃə'nes], *s.* die Marquise.
**mare** [mɛə], *s.* (*Zool.*) die Stute.
**margin** ['mɑ:dʒin], *s.* der Rand.
**marginal** ['mɑ:dʒinəl], *adj.* Rand-, am Rande gelegen.
**marigold** ['mærigould], *s.* (*Bot.*) die Dotterblume.

# marine

marine [mə'ri:n], adj. Marine-, See-.
— s. (Mil.) der Seesoldat; tell that to
the Marines! erzähle das der Großmutter!
mariner ['mærinə], s. der Seemann.
marital ['mæritəl], adj. ehelich.
maritime ['mæritaim], adj. Meeres-,
See-.
mark [ma:k], s. das Zeichen (sign);
(Sch.) die Zensur, Note; (Comm.) die
Marke; wide of the —, auf dem
Holzwege. — v.a. markieren (make
sign on); — my words, merk dir das!
paß auf! (Comm.) — down, den Preis
heruntersetzen; ins Auge fassen
(observe closely); a —ed man, ein
Gezeichneter.
market ['ma:kit], s. der Markt. — v.a.
auf den Markt bringen.
marksman ['ma:ksmən], s. der Schütze.
marl [ma:l], s. der Mergel.
marmalade ['ma:məleid], s. die Oran-
genmarmelade.
marmot ['ma:mət], s. (Zool.) das
Murmeltier.
maroon (1) [mə'ru:n], adj. kastanienbraun, rotbraun.
maroon (2) [mə'ru:n], v.a. aussetzen.
marquee [ma:'ki:], s. das große Zelt.
marquess, marquis ['ma:kwis], s. der
Marquis.
marriage ['mæridʒ], s. die Ehe, Heirat;
die Hochzeit (wedding).
marriageable ['mæridʒəbl], adj.
heiratsfähig.
married ['mærid], adj. verheiratet.
marrow ['mærou], s. (Anat.) das
Mark; (Bot.) der Kürbis.
marry ['mæri], v.a. heiraten; trauen
(perform marriage ceremony); — off,
verheiraten (o.'s daughter). — v.n.
sich verheiraten.
marsh [ma:ʃ], s. der Morast, Sumpf.
marshal ['ma:ʃəl], s. der Marschall.
marshy ['ma:ʃi], adj. morastig, sumpfig.
marten ['ma:tin], s. (Zool.) der Marder.
martial ['ma:ʃəl], adj. Kriegs-, kriegerisch.
martin ['ma:tin], s. (Orn.) die Mauer-
schwalbe.
martyr ['ma:tə], s. der Märtyrer.
martyrdom ['ma:tədəm], s. das
Märtyrertum, der Märtyrertod.
marvel [ma:vl], v.n. staunen (at, über,
Acc.).
marvellous ['ma:v(ə)ləs], adj. wunderbar, erstaunlich.
masculine ['mæskjulin], adj. männlich.
— s. (Gram.) das Maskulinum, das
männliche Geschlecht.
mash [mæʃ], v.a. zerquetschen, zerdrücken. — s. der Brei.
mask [ma:sk], v.a., v.n. maskieren, sich
vermummen. — s. die Maske.
mason ['meisən], s. der Maurer.
masonic [mə'sɔnik], adj. freimaurerisch.
masquerade [mæskə'reid], s. der
Mummenschanz, die Maskerade.
Mass [mæs, ma:s], s. (Eccl.) die Messe;
Low Mass, die stille Messe; High

Mass, das Hochamt; Requiem Mass,
die Seelenmesse.
mass [mæs], s. die Masse; die
Menge. — v.a., v.n. (sich) massen,
ansammeln.
massacre ['mæsəkə], s. das Blutbad.
massive ['mæsiv], adj. massiv, schwer.
mast [ma:st], s. der Mast. — v.a.
(Naut.) bemasten.
Master['ma:stə], s.(Univ.) der Magister;
der junge Herr (before boy's name).
master ['ma:stə], s. der Meister (of a
craft); der Herr, Arbeitgeber (employer); — key, der Hauptschlüssel.
— v.a. meistern, beherrschen.
masticate ['mæstikeit], v.a. kauen.
mastiff ['mæstif], s. (Zool.) der Ketten-
hund, Mastiff.
mat [mæt], s. die Matte.
match (1) [mætʃ], s. das Streichholz,
Zündholz.
match (2) [mætʃ], s. der ebenbürtige
Partner (suitable partner); find o.'s —,
seinesgleichen finden; (Sport) das
Wettspiel, der Wettkampf; Fußball-
kampf; (Cricket) das Cricketspiel. —
v.a., v.n. passen zu, anpassen; ebenbürtig sein (be equal).
matchless ['mætʃlis], adj. unvergleichlich, ohnegleichen.
mate (1) [meit], s. der Gefährte,
Genosse; (Naut.) der Maat, Steuermann; (coll.) Freund. — v.n. sich
paaren, sich verheiraten.
mate (2) [meit], v.a. (Chess) matt setzen.
material [mə'tiəriəl], s. das Material,
der Stoff. — adj. wesentlich (essential); materiell (tangible).
materialism [mə'tiəriəlizm], s. der
Materialismus.
maternal [mə'tə:nəl], adj. mütterlich.
maternity [mə'tə:niti], s. die Mutterschaft; — ward, die Geburtsklinik.
mathematical [mæθə'mætikəl], adj.
mathematisch.
mathematics [mæθə'mætiks], s. die
Mathematik.
matins ['mætinz], s. (Eccl.) die Früh-
mette.
matriculate [mə'trikjuleit], v.n. sich
immatrikulieren (lassen).
matrimonial [mætri'mouniəl], adj.
Ehe-, ehelich.
matrimony ['mætriməni], s. die Ehe.
matron ['meitrən], s. die Oberschwester,
Oberin (in hospital etc.); die Matrone
(older woman).
matter ['mætə], s. der Stoff (substance);
die Sache, der Gegenstand (subject);
die Angelegenheit (case); printed —,
Drucksache; what is the —? was ist
los?; the heart of the —, des Pudels
Kern; as a — of fact, tatsächlich,
ernst gesprochen. — v.n. bedeutsam
sein, wichtig sein.
mattock ['mætək], s. die Haue.
mattress ['mætrəs], s. die Matratze.
mature [mə'tjuə], adj. reif; (fig.)
gereift. — v.a., v.n. reifen, zur Reife
bringen; (Comm.) fällig werden.

**matured** [mə'tjuəd], *adj.* abgelagert.
**maturity** [mə'tjuəriti], *s.* die Reife; (*Comm.*) die Fälligkeit.
**maudlin** ['mɔːdlin], *adj.* rührselig, sentimental.
**maul** [mɔːl], *v.a.* mißhandeln.
**Maundy Thursday** ['mɔːndi'θəːzd(e)i]. der Gründonnerstag.
**mauve** [mouv], *adj.* malvenfarbig, violett.
**maw** [mɔː], *s.* (*Zool.*) der Magen.
**mawkish** ['mɔːkiʃ], *adj.* abgeschmackt, sentimental, rührselig.
**maxim** ['mæksim], *s.* der Grundsatz.
**May** [mei]. der Mai.
**may** (1) [mei], *v.n. aux. irr.* mögen, können; (*permissive*) dürfen.
**may** (2) [mei], *s.* (*Bot.*) der Weißdorn.
**mayor** [mɛə], *s.* der Bürgermeister.
**maypole** ['meipoul], *s.* der Maibaum.
**maze** [meiz], *s.* das Labyrinth.
**me** [miː], *pers. pron.* (*Acc.*) mich; (*Dat.*) mir.
**mead** [miːd], *s.* der Met.
**meadow** ['medou], *s.* die Wiese.
**meagre** ['miːgə], *adj.* mager, karg (*lean, poor*); dürftig.
**meal** (1) [miːl], *s.* das Mahl, Essen, die Mahlzeit.
**meal** (2) [miːl], *s.* das Mehl (*flour*).
**mealy** ['miːli], *adj.* mehlig; — *-mouthed*, frömmelnd; kleinlaut (*shy*).
**mean** (1) [miːn], *v.a. irr.* bedeuten (*signify*); meinen (*wish to express*); vorhaben (*intend*).
**mean** (2) [miːn], *adj.* mittelmäßig, Mittel— (*average*). — *s.* die Mitte.
**mean** (3) [miːn], *adj.* gemein, niedrig (*despicable*); geizig.
**meander** [mi'ændə], *s.* die Windung, das Wellenmuster. — *v.n.* sich winden, fließen.
**meaning** ['miːniŋ], *s.* die Bedeutung (*significance, connotation*); der Sinn.
**meaningless** ['miːniŋlis], *adj.* bedeutungslos.
**means** [miːnz], *s.* das Mittel; *by all* —, auf jeden Fall, unbedingt; *by no* —, keinesfalls; *by* —*of*, mittels (*Genit.*).
**meantime, meanwhile** ['miːntaim, 'miːnwail], *s.* die Zwischenzeit.—*adv.* in der Zwischenzeit, indessen.
**measles** [miːzlz], *s.* (*Med.*) die Masern, *f. pl.*; *German* —, die Röteln, *m. pl.*
**measurable** ['meʒərəbl], *adj.* meßbar.
**measure** ['meʒə], *s.* das Maß; der Maßstab (*scale*); (*Mus.*) der Takt; das Zeitmaß.—*v.a.* messen, abmessen.
**meat** [miːt], *s.* das Fleisch.
**mechanic** [mi'kænik], *s.* der Mechaniker.
**mechanical** [mi'kænikəl], *adj.* mechanisch, automatisch; — *engineering*, der Maschinenbau.
**mechanics** [mi'kæniks], *s.* die Mechanik.
**medal** [medl], *s.* die Medaille, der Orden.
**meddle** [medl], *v.n.* sich einmischen (in, *in, Acc.*).

**mediæval, medieval** [medi'iːvəl], *adj.* mittelalterlich.
**mediate** ['miːdieit], *v.n.* vermitteln, intervenieren. — *adj.* mittelbar.
**mediator** ['miːdieitə], *s.* der Vermittler.
**medical** ['medikəl], *adj.* medizinisch, ärztlich; — *orderly*, der Krankenwärter.
**medicate** ['medikeit], *v.a.* medizinisch behandeln.
**medicine** ['medsən], *s.* die Medizin, Arznei.
**medieval** *see* **mediæval.**
**mediocre** ['miːdioukə], *adj.* mittelmäßig.
**mediocrity** [miːdi'ɔkriti], *s.* die Mittelmäßigkeit.
**meditate** ['mediteit], *v.n.* nachdenken, sinnen.
**meditation** [medi'teiʃən], *s.* das Sinnen, Nachdenken.
**Mediterranean** [meditə'reiniən], *adj.* mittelländisch. — *s.* das Mittelmeer, mittelländische Meer.
**medium** ['miːdjəm], *s.* das Medium; das Mittel (*means*). — *adj.* mittelgroß.
**medlar** ['medlə], *s.* (*Bot.*) die Mispel.
**medley** ['medli], *s.* (*Mus.*) das Potpourri; das Gemisch (*mixture*).
**meek** [miːk], *adj.* sanft, mild.
**meet** [miːt], *v.a., v.n. irr.* treffen (*Acc.*), sich treffen (mit, *Dat.*), begegnen (*Dat.*). — *s.* (*Hunt.*) das Jagd.
**meeting** ['miːtiŋ], *s.* das Zusammentreffen; die Tagung, Sitzung (*conference*).
**melancholy** ['melənkɔli], *adj.* melancholisch, schwermütig. — *s.* die Melancholie, die Schwermut.
**mellifluous** [me'lifluəs], *adj.* lieblich, süß (*of sounds*).
**mellow** ['melou], *adj.* mild, weich, mürbe (*fruit etc.*); freundlich (*mood*). — *v.a.* mürbe machen, reifen lassen. — *v.n.* weich werden.
**melodious** [mə'loudiəs], *adj.* klangvoll, wohlklingend, melodisch.
**melodrama** ['melədrɑːmə], *s.* das Melodrama.
**melody** ['melədi], *s.* die Melodie.
**melon** ['melən], *s.* (*Bot.*) die Melone.
**melt** [melt], *v.a., v.n. reg. & irr.* schmelzen.
**member** ['membə], *s.* das Mitglied (*of club*); (*Parl.*) der Abgeordnete, das Glied.
**membrane** ['membrein], *s.* die Membran; (*Anat.*) das Häutchen.
**memento** [mi'mentou], *s.* das Andenken.
**memoir** ['memwɑː], *s.* die Denkschrift; (*pl.*) die Memoiren, *n. pl.*
**memorable** ['memərəbl], *adj.* denkwürdig.
**memorandum** [memə'rændəm], *s.* das Memorandum, die Denkschrift.
**memorial** [mi'mɔːriəl], *s.* das Denkmal (*monument*). — *adj.* Gedenk-, zum Gedenken, Gedächtnis-.

**memory** ['meməri], s. die Erinnerung; das Gedächtnis (*faculty*); das Andenken (*remembrance*).

**menace** ['menis], s. die Drohung. — *v.a.* bedrohen.

**mend** [mend], *v.a.* reparieren; verbessern, ausbessern. — *v.n.* sich bessern.

**mendacious** [men'deiʃəs], *adj.* lügnerisch, verlogen (*lying*).

**mendacity** [men'dæsiti], s. die Lügenhaftigkeit, Verlogenheit.

**mendicant** ['mendikənt], *adj.* bettlerisch. — s. der Bettler.

**mendicity** [men'disiti], s. die Bettelei.

**menial** ['mi:niəl], *adj.* gemein, grob (*job*).

**mental** [mentl], *adj.* geistig; (*coll.*) geisteskrank.

**mention** ['menʃən], *v.a.* erwähnen; *don't — it*, gern geschehen! — s. die Erwähnung.

**mentor** ['mentə], s. der Ratgeber.

**menu** ['menju:], s. die Speisekarte.

**mercantile** ['mə:kəntail], *adj.* Handels-, kaufmännisch.

**mercenary** ['mə:sənəri], *adj.* für Geld zu haben, käuflich, feil; materiell eingestellt. — s. der Söldner.

**mercer** ['mə:sə], s. der Seidenhändler.

**mercerised** ['mə:səraizd], *adj.* (*Textile*) merzerisiert.

**merchandise** ['mə:tʃəndaiz], s. die Ware.

**merchant** ['mə:tʃənt], s. der Kaufmann.

**merchantman** ['mə:tʃəntmən], s. (*Naut.*) das Handelsschiff, Frachtschiff.

**merciful** ['mə:siful], *adj.* barmherzig, gnädig.

**Mercury** ['mə:kjuəri], (*Myth.*) Merkur, m.

**mercury** ['mə:kjuəri], s. (*Chem.*) das Quecksilber.

**mercy** ['mə:si], s. die Barmherzigkeit, Gnade.

**mere** (1) [miə], *adj.* bloß, allein.

**mere** (2) [miə], s. der Teich.

**meretricious** [meri'triʃəs], *adj.* falsch, täuschend.

**merge** [mə:dʒ], *v.n.* aufgehen lassen, verschmelzen (*combine*).

**merger** ['mə:dʒə], s. (*Comm.*) die Fusion, Vereinigung, Zusammenlegung.

**meridian** [mə'ridiən], s. der Meridian; (*fig.*) der Gipfel.

**merit** ['merit], s. das Verdienst, der Wert. — *v.a.* verdienen.

**meritorious** [meri'tɔ:riəs], *adj.* verdienstlich.

**mermaid** ['mə:meid], s. die Wasserjungfer, Nixe.

**merriment** ['merimənt], s. die Belustigung, das Fröhlichsein, die Fröhlichkeit.

**merry** ['meri], *adj.* froh, fröhlich; — *go-round*, das Karussel.

**mesh** [meʃ], s. das Netz; die Masche (*knitting*). — *v.a.* einfangen.

**mess** (1) [mes], s. (*Mil.*) die Offiziersmesse.

**mess** (2) [mes], s. die Unordnung (*disorder*).

**message** ['mesidʒ], s. die Nachricht, Mitteilung, Botschaft.

**messenger** ['mesindʒə], s. der Bote.

**Messiah** [mi'saiə], s. der Messias.

**metal** [metl], s. das Metall.

**metallurgy** ['metələ:dʒi], s. die Metallurgie, Hüttenkunde.

**metaphor** ['metəfɔ:], s. die Metapher.

**metaphorical** [metə'fɔrikəl], *adj.* bildlich.

**meter** ['mi:tə], s. der Messer, Zähler (*gauge*); (*Am.*) *see* **metre** (1).

**methinks** [mi'θiŋks], *v. impers.* (*obs.*) mich dünkt, ich meine, mir scheint.

**method** ['meθəd], s. die Methode.

**methodical** [mi'θɔdikəl], *adj.* methodisch, systematisch.

**methylate** ['meθileit], *v.a.* (*Chem.*) denaturieren.

**metre** (1) ['mi:tə], s. der *or* das Meter (*unit of measurement*).

**metre** (2) ['mi:tə], s. (*Poet.*) das Versmaß.

**metric** ['metrik], *adj.* metrisch (*system of measurement*).

**metrical** ['metrikəl], *adj.* (*Poet.*) im Metrum, metrisch, Vers-.

**metropolis** [mi'trɔpəlis], s. die Metropole.

**metropolitan** [metrə'pɔlitən], *adj.* hauptstädtisch. — s. (*Eccl.*) der Erzbischof.

**mettle** [metl], s. der Mut (*courage*); *put s.o. on his —*, einen anspornen.

**mew** [mju:], s. das Miauen (*of cat*). — *v.n.* miauen.

**mews** [mju:z], s. *pl.* die Stallung.

**Mexican** ['meksikən], *adj.* mexikanisch. — s. der Mexikaner.

**microphone** ['maikrəfoun], s. das Mikrophon.

**mid-** [mid], *prefix.* mittel, Mittel-, mittler.

**midday** [mid'dei], s. der Mittag.

**middle** [midl], s. die Mitte, das Zentrum.

**middling** ['midliŋ], *adj.* (*coll.*) mittelmäßig.

**midget** ['midʒit], s. der Zwerg (*dwarf*).

**midnight** ['midnait], s. die Mitternacht.

**midriff** ['midrif], s. das Zwerchfell.

**midshipman** ['midʃipmən], s. (*Naut.*) der Seekadett.

**midwife** ['midwaif], s. die Hebamme.

**mien** [mi:n], s. die Miene.

**might** [mait], s. die Macht, Gewalt.

**mighty** ['maiti], *adj.* mächtig, stark.

**mignonette** [minjə'net], s. (*Bot.*) die Reseda.

**migrate** [mai'greit], *v.n.* wandern, migrieren; (*birds*) ziehen.

**migratory** ['maigrətəri], *adj.* Zug-, Wander-.

# miscellaneous

**Milanese** [milə'n:iz], *adj.* mailändisch. — *s.* der Mailänder.

**mild** [maild], *adj.* mild, sanft.

**mildew** ['mildju:], *s.* der Meltau.

**mile** [mail], *s.* die (englische) Meile.

**mileage** ['mailidʒ], *s.* die Meilenzahl.

**milfoil** ['milfɔil], *s.* (*Bot.*) die Schafgarbe (*yarrow*).

**military** ['militəri], *adj.* militärisch. — *s.* das Militär.

**militia** [mi'liʃə], *s.* die Miliz.

**milk** [milk], *v.a.* melken. — *s.* die Milch.

**milksop** ['milksɔp], *s.* die Memme.

**milky** ['milki], *adj.* milchig; *Milky Way,* die Milchstraße.

**mill** [mil], *s.* die Mühle; die Spinnerei (*textile*); *rolling* —, das Walzwerk; *run of the* —, gewöhnlich; *through the* —, wohl erfahren, lebenserfahren. — *v.a.* mahlen (*flour*); rollen, walzen (*steel*); rändern (*coins*); —*ed edge,* die Rändelkante. —*v.n.* — (*around*), sich drängen.

**miller** ['milə], *s.* der Müller.

**millet** ['milit], *s.* die Hirse.

**milliner** ['milinə], *s.* die Modistin, Putzmacherin.

**millinery** ['milinəri], *s.* die Putzwaren, Modewaren, *f. pl.*

**million** ['miljən], *s.* die Million.

**milt** [milt], *s.* die Fischmilch; (*Anat.*) die Milz.

**mimic** ['mimik], *s.* der Mimiker. — *v.a.* nachahmen.

**mimicry** ['mimikri], *s.* die Nachahmung; (*Zool.*) die Anpassung (*in colour*).

**mince** [mins], *v.a.* kleinhacken (*meat*); — *o.'s words,* affektiert sprechen; *not* — *o.'s words,* kein Blatt vor den Mund nehmen. — *s.* gehacktes Fleisch; — *pie,* die Dörrobstpastete.

**mincemeat** ['minsmi:t], *s.* die (gehackte) Dörrobstmischung.

**mincing** ['minsiŋ], *adj.* affektiert; — *steps,* trippelnde Schritte.

**mind** [maind], *s.* der Geist, das Gemüt; die Meinung; der Sinn; der Verstand; *what is on your* —? was bedrückt Sie?; *bear in* —, daran denken; *have a* —, Lust haben; *make up o.'s* —, sich entschließen; *with an open* —, unparteiisch. — *v.a.* beachten, achten (auf, *Acc.*). — *v.n. do you* —? macht es Ihnen etwas aus? *never* —, macht nichts; *I don't* —, mir ist's recht, meinetwegen.

**minded** ['maindid], *adj.* gesinnt, eingestellt.

**mine** (1) [main], *poss. pron.* mein, meinig.

**mine** (2) [main], *s.* das Bergwerk (*general*), die Grube (*coal*). — *v.a.* abbauen, graben (*Acc.,* nach, *Dat.*).

**miner** ['mainə], *s.* der Bergmann, Bergarbeiter; (*coll.*) der Kumpel.

**mineral** ['minərəl], *s.* das Mineral; (*pl.*) Mineralwasser.

**mingle** [miŋgl], *v.a.,v.n.* (sich) mischen.

**minimize** ['minimaiz], *v.a.* (möglichst) klein machen.

**mining** ['mainiŋ], *s.* die Hüttenkunde (*theory*); der Bergbau.

**minion** ['minjən], *s.* der Liebling.

**minister** ['ministə], *s.* (*Pol.*) der Minister; *Prime Minister,* den Ministerpräsident; (*Eccl.*) der Geistliche, Pfarrer. — *v.n.* einen Gottesdienst abhalten; dienen (*to, Dat.*).

**ministration** [minis'treiʃən], *s.* der Dienst, die Dienstleistung.

**ministry** ['ministri], *s.* das Ministerium (*department of state*); (*Eccl.*) der Beruf *or* das Amt des Geistlichen.

**minnow** ['minou], *s.* (*Zool.*) die Elritze.

**minor** ['mainə], *adj.* kleiner, geringer; (*Sch.*) jünger (*after boy's name*). — *s.* (*Law*) der Minderjährige, Unmündige.

**minority** [mai'nɔriti], *s.* die Minorität (*in numbers*); (*Law*) die Unmündigkeit.

**minster** ['minstə], *s.* (*Eccl.*) das Münster.

**minstrel** ['minstrəl], *s.* der Spielmann.

**mint** (1) [mint], *s.* (*Bot.*) die Minze.

**mint** (2) [mint], *s.* die Münzstätte. — *v.a.* münzen.

**minuet** [minju'et], *s.* (*Mus.*) das Menuett.

**minute** (1) ['minit], *s.* die Minute (*time*); (*pl.*) das Protokoll (*of meeting*). — *v.a.* zu Protokoll nehmen, protokollieren.

**minute** (2) [mai'nju:t], *adj.* winzig, klein.

**minutiae** [mai'nju:ʃii], *s.pl.* die Details, *n. pl.,* die Einzelheiten, *f. pl.*

**miracle** ['mirəkl], *s.* das Wunder.

**miraculous** [mi'rækjuləs], *adj.* wunderbar; wundertätig.

**mirage** [mi'rɑ:ʒ], *s.* die Luftspiegelung, die Fata Morgana.

**mire** [maiə], *s.* der Schlamm, Kot.

**mirror** ['mirə], *s.* der Spiegel. — *v.a.* reflektieren, spiegeln.

**mirth** [mə:θ], *s.* der Frohsinn.

**misadventure** [misəd'ventʃə], *s.* das Mißgeschick.

**misalliance** [misə'laiəns], *s.* die Mißheirat, Mesalliance.

**misapply** [misə'plai], *v.a.* falsch anwenden.

**misapprehend** [misæpri'hend], *v.a.* mißverstehen.

**misapprehension** [misæpri'henʃən], *s.* das Mißverständnis.

**misappropriate** [misə'prouprieit], *v.a.* unrechtmäßig erwerben, unterschlagen.

**misbehave** [misbi'heiv], *v.n.* sich schlecht benehmen.

**miscalculate** [mis'kælkjuleit], *v.a.,v.n.* sich verrechnen.

**miscarriage** [mis'kæridʒ], *s.* das Mißlingen; (*Med.*) die Fehlgeburt.

**miscarry** [mis'kæri], *v.n.* mißlingen; (*Med.*) fehlgebären.

**miscellaneous** [misə'leiniəs], *adj.* vermischt.

439

# miscellany

**miscellany** [mi'seləni], *s.* der Sammel-band (*of writers*); die Mischung, das Gemisch.
**mischief** ['mistʃif], *s.* der Unfug; *out to make* —, darauf aus, Unfug zu stiften; — *maker*, der Unheilstifter.
**mischievous** ['mistʃivəs], *adj.* boshaft.
**misconceive** [miskən'siːv], *v.a.* miß-verstehen.
**misconception** [miskən'sepʃən], *s.* das Mißverständnis.
**misconduct** [mis'kɔndʌkt], *s.* das un-korrekte Verhalten; der Fehltritt.
**misconstruction** [miskən'strʌkʃən], *s.* die Mißdeutung.
**misconstrue** [miskən'struː], *v.a.* miß-deuten.
**misdeed** [mis'diːd], *s.* die Missetat.
**misdemeanour** [misdi'miːnə], *s.* (*Law.*) das Vergehen; die Missetat.
**miser** ['maizə], *s.* der Geizhals.
**miserable** ['mizərəbl], *adj.* elend, kläglich (*wretched*); nichtswürdig (*base*).
**miserly** ['maizəli], *adj.* geizig.
**misery** ['mizəri], *s.* das Elend, die Not.
**misfortune** [mis'fɔːtʃən], *s.* das Un-glück.
**misgiving** [mis'givin], *s.* die Befürch-tung, der Zweifel (*doubt*).
**misguide** [mis'gaid], *v.a.* irreführen, verleiten.
**mishap** [mis'hæp], *s.* der Unfall.
**misinform** [misin'fɔːm], *v.a.* falsch informieren, falsch unterrichten.
**misinterpret** [misin'təːprit], *v.a.* miß-deuten.
**misjudge** [mis'dʒʌdʒ], *v.a.* falsch beurteilen.
**mislay** [mis'lei], *v.a. irr.* verlegen.
**mislead** [mis'liːd], *v.a. irr.* verführen, irreführen.
**misnomer** [mis'noumə], *s.* der falsche Name.
**misogynist** [mi'sɔdʒinist], *s.* der Wei-berfeind.
**misplace** [mis'pleis], *v.a.* übel anbrin-gen (*remark*); verlegen (*thing*).
**misprint** [mis'print], *v.a.* verdrucken, falsch drucken. — ['misprint], *s.* der Druckfehler.
**misquote** [mis'kwout], *v.a.* falsch zitieren.
**misrepresent** [misrepri'zent], *v.a.* falsch darstellen.
**misrule** [mis'ruːl], *s.* die schlechte Regierung; die Unordnung (*dis-order*).
**miss** (1) [mis], *s.* das Fräulein.
**miss** (2) [mis], *v.a.* vermissen (*yearn for*); versäumen (*a train, lesson etc.*); verfehlen (*target*); — *the boat*, den Anschluß verpassen; *be missing*, fehlen.
**missal** [misl], *s.* (*Eccl.*) das Meßbuch.
**misshapen** [mis'ʃeipən], *adj.* miß-gestaltet.
**missile** ['misail], *s.* das Geschoß; *ballistic* —, das Raketengeschoß; *guided* —, ferngesteuertes Raketen-geschoss.

**mission** ['miʃən], *s.* die Mission; Sendung; der Auftrag (*task*).
**missionary** ['miʃənəri], *adj.* Missions-. — *s.* der Missionar.
**missive** ['misiv], *s.* das Sendschreiben.
**misspell** [mis'spel], *v.a.* falsch buch-stabieren, falsch schreiben.
**mist** [mist], *s.* der Dunst; Nebel (*fog*).
**mistake** [mis'teik], *s.* der Fehler. — *v.a. irr.* verkennen.
**mistaken** [mis'teikn], *adj.* im Unrecht; irrig; *be* —, sich irren.
**mistimed** [mis'taimd], *adj.* zur Unzeit, unzeitig.
**mistletoe** ['misltou], *s.* (*Bot.*) die Mistel, der Mistelzweig.
**mistress** ['mistrəs], *s.* die Herrin; Hausfrau; Geliebte (*paramour*); Leh-rerin (*Sch.*).
**mistrust** [mis'trʌst], *v.a.* mißtrauen.
**misunderstand** [misʌndə'stænd], *v.a. irr.* mißverstehen.
**misuse** [mis'juːz], *v.a.* mißbrauchen.
**mite** (1) [mait], *s.* (*Zool.*) die Milbe.
**mite** (2) [mait], *s.* das Scherflein (*coin*); (*coll.*) das Kindchen, das Kerlchen.
**mitigate** ['mitigeit], *v.a.* mildern.
**mitre** ['maitə], *s.* die Bischofsmütze, Mitra.
**mitten** [mitn], *s.* der Fäustling, Faust-handschuh.
**mix** [miks], *v.a.* mischen, vermischen. — *v.n.* verkehren.
**mixed** [miksd], *adj. a* — *blessing*, eine fragliche Wohltat.
**mizzle** [mizl], *v.n.* sprühen, rieseln.
**mnemonics** [ni'mɔniks], *s.* die Ge-dächtniskunst.
**moan** [moun], *v.n.* stöhnen (*wail*); klagen (*complain*). — *s.* (*coll.*) die Klage.
**moat** [mout], *s.* der Burggraben, Was-sergraben.
**mob** [mɔb], *s.* der Pöbel.
**mobility** [mo'biliti], *s.* die Beweglich-keit.
**mobilize** ['moubilaiz], *v.a.* mobilisieren.
**mock** [mɔk], *v.a.* verspotten (*tease*); täuschen (*mislead*). — *v.n.* spotten. — *s.* der Spott, die Täuschung. — *adj.* Schein-; — *heroic*, komisch-heroisch.
**modal** [moudl], *adj.* (*Gram.*) modal, der Aussageweise nach; (*Mus.*) dem Modus nach.
**mode** [moud], *s.* (*Mus.*) der Modus, die Art; die Mode (*fashion*).
**model** [mɔdl], *s.* das Modell; das Muster (*pattern*). — *v.a., v.n.* model-lieren.
**moderate** ['mɔdərit], *adj.* mäßig; (*climate*) gemäßigt. — [-reit], *v.a.* mäßigen; abändern.
**modern** ['mɔdən], *adj.* modern.
**modernize** ['mɔdənaiz], *v.a.* moderni-sieren.
**modest** ['mɔdist], *adj.* bescheiden.
**modesty** ['mɔdisti], *s.* die Bescheiden-heit.
**modify** ['mɔdifai], *v.a.* abändern, modifizieren.

# mortise

**modish** [′moudiʃ], *adj.* nach der neuesten Mode, modisch.
**modulate** [′mɔdjuleit], *v.a.* modulieren.
**moil** [mɔil], *v.n.* sich plagen.
**moist** [mɔist], *adj.* feucht.
**moisten** [mɔisn], *v.a.* befeuchten.
**moisture** [′mɔistʃə], *s.* die Feuchtigkeit.
**molasses** [mo′læsiz], *s.* die Melasse.
**mole** (1) [moul], *s.* (*Zool.*) der Maulwurf.
**mole** (2) [moul], *s.* das Muttermal (*skin mark*).
**mole** (3) [moul], *s.* der Seedamm, Hafendamm.
**molecular** [mo′lekjulə], *adj.* molekular.
**molecule** [′mɔl-, ′moulikju:l], *s.* das Molekül.
**molest** [mo′lest], *v.a.* belästigen.
**mollify** [′mɔlifai], *v.a.* besänftigen.
**mollusc** [′mɔləsk], *s.* (*Zool.*) die Molluske.
**molt** *see under* **moult**.
**molten** [′moultən], *adj.* geschmolzen.
**moment** [′moumənt], *s.* der Augenblick, Moment (*instant*); die Wichtigkeit (*importance*).
**momentary** [′mouməntəri], *adj.* momentan, einen Augenblick lang.
**momentum** [mo′mentəm], *s.* das Moment, die Triebkraft.
**monarch** [′mɔnək], *s.* der Monarch.
**monarchy** [′mɔnəki], *s.* die Monarchie.
**monastery** [′mɔnəstri], *s.* das (Mönchs-)kloster.
**monastic** [mə′næstik], *adj.* klösterlich.
**Monday** [′mʌndi], *s.* der Montag.
**money** [′mʌni], *s.* das Geld; *ready —*, bares Geld; *make —*, Geld verdienen; *— order*, die Postanweisung.
**Mongolian** [mɔŋ′goulian], *adj.* mongolisch. *— s.* der Mongole.
**mongrel** [′mʌŋgrəl], *s.* (*Zool.*) der Mischling.
**monitor** [′mɔnitə], *s.* der Ermahner; (*Rad.*) der Abhörer.
**monitoring** [′mɔnitəriŋ], *adj. — service*, der Abhördienst.
**monk** [mʌŋk], *s.* (*Eccl.*) der Mönch.
**monkey** [′mʌŋki], *s.* (*Zool.*) der Affe.
**monomania** [mɔno′meiniə], *s.* die Monomanie, fixe Idee.
**monopolize** [mə′nɔpəlaiz], *v.a.* monopolisieren.
**monopoly** [mə′nɔpəli], *s.* das Monopol.
**monosyllabic** [mɔnəsi′læbik], *adj.* einsilbig.
**monotonous** [mə′nɔtənəs], *adj.* monoton, eintönig.
**monsoon** [mɔn′su:n], *s.* der Monsun.
**monster** [′mɔnstə], *s.* das Ungeheuer.
**monstrance** [′mɔnstrəns], *s.* (*Eccl.*) die Monstranz.
**monstrosity** [mɔns′trɔsiti], *s.* die Ungeheuerlichkeit.
**monstrous** [′mɔnstrəs], *adj.* ungeheuerlich.
**month** [mʌnθ], *s.* der Monat.
**monthly** [′mʌnθli], *adj.* monatlich, Monats-.

**mood** [mu:d], *s.* die Stimmung, Laune; (*Gram., Mus.*) der Modus.
**moodiness** [′mu:dinis], *s.* die Launenhaftigkeit.
**moody** [′mu:di], *adj.* launenhaft.
**moon** [mu:n], *s.* der Mond.
**moonlight** [′mu:nlait], *s.* das Mondlicht, der Mondschein.
**moonshine** [′mu:nʃain], *s.* der Mondschein; (*fig.*) Unsinn.
**moonstruck** [′mu:nstrʌk], *adj.* mondsüchtig; verliebt.
**Moor** [muə], *s.* der Mohr, Neger.
**moor** [muə], *s.* das Moor, Heideland.
**moorage** [′muəridʒ], *s.* der Ankerplatz.
**moorhen** [′mɔ:hen], *s.* (*Orn.*) das Moorhuhn, Wildhuhn.
**moorish** [′muəriʃ], *adj.* maurisch.
**moot** [mu:t], *v.a.* erörtern, besprechen. *— adj. a — point*, ein strittiger Punkt.
**mop** [mɔp], *s.* der Wischlappen, Mop. *— v.a.* aufwischen (*floor*), wischen (*brow*).
**mope** [moup], *v.n.* traurig sein.
**moral** [′mɔrəl], *adj.* moralisch (*high principled*); sittlich (*decent*). *— s.* die Moral (*precept*); (*pl.*) die Sitten, *f. pl.*; die Sittlichkeit.
**moralize** [′mɔrəlaiz], *v.n.* moralisieren, Moral predigen (*Dat.*).
**morass** [mo′ræs], *s.* der Morast.
**morbid** [′mɔ:bid], *adj.* krankhaft.
**more** [mɔ:], *comp. adj., adv.* mehr; *once —*, noch einmal; *all the —*, umso mehr; *the — the better*, je mehr desto besser.
**moreover** [mɔ:′rouvə], *adv.* zudem, überdies, weiterhin.
**morning** [′mɔ:niŋ], *s.* der Morgen, Vormittag; *— coat*, der Cutaway, Frack.
**Moroccan** [mə′rɔkən], *adj.* marokkanisch. *— s.* der Marokkaner.
**Morocco** [mə′rɔkou]. Marokko, *n.*
**morocco** [mə′rɔkou], *s.* der Saffian, das Maroquinleder.
**moron** [′mɔ:rɔn], *s.* der Schwachsinnige.
**morose** [mə′rous], *adj.* mürrisch.
**morrow** [′mɔrou], *s.* (*Poet.*) der Morgen.
**morsel** [mɔ:sl], *s.* der Bissen, das Stück.
**mortal** [mɔ:tl], *adj.* sterblich, tödlich; *— sin*, die Todsünde. *— s.* der Sterbliche, der Mensch.
**mortality** [mɔ:′tæliti], *s.* die Sterblichkeit.
**mortar** [′mɔ:tə], *s.* (*Build.*) der Mörtel; (*Mil.*) der Mörser.
**mortgage** [′mɔ:gidʒ], *s.* die Hypothek. *— v.a.* verpfänden; eine Hypothek aufnehmen (auf, *Acc.*).
**mortgagee** [mɔ:gi′dʒi:], *s.* der Hypothekengläubiger.
**mortician** [mɔ:′tiʃən], *s.* (*Am.*) *see* **undertaker**.
**mortify** [′mɔ:tifai], *v.a.* kasteien (*chasten*); kränken (*humiliate*).
**mortise** [′mɔ:tis], *s.* (*Build.*) das Zapfenloch.

441

# mortuary

**mortuary** ['mɔːtjuəri], *s.* die Leichen-halle.
**mosque** [mɔsk], *s.* (*Rel.*) die Moschee.
**mosquito** [mɔs'kiːtou], *s.* (*Ent.*) der Moskito.
**moss** [mɔs], *s.* (*Bot.*) das Moos.
**most** [moust], *superl. adj.* meist; (*pl.*) die meisten. — *adv.* meist, meistens; höchst (*before adjectives*).
**mostly** ['moustli], *adv.* meistenteils.
**mote** [mout], *s.* das Stäubchen.
**moth** [mɔθ], *s.* (*Ent.*) die Motte.
**mother** ['mʌðə], *s.* die Mutter; — *-in-law*, die Schwiegermutter; —-*of-pearl*, die Perlmutter.
**motherly** ['mʌðəli], *adj.* mütterlich.
**motion** ['mouʃən], *s.* die Bewegung, der Gang; (*Parl.*, *Rhet.*) der Antrag. — *v.a.* bewegen. — *v.n.* zuwinken (*Dat.*).
**motive** ['moutiv], *s.* das Motiv, der Beweggrund.
**motley** ['mɔtli], *adj.* scheckig, bunt.
**motor** ['moutə], *s.* der Motor.
**motoring** ['moutəriŋ], *s.* das Autofahren, der Autosport.
**mottled** [mɔtld], *adj.* gescheckt, gesprenkelt.
**motto** ['mɔtou], *s.* das Motto, der Wahlspruch.
**mould** (1) [mould], *s.* die Form; Guß-form (*casting*); die Schablone. — *v.a.* formen; (*Metall.*) gießen, formen.
**mould** (2) [mould], *s.* der Schimmel (*fungus*); (*Hort.*) die Gartenerde. — *v.n.* schimmeln.
**moulder** (1) ['mouldə], *s.* der Bildner; (*Metall.*) der Gießer.
**moulder** (2) ['mouldə], *v.n.* vermodern.
**mouldy** ['mouldiˑ] *adj.* moderig, schimmelig.
**moult**, (*Am.*) **moᵘt** [moult], *v.n.* (*Zool.*) sich mausern.
**mound** [maund], *s.* der Erdhügel.
**mount** [maunt], *v.a.* besteigen (*horse*, *hill*); montieren, anbringen (*apparatus*). — *v.n.* sich belaufen (*bill*), betragen. — *s.* (*Poet.*) der Berg.
**mountain** ['mauntin], *s.* der Berg.
**mountaineer** [maunti'niə], *s.* der Bergsteiger.
**mountainous** ['mauntinəs], *adj.* gebirgig.
**mourn** [mɔːn], *v.a.*, *v.n.* (be)trauern.
**mourner** ['mɔːnə], *s.* der Leidtragende.
**mournful** ['mɔːnful], *adj.* traurig.
**mourning** ['mɔːniŋ], *s.* die Trauer.
**mouse** [maus], *s.* (*Zool.*) die Maus.
**moustache** [məs'taːʃ], *s.* der Schnurrbart.
**mouth** [mauθ], *s.* (*Anat.*) der Mund; (*Geog.*) die Mündung.
**movable** ['muːvəbl], *adj.* beweglich, verschiebbar.
**move** [muːv], *v.a.* bewegen; (*emotionally*) rühren; den Antrag stellen (*a motion*). — *v.n.* umziehen; übersiedeln (*change residence*).
**movement** ['muːvmənt], *s.* die Bewegung (*motion*); (*Mus.*) der Satz; das Gehwerk (*mechanism*).

**movies** ['muːviz], *s. pl.* (*coll.*) das Kino, der Film.
**mow** [mou], *v.a. irr.* mähen.
**much** [mʌtʃ], *adj.* viel. — *adv.* sehr, bei weitem; *as — as*, ganze . . .; *as — again*, noch einmal so viel.
**mud** [mʌd], *s.* der Schmutz, Schlamm.
**muddle** [mʌdl], *v.a.* verwirren. — *s.* die Verwirrung.
**muff** (1) [mʌf], *s.* der Muff.
**muff** (2) [mʌf], *v.a.* verderben (*mar*).
**muffin** ['mʌfin], *s.* der dünne Kuchen, der Butterkuchen.
**muffle** [mʌfl], *v.a.* umwickeln; dämpfen (*a sound*).
**muffler** ['mʌflə], *s.* das Halstuch; (*Motor.*) der Schalldämpfer.
**mug** [mʌg], *s.* der Krug; (*coll.*) der Tölpel.
**muggy** ['mʌgi], *adj.* schwül; feucht (*humid*).
**mulatto** [mju'lætou], *s.* der Mulatte.
**mulberry** ['mʌlbəri], *s.* (*Bot.*) die Maulbeere.
**mule** [mjuːl], *s.* (*Zool.*) das Maultier, der Maulesel.
**muleteer** [mjuːli'tiə], *s.* der Maulesel-treiber.
**mulish** ['mjuːliʃ], *adj.* störrisch.
**mull** (1) [mʌl], *v.a.* würzen (*add spices to*); *mulled wine*, der Glühwein.
**mull** (2) [mʌl], *v.a.*, *v.n.* — *over*, überlegen, überdenken.
**multifarious** [mʌlti'fɛəriəs], *adj.* mannigfaltig.
**multiple** ['mʌltipl], *s.* das Vielfache. — *adj.* vielfach.
**multiply** ['mʌltiplai], *v.a.*, *v.n.* multiplizieren, (sich) vervielfachen.
**multitude** ['mʌltitjuːd], *s.* die Menge.
**multitudinous** [mʌlti'tjuːdinəs], *adj.* zahlreich, massenhaft.
**mumble** [mʌmbl], *v.a.*, *v.n.* murmeln.
**mummery** ['mʌməri], *s.* der Mummen-schanz.
**mummy** (1) ['mʌmi], *s.* die Mumie.
**mummy** (2) ['mʌmi], *s.* (*coll.*) die Mutti.
**mumps** [mʌmps], *s.* (*Med.*) der Ziegenpeter.
**munch** [mʌntʃ], *v.a.*, *v.n.* kauen.
**mundane** ['mʌndein], *adj.* weltlich.
**municipal** [mju'nisipəl], *adj.* städtisch.
**municipality** [mjunisi'pæliti], *s.* die Stadtgemeinde.
**munificence** [mju'nifisəns], *s.* die Freigebigkeit.
**munificent** [mju'nifisənt], *adj.* freigebig.
**mural** ['mjuərəl], *s.* die Wandmalerei; das Wandgemälde. — *adj.* Wand-.
**murder** ['mɔːdə], *s.* der Mord. — *v.a.* ermorden, morden.
**murderer** ['mɔːdərə], *s.* der Mörder.
**murderous** ['mɔːdərəs], *adj.* mörderisch.
**murky** ['mɔːki], *adj.* trübe, unklar.
**murmur** ['mɔːmə], *s.* das Gemurmel. — *v.a.* murmeln.
**muscle** [mʌsl], *s.* (*Anat.*) der Muskel.
**muscular** ['mʌskjulə], *adj.* (*Anat.*) muskulös, Muskel-.

**muse** (1) [mju:z], *v.n.* nachdenken, sinnen.

**muse** (2) [mju:z], *s.* (*Myth.*) die Muse.

**museum** [mju:'ziəm], *s.* das Museum.

**mushroom** ['mʌʃrum], *s.* (*Bot.*) der (eßbare) Pilz.

**music** ['mju:zik], *s.* die Musik; — *stand*, das Notenpult.

**musician** [mju'ziʃən], *s.* der Musiker.

**musk** [mʌsk], *s.* der Moschus, Bisam.

**musket** ['mʌskit], *s.* die Muskete, Flinte.

**muslin** ['mʌzlin], *s.* der Musselin.

**mussel** [mʌsl], *s.* (*Zool.*) die Muschel.

**must** [mʌst], *v. aux. irr.* müssen; (*with neg.*) dürfen.

**mustard** ['mʌstəd], *s.* der Senf.

**muster** ['mʌstə], *v.a.* mustern. — *v.n.* sich sammeln. — *s.* die Musterung; *pass* —, die Prüfung bestehen.

**musty** ['mʌsti], *adj.* dumpf, dumpfig, muffig.

**mutable** ['mju:təbl], *adj.* veränderlich.

**mutation** [mju'teiʃən], *s.* die Veränderung; (*Maths., Genetics*) die Mutation.

**mute** [mju:t], *adj.* stumm. — *v.a.* (*Mus.*) dämpfen. — *s.* (*Mus.*) der Dämpfer.

**mutilate** ['mju:tileit], *v.a.* verstümmeln.

**mutinous** ['mju:tinəs], *adj.* aufrührerisch.

**mutiny** ['mju:tini], *s.* die Meuterei.

**mutter** ['mʌtə], *v.a., v.n.* murmeln.

**mutton** [mʌtn], *s.* das Hammelfleisch; — *chop*, das Hammelkotelett.

**mutual** ['mju:tjuəl], *adj.* gegenseitig.

**muzzle** [mʌzl], *s.* der Maulkorb (*of dog*); die Mündung (*of rifle*).

**my** [mai], *poss. adj.* mein.

**myrrh** [mə:], *s.* die Myrrhe.

**myrtle** [mə:tl], *s.* (*Bot.*) die Myrte.

**myself** [mai'self], *pron.* ich selbst; (*refl.*) mir, mich.

**mysterious** [mis'tiəriəs], *adj.* geheimnisvoll.

**mystery** ['mistəri], *s.* das Geheimnis.

**mystic** ['mistik], *s.* der Mystiker.

**mystic(al)** ['mistik(əl)], *adj.* mystisch, geheimnisvoll, dunkel.

**mystification** [mistifi'keiʃən], *s.* die Täuschung, Irreführung.

**mystify** ['mistifai], *v.a.* täuschen, verblüffen.

**myth** [miθ], *s.* der Mythos, die Mythe, Sage.

# N

**N** [en]. das N.

**nag** (1) [næg], *v.a.* nörgeln.

**nag** (2) [næg], *s.* der Gaul.

**nail** [neil], *s.* der Nagel. — *v.a.* annageln.

**naïve** ['naii:v], *adj.* naiv.

**naïveté, naïvety** [nai'i:vti], *s.* die Naivität, Einfalt.

**naked** ['neikid], *adj.* nackt.

**name** [neim], *s.* der Name. — *v.a.* nennen, heißen.

**nameless** ['neimlis], *adj.* namenlos.

**namely** ['neimli], *adv.* nämlich.

**namesake** ['neimseik], *s.* der Namensvetter.

**nap** [næp], *s.* das Schläfchen. — *v.n.* schlummern, einnicken.

**nape** [neip], *s.* (*Anat.*) das Genick.

**napkin** ['næpkin], *s.* die Serviette; *Windel* (*baby's*).

**narrate** [nə'reit], *v.a.* erzählen.

**narrative** ['nærətiv], *s.* die Erzählung, Geschichte.

**narrator** [nə'reitə], *s.* der Erzähler; (*Rad.*) der Sprecher.

**narrow** ['nærou], *adj.* eng, schmal; — *gauge*, die Schmalspur; — *minded*, engstirnig.

**nasty** ['nɑ:sti], *adj.* widerlich, unangenehm.

**natal** [neitl], *adj.* Geburts-.

**nation** ['neiʃən], *s.* die Nation, das Volk.

**nationality** [næʃə'næliti], *s.* die Staatsangehörigkeit, Nationalität.

**native** ['neitiv], *adj.* einheimisch, eingeboren. — *s.* der Eingeborene.

**natural** ['nætʃərəl], *adj.* natürlich.

**naturalist** ['nætʃərəlist], *s.* der Naturforscher.

**naturalization** [nætʃərəlai'zeiʃən], *s.* die Naturalisierung, Einbürgerung.

**naturalize** ['nætʃərəlaiz], *v.a., v.n.* naturalisieren, einbürgern.

**nature** ['neitʃə], *s.* die Natur, das Wesen.

**naught** [nɔ:t], *s.* die Null.

**naughty** ['nɔ:ti], *adj.* unartig.

**nausea** ['nɔ:siə], *s.* (*Med.*) der Brechreiz, das Erbrechen.

**nautical** ['nɔ:tikəl], *adj.* nautisch, Schiffs-.

**naval** ['neivəl], *adj.* Marine-.

**nave** [neiv], *s.* (*Archit.*) das Schiff.

**navigable** ['nævigəbl], *adj.* schiffbar.

**navigate** ['nævigeit], *v.a., v.n.* steuern.

**navigation** [nævi'geiʃən], *s.* die Schiffahrt (*shipping*); das Steuern, die Navigation.

**navy** ['neivi], *s.* die Flotte, Marine.

**Neopolitan** [niə'pɔlitən], *adj.* neapolitanisch. — *s.* der Neapolitaner.

**near** [niə], *adj., adv.* nahe, in der Nähe. — *prep.* nahe (an *or* bei).

**nearly** ['niəli], *adv.* beinahe, fast.

**nearness** ['niənis], *s.* die Nähe.

**neat** [ni:t], *adj.* nett, sauber (*tidy*); rein, unvermischt, pur (*unmixed*).

**neatness** ['ni:tnis], *s.* die Sauberkeit.

**necessary** ['nesəsəri], *adj.* notwendig.

**necessity** [ni'sesiti], *s.* die Not, Notwendigkeit; (*pl.*) das zum Leben Nötige.

**neck** [nek], *s.* (*Anat.*) der Hals; *stick o.'s* — *out*, es riskieren. — *v.n.* (*Am. sl.*) knutschen.

**necklace** ['neklis], s. das Halsband, die Halskette.

**necktie** ['nektai], s. der Schlips, die Krawatte.

**need** [ni:d], s. die Not, der Bedarf. — v.a. brauchen, nötig haben.

**needful** ['ni:dful], adj. notwendig.

**needle** [ni:dl], s. die Nadel. — v.a. (coll.) sticheln, ärgern (annoy).

**needy** ['ni:di], adj. in Not befindlich, arm, bedürftig.

**nefarious** [ni'fɛəriəs], adj. nichtswürdig, schändlich.

**negative** ['negətiv], adj. negativ, verneinend. — s. (Phot.) das Negativ; die Verneinung (denial); in the —, verneinend.

**neglect** [ni'glekt], v.a. vernachlässigen, außer acht lassen. — s. die Vernachlässigung.

**neglectful** [ni'glektful], adj. nachlässig.

**negligence** ['neglidʒəns], s. die Nachlässigkeit.

**negotiate** [ni'gouʃieit], v.a., v.n. verhandeln, unterhandeln.

**negotiation** [nigouʃi'eiʃən], s. die Unterhandlung.

**Negro** ['ni:grou], s. der Neger.

**neigh** [nei], v.n. wiehern.

**neighbour** ['neibə], s. der Nachbar.

**neighbourhood** ['neibəhud], s. die Nachbarschaft, Umgebung.

**neighbouring** ['neibəriŋ], adj. Nachbar-, benachbart.

**neighbourliness** ['neibəlinis], s. das gute nachbarliche Verhältnis, die Geselligkeit.

**neither** ['naiðə or 'ni:ðə], adj., pron. keiner (von beiden). — conj. auch nicht; — . . . nor, weder . . . noch.

**Nepalese** [nepə'li:z], adj. nepalesisch. — s. der Nepalese.

**nephew** ['nefju or 'nevju], s. der Neffe.

**nerve** [nə:v], s. der Nerv; der Mut (courage); die Frechheit (impudence); (pl.) die Angst, Nervosität.

**nervous** ['nə:vəs], adj. nervös; — of, furchtsam vor (Dat.), ängstlich wegen (Genit.).

**nest** [nest], s. das Nest; (fig.) — egg, die Ersparnisse, f.pl. — v.n. nisten.

**nestle** [nesl], v.n. sich anschmiegen.

**net** (1) [net], s. das Netz. — v.a. (Fische) fangen, ins Netz bekommen.

**net** (2) [net], adj. netto; ohne Verpackung; — weight, das Nettogewicht.

**nettle** [netl], s. (Bot.) die Nessel. — v.a. sticheln, ärgern.

**neurosis** [njuə'rousis], s. (Med.) die Neurose.

**neutrality** [nju:'træliti], s. die Neutralität.

**never** ['nevə], adv. nie, niemals; — mind, mach Dir (machen Sie sich) nichts draus!

**nevertheless** [nevəðə'les], conj. trotzdem, nichtsdestoweniger.

**new** [nju:], adj. neu; New Year's Day, der Neujahrstag; New Zealander, der

Neuseeländer. — s. (pl.) die Nachrichten, f. pl.

**newspaper** ['nju:speipə], s. die Zeitung.

**next** [nekst], adj. nächst. — adv. danach.

**nib** [nib], s. die Spitze (of pen).

**nibble** [nibl], v.a., v.n. knabbern, nagen (at, an, Dat.).

**nice** [nais], adj. fein (scrupulous); nett, angenehm (pleasant).

**nicety** ['naisəti], s. die Feinheit (of distinction etc.).

**nickel** [nikl], s. das Nickel; (Am.) das Fünfcentstück.

**nickname** ['nikneim], s. der Spitzname.

**niece** [ni:s], s. die Nichte.

**Nigerian** [nai'dʒiəriən], adj. nigerisch. — s. der Nigerier.

**niggardly** ['nigədli], adj. geizig.

**nigh** [nai], adj., adv. (Poet.) nahe.

**night** [nait], s. die Nacht; last —, gestern abend; the — before last, vorgestern abend; at —, nachts.

**nightingale** ['naitiŋgeil], s. (Orn.) die Nachtigall.

**nightmare** ['naitmɛə], s. der Alpdruck.

**nimble** [nimbl], adj. flink; geschickt (deft).

**nine** [nain], num. adj. neun.

**nineteen** [nain'ti:n], num. adj. neunzehn.

**ninety** ['nainti], num. adj. neunzig.

**ninth** [nainθ], num. adj. neunte.

**nip** [nip], v.a. zwicken.

**nipple** [nipl], s. (Anat.) die Brustwarze.

**nitrogen** ['naitrədʒən], s. (Chem.) der Stickstoff.

**no** [nou], part. nein. — adj. kein. — adv. nicht; — one, niemand.

**nobility** [no'biliti], s. der Adel.

**noble** [noubl], adj. edel; großmütig (magnanimous); adlig (well born).

**nobody** ['noubədi], pron. niemand.

**nod** [nɔd], v.n. nicken.

**noise** [nɔiz], s. der Lärm, das Geräusch.

**noiseless** ['nɔizlis], adj. geräuschlos.

**noisy** ['nɔizi], adj. laut, lärmend.

**nominal** ['nɔminəl], adj. nominell.

**nominate** ['nɔmineit], v.a. nennen (name); ernennen (appoint).

**nomination** [nɔmi'neiʃən], s. die Nennung, Ernennung.

**none** [nʌn], pron. keiner, niemand.

**nonsense** ['nɔnsəns], s. der Unsinn.

**nook** [nuk], s. die Ecke, der Winkel.

**noon** [nu:n], s. der Mittag.

**noose** [nu:s], s. die Schlinge.

**nor** [nɔ:], conj. auch nicht; neither . . . —, weder . . . noch.

**normal** ['nɔ:məl], adj. normal.

**normalize** ['nɔ:məlaiz], v.a. normalisieren.

**Norman** ['nɔ:mən], adj. normannisch. — s. der Normanne.

**north** [nɔ:θ], s. der Norden. — adj. nördlich.

**northerly, northern** ['nɔ:ðəli, 'nɔ:ðən], adj. nördlich, von Norden.

**Norwegian** [nɔ:'wi:dʒən], adj. norwegisch. — s. der Norweger.

**nose** [nouz], s. (Anat.) die Nase; — dive, der Sturzflug.

**nosey** ['nouzi], *adj.* (*coll.*) neugierig.
**nostalgia** [nɔs'tældʒə], *s.* das Heimweh, die Sehnsucht.
**nostril** ['nɔstril], *s.* (*Anat.*) das Nasenloch.
**not** [nɔt], *adv.* nicht; — *at all*, keineswegs.
**notable** ['noutəbl], *adj.* berühmt, wohlbekannt; bemerkenswert.
**notary** ['noutəri], *s.* der Notar.
**notch** [nɔtʃ], *s.* die Kerbe. — *v.a.* kerben, einkerben.
**note** [nout], *s.* die Notiz, der Zettel; (*Mus.*) die Note; die Bedeutung; *take* —*s*, Notizen machen; *take* — *of*, zur Kenntnis nehmen. — *v.a.* notieren, aufzeichnen.
**notepaper** ['noutpeipə], *s.* das Briefpapier.
**noteworthy** ['noutwəːði], *adj.* beachtenswert.
**nothing** ['nʌθiŋ], *pron. s.* nichts; *for* —, umsonst; *good for* —, der Taugenichts.
**notice** ['noutis], *s.* die Kenntnis (*attention*); die Anzeige (*in press etc.*); Notiz; Bekanntmachung; *give* —, kündigen. — *v.a.* bemerken.
**noticeable** ['noutisəbl], *adj.* bemerkbar.
**notification** [noutifi'keiʃən], *s.* die Benachrichtigung, Bekanntmachung.
**notify** ['noutifai], *v.a.* benachrichtigen, informieren.
**notion** ['nouʃən], *s.* der Begriff (*concept*); die Idee (*idea*); die Meinung (*opinion*).
**notoriety** [noutə'raiiti], *s.* der üble Ruf.
**notorious** [no'tɔːriəs], *adj.* berüchtigt.
**notwithstanding** [nɔtwið'stændiŋ], *prep.* ungeachtet (*Genit.*). — *adv.* trotzdem, dennoch. — *conj.* — *that*, obgleich.
**nought** [nɔːt], *s.* die Null (*figure 0*); nichts (*nothing*).
**noun** [naun], *s.* (*Gram.*) das Hauptwort, Substantiv.
**nourish** ['nʌriʃ], *v.a.* nähren; ernähren.
**nourishment** ['nʌriʃmənt], *s.* die Nahrung.
**Nova Scotian** ['nouvə'skouʃən], *adj.* neuschottisch.
**novel** [nɔvl], *s.* (*Lit.*) der Roman. — *adj.* neu; neuartig (*modern*).
**novelty** ['nɔvlti], *s.* die Neuheit.
**November** [no'vembə]. der November.
**novice** ['nɔvis], *s.* der Neuling (*greenhorn*); (*Eccl.*) der, die Novize.
**novitiate** [no'viʃiit], *s.* die Lehrzeit; (*Eccl.*) das Noviziat.
**now** [nau], *adv.* nun, jetzt; — *and then*, dann und wann, hin und wieder. — *conj.* — (*that*), da nun.
**nowadays** ['nauədeiz], *adv.* heutzutage.
**nowhere** ['nouhwɛə], *adv.* nirgends.
**noxious** ['nɔkʃəs], *adj.* (*Med., Bot.*) schädlich.
**nozzle** [nɔzl], *s.* die Düse; (*sl.*) die Schnauze.
**nuclear** ['njuːkliə], *adj.* (*Phys.*) nuklear, Kern-.
**nucleus** ['njuːkliəs], *s.* der Kern.

**nude** [njuːd], *adj.* nackt, bloß.
**nudge** [nʌdʒ], *v.a.* leicht anstoßen.
**nudity** ['njuːditi], *s.* die Nacktheit.
**nugget** ['nʌgit], *s.* der Klumpen.
**nuisance** ['njuːsəns], *s.* die Plage, Lästigkeit; das Ärgernis (*annoyance*).
**null** [nʌl], *adj.* null und nichtig; ungültig.
**nullify** ['nʌlifai], *v.a.* annullieren, ungültig machen.
**nullity** ['nʌliti], *s.* die Ungültigkeit.
**numb** [nʌm], *adj.* erstarrt, gefühllos. — *v.a.* erstarren lassen.
**number** ['nʌmbə], *s.* die Zahl, Nummer (*telephone etc.*); die Anzahl (*quantity*); *cardinal* —, die Grundzahl; *ordinal* —, die Ordnungszahl. — *v.a.* nummerieren; zählen (*count*).
**numbness** ['nʌmnis], *s.* die Erstarrung.
**numeral** ['njuːmərəl], *s.* (*Gram.*) das Zahlwort.
**numerical** [njuː'merikəl], *adj.* (*Maths.*) Zahlen-, numerisch.
**numerous** ['njuːmərəs], *adj.* zahlreich.
**numismatics** [njuːmiz'mætiks], *s.* die Münzkunde.
**numskull** ['nʌmskʌl], *s.* der Dummkopf.
**nun** [nʌn], *s.* (*Eccl.*) die Nonne.
**nunnery** ['nʌnəri], *s.* (*Eccl.*) das Nonnenkloster.
**nuptials** ['nʌpʃəlz], *s. pl.* (*Lit., Poet.*) die Hochzeit, das Hochzeitsfest.
**nurse** [nəːs], *s.* die Krankenschwester, Pflegerin; die Amme (*wet nurse*). — *v.a.* pflegen.
**nursery** ['nəːsəri], *s.* das Kinderzimmer; (*Bot.*) die Pflanzschule, Baumschule (*for trees*); — *school*, der Kindergarten.
**nurture** ['nəːtʃə], *v.a.* nähren, aufziehen.
**nut** [nʌt], *s.* (*Bot.*) die Nuß; (*Tech.*) die Schraubenmutter; (*Am. coll.*) *nuts*, verrückt.
**nutcracker** ['nʌtkrækə], *s.* (*usually pl.*) der Nußknacker.
**nutmeg** ['nʌtmeg], *s.* (*Cul.*) die Muskatnuß.
**nutriment** ['njuːtrimənt], *s.* die Nahrung; (*animals*) das Futter.
**nutrition** [njuː'triʃən], *s.* die Ernährung.
**nutritious** [njuː'triʃəs], *adj.* nahrhaft.
**nutshell** ['nʌtʃel], *s.* die Nußschale; (*fig.*) *put in a* —, kurz ausdrücken.
**nymph** [nimf], *s.* (*Myth.*) die Nymphe.

# O

**O** [ou]. das O. — *int.* oh!
**oaf** [ouf], *s.* der Tölpel.
**oak** [ouk], *s.* (*Bot.*) die Eiche.
**oaken** ['oukən], *adj.* eichen, aus Eichenholz.

**oar** [ɔ:], *s.* das Ruder; *put o.'s — in,* sich einmengen.

**oasis** [ou'eisis], *s.* die Oase.

**oath** [ouθ], *s.* der Eid; der Fluch (*curse*); *commissioner for —s,* der öffentliche Notar; *take an —,* einen Eid schwören *or* leisten.

**oats** [outs], *s. pl.* (*Bot.*) der Hafer; *sow o.'s wild —s,* sich austoben, sich die Hörner ablaufen.

**obdurate** ['ɔbdjurit], *adj.* halsstarrig.

**obedience** [o'bi:djəns], *s.* der Gehorsam.

**obedient** [o'bi:djənt], *adj.* gehorsam.

**obeisance** [o'beisəns], *s.* die Verbeugung, Ehrfurchtsbezeigung.

**obese** [o'bi:s], *adj.* fettleibig, beleibt.

**obey** [o'bei], *v.a., v.n.* gehorchen (*Dat.*).

**obituary** [o'bitjuəri], *s.* der Nachruf, der Nekrolog.

**object** ['ɔbdʒikt], *s.* der Gegenstand (*thing*); (*Gram.*) das Objekt; der Zweck (*objective, purpose*). — [əb'dʒekt], *v.n.* — *to,* einwenden (*gainsay*); vorhalten (*remonstrate*).

**objection** [əb'dʒekʃən], *s.* der Einwand.

**objectionable** [əb'dʒekʃənəbl], *adj.* anstößig.

**objective** [əb'dʒektiv], *adj.* objektiv, unparteiisch. — *s.* das Ziel (*aim*).

**obligation** [ɔbli'geiʃən], *s.* die Verpflichtung.

**obligatory** [o'bligətəri, 'ɔblig–], *adj.* verbindlich, obligatorisch.

**oblige** [o'blaidʒ], *v.a.* verpflichten; *much obliged,* vielen Dank; *can you — me?* können Sie mir aushelfen?

**obliging** [o'blaidʒiŋ], *adj.* gefällig, zuvorkommend.

**oblique** [o'bli:k], *adj.* schräg, schief; (*fig.*) indirekt.

**obliterate** [o'blitəreit], *v.a.* auslöschen (*extinguish*); vertilgen (*destroy*).

**oblivion** [o'bliviən], *s.* die Vergessenheit.

**oblivious** [o'bliviəs], *adj.* vergeßlich.

**oblong** ['ɔblɔŋ], *adj.* länglich. — *s.* das Rechteck.

**obloquy** ['ɔbləkwi], *s.* die Schmähung, Schande.

**obnoxious** [ɔb'nɔkʃəs], *adj.* verhaßt, scheußlich.

**obscene** [ɔb'si:n], *adj.* anstößig, obszön.

**obscenity** [ɔb'sen–, ɔb'si:niti], *s.* die Obszönität.

**obscure** [əb'skjuə], *adj.* dunkel (*dark*); unbekannt (*unknown*).

**obscurity** [əb'skjuəriti], *s.* die Dunkelheit (*darkness*); die Unbekanntheit.

**obsequies** ['ɔbsikwiz], *s. pl.* das Leichenbegängnis.

**obsequious** [əb'si:kwiəs], *adj.* unterwürfig.

**observance** [əb'zə:vəns], *s.* die Befolgung, Beobachtung, das Einhalten (*Law etc.*).

**observant** [əb'zə:vənt], *adj.* aufmerksam; achtsam.

**observation** [ɔbzə'veiʃən], *s.* die Beobachtung (*watching*); die Bemerkung (*remark*).

**observatory** [əb'zə:vətri], *s.* die Sternwarte.

**observe** [əb'zə:v], *v.a.* beobachten (*watch*); bemerken (*notice, remark on*).

**obsession** [əb'seʃən], *s.* die Besessenheit, fixe Idee.

**obsolete** ['ɔbsəli:t], *adj.* veraltet.

**obstacle** ['ɔbstəkl], *s.* das Hindernis.

**obstinacy** ['ɔbstinəsi], *s.* die Hartnäckigkeit.

**obstinate** ['ɔbstinit], *adj.* hartnäckig.

**obstruct** [əb'strʌkt], *v.a.* hemmen, hindern.

**obstruction** [əb'strʌkʃən], *s.* das Hindernis, die Hemmung, Verstopfung.

**obtain** [əb'tein], *v.a.* erhalten, erlangen; bekommen (*get*).

**obtrude** [əb'tru:d], *v.n.* sich aufdrängen. — *v.a.* aufdrängen.

**obtrusive** [əb'tru:siv], *adj.* aufdringlich.

**obtuse** [əb'tju:s], *adj.* stumpf; dumm (*stupid*).

**obviate** ['ɔbvieit], *v.a.* vorbeugen (*Dat.*).

**obvious** ['ɔbviəs], *adj.* klar, offenbar, selbstverständlich.

**occasion** [o'keiʒən], *s.* die Gelegenheit (*chance*); der Anlaß; die Veranlassung (*cause*). — *v.a.* veranlassen; verursachen (*cause*).

**occasional** [o'keiʒənəl], *adj.* gelegentlich.

**occident** ['ɔksidənt], *s.* das Abendland, der Westen.

**occult** [ɔ'kʌlt], *adj.* geheim, Okkult–.

**occupancy** ['ɔkjupənsi], *s.* der Besitz, das Innehaben (*holding*).

**occupant** ['ɔkjupənt], *s.* der Inhaber; der Bewohner (*of house*), Insasse.

**occupation** [ɔkju'peiʃən], *s.* die Besetzung; (*Mil.*) *army of —,* die Besatzung; der Beruf, die Beschäftigung (*job*); — *with,* das Befassen mit (*Dat.*).

**occupy** ['ɔkjupai], *v.a.* besetzen, in Besitz nehmen; beschäftigen (*engage*); bekleiden (*office*).

**occur** [ə'kə:], *v.n.* geschehen, sich ereignen; — *to s.o.,* jemandem einfallen.

**occurrence** [ə'kʌrəns], *s.* das Geschehen, Ereignis, der Vorfall.

**ocean** ['ouʃən], *s.* der Ozean, die See, das Meer. — *adj.* Meeres–.

**octagon** ['ɔktəgən], *s.* das Achteck.

**octagonal** [ɔk'tægənəl], *adj.* achteckig.

**October** [ɔk'toubə], *s.* der Oktober.

**octogenarian** [ɔktodʒi'neəriən], *s.* der Achtzigjährige.

**ocular** ['ɔkjulə], *adj.* Augen–.

**oculist** ['ɔkjulist], *s.* (*Med.*) der Augenarzt.

**odd** [ɔd], *adj.* ungerade; seltsam (*queer*); einzeln (*solitary*). — *s.* (*pl.*) die Wahrscheinlichkeit.

**oddity** ['ɔditi], *s.* die Seltenheit, Sonderbarkeit.

**oddment** ['ɔdmənt], *s.* (*pl.*) die Reste, *m. pl.*

**ode** [oud], *s.* (*Poet.*) die Ode.

**odious** ['oudiəs], *adj.* verhaßt, widerwärtig.

**odium** ['oudiəm], s. der Haß.
**odorous** ['oudərəs], adj. duftend, duftig.
**odour** ['oudə], s. der Geruch, Duft.
**of** [ɔv], prep. von (Dat.); aus (out of) (Dat.); — course, natürlich.
**off** [ɔf, ɔ:f], adv. fort, weg; entfernt; make —, sich davonmachen; far —, weit weg; — and on, ab und zu; well —, wohlhabend. — prep. von ( from); fort von; entfernt von (distant from).
**offal** [ɔfl], s. der Abfall.
**offence** [ə'fens], s. (Law) das Vergehen; die Beleidigung (insult).
**offend** [ə'fend], v.a. beleidigen (insult). — v.n. (Law) sich vergehen (gegen, Acc.).
**offensive** [ə'fensiv], adj. beleidigend (insulting); anstößig (indecent). — s. die Offensive, der Angriff (against, auf, Acc.).
**offer** ['ɔfə], v.a. bieten (auction); anbieten (hold out). — s. das Anerbieten; (Comm.) das Angebot, der Antrag.
**offering** ['ɔfəriŋ], s. das Opfer.
**office** ['ɔfis], s. das Amt; die Stellung (position); die Funktion (duties); das Büro; (Eccl.) der Gottesdienst; high —, das hohe Amt; — bearer, der Amtswalter.
**officer** ['ɔfisə], s. (Mil.) der Offizier; der Beamte (functionary); honorary —, der ehrenamtliche Beamte, der Beamte im Ehrenamt.
**official** [ə'fiʃəl], adj. offiziell, amtlich. — s. der Beamte.
**officiate** [ə'fiʃieit], v.n. amtieren; fungieren.
**officious** [ə'fiʃəs], adj. zudringlich, (übertrieben) dienstfertig.
**offing** ['ɔfiŋ], s. (Naut.) die hohe See; in the —, bevorstehend.
**offset** [ɔf'set], v.a. (Comm.) ausgleichen; (Typ.) offset drucken, im Offset drucken; ( fig.) unschädlich machen, wettmachen. — ['ɔfset], s. (Comm.) die Gegenrechnung, der Ausgleich; (Typ.) der Offsetdruck.
**offshoot** ['ɔfʃu:t], s. der Sprößling.
**offspring** ['ɔfspriŋ], s. die Nachkommenschaft.
**often**, (Poet.) **oft** [ɔfn,ɔft], adv.oft, häufig.
**ogle** [ougl], v.a., v.n. äugeln, beäugeln, glotzen, anglotzen.
**ogre** ['ougə], s. der Menschenfresser.
**oil** [ɔil], s. das Öl. — v.a. einölen, einschmieren.
**oilcloth** ['ɔilklɔθ], s. das Wachstuch.
**ointment** ['ɔintmənt], s. die Salbe.
**old** [ould], adj. alt; —fashioned, altmodisch.
**olive** ['ɔliv], s. (Bot.) die Olive; the Mount of Olives, der Ölberg.
**Olympic** [o'limpik], adj. olympisch; the — Games, die Olympischen Spiele.
**omelette** ['ɔmelit], s. (Cul.) das Omelett, der Eierkuchen.
**omen** ['oumən], s. das (böse) Vorzeichen, das Omen.

**ominous** ['ɔminəs], adj. von schlimmer Vorbedeutung, ominös.
**omission** [o'miʃən], s. die Unterlassung; (Typ.) die Auslassung.
**omit** [o'mit], v.a. unterlassen (leave undone); auslassen (leave out).
**omnibus** ['ɔmnibəs], s. der Omnibus, der Autobus.
**omnipotent** [ɔm'nipətənt], adj. allmächtig.
**omniscient** [ɔm'nisiənt], adj. allwissend.
**on** [ɔn], prep. an; auf; über; vor; bei; zu; nach; um; call — (s.o.), vorsprechen (bei, Dat.); — fire, in Flammen; — condition, unter der Bedingung (Comm.); — account, a Konto; — high, hoch oben; — my honour, auf mein Ehrenwort; — purpose, absichtlich; — sale, zum Verkauf. — adv. weiter, fort ( forward); gültig, zutreffend (correct, valid); get —, vorwärtskommen; get — with s.th., weitermachen; get — with s.o., auskommen (mit, Dat.).
**once** [wʌns], adv. einmal; einst (long ago); — more, nochmals, noch einmal; — and for all, ein für alle Mal; at —, sogleich; — in a while, ab und zu. — conj. sobald.
**one** [wʌn], num. adj. ein, eine, ein; — way street, die Einbahnstraße. — pron. man (impersonal). — s. little —, der Kleine; — by —, eins nach dem anderen, einzeln.
**onerous** ['ɔnərəs], adj. beschwerlich.
**onion** ['ʌnjən], s. (Bot.) die Zwiebel.
**onlooker** ['ɔnlukə], s. der Zuschauer.
**only** ['ounli], adj. einzig, allein. — adv. nur, bloß. — conj. jedoch.
**onset** ['ɔnset], s. der Angriff (attack); der Anfang (beginning).
**onslaught** ['ɔnslɔ:t], s. der Angriff, Überfall.
**onward** ['ɔnwəd], adj. fortschreitend. — adv. (also onwards) vorwärts.
**ooze** [u:z], s. der Schlamm. — v.n. träufeln, sickern.
**opacity** [o'pæsiti], s. (Phys.) die Dunkelheit, Undurchsichtigkeit.
**opal** [oupl], s. der Opal.
**opaque** [o'peik], adj. (Phys.) dunkel, undurchsichtig.
**open** [oupn], adj. offen; offenherzig ( frank); — to suggestions, einem Vorschlag zugänglich. — v.a. öffnen; eröffnen (start); — an account, ein Konto eröffnen. — v.n. sich öffnen, sich auftun.
**opening** ['oupniŋ], s. das Öffnen; die freie Stelle; die Gelegenheit (opportunity). — adj. einleitend; — gambit, (Chess) der Eröffnungszug.
**openness** ['oupənnis], s. die Offenheit, Ehrlichkeit ( frankness).
**opera** ['ɔpərə], s. (Mus.) die Oper; comic —, die komische Oper; — hat, der Zylinderhut, Klapphut.
**operatic** [ɔpə'rætik], adj. (Mus.) Opern-.

**operate** ['ɔpəreit], *v.a.*, *v.n.* (*Engin.*) bedienen; (*Med.*) operieren (*on*, *Acc.*).

**operation** [ɔpə'reiʃən], *s.* (*Med.*, *Mil.*) die Operation; die Bedienung (*of engine etc.*).

**operative** ['ɔpərətiv], *adj.* wirksam (*effective*). — *s.* der Arbeiter.

**opiate** ['oupiit], *s.* das Schlafmittel. — *adj.* einschläfernd.

**opine** [o'pain], *v.n.* meinen.

**opinion** [o'pinjən], *s.* die Meinung; *in my* —, meiner Meinung nach.

**opinionated** [o'pinjəneitid], *adj.* von sich eingenommen, selbstgefällig.

**opium** ['oupjəm], *s.* das Opium.

**opponent** [ə'pounənt], *s.* der Gegner.

**opportune** ['ɔpətjuːn], *adj.* gelegen, günstig.

**opportunity** [ɔpə'tjuːniti], *s.* die Gelegenheit, Chance; die Möglichkeit.

**oppose** [ə'pouz], *v.a.* bekämpfen; widerstehen, entgegentreten (*Dat.*).

**opposite** ['ɔpəzit], *adj.* entgegengesetzt; gegenüberliegend; gegensätzlich (*contrary*). — *prep.* gegenüber (*Dat.*). — *s.* das Gegenteil.

**opposition** [ɔpə'ziʃən], *s.* (*Parl.*) die Opposition; der Widerstand.

**oppress** [ə'pres], *v.a.* unterdrücken.

**oppression** [ə'preʃən], *s.* die Unterdrückung.

**oppressive** [ə'presiv], *adj.* drückend, tyrannisch.

**opprobrious** [ə'proubriəs], *adj.* schändlich, schimpflich.

**opprobrium** [ə'proubriəm], *s.* die Schande.

**optician** [ɔp'tiʃən], *s.* der Optiker.

**optics** ['ɔptiks], *s.* die Optik.

**optimism** ['ɔptimizm], *s.* der Optimismus.

**option** ['ɔpʃən], *s.* die Wahl.

**optional** ['ɔpʃənəl], *adj.* Wahl-, frei, beliebig.

**opulence** ['ɔpjuləns], *s.* der Reichtum (an, *Dat.*), die Üppigkeit.

**opulent** ['ɔpjulənt], *adj.* reich, üppig.

**or** [ɔ:], *conj.* oder; noch (*after neg.*); *either* . . . —, entweder . . . oder.

**oracle** ['ɔrəkl], *s.* das Orakel.

**oral** ['ɔ:rəl], *adj.* mündlich. — *s.* die mündliche Prüfung.

**orange** [ɔ'rindʒ], *s.* (*Bot.*) die Orange, Apfelsine.

**oration** [ɔ'reiʃən], *s.* die feierliche Rede, Ansprache.

**orator** ['ɔrətə], *s.* der Redner.

**oratorio** [ɔrə'tɔːriou], *s.* (*Mus.*) das Oratorium.

**oratory** ['ɔrətəri], *s.* (*Eccl.*) die Kapelle; (*Rhet.*) die Redekunst.

**orb** [ɔ:b], *s.* die Kugel; der Reichsapfel; (*Poet.*) der Himmelskörper.

**orbit** ['ɔ:bit], *s.* (*Astron.*) die Bahn (der Gestirne), Planetenbahn.

**orchard** ['ɔ:tʃəd], *s.* der Obstgarten.

**orchestra** ['ɔ:kistrə], *s.* (*Mus.*) das Orchester.

**ordain** [ɔ:'dein], *v.a.* ordinieren, anordnen; (*Eccl.*) zum Priester weihen.

**ordeal** ['ɔ:diəl], *s.* die Feuerprobe; Heimsuchung.

**order** ['ɔ:də], *s.* die Ordnung (*system*); die Verordnung (*command etc.*); (*Mil.*) der Befehl; (*Comm.*) die Bestellung; (*Biol.*) die Ordnung; der Orden (*Eccl.*; *also decoration*); *take* (*holy*) —*s*, ordiniert werden, Priester werden; *in* — *to*, um zu; *in* — *that*, so daß; *by* —, auf (den) Befehl. — *v.a.* befehlen, verordnen, anordnen; (*Comm.*) bestellen.

**orderly** ['ɔ:dəli], *adj.* ordentlich, ruhig. —*s*. (*Mil.*) die Ordonanz; (*Med.*) der Gehilfe, Krankenwärter.

**ordinal** ['ɔ:dinl], *adj.*, *s.* (*number*) die Ordnungszahl.

**ordinance** ['ɔ:dinəns], *s.* die Verordnung.

**ordinary** ['ɔ:dinəri], *adj.* gewöhnlich.

**ordnance** ['ɔ:dnəns], *s.* das schwere Geschütz; (*Mil.*, *Geog.*) — *survey*, die Landesvermessung.

**ore** [ɔ:], *s.* das Erz, Metall.

**organ** ['ɔ:gən], *s.* das Organ; (*Mus.*) die Orgel; — *grinder*, der Leierkastenmann.

**organic** [ɔ:'gænik], *adj.* organisch. edi

**organisation** [ɔ:gənai'zeiʃən], *s.* die Organisation.

**organise** ['ɔ:gənaiz], *v.a.* organisieren.

**organism** ['ɔ:gənizm], *s.* (*Biol.*) der Organismus.

**organist** ['ɔ:gənist], *s.* (*Mus.*) der Organist.

**orgy** ['ɔ:dʒi], *s.* die Orgie.

**oriel** ['ɔ:riəl], *s.* der Erker; — *window*, das Erkerfenster.

**orient** ['ɔ:riənt], *s.* der Orient, Osten.

**oriental** [ɔ:ri'entl], *adj.* östlich.

**orifice** ['ɔrifis], *s.* die Öffnung, Mündung.

**origin** ['ɔridʒin], *s.* der Ursprung, die Herkunft.

**original** [ə'ridʒinl], *adj.* Ursprungs-, ursprünglich; originell (*creative*). — *s.* das Original.

**originality** [əridʒi'næliti], *s.* die Originalität.

**originate** [ə'ridʒineit], *v.n.* entstehen, entspringen. — *v.a.* hervorbringen, entstehen lassen.

**ornament** ['ɔ:nəmənt], *s.* das Ornament; die Verzierung (*decoration*).

**ornate** [ɔ:'neit], *adj.* geziert, geschmückt.

**orphan** ['ɔ:fən], *s.* der, die Waise.

**orphanage** ['ɔ:fənidʒ], *s.* das Waisenhaus.

**orthodoxy** ['ɔ:θədɔksi], *s.* die Orthodoxie, die Rechtgläubigkeit.

**orthography** [ɔ:'θɔgrəfi], *s.* die Rechtschreibung.

**orthopaedic** [ɔ:θə'pi:dik], *adj.* orthopädisch.

**oscillate** ['ɔsileit], *v.n.* oszillieren, schwingen.

**oscillatory** ['ɔsileitəri], *adj.* schwingend, oszillierend.

**osier** ['ouʒə], *s.* (*Bot.*) die Korbweide.

**osprey** ['ɔsprei], *s.* (*Orn.*) der Seeadler.

**ossify** ['ɔsifai], *v.a.* verknöchern lassen; versteinern lassen (*stone*). — *v.n.* verknöchern; versteinern (*stone*).

**ostensible** [ɔs'tensibl], *adj.* scheinbar, anscheinend, vorgeblich.

**ostentation** [ɔsten'teiʃən], *s.* die Großtuerei, der Prunk.

**ostentatious** [ɔsten'teiʃəs], *adj.* großtuerisch, prahlerisch, protzig.

**ostler** ['ɔslə], *s.* (*obs.*) der Stallknecht.

**ostracize** ['ɔstrəsaiz], *v.a.* verbannen, ausschließen.

**ostrich** ['ɔstritʃ], *s.* (*Orn.*) der Strauß.

**other** ['ʌðə], *adj.* ander. — *pron.*, *s.* the —, der, die, das andere.

**otherwise** ['ʌðəwaiz], *conj.* sonst. — *adv.* andernfalls.

**otter** ['ɔtə], *s.* (*Zool.*) die Otter.

**ought** [ɔːt], *v. aux. defect.* sollte, müßte.

**ounce** [auns], *s.* die Unze.

**our** ['auə], *poss. adj.* unser, uns(e)re, unser.

**ours** ['auəz], *poss. pron.* unsrig, unser, uns(e)re, unser.

**ourselves** [auə'selvz], *pers. pron.* wir, wir selbst, uns selbst; (*refl.*) uns.

**ousel** [uːzl], *s.* (*Orn.*) die Amsel.

**out** [aut], *adv.* aus; draußen (*outside*); außerhalb (*outside, externally*); heraus; hinaus (*outward, away from the speaker*). — *prep.* — *of*, aus, von (*Dat.*).

**outer** ['autə], *adj.* äußer.

**outfit** ['autfit], *s.* die Ausrüstung.

**outing** ['autiŋ], *s.* der Ausflug.

**outhouse** ['authaus], *s.* das Nebengebäude, der Anbau.

**outlaw** ['autlɔː], *s.* der Verbannte, der Vogelfreie.

**outlay** ['autlei], *s.* (*Comm.*) die Auslagen, die Spesen, *f. pl.*

**outlet** ['autlit], *s.* der Ausfluß, Abfluß; (*fig.*) das Ventil.

**outline** ['autlain], *s.* der Umriß, Entwurf. — [aut'lain], *v.a.* skizzieren, umreißen, kurz beschreiben.

**outlive** [aut'liv], *v.a.* überleben.

**outlook** ['autluk], *s.* die Aussicht, der Ausblick; die Weltanschauung (*philosophy*).

**outlying** ['autlaiiŋ], *adj.* außenliegend, außerhalb liegend, entlegen.

**outnumber** [aut'nʌmbə], *v.a.* an Zahl übertreffen.

**outpatient** ['autpeiʃənt], *s.* der ambulante Patient.

**outrage** ['autreidʒ], *s.* die Beleidigung (*insult*); die Gewalttat. — [aut'reidʒ], *v.a.* verletzen, beleidigen, schänden.

**outrageous** [aut'reidʒəs], *adj.* schändlich, schimpflich, unerhört; übertrieben (*exaggerated*).

**outright** ['autrait], *adj.* völlig. — [aut'rait], *adv.* gerade heraus, gänzlich.

**outrun** [aut'rʌn], *v.a. irr.* überholen, einholen.

**outset** ['autset], *s.* der Anfang.

**outshine** [aut'ʃain], *v.a. irr.* übertreffen.

**outside** [aut'said], *adv.* außen, draußen. — ['autsaid], *prep.* außerhalb (*Genit.*).

— *adj.* äußere, außenstehend. — *s.* das Äußere, die Außenseite.

**outskirts** ['autskəːts], *s. pl.* die Umgebung, Vorstadt.

**outstanding** [aut'stændiŋ], *adj.* hervorragend (*excellent*); noch unbeglichen (*unpaid*); unerledigt (*undone*).

**outstay** [aut'stei], *v.a.* länger bleiben, zu lange bleiben.

**outvote** [aut'vout], *v.a.* überstimmen.

**outward** ['autwəd], *adj.* äußere, äußerlich, außerhalb befindlich. — *adv.* (*also* **outwards**) auswärts, nach außen.

**outweigh** [aut'wei], *v.a.* schwerer wiegen als, überwiegen.

**outwit** [aut'wit], *v.a.* überlisten.

**oval** [ouvl], *adj.* oval. — *s.* das Oval.

**ovary** ['ouvəri], *s.* (*Anat.*) der Eierstock.

**ovation** [o'veiʃən], *s.* die Huldigung, Ovation.

**oven** [ʌvn], *s.* der Backofen; (kleine) Schmelzofen.

**over** ['ouvə], *prep.* über; oberhalb. — *adv.* über; herüber; drüben; — *there*, drüben; hinüber (*across*); vorüber (*past*).

**overact** [ouvər'ækt], *v.n.* übertreiben.

**overawe** [ouvər'ɔː], *v.a.* einschüchtern.

**overbalance** [ouvə'bæləns], *v.a.* überwiegen. — *v.n.* überkippen.

**overbear** [ouvə'bɛə], *v.a. irr.* überwältigen.

**overbearing** [ouvə'bɛəriŋ], *adj.* anmaßend.

**overboard** ['ouvəbɔːd], *adv.* über Bord.

**overburden** [ouvə'bəːdn], *v.a.* überlasten.

**overcast** [ouvə'kɑːst], *adj.* bewölkt.

**overcharge** [ouvə'tʃɑːdʒ], *v.a.* zu viel berechnen (*pers., Dat.*), übervorteilen; überladen (*overload*). — *s.* die Übervorteilung; (*Tech.*) der Überdruck.

**overcoat** ['ouvəkout], *s.* der Mantel; *light* —, der Überzieher.

**overcome** [ouvə'kʌm], *v.a., v.n. irr.* überwinden.

**overdo** [ouvə'duː], *v.a. irr.* übertreiben.

**overdone** [ouvə'dʌn], *adj.* übergar, zu lange gekocht.

**overdrive** [ouvə'draiv], *v.a. irr.* abhetzen, zu weit treiben. — ['ouvədraiv] *s.* (*Motor.*) der Schnellgang.

**overdue** [ouvə'djuː], *adj.* überfällig, verfallen.

**overflow** [ouvə'flou], *v.a., v.n.* überfließen; überfluten (*banks*). — ['ouvəflou], *s.* der Überfluß (*flood*); die Überschwemmung.

**overgrow** [ouvə'grou], *v.a. irr.* überwachsen, überwuchern. — *v.n.* zu groß werden.

**overhang** [ouvə'hæŋ], *v.a. irr.* überhängen.

**overhaul** [ouvə'hɔːl], *v.a.* überholen. — ['ouvəhɔːl], *s.* die Überholung.

**overhead** [ouvə'hed], *adv.* droben; oben (*above*). — ['ouvəhed], *s.* (*pl.*) (*Comm.*) laufende Unkosten, *pl.*

# overhear

overhear [ouvə'hiə], v.a. irr. zufällig
hören.
overjoyed [ouvə'dʒɔid], adj. entzückt.
overlap [ouvə'læp], v.n. überschneiden,
zusammenfallen (dates etc.).—['ouvə-
læp], s. die Überschneidung, das
Zusammenfallen.
overload [ouvə'loud], v.a. überlasten;
(Elec.) überladen.
overlook [ouvə'luk], v.a. übersehen;
verzeihen (disregard).
overmuch [ouvə'mʌtʃ], adv. allzusehr.
overpay (ouvə'pei], v.a., v.n. zu viel
bezahlen.
overpopulated [ouvə'pɔpjuleitid], adj.
übervölkert.
overpower [ouvə'pauə], v.a. überwältigen.
overrate [ouvə'reit], v.a. überschätzen.
overreach [ouvə'ri:tʃ], v.a. übervorteilen.
override [ouvə'raid], v.a. irr. über-
reiten; unterdrücken (suppress).
overrule [ouvə'ru:l], v.a. nicht gelten
lassen, verwerfen.
overseer ['ouvəsiə], s. der Aufseher.
oversleep [ouvə'sli:p], v.n. irr. sich verschlafen.
overstep [ouvə'step], v.a. überschreiten.
overstrain [ouvə'strein], v.a., v.n.
(sich) zu sehr anstrengen, überanstrengen.
overt [ou'və:t], adj. offenkundig;
öffentlich (public).
overtake [ouvə'teik], v.a. irr. einholen;
(Mot.) überholen.
overtax [ouvə'tæks], v.a. zu hoch
besteuern; (fig.) überanstrengen
(strain).
overthrow [ouvə'θrou], v.a. irr. umstürzen; (Pol.) stürzen. — ['ouvəθrou],
s. der Sturz.
overtime ['ouvətaim], s. Überstunden,
f. pl.
overture ['ouvətjuə], s. die Ouvertüre.
overturn [ouvə'tə:n], v.a. umstürzen.
— v.n. überschlagen.
overweening [ouvə'wi:niŋ], adj. eingebildet.
overweight ['ouvəweit], s. das Über-
gewicht.
overwhelm [ouvə'welm], v.a. überwältigen.
overwork [ouvə'wə:k], v.n. sich überarbeiten.
overwrought [ouvə'rɔ:t], adj. übermäßig erregt, aufgeregt, überreizt.
owe [ou], v.a. schulden. — v.n. verdanken (be in debt).
owing ['ouiŋ], pred. adj. — to, dank
(Dat.), zufolge (Dat.).
owl [aul], s. (Orn.) die Eule.
own (1) [oun], v.a. besitzen (possess).
— adj. eigen.
own (2) [oun], v.a. anerkennen (acknowledge).
owner ['ounə], s. der Besitzer, Eigentümer.
ox [ɔks], s. (Zool). der Ochse.
oxidate ['ɔksideit] see oxidise.

oxide ['ɔksaid], s. (Chem). das Oxyd.
oxidise ['ɔksidaiz], v.a., v.n. (Chem.)
oxydieren.
oxtail ['ɔksteil], s. der Ochsenschwanz.
oxygen ['ɔksidʒən], s. (Chem.) der
Sauerstoff.
oyster ['ɔistə], s. (Zool.) die Auster.
ozone [ou'zoun], s. (Chem.) das Ozon.

# P

P [pi:]. das P.
pa [pɑ:], s. (coll.) Papa, der Vater.
pace [peis], s. der Gang, Schritt (step);
das Tempo (rate). — v.n. — up and
down, auf- und abschreiten. — v.a.
einschulen (horse).
Pacific, The [pə'sifik, ðə]. der Stille
Ozean.
pacific [pə'sifik], adj. friedlich, still.
pacify ['pæsifai], v.a. Frieden stiften,
beruhigen.
pack [pæk], s. das or der Pack; der
Ballen (bale); das Rudel (wolves); das
Spiel (cards); das Paket, die Packung.
— v.a. packen (a case); parteiisch zusammensetzen; die Karten schlecht
mischen (cheat at cards); packed like
sardines, dichtgedrängt, eingepfercht.
— v.n. packen; seine Sachen einpacken.
package ['pækidʒ], s. der Ballen (bale);
das Gepäckstück, Paket.
packet ['pækit], s. das Paket; (Naut.)
— boat, das Paketboot, Postschiff.
pact [pækt], s. der Pakt, Vertrag.
pad [pæd], s. das Polster, Kissen; der
Notizblock (writing block). —
v.a. auspolstern; padded cell, die
Gummizelle.
padding ['pædiŋ], s. (Tail.) das Futter;
(fig.) die (nichtssagende) Ausfüllung,
das leere Geschwätz.
paddle ['pædl], v.a., v.n. rudern, paddeln. — s. das Paddel, (Doppel) ruder,
das Schaufelruder; — steamer, der
Raddampfer.
paddock ['pædɔk], s. der Sattelplatz;
das Gehege.
padlock ['pædlɔk], s. das Vorhängeschloß, Vorlegeschloß.
pagan ['peigən], adj. heidnisch. — s.
der Heide.
paganism ['peigənizm], s. das Heidentum.
page (1) [peidʒ], s. der Page (court
attendant); Hoteljunge (hotel boy). —
v.a. durch Pagen suchen lassen.
page (2) [peidʒ], s. die Seite (of book). —
v.a. paginieren (book).
pageant ['pædʒənt], s. der Aufzug, der
Prunkzug; das Schaustück (dramatic).
pail [peil], s. der Eimer.

**pain** [pein], *s.* der Schmerz, die Pein; (*pl.*) die Mühe; *go to a lot of* —*s*, sich große Mühe geben. — *v.a.* schmerzen; bekümmern (*mentally*).

**paint** [peint], *s.* die Farbe (*dye*); die Schminke (*make-up*). — *v.a.* anstreichen, malen.

**painter** ['peintə], *s.* der Maler.

**painting** ['peintiŋ], *s.* das Gemälde.

**pair** [peə], *s.* das Paar; *two* —*s of shoes*, zwei Paar Schuhe; *a* — *of spectacles*, die Brille; *a* — *of scissors*, die Schere. — *v.a.* paaren. — *v.n.* sich paaren.

**pajamas** [pə'dʒɑ:məz] *see under* **pyjamas**.

**Pakistani** [pɑ:ki'stɑ:ni], *adj.* pakistanisch. — *s.* der Pakistaner.

**palace** ['pæləs], *s.* der Palast.

**palatable** ['pælətəbl], *adj.* schmackhaft.

**palatal** ['pælətl], *adj.* (*Phonet.*) palatal, Gaumen-, Vordergaumen-. — *s.* (*Phonet.*) der Gaumenlaut.

**palate** ['pælit], *s.* der Gaumen.

**Palatinate, The** [pə'lætinit, ðə]. die Pfalz, Pfalzgrafschaft.

**palaver** [pə'lɑ:və], *s.* die Unterredung; das Palaver.

**pale** (1) [peil], *adj.* blaß, bleich.

**pale** (2) [peil], *s.* der Pfahl; *beyond the* —, unkultiviert.

**Palestinian** [pælis'tiniən], *adj.* palästinisch. — *s.* der Palästiner.

**palette** ['pælit], *s.* die Palette (*see also* **pallet** (1)).

**paling** ['peiliŋ], *s.* der Lattenzaun; (*pl.*) der Pfahlbau.

**pall** (1) [pɔ:l], *s.* das Leichentuch.

**pall** (2) [pɔ:l], *v.n.* schal werden (*become stale*).

**pallet** (1) ['pælit], *s.* die Palette (*painter's*); — *knife*, das Streichmesser (*potter's etc.*).

**pallet** (2) ['pælit], *s.* der Strohsack.

**palliative** ['pæliətiv], *s.* linderndes Mittel; (*fig.*) die Beschönigung.

**pallid** ['pælid], *adj.* blaß, bleich.

**pallor** ['pælə], *s.* die Blässe.

**palm** (1) [pɑ:m], *s.* die Handfläche. — *v.a.* — (*off*) *on to s.o.*, an jemanden loswerden, jemandem etwas andrehen.

**palm** (2) [pɑ:m], *s.* (*Bot.*) die Palme; *Palm Sunday*, Palmsonntag.

**palmer** ['pɑ:mə], *s.* (*obs.*) der Pilger (*pilgrim*).

**palmist** ['pɑ:mist], *s.* der Handleser, Wahrsager.

**palmistry** ['pɑ:mistri], *s.* die Handwahrsagerei.

**palmy** ['pɑ:mi], *adj.* glorreich.

**palpable** ['pælpəbl], *adj.* handgreiflich, greifbar, klar.

**palpitate** ['pælpiteit], *v.n.* klopfen (*of heart*).

**palsied** ['pɔ:lzid], *adj.* (*Med.*) gelähmt.

**palsy** ['pɔ:lzi], *s.* (*Med.*) die Lähmung.

**paltry** ['pɔ:ltri], *adj.* erbärmlich, armselig.

**pamper** ['pæmpə], *v.a.* verwöhnen.

**pan** (1) [pæn], *s.* die Pfanne. — *v.n.* —

out, sich ausbreiten, sich weiten.

**pan** (2) [pæn], *v.a.* (*Phot.*) kreisen, im Bogen führen.

**panacea** [pænə'siə], *s.* das Universalmittel.

**pancake** ['pænkeik], *s.* der Pfannkuchen.

**pander** ['pændə], *v.n.* fröhnen (*Dat.*), nachgeben.

**pane** [pein], *s.* die Glasscheibe.

**panel** ['pænl], *s.* die Holzfüllung, Täfelung (*in room*); die Liste; die Kommission (*of experts etc.*).

**pang** [pæŋ], *s.* die Angst, Pein; der Schmerz, Stich (*stab of pain*).

**panic** ['pænik], *s.* die Panik, der Schrecken.

**panoply** ['pænəpli], *s.* (*Poet.*) die Rüstung.

**pansy** ['pænzi], *s.* (*Bot.*) das Stiefmütterchen; (*sl.*) der Weichling, Feigling.

**pant** [pænt], *v.n.* keuchen, schwer atmen.

**pantaloons** [pæntə'lu:nz] (*usually abbr.* **pants** [pænts]), *s. pl.* die Unterhosen, Hosen, *f.pl.*

**panther** ['pænθə], *s.* (*Zool.*) der Panther.

**pantomime** ['pæntəmaim], *s.* die Pantomime, das Weihnachtsstück.

**pantry** ['pæntri], *s.* die Speisekammer.

**pap** [pæp], *s.* der Kinderbrei.

**papacy** ['peipəsi], *s.* das Papsttum.

**papal** ['peipəl], *adj.* päpstlich.

**paper** ['peipə], *s.* das Papier (*material*); die Zeitung (*daily* —); die Abhandlung (*essay*); — *knife*, der Brieföffner. — *v.a.* tapezieren (*a room*).

**paperhanger** ['peipəhæŋə], *s.* der Tapezierer.

**paperweight** ['peipəweit], *s.* der Briefbeschwerer.

**par** [pɑ:], *s.* die Gleichheit, das Pari.

**parable** ['pærəbl], *s.* die Parabel, das Gleichnis.

**parabola** [pə'ræbələ], *s.* (*Geom.*) die Parabel.

**parabolic** [pærə'bɔlik], *adj.* parabolisch, gleichnishaft.

**parachute** ['pærəʃu:t], *s.* (*Aviat.*) der Fallschirm.

**parade** [pə'reid], *s.* die Parade, der Aufmarsch. — *v.a.* herausstellen; zur Schau tragen (*show off*). — *v.n.* (*Mil.*) vorbeimarschieren.

**paradise** ['pærədais], *s.* das Paradies.

**paraffin** ['pærəfin], *s.* das Paraffin.

**paragon** ['pærəgən], *s.* das Musterkind, Musterbeispiel, Vorbild.

**paragraph** ['pærəgrɑ:f], *s.* der Abschnitt, Absatz, Paragraph.

**Paraguayan** [pærə'gwaiən], *adj.* paraguayisch. — *s.* der Paraguayer.

**parallel** ['pærəlel], *adj.* parallel. — *s.* die Parallele.

**paralyse** ['pærəlaiz], *v.a.* lähmen.

**paralysis** [pə'rælisis], *s.* die Lähmung.

**paramount** ['pærəmaunt], *adj.* oberst.

**paramour** ['pærəmuə], *s.* der *or* die Geliebte.

# parapet

**parapet** ['pærəpit], s. das Geländer, die Brüstung.

**paraphrase** ['pærəfreiz], s. die Umschreibung. — v.a. umschreiben.

**parasite** ['pærəsait], s. der Schmarotzer, Parasit.

**parasol** ['pærəsɔl], s. der Sonnenschirm.

**parboil** ['pɑːbɔil], v.a. aufkochen lassen.

**parcel** [pɑːsl], s. das Paket; Bündel (bundle). — v.a. — up, einpacken.

**parch** [pɑːtʃ], v.a. austrocknen.

**parchment** ['pɑːtʃmənt], s. das Pergament.

**pardon** [pɑːdn], v.a. vergeben, verzeihen (Dat.); begnadigen (Acc.) (give amnesty). — s. der Pardon, die Verzeihung; —!, I beg your —! bitte um Entschuldigung; I beg your —? wie bitte?

**pare** [pɛə], v.a. beschneiden (nails); schälen (fruit).

**parent** ['pɛərənt], s. der Vater, die Mutter, (pl.) die Eltern, pl.

**parentage** ['pɛərəntidʒ], s. die Abkunft, Herkunft.

**parenthesis** [pə'renθisis], s. die Parenthese, die Klammer.

**parish** ['pæriʃ], s. das Kirchspiel, die Gemeinde, die Pfarre.

**parishioner** [pə'riʃənə], s. das Gemeindemitglied.

**Parisian** [pə'riziən], adj. parisisch. — s. der Pariser.

**park** [pɑːk], s. der Park; (Motor.) der Wagenpark, Parkplatz. — v.a., v.n. parken.

**parking** ['pɑːkiŋ], s. (Motor.) das Parken; — meter, die Parkuhr, der Parkometer.

**parley** ['pɑːli], s. die Unterredung, Verhandlung. — v.n. verhandeln.

**parliament** ['pɑːləmənt], s. das Parlament.

**parlour** ['pɑːlə], s. das Wohnzimmer, die gute Stube; —maid, das Dienstmädchen; — trick, das Kunststück.

**parochial** [pə'roukiəl], adj. Pfarr–, Gemeinde–; (fig.) engstirnig.

**parody** ['pærədi], s. die Parodie. — v.a. parodieren.

**parole** [pə'roul], s. das Ehrenwort; (Mil.) das Losungswort.

**paroxysm** ['pærəksizm], s. der heftige Anfall.

**parquet** ['pɑːki], s. das Parkett; — floor, der Parkettfußboden.

**parrot** ['pærət], s. (Orn.) der Papagei.

**parry** ['pæri], v.a. parieren, abwehren.

**parse** [pɑːs, pɑːz], v.a. (Gram.) analysieren.

**parsimony** ['pɑːsiməni], s. die Sparsamkeit.

**parsley** ['pɑːsli], s. (Bot.) die Petersilie.

**parson** [pɑːsn], s. der Pastor, Pfarrer.

**parsonage** ['pɑːsənidʒ], s. das Pfarrhaus.

**part** [pɑːt], s. der Teil; Anteil (share); (Theat.) die Rolle; (Mus.) die Stimme;

(Geog.) die Gegend; for his —, seinerseits. — v.n. — (with), sich trennen (von, Dat.); — company, auseinandergehen.

**partake** [pɑː'teik], v.n. teilnehmen, teilhaben (in, an, Dat.).

**partial** [pɑːʃl], adj. Teil–; parteiisch (subjective); — to, eingenommen für.

**participate** [pɑː'tisipeit], v.n. teilnehmen (in, an, Dat.).

**participation** [pɑːtisi'peiʃən], s. die Teilnahme.

**participle** ['pɑːtisipl], s. (Gram.) das Mittelwort, Partizip(ium).

**particle** ['pɑːtikl], s. die Partikel, das Teilchen.

**particular** [pə'tikjulə], adj. besonder (special); einzel (individual); sonderbar (queer); ungewöhnlich; genau. — s. (pl.) die Details, n. pl., Einzelheiten, f. pl.

**parting** ['pɑːtiŋ], s. der Abschied (taking leave); der Scheitel (hair).

**partisan** [pɑː'ti'zæn], s. der Partisane, Parteigänger.

**partition** [pɑː'tiʃən], s. die Teilung (division); die Scheidewand (dividing wall). — v.a. teilen; aufteilen (divide up).

**partly** ['pɑːtli], adv. zum Teil, teils.

**partner** ['pɑːtnə], s. der Partner; Teilhaber (in business etc.).

**partnership** ['pɑːtnəʃip], s. die Partnerschaft.

**partridge** ['pɑːtridʒ], s. (Orn.) das Rebhuhn.

**party** ['pɑːti], s. (Pol.) die Partei; (Law) die Partei, Seite; die Gesellschaft, die Party (social gathering); throw or give a —, einen Gesellschaftsabend (or eine Party) geben; guilty —, der schuldige Teil; (Build.) — wall, die Brandmauer.

**Paschal** ['pɑːskəl], adj. Oster–.

**pass** [pɑːs], v.a. passieren; vorbeigehen (an, Dat.); durchlassen (let through); (Law) — sentence, das Urteil fällen. — v.n. fortgehen, vergehen, geschehen (happen); vorübergehen (of time); — for, gelten; (Sch.) durchkommen (exam); come to —, sich ereignen. — s. der Paß; (Theat.) die Freikarte.

**passable** ['pɑːsəbl], adj. gangbar; (fig.) leidlich, erträglich.

**passage** ['pæsidʒ], s. der Durchgang (thoroughfare); das Vergehen (of time); die Seereise; die Stelle (book).

**passenger** ['pæsindʒə], s. der Reisende, Passagier; — train, der Personenzug.

**passer-by** ['pɑːsəbai], s. der Passant, Vorübergehende.

**passing** ['pɑːsiŋ], s. das Vorbeigehen, das Vorübergehen; (Parl.) das Durchgehen; das Hinscheiden (death). — adj. vorübergehend, zeitweilig.

**Passion** ['pæʃən], s. (Eccl.) das Leiden; (Mus.) die Passion; — Week, die Karwoche; — flower, die Passionsblume.

**passion** ['pæʃən], s. die Leidenschaft;

*fly into a* —, aufbrausen.

**passive** ['pæsiv], *adj.* passiv. — *s.* (*Gram.*) das Passiv(um).

**Passover** ['pɑːsouvə], *s.* (*Rel.*) das Passahfest.

**passport** ['pɑːspɔːt], *s.* der Reisepaß.

**past** [pɑːst], *adj.* vergangen. — *adv.* vorbei. — *prep.* nach (*time*). — *s.* die Vergangenheit; (*Gram.*) das Imperfekt, Präteritum.

**paste** [peist], *s.* die Paste, der Brei; der Kleister (*glue*). — *v.a.* kleben, kleistern.

**pasteboard** ['peistbɔːd], *s.* die Pappe.

**pastime** ['pɑːstaim], *s.* der Zeitvertreib.

**pastor** ['pɑːstə], *s.* (*Rel.*) der Seelsorger, Pfarrer.

**pastoral** ['pɑːstərəl], *adj.* Hirten-, pastoral. — *s.* (*Poet*). das Hirtengedicht.

**pastry** ['peistri], *s.* (*Cul.*) die Pastete; das Gebäck; — *cook*, der Konditor, Zuckerbäcker.

**pasture** ['pɑːstʃə], *s.* die Weide, das Grasland. — *v.n.* weiden, grasen.

**pasty** ['pɑːsti, 'pæsti], *s.* (*Cul.*) die Pastete. — ['peisti], *adj.* teigig.

**pat** [pæt], *s.* der Klaps; der Schlag (*slap*). — *v.a.* leicht schlagen, streicheln (*gently*).

**patch** [pætʃ], *v.a.* flicken, ausbessern. — *s.* der Fleck (*mending material*); der Flecken (*land*); (*coll.*) *no — on him*, kein Vergleich mit ihm; *nicht zu vergleichen mit ihm.*

**patent** ['peitənt *or* 'pætənt], *adj.* offen, klar, patent; — *leather*, das Glanzleder. — *s.* das Patent.

**patentee** [peitən'tiː], *s.* der Patentinhaber.

**paternal** [pə'təːnəl], *adj.* väterlich.

**path** [pɑːθ], *s.* der Pfad, Weg, Fußsteig.

**pathetic** [pə'θetik], *adj.* pathetisch, rührend; armselig.

**pathology** [pə'θɔlədʒi], *s.* (*Med.*) die Pathologie.

**pathway** ['pɑːθwei], *s.* der Fußweg, Fußsteig.

**patience** ['peiʃəns], *s.* die Geduld; die Patience (*card game*).

**patient** ['peiʃənt], *adj.* geduldig. — *s.* (*Med.*) der Patient.

**patrician** [pə'triʃən], *adj.* patrizisch. — *s.* der Patrizier.

**patrimony** ['pætriməni], *s.* das (väterliche) Erbgut.

**patriot** ['peitriət, 'pætriət], *s.* der Patriot.

**patriotism** ['peitriətizm, 'pæt-], *s.* die Vaterlandsliebe, der Patriotismus.

**patrol** [pə'troul], *s.* die Patrouille, Streife. — *v.n.* auf Patrouille gehen.

**patron** ['peitrən], *s.* der Schutzherr, der Gönner; (*Comm.*) der Kunde; — *saint*, der Schutzheilige.

**patronage** ['pætrənidʒ], *s.* die Gönnerschaft, Huld.

**patronize** ['pætrənaiz], *v.a.* besuchen (*frequent*); begünstigen (*favour*).

**patronizing** ['pætrənaiziŋ], *adj.* herablassend.

**patten** [pætn], *s.* (*Archit.*) der Sockel; der Holzschuh (*clog*).

**patter** (1) ['pætə], *s.* das Geplätscher (*rain etc.*). — *v.n.* plätschern.

**patter** (2) ['pætə], *s.* das Geplauder (*chatter*). — *v.n.* schwätzen.

**pattern** ['pætən], *s.* das Muster; die Schablone (*in material*).

**paucity** ['pɔːsiti], *s.* die geringe Anzahl, der Mangel.

**paunch** [pɔːntʃ], *s.* der Wanst.

**pauper** ['pɔːpə], *s.* der Arme.

**pauperize** ['pɔːpəraiz], *v.a.* arm machen, verarmen lassen.

**pause** [pɔːz], *s.* die Pause. — *v.n.* innehalten.

**pave** [peiv], *v.a.* pflastern.

**pavement** ['peivmənt], *s.* das Pflaster; der Bürgersteig, Gehsteig.

**pavilion** [pə'viljən], *s.* das Gartenhaus; der Pavillon.

**paw** [pɔː], *s.* die Pfote; die Tatze. — *v.a.* streicheln, betasten.

**pawn** (1) [pɔːn], *s.* das Pfand. — *v.a.* verpfänden.

**pawn** (2) [pɔːn], *s.* (*Chess*) der Bauer.

**pawnbroker** ['pɔːnbroukə], *s.* der Pfandleiher.

**pay** [pei], *v.a. irr.* zahlen; bezahlen, begleichen (*bill*); — *attention*, aufpassen, Aufmerksamkeit schenken; — *o.'s respects*, Respekt zollen. — *v.n. irr.* sich bezahlt machen, sich lohnen (*it — s to . . .*). — *s.* (*Mil.*) der Sold; (*Comm.*) der Lohn (*wage*), die Bezahlung (*payment*).

**payable** ['peiəbl], *adj.* zahlbar, zu bezahlen.

**payee** [pei'iː], *s.* der Empfänger, Präsentant.

**payer** ['peiə], *s.* der Zahler; (*Comm.*) der Trassat.

**payment** ['peimənt], *s.* die Bezahlung, Begleichung (*of sum*).

**pea** [piː], *s.* (*Bot.*) die Erbse (*see also* peas(e).

**peace** [piːs], *s.* der Friede(n); die Ruhe (*restfulness*).

**peaceable** ['piːsəbl], *adj.* friedlich; friedliebend.

**peaceful** ['piːsful], *adj.* friedlich, ruhig (*restful*).

**peach** [piːtʃ], *s.* (*Bot.*) der *or* (*Austr.*) die Pfirsich.

**peacock** ['piːkɔk], *s.* (*Orn.*) der Pfau.

**peahen** ['piːhen], *s.* (*Orn.*) die Pfauhenne.

**peak** [piːk], *s.* der Gipfel, die Spitze; der Schirm (*of cap*); — *hour*, die Stunde des Hochbetriebs, Hauptverkehrsstunde.

**peal** [piːl], *v.a.* läuten. — *v.n.* erschallen. — *s.* das Läuten, Geläute.

**peanut** ['piːnʌt], *s.* (*Bot.*) die Erdnuß.

**pear** [pɛə], *s.* (*Bot.*) die Birne.

**pearl** [pəːl], *s.* die Perle; — *barley*, die Perlgraupen, *f. pl.*; *mother of* —, die Perlmutter.

peasant

**peasant** ['pezənt], *s.* der Bauer.
**peasantry** ['pezəntri], *s.* das Bauern-volk, die Bauernschaft.
**peas(e)** [pi:z], *s. pl. pease pudding,* der Erbsenbrei, das Erbsenpüree.
**peat** [pi:t], *s.* der Torf.
**pebble** [pebl], *s.* der Kiesel(stein).
**peck** (1) [pek], *s.* der Viertelscheffel (=9 litres.)
**peck** (2) [pek], *s.* das Picken (*of hen*); (*coll.*) der Kuß. — *v.a.* hacken, hauen.
**pecker** ['pekə], *s.* die Picke, Haue; *keep your — up!* Mut bewahren!
**peckish** ['pekiʃ], *adj.* hungrig.
**pectoral** ['pektərəl], *adj.* Brust-. — *s.* das Brustmittel.
**peculiar** [pi'kju:liə], *adj.* eigenartig, eigentümlich (*strange*); — *to,* eigen (*Dat.*); besonder (*special*).
**peculiarity** [pikju:li'æriti], *s.* die Eigen-tümlichkeit, Eigenartigkeit.
**pecuniary** [pi'kju:niəri], *adj.* Geld-, geldlich, finanziell, pekuniär.
**pedagogue** ['pedəgɔg], *s.* der Päda-gog(e), Erzieher.
**pedal** [pedl] *s.* das Pedal; (*Motor.*) der Fußhebel. — *v.n.* radfahren; (*coll.*) radeln.
**pedant** ['pedənt], *s.* der Pedant.
**pedantic** [pi'dæntik], *adj.* pedantisch.
**pedantry** ['pedəntri], *s.* die Pedanterie.
**peddle** [pedl], *v.a.* hausieren.
**peddling** ['pedliŋ], *adj.* kleinlich, un-bedeutend.
**pedestal** ['pedistl], *s.* der Sockel.
**pedestrian** [pi'destriən], *s.* der Fuß-gänger. — *adj.* Fuß-, Fußgänger-.
**pedigree** ['pedigri:], *s.* der Stamm-baum.
**pediment** ['pedimənt], *s.* (*Archit.*) der Ziergiebel.
**pedlar** ['pedlə], *s.* der Hausierer.
**peel** [pi:l], *s.* die Schale (*of fruit*). — *v.a.* schälen. — *v.n.* sich schälen.
**peep** [pi:p], *v.n.* gucken. — *s.* der (schnelle) Blick, das Gucken; — *show,* der Guckkasten.
**peer** (1) [piə], *s.* (*Parl.*) der Pair, Lord; der Ebenbürtige (*equal*).
**peer** (2) [piə], *v.n.* gucken, blicken, schauen.
**peerage** ['piərid3], *s.* der (Reichs)adel.
**peeress** ['piəres], *s.* die Gattin eines Pairs.
**peerless** ['piəlis], *adj.* unvergleichlich.
**peevish** ['pi:viʃ], *adj.* mürrisch.
**pe(e)wit** ['pi:wit], *s.* (*Orn.*) der Kiebitz.
**peg** ['peg], *s.* der Pflock (*stake*); der Holzstift (*in wall*); *clothes —,* die Wäscheklammer. — *v.a.* anpflocken (*to ground*).
**pelican** ['pelikən], *s.* (*Orn.*) der Pelikan.
**pellet** ['pelit], *s.* das Kügelchen.
**pell-mell** ['pel'mel], *adv.* durchein-ander.
**pelt** (1) [pelt], *v.a.* — *with,* bewerfen mit, — *a person with,* werfen nach einem (*Acc.*). — *v.n.* strömen (*rain etc.*); rennen (*hasten*).
**pelt** (2) [pelt], *s.* der Pelz (*of animal*).

**pen** (1) [pen], *s. quill —,* die Feder; *fountain —,* die Füllfeder; *ballpoint —,* der Kugelschreiber. — *v.a.* schrei-ben; verfassen (*compose*).
**pen** (2) [pen], *s.* das Gehege. — *v.a.* einschliessen (*sheep*).
**penal** ['pi:nəl], *adj.* Straf-; — *servitude,* die Zuchthausstrafe.
**penalize** ['pi:nəlaiz], *v.a.* bestrafen.
**penalty** ['penəlti], *s.* die Strafe.
**penance** ['penəns], *s.* die Buße.
**pence** [pens] *see under* **penny.**
**pencil** ['pensl], *s.* der Bleistift; der Stift; (*Geom.*) der Strahl. — *v.a.* niederschreiben, notieren.
**pendant** ['pendənt], *s.* das Ohrgehänge; (*fig.*) das Gegenstück.
**pendent** ['pendənt], *adj.* hängend, schwebend.
**pending** ['pendiŋ], *adj.* in der Schwebe; unentschieden (*undecided*). — *prep.* während (*during*); bis (zu) (*until*).
**pendulum** ['pendjuləm], *s.* das Pendel.
**penetrate** ['penitreit], *v.a.* durch-dringen.
**peninsula** [pi'ninsjulə], *s.* die Halb-insel.
**penitent** ['penitənt], *s.* der Büßer. — *adj.* bußfertig.
**penitentiary** [peni'tenʃəri], *s.* (*Am.*) das Zuchthaus (*prison*).
**penknife** ['pennaif], *s.* das Taschen-messer.
**pennant** ['penənt], *s.* der Wimpel, das Fähnchen.
**penniless** ['penilis], *adj.* mittellos, ohne einen Heller Geld, arm.
**pennon** ['penən] *see* **pennant.**
**penny** ['peni], *s.* (*pl.* **pence** [pens], **pennies** ['peniz]) der Penny; (*Am.*) das Centstück; — *farthing,* das Hoch-rad; — *whistle,* die Blechpfeife; *a pretty —,* hübsches Geld.
**pension** ['penʃən], *s.* die Pension; das Ruhegehalt. — *v.a.* (*off*) pensionieren, in den Ruhestand versetzen.
**pensive** ['pensiv], *adj.* nachdenklich.
**Pentecost** ['pentikɔst]. das *or* (*pl.*) die Pfingsten.
**penthouse** ['penthaus], *s.* das Wetter-dach.
**penurious** [pi'njuəriəs], *adj.* unbe-mittelt, arm (*poor*); dürftig, karg (*meagre*).
**penury** ['penjuəri], *s.* die Not, Armut.
**peony** ['piəni], *s.* (*Bot.*) die Päonie, Pfingstrose.
**people** [pi:pl], *s. pl.* das Volk (*nation*); die Leute, Menschen (*pl.*). — *v.a.* bevölkern.
**pepper** ['pepə], *s.* der Pfeffer. — *v.a.* pfeffern.
**per** [pə:], *prep.* pro; per; durch; *as — account,* laut Rechnung.
**peradventure** [pə:rəd'ventʃə], *adv.* (*obs.*) von ungefähr; vielleicht (*per-haps*).
**perambulator** [pə'ræmbjuleitə] (*abbr. coll.*) **pram** [præm]), *s.* der Kinder-wagen.

454

perceive [pə'si:v], *v.a.* wahrnehmen, merken.

percentage [pə'sentidʒ], *s.* der Prozentsatz (*of interest*); Prozente, *n. pl.*

perceptible [pə'septibl], *adj.* wahrnehmbar, merklich.

perception [pə'sepʃən], *s.* die Wahrnehmung, Empfindung.

perch (1) [pə:tʃ], *v.n.* aufsitzen; sitzen (*of birds*). — *s.* die Stange.

perch (2) [pə:tʃ], *s.* (*Zool.*) der Barsch.

perchance [pə'tʃɑ:ns], *adv.* vielleicht.

percolate ['pə:kəleit], *v.n.* durchsickern, durchtröpfeln.

percolator ['pə:kəleitə], *s.* die Kaffeemaschine.

percussion [pə'kʌʃən], *s.* (*Mus.*) das Schlagzeug.

peremptory ['perəmptəri, pə'remptəri], *adj.* entschieden, bestimmt (*decided*); absprechend.

perennial [pə'reniəl], *adj.* (*Bot.*) perennierend; Dauer-.

perfect ['pə:fikt], *adj.* vollkommen, vollendet, perfekt. — *s.* (*tense*) (*Gram.*) das Perfekt(um). — [pə'fekt], *v.a.* vollenden.

perfection [pə'fekʃən], *s.* die Vollendung, Vollkommenheit; *to* —, vollkommen.

perfidious [pə'fidiəs], *adj.* treulos, untreu; tückisch.

perfidy ['pə:fidi], *s.* die Treulosigkeit.

perforate ['pə:fəreit], *v.a.* durchlöchern, perforieren (*paper*); durchbohren (*pierce*).

perforce [pə'fɔ:s], *adv.* mit Gewalt, notgedrungen.

perform [pə'fɔ:m], *v.a.* ausführen (*carry out*); (*Theat.*) aufführen. — *v.n.* spielen, auftreten (*of actor*).

performance [pə'fɔ:məns], *s.* die Ausführung; Verrichtung (*execution of duty etc.*); (*Theat.*) die Aufführung.

perfume ['pə:fju:m], *s.* das Parfüm; der Duft (*scent*). — *v.a.* parfümieren.

perfunctory [pə'fʌŋktəri], *adj.* nachlässig, oberflächlich, flüchtig.

perhaps [pə'hæps], *adv.* vielleicht.

peril ['peril], *s.* die Gefahr.

period ['piəriəd], *s.* die Periode (*time*); der Zeitraum (*span*); (*Am.*) der Punkt (*full stop*).

periodical [piəri'ɔdikəl], *adj.* periodisch. — *s.* die Zeitschrift.

perish ['periʃ], *v.n.* zugrunde gehen, umkommen.

perishable ['periʃəbl], *adj.* vergänglich; (leicht) verderblich (*of food*).

periwig ['periwig], *s.* die Perücke.

periwinkle (1) ['periwiŋkl], *s.* (*Zool.*) die Uferschnecke.

periwinkle (2) ['periwiŋkl], (*Bot.*) das Immergrün.

perjure ['pə:dʒə], *v.r.* meineidig werden.

perjurer ['pə:dʒərə], *s.* der Meineidige.

perjury ['pə:dʒəri], *s.* der Meineid.

permanence, permanency ['pə:mə-nəns, 'pə:mənənsi], *s.* die Dauer, Beständigkeit.

permanent ['pə:mənənt], *adj.* Dauer-, dauerhaft, beständig; — *wave*, die Dauerwelle.

permeability [pə:miə'biliti], *s.* die Durchdringbarkeit, Durchlässigkeit.

permeable ['pə:miəbl], *adj.* durchdringlich.

permeate ['pə:mieit], *v.a.* durchdringen.

permissible [pə'misibl], *adj.* zulässig, statthaft.

permission [pə'miʃən], *s.* die Erlaubnis.

permit [pə'mit], *v.a.* zulassen, erlauben. — ['pə:mit], *s.* die Erlaubnis; (*official*) die Genehmigung.

permutation [pə:mju'teiʃən], *s.* (*Maths.*) die Permutation.

pernicious [pə'niʃəs], *adj.* verderblich, schädlich, bösartig.

perorate ['perəreit], *v.n.* eine (lange) Rede beschließen.

perpendicular [pə:pən'dikjulə], *adj.* senkrecht. — *s.* die Senkrechte.

perpetrate ['pə:pitreit], *v.a.* begehen (*commit*).

perpetration [pə:pi'treiʃən], *s.* die Verübung, Begehung.

perpetrator ['pə:pitreitə], *s.* der Begeher, Täter.

perpetual [pə'petjuəl], *adj.* (an-)dauernd; ewig.

perpetuate [pə'petjueit], *v.a.* verewigen.

perpetuity [pə:pi'tju:iti], *s.* die Ewigkeit.

perplex [pə'pleks], *v.a.* bestürzen, verblüffen.

perplexity [pə'pleksiti], *s.* die Bestürzung, Verwirrung.

persecute ['pə:sikju:t], *v.a.* verfolgen.

persecution [pə:si'kju:ʃən], *s.* die Verfolgung.

perseverance [pə:si'viərəns], *s.* die Ausdauer, Beharrlichkeit.

persevere [pə:si'viə], *v.n.* beharren (*in*, bei, *Dat.*).

Persian ['pə:ʃən], *adj.* persisch. — *s.* der Perser.

persist [pə'sist], *v.n.* beharren (*in*, auf, *Dat.*).

persistence [pə'sistəns], *s.* die Beharrlichkeit.

person ['pə:sən], *s.* die Person; *in* —, persönlich.

personal ['pə:sənəl], *adj.* persönlich.

personality [pə:sə'næliti], *s.* die Persönlichkeit.

personify [pə'sɔnifai], *v.a.* verkörpern.

personnel [pə:sə'nel], *s.* das Personal; (*Comm.*) — *manager*, der Personalchef.

perspective [pə'spektiv], *s.* die Perspektive. — *adj.* perspektivisch.

perspicacious [pə:spi'keiʃəs], *adj.* scharfsichtig, scharfsinnig.

perspicacity [pə:spi'kæsiti], *s.* der Scharfblick, Scharfsinn.

perspicuity [pə:spi'kju:iti], *s.* die Durchsichtigkeit, Klarheit.

**perspicuous** [pə'spikjuəs], *adj.* deutlich, klar.
**perspiration** [pə:spi'reiʃən], *s.* der Schweiß.
**perspire** [pə'spaiə], *v.n.* schwitzen.
**persuade** [pə'sweid], *v.a.* überreden.
**persuasion** [pə'sweiʒən], *s.* die Überredung.
**persuasive** [pə'sweiziv], *adj.* überzeugend, überredend.
**pert** [pə:t], *adj.* naseweis, keck.
**pertain** [pə'tein], *v.n.* (an)gehören (*to* *Dat.*).
**pertinacious** [pə:ti'neiʃəs], *adj.* beharrlich, halsstarrig.
**pertinacity** [pə:ti'næsiti], *s.* die Beharrlichkeit, Halsstarrigkeit.
**pertinence, pertinency** ['pə:tinəns, 'pə:tinənsi], *s.* die Angemessenheit.
**pertinent** ['pə:tinənt], *adj.* angemessen, passend.
**pertness** ['pə:tnis], *s.* die Keckheit, der Vorwitz.
**perturb** [pə'tə:b], *v.a.* verwirren, stören, beunruhigen.
**perturbation** [pə:tə'beiʃən], *s.* die Verwirrung, Störung, Beunruhigung.
**peruke** [pə'ru:k], *s.* die Perücke.
**peruse** [pə'ru:z], *v.a.* durchlesen.
**Peruvian** [pə'ru:viən], *adj.* peruanisch. — *s.* der Peruaner.
**pervade** [pə'veid], *v.a.* durchdringen.
**perverse** [pə'və:s], *adj.* verkehrt.
**perversion** [pə'və:ʃən], *s.* die Perversion.
**perversity** [pə'və:siti], *s.* die Verdorbenheit, Widernatürlichkeit.
**pervert** [pə'və:t], *v.a.* verkehren, verderben. — ['pə:və:t], *s.* der Verdorbene, der perverse Mensch.
**perverted** [pə'və:tid], *adj.* pervers (*sexually*).
**pervious** ['pə:viəs], *adj.* zugänglich, passierbar; durchlässig.
**pessimist** ['pesimist], *s.* der Pessimist.
**pest** [pest], *s.* (*Med.*) die Pest; (*fig.*) die Plage.
**pester** ['pestə], *v.a.* quälen, auf die Nerven gehen (*Dat.*).
**pestiferous** [pes'tifərəs], *adj.* verpestend.
**pestilence** ['pestiləns], *s.* (*Med.*) die Pest, Seuche.
**pestle** [pesl], *s.* die Mörserkeule.
**pet** [pet], *s.* das Haustier; der Liebling; — *name*, der Kosename. — *v.a.* liebkosen, streicheln.
**petition** [pi'tiʃən], *s.* die Bittschrift. — *v.a.* mit einer Bittschrift herantreten an (*Acc.*).
**petrel** ['petrəl], *s.* (*Orn.*) der Sturmvogel.
**petrification** [petrifi'keiʃən], *s.* die Versteinerung.
**petrify** ['petrifai], *v.a.* versteinern; (*fig.*) starr machen, bestürzen; *petrified with fright*, starr vor Entsetzen. — *v.n.* zu Stein werden.
**petrol** ['petrəl], *s.* das Benzin; (*crude oil*) das Petroleum; — *station*, die Tankstelle.

**petticoat** ['petikout], *s.* der Unterrock.
**pettifogging** ['petifəgiŋ], *adj.* Winkel-, kleinlich, schikanös (*petty*).
**pettiness** ['petinis], *s.* die Kleinlichkeit.
**pettish** ['petiʃ], *adj.* verdrießlich.
**petty** ['peti], *adj.* klein, gering, kleinlich.
**petulance** ['petjuləns], *s.* die Launenhaftigkeit, Gereiztheit.
**petulant** ['petjulənt], *adj.* launenhaft.
**pew** [pju:], *s.* (*Eccl.*) der Kirchensitz; (*coll.*) der Sitz, Stuhl.
**pewit** ['pi:wit] *see* **pe(e)wit**.
**pewter** ['pju:tə], *s.* das Zinn; die Zinnwaren, *f. pl.* (*wares*).
**pewterer** ['pju:tərə], *s.* der Zinngießer.
**phantom** ['fæntəm], *s.* das Phantom, Trugbild; das Gespenst (*ghost*).
**Pharisee** ['færisi:], *s.* der Pharisäer.
**pharmaceutical** [fa:mə'sju:tikəl], *adj.* pharmazeutisch.
**pharmacy** ['fa:məsi], *s.* die Apothekerkunst (*dispensing*); die Apotheke (*dispensary*); die Pharmazeutik (*discipline*).
**phase** [feiz], *s.* die Phase.
**pheasant** ['fezənt], *s.* (*Orn.*) der Fasan.
**phenomenal** [fi'nɔminəl], *adj.* außerordentlich, phänomenal.
**phenomenon** [fi'nɔminən], *s.* das Phänomen.
**phial** ['faiəl], *s.* die Phiole, das Fläschchen.
**philanthropist** [fi'lænθrəpist], *s.* der Philanthrop.
**philanthropy** [fi'lænθrəpi], *s.* die Philanthropie.
**philatelist** [fi'lætəlist], *s.* der Philatelist, Markensammler.
**philately** [fi'lætəli], *s.* das Markensammeln, die Philatelie, Briefmarkenkunde.
**Philippine** ['filipi:n], *adj.* philippinisch.
**Philistine** ['filistain], *s.* der Philister; (*fig.*) der Spießbürger.
**philologist** [fi'bɔlədʒist], *s.* der Philologe.
**philology** [fi'bɔlədʒi], *s.* die Philologie.
**philosopher** [fi'bɔsəfə], *s.* der Philosoph.
**philosophize** [fi'bɔsəfaiz], *v.n.* philosophieren.
**philosophy** [fi'bɔsəfi], *s.* die Philosophie.
**phlegm** [flem], *s.* das Phlegma (*mood*); (*Med.*) der Schleim.
**phlegmatic** [fleg'mætik], *adj.* phlegmatisch, gelassen.
**phone** [foun] *see under* **telephone**.
**phonetics** [fə'netiks], *s.* die Phonetik.
**phosphorescent** [fɔsfə'resənt], *adj.* phosphoreszierend, leuchtend.
**phosphorus** ['fɔsfərəs], *s.* (*Chem.*) der Phosphor.
**photograph** ['foutəgræf *or* -gra:f], *s.* die Photographie, das Lichtbild (*picture*). — *v.a.* photographieren, aufnehmen, (*coll.*) knipsen.
**photographer** [fə'tɔgrəfə], *s.* der Photograph.

**photography** [fə'tɔgrəfi], *s.* die Photographie.

**phrase** [freiz], *s.* die Phrase. — *v.a.* phrasieren, fassen, ausdrücken.

**phrenology** [fre'nɔlədʒi], *s.* die Phrenologie, Schädellehre.

**phthisis** ['θaisis], *s.* (*Med.*) die Schwindsucht.

**physic** ['fizik], *s.* (*obs.*) die Medizin, Arznei.

**physical** ['fizikəl], *adj.* körperlich (*bodily*); physikalisch (*of physics*).

**physician** [fi'ziʃən], *s.* der Arzt.

**physics** ['fiziks], *s.* die Physik.

**physiognomy** [fizi'ɔnəmi *or* -'ɔgnəmi], *s.* die Physiognomie, die Gesichtsbildung.

**physiologist** [fizi'ɔlədʒist], *s.* der Physiolog.

**physiology** [fizi'ɔlədʒi], *s.* die Physiologie.

**piano(forte)** ['pjænou('fɔ:ti)], *s.* das Klavier.

**pick** [pik], *v.a.* pflücken (*flowers*); hacken (*hack*); — *up*, auflesen; auswählen (*select*); gewaltsam öffnen (*a lock*); anfangen (*a quarrel*). — *v.n. why* — *on me?* warum gerade mich auswählen? — *s.* die Picke, Spitzhacke (*axe*); die Auswahl; — *of the bunch*, (*coll.*) das Beste von allen.

**picket** ['pikit], *s.* die Wache; der Streikposten (*of strikers*); der Pflock (*wood*). — *v.a.* bewachen. — *v.n.* Wache stehen.

**pickle** [pikl], *s.* (*Cul.*) der Pökel, das Gepökelte; (*coll.*) die unangenehme Lage (*calamity*). — *v.a.* einpökeln.

**pickpocket** ['pikpɔkit], *s.* der Taschendieb.

**picnic** ['piknik], *s.* das Picknick. — *v.n.* picknicken.

**pictorial** [pik'tɔ:riəl], *adj.* illustriert.

**picture** ['piktʃə], *s.* das Bild; — *book*, das Bilderbuch; — *postcard*, die Ansichtskarte; *pretty as a* —, bildhübsch; der Film; (*pl.*) das Kino. — *v.a.* sich vorstellen.

**picturesque** [piktʃə'resk], *adj.* pittoresk, malerisch.

**pie** (1) [pai], *s.* (*Cul.*) die Pastete (*savoury*); das Törtchen (*sweet*).

**piebald** ['paibɔ:ld], *adj.* scheckig. — *s.* der Schecke (*horse*).

**piece** [pi:s], *s.* das Stück. — *v.a.* — *together*, zusammenflicken (*mend*), zusammensetzen (*compose*).

**piecemeal** ['pi:smi:l], *adv.* stückweise.

**pied** [paid] *see* **piebald**.

**pier** [piə], *s.* der Hafendamm; der Pfeiler (*column*).

**pierce** [piəs], *v.a.* durchstechen, durchbohren.

**pierglass** ['piəglɑ:s], *s.* der Pfeilerspiegel.

**piety** ['paiəti], *s.* die Pietät, Frömmigkeit.

**pig** [pig], *s.* (*Zool.*) das Schwein.

**pigeon** ['pidʒən], *s.* (*Orn.*) die Taube.

**pigeonhole** ['pidʒənhoul], *s.* das Fach.

**pigheaded** [pig'hedid], *adj.* starrköpfig, dickköpfig.

**piglet** ['piglit], *s.* (*Zool.*) das Ferkel.

**pigment** ['pigmənt], *s.* das Pigment, der (natürliche) Farbstoff.

**pigtail** ['pigteil], *s.* der Haarzopf.

**pike** [paik], *s.* (*Zool.*) der Hecht; die Pike (*weapon*).

**pile** (1) [pail], *s.* der Haufen, Stoß (*paper*). — *v.a.* aufhäufen.

**pile** (2) [pail], *s.* (*Archit.*) der Pfahl; Pfeiler (*stone*).

**pile** (3) [pail], *s.* (*Text.*) der Teppichflausch (*carpet*), die Noppe (*cloth*).

**piles** [pailz], *s. pl.* (*Med. coll.*) die Haemorrhoiden, *pl.*

**pilfer** ['pilfə], *v.a.* stehlen, mausen.

**pilferer** ['pilfərə], *s.* der Dieb.

**pilgrim** ['pilgrim], *s.* der Pilger.

**pill** [pil], *s.* (*Med.*) die Pille.

**pillage** ['pilidʒ], *s.* die Plünderung. — *v.a.* ausplündern.

**pillar** ['pilə], *s.* der Pfeiler, die Säule; — *box*, der Briefkasten.

**pillion** ['piljən], *s.* der zweite Sitz, Sozius (*motorcycle*).

**pillory** ['piləri], *s.* der Pranger. — *v.a.* anprangern.

**pillow** ['pilou], *s.* das Kopfkissen.

**pilot** ['pailət], *s.* der Pilot; (*Naut.*) der Lotse. — *v.a.* (*Aviat.*) steuern, (*Naut.*) lotsen.

**pimento** [pi'mentou], *s.* (*Bot.*) der Jamaikapfeffer.

**pimp** [pimp], *s.* der Kuppler.

**pimple** [pimpl], *s.* der Pickel; (*pl.*) der Ausschlag.

**pin** [pin], *s.* die Stecknadel; (*Engin.*) der Bolzen, Stift; (*skittles*) der Kegel. — *v.a.* — *down*, festlegen.

**pinafore** ['pinəfɔ:], *s.* die Schürze, Kinderschürze.

**pincers** ['pinsəz], *s. pl.* die Kneifzange, Zange.

**pinch** [pintʃ], *v.a.* kneifen, zwicken; (*coll.*) klauen, stehlen. — *v.n.* sparen, darben. — *s.* die Prise (*tobacco*); *at a* —, wenn es sein muß.

**pine** (1) [pain], *s.* (*Bot.*) die Kiefer, Föhre.

**pine** (2) [pain], *v.n.* — *for*, schmachten (nach, *Dat.*), sich sehnen.

**pineapple** ['painæpl], *s.* (*Bot.*) die Ananas.

**pinion** ['pinjən], *s.* der Flügel (*wing*); (*Poet.*) die Schwinge; (*Mech.*) das Zahnrad; — *shaft*, die Ritzelwelle; *spindle*, die Zahnradwelle. — *v.a.* binden, fesseln.

**pink** [pink], *adj.* rosa. — *s.* (*Bot.*) die (rosa) Nelke; (*Hunt.*) der (rote) Jagdrock; *in the* — (*of condition*), in bester Gesundheit, in bester Form.

**pinnacle** ['pinəkl], *s.* die Zinne, Spitze; (*fig.*) der Gipfel.

**pint** [paint], *s.* die Pinte (0.57 litre); (*beer*) der Schoppen.

**pioneer** [paiə'niə], *s.* der Pionier. — *v.a.* bahnbrechend sein, bahnen.

**pious** ['paiəs], *adj.* fromm.

**pip** [pip], *s.* der Obstkern; (*Mil. coll.*) der Leutnantsstern.

**pipe** [paip], *s.* die Pfeife; (*Engin.*) das Rohr; die Röhre; (*Mus.*) die Pfeife. — *v.a.* pfeifen; durch Rohre leiten.

**piping** [´paipiŋ], *adj.* — *hot*, kochend heiß.

**pipkin** [´pipkin], *s.* das Töpfchen.

**piquant** [´pi:kənt], *adj.* pikant; scharf (*taste*).

**pique** [pi:k], *s.* der Groll. — *v.a.* reizen.

**piracy** [´pairəsi], *s.* die Seeräuberei.

**pirate** [´pairit], *s.* der Pirat, Seeräuber. — [pai´reit], *v.a.* (*fig.*) plagiieren, ohne Erlaubnis drucken (*books*).

**pistil** [´pistil], *s.* (*Bot.*) der Stempel.

**pistol** [´pistəl], *s.* die Pistole.

**piston** [´pistən], *s.* (*Mech.*) der Kolben.

**pit** [pit], *s.* die Grube; (*Min.*) der Schacht, das Bergwerk; (*Theat., Mus.*) der Orchesterraum; (*Theat.*) das Parterre.

**pitch** (1) [pitʃ], *s.* der Grad, Gipfel (*height*); (*Mus.*) der Ton, die Tonhöhe (*level*); (*Sport*) das Spielfeld. — *v.a.* werfen; feststecken; (*Mus.*) stimmen; befestigen; (*tent*) (ein Zelt) aufschlagen; — *in*, sich ins Zeug legen.

**pitch** (2) [pitʃ], *s.* das Pech (*tar*); — *dark*, pechschwarz.

**pitchblende** [´pitʃblend], *s.* die Pechblende.

**pitcher** [´pitʃə], *s.* der Krug.

**pitchfork** [´pitʃfɔ:k], *s.* die Heugabel.

**piteous** [´pitiəs], *adj.* erbärmlich.

**pitfall** [´pitfɔ:l], *s.* die Falle.

**pith** [piθ], *s.* das Mark; (*fig.*) der Kern, das Wesentliche; die Kraft (*strength*).

**pithy** [´piθi], *adj.* markig, kräftig; prägnant.

**pitiable** [´pitiəbl], *adj.* erbärmlich.

**pitiful** [´pitiful], *adj.* erbärmlich (*pitiable*); mitleidig (*sympathetic*).

**pitiless** [´pitilis], *adj.* erbarmungslos, grausam.

**pittance** [´pitəns], *s.* der Hungerlohn, das Bißchen, die Kleinigkeit.

**pity** [´piti], *s.* das Mitleid. — *v.a.* bemitleiden, bedauern.

**pivot** [´pivət], *s.* (*Mech.*) der Drehpunkt, Zapfen; (*fig.*) der Mittelpunkt, Angelpunkt. — *v.n.* zum Mittelpunkt haben, sich drehen (um).

**placard** [´plækɑ:d], *s.* das Plakat.

**placate** [plə´keit], *v.a.* versöhnen.

**place** [pleis], *s.* der Platz, Ort, die Stelle; — *name*, der Ortsname; (*rank*) der Rang, die Rangstufe. — *v.a.* plazieren (*in a job*); legen, setzen, stellen; — *an order*, einen Auftrag geben.

**placid** [´plæsid], *adj.* gelassen, sanft, gutmütig.

**plagiarism** [´pleidჳiərizm], *s.* das Plagiat, das Plagiieren.

**plague** [pleig], *s.* (*Med.*) die Pest, Seuche; (*fig.*) die Plage. — *v.a.* belästigen, plagen.

**plaice** [pleis], *s.* (*Zool.*) die Scholle.

**plain** [plein], *s.* die Ebene, Fläche. — *adj.* eben, flach (*even*); schlicht,

einfach, klar; — *dealing*, ehrliche Handlungsweise; — *speaking*, offenes Sprechen, aufrichtiges Reden; (*Mus.*) — *song*, der einstimmige Chorgesang, die gregorianische Kirchenmusik.

**plaintiff** [´pleintif], *s.* (*Law*) der Kläger.

**plaintive** [´pleintiv], *adj.* klagend.

**plait** [plæt], *s.* der Zopf, die Flechte. — *v.a.* flechten (*hair*); falten.

**plan** [plæn], *s.* der Plan, Grundriß. — *v.a.* planen, entwerfen.

**plane** (1) [plein], *v.a.* hobeln (*wood*). — *s.* die Fläche (*surface*); die Stufe (*level*); (*coll.*) das Flugzeug (*aeroplane*).

**plane** (2) *see* **plane-tree**.

**planet** [´plænit], *s.* (*Astron.*) der Planet.

**plane-tree** [´pleintri:], *s.* (*Bot.*) die Platane.

**planish** [´plæniʃ], *v.a.* (*woodwork*) polieren, glätten.

**plank** [plæŋk], *s.* die Planke; (*Pol.*) der Programmpunkt.

**plant** [plɑ:nt], *s.* (*Bot.*) die Pflanze; (*Ind.*) die Anlage, der Betrieb. — *v.a.* anpflanzen, anlegen; — *suspicion*, Verdacht einflößen (*of*, *against*, gegen, Acc.).

**plantain** [´plæntein], *s.* (*Bot.*) der Wegerich; (*fruit*) der Pisang.

**plantation** [plæn´teiʃən], *s.* die Pflanzung, Plantage.

**plaster** [´plɑ:stə], *s.* das Pflaster (*adhesive*); (*Build.*) der Mörtel, der Mauerbewurf; — *cast*, der Gipsabdruck; — *of Paris*, der Stuck, der feine Gipsmörtel. — *v.a.* bepflastern, verputzen; (*fig.*) dick auftragen.

**plastic** [´plæstik], *adj.* plastisch; (*malleable*) formbar; — *surgery*, plastische Chirurgie. — *s.* der Kunststoff.

**Plate, River** [pleit, ´rivə]. der La Plata Strom.

**plate** [pleit], *s.* der Teller (*dish*), die Platte, Scheibe; (*coll.*) — *glass*, das Spiegelglas; das Geschirr (*service of crockery*); *gold* —, das Goldgeschirr. — *v.a.* überziehen, versilbern, verchromen.

**platform** [´plætfɔ:m], *s.* (*Railw.*) der Bahnsteig; die Bühne, das Podium.

**platinum** [´plætinəm], *s.* das Platin.

**platitude** [´plætitju:d], *s.* die Plattheit, der Gemeinplatz.

**platitudinous** [plæti´tju:dinəs], *adj.* nichtssagend.

**platoon** [plə´tu:n], *s.* (*Mil.*) der Zug.

**plaudit** [´plɔ:dit], *s.* der Beifall.

**plausible** [´plɔ:zibl], *adj.* wahrscheinlich, glaubwürdig, einleuchtend.

**play** [plei], *s.* das Spiel (*game*); (*Theat.*) das Stück. — *v.a., v.n.* spielen.

**player** [´pleiə], *s.* der Spieler; (*Theat.*) der Schauspieler.

**playful** [´pleiful], *adj.* spielerisch, spielend.

**playground** [´pleigraund], *s.* der Spielplatz.

**playhouse** [´pleihaus], *s.* das Schauspielhaus.

**playmate** ['pleimeit], s. der Spiel-
gefährte.
**playwright** ['pleirait], s. der Dramatiker, Schauspieldichter.
**plea** [pli:], s. die Bitte; das Gesuch; der
Vorwand.
**plead** [pli:d], v.a., v.n. plädieren, sich
berufen auf; vorschützen (claim).
**pleasant** ['plezənt], adj. angenehm,
freundlich.
**pleasantry** ['plezəntri], s. das freund-
liche Wort, der Scherz (joke).
**please** [pli:z], v.a., v.n. gefallen; einen
Gefallen tun (do a favour); — ! bitte,
haben Sie die Güte!; if you —, wenn
Sie nichts dagegen haben.
**pleasing** ['pli:ziŋ], adj. einnehmend,
angenehm.
**pleasure** ['pleʒə], s. das Vergnügen; at
your —, nach Belieben; take — in,
Vergnügen finden an (Dat.).
**pleat** [pli:t], v.a. plissieren. — s. die
Falte, das Plissee.
**pledge** [pledʒ], s. das Pfand, die Bürgschaft (guarantee); das Versprechen
(promise). — v.a. sich verbürgen,
versprechen; zutrinken (drink to).
**plenary** ['pli:nəri], adj. Plenar-, vollständig.
**plenipotentiary** [plenipo'tenʃəri], s.
der Bevollmächtigte.
**plenitude** ['plenitju:d], s. die Fülle.
**plenteous, plentiful** ['plentiəs, 'plenti-
ful], adj. reichlich, in Fülle.
**plenty** ['plenti], s. die Fülle.
**pleurisy** ['pluərəsi], s. (Med.) die
Brustfellentzündung.
**pliable, pliant** ['plaiəbl, 'plaiənt], adj.
geschmeidig, biegsam.
**pliers** ['plaiəz], s. pl. die Drahtzange.
**plight** (1) [plait], s. die Notlage.
**plight** (2) [plait], v.a. feierlich versprechen.
**plod** [plɔd], v.n. schwerfällig gehen
(walk); sich plagen (work hard).
**plot** (1) [plɔt], s. das Stück Land, der
Bauplatz.
**plot** (2) [plɔt], s. das Komplott, die
Verschwörung; die Handlung (book,
play etc.). — v.a. aushecken (ambush
etc.), planen.
**plough, plow** [plau], s. der Pflug. —
v.a. pflügen; (coll.) be —ed, durchfallen (in, in, Dat.).
**ploughshare** ['plauʃɛə], s. die Pflugschar.
**plover** ['plʌvə], s. (Orn.) der Kiebitz,
Regenpfeifer.
**plow** see under **plough**.
**pluck** (1) [plʌk], v.a. pflücken (flowers);
rupfen (feathers); — up courage, Mut
fassen.
**pluck** (2) [plʌk], s. (coll.) der Mut.
**plucky** ['plʌki], adj. mutig.
**plug** [plʌg], s. der Stecker; der
Stöpsel (stopper); sparking —, (Motor.)
die Zündkerze. — v.a. stöpseln,
zustopfen (block); (fig.) betonen,
herausstellen (repeat for advertisement).

**plum** [plʌm], s. (Bot.) die Pflaume;
(coll.) das Beste.
**plumage** ['plu:midʒ], s. (Orn.) das
Gefieder.
**plumb** [plʌm], s. das Senkblei, Lot;
— -rule, die Senkwaage. — adv.
senkrecht, gerade, lotrecht.
**plume** [plu:m], s. die (Schmuck)
feder.
**plump** [plʌmp], adj. dick, drall.
**plunder** ['plʌndə], v.a., v.n. plündern.
— s. die Beute, der Raub.
**plunge** [plʌndʒ], v.a., v.n. untertauchen, stoßen, hinabstürzen.
**plunger** ['plʌndʒə], s. der Taucher;
(Engin.) der Tauchkolben.
**pluperfect** [plu:'pə:fikt], s. (Gram.) das
Plusquamperfektum.
**plural** ['pluərəl], s. (Gram.) der Plural,
die Mehrzahl.
**plurality** [pluə'ræliti], s. die Mehrzahl,
der Plural.
**plus** [plʌs], prep. plus, zuzüglich.
**plush** [plʌʃ], s. (Text.) der Plüsch.
**ply** [plai], s. die Falte (fold), Lage
(layer). — v.a. ausüben (trade).
**plywood** ['plaiwud], s. das Sperrholz,
die Sperrholzplatte.
**pneumonia** [nju:'mouniə], s. (Med.) die
Lungenentzündung.
**poach** (1) [poutʃ], v.n. wildern; — on,
übergreifen auf.
**poach** (2) [poutʃ], v.a. ohne Schale
kochen; poached eggs, verlorene Eier,
n. pl.
**poacher** ['poutʃə], s. der Wilderer,
Wilddieb.
**pocket** ['pɔkit], s. die Tasche; — book,
die Brieftasche; das Taschenbuch;
— money, das Taschengeld.
**pod** [pɔd], s. (Bot.) die Schote.
**poem** ['pouim], s. das Gedicht.
**poet** ['pouit], s. der Dichter.
**poetic(al)** [pou'etik(l)], adj. dichterisch.
**poignancy** ['pɔinjənsi], s. die Schärfe.
**poignant** ['pɔinjənt], adj. scharf, beißend, schmerzlich.
**point** [pɔint], s. der Punkt (of remark,
sentence); die Sache; der Zweck; die
Spitze (of pencil etc.); make a —, es
sich zur Aufgabe machen; in — of
fact, tatsächlich; come to the —, zur
Sache kommen. — v.a., v.n. spitzen,
zuspitzen (pencil); — out, zeigen,
(hin)deuten; — to, hinweisen auf; —
the moral, die Moral erklären.
**pointblank** ['pɔint'blæŋk], adj., adv.
schnurgerade, direkt.
**pointed** ['pɔintid], adj. scharf, spitzig,
deutlich (remark).
**pointer** ['pɔintə], s. der Zeiger; (fig.)
der Fingerzeig (hint).
**poise** [pɔiz], s. das Gleichgewicht; (fig.)
angemessenes Benehmen, die Grazie.
— v.a. abwägen; im Gleichgewicht
halten. — v.n. schweben; —d for
action, tatbereit.
**poison** [pɔizn], s. das Gift. — v.a.
vergiften.

# poke

**poke** (1) [pouk], *v.a.* schüren (*fire*); stoßen; — *fun at,* sich lustig machen über. — *s.* der Stoß; — *in the ribs,* ein Rippenstoß.

**poke** (2) [pouk], *s.* der Sack; *a pig in a* —, die Katze im Sack.

**poker** (1) ['poukə], *s.* der Schürhaken, das Schüreisen.

**poker** (2) ['poukə], *s.* (*Cards*) das Pokerspiel.

**polar** ['poulə], *adj.* (*Geog.*) Polar-; (*Phys.*) polar.

**polarity** [po'læriti], *s.* die Polarität.

**Pole** [poul], *s.* der Pole.

**pole** (1) [poul], *s.* (*Geog.*) der Pol.

**pole** (2) [poul], *s.* die Stange (*rod*); der Pfahl (*upright*).

**poleaxe** ['poulæks], *s.* die Streitaxt.

**polecat** ['poulkæt], *s.* (*Zool.*) der Iltis.

**polemic** [pə'lemik], *s.* die Polemik, der Streit.

**police** [pə'li:s], *s.* die Polizei. — *v.a.* polizeilich beaufsichtigen.

**policeman** [pə'li:smən], *s.* der Polizist.

**policy** (1) ['polisi], *s.* die Politik.

**policy** (2) ['polisi], *s.* (*Insurance*) die Police.

**Polish** ['pouliʃ], *adj.* polnisch.

**polish** ['poliʃ], *v.a.* polieren. — *s.* die Politur, der Glanz.

**polished** ['poliʃd], *adj.* glatt (*smooth*); (*fig.*) wohlerzogen, fein (*manners*).

**polite** [pə'lait], *adj.* höflich.

**politeness** [pə'laitnis], *s.* die Höflichkeit.

**politic** ['politik], *adj.* politisch; schlau (*cunning*).

**political** [pə'litikəl], *adj.* politisch; staatskundig.

**politician** [poli'tiʃən], *s.* der Politiker, Staatsmann.

**politics** ['politiks], *s.* (*sometimes pl.*) die Politik, politische Gesinnung.

**poll** [poul], *s.* die Wahl (*election*). — *v.n.* abstimmen, wählen, seine Stimme abgeben.

**pollard** ['poləd], *s.* (*Bot.*) der gekappte Baum; (*Zool.*) das hornlose Tier.

**pollen** ['polən], *s.* (*Bot.*) der Blütenstaub.

**pollinate** ['polineit], *v.a.* (*Bot.*) bestäuben.

**polling** ['poulin], *s.* die Wahl, der Wahlgang (*election*); — *station,* das Wahllokal.

**pollute** [pə'lju:t], *v.a.* verunreinigen.

**pollution** [pə'lju:ʃən], *s.* die Verunreinigung.

**poltroon** [pol'tru:n], *s.* die Memme.

**poly-** ['poli], *pref.* viel-.

**Polynesian** [poli'ni:ziən], *adj.* polynesisch. — *s.* der Polynesier.

**polytechnic** [poli'teknik], *s.* das Technikum; polytechnische Fachschule.

**pomegranate** ['pom-, 'pʌmgrænit], *s.* (*Bot.*) der Granatapfel.

**Pomeranian** [pomə'reiniən], *adj.* pommerisch. — *s.* der Pommer; der Spitz (*dog*).

**pommel** [paml], *s.* der Sattelknopf; der Knauf (*sword*). — *v.a.* schlagen.

**pomp** [pomp], *s.* der Pomp, das Gepränge.

**pompous** ['pompəs], *adj.* hochtrabend, prahlerisch; (*manner*) schwerfällig, wichtigtuerisch.

**pond** [pond], *s.* der Teich.

**ponder** ['pondə], *v.a., v.n.* bedenken, überlegen.

**ponderous** ['pondərəs], *adj.* schwer, schwerfällig.

**pontiff** ['pontif], *s.* der Hohepriester; der Papst.

**pontifical** [pon'tifikəl], *adj.* bischöflich, päpstlich. — *s. pl.* die bischöfliche Amtstracht.

**pontificate** [pon'tifikit], *s.* das (*or* der) Pontifikat. — [-keit], *v.n.* (*coll.*) predigen.

**pontoon** (1) [pon'tu:n], *s.* die Schiffsbrücke, der Brückenkahn.

**pontoon** (2) [pon'tu:n], *s.* (*cards*) das Einundzwanzig, Vingt-et-un.

**pony** ['pouni], *s.* (*Zool.*) der *or* das Pony.

**poodle** [pu:dl], *s.* (*Zool.*) der Pudel.

**pooh-pooh** [pu:'pu:], *v.a.* verspotten.

**pool** (1) [pu:l], *s.* die Lache, der Pfuhl.

**pool** (2) [pu:l], *s.* (*fig.*) der gemeinsame Einsatz (*money, forces etc.*). — *v.a.* zusammenschließen.

**poop** [pu:p], *s.* (*Naut.*) das Heck, Hinterteil.

**poor** [puə], *adj.* arm, dürftig; *in* — *health,* bei schwacher Gesundheit; (*fig.*) armselig, schlecht.

**pop** [pop], *v.n.* knallen, explodieren. — *v.a.* (*coll.*) schnell versetzen, verpfänden.

**Pope** [poup], *s.* (*Eccl.*) der Papst.

**poplar** ['poplə], *s.* (*Bot.*) die Pappel.

**poppy** ['popi], *s.* (*Bot.*) der Mohn.

**populace** ['popjulis], *s.* der Pöbel.

**popular** ['popjulə], *adj.* volkstümlich, beliebt.

**popularity** [popju'læriti], *s.* die Beliebtheit.

**populate** ['popjuleit], *v.a.* bevölkern.

**population** [popju'leiʃən], *s.* die Bevölkerung.

**populous** ['popjuləs], *adj.* dicht bevölkert.

**porcelain** ['po:slin], *s.* das Porzellan, das Geschirr.

**porch** [po:tʃ], *s.* die Eingangshalle, Vorhalle.

**porcupine** ['po:kjupain], *s.* (*Zool.*) das Stachelschwein.

**pore** (1) [po:], *s.* die Pore.

**pore** (2) [po:], *v.n.* sich vertiefen (*over, in*), brüten (*über*).

**pork** [po:k], *s.* das Schweinefleisch.

**porosity** [po:'rositi], *s.* die Porosität.

**porous** ['po:rəs], *adj.* porös.

**porpoise** ['po:pəs], *s.* (*Zool.*) der Tümmler, das Meerschwein.

**porridge** ['poridʒ], *s.* (*Cul.*) der Haferbrei.

**porringer** ['poridʒə], *s.* (*Cul.*) der Napf.

**port** (1) [po:t], *s.* der Hafen.

**port** (2) [po:t], *s.* der Portwein (*wine*).

**portable** ['pɔːtəbl], *adj.* tragbar; Koffer- (*radio etc.*).
**portcullis** [pɔːt'kʌlis], *s.* das Fallgatter.
**portend** [pɔː'tend], *v.a.* vorbedeuten, ahnen lassen.
**portent** ['pɔːtent], *s.* die Vorbedeutung.
**porter** ['pɔːtə], *s.* (*Railw.*) der Gepäckträger; der Pförtner, Portier (*caretaker, janitor*); das Porterbier (*beer*).
**porterage** ['pɔːtəridʒ], *s.* der Trägerlohn, die Zustellkosten, *f.pl.*
**portfolio** [pɔːt'fouliou], *s.* die Mappe; (*Pol.*) das Ressort; das Portefeuille.
**portico** ['pɔːtikou], *s.* (*Archit.*) die Säulenhalle.
**portion** ['pɔːʃən], *s.* die Portion, der Anteil. — *v.a.* aufteilen, austeilen (*share out*).
**portliness** ['pɔːtlinis], *s.* die Stattlichkeit (*dignity*); Behäbigkeit (*corpulence*).
**portly** ['pɔːtli], *adj.* stattlich (*dignified*); behäbig (*corpulent*).
**portmanteau** [pɔːt'mæntou], *s.* der Handkoffer.
**portrait** ['pɔːtrit], *s.* (*Art*) das Bildnis, Porträt.
**portray** [pɔː'trei], *v.a.* im Bilde darstellen, porträtieren; (*fig.*) schildern, darstellen (*describe*).
**Portuguese** [pɔːtju'giːz], *adj.* portugiesisch. — *s.* der Portugiese.
**pose** [pouz], *s.* die Haltung, Stellung (*of model etc.*). — *v.a.* in Pose stellen; aufwerfen (*question*). — *v.n.* (*as model*) stehen, sitzen; — *as,* posieren, sich ausgeben als (*pretend to be*).
**poser** ['pouzə], *s.* die schwierige Frage.
**position** [pə'ziʃən], *s.* die Lage (*situation*); die Stellung (*job*); der Stand, Rang (*rank*); (*Astron., Mil.*) die Position.
**positive** ['pɔzitiv], *adj.* positiv; (*fig.*) ausdrücklich, sicher (*sure*).
**possess** [pə'zes], *v.a.* besitzen.
**possession** [pə'zeʃən], *s.* der Besitz, Besitztum.
**possessive** [pə'zesiv], *adj.* (*Gram.*) besitzanzeigend, possessiv; (*fig.*) besitzgierig.
**possibility** [pɔsi'biliti], *s.* die Möglichkeit.
**possible** ['pɔsibl], *adj.* möglich.
**post** (1) [poust], *s.* der Pfosten (*pillar*).
**post** (2) [poust], *s.* die Post (*mail*); der Posten (*job*). — *v.a.* zur Post geben; (*coll.*) einstecken (*letter*).
**postage** ['poustidʒ], *s.* das Porto; — *stamp,* die Briefmarke.
**postal** ['poustl], *adj.* Post-.
**poster** ['poustə], *s.* das Plakat.
**posterity** [pɔs'teriti], *s.* die Nachwelt.
**posthumous** ['pɔstjuməs], *adj.* hinterlassen, nach dem Tode, postum.
**postman** ['poustmən], *s.* der Briefträger.
**postmark** ['poustmɑːk], *s.* der Poststempel.
**post-mortem** [poust'mɔːtəm], *s.* — — —

(*examination*), die Obduktion, Leichenschau.
**post-office** ['poustɔfis], *s.* das Postamt.
**postpone** [poust'poun], *v.a.* verschieben, aufschieben.
**postscript** ['poustskript], *s.* die Nachschrift.
**postulate** ['pɔstjuleit], *v.a.* postulieren, voraussetzen.
**posture** ['pɔstʃə], *s.* die Positur, Haltung (*of body*).
**pot** [pɔt], *s.* der Topf; die Kanne (*beer*); (*coll.*) go to —, zugrunde gehen. — *v.a.* einkochen, einmachen; (*fig.*) kürzen.
**potash** ['pɔtæʃ], *s.* (*Chem*) die Pottasche.
**potassium** [pə'tæsiəm], *s.* (*Chem.*) das Kalium.
**potato** [pə'teitou], *s.* (*Bot.*) die Kartoffel.
**potent** ['poutənt], *adj.* kräftig, stark, wirksam.
**potential** [pə'tenʃəl], *s.* das Potential. — *adj.* möglich, potentiell (*possible*).
**potter** ['pɔtə], *s.* der Töpfer.
**pottery** ['pɔtəri], *s.* die Töpferei; die Töpferwaren, Tonwaren, *f. pl.* (*goods*).
**pouch** [pautʃ], *s.* der Beutel.
**poulterer** ['poultərə], *s.* der Geflügelhändler.
**poultice** ['poultis], *s.* der Umschlag.
**poultry** ['poultri], *s.* das Geflügel.
**pounce** (1) [pauns], *s.* (*obs.*) die Klaue. — *v.n.* — *upon,* herfallen (über, *Acc.*).
**pounce** (2) [pauns], *s.* das Bimssteinpulver. — *v.a.* (mit Bimsstein) abreiben.
**pound** (1) [paund], *s.* das Pfund; das Pfund Sterling.
**pound** (2) [paund], *v.a.* zerstoßen.
**poundage** ['paundidʒ], *s.* das Pfundgeld, die Gebühr pro Pfund.
**pour** [pɔː], *v.a.* gießen, schütten, einschenken. — *v.n.* strömen.
**pout** [paut], *v.n.* schmollen.
**poverty** ['pɔvəti], *s.* die Armut.
**powder** ['paudə], *s.* (*Mil.*) das Pulver; der Puder (*face etc.*). — *v.a.* zu Pulver machen, stoßen; (*face*) pudern.
**power** [pauə], *s.* die Macht, Gewalt; Kraft; Fähigkeit; — *of attorney,* die Vollmacht; (*Maths.*) die Potenz; (*Elec.*) der Strom; — *house,* — *station,* das Elektrizitätswerk; — *cut,* die Stromstörung.
**powerful** ['pauəful], *adj.* kräftig, mächtig, einflußreich.
**powerless** ['pauəlis], *adj.* kraftlos, machtlos.
**pox** [pɔks], *s.* (*Med.*) die Pocken, *f. pl.*; die Syphilis.
**practicable** ['præktikəbl], *adj.* ausführbar, tunlich.
**practical** ['præktikəl], *adj.* praktisch.
**practice** ['præktis], *s.* die Ausübung (*doing, carrying out*); die Praxis.
**practise** ['præktis], *v.a.* ausführen, ausüben (*a profession etc.*); üben (*rehearse*). — *v.n.* sich üben.

# practised

**practised** ['præktisd], *adj.* geübt, geschult (in).

**practitioner** [præk'tiʃənə], *s.* (*Med.*) praktischer Arzt; (*Law*) Advokat.

**pragmatic** [præg'mætik], *adj.* pragmatisch.

**prairie** ['preəri], *s.* die Prärie.

**praise** [preiz], *v.a.* preisen, loben. — *s.* das Lob.

**pram** *see under* **perambulator**.

**prance** [prɑ:ns], *v.n.* sich bäumen; (*fig.*) sich brüsten (*brag*).

**prank** [præŋk], *s.* der Streich.

**prate** [preit], *v.n.* plappern, schwatzen.

**prattle** [prætl], *v.n.* plaudern, schwatzen. — *s.* das Geschwätz.

**prawn** [prɔ:n], *s.* (*Zool.*) die Steingarnele.

**pray** [prei], *v.n.* beten. — *v.a.* bitten, ersuchen (*beseech*).

**prayer** [preə], *s.* das Gebet.

**preach** [pri:tʃ], *v.a., v.n.* predigen.

**preacher** ['pri:tʃə], *s.* der Prediger.

**preamble** [pri:'æmbl], *s.* die Vorrede, der Einleitungsparagraph.

**precarious** [pri'kɛəriəs], *adj.* unsicher, prekär.

**precaution** [pri'kɔ:ʃən], *s.* die Vorsichtsmaßregel.

**precede** [pri'si:d], *v.a., v.n.* vorausgehen, den Vortritt haben.

**precedence** [pri'si:dəns *or* 'presidəns], *s.* der Vortritt, Vorrang.

**precedent** ['presidənt], *s.* der Präzedenzfall.

**precept** ['pri:sept], *s.* die Vorschrift, Regel.

**preceptor** [pri'septə], *s.* der Lehrer, Lehrmeister.

**precinct** ['pri:siŋkt], *s.* das Gebiet, der Bezirk; (*pl.*) die Grenzen, *f. pl.*

**precious** ['preʃəs], *adj.* wertvoll, kostbar; — *metal*, das Edelmetall.

**precipice** ['presipis], *s.* der Abgrund.

**precipitous** [pri'sipitəs], *adj.* jäh, abschüssig.

**precise** [pri'sais], *adj.* genau, bestimmt.

**precision** [pri'siʒən], *s.* die Präzision, Genauigkeit; (*Engin.*) — *tool*, das Präzisionswerkzeug.

**preclude** [pri'klu:d], *v.a.* ausschließen.

**precocious** [pri'kouʃəs], *adj.* frühreif.

**preconceive** [pri:kən'si:v], *v.a.* vorher denken.

**preconceived** [pri:kən'si:vd], *adj.* vorgefaßt.

**preconception** [pri:kən'sepʃən], *s.* das Vorurteil.

**precursor** [pri'kə:sə], *s.* der Vorläufer.

**predatory** ['predətəri], *adj.* räuberisch, Raub-.

**predecessor** ['pri:disesə], *s.* der Vorgänger.

**predestin(at)e** [pri:'destin(eit)], *v.a.* vorher bestimmen; (*Theol.*) prädestinieren.

**predicament** [pri'dikəmənt], *s.* die Verlegenheit.

**predicate** ['predikit], *s.* (*Gram.*) das Prädikat. — [-keit], *v.a.* behaupten.

**predict** [pri'dikt], *v.a.* voraussagen, vorhersagen.

**prediction** [pri'dikʃən], *s.* die Vorhersage (*weather etc.*); die Weissagung (*prophecy*).

**predilection** [pri:di'lekʃən], *s.* die Vorliebe.

**predispose** [pri:dis'pouz], *v.a.* vorbereiten; empfänglich machen.

**predominant** [pri'dɔminənt], *adj.* vorherrschend.

**predominate** [pri'dɔmineit], *v.n.* vorherrschen.

**pre-eminence** [pri:'eminəns], *s.* der Vorrang.

**prefabricate** [pri:'fæbrikeit], *v.a.* vorfabrizieren, als Fertigteil herstellen, in der Fabrik herstellen.

**prefabrication** [pri:fæbri'keiʃən], *s.* die Vorfabrizierung.

**preface** ['prefis], *s.* das Vorwort.

**prefatory** ['prefətəri], *adj.* einleitend.

**prefect** ['pri:fekt], *s.* der Präfekt.

**prefer** [pri'fə:], *v.a.* vorziehen.

**preference** ['prefərəns], *s.* der Vorzug; (*Comm.*) — *share*, die Vorzugsaktie.

**preferment** [pri'fə:mənt], *s.* die Beförderung.

**prefix** ['pri:fiks], *s.* die Vorsilbe. — [pri:'fiks], *v.a.* vorsetzen.

**pregnancy** ['pregnənsi], *s.* die Schwangerschaft.

**pregnant** ['pregnənt], *adj.* schwanger.

**prejudge** [pri:'dʒʌdʒ], *v.a.* vorher urteilen, voreilig urteilen.

**prejudice** ['predʒudis], *s.* das Vorurteil. — *v.a.* beeinträchtigen.

**prejudicial** [predʒu'diʃəl], *adj.* schädlich.

**prelate** ['prelit], *s.* (*Eccl.*) der Prälat.

**preliminary** [pri'liminəri], *adj.* vorläufig, Präliminar-. — *s.* (*pl.*) die Vorbereitungen, *f. pl.*

**prelude** ['prelju:d], *s.* das Vorspiel.

**premature** ['premətʃə], *adj.* vorschnell, übereilt, voreilig.

**premeditate** [pri:'mediteit], *v.a.* (*Law*) vorher überlegen.

**Premier** ['premiə], *s.* der Premierminister.

**premise** (1) ['premis], *s.* (*Log.*) die Prämisse; (*pl.*) das Haus, Grundstück; die Stätte, der Ort; das Lokal (*inn etc.*).

**premise** (2) [pri:'maiz], *v.a.* vorausschicken.

**premium** ['pri:miəm], *s.* die Prämie.

**premonition** [pri:mə'niʃən], *s.* die Vorahnung.

**preoccupation** [pri:ɔkju'peiʃən], *s.* die Zerstreutheit.

**preoccupied** [pri:'ɔkjupaid], *adj.* besorgt; zerstreut (*absent-minded*).

**preparation** [prepə'reiʃən], *s.* die Vorbereitung; Zubereitung (*of meals*).

**preparatory** [pri'pærətəri], *adj.* vorbereitend; — *school*, die Vorschule.

**prepare** [pri'pɛə], *v.a., v.n.* vorbereiten (*for*, auf); zubereiten (*meals*).

**prepay** [pri:'pei], *v.a. irr.* vorausbezahlen; (*post*) frankieren.

# principality

**preponderant** [pri'pɔndərənt], *adj.*
überwiegend.
**preponderate** [pri'pɔndəreit], *v.a.,
v.n.* überwiegen.
**preposition** [prepə'ziʃən], *s. (Gram.)*
die Präposition.
**prepossess** [pri:pə'zes], *v.a.* einnehmen,
beeindrucken.
**preposterous** [pri'pɔstərəs], *adj.* töricht,
lächerlich, unerhört.
**prerogative** [pri'rɔgətiv], *s.* das Vorrecht.
**presage** [pri'seidʒ], *v.a.* prophezeien.
— ['presidʒ], *s.* die Prophezeiung.
**prescient** ['presiənt, 'pri:–], *adj.* vorahnend, vorherwissend.
**prescribe** [pri'skraib], *v.a., v.n.* vorschreiben; *(Med.)* verschreiben,
verordnen.
**prescription** [pri'skripʃən], *s.* die
Vorschrift(*precept*); *(Med.)* das Rezept.
**presence** ['prezəns], *s.* die Gegenwart,
Anwesenheit (*attendance*); das Äußere
(*appearance*); — *of mind,* die Geistesgegenwart.
**present** (1) ['prezənt], *adj.* anwesend,
gegenwärtig; jetzig. — *s. (Gram.)* das
Präsens, die Gegenwart; *(time)* die
Gegenwart, heutige Zeit.
**present** (2) [pri'zent], *v.a.* darstellen
(*on stage*); vorstellen (*introduce*);
präsentieren (*arms*); schenken, geben
(*gifts*). — ['prezənt], *s.* das Geschenk
(*gift*).
**presentation** [prezən'teiʃən], *s.* die
Darstellung (*stage, art*); die Vorstellung (*introduction*); die Überreichung (*of gift*).
**presentiment** [pri'zentimənt], *s.* das
Vorgefühl, die Vorahnung.
**presently** ['prezəntli], *adv.* bald, sogleich.
**preservation** [prezə'veiʃən], *s.* die
Erhaltung, Bewahrung.
**preservative** [pri'zə:vətiv], *s.* das Konservierungsmittel.
**preserve** [pri'zə:v], *v.a.* bewahren,
erhalten; (*fruit*) einmachen. — *s.
(Hunt.)* das Jagdgehege, Jagdrevier,
*(pl.)* die Konserven, *f. pl.*
**preside** [pri'zaid], *v.n.* (*over*) den
Vorsitz führen.
**president** ['prezidənt], *s.* der Präsident.
**press** [pres], *v.a., v.n.* drücken (*push*);
bügeln, plätten (*iron*); nötigen (*force*);
dringend bitten (*entreat*). — *s.* die
Presse (*newspapers, printing*); der
Schrank (*cupboard*); das Gedränge
(*crowd*).
**pressing** ['presiŋ], *adj.* dringend.
**pressure** ['preʃə], *s.* der Druck.
**prestige** [pres'ti:ʒ], *s.* das Prestige,
Ansehen.
**presumable** [pri'zju:məbl], *adj.* mutmaßlich, vermutlich.
**presume** [pri'zju:m], *v.a., v.n.* vermuten; — *on,* sich anmaßen.
**presumption** [pri'zʌmpʃən], *s.* die
Annahme; die Anmaßung (*arrogance*).
**presumptive** [pri'zʌmptiv], *adj.* mutmaßlich.

**presumptuous** [pri'zʌmptjuəs], *adj.*
anmaßend, dreist, vermessen.
**presuppose** [pri:sə'pouz], *v.a.* voraussetzen.
**pretence** [pri'tens], *s.* der Vorwand.
**pretend** [pri'tend], *v.a., v.n.* vortäuschen, vorgeben.
**pretension** [pri'tenʃən], *s.* die Anmaßung, der Anspruch (*to, auf*).
**pretentious** [pri'tenʃəs], *adj.* anspruchsvoll.
**preterite** ['pretərit], *s. (Gram.)* das
Präteritum.
**pretext** ['pri:tekst], *s.* der Vorwand.
**pretty** ['priti], *adj.* hübsch, nett. —
*adv. (coll.)* ziemlich.
**prevail** [pri'veil], *v.n.* vorherrschen, die
Oberhand gewinnen.
**prevalence** ['prevələns], *s.* das Vorherrschen.
**prevaricate** [pri'værikeit], *v.n.* Ausflüchte machen.
**prevent** [pri'vent], *v.a.* verhindern.
**prevention** [pri'venʃən], *s.* die Verhinderung.
**preventive** [pri'ventiv], *adj.* vorbeugend.
**previous** ['pri:viəs], *adj.* vorhergehend.
**prey** [prei], *s.* die Beute, der Raub. —
*v.n.* rauben, nachstellen.
**price** [prais], *s.* der Preis, Wert.
**priceless** ['praislis], *adj.* unschätzbar,
unbezahlbar.
**prick** [prik], *s.* der Stachel, Stich (*stab*).
— *v.a.* stechen (*stab*); punktieren
(*puncture*).
**prickle** [prikl], *s. (Bot.)* der Stachel.
**pride** [praid], *s.* der Stolz. — *v.r.* — *o.s.,*
sich brüsten, stolz sein (*on, auf, Acc.*).
**priest** [pri:st], *s. (Eccl.)* der Priester.
**prig** [prig], *s.* der eingebildete Tropf;
Tugendheld.
**priggish** ['prigiʃ], *adj.* dünkelhaft,
selbstgefällig.
**prim** [prim], *adj.* steif, spröde.
**primacy** ['praiməsi], *s.* der, das Primat.
**primæval** [prai'mi:vəl], *adj.* Ur-, anfänglich, ursprünglich.
**primary** ['praiməri], *adj.* erst, ursprünglich; Haupt– (*main*). — *s. (pl.)
(Am.)* die Vorwahlen, *f. pl.* (*Presidential elections*).
**prime** [praim], *adj.* erst, wichtigst. —
*s.* die Blüte, Vollendung, Vollkraft.
**primer** ['praimə], *s.* das Elementarbuch,
die Fibel.
**primitive** ['primitiv], *adj.* primitiv;
ursprünglich (*original*).
**primness** ['primnis], *s.* die Geziertheit,
Steifheit.
**primrose** ['primrouz], *s. (Bot.)* die
Primel.
**prince** [prins], *s.* der Prinz; Fürst
(*rank*).
**princess** [prin'ses], *s.* die Prinzessin.
**principal** ['prinsipl], *s.* der Direktor
(*business*); Rektor (*school etc.*);
*(Comm.)* das Kapital; *(Mus.)* der erste
Spieler. — *adj.* erst, Haupt–.
**principality** [prinsi'pæliti], *s.* das
Fürstentum.

463

# principle

**principle** ['prinsipl], s. das Prinzip, der Grundsatz.

**print** [print], v.a. drucken, abdrucken. — s. (Typ., Art) der Druck; out of —, vergriffen.

**printer** ['printə], s. der Buchdrucker.

**prior** [praiə], adj. früher, eher; — to, vor (Dat.). — s. (Eccl.) der Prior.

**priority** [prai'oriti], s. die Priorität, der Vorrang.

**prise** [praiz], v.a. — open, gewaltsam öffnen, aufbrechen.

**prism** [prizm], s. das Prisma.

**prison** [prizn], s. das Gefängnis.

**prisoner** ['prizənə], s. der Gefangene, Sträfling.

**pristine** ['pristain] adj. ehemalig, vormalig, ursprünglich.

**privacy** ['praivəsi or 'privəsi], s. die Zurückgezogenheit, Stille.

**private** ['praivit], adj. privat, persönlich, vertraulich (confidential). — s. (Mil.) der Gemeine, Landser.

**privation** [prai'veiʃən], s. der Mangel, die Entbehrung (lack); die Beraubung (deprivation).

**privilege** ['privilidʒ], s. das Privileg, Vorrecht. — v.a. ausnehmen, privilegieren.

**privy** ['privi], s. der Abtritt, Abort. — adj. — to, mitwissend; Privy Council, der Staatsrat.

**prize** [praiz], s. der Preis, die Belohnung; — v.a. hochschätzen.

**prizewinner** ['praizwinə], s. der Preisträger; Nobel —, der Nobelpreisträger.

**probability** [probə'biliti], s. die Wahrscheinlichkeit.

**probable** ['probəbl], adj. wahrscheinlich.

**probate** ['proubeit], s. (Law) die Testamentsbestätigung.

**probation** [pro'beiʃən], s. die Bewährung, Bewährungsfrist (period).

**probationary** [pro'beiʃənəri], adj. Bewährungs-.

**probe** [proub], v.a. sondieren, untersuchen. — s. die Sonde, Prüfung.

**probity** ['proubiti], s. die Redlichkeit, Anständigkeit.

**problem** ['probləm], s. das Problem.

**problematic** [problə'mætik], adj. zweifelhaft, problematisch.

**proboscis** [pro'bosis],s.(Ent.)der Rüssel.

**procedure** [prə'si:dʒə], s. der Vorgang, das Verfahren.

**proceed** [prə'si:d], v.n. vorgehen, verfahren.

**proceeds** ['prousi:dz], s. pl. der Ertrag.

**process** (1) ['prouses], s. der Vorgang, Prozeß. — v.a. verarbeiten, fertigen.

**process** (2) [pro'ses], v.n. in einem Zuge gehen.

**procession** [prə'seʃən], s. der (feierliche) Umzug, die Prozession.

**proclaim** [pro'kleim], v.a. (Pol.) proklamieren, ausrufen.

**proclamation** [proklə'meiʃən], s. (Pol.) die Ausrufung, Proklamation.

**proclivity** [prə'kliviti], s. der Hang, die Neigung (tendency).

**procrastinate** [pro'kræstineit], v.a. aufschieben. — v.n. zögern, zaudern.

**procreate** ['proukrieit], v.a. zeugen, hervorbringen.

**procurable** [prə'kjuərəbl], adj. zu verschaffen, erhältlich.

**procure** [pro'kjuə], v.a. verschaffen, besorgen.

**prod** [prod], v.a. stoßen.

**prodigal** ['prodigəl], adj. verschwenderisch, vergeudend; — son, der verlorene Sohn.

**prodigious** [prə'didʒəs], adj. erstaunlich, ungeheuer.

**prodigy** ['prodidʒi], s. das Wunderkind.

**produce** [prə'dju:s], v.a. erzeugen, produzieren. — ['prodju:s], s. das Produkt, Erzeugnis.

**producer** [prə'dju:sə], s. der Erzeuger; (Theat., Cinema) der Regisseur.

**product** ['prodʌkt], s. das Produkt, Erzeugnis.

**production** [prə'dʌkʃən], s. die Produktion; die Erzeugung (industrial); das Zeigen, Vorweisen (of documents); (Theat.) die Regie.

**productive** [prə'dʌktiv], adj. produktiv, schöpferisch (mind); fruchtbar (soil).

**profane** [prə'fein], adj. profan; ruchlos.

**profanity** [prə'fæniti], s. die Profanierung; das Lästern.

**profess** [prə'fes], v.a., v.n. bekennen, erklären, sich bekennen zu.

**profession** [prə'feʃən], s. der (höhere) Beruf; (Eccl.) das Bekenntnis; die Beteuerung (protestation).

**professional** [prə'feʃənəl], adj. beruflich, berufsmäßig.

**professor** [prə'fesə], s. der (Universitäts) Professor.

**professorship** [prə'fesəʃip], s. die Professur.

**proffer** ['profə], v.a. anbieten (offer).

**proficiency** [prə'fiʃənsi], s. die Tüchtigkeit; (skill) die Beherrschung.

**proficient** [prə'fiʃənt], adj. bewandert, tüchtig; (in language) fließend.

**profile** ['proufail], s. das Profil.

**profit** ['profit], s. der Profit, Gewinn, Nutzen. — v.n. Nutzen ziehen. — v.a. von Nutzen sein (Dat.).

**profound** [prə'faund], adj. tief; gründlich (thorough).

**profuse** [prə'fju:s], adj. reichlich, verschwenderisch.

**profusion** [prə'fju:ʒən], s. der Überfluß.

**progeny** ['prodʒəni], s. der Nachkomme; die Nachkommenschaft.

**prognosticate** [prog'nostikeit], v.a. vorhersagen.

**prognostication** [prognosti'keiʃən], s. die Voraussage.

**programme**, (Am.) **program** ['prougræm], s. das Programm.

**progress** ['prougres], s. der Fortschritt. — [pro'gres], v.n. fortschreiten, Fortschritte machen.

**progression** [pro'greʃən], s. (Maths.) die Reihe, Progression.

**progressive** [pro'gresiv], adj. fortschrittlich (modern); fortschreitend (continuous); progressiv.

**prohibit** [prou'hibit], v.a. verbieten.

**prohibition** [proui'biʃən], s. das Verbot.

**project** [prə'dʒekt], v.a. projizieren; entwerfen. — ['prɔdʒekt], s. das Projekt, der Plan.

**projectile** [prə'dʒektail], s. das Geschoß.

**projection** [prə'dʒekʃən], s. die Projektion (film); der Entwurf (plan); der Vorsprung (jutting out).

**proletarian** [prouli'tɛəriən], adj. proletarisch. — s. der Prolet(arier).

**prolific** [prə'lifik], adj. fruchtbar.

**prolix** ['prouliks], adj. weitschweifig.

**prologue** ['proulɔg], s. der Prolog.

**prolong** [prə'lɔŋ], v.a. verlängern, prolongieren.

**prominent** ['prɔminənt], adj. prominent, hervorragend.

**promiscuous** [prə'miskjuəs], adj. unterschiedslos (indiscriminate); vermischt (mixed).

**promise** ['prɔmis], v.a. versprechen. — v.n. Erwartungen erwecken. — s. das Versprechen.

**promissory** ['prɔmisəri], adj. versprechend; (Comm.) — note, der Schuldschein.

**promontory** ['prɔməntəri], s. das Vorgebirge.

**promote** [prə'mout], v.a. befördern; fördern (foster).

**promotion** [prə'mouʃən], s. die Beförderung (advancement); Förderung (fostering); (Am.) die Reklame (publicity).

**prompt** [prɔmpt], adj. prompt, pünktlich. — v.a. (Theat.) soufflieren; treiben (inspire).

**prompter** ['prɔmptə], s. (Theat.) der Souffleur.

**promptitude** ['prɔmptitju:d], s. die Promptheit, Pünktlichkeit.

**promulgate** ['prɔməlgeit], v.a. bekanntmachen, verbreiten.

**prone** [proun], adj. geneigt, neigend.

**prong** [prɔŋ], s. die Zinke, Gabel.

**pronominal** [pro'nɔminəl], adj. (Gram.) pronominal.

**pronoun** ['prounaun], s. das Fürwort, Pronomen.

**pronounce** [prə'nauns], v.a., v.n. aussprechen (words); feierlich erklären (proclaim).

**pronunciation** [prənʌnsi'eiʃən], s. die Aussprache.

**proof** [pru:f], s. der Beweis, die Probe; (Typ.) der Korrekturbogen. — v.a. (Engin., Chem.) imprägnieren.

**prop** [prɔp], s. die Stütze, der Stützpfahl. — v.a. stützen.

**propaganda** [prɔpə'gændə], s. die Propaganda, Reklame.

**propagate** ['prɔpəgeit], v.a. propagieren; (Bot.) fortpflanzen.

**propel** [prə'pel], v.a. forttreiben, vorwärtstreiben.

**propeller** [prə'pelə], s. der Propeller, die Schraube.

**propensity** [prə'pensiti], s. die Neigung, der Hang.

**proper** ['prɔpə], adj. schicklich (manners); eigentümlich, eigen (peculiar).

**property** ['prɔpəti], s. das Eigentum (possession); die Eigenschaft (quality).

**prophecy** ['prɔfisi], s. die Prophezeiung, Weissagung.

**prophesy** ['prɔfisai], v.a. prophezeien.

**propitiate** [prə'piʃieit], v.a. versöhnen.

**propitiation** [prəpiʃi'eiʃən], s. die Versöhnung.

**propitious** [prə'piʃəs], adj. gnädig, günstig, geneigt.

**proportion** [prə'pɔ:ʃən], s. das Verhältnis; die Proportion; der Anteil (portion); das Ebenmaß (in art).

**proportionate** [prə'pɔ:ʃənit], adj. im Verhältnis, verhältnismäßig, proportioniert.

**proposal** [prə'pouzəl], s. der Vorschlag, Antrag.

**propose** [prə'pouz], v.a. antragen, beantragen, vorschlagen. — v.n. — to a lady, einen Heiratsantrag machen.

**proposition** [prɔpə'ziʃən], s. der Vorschlag, Antrag; die Idee.

**propound** [prə'paund], v.a. vorlegen, vorbringen (a theory etc.).

**proprietor** [prə'praiətə], s. der Eigentümer.

**propriety** [prə'praiəti], s. die Schicklichkeit.

**propulsion** [prə'pʌlʃən], s. der Antrieb.

**prorogue** [prə'roug], v.a. vertagen.

**prosaic** [prə'zeiik], adj. prosaisch, nüchtern.

**proscribe** [pro'skraib], v.a. verbieten, ächten.

**proscription** [pro'skripʃən], s. die Verbannung, das Verbot.

**prose** [prouz], s. die Prosa.

**prosecute** ['prɔsikju:t], v.a. verfolgen; (Law) gerichtlich verfolgen, anklagen.

**prosecutor** ['prɔsikju:tə], s. (public) der Staatsanwalt; der Kläger.

**proselyte** ['prɔsəlait], s. der Neubekehrte, Proselyt.

**prospect** ['prɔspekt], s. die Aussicht; (pl.) die Aussichten, Chancen, f.pl. — [prɔs'pekt], v.n. suchen (for, nach, Dat.).

**prospectus** [prə'spektəs], s. der Prospekt.

**prosper** ['prɔspə], v.n. gedeihen, blühen. — v.a. segnen.

**prosperity** [prɔs'periti], s. der Wohlstand; der Reichtum; das Gedeihen (thriving).

**prosperous** ['prɔspərəs], adj. glücklich, wohlhabend.

**prostitute** ['prɔstitju:t], s. die Prostituierte, Dirne. — v.a. erniedrigen.

**prostrate** ['prɔstreit], adj. hingestreckt, niedergeworfen, fußfällig. — [prɔs'treit], v.a. niederwerfen.

prosy

**prosy** ['prouzi], *adj.* prosaisch, weitschweifig, langweilig.
**protect** [prə'tekt], *v.a.* beschützen.
**protection** [prə'tekʃən], *s.* der Schutz; die Protektion (*favour*).
**protective** [prə'tektiv], *adj.* Schutz-, schützend.
**protector** [prə'tektə], *s.* der Beschützer; (*Engin.*) der Schutz.
**protest** [prə'test], *v.a.,* *v.n.* protestieren, einwenden. — ['proutest], *s.* der Protest, Einspruch.
**Protestant** ['protistənt], *adj.* protestantisch. — *s.* der Protestant.
**protestation** [prɔtes'teiʃən], *s.* die Beteuerung, Verwahrung.
**protocol** ['proutəkɔl], *s.* das Protokoll.
**prototype** ['proutotaip], *s.* das Urbild, Modell, der Prototyp.
**protract** [prə'trækt], *v.a.* in die Länge ziehen; hinauszieehen.
**protractor** [prə'træktə], *s.* der Winkelmesser, Transporteur, die Schmiege.
**protrude** [prə'tru:d], *v.n.* herausragen, hervorstehen, vordringen.
**protuberance** [prə'tju:bərəns], *s.* der Höcker, der Auswuchs, die Protuberanz.
**proud** [praud], *adj.* stolz (*of,* auf, *Acc.*).
**prove** [pru:v], *v.a.* beweisen. — *v.n.* sich erweisen (*turn out*).
**provender** ['provində], *s.* das Viehfutter.
**proverb** ['provə:b], *s.* das Sprichwort.
**proverbial** [prə'və:biəl], *adj.* sprichwörtlich.
**provide** [prə'vaid], *v.a.,* *v.n.* vorsehen, versorgen, verschaffen.
**provided** [prə'vaidid], *conj.* vorausgesetzt.
**providence** ['providəns], *s.* die Vorsehung.
**provident** ['providənt], *adj.* vorsorglich.
**providential** [provi'denʃəl], *adj.* von der Vorsehung bestimmt.
**province** ['provins], *s.* die Provinz, das Gebiet (*also fig.*).
**provincial** [prə'vinʃəl], *adj.* ländlich, Provinz-; provinziell.
**provision** [prə'viʒən], *s.* die Versorgung (*supply*); der Vorrat (*stock*); (*pl.*) die Lebensmittel (*victuals*).
**provisional** [prə'viʒənəl], *adj.* vorläufig.
**proviso** [prə'vaizou], *s.* der Vorbehalt.
**provocation** [prɔvə'keiʃən], *s.* die Herausforderung.
**provoke** [prə'vouk], *v.a.* herausfordern, provozieren.
**prow** [prau], *s.* (*Naut.*) der Bug.
**prowess** ['praues], *s.* die Stärke (*physical*); die körperliche Tüchtigkeit; Tapferkeit.
**prowl** [praul], *v.n.* herumstreichen.
**proximity** [prɔk'simiti], *s.* die Nähe.
**proxy** ['prɔksi], *s.* der Stellvertreter.
**prudence** ['pru:dəns], *s.* die Klugheit, Vorsicht.
**prudent** ['pru:dənt], *adj.* klug, vorsichtig.

**prudery** ['pru:dəri], *s.* die Sprödigkeit.
**prudish** ['pru:diʃ], *adj.* prüde, spröde, zimperlich.
**prune** (1) [pru:n], *s.* (*Cul.*) die Backpflaume.
**prune** (2) [pru:n], *v.a.* beschneiden, stutzen.
**Prussian** ['prʌʃən], *adj.* preußisch; — *blue,* das Berlinerblau. — *s.* der Preuße.
**prussic** ['prʌsik], *adj.* blausauer; — *acid,* die Blausäure.
**pry** [prai], *v.n.* spähen, ausforschen.
**psalm** [sɑ:m], *s.* der Psalm.
**psychology** [sai'kɔlədʒi], *s.* die Psychologie.
**pub** [pʌb], *s.* das Wirtshaus, die Kneipe.
**puberty** ['pju:bəti], *s.* die Pubertät, Mannbarkeit.
**public** ['pʌblik], *adj.* öffentlich. — *s.* das Publikum; die Öffentlichkeit.
**publican** ['pʌblikən], *s.* der Gastwirt.
**publication** [pʌbli'keiʃən], *s.* die Veröffentlichung, Herausgabe.
**publicity** [pʌb'lisiti], *s.* die Werbung, die Reklame; — *manager,* der Reklamechef, Werbeleiter.
**publicize** ['pʌblisaiz], *v.a.* weithin bekannt machen, publizieren.
**publish** ['pʌbliʃ], *v.a.* veröffentlichen; verlegen (*books*); —*ing house,* der Verlag.
**publisher** ['pʌbliʃə], *s.* der Verleger.
**pucker** ['pʌkə], *v.a.* falten; runzeln (*wrinkle*). — *s.* die Falte.
**pudding** ['pudiŋ], *s.* der Pudding.
**puddle** [pʌdl], *s.* die Pfütze. — *v.a.* puddeln (*iron*).
**puerile** ['pjuərail], *adj.* kindisch, knabenhaft.
**puff** [pʌf], *v.a.,* *v.n.* puffen, paffen, blasen; —*ed-up,* aufgebläht, stolz. — *s.* der Windstoß; — *pastry,* der Blätterteig.
**pug** [pʌg], *s.* (*Zool.*) der Mops.
**pugnacious** [pʌg'neiʃəs], *adj.* kampfsüchtig, kampflustig.
**puisne** ['pju:ni], *adj.* (*Law*) jünger, Unter-.
**puissant** ['pwi:sənt], *adj.* mächtig, stark.
**puke** [pju:k], *v.n.* sich erbrechen.
**pull** [pul], *v.a.,* *v.n.* ziehen, reißen; zerren. — *s.* der Zug, Ruck.
**pullet** ['pulit], *s.* (*Orn.*) das Hühnchen.
**pulley** ['puli], *s.* der Flaschenzug.
**pulmonary, pulmonic** ['pʌlmənəri, pʌl'mɔnik], *adj.* Lungen-.
**pulp** [pʌlp], *s.* der Brei; das Fleisch (*of fruit*); das Mark (*marrow*); die Pulpa (*tooth*). — *v.a.* zerstampfen, zu Brei stampfen.
**pulpit** ['pulpit], *s.* (*Eccl.*) die Kanzel.
**pulsate** [pʌl'seit], *v.n.* pulsieren, schlagen.
**pulse** (1) [pʌls], *s.* der Puls.
**pulse** (2) [pʌls], *s.* (*Bot.*) die Hülsenfrüchte, *f. pl.*
**pulverize** ['pʌlvəraiz], *v.a.* zu Pulver stoßen, zerstoßen.

466

**pumice** ['pʌmis], *s.* der Bimsstein.
**pump** (1) [pʌmp], *s.* die Pumpe. — *v.a.*, *v.n.* pumpen; ausfragen (*question*).
**pump** (2) [pʌmp], *s.* der Tanzschuh (*dancing shoe*).
**pumpkin** ['pʌmpkin], *s.* (*Bot.*) der Kürbis.
**pun** [pʌn], *s.* das Wortspiel. — *v.n.* Wortspiele machen.
**Punch** [pʌntʃ]. das Kasperle; — *and Judy*, Hanswurst und seine Frau.
**punch** (1) [pʌntʃ], *v.a.* schlagen, boxen (*box*). — *s.* der Schlag (*hit*); der Faustschlag (*boxing*).
**punch** (2) [pʌntʃ], *v.a.* lochen (*card*). — *s.* der Pfriem (*tool*).
**punch** (3) [pʌntʃ], *s.* der Punsch (*drink*).
**punchy** ['pʌntʃi], *adj.* kurz, dick, untersetzt.
**punctilious** [pʌŋk'tiliəs], *adj.* sorgfältig, spitzfindig.
**punctual** ['pʌŋktjuəl], *adj.* pünktlich.
**punctuate** ['pʌŋktjueit], *v.a.* (*Gram.*) interpunktieren; ( *fig.*) betonen.
**punctuation** [pʌŋktju'eiʃən], *s.* (*Gram.*) die Interpunktion.
**puncture** ['pʌŋktʃə], *s.* (*Motor.*) der Reifendefekt, die Panne; (*Med.*) die Punktur, der Einstich. — *v.a.* (*Med.*) punktieren.
**pungent** ['pʌndʒənt], *adj.* scharf, stechend.
**punish** ['pʌniʃ], *v.a.* bestrafen (*s.o.*); strafen.
**punishable** ['pʌniʃəbl], *adj.* strafbar.
**punishment** ['pʌniʃmənt], *s.* die Strafe, Bestrafung.
**punt** [pʌnt],*s.* das kleine Boot, Flachboot.
**puny** ['pju:ni], *adj.* schwach, winzig.
**pup** [pʌp], *s.* der junge Hund; *be sold a* —, einen schlechten Kauf machen. — *v.n.* Junge werfen.
**pupil** (1) ['pju:pil], *s.* der Schüler.
**pupil** (2) ['pju:pil], *s.* die Pupille (*eye*).
**pupil(l)age** ['pju:pilidʒ], *s.* die Minderjährigkeit (*of minor*).
**puppet** ['pʌpit], *s.* die Puppe, Marionette; der Strohmann (*human tool*).
**puppy** ['pʌpi] *see* pup.
**purblind** ['pə:blaind], *adj.* halbblind.
**purchase** ['pə:tʃis], *s.* der Kauf, Einkauf. — *v.a.* kaufen.
**pure** ['pjuə], *adj.* pur, rein.
**purge** [pə:dʒ], *v.a.* reinigen. — *s.* die Reinigung; (*Pol.*) die Säuberung.
**purify** ['pjuərifai], *v.a.* läutern, reinigen.
**purl** (1) [pə:l], *s.* die Borte; (*knitting*) die Häkelkante.
**purl** (2) [pə:l], *v.n.* sich drehen, wirbeln; (*sl.*) umkippen.
**purl** (3) [pə:l], *s.* das Murmeln, Rieseln (*of brook*). — *v.n.* murmeln, rieseln.
**purloin** [pə:'bin], *v.a.* stehlen.
**purple** [pə:pl], *adj.* purpurn; — *patch*, die Glanzstelle. — *s.* der Purpur.
**purport** [pə:'pɔ:t], *v.a.* bedeuten, Sinn haben. — ['pə:pət], *s.* der Sinn, die Bedeutung.
**purpose** ['pə:pəs], *s.* die Absicht, der Zweck.

**purposeful** ['pə:pəsful], *adj.* zweckbewußt, energisch, zielbewußt.
**purr** [pə:], *v.n.* schnurren (*of cat*).
**purse** [pə:s], *s.* die Börse, Geldtasche; das Portemonnaie.
**pursuance** [pə'sju:əns], *s.* (*Law*) die Verfolgung, Ausführung.
**pursuant** [pə'sju:ənt], *adj.* (*Law*) zufolge, gemäß (*to, Dat.*).
**pursue** [pə'sju:], *v.a.* verfolgen.
**pursuit** [pə'sju:t], *s.* die Verfolgung; (*pl.*) die Geschäfte, *n. pl.*; Beschäftigung.
**purvey** [pə'vei], *v.a.* versorgen, liefern.
**purview** ['pə:vju:], *s.* der Spielraum; das Blickfeld.
**push** [puʃ], *v.a.* stoßen, drücken, schieben, drängen; *be —ed for*, in der Klemme sein. — *s.* der Stoß, Schub, das Drängen; *at a —*, wenn absolut nötig.
**pusillanimous** [pju:si'læniməs], *adj.* kleinmütig.
**puss, pussy** [pus, 'pusi], *s.* (*coll.*) die Katze, das Kätzchen, Miezchen.
**put** [put], *v.a. irr.* setzen (*set*),legen(*lay*), stellen (*stand*); — *off*, aufschieben, aus der Fassung bringen (*deflect*); — *on*, anziehen, auflegen; — *it on thickly*, es dick auftragen. — *v.n.* (*Naut.*) — *in*, anlegen.
**putrefy** ['pju:trifai], *v.a.*, *v.n.* faul werden (*rot*), verwesen.
**putrid** ['pju:trid], *adj.* faul (*rotten*).
**puttee** ['pʌti:], *s.* (*Mil.*) die Wickelgamasche.
**putty** ['pʌti], *s.* der Kitt.
**puzzle** [pʌzl], *s.* das Rätsel. — *v.a.* zu denken geben (*Dat.*).
**pygmy** ['pigmi], *s.* der Pygmäe.
**pyjamas**, (*Am.*) **pajamas** [pi'dʒɑ:məz, pə-], *s. pl.* der Schlafanzug.
**pyramid** ['pirəmid], *s.* die Pyramide.
**pyre** [paiə], *s.* der Scheiterhaufen.
**pyrotechnics** [paiərə'tekniks], *s. pl.* das Feuerwerk, die Feuerwerkskunst.
**python** ['paiθən], *s.* (*Zool.*) die Riesenschlange.

# Q

**Q** [kju:]. das Q.
**qua** [kwei], *conj.* als.
**quack** [kwæk], *v.n.* quaken; (*coll.*) quacksalbern. — *s.* der Quacksalber.
**quadrangle** ['kwɔdræŋgl], *s.* (*abbr.* **quad** [kwɔd], das Viereck; der Hof (*in college etc.*).
**quadrant** ['kwɔdrənt], *s.* der Quadrant, Viertelkreis; (*Engin.*) der Winkelmesser.
**quadrille** [kwɔ'dril], *s.* die Quadrille, der Kontertanz.

**quadruped** ['kwɔdruped], *s.* (*Zool.*) das vierfüßige Tier.
**quadruple** ['kwɔdrupl], *adj.* vierfach.
**quaff** [kwæf], *v.a.* schlucken. — *v.n.* zechen (*drink heavily*).
**quagmire** ['kwægmaiə], *s.* der Sumpf.
**quail** (1) [kweil], *s.* (*Orn.*) die Wachtel.
**quail** (2) [kweil], *v.n.* verzagen.
**quaint** [kweint], *adj.* seltsam, wunderlich, eigenartig.
**quake** [kweik], *v.n.* erzittern, beben.
**Quaker** ['kweikə], *s.* der Quäker.
**qualification** [kwɔlifi'keiʃən], *s.* die Befähigung. Qualifikation (*ability*); die Einschränkung (*proviso*).
**qualify** ['kwɔlifai], *v.a.* befähigen (*make able*); beschränken, mäßigen, qualifizieren (*modify*). — *v.n.* sich qualifizieren, das Studium abschließen.
**qualitative** ['kwɔlitətiv], *adj.* qualitätsmäßig, Wert-, qualitativ.
**quality** ['kwɔliti], *s.* die Qualität (*high class*); der Wert (*standard*).
**qualm** [kwɑ:m], *s.* der Skrupel.
**quantitative** ['kwɔntitətiv], *adj.* quantitativ.
**quantity** ['kwɔntiti], *s.* die Quantität, Menge.
**quantum** ['kwɔntəm], *s.* die Menge; das Quantum; — *theory*, die Quantentheorie.
**quarantine** ['kwɔrənti:n], *s.* die Quarantäne.
**quarrel** ['kwɔrəl], *s.* der Streit, Zwist. — *v.n.* streiten, zanken.
**quarry** (1) ['kwɔri], *s.* der Steinbruch.
**quarry** (2) ['kwɔri], *s.* die Beute (*prey*).
**quart** [kwɔ:t], *s.* das Viertelmaß (*1.15 litre*).
**quarter** ['kwɔ:tə] *s.* das Viertel(jahr); (*Arith.*) das Viertel (*also of town*); (*pl.*) das Quartier.
**quartermaster** ['kwɔ:təmɑ:stə], *s.* (*Mil.*) der Feldzeugmeister.
**quartet(te)** [kwɔ:'tet], *s.* das Quartett.
**quarto** ['kwɔ:tou], *s.* das Quartoformat.
**quartz** [kwɔ:ts], *s.* der Quartz.
**quash** [kwɔʃ], *v.a.* unterdrücken (*suppress*); (*Law*) annullieren.
**quaver** ['kweivə], *s.* (*Mus.*) die Achtelnote; der Triller (*trill*). — *v.n.* tremolieren, trillern.
**quay** [ki:], *s.* der Kai, Hafendamm.
**queen** [kwi:n], *s.* die Königin.
**queer** [kwiə], *adj.* seltsam, sonderlich.
**quell** [kwel], *v.a.* unterdrücken.
**quench** [kwentʃ], *v.a.* löschen; stillen (*thirst*).
**querulous** ['kweruləs], *adj.* mürrisch, jämmerlich; zänkisch.
**query** ['kwiəri], *s.* die Frage. — *v.a.* in Frage stellen.
**quest** [kwest], *s.* das Suchen, Streben; die Suche.
**question** ['kwestʃən], *s.* die Frage; — *mark*, das Fragezeichen. — *v.a.* fragen, in Frage stellen; ausfragen (*s.o.*).
**questionable** ['kwestʃənəbl], *adj.* zweifelhaft, fraglich, bedenklich.

**queue** [kju:], *s.* die Schlange, das Anstellen. — *v.n.* Schlange stehen.
**quibble** [kwibl], *s.* das Wortspiel, die Ausflucht. — *v.n.* um Worte streiten.
**quick** [kwik], *adj.* schnell (*fast*); lebendig (*live*).
**quicken** ['kwikən], *v.a.* beleben, anfeuern.
**quicklime** ['kwiklaim], *s.* der ungelöschte Kalk.
**quicksand** ['kwiksænd], *s.* der Flugsand.
**quicksilver** ['kwiksilvə], *s.* (*Chem.*) das Quecksilber.
**quid** (1) [kwid], *s.* (*sl.*) das Pfund Sterling.
**quid** (2) [kwid], *s.* (*Lat.*) etwas; — *pro quo*, Gleiches mit Gleichem.
**quiescence** [kwi'esəns], *s.* die Ruhe.
**quiet** ['kwaiət], *adj.* ruhig.
**quietism** ['kwaiətizm], *s.* der Quietismus.
**quietness** ['kwaiətnis], *s.* die Ruhe, Stille.
**quill** [kwil], *s.* der Federkiel, die Feder. — *v.a.* falten, fälteln.
**quilt** [kwilt], *s.* die Steppdecke.
**quince** [kwins], *s.* (*Bot.*) die Quitte.
**quinine** [kwi'ni:n], *s.* (*Med.*) das Chinin.
**quinquennial** [kwiŋ'kweniəl], *adj.* fünfjährig, fünfjährlich, alle fünf Jahre.
**quinsy** ['kwinzi], *s.* (*Med.*) die Bräune.
**quint** [kwint], *s.* (*Mus.*) die Quinte.
**quintessence** [kwin'tesəns], *s.* die Quintessenz, der Kern, der Inbegriff.
**quintuple** ['kwintjupl], *adj.* fünffach.
**quip** [kwip], *s.* die Stichelei; die witzige Bemerkung.
**quire** [kwaiə], *s.* das Buch Papier.
**quirk** [kwə:k], *s.* die (unerwartete) Wendung; Spitzfindigkeit.
**quit** [kwit], *v.a.*, *v.n.* verlassen; weggehen; (*Am.*) aufhören. — *adj.* (*pl.*) (**quits**) quitt, bezahlt.
**quite** [kwait], *adv.* ganz, völlig.
**quiver** (1) ['kwivə], *s.* der Köcher.
**quiver** (2) ['kwivə], *v.n.* erzittern, schauern.
**quiz** [kwiz], *s.* das Fragespiel, Quizprogramm (*Radio etc.*).
**quoit** [kɔit], *s.* die Wurfscheibe.
**quorum** ['kwɔ:rəm], *s.* die beschlußfähige Anzahl.
**quota** ['kwoutə], *s.* die Quote.
**quotation** [kwo'teiʃen], *s.* das Zitat; (*Comm.*) der Kostenanschlag, die Notierung.
**quote** [kwout], *v.a.* zitieren; (*Comm.*) einen Preis zitieren, notieren.

# R

**R** [ɑ:(r)]. das R.
**rabbet** ['ræbit], *s.* die Fuge, Nute. — *v.a.* einfugen.

**rabbi** ['ræbai], *s.* (*Rel.*) der Rabbiner.
**rabbit** ['ræbit], *s.* (*Zool.*) das Kaninchen.
**rabble** [ræbl], *s.* der Pöbel.
**rabid** ['ræbid], *adj.* wütend, rasend.
**race** (1) [reis], *s.* die Rasse; das Geschlecht (*stock*).
**race** (2) [reis], *s.* das Rennen (*horses etc.*); der Wettlauf (*run*); — *course*, die Rennbahn. — *v.a., v.n.* um die Wette laufen.
**racial** ['reiʃəl], *adj.* rassisch.
**raciness** ['reisinis], *s.* das Rassige, die Urwüchsigkeit.
**rack** [ræk], *s.* die Folterbank; das Reck (*gymnasium*); (*Railw.*) das Gepäcknetz. — *v.a.* recken, strecken; — *o.'s brains*, sich den Kopf zerbrechen.
**racket** (1), **racquet** ['rækit], *s.* der Tennisschläger.
**racket** (2) ['rækit], *s.* der Lärm (*noise, din*).
**racket** (3) ['rækit], *s.* (*coll.*) der Schwindel.
**racketeer** [ræki'tiə], *s.* der Schwindler.
**racy** ['reisi], *adj.* stark; pikant.
**radar**, ['reidɑ:], *s.* das Radar.
**radiance** ['reidiəns], *s.* der Glanz, das Strahlen.
**radiant** ['reidiənt], *adj.* strahlend.
**radiate** ['reidieit], *v.a., v.n.* strahlen, ausstrahlen.
**radiator** ['reidieitə], *s.* der Heizapparat, Heizkörper; (*Motor.*) der Kühler.
**radical** ['rædikəl], *adj.* (*Pol.*) radikal; gründlich (*thorough*). — *s.* (*Pol.*) der Radikale; (*Phonet.*) der Grundlaut, Wurzellaut.
**radio** ['reidiou], *s.* das Radio, der Rundfunk.
**radioactive** [reidiou'æktiv], *adj.* radioaktiv.
**radish** ['rædiʃ], *s.* (*Bot.*) der Rettich.
**radius** ['reidiəs], *s.* der Radius, Halbmesser; (*Phys., Maths.*) der Strahl (*line*).
**raffle** [ræfl], *s.* die Auslosung. — *v.a.* auslosen, ausspielen.
**raft** [rɑ:ft], *s.* das Floß.
**rafter** ['rɑ:ftə], *s.* der Dachsparren.
**rag** (1) [ræg], *s.* der Lumpen.
**rag** (2) [ræg], *v.a.* necken, zum Besten haben (*tease*).
**ragamuffin** ['rægəmʌfin], *s.* der Lumpenkerl.
**rage** [reidʒ], *s.* die Wut, Raserei; die Manie, Mode (*fashion*). — *v.n.* wüten, rasen.
**ragged** ['rægid], *adj.* zerlumpt; zackig, rauh (*rough*).
**ragout** [ra'gu:], *s.* (*Cul.*) das Ragout.
**raid** [reid], *s.* der Streifzug, die Razzia; der Angriff. — *v.a.* überfallen.
**rail** (1) [reil], *s.* (*Railw.*) die Schiene; *by* —, mit der Eisenbahn.
**rail** (2) [reil], *v.n.* schmähen; spotten (*Genit.*).
**railing** ['reiliŋ], *s.* das Geländer, Gitter.
**raillery** ['reiləri], *s.* die Spöttelei, das Schmähen.

**railway**, (*Am.*) **railroad** ['reilwei, 'reilroud], *s.* die Eisenbahn.
**raiment** ['reimənt], *s.* (*Poet.*) die Kleidung.
**rain** [rein], *s.* der Regen. — *v.n.* regnen.
**rainbow** ['reinbou], *s.* der Regenbogen.
**raincoat** ['reinkout], *s.* der Regenmantel.
**raise** [reiz], *v.a.* heben (*lift*); steigern (*prices*); aufbringen (*army, money*); züchten (*breed*); aufziehen (*children*). — *s.* (*Am.*) die Steigerung, Erhöhung (*salary*).
**raisin** ['reizin], *s.* (*Bot.*) die Rosine.
**rake** (1) [reik], *s.* der Rechen (*tool*). — *v.a.* zusammenrechen, harken; bestreichen (*fire at*).
**rake** (2) [reik], *s.* der Schlemmer (*roué*).
**rakish** ['reikiʃ], *adj.* liederlich.
**rally** ['ræli], *v.a.* sammeln, versammeln. — *v.n.* sich versammeln, sich scharen. — *s.* die Massenversammlung, Kundgebung; das Treffen.
**ram** [ræm], *s.* der Widder; (*Mil.*) die Ramme. — *v.a.* rammen.
**ramble** [ræmbl], *v.n.* (im Grünen) wandern; herumschweifen; einen Ausflug machen. — *s.* der Ausflug.
**rambler** ['ræmblə], *s.* der Wanderer (*hiker*); (*Bot.*) die Heckenrose.
**ramification** [ræmifi'keiʃən], *s.* die Verzweigung, Verästelung (*also fig.*); (*pl.*) Zweige, *m. pl.* (*also fig.*).
**ramp** [ræmp], *v.n.* sich ranken (*of plants*). — *s.* die Rampe.
**rampant** ['ræmpənt], *adj.* zügellos, grassierend (*wild*); (*Her.*) sich bäumend.
**rampart** ['ræmpɑ:t], *s.* der Wall.
**ramshackle** ['ræmʃækl], *adj.* wackelig, baufällig.
**rancid** ['rænsid], *adj.* ranzig.
**rancour** ['ræŋkə], *s.* der Groll, die Erbitterung.
**random** ['rændəm], *s. at* —, aufs Geratewohl. — *adj.* zufällig, Zufalls-.
**range** [reindʒ], *s.* die Reihe (*row, series*); (*Geog.*) die Bergkette; der Küchenherd (*stove*); (*Mil.*) die Schießstätte (*shooting ground*); die Schußweite, Reichweite (*distance*). — *v.n.* sich reihen; sich erstrecken (*stretch*). — *v.a.* rangieren, anordnen, durchstreifen.
**rangefinder** ['reindʒfaində], *s.* (*Phot.*) der Entfernungsmesser.
**ranger** ['reindʒə], *s.* der Förster, Forstgehilfe; (*Mil.*) der leichte Reiter.
**rank** (1) [ræŋk], *s.* die Klasse; der Rang (*order*); — *and file*, die Mannschaft (*of members*); die Mitgliedschaft, Masse. — *v.n.* sich reihen; gelten.
**rank** (2) [ræŋk], *adj.* übermäßig, üppig, allzu stark; ranzig (*of fat etc.*).
**rankle** [ræŋkl], *v.n.* nagen.
**ransack** ['rænsæk], *v.a.* plündern.
**ransom** ['rænsəm], *s.* das Lösegeld; *hold to* —, (gegen Lösegeld) gefangen halten. — *v.a.* loskaufen.

# rant

**rant** [rænt], *v.n.* wüten; großtun; groß-
sprechen.
**rap** [ræp], *v.a., v.n.* schlagen, klopfen.
**rapacious** [rəˈpeiʃəs], *adj.* raubgierig.
**rape** (1) [reip], *v.a.* vergewaltigen. — *s.*
die Vergewaltigung.
**rape** (2) [reip], *s.* (*Bot.*) der Raps.
**rapid** [ˈræpid], *adj.* rasch, schnell,
reißend (*river*). — *s.* (*pl.*) die Stromschnelle.
**rapier** [ˈreipiə], *s.* der Degen; (*fencing*)
das Rapier.
**rapine** [ˈræpain], *s.* (*Poet.*) der Raub.
**rapt** [ræpt], *adj.* entzückt; versunken.
**rapture** [ˈræptʃə], *s.* das Entzücken.
**rare** (1) [reə], *adj.* selten.
**rare** (2) [reə], *adj.* (*meat*) rar.
**rarity** [ˈreəriti], *s.* die Seltenheit.
**rascal** [ˈrɑːskəl], *s.* der Schurke.
**rash** (1) [ræʃ], *adj.* unbesonnen.
**rash** (2) [ræʃ], *s.* der Ausschlag (*skin*).
**rasher** [ˈræʃə], *s.* die Speckschnitte.
**rasp** [rɑːsp], *s.* die Raspel, Feile. —
*v.a., v.n.* raspeln; heiser sein (*speech*).
**raspberry** [ˈrɑːzbəri], *s.* (*Bot.*) die
Himbeere.
**rat** [ræt], *s.* (*Zool.*) die Ratte; (*fig.*) der
Verräter.
**ratable** [ˈreitəbl], *adj.* steuerpflichtig.
**rate** (1) [reit], *s.* das Mass; der Tarif;
die Geschwindigkeit (*speed*); Gemein-
deabgabe (*tax*); das Verhältnis (*proportion*). — *v.a.* schätzen (*estimate*);
(*Am.*) einschätzen, halten für.
**rate** (2) [reit], *v.a.* schelten (*berate*).
**rather** [ˈrɑːðə], *adv.* vielmehr, eher,
lieber (*in comparisons*); — *good*, ziemlich gut.
**ratification** [rætifiˈkeiʃən], *s.* die Bestätigung; (*Pol.*) die Ratifizierung.
**ratify** [ˈrætifai], *v.a.* bestätigen; (*Pol.*)
ratifizieren.
**ratio** [ˈreiʃiou], *s.* das Verhältnis.
**ration** [ˈræʃən], *s.* die Ration.
**rational** [ˈræʃənəl], *adj.* Vernunfts-,
rationell, vernunftgemäß.
**rattle** [rætl], *s.* das Geklapper (*noise*);
die Klapper (*toy etc.*); *death* —, das
Todesröcheln. — *v.a.* klappern,
Lärm machen; (*fig.*) aus der Fassung
bringen; — *off*, herunterleiern. —
*v.n.* rasseln, klappern.
**raucous** [ˈrɔːkəs], *adj.* heiser, rauh.
**ravage** [ˈrævidʒ], *v.a.* verheeren. — *s.*
(*pl.*) die Verheerung, Verwüstung.
**rave** [reiv], *v.n.* vernarrt sein (*about*, in);
schwärmen (*für*).
**raven** [reivn], *s.* (*Orn.*) der Rabe.
**ravenous** [ˈrævənəs], *adj.* gefräßig,
gierig.
**ravine** [rəˈviːn], *s.* die Schlucht.
**ravish** [ˈræviʃ], *v.a.* schänden, entehren; (*delight*) entzücken.
**raw** [rɔː], *adj.* rauh (*rough*); roh (*meat*);
jung, grün (*novice*); *a* — *deal*, die
unfaire Behandlung.
**ray** (1) [rei], *s.* (*Phys.*) der Strahl. —
*v.n.* strahlen.
**ray** (2) [rei], *s.* (*Zool.*) der Rochen.
**raze** [reiz], *v.a.* radieren (*erase*); zer-

stören (*destroy*).
**razor** [ˈreizə], *s.* der Rasierapparat;
— *strop*, der Streichriemen.
**re\*** [riː], *pref.* wieder —, noch einmal,
zurück-.

\* In the following pages, only those
compounds are listed in which the
meaning is different from the root
word or where no simple stem exists.

**reach** [riːtʃ], *v.a.* reichen, erlangen
(*attain*); reichen (*hand*); erreichen.
— *s.* der Bereich, ( *fig.*) die Weite.
**react** [riˈækt], *v.n.* reagieren (*to*, auf,
*Acc.*).
**read** (1) [riːd], *v.a., v.n. irr.* lesen; anzeigen (*meter etc.*); — *for a degree,*
studieren.
**read** (2) [red], *adj. well*—, belesen.
**readable** [ˈriːdəbl], *adj.* gut zu lesen,
lesenswert; leserlich (*legible*).
**reader** [ˈriːdə], *s.* der Leser; (*Univ.*)
der außerordentliche Professor; ( *fig.*)
das Lesebuch.
**readiness** [ˈredinis], *s.* die Bereitschaft,
Bereitwilligkeit.
**ready** [ˈredi], *adj.* bereit, fertig; prompt;
— *money*, das Bargeld.
**real** [riəl], *adj.* wirklich, wahr, tatsächlich; echt; — *estate*, der Grundbesitz.
**realistic** [riəˈlistik], *adj.* realistisch.
**reality** [riˈæliti], *s.* die Wirklichkeit.
**realize** [ˈriəlaiz], *v.a.* (*understand*) begreifen; (*sell*) veräußern; verwirklichen.
**realm** [relm], *s.* das Reich.
**reap** [riːp], *v.a.* ernten.
**rear** (1) [riə], *adj.* hinter, nach-. — *s.*
der Hintergrund; (*Mil.*) die Nachhut.
**rear** (2) [riə], *v.a.* aufziehen, erziehen
(*bring up*). — *v.n.* sich bäumen.
**reason** [ˈriːzən], *s.* die Ursache, der
Grund (*cause*); die Vernunft (*reasonableness*). — *v.n.* argumentieren,
debattieren.
**reasonable** [ˈriːzənəbl], *adj.* vernünftig;
verständig.
**reasonably** [ˈriːzənəbli], *adv.* ziemlich,
verhältnismäßig.
**rebate** [ˈriːbeit], *s.* der Rabatt.
**rebel** [rebl], *s.* der Rebell. — [riˈbel],
*v.n.* sich empören.
**rebound** [riˈbaund], *v.n.* zurückprallen.
— [ˈriːbaund], *s.* der Rückprall.
**rebuff** [riˈbʌf], *s.* die Abweisung. —
*v.a.* abweisen, zurückweisen.
**rebuke** [riˈbjuːk], *v.a.* zurechtweisen,
tadeln. — *s.* der Tadel, die Kritik (an).
**rebut** [riˈbʌt], *v.a.* zurückweisen.
**rebuttal** [riˈbʌtl], *s.* die Widerlegung.
**recalcitrant** [riˈkælsitrənt], *adj.* widerspenstig, störrisch.
**recall** [riˈkɔːl], *v.a.* zurückrufen; (*remember*) sich erinnern.
**recant** [riˈkænt], *v.a., v.n.* widerrufen.
**recapitulate** [riːkəˈpitjuleit], *v.a.* re-
kapitulieren, wiederholen.
**recast** [riːˈkɑːst], *v.a.* neu fassen, umarbeiten.
**recede** [riˈsiːd], *v.n.* zurückgehen,
heruntergehen (*prices etc.*).

**receipt** [ri'si:t], *s.* die Empfangsbestätigung, Quittung. — *v.a.* quittieren.
**receive** [ri'si:v], *v.a.* erhalten, empfangen; (*Law*) Diebesgut annehmen.
**receiver** [ri'si:və], *s.* der Empfänger; (*Law*) der Hehler; (*Telephone*) der Hörer; (*Rad.*) der Apparat.
**recent** ['ri:sənt], *adj.* jüngst, neuest.
**recently** ['ri:səntli], *adv.* vor kurzem.
**reception** [ri'sepʃən], *s.* der Empfang.
**receptive** [ri'septiv], *adj.* empfänglich.
**recess** [ri'ses], *s.* (*Parl.*) die Ferien, *pl.*; die Pause; die Nische (*nook*).
**recession** [ri'seʃən], *s.* (*Econ.*) die Rezession, die Baisse.
**recipe** ['resipi], *s.* (*Cul.*) das Rezept.
**recipient** [ri'sipiənt], *s.* der Empfänger (*of donation etc.*).
**reciprocal** [ri'siprəkəl], *adj.* gegenseitig, wechselseitig.
**reciprocate** [ri'siprəkeit], *v.a.,* *v.n.* erwidern, vergelten.
**recital** [ri'saitl], *s.* der Vortrag; (*Mus.*) das Solokonzert, Kammerkonzert.
**recite** [ri'sait], *v.a.* vortragen; (*story*) erzählen, aufsagen.
**reckless** ['reklis], *adj.* leichtsinnig.
**reckon** ['rekən], *v.n.* rechnen (*on*, mit, *Dat.*); dafür halten, denken (*think*).
**reclamation** [reklə'meiʃən], *s.* (*Agr.*) die Urbarmachung; (*fig.*) die Beschwerde, Reklamation.
**recline** [ri'klain], *v.n.* sich zurücklehnen.
**recluse** [ri'klu:s], *s.* der Einsiedler.
**recognition** [rekəg'niʃən], *s.* die Anerkennung.
**recognize** ['rekəgnaiz], *v.a.* anerkennen (als) (*acknowledge*); erkennen (*know again*).
**recoil** [ri'kɔil], *v.n.* zurückprallen, zurückfahren.
**recollect** [rekə'lekt], *v.a.* sich erinnern (an, *Acc.*).
**recollection** [rekə'lekʃən], *s.* die Erinnerung, das Gedächtnis.
**recommend** [rekə'mend], *v.a.* empfehlen.
**recompense** ['rekəmpens], *v.a.* vergelten, entschädigen, belohnen.
**reconcile** ['rekənsail], *v.a.* versöhnen.
**reconciliation** [rekənsili'eiʃən], *s.* die Versöhnung.
**recondite** ['rekəndait], *adj.* dunkel, verborgen, wenig bekannt.
**reconnoitre** [rekə'nɔitə], *v.a.* auskundschaften.
**record** [ri'kɔ:d], *v.a.* notieren, eintragen (*enter*), festhalten; aufnehmen (*tape etc.*). — ['rekɔ:d], *s.* die Aufzeichnung (*in writing*); die Schallplatte (*gramophone*); (*Sports*) der Rekord.
**recorder** [ri'kɔ:də], *s.* der Protokollführer; (*Law*) der Richter; Syndikus, Registrator; (*Mus.*) die Blockflöte.
**recount** [ri'kaunt], *v.a.* erzählen.
**recourse** [ri'kɔ:s], *s.* die Zuflucht.
**recover** [ri'kʌvə], *v.a.* wiedererlangen. — *v.n.* sich erholen.

**recovery** [ri'kʌvəri], *s.* die Wiedererlangung (*regaining*); (*Med.*) die Genesung, Erholung.
**recreation** [rekri'eiʃən], *s.* die Erholung.
**recrimination** [rekrimi'neiʃən], *s.* die Gegenklage.
**recruit** [ri'kru:t], *v.a.* rekrutieren, anwerben. — *s.* der Rekrut.
**rectangle** ['rektæŋgl], *s.* das Rechteck.
**rectify** ['rektifai], *v.a.* richtigstellen; (*Elec.*) gleichrichten, umformen.
**rectilinear** [rekti'liniə], *adj.* geradlinig.
**rectitude** ['rektitju:d], *s.* die Aufrichtigkeit.
**rector** ['rektə], *s.* (*Eccl.*) der Pfarrer; der Rektor, Vorstand (*institution*).
**recuperate** [ri'kju:pəreit], *v.n.* sich erholen.
**recur** [ri'kə:], *v.n.* sich wieder ereignen, sich wiederholen.
**recurrence** [ri'kʌrəns], *s.* die Wiederholung.
**red** [red], *adj.* rot; — *hot*, glühend heiß.
**redbreast** ['redbrest], *s.* (*Orn.*) das Rotkehlchen.
**redeem** [ri'di:m], *v.a.* erlösen.
**redemption** [ri'dempʃən], *s.* die Erlösung.
**redolent** ['redolənt], *adj.* duftend.
**redound** [ri'daund], *v.n.* gereichen, sich erweisen.
**redress** [ri'dres], *v.a.* abhelfen (*Dat.*); wieder herstellen. — *s.* die Abhilfe.
**reduce** [ri'dju:s], *v.a.* vermindern, herabsetzen; (*fig.*) degradieren. — *v.n.* (*weight*) abnehmen.
**reduction** [ri'dʌkʃən], *s.* die Herabsetzung (*price etc.*); die Verminderung (*decrease*); (*Chem.*) die Reduktion.
**redundant** [ri'dʌndənt], *adj.* überflüssig.
**reduplicate** [ri:'dju:plikeit], *v.a.* verdoppeln.
**reed** [ri:d], *s.* (*Bot.*) das Schilfrohr; (*Mus.*) die Rohrpfeife.
**reef** [ri:f], *s.* das Riff, Felsenriff; (*Naut.*) das Reff.
**reek** [ri:k], *v.n.* rauchen, dampfen, riechen. — *s.* der Rauch, Dampf, der Gestank.
**reel** [ri:l], *s.* die Spule, Rolle, Haspel. — *v.a. — off*, abrollen; (*fig.*) mechanisch hersagen. — *v.n.* taumeln.
**refectory** [ri'fektəri], *s.* der Speisesaal; das Refektorium (*in monastery etc.*).
**refer** [ri'fə:], *v.n. — to s.th.*, weiterleiten; überweisen; — *to*, sich beziehen (auf, *Acc.*).
**referee** [refə'ri:], *s.* der Referent; (*Sport*) der Schiedsrichter.
**reference** ['refərəns], *s. with — to*, in or mit Bezug auf; die Referenz, Empfehlung; Verweisung (*to*, auf); — *library*, die Nachschlagebibliothek; — *index*, das (Nachschlags)verzeichnis.
**refine** [ri'fain], *v.a.* (*Chem.*) raffinieren; (*manners*) verfeinern; (*products*) läutern, veredeln.

**reflect** [riˈflekt], *v.a.* widerspiegeln (*mirror*); ein Licht werfen (auf, *Acc.*). — *v.n.* — *on,* überlegen (*think over*).

**reflection, reflexion** [riˈflekʃən], *s.* die Überlegung, das Nachdenken; die Spiegelung, Reflexion.

**reform** [riːˈfɔːm], *s.* die Reform, Verbesserung. — *v.a.* reformieren; [ˈriːˈfɔːm] (sich) neu bilden. — *v.n.* sich bessern.

**refractory** [riˈfræktəri], *adj.* widerspenstig.

**refrain** (1) [riˈfrein], *v.n.* — *from,* sich enthalten (*Genit.*); absehen von (*Dat.*).

**refrain** (2) [riˈfrein], *s.* (*Mus., Poet.*) der Kehrreim.

**refresh** [riˈfreʃ], *v.a.* erfrischen.

**refrigerator** [riˈfridʒəreitə], *s.* der Kühlschrank.

**refuge** [ˈrefjuːdʒ], *s.* die Zuflucht.

**refugee** [refjuˈdʒiː], *s.* der Flüchtling. — *adj.* Flüchtlings-.

**refund** [riːˈfʌnd], *v.a.* ersetzen, zurückzahlen. — [ˈriːfʌnd], *s.* die Rückvergütung.

**refusal** [riˈfjuːzəl], *s.* die Verweigerung.

**refuse** [riˈfjuːz], *v.a.* verweigern, abschlagen. — *v.n.* — *to,* sich weigern. — [ˈrefjuːs], *s.* der Müll.

**refute** [riˈfjuːt], *v.a.* widerlegen.

**regal** [ˈriːgəl], *adj.* königlich.

**regale** [riˈgeil], *v.a.* bewirten.

**regalia** [riˈgeiliə], *s. pl.* die Kronjuwelen, *n. pl.*; (*fig.*) die Amtstracht, der Amtsschmuck.

**regard** [riˈgɑːd], *v.a.* ansehen (*as,* als); beachten (*heed*); *as* —*s,* was ... betrifft. — *s.* die Hochachtung, Achtung (*esteem*); (*pl.*) die Grüsse, *m. pl.*

**regarding** [riˈgɑːdiŋ], *prep.* bezüglich, mit Bezug auf.

**regardless** [riˈgɑːdlis], *adj.* rücksichtslos, ohne Rücksicht auf.

**regency** [ˈriːdʒənsi], *s.* die Regentschaft.

**regent** [ˈriːdʒənt], *s.* der Regent.

**regiment** [ˈredʒimənt], *s.* (*Mil.*) das Regiment. — [-ment], *v.a.* (*fig.*) regimentieren.

**region** [ˈriːdʒən], *s.* die Gegend.

**regional** [ˈriːdʒənəl], *adj.* örtlich, lokal, Bezirks-.

**register** [ˈredʒistə], *s.* das Register, die Liste. — *v.n.* sich eintragen.

**registrar** [ˈredʒistrɑː], *s.* der Registrator; der Standesbeamte (*births etc.*); der Kanzleidirektor (*institution*).

**registry** [ˈredʒistri], *s.* die Registratur.

**regret** [riˈgret], *v.a.* bereuen, bedauern. — *s.* die Reue; das Bedauern (*in formal apology*); *with* —, mit Bedauern.

**regular** [ˈregjulə], *adj.* regelmäßig; (*Am.*) anständig. — *s.* (*Mil.*) der Berufssoldat.

**regulate** [ˈregjuleit], *v.a.* regulieren, regeln.

**regulation** [regjuˈleiʃən], *s.* die Regelung; die Anordung (*order*).

**rehabilitate** [riːhəˈbiliteit], *v.a.* rehabilitieren.

**rehearsal** [riˈhəːsl], *s.* (*Theat., Mus.*) die Probe.

**rehearse** [riˈhəːs], *v.a.* proben, wiederholen.

**reign** [rein], *v.n.* herrschen, regieren. — *s.* die Herrschaft, Regierung.

**rein** [rein], *s.* der Zügel, der Zaum.

**reindeer** [ˈreindiə], *s.* (*Zool.*) das Ren, Rentier.

**reinforce** [riːinˈfɔːs], *v.a.* betonen, verstärken.

**reinforced** [riːinˈfɔːsd], *adj.* verstärkt; — *concrete,* der Eisenbeton.

**reject** [riˈdʒekt], *v.a.* ausschlagen, verwerfen.

**rejection** [riˈdʒekʃən], *s.* die Ablehnung, Verwerfung.

**rejoice** [riˈdʒɔis], *v.n.* sich freuen.

**rejoin** [ˈriːˈdʒɔin], *v.a.* wiedervereinigen. — [riˈdʒɔin], *v.n.* erwidern.

**rejoinder** [riˈdʒɔində], *s.* die Erwiderung.

**relapse** [riˈlæps], *s.* der Rückfall. — *v.n.* fallen, zurückfallen.

**relation** [riˈleiʃən], *s.* die Beziehung (*connexion*); der, die Verwandte (*relative*); (*pl.*) die Verwandtschaft (*family*).

**relative** [ˈrelətiv], *adj.* relativ; verhältnismäßig (*in proportion*). — *s.* der, die Verwandte.

**relax** [riˈlæks], *v.n.* sich ausruhen; nachlassen. — *v.a.* entspannen.

**relay** [riˈlei], *v.a.* (*Rad.*) übertragen. — [ˈriːlei], *s.* — *race,* der Staffellauf.

**release** [riˈliːs], *v.a.* freilassen, freisetzen (*prisoner*); freigeben (*news*). — *s.* die Freigabe (*news etc.*); die Freisetzung (*liberation*).

**relegate** [ˈreligeit], *v.a.* verweisen, zurückweisen.

**relent** [riˈlent], *v.n.* nachgeben.

**relentless** [riˈlentlis], *adj.* unerbittlich, unnachgiebig.

**relevance** [ˈreləvəns], *s.* die Wichtigkeit.

**relevant** [ˈreləvənt], *adj.* wichtig, sachdienlich.

**reliable** [riˈlaiəbl], *adj.* verläßlich, zuverlässig.

**reliance** [riˈlaiəns], *s.* das Vertrauen.

**relic** [ˈrelik], *s.* das Überbleibsel; das Andenken; (*Eccl.*) die Reliquie.

**relief** (1) [riˈliːf], *s.* die Erleichterung, Linderung (*easement*); die Ablösung (*guard etc.*); die Aushilfe (*extra staff etc.*).

**relief** (2) [riˈliːf], *s.* (*Art*) das Relief.

**relieve** [riˈliːv], *v.a.* erleichtern; lindern (*pain*); ablösen (*from duty*).

**religion** [riˈlidʒən], *s.* die Religion.

**religious** [riˈlidʒəs], *adj.* religiös, gläubig, fromm.

**relinquish** [riˈliŋkwiʃ], *v.a.* verlassen, aufgeben.

**relish** ['reliʃ], v.a. Geschmack finden an. — v.n. schmecken. — s. der Geschmack, die Würze.

**reluctance** [ri'lʌktəns], s. der Widerwille, das Zögern.

**reluctant** [ri'lʌktənt], adj. widerwillig, widerstrebend.

**rely** [ri'lai], v.n. sich verlassen (on, auf); vertrauen (auf).

**remain** [ri'mein], v.n. bleiben, zurückbleiben, übrigbleiben.

**remainder** [ri'meində], s. der Rest.

**remand** [ri'mɑ:nd], v.a. — in custody, in die Untersuchungshaft zurückschicken. — s. — home, die Besserungsanstalt.

**remark** [ri'mɑ:k], s. die Bemerkung. — v.a. bemerken.

**remarkable** [ri'mɑ:kəbl], adj. bemerkenswert, außerordentlich.

**remedial** [rə'mi:diəl], adj. Heil-, abhelfend.

**remedy** ['remədi], s. das Heilmittel, Hilfsmittel. — v.a. abhelfen (Dat.).

**remember** [ri'membə], v.a. sich erinnern an; — s.o. to s.o. else, jemanden von jemandem grüßen lassen.

**remembrance** [ri'membrəns], s. die Erinnerung.

**remind** [ri'maind], v.a. erinnern (of, an), mahnen.

**reminiscence** [remi'nisəns], s. die Erinnerung.

**remiss** [ri'mis], adj. nachlässig.

**remission** [ri'miʃən], s. der Nachlaß; (Rel.) die Vergebung (of sins).

**remit** [ri'mit], v.a. (Comm.) überweisen, einsenden; erlassen (forgive).

**remittance** [ri'mitəns], s. (Comm.) die Rimesse, die Überweisung.

**remnant** ['remnənt], s. der Überrest.

**remonstrate** ['remənstreit], v.n. Vorstellungen machen.

**remorse** [ri'mɔ:s], s. die Reue.

**remote** [ri'mout], adj. fern, entlegen.

**removal** [ri'mu:vəl], s. das Wegschaffen (taking away); die Übersiedlung, der Umzug.

**remove** [ri'mu:v], v.a. entfernen. — v.n. umziehen. — s. (Sch.) die Versetzungsklasse; der Verwandtschaftsgrad (relationship).

**removed** [ri'mu:vd], adj. entfernt; cousin once —, der Vetter ersten Grades.

**remuneration** [rimju:nə'reiʃən], s. die Besoldung, Entlöhnung.

**rend** [rend], v.a. reißen, zerreißen.

**render** ['rendə], v.a. leisten (service); übersetzen (translate); wiedergeben; (Comm.) — account, Rechnung vorlegen.

**rendering** ['rendəriŋ], s. die Wiedergabe, der Vortrag (of song etc.); (Comm.) der Vorlage; die Übersetzung (translation).

**renegade** ['renigeid], s. der Abtrünnige.

**renewal** [ri'nju:əl], s. die Erneuerung; die Verlängerung (extension).

**rennet** ['renit], s. das Lab.

**renounce** [ri'nauns], v.a. entsagen (Dat.), verzichten auf (Acc.).

**renown** [ri'naun], s. der Ruhm.

**rent** (1) [rent], v.a. mieten, pachten. — s. die Miete, Pacht (of land, farm).

**rent** (2) [rent], s. der Riß (tear).

**rental** [rentl], s. die Miete.

**renunciation** [rinʌnsi'eiʃən], s. die Entsagung, der Verzicht.

**repair** [ri'pɛə], v.a. ausbessern, reparieren. — s. die Reparatur; beyond —, nicht reparierbar.

**reparations** [repə'reiʃənz], s. pl. (Pol.) die Reparationen, Wiedergutmachungskosten, f. pl.

**repartee** [repɑ:'ti:], s. die treffende Antwort.

**repast** [ri'pɑ:st], s. die Mahlzeit.

**repeal** [ri'pi:l], v.a. (Parl.) aufheben, widerrufen. — s. die Aufhebung.

**repeat** [ri'pi:t], v.a. wiederholen.

**repent** [ri'pent], v.a. bereuen.

**repercussion** [ri:pə'kʌʃən], s. der Rückstoß, die Rückwirkung.

**repertory** ['repətəri], s. (Theat. etc.) das Repertoire, der Spielplan.

**repetition** [repi'tiʃən], s. die Wiederholung.

**replace** [ri:'pleis], v.a. ersetzen.

**replete** [ri'pli:t], adj. voll, angefüllt.

**reply** [ri'plai], v.n. antworten, erwidern. — s. die Antwort.

**report** [ri'pɔ:t], v.a., v.n. berichten. — s. der Bericht; (Sch.) das Zeugnis; der Knall (of explosion).

**repose** [ri'pouz], v.n. ruhen. — v.a. setzen (in, auf). — s. die Ruhe, der Friede.

**repository** [ri'pɔzitəri], s. die Niederlage, Aufbewahrungsstätte, Fundstätte.

**reprehensible** [repri'hensibl], adj. tadelnswert.

**represent** [repri'zent], v.a. repräsentieren, vertreten.

**representative** [repri'zentətiv], adj. repräsentativ, typisch. — s. der Stellvertreter; (Pol.) der Repräsentant.

**repress** [ri'pres], v.a. unterdrücken.

**reprieve** [ri'pri:v], v.a. begnadigen. — s. die Gnadenfrist.

**reprimand** [repri'mɑ:nd], v.a. verweisen, tadeln. — s. der Tadel.

**reprint** [ri:'print], v.a. neu drucken. — ['ri:print], s. der Neudruck.

**reprisal** [ri'praizəl], s. die Vergeltungsmaßregel; (pl.) die Repressalien, f. pl.

**reproach** [ri'proutʃ], v.a. vorwerfen (Dat.), tadeln. — s. der Vorwurf, Tadel.

**reprobate** ['reprəbeit], adj. ruchlos, verworfen.

**reproduce** [ri:prə'dju:s], v.a. reproduzieren, erzeugen.

**reproof** [ri'pru:f], s. der Vorwurf, Tadel.

**reprove** [ri'pru:v], v.a. tadeln, rügen (a person), mißbilligen (a practice).

**republic** [ri'pʌblik], *s.* die Republik.
**repudiate** [ri'pju:dieit], *v.a.* zurückweisen, verwerfen.
**repugnant** [ri'pʌgnənt], *adj.* widerwärtig, ekelhaft.
**repulse** [ri'pʌls], *v.a.* (*Mil.*) zurückschlagen; abweisen (*s.o.*). — *s.* (*Mil.*) das Zurückschlagen; (*fig.*) die Zurückweisung.
**repulsive** [ri'pʌlsiv], *adj.* widerwärtig.
**reputation** [repju'teiʃən], *s.* der (gute) Ruf.
**request** [ri'kwest], *v.a.* ersuchen. — *s.* das Ersuchen, Ansuchen, die Bitte.
**requiem** ['rekwiəm], *s.* (*Eccl.*) das Requiem, die Totenmesse.
**require** [ri'kwaiə], *v.a.* fordern, verlangen, brauchen.
**requirement** [ri'kwaiəmənt], *s.* die Anforderung, das Erfordernis.
**requisite** ['rekwizit], *adj.* erforderlich.
**requisition** [rekwi'ziʃən], *s.* (*Mil.*) die Requisition; die Forderung.
**requite** [ri'kwait], *v.a.* vergelten.
**rescind** [ri'sind], *v.a.* für ungültig erklären, aufheben.
**rescue** ['reskju:], *v.a.* retten. — *s.* die Rettung.
**research** [ri'sə:tʃ], *v.n.* forschen, Forschung treiben. — *s.* die Forschung.
**resemble** [ri'zembl], *v.a.* ähnlich sein (*Dat.*), gleichen (*Dat.*).
**resent** [ri'zent], *v.a.* übelnehmen.
**resentful** [ri'zentful], *adj.* nachträgerisch; empfindlich (*over-sensitive*).
**resentment** [ri'zentmənt], *s.* die Empfindlichkeit; der Groll (*spite*).
**reservation** [rezə'veiʃən], *s.* die Reservierung (*of seat*); der Vorbehalt (*doubt*).
**reserve** [ri'zə:v], *v.a.* reservieren, belegen (*seat*); (*fig.*) vorbehalten (*o.'s position*). — *s.* die Reserve, die Verschlossenheit (*shyness*); die Einschränkung (*limitation*); die Reserven, *f. pl.* (*money*).
**reside** [ri'zaid], *v.n.* wohnen.
**resident** ['rezidənt], *adj.* wohnhaft. — *s.* der Ansässige.
**residual** [ri'zidjuəl], *adj.* übrig bleibend.
**residue** ['rezidju:], *s.* der Rückstand, Rest.
**resign** [ri'zain], *v.a.* abtreten, aufgeben; (ein Amt) niederlegen. — *v.n.* abdanken. — *v.r.* — *o.s. to*, sich in etwas fügen, zurücktreten.
**resignation** [rezig'neiʃən], *s.* die Resignation, der Rücktritt (*from office*); die Fügung, Resignation (*attitude*).
**resin** ['rezin], *s.* das Harz.
**resist** [ri'zist], *v.a., v.n.* widerstehen, Widerstand leisten (*Dat.*).
**resistance** [ri'zistəns], *s.* der Widerstand.
**resolute** ['rezəlju:t], *adj.* entschlossen.
**resolution** [rezə'lju:ʃən], *s.* die Entschlossenheit (*determination*); die Entscheidung (*decision*); der Vorsatz, Entschluß (*vow*).

**resolve** [ri'zɔlv], *v.a.* auflösen (*solve*); beschließen (*conclude*). — *v.n.* entscheiden (*decide*). — *s.* der Beschluß, die Entscheidung.
**resonance** ['rezənəns], *s.* die Resonanz.
**resort** [ri'zɔ:t], *v.n.* — *to*, seine Zuflucht nehmen (zu). — *s. seaside* —, das Seebad, *health* —, der Kurort (*spa*).
**resound** [ri'zaund], *v.n.* widerhallen.
**resource** [ri'sɔ:s], *s.* das Hilfsmittel; (*pl.*) die Mittel, *n. pl.*
**respect** [ri'spekt], *v.a.* respektieren, achten; berücksichtigen (*have regard to*). — *s.* der Respekt, die Achtung; *with* — *to*, mit Bezug auf; *in* — *of*, bezüglich (*Genit.*).
**respectability** [rispektə'biliti], *s.* die Anständigkeit; Achtbarkeit.
**respective** [ris'pektiv], *adj.* respektiv.
**respectively** [ris'pektivli], *adv.* beziehungsweise.
**respiration** [respi'reiʃən], *s.* die Atmung.
**respiratory** [ris'paiərətri *or* 'respireitəri], *adj.* Atmungs-.
**respire** [ris'paiə], *v.n.* atmen.
**respite** ['respit], *s.* die Frist, der Aufschub.
**resplendent** [ri'splendənt], *adj.* glänzend.
**respond** [ri'spɔnd], *v.n.* antworten, eingehen (*to, auf*).
**respondent** [ri'spɔndənt], *s.* (*Law*) der Beklagte.
**response** [ri'spɔns], *s.* die Antwort, Aufnahme, Reaktion; (*fig.*) der Widerhall.
**responsibility** [rispɔnsi'biliti], *s.* die Verantwortung, Verantwortlichkeit.
**responsible** [ri'spɔnsibl], *adj.* verantwortlich.
**responsive** [ri'spɔnsiv], *adj.* empfänglich, zugänglich.
**rest** (1) [rest], *v.n.* ruhen, rasten. — *s.* die Ruhe, Rast; (*Mus.*) die Pause.
**rest** (2) [rest], *v.n.* bleiben (*stay*); — *assured*, sei (seien Sie) versichert. — *s.* der Rest; die übrigen, *pl.*
**restaurant** ['restərã], *s.* das Restaurant.
**restful** ['restful], *adj.* ruhig.
**restitution** [resti'tju:ʃən], *s.* die Wiedergutmachung.
**restive** ['restiv], *adj.* unruhig, ruhelos.
**restless** ['restlis], *adj.* rastlos, unruhig.
**restoration** [restɔ:'reiʃən], *s.* die Wiederherstellung; (*Hist.*) die Restauration.
**restore** [ri'stɔ:], *v.a.* wiederherstellen.
**restrain** [ri'strein], *v.a.* zurückhalten, einschränken.
**restraint** [ri'streint], *s.* die Zurückhaltung.
**restrict** [ri'strikt], *v.a.* beschränken.
**restriction** [ri'strikʃən], *s.* die Einschränkung.
**restrictive** [ri'striktiv], *adj.* einschränkend.

**result** [ri'zʌlt], *v.n.* folgen, sich ergeben; (*come about*) erfolgen. — *s.* das Ergebnis, Resultat; (*consequence*) die Folge.

**resume** [ri'zju:m], *v.a.* wiederaufnehmen; (*narrative*) fortsetzen. — *v.n.* fortfahren.

**résumé** ['rezjumei], *s.* das Resümee, die Zusammenfassung.

**resumption** [ri'zʌmpʃən], *s.* die Wiederaufnahme.

**resurrection** [rezə'rekʃən], *s.* (*Rel.*) die Auferstehung.

**resuscitate** [ri'sʌsiteit], *v.a.* wiederbeleben.

**retail** ['ri:teil], *s.* der Kleinhandel, Einzelhandel. — [ri'teil], *v.a.* im Detail handeln, verkaufen.

**retain** [ri'tein], *v.a.* behalten.

**retainer** [ri'teinə], *s.* der Diener; Gefolgsmann; der Vorschuß (*fee*).

**retake** [ri:'teik], *v.a. irr.* (*Mil.*) wieder erobern; (*Phot., Film*) noch einmal aufnehmen. — *s.* (*Am.*) die Neuaufnahme (*Phot., Film*).

**retaliate** [ri'tælieit], *v.n.* sich rächen, vergelten.

**retard** [ri'tɑ:d], *v.a.* verzögern, verlangsamen.

**retch** [retʃ], *v.n.* sich erbrechen.

**retentive** [ri'tentiv], *adj.* behaltend, gut (*memory*).

**reticent** ['retisənt], *adj.* schweigsam, einsilbig.

**retina** ['retinə], *s.* (*Anat.*) die Netzhaut.

**retinue** ['retinju:], *s.* das Gefolge.

**retire** [ri'taiə], *v.n.* sich zurückziehen (*withdraw*); in den Ruhestand treten (*from work*). — *v.a.* pensionieren.

**retirement** [ri'taiəmənt], *s.* die Pension, der Ruhestand; die Zurückgezogenheit (*seclusion*).

**retort** [ri'tɔ:t], *s.* (*Chem.*) die Retorte; die scharfe Antwort (*debate*). — *v.n.* scharf erwidern.

**retouch** [ri:'tʌtʃ], *v.a.* (*Phot.*) retouchieren.

**retrace** [ri:'treis], *v.a.* zurückverfolgen.

**retreat** [ri'tri:t], *v.n.* sich zurückziehen. — *s.* der Rückzug (*Mil.*); Zufluchtsort.

**retrench** [ri'trentʃ], *v.a.* einschränken (*restrict*); verkürzen (*shorten*). — *v.n.* sich einschränken.

**retribution** [retri'bju:ʃən], *s.* die Vergeltung.

**retrieve** [ri'tri:v], *v.a.* wieder bekommen, wieder gewinnen.

**retriever** [ri'tri:və], *s.* (*Zool.*) der Apportierhund, Stöberhund.

**retrograde** ['retrogreid], *adj.* rückgängig, rückwärts.

**retrospect** ['retrospekt], *s.* der Rückblick.

**retrospective** [retro'spektiv], *adj.* rückblickend.

**return** [ri'tə:n], *v.a.* zurückgeben; erwidern (*reciprocate*); abordnen, entsenden (*to Parl.*); (*figures*) einsenden. — *v.n.* zurückkehren, zurückkommen.

— *s.* die Rückkehr; (*Fin.*) der Gewinn; (*Parl.*) die Entsendung, Mandatierung; (*pl.*) (*figures*) die Einsendung; *by* — *of post*, umgehend, postwendend; — *ticket*, die Rückfahrkarte.

**reunion** [ri:'ju:niən], *s.* die Wiedervereinigung.

**reveal** [ri'vi:l], *v.a.* enthüllen, offenbaren (*show*); verraten (*betray*).

**reveille** [ri'væli], *s.* (*Mil.*) das Wecken Wecksignal.

**revel** [revl], *v.n.* schwelgen.

**revelation** [revə'leiʃən], *s.* die Offenbarung.

**revelry** ['revəlri], *s.* die Schwelgerei.

**revenge** [ri'vendʒ], *s.* die Rache, Revanche. — *v.r.* (also *be revenged*) sich rächen (*on, an, Dat.*).

**revenue** ['revənju:], *s.* das Einkommen; *Inland* —, die Steuereinnahmen.

**reverberate** [ri'və:bəreit], *v.n.* widerhallen.

**revere** [ri'viə], *v.a.* verehren.

**reverence** ['revərəns], *s.* die Ehrerbietung, der Respekt; *show* —, Ehrerbietung zollen.

**Reverend** ['revərənd]. (*abbr.* **Rev.**) (*Eccl.*) *The* —, Seine Ehrwürden; *The Very* —, Seine Hochwürden.

**reverent, reverential** ['revərənt, revə'renʃəl], *adj.* ehrerbietig.

**reverie** ['revəri], *s.* die Träumerei.

**reversal** [ri'və:səl], *s.* die Umkehrung, Umstoßung.

**reverse** [ri'və:s], *v.a., v.n.* umkehren, umdrehen. — *s.* das Gegenteil (*contrary*); die Kehrseite (*of coin*).

**revert** [ri'və:t], *v.a., v.n.* umkehren, zurückkehren.

**review** [ri'vju:], *v.a.* durchsehen, prüfen (*examine*); rezensieren (*book etc.*). — *s.* die Revision; (*Mil.*) die Parade, Truppenmusterung; die Rezension, Besprechung (*book etc.*).

**revile** [ri'vail], *v.a., v.n.* schmähen.

**revise** [ri'vaiz], *v.a.* korrigieren (*correct*); wiederholen (*recapitulate*); umarbeiten (*modify*).

**revision** [ri'viʒən], *s.* die Revision; Korrektur; Umarbeitung; Wiederholung (*recapitulation*).

**revolt** [ri'voult], *v.n.* sich empören, revoltieren. — *v.a.* empören. — *s.* die Empörung.

**revolting** [ri'voultiŋ], *adj.* ekelhaft, empörend.

**revolution** [revə'lju:ʃən], *s.* (*Pol.*) die Revolution; (*Motor.*) die Umdrehung.

**revolve** [ri'vɔlv], *v.n.* rotieren, sich drehen.

**revolver** [ri'vɔlvə], *s.* der Revolver.

**revue** [ri'vju:], *s.* (*Theat.*) die Revue.

**revulsion** [ri'vʌlʃən], *s.* der Ekel; der Umschwung.

**reward** [ri'wɔ:d], *v.a.* belohnen (*person*); vergelten (*deed*). — *s.* die Belohnung.

**rhetoric** ['retərik], *s.* die Redekunst.

**rheumatic** [ru:'mætik], *adj.* (*Med.*)

rheumatisch.
**rheumatism** ['ru:mətizm], s. (Med.) der Rheumatismus.
**Rhodesian** [ro'di:ʃən, -'di:ʒən], adj. rhodesisch. — s. der Rhodesier.
**rhododendron** [roudo'dendrən], s. (Bot.) die Alpenrose.
**rhubarb** ['ru:ba:b], s. (Bot.) der Rhabarber.
**rhyme** [raim], s. der Reim; no — nor reason, sinnlos.
**rhythm** [riðm], s. der Rhythmus.
**rib** [rib], s. (Anat.) die Rippe.
**ribald** ['ribəld], adj. liederlich; (joke) unanständig.
**ribbon** ['ribən], s. das Band.
**rice** [rais], s. der Reis.
**rich** [ritʃ], adj. reich; fruchtbar (fertile).
**rick** [rik], s. der Schober.
**rickets** ['rikits], s. (Med.) die englische Krankheit, die Rachitis.
**rickety** ['rikiti], adj. gebrechlich, wackelig, baufällig.
**rid** [rid], v.a. irr. befreien, freimachen (of, von); — o.s., sich entledigen (of, Genit.); get — of, loswerden (Acc.); be — of, los sein (Acc.).
**riddance** ['ridəns], s. die Befreiung, das Loswerden.
**riddle** (1) [ridl], s. das Rätsel (puzzle).
**riddle** (2) [ridl], s. das grobe Sieb (sieve). — v.a. sieben (sieve); durchlöchern.
**ride** [raid], v.a., v.n. irr. reiten (on horse), fahren (on bicycle etc.); — at anchor, vor Anker liegen. — s. der Ritt (on horse), die Fahrt (in vehicle).
**rider** ['raidə], s. der Reiter (horseman); der Fahrer (cyclist etc.); der Zusatz (addition).
**ridge** [ridʒ], s. der Rücken (edge); die Bergkette; die Furche (furrow). — v.a. furchen.
**ridicule** ['ridikju:l], s. der Spott. — v.a. lächerlich machen.
**ridiculous** [ri'dikjuləs], adj. lächerlich.
**rife** [raif], adj. häufig, weitverbreitet.
**rifle** (1) [raifl], s.die Büchse, das Gewehr.
**rifle** (2) [raifl], v.a. ausplündern.
**rift** [rift], s. der Riß, Spalt, die Spalte. — v.a. spalten.
**rig** [rig], s. (Naut.) die Takelung; (fig.) — out, die Ausstattung. — v.a. (Naut.) (auf)takeln; (Am.) fälschen (fake); — out, ausstatten.
**right** [rait], adj. recht; richtig; wahr; gesund; korrekt; — hand, rechtsseitig; you are —, Sie haben recht; that's —, das stimmt. — s. das Recht; by right(s), rechtmäßig; drive on the —, rechts fahren.
**righteous** ['raitʃəs], adj. rechtschaffen, aufrecht.
**rightful** ['raitful], adj. rechtmäßig.
**rigid** ['ridʒid], adj. steif; unbeugsam; streng (severe).
**rigidity** [ri'dʒiditi], s. die Steifheit, Unnachgiebigkeit; die Strenge.
**rigmarole** ['rigməroul], s. die Salbaderei, das Gewäsch.

**rigorous** ['rigərəs], adj. streng; genau.
**rigour** ['rigə], s. die Strenge; die Härte.
**rill** [ril], s. (Poet.) das Bächlein.
**rim** [rim], s. der Rand, die Felge.
**rime** [raim], s. (Poet.) der Reif.
**rind** [raind], s. die Rinde.
**ring** (1) [riŋ], s. der Ring.
**ring** (2) [riŋ], s. der Schall, das Läuten (bell); der Anruf (telephone); das Geläute (bells). — v.a. irr. läuten, klingeln (bell). — v.n. läuten; ertönen, tönen (call, voice).
**ringleader** ['riŋli:də], s. der Rädelsführer.
**rink** [riŋk], s. die Eisbahn; Rollschuhbahn.
**rinse** [rins], v.a. spülen, waschen. — s. das Abspülen.
**riot** ['raiət], s. der Aufruhr. — v.n. Aufruhr stiften; meutern.
**rip** [rip], v.a. reißen, aufreißen. — s. der Riß.
**ripe** [raip], adj. reif.
**ripen** ['raipən], v.n. reifen. — v.a. reifen lassen.
**ripple** [ripl], s. die Welle, Kräuselwelle (water). — v.n. kräuseln (water); (Bot.) riffeln.
**rise** [raiz], v.n.irr. aufstehen (get up); aufsteigen (ascend); anschwellen (swell); steigen (price). — s. die Erhöhung; (Comm.) der Anstieg; die Steigerung; Erhöhung (salary); der Ursprung (origin).
**rising** ['raiziŋ], s. der Aufstand (rebellion).
**risk** [risk], s. das Risiko. — v.a. wagen, riskieren.
**rite** [rait], s. der Ritus.
**ritual** ['ritjuəl], s. das Ritual.
**rival** [raivl], s. der Rivale, Nebenbuhler. — adj. nebenbuhlerisch, konkurrierend. — v.a. konkurrieren, wetteifern.
**river** ['rivə], s. der Fluß.
**rivet** ['rivit], s. die Niete. — v.a. nieten.
**roach** [routʃ], s. (Zool.) die Plötze.
**road** [roud], s. die Straße; der Weg.
**roam** [roum], v.n. herumstreifen.
**roan** [roun], s. der Rotschimmel (horse).
**roar** [rɔ:], v.n. brüllen (animals); brausen (storm). — s. das Gebrüll (animal); das Getöse, Brausen, Rauschen.
**roast** [roust], v.a., v.n. braten, rösten. — s. der Braten.
**rob** [rɔb], v.a. berauben.
**robbery** ['rɔbəri], s. der Raub, die Räuberei.
**robe** [roub], s. die Robe.
**robin** ['rɔbin], s. (Orn.) das Rotkehlchen.
**rock** [rɔk], s. der Felsen, die Klippe. — v.a. schaukeln, wiegen. — v.n. wackeln, taumeln.
**rocket** ['rɔkit], s. die Rakete; (sl.) die Rüge. — v.n. hochfliegen; hochgehen (prices).
**rocky** ['rɔki], adj. felsig.

**rod** [rɔd], *s.* die Rute; (*fishing*) die Angelrute; die Stange (*pole*).
**rodent** ['roudənt], *s.* (*Zool.*) das Nagetier.
**roe** (1) [rou], *s.* der Fischrogen.
**roe** (2) [rou], *s.* (*Zool.*) das Reh, die Hirschkuh.
**rogation** [ro'geiʃən], *s.* das Gebet, die Litanei; *Rogation Sunday*, der Sonntag Rogate.
**rogue** [roug], *s.* der Schelm.
**role** [roul], *s.* (*Theat., fig.*) die Rolle.
**roll** [roul], *s.* die Liste; — *call*, der Aufruf, die Parade; die Rolle; die Semmel, das Brötchen (*bread*). — *v.a.* rollen; wälzen. — *v.n.* rollen; sich wälzen; sich drehen; schlingen (*ship*); schlenkern (*person*).
**roller** ['roulə], *s.* die Rolle; — *bandage*, das Wickelband; — *skates*, die Rollschuhe.
**rollick** ['rɔlik], *v.n.* herumtollen, lustig sein.
**rolling stock** ['roulin stɔk], *s.* (*Railw.*) der Wagenbestand.
**romance** [rou'mæns], *s.* die Romanze.
**romantic** [rou'mæntik], *adj.* romantisch.
**romp** [rɔmp], *s.* der Wildfang, das Tollen. — *v.n.* toben.
**roof** [ru:f], *s.* das Dach. — *v.a.* decken.
**rook** (1) [ruk], *s.* (*Orn.*) die Saatkrähe.
**rook** (2) [ruk], *s.* (*Chess*) der Turm.
**room** [ru:m, rum], *s.* der Raum, das Zimmer. — *v.n.* (*Am.*) ein Zimmer teilen (*with*, mit).
**roomy** ['ru:mi], *adj.* geräumig.
**roost** [ru:st], *s.* der Hühnerstall. — *v.n.* aufsitzen, schlafen.
**root** [ru:t], *s.* die Wurzel. — *v.n.* wurzeln.
**rooted** ['ru:tid], *adj.* eingewurzelt.
**rope** [roup], *s.* das Seil. — *v.a.* anseilen (*in climbing*); (*coll.*) — *in*, verwickeln, hereinziehen.
**rosary** ['rouzəri], *s.* (*Rel.*) der Rosenkranz.
**rose** [rouz], *s.* (*Bot.*) die Rose.
**Rosemary** ['rouzməri]. Rosemarie.
**rosemary** ['rouzməri], *s.* (*Bot.*) der Rosmarin.
**rosin** ['rɔzin] *see* resin.
**rosy** ['rouzi], *adj.* rosig.
**rot** [rɔt], *v.n.* faulen, modern. — *s.* die Fäulnis, Verwesung; (*coll.*) der Unsinn.
**rotate** [ro'teit], *v.a., v.n.* (sich) drehen, rotieren.
**rote** [rout], *s.* by —, mechanisch, auswendig.
**rotten** [rɔtn], *adj.* faul, verdorben, schlecht.
**rotund** [ro'tʌnd], *adj.* rundlich, rund.
**rough** [rʌf], *adj.* rauh, grob; flüchtig, ungefähr (*approximate*); ungehobelt (*ill-mannered*).
**roughshod** ['rʌfʃɔd], *adj.* rücksichtslos.
**round** [raund], *adj.* rund. — *s.* die Runde. — *prep.* (rund) um; um ... herum. — *adv.* (rings)herum; (*around*) ungefähr; etwa (*approximately*).

**roundabout** ['raundəbaut], *s.* das Karussel. — *adj.* umständlich.
**Roundhead** ['raundhed], *s.* (*Eng. Hist.*) der Puritaner.
**rouse** [rauz], *v.a.* erwecken.
**rout** [raut], *s.* (*Mil.*) die wilde Flucht. — *v.a.* in die Flucht jagen.
**route** [ru:t], *s.* der Weg; die Route.
**rover** ['rouvə], *s.* der Wanderer, ältere Pfadfinder (*scout*); der Seeräuber (*pirate*).
**row** (1) [rou], *s.* die Reihe.
**row** (2) [rau], *s.* der Lärm, Streit. — *v.n.* (*coll.*) lärmend streiten, zanken.
**row** (3) [rou], *v.n.* rudern.
**rowdy** ['raudi], *s.* der Raufbold. — *adj.* laut, lärmend.
**royal** ['rɔiəl], *adj.* königlich.
**royalty** ['rɔiəlti], *s.* das Mitglied des Königshauses, die königliche Hoheit; (*pl.*) (*Law*) die Tantieme.
**rub** [rʌb], *v.a., v.n.* (sich) reiben. — *s.* die Reibung; die heikle Stelle, das Problem.
**rubber** (1) ['rʌbə], *s.* der Gummi; Radiergummi.
**rubber** (2) ['rʌbə], *s.* (*Whist*) der Robber.
**rubbish** ['rʌbiʃ], *s.* der Abfall, Mist; (*fig.*) der Schund (*book*), der Unsinn (*nonsense*).
**ruby** ['ru:bi], *s.* der Rubin.
**rudder** ['rʌdə], *s.* das Steuerruder.
**ruddy** ['rʌdi], *adj.* rötlich.
**rude** [ru:d], *adj.* roh; grob; ungebildet; unhöflich.
**rudiment** ['ru:dimənt], *s.* die Anfangsgründe, die Grundlage.
**rue** (1) [ru:], *s.* (*Bot.*) die Raute.
**rue** (2) [ru:], *v.a.* beklagen, bereuen.
**ruff** [rʌf], *s.* die Halskrause.
**ruffian** ['rʌfiən], *s.* der Raufbold.
**ruffle** [rʌfl], *v.a.* zerzausen (*hair*); verwirren (*muddle*). — *s.* die Krause (*on dress*); die Aufregung.
**rug** [rʌg], *s.* die Wolldecke, der Vorleger.
**rugged** ['rʌgid], *adj.* rauh; uneben.
**ruin** ['ru:in], *s.* die Ruine; (*fig.*) der Zusammenbruch. — *v.a.* ruinieren.
**rule** [ru:l], *s.* die Regel, Vorschrift; die Herrschaft; *slide* —, der Rechenschieber. — *v.a.* beherrschen; regeln; lin(i)ieren (*draw lines on*). — *v.n.* herrschen (*reign; be valid*); lin(i)ieren (*draw lines*); entscheiden (*decide*).
**ruling** ['ru:lin], *s.* die Regelung, Entscheidung.
**rum** (1) [rʌm], *s.* der Rum.
**rum** (2) [rʌm], *adj.* (*sl.*) seltsam.
**Rumanian** [ru:'meiniən], *adj.* rumänisch. — *s.* der Rumäne.
**rumble** [rʌmbl], *v.n.* poltern, rasseln, rumpeln; (*stomach*) knurren.
**ruminate** ['ru:mineit], *v.n.* wiederkäuen; nachsinnen.
**rummage** ['rʌmidʒ], *v.a., v.n.* durchstöbern.
**rumour** ['ru:mə], *s.* das Gerücht.
**rump** [rʌmp], *s.* der Rumpf, Steiß; — *steak*, das Rumpsteak.

# run

run [rʌn], v.n. irr. laufen, rennen; eilen; verkehren (bus); fließen (flow); (Theat.) gegeben werden; lauten (text). — s. der Lauf, das Rennen; (Theat.) die Spieldauer; in the long —, am Ende, auf die Dauer.
runaway ['rʌnəwei], adj. entlaufen. — s. der Ausreißer.
rung [rʌŋ], s. die Sprosse.
runway ['rʌnwei], s. (Aviat.) die Rollbahn, Startbahn, Landebahn.
rupture ['rʌptʃə], s. (Med.) der Leistenbruch.
rural ['ruərəl], adj. ländlich.
rush (1) [rʌʃ], s. (Bot.) die Binse.
rush (2) [rʌʃ], s. der Ansturm, Andrang; die Hetze; der Hochbetrieb. — v.n. stürzen, in Eile sein.
Russian ['rʌʃən], adj. russisch. — s. der Russe.
rust [rʌst], s. der Rost. — v.n. verrosten.
rustic ['rʌstik], adj. ländlich.
rut (1) [rʌt], s. die Spur; das Geleise.
rut (2) [rʌt], s. (animals) die Brunst.
ruthless ['ru:θlis], adj. grausam, rücksichtslos.
rye [rai], s. (Bot.) der Roggen.

# S

S [es]. das S.
sable [seibl], s. der Zobel. — adj. schwarz.
sabotage ['sæbota:ʒ], s. die Sabotage. — v.a. sabotieren.
sabre ['seibə], s. der Säbel.
sack (1) [sæk], s. der Sack; (coll.) die Entlassung (get the —). — v.a. (coll.) entlassen.
sack (2) [sæk], v.a. plündern (pillage).
sack (3) [sæk], s. (obs.) der Weißwein.
sacrament ['sækrəmənt], s. das Sakrament.
sacred ['seikrid], adj. heilig.
sacrifice ['sækrifais], s. das Opfer. — v.a. opfern.
sacrilege ['sækrilidʒ], s. das Sakrileg, der Frevel.
sad [sæd], adj. traurig.
sadden [sædn], v.a. betrüben.
saddle [sædl], s. der Sattel. — v.a. satteln; (coll.) — s.o. with s.th., einem etwas aufhalsen.
safe [seif], adj. sicher (secure); wohlbehalten (arrival etc.). — s. der Geldschrank, das Safe.
safeguard ['seifga:d], v.a. beschützen, garantieren. — s. der Schutz, die Sicherheit.
safety ['seifti], s. die Sicherheit.
saffron ['sæfrən], s. der Safran. — adj. safrangelb.

sagacious [sə'geiʃəs], adj. scharfsinnig.
sagacity [sə'gæsiti], s. der Scharfsinn.
sage (1) [seidʒ], s. (Bot.) der, die Salbei.
sage (2) [seidʒ], s. der Weise. — adj. weise, klug.
sail [seil], s. das Segel. — v.n. segeln, (Naut.) fahren.
sailor ['seilə], s. der Matrose, Seemann.
Saint [seint, sənt]. (abbr. S. or St.) Sankt (before name).
saint [seint], s. der or die Heilige.
sake [seik], s. for my son's —, um meines Sohnes willen; for the — of peace, um des Friedens willen.
salacious [sə'leiʃəs], adj. geil; zotig (joke).
salad ['sæləd], s. der Salat.
salary ['sæləri], s. das Gehalt.
sale [seil], s. der Verkauf; annual —, (Comm.) der Ausverkauf.
salesman ['seilzmən], s. der Verkäufer.
salient ['seiliənt], adj. hervorspringend, wichtig, Haupt–.
saline ['seilain], s. die Salzquelle. — adj. salzhaltig.
saliva [sə'laivə], s. der Speichel.
sallow ['sælou], adj. blaß, bleich.
sally ['sæli], s. der Ausfall, (fig.) der komische Einfall. — v.n. ausfallen; — forth, losgehen.
salmon ['sæmən], s. (Zool.) der Lachs.
saloon [sə'lu:n], s. der Salon; (Am.) das Wirtshaus, die Kneipe.
salt [sɔ:lt], s. das Salz; — cellar, das Salzfäßchen; (coll.) old —, der alte Matrose. — v.a. salzen.
saltpetre [sɔ:lt'pi:tə], s. der Salpeter.
salubrious [sə'lju:briəs], adj. gesund (climate, neighbourhood).
salutary ['sæljutəri], adj. heilsam (lesson, experience).
salute [sə'lju:t], v.a. grüßen. — s. der Gruß, (Mil.) Salut.
salvage ['sælvidʒ], s. die Bergung, Rettung; das Bergegut. — v.a. retten, bergen.
salvation [sæl'veiʃən], s. die Rettung; (Rel.) die Erlösung, das Heil.
salve [sælv, sa:v], v.a. einsalben; heilen. — s. die Salbe.
salver ['sælvə], s. der Präsentierteller.
salvo ['sælvou], s. (Mil.) die Salve.
Samaritan [sə'mæritən], s. der Samariter; (fig.) der Wohltäter.
same [seim], adj. der-, die-, dasselbe.
sample [sa:mpl], s. die Probe, das Muster (test, pack etc.). — v.a. probieren, kosten (food).
sampler ['sa:mplə], s. das Stickmuster.
sanctify ['sæŋktifai], v.a. heiligen.
sanctimonious [sæŋkti'mouniəs], adj. scheinheilig.
sanction ['sæŋkʃən], s. (Pol.) die Sanktion; (fig.) Genehmigung. — v.a. genehmigen, sanktionieren.
sanctuary ['sæŋktjuəri], s. das Heiligtum.
sand [sænd], s. der Sand. — v.a. sanden, bestreuen; (floors) abreiben.
sandal [sændl], s. die Sandale.

# scavenger

**sandwich** ['sænwitʃ], *s.* das belegte (Butter)brot.

**sane** [sein], *adj.* gesund (*mind*); vernünftig.

**sanguine** ['sæŋgwin], *adj.* optimistisch.

**sanitary** ['sænitəri], *adj.* Gesundheits-, Sanitäts-; — *towel,* die (Damen)binde.

**sanity** ['sæniti], *s.* die Vernunft, der gesunde Menschenverstand; (*Law*) die Zurechnungsfähigkeit.

**Santa Claus** [sæntə'klɔːz]. der heilige Nikolaus, Knecht Ruprecht.

**sap** (1) [sæp], *s.* der Saft; (*fig.*) die Lebenskraft.

**sap** (2) [sæp], *v.a.* untergraben, schwächen.

**sapling** ['sæpliŋ], *s.* (*Bot.*) das Bäumchen, der junge Baum.

**sapper** ['sæpə], *s.* (*Mil.*) der Sappeur; der Schanzgräber, Pionier.

**sapphire** ['sæfaiə], *s.* der Saphir.

**sarcasm** ['saːkæzm], *s.* der Sarkasmus.

**sarcastic** [saː'kæstik], *adj.* sarkastisch.

**sash** (1) [sæʃ], *s.* die Schärpe.

**sash** (2) [sæʃ], *s.* — *window,* das Schiebefenster; — *cord,* die Fensterschnur.

**Satan** ['seitən]. der Satan.

**satchel** ['sætʃəl], *s.* die Leder(schul)tasche.

**sate** [seit], *v.a.* sättigen.

**satellite** ['sætəlait], *s.* der Satellit, Trabant.

**satin** ['sætin], *s.* (*Text.*) der Atlas.

**satire** ['sætaiə], *s.* die Satire.

**satisfaction** [sætis'fækʃən], *s.* die Befriedigung, Zufriedenheit.

**satisfactory** [sætis'fæktri], *adj.* befriedigend, genügend; zufriedenstellend.

**satisfy** ['sætisfai], *v.a.* befriedigen, sättigen; (*fig.*) zufriedenstellen.

**saturate** ['sætʃureit], *v.a.* (*Chem.*) saturieren, sättigen.

**Saturday** ['sætədei]. der Samstag, Sonnabend.

**sauce** [sɔːs], *s.* (*Cul.*) die Sauce, Tunke; (*coll.*) die Unverschämtheit.

**saucepan** ['sɔːspæn], *s.* (*Cul.*) der Kochtopf.

**saucer** ['sɔːsə], *s.* die Untertasse.

**saucy** ['sɔːsi], *adj.* (*coll.*) unverschämt, frech.

**saunter** ['sɔːntə], *v.n.* schlendern, spazieren.

**sausage** ['sɔsidʒ], *s.* die Wurst.

**savage** ['sævidʒ], *adj.* wild. — *s.* der Wilde.

**save** [seiv], *v.a.* retten (*life*); (*Theol.*) erlösen; sparen (*money*); sich ersparen (*trouble, labour*); aufheben (*keep*). — *v.n.* sparen, sparsam sein. — *prep., conj.* außer, außer daß, ausgenommen.

**saving** ['seiviŋ], *s.* das Ersparnis; *savings bank,* die Sparkasse.

**saviour** ['seivjə], *s.* der Retter; (*Rel.*) der Heiland.

**savour** ['seivə], *s.* der Geschmack; die Würze. — *v.n.* schmecken (*of,* nach, *Dat.*).

**savoury** ['seivəri], *adj.* schmackhaft. — *s.* pikantes Vor- *or* Nachgericht.

**saw** (1) [sɔː], *v.a.* sägen. — *s.* die Säge.

**saw** (2) [sɔː], *s.* (*obs.*) das Sprichwort.

**sawyer** ['sɔːjə], *s.* der Sägearbeiter, Säger.

**Saxon** ['sæksən], *adj.* sächsisch. — *s.* der Sachse.

**say** [sei], *v.a. irr.* sagen; (*lines, prayer*) hersagen. — *v.n.* (*Am. coll.*) —! sagen Sie mal! — *s.* das entscheidende Wort.

**saying** ['seiiŋ], *s.* das Sprichwort, der Spruch.

**scab** [skæb], *s.* der Schorf, die Krätze.

**scabbard** ['skæbəd], *s.* die Degenscheide.

**scaffold** ['skæfəld], *s.* (*Build.*) das Gerüst; das Schafott (*place of execution*).

**scald** [skɔːld], *v.a.* verbrühen; —*ing hot,* brühheiß.

**scale** (1) [skeil], *s.* die Waagschale (*balance*).

**scale** (2) [skeil], *s.* (*Mus.*) die Skala, Tonleiter.

**scale** (3) [skeil], *s.* (*Geog. etc.*) die Skala, das Ausmaß, der Maßstab; *on a large* —, im großen (Maßstabe). — *v.a.* erklettern (*climb*); — *down,* im Maßstab verringern.

**scale** (4) [skeil], *s.* (*fish etc.*) die Schuppe. — *v.a.* schuppen, abschälen (*remove* —*s*).

**scallop** ['skɔləp], *s.* (*Zool.*) die Kammuschel.

**scalp** [skælp], *s.* (*Anat.*) die Kopfhaut. — *v.a.* skalpieren, die Kopfhaut abziehen.

**scamp** [skæmp], *s.* (*coll.*) der Taugenichts.

**scan** [skæn], *v.a.* (*Poet.*) skandieren; (*Rad.*) absuchen.

**scandalize** ['skændəlaiz], *v.a.* empören, verärgern.

**scant** [skænt], *adj.* selten; knapp, sparsam.

**Scandinavian** [skændi'neivjən], *adj.* skandinavisch. — *s.* der Skandinavier.

**scanty** ['skænti], *adj.* spärlich, knapp.

**scapegoat** ['skeipgout], *s.* der Sündenbock.

**scar** [skaː], *s.* die Narbe.

**scarce** [skɛəs], *adj.* selten, spärlich.

**scarcely** ['skɛəsli], *adv.* kaum.

**scarcity** ['skɛəsiti], *s.* die Seltenheit, Knappheit.

**scare** [skɛə], *v.a.* erschrecken, ängstigen. — *s.* der Schreck.

**scarecrow** ['skɛəkrou], *s.* die Vogelscheuche.

**scarf** [skaːf], *s.* der Schal, das Halstuch.

**scarlet** ['skaːlit], *adj.* scharlachrot. — *s.* der Scharlach.

**scarp** [skaːp], *s.* die Böschung.

**scatter** ['skætə], *v.a., v.n.* (sich) zerstreuen, (sich) verbreiten; streuen.

**scavenge** ['skævindʒ], *v.a.* ausreinigen, auswaschen; säubern.

**scavenger** ['skævindʒə], *s.* der Straßenkehrer; Aasgeier.

479

**scene** [si:n], *s.* die Szene, der Schauplatz; *behind the* —*s,* hinter den Kulissen; — *shifter,* der Kulissenschieber.

**scenery** ['si:nəri], *s.* die Landschaft (*nature*); (*Theat.*) das Bühnenbild, die Kulissen, *f. pl.*

**scent** [sent], *s.* der Geruch, Duft, das Parfüm (*perfume*); die Witterung, Fährte (*trail of hunted animal*).

**sceptic** ['skeptik], *s.* der Skeptiker.

**sceptre** ['septə], *s.* das Zepter.

**schedule** ['ʃedju:l, (*Am.*) 'ske-], *s.* der Plan; die Liste; der (Fahr-, Stunden-)plan; (*Law*) der Zusatz (*in documents*). — *v.a.* (*Am.*) einteilen, zuteilen (*apportion*); aufzeichnen.

**scheme** [ski:m], *s.* das Schema; der Plan; — *of things,* in der Gesamtplanung. — *v.n.* aushecken; Ränke schmieden.

**scholar** ['skɔlə], *s.* der Gelehrte, der Wissenschaftler; der Schuljunge, Schüler; (*Univ.*) der Stipendiat.

**scholarly** ['skɔləli], *adj.* gelehrt.

**scholarship** ['skɔləʃip], *s.* die Gelehrsamkeit (*learning*); das Stipendium (*award*).

**scholastic** [skɔ'læstik], *adj.* scholastisch. — *s.* der Scholastiker.

**school** [sku:l], *s.* die Schule. — *v.a.* abrichten; schulen; erziehen.

**schoolboy** ['sku:lbɔi], *s.* der Schüler.

**schoolgirl** ['sku:lgə:l], *s.* die Schülerin.

**schoolmaster** ['sku:lma:stə], *s.* der Lehrer.

**schoolmistress** ['sku:lmistrəs], *s.* die Lehrerin.

**schooner** ['sku:nə], *s.* (*Naut.*) der Schoner.

**science** ['saiəns], *s.* die Wissenschaft, Naturwissenschaft (*natural* —*s*).

**scientific** [saiən'tifik], *adj.* wissenschaftlich, naturwissenschaftlich.

**scientist** ['saiəntist], *s.* der Gelehrte; Naturwissenschaftler, Naturforscher.

**scintillate** ['sintileit], *v.n.* funkeln, glänzen.

**scion** ['saiən], *s.* der Sprößling.

**scissors** ['sizəz], *s. pl.* die Schere.

**scoff** [skɔf], *v.a.* verspotten, verhöhnen. — *v.n.* spotten. —*s.* der Spott, Hohn.

**scold** [skould], *v.a.* schelten. — *v.n.* zanken.

**scoop** [sku:p], *v.a.* aushöhlen (*hollow out*); ausschöpfen (*ladle out*). — *s.* die Schippe, Schöpfkelle; (*fig.*) die Sensation, Erstmeldung.

**scooter** ['sku:tə], *s.* der (Motor)roller.

**scope** [skoup], *s.* der Wirkungskreis, Spielraum.

**scorch** [skɔ:tʃ], *v.a.* versengen, verbrennen. — *v.n.* versengt werden; (*coll.*) dahinrasen (*speed*).

**score** [skɔ:], *s.* die Zwanzig; die Rechnung; (*Mus.*) die Partitur; das Spielergebnis (*in game*).

**scorn** [skɔ:n], *v.a.* verachten. — *s.* der Spott (*scoffing*); die Geringschätzung, Verachtung.

**Scot, Scotsman** [skɔt, 'skɔtsmən], *s.* der Schotte.

**Scotch** [skɔtʃ], *s.* der Whisky.

**scotch** [skɔtʃ], *v.a.* ritzen; (*fig.*) vernichten.

**Scotswoman** ['skɔtswumən], *s.* die Schottin.

**Scottish** ['skɔtiʃ], *adj.* schottisch.

**scoundrel** ['skaundrəl], *s.* der Schurke.

**scour** ['skauə], *v.a.* scheuern, reinigen.

**scourge** [skə:dʒ], *s.* die Geißel. — *v.a.* geißeln.

**scout** [skaut], *s.* der Kundschafter; (*Boy Scout*) der Pfadfinder.

**scowl** [skaul], *v.n.* finster dreinsehen. — *s.* das finstere Gesicht.

**scraggy** ['skrægi], *adj.* hager, dürr.

**scramble** ['skræmbl], *v.n.* klettern. — *v.a.* verrühren; *scrambled eggs,* das Rührei.

**scrap** [skræp], *s.* das Stückchen, der Brocken, Fetzen; — *merchant,* der Altwarenhändler. — *v.a.* zum alten Eisen werfen, verschrotten.

**scrapbook** ['skræpbuk], *s.* das Sammelbuch, Bilderbuch.

**scrape** [skreip], *v.a., v.n.* (sich) schaben, kratzen; (*coll.*) — *up,* auflesen. — *s.* (*coll.*) die Klemme (*difficulty*).

**scraper** ['skreipə], *s.* der Fußabstreifer.

**scratch** [skrætʃ], *v.a., v.n.* kratzen; sich kratzen; (*Sport*) zurückziehen. — *s.* der Kratzer; *come up to* —, seinen Mann stellen.

**scrawl** [skrɔ:l], *v.a., v.n.* kritzeln (*scribble*); (*coll.*) unleserlich schreiben. — *s.* das Gekritzel.

**scream** [skri:m], *v.n.* schreien; kreischen. — *s.* der Schrei; (*coll.*) zum Schreien, zum Lachen.

**screech** [skri:tʃ], *v.n.* schreien, kreischen (*hoarsely*). — *s.* das Gekreisch.

**screen** [skri:n], *s.* der Schirm (*protection*); (*Cinema*) die Leinwand. — *v.a.* abschirmen (*shade*); (*Film*) durchspielen, vorführen; (*question*) untersuchen; ausfragen.

**screening** ['skri:niŋ], *s.* (*Cinema*) die Vorführung; (*Pol.*) die Befragung, Untersuchung.

**screw** [skru:], *v.a.* schrauben. — *s.* die Schraube.

**screwdriver** ['skru:draivə], *s.* der Schraubenzieher.

**scribble** [skribl], *v.a., v.n.* kritzeln, (unleserlich) schreiben. — *s.* das Gekritzel.

**scribe** [skraib], *s.* der Schreiber.

**script** [skript], *s.* das Manuskript; (*Film*) das Drehbuch.

**scripture** ['skriptʃə], *s.* die Heilige Schrift.

**scroll** [skroul], *s.* die Schriftrolle; (*Typ.*) der Schnörkel; die Urkunde (*document etc.*).

**scrub** [skrʌb], *v.a.* schrubben, reiben, scheuern.

**scruff** [skrʌf], *s.* (*of the neck*) das Genick.

**scruple** [skru:pl], *s.* der Skrupel.

**scrupulous** ['skru:pjuləs], *adj.* genau, gewissenhaft; allzu bedenklich.

**scrutinize** ['skru:tinaiz], *v.a.* genau prüfen, untersuchen.

**scrutiny** ['skru:tini], *s.* die genaue Prüfung; die Untersuchung.

**scuffle** [skʌfl], *v.n.* sich raufen. — *s.* die Balgerei, Rauferei.

**scull** [skʌl], *s.* das kurze Ruder.

**scullery** ['skʌləri], *s.* die Abwaschküche.

**scullion** ['skʌliən], *s.* (*obs.*) der Küchenjunge.

**sculptor** ['skʌlptə], *s.* der Bildhauer.

**sculpture** ['skʌlptʃə], *s.* die Bildhauerei (*activity*); die Skulptur (*piece*).

**scum** [skʌm], *s.* der Abschaum.

**scurf** [skə:f], *s.* der Schorf, Grind.

**scurrilous** ['skʌriləs], *adj.* gemein.

**scurvy** ['skə:vi], *s.* (*Med.*) der Skorbut. — *adj.* niederträchtig.

**scutcheon** ['skʌtʃən] *see* escutcheon.

**scuttle** [skʌtl], *s.* (*Naut.*) die Springluke. — *v.a.* (*Naut.*) ein Schiff zum Sinken bringen, versenken.

**scuttle** (2) [skʌtl], *s.* der Kohleneimer.

**scuttle** (3) [skʌtl], *v.n.* eilen (*hurry*).

**scythe** [saið], *s.* die Sense.

**sea** [si:], *s.* die See, das Meer.

**seal** (1) [si:l], *s.* das Siegel, Petschaft. — *v.a.* (be)siegeln.

**seal** (2) [si:l], *s.* (*Zool.*) der Seehund, die Robbe.

**seam** [si:m], *s.* der Saum; die Naht; (*Min.*) die Ader, das Flöz; (*Metall.*) die Naht. — *v.a.* einsäumen.

**seamstress** ['si:mstrəs], *s.* die Näherin.

**sear** [siə], *v.a.* sengen (*burn*); trocknen; verdorren. — *adj. see* sere.

**search** [sə:tʃ], *v.n.* suchen (*for*, nach, *Dat.*); forschen (*for*, nach, *Dat.*). — *v.a.* untersuchen, durchsuchen (*house, case etc.*). — *s.* die Suche (*for person*); die Untersuchung (*of house etc.*).

**searchlight** ['sə:tʃlait], *s.* der Scheinwerfer.

**seasick** ['si:sik], *adj.* seekrank.

**seaside** ['si:said],*s.* die Küste, der Strand.

**season** [si:zn], *s.* die Jahreszeit, Saison; — *ticket*, die Dauerkarte. — *v.a.* würzen (*spice*). — *v.n.* reifen (*mature*).

**seasoning** ['si:zniŋ], *s.* die Würze.

**seat** [si:t], *s.* der Sitz, Sitzplatz, Stuhl. — *v.a.* setzen; fassen (*of room capacity*); *be* —*ed*, Platz nehmen.

**seaweed** ['si:wi:d], *s.* (*Bot.*) der Seetang.

**secession** [si'seʃən], *s.* die Loslösung, Trennung, Spaltung.

**seclude** [si'klu:d], *v.a.* abschließen, absondern.

**seclusion** [si'klu:ʒən], *s.* die Abgeschlossenheit.

**second** ['sekənd], *num. adj.* zweit; (*repeat*) noch ein. — *s.* die Sekunde (*time*); (*Sport*) der Sekundant. — *v.a.* sekundieren (*Dat.*), beipflichten; [si'kɔnd] abkommandieren (zu).

**secondary** ['sekəndri], *adj.* zweitrangig, sekundär.

**secondhand** ['sekəndhænd], *adj.* antiquarisch, gebraucht.

**secrecy** ['si:krəsi], *s.* die Heimlichkeit; *pledge to* —, die Verschwiegenheit.

**secret** ['si:krit], *s.* das Geheimnis. — *adj.* geheim.

**secretary** ['sekrətəri], *s.* der Sekretär, die Sekretärin.

**secrete** [si'kri:t], *v.a.* ausscheiden, absondern.

**secretion** [si'kri:ʃən], *s.* die Ausscheidung; (*Med.*) das Sekret.

**sect** [sekt], *s.* die Sekte.

**section** ['sekʃən], *s.* die Sektion, Abteilung (*department*); der Teil (*part*); Abschnitt (*in book etc.*).

**secular** ['sekjulə], *adj.* weltlich, säkular.

**secure** [sə'kjuə], *adj.* sicher, gesichert. — *v.a.* sichern (*make safe*); besorgen (*obtain*).

**security** [sə'kjuəriti], *s.* die Sicherheit; (*Comm.*) die Garantie, Bürgschaft; (*pl.*) die Staatspapiere, Wertpapiere, *n. pl.*, Aktien, *f. pl.*

**sedate** [si'deit], *adj.* gesetzt, ruhig (*placid*).

**sedative** ['sedətiv], *adj.* beruhigend. — *s.* das Beruhigungsmittel.

**sedentary** ['sedəntri], *adj.* sitzend, Sitz-.

**sediment** ['sedimənt], *s.* der Bodensatz; (*Geol.*) das Sediment.

**sedition** [si'diʃən], *s.* der Aufstand.

**seditious** [si'diʃəs], *adj.* aufrührerisch.

**seduce** [si'dju:s], *v.a.* verführen.

**sedulous** ['sedjuləs], *adj.* emsig, fleißig.

**see** (1) [si:], *s.* (*Eccl.*) das (Erz)bistum; *Holy See*, der Heilige Stuhl.

**see** (2) [si:], *v.a., v.n. irr.* sehen; einsehen, verstehen (*understand*).

**seed** [si:d], *s.* die Saat; der Same (*grain*). — *v.a.* (*Sport*) aussetzen, setzen.

**seediness** ['si:dinis], *s.* die Schäbigkeit; Armseligkeit, das Elend.

**seedy** ['si:di], *adj.* elend; schäbig.

**seeing** ['si:iŋ], *conj.* — *that*, da doch.

**seek** [si:k], *v.a. irr.* suchen (*object*). — *v.n.* trachten (*to, infin.*).

**seem** [si:m], *v.n.* scheinen, erscheinen.

**seemly** ['si:mli], *adj.* schicklich, anständig.

**seer** [siə], *s.* der Prophet.

**seesaw** ['si:sɔ:], *s.* die Schaukel.

**seethe** [si:ð], *v.n.* kochen, (*fig.*) sieden.

**segment** ['segmənt], *s.* (*Geom.*) der Abschnitt.

**segregate** ['segrigeit], *v.a.* absondern.

**segregation** [segri'geiʃən], *s. racial* —, die Rassentrennung.

**seize** [si:z], *v.a.* ergreifen, packen (*arrest, grasp*); beschlagnahmen (*impound*).

**seizure** ['si:ʒə], *s.* die Beschlagnahme (*of goods*); (*Med.*) der Anfall.

**seldom** ['seldəm], *adv.* selten.

**select** [si'lekt], *v.a.* auswählen; auslesen. — *adj.* auserlesen.

**selection** [si'lekʃən], *s.* die Wahl, Auswahl.

**self** [self], *s.* das Selbst; — — *consciousness*, die Befangenheit; — — *denial*, die Selbstverleugnung, Selbstaufopferung.

selfish

**selfish** ['selfiʃ], *adj.* egoistisch, selbstsüchtig.
**sell** [sel], *v.a. irr.* verkaufen; (*sl.*) —
(*s.o.*) *out*, jemanden verraten.
**semblance** ['sembləns], *s.* der Anschein,
die Ähnlichkeit.
**semi-** ['semi], *pref.* halb.
**semibreve** ['semibri:v], *s.* (*Mus.*) die
ganze Note.
**semicircle** ['semikoulən], *s.* der Halb-
kreis.
**semicolon** ['semikoulən], *s.* der Strichpunkt.
**semiquaver** ['semikweivə], *s.* (*Mus.*)
die Sechzehntelnote.
**senate** ['senit], *s.* der Senat.
**send** [send], *v.a. irr.* senden, schicken;
— *for*, holen lassen; — *-off*, die
Abschiedsfeier.
**Senegalese** [senigə'li:z], *adj.* senegal-.
— *s.* der Senegalese.
**senile** ['si:nail], *adj.* altersschwach.
**senior** ['si:njə], *adj.* älter; dienstälter
(*in position*).
**seniority** [si:ni'ɔriti], *s.* der Rangvor-
tritt, das Dienstalter.
**sensation** [sen'seiʃən], *s.* die Empfindung; Sensation.
**sensational** [sen'seiʃənəl], *adj.* sensationell.
**sense** [sens], *v.a.* fühlen, empfinden.
— *s.* der Sinn; das Empfinden,
Gefühl; *common* —, gesunder Menschenverstand.
**senseless** ['senslis], *adj.* sinnlos.
**sensibility** [sensi'biliti], *s.* die Empfindlichkeit.
**sensible** ['sensibl], *adj.* vernünftig.
**sensitive** ['sensitiv], *adj.* feinfühlend,
empfindlich.
**sensitize** ['sensitaiz], *v.a.* (*Phot. etc.*)
empfindlich machen.
**sensual** ['sensjuəl], *adj.* sinnlich, wollüstig.
**sensuous** ['sensjuəs], *adj.* sinnlich.
**sentence** ['sentəns], *s.* (*Gram.*) der
Satz; (*Law*) das Urteil. — *v.a.* verurteilen.
**sententious** [sen'tenʃəs], *adj.* spruch-
reich; affektiert.
**sentiment** ['sentimənt], *s.* die Empfindung, das Gefühl; die Meinung
(*opinion*).
**sentimental** [senti'mentl], *adj.* sentimental, gefühlvoll; empfindsam.
**sentinel** ['sentinəl], *s.* (*Mil.*) die Schildwache, Wache.
**separable** ['sepərəbl], *adj.* trennbar.
**separate** ['sepəreit], *v.a.* trennen. —
[-rit], *adj.* getrennt.
**separation** [sepə'reiʃən], *s.* die Trennung.
**September** [sep'tembə]. der September.
**sequel** ['si:kwəl], *s.* die Folge, Fortsetzung (*serial*).
**sequence** ['si:kwəns], *s.* die Ordnung,
Reihenfolge, Aufeinanderfolge.
**sequester** [si'kwestə], *v.a.* absondern,
entfernen.

**sere** [siə], *adj.* trocken, dürr.
**serene** [si'ri:n], *adj.* heiter; gelassen,
ruhig (*quiet*).
**serf** [sə:f], *s.* der Leibeigene.
**sergeant** ['sɑ:dʒənt], *s.* (*Mil.*) der
Feldwebel.
**series** ['siəri:z *or* 'siərii:z], *s.* die Reihe.
**serious** ['siəriəs], *adj.* ernst, seriös.
**sermon** ['sə:mən], *s.* die Predigt.
**serpent** ['sə:pənt], *s.* (*Zool.*) die
Schlange.
**serpentine** ['sə:pəntain], *adj.* schlangenartig, sich schlängelnd.
**serrated** [se'reitid], *adj.* (*Bot., Engin.*)
zackig, gezackt.
**serried** ['serid], *adj.* dichtgedrängt.
**servant** ['sə:vənt], *s.* der Bediente,
Diener; die Magd, das Mädchen,
Dienstmädchen.
**serve** [sə:v], *v.a., v.n.* dienen (*Dat.*);
(*Law*) abbüßen, absitzen (*sentence*);
servieren (*food*); (*Tennis*) angeben.
**service** ['sə:vis], *s.* der Dienst, die
Bedienung; (*Mil.*) der Militärdienst;
das Service, Geschirr, Porzellan
(*china*).
**serviceable** ['sə:visəbl], *adj.* brauchbar, dienlich, benutzbar.
**servile** ['sə:vail], *adj.* knechtisch.
**servility** [sə:'viliti], *s.* die Kriecherei.
**servitude** ['sə:vitju:d], *s.* die Knechtschaft.
**session** ['seʃən], *s.* die Sitzung; das
Studienjahr, Hochschuljahr.
**set** [set], *v.a. irr.* setzen; stellen (*stand*);
legen (*lay*); ordnen (— *out*); — *a
saw*, eine Sage schärfen, wetzen;
fassen (*stone*); — *fire to*, in Brand
setzen; — *aside*, beiseitelegen; — *to
music*, vertonen; — *about*, anfangen,
sich anschicken; herfallen über (*s.o.*);
— *up*, einrichten. — *v.n.* — *forth,
forward*, aufbrechen; — *out to*, streben, trachten; (*sun*) untergehen; fest
werden (*solidify*). — *s.* der Satz (*complete collection*); die Garnitur (*gar-
ments*); der Kreis, die Clique (*circle
of people*); (*Theat.*) das Bühnenbild.
**settee** [se'ti:], *s.* das Sofa.
**setter** ['setə], *s.* (*Zool.*) der Vorsteh-
hund; *red* —, der Hühnerhund.
**setting** ['setiŋ], *s.* das Setzen; die
Szene (*of play etc.*); der Sonnenuntergang (*of the sun*); (*Typ.*) — *up*, die
Auslegung, Aufstellung.
**settle** (1) [setl], *v.a.* ordnen, schlichten;
(*Comm.*) begleichen, bezahlen. —
*v.n.* sich niederlassen, siedeln; (*weather*) sich aufklären.
**settle** (2) [setl], *s.* der Ruhesitz.
**settlement** ['setlmənt], *s.* (*Comm.*) die
Begleichung; die Siedlung (*habitation*).
**seven** [sevn], *num. adj.* sieben.
**seventeen** ['sevnti:n], *num. adj.* siebzehn.
**seventh** [sevnθ], *num. adj.* siebente.
**seventy** ['sevnti], *num. adj.* siebzig.
**sever** ['sevə], *v.a.* trennen.
**several** ['sevərəl], *adj. pl.* verschiedene,
mehrere.

**severance** ['sevərəns], *s.* die Trennung.
**severe** [si'viə], *adj.* streng.
**severity** [si'veriti], *s.* die Strenge.
**sew** [sou], *v.a., v.n.* nähen.
**sewage** ['sju:idʒ], *s.* das Abfuhrwasser, Kloakenwasser, Kanalwasser.
**sewer** (1) ['sju:ə], *s.* die Kanalanlage, der Abzugskanal.
**sewer** (2) ['souə], *s.* der Näher, die Näherin.
**sewing** ['souiŋ], *s.* das Nähen; — *machine*, die Nähmaschine.
**sex** [seks], *s.* das Geschlecht.
**sexagenarian** [seksədʒə'neəriən], *s.* der Sechzigjährige.
**sextant** ['sekstənt], *s.* der Sextant.
**sexton** ['sekstən], *s.* (*Eccl.*) der Küster, Totengräber.
**sexual** ['seksjuəl], *adj.* geschlechtlich, sexuell.
**shabby** ['ʃæbi], *adj.* schäbig; (*fig.*) erbärmlich.
**shackle** [ʃækl], *v.a.* fesseln. — *s.* (*usually pl.*) die Fesseln, *f. pl.*
**shade** [ʃeid], *s.* der Schatten; (*pl.*) (*Am.*) die Jalousien, *f. pl.* (*blinds*). — *v.a.* beschatten; (*Art*) schattieren, verdunkeln.
**shadow** ['ʃædou], *s.* der Schatten. — *v.a.* verfolgen.
**shady** ['ʃeidi], *adj.* schattig; (*fig.*) verdächtig.
**shaft** [ʃɑ:ft], *s.* der Schaft (*handle*); (*Min.*) der Schacht; die Deichsel (*cart*); der Pfeil (*arrow*).
**shag** [ʃæg], *s.* der Tabak.
**shaggy** ['ʃægi], *adj.* zottig.
**shake** [ʃeik], *v.a. irr.* schütteln; rütteln; (*fig.*) erschüttern. — *v.n.* zittern (*tremble*); wanken (*waver*). — *s.* das Zittern, Beben; (*Mus.*) der Triller.
**shaky** ['ʃeiki], *adj.* zitternd, wankend; rissig, wackelig (*wobbly*); (*fig.*) unsicher (*insecure*).
**shall** [ʃæl], *v. aux.* sollen (*be supposed to*); werden (*future*).
**shallow** ['ʃælou], *adj.* flach, seicht. — *s.* die Untiefe (*sea*).
**sham** [ʃæm], *adj.* falsch, unecht. — *v.a.* vortäuschen.
**shambles** [ʃæmblz], *s.* die Unordnung; (*fig.*) das Schlachtfeld.
**shame** [ʃeim], *s.* die Scham (*remorse*); die Schande (*dishonour*); *what a —! wie schade! — v.a.* beschämen.
**shamefaced** ['ʃeimfeisd], *adj.* verschämt.
**shameful** ['ʃeimful], *adj.* schändlich (*despicable*).
**shampoo** [ʃæm'pu:], *s.* das Haarwaschmittel. — *v.a.* das Haar waschen.
**shamrock** ['ʃæmrɔk], *s.* (*Bot.*) der irische Klee.
**shank** [ʃæŋk], *s.* der Unterschenkel; (*coll.*) *on Shanks's pony*, zu Fuß.
**shanty** (1) ['ʃænti], *s.* die Hütte.
**shanty** (2) ['ʃænti], *s.* *sea —*, das Matrosenlied.
**shape** [ʃeip], *s.* die Gestalt, Figur, Form. — *v.a.* gestalten, formen. — *v.n.* Gestalt annehmen.

**shapely** ['ʃeipli], *adj.* wohlgestaltet, schön gestaltet.
**share** [ʃɛə], *v.a., v.n.* (sich) teilen. — *s.* der Teil, Anteil; (*Comm.*) die Aktie (*in company*).
**shareholder** ['ʃɛəhouldə], *s.* der Aktionär.
**shark** [ʃɑ:k], *s.* (*Zool.*) der Haifisch, Hai; (*fig.*) der Wucherer (*profiteer*), Hochstapler.
**sharp** [ʃɑ:p], *adj.* scharf; (*fig.*) intelligent. — *s.* (*Mus.*) das Kreuz.
**sharpen** [ʃɑ:pn], *v.a.* schärfen; spitzen (*pencil*).
**sharpener** ['ʃɑ:pnə], *s. pencil —*, der Bleistiftspitzer.
**shatter** ['ʃætə], *v.a.* zerschmettern. — *v.n.* zerbrechen.
**shave** [ʃeiv], *v.a., v.n.* (sich) rasieren; abschaben (*pare*). — *s.* die Rasur, das Rasieren.
**shavings** ['ʃeiviŋz], *s. pl.* die Hobelspäne, *m. pl.*
**shawl** [ʃɔ:l], *s.* der Schal, das Umschlagetuch.
**she** [ʃi:], *pers. pron.* sie.
**sheaf** [ʃi:f], *s.* die Garbe.
**shear** [ʃiə], *v.a. irr.* scheren (*sheep etc.*).
**shears** [ʃiəz], *s. pl.* die Schere.
**sheath** [ʃi:θ], *s.* die Scheide.
**sheathe** [ʃi:ð], *v.a.* in die Scheide stecken.
**shed** (1) [ʃed], *s.* der Schuppen.
**shed** (2) [ʃed], *v.a. irr.* vergießen (*blood, tears*); ausschütten.
**sheen** [ʃi:n], *s.* der Glanz.
**sheep** [ʃi:p], *s.* (*Zool.*) das Schaf.
**sheer** (1) [ʃiə], *adj.* rein, lauter; senkrecht.
**sheer** (2) [ʃiə], *v.n.* (*Naut.*) gieren, abgieren.
**sheet** [ʃi:t], *s.* das Bettuch; das Blatt, der Bogen (*paper*); die Platte (*metal*); *— metal, — iron*, das Eisenblech; *— lightning*, das Wetterleuchten.
**shelf** [ʃelf], *s.* das Brett, Regal; der Sims (*mantel*); (*Geog.*) die Sandbank; (*coll.*) *on the —*, sitzengeblieben.
**shell** [ʃel], *s.* die Schale (*case*); die Muschel (*mussel*); (*Mil.*) die Bombe, Granate. — *v.a.* schälen (*peas*); bombardieren, beschiessen (*town*).
**shelter** ['ʃeltə], *s.* das Obdach (*lodging*); der Unterstand, Schuppen; der Schutz (*protection*). — *v.a.* Obdach gewähren (*Dat.*); beschützen (*protect*). — *v.n.* sich schützen, unterstellen.
**shelve** [ʃelv], *v.a.* auf ein Brett legen; (*fig.*) aufschieben (*postpone*).
**shelving** ['ʃelviŋ], *s.* das Regal.
**shepherd** ['ʃepəd], *s.* der Schäfer, Hirt.
**sheriff** ['ʃerif], *s.* der Sheriff.
**shew** [ʃou] *see* show.
**shield** [ʃi:ld], *s.* der Schild. — *v.a.* schützen.
**shift** [ʃift], *v.a.* verschieben. — *v.n.* die Lage ändern. — *s.* die Veränderung, der Wechsel; (*Industry*) die Schicht.
**shifty** ['ʃifti], *adj.* unstet; durchtrieben.

**shin** [ʃin], s. (*Anat.*) das Schienbein.
**shindy** [ʃindi], s. der Lärm.
**shine** [ʃain], v.n. irr. scheinen (*sun*); glänzen. — s. der Glanz.
**shingle** (1) [ʃiŋgl], s. (*Build.*) die Schindel; (*Hair*) der Herrenschnitt.
**shingle** (2) [ʃiŋgl], s. (*Geol.*) der Kiesel.
**shingles** [ʃiŋglz], s. pl. (*Med.*) die Gürtelrose.
**ship** [ʃip], s. das Schiff. — v.a. verschiffen, (*Comm.*) versenden.
**shipping** [ʃipiŋ], s. die Schiffahrt; (*Comm.*) der Versand, die Verfrachtung, Verschiffung.
**shire** [ʃaiə], s. die Grafschaft.
**shirk** [ʃəːk], v.a. vermeiden, sich drücken (vor, *Dat.*).
**shirt** [ʃəːt], s. das Hemd.
**shirting** [ʃəːtiŋ], s. der Hemdenstoff.
**shiver** [ʃivə], v.n. zittern, beben. — s. der Schauer, Schauder.
**shoal** [ʃoul], s. der Schwarm; (*Naut.*) die Untiefe.
**shock** (1) [ʃɔk], v.a. entsetzen; erschrecken; schockieren. — s. der Schock, das Entsetzen.
**shock** (2) [ʃɔk], s. — of hair, zottiges Haar.
**shoddy** [ʃɔdi], adj. schlecht, wertlos.
**shoe** [ʃuː], s. der Schuh. — v.a. beschuhen; (*horse*) beschlagen.
**shoelace, shoestring** [ʃuːleis, ʃuːstriŋ], s. der Schuhsenkel, (*Austr.*) das Schuhschnürl; on a shoestring, fast ohne Geld.
**shoeshine** [ʃuːʃain], s. (*Am.*) der Schuhputzer.
**shoestring** see under shoelace.
**shoot** [ʃuːt], v.a. irr. schießen. — v.n. sprossen, hervorschießen; (*film*) aufnehmen. — s. (*Bot.*) der Sproß.
**shooting** [ʃuːtiŋ], s. das Schießen; — range, der Schießstand. — adj. — star, die Sternschnuppe.
**shop** [ʃɔp], s. der Laden, das Geschäft; (*work*) die Werkstatt; talk —, fachsimpeln; — window, das Schaufenster. — v.n. einkaufen.
**shopkeeper** [ʃɔpkiːpə], s. der Kaufmann, Krämer.
**shoplifter** [ʃɔpliftə], s. der Ladendieb.
**shore** [ʃɔː], s. das Gestade, die Küste; die Stütze. — v.a. — up, stützen.
**short** [ʃɔːt], adj. kurz, klein, knapp; (*curt*) kurz angebunden; — of money, in Geldnot; run —, knapp werden; —sighted, kurzsichtig; be on — time working, kurz arbeiten. — s. (*Elect.*) (*coll.*) der Kurzschluß (*short circuit*); (*pl.*) die Kniehose, kurze Hose.
**shortcoming** [ʃɔːtkʌmiŋ], s. der Fehler, Mangel.
**shorten** [ʃɔːtn], v.a. verkürzen, abkürzen. — v.n. kürzer werden.
**shorthand** [ʃɔːthænd], s. die Stenographie; — typist, die Stenotypistin.
**shot** [ʃɔt], s. der Schuß; (*man*) der Schütze.

**shoulder** [ʃouldə], s. (*Anat.*) die Schulter. — v.a. schultern, auf sich nehmen, auf die Achsel nehmen.
**shout** [ʃaut], v.n. schreien, rufen. — s. der Schrei, Ruf.
**shove** [ʃʌv], v.a. schieben, stoßen. — s. der Schub, Stoß.
**shovel** [ʃʌvl], s. die Schaufel. — v.a. schaufeln.
**show** [ʃou], v.a. irr. zeigen; (*fig.*) dartun. — v.n. sich zeigen, zu sehen sein; — off, prahlen, protzen. — v.r. — o.s. to be, sich erweisen als. — s. (*Theat.*) die Schau, Aufführung.
**shower** [ʃauə], s. der Schauer (*rain*); (*fig.*) die Fülle, der Überfluß; — (*bath*), die Dusche; take a —(*bath*), brausen. — v.a., v.n. herabregnen; überschütten.
**showing** [ʃouiŋ], s. die Vorführung, der Beweis.
**showy** [ʃoui], adj. protzig, angeberisch.
**shred** [ʃred], s. der Fetzen; (*fig.*) die Spur (*of evidence*). — v.a. zerreißen, zerfetzen.
**shrew** [ʃruː], s. die Spitzmaus; (*fig.*) das zänkische Weib.
**shrewd** [ʃruːd], adj. schlau, verschlagen, listig.
**shriek** [ʃriːk], v.n. kreischen. — s. der Schrei, das Gekreisch.
**shrift** [ʃrift], s. give s.o. short —, mit einem kurzen Prozeß machen.
**shrill** [ʃril], adj. schrill, gellend, durchdringend.
**shrimp** [ʃrimp], s. (*Zool.*) die Garnele.
**shrine** [ʃrain], s. der (Reliquien)-schrein; der Altar.
**shrink** [ʃriŋk], v.n. irr. eingehen, einschrumpfen. — v.a. eingehen lassen.
**shrinkage** [ʃriŋkidʒ], s. das Eingehen (*fabric*); (*Geol.*) die Schrumpfung.
**shrivel** [ʃrivl], v.n. einschrumpfen, sich runzeln.
**shroud** [ʃraud], s. das Leichentuch. — v.a. einhüllen.
**Shrove** [ʃrouv] **Tuesday.** die Fastnacht.
**shrub** [ʃrʌb], s. (*Bot.*) der Strauch, die Staude.
**shrug** [ʃrʌg], v.a. (*shoulders*) die Achseln zucken. — s. das Achselzucken.
**shudder** [ʃʌdə], s. der Schauder. — v.n. schaudern.
**shuffle** [ʃʌfl], v.a. (*cards*) mischen. — v.n. schlürfen, schleppend gehen.
**shun** [ʃʌn], v.a. meiden.
**shunt** [ʃʌnt], v.a., v.n. rangieren.
**shut** [ʃʌt], v.a. irr. schließen. — v.n. sich schließen, zugehen; (*coll.*) — up! halt's Maul!
**shutter** [ʃʌtə], s. der Fensterladen.
**shuttle** [ʃʌtl], s. (*Mech.*) das Weberschiff.
**shuttlecock** [ʃʌtlkɔk], s. der Federball.
**shy** (1) [ʃai], adj. scheu, schüchtern. — v.n. scheuen (*of horses*).
**shy** (2) [ʃai], s. der Wurf.
**sick** [sik], adj. krank; unwohl, übel; leidend (*suffering*); (*fig.*) — of, überdrüssig (*Genit.*).

**sicken** [sikn], v.n. krank werden or sein; sich ekeln (be nauseated). — v.a. anekeln.

**sickle** [sikl], s. die Sichel.

**sickness** ['siknis], s. die Krankheit.

**side** [said], s. die Seite. — v.n. — with, Partei ergreifen für.

**sideboard** ['saidbɔ:d], s. das Büffet, die Anrichte.

**sidereal** [sai'diəriəl], adj. (Maths., Phys.) Sternen-, Stern-.

**sidewalk** ['saidwɔ:k] (Am.) see pavement.

**siding** ['saidiŋ],s.(Railw.)das Nebengleis.

**sidle** [saidl], v.n. — up to, sich heranmachen.

**siege** [si:dʒ], s. die Belagerung.

**sieve** [siv], s. das Sieb. — v.a. sieben.

**sift** [sift], v.a. sieben; (fig.) prüfen.

**sigh** [sai], v.n. seufzen. — s. der Seufzer.

**sight** [sait], s. die Sicht (view); die Sehkraft (sense of); der Anblick; at —, auf den ersten Blick; out of —, out of mind, aus den Augen, aus dem Sinn; (pl.) die Sehenswürdigkeiten, f. pl.; —seeing, die Besichtigung (der Sehenswürdigkeiten). — v.a. sichten.

**sign** [sain], s. das Zeichen; der Wink (hint); das Aushängeschild (of pub, shop etc.). — v.a. unterschreiben, unterzeichnen. — v.n. winken.

**signal** ['signəl], s. das Signal.

**signboard** ['sainbɔ:d], s. das Aushängeschild.

**signet** ['signit], s. das Siegel; — ring, der Siegelring.

**significance** [sig'nifikəns], s. die Bedeutung, der Sinn.

**significant** [sig'nifikənt], adj. bedeutend, wichtig.

**signify** ['signifai], v.a. bedeuten (mean); anzeigen (denote).

**silence** ['sailəns], s. das Schweigen, die Ruhe.

**silent** ['sailənt], adj. still; schweigsam (taciturn).

**Silesian** [sai'li:ʃən], adj. schlesisch. — s. der Schlesier.

**silk** [silk], s. (Text.) die Seide.

**silkworm** ['silkwə:m], s. (Ent.) die Seidenraupe.

**sill** [sil], s. die Schwelle; window —, das Fensterbrett.

**silly** ['sili], adj. albern, dumm.

**silver** ['silvə], s. das Silber. — v.a. versilbern. — adj. silbern.

**similar** ['similə], adj. ähnlich.

**simile** ['simili], s. (Lit.) das Gleichnis.

**simmer** ['simə], v.n., v.a. langsam kochen.

**simper** ['simpə], v.n. lächeln, grinsen.

**simple** [simpl], adj. einfach; (fig.) einfältig.

**simpleton** ['simpltən], s. der Einfaltspinsel, Tor.

**simplicity** [sim'plisiti], s. die Einfachheit; (fig.) die Einfalt.

**simplify** ['simplifai], v.a. vereinfachen.

**simulate** ['simjuleit], v.a. nachahmen, heucheln, vortäuschen.

**simultaneous** [siməl'teinjəs], adj. gleichzeitig.

**sin** [sin], s. die Sünde. — v.n. sündigen.

**since** [sins], prep. seit (Dat.). — conj. seit (time); weil, da (cause). — adv. seither, seitdem.

**sincere** [sin'siə], adj. aufrichtig.

**sincerely** [sin'siəli], adv. yours —, Ihr ergebener (letters).

**sincerity** [sin'seriti], s. die Aufrichtigkeit.

**sine** [sain], s. (Maths.) der Sinus, die Sinuskurve.

**sinecure** ['sainikjuə], s. der Ruheposten, die Sinekure.

**sinew** ['sinju:], s. (Anat.) die Sehne, der Nerv.

**sinful** ['sinful], adj. sündig, sündhaft.

**sing** [siŋ], v.a., v.n. irr. singen; — of, besingen.

**singe** [sindʒ], v.a. sengen.

**Singhalese** [siŋgə'li:z], adj. singhalesisch. — s. der Singhalese, die Singhalesin.

**single** [siŋgl], adj. einzeln; ledig (unmarried); single-handed, allein. — v.a. — out, auswählen.

**singlet** ['siŋglit], s. die Unterjacke.

**singly** ['siŋgli], adv. einzeln (one by one).

**singular** ['siŋgjulə], adj. einzigartig, einzig. — s. (Gram.) die Einzahl.

**sinister** ['sinistə], adj. böse, unheimlich, finster.

**sink** [siŋk], v.a. irr. versenken; (fig.) (differences etc.) begraben. — v.n. versinken; (Naut.) sinken, versinken. — s. das Abwaschbecken, Ausgußbecken.

**sinker** ['siŋkə], s. der Schachtarbeiter (man); (Naut.) das Senkblei.

**sinuous** ['sinjuəs], adj. gewunden.

**sinus** ['sainəs], s. (Anat.) die Knochenhöhle; die Bucht.

**sip** [sip], v.a. schlürfen, nippen. — s. das Schlückchen.

**siphon** ['saifən], s. (Phys.) der Heber; die Siphonflasche. — v.a. auspumpen.

**Sir** (1) [sə:] (title preceding Christian name) Herr von... (baronet or knight).

**sir** (2) [sə:], s. Herr (respectful form of address); dear —, sehr geehrter Herr (in letters).

**sire** [saiə], s. der Ahnherr, Vater. — v.a. zeugen (horses etc.).

**siren** ['saiərən], s. die Sirene.

**sirloin** ['sə:lɔin], s. das Lendenstück.

**siskin** ['siskin], s. (Orn.) der Zeisig.

**sister** ['sistə], s. die Schwester; (Eccl.) Nonne; —in-law, die Schwägerin.

**sit** [sit], v.n. irr. sitzen. — v.a. — an examination, eine Prüfung machen.

**site** [sait], s. die Lage, der Platz.

**sitting** ['sitiŋ], s. die Sitzung; — room, das Wohnzimmer.

**situated** ['sitjueitid], adj. gelegen.

**situation** [sitju'eiʃən], s. die Lage, Situation; der Posten, die Stellung (post).

**six** [siks], *num. adj.* sechs; *be at —es and sevens,* durcheinander, uneinig sein.
**sixteen** [siks'ti:n], *num. adj.* sechzehn.
**sixth** [siksθ], *num. adj.* sechste.
**sixty** ['siksti], *num. adj.* sechzig.
**size** [saiz], *s.* die Größe, das Maß; (*fig.*) der Umfang.
**skate** (1) [skeit], *s.* der Schlittschuh. — *v.n.* Schlittschuh laufen.
**skate** (2) [skeit], *s.* (*Zool.*) der Glattrochen.
**skeleton** ['skelitən], *s.* das Skelett, Knochengerüst; — *key,* der Dietrich.
**sketch** [sketʃ], *s.* die Skizze, der Entwurf. — *v.a.* skizzieren, entwerfen. — *v.n.* Skizzen entwerfen.
**sketchy** ['sketʃi], *adj.* flüchtig.
**skew** [skju:], *adj.* schief, schräg.
**skewer** ['skju:ə], *s.* der Fleischspieß.
**ski** [ski:], *s.* der Schi.
**skid** [skid], *v.n.* gleiten, schleudern, rutschen. — *v.a.* hemmen, bremsen (*wheel*). — *s.* der Hemmschuh, die Bremse (*of wheel*).
**skiff** [skif], *s.* (*Naut.*) der Nachen, Kahn.
**skilful** ['skilful], *adj.* geschickt, gewandt; (*fig.*) erfahren.
**skill** [skil], *s.* die Geschicklichkeit, Gewandtheit; (*fig.*) die Erfahrung.
**skim** [skim], *v.a.* abschöpfen, abschäumen.
**skimp** [skimp], *v.a.* knausern, sparsam sein (mit, *Dat.*).
**skimpy** ['skimpi], *adj.* knapp.
**skin** [skin], *s.* die Haut; die Schale (*fruit*); — *deep,* oberflächlich. — *v.a.* häuten, schinden.
**skinflint** ['skinflint], *s.* der Geizhals.
**skinner** ['skinə], *s.* der Kürschner.
**skip** [skip], *v.n.* springen, hüpfen. — *v.a.* (*coll.*) auslassen, überspringen. — *s.* der Sprung.
**skipper** ['skipə], *s.* (*Naut.*) der Kapitän; (*coll.*) der Chef.
**skipping rope** ['skipiŋ roup], *s.* das Springseil.
**skirmish** ['skə:miʃ], *s.* das Scharmützel. — *v.n.* scharmützeln.
**skirt** [skə:t], *s.* der Rock, Rockschoß (*woman's garment*); der Saum (*edge*). — *v.a.* einsäumen (*seam, edge*); grenzen, am Rande entlang gehen.
**skirting (board)** ['skə:tiŋ (bɔ:d)], *s.* die Fußleiste.
**skit** [skit], *s.* die Stichelei, die Parodie, Satire.
**skittish** ['skitiʃ], *adj.* leichtfertig.
**skulk** [skʌlk], *v.n.* lauern, herumlungern.
**skull** [skʌl], *s.* der Schädel; — *and crossbones,* der Totenkopf.
**skunk** [skʌŋk], *s.* (*Zool.*) das Stinktier; (*coll.*) der Schuft.
**sky** [skai], *s.* der (sichtbare) Himmel.
**skylark** ['skailɑ:k], *s.* (*Orn.*) die Feldlerche.
**skylarking** ['skailɑ:kiŋ], *s.* das Possenreißen, die Streiche.
**skyline** ['skailain], *s.* der Horizont.
**skyscraper** ['skaiskreipə], *s.* der Wolkenkratzer.

**slab** [slæb], *s.* die Platte (*stone*); die Tafel, das Stück.
**slack** [slæk], *adj.* schlaff (*feeble*); locker (*loose*). — *s.* der Kohlengrus. — *v.n.* nachlassen, locker werden, faulenzen.
**slacken** [slækn], *v.a.,* *v.n.* locker werden, nachlassen.
**slackness** ['slæknis], *s.* die Schlaffheit, Faulheit.
**slag** [slæg], *s.* die Schlacke.
**slake** [sleik], *v.a.* dämpfen, löschen, stillen.
**slam** (1) [slæm], *v.a.* zuwerfen, zuschlagen (*door*). — *s.* der Schlag.
**slam** (2) [slæm], *v.a.* (*Cards*) Schlemm ansagen, Schlemm machen. — *s.* (*Cards*) der Stich.
**slander** ['slɑ:ndə], *v.a.* verleumden. — *s.* die Verleumdung.
**slanderer** ['slɑ:ndərə], *s.* der Verleumder.
**slang** [slæŋ], *s.* der Slang.
**slant** [slɑ:nt], *s.* die schräge Richtung, der Winkel (*angle*).
**slap** [slæp], *v.a.* schlagen. — *s.* der Klaps, Schlag.
**slapdash** ['slæpdæʃ], *adj.* oberflächlich.
**slash** [slæʃ], *v.a.* schlitzen, aufschlitzen; (*coll.*) (*Comm.*) herunterbringen (*prices*). — *s.* der Hieb, Schlag.
**slate** [sleit], *s.* der Schiefer. — *v.a.* mit Schiefer decken; (*fig.*) ankreiden, ausschelten (*scold*).
**slattern** ['slætə:n], *s.* die Schlampe.
**slaughter** ['slɔ:tə], *v.a.* schlachten; niedermetzeln. — *s.* das Schlachten; das Gemetzel.
**slave** [sleiv], *s.* der Sklave; — *driver,* der Sklavenaufseher. — *v.n.* — (*away*), sich placken, sich rackern.
**slavery** ['sleivəri], *s.* die Sklaverei.
**slavish** ['sleiviʃ], *adj.* sklavisch.
**slay** [slei], *v.a.* erschlagen, töten.
**sled, sledge** [sled, sledʒ], *s.* der Schlitten.
**sleek** [sli:k], *adj.* glatt. — *v.a.* glätten.
**sleep** [sli:p], *v.n. irr.* schlafen. — *s.* der Schlaf.
**sleeper** ['sli:pə], *s.* der Schläfer; (*Railw.*) die Bahnschwelle; der Schlafwagen (*sleeping car*).
**sleepwalker** ['sli:pwɔ:kə], *s.* der Nachtwandler.
**sleet** [sli:t], *s.* der Graupelregen.
**sleeve** [sli:v], *s.* der Ärmel; der Umschlag (*of record*); *have up o.'s —,* eine Überraschung bereithalten; *laugh in o.'s —,* sich ins Fäustchen lachen.
**sleigh** [slei], *s.* der Schlitten; — *ride,* die Schlittenfahrt.
**sleight** [slait], *s.* — *of hand,* der Taschenspielerstreich; der Trick.
**slender** ['slendə], *adj.* schlank, dünn, gering.
**slice** [slais], *s.* die Schnitte, Scheibe. — *v.a.* in Scheiben schneiden.
**slick** [slik], *adj.* glatt.
**slide** [slaid], *v.n. irr.* gleiten, rutschen (*glide*). — *v.a.* einschieben. — *s.* die Rutschbahn; (*Phot.*) das Dia, Diapositiv; — *rule,* der Rechenschieber.

**slight** [slait], *adj.* leicht (*light*), gering (*small*); (*fig.*) schwach, dünn(*weak*). — *s.* die Geringschätzung, Respektlosigkeit. — *v.a.* mißachten, geringschätzig behandeln.

**slim** [slim], *adj.* schlank.

**slime** [slaim], *s.* der Schleim (*phlegm*); der Schlamm (*mud*).

**sling** [sliŋ], *v.a. irr.* schleudern, werfen. — *s.* die Schleuder; (*Med.*) die Binde; der Wurf (*throw*).

**slink** [sliŋk], *v.n. irr.* schleichen.

**slip** [slip], *v.n.* ausgleiten; — *away*, entschlüpfen; — *up*, einen Fehltritt begehen (*err*). — *v.a.* gleiten lassen, schieben. — *s.* das Ausgleiten; (*fig.*) der Fehltritt; der Fehler (*mistake*); der Unterrock (*petticoat*); *give s.o. the* —, einem entgehen, entschlüpfen.

**slipper** ['slipə], *s.* der Pantoffel, Hausschuh.

**slippery** ['slipəri], *adj.* schlüpfrig, glatt.

**slipshod** ['slipʃɔd], *adj.* nachlässig.

**slit** [slit], *v.a.* schlitzen, spalten. — *s.* der Schlitz, Spalt.

**slither** ['sliðə], *v.n.* gleiten, rutschen.

**sloe** [slou], *s.* (*Bot.*) die Schlehe.

**slogan** ['slougən], *s.* das Schlagwort.

**sloop** [slu:p], *s.* (*Naut.*) die Schaluppe.

**slop** [slɔp], *s.* das Spülicht, Spülwasser.

**slope** [sloup], *s.* der Abhang, die Abdachung. — *v.n.* sich neigen. — *v.a.* abschrägen.

**sloppy** ['slɔpi], *adj.* unordentlich, nachlässig.

**slot** [slɔt], *s.* der Spalt, Schlitz (*slit*); die Kerbe (*notch*); — *machine,* der Automat.

**sloth** [slouθ], *s.* die Trägheit; (*Zool.*) das Faultier.

**slouch** [slautʃ], *v.n.* umherschlendern; sich schlaff halten.

**slough** [slau], *s.* der Morast, Sumpf.

**slovenly** ['slʌvnli], *adj.* schlampig, schmutzig.

**slow** [slou], *adj.* langsam; (*Phot.*) — *motion,* die Zeitlupenaufnahme. — *v.n.* — *down,* langsamer fahren *or* laufen.

**slow-worm** ['slouwə:m], *s.* (*Zool.*) die Blindschleiche.

**sludge** [slʌdʒ], *s.* der Schlamm, Schmutz.

**slug** [slʌg], *s.* (*Zool.*) die Wegschnecke; (*Am.*) die Kugel.

**sluggish** ['slʌgiʃ], *adj.* träg(e).

**sluice** [slu:s], *s.* die Schleuse. — *v.a.* ablassen (*drain*); begießen (*water*).

**slum** [slʌm], *s.* das Elendsviertel; Haus im Elendsviertel.

**slumber** ['slʌmbə], *s.* der Schlummer. — *v.n.* schlummern.

**slump** [slʌmp], *s.* (*Comm.*) der Tiefstand der Konjunktur; der Preissturz. — *v.n.* stürzen.

**slur** [slə:], *v.a.* undeutlich sprechen. — *s.* der Schandfleck, die Beleidigung; das Bindezeichen.

**slush** [slʌʃ], *s.* der Matsch, Schlamm; (*Lit.*) der Kitsch, die Schundliteratur.

**slut** [slʌt], *s.* die Schlampe.

**sly** [slai], *adj.* schlau, listig.

**smack** [smæk], *v.n.* schmecken (*of, nach, Dat.*). — *v.a.* schmatzen, lecken. — *s.* der Klaps. — *adv.* (*coll.*) — *in the middle,* gerade in der Mitte.

**small** [smɔ:l], *adj.* klein; (*fig.*) kleinlich (*petty*); — *talk,* das Geplauder.

**smallpox** ['smɔ:lpɔks], *s.* (*Med.*) die Blattern, *f. pl.*

**smart** [smɑ:t], *adj.* schneidig; elegant, schick (*well-dressed*). — *v.n.* schmerzen. — *s.* der Schmerz.

**smash** [smæʃ], *v.a.* zertrümmern, in Stücke schlagen.— *v.n.* zerschmettern; (*fig.*) zusammenbrechen. — *s.* der Krach.

**smattering** ['smætəriŋ], *s.* die oberflächliche Kenntnis.

**smear** [smiə], *v.a.* beschmieren; (*Am. coll.*) den Charakter angreifen, verleumden. — *s.* die Beschmierung, Befleckung.

**smell** [smel], *v.a. irr.* riechen. — *v.n.* riechen (nach, *Dat.*). — *s.* der Geruch.

**smelt** (1) [smelt], *v.a.* (*Metall.*) schmelzen.

**smelt** (2) [smelt], *s.* (*Zool.*) der Stintfisch.

**smile** [smail], *v.n.* lächeln. — *s.* das Lächeln.

**smirk** [smə:k], *v.n.* grinsen. — *s.* das Grinsen, die Grimasse.

**smite** [smait], *v.a. irr.* treffen, schlagen.

**smith** [smiθ], *s.* der Schmied.

**smitten** [smitn], *adj.* verliebt.

**smock** [smɔk], *s.* der Arbeitskittel.

**smoke** [smouk], *v.a., v.n.* rauchen; räuchern (*fish etc.*). — *s.* der Rauch.

**smoked** [smoukd], *adj.* — *ham,* der Räucherschinken.

**smooth** [smu:ð], *adj.* glatt, sanft (*to touch*); (*fig.*) glatt, geschmeidig, wendig. — *v.a.* glätten, ebnen.

**smother** ['smʌðə], *v.a.* ersticken.

**smoulder** ['smouldə], *v.n.* schwelen.

**smudge** [smʌdʒ], *v.a.* beschmutzen; *v.n.* schmieren, schmutzen. — *s.* der Schmutzfleck, Schmutz.

**smug** [smʌg], *adj.* selbstgefällig.

**smuggle** [smʌgl], *v.a.* schmuggeln.

**smuggler** ['smʌglə], *s.* der Schmuggler.

**smut** [smʌt], *v.a., v.n.* beschmutzen. — *s.* (*fig.*) der Schmutz.

**snack** [snæk], *s.* der Imbiß.

**snaffle** [snæfl], *s.* die Trense.

**snag** [snæg], *s.* die Schwierigkeit; der Haken.

**snail** [sneil], *s.* (*Zool.*) die Schnecke.

**snake** [sneik], *s.* (*Zool.*) die Schlange.

**snap** [snæp], *v.n.* schnappen (*at, nach, Dat.*); (*fig.*) einen anfahren (*shout at s.o.*). — *v.a.* (er)schnappen; (*Phot.*) knipsen. — *s.* (*abbr. for* **snapshot** ['snæpʃɔt]) (*Phot.*) das Photo.

**snare** [snɛə], *s.* die Schlinge. — *v.a. see* **ensnare.**

**snarl** [snɑ:l], *v.n.* knurren (*dog*); — *at s.o.,* einen anfahren, anschnauzen.

# snatch

snatch [snætʃ], *v.a.* erschnappen, erhaschen.

sneak [sni:k], *v.n.* kriechen, schleichen. — *s.* der Kriecher.

sneer [sniə], *v.n.* höhnen, verhöhnen (*at*, *Acc.*). — *s.* der Spott.

sneeze [sni:z], *v.n.* niesen. — *s.* das Niesen.

sniff [snif], *v.a.*, *v.n.* schnüffeln.

snigger ['snigə], *v.n.* kichern. — *s.* das Kichern.

snip [snip], *v.a.* schneiden, schnippeln.

snipe (1) [snaip], *s.* (*Orn.*) die Schnepfe.

snipe (2) [snaip], *v.n.* schießen.

snivel [snivl], *v.n.* schluchzen (*from weeping*); verschnupft sein (*with a cold*).

snob [snɔb], *s.* der Snob.

snobbish ['snɔbiʃ], *adj.* vornehm tuend; protzig, snobistisch.

snooze [snu:z], *v.a.* das Schläfchen. — *v.n.* einschlafen, ein Schläfchen machen.

snore [snɔ:], *v.n.* schnarchen. — *s.* das Schnarchen.

snort [snɔ:t], *v.n.* schnaufen; schnarchen (*snore*).

snout [snaut], *s.* die Schnauze, der Rüssel.

snow [snou], *s.* der Schnee. — *v.n.* schneien.

snowdrift ['snoudrift], *s.* das Schneegestöber.

snowdrop ['snoudrɔp], *s.* (*Bot.*) das Schneeglöckchen.

snub [snʌb], *v.a.* kurz abfertigen; (*fig.*) schneiden (*ignore*). — *adj.* — *nosed*, stumpfnasig. — *s.* die Geringschätzung, das Ignorieren.

snuff [snʌf], *s.* der Schnupftabak. — *v.a.* ausblasen (*candle*).

snug [snʌg], *adj.* behaglich; geborgen (*protected*).

so [sou], *adv.* so, also; *not* — *as*, nicht so wie. — *conj.* so.

soak [souk], *v.a.* einweichen, durchtränken. — *v.n.* weichen, durchsickern (*in(to*), in, *Acc.*). — *s.* der Regenguß.

soap [soup], *s.* die Seife. — *v.a.* einseifen.

soar [sɔ:], *v.n.* sich aufschwingen, schweben.

sob [sɔb], *v.n.* schluchzen. — *s.* das Schluchzen.

sober ['soubə], *adj.* nüchtern. — *v.a.*, *v.n.* — (*down*), (sich) ernüchtern.

sobriety [so'braiəti], *s.* die Nüchternheit.

soccer ['sɔkə], *s.* (*Sport*) das Fußballspiel.

sociable ['souʃəbl], *adj.* gesellig.

social ['souʃəl], *adj.* sozial, gesellschaftlich. — *s.* die Gesellschaft (*party*).

socialism ['souʃəlizm], *s.* (*Pol.*) der Sozialismus.

socialist ['souʃəlist], *adj.* (*Pol.*) sozialistisch, Sozial-. — *s.* der Sozialist.

society [sə'saiəti], *s.* die Gesellschaft (*human* —); der Verein (*association*); (*Comm.*) die (Handels)gesellschaft.

sock (1) [sɔk], *s.* der Strumpf.

sock (2) [sɔk], *v.a.* (*sl.*) schlagen, boxen.

socket ['sɔkit], *s.* *eye* —, die Augenhöhle; (*Elec.*) die Steckdose.

sod [sɔd], *s.* der Rasen, die Erde.

sodden [sɔdn], *adj.* durchweicht.

sofa ['soufə], *s.* das Sofa.

soft [sɔft], *adj.* weich, sanft; einfältig (*stupid*).

soften [sɔfn], *v.a.* weich machen, erweichen. — *v.n.* weich werden, erweichen.

soil [sɔil], *s.* der Boden, die Erde. — *v.a.* beschmutzen.

sojourn ['sɔdʒən *or* 'sɔdʒən], *s.* der Aufenthalt. — *v.n.* sich aufhalten.

solace ['sɔlis], *s.* der Trost.

solar ['soulə], *adj.* Sonnen-.

solder ['sɔldə *or* 'sɔ:də], *v.a.* löten. — *s.* das Lötmittel.

soldier ['souldʒə], *s.* der Soldat. — *v.n.* dienen, Soldat sein.

sole (1) [soul], *s.* (*Zool.*) die Seezunge.

sole (2) [soul], *s.* die Sohle (*foot*).

sole (3) [soul], *adj.* allein, einzig.

solecism ['sɔlisizm], *s.* der Sprachschnitzer.

solemn ['sɔləm], *adj.* feierlich.

solemnize ['sɔləmnaiz], *v.a.* feiern, feierlich begehen.

solicit [sə'lisit], *v.a.* direkt erbitten, angehen, anhalten (*for*, um).

solicitor [sə'lisitə], *s.* (*Law*) der Anwalt, Rechtsanwalt.

solicitous [sə'lisitəs], *adj.* besorgt.

solid ['sɔlid], *adj.* fest; solide; (*fig.*) gediegen; massiv (*bulky*).

solidify [sə'lidifai], *v.a.* verdichten, fest machen. — *v.n.* sich verfestigen.

soliloquy [sə'liləkwi], *s.* das Selbstgespräch, der Monolog.

solitaire [sɔli'tɛə], *s.* der Solitär; (*Am.*) die Patience.

solitary ['sɔlitəri], *adj.* einzeln (*single*); einsam (*lonely*).

solitude ['sɔlitju:d], *s.* die Einsamkeit.

solstice ['sɔlstis], *s.* die Sonnenwende.

soluble ['sɔljubl], *adj.* (*Chem.*) löslich; lösbar.

solution [sə'lju:ʃən], *s.* die Lösung.

solvable ['sɔlvəbl], *adj.* (auf)lösbar (*problem*, *puzzle*).

solve [sɔlv], *v.a.* lösen (*problem*, *puzzle*).

solvent ['sɔlvənt], *adj.* (*Chem.*) auflösend; (*Comm.*) zahlungsfähig. — *s.* das Lösungsmittel.

sombre ['sɔmbə], *adj.* düster; schwermütig, traurig.

some [sʌm], *adj.* irgend ein, etwas; (*pl.*) einige, manche; etliche.

somebody ['sʌmbɔdi], *s.* jemand.

somersault ['sʌməsɔ:lt], *s.* der Purzelbaum.

sometimes ['sʌmtaimz], *adv.* manchmal, zuweilen.

somewhat ['sʌmwɔt], *adv.* etwas, ziemlich.

somewhere ['sʌmwɛə], *adv.* irgendwo(hin).

**somnambulist** [səm'næmbjulist], *s.* der Nachtwandler.
**somnolent** ['sɔmnələnt], *adj.* schläfrig, schlafsüchtig.
**son** [sʌn], *s.* der Sohn; —*-in-law,* der Schwiegersohn.
**song** [sɔŋ], *s.* (*Mus.*) das Lied; der Gesang; *for a* —, spottbillig.
**sonnet** ['sɔnit], *s.* (*Poet.*) das Sonett.
**sonorous** ['sɔnərəs], *adj.* wohlklingend.
**soon** [su:n], *adv.* bald.
**sooner** ['su:nə], *comp. adv.* lieber (*rather*); früher, eher (*earlier*); *no* — *said than done,* gesagt, getan.
**soot** [sut], *s.* der Ruß.
**soothe** [su:ð], *v.a.* besänftigen.
**soothsayer** ['su:θseiə], *s.* der Wahrsager.
**sop** [sɔp], *s.* der eingetunkte Bissen; (*fig.*) die Bestechung (*bribe*).
**soporific** [sɔpə'rifik], *adj.* einschläfernd.
**soprano** [sə'prɑ:nou], *s.* (*Mus.*) der Sopran.
**sorcerer** ['sɔ:sərə], *s.* der Zauberer.
**sorceress** ['sɔ:sərɛs], *s.* die Hexe.
**sorcery** ['sɔ:səri], *s.* die Zauberei, Hexerei.
**sordid** ['sɔ:did], *adj.* schmutzig; gemein.
**sore** [sɔ:], *adj.* wund, schmerzhaft; empfindlich. — *s.* die wunde Stelle.
**sorrel** (1) ['sɔrəl], *s.* (*Bot.*) der Sauerampfer.
**sorrel** (2) ['sɔrəl], *s.* (*Zool.*) der Rotfuchs.
**sorrow** ['sɔrou], *s.* der Kummer, das Leid, der Gram.
**sorry** ['sɔri], *adj.* traurig; *I am* —, es tut mir leid.
**sort** [sɔ:t], *s.* die Art, Gattung, Sorte. — *v.a.* aussortieren.
**sortie** ['sɔ:ti:], *s.* (*Mil.*) der Ausfall.
**sot** [sɔt], *s.* der Trunkenbold.
**soul** [soul], *s.* die Seele; *not a* —, niemand, keine Menschenseele.
**sound** (1) [saund], *v.n., v.a.* tönen, klingen, erklingen lassen. — *s.* der Klang, Ton, Laut.
**sound** (2) [saund], *adj.* gesund; (*fig.*) vernünftig (*plan etc.*); solide.
**soup** [su:p], *s.* die Suppe.
**sour** [sauə], *adj.* sauer; (*fig.*) mürrisch.
**source** [sɔ:s], *s.* die Quelle; der Ursprung (*origin*).
**souse** [saus], *v.a.* einpökeln, einsalzen.
**south** [sauθ], *s.* der Süden.
**South African** [sauθ 'æfrikən], *adj.* südafrikanisch. — *s.* der Südafrikaner.
**southern** ['sʌðən], *adj.* südlich, Süd-.
**sou(th)-wester** [sau(θ)'westə], *s.* (*Naut.*) der Südwester.
**souvenir** ['su:vəniə], *s.* das Andenken.
**sovereign** ['sɔvrin], *s.* der Herrscher (*ruler*); das Goldstück (*£1 coin*). — *adj.* allerhöchst, souverän.
**Soviet** ['souviit], *adj.* sowjetisch. — *s.* der Sowjet.
**sow** (1) [sau], *s.* (*Zool.*) die Sau.
**sow** (2) [sou], *v.a. irr.* säen, ausstreuen (*cast*).

**spa** [spɑ:], *s.* das Bad; der Kurort.
**space** [speis], *s.* der Zwischenraum (*interval*); der Raum, das Weltall, der Kosmos (*interplanetary*); der Platz (*room*). — *v.a.* sperren, richtig plazieren.
**spacious** ['speiʃəs], *adj.* geräumig.
**spade** [speid], *s.* der Spaten; *call a* — *a* —, das Kind beim rechten Namen nennen; (*Cards*) das Pik.
**span** [spæn], *s.* die Spanne (*time*); die Spannweite. — *v.a.* überspannen (*bridge*); ausmessen.
**spangle** [spæŋgl], *s.* der Flitter. — *v.a.* beflittern, schmücken.
**Spaniard** ['spænjəd], *s.* der Spanier.
**spaniel** ['spænjəl], *s.*(*Zool.*) der Wachtelhund.
**Spanish** ['spæniʃ], *adj.* spanisch.
**spanner** ['spænə], *s.* der Schraubenschlüssel.
**spar** (1) [spɑ:], *s.* (*Naut.*) der Sparren.
**spar** (2) [spɑ:], *s.* (*Geol.*) der Spat.
**spar** (3) [spɑ:], *v.n.* boxen.
**spare** [spɛə], *v.a.* schonen (*save*); sparsam sein; übrig haben. — *v.n.* sparen; sparsam sein. — *adj.* übrig (*extra*); mager, hager (*lean*); Reserve- (*tyre etc.*).
**sparing** ['spɛəriŋ], *adj.* sparsam, karg.
**spark** [spɑ:k], *s.* der Funken; (*fig.*) der helle Kopf.
**sparkle** [spɑ:kl], *v.n.* glänzen, funkeln. — *s.* das Funkeln.
**sparrow** ['spærou], *s.* (*Orn.*) der Sperling.
**sparrowhawk** ['spærouhɔ:k], *s.* (*Orn.*) der Sperber.
**sparse** [spɑ:s], *adj.* spärlich, dünn.
**spasm** [spæzm], *s.* der Krampf.
**spasmodic** [spæz'mɔdik], *adj.* krampfhaft; (*fig.*) ab und zu auftretend.
**spats** [spæts], *s. pl.* die Gamaschen, *f.pl.*
**spatter** ['spætə], *v.a.* bespritzen, besudeln.
**spatula** ['spætjulə], *s.* der Spachtel.
**spawn** [spɔ:n], *s.* der Laich, die Brut.
**speak** [spi:k], *v.a., v.n. irr.* sprechen, reden; — *out,* frei herausprechen.
**speaker** ['spi:kə], *s.* der Sprecher.
**spear** [spiə], *s.* der Spieß, Speer, die Lanze. — *v.a.* aufspießen.
**special** [speʃl], *adj.* besonder, speziell, Sonder-.
**specific** [spi'sifik], *adj.* spezifisch, eigentümlich.
**specify** ['spesifai], *v.a.* spezifizieren.
**specimen** ['spesimən], *s.* die Probe; (*Comm.*) das Muster.
**specious** ['spi:ʃəs], *adj.* bestechend, trügerisch.
**speck** [spek], *s.* der Fleck.
**speckle** [spekl], *s.* der Tüpfel, Sprenkel. — *v.a.* sprenkeln.
**spectacle** ['spektəkl], *s.* das Schauspiel, der Anblick; (*pl.*) die Brille.
**spectator** [spek'teitə], *s.* der Zuschauer.
**spectre** ['spektə], *s.* das Gespenst.
**speculate** ['spekjuleit], *v.n.* nachsinnen, grübeln (*ponder*); spekulieren.

# speculative

**speculative** ['spekjulətiv], *adj.* spekulativ; sinnend.

**speech** [spi:tʃ], *s.* die Rede, Ansprache; das Sprechen (*articulation*); *figure of* —, die Redewendung; *make a* —, eine Rede halten.

**speechify** ['spi:tʃifai], *v.n.* viele Worte machen, unermüdlich reden.

**speed** [spi:d], *s.* die Eile; die Geschwindigkeit (*velocity*); (*Mus.*) das Tempo. — *v.a.* (eilig) fortschicken. — *v.n.* eilen, schnell fahren; — *up*, sich beeilen.

**spell** (1) [spel], *s.* der Zauber (*enchantment*). — *v.a.* buchstabieren (*verbally*); richtig schreiben (*in writing*).

**spell** (2) [spel], *s.* die Zeitlang, Zeit (*period*).

**spellbound** ['spelbaund], *adj.* bezaubert, gebannt.

**spend** [spend], *v.a. irr.* ausgeben (*money*); verbringen (*time*); aufwenden (*energy*); erschöpfen (*exhaust*).

**spendthrift** ['spendθrift], *s.* der Verschwender.

**spew** [spju:], *v.a.* speien; ausspeien.

**sphere** [sfiə], *s.* die Sphäre (*also fig.*); (*Geom.*) die Kugel.

**spice** [spais], *s.* die Würze (*seasoning*); das Gewürz (*herb*). — *v.a.* würzen.

**spider** ['spaidə], *s.* (*Zool.*) die Spinne.

**spigot** ['spigət], *s.* (*Mech.*) der Zapfen.

**spike** [spaik], *s.* die Spitze, der lange Nagel; (*fig.*) der Dorn. — *v.a.* durchbohren, spießen; (*Mil.*) vernageln (*a gun*).

**spill** (1) [spil], *v.a. irr.* ausschütten, vergießen; (*Am. coll.*) — *the beans*, mit der Sprache herausrücken, alles verraten; *it's no good crying over spilt milk*, was geschehen ist, ist geschehen.

**spill** (2) [spil], *s.* der Fidibus.

**spin** [spin], *v.a. irr.* spinnen, drehen, wirbeln. — *v.n.* wirbeln, sich schnell drehen; — *dry*, schleudern. — *s.* die schnelle Drehung; — *drier*, die Wäscheschleuder.

**spinach** ['spinidʒ], *s.* (*Bot.*) der Spinat.

**spinal** ['spainəl], *adj.* Rückgrats-.

**spine** [spain], *s.* (*Anat.*) die Wirbelsäule; der Rücken (*of book*).

**spinney** ['spini], *s.* das Gestrüpp.

**spinster** ['spinstə], *s.* die (alte) Jungfer; die unverheiratete Dame.

**spiral** ['spaiərəl], *adj.* Spiral-, gewunden. — *s.* (*Geom.*) die Spirale.

**spirant** ['spaiərənt], *s.* (*Phonet.*) der Spirant.

**spire** [spaiə], *s.* (*Archit.*) die Turmspitze.

**spirit** ['spirit], *s.* der Geist; das Gespenst (*ghost*); der Mut (*courage*); die Stimmung, Verfassung (*mood*); das geistige Getränk (*drink*), (*pl.*) Spirituosen, *pl.*; *in high* —s, in guter Stimmung, Laune. — *v.a.* — *away*, entführen, verschwinden lassen.

**spiritual** ['spiritjuəl], *adj.* geistig (*mental*); (*Rel.*) geistlich. — *s.* (*Mus.*) das Negerlied.

**spit** (1) [spit], *s.* der Spieß, Bratspieß. — *v.a.* aufspießen.

**spit** (2) [spit], *v.n. irr.* ausspucken. — *s.* die Spucke.

**spite** [spait], *s.* der Groll; *in* — *of*, trotz (*Genit.*). — *v.a.* ärgern.

**spiteful** ['spaitful], *adj.* boshaft.

**spittle** [spitl], *s.* der Speichel.

**spittoon**, [spi'tu:n], *s.* der Spucknapf.

**splash** [splæʃ], *s.* der Spritzer; *make a* —, Aufsehen erregen. — *v.a., v.n.* spritzen; (*fig.*) um sich werfen (*money etc.*).

**splay** [splei], *v.a.* ausrenken, verrenken.

**spleen** [spli:n], *s.* (*Anat.*) die Milz; (*fig.*) der Spleen, die Laune, Marotte.

**splendour** ['splendə], *s.* die Pracht, der Glanz.

**splice** [splais], *v.a.* splissen; (*Naut.*) — *the mainbrace*, das Hauptfaß öffnen!

**splint** [splint], *s.* (*Med.*) die Schiene.

**splinter** ['splintə], *s.* der Span; der Splitter (*fragment*).

**split** [split], *v.a. irr.* spalten; (*fig.*) verteilen, teilen (*divide*). — *v.n.* sich trennen; (*coll.*) — *on s.o.*, einen verraten. — *adj.* — *second timing*, auf den Bruchteil einer Sekunde. — *s.* die Spaltung.

**splutter** ['splʌtə], *v.n.* sprudeln. — *s.* das Sprudeln.

**spoil** [spoil], *v.a. irr.* verderben; (*child*) verwöhnen; (*Mil.*) plündern, berauben. — *v.n.* verderben. — *s.* (*pl.*) die Beute.

**spoilsport** ['spoilspo:t], *s.* der Spielverderber.

**spoke** [spouk], *s.* die Speiche; die Sprosse.

**spokesman** ['spouksmən], *s.* der Wortführer, Sprecher.

**sponge** [spʌndʒ], *s.* der Schwamm; — *cake*, die Sandtorte. — *v.a.* mit dem Schwamm wischen. — *v.n.* (*coll.*) schmarotzen (*on, bei, Dat.*).

**sponger** ['spʌndʒə], *s.* (*coll.*) der Schmarotzer (*parasite*).

**sponsor** ['sponsə], *s.* der Bürge (*guarantor*); der Förderer; Pate. — *v.a.* fördern, unterstützen.

**spontaneous** [spon'teiniəs], *adj.* spontan, freiwillig.

**spook** [spuk], *s.* der Spuk, Geist, das Gespenst.

**spool** [spu:l], *s.* die Spule. — *v.a.* aufspulen.

**spoon** [spu:n], *s.* der Löffel. — *v.a.* mit dem Löffel essen, löffeln.

**sport** [spo:t], *s.* der Sport; (*fig.*) der Scherz. — *v.a.* tragen (*wear*). — *v.n.* scherzen.

**spot** [spot], *s.* die Stelle, der Ort, Platz; (*stain*) der Fleck; (*fig.*) der Schandfleck (*on o.'s honour*); *on the* —, sogleich; auf der Stelle; *in a* —, (*Am. coll.*) in Verlegenheit; — *cash*, Barzahlung, *f.* — *v.a.* entdecken, finden.

**spotted** ['spotid], *adj.* — *dick*, der Korinthenpudding.

**spouse** [spauz], *s.* der Gatte; die Gattin.

**spout** [spaut], *v.a.*, *v.n.* ausspeien, sprudeln, sprudeln lassen; (*sl.*) predigen, schwatzen. — *s.* die Tülle (*teapot etc.*); die Abflußröhre.

**sprain** [sprein], *v.a.* (*Med.*) verrenken. — *s.* die Verrenkung.

**sprat** [spræt], *s.* (*Zool.*) die Sprotte.

**sprawl** [sprɔːl], *v.n.* sich spreizen, ausbreiten.

**spray** [sprei], *v.a.*, *v.n.* sprühen spritzen. — *s.* die Sprühe; der Sprühregen.

**spread** [spred], *v.a.*, *v.n. irr.* ausbreiten; verbreiten (*get abroad*); streichen (*overlay with*). — *s.* die Ausbreitung; Verbreitung.

**spree** [spriː], *s.* das Vergnügen, der lustige Abend, Bummel.

**sprig** [sprig], *s.* der Zweig, Sprößling.

**sprightly** ['spraitli], *adj.* munter, lebhaft.

**spring** [spriŋ], *s.* die Quelle (*water*); der Ursprung (*origin*); der Frühling (*season*); (*Mech.*) die Feder, Sprungfeder, Spirale. — *v.n. irr.* springen (*jump*); entspringen (*originate*). — *v.a.* – *a surprise*, eine Überraschung bereiten.

**springe** [sprindʒ], *s.* der Sprenkel.

**sprinkle** ['spriŋkl], *v.a.* (be)sprengen; (*Hort.*) berieseln.

**sprint** [sprint], *s.* der Kurzstreckenlauf, Wettlauf.

**sprite** [sprait], *s.* der Geist, Kobold.

**sprout** [spraut], *s.* (*Bot.*) die Sprosse, der Sprößling; *Brussels —s*, der Rosenkohl.

**spruce** (1) [spruːs], *adj.* sauber, geputzt; schmuck.

**spruce** (2) [spruːs], *s.* (*Bot.*) die Fichte, Rottanne.

**spume** [spjuːm], *s.* der Schaum.

**spur** [spəː], *s.* der Sporn (*goad*); (*fig.*) der Stachel; der Ansporn, Antrieb; (*Geog.*) der Ausläufer (*of range*). — *v.a.* anspornen.

**spurious** ['spjuəriəs], *adj.* unecht, falsch.

**spurn** [spəːn], *v.a.* verschmähen, verachten.

**spurt** [spəːt], *v.a.* spritzen. — *v.n.* sich anstrengen. — *s.* die Anstrengung.

**sputter** ['spʌtə], *v.a.* herausspudeln. — *v.n.* sprühen, sprudeln.

**spy** [spai], *s.* der Spion. — *v.n.* spionieren (*on*, bei, *Dat.*).

**squabble** [skwɔbl], *v.n.* zanken. — *s.* der Zank, Streit.

**squad** [skwɔd], *s.* der Trupp.

**squadron** ['skwɔdrən], *s.* die Schwadron, das Geschwader.

**squalid** ['skwɔlid], *adj.* schmutzig, elend, eklig.

**squall** [skwɔːl], *s.* der Windstoß.

**squalor** ['skwɔlə], *s.* der Schmutz.

**squander** ['skwɔndə], *v.a.* verschwenden, vergeuden.

**square** [skwɛə], *s.* das Quadrat; der Platz; (*coll.*) der Philister, Spießer. — *v.a.* ausrichten; (*coll.*) ins Reine bringen. — *adj.* viereckig; quadratisch; redlich (*honest*); quitt (*quits*).

**squash** (1) [skwɔʃ], *v.a.* zerquetschen, zerdrücken (*press together*). — *s.* das Gedränge (*crowd*); der Fruchtsaft (*drink*).

**squash** (2) [skwɔʃ], *s.* (*Sport*) eine Art Racketspiel.

**squat** [skwɔt], *v.n.* kauern; sich niederlassen. — *adj.* stämmig, untersetzt.

**squatter** ['skwɔtə], *s.* der Ansiedler.

**squaw** [skwɔː], *s.* die Indianerfrau.

**squeak** [skwiːk], *v.n.* quieken, quietschen. — *s.* das Gequiek.

**squeal** [skwiːl], *v.n.* quieken; (*Am. coll.*) verraten, preisgeben.

**squeamish** ['skwiːmiʃ], *adj.* empfindlich, zimperlich.

**squeeze** [skwiːz], *v.a.* drücken, quetschen. — *s.* das Gedränge.

**squib** [skwib], *s.* der Frosch (*firework*); (*Lit.*) das Spottgedicht.

**squint** [skwint], *v.n.* schielen. — *s.* das Schielen.

**squire** [skwaiə], *s.* der Landedelmann, Junker.

**squirrel** ['skwirəl], *s.* (*Zool.*) das Eichhörnchen.

**squirt** [skwəːt], *v.a.* spritzen. — *s.* der Spritzer, Wasserstrahl; (*sl.*) der Wicht.

**stab** [stæb], *v.a.* erstechen, erdolchen. — *s.* der Dolchstich, Dolchstoß.

**stability** [stə'biliti], *s.* die Beständigkeit, Stabilität.

**stable** (1) [steibl], *adj.* fest, beständig; (*Phys.*) stabil.

**stable** (2) [steibl], *s.* der Stall.

**stack** [stæk], *s.* der Stoß (*pile*); der Schornstein (*chimneys*). — *v.a.* aufschichten.

**staff** [stɑːf], *s.* der Stab, Stock; (*Mil.*) der Stab, Generalstab; (*Sch.*) der Lehrkörper; das Personal. — *v.a.* besetzen.

**stag** [stæg], *s.* (*Zool.*) der Hirsch; — *party*, die Herrengesellschaft.

**stage** [steidʒ], *s.* (*Theat.*) die Bühne; die Stufe, das Stadium (*phase*); (*fig.*) der Schauplatz; *fare —*, die Teilstrecke. — *v.a.* (*Theat.*) inszenieren, abhalten (*hold*).

**stagecoach** ['steidʒkoutʃ], *s.* die Postkutsche.

**stagger** ['stægə], *v.n.* schwanken, wanken, taumeln. — *v.a.* (*coll.*) verblüffen (*astonish*); staffeln (*graduate*).

**stagnate** [stæg'neit], *v.n.* stocken, stillstehen.

**staid** [steid], *adj.* gesetzt, gelassen.

**stain** [stein], *s.* der Fleck, Makel. — *v.a.* beflecken; beizen; färben (*dye*).

**stained** [steind], *adj.* – *glass window*, buntes Fenster.

**stainless** ['steinlis], *adj.* rostfrei.

**stair** [stɛə], *s.* die Stufe, Stiege.

**staircase** ['stɛəkeis], *s.* das Treppenhaus; die Treppe.

**stake** [steik], *s.* der Pfahl, Pfosten; Scheiterhaufen; (*Gambling*) der Einsatz; *at —*, auf dem Spiel. — *v.a.* aufs Spiel setzen.

**stale** [steil], *adj.* abgestanden, schal.

# stalemate

**stalemate** ['steilmeit], *s.* (*Chess*) das Patt; der Stillstand.

**stalk** (1) [stɔ:k], *s.* (*Bot.*) der Stengel, Halm.

**stalk** (2) [stɔ:k], *v.n.* stolzieren, steif gehen. — *v.a.* pirschen (*hunt*).

**stall** [stɔ:l], *s.* die Bude (*booth*), der Stand (*stand*); (*Eccl.*) der Chorstuhl; (*Theat.*) der Sperrsitz; Parterresitz. — *v.n.* (*Motor.*) stehenbleiben.

**stallion** ['stæljən], *s.* (*Zool.*) der Hengst.

**stalwart** ['stɔ:lwət], *adj.* kräftig, stark, verläßlich.

**stamina** ['stæminə], *s.* die Ausdauer, Widerstandskraft.

**stammer** ['stæmə], *v.n.* stammeln, stottern.

**stamp** [stæmp], *s.* der Stempel (*rubber* —); die Marke (*postage*); die Stampfe, Stanze (*die* —). — *v.a.* stempeln; (*Mech.*) stanzen; frankieren (*letters*). — *v.n.* stampfen.

**stampede** [stæm'pi:d], *s.* die wilde Flucht. — *v.n.* in wilder Flucht davonlaufen.

**stand** [stænd], *v.n. irr.* stehen. — *v.a.* aushalten, standhalten (*Dat.*). — *s.* der Ständer (*hats etc.*); der Stand (*stall*); (*fig.*) die Stellung.

**standard** ['stændəd], *s.* der Standard (*level*); (*Mil.*) die Standarte; der Maßstab (*yardstick*). — *adj.* normal.

**standing** ['stændiŋ], *s.* der Rang, das Ansehen. — *adj.* — *orders*, die Geschäftsordnung; (*Mil.*) die Vorschriften, *f. pl.*, Dauerbefehle, *m. pl.*

**standpoint** ['stændpɔint], *s.* der Standpunkt (*point of view*).

**standstill** ['stændstil], *s.* der Stillstand.

**stanza** ['stænzə], *s.* (*Poet.*) die Stanze, Strophe.

**staple** ['steipl], *s.* das Haupterzeugnis; der Stapelplatz. — *adj.* Haupt-. — *v.a.* stapeln; heften (*paper*).

**stapler** ['steiplə], *s.* die Heftmaschine.

**star** [sta:], *s.* der Stern; (*Theat. etc.*) der Star. — *v.n.* (*Theat. etc.*) die Hauptrolle spielen.

**starboard** ['sta:bəd], *s.* das Steuerbord.

**starch** [sta:tʃ], *s.* die Stärke (*laundry*). — *v.a.* stärken.

**stare** [stɛə], *v.n.* starren. — *s.* der starre Blick, das Starren.

**stark** [sta:k], *adj.* völlig, ganz.

**starling** ['sta:liŋ], *s.* (*Orn.*) der Star.

**start** [sta:t], *v.n.* anfangen; aufbrechen; auffahren, aufspringen; stutzen (*jerk*); abfahren (*depart*). — *v.a.* starten (*car etc.*), in Gang setzen. — *s.* der Anfang; (*Sport*) der Start, Anlauf; der Aufbruch (*departure*); *by fits and* —*s*, ruckweise.

**starter** ['sta:tə], *s.* (*Sport*) der Starter, Teilnehmer (*participant*); das Rennpferd (*horse*); (*Motor.*) der Anlasser.

**startle** [sta:tl], *v.a.* erschrecken.

**starve** [sta:v], *v.n.* verhungern, hungern. — *v.a.* aushungern.

**state** [steit], *s.* der Zustand, die Lage;

(*Pol.*) der Staat; (*personal*) der Stand (*single etc.*). — *v.a.* erklären, darlegen.

**stately** ['steitli], *adj.* stattlich, prachtvoll.

**statement** ['steitmənt], *s.* die Feststellung; *bank* —, der Kontoauszug.

**statesman** ['steitsmən], *s.* der Staatsmann, Politiker.

**statics** ['stætiks], *s.* die Statik.

**station** ['steiʃən], *s.* (*Railw.*) die Station; der Bahnhof; die Stellung, der Rang (*position*); (*Mil.*) die Stationierung. — *v.a.* (*Mil.*) aufstellen, stationieren; (*fig.*) hinstellen.

**stationary** ['steiʃənri], *adj.* stationär, stillstehend.

**stationer** ['steiʃənə], *s.* der Papierhändler.

**stationery** ['steiʃənri], *s.* das Briefpapier, Schreibpapier; die Papierwaren, *f. pl.*

**statuary** ['stætjuəri], *s.* die Bildhauerkunst.

**statue** ['stætju:], *s.* das Standbild.

**status** ['steitəs], *s.* die Stellung (*rank, position*).

**statute** ['stætju:t], *s.* das Statut; — *law*, das Landesrecht, Gesetzesrecht.

**staunch** [stɔ:ntʃ], *adj.* zuverlässig.

**stave** [steiv], *s.* die Faßdaube (*of vat*); (*Poet.*) die Strophe; (*Mus.*) die Linie. — *v.a.* — *off*, abwehren.

**stay** [stei], *v.n.* bleiben, verweilen, wohnen. — *v.a.* hindern, aufhalten. — *s.* der Aufenthalt; (*pl.*) das Korsett.

**stead** [sted], *s.* die Stelle; *in his* —, an seiner Statt.

**steadfast** ['stedfa:st], *adj.* standhaft, fest.

**steadiness** ['stedinis], *s.* die Beständigkeit.

**steady** ['stedi], *adj.* fest, sicher; beständig, treu.

**steak** [steik], *s.* das Steak.

**steal** [sti:l], *v.a. irr.* stehlen. — *v.n.* sich stehlen, schleichen.

**stealth** [stelθ], *s.* die Heimlichkeit.

**stealthy** ['stelθi], *adj.* heimlich, verstohlen.

**steam** [sti:m], *s.* der Dampf; *get up* —, in Gang bringen *or* kommen; — *boiler*, der Dampfkessel. — *v.n.* dampfen; davondampfen. — *v.a.* dämpfen, (*Cul.*) dünsten.

**steed** [sti:d], *s.* das Schlachtroß.

**steel** [sti:l], *s.* der Stahl. — *adj.* stählern. — *v.n.* — *o.s.*, sich stählen.

**steep** (1) [sti:p], *adj.* steil; (*fig.*) hoch; (*coll.*) gesalzen (*price*).

**steep** (2) [sti:p], *v.a.* einweichen, sättigen.

**steeple** [sti:pl], *s.* (*Archit.*) der Kirchturm.

**steeplechase** ['sti:pltʃeis], *s.* das Hindernisrennen.

**steeplejack** ['sti:pldʒæk], *s.* der Turmdecker.

**steer** (1) [stiə], *s.* (*Zool.*) der junge Stier.

**steer** (2) [stiə], *v.a.* steuern (*guide*).

**steerage** ['stiəridʒ], *s.* die Steuerung; (*Naut.*) das Zwischendeck.

**stellar** ['stelə], *adj.* Stern-, Sternen-.
**stem** (1) [stem], *s.* der Stamm; (*Phonet.*) der Stamm; der Stiel, die Wurzel. — *v.n.* — *from,* kommen von, abstammen.
**stem** (2) [stem], *v.a.* sich entgegenstemmen (*Dat.*); (*fig.*) eindämmen.
**stench** [stentʃ], *s.* der Gestank.
**stencil** ['stensil], *s.* die Schablone, Matrize; *cut a —,* auf Matrize schreiben.
**step** [step], *s.* der Schritt, Tritt; (*of ladder*) die Sprosse; (*of stairs*) die Stufe. — *v.n.* treten, schreiten (*stride*). — *v.a.* (*coll.*) — *up,* beschleunigen.
**step-** [step], *pref.* Stief- (*brother, mother etc.*).
**stereo-** ['stiəriou], *pref.* Stereo-.
**sterile** ['sterail], *adj.* steril.
**sterling** ['stə:liŋ], *adj.* echt, vollwertig; *pound —,* ein Pfund Sterling.
**stern** (1) [stə:n], *adj.* streng.
**stern** (2) [stə:n], *s.* (*Naut.*) das Heck.
**stevedore** ['sti:vədɔ:], *s.* der Hafenarbeiter.
**stew** [stju:], *s.* (*Cul.*) das Schmorfleisch, das Gulasch.
**steward** ['stju:əd], *s.* der Verwalter; der Haushofmeister; (*Naut.*) der Steward.
**stick** [stik], *s.* der Stock, Stecken. — *v.a.* stecken (*insert*); kleben (*glue*). — *v.n.* stecken, haften bleiben; (*fig., coll.*) — *to s.o.,* zu jemandem halten (*be loyal*).
**sticky** ['stiki], *adj.* klebrig; (*fig.*) prekär, schwierig (*difficult*); *come to a — end,* ein böses Ende nehmen.
**stiff** [stif], *adj.* steif; schwer, schwierig (*examination*); formell (*manner*).
**stiffen** ['stifn], *v.a.* steifen, versteifen. — *v.n.* steif werden, sich versteifen.
**stifle** [staifl], *v.a., v.n.* ersticken; (*fig.*) unterdrücken.
**stigmatize** ['stigmətaiz], *v.a.* stigmatisieren, brandmarken.
**stile** [stail], *s.* der Zauntritt, Übergang.
**still** (1) [stil], *adj.* still, ruhig. — *adv.* immer noch. — *conj.* doch, dennoch. — *v.a.* stillen, beruhigen.
**still** (2) [stil], *s.* die Destillierflasche, der Destillierkolben.
**stilt** [stilt], *s.* die Stelze.
**stilted** ['stiltid], *adj.* auf Stelzen; (*fig.*) hochtrabend, geschraubt.
**stimulant** ['stimjulənt], *s.* das Reizmittel. — *adj.* anreizend, anregend.
**stimulate** ['stimjuleit], *v.a.* anreizen, stimulieren, anregen.
**stimulus** ['stimjuləs], *s.* der Reiz, die Anregung.
**sting** [stiŋ], *v.a. irr.* stechen; (*fig.*) kränken, verwunden. — *v.n. irr.* stechen, brennen, schmerzen. — *s.* der Stachel (*prick*); der Stich (*stab*).
**stink** [stiŋk], *v.n. irr.* stinken. — *s.* der Gestank.
**stint** [stint], *s.* die Einschränkung (*limit*); das Maß, Tagespensum. — *v.a.* beschränken, einschränken.

**stipend** ['staipend], *s.* die Besoldung, das Gehalt.
**stipendiary** [stai'pendiəri], *adj.* besoldet, bezahlt.
**stipulate** ['stipjuleit], *v.a.* festsetzen, ausbedingen.
**stir** [stə:], *v.a.* rühren, bewegen. — *v.n.* sich rühren. — *s.* die Aufregung; *cause a —,* Aufsehen erregen.
**stirrup** ['stirəp], *s.* der Steigbügel.
**stitch** [stitʃ], *v.a.* sticken, nähen. — *s.* der Stich; der stechende Schmerz, der Seitenstich (*pain*).
**stoat** [stout], *s.* (*Zool.*) das Hermelin.
**stock** [stɔk], *s.* das Lager; *in —,* auf Lager; vorrätig; der Stamm, die Familie; (*Fin.*) das Kapital; — *exchange,* die Börse; (*pl.*) die Börsenpapiere, *n. pl.,* Aktien, *f. pl.* — *v.a.* halten, führen.
**stockade** [stɔ'keid], *s.* das Staket.
**stockbroker** ['stɔkbroukə], *s.* (*Fin.*) der Börsenmakler.
**stockholder** ['stɔkhouldə], *s.* (*Fin., Am.*) der Aktionär.
**stocking** ['stɔkiŋ], *s.* der Strumpf.
**stocktaking** ['stɔkteikiŋ], *s.* die Inventuraufnahme.
**stoical** ['stouikəl], *adj.* stoisch.
**stoke** [stouk], *v.a.* schüren.
**stoker** ['stoukə], *s.* der Heizer.
**stole** [stoul], *s.* (*Eccl.*) die Stola; der Pelzkragen (*fur*).
**stolid** ['stɔlid], *adj.* schwerfällig, gleichgültig.
**stomach** ['stʌmək], *s.* der Magen; (*fig.*) der Appetit.
**stone** [stoun], *s.* der Stein; der Kern (*fruit*). — *v.a.* steinigen (*throw —s at*); entsteinen (*fruit*).
**stony** ['stouni], *adj.* steinig; (*sl.*) — *broke,* pleite.
**stool** [stu:l], *s.* der Schemel, Hocker; (*Med.*) der Stuhlgang.
**stoop** [stu:p], *v.n.* sich bücken; (*fig.*) sich herablassen.
**stooping** ['stu:piŋ], *adj.* gebückt.
**stop** [stɔp], *v.a.* halten, stoppen; aufhören; aufhalten (*halt*); — *up,* verstopfen, versperren (*block*); (*tooth*) plombieren. — *v.n.* stehen bleiben (*stand*); sich aufhalten (*stay*). — *s.* der Halt, die Haltestelle (*of bus etc.*); das Aufhalten, Innehalten (*stoppage*); das Register (*organ*); (*Gram.*) der Punkt.
**stoppage** ['stɔpidʒ], *s.* die Stockung, Hemmung (*hindrance*); die Arbeitseinstellung (*strike*).
**stopper** ['stɔpə], *s.* der Stöpsel.
**storage** ['stɔ:ridʒ], *s.* das Lagern.
**store** [stɔ:], *s.* der Vorrat, das Lagerhaus, Magazin; (*Am.*) das Kaufhaus; (*fig.*) die Menge (*of anecdotes etc.*). — *v.a.* lagern.
**storey** ['stɔ:ri], *s.* das Stockwerk.
**stork** [stɔ:k], *s.* (*Orn.*) der Storch.
**storm** [stɔ:m], *s.* der Sturm, das Gewitter.
**story** ['stɔ:ri], *s.* die Geschichte, Erzählung (*narrative*).

**stout** [staut], *adj.* fest; stark, kräftig. — *s.* das starke Bier.

**stove** [stouv], *s.* der Ofen.

**stow** [stou], *v.a.* verstauen, packen. — *v.n.* — *away*, als blinder Passagier fahren.

**stowaway** ['stouəwei], *s.* der blinde Passagier.

**straddle** [strædl], *v.n.* rittlings sitzen.

**straggle** [strægl], *v.n.* umherschweifen, streifen; (*Bot.*) wuchern.

**straight** [streit], *adj.* gerade, offen. — *adv.* — *away*, sofort, sogleich.

**straighten** [streitn], *v.a.* ausrichten, gerade richten. — *v.n.* sich ausrichten.

**strain** [strein], *s.* die Anstrengung, Anspannung; (*Mus.*) der Ton, Stil; der Hang. — *v.a.* anstrengen, filtrieren; seihen. — *v.n.* sich anstrengen.

**strainer** ['streinə], *s.* der Seiher, der Filter, das Sieb.

**strait** [streit], *adj.* eng. — *s.* (*usually pl.*) die Enge, Meerenge.

**strand** (1) [strænd], *s.* der Strand.

**strand** (2) [strænd], *s.* die Litze (*of rope, string*).

**strange** [streindʒ], *adj.* fremd (*unknown*); seltsam (*queer*).

**stranger** ['streindʒə], *s.* der Fremdling, Fremde; der Unbekannte.

**strangle** [stræŋgl], *v.a.* erdrosseln, erwürgen.

**strangulation** [stræŋgju'leiʃən], *s.* die Erdrosselung, Erwürgung.

**strap** [stræp], *v.a.* festschnallen, anschnallen. — *s.* der Gurt, Riemen.

**strapping** ['stræpiŋ], *adj.* stark, stämmig.

**strata** *see under* **stratum**.

**stratagem** ['strætədʒəm], *s.* die List, (*Mil.*) der Plan.

**strategy** ['strætədʒi], *s.* die Strategie.

**stratification** [strætifi'keiʃən], *s.* die Schichtung; (*Geol.*) die Lagerung.

**stratum** ['streitəm], *s.* (*pl.* **strata** ['streitə]) die Schicht, Lage.

**straw** [strɔ:], *s.* das Stroh; *that's the last* —, das ist die Höhe!

**strawberry** ['strɔ:bəri], *s.* (*Bot.*) die Erdbeere.

**stray** [strei], *v.n.* irregehen, schweifen; sich verirren. — *adj.* irr, verirrt.

**streak** [stri:k], *s.* der Strich; der Streifen; (*fig.*) der Anflug.

**streaky** [stri:ki], *adj.* gestreift; (*bacon*) durchwachsen.

**stream** [stri:m], *v.n.* strömen, wehen (*in the wind*). — *s.* die Strömung (*flow*); der Bach (*brook*), der Strom (*river*).

**streamer** ['stri:mə], *s.* der Wimpel, das Band, die Papierschlange.

**street** [stri:t], *s.* die Straße; —*s ahead*, weit voraus.

**streetcar** ['stri:tkɑ:], *s.* (*Am.*) *see* **tram**.

**streetlamp** ['stri:tlæmp], *s.* die Straßenlaterne.

**strength** [streŋθ], *s.* die Stärke; die Kraft.

**strengthen** ['streŋθən], *v.a.* stärken; (*fig.*) bekräftigen (*support*).

**strenuous** ['strenjuəs], *adj.* anstrengend.

**stress** [stres], *v.a.* (*Phonet.*) betonen; (*fig.*) hervorheben. — *s.* die Betonung (*emphasis*); der Druck (*pressure*).

**stretch** [stretʃ], *v.a.* spannen; strecken, ausstrecken; — *a point*, eine Ausnahme machen. — *s.* die Strecke (*distance*); (*coll.*) die Zuchthausstrafe (*penal sentence*).

**stretcher** ['stretʃə], *s.* die Tragbahre.

**strew** [stru:], *v.a.* streuen, ausstreuen.

**strict** [strikt], *adj.* streng (*severe*); genau (*exact*).

**stricture** ['striktʃə], *s.* der Tadel, die Kritik; (*pl.*) die kritische Rede.

**stride** [straid], *v.n. irr.* schreiten. — *s.* der Schritt; *take in o.'s* —, leicht bewältigen.

**strident** ['straidənt], *adj.* laut, lärmend; grell.

**strife** [straif], *s.* der Streit, Zank.

**strike** [straik], *v.a., v.n. irr.* schlagen; abmachen (*bargain*); (*Mus.*) — *up*, anstimmen (*song*), aufspielen (*instrument*); beginnen; — *the eye*, auffallen; streiken, in Streik treten. — *s.* der Streik, die Arbeitseinstellung.

**striking** ['straikiŋ], *adj.* auffallend.

**string** [striŋ], *s.* die Schnur; (*Mus.*) die Saite; — *quartet*, das Streichquartett; die Reihe (*series*). — *v.a.* anreihen (*beads etc.*); — *together*, verbinden. — *v.n.* — *along*, sich anschließen.

**stringency** ['strindʒənsi], *s.* die Strenge (*severity*); die Knappheit (*shortage*).

**stringent** ['strindʒənt], *adj.* streng (*severe*); knapp (*short*).

**strip** [strip], *s.* der Streifen. — *v.a., v.n.* abstreifen, (sich) entkleiden; (sich) entblößen.

**stripe** [straip], *s.* der (Farb)streifen; die Strieme (*mark on body*). — *v.a.* streifen, bestreifen.

**strive** [straiv], *v.n. irr.* sich bemühen (*for*, um, *Acc.*), streben (*for*, nach, *Dat.*).

**stroke** (1) [strouk], *v.a.* streicheln.

**stroke** (2) [strouk], *s.* der Strich (*brush*); der Streich (*sword*), der Stoß (*blow*); (*Med.*) der Schlaganfall.

**stroll** [stroul], *v.n.* schlendern.

**strolling** ['stroulin], *adj.* — *players*, die Wandertruppe.

**strong** [strɔŋ], *adj.* stark.

**strongbox** ['strɔŋbɔks], *s.* die Geldkassette.

**strongroom** ['strɔŋrum], *s.* der Geldtresor.

**strop** [strɔp], *s.* der Streichriemen.

**structure** ['straktʃə], *s.* der Bau, Aufbau; die Struktur.

**struggle** [strʌgl], *s.* der Kampf, das Ringen. — *v.n.* kämpfen, ringen.

**strut** [strʌt], *v.n.* stolzieren.

**stub** [stʌb], *s.* der Stumpf, Stummel (*cigarette*). — *v.a.* — *out*, ausmachen, auslöschen (*cigarette etc.*).

**stubble** [stʌbl], *s.* die Stoppel, das Stoppelfeld; die (Bart)stoppeln, *f. pl.* (*beard*).
**stubborn** ['stʌbən], *adj.* eigensinnig, hartnäckig.
**stucco** ['stʌkou], *s.* die Stuckarbeit.
**stud** (1) [stʌd], *s.* der Hemdenknopf, Kragenknopf (*collar* —). — *v.a.* beschlagen (*nail*); besetzen (*bejewel*).
**stud** (2) [stʌd], *s.* das Gestüt (*horses*).
**student** ['stju:dənt], *s.* der Student.
**studied** ['stʌdid], *adj.* geziert, absichtlich (*deliberate*); gelehrt (*learned*).
**studio** ['stju:diou], *s.* (*Phot.*) das Atelier; (*Film, Rad.*) das Studio.
**studious** ['stju:diəs], *adj.* beflissen, fleißig; lernbegierig.
**study** ['stʌdi], *v.a., v.n.* studieren. — *s.* das Studium; das Arbeitszimmer (*room*); (*Mus. etc.*) die Studie; (*Art*) der Entwurf; die Untersuchung (*investigation*).
**stuff** [stʌf], *s.* der Stoff, das Material; (*coll.*) das Zeug (*rubbish*). — *v.a.* stopfen, ausstopfen (*animals*); (*Cul.*) füllen.
**stuffing** ['stʌfiŋ], *s.* die Füllung, das Füllsel.
**stultify** ['stʌltifai], *v.a.* dumm machen.
**stumble** [stʌmbl], *v.n.* stolpern; — *upon,* zufällig stoßen (auf, *Acc.*).
**stumbling** ['stʌmbliŋ], *s.* das Stolpern; — *block,* das Hindernis, der Stein des Anstoßes.
**stump** [stʌmp], *s.* der Stumpf. — *v.a.* verblüffen; abstumpfen. — *v.n.* schwerfällig gehen.
**stun** [stʌn], *v.a.* betäuben, verdutzen.
**stunning** ['stʌniŋ], *adj.* betörend, fabelhaft, überwältigend.
**stunt** (1) [stʌnt], *v.a.* am Wachstum behindern, klein halten.
**stunt** (2) [stʌnt], *s.* der Trick, das Kunststück; (*Aviat.*) der Kunstflug.
**stupefy** ['stju:pifai], *v.a.* betäuben.
**stupendous** [stju:'pendəs], *adj.* erstaunlich.
**stupid** ['stju:pid], *adj.* dumm.
**stupor** ['stju:pə], *s.* die Erstarrung, Lähmung (*of mind*).
**sturdy** ['stə:di], *adj.* derb, stark, stämmig.
**sturgeon** ['stə:dʒən], *s.* (*Zool.*) der Stör.
**stutter** ['stʌtə], *v.n.* stottern.
**sty** [stai], *s.* der Schweinestall.
**sty(e)** [stai], *s.* (*Med.*) das Gerstenkorn (*on eyelid*).
**style** [stail], *s.* (*Lit.*) der Stil; der Griffel (*stylus*); die Mode (*fashion*); die Anrede (*address*). — *v.a.* anreden.
**stylish** ['stailiʃ], *adj.* elegant, modern.
**suave** [sweiv, swɑ:v], *adj.* höflich, gewinnend.
**sub-** [sʌb], *pref.* Unter-.
**subaltern** ['sʌbəltən], *s.* (*Mil.*) der Leutnant, Oberleutnant.
**subject** ['sʌbdʒikt], *s.* (*Gram.*) das Subjekt; (*Pol.*) der Untertan; der Gegenstand. — *adj.* untertan (*to,*

*Dat.*); — *to,* abhängig von. — [sʌb'dʒekt], *v.a.* unterwerfen (*to, Dat.*); aussetzen (*Dat.*).
**subjunctive** [səb'dʒʌŋktiv], *s.* (*Gram.*) der Konjunktiv.
**sublet** [sʌb'let], *v.a.* in Untermiete vermieten, untervermieten.
**sublimate** ['sʌblimeit], *v.a.* sublimieren.
**submarine** ['sʌbməri:n], *s.* das Unterseeboot.
**submission** [səb'miʃən], *s.* die Unterwerfung (*subjection*); der Vorschlag (*suggestion*).
**submit** [səb'mit], *v.a.* unterwerfen (*subjugate*); vorlegen. — *v.n.* sich beugen (*to, Dat.*).
**suborn** [sʌ'bɔ:n], *v.a.* anstiften; bestechen (*corrupt*).
**subpoena** [sʌb'pi:nə], *s.* (*Law*) die Vorladung.
**subscribe** [səb'skraib], *v.a.* unterschreiben. — *v.n.* zeichnen (*to,* zu); abonnieren (*paper*).
**subscription** [səb'skripʃən], *s.* das Abonnement (*to, Genit.*); (*club*) der Beitrag.
**subsequent** ['sʌbsikwənt], *adj.* folgend.
**subservient** [sʌb'sə:viənt], *adj.* unterwürfig.
**subside** [səb'said], *v.n.* sinken; abnehmen (*decrease*).
**subsidence** [sʌb'saidəns, 'sʌbsidəns], *s.* das Sinken, Sichsetzen.
**subsidiary** [sʌb'sidjəri], *adj.* Hilfs-, Neben-.
**subsidize** ['sʌbsidaiz], *v.a.* unterstützen (*with money*), subventionieren.
**subsidy** ['sʌbsidi], *s.* die Unterstützung, Subvention.
**subsist** [səb'sist], *v.n.* leben, existieren.
**subsistence** [səb'sistəns], *s.* das Dasein, Auskommen; der Lebensunterhalt.
**substance** ['sʌbstəns], *s.* das Wesen, der Stoff, die Substanz.
**substantial** [səb'stænʃəl], *adj.* wesentlich, beträchtlich.
**substantiate** [səb'stænʃieit], *v.a.* dartun, nachweisen, bestätigen.
**substantive** ['sʌbstəntiv], *s.* (*Gram.*) das Substantiv, Hauptwort. — *adj.* (*Mil.*) effektiv, wirklich.
**substitute** ['sʌbstitju:t], *v.a.* ersetzen, an die Stelle setzen. — *s.* der Ersatzmann, Vertreter.
**subterfuge** ['sʌbtəfju:dʒ], *s.* die Ausflucht.
**subtle** [sʌtl], *adj.* fein, schlau, subtil.
**subtract** [səb'trækt], *v.a.* abziehen; (*Maths.*) subtrahieren.
**suburb** ['sʌbə:b], *s.* die Vorstadt, der Vorort.
**subversion** [sʌb'və:ʃən], *s.* (*Pol.*) der Umsturz.
**subversive** [səb'və:siv], *adj.* umstürzlerisch, umstürzend.
**subway** ['sʌbwei], *s.* die Unterführung; (*Am.*) die Untergrundbahn.
**succeed** [sək'si:d], *v.n.* erfolgreich sein, Erfolg haben. — *v.a.* nachfolgen (*Dat.*) (*follow*).

success [sək'ses], *s.* der Erfolg.
successful [sək'sesful], *adj.* erfolgreich.
succession [sək'seʃən], *s.* die Nachfolge.
successive [sək'sesiv], *adj.* der Reihe nach, aufeinanderfolgend.
succinct [sək'siŋkt], *adj.* bündig, kurz.
succour ['sʌkə], *v.a.* beistehen (*Dat.*), helfen (*Dat.*).
succulent ['sʌkjulənt], *adj.* saftig.
succumb [sə'kʌm], *v.n.* unterliegen (*to*, *Dat.*).
such [sʌtʃ], *adj.* solch, derartig. — *pron.* ein solcher; — *as*, diejenigen, alle die.
suchlike ['sʌtʃlaik], *pron.* (*coll.*) dergleichen.
suck [sʌk], *v.a.*, *v.n.* saugen.
suckle [sʌkl], *v.a.* säugen, stillen.
suction ['sʌkʃən], *s.* das Saugen; (*Engin.*) Saug-.
Sudanese [su:də'ni:z], *adj.* sudanisch, sudanesisch. — *s.* der Sudan(es)er.
sudden [sʌdn], *adj.* plötzlich.
suds [sʌdz], *s. pl.* das Seifenwasser.
sue [sju:], *v.a.* gerichtlich belangen, verklagen.
suède [sweid], *s.* das Wildleder.
suet ['su:it], *s.* das Nierenfett.
suffer ['sʌfə], *v.a.* ertragen, dulden. — *v.n.* leiden (*from*, an).
sufferance ['sʌfərəns], *s.* die Duldung; *on* —, nur widerwillig.
suffice [sə'fais], *v.n.* genügen, langen, (aus)reichen.
sufficient [sə'fiʃənt], *adj.* genügend, hinreichend.
suffocate ['sʌfəkeit], *v.a.*, *v.n.* ersticken.
suffragan ['sʌfrəgən], *s.* (*Eccl.*) der Weihbischof.
suffrage ['sʌfridʒ], *s.* das Wahlrecht, Stimmrecht.
suffuse [sə'fju:z], *v.a.* übergießen, überfließen.
sugar ['ʃugə], *s.* der Zucker; — *basin*, die Zuckerdose.
suggest [sə'dʒest], *v.a.* vorschlagen, anregen.
suggestion [sə'dʒestʃən], *s.* der Vorschlag.
suggestive [sə'dʒestiv], *adj.* zweideutig.
suicide ['sju:isaid], *s.* der Selbstmord, Freitod.
suit [su:t], *s.* das Gesuch, die Bitte (*request*); die Farbe (*cards*); (*Law*) der Prozeß (*clothes*). — *v.n.* passen (*Dat.*) (*be convenient to*); passen zu (*look well with*). — *v.a.* anpassen (*match*).
suitcase ['su:tkeis], *s.* der Handkoffer.
suitable ['su:təbl], *adj.* passend.
suite [swi:t], *s.* das Gefolge (*following*); die Zimmerflucht (*rooms*); die Reihe (*cards*).
suitor ['su:tə], *s.* der Brautwerber, Freier.
sulk [sʌlk], *v.n.* schmollen.
sullen ['sʌlən], *adj.* düster, mürrisch.
sully ['sʌli], *v.a.* beschmutzen.
sulphur ['sʌlfə], *s.* (*Chem.*) der Schwefel.

Sultan ['sʌltən], *s.* der Sultan.
Sultana [sʌl'tɑ:nə], *s.* die Sultanin.
sultana [sʌl'tɑ:nə], *s.* (*Bot.*) die Sultanine.
sultry ['sʌltri], *adj.* schwül.
sum [sʌm], *s.* die Summe; (*fig.*) der Inbegriff. — *v.a.*, *v.n.* — *up*, zusammenfassen.
summary ['sʌməri], *s.* die Zusammenfassung, der Auszug. — *adj.* summarisch.
summer ['sʌmə], *s.* der Sommer; *Indian* —, der Spätsommer, Altweibersommer, Nachsommer.
summit ['sʌmit], *s.* der Gipfel, die Spitze.
summon(s) ['sʌmən(z)], *v.a.* (*Law*) vorladen. — *s.* (summons) die Vorladung.
sump [sʌmp], *s.* (*Motor.*) die Ölwanne.
sumptuous ['sʌmptjuəs], *adj.* prächtig, mit Aufwand, kostbar.
sun [sʌn], *s.* die Sonne. — *v.r.* sich sonnen.
sunburn ['sʌnbə:n], *s.* der Sonnenbrand.
Sunday ['sʌnd(e)i], *s.* der Sonntag.
sundial ['sʌndaiəl], *s.* die Sonnenuhr.
sundown ['sʌndaun] *see* sunset.
sundry ['sʌndri], *adj.* mehrere, verschiedene. — *s.* (*pl.*) Gemischtwaren, *f. pl.*
sunny ['sʌni], *adj.* sonnig.
sunrise ['sʌnraiz], *s.* der Sonnenaufgang.
sunset ['sʌnset], *s.* der Sonnenuntergang.
sunshade ['sʌnʃeid], *s.* das Sonnendach, der Sonnenschirm (*parasol*).
super ['su:pə], *s.* (*Theat.*) der Statist. — *adj.* (*coll.*) fein, famos.
super- ['su:pə], *pref.* über-, hinzu-.
superannuation [su:pərænju'eiʃən], *s.* die Pensionierung.
superb [su'pə:b], *adj.* hervorragend, herrlich.
supercilious [su:pə'siliəs], *adj.* hochmütig, anmaßend.
superficial [su:pə'fiʃəl], *adj.* oberflächlich.
superfluous [su:'pə:fluəs], *adj.* überflüssig.
superintendent [su:pərin'tendənt], *s.* der Oberaufseher.
superior [su:'piəriə], *adj.* ober, höher. — *s.* der Vorgesetzte.
superiority [su:piəri'oriti], *s.* die Überlegenheit.
superlative [su:'pə:lətiv], *s.* (*Gram.*) der Superlativ. — *adj.* ausnehmend gut.
supermarket ['su:pəmɑ:kit], *s.* das Selbstbedienungsgeschäft, SB-Geschäft, der grosse Lebensmittelladen.
supersede [su:pə'si:d], *v.a.* verdrängen.
superstition [su:pə'stiʃən], *s.* der Aberglaube.
superstitious [su:pə'stiʃəs], *adj.* abergläubisch.
supervise ['su:pəvaiz], *v.a.* beaufsichtigen, überwachen.

**supine** [su'pain], *adj.* auf dem Rücken liegend. — ['su:pain], *s.* (*Gram.*) das Supinum.

**supper** ['sʌpə], *s.* das Abendessen; *Last Supper*, das Heilige Abendmahl.

**supplant** [sə'plɑ:nt], *v.a.* verdrängen.

**supple** [sʌpl], *adj.* geschmeidig, biegsam.

**supplement** ['sʌplimənt], *s.* die Beilage (*paper*); der Zusatz.

**supplementary** [sʌpli'mentri], *adj.* zusätzlich.

**supplier** [sə'plaiə], *s.* der Lieferant.

**supply** [sə'plai], *v.a.* liefern (*s. th.*); beliefern, versorgen (*s.o.*). — *s.* die Versorgung.

**support** [sə'pɔ:t], *v.a.* unterstützen. — *s.* die Stütze (*prop*); die Unterstützung (*financial etc.*).

**suppose** [sə'pouz], *v.a.* annehmen, vermuten.

**supposition** [sʌpə'ziʃən], *s.* die Annahme, Vermutung, Voraussetzung.

**suppress** [sə'pres], *v.a.* unterdrücken.

**suppurate** ['sʌpjureit], *v.n.* eitern.

**supremacy** [su'preməsi], *s.* die Überlegenheit (*pre-eminence*); Obergewalt (*power*).

**supreme** [su'pri:m], *adj.* höchst, oberst.

**surcharge** ['sə:tʃɑ:dʒ], *s.* die Sonderzahlung, der Aufschlag, Zuschlag.

**sure** [ʃuə], *adj.* sicher; *to be —*, sicherlich; *make —*, sich überzeugen.

**surety** ['ʃuəti], *s.* (*Law*) die Kaution.

**surf** [sə:f], *s.* die Brandung.

**surface** ['sə:fis], *s.* die Oberfläche.

**surfeit** ['sə:fit], *s.* die Übersättigung, das Übermaß. — *v.a.* übersättigen.

**surge** [sə:dʒ], *v.n.* wogen, rauschen. — *s.* die Woge, das Aufwallen.

**surgeon** ['sə:dʒən], *s.* (*Med.*) der Chirurg.

**surgery** ['sə:dʒəri], *s.* (*Med.*) die Chirurgie (*subject*); — *hours*, die Sprechstunde.

**surgical** ['sə:dʒikəl], *adj.* chirurgisch.

**surly** ['sə:li], *adj.* mürrisch.

**surmise** [sə:'maiz], *v.a.* mutmaßen, vermuten. — *s.* die Mutmaßung, Vermutung.

**surmount** [sə:'maunt], *v.a.* übersteigen; überwinden (*overcome*).

**surname** ['sə:neim], *s.* der Zuname.

**surpass** [sə'pɑ:s], *v.a.* übertreffen.

**surplice** ['sə:plis], *s.* das Chorhemd.

**surplus** ['sə:pləs], *s.* der Überfluß.

**surprise** [sə'praiz], *s.* die Überraschung. — *v.a.* überraschen.

**surrender** [sə'rendə], *v.a.* übergeben, aufgeben. — *v.n.* sich ergeben. — *s.* die Waffenstreckung, Kapitulation.

**surreptitious** [sʌrəp'tiʃəs], *adj.* heimlich.

**surround** [sə'raund], *v.a.* umgeben, einschließen.

**surroundings** [sə'raundiŋz], *s. pl.* die Umgegend, Umgebung.

**survey** ['sə:vei], *s.* die Übersicht; die Vermessung. — [sə'vei], *v.a.* überblicken; vermessen.

**surveyor** [sə:'veiə], *s.* der Vermesser, Feldmesser.

**survival** [sə'vaivəl], *s.* das Überleben.

**survive** [sə'vaiv], *v.a., v.n.* überleben, überstehen.

**susceptibility** [səsepti'biliti], *s.* die Empfänglichkeit.

**susceptible** [sə'septibl], *adj.* empfänglich, empfindlich.

**suspect** [səs'pekt], *v.a.* verdächtigen. — ['sʌspekt], *adj.* verdächtig. — *s.* die Verdachtsperson, der Verdächtigte.

**suspend** [səs'pend], *v.a.* aufhängen; unterbrechen (*procedure*); einstellen (*work*).

**suspense** [səs'pens], *s.* die Spannung (*tension*); Ungewißheit (*uncertainty*).

**suspension** [səs'penʃən], *s.* (*Law*) die Suspension; die Einstellung (*stoppage*); die Aufhängung, Suspension; (*Motor.*) die Federung; — *bridge*, die Kettenbrücke, Hängebrücke.

**suspicion** [səs'piʃən], *s.* der Verdacht, Argwohn.

**suspicious** [səs'piʃəs], *adj.* verdächtig; argwöhnisch.

**sustain** [səs'tein], *v.a.* erleiden (*suffer*); ertragen (*bear*); aufrechterhalten (*maintain*).

**sustenance** ['sʌstinəns], *s.* der Unterhalt (*maintenance*); die Nahrung (*food*).

**suture** ['sju:tʃə], *s.* (*Med.*) die Naht.

**suzerain** ['sju:zərein], *s.* der Oberherr, Oberlehnsherr.

**swab** [swɔb], *s.* (*Med.*) die Laborprobe, der Abstrich; der Schrubber (*scrubber*). — *v.a.* (*Med.*) eine Probe entnehmen; schrubben (*scrub*).

**swaddle** [swɔdl], *s.* die Windel.

**swaddling** ['swɔdliŋ], *adj.* — *clothes*, die Windeln, *f. pl.*

**swagger** ['swægə], *v.n.* großtun. — *s.* das Großtun, Renommieren.

**swallow** (1) ['swɔlou], *s.* (*Orn.*) die Schwalbe.

**swallow** (2) ['swɔlou], *v.a.* schlucken; verschlingen (*devour*).

**swamp** [swɔmp], *s.* der Sumpf. — *v.a.* versenken; (*fig.*) überschütten.

**swan** [swɔn], *s.* (*Orn.*) der Schwan.

**swank** [swæŋk], *v.n.* großtun, angeben, aufschneiden. — *s.* der Großtuer.

**swap, swop** [swɔp], *v.a.* eintauschen, tauschen. — *v.n.* tauschen. — *s.* der Tausch.

**sward** [swɔ:d], *s.* (*Poet.*) der Rasen.

**swarm** [swɔ:m], *v.n.* schwärmen. — *s.* der Schwarm.

**swarthy** ['swɔ:ði], *adj.* dunkel, dunkelbraun.

**swashbuckler** ['swɔʃbʌklə], *s.* der Aufschneider, Angeber, Renommist.

**swastika** ['swɔstikə], *s.* das Hakenkreuz.

**swathe** [sweið], *v.a.* einhüllen, einwickeln.

**sway** [swei], *v.a.* schwenken; beeinflußen. — *v.n.* schwanken, sich schwingen. — *s.* der Einfluß, die Macht.

**swear** [swɛə], *v.a., v.n. irr.* schwören (*an oath*); fluchen (*curse*).
**sweat** [swet], *v.n.* schwitzen. — *s.* der Schweiß.
**Swede** [swi:d], *s.* der Schwede.
**Swedish** ['swi:diʃ], *adj.* schwedisch.
**sweep** [swi:p], *v.a., v.n. irr.* fegen, kehren; *a new broom — s clean*, neue Besen kehren gut. — *s.* der Schornsteinfeger (*chimney —*).
**sweet** [swi:t], *adj.* süß. — *s.* der Nachtisch; (*pl.*) Süßigkeiten, *f. pl.*
**swell** [swel], *v.a. irr.* anschwellen lassen. — *v.n.* anschwellen. — *adj., adv.* (*Am. sl.*) ausgezeichnet. — *s.* (*sl.*) der feine Kerl.
**swelter** ['sweltə], *v.n.* vor Hitze vergehen.
**swerve** [swə:v], *v.n.* abschweifen, abbiegen.
**swift** (1) [swift], *adj.* schnell, behende, rasch.
**swift** (2) [swift], *s.* (*Orn.*) die Turmschwalbe.
**swill** [swil], *v.a.* spülen (*rinse*); (*sl.*) saufen (*drink heavily*). — *s.* das Spülicht (*dishwater*); (*coll.*) das Gesöff.
**swim** [swim], *v.n. irr.* schwimmen. — *s.* das Schwimmen.
**swindle** [swindl], *v.a.* beschwindeln. — *s.* der Schwindel.
**swine** [swain], *s. pl.* die Schweine; (*sing.*) der Schweinehund, das Schwein.
**swing** [swiŋ], *v.a., v.n. irr.* schwingen, schaukeln. — *s.* der Schwung; die Schaukel.
**swipe** [swaip], *v.a.* schlagen; (*fig.*) stehlen. — *s.* der Schlag.
**swirl** [swə:l], *v.a., v.n.* wirbeln (*in air*). — *s.* der Wirbel.
**Swiss** [swis], *s.* der Schweizer. — *adj.* schweizerisch, Schweizer-.
**switch** [switʃ], *v.a.* (*Elec.*) — *on*, andrehen, einschalten; — *off*, abschalten; (*fig.*) wechseln, vertauschen (*change*). — *v.n.* umstellen, umschalten. — *s.* (*Elec.*) der Schalter.
**switchboard** ['switʃbɔ:d], *s.* die Telephonzentrale, das Schaltbrett.
**switchgear** ['switʃgiə], *s.* (*Elec.*) das Schaltgerät, die Schaltung.
**swivel** [swivl], *v.n.* drehen. — *s.* der Drehring; — *chair*, der Drehstuhl.
**swoon** [swu:n], *v.n.* in Ohnmacht fallen. — *s.* die Ohnmacht.
**swoop** [swu:p], *s.* der Stoß. — *v.n.* (herab)stoßen; stürzen; (nieder)schießen.
**swop** *see* swap.
**sword** [sɔ:d], *s.* das Schwert.
**syllable** ['siləbl], *s.* die Silbe.
**syllabus** ['siləbəs], *s.* das Verzeichnis, der Lehrplan.
**symbol** ['simbəl], *s.* das Symbol, Sinnbild.
**sympathetic** [simpə'θetik], *adj.* mitfühlend, teilnehmend; sympathisch.
**sympathy** ['simpəθi], *s.* die Sympathie, das Mitgefühl.

**symphony** ['simfəni], *s.* (*Mus.*) die Symphonie.
**synchronize** ['siŋkrənaiz], *v.a.* synchronisieren.
**syndicate** ['sindikit], *s.* die Arbeitsgruppe, das Syndikat.
**synod** ['sinəd], *s.* die Synode, Kirchentagung.
**synonymous** [si'nɔniməs], *adj.* synonym.
**synopsis** [si'nɔpsis], *s.* die Zusammenfassung, Übersicht.
**Syrian** ['siriən], *adj.* syrisch. — *s.* der Syrer.
**syringe** ['sirindʒ], *s.* die Spritze.
**syrup** ['sirəp], *s.* der Sirup.
**system** ['sistəm], *s.* das System.
**systematize** ['sistəmətaiz], *v.a.* ordnen, in ein System bringen.

# T

**T** [ti:]. das T.
**tab** [tæb], *s.* das Schildchen, der Streifen.
**tabard** ['tæbəd], *s.* der Wappenrock, Heroldsrock.
**tabby** ['tæbi], *s.* (*cat*) die getigerte Katze.
**table** [teibl], *s.* der Tisch; (*Maths.*) die Tabelle, das Einmaleins. — *v.a.* (*Parl.*) einen Entwurf einbringen; (*Am.*) auf die lange Bank schieben.
**tablecloth** ['teiblklɔθ], *s.* das Tischtuch.
**tablemat** ['teiblmæt], *s.* der Untersatz.
**tablenapkin** ['teiblnæpkin], *s.* die Serviette.
**tablespoon** ['teiblspu:n], *s.* der Eßlöffel.
**tablet** ['tæblit], *s.* die Tablette (*pill*); die Schreibtafel, der Block (*writing*).
**taboo** [tə'bu:], *s.* das Verbot, Tabu.
**tabular** ['tæbjulə], *adj.* tabellarisch; wie eine Tafel.
**tacit** ['tæsit], *adj.* stillschweigend.
**taciturn** ['tæsitə:n], *adj.* schweigsam, einsilbig.
**tack** [tæk], *s.* der Stift; der Stich (*sewing*). — *v.a.* nageln; heften (*sew*).
**tackle** [tækl], *v.a.* (*Naut.*) takeln; (*Footb., fig.*) angreifen; anpacken. — *s.* (*Naut.*) das Takel; (*fig.*) das Zeug; (*Footb.*) das Angreifen.
**tact** [tækt], *s.* der Takt; das Zartgefühl.
**tactics** ['tæktiks], *s. pl.* die Taktik.
**tadpole** ['tædpoul], *s.* (*Zool.*) die Kaulquappe.
**taffeta** ['tæfitə], *s.* (*Text.*) der Taft.
**tag** [tæg], *s.* der Anhängezettel; das Sprichwort (*saying*). — *v.a.* anhängen. — *v.n.* — *on to*, sich anschließen.

**tail** [teil], *s.* der Schwanz; (*fig.*) das Ende; (*pl.*) der Frack (*tailcoat*). — *v.a.* (*Am.*) folgen (*Dat.*).

**tailor** ['teilə], *s.* der Schneider; —*made*, geschneidert, nach Maß gemacht. — *v.a.* schneidern.

**taint** [teint], *v.a.* beflecken; verderben (*corrupt*). — *s.* der Fleck.

**take** [teik], *v.a.* *irr.* nehmen; bringen, ergreifen (*seize*); erfordern (*require*); — *up*, aufnehmen, beginnen; ertragen (*suffer*, *tolerate*); — *breath*, Atem holen; — *care*, sich in acht nehmen; — *offence at*, Anstoß nehmen an; — *place*, stattfinden; — *for*, halten für. — *v.n.* wirken (*be effective*); — *to*, Gefallen finden (an, *Dat.*); — *to flight* or *o.'s heels*, sich aus dem Staube machen; — *after*, ähnlich sein.

**takings** ['teikiŋz], *s.* (*pl.*) die Einnahmen, *f. pl.*

**tale** [teil], *s.* das Märchen, die Geschichte.

**talent** ['tælənt], *s.* das Talent, die Begabung.

**talented** ['tæləntid], *adj.* talentiert, begabt.

**talk** [tɔ:k], *v.a.*, *v.n.* reden, sprechen. — *s.* das Gespräch (*discussion*); der Vortrag (*lecture*); das Reden, Gerede (*speaking*).

**talkative** ['tɔ:kətiv], *adj.* geschwätzig, redselig, gesprächig.

**tall** [tɔ:l], *adj.* hoch (*high*); groß (*grown high*); *a* — *order*, eine schwierige Aufgabe; *a* — *story*, eine Aufschneiderei, das Seemannsgarn.

**tallow** ['tælou], *s.* der Talg.

**tally** ['tæli], *v.n.* passen (*match*); stimmen (*be correct*).

**talon** ['tælən], *s.* die Klaue, Kralle.

**tame** [teim], *adj.* zahm. — *v.a.* zähmen.

**tamper** ['tæmpə], *v.n.* hineinpfuschen (*with*, in, *Acc.*).

**tan** [tæn], *s.* die Lohe, die braune Farbe; der Sonnenbrand (*sun*). — *v.a.* bräunen; (*leather*) gerben; (*fig.*) verbleuen (*beat*).

**tang** [tæŋ], *s.* der Seetang; (*fig.*) der Beigeschmack.

**tangible** ['tændʒibl], *adj.* greifbar.

**tangle** [tæŋgl], *v.a.* verwickeln (*entangle*). — *s.* die Verwirrung, Verwicklung.

**tank** [tæŋk], *s.* der Tank; (*Mil.*) der Panzer; der Wasserspeicher (*cistern*). — *v.a.*, *v.n.* tanken.

**tankard** ['tæŋkəd], *s.* der Maßkrug, Bierkrug.

**tanner** (1) ['tænə], *s.* der Gerber.

**tanner** (2) ['tænə], *s.* (*sl.*) das Sechspencestück.

**tantalize** ['tæntəlaiz], *v.a.* quälen.

**tantamount** ['tæntəmaunt], *adj.* gleich, gleichwertig.

**tap** [tæp], *v.a.* anzapfen (*barrel*); klopfen; tippen (*on shoulder etc.*); (*fig.*) anpumpen (*for money*). — *s.* der Hahn; der Zapfen (*barrel*); der leichte Schlag (*on shoulder etc.*).

**tape** [teip], *s.* das Band; *red* —, die Bürokratie, der Bürokratismus; — *measure*, das Bandmaß; — *recorder*, das Tonbandgerät.

**taper** ['teipə], *v.n.* spitz zulaufen. — *v.a.* spitzen. — *s.* die (spitze) Kerze.

**tapestry** ['tæpistri], *s.* die Tapete, der Wandteppich.

**tapeworm** ['teipwə:m], *s.* der Bandwurm.

**taproot** ['tæpru:t], *s.* die Pfahlwurzel, Hauptwurzel.

**tar** [ta:], *s.* der Teer; (*Naut. sl.*) der Matrose. — *v.a.* teeren.

**tardy** ['ta:di], *adj.* träge (*sluggish*), langsam.

**tare** (1) [teə], das Taragewicht, die Tara (*weight*). — *v.a.* auswägen, tarieren.

**tare** (2) [teə], *s.* (*Bot.*) die Wicke.

**target** ['ta:git], *s.* das Ziel; die Zielscheibe (*board*).

**tariff** ['tærif], *s.* der Tarif.

**tarnish** ['ta:niʃ], *v.a.* trüben. — *v.n.* anlaufen.

**tarpaulin** [ta:'pɔ:lin], *s.* die Persenning.

**tarry** (1) ['tæri], *v.n.* zögern (*hesitate*); warten (*wait*).

**tarry** (2) ['ta:ri], *adj.* teerig.

**tart** (1) [ta:t], *s.* die Torte.

**tart** (2) [ta:t], *adj.* herb, sauer.

**tart** (3) [ta:t], *s.* (*sl.*) die Dirne.

**Tartar** ['ta:tə], *s.* der Tatar; (*fig.*) der Tyrann.

**tartar** ['ta:tə], *s.* (*Chem.*) der Weinstein.

**task** [ta:sk], *s.* die Aufgabe, das Tagewerk; *take to* —, zur Rechenschaft ziehen.

**tassel** [tæsl], *s.* die Quaste.

**taste** [teist], *v.a.* schmecken; versuchen, kosten. — *s.* die Probe (*tasting*); der Geschmack (*flavour*).

**tasteful** ['teistful], *adj.* geschmackvoll.

**tasteless** ['teistlis], *adj.* geschmacklos.

**tasty** ['teisti], *adj.* schmackhaft.

**tatter** ['tætə], *s.* der Lumpen. — *v.a.* in Fetzen reißen, zerfetzen.

**tattle** [tætl], *v.n.* schwatzen. — *s.* das Geschwätz.

**tattoo** (1) [tə'tu:], *s.* (*Mil.*) der Zapfenstreich, das militärische Schaustück, die Parade.

**tattoo** (2) [tə'tu:], *v.a.* tätowieren. — *s.* die Tätowierung.

**taunt** [tɔ:nt], *v.a.* höhnen, schmähen. — *s.* der Hohn, Spott.

**tavern** ['tævən], *s.* die Schenke.

**tawdry** ['tɔ:dri], *adj.* kitschig, flitterhaft.

**tawny** ['tɔ:ni], *adj.* braungelb, lohfarbig.

**tax** [tæks], *s.* die Abgabe, Steuer; Besteuerung (*taxation*). — *v.a.* besteuern; (*fig.*) anstrengen, ermüden (*strain*).

**taxi** ['tæksi], *s.* das Taxi.

**tea** [ti:], *s.* der Tee.

**teach** [ti:tʃ], *v.a.*, *v.n.* *irr.* lehren, unterrichten.

**teacher** ['ti:tʃə], *s.* der Lehrer, die Lehrerin.

499

team

team [ti:m], s. (Sport) die Mannschaft;
das Gespann (horses); (fig.) der Stab;
— spirit, der Korpsgeist.
tear (1) [tɛə], s. der Riß (rent). — v.a. irr.
zerreißen (rend).
tear (2) [tiə], s. die Träne.
tearing ['tɛəriŋ], adj. — hurry, rasende
Eile.
tease [ti:z], v.a. necken (mock); auf-
rauhen (roughen).
teat [ti:t], s. die Brustwarze, Zitze.
technical ['teknikəl], adj. technisch.
technique [tek'ni:k], s. die Technik,
Methode.
techy see tetchy.
tedious ['ti:diəs], adj. langweilig,
lästig.
tedium ['ti:diəm], s. der Überdruß, die
Langeweile.
tee [ti:], s. (Sport) der Golfballhalter.
teem [ti:m], v.n. wimmeln.
teenager ['ti:neidʒə], s. der, die Jugendliche; Teenager.
teeth see under tooth.
teethe [ti:ð], v.n. Zähne bekommen,
zahnen.
teetotal [ti:'toutl], adj. abstinent, anti-
alkoholisch.
teetotaller [ti:'toutlə], s. der Antialkoholiker.
telegram ['teligræm], s. das Telegramm.
telephone ['telifoun], s. (abbr. phone)
das Telephon; — box, die Fernsprech-
zelle; — exchange, das Fernsprechamt.
television [teli'viʒən], s. das Fernsehen; — set, das Fernsehapparat.
tell [tel], v.a. irr. erzählen, berichten
(relate); verraten (reveal).
tell-tale ['telteil], s. der Angeber,
Zuträger. — adj. sprechend; Warn-
ungs-.
teller ['telə], s. der Zähler; der Kassier
(cashier).
temerity [ti'meriti], s. die Verwegenheit, Tollkühnheit.
temper ['tempə], v.a. vermischen
(mix); mäßigen (moderate); (Metall.)
härten. — s. die üble Stimmung, Wut,
Laune; (Metall.) die Härte.
temperance ['tempərəns], s. die Mäßigkeit, Enthaltsamkeit.
temperate ['tempərit], adj. gemäßigt,
temperiert.
temperature ['temprətʃə], s. die Temperatur.
tempest ['tempist], s. der Sturm.
tempestuous [tem'pestjuəs], adj. stürmisch.
temple (1) [templ], s. der Tempel.
temple (2) [templ], s. (Anat.) die
Schläfe (side of brow).
temporal ['tempərəl], adj. weltlich,
zeitlich.
temporary ['tempərəri], adj. zeitweilig,
vorläufig, provisorisch.
temporize ['tempəraiz], v.n. zögern,
Zeit zu gewinnen suchen.
tempt [tempt], v.a. versuchen.
temptation [temp'teiʃən], s. die Versuchung.

ten [ten], num. adj. zehn.
tenth [tenθ], num. adj. zehnte. — s. der
Zehnte.
tenable ['tenəbl], adj. haltbar.
tenacious [ti'neiʃəs], adj. zähe, festhal-
tend, hartnäckig.
tenacity [ti'næsiti], s. die Zähigkeit,
Ausdauer.
tenancy ['tenənsi], s. das Mietver-
hältnis; die Mietdauer.
tenant ['tenənt], s. der Mieter, Pächter.
tench [tentʃ], s. (Zool.) die Schleie.
tend (1) [tend], v.a., v.n. warten,
pflegen (nurse).
tend (2) [tend], v.n. neigen, gerichtet
sein (be inclined).
tendency ['tendənsi], s. die Tendenz,
Neigung.
tender (1) ['tendə], s. das Angebot
(offer); legal —, das Zahlungsmittel.
— v.a. einreichen.
tender (2) ['tendə], adj. sanft (affectionate); zart, zärtlich, weich (delicate).
tender (3) ['tendə], s. (Railw.) der
Tender.
tendon ['tendən], s. (Anat.) die Sehne,
Flechse.
tendril ['tendril], s. (Bot.) die Ranke.
tenement ['tenimənt], s. die Miets-
wohnung, die Mietskaserne.
tenet ['tenit], s. der Grundsatz (principle); die Lehre (doctrine).
tenfold ['tenfould], adj. zehnfach.
tennis ['tenis], s. das Tennis.
tenor ['tenə], s. (Mus.) der Tenor; der
Sinn, Inhalt (meaning).
tense (1) [tens], adj. gespannt; straff
(taut).
tense (2) [tens], s. (Gram.) die Zeitform.
tension ['tenʃən], s. die Spannung.
tent [tent], s. das Zelt.
tentacle ['tentəkl], s. (Zool.) das Fühlhorn, der Fühler.
tentative ['tentətiv], adj. versuchend,
vorsichtig; (fig.) vorläufig.
tenterhooks ['tentəhuks], s. pl. die
Spannhaken, m. pl.; be on —, in
größter Spannung sein.
tenuous ['tenjuəs], adj. dünn, fadenscheinig, spärlich.
tenure ['tenjuə], s. der Mietbesitz, die
Mietvertragslänge, das Mietrecht; —
of office, die Amtsdauer.
tepid ['tepid], adj. lau, lauwarm.
term [tə:m], s. der Ausdruck (expression); die Bedingung (condition); der
Termin, die Frist (period); (Sch.) das
Semester, Trimester; be on good —s
with (s.o.), auf gutem Fuß stehen mit.
— v.a. benennen, bezeichnen.
terminate ['tə:mineit], v.a. beenden,
zu Ende bringen. — v.n. zu Ende
kommen.
terminus ['tə:minəs], s. die Endstation.
terrace ['teris], s. die Terrasse.
terrestrial [te'restriəl], adj. irdisch.
terrible ['teribl], adj. schrecklich,
furchtbar.
terrific [tə'rifik], adj. fürchterlich;
(coll.) ungeheuer.

**terrify** ['terifai], *v.a.* erschrecken.
**territory** ['teritəri], *s.* das Gebiet.
**terror** ['terə], *s.* der Schrecken.
**terse** [təːs], *adj.* bündig, kurz.
**tertiary** ['təːʃəri], *adj.* tertiär.
**test** [test], *s.* die Prüfung; (*Chem.*) die Probe; — *v.a.* prüfen. das Reagensglas *or* Reagenzglas. — *v.a.* prüfen.
**testament** ['testəmənt], *s.* das Testament.
**testator** [tes'teitə], *s.* der Erblasser.
**testicle** ['testikl], *s.* (*Anat.*) die Hode.
**testify** ['testifai], *v.a.* bezeugen.
**testimonial** [testi'mouniəl], *s.* das Zeugnis.
**testimony** ['testiməni], *s.* das Zeugnis, die Zeugenaussage (*oral*).
**testiness** ['testinis], *s.* die Verdrießlichkeit.
**testy** ['testi], *adj.* verdrießlich, reizbar.
**tetanus** ['tetənəs], *s.* (*Med.*) der Starrkrampf.
**tetchy, techy** ['tetʃi], *adj.* mürrisch, reizbar.
**tether** ['teðə], *s.* das Spannseil; (*fig.*) *at the end of o.'s* —, am Ende seiner Geduld. — *v.a.* anbinden.
**text** ['tekst], *s.* der Text, Wortlaut.
**textile** ['tekstail], *s.* die Textilware, der Webstoff.
**textual** ['tekstjuəl], *adj.* textlich, Text-.
**texture** ['tekstʃə], *s.* das Gewebe, die Struktur.
**Thai** [tai], *adj.* Thai-, siamesisch. — *s. pl.* die Thaivölker, *pl.*
**than** [ðæn], *conj.* als (*after comparatives*).
**thank** [θæŋk], *v.a.* danken (*Dat.*). — *s.* (*pl.*) der Dank.
**that** [ðæt], *dem. adj.* der, die, das, jener. — *dem. pron.* der, die, das; (*absolute, no pl.*) das. — *rel. pron.* der, die, das, welcher, was. — *conj.* daß; damit (*in order* —).
**thatch** [θætʃ], *v.a.* decken (mit Stroh). — *s.* das Strohdach.
**thaw** [θɔː], *v.n.* tauen; auftauen. — *s.* das Tauwetter.
**the** [ðə, *before vowel* ði], *def. art.* der, die, das. — *adv.* — *bigger* — *better*, je grösser desto *or* umso besser.
**theatre** ['θiətə], *s.* das Theater; (*fig.*) der Schauplatz.
**theatrical** [θi'ætrikəl], *adj.* bühnenhaft (*of the stage*); theatralisch; Bühnen-, Theater-.
**theft** [θeft], *s.* der Diebstahl.
**their** [ðɛə], *poss. adj.* ihr.
**theirs** [ðɛəz], *poss. pron.* der, die, das ihrige, der, die, das ihre.
**them** [ðem], *pers. pron.* sie, ihnen.
**theme** [θiːm], *s.* das Thema; (*Mus.*) das Thema, Motiv.
**then** [ðen], *adv.* dann, damals; *by* —, *till* —, bis dahin. — *conj.* dann, denn. — *adj.* damalig.
**thence** [ðens], *adv.* von da; daher.
**theology** [θi'ɔlədʒi], *s.* die Theologie.
**theorem** ['θiərəm], *s.* (*Maths.*) der Lehrsatz, Grundsatz.
**theorize** ['θiəraiz], *v.n.* theoretisieren.

**therapeutics** [θerə'pjuːtiks], *s. pl.* die Heilkunde.
**therapy** ['θerəpi], *s.* die Therapie.
**there** [ðɛə], *adv.* dort, da; dorthin, dahin (*thereto*); — *is*, — *are*, es gibt; *here and* —, hier und da.
**thereabout(s)** [ðɛər'ɑːftə(s)], *adv.* ungefähr, da herum.
**thereafter** [ðɛər'ɑːftə], *adv.* hernach, danach.
**thereby** [ðɛə'bai], *adv.* dadurch.
**therefore** ['ðɛəfɔː], *adv.* darum, deshalb.
**thermal, thermic** ['θəːməl, 'θəːmik], *adj.* thermisch; warm; Wärme-.
**thermometer** [θə'mɔmitə], *s.* das Thermometer.
**these** [ðiːz], *dem. adj. & pron. pl.* diese.
**thesis** ['θiːsis], *s.* die These; die Dissertation.
**they** [ðei], *pers. pron. pl.* sie.
**thick** [θik], *adj.* dick; dicht; (*fig.*) dick befreundet; — *as thieves*, wie eine Diebsbande.
**thicken** ['θikən], *v.a.* verdicken. — *v.n.* dick werden.
**thicket** ['θikit], *s.* das Dickicht.
**thickness** ['θiknis], *s.* die Dicke.
**thief** [θiːf], *s.* der Dieb.
**thieve** [θiːv], *v.a.* stehlen.
**thigh** [θai], *s.* (*Anat.*) der Oberschenkel.
**thimble** [θimbl], *s.* der Fingerhut.
**thin** [θin], *adj.* dünn. — *v.a., v.n.* (sich) verdünnen.
**thine** [ðain], *poss. pron.* (*Poet.*) dein, der, die, das deinige.
**thing** [θiŋ], *s.* das Ding; die Sache (*matter*).
**think** [θiŋk], *v.a., v.n. irr.* denken; meinen, glauben.
**thinker** ['θiŋkə], *s.* der Denker.
**third** [θəːd], *num. adj.* der, die, das dritte. — *s.* das Drittel.
**thirdly** ['θəːdli], *adv.* drittens.
**thirst** [θəːst], *s.* der Durst (*for*, nach). — *v.n.* dürsten.
**thirsty** ['θəːsti], *adj.* durstig; *be* —, Durst haben.
**thirteen** [θəː'tiːn], *num. adj.* dreizehn.
**thirty** ['θəːti], *num. adj.* dreißig.
**this** [ðis], *dem. adj.* dieser, diese, dieses. — *dem. pron.* dieser, diese, dieses; dies.
**thistle** [θisl], *s.* (*Bot.*) die Distel.
**thither** ['ðiðə], *adv.* dahin, dorthin.
**tho'** [ðou] *see under* **though.**
**thong** [θɔŋ], *s.* der Riemen (*strap*); die Peitschenschnur.
**thorn** [θɔːn], *s.* (*Bot.*) der Dorn.
**thorough** ['θʌrə], *adj.* gründlich; völlig (*complete*).
**thoroughbred** ['θʌrəbred], *s.* das Vollblut, der Vollblüter. — *adj.* Vollblut-.
**thoroughfare** ['θʌrəfɛə], *s.* der Durchgang (*path*); die Durchfahrt.
**those** [ðouz], *dem. adj. pl.* die, jene. — *dem. pron. pl.* jene, diejenigen.
**thou** [ðau], *pers. pron.* (*Poet.*) du.
**though** [ðou], *conj.* (*abbr.* **tho'**) obgleich, obwohl, wenn auch (*even if*). — *adv.* doch, zwar.

**thought** [θɔːt], _s._ der Gedanke; _also past tense and participle of_ **think** _q.v._

**thoughtful** ['θɔːtful], _adj._ rücksichtsvoll, nachdenklich.

**thoughtless** ['θɔːtlis], _adj._ gedankenlos.

**thousand** ['θauzənd], _num. adj._ a —, tausend. — _s._ das Tausend.

**thrash** [θræʃ], _v.a._ dreschen (_corn_); prügeln (_s.o._).

**thread** [θred], _s._ der Faden. — _v.a._ einfädeln. — _v.n._ sich schlängeln, sich winden.

**threadbare** ['θredbɛə], _adj._ fadenscheinig.

**threat** [θret], _s._ die Drohung.

**threaten** [θretn], _v.a._ drohen, androhen (_Dat._).

**three** [θriː], _num. adj._ drei.

**threescore** ['θriːskɔː], _num. adj._ sechzig.

**thresh** [θreʃ], _v.a._ dreschen (_corn_). — _See also_ **thrash**.

**threshold** ['θreʃould], _s._ die Schwelle (_of door_).

**thrice** [θrais], _num. adv._ dreimal.

**thrift** [θrift], _s._ die Sparsamkeit; (_Bot._) die Grasnelke, Meernelke.

**thrill** [θril], _v.a._ packen (_grip_). — _v.n._ erschauern, zittern (vor, _Dat._). — _s._ der Schauer; die Spannung.

**thriller** ['θrilə], _s._ der Thriller, der spannende Roman _or_ Film etc.

**thrive** [θraiv], _v.n._ gedeihen (_also fig._); (_fig._) gut weiterkommen, Glück haben.

**thriving** ['θraiviŋ], _adj._ blühend, (_Comm._) gut gehend.

**throat** [θrout], _s._ (_Anat._) der Schlund, die Kehle.

**throb** [θrɔb], _v.n._ pochen, klopfen.

**throes** [θrouz], _s. pl._ die Wehen, _f. pl._; die Schmerzen, _m. pl._

**throne** [θroun], _s._ der Thron.

**throng** [θrɔŋ], _s._ die Menge, das Gedränge. — _v.a., v.n._ (sich) drängen.

**throttle** [θrɔtl], _s._ die Kehle, Luftröhre; (_Mech._) das Drosselventil; (_Motor._) open the —, Gas geben.

**through** [θruː], _prep._ durch (_Acc._); mittels (_Genit._) (_by means of_). — _adv._ (mitten) durch.

**throughout** [θruːˈaut], _prep._ ganz (hin)durch (_space_); während, hindurch (_time_). — _adv._ durchaus, in jeder Beziehung.

**throw** [θrou], _v.a. irr._ werfen; — open, eröffnen. — _s._ der Wurf.

**thrush** [θrʌʃ], _s._ (_Orn._) die Drossel.

**thrust** [θrʌst], _v.a._ stoßen, drängen. — _v.n._ stoßen (at, nach); sich drängen. — _s._ der Stoß, Angriff; cut and —, Hieb und Gegenhieb.

**thud** [θʌd], _s._ der Schlag, das Dröhnen, der dumpfe Ton. — _v.n._ dröhnen, aufschlagen.

**thumb** [θʌm], _s._ (_Anat._) der Daumen; rule of —, die Faustregel; (_Am._) — tack see drawing pin. — _v.a._ durchblättern (book); — a lift, per Anhalter fahren.

**thump** [θʌmp], _v.a._ schlagen, puffen. —

_v.n._ schlagen (on, auf; against, gegen). — _s._ der Schlag, Stoß.

**thunder** ['θʌndə], _s._ der Donner. — _v.n._ donnern.

**thunderstruck** ['θʌndəstrʌk], _adj._ wie vom Donner gerührt.

**Thursday** ['θəːzdi]. der Donnerstag.

**Thuringian** [θuəˈrindʒiən], _adj._ thüringisch. — _s._ der Thüringer.

**thus** [ðʌs], _adv._ so, auf diese Weise (in this way).

**thwart** [θwɔːt], _v.a._ vereiteln, durchkreuzen.

**thy** [ðai], _poss. adj._ (_Poet._) dein, deine, dein.

**thyme** [taim], _s._ (_Bot._) der Thymian.

**tic** [tik], _s._ (_Med._) das Zucken.

**tick** (1) [tik], _s._ das Ticken (watch). — _v.n._ ticken.

**tick** (2) [tik], _s._ (_coll._) der Kredit, Borg.

**ticket** ['tikit], _s._ die Fahrkarte (travel); die Eintrittskarte (entry); (_Am._) der Strafzettel (driving).

**ticking** (1) ['tikiŋ], _s._ das Ticken (of watch).

**ticking** (2) ['tikiŋ], _s._ (_Text._) der Zwillich.

**tickle** [tikl], _v.a., v.n._ kitzeln. — _s._ das Kitzeln.

**ticklish** ['tikliʃ], _adj._ kitzlig.

**tidal** [taidl], _adj._ Gezeiten-, Ebbe-, Flut-.

**tide** [taid], _s._ die Gezeiten, _f. pl._, die Ebbe und Flut. — _v.a._ — over, hinweghelfen (über, _Acc._).

**tidiness** ['taidinis], _s._ die Sauberkeit, Ordnung.

**tidings** ['taidiŋz], _s. pl._ (_Poet._) die Nachricht.

**tidy** ['taidi], _adj._ nett, sauber, ordentlich. — _v.a._ — up, sauber machen.

**tie** [tai], _v.a._ binden, knüpfen. — _v.n._ (_Sport_) unentschieden sein. — _s._ die Binde, Krawatte; (_Sport_) das Unentschieden.

**tier** [tiə], _s._ der Rang, die Reihe, Sitzreihe.

**tiger** ['taigə], _s._ (_Zool._) der Tiger.

**tight** [tait], _adj._ fest, eng, dicht (close); (_coll._) betrunken (drunk); — fisted, geizig (stingy). — _s. pl._ die Trikothosen, _f. pl._

**tighten** [taitn], _v.a._ festziehen.

**tile** [tail], _s._ der Ziegel (roof etc.); die Kachel (glazed). — _v.a._ kacheln, ziegeln.

**till** (1) [til], _prep., conj._ bis.

**till** (2) [til], _v.a._ aufbauen, beackern (land).

**till** (3) [til], _s._ die Ladenkasse.

**tilt** [tilt], _v.a._ kippen, neigen, umschlagen (tip over). — _v.n._ sich neigen, kippen, kentern. — _s._ die Neigung.

**timber** ['timbə], _s._ das Holz, Bauholz.

**time** [taim], _s._ die Zeit; (_Mus._) das Tempo, Zeitmaß; in —, zur rechten Zeit; every —, jedesmal; what is the —? wieviel Uhr ist es? — _v.a._ zeitlich messen, rechtzeitig einrichten.

**timely** ['taimli], _adj._ rechtzeitig.

**timetable** ['taimteibl], s. (Railw.) der Fahrplan; (Sch.) der Stundenplan.

**timid** ['timid], adj. furchtsam.

**timpani** ['timpəni], s. pl. (Mus.) die Kesselpauken, f. pl.

**tin** [tin], s. das Zinn, Weißblech; die Dose, Büchse (preserved foods); — opener, der Büchsenöffner.

**tincture** ['tiŋktʃə], s. die Tinktur, das Färbungsmittel.

**tinder** ['tində], s. der Zunder.

**tinfoil** ['tinfɔil], s. das Stanniol.

**tinge** [tindʒ], v.a. färben, anfärben. — s. die Färbung, leichte Farbe; (fig.) die Spur.

**tingle** [tiŋgl], v.n. klingen (bells); (Anat.) prickeln. — s. das Klingen; Prickeln.

**tinker** ['tiŋkə], s. der Kesselflicker. — v.n. basteln.

**tinkle** [tiŋkl], v.a. klingeln.

**tinsel** ['tinsəl], s. das Lametta, Flittergold.

**tint** [tint], v.a. färben. — s. die Farbe; der Farbton.

**tiny** ['taini], adj. winzig.

**tip** (1) [tip], v.a. kippen; (coll.) ein Trinkgeld geben (Dat.). — s. (Sport etc.) (coll.) der Tip; das Trinkgeld (gratuity).

**tip** (2) [tip], s. die Spitze; das Mundstück (cigarette).

**tipple** [tipl], v.n. (viel) trinken, zechen.

**tipsy** ['tipsi], adj. beschwipst.

**tiptoe** ['tiptou], s. on —, auf Zehenspitzen.

**tiptop** ['tiptɔp], adj. (coll.) erstklassig.

**tirade** [ti'reid or tai'reid], s. der Wortschwall, die Tirade.

**tire** (1) [taiə], v.a., v.n. ermüden.

**tire** (2) see under **tyre**.

**tired** ['taiəd], adj. müde.

**tiresome** ['taiəsəm], adj. langweilig (boring); auf die Nerven gehend (annoying).

**tissue** ['tiʃju:], s. das Gewebe; — paper, das Seidenpapier.

**titbit** ['titbit], s. der Leckerbissen.

**tithe** [taið], s. der Zehnte.

**title** [taitl], s. der Titel, die Überschrift; (fig.) der Anspruch (claim).

**titmouse** ['titmaus], s. (Orn.) die Meise.

**titter** ['titə], v.n. kichern. — s. das Kichern.

**tittle** [titl], s. das Tüpfelchen; — tattle, das Geschwätz.

**titular** ['titjulə], adj. Titular-.

**to** [tu], prep. zu (Dat.), gegen (Acc.); bis (until, as far as), nach, an, auf; in order —, um zu. — [tu:], adv. zu; — and fro, hin und her.

**toad** [toud], s. (Zool.) die Kröte.

**toadstool** ['toudstu:l], s. (Bot.) der Giftpilz.

**toady** ['toudi], v.n. kriechen. — s. der Kriecher.

**toast** [toust], s. der Toast, das Röstbrot; der Trinkspruch. — v.a. toasten,

rösten; trinken auf; — s.o., einen Trinkspruch ausbringen auf einen.

**tobacco** [tə'bækou], s. der Tabak.

**toboggan** [tə'bɔgən], s. der Rodel, der Schlitten. — v.n. rodeln, Schlitten fahren.

**tocsin** ['tɔksin], s. die Sturmglocke.

**today** [tə'dei], adv. heute.

**toddle** [tɔdl], v.n. watscheln; abschieben (— off).

**toddler** ['tɔdlə], s. (coll.) das kleine Kind (das gehen lernt).

**toe** [tou], s. (Anat.) die Zehe.

**toffee** ['tɔfi], s. der Sahnebonbon.

**together** [tə'geðə], adv. zusammen.

**toil** [tɔil], v.n. hart arbeiten. — s. die schwere, harte Arbeit.

**toilet** ['tɔilit], s. das Anziehen, Ankleiden; die Toilette, der Abort, das Klosett (lavatory).

**token** ['toukən], s. das Zeichen (sign); der Beweis (proof); das Andenken (keepsake).

**tolerable** ['tɔlərəbl], adj. erträglich, leidlich.

**tolerance** ['tɔlərəns], s. die Toleranz, Duldsamkeit; (Tech.) die Toleranz.

**tolerant** ['tɔlərənt], adj. tolerant, duldsam.

**tolerate** ['tɔləreit], v.a. ertragen, dulden.

**toll** [toul], v.a., v.n. läuten. — s. der Zoll; — gate, — bar, der Schlagbaum.

**tomato** [tə'mɑ:tou], s. (Bot.) die Tomate.

**tomb** [tu:m], s. das Grab, Grabmal.

**tomboy** ['tɔmbɔi], s. der Wildfang.

**tomcat** ['tɔmkæt], s. (Zool.) der Kater.

**tome** [toum], s. der große Band, (coll.) der Wälzer.

**tomfoolery** [tɔm'fu:ləri], s. die Narretei.

**Tommy** ['tɔmi], s. (Mil.) (coll.) der englische Soldat.

**tomorrow** [tə'mɔrou], adv. morgen; — morning, morgen früh; the day after —, übermorgen.

**ton** [tʌn], s. die Tonne.

**tone** [toun], s. der Ton, Klang; (fig.) die Stimmung (mood). — v.a. — down, abtönen, abstimmen.

**tongs** [tɔŋz], s. pl. die Zange.

**tongue** [tʌŋ], s. (Anat.) die Zunge.

**tonic** ['tɔnik], s. das Stärkungsmittel. — adj. tonisch, stärkend.

**tonight** [tu'nait], adv. heute abend, heute nacht.

**tonnage** ['tʌnidʒ], s. die Tonnage, das Tonnengeld.

**tonsil** ['tɔnsil], s. (Anat.) die Mandel.

**tonsilitis** [tɔnsi'laitis], s. (Med.) die Mandelentzündung.

**tonsure** ['tɔnʃə], s. die Tonsur.

**too** [tu:], adv. allzu, zu, allzusehr; auch (also).

**tool** [tu:l], s. das Werkzeug, das Gerät; machine —, die Werkzeugmaschine.

**tooth** [tu:θ], s. (pl. teeth [ti:θ]) der Zahn.

**toothache** ['tu:θeik], s. das Zahnweh.

**toothbrush** ['tu:θbrʌʃ], s. die Zahnbürste.

# toothpaste

**toothpaste** ['tu:θpeist], *s.* die Zahn-paste.

**top** (1) [tɒp], *s.* die Spitze; der Gipfel (*mountain*); der Wipfel (*tree*); der Giebel (*house*); die Oberfläche (*surface*); big —, das Zirkuszeltdach; — hat, der Zylinder. — *v.a.* übertreffen (*surpass*); bedecken (*cover*).

**top** (2) [tɒp], *s.* der Kreisel (*spinning* —).

**topaz** ['toupæz], *s.* der Topas.

**tope** [toup], *v.n.* zechen, saufen.

**toper** ['toupə], *s.* der Zecher.

**topic** ['tɒpik], *s.* das Thema, der Gegenstand.

**topical** ['tɒpikəl], *adj.* aktuell (*up to date*).

**topmost** ['tɒpmoust], *adj.* höchst, oberst.

**topsy-turvy** ['tɒpsi 'tə:vi], *adv.* durcheinander, auf den Kopf gestellt.

**torch** [tɔ:tʃ], *s.* die Fackel; (*Elec.*) die Taschenlampe.

**torment** ['tɔ:ment], *s.* die Qual, Marter. — [tɔ:'ment], *v.a.* quälen, martern, peinigen.

**tornado** [tɔ:'neidou], *s.* der Wirbelsturm.

**torpid** ['tɔ:pid], *adj.* starr, betäubt; (*fig.*) stumpfsinnig.

**torpor** ['tɔ:pə], *s.* die Starre; die Stumpfheit, Stumpfsinnigkeit.

**torrent** ['tɒrənt], *s.* der Gießbach, der (reißende) Strom.

**torrid** ['tɒrid], *adj.* brennend heiß, verbrannt.

**torsion** ['tɔ:ʃən], *s.* die Drehung, Windung.

**tortoise** ['tɔ:təs], *s.* (*Zool.*) die Schildkröte.

**tortoiseshell** ['tɔ:təsʃel], *s.* das Schildpatt.

**tortuous** ['tɔ:tjuəs], *adj.* gewunden.

**torture** ['tɔ:tʃə], *s.* die Folter; (*fig.*) die Folterqualen, *f. pl.* — *v.a.* foltern.

**Tory** ['tɔ:ri], *s.* (*Pol.*) der englische Konservative.

**toss** [tɒs], *s.* der Wurf (*of coin, etc.*); *argue the* —, sich streiten. — *v.a.* werfen. — *v.n.* — *up*, losen.

**total** [toutl], *adj.* ganz, gänzlich, total. — *s.* die Gesamtsumme. — *v.a.* sich (im ganzen) belaufen auf.

**totality** [tou'tæliti], *s.* die Gesamtheit.

**totter** ['tɒtə], *v.n.* wanken, schwanken, torkeln.

**touch** [tʌtʃ], *v.a.* berühren; anfassen; (*coll.*) anpumpen (*for money*); — *up*, auffrischen. — *s.* die Berührung (*contact*); (*Mus.*) der Anschlag.

**touching** ['tʌtʃiŋ], *adj.* rührend, ergreifend.

**touchline** ['tʌtʃlain], *s.* (*Sport*) der Rand des Spielfeldes, die Seitenlinie.

**touchy** ['tʌtʃi], *adj.* empfindlich.

**tough** [tʌf], *adj.* zäh, widerstandsfähig (*resistant*); *get* —, grob werden; — *luck!* Pech! — *s.* (*Am. coll.*) der Grobian.

**tour** [tuə], *s.* die Tour, Reise; (*Theat.*) die Tournee. — *v.a.*, *v.n.* touren, bereisen.

**tourist** ['tuərist], *s.* der Tourist.

**tournament** ['tuə- *or* 'tə:nəmənt], *s.* der Wettkampf, das Turnier.

**tout** [taut], *v.n.* Kunden suchen, anlocken. — *s.* der Kundenfänger.

**tow** [tou], *s.* das Schlepptau. — *v.a.* ziehen, schleppen.

**toward(s)** [tu'wɔ:d(z), tɔ:d(z)], *prep.* gegen; gegenüber; zu . . . hin; auf . . . zu; für.

**towel** ['tauəl], *s.* das Handtuch.

**towelling** ['tauəliŋ], *s.* der Handtuchdrell; *Turkish* —, das Frottiertuch.

**tower** [tauə], *s.* der Turm, Zwinger. — *v.n.* emporragen, hervorragen (über).

**towing path** ['touiŋ pɑ:θ] *see* towpath.

**town** [taun], *s.* die Stadt; — *crier*, der Ausrufer; — *hall*, das Rathaus (*offices*).

**townsman** ['taunzmən], *s.* der Städter.

**towpath** ['toupɑ:θ], *s.* der Treidelpfad.

**toy** [tɔi], *s.* das Spielzeug; (*pl.*) Spielsachen, Spielwaren, *f. pl.*; — *shop*, der Spielwarenladen. — *v.n.* spielen.

**trace** [treis], *s.* die Spur. — *v.a.* suchen, aufspüren; pausen (*through paper*).

**track** [træk], *s.* die Spur, Fährte (*path*); (*Railw.*) das Geleis(e).

**tract** [trækt], *s.* der Traktat (*pamphlet*); die Strecke (*stretch*).

**traction** ['trækʃən], *s.* das Ziehen (*pulling*); (*Tech.*) der Zug.

**tractor** ['træktə], *s.* der Traktor.

**trade** [treid], *s.* der Handel (*commerce*); das Gewerbe (*craft*); — *wind*, der Passatwind; — *union*, die Gewerkschaft. — *v.a.* — *in*, in Zahlung geben. — *v.n.* handeln, Handel treiben; — *in*, eintauschen.

**trademark** ['treidmɑ:k], *s.* die (Schutz-)marke, das Warenzeichen.

**tradesman** ['treidzmən], *s.* der Lieferant.

**traduce** [trə'dju:s], *v.a.* verleumden.

**traffic** ['træfik], *s.* der Verkehr; (*Comm.*) der Handel; — *light*, die Verkehrsampel.

**trafficator** ['træfikeitə], *s.* (*Motor.*) der Winker.

**tragedy** ['trædʒədi], *s.* die Tragödie, das Trauerspiel.

**tragic** ['trædʒik], *adj.* tragisch.

**tradition** [trə'diʃən], *s.* die Tradition.

**traditional** [trə'diʃənəl], *adj.* traditionell.

**trail** [treil], *s.* die Spur, Fährte; (*Am.*) der Pfad. — *v.a.* nach sich ziehen, schleppen; (*Am.*) nachfolgen (*Dat.*).

**trailer** ['treilə], *s.* (*Motor.*) der Anhänger; (*Film*) die Voranzeige.

**train** [trein], *v.a.* ausbilden; (*Sport*) trainieren, abrichten, dressieren (*animal*). — *v.n.* (*Sport*) sich vorbereiten; sich ausbilden (*for profession*). — *s.* (*Railw.*) der Zug; (*Mil.*) der Zug, Transport; die Schleppe (*bridal gown, etc.*); — *of thought*, die Gedankenfolge.

**training** ['treiniŋ], s. die Erziehung;
Ausbildung; — *college*, das Lehrer-
seminar, die pädagogische Hochschule.
**trait** [trei, treit], s. der Zug, Wesenszug.
**traitor** ['treitə], s. der Verräter.
**tram(car)** ['træm(ka:)], s. die Straßenbahn, der Strassenbahnwagen.
**trammelled** [træmld], adj. gebunden,
gefesselt.
**tramp** [træmp], s. der Landstreicher,
Strolch. — v.n. trampeln; (zu Fuß)
wandern.
**trample** [træmpl], v.a. niedertram-
peln. — v.n. trampeln, treten.
**tramway** ['træmwei], s. die Strassen-
bahn.
**trance** [tra:ns], s. die Verzückung.
**tranquil** ['træŋkwil], adj. ruhig, still,
friedlich.
**tranquillizer** ['træŋkwilaizə], s. (Med.)
das Beruhigungsmittel.
**transact** [træn'zækt], v.a. abmachen;
verrichten (conclude); erledigen.
**transaction** [træn'zækʃən], s. die
Verhandlung, Abmachung, Durch-
führung.
**transcend** [træn'send], v.a. übersteigen.
**transcendental** [trænsen'dentl], adj.
transzendental.
**transcribe** [træn'skraib], v.a. übertragen; umschreiben (cipher etc.);
abschreiben.
**transcription** [træn'skripʃən], s. die
Umschrift; die Abschrift (copy).
**transept** ['trænsept], s. (Archit.) das
Querschiff.
**transfer** [træns'fə:], v.a. versetzen,
überführen; übertragen; überweisen
(money). — v.n. verlegt werden.
—['trænsfə:], s. der Wechsel, Transfer;
die Versetzung; Überweisung.
**transfigure** ['trænsfigə], v.a. verklären.
**transfix** [træns'fiks], v.a. durchbohren.
**transform** [træns'fɔ:m], v.a. verwandeln,
umwandeln. — v.r. sich verwandeln.
**transgress** [træns'gres], v.a. überschreiten (trespass on). — v.n. sich
vergehen.
**transient** ['trænsiənt], adj. vergänglich.
**transit** ['trænsit, 'trænzit], s. der
Durchgang; die Durchfahrt, Durchfuhr (travel); (Comm.) der Transit. —
v.n. (Am.) durchfahren (of goods).
**transitive** ['trænsitiv], adj. (Gram.)
transitiv.
**transitory** ['trænsitəri], adj. vergänglich, flüchtig.
**translate** [træns'leit], v.a. übersetzen;
versetzen (office).
**translation** [træns'leiʃən], s. die Übersetzung, die Übertragung.
**translucent** [trænz'lju:sənt], adj. durchscheinend.
**transmission** [trænz'miʃən], s. die
Übersendung, Übermittlung; (Rad.)
die Sendung; (Motor.) die Transmission.
**transmit** [trænz'mit], v.a. übersenden,

übermitteln; (Rad., T.V.) übertragen,
senden.
**transmutation** [trænzmju'teiʃən], s. die
Verwandlung.
**transparent** [træns'pɛərənt], adj.
durchsichtig.
**transpire** [træns'paiə, trænz-], v.n.
bekannt werden.
**transplant** [træns'pla:nt, trænz-], v.a.
verpflanzen; (fig.) entzücken. —
['trænspla:nt], s. die Verpflanzung.
**transport** [træns'pɔ:t], v.a. transportieren; (fig.) entzücken. — ['trænspɔ:t],
s. der Transport; die Versendung
(sending); (fig.) die Entzückung.
**transpose** [træns'pouz], v.a. (Mus.)
transponieren.
**transverse** [trænz'və:s], adj. quer;
schräg (oblique).
**trap** [træp], v.a. in eine Falle führen;
ertappen (detect). — s. die Falle; der
Einspänner (gig).
**trapeze** [trə'pi:z], s. das Trapez.
**trapper** ['træpə], s. der Fallensteller.
**trappings** ['træpiŋz], s.pl. der Schmuck;
(fig.) die Äußerlichkeiten, f. pl.
**trash** [træʃ], s. (Lit.) der Schund; der
Kitsch; das wertlose Zeug.
**trashy** ['træʃi], adj. wertlos, kitschig.
**travail** ['træveil], s. die Wehen, Sorgen,
die Mühe.
**travel** [trævl], v.n. reisen. — v.a. bereisen. — s. das Reisen; — agency, das
Reisebüro.
**traveller** ['trævələ], s. der Reisende;
(Comm.) der Handelsreisende, Vertreter.
**traverse** ['trævə:s], adj. quer. — s. die
Traverse, der Querbalken. — [trə-
'və:s], v.a. durchqueren; (fig.) durchwandern.
**trawl** [trɔ:l], v.n. (mit Schleppnetz)
fischen.
**trawler** ['trɔ:lə], s. das Fischerboot, der
Fischdampfer.
**tray** [trei], s. das Tablett.
**treacherous** ['tretʃərəs], adj. verräterisch; (fig.) gefährlich.
**treachery** ['tretʃəri], s. der Verrat.
**treacle** ['tri:kl], s. der Sirup.
**tread** [tred], v.a., v.n. irr. (be)treten,
auftreten. — s. der Tritt, Schritt;
die Laufflache (of a tyre).
**treason** ['tri:zn], s. der Verrat.
**treasure** ['treʒə], s. der Schatz.
**treasurer** ['treʒərə], s. der Schatzmeister.
**treasury** ['treʒəri], s. die Schatzkammer; (U.K.) the Treasury, das
Schatzamt, Finanzministerium.
**treat** [tri:t], v.a. behandeln; bewirten
(as host). — v.n. (Pol.) unterhandeln
(negotiate). — s. der Genuß (pleasure).
**treatise** ['tri:tis], s. die Abhandlung.
**treatment** ['tri:tmənt], s. die Behandlung.
**treaty** ['tri:ti], s. der Vertrag.
**treble** [trebl], s. (Mus.) die Sopran-
stimme, Knabenstimme, der Diskant;
(Maths.) das Dreifache. — v.a.
verdreifachen.

# tree

**tree** [triː], *s.* (*Bot.*) der Baum.
**trefoil** [ˈtriːfɔil], *s.* (*Bot.*) der dreiblätt(e)rige Klee; das Dreiblatt.
**trellis** [ˈtrelis], *s.* das Gitter.
**tremble** [trembl], *v.n.* zittern. — *s.* das Zittern.
**tremendous** [triˈmendəs], *adj.* ungeheuer (groß); schrecklich.
**tremor** [ˈtremə], *s.* das Zittern; (*Geol.*) das Beben; (*Med.*) das Zucken.
**trench** [trentʃ], *s.* der Graben.
**trenchant** [ˈtrentʃənt], *adj.* einschneidend, scharf.
**trend** [trend], *s.* die Tendenz; (*Comm.*) der Trend.
**trepidation** [trepiˈdeiʃən], *s.* die Angst, das Zittern.
**trespass** [ˈtrespəs], *v.n.* sich vergehen, übertreten (*law*); — *on*, unbefugt betreten. — *s.* die Übertretung.
**tress** [tres], *s.* die Flechte, Haarlocke.
**trestle** [tresl], *s.* das Gestell; — *table*, der Klapptisch.
**trial** [ˈtraiəl], *s.* die Probe, der Versuch; (*Law*) die Verhandlung, der Prozeß, das Verhör.
**triangle** [ˈtraiæŋgl], *s.* das Dreieck; (*Mus.*) der Triangel.
**tribe** [traib], *s.* der Stamm.
**tribulation** [tribjuˈleiʃən], *s.* die Trübsal, Drangsal.
**tribunal** [traiˈbjuːnəl], *s.* das Tribunal, der Gerichtshof.
**tributary** [ˈtribjutəri], *adj.* Neben-. — *s.* der Nebenfluß.
**tribute** [ˈtribjuːt], *s.* der Tribut.
**trice** [trais], *s. in a* —, im Nu.
**trick** [trik], *s.* der Kniff, Trick. — *v.a.* betrügen.
**trickery** [ˈtrikəri], *s.* der Betrug.
**trickle** [trikl], *v.n.* tröpfeln, sickern. — *s.* das Tröpfeln.
**tricky** [ˈtriki], *adj.* verwickelt; (*fig.*) bedenklich, heikel.
**tricycle** [ˈtraisikl], *s.* das Dreirad.
**tried** [traid], *adj.* erprobt, bewährt.
**triennial** [traiˈeniəl], *adj.* dreijährlich.
**trifle** [traifl], *v.n.* scherzen, spielen. — *s.* die Kleinigkeit; (*Cul.*) der süße Auflauf.
**trigger** [ˈtrigə], *s.* der Drücker. — *v.a.* — *off*, auslösen.
**trilateral** [traiˈlætərəl], *adj.* dreiseitig.
**trill** [tril], *s.* (*Mus.*) der Triller. — *v.a., v.n.* trillern.
**trim** [trim], *adj.* niedlich, schmuck; nett (*dress*). — *v.a.* beschneiden; (*Naut.*) — *sails*, einziehen. — *s.* die Ausrüstung; (*Naut.*) das Gleichgewicht.
**trimmer** [ˈtrimə], *s.* die Putzmacherin; (*fig.*) der Opportunist.
**trimmings** [ˈtriminz], *s. pl.* (*fig.*) der Kleinkram; (*Tail.*) der Besatz.
**Trinity** [ˈtriniti], *s.* (*Theol.*) die Dreifaltigkeit, Dreieinigkeit.
**trinket** [ˈtriŋkit], *s.* das Geschmeide; (*pl.*) Schmucksachen, *f. pl.*
**trip** [trip], *s.* der Ausflug, die Reise. —

*v.a.* — *up*, ein Bein stellen (*Dat.*). — *v.n.* stolpern.
**tripe** [ˈtraip], *s.* die Kaldaunen, *f. pl.*; (*fig.*) der Unsinn.
**triple** [tripl], *adj.* dreifach.
**triplet** [ˈtriplit], *s.* der Drilling; (*Mus.*) die Triole; (*Poet.*) der Dreireim.
**tripod** [ˈtraipod], *s.* der Dreifuß.
**tripos** [ˈtraipos], *s.* das Schlußexamen (*Cambridge Univ.*).
**trite** [trait], *adj.* abgedroschen.
**triumph** [ˈtraiʌmf], *s.* der Triumph. — *v.n.* triumphieren.
**triumphant** [traiˈʌmfənt], *adj.* triumphierend.
**trivial** [ˈtriviəl], *adj.* trivial, platt, alltäglich.
**troll** (1) [troul], *v.n.* trällern (*hum*); fischen. — *s.* der Rundgesang (*song*).
**troll** (2) [troul], *s.* der Kobold (*gnome*).
**trolley** [ˈtroli], *s.* der Teewagen (*furniture*); (*Tech.*) die Dräsine, der Karren.
**trollop** [ˈtroləp], *s.* die Schlampe.
**trombone** [tromˈboun], *s.* (*Mus.*) die Posaune.
**troop** [truːp], *s.* der Haufe; (*Mil.*) die Truppe, der Trupp. — *v.n.* sich sammeln. — *v.a. Trooping the Colour*, die Fahnenparade.
**trophy** [ˈtroufi], *s.* die Trophäe, das Siegeszeichen.
**tropic** [ˈtropik], *s.* (*Geog.*) der Wendekreis; (*pl.*) die Tropen, *f. pl.*
**tropical** [ˈtropikəl], *adj.* tropisch.
**trot** [trot], *v.n.* traben. — *s.* der Trab, Trott.
**troth** [trouθ], *s.* (*obs.*) die Treue; *pledge o.'s* —, Treue geloben.
**trouble** [trʌbl], *s.* die Mühe, Sorge (*worry*); der Kummer (*sadness*); die Störung (*disturbance*). — *v.a.* bemühen (*ask favour of*); bekümmern (*worry*); stören (*disturb*).
**troublesome** [ˈtrʌblsəm], *adj.* ärgerlich, schwierig, unangenehm.
**trough** [trof], *s.* der Trog; (*Met.*) das Tief.
**trounce** [trauns], *v.a.* verprügeln.
**trouncing** [ˈtraunsiŋ], *s.* die Tracht Prügel.
**trousers** [ˈtrauzəz], *s. pl.* die Hosen, *f. pl.*
**trout** [traut], *s.* (*Zool.*) die Forelle.
**trowel** [ˈtrauəl], *s.* die Kelle.
**troy(weight)** [ˈtroi(weit)], *s.* das Troygewicht.
**truant** [ˈtruːənt], *s.* (*Sch.*) der Schulschwänzer; *play* —, die Schule schwänzen.
**truce** [truːs], *s.* der Waffenstillstand.
**truck** (1) [trʌk], *s.* (*Rail.*) der Güterwagen; (*Am.*) *see* **lorry**.
**truck** (2) [trʌk], *s. have no* — *with*, nichts zu tun haben mit.
**truculent** [ˈtrakjulənt], *adj.* streitsüchtig.
**trudge** [trʌdʒ], *v.n.* sich schleppen.
**true** [truː], *adj.* wahr; treu (*faithful*); echt (*genuine*); richtig (*correct*).

**truffle** [trʌfl], *s.* die Trüffel.
**truism** ['tru:izm], *s.* der Gemeinplatz, die Binsenwahrheit.
**truly** ['tru:li], *adv. yours* —, Ihr ergebener.
**trump** [trʌmp], *s.* der Trumpf; — *card*, die Trumpfkarte. — *v.a.* — *up*, erfinden, erdichten.
**trumpery** ['trʌmpəri], *s.* der Plunder, Schund. — *adj.* wertlos, belanglos.
**trumpet** ['trʌmpit], *s.* (*Mus.*) die Trompete. — *v.a.* stolz austrompeten, ausposaunen. — *v.n.* trompeten.
**truncate** [trʌŋ'keit], *v.a.* verstümmeln, stutzen.
**truncheon** ['trʌnʃən], *s.* der Knüppel. — *v.a.* durchprügeln.
**trundle** [trʌndl], *v.n.* trudeln; sich wälzen. — *v.a.* — *a hoop*, Reifen schlagen.
**trunk** [trʌŋk], *s.* der Stamm (*tree*); der Rüssel (*of elephant*); der (große) Koffer (*chest*); — *call*, das Ferngespräch.
**truss** [trʌs], *s.* das Band, Bruchband. — *v.a.* zäumen, stützen; aufschürzen.
**trust** [trʌst], *v.a., v.n.* trauen (*Dat.*), vertrauen (*Dat.*); anvertrauen (*Dat., Acc.*). — *s.* das Vertrauen; *in* —, zu treuen Händen, als Treuhänder; (*Comm.*) der Trust.
**trustworthy** ['trʌstwə:ði], *adj.* zuverlässig.
**truth** [tru:θ], *s.* die Wahrheit.
**truthful** ['tru:θful], *adj.* wahrhaftig.
**try** [trai], *v.a., v.n. irr.* versuchen (*s. th.*); (*Law*) verhören; — *on* (*clothes*), anprobieren; — *out*, ausprobieren. — *v.n.* versuchen, sich bemühen. — *s.* der Versuch (*attempt*); (*Rugby*) der Try.
**Tsar** [za:], *s.* der Zar.
**tub** [tʌb], *s.* das Faß; die Wanne (*bath*); (*Naut.*) das Übungsboot.
**tube** [tju:b], *s.* die Tube (*paste etc.*); die Röhre (*pipe, also Elec.*); der Schlauch (*tyre*); das Rohr (*tubing*); (*Transport*) die Londoner Untergrundbahn.
**tuberous** ['tju:bərəs], *adj.* knollenartig, knollig.
**tubular** ['tju:bjulə], *adj.* röhrenförmig.
**tuck** [tʌk], *s.* (*Tail.*) die Falte; (*Sch. sl.*) der Leckerbissen. — *v.a.* — *up*, zudecken; — *in*, einschlagen. — *v.n.* (*sl.*) — *in*, tüchtig zugreifen.
**tucker** ['tʌkə], *s.* (*sl.*) das Essen.
**tuckshop** ['tʌkʃɔp], *s.* der Schulladen.
**Tuesday** ['tju:zdi], der Dienstag.
**tuft** [tʌft], *s.* der Büschel.
**tug** [tʌg], *v.a.* ziehen, zerren. — *s.* (*Naut.*) der Schlepper; — *of war*, das Tauziehen.
**tuition** [tju:'iʃən], *s.* der Unterricht, Privatunterricht.
**tulip** ['tju:lip], *s.* (*Bot.*) die Tulpe.
**tumble** [tʌmbl], *v.n.* purzeln. — *s.* der Sturz, Fall.
**tumbril** ['tʌmbril], *s.* der Karren.
**tumid** ['tju:mid], *adj.* geschwollen.
**tumour** ['tju:mə], *s.* (*Med.*) die Geschwulst, der Tumor.

**tumult** ['tju:mʌlt], *s.* der Tumult, Auflauf; der Lärm (*noise*).
**tun** [tʌn], *s.* die Tonne, das Faß.
**tune** [tju:n], *s.* die Melodie. — *v.a.* stimmen; (*Rad.*) — *in* (*to*), einstellen (auf.)
**tuneful** ['tju:nful], *adj.* melodisch.
**tuner** ['tju:nə], *s.* der (Klavier)stimmer.
**tunic** ['tju:nik], *s.* der Kittel.
**tuning** ['tju:niŋ], *s.* das Stimmen; die Abstimmung (*also Rad.*); — *fork*, die Stimmgabel.
**tunnel** [tʌnl], *s.* der Tunnel. — *v.n.* graben, einen Tunnel bauen.
**turbid** ['tə:bid], *adj.* trüb, dick.
**turbot** ['tə:bət], *s.* (*Zool.*) der Steinbutt.
**turbulence** ['tə:bjuləns], *s.* der Sturm, das Ungestüm; (*Aviat.*) die Turbulenz.
**tureen** [tjuə'ri:n], *s.* die Suppenterrine, Suppenschüssel.
**turf** [tə:f], *s.* der Rasen; (*Sport*) die Rennbahn, der Turf. — *v.a.* mit Rasen belegen; (*sl.*) — *out*, hinausschmeißen.
**turgid** ['tə:dʒid], *adj.* schwülstig (*style*).
**Turk** [tə:k], *s.* der Türke.
**turkey** ['tə:ki], *s.* (*Zool.*) der Truthahn.
**Turkish** ['tə:kiʃ], *adj.* türkisch.
**turmoil** ['tə:mɔil], *s.* die Unruhe, der Aufruhr.
**turn** [tə:n], *v.a.* wenden, drehen, kehren (*to*); — *down*, ablehnen; (*coll.*) — *in*, abgeben (*hand over*); — *on*, andrehen (*tap etc.*); — *off*, ausdrehen; — *out*, produzieren. — *v.n.* sich drehen, sich ändern; werden; — *on s.o.*, jemanden verraten; (*coll.*) — *out*, ausrücken; (*coll.*) — *up*, auftauchen. — *s.* die Drehung, Windung; der Hang; die Reihe; die Nummer (*act*); *it is my* —, ich bin an der Reihe.
**turncoat** ['tə:nkout], *s.* der Überläufer.
**turner** ['tə:nə], *s.* der Drechsler.
**turnip** ['tə:nip], *s.* (*Bot.*) die Rübe.
**turnpike** ['tə:npaik], *s.* der Schlagbaum.
**turnstile** ['tə:nstail], *s.* das Drehkreuz.
**turntable** ['tə:nteibl], *s.* die Drehscheibe.
**turpentine** ['tə:pəntain], *s.* der *or* das Terpentin.
**turquoise** ['tə:kwɔiz *or* 'tə:kɔiz], *s.* der Türkis.
**turret** ['tʌrit], *s.* (*Archit.*) der Turm, das Türmchen.
**turtle** [tə:tl], *s.* (*Zool.*) die Schildkröte; (*Orn.*) — -*dove*, die Turteltaube.
**tusk** [tʌsk], *s.* (*Zool.*) der Stoßzahn.
**tussle** [tʌsl], *s.* der Streit, die Rauferei.
**tutelage** ['tju:tilidʒ], *s.* die Vormundschaft.
**tutor** ['tju:tə], *s.* der Privatlehrer; der Tutor, Studienleiter. — *v.a.* unterrichten.
**twaddle** [twɔdl], *s.* das Geschwätz. — *v.n.* schwätzen.
**twang** [twæŋ], *s.* der scharfe Ton. — *v.n.* scharf klingen.
**tweed** [twi:d], *s.* (*Text.*) der Tweed.
**twelfth** [twelfθ], *num.adj.*zwölft-; *Twelfth Night*, das Fest der Heiligen Drei Könige (*6th January*).

twelve

**twelve** [twelv], *num. adj.* zwölf.
**twenty** ['twenti], *num. adj.* zwanzig.
**twice** [twais], *num. adv.* zweimal, doppelt.
**twig** [twig], *s.* (*Bot.*) der Zweig, die Rute.
**twilight** ['twailait], *s.* das Zwielicht, die Dämmerung.
**twill** [twil], *s.* (*Text.*) der Köper. — *v.a.* köpern.
**twin** [twin], *s.* der Zwilling.
**twine** [twain], *s.* der Bindfaden, die Schnur. — *v.a.* drehen, zwirnen. — *v.n.* sich verflechten; sich winden (*plant*).
**twinge** [twindʒ], *s.* der Zwick, Stich.
**twinkle** ['twiŋkl], *v.n.* blinzeln, blinken. — *s.* das Zwinkern, der Blick.
**twirl** [twə:l], *s.* der Wirbel. — *v.a.* schnell drehen, wirbeln.
**twist** [twist], *v.a.* flechten, drehen; verdrehen. — *s.* die Drehung, Krümmung; das Geflecht; (*fig.*) die Wendung (*sudden change*).
**twitch** [twitʃ], *v.a.* zupfen, zucken. — *v.n.* zucken. — *s.* das Zucken, der Krampf.
**twitter** ['twitə], *v.n.* zwitschern; (*fig.*) zittern. — *s.* das Gezwitscher; (*fig.*) die Angst.
**two** [tu:], *num. adj.* zwei; — *-faced*, falsch.
**twofold** ['tu:fould], *adj.* zweifach.
**tympanum** ['timpənəm], *s.* (*Med.*) das Trommelfell.
**type** [taip], *s.* (*Typ.*) die Type; (*Psych.*) der Typ, Typus. — *v.a.*, *v.n.* tippen; mit der Maschine schreiben.
**typewriter** ['taipraitə], *s.* die Schreibmaschine.
**typhoid** ['taifɔid], *s.* (*Med.*) der (Unterleibs)typhus. — *adj.* typhusartig.
**typist** ['taipist], *s.* der (die) Maschinenschreiber(in).
**typhoon** [tai'fu:n], *s.* der Taifun.
**typical** ['tipikəl], *adj.* typisch, charakteristisch.
**typography** [tai'pɔgrəfi], *s.* die Typographie, Buchdruckerkunst.
**tyrannical** [ti'rænikəl], *adj.* tyrannisch.
**tyranny** ['tirəni], *s.* die Tyrannei.
**tyrant** ['taiərənt], *s.* der Tyrann.
**tyre**, (*Am.*) **tire** [taiə], *s.* der Reifen.
**tyro** ['taiərou], *s.* der Anfänger.
**Tyrolese** [tiro'li:z], *adj.* tirolisch, Tiroler-. — *s.* der Tiroler.

# U

**U** [ju:], *s.* das U.
**ubiquitous** [ju'bikwitəs], *adj.* überall da, überall zu finden.
**udder** ['ʌdə], *s.* (*Zool.*) das Euter.
**ugly** ['ʌgli], *adj.* häßlich.

**Ukrainian** [ju:'kreiniən], *adj.* ukrainisch. — *s.* der Ukrainer.
**ulcer** ['ʌlsə], *s.* (*Med.*) das Geschwür.
**ulcerate** ['ʌlsəreit], *v.n.* (*Med.*) schwären.
**ulcerous** ['ʌlsərəs], *adj.* (*Med.*) geschwürig.
**ulterior** [ʌl'tiəriə], *adj.* weiter, ferner, weiterliegend.
**ultimate** ['ʌltimit], *adj.* letzt, endlich, äußerst.
**ultimatum** [ʌlti'meitəm], *s.* das Ultimatum.
**umbrage** ['ʌmbridʒ], *s.* der Schatten; *take* —, Anstoß nehmen (an, *Dat.*).
**umbrella** [ʌm'brelə], *s.* der Schirm, Regenschirm.
**umpire** ['ʌmpaiə], *s.* (*Sport*) der Schiedsrichter.
**umpteen** ['ʌmpti:n], *adj.* zahlreiche, verschiedene.
**un-** [ʌn], *negating pref.* un-, nicht-; *with verbs*, auf-, ent-, los-, ver-; *where a word is not given, see the simple form.*
**unable** [ʌn'eibl], *adj.* unfähig; *be* —, nicht können.
**unaccustomed** [ʌnə'kʌstəmd], *adj.* ungewohnt.
**unaided** [ʌn'eidid], *adj.* allein, ohne Hilfe.
**unaware** [ʌnə'wɛə], *adj.* unbewußt.
**uncertain** [ʌn'sə:tin], *adj.* unsicher.
**uncle** [ʌŋkl], *s.* der Onkel.
**unconscious** [ʌn'kɔnʃəs], *adj.* bewußtlos; unbewusst.
**uncouth** [ʌn'ku:θ], *adj.* ungehobelt, roh.
**unction** ['ʌŋkʃən], *s.* die Salbung (*anointing*); die Salbe; *Extreme Unction*, (*Eccl.*) die Letzte Ölung.
**unctuous** ['ʌŋktjuəs], *adj.* salbungsvoll.
**under** ['ʌndə], *prep.* unter. — *adv.* darunter, unten (*underneath*); *pref.* (*compounds*) unter-.
**undercarriage** ['ʌndəkæridʒ], *s.* (*Aviat.*) das Fahrwerk.
**underfed** [ʌndə'fed], *adj.* unterernährt.
**undergo** [ʌndə'gou], *v.a. irr.* durchmachen, erdulden.
**undergraduate** [ʌndə'grædjuit], *s.* (*Univ.*) der Student.
**underground** ['ʌndəgraund], *adj.* unterirdisch; — *railway* die Untergrundbahn. — [ʌndə'graund], *adv.* unterirdisch.
**underhand** [ʌndə'hænd], *adj.* heimlich, hinterlistig.
**underline** [ʌndə'lain], *v.a.* unterstreichen.
**undermine** [ʌndə'main], *v.a.* untergraben.
**underneath** [ʌndə'ni:θ], *adv.* unten, darunter. — ['ʌndəni:θ], *prep.* unter.
**undersigned** ['ʌndəsaind], *adj.* unterzeichnet. — *s.* der Unterzeichnete.
**understand** [ʌndə'stænd], *v.a. irr.* verstehen, begreifen.
**understatement** ['ʌndəsteitmənt], *s.* die zu bescheidene Festellung, Unterbewertung.

508

**undertaker** ['ʌndəteikə], *s.* der Leichen-bestatter.
**undertaking** [ʌndə'teikiŋ], *s.* das Unternehmen (*business*); das Versprechen (*promise*).
**undertone** ['ʌndətoun], *s.* der Unterton.
**underwrite** [ʌndə'rait], *v.a. irr.* (*Comm.*) versichern.
**underwriter** ['ʌndəraitə], *s.* (*Comm.*) der Assekurant, Versicherer, Mitversicherer.
**undeserved** [ʌndi'zə:vd], *adj.* unverdient.
**undeserving** [ʌndi'zə:viŋ], *adj.* unwürdig.
**undignified** [ʌn'dignifaid], *adj.* würdelos.
**undiscerning** [ʌndi'zə:niŋ], *adj.* geschmacklos.
**undiscriminating** [ʌndis'krimineitiŋ], *adj.* unterschiedslos, unkritisch.
**undisputed** [ʌndis'pju:tid], *adj.* unbestritten.
**undo** [ʌn'du:], *v.a. irr.* zerstören (*destroy*); öffnen (*open*).
**undoubted** [ʌn'dautid], *adj.* zweifellos.
**undress** [ʌn'dres], *v.a., v.n.* — (sich)ausziehen. — ['ʌndres], *s.* das Hauskleid.
**undue** [ʌn'dju:], *adj.* unangemessen.
**undulate** ['ʌndjuleit], *v.n.* wallen, Wellen schlagen.
**unduly** [ʌn'dju:li], *adv.* ungebührlich, übermäßig.
**unearth** [ʌn'ə:θ], *v.a.* ausgraben.
**unearthly** [ʌn'ə:θli], *adj.* überirdisch.
**uneasy** [ʌn'i:zi], *adj.* unruhig, unbehaglich.
**unemployed** [ʌnim'plɔid], *adj.* arbeitslos.
**unemployment** [ʌnim'plɔimənt], *s.* die Arbeitslosigkeit.
**unending** [ʌn'endiŋ], *adj.* endlos.
**uneven** [ʌn'i:vən], *adj.* uneben; ungerade.
**unexceptionable** [ʌnik'sepʃənəbl], *adj.* tadellos.
**unexpired** [ʌniks'paiəd], *adj.* noch nicht abgelaufen, noch gültig.
**unfair** [ʌn'feə], *adj.* unfair; unehrlich.
**unfeeling** [ʌn'fi:liŋ], *adj.* gefühllos.
**unfit** [ʌn'fit], *adj.* (*Mil., Med.*) untauglich, schwach; (*food etc.*) ungenießbar.
**unfold** [ʌn'fould], *v.a.* entfalten.
**unforeseen** [ʌnfɔ:'si:n], *adj.* unerwartet.
**unfounded** [ʌn'faundid], *adj.* grundlos.
**unfurnished** [ʌn'fə:niʃd], *adj.* unmöbliert.
**ungrudging** [ʌn'grʌdʒiŋ], *adj.* bereitwillig.
**unhappy** [ʌn'hæpi], *adj.* unglücklich.
**unhinge** [ʌn'hindʒ], *v.a.* aus den Angeln heben.
**unicorn** ['ju:nikɔ:n], *s.* (*Myth.*) das Einhorn.
**uniform** ['ju:nifɔ:m], *s.* die Uniform. — *adj.* gleichförmig, einförmig.
**union** ['ju:niən], *s.* die Vereinigung; *trade* —, die Gewerkschaft; *Union Jack*, die britische Nationalflagge.

**unique** [ju'ni:k], *adj.* einzigartig.
**unison** ['ju:nisən], *s.* (*Mus.*) der Einklang, die Harmonie.
**unit** ['ju:nit], *s.* die Einheit (*measure etc.*).
**unite** [ju'nait], *v.a.* vereinen. — *v.n.* sich vereinen, verbünden.
**unity** ['ju:niti], *s.* die Einigkeit.
**universal** [ju:ni'və:səl], *adj.* allgemein.
**universe** ['ju:nivə:s], *s.* das Weltall.
**university** [ju:ni'və:siti], *s.* die Universität, Hochschule; — *degree*, der akademische Grad.
**unkempt** [ʌn'kempt], *adj.* ungekämmt, ungepflegt.
**unleavened** [ʌn'levənd], *adj.* ungesäuert.
**unless** [ʌn'les], *conj.* außer, wenn nicht, es sei denn.
**unlettered** [ʌn'letəd], *adj.* ungebildet.
**unlicensed** [ʌn'laisənsd], *adj.* nicht (für Alkoholverkauf) lizenziert.
**unlike** [ʌn'laik], *adj.* ungleich. — ['ʌnlaik], *prep.* anders als, verschieden von.
**unlikely** [ʌn'laikli], *adj., adv.* unwahrscheinlich.
**unlock** [ʌn'lɔk], *v.a.* aufschließen.
**unmask** [ʌn'mɑ:sk], *v.a.* entlarven.
**unpack** [ʌn'pæk], *v.a., v.n.* auspacken.
**unpleasant** [ʌn'pleznt], *adj.* unangenehm.
**unreliable** [ʌnri'laiəbl], *adj.* unzuverlässig.
**unremitting** [ʌnri'mitiŋ], *adj.* unablässig.
**unrepentant** [ʌnri'pentənt], *adj.* reuelos.
**unrest** [ʌn'rest], *s.* die Unruhe.
**unsafe** [ʌn'seif], *adj.* unsicher.
**unscathed** [ʌn'skeiðd], *adj.* unversehrt.
**unscrew** [ʌn'skru:], *v.a.* abschrauben.
**unscrupulous** [ʌn'skru:pjuləs], *adj.* skrupellos, gewissenlos.
**unseat** [ʌn'si:t], *v.a.* aus dem Sattel heben; absetzen.
**unselfish** [ʌn'selfiʃ], *adj.* selbstlos.
**unsettle** [ʌn'setl], *v.a.* verwirren; (*fig.*) aus dem Konzept bringen.
**unsew** [ʌn'sou], *v.a.* auftrennen.
**unshrinking** [ʌn'ʃriŋkiŋ], *adj.* unverzagt.
**unsophisticated** [ʌnsə'fistikeitid], *adj.* naiv, natürlich.
**unsparing** [ʌn'speəriŋ], *adj.* schonungslos.
**unstable** [ʌn'steibl], *adj.* unsicher; labil.
**unstitch** [ʌn'stitʃ], *v.a.* auftrennen.
**unstop** [ʌn'stɔp], *v.a.* aufstöpseln, öffnen (*a bottle*).
**unstudied** [ʌn'stʌdid], *adj.* ungekünstelt.
**unsuccessful** [ʌnsək'sesful], *adj.* erfolglos.
**unsuspecting** [ʌnsə'spektiŋ], *adj.* arglos.
**untie** [ʌn'tai], *v.a.* losbinden.
**until** [ʌn'til], *prep., conj.* bis.

# untimely

**untimely** [ʌn'taimli], *adj.* vorzeitig, unzeitig.
**untiring** [ʌn'taiəriŋ], *adj.* unermüdlich.
**unto** ['ʌntu], *prep.* (*Poet.*) zu.
**untold** [ʌn'tould], *adj.* ungezählt, unermeßlich.
**untoward** [ʌn'tɔ:d *or* ʌn'touəd], *adj.* unangenehm; widerspenstig (*recalcitrant*).
**untrustworthy** [ʌn'trʌstwə:ði], *adj.* unzuverlässig.
**unveil** [ʌn'veil], *v.a.* enthüllen.
**unwieldy** [ʌn'wi:ldi], *adj.* sperrig, schwerfällig.
**unwind** [ʌn'waind], *v.a.* abwickeln.
**unwitting** [ʌn'witiŋ], *adj.* unwissentlich, unbewusst.
**unwonted** [ʌn'wountid], *adj.* ungewohnt.
**unwrap** [ʌn'ræp], *v.a.* auspacken, auswickeln.
**unyielding** [ʌn'ji:ldiŋ], *adj.* unnachgiebig; hartnäckig.
**unyoke** [ʌn'jouk], *v.a.* ausspannen.
**up** [ʌp], *adv.* auf, aufwärts (*upward*); aufgestanden (*out of bed*); — (*there*), oben; *what's* — *up?* was ist los? — *to*, bis zu; *be — to s.th.*, auf etwas aus sein, etwas im Schilde führen; *it's — to you*, es liegt an dir. — *prep.* auf, hinauf. — *s.* ups *and* downs, das wechselnde Schicksal, Auf und Ab.
**upbraid** [ʌp'breid], *v.a.* tadeln.
**upheaval** [ʌp'hi:vl], *s.* das Chaos, Durcheinander, die Umwälzung.
**uphill** [ʌp'hil], *adv.* bergauf(wärts). — ['ʌphil], *adj.* (an)steigend; (*fig.*) mühsam.
**uphold** [ʌp'hould], *v.a.* aufrechterhalten.
**upholster** [ʌp'houlstə], *v.a.* polstern.
**upholstery** [ʌp'houlstəri], *s.* die Polsterung.
**upon** [ʌ'pɔn] *see* on.
**upper** ['ʌpə], *adj.* ober, höher; — *hand*, die Oberhand.
**uppish** ['ʌpiʃ], *adj.* anmaßend.
**upright** ['ʌprait], *adj.* aufrecht, gerade; (*fig.*) aufrichtig, rechtschaffen.
**uproar** ['ʌprɔ:], *s.* der Lärm, Aufruhr.
**uproot** [ʌp'ru:t], *v.a.* entwurzeln.
**upset** [ʌp'set], *v.a.* umwerfen; (*fig.*) aus der Fassung bringen. — ['ʌpset], *s.* das Umwerfen; (*fig.*) die Bestürzung.
**upshot** ['ʌpʃɔt], *s.* der Ausgang, das Ergebnis.
**upside** ['ʌpsaid], *s.* die Oberseite; — *down*, auf den Kopf gestellt.
**upstairs** [ʌp'stɛəz], *adv.* oben, nach oben.
**upstart** ['ʌpsta:t], *s.* der Parvenü, Emporkömmling.
**upward** ['ʌpwəd], *adj.* steigend, aufwärtsgehend. — *adv.* (*also* **upwards**) aufwärts; — *of*, mehr als.
**urban** ['ə:bən], *adj.* städtisch.
**urbane** [ə:'bein], *adj.* zivilisiert.
**urbanity** [ə:'bæniti], *s.* die Bildung, der Schliff.
**urchin** ['ə:tʃin], *s.* der Schelm; (*Zool.*) *sea* —, der Seeigel.

**urge** [ə:dʒ], *v.a.* drängen. — *s.* der Drang.
**urgent** ['ə:dʒənt], *adj.* dringend, drängend, dringlich.
**urine** ['juərin], *s.* der Urin.
**urn** [ə:n], *s.* die Urne.
**Uruguayan** [ju:ru'gwaiən], *adj.* uruguayisch. — *s.* der Uruguayer.
**us** [ʌs], *pers. pron.* uns.
**usage** ['ju:sidʒ], *s.* der (Sprach)gebrauch; die Sitte.
**use** [ju:z], *v.a.* gebrauchen, benutzen. — [ju:s], *s.* der Gebrauch, die Benutzung; der Nutzen (*usefulness*).
**usher** ['ʌʃə], *s.* der Türhüter, Platzanweiser. — *v.a.* — *in*, anmelden, einführen.
**usherette** [ʌʃə'ret], *s.* die Platzanweiserin, Programmverkäuferin.
**usual** ['ju:ʒuəl], *adj.* gewöhnlich, üblich.
**usurer** ['ju:ʒərə *or* 'ju:zjuərə], *s.* der Wucherer.
**usurp** [ju'zə:p], *v.a.* an sich reißen, usurpieren.
**usury** ['ju:ʒuəri], *s.* der Wucher.
**utensil** [ju'tensil], *s.* das Gerät, Werkzeug.
**utility** [ju:'tiliti], *s.* die Nützlichkeit (*usefulness*); der Nutzen; *public* —, (die) öffentliche Einrichtung.
**utilize** ['ju:tilaiz], *v.a.* nutzbar machen, ausbeuten, ausnützen.
**utmost** ['ʌtmoust], *adj.* äußerst, weitest, höchst. — *s.* das Höchste, Äußerste.
**utter** ['ʌtə], *adj.* äußerst, gänzlich. — *v.a.* äußern, aussprechen.
**utterly** ['ʌtəli], *adv.* äußerst, völlig.
**uvula** ['ju:vjulə], *s.* (*Anat.*) das Zäpfchen.

# V

**V** [vi:]. das V.
**vacancy** ['veikənsi], *s.* die freie Stelle, die Vakanz.
**vacant** ['veikənt], *adj.* frei; leer.
**vacate** [və'keit], *v.a.* frei machen.
**vacation** [və'keiʃən], *s.* die Niederlegung (*of a post*); die Ferien, *pl.* (*school*); der Urlaub (*holiday*).
**vaccinate** ['væksineit], *v.a.* (*Med.*) impfen.
**vaccine** ['væksi:n], *s.* (*Med.*) der Impfstoff.
**vacillate** ['væsileit], *v.n.* schwanken.
**vacuity** [væ'kju:iti], *s.* die Leere.
**vacuous** ['vækjuəs], *adj.* leer.
**vacuum** ['vækjuəm], *s.* das Vakuum; — *cleaner*, der Staubsauger.
**vagabond** ['vægəbɔnd], *s.* der Landstreicher.
**vagary** [və'gɛəri], *s.* die Laune, Grille.

510

**vagrant** ['veigrənt], *adj.* herumstreichend. — *s.* der Landstreicher.
**vague** [veig], *adj.* vage, unbestimmt, unklar.
**vain** [vein], *adj.* nichtig, vergeblich, eitel; *in* —, vergebens, umsonst.
**vale** [veil], *s.* (*Poet.*) das Tal.
**valerian** [və'liəriən], *s.* (*Bot.*) der Baldrian.
**valet** ['vælei, 'vælit], *s.* der Diener.
**valiant** ['væljənt], *adj.* mutig, tapfer.
**valid** ['vælid], *adj.* gültig, stichhaltig.
**valley** ['væli], *s.* das Tal.
**valuable** ['væljuəbl], *adj.* wertvoll, kostbar.
**valuation** [vælju'eiʃən], *s.* die Schätzung.
**value** ['vælju:], *s.* der Wert. — *v.a.* wertschätzen, schätzen.
**valve** [vælv], *s.* (*Mech.*) das Ventil; (*Rad.*) die Röhre.
**vamp** (1) [væmp], *s.* das Oberleder.
**vamp** (2) [væmp], *s.* (*Am. coll.*) der Vamp.
**vampire** ['væmpaiə], *s.* der Vampir.
**van** [væn], *s.* der Lieferwagen.
**vane** [vein], *s.* die Wetterfahne.
**vanguard** ['vængɑ:d], *s.* die Vorhut, der Vortrupp.
**vanilla** [və'nilə], *s.* die Vanille.
**vanish** ['væniʃ], *v.n.* verschwinden.
**vanity** ['væniti], *s.* die Nichtigkeit; die Eitelkeit (*conceit*).
**vanquish** ['væŋkwiʃ], *v.a.* besiegen.
**vantage** ['vɑ:ntidʒ], *s.* der Vorteil; — *point*, die günstige Position.
**vapid** ['væpid], *adj.* leer, schal.
**vapour** ['veipə], *s.* der Dunst; (*Chem.*) der Dampf.
**variable** ['veəriəbl], *adj.* variabel, veränderlich.
**variance** ['veəriəns], *s.* die Uneinigkeit.
**variation** [veəri'eiʃən], *s.* die Variation; die Veränderung, Abweichung.
**varicose** ['værikəs], *adj.* Krampf-, krampfaderig.
**variegated** ['veərigeitid], *adj.* bunt, vielfarbig.
**variety** [və'raiəti], *s.* die Mannigfaltigkeit; (*Bot.*) die Varietät, Abart; (*Theat.*) das Varieté, das Varietétheater.
**various** ['veəriəs], *adj.* verschieden; mannigfaltig.
**varnish** ['vɑ:niʃ], *s.* der Firnis, der Lack. — *v.a.* mit Firnis anstreichen, lackieren.
**vary** ['veəri], *v.a.* abändern. — *v.n.* sich ändern, variieren.
**vase** [vɑ:z], *s.* die Vase.
**vassal** [væsl], *s.* der Vasall, Lehnsmann.
**vast** [vɑ:st], *adj.* ungeheuer, groß.
**vat** [væt], *s.* die Kufe, das große Faß.
**vault** [vɔ:lt], *s.* das Gewölbe; die Gruft (*grave*); (*Sport*) der Sprung, *pole* —, der Stabhochsprung. — *v.n.* springen.
**vaunt** [vɔ:nt], *v.a.* rühmen. — *v.n.* prahlen, sich rühmen. — *s.* die Prahlerei.
**veal** [vi:l], *s.* das Kalbfleisch.

**veer** [viə], *v.n.* sich drehen.
**vegetable** ['vedʒitəbl], *s.* das Gemüse.
**vegetarian** [vedʒi'teəriən], *adj.* vegetarisch. — *s.* der Vegetarier.
**vegetate** ['vedʒiteit], *v.n.* vegetieren.
**vehemence** ['vi:məns], *s.* die Vehemenz, Heftigkeit.
**vehicle** ['vi:ikl], *s.* das Fahrzeug, Fuhrwerk; (*Motor.*) der Wagen.
**veil** [veil], *s.* der Schleier. — *v.a.* verschleiern.
**vein** [vein], *s.* die Ader.
**vellum** ['veləm], *s.* das feine Pergamentpapier.
**velocity** [vi'lɔsiti], *s.* die Geschwindigkeit, Schnelligkeit.
**velvet** ['velvit], *s.* (*Text.*) der Samt.
**venal** ['vi:nəl], *adj.* käuflich.
**vend** [vend], *v.a.* verkaufen; —*ing machine*, der Automat.
**veneer** [və'niə], *s.* das Furnier. — *v.a.* furnieren.
**venerable** ['venərəbl], *adj.* ehrwürdig.
**venerate** ['venəreit], *v.a.* verehren.
**venereal** [və'niəriəl], *adj.* Geschlechts-.
**Venezuelan** [veni'zweilən], *adj.* venezolanisch. — *s.* der Venezolaner.
**vengeance** ['vendʒəns], *s.* die Rache.
**venison** ['venizn *or* venzn], *s.* das Wildpret.
**venom** ['venəm], *s.* das Gift.
**vent** [vent], *v.a.* Luft machen (*Dat.*). — *s.* das Luftloch, die Öffnung.
**ventilate** ['ventileit], *v.a.* ventilieren, lüften.
**ventricle** ['ventrikl], *s.* (*Anat.*) die Herzkammer.
**ventriloquist** [ven'triləkwist], *s.* der Bauchredner.
**venture** ['ventʃə], *s.* das Wagnis, Unternehmen. — *v.a.* wagen, riskieren. — *v.n.* sich erlauben, (sich) wagen.
**venue** ['venju:], *s.* der Treffpunkt, Versammlungsort.
**veracity** [və'ræsiti], *s.* die Glaubwürdigkeit, Wahrhaftigkeit.
**verbose** [və:'bous], *adj.* wortreich, weitschweifig.
**verdant** ['və:dənt], *adj.* grünend, grün.
**verdict** ['və:dikt], *s.* das Urteil, die Entscheidung.
**verdigris** ['və:digri:s], *s.* der Grünspan.
**verdure** ['və:djə], *s.* das Grün.
**verge** [və:dʒ], *s.* der Rand, die Einfassung. — *v.n.* grenzen (*on*, an, *Acc.*).
**verify** ['verifai], *v.a.* bestätigen; (*Law*) beglaubigen.
**verily** ['verili], *adv.* (*Bibl.*) wahrlich.
**veritable** ['veritəbl], *adj.* wahr, echt.
**vermicelli** [və:mi'seli], *s.* die Nudeln, *f. pl.*
**vermilion** [və'miljən], *s.* das Zinnober (*paint*).
**vermin** ['və:min], *s. pl.* das Ungeziefer.
**vermouth** ['və:mu:θ, -mu:t], *s.* der Wermut.
**vernacular** [və'nækjulə], *s.* die Landessprache. — *adj.* einheimisch.
**vernal** ['və:nəl], *adj.* frühlingsartig, Frühlings-.

**versatile** [ˈvəːsətail], *adj.* gewandt; vielseitig.
**verse** [vəːs], *s.* der Vers; (*Poet.*) die Strophe.
**versed** [vəːsd], *adj.* bewandert.
**version** [ˈvəːʃən], *s.* die Version, Fassung, Lesart; (*fig.*) die Darstellung.
**vertebrate** [ˈvəːtibrət], *s.* (*Zool.*) das Wirbeltier. — *adj.* mit Rückenwirbeln versehen.
**vertex** [ˈvəːteks], *s.* der Zenit.
**vertigo** [ˈvəːtigou], *s.* (*Med.*) der Schwindel, das Schwindelgefühl.
**verve** [vəːv], *s.* der Schwung.
**very** [ˈveri], *adv.* sehr. — *adj.* echt, wirklich, wahrhaftig.
**vespers** [ˈvespəz], *s. pl.* (*Eccl.*) der Abendgottesdienst, die Vesper.
**vessel** [vesl], *s.* das Gefäß (*container*); (*Naut.*) das Fahrzeug, Schiff.
**vest** [vest], *s.* das Gewand; (*Tail.*) die Weste; das Unterhemd (*undergarment*). — *v.a.* übertragen.
**vested** [ˈvestid], *adj.* — *interests*, das Eigeninteresse.
**vestige** [ˈvestidʒ], *s.* die Spur.
**vestment** [ˈvestmənt], *s.* (*Eccl.*) das Meßgewand.
**vestry** [ˈvestri], *s.* (*Eccl.*) die Sakristei.
**vetch** [vetʃ], *s.* (*Bot.*) die Wicke.
**veterinary** [ˈvetərinri], *adj.* tierärztlich; — *surgeon*, der Tierarzt.
**veto** [ˈviːtou], *s.* (*Pol.*) der Einspruch, das Veto.
**vex** [veks], *v.a.* quälen, plagen.
**vexation** [vekˈseiʃən], *s.* die Plage, der Verdruß.
**via** [vaiə], *prep.* über.
**vibrate** [vaiˈbreit], *v.n.* schwingen, vibrieren.
**vicar** [ˈvikə], *s.* (*Eccl.*) der Pfarrer, Vikar.
**vicarious** [viˈkɛəriəs], *adj.* stellvertretend.
**vice** (1) [vais], *s.* das Laster (*immorality*).
**vice** (2) [vais], *s.* (*Mech.*) der Schraubstock.
**vice-** [vais], *pref.* Vize-, zweiter (*chairman etc.*).
**vicinity** [viˈsiniti], *s.* die Nachbarschaft, Nähe.
**vicious** [ˈviʃəs], *adj.* böse, bösartig.
**vicissitude** [viˈsisitjuːd], *s.* der Wechsel, Wandel; (*pl.*) Wechselfälle, *m. pl.*
**victim** [ˈviktim], *s.* das Opfer.
**victuals** [vitlz], *s. pl.* die Lebensmittel, *n. pl.*
**vie** [vai], *v.n.* wetteifern.
**Vietnamese** [vjetnəˈmiːz], *adj.* vietnamesisch. — *s.* der Vietnamese.
**view** [vjuː], *s.* der Anblick, die Aussicht (*panorama*); die Ansicht (*opinion*); die Absicht (*intention*). — *v.a.* betrachten; besichtigen (*inspect*).
**vigil** [ˈvidʒil], *s.* die Nachtwache.
**vigilance** [ˈvidʒiləns], *s.* die Wachsamkeit.
**vigorous** [ˈvigərəs], *adj.* kräftig, rüstig, energisch.
**vigour** [ˈvigə], *s.* die Kraft, Energie.
**vile** [vail], *adj.* schlecht, niedrig.

**vilify** [ˈvilifai], *v.a.* beschimpfen, erniedrigen.
**villa** [ˈvilə], *s.* das Landhaus, die Villa.
**village** [ˈvilidʒ], *s.* das Dorf.
**villain** [ˈvilən], *s.* der Schurke.
**villainous** [ˈvilənəs], *adj.* niederträchtig.
**villainy** [ˈviləni], *s.* die Niedertracht, Schändlichkeit.
**vindicate** [ˈvindikeit], *v.a.* behaupten, verteidigen; rechtfertigen (*justify*).
**vindictive** [vinˈdiktiv], *adj.* rachsüchtig.
**vine** [vain], *s.* (*Bot.*) der Weinstock, die Rebe.
**vinegar** [ˈvinigə], *s.* der Essig.
**vintage** [ˈvintidʒ], *s.* die Weinernte; der Jahrgang (*also fig.*).
**vintner** [ˈvintnə], *s.* der Weinbauer, Winzer.
**viola** [viˈoulə], *s.* (*Mus.*) die Viola, Bratsche.
**violate** [ˈvaiəleit], *v.a.* verletzen, schänden.
**violence** [ˈvaiələns], *s.* die Gewalt; die Gewalttätigkeit.
**violent** [ˈvaiələnt], *adj.* gewalttätig (*brutal*); heftig (*vehement*).
**violet** [ˈvaiəlit], *s.* (*Bot.*) das Veilchen. — *adj.* veilchenblau, violett.
**violin** [vaiəˈlin], *s.* (*Mus.*) die Violine, Geige.
**viper** [ˈvaipə], *s.* (*Zool.*) die Viper, Natter.
**virago** [viˈrɑːgou], *s.* das Mannweib.
**virgin** [ˈvəːdʒin], *s.* die Jungfrau.
**virile** [ˈvirail], *adj.* männlich, kräftig.
**virtual** [ˈvəːtjuəl], *adj.* eigentlich.
**virtue** [ˈvəːtjuː], *s.* die Tugend; *by* — *of*, kraft (*Genit.*).
**virtuoso** [vəːtjuˈousou], *s.* der Virtuose.
**virtuous** [ˈvəːtjuəs], *adj.* tugendhaft.
**virulent** [ˈvirulənt], *adj.* bösartig, giftig.
**virus** [ˈvaiərəs], *s.* (*Med.*) das Gift, Virus.
**viscosity** [visˈkɔsiti], *s.* die Zähigkeit, Zähflüssigkeit.
**viscount** [ˈvaikaunt], *s.* der Vicomte.
**viscous** [ˈviskəs], *adj.* zähflüssig, klebrig.
**visibility** [viziˈbiliti], *s.* die Sichtbarkeit, Sicht.
**visible** [ˈvizibl], *adj.* sichtbar.
**vision** [ˈviʒən], *s.* die Sehkraft; (*fig.*) die Vision (*dream*); die Erscheinung (*apparition*).
**visionary** [ˈviʒənri], *s.* der Träumer, (*Poet.*) der Seher. — *adj.* visionär, phantastisch, seherisch.
**visit** [ˈvizit], *s.* der Besuch. — *v.a.* besuchen.
**visitation** [viziˈteiʃən], *s.* die Heimsuchung.
**visor** [ˈvaizə], *s.* das Visier.
**vista** [ˈvistə], *s.* (*Art*) die Aussicht, der Ausblick.
**visual** [ˈviʒuəl], *adj.* visuell, Seh-.
**vital** [vaitl], *adj.* lebenswichtig; (*fig.*) wesentlich.
**vitality** [vaiˈtæliti], *s.* die Lebenskraft, Vitalität.

**vitiate** ['viʃieit], *v.a.* verderben, umstoßen.
**vitreous** ['vitriəs], *adj.* gläsern, glasartig.
**vitrify** ['vitrifai], *v.a.* verglasen.
**vivacious** [vi'veiʃəs], *adj.* lebhaft, munter.
**viva (voce)** ['vaivə ('vousi)], *s.* die mündliche Prüfung.
**vivacity** [vi'væsiti], *s.* die Lebhaftigkeit.
**vivid** ['vivid], *adj.* lebhaft.
**vixen** ['viksən], *s.* (*Zool.*) die Füchsin; (*fig.*) das zänkische Weib.
**vizier** [vi'ziə], *s.* der Wesir.
**vocabulary** [vo'kæbjuləri], *s.* das Vokabular; der Wortschatz.
**vocal** ['voukəl], *adj.* laut; (*Mus.*) Stimm-, Sing-.
**vocation** [vo'keiʃən], *s.* die Berufung (*call*); der Beruf (*occupation*).
**vociferous** [vo'sifərəs], *adj.* schreiend, laut.
**vogue** [voug], *s.* die Mode.
**voice** [vois], *s.* die Stimme.
**void** [void], *adj.* leer (*empty*); ungültig, (*invalid*); *null and* —, null und nichtig. — *s.* die Leere.
**volatile** ['volətail], *adj.* flüchtig.
**volcanic** [vol'kænik], *adj.* vulkanisch.
**volcano** [vol'keinou], *s.* der Vulkan.
**volition** [vo'liʃən], *s.* der Wille.
**volley** ['voli], *s.* (*Mil.*) die Salve; (*Footb.*) der Volleyschuß; (*Tennis*) der Flugball.
**volt** [voult], *s.* (*Elec.*) das Volt.
**voltage** ['voultidʒ], *s.* die Spannung.
**voluble** ['voljubl], *adj.* gesprächig, zungenfertig.
**volume** ['volju:m], *s.* (*Phys.*) das Volumen; der Band (*book*); (*fig.*) der Umfang.
**voluminous** [və'lju:minəs], *adj.* umfangreich.
**voluntary** ['voləntri], *adj.* freiwillig. — *s.* (*Mus.*) das Orgelsolo.
**volunteer** [volən'tiə], *s.* der Freiwillige. — *v.n.* sich freiwillig melden.
**voluptuous** [və'lʌptjuəs], *adj.* wollüstig, lüstern.
**vomit** ['vomit], *v.a., v.n.* (sich) erbrechen, übergeben.
**voracious** [vo'reiʃəs], *adj.* gierig, gefräßig.
**vortex** ['vo:teks], *s.* der Wirbel, Strudel.
**vote** [vout], *v.n.* (*Pol.*) wählen, abstimmen, die Stimme abgeben. — *s.* (*Pol.*) die Stimme.
**voter** ['voutə], *s.* der Wähler.
**votive** ['voutiv], *adj.* (*Eccl.*) geweiht, gelobt; Votiv-.
**vouch** [vautʃ], *v.a., v.n.* (sich) verbürgen, einstehen(für).
**voucher** ['vautʃə], *s.* der Beleg; (*Comm.*) der Gutschein.
**vouchsafe** [vautʃ'seif], *v.a.* bewilligen, gewähren. — *v.n.* geruhen, sich herablassen.
**vow** [vau], *s.* das Gelübde. — *v.a.* schwören, geloben.

**vowel** ['vauəl], *s.* der Vokal.
**voyage** ['voiidʒ], *s.* die Seereise. — *v.n.* zur See reisen.
**vulcanize** ['vʌlkənaiz], *v.a.* vulkanisieren.
**vulgar** ['vʌlgə], *adj.* gemein, pöbelhaft, ordinär, vulgär.
**vulnerable** ['vʌlnərəbl], *adj.* verwundbar, verletzbar.
**vulture** ['vʌltʃə], *s.* (*Orn.*) der Geier.

# W

**W** ['dʌblju:]. das W.
**wabble** *see* **wobble**.
**wad** [wod], *s.* das Bündel (*notes*); der Bausch (*cotton wool*).
**waddle** ['wodl], *v.n.* watscheln.
**wade** [weid], *v.n.* waten, durchwaten.
**wafer** ['weifə], *s.* die Oblate, die Waffel; (*Eccl.*) die Hostie.
**waffle** ['wofl], *s.* (*Cul.*) die Waffel. — *v.n.* (*coll.*) schwafeln.
**waft** [wæft], *v.a.* wegwehen.
**wag** (1) [wæg], *v.a.* wedeln, schütteln.
**wag** (2) [wæg], *s.* der Spaßvogel.
**wage** (1) [weidʒ], *v.a.* unternehmen; — *war*, Krieg führen.
**wage** (2) ['weidʒ], *s.* (*often in pl.*) der Lohn.
**wager** ['weidʒə], *v.a.* wetten. — *s.* die Wette.
**waggish** ['wægiʃ], *adj.* spaßhaft, mutwillig, schelmisch.
**wag(g)on** ['wægən], *s.* der Wagen, Güterwagen.
**wagtail** ['wægteil], *s.* (*Orn.*) die Bachstelze.
**waif** [weif], *s.* das verwahrloste Kind; das herrenlose Gut.
**wail** [weil], *v.n.* wehklagen. — *s.* das Wehklagen, die Klage.
**waist** [weist], *s.* (*Anat.*) die Taille.
**waistcoat** ['weiskout, 'weskət], *s.* die Weste, das Wams.
**wait** [weit], *v.n.* warten; — *for*, warten auf; — *upon*, bedienen. — *v.a.* erwarten.
**waiter** ['weitə], *s.* der Kellner; *head* —, der Oberkellner, (*coll.*) der Ober.
**waiting room** ['weitiŋ rum], *s.* das Wartezimmer; (*Railw.*) der Wartesaal.
**waive** [weiv], *v.a.* aufgeben, verzichten (auf, *Acc.*).
**wake** (1) [weik], *v.n. irr.* wachen, aufwachen, wach sein. — *v.a.* aufwecken.
**wake** (2) [weik], *s.* (*Naut.*) das Kielwasser; (*fig.*) die Spur; *in the* — *of*, in den Fußstapfen (*Genit.*).
**waken** ['weikən], *v.a.* aufwecken. — *v.n.* aufwachen.
**walk** [wo:k], *v.n.* (zu Fuß) gehen. — *s.* der Gang (*gait*); der Spaziergang.

# wall

**wall** [wɔ:l], _s._ die Wand, Mauer.
**wallet** ['wɔlit], _s._ die Brieftasche.
**wallflower** ['wɔ:lflauə], _s._ (_Bot._) der Goldlack; (_fig._) das Mauerblümchen.
**wallow** ['wɔlou], _v.n._ schwelgen; sich wälzen.
**walnut** ['wɔ:lnʌt], _s._ (_Bot._) die Walnuß.
**walrus** ['wɔ:lrəs], _s._ (_Zool._) das Walroß.
**waltz** [wɔ:lts], _s._ der Walzer.
**wan** [wɔn], _adj._ blaß, bleich.
**wand** [wɔnd], _s._ der Stab.
**wander** ['wɔndə], _v.n._ wandern, durchwandern; (_fig._) — _from the subject_, vom Thema abkommen.
**wane** [wein], _v.n._ abnehmen, verfallen.
**want** [wɔnt], _v.a._ brauchen, wollen, nötig haben, wünschen. — _v.n._ mangeln, fehlen. — _s._ die Not.
**wanton** ['wɔntən], _adj._ mutwillig, ausgelassen.
**war** [wɔ:], _s._ der Krieg.
**warble** [wɔ:bl], _v.a., v.n._ singen; (_Mus._) trillern.
**warbler** ['wɔ:blə], _s._ (_Orn._) der Singvogel.
**ward** [wɔ:d], _s._ die Verwahrung; das _or_ der Mündel (_child in care_); (_Pol._) der Wahlbezirk; die Station (_hospital_). — _v.a._ — _off_, abwehren.
**warden** [wɔ:dn], _s._ der Vorstand, Vorsteher; Rektor.
**warder** ['wɔ:də], _s._ der Wächter; (_in prison_) der Wärter, Gefängniswärter.
**wardrobe** ['wɔ:droub], _s._ der Kleiderschrank.
**ware** [weə], _s._ die Ware.
**warehouse** ['weəhaus], _s._ das Warenlager.
**warfare** ['wɔ:fɛə], _s._ der Krieg, die Kriegsführung.
**warlike** ['wɔ:laik], _adj._ kriegerisch.
**warm** [wɔ:m], _adj._ warm.
**warn** [wɔ:n], _v.a._ warnen, ermahnen.
**warning** ['wɔ:niŋ], _s._ die Warnung.
**warp** [wɔ:p], _v.a._ krümmen, verziehen (_of wood_); (_fig._) verderben; verzerren, verdrehen. — _v.n._ sich werfen, krümmen.
**warrant** ['wɔrənt], _s._ (_Law_) der Haftbefehl; — _officer_, der Unteroffizier; (_Comm._) die Vollmacht, Bürgschaft. — _v.a._ garantieren (_vouch for_); versichern (_assure_).
**warranty** ['wɔrənti], _s._ (_Law_) die Gewähr; Garantie.
**warren** ['wɔrən], _s._ das Gehege.
**warrior** ['wɔriə], _s._ der Krieger.
**wart** [wɔ:t], _s._ (_Med._) die Warze.
**wary** ['wɛəri], _adj._ vorsichtig, achtsam (_careful_).
**wash** [wɔʃ], _v.a., v.n._ (sich) waschen; — _up_, spülen, abwaschen. — _s._ die Wäsche (_laundry_).
**wasp** [wɔsp], _s._ (_Ent._) die Wespe.
**waspish** ['wɔspiʃ], _adj._ reizbar, zänkisch, bissig.
**wassail** [wɔsl], _s._ das Trinkgelage. — _v.n._ zechen.
**waste** [weist], _v.a._ zerstören, verwüsten;

verschwenden. — _adj._ wüst, öde. — _s._ die Verschwendung (_process_); der Abfall (_product_); — _paper_, die Makulatur; — _paper basket_, der Papierkorb.
**wasteful** ['weistful], _adj._ verschwenderisch.
**watch** [wɔtʃ], _v.a._ bewachen; beobachten (_observe_); hüten (_guard_). — _s._ die Wache (_guard_); die Uhr, Taschenuhr (_time-piece_).
**watchful** ['wɔtʃful], _adj._ wachsam.
**watchman** ['wɔtʃmən], _s._ der Nachtwächter.
**water** ['wɔ:tə], _s._ das Wasser; (_pl._) die Kur; — _colour_, das Aquarell; — _gauge_, der Pegel. — _v.a._ wässern; begießen (_flowers_).
**watercress** ['wɔ:təkres], _s._ (_Bot._) die Brunnenkresse.
**waterproof** ['wɔ:təpru:f], _adj._ wasserdicht.
**watt** [wɔt], _s._ (_Elec._) das Watt.
**wattle** [wɔtl], _s._ (_Bot._) die Hürde.
**wave** [weiv], _s._ die Welle; _permanent_ —, die Dauerwelle. — _v.n._ zuwinken (_Dat._); wehen; winken. — _v.a._ schwenken (_handkerchief_).
**waver** ['weivə], _v.n._ schwanken, unentschlossen sein.
**wax** [wæks], _s._ das Wachs, der Siegellack. — _v.a._ wachsen, bohnern.
**waxen** [wæksn], _adj._ aus Wachs, wächsern.
**way** [wei], _s._ der Weg (_road etc._); die Strecke; Richtung; _in no_ —, keineswegs; (_pl._) die Art und Weise; _Milky Way_, die Milchstraße.
**wayward** ['weiwəd], _adj._ eigensinnig.
**we** [wi:], _pers. pron._ wir.
**weak** [wi:k], _adj._ schwach, kraftlos.
**weaken** ['wi:kən], _v.a._ schwächen. — _v.n._ schwach werden.
**weakling** ['wi:kliŋ], _s._ der Schwächling.
**wealth** [welθ], _s._ der Wohlstand, Reichtum.
**wealthy** ['welθi], _adj._ wohlhabend, reich.
**wean** [wi:n], _v.a._ entwöhnen.
**weapon** ['wepən], _s._ die Waffe.
**wear** [wɛə], _v.a. irr._ tragen (_clothes_). — _v.n._ — _off_, sich abtragen, schäbig werden; — _out_, sich erschöpfen. — _s._ die Abnutzung.
**weariness** ['wiərinis], _s._ die Müdigkeit, der Überdruß.
**weary** ['wiəri], _adj._ müde, überdrüssig.
**weasel** ['wi:zl], _s._ (_Zool._) das Wiesel.
**weather** ['weðə], _s._ das Wetter. — _v.a._ überstehen. — _v.n._ (_Geol._) verwittern.
**weatherbeaten** ['weðəbi:tn], _adj._ abgehärtet, wetterhart.
**weathercock** ['weðəkɔk], _s._ der Wetterhahn; (_fig._) wetterwendischer Mensch.
**weave** [wi:v], _v.a. irr._ (_Text._) weben, — _s._ das Gewebe.
**web** [web], _s._ das Gewebe.
**wed** [wed], _v.a._ heiraten; trauen (_a couple_). — _v.n._ (sich ver)heiraten.
**wedding** ['wediŋ], _s._ die Hochzeit; Trauung (_ceremony_).

**wedge** [wedʒ], s. der Keil. — v.a. keilen.

**wedlock** ['wedlɔk], s. die Ehe.

**Wednesday** ['wenzd(e)i]. der Mittwoch.

**wee** [wi:], adj. (Scot.) winzig, klein.

**weed** [wi:d], s. das Unkraut. — v.a. ausjäten, jäten.

**week** [wi:k], s. die Woche.

**weep** [wi:p], v.n. irr. weinen; —ing willow, die Trauerweide.

**weigh** [wei], v.a. wiegen, wägen; (fig.) abwägen, beurteilen; (Naut.) — anchor, den Anker lichten. — v.n. wiegen.

**weighing machine** ['weiiŋ mə'ʃi:n], s. die Waage.

**weight** [weit], s. das Gewicht; gross —, das Bruttogewicht; net —, das Nettogewicht.

**weighty** ['weiti], adj. (ge)wichtig; (fig.) schwer.

**weir** [wiə], s. das Wehr.

**weird** [wiəd], adj. unheimlich.

**welcome** ['welkəm], adj. willkommen. — s. der or das Willkommen. — v.a. willkommen heißen, begrüßen.

**weld** [weld], v.a. schweißen.

**welfare** ['welfeə], s. die Wohlfahrt, soziale Fürsorge.

**well** (1) [wel], s. der Brunnen. — v.n. hervorsprudeln.

**well** (2) [wel], adv. gut, wohl; durchaus; — bred, wohlerzogen. — pred. adj. gesund, wohl.

**Welsh** [welʃ], adj. walisisch. — s. pl. die Waliser, m.pl.

**Welshman** ['welʃmən], s. der Waliser.

**welt** [welt], s. der Rand, die Einfassung.

**welter** ['weltə], s. die Masse, das Chaos. — v.n. sich wälzen.

**wen** [wen], s. (Med.) die Schwellung.

**wench** [wentʃ], s. die Magd, das Mädchen.

**west** [west], s. der Westen. — adj. (also **westerly, western** ['westəli, 'westən]) westlich.

**Westphalian** [west'feiliən], adj. westfälisch. — s. der Westfale.

**wet** [wet], adj. naß, feucht; — paint, frisch gestrichen. — v.a. anfeuchten, benetzen, naß machen.

**whack** [hwæk], v.a. durchprügeln. — s. die Tracht Prügel, der Schlag.

**whale** [hweil], s. (Zool.) der Walfisch.

**whalebone** ['hweilboun], s. das Fischbein.

**wharf** [hwɔ:f], s. der Kai.

**wharfinger** ['hwɔ:findʒə], s. der Kaimeister.

**what** [hwɔt], rel. & interr. pron. was; welcher, welche, welches; was für.

**what(so)ever** [hwɔt(sou)'evə], rel. pron. was auch immer. — adj. einerlei welche-r, -s, -n.

**wheat** [hwi:t], s. (Bot.) der Weizen.

**wheedle** ['hwi:dl], v.a. beschwatzen.

**wheel** [hwi:l], s. das Rad; die Umdrehung, Drehung. — v.a., v.n. drehen, sich drehen, schieben.

**wheelbarrow** ['hwi:lbærou], s. der Schubkarren.

**wheeze** [hwi:z], v.n. keuchen, schnaufen. — s. das Keuchen.

**whelp** [hwelp], s. (Zool.) das Junge, der junge Hund. — v.n. Junge werfen.

**when** [hwen], adv. (interr.) wann? — conj. als (in past), wenn, während.

**whence** [hwens], adv. woher, von wo.

**where** [hweə], adv. wo, wohin; (interr.) wo? wohin?

**whereabout(s)** ['hwɛərəbaut(s)], adv. wo, wo etwa. — s. (**whereabouts**) der zeitweilige Aufenthalt or Wohnort.

**whereas** [hwɛər'æz], conj. wohingegen, während.

**whereupon** [hwɛərə'pɔn], conj. woraufhin.

**wherewithal** ['hwɛəwiðɔ:l], s. die gesamte Habe, das Nötige. — adv. (obs.) womit.

**whet** [hwet], v.a. wetzen, schleifen.

**whether** ['hweðə], conj. ob.

**whey** [hwei], s. die Molke.

**which** [hwitʃ], rel. & interr. pron. welcher, welche, welches; der, die, das.

**whiff** [hwif], s. der Hauch, Luftzug.

**while** [hwail], s. die Weile, Zeit. — v.a. — away the time, dahinbringen, vertreiben. — conj. (also **whilst**) während, so lange als.

**whim** [hwim], s. die Laune, Grille.

**whimper** ['hwimpə], v.n. winseln.

**whimsical** ['hwimzikəl], adj. grillenhaft.

**whine** [hwain], v.n. weinen, wimmern, klagen. — s. das Gewimmer, Gejammer.

**whinny** ['hwini], v.n. wiehern.

**whip** [hwip], s. die Peitsche; (Pol.) der Einpeitscher. — v.a. peitschen.

**whir** [hwə:], v.n. schwirren. — s. das Schwirren.

**whirl** [hwə:l], s. der Wirbel, Strudel. — v.a., v.n. wirbeln.

**whirligig** ['hwə:ligig], s. das Karussel.

**whirlpool** ['hwə:lpu:l], s. der Strudel.

**whirr** see whir.

**whisk** [hwisk], v.a. fegen; schlagen; —away or off, schnell wegtun (a th.), schnell fortnehmen (a p.). — v.n. — away, dahinhuschen. — s. der Schläger.

**whiskers** ['hwiskəz], s. der Backenbart, Bart.

**whisky** ['hwiski], s. der Whisky.

**whisper** ['hwispə], s. das Geflüster. v.a., v.n. flüstern.

**whistle** [hwisl], s. die Pfeife (instrument); der Pfiff (sound). — v.a., v.n. pfeifen.

**whit** [hwit], s. die Kleinigkeit; not a —, nicht im geringsten.

**white** [hwait], adj. weiß; — lead, das Bleiweiß; — lie, die Notlüge.

**whitebait** ['hwaitbeit], s. (Zool.) der Breitling.

**whiten** [hwaitn], v.a. weißen, bleichen.

**whitewash** ['hwaitwɔʃ], s. die Tünche. — v.a. reinwaschen.

whither ['hwiðə], adv. wohin; dahin wo.

whiting ['hwaitiŋ], s. (Zool.) der Weißfisch; die Schlämmkreide (chalk).

whitlow ['hwitlou], s. (Med.) das Nagelgeschwür.

Whitsun(tide) ['hwitsən(taid)], s. (das) Pfingsten; Whit Sunday, der Pfingstsonntag.

whittle [hwitl], v.a. schnitzen, abschaben.

whiz [hwiz], v.n. zischen; (fig.) vorbeiflitzen.

who [hu:], interr. pron. wer?, welcher?, welche? — rel. pron. welcher, welche, welches, der, die, das.

whoever [hu:'evə], rel. pron. wer auch immer.

whole [houl], adj. ganz, völlig. — s. das Ganze.

wholesale ['houlseil], adv. im Engros. — adj. Engros-, Großhandels-.

wholesome ['houlsəm], adj. gesund.

whoop [hu:p], s. das Geschrei; — v.n. laut keuchen; —ing cough, der Keuchhusten.

whortleberry ['hwə:tlbəri], s. (Bot.) die Heidelbeere.

whose [hu:z], pron. wessen, dessen, deren.

whosoever [hu:sou'evə] see whoever.

why [hwai], rel. & interr. adv. warum?

wick [wik], s. der Docht.

wicked ['wikid], adj. böse, schlecht.

wicker ['wikə], adj. Rohr-, geflochten.

wicket ['wikit], s. das Pförtchen.

wide [waid], adj. weit, breit; (fig.) schlau; (Am.) schlau, gerieben. — adv. far and —, weit und breit; — awake, völlig wach.

widen [waidn], v.a. erweitern.

widgeon ['widʒən], s. die Pfeifente.

widow ['widou], s. die Witwe.

widower ['widouə], s. der Witwer.

width [widθ], s. die Weite, Breite.

wield [wi:ld], v.a. schwingen; — power, die Macht ausüben.

wife [waif], s. die Frau, Gattin.

wig [wig], s. die Perücke.

wild [waild], adj. wild.

wilderness ['wildənis], s. die Wildnis.

wildfire ['waildfaiə], s. das Lauffeuer.

wilful ['wilful], adj. absichtlich; vorsätzlich.

wiliness ['wailinis], s. die Schlauheit, Arglist.

will [wil], s. der Wille; (Law) der letzte Wille, das Testament. — v.n. wollen. — v.a. (Law) vermachen, hinterlassen.

willing ['wiliŋ], adj. bereitwillig.

will-o'-the-wisp [wiləðə'wisp], s. das Irrlicht.

willow ['wilou], s. (Bot.) die Weide.

wily ['waili], adj. schlau, verschmitzt.

wimple [wimpl], s. der Schleier.

win [win], v.a., v.n. irr. gewinnen, siegen, erringen.

wince [wins], v.n. zucken, zusammenzucken.

winch [wintʃ], s. die Kurbel, Winde.

wind (1) [wind], s. der Wind; der Atem (breath); get — of s.th., von etwas hören.

wind (2) [waind], v.a. irr. winden; wenden, drehen (turn); —(up), aufziehen (timepiece); — up, (business, debate) beenden. — v.n. sich schlängeln, winden.

windfall ['windfɔ:l], s. das Fallobst (fruit); (fig.) der Glücksfall.

windlass ['windləs], s. die Winde.

window ['windou], s. das Fenster; — sill, das Fensterbrett.

windpipe ['windpaip], s. (Anat.) die Luftröhre.

windscreen ['windskri:n], s. (Motor.) die Windschutzscheibe.

windshield ['windʃi:ld] (Am.) see windscreen.

windy ['windi], adj. windig.

wine [wain], s. der Wein; — merchant, der Weinhändler.

wing [wiŋ], s. der Flügel; (Poet.) die Schwinge.

wink [wiŋk], s. das Zwinkern; der Augenblick. —v.n. blinzeln, zwinkern.

winner ['winə], s. der Sieger, Gewinner.

winning ['winiŋ], adj. einnehmend.

winsome ['winsəm], adj. reizend, einnehmend.

winter ['wintə], s. der Winter.

wintry ['wintri], adj. winterlich.

wipe [waip], v.a. wischen, abwischen.

wire [waiə], s. der Draht; (coll.) das Telegramm; barbed —, der Stacheldraht. — v.a. verbinden; (fig.) telegraphieren. — v.n. telegraphieren.

wireless ['waiəlis], s. das Radio. — adj. drahtlos.

wirepuller ['waiəpulə], s. der Puppenspieler; (fig.) der Intrigant.

wiry ['waiəri], adj. zäh, stark.

wisdom ['wizdəm], s. die Weisheit.

wise [waiz], adj. weise, verständig, klug.

wiseacre ['waizeikə], s. der Allzuschlaue, Naseweis.

wish [wiʃ], v.a., v.n. wünschen. — s. der Wunsch.

wistful ['wistful], adj. nachdenklich (pensive); wehmütig (sad).

wit [wit], s. der Witz; Geist; Verstand; der witzige Mensch; der Witzbold.

witch [witʃ], s. die Hexe, Zauberin.

witchcraft ['witʃkrɑ:ft], s. die Zauberkunst, Hexerei.

with [wið], prep. mit, mitsamt, bei, durch, von.

withal [wi'ðɔ:l], adv. obendrein.

withdraw [wið'drɔ:], v.a., v.n. irr. (sich) zurückziehen; widerrufen; abheben (money from bank).

withdrawal [wið'drɔ:əl], s. der Rückzug; (Comm. etc.) die Widerrufung; Abhebung (bank).

wither ['wiðə], v.a. welk machen. — v.n. verwelken; ausdorren, verdorren (dry up); (fig.) vergehen.

withhold [wið'hould], v.a. irr. zurückhalten, vorenthalten.

**within** [wi'ðin], *prep.* innerhalb; *(time)* binnen *(Genit.)*. — *adv.* darin, drinnen.

**without** [wi'ðaut], *prep.* ohne; *(obs.)* außerhalb *(outside)*; do —, entbehren. — *adv.* draußen, außen.

**withstand** [wið'stænd], *v.a. irr.* widerstehen *(Dat.)*.

**withy** ['wiði], *s.* der Weidenzweig.

**witless** ['witlis], *adj.* einfältig.

**witness** ['witnis], *s.* der Zeuge. — *v.a.* bezeugen, Zeuge sein von. — *v.n.* zeugen, Zeuge sein.

**witticism** ['witisizm], *s.* das Bonmot, die witzige Bemerkung.

**witty** ['witi], *adj.* witzig, geistreich.

**wizard** ['wizəd], *s.* der Zauberer.

**wizened** ['wizənd], *adj.* verwelkt, vertrocknet, runzlig.

**wobble** [wɔbl], *v.n.* wackeln.

**woe** [wou], *s. (Poet.)* das Weh, Leid.

**wolf** [wulf], *s. (Zool.)* der Wolf.

**woman** ['wumən], *s.* die Frau, das Weib.

**womanly** ['wumənli], *adj.* weiblich.

**womb** [wu:m], *s.* der Mutterleib, Schoß; *(Anat.)* die Gebärmutter.

**wonder** ['wʌndə], *s.* das Wunder. — *v.n.* sich wundern *(be amazed)*; gern wissen mögen *(like to know)*; sich fragen.

**wonderful** ['wʌndəful], *adj.* wunderbar.

**wondrous** ['wʌndrəs], *adj. (Poet.)* wunderbar.

**wont** [wount], *s.* die Gewohnheit. — *pred. adj.* gewohnt.

**won't** [wount] = **will not.**

**woo** [wu:], *v.a.* freien, werben (um).

**wood** [wud], *s.* das Holz *(timber)*; der Wald *(forest)*.

**woodbine** ['wudbain], *s.* das Geißblatt.

**woodcock** ['wudkɔk], *s. (Orn.)* die Waldschnepfe.

**woodcut** ['wudkʌt], *s. (Art)* der Holzschnitt.

**wooded** ['wudid], *adj.* bewaldet.

**wooden** [wudn], *adj.* hölzern, Holz-.

**woodlark** ['wudla:k], *s. (Orn.)* die Heidelerche.

**woodpecker** ['wudpekə], *s. (Orn.)* der Specht.

**woodruff** ['wudrʌf], *s. (Bot.)* der Waldmeister.

**woof** [wu:f], *s. (Text.)* der Einschlag, das Gewebe.

**wool** [wul], *s.* die Wolle; — *gathering*, zerstreut.

**woollen** ['wulən], *adj.* wollen, aus Wolle.

**woolly** ['wuli], *adj.* wollig; *(fig.)* unklar, verschwommen.

**word** [wə:d], *s.* das Wort; *send* —, Botschaft senden. — *v.a.* ausdrücken.

**wording** ['wə:diŋ], *s.* die Fassung, der Stil.

**work** [wə:k], *s.* die Arbeit; *out of* —, arbeitslos; das Werk *(opus)*; *(pl.)* die Fabrik. — *v.a., v.n.* arbeiten, bearbeiten; *(engine)* funktionieren.

**worker** ['wə:kə], *s.* der Arbeiter.

**workhouse** ['wə:khaus], *s.* das Armenhaus.

**workshop** ['wə:kʃɔp], *s.* die Werkstatt.

**world** [wə:ld], *s.* die Welt.

**worldly** ['wə:ldli], *adj.* weltlich, zeitlich.

**worm** [wə:m], *s. (Zool.)* der Wurm. — *v.a.* — *o.'s way*, sich einschleichen. — *v.n.* sich einschleichen.

**wormeaten** ['wə:mi:tn], *adj.* wurmstichig.

**worry** ['wʌri], *v.a., v.n.* plagen, quälen, sorgen, ängstigen; sich beunruhigen; *don't* —, bitte machen Sie sich keine Mühe. — *s.* die Plage, Mühe, Qual, Sorge *(about,* um, *Acc.)*.

**worse** [wə:s], *comp. adj., adv.* schlechter, schlimmer.

**worship** ['wə:ʃip], *s.* die Verehrung; der Gottesdienst *(divine —)*.

**worst** [wə:st], *superl. adj.* schlechtest, schlimmst. — *[adv.* am schlimmsten *or* schlechtesten. — *s.* das Schlimmste.

**worsted** ['wustid], *s. (Text.)* das Kammgarn.

**worth** [wə:θ], *adj.* wert. — *s.* der Wert.

**worthy** ['wə:ði], *adj.* würdig, wert, verdient.

**would** [wud] *past tense of* **will,** *q.v.*

**wound** [wu:nd], *s.* die Wunde. — *v.a.* verwunden.

**wraith** [reiθ], *s.* das Gespenst.

**wrangle** [ræŋgl], *v.n.* zanken, streiten. — *s.* der Zank, Streit.

**wrap** [ræp], *v.a.* einwickeln, einhüllen. — *s. (Am.)* der Mantel *(coat)*, Pelz *(fur)*, Schal *(stole)*.

**wrapper** ['ræpə], *s.* der Umschlag, die Hülle.

**wrath** [rɔ:θ], *s.* der Zorn, Grimm.

**wreak** [ri:k], *v.a. (Lit.)* auslassen, üben.

**wreath** [ri:θ], *s.* der Kranz.

**wreathe** [ri:ð], *v.a.* winden, bekränzen.

**wreck** [rek], *s.* der Schiffbruch; das Wrack *(debris)*. — *v.a.* zerstören, zertrümmern, *(fig.)* verderben.

**wren** [ren], *s. (Orn.)* der Zaunkönig.

**wrench** [rentʃ], *v.a.* entreißen *(tear from)*; verdrehen. — *s.* heftiger Ruck; *(fig.)* der *(Trennungs)*schmerz.

**wrest** [rest], *v.a.* zerren.

**wrestle** [resl], *v.n.* ringen, im Ringkampf kämpfen.

**wrestling** ['resliŋ], *s.* der Ringkampf.

**wretch** [retʃ], *s.* der Schuft, Lump *(scoundrel)*.

**wretched** ['retʃid], *adj.* elend.

**wriggle** [rigl], *v.n.* sich winden, schlängeln.

**wring** [riŋ], *v.a. irr.* auswinden, ausringen.

**wrinkle** [riŋkl], *s.* die Hautfalte, Runzel. — *v.a.* runzeln *(brow)*; rümpfen *(nose)*.

**wrist** [rist], *s. (Anat.)* das Handgelenk.

**wristwatch** ['ristwɔtʃ], *s.* die Armbanduhr.

**writ** [rit], *s.* die Schrift; *(Law)* die Vorladung.

**write** [rait], *v.a.*, *v.n. irr.* schreiben, verfassen.
**writer** ['raitə], *s.* der Schreiber; (*Lit.*) der Schriftsteller.
**writhe** [raið], *v.n.* sich winden.
**writing** ['raitiŋ], *s.* die Schrift; der Stil (*style*).
**wrong** [rɔŋ], *adj.* falsch, verkehrt; *to be —,* unrecht haben. *— s.* das Unrecht. *— v.a.* Unrecht *or* Schaden tun (*Dat.*).
**wrongful** ['rɔŋful], *adj.* unrechtmäßig.
**wrongheaded** [rɔŋ'hedid], *adj.* querköpfig.
**wroth** [rouθ], *adj.* (*Lit.*) zornig.
**wrought** [rɔːt], *adj.* (*work*) gearbeitet; *— iron,* das Schmiedeeisen.
**wry** [rai], *adj.* verkehrt, krumm, schief, verdreht.

# X

**X** [eks]. das X.
**X-ray** ['eksrei], *s.* (der) Röntgenstrahl.
**xylophone** ['zailəfoun], *s.* (*Mus.*) das Xylophon.

# Y

**Y** [wai]. das Y, Ypsilon.
**yacht** [jɔt], *s.* (*Naut.*) die Jacht.
**yachtsman** ['jɔtsmən], *s.* (*Naut.*) der Segelsportler.
**yap** [jæp], *v.n.* kläffen.
**yard** (1) [jɑːd], *s.* der Hof.
**yard** (2) [jɑːd], *s.* die englische Elle, der Yard.
**yarn** [jɑːn], *s.* das Garn; (*coll.*) die Geschichte (*tale*).
**yarrow** ['jærou], *s.* (*Bot.*) die Schafgarbe.
**yawl** [jɔːl], *s.* (*Naut.*) die Yawl.
**yawn** [jɔːn], *v.n.* gähnen. *— s.* das Gähnen.
**ye** [jiː], *pron.* (*obs.*) *see* you.
**year** [jə: *or* jiə], *s.* das Jahr; *every other —,* alle zwei Jahre.
**yearly** ['jiəli], *adj., adv.* jährlich.
**yearn** [jəːn], *v.n.* sich sehnen (nach, *Dat.*).
**yeast** [jiːst], *s.* die Hefe.
**yell** [jel], *v.n.* gellen, schreien. *— s.* der Schrei.
**yellow** ['jelou], *adj.* gelb; (*sl.*) feige.
**yelp** [jelp], *v.n.* kläffen, bellen. *— s.* das Gebelle.
**yeoman** ['joumən], *s.* der Freisasse; (*Mil.*) der Leibgardist (*Yeoman of the Guard*).

**yes** [jes], *adv.* ja; jawohl.
**yesterday** ['jestəd(e)i], *adv.* gestern; *the day before —,* vorgestern.
**yet** [jet], *conj.* doch, dennoch. *— adv.* noch, außerdem; *as —,* bisher; *not —,* noch nicht.
**yew** [juː], *s.* (*Bot.*) die Eibe.
**yield** [jiːld], *v.a.* hervorbringen, ergeben; abwerfen (*profit*). *— v.n.* nachgeben (*to, Dat.*). *— s.* der Ertrag.
**yoke** [jouk], *s.* das Joch (Ochsen). *— v.a.* einspannen, anspannen.
**yolk** [jouk], *s.* das Eidotter.
**yon, yonder** [jɔn, 'jɔndə], *dem. adj.* (*obs.*) jener, jene, jenes; der *or* die *or* das da drüben.
**yore** [jɔː], *adv.* (*obs.*) *of —,* von damals; ehedem.
**you** [juː], *pers. pron.* du, dich, ihr, euch; (*formal*) sie (*in letters*, Du, Dich *etc.*).
**young** [jʌŋ], *adj.* jung. *— s.* (*Zool.*) das Junge.
**your** [juə], *poss. adj.* dein, deine, dein; euer, eure, euer; (*formal*) ihr, ihre, ihr (*in letters* Dein, Euer *etc.*).
**yours** [jɔːz], *poss. pron.* deinig, eurig; der, die *or* das ihrige (*in letters* Deinig, Ihrige *etc.*).
**yourself** [juə'self], *pers. pron.* du selbst, Sie selbst; ihr selbst; dich (selbst), euch (selbst) (*in letters* Du selbst; Dich (selbst) *etc.*).
**youth** [juːθ], *s.* die Jugend.
**youthful** ['juːθful], *adj.* jugendlich.
**Yugoslav** [ju:go'slɑːv], *adj.* jugoslawisch. *— s.* der Jugoslawe.
**Yule, Yuletide** [juːl, 'juːltaid], *s.* das Julfest, die Weihnachtszeit.

# Z

**Z** [zed, (*Am.*) ziː]. das Z.
**zany** ['zeini], *s.* der Hanswurst.
**zeal** [ziːl], *s.* der Eifer.
**zealous** ['zeləs], *adj.* eifrig.
**zebra** ['ziːbrə], *s.* (*Zool.*) das Zebra.
**zenith** ['zeniθ], *s.* der Zenit, Scheitelpunkt.
**zero** ['ziərou], *s.* der Nullpunkt, die (Ziffer) Null; *— hour,* die festgesetzte Stunde; festgesetzter Zeitpunkt.
**zest** [zest], *s.* die Lust; der Genuß; die Würze.
**zigzag** ['zigzæg], *s.* der Zickzack. *— adj.* Zickzack-.
**zinc** [ziŋk], *s.* das Zink.
**zip(per)** ['zip(ə)], *s.* der Reißverschluß (*zip fastener*).
**zone** [zoun], *s.* die Zone.
**zoological gardens** [zouə'lɔdʒikəl gɑːdnz], *s.* (*abbr.* **zoo** [zuː]) zoologischer Garten, der Zoo, Tiergarten.

# German Irregular Verbs

| Infin. | Pres. Indic. 3rd Pers. Sing. | Imperf. Indic. | Imperf. Subj. |
|---|---|---|---|
| backen | bäckt | backte (buk) | backte |
| befehlen | befiehlt | befahl | beföhle |
| beginnen | beginnt | begann | begönne |
| beißen | beißt | biß | bisse |
| bergen | birgt | barg | bürge |
| bersten | birst | barst | börste |
| bewegen | bewegt | bewog | bewöge |
| biegen | biegt | bog | böge |
| bieten | bietet | bot | böte |
| binden | bindet | band | bände |
| bitten | bittet | bat | bäte |
| blasen | bläst | blies | bliese |
| bleiben | bleibt | blieb | bliebe |
| braten | brät | briet | briete |
| brechen | bricht | brach | bräche |
| brennen | brennt | brannte | brennte |
| bringen | bringt | brachte | brächte |
| denken | denkt | dachte | dächte |
| dreschen | drischt | drosch | drösche |
| dringen | dringt | drang | dränge |
| dürfen | darf | durfte | dürfte |
| empfangen | empfängt | empfing | empfinge |
| empfehlen | empfiehlt | empfahl | empföhle |
| empfinden | empfindet | empfand | empfände |
| erlöschen | erlischt | erlosch | erlösche |

| Imper. | Past Participle | English |
|---|---|---|
| backe | gebacken | bake |
| befiehl | befohlen | order, command |
| beginn(e) | begonnen | begin |
| beiß(e) | gebissen | bite |
| birg | geborgen | save, conceal |
| birst | geborsten | burst |
| beweg(e) | bewogen | induce |
| bieg(e) | gebogen | bend |
| biet(e) | geboten | offer |
| bind(e) | gebunden | tie, bind |
| bitte | gebeten | request |
| blas(e) | geblasen | blow |
| bleib(e) | geblieben | remain |
| brat(e) | gebraten | roast |
| brich | gebrochen | break |
| brenne | gebrannt | burn |
| bring(e) | gebracht | bring |
| denk(e) | gedacht | think |
| drisch | gedroschen | thrash |
| dring(e) | gedrungen | press forward |
|  | gedurft | be permitted |
| empfang(e) | empfangen | receive |
| empfiehl | empfohlen | (re)commend |
| empfind(e) | empfunden | feel, perceive |
| erlisch | erloschen | be extinguished |

# German Irregular Verbs

| Infin. | Pres. Indic. 3rd Pers. Sing. | Imperf. Indic. | Imperf. Subj. |
|---|---|---|---|
| erschrecken (*v.n.*) | erschrickt | erschrak | erschräke |
| essen | ißt | aß | äße |
| fahren | fährt | fuhr | führe |
| fallen | fällt | fiel | fiele |
| fangen | fängt | fing | finge |
| fechten | ficht | focht | föchte |
| finden | findet | fand | fände |
| flechten | flicht | flocht | flöchte |
| fliegen | fliegt | flog | flöge |
| fliehen | flieht | floh | flöhe |
| fließen | fließt | floß | flösse |
| fressen | frißt | fraß | fräße |
| frieren | friert | fror | fröre |
| gebären | gebiert | gebar | gebäre |
| geben | gibt | gab | gäbe |
| gedeihen | gedeiht | gedieh | gediehe |
| gehen | geht | ging | ginge |
| gelingen (*impers.*) | (mir) gelingt | gelang | gelänge |
| gelten | gilt | galt | gälte |
| genesen | genest | genas | genäse |
| genießen | genießt | genoß | genösse |
| geschehen (*impers.*) | (mir) geschieht | geschah | geschähe |
| gewinnen | gewinnt | gewann | gewönne |
| gießen | gießt | goß | gösse |
| gleichen | gleicht | glich | gliche |
| gleiten | gleitet | glitt | glitte |
| graben | gräbt | grub | grübe |
| greifen | greift | griff | griffe |

| *Imper.* | *Past Participle* | *English* |
|---|---|---|
| erschrick | erschrocken | be frightened |
| iß | gegessen | eat |
| fahr(e) | gefahren | travel |
| fall(e) | gefallen | fall |
| fang(e) | gefangen | catch |
| ficht | gefochten | fight |
| find(e) | gefunden | find |
| flicht | geflochten | twine together |
| flieg(e) | geflogen | fly |
| flieh(e) | geflohen | flee |
| fließ(e) | geflossen | flow |
| friß | gefressen | eat (of animals) |
| frier(e) | gefroren | freeze |
| gebier | geboren | give birth to |
| gib | gegeben | give |
| gedeih(e) | gediehen | thrive |
| geh(e) | gegangen | go |
| geling(e) | gelungen | succeed |
| gilt | gegolten | be worth, be valid |
| genese | genesen | recover |
| genieß(e) | genossen | enjoy |
|  | geschehen | happen |
| gewinn(e) | gewonnen | win |
| gieß(e) | gegossen | pour |
| gleich(e) | geglichen | equal, resemble |
| gleit(e) | geglitten | glide |
| grab(e) | gegraben | dig |
| greif(e) | gegriffen | grasp |

# German Irregular Verbs

| Infin. | Pres. Indic. 3rd Pers. Sing. | Imperf. Indic. | Imperf. Subj. |
|---|---|---|---|
| haben | hat | hatte | hätte |
| halten | hält | hielt | hielte |
| hangen (*v.n.*) | hängt | hing | hinge |
| heben | hebt | hob | höbe |
| heißen | heißt | hieß | hieße |
| helfen | hilft | half | hülfe |
| kennen | kennt | kannte | kennte |
| klimmen | klimmt | klomm | klömme |
| klingen | klingt | klang | klänge |
| kneifen | kneift | kniff | kniffe |
| kommen | kommt | kam | käme |
| können | kann | konnte | könnte |
| kriechen | kriecht | kroch | kröche |
| laden | lädt | lud | lüde |
| lassen | läßt | ließ | ließe |
| laufen | läuft | lief | liefe |
| leiden | leidet | litt | litte |
| leihen | leiht | lieh | liehe |
| lesen | liest | las | läse |
| liegen | liegt | lag | läge |
| lügen | lügt | log | löge |
| mahlen | mahlt | mahlte | mahlte |
| meiden | meidet | mied | miede |
| messen | mißt | maß | mäße |
| mißlingen (*impers.*) | (mir) mißlingt | mißlang | mißlänge |
| mögen | mag | mochte | möchte |
| müssen | muß | mußte | müßte |
| nehmen | nimmt | nahm | nähme |

| Imper. | Past Participle | English |
|---|---|---|
| habe | gehabt | have |
| halt(e) | gehalten | hold |
| häng(e) | gehangen | hang |
| hebe | gehoben | lift |
| heiß(e) | geheißen | be called |
| hilf | geholfen | help |
| kenn(e) | gekannt | know |
| klimm(e) | geklommen | climb |
| kling(e) | geklungen | ring, sound |
| kneif(e) | gekniffen | pinch |
| komm(e) | gekommen | come |
| | gekonnt | be able |
| kriech(e) | gekrochen | creep |
| lad(e) | geladen | load |
| laß | gelassen | let |
| lauf(e) | gelaufen | run |
| leid(e) | gelitten | suffer |
| leih(e) | geliehen | lend |
| lies | gelesen | read |
| lieg(e) | gelegen | lie |
| lüg(e) | gelogen | lie, be untruthful |
| mahle | gemahlen | grind |
| meid(e) | gemieden | avoid |
| miß | gemessen | measure |
| | mißlungen | fail |
| | gemocht | wish, be willing |
| | gemußt | have to |
| nimm | genommen | take |

# German Irregular Verbs

| Infin. | Pres. Indic. 3rd Pers. Sing. | Imperf. Indic. | Imperf. Subj. |
|---|---|---|---|
| nennen | nennt | nannte | nennte |
| pfeifen | pfeift | pfiff | pfiffe |
| preisen | preist | pries | priese |
| quellen (*v.n.*) | quillt | quoll | quölle |
| raten | rät | riet | riete |
| reiben | reibt | rieb | riebe |
| reißen | reißt | riß | risse |
| reiten | reitet | ritt | ritte |
| rennen | rennt | rannte | rennte |
| riechen | riecht | roch | röche |
| ringen | ringt | rang | ränge |
| rinnen | rinnt | rann | rönne |
| rufen | ruft | rief | riefe |
| saufen | säuft | soff | söffe |
| saugen | saugt | sog | söge |
| schaffen | schafft | schuf | schüfe |
| scheiden | scheidet | schied | schiede |
| scheinen | scheint | schien | schiene |
| schelten | schilt | schalt | schölte |
| schieben | schiebt | schob | schöbe |
| schießen | schießt | schoß | schösse |
| schinden | schindet | schund | schünde |
| schlafen | schläft | schlief | schliefe |
| schlagen | schlägt | schlug | schlüge |
| schleichen | schleicht | schlich | schliche |
| schleifen | schleift | schliff | schliffe |
| schließen | schließt | schloß | schlösse |
| schlingen | schlingt | schlang | schlänge |

| Imper. | Past Participle | English |
| --- | --- | --- |
| nenne | genannt | name |
| pfeif(e) | gepfiffen | whistle |
| preis(e) | gepriesen | praise |
| quill | gequollen | spring |
| rat(e) | geraten | counsel |
| reib(e) | gerieben | rub |
| reiß(e) | gerissen | tear |
| reit(e) | geritten | ride |
| renn(e) | gerannt | run |
| riech(e) | gerochen | smell |
| ring(e) | gerungen | struggle |
| rinn(e) | geronnen | flow |
| ruf(e) | gerufen | call |
| sauf(e) | gesoffen | drink (to excess) |
| saug(e) | gesogen | suck |
| schaff(e) | geschaffen | create |
| scheid(e) | geschieden | separate |
| schein(e) | geschienen | appear |
| schilt | gescholten | scold |
| schieb(e) | geschoben | shove |
| schieß(e) | geschossen | shoot |
| schind(e) | geschunden | skin |
| schlaf(e) | geschlafen | sleep |
| schlag(e) | geschlagen | beat |
| schleich(e) | geschlichen | slink, creep |
| schleif(e) | geschliffen | slide, polish |
| schließ(e) | geschlossen | shut, close |
| schling(e) | geschlungen | wind, devour |

# German Irregular Verbs

| Infin. | Pres. Indic. 3rd Pers. Sing. | Imperf. Indic. | Imperf. Subj. |
|---|---|---|---|
| schmeißen | schmeißt | schmiß | schmisse |
| schmelzen (v.n.) | schmilzt | schmolz | schmölze |
| schneiden | schneidet | schnitt | schnitte |
| schrecken (v.n.) | schrickt | schrak | schräke |
| schreiben | schreibt | schrieb | schriebe |
| schreien | schreit | schrie | schriee |
| schreiten | schreitet | schritt | schritte |
| schweigen | schweigt | schwieg | schwiege |
| schwellen | schwillt | schwoll | schwölle |
| schwimmen | schwimmt | schwamm | schwömme |
| schwinden | schwindet | schwand | schwände |
| schwingen | schwingt | schwang | schwänge |
| schwören | schwört | schwur | schwüre |
| sehen | sieht | sah | sähe |
| sein | ist | war | wäre |
| senden | sendet | sandte or sendete | sendete |
| singen | singt | sang | sänge |
| sinken | sinkt | sank | sänke |
| sinnen | sinnt | sann | sänne |
| sitzen | sitzt | saß | säße |
| sollen | soll | sollte | sollte |
| speien | speit | spie | spiee |
| spinnen | spinnt | spann | spönne |
| sprechen | spricht | sprach | spräche |
| sprießen | sprießt | sproß | sprösse |
| springen | springt | sprang | spränge |
| stechen | sticht | stach | stäche |
| stehen | steht | stand | stände |

| Imper. | Past Participle | English |
|---|---|---|
| schmeiß(e) | geschmissen | hurl |
| schmilz | geschmolzen | melt |
| schneid(e) | geschnitten | cut |
| schrick | (erschrocken) | frighten |
| schreib(e) | geschrieben | write |
| schrei(e) | geschrien | cry |
| schreit(e) | geschritten | stride |
| schweig(e) | geschwiegen | be silent |
| schwill | geschwollen | swell |
| schwimm(e) | geschwommen | swim |
| schwind(e) | geschwunden | vanish |
| schwing(e) | geschwungen | swing |
| schwör(e) | geschworen | swear |
| sieh | gesehen | see |
| sei | gewesen | be |
| send(e) | gesandt *or* gesendet | send |
| sing(e) | gesungen | sing |
| sink(e) | gesunken | sink |
| sinn(e) | gesonnen | meditate |
| sitz(e) | gesessen | sit |
| | gesollt | be obliged |
| spei(e) | gespieen | spit |
| spinn(e) | gesponnen | spin |
| sprich | gesprochen | speak |
| sprieß(e) | gesprossen | sprout |
| spring(e) | gesprungen | leap |
| stich | gestochen | prick |
| steh(e) | gestanden | stand |

# German Irregular Verbs

| Infin. | Pres. Indic. 3rd Pers. Sing. | Imperf. Indic. | Imperf. Subj. |
|---|---|---|---|
| stehlen | stiehlt | stahl | stöhle |
| steigen | steigt | stieg | stiege |
| sterben | stirbt | starb | stürbe |
| stinken | stinkt | stank | stänke |
| stoßen | stößt | stieß | stieße |
| streichen | streicht | strich | striche |
| streiten | streitet | stritt | stritte |
| tragen | trägt | trug | trüge |
| treffen | trifft | traf | träfe |
| treiben | treibt | trieb | triebe |
| treten | tritt | trat | träte |
| trinken | trinkt | trank | tränke |
| trügen | trügt | trog | tröge |
| tun | tut | tat | täte |
| verderben | verdirbt | verdarb | verdürbe |
| verdrießen | verdrießt | verdroß | verdrösse |
| vergessen | vergißt | vergaß | vergäße |
| verlieren | verliert | verlor | verlöre |
| wachsen | wächst | wuchs | wüchse |
| wägen | wägt | wog | wöge |
| waschen | wäscht | wusch | wüsche |
| weichen | weicht | wich | wiche |
| weisen | weist | wies | wiese |
| werben | wirbt | warb | würbe |
| werden | wird | wurde | würde |
| werfen | wirft | warf | würfe |
| wiegen | wiegt | wog | wöge |
| winden (v.a.) | windet | wand | wände |

# German Irregular Verbs

| Imper. | Past Participle | English |
|---|---|---|
| stiehl | gestohlen | steal |
| steig(e) | gestiegen | climb |
| stirb | gestorben | die |
| stink(e) | gestunken | stink |
| stoß(e) | gestoßen | push |
| streich(e) | gestrichen | stroke, touch |
| streit(e) | gestritten | quarrel, fight |
| trag(e) | getragen | carry |
| triff | getroffen | meet |
| treib(e) | getrieben | drive |
| tritt | getreten | step |
| trink(e) | getrunken | drink |
| trüg(e) | getrogen | deceive |
| tu(e) | getan | do |
| verdirb | verdorben (and verderbt) | spoil |
| verdrieß(e) | verdrossen | grieve |
| vergiß | vergessen | forget |
| verlier(e) | verloren | lose |
| wachs(e) | gewachsen | grow |
| wäg(e) | gewogen | weigh |
| wasch(e) | gewaschen | wash |
| weich(e) | gewichen | yield |
| weis(e) | gewiesen | show |
| wirb | geworben | court |
| werde | geworden | become |
| wirf | geworfen | throw |
| wieg(e) | gewogen | weigh |
| wind(e) | gewunden | wind |

# German Irregular Verbs

| Infin. | Pres. Indic. 3rd. Pers. Sing. | Imperf. Indic. | Imperf. Subj. |
|---|---|---|---|
| wissen | weiß | wußte | wüßte |
| wollen | will | wollte | wollte |
| zeihen | zeiht | zieh | ziehe |
| ziehen | zieht | zog | zöge |
| zwingen | zwingt | zwang | zwänge |

# German Irregular Verbs

| Imper. | Past Participle | English |
|---|---|---|
| wisse | gewußt | know |
| wolle | gewollt | wish, want |
| zeih(e) | geziehen | accuse |
| zieh(e) | gezogen | draw, pull |
| zwing(e) | gezwungen | force, compel |

# English Irregular Verbs

| Infin. | Past Indic. | Past Participle | German |
|--------|-------------|-----------------|--------|
| abide | abode | abode | bleiben |
| arise | arose | arisen | aufstehen |
| awake | awoke | awoke | aufwecken |
| be | was, were | been | sein |
| bear | bore | borne | tragen |
| beat | beat | beaten | schlagen |
| become | became | become | werden |
| beget | begot | begotten | zeugen |
| begin | began | begun | beginnen |
| bend | bent | bent | biegen |
| bereave | bereaved, bereft | bereaved, bereft | berauben |
| beseech | besought | besought | bitten |
| bid | bade, bid | bidden, bid | gebieten |
| bide | bided, bode | bided | verbleiben |
| bind | bound | bound | binden |
| bite | bit | bitten | beißen |
| bleed | bled | bled | bluten |
| blow | blew | blown | blasen |
| break | broke | broken | brechen |
| breed | bred | bred | zeugen |
| bring | brought | brought | bringen |
| build | built | built | bauen |
| burn | burnt, burned | burnt, burned | brennen |
| burst | burst | burst | bersten |
| buy | bought | bought | kaufen |

| Infin. | Past Indic. | Past Participle | German |
|---|---|---|---|
| can (*pres. indic.*) | could | — | können |
| cast | cast | cast | werfen |
| catch | caught | caught | fangen |
| chide | chid | chidden, chid | schelten |
| choose | chose | chosen | wählen |
| cleave | cleft, clove | cleft, cloven | spalten |
| cling | clung | clung | sich anklammern |
| clothe | clothed, clad | clothed, clad | kleiden |
| come | came | come | kommen |
| cost | cost | cost | kosten |
| creep | crept | crept | kriechen |
| crow | crowed, crew | crowed | krähen |
| cut | cut | cut | schneiden |
| dare | dared, durst | dared | wagen |
| deal | dealt | dealt | austeilen, handeln |
| dig | dug | dug | graben |
| do | did | done | tun |
| draw | drew | drawn | ziehen |
| dream | dreamt, dreamed | dreamt, dreamed | träumen |
| drink | drank | drunk | trinken |
| drive | drove | driven | treiben |
| dwell | dwelt | dwelt | wohnen |
| eat | ate | eaten | essen |
| fall | fell | fallen | fallen |
| feed | fed | fed | füttern |
| feel | felt | felt | fühlen |
| fight | fought | fought | kämpfen |
| find | found | found | finden |

# English Irregular Verbs

| Infin. | Past Indic. | Past Participle | German |
|---|---|---|---|
| flee | fled | fled | fliehen |
| fling | flung | flung | schleudern |
| fly | flew | flown | fliegen |
| forbid | forbad(e) | forbidden | verbieten |
| forget | forgot | forgotten | vergessen |
| forgive | forgave | forgiven | vergeben |
| forsake | forsook | forsaken | verlassen |
| freeze | froze | frozen | frieren |
| get | got | got | bekommen |
| gird | girded, girt | girden, girt | gürten |
| give | gave | given | geben |
| go | went | gone | gehen |
| grind | ground | ground | mahlen |
| grow | grew | grown | wachsen |
| hang | hung | hung | hängen |
| have | had | had | haben |
| hear | heard | heard | hören |
| heave | heaved, hove | heaved, hove | heben |
| hew | hewed | hewn, hewed | hauen |
| hide | hid | hidden, hid | verstecken |
| hit | hit | hit | schlagen |
| hold | held | held | halten |
| hurt | hurt | hurt | verletzen |
| keep | kept | kept | halten |
| kneel | knelt | knelt | knien |
| knit | knitted, knit | knitted, knit | stricken |
| know | knew | known | kennen, wissen |
| lay | laid | laid | legen |

| Infin. | Past Indic. | Past Participle | German |
|---|---|---|---|
| lead | led | led | führen |
| lean | leant, leaned | leant, leaned | lehnen |
| leap | leaped, leapt | leaped, leapt | springen |
| learn | learned, learnt | learned, learnt | lernen |
| leave | left | left | lassen |
| lend | lent | lent | leihen |
| let | let | let | lassen |
| lie (=recline) | lay | lain | liegen |
| light | lit, lighted | lit, lighted | beleuchten |
| lost | lost | lost | verlieren |
| make | made | made | machen |
| may (*pres. indic.*) | might | — | mögen |
| mean | meant | meant | meinen |
| meet | met | met | treffen, begegnen |
| melt | melted | melted, molten | schmelzen |
| mow | mowed | mown | mähen |
| must (*pres. indic.*) | — | — | müssen |
| pay | paid | paid | zahlen |
| put | put | put | stellen |
| quit | quit(ted) | quit(ted) | verlassen |
| — | quoth | — | sagte |
| read | read | read | lesen |
| rend | rent | rent | reissen |
| rid | rid | rid | befreien |
| ride | rode | ridden | reiten, fahren |
| ring | rang | rung | klingeln |
| rise | rose | risen | aufstehen |
| run | ran | run | laufen |

# English Irregular Verbs

| Infin. | Past Indic. | Past Participle | German |
|--------|-------------|-----------------|--------|
| saw | sawed | sawn | sägen |
| say | said | said | sagen |
| see | saw | seen | sehen |
| seek | sought | sought | suchen |
| sell | sold | sold | verkaufen |
| send | sent | sent | senden |
| set | set | set | setzen |
| shake | shook | shaken | schütteln |
| shall (*pres. indic.*) | should | — | werden, sollen |
| shape | shaped | shaped, shapen | formen |
| shear | sheared | shorn | scheren |
| shed | shed | shed | vergiessen |
| shine | shone | shone | scheinen |
| shoe | shod | shod | beschuhen |
| shoot | shot | shot | schiessen |
| show | showed | shown | zeigen |
| shrink | shrank | shrunk | schrumpfen |
| shut | shut | shut | schliessen |
| sing | sang | sung | singen |
| sink | sank | sunk | sinken |
| sit | sat | sat | sitzen |
| slay | slew | slain | erschlagen |
| sleep | slept | slept | schlafen |
| slide | slid | slid | gleiten |
| sling | slung | slung | schleudern |
| slink | slunk | slunk | schleichen |
| slit | slit | slit | schlitzen |
| smell | smelt | smelt | riechen |

| Infin. | Past Indic. | Past Participle | German |
|---|---|---|---|
| smit | smote | smitten | schlagen |
| sow | sowed | sown, sowed | säen |
| speak | spoke | spoken | sprechen |
| speed | sped, speeded | sped, speeded | eilen |
| spell | spelt, spelled | spelt, spelled | buchstabieren |
| spend | spent | spent | ausgeben |
| spill | spilled, spilt | spilled, spilt | verschütten |
| spin | spun, span | spun | spinnen |
| spit | spat | spat | speien |
| split | split | split | spalten |
| spread | spread | spread | ausbreiten |
| spring | sprang | sprung | springen |
| stand | stood | stood | stehen |
| steal | stole | stolen | stehlen |
| stick | stuck | stuck | stecken |
| sting | stung | stung | stechen |
| stink | stank, stunk | stunk | stinken |
| strew | strewed | strewed, strewn | streuen |
| stride | strode | stridden | schreiten |
| strike | struck | struck, stricken | schlagen |
| string | strung | strung | (auf)reihen |
| strive | strove | striven | streben |
| swear | swore | sworn | schwören |
| sweep | swept | swept | kehren |
| swell | swelled | swollen | schwellen |
| swim | swam | swum | schwimmen |
| swing | swung | swung | schwingen |
| take | took | taken | nehmen |

# English Irregular Verbs

| Infin. | Past Indic. | Past Participle | German |
|---|---|---|---|
| teach | taught | taught | lehren |
| tear | tore | torn | zerreißen |
| tell | told | told | erzählen |
| think | thought | thought | denken |
| thrive | thrived, throve | thrived, thriven | gedeihen |
| throw | threw | thrown | werfen |
| thrust | thrust | thrust | stoßen |
| tread | trod | trodden | treten |
| wake | woke, waked | waked, woken woke | wachen |
| wear | wore | worn | tragen |
| weave | wove | woven | weben |
| weep | wept | wept | weinen |
| will | would | — | wollen |
| win | won | won | gewinnen |
| wind | wound | wound | winden |
| work | worked, wrought | worked, wrought | arbeiten |
| wring | wrung | wrung | ringen |
| write | wrote | written | schreiben |

# Numerical Tables

## Cardinal Numbers

| 0 | nought, zero | null |
|---|---|---|
| 1 | one | eins |
| 2 | two | zwei |
| 3 | three | drei |
| 4 | four | vier |
| 5 | five | fünf |
| 6 | six | sechs |
| 7 | seven | sieben |
| 8 | eight | acht |
| 9 | nine | neun |
| 10 | ten | zehn |
| 11 | eleven | elf |
| 12 | twelve | zwölf |
| 13 | thirteen | dreizehn |
| 14 | fourteen | vierzehn |
| 15 | fifteen | fünfzehn |
| 16 | sixteen | sechzehn |
| 17 | seventeen | siebzehn |
| 18 | eighteen | achtzehn |
| 19 | nineteen | neunzehn |
| 20 | twenty | zwanzig |
| 21 | twenty-one | einundzwanzig |
| 22 | twenty-two | zweiundzwanzig |
| 25 | twenty-five | fünfundzwanzig |
| 30 | thirty | dreißig |
| 36 | thirty-six | sechsunddreißig |
| 40 | forty | vierzig |
| 50 | fifty | fünfzig |
| 60 | sixty | sechzig |
| 70 | seventy | siebzig |
| 80 | eighty | achtzig |
| 90 | ninety | neunzig |
| 100 | (one)hundred | hundert |
| 101 | (a)hundred and one | hundert(und)eins |
| 102 | (a)hundred and two | hundert(und)zwei |
| 200 | two hundred | zweihundert |
| 300 | three hundred | dreihundert |
| 600 | six hundred | sechshundert |
| 625 | six hundred and twenty-five | sechshundertfünfundzwanzig |
| 1000 | (a)thousand | tausend |
| 1965 | nineteen hundred and sixty-five | neunzehnhundertfünfundsechzig |
| 2000 | two thousand | zweitausend |
| 1,000,000 | a million | eine Million |
| 2,000,000 | two million | zwei Millionen |

Various suffixes may be added to German numerals, the commonest of which are cited in the following examples:

| | |
|---|---|
| zehnfach | tenfold |
| dreisilbig | trisyllabic |
| vierstimmig | four-part (*i.e.* for four voices) |
| sechsteilig | in six parts |

## Ordinal Numbers

| 1st | first | erste (abbr. 1.) |
|---|---|---|
| 2nd | second | zweite (abbr. 2.) |
| 3rd | third | dritte (abbr. 3.) |
| 4th | fourth | vierte |
| 5th | fifth | fünfte |
| 6th | sixth | sechste |
| 7th | seventh | siebte |
| 8th | eighth | achte |
| 9th | ninth | neunte |
| 10th | tenth | zehnte |
| 11th | eleventh | elfte |
| 12th | twelfth | zwölfte |
| 13th | thirteenth | dreizehnte |
| 14th | fourteenth | vierzehnte |
| 15th | fifteenth | fünfzehnte |
| 16th | sixteenth | sechzehnte |
| 17th | seventeenth | siebzehnte |
| 18th | eighteenth | achtzehnte |
| 19th | nineteenth | neunzehnte |
| 20th | twentieth | zwanzigste |
| 21st | twenty-first | einundzwanzigste |
| 22nd | twenty-second | zweiundzwanzigste |
| 25th | twenty-fifth | fünfundzwanzigste |
| 30th | thirtieth | dreißigste |
| 40th | fortieth | vierzigste |
| 50th | fiftieth | fünfzigste |
| 60th | sixtieth | sechzigste |
| 70th | seventieth | siebzigste |
| 80th | eightieth | achtzigste |
| 90th | ninetieth | neunzigste |
| 100th | hundredth | hundertste |
| 102nd | hundred and second | hundert(und)zweite |
| 200th | two hundredth | zweihundertste |
| 300th | three hundredth | dreihundertste |
| 625th | six hundred and twenty-fifth | sechshundertfünfundzwanzigste |
| 1000th | thousandth | tausendste |
| 2000th | two thousandth | zweitausendste |
| 1,000,000th | millionth | millionste |

## Fractions etc.

| $\frac{1}{4}$ | a quarter | ein Viertel |
|---|---|---|
| $\frac{1}{3}$ | a third | ein Drittel |
| $\frac{1}{2}$ | a half | (ein)halb |
| $\frac{2}{3}$ | two thirds | zwei Drittel |
| $\frac{3}{4}$ | three quarters | drei Viertel |
| $1\frac{1}{4}$ | one and a quarter | ein ein Viertel |
| $1\frac{1}{2}$ | one and a half | anderthalb |
| $5\frac{1}{2}$ | five and a half | fünfeinhalb |
| $7\frac{2}{5}$ | seven and two-fifths | sieben zwei Fünftel |
| $\frac{15}{20}$ | fifteen-twentieths | fünfzehn Zwanzigstel |
| .7 | point seven | 0,7 Null Komma sieben |

541